BAKER'S
BIOGRAPHICAL DICTIONARY OF
MUSICIANS

CREDITS

Laura Kuhn
Classical Editor

Dennis McIntire
Associate Classical Editor

Lewis Porter
Jazz Editor

William Ruhlmann
Pop Editor

Key to Contributors

AB	Andrew Barlett	ETA	E. Taylor Atkins	NAL	Nancy Ann Lee
AG	Andrew Gilbert	GB	Greg Baise	NC	Norene Cashen
BH	Brock Helander	GBr	Gig Brown	NS	Nicolas Slonimsky
BJH	B. J. Huchtemann	GJ	Gregg Juke	PK	Peter Keepnews
BM	Bill Moody	GK	Gregory Kiewiet	PM	Patricia Myers
BP	Bret Primack	GM	Garaud MacTaggart	PMac	Paul MacArthur
BR	Bryan Reesman	HB	Hank Bordowitz	RB	Ralph Burnett
BW	Bill Wahl	JB	Joshua Berrett	RC	Richard Carlin
CH	Chris Hovan	JC	John Chilton,	RI	Robert Iannapolto
DB	Dan Bindert		*Who's Who of Jazz*	SC	Safford Chamberlain
DCG	David C. Gross	JC-B	John Chilton,	SH	Steve Holtje
DD	David Demsey		*Who's Who of British Jazz*	SKB	Susan K. Berlowitz
DDD	Dean D. Dauphinais	JE	James Eason	SP	Sam Prestianni
DK	Dan Keener	JM	Jeff McMillan	TP	Ted Panken
DM	Dennis McIntire	JO	Jim O'Rourke	TS	Tom Smith
DO	David Okamoto	JTB	John T. Bitter	WB	Will Bickart
DPe	Damon Percy	LK	Laura Kuhn	WF	Walter Faber
DPr	David Prince	LP	Lewis Porter	WKH	W. Kim Heron
DR	Dennis Rea	MF	Michael Fitzgerald	WR	William Ruhlmann
ED	Eric Deggans	MM	*Music Master Jazz*		
EH	Ed Hazell		*and Blues Catalogue*		
EJL	Eric J. Lawrence	MS	Matthew Snyder		

BAKER'S
BIOGRAPHICAL DICTIONARY OF
MUSICIANS

VOLUME 2

CONF - GYSI

Centennial Edition

NICOLAS SLONIMSKY

Editor Emeritus

LAURA KUHN

Baker's Series Advisory Editor

Schirmer Books

an imprint of the Gale Group

New York • Detroit • San Francisco • London • Boston • Woodbridge, CT

Schirmer Books
1633 Broadway
New York, New York 10019

Gale Group
27500 Drake Road
Farmington Hills, Michigan 48331-3535

Library of Congress Catalog Card Number: 00-046375

Printed in the United States of America

Printing number
1 2 3 4 5 6 7 8 9 10

Library of Congress Cataloging-in-Publication Data

Baker's biographical dictionary of musicians.—Centennial ed. / Nicolas Slonimsky, editor emeritus.
  p. cm.
Includes bibliographical references and discographies.
Enl. ed. of: Baker's biographical dictionary of musicians. 8th ed. / rev. by Nicolas Slonimsky.
ISBN 0-02-865525-7 (set : alk. paper) — ISBN 0-02- 865526-5 (vol. 1) — ISBN 0-02-865527-3 (vol. 2) — ISBN 0-02-865528-1 (vol. 3) — ISBN 0-02-865529-X (vol. 4) — ISBN 0-02-865530-3 (vol. 5) — ISBN 0-02-865571-0 (vol. 6)
  1. Music—Bio-bibliography—Dictionaries. I. Slonimsky, Nicolas, 1894-
II. Slonimsky, Nicolas, 1894- Baker's biographical dictionary of musicians.

ML105.B16 2000
780'.92'2—dc21
  [B]
                                                                      00-046375

ABBREVIATIONS

A.B.	Bachelor of Arts
ABC	American Broadcasting Company
A.M.	Master of Arts
ASCAP	American Society of Composers, Authors, and Publishers
assn./Assn.	association/Association
assoc.	associate
aug.	augmented
b.	born
B.A.	Bachelor of Arts
bar.	baritone
BBC	British Broadcasting Corporation
bjo.	banjo
B.M.	Bachelor of Music
brs.	brass
bs.	bass
CBC	Canadian Broadcasting Corporation
CBS	Columbia Broadcasting System
Coll.	College
cons./Cons.	conservatory/Conservatory
d.	died
dept./Dept.	department/Department
diss.	dissertation
D.M.A.	Doctor of Musical Arts
drm.	drums
ed(s).	edit(ed), editor(s), edition(s)
enl.	enlarged
f.	formed
flt.	flute
gtr.	guitar
har.	harmonica
H.S.	High School
IRCAM	Institut de Recherche et de Coordination Acoustique/Musique
ISCM	International Society for Contemporary Music
inst./Inst.	institute/Institute

kybd.	keyboards
M.A.	Master of Arts
mdln.	mandolin
M.M.	Master of Music
MS(S)	manuscript(s)
Mus.B.	Bachelor of Music
Mus.D.	Doctor of Music
Mus.M.	Master of Music
NAACP	National Association for the Advancement of Colored People
NBC	National Broadcasting Company
n.d.	no date
NEA	National Endowment for the Arts
NHK	Japan Broadcasting Company
no(s).	number(s)
N.Y.	New York
org.	organ
op(p).	opus
orch./Orch.	orchestra/Orchestra
p(p).	page(s)
PBS	Public Broadcasting Service
perc.	percussion
perf.	performance
Ph.D.	Doctor of Philosophy
phil./Phil.	philharmonic/Philharmonic
pno.	piano
posth.	posthumously
prof.	professor
publ.	publish(ed)
RAI	Radiotelevisione Italiana
rds.	reeds
rec.	recorded
rel.	released
rev.	revised
RIAS	Radio in the American Sector
S.	San, Santo, Santa
sax.	saxophone
sop.	soprano
Ss.	Santi, Sante
St(e).	Saint(e)
sym(s).	symphony (-ies)
synth.	synthesizer
tamb.	tamborine
ten.	tenor
tr.	translate(d), translation
trmb.	trombone
trpt.	trumpet
univ./Univ.	university/University
vln.	violin
voc.	vocals
vol(s).	volume(s)
WDR	Westdeutscher Rundfunk (West German Radio)
wdwnd.	woodwinds

C

(CONTINUED)

Conforti (Conforto), Giovanni Luca, Italian theorist; b. Mileto (Calabria), c. 1560; d. date and place unknown. He entered the Papal Choir in 1580 and remained there until Oct. 31, 1585, when he returned to Mileto. He was chorister at the Papal Chapel again from Nov. 4, 1591. According to Baini, he was the first of his period to restore the "trillo."

WRITINGS: *Breve et facile maniera d'essercitarsi ad ogni scolaro...a far passaggi...* (Rome, 1593; facsimile ed., with tr., edited by J. Wolf, Berlin, 1922); *Passaggi sopra tutti li salmi...* (Venice, 1607; contains a set of vocal ornamentations to be used in the singing of the Psalms employed on Sundays and holidays throughout the year).—**NS/LK/DM**

Conlon, James (Joseph), American conductor; b. N.Y., March 18, 1950. He studied at the H.S. of Music and Art in N.Y., and then was a pupil in conducting of Morel at the Juilliard School of Music in N.Y. (B.M., 1972). After making his formal conducting debut with *Boris Godunov* at the Spoleto Festival in 1971, he conducted at the Juilliard School (1972–75). On April 12, 1974, he became the youngest conductor ever to lead a subscription concert of the N.Y. Phil. On Dec. 11, 1976, he made his Metropolitan Opera debut in N.Y. conducting *Die Zauberflöte*, and remained on its roster until 1980; was again on its roster from 1981 to 1983. He served as music director of the Cincinnati May Festival (from 1979) and chief conductor of the Rotterdam Phil. (1983–91). In 1989 he became chief conductor of the Cologne Opera; in 1991 he also was made Generalmusikdirektor of the city of Cologne and chief conductor of the Gürzenich Orch. there. He likewise was music advisor (1995–96) and principal conductor (from 1996) of the Opéra de la Bastille in Paris.—**NS/LK/DM**

Connell, Elizabeth, Irish mezzo-soprano, later soprano; b. Port Elizabeth, South Africa, Oct. 22, 1946. She was a student of Otakar Kraus at the London Opera Centre. In 1972 she won the Maggie Teyte Prize and made her operatic debut at the Wexford Festival as Varvara in *Kát'a Kabanová*. In 1975 she sang with the Australian Opera in Sydney, and from 1975 to 1980 she was a member of the English National Opera in London, where she won notice as Eboli and Herodias. In 1976 she made her debut at London's Covent Garden as Verdi's Viclinda, and in 1980 at the Bayreuth Festival as Ortrud. In 1983 she turned to soprano roles, and in 1984 appeared as Electra at the Salzburg Festival and as Norma in Geneva. On Jan. 7, 1985, she made her Metropolitan Opera debut in N.Y. as Vitellia, and then returned to Covent Garden to sing Leonora in *Il Trovatore* and Leonore in *Fidelio*. In 1990 she portrayed Lady Macbeth in Bonn, a role she reprised in Cologne in 1992. She appeared as Isolde at the Royal Festival Hall in London in 1993. In 1997 she was engaged as Elektra at the San Francisco Opera, and returned there as Isolde in 1998. On March 21, 1999, she sang Senta at the opening of the new Macau Cultural Centre.—**NS/LK/DM**

Connick, Harry Jr., jazz pianist, singer, songwriter; b. New Orleans, La., Sept. 11, 1967. He played in Bourbon Street clubs from the age of 13 and turned professional as a teenager. In 1983, he was one of the five winners of the IAJE Young Talent Program and was reportedly discovered there by George Butler, head of Columbia Records' Jazz Division at that time. Connick moved to N.Y. for a season as house pianist at Algonquin Hotel. He rapidly achieved fame as vocalist in the Sinatra/Torme mode and as an eclectic pianist with elements of Monk, Ellington, and Garner integrated into his admired style. He has made many successful albums for Columbia since 1987. Connick played and sang on the soundtrack for *When Harry Met Sally* (1989); the album went platinum, as did his 1990 follow-up, *We Are in Love*. Also in 1990, Connick released *Lofty's Roach Souffle*, an album recorded with his jazz trio; although it got mixed reviews from jazz critics, it broke the Top 100 pop album chart, a rare feat for a jazz record. He then performed with his own big band for concert, TV, and

707

festival appearances, before deciding to form a funk band (1994). He has since led a big band and also expanded his career into film acting, landing supporting roles in several feature films.

DISC.: *11* (1978); *Harry Connick Jr.* (1987); *When Harry Met Sally* (1989); *20* (1989); *We Are in Love* (1990); *Singin' & Swingin'* (1990); *Lofty's Roach Souffle* (1990); *Swinging out Live* (1991); *25* (1992); *When My Heart Finds Christmas* (1993); *She* (1994); *Whisper Your Name* (1995); *Star Turtle* (1995); *To See You* (1997); *Come by Me* (1999).—**MM/LP**

Conniff, Ray, American bandleader, arranger, and trombonist; b. Attleboro, Mass., Nov. 6, 1916. Conniff maintained the popularity of big band music long after the music's heyday. Adopting a formula combining swing arrangements with choruses performing well-known songs, he charted 53 albums between 1957 and 1974, including the million-sellers *We Wish You a Merry Christmas*, *Somewhere My Love*, and 13 other LPs that reached the Top Ten.

Conniff's father, John Lawrence Conniff, was a trombonist and the leader of the Attleboro Jewelry City Band; his mother, Maude Angela Conniff, played piano. He received musical instruction from his father. He formed his first band with friends while a junior in high school, playing trombone. He taught himself arranging with a mail-order course. After graduating from high school in 1934, he went to Boston, where he joined Dan Murphy's Musical Skippers. Two years later, he switched to Hank Biagini's band in 1936. That same year he moved to N.Y., and in 1938 he joined the orchestra of Bunny Berigan, moving to Bob Crosby in 1939 and Artie Shaw in 1940. During this period he also studied at the Juilliard School of Music. On Feb. 14, 1938, he married Emily Jo Ann Imhof. They had two children.

After Shaw temporarily disbanded his orchestra, Conniff led his own small band in the spring of 1941, then worked with Vaughn Monroe before rejoining Shaw in the fall and staying into 1942. He worked with Bobby Hackett in 1943 and with Cozy Cole and Art Hodes in 1944, then returned to Shaw, doing a notable arrangement of George Gershwin's "'S Wonderful." He joined the army and worked for the Armed Forces Radio Services until his discharge in 1946, when he went to work for Harry James, also doing arrangements for Shaw, Sonny Burke, and Frank DeVol. On Aug. 23, 1947, he married Ann Marie Engberg.

With the decline in popularity of swing music and the rise of bebop jazz in the late 1940s, Conniff became disillusioned and worked outside music for a number of years. He occasionally worked as a freelance and studio musician. He also made a study of popular music to better understand what it took to make a commercial success.

Conniff's arrangement of "Castle Rock" (music by Al Sears, lyrics by Ervin Drake and Jimmy Shirl) was recorded by Frank Sinatra and Harry James and peaked in the Top Ten in September 1951. In 1954 he worked as a staff trombonist at ABC and NBC, and in 1955 he was hired by Columbia Records as an arranger-conductor. He wrote an arrangement of "Band of Gold" (music by

Jack Taylor, lyrics by Bob Musel) for Don Cherry, whose Columbia recording reached the Top Ten in January 1956. The Columbia singers, often backed by the Ray Conniff Orch., recorded various Conniff arrangements including the Top Ten hits: "Just Walking in the Rain" (music and lyrics by Johnny Bragg and Robert S. Riley), a million-seller for Johnnie Ray, in October 1956; the million-selling "Singing the Blues" (music and lyrics by Melvin Endsley), which topped the charts for Guy Mitchell in December 1956; "Moonlight Gambler" (music by Phil Springer, lyrics by Bob Hilliard), a million-seller for Frankie Laine, in January 1957; "You Don't Owe Me a Thing" (music and lyrics by Marty Robbins), for Johnnie Ray, in February 1957; "A White Sport Coat (And a Pink Carnation)" (music and lyrics by Marty Robbins), for Marty Robbins, in May 1957; and two million-sellers for Johnny Mathis, with music by Robert Allen and lyrics by Al Stillman—"It's Not for Me to Say," in July 1957, and "Chances Are," in September 1957.

Meanwhile, Conniff himself turned recording artist. *'S Wonderful!*, his debut album, released in December 1956, was credited to Ray Conniff and His Orch. and featured swing arrangements of pop standards performed by a big band and a chorus wordlessly voicing instrumental parts. The LP charted and led to a long series of successful albums. *'S Marvelous*, released in November 1957, reached the Top Ten and went gold. *'S Awful Nice*, released in June 1958, made the Top Ten.

Concert in Rhythm, featuring adaptations of classical pieces, was released in September 1958; it made the Top Ten and went gold. *Broadway in Rhythm*, released in March 1959, reached the Top Ten. *It's the Talk of the Town*, the first album on which his singers sang lyrics, was released in July 1959 and hit the Top Ten. *Conniff Meets Butterfield*, featuring trumpeter Billy Butterfield, was released in October 1959 and reached the Top Ten. *Christmas with Conniff*, released in December 1959, went gold. With the success of his recordings, Conniff began performing live with his "Concert in Stereo" in Santa Monica in July 1959. A TV special followed in May 1960.

Conniff released at least three albums a year during the 1960s. *Young at Heart*, a vocal album, was released in July 1960 and made the Top Ten. *Say It with Music (A Touch of Latin)*, an instrumental collection, was released in August 1960 and reached the Top Ten. The January 1961 instrumental LP *Memories Are Made of This* hit the Top Ten and went gold. *So Much in Love*, a vocal album released in January 1962, hit the Top Ten and went gold. *'S Continental*, an instrumental album released in April 1962, reached the Top Ten. A second holiday collection, *We Wish You a Merry Christmas*, released in October 1962, eventually sold a million copies.

Conniff's sales fell off after 1962, but in May 1966 he released a choral rendition of "Somewhere My Love" (music by Maurice Jarre, lyrics by Paul Francis Webster), also known as "Lara's Theme" from the motion picture *Dr. Zhivago*. It hit #1 on the easy-listening charts, reached the Top Ten of the pop charts, and won the Grammy Award for Best Performance by a Chorus. Conniff's *Somewhere My Love* LP hit the Top Ten and sold a million copies.

On Aug. 24, 1968, Conniff married Vera Schmidheiny. They had one child. By the late 1960s he had turned to recording contemporary songs, which led to a rise in his record sales. The vocal album *It Must Be Him*, released in January 1968, went gold, as did another vocal album, *Honey*, released in April 1968. The title song from that album, written by Bobby Russell, earned the Ray Conniff Singers a Grammy nomination for Best Contemporary Pop Performance by a Chorus. They were nominated again the following year for "Jean" (music and lyrics by Rod McKuen), from the album of the same name, which was released in December 1969.

From the 1960s on, Conniff was also popular beyond the U.S. His *Hi-Fi Companion* album reached the U.K. Top Ten in 1960, and the LP *His Orch., His Chorus, His Singers, His Sound* topped the British charts in June 1969. As he toured internationally, his instrumental music found appeal all over the world, especially in Latin America, and he recorded many albums exclusively for the Latin market.

Conniff continued to reach the U.S. album charts through 1974 and the easy- listening charts through 1977. He recorded for Columbia until 1995, then began releasing albums on his own Ivy Music label in the U.S., with international distribution through PolyGram. In 1997 he released his 100th album, *I Love Movies. My Way*, a recording of songs associated with Frank Sinatra, was released on Oct. 6, 1998.

Disc.: *'S Wondeful* (1957); *Dance the Bop* (1957); *'S Marvelous* (1957); *'S Awful Nice* (1958); *Broadway in Rhythum* (1959); *Hollywood in Rhythm* (1959); *Conniff Meets Butterfield* (1959); *Christmas with Conniff* (1959); *It's the Talk of the Town* (1960); *Young at Heart* (1960); *Say It with Music (A Touch of Latin)* (1960); *Somebody Loves Me* (1961); *Christmas Album* (1961); *So Much in Love* (1962); *'S Continental* (1962); *Rhapsody in Rhythm* (1962); *We Wish You a Merry Christmas* (1962): *Just Kiddin' Around* (1963); *You Make Me Feel So Young* (1964); *Speak to Me of Love* (1964); *Invisible Tears* (1964); *Friendly Persuasion* (1965); *Love Affair* (1965); *Happiness Is* (1966); *Somewhere My Love* (1966); *This Is My Song* (1967); *Ray Conniff's Hawaiian Album* (1967); *It Must Be Him* (1968); *Honey* (1968); *Turn Around Look at Me* (1968); *I Love How You Love Me* (1969); *Jean* (1969); *Bridge Over Troubled Water* (1970); *We've Only Just Begun* (1970); *Love Story* (1971); *I'd Like to Teach the World to Sing* (1972); *I Can See Clearly Now* (1973); *You Are the Sunshine of My Life* (1973); *Harmony* (1973); *Send in the Clowns* (1976); *Always in My Heart* (1978); *Amor, Amor, Amor* (1984); *Plays Broadway* (1991); *Christmas Caroling* (1995); *Pure Country* (1996); *I Love Movies* (1997); *Tico Tico* (1998); *My Way* (1998).—**WR**

Connolly, Justin (Riveagh),

English composer and teacher; b. London, Aug. 11, 1933. He was a student of Fricker and Boult at the Royal Coll. of Music in London. He then held a Harkness fellowship at Yale Univ., where he studied with Powell (1963–65) and also taught. Returning to London, he was prof. of theory and composition at the Royal Coll. of Music (1966–89). As a composer, Connolly has followed the structural techniques of the avant-garde, with notable influence from Babbitt and Carter.

Works: DRAMATIC: *Chimaera* for Dancer, Alto, Baritone, Chorus, Piano, Percussion, and Cello (1979; rev. 1981). **ORCH.:** *Antiphonies* (Norfolk, Conn., Aug. 10, 1966); *Rebus* (1970); *Anima* for Viola and Orch. (1974; London, March 9, 1975); *Diaphony* for Organ and Orch. (1977; Winchester, Aug. 31, 1978); Sym. (1991). **CHAMBER:** *Triad I* for Trumpet, Viola, and Piano (1964), *II* for Double Bass, Percussion, and Piano (1965), *III* for Oboe, Viola, and Cello (1966), *IV* for Flute, Percussion, and Tape (1969), and *V* for Clarinet, Violin, and Cello (1971); *Cinquepaces* for Brass Quintet (1965; Cheltenham, July 6, 1968); *Tesserae B* for Flute and Piano (1970), *C* for Cello (1971), *D* for Trumpet and Tape (1971), *E* for Flute and Double Bass (1972), and *F* for Clarinet (Leeds, May 30, 1981); *Sestina B* for Harpsichord, Flute, Oboe, Clarinet, Violin, and Cello (1972; rev. 1978); *Ceilidh* for 4 Violins (1976); *Nocturnal* for Flute Quartet, Piano, Double Bass, and Percussion (1991; London, Jan. 20, 1992). **KEYBOARD: P i a n o :** Sonatina (1962; rev. 1983); *Garden of Forking Paths—Fourfold* for Piano Duet (1983; London, Jan. 9, 1984); *Ennead, Night Thoughts* (1983; London, Jan. 12, 1984). **VOCAL:** *Prose* for Chorus (1967); *Poems of Wallace Stevens I* for Soprano and 7 Players (1967) and *II* for Soprano, Clarinet, and Piano (London, April 10, 1970); *Verse* for Chorus (London, March 23, 1969); *Poems of Henry Vaughan, No. 1, The Evening Watch* for Chorus (1970); *Waka* for Mezzo-soprano and Piano (1972; rev. version, London, Jan. 29, 1988); *Spelt from Sybil's Leaves* for 5 Soloists and Chamber Ensemble (London, June 15, 1989).—**NS/LK/DM**

Connor, Chris,

jazz singer; b. Kansas City, Mo., Nov. 8, 1927. She started out on clarinet, then began singing at the Univ. of Mo. with a band led by Bob Brookmeyer. She moved to N.Y. in 1949 to sing with Claude Thornhill's vocal group, the Snowflakes, then went solo and joined Stan Kenton (January–July 1953), establishing a reputation in the line of Kenton singers Anita O'Day and June Christy as a stylist in the cool school. Connor signed with Bethlehem (1953) and released several albums, including one with Carmen McRae. She was very successful in the mid-1950s, enjoying large record sales and sold-out appearances. Her career slowed considerably in the 1960s with the coming of rock and roll, and she was less active for awhile. She reemerged on record in the mid-1970s and has been touring and recording since on the nightclub circuit. In 1991, she participated in a Kenton reunion concert in Calif.

Disc.: *Lullabies at Birdland* (1953); *Chris Connor with Ellis Larkin* (1954); *This Is Chris* (1955); *Chris* (1955); *Chris Connor* (1956); *Chris Craft* (1958); *Witchcraft* (1959); *Chris in Person* (1959); *Ballads of the Sad Cafe* (1959); *Portrait of Chris* (1960); *Double Exposure* (1960); *Free Spirits* (1961); *Chris Connor at the Village Gate* (1963); *Sings Gentle Bossa Nova* (1965); *Now* (1967); *Sweet and Swinging* (1978); *Love Being Here with You* (1983); *Chris Connor with Helen Forrest* (1983); *Classic* (1986); *New Again* (1987); *As Time Goes By* (1991); *Lover Come Back to Me* (1995). —**MM/LP**

Connors, Norman,

American drummer, singer, composer, producer; b. Philadelphia, Pa., March 1, 1948. He has built a career to confound those who would limit drummers to work behind the trap set. Early on, he became one of jazz fusion's first artists, moving from work recording with John Coltrane, Pharoah Sanders, and Archie Shepp to leading a crack band featuring Stanley Clarke, Ron Carter, and Hubert Laws. A drummer since age five, Connors began recording as a teen with stars such as Coltrane and "Brother" Jack McDuff. Joining Sanders's band shortly after a move to N.Y. in 1971, he was eventually offered contracts with two record labels. Choosing musical freedom over a company that wanted to mold him into yet another soul/jazz artist, he embarked on a series of records for Buddah subsidiary Cobblestone Records that helped define the fusion jazz movement. Aided by bandmates Clarke, Herbie Hancock, and Airto, he stirred funk, jazz, and soul rhythms into a heady stew of albums. But his biggest success would come with a more conventional tune, "You Are My Starship," a ballad smash he recorded in 1976 that would be his biggest hit. As the advent of disco made his type of soul more obsolete, he turned to producing and discovering other artists, including Dee Dee Bridgewater (who wrote "Starship"), Angela Bofill, Phyllis Hyman, Glenn Jones, Norman Brown, and Marion Meadows. Even now, Connors continues to tour with his Starship Orch., producing records for several artists on Motown's jazz label, MoJazz.

Disc.: *Slewfoot* (1974); *Love from the Sun* (1974); *Saturday Night Special* (1975); *Aquarian Dream* (1976); *This Is Your Life* (1977); *You Are My Starship* (1977); *Invitation* (1979); *Passion* (1988); *Just between Us* (1992); *Remember Who You Are* (1993); *Romantic Journey* (1994); *The Best of Norman Connors* (1995); *Dark of Light/Dance of Magic* (1996); *Easy Living* (1997); *The Best of Norman Connors and Friends* (1997).—**ED**

Conradi, Johann Georg, German composer; b. place and date unknown; d. Oettingen, May 22, 1699. He may have studied with his father, the Oettingen organist Caspar Conrad. He was a member of the Oettingen court chapel choir before becoming director of music at the court in 1671. From 1683 to 1686 he was Kapellmeister at the Ansbach court, and then to Duke Heinrich of Saxe- Gotha in Römhild from 1687 to 1690. In 1690 he became music director of the Hamburg Opera. About 1698 he returned to Oettingen as Kapellmeister. Conradi composed at least 9 operas. His only extant opera, *Die schöne und gretreue Ariadne* (Hamburg, 1691), exemplifies the French style he introduced to that city. He also wrote sacred and ceremonial music for the Protestant courts he served. His son, Johann Melchior Conradi (b. Oettingen [baptized], Feb. 17, 1675; d. Heroldingen, near Oettingen, March 13, 1756), was also a composer. In 1699 he succeeded his father as Kapellmeister in Oettingen, a post he held until 1732. Among his extant works are serenades and cantatas.—**LK/DM**

Conrad von Zabern, German music theorist; b. Zabern, date unknown; d. c. 1478. He was educated at the Univ. of Heidelberg (B.A., 1410; M.A., 1414), where he later taught, and then at the univs. of Frieburg im Breisgau, Basel, and Ingolstadt. His extant treatises comprise *Novellus musicae artis tractatus* (c. 1465), *Opusculum de monochordo* (Mainz, c. 1470), *De modo bene cantandi choralem cantum* (Mainz, 1474), and *Lere von Koergesanck* (c. 1474). They have been ed. by K.-W. Gümpel as *Die Musiktraktate C.s v. Z.* (Mainz, 1956). —**LK/DM**

Conried (real name, **Cohn**), **Heinrich,** Austrian-American operatic impresario; b. Bielitz, Sept. 13, 1848; d. Meran, Tirol, April 27, 1909. He started as an actor in Vienna. In 1877 he managed the Bremen Municipal Theater, and then went to the U.S. in 1878 and took over the management of the Germania Theater in N.Y.; then was in charge of various theatrical enterprises. From 1892 he was director of the Irving Place Theater in N.Y., which he brought to a high degree of efficiency. From 1903 till 1908 he was the manager of the Metropolitan Opera and was instrumental in engaging numerous celebrated artists, including Caruso. During his first season he gave the first American production of *Parsifal*, despite the heated controversy regarding the rights of Wagner's heirs. His decision to produce the opera *Salome* by Richard Strauss in 1907 also aroused a storm of protests. Conried resigned in 1908 because of dissension within the management of the Metropolitan, and retired in Europe. He was decorated by several European governments, and also received an honorary M.A. from Harvard Univ.

Bibl.: M. Moses, *H. C.* (N.Y., 1916).—**NS/LK/DM**

Consoli, Marc-Antonio, Italian-born American composer and teacher; b. Catania, May 19, 1941. He studied with Rieti at the N.Y. Coll. of Music (B.M., 1966), with Krenek at the Peabody Cons. of Music in Baltimore (M.M., 1967), and with Goehr at the Yale Univ. School of Music (M.M., 1971; D.M.A., 1977), and also took courses with Schuller and Crumb at the Berkshire Music Center in Tanglewood, with Donatoni at the Accademia Musicale Chigiana in Siena, and at the Warsaw Cons. He became a naturalized American citizen in 1967. He was founder-director of the Musica Oggi Ensemble (1978–80) and served as a church music director and organist (from 1988). He was also ed. of the Hargail Music Press (1978–84) and ed. and publisher of Rinaldo Music Press (from 1983). From 1990 he was adjunct asst. prof. at N.Y.U. His honors include Guggenheim fellowships (1971, 1979), NEA grants (1979, 1981, 1985), and an award from the American Academy and Inst. of Arts and Letters (1975). In several of his works, Consoli has found inspiration in Italian folk elements which he has utilized in writing scores marked by a fine abstract lyricism.

Works: DRAMATIC: B a l l e t : *Naked Masks: Three Frescoes from a Dream* (N.Y., Dec. 13, 1980); *The Last Unicorn* (1981; N.Y., Feb. 24, 1989). **ORCH.:** *Profiles* (1973); *Music for Chambers* (1974; Hilversum, Sept. 13, 1975); *Odefonia* (1976; N.Y., May 23, 1978); *Afterimages* (1982; N.Y., June 2, 1983); Cello Concerto (N.Y., May 9, 1988); *Arie Mutate* (1990); *Musiculi III* (1992–94). **CHAMBER:** *Brazilian Fantasy* for Clarinet and Piano (1965); Sonatina for Tenor Saxophone and Piano (1965); *Interactions I* for 6 Instruments (Tanglewood, Aug. 12, 1970), *II* for Flute and Harp (New Haven, Conn., April 30, 1971), *III* for Violin, Cello, and Piano (College Park, Md., March 22, 1971), *IV: The Aftermath* for 5 Instruments (New Haven, Conn., Dec. 12, 1971), and *V: The Consequence* for Flute and String Quartet (1972); *Sciuri Novi I* for Flute (Siena, Aug. 28, 1974), *II* for Contrabass and Tape (1975; Royan, March 23, 1976), and *III* for Clarinet and Tape or 2 Clarinets (N.Y., March 13, 1997); *Music for Chambers* for 3 Groups of Instruments (1974; Helsinki, May 10, 1978); *Ellipsonics* for 1 to 4 Players and Optional Slides,

Lights, Mimes, and/or Dancers (1974; Pamparato, Italy, July 10, 1975); *Tre Fiori Musicali* for Flute and Guitar (1978; N.Y., April 30, 1980); *Orpheus's Meditation* for Guitar (1981; N.Y., May 4, 1982); *Saxlodie* for Alto Saxophone and Piano (Warsaw, Oct. 20, 1981); 2 string quartets: No. 1 (1983; N.Y., April 25, 1984) and No. 2 (1990); *Sans Parole I* for Cello (1983) and *II* for Violin (N.Y., Nov. 10, 1988); *Lauda* for Violin, Cello, and Piano (San Diego, Dec. 7, 1985); *Reflections* for Clarinet, Alto Saxophone, Trombone, Contrabass, and Percussion (N.Y., March 10, 1986); *Games for 2* for Flute and Bassoon (1994); *Games for 3* for Flute, Horn, and Bassoon (1994); *Di-Ver-Ti-Mento* for Clarinet, Alto Saxophone, Horn, and Trombone (1995); *Varie Azioni I* for Violin and Piano (1995; N.Y., March 13, 1997), *II* for Clarinet and Piano (1998), and *III* for Violin, Horn, and Piano (1999); *Cantiones Vulgares* for Flute and Clarinet (1996); *Pensieri Sospesi* for Flute, Clarinet, Violin, Viola, Cello, and Piano (Mexico City, Nov. 13, 1997); *Four Shades of Tango* for Violin, Horn, and Piano (1998–99). KEYBOARD: P i a n o : *Pezzo* (1969; New Haven, Feb. 13, 1971); *Memorie Pie* (Royan, March 24, 1976); *Collected Moments* (1996; N.Y., March 13, 1997); *Rounds & Relays* for 2 Pianos (1997). VOCAL: *Two Accounts of Childhood* for Soprano or Mezzo-soprano and Piano (1964); *Ité* for Chorus (1964–88); *Save Me, O God* for Chorus (1965); *Apodoses* for Baritone and Piano (1966); *O God, My Heart is Fixed* for Chorus (1966); *Equinox I* (Baltimore, May 23, 1967) and *II* (Tanglewood, Aug. 14, 1968) for Soprano Ensemble; *Isonic* for Soprano, Flute, 2 Pianos, and Percussion (Graz, Oct. 26, 1970); *Lux Aeterna* for Chorus (1972); *Canti Trinacriani* for Baritone, Orch., and Tape (1975; Royan, March 2, 1976); *Tre Canzoni* for Soprano or Mezzo-soprano, Flute, and Cello (N.Y., May 18, 1976); *Vuci Siculani* for Mezzo-soprano, Flute, Clarinet, Guitar, and String Quartet (N.Y., Dec. 12, 1979); *Fantasia Celeste* for Soprano, Flute, Clarinet, Violin, Cello, Piano, and Percussion (Boston, April 4, 1983); *Six Ancient Greek Lyrics* for Soprano or Mezzo-soprano, Flute, Cello, and Piano (N.Y., Dec. 10, 1984); *Musiculi II* for Women's Voices and Orch. (1985–86; N.Y., Feb. 19, 1991) and *IV* for Chorus and Orch. (1990–92); *Eyes of the Peacock* for Soprano and Piano (1988); *I Shall Know Why* for Soprano or Mezzo-soprano, Chorus, and Piano (1988); *The Light of Heaven* for Soprano or Mezzo-soprano, Chorus, and Piano (1988); *Come Sing* for Chorus and Piano (1988); *O Blesed Bodie!* for Chorus (1988); *Greek Lyrics* for Soprano, Chorus, Piano, and Strings (N.Y., June 5, 1988); *Cinque Canti* for Baritone and Piano (1995; N.Y., March 13, 1997).—NS/LK/DM

Constant, Franz, Belgian composer and pianist; b. Montignies-le-Tilleul, Nov. 17, 1910. He studied at the Charleroi Academy of Music and at the Brussels Cons. with M. Maas, L. Jongen, Bourguignon, and Absil; he also studied with Tomasi in Paris. He became a concert pianist and formed a successful duo with his wife, Jeanne Pellaerts. In 1947 he was appointed to the faculty of the Brussels Cons. As a composer, Constant blends the modalities of the classical Belgian School with coloristic harmonies.

WORKS: ORCH.: *Rhapsodie* for Violin and Orch. (1962); Saxophone Concerto (1963); Trumpet Concerto (1965); Sinfonietta for Flute, Oboe, and Strings (1968); *Fantasia* for Saxophone and Orch. (1969); Concertino for Flute and Strings (1970); Violin Concerto (1971); *Rhapsodie* (1973); *Expressions* for Violin, Piano, and Strings (1973); Clarinet Concertino (1975); *Ballade du sud* for 2 Pianos and Orch. (1979); *Mouvement rhapsodie* for Double Bass and Orch. (1980); *Musique* for Saxophone Quartet and Strings (1981); *Quattro movimenti sinfonici* (1983); Concerto

for Accordion and Wind Orch. (1985); Concerto for Brass and Wind Orch. (1987). CHAMBER: *Allegro* for Trumpet and Piano (1959); *4 séquences* for 4 Saxophones (1962); *Impressions* for 4 Clarinets (1964); Flute Sonata (1967); *Évocation* for Flute and Piano (1969); *Suo tempore* for Violin and Piano (1969); *Dialogue* for Clarinet and Piano (1970); *Sonatine picturale* for Clarinet and Piano (1970); *Couleur provençale* for Horn and Piano (1970); *Pour la guitare I* and *II* (1971); *5 Miniatures* for Violin, Flute, and Piano (1971); Piano Quartet (1971); *Divertissement* for Bassoon and Piano (1972); *Rythme et expression* for Violin, Saxophone, Piano, and Percussion (1972); *Musique à deux* for Flute and Guitar (1973); *Musica lyrica* for Flute, Violin, and Piano or Harpsichord (1976); *Suite en trio* for Flute, Violin, and Piano (1977); *Rhapsodie d'été* for Clarinet Octet and Percussion (1977); *Odyssée* for Cello and Piano (1982); *Sonate a trois* for 2 Violins and Piano (1983); *Triptyque* for 2 Pianos and Percussion (1984); String Quartet (1985); *Impromptu* for Alto Saxophone and Piano (1987); many piano pieces. VOCAL: *Jeanne de Naples*, cantata for Soprano, Narrator, Children's Voices, Speaking and Singing Choruses, and Orch. (1972); *Histoires du dimanche* for Children's Chorus, and Piano or Ensemble of 11 Instruments (1973); songs. —NS/LK/DM

Constant, Marius, Romanian-born French conductor, composer, and teacher; b. Bucharest, Feb. 7, 1925. He first studied at the Bucharest Cons., where he took prizes in piano, harmony, counterpoint, and composition. In 1946 he settled in Paris and eventually became a naturalized French citizen. He was a student of Honegger, and also at the Cons. of Messiaen, Aubin, and Boulanger (premiers prix in composition and analysis, 1949), and at the École Normale de Musique of Fournet (conducting degree, 1949). He was active with the Groupe de Recherches Musicales du Club d'Essai de la Radio (1952–54), and was co-founder and director of the program France-Musique (1954–66). He also was chief conductor of the Ballets de Roland Petit (1957–63). In 1963 he founded Ars Nova, a contemporary music ensemble, which he served as music director until 1971. From 1973 to 1978 he was director of dance at the Paris Opéra. He was prof. of orchestration at the Paris Cons. (1979–88), and also taught composition and analysis at Stanford Univ. in Calif. Constant has won a number of honors for his compositions, including the Italia Prize (1952, 1987), the Koussevitzky Prize (1962), the Grand Prix National de la Musique (1969), and the "Victoires" de la Musique (1991). In 1993 he was elected a member of the Académie des Beaux-Arts, succeeding to the chair of Messiaen. In his compositions, Constant at first wrote along impressionistic lines. He later adopted a more advanced style in which he often made use of both serial and aleatory procedures.

WORKS: DRAMATIC: O p e r a : *Le Souper* (Besançon, Sept. 9, 1969); *Le jeu de Sainte Agnès* (Besançon, Sept. 6, 1974); *La Tragédie de Carmen* (Paris, Nov. 5, 1981); *Impressions de Pélléas* (Paris, Nov. 13, 1992); *Sade-Teresa* (1995); *Des Saisons en enfer* (Monte Carlo, April 28, 1999). B a l l e t : *Cyrano de Bergerac* (Paris, April 17, 1959); *Eloge de la folie* (Paris, March 11, 1966); *Paradis perdu* (London, Feb. 27, 1967); *Candide* (1970; Hamburg, Jan. 20, 1971); *Septentrion* (Marseilles, May 15, 1975); *Nana* (Paris, May 6, 1976); *L'Ange bleu* (Berlin, June 8, 1985). F i l m : *Napoléon* (1992). T e l e v i s i o n : *Twilight Zone*, signature theme (1959). ORCH.: *Musique de concert* for Alto Saxophone and Chamber Orch. (1955); *24 Préludes* (Paris, March 24, 1959);

Turner, 3 essays (Aix-en-Provence, July 17, 1961); *Chants de Maldoror* for Narrator and Orch. (Vicenza, Sept. 17, 1962); *Chaconne et Marche militaire* (Philadelphia, March 28, 1968); *Winds* for 14 Instruments (Aix-en-Provence, July 11, 1968); *Strings* for Electric Guitar and 12 Strings (1969; also for Harpsichord and 12 Strings, 1972); *Candide* for Harpsichord and Orch. (1970; Geneva, May 5, 1971); *Faciebat Anno 1973* for 24 Violins and Orch. (Aix-en-Provence, July 17, 1973); 3 syms.: No. 1, *Nana-Symphonie* (1976–80; Besançon, Sept. 12, 1980), No. 2, Sym. for Winds (Montreal, March 17, 1978), and No. 3, *Brevissima* (Madrid, Feb. 27, 1992); *Concerto Gli Elementi* for Trombone and Orch. (1977); *Stress* for Jazz Trio and Orch. (Châteauvallon, Aug. 21, 1977; in collaboration with M. Solal); Concertante for Alto Saxophone and Orch. (1978); *Harpalycée* for Harp and Strings (1980; also for Harp and String Quartet); *103 Regards dans l'eau* for Violin and Orch. (1981; also for Violin and 12 Instruments, 1983); *Perpetuo* (1986); *Texas Twilight* (1986); *Choruses and Interludes* for Horn, Orch., and Jazz Quartet (1987; Rheims, June 3, 1988); Barrel Organ Concerto (Cannes, April 10, 1988); *Konzertstück* for Oboe and Orch. (Toulon, May 30, 1990); *Hämeenlinna: An Imaginary Landscape* (Helsinki, May 23, 1991). **B a n d :** *L'inaguration de la maison* (1985). **CHAMBER:** Trio for Oboe, Clarinet, and Bassoon (1950); *Trois complexes* for Double Bass and Piano (1951); *Moulins à prières* for 2 Harpsichords (1969); *Equal* for 5 Percussionists (1970); *Quatorze stations* for Percussionist (1970); *9 Mars 1971: Hommage à Jean-Pierre Guezec* for Piccolo and Glockenspiel (1971); *Pour flûte et un instrument* (1972); *Silètes* for Harpsichord (1973); *Psyché* for 2 Pianos and 2 Percussion (1975); *For Clarinet* (1975); *9 Pièces* for Flute and Piano (1978); *Alleluias* for Trumpet and Organ (1980); *D'une élégie slave* for Guitar (1981); *Recitativo* for Viola (1983); *Pierres-Jewels* for 3 Cellos (1984); *Die Trennung* for String Quartet (1990); *Phantasma* for Violin and Piano (1990); *Blues-Variations* for Guitar and Electric Guitar (1990); *Matines* for Organ (1992). —NS/LK/DM

Constantinescu, Dan, Romanian composer and teacher; b. Bucharest, June 10, 1931; d. there, Feb. 6, 1993. He studied at the Bucharest Cons. (1950–55), where he then taught from 1956 to 1992.

WORKS: ORCH.: *Divertisment în stil clasic* for Strings (1954; Iaşi, Nov. 1, 1957); *Toma Alimos* (1955); Overture (1956); *Partita* (1957; Bucharest, Nov. 2, 1963); Concerto for Piano and Strings (1963; Cluj-Napoca, Dec. 3, 1966); *Simfonie de cameră* (1968; Cluj-Napoca, Feb. 1970); *Simfonie concertantă* (1970; Cluj-Napoca, Oct. 1975); Concerto for 2 Pianos and Orch. (1972; Cluj-Napoca, June 14, 1974); Sym. for Strings (1973); Sym for Winds (1975); Concerto for Harpsichord, Harp, and Winds (1979); *Concert de cameră* (1983). **CHAMBER:** 2 violin sonatas (1953, 1962); 2 string quartets (1955, 1967); Flute Sonata (1964); Trio for Piano, Clarinet, and Percussion (1964); Cello Sonata (1964); Clarinet Sonata (1965); *Variations* for Violin, Viola, Cello, and Piano (1966); *Mişcări* for Clarinet and String Trio (1974); String Sextet (1976); *Serenade* for String Quintet (Craiova, June 20, 1978); Quarter for Harp, Flute, Clarinet, and Bassoon (1979); Quartet for Harpsichord, Trumpet, Horn, and Trombone (1979). **KEYBOARD: P i a n o :** 2 sonatas (1953, 1961) and other pieces. **VOCAL:** Choral works and songs.—NS/LK/DM

Constantinescu, Paul, eminent Romanian composer and pedagogue; b. Ploieşti, July 13, 1909; d. Bucharest, Dec. 20, 1963. He studied with Castaldi, Jora, Cuclin, and Brăiloiu at the Bucharest Cons. (1928–33) and with Schmidt and Marx in Vienna (1934–35). Re-

turning to Bucharest, he taught at the academy for religious music (1937–41) and then was a prof. of composition at the Cons. from 1941 until his death. In 1932 he received the Enesco prize and in 1956 the Romanian Academy prize. Constantiescu made use of folk and liturgical elements in his works, developing a style marked by an assured command of form and modal harmony. He did much to chart the course for the post-Enesco generation of Romanian nationalist composers.

WORKS: DRAMATIC: *O noapte furtunoasă*, comic opera (1934; rev. 1950; Bucharest, May 19, 1951); *Nunta în Carpaţi*, choreographic poem (Bucharest, May 5, 1938); *Pană Lesnea Rusalim*, opera (1954–55; Cluj-Napoca, June 26, 1956). **ORCH.:** *Suită românească* (1930–36; rev. 1942); *Jocuri româneşti* (1936); *Burlescă* for Piano and Orch. (1937; Bucharest Radio, March 7, 1938); *Simfonietă* (1937; Bucharest Radio, March 16, 1938); 2 syms.: No. 1 (1944; Bucharest, May 18, 1947; rev. 1955) and No. 2, *Simfonie ploieşteană* (Ploieşti, Sept. 29, 1961); *Variatuni libere asupra unei melodii bizantine din sec. XIII* for Cello and Orch. (1946; rev. 1951); Concerto for Strings (1947; rev. 1955; Bucharest, Feb. 16, 1956); *Rapsodia II* (1949; Bucharest, Oct. 15, 1950); *Baladă haiducească* for Cello and Orch. (1950; Bucharest, Dec. 23, 1951); *Suită bucovineană* (1951); Piano Concerto (1952; Bucharest, May 16, 1953); *Juventus*, overture (1952); *Rapsodie oltenească* (1957); Violin Concerto (1957; Brasov, May 21, 1958); *Înfrăţire*, choreographic rhapsody (Bucharest, Aug. 20, 1959); Harp Concerto (1960; Bucharest, May 4, 1961); Triple Concerto for Violin, Cello, Piano, and Orch. (Bucharest, Dec. 28, 1963). **CHAMBER:** *2 Studii în stil bizantin* for Violin, Viola, and Cello (1929); Quintet (1932); Violin Sonatina (1933); *Sonatină bizantină* for Solo Cello or Viola (1940); *Cîntec vechi pe 2 melodii din Anton Pann* for Cello and Piano (1952); piano pieces. **VOCAL:** *Isarlîk* for Soprano and Orch. (1936); *Ryga Crypto şi Lapona Enigel* for Soli, Reciter, and Orch. (1936; rev. 1951; Bucharest, June 1, 1966); *Byzantinisches Passions und Osteroratorium* for Soli, Chorus, and Orch. (1943; Bucharest, March 3, 1946; rev. 1948); *Byzantinisches Weihnachtoratorium* for Soli, Chorus, and Orch. (Bucharest, Dec. 21, 1947); *Uliţa noastră*, 7 songs for Baritone and orch. (1960); other songs.

BIBL.: V. Tomescu, *P. C.* (Bucharest, 1967).—NS/LK/DM

Conti, Carlo, Italian composer and pedagogue; b. Arpino, Oct. 14, 1796; d. there, July 10, 1868. He studied in Naples with Zingarelli at the Reale Collegio di Musica di S. Sebatiano, where his opera *Le truppe in Franconia* was premiered while he was still a student in 1819 and won the high praise of Rossini. He also studied with J.S. Mayr. After teaching at the Reale Collegio di Musica di S. Sebastiano from 1819 to 1821, he pursued a career as a composer of operas, garnering his most popular success with *L'Olimpia* (Naples, oct. 28, 1826). In 1831 he gave up composing and settled in Arpino. From 1846 to 1858 he again taught at the Reale Collegio di Musica di S. Sebastiano, where he was made its asst. director in 1862. Conti was an honorary member, and later president, of the Royal Academy of Arts in Naples. He was also elected an assoc. member of the Institut de France in Paris. His operas, in the style of Rossini, are the work of a fine craftsman.

WORKS: DRAMATIC: O p e r a (all 1st perf. in Naples unless otherwise given): *Le truppe in Franconia* (1819); *La pace desiderata* (1820); *Misantropia e pentimento* (Feb. 4, 1823); *Il trionfo* *della giustizia* (1823); *L'Olimpia* (Oct. 28, 1826); *L'audacia fortunata* (Rome, Carnival 1827); *I finti sposi* (Rome, Carnival 1827); *Bartolomeo dela Cavalla, overo L'innocente in periglio* (Rome, Sept. 10, 1827); *Gli Aragonesi in Napoli* (Dec. 29, 1827); *Alexi* (July 6, 1828; in collaboration with N. Vaccai); *Giovanna Shore* (Milan, Oct. 31, 1829).—**NS/LK/DM**

Conti, Francesco Bartolomeo, eminent Italian composer, theorbist, and mandolinist; b. Florence, Jan. 20, 1681; d. Vienna, July 20, 1732. He settled in Vienna, and was assoc. theorbist (1701–06; 1707–08) and principal theorbist (1708–26) at the court. In 1713 he also became court composer. After the death of his first wife in 1711, he married the court prima donna Maria Landini, who sang the principal roles in his operas between 1714 and 1721. Following her death in 1722, he married the court prima donna Maria Anna Lorenzani in 1725, who also sang the principal roles in his operas. Conti was an outstanding composer of both secular and sacred dramatic works. His tragicommedia, *Don Chisciotte in Sierra Morena* (Vienna, Carnival 1719), was one of his most remarkable works. His son, Ignazio Maria Conti (b. probably in Florence, 1699; d. Vienna, March 28, 1759), was a theorbist and composer who was active at the court in Vienna from 1719. Among his works were operas, oratorios, masses, and cantatas.

WORKS: DRAMATIC (all 1st perf. in Vienna unless otherwise given): *Clotilde* (1706); *Il trionfo dell'amicizia e dell'amore* (Carnival 1711; rev. as *Il trionfo dell'amore e della costanza,* Hamburg, Jan. 1718); *Circe fatta saggia* (Aug. 28, 1713); *Alba Cornelia* (Carnival 1714; rev. version, Breslau, Carnival 1726); *I Sattiri in Arcadia* (Aug. 28, 1714); *Il Ciro* (Carnival 1715; in collaboration with Bagatella, Mamalucca, and Pattatocco); *Teseo in Creta* (Aug. 28, 1715; in collaboration with Galantina and Pampalugo); *Il finto Policare* (Jan. 24, 1716); *Sesostri, re di Egitto* (Jan. 24, 1717; in collaboration with Grilletta and Pimpinone); *Astarto* (Carnival, 1718; in collaboration with Farfalletta, Lirone, and Terremoto); *Amore in Tessaglia* (Aug. 28, 1718); *Don Chisciotte in Sierra Morena* (Carnival 1719; rev. version, Hamburg, 1720); *Cloris und Thyrsis* (Hamburg, April 26, 1719); *Galatea vendicata* (Nov. 19, 1719); *Alessandro in Sidone* (Carnival 1721; rev. version, Braunschweig, Aug. 1726); *La via del saggio* (Oct. 1, 1721); *Archelao, re di Cappadocia* (Carnival 1722); *Pallade trionfante* (Nov. 19, 1722); *Creso* (Carnival 1723); *Il trionfo della fama* (Prague, Nov. 4, 1723); *Penelope* (Carnival 1724); *Meleagro* (Nov. 19, 1724); *Griselda* (Carnival 1725; in collaboration with Erighetta and Don Chilone); *Isicratea* (Nov. 19, 1726); *Issipile* (Carnival 1732; rev. version, Hamburg, Feb. 20, 1737). **OTHER:** 10 oratorios; many cantatas and other sacred works; instrumental pieces.

BIBL.: J. Schneider, *F. C. als dramatischer Componist* (diss., Univ. of Vienna, 1902); H. Williams, *F.B. C.: His Life and Operas* (diss., Columbia Univ., 1964); H. Williams, *F.B. C.: His Life and Music* (Brookfoeld, Vt., 1999).—**NS/LK/DM**

Conti, Gioacchino, celebrated Italian castrato soprano, known as "Gizziello" and "Egizziello," after his teacher; b. Arpino, Feb. 28, 1714; d. Rome, Oct. 25, 1761. He began study at the age of eight with Domenico Gizzi in Naples, making his debut in Vinci's *Artaserse* in Rome (Feb. 4, 1730), where he scored a triumph. He subsequently sang in various Italian music centers, and also appeared in Vienna. Handel then called him to London,

where he made his debut in *Ariodante* at Covent Garden (May 5, 1736; he had no time to learn the title role, however, and was compelled to sing Italian arias); he then created the roles of Meleager in *Atalanta* (May 12, 1736), Sigismondo in *Arminio* (Jan. 12, 1737), Anastasio in *Giustino* (Feb. 16, 1737), and Alessandro in *Berenice* (May 18, 1737), all of which were composed for him by Handel. Returning to Italy, he sang in Rome (1738, 1741), Padua (1739), and Florence (1742); after a sojourn in Lisbon (from 1743), he returned to Italy and sang in Naples (1747–50), Lucca (1749), and Padua (1751). He appeared at the court theater of Lisbon (1752–55) before retiring in Italy. Conti possessed a brilliant voice with a compass of 2 octaves.—**NS/LK/DM**

Contiguglia, Richard and John, brilliant American duo-pianists; b. identical twins, N.Y., April 13, 1937. They began taking piano lessons in early childhood, and grew in parallel congruence. They played in a duo recital in public when they were six, and continued to develop in close consanguinity; they composed music for two pianos and transcribed solo works for their concerts. When they were 12, Percy Grainger invited them to play at one of his recitals; he subsequently befriended them and gave them valuable advice. Later they took piano lessons with Jean Wilder and with Bruce Simonds at Yale Univ., and upon graduation received a Ditson Fellowship, which enabled them to study with Dame Myra Hess in London. They made their professional debut in London in 1962, playing piano Four-Hands; in 1964 they made a major European tour. In addition to the standard literature for duo-pianos, they performed piano transcriptions for two pianos and for piano Four-Hands of obscure works. In 1971 they gave an all-Liszt concert in London, which included his piano transcription of his symphonic poems *Mazeppa* and *Orpheus,* and of his arrangements of excerpts from Bellini's *Norma* and *La Sonnambula* and Mozart's *Don Giovanni.* In 1972 they played Liszt's transcriptions of Beethoven's Ninth Sym. in London, arousing considerable curiosity, and repeated this exhibition in N.Y. in 1974. They gave the first performance of Liszt's *Grosses Konzertstück über Mendelssohn's "Lieder ohne Worte"* for two Pianos, composed in 1834, in Utrecht on Oct. 19, 1986. They further played duo-piano works by Bartók and Grainger. For a brief period, they split their original fetal name into two fungible parts, Conti-Guglia.—**NS/LK/DM**

Conus, Georgi (Eduardovich), Russian composer, pedagogue, and music theorist, brother of **Julius Conus;** b. Moscow, Sept. 30, 1862; d. there, Aug. 29, 1933. After studies with his father, he was a student of Pabst (piano) and Arensky and Taneyev (composition) at the Moscow Cons., where he then taught theory (1891–99). He was prof. of composition (1902–06) and director (1904–05) of the music and drama institute of the Moscow Phil. Soc. After serving as prof. of composition (1902–19) and rector (1917–19) at the Saratov Cons., he was a prof. at the Moscow Cons. (from 1920). Among his pupils were Scriabin, Vasilenko, Medtner, Kabalevsky, and Khachuturian. He originated a theory of metric analysis (metrotectonism, i.e. measured structure), which he outlined in his writings (Moscow, 1932, 1933). He composed symphonic scores, a ballet, piano pieces, and songs.

BIBL.: P. Krilov, *G.E. C.* (Moscow, 1932); G. Golovinsky, ed., *G.E. C.: Stati, materiali, vospominaniya* (G.E. C.: Articles, materials, reminiscences; Moscow, 1965).—**NS/LK/DM**

Conus, Julius, Russian violinist and composer, brother of **Georgi (Eduardovich) Conus** and father of **Sergei Conus;** b. Moscow, Feb. 1, 1869; d. Malenki, Ivanov District, Jan. 3, 1942. He studied at the Moscow Cons., where he later taught violin. He was a friend of Tchaikovsky and was greatly esteemed in Moscow musical circles. His Violin Concerto, first performed by him in Moscow in 1898, has retained its popularity in Russia.—**NS/LK/DM**

Conus, Sergei, Russian-American pianist and composer, son of **Julius Conus;** b. Moscow, Oct. 18, 1902. He studied music with his father and his uncle, Leo Conus, and with Oskar Riesemann. In 1920 he went to Paris, where he studied piano with Cortot and Philipp; then lived in Serbia, Bulgaria, and Poland. He was again in France from 1937 to 1949, and in Morocco from 1949 to 1959. He then settled in America, where he taught piano at the Boston Cons. His compositions are mostly for piano (24 preludes, many miniatures, a concerto); he also wrote a Sym. His style is characteristically Russian, closely resembling that of Rachmaninoff.—**NS/LK/DM**

Converse, Frederick Shepherd, distinguished American composer and teacher; b. Newton, Mass., Jan. 5, 1871; d. Westwood, Mass., June 8, 1940. After graduating from Harvard Univ. (1893), he studied music in Boston with Carl Baermann and Chadwick (1894–96), then in Munich at the Royal Academy of Music with Rheinberger (graduated, 1898). Returning to Boston, he taught harmony at the New England Cons. of Music (1900–1902; 1920–36; dean, 1931–37) and was a composition instructor at Harvard Univ. (1901–07). He received a Mus.Doc. from Boston Univ. (1933); became a member of the American Academy of Arts and Letters (1937). His early works reflect the influence of academic German training; later he began to apply more advanced harmonies; in his *Flivver 10 Million*, written to glorify the 10 millionth Ford car, he adopted a frankly modern idiom, modeled after Honegger's *Pacific 231*. He sketched some material for a fifth Sym. in 1937, but did not complete it. He renumbered his syms. in 1936, calling his previously unnumbered Sym. No. 1 and upping Nos. 1, 2, and 3 by one, giving the title of Sym. No. 5 to the undeveloped sketches for that work. But his Syms. Nos. 2, 3, and 4 were premiered, respectively, as Nos. 1, 2, and 3.

WORKS: DRAMATIC: O p e r a : *The Pipe of Desire* (1905; Boston, Jan. 31, 1906); *The Sacrifice* (1910; Boston, March 3, 1911); *Sinbad the Sailor* (1913); *The Immigrants* (1914). ORCH.: Syms.: D minor (Munich, July 14, 1898), No. 1 (c. 1919; Boston, Jan. 30, 1920), No. 2 (1921; Boston, April 21, 1922), No. 3 (1936), and No. 6 (Indianapolis, Nov. 29, 1940); *Youth*, overture (1895; rev. 1897); *Festival March* (1899); *Festival of Pan* (1899; Boston, Dec. 21, 1900); *Endymion's Narrative* (1901; Boston, April 9,

1903); *Night and Day* (1901; Boston, Jan. 21, 1905); Violin Concerto (1902); *Euphrosyne*, overture (1903); *The Mystic Trumpeter* (1904; Philadelphia, March 3, 1905); *Ormazd*, tone poem (1911; St. Louis, Jan. 26, 1912); *Ave atque vale*, tone poem (1916; St. Louis, Jan. 26, 1917); *Fantasia* for Piano and Orch. (1922); *Song of the Sea*, tone poem (1923; Boston, April 18, 1924); *Elegiac Poem* (1925; Cleveland, Dec. 2, 1926); *Flivver 10 Million*, epic tone poem (1926; Boston, April 15, 1927); *California*, descriptive tone poem (1927; Boston, April 6, 1928); *American Sketches*, symphonic suite (1928; Boston, Feb. 8, 1935); Piano Concertino (1932); *Salutation*, concert march (1935); *3 Old-fashioned Dances* for Chamber Orch. (1938); *Rhapsody* for Clarinet and Orch. (1938); *Haul Away, Jo!*, variations on an American sea shanty (1939). CHAMBER: 3 string quartets (1896, rev. 1901; 1904; 1935); Septet for Clarinet, Bassoon, Horn, Piano, and String Trio (1897); Piano Trio (1932); *Prelude and Intermezzo* for Brass Sextet (1938); *2 Lyric Pieces* for Brass Quintet (1939); piano pieces. VOCAL: O r a t o r i o s : *Job*, dramatic poem for Soli, Chorus, and Orch. (Worcester Festival, Oct. 2, 1907); *Hagar in the Desert*, dramatic narrative for Low Voice and Orch. (Hamburg, 1908). C a n t a t a s : *The Peace Pipe* (1914); *The Answer of the Stars* (1919); *The Flight of the Eagle* (1930). O t h e r : *La Belle Dame sans merci*, ballade for Baritone with Orch. (1902); *Psalm, I Will Praise Thee, O Lord* (1924); choruses; songs.

BIBL.: R. Severence, *The Life and Works of F.S. C.* (diss., Boston Univ., 1932); R. Garofalo, *The Life and Works of F.S. C. (1871–1940)* (diss., Catholic Univ. of America, Washington, D.C., 1969).—**NS/LK/DM**

Conway, Patrick, American bandmaster, conductor, and music educator; b. near Troy, N.Y., July 4, 1867; d. Ithaca, N.Y., June 10, 1929. He received training in cornet from Charles Bates. As a youth, he played in the Homer Band, becoming its director while still in his teens. After attending the Ithaca Cons. of Music and Cornell Univ., he conducted the latter's Cadet Band (1895–1908). He also founded his own band, which took the name Patrick Conway and his Band in 1908. From 1914 to 1916 he was conductor of the Syracuse (N.Y.) Sym. Orch. In 1916 he became a captain in the U.S. Army Air Service, where he supervised its music program and founded its band. In 1922 he founded the Conway Military Band School of the Ithaca Cons. of Music. Conway was highly regarded as one of America's leading bandmasters.—**LK/DM**

Cooder, Ry, arguably one of the best all-around guitarists in rock music, has played innumerable sessions and recorded a series of modest-selling albums that explored a diverse set of material, from folk to blues, from country to gospel and rock, as well as Dixieland and TexMex and Hawaiian music; b. Los Angeles, March 15, 1947. An outstanding bottleneck guitarist, Cooder won his first widespread acclaim as lead guitarist with Little Village, along with fellow musical iconoclasts Nick Lowe and John Hiatt.

Ry Cooder took up guitar at age ten and began frequenting Los Angeles's Ash Groove folk club as a teenager. Self-taught on mandolin, banjo, and bottleneck guitar, Cooder briefly worked with singer-songwriter Jackie De Shannon in 1963 and formed the Rising Sons with Taj Mahal and Jesse Ed Davis in 1965. The group recorded one single for Columbia before breaking up. Cooder subsequently joined Captain Beefheart, recording on his album *Safe as Milk* and performing on one tour before pursuing session work with Taj Mahal, Neil Young, Paul Revere and the Raiders, the Rolling Stones, Longbranch Pennywhistle (with J. D. Souther and future Eagle Glenn Frey), Randy Newman, and Gordon Lightfoot, among others.

Signed to Reprise Records, Ry Cooder initiated his solo recording career with a self-named debut album. Through 1972 he recorded two more solo albums and worked on the debut albums of Little Feat, Rita Coolidge, and Crazy Horse. He also assisted the Rolling Stones with the recordings of the soundtrack *Performance*, *Sticky Fingers*, and *Jammin' with Edward*. Cooder began working with gospel singer Bobby King, who guested on Cooder's classic album *Paradise and Lunch*, which featured "Mexican Divorce," "If Walls Could Talk," and "Jesus on the Mainline." Terry Evans joined Bobby King for gospel backups for *Chicken Skin Music*, which included Cooder's idols Hawaiian guitarist Gabby Pahinui on two songs and Tex-Mex accordionist Flaco Jimenez on three others. Cooder's session work continued with Randy Newman, Arlo Guthrie, Maria Muldaur, John Sebastian, and Gabby Pahinui.

Cooder made a series of radical changes in style, beginning with his album *Jazz*, which explored Dixieland. The follow-up *Bop Till You Drop* celebrated early rock and roll. It was probably Cooder's best-seller, featuring another guitar god, David Lindley, and including the favorites "Little Sister," "The Very Thing That Makes You Rich," and "Down in Hollywood," cowritten by Cooder. Cooder returned to an eclectic mixture of material on his next two albums, *Borderline*, which featured John Hiatt's "The Way We Make a Broken Heart" and Cooder's title song, and *The Slide Area*, which included two songs written by Cooder and session drummer Jim Keltner (most notably "I'm Drinking Again") and three others cowritten by Cooder.

During the 1980s Ry Cooder found a new outlet for his talents: composing, arranging, and performing soundtracks for films, including *The Long Riders* (1980), *The Border* (1982), *Paris, Texas* and *Alamo Bay* (1985), *Blue City* and *Crossroads* (1986), and *Johnny Handsome* (1989). In 1983 he guested on Eric Clapton's *Money and Cigarettes* album and subsequent tour, inspiring some of Clapton's best guitar playing in a number of years. In 1987 Cooder joined Nick Lowe and Jim Kelnher in the recording of John Hiatt's breakthrough album, *Bring the Family*. The following year backup gospel singers Bobby King and Terry Evans began recording for Rounder Records. After more than 25 years of recording, Ry Cooder finally received a modicum of recognition with the group, tour, and album *Little Village*, a collaborative effort recorded with Hiatt, Lowe, and Keltner. However, the band soon dissolved due to the clash of egos among the individual members. Cooder next recorded the outstanding *Talking Timbuktu* with Ali Farka Touré from the African nation of Mali, a unique cross-cultural exploration.

DISC.: **THE RISING SONS:** *The Rising Sons Featuring Taj Mahal and R. C.* (1992). **RY COODER:** *R. C.* (1970); *Into the Purple Valley* (1971); *Boomer's Story* (1972); *Paradise and Lunch* (1974); *Chicken Skin Music* (1976); *Showtime* (1977); *Jazz* (1978); *Bop Till You Drop* (1979); *Borderline* (1980); *The Slide Area* (1982); *Get Rhythm* (1987). **RY COODER SOUNDTRACKS:** *Paris, Texas* (1985); *Blue City* (1986); *Crossroads* (1986); *Johnny Handsome* (1989); *Trespass* (1992); *Geronimo* (1993); *Music by R. C.* (1995). **BOBBY KING AND TERRY EVANS:** *Live and Let Live!* (1988); *Rhythm, Blues, Soul and Grooves* (1990). **TERRY EVANS:** *Blues for Thought* (1994); *Puttin' It Down* (1995). **LITTLE VILLAGE:** *Little Village* (1992). **ALI FARKA TOURÉ WITH RY COODER:** *Talking Timbuktu* (1994). —BH

Cook, Doc (originally, **Cooke, Charles L.**), jazz pianist, band leader, arranger; b. Louisville, Ky., Sept. 3, 1891; d. Wurtsboro, N.Y., Dec. 25, 1958. In 1909 he was working as a composer–arranger in Detroit; he subsequently moved to Chicago where he led his own bands at several venues, while acting as musical director for Riverview Park. From 1922 led his own ten-piece band at Harmon's Dreamland, Chicago, and played there regularly for almost six years. This band featured many leading Chicago jazz luminaries, including Freddie Keppard and Jimmie Noone; the full band recorded on several occasions, as did a smaller group drawn from the orch. called Cook's Gingersnaps. After the Dreamland job ended, Cook worked at other area theaters and clubs until moving to N.Y. in 1930. During the 1930s he was a staff arranger at R.K.O, and at Radio City Music Hall, occupied similar positions during the early 1940s, then left full-time music and retired to N.J. Cook was a Doctor of Music, having gained this honor at the Chicago Coll. of Music in 1926, having previously received a Bachelor of Music at Chicago Musical Coll. For this reason, he was usually billed as "Doc" Cook. —JC/LP

Cook, Thomas (Aynsley), English bass; b. London, July 1831 or 1836; d. Liverpool, Feb. 16, 1894. He was a pupil of Hopkins at the City Temple in London, and of Staudigl in Munich. After singing in Germany, he made his British debut as a member of Lucy Escott's National English Opera Co. in Manchester in 1856. Following a tour of the U.S. with Escott, he joined the Pyne-Harrison Co. in London in 1862. After singing with the English Opera Co., he appeared at the Gaiety Theatre from 1870 to 1872. From 1875 he was a member of the Carl Rosa Opera Co. Cook was the maternal grandfather of **Sir Eugene, Marie, Leon,** and **Sidonie Goossens.**—NS/LK/DM

Cook, Will Marion, black American conductor and composer; b. Washington, D.C., Jan. 27, 1869; d. N.Y., July 19, 1944. He entered the Oberlin (Ohio) Cons. to study violin when he was 13, continuing his studies with Joachim in Germany and at the National Cons. in N.Y. He had a brief career as a concert violinist before devoting himself to composition for the black musical theater in N.Y.; he was director and composer for the Bert Williams-George Walker productions (1900–1908) and founded his own "syncopated" sym. orch. (1918), with which he toured extensively. In his later years, he was active mainly as a conductor and teacher in N.Y.

WORKS: DRAMATIC: Musicals (all 1st perf. in N.Y.): *Clorindy, or the Origin of the Cakewalk* (July 5, 1898); *Jes' Lak White Fo'ks* (1899); *The Cannibal King* (1901); *In Dahomey* (Feb. 18, 1903; in collaboration with others); *The Southerners* (May 23, 1904); *Abyssinia* (Feb. 10, 1906; in collaboration with others); *Bandana Land* (Feb. 3, 1908; in collaboration with others); *The Traitor* (March 1913; in collaboration with others); *Darkeydom* (Oct. 23, 1915; in collaboration with others); *Swing Along* (1929; in collaboration with W. Vodery). **OTHER:** Choral works; songs.—**NS/LK/DM**

Cooke, Arnold (Atkinson), English composer and pedagogue; b. Gomersal, Yorkshire, Nov. 4, 1906. He studied with Dent at Caius Coll., Cambridge (B.A., 1928; B.Mus., 1929), returning there to take his D.Mus. in 1948; he also studied with Hindemith at the Berlin Hochschule für Musik (1929–32). He served as prof. of harmony, counterpoint, and composition at the Royal Manchester Coll. of Music (1933–38), and later at Trinity Coll. of Music in London (1947–77); in 1953 he also was chairman of the Composers Guild of Great Britain. His works are composed in an agreeable tonal idiom.

WORKS: DRAMATIC: Opera: *Mary Barton* (1949–52); *The Invisible Duke* (1975). **Ballet:** *Jabez and the Devil* (1962). **ORCH.:** *Concert Overture No. 1* (1934) and *No. 2, The Processional* (1946); Piano Concerto (1939–40); 6 syms. (1946–47; 1963; 1967; 1974; 1978–79, London, July 17, 1981; 1983–84); Concerto for Strings (1948); Concerto for Oboe and Strings (1954); Sinfonietta for Chamber Orch. (1954); Concerto for Clarinet and Strings (1955); Concerto for Recorder or Flute and Strings (1956); Violin Concerto (1958); Concerto for Small Orch. (1966); *Variations on a Theme of Dufay* (1966); *York Suite* (1972); Cello Concerto (1972–73); *Repton Fantasia* (1984); *Concerto for Orchestra* (1986). **CHAMBER:** Cello Sonata (1925–26); 2 numbered cello sonatas (1941; 1979–80); String Quartet (1927–28); 5 numbered string quartets (1933, 1947, 1967, 1976, 1978); Quintet for Harp, Flute, Clarinet, Violin, and Cello (1932); Quartet for Flute and String Trio (1936); Viola Sonata (1936–37); 2 violin sonatas (1939, 1951); Piano Trio (1944); Quartet for Oboe and String Trio (1948); Piano Quartet (1949); String Trio (1950); Quintet for Horn, Violin, 2 Violas, and Piano (1955); 3 oboe sonatas (1957, 1959, 1962); Clarinet Sonata (1959); Wind Quintet (1961); Quintet for Clarinet and String Quartet (1962); Quartet for Flute, Clarinet, Cello, and Piano (1964); Quartet-Sonata for Recorder, Violin, Cello, and Harpsichord (1964); Trio for Clarinet, Cello, and Piano (1965); Quintet for Piano and String Quartet (1969); Harmonica Sonata (1970); Septet for 7 Clarinets (1971); Quartet for 4 Clarinets (1977); Trio for Oboe, Clarinet, and Bassoon (1984); Alto Flute Sonata (1985); Bassoon Sonata (1987); Sonata for Flute and Harp (1988); also piano and organ music. **VOCAL:** Cantatas: *Holderneth* (1933–34) and *Ode on St. Cecilia's Day* (1964); anthems; choruses; songs.—**NS/LK/DM**

Cooke, Benjamin, English organist and composer; b. London, 1734; d. there, Sept. 14, 1793. He studied with Pepusch, whom he succeeded in 1752 as conductor at the Academy of Ancient Music. In 1757 he became choirmaster (after Gates), in 1758 lay vicar, and in 1762 organist, of Westminster Abbey. He received a Mus.Doc. from Cambridge (1775) and from Oxford (1782). He became organist of St. Martin-in-the-Fields in 1782, resigning the Academy conductorship in 1789 in favor of Arnold. His best works are in the form of glees,

canons, and catches, for which he took several Catch Club prizes (*Collection of 20 Glees, Catches, and Canons for 3–6 Voices in Score*, London, 1775; *9 Glees and 2 Duets*, 1795). He also wrote odes, instrumental concertos, church music, pieces for organ and harpsichord, etc., and added choruses and accompaniments to Pergolesi's *Stabat Mater* (1759) and Galliard's *Morning Hymn* (1772) for the Academy of Ancient Music. His son Robert Cooke (b. Westminster, 1768; d. Aug. 13, 1814) became organist of St. Martin-in-the-Fields after his father's death in 1793, and on the death of Arnold, in 1802, was appointed organist and choirmaster of Westminster Abbey. He ended his life by drowning himself in the Thames. He publ. a collection of glees in 1805. —**NS/LK/DM**

Cooke, Deryck (Victor), English writer on music; b. Leicester, Sept. 14, 1919; d. Thornton Heath, Oct. 26, 1976. He studied composition with Hadley and Orr at the Univ. of Cambridge (B.A., 1940; M.A., 1943; Mus.B., 1947) and then worked in the BBC music dept. (1947–59; 1965–76). He prepared a performing version of the odd-numbered movements of Mahler's Tenth Sym. for a BBC broadcast on Dec. 19, 1960. The composer's widow, Alma, forbade any further broadcasts or performances, but was eventually convinced of the merits of the score and supplied Cooke with 24 unpubl. pages of fragments with which he completed the sym. (new version, London, Aug. 13, 1964). Further revisions were made with the assistance of Colin and David Matthews before the work was publ. in 1976. Since then the Mahler-Cooke version has been performed throughout the world.

WRITINGS (all publ. in London): *The Language of Music* (1959); *Mahler 1860–1911* (1960; rev. and enl. ed., 1980, as *Gustav Mahler: An Introduction to His Music*); *I Saw the World End: A Study of Wagner's Ring* (1979); *Variations: Essays on Romantic Music* (1982).—**NS/LK/DM**

Cooke, Henry, English bass, choirmaster, and composer; b. probably in Lichfield, c. 1615; d. Hampton Court, July 13, 1672. He was a member of the Chapel Royal before serving in the royalist army during the Civil War, in which he attained the rank of captain. Thereafter, he was known as Captain Cooke. During the Cromwellian era, he was a singer and composer for the London stage. At the Restoration in 1660, he was made a singer and composer in the King's Private Musicke and master of the boys there. In 1660 he was also charged with organizing the children of the Chapel Royal, whose choir became deservedly renowned under his direction. Among his pupils were Blow, Humfrey, Tudway, and Wise. His extant works include 13 anthems, three court odes, and songs.

BIBL.: H. Dussauze, *"Captain" C. and His Choirboys* (diss., Univ. of Paris, 1911).—**LK/DM**

Cooke, Sam, one of the most popular and influential black singers to emerge in the late 1950s; b. Clarksdale, Miss., Jan. 2 or 22, 1931 (although some claim Chicago, Jan. 2 or 22, 1935); d. Los Angeles, Calif., Dec. 11, 1964. The son of Reverend Charles Cooke, Sam

Cooke was raised in Chicago where he was a member of the family gospel quartet, the Singing Children, at age nine. Performing in the gospel group The Highway Q.C.s in high school, Cooke joined the Soul Stirrers, one of the most popular and influential gospel quartets of the 1940s, as lead vocalist around 1950. He remained with the Soul Stirrers until 1956. Cooke also briefly manned the Pilgrim Travelers with Lou Rawls.

In 1956 Sam Cooke, under the name Dale Cook, began recording pop material for Specialty Records. In late 1957 he scored a top R&B and pop hit on Keen Records with "You Send Me," written by his brother Charles "L.C." Cooke. Subsequent smash R&B and major pop hits through 1960 included "I'll Come Running Back to You" on Specialty and "You Were Made For Me," "Win Your Love for Me," "Everybody Loves to Cha Cha Cha," the classic "Only Sixteen" and "Wonderful World" on Keen.

In 1960 Sam Cooke accepted a lucrative offer to join RCA Records. Recorded with cloying pop arrangements featuring strings and horns under producers Hugo (Peretti) and Luigi (Creatore), Cooke scored a series of hits between 1960 and 1964. These included the pop and R&B smashes "Chain Gang," "Twistin' the Night Away" and "Another Saturday Night"; the hits "Cupid," "Bring It on Home to Me" backed with "Having a Party," "Nothing Can Change This Love," "Send Me Some Lovin'," "Frankie and Johnny," and "Little Red Rooster. "(Ain't That) Good News" and "Good Times" became major R&B and pop hits.

In 1961 Sam Cooke launched Sar Records, followed by Derby Records in 1963. R&B/pop hits on Sar included "Lookin' for a Love" (1962) and "It's All Over Now" (1964) by the Valentinos (later covered by the J. Geils Band and the Rolling Stones, respectively), "Soothe Me" by the Sims Twins (1961), and "Meet Me at the Twistin' Place" by Johnnie Morisette (1962). "When a Boy Falls in Love" became a moderate hit for Mel Carter on Derby in 1963.

In early 1964 Cooke announced that he was going to cut back on his touring to concentrate on running his record labels. Later that year the live set *At the Copa* was issued, but a far more representative set, *Feel It! Live at the Harlem Square Club, 1963*, recorded with saxophonist King Curtis, was eventually released in 1985.

Sam Cooke's career was secure by 1964, with enormous promise for the future, but on Dec. 11, 1964, he was shot to death in Los Angeles. Posthumously, his "Shake" (covered by Otis Redding in 1967) became a near-smash hit in 1965, followed by his most enduring composition, "A Change Is Gonna Come," only a few days later.

Cooke was one of the first black recording artists to successfully synthesize a popular blend of gospel music styling and secular themes. Eschewing the harsher shouting style of Ray Charles and emphasizing his high, clear, sensual tenor voice, Cooke, along with Charles, helped pioneer the sound that became known as soul music, influencing black singers from Smokey Robinson to Al Green, and Otis Redding to Aretha Franklin, and white British singers such as Mick Jagger and Rod Stewart. Along with James Brown, Cooke was one of the first black artists to write his own songs and gain control over his recording career (also founding two record labels). He demonstrated a growing sense of social consciousness with the moving "A Change Is Gonna Come." Cooke was inducted into the Rock and Roll Hall of Fame in its inaugural year, 1986, and the Soul Stirrers were inducted into the Hall as Early Influences in 1990.

DISC.: SAM COOKE: *Two Sides of Sam Cooke* (1957); *Sam Cooke Sings* (1958); *Encore* (1958); *Tribute to the Lady* (1959); *Encore, Vol. 2* (1959); *Hit Kid* (1960); *I Thank God* (1960); *Wonderful World* (1960); *Cooke's Tour* (1960); *One and Only* (1960); *Sam's Songs* (1961); *Only Sixteen* (1961); *So Wonderful* (1961); *Sam Cooke—Swing Low* (1961); *My Kind of Blues* (1961); *You Send Me* (1962); *Cha Cha Cha* (1962); *Twistin' the Night Away* (1962); *Mister Soul* (1963); *Night Beat* (1963); *Ain't That Good News* (1964); *At the Copa* (1964); *Shake* (1965); *Try a Little Love* (1965); *The Unforgettable Sam Cooke* (1966); *The Man Who Invented Soul* (1968); *One and Only* (1968); *This Is Sam Cooke* (1970); *Sam Cooke* (1970); *The Unforgettable Sam Cooke* (1973); *Golden Sound* (1973); *Sings the Billie Holiday Story* (1973); *Interprets Billie Holiday* (1975); *You Send Me* (1975); *Right On* (1975); *Feel It! Live at the Harlem* (1985); *Forever* (1986); *The Man and His Music* (1986); *The Rhythm and the Blues* (1995). **SOUL STIRRERS:** *Sam Cooke and the Soul Stirrers* (1959); *The Gospel Soul of Sam Cooke, Vol. 1* (1970); *The Gospel Soul of Sam Cooke, Vol. 2* (1971), *The Original Soul Stirrers* (1971); *That's Heaven to Me* (1972); *In the Beginning* (1989); *Jesus Gave Me Water* (1992); *Heaven Is My Home* (1993); *The Last Mile of the Way* (1994).

BIBL.: J. McEuen, *S. C.: A Biography in Words and Pictures* (N.Y., 1977); D. Wolff with S. R. Crain, C. White and G. David Tenenbaun, *You Send Me: The Life and Times of S. C.* (N.Y., 1995). **—BH**

Cooke, Tom (actually, **Thomas Simpson**), Irish tenor, instrumentalist, and composer; b. Dublin, 1782; d. London, Feb. 26, 1848. He studied with his father, the oboist Bartlett Cooke, and appeared in public playing a violin concerto when he was seven. He then studied with Giordani. At age 15, he became concertmaster of Dublin's Crow Street Theatre orch. He also ran a music shop (1806–12). In 1813 he settled in London, where he became a dominant figure at the Drury Lane Theatre as a singer, concertmaster, versatile instrumentalist (on some nine instruments), manager, and composer. He also taught voice. Cooke composed many stage pieces. He also wrote the treatises *Singing Exemplified in a Series of Solfeggi* and *Singing in Parts* (London, 1842).—**NS/LK/DM**

Coolidge, Elizabeth (Penn) Sprague, generous American music patronesss; b. Chicago, Oct. 30, 1864; d. Cambridge, Mass., Nov. 4, 1953. In 1918 she established the Berkshire Festivals of Chamber Music in Pittsfield, Mass., which were held annually under her auspices; she later sponsored the Elizabeth Sprague Coolidge Foundation in the Library of Congress in Washington, D.C., created in 1925 for the purpose of producing concerts and music festivals, awarding prizes, etc., under the administration of the Music Division of the Library. Numerous composers were commissioned to write music for it. The auditorium of the Library of Congress was likewise her gift. In 1932 she founded the Elizabeth Sprague Coolidge Medal "for eminent services to chamber music," awarded annually (until 1949). She also initiated performances of modern and classical chamber music throughout the U.S. and Europe. Her sponsorship of the appearances of artists in the U.S. and abroad (the Pro Arte, Coolidge, Roth quartets, etc.) was an important factor in the development of musical life in the U.S. In recognition of her many cultural contributions, she was made honorary M.A. (Yale Univ., Smith Coll., Mills Coll.), L.D. (Mt. Holyoke Coll.), Mus.Doc. (Pomona Coll.), and LL.D. (Univ. of Calif.). She also received the Cobbett Medal and various foreign decorations.

BIBL.: W. Bedford, *E.S. C.: The Education of a Patron of Chamber Music: The Early Years* (diss., Univ. of Mo., 1964); J. Rosenfeld, *E.S. C.: A Tribute on the One Hundredth Anniversary of Her Birth* (n.p., 1964); C. Barr, *E.S. C.: American Patron of Music* (N.Y., 1998).—NS/LK/DM

Coolidge, Rita, a vocalist-pianist who emerged from session work, toured with Delaney and Bonnie and Joe Cocker's infamous Mad Dogs and Englishmen tour before launching a solo career as a cover artist; b. Nashville, Tenn., May 1, 1944. Known as the Delta Lady (Leon Russell wrote the song for her), Coolidge collaborated with and was married to Kris Kristofferson from 1973 to 1980.

Rita Coolidge and her sisters Priscilla and Linda grew up in Lafayette, Tenn. The sisters began performing in high school, and Priscilla and Rita moved to Los Angeles in 1968. Priscilla later married Booker T. Jones, while Rita met producer Leon Russell and folk-rock singers Delaney and Bonnie. Over the next two years she recorded with Delaney and Bonnie, Russell, Joe Cocker, Eric Clapton, Steve Stills, and Dave Mason as a backup vocalist. She toured several times with Delaney and Bonnie and became a member of the Mad Dogs and Englishmen—Joe Cocker tour of the United States and Europe. On that tour she performed the Delaney Bramlett—Leon Russell composition "Superstar," later popularized by the Carpenters. Signed to A&M Records in late 1970, Coolidge recorded a number of excellent songs by Marc Benno on her early albums, including "Second Story Window," "(I Always Called Them) Mountains," "Nice Feelin'," and "Inside of Me." In 1973 she married and toured and recorded with Kris Kristofferson. Their *Full Moon* album contained a number of fine compositions such as "I Never Had It So Good," "Take Time to Love," and "Loving Arms," a minor hit. They later recorded *Breakaway* (1974) and *Natural Act* (1979).

Rita Coolidge achieved her greatest success with her *Anytime ...Anywhere* album, scoring three hits with Jackie Wilson's "Higher and Higher," Boz Scaggs's "We're All Alone," and the Motown classic "The Way You Do the Things You Do." Later hits included 1979's "I'd Rather Leave While I'm in Love" and 1983's "All Time High" but by the late 1980s she was without a record label. For a while Coolidge pursued a country career, after her laid-back vocal style became passé on the pop/rock charts. In 1992 Rita Coolidge returned to recording with *Love Sessions* for Critique/Caliber. The album included a duet with Lee Greenwood, "Heart Don't Fail Me Now,"

which was used as the love theme for the CBS television soap opera *As the World Turns,* and "Cherokee," a tribute to her half-Cherokee father, sung with her sister Priscilla.

DISC.: RITA COOLIDGE: *R. C.* (1971); *Nice Feelin'* (1971); *The Lady's Not for Sale* (1972); *Fall into Spring* (1974); *It's Only Love* (1975); *Anytime ... Anywhere* (1977); *Love Me Again* (1978); *Satisfied* (1979); *Greatest Hits* (1981); *Heartbreak Radio* (1981); *Never Let You Go* (1983); *Inside the Fire* (1984); *Love Sessions* (1992). **RITA COOLIDGE AND KRIS KRISTOFFERSON:** *Full Moon* (1973); *Natural Act* (1979); *Breakaway* (1974).—BH

Coolio (originally, **Ivey, Artis**), popular gangsta rapper; b. Compton, Calif., Aug. 1, 1963. While he generally gets classified with the Calif. gangsta rappers, Coolio seems somehow safer, probably due to the combination of his sense of humor and prevailing attitude that there is a better life than street life. The tension between street and safety, however, made him an enormously popular artist through the mid-1990s.

In his teens, Artis Ivey hung with gangs, did drugs, and did time. After getting out of prison and kicking his crack habit, he became a fire fighter, which he likened to boot camp. He pursued his interest in hip-hop during his off-hours, performing free rap shows for radio station KDAY in LA. His carefully cultivated looks included his now trademark Medusa-like dreadlocks.

Coolio signed to Tommy Boy records and in 1994 released the single "Fantastic Voyage," which went to #3 in the charts, selling platinum. The album *It Takes a Thief* debuted at a peak of #5 on the pop charts and also went platinum.

Coolio followed this up with the double platinum *Gangsta's Paradise* the following year. The title track, featured in the film *Dangerous Minds,* heavily sampled Stevie Wonder's "Pastime Paradise." It went to #1 and sold triple platinum. However, the follow-up, "Too Hot," only hit #24. Coolio returned to chart success with a remixed version of the track "Sumpin' New" titled "1,2,3,4 (Sumpin' New)." The single reached #5 pop and sold gold. The album went to #9 and Coolio won the best solo rap Grammy for the song "Gangsta's Paradise" in 1996.

Coolio contributed the track "All The Way Live (Now)" for the soundtrack to the Whoopie Goldberg film *Eddie.* The tune went gold, although it only hit #29. He made appearances on television shows like *Sabrina the Teenaged Witch,* solidifying his popularity among pre-teens to the extent that he won two Nickelodeon Kid's Choice awards. He also started appearing in films, including a cameo appearance in *Batman and Robin.*

Coolio's gold single "C U When U Get There," built around samples of Pachabel's Canon In D, was released late in the summer of 1997. From the soundtrack to the film *Nothing to Lose,* it reached #12 and went gold. Considering how successful his previous singles were, that was considered a disappointment, as was the performance of the *My Soul* album, which also only went gold, topping out at #39.

A dispute with Tommy Boy kept Coolio out of the recording studios after that. He has considered releasing his music via the Internet and started his own label, Crowbar Records.

Disc.: *It Takes a Thief* (1994); *Gangsta's Paradise* (1995); *My Soul* (1997).—HB

Coolman, Todd (Francis), jazz bassist, educator, pianist; b. Gary, Ind., July 14, 1954. After receiving a B.M. from Ind. Univ. (1975), he moved to N.Y. (1978) and has become one of the most in-demand bassists, performing with Horace Silver, Gerry Mulligan, Stan Getz, Benny Golson, Art Farmer, Tommy Flanagan, Lionel Hampton, Benny Goodman, and numerous others. In the mid-1990s, he worked with James Moody, Ahmad Jamal, Slide Hampton, Jimmy Heath, and The Carnegie Hall Jazz Band. Coolman earned an M.M. at Manhattan School of Music (1986), and Ph.D. from N.Y.U. School of Education jazz program (1997). A dedicated educator and author, he has taught at William Paterson Coll. (1981–88), SUNY at Stony Brook (1994–98), City Coll. of N.Y. (1998), and joined the full-time faculty at the Purchase Coll. Cons. of Music (September 1998).

Disc.: *Tomorrows* (1990); *Lexicon* (1991).—LP

Coon, Carleton (A. Sr.), jazz drummer, leader, singer; b. Rochester, Minn., Feb. 5, 1894; d. Chicago, Ill., May 4, 1932. He grew up in Lexington, Mo., where he became interested in black music by hanging out with dock workers. He formed a band in high school and met pianist and singer Joe Sanders at a music store in Kansas City around the end of World War I; they formed a band (1920) that performed there for several years; Sanders wrote much of the material for the group of nine to ten pieces. They achieved wider fame during the mid-1920s due to late night radio broadcasts throughout the Midwest from the Muehlebach Hotel. Known as the Coon-Sanders Nighthawks, the band was heard nationwide and in Canada, and their program had popular features such as a telegraph site near the band to which listeners could send in requests, comments, and greetings to friends, which would be read during the show. They performed at Lincoln Tavern and Congress Hotel in Chicago (1924), and later returned for a long stint at the Blackhawk Restaurant (1926), from which they made nightly radio broadcasts; this led to a recording contract with Victor and some 80 recorded songs. They also had their own NBC radio show for a while. Keeping their home base in Kansas City, they frequently toured college dances and other one-night gigs, traveling flamboyantly in a caravan of colorful sports cars, one to each musician. From late 1931 through March 1932 or longer, they were at the Hotel New Yorker in N.Y. Soon after, the band was performing at Hotel Sherman's Coll. Inn, Chicago, when Coon was suffering from a jaw abscess due to an infected tooth and checked in to Henrotin Memorial Hospital. He suddenly died, and the band broke up a year later.

Disc.: "Sluefoot" (1927); "Here Comes My Ball and Chain" (1928).—LP

Cooper, Alice both the name of the 1970s rock group and the pseudonym of its protagonist-vocalist, established their reputation through the onstage simu-

lation of acts of violence. **Membership:** Alice (real name, Vincent Furnier) Cooper, lead voc. (b. Detroit, Mich., Feb. 4, 1948); Glen Buxton, lead gtr. (b. Washington, D.C., June 17, 1947); Michael Bruce, gtr., kybd. (b. Calif., Nov. 21, 1948); Dennis Dunaway, bs. (b. Cottage Grove, Ore., March 15, 1946); Neal Smith, drm. (b. Washington, D.C., Jan. 10, 1946).

Group leader Cooper, often dressed in clothes intended to suggest bisexuality and transvestism, acted out such fantasies as necrophilia, infanticide, and execution. Initially rejected en masse by audiences, the group cultivated a perverse and repulsive image, and profited from sensationalized adverse publicity. Thus Alice Cooper became the first rock act to achieve widespread popularity *because of* a carefully perpetrated distasteful image, predating the wave of late–1970s punk groups and antedated by groups such as Iggy Pop and the Stooges. Moreover, Alice Cooper was one of the first rock acts to utilize extravagant stage sets, and group leader Cooper was one of the first to use garish makeup, both practices taken up by groups from Kiss to Gwar. The group did produce a number of classic rock songs with "Eighteen," "School's Out," "Elected," and "No More Mr. Nice Guy." Protagonist Cooper disbanded the group in 1974 and assembled a new group for his classic *Welcome to My Nightmare* tour of 1975. Out of action for much of the 1980s, Alice Cooper staged a remarkable comeback with his 1989 *Trash* album and tour. He also made a humorous appearance in the 1992 film *Wayne's World*, in which he parodied his badder-than-bad image.

Group protagonist Vincent Furnier traveled extensively with his family in early childhood, eventually settling in Phoenix, Ariz., in the early 1960s. In 1964, while still in high school, he formed his first band, the Earwigs, with friends Glen Buxton and Dennis Dunaway. By fall 1965 the group had changed its name to the Spiders and added Michael Bruce. Playing local engagements in 1966, the band next adopted the name the Nazz and added Neal Smith.

Making forays into Los Angeles in search of club dates and a recording contract, the group again changed its name when they discovered that a Philadelphia band led by Todd Rundgren was also using the name the Nazz. Vincent Furnier became Alice Cooper and the group as a whole took on the name. They achieved their first notoriety in Los Angeles by performing at a memorial birthday party for the controversial comedian Lenny Bruce. Thousands of people left the show shortly after the band took the stage, but two important individuals stayed: Frank Zappa and Shep Gordon. Zappa signed Alice Cooper to his new label, Straight Records, and Gordon became the group's manager. They moved to Los Angeles in 1968, but their first two albums were virtually ignored.

Alice Cooper moved to Detroit in 1969, and during 1970 the group began playing engagements across the country. Switching to Warner Bros. Records, the group scored their first major hit with the alienated "Eighteen." Receiving intense publicity for their outrageous stage act, the group achieved a near-smash with 1972's "School's Out." *Billion Dollar Babies* in 1973 yielded the hits "Elected," "Hello, Hurray," and "No More Mr. Nice Guy." Their subsequent tour was one of the biggest moneymakers of its time.

Unable to match the Billion Dollar Babies tour, Cooper disbanded the group in 1974, replacing them with musicians who had earlier backed Lou Reed. Cooper switched to Atlantic Records for 1975's *Welcome to My Nightmare*, which formed the basis for an hour-long television special and perhaps the definitive tour of his career. The album yielded a major hit with the uncharacteristic ballad "Only Women (Bleed)." Cooper returned to Warner Bros., scoring other mid-1970s hits including the ballads "I Never Cry" and "You and Me." In 1978 Cooper served a stint in a psychiatric hospital for treatment for chronic alcoholism, and the experience served as the basis for his *From the Inside* album of the same year, and his Madhouse Rock tour.

Weary from years of touring and inundated by the wave of disco groups then popular, Alice Cooper withdrew from the music scene in 1980. He eventually reemerged in 1986 with a new band and a new record label, MCA. The comeback failed, but in 1989 he proved successful, scoring a near-smash with "Poison" from *Trash*, his best-selling album in more than a decade.

DISC.: ALICE COOPER: *Live at the Whisky* (1992); *Pretties for You* (1969); *Easy Action* (1970); *Love It to Death* (1971); *Killer* (1971); *School's Out* (1972); *Billion Dollar Babies* (1973); *Muscle of Love* (1973); *Greatest Hits* (1974); *Welcome to My Nightmare* (1975); *A. C. Goes to Hell* (1976); *Lace and Whiskey* (1977); *The A. C. Show* (1977); *From the Inside* (1978); *Flush the Fashion* (1980); *Special Forces* (1981); *Zipper Catches Skin* (1982); *Da Da* (1983); *Constrictor* (1986); *Raise Your Fist and Yell* (1987); *Prince of Darkness* (1989); *Trash* (1989); *Hey Stoopid* (1991); *The Last Temptation* (1994); *The Last Temptation: Comic Book Version* (1994). **BILLION DOLLAR BABIES:** *Battle Axe* (1977).

BIBL.: Steve Demorest, *A. C.* (N.Y., 1974); Bob Greene, *Billion Dollar Baby* (N.Y., 1974).—**BH**

Cooper, Bob (actually, Robert William),

jazz tenor saxophonist, saxophonist, oboist; b. Pittsburgh, Pa., Dec. 6, 1925; d. Los Angeles, Calif., Aug. 5, 1993. He played with Stan Kenton (1945–51) and married Kenton's vocalist, June Christy. Cooper performed and recorded with Howard Rumsey's Lighthouse All-Stars with Kenton, Christy, and others well in to 1960s, including several albums as band leader. Like many West Coast jazzmen of that era, Cooper disappeared to do studio work during lean years for jazz, and became especially noted for the quality of his work using oboe improvisation. He briefly found a degree of interest in his work during the late 1980s. In 1989, he was honored with a tribute by the L.A. Jazz Society.

DISC.: *Shifting Winds* (1955); *Flute and Oboe of Bud Shank and B. C.* (1956); *Milano Blues* (1957); *Coop! the Music of Bob Cooper* (1958); *Tenor Sax Jazz Impressions* (1979); *Music of Michel Legrand, Vols. 1, 2* (1980); *Tenor Sax Impressions* (1981); *In a Mellotone* (1985); *For All We Know* (1990).—**MM/LP**

Cooper, Emil (Albertovich),

respected Russian conductor of English descent; b. Kherson, Dec. 20, 1877; d. N.Y., Nov. 16, 1960. He studied at the Odessa Cons., with Hellmesberger Jr., and Nikisch in Vienna, and with Taneyev in Moscow. In 1896 he made his conducting debut in Odessa. He then conducted in Kiev (1899–1906), and at Moscow's Bolshoi and Zimin theaters (1904). On Oct. 7, 1909, he conducted the premiere of Rimsky-Korsakov's *The Golden Cockerel* in Moscow. From 1909 to 1911 he conducted Diaghilev's Russian seasons in Paris, and also appeared at London's Covent Garden. He continued to conduct in Russia until 1923, and then in Riga (1925–28). From 1929 to 1932 he conducted at the Chicago Opera, and then in Europe. In 1939 he returned to the Chicago Opera, remaining with it until his Metropolitan Opera debut in N.Y. on Jan. 26, 1944, conducting *Pelléas et Mélisande*. He remained on the roster there until 1950, and then conducted the Montréal Opera Guild. In addition to the Russian repertory, he was esteemed for his interpretations of Wagner.—**NS/LK/DM**

Cooper, Harry (R.),

jazz trumpeter; b. Lake Charles, La., 1903; d. Paris, France, 1961. He left La. as a child and moved with family to Kansas City, Mo. Where he attended Lincoln H.S. and took up trumpet in Reserve Officers' Training Corps Band. While at high school, Cooper gigged with Bennie Moten, George E. Lee, and bassist James Smith Leaving Kansas City in 1922, Cooper studied architecture at Hampton Inst., Va., and gigged with local bands. He then moved on to Baltimore, Md., and joined a band accompanying singer Virginia Listen, travelling with this group to N.Y. for their first recordings (OKeh). With augmented personnel (among the players was Prince Robinson), this band became the Seminole Syncopators (led by pianist Graham Jackson). They played a three-month residency at the 81 Theatre in Atlanta, Ga., then Cooper returned to N.Y. and joined Billy Fowler (late 1924). He gigged with Elmer Snowden, led own band at the Blackbottom Club, and worked with violinist Andrew Preer's Cotton Club Orch. (1925). His quartet, Harry's Happy Four, made recordings in 1925 and accompanied Sara Martin. Cooper was with Billy Fowler (1926), worked on and off with Duke Ellington in 1926, and led his own band before joining Leon Abbey. He worked in Europe with Leon Abbey from early 1928 and then joined Sam Wooding in late 1929. Cooper remained in Europe for the rest of his life, occasionally working for other leaders such as Hubert Rostaing, but usually leading his own bands. He recorded in Paris during the Nazi occupation.

DISC.: "Blues 1943" (1943); "Nuages" (1943).—**JC/LP**

Cooper, Imogen,

English pianist, daughter of **Martin (Du Pré) Cooper**; b. London, Aug. 28, 1949. She went to Paris at age 12 to study at the Cons. with Jacques Février and Yvonne Lefébure, taking the premier prix in 1967. She then went to Vienna to pursue training with Alfred Brendel, Paul Badura-Skoda, and Jörg Demus. In 1969 she won the Mozart Memorial Prize in London. In 1973 she made her first appearance at the London Promenade Concerts, and subsequently appeared as a soloist with various British orchs., as a recitalist, and as a chamber music player. Her engagements as a soloist led to appearances with the Vienna

Phil., the Berlin Phil., the Dresden State Orch., the N.Y. Phil., the Boston Sym. Orch., the Los Angeles Phil., and many other orchs. She has played lieder recitals with Wolfgang Holzmair in leading cities, including London, Vienna, and Paris. In 1996 she became a member of a chamber music group founded with members of the Berlin Phil. In 1997 she organized a trio with Raphael Oleg and Sonia Wieder-Ahterton. Her repertoire ranges from the classics to contemporary scores, from Mozart to Adès.—NS/LK/DM

Cooper, Jerome (D.), avant-garde jazz drummer, percussionist; b. Chicago, Ill., Dec. 14, 1946. He began playing drums as a teenager, taking lessons in high school, and then attended the American Cons. (1967–68). At the same time, he gigged with local R&B and jazz bands. In 1969 he moved to Europe to work with Steve Lacy; a year later, he played in Gambia and Senegal with Lou Bennett. Cooper accompanied Rahsaan Roland Kirk on Kirk's European tour of 1970–71. In 1971 he returned to the U.S. and formed the Revolutionary Ensemble with Leroy Jenkins; he played piano, bugle, and flute, in addition to drums and percussion, with the group. They disbanded in 1977; during this same period, Cooper also gigged and recorded with various leaders, including Sam Rivers (1973) and Maurice McIntyre (1974–80s). From 1977, he has worked as an unaccompanied soloist; in 1980 he recorded with Cecil Taylor.

DISC.: *For the People* (1979); *Toot Assumptions* (1978); *The Unpredictability of Predictability* (1979). Revolutionary Ensemble: *Vietnam* (1972); *Manhattan Cycles* (1972); *Positions 369* (1977). S. Lacy: *Wordless* (1971). A. Braxton: *New York, Fall 1974* (1974). C. Taylor: *It Is in the Brewing Luminous* (1980).—LP

Cooper, Kenneth, versatile American harpsichordist, pianist, fortepianist, conductor, musicologist, and pedagogue; b. N.Y., May 31, 1941. He studied at N.Y.'s H.S. of Music and Art (1954–58), where he received instruction in harpsichord from Fernando Valenti. He then entered Columbia Coll. (B.A., 1962), where his mentors included Jack Beeson, Otto Luening, and Douglas Moore, and pursued his education at Columbia Univ. (M.A., 1964; Ph.D. in musicology, 1971), where he studied with Paul Henry Lang and Denis Stevens. He also studied harpsichord with Sylvia Marlowe at the Mannes Coll. of Music (1960–63). On July 6, 1965, he made his London recital debut at Wigmore Hall, followed by his U.S. recital debut at N.Y.'s Alice Tully Hall on Feb. 2, 1973. He was an instructor at Barnard Coll. (1967–71) and an adjunct prof. of music at Brooklyn Coll. of the City Univ. of N.Y. (1971–73). From 1975 to 1984 he was prof. of harpsichord and director of the Collegium Musicum at the Mannes Coll. of Music. He appeared as a chamber music artist at the Spoleto Festival U.S.A. in Charleston, S.C., from 1979 to 1992, and also at the Grand Canyon Chamber Music Festival from 1985. In 1983 he became artist-in-residence and assoc.-in-performance at Columbia Univ. He also was director of the Baroque Orch. (1984–92) and of the Baroque Aria Ensemble (from 1992) at the Manhattan School of Music, where he also was chairman of the harpsichord dept., a teacher at the Peabody Cons. of

Music in Baltimore (1986–90), and founder-director of the Berkshire Bach Ensemble (from 1989). He ed. the anthology *Three Centuries of Music in Score* (13 vols., 1988–90), prepared editions of Monteverdi's *Tirsi e Clori* (1967) and Giardini's *"Billiard" Sonata* (1998), and made reconstructions of several works. As both a performer and scholar, his interests range from early music to contemporary scores.—NS/LK/DM

Cooper, Martin (Du Pré), English music writer on music, father of **Imogen Cooper;** b. Winchester, Jan. 17, 1910; d. Richmond, Surrey, March 15, 1986. He studied at Hertford Coll., Oxford (B.A., 1931) and with Wellesz in Vienna (1932–34). He then was music critic for the London *Mercury* (1935–38), *Daily Herald* (1946–50), and the *Daily Telegraph* (1950–54; chief music critic, 1954–76)6); also was ed. of the *Musical Times* (1953–56).

WRITINGS (all publ. in London unless otherwise given): *Gluck* (1935); *Bizet* (1938); *Opéra comique* (1949); *Profils de musiciens anglais* (Paris, 1950); *French Music from the Death of Berlioz to the Death of Fauré* (1951); *Russian Opera* (1951); ed. *The Concise Encyclopedia of Music and Musicians* (1958; 3rd ed., rev., 1975); ed. vol. X, *The Modern Age 1890–1960,* in *The New Oxford History of Music* (1974); D. Cooper, ed., *Judgements of Value: Selected Writings on Music* (Oxford, 1988; includes many of Cooper's writings).—NS/LK/DM

Cooper, Paul, American composer and teacher; b. Victoria, Ill., May 19, 1926; d. Houston, April 4, 1996. He received instruction from Kanitz, Stevens, and Sessions at the Univ. of Southern Calif. in Los Angeles (B.S., 1950; M.A., 1953; D.M.A., 1956), and from Boulanger in Paris at the Cons. and the Sorbonne (1953–54). He was a teacher (1955–65) and a prof. (1965–68) of music at the Univ. of Mich., where he also was chairman of the music dept. (1966–68), and then was prof. of composition at the Univ. of Cincinnati Coll.-Cons. of Music (1969–74) and subsequently at the Shepherd School of Music at Rice Univ. in Houston (1974–96). Cooper held Guggenheim fellowships (1965, 1972). He publ. *Perspectives in Music Theory* (1973; 2nd ed., 1981). In his works, Cooper followed an eclectic course in which he utilized various styles in an original manner.

WORKS: DRAMATIC: *Mysterion* for Soprano, Narrator, Chamber Orch., and Optional Dancers (1988). **ORCH.:** 6 syms.: No. 1, *Concertant,* for Solo Woodwind, Brass, String Quartet, Percussion, and Strings (1966), No. 2, *Antiphons,* for Oboe and Symphonic Winds (1971), No. 3, *Lamentations,* for Strings (1971), No. 4, *Landscape,* for Flute, Trumpet, Viola, and Orch. (1973–75), No. 5, *Symphony in 2 Movements* (1982–83; Houston, Sept. 10, 1983), and No. 6, *In Memoriam* (1987); 2 violin concertos (1967; 1980–82); *Liturgies* for Symphonic Woodwinds, Brass, and Percussion (1968); *A Shenandoah: For Ives' Birthday* for Flute, Trumpet, Viola, and Orch. (1974); *Descants* for Viola and Orch. (1975); *Homage* for Flute, Trumpet, Viola, and Orch. (1976); Cello Concerto (1976–78); *Variants* (1978); Flute Concerto (1980–81); Organ Concerto (1982); Saxophone Concerto (1982); Duo Concertante for Violin, Viola, and Orch. (1985); *Jubilate* for Symphonic Woodwinds, Brass, and Percussion (1985–86); Double Concerto for Violin, Viola, and Orch. (1985–87). **CHAMBER:** 6 string quartets (1952, rev. 1978; 1954, rev. 1979; 1959; 1963–64; 1973; 1977); Viola Sonata (1961); Violin Sonata

(1962); Sonata for [3] Flutes [1 Player] and Piano (1962–63); 2 cello sonatas (1962–63; 1965); Double Bass Sonata (1964); Concert for 4 for Flute, Oboe, Harpsichord, and Double Bass (1965); Concert for 5 for Wind Quintet (1965); Epitaphs for Alto Flute, Harp, and Double Bass (1969); Soliloquies for Violin and Piano (1970); Variants II for Viola and Piano (1972); Chimera for Violin, Viola, Cello, and Piano (1973); Concert for 3 for Clarinet, Cello, and Piano (1977); Canons d'Amour for Violin and Viola (1981); Canti for Viola and Piano (1981); Chamber Music I for 6 Instruments (1982; rev. as Chamber Music II, 1983); 4 Impromptus for Alto Saxophone and Piano (1983); Variants IV for Alto Saxophone and Piano (1986); Tre voci, trio for Violin, Cello, and Piano (1986); also piano pieces and organ music. VOCAL: Credo for Double Chorus and Orch. (1970); Cantigas for Soprano, Double Chorus, and Orch. (1972); Refrains for Soprano, Baritone, Double Chorus, and Orch. (1976); Celebration for Chamber Chorus, Organ, Speaker, and Congregational Singing (1983); Voyagers for Chorus and Orch. (1983); Omnia tempus habent for Chorus and Organ (1987); song cycles.—NS/LK/DM

Coover, James B(urrell), American music librarian and pedagogue; b. Jacksonville, Ill., June 3, 1925. He was educated at the Univ. of Northern Colo. (B.A., 1949; M.A., 1950) and the Univ. of Denver (M.A., 1953). He was associated with the Bibliographical Center for Research in Denver (1951–53), where he was its asst. director (1952–53). From 1953 to 1967 he was director of the George Sherman Dickinson Music Library at Vassar Coll. He was prof. of music and director of the music library (1967–75), Birge-Cary Prof. of Music (1975–81), Ziegele Prof. (1981–2000) and Distinguished Service Prof. (from 1992) at the State Univ. of N.Y. at Buffalo. He also was president (1959–60) and an executive board member (1987–90) of the Music Library Assn.

WRITINGS: Music Lexicography (1952; 3rd ed., rev. and enl., 1971); Provisional Checklist of Priced Antiquarian Catalogues Containing Musical Materials (1981; rev. ed., 1987, as Antiquarians' Catalogues of Musical Interest): Musical Instrument Collections (1981); Music Publishing, Copyright and Piracy in Victorian England, 1881–1906 (1985); ed. with C. Bradley, Richard S. Hill: Tributes from Friends (1987); Music at Auction: Puttick & Simpson (of London), 1794–1971 (1988).—NS/LK/DM

Cope, David (Howell), innovative American writer, composer, programmer, and teacher; b. San Francisco, May 17, 1941. He was educated at Ariz. State Univ. and the Univ. of Southern Calif. in Los Angeles, numbering among his mentors George Perle, Halsey Stevens, Ingolf Dahl, and Grant Fletcher. He then served on the faculties of Miami Univ. of Ohio and at the Univ. of Calif. at Santa Cruz. Cope is well known for his scholarly books on contemporary composition, several of which describe and document the computer program Experiments in Musical Intelligence he created in 1982. Select works created with this program are available on the CD recordings Bach by Design, Classical Music Composed by Computer, and Virtual Mozart.

WORKS: DRAMATIC: Opera: Cradle Falling (1985); Mozart Opera (1992). OTHER: Out, filmscore (1981); Richard II, incidental music (1986). ORCH.: Tragic Overture for Strings (1960); Contrasts (1966); Music for Brass and Strings (1967); Streams (1973); Concerto (1976); Threshold and Visions (1977); Concert for Piano and Orchestra (1980); Afterlife (1982); Dedications

(1994); Horizons (1994). WIND ENSEMBLE/BRASS CHOIR: Variations for Piano and Wind Orch. (1965); Requiem for Bosque Redondo (1974); Re-Birth (1975). CHAMBER: Ensemble: Five Pieces (1965); Towers (1968); The Deadliest Angel Revision (1970); Dragoon (1972); Margins (1972); Koosharem (1973); Vortex (1976); Vectors (1976); The Way (1981); Corridors of Light (1983). Other: 2 string quartets (1960, 1963); Sonata for Solo Cello (1964); Sonata for Solo Horn (1964); Three Pieces for Clarinet (1965); Three Pieces for Bassoon (1966); Three Pieces for Trombone (1966); Alternatives for Contrabass (1969); Cycles for Flute and Contrabass (1969); Obelisk for Percussion (1970); B.T.R.B. for Trombone (1971); Probe 3 for Saxophone (1971); Angel's Camp II for Violin (1972); Bright Angel for Trumpet (1972); Cedar Breaks for Contrabass (1972); Spirals for Tuba (1972); Extensions for Trumpet (1973); Indices for Oboe (1973); Triplum for Flute (1973); Arena for Cello (1974); Paradigm for Violin (1974); Clone for Saxophone (1975); FMS for Trumpet (1975); Rituals for Cello (1976); In Memoriam for String Quartet (1991). KEYBOARD: Piano: Soundpiece (1959); Three 2-Part Inventions (1960); 4 sonatas (1960, 1960, 1962, 1967); Iceberg Meadow (1968); Parallax (1974); Glassworks (1978); The Well-Tempered Disklavier (1991). Organ: Or (1976). VOCAL: A Christmas for Dismas for Chorus (1967); Ashes for Voice and Percussion (1972); Tyger, Tyger for Chorus (1985). ELECTRONIC: The Birds (1968); Teec Nos Pos (1975); K (1972); Weeds (1972). OTHER: Various works composed with Experiments in Musical Intelligence, including 15 Bach Inventions (1987), Chopin Mazurkas (1987), Joplin Rag 1 (1988) and 2 (1996), Beethoven Sonata (1993), Rachmaninoff Suite (1994), Mozart Concerto for Piano and Orchestra (1995), and Five Songs (Bach, Mozart, Schubert, Strauss, Puccini) (1996).

WRITINGS: Notes in Discontinuum (1970); New Directions in Music (Dubuque, 1971; 7th ed., rev., 2000); New Music Notation (1976); New Music Composition (N.Y., 1977); Computers and Musical Style (Madison, Wisc., 1991); Experiments in Musical Intelligence (Madison, Wisc., 1996); Techniques of the Contemporary Composer (1997); The Algorithmic Composer (Madison, Wisc., 2000); Virtual Music (Cambridge, Mass., 2000).—NS/LK/DM

Copeland, Keith (Lamont), jazz drummer, son of Ray Copeland; b. N.Y., April 18, 1946. A protégé of Alan Dawson, Copeland has developed his own drum method and taught at Berklee himself from 1975–78. He played with Johnny Griffin, The Heath Brothers (1978–79), Sam Jones (recording 1979), Charlie Rouse, and Kenny Barron. He toured with Billy Taylor for most of the 1980s. In 1993 he accepted a full-time performing and teaching position in Cologne, Germany. He is a hard swinging player and truly inspired teacher.

DISC.: On Target (1993); Round Trip (1996); The Irish Connection (1996); Postcard from Vancouver (1998).—LP

Coperari, Giovanni
See **Coprario, Giovanni**

Copland, Aaron, greatly distinguished and exceptionally gifted American composer; b. N.Y., Nov. 14, 1900; d. North Tarrytown, N.Y., Dec. 2, 1990. He was educated at the Boys' H.S. in Brooklyn, and began piano study with Leopold Wolfsohn, Victor Wittgenstein, and Clarence Adler as a young child. In 1917 he commenced lessons in harmony and counterpoint with Rubin Goldmark in N.Y., and soon began to compose. His first publ. piece, *The Cat and the Mouse* for Piano (1920), subtitled *Scherzo humoristique*, shows the influence of Debussy. In 1920 he entered the American Cons. in Fontainebleau, where he studied composition and orchestration with Boulanger. Returning to America in 1924, he lived mostly in N.Y.; became active in many musical activities, not only as a composer but also as a lecturer, pianist, and organizer in various musical societies. He attracted the attention of Koussevitzky, who gave the first performance of his early score *Music for the Theater* with the Boston Sym. Orch. in 1925; Koussevitzky then engaged Copland as soloist in his Piano Concerto in 1927; the work produced a considerable sensation because of its jazz elements, and there was some subterranean grumbling among the staid subscribers to the Boston Sym. concerts. Koussevitzky remained Copland's steadfast supporter throughout his tenure as conductor of the Boston Sym., and later as the founder of the Koussevitzky Music Foundation. In the meantime, Walter Damrosch conducted in N.Y. Copland's Sym. for Organ and Orch., with Boulanger as soloist. Other orchs. and their conductors also performed his music, which gained increasing recognition. Particularly popular were Copland's works based on folk motifs; of these the most remarkable are *El Salón México* (1933–36) and the American ballets *Billy the Kid* (1938), *Rodeo* (1942), and *Appalachian Spring* (1944). A place apart is occupied by Copland's *Lincoln Portrait* for Narrator and Orch. (1942), with texts arranged by the composer from speeches and letters of Abraham Lincoln; this work has had a great many performances, with the role of the narrator performed by such notables as Adlai Stevenson and Eleanor Roosevelt. His patriotic *Fanfare for the Common Man* (1942) achieved tremendous popularity and continued to be played on various occasions for decades; Copland incorporated it in toto into the score of his Third Sym. He was for many years a member of the board of directors of the League of Composers in N.Y.; with Roger Sessions, he organized the Copland-Sessions Concerts (1928–31), and was also a founder of the Yaddo Festivals (1932) and of the American Composers' Alliance (1937); was also a participant in such organizations as the Koussevitzky Music Foundation, the Composers Forum, the Cos Cob Press, etc. He was head of the composition dept. at the Berkshire Music Center at Tanglewood from 1940 to 1965, and from 1957 to 1965 was chairman of the faculty. He lectured extensively and gave courses at The New School for Social Research in N.Y. and at Harvard Univ. (1935 and 1944); was the Charles Eliot Norton Lecturer at Harvard in 1951–52. He was the recipient of many awards: Guggenheim fellowship (1925–27); RCA Victor award of $5,000 for his *Dance Symphony*; Pulitzer Prize in Music and N.Y. Music Critics' Circle Award for *Appalachian Spring* (1945); N.Y. Music Critics' Circle Award for the Third Sym. (1947); Oscar award for the film score *The Heiress* from the Academy of Motion Picture Arts and Sciences (1950); Gold Medal for Music from the American Academy of Arts and Letters (1956); Presidential Medal of Freedom (1964); Howland Memorial Prize of Yale Univ. (1970); he was also decorated with a Commander's Cross of the Order of Merit in

West Germany; was elected to honorary membership of the Accademia di Santa Cecilia in Rome. He held numerous honorary doctor's degrees: Princeton Univ. (1956); Brandeis Univ. (1957); Wesleyan Univ. (1958); Temple Univ. (1959); Harvard Univ. (1961); Rutgers Univ. (1967); Ohio State Univ. (1970); N.Y.U. (1970); Columbia Univ. (1971). About 1955 Copland developed a successful career as a conductor, and led major sym. orchs. in Europe, the U.S., South America, and Mexico; he also traveled to Russia under the auspices of the State Dept. In 1982 the Aaron Copland School of Music was created at Queens Coll. of the City Univ. of N.Y. In 1983 he made his last appearance as a conductor in N.Y. His 85th birthday was widely celebrated; Copland attended a special concert given in his honor by Zubin Mehta and the N.Y. Phil., which was televised live by PBS. He was awarded the National Medal of Arts (1986). As a composer, Copland made use of a broad variety of idioms and techniques, tempering dissonant textures by a strong sense of tonality. He enlivened his musical textures by ingenious applications of syncopation and polyrhythmic combinations; but in such works as Piano Variations, he adopted an austere method of musical constructivism. He used a modified 12-tone technique in his Piano Quartet (1950) and an integral dodecaphonic idiom in the score of *Connotations* (1962).

WORKS: DRAMATIC: *Grohg*, ballet (1922–25; not perf.; material incorporated into *Dance Symphony*); *Hear Ye! Hear Ye!*, ballet (Chicago, Nov. 30, 1934); *The 2nd Hurricane*, play-opera for high school (1936; N.Y., April 21, 1937); *Billy the Kid*, ballet (Chicago, Oct. 16, 1938); *From Sorcery to Science*, music for a puppet show (N.Y., May 12, 1939); *Rodeo*, ballet (N.Y., Oct. 16, 1942); *Appalachian Spring*, ballet (Washington, D.C., Oct. 30, 1944); *The Tender Land*, opera (N.Y., April 1, 1954); *Dance Panels*, ballet (1959; rev. 1962; Munich, Dec. 3, 1963; arranged for Piano, 1965). **Film Music:** *The City* (1939); *Of Mice and Men* (1939); *Our Town* (1940); *North Star* (1943); *The Cummington Story* (1945); *The Red Pony* (1948); *The Heiress* (1948); *Something Wild* (1961). **Incidental Music to Plays:** *Miracle at Verdun* (1931); *The 5 Kings* (1939); *Quiet City* (1939). **ORCH.:** *Music for the Theater* (Boston, Nov. 20, 1925); Sym. for Organ and Orch. (N.Y., Jan. 11, 1925; rev. version without organ, designated as Sym. No. 1, 1928; Berlin, Dec. 9, 1931; also as *Prelude for Chamber Orch.*, 1934); Piano Concerto (1926; Boston, Jan. 28, 1927); *Symphonic Ode* (1927–29; composed for the 50th anniversary of the Boston Sym. Orch.; Boston, Feb. 19, 1932; rev. 1955 for the 75th anniversary of the Boston Sym. Orch. and rededicated to the memory of Koussevitzky; Boston, Feb. 3, 1956); *A Dance Symphony* (1930; based on the ballet *Grohg*; Philadelphia, April 15, 1931); *Short Symphony* (Sym. No. 2) (1932–33; Mexico City, Nov. 23, 1934); *Statements* (1932–35; 1st complete perf., N.Y., Jan. 7, 1942); *El Salón México* (1933–36; Mexico City, Aug. 27, 1937); *Music for Radio (Prairie Journal)*, subtitled *Saga of the Prairie* (CBS, N.Y., July 25, 1937); *An Outdoor Overture* (N.Y., Dec. 16, 1938; arr. for Band, 1941); *Quiet City*, suite from the film for English Horn, Trumpet, and Strings (1939; N.Y., Jan. 28, 1941); *John Henry* for Chamber Orch. (CBS, N.Y., March 5, 1940; rev. 1952); *Our Town*, suite from the film (CBS, N.Y., June 9, 1940); *Billy the Kid*, suite from the ballet (NBC, N.Y., Nov. 9, 1940); *Lincoln Portrait* for Speaker and Orch. (Cincinnati, May 14, 1942); *Rodeo*, 4 dance episodes from the ballet (1942; Boston, May 28, 1943); *Music for Movies* for Chamber Orch. (from the films *The City*, *Of Mice and Men*, and *Our Town*; 1942; N.Y., Feb.

17, 1943); *Fanfare for the Common Man* for Brass and Percussion (1942; Cincinnati, March 12, 1943); *Letter from Home* (N.Y. broadcast, Oct. 17, 1944; rev. 1962); *Variations on a Theme by Eugene Goossens* (with 9 other composers; 1944; Cincinnati, March 23, 1945); *Appalachian Spring,* suite from the ballet (N.Y., Oct. 4, 1945); *Danzón Cubano* (orig. for 2 Pianos, 1942; orch. version, 1944; Baltimore, Feb. 17, 1946); Sym. No. 3 (1944–46; Boston, Oct. 18, 1946); Concerto for Clarinet, Strings, Harp, and Piano (1947–48; N.Y., Nov. 6, 1950); *The Red Pony,* suite from the film (Houston, Nov. 1, 1948); *Preamble for a Solemn Occasion* for Speaker and Orch. (N.Y., Dec. 10, 1949; arr. for Organ, 1953; arr. for Band, 1973); *Orchestral Variations* (orch. version of the *Piano Variations;* 1930; 1957; Louisville, March 5, 1958); *Connotations* (commissioned for the opening of Phil. Hall, Lincoln Center, N.Y., Sept. 23, 1962); *Music for a Great City* (symphonic suite descriptive of life in N.Y.C.; London, May 26, 1964); *Emblems* for Band (1964); *Down a Country Lane* for School Orch. (London, Nov. 20, 1964); *Inscape* (commissioned by the N.Y. Phil. and 1st perf. by that orch. at the Univ. of Mich., Ann Arbor, Sept. 13, 1967); *Inaugural Fanfare* (Grand Rapids, Mich., June 1969; rev. 1975); *3 Latin American Sketches: Estribillo, Paisaje mexicano, Danza de Jalisco* (N.Y., June 7, 1972); *Proclamation* (1982; orchestrated by P. Ramey, 1985; N.Y., Nov. 14, 1985). **CHAMBER:** *Capriccio* for Violin and Piano; *Poem* for Cello and Piano; *Lament* for Cello and Piano; *Preludes* for Violin and Piano; String Quartet (unfinished); Piano Trio (unfinished); *Rondino* for String Quartet (1923; N.Y., Oct. 18, 1984); *Nocturne* for Violin and Piano (1926); *Ukelele Serenade* for Violin and Piano (1926); *Lento molto* for String Quartet (1928); *Vitebsk, Study on a Jewish Theme* for Piano Trio (1928; N.Y., Feb. 16, 1929); *Elegies* for Violin and Viola (1932); Sextet for Clarinet, Piano, and String Quartet (arranged from *Short Symphony;* 1932–33; 1937; N.Y., Feb. 26, 1939); Violin Sonata (1942–43); Quartet for Piano and Strings (Washington, D.C., Oct. 29, 1950); *Nonet* for 3 Violins, 3 Violas, and 3 Cellos (1960; Washington, D.C., March 2, 1961); *Duo* for Flute and Piano (1971); *Threnody I: Igor Stravinsky, In Memoriam* for Flute and String Trio (1971) and *II: Beatrice Cunningham, Im Memoriam* for G-Flute and String Trio (1973); *Vocalise* for Flute and Piano (arrangement of *Vocalise;* 1928; 1972). **KEYBOARD: P i a n o :** *Moment musical* (1917); *Danse caracteristique* for Piano Duet or Orch. (1918); *Waltz Caprice* (1918); *Sonnets, 1–3* (1918–20); *Moods (3 esquisses): Amertume, pensif, jazzy* and *Petit portrait,* a supplement (1920–21); Piano Sonata in G major (1920–21); *Scherzo humoristique: Le Chat et la souris* (1920); *Passacaglia* (1921–22); *Sentimental Melody* (1926); *4 Piano Blues* (1926–48); *Piano Variations* (1930; orch. version, 1957); *Sunday Afternoon Music (The Young Pioneers)* (1935); Piano Sonata (1939–41; Buenos Aires, Oct. 21, 1941, composer pianist); *Piano Fantasy* (1952–57); *Down a Country Lane* (1962); *Rodeo* (arrangement from the ballet; 1962); *Danza de Jalisco* for 2 Pianos (1963; orch. version, 1972); *Dance Panels* (arrangement from the ballet; 1965); *In Evening Air* (excerpt arranged from the film score *The Cummington Story;* 1969); *Night Thoughts (Homage to Ives)* (1972); *Midsummer Nocturne* (1977); *Midday Thoughts* (1982); *Proclamation* (1982). **VOCAL: C h o r a l :** 4 Motets (1921); *The House on the Hill* for Women's Voices (1925); *An Immorality* for Soprano, Women's Voices, and Piano (1925); *What Do We Plant?* for Women's Voices and Piano (1935); *Lark* for Bass and Chorus (1938); *Las agachadas* for Chorus (1942); *Song of the Guerrillas* for Baritone, Men's Voices, and Piano (1943); *The Younger Generation* for Chorus and Piano (1943); *In the Beginning* for Mezzo-soprano and Chorus (commissioned for the Harvard Symposium; Cambridge, Mass., May 2, 1947); *Canticle of Freedom* (1955;

rev. 1965). **S o n g s :** *Melancholy* (1917); *Spurned Love* (1917); *After Antwerp* (1917); *Night* (1918); *A Summer Vacation* (1918); *My Heart Is in the East* (1918); *Simone* (1919); *Music I Heard* (1920); *Old Poem* (1920); *Pastorale* (1921); *As It Fell upon a Day* (1923); *Poet's Song* (1927); *Vocalise* (1928); *12 Poems of Emily Dickinson* (1949–50); *Old American Songs* for Voice and Orch. (arrangements in 2 sets, 1950 and 1952); *Dirge in Woods* (1954).

WRITINGS: *What to Listen for in Music* (N.Y., 1939; 2nd ed., 1957; tr. into German, Italian, Spanish, Dutch, Arabic, and Chinese); *Our New Music* (N.Y., 1941; 2nd ed., rev. and enl. as *The New Music, 1900–1960,* N.Y., 1968); *Music and Imagination,* a collection of lectures delivered at Harvard Univ., 1951–52 (Cambridge, Mass., 1952); *Copland on Music* (N.Y., 1960); an autobiography, *Copland* (with V. Perlis; 2 vols., N.Y., 1984, 1989).

BIBL.: P. Rosenfeld, *An Hour with American Music* (Philadelphia, 1929); A. Berger, *A. C.* (N.Y., 1953); J. Smith, *A. C.: His Work and Contribution to American Music* (N.Y., 1955); C. Peare, *A. C. His Life* (N.Y., 1969); Q. Hilliard, *A Theoretical Analysis of the Symphonies of A. C.* (diss., Univ. of Fla., 1984); N. Butterworth, *The Music of A. C.* (N.Y., 1985); J. Skowronski, *A. C.: A Bio-Bibliography* (Westport, Conn., 1985); V. Perlis, *C: 1900–1942* (N.Y., 1987); idem., *C.: Since 1943* (N.Y., 1990); H. Pollalack, *A. C.: The Life and Work of an Uncommon Man* (N.Y., 1999); M. Robertson and R. Armstrong, *A. C.: A Guide to Research* (N.Y., 2000).—NS/LK/DM

Copland, Marc (originally, **Cohen, Marc**), jazz pianist, alto saxophonist; b. Philadelphia, Pa., May 27, 1948. He originally used alto as his main instrument, playing it with Chico Hamilton and others (1970–72). By 1972, he was beginning to gig more on piano, and soon decided to concentrate solely on it with John Abercrombie and others. From the early 1990s on, he played regularly with James Moody, as well as leading his own groups. He changed his name to Copland to avoid confusion with other Marc Cohens in other fields of music.

DISC.: *At Night* (1991); *Stompin' with Savoy* (1995); *Second Look* (1996); *Paradiso (1997); Softly* (1998).—LP

Copley, John (Michael), English opera director; b. Birmingham, June 12, 1933. He studied with Joan Cross at the National School of Opera in London. He was active in London as a stage manager at the Sadler's Wells Opera, where he first turned to directing with his staging of *Il Tabarro* in 1957; he then worked at Covent Garden, where he garnered success with his production of *Così fan tutte* in 1968; from 1971 to 1988 he was resident opera director there, and also was active at the English National Opera. As a guest opera director, he staged works at the San Francisco Opera, the Australian Opera in Sydney, the Santa Fe Opera, and the Metropolitan Opera in N.Y. His respect for the score at hand and the singers engaged, combined with imaginative direction, have made Copley's productions notably successful.—NS/LK/DM

Coppens, Claude A(lbert), Belgian pianist, teacher, and composer; b. Schaerbeek, Dec. 23, 1936. He studied at the Brussels Cons. (1944–52), and with Jacques Fevrier and Marguerite Long in Paris, completing his education at the Univ. of Brussels (doctorate in law, 1960). He was active as a teacher at the conservatories in Brussels, Antwerp, and Ghent.

WORKS: *Symetries A* for 9 Instruments (1960–61); Piano Sonata (1964); *Due sinfonie per tre gruppi* (1965–66); *Concerting Variations* for Violin and 9 Instruments (1970); *Gedichtje van St. Niklaas*, cantata for Boy's Chorus and Small Orch. (1970–71); *The Horn of Plenty*, musical play (1978); Saxophone Quartet (1979–80); Sonata for Flute and Cello (1981–82); *Skiai* for Trombone and Percussion (1982); *XIII Pages for XIII Clarinets: Portrait of the Artist as a Young-Old Man* for Clarinet Orch. (1982–83); *...un coup de des jamais n'abolira le hasard...* for Marimba and Clarinet Orch. (1984; also for Harpsichord and String Orch.); *Logoganic Patterns* for Double Percussion (1984).—**NS/LK/DM**

Coppini, Alessandro, Italian organist, composer, and theologian; b. probably in Florence, c. 1465; d. there, 1527. He began training for the priesthood in Florence in 1475. Following studies in Bologna (Master of Sacred Theology, 1502), he obtained a doctorate in theology. From 1489 to 1497 he was a musician at the church of the Ss. Annunziata in Florence, and then was an organist in various churches until 1516. In 1517 he became a deacon at the Coll. of Theologians. In 1522 he went to Rome as a singer in the papal choir. Coppini was an accomplished composer of both sacred and secular vocal music.—**LK/DM**

Coppola, Piero, admired Italian conductor; b. Milan, Oct. 11, 1888; d. Lausanne, March 13, 1971. He studied at the Milan Cons. (graduated, 1909). After conducting in various Italian operatic centers, he conducted in London in 1914. During World War I, he pursued his career in Scandinavia. In 1921 he went to Paris, where he won distinction as music director of the recording firm La Voix de son Maître (1923–34), with whom he made a number of pioneering recordings. In 1930 he was awarded the Chevalier of the French Legion d'honneur for his services to French music. He conducted throughout Europe until World War II; after the War, he conducted in Switzerland and Italy. He also composed, producing two operas, *Sirmione* and *Nikita* (1914), a Sym. (Paris, Nov. 13, 1924, composer conducting), and the symphonic sketch *La Ronde sous la cloche* (1924).—**NS/LK/DM**

Coppola, Pietro Antonio (Pierantonio), Italian composer; b. Castrogiovanni, Sicily, Dec. 11, 1793; d. Catania, Nov. 13, 1877. For a short time he studied at the Naples Cons. He then began to compose operas, which obtained sufficient success to enable his friends and admirers to present him as a rival to Rossini. From the time he was 19, he produced one opera after another, but without much success until he composed *La Pazza per amore* (Rome, Feb. 14, 1835). This was his fourth opera and it became popular all over Europe (presented in Paris under the title *Eva*). From 1839 to 1843, and again from 1850 to 1871, he was conductor of the Lisbon Royal Opera. His other operas were *Gli Illinesi* (Turin, Dec. 26, 1835), *Enrichietta di Baienfeld* (Vienna, June 29, 1836), *La bella Celeste degli Spadari* (Milan, June 14, 1837), *Giovanna prima di Napoli* (Lisbon, Oct. 11, 1840), and *Il Folletto* (Rome, June 18, 1843). He

also wrote church music, notably a *Salve Regina*, which was highly regarded.

BIBL.: U. Coppola, *P.A. C.* (Catania, 1898).—**NS/LK/DM**

Coprario or **Coperario, Giovanni** (real name, **John Cooper**), famous English lutenist, viola da gambist, and composer; b. c. 1575; d. London, 1626. He went to Italy about 1600, and upon his return to England he adopted the Italianized name Giovanni Coprario. With the patronage of Sir Robert Cecil and Edward Seymour, Earl of Hertford, he gained renown in his homeland as an instrumentalist and composer. According to tradition, he was the music teacher of James I's children; he also was the teacher of Henry and William Lawes. His works are patterned closely on Italian models. He wrote a fine series of fantasias for viols, many with organ, music for two masques, anthems, and songs (*Funeral Teares for the Death of Right Honorable the Earle of Devonshire*, London, 1606, and *Songs of Mourning: Bewailing the Untimely Death of Prince Henry*, London, 1613). See R. Charteris, *John Coprario (Cooper) c. 1575–1626: A Study and Complete Critical Edition of His Instrumental Music* (diss., Univ. of Canterbury, New Zealand, 1976). He wrote the treatise *Rules How to Compose* (c. 1610; facsimile ed. by M. Bukofzer, Los Angeles, 1951).

BIBL.: R. Charteris, *John C.: A Thematic Catalogue of His Music with a Biographical Introduction* (N.Y., 1977).—**NS/LK/DM**

Coquard, Arthur (-Joseph), French writer on music and composer; b. Paris, May 26, 1846; d. Noirmoutier, Vendée, Aug. 20, 1910. He studied with Franck (1862–66), then practiced law. He also was a music critic for *Le Monde* and *Echo de Paris*. In addition to composing original works for the stage, he completed Lalo's opera *La Jacquerie* (Monte Carlo, March 9, 1895).

WORKS: DRAMATIC: *L'Epée du roi* (Angers, March 20, 1884); *La Mari d'un jour* (Paris, Feb. 4, 1886); *L'Oiseau bleu* (Paris, March 6, 1894); *Jahel* (Lyons, May 24, 1900); *La Troupe Joilicouer* (Paris, May 30, 1902). **VOCAL:** *Jeanne d'Arc*, oratorio.

WRITINGS: *César Franck* (Paris, 1890); *De la musique en France depuis Rameau* (Paris, 1891); *Berlioz* (Paris, 1909).

BIBL.: N. Dufourcq, *Autuour de C., César Franck et Vincent d'Indy* (Paris, 1952).—**NS/LK/DM**

Corbett, William, English violinist and composer; b. c. 1675; d. probably in London, March 7, 1748. He was concertmaster of the orch. at the Queen's Theatre in London (1705–11), and also made successful appearances as a soloist and composed music for the stage. In 1716 he became a member of the royal orch. but soon went to Italy to pursue his career, where he also acquired a valuable music and instrument collection. About 1740 he returned to London. In 1751 his collection was sold at auction.

WORKS: INSTRUMENTAL (all publ. in London unless otherwise given): *12 sonate à tre* for 2 Violins, Cello, and Basso Continuo (organ) (Amsterdam, c. 1700); *6 Sonatas* for 2 Flutes and Basso Continuo (1705); *6 Sonatas with an Overture and Aires in 4 Parts* for Trumpet, 2 Violins, 2 Oboes, Flute, and Bassoon or Harpsichord (c. 1708); *6 Sonatas a 3* for 2 Recorders or Flutes and

Basso Continuo, *libro primo* (c. 1713); *6 Sonatas a 3* for 2 Violins and Basso Continuo, *libro secondo* (c. 1713); *Le bizzarie universali a 4* for 2 Violins, Viola, and Basso Continuo (1728). **VOCAL:** *Lost is My Love*, cantata for Tenor and Orch. (c. 1725); songs for plays and in contemporary collections.—**LK/DM**

Corbetta, Francesco, distinguished Italian composer; b. Pavia, c. 1615; d. Paris, 1681. He was in Bologna as a guitar teacher by 1639. About 1643 he entered the service of the Duke of Mantua. He entered the service of the Archduke of Austria about 1648. He was taken to Paris by Cardinal Mazarin, where he was guitar master to King Louis XIV. Following a sojourn in London as teacher to the king and the nobility, he returned to Paris in 1671 as guitar master to the dauphin. After another sojourn in London in 1675, he settled in Paris. As a composer, Corbetta was an outstanding master of the Baroque guitar genre. His collections *Scherzi armonici* (Bologna, 1639), *Varii capricii* (Milan, 1643), and *Varii scherzi di sonate* (Brussels, 1648) are the embodiment of the Italian style of guitar writing of his era. In his collections *La guitarre royal dédiée au roy de la Grande Bretagne* (Paris, 1671) and *La guitarre royale dédiée a roy* (Paris, 1674), he also demonstrated a mastery of the French style of guitar writing.

BIBL.: R. Pinnell, *The Role of F. C. (1615–1681) in the History of Music for the Baroque Guitar* (diss., Univ. of Calif. at Los Angeles, 1976; includes transcriptions of his works).—**LK/DM**

Corboz, Michel (-Jules), Swiss conductor; b. Marsens, Feb. 14, 1934. He was educated at the École Normale in Fribourg; then became a director of church music in Lausanne (1953), where he organized the Ensemble Vocal et Instrumental de Lausanne (1968), with which he has given numerous performances of Baroque vocal and orch. music.—**NS/LK/DM**

Corcoran, Frank, Irish composer and teacher; b. Tipperary, May 1, 1944. He began his training in Dublin, and then studied in Rome (1964–67). After further studies in Dublin (1967–69), he completed his training with Boris Blacher in Berlin (1969–71). From 1971 to 1979 he was a music inspector for the Irish Dept. of Education. He was made a member of Aosdána, Ireland's state-sponsored academy of creative artists. After receiving a composition fellowship in Berlin, he settled in Germany and taught in Berlin (1981) and Stuttgart (1982). In 1983 he became a prof. of composition and theory at the Hamburg Hochschule für Musik. In 1989–90 he was a guest lecturer in the U.S.

WORKS: DRAMATIC: Opera: *Gilgamesh* (1990). **ORCH.:** Sonata for Strings (1971); *3 Pieces: Pictures from My Exhibition* (1974; rev. 1976); Chamber Sym. No. 1 (1976); *Caoine* (1978); 4 numbered syms. (*Symphonies of Wind Instruments*, 1980–81; 1982–87; 1994; 1996); Concerto for Strings (1982); *Farewell Symphonies* for Speaker, Tape, and Orch. (1982); *Shadows of Gilgamesh* (1988); *Cantus de Calamitate Hiberniorum in Patria Antiqua* (1991); *Mikrokosmoi: Scenes from My Receding Past* for Chamber String Orch. (1994). **CHAMBER:** Chamber Sonata for Oboe, String Trio, and Percussion (1975); 2 string quartets (1976, 1978); Piano Trio (1978); 3 wind quintets (1978, 1978, 1999); *Music from the Book of Kells* for Piano and 5 Percussionists

(1990); *Four Concertini of Ice* for Octet (1993); *Rhapsodic Thinking* for 4 Violins (1994); *Trauerfelder* for 4 Percussionists (1995); *Ice Etchings No. 1* for 9 Instruments (1996) and *No. 2* for Cello (1996); *Mad Sweeney* for Speaker and Chamber Ensemble (1996). **TAPE:** *Balthazar's Dream* (1980); *Sweeney's Vision* (1997); *Sweeney's Last Poem* (1998); *Quasi una Missa* (1999). **OTHER:** Piano pieces; Organ Sonata (1973); several choral pieces.—**LK/DM**

Corder, Frederick, English composer and teacher, father of **Paul Corder;** b. London, Jan. 26, 1852; d. there, Aug. 21, 1932. He was a pupil at the Royal Academy of Music in London (1873–75), and in 1875 won the Mendelssohn Scholarship. He studied with Ferdinand Hiller at Cologne (1875–78). He was conductor of the Brighton Aquarium Concerts from 1880 to 1882, and greatly improved their quality. From 1886 he was a prof. of composition at the Royal Academy of Music and, from 1889, also curator. In 1905 he founded the Soc. of British Composers. He was remarkably successful as a teacher, many prominent British composers having been his pupils. A zealous apostle of Wagner, Corder and his wife made the first Eng. tr. of *The Ring of the Nibelung, Die Meistersinger,* and *Parsifal.*

WORKS: DRAMATIC: Opera: *Morte d'Arthur* (1877); *Nordisa* (Liverpool, Jan. 26, 1887); *Ossian* (1905). **Operettas:** *Philomel* (1880); *A Storm in a Teacup* (1880); *The Nabob's Pickle* (1883); *The Noble Savage* (1885). **Incidental Music to Plays:** *The Tempest* (1886); *The Termagant* (1898); *The Black Tulip* (1899). **ORCH.:** *Evening on the Sea Shore,* idyll (1876); *Im Schwarzwald,* suite (1876); *Ossian,* overture (1882); *Nocturne* (1882); *Prospero,* overture (1885); *Roumanian Suite* (1887); *Pippa Passes,* orch. poem (1897); *A Fairy Tale* (1913). **CHAMBER:** *Roumanian Dances* for Violin and Piano (1883); *Elegy* for 24 Violins (1908). **VOCAL: Cantatas:** *The Cyclops* (1881); *The Bridal of Triermain* (1886); *The Blind Girl of Castel-Cuille* (1888); *The Sword of Argantyr* (1889). **Other:** *Dreamland,* ode for Chorus and Orch. (1883); *The Minstrel's Curse,* ballad for declamation, with Orch. (1888); *True Thomas,* musical recitation (1895); *The Witch's Song* (1904); *Empire Pageant Masque* (1910); *The Angels,* biblical scene for 6 Choirs (1911); *Sing unto God,* 50-part motet (1912).

WRITINGS: *Exercises in Harmony and Musical Composition* (1891); *The Orchestra and How to Write for It* (1895); *Modern Composition* (1909); *Musical Encyclopaedia* (1915); *History of the Royal Academy of Music* (1922).—**NS/LK/DM**

Corder, Paul, English composer, son of **Frederick Corder;** b. London, Dec. 14, 1879; d. there, Aug. 6, 1942. He entered the Royal Academy of Music in London in 1895, studying piano with Oscar Beringer and Tobias Matthay, and composition with his father. He was appointed a prof. of harmony and composition there in 1907.

WORKS: 2 operas: *Grettir the Strong* and *Rapunzel* (1917); *The Moon Slave,* terpsichorean fantasy; *Cyrano de Bergerac,* overture; *Dross,* music drama without words; op.8, *Morar,* a "Gaelic fantasy"; *The Dryad,* ballet; *Prelude and Fugue; Sea-Songs;* 2 *Choral Songs; Heroic Elegy;* many piano works (*Transmutations,* 9 *Preludes, Passacaglia,* etc.); songs.—**NS/LK/DM**

Cordero, Roque, Panamanian composer, teacher, and conductor; b. Panama, Aug. 16, 1917. After training in Panama, he won a scholarship in 1943 to the Univ. of Minn., where he had lessons in conducting from Mitropoulos. He also studied counterpoint and composition with Krenek at Hamline Univ. in St. Paul, and pursued training in conducting with Chappel at the Berkshire Music Center in Tanglewood and with Barzin in N.Y. Returning to Panama, he was prof. of composition at the National Inst. of Music (1950–66), where he served as its director (1953–64). He also was conductor of the National orch. (1964–66). He taught at Ind. Univ. in Bloomington (1966–69) and at Ill. State Univ. in Normal (1972–99). As a conductor, he toured internationally. Cordero received various awards and commission as a composer, and in 1949 he received a Guggenheim fellowship. After composing in a basically tonal idiom, he developed a modified 12-tone technique in 1946.

WORKS: DRAMATIC: 2 ballets. **ORCH.:** *8 Miniatures* (1944; rev. 1948); *Obertura panamena No. 2* (1944); Piano Concerto (1944); 4 syms. (1945, 1946, 1965, 1986); *Movimento sinfonico* for Strings (1946); *Rapsodia campesina* (1949); *5 mensajes breves* (1959); Violin Concerto (1962); *Circunvoluciones y moviles* for 57 Instruments (1967); Concertino for Viola and Strings (1968); *Elegy* for Strings (1973); *Momentum jubilo* (1973); *6 Mobiles* (1974–75); *Overture of Salutation* (1980); *Centennial Symphonic Tribute* (1997). **CHAMBER:** Violin Sonatine (1946); Quintet for Flute, Clarinet, Violin, Viola, and Piano (1949); 4 string quartets (1960, 1968, 1973, 1983); Cello Sonata (1962); *3 Short Messages* for Viola and Piano (1966); *Permutaciones 7* for Clarinet, Trumpet, Timpani, Piano, Violin, Viola, and Double Bass (1967); *Paz, Paix, Peace* for 4 Trios and Harp (1969); *Variations and Theme for 5* for Wind Quartet and Horn (1975); *Soliloquios No. 1* for Flute (1975), *No. 2* for Saxophone (1976), *No. 3* for Clarinet (1976), *No. 4* for Percussion (1981), *No. 5* for Double Bass (1981), and *No. 6* for Cello (1992); *Double Concerto without Orchestra* for Violin and Piano (1978); *Music for 5 Brass* (1980); *Poetic Nocturne of the Min River* for Chamber Ensemble (1981); *Petite Mobiles* for Bassoon and Trios (1983); *Three Miniminiatures for Ernst* for Flute and Clarinet (1985); *Serenatas* for Flute, Clarinet, Viola, and Harp (1987); *Duos* for Oboe and Bassoon (1996). **KEYBOARD: Piano:** *Sonatina ritmíca* (1943); *Rhapsody* for 2 Pianos (1945); *Sonata breve* (1966); *3 Piececillas para Alina* (1978); *Five New Preludes* (1983); Sonata (1985); *Tres Meditaciones Poéticas* (1995). **VOCAL:** *Cantata for Peace* (1975–79); choral pieces. —NS/LK/DM

Cordon, Norman, American baritone; b. Washington, N.C., Jan. 20, 1904; d. Chapel Hill, N.C., March 1, 1964. He attended the Fishburne Military School, and later studied at the Univ. of N.C. and at the Nashville Cons. of Music. He was a voice student of Gaetano de Lucas and Hadley Outland. He sang with the San Carlo Opera Co.; in 1933 he made his debut as Scarpia at the Civic Opera in Chicago, of which he was a member until 1936; on May 13, 1936, he made his Metropolitan Opera debut in N.Y. as Monterone, remaining on its roster until 1946; he also appeared with the San Francisco Opera, the Cincinnati Summer Opera, and on Broadway. —NS/LK/DM

Corea, Chick (Armando Anthony), influential jazz–fusion pianist, composer; b. Chelsea, Mass., June 12, 1941. His father was a Latin percussionist of

Portuguese origin who took Chick to hear live jazz. Chick began piano at four; Bud Powell was his first jazz inspiration. He studied classical piano as a teenager. In the 1950s in Boston, he played at Wally's Jazz Club, in Phil Barboza's Latin band, and had a trio with Tony Williams and Don Alias. He began studying liberal arts at Columbia Univ. (1958), but decided to become a full-time musician after seeing the Miles Davis group with Coltrane at Birdland (January 1959). Joe Farrell helped introduce him and he began working and recording with Mongo Santamaria, Willie Bobo, and Cal Tjader. In the early 1960s, he worked with Blue Mitchell and Herbie Mann and spent a year accompanying Sarah Vaughan. In March 1968 he recorded *Now He Sings, Now He Sobs* with Miroslav Vitous and Roy Haynes, which was widely influential; his solo on "Matrix" was transcribed, studied, and performed by Lee Konitz and others. He joined Miles Davis's band (mid-1968–mid-1970; recording 1972), playing first acoustic, then electric piano at the insistence of the leader. During his tenure, he also became more involved in free improvisation, recording the album *Is*, on which he also played percussion. After Davis, he led Circle (1970–71) with Dave Holland, Barry Altschul, and Anthony Braxton, and also performed and recorded solo (1971). During this time, he was introduced to Scientology and decided that he wanted his music to be more accessible, "melodic and lyrical with more traditional rhythms" and with occasional vocals; he has concentrated heavily since then on composition. Corea has created a distinct musical identity by a conscious incorporation of his Latin roots and experiences and of modern classical music, particularly Bartok.

Corea performed at the Village Vanguard (January 1972) and recorded the album *Return to Forever*, which became the title of the band that included Farrell, Stanley Clarke, Airto Moreira, and Flora Purim. He, Clarke, and Tony Williams toured with Stan Getz (1972), before turning to full-time touring with Return to Forever. By 1973, the band featured Clarke, Lenny White, and Bill Connors, replaced by Al DiMeola in 1974. Corea began using a broader range of keyboards, including the Moog synthesizer. He settled in Los Angeles in the mid- 1970s and added his friend and eventual wife, singer Gayle Moran, to the group. Return to Forever had six albums reach the Billboard pop album chart in the 1970s, three in the Top 40. He continued using the Return to Forever title for his bands through 1977. Corea then delved into a diverse series of recordings: electronic ensembles, solo piano, chamber music, reunions with Vitous and Haynes (occasionally for tours and recordings since 1981), and acoustic duos with Herbie Hancock (1978, on tour and on recordings) and Gary Burton (occasionally since 1972). Other projects include the Grammy winning *Leprechaun*, and tours and recordings with Joe Henderson and Freddie Hubbard (1979–82). In June 1982 he recorded duets with European pianists accomplished in both classical music and jazz, Friedrich Gulda and Nicolas Economou, the latter including some music of Bartok. He has also recorded Mozart's *Concerto for Two Pianos and Orch.* (with Gulda); his own piano concerto was premiered in 1986, but not recorded.

Corea began an association with GRP Records in 1985 that was marked by the release of a recording with his new group, the Elektric Band; this also was the beginning of his collaboration with John Patitucci and Dave Weckl, who recorded and performed acoustic trio music as the Akoustic Band. In 1992 he and his manager, Ron Moss, formed Stretch Records. Among its early releases have been projects by Bob Berg, Patitucci, Eddie Gomez, and Robben Ford. He also runs the Mad Hatter studio in Los Angeles. He toured in 1996 with his Time Warp quartet in the U.S. and Europe. Also that year, he performed with Bobby McFerrin and the St. Paul Chamber Orch., playing two Mozart concerti and some duets and then made a recording. In 1996 he also toured and recorded with Joshua Redman, Roy Haynes, and others to celebrate the legacy of Bud Powell. He recorded on drums with Wayne Shorter on his record *Super Nova*. He holds an honorary doctorate from Berklee (1997). He studied martial arts with Portland, Ore. native Fred King some years ago and performed "Sifu" for him with his latest group, Origin (1998).

Besides his many influential albums, many of Corea's compositions have become new standards in the jazz–fusion movement. These include "Crystal Silence," "Tones for Joan's Bones," "500 Miles High," "Spain," and "La Fiesta," among others.

Disc.: *Now He Sings, Now He Sobs* (1968); *Sundance* (1969); *Is* (1969); *Song of Singing* (1970); *Early Circle* (1970); *Circulus* (1970); *Circling In* (1970); *Piano Improvisations, Vols. 1, 2* (1971); *A.R.C.* (1971); *Return to Forever* (1972); *Light As a Feather* (1972); *Crystal Silence* (1972); *Children of Forever* (1972); *Seven Songs for Quartet and Chamber Group* (1973); *Hymn of the Seventh Galaxy* (1973); *Leprechaun* (1975); *Dreams So Real* (1975); *Romantic Warrior* (1976); *Passengers* (1976); *My Spanish Heart* (1976); *Return to Forever Live* (1977); *Music Magic* (1977); *Tap Step* (1978); *Secret Agent* (1978); *R.T.F. Live* (1978); *Mad Hatter* (1978); *Homecoming: Corea and Hancock* (1978); *Friends* (1978); *Evening with Herbie Hancock* (1978); *Duet* (1978); *Delphi I, II, III: Solo Piano Improvisations* (1978); *In Concert* (1979); *Duet* (1979); *An Evening With* (1980); *Trio Music* (1981); *Three Quartets* (1981); *Touchstone* (1982); *Meeting* (1982); *Lyric Suite for Sextet* (1982); *Chick and Lionel* (1982); *Children's Songs* (1983); *Voyage* (1984); *Trio Music: Live in Europe* (1984); *Septet* (1984); *Sea Journey* (1985); *Elektric Band* (1986); *Light Years* (1987); *Times Like These* (1988); *Eye of the Beholder* (1988); *Akoustic Band* (1989); *Right Time, Right Place* (1990); *Inside Out* (1990); *Expressions* (1993); *Time Warp* (1995); *A Week at the Blue Note* (1998); *Origin* (1998).

Writings: *Music Poetry: Thoughts on Music and Art* (Hollywood, 1980).—LP

Corelli, Arcangelo,

celebrated Italian composer, violinist, and teacher; b. Fusignano, Feb. 17, 1653; d. Rome, Jan. 8, 1713. He was born into a family of well-to-do landowners. After musical training in Faenza and Lugo, he went to Bologna in 1666 to pursue his studies in earnest. At the age of 17, he was made a member of Bologna's Accademia Filarmonica. By 1675 he was in Rome, where he worked as a violinist in churches and theaters. He acquired a distinguished reputation, and soon found a patron in Queen Christina of Sweden, who made him a chamber musician in her service. His 12 trio sonatas, op.1 (Rome, 1681), were dedicated to her. In 1684 Corelli became a regular performer in the Sunday academies of Cardinal Benedetto Pamphili given at his Palazzo al Corso, and was soon asked to assume their directorship. He also was made a member of the Congregazione dei Virtuosi de S. Cecilia in 1684, and he became director of the instrumental ensemble in 1700. Corelli dedicated his 12 chamber trios, op.2 (Rome, 1685), to Cardinal Pamphili, who made him his music master in 1687, where he took up his residence. His next set of 12 chamber trios, op.3 (Rome, 1689), were dedicated to Francesco II, the Duke of Modena. Corelli remained in Cardinal Pamphili's service until 1690. He then found a new patron in Cardinal Pietro Ottoboni, in whose palace, the Cancelleria, he lived and oversaw the Monday academies and the opera performances. Cardinal Ottoboni became the dedicatee of Corelli's 12 chamber trios, op.4 (Rome, 1694). His famous set of 12 violin sonatas, op.5 (Rome, 1700), were dedicated to Sophie Charlotte, the Electress of Brandenburg. In 1706 he was made a member of the Accademia dell'Arcadia, where he was given the name of Arcomelo Erimanteo. Corelli made his final public appearance in 1708, and then lived at the Cancelleria until settling in the Palazzetto Ermini in 1712. He died a famous and wealthy man, and was given interment in S. Maria della Rotonda, the Pantheon. His former pupil, Matteo Fornari, oversaw the publication of Corelli's 12 Concerti grossi, op.6 (Amsterdam, 1714), which added luster to the composer's renown. Corelli was one of the outstanding instrumental composers of his era. His sonatas and concerti grossi became paradigms of the Baroque era, being particularly esteemed for their assured command of counterpoint and harmony, and for their idiomatic string writing. His works were widely distributed and emulated. As a performing musician, he was also held in high regard. His influence as a violin teacher was profound, for he numbered among his students such native musicians as Carbonelli, Castrucci, Gasparini, Geminiani, and Somis, and such foreign musicians as Anet, Herrando, and Störl.

Works: (12) *Sonate a tre* for 2 Violins, Violone or Archlute, and Organ, op.1 (Rome, 1681); (12) *Sonate da camera a tre* for 2 Violins and Violone or Harpsichord, op.2 (Rome, 1685); (12) *Sonate a tre* for 2 Violins, Violone or Archlute, and Organ, op.3 (Rome, 1689); (12) *Sonate a tre* for 2 Violins and Violone, op.4 (Rome, 1694); (12) *Sonate* for Violin and Violone or Harpsichord, op.5 (Rome, 1700); (12) *Concerti grossi*, op.6 (Amsterdam, 1714); (6) *Sonate a tre* for 2 Violins and Basso Continuo, op.posthumous (Amsterdam, 1715). Also 2 sonatas for 2 Violins, Viola, and Bass (n.d.) and the overture to G. Lulier's oratorio *S. Beatrice d'Este* (1689). See J. Joachim and F. Chrysander, eds., *Les oeuvres de A. C.*, Denkmäler der Tonkunst, III (1871), and H. Marx et al. eds., *A. C.: Historisch-kritische Gesamtausgabe der musikalischen Werke* (Cologne, 1976 et seq.).

Bibl.: C. Piancastelli, *In onore di A. C.: Fusignano ad A. C. nel secondo centenario dalla morte, 1913* (Bologna, 1914); M. Pincherle, *C.* (Paris, 1933; 2nd ed., rev. and enl., 1954 as *C. et son temps*; Eng. tr., 1956); M. Rinaldi, *A. C.* (Milan, 1954); *Studi c.ani: 1[00aa] congresso internazionale: Fusignano 1968* (Fusignano, 1968); *Nuovi studi c.ani: 2[00aa] congresso internazionale: Fusignano 1974* (Fusignano, 1974); *Nuovissimi studi c.ani: 3[00aa]* *congresso internazionale: Fusignano 1980* (Fusignano, 1980); G. Morelli, ed., *L'invenzione del gusto: C. e Vivaldi: Mutazioni culturali, a Roma e Venezia, nel periodo post- barocco* (Milan, 1982). —NS/LK/DM

Corelli, Franco, outstanding Italian tenor; b. Ancona, April 8, 1921. He studied naval engineering at the Univ. of Bologna; in 1947 he entered the Pesaro Cons. to study voice; dissatisfied with the academic training, he left the Cons. and proceeded to learn the repertoire by listening to recordings of great singers. He made his operatic debut at the Spoleto Festival in 1952 as Don José; then sang at the Rome Opera in 1953 and at Milan's La Scala in 1954; he appeared at London's Covent Garden in 1957. On Jan. 27, 1961, he made his Metropolitan Opera debut in N.Y. as Manrico in *Il Trovatore*; while continuing on its roster until 1975, he also appeared with major opera houses worldwide. Among his finest roles were Radames, Ernani, Don Alvaro, Raoul, and Calaf.

BIBL.: M. Boagno, *F. C.: Un uomo, una voce* (Parma, 1990; Eng. tr., 1996, as *F. C.: A Man, a Voice*).—NS/LK/DM

Corena, Fernando, Swiss bass; b. Geneva, Dec. 22, 1916; d. Lugano, Nov. 26, 1984. He studied in Geneva and with Enrico Romani in Milan. After making his operatic debut in 1937, he sang with the radio and municipal theater in Zürich. He first gained wide notice as Varlaam in Trieste in 1947, and subsequently was invited to sing with major opera houses in Europe and the U.S.; he made his Metropolitan Opera debut in N.Y. as Leporello (Feb. 6, 1954), and remained on its roster until 1979. He first appeared at London's Covent Garden on May 16, 1960, as Dr. Bartolo in *Il Barbiere di Siviglia*. He was particularly known for his buffo roles. Among his other roles were Don Pasquale, Dulcamare, Alfonso, Osmin, and Gianni Schicchi.—NS/LK/DM

Corigliano, John, American violinist, father of **John (Paul) Corigliano;** b. N.Y., Aug. 28, 1901; d. Norfolk, Conn., Sept. 1, 1975. He was a student of Giacomo Quintano, Alois Trnka, and Auer. After making his N.Y. debut in 1919, he toured as a soloist. He was concertmaster of the CBS Sym. Orch. (1934–35), and then asst. concertmaster (1935–43) and concertmaster (1943–66) of the N.Y. Phil.; thereafter he was concertmaster of the San Antonio Sym. Orch.—NS/LK/DM

Corigliano, John (Paul), notable American composer and teacher, son of **John Corigliano;** b. N.Y., Feb. 16, 1938. While still a child, he began to play the piano and to try his hand at composing. During his high school years, he studied orchestration on his own by listening to recordings with scores in hand. He then was a student of Luening at Columbia Univ. (B.A., 1959) and of Giannini at the Manhattan School of Music. He worked as a music programmer in N.Y. for WQXR-FM and WBAI-FM (1959–64), as an assoc. producer of music programs for CBS-TV (1961–72)2), and as music director of the Morris Theater in N.J. (1962–64). After teaching at the Coll. of Church Musicians in Washington, D.C. (1968–71), he was on the faculties of the Manhattan School of Music (from 1971) and of Lehman Coll. of the City Univ. of N.Y. (from 1973), where he later held the title of Distinguished Prof. (from 1986). He also taught at the Juilliard School in N.Y. (from 1991). Corigliano established his considerable reputation as a composer with his Clarinet Concerto (N.Y., Dec. 6, 1977). From 1987 to 1990 he served as the first composer-in- residence of the Chicago Sym. Orch. His deeply felt Sym. No. 1, dedicated to the victims of AIDS, was premiered by that orch. under Barenboim's direction on March 15, 1990. The highly successful premiere and subsequent recording of the score brought Corigliano international acclaim. His opera, *The Ghosts of Versailles*, added further lustre to his reputation at its critically acclaimed premiere by the Metropolitan Opera in N.Y. under Levine's direction on Dec. 19, 1991. Corigliano has won many honors and awards and received major commissions. In 1968–69 he held a Guggenheim fellowship. In 1989 the American Academy and Inst. of Arts and Letters gave him its award for music, and in 1991 he was elected to its membership. He also won the Grawemeyer Award in 1991 from the Univ. of Louisville for his Sym. No. 1. In 1993 he served as Distinguished Artist-in-Residence of the Winnipeg Sym. Orch. He was Distinguished Composer-in-Residence of the Helsinki Biennale in 1997. In his diverse output, Corigliano has produced a body of music notable for its remarkable originality and craftsmanship. Despite the apparent dissonant freedom of his polyphonic writing, his music retains a firm tonal anchorage.

WORKS: DRAMATIC: *The Naked Carmen*, electric rock opera (1970; transcription of Bizet's *Carmen*); *The Ghosts of Versailles*, grand opera buffa (N.Y., Dec. 19, 1991); incidental music for plays; film scores, including *The Red Violin* (1998). **ORCH.:** *Elegy* (1965; San Francisco, June 1, 1966); *Tournaments* (1965; Louisville, Jan. 11, 1980); Piano Concerto (San Antonio, April 7, 1968); *Gazebo Dances* for Concert Band (Evansville, Ind., May 6, 1973; also for Orch., 1974; Woodbury, N.J., Feb. 20, 1981; also for Piano, 4-Hands, 1972); *Aria* for Oboe and Strings (1975; 4th movement of the Oboe Concerto, 1975; also for Oboe and String Quintet, 1985); Oboe Concerto (N.Y., Nov. 9, 1975); *Voyage* for Strings (1976; Rockland County, N.Y., April 22, 1977; also for Flute and Strings, London, Nov. 26, 1983; also for Flute and String Quintet, 1988); Clarinet Concerto (N.Y., Dec. 6, 1977); *Pied Piper Fantasy*, flute concerto (1981; Los Angeles, Feb. 4, 1982); *Promenade Overture* (Boston, July 10, 1981); *3 Hallucinations* (1981; Syracuse, N.Y., Jan. 22, 1982; based on the film score for *Altered States*); *Summer Fanfare: Echoes of Forgotten Rites* (Miami, June 21, 1982); *Fantasia on an Ostinato* (N.Y., Sept. 18, 1986; also for Piano, 1985); *Campagne di Ravello: A Celebration Piece for Sir Georg Solti* (Chicago, Oct. 9, 1987); Sym. No. 1 (1988–89; Chicago, March 15, 1990); *Troubadours: Variations* for Guitar and Chamber Orch. (St. Paul, Minn., Oct. 8, 1993); *Fanfares to Music* (1994; also for 11 Instruments, 1993); *Chaconne* for Violin and Orch. (1997; used in the film score *The Red Violin*, 1998; as a suite for Violin and Orch., N.Y., June 3, 1999); *Nocturne* (1997); *D.C. Fanfare* (1997). **CHAMBER:** Violin Sonata (1963; Spoleto, July 10, 1964); *Scherzo* for Oboe and Percussion (1975); *Aria* for Oboe and String Quintet (1985; also for Oboe and String Orch., 1975); *Phantasmagoria* for Cello and Piano (Washington, D.C., May 1993); *Fanfare to Music* for 11 Instruments (N.Y., Oct. 20, 1993; also for Orch., 1994); *Amen* for Double Brass Ensemble (1994; also for Chorus); String Quartet

(1995). **KEYBOARD: P i a n o :** *Kaleidoscope* for 2 Pianos (1959; Spoleto, June 28, 1961); *Gazebo Dances* for Piano, 4-Hands (1972; N.Y., Feb. 24, 1985; also for Concert Band, 1973, and for Orch., 1974); *Étude Fantasy* (Washington, D.C., Oct. 9, 1976); *Fantasia on an Ostinato* (Fort Worth, May 24, 1985; also for Orch., 1986). **VOCAL:** *Petit Fours* for Voice and Piano (1959); *Fern Hill* for Mezzo- soprano, Chorus, and Orch. (1960–61; Washington, D.C., Dec. 11, 1965; alsoso for String Orch., N.Y., Dec. 19, 1961); *Poem in October* for Tenor and 8 Instruments (N.Y., Oct. 25, 1970; also for Tenor and Orch., Washington, D.C., April 24, 1976); *Poem on His Birthday* for Baritone, Chorus, and Orch. (Washington, D.C., April 14, 1976; also for Baritone, Chorus, and Piano); the preceding 3 works constitute *A Dylan Thomas Trilogy,* choral sym. for Soloists, Chorus, and Orch. (1st complete perf., Washington, D.C., April 24, 1976); *What I Expected Was...* for Chorus, Brass, and Percussion (Tanglewood, Aug. 16, 1962); *The Cloisters* for Voice and Piano (N.Y., Nov. 15, 1965; also for Voice and Orch., Washington, D.C., May 2, 1976); *Christmas at the Cloisters* for Chorus and Organ or Piano (1966; NBC-TV, Dec. 25, 1967); *L'Invitation au Voyage* for Chorus (1971; San Antonio, May 13, 1972); *Wedding Song* for Medium Voice, Melody Instrument, and Organ (1971); *Creations* for Narrator and Orch. (1972; rev. version, Milwaukee, Oct. 3, 1984); *A Black November Turkey* for Chorus (1972; San Antonio, Jan. 20, 1973); *Psalm No. 8* for Chorus and Organ (San Antonio, Oct. 18, 1976); *3 Irish Folksong Settings* for Voice and Flute (N.Y., June 18, 1988); *Of Rage and Remembrance* for Mezzo-soprano, Men's Chorus with 12 Chimes, Timpani, 8 Cellos, and 4 Double Basses (Seattle, March 29, 1991); *Amen* for Chorus (Montreat, N.C., June 19, 1994; also for Double Brass Ensemble); *Vocalise* for Soprano, Electronics, and Orch. (1999).

BIBL.: M. Humphrey, *J. C.* (N.Y., 1989; rev. ed., 1994). —NS/LK/DM

Cornelius, Peter (real name, **Lauritz Peter Corneliys Petersen**), esteemed Danish tenor; b. Labjerggaard, Jan. 4, 1865; d. Snekkersten, near Copenhagen, Dec. 30, 1934. He studied with Nyrop in Copenhagen, making his operatic debut there in the baritone role of Escamillo (1892). After further appearances as a baritone, he then studied with Lieban, Revilliers, and Spiro in Berlin and made his tenor debut as the Steersman in *Der fliegende Holländer* in Copenhagen (1899), where he was subsequently a principal member of the Royal Danish Theater until 1922. He also sang at the Bayreuth Festival in 1906 and at London's Covent Garden (1907–14), and made guest appearances in Paris, Stockholm, and Oslo. Although he returned briefly to the stage in 1927, his later years were devoted mainly to teaching. He was particularly known for his Wagnerian roles, which included Tannhäuser, Siegfried, Lohengrin, Siegmund, and Tristan.

BIBL.: C. Cornelius, *P. C.* (1925).—NS/LK/DM

Cornelius, Peter, important German composer and writer on music; b. Mainz, Dec. 24, 1824; d. there, Oct. 26, 1874. A nephew of the painter Peter von Cornelius, he at first became an actor, but after an unsuccessful debut, changed his mind; he studied theory with Dehn at Berlin (1845–52) and then joined Liszt's following in Weimar as a champion of Wagner, contributing frequent articles to the *Neue Zeitschrift für Musik.* His masterpiece, the opera *Der Barbier von Bagdad,* was premiered at Weimar (Dec. 15, 1858) under the direction of Liszt, who resigned his position there because of hostile demonstrations while he was conducting the opera. In 1861 Cornelius went to Wagner at Vienna, and followed him to Munich (1865), where he was appointed reader to King Ludwig II, and prof. of harmony and rhetoric at the Royal Music School. A second opera, *Der Cid,* was premiered at Weimar on May 21, 1865; a third, *Gunlöd* (from the Edda), remained unfinished (completed by Lassen and premiered at Weimar, May 6, 1891). *Der Barbier von Bagdad* was revived at Karlsruhe on Feb. 1, 1884, in a drastically altered version by Mottl. Cornelius publ. *Lieder-Cyclus* (op.3), duets for Soprano and Baritone (op.6), *Weihnachtslieder* (op.8), and *Trauerchöre* for Men's Chorus (op.9). A vol. of *Lyrische Poesien* was issued in 1861. A complete ed. of Cornelius's works was issued by Breitkopf & Härtel (1905–06).

BIBL.: A Sandberger, *Leben und Werke des Dichtermusikers P. C.* (Leipzig, 1887); E. Istel, *P. C.* (Leipzig, 1904); E. Sulger-Gebing, *P. C. als Mensch und Dichter* (Munich, 1908); M. Hasse, *Der Dichtermusiker P. C.* (2 vols., Leipzig, 1923); A. Cherbuliez, *P. C.* (Zürich, 1925); C. Cornelius, *P. C., der Wort- und Tondichter* (2 vols., Regensburg, 1925); P. Egert, *P. C.* (Berlin, 1940); G. Wagner, *P. C.: Verzeichnis seiner musikalischen und literarischen Werke* (Mainz, 1986); R. Chraska, *Der Mainzer Dichter-Komponist P. C. in Salzburg und Trier* (Trier, 1992).—NS/LK/DM

Cornelys, T(h)eresa (née **Imer**), colorful Italian singer; b. Venice, 1723; d. London, Aug. 19, 1797. After making her debut in Venice (c. 1741), she pursued her career in Vienna, Hamburg, Copenhagen, and the Low Countries; while in the latter, she married the dancer Pompeati but generally used the professional name of Cornelys. In 1746 she made her London debut in Gluck's *Caduta de' giganti.* In 1759 she settled in London, where she received the support of Casanova, with whom she was intimate. In 1760 she began giving concerts at Carlisle House in Soho Square, but these came to an inglorious end when she was indicted in 1771 for running an establishment of ill repute. She was convicted and spent her remaining years in the Fleet Street prison, being survived by a daughter born out of wedlock to Casanova. Although her contemporaries considered her a gifted singer, her reputation suffered as a result of the vagaries of her private life.—NS/LK/DM

Corner, Philip (Lionel), American composer, performer, and teacher; b. N.Y., April 10, 1933. He studied with Mark Brunswick at the City Coll. of N.Y. (B.A., 1955), then pursued training in philosophy with Messiaen at the Paris Cons. (2nd prix, 1957), composition with Luening and Cowell at Columbia Univ. (M.A., 1959), and piano with Dorothy Taubman (1961–75). While serving in the U.S. Army in South Korea (1959–60), he became immersed in Asian music; upon his discharge, he was active with various avant-garde groups in N.Y., and also taught at Rutgers Univ. (from 1972). One of the earliest minimalists, Corner has extended his compositional horizon to include both Western and non-Western forms of expression, carefully recorded in his own graphic notation. He publ. *I Can Walk through the World as Music* (1980).

WORKS: ORCH.: *This Is It...This Time* (1959). **INSTRU-MENTAL:** *Sang-teh* (1959); *Air Effect* (1961); *Certain Distilling Processes* (1962); *Pond* (1968); *OM Emerging* (1970); *OM series* (1970–74); *Elementals* (1976). **GAMELAN** (works in open score): *Gamelan* (1975); *Gamelan II* (1975); *Gamelan IX* (1975); *The Barcelona Cathedral* (1978); *Gamelan P. C.* (1979); *Gamelan LY* for Gamelan Ensemble, Erhu, and Clarinet (1979); *Gamelan IRIS* for Gamelan Ensemble and Flute (1980); *Gamelan CONCERT!O* for Gamelan Ensemble, Harpsichord, and Electric Guitar (1980); *Gamelan CORN* for Violin (1982); *Gamelan ANTIPODE* for Violin (1984). **OTHER:** Theater pieces; electronic works; piano music.—**NS/LK/DM**

Cornet, Peeter, Flemish organist and composer; b. probably in Brussels, c. 1575; d. there, March 27, 1633. He was born into a musical family and spent his entire career in Brussels. From 1603 to 1606 he was organist at St. Nicolas, and then was in the service of the court of Archduke Albert. Cornet excelled as a composer of extended keyboard fantasias. W. Apel ed. *P. C.: Collected Keyboard Works*, Corpus of Early Keyboard Music, XXVI (1969).

BIBL.: M. Ferrand, *P. C. (?–1633), organiste à la cour d'Albert et Isabelle à Bruxelles* (Brussels, 1973).—**LK/DM**

Cornysh or **Cornyshe, William,** English composer, poet, dramatist, and actor; b. place and date unknown; d. probably in Hylden, Kent, c.Oct. 1523. He was active at the court from 1494, and was made a Gentleman of the Chapel Royal. From 1509 he served as Master of the Children there. He was the most prominent figure in the production of the court dramas and entertainments, and he also accompanied the Chapel Royal to France on several occasions in the retinue of King Henry VIII. Some of his sacred vocal works are found in the Eton Choirbook. In addition to his Magnificats, *Stabat mater, Ave Maria Mater Dei,* and motets, he distinguished himself as a composer of part songs.
—**LK/DM**

Coronaro, family of Italian musicians, all brothers:

(1) Antonio Coronaro, organist, teacher, and composer; b. Vicenza, June 29, 1851; d. there, March 24, 1933. He was trained in Vicenza, where he served as organist at the Cathedral from 1885 until his death. His first opera, *Seila* (Vicenza, Jan. 18, 1880), was well received. He also wrote the operas *La maliarda* (Vicenza, Carnival 1884), *Il falco di Calabria* (Vicenza, Jan. 15, 1903), *Edward*, and *Olinta e Simone*. Among his other works were piano pieces, sacred music, and songs.

(2) Gaetano Coronaro, conductor, pedagogue, and composer; b. Vicenza, Dec. 18, 1852; d. Milan, April 5, 1908. Following initial training in Vicenza, he pursued his studies with Faccio at the Milan Cons. (1871–73). His graduation piece, the eclogue *Un tramonto* (Aug. 8, 1873), was awarded the Giovannina Lucca prize and subsequently was heard with success in many other music centers. After further studies abroad, he settled in Milan in 1876. In 1879 he became a teacher at the Cons., where he was made a prof. of composition in 1894. He also conducted at La Scala. Coronaro wrote five operas, but only the first, *La creole* (Bologna, Nov. 27, 1878),

attained real success. His other operas were *Il malacarne* (Brescia, Jan. 20, 1894), *Un curioso accidente* (Turin, Nov. 11, 1903), *Enoch Arden* (1905), and *La signora di Challant*. He also composed orch. pieces, sacred works, and chamber music.

BIBL.: E. Oddone, *G. C.* (Rome, 1922).

(3) Gellio (Benevenuto) Coronaro, pianist, conductor, and composer; b. Vicenza, Nov. 30, 1863; d. Milan, July 26, 1916. He made his debut as a pianist at age 8, and was only 13 when he became a theater conductor in Marosteca. At 19, he entered the Bologna Cons. and studied with Busi, Parisini, and Mancinelli, graduating with a prize for his first opera, *Jolanda*, which was premiered there on June 24, 1883. His next opera, *La festa a marina*, won 1st prize in the Sonzogno competition and was successfully premiered in Venice on March 21, 1893. His other stage works included *Minestrone napoletano* (Messina, 1893), *Claudia* (Milan, Nov. 5, 1895), and *Bertoldo* (Milan, March 2, 1910). Among his other works were chamber music, sacred pieces, and songs.—**LK/DM**

Corradini, Francesco, Italian composer; b. Venice, c. 1700; d. Madrid, Oct. 14, 1769. After composing three stage works for Naples, he went to Spain about 1726 and became maestro di capilla to the viceroy Prince of Campoflorido in Valencia. In 1729 he settled in Madrid, where he became the leading composer for the stage. With Mele and Corselli, he became a director of the orch. of the royal theater in the palace of Buen Retiro in 1747. That same year, he assumed the position of maestro de musica de camera of the queen dowager, Isabella Farenese. Upon her death in 1766, he retired on a royal pension. Corradini composed at least 45 stage works in such genres as opera, opera buffa, comedia, zarzuela, and auto sacramentale.—**LK/DM**

Correa de Arauxo, Francisco, important Spanish organist; b. Seville, c. 1576; d. Segovia, Oct. 31, 1654. He held the post of organist at the Church of San Salvador in Seville (1599–1636), at the Cathedral of Jaen (1636–40), and at Segovia (from 1640 until his death). His *Facultad orgánica* (orig. publ. in Alcalá de Henares, 1626) contains 70 pieces for organ in tablature (most of them his own compositions), reproduced in the series Monumentos de la Musica Española, ed. by S. Kastner (Madrid, 1950).

BIBL.: C. Jacobs, *F. C.d.A.* (The Hague, 1973); J. Ayarra Jarne, *F. C.d.A., organista sevillano del siglo XVII* (Seville, 1986).
—**NS/LK/DM**

Corrette, Michel, French organist, composer, and writer on music; b. Rouen, 1709; d. Paris, Jan. 22, 1795. He was the son of the organist Gaspard Corrette. He was active in Paris as an organist in several churches and also in the service of several patrons of music. He was a prolific composer, producing concertos for harpsichord, organ, flute, and hurdy-gurdy, sonatas, organ works, and a large output of sacred music. He also prepared 17 methods on performing practice, 6 of which are lost.

BIBL.: H. Eliza, *The Organ Masses, Hymns, and Magnificats of Gaspard and M. C.* (diss., Ind. Univ., 1967).—**NS/LK/DM**

Corri, Domenico, Italian composer; b. Rome, Oct. 4, 1744; d. London, May 22, 1825. He was a pupil of Porpora in Naples. In 1771 went to Edinburgh as an opera conductor. His attempt to organize his own opera company and a publishing firm there was a failure, and he sought better fortune in London (1790). There he engaged in various enterprises as a publisher, composer, and impresario. His opera, *The Travelers, or Music's Fascination*, was given at Drury Lane on Jan. 22, 1806, with little success. He publ. four music manuals in Eng.: *A Complete Musical Grammar* (1787), *A Musical Dictionary* (1798), *The Art of Fingering* (1799), and *The Singer's Preceptor* (1810). His daughter, Sophia Giustina Corri Dussek (b. Edinburgh, May 1, 1775; d. after 1828), a talented pianist and singer, married Dussek. His sons, Montague Corri (1784–1849) and Haydn Corri (1785–1860), were also musicians.—NS/LK/DM

Corsaro, Frank (Anthony), American theater, musical, and opera producer and administrator; b. N.Y., Dec. 22, 1924. He studied at City Coll. in N.Y., the Yale Univ. School of Drama (graduated, 1947), and the Actors' Studio in N.Y. In 1952 he made his debut as a theater director, and from 1955 he was active on Broadway. In 1958 he made his debut as an opera producer with his staging of Floyd's *Susannah* at the N.Y.C. Opera, where his subsequent productions included *Don Giovanni, Rigoletto, Faust, Pelléas et Mélisande, A Village Romeo and Juliet, The Cunning Little Vixen,* and *The Makropulos Affair.* He staged the premieres of Floyd's *Of Mice and Men* in Seattle (1970), Hoiby's *Summer and Smoke* in St. Paul (1971), and Pasatieri's *The Seagull* in Houston (1974). In 1977 he was named artistic director of the Actors' Studio in N.Y. His production of Handel's *Rinaldo* was seen at the Metropolitan Opera in N.Y. in 1984. In 1992 he oversaw the U.S. stage premiere of Busoni's *Doktor Faust* at the N.Y.C. Opera. He staged *Faust* at the Lyric Opera in Chicago in 1996. Corsaro's dramatically compelling opera productions have also been seen in Europe and Australia.—NS/LK/DM

Corselli (real name, **Courcelle**), **Francesco,** Italian composer; b. Piacenza, c. 1702; d. Madrid, April 3, 1778. He became an accomplished tenor, violinist, and harpsichordist. He then went to Parma, where he was made maestro di cappella at the Steccata Church (1727), a position that extended to include the period of rule by the Duke of Parma (1727–33). He was then called to Madrid (1734), where he was appointed suffragan royal maestro de capilla and music teacher to the royal children. In 1737 he was named coadjutor of the royal chapel, serving as its titular maestro from 1738; he also was rector of the choir school.

WORKS: DRAMATIC: O p e r a (all 1st perf. in Madrid unless otherwise given): *Venere placata* (Venice, 1731); *Nino* (Venice, Carnival 1732); *La Cautela en la amistad y el robo de las Sabinas* (1735); *Alessandro nelle Indie* (May 9, 1738); *Farnace* (Nov. 4, 1739); *Achille in Sciro* (Dec. 8, 1744); *La clemencia de Tito* (Carnival 1747; Act 1 by Corselli, Act 2 by F. Corradini, and Act 3 by G.B. Mele); *El Polifemo* (Carnival 1748; Act 1 by Corselli, Act 2 by Corradini, and Act 3 by Mele). **OTHER:** Much sacred music.—NS/LK/DM

Corsi (Corso), Giuseppe (called **Celano** after his birthplace), Italian composer; b. Celano, May 1630; d. Dec. 1690. He studied with Carissimi. He served as maestro di cappella at S. Maria Maggiore in Rome (1659–61), at the Lateran Palace chapel (1661–65), and at S. Casa di Loreto (1668–75). He then returned to Rome, but because of his dissemination of books placed on the Church Index, he was persecuted and forced to leave (1678). From 1681 to 1688 he was at the court of the Duke of Parma. Among his pupils were Jacopo Perti (at Parma) and Petronio Franceschini. He publ. *Motetti a 2, 3 e 4 voci* (Rome, 1667), *Miserere a 5,* and *Motetti a 9,* as well as various other works in MS. Several of his works appeared in collections of the time. He is mentioned in Giuseppe Pitoni's *Guida armonica.*—NS/LK/DM

Corsi, Jacopo, Italian nobleman and patron of art; b. Florence, July 17, 1560; d. there, Dec. 29, 1602. In his palace, as in Bardi's, were held the memorable meetings of the "Camerata" in which Peri, Caccini, Emilio del Cavaliere, Galilei, the poet Rinuccini, and others took part, leading to the creation of the earliest operas. Corsi was a good musician, a skillful player on the harpsichord, and a composer. He wrote the concluding two numbers of the first opera by Peri, *Dafne,* which was performed at his home in 1598. These settings are preserved in the library of the Brussels Cons., and were publ. in Solerti's *Albori del Melodramma* (Milan, 1905). —NS/LK/DM

Corso, Giuseppe
 See **Corsi, Giuseppe**

Corte, Andrea della
 See **Della Corte, Andrea**

Corteccia, (Pier) Francesco, Italian composer and organist; b. Florence, July 27, 1502; d. there, June 27, 1571. He sang at S. Giovanni Battista in Florence. He later studied for the priesthood, and also received instruction in music from Bernardo Pisano. After serving as chaplain at S. Giovanni Battista (1527–31), he was organist at S. Lorenzo (1531–32) and at S. Giovanni Battista (1535–39). He subsequently was maestro di cappella there and at the Florence Cathedral until his death, and also was in the service of Duke Cosimo the Great. His musical intermezzi to various stage works (e.g. to Francesco d'Ambra's *Il furto,* 1544) are noteworthy in the development of opera. He also composed wedding music for Duke Cosimo, nine pieces for 4, 6, and 8 Voices (Venice, 1539), three books of madrigals for 4, 4, and 5 to 6 Voices, respectively (Venice, 1544, 1547, 1547), a Passion, two books of music for Tenebrae services (1570), motets, and hymns. Several of his works have been publ. in modern editions.—NS/LK/DM

Cortellini, Camillo, Italian trombonist and composer; b. Bologna, c. 1560; d. there, March 1630. He spent his entire life in his native city. After studies with his father, he received instruction in trombone, singing, and counterpoint from Alfonso Ganassi. In 1573 he became a member of the concerto palatino, a distinguished instrumental ensemble, and served as its director from 1613. From 1593 he was also active at S. Petronio. He publ. seven books of sacred music (1595–1626) and three books of madrigals (1583–86).—**LK/DM**

Cortés, Ramiro Jr., American composer and teacher; b. Dallas, Nov. 25, 1933; d. Salt Lake City, July 2, 1984. He was a student of Cowell in N.Y. (1952), of Donovan at Yale Univ. (1953–54), and of Stevens and Dahl at the Univ. of Southern Calif. in Los Angeles (B.M., 1955); after training with Petrassi in Rome on a Fulbright fellowship (1956–58), he completed his studies with Sessions at Princeton Univ. (1958) and with Giannini at the Juilliard School of Music in N.Y. (M.M., 1962). He taught in Los Angeles at the Univ. of Calif. (1966–67), and at the Univ. of Southern Calif. (1967–72); in 1972–73 he was composer-in-residence at the Univ. of Utah, where he subsequently served as a teacher and chairman of its theory and composition dept. (1973–84). In his works to the late 1960s, he followed strict serial procedures; later he became less dogmatic in approach.

WORKS: DRAMATIC: O p e r a : *The Christmas Garden*, children's opera (1955); *Prometheus* (1960); *The Eternal Return* (1981). M u s i c a l s : *The Patriots* (1975–76; rev. 1978). Also incidental music and dance scores. ORCH.: *Night Music* for Chamber Orch. (1954); *Sinfonia sacra* (1954; N.Y., April 9, 1955; rev. 1959); *Yerma*, symphonic portrait (1955); *Xochitl* (1955; Los Angeles, April 22, 1956); Chamber Concerto for Cello and 12 Winds (1957–58; rev. 1978); Sym. (1953–58); *Sinfonia breve* (1955–58); *Meditation* for Strings (1961); *The Eternal Return* (1963; rev. 1965); Concerto for Violin and Strings (1964–65; rev. 1983); *Charenton*, suite for Chamber Orch. (1968–71); Concerto for Harpsichord and Strings (1970–71); *Movements in Variation* (1972); Piano Concerto (1975); *Symphonic Celebration* (1979); *Contrasts* for Symphonic Band (1979–80); *Music* for Strings (1983). CHAMBER: *Elegy* for Flute and Piano (1952); *Divertimento* for Flute, Clarinet, and Bassoon (1953); Piano Quintet (1953); Piano Trio (1959; rev. 1965); 2 string quartets (1962, 1983); *The Brass Ring* for 2 Trumpets and 3 Trombones (1967); Duo for Flute and Oboe (1967); Wind Quintet (1967–68); *3 Movements* for 5 Wind Instruments (1968); Capriccio for Woodwind Quintet (1971); Violin Sonata (1971–72); Cello Sonata (1976–77); *Charenton Variations* for 11 Instruments (1978); *Little Suite* for 8 Instruments (1978); Trumpet Sonata (1978); Suite for Violin and Piano (1980); Trio for Clarinet, Cello, and Piano (1981); *Bridges* for Wind Ensemble (1982); piano pieces, including 3 sonatas (1954–79). VOCAL: Choral works; song cycles.—**NS/LK/DM**

Cortis, Antonio, Spanish tenor; b. on a ship between Oran and Altea, Aug. 12, 1891; d. Valencia, April 2, 1952. He went to Madrid, where he sang in the children's (1901–05) and adult (from 1911) choruses at the Teatro Real; he was soon singing operatic roles in Barcelona and Valencia. He made appearances in South America (from 1917) and in Italy (1919), and was a member of the Chicago Opera (1924–32) and the San Francisco Opera (1925–26). In 1931 he sang at London's Covent Garden, and from 1935 pursued his career in Spain; he made his farewell appearance as Cavaradossi in Saragossa (1951). Held in high esteem in his homeland, Cortis became known as the Spanish Caruso. Among his most prominent roles were Radames, Canio, Don José, Edgardo, and Andrea Chénier.—**NS/LK/DM**

Cortot, Alfred (Denis), famous French pianist, conductor, and teacher; b. Nyon, Switzerland (of a French father and a Swiss mother), Sept. 26, 1877; d. Lausanne, June 15, 1962. He was a pupil at the Paris Cons., and studied with Decambes, Rouquou, and Diémer; he won the first prize for piano in 1896; the same year he made his debut in Paris, playing Beethoven's C-minor Concerto at one of the Colonne concerts, and won signal success; he went to Bayreuth (1898) and studied Wagner's works with J. Kniese, and acted as répétiteur at the festivals from 1898 to 1901. Returning to Paris, he began a most active propaganda for the works of Wagner; on May 17, 1902, he conducted the French premiere of *Götterdämmerung* at the Théâtre du Château d'Eau, and in the same year established the Association des Concerts A. Cortot, which he directed for two years, educating the public to an appreciation of Wagner; in 1904 he became conductor of the orch. concerts of the Societe Nationale and of the Concerts Populaires at Lille (until 1908). In 1905, together with Jacques Thibaud (violin) and Pablo Casals (cello), he formed a trio, which soon gained a great European reputation, and which continued to perform until 1937. From 1907 to 1918 he was a prof. of piano at the Paris Cons. With A. Mangeot, he founded the École Normale de Musique in Paris in 1919, and subsequently served as its director. Cortot toured widely as a soloist and recitalist in Europe and the U.S. until the outbreak of World War II. During the German occupation of France, he was a highly visible artist and was associated with the cultural policies of the Vichy regime. After the liberation, he was compelled to make an accounting of his activities, but was soon allowed to resume his concert career. He subsequently gave numerous concerts until his farewell appearance at the Prades Festival in 1958. He was awarded the Gold Medal of the Royal Phil. Soc. of London in 1923 and was made a Commandeur de la Légion d'Honneur of France in 1934. Among his outstanding pupils were Haskil, Solomon, Bachauer, and Lipatti. Although Cortot was technically a highly wayward pianist, he succeeded in infusing his readings of the Romantic repertory with a rare insight and poetic patina.

WRITINGS: *Principes rationnels de la technique pianistique* (French and Eng., Paris, 1928; American ed., Boston, 1930); *La Musique française de piano* (vol. I, 1930; Eng. tr., 1932; vol. II, 1932); *Cours d'interpretátion* (vol. I, Paris, 1934; Eng. tr., 1937); *Aspects de Chopin* (Paris, 1949; Eng. tr., 1951).

BIBL.: B. Gavoty, *A. C.* (Paris, 1977); T. Manshardt, *Aspects of C.* (Hexham, 1994).—**NS/LK/DM**

Coryell, Larry, American jazz musician; b. Galveston, Tex., April 2, 1943. A founding father of the fusion movement, an amazing live musician, and one of the most important jazz musicians to emerge in the 1960s, he is an influential though often underrated and sometimes inconsistent guitarist. His playing contains more blues influence than most jazz/rock players and he is probably the most lyrical jazz/rock guitarist spawned from that era (few guitarists have ever written anything as catchy as "Bicentennial Headfest"). Like fellow fusion pioneer John McLaughlin, he has stunning technique and grows restless playing any one style.

Shortly after his recording debut with Chico Hamilton in 1966, he co-founded the Free Spirits, a Byrds-influenced rock band with jazz undertones. He joined Gary Burton in 1967, and while his reputation as a versatile rock-influenced jazz player grew with Burton, it was in 1969, when he recorded his first two ground-breaking solo albums—*Lady Coryell* and the out-of-print *Coryell*—that he became recognized as a world-beater. Both albums combine rock, jazz, folk, classical, and country influences, have a sense of experimentation that was typical of that era, and are filled with some wild guitar playing. During the 1970s he was all over the road stylistically. He kicked off the decade by recording the legendary *Spaces* album with John McLaughlin, which pretty much guaranteed both guitarists a place in jazz history. From there, the 1970s saw him form his own fusion band, the Eleventh House (with Alphonze Mouzon and Mike Mandel); record a classic album, *The Restful Mind* with Ralph Towner (currently out of print); make several solo albums that ranged from jazz-rock to challenging acoustic adventures; and record two excellent duets with guitarist Philip Catherine, *Twin House* and *Splendid* (both are out of print). He also recorded with Joe Beck and John Scofield and in 1979 formed the first version of the Acoustic Guitar Super Trio with McLaughlin and Paco de Lucia. He showed he was also an adept flamenco player as the trio barnstormed Europe and made an excellent live video from Royal Albert Hall. However, by the time the trio hit he United States, Coryell was replaced by Al Di Meola, though accounts vary as to why.

In the early 1980s, Coryell embarked on the ambitious project of scoring and recording famous orchestral works by Stravinsky and Rimsky-Korsakov for solo acoustic guitar (*The Rite of Spring* and *Scherazade*); he has scored and recorded works by Ravel and Gershwin. The 1980s also saw him form a partnership with Brian Keane, record an indispensable duet album with Emily Remler, and embark on a number of straight-ahead albums. In the 1990s he has recorded albums in the smooth jazz and world genres, made acoustic dates with heavy folk influences, and most recently has revisited the fusion landscape he mapped out over 27 years ago.

Coryell has been active in education, had a regular guitar column in the magazine *Guitar Player* for several years, and has two sons who are also musicians. Despite his status as one of the most important jazz guitarists of the past 30 years, the current state of his catalog is a disgrace. Despite making over 50 recordings as leader, only a small percentage are in print and the record companies are not making a concerted effort to reissue his material on CD. This is problematic, as while his catalog has its share of inconsistent dates, there are a number of historic recordings sitting on the shelves.

DISC.: *Coryell* (1969); *Lady Coryell* (1969); *Spaces* (1970); *Introducing the Eleventh House* (1974); *The Essential Larry Coryell* (1975); *Planet End* (1975); *Larry Coryell & the Eleventh House at Montreux* (1978); *Just Like Being Born* (1985); *Together* (1985); *Dragon Gate* (1989); *Twelve Frets to One Octave* (1991); *Live from Bahia* (1992); *Bolero* (1993); *Sketches of Coryell* (1996); *Spaces Revisited* (1997); *Major Jazz Minor Blues* (1998); *Cause and Effect* (1998); *Monk, 'Trane, Miles & Me* (1999); *Coryells* (2000).—**PMac**

Cosma, Viorel, Romanian musicologist, lexicographer, music critic, and pedagogue; b. Timişoara, March 30, 1923. He studied at the Timişoara Cons. (1929–31) and the Bucharest Cons. (1945–50), and later attended the musicology seminars under Martin Runcke in Erlangen and Nuremberg (1972–73). In 1951 he joined the faculty of the Bucharest Cons., where he was a lecturer (1964–85) and an assoc. prof. (1996–99). From 1993 to 1996 he also was prof. of music history at the Hyperionon Univ. in Bucharest. Cosma has contributed numerous articles to journals, books, and reference works. Among his own books (all publ. in Bucharest) are *Compozitori si muzicologi români: Mic Lexicon* (1965), *Muzicieni români: Lexicon* (1970), *A Concise History of Romanian Music* (1982), *Exegeze muzicologice* (1984), *40 de ani în fotoliul de orchestră: Eseuri, studii, cronici muzicale (1946–1976)* (Vol. I, 1986), *Muzicieni din România: Lexicon* (A-E, 2 vols., 1989, 1999), *Interpreti din România* (Vol. I, A-F, 1996), and *Enciclopedia marilor personalităti din istoria, stiinta si cultura românească de—a lungul timpului* (1998).—**NS/LK/DM**

Cossa, Dominic, American baritone and teacher; b. Jessup, Pa., May 13, 1935. He studied at the Univ. of Scranton (B.S. in psychology, 1959), the Univ. of Detroit (M.A., 1961), the Detroit Inst. of Musical Arts, and the Philadelphia Academy of Vocal Arts, his principal vocal mentors being Anthony Marlowe, Robert Weede, and Armen Boyajin. On Oct. 13, 1961, he made his first appearance at the N.Y.C. Opera as Morales in *Carmen*, and subsequently sang leading baritone roles there. On Jan. 30, 1970, he made his Metropolitan Opera debut in N.Y. as Silvio, and remained on its roster until 1975; he returned for the 1978–79 season. He also appeared as a guest artist with other U.S. opera companies and in Europe. He taught at the Manhattan School of Music in N.Y. and at the Univ. of Md. Among his best roles were Rossini's Figaro, Lescaut, Germont, Marcello, Rigoletto, and Dr. Malatesta.—**NS/LK/DM**

Cossira (real name, **Coussival**), **Emil,** French tenor; b. Orthez, 1854; d. Quebec, Feb. 1923. After training in Bordeaux, he made his operatic debut as Grétry's Richard Coeur de Leon at the Paris Opéra-Comique in 1883, where he was chosen to create the title role in Saint-Saëns's *Ascanio* (March 21, 1890). In 1891, 1894, and 1900 he appeared at London's Covent Garden, where he sang Faust, Roméo, Raoul, and Don José. In addition to the French repertoire, he appeared as a Wagnerian. He was the first to sing Tristan in Brussels (1894) and Walther von Stolzing in Lyons (1896). —**NS/LK/DM**

Cossmann, Bernhard, German cellist and teacher; b. Dessau, May 17, 1822; d. Frankfurt am Main, May 7, 1910. He was a student of Drechsler in Dessau, Theodor Müller in Braunschweig, and Kummer in Dresden. After playing in orchs. in Paris (1840–46), London (1841), Leipzig (1847–48), and Weimar (1850–66), he taught at the Moscow Cons. (1866–70), in Baden-Baden (1870–78), and at the Frankfurt am Main Cons. (from 1878).—**NS/LK/DM**

Cossotto, Fiorenza, distinguished Italian mezzo-soprano; b. Crescentino, April 22, 1935. After training at the Turin Cons., she studied in Milan at the La Scala opera school with Ettore Campogalliani. While still a student, she sang at La Scala before making her formal operatic debut there as Sister Mathilde in *Les Dialogues des Carmélites* on Jan. 26, 1957; continued to sing there regularly until 1973, winning special praise for her Verdi roles and as Donizetti's Leonora. In 1958 she commenced an international career with her appearance in Wexford as Donizetti's Giovanna Seymour; she then made debuts at the Vienna State Opera (as Maddalena, 1958), London's Covent Garden (as Néris in *Médée,* 1959), and the Chicago Lyric Opera (as Donizetti's Leonora, 1964). On Feb. 6, 1968, she made her Metropolitan Opera debut in N.Y. as Amneris, and continued to sing there with distinction in succeeding years in such roles as Adalgisa, Eboli, Mistress Quickly, Laura, and Carmen. In 1958 she married **Ivo Vinco.** —NS/LK/DM

Cossutta, Carlo, Italian tenor; b. Trieste, May 8, 1932; d. Udine, Jan. 22, 2000. He was a student of Manfredo Miselli, Mario Melani, and Arturo Wolken in Buenos Aires, where he made his operatic debut as Alfredo in 1956. In 1958 he made his first appearance at the Teatro Colón in Buenos Aires as Cassio, and created the title role in Ginastera's *Don Rodrigo* there in 1968. In 1963 he appered as Cassio at his Chicago Lyric Opera debut, and, in 1964, as the Duke of Mantua at his debut at London's Covent Garden. On Feb. 17, 1973, he made his first appearance at the Metropolitan Opera in N.Y. as Pollione, where he sang for one season and then returned for the 1978–79 season. He also sang in Milan, Paris, Berlin, Munich, Hamburg, Philadelphia, Boston, and San Francisco. Among his other roles were Otello, Don Carlos, Turiddu, Cavaradossi, and Manrico. —NS/LK/DM

Costa, Johnny, jazz pianist; b. Arnold, Pa., Jan. 18, 1922; d. Pittsburgh, Pa., Oct. 11, 1996. Studied piano at Carnegie Tech (B.A., comp., 1951). He was an active freelancer in the Pittsburgh area, where he did club and radio and TV work. From the early 1970s until his death, Costa was the pianist, mostly behind the scenes, for the public television children's show *Mister Rogers' Neighborhood.* He added a touch of Art Tatum to the musical interludes that accompanied the sunny children's personality.

DISC.: *Neighborhood* (1955); *Amazing J. Costa and This Trio* (1955); *In My Own Quiet Way* (1959); *Classic Costa* (1990); *Flying Fingers* (1991). —LP

Costa, Mary, American soprano; b. Knoxville, Tenn., April 5, 1932. She was trained at the Los Angeles Cons. of Music. She pursued work in films (was the voice of Walt Disney's Sleeping Beauty) and television commercials before taking up a serious vocal career. In 1958 she made her operatic debut with the Los Angeles Opera, and in 1959 she made her first appearance with the San Francisco Opera. On Jan. 6, 1964, she made her Metropolitan Opera debut in N.Y. as Violetta, and returned there for occasional appearances until 1978. She also sang at the Glyndebourne Festival, London's Covent Garden, the Leningrad Opera, the Bolshoi Theater in Moscow, the Cincinnati Opera, the Philadelphia Opera, et al. She also appeared as a soloist with orchs. and as a recitalist around the world. In 1972 she starred in the film *The Great Waltz.* She founded the Knoxville (Tenn.) Opera Co. in 1978. In 1979 the Mary Costa Scholarship was established at the Univ. of Tenn. Among her best known roles were Manon, Rosalinde, Musetta, and Alice Ford. —NS/LK/DM

Costa, Sir Michael (Andrew Agnus) (actually, **Michele Andrea Agniello**), Italian-born English conductor of Spanish descent; b. Naples, Feb. 4, 1806; d. Hove, England, April 29, 1884. He studied with his maternal grandfather, **Giacomo Tritto,** with his father, Pasquale Costa (a composer of church music), and with Giovanni Furno. He then studied at the Naples Cons. with Crescentini (singing) and Zingarelli (composition). His operas *Il sospetto funesto* (Naples, 1826), *Il delitto punito* (1827), *Il carcere d'Ildegonda* (Naples, 1828), and *Malvina* (Naples, 1829) were well received; when Zingarelli was commissioned to write a Psalm (*Super Flumina Babilonis*) for the Music Festival at Birmingham, England, he sent Costa to conduct it. When Costa arrived in Birmingham, the directors of the Festival refused to accept him as a conductor owing to his extreme youth, but offered to pay him a similar fee for performance as tenor in Zingarelli's Psalm and in other works. He was compelled to accept, but his debut as a singer was disastrous. Despite this setback, he decided to remain in England, a decision in which he was encouraged by Clementi, who was impressed by Costa's scoring of a Bellini aria. In 1830 Costa was engaged as maestro al cembalo at the King's Theatre in London; from 1833 to 1846 he was director and conductor of the Italian Opera there. During this time, he produced three of his ballets, *Kenilworth* (1831), *Une Heure a Naples* (1832), and *Sir Huon* (1833). From 1846 to 1854 he was conductor of the Phil. Soc. concerts; in 1847 he organized the Royal Italian Opera at Covent Garden, conducting it until 1868. He was conductor of the Handel Festivals at the Crystal Palace (1847–80), the Sacred Harmonic Soc. (1848–82), and the Birmingham Festivals (1849–82). From 1868 to 1871 he conducted opera at Her Majesty's Theatre, and then was its music director from 1871 to 1881. In 1869 he was knighted. Costa was generally acknowledged as the leading conductor in England in his day. He produced two operas in London: *Malek Adel* (May 18, 1837; a revision of *Malvina*) and *Don Carlos* (June 20, 1844). —NS/LK/DM

Coste, Napoléon, outstanding French guitarist and composer; b. Doubs, June 28, 1806; d. Paris, Feb. 17, 1883. He studied guitar with his mother and began his career in Valenciennes while still a teenager. In 1828 he went to Paris to study harmony and counterpoint, and thereafter pursued a career as a guitar virtuoso. In 1863 he fractured an arm in an accident and was compelled to abandon his brilliant career. He composed much music for his instrument, including a famous set of études, op.38. —LK/DM

Costeley, Guillaume, French organist and composer; b. c. 1531; d. Évreux, Jan. 28, 1606. Theories that he was an Irishman named Costello who settled in France, or that he was of Scottish extraction, have been discarded. He was court organist to Charles IX of France. In 1570 he became the first annually elected "prince" or "maître" of a society organized in honor of St. Cecilia, which, beginning in 1575, awarded a prize each year for a polyphonic composition. Costeley excelled as a composer of polyphonic chansons. His *Musique,* a book of such works for four to six voices, appeared in 1570. Modern eds. of some of those for four voices are in H. Expert, Maîtres Musiciens de la Renaissance Française (vols. III, XVIII, XIX, 1896–1904). An example for five voices is in Cauchie's *Quinze chansons.*

BIBL.: I. Godt, *G. C., Life and Works* (diss., N.Y.U., 1969). —NS/LK/DM

Costello, Elvis (originally **McManus, Declan**), one of the most lyrically intelligent and musical ambitious singer-songwriters to emerge in the late 1970s; b. Liverpool, England, Aug. 25, 1954. Along with the Clash, Elvis Costello was the British punk or New Wave act that persevered long enough to achieve both acclaim and notoriety in the United States. Certainly a prolific songwriter of the New Wave movement, perhaps even the most productive songwriter of his generation regardless of genre. Costello's biting, incisive, and literate songs and his basic, unadorned rock music served as a stark and refreshing contrast to both the overproduced, pretentious music of British compatriots such as Genesis and Pink Floyd, and the mindless, contrived dance music of disco.

Initially favoring vituperative, sarcastic, and angry songs (witness his stunning *My Aim Is True*), Costello developed into a profound and compassionate songwriter by the early 1980s without abandoning his fire and rage. His early caustic, aloof manner in performance evolved into a sincere, almost congenial style that ingratiated him to fans. Although criticized for his perceived lack of vocal range, he possessed one of the most emotionally evocative voices performing in rock.

Remarkably eclectic from the very beginning—utilizing the sound of reggae, soul, country, jazz, and even pop in his music—Costello produced the most diverse catalog of songs imaginable. He even recorded an album of country standards in the early 1980s, and in the early 1990s an album for voice and classical string quartet.

Elvis Costello grew up in a musical household. His father, Ross McManus, was a big-band singer. Playing guitar and writing songs as a youth, he took the name Elvis Costello to perform as a country act in pubs around London. He was the first artist to submit a demonstration tape to England's Stiff Records, a small, independent label formed in 1976 to record punk music. His debut album, recorded with the northern Calif.-based country-rock group Clover under producer Nick Lowe, was released in Great Britain in the spring of 1977. That fall Costello completed his first British tour with the Attractions, comprised of keyboardist Steve Nieve, bassist Bruce Thomas, and drummer Pete Tho-

mas (no relation).

When the cofounders of Stiff Records split up in late 1977, Elvis Costello switched to Columbia Records. The company issued the brilliant album *My Aim Is True* on the verge of his American debut in San Francisco. The first New Wave album to sell well in the United States, it featured a number of compelling songs, such as "Watching the Detectives," "Red Shoes," "Mystery Dance," "I'm Not Angry," and "Waiting for the End of the World," plus the uncharacteristic love ballad "Alison." The latter song was recorded by Linda Ronstadt for her 1978 *Living in the U.S.A.* album, giving a further boost to Costello's career.

Without a hit single, Elvis Costello quickly achieved an underground following with his early American tours. His enigmatic reputation was bolstered by *This Year's Model,* recorded with the Attractions under producer Nick Lowe. The album included "No Action," "Pump It Up," "Lipstick Vogue," and "Radio Radio." Costello's early 1979 American tour was equivocal at best, frequently alienating curious American rock artists, promoters, and audiences alike. A strange incident in Columbus, Ohio, when an apparently drunken Costello attacked singers Steve Stills and Bonnie Bramlett and reportedly made racist remarks about Ray Charles, was widely covered in the press, doing little to help his career. Nonetheless, *Armed Forces* became a best-seller, featuring "Accidents Will Happen," "Party Girl," and Nick Lowe's "(What's So Funny About) Peace, Love and Understanding," a minor hit.

Costello continued to pump out albums, with two releases in 1980. *Get Happy!!* included 20 songs, and was quickly followed by *Taking Liberties,* which contained B-sides to singles and previously unreleased recordings such as "Girls Talk" (a minor hit for Dave Edmunds in 1979), "Talking in the Dark" (recorded by Linda Ronstadt), and "Stranger in the House" (recorded by country star George Jones). *Trust,* released in 1981, included "Clubland," "Pretty Words," and "Different Finger." It was followed by an entirely new style on *Almost Blue,* recorded in Nashville and produced by country veteran Owen Bradley, revealing Costello's country music bent with performances of country standards by Hank Williams, Merle Haggard, and George Jones, and two Gram Parsons songs.

Costello returned to his own songwriting on 1982's *Imperial Bedroom,* regarded by many as his masterpiece. Exploring the anguish of love in a variety of styles, the album featured "The Long Honeymoon," "Human Hands," "Pidgin English," and the moving ballad "Almost Blue." A U.S. tour followed, as did two more albums: *Punch the Clock* included the antiwar "Shipbuilding" and yielded Costello's first (moderate) hit with "Everyday I Write the Book," while *Goodbye Cruel World* produced a minor hit with "The Only Flame in Town."

In spring 1984 Elvis Costello toured America again, this time as a solo artist performing primarily acoustic music. Without the din of the Attractions his lyrics were far easier to appreciate, and he revealed a warm and lighter side, unlike his tours of the 1970s. Dominated by country ballads, *King of America* was recorded without the Attractions (save one song), and Costello played acoustic guitar for producer T-Bone Burnett. The Attractions and producer Nick Lowe were back for *Blood and Chocolate*, which included "I Hope You're Happy Now," "Honey, Are You Straight or Are You Blind?," and the ballad "I Want You."

In May 1986 Elvis Costello married Cait O'Riordan, bassist of the Pogues, which she left late in the year. In 1987 the Attractions split up, and for a time Costello was without a record label. Signed to Warner Bros., he reemerged in 1989 with *Spike*, his best-selling album in years. Recorded with Paul McCartney, Roger McGuinn, coproducer T-Bone Burnett, and the Dirty Dozen Brass Band, the album featured "Baby Plays Around," "God's Comic," and Costello's first major hit single, "Veronica," cowritten with McCartney. At the same time, McCartney scored a major hit with "My Brave Face," cowritten with Costello. Costello toured again in 1989, with the Rude 5, who included guitarist Marc Ribot (who worked with Tom Waits), ace session keyboardist Larry Knechtel, bassist Jerry Scheff (who worked with Elvis Presley), and Attractions drummer Pete Thomas. The Rude 5 helped Costello record *Mighty Like a Rose* in Los Angeles. It included "Broken" (written by O'Riordan), "So Like Candy," and "Playboy to a Man" (cowritten with McCartney), plus "The Other Side of Summer" and "Hurry Down Doomsday."

In 1992 Elvis Costello made perhaps the boldest move of his career, recording *The Juliet Letters* with the Brodsky Quartet, a respected British classical string quartet. Sharing songwriting credit with the Quartet on more than half the songs, Costello bore sole responsibility for the vocals. The album, comprised largely of ballads, featured "Taking My Life in Your Hands" and "I Almost Had a Weakness." In 1994 Costello reassembled the Attractions to make the album *Brutal Youth* and for their first tour in eight years. Taking another right turn, Costello then issued an album of cover songs, *Kojak Variety*, ranging from Mose Allison's "Everybody's Crying Mercy" to Randy Newman's "I've Been Wrong Before" and Jesse Winchester's "Payday."

DISC.: ELVIS COSTELLO (Beginning in 1990, Rykodisc began reissuing Elvis Costello's early albums with additional studio and live tracks, so the Rykodisc recordings do not correspond exactly to the original U.S. issues): *My Aim Is True* (1977); *This Year's Model* (1978); *Armed Forces* (1979); *Get Happy!!* (1980); *Taking Liberties* (1980); *Trust* (1981); *Almost Blue* (1981); *Imperial Bedroom* (1982); *Punch the Clock* (1983); *Goodbye Cruel World* (1984); *The Best of Elvis Costello and the Attractions, 1977–1984* (1985); *King of America* (1986); *Blood and Chocolate* (1986); *Girls, Girls, Girls* (1990); *Spike* (1989); *Mighty Like a Rose* (1991); *Brutal Youth* (1994); *Kojak Variety* (1995); *All This Useless Beauty* (1996); *2 1/2 Years* (1993); *The Very Best of Elvis* (1994). ELVIS COSTELLO AND THE BRODSKY QUARTET: *The Juliet Letters* (1993).

BIBL.: Krista Reese, *E. C.* (N.Y., 1981); Mick St. Michael, *E. C.* (London, 1986); David Gouldstone, *E. C.: A Man Out of Time* (London, 1989); Bruce Thomas, *The Big Wheel* (N.Y., 1990).—**BH**

Cosyn, Benjamin, English organist and composer; b. c. 1570; d. probably in London, after 1652. He pursued his career in London, serving as organist at Dulwich Coll. (1622–24) and at the Charterhouse (1626–43). His distinguished keyboard works, which call for virtuoso technique, are modeled after the music of Bull. Cosyn included 32 keyboard pieces in what has become known as the Cosyn Virginal Book (MS, c. 1620), which also includes works by Bull, Byrd, Gibbons, and Tallis. Another MS collection (1652) includes some 50 works by Cosyn, along with works by others.

BIBL.: O. Memed, ed., *Seventeenth-Century English Keyboard Music: B. C.* (2 vols., N.Y. and London, 1993).—**LK/DM**

Cotogni, Antonio, notable Italian baritone and pedagogue; b. Rome, Aug. 1, 1831; d. there, Oct. 15, 1918. He was a pupil of Fontemaggi and Faldi. After making his operatic debut in Rome in 1852 as Belcore, he sang in various Italian opera centers until joining Milan's La Scala in 1860. In 1867 he made his debut at London's Covent Garden as Valentine, and continued to appear there regularly until 1889. He also sang in Paris, Madrid, Lisbon, and Barcelona. From 1893 to 1898 he sang in St. Petersburg, where he also was active as a teacher. Upon returning to Rome, he became a prof. of voice at the Accademia di Santa Cecilia. His repertoire included over 125 roles. Among his students were Jean de Reszke, Battistini, Lauri-Volpi, Gigli, and Stabile.
—**NS/LK/DM**

Cotrubaș, Ileana, outstanding Romanian soprano; b. Galați, June 9, 1939. After studies at the Scolǎ Specialǎ de Muzicǎ (1952–57) and with Eugenia Elinescu and Constantin Stroescu at the Bucharest Cons. (1957–63), she made her operatic debut as Yniod in *Pelléas et Mélisande* in Bucharest (1964). She took first prize in both the 's-Hertogenbosch (1965) and Munich Radio (1966) competitions, and then completed her studies at the Vienna Academy of Music (1967). She appeared at the Salzburg Festival in 1967, then was a member of the Frankfurt am Main Opera (1968–71). In 1969 she appeared as Mélisande at the Glyndebourne Festival and as Pamina at the Vienna State Opera, where she subsequently appeared regularly. She was made an Austrian Kammersängerin in 1981. In 1973 she made her U.S. debut as Mimi at the Chicago Lyric Opera. She then sang in Paris (1974) and at Milan's La Scala (1975). On March 23, 1977, she made her Metropolitan Opera debut in N.Y. in the role of Mimi. In addition to her appearances at the world's leading opera houses and festivals, she also toured extensively as a concert artist until her retirement in 1989. Among her other notable roles were Amina, Susanna, Norina, Adina, Violetta, Gilda, Marguerite, Elisabetta, Antonia, and Micaëla. Her career is recounted in her book *Opernwahrheiten* (Vienna, 1998).
—**NS/LK/DM**

Cotton, John (or **Johannis Cottonis**; also **Joannes Musica, Johannes filius Dei,** and **Johannes of Afflighem**), music theorist who flourished in the late 11th and early 12th centuries. He wrote the treatise *Epistola ad Fulgentium* (printed by Gerbert in Scriptores, vol. II), a valuable work on music describing the modal system of the time and a phase of the development of organum. Six MS copies are preserved: one each in Leipzig, Paris, Antwerp, and the Vatican Library, and two in Vienna. Various theories have been advanced concerning its authorship. In the copies at Antwerp and Paris, the author is referred to as Cotton or Cottonius, while two others give the author's name as Joannes Musica. In an anonymous work, *De script. eccles.*, quoted by Gerbert, there is a reference to a certain Joannes, an erudite English musician; the dedication of this vol., "Domino et patri sua venerabili Anglorum antistiti Fulgentio," adds further strength to the contention that the author of the *Epistola* was English. However, J. Smits van Waesberghe identifies him with the Flemish theorist Johannes of Afflighem, author of the treatise *De Musica cum tonario* (reprinted Rome, 1950). Other sources suggest that Cotton was also one Johannes filius Dei.—NS/LK/DM

Cottrell, Louis (Albert) Jr., jazz clarinetist, tenor saxophonist; b. New Orleans, La., March 7, 1911; d. there, March 21, 1978. He was the son of the famous drummer Louis Cottrell Sr. (b. New Orleans, La., Dec. 25, 1878; d. there, Oct. 17, 1927). Louis Jr. worked regularly with The Young Tuxedo Orch. from the mid-1920s, and also played for The Golden Rule Band, Sidney Desvigne, and William Ridgely, among others. He left New Orleans to join a band led by Don Albert, with whom he worked throughout the 1930s, then returned to New Orleans. He worked again with Sidney Desvigne in the 1940s, and became president of the local (black) musician's union. He participated in occasional parades with Kid Howard's Brass Band in the 1950s; also did regular work and recordings with Paul Barbarin during that period. He worked in Pete Bocage's Creole Serenaders in the early 1960s. Primarily playing on clarinet, he was featured with his own trio at the New Orleans Jazz Fest in June 1969.

DISC.: *Bourbon Street Parade* (1961); *New Orleans: The Living Legends* (1994).—JC/LP

Coulthard, Jean, Canadian composer and teacher; b. Vancouver, Feb. 10, 1908; d. Vancouver, March 9, 2000. She began her studies with her mother, Jean (Blake; née Robinson) Coulthard (b. Moncton, New Brunswick, Aug. 13, 1882; d. Vancouver, July 16, 1933), a pianist and teacher. Following lessons with Jan Cherniavsky (piano) and Frederick Chubb (theory) in Vancouver (1924–28), she continued her training on scholarship at the Royal Coll. of Music in London (1928–30), where she was a composition student of R.O. Morris and Vaughan Williams; still later she worked with Arthur Benjamin (1939), Bernard Wagenaar (1945, 1949), and Gordon Jacob (1965–66). After serving as head of the music dept at St. Anthony's Coll. (1934–36) and Queen's Hall School (1936–37) in Vancouver, she was a lecturer (1947–57) and senior instructor (1957–73) in composition at the Univ. of British Columbia. In 1978 she was named an Officer of the Order of Canada. Coulthard's well-crafted works follow along traditional lines.

WORKS: DRAMATIC: *Excursion,* ballet (1940); *The Return of the Native,* opera (1956–79); *The Devil's Fanfare,* ballet (1958). **ORCH.:** *A Winter's Tale* for Strings (1940); *Convoy,* later retitled *Song to the Sea,* overture (1941); 4 syms.: No. 1 (1951),

No. 2, *This Land,* choral sym. for Soli, Chorus, and Orch. (1966–67), No. 3, *Lyric Symphony,* for Bassoon and Chamber Orch. (1975), and No. 4, *Autumn Symphony,* for Strings (originally titled *Symphonic Images;* 1984–85); *A Prayer for Elizabeth* for Strings (1953); *Rider on the Sands* (1953); *The Bird of Dawning Singeth All Night Long* (1960); *Fantasy* for Violin, Piano, and Orch. (1961); *Serenade or a Meditation and 3 Dances* for Strings (1961); Piano Concerto (1963); *Endymion* (1964); *Kalamalka: Lake of Many Colors* (1974); *Canada Mosaic* (1974); *Burlesca* for Piano and Strings (1977); Symphonic Ode for Violin and Chamber Orch. (1977); *Symphonic Image: Vision of the North* for Strings (1989). **CHAMBER:** 2 violin sonatinas (1945); *Music on a Quiet Song* for Flute and Strings (1946); Cello Sonata (1947); Oboe Sonata (1947); 3 string quartets: No. 1 (1948; rev. 1952), No. 2, *Threnody* (1954; rev. 1969), and No. 3 (1981); 3 violin sonatas: No. 1, *Duo Sonata* (1952), No. 2, *Correspondence* (1964), and No. 3, *Á la jeunesse* (1981); Piano Quartet, *Sketches from a Mediaeval* (1957); *Sonata Rhapsody* for Viola and Piano (1962); *Ballad of the North* for Violin and Piano (1965–66); *Divertimento* for Flute, Oboe, Clarinet, Horn, Bassoon, and Piano (1968); *Lyric Trio* for Piano Trio (1968); *Lyric Sonatina* for Bassoon and Piano (1969); *Lyric Sonatina* for Flute and Piano (1971); *The Birds of Lansdowne* for Piano Trio and Tape (1972); *12 Essays on a Cantabile Theme* for 2 String Quartets (1972); *Music on a Scottish Folk Song* for Violin and Guitar (1974); *Lyric Sonatina* for Clarinet and Piano (1976); *Fanfare Sonata* for Trumpet and Piano (1978); *Shizen: 3 Nature Sketches from Japan* for Oboe and Piano (1979); *Pas de Deux,* sonatina for Flute and Bassoon (1980); *Fantasy Sonata* for Horn and Piano (1983); *Lyric Sonatina* for Guitar (1984); *Dopo Botticelli* for Cello and Piano (1985); *Duo Sonata* for Violin and Cello (1989); numerous piano pieces, including 2 sonatas (1947, 1986). **VOCAL:** *Night Wind* for Alto and Piano (1951; rev. for Soprano and Orch.); *2 Visionary Songs* for Soprano, Flute, and Strings (1968); *Songs from the Distaff Muse I* for Soprano, Alto, and Cello (1972) and *II* for Soprano, Alto, and Piano (1974); *Serenade* for Alto and Violin (1977); *Vancouver Lights: A Soliloquy* for Soprano, Baritone, Chorus, and Orch. (1980); *Fanfare Overture* for Chorus and Orch. (1985); *Shelley Portrait* for Alto, Flute, Clarinet, Cello, and Piano (1987); *When Tempests Rise,* cantata for Soli, Chorus, and Orch. (based on the opera *The Return of the Native,* 1988); choruses; other songs.—NS/LK/DM

Couperin, renowned family of French musicians. Its musical prominence dates from the three sons of **Charles Couperin,** merchant and organist of Chaume, in the dept. of Brie, and his wife, Marie Andry. The eldest of these, **Louis,** established the family in Paris, where it remained until the extinction of the male line in 1826. He was also the first of his name to hold the post of organist at St.-Gervais in Paris. He was followed in this position by his youngest brother, **Charles; François le Grand,** son of Charles, and the family's most illustrious representative; **Nicolas,** son of **François** (called **Sieur de Crouilly); Armand-Louis,** son of Nicolas; and by the two sons of Armand-Louis, **Pierre-Louis** and **Gervais-François.** The following articles, arranged alphabetically, give the individual histories of the members of the Couperin family.—NS/LK/DM

Couperin, Armand-Louis, organist and composer, son of **Nicolas Couperin;** b. Paris, Feb. 25, 1727; d. there, Feb. 2, 1789. His virtuosity on the organ was extraordinary. In 1748 he succeeded his father as organist at St.-Gervais. He was also organist to the King (1770–89), and held appointments at St.-Barthélemy, Ste.-Marguerite, Ste.-Chapelle, St.- Jean-en-Grève, et al. He was one of the four organists of Notre-Dame. He died a violent death, having been knocked down by a runaway horse. His compositions include sonatas, a trio, motets, and other church music. His wife, Elisabeth-Antoinette (née Blanchet; b. Paris, Jan. 14, 1729), was also a remarkable organist and harpsichord-ist, still playing in public at the age of 81 (in 1810). She was the daughter of Blanchet, the famous harpsichord maker, and sister-in-law to **Pascal Joseph Taskin**, the court instrument keeper under Louis XV. D. Fuller ed. *A.-L. Couperin: Selected Works for Keyboard* (Madison, Wisc., 1975).—NS/LK/DM

Couperin, Charles, organist; b. Chaumes (baptized), April 9, 1638; d. Paris, between Jan. 15 and Feb. 26, 1679. He succeeded his brother **Louis** as organist at St.-Gervais in 1661. He married Marie Guérin (Feb. 20, 1662), and is principally remembered as being the father of the celebrated **François le Grand.**—NS/LK/DM

Couperin, François, (surnamed **le Grand**), the most illustrious member of the distinguished family and one of the greatest of French composers, son of **Charles Couperin;** b. Paris, Nov. 10, 1668; d. there, Sept. 11, 1733. He studied with his father, and later was a pupil of Jacques-Denis Thomelin, organist of the King's chapel. In 1685 he became organist of St.-Gervais, which post he held until his death. On Dec. 26, 1693, after a successful competition, he succeeded Thomelin as organist of the Chapelle Royale, receiving the title of "organiste du roi". In 1701 he was appointed "clavecin-iste de la chambre du roi, et organiste de sa chapelle," and in 1717 he received the title "Ordinaire de la musique de la chambre du roi". He also was made a chevalier of the Order of Latran. He was music master to the Dauphin and other members of the royal family, and ranked high in the favor of King Louis XIV, for whom he composed the *Concerts royaux*, which, during 1714–15, were played in Sunday concerts in the royal apartments. He married Marie-Anne Ansault (April 26, 1689), by whom he had two daughters: Marie-Madeleine (b. Paris, March 9, 1690; d. Montbuisson, April 16, 1742), who became organist of the Abbey of Montbuisson, and Marguerite-Antoinette (b. Paris, Sept. 19, 1705; d. there, 1778), who was a talented harpsi-chordist; from 1731 to 1733, she substituted for her father as harpsichordist to the King, being the first woman to hold this position. There were also 2 sons, Nicolas-Louis (b. July 24, 1707), who died young, and François-Laurent (b. c. 1708). Famed as an organist, Couperin also acquired a high reputation for his re-markable ability as a performer on the harpsichord.

WORKS: Couperin's compositions may be conveniently divided into 3 categories: those written for the church, those for the King, and those for the general public. More than half of his creative life was taken up with the religious compositions of the first 2 periods. These include *Pièces d'orgue consistantes en deux Messes* (1690; 42 pieces), formerly attributed to his uncle François, and, indeed, publ. under the latter's name in Vol. five

of *Archives des maîtres de l'orgue*, ed. by Guilmant, but now established, through the researches of A. Tessier and P. Brunold, as the early work of Couperin le Grand; motets; *Elévations*; *Leçons de ténèbres*; etc. Couperin's last and most prolific period was concerned exclusively with instrumental works, and in this field he achieved his greatest and most enduring distinction. In 1713, 1716, 1722, and 1730, he publ. the 4 vols. of his *Pièces de clavecin*, consisting of about 230 pieces or 27 "Ordres" or Suites, each suite being a series of dance forms, programmatic in title and content (*La Majes tueuse, La Nanette, Les Petits Moulins à vent, Le Carillon de Cythère, Les Barricades mystérieuses, Les Tic-Toc-Choc ou Les Maillotins*, et al.). In 1716 he publ. an expository work pertaining to the execution of his harpsichord pieces, *L'Art de toucher le clavecin*, which attained wide celebrity, and which influenced the keyboard style of Couperin's great contemporary, J.S. Bach. Couperin also introduced the trio sonata to France, his first works in this form being an imitation of Corelli. Later, in 1726, he publ. 4 sonatas, *Les Nations*, described as "Sonades" or "Suites de symphonies en trio," three of which are partial reworkings of earlier pieces. They are composed alternately in the strict form, *sonata de chiesa*, and the more flexible composite of dance forms, *sonata de camera*. The 3rd of the series, *L'Impériale*, perhaps represents his most mature and inspired style. Living at a time during which the rivalry between French and Italian music reached its climax, Couperin sought to adapt the new Italian forms to his own personal, and essentially French, style. In his *Les Goûts réunis* (1724), a series of concerted pieces with strings very similar in form and spirit to the *Pièces de clavecin*, one finds titles such as *Sicilienne* and *Ritratto dell' amore*. In the following year he publ. an *Apothéose de Lully*, in which the rivals Lully and Corelli are made to unite for the furtherance of art. Couperin's style of composition was based on the basso continuo, the most important voices usually being the uppermost, carrying the melody, and the bass. Nevertheless, his music sometimes attains considerable com-plexity (on occasion requiring as many as three harpsichordists for its proper execution). His melodic invention, particularly in his use of the rondeau, was virtually inexhaustible, his themes swift and expressive. An outstanding feature was his inventive mode of ornamentation, in the "gallant style" of the period. In 1933 the Lyrebird Press in Paris publ. a "complete" ed. of Couperin's works, in 12 vols., under the chief editorship of Maurice Cauchie, assisted by P. Brunold, A. Gastoué, A. Tessier, and A. Schaeffner. The contents are as follows: Vol. I, Didactic works: *Règle pour l'accompagnement* and *L'Art de toucher le clavecin*; Vols. II-V, the 4 books of *Pièces de clavecin*; Vol. VI, *Pièces d'orgue consistantes en deux Messes*; Vols. VII-X, chamber music, including *Concerts royaux, Les Goûts réunis ou Nouveaux Concerts à l'usage de toutes les sortes d'instruments de musique, Les Nations, Le Parnasse ou l'Apothéose de Corelli, Apothéose de Lully, Pièces de violes avec la basse chiffrée*, and *Sonades inédites*; Vols. XI and XII, secular vocal music and religious music I and II. More recent eds. are in the Le Pupitre series, vols. 8 (*Leçons de ténèbres*; 1968), 21–24 (*Pièces de clavecin*, books 1–4; 1969–72), 45 (9 motets; 1972), and 51 (*Pièces de violes*; 1974); also separate eds. of *Pièces de clavecin*, edited by M. Cauchie (1968–72) and by K. Gilbert (1969–72).

BIBL.: H. Quittard, *Les C.* (Paris, 1913); C. Bouvet, *Une Dynastie de musiciens français: Les C....* (Paris, 1919); J. Llongueras, *C. o la Gracia* (1925); A. Tessier, *C.* (Paris, 1926); J. Tiersot, *Les C.* (Paris, 1926); P. Brunold, *F. C.* (Eng. tr., Monaco, 1949); M. Cauchie, *Thematic Index of the Works of C.* (Monaco,

1949); W. Mellers, *F. C. and the French Classical Tradition* (London, 1950; second ed., rev., 1986); P. Citron, *C.*(Paris, 1956); D. Tunley, *C.*(London, 1982); P. Citron, *C.* (Paris, 1996); C. Giglio, *F. C.* (Palermo, 1998).—NS/LK/DM

Couperin, François, Sieur de Crouilly, organist and teacher; b. Chaumes, c. 1631; d. Paris, after 1708. He was a pupil of Chambonnières in harmony and harpsichord. He was active as a music teacher and organist. His daughter, Marguerite Louise (b. Paris, 1676; d. Versailles, May 30, 1728), was a well-known singer and harpsichordist. She was a fellow member of the Chambre du Roi with her cousin **François le Grand,** who wrote for her the verset *Qui dat nivem* and other pieces.—NS/LK/DM

Couperin, Gervais-François, organist and composer, second son of **Armand-Louis Couperin;** b. Paris, May 22, 1759; d. there, March 11, 1826. He succeeded his brother, **Pierre-Louis,** as organist at St.-Gervais in 1789, also taking over his otheher appointments. He composed sonatas, variations, etc. He was the last of the Couperins to serve as organist at St.-Gervais, although his daughter, Céleste (b. 1793; d. Belleville, Feb. 14, 1860), played there at the time of her father's death. She was a teacher of singing and piano at Beauvais for about ten years.—NS/LK/DM

Couperin, Louis, organist, violinist, violist, and composer; b. Chaumes, c. 1626; d. Paris, Aug. 29, 1661. He went to Paris with his teacher, Chambonnières, and in 1653 became organist of St.-Gervais, a post in which he was succeeded, without interruption, by other members and descendants of the Couperin family until 1826. From 1656 he was a violinist and violist in the orchs. of the court ballets, and musician of the Chambre du Roi. He composed *Pièces de clavecin, Carillons* for Organ, violin pieces, etc. He was one of the earliest of French composers for the harpsichord in the new harmonic style employing the basso continuo, possibly being preceded only by his teacher, Chambonnières. The Lyrebird Press in Paris publ. a "complete" edition of his works, ed. by P. Brunold. His *Pièces de clavecin* is publ. as Vol. 18 of Le Pupitre (1970).—NS/LK/DM

Couperin, Nicolas, organist, son of **François Couperin, Sieur de Crouilly;** b. Paris, Dec. 20, 1680; d. there, July 25, 1748. In 1733 he succeeded his cousin **François le Grand** as organist at St.-Gervais.—NS/LK/DM

Couperin, Pierre-Louis, organist and composer, known as **M. Couperin l'aîné** or **Couperin fils,** son of **Armand-Louis Couperin;** b. Paris, March 14, 1755; d. there, Oct. 10, 1789. He was organist to the King, and later at Notre-Dame, St.-Jean, St.-Merry, and St.-Gervais, succeeding his father at the latter earlrly in 1789. He died 8 months later. Some of his compositions were publ. in contemporary collections; others are in MS. —NS/LK/DM

Courtois, Jean, Franco-Flemish composer who flourished in the first half of the 16th century. He was maître de chapelle at Cambrai Cathedral in 1540, when a four-part motet of his, *Venite populi terrae,* was performed before Charles V of Spain. His extant works comprise two masses, 14 motets, and 19 chansons. —NS/LK/DM

Coussemaker, (Charles-) Edmond (-Henri) de, French music scholar; b. Bailleul, Nord, April 19, 1805; d. Bourbourg, Jan. 10, 1876. He studied music as a child. His main profession was the law; while studying law at the Univ. of Paris, he took private lessons with Pellegrini in singing and Anton Reicha in harmony. He continued his studies with Lefebvre in Douai, after becoming a practicing lawyer. At this time (1831–35) he found leisure to compose music of the most varied description, all of which, with the exception of a few *romances* and two sets of songs, is unpubl., and apparently lost. His interest in history and archaeology led him to the study of the authentic documents of music; he was also influenced by the scholarly articles in *La Gazette et Revue Musicale* (then ed. by Fétis). During successive terms as judge in Hazebrouck, Dunkirk, and Lille, he continued to accumulate knowledge of musical documentation; he assembled a vast library; 1,075 items in his library are listed in the *Catalogue des livres, manuscrits et instruments de musique du feu M. Charles Coussemaker* (Brussels, 1877; issued for an auction).

WRITINGS: *Mémoire sur Hucbald* (1841); *Notice sur les collections musicales de la bibliothèque de Cambrai...* (1843); *Histoire de l'harmonie au moyen-âge* (1852); *Trois chants historiques* (1854); *Chants populaires des Flamands de France* (1856); *Drames liturgiques du moyen-âge* (1860); *Les Harmonistes des XIIe et XIII siècles* (1865); *Scriptorum de musica medii aevi nova series* (4 vols., 1864–76; new ed., Graz, 1908); *L'Art harmonique aux XIIe et XIIIe siècles*(1865); *OEuvres completes d'Adam de la Halle* (1872); etc.

BIBL.: A. Desplanque, *Étude sur les travaux d'historie et d'archéologie de M. E. d.C.* (Paris, 1870).—NS/LK/DM

Coward, Sir Noël (Peirce), witty English writer, actor, and composer; b. Teddington, Middlesex, England, Dec. 16, 1899; d. Port Maria, Jamaica, March 26, 1973. Coward found his greatest recognition as a playwright, his most successful plays being comedies such as *Private Lives, Design for Living,* and *Blithe Spirit,* but he also wrote screenplays, fiction, and poetry, and he sometimes acted in, directed, and produced his own works and those of others. He also distinguished himself as a successful singer and songwriter. His most popular songs included sentimental ballads like "I'll See You Again" and characteristically droll tunes such as "Mad Dogs and Englishmen" and "Mad About the Boy."

Coward's father, Arthur Sabin Coward, was a piano salesman; though Coward had no musical training, he began playing piano by ear at age seven. He attended private schools only until the age of ten, when he went into the theater. He had his first acting role in the play *The Goldfish* in London during the 1911 Christmas season. He wrote his first song, "Forbidden Fruit," at age 16 and placed his first song in a show when the revue *Tails-Up* featured "Peter Pan" (music by Doris Joel) in June 1918.

In 1923, Coward wrote the songs, cowrote the libretto, and appeared in the revue *London Calling*; it ran 316 performances and included his first published song, "Parisian Pierrot." That song was used along with two other Coward compositions in the American production *André Charlot's Revue of 1924* (N.Y., 1924), which marked his musical introduction to the U.S.

Coward wrote the songs and libretto for *On with the Dance* in 1925. It ran for 229 performances in London and included "Poor Little Rich Girl" (music by Philip Braham), which, along with six other Coward songs and many interpolations, was used in the *Charlot Revue of 1926* on Broadway. The show, the first N.Y. musical production to bear Coward's name, ran 140 performances, and "Poor Little Rich Girl" became a hit for Gertrude Lawrence, who sang it onstage, in April 1926.

After several plays, Coward returned to musical theater work in 1928 with *This Year of Grace!*, for which he wrote the songs and the libretto and which he directed and starred in on Broadway. The show ran 316 performances in London and 158 in N.Y. Two of its songs became hits in the U.S. in the late winter of 1929—"A Room with a View," recorded by Ben Selvin and His Orch., and "Dance, Little Lady," by the orchestra of Roger Wolfe Kahn.

Bitter Sweet, Coward's 1929 show, was a full-fledged operetta. Coward wrote the libretto and directed the show in both its London and N.Y. productions. His most successful musical work, it ran 697 performances in the West End, 159 on Broadway, and gave Coward his biggest song success yet when "I'll See You Again" was recorded by Leo Reisman and His Orch. for a hit in January 1930.

Coward contributed songs to two Broadway revues, the comic comment on colonialism "Mad Dogs and Englishmen (Go Out in the Mid-Day Sun)," sung by Beatrice Lillie in *The Third Little Show* (N.Y., 1931), and "Half Caste Woman," sung by Helen Morgan in the *Ziegfeld Follies of 1931* (N.Y., 1931). Several new Coward songs, along with many period songs, were featured in *Cavalcade* (1931), Coward's patriotic pageant about the first three decades of the century in England. (Though the show was not produced in the U.S., an American film version released in 1933 was a substantial success, winning the Academy Award for Best Picture.)

The U.K.-only revue *Words and Music* (1932) was written and directed by Coward and marked the introduction of "Mad About the Boy," a song often cited as reflecting his homosexuality. The show ran 164 performances.

Conversation Piece (1934), a "play with music," was Coward's first musical work to play in both N.Y. and London in five years. In the West End, where Coward also starred in the show, it was a hit, but on Broadway, where he did not, it ran a mere 55 performances. Nevertheless, Ray Noble and His Orch. recorded "I'll Follow My Secret Heart" from the score for a hit in November. The following August, Noble made a U.S. hit out of "Mad About the Boy," which had not yet been performed in an American show.

Though Coward did not have a new musical ready in 1935, he did publish one of his most memorable comic songs, "Mrs. Worthington (Don't Put Your Daughter on the Stage)," the ultimate rejection letter to a stage mother. Opening in London in January 1936, *Tonight at 8:30* consisted of nine one-act plays, several of which contained songs. Coward appeared in both the West End and Broadway productions, with the former running 157 performances and the latter 113.

At the end of the 1930s, Coward alternated between N.Y. and London, first writing and directing the musical *Operette* for the West End in 1938. The show ran 133 performances but failed to pay back its investment. Coward used some of its songs in a revised version of *Words and Music* called *Set to Music* in N.Y. in 1939. Featuring the American stage premieres of such songs as "Mad About the Boy" and the comic "The Stately Homes of England," the revue ran 129 performances.

With the onset of World War II, Coward devoted much of his time to the war effort. Though he did not spend much time on music during this period, he did write individual songs reflecting patriotic and war sentiments, such as "London Pride" (1941), which was used in the West End revue *Up and Running*, and the satiric "Don't Let's Be Beastly to the Germans" (1943). In addition to writing, codirecting, producing, and starring in the award-winning patriotic film *In Which We Serve* (1942), he also composed its music.

Coward's first post-war musical theater work came in 1945 with the revue *Sigh No More*, which ran 213 performances, followed by 1946's *Pacific 1860*, an operetta that starred Mary Martin and had a run of 129 performances, though it failed financially. The musical *Ace of Clubs* (1950) was a flop, while *After the Ball* (1954) ran 188 performances. In the 1950s, Coward turned increasingly to nightclub performing and cameo appearances in films. His cabaret act resulted in the album *Noël Coward at Las Vegas*, recorded in June 1955. It reached the U.S. charts in January 1956. *Together with Music*, a 90-minute television special featuring material from the act and costarring Martin, had been broadcast in the U.S. in October.

Coward returned to musical theater in 1961, when *Sail Away* ran for 167 performances on Broadway and the cast album spent five months on the charts. *The Girl Who Came to Supper* (1963) featured songs by Coward, though he did not write the book or direct; it ran 112 performances and the cast album charted for three months. Coward *did* direct the musical *High Spirits* (N.Y., 1964), based on his play, *Blithe Spirit*, but he did not write the music. Richard Rodgers wrote the songs for the television musical *Androcles and the Lion*, in which Coward appeared when it was broadcast on American TV on Nov. 15, 1967.

Toward the end of Coward's life, his stature was reflected in awards and revivals. He was knighted in 1970, the same year he received a special Tony Award. His songs were anthologized in the Broadway shows *Noël Coward's Sweet Potato* (1968) and *Oh Coward!* (1972) and the West End revue *Cowardy Custard* (1972). He died at the age of 73.

WRITINGS: *Present Indicative* (N.Y., 1937); *The N. C. Song Book* (London, 1953); *Future Indefinite* (London, 1954); *The Lyrics of N. C.* (London, 1965); *The Wit of N. C.* (London, 1968); *A Last*

Encore (Boston, 1973); G. Payn and S. Morley, eds., *The N. C. Diaries* (London, 1982); S. Morley, ed. *Autobiography (Present Indicative, Future Indefinite, Past Conditional)* (London, 1986).

DISC.: *Together with Music* (1955); *Noel Coward at Las Vegas [live]* (1955).

WORKS (only works for which Coward was the primary, credited songwriter or composer are listed): **MUSICALS/ REVUES/OPERETTAS:** *London Calling* (London, 1923); *On with the Dance* (London, 1925); *Charlot Revue of 1926* (N.Y., 1925); *This Year of Grace!* (London, 1928); *Bitter Sweet* (London, 1929); *Cavalcade* (London, 1931); *Words and Music* (London, 1932); *Conversation Piece* (London, 1934); *Tonight at 8:30* (London, 1936); *Operette* (London, 1938); *Sigh No More* (London, 1945); *Pacific 1860* (London, 1946); *Ace of Clubs* (London, 1950); *After the Ball* (London, 1954); *Sail Away* (N.Y., 1961); *The Girl Who Came to Supper* (N.Y., 1963); *N. C.'s Sweet Potato* (N.Y., 1968); *Cly Custard* (London, 1972); *Oh C.!* (N.Y., 1972). **FILMS:** *Cavalcade* (1933); *Bitter Sweet* (1933); *Bitter Sweet* (1940); *In Which We Serve* (1942); *The Astonished Heart* (1950).

BIBL.: P. Braybrooke, *The Amazing Mr. N. C.* (London, 1933); R. Greacen, *The Art of N. C.* (Aldington, England, 1953); J. Mander and R. Mitchenson, *Theatrical Companion to C.* (London, 1957); M. Levin, *N. C.* (Boston, 1958); S. Morley, *A Talent to Amuse: A Biography of N. C.* (London, 1969); C. Castle, *N.* (London, 1972); J. Hadfield, ed., *Cly Custard: The World of N. C.* (London, 1973); W. Marchant, *The Privilege of His Company* (N.Y., 1975); C. Lesley, *Remembered Laughter: The Life of N. C.* (London, 1976); C. Lesley, G. Payn, and S. Morley, *N. C. and His Friends* (London, 1979); J. Lahr, *C. the Playwright* (N.Y., 1982); C. Citron, *N. and Cole: The Sophisticates* (London, 1992); C. Fisher, *N. C.: A Biography* (N.Y., 1992); S. Cole, *N. C.: A Bio-Bibliography* (Westport, Conn., 1993); G. Payn with B. Day, *My Life with N. C.* (N.Y., 1994); P. Hoare, *N. C.: A Biography* (N.Y., 1995); J. Morella and G. Mazzei, *Genius & Lust: The Creative and Sexual Lives of Cole Porter and N. C.* (N.Y., 1995).—**WR**

Cowell, Henry (Dixon),

remarkable and innovative American composer; b. Menlo Park, Calif., March 11, 1897; d. Shady, N.Y., Dec. 10, 1965. His father, of Irish birth, was a member of a clergyman's family in Kildare; his mother was an American of progressive persuasion. Cowell studied violin with Henry Holmes in San Francisco; after the earthquake of 1906, his mother took him to N.Y., where they were compelled to seek support from the Soc. for the Improvement of the Condition of the Poor; they returned to Menlo Park, Calif., where Cowell was able to save enough money, earned from menial jobs, to buy a piano. He began to experiment with the keyboard by striking the keys with his fists and forearms; he named such chords "tone clusters" and at the age of 13 composed a piece called *Adventures in Harmony*, in which they appear. Later he began experimenting in altering the sound of the piano by placing various objects on the strings, and also by playing directly under the lid of the piano *pizzicato* and *glissando*, thus the later development of the "prepared piano." He first exhibited these startling innovations on March 5, 1914, at the San Francisco Musical Soc. at the St. Francis Hotel, much to the consternation of its members. The tone clusters per se were not new; they were used for special sound effects by composers in the 18th century to imitate thunder or cannon fire. Vladimir Rebikov applied them, for example, in his piano piece *Hymn to Inca*,

and Charles Ives used them in his *Concord Sonata* to be sounded by covering a set of white or black keys with a wooden board. However, Cowell had a priority by systematizing tone clusters as harmonic amplifications of tonal chords, and he devised a logical notation for them. These tone clusters eventually acquired legitimacy in the works of many European and American composers. Cowell also extended the sonorities of tone clusters to instrumental combinations and applied them in several of his symphonic works. In the meantime, Cowell began taking lessons in composition with E.G. Strickland and Wallace Sabin at the Univ. of Calif. at Berkeley, and later with Frank Damrosch at the Inst. of Musical Art in N.Y., and, privately, with Charles Seeger (1914–16). After brief service in the U.S. Army in 1918, where he was employed first as a cook and later as arranger for its Band, he became engaged professionally to give a series of lectures on new music, illustrated by his playing his own works on the piano. In 1928 he became the first American composer to visit Russia, where he attracted considerable attention; some of his pieces were publ. in a Russian ed., the first such publications by an American. Upon his return to the U.S., he was appointed lecturer on music at the New School for Social Research in N.Y.

In 1931 Cowell received a Guggenheim fellowship, and went to Berlin to study ethnomusicology with Hornbostel. This was the beginning of his serious study of ethnic musical materials. He had already experimented with Indian and Chinese devices in some of his works; in his *Ensemble for Strings* (1924), he included Indian thundersticks. In 1931 he formed a collaboration with Leon Theremin, then visiting the U.S.; with his aid he constructed an ingenious instrument, the Rhythmicon, which made possible the simultaneous production of 16 different rhythms on 16 different pitch levels of the harmonic series. He demonstrated the Rhythmicon at a lecture-concert in San Francisco on May 15, 1932. He also composed an extensive work entitled *Rhythmicana* for it, but it did not receive a performance until Dec. 3, 1971, at Stanford Univ., using advanced electronic techniques. In 1927 Cowell founded the *New Music Quarterly* for publication of ultramodern music, mainly by American composers.

Cowell's career was brutally interrupted in 1936, when he was arrested in Calif. on charges of homosexuality (then a heinous offense) involving the impairment of the morals of a minor. Lulled by the deceptive promises of a wily district attorney of a brief confinement in a sanatorium, Cowell pleaded guilty to a limited offense; he was vengefully given a maximum sentence of imprisonment, up to 15 years. Incarcerated at San Quentin, he was assigned to work in a jute mill, but indomitably continued to write music. Thanks to interventions on his behalf by a number of eminent musicians, he was paroled in 1940 to Percy Grainger as a guarantor of his good conduct; he obtained a full pardon on Dec. 9, 1942, from the governor of Calif., Earl Warren, after it was discovered that the evidence against him was largely contrived. On Sept. 27, 1941, he married Sidney Robertson, a noted ethnomusicologist. He then resumed his full activities as an ed. and instructor; he held teaching positions at the New School for Social Research in N.Y. (1940–62), the Univ. of Southern Calif. in Los Angeles, Mills Coll. in Oakland, Calif., and the Peabody Cons. of Music in Baltimore (1951–56); he was also appointed adjunct prof. at summer classes at Columbia Univ. (1951–65). In 1951 Cowell was elected a member of the National Academy of Arts and Letters; he received an honorary Mus.D. from Wilmington Coll. (1953) and from Monmouth (Ill.) Coll. (1963). In 1956–57 he undertook a world tour with his wife through the Near East, India, and Japan, collecting rich prime materials for his compositions, which by now had acquired a decisive turn toward the use of ethnomusicological melodic and rhythmic materials, without abandoning, however, the experimental devices which were the signposts of most of his works. In addition to his symphonic and chamber music, Cowell publ. in 1930 an important book, *New Musical Resources*. He also ed. a symposium, *American Composers on American Music* (Stanford, Calif., 1933). In collaboration with his wife, he wrote a biography of Charles Ives (1955).

WORKS: DRAMATIC: *The Building of Bamba*, pageant (Halcyon, near Pismo Beach, Calif., Aug. 18, 1917). *O'Higgins of Chile*, opera (1949; unifnished); *The Commission*, "operatic episode" (1954; Woodstock, N.Y., Sept. 26, 1992). **16 HYMN AND FUGUING TUNES** (based on fuguing tunes of William Billings): No. 1 for Band (1943); No. 2 for String Orch. (1944); No. 3 for Orch. (1944); No. 4 for 3 Instruments (1944); No. 5 for String Orch. (1945; version for Orch. incorporated into Sym. No. 10); No. 6 for Piano (1946); No. 7 for Viola and Piano (1946); No. 8 for String Quartet or String Orch. (1947–48); No. 9 for Cello and Piano (1950); No. 10 for Oboe and Strings (1955); No. 11, became *7 Rites of Music* for Men's Chorus and Orch. (1956); No. 12 for 3 Horns (1957); No. 13 for Trombone and Piano (1960); No. 14 for Organ (1961); No. 15A, a duet for the anniversary of his marriage (Sept. 27, 1961); No. 15B for 2 Violins or Any Combination (2 versions, 1 with a more extended ground bass); No. 16 for Violin and Piano (1965; N.Y., Oct. 6, 1966; also for Violin and Orch.). **20 SYMS:** No. 1 (1916–17); No. 2, *Anthropos* (Mankind; 1938); No. 3, *Gaelic Symphony* (1942); No. 4, *Short Symphony* (1946; Boston, Oct. 24, 1947); No. 5 (1948; Washington, D.C., Jan. 5, 1949); No. 6 (1950–55; Houston, Nov. 14, 1955); No. 7 (Baltimore, Nov. 25, 1952); No. 8, *Choral*, for Chorus and Orch. (1952; Wilmington, Ohio, March 1, 1953); No. 9 (1953; Green Bay, Wisc., March 14, 1954); No. 10 for Chamber Orch. (1953; U.S. premiere, N.Y., Feb. 24, 1957); No. 11, *The 7 Rituals of Music* (1953; Louisville, May 29, 1954); No. 12 (1955–56; Houston, March 28, 1960); No. 13, *Madras Symphony*, for Small Orch. and 3 Indian Instruments (1957–58; Madras, India, March 3, 1959); No. 14 (1960–61; Washington, D.C., April 27, 1961); No. 15, *Thesis* (Bowling Green, Ky., Oct. 7, 1961); No. 16, *Icelandic Symphony* (1962; Reykjavík, March 21, 1963); No. 17 (1962–63; 1st movement perf. as *Lancaster Overture*, Lancaster, Pa., 1963); No. 18 (1964); No. 19 (Nashville, Tenn., Oct. 18, 1965); No. 20 (1965). **OTHER WORKS FOR ORCH.:** *Vestiges* (1914–20); *Some Music* (1915); *Some More Music* (1915–16); *Communication* (1920); Sinfonietta for Small Orch. (1924–28; Boston, Nov. 23, 1931, Slonimsky conducting); *Irish Suite* for Solo String, Percussion, and Piano (1928; Boston, March 11, 1929, Slonimsky conducting; a scoring of the piano pieces *The Banshee, Leprechaun,* and *Fairy Bells* with Chamber Orch. accompaniment); Piano Concerto (1929; Havana, Dec. 28, 1930; 1st complete U.S. perf., Omaha, Oct. 12, 1978); *Polyphonica* for 12 Instruments (1930); Synchrony

(1930; Paris, June 6, 1931, Slonimsky conducting); *Reel No. 1* and *No. 2* (1930, 1932); *2 Appositions* for Strings (1931); *Rhythmicana*, Concerto for Rhythmicon and Orch. (1931; Palo Alto, Calif., Dec. 3, 1971); 3 pieces for Chamber Orch.: *Competitive Sport, Steel and Stone,* and *Heroic Dance* (1931); *4 Continuations* for Strings (1933); *Old American Country Set* (1937; Indianapolis, Feb. 28, 1940); *Celtic Set* (Selinsgrove, Pa., May 6, 1938); *American Melting Pot* (1939); *Symphonic Set* (1939; orchestration of *Toccanta*); *Shoonthree* (Sleep Music; 1939; also for Band); *Pastoral & Fiddler's Delight* (1940; N.Y., July 26, 1949, Stokowski conducting); *Ancient Desert Drone* (1940); *Tales of Our Countryside* for Piano and Orch. (1940; Atlantic City, May 11, 1941; composer soloist, Stokowski conducting; based on piano pieces written 1922–30); *Vox Humana* (1940); *Little Concerto* for Piano and Orch. or Band (1942; also known as *Concerto piccolo*); Suite for Piano and Strings (1943); *American Pipers* (1943); *United Music* (1944); *Big Sing* (1945); *Festival Overture* for 2 Orchs. (1946); *Saturday Night at the Firehouse* (1948); *Aria* for Violin and Strings (1952); *Rondo* (1953); *Ballad* for Strings (1955); *Variations* (1956); *Persian Set* for 12 Instruments (1956–57); *Music 1957* (1957); *Ongaku* (1957; Louisville, March 26, 1958); *Antiphony* for 2 Orchs. (1958; Kansas City, Mo., Nov. 14, 1959); Percussion Concerto (1958; Kansas City, Jan. 7, 1961); *Mela and Fair* (New Delhi, India, Dec. 11, 1959); *Characters* (1959); *Chiaroscuro* (1960; Guatemala City, Oct. 13, 1961); *Variations on Thirds* for 2 Solo Violas and Strings (1960); *Concerto brevis* for Accordion and Orch. (1960); Harmonica Concerto (1960); *Air and Scherzo* for Saxophone and Small Orch. (1961); *Duo concertante* for Flute, Harp, and Orch. (Springfield, Ohio, Oct. 21, 1961); two koto concertos: No. 1 (1963; Philadelphia, Dec. 18, 1964) and No. two (Hanover, N.H., May 8, 1965); *Concerto grosso* for five Instruments and Orch. (1963; Miami Beach, Jan. 12, 1964); Harp Concerto (1965); Carol (1965; new orchestration of slow movement of Koto Concerto No. 1). **OTHER WORKS FOR BAND:** *A Curse and a Blessing* (1938); *Shoonthree* (1940; also for Orch.); *Celtic Set* (1943; orig. for Orch., 1938); *Animal Magic* (1944); *Grandma's Rumba* (1945); *Fantasie* (West Point, N.Y., May 30, 1952); *Singing Band* (1953). **OTHER WORKS FOR VOICE:** *The Thistle Flower* for Women's Voices (1928); *Vocalise* for Voice, Flute, and Piano (1937); *Chrysanthemums* for Soprano, 2 Saxophones, and 4 Strings (1937); *Toccanta* for Soprano, Flute, Cello, and Piano (1938); *The Coming of Light* for Chorus (1939); *Fire and Ice*, after Frost, for four Male Soloists and Orch. or Band (1942); Sonatina for Baritone, Violin, and Piano (1942); *American Muse* for Soprano, Alto, and Piano (1943); *To America* for Chorus (1947); *The Commission*, cantata for four Soloists and Orch. (1954); *...if He Please* for Mixed and either Boys' or Women's Choruses and Orch. (1954); Septet for five Voices without words, Clarinet, and Piano (1955–56); *A Thanksgiving Psalm from the Dead Sea Scrolls* for Men's Chorus and Orch. (1956; orig. *Hymn and Fuguing Tune No. 11*); *Edson Hymns and Fuguing Tunes* for Chorus and Orch. (1960); *The Creator* for Chorus and Orch. (1963); *Ultima Actio* for Chorus (1965). **OTHER CHAMBER WORKS:** *Quartet Romantic* for 2 Flutes, Violin, and Viola (1915–17); five string quartets: No. 1, *Pedantic* (1915–16), No. 2, *Movement* (1928), No. 3, *Mosaic* (1935), No. 4, *United* (1936), and No. five (1956; rev. 1962); also the unnumbered *Quartet Euphometric* (1916–19); other pieces; also unnumbered *Ensemble* for 2 Violins, Viola, 2 Cellos, and 3 Thundersticks (1924; version for String Orch. without Thundersticks, 1959); *7 Paragraphs* for String Trio (1925); Suite for Violin and Piano (1927); *Exultation* for 10 Strings (1928); Suite for Wind Quintet (1930); 3 works for Percussion: *Pulse, Return,* and *Ostinato Pianissimo* (1930–34); *6 Casual Developments* for Clarinet and Piano (1935); *Sound-form* for Dance for Flute, Clarinet, Bassoon, and Percussion (1936); *Sarabande* for Oboe, Clarinet, and Percussion (1937); *Trickster Coyote* for Flute and Percussion (1941); *Action in Brass* for five Brasses (1943); Violin Sonata (1945; rev. 1947); Saxophone Quartet (1946); *Tall Tale* for Brass Sextet (1947); *Set for 2* for Violin and Piano (1948); *4 Declamations and Return* for Cello and Piano (1949); *Set of 5* for Violin, Piano, and Percussion (1951); *Set for Harpsichord, Flute, Oboe, and Cello* (1953); *Set of 2* for Harp and Violin (1955); *Homage to Iran* for Violin and Piano (1957); *Iridescent Rondo* for Accordion (1959); *Air and Scherzo* for Saxophone and Piano (1961); Quartet for Flute, Oboe, Cello, and Harp (1962); *Gravely and Vigorously*, in memory of John F. Kennedy, for Cello (1963; orig. the *Hymn and Fuguing Tune* No. 17); *26 Simultaneous Mosaics* for Violin, Cello, Clarinet, Piano, and Percussion (N.Y., Dec. 1, 1964); Piano Trio (1965); *Cleistogamy* (self-pollinating flowerlets), a collection of pieces written between 1941 and 1963. **KEYBOARD: P i a n o :** *The Tides of Manaunaun* (1912); *Advertisements* (1914; rev. 1959); *Dynamic Motion* (1914); *6 Ings: Floating-Fleeting-Wafting-Seething-Frisking-Scooting* (1916); *It Isn't It* (1922); *The Snows of Fujiyama* (1922); *Aeolian Harp* (1923); *Piece* for Piano with Strings (Paris, 1924); *The Banshee* (1925); *Lilt of the Reel* (1925); *Sinister Resonance* (1925); *Tiger* (1927); *2 Woofs* (1930); *Hilarious Curtain Opener and Ritournelle* (1937); hundreds of other pieces with similar fanciful titles; also some organ pieces.

WRITINGS: *New Musical Resources* (N.Y., 1930); ed., *American Composers on American Music: A Symposium* (Stanford, Calif., 1933); with S. Cowell, *Charles Ives and His Music* (N.Y., 1955).

BIBL.: R. Mead, *H. C.'s New Music, 1925–1936* (N.Y., 1981); M. Manion, *Writings about H. C.: An Annotated Bibliography* (N.Y., 1982); W. Lichtenwanger, *The Music of H. C.: A Descriptive Catalog* (Brooklyn, 1986).—NS/LK/DM

Cowell, Stanley (A.), jazz pianist, composer; b. Toledo, Ohio; b. May 5, 1941. He studied classical piano with two noted teachers, Mary Belle Shealy and Elmer Gertz; and pipe organ with William Harter. By 14, he was featured soloist with the Toledo Youth Orch., a church organist/choir director, and a budding jazz pianist. He attended Oberlin (B.M.) and Univ. of Mich. (M.M.). He also did undergraduate work at the Mozarteum Akademie, Salzburg, Austria, and graduate study at Wichita State Univ. and the Univ. of Southern Calif. After completing his studies, Cowell headed for N.Y. (1966) and worked with Max Roach, Abbey Lincoln, Rahsaan Roland Kirk, Herbie Mann, Miles Davis, Stan Getz, and the Bobby Hutcherson–Harold Land groups. For several years, he was part of Music Inc., along with Charles Tolliver, with whom he formed the innovative musician-owned record company Strata-East (1971). He organized the Piano Choir (1972), a group of seven N.Y.-based keyboardists, and he became a founding member of Collective Black Artists, Inc., a non-profit company devoted to bringing African American music and musicians to the public. He served as conductor of the CBA Ensemble (1973–74). In 1974 he was the musical director of the N.Y. Jazz Repertory Company at Carnegie Hall, along with Gil Evans, Billy Taylor, and Sy Oliver.

During the 1970s, Cowell established his reputation as a versatile and sensitive pianist/composer, performing and recording with Sonny Rollins, Clifford Jordan, Oliver Nelson, Donald Byrd, Roy Haynes, Richard

Davis, Art Pepper, Jimmy Heath and others. From 1974–84, he toured, recorded and did workshops with the Heath Brothers. He received an Ohio Arts Council Grant for choral composition with jazz ensemble which was later performed in 1987. He taught jazz piano at New England Cons., Boston (1988–89). He did the score for *The Dream Keeper: Langston Hughes*, a one hour documentary aired on PBS (1988). He did a six-week residency with the Toledo Symphony Orch. consisting of lectures, workshops, interviews, and performances in area schools, colleges, public libraries, and media (1992). He was a recipient of a Meet the Composer/Rockefeller Foundation/AT&T Jazz Program grant (1990–91), for which he created "Piano Concerto No. 1" (1992). He served on the board of the Charlin Jazz Society, producer of jazz concerts in Washington, D.C. (1990–96), and has been featured in many "third stream" works, conducted by Gunther Schuller and Larry Newland. For many years he lived in D.C. and commuted to teach at Lehman Coll. in the Bronx. During the 1999–2000 school year he began teaching at Rutgers Univ. in New Brunswick, N.J.

DISC.: *Brilliant Circles* (1969); *Blues for the Viet Cong* (1969); *Illusion Suite* (1972); *Questions and Answers* (1973); *Musa Ancestral Streams* (1973); *Regeneration* (1975); *Waiting for the Moment* (1977); *Talkin' 'bout Love* (1978); *Equipoise* (1978); *We Three* (1987); *Sienna* (1989); *Back to the Beautiful* (1989); *Live at Maybeck Recital Hall, V* (1990); *Close to You Alone* (1990); *Angel Eyes* (1994); *Setup* (1994); *Piano Jazz* (1995); *Live at Copenhagen Jazz House* (1995); *Mandara Blossoms* (1996); *Hear Me One* (1997); *Piano Choir: Handscapes, Vols. 1 & 2* (1974).—LP

Cowen, Sir Frederic (Hymen), English conductor and composer; b. Kingston, Jamaica, Jan. 29, 1852; d. London, Oct. 6, 1935. His evident talent for music caused his parents to take him to England to study at the age of four. He was a pupil of Benedict and Goss in London; studied at the Leipzig Cons. under Hauptmann, Moscheles, Reinecke, Richter, and Plaidy (1865–66); in Berlin under Kiel at the Stern Cons. (1867–68). He was conductor of the Phil. Soc. of London (1888–92; 1900–07), the Liverpool Phil. (1895–1913), the Hallé Orch. in Manchester (1896–99), the Scottish Orch. in Glasgow (1900–10) and the Handel Triennial Festivals in London (1902–23). In 1911 he was knighted. He publ. his memoirs as *My Art and My Friends* (London, 1913), and an amusing glossary of musical terms, *Music as She Is Wrote* (London, 1915); also books on Haydn, Mozart, Mendelssohn, and Rossini.

WORKS: DRAMATIC: O p e r a : *Pauline* (London, Nov. 22, 1876); *Thorgrim* (London, April 22, 1890); *Signa* (Milan, Nov. 12, 1893); *Harold, or The Norman Conquest* (London, June 8, 1895). **ORCH.:** 6 syms.: No. 1 (1869), No. 2 (1872), No. 3, *Scandinavian* (1880), No. 4, *Welsh* (1884), No. 5 (1887), and No. 6, *Idyllic* (1897); three suites: *The Language of Flowers, In the Olden Time,* and *In Fairyland;* Sinfonietta; Piano Concerto; four overtures; *Of Life and Love,* fantasy. **CHAMBER:** 2 piano trios; 2 string quartets; piano pieces. **VOCAL: O r a t o r i o s :** *The Deluge* (1878); *St. Ursula* (1881); *Ruth* (1887); *The Veil* (Cardiff, Sept. 20, 1910). **O t h e r :** Cantatas; over 250 songs. —NS/LK/DM

Cowie, Edward, English-born Australian composer, conductor, teacher, and painter; b. Birmingham,

Aug. 17, 1943. He studied with Fricker and took his B.Ed. at the Univ. of London (1964); after training from A. Goehr (1964–68), he worked with Lutoslawski in Poland (1971); he also studied at the Trinity Coll. of Music in London (L.T.C.L., 1968), and at the univs. of Southampton (B.Mus., 1970; D.Mus., 1979) and Lancaster (Ph.D., 1983). From 1974 to 1983 he was senior lecturer at the Univ. of Lancaster; in 1979 he also was a visiting prof. at the Univ. of Kassel. From 1983 to 1986 he was composer-in- residence at the Royal Liverpool Phil., and from 1983 to 1989 prof. of creative arts at the Univ. of Wollongong in New South Wales. In 1988 he became a naturalized Australian citizen. In 1989–90 he was prof. of creative arts at James Cook Univ. in Queensland. He then served as artistic director and prof. of arts fusion of the Australian Arts Fusion Centre in Brisbane (from 1991). He also was active as a conductor. His talent as a painter has been highlighted in various exhibitions. As a composer, his technique ranges from static triadic tonality to serialistic atonality; reflections of nature, including birdsong, and a preoccupation with form, are pervasive aspects of his works.

Works: DRAMATIC: *Commedia*, opera (1976–78); *Kate Kelly's Roadshow*, music theater (1982). **ORCH.:** 2 clarinet concertos (1969, 1975); *Moon, Sea, and Stars* (1974); *Leviathan*, symphonic poem (1975); *Columbine* (1976); Piano Concerto (1976–77); *L'Or de la trompette d'ete* for 18 Strings (1977); *Concerto for Orchestra* (1980–81); *Leonardo* for Strings (1980–81); two numbered syms.: No. 1, *The American* (1980–81; Liverpool, Feb. 1, 1984) and No. 2, *The Australian* (1982); *Choral Symphony: Symphonies of Rain, Sea, and Speed* for Baritone, Chorus, and Orch. (1981–82); Concerto for Harp and Strings (1983); *Atlas* (1984; Liverpool, May 13, 1986); *15-Minute Australia* for Youth Orch. (1985); Cello Concerto (1992). **CHAMBER:** four string quartets (1973, 1976, 1980, 1981); *Cathedral Music* for Brass (1976); *Harlequin* for Harp (1977); *Commedia Lazzis* for Guitar (1977); *Kelly-Nolan-Kelly* for Clarinet (1980); *Cartoon Music* for Percussion, Keyboard, Violin, and Cello (1984); Flute Quartet (1991). **KEYBOARD: Piano:** *Piano Variations* (1976; rev. 1981); *The Falls of Clyde* for two Pianos (1976); *Kelly Variations* (1980); Sonata (1985). **VOCAL:** *Shinko-Kinshu* for High Voice and Instruments (1968; rev. 1972); *Gesangbuch* for 24 Voices Unaccompanied or With Instruments (1971); *Endymion Nocturnes* for Tenor and String Quartet (1973; also for Tenor, Horn, and Strings, 1981); *A Charm of Finches* for Soprano and three Flutes (1973); *Leighton Moss* for Chorus and Chamber Orch. (1974–75); *Columbine* for Soprano and Chamber Orch. (1979); *Missa Brevis* for Chorus and Organ (1982); *Avium Cencentus* for Chorus (1988); *The Roof of Heaven* for Tenor, two Oboes, two Horns, and Strings (1988); *'48* for High Voice and Chamber Ensemble (1992).—NS/LK/DM

Cox, Ida (nee Prather), jazz–blues singer; b. Toccoa, Ga., Feb. 25, c. 1896; d. Knoxville, Tenn., Nov. 10, 1967. She sang in her local African Methodist Choir during childhood, and later ran away from home to tour with White and Clark's Minstrels on the T.O.B.A. circuit. She became a solo artist and began recording in 1923. She worked with Jelly Roll Morton and King Oliver, among many other jazz musicians. During the 1920s and early 1930s, she toured with her own "Raisin' Cain" show, then headed the "Darktown Scandals" company. Cox recorded with Hot Lips Page and Fletcher Henderson. After playing solo residencies in N.Y. (1939; at this time managed by blues singer Big Bill Broonzy), she appeared at "Spirituals to Swing" concert at Carnegie Hall (December 1939). She continued to work regularly until suffering a stroke in Buffalo, N.Y. (1945); she eventually retired to Knoxville (1949). Cox was rediscovered in late 1959 after John Hammond placed an ad in *Variety*. She hadn't sang in five years but resumed recording in 1961 with an album featuring all-star jazz accompaniment. She died of cancer in 1967. She was the wife of Tex. pianist- organist Jesse "Tiny" Crump.

Disc.: *Wild Women Don't Have the Blues* (1961); *Moanin' Groanin' Blues* (1961); *Blues for Rampart Street* (1961).—JC/LP

Cox, Jean, American tenor; b. Gadsen, Ala., Jan. 16, 1922. After attending the Univ. of Ala. and the New England Cons. of Music in Boston, he studied with Kitsamer in Frankfurt am Main, Ricci and Bertelli in Rome, and Lorenz in Munich. In 1951 he made his operatic debut as Lensky with the New England Opera Theater in Boston. In 1954 he made his European operatic debut as Rodolfo in Spoleto, and then sang in Kiel (1954–55) and Braunschweig (1955–59). He appeared at the Bayreuth Festivals (1956–75), at the Hamburg State Opera (1958–73), and at the Mannheim National Theater (from 1959). As a guest artist, he sang with various European opera houses, including the Paris Opéra (as Siegmund, 1971) and at London's Covent Garden (as Siegfried, 1975). In the U.S. he appeared at the Chicago Lyric Opera (1964, 1970, 1973) and made his Metropolitan Opera debut in N.Y. as Walther von Stolzing on April 2, 1976, where he sang for the season before concentrating his career in Europe. He sang various Wagnerian roles, as well as Fra Diavolo, Don Carlos, Othello, Strauss's Herod and Bacchus, and the Cardinal in *Mathis der Maler*.—NS/LK/DM

Cox, John, English opera director and administrator; b. Bristol, March 12, 1935. He was educated at Oxford, where he produced the first British staging of *L'enfant et les sortilèges* in 1958. In 1959 he was an assistant at the Glyndebourne Festival. In 1965 he launched his professional career with his staging of *L'enfant et les sortilèges* at the Sadler's Wells Opera in London, and worked there regularly from 1969. From 1971 to 1981 he was director of production at the Glyndebourne Festival, where he excelled in the staging of operas by Richard Strauss. Following his tenure as general administrator and artistic director of Glasgow's Scottish Opera (1981–86), he was director of production at Covent Garden from 1988. His inventive productions have been seen on the Continent, in the U.S., and Australia.—NS/LK/DM

Crabbé, Armand (Charles), Belgian baritone; b. Brussels, April 23, 1883; d. there, July 24, 1947. He studied with Demest and Gilles at the Brussels Cons. (1902–04), and then with Cottone in Milan. In 1904 he made his operatic debut as the Nightwatchman in *Die Meistersinger von Nürnberg* at the Théâtre Royal de la Monnaie in Brussels. From 1906 to 1914 he sang at London's Covent Garden, and returned there in 1937. On Nov. 5, 1907, he made his U.S. debut as Escamillo at

N.Y.'s Manhattan Opera; after appearances with the Chicago Grand Opera (1910–14), he sang at Milan's La Scala (1915–16; 1928–31), in Buenos Aires (1916–26), and in Belgium. In his last years, he taught voice in Brussels. With Auguste Maurage, he composed the opera *Les Noces d'or*. He publ. the books *Conseils sur l'art du chant* (Brussels, 1931) and *L'art d'Orphée* (Brussels, 1933). Among his many roles were Rossini's Figaro, Silvio, Beckmesser, Rabaud's Mârouf, Ford, and Valentin. —NS/LK/DM

Craft, Robert (Lawson), American conductor and writer on music; b. Kingston, N.Y., Oct. 20, 1923. He studied at the Juilliard School of Music in N.Y. (B.A., 1946) and the Berkshire Music Center in Tanglewood; took courses in conducting with Monteux. In 1947 he conducted the N.Y. Brass and Woodwind Ensemble. He was conductor of the Evenings-on-the-Roof and the Monday Evening Concerts in Los Angeles (1950–68). A decisive turn in his career was his encounter with Stravinsky in 1948, whom he greatly impressed by his precise knowledge of Stravinsky's music; gradually he became Stravinsky's closest associate. He was also instrumental in persuading Stravinsky to adopt the 12-tone method of composition, a momentous turn in Stravinsky's creative path. He collaborated with Stravinsky on six vols. of a catechumenical and discursive nature: *Conversations with Igor Stravinsky* (N.Y., 1959); *Memories and Commentaries* (N.Y., 1960); *Expositions and Developments* (N.Y., 1962); *Dialogues and a Diary* (N.Y., 1963); *Themes and Episodes* (N.Y., 1967); *Retrospections and Conclusions* (N.Y., 1969). Resentful of frequent referral to him as a musical Boswell, Craft insists that his collaboration with Stravinsky was more akin to that between the Goncourt brothers, both acting and reacting to an emerging topic of discussion, with Stravinsky evoking his ancient memories in his careful English, or fluent French, spiced with unrestrained discourtesies toward professional colleagues on the American scene, and Craft reifying the material with an analeptic bulimia of quaquaversal literary, psychological, physiological, and culinary references in a flow of finely ordered dialogue. His other publications include *Prejudices in Disguise* (N.Y., 1974); *Stravinsky in Photographs and Documents* (with Vera Stravinsky; London, 1976; N.Y., 1978); *Current Convictions: Views and Reviews* (N. Y., 1977); *Present Perspectives* (N.Y., 1984); *Stravinsky: Glimpses of a Life* (N.Y., 1992). He also tr. and ed. *Stravinsky, Selected Correspondence* (2 vols., N.Y., 1982, 1984).—NS/LK/DM

Craighead, David, highly regarded American organist and pedagogue; b. Strasburg, Pa., Jan. 24, 1924. He was a student of Alexander McCurdy at the Curtis Inst. of Music in Philadelphia (B.M., 1946). He began his career as a church organist, then taught at Westminster Choir Coll. in Princeton, N.J. (1945–46) and at Occidental Coll. in Los Angeles (1948–55). From 1955 to 1992 he was prof. of organ and chairman of the organ dept. at the Eastman School of Music in Rochester, N.Y., where he taught again in 1993. He made extensive tours of the U.S. as a concert artist, giving numerous world premieres.—NS/LK/DM

Cramer, Johann Baptist, famous German pianist and pedagogue, son of **Wilhelm Cramer;** b. Mannheim, Feb. 24, 1771; d. London, April 16, 1858. He was taken to London as an infant, and throughout his life regarded it as his home. He received a fine musical education, first from his father, then from Clementi (1783–84) and C.F. Abel (1785). He began to travel as a concert pianist in 1788; visited Vienna, where he met Beethoven (1799–1800); in later years (1835–45) spent considerable time as a teacher in Munich and Paris, finally returning to London. His greatest work is his piano method, *Grosse Praktische Pianoforte Schule* (1815) in five parts, the last of which, *84 Studies* (op.50; later rev. and publ. as op.81, including 16 nouvelles etudes) is famous in piano pedagogy. Hans von Bülow made a selection of 50 studies from this collection, later revised and annotated in collections of 52 and 60; Henselt issued a different selection, with accompaniment of a second piano; other eds. of Cramer's studies are by Coccius, Riemann, Pauer, Lack, and Lickl; *100 Progressive Etudes* is also well known. Apart from his pedagogic collections, Cramer wrote nine piano concertos, over 50 piano sonatas, two piano quartets, two piano quintets, and numerous piano pieces of the salon type; but all these are quite forgotten, while his piano studies, with those of Czerny, maintained their value for more than a century. He first entered the music publishing business in 1805, as head of the firm Cramer & Keys; was in partnership with Samuel Chappell (1810–19). In 1824, together with R. Addison and T.F. Beale, Cramer established a music publishing house (now J.B. Cramer & Co., Ltd.), of which he was director until 1842; in 1844 Addison retired and was succeeded by W. Chappell, the firm then becoming Cramer, Beale & Chappell; after Cramer's death in 1858, and Chappell's retirement in 1861, G. Wood became Beale's partner; about 1862 the firm began to devote much attention to the manufacture of pianos; on Beale's death in 1863, Wood became sole director, continuing it successfully until his death in 1893, although devoting more consideration to piano manufacture than to music publishing. His two nephews succeeded him. In 1897 the firm became a limited company.

BIBL.: J. Pembaur, *Die 84 Etuden von J.B. C.; Anleitung zu gründlichem Studieren und Analysieren derselben* (Leipzig, 1901); T. Schlesinger, *J.B. C. und seine Klavier-Sonaten* (Munich, 1928). —NS/LK/DM

Cramer, Wilhelm, German violinist and composer, father of **Johann Baptist Cramer;** b. Mannheim (baptized), June 2, 1746; d. London, Oct. 5, 1799. He received his musical training from his father, Jacob Cramer (1705–70), who was a violinist in the Mannheim Orch., and also studied with Johann Stamitz and Cannabich. From 1752 to 1769 he was a member of the Mannheim Orch. He then went to Paris, and in 1772 to London, where he became a successful violinist and conductor. He was concertmaster of the orch. of the Anacreontic Soc. during its most prestigious years (1773–91). He was also chamber musician to the King. He wrote 11 violin concertos, six string quartets, six violin sonatas, and other string music.—**NS/LK/DM**

Cranberries, The, political-flavored Irish band fronted by strong- lunged singer Delores O'Riordan. **MEMBERSHIP:** Delores O'Riordan, voc. (b. Limerick, Ireland, Sept. 6, 1971); Noel Hogan, gtr. (b. Limerick, Ireland, Dec. 25, 1971); Mike Hogan, bs. (b. Limerick, Ireland, April 29, 1973); Fergal Lawler, drm. (b. Limerick, Ireland, March 4, 1971). Unlike fellow Irish musicians with worldwide hits, the Cranberries had only minimal popular acceptance in Europe before their debut album, *Everyone Else Is Doing It, So Why Can't We* took off in America. They had, however, made some pretty powerful allies.

Brothers Mike and Noel Hogan started the band in Limerick as The Cranberry Saw Us. Their original singer left, complaining that the songs were "too feminine" for him. They put an ad in the local paper. Among those who answered it was Delores O'Riordan. Although she had never sang in a band, she had sung in church most of her life. The band had her write lyrics to some tapes they made. She came back with a rough version of a song called "Linger" and was immediately made a member of the group. They cut a tape at a local studio, and the owner of the studio was so impressed that he became their manager. The tape spurred a bidding war among labels, but Island records eventually won. They cut their first, tentative EP, called *Uncertain*, which garnered poor reviews. Upon discovering that their manager had used them as leverage to coerce Island into refitting his studio, they fired him.

A new manager hooked them up with producer Stephen Street, best known for his work with The Smiths. They cut *Everybody Else Is Doing It, So Why Can't We*. The initial single, "Dreams" met with widespread indifference, as did the initial release of "Linger." The band went on tour, supporting bands like The The and Suede. By the end of the Suede tour, the headliners gave up and left the rest of the tour to The Cranberries. The show impressed the powers at MTV, who put "Linger" into "power rotation." Suddenly the song became a U.S. hit, rising to #8, selling gold, and propelling the album to #18, and eventual quintuple platinum. Only then did it start to make waves in Britain, where the album eventually topped the charts.

With her keening, athletic voice, O'Riordan became the focal point of the band. On the group's second album, *No Need to Argue*, the band's sound got harder but more focused. The album debuted at its peak of #6, and while there were no Top 40 hits, the band got considerable modern rock airplay for tunes like "Zombie" and "Ode to My Family." The album eventually sold over eight million copies in the U.S. alone.

The Cranberries took a couple of years off after the tour to support *No Need to Argue*. O'Riordan started a family. Rumors ran rampant that the band was going to break up and O'Riordan would start a solo career. Instead, they all went back into the studio with hard-pop producer Bruce Fairburn and recorded *To the Faithful Departed*, a more overtly political and harder rocking record than anything they had done previously. The album entered the charts at a peak of #4. The singles did not fare well, although "When You're Gone/Free To Decide" did chart at #22. The album only went double

platinum, a definite disappointment after the previous two hits.

Once again rumors abounded that O'Riordan would start a solo career, and once again they were quashed as the band went into the studio. They released *Bury the Hatchet* in the spring of 1999. It entered the chart at its peak position of #13 and went gold by the summer. With this success, O'Riordan was rumored to be the fifth richest woman in the British Isles.

DISC.: *Everybody Else Is Doing It, So Why Can't We* (1993); *No Need to Argue* (1994); *To the Faithful Departed* (1996); *Bury the Hatchet* (1999); *Promises* (U.K. 1, 2; live; 1999).—**HB**

Crass, Franz, German bass-baritone; b. Wipperfurth, Feb. 9, 1928. He was a student of Glettenberg at the Cologne Hochschule für Musik. In 1954 he made his operatic debut as Amonasro in Krefeld, and then sang in Hannover (1956–62), Bayreuth (1959–73), and Cologne (1962–64). He was a member of the Hamburg State Opera (from 1964), and also appeared at the Vienna State Opera, the Bavarian State Opera in Munich, at La Scala in Milan, and at Covent Garden in London. He was particularly known for his roles in operas by Mozart and Wagner, as well as for his appearances as a concert artist.—**NS/LK/DM**

Crawford, Jimmy (actually, **James Strickland**; aka **Jimmie**), jazz drummer; b. Memphis, Tenn., Jan. 14, 1910; d. N.Y., Jan. 28, 1980. His first instrument was the alto horn, then he switched to drums. Crawford attended LeMoyne Coll., then met Jimmie Lunceford while studying at Manassas H.S. He began doing local work with Lunceford and made his professional debut with the band in Lakeside, Ohio (summer 1928). He remained with Lunceford until early 1943, then had a short spell with Ben Webster; he then led his own group at the Three Deuces, N.Y., until serving in the U.S. Army from summer 1943–August 1945. Crawford played in an all-star service band with Sy Oliver, Buck Clayton, etc., also mainly with Edmond Hall's Walter Gross Service Band (1945). He played in a sextet from late 1945 until 1949, briefly with Harry James in mid-1946, with Ed Hall in N.Y. and Boston, and then played in Fletcher Henderson's last group in December 1950. Crawford did a long spell with the Broadway show *Pal Joey* during the early 1950s, and played for many other Broadway shows in the 1950s and 1960s. He then took part in Henderson Reunion Band in summer of 1957 and toured with Lena Horne's show *Jamaica* in 1958. He continued to work in clubs and show bands through the mid-1970s, when ill health slowed him down.

Crawford was the mainstay of the Jimmy Lunceford band and an early proponent of the high-hat, saying "You can hold everything together with that snap." —**JC/LP**

Crawford, Ray (Holland), bebop-flavored jazz guitarist; b. Pittsburgh, Pa., Feb. 7, 1924. He was a clarinet and saxophonist who played with Fletcher Henderson's orch. in the early 1940s, but then contracted tuberculosis, which forced him to switch to guitar. He became a good player in bop style and attained popularity as part of Ahmad Jamal's influential 1950s combos. Crawford stayed with Jamal until 1956, then played with Jimmy Smith and Gil Evans in the late 1950s and early 1960s. After recording and working with Tony Scott, Crawford moved from N.Y. to Los Angeles in 1961, heading a sextet that also included Johnny Coles and Cecil Payne. He recorded with this band, and later performed with Sonny Stitt and Sonny Criss. Crawford worked extensively in the 1960s, 1970s, and 1980s with Jimmy Smith. In 1983 he began playing tenor sax again on occasion, although he primarily worked on guitar. Since 1990 he has lived in Pasadena, Calif., where he teaches privately and continues to record, perform, and compose.

DISC.: *Smooth Groove* (1961).—LP

Crawford, Ruth
See **Seeger, Ruth Crawford**

Cray, Robert, revitalized and popularized guitar-based blues music in the 1980s, along with George Thorogood and the Vaughan brothers Stevie Ray and Jimmie (Fabulous Thunderbirds); b. Columbus, Ga., Aug. 1, 1953. With his rich tenor voice, economical yet fluid guitar style, and original material, Cray broke through into mass popularity with 1986's *Strong Persuader* album, the best-selling blues album since the blues revival of the late 1960s and perhaps the best-selling blues recording in history.

Robert Cray moved often with his Army family, eventually settling in Tacoma, Wash. He studied classical piano as a child, and took up guitar at age 12. In 1969 he met bassist Richard Cousins and formed his first group, One Way Street, performing locally. Around 1974 the two moved to Eugene, Ore., and formed the Robert Cray Band. Playing local honky-tonks through 1976 and then touring tirelessly up and down the West Coast, the band gained its first recognition at the San Francisco Blues Festival in 1977. Between 1976 and 1978 Cray and Cousins toured in support of Cray' guitar idol, Albert Collins. Signed to Tomato Records, the group recorded their debut album, *Who's Been Talkin'* (reissued as *Too Many Cooks*) in 1978, but Tomato soon went out of business and the album wasn't released until 1980.

Playing 250 engagements a year, the Robert Cray Band recorded *Bad Influence* for the small, independent Bay Area label Hightone in 1983. The album, recorded with saxophonists Mike Vannice and Warren Rand, revealed the group's penchant for the sound of Memphis's Stax/Volt Records. It was hailed as the first major stylistic advance for the blues in years and brought the group's first recognition. By 1985's *False Accusations* Vannice and Rand had left the band and keyboardist Peter Boe had been added. The album included "Last Time (I Get Burned Like This)" and "Playin' in the Dirt." Cray' first national recognition came with *Showdown!*, recorded with blues guitarists Albert Collins and Johnny Copeland and released on the small Chicago-based Alligator label in 1986.

A new contract with Polygram (Mercury) Records gave Hightone complete control over the production of *Strong Persuader*, the Robert Cray Band' breakthrough album. The album yielded a major hit with "Smoking Gun" and a minor hit with "Right Next Door (Because of Me)," and became the best-selling blues album since B. B. King's *Completely Well* —and perhaps the best-selling blues recording of all time. In 1986 Eric Clapton recorded Cray's "Bad Influence" for his *August* album, and the Robert Cray Band toured in support of Clapton in 1987. *Don't Be Afraid of the Dark* was recorded with saxophonist David Sanborn, and in 1989 Cray assisted in the recording of John Lee Hooker' comeback album *The Healer* along with Bonnie Raitt, George Thorogood, and Carlos Santana, among others.

Cray subsequently regrouped his band, retaining Richard Cousins and bringing in guitarist Tim Kaihatsu, keyboardist Jimmy Pugh, and drummer Kevin Hayes for *Midnight Stroll*, which featured the Memphis Horns, Wayne Jackson (trumpet) and Andrew Love (saxophone). The Robert Cray Band cut their touring schedule to about a hundred dates in 1992, recording *I Was Warned* with new bassist Karl Sevareid under producer Dennis Walker, who cowrote seven of the album's ten songs. Tim Kaihatsu was dismissed before the band' next album, *Shame + a Sin. Some Rainy Morning* followed in 1995.

DISC.: THE ROBERT CRAY BAND: *Too Many Cooks* (1980); *Bad Influence* (1983); *False Accusations* (1985); *Strong Persuader* (1986); *Don't Be Afraid of the Dark* (1988); *Midnight Stroll* (1990); *I Was Warned* (1992); *Shame + a Sin* (1993); *Some Rainy Morning* (1995). ROBERT CRAY, ALBERT COLLINS, AND JOHNNY COPELAND: *Showdown* (1986).—BH

Cream, the original "power trio," and perhaps the second most influential British group of the 1960s. **MEMBERSHIP:** Eric Clapton (real name, Eric Clapp), lead gtr., voc. (b. Rippley, Surrey, England, March 30, 1945); Jack Bruce, bs., kybd., har., voc. (b. Glasgow, Scotland, May 14, 1943); Peter "Ginger" Baker, drm., voc. (b. Lewisham, London, Aug. 19, 1939).

Cream was formed in June 1966 by lead guitarist Eric Clapton, bassist Jack Bruce, and drummer Peter "Ginger" Baker. Clapton had previously played with the Yardbirds and John Mayall's Bluesbreakers, whereas Baker had played with Alexis Korner and Graham Bond, and Bruce with Bond, Mayall, and Manfred Mann. Signed almost immediately by Atlantic Records, Cream's first album, *Fresh Cream*, was issued in early 1967. Although the album contained little of the improvisation that characterized the group in performance, it included the British hit "I Feel Free," written by Bruce and lyricist Peter Brown, and Baker's "Toad," as well as Muddy Waters's "Rollin' and Tumblin'" and Skip James "I'm So Glad."

Undeniably more exciting in concert than on records, Cream soon completed enormously successful tours of Great Britain and the United States. Produced by Felix Pappalardi, *Disraeli Gears* established Cream's improvisational format. Rather that playing a song straight through, Clapton, Bruce, and Baker would set up the basic "riff" to a song, then take off into individual improvisatory jams. The album consisted of standard blues fare plus original songs composed by Bruce and Clapton, often with Peter Brown, with Bruce handling most of the lead vocals. "Sunshine of Your Love," written by Clapton, Bruce, and Brown, was a moderate hit from the album, later to become a major hit when rereleased in the summer of 1968. Other outstanding cuts included "Strange Brew" (written by Clapton, Pappalardi, and his wife-to-be, Gail Collins), "Tales of Brave Ulysses," "Take It Back," and "S.W.L.A.B.R.," again by Bruce and Brown.

Wheels of Fire, produced by Felix Pappalardi, was a double-record set, one from the studio and one recorded live at the Fillmore Auditorium in San Francisco. Among the extended live pieces were Robert Johnson's "Crossroads" (a major hit), Willie Dixon's "Spoonful," and "Toad," on which Baker soloed for more than ten minutes. Pappalardi played on the studio record, which contained Booker T. Jones's "Born Under a Bad Sign" as well as "Politician" and "White Room" (a near-smash hit), both written by Bruce and Brown. By mid-1968, strains within the group became increasingly evident and, coupled with the limited amount of mutually acceptable material, Cream announced their intention to disband. After a farewell tour of America in October and November and a final album, *Goodbye* (which included "Badge," written by Clapton and George Harrison), Cream made their final appearance at London's Royal Albert Hall on Nov. 26, 1968.

Although all three members of Cream demonstrated exceptional talent on their respective instruments, Jack Bruce was the real musical pioneer—he established the use of the repeated musical figure or ostinato (the so-called "heavy riff") on bass, around which he played lead lines, thus liberating the instrument from its strictly rhythmic role. Additional credit for Cream's success must be given to lyricist Peter Brown, who wrote many of the group's best remembered songs, often with Bruce. Ginger Baker instituted the long drum solo into rock and Eric Clapton unwittingly created the cult of the superstar lead guitarist. In openly acknowledging their debt to many obscure black American bluesmen (Robert Johnson, in particular), Cream helped inspire the blues revival of the late 1960s. As the first major rock group to utilize the power trio format, Cream established the viability of the three-man instrumental lineup. Cream was inducted into the Rock and Roll Hall of Fame in 1993.

Almost immediately after Cream ended, Eric Clapton and Ginger Baker formed the "supergroup" Blind Faith with Traffic's Stevie Winwood (kybd.) and Family's Rick Grech (bs.). Completing one British and one American tour, the group recorded an interesting, if flawed, album. It included Winwood's "Sea of Joy" and "Can't Find My Way Home" and Clapton's "In the Presence of the Lord." Clashes between Winwood and Baker tore the group apart, and Blind Faith disbanded at the end of 1969. Clapton subsequently performed sessions work, formed Derek and the Dominoes, and pursued a spectacular solo career.

Jack Bruce, the odd-man-out in the formation of Blind Faith, briefly toured with keyboardist Mike Mandel, guitarist Larry Coryell, and drummer Mitch Mitchell before pursuing a solo career in conjunction with lyricist Peter Brown, recording two albums for Atco, including *Songs for a Tailor*, and two albums for RSO. (Material from these albums and 1978's unreleased *Jet Set Jewel* were issued on 1989's *Willpower* album.) Bruce also joined Tony Williams Lifetime with former Miles Davis drummer Tony Williams, organist Larry Young, and guitarist extraordinaire John McLaughlin for touring and the album *Turn It Over*. Peter Brown later formed Battered Ornaments (with Chris Spedding) and Piblokto!, and worked with British blues pioneer Graham Bond in Bond and Brown. He reunited with Bruce for 1989's *A Question of Time*.

Producer-bassist Felix Pappalardi, who produced the Youngblood's first two albums, was assigned by Atlantic Records to produce the N.Y. group the Vagrants in 1968. Although recordings proved unsuccessful, Pappalardi was sufficiently impressed by the group's lead guitarist Leslie West to produce his debut solo album. In 1969, Pappalardi and West formed Mountain with keyboardist Steve Knight and drummer Corky Laing. They scored a major hit in 1970 with "Mississippi Queen," but disbanded in 1972. West and Laing then joined former Cream bassist Jack Bruce for West, Bruce, and Laing. That group broke up in 1973, and West and Pappalardi briefly reformed Mountain in 1974. Pappalardi later organized and produced the Japanese heavy-metal group Creation around 1975. On April 17, 1983, Felix Pappalardi was shot and killed by his wife Gail in their N.Y. apartment.

At the beginning of 1970, drummer Ginger Baker formed Ginger Baker's Air Force with Stevie Winwood, Rick Grech, Chris Wood, and a host of others. Recordings by the group were reissued in 1989. Baker later pursued an interest in African music, building a recording studio in Nigeria, which opened in January 1973, and recording with Fela Kuti. From late 1974 until 1976, he manned the Baker-Gurvitz Army with Gurvitz brothers Adrian and Paul. Baker was out of the limelight during the first half of the 1980s, having settled in Italy. He eventually relocated to Calif. and reemerged with *Horses and Trees*, later recording *Middle Passage* with former George Clinton/Talking Heads keyboardist Bernie Worrell and forming the hard-rock group Masters of Reality.

In addition to his solo albums, Jack Bruce recorded with a number of jazz artists during the 1970s, including Carla Bley and Mike Mantler, while playing sessions for Lou Reed, John McLaughlin, and Frank Zappa. In the early 1980s, he recorded *B.L.T.* and *Truce* with erstwhile Procol Harum lead guitarist Robin Trower. *No Stopping Anytime*, from 1989, compiled these recordings. Jack Bruce recorded *A Question of Time* for Epic in 1989 and *Somethinels* for Creative Music in 1993. In 1994, Ginger Baker recorded with Bill Frisell and Charlie Haden as the Ginger Baker Trio and formed BBM with Jack Bruce and Gary Moore for *Around the Next Dream*.

DISC.: *Fresh Cream* (1967); *Disraeli Gears* (1967); *Wheels of Fire* (1968); *Goodbye* (1969); *Live Cream, Vol. 1* (1970); *Live Cream,*

Vol. 2 (1972); *Heavy Cream* (1973); *Off the Top* (1973). Blind Faith: *Blind Faith* (1969). Ginger Baker: *Ginger Baker's Air Force* (1970); *Ginger Baker's Air Force–2* (1970); *Stratavarious* (1972); *Fela Ransome-Kuti and Africa '70 with Ginger Baker—Live!* (1972); *At His Best* (1972); *11 Sides of Baker* (1977); *Horses and Trees* (1986); *Middle Passage* (1989). Baker-Gurvitz Army: *Baker-Gurvitz Army* (1975); *Elysian Encounters* (1975); *Hearts on Fire* (1976). Masters of Reality: *Masters of Reality* (1990); *Sunrise on the Sufferbus* (1993). The Ginger Baker Trio: *Going Back Home* (1994). Jack Bruce: *Songs for a Tailor* (1969); *Harmony Row* (1971); *At His Best* (1972); *Out of the Storm* (1974); *How's Tricks* (1977); *I've Always Wanted to Do This* (1980); *Things We Like* (1988); *A Question of Time* (1989); *Somethinels* (1993); *Monkjack* (1996). Tony Williams's Lifetime (with Jack Bruce): *Turn It Over* (1970); *Once in a Lifetime* (1983). Mountain (Felix Pappalardi, Leslie West, Corky Laing): *Mountain* (1969); *Mountain Climbing* (1970); *Nantucket Sleighride* (1971); *Flowers of Evil* (1971); *The Road Goes Ever On* (1972); *Twin Peaks* (1974); *Avalanche* (1974); *Why Dontcha* (1972); *Whatever Turns You On* (1973); *Live 'N' Kickin* (1974). Carla Bley (with Jack Bruce): *Escalator Over the Hill* (1973). Jack Bruce, Bill Lordan and Robin Trower: *B.L.T.* (1981). Jack Bruce and Robin Trower: *Truce* (1982); *No Stopping Anytime* (1989).—**BH**

Creath, Charlie (actually, Charles Cyril),

trumpeter, leader, saxophonist, accordion player; b. Ironton, Mo., Dec. 30, 1890; d. Chicago, Ill., Oct. 23, 1951. He was the brother of pianist Marge (who was married to Zutty Singleton); another sister, Pauline, also played piano. Started on alto saxophone, then switched to trumpet in his early teens. At 16 Creath worked in Pop Adams's Circus Band, then toured with P. G. Lowry's troupe. Later he toured with Drake and Walker's Musical Comedy Show and the Hagen Beck–Wallace Circus Band. He did theatre work, then led his own band in Seattle, returning to St. Louis c. 1918. He took over the band led by pianist Marcella Kyle c. 1921 and led that band at Alamac Hall. Several bands worked under Creath's name in and around St. Louis during the early 1920s. Creath himself played many residencies including long stay at Jazzland. He joined Fate Marable on S. S. *Capitol* in late 1926, but was inactive through illness from 1928–30, from that date he doubled sax and accordion. Creath then worked with Harvey Lankford's Synco High-Hatters (1933), then co-led a band with Fate Marable during the mid-1930s. He subsequently moved to Chicago, ran his own night club for awhile, then worked as an inspector in an aircraft factory (1944). Creath was ill for several years before dying in 1951. —**JC/LP**

Crecquillon, Thomas, Franco-Flemish com-

poser; b. c. 1490; d. probably in Béthune, 1557. He was in the chapel of Emperor Charles V in Béthune by 1540, where he later may have been maître de chapelle. He held benefices in Béthune, Termonde, and Louvain, and was a canon at St. Aubin in Termonde. In 1555 he became a canon in Béthune. Crecquillon composed almost 200 distinguished chansons for four, five, and six Voices. He publ. of vol. of chansons (1544), and many others appeared in collections of his day. He also wrote 12 masses for four, five, and six Voices, over 100 motets, many of which were publ. (two vols., 1559, 1576), and two cycles of Lamentations. Other works were ed. by N.

Bridgman and B. Hudson in the Corpus Mensurabilis Musicae series, LXIII/1 (1974 et seq.).

BIBL.: W. Lueger, *Die Messen der T. C.* (diss., Univ. of Bonn, 1948).—**NS/LK/DM**

Creedence Clearwater Revival, popular

American rock band of the late 1960s. **MEMBERSHIP:** John Fogerty, lead gtr., lead voc., kybd., har. (b. Berkeley, Calif., May 28, 1945); Tom Fogerty, rhythm gtr., pno., voc. (b. Berkeley, Calif., Nov. 9, 1941; d. Scottsdale, Ariz., Sept. 6, 1990); Stu Cook, bs., pno. (b. Oakland, Calif., April 24, 1945); Doug Clifford, drm. (b. Palo Alto, Calif., April 24, 1945).

John Fogerty got his first guitar at age 12. With fellow El Cerrito, Calif., junior high school students Stu Cook and Doug Clifford, he formed The Blue Velvets in 1959. Joined by John's brother Tom, the band played local engagements for years and recorded unsuccessfully for the Orch. label before securing a recording contract with Berkeley's Fantasy Records in 1964. With a name change to the Golliwogs, the group released a series of singles between 1965 and 1967, including "Brown-Eyed Girl" and "Walking on the Water." Subsequently, Saul Zaentz took over Fantasy Records and the group changed their name to Creedence Clearwater Revival (CCR).

CCR's self-titled debut album, released in the middle of 1968, was a mixture of rock standards and John Fogerty originals. The first single release, a reworking of Dale Hawkins's "Suzie Q," became a major hit and launched the band on its successful career as a singles band. Their breakthrough album *Bayou Country* produced the smash hit classic "Proud Mary" (covered by Ike and Tina Turner in 1971) and included "Born on the Bayou." CCR played at the Woodstock Music and Art Fair in August 1969, when *Green River* was released. It contained the ballad "Wrote a Song for Everyone" and yielded two smash two-sided hits, "Bad Moon Rising" (a top British hit) backed with the classic "Lodi," and "Green River" backed by "Commotion." The hits continued with "Down on the Corner"/"Fortunate Son" and three two-sided hits from *Cosmo's Factory*: "Travelin' Band"/"Who'll Stop the Rain," "Up Around the Bend"/"Run Through the Jungle" and "Lookin' Out My Back Door"/"Long as I See the Light." "Have You Ever Seen the Rain"/"Hey Tonight" nearly became a smash hit in early 1971.

John Fogerty's creative dominance of the group led to dissension among the other members, and Tom Fogerty left in Feb. 1971. The remaining trio subsequently toured and recorded *Mardi Gras*, which yielded the hit singles "Sweet Hitchhiker" and "Someday Never Comes." In October 1972, Creedence Clearwater Revival disbanded. The group was inducted into the Rock and Roll Hall of Fame in 1993.

During the 1970s, the members of CCR pursued a variety of projects. Tom Fogerty recorded five solo albums and two albums with Ruby. He moved to Ariz. in the mid-1980s and died of respiratory failure in Scottsdale on Sept. 6, 1990. Doug Clifford recorded a solo album and two albums with the Don Harrison Band, which included Stu Cook. Only John Fogerty enjoyed any measure of success. He played all instruments and sang all parts on *Blue Ridge Rangers*, an album comprising primarily country material. It yielded two hits with "Hearts of Stone" and Hank Williams's "Jambalaya." He later recorded an album for Asylum Records that produced the major hit "Rockin' All Over the World" and the minor hit "Almost Saturday Night."

Embroiled in lawsuits with the group's accountants and Fantasy Records for years, John Fogerty withdrew to a family farm in Ore. for ten years. He eventually emerged in 1985, playing all instruments on *Centerfield*, which contained the baseball classic "Centerfield" and the major hits "The Old Man Down the Road" and "Rock and Roll Girls." He toured between 1985 and 1986 for the first time since 1972, but the follow-up album *Eye of the Zombie* sold only moderately.

Stu Cook joined the country-rock band Southern Pacific after their debut album, which had yielded the country-only hits "Thing About You" (written by Tom Petty), "Perfect Stranger," and "Reno Bound." The group included John McFee (gtr., pedal steel gtr., fdl.) and Keith Knudsen (drm.), formerly with the Doobie Brothers. Featuring intricate, multipart harmonies, Southern Pacific scored major country-only hits with "A Girl Like Emmylou" and "Midnight Highway," and the country smashes "New Shade of Blue," "Honey I Dare You," and "Any Way the Wind Blows" through 1989. The group disbanded in 1991. Cook joined Doug Clifford and three others in the formation of Creedence Clearwater Revisited in 1995.

After another hiatus, John Fogerty spent more than four years recording 1997's *Blue Moon Swamp*, which featured "Walking in a Hurricane" and "A Hundred and Ten in the Shade." He toured in support of the album with a four-piece band, performing Creedence Clearwater Revival material for the first time in 25 years.

DISC.: *Creedence Clearwater Revival* (1968); *Bayou Country* (1969); *Green River* (1969); *Willy and the Poor Boys* (1969); *Cosmo's Factory* (1970); *Pendulum* (1970); *Mardi Gras* (1972); *Creedence Gold* (1972); *More Creedence Gold* (1973); *Live in Europe* (1973); *Chronicle* (1976). **TOM FOGERTY:** *Tom Fogerty* (1972); *Excalibur* (1973); *Zephyr National* (1974); *Myopia* (1974); *Deal It Out* (1981). **RUBY (WITH TOM FOGERTY):** *Ruby* (1977); *Rock and Roll Madness* (1978). **TOM FOGERTY/KEVIN ODA:** *Sidekicks* (1993). **DOUG CLIFFORD:** *Cosmo* (1972). **THE DON HARRISON BAND (WITH DOUG CLIFFORD AND STU COOK):** *The Don Harrison Band* (1976); *Red Hot* (1977). Southern Pacific (with Stu Cook): *Killbilly Hill* (1986); *Zuma* (1988); *Country Line* (1990). **JOHN FOGERTY:** *Blue Ridge Rangers* (1973); *John Fogerty* (1975); *Hoodoo* (1976); *Centerfield* (1985); *Eye of the Zombie* (1986); *Blue Moon Swamp* (1997).

BIBL.: H. Bordowitz, *Bad Moon Rising: The Unofficial History of Creedence Clearwater Revival* (N.Y., 1998); J. Hallowell, *Inside Creedence* (N.Y., 1971).—**BH**

Crescentini, Girolamo,

notable Italian castrato mezzo-soprano; b. Urbania, near Urbino, Feb. 2, 1762; d. Naples, April 24, 1846. He studied singing with Gibelli at Bologna. He began his career in Padua in 1782 and then sang in Rome in 1783; subsequent successes in other European capitals earned him the surname of "Orfeo Italiano." He sang at Livorno, Padua, Venice, Turin, London (1786), Milan, and Naples (1788–89). Napoleon, having heard him in 1805, decorated him with the Iron Crown, and engaged him to teach singing to his family from 1806 to 1812; Crescentini then retired from the stage and left Paris, on account of vocal disorders induced by the climate. In 1816 he became a prof. of singing in the Royal Cons. in Naples. Cimarosa wrote his *Orazi e Curiazi* for him. Crescentini publ. several collections of Ariette (Vienna, 1797) and a *Treatise on Vocalization in France and Italy*, with vocal exercises (Paris, 1811).—**NS/LK/DM**

Crespin, Régine,

outstanding French soprano, later mezzo-soprano; b. Marseilles, Feb. 23, 1927. She studied pharmacology, and then began taking voice lessons with Suzanne Cesbron-Viseur and Georges Jouatte in Paris. She made her debut in Mulhouse as Elsa in 1950 and then sang at the Paris Opéra from 1951, where she quickly rose to prominence. She acquired a reputation as one of the best Wagnerian singers of her era. Crespin sang Kundry at the Bayreuth Festivals (1958–60). She appeared also at La Scala in Milan, at Covent Garden in London, and on Nov. 19, 1962, made her debut with the Metropolitan Opera in N.Y. in the role of the Marschallin; she remained with the Metropolitan until her farewell appearance as Mme. De Croissy in *Les Dialogues des Carmélites* on April 16, 1987. From 1977 until her retirement in 1991 she sang mezzo-soprano roles. Her memoires were publ. as *La vie et l'amour d'une femme* (Paris, 1980; 2nd ed., rev. and aug., 1997, as *A la scène, à la ville*; rev. Eng. tr., 1997, as *On Stage, Off Stage: A Memoir*). She sang the parts of Elsa in *Lohengrin*, Sieglinde in *Die Walküre*, and Amelia in *Un ballo in maschera*; also appeared as a concert singer. Her sonorous, somewhat somber voice suited dramatic parts excellently.

BIBL.: B. Durup, *R. C.: La voix de velours* (Paris, 1998). —**NS/LK/DM**

Cresswell, Lyell (Richard),

New Zealand composer; b. Wellington, Oct. 13, 1944. He was educated at Victoria Univ. of Wellington (B.Mus., 1968), the Univ. of Toronto (Mus.M., 1970), the Univ. of Aberdeen (Ph.D., 1974), and the Inst. of Sonology at the Univ. of Utrecht (1974–75). After teaching at the Univ. of Glasgow, he was music organizer for the Chapter Arts Centre in Cardiff (1978–80). He was the Forman Fellow in Composition at the Univ. of Edinburgh (1980–82) and the Cramb Fellow in Composition at the Univ. of Glasgow (1982–85). In 1978 he won the Ian Whyte Award and in 1979 the Australasian Performing Rights Assn. Silver Scroll for his contributions to New Zealand music. His works were selected as outstanding compositions by the UNESCO International Rostrum of Composers in 1979, 1981, and 1988. He was the featured composer at Musica Nova in Glasgow (1984), the Sonorities Festival of 20th Century Music in Belfast (1985), the Asian Music Festival in Tokyo (1990), and the New Zealand International Festival of the Arts (1990, 1994). While Cresswell utilized aleatoric methods and electronic means in his early works, he later developed a style in which textural and structural components became the focus of attention. He also found inspiration in New Zealand and Scottish sources, and extended his reach to include various folk and ethnic materials. In some of his works, he displayed an engaging wit and humor.

WORKS: ORCH.: *Salm* (1977; Aberdeen, Jan. 30, 1979); *The Magical Wooden Head* (Denedin, Sept. 20, 1980); *O!* (1983, Wellington, March 12, 1983); Cello Concerto (Glasgow, Sept. 22, 1984); *Speak for us, great sea* (Belfast, April 28, 1985); *Akarana Karaka* (1989; Auckland, June 7, 1990); *Ixion* (Edinburgh, Aug. 12, 1989); *Ylur* (1990–91; Kirkwall, June 23, 1991); *Major Ricketts* for Brass Band (1991; Manchester, Feb. 16, 1992); *Dragspil*, accordion concerto (London, Aug. 7, 1995); String Quartet Concerto (1996; Aberdeen, Feb. 5, 1997); *Kaea*, trombone concerto (1997; St. Andrews, Feb. 18, 1998). **CHAMBER:** String Quartet (Edinburgh, Dec. 3, 1981); *Le Sucre du Printemps* for six Bass Clarinets and 3 Contrabass Clarinets (1982; Amsterdam, Jan. 19, 1983); *The Pumpkin Massacre* for 12 Solo Strings (1987; Napier, April 15, 1989); *Passacagli* for Large Chamber Ensemble (1988; Edinburgh, April 16, 1989); Brass Sextet (1988; Edinburgh, March 9, 1989); *Atta* for Cello (Ferrara, Oct. 3, 1993); *Whira* for Violin (Nelson, April 22, 1997); *Of Whirlwind Underground* for E-flat Clarinet, Bass Clarinet, Bass Trombone, Cello, and Double Bass (Auckland, Nov. 21, 1999); *And Every Sparke Shivering* for Piano Quintet (Auckland, Oct. 25, 2000). **KEYBOARD: Piano:** *The Grammar of Solitude* (1985–88; Paris, May 25, 1989); *Who's Afraid of Red, Yellow, and Blue* (Middelburg, July 7, 1993); *Acquerello* (Gijón, Oct. 15, 1995). **Harpsichord:** *Bisbigliando* (1993; Viitasaari, July 10, 1994). **VOCAL:** *Prayer for the cure of a sprained back* for Mezzo-soprano (1979; Christchurch, March 12, 1982); *7 Shaker Songs* for Baritone and Piano (Stroud, Oct. 16, 1980); *O Let the Fire Burn* for Chorus (Wellington, April 25, 1981); *8 Shaker Songs* for Soprano and Piano (1985; London, June 17, 1986); *To Aspro Pano Sto Aspro* for Chorus (1985; Glasgow, May 12, 1986); *A Modern Ecstasy* for Mezzo-soprano, Baritone, and Orch. (1986; Glasgow, May 6, 1989); *Words for Music* for Mezzo-soprano (1989; London, Feb. 6, 1990); *Voices of Ocean Winds* for Chorus and Orch. (1989; Wellington, March 23, 1990); *Il Suono di Enormi Distanze* for Mezzo-soprano and Large Ensemble (1992–93; Glasgow, May 7, 1993); *Snatches from Baptized Generations* for Tenor and Piano (Aberdeen, Sept. 28, 1995); *The Belly of the Whale* for Chorus (1996; Glasgow, Feb. 20, 1997).—**NS/LK/DM**

Creston, Paul (real name, Giuseppe Guttoveggio),

American composer, organist, and teacher; b. N.Y., Oct. 10, 1906; d. San Diego, Aug. 24, 1985. He received training in piano from Randegger and Déthier and in organ from Yon, but lacked formal instruction in theory or composition. Although he composed tentatively in his youth, he did not embark upon a serious career as a composer until he was 26 when he wrote his *Five Dances* for Piano. From 1934 to 1967 he was organist at St. Malachy's Church in N.Y. In 1938 he held a Guggenheim fellowship. In 1941 his first sym. won the N.Y. Music Critics' Circle Award, and thereafter he received various awards and commissions. He taught at the N.Y. Coll. of Music (1963–67), and then was a prof. of music and composer-in-residence at Central Washington State Coll. in Ellensburg (1968–75). Among his writings were *Principles of Rhythm* (1964), *Creative Harmony* (1970), and *Rational Metric Notation* (1979). Creston's large output was marked by a harmonic and rhythmic idiom of considerable complexity, principally in his instrumental writing. He avoided illogical binary meters and proposed such time signatures as 6/12 or 3/9 in several of his works.

WORKS: ORCH.: *Partita* for Flute, Violin, and Strings (1937); *Threnody* (1938); *2 Choric Dances* (1938); six syms.: No. 1 (1940; N.Y., Feb. 22, 1941), No. 2 (1944; N.Y., Feb. 15, 1945), No. 3 (Worcester Festival, Oct. 27, 1950), No. 4 (1951; Washington, D.C., Jan. 30, 1952), No. 5 (1955; Washington, D.C., April 4, 1956), and No. six for Organ and Orch. (1981; Washington, D.C., June 28, 1982); Marimba Concertino (1940); Saxophone Concerto (1941; N.Y., Jan. 27, 1944); *A Rumor*, symphonic sketch (N.Y., Dec. 13, 1941); *Fantasy* for Piano and Orch. (1942); *Frontiers* (Toronto, Oct. 14, 1943); *Poem* for Harp and Orch. (1945); *Fantasy* for Trombone and Orch. (1947; Los Angeles, Feb. 12, 1948); Piano Concerto (1949); Concerto for 2 Pianos and Orch. (1951; Montevallo, Ala., Nov. 18, 1968); *Walt Whitman*, symphonic poem (1952); *Invocation and Dance* (1953; Louisville, May 15, 1954); *Dance Overture* (1954); 2 violin concertos: No. 1 (1956; Detroit, Jan. 14, 1960) and No. 2 (Los Angeles, Nov. 17, 1960); *Lydian Ode* (1956); *Toccata* (1957); Accordion Concerto (1958); *Janus* (Denver, July 17, 1959); *Corinthians: XIII*, symphonic poem (1963; Phoenix, March 30, 1964); *Choreografic Suite* (1965); *Pavane Variations* (La Jolla, Calif., Aug. 21, 1966); *Chthonic Ode* (1966; Detroit, April 6, 1967); *Thanatopsis* (1971); *Square Dance 76* for Wind Sym. Orch. (1975); Suite for Strings (1978); *Sadhana* for Cello and Orch. (Los Angeles, Oct. 3, 1981). **CHAMBER:** *3 Poems from Walt Whitman* for Cello and Piano (1934); Suite for Saxophone and Piano (1935); Strin Quartet (1936); Suite for Viola and Piano (1937); Suite for Violin and Piano (1939); Saxophone Sonata (1939); Suite for Flute, Viola, and Piano (1952); Suite for Cello and Piano (1956); Concertino for Piano and Wind Quintet (1969); *Ceremonial* for Percussion Ensemble (1972); *Rapsodie* for Saxophone and Piano or Organ (1976); Suite for Saxophone Quartet (1979); Piano Trio (1979); piano works. **VOCAL:** three chorales, after Tagore (1936); Requiem for Tenor, Bass, and Organ (1938); *Dance Variations* for Soprano and Orch. (1942); *Psalm XXIII* for Soprano, Chorus, and Piano (1945); Missa solemnis for Chorus and Organ or Orch. (1949); *Adoro te*, mass for Women's or Mixed Chorus and Piano (1952); *The Celestial Vision* for Men's Chorus (1954); *Isaiah's Prophecy*, Christmas oratorio (1962); *Nocturne* for Soprano, Wind Quintet, String Quintet, and Piano (1964); *The Psalmist* for Alto and Orch. (1967); *Cum jubilo*, mass for Chorus (1968); *Hyas Illahee* for Chorus and Orch. (1969); *Leaves of Grass* for Chorus and Piano (1970); *Thanksgiving Anthem* for Chorus and Orch. (1982).—**NS/LK/DM**

Crew Cuts, The,

caucasian Canadian quartet that made their fortune emulating the music of African-American vocal groups. **MEMBERSHIP:** John Perkins, lead voc. (b. 1931); Pat Barrett, tenor voc.; Rudi Maugeri, baritone voc. (b. Jan. 27, 1931); Ray Perkins, bass voc.

Originally cast in the mold of the Four Lads, who attended the same Toronto school, the Perkins brothers formed a vocal group called the Canadians. They worked live and on the radio. After one show in Cleveland, a DJ advised a name change to the Crew Cuts and then referred them to Mercury records.

They debuted auspiciously at #8 in the spring of 1954 with their own song "Crazy 'Bout You Baby." A month later they released a track originally by an R&B group called the Chords, using what was then standard operating procedure for a pop vocal group of working with a small orchestra (in this case, David Carroll's). That tune, "Sh-Boom" zoomed to #1 and stayed there for nine weeks, starting a trend of white performers singing R&B tunes for white audiences, an early hallmark of commercial rock and roll. Some historians actually cite this record as the first hit of the rock and roll era. Continuing in this vein, they covered another R&B novelty, "Oop Shoop," which peaked at #13. Their album *The Crew Cuts on Campus* topped out at #14, their only album to chart.

Ushering in the rock and roll era in the winter of 1955, they took the Penguins' R&B chart topper (#8 pop) "Earth Angel" and eclipsed the original by five chart positions, though the Penguins' version is the one that stood the test of time. Another cover, of Gene and Eunice's R&B #6 tune "Ko Ko Mo," reached #6. In the spring of that year, the Cuts took Nappy Brown's #25 hit "Don't Be Angry" to #14. The B-side, a take on the Danderliers' #10 R&B tune "Chop Chop Boom," was a simultaneous hit. To capitalize on this success, their version of the Nutmegs' #2 R&B hit "A Story Untold" was rush released and rose to #16 in June. The Charms' "Gum Drop" was their next hit in Aug., rising to #10.

The Crew Cuts dug into another mine for their next hit, covering Tony Martin's "Angels in the Sky" which hit #11, then Larry Clinton's "Mostly Martha" a #2 hit for that singer in 1938. In Feb. 1956, they did Clyde McPhatter's "Seven Days," taking it to #18. However, the group didn't have another Top 40 hit for nearly a year, finally scoring with a version of Sonny James's country hit, "Young Love," which they took to #17. By this time, however, the original versions of the R&B and country hits, at first deemed too raw for middle-of-the-road audiences, started to become pop hits in their own right. This acceptance was the death knell for the Crew Cuts and their ilk. It took them nearly six hitless years to get the idea, but they finally broke up in 1963.

Disc.: *Crew Cut Capers* (1954); *The Crew Cuts on the Campus* (1954); *Music a la Carte* (1955); *Surprise Package* (1958); *You Must Have Been a Beautiful Baby* (1960); *The Crew Cuts Sing Out!* (1960); *High School Favorites* (1962); *The Crew Cuts Sing Folk* (1963).—HB

Crispell, Marilyn, American classical pianist: b. Philadelphia, Pa., March 30, 1947. She played classical piano from age seven and graduated from the New England Cons. in 1968, having focused on piano and composition. Yet, she was much more attracted to improvisation, although in a non-jazz context. She gave up music in favor of medicine for six years, but after the breakup of her marriage began singing blues in a folk-rock group for the catharsis it offered. After a pianist turned her on to some jazz albums, she experienced a personal revelation upon listening to John Coltrane's *A Love Supreme* and decided to learn to play jazz. Eventually this led her to move to Woodstock, where she studied and then taught at Karl Berger's Creative Music Studio until it shut down in the early 1980s. During this time she worked in the groups of Anthony Braxton, Roscoe Mitchell, and Leo Smith, with the Braxton association proving particularly lasting. Cecil Taylor was both an inspiration and an influence,

and it is to his playing that hers is most often compared, though she has developed a style of her own over the years.

Disc.: *Spirit Music* (1982); *Live in Berlin* (1983); *Live in San Francisco* (1990); *Marilyn Crispell & Gerry Hemingway Duo* (1992); *Marilyn Crispell Trio* (1993); *Labyrinths* (1995); *Live at Mills College 1995* (1996); *Contrasts: Live at Yoshi's* (1996); *Woodstock Concert* (1996); *Nothing Ever Was, Anyway: The Music of Annette Peacock* (1997); *Quartet* (1997).—WF

Crist, Bainbridge, American composer and teacher; b. Lawrenceburg, Ind., Feb. 13, 1883; d. Barnstable, Mass., Feb. 7, 1969. He studied piano and flute; later law at George Washington Univ. (LL.B.). He went to Europe to complete his musical training (theory with P. Juon in Berlin and C. Landi in London, and singing with William Shakespeare. He taught singing in Boston (1915–21) and Washington, D.C. (1922–23); returned to Europe (1923) and spent four years in Florence, Paris, Lucerne, and Berlin; then settled in Washington, D.C. Crist devoted much time to teaching. He was the author of *The Art of Setting Words to Music* (N.Y., 1944).

Works: DRAMATIC: *Le Pied de la momie*, choreographic drama (1915); *Pregiwa's Marriage*, Javanese ballet (1920); *The Sorceress*, choreographic drama (1926). **ORCH.:** *Egyptian Impressions*, suite (Boston Pops, June 22, 1915); *Abhisarika* for Violin and Orch. (1921); *Intermezzo* (1921); *Chinese Dance* (1922); *Arabian Dance* (1922); *Nautch Dance* (1922); *Dreams* (1924); *Yearning* (1924); *Nocturne* (1924); *An Old Portrait* (1924); *La Nuit revécue* (1933; N.Y., March 8, 1936); *Vienna 1913* (1933); *Frivolité* (1934); *Hymn to Nefertiti* (1936); *Fête espagnole* (1937); *American Epic 1620*, tone poem (Washington, D.C., Feb. 28, 1943). **CHAMBER:** Piano pieces. **VOCAL: Voice and Orch.:** *A Bag of Whistles* (1915); *The Parting*, poem (1916); *Rhymes* (1917); *O Come Hither!* (1918); *Drolleries* (1920); *Colored Stars*, suite of four songs (1921); *Remember* (1930); *The Way That Lovers Use* (1931); *Noontime* (1931); *Evening* (1931); *By a Silent Shore* (1932). **Other:** Choral works; songs.

Bibl.: J. Howard, *B. C.* (N.Y., 1929).—NS/LK/DM

Cristiani, Lisa (Barbier), famous French cellist; b. Paris, Dec. 24, 1827; d. Tobolsk, 1853. She launched her career at an early age, and soon became renowned via many European tours. Her brilliant renditions of the salon repertory so impressed the King of Denmark that he made her a chamber virtuosa. Her early death was the result of contracting cholera while on a tour of Russia. She played a Stradivari cello of 1720, which instrument still bears her name.—LK/DM

Cristoforeanu, Florica, Romanian soprano; b. Rimnicu-Sarat, Aug. 16, 1887; d. Rio de Janeiro, March 1, 1960. She studied at the Milan Cons. with Filippi and Bodrilla; made her debut in Capodistria in 1908 as Lucia; then sang operetta in Bucharest and Milan (1909–19). From 1927 to 1932 she appeared at Milan's La Scala; also sang in Rome (1928–34) and in South America. She retired in 1940. In addition to her classical roles, she was known for her performances of works by contemporary Italian composers.—NS/LK/DM

Cristofori, Bartolomeo, celebrated Italian instrument maker; b. Padua, May 4, 1655; d. Florence, Jan.

27, 1731. He was the inventor of the first practical piano as opposed to the clavichord, although two-keyed instruments called "Piano e Forte" are known to have exiixisted in Modena in 1598, and a four-octave keyboard instrument shaped like a dulcimer, with small hammers and no dampers, dating from 1610, is yet in existence. He was a leading maker of clavicembali in Padua; about 1690 he went to Florence, where he was instrument maker to Ferdinando de' Medici; on the latter's death in 1713, he was made custodian of the court collection of instruments by Cosimo III. According to an article by Maffei (*Giornale dei Letterati d'Italia*, 1711), Cristofori had up to that year made three "gravecembali col piano e forte," these having, instead of the usual jacks plucking the strings with quills, a row of little hammers striking the strings from below. The principle of this hammer action was adopted, in the main, by Gottfried Silbermann, the Streichers, and Broadwood (hence called the "English action"). Following the designation by its inventor, the new instrument was named piano-forte. Only three of Cristofori's pianos are extant; one built in 1720 is in the Metropolitan Museum of Art in N.Y. A double- string spinet (1693) and a harpsichord (1722) are also extant.

BIBL.: F. Casaglia, *B. C.* (Florence, 1894); B. Bonetti and A. Damerini, *B. C., inventore del pianoforte* (Padua, 1957); K. Restle, *B. C. und die Anfänge des Hammerclaviers: Quellen, Dokumente und Instruments des 15. bis 18. Jahrhunderts* (Munich, 1991). —**NS/LK/DM**

Crivelli, Gaetano, Italian tenor; b. Brescia, Oct. 20, 1768; d. there, July 10, 1836. He made his debut in Brescia in 1794, and then sang in Verona, Palermo, Venice, and Naples. After studies in Naples with Nozzari and Aprile, he made his first appearance at Milan's La Scala in 1805. On Jan. 19, 1811, he made his Paris debut in Paisiello's *Pirro*. He made his London debut at the King's Theatre as Ulysses in Cimarosa's *Penelope* on Jan. 11, 1817. On March 7, 1824, he created the role of Adriano in Meyerbeer's *Il Crociato in Egitto* in Venice, which role he made his own and which he chose for his farewell performance in 1831. He also sang in operas by Mozart and Paër. His son, Domenico Crivelli (b. Brescia, June 7, 1793; d. London, Nov. 11, 1851), was a singing teacher and composer who pursued his career in London. He publ. *The Art of Singing and New Solfeggios for the Cultivation of the Bass Voice* (London, 2nd ed., 1844). —**NS/LK/DM**

Crivelli, Giovanni Battista, Italian composer; b. Scandiano, Modena, date unknown; d. Modena, March 1652. He was organist at the Reggio Emilia Cathedral (1614–19); then served as maestro di cappella at the Accademia dello Spirito Santo in Ferrara (1626); subsequently was organist at the electoral court in Munich. He was maestro di cappella at the Milan Cathedral (1638–42), at S. Maria Maggiore in Bergamo (1642–48), and at the ducal court in Modena (1651–52). He publ. *Il primo libro delli motetti concertati* for two to five Voices and Basso Continu (Venice, 1626) and *Il primo libro delli madrigali concertati* for two to four Voices and Basso Continuo (Venice, 1626).—**NS/LK/DM**

Croce, Giovanni, esteemed Italian composer, known as **Il Chiozzotto** after his birthplace; b. Chioggia, c. 1557; d. Venice, May 15, 1609. He went to Venice at an early age and was a pupil of Zarlino, who placed him in the choir of S. Marco. After taking holy orders in 1585, he was active at the church of S. Maria Formosa. In 1590 he was made vice-maestro di cappella at S. Marco, where he taught singing at its seminary from 1593. In 1603 he became maestro di cappella at S. Marco. Croce was one of the principal Venetian composers of sacred and secular music of his time. In all, he publ. 14 vols. of sacred music, including three vols. of masses (Venice, 1596, 1596, 1599), and 10 vols. of secular music, including two notable vols. of canzonette (Venice, 1588, 1601), and four vols. of madrigals (Venice, 1585, 1590, 1592, 1607). Several of his works have been publ. in modern editions.

BIBL.: L. Putz, *Die Tonsymbolik im Madrigalwerk G. C.s* (Graz, 1976); D. Gustafson, *G. C.'s Mascarate piacevoli et ridicolose per il carnevale: A Contextual Study and Critical Edition* (diss., Univ. of Minn., 1992).—**NS/LK/DM**

Croce, Jim, one of America's finest singer-songwriters of the early 1970s, was known for his amusing character songs and gentle love songs; b. Philadelphia, Pa., Jan 10, 1943; d. near Natchitoches, La., Sept. 20, 1973. Jim Croce died in an airplane crash just as he was beginning to receive much- deserved recognition. His son, A. J. Croce, has recently begun his own recording career.

Raised in Philadelphia, Jim Croce began playing music professionally at Villanova Univ. in 1964. Recording an album on his own Croce label in 1966, he moved to N.Y., where he played coffeehouses on the advice of college friend Tommy West. Signed to Capitol Records, he recorded an album with his wife Ingrid before returning to Pa. Joined by lead guitarist Maury Muehleisen, Croce recorded a demonstration tape under producers Tommy West and Terry Cashman that lead to a recording contract with ABC Records.

Jim Croce's debut album for ABC yielded two major hits, "You Don't Mess Around with Jim" and "Operator (That's Not the Way It Feels)," and included the love song "Time in a Bottle," which became a top hit when it was issued in late 1973. Croce was established as a singer-songwriter with his second ABC album, *Life and Times*, which produced the moderate hit "One Less Set of Footsteps" and the top hit "Bad, Bad Leroy Brown." Croce and Muehleisen were killed on Sept. 20, 1973, when their chartered plane crashed on takeoff near Natchitoches, La. *I Got a Name*, released posthumously, yielded three hits: "I Got a Name," "I'll Have to Say I Love You in a Song," and "Workin' at the Car Wash Blues."

Born in 1971 near Philadelphia, Adrian James "A. J." Croce began playing piano at six and started playing professionally at 12. Raised in San Diego, he performed for years at his mother Ingrid's nightclub, Croce's, before winning a recording contract with Private Music in 1993.

DISC.: JIM AND INGRID CROCE: *Jim and Ingrid Croce* (1969); *Another Day, Another Town* (1976). **MAURY**

MUEHLEISEN: *Gingerbread* (1970). **JIM CROCE:** *You Don't Mess Around with Jim* (1972); *Life and Times* (1973); *I Got a Name* (1973); *Photographs and Memories: His Greatest Hits* (1974); *The Faces I've Been* (1975); *Time in a Bottle: J. C.'s Greatest Love Songs* (1977); *Bad, Bad Leroy Brown: J. C.'s Greatest Character Songs* (1978); *Down the Highway* (1985); *J. C. Live: The Final Tour* (1990); *The 50th Anniversary Collection* (1992). **A. J. CROCE:** *A. J. Croce* (1993); *That's Me in the Bar* (1995).—**BH**

Crocker, Richard L(incoln), American music historian; b. Roxbury, Mass., Feb. 17, 1927. He studied with Schrade at Yale Univ. (B.A., 1950; Ph.D., 1957, with the diss. *The Repertoire of Proses at St. Martial de Limoges*), and later conducted research in England and France on a Guggenheim fellowship (1969–70). From 1955 to 1963 he taught at Yale Univ., and then at the Univ. of Calif. at Berkeley from 1963. He publ. *A History of Musical Style* (N.Y., 1966), with A. Basart, *Listening to Music* (N.Y., 1971), *The Early Medieval Sequence* (Berkeley and Los Angeles, 1977), and *Introduction to Gregorian Chant* (London and New Haven, 2000). He also ed., with D. Hiley, Vol. II: *The Early Middle Ages to 1300 in The New Oxford History of Music* (Oxford, 1990).—**NS/LK/DM**

Crockett, Donald, American composer, conductor, and teacher; b. Pasadena, Calif., Feb. 18, 1951. He studied composition at the Univ. of Southern Calif. in Los Angeles (B.M., 1974; M.M., 1976) and at the Univ. of Calif. at Santa Barbara (Ph.D., 1981). From 1981 to 1984 he was composer-in- residence of the Pasadena Chamber Orch. In 1981 he joined the faculty of the Univ. of Southern Calif. as an asst. prof., and subsequently was named an assoc. prof. in 1984 and a prof. of composition in 1994. He also was made music director of its Contemporary Music Ensemble in 1984. From 1991 to 1997 he was composer-in-residence of the Los Angeles Chamber Orch. In 1992 he became artistic director and conductor of Xtet. In 1991 he received a Kennedy Center Friedheim Award, in 1994 the Goddard Lieberson Fellowship of the American Academy of Arts and Letters, and in 1998 the Aaron Copland Award of the Copland Soc. As a conductor, Crockett has championed the cause of contemporary music.

WORKS: ORCH.: *Melting Voices* (1986; N.Y., March 2, 1990); Concerto for Piano and Wind Ensemble (1988; Los Angeles, March 8, 1989); *Wedge* (1990; Los Angeles, April 26, 1991); *Antiphonies* for Chamber Orch. (1992; Los Angeles, March 19, 1993); Cello Concerto (1993; Chatham, N.J., May 6, 1994); *Roethke Preludes* (1994; Los Angeles, Feb. 2, 1995); *Aubade* (1996; Los Angeles, Feb. 26, 1997, composer conducting); *Island* for Wind Ensemble (East Lansing, Mich., Nov. 21, 1998). **CHAMBER:** Trio for Flute, Cello, and Harp (1980; Boston, May 10, 1981); *Four Songs of a Nomad Flute* for Harpsichord (N.Y., Nov. 7, 1984); *The Melting Voice* for 17 Instruments (1986; Los Angeles, March 10, 1987); two string quartets: No. 1, *Array* (1987; San Francisco, Jan. 12, 1989) and No. two (1993; Palo Alto, Calif., March 12, 1994); *Pilgrimage* for Piano (San Diego, Oct. 9, 1988); *to be sung on the water* for Violin and Viola (1988; Basel, March 1989); *Still Life with Bell* for 14 Instruments (Los Angeles, April 3, 1989); *Celestial Mechanics* for Oboe and String Quartet (1990; Los Angeles, March 15, 1991); *Short Stories* for Flute, Viola, and Harp (1995; Eugene, Ore., May 4, 1997); *Extant* for Bassoon and 8 Instruments (Pittsburgh, Sept. 22, 1997); *Scree* for Cello, Piano,

and Percussion (Bowling Green, Ohio, Oct. 15, 1997); *Whistling in the Dark* for Chamber Ensemble (Los Angeles, May 12, 1999); Horn Quintet, *La Barca* (Angel Fire, N.Mex., Sept. 3, 1999). **VOCAL:** *Occhi dell'alma mia* for High Voice and Guitar (1977; Los Angeles, March 31, 1978); *Lyrikos* for Tenor and Orch. (Pasadena, May 29, 1979; also for Tenor and 8 Instruments, Los Angeles, Oct. 15, 1985); *The Pensive Traveller* for High Voice and Piano, after Thoreau (1981; Los Angeles, April 1982); *Vox in Rama* for Double Chorus and Orch. (Los Angeles, Oct. 23, 1983); *White Night* for Chorus (1984; Portland, Ore., May 1985); *The Tenth Muse* for Soprano and Orch. (Pasadena, June 17, 1986); *Ecstatic Songs* for High Voice and Piano, after Whitman (Part 1, Los Angeles, July 3, 1989; Part 2, 1995, Los Angeles, Feb. 28, 1996; Part 3, 1995, Los Angeles, Feb. 28, 1996); *The Cinnamon Peeler* for Mezzo-soprano and Chamber Ensemble, after Michael Ondaatje (1993; Los Angeles, Feb. 7, 1994). —**NS/LK/DM**

Crosby, Bing (actually, **Harry Lillis**), versatile popular singer and actor; b. Tacoma, Wash., May 3, 1903; d. near Madrid, Spain, Oct. 14, 1977. Crosby was the most successful singer of the first half of the 20th century, dominating several fields of entertainment especially during the 1930s and 1940s. Of his thousands of recordings, hundreds became hits, including 30 that were best-sellers and 22 that sold at least a million copies each. "White Christmas" and "Silent Night" are among the biggest selling records of all time; his other big hits include "Sweet Leilani," "Pennies from Heaven," and "Swinging on a Star." Crosby also was a major motion picture actor, with leading roles in 51 feature films between 1932 and 1962, frequently placing among the top box office stars and winning the Academy Award for Best Actor. His radio shows, broadcast from 1931 to 1962, earned consistently high ratings.

Crosby was born into a large, poor Irish-American family; his younger brother **Bob** (1913–93) became a singer, bandleader, and actor. His father, Harry Lowe Crosby, was a bookkeeper. The family moved to Spokane when Crosby was three. He acquired his nickname from his interest in a comic strip, *The Bingville Bugle*. By age 15 he was playing drums in a band. He attended Gonzaga Univ. as a pre-law student from 1921 to 1925, quitting in his senior year as he began to earn money singing. On Oct. 15, 1925, he and friend Al Rinker, brother of singer Mildred Bailey, left Spokane for Los Angeles, where Bailey found them work as a duo. By the end of the year they had joined a West Coast vaudeville tour.

Crosby and Rinker made their recording debut singing with Don Clark and His Los Angeles Biltmore Hotel Orch. on "I've Got the Girl" (music and lyrics by Walter Donaldson) on Oct. 18, 1926. On Dec. 15 they joined Paul Whiteman and His Orch. Initially successful on tour, they failed in N.Y. in January 1927, and Whiteman added Harry Barris to form the Rhythm Boys trio. The first popular Whiteman recording to feature Crosby was "Muddy Water" (music by Peter DeRose and Harry Richman, lyrics by Jo Trent), which became a hit in June 1927. From August 1927 to June 1928 the Rhythm Boys toured in vaudeville under Whiteman's sponsorship but separate from the band. Whiteman scored a best-selling record in November 1927 with "My Blue

Heaven" (music by Donaldson, lyrics by George Whiting), which contained a vocal chorus by a quintet that included Crosby. Crosby sang lead on a Whiteman recording of "Ol' Man River" (music by Jerome Kern, lyrics by Oscar Hammerstein II), which became a best-seller in April 1928.

In November 1929 the Whiteman orchestra including Crosby began shooting the film *King of Jazz* at Universal Studios in Hollywood. Whiteman's recording of "Great Day" (music by Vincent Youmans, lyrics by Billy Rose and Edward Eliscu) featuring Crosby's solo vocal became a best-seller in December. In May 1930, shortly after the release of *King of Jazz*, the Rhythm Boys left Whiteman. They recorded "Three Little Words" (music by Harry Ruby, lyrics by Bert Kalmar) with Duke Ellington and His Famous Orch.; it became a best-seller in November after being featured in the film *Check and Double Check*.

Crosby married actress Dixie Lee (real name Wilma Winfred Wyatt) on Sept. 20, 1930. They had four sons, Gary, twins Phillip and Dennis, and Lindsay, all of whom became singers.

The Rhythm Boys began singing with Gus Arnheim and His Orch. at the Cocoanut Grove nightclub in Los Angeles in September 1930. Crosby made his first feature film appearance apart from the group in December, singing a song in *Reaching for the Moon*. The group broke up in the spring of 1931 and Crosby went solo, signing a contract with Brunswick Records and forming an association with its recording director, Jack Kapp, that would last until Kapp's death 18 years later. (He moved with Kapp to the newly formed American Decca label in 1934.) "Out of Nowhere" (music by John Green, lyrics by Edward Heyman), Crosby's initial solo recording, became a best-seller in May, followed by "Just One More Chance" (music by Arthur Johnston, lyrics by Sam Coslow) in June and "At Your Command" (music and lyrics by Harry Barris, Bing Crosby, and Harry Tobias) in August.

Crosby launched his solo radio career with a 15-minute program on CBS on Sept. 2. Starting in November he played an extended engagement at the Paramount Theatre in N.Y. In January 1932 he scored another best-seller with "Dinah" (music by Harry Akst, lyrics by Sam M. Lewis and Joe Young), a duet with the Mills Brothers.

Signed to Paramount Pictures, Crosby began filming his first starring role in *The Big Broadcast* in June 1932. Following the film's successful release in October, he was signed to a long-term contract with the studio and stayed there for 24 years. In July he went on an extensive concert tour, the only one of his career. "Please" (music by Ralph Rainger, lyrics by Leo Robin), which he introduced in *The Big Broadcast*, became his next top-seller in October, followed in November by "Brother, Can You Spare a Dime?" (music by Jay Gorney, lyrics by E. Y. Harburg).

In 1933, Crosby settled into a pattern he would follow with only minor variations for the next two decades. Living in Los Angeles, he appeared on his own radio show while shooting two or three movies a year. The films usually were light romantic musical comedies

in which he sang several specially written songs, which he also recorded, resulting in a stream of hits.

"You're Getting to Be a Habit with Me" (music by Harry Warren, lyrics by Al Dubin), Crosby's next best-seller in March 1933, found him accompanied by Guy Lombardo and His Royal Canadians. Another Warren-Dubin composition, "Shadow Waltz," became a top hit for Crosby in July. On it, and his next big hit, "Little Dutch Mill" (music by Harry Barris, lyrics by Ralph Freed), in April 1934, he was accompanied by Jimmie Grier and His Orch. The Rainger-Robin song "Love in Bloom," a best-seller in August, was featured in Crosby's film *She Loves Me Not*, released in September. Rainger and Robin's "June in January" was a major hit in December, the same month Crosby sang it in *Here Is My Heart*.

Crosby had two best-sellers from the Richard Rodgers-Lorenz Hart score of *Mississippi*, released in April 1935, "Easy to Remember" and "Soon." But he lost ground to the swing bands, and his next #1 on the hit parade did not come until December 1936 with "Pennies from Heaven" (music by Arthur Johnston, lyrics by Johnny Burke), the title song from a film released that month. His first million-selling record was "Sweet Leilani" (music and lyrics by Harry Owens), from the March 1937 film *Waikiki Wedding*, which was in the hit parade for 12 weeks that spring and summer. "Remember Me?" (a Warren-Dubin song) topped the hit parade for Crosby in November 1937. In October 1938, "I've Got a Pocketful of Dreams" (music by James V. Monaco, lyrics by Johnny Burke), from the August film release *Sing, You Sinners*, led the hit parade for four weeks, becoming the second-biggest hit of the year. In December 1938 and Jan. 1939, Crosby again reached the top of the hit parade with "You Must Have Been a Beautiful Baby" (music by Harry Warren, lyrics by Johnny Mercer).

Crosby's hits of the 1930s were enough to make him the most successful recording artist of the decade. He repeated this feat in the 1940s, starting with two chart-toppers, a revival of the 1916 song "Sierra Sue" (music and lyrics by Joseph Buell Carey) in September 1940 and the Monaco-Burke composition "Only Forever" from his August film release *Rhythm on the River* in October. A revival of Bob Wills's "San Antonio Rose," released as "New San Antonio Rose" in early 1941, on which Crosby was backed by his brother Bob's orchestra, became his second million-seller.

Crosby's third million-seller was "White Christmas" (music and lyrics by Irving Berlin), recorded on May 29, 1942, and featured in the August 1942 film *Holiday Inn*. Topping the charts in October, it became the biggest hit of the year. It returned to the top of the charts in the holiday seasons of 1945 and 1946, and continued to reach the charts yearly through 1962. With worldwide sales estimated as high as a hundred million copies, it was the best-selling single record of all time. On June 8, 1942, Crosby made a commercial recording of the 1818 Christmas song "Silent Night" (music by Franz Gruber, lyrics by Joseph Mohr); he had previously recorded the song with Whiteman in 1928 and for a charity album in 1935. It went on to become one of his biggest selling singles, with sales estimated at seven million copies.

The success of his Christmas recordings propelled Crosby to a new level of popularity, and he dominated the record charts and the box office rankings in the mid-1940s. His next chart-topper and million-seller came in September 1943 with "Sunday, Monday or Always" (music by James Van Heusen, lyrics by Johnny Burke) from the film *Dixie*. That month he recorded two more million-sellers in duets with the Andrews Sisters, "Pistol Packin' Mama" (music and lyrics by Al Dexter) and the 1857 Christmas song "Jingle Bells" (music and lyrics by J. S. Pierpont), and the following month yet another, "I'll Be Home for Christmas" (music and lyrics by Walter Kent, Kim Gannon, and Buck Ram).

Crosby's remarkable chart performance in 1943–44 is partially due to his being the flagship artist for the one major recording label that settled a dispute with the musicians' union a year ahead of its rivals, allowing its artists to record freely. He topped the charts with six records during 1944: in April with "San Fernando Valley" (music and lyrics by Gordon Jenkins); in May with "I Love You" (music and lyrics by Cole Porter); in July with a revival of the 1938 song "I'll Be Seeing You" (music by Sammy Fain, lyrics by Irving Kahal); in August with the biggest hit of the year and his ninth million-seller, "Swinging on a Star" (music by James Van Heusen, lyrics by Johnny Burke), from his May motion picture release *Going My Way*, the biggest box office hit of the year, for which he won the Academy Award for Best Actor; in Oct. with "(There'll Be a) Hot Time in the Town of Berlin (When the Yanks Go Marching In)" (music by Joe Bushkin, lyrics by John De Vries), a duet with the Andrews Sisters; and in December with another Andrews Sisters duet, "Don't Fence Me In" (music and lyrics by Cole Porter), which became his 11th million-seller. (His tenth, the 1914 Irish song "Too-Ra- Loo-Ra-Loo-Ral" [music and lyrics by James Royce Shannon] also was heard in the film *Going My Way*.)

With Columbia and RCA Victor back to making records in 1945, Crosby was not able to rule the record industry as he had the year before, but he remained the top-selling artist, scoring chart-topping hits with "It's Been a Long, Long Time" (music by Jule Styne, lyrics by Sammy Cahn) and "I Can't Begin to Tell You" (music by James V. Monaco, lyrics by Mack Gordon), his 12th million-seller, in December. He also topped the album charts with *Going My Way* in October and *Merry Christmas* in November. (Initially released as an eight-song collection on four 78 rpm discs, *Merry Christmas* became a perennial holiday seller, topping the charts again every year through 1950 and again in 1957. Upon its reissue as an LP, four tracks were added. In 1970, *Merry Christmas* became Crosby's only record to be certified gold by the R.I.A.A.) And, for the second time in a row, he starred in the year's box office champ, the *Going My Way* sequel, *The Bells of St. Mary's*, which earned him an Academy Award nomination.

Crosby topped the album charts with *The Bells of St. Mary's* in March 1946. He had more million-selling singles that year with the Irish song "McNamara's Band" (music by Shamus O'Connor, lyrics by John J.

Stamford) and another Andrews Sisters duet, "South America, Take It Away" (music and lyrics by Harold Rome). *Blue Skies*, costarring Fred Astaire, was one of the most successful films of the year. To commemorate St. Patrick's Day 1947, Crosby released a *St. Patrick's Day* album, which charted over the next three years, hitting #1 in March 1948. He had four more million-selling singles during 1947: a coupling of "Alexander's Ragtime Band" (music and lyrics by Irving Berlin) and "The Spaniard That Blighted My Life" (music and lyrics by Billy Merson), both vintage songs, recorded as duets with Al Jolson; "The Whiffenpoof Song" (music by Tod B. Galloway, lyrics by Meade Minnigerode and George S. Pomeroy); "Now Is the Hour" (music and lyrics by Maewa Kaihan, Clement Scott, and Dorothy Stewart), which topped the charts in April 1948; and "Galway Bay" (music and lyrics by Dr. Arthur Colahan). He also starred in the year's most successful film, *Welcome Stranger*, in which he was again teamed with *Going My Way* costar, Barry Fitzgerald.

Another of Crosby's holiday albums, *St. Valentine's Day*, topped the charts in February 1948. He enjoyed his 20th million-selling single with "Dear Hearts and Gentle People" (music by Sammy Fain, lyrics by Bob Hilliard), released in fall 1949. Though he didn't hit #1 on the singles charts in 1950, his nine chart entries, four of them Top Ten hits, made him the most successful recording artist of the year; his biggest single and 21st million-seller was the duet with his son Gary, "Play a Simple Melody" (music and lyrics by Irving Berlin).

Crosby began to cut back in the 1950s, making only one or two films a year, and his record sales declined. On Nov. 11, 1952, his wife died of cancer. In his films he took on more serious roles, notably playing an alcoholic singer in *The Country Girl* (1954), which earned him his third Oscar nomination. His greatest popular success came with efforts that hearkened back to earlier triumphs, such as the 1954 film *White Christmas* and the Top Ten, five-LP boxed set *Bing: A Musical Autobiography* (1954), on which he rerecorded many of his old hits. His Paramount contract ended in 1954, and his Decca contract in 1955, after which he made records and films on a freelance basis. The popular movie *High Society*, released in August 1956, featured his duet with Grace Kelly on "True Love" (music and lyrics by Cole Porter), his 22nd and last million-selling record.

Crosby married actress/singer Kathryn Grant (real name Grandstaff) on Oct. 24, 1957. They had three children, each of whom performed with their parents; Mary Crosby went on to become a successful actress.

During the last 20 years of his life, Crosby worked steadily in a variety of media, though with less public exposure and commercial success. In films like *Say One for Me* (1959) and *High Time* (1960), he was paired with much younger costars. His last starring role came with *The Road to Hong Kong* (1962), the seventh of his popular series of comedies with Bob Hope, though he made supporting appearances in *Robin and the Seven Hoods* (1964) and *Stagecoach* (1966). He worked extensively on television, frequently hosting the variety series *The Hollywood Palace* between 1964 and 1970 and starring in his own situation comedy, *The Bing Crosby Show*, during the 1964–65 season and hosting his annual Christmas specials.

Following a successful operation to remove a tumor from his left lung in 1974, Crosby became more active as a recording artist and concert performer during the last few years of his life, cutting a series of albums and touring with his family and Rosemary Clooney. He died of a heart attack at age 74 just after performing a series of shows at the London Palladium and recording a final album, *Seasons*.

Crosby's reputation was tarnished in the early 1980s by the publication of the scandalous biography, *Bing Crosby: The Hollow Man* (1981) and a harsh memoir by his son Gary, *Going My Own Way* (1983). Though neither book dug up much real dirt on the star or even fully justified what little it did, his image had been so saintly that any criticism was magnified. The suicides of his sons Lindsay (1989) and Dennis (1991) tended to reinforce the sense that, as a father at least, Crosby was more stern than his public persona suggested, something he had admitted in his 1953 autobiography *Call Me Lucky*. Nevertheless, the controversy did not diminish Crosby's overwhelming impact on popular music, one reinforced every Christmas season, and by the mid-1990s many of his recordings were coming back into print (notably the four-CD boxed set *Bing! His Legendary Years* in 1993) and many of his films were becoming available on video.

Crosby differed from most singers in that he performed relatively few concerts; instead he was an early master of the various electronic media that rose up in the late 1920s. Although he was not the first performer to tailor his approach to the microphone, he was the most effective and the most successful, evolving an intimate, relaxed persona through a warm, supple baritone, employing apparently casual phrasing that nevertheless evoked the swing rhythm of jazz. His influence as a singer was felt by his immediate successors such as Perry Como as well as James Taylor. The breadth of his repertoire, embracing everything from Hawaiian to country music, expanded popular music and its audience to an unprecedented degree.

Disc.: *Jerome Kern Songs* (1949); *Stephen Foster Songs* (1949); *Bing Crosby* (1950); *Bing Sings George Gershwin* (1950); *Bings Sings Cole Porter* (1950); *Blue of the Night* (1950); *Christmas Greetings* (1950); *Cowboys Songs* (1950); *Cowboy Songs, Vol. 2* (1950); *Don't Fence Me In* (1950); *Drifting and Dreaming* (1950); *El Bingo* (1950); *Foster* (1950); *St. Patrick's Day* (1950); *St. Valentine's Day* (1950); *Stardust* (1950); *Top o' the Morning* (1950); Auld Lang Syne (1950); *Going My Way* (1950); *Cole Porter Songs* (1950); *Songs by Gershwin* (1950); *Hawaiian Songs* (1950); *Mr. Music* (1950); *Blue Skies* (1950); *Holiday Inn* (1950); *Bing and the Dixieland Bands* (1951); *Country Style* (1951); *Down Memory Lane* (1951); *Down Memory Lane, Vol. 2* (1951); *Favorite Hawaiian Songs* (1951); *Go West, Young Man* (1951); *Way Back Home* (1951); *Yours Is My Heart Alone* (1951); *Beloved Hymns* (1951); *Bing Sings Victor Herbert* (1951); *Bing and Connee* (1951); *Road to Bali* (1952); *Country Girl* (1953); *Old Masters* (1954); *Ichabod Crane* (1955); *Bing Sings Whilst Bregman Swings* (1956); *Blue Hawaii* (1956); *High Society* (1956); *Home on the Range* (1956); *Lullabye Time* (1956); *A Man without a Country* (1956); *The Road to Sinapore* (1956); *The Star Maker* (1956); *Waikiki Wedding* (1956); *Two for Tonight* (1956); *Shillelaghs and Shamrocks* (1956); *White Christmas*

(1956); *Bing with a Beat* (1957); *The Christmas Story* (1957); *Around the World* (1958); *Bing in Paris* (1958); *New Tricks* (1958); *Some Fine Old Chestnuts* (1958); *Songs I Wish I Had Sung* (1958); *Twilight on the Trail* (1958); *Fancy Meeting You Here* (1958); *That Travelin' Two-Beat* (1958); *A Christmas Sing with Bing around the World* (1958); *That Christmas Feeling* (1958); *In a Little Spanish Town* (1959); *Der Bingle* (1959); *Join with Bing and Sing Along* (1960); *Bing and Satchmo* (1960); *High Time* (1960); *101 Gang Songs* (1961); *Senor Bing* (1961); *Accentuate the Positive* (1962); *But Beautiful* (1962); *Cool of the Evening* (1962); *East Side of Heaven* (1962); *Easy to Remember* (1962); *Holiday in Europe* (1962); *I Wish You a Very Merry Christmas* (1962); *On the Happy Side* (1962); *Only Forever* (1962); *The Road Begins* (1962); *Sunshine Cake* (1962); *Zing a Little Zong* (1962); *Swingin' on a Star* (1962); *The Great Standards* (1963); *Return to Paradise Island* (1964); *Songs Everybody Knows* (1964); *Blue Skies* (1965); *Wrap Your Troubles in Dreams* (1972); *Bing & Basie* (1972); *That's What Life Is All About* (1976); *Feels Good, Feels Right* (1976); *Bing Crosby at the London Palladium* (1976).

BIBL.: T. and L. Crosby (his brothers), *The Story of B. C.* (Cleveland, Ohio, 1937); J. Mize, *B. C. and the B. C. Style: Crosbyana thru Biography-Photography-Discography* (Chicago, 1946); E. Mello and T. McBride, *B. C. Discography* (San Francisco, 1947); B. Ulanov, *The Incredible C.* (N.Y., 1948); K. Crosby (his wife), *B. and Other Things* (1967); K. Crosby, *My Life with B.* (Wheeling, Ill., 1983); J. Bassett, et al., *The B. C. LP-ography* (1973); C. Thompson, *B.: The Authorized Biography* (London, 1975); B. Bauer, *B. C.* (N.Y., 1977); R. Bookbinder, *The Films of B. C.* (Seacaucus, N.J., 1977); G. Carpozi Jr., *The Fabulous Life of B. C.* (N.Y., 1977); J. Koenig, *B.* (N.Y., 1977); B. Thomas, *The One and Only B.* (N.Y., 1977); L. Zwisohn, *B. C.: A Lifetime of Music* (Los Angeles, 1978); K. Barnes, *The C. Years* (London, 1979); B. Bishop and J. Bassett, compilers, *B.—Just for the Record: The Complete Encyclopedia of Commercial Recordings, 1926–77* (Gateshead, England, 1980); D. Shepherd and R. Slatzer, *B. C.: The Hollow Man* (N.Y., 1981); G. Crosby (his son) and R. Firestone, *Going My Own Way* (N.Y., 1983); F. Reynolds, *Road to Hollywood: The B. C. Films Book* (Gateshead, England, 1986); T. Morgereth, *B. C.: A Discography, Radio Program List and Filmography* (Jefferson, N.C., 1987); C. Pugh, *Alternate B. C.: The Book of "Alternate" B. C. Takes* (Montpelier, England, 1988); F. Reynolds, *The Crosby Collection, 1926–77: A Review of the Commercial Recordings Made by B. C.* (five volumes; England, 1991–97); J. Osterholm, *B. C.: A Bio-Bibliography* (Westport, Conn., 1994); G. Hamann, ed., *B. C. in the 1930s* (Hollywood, 1996).—WR

Crosby, Bob (actually, George Robert),

singer, leader, brother of **Bing Crosby;** b. Spokane, Wash., Aug. 25, 1913; d. La Jolla, Calif., March 9, 1993. Attending Gonzaga Coll. with the intention of taking up law, he instead became a professional singer with Anson Weeks' Orch. (1932). Two years later, he joined the Dorsey Brothers' Orch. Early in 1935, Crosby was chosen as the front man for a new band put together by Gil Rodin, comprising of ex-Ben Pollack musicians. For the next seven years, the Bob Crosby Orch. (and the smaller band-within-a-band, The Bobcats) achieved great touring and recording success. The original lineup included Yank Lawson, Bob Haggart, Ray Baudoc, Nappy Lamare, arranger Deane Kincaide, Matty Matlock, and Eddie Miller. Others passing through included many of the best white musicians of the era. The band had dozens of hits, including "South Rampart Street Parade" and "Dogtown Blues," both written by Haggart.

Crosby couldn't conduct, but was a good pop singer who got better, and valued the company he was keeping; the band was satisfied with the deal. The original band broke up in late1942; Bob Crosby served in the U.S. Marines (1944–45). After an acting role in *The Singing Sheriff*, he formed a new band and featured them on his radio series. During the 1950s, he was mainly active as a solo artist with his own TV and radio shows and occasionally re-formed the band for specific engagements, often using many of his original sidemen. From 1960, he was mainly occupied with business interests outside of music, but regularly led reunion bands for jazz festivals, residencies in N.Y. and Las Vegas, and tours of Japan and the Far East (late 1964). Films that feature the Bob Crosby Band include *Sis Hopkins* (1941), *Presenting Lily Mars* (1942), and *As Thousands Cheer*. The band also did the soundtrack for *Holiday Inn* (1942). Crosby led his band on several concert tours during the 1970s and appeared at the Reagan White House (1985).

DISC.: *South Rampart Street Parade* (1936); *I Remember You* (1941); *Bob Crosby's Bob Cats* (1954); *Bobcats on Parade* (1957); *Bob Crosby's Bobcats in Hi Fi* (1957); *Mardi Gras Parade* (1966).

BIBL.: C. Jones, *Bob Crosby Band* (London, 1946); J. Chilton, *Stomp Off, Let's Go! The Story of Bob Crosby's Bob Cats and Big Band* (London, 1983).—**JC/MM**

Crosby, Israel (Clem), bassist; b. Chicago, Ill., Jan. 19, 1919; d. there, Aug. 11, 1962. He played trumpet from the age of five, changed to trombone and tuba, and at 13 was gigging regularly on these instruments. He changed to string bass in 1934, with Johnny Long, Anthony Frambro, then with Albert Ammons in the Club DeLisa in Chicago. After making his record debut with Gene Krupa, he spent two years with Fletcher Henderson (1936–38). He left in 1939 to spend a year working with Three Sharps and a Flat. He joined Horace Henderson in September 1940, but left the following May to spend two years in the Teddy Wilson Band. In the summer of 1944 he joined Raymond Scott at CBS where he spent several years as a freelance studio musician, also with James P. Johnson (1945). From 1951–53 he was with pianist Ahmad Jamal, briefly with Teddy Wilson Trio, then worked with Benny Goodman (late 1956–early 1957 tour of Asia) Crosby returned to work with Ahmad Jamal Trio until the trio disbanded in the spring of 1962, then joined pianist George Shearing; his last recordings were made with Shearing in June 1962. During the following month he returned to Chicago for a medical check-up, and died of a blood clot on the heart.—**JC/LP**

Crosby, John (O'Hea), American conductor, opera impresario, and music educator; b. N.Y., July 12, 1926. He received instruction in violin and piano from his mother, and later studied composition with Hindemith at Yale Univ. (B.A., 1950) and conducting with Rudolph Thomas at Columbia Univ. and Monteux in Hancock, Maine. From 1951 to 1956 he was on the staff of the N.Y.C. Opera. In 1956 he founded the Opera Assn. of N.Mex., later renamed the Santa Fe Opera. During his long tenure as its general director and resident conduc-

tor, he gave premiere performances of numerous operas by American and foreign composers. Crosby was also president of the Manhattan School of Music in N.Y. (1976–85) and of Opera America (from 1976). —**NS/LK/DM**

Crosby, Stills, Nash (and Young), the quintessential close harmony, acoustic-guitar, songwriting trio of the late 1960s and early 1970s. **MEMBERSHIP:** David Crosby (real name, David Van Cortland), gtr., tenor voc. (b. Los Angeles, Aug. 14, 1941); Stephen Stills, gtr., kybd., voc. (b. Dallas, Jan. 3, 1945); Graham Nash, gtr., high tenor voc. (b. Blackpool, Lancashire, England, Feb. 2, 1942); Neil Young, gtr., voc. (b. Toronto, Ontario, Canada, Nov. 12, 1945).

Ex-Byrd David Crosby and former member of Buffalo Springfield, Stephen Stills, met Graham Nash of the Hollies in 1968. An informal jam session in Los Angeles that July so impressed the three that they decided to form a group as soon as Nash could sever relations with the English group. Nash performed his last engagement with the Hollies on Dec. 8, 1968. Signing with Atlantic Records in January 1969, their debut album *Crosby, Stills and Nash* yielded two moderate hits with Nash's "Marrakesh Express" and Stills's "Suite: Judy Blue Eyes," written about Judy Collins. With Crosby on rhythm guitar and Stills overdubbing lead guitar, organ, and bass, the album featured precise three-part harmonies. Included were two Crosby songs, "Long Time Gone" and "Guinnevere," Nash's "Lady of the Island," Stills's "Helplessly Hoping," and the mystical "Wooden Ships," composed by Crosby, Stills, and (uncredited) Paul Kantner.

In an effort to fill out their acoustic sound, Crosby, Stills and Nash recruited Neil Young, another former member of Buffalo Springfield who was pursuing a successful solo career. They debuted at N.Y.'s Fillmore East less than a month before the quartet's celebrated appearance at the Woodstock Music and Art Fair in August 1969. By the end of the year, however, the "good vibes" that had produced the magnificent results on the first album were dashed, as Stills broke up with Judy Collins, Nash broke up with Joni Mitchell, and Crosby's girlfriend Christine Hinton was killed in an auto crash. Young admirably took up the slack for *Deja Vu*, the group's most successful album. It featured three hits, an electric version of Joni Mitchell's "Woodstock" and two Nash songs, "Teach Your Children" and "Our House." The album also included Crosby's title song and "Almost Cut My Hair," Stills's "Carry On" and "4 and 20," and Young's three-part production effort "Country Girl." By fall 1970, the group had split, but not before issuing Young's brilliant "Ohio," an outraged response to the Kent State student murders of May 1970. Nash subsequently compiled the double-record live set *Four Way Street*, which included Young classics such as "On the Way Home," "Cowgirl in the Sand," and "Southern Man," and two beautiful Crosby songs, "Triad" and "The Lee Shore."

Stephen Stills had already recorded one side of the *Super Session* album with Al Kooper. Stills's debut solo album, consisting entirely of his own songs, yielded his only major hit with "Love the One You're With" and the moderate hit "Sit Yourself Down." The album also featured "We Are Not Helpless" and the inebriated "Black Queen," plus the instrumental "Old Times, Good Times" (featuring Jimi Hendrix) and "Go Back Home" (with Eric Clapton on second lead guitar). Stills's second solo album included "Sugar Babe" and "Singin' Call" and yielded moderate hits with "Change Partners" and "Marianne." Conducting his first major solo tour in July 1971, in Oct. Stills formed Manassas with former Byrd and Flying Burrito Brother Chris Hillman and pedal steel guitarist Al Perkins. The group toured extensively and recorded two albums before breaking up in September 1973.

Meanwhile, David Crosby recorded his debut solo album *If I Could Only Remember My Name*. Featuring several songs composed of wordless vocal harmonies, the album contained Crosby's "Laughing" and "Traction in the Rain," as well as Nash, Young, and Crosby's "Music Is Love" and the conspiratorial "What Are Their Names." Graham Nash's debut solo album, *Songs for Beginners*, produced moderate hits with the political songs "Chicago" and "Military Madness," and included Nash's "Better Days" and the old Hollies' song "I Used to Be a King."

In 1972, Crosby and Nash teamed for touring and an album that yielded a moderate hit with Nash's "Immigration Man." Nash recorded a second solo album in 1973, and Crosby, Stills, Nash and Young conducted a summer-long stadium tour in 1974. Crosby and Nash subsequently recorded *Wind on the Water* and *Whistling Down the Wire* for ABC (later MCA), whereas Stills recorded three albums for Columbia through 1978. During 1976, Stills and Young formed the short-lived Stills-Young Band for one album on Reprise and an aborted tour. Crosby, Stills and Nash then regrouped for touring and 1977's *CSN*, which included Stills's "Dark Star" and the near-smash "Just a Song Before I Go" by Nash. Nash was a founding director of the antinuclear power Musicians United for Safe Energy (MUSE) and organizer of the "No Nukes" concerts of September 1979.

Crosby, Stills and Nash regrouped in 1982 for touring and *Daylight Again*, which yielded the near-smash hit "Wasted on the Way" and the major hit "Southern Cross." The three continued to tour and record, while Stills recorded *Right By You*. Nash reunited with the Hollies' Allan Clarke, Tony Hicks, and Bobby Elliott for the album *What Goes Around* in 1983 and solo-recorded *Innocent Eyes* in 1986. Crosby, Stills, Nash and Young appeared at Live Aid in 1985.

David Crosby was arrested several times on drug and weapons charges in the early 1980s, leading to his imprisonment in Tex. in 1985 and 1986. Breaking his addiction to cocaine while in prison, he was paroled in September 1986 and exonerated of charges in November 1987. Putting his life back together, Crosby married longtime girlfriend Jan Dance in May 1987 and published the autobiography *Long Time Gone* in 1988.

Crosby, Stills, Nash and Young subsequently recorded their first studio release in 18 years, *American Dream*, and later Crosby recorded *Oh Yes I Can* solo for

A&M Records. During the 1990s, Crosby, Stills and Nash recorded *Live It Up* and *After the Storm* and conducted an all-acoustic tour in 1992. Crosby recorded *Thousand Roads*, which included "Yvette in English," cowritten with Joni Mitchell, and "Hero," a moderate hit cowritten with Phil Collins. He underwent a liver transplant operation in November 1994. Crosby, Stills and Nash toured again in 1996 and 1997, the year they were inducted into the Rock and Roll Hall of Fame.

In 1995, David Crosby met his heretofore unknown son, James Raymond, with whom he formed the ironically named group CPR with Jeff Pevar. In 1998, Steve Stills's son by actress Veronique Sanson, Chris, launched his solo recording career with *100 Year Thing* on Atlantic Records.

DISC.: CROSBY, STILLS AND NASH: *Crosby, Stills and Nash* (1969); *Daylight Again* (1982); *Live It Up* (1990). **CROSBY, STILLS, NASH AND YOUNG:** *Deja Vu* (1970); *4 Way Street* (1971); *So Far* (1974); *American Dream* (1988). **KOOPER, BLOOMFIELD, AND STILLS:** *Super Session* (1968). **STEPHEN STILLS:** *Stephen Stills* (1970); *Down the Road* (1973); *Stills* (1975); *Thoroughfare Gap* (1978); *Live* (1979); *Right by You* (1984); *Stills Alone* (1991). **MANASSAS:** *Manassas* (1972). **THE STILLS-YOUNG BAND:** *Long May You Run* (1976). **CHRIS STILLS:** *100 Year Thing* (1998). **DAVID CROSBY:** *If I Could Only Remember* (1971); *Oh Yes I Can* (1989); *Thousand Roads* (1993); *It's All Coming Back to Me Now...* (1995). **CPR:** *CPR* (1998). **GRAHAM NASH:** *Songs for Beginners* (1971); *Earth and Sky* (1980); *Innocent Eyes* (1986). **THE HOLLIES (WITH GRAHAM NASH):** *What Goes Around* (1983). **DAVID CROSBY AND GRAHAM NASH:** *Graham Nash/David Crosby* (1972); *Live* (1975); *Wind on the Water* (1975); *Whistling Down the Wire* (1976).

WRITINGS: D. C. and C. Gottlieb, *Long Time Gone: The Autobiography of D. C.* (N.Y., 1988).

BIBL.: D. Zimmer, *Crosby, Stills and Nash: The Authorized Biography* (N.Y., 1984).—BH

Cross, Joan, English soprano, opera producer, and teacher; b. London, Sept. 7, 1900; d. Aldeburgh, Dec. 12, 1993. She received training from Holst at St. Paul's Girls School and from Dawson Freer at Trinity Coll. of Music in London. In 1924 she became a member of the chorus at the Old Vic Theatre in London; in 1931 she joined the Sadler's Wells Opera in London, where she was principal soprano until 1946. In 1946 she helped to found the English Opera Group, with which she was active as both a soprano and producer. In 1948 she co-founded the Opera School, which became the National School of Opera in 1955. In 1951 she was made a Commander of the Order of the British Empire. Cross became particularly known for her roles in Britten's operas, in which she created Ellen Orford in *Peter Grimes* (1945), the Female Chorus in *The Rape of Lucretia* (1946), Lady Billows in *Albert Herring* (1947), Elizabeth I in *Gloriana* (1953), and Mrs. Grose in *The Turn of the Screw* (1954). —NS/LK/DM

Cross, Lowell (Merlin), American composer and electro-musicologist; b. Kingsville, Tex., June 24, 1938. He studied mathematics and music at Tex. Tech. Univ., graduating in 1963; then entered the Univ. of

Toronto, obtaining his M.A. in musicology in 1968; attended classes of Marshall McLuhan in environmental technology there; took a course in electronic music with Myron Schaeffer and Gustav Ciamaga. After teaching electronic music and working as a research assoc. at the electronic music studio there (1967–68), he was director and a teacher at the Mills Tape Music Center (1968–69) and a consulting artist and engineer with Experiments in Art and Technology, Inc. (1968–70). In 1971 he joined the faculty of the Univ. of Iowa, where he served as a prof. from 1981. Eschewing any preliminary serial experimentation, Cross espoused a cybernetic totality of audiovisual, electronic, and theatrical arts. He compiled a manual, *A Bibliography of Electronic Music* (Toronto, 1967; 3rd ed., rev., 1970). As a pioneer in astromusicology, he created the selenogeodesic score *Lunar Laser Beam* (broadcast as a salutatory message on Nicolas Slonimsky's 77th birthday, April 27, 1971, purportedly via Leningrad, the subject's birthplace; the Sea of Tranquillity on the moon; and the Ciudad de Nuestra Señora Reina de Los Angeles in Calif.).

WORKS: *4 Random Studies* for Tape (1961); *0.8 Century* for Tape (1962); *Eclectic Music* for Flute and Piano (1964); *Antiphonies* for Tape (1964); *After Long Silence* for Soprano and Tape (1964); *3 Etudes* for Tape (1965); *Video I* and *II* for Variable Media, including Tape, Audio System, Oscilloscope, and Television (1965–68); *Musica Instrumentalis* for Acoustical Stereophonic Instruments, Monochrome and Polychrome Television (1965–68); *Video III* for Television and Phase-derived Audio System (1968); *Reunion* for Electronic Chessboard (constructed by Cross and first demonstrated in Toronto, March 5, 1968, the main opponents in the chess game being John Cage and Marcel Duchamp, who won readily); *Video/Laser I-IV* for Laser Deflection System (1969–80); *Electro-Acustica* for Instruments, Laser Deflection System, Television, and Phase-derived Audio System (1970–71).—NS/LK/DM

Crosse, Gordon, English composer; b. Bury, Lancashire, Dec. 1, 1937. He studied music history with Wellesz at the Univ. of Oxford (graduated, 1961), where he continued his research under Frank Harrison in 1961–62; he then studied with Petrassi at the Accademia di Santa Cecilia in Rome (1962). After working as senior music tutor in the extra-mural dept. at the Univ. of Birmingham (1964–66), he served as its Haywood fellow in music (1966–69). From 1969 to 1976 he was a fellow in music at the Univ. of Essex, and in 1973 composer-in-residence at King's Coll., Cambridge. In 1976 he was awarded the Cobbett Medal. In subsequent years, Crosse devoted himself to composition. His research into early music, combined with his love of literature, resulted in dramatic, vocal, and instrumental works notable for their rich expressivity in a strongly defined personal style.

WORKS: DRAMATIC: Opera: *Purgatory* (Cheltenham, July 7, 1966); *The Grace of Todd* (1967–68; Aldeburgh, June 7, 1969); *The Story of Vasco* (1968–73; London, March 13, 1974); *Potter Thompson* (1972–73; London, Jan. 9, 1975). **Ballet:** *Wildboy* (Washington, D.C., Dec. 12, 1980); *Young Apollo* (London, Nov. 17, 1984). **ORCH.:** *Elegy* for Small Orch. (1959–61; Manchester, April 1962); two violin concertos: No. 1, *Concerto da camera* (1962; BBC, 1966; 1st concert perf., London, Feb. 18, 1968) and No. 2 (1969; Oxford, Jan. 29, 1970); Concerto for Chamber Orch. (1962; Budapest, July 3, 1968); *Symphonies* for Chamber Orch. (1964; Birmingham, Feb. 13, 1965); Sinfonia concertante (Cheltenham, Feb. 13, 1965; rev. as Sym. No. 1, 1975–76); *Ceremony* for Cello and Orch. (London, Aug. 4, 1966); *Ouvert: Clos* for Chamber Orch. (London, Sept. 15, 1969); *Some Marches on a Ground* (Norwich, Oct. 14, 1970); *Ariadne* for Oboe and Small Orch. (1971–72; Cheltenham, July 11, 1972); *Thel* for Flute, two Horns, and Strings (1974–76; Aldeburgh, June 27, 1978); *Epiphany Variations* or *Mag and Nunc* (1975); *Play Ground*, ballet suite (Manchester, March 2, 1978); *Dreamsongs* (Edinburgh, Aug. 20, 1979; based on the chamber piece, 1973); Cello Concerto, *In Memoriam Luigi Dallapiccola* (Cheltenham, July 7, 1979); *Elegy and Scherzo alla Marcia* for Strings (1980; Snape, June 24, 1981; adapted from the String Quartet, 1979); *Array* for Trumpet and Strings (London, Aug. 9, 1986); *Quiet!* for Wind Band (1987). **CHAMBER:** *Villanelles* for Wind Quintet, Violin, and Cello (1959; rev. version, London, Nov. 23, 1974); *3 Inventions* for Flute and Clarinet (1959); *Canto* for six Instruments (1961; rev. 1963); two sets of *Studies* for String Quartet (1972–73; 1977); *Dreamsongs* for Clarinet, Oboe, Bassoon, and Piano (1973; also for Orch., 1979); String Quartet (1979; London, Nov. 24, 1980); *Rhymes and Reasons*, trio for Clarinet, Cello, and Piano (1980; Huntingdon, Nov. 17, 1982); *Peace for Brass* for 10 Instruments (1980; King's Lynn, July 29, 1981); *Fear No More* for Oboe, Oboe d'amore, and English Horn (1980; London, Oct. 5, 1981); *A Wake* for Flute, Clarinet, Cello, and Piano (Aldeburgh, June 16, 1982); *Watermusic* for Treble, Descant, and Sopranino Recorders and Piano (Glasgow, Dec. 3, 1982); *Wavesongs* for Cello and Piano (Oxford, Oct. 30, 1983); *Chime* for two Trumpets, Trombone, Horn, and Tuba (1983); Trio for Violin, Cello, and Piano (1985; London, April 4, 1986); Oboe Quintet (Birmingham, Dec. 3, 1988). **VOCAL:** *Corpus Christi Carol* for Soprano or Tenor, Clarinet, and String Quartet (1961; London, Dec. 18, 1964); *For the Unfallen* for Tenor, Horn, and Strings (1963; Liverpool, Sept. 17, 1968); *Changes: A Nocturnal Cycle* for Solo Voices and Orch. (1965–66); *The Covenant of the Rainbow* for Chorus, Organ, and Piano, 4-Hands (Northampton, Sept. 20, 1968); *Memories of Morning: Night* for Mezzo-soprano and Orch. (London, Dec. 8, 1971); *Celebration* for Unison Voices, Mixed Chorus, and Orch. (1972; London, Sept. 16, 1974); *World Within* for Narrator, Mezzo-soprano, and 10 Instruments (1976; London, April 17, 1977); *Verses in Memoriam David Munrow* for Countertenor, Recorder, Cello, and Harpsichord (1979); *Voices from the Tomb* for Medium Voice and Piano (1979; London, Oct. 21, 1980); *Harvest Songs* for Double Chorus, Junior Chorus, and Orch. (Manchester, July 18, 1980); *Dreamcanon* for Alto, Chorus, Piano, Electric Piano, and Percussion (London, Nov. 11, 1981); *Wintersong* for six Soloists and Optional Percussion (London, Nov. 26, 1982); *A Wake Again* for two Countertenors, two Recorders, Cello, and Harpsichord (1985; N.Y., April 13, 1986); *Armada Echoes* for two Countertenors, Tenor, two Baritones, and Bass (Plymouth, July 10, 1988). **OTHER:** *Meet My Folks!* for Speaker, Children's Voices, and 8 Instruments (1964); *Rats Away!* for Children's Voices and six Instruments (1964); *Ahmet the Woodseller* for Unison Voices, Percussion, and 8 Instruments (1964–65); *The Demon of Adachigahara* for Narrator, Children's Voices, and Orch. (1967); *Wheel of the World*, entertainment (1969–72; Aldeburgh, June 5, 1972); *The History of the Flood* for Children's Voices and Harp (1970); *Matthew Mark Luke and John* for Children's Chorus and Harp (London, Dec. 6, 1970); *Holly from the Bongs*, nativity (1973; Manchester, Dec. 9, 1974).—NS/LK/DM

Crossley, Paul (Christopher Richard), English pianist; b. Dewsbury, Yorkshire, May 17, 1944. He was an organ scholar at Mansfield Coll., Oxford, and also studied piano with Fanny Waterman in Leeds. In 1967 he received a scholarship from the French government to continue his studies with Messiaen and Yvonne Loriod. In 1968 he made his first major tour, garnering praise in England and on the Continent. In subsequent years, he performed regularly in England, and also made tours of Europe, North America, and Japan, often in programs of contemporary works. From 1988 to 1994 he was joint artistic director of the London Sinfonietta. In 1993 he was made a Commander of the Order of the British Empire. Among composers whose works he has championed are Fauré, Ravel, Berg, Janáček, Poulenc, Messiaen, and Tippett.—NS/LK/DM

Crossley-Holland, Peter, English ethnomusicologist and composer; b. London, Jan. 28, 1916. He studied physiology (B.A., 1936; M.A., 1941) and music (B.Mus., 1943) at the Univ. of Oxford. He also studied at the Royal Coll. of Music in London (1937–39), where he worked under John Ireland and gained a Foli Scholarship (1938). Following guidance from Mátyás Seiber, Julius Harrison, and Edmund Rubbra, he pursued postgraduate work at the Univ. of London School of Oriental and African Studies. From 1948 to 1963 he was a member of the music production staff of the BBC in London. A growing interest in the music of the East and a Rockefeller Grant took him to the Himalayan borderlands of Tibet, where he studied Buddhist liturgical music in various monasteries. His field recordings won a Golden Disc Award from the Japanese Ministry of Education (1966), and a Gold Medal (Preis der Deutsche Schallplatten Kritik), and were retained by the International Inst. of Comparative Music Studies and Documentation in West Berlin. In 1966 he taught at the Univ. of Ill. and in 1968–69 he was a visiting prof. at the Univ. of Hawaii. In 1969 he joined the faculty of the Univ. of Calif. at Los Angeles, where he became a prof. in 1972 and chairman of the Council of Ethnomusicology in 1976. After his retirement in 1983, he was briefly recalled in 1984 and then settled in Wales, where he served as an external examiner for the Univ. of Wales at Aberystwyth (1989–93), and at Bangor. He also continued to make field recordings in Celtic-speaking countries, and in Japan, India, and Iran. He contributed numerous articles to scholarly journals, including valuable ones on traditional Celtic music, Tibetan music, and musical instruments of pre-Hispanic Mexico. Crossley-Holland was honored on his 65th birthday with a vol. of essays (*Selected Reports in Ethnomusicology,* IV, 1983). The Univ. of Wales at Aberystwyth conferred upon him two honorary fellowships (Lampeter, 1986; Bangor, 1992) and an honorary professorship (of philosophy, Lampeter, 1987). His music is deeply rooted in European tradition, and many works have been enriched by his love of Celtic and Oriental music.

WORKS: DRAMATIC: Incidental music for five radio plays (1951–59). **ORCH.:** Suite for Strings (1939); *Maguire's Lamentation* for Strings (1944); *Suite, Ulick, and Soracha* for Chamber Orch. (1956); *The Land Beyond* for Small Orch. (1988); *Symphonic Adventure* (1989); *Pilgrimage* (1989); *The Golden Pathway* (1990); Sym. (1994). **CHAMBER:** *Romance* for Cello and Piano (1937); Violin Sonata (1938); Trio for two Violins and Violas (1939); Trio for Flute, Oboe, and Viola (1940); *A Little Suite* for Descant Recorder and Piano (1957; also for Descant and two Trebles [1 Alto Tenor] with or without Piano); *Irish Tunes* for Descant and two Trebles (1957); Albion for Descant, Treble, Tenor (Alto Bass), and Harpsichord (1959); *Breton Tunes* for Descant and Piano (1960; also for Descant and Treble Recorders with or without Piano); *Invocation at Midsummer* for Tenor Recorder (1993); *Tribute to Manannan* for Treble Recorder (Alto Bass) and Piano (1999). **KEYBOARD: P i a n o :** Sonata (1940); *The Distant Isle* (1946). **O r g a n :** *Introit* (1996). **VOCAL:** *2 Mystical Songs* for Baritone and Orch. (1945); *The Sacred Dance,* cantata for Baritone, Chorus, and Orch. (1952); *6 Carols for Sundry Seasons* for Soloists and Chorus (1952); *Des Puys d'Amors,* song-cycle for Baritone and String Orch. (1956); *The Visions of Saint Godric,* cantata for Soprano, Alto, Baritone, Chorus, and Orch. (1959); *Ubi caritas,* anthem for Chorus and Organ (1995); *Missa Brevis* for Chorus and Organ (1997); *Collected Songs* (1998).

WRITINGS: Ed. *Music in Wales* (London, 1948); *Secular Medieval Music in Wales* (Cardiff, 1962); ed. *Artistic Values in Traditional Music* (Berlin, 1966); ed. *Proceedings of the Centennial Workshop on Ethnomusicology* (2 vols., Victoria, 1968, 1978); *Musical Artifacts from Pre-Hispanic West Mexico* (Los Angeles, 1980); *Musical Instruments in Tibetan Legend and Folklore* (Los Angeles, 1982); *Some Musical Traditions of the Celtic-Speaking Peoples* (Bangor, 1996); *Musical Learning and Creativity: A Cross-Cultural Perspective* (Bangor, 1997); *Telyn Teirtu: Myth and Magic in Medieval Wales* (Bangor, 1997); *The Composers in the Robert ap Huw Manuscript* (Bangor, 1998).—NS/LK/DM

Crotch, William, eminent English organist, teacher, and composer; b. Norwich, July 5, 1775; d. Taunton, Dec. 29, 1847. His extraordinary precocity may be measured by the well-authenticated statement (C. Burney, "Account of an Infant Musician," *Philosophical Transactions,* 1779) that when two and a half years old he played on a small organ built by his father, a master carpenter. In Nov. 1778 he began to tour under his mother's guidance. On Jan. 1, 1779, he played before the king and queen at Buckingham Palace. In 1786 he became assistant to Randall, organist of Trinity and King's colleges at Cambridge; at 14, he composed an oratorio, *The Captivity of Judah* (Cambridge, June 4, 1789); he then studied for the ministry (1788–90). Returning to music, he was made organist of Christ Church, Oxford, in 1790. He graduated from Oxford with a Mus.Bac. in 1794, and received a Mus.Doc. in 1799. In 1797 he succeeded Hayes as prof. of music at Oxford and as organist of St. John's Coll. Crotch lectured in the Music School (1800–04), and in the Royal Institution in London (1804, 1805, 1807, and again from 1820). He was principal of the new Royal Academy of Music from 1822 to 1832. Crotch was most successful as a composer of oratorios and organ concertos. His finest work was the oratorio *Palestine* (London, April 21, 1812). His third oratorio, *The Captivity of Judah* (Oxford, June 10, 1834) should not be confused with his juvenile effort of the same title of 1789. Among his other works were five sonatas for Piano or Harpsichord; anthems: ten (1797–1803), ten (1798), and two (1825); odes; chants; Psalm tunes; hymn tunes; songs. He also brought out *Specimens of Various Styles of Music* (c. 1808–15) and various manuals, including *Elements of Musical Composition* (London, 1812; second ed., 1856). In addition,

Crotch revealed talent as a painter.

BIBL.: J. Rennert, *W. C.* (London, 1975).—**NS/LK/DM**

Crothers, Connie, jazz pianist; b. Palo Alto, Calif., June 2, 1941. She was raised in Calif., but moved in N.Y. in 1962; she spent the next decade and a half working with legendary pianist Lennie Tristano. After his death in 1979, she became executor of his estate and also co-founded a foundation in his name. Since the early 1970s, Crothers has been making capable, often impressive albums and showcasing her own pieces rather than reworking standards, although on solo dates she has demonstrated her interpretative abilities. Since the late 1980s, she's worked extensively with saxophonist Lenny Popkin. Although she is a disciple of Tristano, Crothers's style consists more of chordal clusters than of his long lines.

DISC.: *Solo* (1980); *Swish* (1982); *Concert at Cooper Union* (1984). **ROGER MANCUSO:** *Duo Dimensions* (1987); *Music from Everyday Life* (1997). **LENNY POPKIN:** *Love Energy* (1988); *N.Y. Night* (1989); *In Motion* (1989); *Jazz Spring* (1993). —**LP**

Crouch, Stanley, jazz author, drummer; b. Los Angeles, Calif., Dec. 14, 1945. Early in his career, he was associated with David Murray and Arthur Blythe, recording a demo tape with them in 1973 that was never issued. He gave up drums, moved to N.Y., and has since become one of the best-known jazz critics, as well as a provocative commentator on race and politics. He also has been an active mentor to Wynton Marsalis.—**LP**

Crow, Bill (actually, **William Orval**), jazz bassist, author, tuba player; b. Othello, Wash., Dec. 27, 1927. His mother sang professionally on Seattle Radio in the 1930s. He first played trumpet, then switched to drums and valve trombone, working in army bands in the 1940s. After leaving the army, he continued to work in the Seattle area before taking up bass in 1950, the same year he moved to N.Y. Throughout his long career, he has played in the big bands of Claude Thornhill, Gerry Mulligan, and Benny Goodman, as well as in small groups including the Stan Getz Quintet, Gene DiNovi Trio, Marian McPartland Trio, Gerry Mulligan Sextet and Quartet, Al Cohn and Zoot Sims Quintet, Bob Brookmeyer and Clark Terry Quintet, Jay and Kai, and the Terry Gibbs quartet. He toured Europe and Japan with Mulligan during the 1950s and 1960s; he played with the Goodman band at the Seattle World's Fair and during Goodman's Russian tour (1962); he later served as a member of the house bands at Eddie Condon's and at the Playboy Club, both in N.Y. During the 1970s and 1980s, Crow played Broadway shows, including *The King and I* and *42nd Street*, doubling on string bass and tuba. He is currently an active freelancer in N.Y., playing clubs, concerts, jazz cruises, and festivals. He has been a featured sideman on many jazz recordings. He has recorded two albums with his own quartet. He is also the author of two books and writes articles and reviews for jazz magazines, and liner notes for record albums.

DISC.: *From Birdland to Broadway* (1996); *Jazz Anecdotes* (1997).

WRITINGS: *Jazz Anecdotes* (N.Y., 1990); *From Birdland to Broadway* (N.Y., 1992).—**LP**

Crow, Sheryl, talented, hit-making singer/songwriter and producer; b. Kennett, Miss., Feb. 11, 1963. Crow's father was a trumpet player who went to law school (and whose tale became fodder for one of her songs). Her mother taught piano. Crow studied piano and voice at the Univ. of Mo. while playing in a variety of bands.

When her born-again Christian fiancé suggested that she might be better off singing for the Lord, she fled to Los Angeles. There, she became a backing vocalist on Michael Jackson's *Bad* tour for two years. She learned that she loved performing and loved the road. She also learned that a high-profile gig led to high exposure: she was pictured on the cover of supermarket tabloids as the bearer of Jackson's "love child." When the tour finally ended, the press proved a detriment to getting her own songs heard and to securing her own recording contract, at least on her terms. Because Crow had worked with a dance pop artist like Jackson, every record company she went to assumed she was the next Paula Abdul. When she played her soulful, bluesy pop for them, they couldn't hear it.

Instead, Crow sold her songs to other artists, placing them with Eric Clapton and Wynonna Judd, among others. She also continued to sing on sessions. One of these was a session for Sting. Producer Hugh Padgham was so impressed by Crow, he urged A&M to sign her. He then produced an album with her that Crow felt was far too slick. She asked A&M to shelve it, and went to work with producer Bruce Bottrell and a variety of her L.A. studio scene cronies. They eventually came up with *Tuesday Night Music Club*. The first single, "Leaving Las Vegas" did well on rock radio, but made few inroads into pop. The second single, "All I Wanna Do" (based on a poem) became the surprise hit of the summer of 1994, spending six weeks at #2 and going gold. Crow followed this with the #5 "Strong Enough" and "Can't Cry Anymore," which topped out at #26. Suddenly, people were discovering the *Tuesday Night Music Club* and it rose to #8, eventually going septuple platinum. She won three Grammy Awards that year: Record of the Year and Best Pop Performance, Female for "All I Wanna Do," and Best New Artist.

Crow's next album, an eponymous sophomore effort, continued the climb. It entered the charts at its peak of #6, producing the #10 single "If It Makes You Happy." This was followed by "Everyday Is a Winding Road," which topped out at #11. The album went triple platinum and earned her Grammy Awards for Best Female Rock Vocal and Best Rock Album.

Crow moved to N.Y. and took up professional residence in the Globe Recording studios. The product of this work was 1998's *The Globe Sessions* which entered the charts at #5, almost immediately going platinum. The hits, however, were farther apart. "My Favorite Mistake" topped out at #20. The follow-up, "Anything But Down," peaked at a distressingly low #49. She still won Best Rock Album, Female, at the 1998 Grammies. Crow continued to tour, including making appearances with the 1998 and 1999 versions of Lillith Fair.

Even if her records never sell like *Tuesday Night Music Club* again, Crow has demonstrated appealing taste in her music. She also embarked on a new offshoot of her career, producing songs for one of her musical heroines, Stevie Nicks.

DISC.: *Sheryl Crow* (1992); *Tuesday Night Music Club* (1993); *Sheryl Crow* (1996); *The Globe Sessions* (1998).—**HB**

Crowell, Rodney, the first of the new wave of country-rock singer- songwriter-guitarists to emerge in the 1980s, gained his earliest recognition as leader of Emmylou Harris's Hot Band in the late 1970s; b. Houston, Tex., Aug. 7, 1950.

Recognized as a songwriter and producer by the early 1980s, Crowell utilized both rock and country instrumentation and arrangements on his own recordings of songs either joyously amusing or profoundly honest, insightful, and emotive. He inspired country-style singer-songwriter-guitarists such as Jimmie Dale Gilmore and Robert Earl Keen, advanced the careers of others such as Guy Clark, produced much of the best work of his then-wife Rosanne Cash, and eventually broke through in the country field with 1988's *Diamonds and Dirt*.

Rodney Crowell began playing in his father's weekend honky-tonk band around age 11. In 1972 he moved to Nashville, where he met songwriters Guy Clark, Townes Van Zandt, and Steve Young. In 1974 Crowell moved to Los Angeles to join Emmylou Harris's Hot Band with electric guitarist James Burton (and later Albert Lee), pedal steel guitarist Hank DeVito, pianist Glen D. Hardin, and bassist Emory Gordy. He toured and recorded with Harris through 1977, contributing compositions such as "'Til I Gain Control Again," "Tulsa Queen," "Leaving Louisiana in the Broad Daylight," "I Ain't Living Long Like This," "Even Cowgirls Get the Blues," and "Amarillo" (cowritten with Harris). During the late 1970s Jerry Jeff Walker recorded his "Song for the Life" and Bobby Bare recorded his "On a Real Good Night." Crowell also produced albums by Bare and Guy Clark. In 1977 he met singer Rosanne Cash; he married her two years later. The two worked together on Cash's solo albums (and recorded a number of duets) through much of the 1980s.

Rodney Crowell's 1978 debut album for Warner Bros. contained a number of these songs, but other artists made hits out of them: The Oak Ridge Boys and Waylon Jennings scored top country hits with "Leaving Louisiana in the Broad Daylight" and "I Ain't Living Long Like This," respectively, and the Nitty Gritty Dirt Band scored a major pop hit with "American Dream," all in 1980. Crowell garnered a cult following with *But What Will the Neighbors Think*, which included his "It's Only Rock 'n' Roll," "On a Real Good Night," and "Ashes by Now" (a moderate pop hit), plus Guy Clark's "Heartbroke" and Hank DeVito's "Queen of Hearts." *Rodney Crowell*, from 1981, featured his "Stars on the Water," "Victim or a Fool,"" 'Til I Gain Control Again," and "Shame on the Moon." In 1983 Bob Seger scored a major country and smash pop hit with "Shame on the Moon," but Crowell's next album was rejected by

Warner Bros.

Crowell switched to Columbia for *Street Language*, which yielded the minor country hits "When I'm Free Again," "She Loves the Jerk," and "Looking for You." Finally, in 1988 he was established as a country recording artist with *Diamonds and Dirt*, which produced five hit singles, including the top country hits "It's Such a Small World" (in duet with Rosanne Cash), "I Couldn't Leave You If I Tried," "She's Crazy for Leaving" (cowritten with Guy Clark), and "After All This Time." Still, Crowell remained primarily a fringe figure in country music, with a more eccentric, personal outlook than the hunks in hats who dominated the charts. *Keys to the Highway* featured "Soul Searchin'," "The Faith Is Mine," and "Tell Me the Truth" and was followed in 1992 with *Life Is Messy*, which reflected the breakup of his marriage to Rosanne Cash. He left Columbia in 1994 and has since issued an album on MCA.

DISC.: RODNEY CROWELL: *Ain't Living Long Like* (1978); *But What Will the Neighbors Think* (1980); *R. C.* (1981); *The R. C. Collection* (1989); *Street Language* (1986); *Diamonds and Dirt* (1988); *Keys to the Highway* (1990); *Life Is Messy* (1992); *Greatest Hits* (1993); *Jewel of the South* (1995).—**BH**

Crozier, Catharine, esteemed American organist and pedagogue; b. Hobart, Okla., Jan. 18, 1914. She was educated at the Eastman School of Music in Rochester, N.Y. (B.M., 1936; artist's diploma, 1938; M.M., 1941), numbering among her mentors Joseph Bonnet, Yella Pessl, and **Harold Gleason**, to whom she was later married. In 1941 she made her formal debut at the Washington (D.C.) National Cathedral. After World War II, she pursued an international career as a concert organist. She taught organ (1938–55) and was head of the organ dept. (1953–55) at the Eastman School of Music; then served as prof. of organ at Rollins Coll. in Winter Park, Fla. (1955–69). She maintained an exhaustive repertory, which she fully committed to memory. She particularly championed the cause of contemporary organ music.—**NS/LK/DM**

Crüger, Johann, noted German composer; b. Grossbreesen, near Guben, April 9, 1598; d. Berlin, Feb. 23, 1662. A student of divinity at Wittenberg in 1620, he had received thorough musical training at Regensburg under Paulus Homberger. He then traveled in Austria and Hungary. He spent some time in Bohemia and Saxony before settling in Berlin, where he was cantor at the Nicolaikirche from 1622 until his death. His fame rests on the composition of many fine chorales (*Jesu, meine Freude; Jesu, meine Zuversicht; Nun danket alle Gott;* et al.), which were orig. publ. in the collection *Praxis pietatis melica* (Berlin, 1644; reprinted in 45 eds. before 1736). In addition, he publ. the following collections: *Neues vollkömmliches Gesangbuch Augsburgischer Konfession...* (1640), *Geistliche Kirchenmelodeyen...* (1649), *Dr. M. Luthers wie auch andrer gottseliger christlicher Leute Geistliche Lieder und Psalmen* (1657), and *Psalmodia sacra...* (1658). He also publ the valuable theoretical works *Synopsis musica* (1630; enl. 1634), *Praecepta musicae figuralis* (1625), and *Quaestiones musicae practicae* (1650).

BIBL.: E. Langbecker, *J. C.s Choral-Melodien* (Berlin, 1835); J. Hoffmeister, *Der Kantor zu St. Nicolai: Beschreibung des Lebens von J. C.* (Berlin, 1964).—NS/LK/DM

Crumb, George (Henry Jr.), distinguished and innovative American composer; b. Charleston, W.Va., Oct. 24, 1929. He studied music at home. He began composing while in school, and had some of his pieces performed by the Charleston Sym. Orch. He took courses in composition at Mason Coll. in Charleston (B.M., 1950), pursued training at the Univ. of Ill. (M.M., 1952), and continued his studies in composition with Finney at the Univ. of Mich. (D.M.A., 1959). In 1955 he received a Fulbright fellowship for travel to Germany, where he studied with Blacher at the Berlin Hochschule für Musik. He further received grants from the Rockefeller (1964), Koussevitzky (1965), and Coolidge (1970) foundations. In 1967 he held a Guggenheim fellowship, and also was given the National Inst. of Arts and Letters Award. In 1968 he was awarded the Pulitzer Prize in Music for his *Echoes of Time and the River.* From 1959 to 1964 he taught piano and occasional classes in composition at the Univ. of Colo. in Boulder. In 1965 he joined the music dept. of the Univ. of Pa. where he was subsequently the Annenberg Prof. of the Humanities (1983–96). In his music, Crumb is a universalist. Nothing in the realm of sound is alien to him; no method of composition is unsuited to his artistic purposes; accordingly, his music can sing as sweetly as the proverbial nightingale, and it can be as rough, rude, and crude as a primitive man of the mountains. His vocal parts especially demand extraordinary skills of lungs, lips, tongue, and larynx to produce such sound effects as percussive tongue clicks, explosive shrieks, hissing, whistling, whispering, and sudden shouting of verbal irrelevancies, interspersed with portentous syllabification, disparate phonemes, and rhetorical logorrhea. In startling contrast, Crumb injects into his sonorous kaleidoscope citations from popular works, such as the middle section of Chopin's *Fantaisie- Impromptu,* Ravel's *Bolero,* or some other "objet trouvé." In his instrumentations, Crumb is no less unconventional. Among the many unusual effects to be found in his scores is an instruction to the percussion player to immerse the loudly sounding gong into a tub of water, having an electric guitar played with glass rods over the frets, or telling wind instrumentalists to blow soundlessly through their tubes. Spatial distribution also plays a role: instrumentalists and singers are assigned their reciprocal locations on the podium or in the hall. Like many composers who began their work around the middle of the 20th century, Crumb first adopted the Schoenbergian idiom, seasoned with pointillistic devices. After these preliminaries, he wrote his unmistakably individual *Madrigals,* to words by Federico García Lorca, scored for voice and instrumental groups. There followed his extraordinary *Ancient Voices of Children,* performed for the first time at a chamber music festival in Washington, D.C., on Oct. 31, 1970; the text is again by García Lorca; a female singer intones into the space under the lid of an amplified grand piano; a boy's voice responds in anguish; the accompaniment is supplied by an orch. group and an assortment of exotic percussion instruments, such as Tibetan prayer stones, Japanese temple bells, a musical saw, and a toy piano. His equally remarkable *Makrokosmos* calls for equally unusual effects; in several movements, the pianist is instructed to vocalize at specified points of time. Crumb's most grandiose creation is *Star-Child,* which calls for gargantuan forces, including a large orch., two children's choruses, and eight additional percussion players performing on all kinds of utensils, such as pot lids, and also iron chains and metal sheets, as well as ordinary drums; it had its first performance under the direction of Pierre Boulez with the N.Y. Phil. on May 5, 1977.

WORKS: Sonata for Solo Cello (1955); *Variazioni* for Orch. (1959; Cincinnati, May 8, 1965); *5 Pieces* for Piano (1962); *Night Music I* for Soprano, Piano or Celesta, and Percussion, after García García Lorca (1963; Paris, Jan. 30, 1964); *4 Nocturnes (Night Music II)* for Violin and Piano (1963; Buffalo, N.Y., Feb. 3, 1965); *Madrigals, Book I* for Soprano, Contrabass, and Vibraphone, after García Lorca (1965; Philadelphia, Feb. 18, 1966); *Madrigals, Book II* for Soprano, Flute, and Percussion, after García Lorca (1965; Washington, D.C., March 11, 1966); *11 Echoes of Autumn, 1965 (Echoes I)* for Violin, Alto Flute, Clarinet, and Piano (Brunswick, Maine, Aug. 10, 1966); *Echoes of Time and the River (Echoes II: four Processionals)* for Orch. (Chicago, May 26, 1967); *Songs, Drones, and Refrains of Death* for Baritone, Electric Guitar, Electric Contrabass, Amplified Piano (and Amplified Harpsichord), and two Percussionists, after García Lorca (1968; Iowa City, Iowa, March 29, 1969); *Madrigals, Book III* for Soprano, Harp, and 1 Percussion Player, after García Lorca (1969; Seattle, March 6, 1970); *Madrigals, Book IV* for Soprano, Flute, Harp, Contrabass, and Percussion, after García Lorca (1969; Seattle, March 6, 1970); *Night of the Four Moons* for Alto, Alto Flute, Banjo, Electric Cello, and Percussion, after García Lorca (Washington, Pa., Nov. 6, 1969); *Black Angels (13 Images from the Dark Land: Images I)* for Electric String Quartet (Ann Arbor, Oct. 23, 1970); *Ancient Voices of Children* for Soprano, Boy Soprano, Oboe, Mandolin, Harp, Electric Piano (and Toy Piano), and three Percussionists, after García Lorca (Washington, D.C., Oct. 31, 1970); *Lux aeterna* for five Masked Players for Soprano, Bass Flute (and Soprano Recorder), Sitar, and two Percussionists (1971; Richmond, Va., Jan. 16, 1972); *Vox balaenae (Voice of the Whale)* for three Masked Players for Electric Flute, Electric Cello, and Amplified Piano (1971; Washington, D.C., March 17, 1972); *Makrokosmos, Vol. I (12 Fantasy- Pieces after the Zodiac)* for Amplified Piano (1972; Colorado Springs, Feb. 8, 1973); *Makrokosmos, Vol. II (12 Fantasy-Pieces after the Zodiac)* for Amplified Piano (1973; N.Y., Nov. 12, 1974); *Music for a Summer Evening (Makrokosmos III)* for two Amplified Pianos and two Percussionists (Swarthmore, Pa., March 30, 1974); *Dream Sequence (Images II)* for Violin, Cello, Piano, Percussion, and 2 Offstage Musicians playing Glass Harmonica (1976); *Star-Child,* parable for Soprano, Antiphonal Children's Voices, Men's Speaking Chorus, Bell Ringers, and Large Orch., demanding the coordinating abilities of four conductors (N.Y., May 5, 1977, under the general direction of Pierre Boulez); *Celestial Mechanics (Makrokosmos IV),* cosmic dances for Amplified Piano, 4-Hands (N.Y., Nov. 18, 1979); *Apparition,* elegiac songs and vocalises for Soprano and Amplified Piano, after Walt Whitman (1979; N.Y., Jan. 13, 1981); *A Little Suite for Christmas, A.D. 1979* for Piano (Washington, D.C., Dec. 14, 1980); *Gnomic Variations* for Piano (1981); *Pastoral Drone* for Organ (1982); *Processional* for Piano (1983); *A Haunted Landscape* for Orch. (N.Y., June 7, 1984); *The Sleeper* for Mezzo-soprano and Piano, after Poe (N.Y., Dec. 4, 1984); *An Idyll for the Misbegotten* for Amplified Flute and three

Percussionists (1985; Toronto, Nov. 16, 1986); *Federico's Little Songs for Children* for Soprano, Flute, and Percussion, after García Lorca (1986; Philadelphia, June 12, 1988); *Zeitgeist* for two Amplified Pianos (1987; Duisburg, Jan. 17, 1988); *Quest* for Guitar, Soprano Saxophone, 2 Percussion, Harp, and Contrabass (1990; rev. version, Vienna, Oct. 31, 1994); *Easter Dawning* for Carillon (1991; Dayton, Ohio, June 12, 1992); *Mundus Canis: 5 Humoresques* for Guitar and Percussion (1998).

BIBL.: D. Cope, *G. C.: A Biography* (N.Y., 1984; with annotated list of works compiled by D. Gillespie); D. Gillespie, ed., *G. C.: Profile of a Composer* (N.Y., 1986).—NS/LK/DM

Crumbley, Elmer (E.), jazz trombonist, singer; b. Kingfisher, Okla., Aug. 1, 1908; d. Brooklyn, N.Y., Sept. 17, 1993. Brother George was a trumpeter. Family moved to Denver, Colo., in 1910, then to Omaha, Nebr., in 1915. He joined Lloyd Hunter in 1923, and worked with him until 1929, except six months in 1927 with the Dandie Dixie Minstrels. Crumbley worked with various leaders in Kansas City, Omaha, and Lincoln, Nebr., through late 1931, and then rejoined Hunter until September 1932. He worked with various other leaders in the area, and then led his own band in 1934. He joined Jimmie Lunceford in December 1934 and, except for short periods of absence, remained until the leader's death in 1947; subsequently worked with Eddie Wilcox Band. Crumbley was with Lucky Millinder during the early 1950s, then played in Erskine Hawkins' Band. He went to Europe in October 1958 with Sammy Price and then worked with Reuben Phillips Band at Apollo during late 1950s and early 1960s. He continued to play regularly through mid-1960s, including with big bands specially re-formed by Cab Calloway and Earl Hines.—JC/LP

Crusell, Bernhard Henrik, noted Finnish clarinetist and composer; b. Uusikaupunki, near Turku, Oct. 15, 1775; d. Stockholm, July 28, 1838. He took clarinet lessons from a member of the military band at Svaeborg Castle, then moved to Stockholm in 1791, where he studied with Abbé Vogler. While improving his general knowledge of music, Crusell continued to play the clarinet. In 1798 he went to Berlin to study with Franz Tausch. In 1803 he went to Paris, where he studied composition with Berton and Gossec. In his instrumental music, Crusell followed the tradition of Gluck. His vocal works reveal Nordic traits. In Sweden he acted as translator of opera librettos for Stockholm productions. The Swedish Academy awarded him its gold medal shortly before his death.

WORKS: ORCH.: three clarinet concertos (1811, 1818, 1828); Concertante for Horn, Bassoon, Clarinet, and Orch. (1816); *Introduction et air suedois* for Clarinet and Orch. (1830); Concertino for Bassoon and Orch. **CHAMBER:** three quartets for Clarinet and Strings (1811, 1817, 1823); three clarinet duos (1821); *Divertimento* for Oboe and Strings (1823). **VOCAL:** 37 songs for Chorus; *Den lilla slavinnan* (The Little Slave Girl; Stockholm, Feb. 18, 1824).—NS/LK/DM

Cruvelli, Sofia (real name, **Johanne Sophie Charlotte Crüwell**), esteemed German soprano; b. Bielefeld, Aug. 29, 1824; d. Nice, Nov. 6, 1907. She studied in Paris with Piermarini, and completed her training with Bordogni and Lamperti. In 1847 she made her operatic debut in Venice as Odabella in Verdi's *Attila*, and then appeared as Elvira and Abigaille at Her Majesty's Theatre in London in 1848. After singing in Milan (1850), she sang at the Théâtre-Italien in Paris (1851–53), where she appeared as Elvira, Norma, Semiramide, and Leonore. In 1854 she sang Donna Anna, Leonore, and Rossini's Desdemona at London's Covent Garden, and that same year she joined the Paris Opéra, where she was notably successful as Valentine, Rachel, Giulia, and Hélène in Verdi's *Les Vêspres siciliennes*, which role she created on June 13, 1855. Upon her marriage to Comte Vigier in 1856, she retired from the operatic stage. Her sister was Friederike Marie Crüwell (1824–68), a mezzo-soprano who studied with Roger and then pursued her career in France and Italy.—NS/LK/DM

Cruz, Celia, Cuban salsa singer; b. Havana, Cuba, Oct. 21, 1924. Considered by many to be the "Queen of Salsa," she is a feminine icon in a notoriously macho field. She has been performing for well over four decades, but her voice transcends matters of age, however, and while not quite as flexible in the 1990s as it was during her artistic heyday in the early 1950s, Cruz has proven that she still carries surprising power in her singing.

In 1950 she became the lead singer for Sonora Matancera, one of the leading Cuban orchestras of the time. This was the start of her "classic" period, when she was cementing her reputation as the most popular female singer in Cuba. Her recordings from the period she spent with Sonora Matancera (until 1965) were originally released through Seeco Records and some have been reissued through Palladium and PolyGram Latino. It was also during this time that Cruz and the band left Cuba for a tour that never made it back to their homeland, applying for residency in the United States when they were able to secure a long-term gig at the Hollywood Palladium. Cruz had a commercial downturn from the mid-1960s through the early 1970s as the Latin audience turned to newer Latin styles like bugálu.

By the mid-1970s she was making the climb back into popularity with a performance at Carnegie Hall in 1973, and a series of releases with Johnny Pacheco that were big sellers within the Hispanic community. By the late 1980s, her role as "Queen of Salsa" was the real deal. She received an honorary doctorate degree in music from Yale in 1989 and her album with Ray Barretto (*Ritmo en el Corazón*) won a Grammy Award in 1990, the same year her star appeared on the Hollywood Walk of Fame. She has also made cinematic appearances in the movies the *Mambo Kings Play Songs of Love* and *The Perez Family*. Cruz's later albums on RMM still carry some Latin-jazz punch but, in general, they target salsa fans.

DISC.: *Ritmon en el Corazón* (1988); *La Dinamica Celia Cruz* (1991); *Canciones Premiadas* (1994); *Irrepetible* (1994); *Homenaje a los Santos* (1994); *The Best of Celia Cruz* (1994); *Las Guaracheras de la Guaracha* (1994); *Mi Llaman la Reina (They Call Me the Queen)* (1996).—GM

Cruz-Romo, Gilda, Mexican soprano; b. Guadalajara, Feb. 12, 1940. She studied at the Cons. of Mexico, making her debut there in 1962. On May 8, 1970, she appeared at the Metropolitan Opera in N.Y. as Maddalena in *Andrea Chénier*; continued to sing there in subsequent seasons; also sang in Chicago, Houston, and Dallas. In Europe, she appeared in London, Milan, Moscow, Paris, and Vienna. Her large repertory included both Verdi Leonoras, Violetta, Amelia, Aida, Elisabeth de Valois, Cherubini's Medea, Donna Anna, Cio-Cio-San, Manon, Suor Angelica, and Tosca. —NS/LK/DM

Crzellitzer, Franz, German-born Israeli composer; b. Berlin- Charlottenburg, Nov. 1, 1905; d. Tel Aviv, Jan. 27, 1979. In 1934 he settled in Tel Aviv.

WORKS: DRAMATIC: B a l l e t - p a n t o m i m e: *The Pied Piper of Hamelin* (1944–46). ORCH.: *Charaktermarsch* (1939); two unnumbered syms. (1940–41; 1968–70); *Improvisation* (1951); *3 Suites* for Strings (1952; 1968–74; 1974); *2 Symphonic Fantasies* (1958, 1959); *Fantasy* for Violin and Orch. (1960); *Fantasy* for Cello and Orch. (1962); Concerto for two Pianos and Orch. (1966); Trumpet Concerto (1967); Viola Concerto (1967); *Capriccio* for Piano and Chamber Orch. (1970); Concertino for Clarinet and Strings (1971); *Concert Piece* for Trombone and Orch. (1971); Sinfonietta (1972); *Concert Piece* for Horn, Clarinet, and Strings (1972); *Die Wüste* (1974); Concertino for Bassoon and Strings (1975); Concertino for Flute and Strings (1975); Concertino for Violin and Strings (1976); *Concert Piece* for Organ and Orch. (1976); *Concert Piece* (1977). CHAMBER: 2 violin sonatas (1948); Piano Quintet (1949); two string quartets (1954, 1963); Oboe Quartet (1955); Wind Quintet (1966); two piano trios (1968, 1971); Cello Sonata (1971); Flute Sonata (1972); Trio for Horn, Violin, and Piano (1973); Viola Sonata (1974); Brass Quintet (1975). KEYBOARD: P i a n o: *5 Preludes* (1947); *7 Preludes* (1968–69); *Theme and Variations* (1973); *Toccata and two Études* (1976). O r g a n: *Passacaglia* (1972).—NS/LK/DM

Ctesibius or **Ktesibios,** known as **Ctesibius of Alexandria,** Greek physicist and inventor who flourished c.270 B.C. He was celebrated as an inventor of mechanical devices which performed by air or water pressure. He is the reputed inventor of the hydraulis, the organ of antiquity which comprised a keyboard device, pipes, and a wind mechanism activated by water to regulate the air pressure.—NS/LK/DM

Cuberli, Lella (Alice), American soprano; b. Austin, Tex., Sept. 29, 1945. She was educated at Southern Methodist Univ. (B.Mus., 1974). In 1975 she made her operatic debut as Violetta in Budapest. Following her first appearance at Milan's La Scala as Mozart's Constanze in 1978, she sang there frequently in later years. She also toured with the company to the Edinburgh Festival in 1982 in Handel's *Ariodante*. In 1985 she made her debut as a soloist at the Berlin Festival. She sang Mozart's Countess at her first appearance at the Salzburg Festival in 1986. After an engagement as Violetta in Brussels in 1987, she made her debut at the Vienna State Opera in 1988 in *Il viaggio a Reims*. On Nov. 30, 1990, she made her Metropolitan Opera debut in N.Y. as Rossini's Semiramis. She sang Antonia in *Les Contes d'Hoffmann* at the Opéra de la Bastille in Paris in 1992, and that same year appeared as Mozart's Countess with the Royal Opera, Covent Garden, London, on the company's visit to Japan. In 1996 she was engaged as Donna Anna at the Salzburg Festival. As a concert artist, she sang with many major orchs.—NS/LK/DM

Cuclin, Dimitrie, Romanian composer and pedagogue; b. Galaţi, April 5, 1885; d. Bucharest, Feb. 7, 1978. He studied with Kiriac, Castaldi, and Dinicu at the Bucharest Cons. (1904–07), and then in Paris at the Cons. and at the Schola Cantorum with Widor and d'Indy (1908–14). After teaching at the Brooklyn Coll. of Music (1922–30), he returned to his homeland to serve as a prof. at the Bucharest Cons. (1930–48). His prolific output reflected the influence of the French and German Romantic tradition.

WORKS: DRAMATIC: O p e r a: *Soria* (1910–11); *Traian şi Dochia* (1921); *Agamemnon* (1922); *Bellérophon* (1925); *Meleagridele* (1958). B a l l e t: *Tragedie în pădure* (1962). ORCH.: 20 syms. (1910–32; 1938; 1942; 1944; 1947; 1948; 1948; 1948; 1949; 1949; 1950; 1951; 1951; 1952; 1954; 1959; 1965; 1967; 1971; 1972); *Triptic* (1928); *Suite Miscellanea* (1932); Piano Concerto (1939); *Rapsodie prahoveană* (1944); *Dansuri româneşti* (1961); Clarinet Concerto (1968). CHAMBER: three string quartets (1913, 1948, 1949); Violin Sonata (1923); Trio for Piano, Violin, and Cello (1924); Sonata for Flute and Cello (1953); Trio for Clarinet, Trumpet, and Bassoon (1954); Quintet for Flute, English Horn, Piano, Trombone, and Tuba (1955); Quartet for two Violins, Viola, and Clarinet (1955); Trio for Harp, Cello, and Double Bass (1955); various suites; five piano sonatas (1909–57). VOCAL: *David şi Goliath*, oratorio (1928); *Cetatea-i pe stîncă*, cantata (1959); many songs.—NS/LK/DM

Cuellar y Altarriba, Ramón Felix, Spanish organist and composer; b. Saragossa, Sept. 20, 1777; d. Santiago de Compostela, Jan. 7, 1833. He was a chorister at the church of La Seo in Saragossa, where he received instruction from its maestro de capilla, Francisco Javier García, and whom he succeeded in that position in 1812. From 1815 he also was an honorary musician in the royal household. In 1817 he became maestro de capilla at Oviedo Cathedral, but his espousal of political liberalism forced him to flee to Madrid in 1823. He then lived in destitution until securing the position of first organist at the basilica of Santiago de Compostela in 1828. His output included many fine sacred vocal works, among them 16 masses, and several instrumental pieces.

BIBL.: J. La Puente y Vilanúa, *Biografia del presbitero Don R.F. C. y A.* (Oviedo, 1854).—LK/DM

Cuénod, Hugues (-Adhémar), notable Swiss tenor; b. Corseaux-sur-Vevey, June 26, 1902. He received training at the Ribaupierre Institut in Lausanne, at the conservatories in Geneva and Basel, and in Vienna. He commenced his career as a concert singer. In 1928 he made his stage debut in *Jonny spielt auf* in Paris, and in 1929 he sang for the first time in the U.S. in *Bitter Sweet*. From 1930 to 1933 he was active in Geneva, and then in Paris from 1934 to 1937. During the 1937–39 seasons, he made an extensive concert tour of North America. From 1940 to 1946 he taught at the Geneva Cons. In 1943 he resumed his operatic career singing in *Die Fledermaus* in Geneva. He subsequently sang at Milan's La Scala (1951), the Glyndebourne Festival (from 1954), and London's Covent Garden (1954, 1956, 1958). Cuénod pursued his career into old age, making his belated debut at the Metropolitan Opera in N.Y. as the Emperor in *Turandot* just 3 months before his 85th birthday. In his 87th year, he appeared as Monsieur Taupe in *Capricuio* at the Geneva Opera in 1989. Among his finest roles were Mozart's Basilio, the Astrologer in *The Golden Cockerel*, and Sellem in *The Rake's Progress*. He was particularly known for his championship of early music and of the French song repertory.—NS/LK/DM

Cuffee, Ed(ward Emerson), trombonist; b. Norfolk, Va., June 7, 1902; d. N.Y., Jan. 3, 1959. He was a boyhood friend of Jimmy Archey. He moved to N.Y. in the mid-1920s; shortly afterwards he became a regular on Clarence Williams's recording sessions. He worked with pianist LeRoy Tibbs at Connie's Inn in 1929, then worked with Bingie Madison before working with McKinney's Cotton Pickers (1930–34). During this period Cuffee worked briefly in Ellsworth Reynolds–Kaiser Marshall Bostonians. He was with Fletcher Henderson (1936–39) and gigged in N.Y. before joining Leon Abbey (1940). He joined Count Basie in January 1941, left seven months later, worked occasionally with Leon Abbey, and then regularly in the Chris Columbus Band in 1944. He gigged and recorded with Bunk Johnson in late 1947 but left full-time music to work as an electrician, although he continued gigging in the 1950s. Ed Cuffee's name was once printed as Cuffee Davidson. The error snowballed and for over 30 years he has been mistakenly referred to by this name.—JC/LP

Cui, César (Antonovich), Russian composer; b. Vilnius, Jan. 18, 1835; d. Petrograd, March 26, 1918. He was the son of a soldier in Napoleon's army who remained in Russia, married a Lithuanian noblewoman, and settled as a teacher of French in Vilnius. Cui learned musical notation by copying Chopin's mazurkas and various Italian operas, then tried his hand at composition on his own. In 1849 he took lessons with Moniuszko in Vilnius. In 1850 he went to St. Petersburg, where he entered the Engineering School in 1851 and later the Academy of Military Engineering (1855). After graduation in 1857, he became a topographer and later an expert in fortification. He participated in the Russo-Turkish War of 1877; in 1878 he became a prof. at the Engineering School and was tutor in military fortification to Czar Nicholas II. In 1856 Cui met Balakirev, who helped him master the technique of composition. In 1858 he married Malvina Bamberg; for her he wrote a scherzo on the theme *BABEG* (for the letters in her name) and *CC* (his own initials). In 1864 he began writing music criticism in the St. Petersburg *Vedomosti* and later in other newspapers, continuing as music critic until 1900. Cui's musical tastes were conditioned by his early admiration for Schumann. He opposed Wagner, against whom he wrote vitriolic articles, and he attacked Strauss and Reger with even greater violence. He was an ardent propagandist of Glinka and the Russian national school, but was somewhat critical toward Tchaikovsky. He publ. the first comprehensive book on Russian music, *Musique en Russie* (Paris, 1880). Cui was grouped with Rimsky-Korsakov, Mussorgsky, Borodin, and Balakirev as one of the "Moguchaya Kuchka" (Mighty 5); the adjective in his case, however, is not very appropriate, for his music lacks grandeur. He was at his best in delicate miniatures, e.g., *Orientale*, from the suite *Kaleidoscope*, op.50. Editions of his selected articles were publ. in Petrograd (1918) and Leningrad (1952), and of his selected letters in Leningrad (1955).

WORKS: DRAMATIC: O p e r a : *Kavkazskiy plennik* (The Prisoner of the Caucasus; 1857–58, 1881–82; St. Petersburg, Feb. 16, 1883); *Sïn mandarina* (The Mandarin's Son), comic opera (1859; St. Petersburg, Dec. 19, 1878); *William Ratcliff* (1861–68; St. Petersburg, Feb. 26, 1869); *Angelo* (1871–75; St. Petersburg, Feb. 13, 1876; rev. version, Moscow, Jan. 17, 1901); *Mlada*, opera-ballet (1872; concert perf., Petrograd, Feb. 1917; in collaboration with Borodin, Minkus, Mussorgsky, and Rimsky-Korsakov); *Le flibuestier* (1888–89; Paris, Jan. 22, 1894); *Pir vo vremya chumï* (A Feast in Time of Plague; 1895–97, 1900; Moscow, Nov. 24, 1901). *Saratsïn* (The Saracen; 1896–98; St. Petersburg, Nov. 14, 1899); *Mademuazel Fifi* (1902–03; Moscow, Nov. 17, 1903); *Snezhnïy bogatïr* (Hero of the Snows), children's opera (Yalta, May 28, 1906); *Mateo Falcone* (Moscow, Dec. 27, 1907); *Kapitanskaya dochka* (The Captain's Daughter; 1907–09; St. Petersburg, Feb. 27, 1911); *Krasnaya shapochka* (Little Red Riding Hood), children's fairly tale opera (1911); *Kot v sapogakh* (Puss in Boots), children's fairy tale opera (1913; Tiflis, Jan. 12, 1916); *Ivanushka-durachok* (Ivanushka the Little Fool), children's fairy tale opera (1913). ORCH.: 2 scherzos (both 1857; orchestrated from piano pieces); *Tarantella* (1859); *Marche solennelle* (1881); *Suite miniature* (1882); *Deux morceaux* for Violin and Orch. (1884; also for Violin and Piano); *Suite concertante* for Violin and Orch. (1884; also for Violin and Piano); *Deux morceaux* for Cello and Orch. (1886; also for Cello and Piano); Suites Nos. two (1887), three (1890), and four (1887); *Waltz* (1904); *3 Scherzos* (1910). CHAMBER: Violin Sonata (c. 1865); *Petite suite* for Violin and Piano (1879); *12 Miniatures* for Violin and Piano (1882); *7 Miniatures* for Violin and Piano (1886); three string quartets (1890, 1907, 1913); *Kaleidoscope*, 24 pieces for Violin and Piano (1893); *Tarantelle* for Violin and Piano (1893); *6 Bagatelles* for Violin and Piano (c. 1893); *5 Little Duets* for Flute and Violin (1897); *Barcarolle* for Cello and Piano (1910); many solo piano pieces. VOCAL: Choral works; numerous songs.

BIBL.: L. Mercy-Argenteau, *C. C.: Esquisse critique* (Paris, 1888); S. Neef, *Die Russischen Fünf: Balakirew, Borodin, C., Mussorgski, Rimski-Korsakow: Monographien, Dokumente, Briefe, Programme, Werke* (Berlin, 1992).—NS/LK/DM

Culp, Julia, Dutch contralto; b. Groningen, Oct. 6, 1880; d. Amsterdam, Oct. 13, 1970. She first studied violin as a child; then became a voice pupil of Cornelia van Zanten at the Amsterdam Cons. (1897), and later of Etelka Gerster in Berlin. She made her formal debut in Magdeburg in 1901; her tours of Germany, Austria, the Netherlands, France, Spain, and Russia were highly successful, establishing her as one of the finest singers of German lieder. Her American debut took place in N.Y. on Jan. 10, 1913; for many years, she visited the U.S. every season.—NS/LK/DM

Culshaw, John (Royds), English recording producer; b. London, May 28, 1924; d. there, April 27, 1980.

He studied music while serving in the British army. From 1954 to 1967 he was manager and chief producer with the Decca Record Co.; from 1967 to 1975 he held the same post with the BBC. He was awarded the rank of Officer of the Order of the British Empire in 1966. He made a mark in the recording industry by introducing the stereo-reproduction process, which created a three-dimensional effect. His principal achievement was the stereophonic recording of *Der Ring des Nibelungen*, issued by Decca under the direction of Solti. Culshaw related the background of this undertaking in his books *Ring Resounding* (London, 1967) and *Reflections on Wagner's Ring* (London, 1976). His other publications are *Sergei Rachmaninov* (London, 1949) and *A Century of Music* (London, 1952). He also publ. an autobiography, *Odyssey of a Recording Pioneer: Putting the Record Straight* (N.Y., 1981).—**NS/LK/DM**

Culture Club, gentle, gender-bending band that topped the charts. **MEMBERSHIP:** Boy George (real name, George O'Dowd), voc. (b. London, England, June 14, 1961); Mikey Craig, bs. (b. London, England, Feb. 15, 1960); Jon Moss, drm. (b. London, England, Sept. 11, 1957); Roy Hay, gtr. (b. Essex, England, Aug. 12, 1961).

George O'Dowd seemed like a normal working-class London kid. His father managed a boxing club. George was a Boy Scout. Then, in his teens, things got twisted: George began wearing make-up and hanging out all night in clubs. He was thrown out of school at age 15 and started working in London boutiques. He became known for his wild clothes and heavy makeup. Fashion mogul and music impresario Malcolm McLaren—who assembled the Sex Pistols—thought he had just the right image for a new band he was putting together, Bow Wow Wow. George spent the next three months singing backgrounds as "Lieutenant Lush."

Sensing that music was a better way of making a living than being a fixture at the discos, George formed his own band, In Praise of Lemmings, with bass player Mikey Craig. By this time, he was known as Boy George. They added guitarist John Suede and changed their name to Sex Gang Children. They added former Adam and the Ants drummer Jon Moss, and George and Moss began a torrid affair. With the addition of Roy Hay to replace Suede, the group became Culture Club. The band recorded a set of demos that got them signed to Virgin Records in 1981. Though their first two singles didn't attract much attention, their third, a gently reggaefied confection "Do You Really Want to Hurt Me" zoomed to the top of the English charts, and went on to become an international sensation, topping the charts in 23 countries. The group's debut album *Kissing to be Clever* followed soon after.

The album came out in the U.S., along with "Do You Really Want to Hurt Me," which reached #2 on the charts. "Time (Clock of the Heart)" soon followed and also rose to #2. When "I'll Tumble 4 Ya" came in at #9, Culture Club became the first band since the Beatles to have three Top Ten singles from a debut record. The album peaked at #14 and went platinum. When the band won the Grammy Award that year for best new Artist, George accepted it, saying, "You sure know a

good drag queen when you see one."

In the U.S., the group led off their next album *Colour by Numbers* with the infectious "Karma Chameleon." The single topped the charts and sold platinum. The album produced three more hit singles, reached #2 on the charts, and sold quadruple platinum.

Things started to fall apart after that, but slowly, as O'Dowd's and Moss's affection for each other wavered. Their 1984 album *Waking Up with the House On Fire* did well in England, but only reached #26 in the U.S., although the band still had some momentum. In the U.S., the album sold platinum and produced three lesser hits. However, the freshness of the group had expired. The band took a break in 1985, during which time George started experimenting with heroin. When they went back into action in the winter of 1986, they created *From Luxury to Heartache*. The single "Move Away" managed to hit #12, but the album didn't even make the gold mark. That summer George was arrested for possession of drugs. Then the keyboard player from the album was found dead of an overdose in George's home. The band broke up and George released his first solo project, *Sold*. While his reggae version of Bread's "Everything I Own" topped the English charts, the album didn't even chart in the U.S., although one single, "Live My Life" did hit #40 on the charts. His next album, 1988's *Tense Nervous Headache*, didn't chart on either side of the Atlantic.

In 1989, George started working with the band Jesus Loves You, which released one album, *The Martyr Mantra*. Again, it failed to chart in the U.S. Culture Club came back together briefly in 1990, but the work offered nothing new, so George bailed out. He made a slight comeback in 1992 with the theme music of the film *The Crying Game*. His version of the song peaked at #15. However, his next release, 1995's *Cheapness and Beauty*, failed to chart in the U.S., despite its cross marketing with the concurrent release of George's autobiography *Take It Like a Man*. By this time, George had become quite outspoken about his homosexuality, and the songs on the album were all couched in homoerotic terms.

George kept busy, nonetheless, running his More Protein record company, deejaying, and writing a column for a London newspaper. In 1998, VH–1 profiled Culture Club in their *Behind the Music* series. They then asked the band to regroup for an episode of their show *Storytellers*. The band got back together, and even wrote a couple of new songs. In 1998, they put out a greatest hits record with a bonus disc of the *Storytellers* performances. However, the album stiffed. The subsequent tour that put them on the road with The Human League and Howard Jones played to half-empty houses. It seemed that the world had just lost interest.

WRITINGS: *Take It Like a Man* (N.Y., 1995).

DISC.: *Kissing to Be Clever* (1982); *Colour by Numbers* (1983); *Waking Up with the House on Fire* (1984); *From Luxury to Heartache* (1986). **BOY GEORGE:** *Sold* (1987); *Tense Nervous Headache* (1988); *Cheapness and Beauty* (1995). **JESUS LOVES YOU (WITH BOY GEORGE):** *The Martyr Mantra* (1991). —**HB**

Culver, (David) Andrew, inventive American-Canadian composer, instrument maker, and performer; b. Morristown, N.J., Aug. 30, 1953. He studied composition with John Rea and Bengt Hambraeus, electronic music with Alcides Lanza, and sound recording with Wieslaw Woczcyk at McGill Univ. in Montreal (B.M., 1977; M.M., 1980). He subsequently was a founding member of SONDE, a Canadian music design and performance ensemble. He pioneered the musical application of R. Buckminster Fuller's tensegrity structural principle, devising richly resonant music sculptures that vibrate synergistically. His output of more than 60 works takes four forms: stage performances by music sculpture ensemble, interactive music sculpture installations, computer-displayed text and electroacoustic music projections, and scores for traditional instruments. His solo stage works include *Viti* (1981) and *Music with Tensegrity Sound Source #5* (1983), which he has performed in Europe, Canada, and the U.S.; his *Hard Lake Frozen Moon* (1989), for two performers active in an elaborate stage environment built up of 19 sound sources, was commissioned by Toronto's New Music Concerts and the Laidlaw Foundation. His *Quasicrystals...* (1989), developed with pianist Thomas Moore at the Yellow Springs Inst. for Contemporary Studies and the Arts, is a work for two performers on separate and complex itineraries within a field of 21 amplified, hanging music sculptures. Chance-composed lighting is an essential, determining element of these and other works. Culver has also created public installations of interactive music sculptures, including those at the Staten Island Children's Museum (1983) and the Children's Museum of Manhattan (1989–91). From 1984 to 1992, Culver worked with John Cage, developing computer programs toward the realization of Cage's musical and poetic processes. His programs ic and tic, computer simulations of the coin oracle of the *I Ching*, were used in all aspects of the composition and direction of Cage's *Europeras 1 & 2* (1987). He composed *Ocean 1–95* for 112 Instrumental Soloists (1993) for the posthumous realization of Cage's final collaboration with Merce Cunningham, *Ocean*.—NS/LK/DM

Cummings, Conrad, American composer and teacher; b. San Francisco, Feb. 10, 1948. He studied with Bulent Arel at Yale Univ., took courses at the State Univ. of N.Y. at Stony Brook, was a student of Davidovsky and Ussachevsky at Columbia Univ., attended the Berkshire Music Center at Tanglewood, and pursued training at Stanford Univ. After teaching at the Columbia-Princeton Electronic Music Center (1974–76), he was electronic music coordinator at Brooklyn Coll. of the City Univ. of N.Y. (1976–79). From 1980 he taught at the Oberlin Coll.-Cons. of Music. His dramatic works include *Eros and Psyche* (Oberlin, Nov. 16, 1983), *Cassandra* (1984–85; rev. 1986), *Positions 1956* (N.Y., March 11, 1988), *Insertions* (N.Y., March 18, 1988), *Photo-Op* (N.Y., May 19, 1989), and *Tonkin* (Wilmington, Nov. 27, 1993). He also wrote orch. works, chamber music, and vocal pieces.—NS/LK/DM

Cummings, David (Michael), intrepid English music lexicographer; b. London, Oct. 10, 1942. After taking his B.Ed. degree at Sidney Webb Coll. in London (1975), he entered the mundane profession of British schoolteacher. His passion for music and its elucidation led him to wade perilously in the backwaters of musicography with the ineluctable mission to correct the errors of his predecessors and contemporaries. From 1980 he served as an advisor and contributor to various standard music reference works, and also wrote articles and reviews for music journals. He was ed. of *The New Everyman Dictionary of Music* (6th ed., 1988; new ed., rev., 1995 as *The Hutchinson Encyclopedia of Music*). With D. McIntire, he was co-consultant ed. of the *International Who's Who in Music* (12th ed., 1990), and subsequently served as its ed. (14th to 17th eds., 1992–2000). —NS/LK/DM

Cummings, W(illiam) H(ayman), English tenor and music antiquarian; b. Sidbury, Devonshire, Aug. 22, 1831; d. London, June 6, 1915. He was a chorister in London at St. Paul's and at the Temple Church, organist of Waltham Abbey (1847), tenor in the Temple, Westminster Abbey, and Chapel Royal, and a prof. of singing at the Royal Academy of Music (1879–96). From 1882 to 1888 he was conductor of the Sacred Harmonic Soc., then precentor of St. Anne's, Soho (1886–98) and principal of the Guildhall School of Music (1896–1910). He received an honorary degree of Mus.D. from Trinity Coll. in Dublin (1900). He was a cultivated singer and a learned antiquarian, and also instrumental in founding the Purcell Soc. He edited its first publications. He was the author of a biography of Purcell (London, 1882; 2nd ed., 1911); also publ. *Primer of the Rudiments of Music* (1877) and *Biographical Dictionary of Musicians* (1892). His library of 4,500 vols. contained many rare autographs. He composed a cantata, *The Fairy Ring* (1873), sacred music, glees, part-songs, et al., and adapted the tune of the second number of Mendelssohn's *Festgesang* to the hymn *Hark the Herald Angels Sing*, publishing in 1856 his version, which became universally popular.—NS/LK/DM

Cunningham, Arthur, black American composer; b. Piermont, N.Y., Nov. 11, 1928. He commenced piano studies at the age of six and was composing for his own jazz group when he was 12; he later received formal training at Fisk Univ. (B.A., 1951), Columbia Univ. Teachers Coll. (M.A., 1957), and the Juilliard School of Music. In addition to composing, he was active as a teacher and conductor. His output runs the gamut of styles and techniques, ranging from serious to rock.

WORKS: *Adagio* for Oboe and Strings (1954); *Night Lights* for Orch. (1955); *Lights across the Hudson*, tone poem (1956); *The Beauty Part*, musical (1963); *Violetta*, musical (1963); *Dialogues* for Piano and Chamber Orch. (1966); *Ballet* for String Quartet and Jazz Quartet (1968); *His Natural Grace*, rock opera (1969); *Harlem Suite*, ballet (1971); Double-bass Concerto (1971); *The Prince* for Baritone and Orch. (1973); *Rooster Rhapsody* for Narrator and Orch. (1975); *Crispus Attucks* for Band (1976); *Night Bird* for Voice, Jazz Quintet, and Orch. (1978); also chamber pieces, piano pieces, choral part songs and suites, and songs.—NS/LK/DM

Cupido, Alberto, Italian tenor; b. Portofino, March 19, 1948. He studied at the Milan Cons. and at the Accademia Musicale Chigiana in Siena. In 1977 he made his operatic debut in Genoa as Pinkerton, and then his German debut as Rodolfo in Frankfurt am Main. He made his British debut in 1978 as Rodolfo at the Glyndebourne Festival. Following an engagement as Faust at the Bavarian State Opera in Munich in 1982, he made his U.S. debut in San Francisco in 1983. He portrayed Edgardo at his first appearance at Milan's La Scala in 1983, a role he reprised in Monte Carlo in 1987. He sang Faust in Geneva in 1988 and in Rome in 1990. Following an appearance as Faust at the Lyric Opera in Chicago in 1991, he portrayed Cavaradossi at London's Covent Garden in 1993. In 1995 he sang Reyer's Sigurd in Marseilles, and then appeared as Rodolfo in Genoa in 1996.—NS/LK/DM

Cura, José, Argentine tenor, conductor, and composer; b. Rosario, Dec. 5, 1962. He began to take lessons in voice and guitar when he was 12. At 15, he made his debut as a conductor at an open-air choral concert in Rosario. After training in composition at the Univ. of Rosario and in voice at the singing school at the Teatro Colón in Buenos Aries, he pursued vocal studies with Horacio Amauri. In 1991 he went to Italy and completed his vocal training with Vittorio Terranova. On Feb. 1, 1992, he made his operatic debut as the Father in Henze's *Pollicino* in Verona. In 1993 he sang Jean in Bibalo's *Miss Julie* in Trieste and Albert Gregor in *The Makropoulos Affair* in Turin. In 1994 he won a prize in the Operalia Competition and made his U.S. debut as Loris in *Fedora* at the Lyric Opera in Chicago. In 1995 he was engaged as Paolo in Zandonai's *Francesca da Rimini* in Palermo, as Stiffelio at London's Covent Garden, and as Ismaele in *Nabucco* at the Opéra de la Bastille in Paris. He returned to Covent Garden in 1996 as Samson and as Cavaradossi, and also sang Osaka in Mascagni's *Iris* in Rome, the title role in *Il corsaro* in Turin, and Pollione in Los Angeles. In 1997 he portrayed Enzo in *La Gioconda* at Milan's La Scala, Turiddu in Bologna, and Otello and Samson in Turin. He sang Radamès in the reopening of the Teatro Massimo in Palermo in 1998, and also appeared as Des Grieux at La Scala and as Samson at the Washington (D.C.) Opera. In 1999 he appeared as both a singer and a conductor at London's Royal Festival Hall. He made his Metropolitan Opera debut in N.Y. as Turiddu on Sept. 26, 1999. Cura was engaged to sing Don Carlos in Zürich and Turiddu at Covent Garden in 2001. Among his compositions are a Requiem (1984), a Stabat Mater (1989), and various songs.—NS/LK/DM

Cure, The, doom-and-gloom gothic pop band. **MEMBERSHIP:** Robert Smith, voc., gtr. (b. Blackpool, England, April 21, 1959); Michael Dempsey, bs. (b. Salisbury, Southern Rhodesia, Nov. 29, 1958); Laurence "Lol" Tolhurst, drm. (b. Horley, England, Feb. 3, 1959); Porl Thompson, gtr. (b. Wimbledon, England, Nov. 8, 1957); Simon Gallup, bs. (b. Duxhurst, England, June 1, 1960); Mathieu Hartley, kybd. (b. Smallfield, England, Feb. 4, 1960); Boris Williams, drm. (b. Versailles, France, April 24, 1957); Roger O'Donnell, kybd. (b. Oct. 29, 1955); Perry Bamonte, gtr., kybd. (b. London, England,

Sept. 3, 1960); Jason Cooper, drm. (b. London, England, Jan. 31, 1967).

Brought up in suburban Crawley, Robert Smith started learning guitar from his older brother at the age of six. Ten years later, he formed the Easy Cure with a couple of schoolmates, including drummer Lol Tolhurst. Although they came together with a typical punk format at the tail end of the punk explosion, they took another route, creating atmospheric songs with bite, flavored by Smith's distinctive vocals. That, and his distinctive look—he wore pale make-up, bright red lipstick, and his hair looked like a pitch-black haystack—set the band way apart from their contemporaries. Smith has been described as looking like an advance man for the apocalypse, but he has an unerring way of turning pain into pop, despite being happily married to a woman he has been with since they met in drama class when they were both 13 years old.

With the erudite irony that would inform Smith's music over the next two decades, one of the group's first demos drew inspiration from Camus's existential classic *The Stranger*. Called "Killing an Arab," the song came to the attention of Chris Parry, an A&R representative for Polydor. He saw to it that the record was released, and when he left Polydor to form his own label, Fiction, in 1979 he took the band—their sobriquet shortened to The Cure—with him as his first act.

In spring 1979, the band's first album *Three Imaginary Boys* came out. It reached #44 in the U.K. After cutting a couple more singles, "Boys Don't Cry" and "Jumping Someone Else's Train," the band hit the road with Siouxsie and the Banshees. Smith found himself playing both ends of the bill, as he filled in when Banshee guitarist John McKay left the band. It began a long-standing relationship with the band.

The decidedly dark album *17 Seconds* came out in the spring of 1980. Bolstered by the single "A Forest" which landed them on the English TV show *Top of the Pops* and peaked at #31, the album rose to #20. In America, however, the Cure's records were only available as imports. Between tours, they did some soundtrack work.

Almost a year to the day after *17 Seconds* came out, the band released the even darker album, *Faith*. Building their base around fans of music now being called gothic, the album hit #14 on the U.K. charts.

Almost a year to the day after *Faith* came out, the band released *Pornography*, another salvo of gloom to darken the English spring. Regarded as one of the band's masterpieces, it reached #8. And just when people thought the band couldn't get any creepier, they unleashed the poppy, snappy, one-off single "Let's Go to Bed." While it stalled at #44, it attracted some attention in the burgeoning U.S. dance-rock clubs and among alternative radio stations. Through July 1983, the band released a spate of singles that did fairly well. "The Walk" hit #12 on the U.K. charts, and the light, jazzy tune "The Love Cats" rose to #7. All three singles were collected on the mini-album *Japanese Whispers* in December. The EP topped out at #26.

Meanwhile, Smith found himself working once more with Siouxsie and the Banshees. He recorded two albums as a spot replacement for John McGeoch, the studio album *Hyena* and the live *Nocturne*. When The Cure regrouped in 1984, Smith and Tolhurst were the only original members remaining, and Tolhurst had switched from drums to keyboards.

After two years, they once again brought a salvo of sonic storm to the English spring with *The Top*. The single, "The Caterpillar" hit #14 and the album reached #10. In the fall, they put out a live greatest hits collection that hit #26.

The Cure had achieved cult status in the U.S., but never the acclaim that was theirs at home. That began to change when they got a new U.S. distributor for 1985's *The Head on the Door*. The single "In Between Days" hit #15 on the U.K. charts that summer, and skimmed the Hot 100 in the U.S. that winter (coming in at #99) their first single to chart at all in the U.S. The album reached #7 in the U.K. and hit a respectable #59 in the U.S.

With their initial foray into American pop consciousness, the record company collected some of the band's greatest hits and released *Standing on a Beach*. The record hit #4 in the U.K. and rose to #48 in the U.S., eventually going double platinum.

With their next album, 1987's *Kiss Me, Kiss Me, Kiss Me*, the Cure sprang from cult status to a headlining act in arenas. The double album ran the gamut from pop to outright horror. "Just Like Heaven" actually hit #40 pop. The album rose to #33 in the U.S. and sold platinum. In the U.K., it spun off three more hit singles and topped out at #6.

Tolhurst, who had been with the band from the beginning, left in anger early in 1989, leaving Smith as the lone remaining original member. Tolhurst sued the group, claiming that as a founding member, he was entitled to more royalties than he was getting. That same year, the band released the downhearted *Disintegration*. The single "Love Song" rose to #2 in the U.S. charts, for the first time eclipsing their #18 success at home. They toured the U.S. extensively to promote the album. In 1990 the Cure put out one of the first dance remix albums. Called *Mixed Up*, it featured extended dance versions of all their previous U.S. hits and many of their U.K. successes.

In 1992, they put out perhaps their finest record, *Wish*. Propelled by the remarkable pop single "Friday I'm in Love," which hit #18 in the U.S. The album topped the U.K. charts, hit #2 in the U.S., and went platinum. While touring *Wish*, they recorded concerts in the U.S. and Europe. These came out as *Show* and *Paris* in fall 1993.

By this time, Smith had become Robert Smith, Esq., appearing in Debrett's peerage. The band went on hiatus for a few years after that. In 1994, the Tolhurst case came to a conclusion, with the British High Court finding in favor of Smith, the Cure, and Fiction Records. As this blew over, the group's drummer, Boris Williams, left. Smith placed an ad that read "...famous group requires drummer—no metal heads." The album in progress, *Wild Mood Swings* was completed with seven separate drummers and released in 1996. The band performed on *Saturday Night Live* and *David Letterman*.

The album debuted at its peak of #12 and went gold. Their effect on popular culture became the subtext of the film *Career Girls*.

In 1998, the band put out yet another greatest hits collection, *Galore*, which compiled 18 of the group's best-known tunes. Robert Smith threatened that he would disband the Cure on his 40th birthday, but they continue to tour and record.

DISC.: *Three Imaginary Boys* (1979); *Seventeen Seconds* (1980); *Boys Don't Cry* (1980); *...Happily Ever After* (1981); *Carnage Visors* (1981); *Faith* (1981); *Pornography* (1982); *Concert/Curiosity* (live; 1984); *The Top* (1984); *Concert: Live* (1984); *The Head on the Door* (1985); *Standing on a Beach* (1986); *Kiss Me, Kiss Me, Kiss Me* (1987); *Peel Sessions* (1988); *Disintegration* (1989); *Integration* (1990); *Mixed Up* (1990); *Entreat* (live; 1990); *Wish* (1992); *Show* (live; 1993); *Paris* (live; 1993); *Wild Mood Swings* (1996); *Galore* (1998); *Bloodflowers* (2000).—HB

Curran, Alvin, American composer and teacher; b. Providence, R.I., Dec. 13, 1938. He studied piano and trombone in his youth, later receiving training in composition from Ron Nelson at Brown Univ. (B.A., 1960) and from Carter and Powell at Yale Univ. (M.Mus., 1963). Following a year of study with Carter in Berlin on a Ford Foundation grant, he went to Rome in 1965, wher he founded the Musica Elettronica Viva ensemble for the performance of live electronic music with Richard Teitelbaum and Frederic Rzewski; the ensemble later evolved to include all manner of avant-garde performance practices. From 1975 to 1980 he taught vocal improvisation at the Accademia Nazionale d'Arte Drammatien in Rome, and in 1992 he joined the faculty of Mills Coll., becoming its Milhaus Prof. of Composition. In the 1970s he created a series of solo performances, and in the 1980s he composed numerous large-scale environments works on lakes, rivers, caverns, and public buildings. His *A Piece for Peace* (1985) uses the radio as a geographical music instrument and incorporates performances by musicians spread all over Europe; his *Crystal Psalms* (1988) and *Erat Verbum (Finale)* (1997) are Holocaust commemorations. Curran has also contributed articles on a wide variety of musical topics to primary new music journals.

WORKS: *Music for Every Occasion*, 50 monodic pieces for Any Use (1967–77); *Songs and Views from the Magnetic Garden* for Voice, Flugelhorn, Synthesizer, and Tape (1973–75); *Light Flowers, Dark Flowers* for Piano, Ocarina, Synthesizer, and Tape (1974–77); *The Works* for Voice, Piano, Synthesizer, and Tape (1977–80); *The Crossing* for four Sopranos, Chorus, seven Instruments, and Tape (1978); *Maritime Rites*, environmental concerts for Choruses in Rowboats, Ship, and Foghorns (1981); *Natural History* for Tape (1984); *Maritime Rites Satellite Music*, 10 radio concerts for the Sounds of the Eastern U.S. Seaboard and Soloists (1984–85); *Electric Rags I* for Piano and Computer-controlled Synthesizers (1985) and *II* for Saxophone Quartet and Computer Electronics (1989); *For Four or More* for Amplified String Quartet and Computer-controlled Synthesizers (1986); *Waterworks* for 22 Computer-controlled Ship Horns, Brass Bands, and Fireworks (1987); *Edible Weeds* for String Quartet, Flute, Oboe, Clarinet, Bassoon, Trombone, Electric Bass, and Keyboards (1988); *Crystal Psalms* for six Choruses, Percussion, Instrumental Ensembles, Accordions, Shofars, and Tape (1988); *Vsto for Giacinto* for String Quartet (1989); *7 Articles*

for 10 Instruments (1989); *Via Delle Terme Di C.* for Tape (1994); *Inner Cities I, II,* and *III* for Piano (1994); *Theme Park/Bang Zoom* for Solo Percussion and Percussion Quartet (1994–95); *A Beginner's Guide to Looking at Birds* for Tape (1995); *My Body in the Course of a Dream* for Chorus, after John Cage (1995–96); *Music is Not Music* for Chorus, after John Cage (1995–96); *Fault* for Tape (1996); *In Hora Mortis* for 25 Instruments (1996); *Land im Klang* for four Percussion, MIDI Grand Piano, Electric Violin, and Multiple Projections (1996); *The Twentieth Century* for MIDI Grand Piano (1996); *Footprint of War* for Chamber Ensemble (1997); *Erat Verbum (Finale)* (1997); *Everybody Dreams Their Own Music,* installation/performance piece (1997); *Endangered Species* for MIDI Grand Piano, Sampler, and Computer (1998); *Kaboom,* installation (1998; in collaboration with M. Gould).
—NS/LK/DM

Curson, Ted (actually, Theodore),

trumpeter; b. Philadelphia, Pa., July 3, 1935. After attending the Granoff school and taking private lessons with Jimmy Heath, he worked locally with John Coltrane and others. After moving to N.Y. in 1956, he worked with Mal Waldron, Red Garland, Philly Joe Jones, and Cecil Taylor. Curson says he rehearsed every day for a year with Taylor, but they were only able to get one record date and one concert. He had a chance to play with Art Blakey, but turned him down to work with Charles Mingus and Eric Dolphy, including an acclaimed quartet recording in 1960. Curson then co-led a band with Bill Barron, playing with Max Roach, Maynard Ferguson, Charlie Ventura, and his own groups. He worked frequently in Canada (1962–63), then spent most of the late 1960s and 1970s in Europe. He is less well known than he should be at home because he has spent so much time in Europe. His playing displays his natural wit and charm.

DISC.: *Plenty of Horn* (1961); *Live at La Tete de L'Art* (1962); *Fire Down Below* (1962); *Tears for Dolphy* (1964); *Flip Top* (1964); *New Thing and the Blue Thing* (1965); *Ode to Booker Ervin* (1970); *Cattin' Curson* (1973); *Ted Curson and Co.* (1976); *Jubilant Power* (1976); *'Round About Midnight* (1992).—LP

Curtin, Phyllis (née Smith),

esteemed American soprano and teacher; b. Clarksburg, W.Va., Dec. 3, 1921. She studied at Wellesley Coll. (B.A., 1943) and received vocal instruction from Olga Avierino, Joseph Regnaeas, and Goldovsky. In 1946 she made her operatic debut as Lisa in *The Queen of Spades* with the New England Opera Theatre in Boston. Her recital debut followed in 1950 at N.Y.'s Town Hall. On Oct. 22, 1953, she made her first appearance with the N.Y.C. Opera as Fräulein Burstner in Gottfried von Einem's *The Trial,* where she remained on the roster until 1960; then returned in 1962, 1964, and 1975–76. She also made appearances at the Teatro Colón in Buenos Aires (1959), the Glyndebourne Festival (1959), the Vienna State Opera (1960–61), and at La Scala in Milan (1962). On Nov. 4, 1961, she made her Metropolitan Opera debut in N.Y. as Fiordiligi, remaining on its roster for the season; she returned for the 1966–70 and 1972–73 seasons. Her tours as a soloist with orchs. and as a recitalist took her all over the globe until her retirement in 1984. She taught at the Aspen (Colo) School of Music and the Berkshire Music Center in Tanglewood. After serving as

prof. of voice at the Yale Univ. School of Music (1974–83), she was prof. of voice and dean of the school of the arts at Boston Univ. (from 1983); in 1992 she retired as its dean but continued to teach there. Curtin became well known for such roles as Mozart's Countess, Donna Anna, Rosalinde, Eva, Violetta, Alice Ford, Salome, and Ellen Orford. She also created Floyd's Susannah (1955) and Cathy in *Wuthering Heights* (1958).
—NS/LK/DM

Curtis-Smith, Curtis O(tto) B(ismarck),

American composer, pianist, and teacher; b. Walla Walla, Wash., Sept. 9, 1941. He studied piano with David Burge at Whitman (Wash.) Coll. (1960–62) and Gui Mombaerts at Northwestern Univ. (B.M., 1964; M.M., 1965), and composition with Kenneth Gaburo (1966) and Bruno Maderna (1972) at the Berkshire Music Center in Tanglewood. He taught at Western Mich. Univ. in Kalamazoo (from 1968), making concurrent appearances as a recitalist and soloist with various orchs. Among his honors are the Koussevitzky Prize (1972), the Gold Medal of the Concorso Internazionale di Musica e Danza G.B. Viotti (1975), NEA grants (1975, 1980), the Prix du Francis Salabert (1976), annual AS-CAP awards (from 1977), a Guggenheim fellowship (1978–79), an American Academy and Inst. of Arts and Letters award (1978), and Mich. Council for the Arts grants (1981, 1984). In 1972 he developed the technique of "piano bowing," heard in his *Rhapsodies* and *Unisonics,* in which a fishing line is drawn across the strings of the instrument to produce continuous single and clustered pitches. He later utilized Sub-Saharan African polyrhythms and melodies.

WORKS: ORCH.: *(Bells) Belle de Jour* for Piano and Orch. (1974–75); two syms.: No. 1, *The Great American Symphony (GAS!)* (1981) and No. 2, *African Laughter* (1996); *Songs and Cantillations* for Guitar and Orch. (1983); *Chaconne à son goût* (1984); *Celebration* (1986); *Passacaglia* (1986); *"...Float Wild Birds, Sleeping"* (1988); Concerto for Piano, Left-Hand, and Orch. (1990); *Anthem* for Piano and Strings (1996); Violin Concerto (Columbus, Ohio, March 6, 1999). CHAMBER: three string quartets (1964, 1965, 1980); *A Song of the Degrees* for two Pianos and Percussion (1972); *5 Sonorous Inventions* for Violin and Piano (1973); *Unisonics* for Alto Saxophone and Piano (1977); *Partita* for Chamber Ensemble (1977); *Ensembles/Solos* for Piano and Chamber Ensemble (1977); *Plays and Rimes* for Piano and Brass Quintet (1979); *Sundry Dances* for Winds and Brass (1979–80); *Black and Blue* for Brass Quintet (1979); two piano trios (1982, 1992); *Sardonic Sketches* for Wind Quintet (1986); *Fantasy Pieces* for Violin and Piano (1987); *5 Pieces* for Piano and Percussion (1988); Sextet for Piano and Winds (1991); *African Laughter,* sextet for Flute, Oboe, Clarinet, Violin, Viola, Cello, and Piano (1994); *Masques d'Afrique* for Organ, Trumpet, and Percussion (1997); Trio for Violin, Clarinet, and Piano (2000); pieces for solo instrument. KEYBOARD: P i a n o : *Pianacaglia* (1967); *Trajectories* (1967–68); *Piece du jour* (1971); *Rhapsodies* (1973); *Tristana Variations* (1975–76); *For Gatsby (Steinway #81281)* (1982); *Collusions* (1998; in collaboration with W. Bolcom); *12 Etudes* (2000). VOCAL: *Till Thousands Thee. Lps. A Secular Alleluia without...* for 6 Sopranos, two Trumpets, and Percussion (1969); *Passant. Un. Nous passons. Deux. De notres somme passons. Trois.* for 19 Voices, Chamber Ensemble, and Electronics (1970); *Cnticum Novum/Desideria* for six Sopranos, four Tenors, and Chamber Ensemble (1971); *Comedie* for two Sopranos and Chamber Orch. (1972); *Beastly Rhymes* for Chorus (1983–84); *Chansons innocentes* for Soprano and Piano (1987); *A Civil War Song Cycle* for Mezzo-soprano or Soprano and Piano (1987); *The Shimmer of Evil* for Baritone and Chamber Ensemble or Piano (1989); *The Mystic Trumpeter* for Baritone, Men's Chorus, Trumpet, and Organ (1991); *Gold Are My Flowers,* cantata/melodrama for Soprano, Baritone, and Chamber Group (Houston, Dec. 5, 1992).—NS/LK/DM

Curzon, Sir Clifford (Michael), eminent English pianist; b. London, May 18, 1907; d. there, Sept. 1, 1982. His father and mother were music- lovers and they encouraged their son's studies, first as a violinist, and then as a pianist. In 1919 he enrolled at the Royal Academy of Music in London, where he studied piano with Charles Reddie and Katharine Goodson; he won two scholarships and the Macfarren Gold Medal. At the age of 16, he garnered praise as a soloist in Bach's Triple Concerto at a Henry Wood Promenade Concert in London. He was only 19 when he was given a post as a teacher at the Royal Academy of Music, but he decided to continue his studies and went to Berlin (1928), where he was tutored by Schnabel, and then to Paris (1930), where he took courses with Landowska in harpsichord and with Boulanger in general music culture. In 1932 he returned to England and pursued a distinguished concert career. On Feb. 26, 1939, he made an auspicious U.S. debut in N.Y., and in subsequent years made regular concert tours in the U.S. Curzon was a scholarly virtuoso with a formidable technique. His interpretations of Mozart and Beethoven were particularly notable, but he also was praised for his congenial interpretations of works by Romantic composers, especially Schubert, Schumann, and Brahms. In 1958 he was made a Commander of the Order of the British Empire. He received the degree of D.Mus. *honoris causa* from the Univ. of Leeds in 1970. He was knighted in 1977. In 1980 he received the Gold Medal of the Royal Phil. Soc. in London. In 1931 he married **Lucille Wallace.** —NS/LK/DM

Cusins, Sir William (George), English organist, pianist, conductor, pedagogue, and composer; b. London, Oct. 14, 1833; d. Remouchamps, Ardennes, Aug. 31, 1893. He was a pupil of Fetis at the Brussels Cons. (1844), and of Bennett, Potter, Lucas, and Sainton at the Royal Academy of Music in London (1847). He took the King's Scholarship in 1847 and 1849; in the latter year he was appointed organist of the Queen's private chapel, and became a violinist in the Italian Opera orch. In 1851 he became prof. at the Royal Academy of Music; succeeded Bennett (1867–83) as conductor of the Phil. Soc., and also became conductor of the Royal Band in 1870; served as Master of the Queen's Musick from 1870 until his death. He also succeeded Bennett as examining prof. at Queen's Coll. (1875), and was a prof. at Trinity Coll. and a prof. of piano at the Guildhall School of Music (1885). He was knighted in 1892.

WORKS: *Royal Wedding Serenata* (1863); two concert overtures: *Les Travailleurs de la mer* (1869) and *Love's Labour's Lost* (1875); oratorio, *Gideon* (Gloucester Festival, 1871); Piano Concerto; Septet for Winds and Double Bass; piano pieces; songs. —NS/LK/DM

Custer, Arthur, American composer; b. Manchester, Conn., April 21, 1923. He studied engineering at the Univ. of Hartford (1940–42). After graduating in music from the Univ. of Conn. at Storrs (1949), he pursued training with Pisk at the Univ. of Redlands in Calif. (1949–51), Bezanson at the Univ. of Iowa (1952–55), and Boulanger (1960–62). He taught at Kansas Wesleyan Univ. (1952–55) and the Univ. of Omaha (1955–58); then was asst. dean of fine arts at the Univ. of R.I. (1962–65) and dean of the Philadephia Musical Academy (1965–67). After serving as director of the St. Louis Metropolitan Educational Center for the Arts (1967–70), he was director (1970–73) and composer-in-residence (1973–75) of the Arts in Education Project of the R.I. State Council on the Arts.

WORKS: Sextet for Woodwinds and Piano (1959); *Colloquy* for String Quartet (1961); *Sinfonia de Madrid* (Madrid, April 28, 1962); *Cycle* for a Heterogeneous Ensemble (1963); Concertino for 2nd Violin and Strings, in reality his String Quartet No. two (1964); *2 Movements* for Wind Quintet (1964); *Permutations* for Violin, Clarinet, and Cello (1967); Concerto for Brass Quintet (1968); *Rhapsodality Brass!* for Orch. (1969); *Interface I* for String Quartet and 2 Recording Engineers, being his String Quartet No. 3 (1969) and *II* for Ensemble, Slide Projectors, and Audience (1976); *Rhapsodality Brown!* for Piano (1969); *Parabolas* for Trombone and Percussion (1969); *Parabolas* for Viola and Piano (1969); *Doubles* for Violin and Chamber Orch. (1972; rev. 1975); *Eyepiece* for Oboe and Tape (1974); *Sweet 16* for Clarinet and Piano (1976).—NS/LK/DM

Cutler, Henry Stephen, American organist and composer; b. Boston, Oct. 13, 1824; d. there, Dec. 5, 1902. He was a pupil of George F. Root in Boston. After further training in Frankfurt am Main, he was active as a church organist in Boston, N.Y., Philadelphia, and other cities. He publ. five vols. of sacred music and composed some 20 organ pieces. His best known works are the hymns *The Son of God Goes Forth to War* and *Brightest and Best of the Sons of Morning.*—NS/LK/DM

Cuyler, Louise (Elvira), American musicologist; b. Omaha, March 14, 1905; d. Carmel-by-the-Sea, Calif., Jan. 3, 1998. She was educated at the Eastman School of Music in Rochester, N.Y. (B.M., 1929; Ph.D., 1948) and the Univ. of Mich. (M.M., 1933). With the exception of her service with the American Red Cross in the Pacific during World War II (1942–45), she was on the faculty of the Univ. of Mich. (1929–42; 1945–75). In 1975 she became the Neilson Distinguished Prof. at Smith Coll. Cuyler publ. the vols. *The Emperor Maximilian I and Music* (London, 1973) and *The Symphony* (N.Y., 1973; 2nd ed., 1995). She also contributed articles to various scholarly publications and ed. works by Heinrich Isaac.

BIBL.: E. Borroff, ed., *Notations and Editions: A Book in Honor of L. C.* (Dubuque, 1974).—NS/LK/DM

Cuzzoni, Francesca, celebrated Italian soprano; b. Parma, c. 1700; d. Bologna, 1770. She studied with

Lanzi. She sang in Parma, Bologna, Genoa, and Venice (1716–18), then was engaged at the Italian opera in London, making her debut as Teofane in Handel's opera *Ottone* (Jan. 12, 1723). She made a profound impression on London opera lovers, and was particularly distinguished in lyric roles, but later her notorious rivalry with Faustina Bordoni nearly ruined her career. Following some appearances in Venice, she returned to London (1734); after several seasons she went to the Netherlands, where she became impoverished and was imprisoned for debt. Eventually, she returned to Bologna, where she subsisted by making buttons.
—NS/LK/DM

Cyrille, Andrew (Charles), avant-garde jazz drummer, composer; b. Brooklyn, N.Y., Nov. 10, 1939. He was playing in a drum and bugle corps at St. Peter Claver Church, Brooklyn, at age 11; at 15, he was performing in a local trio with Eric Gale. He chose a career in music over chemistry and enrolled at Julliard (1960–64); around then, he worked with Freddie Hubbard. Cyrille made his professional debut with Nellie Lutcher, then played with Mary Lou Williams. In 1964 he replaced Sonny Murray in Cecil Taylor's ensemble. This association lasted until 1975, including a period as artist-in-residence at Antioch Coll. In the mid-1970s he performed Dialogue of the Drums, a series of all-percussion concerts with Milford Graves and Rashied Al; he also recorded with them, Taylor, and Marion Brown. He taught and led his own group, Maono (1975–80), which included David Ware, Sonny Smith, Ted Daniel, Lisle Atkinson, and Nick DiGeronimo. During the 1980s, Cyrille played with the Group (featuring Billy Bang, Fred Hopkins, Sirone, Ahmed Abdullah, and Marion Brown) and Pieces of Time (which included Don Moye, Kenny Clarke, and Milford Graves). He also did sessions with Muhal Richard Abrams and John Carter. He has worked with the Jazz Composers Orch. and with Jimmy Lyons. He has taught at the New School since 1986. He toured the U.K. (1990) with a trio that played a wide range of music. He is a brilliant avant-garde jazz percussionist and composer who incorporates his voice, as well as Eastern influences, into his soloing.

DISC.: *What About* (1971); *Dialogue of the Drums* (1974); *Metamusicians' Stomp* (1978); *Loop* (1978); *Nuba* (1979); *Special People* (1980); *Junction* (1980); *Celebration* (1980); *Navigator* (1982); *Andrew Cyrille Meets Peter Brotzmann* (1982); *Galaxies* (1990); *My Friend Louis* (1991); *X Man* (1993).—**LP/MM**

Czernohorsky (actually, **Černohorský**), **Bohuslav Matčj,** distinguished Bohemian composer, organist, and teacher; b. Nimburg, Feb. 16, 1684; d. Graz, July 1, 1742. He studied at the Univ. of Prague. A Minorite monk, he was organist at Assisi from 1710 to 1715 (Tartini was one of his pupils) and choirmaster at S. Antonio in Padua from 1715 to 1720. Returning to Bohemia, he was Kapellmeister at the Teinkirche in Prague, and (1735) at St. Jacob's (Gluck was among his pupils); he was again organist in Padua from 1731 to 1741. Many of his MSS were lost at the burning of the Minorite monastery (1754). An offertory and several organ fugues and preludes were publ. by O. Schmid in *Orgelwerke altböhmischer Meister;* five organ fugues have been ed. by K. Pietsch; a *Regina Coeli* for Soprano, Organ, and Cello obbligato, and a motet, *Quem lapidaverunt,* are also extant; *Composizioni per organo* constitute vol. three of *Musica antiqua Bohemica* (Prague, 1968). The contrapuntal skill of Czernohorsky's fugal writing is remarkable. Czech writers refer to him as "the father of Bohemian music" despite the fact that Czernohorsky never made thematic use of native rhythms or melodies.
—NS/LK/DM

Czerny, Carl, celebrated Austrian pianist, pedagogue, writer on music, and composer; b. Vienna, Feb. 20, 1791; d. there, July 15, 1857. He was born into a musical family, and began his training at the age of three with his father. At nine, he made his first public appearance as a pianist in Vienna playing Mozart's C minor Concerto, K.491. When he was ten, he played for Beethoven who agreed to take him on an his pupil. Czerny's devotion to Beethoven led him to memorize all of his mentor's piano works. In 1806 he performed Beethoven's C major Concerto, and in 1812 his *Emperor Concerto.* However, Czerny opted to forego the career of a virtuoso and instead began to accept pupils when he was only 15. He eventually established himself as one of the foremost piano pedagogues of his day, numbering among his students Döhler, T. Kullak, Jaëll, Thalberg, Heller, and Liszt. Although he pursued a demanding teaching schedule, he managed to find the time to compose prolifically. According to his own account, his output included hundreds of scores. In his lifetime, he publ. 861 opus numbers. In addition, he brought out innumerable studies and exercises for piano which remained the bane of students for generations. He also prepared editions of works by J.S. Bach and D. Scarlatti, and numerous arrangements of works by Handel, Haydn, Mozart, Beethoven, Schubert, Mendelssohn et al. Czerny's serious works included operas, seven syms., six overtures, six piano concertos, much chamber music, and numerous sacred vocal pieces, including masses, cantatas, and two Te Deum settings. With the exception of his piano sonatas, almost all of his serious music was left in MS. In recent years, recordings of a number of his more ambitious scores have revealed him to be a composer of considerable talent. Indeed, his Sym. No. 1, while owing much to Beethoven, nevertheless is a notable example of his assured handling of symphonic form. His publications included the *School of Extemporaneous Performance* (2 vols.), *Complete Theoretical and Practical Pianoforte School,* and *School of Practical Composition* (3 vols.). He also wrote an autobiography, *Erinnerungen aus meinem Leben* (MS, 1842; ed. by W. Kolneder, Baden-Baden, 1968; partial Eng. tr. in the *Musical Quarterly,* July 1956).

BIBL.: H. Steger, *Beiträge zu K. C.s Leben und Schaffen* (diss., Univ. of Munich, 1924); P. Badura-Skoda, ed., *C. C.:Über den richtigen Vortrag der sämtlichen Beethoven'schen Klavierwerke* (Vienna, 1963); G. Wehmeyer, *C. C. u. d. Einzelhaft am Klavier* (Kassel and Zürich, 1983).—**NS/LK/DM**

Czerwenka, Oskar, Austrian bass; b. Vöcklabruck bei Linz, July 5, 1924. He was a student of O. Iro in Vienna. In 1947 he made his operatic debut as the Hermit in *Der Freischütz* in Graz. He joined the Vienna State Opera in 1951, where he became successful in such roles as Baron Ochs, Osmin, and Kecal in *The Bartered Bride*, and in operas by Lortzing; in 1961 he was made an Austrian Kammersänger. From 1953 he also appeared at the Salzburg Festival. In 1959 he sang Baron Ochs at the Glyndebourne Festival and, on Dec. 26 of that year, made his Metropolitan Opera debut in N.Y. in the same role. He also appeared in Hamburg, Berlin, Munich, Frankfurt am Main, Cologne, and Stuttgart. He also appeared widely as a concert artist. He publ. the book *Lebenszeiten-Ungebetene Briefe* (Vienna, 1987). —NS/LK/DM

Czibulka, Alphons, Hungarian conductor and composer; b. Szepes-Várallya, May 14, 1842; d. Vienna, Oct. 27, 1894. After a brief career as a pianist, he was active as a theater conductor and military bandmaster. He composed and arranged much dance music, and also the successful operettas *Pfingsten in Florenz* (Vienna, Dec. 20, 1884) and *Der Glücksritter* (Vienna, Dec. 22, 1887), which were performed abroad. Among his other operettas were *Der Jagdjunker der Kaiserin* (Berlin, Dec. 3, 1885; rev. version, Vienna, March 20, 1886), *Gil Blas von Santillana* (Hamburg, Nov. 23, 1888), *Der Bajazzo* (Vienna, Dec. 7, 1892), and *Monsieur Hannibal* (Munich, Sept. 5, 1893).—NS/LK/DM

Cziffra, György, noted Hungarian-born French pianist; b. Budapest, Sept. 5, 1921; d. Morsang-sur-Orge, Jan. 15, 1994. He studied with Dohnányi at the Budapest Academy of Music, but his education was interrupted by World War II, when he served in the Hungarian army. After the war, he continued his studies at the Budapest Academy of Music with Ferenczi, but was once more distracted from music when he was arrested in 1950 for his rebellious political views. He was released from jail in 1953, but was again endangered by the abortive Hungarian revolt in 1956. Convinced that he could have no peace under Communist rule, he went to Paris, where he made successful appearances as a pianist; in 1968 he became a naturalized French citizen. In 1973 he founded the St.-Frambourg Royal Chapel Foundation in Senlis to assist young musicians and artists. He was best known for his interpretations of works of the Romantic repertoire; especially brilliant were his renditions of the music of Liszt. He publ. *Des canons et des fleurs* (Paris, 1977).—NS/LK/DM

Czukay, Holger, German new-wave composer; b. Danzig, March 24, 1938. A musical iconoclast, Czukay fell through the cracks of both jazz and classical instruction until he studied with Stockhausen (1962). He subsequently went to Switzerland, where he encountered rock music through the guitarist Michael Karoli, with whom he formed the pioneer new-wave group Can (1968–78). Can followed the early Stockhausen aesthetic, utilizing "found" music from shortwave radio as well as the techniques of tape splicing and the collage of ethnic music. Czukay anticipated trends in alternative pop music not apparent to most people until well into the 1980s; the ethnic-based constructions in his Forgery series of the 1970s were acknowledged by David Byrne and Brian Eno as an influence in their collaboration, *My Life in the Bush of Ghosts*.—NS/LK/DM

Czyż, Henryk, Polish conductor and composer; b. Grudziadz, June 16, 1923. He studied law at Torun Univ.; then went to the Poznán Academy of Music, where he studied conducting with Bierdiajew and composition with Szeligowski. In 1952 he was appointed conductor at the Poznán Opera; from 1953 to 1956 he conducted the Polish Radio and Television Sym. Orch. in Katowice. He was subsequently chief conductor of the ód Phil. (1957–60); from 1964 to 1968 he conducted the Kraków Phil.; from 1971 to 1974 served as Generalmusikdirektor of the Düsseldorf Sym. Orch.; from 1972 to 1980 he was again chief conductor of the ód Phil. He made his American debut with the Minn. Orch. in 1973. In 1980 he became a prof. at the Warsaw Academy of Music. Among his works were the stage pieces *Biaowosa* (The Girl with the Flaxen Hair; Warsaw, Nov. 24, 1962; rev. version, ód, Oct. 2, 1971); *Knyolog w rozterce* (Cynologist at a Loss; Polish TV, 1965; stage premiere, Karków, Nov. 19, 1967), and *Inge Bartsch* (Warsaw, Dec. 11, 1982); several orch. works, including *Étude* (1949) and Symphonic Variations (1952), etc.—NS/LK/DM

Dabadie, Henri-Bernard, French baritone; b. Pau, Jan. 19, 1797; d. Paris, May 1853. He received training at the Paris Cons., and in 1819 made his operatic debut as Cinna in *La Vestale* at the Paris Opéra, where he sang until 1835. He became especially well known there for his roles in Rossini's operas, creating Pharaon in *Moïse et Pharaon* (March 26, 1827), Raimbaud in *Le Comte Ory* (Aug. 20, 1828), and the title role in *Guillaume Tell* (Aug. 3, 1829). He also created the role of Belcore in Donizetti's *L'elisir d'amore* in Milan (May 12, 1832). His wife was the soprano Louise Zulme Léroux (b. Boulogne, Oct. 4, 1796; d. Paris, Nov. 1877), who sang at the Paris Opéra (1824–35), where she created the roles of Sinaïde in *Moïse et Pharaon* and Jemmy in *Guillaume Tell*.—**NS/LK/DM**

D'Accone, Frank (Anthony), American musicologist; b. Somerville, Mass., June 13, 1931. He was a student of Geiringer, Read, and Norden at Boston Univ. (B.M., 1952; M.M., 1953) and of Pirrotta, Merritt, Thompson, Piston, and Dart at Harvard Univ. (M.A., 1955; Ph.D., 1960, with the diss. *A Documentary History of Music at the Florentine Cathedral and Baptistry*). He was an asst. prof. (1960–63) and assoc. prof. (1963–68) of music at the State Univ. of N.Y. at Buffalo. In 1966–67 he was a visiting prof. of music at the Univ. of Calif. at Los Angeles, where he then was a prof. of music (1968–94) and chairman of its depts. of music (1973–76) and musicology (1989–92). In 1972–73 he also was a visiting prof. of music at Yale Univ. He was general ed. of the Corpus Mensurabilis Musicae series, co-ed. of *Musica Disciplina*, and a contributor to scholarly books and journals. In 1974 he was named a Cavaliere della Repubblica d'Italia, in 1980–81 he held a Guggenheim fellowship, in 1997 he was awarded the International Galileo Galilei Prize of the Univ. of Pisa, and in 1998 he was made a Fellow of the American Academy of Arts and Sciences.

WRITINGS: *The History of a Baroque Opera: Alessandro Scarlatti's Gli equivoci nel sembiante* (N.Y., 1985); *The Civic Muse: Music and Musicians in Siena during the Middle Ages and the Renaissance* (Chicago, 1997).

BIBL.: I. Alm, A. McLamore, and C. Reardon, eds., *Musica Franca: Essays in Honor of F. A. D.* (Stuyvesant, N.Y., 1996). —**NS/LK/DM**

Dachs, Joseph, Austrian pianist and pedagogue; b. Regensburg, Sept. 30, 1825; d. Vienna, June 6, 1896. He studied in Vienna with Czerny and Sechter. In 1861 was appointed prof. of piano at the Vienna Cons. Dachs had numerous distinguished pupils, among them Vladimir de Pachmann, Laura Rappoldi, and Isabelle Vengerova. He also gave concerts that were well received in Vienna. —**NS/LK/DM**

Dadelsen, Georg von, distinguished German musicologist; b. Dresden, Nov. 7, 1918. He studied musicology at the Univ. of Kiel at Humboldt Univ. in Berlin, and at the Free Univ. of Berlin (Ph.D., 1951, with the diss. *Alter Stil und alte Techniken in der Musik des 19. Jahrhunderts*); completed his Habilitation at the Univ. of Tübingen in 1958 with his *Beiträge zur Chronologie der Werke J.S. Bachs* (publ. in Trossingen, 1958). He was an asst. lecturer at the Univ. of Tübingen (1952–58); was then prof. of musicology at the Univ. of Hamburg (1960–71); from 1971 he held the same title at the Univ. of Tübingen. He is particularly noted for his valuable contributions to the study of Bach's music.

WRITINGS: *Bemerkungen zur Handschrift J.S. Bachs, seiner Familie und seines Kreises* (Trossingen, 1957); *Editionsrichtlinien musikalischer Denkmäler und Gesamtausgaben* (Kassel, 1967); A. Feil and T. Kohlhase, eds., *Über Bach und anderes: Aufsätze und Vortrage, 1957–1982* (Laaber, 1983).

BIBL.: *Acht klein Präludien und Studien über Bach: G. v. D. zum 70. Geburtstag am 17. November 1988* (Wiesbaden, 1992). —**NS/LK/DM**

Daffner, Hugo, German composer and musicologist; b. Munich, June 2, 1882; d. in the concentration camp in Dachau, Oct. 9, 1936. He studied composition with Thuille and musicology with Sandberger and Kroyer at the Royal Academy in Munich (Ph.D., 1904, with the diss. *Die Entwicklung des Klavierkonzerts bis Mozarts*; publ. in Leipzig, 1908); subsequently took private lessons with Reger. He conducted opera in Munich from 1904 to 1906; was active as a music critic in Königsberg and Dresden; decided to study medicine, and obtained the degree of M.D. in 1920; in 1924 he went to live in Berlin as a practicing physician. He became a victim of the Nazi program of extermination of Jews. Among his works were the operas *Macbeth*, *Truffaldino*, and *Der eingebildete*, 2 syms., 2 string quartets, 2 piano trios, and 2 piano quintets.—NS/LK/DM

Dagincour, François, French organist, harpsichordist, and composer; b. Rouen, 1684; d. there, April 30, 1758. He was a pupil of Jacques Boyvin in Rouen and of Nicolas Lebègue in Paris. From 1691 to 1696 he was organist at Ste. Madeleine-en-la-cité in Paris, and then returned to Rouen to assume the post of organist at Notre Dame in 1696, which he held for the rest of his life. He also was organist at the royal abbey of St. Ouen and then at St. Jean in Rouen. In 1714 he was named one of the four organists of the royal chapel. Notable among his works were the *Pièces de clavecin* (Paris, 1733; ed. by H. Ferguson, 1969). Forty-six of his organ pieces were ed. by L. Panel (Paris, 1956).—LK/DM

Dahl, Ingolf, distinguished German-born American pianist, conductor, pedagogue, and composer of German-Swedish descent; b. Hamburg, June 9, 1912; d. Frutigen, near Bern, Aug. 6, 1970. After composition training with Jarnach at the Cologne Hochschule für Musik (1930–32), he went to Zürich and studied musicology at the Univ. and conducting with Andreae at the Cons. (1932–36). In 1938 he emigrated to the U.S., becoming a naturalized American citizen in 1943. In 1944 he received additional training from Boulanger. In 1945 he joined the faculty of the Univ. of Southern Calif. in Los Angeles, where he also conducted its sym. orch. until 1958, and again in 1968–69. During the summers from 1952 to 1957, he oversaw his own Tanglewood Study Group at the Berkshire Music Center. During the summers from 1964 to 1966, he served as director and conductor of the Ojai Festival. In 1954 and 1968 he held Guggenheim fellowships, and in 1964 he received the Alice M. Ditson Award. As a performer, Dahl was an active champion of contemporary music. He became associated with Stravinsky, who influenced him in his direction as a composer. With his Piano Quartet (1957), Dahl adopted serial techniques that he utilized inventively in such works as his *Sinfonietta for Concert Band* (1961) and his *Aria Sinfonica* (1965).

WORKS: ORCH.: Concerto for Alto Saxophone and Wind Orch. (1949; rev. 1953); Symphony concertante for 2 Clarinets and Orch. (1952); *The Tower of Saint Barbara*, symphonic legend (1954; Louisville, Jan. 29, 1955); Sinfonietta for Concert Band (1961); *Aria sinfonica* (Los Angeles, April 15, 1965); *Quodlibet on American Folktunes* (1965; arranged from the piece for 2 Pianos, 8-Hands, 1953); 4 *Intervals* for Strings (1967; arranged for Piano, 4-Hands, 1967); *Elegy Concerto* for Violin and Chamber Orch. (1970; completed by D. Michalsky, 1971).

CHAMBER: *Allegro and Arioso* for Woodwind Quartet (1942); *Music for Brass Instruments*, brass quintet (1944); *Variations on a Swedish Folktune* for Flute (1945; rev. 1962; arranged for Flute and Alto Flute, 1970); *Concerto a tre* for Violin, Cello, and Clarinet (1946); Duo for Cello and Piano (1946; rev. 1948); *Notturno* for Cello and Piano (1946); *Divertimento* for Viola and Piano (1949); *Couperin Variations* for Recorder or Flute and Harpsichord or Piano (1957); Piano Quartet (1957); *Serenade* for 4 Flutes (1960); Piano Trio (1962); *Duettino concertante* for Flute and Percussion (1966); *IMC Fanfare* for 3 Trumpets and 3 Trombones (1968); *Fanfare on A and C* [for Aaron Copland] for 3 Trumpets, Horn, Baritone, and Trombone (1969); *Sonata da camera* for Clarinet and Piano (1970); 5 duets for 2 Clarinets (1970); *Little Canonic Suite* for Violin and Viola (1970); *Variations on a French Folksong* for Flute and Piano (1970). **PIANO:** *Rondo* for Piano, 4-Hands (1938); *Prelude and Fugue* (1939); *Pastorale montano* (1943); *Hymn and Toccata* (1947); *Quodlibet on American Folktunes* for 2 Pianos, 8-Hands (1953; arranged for Orch., 1965); *Sonata seria* (1953); *Sonatina alla marcia* (1956); *Fanfares* (1958); *Sonata pastorale* (1959); *Reflections* (1967). **VOCAL:** Choruses and songs.

BIBL.: J. Berdahl, *I. D.: His Life and Works* (diss., Univ. of Miami, 1975).—NS/LK/DM

Dahl, Viking, Danish organist and composer; b. Osby, Oct. 8, 1895; d. Stockholm, Jan. 5, 1945. He studied organ at the Stockholm Cons. (1915–19), and concurrently took courses in art history. In 1920 he went to Paris, where he had lessons in modern dance with Isadora Duncan and in composition with Koechlin; he later completed his studies in Copenhagen and Berlin. In 1921 he went to Lund as a music teacher, and from 1926 he served as organist of Varberg Church. After composing in both impressionist and expressionist styles, he turned to Swedish folk music for inspiration. His first work, the *Oriental Suite for Orch.* (1919), was followed by his choreographic poem *Maison de fous* (Paris, 1920), which attracted considerable attention. His early promise as a composer, however, was not fulfilled.—NS/LK/DM

Dahlhaus, Carl, eminent German musicologist and editor; b. Hannover, June 10, 1928; d. Berlin, March 13, 1989. He studied musicology at the Univ. of Göttingen with Gerber; also at the Univ. of Freiburg with Gurlitt; received his Ph.D. from the Univ. of Göttingen in 1953 with the diss. *Studien zu den Messen Josquins des Prés*. He was a dramatic adviser for the Deutsches Theater in Göttingen from 1950 to 1958; from 1960 to 1962, was an ed. of the *Stuttgarter Zeitung*; then joined the Inst. für Musikalische Landesforschung of the Univ. of Kiel; completed his Habilitation there in 1966 with his *Untersuchungen uber die Entstehung der harmonischen Tonalität* (publ. in Kassel, 1968; Eng. tr., 1991, as *Studies on the Origin of Harmonic Tonality*). In 1966–67 he was a research fellow at the Univ. of Saarbrücken; in 1967 he became prof. of music history at the Technical Univ. of Berlin. In 1984 he was made a corresponding member of the American Musicological Soc. He was the ed.-in-chief of the complete edition of Wagner's works, which began publication in 1970; he was also an ed. of the Supplement to the 12th edition of the *Riemann Musik-Lexikon* (2 vols., Mainz, 1972, 1975); with Hans Eggebrecht, of the

Brockhaus-Riemann Musik-Lexikon (2 vols., Wiesbaden and Mainz, 1978–79); and of *Pipers Enzyklopadie des Musiktheaters* (from 1986); in addition, he was co-ed. of the *Neue Zeitschrift für Musik* (1972–74), *Melos/NZ für Musik* (1975–78), *Musik und Bildung* (1978–80), and *Musica* (from 1981). He was one of the foremost musicologists of the second half of the 20th century. A scholar of great erudition, he wrote authoritatively and prolifically on a vast range of subjects, extending from the era of Josquin to the present day.

WRITINGS: *Musikästhetik* (Cologne, 1967; 4th ed., 1986; Eng. tr., 1982, as *Aesthetics of Music*); *Studien zur Trivialmusik des 19. Jahrhunderts* (Regensburg, 1967); *Analyse und Werturteil* (Mainz, 1970; Eng. tr., 1983, as *Analysis and Value Judgment*); *Das Drama Richard Wagners als musikalisches Kunstwerk* (Regensburg, 1970); *Richard Wagner: Werk und Wirkung* (Regensburg, 1971); *Wagners Konzeption des musikalischen Dramas* (Regensburg, 1971); *Richard Wagners Musikdramen* (Velber, 1971; 2nd ed., 1985; Eng. tr., 1979, as *Richard Wagner's Music Dramas*); *Wagner's Ästhetik* (Bayreuth, 1971); *Zwischen Romantik und Moderne: Vier Studien zur Musikgeschichte des späteren 19. Jahrhunderts* (Munich, 1974; Eng. tr., 1980, as *Between Romanticism and Modernism: Four Studies in the Music of the Later Nineteenth Century*); *Grundlagen der Musikgeschichte* (Cologne, 1977; Eng. tr., 1983, as *Foundations of Music History*); *Die Idee der absoluten Musik* (Kassel, 1978; Eng. tr., 1989, as *The Idea of Absolute Music*); *Schönberg und andere: Gesammelte Aufsätze zur Neuen Musik* (Mainz, 1978; Eng. tr., 1988, as *Schoenberg and the New Music*); *Die Musik des 19. Jahrhunderts* (Wiesbaden, 1980; 2nd ed., 1988; Eng. tr., 1989, as *Nineteenth Century Music*); *Musikalischer Realismus: Zur Musikgeschichte des 19. Jahrhunderts* (Munich and Zürich, 1982; Eng. tr., 1985, as *Realism in Nineteenth Century Music*); with H. de la Motte-Haber, *Systematische Musikwissenschaft* (Laaber, 1982); *Vom Musikdrama zur Literaturoper: Aufsätze zur neueren Operngeschichte* (Munich and Salzburg, 1983); with J. Deathridge, *Wagner* (London, 1984); *Die Musiktheorie im 18. und 19. Jahrhundert: Erster Teil: Grundzüge einer Systematik* (Darmstadt, 1984); *Die Musik des 18. Jahrhunderts* (Laaber, 1985); with R. Katz, *Contemplating Music: Source Readings in the Aesthetics of Music* (N.Y., 1987); *Ludwig van Beethoven und seine Zeit* (Laaber, 1987; 2nd ed., 1988; Eng. tr., 1991, as *Ludwig van Beethoven: Approaches to His Music*); *Klassische und romantische Musikästhetik* (Laaber, 1988).

BIBL.: H. Danuser et al., eds., *Das musikalische Kunstwerk: Geschichte, Ästhetik, Theorie: Festschrift C. D. zum 60. Geburtstag* (Laaber, 1988); M. Zimmermann, ed., *Oper nach Wagner: In memoriam C. D.* (Laaber, 1993).—**NS/LK/DM**

Dalayrac, Nicolas(-Marie), French composer; b. Muret, Haute-Garonne, June 8, 1753; d. Paris, Nov. 26, 1809. (He signed his name d'Alayrac, but dropped the nobiliary particle after the Revolution.) His early schooling was in Toulouse. Returning to Muret in 1767, he studied law and played violin in a local band. He then entered the service of the Count d'Artois in his Guard of Honor, and at the same time took lessons in harmony with François Langlé at Versailles; he also received some help from Grétry. His first theater work was a 1-act comedy, *L'Eclipse totale* (Paris, March 7, 1782). From then on, he devoted most of his energies to the theater. He wrote over 56 operas; during the Revolution, he composed patriotic songs for special occasions. He also enjoyed Napoleon's favors later on. During his lifetime, and for some 3 decades after his death, many of his operas were popular not only in France but also in Germany, Italy, and Russia; then they gradually disappeared from the active repertoire, but there were several revivals. Dalayrac's natural facility enabled him to write successfully in all operatic genres.

WORKS: DRAMATIC: O p e r a (most first perf. in Paris, most at the Opéra-Comique): *Le Petit Souper, ou L'Abbé qui veut parvenir* (1781); *Le Chevalier à la mode* (1781); *Nina* (May 15, 1786); *Sargines* (May 14, 1788); *Les Deux Petits Savoyards* (Jan. 14, 1789); *Raoul, Sire de Créqui* (Oct. 31, 1789); *La Soirée orageuse* (May 29, 1790); *Camille* (March 19, 1791); *Philippe et Georgette* (Dec. 28, 1791); *Ambroise* (Jan. 12, 1793); *Adèle et Dorsan* (April 27, 1795); *Marianne* (July 7, 1796); *La Maison isolée* (May 11, 1797); *Gulnare* (Dec. 30, 1797); *Alexis* (Jan. 24, 1798); *Adolphe et Clara* (Feb. 10, 1799); *Maison à vendre* (Oct. 23, 1800); *Léhéman* (Dec. 12, 1801); *L'Antichambre* (Feb. 26, 1802); *La Jeune Prude* (Jan. 14, 1804); *Une Heure de mariage* (March 20, 1804); *Gulistan* (Sept. 30, 1805); *Deux mots* (June 9, 1806); *Koulouf* (Dec. 18, 1806); *Le Poète et le musicien* (Paris, May 30, 1811).

BIBL.: R. de Pixérécourt, *Vie de D.* (Paris, 1810); A. Fourgeaud, *Les Violons de D.* (Paris, 1856); F. Karro-Péleisson, ed., *N. D.: Musicien murétain, homme des lumières* (Muret, 1991).—**NS/LK/DM**

Dal Barba, Daniel, Italian singer, violinist, teacher, and composer; b. Verona, May 5, 1715; d. there, July 16, 1801. He made his debut as a singer in Chiarini's *I fratelli riconosciuti* in Venora in 1743. After singing in his own opera *Il Tigrane* (1744) and others, he devoted himself to a career as a violinist, teacher, and composer in his native city. He became maestro di cappella of the Filarmonica and Filotima academies, posts he retained for the next 30 years. He also was temporary maestro di cappella (1762–70) and maestro di cappella (1770–79) at the Cathedral. Among his works were 7 operas, a Flute Concerto, an accomplished set of 12 violin sonatas, and many sacred works.

BIBL.: M. Dubiaga Jr. *The Life and Works of D.P. D.B. (1715–1801)* (diss., Univ. of Colo., 1977).—**NS/LK/DM**

Dalberg, Johann Friedrich Hugo, German pianist, composer, and writer on music; b. Aschaffenburg, May 17, 1760; d. there, July 26, 1812. He studied theology, and became a canon in Trier; was also counsellor to the Elector of Trier at Coblenz. He traveled in Italy (1775) and England (1798), and also gave private concerts as a pianist. Although he was not a professional musician, his compositions and particularly his writings reveal considerable musical culture. He publ. many vocal works, including songs to Eng. and Fr. texts. He set to music Schiller's *Ode an die Freude* (1799). In addition to the publs. listed below, he also tr. Jones's *The Musical Modes of the Hindus* (1802).

WRITINGS: *Blicke eines Tonkünstlers in die Musik der Geister* (Mannheim, 1787); *Vom Erfinden und Bilden* (Frankfurt am Main, 1791); *Untersuchungen über den Ursprung der Harmonie* (Erfurt, 1800); *Die Äolsharfe, Ein allegorischer Traum* (Erfurt, 1801); etc. —**NS/LK/DM**

D'Albert, Eugène
    See **Albert, Eugen d'**

Dalberto, Michel (Jean Jacques), French pianist; b. Paris, June 2, 1955. He was a student at the Paris

Cons., his principal mentors being Vlado Perlemuter, Raymond Trouard, and Jean Hubeau. In 1975 he won the Clara Haskil prize and the Salzburg Mozart competition, and in 1978 captured first prize in the Leeds competition. After making his formal debut as soloist with Leinsdorf and the Orchestre de Paris in 1980, he pursued a global career as a soloist with orchs., recitalist, and chamber music player.—NS/LK/DM

Dalby, (John) Martin, Scottish composer and broadcasting administrator; b. Aberdeen, April 25, 1942. He was a violist in the National Youth Orch. of Great Britain before attending the Royal Coll. of Music in London on scholarship, where he studied viola with Riddle and composition with Howells (1960–63); additional scholarships allowed him to pursue studies in Italy (1963–65). From 1965 to 1971 he was a music producer with the BBC in London. After serving as the Cramb Research Fellow in composition at the Univ. of Glasgow (1971–72), he held the position of head of music with the BBC in Scotland (from 1972), where he was executive music producer (from 1990).

WORKS: ORCH.: *Waltz Overture* (Glasgow, Nov. 29, 1965); 2 syms.: No. 1 (Aberdeen, March 10, 1970) and No. 2, Chamber Sym., *O Bella e Vaga Aurora* (Edinburgh, Sept. 10, 1982); *Concerto Martin Pescatore* for Strings (Cheltenham, July 6, 1971); *The Tower of Victory* (Glasgow, Sept. 22, 1973); Viola Concerto (London, Sept. 6, 1974); *El Ruiseñor* (London, Oct. 27, 1979); *Nozze di Primavera* (Kirkwall, June 19, 1984); *The Mary Bean* (London, Aug. 17, 1991). SYMPHONIC WIND BAND: *A Plain Man's Hammer* (1984; Glasgow, June 19, 1985); *Flight Dreaming* (Glasgow, Sept. 22, 1990). BRASS BAND: *Lively Man* (Stirling, Aug. 6, 1988). CHAMBER: Piano Trio (1967); *Pindar is Dead* for Clarinet and Piano (1968); Oboe Sonatina (1969); *Commedia* for Clarinet, Violin, Cello and Piano (London, May 5, 1969); *Whisper Music* for Flute, Piccolo Clarinet, Bass Clarinet, Trumpet, Percussion, Harp, and Cello (London, May 5, 1971); *Cancionero para una Mariposa* for Flute, 2 Bassoons, 2 Trumpets, 2 Trombones, and 2 Cellos (Cardiff, March 13, 1971); String Quintet (London, Oct. 27, 1972); *Yet Still She is the Moone* for 3 Trumpets, 3 Trombones, and Tuba (London, April 30, 1973); *Paginas* for Treble Recorder and Harpsichord (London, March 1, 1973); *Unicorn* for Violin and Piano (1975); *Aleph* for 2 Flutes, Horn, Trumpet, Trombone, Cimbalom or Harpsichord, and 2 Double Basses (Royan, March 25, 1975); *Almost a Madrigal* for Flute, Horn, 2 Trumpets, Trombone, Tuba, and 2 Percussion (Glasgow, April 28, 1977); *The Dancer Eduardova* for 6 Players (Orkney, June 20, 1978); *Man Walking,* serenade for Octet (London, June 4, 1981); *Scotch Rhapsody* for Viola and Piano (1983; London, Jan. 11, 1984); *Songs My Mother Taught Me* for Chamber Ensemble (1986; Glasgow, Feb. 16, 1987); *Rose of Gazing* for Recorder and Harpsichord (1987); *De Patre ex Filio* for Clarinet, Bassoon, Horn, 2 Violins, Viola, Cello, and Double Bass (Edinburgh, March 13, 1988). PIANO: 2 sonatas: No. 1 (Lower Machen, South Wales, July 21, 1985) and No. 2 (1989; Edinburgh, Oct. 30, 1990). VOCAL: *Laudate Dominum* for Tenor or Soprano, Chorus, and Organ or Orch. (1964; Aberdeen, May 17, 1965); *Wanderer* for Mezzo-soprano and Piano (Edinburgh, Aug. 22, 1965); *Requiem for Philip Sparrow* for Mezzo-soprano, Chorus, and Orch. (1967; London, March 10, 1968); *The Fiddler* for Soprano or Tenor and Violin (1967; Glasgow, Jan. 18, 1971); *Cantica* for Soprano or Tenor, Clarinet, Viola, and Piano (London, June 4, 1969); *The Keeper of the Pass* for Soprano and

Chamber Ensemble (Edinburgh, Sept. 4, 1971); *Orpheus* for Chorus, Optional Narrator, and 11 Instruments (Stirling, April 16, 1972); *Cantigas del Cancionero* for 2 Tenors, 2 Baritones, and Bass (Glasgow, Feb. 9, 1972); *El Remanso del Pitido* for 12 Solo Voices (London, April 5, 1974); *Ad Flumina Babyloniae,* motet for Chorus (Ghent, Sept. 17, 1975); *Beauty a Cause* for 12 or 16 Voices and Instrumental Ensemble (1977; Glasgow, Feb. 13, 1978); *Coll for the Hazel Tree* for Soprano, Alto, Tenor, and Bass with Amplification (1979; Fife, Feb. 27, 1980); *Antoinette Alone* for Mezzo-soprano and Piano (1980; BBC Radio 3, Sept. 19, 1981); *Magnificat and Nunc Dimittis* for Chorus and Organ (Paisley Abbey, Nov. 30, 1980); *My Heart Aflame,* motet for Chorus (Glasgow, Oct. 29, 1983); *5 Sonnets from Scotland* for Soprano, Tenor, and Piano (1985; Aberdeen, March 17, 1986); *Celebration in Psalms* for Chorus, Brass, Percussion, and Organ (Aberdeen, Dec. 8, 1985); *The Sower,* anthem for Chorus (Radio Scotland, Nov. 20, 1988); *Nec Tamen Consumebater,* anthem for Chorus and Organ (Glasgow, June 26, 1989); *Et Resurrexit* for Chorus and Organ (Glasgow, June 22, 1990).—NS/LK/DM

Dalcroze, Émile Jaques
See **Jaques- Dalcroze, Émile**

Dale, Benjamin (James), English composer and teacher; b. Crouch Hill, July 17, 1885; d. London, July 30, 1943. He studied at the Royal Academy of Music in London with F. Corder. After serving as organist at St. Stephen's, Ealing, he taught composition at the Royal Academy of Music.

WORKS: *The Tempest,* overture (1902); Piano Sonata (1905); suites for Piano and Viola (1907); *Before the Paling of the Stars* for Chorus and Orch. (1912); *Songs of Praise* for Chorus and Orch. (1923); *The Flowing Tide* for Orch. (1924; 1943); *Rosa mystica* and *Cradle Song* for Chorus; 2 songs (after Shakespeare) for Voice and Viola obbligato; Sextet for Violas; Violin Sonata; piano pieces; songs; etc.—NS/LK/DM

Dale, Clamma, black American soprano; b. Chester, Pa., July 4, 1948. She studied at the Philadelphia Settlement Music School, and later with Hans Heinz, Alice Howland, and Cornelius Reed at the Juilliard School of Music in N.Y. (B.Mus., 1970; M.S., 1975). On Feb. 20, 1973, she appeared as St. Teresa I in *4 Saints in 3 Acts* in the Mini-Met staging at N.Y.'s Manhattan Forum. On Sept. 30, 1975, she made her N.Y.C. Opera debut as Antonia in *Les Contes d'Hoffmann,* and subsequently appeared with opera companies throughout North America and abroad; she also toured extensively as a concert artist. In 1988 she sang Gershwin's Bess at the Theater des Westens in Berlin, and in 1989 she sang Puccini's Liù at the Deutsche Oper there. Among her other principal roles were Pamina, Countess Almaviva, Nedda, and Musetta.—NS/LK/DM

D'Alembert, Jean le Rond
See **Alembert, Jean le Rond d'**

D'Alheim, Marie (Alexeievna) Olénine
See **Olénine d'Alheim, Marie (Alexeievna)**

Dalis, Irene, American mezzo-soprano, teacher, and operatic administrator; b. San Jose, Calif., Oct. 8,

1925. She studied at San Jose State Univ. (A.B., 1946; M.S., 1957) and at Columbia Univ. Teachers Coll. (M.A., 1947); received vocal training from Edyth Walker (1947–50) and Paul Althouse (1950–51) in N.Y., and from Otto Müller (1952) in Milan. In 1953 she made her operatic debut as Eboli in *Don Carlo* at the Oldenburg Landestheater; sang with the Städtische Oper in Berlin (1955–60). On March 16, 1957, she made her Metropolitan Opera debut in N.Y. as Eboli, and continued to sing there regularly until 1977. She also made guest appearances at Covent Garden in London, the Chicago Lyric Opera, and the Bayreuth Festivals. In 1976 she became a prof. of music at San Jose State Univ.; she also directed its opera workshop, which served as the nucleus for the fully professional Opera San Jose, with Dalis as executive director (1984–88) and artistic director (from 1988). —NS/LK/DM

Dall'Abaco, Evaristo Felice, Italian cellist, violinist, and composer, father of **Joseph-Marie-Clément Dall'Abaco;** b. Verona, July 12, 1675; d. Munich, July 12, 1742. He received training in violin and cello in Verona. From 1696 to 1701 he was in the service of the Modena court of Duke Rinaldo d'Este. In 1704 he entered the service of the Bavarian court in Munich of the Elector Maximilian II Emanuel, where he was a cellist and chamber musician. The outbreak of the War of the Spanish Succession that same year compelled the elector to flee, and Dall'Abaco followed his patron to the Low Countries and later to France. Upon the return of the elector to Munich in 1715, Dall'Abaco was made Konzertmeister of the Bavarian court orch. In 1717 he was also made electoral councillor. He remained in the service of the court when Karl Albert became elector in 1726, retiring in 1740. In his adept and imaginative concerto writing, Dall'Abaco moved from the Italian Baroque style to the stile misto of Italian and French elements to the galant style of early classicism.

WORKS (all publ. in Amsterdam): *XII sonate da camera* for Violin and Cello or Harpsichord, op.1 (c. 1708); (12) *Concerti a quattro da chiesa,* op.2 (1712); *XII sonate da chiesa e da camera a tre,* op.3 (1712); (12) *Sonate da camera* for Violin and Cello, op.4 (1716); (6) *Concerti a più istrumenti...libro primo,* op.5 (c. 1719); (12) *Concerti a più istrumenti,* op.6 (1735).—NS/LK/DM

Dall'Abaco, Joseph-Marie-Clément, Italian cellist and composer, son of **Evaristo Felice Dall'Abaco;** b. Brussels (baptized), March 27, 1710; d. Arbizzano di Valpolicella, near Verona, Aug. 31, 1805. He studied with his father. At 19, he entered the service of the electoral chapel in Bonn as a chamber music cellist. In 1738 he was made director of the court orch. In 1740 he visited London, and in 1749 Vienna. In 1766 he was made a baron by the Munich court. Among his works were many cello sonatas.—NS/LK/DM

Dallapiccola, Luigi, eminent Italian composer and pedagogue; b. Pisino, Istria, Feb. 3, 1904; d. Florence, Feb. 19, 1975. He took piano lessons at an early age in Pisino. After training in piano and harmony in Trieste (1919–21), he studied with Ernesto Consolo (piano diploma, 1924) and Vito Frazzi (composition

diploma, 1931) at the Florence Cons., where he subsequently was a distinguished member of the faculty (1934–67). A collection of his essays appeared as *Appunti incontri meditazioni* (Milan, 1970). As a composer, Dallapiccola adopted dodecaphonic procedures but added considerable innovations, such as the use of mutually exclusive triads and thematic structure and harmonic progressions. He particularly excelled in his handling of vocal lines in a complex modern idiom.

WORKS: DRAMATIC: O p e r a : *Volo di notte* (1937–39; Florence, May 18, 1940); *Il Prigioniero* (1944–48; rev. version, Turin Radio, Dec. 4, 1949; stage premiere, Florence, May 20, 1950); *Ulisse* (1959–68; in Ger. as *Odysseus,* Berlin, Sept. 29, 1968. B a l l e t : *Marsia* (1942–43; Venice, Sept. 9, 1948). ORCH.: *Partita* (1930–32; Florence, Jan. 22, 1933); *Piccolo Concerto per Muriel Couvreaux* for Piano and Chamber Orch. (1939–41; Rome, May 1, 1941); *Due pezzi* (1947; based on the *Due studi* for Violin and Piano); *Tartiniana* for Violin and Chamber Orch. (1951; Bern, March 4, 1952); *Variazioni per orchestra* (1953–54; Louisville, Oct. 2, 1954); orchestration of *Quaderno musicale di Annalibera* for Piano); *Piccola musica notturna* (Hannover, June 7, 1954; also for 8 Instruments, 1961); *Tartiniana seconda* for Violin and Chamber Orch. (1956; Turin Radio, March 15, 1957; orchestration of the piece for Violin and Piano); *Dialoghi* for Cello and Orch. (1959–60; Venice, Sept. 17, 1960); *3 Questions with 2 Answers* (1962; New Haven, Conn., Feb. 5, 1963; based on *Ulisse*). CHAMBER: *Ciaccona, Intermezzo e Adagio* for Cello (1945); *Due studi* for Violin and Piano (1946–47; also used in the *Due pezzi* for Orch.); *Tartiana seconda* for Violin and Piano (1955–56; also for Violin and Chamber Orch.); *Piccola musica notturna* for 8 Instruments (1961; also for Orch.). P i a n o : *Musica* for 3 Pianos (1935); *Sonatina canonica* (1942–43); *Quaderno musicale di Annalibera* (1952, rev. 1953; also for Orch.; transcribed for organ by R. Shackelford, 1970). VOCAL: *Due canzoni di Grado* for Mezzo-soprano, Small Women's Chorus, and Small Orch. (1927); *Dalla mia terra,* song cycle for Mezzo-soprano, Chorus, and Orch. (1928); *Due laudi di Fra Jacopone da Todi* for Soprano, Baritone, Chorus, and Orch. (1929); *La Canzone del Quarnaro* for Tenor, Men's Chorus, and Orch. (1930); *Due liriche del Kalevala* for Tenor, Baritone, Chamber Chorus, and 4 Percussion (1930); *3 studi* for Soprano and Chamber Orch. (1932); *Estate* for Men's Chorus (1932); *Rhapsody* for Voice and Chamber Orch. (1934); *Divertimento in quattro esercizi* for Soprano, Flute, Oboe, Clarinet, Viola, and Cello (1934); *Cori di Michelangelo I* for Chorus (1933), *II* for Women's Chorus and 17 Instruments (1935), and *III* for Chorus and Orch. (1936); *3 laudi* for Soprano and Chamber Orch. (1936–37); *Canti di prigionia* for Chorus, 2 Pianos, 2 Harps, and Percussion (1938–41; 1st complete perf., Rome, Dec. 11, 1941); *Liriche greche I: Cinque frammenti di Saffo* for Voice and 15 Instruments (1942), *II: Due liriche di Anacreonte* for Soprano, 2 Clarinets, Viola, and Piano (1945), and *III: Sex carmina Alcaei* for Soprano and 11 Instruments (1943); *Roncesvals* for Voice and Piano (1946); *Quattro liriche di Antonio Machado* for Soprano and Piano (1948; also for Soprano and Chamber Orch., 1964); *3 poemi* for Soprano and Chamber Ensemble (1949); *Job,* biblical drama for 5 Singers, Narrator, Chorus, Speaking Chorus, and Orch. (1949–50; Rome, Oct. 30, 1950); *Canti di liberazione* for Chorus and Orch. (1951–55; Cologne, Oct. 28, 1955); *Goethe-Lieder* for Woman's Voice and 3 Clarinets (1953); *An Mathilde,* cantata for Woman's Voice and Orch. (1955); *5 canti* for Baritone and 8 Instruments (1956); *Concerto per la notte di Natale dell'anno 1956* for Soprano and Chamber Orch. (1956; Tokyo, Oct. 11, 1957); *Requiescant* for Chorus, Children's Chorus, and Orch. (1957–58; North German

Radio, Hamburg, Nov. 17, 1959); *Preghiere* for Baritone and Chamber Orch. (Berkeley, Calif., Nov. 10, 1962); *Parole di San Paolo* for Medium Voice and Chamber Ensemble (Washington, D.C., Oct. 10, 1969); *Sicut umbra...* for Mezzo-soprano and 4 Instrumental Groups (1969–70; Washington, Oct. 30, 1970); *Tempus destruendi/Tempus aedificandi* for Chorus (1970–71); *Commiato* for Soprano and Chamber Ensemble (Murau, Austria, Oct. 15, 1972).

BIBL.: B. Zanolini, *L. D.: La conquista di un linguaggio* (Padua, 1974); D. Kamper, *Gefangenschaft und Freiheit: Leben und Werk des Komponisten L. D.* (Cologne, 1984); A. Quattrocchi, ed., *Studi zu L. D.: Un Seminario* (Lucca, 1993); M. De Santis, ed., *Fondo L. D.: Autografi, scritti a stampa, bibliografia critica con un elenco dei corrispondenti* (Florence, 1995); idem, ed., *D.: Letture e prospettive* (Milan, 1997).—**NS/LK/DM**

Dallapozza, Adolf, Italian-born Austrian tenor; b. Bolzano, March 14, 1940. His parents settled in Austria when he was 5 months old. He received his musical education at the Vienna Cons.; then joined the Chorus of the Volksoper; in 1962 he made his debut as soloist in the role of Ernesto in Donizetti's *Don Pasquale*. In 1967 he became a member of the Vienna State Opera; also sang with the Bavarian State Opera in Munich and made appearances in Milan, Basel, Hamburg, Zürich, and Buenos Aires. In 1976 the President of Austria made him a Kammersänger. He is highly regarded for his versatility, being equally competent in opera, oratorio, and operetta.—**NS/LK/DM**

Dalla Rizza, Gilda, Italian soprano; b. Verona, Oct. 2, 1892; d. Milan, July 4, 1975. She received her musical training in Bologna where she made her operatic debut as Charlotte in *Werther* in 1912; in 1915 she sang at La Scala in Milan; Puccini so admired her singing that he created the role of Magda in *La Rondine* for her (Monte Carlo, March 27, 1917). She sang in Rome (1919), at London's Covent Garden (1920), and again at La Scala (1923–39); then taught voice at the Venice Cons. (1939–55). Her students included Anna Moffo and Gianna d'Angelo. She was married to the tenor Agostino Capuzzo (1889–1963). Her most famous role was Violetta.

BIBL.: P. Badoer, *G. d. R.: La cantante prediletta di Giacomo Puccini* (Abano Terme, 1991).—**NS/LK/DM**

Dalla Viola, Alfonso, Italian instrumentalist and composer; b. Ferrara, c. 1508; d. there, c. 1573. He was in the service of the Este family in Ferrara from 1528. He acquired a fine reputation as an instrumentalist and composer. He was also maestro di cappella at Ferrara Cathedral (c. 1563–72). Among his extant works are the vols. *Primo libro di madrigali* for 4 Voices (Ferrara, 1539) and *Il secondo libro di madrigali* for 4 Voices (Ferrara, 1540).—**NS/LK/DM**

Dalla Viola, Francesco, Italian composer; b. Ferrara, date unknown; d. there, March 1568. He sang at Ferrara Cathedral (c. 1522–26). A teacher of Ercole II, he also found a patron in the latter's brother, Cardinal Ippolito II; he was given a benefice by Ercole II in 1553.

He served as maestro di cappella at the Ferrara court (from 1559). He publ. *Il primo libro di madrigali* for 4 Voices (Venice, 1550); several of his sacred works are also extant.—**NS/LK/DM**

Dal Monte, Toti (real name, **Antonietta Meneghelli**), outstanding Italian soprano; b. Mogliano, near Treviso, June 27, 1893; d. Pieve di Soligo, Treviso, Jan. 26, 1975. She studied piano at the Venice Cons., then voice with Barbara Marchisio. She made her operatic debut at La Scala in Milan as Biancafiore in Zandonai's *Francesca da Rimini* in 1916, and then sang throughout Italy. After a brilliant appearance as Gilda at La Scala in 1922, she pursued a notably acclaimed career in Europe, singing in Paris, Vienna, London, and Berlin with extraordinary success. On Dec. 5, 1924, she made her Metropolitan Opera debut in N.Y. as Lucia, remaining on its roster for 1 season; she also sang at the Chicago Civic Opera (1924–28) and at London's Covent Garden (1926). She continued to sing in opera until World War II, after which she made her farewell performance at the Verona Arena in 1949; thereafter she taught voice. She publ. an autobiography, *Una voce nel mondo* (Milan, 1962). Her other remarkable roles included Cio-Cio-San, Mimi, and Stravinsky's Nightingale. —**NS/LK/DM**

Dalmorès, Charles (real name, **Henry Alphonse Boin**), French tenor; b. Nancy, Jan. 1, 1871; d. Los Angeles, Dec. 6, 1939. After taking first prizes at the local Cons. for solfeggio and horn at 17, he received from the city of Nancy a stipend for study at the Paris Cons., where he took first prize for horn at 19; played in the Colonne Orch. and the Lamoureux Orch.; at 23, became a prof. of horn at the Lyons Cons. His vocal teacher was Dauphin. His stage debut as a tenor took place on Oct. 6, 1899, at Rouen as Siegfried; later he sang at the Théâtre Royal de la Monnaie in Brussels (1900–06) and at London's Covent Garden (1904–05; 1909–11). On Dec. 7, 1906, he made his debut as Faust at the Manhattan Opera House in N.Y., then was with the Chicago Opera Co. (1910–18). His repertoire was large, and included Wagnerian as well as French operas; in Chicago he sang Tristan and the title role in the first performance of *Parsifal* to be presented there. —**NS/LK/DM**

Dal Pane, Domenico, noted Italian castrato soprano and composer; b. probably in Rome, c. 1630; d. there, Dec. 10, 1694. He became a treble at S. Maria Maggiore in Rome in his youth. After studies with Abbatini, he went to Vienna as a singer at the imperial court about 1650. Upon his return to Rome in 1654, he became active at the Sistine Chapel, where he later was its maestro di cappella (1669–79). He also was in the service of the Pamphili family. Among his finest works are 2 vols. of madrigals for 5 Voices and Basso Continuo (Rome, 1652, 1678) and the vol. *Sagri concerti ad honore del Ss. Sagramento* for 2–5 Voices and Basso Continuo (Rome, 1675).—**NS/LK/DM**

Dalvimare (real name, **d'Alvimare**), **(Martin-) Pierre,** French harpist and composer; b. Dreux, Eure-et-Loire, Sept. 18, 1772; d. Paris, June 13,

1839. In 1800 he was harpist at the Paris Opéra. In 1806 he became harpist to Napoleon, and in 1807 harp teacher to the Empress Josephine (1807); retired to his estate at Dreux in 1812. He wrote several sonatas for harp and violin, duets for 2 harps, for harp and piano, and for harp and horn, fantasies, variations, etc. —NS/LK/DM

Damase, Jean-Michael, French composer and pianist; b. Bordeaux, Jan. 27, 1928. His mother was the harpist Micheline Kahn. He was taken to Paris, where he was enrolled at the École Samuel-Rousseau at age 5 to receive rudimentary training in piano and theory. He wrote his first work at age 9 and appeared as a pianist at the Children's Pavilion at the Universal Exhibition. When he was 12 he became a student of Cortot at the École Normale de Musique. He pursued training at the Cons., where he was a student of Armand Ferté (premier prix in piano, 1943), Henri Büsser (premier prix in composition, 1947), and Marcel Dupré (harmony and counterpoint). In 1947 he was awarded the Premier Grand Prix de Rome for his cantata *Et la belle se réveilla*. While he subsequently made appearances as a pianist, he devoted himself principally to composition. Damase has become best known for his dramatic and chamber works in an appealing tonal style.

WORKS: DRAMATIC: *La croqueuse de diamants*, ballet (1950); *Piège de lumière*, ballet (1952); *Balance a trois*, ballet (1955); *Colombe*, opera (Bordeaux, Nov. 1956); *La Boucle*, ballet (1957); *La tendre Éléonore*, opera bouffe (1958; Marseilles, March 10, 1962); *Silk Rhapsody*, ballet (1966); *Madame de*, opera (1970); *Euridyce*, opera (Bordeaux, May 26, 1972); *L'Escarpolette*, comic opera (French TV, March 1982); *Ochelata's Wedding*, opera bouffe (1999). ORCH.: Concertino for Harp and Strings (1951); Violin Concerto (Paris, Dec. 1956); *Sérénade* for Flute and Strings (1956); *La valse mauve* (1959); *Guitare* (1961); *Rondeau* (1962); *Cavatine* (1963); *Souvenir* (1964); *Méandres* for Oboe and Strings (1978); *Suite concertante* for Oboe and Chamber Orch. (1978); Double Bass Concerto (1979); *Concert* for Chamber Orch. (1984); *Rhapsodie* for Horn and Orch. (1986); Concertino for Piano and Strings (1989; Rueil-Malmaison, March 11, 1995); Concerto for Viola, Harp, and Orch. (Paris, June 1990); Flute Concerto (Paris, Nov. 1993); *Ballade* for Harp and Strings (1994); *Rhapsodie juvénile* for Guitar and Strings (1994); *Suite en ut* for Chamber Orch. (Paris, Dec. 1994); *Variations on a Theme by Mozart* for 2 Pianos and Orch. (Bartlesville, Okla., June 1994); Horn Concerto (1995). CHAMBER: Trio for Flute, Harp, and Cello (1946); Quintet for Flute, Harp, Violin, Viola, and Cello (1948); *Rhapsodie* for Oboe and Piano (1948); *Étude de concert* for Harp (1951); *Sonata en concert* for Flute, Cello, and Piano (1952); Sonata for Flute and Harp (1964); Trio for Violin, Viola, and Cello (1965; Paris, Dec. 1970); Sonata for Flute or Violin and Piano (1976); Saxophone Quartet (1978); *Suite pour quatre* for 2 Oboes, Bassoon, and Harpsichord (1981); *Early Morning*, variations for Flute and Harp (Bartlesville, Okla., June 1982); Trio for Trumpet, Trombone, and Piano (1983); *Quatre à quatre* for 4 Clarinets (1986); *Quatre divertissements* for Flute and Piano (1986); *Aspects* for Horn and Piano or Harp (1987); *Variations* for Flute and Piano (1987); Flute Quartet (1989); Trio for Oboe, Horn, and Piano (1990); Flute Quartet (Bartlesville, Okla., June 1992); *Cinq petits dialogues* for Marimba and Harp or Piano (1994); *Thème et Variations* for Harp (Cardiff, June 1994); *Trois Prières sans paroles* for Trumpet and Organ (1994); Clarinet Sonata (Tokyo, March 1995); Horn Sonata (Paris, April 1996); *Quatre facettes* for Flute

and Guitar (1997). PIANO: *Pastorale* (1949); *Thème et Variations* (Paris, Nov. 1955); Sonatine (Bartlesvilles, Okla., June 1992). Organ: *Quatre Pastorales* (1993). VOCAL: *Ouverture, confiture, fermeture* for Soprano, Baritone, and Orch. (1959); *Hymne pour la jeunesse* for Chorus and Orch. (1965); *Onze psaumes de David* for Baritone, Chorus, and Orch. (Auvers-sur-Oise, June 16, 1985); songs.—NS/LK/DM

Dameron, Tadd (actually, **Tadley Ewing Peake**), bebop composer, arranger, leader, pianist; b. Cleveland, Ohio, Feb. 21, 1917; d. N.Y., March 8, 1965. He was inspired to follow a career as a jazz musician by his brother Caesar, a saxophonist. His first important job was with Freddie Webster's Band in Cleveland; he then worked with Zach Whyte and Blanche Calloway. During the 1940s he was highly active as an arranger in Chicago and N.Y., writing for many bands, including Harland Leonard's, Dizzy Gillespie's, Jimmie Lunceford's, and George Auld's, among others; he also continued to play piano regularly, often with his own small band. In 1948 he led a small group at the Royal Roost that featured Fats Navarro, Allen Eager, Curly Russell, and Kenny Clarke. Among his compositions are "Hot House," "Good Bait," "Lady Bird," and "Our Delight." His ballad "If You Could See Me Now" came out of a phrase from a Dizzy Gillespie solo. In May 1949 he went to Paris to play with Miles Davis, then remained in Europe and briefly worked as staff arranger for the English bandleader Ted Heath. He returned to the U.S., and during the early 1950s worked with Benjamin "Bull Moose" Jackson and then led his own band. At a show in Atlantic City in 1953, Clifford Brown and Philly Joe Jones were part of his band; this date was recorded. He wrote arrangements for Carmen McRae and Sarah Vaughan. His career was plagued by drug addiction, as a result he served time in federal prison in Lexington, Ky. (1958–60). In the early 1960s he returned to full-time music, doing arrangements for many famous bands until his activities were curtailed by the onset of cancer, which eventually led to his death. In the early 1980s, the groups Dameronia (9 or 10 pieces led by Philly Joe Jones) and Continuum (a quintet with Jimmy Heath and Slide Hampton) performed and recorded his pieces.

DISC.: Broadcast fragment, Atlantic City (1953); *Study in Dameronia* (1953); *Fontainebleau* (1956); *Mating Call* (1956); *Magic Touch of Tadd Dameron* (1962); *Dameronia* (1963). DAMERONIA: *To Tadd with Love* (his compositions; 1983). BARRY HARRIS: *Barry Harris* (plays Dameron compositions; 1975). —JC/MM/LP

Da Motta, José Vianna
See **Vianna da Motta, José**

Damrosch, Frank (Heino), German-American conductor and teacher, son of **Leopold Damrosch** and brother of **Walter (Johannes) Damrosch;** b. Breslau, June 22, 1859; d. N.Y., Oct. 22, 1937. He studied piano and composition in his youth; in 1871 he went with his family to N.Y., then went to Denver, where he conducted the Chorus Club (1882–85) and was supervisor of music in the public schools (1884–85). Returning to N.Y., he was chorus master and asst. conductor at the

Metropolitan Opera (1885–91). After studying composition with Moszkowski in Berlin (1891), he returned to N.Y. and organized the People's Singing Classes in 1892, which he conducted as the People's Choral Union (1894–1909). In 1893 he founded the Musical Art Soc., a professional chorus devoted to the performance of a cappella choral works, which he led until 1920; he also conducted the Oratorio Soc. (1898–1912). From 1898 to 1912 he conducted a series of sym. concerts for young people that were continued by his brother Walter; he also served as supervisor of music in N.Y. public schools (1897–1905). In 1905 he established the splendidly equipped Inst. of Musical Art, which, in 1926, became affiliated with the Juilliard School of Music; he retained his position as dean until his retirement in 1933. He received the degree of D.Mus. (honoris causa) from Yale Univ. in 1904. He publ. *Popular Method of Sight-Singing* (N.Y., 1894), *Some Essentials in the Teaching of Music* (N.Y., 1916), and *Institute of Musical Art, 1905–1926* (N.Y., 1936).

BIBL.: L. and R. Stebbins, *F. D.* (1945); G. Martin, *The D. Dynasty: America's First Family of Music* (N.Y., 1983). —NS/LK/DM

Damrosch, Leopold, eminent German-American conductor and violinist, father of **Frank (Heino) Damrosch** and **Walter (Johannes) Damrosch;** b. Posen, Oct. 22, 1832; d. N.Y., Feb. 15, 1885. He took the degree of M.D. at the Univ. of Berlin in 1854, but then, against his parents' wishes, embraced the career of a musician, studying with Ries, Dehn, and Bohmer. He appeared at first as a solo violinist in several German cities, later as a conductor at minor theaters, and in 1857 procured, through Liszt, the position of solo violinist in the Weimar Court Orch. While there, he was a close friend of Liszt and many of his most distinguished pupils, and won Wagner's lifelong friendship; in Weimar, too, he married the singer Helene von Heimburg (b. Oldenburg, 1835; d. N.Y., Nov. 21, 1904). From 1858 to 1860 Damrosch was conductor of the Breslau Phil. Concerts. He gave up the post to make tours with Bülow and Tausig; organized the Breslau Orch. Soc. in 1862. Besides this, he founded quartet *soirées*, and a choral society; conducted the Soc. for Classical Music, and a theater orch.; frequently appeared as a solo violinist. In 1871 he was called to N.Y. to conduct the Arion Soc., and made his debut, in April 1871, as conductor, composer, and violinist. He continued as its conductor until 1883. In 1873 he founded the Oratorio Soc., which he conducted until his death. In 1876–77 he was conductor of the N.Y. Phil., and then conducted his own orch. in 1877–78, which became the Sym. Soc. of N.Y. in the latter year. He continued as its conductor until his death, taking it on major tours in 1882 and 1883. During the 1884–85 season, he served as general manager of the Metropolitan Opera in N.Y., dying just 6 days before the close of the season. In 1880 he received an honorary D.Mus. degree from Columbia Coll. Damrosch was one of the most important figures in the musical life of N.Y. during his era, leaving a worthy heritage as performing artist and administrator. He also tried his hand at composing, producing a large output of music of little lasting value.

BIBL.: G. Martin, *The D. Dynasty: America's First Family of Music* (N.Y., 1983).—NS/LK/DM

Damrosch, Walter (Johannes), distinguished German- American conductor, music educator, and composer, son of **Leopold Damrosch** and brother of **Frank (Heino) Damrosch;** b. Breslau, Jan. 30, 1862; d. N.Y., Dec. 22, 1950. He received lessons in piano and composition before going to N.Y. with his family in 1871, where he continued his music studies. During the 1884–85 season of the Metropolitan Opera, he served as his father's assistant. When his father fell ill, he received some deathbed coaching from him and made his Metropolitan Opera debut conducting *Tannhäuser* on Feb. 11, 1885, just 4 days before his father succumbed. He remained on the roster of the Metropolitan Opera until 1891, and also served as his father's successor as conductor of the Oratorio Soc. of N.Y. (1885–98) and the Sym. Soc. of N.Y. (from 1885). In 1887 he pursued training in conducting with Bülow in Frankfurt am Main. In 1894 he founded the Damrosch Opera Co. in N.Y., which he conducted in performances of German operas until 1899, both there and in other major U.S. cities. From 1900 to 1902 he was again on the roster of the Metropolitan Opera. He was conductor of the N.Y. Phil. in 1902–03. After the reorganization of the Sym. Soc. of N.Y. in 1903, he was its conductor until it merged with the N.Y. Phil. in 1928. In 1920 he conducted the Sym. Soc. of N.Y. on a major tour of Europe. In 1912 he took over the sym. concerts for young people originally organized by his brother, and he also conducted young people's concerts with the Sym. Soc. of N.Y. His interest in music education prompted him to use the medium of radio to further the cause of music appreciation; on Oct. 19, 1923, he conducted the Sym. Soc. of N.Y. in its first radio broadcast from Carnegie Hall. In 1926 he inaugurated a regular series of radio broadcasts, which were later aired as the "NBC Music Appreciation Hour" throughout the U.S. and Canada from 1928 to 1942. He also served as musical counsel to NBC from 1927 to 1947. Damrosch conducted the U.S. premieres of Tchaikovsky's Fourth and Sixth syms. as well as scores by Wagner, Mahler, and Elgar. He also conducted premieres of works by American composers, including Gershwin's *An American in Paris*. He received honorary doctorates from Columbia Univ. (1914), Princeton Univ. (1929), N.Y.U. (1935) etc. In 1929 he was awarded the David Bispham medal. In 1932 he was elected to membership in the American Academy of Arts and Letters, and in 1938 he received the gold medal. His autobiography was publ. as *My Musical Life* (N.Y., 1923; 2nd ed., 1930).

WORKS: DRAMATIC: Opera: *The Scarlet Letter* (Boston, Feb. 10, 1896); *The Dove of Peace*, comic opera (Philadelphia, Oct. 15, 1912); *Cyrano de Bergerac* (N.Y., Feb. 27, 1913; rev. 1939); *The Man without a Country* (May 12, 1937); *The Opera Cloak* (N.Y., Nov. 3, 1942). **Incidental Music To:** Euripides' *Iphigenia in Aulis* (Berkeley, 1915) and *Medea* (Berkeley, 1915); Sophocles' *Electra* (N.Y., 1917). **OTHER:** *Manila Te Deum* (N.Y., 1898); *An Abraham Lincoln Song* for Baritone, Chorus, and Orch. (1935); *Dunkirk* for Baritone, Men's Chorus, and Chamber Orch. (NBC, May 2, 1943); chamber music; songs.

BIBL.: G. Damrosch Finletter, *From the Top of the Stairs*

(Boston, 1946); F. Himmelein, *W. D.: A Cultural Biography* diss., Univ. of Va., 1972); M. Goodell, *W. D. and his Contributions to Music Education* (diss., Catholic Univ. of America, 1973); G. Martin, *The D. Dynasty: America's First Family of Music* (N.Y., 1983).—**NS/LK/DM**

Dan, Ikuma, Japanese composer; b. Tokyo, April 7, 1924. He studied at the Tokyo Music Academy with K. Shimofusa and S. Moroi. After teaching at the Tokyo Music School (1947–50), he was active as a film music director and composer.

WORKS: DRAMATIC: O p e r a : *Yûzuru* (The Twilight Crane; 1950–51; Tokyo, Jan. 30, 1952; rev. 1956); *Kikimimi- zukin* (The Listening Cap; 1954–55; Tokyo, March 18, 1955); *Yang Kwei- fei* (1957–58; Tokyo, Dec. 11, 1958); *Chanchiki* (Cling-Clang; 1961–63); *Hikarigoke* (1972; Osaka, April 27, 1972). D a n c e D r a m a : *Futari Shizuka* (1961). ORCH.: Symphonic Poem (1948); 6 syms. (1949–50; 1955–56; 1959–60; 1964–65; 1965; 1970); *Sinfonia burlesca* (1953; Tokyo, Jan. 26, 1959); *The Silken Road,* dance suite (1953–54; Tokyo, June 23, 1955); *Journey through Arabia,* symphonic suite (1958); *Olympic Games Overture* (1964); *Festival Overture* (1965); Concerto Grosso for Harpsichord and Strings (1965); *Japanese Poem No. 1* (Tokyo, Sept. 25, 1967); *A Letter from Japan No. 2* (1969); *Rainbow Tower* (1970). CHAMBER: String Trio (1947); Piano Sonata (1947); String Quartet (1948); *Divertimento* for 2 Pianos (1949). VOCAL: *Hymn to the Sai-kai* for Chorus and Orch. (1969); choruses.—**NS/LK/DM**

Danckert, Werner, German musicologist; b. Erfurt, June 22, 1900; d. Krefeld, March 5, 1970. He studied natural science and mathematics at the Univ. of Jena, then musicology at the Univ. of Leipzig with Riemann and Abert, at the Univ. of Erlangen with Becking, and at the Leipzig Cons. with Schering. He received his Ph.D. in 1924 at the Univ. of Erlangen with the diss. *Geschichte der Gigue* (publ. in Leipzig, 1924); he completed his Habilitation at the Univ. of Jena in 1926 with his *Personale Typen des Melodiestils* (publ. in an enl. ed. as *Ursymbole melodischer Gestaltung* in Kassel, 1932). He was Becking's assistant at the Univ. of Erlangen (1924–25); then taught piano at the Weimar Academy of Music (1929–32) and was a music critic in Erfurt (1932–37). He became a lecturer at the Univ. of Berlin in 1937, prof. in 1939, and head of the musicology dept. in 1943; then was in Graz (1943–45). He was a prof. at the Univ. of Rostock in 1950, but returned to West Germany that same year.

WRITINGS: *Beiträge zur Bachkritik* (Kassel, 1934); *Das europäische Volkslied* (Berlin, 1939; 2nd ed., 1970); *Grundriss der Volksliedkunde* (Berlin, 1939); *Claude Debussy* (Berlin, 1950); *Goethe: Der mythische Urgrund seiner Weltenschau* (Berlin, 1951); *Offenes und geschlossenes Leben: Zwei Daseinsaspekte in Goethes Weltenschau* (Bonn, 1963); *Unehrliche Leute: Die verfemten Berufe* (Bern and Munich, 1964); *Das Volkslied im Abendland* (Bern and Munich, 1966); *Tonreich und Symbolzahl in Hochkulturen und in der Primitivenwelt* (Bonn, 1966); *Symbol, Metaphor, Allegorie im Lied der Völker* (Bonn, 1977).—**NS/LK/DM**

Danckerts, Ghiselin, Flemish composer and music theorist; b. Tholen, Zeeland, c. 1510; d. after Aug. 1565. He entered the Papal Chapel in Rome as a chorister in 1538, and was pensioned in 1565. Although collections of his works were publ., they are lost; however, single works are extant. His ingenuity in counterpoint is demonstrated in the so-called Chessboard Canon for 4 voices with alternating black and white notes. His treatise (c. 1551) pronouncing judgment on the theoretical dispute between Vincentino and Lusitano on the nature of ancient modes subsequently appeared in 2 versions (c. 1555–56 and 1559–60).—**NS/LK/DM**

Dancla, Arnaud Phillipe, French cellist and composer, brother of **(Jean Baptiste) Charles Dancla** and **(Jean Pierre) Léopold Dancla;** b. Bagnères-de-Bigorre, Jan. 1, 1819; d. there, Feb. 1, 1862. He studied cello with Norblin at the Paris Cons. (premier prix, 1841) and was a cellist in the orch. of the Société des Concerts du Conservatoire (1847–61); he was also in the orch. of the Opéra-Comique. He was the author of a method for cello. He also composed études, duos, and melodies for his instrument.—**NS/LK/DM**

Dancla, (Jean Baptiste) Charles, French violinist, teacher, and composer, brother of **Arnaud Phillipe Dancla** and **(Jean Pierre) Léopold Dancla;** b. Bagnères-de-Bigorre, Dec. 19, 1817; d. Tunis, Nov. 9, 1907. He studied violin with Dussert in Bagnères-de-Bigorre, then entered the Paris Cons. (1828), where he studied violin with Guerin and Baillot (premier prix, 1833), counterpoint and fugue with Halévy, and composition with Berton (graduated, 1840). He joined the orch. of the Société des Concerts du Conservatoire in 1834, serving as its principal violinist (1841–63). He also taught at the Paris Cons. (from 1855), where he was prof. of violin (1860–92). His quartet *soirées* were famous. Besides 4 syms., he composed some 130 works for violin, 14 string quartets, and 4 piano trios.

WRITINGS: *Méthode élémentaire et progressive pour le violon; École du mécanisme; L'École de la mélodie; École de l'expression;* and (with Panseron) *L'Art de moduler sur le violon;* also books of essays, *Les Compositeurs chefs d'orchestre* (1873) and *Miscellanées musicales* (1876).

BIBL.: C. D., *Notes et souvenirs* (Paris, 1893; 2nd ed., 1898). —**NS/LK/DM**

Dancla, (Jean Pierre) Léopold, French violinist and composer, brother of **Arnaud Phillipe Dancla** and **(Jean Baptiste) Charles Dancla;** b. Bagnères-de-Bigorre, June 1, 1822; d. Paris, April 29, 1895. He studied violin with Dussert in Bagnères-de- Bigorre, then entered the Paris Cons., where he studied cornet with Meifred (premier prix, 1838) and violin with Baillot (premier prix, 1842). He became a violinist in the orch. of the Société des Concerts du Conservatoire (1846), and also joined the orchs. of the Paris Opéra (1853) and the Théâtre-Italien (1858). He wrote much chamber music, works for violin, and vocal pieces.—**NS/LK/DM**

Danco, Suzanne, admired Belgian soprano; b. Brussels, Jan. 22, 1911. She began her training at the Brussels Cons.; after winning the Vienna vocal competition (1936), she studied with Fernando Carpi in Prague. She then went to Italy, where she made her debut as a concert artist in 1940. In 1941 she made her operatic debut as Fiordiligi in Genoa, and later sang in various Italian operatic centers. She had much success at Milan's La Scala, where she sang in the local premieres of *Peter Grimes* (as Ellen Orford, 1947) and *Oedipus Rex* (as Jocasta, 1948). From 1948 to 1951 she appeared at the Glyndebourne Festivals. She sang in the U.S. for the first time in 1950. In 1951 she appeared as Mimi at London's Covent Garden. In later years, she concentrated on concert engagements and also was active as a teacher at the Accademia Musicale Chigiana in Siena. Among her other notables roles were Donna Anna, Mélisande, and Berg's Marie. She was especially praised as a concert artist, excelling in the French repertory, particularly in works by Berlioz, Debussy, and Ravel.—NS/LK/DM

Dandara, Liviu, Romanian composer; b. Miorcani, Dec. 3, 1933; d. Bucharest, July 22, 1991. He studied at the Bucharest Cons. (1952–58), and later attended the summer courses in new music in Darmstadt (1967, 1978).

WORKS: DRAMATIC: *Fata Babei si fata Mosneagului*, music theater (Bucharest, May 5, 1976); *Fratii Cris*, music theater (Bucharest, May 7, 1977); film music. **ORCH.:** *Sinfonietta lirică* (1958; Galati, Feb. 1959); *Uvertura festivă* (1958; Focșani, Jan. 1959); Suite (1962); *Divertisment* (1964); *Expresii umane* (1968); *Spatii*, stereophonic piece for 32 Instruments and Amplification (1971); Piano Concerto (1972). **CHAMBER:** *Trei miscări lente* for Clarinet and Piano (1963); *Ipostaze* for Flute, Oboe, Clarinet, and Bassoon (1966); Sonata for Solo Clarinet (1966); *Dialoguri cu axa timpului* for Flute, Violin, Piano, and Percussion (1968); *Pentaedre por la "Musica nova"* for Clarinet, Violin, Viola, Cello, and Piano (1969); *Quadriforium* for Piano and Electronics (1970); *Bamba* for Winds or Voice and Percussion (1971); *Incantatii* for Flute (1971); *Trei stări despre liniste* for Violin and Piano (1980); Suite for Violin and Piano (1981); *Multiversum* for Violin (1983). **OTHER:** Choral pieces; songs; electronic music.—NS/LK/DM

Dandelot, Georges (Edouard), French composer and teacher; b. Paris, Dec. 2, 1895; d. St.-Georges de Didonne, Charente-Maritime, Aug. 17, 1975. He studied with Widor at the Paris Cons., and later took lessons with Dukas and Roussel. He was in the French army during World War I, and received the Croix de Guerre for valor. In 1919 he became an instructor at the École Normale de Musique in Paris, and in 1942 he was appointed a prof. at the Paris Cons. Dandelot composed an oratorio, *Pax* (1st prize at the International Exposition in Paris, 1937); 2 operas: *Midas* (1947) and *L'Ennemi* (1948); 3 ballets: *Le Souper de famine* (1943), *Le Jardin merveilleux* (1944), and *Pierrot et la rose* (1948); Sym. (1941); Piano Concerto (Paris, Jan. 7, 1934); *Concerto romantique* for Violin and Orch. (1944); chamber music; songs.—NS/LK/DM

Dandrieu, Jean François, French organist and composer; b. Paris, 1682; d. there, Jan. 17, 1738. He was organist at Saint- Merry, Paris, in 1704, and in 1721 became organist at the Royal Chapel. He publ. *Livre de*

sonates en trio (1705), *Livre de sonates* for Solo Violin (1710), *Principes de l'accompagnement du clavecin* (1718), *Pièces de clavecin* (3 albums, 1724), organ pieces, and airs. His importance lies in his works for clavecin, written in a style closely resembling Couperin's.

BIBL.: P. Brunold, *D.* (Paris, 1954).—NS/LK/DM

Daneau, Nicolas, Belgian composer; b. Binche, June 17, 1866; d. Brussels, July 12, 1944. He studied at the Ghent Cons. with Adolphe Samuel, graduating in 1892, and winning the second Prix de Rome in 1895. He was director of the Cons. of Tournai (1896–1919), and of the Cons. of Mons (1919–31). His daughter, Suzanne Daneau (b. Tournai, Aug. 17, 1901; d. there, Nov. 29, 1971), was his pupil. She wrote orch. works, chamber music, and piano pieces, mostly based on native folk songs.

WORKS: DRAMATIC: *Linario*, lyric drama (Tournai, 1906); *Myrtis*, opera-idyll (Tournai, 1910); *Le Sphynx*, opera; *La Brute*, lyric drama. **ORCH.:** *Villes d'Italie*; *Adima et Hevah*; *Arles*; *Mardi-Gras*; *Petite suite*. **CHAMBER:** Suite for Violin and Piano; String Quartet; Piano Quintet.

BIBL.: L. Beatrice, *D.*; *Histoire d'une famille d'artistes* (Brussels, 1944).—NS/LK/DM

D'Angeri, Anna (real name, **Anna von Angermayer de Redernburg**), Austrian soprano; b. Vienna, Nov. 14, 1853; d. Trieste, Dec. 14, 1907. She studied with Marchesi in Vienna. In 1872 she made her operatic debut as Selika in Mantua, and then appeared at London's Covent Garden (1874–77). She was admired as a Wagnerian, and was the first to sing Ortrud and Venus in London (1875–76). After singing at the Vienna Court Opera (1878–79), she appeared at Milan's La Scala (1879–81), where she sang Amelia in the rev. version of *Simon Boccanegra* in 1881. She then married Vittorio Dalem, director of the Teatro Rossetti in Trieste, and retired from the stage.—NS/LK/DM

D'Anglebert, Jean-Henri, significant French harpsichordist, organist, and composer; b. Paris, 1635; d. there, April 23, 1691. He was a pupil of Chambonnières. After serving in the position of first organist to the Duke of Orléans and to the Jacobins in the rue St. Honoré in Paris, he was made ordinaire de la chambre du Roy pour le clavecin by King Louis XIV in 1662. He publ. *Pièces de clavecin avec la manière de les jouer* (Paris, 1689), which contains 4 dance suites, 5 organ fugues, transcriptions of popular tunes, arrangements of works by Lully, a treatise on keyboard harmony, and a table of ornaments, with many new signs that were widely accepted. The vol. stands as a major source for the French Classical style. A modern ed. of his works was publ. in Le pupitre, LIV (1975). His son, Jean-Baptiste Henri D'Anglebert (b. Paris, Sept. 5, 1661; d. there, Nov. 1735), succeeded him at the court.

BIBL.: B. Seibert, *J.-H. d'A. and the Seventeenth Century Clavecin School* (Bloomington, Ind., 1986).—NS/LK/DM

Dang Thai Son (actually, **Son Thai Dang**), Vietnamese pianist; b. Hanoi, July 2, 1958. He began piano lessons at age 5 with his mother, a piano teacher at the Hanoi Cons., where he became a student in 1965. His studies were interrupted by the American bombing campaign during the Vietnam War, and he and his mother fled to the village of Xuan Phu, where he continued his training. After the War, he took his degree at the Hanoi Cons. (1976). He then went to Moscow to pursue his studies at the Cons. with Natanson, graduating in 1983; subsequently completed his training with Bashkirov (1983–86). In 1980 he won first prize in the Chopin Competition in Warsaw in the wake of the controversial decision by the jury to eliminate his fellow competitor Ivo Pogorelich in the final round. Dang's victory was significant, since with it he became the first Asian pianist to win first prize in such a prestigious competition. In 1981 he made his debut in Paris, followed by debuts in London in 1984 and in Berlin in 1985. In 1989 he made his U.S. debut in a recital at N.Y.'s 92nd Street Y. In 1991 he settled in Canada while continuing to pursue an international career. His repertoire ranges from Haydn to Prokofiev.—NS/LK/DM

Danhauser, Adolphe-Léopold, French composer and teacher; b. Paris, Feb. 26, 1835; d. there, June 9, 1896. He studied at the Paris Cons. with Halévy and Reber, winning first prize in harmony (1857), first prize in fugue (1859), and second Prix de Rome (1862). He was chief inspector of instruction in singing in the communal schools in Paris and prof. of solfeggio at the Cons. He wrote *Théorie de la musique*, and also publ. *Soirées orphéoniques*, a collection of 3-part choruses for equal voices. He composed *Le Proscrit*, a musical drama with choruses, which was produced (1866) in a religious institution at Auteuil, and a 3-act opera, *Maures et Castillans* (not perf.). His *Solfège des solfèges* (3 vols.; tr. into Eng. and Sp.) was used throughout the U.S. and South America.—NS/LK/DM

Daniel, Minna (née **Lederman**), legendary American editor and writer on music; b. N.Y., March 3, 1896; d. N.Y., Oct. 29, 1995. She studied music and dance professionally before taking a degree at Barnard Coll. (1917) and beginning her career as a journalist. In 1923 she joined the newly formed League of Composers, and in 1924 helped launch its *Review*, which in 1925 became *Modern Music*, the first American journal to serve as a literary forum for contemporary composers. During her tenure as its sole editor (1924–46), she encouraged a generation of American composer-critics, publishing essays and reviews by such musical activists as Thomson, Cage, Carter, Blitzstein, and Bowles; she also publ. articles by Berg, Schoenberg, and Bartók. The journal attained an international reputation. In 1975 she established the Archives of Modern Music at the Library of Congress in Washington, D.C. In 1983 she publ. the informative chronicle *The Life and Death of a Small Magazine*. She also ed. *Stravinsky in the Theatre* (N.Y., 1949; 3rd ed., 1975).—NS/LK/DM

Daniel, Oliver, American music administrator and writer on music; b. De Pere, Wisc., Nov. 24, 1911; d. Scarsdale, N.Y., Dec. 30, 1990. He attended St. Norbert Coll. in West De Pere (1925–29), then studied piano in Europe and at the New England Cons. of Music in Boston. He was active as a pianist and as a piano teacher until becoming music director of the educational division of CBS radio in 1942; he was head of the concert-music division of BMI (1954–77) and was associated with the International Music Council of UNESCO (from 1958). With Stokowski, he founded the Contemporary Music Soc. in 1952; later was active with various other organizations, including the American Music Center, the Charles Ives Soc., and the American Composers Orch. He wrote a column for the *Saturday Review* (1957–68); also contributed to other journals. He ed. various collections of works by early American composers and publ. the study *Leopold Stokowski: A Counterpoint of View* (1982).—NS/LK/DM

Daniel, Paul (Wilson), English conductor; b. Birmingham, July 1, 1958. He was a chorister at Coventry Cathedral, and pursued his musical training at King's Coll., Cambridge (1976–79) and at the Guildhall School of Music and Drama in London (1979–80). His mentors in conducting were Boult and Downes in England, and Ferrara in Italy. He was on the staff of the English National Opera in London from 1980 to 1985. In 1982 he made his debut as an operatic conductor with *The Beggar's Opera* with the Opera Factory in London. In 1985 he joined its staff, subsequently serving as its music director from 1987 to 1990. In 1988 he made his U.S. debut in N.Y. with the London Sinfonietta. From 1990 to 1997 he was artistic director of Opera North in Leeds, where he concurrently served as principal conductor of the English Northern Philharmonia. He made his first appearance at London's Covent Garden in 1993 conducting *Mitridate*. In 1997 he became music director of the English National Opera. As a guest conductor, his engagements took him all over England and Europe in appearances with major opera houses and orchs. In 1988 he married **Joan Rodgers**. Daniel's operatic repertoire is an expansive one, ranging from Cavalli, Mozart, and Verdi to Birtwistle, Maxwell Davies, and Böse. —NS/LK/DM

Daniel, Salvador (real name, **Francisco Daniel**; also known as **Salvador-Daniel**), French composer and political revolutionary; b. Bourges, Feb. 17, 1831; killed during the Paris Commune, May 23, 1871. For a brief time he was director of the Paris Cons. under the Commune. He taught music in an Arab school in Algiers, and studied native folk songs of North Africa. He wrote a valuable book, *La Musique arabe* (Algiers, 1863; Eng. tr., 1915, as *The Music and Musical Instruments of the Arabs*).—NS/LK/DM

Daniel-Lesur, Jean Yves (real name, **Daniel Jean Yves Lesur**), prominent French composer and pedagogue; b. Paris, Nov. 19, 1908. He spent his entire life in Paris, where he studied at the Cons. (1919–29) with J. Gallon and Caussade (harmony and fugue), Armand Ferté (piano), and Tournemiere (organ and composition). He was asst. organist at St. Clotilde (1927–37) and organist at the Benedictine Abbey (1935–39; 1942–44). With Messiaen, Baudrier, and

Jolivet, he founded the Groupe Jeune France in 1936. He taught counterpoint (1935–64) and was director (1957–62) of the Schola Cantorum. He was responsible for music information for the French Radio (from 1939) and was music councilor for the French TV (from 1968). From 1969 to 1971 he was inspector general of music for the Ministry of Culture. He was administrator of the Réunion des Théâtres Lyriques Nationaux from 1971 to 1973. With B. Gavoty, he publ. *Pour ou contre la musique moderne* (Paris, 1957). He was made a Commandeur de la Légion d'honneur and a Commander de l'Ordre National du Merité et Commandeur des Arts et Lettres. In 1982 he was made a member of the Académie des Beaux-Arts. In his compositions, Daniel- Lesur perfected an ascetic modal style.

WORKS: DRAMATIC: O p e r a : *Andrea del Sarto* (1968; Marseilles, Jan. 24, 1969); *Ondine* (Paris, April 26, 1982); *La Reine morte* (1987). **B a l l e t :** *L'Infante et le Monstre* (1938; in collaboration with A. Jolivet); *Le bal du destin,* after the *Symphonie de danses* (1954); *Metaforen* (1965; The Hague, Jan. 17, 1966); *Un jour un enfant,* after the Suite for String Trio and Piano (Tours, Nov. 29, 1969). **O t h e r :** Film scores. **ORCH.:** *Hommage à J.S. Bach* for Strings (1933); *Suite française* (Paris, March 17, 1935); *Passacaille* for Piano and Orch. (Paris, June 4, 1937); *Pastorale* for Chamber Orch. (1938); *Ricercare* (1939; Radio Geneva, May 11, 1941); *L'Étoile de Seville,* suite for Chamber Orch. (1941); *Variations* for Piano and Strings (1943); *Andrea del Sarto,* symphonic poem (Paris, June 21, 1949); *Ouverture pour un festival* (Toulouse, June 6, 1951); *Concerto da camera* for Piano and Chamber Orch. (1953; Strasbourg, June 14, 1954); *Sérénade* for Strings (1954); *Le bal du destin,* suite after the ballet (1956; Paris, Jan. 10, 1957); *Symphonie de danses* for Piano, Timpani, and Strings (Paris, Dec. 4, 1958); *Nocturne* for Oboe and Strings (1974); *Symphonie d'ombre et de lumière* (1974; Paris, May 7, 1975); *Mélodrame* for Tuba and Orch. (1991); *Stèle à la mémoire d'une jeune fille* for Flute and Strings (1991; Fresnes, Jan. 16, 1992); *Fantaisie concertante* for Cello and Orch. (1992; Paris, Sept. 1994); *Impromptu* for Flute, Harp, and Strings (1993); *Lamento* for Harp and Strings (1995). **CHAMBER:** *Cinq Interludes* for 4 Horns (1935); Suite for 3 Woodwinds (1939); Suite for String Quartet (1940); Suite for Piano Quartet (1943); *Suite médiévale* for Flute, Harp, and String Trio (1946); Sextet for Flute, Oboe, Violin, Viola, Cello, and Harpsichord (1948); *Élégie* for 2 Guitars (1956); *Nocturne* for Oboe and Piano (1974); *Intermezzo* for Violin and Piano (1977); *Novellete* for Flute and Piano (1977). **KEYBOARD: P i a n o :** *Soirs* (1922–29); *Les carillons,* suite (1930); *Bagatelle* (1934); *Suite Française* (1935); *Pavane* (1938); *Deux Noëls* (1939–40); *Le village imaginaire* for 2 Pianos (1947); *Pastorale variée* (1947); *Ballade* (1948); *Nocturne* (1953); *Le bal* (1954); *Fantaisie* for 2 Pianos (1962); *Trois études* (1962); *Contre-fugue for* 2 Pianos (1970). **O r g a n :** *Scène de la passion* (1931); *La vie intérieure* (1932); *In paradisum* (1933); *Hymnes* (1935); *Quatre hymnes* (1937–39). **VOCAL: V o i c e a n d P i a n o :** *Les harmonies intimes* (1931); *La mort des violes* (1931); *Les yeux fermés* (1932); *La mouette* (1932); *Trois poèmes de Cécile Sauvage* (1939); *L'enfance de l'art* (1942); *Clair comme le jour* (1945); *Berceuses à tenir éveillé* (1947). **OTHER:** *Quatre lieder* for Voice and Orch. (1933–39; N.Y., Nov. 30, 1948); *Deux chansons de l'Etoile de Seville* for Voice and Orch. (1941); *Anne et le dragon* for Chorus and Chamber Ensemble (1945); *Chansons Cambodgiennes* for Voice and Orch. (1947); *Dialogues dans la nuit* for Soprano, Baritone, and Orch. (1950–87); *L'Annonciation,* oratorio for Tenor, 2 Reciters, Chorus, and Chamber Orch. (1951); *Le Cantique des Cantiques,* cantata for Chorus (Bordeaux, May 1, 1953); *Le Cantique*

des Colonnes for Women's Chorus and Orch. (1953–57); *Messe du jubilé* for Chorus, Organ, and Orch. (1960); *Chanson de mariage* for Women's Chorus (1964); *Encore un instant de bonheur,* cantata for Vocal Ensemble and Chamber Orch. (1989); *Le voyage d'automne* for Voice and Orch. (1990); *Permis de séjour* for Voice and Strings (1990); *A la lisière du temps* for Voice, Flute, Harp, and Strings (1991); *Dialogues imaginaires* for Soprano, Baritone, and Orch. (1991).—NS/LK/DM

Daniélou, Alain, French musicologist; b. Paris, Oct. 4, 1907; d. Lausanne, Jan. 27, 1994. He devoted himself mainly to the study of Asian music. He lectured at the Univ. of Benares (1949–54), and was director of research in Madras (1954–56) and at the Inst. of Indology in Pondicherry (1956–59). In 1959 he was appointed instructor at the École Française d'Extrême Orient in Paris. In 1963 he assumed the post of director of the International Inst. for Comparative Studies.

WRITINGS: *Introduction to the Study of Musical Scales* (London, 1943); *Northern Indian Music* (2 vols., Calcutta, 1949, 1953; 2nd ed., rev., 1968, as *The Ragas of Northern Indian Music*); *La Musique du Cambodge et du Laos* (Pondicherry, 1957); *Traité de musicologie comparée* (Paris, 1959); *Purānas: Textes des Purānas sur la théorie musicale* (Pondicherry, 1959); *Bharata, Muni, Le Gītālamkāra* (Pondicherry, 1960); *Inde* (Paris, 1966); *Sémantique musicale* (Paris, 1967); *La Situation de la musique et des musiciens dans les pays d'orient* (Florence, 1971; Eng. tr., 1971). —NS/LK/DM

Danielpour, Richard, American composer; b. N.Y., Jan. 28, 1956. He studied at Oberlin (Ohio) Coll., then at the New England Cons. of Music in Boston (B.M., 1980) before pursuing graduate studies in composition with Mennin and Persichetti at the Juilliard School in N.Y. (M.M., 1982; D.M.A., 1986) and piano studies with Hollander and Lettvin. He taught at the Coll. of New Rochelle and Marymount Manhattan Coll. (1984–88). In 1989 he was a guest composer at the Accademia di Santa Cecilia in Rome. In 1991–92 he was composer-in-residence of the Seattle Sym. Orch., and in 1994 of the Santa Fe (N.Mex.) Chamber Music Festival. He currently teaches on the composition faculty at the Curtis Inst. and at the Manhattan School of Music, and is completing a 3- year composer residency with the Pacific Sym. His awards include a Guggenheim fellowship, a Rockefeller Foundation grant, and two awards from the American Academy of Arts and Letters. Danielpour's widely performed music exhibits a modern Romantic tenor and is often programmatically derived.

WORKS: DRAMATIC: B a l l e t : *Anima Mundi* (1995; also a concert suite); *Urban Dances: Dance Suite in Five Movements* (1996). **ORCH.:** 4 syms.: No. 1, *Dona Nobis Pacem* (1984–85), No. 2, *Visions,* for Soprano, Tenor, and Orch., after Dylan Thomas (1986; San Francisco, Dec. 19, 1986), No. 3, *Journey Without Distance,* for Soprano, Chamber Chorus, and Orch., after Schumann (1989–90; Akron, Feb. 24, 1990), and No. 4, *Celestial Night* (1997); *First Light* for Chamber Orch. (1988; also for Orch., 1989); *The Awakened Heart* (1990); 2 piano concertos: No. 1, *Metamorphosis* (N.Y., April 21, 1990) and No. 2 (1993; N.Y., March 30, 1994); *Song of Remembrance* (1991); *Toward the Splendid City* (1992); Cello Concerto (San Francisco, Sept. 14, 1994); *Concerto for Orchestra:"Zoroastrian Riddles"* (1996); *Elegies* (1997);

Vox Populi (1998); *The Night Rainbow* (1999); Violin Concerto, *A Fool's Paradise* (1999); *Voices of Remembrance,* concerto for String Quartet and Orch. (2000). **CHAMBER:** 3 string quartets (n.d., withdrawn; *Shadow Dances,* 1992; *Psalms of Sorrow* for Baritone and String Quartet, 1994); *Urban Dances I* (1989) and *II* (1993) for Brass Quintet; Piano Quintet (1988); *Fantasy Variation* for Cello and Piano (1997); *Feast of Fools* for Bassoon and String Quartet (1998); *A Child's Reliquary,* piano trio (1999). **PIANO:** *Piano Fantasy* (1980); *The Enchanted Garden* (1992). **VOCAL:** *Prologue and Prayer* for Chorus and String Orch. (1982; rev. 1988); *Sonnets to Orpheus I* for Soprano and Ensemble (1991) and *Book II* for Baritone and Ensemble (1994); *Songs of the Night* for Tenor, Violin, Cello, and Piano (1993); *Canticle of Peace* for Baritone Solo and Chorus (1995); *I Am Not Prey* for Soprano and Piano, 4-Hands (1996); *Sweet Talk: Four Songs on Texts by Toni Morrison* for Soprano, Cello, Double Bass, and Piano (1997); *Spirits in the Well,* song cycle for Soprano and Orch. after Toni Morrison (1998).—**NS/LK/DM**

Daniels, Barbara, American soprano; b. Newark, Ohio, May 7, 1946. She studied at Ohio State Univ. (B.Mus., 1969) and the Univ. of Cincinnati Coll.-Cons. of Music (M.A., 1971). In 1973 she made her operatic debut as Susanna in *Le nozze di Figaro* at the West Palm Beach (Fla.) Opera; then was a member of the Innsbruck Landestheater (1974–76), Kassel Staatstheater (1976–78), and Cologne Opera (1978–82). In 1978 she appeared as Rosalinde at London's Covent Garden, and on Sept. 30, 1983, she made her Metropolitan Opera debut in N.Y. as Musetta, also making guest appearances at the Vienna State Opera, the Chicago Lyric Opera, the Paris Opéra, and the Bavarian State Opera in Munich. Among her other roles are Violetta, Alice Ford, Massenet's Manon, and Micaëla.—**NS/LK/DM**

Daniels, David, extraordinary American counter-tenor; b. Spartanburg, S.C., March 12, 1966. He was reared in a musical family. Following studies at the Univ. of Cincinnati Coll.-Cons. of Music, he pursued graduate training with George Shirley at the Univ. of Mich. (M.A., 1992). He sang minor roles with the Los Angeles Opera and appeared in oratorios before attracting notice as Nerone in *L'incoronazione di Poppea* at the Glimmerglass Opera in Cooperstown, N.Y., in 1994. In 1995 he returned there to great critical acclaim as Handel's Tamerlano. He sang Arsamene in Handel's *Xerxes* with the Boston Lyric Opera, Didymus in Handel's *Theodora* at the Glyndebourne Festival, and Oberon in his London debut in 1996. On Dec. 2, 1996, he made his N.Y. recital debut at Lincoln Center. In 1997 he won the Richard Tucker Music Foundation Award, and sang Sesto in Handel's *Giulio Cesare* at London's Covent Garden, Nerone in Munich, and Arsamene at the N.Y.C. Opera. He was engaged to make his Metropolitan Opera debut in N.Y. as Arsamene on April 10, 1999. Daniels's remarkable artistry combines a mastery of vocal splendor and dramatic power.—**NS/LK/DM**

Daniels, Eddie (actually, **Edward Kenneth**), tenor saxophonist, clarinetist; b. N.Y., Oct. 19, 1941. He studied at N.Y.'s H.S. of Performing Arts, and was a member of Marshall Brown's Youth Band which performed at the 1957 Newport Jazz Festival. He took a masters degree in clarinet from Julliard in 1966. He first attracted attention in the jazz world as a member of the Thad Jones–Mel Lewis band in 1966, remaining with it until 1972. In the late 1960s and early 1970s he also recorded with Freddie Hubbard, Richard Davis, Don Patterson, and Bucky Pizzarelli, as well as leading his own projects. Daniels had always played clarinet, but was mainly a tenor player during this period. However, he stopped playing saxophone in the early 1980s and began concentrating on clarinet. Beginning in the mid-1980s, Daniels recorded several albums for GRP. These releases helped make him one of the most popular and publicly known jazz clarinetists in decades and created renewed interest in the instrument. In the late 1990s he returned to doubling on tenor. He has appeared on *The Tonight Show* and his Benny Goodman tribute with Gary Burton was featured in a one-hour video.

DISC.: *First Prize* (1966); *Blue Bossa* (1972); *Flower for All Seasons* (1973); *Brief Encounter* (1977); *Morning Thunder* (1978); *Breakthrough* (1986); *Collection* (1986); *Memos from Paradise* (1987); *To Bird with Love* (1987); *Blackwood* (1989); *Nepenthe* (1989); *This Is Now* (1991); *Benny Rides Again* (Goodman tribute, with Gary Burton; 1992); *Under the Influence* (1993); *Eddie Daniels Collection* (1994); *Real Time* (1994); *Five Seasons* (1996); *Beautiful Love* (1997).—**LP**

Daniels, Mabel Wheeler, American composer; b. Swampscott, Mass., Nov. 27, 1878; d. Boston, March 10, 1971. She studied at Radcliffe Coll. (B.A., 1900), with Chadwick in Boston, and with Thuille in Munich (1904–05). She was director of the Radcliffe Glee Club (1911–13) and head of music at Simmons Coll. in Boston (1913–18). In 1931 she held a MacDowell fellowship, and was awarded honorary doctorates from Boston Univ. (1939), Wheaton Coll. (1957), and the New England Cons. of Music (1958). Daniels became best known as a composer of choral music. Her experiences abroad were captured in her *An American Girl in Munich: Impressions of a Music Student* (Boston, 1905).

WORKS: DRAMATIC: Operettas: *A Copper Complication* (1900); *The Court of Hearts* (1900; Cambridge, Mass., Jan. 2, 1901); *The Show Girl* (1902; in collaboration with D. Stevens). **Opera Sketch:** *Alice in Wonderland Continued* (Brookline, Mass., May 20, 1904). **ORCH.:** Suite for Strings (1910); *Deep Forest* for Small Orch. (N.Y., June 3, 1931; arranged for Full Orch., 1934; Boston, April 16, 1937); *Pirates' Island* (1934; Harrisburg, Pa., Feb. 19, 1935); *Im memoriam* (1945); *Digressions,* ballet for Strings (1947); Overture (1951). **CHAMBER:** *Pastoral Ode* for Flute and Strings (1940); *3 Observations* for 3 Woodwinds (1943); *4 Observations* for 4 Strings (1945); Violin Sonata (n.d.). **VOCAL: Choral with Orch.:** *The Desolate City,* with baritone solo (1913); *Peace with a Sword* (1917); *Songs of Elfland* (St. Louis, Feb. 2, 1924); *The Holy Star* (1928); *A Holiday Fantasy* (1928); *Exultate Deo* (Boston, May 31, 1929); *The Song of Jael,* with soprano solo (1937; Worcester, Oct. 5, 1940); *A Psalm of Praise* (Cambridge, Mass., Dec. 3, 1954). **Other Choral:** *In Springtime,* cycle for Women's Voices (1910); *Eastern Song* and *The Voice of My Beloved* for Women's Voices, Piano, and 2 Violins (both 1911); *Flowerwagon* for Women's Chorus and Piano (1914); *The Girl Scouts Marching*

Song (1918); *Oh God of all our Glorious Past* (1930); *Through the Dark the Dreamers Came* for Women's or Mixed Chorus (c. 1930; rev. 1961); *The Christ Child* for Chorus and Piano (1931); *A Night in Bethlehem* (1954). Also numerous songs.—NS/LK/DM

Danjou, Jean-Louis-Félix, French music teacher; b. Paris, June 21, 1812; d. Montpellier, March 4, 1866. He studied organ with Francois Benoist at the Paris Cons., then played organ at various churches from 1830; was organist at Notre Dame from 1840 until 1847. With his essay *De l'état de l'avenir du chant ecclésiastique* (1844), he became the pioneer in the movement for reforming plainchant. Further, his journal *Revue de la Musique Religieuse, Populaire et Classique* (1845–49) showed profound erudition gained by assiduous historical research. He was the discoverer (1847) of the celebrated "Antiphonary of Montpellier." He labored to promote organ building in France, and made a special study of organ manufacture in Germany and the Netherlands. He entered into partnership with the organ builders Daublaine & Callinet of Paris, but lost his entire capital, gave up music, and in 1849 became a political journalist in Marseilles and Montpellier.—NS/LK/DM

Dankevich, Konstantin, eminent Ukrainian composer and teacher; b. Odessa, Dec. 24, 1905; d. Kiev, Feb. 26, 1984. He studied with Zolotarev at the Odessa Cons., graduating in 1929. In 1942 he was made artistic director of the Red Army Ensemble of Songs and Dance in Tbilisi. From 1944 to 1953 he was a prof. of composition at the Odessa Cons.; in 1953 he was appointed to the faculty of the Kiev Cons. In his works, Dankevich utilized motifs of Ukrainian and Russian folk songs. He first attracted attention with his opera *Bogdan Khmelnitsky* (Kiev, Jan. 29, 1951), on a subject from Ukrainian history, which was attacked for its libretto and its unsuitable music; Dankevich revised the score, after which it gained favorable notices in Russia. He also wrote the opera *Nazar Stodolya* (Kharkov, May 28, 1960). His most popular score was *Lileya*, a ballet (1939). Other works included 2 syms. (1937, 1945), several overtures, and patriotic choruses, including *Poem of the Ukraine* (1960) and the ideological cantata to his own words, *The Dawn of Communism Has Risen over Us* (1961). A monograph on him was publ. in Ukrainian in Kiev (1959). —NS/LK/DM

Dannreuther, Edward (George), pianist and music scholar, brother of **Gustav Dannreuther;** b. Strasbourg, Nov. 4, 1844; d. London, Feb. 12, 1905. He went with his parents in 1849 to Cincinnati, where he was taught by F.L. Ritter; then studied at the Leipzig Cons. with Richter, Moscheles, and Hauptmann (1859–63). On April 11, 1863, he made his debut in London, playing Chopin's Concerto in F minor. He introduced into England the piano concertos of Liszt, Grieg, and Tchaikovsky. In 1872 he founded the London Wagner Soc., and conducted its concerts in 1873–74; was an active promoter of the Wagner Festival (1877). He was appointed a prof. at the Royal Academy of Music in 1895. An indefatigable champion of the new composers, Dannreuther was equally active on behalf of the older masters; the chamber music concerts that he gave at his home (1874–93) were famous. Dannreuther visited the U.S. several times.

WRITINGS: "Richard Wagner and the Reform of the Opera," *Monthly Musical Record* (separately, London, 1873; 2nd ed., rev., 1904); *Richard Wagner, His Tendencies and Theories* (London, 1873); *Musical Ornamentation* (2 vols., London, 1893–95); *The Romantic Period,* Vol. VI of the *Oxford History of Music* (London, 1905; 3rd ed., 1931).—NS/LK/DM

Dannreuther, Gustav, American violinist, brother of **Edward (George) Dannreuther;** b. Cincinnati, July 21, 1853; d. N.Y., Dec. 19, 1923. He studied at the Berlin Hochschule für Musik under de Ahna and Joachim (violin) and Heitel (theory). He then lived in London, and in 1877 joined the Mendelssohn Quintette Club of Boston, traveling through the U.S., Canada, and Newfoundland. From 1882 to 1884 he was director of the Buffalo Phil. Soc. (a chamber music organization). In 1884 he founded the Beethoven String Quartet of N.Y. (renamed the Dannreuther Quartet in 1894). From 1907 he taught violin at Vassar Coll.—NS/LK/DM

Danon, Oskar, Serbian conductor; b. Sarajevo, Feb. 7, 1913. He was educated at the Prague Cons. and the Univ. of Prague (Ph.D., 1938). In 1940 he became a conductor at the Belgrade Opera; was its director (1945–60). He also conducted throughout Europe, both opera and sym. concerts.—NS/LK/DM

Danuser, Hermann, learned Swiss-born German musicologist; b. Frauenfeld, Oct. 3, 1946. He studied at the Hochschule für Musik (concert diploma in piano, 1971) and at the Univ. (Ph.D., 1973, with the diss. *Musikalische Prosa;* publ. in Regensburg, 1975) of Zürich. In 1973–74 he held a Deutscher Akademischer Austauschdienst scholarship in Berlin, where he then was an assistant at the Staatlichen Institut für Musikforschung (1974–75) and the Hochschule der Künste (1975–82). In 1982 he completed his Habilitation at the Technical Univ. there with his *Die Musik des 20. Jahrhunderts* (publ. in Laaber, 1984). From 1982 to 1988 he was a prof. of musicology at the Hannover Hochschule für Musik und Theater, and then at the Albert-Ludwigs-Univ. in Freiburg im Breisgau from 1988 to 1993. He was active with the Paul Sacher Foundation in Basel from 1988, becoming its coordinator of research in 1992. In 1991 he was a visiting prof. at Stanford Univ. In 1993 he became prof. of historical musicology at the Humboldt Univ. in Berlin. He became a member of the Berlin-Brandenburg Akademie der Wissenschaften in 1998. Danuser is an authority on the music of the 20th century. He served as ed. of the series Neues Handbuch der Musikwissenschaft (Laaber, 1989–95), Meisterwerke der Musik (Munich, from 1993), and Freiburger Beiträge zur Musikwissenschaft (Laaber, from 1993). His articles have appeared in various scholarly books and journals.

WRITINGS: *Gustav Mahler: Das Lied von der Erde* (Munich, 1986); ed. *Gattungen der Musik und ihre Klassiker* (Laaber, 1988; 2nd ed., 1998); *Gustav Mahler und seine Zeit* (Laaber, 1991); ed. *Neue Musik im politischen Wandel* (Mainz, 1991); ed. *Gustav Mahler* (Darmstadt, 1992); ed. *Musikalische Interpretation* (Laaber,

1992); ed. *Igor Strawinsky: Trois pièces pour quatuor à cordes: Skizzen, Fassungen, Dokumente, Essays* (Winterthur, 1994); ed. *Die klassizistische Moderne in der Musik des 20. Jahrhunderts: Internationales Symposion der Paul Sacher Stiftung Basel 1996* (Winterthur, 1997).—**NS/LK/DM**

Danzi, Franz (Ignaz), German composer and teacher; b. Schwetzingen, June 15, 1763; d. Karlsruhe, April 13, 1826. He received primary instruction in music from his father, Innocenz Danzi, a cellist, and later took theory lessons with Abbé Vogler. He became a cellist in the Mannheim Court Orch. After the orch. removed to Munich in 1778, he remained in Mannheim as a member of the orch. of the new National Theater. In 1783 he went to Munich as successor of his father in the Court Orch. In 1798 he became asst. Kapellmeister. From 1807 to 1812 he was Kapellmeister in Stuttgart, where he was the teacher of Weber. He then settled in Karlsruhe. He was an excellent singing teacher, and wrote vocal exercises of practical value.

WORKS: DRAMATIC: *Cleopatra,* duodrama (Mannheim, Jan. 30, 1780); *Azakia,* comedy (Mannheim, June 6, 1780); *Die Mitternachtsstunde,* Singspiel (Munich, April 1788); *Der Sylphe,* Singspiel (Munich, 1788); *Der Triumph der Treue,* melodrama (Munich, Feb. 1789; not extant); *Der Quasi-Mann,* comedy (Munich, Aug. 1789; not extant); *Deucalion et Pirrha,* opera (c. 1795); *Der Kuss,* comedy (Munich, June 27, 1799); *El Bondocani,* Singspiel (Munich, 1802; not extant); *Iphigenie in Aulis,* grand opera (Munich, Jan. 27, 1807); *Dido,* melodrama (Stuttgart, 1811; not extant); *Camilla und Eugen oder Der Gartenschlüssel,* comedy (Stuttgart, March 15, 1812); *Rübezahl,* Singspiel (Karlsruhe, April 19, 1813); *Malvina,* Singspiel (Karlsruhe, Dec. 20, 1814); *Turandot,* Singspiel (Karlsruhe, Feb. 9, 1817); *Die Probe,* opera (Karlsruhe, Oct. 1817); *L'Abbe de Attaignant oder Die Theaterprobe,* opera (Karlsruhe, Sept. 14, 1820). **OTHER:** Oratorios; cantatas; masses; the 128th Psalm for Chorus and Orch.; syms.; concertos; chamber music.

BIBL.: E. Reipschläger, *Schubaur, D. und Poissl als Opernkomponisten* (diss., Univ. of Rostock, 1911); M. Herre, *F. D.* (diss., Univ. of Munich, 1924); T. Gebhard, *Studien zum Klarinettensatz und - stil in den konzertanten Werken von Georg-Friedrich Fuchs, Peter von Winter und F. D.* (Hildesheim, 1998).—**NS/LK/DM**

Da-Oz, Ram (real name, **Avraham Daus**), German- born Israeli composer; b. Berlin, Oct. 17, 1929. He went to Palestine as a child in 1934. He studied oboe and piano at the Cons. in Tel Aviv, and composition with André Hajdu at the Music Academy there. He lost his eyesight during the Israeli war for independence in 1948.

WORKS: ORCH.: *Von Trauer und Trost* (1960); Concerto for Violin and Strings (1961); *Dmuyoth umassechot* (Changing Phantoms), movements for Chamber Ensemble (1967); *Quartet* for Narrator and Small Orch. (1970); *Rhapsody on a Jewish Yemenite Song* for Piano and Strings (1971); *3 Romances* for Violin and Small Orch. (1975); *Introduction and Passacaglia* (1981). **CHAMBER:** 4 string quartets (1955–70); Violin Sonata (1960); String Trio (1961); Suite for Harpsichord, Flute, Oboe, and Cello (1963); Piano Trio (1963); Dialogue for 2 Clarinets (1965); *Illumination* for Violin (1966); *Improvisation on a Song* for 10 Instruments (1968); *4 Miniatures* for Recorders and Piano (1975);

Divertimento for Brass Quartet (1977). **P i a n o :** 2 sonatas (1955; *Movimenti quasi una sonata,* 1963); *5 Contrasts* (1958); *Capriccio* (1960); *8 Little Pictures* (1962); *Aspects* (1969); *Bells* (1973); *Mood Ring* (1976); *Pictures in Procession* (1979); *Ru-TaNoWa* (1980). **VOCAL:** Songs.—**NS/LK/DM**

Da Ponte, Lorenzo (real name, **Emanuele Conegliano**), famous Italian librettist; b. Ceneda, near Venice, March 10, 1749; d. N.Y., Aug. 17, 1838. He was of a Jewish family, but was converted to Christianity at the age of 14, and assumed the name of his patron, Lorenzo da Ponte, Bishop of Ceneda. He then studied at the Ceneda Seminary and at the Portogruaro Seminary, where he taught from 1770 to 1773; in 1774 obtained a post as prof. of rhetoric at Treviso, but was dismissed in 1776 for his beliefs concerning natural laws. He then went to Venice, where he led an adventurous life, and was banished in 1779 for adultery; subsequently lived in Austria and in Dresden, and in 1782 settled in Vienna and became official poet to the Imperial Theater. He met Mozart and became his friend and librettist of his most famous operas, *Le nozze di Figaro, Don Giovanni,* and *Così fan tutte.* From 1792 to 1798 he was in London, then traveled in Europe, and went to N.Y. in 1805. After disastrous business ventures, with intervals of teaching, he became interested in various operatic enterprises. In his last years he was a teacher of Italian at Columbia Coll. He publ. *Memorie* (4 vols., N.Y., 1823–27; Eng. tr., London, 1929, and Philadelphia, 1929).

BIBL.: A. Marchesan, *Della vita e delle opere di L. d.P.* (Treviso, 1900); J. Russo, *L. d.P., Poet and Adventurer* (N.Y., 1922); A. Fitzlyon, *The Libertine Librettist* (London, 1955); S. Hodges, *L. d.P.: The Life and Times of Mozart's Librettist* (London, 1985); A. Steptoe, *The Mozart-D.P. Operas: The Cultural and Musical Background to Le nozze di Figaro, Don Giovanni, and Così fan tutte* (Oxford, 1988); M. Siniscalchi and P. Spedicato, eds., *Omaggio a L. D. P.* (Rome, 1992).—**NS/LK/DM**

Daquin, Louis-Claude, French organist and composer; b. Paris, July 4, 1694; d. there, June 15, 1772. He was a pupil of Marchand. At the age of 6 he played on the clavecin before Louis XIV, and at 12 he became organist at St.-Antoine, where his playing attracted crowds of curious listeners. From 1727 until his death he was organist at St.-Paul, having won the position in competition with Rameau. He publ. a book of *Pièces de clavecin* (Paris, 1735; contains the celebrated piece *Le Coucou;* first complete modern ed. by C. Hogwood, London, 1983), a collection of *Noëls pour l'orgue ou le clavecin* (reprinted by Guilmant in *Archives des Maîtres de l'Orgue*), and a cantata, *La Rose.*—**NS/LK/DM**

D'Arányi, Jelly
See d'Arányi, Jelly

Darasse, Xavier, French composer, pedagogue, and organist; b. Toulouse, Sept. 3, 1934; d. there, Nov. 24, 1992. He was reared in a musical family. His mother was an organist, and it was the organ that Darasse studied before pursuing training at the Paris Cons. Among his mentors there was Olivier Messiaen, with whom he studied analysis. Darasse was active as an organist until

791

an accident in 1976 compelled him to concentrate on composition and teaching. From 1985 to 1991 he was prof. of organ at the Lyons Cons. In 1991 he became director of the Paris Cons. The organ played an important role in Darasse's approach to composition. It was his intent to explore its capacities as a wind instrument with a judicious handling of registration and color. He also wrote much vocal music of estimable quality. His opera *Portrait de Dorian Gray* was left unfinished at his death.

WORKS: DRAMATIC: *Monsieur Bonhomme et les Incendiaires*, musique de scène after Max Frisch (Toulouse, May 15, 1967); *Les Violettes*, musique de scène after Georges Schéhadé (1967); *Rugby dans le cuir*, film music (1987); *Portrait de Dorian Gray*, opera after Wilde (1990–92; unfinished). **ORCH.**: *Antagonisme III* (Toulouse, June 27, 1968); *L'Instant d'après*, sym. for 23 Winds (1977; Radio France, Paris, Feb. 11, 1978); *Instants éclatés* (Schweinfurt, Nov. 16, 1983); *Instants passés* (Paris, April 7, 1989). **CHAMBER**: *Antagonisme II* for 6 Instruments (Paris, June 1966) and *IV* for 2 Trumpets and 3 Trombones (1972; also for Horn, 2 Trumpets, and Trombone, 1976); *Organum VIII-In memoriam Jean-Pierre Guézec* for Wind Quintet, Organ, and Percussion (Metz, Nov. 25, 1972) and *IV* for 2 Percussionists and Organ (1981; also for Organ and 3 Percussionists, Le Havre, May 30, 1981); *Étude concertée* for 2 Violins and Vibraphone (Boulogne sur Seine, June 20, 1979); *Per sonare* for Trumpet, Trombone, and Percussion (Toulouse, Oct. 3, 1979); *Belles "Bells"* for Carillon (1980); *Dont'Lose Toulouse* for String Quartet and Piano (Toulouse, July 1980); Trio for Violin, Viola, and Cello (1981; Radio France, Paris, Jan. 25, 1982); *Carillons-De plus en plus loin* for Clarinet and Piano (Blanc-Mesnil, Feb. 1982); *Concert...tôt ou tard* for Piano and Percussion (Paris, Dec. 6, 1984); *Magnificat* for Organ and Chorus ad libitum or 2 Instruments (1986); *Grazioso, hommage à Maurice Ravel* for Cello (Montpellier, July 1987); *Musiques pour Santi-Paul Cap de Joux* for Trumpet, 4 Trombones, and Percussionist (Saint-Paul Cap de Joux, Aug. 8, 1987); *Septembre* for String Sextet (Villeneuve d'Ascq, April 13, 1989); *Actions* for Wind Quintet (Eglise Saint-Jacques de Muret, Dec. 15, 1990). **KEYBOARD: P i a n o**: *Étude* (1978; Saint-German en Laye, April 8, 1979). **H a r p s i c h o r d**: *Masques I* (Paris, Dec. 3, 1985) and *III* (1992). **O r g a n**: *Trois Pièces* (1961–62); *Organum I* (Royan, March 24, 1970), *II* (Paris, May 19, 1978), *III* (1979; Chartres, Sept. 21, 1980), *V* (Orléans, Oct. 30, 1983), *VI* (Paris, March 15, 1987), and *IX* (1991); *Pedal-exercitum* (1985). **VOCAL**: *Le Charmeur de serpent* for Voice and Piano (1945); *Deux Mélodies de Boris Pasternak* for Soprano and Piano (1959); *Quatre Discors d'amor* for Soprano and Piano (1960); *Les Rois mages*, cantata for Tenor, Bass, and Orch. (Paris, July 4, 1964); *Antagonisme I* for Reciter, Piano, Marimba, Vibraphone, and Violin (Paris, June 1965); *Les Visions de Cassandre*, cantata for Mezzo-soprano, Bass, Chorus, and Orch. (Paris, July 3, 1965); *Psalmus* for Chorus (1970; Innsbruck, July 1971); *Messe des Jacobins* for Voice, Chorus, Winds, and 2 Percussionists (Toulouse, Oct. 27, 1974); *Musique d'ouverture "Paix et joie"* for Soprano and Chorus (Paris, July 2, 1977); *A propos d'Orphée I* for Mezzo-soprano, Violin, and Percussion (Radio France, Paris, March 13, 1978), *II* for 3 Sopranos, Chorus, and 6 Percussionists (Breme, Oct. 10, 1984), and *III* for Mezzo-soprano, Horn, Percussion, and Piano 4-Hands (Radio France, Paris, June 2, 1987); *Messe pour Montserrat* for Soprano, Chorus, and 2 Pianos or Organ (Liverpool, July 15, 1978); *Romanesques*, "cantate nocturne" for 6 Soloists, Horn, 2 Percussion, and Chorus (Paris, Nov. 4, 1980); *Psaume XXXII, Exultate* for 6 Soloists and 15 Instruments (Paris, Nov.

15, 1985); *Odes élémentaires "aux enfants de l'Essone"* for Chorus and Percussion (1986); *Organum VII* for Chorus (1988; also for Organ and Soprano ad libitum); *Mélodies pour le "Psautier des dimanches"* for Chorus (1988); *Messe pour les Paroisses* for Chorus, Congregation, and Organ (Auch, Oct. 1989; rev. 1990 and 1991).—**LK/DM**

Darbellay, Jean-Luc, Swiss composer and conductor; b. Bern, July 2, 1946. He obtained a diploma as a physician before studying clarinet at the Bern Cons. (1974–79). He then pursued training in composition with Cristóbal Halffter and Demitri Terzakis. He later attended the master classes of Edison Denisov (1993) and Klaus Huber at the Lucerne Cons., workshops with Pierre Boulez in Paris, and conducting sessions with Pierre Dervaux. In 1978 Darbellay founded the Ludus Ensemble of the Bern Cons., and subsequently served as its conductor. While in Denisov's master class, he and 4 other composers living in Switzerland and Germany formed the Groupe Lacroix to promote a mutually beneficial contact between composers. By 1996 two more composers had joined the group. In 1995 Darbellay became president of the Swiss section of the ISCM. His music often explores the complementary sonic properties of simultaneously sounding instruments. A significant number of his works feature the horn and basset horn in solo roles, due to the fact that his son Olivier (b.1974) and wife Elizabeth are virtuosos on those respective instruments.

WORKS: DRAMATIC: *C'est un peu d'eau qui nous separe*, chamber opera (1989). **ORCH.**: *Espaces* for Horn or Basset Horn and Strings (1984); Cello Concerto (1989); *Pranam III* for Solo Cello, 2 Flutes, Horn, and Strings (1992) and *IV* for Horn and Strings (1995); *Orion* (1994); *Elégie* (1994); *Incanto* for Horn and Orch. (1995). **CHAMBER**: *Vestiges* for Bassoon (1982); *Amphores* for Clarinet and Harp (1983); *Plages* for English Horn or Alto Saxophone (1985); *Miroir* for 3 Basset Horns (1988); Saxophone Quartet (1988); Wind Octet (1991); *Vormittagsspuk* for Chamber Ensemble (1991); *Interférences* for Flute, Oboe, and Natural Horn (1993); *Andromède* for Guitar, Vibraphone, and Harp (1991); *Spectrum* for Natural Horn (1993); *Cantus* for Horn and Organ (1993); *Oréade* for Clarinet and String Trio (1993); *à la recherche* for Chamber Ensemble (1994); String Quartet (1994); *Images perdues* for Cello and Piano (1995); *Solo* for Cello (1995); *Ecumes* for String Quartet (1996); *Ein Garten für Orpheus* for Horn, Basset Horn, and String Quartet, after the Klee painting (1996); *Néva* for String Quartet (1996); *Chandigarh* for 17 Instruments (1996); *Empreintes* for Piano Trio (1996); *Accents* for Saxophone and Horn (1997); *Luce* for Saxophone and Cello (1997); *Valère* for Violin and Piano (1997); *Sospeso* for Clarinet and String Quartet (1997); *Sozusagen* for Oboe, Viola, Bassoon, and Guitar, after the Klee painting (1997–99); *Trajectoire* for 12 Winds and Double Bass (1998); *Kantha Bopha* for Solo Cello and 32 Tutti-Cellos (1999); String Trio (1999); Trio for Bass Clarinet, Cello, and Piano (1999). **VOCAL**: *Envols* for Mezzo-soprano, Flute, Clarinet, and Basset Horn (1985); *7 poèmes romands* for Mezzo-soprano, Flute, Clarinet, and Basset Horn (1986); *Elan*, chamber cantata for Mezzo-soprano, Clarinet, Basset Horn, and Harp (1987).—**LK/DM**

Darclée, Hariclea (real name, Haricly Hartulary), Romanian soprano; b. Braila, June 10, 1860; d. Bucharest, Jan. 10, 1939. She studied in Bucharest and Paris; made her debut as Marguerite at the Paris Opéra in 1888; then sang at La Scala in Milan, creating La Wally on Jan. 20, 1892; also sang in Rome, N.Y., St. Petersburg, Moscow, and in South America before retiring in 1918. She was particularly distinguished for her Italian repertoire; she created the role of Tosca (Rome, Jan. 14, 1900); also was known for her performances of roles in Wagner's operas.—NS/LK/DM

Darcy, Robert, French-born Belgian cellist and composer; b. Paris, Nov. 10, 1910; d. Schaerbeek, near Brussels, June 6, 1967. He obtained the Premier Prix in cello at the Lyons Cons. (1928); studied composition with Francis Bousquet and Paul Vidal. He played the cello in orchs. in Paris and Brussels. Mobilized in 1939, he was taken prisoner of war in June 1940; while in captivity, he organized a prisoners' orch.; after his release he returned to Belgium, becoming a naturalized citizen in 1949. His style is rooted in neo-Classicism, with an admixture of atonal elements.

WORKS: ORCH.: *Scherzo* (1923); *Rêverie* (1931); *7 Sketches* for Small Orch. (1933); Suite for Wind Orch. (1935); Suite for Strings (1936); Concerto for 4 Cellos and Wind Orch. (1936); *Piece* for 2 Cellos and Orch. (1937); *Fantasie* for Cello and Orch. (1937); *3 Marines* (1939); Concerto for 4 Saxophones and Orch. (1939); *Danses mosanes* (1943); Trumpet Concerto (1948); Piano Concerto (1951); Sym. (1953); *Concerto for Orchestra* (1965). **CHAMBER:** 3 quartets for 4 Cellos (1935–37); 3 string quartets (1936–50); *Caprice* for Wind Quintet (1936); Sextet for Winds (1937); *6 Pieces* for 4 Cellos (1937); Trio for Oboe, Clarinet, and Bassoon (1938); Quartet for 4 Saxophones (1938); Bassoon Sonata (1948); Piece for Wind Quintet (1962). **VOCAL:** Songs. —NS/LK/DM

Dargomyzhsky, Alexander (Sergeievich), outstanding Russian composer; b. in Tula province, Feb. 14, 1813; d. St. Petersburg, Jan. 17, 1869. From 1817 he lived in St. Petersburg, where he studied piano with Schoberlechner and Danilevsky and violin with Vorontsov. At 20 he was a brilliant pianist. From 1827 to 1843 he held a government position, but then devoted himself exclusively to music, studying assiduously for 8 years. He visited Germany, Brussels, and Paris in 1845. At Moscow (Dec. 17, 1847) he produced an opera, *Esmeralda* (after Victor Hugo's *Notre-Dame de Paris*), with great success (excerpts publ. in piano score, Moscow, 1848). From 1845 to 1855 he publ. over 100 minor works (vocal romances, ballads, airs, and duos; waltzes, fantasies, etc.). On May 16, 1856, he brought out his best opera, *Rusalka*, at St. Petersburg (vocal score, with indications of instruments, publ. at Moscow, 1937), and in 1867, an opera-ballet, *The Triumph of Bacchus* (written in 1845; perf. in Moscow, Jan. 23, 1867). A posthumous opera, *Kamennyi gost* (The Stone Guest, after Pushkin's poem of the same title), was scored by Rimsky-Korsakov and produced at St. Petersburg on Feb. 28, 1872. Of *Rogdana*, a fantasy-opera, only a few scenes were sketched. At first a follower of Rossini and Auber, Dargomyzhsky gradually became convinced that dramatic realism with nationalistic connotations was the destiny of Russian music. He applied this realistic method in treating the recitative in his opera *The Stone*

Guest and in his songs (several of these to satirical words). His orch. works (*Finnish Fantasia, Cossack Dance, Baba-Yaga,* etc.) enjoyed wide popularity. In 1867 he was elected president of the Russian Music Soc.

BIBL.: N. Findeisen, *A. S. D.: His Life and Work* (Moscow, 1902); S. Fried, *A.S. D.* (St. Petersburg, 1913); A. Drozdov, *A. S. D.* (Moscow, 1929); M. Pekelis, *A. D. and His Circle* (2 vols., Moscow, 1966, 1973).—NS/LK/DM

Darin, Bobby (originally, **Cassotto, Walden Robert**), one of the most popular rock 'n' roll teen idols of the late 1950s; b. Bronx, N.Y., May 14, 1936; d. Los Angeles, Dec. 20, 1973. As he matured, he moved into the pop mainstream and nightclub circuit with the definitive version of "Mack the Knife" in 1959. Embarking on a film career in the 1960s, Darin later explored both country and folk music and formed his own record label, Direction, before ending his career at Motown Records. A childhood victim of rheumatic fever, Darin was not expected to live beyond 25, yet he persevered until 1973, when he died at the age of 37.

Robert Cassotto learned to play drums, piano, and guitar as a child and studied drama for a time at Hunter Coll. in N.Y. Rheumatic fever has struck him at the age of eight and he suffered health problems throughout his life. Changing his name to enter show business, Darin recorded unsuccessfully for Decca Records in 1956, switching to the Atco subsidiary of Atlantic Records in 1957. He eventually broke through in mid 1958 with his own novelty composition "Splish Splash," a R&B/pop/country smash, followed by the pop/R&B hit "Queen of the Hop." He also recorded his composition "Early in the Morning" for Brunswick as the Ding Dongs, and the song later became a major hit on Atco under the name the Rinky-Dinks. It was also successfully covered by Buddy Holly. In late 1958 Ruth Brown scored a R&B/pop hit with Darin's "This Little Girl's Gone Rockin'." In 1959 he achieved a smash pop/R&B hit with his composition "Dream Lover."

Darin moved decisively into the popular mainstream with his album *That's All*, which produced a top pop hit with "Mack the Knife," based on Kurt Weill's 1928 "Moritat," from *The Threepenny Opera*, and a smash pop hit with "Beyond the Sea." His shift was completed with a live album recorded at the Copacabana and *Two of a Kind*, recorded with singer-lyricist Johnny Mercer. Subsequent pop hits included "Artificial Flowers," "Irresistible You" (backed with "Multiplication"), and the smash "Things," which he wrote. Darin also initiated an acting career in the 1960s, garnering an Academy Award nomination as best supporting actor for his role in 1963's *Captain Newman, M.D.* He was married to actress Sandra Dee from 1960 to 1967.

In 1962 Darin signed with Capitol Records, scoring a smash pop/R&B hit with the country-styled "You're the Reason I'm Living" and a smash pop hit with "18 Yellow Roses" in 1963. Subsequent Capitol releases proved relative failures, yet his concerts often featured guitarist Roger McGuinn, who later formed the Byrds. Darin returned to Atlantic and rebounded with a near-smash version of Tim Hardin's folk song "If I Were a Carpenter" in 1966. He formed Direction Records in

1968, recording for the label, and worked extensively for Robert Kennedy during the 1968 presidential campaign. He moved to Motown Records in 1971, where he managed his last minor hit with "Happy," the love theme from the movie *Lady Sings the Blues*. On Dec. 20, 1973, Darin died in L.A. of heart failure while undergoing an operation. He was inducted into the Rock and Roll Hall of Fame in 1990.

DISC.: *B.D.* (1958); *Darin at the Copa* (1960); *For Teenagers Only* (1960); *The 25th Day of December* (1960); *This Is Darin* (1960); *Darin Live at the Copa* (1961); *Love Swings* (1961); *The B.D. Story* (1961); *Two of a Kind* (with Johnny Mercer; 1961); *Oh! Look at Me Now* (1962); *Sings Ray Charles* (1962); *Things and Other Things* (1962); *Earthy* (1963); *Golden Folk Hits* (1963); *It's You or No One* (recorded 1960; 1963); *18 Yellow Roses* (1963); *You're the Reason I'm Living* (1963); *Clementine* (1964); *From Hello Dolly to Goodbye Charlie* (1964); *Winners* (1964); *Venice Blue* (1965); *Best* (1966); *In a Broadway Bag* (1966); *Sings the Shadow of Your Smile* (1966); *If I Were a Carpenter* (1967); *Inside Out* (1967); *Sings Doctor Doolittle* (1967); *Born Walden Robert Cassotto* (1968); *Commitment* (1969); *B. D.* (1972); *The Legendary B. D.* (1974); *Darin 1936–1973* (1974); *Live at the Desert Inn* (1987); *B. D.* (1989); *Best* (1990); *Splish Splash: The Best of B. D., Vol. One* (1991); *Mack the Knife: The Best of B. D., Vol. Two* (1992); *Spotlight on Bobby Darin* (1994); *That's All* (1994); *As Long As I'm Singing: The B. D. Collection* (1995).

BIBL.: Al DiOrio, *Borrowed Time: The 37 Years of B.D.* (Philadelphia, 1981); Dodd Darin, *Dream Lovers: The Magnificent Shattered Lives of B.D. and Sandra Dee* (N.Y., 1994).—**BH**

Darke, Harold (Edwin), English organist, teacher, and composer; b. London, Oct. 29, 1888; d. Cambridge, Nov. 28, 1976. He studied with Parratt (organ) and Stanford (composition) at the Royal Coll. of Music in London, where he served as a prof. of organ (1919–69); he also was organist at St. Michael's Church, Cornhill (1916–41; 1945–66) and at King's Coll., Cambridge (1941–45). In 1966 he was made a Commander of the Order of the British Empire. He wrote sacred music, organ and piano pieces, and songs.—**NS/LK/DM**

Darnton, (Philip) Christian, English composer; b. near Leeds, Oct. 30, 1905; d. Hove, April 14, 1981. He began piano lessons at the age of 4 and began composing at 9. After studies with F. Corder Sr. at the Brighton School of Music, he went to London for studies with Craxton (piano) at the Matthay School and Dale (composition) at the Royal Academy of Music. He later was a student of Wood (composition) and Rootham (theory) at Caius Coll., Cambridge (1923–26), Jacob at the Royal Coll. of Music, London (1927), and Butting in Berlin (1928–29). He publ. *You and Music* (Harmondsworth, 1939; 2nd ed., 1946).

WORKS: *Fantasy Fair*, opera; 3 syms.; 2 piano concertos; *Suite concertante* for Violin and Chamber Orch. (1938); *5 Orchestral Pieces* (Warsaw, April 14, 1939); *Jet Pilot*, cantata (1950); *Concerto for Orchestra* (1970–73).—**NS/LK/DM**

Darré, Jeanne-Marie, French pianist and teacher; b. Givet, July 30, 1905. She studied with Marguerite Long and Isidor Philipp in Paris. After numerous concerts in France and elsewhere in Europe, she made her U.S. debut in N.Y. (1962). She then made a successful series of tours in the U.S., appearing with major American orchs. In 1958 she became a teacher at the Paris Cons. A virtuoso in the grand manner, Darré produced a sensation by playing several piano concertos on a single night.—**NS/LK/DM**

Dart, (Robert) Thurston, eminent English musicologist and keyboard player; b. London, Sept. 3, 1921; d. there, March 6, 1971. He studied keyboard instruments at the Royal Coll. of Music in London (1938–39), and also took courses in mathematics at Univ. Coll., Exeter (B.Sc., 1942). In 1947 he became an asst. lecturer in music at the Univ. of Cambridge, a full lecturer in 1952, and finally a prof. of music in 1962. In 1964 he was named King Edward Prof. of Music at King's Coll. of the Univ. of London. As a performing musician, he made numerous appearances on the harpsichord; also appeared as organist and performer on Baroque keyboard instruments. He served as ed. of the *Galpin Society Journal* (1947–54) and secretary of the documentary ed. Musica Britannica (1950–65). His magnum opus was *The Interpretation of Music* (London, 1954; 5th ed., 1984; Ger. tr., 1959, as *Practica musica*; Swedish tr., 1964). He also ed. works by Morley, Purcell, John Bull, and others.

BIBL.: I. Bent, ed., *Source Materials and the Interpretation of Music: A Memorial Volume to T. D.* (London, 1981).—**NS/LK/DM**

Darvos, Gábor, Hungarian composer; b. Szatmárnémeti, Jan. 18, 1911; d. Budapest, Feb. 18, 1985. He studied bassoon and composition (with Kodály) at the Budapest Academy of Music (1926–32). After a South American sojourn (1939–48), he returned to Budapest and worked at the Hungarian Radio (1949–60); he also was ed.-in-chief of Editio Musica Budapest (1955–57) and artistic director of Hungaroton Records (1957–59); subsequently he was music advisor to Artisjus, the Hungarian Copyright Office (1960–72). In 1955 he was awarded the Erkel Prize.

WORKS: ORCH.: *Improvisations symphoniques* for Piano and Orch. (1963; rev. as *Fantázia* for Piano and Chamber Ensemble, 1983); *Szimfonikus etüdök* (Symphonic Etudes; 1984). **CHAMBER:** *Rotation for 5* for Vibraphone, Marimbaphone, Guitar, Cimbalom, and Piano (1967); *Magánzárka* (Solitary Confinement) for Pecussion and Tape (1970). **VOCAL:** *Medália* (Medal) for Soprano, Percussion, Keyboard Instruments, and Tape (1965); *A Torony* (The Tower) for Voices and Instruments (1967; also for Chorus and Tape, 1984); *Passiózene* (Passion Music) for Voices and Tape (1974–78); *Bánat* (Grief) for Baritone, Orch., and Tape (1978). **TAPE:** *Preludium* (1970); *Reminiszcenciák* (Reminiscences; 1979); *Poèmes électroniques* (1982–83).
—**NS/LK/DM**

D'Ascoli, Bernard, blind French pianist; b. Aubagne, Nov. 18, 1958. He was stricken with blindness at the age of 3, but by the time he was 11 he was able to read music via Braille, which allowed him to pursue studies at the Marseilles Cons. (1973–77). In 1978 he won first prize in the Maria Canals competition in Barcelona, and in 1981 he took third prize in the Leeds competition. In 1981 he made his Paris debut at the Salle Cortot, followed by his first appearance in London in 1982. In 1983 he made his Australian debut in Sydney, and in 1985 his U.S. debut as soloist with the Houston Sym. Orch. He played for the first time in Vienna in 1986 and in Tokyo in 1988. In addition to his engagements with leading orchs. of the day, he also appeared widely as a recitalist.—NS/LK/DM

Daser (Dasser, Dasserus), Ludwig, German composer; b. Munich, c. 1525; d. Stuttgart, March 27, 1589. He preceded Orlando di Lasso as Kapellmeister at Munich to Duke Albert V of Bavaria, holding that post until 1559. He publ. a Passion *a* 4 (1578), plus motets in the *Orgeltabulaturbuch* of J. Paix.—**NS/LK/DM**

Dashow, James (Hilyer), American composer; b. Chicago, Nov. 7, 1944. After studies with Babbitt, Cone, Kim, and Randall at Princeton Univ. (B.A., 1966), with Berger, Boykan, and Shifrin at Brandeis Univ. (M.F.A., 1969), and with Petrassi at the Accademia di Santa Cecilia in Rome (diploma, 1971), he founded the Forum Players (1971–75), a contemporary chamber music group. He served as director of the Studio di Musica Elettronica Sciadoni in Rome (from 1975). From 1982 to 1989 he taught computer music at the Centro di Sonologia Computazionale at the Univ. of Padua, and also was guest lecturer in various European and U.S. cities. He was a producer of contemporary music programs for the RAI from 1985 to 1992. He held a Fulbright fellowship (1969), grant from he NEA (1976, 1981) and the Rockefeller Foundation (1982), an award from the American Academy and Inst. of Arts and Letters (1984), a Guggenheim fellowship (1989), commissions from the Fromm (1992) and Koussevitzky (1998) foundations, and won the Prize of Distinction at the Linz Ars Electronica Festival (1996). He wrote the MUSIC30 computer language for digital sound synthesis (1991–93). As a composer, Dashow finds his role far more interesting, challenging, and culturally relevant to continue deepening the musical tradition of the 20th century rather than that of the Baroque, Classical, and Romantic eras.

WORKS: *Songs of Despair* for Soprano and 11 Instruments (1968–69); *Transformations* for Dance and Electronics (1969); *Astrazioni Pomeridiane* for Orch. (1970–71); *BURST!* for Soprano and Electronics (1971); *Maximus* for Soprano, 3 Wind Players, Piano, and Percussion (1972–73); *At Delphi* for Soprano and Electronics (1975); *Whispers out of Time* for Electronics (1975–76); *Effetti collaterali* for Clarinet and Computer-generated Electronics (1976); *Il piccolo principe*, opera (1981–82); *Songs from a Spiral Tree* for Mezzo-soprano, Flute, and Harp (1984–86); *Oro, argento, and legno* for Flute and Computer (1987); *Archimede*, theater piece (1988); *Disclosures* for Cello and Computer (1988–89); *4/3*, trio for Violin, Cello, and Piano (1989–91); *Ritorno a Delfi* for Alto Flute and Electronics (1990); *Reconstructions* for Harp and Computer (1992); *A Sheaf of Times*, septet for Flute, Clarinet, Harp, Percussion, Piano, Violin, and Cello (1992–94); *Morfologie* for Trumpet and Computer (1993); *Le Tracce di Kronos, i Passi* for Clarinet, Dancer, and Computer (1995); *Media Survival Kit*, lyric satire for Electrified Voices, Electrified Instruments, and Electronic Sounds (1995–96); *First Tangent to the Given Curve* for Piano and Computer (1995–97); *Personnagi ed Interpreti* for Flute, Clarinet, Violin, and Piano (1997); *Far Sounds, Broken Cries* for 12 Instruments and Quadraphonic Sounds (1998–99); *"...at other times, the distances,"* quadraphonic electronic piece for Tape (1999; reworking of the electronic sounds from *Far Sounds, Broken Cries*); *Sul Filo dei Tramonti* for Soprano, Piano, and Electronic Sounds (1999–2000); *Archimedes*, opera (1999–2000). —NS/LK/DM

Daube, Johann Friedrich, important German music theorist; b. probably in Hesse, c. 1730; d. Vienna, Sept. 19, 1797. He became a theorist at the court of Friedrich the Great in Berlin when he was 11. In 1744 he was made Cammer-Theorist to the Prince of Württemberg in Stuttgart, and later was his chamber flutist (1750–55); from 1756 he was a flutist in the court orch. By 1770 he was in Vienna as council and first secretary to the royal Franciscan Academy of Free Arts and Sciences. His writings are invaluable sources on the musical aesthetics and compositional practices of the Classical era. He also was a composer of orch. works, chamber music, and vocal pieces.

WRITINGS: *General-Bass in drey Accorden, gegründet in den Regeln der alt- und neuen Autoren* (Leipzig, 1756); *Der musikalische Dillettant* (3 vols., Vienna, 1770, 1771, and 1773; ed. by S. Snook-Luther as *The Musical Dilettante: A Treatise on Composition by J.F. Daube*, Cambridge, 1992); *Beweis, dass die gottesdienstliche Musik von den allerältesten Zeiten an unter allen Völkern des Erdbodens fortgewährt und ach in Eweigkeit dauern werde* (Vienna, 1782); *Anleitung zur Erfindung der Melodie und ihrer Fortsetzung*, I (Vienna, 1797), and *welcher die Composition enthält*, II (Vienna, 1798); preceding 2 vols. also publ. as *Anleitung zum Selbstunterricht in der musikalischen Composition, sowolf für die Instrumental-als Vocalmusik* (Vienna, 1798).

BIBL.: M. Karbaum, *Das theoretische Werk F. D.s: Der Theoretiker J. F. D.: Ein Beitrag zur Kompositionslehre des 18. Jahrhunderts* (diss., Univ. of Vienna, 1968).—**LK/DM**

Daugherty, Michael, innovative American composer; b. Cedar Rapids, Iowa, April 28, 1954. His father was a dance band drummer and all four of his brothers became professional musicians. He grew up playing in rock, jazz, and funk bands in Iowa, and composed his first orchestral piece while attending North Tex. State Univ. (1972–76). He then went to N.Y., where he studied with Wuorinen at the Manhattan School of Music (M.A., 1976) and with Druckman, Brown, Reynolds, Rands, and Evans at Yale Univ. (M.M.A., 1982; D.M.A., 1986). He then traveled to Hamburg, where he studied with Ligeti at the Hochschule für Musik (1982–84). He also studied at IRCAM on a Fulbright fellowship (1978–80). He received an NEA Composition Fellowship in 1980, and from 1986 to 1991 was on the faculty at the Oberlin (Ohio) Coll. Cons. of Music, serving as director of its Summer Electronic Music Workshop. In 1991 he joined the faculty of the Univ. of Mich. in Ann Arbor. Daugherty's music is often inspired by contemporary American popular culture. His *Snap!—Blue Like an Orange* (1987) won a Kennedy Friedheim Award.

WORKS: DRAMATIC: O p e r a : *Jackie O* (1997). ORCH.: *5 Seasons* (1980); *Metropolis Symphony* (1988–93); *Mxyzptlk* for 2 Flute Soloists and Chamber Orch. (1988; Cleveland, Feb. 6, 1989); *Oh Lois!* (St. Paul, Minn., April 4, 1989); *Lex* (1990); *Desi* for Symphonic Winds (1991); *Bizarro* for Symphonic Winds (1993). CHAMBER ENSEMBLE: *Future Music, Part I* (1984); *Future Funk* (1985); *Piano Plus* (1985); *Re: Percussion* (1986); *Blue Like an Orange* (1987); *Snap!—Blue Like an Orange* (1987); *Bounce*

I (1988); *Lex* (1989); *Sing Sing: J. Edgar Hoover* for String Quartet (1992); *Elvis Everywhere* for 3 Elvis Impersonators and String Quartet (1993). **OTHER**: Synthesizer and computer pieces. —**NS/LK/DM**

Dauprat, Louis-François, celebrated French horn player and composer; b. Paris, May 24, 1781; d. there, July 16, 1868. He studied with Kenn at the Paris Cons. He joined the band of the Garde Nationale, and in 1799 the band of the Garde des Consuls, with which he passed through the Egyptian campaign. From 1801 to 1805 he studied theory at the Cons. under Catel and Gossec, and studied again with Reicha from 1811 to 1814. From 1806 to 1808 he was first horn at the Bordeaux Theater. He succeeded Kenn in the Opéra orch. in Paris, and Duvernoy (as *cor solo*), retiring in 1831. He was chamber musician to Napoleon (1811) and Louis XVIII (1816). In 1816 he was appointed prof. of horn in the Cons., resigning in 1842.—**NS/LK/DM**

Daussoigne-Méhul, Louis-Joseph, French composer, nephew and foster son of **Etienne-Nicolas Méhul;** b. Givet, Ardennes, June 10, 1790; d. Liège, March 10, 1875. He studied under Méhul and Catel at the Cons., taking the Grand Prix de Rome in 1809. After writing 4 operas, which were rejected, he at length produced his 1-act *Aspasie* at the Grand Opéra (1820) with moderate success. He did still better with *Valentine de Milan*, a 3-act opera left unfinished by his foster father which he completed. In 1827 he accepted the directorship of the Liège Cons., which he retained, with great benefit to the school, until 1862. Daussoigne-Méhul was an associate of the Royal Academy, Brussels. He brought out a cantata with full orch. in 1828, and a choral sym., *Une Journée de la Révolution*, in 1834.—**NS/LK/DM**

Dauvergne, Antoine, French composer, violinist, and conductor; b. Moulins, Oct. 3, 1713; d. Lyons, Feb. 11, 1797. He received his first instruction from his father, then went for further study to Paris, where he was appointed a violinist in the chambre du roi (1739) and in the orch. of the Opéra (1744). In 1755 he was appointed composer to the court and in 1762 became conductor and one of the directors of the Concerts Spirituels. He was one of the directors of the Opéra (1769–76; 1780–82; 1785–90) before retiring to Lyons. He introduced into France the forms of the Italian intermezzo, substituting spoken dialogue for the recitative, and thus was the originator of a style that soon became typical of French dramatic composition. He composed 18 stage works, the first being *Les Troqueurs* (Paris, July 30, 1753), which is regarded as the first opéra-comique, as well as 2 books of syms. (1751), 12 sonatas for Violin and Basso Continuo (1739), 6 sonatas for 2 Violins and Basso Continuo (c. 1739), choral music, etc.—**NS/LK/DM**

d'Avalos, Francesco, Italian composer, conductor, and teacher; b. Naples, April 11, 1930. He received lessons in piano from age 12 from Vincenzo Vitale, and then studied composition and orchestration with Renato Parodi at the Cons. of San Pietro a Majella in Naples (diploma with high honors, 1955). He later

studied conducting with Kempen, Celibidache, and Ferrara in Siena, and also philosophy at the Univ. of Naples. After making his conducting debut with the RAI Orch. in Rome in 1964, he appeared as a guest conductor in Italy and Europe. He taught at the Bari Cons. before joining the faculty of the Cons. of San Pietro a Majella in 1979. As a composer, d'Avalos followed an avant-, later post-avant-, garde path. As a conductor, he strives to preserve the composer's intentions even in the face of received tradition. He has won particular distinction for his performances of the Italian symphonic repertoire of the 19th and early 20th centuries. His recordings won the Grand Prix International du disque de l'Académie Charles Cros of Paris in 1990, and the Discothèque Ideale of Paris in 1991.

WORKS: MUSIC DRAMA: *Maria di Venosa* (1992); *Qumrān* (2000). **ORCH.:** *Psyché and Eros*, suite (1947); *Music for Orch. and Piano Concertante* (1948); *Music for Imaginary Drama* (1951); 2 syms.: No. 1 for Soprano and Orch. (1955) and No. 2 for Soprano and Orch. (1991); *Studio sinfonico* (1956; rev. 1982); *Hymne an die Nacht* (1958); *Qumrān* (1966). **CHAMBER:** String Quintet (1960); Quintet for Piano and Strings (1967). **VOCAL:** *3 Songs on Japanese Poems* for Soprano and Orch. (1953); *Vexilla Regis* for Chorus and Orch. (1960); *The River Wang* for Soprano, Double String Orch., and 2 Flutes (1961); *Lines* for Soprano and Orch. (1963); *Die stille Stadt* for Soprano, String Orch., and Timpani (1995); *In Morte di due nobilissimi amanti* for 5 Voices and 3 Instruments (1996).—**NS/LK/DM**

Davaux, Jean-Baptiste, prominent French composer; b. La Côte-St. André, July 19, 1742; d. Paris, Feb. 2, 1822. He studied music with his parents, then settled in Paris, where he made a name for himself as a violinist and composer. Although he continued to be active as a composer in subsequent years, he found employment in the Ministry of War; upon retiring, he was made a member of the Légion d'honneur (1814). Davaux was highly regarded as a composer of orch. and chamber music. In his *Trois simphonies à grand orchestre*, op.11 (1784), he included his chronometre, thus anticipating Maelzel's invention.

WORKS: DRAMATIC: Opera: *Théodore, ou Le Bonheur inattendu*, comic opera (Fontainebleau, March 4, 1785; not extant); *Cécilia, ou Les Trois Tuteurs*, comic opera (Paris, Dec. 14, 1786). **ORCH.:** 8 syms. concertantes (c. 1772–85); *Sinfonie concertante mêlée d'airs patriotiques* (1794); *Simphonie concertante* (1800); 4 violin concertos (1769–71); 3 simphonies for Strings (1784). **CHAMBER:** 6 quatuors concertants for String Quartet (1779); 6 quatuors d'airs connus for String Quartet (1780); 6 duos for 2 Violins (1788); 4 quartetti for String Quartet (London, 1790); 6 trios for 2 Violins and Viola (c. 1792); 3 quatuors concertants for 2 Violins, Cello, and Bass (c. 1800); 4 Quintettos for 2 Violins, 2 Violas, and Cello.—**NS/LK/DM**

Dave Clark Five, hit-making British invasion-era combo. **MEMBERSHIP:** Dave Clark, drm. (b. Tottenham, London, England, Dec. 15, 1942); Mike Smith, kybd., lead voc. (b. Edmonton, London, Dec. 12, 1943); Lenny Davidson, lead gtr. (b. Enfield, Middlesex, May 30, 1944); Denny Payton, sax., har., gtr. (b. Walthamstow, London, Aug. 11, 1943); Rick Huxley, rhythm gtr., bs. (b. Dartford, Kent, Aug. 5, 1942).

One of the few 1960s rock groups led by a drummer, the Dave Clark Five were an enormously successful singles band from 1964 to 1966, briefly challenging the Beatles in popularity, particularly in the U.S. Despite featuring three songwriters and a potent lead vocalist, the Dave Clark Five never progressed beyond their raucous rockers and gentle ballads, disbanding in 1970, although principals Mike Smith and Dave Clark continued to perform until 1973.

Originally formed as a semiprofessional band in 1958 by Dave Clark and Rick Huxley, the Dave Clark Five comprised Clark, Huxley, Mike Smith, Lenny Davidson, and Denny Payton by 1961. Debuting in Tottenham, London, in early 1962, the group first recorded for the Pye subsidiary of Picadilly Records later that year. The group switched to Columbia Records (Epic in the U.S.) in 1963.

With Clark, Smith, and Davidson providing many of the songs, the Dave Clark Five achieved more than 20 British and American hits in the 1960s. They began their string of successes with the smash British and American hits "Glad All Over," "Bits and Pieces," and "Can't You See That She's Mine," written by Clark and Smith. Conducting a highly successful American tour in the spring of 1964, the group made the first of 18 appearances on the *Ed Sullivan Show* on May 31. They scored major American hits with the ballads "Because" (by Clark) and "Everybody Knows," and the originals "Anyway You Want It" and "Come Home" became major British and American hits. The group appeared in the 1965 film *Having a Wild Weekend* and toured America during the summer.

Later in 1965, the Dave Clark Five scored a smash British and American hit with "Catch Us if You Can" (by Clark and Davidson) and a top American hit with Bobby Day's "Over and Over." Major American hits continued with "At the Scene" and "Try Too Hard," and the group once again toured the U.S. in the summer of 1966. The hits subsequently slowed down, and after the smash American hit "You Got What It Takes" in the spring of 1967, the Dave Clark Five never achieved another major American hit. Major British hits continued into 1970 with "Red Balloon," "Good Old Rock and Roll," and Everybody Get Together."

The Dave Clark Five announced their intention to disband in August 1970, yet Clark and Smith continued to perform as Dave Clark and Friends until 1973. Mike Smith recorded a British-only album with former Manfred Mann vocalist Mike D'Abo in 1975, as Dave Clark concentrated on business activities that included music publishing. In 1986 Clark co-wrote and produced the modestly successful London stage musical *Time*. The original cast recording of the show included performances by Cliff Richard, Dionne Warwick, Leo Sayer, and Freddie Mercury. The hit recordings of the Dave Clark Five, unavailable for years, were eventually issued on the 1993 anthology set *The History of the Dave Clark Five.*

DISC.: *American Tour* (1964); *Glad All Over* (1964); *Return!* (1964); *Coast to Coast* (1965); *Having a Wild Weekend* (soundtrack, 1965); *I Like It Like That* (1965); *Weekend in London* (1965); *Greatest Hits* (1966); *More Greatest Hits* (1966); *Satisfied with You* (1966); *Try Too Hard* (1966); *5 by 5* (1967); *You Got What It Takes* (1967); *Everybody Knows* (1968); *The Dave Clark Five* (1971).—**BH**

Dave Matthews Band, cosmopolitan roots rock band; formed Charlottesville, Va., 1991. **MEMBERSHIP:** Dave Matthews, voc., gtr. (b. Johannesburg, South Africa, Jan. 9, 1967); Boyd Tinsley, vln.; LeRoi Moore, sax.; Stefan Lessard, bs.; Carter Beauford, drm.

Dave Matthews, a regular-joe musician who initially played clubs on the Univ. of Va. campus, has used constant touring and a hypnotic jazz-rock sound to become one of the biggest rock stars of recent years. At age two, he and his family moved from racially divided Johannesburg to the N.Y.C. suburb of Yorktown Heights. After relocating to Charlottesville as an adult, he put together a band, picking up Carter Beauford and LeRoi Moore (regular performers at Miller's, a jazz club where Matthews tended bar), then-16-year-old bass prodigy Stefan Lessard, and violinist Boyd Tinsley. Dave Matthews Band played its first gig in front of 40 people on May 11, 1991, on the roof of a Charlottesville apartment building. After performing as part of a 1991 Earth Day festival, the band found a permanent place to play: the Eastern Standard, a small restaurant, on Tuesday nights. Eventually, the band moved on to a club called Trax and its Tuesday night shows became a "must see." Because the band allows fans to tape shows, Dave Matthews Band's first recordings were bootlegs; its first official album was the live *Remember Two Things*. From those small beginnings, DMB won opening concert slots from fellow jam-rockers such as The Samples, then made smash hits out of catchy, bouncy numbers from its breakthrough 1994 album, *Under the Table and Dreaming*. Ambitious but unpretentious, Matthews's open-minded music found its moment with later-1990s youth's peace-craving outlook and genre-crossing tastes, and the band has been turning arenas and stadia into the intimate clubs of their ascension ever since.

DISC.: *Remember Two Things* (1993); *Under the Table and Dreaming* (1994); *Crash* (1996); Live at Red Rocks 8.15.95 (1997); *Before These Crowded Streets* (1998); *Listener Supported* (1999). **DAVE MATTHEWS AND TIM REYNOLDS:** *Live at Luther College* (1999).

Davenport, "Cow Cow" (actually, **Charles Edward**), distinctive boogie-woogie pianist, singer; b. Anniston, Ala., April 23, 1894; d. Cleveland, Ohio, Dec. 2, 1955. One of eight children, the son of a preacher, Davenport began studying at a theological school, but was expelled for playing ragtime piano. On his way back to Anniston he began working in Birmingham. He joined a traveling carnival troupe, later leaving to work as a solo act. He then teamed with singer Dora Carr, and they appeared in vaudeville as "Davenport & Co." The partnership ended when Dora Carr married. "Cow Cow" worked as a single in Chicago, then temporarily teamed up with Ivy Smith. During the mid-1920s he acted as talent scout for Vocalion Record Company, while continuing to tour in vaudeville. After a disastrous tour, he spent six months in prison in Montgomery, Ala. In the early 1930s, he moved to Cleveland where he made an unsuccessful attempt to run a music and record shop. He returned to theater work until 1935 when he opened his own cafe in Cleveland. He suffered a stroke in 1938, which temporarily affected his right hand; during that year he was featured as a vocalist with a pick-up recording unit. After his health returned, he moved to N.Y. and worked for a time as the washroom attendant at the Onyx Club, but was helped by Art Hodes who featured him on WNYC broadcasts. In the mid-1940s, he recorded for several small N.Y. labels. He left N.Y. and worked for a time at the Plantation Club in Nashville, then returned to Cleveland to play at the Starlite Grill. Late in his life (with Art Hodes's help) he gained ASCAP ratings for his part in the compositions "Mama Don't Allow" and "I'll Be Glad When You're Dead You Rascal You." He also composed the famous "Cow Cow Boogie," which was a swing hit in the 1940s, and was associated with the boogie-woogie classic "Cow Cow Blues," with its distinctive imitation of a freight train. During the last year of his life, he played at the Pin Wheel Club in Cleveland.

DISC.: *Cow Cow Blues* (1978); *Alabama Strut* (1979); *Cow Cow Davenport 1926–38* (1988); *Cow Cow Davenport 1927–29* (1989); *The Accompanist 1924–29* (1993).—JC/LP

Davenport, Francis William, English composer; b. Wilderslowe, near Derby, April 9, 1847; d. Scarborough, April 1, 1925. He studied law at Oxford, but preferred music, and became the pupil (later son-in-law) of G.A. Macfarren. In 1879, he became a prof. at the Royal Academy of Music, and in 1882 at the Guildhall School of Music.

WORKS: 2 syms.; *12th Night*, overture; 6 pieces for Piano and Cello; *Pictures on a Journey*, a series of piano pieces; part-songs and songs.—NS/LK/DM

Daverio, John, American musicologist and violinist; b. Sharon, Pa., Oct. 19, 1954. He was a violin fellow at the Tanglewood Music Center (1971–73) before pursuing his education at Boston Univ. (B.M., violin, 1975; M.M., violin, 1976; Ph.D., musicology, 1983, with the diss. *Formal Design and Terminology in the Pre-Corellian Sonata*). After serving as a lecturer at the Longy School of Music (1981–83), he was an asst. prof. (1983–89), chairman of the dept. of musicology (from 1987), assoc. prof. (1989–98), and prof. of music (from 1998) at Boston Univ. He was also active as a violinist in recitals and as a member of new music groups. Daverio publ. *Nineteenth-Century Music and the German Romantic Ideology* (1993) and *Robert Schumann: Herald of a "New Poetic Age"* (1997), the latter a particularly valuable addition to the Schumann literature.—LK/DM

Davico, Vincenzo, Italian composer; b. Monaco, Jan. 14, 1889; d. Rome, Dec. 8, 1969. He was a student of Cravero in Turin and of Reger in Leipzig. After living in Paris (1918–40), he settled in Rome.

WORKS: DRAMATIC: Opera: *La dogaressa* (1919; Monte Carlo, Feb. 26, 1920); *Berlingaccio* (1931); *La principessa prigioniera* (Bergamo, Sept. 29, 1940). **Ballet:** *L'agonia della rosa* (Paris, May 2, 1927); *Narciso* (San Remo, Feb. 19, 1935). **ORCH.:** *Polifemo* (1910); *La principessa lontana*, suite (1911); *Impressioni pagane* (1916); *Poema erotico* (1913); *Impressioni romane* (1913); *Impressioni antiche* (1916); *Poemetti pastorali* (1926). **CHAMBER:** Cello Sonata (1909); Piano Trio (1911); *Sonatina rustica* for Violin and Piano (1926); *10 variazioni senza tema* for Cello and Piano (n.d.); *Soliloqui* for Cello and Piano (1945);

piano pieces. **VOCAL:** *La tentazione di San Antonio* for Soloists, Chorus, and Orch. (1921); *Cantata breve* for Baritone, Chorus, and Orch. (1945); *Requiem per la morte d'un povero* for Soloists, Chorus, and Orch. (1949–50); songs.

BIBL.: C. Valabrega, *La lirica da camera di V. D.* (Rome, 1953).—NS/LK/DM

David, Félicien (-César), French composer; b. Cadenet, Vaucluse, April 13, 1810; d. St.-Germain-en-Laye, Aug. 29, 1876. After the death of his parents, he was sent to be a chorister at the cathedral of St. Sauveur in Aix-en-Provence. He entered the Paris Cons. in 1830, where he studied with F. Fétis (fugue) and F. Benoist (organ); he also studied privately with H. Reber. In 1831 he joined the St. Simonians, a messianic socialistic cult patterned after the ideas of Claude-Henri de Rouvroy, Count of St.-Simon (1760–1825). After its forced disbanding in 1832, he made a pilgrimage to Egypt and the Near East, where he absorbed the flavor of the Orient. Returning to Paris in 1836, he produced a number of works based upon his travels, many with titles reflecting oriental exoticism. His first success came in 1844 with the symphonic ode *Le Désert* for Soloists, Men's Chorus, and Orch. After visiting Mendelssohn and Meyerbeer in Germany in 1845, he turned his attention to opera. He achieved little success, with the exception of his *Lalla-Roukh* (1862), which retained its popularity for many years. Although he received many awards, including the rank of Officier de la Legion d'Honneur (1862) and membership into the Académie des Beaux Arts (succeeding Berlioz, 1869), his music virtually disappeared; occasional revivals are fostered by those with an interest in the exoticism of the period.

WORKS (all 1st perf. in Paris): **DRAMATIC: Opera:** *La Perle du Brésil* (Nov. 22, 1851); *Le Fermier de Franconville* (1857); *Herculanum* (March 4, 1859); *Lalla-Roukh* (May 12, 1862); *La Captive* (1860–64); *Le Saphir*, after Shakespeare's *All's Well That Ends Well* (March 8, 1865). **Incidental Music:** *Le Jugement dernier, ou La Fin du monde* (1849). **ORCH.:** 4 syms. (1837, 1838, 1846, 1849). **CHAMBER:** 2 nonets (1839, lost; 1839); *Les Quatre Saisons*, 24 miniature string quintets (1845–46); String Quartet (1868); 3 piano trios (1857); many piano works. **VOCAL: Orch. with Chorus** *Le Désert*, symphonic ode (Dec. 8, 1844); *Moïse au Sinai*, oratorio (March 24, 1846); *Christophe Colomb*, symphonic ode (March 7, 1847); *L'Eden*, oratorio (Aug. 25, 1848; full score lost). **Other:** Choruses; songs.

BIBL.: S. St-Etienne, *Biographie de F. D.* (Marseilles, 1845); A. Azevedo, *F. D.* (Paris, 1863); R. Brancour, *F. D.* (Paris, 1911); M. Achter, *F. D., Ambroise Thomas and French Opéra Lyrique* (diss., Univ. of Mich., 1972); R. Locke, *Music and the St. Simonians: The Involvement of F. D. and Other Musicians in a Utopian Socialist Movement* (diss., Univ. of Chicago, 1980); D. Hagan, *F. D. 1810–1876: A Composer and a Cause* (Syracuse, N.Y., 1985). —NS/LK/DM

David, Ferdinand, noted German violinist, pedagogue, and composer; b. Hamburg, Jan. 19, 1810; d. near Klosters, Switzerland, July 18, 1873. In 1823–24 he studied with Spohr and Hauptmann at Kassel, then played in the Gewandhaus Orch. in Leipzig in 1825. From 1826 to 1829 he was a member of the Königstadt Theater in Berlin. In 1829 he became the first violinist in the private string quartet of the wealthy amateur Baron von Liphardt of Russia, whose daughter he married. He remained in Russia until 1835, giving concerts in Riga, Moscow, and St. Petersburg with great acclaim. In 1836 he was appointed first violinist of the Gewandhaus Orch., of which Mendelssohn was the conductor. They became warm friends; Mendelssohn had a great regard for him, and consulted him while writing his Violin Concerto; it was David who gave its first performance (Leipzig, March 13, 1845). When the Leipzig Cons. was established in 1843, David became one of its most important teachers. His class was regarded as the finishing school of the most talented violinists in Europe, and among his pupils were Joachim and Wilhelmj. He publ. many valuable eds. of violin works by classical composers, notably *Die hohe Schule des Violinspiels*, containing French and Italian masterpieces of the 17th and 18th centuries. His pedagogical activities did not interfere with his concert career. He played in England in 1839 and 1841 with excellent success and was compared with Spohr as a virtuoso, and he also made occasional appearances on the Continent. Among his works were 5 violin concertos and many other pieces for violin, an opera, *Hans Wacht* (Leipzig, 1852), 2 syms., and string quartets and other chamber music. His violin pieces, *Bunte Reihe*, were transcribed for piano by Liszt.

BIBL.: J. Eckardt, *F. D. und die Familie Mendelssohn- Bartholdy* (Leipzig, 1888).—NS/LK/DM

David, Giacomo,

Italian tenor, father of **Giovanni David**; b. Presezzo, near Bergamo, 1750; d. Bergamo, Dec. 31, 1830. He studied in Naples, and made his debut in 1773 in Milan. He then made many appearances at La Scala in Milan (1782–83; 1799–1800; 1802–03; 1806–08), and also sang in concert in London (1791). David was a featured singer at the first performances given at the Teatro Nuovo in Trieste (1801) and at the Teatro Carcano in Milan (1803).—NS/LK/DM

David, Giovanni,

Italian tenor, son of **Giacomo David**; b. Naples, Sept. 15, 1790; d. St. Petersburg, 1864. He studied with his father, making his debut in 1808 in Siena. He created the role of Narciso in Rossini's *Il Turco in Italia* at La Scala in Milan on Aug. 14, 1814, as well as created other roles in Rossini operas. He sang in London in 1818 and 1831. In 1839 he quit the stage and later became manager of the St. Petersburg Opera. —NS/LK/DM

Dávid, Gyula,

Hungarian composer and teacher; b. Budapest, May 6, 1913; d. there, March 14, 1977. He studied with Kodály at the Budapest Academy of Music (graduated, 1938). He was a violist in several orchs. (1938–45), and also a conductor at the National Theater in Budapest (until 1949); then taught chamber music at the Academy of Music (1950–60; 1967–77) and the Béla Bartók Music School (1964–67). In 1952 and 1955 he received the Erkel Prize, and in 1957 the Kossuth Prize. His compositional practices ranged from free use of folk melodies to strict 12-tone procedures.

WORKS: D R A M A T I C : *Nádasban* (In the Reeds), ballet (1961); much incidental music. O R C H . : 4 syms. (1948, 1958, 1960, 1970); *Balettzene* (Ballet Music; 1948); *Tánczene* (Dance Music; 1950); Viola Concerto (1950); *Színházi zene* (Theater Music; 1955); *Sinfonietta* (1960); Concerto Grosso for Viola and Strings (1963); Violin Concerto (1966); Horn Concerto (1971); *Ünnepi nyitány* (Festive Overture; 1972). C H A M B E R : 5 wind quintets (1949, 1955, 1964, 1967, 1968); Flute Sonata (1954); 2 string quartets (1962, 1973); *Preludio* for Flute and Piano (1964); *Miniat&ubdlac;rök* (Miniatures) for Brass Sextet (1968); Viola Sonatina (1969); Trio for Violin, Cello, and Piano (1972); *Pezzo* for Viola and Piano (1974). P i a n o : Sonata (1955). V O C A L : *Felhőtlen ég* (Cloudless Skies), cantata for Chorus and Orch. (1964); *A rózsa lágolás* (The Rose is Aflame) for Woman's Voice, Flute, and Viola (1966); *Égő szavakkal* (With Flaming Words), cantata for Chorus and Orch. (1969); choruses.

BIBL.: J. Breuer, *D. G.* (Budapest, 1966).—NS/LK/DM

David, Hal,

American lyricist; b. N.Y., May 25, 1921. David wrote literate, romantic lyrics, primarily to the complex melodies of Burt Bacharach, that made him one of the most successful lyricists of the 1960s and resulted in such hits as "This Guy's in Love with You," "Raindrops Keep Fallin' on My Head," "(They Long to Be) Close to You," and a string of popular songs written for Dionne Warwick. Though primarily a creator of independent songs, David also wrote the lyrics for one long-running Broadway musical, *Promises, Promises*, and for songs used in at least 32 motion pictures between 1952–80.

David was the son of Gedalier David, who ran a delicatessen, and Lina Goldberg David. His older brother Mack David was also a successful lyricist. He studied violin as a child and played in local bands, but he was also interested in writing, and after graduating from high school he enrolled in the School of Journalism at N.Y.U. Dropping out after his sophomore year, he worked as a copywriter for the *New York Post* then went into the armed forces when the U.S. entered WW II. He served in the Special Services division, where he wrote songs and sketches, gaining enough recognition to be admitted into ASCAP in 1943. He returned to N.Y. after the war to pursue songwriting. On Dec. 24, 1947, he married Anne Rauchman, a schoolteacher, with whom he would have two children.

David enjoyed his first song success with "The Four Winds and the Seven Seas" (music by Don Rodney), which peaked in the Top Ten for Sammy Kaye in September 1949. His second came with "American Beauty Rose" (music and lyrics by David, Redd Evans, and Arthur Altman), a chart entry for Eddy Howard in July 1950. "Wonderful, Wasn't It?" (music by Don Rodney) was performed by Frankie Laine in the film *Rainbow 'Round My Shoulder*, released in August 1952, and Laine's recording turned up in the charts in September. Teresa Brewer had a chart entry in February 1954 with David's "Bell Bottom Blues" (music by Leon Carr).

David met Burt Bacharach in 1957 and they began to collaborate, first placing the song "Warm and Tender" in the film *Lizzie* (April 1957), where it was sung by Johnny Mathis, who also recorded it. Marty Robbins then recorded their song "The Story of My Life," which reached the pop Top 40 in November 1957 and hit #1 in the country charts in January 1958. Perry Como cut

"Magic Moments," which entered the pop Top Ten in January 1958. (In the U.K., Michael Holliday's version of "The Story of My Life" hit #1 in February, followed by Perry Como's "Magic Moments.") Notwithstanding these successes, Bacharach accepted an offer from Marlene Dietrich to become her musical director, and he toured with her for the next several years. Back in N.Y., he collaborated with various lyricists, including David, who also worked with other composers.

David scored his next hit with Lee Pockriss; the two wrote "My Heart Is an Open Book," which hit the Top Ten for Carl Dobkins Jr. in July 1959. That month, "Broken-Hearted Melody" (music by Sherman Edwards) hit the charts for Sarah Vaughan. It reached the Top Ten in August and became David's first million-seller. Also in August, "With Open Arms," a collaboration with Bacharach, reached the Top 40 for Jane Morgan.

David worked steadily during the late 1950s and early 1960s, often writing English lyrics to popular foreign songs and title or "exploitation" (i.e., promotional) songs for motion pictures. His next notable success came with "Sea of Heartbreak" (music by Paul Hampton), a Top 40 pop hit and Top Ten country hit for Don Gibson in July 1961. By 1962, Bacharach was spending more time in N.Y., and he and David began to collaborate more frequently. Their exploitation song "(The Man Who Shot) Liberty Valance," promoting but not actually heard in the film of the same name, became a Top Ten hit for Gene Pitney in June 1962. That same month, David's "Johnny Get Angry" (music by Sherman Edwards) reached the Top 40 for Joanie Sommers, but this was his last hit without Bacharach for more than a decade. Bacharach and David returned to the Top 40 in August with Jerry Butler's recording of "Make It Easy on Yourself" and in October with Gene Pitney's "Only Love Can Break a Heart," which also topped the easy-listening chart.

Bacharach and David discovered Dionne Warwick as a backup singer at a recording session and used her as a demo singer on their songs, then arranged to have her signed to Scepter Records and became her producers. Their first record together was "Don't Make Me Over," which reached the Top 40 in December 1962. The songwriters' string of hits continued in 1963: Bobby Vinton's recording of "Blue on Blue" reached the Top Ten in June; and Gene Pitney scored a Top 40 hit with "True Love Never Runs Smooth" in August and another with "Twenty Four Hours from Tulsa" in November. That same month, Bacharach and David scored a second Top 40 hit with "Wives and Lovers," an exploitation song recorded by Jack Jones that earned them a Grammy nomination for Song of the Year.

Warwick scored her first Top Ten hit with a Bacharach-David song in February 1964 with "Anyone Who Had a Heart." Cilla Black bested her that same month in the U.K., going all the way to #1 with the song. Warwick followed up with a second Top Ten hit in the team's "Walk on By" in May. By this point Bacharach and David were so prolific that artists began to score hits with songs the songwriters failed to have hits with earlier, or that had been placed on the B-sides of

successful records. Dusty Springfield reached the Top Ten in July 1964 with "Wishin' and Hopin'," a song that had appeared on the B-side of a single by Warwick the year before. That same month, Springfield hit the Top Ten in the U.K. with "I Just Don't Know What to Do with Myself," which did not become an American hit until later. Warwick returned to the Top 40 in September with "You'll Never Get to Heaven (If You Break My Heart)" and in November with Bacharach and David's 1963 song "Reach Out for Me." Meanwhile, "(There's) Always Something There to Remind Me" missed the American Top 40 but hit #1 for Sandie Shaw in the U.K. in October. Similarly, Billy J. Kramer and the Dakotas' rendition of "Trains and Boats and Planes" made the British Top 40 in May 1965, but did not climb as high in the U.S.

Bacharach and David wrote and produced "What the World Needs Now Is Love" for Jackie DeShannon, and the record hit the Top Ten in July 1965. They wrote the songs for the comic film *What's New Pussycat?* featuring Peter Sellers and released in June, among them the Oscar-nominated title song, a Top Ten hit for Tom Jones in July. The film was one of the year's biggest hits, and the soundtrack album spent five months in the charts. The Walker Brothers revived "Make It Easy on Yourself," topping the U.K. charts in September and reaching the U.S. Top 40 in November. Warwick's recording of "Are You There (With Another Girl)" entered the charts in December, reaching the Top 40 in January 1966.

Bacharach and David devoted much of 1966 to writing music for films and television. Their title song for the motion picture *Alfie* was first heard in a version by Cilla Black that hit the U.K. Top Ten in April, then was sung on the soundtrack by Cher when the film opened in August; her recording reached the U.S. Top 40. Bacharach and David scored an original TV musical, *On the Flip Side*, starring Rick Nelson, that was broadcast in December, as well as another Peter Sellers movie, *After the Fox*, released the same month. Meanwhile, their catalog was mined for hits, especially by Warwick, in recordings produced by the songwriters themselves. She altered the 1964 song "Kentucky Bluebird (Send a Message to Martha)" to "Message to Michael" and took it into the Top Ten in May, revived "Trains and Boats and Planes" for a Top 40 hit in July, and put "I Just Don't Know What to Do with Myself" into the American Top 40 for the first time in October. In June, a year after the release of *What's New Pussycat?*, the rock band Love made a Top 40 hit out of "My Little Red Book," a song from the movie's score.

"Alfie" was nominated for the Academy Award for Best Song in early 1968, which may have prompted Warwick to record a new version produced by Bacharach and David. She sang it at the Oscar ceremony, and her rendition reached the Top 40. The songwriters did their third score for a Peter Sellers film comedy, the James Bond spoof *Casino Royale*, released in April. The title tune was performed by Herb Alpert and the Tijuana Brass as an instrumental on the soundtrack and became a Top 40 hit, earning Bacharach and David a Grammy nomination for Best Instrumental Theme. "The Look of

Love" was sung on the soundtrack by Dusty Springfield and also became a Top 40 hit. The film was one of the year's biggest box office successes, and the soundtrack album spent five months in the charts, earning a Grammy nomination for Best Original Score Written for a Motion Picture or TV Show.

Their film work completed, Bacharach and David again had time to write and produce for Warwick. She took their socially conscious song "The Windows of the World" into the Top 40 in August, then scored her biggest hit ever with a Bacharach-David song, hitting the Top Ten with the gold-selling "I Say a Little Prayer" in November. She followed it with "Do You Know the Way to San José," which hit the Top Ten in May 1968.

As with "Alfie" the year before, the Academy Award nomination for "The Look of Love" in early 1969 may have inspired Sergio Mendes and Brasil '66 to revive the song with a version that bested Dusty Springfield's original in the charts, reaching the Top Ten in 1968. Meanwhile, Herb Alpert debuted as a singer, recording Bacharach and David's "This Guy's in Love with You" for a million-selling #1 hit the same month. The songwriters also provided a follow-up, their 1964 song "To Wait for Love," which Alpert took into the Top 40 in September. Warwick returned to the Top 40 with the songwriters' "Who Is Gonna Love Me?" in September, and "I Say a Little Prayer" became a million-selling Top Ten hit for the second time within a year in October as a recording by Aretha Franklin.

Bacharach and David spent the better part of 1968 writing songs for the Broadway musical *Promises, Promises*, playwright Neil Simon's stage adaptation of the film *The Apartment*. Warwick provided a preview of the show in a recording of the title song that reached the Top 40 in November. When *Promises, Promises* opened the following month, it became an enormous hit, running 1,281 performances, winning the Tony Award for Best Musical, and spawning a cast album that spent three months in the charts and won the Grammy for Best Score from an Original Cast Show Album.

Warwick again achieved a quick revival with a Bacharach-David song, altering the title of their earlier hit to "This Girl's in Love with You" and returning it to the Top Ten in March 1969. She followed with the songwriters' title song for the motion picture *The April Fools*, reaching the Top 40 in June. Tom Jones hit #1 on the easy-listening charts in September with "I'll Never Fall in Love Again," a song drawn from the score of the still-running *Promises, Promises*. The song went on to become a standard: Bobbie Gentry topped the U.K. charts with it in October; Warwick returned it to #1 on the easy-listening charts and took it into the pop Top Ten in early 1970; it was also nominated for a Grammy for Song of the Year.

Also in September 1969, Bacharach and David enjoyed a Top 40 hit with Engelbert Humperdinck's recording of "I'm a Better Man," and in October. Isaac Hayes took a revival of "Walk on By" into the Top 40. The duo's major effort for the fall was the music for the Western film *Butch Cassidy and the Sundance Kid*. It became the biggest box office hit of 1969 with a gold-selling soundtrack album that spent more than a year in

the charts, featuring the #1 million-selling single "Raindrops Keep Fallin' on My Head," sung by B. J. Thomas in a recording produced by Bacharach and David. The song won the Academy Award for Best Song and earned Grammy nominations for Song of the Year and Best Contemporary Song.

As the Bacharach-David songwriting partnership reached a peak of success in late 1969, however, David engaged in his most prominent work outside the team since the early 1960s, collaborating with John Barry on the songs used in the James Bond film *On Her Majesty's Secret Service*, released in December, and one of the year's biggest box office successes, with a soundtrack album that spent three months in the charts.

By now, Bacharach had established a career as a recording artist and performer that was taking up much of his time. Nevertheless, in 1970 the two collaborated on a follow-up to "Raindrops Keep Fallin' on My Head" for B. J. Thomas, who took their "Everybody's Out of Town" into the Top 40 in April, and they continued to produce new material for Warwick, who enjoyed Top 40 hits with "Let Me Go to Him" in May and "Paper Mache" in August. Most of the team's hits during the year, however, came with revivals of earlier songs. R. B. Greaves reached the Top 40 in February with "(There's) Always Something There to Remind Me." In July, the Carpenters hit #1 with the gold-selling "(They Long to Be) Close to You," a 1963 song that had been recorded unsuccessfully several times before. Warwick reached the Top 40 with a revival of "Make It Easy on Yourself" in October. And the 5th Dimension took a 1967 Bacharach-David song, "One Less Bell to Answer," into the Top Ten in December. The record sold a million copies and topped the easy-listening charts in January 1971.

Bacharach and David were not heard from much in 1971 and 1972 while they worked on a film musical adaptation of the James Hilton novel *Lost Horizon*. Still, they continued to write songs for Warwick and Thomas that became minor chart entries. The most notable revival of one of their songs during this period was Tom Clay's medley of "What the World Needs Now Is Love" and "Abraham, Martin and John" (music and lyrics by Dick Holler), which hit the Top Ten in July 1971. The first hearing of music from *Lost Horizon* came in December 1972 with the release of "Living Together, Growing Together," a song from the score recorded by the 5th Dimension. It reached the Top 40 in February 1973. The original motion picture soundtrack, released in January, spent more than four months in the charts. But the film, which opened in March, was a failure, leading to the breakup of the Bacharach-David partnership.

The Stylistics revived "You'll Never Get to Heaven (If You Break My Heart)," reaching the Top 40 in June 1973. David had songs in two films released that spring. Marty Robbins sang "A Man and a Train" (music by Frank DeVol) in *Emperor of the North Pole*, released in May, and his recording made the country charts in June. Anne Murray sang "Send a Little Love My Way" (music by Henry Mancini) in *Oklahoma Crude*, released in June, and her recording made both the pop and country charts in August. Teaming with Michel Legrand, David wrote songs for the stage musical *Brainchild*, which opened a tryout in Philadelphia on March 25, 1974, but closed on April 16 without going to Broadway. Lena Horne recorded three of the show's songs with the composer for her 1975 album *Lena and Michel*. David joined the board of directors of ASCAP in 1974, a position he continued to hold 25 years later; he served as the organization's president from 1980–86.

In April 1975, Albert Hammond reached the charts with "99 Miles from L.A." (music by Albert Hammond, lyrics by David); the song topped the easy-listening charts in May. That month, "The Greatest Gift" (music by Henry Mancini, lyrics by David) was featured in the Peter Sellers film *The Return of the Pink Panther*. Warwick sued Bacharach and David in the fall of 1975 for failing to write and produce an album for her; they in turn sued each other. The suits were settled out of court in 1979. David collaborated with Archie Jordan in 1977 for "It Was Almost Like a Song"; Ronnie Milsap's recording topped the country charts in July and crossed over to the pop charts, reaching the Top 40 in August. It was nominated for a Grammy for Best Country Song.

David again collaborated with John Barry for the title song of the James Bond film *Moonraker*, released in June 1979. Naked Eyes revived "(There's) Always Something There to Remind Me" for a Top Ten hit in June 1983. Julio Iglesias and Willie Nelson's recording of "To All the Girls I've Loved Before" (music by Albert Hammond, lyrics by David) reached the Top Ten of the pop charts in April 1984 and topped the country charts in May, selling a million copies. Sybil revived "Don't Make Me Over" for a million-selling Top 40 hit in November 1989.

David reunited with Bacharach in 1992 and wrote "Sunny Weather Lover," which Warwick recorded for her album *Friends Can Be Lovers*. *Back to Bacharach and David* featuring the team's songs opened Off- Broadway on March 25, 1993, and ran 69 performances. The songwriters again teamed to write a new song, "You've Got It All Wrong," for inclusion in a showcase performance of *Promises, Promises* in N.Y. in the spring of 1997. Bacharach-David songs were prominently featured in the 1997 films *Austin Powers: International Man of Mystery*, released in May, and *My Best Friend's Wedding*, released in June. The latter had a gold- selling soundtrack album.

David continued to write lyrics in the late 1990s, notably working with Charles Strouse on a stage musical called *Times Square* and again teaming with Bacharach on songs for the film *Isn't She Great?* starring Bette Midler.

WORKS (only works for which David was a primary, credited lyricist are listed): **FILMS:** *What's New Pussycat?* (1965); *After the Fox* (1966); *Casino Royale* (1967); *Butch Cassidy and the Sundance Kid* (1969); *On Her Majesty's Secret Service* (1969); *Lost Horizon* (1973). **MUSICALS/REVUES:** *Promises, Promises* (Dec. 1, 1968). **TELEVISION:** *On the Flip Side* (Dec. 7, 1966).—**WR**

David, Hans T(heodor), German-American musicologist; b. Speyer, Palatinate, July 8, 1902; d. Ann Arbor, Mich., Oct. 30, 1967. He was educated at the univs. of Tübingen, Göttingen, and Berlin (Ph.D., 1928, with the diss. *Johann Schobert als Sonatenkomponist*; publ. in Borna, 1928). In 1933 he went to the Netherlands, and in 1936 he emigrated to the U.S. In 1937 he joined the staff at the N.Y. Public Libary, and in 1939 became a lecturer at N.Y.U. After serving as a prof. and head of the musicology dept. at Southern Methodist Univ. in Dallas (1945–50), he was prof. of music history at the Univ. of Mich. at Ann Arbor (from 1950). He was highly regarded as a Bach scholar.

WRITINGS: With A. Rau, *A Catalog of Music of American Moravians, 1742–1842, from the Archives of the Moravian Church at Bethlehem* (Bethlehem, Pa., 1938); *Bach's 'Musical Offering': History, Interpretation and Analysis* (N.Y., 1945); ed. with A. Mendel, *The Bach Reader* (N.Y., 1945; 2nd ed., rev., 1966; rev. and enl. ed., 1998, by C. Wolff as *The New Bach Reader*).—**NS/LK/DM**

David, Johann Nepomuk, outstanding Austrian composer and teacher, father of **Thomas Christian David;** b. Eferding, Nov. 30, 1895; d. Stuttgart, Dec. 22, 1977. He studied with Joseph Marx at the Vienna Academy of Music (1921–22). After serving as a schoolteacher, organist, and choirmaster in Wels (1924–34), he joined the faculty of the Leipzig Landeskonservatorium (later the Hochschule für Musik) in 1934, becoming its director in 1942. He was subsequently director at the Salzburg Mozarteum (1945–48). In 1948 he was appointed prof. of composition at the Musikhochschule in Stuttgart, serving until 1963. In 1978 the International Johann Nepomuk David Soc. was organized in Stuttgart. His mastery of counterpoint is revealed in all of his works, which are polyphonic in structure.

WRITINGS (all publ. in Göttingen unless otherwise given): *Die Jupitersymphonie* (1953); *Die zweistimmigen Inventionen von Johann Sebastian Bach* (1957); *Die dreistimmigen Inventionen von Johann Sebastian Bach* (1959); *Das wohltemperierte Klavier: Versuch einer Synopsis* (1962); *Der musikalische Satz im Spiegel der Zeit* (Graz, 1963).

WORKS: ORCH.: Concerto Grosso for Chamber Orch. (1923); Flute Concerto (1934); 2 partitas (1935, 1939); 8 numbered syms.: No. 1 in A minor (1936), No. 2 (1938), No. 3 (1940), No. 4 (1945), No. 5 (1951; Stuttgart, May 3, 1952), No. 6 (1954; Vienna, June 22, 1955), No. 7 (1956; Stuttgart, Oct. 10, 1957), and No. 8 (1964–65; Stuttgart, Nov. 20, 1965); *Kume, kum, geselle min*, divertimento on old folk songs (1938); *Variationen über ein Thema von Johann Sebastian Bach* (1942); *Symphonische Variationen über ein Thema von Heinrich Schütz* (1942); 3 concertos for Strings: No. 1 (1950), No. 2 (1951) and No. 3 (1974; Berlin, Feb. 20, 1975); 2 violin concertos: No. 1 (1952; Stuttgart, April 25, 1954) and No. 2 (1957; Munich, April 22, 1958); *Deutsche Tänze* for Strings (1953; Wiesbaden, July 7, 1954); *Sinfonia preclassica super nomen H-A-S-E* (1953; St. Veit, Carinthia, Oct. 16, 1954); *Sinfonia breve* (1955; Baden-Baden, March 4, 1956); *Melancholia* for Viola and Chamber Orch. (1958; Lucerne, Aug. 31, 1961); *Magische Quadrate* (1959; Recklinghausen, March 23, 1960); *Sinfonia per archi* (1959; Linz, Nov. 30, 1960); *Spiegelkabinett*, waltz (Dresden, Nov. 20, 1960); Organ Concerto (1965; Cologne, Nov. 28, 1966); *Variationen über ein Thema von Josquin des Prés* for Flute, Horn, and Strings (1966; Munich, April 17, 1969); Concerto for Violin, Cello, and Small Orch. (1969); *Chaconne* (1972). **CHAMBER:** String Trio (1935); *Duo concertante* for Violin and Cello (1937); Sonata for Flute, Viola, and Guitar (1940); Trio for Flute, Violin, and Viola (1942); solo sonatas for Flute (1942), Violin (1943),

Viola (1943), Cello (1944), and Lute (1944); Sonata for Flute and Viola (1943); Sonata for 2 Violins (1945); 4 string trios (1945, 1945, 1948, 1948); Clarinet Sonata (1948); Sonata for 3 Cellos (1962); Sonata No. 2 for Solo Violin (1963); Trio for Flute, Violin, and Cello (1974). **O r g a n :** *Ricercare* (1925); *Chaconne* (1927); *2 Hymnen* (1928); *Passamezzo and Fugue* (1928); *Toccata and Fugue* (1928); *Fantasia super "L'homme armé"* (1929); *Preambel und Fuge* (1930); *Das Choralwerk* (21 vols., 1932–73); *2 Fantasias and Fugue* (1935); *Ricercare* (1937); *Introitus, Chorale and Fugue on a Theme of Bruckner* for Organ and 9 Wind Instruments (1939); *Chaconne and Fugue* (1962); *Toccata and Fugue* (1962); *Partita über B-A-C-H* (1964); *12 Orgelfugen durch alle Tonarten* (1968); *Partita* (1970); *Partita* for Violin and Organ (1975). **SACRED VOCAL:** *Stabat Mater* for 6-part Chorus (1927); *Deutsche Messe* for Chorus (1952; Leipzig, Feb. 19, 1953); *Missa choralis (de Angelis) ad quattuor voces inaequales* (1953; Linz, Jan. 17, 1954); *Requiem chorale* for Soloists, Chorus, and Orch. (1956; Vienna, June 11, 1957); *Ezzolied*, oratorio for Soloists, Chorus, and Orch. (1957; Berlin, May 17, 1960); *O, wir armen Sunder*, cantata for Alto, Chorus, and Organ (1966); *Mass* (1968); *Komm, Heiliger Geist*, cantata for 2 Choruses and Orch. (1972; Linz, March 26, 1974); also motets.

BIBL.: R. Klein, *J. N. D.* (Vienna, 1964); H. Bertram, *Material—Struktur—Form: Studien zur musikalischen Ordnung bei J. N. D.* (Wiesbaden, 1965); H. Stuckenschmidt, *J. N. D.* (Wiesbaden, 1965); G. Sievers, ed., *Ex Deo nascimur: Festschrift zum 75. Geburtstag von J. N. D.* (Wiesbaden, 1970); W. Dallmann, *J. N. D.: Das Choralwerk für Orgel* (Bern, 1994); W. Dallmann, *J. N. D.: Das Chorwerk für Orgel: Versuch einer hinfurhrenden Analyse* (Frankfurt am Main, 1994).—**NS/LK/DM**

David, José, French composer, son of **Léon David;** b. Sables-d'Olonne, Jan. 6, 1913. He entered the Paris Cons. in 1933. He studied with Fauchet, Jacques de la Presle, and Büsser; also had lessons with Dupré (organ) and Emmanuel (music history). He collaborated with N. Obouhov in *Traité d'harmonie tonale et atonale* (Paris, 1947).

WORKS: *Impressions de Vendée* for Piano (1944; also for Orch.); *La Ballade de Florentin Prunier* for Voice, Violin, Cello, and Piano (1947); *Symphonie* for Ondes Martenot and Orch. (1948); *Jacquet le Prioux*, ballet (1950); Violin Sonata (1955); *Laudate dominum* for 3 Men's Voices and Organ (1960); *2 Poems* for Voice and Piano (1973).—**NS/LK/DM**

David, Karl Heinrich, Swiss composer; b. St. Gallen, Dec. 30, 1884; d. Nervi, Italy, May 17, 1951. He studied in Cologne and Munich; taught at the Basel Cons. (1910–14), then at Cologne and Berlin (1914–17); in 1918, returned to Switzerland. He was the ed. of the *Schweizer Musikzeitung* in Zürich (1928–41).

WORKS: DRAMATIC: O p e r a : *Aschenputtel* (Basel, Oct. 21, 1921); *Der Sizilianer* (Zürich, Oct. 22, 1924); *Jugendfestspiel* (Zürich, June 8, 1924); *Traumwandel* (Zürich, Jan. 29, 1928); *Weekend*, comic opera (1933). **ORCH.:** Piano Concerto (1929); *Ballet* (1931); *Pezzo sinfonico* (1945); Concerto for Saxophone and Strings (1947); *Symphonie de la côte d'argent* (1948); *Mascarade*, overture (1950); *Andante and Rondo* for Violin and Chamber Orch. **CHAMBER:** *2 Pieces* for Piano and 9 Woodwinds; Viola Suite; Piano Trio; Quartet for Saxophone, Violin, Cello, and Piano (1946); Duet for Horn and Piano (1951). **VOCAL:** *Das hohe Lied Salomonis* for Soprano, Tenor, Women's Chorus, and Orch.; songs.—**NS/LK/DM**

David, Léon, French tenor, father of **José David;** b. Sables-d'Olonne, Dec. 18, 1867; d. there, Oct. 27, 1962. He studied at the Nantes Cons. and later at the Paris Cons. He made his debut at the Opéra-Comique in Paris in 1892, appearing subsequently in Brussels, Monte Carlo, Marseilles, Bordeaux, Cairo, Lisbon, Bucharest, and other cities. From 1924 to 1938 he was a prof. of singing at the Paris Cons.—**NS/LK/DM**

David, Samuel, French composer; b. Paris, Nov. 12, 1836; d. there, Oct. 3, 1895. He studied at the Paris Cons. with Halévy. He won the Grand Prix de Rome (1858) for his cantata *Jephté*, and another prize for a work for Men's Chorus and Orch., *Le Génie de la terre*, performed by a chorus of 6,000 singers (1859). David was a prof. at the Coll. de Sainte-Barbe (1861) and a music director in Paris synagogues (1872). Other works include several operas, 4 syms., choruses, and songs. —**NS/LK/DM**

David, Thomas Christian, noted Austrian composer and teacher, son of **Johann Nepomuk David;** b. Wels, Dec. 22, 1925. He was a choirboy at Leipzig's Thomaskirche and studied with his father at the Leipzig Hochschule für Musik before studying musicology at the Univ. of Tübingen (1948). He taught flute at the Salzburg Mozarteum (1945–48) and was founder-director of the South German Madrigal Choir (1952–57); he then went to Vienna, where he taught harmony and composition at the Academy of Music (from 1957), later serving as prof. of harmony at the Hochschule für Musik (from 1973) and director of the Austrian Composers Soc. (from 1986). He also taught at the Univ. of Teheran and was director of the Iranian Television Orch. (1967–73). He made various appearances as a flutist, harpsichordist, pianist, choral director, and conductor. David received several awards for his compositions, which are noted for their innovative, modernistic uses of contrapuntal devices.

WORKS: DRAMATIC: O p e r a : *Atossa* (1968); *Der Weg nach Emmaus* (Alpbach, Aug. 28, 1982); *Als Oedipus kam* (1986). **ORCH.:** *Divertimento* for Strings (1951); *Serenade* for Strings (1957); Concerto No. 1 for Strings (1961; Munich, Sept. 20, 1962); Concerto for 12 Strings (1964); Sym. No. 1 (1965); Concerto (1967); Concerto No. 2 for Strings (1971; Teheran, Jan. 10, 1973); Concerto No. 3 for Strings (1974; Linz, Nov. 30, 1975); *Entrada* (1975); *Sinfonia giacosa* (1975); Concerto grosso (1978; Prague, Feb. 21, 1982); *Duplum* for Wind Orch. (East Lansing, Mich., June 3, 1983); *Festival Prologue* (1982). **CONCERTOS WITH ORCH.:** Piano (1960); Clarinet (1961); 5 Brass Instruments and Strings (1962); Violin (1962; Munich, May 26, 1965); Violin (No. 1, 1962; Munich, May 26, 1965; No. 2, 1986); Guitar and Chamber Orch. (1963); Violin and Strings (Teheran, Sept. 3, 1970); Oboe (1975; Hagen, March 18, 1976); Organ (1976; Vienna, Dec. 11, 1981); 2 Violins and Strings (1977; Hagen, March 8, 1979); Bass (1979; Hagen, Oct. 16, 1980); 3 Violins and Strings (1981); Flute (1982; Vienna, March 3, 1983); Cello (1983; Vienna, March 20, 1987); Violin, Clarinet, and Piano (1983; N.Y., May 1, 1984); Sinfonia Concertante for Violin, Clarinet, Piano, and Wind Orch. (1986). **CHAMBER:** 5 string quartets (1952, 1953, 1954, 1965, 1967); Quartet for Flute and String Trio (1958); Concerto for 9 Instruments (1961; Vienna, Feb. 28, 1962); Quintet for Clarinet and String Quartet (1963); 3 Intermezzi for

Violin and Piano (1964); 2 wind quintets (1966, 1979); Cello Sonata (1970); Trio for Violin, Clarinet, and Piano (1977); *Tricinium* for Flute, English Horn or Viola, and Cello (1977); Quartet for Oboe and String Trio (1979); Sonata for Violin and Viola (1980); Sonata for Clarinet and Violin (1980); Sonata for Flute and Clarinet (1980); Sonata for Cello and Guitar (1982); Trio for Violin, Viola, and Cello (1984); Toccata for 9 Flutes (1985); Trio for Violin, Cello, and Piano (1985); Trio for Flute, Viola, and Guitar (1985); Quintet for 2 Flutes, Violin, Cello, and Piano (1987); many works for solo instruments. **VOCAL:** 10 madrigals (1950–82); *Wer ist es*, motet (1960); *Missa in honorem Mariae* (1965); *Das Lied des Menschen*, oratorio (1975; Gumersbach, May 1978); *Die Vogel*, cantata for Soprano, Flute, Clarinet, and Piano (1981); *Und wir haben erkannt*, motet (1982); also 15 songs (1963–86).—**NS/LK/DM**

Davidenko, Alexander, Russian composer; b. Odessa, April 13, 1899; d. Moscow, May 1, 1934. He organized, with Bely, the Procoll (Production Collective of Composers) in Russia in 1925. His most important work is the opera *1905* (1929–33; with B. Shekhter); another opera, *Down the Cliff*, was left incomplete. He also composed workers's songs.

BIBL.: N. Martynov, ed., *A. D.* (Leningrad, 1968). —**NS/LK/DM**

Davidov, Carl, outstanding Russian cellist; b. Goldingen, Latvia, March 15, 1838; d. Moscow, Feb. 26, 1889. He studied cello in Moscow with Heinrich Schmidt and in St. Petersburg with K. Schuberth. In 1859 he went to Leipzig, where he studied composition with Hauptmann. In 1860, at the age of 22, he was appointed an instructor at the Leipzig Cons; also played in the Gewandhaus Orch. In 1862 he returned to Russia, and from 1862 to 1887 he was a prof. at the St. Petersburg Cons., and acting director from 1876 to 1887. He made several European tours, during which he played recitals with Anton Rubinstein, Saint-Saëns, and Liszt. Davidov was also a reputable composer, numbering among his works 4 cello concertos, a fantasy on Russian songs for Cello and Orch., a symphonic poem, *The Gifts of the Terek River*, String Quartet, String Sextet, Piano Quintet, and songs. He also publ. a cello method (Leipzig, 1888; Russian ed., supervised by L. Ginsburg, Moscow, 1947).

BIBL.: V. Hutor, *C. D. und seine Art das Violoncell zu behandeln* (Moscow, 1899); S. Ginsburg, *C. D.* (Moscow, 1950). —**NS/LK/DM**

Davidov, Stepan Ivanovich, Russian composer; b. 1777; d. St. Petersburg, May 22, 1825. He studied with Giuseppe Sarti in St. Petersburg and was subsequently active as a singing teacher, répétiteur, and composer at the Drama School there. After serving as music director to Count Sheremetev, he was a singing teacher at the Moscow Drama School. He was one of the leading Russian composers of music for the stage in his day.

WORKS: DRAMATIC: O p e r a : *Lesta, the Dnepr Water Nymph* (St. Petersburg, Nov. 6, 1805); *Rusalka* (St. Petersburg, 1807); also numbers for Kauer's *Das Donauweibchen*, given in Russian as *Rusalka* (St. Petersburg, Nov. 7, 1803). **B a l l e t :** *Virtue Crowned* (St. Petersburg, Oct. 7, 1801); *Thank Offering* (St. Petersburg, 1802); *The Victory Celebration* (1814). Also several

comical divertissements; incidental music; sacred works. **O t h e r :** Several comical divertissements and incidental music. **VOCAL:** Sacred works.—**NS/LK/DM**

Davidovich, Bella, esteemed Russian-born American pianist and pedagogue, mother of **Dmitry Sitkovetsky**; b. Baku, July 16, 1928. Her maternal grandfather was concertmaster of the Baku opera orch. and her mother was a pianist. She began formal piano training when she was 6; at age 9 she appeared as soloist in the Beethoven First Piano Concerto in Baku. In 1939 she was sent to Moscow to pursue studies with Igumnov, with whom she subsequently studied at the Cons. (1946–48), where she completed her training with Yakov Flier (1948–54). In 1949 she captured joint first prize at the Chopin Competition in Warsaw, which launched her upon a highly successful career in Russia and Eastern Europe; she was a soloist each season with the Leningrad Phil. (1950–78) and taught at the Cons. (1962–78). In 1967 she made her first appearance outside Russia, playing in Amsterdam; in 1971 she made a tour of Italy. Following the defection of her son to the West in 1977, she was refused permission to perform there by the Soviet government. In 1978 she emigrated to the U.S., becoming a naturalized American citizen in 1984. In 1979 she made an acclaimed debut in a recital at N.Y.'s Carnegie Hall. In 1982 she joined the faculty of the Juilliard School in N.Y. but continued to pursue an international career. In 1988 she and her son visited Russia, being the first émigrés to be invited to perform there by Goskontsert since the Gorbachev era of reform was launched.—**NS/LK/DM**

Davidovsky, Mario, Argentine composer and teacher; b. Buenos Aires, March 4, 1934. He studied composition and theory with Guillermo Graetzer in Buenos Aires and also took courses with Teodor Fuchs, Erwin Leuchter, and Ernesto Epstein; then continued his training with Babbitt at the Berkshire Music Center in Tanglewood (summer, 1958). He worked at the Columbia- Princeton Electronic Music Center (from 1960) and taught at the Univ. of Mich. (1964), the Di Tella Inst. of Buenos Aires (1965), the Manhattan School of Music in N.Y. (1968–69), Yale Univ. (1969–70), City Coll. of the City Univ. of N.Y. (1968–80), Columbia Univ. (1981–94), where he served as director of the Columbia-Princeton Electronic Music Center, and Harvard Univ. (from 1994). He held 2 Guggenheim fellowships (1960, 1971) and in 1971 received the Pulitzer Prize in Music for his *Synchronisms No. 6* for Piano and Electronics. In 1982 he was elected a member of the Inst. of the American Academy and Inst. of Arts and Letters. Davidovsky's method of composition tends toward mathematical parameters; his series of 8 compositions entitled *Synchronisms* derives from the numerical coordinates of acoustical elements; electronic sound is integral to most of his work.

WORKS: ORCH.: Concertino for Percussion and Strings (1954); *Suite sinfonica para "El payaso"* (1955); *Serie sinfonica* (1959); *Contrastes No. 1* for Strings and Electronics (1960); *Pianos* (1961); *Transientes* (1972); *Synchronisms No. 7* for Orch. and Electronics (1973); *Consorts* for Symphonic Band (1980); *Divertimento* for Cello and Orch. (1984); Concertante for String

Quartet and Orch. (Philadelphia, March 8, 1990). **CHAMBER:** 4 string quartets (1954, 1958, 1976, 1980); Quintet for Clarinet and Strings (1955); *3 Pieces* for Woodwind Quintet (1956); *Noneto* for 9 Instruments (1956); Trio for Clarinet, Trumpet, and Viola (1962); *Synchronisms No. 1* for Flute and Electronics (1963), *No. 2* for Flute, Clarinet, Violin, Cello, and Electronics (1964), *No. 5* for Percussion Ensemble and Electronics (1969), *No. 6* for Piano and Electronics (1970), and *No. 8* for Woodwind Quintet and Electronics (1974); *Inflexions* for Chamber Ensemble (1965); *Junctures* for Flute, Clarinet, and Violin (1966); *Music* for Violin (1968); *Chacona* for Violin, Cello, and Piano (1971); *Pennplay* for 16 Players (1978); String Trio (1982); *Capriccio* for 2 Pianos (1985). **VOCAL:** *Synchronisms No. 4* for Men's Voices or Mixed Chorus and Electronics (1967); *Scenes from Shir-ha-shirim* for Soprano, 2 Tenors, Baritone, and Chamber Orch. (1975); *Romancero* for Soprano, Flute, Clarinet, Violin, and Cello (1983). **TAPE:** 3 studies (1961, 1962, 1965).—**NS/LK/DM**

Davidson, Lyle, American composer; b. Randolph, Vt., Feb. 25, 1938. He studied at the Univ. of Vt. (1956–58), the New England Cons. of Music in Boston (B.M., 1962; M.M., 1964), Brandeis Univ., and Boston Univ. He was active in avant-garde circles, composing pieces for the theater, dance, and films. His output utilized various contemporary techniques, including the use of electronics.—**NS/LK/DM**

Davidson, Randall, American composer; b. Pueblo, Colo., July 31, 1953. His mother was a church secretary and his father the son of the minister, and when Randall was 12 the family settled in Columbia, Mo. He studied with Dominick Argento, Eric Stokes, Susan McClary, and Paul Fetler at the Univ. of Minn. School of Music and with Alf Houkon, Olivier Messiaen, and Ned Rorem at Cornell Coll. He then had training with Sandy Goehr in London. He settled in Minneapolis, where he devoted himself to composition. Davidson has enjoyed a lengthy collaborative relationship with the celebrated radio humorist Garrison Keillor, for whom he has composed numerous works, including *The Young Lutheran's Guide to the Orchestra* (1988). He hosts a regular chamber concert series for the Schubert Club in Minneapolis, and in 1993 was commissioned by NIKE International for 4 grand opera commercials that were shown in cinemas and on commercial television around the world. One of these, *Don Quincy,* received a Gold Lion award at the 1993 Cannes Film Festival. Davidson has received numerous other honors and awards, including grants from Meet the Composer and American Composers Forum. From 1996 to 2000 he served as president of the American Music Center.

WORKS: ORCH.: *Black and Blues* (1984); *Mexico- Bolivar Tango* (1987); *The Young Lutheran's Guide to the Orchestra* (1988). **CHAMBER:** *Chamber Music (for these distracted times)* for Clarinet, Viola, and Cello (1979); *Three Ways of the Sacred & Profane* for Cello (1979); *Johann & Joe* for Violin (1984); *Song & Dance* for Cello Trio (1984); *Fanfare for the Union Depot* for Brass Choir (1985); *Around Columbia* for String Trio (1987); *Kittyhawk* for Violin or Flute and Piano (1987); *Mexico-Bolivar Tango* for Oboe, Violin, and Piano (1989; also for String Trio); *Anniversary Sonata* or Oboe and Guitar (1992); *Ya Ribon* for Cello, Folk and Classical Harp, and Percussion (1994); *How Can I Keep from Singing* for Oboe, Cello, and Piano (1995). **Piano:** *It's All Right* for Piano, 5-Hands (1987); *Concerning One Summer: a Fantasy on Newfoundland Folk Melodies* (1997). **VOCAL: Chorus:** *Psalm 118:22–3* for Chorus and Handbells (1980); *Christ is the King* (1985); *We Three Kings* for 3 Male Soloists, Chorus, and Organ (1985; also for Chorus, Harp, Psalter, and Strings); *Moving, at a Distance* for Chorus and Orch. (1988); *Lord, Whose Love in Humble Service* for Chorus and Organ or String Trio (1989); *O Lux Trinitas* for Vocal Soloists, Chorus, and Organ (1989); *Good Night...* for Chorus and Piano (1990); *Lover's Lament* for Chorus and Guitar (1991); *Christ Was Born on Christmas Day* for Chorus and Percussion and/or Organ (1992); *Come Rejoicing* for Chorus and Percussion (1992); *Gloria* for Chorus and Piano (1992); *Love is a Thread* for Chorus, Drum, and Organ (1992); *These Children of Both God and Earth—Mamrelund* for Chorus and Organ (1992); *Pour Out the Spirit* for Chorus and Organ (1993); *Jesus Leads the Way* for Baritone Solo, Chorus, and Organ (1994); *The Fourth Wise Man* for 4 Men's Voices, Mezzo-soprano, Treble Trio, Choruses, and Chamber Orch. (1995); *Beatitudes* for Tenor and Baritone Soloists, Chorus, and Organ, from *The Fourth Wise Man* (1997). **Other Vocal:** *Three Songs on texts by Emily Dickinson* for Mezzo-soprano and Viola (1978); *Simple Gifts* for Soprano, Oboe, Violin, Viola, and Cello (1982); *The Land Where One Never Dies* for Narrator and Piano Trio (1982); *Lord Thomas & Ellender* for Soprano, Oboe, Violin, Viola, and Cello (1983); *Part Song* for Tenor, Baritone, Bass, and Piano (1991); *Pete Seeger's Old Devil Time* for Mezzo-soprano and Chamber Ensemble (1993). **OTHER:** Numerous arrangements and original compositions for Garrison Keillor's repertoire; arrangement of Schubert's Fantasy in F minor, op.103 (1993).—**LK/DM**

Davidson, Tina, American composer; b. Stockholm (of American parents), Dec. 30, 1952. She studied piano at the State Univ. of N.Y. at Oneonta (1962–70) and at the School of Music in Tel Aviv (1971), and composition with Brant, Fine, and Nowak at Bennington (Vt.) Coll. (1972–76). From 1978 to 1989 she was assoc. director of RELÂCHE, a Philadelphia-based ensemble for the performance of contemporary music. From 1981 to 1985 she taught piano at Drexel Univ. She was composer-in-residence of the Orch. Soc. of Philadelphia (1992–94), of Opera-Delaware in Wilmington (1994–97), and the Fleisher Art Memorial (1998–2000). Her music is replete with colorful sonoric effects and extra-musical influences.

WORKS: DRAMATIC: Opera: *Billy and Zelda* (Wilmington, Del., Dec. 11, 1998). **ORCH.:** *Complex* for Wind Orch. (1977); *Dancers* (Philadelphia, May 25, 1980); Piano Concerto (1981; Philadelphia, Feb. 28, 1983); *Blood Memory: A Long Quiet after the Call* for Cello and Orch. (1985; Bennington, Vt., June 1, 1986); *In the Darkness I Find a Face (It is Mine)* (1989); *The Selkie Boy* (1991); *They Come Dancing* (1994; Roanoke, Va., Jan. 23, 1995). **CHAMBER:** *Recollections of Darkness,* string trio (1975); Quintet for Alto Flute, Bass Clarinet, Viola, Cello, and Double Bass (1981); *Wait for the End of Dreaming* for 2 Baritone Saxophones and Double Bass (1983–85); *Day of Rage* for Piano (1984); *Never Love a Wild Thing* for Variable Ensemble (1986); *Star Myths* for Piano or Variable Ensemble (1987); *Cassandra Sings* for String Quartet (1988); *Blue Dawn (The Promised Fruit)* for 3 Winds and Piano (1989); *In that Early Light* for Glass Harmonica and Cello (WHYY-TV, Philadelphia, Dec. 1, 1999); Piece for Triple String Quartet (Philadelphia, April 28, 2000).

VOCAL: *2 Beasts from the Forest of Imaginary Beings* for Narrator and Orch. (1975; Bennington, Vt., April 20, 1976); *Man-Faced-Scarab* for Soprano, Flute, Clarinet, and Oboe (1978); *Witches' Hammer* for Voice and Percussion (1979); *Unicorn/Tapestry* for Voice, Cello, and Tape (1982).—**NS/LK/DM**

Davie, Cedric Thorpe
See **Thorpe Davie, Cedric**

Davies, (Albert) Meredith, English organist, conductor, and music educator; b. Birkenhead, July 30, 1922. He studied at the Royal Coll. of Music in London and was an organ scholar at Keble Coll., Oxford, later becoming organist at St. Albans Cathedral (1947) and at Hereford Cathedral (1949). He then pursued conducting studies with Previtali at the Accademia di Santa Cecilia in Rome (1954, 1956). He was organist at New Coll., Oxford (1956–60), assoc. conductor (1957–59) and deputy music director (1959–60) of the City of Birmingham Sym. Orch., and director of the City of Birmingham Choir (1957–64). Davies was music director of the English Opera Group in London (1963–65) and of the Vancouver (B.C.) Sym. Orch. (1964–71), and also chief conductor of the BBC Training Orch. in London (1969–72). He was conductor of the Royal Choral Soc. of London (1972–85) and of the Leeds Phil. (1975–84). From 1979 to 1988 he was principal of Trinity Coll. of Music in London. In 1982 he was made a Commander of the Order of the British Empire.—**NS/LK/DM**

Davies, Arthur, Welsh tenor; b. Wrexham, April 11, 1941. He was a student at the Royal Northern Coll. of Music in Manchester. After appearing with Opera for All and singing in the Welsh National Opera chorus in Cardiff, he made his formal operatic debut as Squeak in *Billy Buddy* with the Welsh National Opera. In subsequent seasons, he sang such roles there as Nero, Nadir, Nemorino, Lensky, Rodolfo, Don José, Pinkerton, and Števa. In 1976 he made his first appearance at London's Covent Garden in the premiere of Henze's *We Come to the River*, and returned in later seasons to sing such roles as Alfredo, the Italian Singer in *Der Rosenkavalier*, Pinkerton, Števa, and Walton's Troilus. He also made guest appearances with the Scottish Opera in Glasgow, the Edinburgh Festival, the English National Opera in London, and in Leipzig, Chicago, Moscow, and Buenos Aires. As a concert artist, he was known for his performances in works by Elgar.—**NS/LK/DM**

Davies, Ben(jamin) Grey, Welsh tenor; b. Pontardawe, near Swansea, South Wales, Jan. 6, 1858; d. Bath, England, March 28, 1943. After winning first prize for solo singing at the Swansea Eisteddfod in 1877, he studied at the Royal Academy of Music in London (1878–80) under Randegger Sr., and Fiori, winning the bronze, silver, and gold medals for best declamatory English singing. His debut was in Birmingham, Oct. 11, 1881, in *The Bohemian Girl*. He created the title role in Sullivan's *Ivanhoe* (London, Jan. 31, 1891). In 1892 he made his debut at London's Covent Garden as Faust. He made his first appearance in the U.S. at the Chicago World's Fair in 1893, then was mainly active as a concert and oratorio singer. He sang regularly at the Handel Festivals until 1926.—**NS/LK/DM**

Davies, Cecilia, English soprano; b. c. 1755; d. London, July 3, 1836. A precocious child, she toured with her parents and her sister, Marianne Davies (b. 1743 or 1744; d. c. 1818), who played the harpsichord and flute, and then the glass harmonica from 1762. Cecilia appeared in Ireland in 1763, and then with her sister in London in 1767 before touring throughout Europe. During their stay in Vienna, Cecilia studied with Hasse, in whose *Ruggiero* she appeared in Naples in 1772. Following appearances in other Italian cities, she sang in London (1773–74; 1776–77) before pursuing her career on the Continent. She gave concerts in London and other British cities in 1787 and 1791, but her career then waned and she ended her days in poverty. —**NS/LK/DM**

Davies, Dennis Russell, significant American conductor; b. Toledo, Ohio, April 16, 1944. He studied piano with Lonny Epstein and Sascha Gorodnitzki and conducting with Morel and Mester at the Juilliard School of Music in N.Y. (B.Mus., 1966; M.S., 1968; D.M.A., 1972), where he also taught (1968–71) and was co-founder (with Berio) of the Juilliard Ensemble (1968–74). He was music director of the Norwalk (Conn.) Sym. Orch. (1968–73), the St. Paul (Minn.) Chamber Orch. (1972–80), the Cabrillo (Calif.) Music Festival (1974–91), and the American Composers Orch. in N.Y. (1977–2001). In 1978 he made his first appearance at the Bayreuth Festival, conducting *Der fliegende Holländer*. He was Generalmusikdirektor of the Württemberg State Theater in Stuttgart (1980–87), principal conductor and director of Classical music programming at the Saratoga (N.Y.) Performing Arts Center (1985–88), and Generalmusikdirektor of Bonn (1987–95), where he was chief conductor of the Orchester der Beethovenhalle and of the Opera. In 1994 he led the orch. on a tour of North America. From 1991 to 1996 he was music director of the Brooklyn Academy of Music and principal conductor of the Brooklyn Phil. He likewise was chief conductor of the Stuttgart Chamber Orch. (from 1995) and the Austrian Radio Sym. Orch. in Vienna (from 1996). In 1998 he became a prof. at the Salzburg Mozarteum. In 2002 he was to assume the positions of chief conductor of the Bruckner Orch. and of the Opera in Linz. In 1987 he received the Alice M. Ditson conductor's award. Davies has acquired a notable reputation as a champion of contemporary music. He has conducted numerous premieres in the U.S. and Europe. —**NS/LK/DM**

Davies, Fanny, English pianist; b. Guernsey, June 27, 1861; d. London, Sept. 1, 1934. She studied at the Leipzig Cons. with Reinecke and Paul (piano) and Jadassohn (theory) in 1882–83, and at the Hoch Cons. in Frankfurt am Main with Clara Schumann (1883–85). She also was a pupil of Scholz in fugue and composition. Her London debut took place at the Crystal Palace on Oct. 17, 1885, after which she made successful tours in England, Germany, France, and Italy.—**NS/LK/DM**

Davies, Hugh (Seymour), English composer and instrument inventor; b. Exmouth, April 23, 1943. He was a pupil of Rubbra at the Univ. of Oxford (1961–64) and subsequently an assistant to Stockhausen as well as a member of his electronic music group (1964–66); then was director of the electronic music studio at Goldsmiths' Coll., Univ. of London (1967–86), and subsequently was active as a consultant researcher. In addition to works for traditional instruments, he wrote music utilizing instruments of his own invention, tape, and electronics.

WORKS: *Contact* for Piano (1963); *Vom ertrunkenen Mädchen* for Soprano, Flute, Clarinet, and Piano (1964); Quintet for Electronics (1967–68); *Interfaces* for Tape and Electronics (1967–68); *Kangaroo* for Organ (1968); *Beautiful Seaweeds* for Players, Dancers, and Slides (1972–73); Wind Trio (1973–75); *The Musical Educator* for Speaker, Players, Dancers, and Slides (1974); *Natural Images* for Tape (1976); *Melodic Gestures* for Flute, Violin, Cello, and Piano (1978); *Ex una voce* for Tenor and Synthesizer (1979). **SPECIALLY CONSTRUCTED INSTRUMENTS:** *Shozyg I, II, I + II* (1968); *Spring Song* (1970); *Gentle Springs* (1973); *Music for Bowed Diaphragms* (1973); *My Spring Collection* (1975); *Salad* (1977); *The Search for the Music of the Spheres* (1978); *At Home* (1978).—NS/LK/DM

Davies, Ryland, Welsh tenor; b. Cwm, Ebbw Vale, Feb. 9, 1943. He studied at the Royal Manchester Coll. of Music. He made his operatic debut as Almaviva in 1964 with the Welsh National Opera; then sang in Glasgow, Glyndebourne, and London (1969). He sang in San Francisco in 1970; made his Metropolitan Opera debut in N.Y. on Oct. 15, 1975, as Ferrando in *Così fan tutte*. He appeared in major European operatic centers, and also toured widely as a concert singer. Among his best known roles were Tamino, Don Ottavio, Belmonte, Lensky, Nemorino, and Pelléas. From 1966 to 1981 he was married to **Anne Howells.**—NS/LK/DM

Davies, Sir (Henry) Walford, eminent Welsh organist, educator, and composer; b. Oswestry, Sept. 6, 1869; d. Wrington, Somerset, March 11, 1941. He was a pupil of Walter Parratt at St. George's Chapel in Windsor, where he served as his assistant (1885–90), and then studied with Parry and Stanford at the Royal Coll. of Music in London, where he subsequently taught (1895–1903). He was conductor of the Bach Choir (1903–07), and also held positions as organist at Christ Church, Hampstead (1891–98), Temple Church (1898–1918), and St. George's Chapel (1927–32). He was a prof. of music at the Univ. of Wales (1919–26). Between 1924 and 1934 he led the novel broadcasting series "Music Lessons in Schools." He was knighted in 1922, and in 1934 he was appointed Master of the King's Musick. He publ. *The Musical Outlook in Wales* (London, 1926), *The Pursuit of Music* (London, 1935), and *Music and Worship* (with Harvey Grace, London, 1935). As a composer, Davies is remembered for his *Solemn Melody* for Organ and Strings (1908) and his march for the Royal Air Force (1917). He also wrote a Sym. (1911), *Conversations* for Piano and Orch. (London, Oct. 14, 1914), overtures, choral music, chamber music, songs, and many pieces for school performance.

WORKS: ORCH.: O v e r t u r e s : *Dedication Overture* (1893); *Festal Overture* (1910). **O t h e r :** *Conversations* for Piano and Orch. (London, Oct. 14, 1914). **CHAMBER:** 2 violin sonatas (1894, 1896); *Peter Pan* for String Quartet (1909). **VOCAL: C h o r u s :** *The Temple* (1902); *Lift Up Your Hearts* (1906); *5 Sayings of Jesus* (1911); *Heaven's Gate* (1916); *Men and Angels* (1925); *Christ in the Universe* (1929). **O t h e r Vo c a l :** Numerous part-songs. **OTHER:** Many works for school performance, including *A Children's Symphony* (1927) and *London Calling the Schools* for Piano, Orch., and Radio Announcer (1932).

BIBL.: H.C. Colles, *W. D., A Biography* (London, 1942). —NS/LK/DM

Davies, Sir Peter Maxwell, eminent English composer and conductor; b. Manchester, Sept. 8, 1934. He was educated at the Royal Manchester Coll. of Music (graduated, 1952) and at the Univ. of Manchester (Mus.B., 1956). In 1957 he won an Italian government scholarship to study with Petrassi in Rome. After serving as director of music at Cirencester Grammar School (1959–62), he studied with Sessions and Babbitt on a Harkness fellowship at Princeton Univ. (1962–64). In 1967 he founded the Pierrot Players in London, serving as co-director with Birtwistle until 1971. In 1971 Davies founded the Fires of London, which he led as artistic director until 1987. In 1970 he settled in the Orkney Islands, where he founded the St. Magnus Festival in 1977 and for which he served as artistic director until 1986, and then as its president. From 1979 to 1983 he was artistic director of the Dartington Summer School of Music. In 1985 he was the Visiting Fromm Prof. of Composition at Harvard Univ. From 1985 to 1994 he served as assoc. composer/conductor of the Scottish Chamber Orch. in Glasgow, and then was its composer laureate. He was president of the Composers' Guild of Great Britain from 1986. In 1992 he became conductor/composer of the BBC Phil. in Manchester and assoc. conductor/composer of the Royal Phil. in London. He left his Manchester position in 2000. He was president of the Soc. for the Promotion of New Music from 1995. Davies has received numerous honors, including various honorary doctorates. In 1981 he was made a Commander of the Order of the British Empire, and in 1987 he was knighted. In 1988 he was named an Officier dans l'Ordre des Arts et des Lettres de France. He was awarded the Cobbett Medal for his services to chamber music in 1989. In 1998 he was made a member of the Bayerische (Bavarian) Akademie der Schöne Künste in Munich.

Davies is a prolific composer who has written significant scores in all of the major genres. Following an early period in which he was influenced by both Western and non-Western currents, he turned to an expressionist mode as exemplified in his music theater pieces. After settling in the Orkney Islands, he drew great inspiration from its landscape and literary history.

WORKS: DRAMATIC: O p e r a : *Taverner* (1962–70; London, July 12, 1972); *The Martyrdom of St. Magnus* (1976; Orkney, June 18, 1977); *The Lighthouse* (1979; Edinburgh, Sept. 2, 1980); *Resurrection* (1987; Darmstadt, Sept. 18, 1988); *Redemption* (1988); *The Doctor of Myddfai* (1993–96; Cardiff, July 5, 1996). **M u s i c T h e a t e r :** *8 Songs for a Mad King* for Baritone, Flute, Clarinet, Keyboards, Percussion, Violin, and Cello (London, April 22, 1969); *Vesalii Icones* for Dancer, Cello, Flute, Clarinet, Piano, Percussion, and Viola (London, Dec. 9, 1969); *Blind Man's Bluff* for Mime, Soprano, Mezzo- soprano, and Small Orch. (London, May 29, 1972); *Miss Donnithorne's Maggot* for Female Singer, Flute, Clarinet, Violin, Cello, Piano, Percussion, and 4 Mechanical Metronomes (Adelaide, March 9, 1974); *Salome*, ballet (Copenhagen, Nov. 10, 1978; concert suite, London, March 16, 1979); *Le Jongleur de Notre Dame* for Mime, Baritone, Flute, Clarinet, Violin, Cello, Piano, Percussion, and Children's Band (Orkney, June 18, 1978); *The Yellow-Cake Revue*, anti-nuclear cabaret for Singer and Piano (Orkney, June 21, 1980); *The Medium*, monodrama for Mezzo-soprano (Orkney, July 21, 1981); *The No. 11 Bus* for Mime, 2 Dancers, Mezzo-soprano, Tenor, Baritone, Flute, Clarinet, Violin, Cello, Piano, and Percussion (London, March 20, 1984); *Caroline Mathilde*, ballet (1990). **ORCH.:** *Prolation* (1958; Rome, June 10, 1959); 2 fantasias on an In Nomine of John Taverner (London, Sept. 13, 1962; London, April 30, 1965); *Sinfonia* for Chamber Orch. (London, May 1962); *St. Thomas Wake Foxtrot for Orchestra on a Pavan by John Bull* (Dortmund, June 2, 1969); *Wordles Blis* (London, Aug. 28, 1969); *The Boy Friend*, film suite (London, Dec. 11, 1971); 6 syms.: No. 1 (1976; London, Feb. 2, 1978), No. 2 (1980; Boston, Feb. 26, 1981), No. 3 (1984; Manchester, Feb. 19, 1985), No. 4 (London, Sept. 10, 1989), No. 5 (1993–94; London, Aug. 10, 1994), and No. 6 (1996); Sinfonia Concertante for Wind Quintet and Chamber Orch. (1982; London, Aug. 12, 1983); *Sinfonietta accademica* (Edinburgh, Oct. 6, 1983); *An Orkney Wedding, with Sunrise* for Bagpipes and Orch. (Boston, May 10, 1985); Violin Concerto (1985; Kirkwall, Orkney, June 21, 1986); *Jimmack the Postie* (Kirkwall, June 22, 1986); 10 *Strathclyde* concertos: No. 1 for Oboe and Orch. (Glasgow, April 29, 1987), No. 2 for Cello and Orch. (1988; Glasgow, Feb. 1, 1989), No. 3 for Horn, Trumpet, and Orch. (1989; Glasgow, Jan. 19, 1990), No. 4 for Clarinet and Orch. (1990), No. 5 for Violin, Viola, and Orch. (Glasgow, March 13, 1991), No. 6 for Flute and Orch. (1991), No. 7 for Double Bass and Orch. (Glasgow, Nov. 25, 1992), No. 8 for Bassoon and Orch. (Glasgow, Nov. 24, 1993), No. 9 for Chamber Orch. (1994), and No. 10 for Chamber Orch. (1995); Trumpet Concerto (Hiroshima, Sept. 21, 1988); *Ojai Festival Overture* (Ojai, Calif., June 1, 1991); *Sir Charles: His Pavan* (1992); *A Spell for Green Corn: The MacDonald Dances* (Glasgow, Nov. 24, 1993); *Chat Moss* (1993; Liverpool, March 15, 1994); *Carolisma*, serenade for Chamber Orch. or Instrumental Ensemble (1994); *Cross Lane Fair* for Northumbrian Bagpipes and Orch. (Kirkwall, Orkney, June 18, 1994); *The Beltane Fire*, choreographic poem (1995); *Time and the Raven* (Nottingham, June 12, 1995); *Throstle's Nest Junction* (Manchester, Nov. 16, 1996); Piccolo Concerto (1996; Nottingham, April 23, 1997); *Mavis in Las Vegas* (Manchester, March 13, 1997); Piano Concerto (Nottingham, Nov. 7, 1997); *Sails in St. Magnus I: Fifteen keels laid in Norway for Jerusalem-farers* (1997), *II: In Kirkwall, the first red Saint Magnus Stones* (1997), and *III: An Orkney wintering. Stone poems in Orkahowe:"great treasure..."* (1999); *A Reel of Seven Fishermen* (1998); *Maxwell's Reel, with Northern Lights* (London, May 23, 1998); *Roma Amor Labyrinth* (1998); *Swinton Jig* (York, Nov. 27, 1998); *Temenos, with Mermaids and Angels* (1998; Dublin, May 17, 1999); *High on the Slopes of Terror* (1999); *Spinning Jenny: A Portrait of Leigh, Lancashire, circa 1948* (1999). **CHAMBER:** Movement for String Quartet (1952; London, May 23, 1983); Trumpet Sonata (1955); *Stedman Doubles* for Clarinet and Percussion for 1 Player (1956; rev. 1968); Clarinet Sonata (1956; Darmstadt, July 20, 1957); *Alma redemptoris mater* for Flute, Oboe, 2 Clarinets, Bassoon, and Horn (Dartington, Aug. 7, 1957); *St. Michael* for 17 Wind Instruments (1957; London, July 13, 1959); Sextet for

Flute, Clarinet, Harpsichord, Percussion, Viola, and Cello (1958; rev. as a Septet with the addition of a guitar, 1972); *Ricercar and Doubles on "To Many a Well"* for Flute, Oboe, Clarinet, Bassoon, Horn, Harpsichord, Viola, and Cello (1959); String Quartet (London, Nov. 1961); *Shakespeare Music* for 11 Instruments (London, Dec. 8, 1964); *7 in Nomine* for 10 Instruments (London, Dec. 3, 1965); *Antechrist* for Piccolo, Bass Clarinet, 3 Percussionists, Violin, and Cello (London, May 30, 1967); *Hymnos* for Clarinet and Piano (1967); *Stedman Caters* for Flute, Clarinet, Harpsichord, Viola, Cello, and Percussion (London, May 30, 1968); *Eram quasi agnus* for 7 Wind Instruments, Handbells, and Harp (London, June 10, 1969); *Canon in memoriam Igor Stravinsky* for Flute, Clarinet, Harp, and String Quartet (broadcast, April 6, 1972); *Hymn to St. Magnus* for Flute, Clarinet, Piano, Viola, Cello, and Percussion (London, Oct. 13, 1972); *Renaissance Scottish Dances* for Flute, Clarinet, Guitar, Violin, Cello, and Percussion (Dartington, July 29, 1973); *Si quis diligit Me* for Alto Flute, Clarinet, Celesta, Crotales, Viola, and Cello (Dartington, July 29, 1973); *All Sons of Adam* for Alto Flute, Clarinet, Celesta, Guitar, Marimba, Viola, and Cello (London, Feb. 20, 1974); *Psalm 124* for Flute, Bass Clarinet, Glockenspiel, Marimba, Guitar, Violin, and Cello (Dartington, July 28, 1974); *Ave Maris Stella* for Flute, Clarinet, Piano, Marimba, Viola, and Cello (Bath, May 27, 1975); *3 Studies for Percussion* for 11 Players (1975); *My Lady Lothian's Lilt* for Alto Flute, Bass Clarinet, Viola, Cello, Percussion, and Mezzo-sorpano Obbligato (Dartington, Aug. 20, 1975); *Kinloche His Fantassie* for Flute, Clarinet, Harpsichord, Glockenspiel, Violin, and Cello (Dartington, Aug. 19, 1976); *Runes from a Holy Island* for Alto Flute, Clarinet, Celesta, Percussion, Viola, and Cello (broadcast, Nov. 6, 1977); *A Mirror of Whitening Light* for 14 Instruments (London, March 23, 1977); *Our Father Whiche in Heaven Art* for Flute, Clarinet, Celesta, Marimba, Violin, and Cello (Dartington, Aug. 18, 1977); *Little Quartet No. 2* for String Quartet (1977; rev. version, Canton, N.Y., Nov. 12, 1987); *A Welcome to Orkney* for Flute, Oboe, Clarinet, Bassoon, Horn, 2 String Quartets, and Double Bass (Orkney, June 20, 1980); *Little Quartet No. 1* for String Quartet (1980; Dartington, July 26, 1982); *The Bairns of Brugh* for Piccolo, Bass Clarinet, Piano, Marimba, Viola, and Cello (Bergen, May 30, 1981); Quintet for 2 Trumpets, Horn, Trombone, and Tuba (1981; Boston, March 19, 1982); *Image, Reflection, Shadow* for Flute, Clarinet, Cimbalom, Piano, Violin, and Cello (Lucerne, Aug. 22, 1981); *The Pole Star*, march for 2 Trumpets, Horn, Trombone, and Tuba (1982; Dartington, Aug. 18, 1983); *Birthday Music for John* for Flute, Viola, and Cello (Swansea, Oct. 13, 1983); Sonatine for Violin and Cimbalom (London, June 8, 1984); *Unbroken Circle* for Alto Flute, Bass Clarinet, Piano, Viola, and Cello (Bath, June 1, 1984); *Dowland: Farewell—A Fancye* for Alto Flute, Bass Clarinet, Viola, Cello, Piano, and Marimba (1986; London, Jan. 20, 1987); *Thaw* for Instrumental Ensemble (1995); *Fanfare* for Brass Ensemble (1998); *Mishkenot* for 9 Players (London, May 3, 1988); Trumpet Quintet (Aberdeen, Feb. 25, 1999). **Solo Instruments:** *Solita* for Flute (1969); *Turris campanarum sonatium* for Percussion (1971); *The Door of the Sun* for Viola (1975); *The Kestrel Paced Round the Sun* for Flute (1975); *The 7 Brightnesses* for Clarinet (1975); *3 Organ Voluntaries* (1976); *Nocturne* for Alto Flute (1979); Piano Sonata (1981); *Hill Runes* for Guitar (1981); *Sea Eagle* for Horn (1982); Organ Sonata (1982); Guitar Sonata (1984); *First Grace of Light* for Oboe (1991); *6 Secret Songs* for Piano (1993); *Reliqui Domum Meum* for Organ (1996); *Mrs. Linklater's Tune* for Violin (1998); *Litany—for a Ruined Chapel between Sheep and Shore* for Trumpet (1999). **VOCAL:** *5 Motets* for Soprano, Alto, Tenor, Bass, Chorus, and 16 Instruments (1959; London, March 1, 1965); *O* *magnum mysterium* for Chorus, Organ, and Ensemble (Cirencester, Dec. 8, 1960); *Ave Maria, Hail Blessed Flower* for Chorus (1961); *Te lucis ante terminum* for Chorus and 12 Instruments (Cirencester, Nov. 30, 1961); *Leopardi Fragments* for Soprano, Mezzo-soprano, and 8 Instruments (London, July 1962); *Veni sancte spiritus* for Soprano, Alto, Tenor, Bass, Chorus, and Orch. (1963; Cheltenham, July 10, 1964); *Ecce manus tradentis* for Soprano, Alto, Tenor, Bass, Chorus, and Ensemble (Wiltshire, Aug. 20, 1965); *Revelation and Fall* for Soprano and 16 Instruments (1965; London, Feb. 26, 1968; rev. 1980); *Notre Dame des Fleurs* for Soprano, Mezzo-soprano, Countertenor, and 6 Instruments (1966; London, March 17, 1973); *Missa super L'Homme Armé* for Voice and 6 Players (1968; London, April 22, 1969); *From Stone to Thorn* for Mezzo-soprano and 4 Instruments (Oxford, June 30, 1971); *Stone Litany: Runes from a House of the Dead* for Mezzo-soprano and Orch. (Glasgow, Sept. 22, 1973); *Fiddlers at the Wedding* for Mezzo-soprano and 4 Instruments (1973; Paris, May 3, 1974); *Dark Angels* for Mezzo-soprano and Guitar (1974); *Anakreontika* for Mezzo-soprano and 4 Instruments (London, Sept. 17, 1976); *The Blind Fiddler* for Mezzo-soprano and 6 Instruments (Edinburgh, Feb. 20, 1976); *Norn pater noster* for Chorus and Organ (1977); *Westerlings* for Chorus (1977); *Black Pentecost* for Baritone, Mezzo-soprano, and Orch. (1979; London, May 11, 1982); *Solstice of Light* for Tenor, Chorus, and Organ (Orkney, June 18, 1979); *Into the Labyrinth* for Tenor and Chamber Orch. (Kirkwall, June 22, 1983); *1 Star, at Last* for Chorus (Cambridge, Dec. 24, 1984); *Excuse Me* for Mezzo-soprano and 5 Instruments (1985; London, Feb. 26, 1986); *House of Winter* for Chorus (Orkney, June 23, 1986); *Sea Runes* for Chorus (N.Y., Nov. 16, 1986); *Winterfold* for Mezzo-soprano and 7 Instruments (1986; London, Jan. 20, 1987); *Hallelujah! The Lord Almightie* for Chorus and Organ (Edinburgh, June 11, 1989); *Hymn to the Word of God* for Soloists and Chorus (1990); *Corpus Christi, with Cat and Mouse* for Chorus (Oxford, Nov. 30, 1993); *A Hoy Calendar* for Chorus (Liverpool, March 15, 1994); *Invocation to Mercurius* for Chorus and Crotales (Edinburgh, Nov. 6, 1994); *The Three Kings* for Soprano, Mezzo-soprano, Tenor, Baritone, Chorus, and Orch. (London, Oct. 15, 1995); *A Birthday Card for Hans* for Mezzo-soprano and Instrumental Ensemble (1996); *Job*, oratorio for Soprano, Alto, Tenor, Bass, Chorus, and Orch. (Vancouver, British Columbia, May 11, 1997); *Il rozzo martello* for Chorus (1997); *The Jacobite Rising* for Soprano, Alto, Tenor, Bass, Chorus, and Orch. (1997); *Sea Elegy* for Soprano, Alto, Tenor, Bass, Chorus, and Orch. (1998). **OTHER:** Various works for young people.

BIBL.: P. Griffiths, *P. M. D.* (London, 1982); M. Seabrook, *Max: The Life and Music of P. M. D.* (London, 1994).—**NS/LK/DM**

Davies, Tudor, Welsh tenor; b. Cymmer, Nov. 12, 1892; d. London, April 2, 1958. He studied in Cardiff and at the Royal Academy of Music in London. He appeared at the Old Vic; joined the British National Opera Co. in 1922; created the title role in *Hugh the Drover* by Vaughan Williams (London, July 14, 1924); in 1928 he sang in the U.S. with the Civic Opera in Philadelphia. He then was a principal singer with the Old Vic and the Sadler's Wells Opera (1931–41); was a member of the Carl Rosa Opera Co. (1941–46); also appeared in concerts.—**NS/LK/DM**

Davis, Anthony, progressive jazz pianist, composer; b. Paterson, N.J., Feb. 20, 1951. His father, Charles T. Davis, is a professor of African-American literature.

He studied at Yale Univ. (B.A., 1975) and proved himself to be an extremely facile jazz pianist. He was co-founder of Advent (1973), a free jazz ensemble which included trombonist George Lewis; then played in trumpeter Leo Smith's New Delta Ahkri band (1974–77). He played in N.Y. with violinist Leroy Jenkins (1977–79) and with flutist James Newton, who are both active proponents of the Assoc. for the Advancement of Creative Musicians. His compositions, while strictly notated, are improvisational in tone. His opera *X*, based on the life of Malcolm X, was produced in Philadelphia (1985) and at N.Y.C. Opera (1986). In 1998 he premiered another opera, *Amistad*. He often collaborates with his sister, a poet.

DISC.: *Of Blues and Dreams* (1978); *Past Lives* (1978); *Song for the Old World* (1978); *Hidden Voices* (with J. Newton; 1979); *Lady of the Mirrors* (1980); *Episteme* (1981); *Under the Double Moon* (with J. Hoggard; 1982); *I've Known Rivers* (1982); *Mystic Winds, Tropic Breezes* (1982); *Variations in Dreamtime* (1982); *Hemispheres* (1983); *Middle Passage* (1984); *Ghost Factory* (1987); *Trio, Vol. 2* (1989); *Trio, Vol. 1* (1990); *X: The Life and Times of Malcolm X* (1992).—**NS/LP**

Davis, Art(hur D.), jazz bassist; b. Harrisburg, Pa., Dec. 5, 1934. He initially studied piano and tuba, winning a national competition on the latter before starting on bass in 1951. A prodigious talent, he was rated the top bass and tuba player for two years at William Penn H.S. He led his own quintet that, by 1956, had been featured on radio, TV, and at major colleges and clubs throughout the Pa. area. At this time, he worked in the Harrisburg Symphony, studied at the Curtis Inst., and was offered scholarships to three of the leading music conservatories—the Eastman, Juilliard, and Manhattan schools. He selected the latter two and by 1958 was also working around N.Y. He studied with Anselme Fortier, and learned by watching and listening to Oscar Pettiford. He played with Max Roach in 1958–59. The group debuted at the Newport festival on July 6, 1958. Davis had to play with an injured plucking finger—another musician had accidentally shut the car door on it—and his bandage is clearly visible in the photographs on the resulting live album. He toured Europe with Dizzy Gillespie from 1959 through early 1961, then worked with Lena Horne for a month in London. By the early 1960s had symphonic work in N.Y.C., and extensive employment in theatres, studios, and with singers and jazz groups. He played bass with Coltrane, usually in tandem with Reggie Workman, intermittently from May through about October 1961, and on some later occasions including the 1965 recordings the *Quartet Plays* and *Ascension*. (In interviews, Coltrane said that Davis was his first-choice for bass player with his quartet, but Davis was often unavailable when Coltrane offered him the position.) At various times Davis also performed or recorded with O. Coleman, Count Basie, Duke Ellington, Clark Terry-Bob Brookmeyer Quintet, Gene Ammons, Lee Morgan, Aretha Franklin, Gigi Gryce, Booker Little, Quincy Jones, Roland Kirk, Oliver Nelson, Freddie Hubbard, Roach Presents Hassan Ibn Ali, Leo Wright, Abbey Lincoln, Al Grey-Billy Mitchell, and Art Blakey. He made appearances on albums by Bob Dylan, John Denver, Judy Garland, Bob Gibson, Peter, Paul & Mary,

Nancy Ames, Buffy Ste. Marie, and others. He was a member of the NBC, CBS, and Westinghouse television orchestras from 1962 through 1970, breaking the race barrier, and was prominently featured on the Merv Griffin show in the late 1960s. In 1969, after having been turned down for the N.Y. Philharmonic four times, he (along with cellist Earl Madison) brought a historic lawsuit against the orchestra and its conductor Leonard Bernstein for racial discrimination. After 15 months the N.Y. Commission on Human Rights maintained that discrimination had not been proved for permanent jobs (which was challenged by Davis, who maintained that auditions should be held behind a screen), but that the orchestra had discriminated by avoiding black artists when short-term and substitute musicians were needed. From around 1970 he was primarily involved in teaching. He taught at Manhattan Community Coll. from 1971 to 1973. He earned a B.A. from Hunter Coll. in 1972, M.A. degrees from C.U.N.Y. and N.Y.U. in music and psychology in 1976, and a doctorate in psychology in 1981. Moving to the L.A. area in the early 1980s, Davis has since worked as a psychologist, while continuing with his first profession, doing studio sessions, playing in a duo with Hilton Ruiz (1985 and 1986), and recording as a leader (1984 and 1995). He performed in Brooklyn in July 1997 and was interviewed on WKCR radio prior to the concert.

DISC.: *Reemergence* (1980); *Live* (1984); *Life* (1985); *A Time Remembered* (1995). **MAX ROACH:** *Deeds, Not Words* (1958); *Live at Newport* (1958); *Award-Winning Drummer* (1959); *Many Sides of Max Roach* (1959); *Percussion Bitter Sweet* (1961); *It's Time* (1962). **DIZZY GILLESPIE:** *Copenhagen Concert* (1959); *Live at Newport 1960; Gillespiana* (1960); *Carnegie Hall Concert* (1961). **ABBEY LINCOLN:** *Straight Ahead* (1961). **BOOKER LITTLE:** *Out Front* (1961). **JOHN COLTRANE:** *Africa/Brass* (1961); *Olé Coltrane* (1961); *J.C. Quartet Plays* (1965); *Ascension* (1965).—**LP**

Davis, Carl, American conductor and composer; b. N.Y., Oct. 28, 1936. He was educated at the New England Cons. of Music in Boston and at Bard Coll. (B.A.), his mentors in composition in the U.S. being Paul Nordoff and Hugo Kauder; also studied with Per Nørgård in Copenhagen. He became active in England as a conductor and composer. From 1984 to 1987 he was principal conductor of the Bournemouth Pops. In 1987–88 he was assoc. conductor of the London Phil. He composed much stage, film, and television music. He also collaborated with Paul McCartney on the *Liverpool Oratorio* (1991).

WORKS: DRAMATIC: O p e r a : *Peace* (1978). **T e l e-v i s i o n O p e r a :** *The Arrangement* (1967); *Orpheus in the Underground* (1976). **M u s i c a l s :** *The Projector* (1971); *Pilgrim* (1975); *Cranford* (1976); *Alice in Wonderland* (1977); *The Wind in the Willows* (1986); *Kip's War* (1987). **B a l l e t :** *Dances of Love and Death* (1981); *Fire and Ice* (1986); *The Portrait of Dorian Gray* (1987); *A Simple Man* (1987); *Liaisons Amoureuses* (1989); *Lipizzaner* (1989); *A Christmas Carol* (1992); *Savoy Suite* (1993). **F i l m :** *The French Lieutenant's Woman* (1981); *Champions* (1984); *King David* (1985); *Girl in a Swing* (1988); *Scandal* (1988); *The Rainbow* (1988); *Frankenstein Unbound* (1989); *Fragments of Isabella* (1990); *Crucifer of Blood* (1991); *Raft of the Medusa* (1992); *The Voyage* (1993); *The Trial* (1993); also scores for various silent films,

including *Napoleon* (1980), *Thief of Baghdad* (1984), *Ben Hur* (1987), and *City Lights* (1988). **ORCH.:** *Lines on London*, sym. (1980); *Overture on Australian Themes* (1981); Clarinet Concerto (1984); *Fantasy for Flute, Strings, and Harpsichord* (1985); *Glenlivet Fireworks Music* (1987); *The Pigeon's Progress* for Narrator and Orch. (1988); *A Duck's Diary* for Narrator and Orch. (1990); *The Town Fox* for Narrator and Orch. (1990). **VOCAL:** *The Most Wonderful Birthday of All* for Soprano and Orch. (1985); *Liverpool Oratorio* for Voices and Orch. (1991; in collaboration with P. McCartney).—**NS/LK/DM**

Davis, Charles (A.), baritone saxophonist, soprano and tenor saxophonist; b. Goodman, Miss., May 20, 1933. Best known as a superb baritone saxophonist, he is a versatile artist who plays the other saxophones in a variety of musical settings. His father was Lindsey Davis, his mother Vernell Coleman Davis. He was raised in Chicago from 1936 and graduated from DuSable H.S.; he studied at the Chicago School of Music from 1948 to 1950, and was a private student of John Hauser. He had an extensive musical relationship with Sun Ra, first working with him in 1954. Pat Patrick, his Sun Ra band mate, sold him his first baritone. He was a full-time Arkestra member for two years, and would periodically perform, record, and tour with Sun Ra into the 1980s. He worked with Jack McDuff, Ben Webster, Billie Holiday, and Dinah Washington in the mid and late 1950s, before spending three years in Kenny Dorham's group, a period that helped to establish his reputation and forged a musical association that would last for many years. Davis played with John Coltrane at the Cork 'n Bib, Westbury, Long Island, N.Y., probably in October 1962. He also played with Illinois Jacquet and Lionel Hampton in the early 1960s. In 1964 he won *Down Beat* magazine's International Jazz Critics Poll for the baritone saxophone. He formed his own band in 1965 and 1966. In the 1960s he performed in the musical production of *The Philosophy of the Spiritual—A Masque of the Black* under the direction of Willie Jones and the auspices of Nadi Qumar.

He taught at PS 179 in Brooklyn and was musical director of The Turntable, a nightclub owned by Lloyd Price. He performed for 10 years from the mid-1960s with the Jazz Composer's Orch. He continued to freelance with Blue Mitchell, Erskine Hawkins, Clifford Jordan, and others. In the 1970s he was a member of the cooperative group "Artistry in Music" with Hank Mobley, Cedar Walton, Sam Jones, and Billy Higgins; was the co-leader and composer/arranger for the Baritone Saxophone Retinue, a group featuring six baritone saxophones; made European tours of major jazz festivals and concerts with the Clark Terry Orch.; and toured the USA with Duke Ellington's Orch. under the direction of Mercer Ellington, and in 1978 the Thad Jones-Mel Lewis Orch. He was musical director of the Home of the Id nightclub, presenting Gene Ammons, Randy Weston, and Max Roach; and was producer of Monday Night Boat Ride up the Hudson presenting Art Blakey, George Benson, and Etta Jones; and made TV appearances with Archie Shepp, Lucky Thompson, Ossie Davis, and Ruby Dee. In the 1980s he performed and recorded with the Philly Joe Jones Quartet and Jones's Dameronia and with Abdullah Ibrahim's Ekaya in the United States,

Europe, and Africa; toured Europe with the Savoy Seven Plus 1: A Salute to Benny Goodman. With his own quartet, he performed in Rome, at the Bologna Jazz Festival, Jazz in Sardinia Festival, and the La Spezia Festival. He was the musical director of the Syncopation nightclub. He performed in the movie *The Man with Perfect Timing* with Abdullah Ibrahim. In 1984 he was named a "BMI Jazz Pioneer."

In the 1990s he was musical librarian for Spike Lee's *Mo Better Blues;* performed at the Jamaica Jazz Festival with Dizzy Reece and returned to perform with Roy Burrowes; and was in the Apollo Hall of Fame Band accompanying Ray Charles, Joe Williams, Nancy Wilson, and others. He toured Holland saluting the music of Kenny Dorham; and was the guest artist at the 12th Annual N.C. Jazz Festival at Duke Univ. He was featured soloist of the Barry Harris Jazz Ensemble and performs in clubs with the Barry Harris/Charles Davis Quartet. He recorded and toured Europe and Japan with the Clifford Jordan Big Band. He is the tenor saxophonist and a major contributor of musical arrangements with Larry Ridley's Jazz Legacy Ensemble, which appeared at the Senegal Jazz Festival, and performs concerts and conducts clinics, seminars, and master classes. This ensemble also appears in an ongoing concert series at the Schomberg Center for Research in Black Culture in Harlem. He was a featured artist at the Amman, Jordan Jazz Festival, arranged by the American Embassy; also the featured artist in clubs and concerts in Paris, Toulouse, and Hamburg. He appeared at the Williamstown Theatre Festival in an original production of Eduardo Machado's *Stevie Wants to Play the Blues,* directed by Jim Simpson. He performs in the Three Baritone Saxophone Band with Ronnie Cuber and Gary Smulyan. His group appeared in 1998 at the New Orleans Jazz Festival, toured Italy, appeared at the JVC Jazz Image Festival at Villa Celimontana in Rome and in Oslo. Charles was also a featured soloist at the 1998 Chicago Jazz Festival. In June 1999, he performed with Aaron Bell and the Duke Ellington Tribute Orch. at the Jackie Robinson "Afternoon in Jazz Festival" in Norwalk, Conn. He teaches private students through the New School, is a teacher at the Lucy Moses School, and for over 20 years has been an instructor at the Jazzmobile Workshops. He has made four albums as a leader and is featured on over 50 as a sideperson.

DISC.: *Dedicated to Tadd* (1980); *Super 80* (1982); *Reflections* (1990). **DORHAM:** *Elvin Jones: Illuminations* (1966).—**LP**

Davis, Eddie "Lockjaw,"
jazz tenor saxophonist; b. N.Y., March 2, 1922; d. Culver City, Calif., Nov. 3, 1986. He was a unique tenor-sax stylist, who employed rasps and squeals more characteristic of R&B players and filtered them through his own highly original harmonic conception. He taught himself to play the tenor saxophone and began his career as a musician in Harlem; later worked with Cootie Williams (first recording in 1944), Andy Kirk, Lucky Millinder, Louis Armstrong; and subsequently led his own combos. Popular in Harlem, he worked regularly in clubs there throughout the 1940s and 1950s. His nickname came from a late 1940s session where all the tunes were named for illnesses. His 1950s recordings often included an organ-

ist (Bill Doggett, Doc Bagby, or, most frequently, Shirley Scott). In 1952 he joined the Count Basie Orch. and for the next 20 years played intermittently with the band, including a London TV broadcast in the mid-1960s. His longest unbroken period with Basie was from 1966–73. He co-led a quintet with saxophonist Johnny Griffin (1960–62) and then retired from music for a period in 1963 and worked as a booking agent. During the 1970s he was often featured in a group with trumpeter Harry Edison. He frequently recorded in Europe, where he had always enjoyed popularity.

DISC.: *Jaws N' Stitt at Birdland* (1954); *Uptown* (1955); *Count Basie Presents Eddie Davis* (1957); *Eddie Davis Trio* (1958); *Eddie Lockjaw Davis Cookbook, Vols. 1–3* (1958); *Jaws* (1958); *Smokin'* (1958); *Jaws in Orbit* (1959); *Very Saxy* (1959); *Battle Stations* (1960); *Eddie Lockjaw Davis with Shirley Scott* (1960); *Griff and Lock* (1960; with Griffin); *Tough Tenors* (1960); *Trane Whistle* (1960); *At Minton's Playhouse* (1961); *Blues up and Down* (1961); *First Set* (1961); *Live at Minton's* (1961); *Live! The Breakfast Show* (1961); *Live! The Late Show* (1961); *Live! The Midnight Show* (1961); *Lookin' at Monk* (1961); *Tenor Scene* (1961); *Jawbreakers* (1962); *Fox and the Hounds* (1966); *Lock the Fox* (1966); *Tough Tenors Again 'n Again* (1970); *Leapin' on Lennox* (1976); *Montreux '77* (1977); *Jaw's Blues* (1981); *Live at the Widder* (1982); *Sonny, Sweets and Jaws* (1982); *Hey Lock!* (1983).—**LP**

Davis, Ivan,
American pianist and teacher; b. Electra, Tex., Feb. 4, 1932. He studied piano with Silvio Scionti at North Tex. State Univ. in Denton and later at the Accademia di Santa Cecilia in Rome with Carlo Zecchi. He also took private lessons with Horowitz, beginning in 1961. He obtained first prizes at the Busoni Competition in Bolzano (1958), the Casella Competition at Naples (1958), and the Franz Liszt Competition in N.Y. (1960). On Oct. 21, 1959, he made his N.Y. recital debut at Town Hall, and subsequently toured throughout the U.S. After making his London debut in 1966, he played on the Continent. In addition to serving on the faculty of the Univ. of Miami in Coral Gables (from 1966), he was a visiting prof. at the Ind. Univ. School of Music in Bloomington (1971–72); he also gave master classes in various locales throughout the U.S. His repertoire ranges from Scarlatti to Gershwin, showing special affinity for the works of Schumann, Chopin, Liszt, and Tchaikovsky.—**NS/LK/DM**

Davis, Miles (actually, Dewey III),
innovative American jazz trumpeter, bandleader, and composer; b. Alton, Ill., May 25, 1926; d. Santa Monica, Calif., Sept. 28, 1991. Though Davis maintained the same restrained, intimate approach to his trumpet playing throughout his career, the contexts in which he played could hardly have been more varied, and he triggered a series of stylistic developments in jazz. A central figure in the bebop scene of the 1940s, he pioneered the cool style of the 1950s, undertook orchestral experiments with arranger Gil Evans at the end of that decade, led the premier small jazz group of the 1960s, and initiated the jazz-and-rock hybrid of fusion music in the late 1960s and early 1970s. His appeal transcended jazz to the extent that he placed 28 albums in the pop charts between 1961 and 1992, his most

successful recording, *Bitches Brew*, being one of his most challenging.

As the son of Dr. Miles Dewey Davis Jr., a dental surgeon, and Cleota Mae Henry Davis, a former music teacher, Davis had a comfortable upbringing in East St. Louis, where the family moved when he was an infant. He began taking trumpet lessons at 12, his principal teacher being Elwood Buchanon, and played in his high school band. By 1941 he was playing professionally with Eddie Randall's group in St. Louis. In 1944 he sat in with Billy Eckstine's band for two weeks, encountering bebop masters Dizzy Gillespie and Charlie Parker, and after graduating from high school he moved to N.Y. to attend the Juilliard School of Music but spent much of his time playing in clubs with Parker. He had left behind Irene Davis, his common-law wife, who later joined him in N.Y.; they had three children.

Davis left Juilliard in 1945 and joined Benny Carter's band. He made his first recordings that year as a sideman with Charlie Parker. He played with Billy Eckstine's band in 1946–47 and with Parker's group in 1947–48. He made his first recordings under his own name in 1947 with a quintet that included Parker. In 1948 he organized a nine-piece group featuring instruments unusual to jazz, such as French horn and tuba, and using unusual arrangements by Gil Evans and others. The group played very few shows, but it did a series of recordings for Capitol Records later compiled by the label into the 1957 album *Birth of the Cool*, music that fostered the post-bebop style of more relaxed cool jazz.

Davis's progress was interrupted in the late 1940s by his addiction to heroin, which made him only an intermittent presence in jazz for the first half of the 1950s, though he recorded frequently for the independent Prestige Records label. By 1954 he had succeeded in giving up heroin, and he made a strong comeback with an appearance at the Newport Jazz Festival in 1955 that convinced the major label Columbia Records to sign him.

Davis organized a permanent group featuring saxophonist John Coltrane and made a series of recordings in the late 1950s that propelled jazz into new directions. With the group, these included the modal experiment *Kind of Blue* (1959), a critically acclaimed album that became a perennial seller. He also teamed again with Gil Evans for a series of recordings with a larger studio group, including *Miles Ahead* (1958), *Porgy and Bess* (1959), and *Sketches of Spain* (1960). The attention given these recordings may be illustrated by the recognition given them by NARAS. *Miles Ahead* was enrolled in the Grammy Hall of Fame, and *Sketches of Spain* won Davis and Evans a Grammy for Best Jazz Composition, while Davis also earned a nomination for Best Jazz Performance, Large Group, for the album. (He also earned a nomination for Best Jazz Performance, Small Group, for the album *Jazz Track*, which contained music from his score for the film *L'Ascenseur pour l'Echafaud [Elevator to the Gallows]*.) Davis and Evans also earned Grammy nominations in the large group jazz performance category in 1962 for *M.D. at Carnegie Hall* and in 1964 for *Quiet Nights*, and in 1996 the box set compilation *The*

Complete Columbia Studio Recordings of all the Davis/Evans collaborations won the Grammy for Best Historical Album.

On Dec. 21, 1960, Davis married Frances Taylor, a dancer; they later divorced. Coltrane left the group, but Davis continued to perform and record extensively with changing personnel in his band. In 1961, *M. D. in Person (Friday & Saturday Nights at the Blackhawk, San Francisco)*, a double live album, became his first to reach the pop charts. He earned another Grammy nomination for Best Jazz Performance, Large Group, for *Seven Steps to Heaven* in 1963. That year he assembled most of the members of what is generally considered his greatest group: drummer Tony Williams, bassist Ron Carter, and pianist Herbie Hancock, joined the following year by saxophonist Wayne Shorter. With this group he largely abandoned playing standards in favor of originals, usually written by members of the group. He earned a Grammy nomination for Best Jazz Performance, Small Group, for *M. D. in Europe* in 1964.

The Davis quintet of the mid-1960s made a series of highly regarded albums including *E. S. P.* (1965), *Miles Smiles* (1967; Grammy nomination for Best Jazz Performance, Small Group), *Sorcerer* (1967), *Nefertitti* (1968), *Miles in the Sky* (1968; Grammy nomination for Best Jazz Performance, Small Group), and *Filles de Kilimanjaro* (1969). Appreciated by jazz fans, these albums did not reach the pop charts. Davis had begun to experiment with electrified instruments by 1968, and in 1969 *In a Silent Way* employed electric keyboards played by Hancock, Chick Corea, and Joe Zawinul, as well as electric guitar by John McLaughlin; it earned a small group jazz performance Grammy nomination and returned Davis to the pop charts for the first time in more than four years. With the demise of the quintet (all of whose members became bandleaders themselves), he moved toward a closer association between jazz and rock music.

The result was *Bitches Brew* (March 1970), a double album of jazz-rock that went gold, earned a Grammy nomination for Best Instrumental Arrangement, and won Davis his second Grammy for Large Group Jazz Performance. It also alienated traditional jazz fans. For the next five years Davis recorded extensively in his new style, creating such chart albums as *M.D. at Fillmore East* (1970; Grammy nomination), *A Tribute to Jack Johnson* (1971; soundtrack to the film *Jack Johnson*), *Live-Evil* (1971), *On the Corner* (1972), *In Concert* (1973), *Big Fun* (1974), and *Get Up with It* (1974), most of them double albums containing lengthy compositions, themselves edited down from even longer performances to fit onto LPs. In the meantime, several of his former sidemen formed bands in the new fusion style: Corea's Return to Forever, Zawinul and Shorter's Weather Report, and McLaughlin's Mahavishnu Orch.

Davis eventually was overcome by injury and illness. He broke both ankles in a car accident in October 1972, and in late 1975 he underwent surgery for hip replacement. He was out of action for the next several years. In November 1981 he married actress Cicely Tyson; they divorced in 1989. He finally returned to music in 1981, by which time opinion about his work had calmed, but also solidified. Traditional jazz fans disdained him, but he continued to find favor with more general music fans.

In the last decade of his life, Davis performed regularly on the music festival circuit and recorded a series of albums that usually sold well enough to reach the pop charts for a few weeks and earned Grammy nominations, especially in the jazz fusion category that had been created in his absence. They included: *The Man with the Horn* (1981), *We Want Miles* (1982; Grammy winner for Best Jazz Instrumental Performance by a Soloist), *Star People* (1983), *Decoy* (1984), *You're Under Arrest* (1985), *Tutu* (1986; his first album under a new contract with Warner Bros. Records; Grammy winner for Best Jazz Instrumental Performance), *Music from Siesta* (1988; a soundtrack), *Amandla* (1989), *Aura* (recorded in 1984, released by Columbia in 1989; Grammy winner for Best Jazz Instrumental Performance by a Soloist [on a Jazz Recording]), and *The Hot Spot* (1990; soundtrack performed with John Lee Hooker and others).

During his final concert appearance, at the Montreux Jazz Festival in Switzerland on July 8, 1991, Davis surprisingly agreed to re-create recordings with Gil Evans of *Sketches of Spain* and *Porgy and Bess* in combination with a band conducted by Quincy Jones. Less than three months later, he died of pneumonia, respiratory failure, and a stroke at 65. In 1992, Warner Bros. released *Doo-Bop*, his final studio album, on which he performed with rapper Easy Mo Bee. It won him his sixth Grammy, for Best Rhythm & Blues Instrumental Performance. He won his seventh Grammy along with Quincy Jones for Best Large Jazz Ensemble Performance for *Miles & Quincy Live at Montreux*.

WRITINGS: With Q. Troupe, M.: *The Autobiography* (N.Y., 1989).

DISC.: *Birth of the Cool* (1957); *Miles Ahead* (1957); *Jazz Track* (1958); *Kind of Blue* (1959); *Porgy and Bess* (1959); *Sketches of Spain* (1960); *Miles Davis in Person* (1961); *Miles Davis at Carnegie Hall* (1962); *Seven Steps to Heaven* (1963); *Miles Davis in Europe* (1964); *Quiet Nights* (1964); *E. S. P.* (1965); *Miles Smiles* (1967); *Sorcerer* (1967); *Nefertiti* (1968); *Miles in the Sky* (1968); *Filles de Kilimanjaro* (1969); *In a Silent Way* (1969); *Bitches Brew* (1970); *Miles Davis at Fillmore East* (1970); *A Tribute to Jack Johnson* (1971); *Live-Evil* (1971); *On the Corner* (1972); *In Concert* (1973); *Big Fun* (1974); *Get Up with It* (1974); *The Man with the Horn* (1981); *We Want Miles* (1982); *Star People* (1983); *Decoy* (1984); *You're Under Arrest* (1985); *Tutu* (1986); *Music from Siesta* (1988); *Amandla* (1989); *Aura* (recorded in 1984; released in 1989); *The Hot Spot* (1990); *Miles & Quincy Live at Montreux* (1991); *Doo-Bop* (1992); *The Complete Columbia Studio Recordings* (with Gil Evans; 1996).

BIBL.: M. James, *M. D.* (London, 1961); B. Cole, *M. D.: A Musical Biography* (N.Y., 1974; repr., as *M. D.: The Early Years*, N.Y., 1994); I. Carr, *M. D.: A Critical Biography* (London, 1982; U.S. ed., 1982, as *M. D.: A Biography*); E. Nisenson, *'Round About Midnight: A Portrait of M. D.* (N.Y., 1982); J. Chambers, *Milestones 1: The Music and Times of M. D. to 1960* (Toronto, 1983); Chambers, *Milestones 2: The Music and Times of M. D. Since 1960* (Toronto, 1985); B. McRae, *M. D.* (London, 1988); D. Long, *M. D. for Beginners* (N.Y., 1992); G. Carner, ed., *The M. D. Companion: Four Decades of Commentary* (N.Y., 1996); B. Kirchner, ed., *A M. D. Reader* (Washington, D.C., 1997).—WR

Davis, Reverend Gary D., influential American blues, folk, and gospel singer, songwriter, and guitarist; b. Laurens County, S.C., April 30, 1896; d. Hammonton, N.J., May 5, 1972. Davis's original mixture of blues, gospel, and folk made him a major influence on a generation of folk and rock performers.

The son of John and Evelina Davis, Davis suffered from ulcerated eyes and was partially blind by the age of two, losing his sight completely by his twenties. He taught himself to play guitar, banjo, and harmonica as a child and began performing before he reached his teens. He attended the Cedar Springs School for Blind People in Spartanburg, S.C., in the mid-1910s.

Davis traveled extensively through the upper South during the 1920s and 1930s, although he was based in Durham, N.C. He was ordained a Baptist minister in Washington, D.C., in 1933. He made his first recordings in 1935. He had been married during the 1920s; in 1937 he married his second wife, Annie Bell Wright. Around 1940 he moved to N.Y., where he gradually became known in folk music circles. He performed at the first Newport Folk Festival in 1959 and at several subsequent editions of the festival, as well as at other folk festivals during the 1960s.

Among Davis's many recordings, the most influential was the 1960 Prestige Records album *Pure Religion!*, which featured a series of songs written by or associated with him that were taken up by other artists. "Samson and Delilah" was recorded by Peter, Paul and Mary on their self-titled debut album in 1962 under the title "If I Had My Way" and became a regular part of the Grateful Dead's repertoire. "Let Us Get Together Right Down Here" was one of many Davis songs recorded by Hot Tuna, whose guitarist, former Jefferson Airplane member Jorma Kaukonen, took lessons from Davis. Another was "Death Don't Have No Mercy," which also was played extensively by the Dead. Davis's songs were performed by such other folk artists as Bob Dylan, Donovan, Taj Mahal, Dave Van Ronk, David Bromberg, and Ry Cooder, some of whom studied with Davis. Other notable songs he wrote or popularized include "Candyman," "Cocaine Blues," "Delia," "I Am the Light of This World," "Twelve Gates to the City," and "You've Got to Move."

WRITINGS: *The Holy Blues* (1970); S. Grossman, ed., *Rev. Gary Davis/Blues Guitar* (1974).—WR

Davis, Sammy, Jr., dynamic American singer, actor, and dancer; b. N.Y., Dec. 8, 1925; d. Beverly Hills, Calif., May 16, 1990. A nightclub entertainer with a background in vaudeville who could sing, dance, act, play several instruments, and do impressions, Davis found success in recordings, film, television, and personal appearances during a career that lasted virtually his entire life. As an African-American, he broke down racial restrictions while simultaneously challenging assumptions about what a black performer should be. As such he was both a throwback to an earlier time in entertainment and a precursor of a less race-conscious future.

Davis's parents, Sammy Davis Sr. and Elvera Sanchez Davis, were members of *Holiday in Dixieland*, a vaudeville troupe led by Will Mastin. Davis began appearing onstage with the troupe when scarcely out of infancy. His parents separated when he was two, and he remained with his father in the act, which diminished during the Depression to a trio of himself, his father, and Mastin. He made his film debut in the short *Rufus for President* in September 1933.

Davis was drafted in 1943 and served in the army until 1945, when he rejoined the Will Mastin Trio. After World War II, the group, which Davis dominated with his singing, dancing, and impressions, broke into the upper echelon of nightclubs and hotels. Davis was signed as a solo act to Capitol Records and made his first recordings for the label in 1949. In 1954 he joined Decca Records, first reaching the charts in August with "Hey There" (music and lyrics by Richard Adler and Jerry Ross). He was appearing with the Mastin Trio at the New Frontier Hotel in Las Vegas when, on Nov. 19, 1954, he was severely injured in an automobile accident, losing his left eye. Nevertheless, he was back performing in January 1955.

Davis's career took off in 1955. His album *Starring Sammy Davis Jr.* topped the charts in June, he had a Top Ten single in "Something's Gotta Give" (music and lyrics by Johnny Mercer), followed by Top 40 hits with "Love Me or Leave Me" (music by Walter Donaldson, lyrics by Gus Kahn) and "That Old Black Magic" (music by Harold Arlen, lyrics by Johnny Mercer), and the LP *Just for Lovers* reached the Top Ten in the fall. At the end of the year he made his adult acting debut playing Fletcher Henderson in the film biography *The Benny Goodman Story.* He then made his Broadway debut starring in the musical *Mr. Wonderful* (N.Y., March 22, 1956), which ran 383 performances.

In 1957 the Will Mastin Trio broke up, leaving Davis to work as a solo performer. On Jan. 10, 1958, he married Loray White, a singer; they divorced on April 23, 1959. He made his television acting debut on an episode of *G. E. Theatre* on Oct. 5, 1958, and the following month appeared in the film *Anna Lucasta.* In July 1959 he portrayed Sportin' Life and sang "It Ain't Necessarily So" (music by George Gershwin, lyrics by Ira Gershwin) in a film version of *Porgy and Bess.* A friend of Frank Sinatra's and member of Sinatra's "Rat Pack" of fellow entertainers, he appeared in a series of films with them, beginning in August 1960 with *Ocean's Eleven* and continuing with *Sergeants Three* (1962) and *Robin and the 7 Hoods* (1964).

On Nov. 13, 1960, Davis married Swedish actress Mai Britt; they had one daughter and adopted two sons. They divorced on Dec. 19, 1968. Having signed to Frank Sinatra's Reprise Records label, Davis returned to the Top 40 in the fall of 1962 with "What Kind of Fool Am I?" (music and lyrics by Leslie Bricusse and Anthony Newley), from the musical *Stop the World—I Want to Get Off*, and his album *What Kind of Fool Am I and Other Show- Stoppers* spent five months in the charts.

By now Davis was appearing regularly in motion pictures, only some of which featured his singing. One was the West German production *Die Dreigroschenoper*, released in the U.S. in March 1963 under its English title *The Threepenny Opera*, in which he played the Street Singer and sang "Mack the Knife" (music by Kurt Weill, lyrics by Bertolt Brecht). He starred in his first television special, *S. D. and the Wonderful World of Children*, on Nov. 25, 1963, and reached the Top 40 at the end of the year with "The Shelter of Your Arms" (music and lyrics by Jerry Samuels).

Davis returned to Broadway with the musical *Golden Boy* (N.Y., Oct. 20, 1964), which ran 569 performances. In 1965 he appeared in another TV special and made an album, *Our Shining Hour*, with Count Basie. He had his own television series, *The S.D. Jr. Show*, from January to April 1966, and in June starred in the film drama *A Man Called Adam*, playing a jazz musician. He reached the Top 40 with the spoken-word recording "Don't Blame the Children" (music by H. B. Barnum, lyrics by Ivan Reeve) in 1967. In 1968 he performed *Golden Boy* in London and appeared in the comic spy film *Salt and Pepper* with fellow Rat Pack member Peter Lawford; they did a sequel, *One More Time*, in 1970. At the end of 1968 he scored his biggest hit single since 1955 with "I've Gotta Be Me" (music and lyrics by Walter Marks), which topped the easy-listening charts. He made a musical appearance in the film version of the musical *Sweet Charity*, released in January 1969.

On May 11, 1970, Davis wed dancer Altovise Gore, to whom he remained married for the rest of his life; they later adopted a son. Davis was hospitalized with cirrhosis of the liver in 1971, but he recovered. Signing to MGM Records, he released "The Candy Man" (music and lyrics by Leslie Bricusse and Anthony Newley) in December 1971; it hit #1 in June 1972 and sold a million copies. The LP *S. D. Jr. Now*, on which it appeared, spent six months in the charts. He appeared in the concert film *Save the Children*, released in September 1973, and the same month began making regular appearances on the TV variety series *NBC Follies*, which ran through December. In April 1974 he was back on the N.Y. stage in his own revue, *Sammy on Broadway.* He hosted a syndicated TV talk show, *Sammy and Company*, during the 1975–76 and 1976–77 seasons. In August 1978 he appeared at Lincoln Center in N.Y. in a production of *Stop the World—I Want to Get Off* that was filmed and released as *Sammy Stops the World* in December.

Davis was less active in the 1980s, suffering a recurrence of his liver problems in 1983 and having to undergo hip replacement surgery in 1985. But he was working more frequently by the late 1980s, appearing in the films *Moon Over Parador* (1988) and *Tap* (1989), and touring internationally with Frank Sinatra and Liza Minnelli. He contracted throat cancer in 1989 and died of it in 1990 at age 64.

WRITINGS: With J. and B. Boyar, *Yes I Can* (N.Y., 1965); *Hollywood in a Suitcase* (N.Y., 1980); *Why Me?* (N.Y., 1989).

DISC.: *Starring Sammy Davis Jr.* (1955); *Just for Lovers* (1955); *Mr. Wonderful* (1956); *Porgy and Bess* (1959); *What Kind of Fool Am I and Other Show Stoppers* (1962); *Threepenny Opera* (1964); *Golden Boy* (1964); *Our Shining Hour* (with Count Basie; 1965); *Sammy Davis Jr. Now* (1972); *Stop the World I Want to Get Off* (1978).

BIBL.: T. Davis with D. Barclay, *S. D. Jr., My Father* (L.A., 1996).—WR

Davis, Sir Andrew (Frank), esteemed English conductor; b. Ashridge, Hertfordshire, Feb. 2, 1944. He studied piano at the Royal Academy of Music in London, and after taking organ lessons with Peter Hurford and Piet Kee, was an organ scholar at King's Coll., Cambridge (1963–67). He then received instruction in conducting from Franco Ferrara at the Accademia di Santa Cecilia in Rome. Following a successful guest conducting engagement with the BBC Sym. Orch. in London in 1970, he served as asst. conductor of the BBC Scottish Sym. Orch. in Glasgow until 1973, making his debut as an opera conductor that same year at the Glyndebourne Festival. He was assoc. conductor of the New Philharmonia Orch. in London (1973–75) and principal guest conductor of the Royal Liverpool Phil. (1974–76). In 1974 he made his North American debut as a guest conductor with the Detroit Sym. Orch. He then was music director of the Toronto Sym. (1975–88), which, under his guidance, acquired a fine international reputation via major tours of North America, Europe, the People's Republic of China, and Japan. In 1982 he inaugurated the orch.'s new home, the Roy Thomson Hall in Toronto, in a gala concert. After completing his tenure, he served as the orch.'s conductor laureate from 1988 to 1990. In 1988 he was named chief conductor of the BBC Sym. Orch. in London and music director of the Glyndebourne Festival. He left these positions in 2000 to become music director of the Lyric Opera of Chicago. However, he retained his association with the BBC Sym. Orch. as its first conductor laureate from 2000. His third marriage was to **Gianna Rolandi**. In 1992 he was made a Commander of the Order of the British Empire. He was knighted in 1999. His vast repertoire encompasses works from virtually every era, all of which display his wide sympathies, command of technique, and musical integrity.—**NS/LK/DM**

Davis, Sir Colin (Rex), eminent English conductor; b. Weybridge, Sept. 25, 1927. He studied clarinet at the Royal Coll. of Music in London, and played in the band of the Household Cavalry while serving in the army. He began his conducting career with the Kalmar Chamber Orch. and the Chelsea Opera Group; in 1958 he conducted a performance of *Die Entführung aus dem Serail* in London; from 1961 to 1965 he served as music director of Sadler's Wells. He made his U.S. debut as a guest conductor with the Minneapolis Sym. Orch. on Dec. 30, 1960; subsequently had engagements with the N.Y. Phil., the Philadelphia Orch., and the Los Angeles Phil. From 1972 to 1983 he served as principal guest conductor of the Boston Sym. Orch. On Jan. 20, 1967, he made his Metropolitan Opera debut in N.Y. conducting *Peter Grimes*. From 1967 to 1971 he was chief conductor of the BBC Sym. Orch. in London. In 1965 he conducted at the Royal Opera at Covent Garden; he succeeded Solti as its music director in 1971. Among his notable achievements was a production at Covent Garden of the *Ring* cycle between 1974 and 1976; in 1977 he became the first British conductor to appear at the Bayreuth Festival, conducting *Tannhäuser*. He conducted the Royal Opera during its tours in South Korea and Japan in 1979, and in the U.S. in 1984. In 1983 he was appointed chief conductor of the Bavarian Radio Sym.

Orch. in Munich, which he led on a tour of North America in 1986. In 1986 he stepped down as music director at Covent Garden to devote himself fully to his duties in Munich and to pursue far-flung engagements as a guest conductor with major orchs. and opera houses of the world. In 1988 he was named to an international chair at the Royal Academy of Music. In 1993 he stepped down from his Munich position. In 1995 he became principal conductor of the London Sym. Orch. Davis is an authoritative interpreter of such masters as Mozart, Berlioz, Sibelius, and Stravinsky. He has also championed the cause of his British contemporaries, most notably Sir Michael Tippett. He was made a Commander of the Order of the British Empire in 1965, and was knighted in 1980. From 1949 to 1964 he was married to **April Cantelo**.

BIBL.: A. Blyth, *C. D.* (London, 1972).—**NS/LK/DM**

Davis, Steve (actually, **Stephen**; aka **Syeed/Saeed, Luquman Abdul**), bassist; b. Philadelphia, Pa., 1929; d. there, Aug. 21, 1987. He was married to the singer Khadijah (making him brother-in-law to Aisha Tyner) and they were close friends of Naima before she met Coltrane. Davis was playing professionally around Philadelphia as early as 1947 with Joe Sewell, Chas. Coker, and Calvin Todd. He was arrested for heroin possession the same weekend as Jimmy Heath in January 1955. In late April 1960 he joined Coltrane's quartet, but left by the end of the year (or perhaps early 1961) and returned to Philadelphia, where he remained in obscurity. He spent perhaps ten years in Rochester, N.Y. during the 1970s and 1980s, often using a Fender bass with a group of younger players led by Joe Locke; sometimes Khadijah would sit in. In the mid-1980s, Locke and some others left for N.Y., and Davis seems to have returned to Philadelphia, where he died after a long struggle with emphysema. —**LP**

Davison, A(rchibald) T(hompson), eminent American music educator; b. Boston, Oct. 11, 1883; d. Brant Rock, Mass., Feb. 6, 1961. He studied at Harvard Univ. (B.A., 1906; M.A., 1907; Ph.D., 1908, with the diss. *The Harmonic Contributions of Claude Debussy*); then took lessons in organ with Widor in Paris (1908–09). Returning to America, he was organist and choirmaster at Harvard Univ. (1910–40); conducted the Harvard Glee Club (1912–33) and the Radcliffe Choral Soc. (1913–28); he began teaching at Harvard in 1917 as asst. prof.; subsequently he was assoc. prof. (1920–29), prof. of choral music (1929–40), and the James Edward Ditson Prof. of Music (1940–54). He held numerous honorary degrees, including those of D.Mus. at Williams Coll. and the Univ. of Oxford; Fellow of the Royal Coll. of Music, London; Litt.D. from Washington Univ. (1953); and L.H.D. from Temple Univ. (1955). He wrote 2 comic operas, the musical comedy *The Girl and the Chauffeur* (Boston, April 16, 1906), the *Tragic Overture*, and the symphonic poem *Hero and Leander*. His greatest achievement, however, was as an educator and popularizer of musical subjects: his lectures on music appreciation were broadcast and enjoyed considerable success among radio listeners. He was assoc. ed., with T. Surette, of a multi-vol. collection of vocal and instrumental pieces, the Concord Series of Educational Music, for which he made numerous arrangements.

WRITINGS (all publ. in Cambridge, Mass., unless otherwise given): *Protestant Church Music in America* (Boston, 1920; 2nd ed., enl., 1933); *Music Education in America* (N.Y., 1926); *Choral Conducting* (1940); *The Technique of Choral Composition* (1946); ed. with W. Apel, *Historical Anthology of Music* (vol. I, 1946; 2nd ed., rev., 1950; vol. II, 1950); *Bach and Handel: The Consummation of the Baroque in Music* (1951); *Church Music: Illusion and Reality* (1952); *Words and Music: A Lecture Delivered to the Whittal Pavilion of the Library of Congress* (Washington, D.C., 1954).

BIBL.: *Essays on Music in Honor of A. T. D. by his Associates* (Cambridge, Mass., 1957); D. Tovey, *A. T. D.: Harvard Musician and Scholar* (diss., Univ. of Mich., 1979).—NS/LK/DM

Davison, J(ames) W(illiam),

renowned English music critic; b. London, Oct. 5, 1813; d. Margate, March 24, 1885. He was founder and ed. of the *Musical Examiner* (1842–44) and ed. of the *Musical World* (1844–85), as well as a contributor to the *Saturday Review, Pall Mall Gazette,* and *Graphic.* From 1846 to 1878 he was the influential critic of the *Times.* In 1859 he married his pupil Arabella Goddard. He wrote the analytical program books for the Popular Concerts and the Halle recitals. He also composed a few songs, several piano pieces, and a dramatic overture (for Piano Duet) to *Fortunatus,* a fairy tale. His memoirs were publ. by H. Davison as *From Mendelssohn to Wagner* (1912).

BIBL.: C. Reid, *The Music Monster: A Biography of J. W. D., Music Critic of the Times of London, 1846–78, with Excerpts from His Critical Writings* (London, 1984).—NS/LK/DM

Davison, Wild Bill (actually, William Edward),

jazz cornetist, band leader; b. Defiance, Ohio, Jan. 5, 1906; d. Santa Barbara, Calif., Nov. 14, 1989. His parents died when he was very young; he was raised by his grandparents, the town librarians. He began on mandolin, banjo, and guitar, and then switched to mellophone and cornet. He worked in local groups the Ohio Lucky Seven and James Jackson's Band, then with Roland Potter's players in Cincinnati. He joined the Chubb-Steinberg Orch., which recorded in April 1924. This band was subsequently jointly led by Art Hicks and Paul Omer, and as the Omer-Hicks Orch. it played in N.Y. in early 1926. Wild Bill left the band, returned to his home town, then joined Seattle Harmony Kings, and traveled to Chicago with them. He worked mostly in and around Chicago during the five- year period 1927–32, including a long spell with Benny Meroff, also worked with Charles Dornberger and Ray Miller, etc. He came under the influence of the young generation of Chicago musicians, and was particularly impressed by the playing of Louis Armstrong. In late 1931, he began organizing his own big band. After intensive rehearsals the band worked briefly at Guyon's. Davison's Chicago career was cut short in 1932 by a car accident that killed his fellow bandmember, Frank Teschemacher (Some have blamed Davison for Teschemacher's death). He moved to Milwaukee and worked there for most of the

time between 1933 and 1941, leading his own small groups at various clubs including East Side Spa and Schmitz's, and also worked for other leaders, including Charles "Murph" Podolsky. During these eight years Wild Bill occasionally doubled on valve trombone. He overcame a lip injury in 1939 caused when a fan flung a beer mug at his face. He moved to N.Y. in the spring of 1941, and led his own band at several small clubs. Dancer Katherine Dunham launched a revue during 1943 which included a recreation of the Original Jazz Band; Davison was enlisted for the group. This resulted in a 1944 recording session and paved the way for a switch from a Chicago-style approach to a New Orleans-traditional approach. He served in the army from 1943–mid-1945, and then worked with Art Hodes and led his own band in St. Louis, before becoming a regular at Eddie Condon's Club from December 1945 in N.Y. He toured Britain with Eddie Condon in February 1957. Davison moved to the West Coast in 1960, where he played at the 400 Club, Los Angeles. Through the 1960s, he alternated between touring with his own bands and working with other Dixieland-revival groups. He was very popular in Europe, and spent the early 1970s living in Denmark. He was back to working at Condon's club from 1975–85, while continuing to tour with various ensembles. Davison continued to play and record through the end of his life.

DISC.: *This Is Jazz, Vol. 1* (1947); *S' Wonderful* (1962); *That's a Plenty* (1943); *Sweet and Hot* (1947); *Individualism Of...* (1951); *Ringside at Condon's* (1951); *Showcase* (1951); *Live! Miami Beach* (1955; 1956); *Blowin' Wild* (1965); *Nick's* (1974); *Plays Hoagy Carmichael* (1981); *Wild Bill Davidson and Eddie Miller* (1982); *All-Stars* (1986).

BIBL.: Hal Willard, *The Wildest One: The Life of Wild Bill Davison* (Monkton, Md., 1996).—JC/LP

Davy, Gloria,

black American soprano; b. N.Y., March 29, 1931. She was a student of Belle Julie Soudent at the Juilliard School of Music in N.Y. (1948–53) and of Victor de Sabata in Milan. In 1953 she sang in the touring production of *Porgy and Bess.* On April 2, 1954, she appeared as the Countess in the U.S. premiere of *Capriccio* in N.Y. She made her European operatic debut in Nice as Aida in 1957, a role she repeated for her Metropolitan Opera debut in N.Y. on Feb. 12, 1958. She remained on the Metropolitan roster until 1961, appearing as Pamina, Nedda, and Leonora in *Il Trovatore.* Aida was her debut role at the Vienna State Opera in 1959 and at London's Covent Garden in 1960. From 1961 she appeared at the Berlin Deutsche Oper, singing such roles as Aida, Fiordiligi, Donna Anna, Cio-Cio-San, Donna Elvira, and Salome. She also pursued guest engagements in other European operatic centers (1963–69). From 1975 to 1985 she made regular concert tours in Europe. In 1983 she made her London recital debut at Wigmore Hall. She served as a prof. at the Ind. Univ. School of Music in Bloomington from 1985 to 1993.—NS/LK/DM

Davy, John,

English song composer and violinist; b. Upton-Helions, near Exeter, Dec. 23, 1763; d. London, Feb. 22, 1824. He studied at Exeter, and then settled in

London, where he played the violin at Covent Garden. He wrote the music to a number of plays: *A Pennyworth of Wit* (London, April 18, 1796), *Alfred the Great*, a "grand historical ballet" (London, June 4, 1798), etc. "The Bay of Biscay, O!," one of the songs from his incidental music to a play, *Spanish Dollars*, was extremely popular. He also composed an opera, *The Caffres, or Buried Alive* (Covent Garden, London, June 2, 1802).—NS/LK/DM

Davy, Richard, English composer; b. c. 1465; d. probably in Exeter, c. 1507. He was a scholar at Magdalen Coll., Oxford (from c. 1483), where he was joint Informator choristarum and organist with William Bernard in 1490–91, and then sole Informator and organist in 1492. From 1497 to 1506 he was a member of the college of vicars-choral at Exeter Cathedral. He was a distinguished composer of sacred music. Among his extant compositions are a St. Matthew Passion for 4 Voices, a Magnificant, and 7 antiphons.—LK/DM

Dawson, Frederick, English pianist and teacher; b. Leeds, July 16, 1868; d. Lymm, Cheshire, Oct. 23, 1940. He studied with his father, and later with Hallé and Dannreuther, and by age 10 he could play the complete Bach "48" from memory. After additional guidance from A. Rubinstein, he pursued a successful career in his homeland and in Europe. He also taught at the Royal Manchester Coll. of Music (from 1893) and at London's Royal Coll. of Music. Dawson's repertory was extensive, embracing the early English virginalists through the French Impressionists of his own era. He publ. the study *The Pianoforte* (Glasgow, 1922).—NS/LK/DM

Dawson, Lynne, English soprano; b. York, June 3, 1953. She received vocal training at the Guildhall School of Music and Drama in London. In 1975 she began to make regular appearances in the Baroque repertoire, with which she became closely identified. In 1986 she made her formal operatic debut with the Kent Opera as Mozart's Countess. After appearing in Florence as Monteverdi's Orfeo in 1987, she sang Pamina with the Scottish Opera in Glasgow and Zdenka in *Arabella* at the Théâtre du Châtelet in Paris in 1988. In 1990 she sang in Monteverdi's *Orfeo* at the Salzburg Festival and as Mozart's Countess in Brussels. She appeared as Cornelia in Graun's *Cesare e Cleopatra* at the Berlin State Opera in 1992. In 1996 she was a soloist in Handel's *Belshazzar* in Göttingen. Her performances of Monteverdi, Purcell, Handel, Gluck, Mozart, and Rossini have won her well-deserved accolades.—NS/LK/DM

Dawson, Ted, Canadian composer and teacher; b. Victoria, British Columbia, April 28, 1951. After training in violin, piano, and composition at the Victoria School of Music, he studied composition with Brian Cherney and Rudolf Komorous at the Univ. of Victoria (B.Mus., 1972); concurrently played viola in the Victoria Sym. Orch. He then pursued graduate studies in electronic music and composition with Gustav Ciamaga at the Univ. of Toronto (1972); he was also a student of Hambraeus and Lanza at McGill Univ. in Montreal

(M.M.A., 1974) and took courses in music and visual arts at the Univ. of Toronto (1984), where he obtained his honors specialist certificate in music (1987). His advanced education was completed at the State Univ. of N.Y. at Buffalo (Ph.D., 1994). He taught at Concordia Univ. (1974–78) and Vanier Coll. (1978–80) in Montreal, and then was asst. prof. at Queen's Univ. in Kingston, Ontario (1987–88) and at Brock Univ. in St. Catharines, Ontario (1988–90). In 1988 he founded the ComPoster Project, which included the creation of a comprehensive audiovisual kit with text to promote Canadian music via education. He served as director of Canadian Music Days at the invitation of the Estonia Music Council in 1993, and oversaw concerts and a film series in four Estonian cities. In 1995 he was awarded the SOCAN Prize. As director of the True North Foundation of Toronto, he oversaw the True North Festival in Taiwan in 1998. Dawson's compositional style has evolved from an experimental abstract modernism with links to multimedia into an amalgam of both modernist and expressive styles that reflects his sense of living in the northern environment of Canada.

WORKS: *Pentad* for String Quartet (1971); *Concerto grosso I* for Quadraphonic Tape or Amplified Viola, Amplified Bassoon, Trombone, Percussion, and Stereo Tape (1973–74) and *II* for 5 Instrumental Soloists and Orch. (1973); *Chameleon* for Amplified Flute (1974–75); *The Land of Nurr* for Electronics (1975); *The Clouds of Magellan* for 3 Slide Projectors, Computerized Dissolver, Synchronization Tape, and Quadraphonic Audiotape (1976–77); *Binaries* for 4 Dancers, 2 Amplified Percussion, and Amplified Piano (1980); *Joint Actions* for Female Dancer and Double Bass (1980–81); *Traces in Glass* for Orch. (1986–92); *Portraits in a Landscape* for Tape (1988); *Topographical Sonata* for Amplified Piano and Tape (1992–96); Sym. No. 1 (1993–96); *Dragon Songs* for Bass-baritone and Orch., after Li Ho and Li Shang-Yin (1995–98).—NS/LK/DM

Dawson, William Levi, black American composer; b. Anniston, Ala., Sept. 26, 1898; d. Tuskegee, Ala., May 2, 1990. He ran away from home at 13 to enter the Tuskegee Inst., and later played trombone on the Redpath Chautauqua Circuit. After graduating from the Tuskegee Inst. in 1921, he studied with Carl Busch in Kansas City and at the American Cons. in Chicago (M.A., 1927). He played first trombone in the Chicago Civic Orch. (1926–30), and then conducted the Tuskegee Choir. Among his works was a *Negro Folk Symphony* (Philadelphia, Nov. 16, 1934; rev. 1952), *Out in the Fields* for Soprano and Orch. (1928), *Scherzo* for Orch. (1930), *A Negro Work Song* for Orch. (1940), Piano Trio (1925), Violin Sonata (1927), many choral part songs, and numerous arrangements of spirituals and black folk songs.

BIBL.: J. Spady, *W. L. D.: A Umum Tribute* (Philadelphia, 1981).—NS/LK/DM

Day, Doris (originally, **Doris Mary Anne von Kappelhoff**), refreshing American singer and actress; b. Cincinnati, Ohio, April 3, 1922. Day's warm and intimate singing style proved well suited to the romantic ballads she recorded with Les Brown's orch. and on her own, including "Sentimental Journey," "Se-

817

cret Love," and "Whatever Will Be, Will Be (Que Sera, Sera)," the most popular of the 59 chart records she scored between 1945 and 1962. Her appealing physical appearance and personality allowed her to become one of the few popular singers of her time to cross over to a career as a movie star, appearing in 39 feature films between 1948 and 1968. Initially she performed in movie musicals, but she achieved her greatest popularity in a series of romantic comedies in the late 1950s and early 1960s.

Day was the daughter of Frederick William von Kappelhoff, a church choral master and piano teacher, and Alma Sophia von Kappelhoff. She sang and danced as a child, and attended Pep's Golden Dance School, among other institutions. By her early teens she was performing in a dance act with partner Jerry Dougherty, with whom she won a local dance contest. The two performed on a vaudeville circuit and made a trip to L.A., where they planned to settle. But on Oct. 13, 1937, she was seriously injured in an automobile accident and forced to convalesce for more than a year. She switched her ambition to singing and took lessons from Grace Raine, who helped her gain exposure singing on local radio. This led to her first professional job singing with Barney Rapp and His New Englanders. Rapp suggested she adopt Day as her stage name, inspired by the 1938 song "Day After Day" (music by Richard Himber, lyrics by Bud Green).

Day quickly moved to the more prominent Bob Crosby Orch., then, in August 1940, to Les Brown and His Band of Renown, with whom she made her recording debut in November. But she quit the band in April 1941 to marry trombonist Al Jorden and retire from music. On Feb. 8, 1942, she bore a son, Terrence, who, as Terry Melcher, grew up to be a record producer, recording artist, and songwriter. In 1943 she divorced Jorden and moved back to Cincinnati, then rejoined Brown. With the end of the musicians' union recording ban in the fall of 1944, Brown was able to return to the recording studio and cut the ballad "Sentimental Journey" (music by Les Brown and Ben Homer, lyrics by Bud Green) with Day on vocals. The Columbia Records single hit #1 in May and sold a million copies. It was actually preceded to the top of the charts by its follow-up, "My Dreams Are Getting Better All the Time" (music by Vic Mizzy, lyrics by Mann Curtis), another Day vocal, in April. Before the end of 1945, two additional Brown-Day collaborations had reached the Top Ten, and Day sang on four more Brown recordings that reached the Top Ten between early 1946 and January 1947.

On March 30, 1946, Day married George Weidler, a saxophonist in Les Brown's orch. When Weidler left the band later in the year, she went with him, and the couple settled in Santa Monica, Calif. They divorced on May 31, 1949. Day had appeared on radio in N.Y., and she found more radio work in L.A., initially on the comedy series *Sweeney and March*, then on *Your Hit Parade* in 1947 and *The Bob Hope Show* in 1948. She also made personal appearances, and it was while performing at the Little Club in N.Y. in March 1947 that she was spotted by a talent scout and brought back to Calif. for

an audition with film director Michael Curtiz at Warner Bros. Curtiz cast her in the film musical *Romance on the High Seas*. Released in June 1948, the movie was sufficiently successful that she was signed to a seven-year contract at Warner Bros.

At the same time her solo recording career took off, as both sides of her duet single with Buddy Clark, "Love Somebody" (music and lyrics by Joan Whitney and Alex Kramer) and "Confess" (music and lyrics by Bennie Benjamin and George David Weiss), became million-sellers, with "Love Somebody" hitting #1 in August. Columbia Records, still her label, followed it with a version of "It's Magic" (music by Jule Styne, lyrics by Sammy Cahn), which she had sung in *Romance on the High Seas*, and it peaked in the Top Ten in September.

For the next six years, Day worked steadily at Warner Bros., appearing in an average of two movie musicals a year, and at Columbia, where she scored an additional ten Top Ten singles through 1954, among them the chart-toppers "A Guy Is a Guy" (music and lyrics by Oscar Brand, adapted from the World War II soldiers' parody "A Gob Is a Slob," in turn based on the 1719 song "I Went to the Alehouse [A Knave Is a Knave]") in May 1952; the million-selling "Secret Love" (music by Sammy Fain, lyrics by Paul Francis Webster), from her film *Calamity Jane*, in February 1954; and "If I Give My Heart to You" (music and lyrics by Jimmie Crane, Al Jacobs, and Jimmy Brewster) in November 1954; and seven Top Ten albums, *You're My Thrill* (1949), *Tea for Two* (1950), *Lullaby of Broadway* (1951), *Moonlight Bay* (1951), the chart-topping *I'll See You in My Dreams* (1952), *By the Light of the Silvery Moon* (1953), and *Calamity Jane* (1954), most of them featuring songs she sang in similarly titled films. She also hosted her own weekly network radio series, *The Doris Day Show*, from 1952–53. On April 3, 1951, she married her manager, Martin Melcher, who adopted her son the following year.

Day completed her commitment to Warner Bros. with *Young at Heart*, released in January 1955, after which she freelanced for different studios and focused more on nonsinging dramatic or comic roles. While technically a musical, her next film, *Love Me or Leave Me*, released in May 1955, was actually a dramatic film biography of Ruth Etting, in which Day performed songs associated with the singer. The soundtrack album topped the charts in July, becoming the most successful LP of the year. Her next film was the thriller *The Man Who Knew Too Much*, directed by Alfred Hitchcock, a box office hit released in May 1956. In it she sang "Whatever Will Be, Will Be (Que Sera, Sera)" (music and lyrics by Jay Livingston and Ray Evans). Her recording of the song reached the Top Ten and sold a million copies.

Day continued to record independent material for Columbia, and her album *Day by Day* reached the Top Ten in February 1957. In August she starred in the film adaptation of the Richard Adler—Jerry Ross Broadway musical *The Pajama Game*, and the soundtrack album was a Top Ten hit. For the most part, however, she tended to appear in nonmusical films in which she frequently would be heard on the soundtrack singing a title song under the credits. She scored her final U.S. Top Ten hit in July 1958 with "Everybody Loves a Lover" (music by Robert Allen, lyrics by Richard Adler). It earned her a Grammy nomination for Best Vocal Performance, Female. Also in 1958, Columbia released *Doris Day's Greatest Hits*, which eventually went gold.

Day's movement away from film musicals and toward nonsinging roles was bolstered by the success of the romantic comedy *Pillow Talk*, released in October 1959, in which she costarred with Rock Hudson. It became one of the biggest box office hits of the year and earned her an Academy Award nomination for Best Actress. For the next five years, she was arguably the biggest film star in the world, repeating her portrayal of a virginal woman tempted into romance in a series of enormously successful comedies including *Please Don't Eat the Daisies* (1960), *Lover Come Back* (1961), *That Touch of Mink* (1962), *Move Over, Darling* (1963), and *Send Me No Flowers* (1964). She made one more film musical, an adaptation of Richard Rodgers and Lorenz Hart's *Jumbo*, in 1962, and she continued to record for Columbia with diminishing success, though her 1960 single "Sound of Music" (music by Richard Rodgers, lyrics by Oscar Hammerstein II) earned a Grammy nomination for Best Vocal Performance, Record or Track, Female, and her 1964 recording of the title song from *Move Over, Darling* (music by Joe Lubin, lyrics by Hal Kanter and Terry Melcher) became a Top Ten hit in the U.K.

Day worked less frequently in films and on records after the mid-1960s, doing her final work in each medium in 1967. Her husband, Martin Melcher, died of a stroke on April 20, 1968, after which she discovered that he and her lawyer had squandered her money, leaving her with a tax debt, and that he had committed her to a network television series. She sued the lawyer, eventually winning a multi- million-dollar judgment, and went ahead with the television series, a situation comedy called *The Doris Day Show*, which premiered on Sept. 24, 1968. A ratings success, it ran for five seasons. She also did two television specials, *The Doris Mary Ann Kappelhoff Special* on March 14, 1971, and *Doris Day Today* on Feb. 19, 1975. On April 14, 1976, she married restaurant owner Barry Comden; they divorced in 1981. In 1977 she founded the Doris Day Pet Foundation, followed by the politically oriented Doris Day Animal League, and she spent most of her time caring for animals and working for antivivisection causes.

In the mid-1980s, Day returned to television for a season on the Christian Broadcasting Network cable channel with the show *Doris Day's Best Friends*, which was oriented toward animals. In 1995, Terry Melcher located her last, unreleased recordings from the 1960s, and they were released as *The Love Album*, but she resisted offers to return to singing or acting.

WRITINGS: With A. E. Hotchner, *D. D.: Her Own Story* (Boston, 1975).

DISC.: "Sentimental Journey" (1944); "My Dreams Are Getting Better All the Time" (1944); "Love Somebody" (1948); "Confess" (1948); "It's Magic" (1948); *You're My Thrill* (1949); *Tea for Two* (1950); *Lullaby of Broadway* (1951); *Moonlight Bay* (1951); *I'll See You in My Dreams* (1952); "A Guy Is a Guy" (1952); *By the Light of the Silvery Moon* (1953); "Secret Love" (1954);

Calamity Jane (1954); "If I Give My Heart to You" (1954); "Whatever Will Be, Will Be (Que Sera Sera)" (1956); *Day by Day* (1957); *The Pajama Game* (1957); "Everybody Loves a Lover" (1958); *Doris Day's Greatest Hits* (1958); *Jumbo* (with Jimmy Durante, Steven Boyd, and Martha Raye; 1962); "Move Over, Darling" (1964); *The Love Album* (1995).

BIBL.: G. Morris, *D. D.* (N.Y., 1976); A. Gelb, *The D. D. Scrapbook* (N.Y., 1977); C. Young, *Films of D. D.* (Secaucus, N.J., 1977); E. Braun, *D. D.* (1991).—**WR**

Deák, Csaba, Hungarian-born Swedish composer; b. Budapest, April 16, 1932. He studied clarinet and composition at the Béla Bartók Cons. in Budapest (1949–55) and composition with Ferenc Farkas at the Budapest Academy of Music (1955–56), and subsequently went to Sweden, where he took composition lessons with Hilding Rosenberg. He also studied composition, clarinet, and conducting at the Ingesund School of Music in Arvika, and received his music teacher's certification from the Stockholm Musikhögskolan (1969). He taught at the Swedish State School of the Dance in Stockholm (from 1969) and at the Univ. of Göteborg (1971–74).

WORKS: DRAMATIC: *Fäderna* (The Fathers), chamber opera (Stockholm, Oct. 16, 1968); *Etude on Spring*, electronic ballet (1970); *Lucie's Ascent into Heaven*, an "astrophonic minimelodrama" (1973); *Bye-bye, Earth, A Play about Death* (1976–77); theater music. **ORCH.:** *Eden* for Symphonic Band (1978); *The Piper's Wedding* for Wind Quintet and Symphonic Band (1979); *Vivax* (1982); *5 Short Pieces* for Symphonic Band (1983); *Farina Pagus* for Symphonic Band (1983); *Concerto Maeutro* (1989); *Gustadolphory* for Symphonic Band (1989); *Ad Nordiam Hungarica* for Chamber Orch. (1991); Concerto for Clarinet and Wind Orch. (1992); Sym. for Wind Orch. (1995). **CHAMBER:** 2 string quartets (1959, 1967); *Duo Suite* for Flute and Clarinet (1960); *Air* for Violin and Piano (1961); *121* for Winds, Percussion, and Double Bass (1969); Trio for Flute, Cello, and Piano (1971); *Andante och Rondo* for Wind Quintet (1973); *Verbunk* for Brass Sextet (1976); *Hungarian Dances* for Wind Quintet (1977); Octet for Wind Quintet and String Trio (1977); *Herykon* for Brass Quintet (1981); *Massallians* for Trumpet, Trombone, Brass Ensemble, and Percussion (1985); Saxophone Quartet (1986); Saxophone Quintet (1988); Quartet for Tubas (1990); *Magie noire* for Clarinet and String Quartet (1993); *Novem* for Saxophone Quartet and Brass Quintet (1994); *Gratulatio* for Cello and Double Bass (1995); Octet for Saxophone Quartet and String Quartet (1998); *Sax Appeal* for Saxophone Quartet (1999); piano pieces. **VOCAL:** Choral works; songs. —**NS/LK/DM**

De Amicis, Anna Lucia, outstanding Italian soprano; b. Naples, c. 1733; d. there, 1816. She began her career singing with her family in comic operas in Italy, Paris, and Brussels. In 1762 she made her London debut at the King's Theatre. In 1763 she appeared in J.C. Bach's *Orione* in London, and then devoted herself to serious operas. She sang in Venice (1764; 1768–69; 1770–71), Milan (1764–65; 1772), Innsbruck (1765), Naples (1766; 1769–70; 1771–72), Turin (1776–79), and Bologna (1778). After appearing in private opera performances in Naples from about 1778 to 1788, she retired. De Amicis won great praise for her remarkable vocal and acting gifts. Mozart was much taken by her extraordinary talents.—**NS/LK/DM**

Dean, Stafford (Roderick),

English bass; b. Kingswood, Surrey, June 20, 1937. He studied at Epsom Coll. and at the Royal Coll. of Music in London; also received private lessons from Howell Glynne and Otakar Kraus. He first sang with Opera for All (1962–64); in 1964 he made his debut at the Glyndebourne Festival as Lictor in *L'incoronazione de Poppea*, and at Sadler's Wells in London as Zuniga, where he appeared regularly until 1970; in 1969 he made his debut at London's Covent Garden as Masetto, and remained on its roster. On Feb. 6, 1976, he made his Metropolitan Opera debut in N.Y. as Figaro. He also sang opera in Chicago, San Francisco, Toronto, Hamburg, Berlin, Vienna, Paris, and other cities, and likewise toured widely as a concert artist. His extensive repertoire includes such roles as Sarastro, Leporello, Osmind, Sparafucile, and King Philip. He married **Anne Howells**.—NS/LK/DM

Dean, Winton (Basil),

English musicologist; b. Birkenhead, March 18, 1916. He pursued studies in the liberal arts at King's Coll., Cambridge (B.A., 1938; M.A., 1941) and took private music lessons from Philip Radcliffe. In 1965 he became a member of the council and in 1970 vice president of the Royal Musical Assn. In 1965–66 he was the Ernest Bloch Prof. of Music and in 1977 the Regent's Lecturer at the Univ. of Calif. at Berkeley. He was the Matthew Vassar Lecturer at Vassar Coll. in Poughkeepsie, N.Y., in 1979. In 1979 he became a member of the management committee of the Halle Handel Soc., of which he was vice president from 1991 until being made an honorary member in 1999. In 1975 he was made a Fellow of the British Academy and in 1989 a corresponding member of the American Musicological Soc. He was awarded an honorary doctorate in music from the Univ. of Cambridge in 1996. In addition to his valuable books, he has contributed articles to various scholarly journals and music periodicals.

WRITINGS: *Bizet* (London, 1948; 2nd ed., rev., 1965, as *Georges Bizet: His Life and Work*; 3rd ed., 1976); *Carmen* (London, 1949); *Franck* (London, 1950); *Introduction to the Music of Bizet* (London, 1950); *Handel's Dramatic Oratorios and Masques* (London, 1959; rev. ed., 1990); *Handel and the Opera Seria* (Berkeley, 1969); with J. Knapp, *Handel's Operas 1704–1726* (Oxford, 1987; 2nd ed., rev., 1995); *Essays on Opera* (Oxford, 1990).

BIBL.: N. Fortune, ed., *Music and Theatre: Essays in Honour of W. D.* (Cambridge, 1987).—NS/LK/DM

Deane, Raymond,

Irish composer and pianist; b. Dublin, Jan. 27, 1953. He studied at Univ. Coll., Dublin (graduated, 1974) before pursuing training in composition with Stockhausen and Yun in Cologne and Berlin (1974–79). After teaching composition in Oldenburg (1984–87) and Paris (1990–94), he returned to Dublin as a composer and pianist.

WORKS: DRAMATIC: *The Poet and His Double*, chamber opera (Dublin, Oct. 17, 1991); *The Wall of Cloud*, chamber opera (1997). **ORCH.:** *Embers* for Strings (1973–81; also for String Quartet); *Compact* (1976); *Enchantment* (1981–82); *de/montage* (1984); *Quaternion* (1988); *Krespel's Concerto: Fantasia on E. T. A. Hoffmann* (1990); Oboe Concerto (1993–94); *Dekatriad* (1995); *Ripieno* (1999–2000). **CHAMBER:** *Aliens* for Clarinet, Trombone, Viola, Organ, and Harpsichord (1971–72); *Equivoke* for Flute, Horn, Organ, Piano, and Cello (1972); *Embers* for String Quartet (1973–81; also for String Orch.); *Aprèslude* for Flute, Cello, Percussion, Harp, Viola, and Cello (1979); *Silhouettes* for String Quartet or Wind Quintet (1981–95); *Catenae* for Chamber Ensemble (1991); *Seachanges (with Danse Macabre)* for Flute, Piano, Percussion, Violin, and Cello (1993); *Catacombs* for Clarinet, Violin, Cello, and Piano (1994); *Fügung* for Bass Clarinet and Harpsichord (1995); *Brown Studies* for String Quartet (1997–98). **PIANO:** *Orphica: 4 Orphic Pieces* (1969–81); 2 sonatas (1974, rev. 1980; 1981); *Avatars* (1982); *Contretemps* for 2 Pianos (1989); *After- Pieces* (1989–90); *Rahu's Rounds* (1998). **Organ:** *Idols* (1971; rev. 1996).—LK/DM

De Angelis, Nazzareno,

noted Italian bass; b. Aquila, Nov. 17, 1881; d. Rome, Dec. 14, 1962. As a boy, he sang in the Sistine and Justine chapel choirs in Rome. He made his operatic debut in Aquila in 1903; then appeared with major Italian opera houses. In 1909–10 he was on the roster of the Manhattan Opera House in N.Y.; then of the Chicago Opera (1910–11; 1915–20); later made appearances with the Rome Opera (until 1938); also gave song recitals. He was regarded as one of the most cultured bass singers of the Italian school of opera, and he was equally appreciated in Wagnerian roles. —NS/LK/DM

Debain, Alexandre-François,

French inventor of the harmonium; b. Paris, 1809; d. there, Dec. 3, 1877. He established a factory of pianos and organs in Paris (1834), and after long experimentation with free reeds patented his harmonium in 1840. He also invented the antiphonel and the harmonichorde, and improved the accordion.—NS/LK/DM

DeBarge,

the family vocal group touted as the new-jack Jacksons; they didn't quite live up to the hype. **MEMBERSHIP:** Randy DeBarge, voc. (b. Grand Rapids, Mich., Aug. 6, 1958); Bunny DeBarge, voc. (b. Grand Rapids, Mich., March 10, 1955); Bobby DeBarge (b. Grand Rapids, Mich., March 5, 1956, d. Aug. 16, 1995 in Mansfield, Ohio); El DeBarge, voc., keybd. (b. Eldra DeBarge, Grand Rapids, Mich., June 4, 1961); Marty DeBarge, voc. (b. Mark DeBarge, Grand Rapids, Mich., June 19, 1959).

When the DeBarge family grew to ten children, their father left them. They were, however, able to capitalize on their great musical talent. They started singing in the Pentecostal church, before brothers Bobby and Tommy became secular recording artists as members of the funk band Switch, which had a Top 40 hit in 1978 with "There'll Never Be." Hoping to piggyback on their brothers' success, five of the other DeBarge children went to L.A. After an audition with their older brother's mentor, Jermaine Jackson, the band signed to Motown. The company released their eponymous debut, but it disappeared without a whisper.

The group rehearsed and refined their sound, recording *All This Love*. Although it was released in September of 1982, the album didn't really start selling until the single "I Like It" began to get airplay the following spring. It reached #31 and was followed by the title track, which rose to top the adult contemporary charts and to #17 on the pop charts. The album peaked at #24 and went gold.

Although it followed *All This Love* by more than a year, the group's third album, *In a Special Way*, seemed to come out on the heels of their previous success. The first single, "Time Will Reveal," topped the R&B chart and went to #18 pop. The band toured as a quartet with Luther Vandross, leaving their pregnant sister Bunny at home. They also made an appearance in the Motown film *The Last Dragon*, which featured the group singing "Rhythm of the Night." *In a Special Way* peaked at #36, but went gold.

"Rhythm of the Night" became the title track of their next album. The song topped the Adult Contemporary and R&B charts, reaching #3 on the pop charts. The follow-up single, "Who's Holding Donna Now," also topped the R&B and Adult Contemporary charts, hitting #6 pop. The album went gold; it topped out at #19. Flush with the group's success, James married their mentor's sister, Janet Jackson. It was annulled seven months later.

One of the brothers, El, had become the focal point of the group. In 1986, he left the band to go solo. Another brother, Jonathan (Chico) DeBarge, who was too young to join the band initially, signed as a solo with Gordy as well, bringing the number of DeBarges signed to the label to eight of ten. El's solo debut, "Who's Johnny" was featured in the hit movie *Short Circuit*. It rose to #3 in the charts. His debut album, *El DeBarge*, rose to #24 and went gold.

The band went on as a quartet to limited success. Bunny went solo in 1987. Her debut album topped out at #172. Chico's eponymous debut produced the hit "Talk to Me," which rose to #21. Motown dropped the group, though. Two of the remaining brothers, Bobby and James, recorded an independent album *Bad Boys* under the group name, but it went nowhere.

In 1988, Bobby and Chico were arrested for drug trafficking. Both went to jail, where Bobby died of AIDS. The rest of the group fell into professional limbo, with El resurfacing on Quincy Jones's "The Secret Garden" in 1990, along with Al B. Sure!, James Ingram, and Barry White. The single topped the R&B chart, hit #31 pop, and went gold.

By the late 1990s, however, the only DeBarge actively recording was Chico. After serving six years, he staged a comeback with the album *Long Time No See*. Ironically, the music of the family band made something of a comeback in the late 1990s, being sampled in songs by hot acts like Blackstreet, 2 Pac, and Notorious B.I.G.

DISC.: *The DeBarges* (1981); *All This Love* (1982); *In a Special Way* (1983); *Rhythm of the Night* (1985); *Back on Track*; *DeBarge Family.* **EL DEBARGE:** *E.D.* (1986); *Gemini* (1989); *In the Storm* (1992); *Heart Mind & Soul* (1994). **BAD BOYS:** *Bad Boys* (1988). **BUNNY DEBARGE:** *In Love* (1987). **BOBBY DE-BARGE:** *It's Not Over* (1995). **CHICO DEBARGE:** *Talk to Me* (1986); *C.D.* (1986); *Kiss Serious* (1988); *Long Time, No See* (1997).—HB

De Bassini (real name, **Bassi), Achille,** Italian baritone; b. Milan, May 5, 1819; d. Cavadei Tirreni, July 3, 1881. He studied with Perelli, and then made his operatic debut in Voghera (c. 1837). He won the admiration of Verdi, who chose him to create the roles of Francisco in *I due Foscari* (Rome, Nov. 3, 1844), Corsaro (Trieste, Oct. 25, 1848), Miller in *Luisa Miller* (Naples, Dec. 8, 1849), and Melitone in *La forza del destino* (St. Petersburg, Nov. 10, 1862). In 1859 he sang at London's Covent Garden. In addition to his Verdi roles, he won distinction in operas by Bellini and Donizetti. His wife, Rita (Gabriella) Gabussi (b. Bologna, c. 1815; d. Naples, Jan. 26, 1891), was also a singer. After making her operatic debut as Rosina in Milan in 1830, she sang widely in Italy. In 1851 she created the title role in Mercadante's *Medea* in Naples and then retired. Their son, Alberto De Bassini (b. Florence, July 14, 1847; place and date of death unknown), was also a singer. In 1869 he made his operatic debut in *Belisario* in Venice. After singing mainly French roles, he appeared with the Royal Italian Grand Opera Co. on tour in the U.S. in 1898. He later taught voice.—NS/LK/DM

Debriano, Santi, jazz bassist, composer, leader; b. Colon, Panama, June 27, 1955. His father, Alonso Wilson Debriano, a pianist and composer, moved to Harlem, and after finding a place to live, the family followed. Santi, age two, became very ill and was brought back to Panama to stay with his grandmother. He returned to N.Y. in 1959. From the age of 7 to 17 he lived with his family in the East N.Y. section of Brooklyn; attended Union Coll., studying political science and music (B.A. 1976); then began a Masters program at New England Cons. in the fall of 1976, where he had a few bass lessons with Tiny Martin and a few with Miroslav Vitous. In early 1978 he left the program to tour with Archie Shepp. He recorded with the Don Pullen Trio, the George Adams Quartet, the Sonny Fortune Group, and the Billy Hart Band, among others. He has had long-standing affiliations with Sam Rivers, Danilo Perez, Oliver Lake, Kirk Lightsey, Jerry Gonzalez, and Kenny Barron. He has also recorded with Freddie Hubbard, Chico Freeman, Joe Chambers, Charlie Rouse, George Cables, Sonny Fortune, David Murray, Red Rodney, Larry Willis, Bill Pierce, Karl Berger, George Adams, Ravi Coltrane, and Antoine Roney. On tour with his bands in Europe and Japan, he has performed original modern jazz and Latin-influenced compositions. He often appears in N.Y.C. with his band, the Panamaniacs, which usually includes Donny McCaslin, saxophones and flute (who has recorded and toured with Steps Ahead), Alan Mallet, piano, Tommy Campbell, drums (formerly with the Mahavishnu Orch.), Raul Jorena, bandoneon master, and Horacio Hernandez, Latin percussionist (from Gonzalo Rubalcaba). He also performs in duet with Cecilia Engelhart Lopez (vocalist, percussionist, composer and lyricist). He completed an MA in ethnomusicology at Wesleyan Univ. (1989–91). During 1996 he worked on a documentary film, *Check the Changes*, about the N.Y.C. jazz scene with director Marc Hureaux and others.

DISC.: *Obeah* (1987); *Soldiers of Fortune* (1989); *Panamaniacs* (1997); *Circle Chant* (1999).—LP

Debussy, (Achille-)Claude, great French composer whose music created new poetry of mutating tonalities and became a perfect counterpart of new painting in France; b. St.-Germain-en-Laye, Aug. 22, 1862; d. Paris, March 25, 1918. Mme. Mauté de Fleurville, the mother-in-law of the poet Verlaine, prepared him for the Paris Cons.; he was admitted at the age of 10 and studied piano with Marmontel (second prize, 1877) and solfège with Lavignac (third medal, 1874; second, 1875; first, 1876). He further took courses in harmony with Emile Durand (1877–80) and practiced score reading under Bazille. In 1880 Marmontel recommended him to Mme. Nadezhda von Meck, Tchaikovsky's patroness. She summoned him to Interlaken, and they subsequently visited Rome, Naples, and Fiesole. During the summers of 1881 and 1882, Debussy stayed with Mme. von Meck's family in Moscow, where he became acquainted with the syms. of Tchaikovsky; however, he failed to appreciate Tchaikovsky's music and became more interested in the idiosyncratic compositions of Mussorgsky. Back in France, he became friendly with Mme. Vasnier, wife of a Paris architect and an amateur singer.

Debussy made his earliest professional appearance as a composer in Paris on May 12, 1882, at a concert given by the violinist Maurice Thieberg. In Dec. 1880 he enrolled in the composition class of Guiraud at the Paris Cons. with the ambition of winning the Grand Prix de Rome; after completing his courses, he won the second Prix de Rome in 1883. Finally, on June 27, 1884, he succeeded in obtaining the Grand Prix de Rome with his cantata L'Enfant prodigue, written in a poetic but conservative manner reflecting the trends of French romanticism. During his stay in Rome, he wrote a choral work, Zuleima (1885–86), after Heine's Almanzor, and began work on another cantata, Diane au bois. Neither of these 2 incunabulae was preserved. His choral suite with orch., Printemps (1887), failed to win formal recognition. He then set to work on another cantata, La Damoiselle élue (1887–89), which gained immediate favor among French musicians.

In 1888 Debussy visited Bayreuth, where he heard Parsifal and Die Meistersinger von Nürnberg for the first time, but Wagner's grandiloquence never gained his full devotion. What thoroughly engaged his interest was the oriental music that he heard at the Paris World Exposition in 1889. He was fascinated by the asymmetric rhythms of the thematic content and the new instrumental colors achieved by native players; he also found an inner valence between these oriental modalities and the verses of certain French impressionist poets, including Mallarmé, Verlaine, Baudelaire, and Pierre Louÿs. The combined impressions of exotic music and symbolist French verses were rendered in Debussy's vocal works, such as Cinq poèmes de Baudelaire (1887–89), Ariettes oubliées (1888), Trois mélodies (1891), and Fêtes galantes (1892). He also wrote Proses lyriques (1892–93) to his own texts. For the piano, he composed Suite bergamasque (1890–1905), which includes the famous Clair de lune. In 1892 he began work on his instrumental Prélude à l'après-midi d'un faune, after Mallarmé, which comprises the quintessence of tonal painting with its free modal sequences under a subtle umbrage of oscillating instrumentation. The work was first heard in Paris on Dec. 22, 1894; a program book cautioned the audience

that the text contained sensuous elements that might be distracting to young females. It was about that time that Debussy attended a performance of Maeterlinck's drama Pelléas et Mélisande, which inspired him to begin work on an opera on that subject. In 1893 there followed Trois chansons de Bilitis, after prose poems by Louÿs, marked by exceptional sensuality of the text in a musical context of free modality; a later work, Les Chansons de Bilitis for 2 harps, 2 flutes, and celesta, was heard in Paris in 1901 as incidental music to accompany recited and mimed neo-Grecian poetry of Louÿs. Between 1892 and 1899 Debussy worked on 3 Nocturnes for orch.: Nuages, Fêtes, and Sirènes.

As the 20th century dawned, Debussy found himself in a tangle of domestic relationships. A tempestuous liaison with Gabrielle Dupont (known as Gaby Lhéry) led to a break, which so distressed Gaby that she took poison. She survived, but Debussy sought more stable attachments; on Oct. 19, 1899, he married Rosalie Texier, with whom he made his first attempt to form a legitimate union. But he soon discovered that like Gaby before her, Rosalie failed to satisfy his expectations, and he began to look elsewhere for a true union of souls. This he found in the person of Emma Bardac, the wife of a banker. He bluntly informed Rosalie of his dissatisfaction with their marriage. Like Gaby 7 years before, Rosalie, plunged into despair by Debussy's selfish decision, attempted suicide; she shot herself in the chest but missed her suffering heart. Debussy, now 42 years old, divorced Rosalie on Aug. 2, 1905. Bardac and her husband were divorced on May 4, 1905; Debussy married her on Jan. 20, 1908. They had a daughter, Claude-Emma (known as "Chouchou"), born Oct. 15, 1905; she was the inspiration for Debussy's charming piano suite, Children's Corner (the title was in English, for Chouchou had an English governess). She survived her father by barely a year, dying of diphtheria on July 14, 1919.

With his opera Pelléas et Mélisande, Debussy assumed a leading place among French composers. It was premiered at the Opéra-Comique in Paris on April 30, 1902, after many difficulties, including the open opposition of Maeterlinck, who objected to having the role of Mélisande sung by the American soprano Mary Garden, whose accent jarred Maeterlinck's sensibilities; he wanted his mistress, Georgette Leblanc, to be the first Mélisande. The production of the opera aroused a violent controversy among French musicians and littérateurs. The press was vicious in the extreme: "Rhythm, melody, tonality, these are 3 things unknown to Monsieur Debussy, " wrote the doyen of the Paris music critics, Arthur Pougin. "What a pretty series of false relations! What adorable progressions of triads in parallel motion and fifths and octaves which result from it! What a collection of dissonances, sevenths and ninths, ascending with energy!...No, decidedly I will never agree with these anarchists of music!" Camille Bellaigue, who was Debussy's classmate at the Paris Cons., conceded that Pelléas et Mélisande "makes little noise," but, he remarked, "it is a nasty little noise." The English and American reports were no less vituperative, pejorative, and deprecatory. "Debussy disowns melody and despises harmony with all its resources," opined the critic of the Monthly Musical Record of London. Echoing such judgments, the *Musical Courier* of N.Y. compared Debussy's "disharmony" with the sensation of "an involuntary start when the dentist touches the nerve of a sensitive tooth." And the American writer James Gibbons Huneker exceeded all limits of permissible literary mores by attacking Debussy's physical appearance. "I met Debussy at the Café Riche the other night," he wrote in the N.Y. *Sun*, "and was struck by the unique ugliness of the man...[H]e looks more like a Bohemian, a Croat, a Hun, than a Gaul." These utterances were followed by a suggestion that Debussy's music was fit for a procession of head-hunters of Borneo, carrying home "their ghastly spoils of war."

Debussy's next important work was *La Mer*, which he completed during a sojourn in England in 1905. It was first performed in Paris on Oct. 15, 1905. Like his String Quartet, it was conceived monothematically; a single musical idea permeated the entire work despite a great variety of instrumentation. It consists of 3 symphonic sketches: *De l'aube à midi sur la mer*, *Jeux de vagues*, and *Dialogue du vent et de la mer*. *La Mer* was attacked by critics with even greater displeasure than *Pelléas et Mélisande*. The American critic Louis Elson went so far as to suggest that the original title was actually "Le Mal de mer," and that the last movement represented a violent seizure of vomiting. To summarize the judgment on Debussy, a vol. entitled *Le Cas Debussy* was publ. in Paris in 1910. It contained a final assessment of Debussy as a "déformateur musical," suffering from a modern nervous disease that affects one's power of discernment.

Meanwhile, Debussy continued to work. To be mentioned is the remarkable orch. triptych, *Images* (1906–12), comprising *Gigues*, *Ibéria*, and *Rondes de printemps*. In 1908 he conducted a concert of his works in London; he also accepted engagements as conductor in Vienna (1910), Turin (1911), Moscow and St. Petersburg (1913), and Rome, Amsterdam, and The Hague (1914). Among other works of the period are the piano pieces, *Douze préludes* (2 books, 1909–10; 1910–13) and *Douze études* (2 books, 1915). *En blanc et noir*, for 2 pianos, dates from 1915. On May 15, 1913, Diaghilev produced Debussy's ballet *Jeux* in Paris. On May 5, 1917, Debussy played the piano part of his Violin Sonata at its premiere in Paris with violinist Gaston Poulet. But his projected tour of the U.S. with the violinist Arthur Hartmann had to be abandoned when it was discovered that Debussy had irreversible colon cancer. Surgery was performed in Dec. 1915, but there was little hope of recovery. The protracted First World War depressed him; his hatred of the Germans became intense as the military threat to Paris increased. He wrote the lyrics and the accompaniment to a song, *Noël des enfants*, in which he begged Santa Claus not to bring presents to German children whose parents were destroying the French children's Christmas. To underline his national sentiments, he emphatically signed his last works "musicien français." Debussy died on the evening of March 25, 1918, as the great German gun, "Big Bertha," made the last attempt to subdue the city of Paris by long-distance (76 miles) bombardment.

Debussy emphatically rejected the term "impressionism" as applied to his music. But it cannot alter the essential truth that like Mallarmé in poetry, he created a style peculiarly sensitive to musical mezzotint, a palette of half-lit delicate colors. He systematically applied the oriental pentatonic scale for exotic evocations, as well as the whole-tone scale (which he did not invent, however; earlier samples of its use are found in works by Glinka and Liszt). His piece for piano solo, *Voiles*, is written in a whole-tone scale, while its middle section is set entirely in the pentatonic scale. In his music, Debussy emancipated discords; he also revived the archaic practice of consecutive perfect intervals (particularly fifths and fourths). In his formal constructions, the themes are shortened and rhythmically sharpened, while in the instrumental treatment the role of individual solo passages is enhanced and the dynamic range made more subtle.

WORKS: CHORAL, DRAMATIC, AND LITERARY: *Hymnis*, cantata (1880; unfinished); *Daniel*, cantata for 3 Voices (1880–84); *Printemps* for Women's Chorus and Orch. (1882; publ. as *Salut printemps*, 1928); *Le Gladiateur*, cantata (June 22, 1883); *Invocation* for 4 Men's Voices and Orch. (1883; publ. 1957); *L'Enfant prodigue*, cantata for Soprano, Tenor, Baritone, Chorus, and Orch. (Paris, June 27, 1884; reorchestrated 1905 and 1908); *Printemps* for Chorus (1884); *Diane au bois*, cantata (1884–86; unfinished); *La Damoiselle élue*, cantata for Soprano, Mezzo-soprano, Women's Chorus, and Orch. (1887–89; Paris, April 7, 1893); *Axel*, music for a scene to Villiers de l'Isle Adam's drama (1889); *Rodrigue et Chimène*, opera (1890–92; piano score only, partially lost; reconstructed by Richard Smith and orchestrated by Edison Denisov; Lyons, May 14, 1993); *Pelléas et Mélisande*, opera (1893–95; 1901–02; Paris, April 30, 1902, Messager conducting); *F.E.A. (Frères en art)*, play written with René Peter (1896–1900; unfinished); *Esther et la maison des fous*, text for a dramatic work (1900); *Le Diable dans le beffroi*, opera after Poe's *The Devil in the Belfry* (1902–03; unfinished; only notes for the libretto and sketch for Scene I extant); *Trois chansons de Charles d'Orléans* for Chorus (2 pieces composed in 1898 incorporated into score of 1908; Paris, April 9, 1909, composer conducting); *Masques et Bergamasques*, scenario for a ballet (1910); *La Chute de la maison Usher*, opera after Poe's *The Fall of the House of Usher* (1908–18; unfinished; only sketches and final version of the libretto and incomplete vocal score extant); *Le Martyre de Saint-Sébastien*, incidental music to the mystery play by d'Annunzio for Soprano, 2 Contraltos, Chorus, and Orch. (Paris, May 22, 1911); *Jeux*, ballet (1912; Paris, May 15, 1913, Monteux conducting); *Khamma*, ballet (1912; Paris, Nov. 15, 1924, Pierné conducting); *Ode à la France*, cantata for Solo, Chorus, and Orch. (1916; completed from the sketches by M. F. Gaillard; piano score, 1928; orch. score, 1954). **ORCH.:** *Intermezzo*, after Heine's *Intermezzo* (1882); *Suite d'orchestre* (1883–84); *Printemps*, symphonic suite for Orch. and Chorus (1887; full score destroyed in a fire; later reduction for Voices and Piano, 5-Hands, by Durand, 1904; definitive version reorchestrated by Büsser, 1913; Paris, April 18, 1913, Rhené-Baton conducting); *Fantaisie* for Piano and Orch. (1889; London, Nov. 20, 1919, Coates conducting); *Prélude à l'après-midi d'un faune* (1892–94; Paris, Dec. 22, 1894, Doret conducting); *Nocturnes: Nuages; Fêtes; Sirènes* (the latter with wordless women's chorus; 1892–99; *Nuages* and *Fêtes*, Paris, Dec. 9, 1900, Chevillard conducting; first complete perf., Paris, Oct. 27, 1901, Chevillard conducting); *Danse sacrée* and *Danse profane* for Harp and Strings (1903; Paris, Nov. 6, 1904); *La Mer*, 3 symphonic sketches: 1, *De l'aube à midi* sur la mer; 2, *Jeux de vagues*; 3, *Dialogue du vent et de la mer* (1903–05; Paris, Oct. 15, 1905, Chevillard conducting); *King Lear*, incidental music to Shakespeare's play: *Fanfare* and *Sommeil de Lear* (1904; Paris, Oct. 30, 1926, Wolff conducting; also notes in MS for 6 other pieces); *Images: Gigues* (1909–12); *Ibéria* (1906–08); *Rondes de printemps* (1908–09) (orchestration of *Gigues* completed by Caplet; *Gigues*, Paris, Jan. 26, 1913, Pierné conducting; *Ibéria*, Paris, Feb. 20, 1910, Pierné conducting; *Rondes de printemps*, Paris, March 2, 1910, composer conducting). **CHAMBER:** Trio in G major for Piano, Violin, and Cello (1880); *Intermezzo* for Cello and Piano (1882); *Scherzo* for Cello and Piano (1882); String Quartet (Paris, Dec. 29, 1893); *Chansons de Bilitis*, incidental music for the poems of Louÿs for 2 Flutes, 2 Harps, and Celesta (1900; Paris, Feb. 7, 1901); *Rapsodie* for Saxophone and Piano (1903–05; unfinished; piano accompaniment orchestrated by Roger-Ducasse; Paris, May 14, 1919, Caplet conducting); *Prèmiere rapsodie* for Clarinet and Piano (1909–10; Paris, Jan. 16, 1911; orchestrated by the composer, 1910); *Petite pièce* for Clarinet and Piano (1910); *Syrinx* for Flute (Paris, Dec. 1, 1913); Cello Sonata (1915; first confirmed perf., London, March 4, 1916); Sonata for Flute, Viola, and Harp (1915; Paris, Dec. 10, 1916 [private perf.]); Sonata for Piano and Violin (1916–17; Paris, May 5, 1917, composer pianist, Poulet violinist). **PIANO: Solo Piano:** *Danse bohémienne* (1880); *Deux arabesques* (1880); *Rêverie; Ballade; Danse* (orchestrated by Ravel); *Valse romantique; Nocturnes* (1890); *Suite bergamasque: Prélude; Menuet; Clair de lune; Passepied* (1890–1905); *Mazurka* (1891); *Pour le piano: Prélude; Sarabande* (orchestrated by Ravel); *Toccata* (1896–1901; Paris, Jan. 11, 1902, Viñes pianist); *Estampes: Pagodes; Soirée dans Grenade; Jardins sous la pluie* (1903; first complete perf., Paris, Jan. 9, 1904, Viñes pianist); *D'un cahier d'esquisses* (1903; Paris, April 20, 1910, Ravel pianist); *Masques* (1904) and *L'Isle joyeuse* (1904; orchestrated by B. Molinari; Paris, Feb. 18, 1905, Viñes pianist); *Images*, first series: *Reflets dans l'eau; Hommage à Rameau; Mouvement* (1905; Paris, March 3, 1906, Viñes pianist); *Children's Corner: Doctor Gradus ad Parnassum; Jimbo's Lullaby; Serenade for the Doll; Snow Is Dancing; The Little Shepherd; Golliwog's Cake-walk* (1906–08; Paris, Dec. 18, 1908, Harold Bauer, pianist; orchestrated by Caplet); *Images*, 2nd series: *Cloches à travers les feuilles; Et la lune descend sur le temple qui fut; Poissons d'or* (1907–08; Paris, Feb. 21, 1908, Viñes pianist); *Le Petit Nègre* (1909); *Hommage à Haydn* (1909; Paris, March 11, 1911); *Douze préludes*, Book I: *Danseuses de Delphes* (Paris, May 25, 1910, composer pianist); *Voiles* (Paris, May 25, 1910, composer pianist); *Le Vent dans la plaine; Les Sons et les parfums tournent dans l'air du soir; Les Collines d'Anacapri* (Paris, Dec. 26, 1909, Viñes pianist); *Des Pas sur la neige; Ce qu'a vu le Vent d'Ouest; La Fille aux cheveux de lin; La Sérénade interrompue* (Paris, Jan. 14, 1911, Viñes pianist); *La Cathédrale engloutie* (Paris, May 25, 1910, composer pianist); *La Danse de Puck; Minstrels* (1909–10); *La Plus que lente* (1910; orchestrated by the composer, 1912); *Douze préludes*, Book II: *Brouillards; Feuilles mortes; La Puerta del Vino; Les Fées sont d'exquises danseuses; Bruyères; General Lavine—eccentric; La Terrasse des audiences du clair de lune; Ondine; Hommage à S. Pickwick, Esq., P.P.M.P.C.; Canope; Les Tierces alternées; Feux d'artifice* (1910–13); *La Boîte a joujoux*, children's ballet (1913; Paris, Dec. 10, 1919, Inghelbrecht conducting); *Berceuse héroïque pour rendre hommage à S.M. le Roi Albert I de Belgique et à ses soldats* (1914; orchestrated by the composer, 1914; Paris, Oct. 26, 1915, Chevillard conducting); *Douze études*, Book I: *Pour les cinq doigts; Pour les tierces; Pour les quartes; Pour les sixtes; Pour les octaves; Pour les huit doigts* (1915); *Douze études*, Book II: *Pour les degrés chromatiques; Pour les agréments; Pour les notes répétées; Pour les sonorités opposées; Pour*

les arpèges; *Pour les accords* (1915; both books perf. Dec. 14, 1916, Walter Morse Rummel pianist). **Piano Duet:** *Symphonie en si* (1 movement, 1880; intended for orch.; Paris, Jan. 27, 1937); *Triomphe de Bacchus* (1882; intended as an orch. interlude; orchestrated by Gaillard, 1927); *Petite suite: En bateau; Cortège; Menuet; Ballet* (1889); *Marche écossaise sur un thème populaire* (The Earl of Ross March; 1891; orchestrated by the composer, Paris, Oct. 22, 1913, Inghelbrecht conducting); *Six epigraphes antiques: Pour invoquer Pan, dieu du vent d'été; Pour un tombeau sans nom; Pour que la nuit soit propice; Pour la danseuse aux crotales; Pour l'Egyptienne; Pour remercier la pluie au matin* (1900–1914; also for piano solo; orchestrated by Ansermet). **2 Pianos:** *Lindaraja* (1901; Paris, Oct. 28, 1926); *En blanc et noir* (3 pieces; 1915; Paris, Dec. 21, 1916, composer and Roger-Ducasse pianists). **SONGS** (author of text precedes date of composition): *Ballade à la lune* (Alfred de Musset; 1876?); *Beau soir* (Paul Bourget; 1876?); *Fleur des eaux* (Maurice Bouchor; 1876?); *Nuit d'étoiles* (Théodore de Banville; 1876?); *Fleur des blés* (André Girod; 1877); *Mandoline* (Paul Verlaine); *La Belle au bois dormant* (Vincent Hypsa); *Voici que le printemps* (Bourget); *Paysage sentimental* (Bourget; all composed 1880–83); *L'Archet* (Charles Cros); *Séguedille* (J.L. Vauthier); *Les Roses; Chanson espagnole* (for 2 voices); *Rondel chinois*; 3 songs on poems by Gourget: *Regret; Romance d'Ariel; Musique*; 6 songs on poems by Banville: *Caprice; Aimons-nous; O floraison divine des lilas; Souhait; Sérénade; Fête galante*; 3 songs on poems by Leconte de Lisle: *La Fille aux cheveux de lin; Jane; Eclogue* (for soprano and tenor); *Il dort encore* (from Banville's *Hymnis*); *Coquetterie posthume* (Théophile Gautier); *Flots, palmes, sables* (Armand Renaud; all composed 1880–84); *Zéphyr* (Banville; 1881); *En sourdine* (Verlaine; 1st version, 1882); *Rondeau* (Musset; 1882); *Pantomime* (Verlaine); *Clair de lune* (Verlaine); *Pierrot* (Banville); *Apparition* (Stéphane Mallarmé; all composed 1882–84); *Cinq poèmes de Baudelaire: Le Balcon; Harmonie du soir; Le Jet d'eau* (piano accompaniment orchestrated by the composer); *Recueillement; La Mort des amants* (all composed 1887–89); *Ariettes oubliées* (Verlaine): *C'est l'extase...; Il pleure dans mon coeur...; L'ombre des arbres...; Chevaux de bois; Green; Spleen* (all composed 1888); *Deux romances* (Bourget): *Romances; Les Cloches* (1891); *Les Angélus* (G. le Roy; 1891); *Dans le jardin* (Paul Gravolet; 1891); *Trois mélodies* (Verlaine): *La mer est plus belle...; Le Son du cor s'afflige...; L'Echelonnement des haies* (1891); *Fêtes galantes* (Verlaine), 1st series: *En sourdine; Fantoches; Clair de lune* (1892); *Proses lyriques* (composer): *De rêve; De grève; De fleurs; De soir* (1892–93); *Trois chansons de Bilitis* (Pierre Louÿs): *La Flûte de Pan; La Chevelure; Le Tombeau des Naïades* (1897); *Fêtes galantes* (Verlaine), 2nd series: *Les Ingénus; Le Faune; Colloque sentimental* (1904); *Trois chansons de France: Rondel: Le temps a laissé son manteau...* (Charles d'Orléans); *La Grotte* (Tristan Lhermite; identical to *Auprès de cette grotte sombre*, below); *Rondel: Pour ce que plaisance est morte...* (Charles d'Orléans; all composed 1904); *Le Promenoir des deux amants* (Lhermite): *Auprès de cette grotte sombre...; Crois mon conseil...; Je tremble en voyant ton visage* (1910); *Trois ballades de François Villon* (orchestrated by the composer); *Ballade de Villon à s'amye; Ballade que feit Villon à la requeste de sa mère pour prier Nostre-Dame; Ballade des femmes de Paris* (1910); *Trois poèmes de Stéphane Mallarmé: Soupir; Placet futile; Eventail* (1913); *Noël des enfants qui n'ont plus de maison* (composer; 1915).

WRITINGS: Debussy contributed numerous critical articles to *La Revue Blanche, Gil Blas, Musica, La Revue S.I.M.* et al. A selection of these, some abridged, appeared as *Monsieur Croche, antidilettante* (Paris, 1921; 2nd ed., 1926; Eng. tr., 1927, as *Monsieur Croche the Dilettante-Hater*; 2nd ed., 1962; new ed. by F. Lesure as *Monsieur Croche et autres écrits*, Paris, 1971; Eng. tr., 1977, as *D. on Music: The Critical Writings of the Great French*

Composer C. D.).

BIBL.: SOURCE MATERIAL: F. Lesure has prepared a *Catalogue de l'oeuvre de C. D.* (Geneva, 1977). The *Oeuvres complètes* began publication in 1986. Other sources include the following: A. Martin, *C. D.: Chronologie de sa vie et de ses oeuvres* (Paris, 1942); A. Gauthier, *D.: Documents iconographiques* (Geneva, 1952); *Catalogue de la collection Walter Straram: Manuscrits de C. D.* (Rambouillet, 1961); F. Lesure, *C. D., Catalogue de l'Exposition* (Paris, 1962); C. Abravanel, *C. D.: A Bibliography* (Detroit, 1974); F. Lesure, *Iconographie musicale: D.* (Geneva, 1974); J. Briscoe, *C. D.: A Guide to Research* (N.Y., 1990). **CORRESPONDENCE:** J. Duran, ed., *Lettres de C. D. à son éditeur* (Paris, 1927); *Correspondance de C. D. et P. J. Toulet* (Paris, 1929); J. André-Messager, ed., *La Jeunesse de Pelléas: Lettres de C. D. à André Messager* (Paris, 1938); *C. D.: Lettres à deux amis:78 lettres inédites à Robert Godet et G. Jean-Aubry* (Paris, 1942); H. Borgeaud, ed., *Correspondance de C. D. et Pierre Louÿs* (Paris, 1945); E. Lockspeiser, ed., *Lettres inédites de C. D. à André Caplet* (Monaco, 1957); P. Vallery-Radot, ed., *Lettres de C. D. à sa femme Emma* (Paris, 1957); F. Lesure, ed., *C. D.: Correspondance 1884–1918* (Paris, 1980; rev. ed., 1993) **BIOGRAPHICAL:** L. Liebich, *C.-A. D.* (London, 1908); L. Laloy, *C. D.* (Paris, 1909; 2nd ed., aug., 1944); E. Vuillermoz, *C. D.* (Paris, 1920); R. Jardillier, *C. D.* (Dijon, 1922); A. Suarés, *D.* (Paris, 1922; 2nd ed., aug., 1936); R. Paoli, *D.* (Florence, 1924; 2nd ed., 1947); F. Shera, *D. and Ravel* (London, 1925); F. Gysi, *C. D.* (Zürich, 1926); R. van Santen, *D.* (The Hague, 1926; 2nd ed., 1947); C. Koechlin, *D.* (Paris, 1930); R. Peter, *C. D.* (Paris, 1931; 2nd ed., aug., 1944); L. Vallas, *C. D. et son temps* (Paris, 1932; 2nd ed., 1958; Eng. tr., 1973); E. Decsey, *C. D.* (Graz, 1936); E. Lockspeiser, *D.* (London, 1936; 5thth ed., rev., 1980); O. Thompson, *D., Man and Artist* (N.Y., 1937); H. Strobel, *C. D.* (Zürich, 1940; 3rd ed., rev., 1948); L. Vallas, *A.-C. D.* (Paris, 1944); R. Paoli, *D.* (Florence, 1947; 2nd ed., 1951); G. Ferchault, *C. D., musicien français* (Paris, 1948); H. Harvey, *C. of France: The Story of D.* (N.Y., 1948); R. Malipiero, *D.* (Brescia, 1948); J. van Ackere, *C. D.* (Antwerp, 1949); R. Myers, *D.* (London, 1949); W. Danckert, *C. D.* (Berlin, 1950); G. and D.-E. Inghelbrecht, *C. D.* (Paris, 1953); V. Seroff, *D., Musician of France* (N.Y., 1956); E. Vuillermoz, *C. D.* (Geneva, 1957); J. Barraqué, *D.* (Paris, 1962; Eng. tr., 1972); E. Lockspeiser, *D.: His Life and Mind* (2 vols., London, 1962, 1965; rev. ed., Cambridge, 1978); Y. Tiénot and O. d'Estrade-Guerra, *D.: L'Homme, son oeuvre, son milieu* (Paris, 1962); A. Goléa, *D.* (Paris, 1965); P. Young, *D.* (London, 1966); G. Gourdet, *D.* (Paris, 1970); R. Nichols, *D.* (London, 1973); C. Goubault, *C. D.* (Paris, 1986); L. Knödler, *D.* (Haarlem, 1989); R. Nichols, *D. Remembered* (London and Boston, 1992); F. Lesure, *C. D.: Biographie critique* (Paris, 1994); R. Langham Smith, ed., *D. Studies* (Cambridge, 1997); R. Nichols, *The Life of D.* (Cambridge, 1998). **CRITICAL, ANALYTICAL:** L. Gilman, *D.'s "Pelléas et Mélisande"* (N.Y., 1907); F. Santoliquido, *Il Dopo-Wagner, C. D. e Richard Strauss* (Rome, 1909); C. Caillard and J. de Bérys, *Le Cas D.* (Paris, 1910); G. Setaccioli, *D. é un innovatore?* (Rome, 1910); D. Chennevière, *C. D. et son oeuvre* (Paris, 1913); C. Paglia, *Strauss, D., e compagnia bella* (Bologna, 1913); M. Emmanuel, *Pelléas et Mélisande* (Paris, 1926); L. Vallas, *Les Idées de C. D., musicien français* (Paris, 1927; Eng. tr., 1929, as *The Theories of C. D.*); M. Dumesnil, *How to Play and Teach D.* (N.Y., 1932); A. Liess, *C. D. Das Werk in Zeitbild* (2 vols., Strasbourg, 1936); H. Kolsch, *Der Impressionismus bei D.* (Düsseldorf, 1937); E. Lockspeiser, "D.'s Unpublished Songs," *Radio Times* (Sept. 23, 1938); A. Liess, *C. D. und das deutsche Musikschaffen* (Würzburg, 1939); A. Jakobik, *Die assoziative Harmonik in den Klavier-Werken C. D.s* (Würzburg, 1940); G. Schaeffner, *C. D. und das Poetische* (Bern, 1943); A. Gauthier, *Sous l'influence de Neptune: Dialogues avec D.* (Paris, 1945); J. d'Almendra, *Les Modes grégoriens dans l'oeuvre de C. D.* (Paris, 1948); E. Decsey, *D.s Werke* (Graz, 1949); V. Jankélévitch, *D. et le mystère* (Neuchâtel, 1949; 2nd ed., 1962); E. Robert Schmitz, *The Piano Works of C. D.* (N.Y., 1950; 2nd ed., 1966); J. van Ackere, *Pelléas et Mélisande* (Brussels, 1952); A. Goléa, *Pelléas et Mélisande, analyse poetique et musicale* (Paris, 1952); H. Büsser, *De Pelléas aux Index galantes* (Paris, 1955); M. Long, *Au piano avec C. D.* (Paris, 1960; Eng. tr., 1972); M. Dietschy, *La Passion de C. D.* (Neuchâtel, 1962; Eng. tr., 1990, as *A Portrait of C. D.*); E. Lockspeiser, *D. et Edgar Poe* (Monaco, 1962); S. Jarocinski, *D., a impresionizm i synmbolizm* (Kraków, 1966; French tr., 1971; Eng. tr., 1976, as *D.: Impressionism and Symbolism*); P. Ruschenburg, *Stilkritische Untersuchungen zu den Liedern C. D.s* (diss., Univ. of Hamburg, 1966); E. Hardeck, *Untersuchungen zu den Klavierliedern C. D.s* (Regensburg, 1967); R. Park, *The Later Style of C. D.* (diss., Univ. of Mich., 1967); V. Jankélévitch, *La Vie et la mort dans la musique de D.* (Neuchâtel, 1968); F. Dawes, *D. Piano Music* (London, 1969); W. Austin, ed., *D.: Prelude to "The Afternoon of a Faun"* (Norton Critical Score ed., containing background, criticism, and analysis; N.Y., 1970); D. Cox, *D.'s Orchestral Music* (London, 1974); C. Zenck, *Versuch über die wahre Art D. zu analysieren* (Munich, 1974); V. Jankélévitch, *D. et le mystère de l'instant* (Paris, 1976); A. Wenk, *D. and the Poets* (Berkeley and Los Angeles, 1976); R. Holloway, *D. and Wagner* (London, 1979); M. Cobb, ed., *The Poetic D.: A Collection of His Song Texts and Selected Letters* (annotated; Boston, 1982); E. Lang-Becker, *D. Nocturnes* (Munich, 1982); R. Orledge, *D. and the Theatre* (Cambridge, 1982); R. Howat, *D. in Proportion: A Musical Analysis* (Cambridge, 1983); J. Trilling, *Untersuchungen zur Rezeption C. D.s in der zeitgenössischen Musikkritik* (Tutzing, 1983); A. Wenk, *C. D. and Twentieth-Century Music* (Boston, 1983); G.-P. Biasih, *Montale, D., and Modernism* (Princeton, 1989); R. Nichols and R. Smith, *C. D.: Pelléas et Mélisande* (Cambridge, 1989); R. Parks, *The Music of C. D.* (New Haven and London, 1989); R. Beyer, *Organale Satztechniken in den Werken von C. D. und Maurice Ravel* (Wiesbaden, 1992); F. Lesure, *C. D. avant "Pelléas" ou Les Années symbolistes* (Paris, 1992); J. Arndt, *Der Einfluss der javanischen Gamelan-Musik auf Kompositionen von C. D.* (Frankfurt am Main, 1993); idem, *Einheitlichkeit versus Widerstreit: Zwei gründsätzlich verschiedene Gestaltungsarten in der Musik C. Ds* (Frankfurt am Main, 1993); A Penesco, ed., *Études sur la musique française: Autour de D., Ravel et Paul de Flem* (Lyons, 1994); V. Raad, *The Piano Sonority of C. D.* (Lewiston, N.Y., 1994); P. Roberts, *Images: The Piano Music of C. D.* (Portland, Ore., 1996); S. Bruhn, *Images and Ideas in Modern French Piano Music: The Extra-Musical Subtext in Piano Works by Ravel, D., and Messiaen* (Stuyvesant, N.Y., 1997); J.-F. Gautier, *C. D.: La musique et le mouvant* (Arles, 1997); A. Boucourechliev, *D.: La révolution subtile* (Paris, 1998). —NS/LK/DM

Decadt, Jan, Belgian composer; b. Ypres, June 21, 1914. He studied with Joseph Ryelandt at the Ghent Cons., and later with Jean Absil in Brussels. He was director of the music school in Harelbeke from 1945, and in 1957 was appointed prof. of fugue at the Antwerp Cons. From 1971 he taught composition at the Ghent Cons. His musical style is marked by strong polyphonic structures with impressionistic coloration.

WORKS: *Variations on "Sir Halewijn"* for Orch. (1943); *Ballada op een boom* (Ballade on a Tree) for Soprano, Flute, Oboe, and String Trio (1945); *Habanera* for Orch. (1947); Piano Concerto (1953); Sym. No. 1 (1958); *Constant Permeke*, cantata (1963); *Monographie musicale d'un grand peintre* for Orch. (Johannesburg,

Nov. 17, 1964); *Concerto Overture* for Flute, Oboe, and String Orch. (1964); Suite for Trumpet and Chamber Orch. (1967); *Petite planète* for Narrator, Soprano, Flute, Viola, and Cello (1967); *Concertante Fantasia* for Oboe and Piano (1970); *Introduction and Capriccio* for Clarinet and Piano (1972); Saxophone Concerto (1973); Quartet for Saxophones (1974); *Wens- album* for Flute and Clarinet (1976); *Kleine fanfare* for Brass Band (1981); *Naar Wiegeland* for Voice and Piano (1986).—NS/LK/DM

Decaux, Abel, French organist, teacher, and composer; b. Auffay, 1869; d. Paris, March 19, 1943. He studied organ with Widor and Guilmant and composition with Massenet at the Paris Cons. He served as organist at the church of Sacré-Coeur in Montmartre; then was prof. of organ at the Paris Schola Cantorum; from 1923 to 1937 he taught organ at the Eastman School of Music in Rochester, N.Y. Decaux composed very little, but he attracted posthumous attention by the discovery, and performance, of his group of piano pieces under the title *Clairs de lune* (the plural being of the essence): *Minuit passe, La Ruelle, Le Cimétière,* and *La Mer,* written between 1900 and 1907 and publ. in 1913, which seem to represent early examples of piano writing usually associated with Debussy and Ravel; the similarity of styles is indeed striking, which indicates that Impressionism was "in the air," and in the ears, of impressionable French musicians early in the new century.—NS/LK/DM

Decker, Franz-Paul, German conductor; b. Cologne, June 23, 1923. He was a student of Jarnach and Papst at the Cologne Hochschule für Musik (1941–44) and of Bücken and Fellerer at the Univ. of Cologne. After conducting in Gniessen (1944–46), he was music director in Krefeld (1946–50), 1st conductor (1950–53) and city music director (1953–56) in Wiesbaden, and Generalmusikdirektor in Bochum (1956–64). From 1962 to 1968 he was chief conductor of the Rotterdam Phil. From 1967 to 1975 he was music director of the Montreal Sym. Orch. He served as principal guest conductor and music adviser of the Calgary (Alberta) Phil. (1975–77), as artistic adviser of the Winnipeg Sym. Orch. (1981–82), and as principal guest conductor of the New Zealand Sym. Orch. in Wellington (1984–85; 1986–88). From 1986 to 1992 he was principal conductor of the Orquestra Ciutat de Barcelona, which position he held again from 1994 to 1996. He also was principal guest conductor of the National Arts Centre Orch. in Ottawa from 1991 to 1997. He has appeared widely as a guest conductor with both orchs. and opera houses.—NS/LK/DM

Decoust, Michel, French composer and administrator; b. Paris, Nov. 19, 1936. He studied at the Paris Cons. (1949–50; 1956–65), where he took courses with Dandelot (premier prix in harmony), Desportes (counterpoint), Milhaud and Rivier (composition), Fourestier (premier prix in conducting), and Messiaen (premier prix in analysis), and where he won the Grand Prix de Rome (1963). He also attended courses in new music given by Stockhausen and Pousseur in Cologne (1964–65) and studied conducting with Boulez in Basel (1965). From 1967 to 1969 he was a prof. at Dartington

Coll. in England. In 1967 he founded the Orchestre Philharmonique des Pays de la Loire in Angers, which he administered until 1970. From 1970 to 1972 he was in charge of musical activities of the Maison de la Culture in Rennes and Nevers. In 1972 he founded the Pantin Cons., serving as its director until 1976. From 1976 to 1978 he was president of the ISCM, and from 1976 to 1979 also in charge of its pedagogical dept. in Paris. From 1979 to 1991 he served as inspector general for the French Ministry of Culture, and then was director general for the district of Montpellier from 1991 to 1994. In 1980 he made a Chevalier de l'ordre des Arts et des Lettres, and in 1987 he was made a Chevalier de la Légion d'honneur in 1987. In 1998 he was awarded the Grand Prix of the SACEM. He was made an Officier dans l'ordre National du Mérite in 1991.

WORKS: DRAMATIC: Music Theater: *L'enterreur* (1970; Rennes, Feb. 1971); *Quais* (1985; Paris, April 1986). **ORCH.:** *Polymorphie* (Royan, April 1967); *Si et si seulement* (1971; Paris, Jan. 1972); *Inférence* (Metz, Nov. 1974); *Spectre* (1978); *T.H.T.* (1982; Orléans, Dec. 1984); *Lierre* for Strings (1986); *De la gravitation suspendue des mémoires* (1986; Paris, March 1987); *Symétrie* (1986; Strasbourg, March 5, 1989); *Hommage à Maurice Ravel* (Montpellier, July 1987); *Synopsis* (d'Evry, June 1989); Violin Concerto (1990; Paris, Jan. 1991); *Onyx* (1990; Cannes, Feb. 1991). **CHAMBER:** *Distorsion* for 3 Flutes (1965); *Mobile* for Percussion (1965; Rome, June 1982); *Intéraction* for String Trio (Paris, Oct. 1967); *Aentre* for Horn, Trumpet, Trombone, and Tape (Sion, Aug. 1971); *Sun* for Viola or Viola and 12 Strings (1971; Marseilles, May 1975); *C.H.9.A.M.J.* for Chamber Ensemble (1971); *8.393.574.281* for Variable Chamber Ensemble (1972; also for Chorus); *Actions* for 2 Instruments (Angers, April 1972); *Iambe* for Chamber Ensemble (1976); *Pour 70 doigts* for 7 Players (1980; Toulouse, Dec. 1982); *Onde,* wind quintet (1982; Paris, Jan. 1983); *Le Cygne* for Flute (1982); *Sinfonietta* for 10 Players (Metz, Nov. 1983); *Olos* for Tenor Saxophone and Electronics (1983; Zagreb, Oct. 1984); *Folio 4* for Percussion Quartet (Strasbourg, June 1984); *Les Galeries de pierres* for Viola (Lugano, March 1984); *Xelis* for Percussionist (1984; Paris, June 1985); *Eole* for Flute Quartet (Paris, June 1985); *Sonnet* for 12 Players (Paris, April 1985); *Cantilène* for Oboe (1985; Geneva, July 1986); *Figures II* for Bassoon and Double Bass (Erlangen, Nov. 1986); *Ombres portées* for 8 Players (Angers, Oct. 1986); *Ouverture* for 5 Players (1986; Toulouse, Jan. 1987); *Les Fruits de la passion* for 10 Players (Champigny, April 1987); *1+ 1=4* for Piano and Percussion (Nice, April 1988); *Travelling Ariane* for Flute and Harp (1988); *Lignes* for Clarinet and String Quartet (1992; N.Y., Feb. 4, 1993); Octet for 8 Cellos (1996); *Les Pas du temps* for Violin, Viola, Cello, Flute, and Harp (2000). **Piano:** *Et/Ou* (Paris, June 1972); *Le Temps d'écrire* (Nevers, Nov. 1988). **VOCAL:** *Le Grand yacht Despair* for Voice and Orch. (Paris, June 1962); *Les Hommes sur la terre* for Tenor, Baritone, and Orch. (Paris, June 1963); *Horizon remarquable* for Soprano and Orch. (Paris, June 1964); *Les Rois mages* for Voice and Orch. (Paris, June 1964); *Relevé d'esquisse* for Soprano and 4 Players (1964–82; Rome, June 1981); *Etat* for Chorus (Clermont-Ferrand, Feb. 1968); *M.U.R.* for Chorus (Nantes, March 1971); *8.393.574.281* for Chorus (Nevers, April 1972; also for Variable Chamber Ensemble); *T'aï* for Voice, Harpsichord, Electric Guitar, Percussion, and Double Bass (Paris, Jan. 1972); *Ion* for Soprano and Tape (1973; Champigny, Feb. 1974); *Et ée ou é ée* for Chorus and orch. (Paris, July 1973); *L'application des lectrices aux champs* for Soprano and Orch. (1977; Paris, March 1978); *Traits* for Soprano and 5 Players (1982); *Café-Théâtre* for Soprano and Piano (1984;

Fontenay Bois, Jan. 1986); *Aubes incendiées* for Reciter and 12 Players (Montpellier, July 1985); *5 Mélodies (Bleus)* for Soprano and Piano (Paris, Dec. 1986); *Sept Chansons érotiques* for Soprano and Piano (1986; Paris, Jan. 1987); *Je qui d'autre* for Soprano, Tenor, Bass, and 14 Players (Paris, March 1987); *Dodici voci* for 3 Sopranos, 3 Altos, 3 Tenors, 2 Baritones, and Bass (1989); *Duo pour trois* for Mezzo-soprano, Flute, and Piano (Nice, July 1989); *Ryôjin' hishô* for Soprano and Piano (Paris, Nov. 1989); *Mélodies en trio* for Bass, Bass Clarinet, and Piano (Budapest, April 1991); *L'oree des ajours* for Voice and Instrumentalists (1994); *A Jamais d'ombre* for Voice and String Quartet (1997); *Les Mains deliees* for Reciter, Soprano, Chorus, and Orch. (1998); *Cabaret X* for Voice and Piano (1998). ELECTROACOUSTIC: *Solstice* (1968); *7.854.693.286* (Royan, April 1972); *Interphone* (1977); *Marbres* (Utrecht, April 1986).—NS/LK/DM

Decsényi, János, Hungarian composer; b. Budapest, March 24, 1927. He studied in Budapest with Sugár at the Cons. (1948–52) and with Szervánszky at the Academy of Music (1952–56). From 1951 he was active with the Hungarian Radio, becoming head of its dept. of serious music and director of its electronic music studio. In 1986 he was made a Merited Artist by the Hungarian government. He was awarded the Bartók Pásztory Prize in 1999.

WORKS: DRAMATIC: *Képtelen történet* (An Absurd Story), ballet (1962); *Az orr* (The Nose), pantomime (1979). ORCH.: *Divertimento* for Harpsichord and Chamber Orch. (1959); *Csontváry-képek* (Csontváry Pictures; 1967); *Melodiae hominis* for Chamber Orch. (1969); *Gondolatok—nappal, éjszaka* (Thoughts—by Day, by Night; 1971); *Kommentárok Marcus Aureliushoz* (Commentaries on Marcus Aurelius) for 16 Solo Strings (1973); *Double* for Chamber Orch. (1974); *Variations* for Piano and Orch. (1976); *Concerto boemo* (1976); *Concerto grosso* for Chamber Orch. (1978); *A tücsökszót ki érti meg?* (Who Understands the Speech of Crickets?) for Chamber Orch. and Tape (1983); Cello Concerto (1984); *A harmadik* (The 3rd One) for 15 Solo Strings (1985); 2 syms. (1986, 1993). CHAMBER: String Trio (1955); *Sonatina pastorale* for Flute and Piano (1956); String Quartet (1978); Cello Sonata (1991). VOCAL: *Szerelem* (Love) for Soprano and Orch. (1957); *A gondolat játékai* (The Plays of Thought), cantata for Soprano and Chamber Orch. (1972); *Sirfelirat Aquincumból* (Epitaph from Aquincum) for Soprano, Electric Organ, and 16 Solo Strings (1979); *Weöres Sándor tizenkettedik szimfóniája* (The 12th Symphony of Sandor Weöres) for Soprano and Percussion (1980); *Old Hungarian Texts*, oratorio for Soprano, Bass, and Chamber Ensemble (1991); *Keepsake Album*, oratorio for Soprano, Bass, Chamber Chorus, Chamber Ensemble, Electronics, and Projected Images (1998). ELECTRONIC: *Kövek* (Stones; 1987); *Prospero szigete* (Prospero's Island; 1989); *Birds of the Cathedral* (1991); *Book of Verses* (2000). —NS/LK/DM

Decsey, Ernst (Heinrich Franz), German-born Austrian writer on music; b. Hamburg, April 13, 1870; d. Vienna, March 12, 1941. He studied law in Vienna (doctorate, 1894), then composition with Bruckner and Robert Fuchs at the Vienna Cons. He was active as a music critic in Graz and in Vienna. He was the author of a major biography of Hugo Wolf (4 vols., Berlin, 1903–06; abridged 1-vol. ed., 1921). He also wrote *Anton Bruckner* (Berlin, 1920), *Johann Strauss* (Berlin,

1922; 2nd ed., 1947), *Franz Lehár* (Vienna, 1924), *Franz Schubert* (Vienna, 1924), *Maria Jeritza* (Vienna, 1931), *Claude Debussy* (2 vols., Graz, 1936), and *Debussys Werke* (Graz and Vienna, 1948).—NS/LK/DM

Deering (or Dering), Richard, English organist and composer; b. Kent, c. 1580; d. London (buried, March 22), 1630. He was educated in Italy; returned to England as a well-known musician and practiced in London; in 1610, took the degree of B.Mus. at Oxford; in 1617, became organist at the convent of English nuns at Brussels; in 1625, was appointed organist to Queen Henrietta Maria.

WORKS: *Cantiones sacrae sex vocum cum basso continuo ad organum* (Antwerp, 1597); *Cantiones sacrae quinque vocum* (1617); *Cantica sacra ad melodium madrigalium elaborata senis vocibus* (Antwerp, 1618); *Cantiones sacrae quinque vocum* (1619); 2 books of Canzonette, one for 3 Voices and one for 4 (1620; author's name given as Richardo Diringo Inglese); *Cantica sacra ad duos et tres voces, composita cum basso continuo ad organum* (London, 1662).—NS/LK/DM

DeFabritiis, Oliviero (Carlo), Italian conductor; b. Rome, June 13, 1902; d. there, Aug. 12, 1982. He studied with Setaccioli and Refice. He made his conducting debut at the Teatro Adriano in Rome in 1920, and subsequently was a conductor at the Rome Opera (1934–61). He made numerous guest appearances with major European opera houses, and also conducted in the U.S.—NS/LK/DM

Defauw, Désiré, Belgian conductor; b. Ghent, Sept. 5, 1885; d. Gary, Ind., July 25, 1960. He was a violin pupil of Johan Smit. From 1914 to 1918 he led his own quartet, the Allied Quartet of London. He was prof. of conducting at the Brussels Cons. and conductor of its concerts (from 1926); he also conducted his own concert series in Brussels and was founder-conductor of the Orchestre National de Belgique there in 1937. In 1940 he went to Canada, where he was music director of the Montreal Sym. Orch. (1941–53). He was also music director of the Chicago Sym. Orch. (1943–47) and then of the Gary (Ind.) Sym. Orch. (1950–58).

BIBL.: M. Herzberg, *D. D.* (Brussels, 1937).—NS/LK/DM

De Ferrari, Serafino (Amedeo), Italian pianist, organist, conductor, and composer; b. Genoa, 1824; d. there, March 27, 1885. He was a pupil of Bevilacqua, Sciorati, and Serra in Genoa and of Mandanici in Milan. In 1852 he went to Amsterdam as an opera conductor. After serving as director of singing at the Teatro Carlo Felice in Genoa, he held that position at the Teatro Carignano in Turin. In 1873 he became director of the Civico Istituo de Musica in Genoa.

WORKS: DRAMATIC: O p e r a : *Catilina* (1852); *Don Carlo* (Genoa, Feb. 12, 1854); *Pipelet, o Il portinaio di Parigi* (Venice, Nov. 25, 1855); *Il matrimonio per concorso* (Venice, Aug. 7, 1858); *Il menestrello* (Genoa, April 17, 1859); *Il cadetto di Guascogna* (Genoa, Nov. 9, 1864); also a ballet. OTHER: Chamber music, 3 cantatas, sacred music, and songs.—LK/DM

De Fesch (also Defesch, du Feche, de Feghe, de Veg), Willem, prominent Dutch violinist and composer; b. Alkmaar, 1687; d. London, c.

1757. He married the daughter of the violinist Karel Rosier, vice- Kapellmeister at the court of the Elector of Cologne in Bonn, in 1711. He most likely studied with Rosier. He was active in Amsterdam (1710–25), and, after serving as Kapelmeester of Antwerp Cathedral (1725–31), he settled in London, where he pursued a career as a violinist and composer until about 1750. He was an accomplished composer, following in the pathway marked out by Vivaldi, Corelli, and Handel. His 2 sets of sonatas, opp. 8a and 8b, are particularly notable.

WORKS (all publ. in London unless otherwise given): **VOCAL:** *Canzonette ed arie* for Soprano, Basso Continuo, and Violin or Flute (1739); *XX canzonette* for Soprano, Basso Continuo, and Violin, Flute, or Mandolin (c. 1745); *VI English Songs* for Voice, Violins, Flutes, and Harpsichord (c. 1748); *6 New English Songs* for Voice, Violin, Flute, and Harpsichord (1749); *Mr. Defesch's Songs Sung at Marybon-Gardens* (1753); various other songs publ. separately; also 3 oratorios (all lost) and a cantata. **INSTRUMENTAL:** *VI duetti* for 2 Violins, op.1a (Amsterdam, 1716; 2nd ed., Paris, 1738); *VI concerti* for 4 Violins, Viola, Cello, and Organ, op.2a (Amsterdam, 1716–17); *VI concerts*: 4 for 4 Violins, Viola, and Basso Continuo and 2 for Oboe, 2 Violins, Cello, and Basso Continuo, op.3a (Amsterdam, 1716–17); *XII sonate*: 6 for Violin, Violone, and Harpsichord and 6 for 2 Cellos, op.4 (Amsterdam, 1725); *VI concerti*: 4 for 2 Flutes, 2 Violins, Viola, and Organ and 2 for 4 Violins, Viola, Cello, and Organ, op.5 (Amsterdam, c. 1725–31); *VI sonate* for Violin or Flute and Organ, op.6 (Brussels, 1725–31); *X sonate a tre* for 2 Flutes or Violins and Cello or Basso Continuo, op.7 (Amsterdam, 1733); *XII Sonatas*: 6 for Violin and Basso Continuo and 6 for 2 Cellos, op.8a (1733; nos. 1–6 ed. in Hortus Musicus, CXXVII–CXXVIII, 1958; nos 7–12 ed. in Moeck's Kammermusik, XIX–XX, Celle, 1940); *6 Sonatas* for Cello and Harpsichord, op.8b (1736); *Sonatas* for 2 Cellos, Bassoons, or Viols, op.1b (Paris, 1738); *VI Sonatas* for 2 Flutes, op.9 (1739); *VIII Concertos* in 7 Parts: 6 for 2 Violins, Viola, and Cello, with 2 others for Violin, 1 for Flute with all the other Instruments, and 1 for 2 Flutes, 2 Violins, Viola, Cello, and Harpsichord, op.10 (1741); *Musical Amuzements* (1744; also as *30 Duets* for 2 Flutes, op.11, 1747); *12 Sonatas* for 2 Flutes or Violin and Cello or Harpsichord, op.12 (1748); *VI Sonatas* for Cello and Harpsichord, op.13 (c. 1750).

BIBL.: F. van den Bremt, *W. d. F. (1687–1757), Nederlands componist en virtuoos: Leven en werk* (Louvain and Brussels, 1949).—**NS/LK/DM**

Def Leppard, the band that helped define 1980s pop-metal, formed 1977, in Sheffield, England. **MEMBERSHIP:** Joe Elliott, lead voc. (b. England, Aug. 1, 1959); Pete Willis, gtr. (b. England, Feb. 16, 1960); Rick Savage, bs. (b. England, Dec. 2, 1960); Rick Allen, drm. (b. England, Nov. 1, 1963); Steve Clark, gtr. (b. England, April 23, 1960; d. London, Jan. 8, 1991).

When Def Leppard were coming together in Sheffield in the late 1970s, their sound was inspired by the "new wave of heavy metal" bands like Saxon, but Def Leppard had more pop sense than most of their brethren. This has made them more than a bunch of working-class kids from a steel town. All were working blue-collar jobs in England when the band formed, except drummer Rick Allen, who was just 15 and still in school—although *he* even claims to have been a truck driver at one point. All of them were less than 20 years old.

The group started playing gigs at local clubs in 1978, and in 1979, they put out an EP, *Getcha Rocks Off*, on their own Bludgeon Riffola label. The name of the label was appropriate, as the record was raw, but not thrashy or stark. The disc sold 24,000 copies aided by some BBC airplay. This helped them land a management deal and got them signed to Phonogram. They released *On Through the Night* in 1980, which had a trucking motif. On the strength of the songs "Hello America" and "Wasted," the group gained quite a bit of notoriety on both sides of the Atlantic, as much for their two- guitar attack as for their youthful exuberance.

It was the next album, 1981's *High & Dry*, that blew the band wide open, largely on the strength of the hit "Bringin' on the Heartbreak," a tune that added the phrase "heavy metal ballad" to the lexicon of popular music criticism. Sparked by play on MTV and AOR radio, it was a mega-hit. It grabbed hold instantly with the Bad Company-inspired, double-guitar intro. The guitar work of Steve Clark and Pete Willis was rooted in the standard heavy-metal crunch: riff and speed. But the group vocals were the most distinctive and overlooked aspect of the Def Leppard sound. Essentially, *High and Dry* presented Def Leppard as a better then average, radio ready, hard-rock band, but while the album hinted at it, they had yet to find that niche that made them stand out from the crowd. The album topped out at #38, but still sold double platinum.

The group's potential was realized on their next release, 1983's *Pyromania*. The album effectively (perhaps in concert with Van Halen) ushered in the revolutionary idea of pop-metal. In large part, this was due to the departure of one of the group's founders, guitarist Pete Willis, who was fired because of his drinking problem. He was replaced by Phil Collen (b. Dec. 8, 1957), formerly of Girl, a band with a decidedly glam image. There was musical chemistry between Collen and Clark right from the start, borne out by *Pyromania*. "Rock of Ages" reached #16 pop, "Photograph" catapulted to #12, and the power ballad "Foolin'," one of their songs to feature an acoustic guitar, got up to #28, an unprecedented third hit single from a hard-rock album. Def Leppard was finding their sound, and it was a sound that people liked. The only thing that kept *Pyromania* from the top of the charts was the pop juggernaut of Michael Jackson's *Thriller*. The album eventually went nine times platinum.

Between the overwhelming success of *Pyromania* and 1987's *Hysteria*, Def Leppard went through the trials of Job. Mutt Lange, the producer who guided them to success, had other commitments, so they enlisted two other producers, but neither worked out. By the time they had scrapped the two aborted versions of *Hysteria*, Lange was available, but then suffered a car accident that nearly cost him the use of his legs. When he finally got back on his feet and the band was about to go into the studio, Joe Elliot came down with the mumps. The most devastating blow came on New Year's Eve 1985, when drummer Rick Allen's Corvette went off the road. It could have cost him his life, but he deems himself lucky to have only lost his arm. Through ingenuity, dedication, and hard work, Allen and his drum technician developed a set that allowed him to have his left leg do the work his left arm used to do.

But the result of all these trials was an album that went 12 times platinum (and counting), spinning off six separate Top 40 singles. The Def Leppard on *Hysteria* is a band that has found its expression. Joe Elliot sounded more comfortable using the lower end of his voice. The overall sound became slicker. With the pop success of *Pyromania*, Def Leppard could get beyond the cliches of being a metal band without the fear of losing their audience. The album's hits showcased the band's many different sides. "Animal," which peaked at #19, wouldn't have sounded out of place on a Cars album. "Pour Some Sugar on Me," which spent a couple of weeks at #2, effectively revived the glam-rock sound. The power ballad "Love Bites," the band's first chart-topping single, established a more vulnerable feel. "Armageddon It," which rose to #3, displayed their sense of humor. "Rocket," which hit #12 fully two years after the album came out, kicked off with the beat that made Gary Glitter famous.

Again, tragedy struck between *Hysteria* and their next album. Steve Clark, whose drinking had only been slightly less troublesome than Willis's, died when he mixed pain medicine he was taking for cracked ribs with his libations. The band vowed to continue on without him, and recorded *Adrenalize* as a quartet. The 1992 record produced such anthemic tunes as the #15 "Let's Get Rocked," the #36 "Make Love Like a Man," the #12 "Have You Ever Needed Someone So Bad," and "Stand Up (Kick Love in Motion)." Despite spending five weeks atop the album charts and selling triple platinum, the album was regarded as a commercial and critical disappointment.

Before hitting the road for *Adrenalize*, the band added veteran metal guitarist Vivian Campbell (b. Belfast, N. Ireland, Aug. 25, 1962) to their lineup. Beyond touring extensively over the next couple of years, they recorded the #12 single "Two Steps Behind" for the movie *The Last Action Hero*. That tune found its way onto *Retro Active*, a collection of non- album B-sides, other rarities, and the new single "Miss You in a Heartbeat," which peaked at #39. In 1995, they put out their greatest hits record, *Vault*, which they saw as closing an old chapter and starting a new one. The record peaked at #15 and sold double platinum.

The new chapter started with *Slang* in 1996. The album was more raw, practically devoid of the vocal harmonies that characterized the band's previous albums. They used Indian instruments, funk, and even industrial sounds, trying to move with the times. Allen brought back his acoustic drum kit. The album met with great indifference, hitting #15 but only going gold. They remained popular live, however, and in 1999 released *Euphoria*, an album that harked back to their earlier records, reuniting them with producer Mutt Lange. It entered the charts at a peak of #11 and went gold almost immediately.

DISC.: *Getcha Rocks Off* (1979); *On Through the Night* (1980); *High 'n' Dry* (1981); *Pyromania* (1983); *First Strike Flash* (1985); *Hysteria* (1987); *Adrenalize* (1992); *Retro Active* (1993); *Mega Edition* (1994); *Slang* (1996); *Euphoria* (1999).—HB

Defossez, René, Belgian conductor, pedagogue, and composer; b. Spa, Oct. 4, 1905; d. Brussels, May 20, 1988. He studied with Rasse at the Liège Cons., winning the Belgian Prix de Rome in 1935 with his opera-cantata *Le Vieux Soudard.* He was conductor at the Théâtre Royal de la Monnaie in Brussels (1936–59) and prof of conducting at the Brussels Cons. (1946–71). In 1969 he was elected a member of the Royal Belgian Academy.

WORKS: DRAMATIC: O p e r a : *Le Subterfuge improvisé* (1938). **O p e r a - c a n t a t a :** *La Conversion de St. Hubert* (1933); *Le Vieux Soudard* (1935). **B a l l e t :** *Floriante* (1942); *Le Sens du divin* (1947); *Le Rêve de l'astronome* (1950); *Les Jeux de France* (1959); *Le Regard* (1970). **B a l l e t - c a n t a t a :** *Le Pêcheur et son âme* (1965). **H i s t o r i c F r e s c o :** *Lièges libertes* (1981). **O r a t o r i o :** *Bê Pretimps d'amour* (1939); *La Frise empourprée* (1939). **ORCH.:** *Aquarium* (1927); *Images sous-marines* (1930); *Symphonie wallonne* (1935); *Poème romantique* for Strings (1935); *Amaterasu* (1935); *Variations* for Piano and Orch. (1939); *Adagio et Scherzo* for Flute and Orch. (1941); *Recitativo et Allegro* for Trumpet and Orch. (1945); *Marche funebre* (1946); Trombone Concerto (1948); Violin Concerto (1951); Piano Concerto (1956; rev. for 2 Pianos, 1963); *La Chasseur d'images* (1966); *Sinfonietta de printemps* (1975). **CHAMBER:** 2 string quartets (1934, 1950); Wind Trio (1946); *Petit quartet* for Violin, Piano, Saxophone, and Percussion (1973); piano pieces. **VOCAL:** Choruses and songs.—NS/LK/DM

De Francesco, Joey, jazz organist, keyboard player, trumpeter; b. Springfield, Pa., April 10, 1971. His father, Papa John De Francesco, is also an organist; his brother Johnny De Francesco is a guitarist. He began playing when he was just four years old. Miles Davis, in the course of being interviewed on Bill Boggs's "Time Out" (Philadelphia TV) in 1986, heard the keyboard player in the house trio and asked for his name on the air. Davis later recommended De Francesco to Columbia Records. He worked with the Davis band in the mid-1980s, recording with them on the album *Amandla.* He won the Philadelphia Jazz Society's McCoy Tyner Scholarship and was a finalist in the first Thelonious Monk Jazz Piano Competition in 1987. Since the late 1980s, he has led various small groups, and also continues to record as a sideman. Although primarily a keyboard player, he also plays trumpet, although not to the same level of capability. His brother, Johnny, works in the jazz, funk, and blues genres. Johnny has had numerous concert and club performances with artists including George Benson, Ike Turner, his father and brother, John Lee Hooker, and others. He is Assistant Professor of Guitar (part time), at Berklee Coll. of Music.

DISC.: *All of Me* (1989); *Where Were You?* (1990); *Port III* (1991); *Reboppin'* (1992); *Live at the 5 Spot* (1993); *All About My Girl* (1994); *Street of Dreams* (1995).—LP

DeFranco, Buddy (actually, **Boniface Ferdinand Leonardo**), clarinetist; b. Camden, N.J., Feb. 17, 1923. He took up the clarinet at the age of 12 (in

Philadelphia) and was classically trained. He attended the Mastbaum Vocational School, where his classmates included Joe Wilder, John LaPorta, Johnny Coles, and Red Rodney. Upon hearing Benny Goodman, DeFranco became interested in jazz; he has said his other influences were Artie Shaw, Art Tatum, and from the midforties, Charlie Parker. He can be heard making use of polytonal ideas by the late 1940s, and has said that Parker gave him credit for Parker's innovations in this area. Early in his career DeFranco was faulted by some for an over-technical, cold sound and approach, but the ideas and energy in his playing have always proved him a jazz musician of the first order. During the 1940s, he worked with many leading jazz bands, sometimes doubling on alto, including Gene Krupa (1941–42), Charlie Barnet (1943–44), Boyd Raeburn, and Tommy Dorsey (1944–46). From 1950–51, he played with the Count Basie septet. He organized his own big band (1951) and quartet (from 1952 on; at various times with Art Blakey, Kenny Drew, Milt Hinton, Sonny Clark, Eugene Wright, and Tal Farlow). In 1955 he settled in Calif., and used Don Friedman in his quartet for gigs around L.A. and a tour that came to N.Y. In the early 1960s, he led a quartet with accordionist Tommy Gumina. He led the Glenn Miller Orch. from 1966 to 1974; then resumed touring on his own. In the 1980s, he worked frequently with Terry Gibbs and guitarist Joe Beck. His quintet toured the U.K. in 1985. In 1950–51 he appeared with Basie in several film shorts, and in four of them he appears onscreen. In a different short film with Billie Holiday, Marshall Royal is seen but his music was reportedly dubbed by DeFranco because the producer or perhaps the director (Will Cowan) didn't want to show an interracial band and left DeFranco, the only white, off camera.

DISC.: *A Bird in Igor's Yard* (1949); *Buddy DeFranco with Strings* (1952); *King of the Clarinet* (1952); *Mr. Clarinet* (1953); *Progressive Mr. DeFranco* (1953); *With Tatum* (1953); *Cooking the Blues* (1955); *Buddy DeFranco Meets the Oscar Peterson Trio* (1956); *Jazz Tones* (1956); *Odalisque* (1956); *Bravura* (1957); *Buddy De-Franco Wailers* (1957); *Closed Session* (1957); *Generalissimo* (1957); *Cross-Country Suite* (1959); *Presenting the Buddy DeFranco–Tommy Gumina Quartet* (1961) *Kaleidoscope* (1962); *Polytones* (1963); *Tommy Gumina Quintet* (1962); *Blues Bag* (1964); *Girl from Ipanema* (1964); *Free Sail* (1974); *Buddy DeFranco* (1977); *Like Someone in Love* (1977); *Waterbed* (1977); *Mr. Lucky* (1982); *On Tour: U.K.* (1983); *Born to Swing!* (1988) *Holiday for Swing* (1988); *Garden of Dreams* (1989); *Chip off the Old Bop* (1992).

BIBL.: John Kuehn and Arne Astrup, *Buddy DeFranco: A Biographical Portrait and Discography* (New Brunswick, N.J., 1993).—**LP/MS**

DeGaetani, Jan(ice), remarkable American mezzo-soprano; b. Massillon, Ohio, July 10, 1933; d. Rochester, N.Y., Sept. 15, 1989. She studied at the Juilliard School of Music in N.Y. with Sergius Kagan. Upon graduation, she joined the Contemporary Chamber Ensemble, with which she developed a peculiar technique essential for performance of ultramodern vocal works. She devoted herself to a detailed study of Schoenberg's *Pierrot lunaire*, which became one of her finest interpretations. She mastered the most challenging techniques of new vocal music, including fractional intervals. She also mastered foreign languages to be able to perform a wide European repertoire. She became a faithful interpreter of the most demanding works by modern composers, among them Boulez, Crumb, Druckman, Maxwell Davies, Ligeti, Carter, and Davidovsky. She also developed a fine repertoire of Renaissance songs, and soon became a unique phenomenon as a lieder artist, excelling in an analytical capacity to express the most minute vocal modulations of the melodic line while parsing the words with exquisite intellectual penetration of their meaning, so that even experienced critics found themselves at a loss of superlatives to describe her artistry. From 1973 she taught at the Eastman School of Music. With N. and R. Lloyd, she publ. the useful vol. *The Complete Sightsinger* (1980). —**NS/LK/DM**

Degen, Helmut, German composer and teacher; b. Aglasterhausen, near Heidelberg, Jan. 14, 1911; d. Trossingen, Oct. 2, 1995. He studied piano, composition, and conducting at the Hochschule für Musik in Cologne, then took courses at the Univ. of Bonn with Schiedermair and Schrade. He taught at the Duisburg Cons., and at the Trossingen Hochschulinstitut für Musik. His music was couched in a well-defined, neo-Classical idiom, with strong points of reference to Baroque forms. He publ. a *Handbuch der Formenlehre* (Regensburg, 1957).

WORKS: ORCH.: Piano Concerto (1940); Organ Concerto (1943); Concertino for 2 Clarinets and Orch. (1944); Cello Concerto (1945); 3 syms. (1945, 1947, 1948); *Symphonisches Spiel I* (1956), *II* for Violin, Cello, Piano, and Orch. (1957), and *III* (1960); *Triptychon* (1952). **CHAMBER:** 2 string quartets (1941, 1950); Piano Trio (1943); Concerto for Harpsichord and 6 Instruments (1945); Trio for Flute, Viola, and Clarinet (1950); Saxophone Sonata (1950); Nonet for Wind Instruments and Strings (1951); 4 piano sonatas; numerous concert studies. **VOCAL:** Choruses.—**NS/LK/DM**

Degeyter, Pierre, French wood-carver and author of the famous workers' song *Internationale* (1888); b. Ghent, Oct. 8, 1848; d. St. Denis, near Paris, Sept. 27, 1932. The authorship of the song was contested by Pierre's brother, Adolphe, a blacksmith (b. 1858; d. Lille, Feb. 15, 1917), but after 18 years of litigation, the Paris Appellate Court decided in favor of Pierre.—**NS/LK/DM**

De Giosa, Nicola, Italian conductor and composer; b. Bari, May 3, 1819; d. there, July 7, 1885. He was a student at the Naples Cons. (1834–41), where his teachers included Zingarelli, Donizetti, and Pietro Raimondi. He began to compose operas forthwith, most of them first performed in Naples. His most celebrated work was the opera buffa *Don Checco*, which was premiered at the Teatro Nuovo in Naples to extraordinary acclaim on July 11, 1850. While he continued to compose mainly comic operas, he never succeeded in duplicating this success. In 1860 he began to devote most of his time to conducting opera, and subsequently was engaged in Naples, Venice, Cairo, and in Buenos Aires before returning to Naples in 1876. He resumed composing for the stage and obtained a modest success with his opera buffa *Napoli di carnevale*, which was first performed at the Teatro Nuovo on Dec. 28, 1876. In all, he wrote over 20 operas. He also composed some orch. pieces and church music, but it is as a composer of songs in a salon style that he remains best known. **—LK/DM**

Degli Antoni, Pietro, Italian composer; b. Bologna, May 16, 1639; d. there, 1720. He pursued his career in his native city, where he was active as an instrumentalist. In 1666 he became a charter member of its Accademia Filarmonica, and later served as its principe (1676, 1684, 1696, 1700, 1705, 1708). He served as maestro di cappella at S. Maria Maggiore (from 1680) and at S. Stefano (1686–96). He played an important role in the development of the sonata da camera and the sonata da chiesa, of which notable examples may be found in his sonatas for Violin and Basso Continuo, opp. 4 and 5 (Bologna, 1676, 1686). He also wrote sacred music, including the oratorio *L'innocenza depressa*. His brother, Giovanni Battista Degli Antoni (b. Bologna, 1636; d. there, after 1696), was an organist and composer. After studies with Giacomo Predieri, he became a member of Bologna's Accademia Filarmonica in 1684 and later served as organist at that city's S. Giacomo Magiore. His *Ricercate* for Cello or Harpsichord, op.1 (Bologna, 1687), anticipate J.S. Bach's solo suites.**—LK/DM**

Degrada, Francesco, esteemed Italian musicologist; b. Milan, May 23, 1940. He studied piano, composition, and conducting at the Milan Cons., obtaining a simultaneous arts degree from the Univ. of Milan (1964). He joined the music history faculty of the Univ. of Milan in 1964, where he was prof. (from 1976) and director of the arts dept. (from 1983). He also taught at the Milan Cons. (1966–73) and gave lectures at various European and U.S. univs., including N.Y.U. (1986). His interest in Baroque music led him to organize the chamber group Complesso Barocco di Milan in 1967, with which he was associated as director and harpsichordist until 1976. His research ranges from the Renaissance period to the contemporary era. In addition to numerous scholarly articles in various publications, he has also ed. works by Pergolesi, Vivaldi, Durante, D. Scarlatti, and Sarti.

WRITINGS: *Al gran sole carico d'amore. Per un nuovo teatro musicale* (Milan, 1974; 2nd ed., 1977); *Sylvano Bussotti e il suo teatro* (Milan, 1976); *Antonio Vivaldi da Venezia all'Europa* (Milan, 1977); *Il palazzo incantato. Studi sulla tradizione del melodramma dal Barocco al Romanticismo* (2 vols., Florence, 1979); *Vivaldi veneziano europeo* (Florence, 1980); ed., *Studi Pergolesiani/Pergolesi Studies* (4 vols., N.Y., 1986, 1988, 1999, 2000); *Andrea Gabrieli e il suo tempo* (Florence, 1988); *Illusione e disincanto: Mozart e altri percorsi settecenteschi* (Florence, 2000). **—NS/LK/DM**

Degtiarev, Stepan (Anikievich), Ukrainian composer; b. Borisovka, Kursk District, 1766; d. Kursk, May 5, 1813. He was a serf bonded to the Sheremetev family. Trained as a chorister, he became musical director of Sheremetev's domestic and theatrical ensembles, including the opera troupe of the summer theater-palace at Ostankino, near Moscow. In 1805 he publ. a

Russian tr. of F. Manfredini's *Regole armoniche*. In addition to at least 76 Orthodox choral concerti and various liturgies and cantatas, he composed a dramatic patriotic oratoria, *Minin i Pozharskii, ili Osvobozhdenie Moskvy* (Minin and Pozharskii, or the Freeing of Moscow; 1811).

BIBL.: C. Hughes, *The Origins of the First Russian Patriotic Oratorio: S.A. D.'s "Minin i Pozharskii" (1811)* (diss., Univ. of N.C., 1984).**—NS/LK/DM**

De Guide, Richard, Belgian composer and pedagogue; b. Basècles, March 1, 1909; d. Brussels, Jan. 12, 1962. He was a student of Gilson and Absil. After working at the Institut National de Radiodiffusion (1938–45), he was director of the music academy of Woluwé-St. Pierre in Brussels (1946–61); he also taught at the Liège Cons. (1950–53) and the Mons Cons. (1961). He publ. *Jean Absil: Vie et oeuvre* (Tournai, 1965).

WORKS: D R A M A T I C : B a l l e t : *Les Danaïdes* (1956). **ORCH.:** *Mouvements symphoniques* (1938); 3 syms.: No. 1 (1943), No. 2 for Organ and Orch. (1951), and No. 3 for Strings, Harp, and Timpani (1957); *Vincti non devicti*, symphonic poem (1948); Piano Concerto, *Le Téméraire* (1952); *Le Tombeau de Montaigne*, suite (1955); *Hommage à Hindemith* for Chamber Orch. (1958). **CHAMBER:** *Concerto for 11* for Winds and Percussion (1940); Duo for 2 Trumpets (1944); Duo for 2 Violins (1945); *Speciosa miracula*, sextet for Winds and Piano (1948); *2 nomes* for Flute (1951); *Les caractères du trombone*, suite for Trombone and Piano (1958). **KEYBOARD: P i a n o :** *Humoresque* (1927); *Préludes and Toccata* (1949); *4 symptômes* for Piano, Left-Hand (1960). **O r g a n :** *Préludes* (1942). **VOCAL:** *Illustration pour un Jeu de l'Oie* for Voice and Piano or Orch. (1939–41).**—NS/LK/DM**

Dehn, Siegfried (Wilhelm), famous German music theorist and teacher; b. Altona, Feb. 24, 1799; d. Berlin, April 12, 1858. He was a law student at Leipzig from 1819 to 1825, and also studied harmony and cello. He studied theory assiduously with Bernhard Klein in Berlin. At Meyerbeer's insistence he was appointed librarian of the music dept. of the Royal Library in 1842. From 1842 to 1848 he was also ed. of the *Caecilia*. He then was a prof. at the Royal Academy of Arts (1849–58). Dehn was a profound theorist, and very successful as a teacher of theory, numbering among his pupils Anton Rubinstein and Glinka.

WRITINGS: *Theoretisch-praktische Harmonielehre* (Berlin, 1840; 2nd ed., Leipzig, 1860); *Analyse dreier Fugen aus J.S. Bachs Wohltemperiertem Clavier und einer Vokaldoppelfuge G.M. Buononcinis* (Leipzig, 1858); *Lehre vom Kontrapunkt, dem Kanon und der Fuge* (Berlin, 1859; 2nd ed., 1883).**—NS/LK/DM**

Deiters, Hermann (Clemens Otto), German writer on music; b. Bonn, June 27, 1833; d. Koblenz, May 11, 1907. He studied jurisprudence in Bonn, where he took the degrees of Dr.Jur. (1854) and Dr.Phil. (1858). He taught in the gymnasia at Bonn (1858) and Duren (1869), was director of gymnasia at Konitz (1874), Posen (1878), and Bonn (1883), "Provincial- Schulrath" at Koblenz (1885–93), and assistant in the Ministry of Public Worship at Berlin (1890); he retired in 1903, living thereafter in Koblenz. Deiters wrote many articles for journals. His greatest achievement was his masterly tr. into German of *Thayer's Life of Beethoven*, with critical comments by Deiters (3 vols., Berlin, 1866–77; 2nd ed., with 2 additional vols. ed. by Riemann, Leipzig, 1907–08; Vols. I, II, and III re-ed. by Riemann, Leipzig, 1910–17).—**NS/LK/DM**

DeJohnette, Jack, jazz drummer, pianist, composer, band leader; b. Chicago, Ill., Aug. 9, 1942. He is a unique, powerful, and brilliant drummer, one of the most inspiring since the mid-1960s; he is also a superb pianist and composer. He was a classical piano student for over a decade and an American Music Cons. graduate, but it was the drums that became his instrument of choice. His background in R&B and free jazz got him regular work in Chicago (where he played alongside Rashied Ali in Coltrane's group at least once) before he moved to N.Y. in 1966. He soon worked with John Patton, Jackie McLean, Abbey Lincoln, and Betty Carter. He became well-known touring with Charles Lloyd (1966–69). He toured with Bill Evans, and worked with Joe Henderson. He played on Miles Davis's *Bitches Brew* in 1969 and worked with Davis again in 1970–71. He led the group Complex, which made an album on CBS in 1969. He has recorded for ECM as a leader since 1976; from 1979 worked with varying personnel as Jack DeJohnette's Special Edition. His own groups have featured Arthur Blythe, John Purcell, Greg Osby, Benny Maupin. Since the early 1980s, he has been based in Woodstock, N.Y., where he can often be seen performing in informal settings. He has continued to be associated with his Lloyd bandmate Keith Jarrett, and since 1983 has toured regularly in a trio with Jarrett and Gary Peacock, playing standards.

WRITINGS: *The Jack DeJohnette Collection* (14 contemporary jazz compositions, melodies, harmonies, bass lines, vamps, and drum parts: "Ahmad the Terrible," "Ebony," "Herbie's Hand Cocked," "Indigo Dreamscapes," "Irresistible Forces," "Jack In," "Lydia," "Milton," "Monk's Plumb," "One for Eric," "Oneness," "Silver Hollow," "Where Or Wayne," "Zoot Suite"; Milwaukee, Wisc., 1997); Jack DeJohnette and Charlie Perry, *The Art of Modern Jazz Drumming* (Merrick, N.Y., 1981).

DISC.: *De Johnette Complex* (1968); *Have You Heard?* (1970); *Compost* (1972); *Sorcery* (1974); *Cosmic Chicken* (1975); *Gate Way* (1975); *Ruta and Daitya* (1975); *Works* (1975); *Directions* (1976); *Pictures* (1976); *New Rags* (1977); *Tales of Another* (1977); *New Directions* (1978); *Special Edition* (1979); *New Directions in Europe* (1979); *Tin Can Alley* (1980); *Inflation Blues* (1982); *Album, Album* (1984); *Jack Dejohnette Piano Album* (1985); *Zebra* (1985); *Irresistible Force* (1987); *Audio-Visualscapes* (1988); *Parallel Realities* (1990); *Earthwalk* (1991); *Music for the Fifth World* (1992); *Extra Special Edition* (1994); *Dancing with Nature Spirits* (1995); *Oneness* (1997).—**LP**

Dejoncker, Theodore, Belgian composer; b. Brussels, April 11, 1894; d. Asse, July 10, 1964. He studied with Gilson. In 1925 he founded, with 7 other composers, the progressive Groupe des Synthétistes.

WORKS: *Sinfonia la classica* (1939); *Symphonie burlesque*; *Symphonie romantique*; *Brutus*, overture; *Prologue symphonique*; *Portrait de Bernard Shaw* for Orch.; String Quartet; Saxophone Quartet; String Trio (1960).—**NS/LK/DM**

De Jong, Conrad J(ohn), American composer; b. Hull, Iowa, Jan. 13, 1934. He studied trumpet at North Tex. State Univ. in Denton, majoring in music education (B.M.Ed., 1954), and later studied composition with Heiden at Ind. Univ. in Bloomington (M.M., 1959); subsequently took lessons with Ton de Leeuw in Amsterdam (1969). He was appointed to the music faculty of the Univ. of Wisc. in River Falls in 1959.

WORKS: *Unicycle* for Harpsichord or Piano (1960); 3 *Studies* for Brass Septet (1960); *Music* for 2 Tubas (1961); *Essay* for Brass Quintet (1963); String Trio (1964); *Fun and Games* for Any Instrument with Piano (1966; rev. 1970); *Aanraking* (Contact) for Trombone (1969); *Hist Whist* for Soprano, Flute, Viola, and Percussion (1969); *Grab Bag* for Tuba Ensemble (1970); *Resound*, trio for Flute, Guitar, and Percussionist or Half-Track Stereo Tape with Tape Delay System and 35mm Slide Projection (1974); 3 Short Variation Fanfares for Brass Quintet (1980); *La Dolorosa* for English Horn (1982).—**NS/LK/DM**

De Jong, Marinus
See **Jong, Marinus de**

De Koven, (Henry Louis) Reginald, American composer; b. Middletown, Conn., April 3, 1859; d. Chicago, Jan. 16, 1920. He was educated in Europe from 1870, taking his degree at St. John's Coll., Oxford, in 1879. Before this he studied piano under W. Speidel at Stuttgart, and after graduation studied there another year under Lebert (piano) and Pruckner (harmony). After a 6-month course in Frankfurt am Main under Hauff (composition), he studied singing with Vannuccini at Florence, and operatic composition under Genee in Vienna and Delibes in Paris. In 1902 he organized the Phil. Orch. at Washington, D.C., which he conducted for 3 seasons. He was music critic for the *Chicago Evening Post* (1889–90), *Harper's Weekly* (1895–97), *N.Y. World* (1898–1900; 1907–12), and later for the *N.Y. Herald*. His best know work was the operetta *Robin Hood* (Chicago, June 9, 1890), in which the celebrated song "O Promise Me," originally publ. in 1899 and introduced into the short after its first performance, is featured.

WORKS: DRAMATIC: O p e r a : *The Canterbury Pilgrims* (N.Y., March 8, 1917); *Rip van Winkle* (Chicago, Jan. 2, 1920). O p e r e t t a : *The Begum* (Philadelphia, Nov. 7, 1887); *Don Quixote* (Boston, Nov. 18, 1889); *Robin Hood* (Chicago, June 9, 1890; as *Maid Marian*, London, Jan. 5, 1891); *The Fencing Master* (Boston, 1892); *The Knickerbockers* (Boston, 1893); *The Algerian* (Philadelphia, 1893); *Rob Roy* (Detroit, 1894); *The Tzigane* (N.Y., 1895); *The Mandarin* (Cleveland, 1896); *The Paris Doll* (Hartford, Conn., 1897); *The Highwayman* (New Haven, 1897); and the following, all of which had their premieres in N.Y.: *The 3 Dragoons* (1899); *Red Feather* (1903); *Happyland* (1905); *Student King* (1906); *The Golden Butterfly* (1907); *The Beauty Spot* (1909); *The Wedding Trip* (1911); *Her Little Highness* (1913). O T H E R : Some 400 songs; a Piano Sonata.

BIBL.: A. de Koven, *A Musician and His Wife* (N.Y., 1926).
—**NS/LK/DM**

Dela, Maurice (real name, **Albert Phaneuf**), Canadian composer and organist; b. Montreal, Sept. 9, 1919; d. there, April 28, 1978. He studied organ and theory with Raoul Paquet before taking courses in theory and composition with Séverin Moisse and Claude Champagne at the Cons. de Musique du Quebec à Montreal (1943–47). He also studied orchestration with Sowerby in Chicago and J.-J. Gagnier in Montreal. He subsequently was a church organist in the province of Quebec, a composer and arranger for the CBC (1951–65), and a teacher in Montreal. His music is pragmatic in style and idiom, tending toward Baroque consistency but energized by an injection of euphonious dissonance.

WORKS: ORCH.: *Ballade* for Piano and Orch. (1945); Piano Concerto (1946); *Le Chat, la belette et le petit lapin* for Narrator and Orch. (1950; rev. 1965); *Les Fleurs de Glais* for Narrator and Orch. (1951); *Scherzo* (1952); *Adagio* for Strings (1956); Piano Concertino (1962); *2 esquisses* (1962); *Projection* (1966); 2 syms. (1968, 1972); *3 Dances* (1971); *Triptyque* (1973); *Suite 437* for Band (1977). **CHAMBER:** *Petite suite maritime* for Wind Instruments (1946); Suite for Flute, Cello, and Piano (1953–54); 2 string quartets (1960, 1963); *Divertissement* for Brass Quintet (1962); *Miniatures* for 3 Recorders (1968). **PIANO:** *Hommage* (1950); *2 Impromptus* (1964). **VOCAL:** *Ronde* for Soprano and Small Orch. or Piano (1949); songs; arrangements of folk songs of Quebec province.—NS/LK/DM

Delaborde, Elie (Miriam) (né Elie Miriam), eccentric French pianist, pedagogue, and composer; b. Paris, Feb. 8, 1839; d. there, Dec. 9, 1913. Though no official documents exist to authenticate the claim, evidence is substantial that he was the natural son of **Charles-Valentin Alkan**, his teacher, and Lina Eraim Miriam, a lady of means. He also studied with Moscheles and Henselt, and subsequently made successful tours of England, Germany, and Russia. During the Franco-Prussian War in 1870, he fled with 121 parrots and cockatoos (later also kept 2 apes, named Isidore and Sara, in his apartment) to London, where he introduced some of his father's works for piano with pédalier. In 1873 he was appointed prof. of piano at the Paris Cons., numbering among his students Olga Samaroff. He was reputed to have had an affair with Bizet's wife, which was substantiated by the announcement of their marriage shortly following Bizet's death. Indeed, he was a close friend of Bizet, having been his swimming companion in the Seine when Bizet caught his fatal illness. He wrote an opéra-comique, *La Reine dort*, an overture, *Attila*, a Piano Quintet, 12 Preludes, Études, and Fantaisies for Piano, and a number of songs.

BIBL.: R. Smith, *Alkan: The Enigma* (London, 1976). —NS/LK/DM

Delacôte, Jacques, French conductor; b. Remiremont, Aug. 16, 1942. He studied at the Nancy Cons. (1956–60) and at the Paris Cons. (1960–63) before pursuing training in conducting with Swarowsky at the Vienna Academy of Music (1965–70). In 1971 he took first prize at the Mitropoulos Competition in N.Y., which led to his appointment as an assistant to Leonard Bernstein at the N.Y. Phil., with which he appeared as a conductor in 1972. In 1973 he made an impressive debut with the London Sym. Orch. when he was engaged on short notice to conduct Mahler's 3rd Sym. He subsequently appeared as a guest conductor with many of the major European orchs. In 1981 he conducted Massenet's *Cendrillon* in Paris, and thereafter was regularly en-

gaged as a conductor with leading Paris opera theaters. He conducted *Carmen* at London's Earls Court, *Samson et Dalila* in Barcelona, and *Faust* in Montreal in 1989. In 1990 he returned to London to conduct *Faust* at the English National Opera, and in 1991 he returned once more to that city to conduct *Samson et Dalila* at Covent Garden and *Tosca* at Earls Court. He was engaged to conduct *Roméo et Juliette* in Toronto in 1992. After conducting *Le Cid* at the Lyric Opera in Chicago in 1993, he returned to London in 1994 to conduct *Carmen* at Covent Garden. In 1996 he returned to Covent Garden to conduct *Samson et Dalila*. Delacôte is particularly known for the refinement and elegance he brings to his interpretations of the French operatic and symphonic masterworks.—NS/LK/DM

Delage, Maurice (Charles), French composer; b. Paris, Nov. 13, 1879; d. there, Sept. 19, 1961. He took lessons with Ravel. Subsequently he made voyages to the Orient, and was greatly impressed with Japanese art. His music reveals oriental traits in subject matter as well as in melodic progressions. An ardent follower of Debussy's principles, Delage wrote music in a highly subtilized manner with distinctive instrumental colors. Among his compositions were *Conte par la mer*, symphonic poem (1908), songs with Small Orch.: *4 poèmes hindous* (1921), *Roses d'Octobre* (1922), *7 Hai-Kaï* (1923), *3 chants de la jungle* (1935), *2 fables de La Fontaine* (1949), and *In Morte* (1951), and String Quartet (1948). —NS/LK/DM

Delalande (also **de La Lande, Lalande,** etc.), **Michel-Richard,** noted French organist, harpsichordist, and composer; b. Paris, Dec. 15, 1657; d. Versailles, June 18, 1726. He was the 15th child of a Paris tailor. He joined the choir of the royal church of St.-Germain-l'Auxerrois about 1666 and sang there until his voice broke at age 15. He became a distinguished organist and harpsichordist, giving instruction on the latter to 2 of the daughters of Louis XIV by his mistress Mme. de Montespan. He was also active as a church organist in Paris. In 1683 he became one of the 4 sous-maîtres of the Royal Chapel; he was in sole charge from 1714 until 1723, when Louis XV restored the other 3 positions. He then was joined by Campra, Bernier, and Gervais. In 1685 he was named compositeur de la musique de la chambre, a title he solely held from 1709 to 1718. He also was surintendant de la musique de la chambre from 1689 to 1719. He was made a Chevalier of the Order of St. Michel by Louis XV in 1722. Delalande's grand motets are outstanding, being notable for their mastery of the Versailles style. He is also distinguished by his music for the stage. He deftly used music from his ballets and divertissements in his *Sinfonies pour les soupers du Roi*, which were played at the dinners of Louis XIV and Louis XV.

WORKS: DRAMATIC: OperaBallet: *Les Éléments* (Tuileries Palace, Paris, Dec. 31, 1721; major portion by Destouches; ed. by d'Indy, 1883). **Ballet Pastorales, Divertissements:** *La Sérénade* (Fontainebleau, 1682); *L'Amour berger* (Paris, 1683); *Les Fontaines de Versailles* (Versailles, April 5, 1683); *Epithalame* (Versailles, June

25, 1685; music not extant); *Le Ballet de la jeunesse* (Versailles, Jan. 28, 1686); *Le Palais de Flore* (Versailles, Jan. 5, 1689); *Ballet de M. de La Lande* (Versailles, Aug. 25, 1691); *Adonis* (1696); *L'Amour, fléchy par la constance* (Fontainebleau, 1697); *La Noce de village* (Sceaux, Feb. 21, 1700); *L'Hymen champestre* (Marly, 1700); *Ode à la louange du Roy* (Sceaux, Oct. 24, 1704; music not extant); *Ballet de la paix* (Marly, July 1713); *L'Inconnu* (Paris, Feb. 1720); *Les Folies de Cardenio* (Paris, Dec. 30, 1720); etc. **INSTRUMEN-TAL:** *Sinfonies pour les soupers du Roi* (Suite No. 1 ed. by R. Desormière, Paris, 1947; Suite No. 4 ed. by Clerisse, Paris, 1954; 2 Caprices ed. by Paillard, Paris, 1965); *Symphonies des Noëls* (more than 20 in all; Nos. 1–4 ed. by A. Cellier, Paris, 1937); 18 suites, etc. **OTHER:** His grand motets number more than 70; Philidor prepared a manuscript copy of 27 motets (1689–90), Hue publ. 40 motets (Paris, 1729–33), and the so-called Cauvin manuscript of the mid-18th[th] century contains 41 motets. A number of these have appeared in modern eds.

BIBL.: J. Richards, *The "Grand Motet" of the Late Baroque in France as Exemplified by M.-R. d.L.* (diss., Univ. of Southern Calif., 1950).—NS/LK/DM

De Lamarter, Eric, American organist, conductor, music critic, teacher, and composer; b. Lansing, Mich., Feb. 18, 1880; d. Orlando, Fla., May 17, 1953. He studied organ with Fairclough in St. Paul, Middelschulte in Chicago, and Guilmant and Widor in Paris (1901–02), and was a graduate of Albion Coll. in Mich. (1900). He then held several organ positions in Chicago, notably with the Fourth Presbyterian Church (1914–36). He was music critic for the *Chicago Inter-Ocean* (1901–14), the *Chicago Record-Herald* (1905–08), and the *Chicago Tribune* (1909–10); he also taught at Olivet Coll. (1904–05), Chicago Musical Coll. (1909–10), Univ. of Mo., Ohio State Univ., and the Univ. of Tex. He was asst. conductor of the Chicago Sym. Orch. and conductor of the Chicago Civic Orch. (1918–36).

WORKS: DRAMATIC: *The Betrothal*, incidental music (N.Y., Nov. 19, 1918); ballet music. **ORCH.:** 4 syms.: No. 1 (1913; Chicago, Jan. 23, 1914), No. 2 (Philadelphia, June 5, 1925), No. 3 (1931; Chicago, Feb. 16, 1933), and No. 4 (1932); *The Faun*, overture (Chicago, Nov. 18, 1913); *Serenade* (1915); *Masquerade*, overture (1916); *Fable of the Hapless Folktune* (Chicago, April 6, 1917); 2 organ concertos: No. 1 (Chicago, April 2, 1920) and No. 2 (Chicago, Feb. 24, 1922); *Weaver of Tales* for Organ and Chamber Orch. (1926); *The Black Orchid*, suite from *The Dance of Life*, ballet (Chicago, Feb. 27, 1931); *Serenade near Taos* (N.Y., Jan. 11, 1938); *The Giddy Puritan*, overture (original title, *They, Too, Went t'Town*, 1921; NBC, June 6, 1938); *Huckleberry Finn*, overture (1948); *Ol' Kaintuck*, overture (1948); *Cluny*, dialogue for Viola and Orch. (1949). **OTHER:** Chamber music; organ works; songs.—NS/LK/DM

Delamont, Gordon (Arthur), Canadian composer; b. Moose Jaw, Saskatchewan, Oct. 27, 1918; d. Toronto, Jan. 16, 1981. He studied trumpet and played in his father's band in Vancouver; played in dance orchs. and led his own dance band (1945–49). His works are all in the jazz idiom. For jazz orch., he wrote *Allegro and Blues* (1962), *Ontario Suite* (1965), *Centum* (1966), *Song and Dance* (1967), and *Collage No. 3* (1967). He also wrote *Portrait of Charles Mingus* for Octet (1963), *3 Entertainments* for Saxophone Quartet (1969), *Moderato and Blues* for Brass Quintet (1972), and *Conversation* for Flugelhorn

and Alto Saxophone (1977). He publ. *Modern Arranging Techniques* (N.Y., 1965), *Modern Harmonic Techniques* (2 vols., N.Y., 1965), *Modern Contrapuntal Techniques* (N.Y., 1969), *Modern Twelve-Tone Techniques* (N.Y., 1973), and *Modern Melodic Techniques* (N.Y., 1976).—NS/LK/DM

De Lancie, John (Sherwood), prominent American oboist and teacher; b. Berkeley, Calif., July 26, 1921. His father was an electrical engineer and an amateur clarinet player; his brother played the violin. In 1935 he won an audition for the Philadelphia Orch., and was also accepted to study oboe in the class of Tabuteau at the Curtis Inst. of Music in Philadelphia (1936–40). He was engaged as oboist with the Pittsburgh Sym. Orch. (1940–42). In 1942 he was drafted into the U.S. Army as a member of the U.S. Army Band. De Lancie was sent to Algiers, to Eisenhower's headquarters; he was subsequently employed by the Office of Strategic Services. After World War II, De Lancie joined the Philadelphia Orch. (1946), serving as its principal oboist (1954–74). In 1977 he was appointed director of the Curtis Inst. of Music, retiring in 1985. He rapidly advanced to the position of one of the greatest virtuosos on his instrument. An interesting episode in his career concerns his meeting with Richard Strauss in Munich in 1945, during which he asked Strauss why he had not composed an oboe concerto, in view of the fact that there were so many beautiful oboe solos in many of his works. This suggestion bore fruit, but De Lancie was not the first to play it; the first performance was given by Marcel Saillet on Feb. 26, 1946, in Zürich. De Lancie did, however, commission and give first performances of a number of works, including Jean Françaix's *L'Horloge de Flore* and Benjamin Lee's Oboe Concerto.—NS/LK/DM

Delaney, Robert (Mills), American composer and teacher; b. Baltimore, July 24, 1903; d. Santa Barbara, Calif., Sept. 21, 1956. He studied music in the U.S., in Italy, and in Paris (1922–27) with Capet (violin) and Boulanger and Honegger (composition). He held a Guggenheim fellowship in 1929, and in 1933 he received a Pulitzer Traveling Fellowship for his music to Stephen Vincent Benet's *John Brown's Body*. He then occupied various teaching posts.

WORKS: *Don Quixote Symphony* (1927); *John Brown's Song*, choral sym. (1931); *Night* for Chorus, String Orch., and Piano (1934); *Adagio* for Violin and Strings (1935); *Work 22*, overture (1939); Sym. No. 1 (1942); *Western Star* for Chorus and Orch. (1944); orch. suites; 3 string quartets.—NS/LK/DM

Delannoy, Marcel, French composer; b. La Ferté-Alais, July 9, 1898; d. Nantes, Sept. 14, 1962. He took lessons with Gédalge and Honegger. He wrote an effective stage work, *Poirier de Misère* (Paris, Feb. 21, 1927), which obtained excellent success. Other works are the ballet-cantata *Le Fou de la dame* (concert perf., Paris, Nov. 9, 1928; stage perf., Geneva, April 6, 1929), *Cinderella*, ballet (Chicago, Aug. 30, 1931; rev. as *La Pantoufle de vair*, Paris, May 14, 1935), Sym. (Paris, March 15, 1934), *Ginevra*, comic opera (Paris, July 25, 1942), *Arlequin radiophile*, chamber opera (Paris, April 1, 1946), *Puck*, fairy opera after Shakespeare (Strasbourg,

Jan. 29, 1949), *Concerto de mai* for Piano and Orch. (Paris, May 4, 1950), *Travesti*, ballet (Enghien-les-Bains, June 4, 1952), Sym. for Strings and Celesta (1952–54), *Les Noces fantastiques*, ballet (Paris, Feb. 9, 1955), and *Le Moulin de la galette*, symphonic poem (1958).—NS/LK/DM

De Lara (real name, **Cohen**), **Isidore,** English composer; b. London, Aug. 9, 1858; d. Paris, Sept. 2, 1935. He began to study the piano at the age of 10 with H. Aguilar, and he also studied singing with Lamperti and composition with Mazzucato at the Milan Cons. He then went to Paris to study with Lalo. Returning to London, he wrote one opera after another, and easily secured performances. His most successful work was *Messalina* (Monte Carlo, March 21, 1899).

WORKS: DRAMATIC: O p e r a : *The Light of Asia* (1892); *Amy Robsart* (London, July 20, 1893); *Moina* (Monte Carlo, March 14, 1897); *Messalina* (Monte Carlo, March 21, 1899); *Sanga* (Nice, Feb. 21, 1906); *Solea* (Cologne, Dec. 12, 1907); *Les Trois Masques* (Marseilles, Feb. 24, 1912); *Nail* (Paris, April 22, 1912); *Les Trois Mousquetaires* (Cannes, March 3, 1921). —NS/LK/DM

DeLay, Dorothy, greatly respected American violin pedagogue; b. Medicine Lodge, Kans., March 31, 1917. Her father was a cellist and her mother a pianist. She attended Oberlin Coll. (1933–34) before pursuing violin studies with Michael Press at Mich. State Univ. (B.A., 1937) and Louis Persinger and Raphael Bronstein at the Juilliard Graduate School of Music in N.Y. (diploma, 1941). She established herself as one of the foremost violin teachers in the world; after working as an assistant to Ivan Galamian, she taught at the Juilliard School of Music (from 1947), Sarah Lawrence Coll. (1948–87), the Meadowmount School of Music in Westport, N.Y. (1948–70), the Aspen (Colo.) Music School (from 1971), the Univ. of Cincinnati Coll.-Cons. of Music (from 1974), the Philadelphia Coll. of the Performing Arts (1977–83), and the New England Cons. of Music in Boston (1978–87). She also conducted master classes all over the world. Among her most celebrated pupils were Itzhak Perlman, Shlomo Mintz, and Cho-Liang Lin. —NS/LK/DM

Delcroix, Léon Charles, Belgian composer; b. Brussels, Sept. 15, 1880; d. there, Nov. 14, 1938. He studied piano with J. Wieniawski, organ with A. Mailly, and composition with Ysaÿe in Brussels and d'Indy in Paris. He conducted theater orchs. in Belgium (1909–27); then devoted himself to composition. He wrote a biography of J. Wieniawski (Brussels, 1908).

WORKS: DRAMATIC: *Ce n'était qu'un rêve*; *La Bacchante*, ballet (Ghent, 1912); *Le Petit Poucet*, opera (Brussels, Oct. 9, 1913). ORCH.: Sym. (won the award of the Belgian Academy); *Le Roi Harald*; *Çunacépa*; *Soir d'été à Lerici*; *Le Val harmonieux*; *Rapsodie languedocienne*; *Marche cortège*; *Sérénade* for Clarinet, Piano, and Orch.; *Elégie et Poème* for Violin and Orch. OTHER: Many chamber music works (quartets, quintets, sonatas, etc.); piano pieces; church music; songs.—NS/LK/DM

Delden, Lex van, Dutch composer and writer on music; b. Amsterdam, Sept. 10, 1919; d. there, July 1,

1988. He studied medicine at the Univ. of Amsterdam and was autodidact in composition. He contributed articles to various Dutch and foreign publications, and also served as music ed. of the newspaper *Het Parool* (from 1947); he likewise was president of the Soc. of Dutch Composers. He was a prolific composer who wrote in a basically tonal style.

WORKS: ORCH.: 8 syms.: No. 1, *De stroom, Mei 1940* (The Torrent; May 1940) for Soprano, Chorus, 8 Instruments, and Percussion (1952; for Orch., 1954), No. 2, *Sinfonia giocosa* (1953), No. 3, *Facetten* (Facets; 1955), No. 4 (1957), No. 5 (1959), No. 6 (1963), No. 7, *Sinfonia concertante*, for 11 Winds (1964), and No. 8 for Strings (1964); Harp Concerto (1951–52); Trumpet Concerto (1956); Concerto for 2 Oboes and Orch. (1959); Piano Concerto (1960); Concerto for 2 String Orchs. (1961); Flute Concerto (1965); Concerto for Violin, Viola, Double Bass, and Orch. (1965); Concerto for 2 Soprano Saxophones and Orch. (1967); *Musica sinfonica* (1967); Concerto for Percussion, Celesta, and Strings (1968); Concerto for Electronic Organ and Orch. (1973); Concerto for Violin, 15 Winds, and Percussion (1978); *Musica di catasto* for Strings (1981; also for String Quintet). **CHAMBER:** Trio for Piano, Violin, and Viola (1944); Piano Sonata (1949); *Kleine Suite* for 12 Harps (1951; in collaboration with M. Flothius); 3 string quartets (1954, 1965, 1979); Quartet for Flute, Violin, Viola, and Cello (1957); Sonata for Solo Cello (1958); Violin Sonata (1964); *Fantasia* for Harp and 8 Winds (1965); 2 trios for Violin, Cello, and Piano (1969, 1988); *Sestetto* for String Sextet (1971); *Nonetto per Amsterdam* for Clarinet, Bassoon, Horn, 2 Violins, Viola, Cello, Double Bass, and Piano (1975); *Quintetto* for Brass Quintet (1981); *Tomba* for 4 Saxophones (1985). **VOCAL: O r a t o r i o s :** *De Vogel Vrijheid* (The Bird of Freedom; 1955); *Anthropolis* (1962); *Icarus* (1963). **O t h e r :** Choral pieces; songs.—NS/LK/DM

Deldevez, Edouard (-Marie-Ernest), French conductor and composer; b. Paris, May 31, 1817; d. there, Nov. 6, 1897. He studied violin with Habeneck and music theory with Halévy and Berton at the Paris Cons. He was asst. conductor (1859–73) and then principal (1873–77) conductor at the Paris Opéra, as well as asst. (1860–72) and then principal (1872–75) conductor of the Société des Concerts du Conservatoire. He taught orch. playing at the Paris Cons. (1874–85).

WORKS: DRAMATIC: O p e r a : *Samson*; *Le Violon enchanté*. **B a l l e t :** *Eucharis* (1844); *Paquita* (1846); *Vert-Vert* (1851, with Tolbecque). **OTHER:** 3 syms.; chamber music; sacred choruses and songs.

WRITINGS: *Curiosités musicales* (1873); *La Notation de la musique classique comparée à la notation de la musique moderne, et de l'exécution des petites notes en général*; *L'Art du chef d'orchestre* (1878); *La Société des Concerts de 1860 à 1885* (1887); *De l'exécution d'ensemble* (1888); *Le Passé à propos du présent* (1892), a continuation of his personal recollections publ. in 1890 as *Mes mémoires*. —NS/LK/DM

Delfs, Andreas, German conductor; b. Flensburg, Aug. 30, 1959. He received training in piano and theory as a child. He studied conducting with Dohnányi and Ceccato at the Hamburg Hochschule für Musik, graduating in 1981. At 20, he became music director of the Univ. of Hamburg Sym. Orch. and an assistant at the Hamburg State Opera. He completed his training in conducting with Mester and Ehrling at the Juilliard

School in N.Y., where he was awarded his M.A. degree in 1984. After serving as conductor of the Pittsburgh Youth Sym. Orch. (1984–86), he was resident conductor of the Pittsburgh Sym. Orch. from 1986 to 1990. From 1986 to 1995 he also was music director of the Orchestre Suisse des Jeunes, and from 1991 to 1994 of the Bern City Theater. In 1995 he won critical accolades when he conducted *Carmen* at his debut with the N.Y.C. Opera. From 1997 to 2000 he was Generalmusikdirektor of the Niedersächsische State Theater and Orch. in Hannover. He became music director of the Milwaukee Sym. Orch. in 1997. In 1998 he made his debut in Carnegie Hall as a guest conductor with the Philadelphia Orch. He has also appeared as a guest conductor with many other orchs. and opera companies, and at various festivals on both sides of the Atlantic. In addition to the standard repertoire, Delfs has ventured forth to program scores by many contemporary composers.—LK/DM

Delgadillo, Luis (Abraham), Nicaraguan composer; b. Managua, Aug. 26, 1887; d. there, Dec. 20, 1961. He studied at the Milan Cons. Returning to Nicaragua, he became a band conductor and opened a music school, which later became a cons. His music is permeated with native rhythm and melos; virtually all of his output is descriptive of some aspect of Latin American culture and history.

WORKS: ORCH.: *Sinfonia indigena* (1921); *Sinfonia mexicana* (1924); *Teotihuacan* (1925); *Sinfonia incaica* (1926; Caracas, May 20, 1927); *Sinfonia serrana* (1928); 12 short syms. (all 1953); *Obertura Debussyana* (1955); *Obertura Schoenbergiana* (1955). OTHER: 7 string quartets; piano pieces; church music. —NS/LK/DM

Delibes, (Clément-Philibert-)Léo, famous French composer; b. St.-Germain-du-Val, Sarthe, Feb. 21, 1836; d. Paris, Jan. 16, 1891. He received his early musical training with his mother and an uncle, then enrolled in the Paris Cons. in 1847 as a student of Tariot. He won a premier prix in solfège in 1850, and also studied organ with Benoist and composition with Adam. In 1853 he became organist of St. Pierre de Chaillot and accompanist at the Théâtre-Lyrique. In 1856 his first work for the stage, *Deux sous de charbon*, a one-act operetta, humorously designated an "asphyxie lyrique," was produced at the Folies-Nouvelles. His second work, the opérette bouffe *Deux vieilles gardes,* won considerable acclaim at its premiere at the Bouffes-Parisiens on Aug. 8, 1856. Several more operettas were to follow, as well as his first substantial work for the stage, *Le Jardinier et son seigneur*, given at the Théâtre-Lyrique on May 1, 1863. In 1864 he became chorus master of the Paris Opéra. With Louis Minkus, he collaborated on the ballet score *La Source*, which was heard for the first time at the Paris Opéra, on Nov. 12, 1866. It was with his next ballet, *Coppélia, ou La Fille aux yeux d'email*, that Delibes achieved lasting fame after its premiere at the Paris Opéra on May 25, 1870. Another ballet, *Sylvia, ou La Nymphe de Diane* (Paris Opéra, June 14, 1876), was equally successful. He then wrote a grand opera, *Jean de Nivelle* (Opéra-Comique, March 8, 1880), which was moderately successful; it was followed by his triumphant masterpiece, the opera *Lakmé* (Opéra-

Comique, April 14, 1883), in which he created a most effective lyric evocation of India; the "Bell Song" from *Lakmé* became a perennial favorite in recitals. In 1881 he was appointed prof. of composition at the Paris Cons.; in 1884, was elected a member of the Inst. His last opera, *Kassya*, was completed but not orchestrated at the time of his death; Massenet orchestrated the score, and it was premiered at the Opéra-Comique on March 24, 1893. Delibes was a master of melodious elegance and harmonious charm; his music possessed an autonomous flow in colorful timbres, and a finality of excellence that seemed effortless while subtly revealing a mastery of the Romantic technique of composition.

WORKS: DRAMATIC (all first perf. at the Bouffes-Parisiens in Paris unless otherwise given): *Deux sous de charbon, ou Le Suicide de Bigorneau*, asphyxie lyrique (Folies-Nouvelles, Feb. 9, 1856); *Deux vieilles gardes*, opérette bouffe (Aug. 8, 1856); *Six demoiselles à marier*, opérette bouffe (Nov. 12, 1856); *Maître Griffard*, opéra-comique (Théâtre- Lyrique, Oct. 3, 1857); *La Fille du golfe*, opéra-comique (publ. 1859); *L'Omelette à la Follembuche*, opérette bouffe (June 8, 1859); *Monsieur de Bonne-Etoile*, opéra-comique (Feb. 4, 1860); *Les Musiciens de l'orchestre*, opérette bouffe (Jan. 25, 1861; in collaboration with Offenbach, Hignard, and Erlanger); *Les Eaux d'Ems*, comédie (1861); *Mon ami Pierrot*, operette (1862); *Le Jardinier et son seigneur*, opéra-comique (Théâtre- Lyrique, May 1, 1863); *La Tradition*, prologue en vers (Jan. 5, 1864); *Grande nouvelle*, operette (publ. 1864); *Le Serpent à plumes*, farce (Dec. 16, 1864); *Le Boeuf Apis*, opéra bouffe (April 25, 1865); *La Source, ou Naila*, ballet (Opéra, Nov. 12, 1866; in collaboration with Louis Minkus); *Valse, ou Pas de fleurs*, divertissement (Opéra, Nov. 12, 1867; for Adam's *Le Corsaire*); *Malbrough s'en va-t-en guerre*, Act 4, opérette bouffe (Athénée, Dec. 13, 1867; Act 1 by Bizet, 2 by E. Jonas, and 3 by Legouix); *L'Écossais de Chatou*, operette (Jan. 16, 1869); *La Cour du roi Petaud*, opéra bouffe (Variétés, April 24, 1869); *Coppélia, ou La Fille aux yeux d'email*, ballet (Opéra, May 25, 1870); *Le Roi l'a dit*, opéra-comique (Opéra-Comique, May 24, 1873); *Sylvia, ou La Nymphe de Diane*, ballet (Opéra, June 14, 1876); *Jean de Nivelle*, opera (Opéra-Comique, March 8, 1880); *Le Roi s'amuse, six airs de danse dans le style ancien*, incidental music to Hugo's play (Comédie-Française, Nov. 22, 1882); *Lakmé*, opera (Opéra-Comique, April 14, 1883); *Kassya*, drame lyrique (Opéra-Comique, March 24, 1893; orchestrated by Massenet); also sketches for *Le Roi des montagnes*, opéra- comique; 2 works not extant: *Le Don Juan suisse*, opéra bouffe, and *La Princesse Ravigote*, opéra bouffe. OTHER: *Alger*, cantata (1865); choral works; songs; duets; pieces for organ and piano; etc.

BIBL.: E. Guiraud, *Notice sur la vie et les oeuvres de L. D.* (Paris, 1892); H. de Curzon, *L. D.* (Paris, 1926); A. Coquis, *L. D.: Sa vie et son oeuvre (1836–1891)* (Paris, 1957); W. Studwell, ed., *Adolphe Adam and L. D.: A Guide to Research* (N.Y., 1987). —NS/LK/DM

DeLio, Thomas, American composer and music theorist; b. N.Y., Jan. 7, 1951. He studied composition at the New England Cons. of Music in Boston (B.M., 1972) and at Brown Univ., in an interdisciplinary program involving music, mathematics, and visual art (Ph.D., 1979, with the diss. *Structural Pluralism*). He taught at Clark Univ. (1977), the New England Cons. of Music (1977–80), and the Univ. of Md. (from 1980). He was co-founder and co-ed. of the journal *Sonus* (1980–85); his articles have appeared in various other art and music journals. His research focuses on open structures and mathematical concepts in composition. As a composer, he has created live electronic sound installations and computer-aided compositions; among his works are *Text* for Piano (1985), *Against the silence...* for Percussion and Tape (1985), and *contrecoup...* for Chamber Ensemble (1989). He publ. *Circumscribing the Open Universe* (Lanham, Md., 1983); ed. *Contiguous Lines: Issues and Ideas in the Music of the '60s and '70s* (Lanham, Md., 1985).—NS/LK/DM

Delius, Frederick (actually, Fritz Theodor Albert), significant English composer of German parentage; b. Bradford, Jan. 29, 1862; d. Grez-sur-Loing, France, June 10, 1934.

His father was a successful merchant, owner of a wool company; he naturally hoped to have his son follow a career in industry, but did not object to his study of art and music. Delius learned to play the piano and violin. At the age of 22 he went to Solano, Fla., to work on an orange plantation owned by his father; a musical souvenir of his sojourn there was his symphonic suite *Florida*. There he met an American organist, Thomas F. Ward, who gave him a thorough instruction in theory; this study, which lasted 6 months, gave Delius a foundation for his further progress in music. In 1885 he went to Danville, Va., as a teacher. In 1886 he enrolled at the Leipzig Cons., where he took courses in harmony and counterpoint with Reinecke, Sitt, and Jadassohn. It was there that he met Grieg, becoming his friend and admirer. Indeed, Grieg's music found a deep resonance in his own compositions. An even more powerful influence was Wagner, whose principles of continuous melodic line and thematic development Delius adopted in his own works. Euphonious serenity reigns on the symphonic surface of his music, diversified by occasional resolvable dissonances. In some works, he made congenial use of English folk motifs, often in elaborate variation forms. Particularly successful are his evocative symphonic sketches *On Hearing the 1st Cuckoo in Spring, North Country Sketches, Brigg Fair,* and *A Song of the High Hills*. His orch. nocturne *Paris: The Song of a Great City* is a tribute to a city in which he spent many years of his life. Much more ambitious in scope is his choral work *A Mass of Life*, in which he draws on passages from Nietzsche's *Also sprach Zarathustra*.

Delius settled in Paris in 1888; in 1897 he moved to Grez-sur-Loing, near Paris, where he remained for the rest of his life, except for a few short trips abroad. In 1903 he married the painter Jelka Rosen. His music began to win recognition in England and Germany; he became a favorite composer of Sir Thomas Beecham, who gave numerous performances of his music in London. But these successes came too late for Delius; a syphilitic infection that he had contracted early in life eventually grew into an incurable illness accompanied by paralysis and blindness; as Beecham phrased it, "Delius had suffered a heavy blow in the defection of his favorite goddess, Aphrodite Pandemos, who had returned his devotions with an affliction that was to break out many years later." Still eager to compose, he engaged as his amanuensis the English musician Eric Fenby, who wrote down music at the dictation of Delius, including complete orch. scores. In 1929 Beecham orga-

nized a Delius Festival in London (6 concerts; Oct. 12 to Nov. 1, 1929) and the composer was brought from France to hear it. In the same year Delius was made a Companion of Honour by King George V and an Hon.Mus.D. by Oxford. A film was made by the British filmmaker Ken Russell on the life and works of Delius. However, he remains a solitary figure in modern music. Affectionately appreciated in England, in America, and to some extent in Germany, his works are rarely performed elsewhere.

WORKS: DRAMATIC: *Zanoni,* incidental music after Bulwer Lytton (1888; unfinished); *Irmelin,* opera (1890–92; Oxford, May 4, 1953); *The Magic Foundation,* lyric drama (1893–95; BBC, London, Nov. 20, 1977); *Koanga,* lyric drama (1895–97; Elberfeld, March 30, 1904); *Folkeraadet,* incidental music to G. Heiberg's drama (Christiania, Oct. 18, 1897); *A Village Romeo and Juliet,* lyric drama (1899–1901; Berlin, Feb. 21, 1907); *Margot la Rouge,* lyric drama (1902; concert perf. BBC, London, Feb. 21, 1982; stage perf., St. Louis, June 8, 1983); *Fennimore and Gerda,* opera (1908–10; Frankfurt am Main, Oct. 21, 1919); *Hassan, or The Golden Journey to Samarkand,* incidental music to J. Flecker's drama (1920–23; Darmstadt, June 1, 1923; full version, London, Sept. 20, 1923). **ORCH.:** *Florida,* suite (1887; private perf., Leipzig, 1888; rev. 1889; public perf., London, April 1, 1937); *Hiawatha,* tone poem (1888; unfinished; excerpt, Norwegian TV, Oslo, Jan. 13, 1984); *Suite* for Violin and Orch. (1888; BBC, Feb. 28, 1984); *Rhapsodic Variations* (1888; unfinished); *Idylle de Printemps* (1889); *Suite d'orchestre* (1889); 3 *Small Tone Poems: Summer Evening, Winter Night [Sleigh Ride],* and *Spring Morning* (1889–90; Westminster, Nov. 18, 1946); *Légendes* for Piano and Orch. (1890; unfinished); *Petite suite d'orchestre* for Small Orch. (1890; Stratford-upon-Avon, May 13, 1978); *Paa vidderne* (On the Heights), symphonic poem after Ibsen (1890–91; Christiania, Oct. 10, 1891); *Légende* for Violin and Orch. (1895?; London, May 30, 1899); *Over the Hills and Far Away,* fantasy overture (1895–97; Elberfeld, Nov. 13,1897); *Appalachia: American Rhapsody* (1896; London, Dec. 10, 1986; rev. as *Appalachia: Variations on an Old Slave Song* for Baritone, Chorus, and Orch.; 1902–03; Elberfeld, Oct. 15, 1904); Piano Concerto in C minor (1st version in 3 movements, 1897; Elberfeld, Oct. 24, 1904; 2nd version in 1 movement, 1906; London, Oct. 22, 1907); *La Ronde se deroule,* symphonic poem after H. Rode (London, May 30, 1899; rev. 1901, as *Lebenstanz* [Life's Dance]; Düsseldorf, Jan. 21, 1904; 2nd rev., 1912; Berlin, Nov. 15, 1912); *Paris: A Nocturne (The Song of a Great City)* (1899; Elberfeld, Dec. 14, 1901); *Brigg Fair: An English Rhapsody* (Basel, 1907); *In a Summer Garden,* rhapsody (London, Dec. 11, 1908; rev., Boston, April 19, 1912); *A Dance Rhapsody,* No. 1 (1908; Hereford, Sept. 8, 1909) and No. 2 (1916; London, Oct. 20, 1923); 2 *Pieces* for Small Orch: *On Hearing the 1st Cuckoo in Spring* (1912) and *Summer Night on the River* (1911; Leipzig, Oct. 23, 1913); *North Country Sketches* (1913–14; London, May 10, 1915); *Air and Dance* for Strings (private perf., London, 1915; public perf., London, Oct. 16, 1929); Double Concerto for Violin, Cello, and Orch. (1915–16; London, Feb. 21, 1920); Violin Concerto (1916; London, Jan. 30, 1919); *Eventyr (Once upon a Time),* ballad after Asbjrnsen (1917; London, Jan. 11, 1919); *A Song before Sunrise* for Small Orch. (1918; London, Sept. 19, 1923); *Poem of Life and Love* (1918); Cello Concerto (1920–21; Frankfurt am Main, Jan. 30, 1921); *A Song of Summer* (1929–30; London, Sept. 7, 1931); *Caprice and Elegy* for Cello and Chamber Orch. (1930); *Irmelin Prelude* (1931; London, Sept. 23, 1935); *Fantastic Dance* (1931; London, Jan. 12, 1934). **CHAMBER:** 2 string quartets: No. 1 (1888; unfinished) and No. 2 (original version in 3 movements, London, Nov. 17, 1916; rev.

version in 4 movements, London, Feb. 1, 1919); *Romance* for Violin and Piano (1889); Violin Sonata in B major (1892; private perf., Paris, 1893); 3 numbered violin sonatas: No. 1 (1905, 1914; Manchester, Feb. 24, 1915), No. 2 (1923; London, Oct. 7, 1924), and No. 3 (London, Nov. 6, 1930); *Romance* for Cello and Piano (1896; Helsinki, June 22, 1976); Cello Sonata (1916; London, Oct. 31, 1918); *Dance* for Harpsichord (1919). **PIANO:** *Zum Carnival Polka* (1885); *Pensées mélodieuses* (1885); *Valse* and *Rêverie* (1889–90; unfinished); *Badinage* (1895?); *5 Pieces* (1922–23); *3 Preludes* (1923; London, Sept. 4, 1924). **VOCAL:** *6 German Partsongs* for Chorus (1885–87); *Paa vidderne* (On the Heights) for Reciter and Orch., after Ibsen (1888; Norwegian TV, Oslo, May 17, 1983); *Sakuntala* for Tenor and Orch. (1889); *Twilight Fancies* for Voice and Piano (1889; orchestrated 1908; Liverpool, March 21, 1908); *The Bird's Story* for Voice and Piano (1889; orchestrated 1908; Liverpool, March 21, 1908); *Maud,* 5 songs for Tenor and Orch., after Tennyson (1891); *2 songs* for Voice and Piano, after Verlaine (1895; later orchestrated); *7 Danish Songs* for Voice and Orch. or Piano (1897; 5 songs, London, March 30, 1899); *Mitternachtslied Zarathustras* for Baritone, Men's Chorus, and Orch., after Nietzsche (1898; London, May 30, 1899); *The Violet* for Voice and Piano (1900; orchestrated 1908; Liverpool, March 21, 1908); *Summer Landscape* for Voice and Piano (1902; orchestrated 1903); *Appalachia: Variations on an Old Slave Song* for Baritone, Chorus, and Orch. (1902–03; Elberfeld, Oct. 15, 1904; rev. of *Appalachia: American Rhapsody* for Orch., 1896; London, Dec. 10, 1986); *Sea Drift* for Baritone, Chorus, and Orch., after Whitman (1903–04; Essen, May 24, 1906); *A Mass of Life* for Soprano, Alto, Tenor, Baritone, Chorus, and Orch., after Nietzsche's *Also sprach Zarathustra* (1904–05; partial perf., Munich, June 4, 1908; complete perf., London, June 7, 1909); *Songs of Sunset* for Mezzo-soprano, Baritone, Chorus, and Orch., after E. Dowson (1906–07; London, June 16, 1911); *Cynara* for Baritone and Orch. (1907, 1929; London, Oct. 18, 1929); *On Craig Ddu* for Chorus (1907; Blackpool, 1910); *Wanderer's Song* for Men's Chorus (1908); *Midsummer Song* for Chorus (1908); *La Lune blanche* for Voice and Orch. or Piano, after Verlaine (1910); *An Arabesque* for Baritone, Chorus, and Orch. (1911; Newport, Monmouthshire, May 28, 1920); *The Song of the High Hills* for Wordless Chorus and Orch. (1911–12; London, Feb. 26, 1920); *2 Songs for Children* (1913); *I-Brasîl* for Voice and Orch. or Piano (1913; Westminster, Nov. 21, 1946); *Requiem* for Soprano, Baritone, Chorus, and Orch. (1913–14; London, March 23, 1922); *To Be Sung of a Summer Night on the Water,* 2 songs for Wordless Chorus (1917; London, June 28, 1921); *The splendour falls on castle walls* for Chorus, after Tennyson (1923; London, June 17, 1924); *A Late Lark* for Tenor and Orch. (1924, 1929; London, Oct. 12, 1929); *Songs of Farewell* for Chorus and Orch., after Whitman (1930; London, March 21, 1932); *Idyll: Once I passed through a populous city* for Soprano, Baritone, and Orch., after Whitman (1932; London, Oct. 3, 1933; based on *Margot la Rouge*). **Solo Songs:** *Over the Mountains High* (1885); *Zwei braune Augen* (1885); *Der Fichtenbaum* (1886); *5 Songs from the Norwegian: Slumber Song, The Nightingale, Summer Eve, Longing,* and *Sunset* (1888); *Hochgebirgsleben* (1888); *O schneller, mein Ross* (1888); *Chanson de Fortunio* (1889); *7 Songs from the Norwegian: Cradle Song, The Homeward Journey, Evening Voices, Sweet Venevil, Minstrel, Love Concealed,* and *The Bird's Story* (1889–90; Nos. 3 and 7 orchestrated); *Skogen gir susende, langsom besked* (1890–91); *4 Songs,* after Heine: *Mit deinen blauen Augen, Ein schöner Stern, Hör' ich das Liedchen klingen,* and *Aus deinen Augen* (1890–91); *3 Songs,* after Shelley: *Indian Love Song, Love's Philosophy,* and *To the Queen of My Heart* (1891); *Lyse Naetter* (1891); *Jeg havde en nyskaare Seljefljte* (1892–93); *Nuages* (1893); *2 Songs,* after Ver-

laine: *Il pleure dans mon coeur* and *Le ciel est, pardessus le toit* (1895; also orchestrated); *The page sat in the lofty tower* (1895?); *7 Danish Songs: Summer Nights, Through Long, Long Years, Wine Roses, Let Springtime Come, Irmelin Rose, In the Seraglio Garden,* and *Silken Shoes* (1896–97; also orchestrated); *Traum Rosen* (1898?); *Im Glück wir lachend gingen* (1898?); *4 Songs,* after Nietzsche: *Nach neuen Meeren, Der Wanderer, Der Einsame,* and *Der Wanderer und sein Schatten* (1898); *The Violet* (1900; also orchestrated); *Autumn* (1900); *Black Roses* (1901); *Jeg hrer i Natten* (1901); *Summer Landscape* (1902; also orchestrated); *The nightingale has a lyre of gold* (1910); *La Lune blanche,* after Verlaine (1910; also orchestrated); *Chanson d'automne,* after Verlaine (1911); *I-Brasîl* (1913; also orchestrated); *4 Old English Lyrics: It was a lover and his lass, So white, so soft is she, Spring, the sweet spring,* and *To Daffodile* (1915–16); *Avant que tu ne t'en ailles,* after Verlaine (1919, 1932).

BIBL.: P. Heseltine, *F. D.* (London, 1923; 2nd ed., rev., 1952); R. Hull, *F. D.* (London, 1928); C. Delius, *F. D., Memories of My Brother* (London, 1935); E. Fenby, *D. as I Knew Him* (London, 1936; 3rd ed., 1966); A. Hutchings, *D., A Critical Biography* (London, 1948); T. Beecham, *F. D.* (London, 1959; 2nd ed., rev., 1975); G. Jahoda, *The Road to Samarkand: F. D. and His Music* (N.Y., 1969); E. Fenby, *D.* (London, 1971); L. Carley and R. Threlfall, *D. and America* (London, 1972); A. Jefferson, *D.* (London, 1972); R. Lowe, *F. D., 1862–1934; A Catalogue of the Music Archives of the D. Trust, London* (London, 1974); L. Carley, *D.: The Paris Years* (London, 1975); C. Palmer, *D.: Portrait of a Cosmopolitan* (London, 1976); C. Redwood, ed., *A D. Companion* (London, 1976; 2nd ed., 1980); L. Carley and R. Threlfall, *D.: A Life in Pictures* (London, 1977; 2nd ed., 1984); R. Threlfall, *F. D. (1862–1934): A Catalogue of the Compositions* (London, 1977); C. Redwood, *Flecker and D.: The Making of "Hassan"* (London, 1978); L. Carley, *D.: A Life in Letters:* vol. I, *1862–1908* (London, 1983; Cambridge, Mass., 1984) and vol. II, *1909–1934* (Aldershot, 1988); *D. 1862–1934* (50th anniversary brochure by the D. Trust, London, 1984); R. Threlfall, *F. D.: A Supplementary Catalogue* (London, 1986); P. Jones, *The American Source of D.' Style* (N.Y., 1989); L. Carley, ed., *Grieg and D.: A Chronicle of their Friendship in Letters* (N.Y., 1993).—**NS/LK/DM**

Della Casa, Lisa, outstanding Swiss soprano; b. Burgdorf, near Bern, Feb. 2, 1919. She was 15 when she commenced vocal studies with Margarete Haeser in Zürich. In 1941 she made her operatic debut as Cio-Cio-San in Solothurn-Biel. From 1943 to 1950 she was a member of the Zürich Opera, where her roles included Pamina, Gilda, and Gershwin's Serena and where she created the Young Woman in Burkhard's *Die schwarze Spinne* on May 28, 1949. In 1947 she made her first appearance at the Salzburg Festival as Zdenka, where she created 3 roles in Einem's *Per Prozess* on Aug. 17, 1953. She made her debut at the Glyndebourne Festival as Mozart's Countess in 1951, and she also appeared that year in Munich as Arabella, her most celebrated role. In 1952 she made her first appearance at the Bayreuth Festival as Eva, the same year that she joined the Vienna State Opera. She was a leading singer at the latter until her farewell appearance as Arabella in 1973. In 1953 she sang Arabella at London's Covent Garden with the visiting Bavarian State Opera in Munich. On Nov. 20, 1953, she made her Metropolitan Opera debut in N.Y. as Mozart's Countess, where she remained on the roster until her final appearance as that composer's Rosina on Dec. 9, 1967. In 1960 she was chosen to sing the Marschallin at the opening of the new Salzburg Festspielhaus. She returned to Covent Garden as Arabella in 1965. Her guest engagements also took her to Paris, Rome, Chicago, and Buenos Aires. Della Casa was one of the most remarkable Mozart and Strauss interpreters of her era. In addition to Mozart's Pamina and Countess, she was acclaimed for her portrayals of his Fiordiligi, Donna Anna, Donna Elvira, and Ilia. While her characterization of Strauss's Arabella was unsurpassed in her day, she was no less compelling as his Salome, Octavian, Sophie, the Marschallin, Zdenka, and the Countess in *Capriccio*. She was also a luminous interpreter of his *Vier letzte Lieder*.

BIBL.: D. Debeljević, *Ein Leben mit L. D. C.* (Zürich, 1975). —NS/LK/DM

Della Ciaia, Azzolino Bernardino, Italian organist, organ builder, and composer; b. Siena, March 21, 1671; d. Pisa, Jan. 15, 1755. He constructed a large organ with 4 manuals and 100 stops for the St. Stephen Church in Pisa. He publ. *Salmi concertati* for 4 Voices, with Instruments (Bologna, 1700), *Cantate da camera* (Lucca, 1701), and *Sonate per cembalo* (Rome, 1727). Much of his church music is extant in MS. He is regarded by some as an Italian originator of the sonata form, but his instrumental music is more interesting for its florid ornamentation than for strict formal development.

BIBL.: F. Baggiani, *L'organo di A. B. D. C.* (Pisa, 1974). —NS/LK/DM

Della Corte, Andrea, eminent Italian musicologist; b. Naples, April 5, 1883; d. Turin, March 12, 1968. He was self-taught in music; devoted himself mainly to musical biography and analysis. He taught music history at the Turin Cons. (1926–53) and at the Univ. of Turin (1939–53). From 1919 till 1967 he was music critic of *La Stampa*.

WRITINGS: *Paisiello* (Turin, 1922); *Saggi di critica musicale* (Turin, 1922); *L'opera comica italiana del 1700* (2 vols., Bari, 1923); *Piccola antologia settecentesca, XXIV pezzi inediti o rari* (Milan, 1925); with G. Gatti, *Dizionario di musica* (Turin, 1925; 6th ed., 1959); *Disegno storico dell'arte musicale* (Turin, 1927; 5th ed., 1950); *Antologia della storia della musica* (2 vols., Turin, 1927–29; 4th ed., 1945); *Niccolò Piccinni* (Bari, 1928); *Scelta di musiche per lo studio della storia* (Milan, 1928; 3rd ed., 1949); *La vita musicale di Goethe* (Turin, 1932); with G. Pannain, *Storia della musica* (Turin, 1936; 4th ed., 1964); with G. Pannain, *Vincenzo Bellini* (Turin, 1936); *Ritratto di Franco Alfano* (Turin, 1936); *Pergolesi* (Turin, 1936); *Un Italiano all'estero: Antonio Salieri* (Turin, 1937); *Tre secoli di opera italiana* (Turin, 1938); *Verdi* (Turin, 1939); *Toscanini* (Vicenza, 1946); *Satire e grotteschi di musiche e di musicisti d'ogni tempo* (Turin, 1947); *Le sei più belle opere di Verdi: Rigoletto, Il Trovatore, La Traviata, Aida, Otello, Falstaff* (Milan, 1947); *Gluck* (Florence, 1948); *Baldassare Galuppi* (Siena, 1949); *Arrigo Serato* (Siena, 1949); *L'interpretazione musicale e gli interpreti* (Turin, 1951).—NS/LK/DM

Della Maria, (Pierre-Antoine-)Dominique, French opera composer; b. Marseilles, June 14, 1769; d. Paris, March 9, 1800. Son of an Italian mandolinist, he was remarkably precocious. He played the mandolin and cello at an early age, and at 18 produced a grand opera at Marseilles. He then studied composition in Italy (for a time with Paisiello) and produced in Naples a successful opera, *Il maestro di cappella* (1792). He went to Paris in 1796; obtaining a libretto (*Le Prisonnier*) from Duval, he set it to music in 8 days, brought it out at the Opéra-Comique (Jan. 29, 1798), and was at once famous. Before his death he finished 6 more operas, 4 of which were produced during his lifetime; a posthumous opera, *La Fausse Duegne* (completed by Blangini), was produced at Paris in 1802.—NS/LK/DM

Della Valle, Pietro, Italian man of letters and composer, known as "Il Pellegrino"; b. Rome, April 11, 1586; d. there, April 21, 1652. He studied harpsichord with Stefano Tavolaccio, Quinzio Solini, and Paolo Quagliati, counterpoint, continuo playing, and theorbo with Solini, and viola da gamba with Marco Fraticelli. After extended travel abroad (1614–26), he returned to Rome, becoming a significant figure in the cultural life of the city. He publ. an account of his adventures as *Viaggi descritti in 54 lettere famigliari* (4 vols., Rome, 1650–58). Almost all of his music is lost, but his valuable *Della musica dell'età nostra che non è punto inferiore, anzi è migliore di quella dell'età* (Jan. 16, 1640) may be found in A. Gori, *G.B. Doni: Trattati di musica*, II (Florence, 1763).

BIBL.: V. Losito, *P. d. V.* (Varese, 1928).—NS/LK/DM

Deller, Alfred (George), English countertenor; b. Margate, May 31, 1912; d. Bologna, July 16, 1979. He studied voice with his father; began singing as a boy soprano, later developing the alto range. He sang in the choirs of the Canterbury Cathedral (1940–47) and at St. Paul's in London. In 1950 he formed his own vocal and instrumental ensemble, the Deller Consort, acting as conductor and soloist in a repertoire of early English music. This unique enterprise led to a modest revival of English madrigals of the Renaissance. In 1963 he founded the Stour Music Festival in Kent. Britten wrote the part of Oberon in his *A Midsummer Night's Dream* for him. In 1970 Deller was named a Commander of the Order of the British Empire.

BIBL.: M. and M. Hardwick, *A. D.: A Singularity of Voice* (London, 1968; 2nd ed., rev., 1982); J.-L. Tingaud, *A. D.: Le contre-ténor* (Paris, 1996).—NS/LK/DM

Deller, Florian Johann, Austrian violinist and composer; b. Dorsendorf (baptized), May 2, 1729; d. Munich, April 19, 1773. He became a ripieno violinist in the Stuttgart Hofkapelle in 1751, and from 1756 he studied counterpoint and composition with Jommelli. Between 1761 and 1767 he composed 6 ballets for the court, thereby winning notable distinction. His most famous ballet was *Orfeo ed Euridice* (1763). In 1771 he went to Vienna, and shortly afterward settled in Munich. Among his other works were several comic operas, 5 syms., 2 flute concertos (not extant), and 6 sonatas for 2 Violins, Cello, and Harpsichord.—LK/DM

Delle Sedie, Enrico, Italian baritone and singing teacher; b. Livorno, June 17, 1822; d. La Garennes-

Colombes, near Paris, Nov. 28, 1907. His teachers were Galeffi, Persanola, and Domeniconi. After imprisonment as a revolutionist (1848), he resumed the study of singing and made his debut in San Casciano (1851) in Verdi's *Nabucco*. Until 1861 he sang in the principal Italian cities; appeared in London in 1861, and then was engaged at the Théâtre-Italien, Paris, and was prof. of singing in the Cons. (1867–71); was regarded as one of the best singing teachers in Paris. His basic manuals, *Arte e fisiologia del canto* (Milan, 1876; in French as *L'Art lyrique*, Paris, 1876) and *L'estetica del canto e dell'arte melodrammatica* (Milan, 1886), were publ. in N.Y. in Eng. as *Vocal Art* (3 parts) and *Esthetics of the Art of Singing, and of the Melodrama* (4 vols.). A condensation (by the author) of both manuals was publ. in 1 vol. as *A Complete Method of Singing* (N.Y., 1894).—NS/LK/DM

Dello Joio, Norman, distinguished American composer and teacher; b. N.Y., Jan. 24, 1913. His family's original name was Ioio. His father, grandfather, and great-grandfather were church organists. Dello Joio acquired skill as an organist and pianist at home. At the age of 12, he occasionally substituted for his father on his job at the Church of Our Lady of Mount Carmel in N.Y. He took additional organ lessons from his well-known godfather, **Pietro Yon**, and studied piano with Gaston Déthier at the Inst. of Musical Art in N.Y. (1933–38). In the meantime, he played jazz piano in various groups in N.Y. From 1939 to 1941 he studied composition with Wagenaar at the Juilliard School of Music in N.Y. In 1941 he enrolled in the summer class of composition led by Hindemith at the Berkshire Music Center in Tanglewood. He continued to attend Hindemith's courses at Yale Univ. from 1941 to 1943. During this period, he wrote several works of considerable validity, among them a piano trio, a ballet entitled *The Duke of Sacramento*, a Magnificat, a Piano Sonata, and other pieces. In 1944 and 1945 he held Guggenheim fellowships. From 1945 to 1950 he taught at Sarah Lawrence Coll. All the while, he continued to compose music with utmost facility and ingratiating felicity. His *Concert Music* was premiered by the Pittsburgh Sym. Orch., conducted by Fritz Reiner, on Jan. 4, 1946, and his *Ricercari* for Piano and Orch. was introduced by the N.Y. Phil. on Dec. 19, 1946, with George Szell conducting, with the piano part played by Dello Joio himself. There followed a number of major works in a distinctive Joioan manner, some of them deeply rooted in medieval ecclesiasticism, profoundly liturgical, and yet overtly modern in their neo-modal moderately dissonant counterpoint. He also exhibited a flair for writing on topical American themes, ranging from impressions of the Cloisters in N.Y. to rhythmic modalities of Manhattan's Little Italy. On May 9, 1950, at Sarah Lawrence Coll., he produced his first opera, *The Triumph of Joan*; he later used its thematic material in a sym. in 3 movements, *The Triumph of St. Joan*, originally titled *Seraphic Dialogue*. He then wrote another opera on the subject of St. Joan, to his own libretto, *The Trial of Rouen*, first performed on television, by the NBC Opera Theater, April 8, 1956; still another version of the St. Joan theme was an opera in which Dello Joio used the original title, *The Triumph of St. Joan*, but composed the music anew; it had its

premiere at the N.Y.C. Opera on April 16, 1959. In 1957 Dello Joio received the Pulitzer Prize in Music for his *Meditations on Ecclesiastes*, scored for string orch.; it was first performed in Washington, D.C., on Dec. 17, 1957, but the material was used previously for a ballet, *There Is a Time*. His opera *Blood Moon* was premiered at the San Francisco Opera on Sept. 18, 1961, to a scenario dealing with the life and times of an adventurous actress, Adah Menken, who exercised her charms in New Orleans at the time of the Civil War. Returning to liturgical themes, Dello Joio composed three masses (1968, 1975, 1976). He continued his activities as a teacher; from 1956 to 1972 he was on the faculty of the Mannes Coll. of Music in N.Y.; from 1972 to 1979 he taught at Boston Univ. He held honorary doctorates in music from Lawrence Coll. in Wisc. (1959), Colby Coll. in Maine (1963), and the Univ. of Cincinnati (1969). He received the N.Y. Music Critics' Circle Award in 1947 and 1959. His music for the NBC-TV program *The Louvre* (1965) garnered him an Emmy Award.

WORKS: DRAMATIC: *Prairie*, ballet (1942; arranged from the Sinfonietta, 1941); *The Duke of Sacramento*, ballet (1942); *On Stage*, ballet (1945); *Diversion of Angels*, ballet (New London, Conn., Aug. 13, 1948; for Martha Graham); *The Triumph of Joan*, opera (1949; Bronxville, N.Y., May 9, 1950; withdrawn); *The Triumph of St. Joan Symphony*, ballet (Louisville, Dec. 5, 1951; based on the opera *The Triumph of St. Joan*; rechoreographed as *Seraphic Dialogue* [by Martha Graham], 1955); *The Ruby*, opera (1953; Bloomington, Ind., May 13, 1955); *The Tall Kentuckian*, incidental music to B. Anderson's play (Louisville, June 15, 1953); *The Trial at Rouen*, opera (1955; NBC- TV, April 8, 1956; rev. as *The Triumph of St. Joan*, N.Y., April 16, 1959); *There is a Time*, ballet (1956; arranged from *Meditations on Ecclesiastes* for Strings, 1956); *Air Power*, television music (1956–57; arranged as a symphonic suite, 1957); *Profile of a Composer*, television music (CBS-TV, Feb. 16, 1958; includes *Ballad of the 7 Lively Arts*); *Here Is New York*, television music (1959; includes excerpts from *New York Profiles*; arranged as an orch. suite); *The Saintmaker's Christmas Eve*, television music (1959); *Vanity Fair*, television music (1959); *Women's Song*, ballet (1960; arranged from the Harp Concerto, 1945); *Anthony and Cleopatra*, incidental music to Shakespeare's play (1960); *Blood Moon*, opera (San Francisco, Sept. 18, 1961); *Time of Decision*, television music (1962); *The Louvre*, television music (1965; arranged for Band, 1965); *A Time of Snow*, ballet (1968; arranged for Band as *Songs of Abelard*, 1969); *The Glass Heart*, ballet (1968; arranged from *Meditations on Ecclesiastes* for Strings, 1956); *Satiric Dances for a Comedy by Aristophanes* for Band (1974; Concord, Mass., July 17, 1975); *As of a Dream*, masque (1978). **ORCH.:** Piano Concertino (1938; withdrawn); Flute Concertino (1938; withdrawn); *Ballad for Strings* (1940; withdrawn); Concerto for 2 Pianos and Orch. (1941; withdrawn); Sinfonietta (1941; arranged as the ballet *Prairie*, 1942); Harmonica Concerto (1942; withdrawn); *Magnificat* (1942); *To a Lone Sentry* for Chamber Orch. (1943); *Concert Music* (1944; Pittsburgh, Jan. 4, 1946); *On Stage* (Cleveland, Nov. 23, 1945; arranged from the ballet); Harp Concerto (1945; N.Y., Oct. 20, 1947; arranged as the ballet *Women's Song*, 1960); *3 Ricercari* for Piano and Orch. (N.Y., Dec. 19, 1946); *Serenade* (1947–48; Cleveland, Oct. 20, 1949; arranged as the ballet *Diversion of Angels*, 1948); *Variations, Chaconne and Finale (3 Symphonic Dances)* (1947; Pittsburgh, Jan. 30, 1948); *Concertato for Clarinet and Orch.* (Chautauqua, May 22, 1949; arranged for Clarinet and Piano, 1949); *New York Profiles* (La Jolla, Calif., Aug. 21, 1949); *Epigraph* (1951; Danver, Jan. 29, 1952); *Meditations on*

Ecclesiastes for Strings (1956; Washington, D.C., Dec. 17, 1957; arranged as the ballets *There is a Time,* 1956, and *The Glass Heart,* 1968); *A Ballad of the 7 Lively Arts* for Piano and Orch. (1957); *Fantasy and Variations* for Piano and Orch. (1961; Cincinnati, March 9, 1962); *Variants on a Medieval Tune* for Band (Durham, N.C., May 8, 1963); *From Every Horizon* for Band (1964); *Antiphonal Fantasy on a Theme of Vincenzo Albrici* for Organ, Brass, and Strings (1965); *Air* for Strings (1967); *Fantasies on a Theme by Haydn* (1968; Little Rock, Ark., June 3, 1969); *Homage to Haydn* (1968–69); *Songs of Abelard* for Band (1969; arranged from the ballet *A Time of Snow,* 1968); *Choreography* for Strings (1972); *Concertante* for Band (1973); *Lyric Fantasies* for Viola and Strings (1973); *Colonial Ballads* for Band (1976); *Colonial Variants: 13 Profiles of the Original Colonies* (Philadelphia, May 27, 1976); *Arietta* for Strings (1978); *Caccia* for Band (1978); *Ballabili* (1981); *Air and Roulade* for Band (1984); *East Hampton Sketches* for Strings (1984); *Variants on a Bach Chorale* (1985); *Lyrical Movement* for Strings (1993); *Reflections on an Ancient Hymn* for Chamber Orch. (1996); *Divertimento* for Chamber Orch. (1997). **CHAMBER:** Piano Trio (1937; withdrawn); Quartet for 4 Bassoons (1937; withdrawn); Cello Sonata (1937; withdrawn); Violin Sonata (1937; withdrawn); *Colloquy* for Violin and Piano (1938; withdrawn); Violin Sonata (1938; withdrawn); Woodwind Quintet (1939; withdrawn); Woodwind Trio (1940; withdrawn); *Fantasia on a Gregorian Theme* for Violin and Piano (1942); Sextet for 3 Recorders and String Trio (1943); Trio for Flute, Cello, and Piano (1944); *Duo concertante* for Cello and Piano or 2 Pianos (1945); *Variations and Capriccio* for Violin and Piano (1948); *Concertante* for Clarinet and Piano (1949; arranged from the *Concertato* for Clarinet and Orch., 1949); *Colloquies* for Violin and Piano (1963); *Bagatelles* for Harp (1968); *The Developing Flutist* for Flute and Piano (1972); *3 Essays* for Clarinet and Piano (1974); 2 string quartets: No. 1 (1974) and No. 2, *Lyrical Interludes* (1997); Trumpet Sonata (1979); *Reflections on a Christmas Tune* for Woodwind Quintet (1981). **Piano:** 3 sonatas (1933, 1944, 1948); *Prelude to a Young Dancer* (1943); *Prelude to a Young Musician* (1943); 2 *Nocturnes* (1946); *Aria and Toccata* for 2 Pianos (1952); *Family Album* for Piano, 4-Hands (1962); *Night Song* (1963); *5 Images* for Piano, 4-Hands (1967); *Capriccio on the Interval of a Second* (1968); *Stage Parodies* for Piano, 4-Hands (1974); *Diversions* (1975); *Salute to Scarlatti* (1979; also for Harpsichord); *Concert Variations* (1980); *Song at Springtide* for Piano, 4-Hands (1984). **VOCAL:** *Chicago* for Chorus, after Sandburg (1939; withdrawn); *Vigil Strange* for Chorus and Piano, 4-Hands (1941); *The Mystic Trumpeter* for Chorus and Horn, after Whitman (1943); *A Jubilant Song* for Women's Voices and Piano, after Whitman (1945); *Symphony for Voices* for Chorus, after Benet (1945; rev. as *Song of Affirmation* for Soprano, Narrator, Chorus, and Orch., 1953); *A Fable* for Chorus and Piano, after Lindsay (1946); *Madrigal* for Chorus and Piano, after Rossetti (1947); *The Bluebird* for Chorus and Piano (1950); *A Psalm of David* for Chorus, Strings, Brass, and Percussion (1950); *Song of the Open Road* for Chorus, Trumpet, and Piano, after Whitman (1952); *The Lamentation of Saul* for Baritone and Orch. or Sextet, after D.H. Lawrence (1954); *O Sing Unto the Lord (Psalm 98)* for Men's Voices and Organ (1958); *To St. Cecilia* for Chorus and Piano or Brass, after Dryden (1958); *Prayers for Cardinal Newman* for Chorus and Organ (1960); *The Holy Infant's Lullaby* for Unison Voices and Organ (1961); (4) *Songs of Walt Whitman* for Chorus and Orch. (1966); *Proud Music of the Storm* for Chorus, Brass, and Organ, after Whitman (1967); *Years of the Modern* for Chorus, Brass, and Percussion, after Whitman (1968); *Mass* for Chorus, Brass, and Organ or Piano (1969); *Evocations: Visitation at Night* for Chorus, Optional Children's Voices, and Orch. or

Piano (1970); *Evocations: Promise of Spring* for Chorus, Optional Children's Voices, and Orch. or Piano (1970); *O Come to Me, My Love* for Chorus and Piano, after Rossetti (1972); *Psalm of Peace* for Chorus, Trumpet, Horn, and Organ or Piano (1972); *The Poet's Song* for Chorus and Piano, after Tennyson (1973); *Mass in Honor of the Eucharist* for Chorus, Cantor, Congregation, Brass, and Organ (1975); *Songs of Remembrance* for Baritone and Orch. (1977); *The Psalmist's Meditation* for Chorus and Organ or Piano (1979); *Hymns Without Words* for Chorus and Piano or Orch. (1980); *Love Songs at Parting* for Chorus and Piano (1981); *I Dreamed of an Invincible City* for Chorus and Piano or Organ (1984); *The Vigil* for Chorus, Brass, and Percussion (1985); *Nativity* for Soloists, Chorus, and Orch. (1987).

BIBL.: T. Bumgardner, *N. D. J.* (Boston, 1986). —NS/LK/DM

Dell'Orefice, Giuseppe,

Italian composer; b. Fara, Abruzzio Chietino, Aug. 22, 1848; d. Naples, Jan. 3, 1889. He was a pupil of Fenaroli and Miceli at the Naples Cons. From 1878 he was conductor at the San Carlo Theater in Naples. He wrote the ballet *I fantasmi notturni* (Naples, 1872), the operas *Romilda de' Bardi* (Naples, 1874), *Egmont* (Naples, 1878), *Il segreto della Duchesa* (Naples, 1879), and *L'oasi* (Vicenza, 1886), songs, and piano pieces.—NS/LK/DM

Dells, The,

one of the longest running groups in pop music, with only one personnel change in nearly 50 years together, and the inspiration for the movie *The Five Heartbeats,* formed 1952 in Harvey, Ill. **MEMBERSHIP:** Johnny Funches, voc.; Marvin Junior, voc.; Verne Allison, voc.; Mickey McGill, voc.; Chuck Barksdale, voc.

Those who agree with Oscar Wilde's notion that "American lives have no second act" should consider The Dells. With the exception of Johnny Funches, who left the band in 1960 and was replaced by former Flamingo Johnny Carter, the Dells lineup has remained unchanged since 1952. Even their style hasn't so much changed as evolved with the styles of African-American vocal music, segueing from doo-wop to vocal group soul with seamless elegance, eloquence, and extraordinary harmony. They have endured and recorded for most of that time, even scoring an R&B hit in 1991. Every time the band seemed like it was over, something came along to keep them going.

The El-Rays, as they called themselves in the beginning, started singing in high school mostly as a way to get into parties and meet girls. When they started to get good, they took a stroll down Chicago's musical Mecca, Michigan Ave. When Vee-Jay records didn't want them, they crossed the street and signed with Checker. Checker put out their first single, "Darling Dear, I Know" which netted them a whopping $56 dollars and sold dozens. But they met Harvey Fuqua of the Moonglows, who helped them sort out their harmonies. Vee-Jay took another look and signed them in 1955. They recorded their breakthrough record "Oh What a Night" a year later. That record sold millions of copies. Still, one member recalled that their first album showed a white band on the cover!

Over the next years, the Dells recorded and toured. They had several minor hits, including a 1965 Vee-Jay release of "Stay in My Corner" that hit #23 on the R&B charts. However, it took the group until 1968 to score another major hit. By then, they had returned to Chess subsidiary Cadet. They recorded the *There Is* album. The title track went to #20. A re-recorded version of "Stay in My Corner" hit #10, pop and topped the R&B charts. Through 1973, they scored another half-dozen pop hits, including "Always Together" (#18, 1968), "Does Anyone Know I'm Here" (#38, 1969) and "I Can Sing a Rainbow/Love Is Blue" (#22, 1969). A new, extended version of "Oh What a Night" topped the R&B charts in 1969, rising to #10 on the pop charts. They followed this with the 1971 #30 hit "The Love We Had (Stays on My Mind)" and the 1973 gold record "Give Your Baby a Standing Ovation," which topped out at #34 pop.

Despite all their years together, the Dells rarely traded on nostalgia, recording low level R&B hits through the 1980s for Epic and other labels, and spending much of their year on the road. In 1990, Robert Townsend hired the band as "technical consultants" for a comedy he was thinking of doing about a vocal group. His time with the Dells convinced him that a drama would be more appropriate, and the film became *The Five Heartbeats*. In addition to being very nearly a biopic, the soundtrack produced the group's #13 R&B hit "A Heart Is a House for Love." In the wake of this, they hooked up with the legendary production team of Gamble and Huff for the tune "Oh My Love" and signed to Zoo records.

While the hits stopped coming, the Dells keep going. Working on 50 years together, they continue to play out, indefatigable and still in fabulous voice.

DISC.: *It's Not Unusual* (1965); *Stay in My Corner* (1968); *Musical Menu* (1968); *There Is* (1968); *The Dells* (1969); *Love Is Blue* (1969); *Musical Menu/Always Together* (1969); *Like It Is, Like It Was* (1970); *Oh, What a Night* (1970); *Freedom Means* (1971); *Come Together* (soundtrack; 1971); *Sweet As Funk Can Be* (1972); *Give Your Baby a Standing Ovation* (1973); *The Mighty Mighty Dells* (1974); *The Dells Vs. Dramatics* (1974); *We Got Together* (1975); *No Way Back* (1975); *Love Connection* (1977); *They Said It Couldn't Be Done But We Did It* (1977); *New Beginnings* (1978); *Face to Face* (1979); *I Touched a Dream* (1980); *Whatever Turns You On* (1981). —HB

Delmar, Dezso, Hungarian-American composer; b. Timişoara, July 14, 1891; d. Contra Costa Co., Calif., Oct. 20, 1985. He studied piano with Bartók and theory with Kodály at the Royal Academy of Music in Budapest, graduating in 1913; concurrently took courses in jurisprudence, obtaining a law degree. He served in the Austro-Hungarian army in World War I; after demobilization, he devoted himself entirely to music. He went to the U.S. in 1922; lived in N.Y. until 1929, then moved to Los Angeles; in 1946 he settled in Sacramento as a teacher of piano and theory. His works include *Hungarian Sketches* for Orch. (1947), Sym. (1949), 3 string quartets, String Trio, Violin Sonata, choral music, many piano pieces, and songs. His works reflect the melorhythmic modalities of Hungarian folk music. —NS/LK/DM

Del Mar, Jonathan (Rene), English conductor and musicologist, son of **Norman (René) Del Mar;** b.

London, Jan. 7, 1951. He was awarded a music scholarship to Christ Church, Oxford, when he was 17, and took his M.A. there in 1972. In 1976 he received his diploma from the Royal Coll. of Music in London. He then attended Ferrara's conducting courses in Venice (1976–77) and at the Accademia di Santa Cecilia in Rome (1977), and also studied with Kondrashin in the Netherlands. In 1977 he was a finalist in the Karajan competition, and then won prizes in the Malko (1980) and Leeds (1984) competitions. In 1984 he made his debut with the London Sym. Orch., and subsequently appeared as a guest conductor with many of the leading British orchs. His interest in the major orch. works of Beethoven led him to pursue a diligent search of all relevant extant sources as well as evaluating every aspect of 19th century historical performance practice. In 1995 he prepared the Urtext Edition of Beethoven's *Emperor Concerto*, which was followed by the invaluable New Bärenreiter Urtext Edition of Beethoven's 9 syms. (Kassel, 1996–2000). In addition to his articles in journals, he publ. *Indicatore Anagrafico di Venezia* (1996) and ed. his father's *Conducting Berlioz* (1997), *Conducting Elgar* (1998), and *Conducting Favourite Concert Pieces* (1998).—LK/DM

Del Mar, Norman (René), English conductor, teacher, and writer on music, father of **Jonathan (Rene) Del Mar;** b. London, July 31, 1919; d. Bushey, Feb. 6, 1994. He studied composition with Morris and Vaughan Williams at the Royal Coll. of Music in London, and also had lessons in conducting with Lambert. In 1944 he founded the Chelsea Sym. Orch., with which he championed rarely performed works in England. He also played horn in and was asst. conductor of the Royal Phil. in London (1947–48). From 1949 to 1955 he was principal conductor of the English Opera Group, and from 1953 to 1960 conductor and prof. at the Guildhall School of Music and Drama in London. In 1954–55 he was conductor with the Yorkshire Sym. Orch. After serving as principal conductor of the BBC Scottish Sym. in Glasgow (1960–65), he was principal guest conductor of the Göteborg Sym. Orch. (1969–73). In 1972 he joined the faculty of the Royal Coll. of Music, where he taught conducting and conducted its First Orch. He also conducted the chamber orch. of the Royal Academy of Music in London (1973–77) and was principal conductor of the Academy of the BBC (1974–77), a training ensemble. After serving as principal guest conductor of the Bournemouth Sinfonietta (1982–85), he was artistic director of the Århus Sym. Orch. (1985–88). In 1990 he retired from the faculty of the Royal Coll. of Music. In 1975 he was made a Commander of the Order of the British Empire.

WRITINGS: *Paul Hindemith* (London, 1957); *Modern Music and the Conductor* (London, 1960); *Richard Strauss: A Critical Commentary of His Life and Works* (3 vols., London, 1962, 1968, 1972); *Mahler's Sixth Symphony: A Study* (London, 1980); *Anatomy of the Orchestra* (London, 1981); *A Companion to the Orchestra* (London, 1987); *Conducting Beethoven: Volume I: The Symphonies* (Oxford, 1992) and *Volume 2: Overtures, Concertos, Missa Solemnis* (Oxford, 1993); *Conducting Brahms* (Oxford,

1993); J. Del Mar, ed., *Conducting Berlioz* (Oxford, 1997); J. Del Mar, ed., *Conducting Elgar* (Oxford, 1998); J. Del Mar, ed., *Conducting Favourite Concert Pieces* (Oxford, 1998). —NS/LK/DM

Delmas, Jean-François, famous French bass-baritone; b. Lyons, April 14, 1861; d. St. Alban de Monthel, Sept. 29, 1933. He was a pupil of Bussine and Obin at the Paris Cons., where he won the premier prix for singing in 1886. He made his operatic debut at the Paris Opéra in 1886 as St.-Bris in *Les Huguenots.* He was a regular member there until his retirement in 1927, idolized by the public, and unexcelled as an interpreter of Wagner, in whose works he created the principal bass parts in several French premieres. He created also the chief roles in Massenet's *Le Mage* (1891) and *Thaïs* (1894), Leroux's *Astarté* (1901), Saint-Saëns's *Les Barbares* (1901), and Erlanger's *Le Fils de l'étoile* (1904). In addition to his enormous French repertoire, Delmas also sang in the operas of Gluck, Mozart, and Weber.—NS/LK/DM

Delmas, Marc-Jean-Baptiste, talented French composer; b. St. Quentin, March 28, 1885; d. Paris, Nov. 30, 1931. He was a pupil of Vidal and Leroux, winning the Prix de Rossini (1911), the Grand Prix de Rome (1919), the Chartier Prix for chamber music, the Prix Cressent, and other awards for various compositions. He wrote the books *Georges Bizet* (Paris, 1930), *Gustave Charpentier et le lyrisme française* (Coulommiers, 1931), and *Massenet, sa vie, ses oeuvres* (Paris, 1932).

WORKS: DRAMATIC: O p e r a : *Jean de Calais* (1907); *Laïs* (1909); *Stéfano* (1910); *Cyrca* (1920); *Iriam* (1921); *Anne-Marie* (1922); *Le Giaour* (1925). ORCH.: *Les Deux Routes* (1913); *Au pays wallon* (1914); *Le Poète et la fée* (1920); *Le Bateau ivre* (1923); *Penthésilée* (1922); *Rapsodie ariegéoise* for Cello and Orch. OTHER: Chamber music; piano pieces.—NS/LK/DM

Del Monaco, Giancarlo, Italian opera producer and administrator, son of **Mario Del Monaco;** b. Venice, Dec. 27, 1943. He received training in languages and music in Lausanne. In 1964 he staged his first opera, *Samson et Dalila,* in Siracusa, and then was an assistant to Günter Rennert, Wieland Wagner, and Walter Felsenstein (1965–68). After serving as personal assistant to the general director of the Vienna State Opera (1968–70), he was principal stage director in Ulm (1970–73). From 1980 to 1982 he was Intendant of the Kassel State Theater, and then was director of the Macerata Festival from 1986 to 1988. In 1989 he staged *La forza del destino* at the Vienna State Opera, *La Fille du régiment* in Zürich, and *Samson et Dalila* in Barcelona. His production of *Les Huguenots* opened the new opera house in Montpellier in 1990. In 1991 he staged *La fanciulla del West* at the Metropolitan Opera in N.Y. From 1992 to 1997 he was Intendant of the Bonn Opera, where his productions included *Cavalleria rusticana* and *Pagliacci* (1993), *Les Contes d'Hoffmann* (1994), and *Manon Lescaut* (1995). In 1997 he staged *Aida* in Cologne. He became general director of the Nice Opera in 1997.—NS/LK/DM

Del Monaco, Mario, renowned Italian tenor, father of **Giancarlo Del Monaco;** b. Florence, July 27, 1915; d. Mestre, near Venice, Oct. 16, 1982. His father was a government functionary, but his mother loved music and sang. Del Monaco haunted provincial opera theaters, determined to be a singer; indeed, he sang a minor part in a theater in Mondolfo, near Pesaro, when he was only 13. Rather than take formal voice lessons, he listened to operatic recordings; at 19 he entered the Rossini Cons. in Pesaro, but left it after an unhappy semester of academic vocal training with unimaginative teachers. In 1935 he won a prize in a singing contest in Rome. In 1939 he made his operatic debut as Turriddu in Pesaro. On Jan. 1, 1941, he made his Milan debut as Pinkerton, but had to serve time in the Italian army during World War II. After the War's end, he developed a busy career singing opera in a number of Italian theaters, including La Scala of Milan. In 1946 he sang at the Teatro Colón in Buenos Aires, and also in Rio de Janeiro, Mexico City, and at London's Covent Garden. On Sept. 26, 1950, he sang the role of Radames at the San Francisco Opera in his first appearance in the U.S.; on Nov. 27, 1950, he made his Metropolitan Opera debut in N.Y. as Des Grieux in *Manon Lescaut;* he continued to sing at the Metropolitan until 1958 in virtually every famous tenor part, including Don José, Manrico, Cavaradossi, Canio, Andrea Chénier, Otello, etc. In 1973 he deemed it prudent to retire, and he spent the rest of his life in a villa near Venice, devoting his leisure to his favorite avocations, sculpture and painting. Del Monaco was buried in his Otello costume, while the funeral hymns were intoned in his own voice on a phonograph record.—NS/LK/DM

Delmotte, Roger, French trumpeter; b. Roubaix, Sept. 20, 1925. He studied with M. Leclercq at the Roubaix Cons., and then with E. Foveau at the Paris Cons., where he won the premier prix for trumpet. After winning first prize in the Geneva competition in 1950, he became first trumpeter in the Opéra orch. and the Concerts Lamoureux in Paris in 1951. He soon established himself as a soloist with orchs. and as a recitalist; also was active as a teacher. While he won particular distinction for his performances of the Baroque repertory, Delmotte did much to further the cause of the contemporary trumpet literature through commissions and first performances.—NS/LK/DM

Delna (real name, **Ledan**), **Marie,** French contralto; b. Meudon, near Paris, April 3, 1875; d. Paris, July 23, 1932. She was a pupil of Laborde and Savary in Paris, where she made her debut at the Opéra-Comique on June 9, 1892, as Dido in Berlioz's *Les Troyens;* sang there for 6 years with great success; she also appeared at London's Covent Garden in 1894. She sang at the Paris Opéra (1898–1901) and at Milan's Teatro Lirico (1898–1901); then again at the Opéra-Comique. In 1903 she married a Belgian, A.H. de Saone, and retired temporarily from the stage; her reappearance at the Opéra-Comique in 1908 was greatly acclaimed and after that she was a prime favorite. On March 5, 1910, she sang Gluck's *Orfeo* at her Metropolitan Opera debut in N.Y. and later Marcelline in Bruneau's *L'Attaque du* *moulin* at the New Theater, making a deep impression. She then returned to Paris, where she continued to sing at the Opéra-Comique until her retirement in 1922. —NS/LK/DM

Delogu, Gaetano, Italian conductor; b. Messina, April 14, 1934. He studied violin as a child, then music and law (degree 1958) at the Univ. of Catania. He also studied conducting with Ferrara in Rome and Venice. After winning first prize in the Florence (1964) and Mitropoulos (1968) competitions, he appeared as a guest conductor in Europe and the U.S. He was music director of the Teatro Massimo in Palermo (1975–78) and the Denver Sym. Orch. (1979–86).—NS/LK/DM

De Los Angeles, Victoria
See **Los Angeles (real name, Gómez Cima), Victoria de**

Delsart, Jules, French cellist, bass viol player, and pedagogue; b. Valenciennes, 1844; d. Paris, July 3, 1900. He studied cello at the Valenciennes Cons. and with Franchomme at the Paris Cons., where he graduated with the premier prix in 1866. He subsequently made successful tours of Europe as a cellist. He also mastered the bass viol and played in the Société des Instruments Anciens. In 1884 he became a prof. at the Paris Cons. —LK/DM

Del Tredici, David (Walter), outstanding American composer and teacher; b. Cloverdale, Calif., March 16, 1937. He studied piano with Bernhard Abramowitsch (1954–60); also composition with Shifrin and Elston at the Univ. of Calif. at Berkeley (B.A., 1959). In the summer of 1958, he pursued training in piano at the Aspen (Colo.) Music School, where he also attended Milhaud's composition seminar. He continued his studies in composition with Kim and Sessions at Princeton Univ. (M.F.A., 1963) and had private lessons with Helps in N.Y. In 1964 he completed his graduate studies at Princeton Univ., and also attended the Berkshire Music Center in Tanglewood that summer, returning there in 1965. In 1966–67 he held a Guggenheim fellowship, and during those summers he was composer-in-residence at the Marlboro (Vt.) Festival. From 1968 to 1972 he taught at Harvard Univ. In 1973 he taught at the S.U.N.Y. at Buffalo, and later that year became a teacher at Boston Univ. In the summer of 1975 he also was composer-in-residence at Aspen. In 1984 he became a teacher at City Coll. of the City Univ. of N.Y. He also was composer-in-residence at the American Academy in Rome in 1985, and from 1988 to 1990 he held that title with the N.Y. Phil. In 1991 he was made a prof. at the Manhattan School of Music in N.Y. In 1992 he was the featured composer at the Pacific Music Festival in Sapporo, Japan. Del Tredici has received various awards, commissions, and honors. In 1968 he received an award from the American Inst. of Arts and Letters. In 1973 and 1974 he held NEA grants. In 1980 he was awarded the Pulitzer Prize in Music for his *In Memory of a Summer Day* for Amplified Soprano and Orch. His *Happy Voices*

for Orch. won a Friedheim Award in 1982. In 1984 he was elected a member of the American Academy and Inst. of Arts and Letters. Among Del Tredici's first scores to attract notice were those inspired by James Joyce, including *I Hear an Army* for Soprano and String Quartet (Tanglewood, Aug. 12, 1964), which immediately caught the fancy of the cloistered but influential cognoscenti, literati, and illuminati, and *Night Conjure-Verse* for Soprano, Mezzo-soprano, and Chamber Ensemble, which Del Tredici conducted in its San Francisco premiere on March 2, 1966. In these and other Joyce-inspired works, he plied a modified dodecaphonic course in a poly-rhythmic context, gravid with meaningful pauses without fear of triadic encounters. However, Del Tredici achieved his greatest fame with a series of brilliant tone pictures after Lewis Carroll's *Alice in Wonderland*, in which he projected, in utter defiance of all modernistic conventions, overt tonal proclamations, fanfares, and pretty tunes that were almost embarrassingly attractive, becoming more melodious and harmonious with each consequent tone portrait. His *Final Alice* for Amplified Soprano, Folk Group, and Orch. (Chicago, Oct. 7, 1976) secured his international reputation as a composer of truly imaginative gifts, whose embrace of tonality is evinced in scores replete with brilliant harmonies and resplendent colors.

WORKS: *Soliloquy* for Piano (Aspen, Colo., Aug. 1958); *4 Songs on Poems of James Joyce* for Voice and Piano (1958–60; Berkeley, March 1, 1961); *2 Songs on Poems of James Joyce* for Voice and Piano (1959; rev. 1978; Washington, D.C., Feb. 11, 1983); String Trio for Violin, Viola, and Cello (Berkeley, May 21, 1959); *Fantasy Pieces* for Piano (1959–60); *Scherzo* for Piano, 4-Hands (1960); String Quartet (1961–63; unfinished); *I Hear an Army* for Soprano and String Quartet (Tanglewood, Aug. 12, 1964); *Night Conjure-Verse* for Soprano, Mezzo- soprano or Countertenor, and Chamber Ensemble, after Joyce (1965; San Francisco, March 2, 1966); *Syzygy* for Soprano, Horn, and Orch., after Joyce (1966; N.Y., July 6, 1968); *The Last Gospel* for Woman's Voice, Rock Group, Chorus, and Orch. (1967; San Francisco, June 15, 1968; rev. version, Milwaukee, Oct. 3, 1984); *Pop-Pourri* for Amplified Soprano, Rock Group, Chorus, and Orch., after Carroll (La Jolla, Calif., July 28, 1968; rev. 1973); *An Alice Symphony* for Amplified Soprano, Folk Group, and Orch., after Carroll (1969; rev. 1976; movements 1 and 4, *Illustrated Alice*, for Amplified Soprano and Orch., San Francisco, Aug. 8, 1976; movements 2 and 3, *In Wonderland*, for Amplified Soprano, Folk Group, and Orch., Aspen, July 29, 1975; 1st complete perf., Tanglewood, Aug. 7, 1991); *Adventures Underground* for Amplified Soprano, Folk Group, and Orch., after Carroll and Isaac Watts (1971; Buffalo, N.Y., April 13, 1975; rev. 1977); *Vintage Alice: Fantascene on A Mad Tea Party* for Amplified Soprano, Folk Group, and Orch., after Carroll, Jane Taylor, and *God Save the Queen* (Saratoga, Calif., Aug. 5, 1972); *Final Alice* for Amplified Soprano, Folk Group, and Orch., after Carroll, William Mee, and an unknown author (1974–75; Chicago, Oct. 7, 1976); *Child Alice* for Amplified Soprano(s) and Orch., after Carroll (1977–81; part 1, *In Memory of a Summer Day*, St. Louis, Feb. 23, 1980; part 2, *Quaint Events*, Buffalo, Nov. 19, 1981, *Happy Voices*, San Francisco, Sept. 16, 1980, and *All in the Golden Afternoon*, Philadelphia, May 8, 1981; 1st complete perf., N.Y., April 27, 1986); *Acrostic Song* from *Final Alice* for High Voice and Piano (Lenox, Mass., Aug. 21, 1982; also for Medium Voice and Piano, 1982; Chorus and Piano, N.Y., Nov. 19, 1983; Flute and Piano,

N.Y., Feb. 12, 1985; Chorus and Piano or Harp, N.Y., May 16, 1986; Soprano and 10 Instruments, N.Y., Dec. 15, 1987; etc.); *Acrostic Paraphrase* for Harp, after the *Acrostic Song* from *Final Alice* (Tempe, Ariz., June 22, 1983); *Virtuoso Alice*, grand fantasy on a theme from *Final Alice* for Piano (1984; N.Y., Nov. 10, 1987); *March to Tonality* for Orch. (Chicago, June 13, 1985; *Haddock's Eyes* for Amplified Soprano and 10 Instruments, after Carroll and Thomas Moore (1985; N.Y., May 2, 1986); *Tattoo* for Orch. (1986; Amsterdam, Jan. 30, 1987); *Steps* for Orch. (N.Y., March 8, 1990); *Brass Symphony* for Brass Quintet (1992); *Dum Dee Tweedle* for Voices and Orch., after Carroll (1993).—**NS/LK/DM**

De Luca, Giuseppe, notable Italian baritone; b. Rome, Dec. 25, 1876; d. N.Y., Aug. 26, 1950. He studied with Vinceslao Persichini at the Accademia di Santa Cecilia in Rome. He made his first professional appearance in Piacenza (Nov. 6, 1897) as Valentine in *Faust*; then sang in various cities of Italy; from 1902, was chiefly in Milan at the Teatro Lirico, and from 1903 at La Scala; he created the principal baritone role in the premieres of *Adriana Lecouvreur* at the Teatro Lirico (Nov. 6, 1902) and *Madama Butterfly* at La Scala (Feb. 17, 1904). He made his Metropolitan Opera debut in N.Y. as Figaro in *Il Barbiere di Siviglia* on Nov. 25, 1915, with excellent success, immediately establishing himself as a favorite; on Jan. 28, 1916, he sang the part of Paquiro in the premiere of *Goyescas* by Granados, at the Metropolitan, of which he was a member until 1935. After a sojourn in Italy, he returned to the U.S. in 1940, and made a few more appearances at the Metropolitan, his vocal powers undiminished by age; he made his farewell appearance in a concert in N.Y. in 1947. He sang almost exclusively the Italian repertoire; his interpretations were distinguished by fidelity to the dramatic import of his roles and he was praised by critics for his finely graduated dynamic range and his mastery of *bel canto*.—**NS/LK/DM**

De Lucia, Fernando, famous Italian tenor; b. Naples, Oct. 11, 1860; d. there, Feb. 21, 1925. He made his debut in Naples on March 9, 1885, as Faust, then appeared in London at Drury Lane (1887). On Oct. 31, 1891, in Rome he created the role of Fritz in Mascagni's *L'Amico Fritz*; on Jan. 10, 1894, he made his American debut at the Metropolitan Opera in N.Y., again as Fritz in Mascagni's opera; then returned to Europe. He retired from the stage in 1917, singing for the last time in public at Caruso's funeral (1921). De Lucia was one of the finest representatives of the *bel canto* era, being especially praised for his authentic interpretations of Italian operatic roles, excelling in operas by Rossini, Bellini, and Verdi.—**NS/LK/DM**

Delune, Louis, Belgian composer; b. Charleroi, March 15, 1876; d. Paris, Jan. 5, 1940. He studied with Tinel at the Brussels Cons., and won the Belgian Prix de Rome with his cantata *La Mort du roi Reynaud* (1905); then traveled as accompanist for César Thomson. He lived for many years in Paris, and wrote most of his works there, including *Symphonie chevaleresque*, the opera *Tania*, a ballet, *Le Fruit défendu*, Piano Concerto, and violin pieces.—**NS/LK/DM**

Delvaux, Albert, Belgian composer; b. Louvain, May 31, 1913. He studied at the Louvain Cons. and then completed his training with Joseph Leroy at the Liège Cons. He won a third prize (1957, for *Esquisses*) and a first prize (1961, for *Sinfonia burlesca*) in the Queen Elisabeth International Composition Competition in Brussels.

WORKS: ORCH.: *5 Pieces* for Strings (1942); *Scherzo* (1942); Symphonic Poem (1943); Symphonic Suite (1948); Symphonic Variations (1948); *Sinfonietta* (1952); Concerto for Cello and Chamber Orch. (1957); *Concerto da camera* for Chamber Orch. (1957); *Sinfonia burlesca* (1960); *5 Bagatelles* for Chamber Orch. (1960); *Miniatures* (1960); 2 violin concertos (1961, 1974); *Sinfonia concertante* for Violin, Viola, and Strings (1963); *Mouvement symphonique* (1966); Concerto for Flute, Oboe, Clarinet, Bassoon, and Chamber Orch. (1967); *Sinfonia* (1969); Concerto for Violin, Cello, and Strings (1970); *Introduction et Allegro* for Strings (1971); *Divertimento* for Strings (1981); Concerto for Viola and Chamber Orch. (1984); *Sinfonia in Sol* (1986); *Capriccio* (1988). **CHAMBER:** 2 string trios (1939, 1961); Sonata for Flute, Oboe, Clarinet, and Bassoon (1940); 4 string quartets (1943, 1945, 1955, 1961); Trio for Oboe, Clarinet, and Bassoon (1948); *5 Impromptus* for Flute, Oboe, Clarinet, and Piano (1959); Violin Sonata (1962); *Sonata a 4* for 4 Clarinets or Flute, Oboe, Clarinet, and Bassoon (1964); *Walliser Suite* for Wind Quintet (1966); *Cassazione* for Violin, Oboe, Clarinet, and Cello (1966); *Andante e Scherzando* for Violin and Piano (1972); Cello Sonatine (1978); Sonatine for Guitar and Flute (1981); Saxophone Quartet (1982); *Adagio-Scherzo* for Violin, Flute, Viola, Cello, and Harp (1982); Duo for Flute and Harp (1985); Duo for Clarinets (1987). **VOCAL:** *Hero et Léandre* for Soloists, Chorus, and Orch. (1941); choruses; songs.—**NS/LK/DM**

Del Vikings, The, one of the first integrated groups of the rock era to make it big on the charts, formed 1956, in Pittsburgh, Pa. **MEMBERSHIP:** Clarence Quick, voc. (b. Brooklyn, N.Y., d. c. 1985); Dave Lerchey, voc. (b. New Albany, Ind.); Norman Wright, voc. (b. Philadelphia, Oct. 21, 1937); Don Jackson, voc.; Corinthian "Kripp" Johnson, voc. (b. Cambridge, Mass., c. 1933; d. June 22, 1990).

Formed at the Pittsburgh Air Force Base among enlisted men who liked to sing, the Del Vikings (named after a basketball team from Clarence Quick's area of Brooklyn) had a fairly fluid lineup during their early years as airmen were transferred from one base to another. The addition of baritone David Lerchey had less to do with integration and more to do with available talent; he was the best singer for the job at the time.

The group performed at local talent shows and came to the attention of local DJ Barry Kaye. He recorded a demo of them singing nine songs a cappella, including a Quick composition called "Come and Go with Me." When the majors passed on the group, a small local label picked them up and put them into the studio. There, they cut a version of "Come and Go with Me" with a band. When the single took off, the small label leased it to Dot Records. The Dot release came out in 1957 and went to #4 in the charts, selling gold. They followed that with another Quick composition, "Whispering Bells, " which climbed to #9.

With two hits, the group's manager saw an opportunity to make lots of money and soon there was a "Del

Vikings" and a "Dell Vikings," one signed to the local label, the other to major label Mercury. The Mercury Vikings were still in the Air Force and could not tour. The local label Vikings were discharged and could tour as they pleased. The Mercury Vikings released "Cool Shake" at the same time as "Whispering Bells" was climbing the charts. It reached #12.

A third group of original members using a Viking variation formed, appearing in the movie *The Big Beat.* Eventually, the Mercury version won the rights to the name. Within two years, Kripp Johnson was back with the Mercury Vikings, and the original lineup once again intact. Unfortunately, their day in the pop sun had passed. They continued to make quality music, but no one really cared. Variations of the group, however, continue to tour the oldies circuit.

DISC.: *Come Go with the Del-Vikings* (1957); *They Sing—They Swing* (1957); *A Swinging, Singing Record Session* (1958); *And the Sonnets* (1963); *The Dell Vikings and the Sonnets* (1963); *Come Go with Us* (1960); *Cool Shake Buffalo Bop* (1988).—HB

Delvincourt, Claude, outstanding French composer and music educator; b. Paris, Jan. 12, 1888; d. in an automobile accident in Orbetello, Italy, April 5, 1954. He studied with Boellmann, Büsser, Caussade, and Widor at the Paris Cons.; in 1913 he received the Prix de Rome for his cantata *Faust et Hélène* (sharing the prize with Lili Boulanger). He was in the French army during World War I, and on Dec. 31, 1915, suffered a crippling wound. He recovered in a few years, and devoted himself energetically to musical education and composition. In 1931 he became director of the Versailles Cons.; in 1941 he was appointed director of the Paris Cons. His music was distinguished by strong dramatic and lyric qualities; he was most successful in his stage works.

WORKS: *Offrande à Siva,* choreographic poem (Frankfurt am Main, July 3, 1927); *La Femme à barbe,* musical farce (Versailles, June 2, 1938); *Lucifer,* mystery play (Paris, Dec. 8, 1948); 2 orch. suites from the film score *La Croisière jaune: Pamir* (Paris, Dec. 8, 1935) and *Films d'Asie* (Paris, Jan. 16, 1937); *Ce monde de rosée* for Voice and Orch. (Paris, March 25, 1935); chamber music; piano pieces.

BIBL.: W. Landowski, *L'Oeuvre de C. D.* (Paris, 1947).—NS/LK/DM

Delz, Christoph, Swiss-born German composer and pianist; b. Basel, Jan. 3, 1950; d. there, Sept. 13, 1993. He began studies in performance and counterpoint early, completing a concert pianist diploma before finishing school. He then studied with Stockhausen (composition), Aloys Kontarsky (piano), and Wangenheim (conducting) at the Cologne Hochschule für Musik (1974–81). His compositions involved musical collage, theatrical gestures, eclectically combined styles, and revolutionary agendas, and were performed at ISCM World Music Days in Cologne, Paris, Donaueschingen, Venice, and London. In 1983 he received the Music Prize of the City of Cologne.

WORKS: Piano Quartet (1975–76; Bonn, Nov. 25, 1977); *Kölner Messe* for Tape and Chorus (1977–81; Cologne, Nov. 4, 1983); *Im Dschungel, Ehrung für Rousseau den Zöllner* for Large Orch. (1981–82; Donaueschingen, Oct. 16, 1983); String Quartet (1982; Witten, April 28, 1985); *Arbeitslieder* for Soli, Chorus, Piano, and Wind Quintet (1983–84; Venice, Nov. 23, 1985); Piano Concerto (1984–85; London, Feb. 22, 1986); *Solde, Lecture d'après Lautréamont* for Soli, Chorus, and Percussion (1985–86); 2 Nocturnes for Piano and Orch. (1986); *Jahreszeiten* for Piano, Small Orch., and Tape (1988–89); *Joyce-Fantasy* for Soprano, Chorus, 2 Pianos, and Harmonium (1990).—NS/LK/DM

De Main, John (Lee), American conductor; b. Youngstown, Ohio, Jan. 11, 1944. He studied with Adele Marcus (piano; B.A., 1966) and Jorge Mester (conducting; M.S., 1968) at the Juilliard School of Music in N.Y. He was an asst. conductor at the WNET opera project in N.Y. and in 1972 at the N.Y.C. Opera. After serving as assoc. conductor of the St. Paul (Minn.) Chamber Orch. (1972–74), he became music director of the Tex. Opera Theater in 1975, the touring company of the Houston Grand Opera. In 1978 he was appointed principal conductor of the Houston Grand Opera, serving as its music director from 1980 to 1994; he also was principal conductor of the Chatauqua (N.Y.) Opera (1982–87) and music director of Opera Omaha (1983–91). He was music director of the Madison (Wisc.) Sym. Orch. and artistic director of the Madison (Wisc.) Opera from 1994. From 1997 he also was music director of Opera Pacific in Costa Mesa, Calif. In addition to conducting rarely heard works, De Main gave many premiere performances of contemporary operas.—NS/LK/DM

Demantius, (Johannes) Christoph, German composer; b. Reichenberg, Dec. 15, 1567; d. Freiberg, Saxony, April 20, 1643. He became cantor at Zittau in 1597, and was at Freiberg from 1604 to 1643. A prolific composer of sacred and secular music, he ranks with Hassler, M. and H. Prätorius, and Eccard. He wrote *Deutsche Passion, nach dem Evangelisten S. Iohanne* (1631; ed. and publ. by F. Blume, 1934), *Triades precum vespertinarum* (1602), etc. He was the author of an instruction book, *Isagoge artis musicae* (Nuremberg, 1605; 10th ed., 1671).—NS/LK/DM

DeMarinis, Paul, American composer; b. Cleveland, Oct. 6, 1948. He was educated at Antioch (Ohio) Coll. (B.A., 1971) and Mills Coll. in Oakland, Calif., where he studied with Robert Ashley (M.F.A., 1973) and subsequently taught composition and computer art (1973–78). He also taught at Wesleyan Univ. (1979–81) and San Francisco State Univ. (1987–89), and was a sound designer for Atari video games (1982–84). As a performer, he has appeared solo and in collaboration with such artists as Ashley and David Tudor. He is best known for his performance works, computer/sound installations, and interactive electronic inventions. His computer audio-graphics systems have been installed at the Museum of Contemporary Art in Chicago and at the Wadsworth Athenaeum; he has also created permanent audio installations at the Exploratorium in San Francisco and at the Boston Children's Museum. Much of his later work, such as *Kokole* (1985) and *I Want You* (1986), involves computer-processed speech. Among his installations are *Pygmy Gamelan* (Paris, N.Y., Los Angeles, 1976–80), *Music Room/Faultless Jamming* (San Francisco, Boston, 1982), and *Laser Disk* (Eindhoven, Netherlands, 1989).—**NS/LK/DM**

Demarquez, Suzanne, French composer and writer on music; b. Paris, July 5, 1899; d. there, Oct. 23, 1965. She studied at the Paris Cons. She composed chamber music, including a sprightly Flute Sonatine (1953). She publ. *André Jolivet* (Paris, 1958), *Manuel de Falla* (Paris, 1963; Eng. tr., 1968), and *Hector Berlioz* (Paris, 1969).—**NS/LK/DM**

Demény, Desiderius, Hungarian composer; b. Budapest, Jan. 29, 1871; d. there, Nov. 9, 1937. He was a pupil of V. Herzfeld and S. von Bacho; was ordained as a priest at Gran in 1893; became court chaplain (1897). On three different occasions he won the Géza Zichy Prize (with *Ungarische Tanzsuite, Festouvertüre,* and *Rhapsodie*). In 1902 he founded *Zeneközlöny,* an important Hungarian music journal. Among his compositions were 8 masses, *Hungarian Suite* for Chorus, *Scherzo* for Men's Chorus, *2 Bilder aus Algier, Serenata sinfonica, Der sieghafte Tod,* operetta, several melodramas, and many other choral and vocal works, including about 100 songs (most to German texts).—**NS/LK/DM**

Demessieux, Jeanne, distinguished French organist and pedagogue; b. Montpellier, Feb. 14, 1921; d. Paris, Nov. 11, 1968. At the age of 12, she played organ at the church of St.-Esprit. She studied at the Paris Cons. with Tagliaferro, J. and N. Gallon, and Dupré, winning premiers prix in harmony (1937), piano (1938), and fugue and counterpoint (1940). She gave her first public recital in Paris in 1946, then toured widely in Europe and made her first highly successful visit to the U.S. in 1953. In 1952 she became a prof. at the Liège Cons. She also served as organist at the Madeleine in Paris from 1962. She possessed a phenomenal technique and was regarded as one of the most brilliant improvisers on the organ.—**NS/LK/DM**

Demidenko, Nikolai, Russian pianist; b. Aniskino, July 1, 1955. He was a pupil of Bashkirov at the Moscow Cons. After winning second prize at the Montreal competition in 1976 and third prize at the Tchaikovsky competition in Moscow in 1978, he toured throughout his homeland as a soloist with orchs. and as a recitalist. In 1985 he made his British debut as soloist on tour with the Moscow Radio Sym. Orch.; subsequently returned to appear as soloist with the principal British orchs. In 1990 he settled in England and became a teacher at the Yehudi Menuhin School. In 1992 he made his first appearance at the London Promenade Concerts as soloist in Rachmaninoff's fourth Piano Concerto. In 1993 he won critical acclaim for a series of 6 recitals at London's Wigmore Hall in which he surveyed the piano repertoire from the standard literature to contemporary works with virtuosic aplomb and interpretative insight.—**NS/LK/DM**

Demougeot, (Jeanne Marguerite) Marcelle (Decorne), remarkable French soprano; b. Dijon, June 18, 1871; d. Paris, Nov. 24, 1931. She studied

in Dijon and Paris. She made her operatic debut at the Paris Opéra in 1902 as Donna Elvira; continued to sing there until 1925. She was one of the foremost French Wagnerian sopranos of her time, noted for her fine renditions as Brünnhilde, Elisabeth, Kundry, and Venus. —**NS/LK/DM**

Dempster, Stuart (Ross), American trombonist and composer; b. Berkeley, Calif., July 7, 1936. He studied at San Francisco State Coll. (B.A. in perf., 1958; M.A. in composition, 1967) and also had private trombone instruction from A.B. Moore, Orlando Giosi, and John Klock. He taught at the San Francisco Cons. of Music (1961–66) and at Calif. State Coll. at Hayward (1963–66); in 1968 he joined the faculty of the Univ. of Wash. in Seattle. From 1962 he made tours as a trombone virtuoso. He received a Fulbright-Hays Award as a senior scholar in Australia (1973) and a Guggenheim fellowship (1981). He has made a special study of trombone music, both past and present, and has commissioned and premiered many works for his instrument. His interests also include non-Western instruments, especially the Australian didjeridu. He publ. the study *The Modern Trombone: A Definition of Its Idioms* (Berkeley, Calif., 1979).

WORKS: 5 pieces for Brass Quintet (1957–59); Bass Trombone Sonata (1961); *Adagio and Canonic Variations* for Brass Quintet (1962); *Chamber Music 12* for Voice and Trombones (1964); *The Road Not Taken* for Voice, Chorus, and Orch. (1967); *10 Grand Hosery,* mixed media ballet (1971–72); *Life Begins at 40,* concert series and musical gallery show (1976); *Didjeridervish* for Didjeridu (1976); *Hornfinder* for Trombone and Audience (1982); *Aix en Providence* for Multiple Trombones (1983); *JDBBBDJ* for Didjeridu and Audience (1983); *Sound Massage Parlor* for Didjeridu, Garden Hoses, Shell, and Audience (1986); *SWAMI* (State of Washington as a Musical Instrument), performance piece for the state of Washington centennial (1987–89). —**NS/LK/DM**

Demus, Jörg (Wolfgang), noted Austrian pianist; b. St. Polten, Dec. 2, 1928. At the age of 11, he entered the Vienna Academy of Music. He also took lessons in conducting with Swarowsky and Josef Krips and in composition with Joseph Marx, and continued his piano studies with Gieseking at the Saarbrücken Cons. He then worked with Kempff, Michelangeli, Edwin Fischer, and Nat. He made his debut as a concert pianist at the age of 14 in Vienna, and his London debut in 1950. He then toured South America (1951). In 1956 he won first prize in the Busoni Competition in Bolzano. Apart from his solo recitals, he distinguished himself as a lieder accompanist to Dietrich Fischer-Dieskau and other prominent singers. Demus assembled a large collection of historic keyboard instruments; publ. a book of essays, *Abenteuer der Interpretation* (1967), and, with Paul Badura-Skoda, an analysis of Beethoven's piano sonatas (1970). In 1977 he was awarded the Beethoven Ring and in 1979 the Mozart Medal of Vienna. —**NS/LK/DM**

Demuth (real name, **Pokorný**), **Leopold,** esteemed Austrian baritone; b. Brunn, Nov. 2, 1861; d. while giving a concert in Czernowitz, March 4, 1910. He studied with Joseph Gänsbacher in Vienna, making his debut in 1889 in Halle as Hans Heiling. He sang in Leipzig (1891–95) and Hamburg (1895–97), then joined the Vienna Court Opera, remaining on its roster until his death. He also sang at Bayreuth (1899), where he gained recognition as a fine Wagnerian.—NS/LK/DM

Demuth, Norman, English composer, writer on music, and teacher; b. South Croydon, July 15, 1898; d. Chichester, April 21, 1968. He was a student of Parratt and Dunhill at the Royal Coll. of Music in London, and then continued private studies with Dunhill. After military service during World War I (1915–17), he was active as a church organist and later conducted in provincial music centers. He became prof. of composition at the Royal Academy of Music in London in 1930; with the exception of his military service in World War II, he retained this post throughout his life. Demuth's high regard for French music led to his being made a corresponding member of the Institut. In 1951 he became an officer of the French Académie and in 1954 a chevalier of the Légion d'honneur. In his compositions, he followed a course set by d'Indy and Roussel.

WORKS: DRAMATIC: O p e r a : *Conte venitien* (1947); *Le Flambeau* (1948); *Volpone* (1949); *The Oresteia* (1950); *Rogue Scapin* (1954). B a l l e t : *The Temptation of St. Anthony* (1937); *Planetomania* (1940); *Complainte* (1946); *Bal des fantômes* (1949); *La débutante* (1949). O t h e r : Incidental music and film scores. ORCH.: *Cortège* (1931); *Introduction and Allegro* (1936); Violin Concerto (1937); 2 partitas (1939, 1958); *2 War Poems* for Piano and Orch. (1940); *Valse graves et gaies* (1940); Concertino for Flute and Strings (1941); *Fantasy and Fugue* (1941); *Divertimento No. 1* for Strings (1941) and *No. 2* (1943); *Elegiac Rhapsody* for Cello and Small Orch. (1942); *Threnody* for Strings (1942); *Overture for a Victory* (1943); Piano Concerto (1943); *Suite champêtre* (1945); *Overture for a Joyful Occasion* (1946); Concertino for Piano and Small Orch. (1947); Concerto for Piano, Left-hand, and Orch. (1947); *Legend* for Piano, Left- hand, and Orch. (1949); 4 syms.: No. 1 (1949), No. 2 (1950), No. 3 for Strings (1952), and No. 4 (1956–57); 2 symphonic studies (1949, 1950); *Mouvement symphonique* for Ondes Martenot and Orch. (1952); *Ouverture à la française* (1952); *Ballade* for Viola and Orch. (1953); *Variations symphonique* (1954); *François Villon* (1956); Cello Concerto (1956); Concert Overture (1958); *Sinfonietta* (1958). M i l i t a r y B a n d : Saxophone Concerto (1938); *The Sea* (1939); *Regimental March of the Royal Pioneer Corps* (1943). CHAMBER: 3 violin sonatas (1937, 1938, 1948); *Serenade* for Violin and Piano (1938); Flute Sonata (1938); Cello Sonata (1939); Sonatina for 2 Violins (1939); Sonatine for Flute, Oboe, and Piano (1946); *Capriccio* for Violin and Piano (1948); Trio for Flute, Oboe, and Bassoon (1949); String Trio (1950); String Quartet (1950); *Lyric Trio* for Flute, Oboe, and Piano (1953); Suite for Flute, Oboe, and Harpsichord (1954); Quartet for Flute and Piano Trio (1955); *Suite de printemps* for Violin and Piano (1955); *Le souper du roi* for Wind, Drums, and Harpsichord (1956); *Divertissement* for Flute and Piano Trio (1957); *Pastoral Fantasy* for Piano Quartet (1957); *Primavera* for Flute and Piano Trio (1958); piano pieces; organ works. VOCAL: *3 Poems* for Soprano and Strings (1941); *3 Poems* for Voice and Strings (1944); *Pan's Anniversary* for Chorus and Orch. (1952); *Sonnet* for Baritone, Chorus, and Orch. (1953); *Requiem* for Chorus (1954); numerous part songs; many solo songs. WRITINGS (all publ. in London unless otherwise given): *The Gramophone and How to Use it* (1945); *Albert Roussel* (1947);

Ravel (1947); *An Anthology of Musical Criticism* (1948); *César Franck* (1949); *Paul Dukas* (1949); *The Symphony: Its History and Development* (1950); *A Course in Musical Composition* (1950–58); *Gounod* (1951); *Musical Trends in the 20th Century* (1952); *Musical Forms and Textures* (1953); *French Piano Music* (1958); *French Opera: Its Development to the Revolution* (Horsham, 1963). —NS/LK/DM

Dencke, Jeremiah, American Moravian minister, organist, and composer; b. Langenbilau, Silesia, Oct. 2, 1725; d. Bethlehem, Pa., May 28, 1795. In 1748 he became organist at Herrnhut, the center of the European Moravians. He went to the U.S. in 1761 and served the Moravian settlements in Pa. in various capacities. During the Revolutionary War he was warden of the Bethlehem congregation. Dencke was apparently the first individual to compose vocal concerted church music in the Moravian settlements in Pa., and possibly the first to write such music in colonial America. He was an able composer. The earliest work he is known to have composed in America is a simple anthem for chorus, strings, and figured bass, written for a *Liebesmahl* ("love feast," a service of spiritual devotion and earthly fraternalism, composed of hymn singing and a light meal of a roll and beverage) on Aug. 29, 1765. His finest works are 3 sets of sacred songs for soprano, strings, and organ, composed in 1767–68. The first, written for the annual festival of the "choir" of small girls, is included in the first vol. of the series Music of the Moravians in America, issued by the N.Y. Public Library in 1938. The other sets of solos were written for Christmas services. Dencke's compositions are listed in A.G. Rau and H.T. David, *A Catalogue of Music by American Moravians, 1742–1842, from the Archives of the Moravian Church at Bethlehem, Pa.* (Bethlehem, Pa., 1938).—NS/LK/DM

Denefve, Jules, Belgian cellist, conductor, pedagogue, and composer; b. Chimay, 1814; d. Mons, Aug. 19, 1877. He studied cello with Platel and De Munck (second prix, 1836) and composition with Fétis at the Brussels Cons. After settling in Mons, he taught at and later was director of the Cons. He also was founder-conductor of the Roland de Lattre Choral Soc. (from 1841) and conductor of the Société des Concerts. He composed the operas *Kettly, ou Le retour en suisse* (1838), *Léchevin Brassart* (1845), *Marie de Brabant* (1850), and *Séguille* (1854), as well as syms., overtures, many pieces for 4-voice Men's Chorus, and songs.—LK/DM

Denéréaz, Alexandre, Swiss composer and musicologist; b. Lausanne, July 31, 1875; d. there, July 25, 1947. He studied at the Lausanne Cons. with Blanchet and at the Dresden Cons. with Draeseke and Doring. In 1896 he was appointed a prof. at the Lausanne Cons.; also taught musicology at the Univ. of Lausanne. He publ. an original theory of harmony. He was also the author, with C. Bourgues, of *La Musique et la vie intérieure: Histoire psychologique de l'art musical* (appendix entitled *L'Arbre généalogique de l'art musical*; 1919). Among his compositions were 3 syms., many symphonic poems, cantatas, Concerto Grosso for Orch. and Organ, string quartets, organ works, and music to René Morax's *La Dime*.—NS/LK/DM

Denis, Didier, French composer; b. Paris, Nov. 5, 1947. He studied at the Paris Cons. (1958–71) with Simone Petit (solfège), Henri Challan (harmony), Marcel Bitsch (counterpoint and fugue), and Olivier Messiaen (analysis and composition). In 1969 and 1971 he won the Lili Boulanger Prize, in 1971 the Prix Van Zeeland de l'Académie des beaux arts, and in 1972 the prize of the SACEM. From 1971 to 1973 he was in residence at the Villa Medici in Rome under the auspices of the Académie des beaux arts. From 1982 to 1991 he was an inspector of music for the French Ministry of Culture. After teaching composition at the Toulouse Cons. (1991–95), he was again an inspector of music for the French Ministry of Culture.

WORKS: DRAMATIC: *Ubicande,* opera (1983–98); incidental music. **ORCH.:** *Chants de Tse Yeh* for Piano and Chamber Ensemble (1969); *Levres, rouge* for Viola and Orch. (1973); *T'aimer beaucoup, t'aimer d'amour, sept fois d'amour* for Horn and Large String Orch. (1985); *Ivre de t'aimer beaucoup, ivre de t'aimer d'amour, ivre de t'aimer trente et une fois d'amour* for Cello and Wind Orch. (19897). **CHAMBER:** Trio for Flute, Clarinet, and Bassoon (1966); *Fugue indoue* for 2 Percussion Groups (1968); *Triangle au soleil à 7 branches* for Jazz Quartet and 11 Players (1969); *Lévres, rouge* for Viola (1972); *Le fleuvre, le serpent, le serin et l'épervier* for Flutes (1974); *Amore stelle* for Flute and Viola (1983); *L'état des lieux* for Oboe (1992); *Chansons obscures* for Guitar (1994); *Les toiles—l'indiscible du passage* for 11 Players (1996); *La nuit des aveugles* for Violin and Piano (1999); *Un regard blessé (par les soleils de la mort)* for Clarinet (1999). **VOCAL:** *Sagesse, froce, beauté, l'amour* for Soprano and 18 Players (1967); *Cinq fois je t'aimes* for Reciter, Soprano, and Orch. (1968); *Chansons de la plus haute tour* for Soprano (1969); *Puzzle* for Voice, Guitar, and Percussion (1970); *C'est pas une raison* for Soprano, Tenor, Jazz Ensemble, 10 Players, and Tape (1970); *La vieille danse* for Soprano and 6 Players (1972); *Le coq* for 12 Voices (1972); *Obscur et foncé comme un oeillet violet* for 2 Sopranos, Chorus, and 6 Players (1972); *Les herbes folles de la campagne* for Soprano, Lute, and 71 Guitars (1975); *Khamaïleôn* for Soprano and 3 Clarinets (1986); *Les temps sont révolus—un carousel sur la rive nord* for Voice and Instrument (1991); *A la grâce de Dieu* for Soprano, Children's Chorus, and 10 Players (1992).
—NS/LK/DM

Denisov, Edison, notable Russian composer and teacher; b. Tomsk, April 6, 1929; d. Paris, Nov. 23, 1996. He received training in mathematics before studying at the Moscow Cons. with Shebalin (composition), Rakov (orchestration), Zuckerman (analysis), and Belov (piano). In 1959 he joined its faculty as a teacher of form and orchestration, becoming a composition teacher in 1992. He became director of the Assn. of Contemporary Music in Moscow in 1990. In 1990–91 he worked at IRCAM in Paris. He was made an Officier des Arts et Lettres of France in 1986, and in 1993 he was awarded the Grand Prize of the City of Paris. In his extensive output, Denisov demonstrated a remarkable command of a wide variety of contemporary techniques and procedures in creating scores of a pronounced individuality.

WORKS: DRAMATIC: *Soldier Ivan,* opera (1959); *L'écume des jours,* opera (1981; Paris, March 15, 1986); *Confession,* ballet (Tallinn, Nov. 30, 1984); *Quatre Jeunes filles,* opera (1986; Moscow, May 24, 1990); incidental music to plays; film music.

ORCH.: 2 syms.: No. 1 (1955) and No. 2 (1987; Paris, March 2, 1988); *Sinfonietta on Tadzhik Themes* (1957); *Crescendo e diminuendo* for Harpsichord and 12 Strings (1965; Zagreb, May 14, 1967); *Peinture* (Weiz, Oct. 30, 1970); Cello Concerto (1972; Leipzig, Sept. 25, 1973); *Aquarelle* for 24 Strings (1974; Paris, June 12, 1975); Piano Concerto (1974; Leipzig, Sept. 5, 1978); Flute Concerto (1975; Dresden, May 22, 1976); Violin Concerto (1977; Milan, July 18, 1978); Concerto for Flute, Oboe, and Orch. (Cologne, March 24, 1979); *Partita* for Violin and Orch. (Moscow, March 23, 1981); *Tod ist ein langer Schaf* for Cello and Orch. (Moscow, May 30, 1982); *Musique de chambre* for Viola, Harpsichord, and Strings (1982; Moscow, May 7, 1983); 2 chamber syms.: No. 1 (1982; Paris, March 7, 1983) and No. 2 (Tokyo, July 13, 1994); Concerto for Bassoon, Cello, and Orch. (1982; Como, Sept. 24, 1984); *Épitaphe* for Chamber Orch. (Reggio Emilia, Sept. 11, 1983); Concerto for 2 Violas, Harpsichord, and Strings (1984; Amsterdam, June 24, 1991); *Confession,* suite after the ballet (Moscow, Oct. 22, 1985); *Caprices de Paganini* for Violin and Strings (1985; Moscow, Feb. 5, 1986); *Happy End* for 2 Violins, Cello, Double Bass, and Strings (1985; Kaliningrad, Dec. 4, 1989); Viola Concerto (Berlin, Sept. 2, 1986); Oboe Concerto (1986; Cologne, March 4, 1988); *Es ist genug* for Viola and Chamber Orch. (1986; Lucerne, Sept. 3, 1989; also for Viola and Piano); *Glocken im Nebel* (Moscow, Aug. 19, 1988); Clarinet Concerto (Lübeck, July 9, 1989); Guitar Concerto (Stuttgart, Nov. 30, 1991); Concerto for Flute, Vibraphone, Harpsichord, and Strings (Lucerne, Aug. 17, 1993); *Postludio (in memoriam Witold Lutosławski)* for Chamber Orch. (Warsaw, Sept. 21, 1994). **CHAMBER:** Flute Sonata (1960; Moscow, March 27, 1962); String Quartet No. 2 (1961); *Music* for 11 Winds and Timpani (1961; Leningrad, Nov. 15, 1965); Concerto for Flute, Oboe, Piano, and Percussion (1963; Warsaw, Sept. 24, 1964); Violin Sonata (1963; Moscow, April 11, 1972); *Ode* for Clarinet, Piano, and Percussion (1967; Moscow, Jan. 22, 1968); 3 Pieces for Cello and Piano (1967; Moscow, May 11, 1968); *Musique romantique* for Oboe, Harp, and String Trio (1968; Zagreb, May 16, 1969); *D.S.C.H.* for Clarinet, Trombone, Cello, and Piano (Warsaw, Sept. 26, 1969); *Silhouettes* for Flute, 2 Pianos, and Percussion (Baden-Baden, Oct. 5, 1969); Wind Quintet (Amsterdam, Oct. 10, 1969); String Trio (Paris, Oct. 23, 1969); Alto Saxophone Sonata (Chicago, Dec. 14, 1970); *Canon in Memory of Igor Stravinsky* for Flute, Clarinet, and Harp (1971); Solo for Oboe (1971); Cello Sonata (Royan, April 8, 1971); Trio for Violin, Cello, and Piano (1971; Moscow, Oct. 30, 1972); Solo for Flute (1971; Witten, April 29, 1973); Solo for Trumpet (1972); Sonata for Solo Clarinet (1972; Moscow, Jan. 24, 1974); 3 Pieces for Harpsichord and Percussion (1972; Moscow, Oct. 8, 1983); *Prélude et air* for Flute and Piano (1973); 4 Pieces for Alto Saxophone and Piano (Bordeaux, June 1974); *Choral varié* for Trombone and Piano (1975; Venice, Aug. 27, 1976); 4 Pieces for Flute and Piano (1977; Paris, April 21, 1978); Sonata for Flute and Guitar (1977; Moscow, Dec. 25, 1978); *Concerto piccolo* for 4 Saxophones and Percussion (1977; Bordeaux, April 28, 1979); Sonata for Solo Violin (Hamburg, Oct. 19, 1978); 3 Pieces for 3 Instruments (1978; London, July 3, 1984); Sonata for Solo Guitar (Moscow, Dec. 14, 1981); Trio for Oboe, Cello, and Harpsichord (Donaueschingen, Oct. 1981); Sonata for Solo Bassoon (Moscow, Nov. 1, 1982); Sonata for Violin and Organ (1982; Leningrad, March 26, 1983); Sonata for Solo Flute (1982; Münster, Feb. 15, 1984); 5 *Études* for Bassoon (1983); Sonata for Flute and Harp (1983; Moscow, Jan. 7, 1984); 4 Pieces for Flute (1984); 3 *Pictures of Paul Klee* for Viola and 5 Instruments (1984; Moscow, Jan. 27, 1985); *In deo speravit cor meum* for Violin, Guitar, and Organ (Kassel, Nov. 1, 1984); Sextet for Flute, Oboe, Clarinet, Violin,

Viola, and Cello (1984; Cheltenham, July 15, 1985); *Es ist genug* for Viola and Piano (1984; also for Viola and Chamber Orch., Lucerne, Sept. 3, 1989); *Paysage au Clair de Lune* for Clarinet and Piano (1985; Saarbrücken, May 30, 1987); Duo for Flute and Viola (1985; Moscow, March 28, 1990); *Variations on a Theme of Schubert* for Cello and Piano (Moscow, March 8, 1986); *Paysage Hivernal* for Harp (1987); Quintet for 2 Violins, Viola, Cello, and Piano (Bristol, May 24, 1987); Quintet for Clarinet, 2 Violins, Viola, and Cello (Saarbrücken, May 30, 1987); 3 Pieces for 3 Percussionists (Moscow, April 14, 1989); Quartet for Flute, Violin, Viola, and Cello (Trento, Nov. 7, 1989); *Variations on a Theme of Mozart* for 8 Flutes (1990; Munich, Jan. 25, 1991); 4 Pieces for String Quartet (1991); *Dedicace* for Flute, Clarinet, 2 Violins, Viola, and Cello (1991; London, Feb. 6, 1992); Quintet for 4 Saxophones and Piano (1991; Paris, Feb. 20, 1993); Clarinet Sonata (Cologne, Dec. 27, 1993). **KEYBOARD: P i a n o :** *Variations* (1961; Copenhagen, March 28, 1965); Pieces for Piano, 4-Hands (1967; London, Feb. 16, 1968); *Signes en blanc* (Warsaw, Sept. 26, 1974); *Variations on a Theme of Handel* (1986; Leningrad, March 26, 1987); *Points et lignes* for 2 Pianos, 8-Hands (Amsterdam, Oct. 2, 1988); *Pièces pour enfants* (1989); *Pour Daniel* (1989); *Reflets* (Glasgow, Nov. 23, 1989). **H a r p s i c h o r d :** *Feuilles mortes* (1980; Berlin, Oct. 8, 1983). **VOCAL:** *Canti di Catullo* for Bass and 3 Trombones (1962; Moscow, March 18, 1982); *Chansons italiennes* for Soprano, Flute, Horn, Violin, and Harpsichord (1964; Leningrad, May 10, 1966); *Le Soleil des Incas* for Soprano and Ensemble, after Mistral (1964; Leningrad, Nov. 30, 1966); 5 *Geschichten vom Herrn Keuner* for Tenor and 7 Instruments, after Brecht (1966; Berlin, Feb. 20, 1968); *Les Pleurs* for Soprano, Piano, and 3 Percussionists (1966; Brussels, Dec. 17, 1968); *Automne* for 13 Solo Voices (1968; Royan, March 30, 1969); 2 *Poems of Ivan Bounine* for Soprano and Piano (1970; Halle, April 3, 1971); *Chant d'automne* for Soprano and Orch., after Baudelaire (Zagreb, May 16, 1971); *La Vie en rouge* for Voice, Flute, Clarinet, Violin, Cello, and Piano (Zagreb, May 1973); *Blätter* for Soprano and String Trio (1978; Moscow, Jan. 28, 1980); 5 *Poems of Baratynsky* for Voice and Piano (1979; Moscow, Jan. 28, 1980); *Douleur et silence* for Mezzo-soprano, Clarinet, Viola, and Piano, after Mandelstam (1979; Moscow, Jan. 28, 1980); *Requiem* for Soprano, Tenor, Chorus, and Orch. (Hamburg, Oct. 30, 1980); *Ton image charmante* for Voice and Piano, after Pushkin (Moscow, Dec. 8, 1980; also for Voice and Orch., Moscow, Oct. 30, 1984); *For Flore* for Voice and Piano (1980; Moscow, Nov. 1, 1982); *Sur le bûcher de neige* for Voice and Piano, after Blok (1981; Moscow, April 12, 1982); *Colin et Chloé*, suite for Soprano, Mezzo-soprano, Tenor, Chorus, and Orch., after the opera *L'ecume des jours* (1981; Moscow, Oct. 17, 1983); *Le Cahier bleu* for Soprano, Reciter, Violin, 2 Cellos, and Piano (1984; Rostov-na-Donau, April 11, 1985); *Venue du printemps* for Chorus (1984; Moscow, Nov. 7, 1986); *Wishing Well* for Mezzo-soprano, Clarinet, Viola, and Piano (N.Y., March 1, 1986); *Au plus haut des cieux* for Voice and Chamber Orch. (1986; Paris, May 11, 1987); *Eternal Light* for Chorus (1988; Tallinn, Jan. 30, 1989); *Légends des eaux souterraines* for 12 Solo Voices (1989); *4 Poèmes de Gérard de Nerval* for Voice, Flute, and Piano (Davos, July 22, 1989); *Étoile de noël* for Voice, Flute, and String Orch., after Pasternak (Moscow, Dec. 28, 1989); 3 *Extraits du nouveau testament* for Countertenor, 2 Tenors, Baritone, Flute, and Bells (1989; Bale, Dec. 7, 1990); *The Story of the Life and Death of Our Saviour Jesus Christ* for Tenor, Bass, Chorus, and Orch. (1992; Frankfurt am Main, Sept. 14, 1994); *Morgenstraum* for Soprano, Chorus, and Orch. (1993; Düsseldorf, Jan. 19, 1995). **E l e c t r o a c o u s - t i c :** *Chant des oiseaux* for Prepared Piano and Tape (1969; Dubna, Dec. 20, 1970); *Sur la nappe d'un étang glacé* for 9 Instruments and Tape (1991; Paris, Feb. 24, 1992). **O r c h e s - t r a t i o n s :** Works by Beethoven, Schubert, Chopin, Mussorgsky, Mossolov, and Debussy, including the latter's unfinished opera *Rodrique et Chimène* (Lyons, May 15, 1993).

BIBL.: J. P. Armengaud, *Entretiens avec E. D.: Un compositeur sous le regime communist* (Paris, 1993); I. Kholopov, *E. D.* (Moscow, 1993).—**NS/LK/DM**

Denny, William D(ouglas),

American composer, teacher, violist, and conductor; b. Seattle, July 2, 1910; d. Berkeley, Calif., Sept. 2, 1980. He studied at the Univ. of Calif. at Berkeley (B.A., 1931; M.A., 1933) before pursuing training in composition with Dukas in Paris (1933–35) and as a Horatio Parker Fellow at the American Academy in Rome (1939–41). He taught at his alma mater (1938–39), at Harvard Univ. (1941–42), and at Vassar Coll. (1942–44); returning to his alma mater, he served as a prof. (1945–78) and as chairman of the music dept. (1972–75). In his well- crafted output, he favored complex contrapuntal textures and dissonant harmonies.

WORKS: ORCH.: *Bacchanale* (1935); *Concertino* (1937; San Francisco, April 25, 1939); 3 syms.: No. 1 (CBS, May 1939), No. 2 (1949; San Francisco, March 22, 1951), and No. 3 (1955–57; San Francisco, Jan. 16, 1963); *Sinfonietta* (1940); Suite for Chamber Orch. (1940); Overture for Strings (1945; San Francisco, May 2, 1946); *Praeludium* (1946; San Francisco, Feb. 5, 1947); *Introduction and Allegro* (1956). **CHAMBER:** 3 string quartets (1937–38; 1952; 1955); Viola Sonata (1943–44); String Trio (1965). **O r g a n :** *Partita* (1958); *Toccata, Aria, and Fugue* (1966). **CHO-RAL:** *Most Glorious Lord of Life*, cantata (1943); 3 motets (1946–47).—**NS/LK/DM**

Densmore, Frances,

American ethnomusicologist; b. Red Wing, Minn., May 21, 1867; d. there, June 5, 1957. She studied at the Oberlin (Ohio) Cons. (hon. M.A., 1924), then took courses with Leopold Godowsky (piano) and J. K. Paine (counterpoint). She began the study of Indian music in 1893 at the World's Fair in Chicago, continuing privately until 1907, when she began systematic research for the Bureau of American Ethnology (Smithsonian Inst.), including an exhaustive study of the Cheyenne, Arapaho, Maidu, Santo Domingo Pueblo, and New Mexican Indian tribes. She lectured extensively on Indian music, and publ. a number of books and articles on the subject. A Frances Densmore ethnological library has been established at Macalester Coll. in St. Paul, Minn.

WRITINGS: *Chippewa Music*, a collection of Indian songs in 2 vols. (1910–13); *Poems from Sioux and Chippewa Songs* (words only; 1917); *Tetom Sioux Music* (1918); *Indian Action Songs* (1921); *Northern Ute Music* (1922); *Mandan and Hidatfa Music* (1923); *The American Indians and Their Music* (1926; 2nd ed., 1936); *The Music of the Tule Indians of Panama* (1926); *Some Results of the Study of American Indian Music* (reprinted from the *Journal of the Washington Academy of Sciences*, XVIII/14; 1928); *Pawnee Music* (1929); *Papago Music* (1929); *What Intervals Do Indians Sing?* (reprinted from the *American Anthropologist*, April/June, 1929); *Yaman and Yaqui Music* (U.S. Bureau of American Ethnology, Bulletin 110; 1932); *Menominee Music* (ibid., Bulletin 102; 1932); *Cheyenne and Arapaho Music* (Southwest Museum, 1936); *Alabama Music* (Tex. Folk-Lore Soc., 1937); *Music of Santo Domingo Pueblo, New*

Mexico (Southwest Museum, 1938); *Nootka and Quileute Music* (Washington, D.C., 1939); *Music of the Indians of British Columbia* (Washington, 1943); *Choctaw Music* (1943); *Seminole Music* (1956).—**NS/LK/DM**

Dent, Edward J(oseph), eminent English musicologist, teacher, and music critic; b. Ribston, Yorkshire, July 16, 1876; d. London, Aug. 22, 1957. He studied with C. H. Lloyd at Eton Coll., then went to Cambridge to continue his studies with Charles Wood and Stanford (Mus.B., 1899; M.A., 1905). He was elected a Fellow of King's Coll. there in 1902, and subsequently taught music history, harmony, counterpoint, and composition until 1918. He was also active in promoting operatic productions in England by preparing translations of libretti for performances at Cambridge, particularly of the operas of Mozart. From 1918 he wrote music criticism in London. In 1919 he became one of the founders of the British Music Soc., which remained active until 1933. The ISCM came into being in 1922 largely through his efforts, and he served as its president until 1938 and again in 1945; he also was president of the Société Internationale de Musicologie from 1931 until 1949. In 1926 he was appointed prof. of music at Cambridge, a position he held until 1941. He was made an honorary Mus.D. at the Univ. of Oxford (1932), Harvard (1936), and Cambridge (1947). In 1937 he was made a corresponding member of the American Musicological Soc. After his death, the Royal Musical Assn. created, in 1961, the Dent Medal, which is given annually to those selected for their important contributions to musicology. A scholar of the widest interests, Dent contributed numerous articles to music journals, encyclopedias, dictionaries, and symposia.

WRITINGS: *Alessandro Scarlatti* (London, 1905; 2nd ed., rev. by F. Walker, 1960); *Mozart's Operas: A Critical Study* (London, 1913; 3rd ed., rev., 1955); *Terpander, or Music and the Future* (London, 1926); *Foundations of English Opera: A Study of Musical Drama in England during the Seventeenth Century* (Cambridge, 1928); *Ferruccio Busoni* (London, 1933; 2nd ed., 1966); *Handel* (London, 1934); *Opera* (Harmondsworth, 1940; 5th ed., rev., 1949); *Notes on Fugue for Beginners* (Cambridge, 1941); *A Theatre for Everybody: The Story of the Old Vic and Sadler's Wells* (London, 1945; 2nd ed., rev., 1946); *The Rise of Romantic Opera* (ed. by W. Dean; Cambridge, 1976); *Selected Essays* (ed. by H. Taylor; Cambridge, 1979).

BIBL.: P. Radcliffe, *E. J. D.: A Centenary Memoir* (Rickmansworth, 1976).—**NS/LK/DM**

Denver, John (originally, **Deutschendorf, Henry John**), pleasant-voiced singer/songwriter and movie actor; b. Roswell, N.Mex., Dec. 31, 1943; d. in a small-plane crash that he was piloting, near L.A., Oct. 12, 1997. Denver was a folk-country singer/songwriter who had his greatest success in the mid-1970s with his back-to-nature hymns "Rocky Mountain High" and "Thank God I'm a Country Boy." Denver's bland tenor vocals and golly-gosh manners made him popular both in films and as a middle-of-the-road popster.

Denver was the son of a career Air Force pilot. He performed with the Chad Mitchell Trio in the early 1960s, one of the more topically oriented of the folk-revival groups. In 1965, he replaced leader Chad Mitchell in the group, continuing to record with them until 1969 when the trio dissolved. Denver was signed to RCA as a solo artist, recording his first album combining self-penned satirical songs attacking then-president Nixon and the war in Vietnam along with his sentimental pop songs like "(Leaving on a) Jet Plane," which had been a hit for Peter, Paul and Mary.

Denver's big break came in 1971 with his recording of "Take Me Home, Country Roads," followed by a string of country-flavored pop hits, including the sappy ballad "Annie's Song" and the up-tempo, enthusiastic "Thank God I'm a Country Boy." Denver began a film-acting career in 1977, showing himself to be an affable comedian. He continued to record his own material through the mid-1980s with limited success, forming his own label later to promote a country album *Higher Ground* in 1988, featuring the title hit. Denver died while piloting a small airplane in 1997.

DISC.: *Rhymes and Reasons* (1969); *Rocky Mountain High* (1972); *John Denver's Greatest Hits* (1973); *Back Home Again* (1974); *An Evening with John Denver* (1975); *Windsong* (1975); *Spirit* (1976); *John Denver* (1979); *A Christmas Together* (with the Muppets; 1979); *Autograph* (1980); *Wildlife Concert* (1995); *The Rocky Mountain Collection* (1996); *The Country Roads Collection* (1997).—**RC**

Denza, Luigi, Italian composer; b. Castellammare di Stabia, Feb. 24, 1846; d. London, Jan. 26, 1922. He studied with Serrao and Mercadante at the Naples Cons. Besides the opera *Wallenstein* (Naples, May 13, 1876), which was not especially successful, he wrote about 600 songs (some in Neapolitan dialect), many of which won great popularity. In 1879 he settled in London, where he was appointed prof. of singing at the Royal Academy of Music (1898); was made a Chevalier of the order of the Crown of Italy. His most famous song is *Funiculi-Funicula*, which was used (under the mistaken impression that it was a folk song) by Richard Strauss in *Aus Italien*.—**NS/LK/DM**

Denzler, Robert, Swiss conductor and composer; b. Zürich, March 19, 1892; d. there, Aug. 25, 1972. He studied with Andreae at the Zürich Cons., and after further training in Cologne, he was an assistant at Bayreuth. He was music director of the Lucerne (1912–15) and then of the Zürich Opera (1915–27); after serving as first conductor of the Berlin Städtische Oper (1927–32), he was again music director of the Zürich Opera (1934–47). He composed a Piano Concerto, suites, and songs.—**NS/LK/DM**

DeParis, Wilbur, leader, trombonist, occasionally drummer; b. Crawfordsville, Ind., Jan. 11, 1900; d. N.Y., Jan. 3, 1973. His brother, Sidney, was a trumpeter; their father was a bandmaster and music teacher. He began on alto horn at the age of 7, and was soon working with his father's carnival band. Later he played tent shows and toured on the T.O.B.A, circuit. He traveled to New Orleans (c. 1922) with Mack's Merrymakers, and sat in on 'C' melody sax with Louis Armstrong. From 1925 he regularly led his own band in Philadelphia, and also worked with various other local bands. In 1927–28, he managed the big band resident at the Pearl Theatre, Philadelphia. He relocated to N.Y. toward the end of the decade, and during the 1930s worked with various groups, including Noble Sissle (for a European tour in 1931), and Mills Blue Rhythm Band (recording in 1937). He was with Teddy Hill from late 1936–37, including a trip to Europe, then with Louis Armstrong (November 1937 until September 1940). Briefly with the Ella Fitzgerald Orch., DeParis then worked in the pit band for the Broadway show *The Pirate* (1942). During spring 1943, he toured with the Roy Eldridge Big Band, and then led his own small band, before joining Duke Ellington from late 1945 until May 1947. He also recorded with Sidney Bechet in 1946, 1949, and 1950. He reformed his own highly successful small band (with brother Sidney DeParis and Omer Simeon), mainly resident at Jimmy Ryan's in N.Y. from 1951 until early 1962 (he toured Africa in the spring of 1957, a U.S. State-Department sponsored trip). The band continued to work various clubs through the 1960s. He led his own rehearsal studio in N.Y. (1971), and worked as both leader and arranger until 1972.

DISC.: *Evening at Jimmy Ryan's* (1951); *And His Rampart Street Ramblers* (1952); *Wilbur DeParis, Vol. 2* (1952); *New New Orleans Jazz* (1955); *At Symphony Hall* (1956); *Marchin' and Swingin'* (1956); *New Orleans Blues* (1957); *That's Aplenty* (1958); *On the Riviera* (1960); *Wild Jazz Age* (1960).—**JC/LP**

Depeche Mode,

popularizers of the post-punk synth-pop sound, formed 1980, is Basildon, England. **MEMBERSHIP:** Andrew John Fletcher, synth. (b. Nottingham England, July 8, 1961); Martin Lee Gore, synth. (b. London, England, July 23, 1961); Vincent Clarke, synth. (b. Basildon, England, July 3, 1961); David Gahan, voc. (b. Epping, England, May 9, 1962).

Andrew Fletcher and Vince Clarke met as children in an organization called Boys Brigade. In 1977, they got caught up in the wave of punk. Fletcher bought a bass, Clarke a guitar, and they formed a band. They met Martin Gore during a show, shared several bills with his band, and became friendly. Together, they formed a trio called Composition of Sound. Fletcher took up the synthesizer, and eventually all three were playing synthesizers. They found lead vocalist Gahan working in a cover band and asked him to join their group. Gahan, whose father had left home when he was young, had a history of petty crime and once went through a period of going through 20 jobs in six months.

With the new sound, they decided they needed a new name. They selected one from a French fashion magazine, *Depeche Mode*, which translated as "fast fashion." Their sound, a catchy, totally electronic, melodic rendering of Vince Clarke songs was unique for the time. After one release on Some Bizarre records, they came to the attention of the U.K.'s Mute records. After a pair of singles that generated little attention, they recorded one of the anthems of early synth-pop, "Just Can't Get Enough." It broke the Top Ten in the U.K. and became a substantial dance hit in the U.S., first as an import, and even more so after Sire records took on the group in the U.S. Their debut album *Speak and Spell*

featured several more Clarke gems and a pair of tunes by Gore. It became a fair-sized hit in the U.K., while garnering a substantial cult following in the U.S.

However, after the acclaim, Clarke took his songs and synthesizer and started working with Alison Moyet in a new venture called Yazoo (Yaz in the U.S. to avoid confusion with the blues label of the same name). They went on to record the monster hit "Only You." Depeche Mode decided to continue, adding Alex Wilder (b. England, June 1, 1959) to fill Clarke's sonic space, first just as a live adjunct. Gore took over the songwriting chores. The band went into the studio to record *A Broken Frame*, and announced that Wilder had become a full-time member. The album produced the U.K. hit "The Meaning of Love." Their third album, *Construction Time Again* spawned "Everything Counts," a #6 hit in the U.K. and a substantial new wave and dance hit in the U.S.

With the release of *Some Great Reward* in 1984, Gore began to hit his stride as a songwriter. "People Are People" became a major hit in the U.K., and finally broke the band pop in the U.S., hitting #13 on the pop charts. The follow-up singles, "Master and Servant" and "Blasphemous Rumours" also did well on the U.K. charts and on the new-wave stations in the U.S. The album eventually went platinum in the U.S.

With the sudden rise to visibility in the U.S., Sire mined the band's back catalog, releasing a collection of their previous hit singles and an album aptly called *Catching Up with Depeche Mode*. With everyone up to speed, the band released *Black Celebration* in 1986. Again, the modern rock stations picked up on English hits like "Stripped," "A Question of Lust," and "A Question of Time." Similarly, their next album *Music for the Masses* generated "Strangelove," "Never Let Me Down Again," "Behind the Wheel," and "Little 15." U.K. hits all, they only garnered modern rock radio play in the U.S., but that was enough for the album to chart in the U.S. at #35 and go platinum.

One of the few totally synthesizer-based bands to have a regular touring schedule, their tour for *Music for the Masses* sold out across America. The band released the double-live *101* in 1989, along with a concert film by D.A. Pennebaker documenting that tour.

Even with all this adulation, the band was still regarded as mostly an underground phenomenon. Their next album, 1990's *Violator*, changed that perception. The album became enormously popular, spinning four Top 20 singles in the U.K. Three of them became pop hits in the U.S. as well: "Personal Jesus" hit #28 and went gold, "Enjoy the Silence" rose as high as #8, also going gold, and "Policy of Truth" became the band's first single to chart higher in the U.S. (#15) than it did in the U.K. (#16). The album eventually topped triple platinum and rose to #7.

They took some time off and their absence whetted fans' appetites for a new Depeche Mode record to such an extent that their 1993 release *Songs of Faith and Devotion* entered the U.S. chart at #1. Although it only hit #37, the single "I Feel You" went gold. The album shipped platinum.

By 1995, however, things looked bleaker for Depeche Mode than they had since Clarke's exit. Wilder left the band. Then, Gahan attempted suicide and went into drug rehabilitation to kick a heroin habit. For over a year, there was a question as to whether the band existed anymore. Then they went into the studio and cut *Ultra*. Again eager fans rushed to pick up the first Depeche Mode album in four years. However, over the course of four years, there were fewer eager fans. The album entered the charts at #5 with an anchor and only went gold in the U.S., producing only one meager hit, the #38 "It's No Good." In the U.K., however, the band seemed as strong as ever, with two Top Ten hits, a Top 20, and a Top 30 tune off the album.

DISC.: *Speak & Spell* (1981); *A Broken Frame* (1982); *Construction Time Again* (1983); *People Are People* (U.S.; 1984); *Some Great Reward* (1984); *Catching Up with Depeche Mode* (1985); *Black Celebration* (1986); *Music for the Masses* (1987); *Une Nuit a La Mode, Vol.1* (live; 1990); *Une Nuit a La Mode, Vol. 2* (1990); *Violator* (1990), *We Just Can't Get Enough* (live; 1991); *Songs of Faith & Devotion* (1993); *Songs of Faith & Devotion Live* (1993); *Depeche Mode* (1995); *Ultra* (1997); *Singles 81–85* (1998).—**HB**

De Peyer, Gervase (Alan), English clarinetist, conductor, and teacher; b. London, April 11, 1926. He studied with Frederick Thurston at the Royal Coll. of Music in London and with Louis Cahuzac in Paris (1949). He then pursued an international career as a clarinet virtuoso; served as first clarinetist of the London Sym. Orch. (1955–72), was founder- conductor of the Melos Sinfonia, and assoc. conductor of the Haydn Orch. in London. He taught at the Royal Academy of Music in London (from 1959) and performed with the Chamber Music Soc. of Lincoln Center in N.Y. (1969–89). He gave master classes all over the globe and also commissioned a number of works for clarinet. —**NS/LK/DM**

Deppe, Ludwig, famous German piano pedagogue; b. Alverdissen, Lippe, Nov. 7, 1828; d. Bad Pyramont, Sept. 5, 1890. He was a pupil of Marxsen at Hamburg in 1849, and later of Lobe at Leipzig. He settled in Hamburg in 1857 as a music teacher, and founded a singing society, which he conducted until 1868. He went to Berlin in 1874, and from 1886 to 1888 was court conductor; also conducted the Silesian Musical Festivals established by Count Hochberg in 1876. He wrote a sym. and overtures, *Zriny* and *Don Carlos*.

BIBL.: H. Klose, *D.sche Lehre des Klavierspiels* (Hamburg, 1886); E. Caland, *Die D.sche Lehre des Klavierspiels* (Stuttgart, 1897; 5th⁺ʰ ed., 1921; Eng. tr., 1903, as *Artistic Piano Playing*). —**NS/LK/DM**

Déré, Jean, French composer; b. Niort, June 23, 1886; d. Sainte Suzanne, Mayenne, Dec. 6, 1970. He studied at the Paris Cons. with Caussade, Diémer, and Widor, winning the second Prix de Rome (1919). Among his works were the symphonic poem *Krischna*, incidental music for Marlowe's *Faustus*, *3 esquisses* for Piano and Orch., chamber music, piano pieces, and songs. —**NS/LK/DM**

De Reszke, Jean (actually, **Jan Mieczislaw**), celebrated Polish tenor, brother of Edouard de Reszke and **Josephine de Reszke;** b. Warsaw, Jan. 14, 1850; d. Nice, April 3, 1925. His mother gave him his first singing lessons; he then studied with Ciaffei and Cotogni. He sang at the Warsaw Cathedral as a boy; then went to Paris, where he studied with Sbriglia. He was first trained as a baritone, and made his debut in Venice (1874) as Alfonso in *La Favorite* under the name of Giovanni di Reschi. He continued singing in Italy and France in baritone parts; his first appearance as a tenor took place in Madrid on Nov. 9, 1879, in *Robert le Diable*. He created the title role in Massenet's *Le Cid* at the Paris Opéra (Nov. 30, 1885) and became a favorite tenor there. He appeared at Drury Lane in London as Radames on June 13, 1887 (having previously sung there as a baritone in 1874). He then sang at Covent Garden (until 1900). On Nov. 9, 1891, he made his American debut in Chicago as Lohengrin; he made his Metropolitan Opera debut in N.Y. on Dec. 14, 1891, as Romeo; he remained with the Metropolitan for 11 seasons. In order to sing Wagnerian roles, he learned German, and made a sensationally successful appearance as Tristan (N.Y., Nov. 27, 1895). His last appearance at the Metropolitan was as Tristan on April 29, 1901, in Act 2 during a post-season gala performance. The secret of his success rested not so much on the power of his voice (some baritone quality remained in his singing to the end) as on his controlled interpretation, musical culture, and fine dynamic balance. When he retired from the stage in 1902, settling in Paris as a voice teacher, he was able to transmit his method to many of his students, several of whom later became famous on the opera stage.

BIBL.: C. Leiser, *J. d.R. and the Great Days of Opera* (London, 1933).—**NS/LK/DM**

De Reszke, Josephine, Polish soprano, sister of **Jean (Jan Mieczislaw) de Reszke** and Edouard de Reszke; b. Warsaw, June 4, 1855; d. there, Feb. 22, 1891. She studied at the St. Petersburg Cons., first appearing in public under the name of Giuseppina di Reschi at Venice in 1874. She sang Marguerite in Gounod's *Faust* (Aug. 1, 1874), with her brother Jean as Valentin; then was engaged at the Paris Opéra, where she made her debut as Ophelia in *Hamlet* by Ambroise Thomas (Paris, June 21, 1875); later sang in Madrid and Lisbon, and appeared as Aida at Covent Garden in London on April 18, 1881. She retired from the stage upon her marriage in 1885 and settled in Poland.—**NS/LK/DM**

Dering, Richard
See **Deering, Richard**

Dérivis, Henri Etienne, French bass, father of **Prosper Dérivis;** b. Albi, Aug. 2, 1780; d. Livry, Feb. 1, 1856. He made his debut at the Paris Opéra as Sarastro in the French version of *Die Zauberflöte* under the title of *Les Mystères d'Isis* in 1803. During the next 25 years he was a principal singer there, creating roles in works by Spontini (*La Vestale, Fernand Cortez,* and *Olympie*), Cherubini (*Les Abencérages*), Rossini (*Le Siège de Corinthe*), and others.—**NS/LK/DM**

Dérivis, Prosper, distinguished French bass, son of **Henri Etienne Dérivis;** b. Paris, Oct. 28, 1808; d. there, Feb. 11, 1880. He studied with Pellegrini and Nourrit in Paris, making his debut at the Paris Opéra in 1831. He subsequently created roles there in operas by Berlioz (*Benvenuto Cellini*), Meyerbeer (*Les Huguenots*), Donizetti (*Les Martyrs*), and others. He appeared at La Scala in Milan (1842–43), singing in the premieres of Verdi's *Nabucco* and *I Lombardi;* also sang in the first performance of Donizetti's *Linda di Chamounix* in Vienna in 1842. After his retirement from the stage in 1857, he taught voice in Paris.—**NS/LK/DM**

Dermota, Anton, Austrian tenor of Slovenian descent; b. Kropa, June 4, 1910; d. Vienna, June 22, 1989. After training at the Ljubljana Cons., he was a student in Vienna of Elisabeth Rado. In 1934 he made his operatic debut in Cluj; in 1936 he joined the Vienna State Opera, where he sang regularly during the next 40 years; in 1946 he was made a Kammersänger and in 1955 he sang Florestan at the reopening celebration of the restored Vienna State Opera house. He also sang at the Salzburg Festival, Milan's La Scala, the Paris Opéra, and London's Covent Garden, and appeared as a concert artist. In 1966 he became a prof. at the Vienna Academy of Music. He was best known for his roles in Mozart's operas, but he also was admired as Des Grieux, Lensky, Rodolfo, and Palestrina.—**NS/LK/DM**

Dernesch, Helga, Austrian soprano; b. Vienna, Feb. 3, 1939. She was educated at the Vienna Cons. She made her operatic debut at the Bern Stadttheater in 1961; then sang in Wiesbaden and Cologne; subsequently appeared at the Bayreuth Festivals. In 1969 Herbert von Karajan chose her for his Salzburg Easter Festival; in 1970 she made her debut at Covent Garden, London; also sang with the Hamburg State Opera, the Berlin Städtische Oper, and the Vienna State Opera. She sang many Wagnerian dramatic roles and those of Richard Strauss; from 1979 she turned her attention to mezzo-soprano parts. From 1982 she sang at the San Francisco Opera. On Oct. 14, 1985, she made her Metropolitan Opera debut in N.Y. as Mussorgsky's Marfa. In 1990 she appeared as Verdi's Mistress Quickly in Los Angeles. She sang Strauss's Clytemnestra at the Opéra de la Bastille in Paris in 1992. In 1996 she appeared as Frau von Luber in Weill's *Silbersee* at the London Promenade Concerts. She married **Werner Krenn.** —**NS/LK/DM**

De Rogatis, Pascual, Argentine composer and teacher; b. Teora, Italy, May 17, 1880; d. Buenos Aires, April 2, 1980. He studied piano and composition with Alberto Williams and violin with Pietro Melani and Rafael Albertini in Buenos Aires, where he then devoted himself to teaching and composing.

WORKS: DRAMATIC: *Huemac,* lyric drama (1913–14; Buenos Aires, July 22, 1916); *La novia del hereje* or *La Inquisición en Lima,* opera (c. 1924; Buenos Aires, June 13, 1935); incidental music; dance scores. ORCH.: *Suite árabe* (1902; Buenos Aires, Oct. 10, 1904); *Danza de las dríades* (1902); *Preludio sinfónico* (1903; Buenos Aires, Oct. 10, 1904); *Oriental* (1903; Buenos Aires, Nov.

20, 1905); *Marcha heroica* (1904); symphonic poems: *Marko y el hada* (1905), *Paisaje otoñal* (1905), *Belkiss en la selva* (1906), *Zupay* (1910), *Atipac: Escenas de la selva americana* (c. 1920), and *La fiesta del Chiqui* (1935); *Segunda oda de Safo* (1906); *América* c. 1920); *Fantasía indígena* (1920); *Suite americana* (1924; Buenos Aires, Aug. 24, 1926); *Estampas argentinas* (1942). OTHER: Chamber music, mostly for Solo Piano; *Oratorio laico* for Soprano, Tenor, Chorus, and Orch. (1910; Buenos Aires, May 5, 1928); many songs with piano.—**NS/LK/DM**

DeRose, Dena, pianist, singer; b. Binghamton, N.Y., Feb. 15, 1966. She began her formal piano training at the age of three after her mother heard her pick out simple melodies on a toy chord organ. She studied classical music through her early teens and, in high school, began to explore other styles of music. In college, she began to build a career as a jazz pianist, performing with bassists Slam Stewart and Major Holley, and appearing as a leader in and around upstate N.Y. In the mid-1980s, a series of hand surgeries interrupted her musical career. Unable to play the piano, she began to sing. For about a year and a half she worked exclusively as a vocalist, and after making a full recovery, began to integrate her piano playing with her singing. Since moving to N.Y.C. in 1992, she has performed on piano with Randy Brecker, Bob Moses, Peter Washington, Billy Drummond, Virginia Mayhew, Bruce Forman, Terry Clarke, Ingrid Jensen, and Dottie Dodgion, among others. She also appears frequently as both pianist and vocalist with her own quartet in N.Y. She has been teaching privately since the early 1980s. She conducts seminars and master classes at community music centers, high schools, and colleges, and is a member of the piano and voice faculty of Stanford Univ.'s Stanford Jazz Workshop (summer program). She also serves as accompanist and vocal coach for the Actors' Guild at the New School for Social Research in N.Y. She is on the faculty at The N.J. Performing Arts Center's Jazz for Teens programs under the direction of Rufus Reid. In 1999, she was chosen as the jazz vocal adjudicator for The Star-Ledger Award Scholarship given by The N.J. Performing Arts Center in Newark, N.J.

DISC.: *Introducing Dena DeRose* (1996); *Another World* (1999); *Rob Bargad: The Shadow of Your Smile* (1998).—**LP**

Dervaux, Pierre, noted French conductor and teacher; b. Juvisy-sur-Orge, Jan. 3, 1917; d. Marseilles, Feb. 20, 1992. He studied at the Paris Cons. with Philipp, Armand Ferté, Nat, J. and N. Gallon, and Samuel-Roussel. After conducting at the Paris Opéra-Comique (1945–53), he was permanent conductor at the Paris Opéra (1956–70); from 1958 he was also president and chief conductor of the Concerts Colonne in Paris. He was music director of the Orchestre Symphonique de Québec (1968–71), the Orchestre Philharmonique des Pays de la Loire (1971–78), and in Nice (1979–82). He taught at the École Normale de Musique in Paris (1964–86), the Montreal Cons. (1965–72), and the Nice Academy (1971–82). Dervaux was especially admired for his brilliant and colorful interpretations of the French repertoire. He also composed, producing 2 syms., concertos, chamber music, and piano pieces. —**NS/LK/DM**

Derzhinskaya, Xenia (Georgievna), notable Russian soprano; b. Kiev, Feb. 6, 1889; d. Moscow, June 9, 1951. She was a pupil of F. Pash and M. Marchesi in Kiev. After appearing in concerts there, she settled in Moscow and sang at the Narodniy Dom Opera (1913–15), and subsequently was a leading member of the Bolshoi Theater (1915–48); also pursued a concert career, and taught voice at the Moscow Cons. (1947–51). In 1937 she was named a People's Artist of the USSR. She won high praise in her homeland for her compelling portrayals of roles in Russian operas.

BIBL.: E. Grosheva, *X. G. D.* (Moscow, 1952).—**NS/LK/DM**

De Sabata, Victor (actually, Vittorio), outstanding Italian conductor and composer; b. Trieste, April 10, 1892; d. Santa Margherita Ligure, Dec. 11, 1967. He studied with Michele Saladino and Giacomo Orefice at the Milan Cons. (1901–11). An extremely versatile musician, he could play piano with considerable élan, and also took lessons on cello, clarinet, oboe, and bassoon. He was encouraged in his career as a conductor by Toscanini; at the same time, he began to compose operas. His first production was *Il Macigno*, which was first performed at La Scala in Milan on March 30, 1917. His symphonic poem *Juventus* (1919) was conducted at La Scala by Toscanini. De Sabata's style of composition involved Romantic Italian formulas, with lyric and dramatic episodes receiving an equal share of attention. In the meantime, he filled engagements as an opera and sym. conductor in Italy. In 1927 he conducted concerts in N.Y. and Cincinnati, in 1936 he conducted at the Vienna State Opera, in 1939 he was a guest conductor with the Berlin Phil., and in 1946 he conducted in Switzerland. On April 21, 1946, he was invited to conduct a sym. concert in London, the first conductor from an "enemy country" to conduct in England after World War II. He then was a guest conductor with the Chicago Sym. Orch. in 1949, and with the N.Y. Phil. and the Boston Sym. Orch. in 1950. He became popular with American audiences, and in 1952 was engaged to conduct in N.Y., Philadelphia, Washington, D.C., Baltimore, St. Louis, and Detroit. In 1953 he conducted in Philadelphia, Los Angeles, San Francisco, and Santa Barbara, Calif. On Feb. 18, 1957, he conducted at the funeral of Toscanini; this was his last appearance on the podium. He was the father-in-law of **Aldo Ceccato.** As a conductor, De Sabata acquired a brilliant reputation in both operatic and symphonic repertoire. He was an impassioned and dynamic conductor who excelled particularly in the works of Verdi and Wagner.

WORKS: DRAMATIC: *Il Macigno*, opera (Milan, March 30, 1917; 2nd version, Driada, Turin, Nov. 12, 1935); *Lisistrata*, opera (1920); *Le mille e una notte*, ballet (Milan, Jan. 20, 1931); theater music for Max Reinhardt's production of *The Merchant of Venice* (Venice, July 18, 1934). **ORCH:** 3 symphonic poems: *Juventus* (1919), *La notte di Platon* (1924), and *Gethsemani* (1925).

BIBL.: R. Mucci, *V. d.S.* (Lanciano, 1937); T. Celli, *L'arte di V. d.S.* (Turin, 1978).—**NS/LK/DM**

De Santi, Angelo, distinguished Italian music scholar; b. Trieste, July 12, 1847; d. Rome, Jan. 28, 1922. He became a Jesuit at age 16, and after studies in Italy and France, he completed his training at the Univ. of Innsbruck (ordained, 1877). He taught at the Zara Episcopal Seminary before being called to Rome in 1887 by Pope Leo XIII to take part in the reform of church music; he also taught music at the Vatican Seminary, where he founded a schola cantorum. His reformist zeal encountered opposition and he quit his position in 1893. However, Pope Pius X's encyclical *Motu proprio* (1903) reflects De Santi's views. In 1910 he founded the Scuola Superiore di Musica Sacra. With C. Respighi, he founded the *Rassegna gregoriana* in 1902.

WRITINGS (all publ. in Rome unless otherwise given): *Il maestro Filippo Capocci e le sur composizioni per organo* (1888); *Intorno al metodo di canto ecclesiastico* (Prato, 1888); *S. Gregorio Magno, Leone XIII e il canto liturgico* (1891); *A Solesmes fra i monaci esiliati all'Isola di Wight* (1901); *Il "cursus" nella storia letteraria e nella liturgia* (1903); *L'origine delle feste natalizie* (1907); *Il primo decennio della Pontificia scuola superiore di musica sacra* (1920); *Le "Laudes" nell'incoronazione de Sommo Pontefice* (n.d.).—**LK/DM**

Desarzens, Victor, Swiss conductor; b. Château d'Oex, Oct. 27, 1908; d. Lausanne, Feb. 13, 1986. After studies with Porta (violin) and Hoesslin (conducting) at the Lausanne Cons., he completed his training with Enesco. He began his career as first violinist in the Orchestre de la Suisse Romande in Geneva and as a chamber music player. In 1942 he founded a chamber ensemble in Lausanne, which later became the Lausanne Chamber Orch., which he led until 1973 in radio broadcasts and tours of Europe. He also was music director of the Winterthur Musikkollegium (1945–76).

BIBL.: J.-M. Pittier, *The Musician and the Man: Portrait of V. D., 1908–1986* (Vevey, 1992).—**NS/LK/DM**

Deschamps-Jehin, (Marie-)Blanche, outstanding French contralto; b. Lyons, Sept. 18, 1857; d. Paris, June 1923. She studied at the Cons. in Lyons and later at the Paris Cons., making her debut in Brussels in *Giroflé-Girofla* in 1874. She then sang at the Théâtre Royal de la Monnaie in Brussels (1879–85), during which tenure she created the role of Hérodiade in Massenet's opera (1881); then sang in Paris at the Opéra-Comique (1885–91) and the Opéra (1891–1902), and at Covent Garden in London (1891). In later years she appeared at the Monte Carlo Opera and then mainly in concerts. She was married to **Léon Jehin.**—**NS/LK/DM**

Desderi, Ettore, Italian composer and pedagogue; b. Asti, Dec. 10, 1892; d. Florence, Nov. 23, 1974. He studied with Luigi Perrachio at the Turin Cons. and then with Franco Alfano in Bologna. From 1933 to 1941 he was director of the Liceo Musicale in Alessandria and, from 1941 to 1951, a teacher of composition at the Milan Cons. From 1951 to 1963 he was director of the Bologna Cons. He publ. *La musica contemporanea* (Turin, 1930) and numerous articles in Italian and German journals.

WORKS: *Intermezzi all' Antigone* for Orch. (1924); *Job*, biblical cantata (1927); *Sinfonia davidica* for Soloists, Chorus, and Orch. (1929); Violin Sonata; Cello Sonata; many choral works.

BIBL.: M. Rinaldi, *E. D.* (Tivoli, 1943); *A E. D. nel suo 70 compleanno* (Bologna, 1963).—**NS/LK/DM**

De Segurola, Andrés (Perello), Spanish bass; b. Valencia, March 27, 1874; d. Barcelona, Jan. 22, 1953. He studied with Pietro Farvaro in Barcelona, where he made his operatic debut in 1898 at the Teatro Liceo. On Oct. 10, 1901, he made his first appearance with the Metropolitan Opera in a concert during the company's visit to Toronto, and 2 days later sang Laurent in *Roméo et Juliet* there; his debut with the company in N.Y. came on March 3, 1902, as the King in *Aida*, and he remained on its roster until the end of the season; then was again on its roster from 1909 to 1920. He later appeared in films and taught in Hollywood (1931–51) before settling in Barcelona. Among his most prominent roles were Basilio, Alvise, Varlaam, Colline, Sparafucile, and Geronte in *Manon Lescaut*. G. Creegan ed. *Through My Monocle: Memoirs of the Great Basso Andreas de Segurola* (Steubenville, Ohio, 1991).—**NS/LK/DM**

DeShannon, Jackie (originally, **Sharon Lee Myers**), one of the most versatile artists in pop music who never got her full measure of success; b. Hazel, Ky., Aug. 21, 1944. Sharon Lee Myers was performing rockabilly by the time she was 15 around her native Ky. A year later, she migrated to L.A. and started recording for a series of small labels. Her first album was a cover of Ray Charles's tunes so raw and gritty that her label wouldn't release it. She also started getting known as a songwriter, creating or collaborating on hits for artists like Brenda Lee, the Kalin Twins, the Searchers, Marianne Faithfull, the Fleetwoods, and Irma Thomas. The Byrds covered her tune "Don't Doubt Yourself, Babe.'

As a performer, ironically, DeShannon became best known for singing other people's songs. Sonny Bono wrote "Needles and Pins" for her, soon a hit for the Searchers (as was her "When You Walk in the Room"). Her first hit was a cover of Burt Bacharach's "What the World Needs Now Is Love," which she took to #7 in 1965. She was one of the opening acts for The Beatles on their first major tour of the U.S.

Four years later, DeShannon had her second substantial hit, one of her own compositions this time. She took her tune "Put a Little Love in Your Heart" to gold status. It peaked at #4. She followed this with the #40 "Love Will Find a Way" several months later. That same year she was given a recurring role on the television show *The Virginian*.

Many of DeShannon's songs became hits for other artists. Al Green and Annie Lennox did a version of "Put a Little Love in Your Heart" for the soundtrack to the movie *Scrooged* that went to #9. Her song "Bette Davis Eyes" became a chart-topping hit for another songwriter who did well with outside material, Kim Carnes. For her own albums, she recorded her own tunes and songs by the likes of Warren Zevon, Robbie Robertson, and Tim Hardin, and collaborated with folks like Randy Newman and Jack Nitzsche. She married successful soundtrack composer Randy Edelman.

DISC.: *Jackie DeShannon* (1963); *Surf Party* (soundtrack; 1963); *Breakin' It Up on the Beatles Tour!* (1964); *This Is Jackie DeShannon* (1965); *In the Wind* (1965); *C'mon Let's Live a Little* (soundtrack; 1965); *Are You Ready for This?* (1966); *New Image* (1967); *Here's Jackie, You Won't Forget Me* (1965); *For You* (1967);

What the World Needs Now Is Love (1968); *Laurel Canyon* (1968); *Me about You* (1968); *Lonely Girl* (1968); *Put a Little Love in Your Heart* (1969); *To Be Free* (1970); *Songs* (1971); *Jackie* (1972); *Your Baby Is a Lady* (1974); *New Arrangement* (1975); *You're the Only Dancer* (1977); *Sky High* (1985); *The Very Best of Jackie DeShannon* (1988); *Good As Gold!* (1990); *Trouble with Jackie Dee* (1991); *The Best of Jackie DeShannon* (1991); *What the World Needs Now* (1992); *What the World Needs Now...: The Definitive...* (1994); *You're the Only Dancer/Quick Touches* (1995); *The Very Best of Jackie DeShannon...* (1996).—**HB**

Deslandres, Adolphe - Edouard - Marie, French organist and composer; b. Batignolles, Monceaux, Jan. 22, 1840; d. Paris, July 30, 1911. He was a pupil of Leborne and Benoist at the Paris Cons., and in 1862 was appointed organist at Ste.-Marie. He wrote the operas *Dimanche et lundi* (1872), *Le Chevalier Bijou* (1875), and *Fridolin* (1876), as well as *Ode à l'harmonie*, *La Banque brisée*, a patriotic dirge, *Les Sept Paroles*, and many sacred choruses.—**NS/LK/DM**

Des Marais, Paul (Emile), American composer; b. Menominee, Mich., June 23, 1920. He studied with Sowerby in Chicago (1937–41), Boulanger in Cambridge, Mass. (1941–42) and Paris (1949), and Piston at Harvard Univ. (B.A., 1949; M.A., 1953). He received the Lili Boulanger prize (1947–48), the Boott prize in composition from Harvard (1949), and a John Knowles Paine Traveling Fellowship (1949–51). After teaching at Harvard (1953–56), he was on the faculty of the Univ. of Calif. at Los Angeles (from 1956), where he received the Inst. of Creative Arts Award (1964–65); he later received the Phoebe Ketchum Thorne award (1970–73). He publ. the study *Harmony* (1962) and contributed articles to *Perspectives of New Music*. His early music was oriented toward neo-Classicism, with pandiatonic excrescences in harmonic structures. He later moved to a free combination of serial and non-serial elements, functioning on broad tonal planes.

WORKS: DRAMATIC: *Epiphanies*, chamber opera (1968); *Orpheus*, theater piece for Narrator and Instruments (1987); incidental music to Dryden's *A Secular Masque* (1976), Shakespeare's *A Midsummer Night's Dream* (1976), Sophocles' *Oedipus* (1978), G.B. Shaw's *St. Joan* (1980), Dryden's *Marriage à la Mode* (1981), Shakespeare's *As You Like It* (1983), and G. Etherege's *The Man of Mode* (1984). **Dance:** *Triplum* for Organ and Percussion (1981); *Touch* for 2 Pianos (1984). **CHAMBER:** 2 piano sonatas (1947, 1952); *Theme and Changes* for Harpsichord (1953); *Capriccio* for 2 Pianos and Percussion (1962); *2 Movements* for 2 Pianos and Percussion (1972; rev. and enl. as *3 Movements*, 1975); *Baroque Isles: The Voyage Out* for 2 Keyboard Percussionists (1986); *The French Park* for 2 Guitars (1988). **CHORAL:** *Polychoric Mass* for Voices (1949); *Motet* for Voices, Cellos, and Double Basses (1959); *Psalm 121* for Chorus (1959); *Organum 1–6* for Chorus, Organ, and Percussion (1972; rev. and enl. 1980); *Brief Mass* for Chorus, Organ, and Percussion (1973); *Seasons of the Mind* for Chorus, Piano 4-Hands, and Celesta (1980–81). **VOCAL:** *Le Cimetière marin* for Voice, Keyboards, and Percussion (1971); solo songs.—**NS/LK/DM**

Desmarets, Henri, important French composer; b. Paris, Feb. 1661; d. Lunéville, Sept. 7, 1741. He was a boy soprano in the Paris royal chapel, subsequently becoming one of the most highly regarded musicians of his day. Many of his works were performed at the court of Louis XIV. He served as maître de chapelle at the Jesuit Coll. of Louis-le-Grand. His personal life was stormy. After the death of his wife, he became involved with one of his students; when the girl's father objected, the lovers fled to Brussels in 1699. In 1701 he was made maître de musique de la chambre to Philip V in Madrid, and in 1707 became surintendant de la musique to Leopold I, Duke of Lorraine, in Lunéville. Having been sentenced to death in absentia for personal indiscretions, he was unable to return to France until he was pardoned by the regent in 1720. For the most part, he spent his remaining years in Lunéville.

WORKS: DRAMATIC: O p e r a (all 1st perf. in Paris): *Didon* (Sept. 11, 1693); *Circé* (Oct. 1, 1694); *Venus et Adonis* (March 7, 1697); *Théagène et Cariclée* (Feb. 3, 1695); *Iphigénie en Tauride* (May 6, 1704); *Renaud, ou La Suite d'Armide* (March 5, 1722). **B a l l e t** : *Les Amours de Momus* (May 25, 1695); *Les Fêtes galantes* (May 10, 1698).

BIBL.: M. Antoine, *Henry D.* (Paris, 1965).—NS/LK/DM

Desmazures, Laurent, famous French organist; b. Marseilles, Nov. 10, 1714; d. while playing the organ at the church of St. Férréol there, April 29, 1778. He was the son of Charles Desmazures (b. 1670; d. Marseilles, Feb. 13, 1736), an organist and composer who served as organist at Marseilles Cathedral. In 1737 he began his career as an organist at the Moissac Abbey, and subsequently was organist at the Cathedral of St. Lazare d'Autun (1750–52), at Notre Dame Cathedral in Rouen (1758–77), and at the church of St. Férréol in Marseilles (from 1777). Although he lost 3 of his fingers on his left hand, he overcame this handicap by learning to play with false fingers that in no way diminished his dexterity as a virtuoso. He also was a composer and wrote the opéra- ballet *Les fêtes de Grenade* (Dijon, Jan. 12, 1752). —LK/DM

Desmond, Astra, English mezzo-soprano and teacher; b. Torquay, April 10, 1893; d. Faversham, Aug. 16, 1973. She studied in London at Westfield Coll. and with Blanche Marchesi at the Royal Academy of Music. Following additional training in Berlin, she returned to London and made her recital debut in 1915. While she made some appearances with the Carl Rosa Opera Co., she devoted herself principally to the concert and oratorio repertory; was a prof. of voice at the Royal Academy of Music (from 1947). In 1949 she was made a Commander of the Order of the British Empire. Her interpretations of English music, particularly works by Elgar and Vaughan Williams, were outstanding. Having mastered 12 languages, she also excelled as an interpreter of the Scandinavian song literature.—NS/LK/DM

Desmond, Paul (originally, **Emil Breitenfeld**), alto saxophonist; b. San Francisco, Nov. 25, 1924; d. N.Y., May 30, 1977. He chose his surname at random from a telephone book. He was given the nickname "The Stork," because he would stand on one leg and lean on the piano when he played. He learned the rudiments of music from his father, who played the organ for silent movies; Desmond played clarinet in the school orch. and then at San Francisco State Univ., but eventually concentrated on the alto saxophone. He named Pete Brown and Willie Smith as influences. He played clarinet in the big bands of Jack Fina and Alvino Rey. He idolized Charlie Parker, but never imitated him. He interviewed Parker on Boston radio (a tape survives), and the two would play chess together; he said that the one time he beat Parker was the proudest moment of his life. Though he had been married early in life, he never remarried and gained a reputation as a ladies' man. In 1948 he joined Dave Brubeck's octet, staying until 1950; he rejoined Brubeck, playing with his new quartet from 1951 to 1967. In 1956 when Joe Morello joined the Quartet, Desmond, who disliked Morello's crowd- pleasing performances, threatened to quit. Desmond stayed and, though they shared the same concert stage nearly every night, did not speak to Morello for a year. Eventually they became friends, but Desmond would often go backstage and read a book during Morello's extended drum solo on "Take Five." The group toured the world, playing 300 concerts a year, and had a Columbia recording contract that called for four albums a year. In 1959 Desmond penned the first million-seller jazz single, "Take Five." It became the Quartet's theme, performed at all their concert appearances, and made Desmond a small fortune in royalties. His lyrical style and light, airy tone was liked even by people who were not Brubeck fans. In 1953 *Down Beat* proclaimed, "It is again a case where the sideman (in this instance Desmond) seems to be quite superior to the leader as a jazzman."

When the Quartet split up in 1967, Desmond unofficially retired and didn't play his horn for three years. Eventually he was coaxed out of retirement to play occasional gigs with his friends. He fronted a quartet featuring guitarist Jim Hall for two weeks at the Half Note in N.Y.C., breaking the club's attendance record. At the New Orleans Jazz Festival he played a soaring set with Gerry Mulligan. As guest soloist he played with the Modern Jazz Quartet for a 1971 Christmas concert. He played on several albums with his long- time friend Chet Baker. When Brubeck led a group with Jack Six, Alan Dawson, and Gerry Mulligan, Desmond often joined them. He appeared with Brubeck in a series of concerts called "Two Generations of Brubeck" in which Dave played with his sons, and in 1976, the Quartet reunited for the Silver Anniversary Tour. They were greeted with enthusiasm wherever they played but the deteriorating eyesight of Joe Morello cut the tour short. In 1975 Jim Hall talked him into playing with Ed Bickert at Toronto's Bourbon Street club. After the first two weeks Desmond rushed back to N.Y. and talked producer Creed Taylor into flying Bickert in to record. Don Thompson, bassist on the gig, also recorded a number of the club dates, which were released. The group appeared on CBC-TV's "Take 30," were recorded at the Edmonton Jazz Festival, played the Monterey Jazz festival, and at a club in San Francisco called the Matador; they even closed the Matador. Desmond's tune "Wendy," written for these gigs, was named for the daughter of one of his old girlfriends in the San Francisco area. His last concert was with Dave Brubeck in

February 1977 at N.Y.'s Avery Fisher Hall. He was only able to play the second half due to shortness of breath and took no encore. Though his drinking was legendary, it was his smoking three packs of cigarettes a day that caught up with him and he died of lung cancer. He said he was writing a humorous memoir of his years on the road with the Quartet, to be titled *How Many of You Are There in the Quartet?*—a question frequently asked by airline stewardesses—but he never did. Paul left his alto in his will to Dave's son, Michael Brubeck. His Steinway piano went to Bradley's, a small jazz club in Manhattan. *Pure Desmond: The Wit & Music of Paul Desmond* is a one-hour documentary film, currently in development by Paul Caulfield.

DISC.: *Paul Desmond* (1954); *Paul and Dave's Jazz Interwoven* (1954); *Featuring Don Elliot* (1956); *Blues in Time* (1957); *East of the Sun* (1959); *First Place Again* (1959); *Paul Desmond and Friends* (1959); *Desmond Blue* (1961); *Late Lament* (1961); *Two of a Mind* (1962); *Glad to Be Unhappy* (1963); *Take Ten* (1963) *Bossa Antigua* (1964); *Summertime* (1968); *Bridge over Troubled Water* (1969); *In Concert at Town Hall* (1971); *Skylark* (1973); *Pure Desmond* (1974). **BRUBECK AND DESMOND:** *Duets* (1975); *Paul Desmond Quartet Live* (1975; unissued titles exist); *The Duets: 1975* (1975). **—LP**

Désormière, Roger, brilliant French conductor; b. Vichy, Sept. 13, 1898; d. Paris, Oct. 25, 1963. He studied with Koechlin in Paris. After serving as music director of the Paris Ballets Suédois (1924–25) and the Ballets Russes (1925–29), he was conductor (from 1936) and director (1944–46) of the Opéra-Comique; in 1945–46 he also was assoc. director of the Paris Opéra. In 1946–47 he was a guest conductor with the BBC Sym. Orch. in London, and in 1949 he returned to that city with the Opéra-Comique to conduct *Pelléas et Mélisande* at Covent Garden. He also appeared as a guest conductor of opera and sym. throughout Europe. Désormière was an outstanding interpreter of the French repertory. He also championed 20th-century French music, conducting premieres of works by Satie, Koechlin, Roussel, Milhaud, Poulenc, Messiaen, Boulez et al. After being stricken with aphasia and other disorders, he abandoned his career in 1952.

BIBL.: D. Mayer and P. Souvchinsky, *R. D. et son temps* (Monaco, 1966).**—NS/LK/DM**

Des Prez, Josquin, great Franco-Flemish composer; b. probably in Hainaut, c. 1440; d. Conde-sur-Escaut, near Valenciennes, Aug. 27, 1521. His surname was variously spelled: *Després, Desprez, Deprés, Depret, Deprez, Desprets, Dupré,* and by the Italians *Del Prato* (Latinized as *a Prato, a Pratis, Pratensis*), etc.; while Josquin (contracted from the Flemish Jossekin, "little Joseph") appears as *Jossé, Jossien, Jusquin, Giosquin, Josquinus, Jacobo, Jodocus, Jodoculus,* etc. His epitaph reads *Jossé de Prés.* However, in the motet *Illibata Dei Virgo Nutrix* (contained in Vol. 9 of the Josquin ed.), of which the text is quite likely of Josquin's authorship, his name appears as an acrostic, thus: I, O, S, Q, V, I, N, D[es], P, R, E, Z; this seems to leave little doubt as to its correct spelling. Few details of Josquin's early life are known. He may have been a boy chorister of the

Collegiate Church at St.-Quentin, later becoming canon and choirmaster there. He possibly was a pupil of Ockeghem, whom he greatly admired (after Ockeghem's death, in 1497, he wrote *La Déploration de Johan Okeghem*). From 1459 to 1472 he sang at the Milan Cathedral, and by July 1474 he was at the Court of Duke Galeazzo Maria Sforza, Milan, as a chorister. After the Duke's assassination he entered the service of the Duke's brother, Cardinal Ascanio Sforza. From 1486 to 1494 he was a singer in the papal choir under the Popes Innocent VIII and Alexander VI. He was also active, for various periods, in Florence, where he met the famous theorist Pietro Aron, Modena, and in Ferrara (where Isaac was also) as maestro di cappella in 1503–04. Later Josquin returned to Burgundy, settling in Conde-sur-Escaut (1504), where he became provost of Notre Dame. As a composer, he was considered by contemporary musicians and theorists to be the greatest of his period, and he had a strong influence on all those who came into contact with his music or with him personally, as a teacher; Adriaan Petit Coclicus, who may have been one of Josquin's pupils, publ. a method in 1552 entitled *Compendium musices,* based on Josquin's teaching. He described Josquin as "princeps musicorum." His works were sung everywhere, and universally admired. In them he achieves a complete union between word and tone, thereby fusing the intricate Netherlandish contrapuntal devices into expressive and beautiful art forms. Two contrasting styles are present in his compositions: some are intricately contrapuntal, displaying the technical ingenuity characteristic of the Netherlands style; others, probably as a result of Italian influence, are homophonic.

WORKS: Masses (In Petrucci's Lib. I, Venice, 1502): *L'Omme armé; La sol fa re mi; Gaudeamus; Fortunata desperata; L'Omme armé, sexti toni.* (Ibid., II, 1505): *Ave Maris stella; Hercules, dux Ferrarae; Malheur me bat; Lami Baudichon; Una musque de Buscaya; Dung aultre amor.* (Ibid., III, 1514): *Mater patris; Faysans regrets; Ad fugam; Di dadi; De Beata Virgine; Sine nomine.* Petrucci's vols. contain all but 1 of the extant masses. (In Graphäus's *Missae III*): *Pange lingua; Da pacem; Sub tuum praesidium.* Some of these are scattered in other collections, and fragments are found in still others. Motets were publ. by Petrucci (8 in the *Odhecaton,* 1501; others in his books of motets); by Peutinger (*Liber selectarum cantionum,* 1520); and by others of the period. French chansons were publ. by T. Susato (1545), P. Attaignant (1549), and Du Chemin (1553). A complete ed. of Josquin's works was issued (1921–69; 55 vols.) by the Vereeniging voor Nederlandsche Muziekgeschiedenis under the general editorship of A. Smijers, M. Amlonowycz, and W. Elders. The New Josquin Edition, under general ed. W. Elders, was launched in 1988. The International Josquin Festival Conference was held in N.Y. from June 21 to 25, 1971; reports appeared in *Journal of the American Musicological Society* (Fall 1971), *Die Musikforschung* (Oct.–Dec. 1971), and *Current Musicology,* 14 (1972); papers presented at the conference were ed. by E. Lowinsky (London, 1976).

BIBL.: F. de Ménil, *Les Grands Musiciens du Nord: J. de Prés* (Paris, 1897); A. Schering, *Die niederländische Orgelmesse im Zeitalter des J.* (Leipzig, 1912); M. Antonowitsch, *Die Motette "Benedicta Es" von J. D. P.* (Utrecht, 1951); H. Osthoff, *J. Desprez* (2 vols., Tutzing, 1962, 1965); A. Ghislanzoni, *J. D. P. (Joducus*

Pratensis) (Frosinone, 1976); S. Charles, *J. des Pres.: A Guide to Research* (N.Y. and London, 1983); J.-P. Ouvrard, *J. Desprez et ses contemporains: De l'écrit au sonore, guide pratique d'interprétation* (Arles, 1986).—**NS/LK/DM**

Dessau, Bernhard, German violinist and composer; b. Hamburg, March 1, 1861; d. Berlin, April 28, 1923. He studied violin with Joachim and Wieniawski, then held various posts as concertmaster in Germany and the Netherlands. In 1906 he was appointed a prof. at the Berlin Cons. He was a prolific composer, his Violin Concerto "im alten Stil" becoming widely known.—**NS/LK/DM**

Dessau, Paul, prominent German composer; b. Hamburg, Dec. 19, 1894; d. Königs Wusterhausen, near Berlin, June 27, 1979. He studied violin with Florian Zajic at the Klindworth-Scharwenka Cons. in Berlin (1910–12), and then returned to Hamburg to study piano and score reading with Eduard Behm and composition with Max Loewengard. In 1912 he became co-répétiteur at the Hamburg City Theater, and then went to Bremem in 1913 as an operetta conductor at the Tivoli Theater. After military service during World War I, he returned to Hamburg in 1918 as conductor and composer at the Kammerspiele. He was co-répétiteur and conductor at the Cologne Opera (1919–23) and at the Mainz City Theater (1923–25), and then was first conductor at the Berlin Städtische Oper from 1925. When the Nazis came to power in 1933, Dessau lost his post and made his way to Paris, where he came into contact with René Leibowitz and 12-tone music. In 1939 he went to the U.S. While in N.Y., he commenced a long collaboration with Bertolt Brecht. In 1944 he went to Hollywood, where he composed for films. He also composed the music for his most successful collaboration with Brecht, *Mutter Courage und ihre Kinder* (1946). In 1948 he settled in East Germany, where he continued to work with Brecht until the latter's death in 1956. In 1952 Dessau was made a member of the German Academy of Arts, becoming vice-president and prof. there in 1959. He taught at the Zeuthen school, near Berlin, from 1960. In 1953, 1956, 1965, and 1974 he was awarded state prizes by the German Democratic Republic, and in 1964 he received its National Order of Merit. His wife was **Ruth Berghaus.** In his earliest scores, Dessau pursued expressionist and neo-Classical precepts. He then developed an interest in Jewish folk music while exploring 12-tone music. His association with Brecht led him into more popular modes of expression. His works after settling in East Germany are imbued with the progressive ideals of socialist realism, but with increasing serial applications.

WORKS: DRAMATIC: O p e r a : *Giuditta* (1910–12; unfinished); *Orpheus 1930/31,* radio operetta (Berlin, 1931; rev. as *Orpheus und der Bürgermeister*); *Die Reisen des Glücksgotts* (1945; unfinished); *Das Verhöor des Lukullus* (1949; Berlin, March 17, 1951; rev. version as *Die Verurteilung des Lukullus,* Berlin, Oct. 12, 1951); *Puntila* (1956–59; Berlin, Nov. 15, 1966); *Lanzelot* (1967–69; Berlin, Dec. 19, 1969); *Einstein* (1971–73; Berlin, Feb. 16, 1974); *Leonce und Lena* (1977–78; Berlin, Nov. 24, 1979). **I n c i d e n - t a l M u s i c T o :** Brecht's *99%,* later retitled *Furcht und Elend des Dritten Reiches* (1938), *Mutter Courage und ihre Kinder*

(1946), *Der gute Mensch von Sezuan* (1947), *Herr Puntila und sein Knecht* (1949), *Mann ist Mann* (1951), and *Der kaukasische Kreide-kreis* (1953–54); also Goethe's *Faust,* part I (1949) and *Urfaust* (1952), F. Wolf's *Der arme Konrad* (1951), J. Becher's *Der Weg nach Fussen* (1956), Shakespeare's *Coriolanus* (1964), Weiss's *Vietnam-Diskurs* (1968), and Müller's *Zement* (1973). Also film scores, tanzscenen, lehrstücke, and schulstücke. **ORCH.:** 2 syms.: No. 1 (1926) and No. 2 (1934; rev. 1962); *Trauermarsch* for Winds (1953); *Sinfonischer Marsch,* retitled *Sozialistische Festouvertüre* (1953; rev. 1963); 4 sets of *Orchestermusik:* No. 1, *1955* (1955), No. 2, *Meer dur Stürme* (1967), No. 3, *Lenin* (1970), and No. 4 (1973); *In memoriam Bertolt Brecht* (1957); *Bach-Variationen* (1963); *Divertimento* for Chamber Orch. (1964). **CHAMBER:** Concertino for Violin, Flute, Clarinet, and Horn (1924); *Lustige Variationen über Hab mein' Wagen vollgeladen* for Clarinet, Bassoon, and Harpsichord (1928; rev. for Clarinet, Bassoon, and Piano, 1953); 5 string quartets (1932; 1942–43; 1943–46; 1948; 1955); *Hebräische Melodie* for Violin and Piano (1935); *Burleske* for Cello and Piano (1932); Suite for Saxophone and Piano (1935); *Jewish Dance* for Violin and Piano (1940); *2 Kanons* for Flute, Clarinet, and Bassoon (1942); *Arie* for Cello and Piano (1950); *5 Tanzstücke* for Mandolin, Guitar, and Accordion (1951); *Quattrodramma 1965* for 4 Cellos, 2 Pianos, and 2 Percussion (1965); *3 Stücke* for 2 Trumpets or Clarinets and Trombone or Bassoon (1975). **P i - a n o :** Sonata (1914; rev. 1948); *12 Studien* (1932); *10 Kinder-stücke* (1934; rev. 1953); *Zwölfton Versuche* (1937); *Guernica* (1938); *11 Jüdische Volktänze* (1946); *Klavierstück über BACH* (1948); *5 Studien für Anfänger* (1948); Sonatine (1955); *3 Intermezzi* (1955); *Klavierstücke für Maxim* (1955–63). **VOCAL: O r a t o r i o s a n d C a n t a t a s :** *Haggada* for Soli, Chorus, Children's Chorus, and Orch. (1936; rev. 1962); *2 Gebete* for Voice, Chorus, and Organ (1939); *Jeworechecho* for Baritone, Chorus, and Organ (1941); *Internationale Kriegsfibel* (1944–45); *Deutsches Miserere* for Soli, Chorus, Children's Chorus, Orch., Organ, and Trautonium (1944–47); *An die Mütter und an die Lehrer* for Mezzo- soprano, Speaker, Chorus, 3 Trumpets, 2 Pianos, and Timpani (1950); *Die Appell* for Soli, Speaker, Chorus, Children's Chorus, and Orch. (1951–52); *Die Erziehung der Hirse* for Baritone, Speaker, Chorus, Youth Chorus, and Orch. (1952; rev. 1954); *Lilo Herrmann* for Sprechstimme, Small Chorus, Flute, Clarinet, Trumpet, Violin, Viola, and Cello (1953); *Hymne auf den Beginn einer neuen Geschichte der Menschheit* for Soprano, Speaker, Chorus, 3 Pianos, 2 Harps, Double Bass, Timpani, and Percussion (1959; rev. 1964); *Jüdische Chronik* for Baritone, Speaker, Chamber Chorus, and Small Orch. (1960; in collaboration with Blacher, Hartmann, Henze, and Wagner-Régeny); *Margurer Bericht* for Baritone, Chorus, Children's Chorus, and Orch. (1961); *Appell der Arbeiterklasse* for Alto, Tenor, Chorus, and Orch. (1961); *Requiem für Lumumba* for Soprano, Baritone, Speaker, Chorus, and Instruments (1963); *Geschäftsbericht* for 4 Soli, Speaker, Chorus, and Instruments (1967). **O t h e r V o c a l :** *Psalm XV* (1927); *Psalm XIII* (1930–31); *Chormusik mit Schlagzeug* (1930–31); *Aus-marsch* (1933); *Hawel Hawalim* for Chorus and Piano or Organ (1939); *Grabschrift für Gorki* for Unison Men's Voices and Winds (1947); *Grabschrift für Rosa Luxemburg* for Chorus and Orch. (1948); *Grabschrift für Karl Liebknecht* for Chorus and Orch. (1948); *Proletarier aller Länder, vereinigt euch!* (1948); *3 Chorlieder* for Chorus and Orch. (1949); *Grabschrift für Lenin* for Chorus and Orch. (1951); *Dreistimmiger Kanon für Otto Nagel* (1959); *Sang der Gesänge* for Chorus and Percussion (1963); much solo vocal music.

WRITINGS: *Musikarbeit in der Schule* (Berlin, 1968); *Aus Gesprächen* (Leipzig, 1975); *Notizen und Noten* (Leipzig, 1974); F. Hennenberg, ed., *Opern* (Berlin, 1976).

BIBL.: F. Hennenberg, *D. Brecht: Musikalische Arbeiten* (Berlin, 1963); idem, *P. D.: Eine Biographie* (Leipzig, 1965); idem, *Für Sie porträtiert: P. D.* (Leipzig, 1974; 2nd ed., 1981); K. Angermann, ed., *Symposion P. D.* (Hofheim, 1994).—NS/LK/DM

Dessauer, Josef, Bohemian composer; b. Prague, May 28, 1798; d. Mödling, near Vienna, July 8, 1876. He studied piano with Tomaschek and composition with Dionys Weber in Prague. He wrote several operas: *Lidwina* (Prague, 1836), *Ein Besuch in Saint-Cyr* (Dresden, May 6, 1838; his best work), *Paquita* (Vienna, 1851), *Domingo* (1860), and *Oberon* (not perf.); also overtures, string quartets, piano pieces, etc.

BIBL.: O. Sestl, *J. D. (1798–1876): Ein Liedermeister des Wiener Biedermeier* (diss., Univ. of Innsbruck, 1951). —NS/LK/DM

Dessay, Natalie, remarkable French soprano; b. Lyons, April 19, 1965. Following training at the Bordeaux Cons., she completed her studies in Paris. In 1990 she won the Mozart Competition in Vienna. After singing Bizet's Don Procopio at the Opéra-Comique in Paris in 1990, she appeared as Adele in Geneva in 1991. She sang at the Lyons Opera from 1991, where she won notable success for her Mozart roles. In 1992 she was engaged as Olympia in *Les Contes d'Hoffmann* at the Opéra de la Bastille in Paris and as Blondchen in Lausanne. In 1993 she portrayed Olympia at the Vienna State Opera. On Oct. 13, 1994, she made her debut at the Metropolitan Opera in N.Y. as Fiakermilli in *Arabella*. In 1995 she appeared as Lakmé at the Opéra-Comique. Her portrayal of Ophélie in Thomas's *Hamlet* was acclaimed in Geneva in 1996, the same year she sang Aminta at the Vienna State Opera. In 1997 she appeared as Stravinsky's Nightingale at the Théâtre du Châtelet in Paris. In 1999 she made her first appearance at the Lyric Opera of Chicago as Morgana in *Alcina*. She was also highly successful as a concert artist.—NS/LK/DM

Dessoff, (Felix) Otto, eminent German conductor; b. Leipzig, Jan. 14, 1835; d. Frankfurt am Main, Oct. 28, 1892. He studied at the Leipzig Cons. with Moscheles, Hauptmann, and Rietz, and then was a theater conductor in various German cities (1854–60). From 1860 to 1875 he was a conductor of the Vienna Court Opera. He also conducted the Vienna Phil., and taught at the Vienna Cons. From 1875 to 1881 he occupied similar posts at Karlsruhe. In 1881 he became conductor in Frankfurt am Main. He was greatly esteemed by his many celebrated friends for his musicianship. His correspondence with Brahms was publ. by the Brahms Soc. He also wrote chamber music.—NS/LK/DM

Dessoff, Margarethe, Austrian choral conductor; b. Vienna, June 11, 1874; d. Locarno, Switzerland, Nov. 19, 1944. She was trained at the Frankfurt am Main Cons. After championing the cause of early vocal music in Europe, she went to N.Y. and in 1924 founded the Adesdi Chorus, a women's chorus, and in 1928 a mixed chorus; they were amalgamated under her direction in 1930 as the Dessoff Choirs. In 1936 she settled in Switzerland.—NS/LK/DM

Destinn, Emmy (real name, **Emilie Pavlína Kittlová**), famous Czech soprano; b. Prague, Feb. 26, 1878; d. ČEské Budějovice, Jan. 28, 1930. She first studied the violin; her vocal abilities were revealed later by Marie Loewe-Destinn, whose surname she adopted as a token of appreciation. She made her debut as Santuzza at the Kroll Opera in Berlin (July 19, 1898) and was engaged at the Berlin Royal Opera as a regular member until 1908. She specialized in Wagnerian operas, and became a protégée of Cosima Wagner in Bayreuth, where she sang for the first time in 1901 as Senta; because of her ability to cope with difficult singing parts, Richard Strauss selected her for the title role in the Berlin and Paris premieres of his *Salome*. She made her London debut at Covent Garden on May 2, 1904, as Donna Anna; her success in England was spontaneous and unmistakable, and she continued to sing opera in England until the outbreak of World War I. She made her American debut in *Aida* with the Metropolitan Opera in N.Y. on Nov. 16, 1908, and remained with the company until 1916, and then was on its roster again from 1919 to 1921. She retired from the opera stage in 1926 but continued to make concert appearances until shortly before her death. For a few years following World War I, she used her Czech name, Ema Destinnová, but later dropped it. She was a versatile singer with a pure soprano voice of great power; her repertoire included some 80 parts. A film biography of her life, *The Divine Emma*, was produced in Czechoslovakia in 1982.

BIBL.: A. Rektorys, *Ema D.ová* (Prague, 1936); M. Martínková, *Život Emy D.ová* (Pilzen, 1946); V. Holzknecht and B. Trita, *E. D.ová ve slovech a obrazech* (E. D. in Words and Pictures; Prague, 1972); M. Pospíšil, *Veliké srdce:Život a umění Emy Destinové* (A Great Heart: The Life and Art of E. D.; Prague, 1974).—NS/LK/DM

Destouches, André-Cardinal, French composer; b. Paris (baptized), April 6, 1672; d. there, Feb. 7, 1749. After attending a Jesuit school in Paris, he went as a boy to Siam with his teacher, the missionary Gui Tachard (1686). He returned to France in 1688. He served in the Royal Musketeers (1692–94), and later took lessons from André Campra, contributing 3 airs to Campra's opera-ballet *L'Europe galante* (1697). After this initiation, Destouches produced his first independent work, *Issé*, a "heroic pastorale" in 3 acts (Fontainebleau, Oct. 7, 1697); its popularity was parodied in several productions of a similar pastoral nature (*Les Amours de Vincennes* by P.F. Dominique, 1719; *Les Oracles* by J.A. Romagnesi, 1741). Among his other operas, the following were produced in Paris: *Amadis de Grèce* (March 22, 1699), *Omphale* (Nov. 10, 1701), and *Callirhoé* (Dec. 27, 1712). With Delalande, he wrote the ballet *Les Eléments*, which was produced at the Tuileries Palace in Paris on Dec. 22, 1721. In 1713 Louis XIV appointed him inspector general of the Académie Royale de Musique. In 1728 he became its director, retiring in 1730. A revival of *Omphale* in 1752 evoked Baron Grimm's famous *Lettre sur Omphale*, inaugurating the so-called "Guerre des Bouffons" between the proponents of the French school, as exemplified by Destouches, and Italian opera buffa.

BIBL.: K. Dulle, *A. C. D.* (Leipzig, 1908).—NS/LK/DM

Destouches, Franz (Seraph) von, German conductor and composer; b. Munich, Jan. 21, 1772; d. there, Dec. 10, 1844. He was a pupil of Haydn in Vienna in 1787. He was appointed music director at Erlangen (1797), and then was second concertmaster at the Weimar theater (1799), later becoming first concertmaster and director of music (1804–08). In 1810 he was a prof. of theory at Landshut Univ. He then was a conductor at Homburg (1826–42), retiring to Munich in 1842.

WORKS: DRAMATIC: O p e r a : *Die Thomasnacht* (Munich, Aug. 31, 1792); *Das Missverständniss*, operetta (Weimar, April 27, 1805); *Der Teufel und der Schneider*, comic opera (1843; not perf.). I n c i d e n t a l M u s i c T o : Schiller's version of *Gozzi's Turandot* (1802); Schiller's *Die Braut von Messina* (1803), *Die Jungfrau von Orleans* (1803), and *Wilhelm Tell* (1804); Kotzebue's *Die Hussiten vor Naumburg* (1804); Zacharias Werner's play *Wanda, Königin der Sarmaten* (1808). OTHER: Piano Concerto; piano sonatas; fantasias; variations for piano; Piano Trio; Clarinet Concerto; Mass; oratorio, *Die Anbetung am Grabe Christi.*

BIBL.: E. von Destouches, *F. v. D.* (Munich, 1904). —NS/LK/DM

Deswert, Jules
See **Swert, Jules de**

De Sylva, B. G. (actually, **George Gard**; aka **"Bud"** or **"Buddy"**), American lyricist, librettist, and producer; b. N.Y., Jan. 27, 1895; d. Hollywood, Calif., July 11, 1950. As a lyricist, De Sylva is best known for the series of songs he wrote for Al Jolson, among them "I'll Say She Does," "April Showers," and "California, Here I Come," and for his partnership with lyricist Lew Brown and composer Ray Henderson, which resulted in successful Broadway musicals and Hollywood films, including such hits as "The Birth of the Blues," "Sonny Boy," and "Button Up Your Overcoat." He also worked with such composers as Victor Herbert, Jerome Kern, and George Gershwin. De Sylva's lyrics typify the upbeat style of 1920s popular music. By the early 1930s he had turned away from songwriting and launched a career as a producer. In the early 1940s he had three shows running on Broadway simultaneously, he ran one of the major film studios, and he co-founded Capitol Records.

De Sylva was the son of Aloysius De Sylva, a vaudeville actor who performed under the name Hal De Forest but gave up the stage to become a lawyer after marrying Georgetta Gard. Nevertheless, the marriage broke up when De Sylva was an infant, and his mother took him to her family home in Azusa, Calif., where he grew up. After he performed in a benefit show at the Grand Opera House in L.A. as "Baby Gard" at the age of four, he was offered a contract by the B. F. Keith vaudeville circuit, but his family declined. De Sylva's talent as an entertainer was furthered by violin lessons as a child, and by his college years he was writing songs. He attended the Univ. of Southern Calif. in 1915 and 1916, dropping out to sing and play ukulele in a supposedly Hawaiian band. In the summer of 1917, Jolson, who was on tour with his show *Robinson Crusoe Jr.*, heard one of De Sylva's songs, "'N' Everything." By the time Jolson recorded it on Dec. 27, 1917, the song was credited to De Sylva, Jolson, and Gus Kahn. Jolson introduced it in his next show, *Sinbad* (N.Y., Feb. 14, 1918), and it became a record hit for him in June. Reopening the show after a summer break, Jolson interpolated "I'll Say She Does," also credited to De Sylva/Jolson/Kahn; his recording was the most successful of several.

De Sylva moved to N.Y., where he became a staff writer for music publisher Jerome H. Remick. There he met George Gershwin, with whom he collaborated in 1919 on *La-La-Lucille* (lyrics also by Arthur Jackson), which ran for 104 performances, and on *Morris Gest's Midnight Whirl* (lyrics also by John Henry Mears), which ran for 110 performances. His next hits came from further Jolson interpolations into the road tour of *Sinbad*. Using Jolson's catch phrase, "You ain't heard nothin' yet," De Sylva, Jolson, and Kahn constructed a song that Jolson introduced for the fall tour of 1919 and recorded for a hit in the spring of 1920. At the same time, Jolson introduced two songs written solely with De Sylva—"I Gave Her That" and "Chloe"—for two more hits.

In 1920, De Sylva wrote music and lyrics for the musical *I'll Say She Does*, which closed during tryouts. A second abortive project was *Zip Goes a Million*, for which De Sylva wrote lyrics to music by Kern. The show was reworked into the successful *Sally* (N.Y., Dec. 21, 1920), with two of the earlier songs retained, both of which became hits: "Whip-Poor-Will" in an instrumental recording by Isham Jones and His Orch., and "Look for the Silver Lining" in a best-selling record for Marion Harris among others. Meanwhile, De Sylva had contributed "Just Snap Your Fingers at Care" (music by Louis Silvers) to the *Greenwich Village Follies* (N.Y., Aug. 30, 1920); it became a hit for Bert Williams. And Jolson continued to interpolate De Sylva songs into *Sinbad*—for the fall 1920 tour he introduced "Avalon" (music and lyrics by Vincent Rose, Jolson, and De Sylva) and recorded it for a hit at the end of the year. ("Avalon" later was the subject of successful plagiarism suit brought by Puccini's publishers, who charged the melody came from the aria "E lucevan le stelle" in *Tosca*.)

Jolson finally finished the road tour of *Sinbad* in the spring of 1921 and immediately began preparing his next show, *Bombo*, for the fall. Though composer Sigmund Romberg and lyricist Harold Atteridge were engaged to write the songs, De Sylva was heavily involved, contributing several songs. These included "April Showers" (music by Silvers), "Give Me My Mammy" (music by Walter Donaldson), and "Yoo-Hoo" (music by Jolson), all of which Jolson recorded for hits.

De Sylva teamed again with Gershwin early in 1922 for the risqué "Do It Again!" which was used in the play *The French Doll* (N.Y., Feb. 20, 1922) and recorded by Paul Whiteman and His Orch. as an instrumental that became a best-seller in July. That month De Sylva and Gershwin contributed "Yankee Doodle Blues" (lyrics also by Irving Caesar) to the revue *Spice of 1922* (N.Y., July 6, 1922); it became a hit for Billy Murray and Ed Smalle in February 1923. De Sylva, lyricist E. Ray Goetz, and Gershwin were hired to provide songs for the 1922 edition of *George White's Scandals*. The hit of the show was De Sylva and Gershwin's "I'll Build a Stairway to Paradise" (lyrics also by Ira Gershwin), which was recorded for a best-selling instrumental by Whiteman (who appeared in the show) in January 1923.

De Sylva next wrote lyrics for *Orange Blossoms*, with music by Victor Herbert, and the two scored a hit with "A Kiss in the Dark," with which both Metropolitan Opera star Amelita Galli-Curci and violin virtuoso Fritz Kreisler enjoyed successful recordings. De Sylva also scored a hit with Jolson's recording of "Coo Coo," for which the two were co-credited as songwriters.

De Sylva shared lyric-writing chores with Goetz and Ballard MacDonald on the George Gershwin-composed songs for the 1923 edition of *George White's Scandals*, none of which became hits. But De Sylva had three more hits thanks to Jolson when the singer recorded "Morning Will Come" (music and lyrics by De Sylva, Jolson, and Con Conrad) and interpolated "Arcady" (music and lyrics by Jolson and De Sylva) and "California, Here I Come" (music and lyrics by Jolson, De Sylva, and Joseph Meyer) into the fall tour of *Bombo*. When Jolson got around to recording the latter in Chicago in January 1924 with Isham Jones's Orch., De Sylva sat in on ukulele; the record became a best-seller.

In early 1924, De Sylva and Gershwin collaborated on *Sweet Little Devil*, a modest success that included "Virginia (Don't Go Too Far)," a hit in Carl Fenton and His Orch.'s instrumental recording. The 1924 edition of *George White's Scandals* produced a hit for De Sylva, MacDonald, and George Gershwin in "Somebody Loves Me," given its best-selling recording by Whiteman. And De Sylva scored an independent hit with "Memory Lane" (music by Larry Spier and Conrad), recorded for a best-seller by Fred Waring's Pennsylvanians in October 1924.

De Sylva was the credited lyricist for Jolson's next show, *Big Boy*, the biggest initial hit from which was "Hello, 'Tucky" (music by Joseph Meyer), recorded by Jolson, though Eddie Cantor made a bigger hit out of a castoff from the show, "If You Knew Susie (Like I Know Susie)" (music by Meyer), which he recorded for a best-seller in August and thereafter used as his signature song. De Sylva next worked with the Gershwin brothers on *Tell Me More!*, which opened two days after his marriage to former *Ziegfeld Follies* girl Marie Wallace on April 11. He then collaborated with lyricist Bud Green and composer Ray Henderson on the independent song "Alabamy Bound," which became a hit for Blossom Seely in May.

George Gershwin bowed out of *George White's Scandals* for 1925, and White replaced him with the team of Henderson and Brown, while retaining De Sylva. The new team did not have an auspicious beginning with the show, which produced no hits. De Sylva went on to collaborate with composer Lewis E. Gensler and lyricist Stephen Jones on the modestly successful show *Captain Jinks*, and to work with composer Al Sherman on the independent song "Save Your Sorrow (For Tomorrow)," the most successful recording of which was by the Shannon Four in November.

Typically, Jolson interpolated new songs into *Big Boy* when the show reopened for the fall of 1925, and one of these was "Miami" (music and lyrics by De Sylva, Jolson, and Conrad), which he recorded for a hit in the spring of 1926. That same season "Just a Cottage Small (By a Waterfall)" (music by James F. Hanley) was popular on records, primarily by John McCormack. De Sylva returned to his partnership with Brown and Henderson for the 1926 edition of *George White's Scandals*, which finally established the team, running 424 performances and producing three hits: "Lucky Day" (for George Olsen and His Orch.); "The Birth of the Blues" (a best-seller for Whiteman in December); and the dance sensation "Black Bottom" (an instrumental for Johnny Hamp and His Orch.).

Within months, De Sylva was back on Broadway with *Queen High!*, for which he wrote lyrics to Gensler's music and co-wrote the libretto with Laurence Schwab. Among the songs were "Cross Your Heart," a hit for the orch. of Roger Wolfe Kahn with a vocal by Henry Burr, and "Gentlemen Prefer Blondes," a hit for Ernest Hare and Billy Jones. Jolson interpolated a De Sylva/Brown/Henderson song, "It All Depends on You," into *Big Boy* for the fall 1926 tour, but the biggest hit recording, an instrumental, was by Whiteman.

The next De Sylva/Brown/Henderson hit was an independent song, "So Blue," for Whiteman in July 1927. In September, Paul Whiteman's Concert Orch., as it was billed, had the biggest hit version of "When Day Is Done," a German song by Robert Katscher for which De Sylva had written English lyrics; Whiteman's 12-inch disc was an instrumental, however, and the most popular record to use De Sylva's words was the one by Harry Archer and His Orch. Whiteman employed a vocal trio to sing the independent De Sylva/Brown/Henderson song "Broken Hearted," also a hit in September.

Given the success of the 1926 edition, George White did not mount a 1927 edition of his *Scandals*, leaving De Sylva, Brown, and Henderson free to write two book musicals. The first, with a libretto written by De Sylva and Schwab, was their look at college life, *Good News!*, which ran 551 performances and featured four hits, all of them recorded by George Olsen and His Orch., who appeared in the show: "The Best Things in Life Are Free," "The Varsity Drag," "Lucky in Love," and the title song. The second, not as successful but still running a healthy 264 performances, was *Manhattan Mary*, produced and directed by White. Written independently but interpolated into the show was the hit "Just a Memory," recorded by Whiteman.

The next De Sylva/Brown/Henderson hit was also an independent song, "Together," a best-seller for Whiteman in April 1928. The team's final *Scandals* ran 240 performances and generated only one hit, "I'm on the Crest of a Wave," the most popular recording made by Whiteman in September. They were in Atlantic City preparing their next show when a call came from Jolson in Hollywood, asking for a song for his second motion picture, *The Singing Fool*. The result was the maudlin "Sonny Boy," which Jolson made into a million-seller on records and in sheet music. The next De Sylva/

Brown/Henderson musical was *Hold Everything!*, for which De Sylva co-wrote the libretto with John McGowan. It ran 413 performances and introduced the hit "You're the Cream in My Coffee," recorded by Ben Selvin and His Orch. among others. *Three Cheers* was nominally a De Sylva/Henderson musical, but several songs with lyrics co-written by Brown were included. One of these was the hit "Pompanola," recorded by Selvin. The show ran 210 performances. The last De Sylva/Brown/Henderson hit of 1928 was the independent song "For Old Times' Sake," recorded by Annette Hanshaw in November.

De Sylva, Brown, and Henderson began 1929 with a new musical, *Follow Thru*, for which De Sylva co-wrote the libretto with Schwab. The show ran 403 performances and featured three hits: "Button Up Your Overcoat" and "I Want to Be Bad," both recorded by Helen Kane, and "My Lucky Star," recorded by Whiteman. After writing two independent hits, "The Song I Love" for Fred Waring and "My Sin" for Ben Selvin, the team took off for Hollywood to write songs for the next Jolson picture. This was *Say It with Songs*, and Jolson scored four hits from it, earning co-writing credits with De Sylva, Brown, and Henderson on each: "Little Pal," a follow-up to "Sonny Boy" that was a best-seller in August; "I'm in Seventh Heaven"; "Why Can't You?"; and "Used to You."

The onset of talking pictures led to a plethora of movie musicals at the turn of the decade, and songs with De Sylva lyrics turned up in 11 films released in 1929. Five of these contained previously written songs, such as "Look for the Silver Lining," retained in the movie adaptation of *Sally*. But De Sylva, Brown, and Henderson contributed "My Tonia" to *In Old Arizona*, and it was recorded for a hit by Nick Lucas. They also wrote songs for such films as *A Man's Man*, *Why Bring That Up?*, and *The Song of Love*. For the last, their work was credited to "Elmer Colby," perhaps because it was a Columbia picture and by the time of its release they had signed to Fox, for which they wrote songs for the original movie musical *Sunny Side Up*. The film contained seven songs, four of which became hits: "I'm a Dreamer, Aren't We All?" and "If I Had a Talking Picture of You" for Whiteman, the latter with a vocal by Bing Crosby; and "Sunny Side Up" and "Turn on the Heat" for Earl Burtnett and His L.A. Biltmore Hotel Orch.

De Sylva, Brown, and Henderson returned to Broadway with *Flying High*, for which De Sylva and Brown collaborated on the libretto with John McGowan. It ran for 355 performances but generated only one hit, "Thank Your Father," recorded by Al Goodman and His Orch. The team then returned to Hollywood, where several of their stage musicals were being filmed: *Hold Everything* by Warner Brothers, *Good News* by MGM, and *Follow Thru* by Paramount. Paramount also made *Follow the Leader*, based on *Manhattan Mary*. While they worked on *Just Imagine*, their next original movie musical for Fox, "Don't Tell Her What Happened to Me," an independent song, became a hit for Ruth Etting in October. *Just Imagine*, a science-fiction film on which the team also served as screenwriters and producers, was a

failure. In 1931 they had two songs in the nonmusical film *Indiscreet*, including "Come to Me," which became a hit for the High Hatters, and they wrote two ironically titled independent hits, "One More Time" for Gus Arnheim and His Orch. with a vocal by Bing Crosby, and "You Try Somebody Else" for Guy Lombardo and His Royal Canadians. Then De Sylva split from Brown and Henderson, who continued to work together.

Initially, De Sylva remained in Hollywood, where he wrote four songs for Paramount's *One Hour with You* with composer Richard A. Whiting. But in the backlash against movie musicals, the studio cut all the songs before the film was released. De Sylva returned to N.Y. and put together the musical *Take a Chance*. He and Laurence Schwab co-wrote the libretto and co-produced the show, and he co-wrote the songs with Whiting, Nacio Herb Brown, and Vincent Youmans. It ran 243 performances and featured three hits: "Eadie Was a Lady" (music by Whiting and Brown) recorded by Ethel Merman, who appeared in the show; and "You're an Old Smoothie" (music and lyrics by De Sylva, Whiting, and Brown) and "Rise 'n' Shine" (music by Youmans), recorded by Whiteman.

The success of *42nd Street* in the spring of 1933 renewed Hollywood's interest in musicals. On April 11, Fox announced that De Sylva had been signed to the studio as a producer. His first production was *My Weakness*, for which he also co-wrote the songs and the screenplay. In 1934 he produced and co-wrote the screenplay for *Bottoms Up* at Fox and co-wrote the screenplay for *Have a Heart* at MGM. He had five productions at what was now 20th Century–Fox in 1935—two Shirley Temple films, *The Little Colonel* and *The Littlest Rebel*, plus *Doubting Thomas*, *Under the Pampas Moon*, and *Welcome Home*, also writing songs for the last two. He produced another Temple film, *Stowaway*, in 1936. In 1937 he moved to Universal and produced *Merry-Go-Round of 1938*, followed in 1938 by *You're a Sweetheart* and *The Rage of Paris*. Moving to RKO in 1939, he wrote music and lyrics to "Wishing," used in *Love Affair*; it topped the hit parade in June and July for Glenn Miller and His Orch. He produced *Bachelor Mother* in the summer.

On Nov. 15, 1939, De Sylva started work as a producer at Paramount. *DuBarry Was a Lady*, a musical with songs by Cole Porter, opened on Broadway on Dec. 6. De Sylva produced it and co-wrote the libretto. *Louisiana Purchase*, with songs by Irving Berlin, followed on May 28, 1940. De Sylva again produced, and the show was based on his original story. When *Panama Hattie*, with songs by Porter and a libretto by De Sylva, opened on Oct. 30, De Sylva became the first producer since Ziegfeld to have three shows running simultaneously on Broadway.

On Feb. 5, 1941, De Sylva was named head of production at Paramount, responsible for the studio's 50-film-per-year schedule. During the year, he personally produced two films, *Birth of the Blues* and *Caught in the Draft*. In 1942 he joined with songwriter Johnny Mercer and record store owner Glenn Wallichs to form Capitol Records, which became the leading label for popular singers especially after World War II. De Sylva personally produced two films in 1944, *Lady in the Dark* and *Frenchman's Creek*. The release of MGM's *Since You Went Away*, featuring "Together" revived interest in the song, and the most successful of several new recordings was Dick Haymes and Helen Forrest's Top Ten hit. (In 1961 it became a gold-selling Top Ten hit in the hands of Connie Francis.)

But such professional triumphs belied personal difficulties. De Sylva fathered a son by his secretary, Marie Ballentine, as he was later forced to acknowledge. In August he and his wife separated. On Sept. 15 he left Paramount due to ill health. In 1945 he made *The Stork Club* as an independent production released by Paramount, producing and co-writing the screenplay, but he retired after suffering a heart attack.

Al Jolson's comeback in 1946 as a result of *The Jolson Story* allowed him to revive several songs written with De Sylva, including "April Showers" (also a Top Ten hit for Guy Lombardo) and "Sonny Boy," for gold-selling hits. MGM remade *Good News* in 1947, retaining much of the original score.

De Sylva died at 55 after suffering another heart attack. In the years following his death, Ballentine and their son fought his widow in the courts for the right to participate in his song copyright renewals and thus share in his publishing income. Eventually they won a unanimous Supreme Court decision.

The Best Things in Life Are Free was a film biography of De Sylva, Brown, and Henderson.

WORKS (only works for which De Sylva was one of the primary, credited lyricists are listed): **MUSICALS/REVUES** (all dates refer to N.Y. openings): *La-La-Lucille* (May 26, 1919); *Morris Gest's Midnight Whirl* (Dec. 27, 1919); *George White's Scandals* (Aug. 28, 1922); *Orange Blossoms* (Sept. 19, 1922); *The Yankee Princess* (Oct. 2, 1922); *George White's Scandals* (June 18, 1923); *Sweet Little Devil* (Jan. 21, 1924); *George White's Scandals* (June 30, 1924); *Big Boy* (Jan. 7, 1925); *Tell Me More!* (April 13, 1925); *George White's Scandals* (June 22, 1925); *Captain Jinks* (Sept. 8, 1925); *George White's Scandals* (June 14, 1926); *Queen High!* (Sept. 5, 1926); *Good News!* (Sept. 6, 1927); *Manhattan Mary* (Sept. 26, 1927); *George White's Scandals* (July 2, 1928); *Hold Everything!* (Oct. 10, 1928); *Three Cheers* (Oct. 15, 1928); *Follow Thru* (Jan. 9, 1929); *Flying High* (March 3, 1930); *Take a Chance* (Nov. 26, 1932). **FILMS:** *The Singing Fool* (1928); *Say It with Songs* (1929); *Sunny Side Up* (1929); *Good News* (1930); *Follow Thru* (1930); *Just Imagine* (1930); *A Holy Terror* (1931); *Indiscreet* (1931); *My Weakness* (1933); *Good News* (1947); *The Best Things in Life Are Free* (1956). —WR

Detoni, Dubravko, Croatian pianist and composer; b. Križevci, Feb. 22, 1937. He graduated in piano from the Zagreb Academy of Music in 1960, and studied with Cortot in Siena (1960–61). He then took lessons in composition with Šulek at the Zagreb Academy of Music, graduating in 1965, and had advanced studies with Bacewicz and Lutosławski at the experimental studio of the Polish Radio in Warsaw (1966–67) and with Stockhausen and Ligeti in Darmstadt. He was the founder and artistic leader of ACEZANTEZ, the Ensemble of the Center for New Tendencies in Zagreb. His music rejects all established formulas and seeks new conceptions in sound through serial, aleatory, and musical-theater resources.

WORKS: ORCH.: *Musica a cinque* (1962); *Passacaglia* for 2 Pianos and Strings (1962); *Preobrazbe* (Transfigurations; 1963; Zagreb, June 7, 1965); *Dramatski prolog* (1965); *Likovi i plohe* (Forms and Surfaces) for Chamber Orch. (1967; Graz, Sept. 26, 1968); *Assonanze No. 2* for Cello and Orch. (1971); *Elucubrations* for Piano and Orch. (1969; Zagreb, Jan. 7, 1970); *Einflüsse* for 2 Cellos and Orch. (1971); Piano Concerto (1989; Ljubljana, April 5, 1990). **CHAMBER:** *Stravaganze* for Wind Quintet (1966); *Phonomorphia 1* for Electronic and Concrete Sounds (1967) and *2* for Piano and Tape (1968); *Grafika I* for Organ (1968), *II* for Chamber Ensemble (1968), *IV* for ad libitum Chamber Ensemble (1971), and *V*, instrumental "theater" for Chamber Ensemble (1972; Graz, Oct. 14, 1973); *Assonanze No. 1* for Cello and Piano (1968); *Forte-Piano, Arpa, Crescendo* for 2 Pianos and Percussion (1969); *Monos 1–3*, cycle for variable orchestration (1970–72); *10 Beginnings* for String Quartet (1973); *Dokument 75* for Chamber Ensemble (1975); *Fragment 75* for Chamber Ensemble (Graz, Oct. 11, 1975); *Ispadi* (Outbursts) for 2 Double Basses and Electronic Sound (1997). **VOCAL:** *Phonomorphia 3* for Voices, Instrumental Ensemble, and Tape (1969); *Grafika III* for Vocal Ensemble, 6 Flutes, Ondes Martenot, Organ, and Piano (1969), *Notturni* for 4 Vocal Groups, 4 Instrumental Ensembles, Organ, and Tape (1970); *Music, or Tract about the Superfluous* for Narrating Actor, Organ, Piano, Percussion, Clarinet, and Orch. (1973).—NS/LK/DM

Dett, R(obert) Nathaniel, distinguished black American composer, conductor, and anthologist; b. Drummondville, Quebec, Oct. 11, 1882; d. Battle Creek, Mich., Oct. 2, 1943. He came from a musical family; both his parents were amateur pianists and singers. In 1893 the family moved to Niagara Falls, N.Y., where Dett studied piano with local teachers. He earned his living by playing at various clubs and hotels, then enrolled at the Oberlin (Ohio) Cons., where he studied piano with Howard Handel Carter and theory with Arthur E. Heacox and George Carl Hastings (B.Mus., 1908). He also conducted a school choir; eventually, choral conducting became his principal profession. He taught at Lane Coll. in Jackson, Tenn. (1908–11), the Lincoln Inst. in Jefferson, Mo. (1911–13), the Hampton Inst. in Va. (1913–32), and Bennett Coll. in Greensboro, N.C. (1937–42). Concerned about his lack of technical knowledge in music, he took lessons with Karl Gehrkens at Oberlin in 1913; also attended classes at Columbia Univ., the American Cons. of Music in Chicago, Northwestern Univ., the Univ. of Pa., and, during the academic year 1919–20, at Harvard Univ., where he studied composition with Foote. In 1929 he pursued training with Boulanger at the American Cons. in Fontainebleau; during 1931–32, he attended the Eastman School of Music in Rochester, N.Y. (M.Mus., 1932). In the meantime, he developed the Hampton Choir, which toured in Europe in 1930 with excellent success, receiving encomiums in England, France, Belgium, the Netherlands, Germany, and Switzerland. He also periodically led his choir on the radio; in 1943 he became a musical adviser for the USO, and worked with the WAC (Women's Army Corps) on service duty at Battle Creek. His dominating interest was in cultivating Negro music, arranging Negro spirituals, and publishing collections of Negro folk songs. All of his works were inspired by black melodies and rhythms; some of his piano pieces in the Negro idiom became quite popular, among them the suite *Magnolia* (1912), *In the Bottoms* (1913), which contained the rousing *Juba Dance*, and *Enchantment* (1922). He also wrote a number of choral pieces, mostly on biblical themes, such as the oratorios *The Chariot Jubilee* (1921) and *The Ordering of Moses* (Cincinnati, May 7, 1937). His choruses *Listen to the lambs*, *I'll never turn back no more*, and *Don't be weary, traveler* became standards in the choral repertoire. He publ. the anthologies *Religious Folk Songs of the Negro* (1926) and *The Dett Collection of Negro Spirituals* (4 vols., 1936). His piano compositions were ed by D.-R. de Lerma and V. McBrier (Evanston, Ill., 1973).

BIBL.: V. McBrier, *R.N. D.: His Life and Works: 1882–1943* (Washington, D.C., 1977); A. Simpson, *Follow Me: The Life and Music of R.N. D.* (Metuchen, N.J., 1993).—**NS/LK/DM**

Deutekom, Cristina (real name, **Stientje Engel**), notable Dutch soprano; b. Amsterdam, Aug. 28, 1931. She was a student of Johan Thomas and Coby Riemersma at the Amsterdam Cons. In 1962 she made her operatic debut as the Queen of the Night in Amsterdam, a role she subsequently sang with great distinction at her Metropolitan Opera debut in N.Y. on Sept. 28, 1967; was again on its roster (1973–75). She subsequently sang in principal opera houses of the world, becoming equally adept in both coloratura and dramatic roles. Deutekom excelled particularly in the operas of Mozart, Rossini, Bellini, Donizetti, and Verdi. —**NS/LK/DM**

Deutsch, Diana, significant English-born American music psychologist; b. London, Feb. 15, 1938. She studied theory and composition in London; received first-class honors B.A. in psychology from Oxford (1959) and a Ph.D. in psychology from the Univ. of Calif. at San Diego (1970), where she became a research psychologist at its Center for Human Information Processing. In 1989 she obtained professorial status there. She conducted highly creative research in psychoacoustics and the psychology of music. Her work has included extensive study of auditory illusions and paradoxes; she also created a model of the process of analyzing musical shape that received widespread attention. She ed. *The Psychology of Music* (N.Y., 1982), and in 1983 founded the journal *Music Perception*, of which she served as ed. Among her important articles are "An Auditory Illusion," *Nature*, 1251 (1974), "Internal Representation of Pitch Sequences in Tonal Music," *Psychological Review*, lxxxviii (1981), and "Pitch Class and Perceived Height: Some Paradoxes and Their Implications," *Explorations in Music, the Arts and Ideas*, ed. by Narmour and Solie (N.Y., 1988).—**NS/LK/DM**

Deutsch, Max, Austrian-born French composer, conductor, and pedagogue; b. Vienna, Nov. 17, 1892; d. Paris, Nov. 22, 1982. He studied composition privately with Schoenberg; also took courses at the Univ. of Vienna. He began his career conducting operetta in Vienna; in 1923 he went to Berlin, where he organized his own orch. group concentrating mainly on modern music, emulating Schoenberg's Soc. for Private Performances of Vienna. In 1925 he settled in Paris, where he founded a Jewish theatrical ensemble, Der Jiddische Spiegel; also conducted concerts of modern music. From 1933 to 1935 he was in Madrid, where he was in charge of a film enterprise; in 1939 he went to France; after service in the Foreign Legion (until 1945), he returned to Paris, where he devoted himself to teaching, using Schoenberg's method. In 1960 he founded the Grands Concerts de la Sorbonne. In his compositions, Deutsch pursued novel ideas; he was the first to write a complete film sym., in 5 movements, for the production of the German film *Der Schutz* (1923); he furthermore composed 2 syms. and a choral sym., *Prière pour nous autres mortels.*—**NS/LK/DM**

Deutsch, Otto Erich, eminent Austrian musicologist; b. Vienna, Sept. 5, 1883; d. there, Nov. 23, 1967. He studied literature and art history at the univs. of Vienna and Graz; was art critic of Vienna's *Die Zeit* (1908–09); then served as an assistant at the Kunsthistorisches Institut of the Univ. of Vienna (1909–12); later was a bookseller, and then music librarian of the important collection of Anthony van Hoboken in Vienna (1926–35). In 1939 he emigrated to England and settled in Cambridge; in 1947 he became a naturalized British subject, but returned to Vienna in 1951. A scholar of impeccable credentials, Deutsch was an acknowledged authority on Handel, Mozart, and Schubert; his documentary biographies of these composers constitute primary sources; he was also responsible for initiating the critical edition of Mozart's letters, which he ed. with W. Bauer and J. Eibl as *Mozart: Briefe und Aufzeichnungen* (7 vols., Kassel, 1962–75).

WRITINGS: *Schubert-Brevier* (Berlin, 1905); *Beethovens Beziehungen zu Graz* (Graz, 1907); *Franz Schubert: Die Dokumente seines Lebens und Schaffens* (in collaboration, first with L. Scheibler, then with W. Kahl and G. Kinsky), which was planned as a comprehensive work in 3 vols. containing all known documents, pictures, and other materials pertaining to Schubert, arranged in chronological order, with a thematic catalog, but of which only 2 vols. were publ.: vol. III, *Sein Leben in Bildern* (Munich, 1913), and vol. II, part 1, *Die Dokumente seines Lebens* (Munich, 1914; Eng. tr. 1946, by E. Blom, as *Schubert: A Documentary Biography*; American ed., 1947, as *The Schubert Reader: A Life of Franz Schubert in Letters and Documents*; 2nd German ed., 1964, enl., in the *Neue Ausgabe sämtlicher Werke of Schubert*); *Franz Schuberts Briefe und Schriften* (Munich, 1919; Eng. tr., 1928; 4th German ed., Vienna, 1954); *Die historischen Bildnisse Franz Schuberts in getreuen Nachbildungen* (Vienna, 1922); *Die Originalausgaben von Schuberts Goethe- Liedern* (Vienna, 1926); *Franz Schubert: Tagebuch: Faksimile der Originalhandschrift* (Vienna, 1928); *Mozart und die Wiener Logen* (Vienna, 1932); with B. Paumgartner, *Leopold Mozarts Briefe an seine Tochter* (Salzburg, 1936); *Das Freihaustheater auf der Wieden 1787–1801* (Vienna, 1937); *Wolfgang Amadé Mozart: Verzeichnis aller meiner Werke. Faksimile der Handschrift mit dem Beiheft "Mozarts Werkverzeichnis 1784–1791"* (Vienna, 1938; Eng. tr., 1956); *Schubert: Thematic Catalogue of All His Works in Chronological Order* (with D. Wakeling; London, 1951; Ger tr. as *Franz Schubert: Thematisches Verzeichnis seiner Werke*, in the *Neue Ausgabe samtlicher Werke of Schubert* in a rev. ed., 1978); *Handel: A Documentary Biography* (N.Y., 1954; London, 1955); *Franz Schubert: Die Erinnerungen seiner Freunde* (Leipzig, 1957; Eng. tr.,

1958); *Mozart: Die Dokumente seines Lebens* (Kassel, 1961; Eng. tr., 1965, as *Mozart: A Documentary Biography*; 2nd ed., 1966; suppl., 1978); *Mozart und seine Welt in zeitgenössischen Bildern* (completed by M. Zenger, Kassel, 1961).

BIBL.: *O. E. D. zum 75. Geburtstag* (Vienna, 1958); W. Gerstenberg, J. LaRue, and W. Rehm, eds., *Festschrift O. E. D.* (Kassel, 1963).—NS/LK/DM

Devienne, François,

versatile French musician; b. Joinville, Haute-Marne, Jan. 31, 1759; d. in the insane asylum at Charenton, Sept. 5, 1803. A flutist and bassoonist, member of the band of the Gardes Suisses, bassoonist at the Théâtre de Monsieur (1789–1801), and a prof. at the Paris Cons. (from 1795), he was an extraordinarily prolific composer of peculiar importance from the impulse that he gave to perfecting the technique of wind instruments. He also wrote a valuable *Méthode de flûte* (Paris, 1795), which went through several eds.

WORKS: 12 operas; many concerted pieces for various wind instruments, with orch.; overtures; concertos, quartets, trios, sonatas, etc., for flute, piano, and other instruments; *12 suites d'harmonies à 8 et 12 parties*; numerous romances, chansons, etc.

BIBL.: W. Montgomery, *The Life and Works of F. D., 1759–1803* (diss., Catholic Univ. of America, 1975). —NS/LK/DM

De Vito, Gioconda,

Italian violinist; b. Martina Franca (Lecce), July 26, 1907. She studied at the Liceo Musicale in Pesaro, graduating in 1921, then performed throughout Europe. She taught at the Bari Cons., retiring in 1961.—NS/LK/DM

Devlin, Michael (Coles),

American bass-baritone; b. Chicago, Nov. 27, 1942. He studied at La. State Univ. (B.Mus., 1965) and received vocal training from Norman Treigle and Daniel Ferro in N.Y. In 1963 he made his operatic debut as Spalanzani in *Les Contes d'Hoffmann* in New Orleans, and in 1966 he made his first appearance at the N.Y.C. Opera as the Hermit in the U.S. premiere of Ginastera's *Don Rodrigo*, continuing on its roster until 1978. In 1974 he made his British debut at the Glyndebourne Festival as Mozart's Almaviva; he first sang at London's Covent Garden in 1975, then appeared at the Holland Festival, the Frankfurt am Main Opera, and the Bavarian State Opera in Munich in 1977. On Nov. 23, 1978, he made his Metropolitan Opera debut in N.Y. as Escamillo, and subsequently returned there regularly. In later years, he sang with opera companies in San Francisco, Hamburg, Paris, Monte Carlo, Dallas, Chicago, Los Angeles, and other cities. He also appeared as a soloist with the world's major orchs. —NS/LK/DM

Devo,

the misunderstood, subversive, funny band that changed rock perceptions of nerds forever, formed in Akron, Ohio, 1972. **MEMBERSHIP:** Mark Mothersbaugh, synth., voc. (b. May 18); Jerry Casale, bs. (b. July 28); Bob Mothersbaugh, gtr., voc. (b. Aug. 11); Bob Casale, gtr. (b. July 14); Alan Myers, drm. (b. Dec. 29).

While they were attending Kent State Univ., Mark Mothersbaugh and Gerald Casale became increasingly disillusioned by the social scene. As Mark succinctly put it, "We didn't have enough money for drugs, we didn't have a van and we didn't like to bowl." So they put together a band to entertain each other. With the band came a cosmology, based on their view of humanity from Kent State: Evolution was a myth to make people feel superior. Actually, the band maintained, humanity was on the skids, rapidly devolving. While they meant it as a joke, the infamous riots at Kent State left them less sure that it was funny. They wore uniforms that included yellow jump suits with red plastic flowerpots as hats.

Devo created a movie, *The Truth About De-evolution*, that featured the band and their music. At the Cleveland stop on Iggy Pop's *Idiot* tour, they enlisted a pretty girl of their acquaintance to bring a tape backstage to Pop and David Bowie, who was playing with Pop on the tour. After the tour, the tape went with Iggy and Bowie to Germany, where Bowie was making a new album. Between sessions, when things got boring, they played the Devo tape. They found the music so intriguing, they started to learn the songs to pass the time, not really believing that this was the product of a band, but more of an elaborate hoax.

When Pop got back to Calif., he discovered they were a band when he caught them in concert. Overflowing with enthusiasm, Pop came backstage singing their songs. When the band played N.Y., Bowie, Brian Eno, and Robert Fripp attended the show. Later that year, Eno put the band up in a studio in Germany and produced the group's debut album *Q: Are We Not Men? A: We Are Devo!* The songs defied rock convention. A cover of "Satisfaction" disassembled the song. Parts of the title track were in 9/4. They sang about mongoloids and space junk falling from the sky. Naturally, Devo became a major cult success in the burgeoning new wave of 1978.

Devo followed this effort with *Duty Now for the Future*. The album was strong, with tunes like "Wiggly World" and "The Day My Baby Gave Me a Surprize," but lacked the shock value of the debut. The band made a guest appearance in Neil Young's film *Rust Never Sleeps*, supplying the title of the project from an advertising campaign.

Devo's 1980 release, *Freedom of Choice*, expanded their reach a little. Even more informed by Mothersbaugh's keyboards, the album actually produced a hit, "Whip It." The single hit #14 and went gold. The album went platinum and hit #22. The follow-up, *New Traditionalists*, was less: not as funny, not as idiosyncratic, not as idea-driven. It hit #24 on the charts on the momentum from the previous record, but the material was not as strong.

The band soldiered on despite this disappointment. The animated move *Heavy Metal* featured the band on the soundtrack doing a version of Lee Dorsey's "Workin' in a Coal Mine" that got alternative radio and rock play, but failed to chart. Their next album, 1982's *Oh No! It's Devo*, had a similar hit, the unusual "Speed Racer," featuring the undying line "I'm a Barbie Doll and I like sex, I've got brains and I like sex." Next, they cut the title track for the Dan Akroyd film *Dr. Detroit,* but neither the film nor the song made much noise. Similarly, the 1984 album *Shout* only touched the lower reaches of the charts, and, four years later, their indie label debut *Total Devo* didn't chart at all. When the follow-up, 1990's *Smooth Noodle Maps,* didn't chart either, the band called it a day—sort of.

Actually, they had found a far more subversive way to spread their message. In the mid-1970s, Motherbaugh's friend, actor Paul Reubens, landed a children's television show for his character Pee-Wee Herman. He asked Mothersbaugh to write the theme and soundtrack music. This started a profitable sideline for Mothersbaugh. He did music for Nickelodeon's *Rugrats, Beakman's World,* and various other shows, created the music for the video game *Crash Bandicoot 2,* and even produced a Saturday morning TV show. He won awards for his music in commercials. His brother and Bob Casale frequently worked with him. They opened a studio called Mutato Muzika in Hollywood. Jerry Casale became an in-demand director of music videos.

Additionally, artists as far ranging as Robert Palmer and Nirvana saw fit to cover Devo songs. While none of the band members stopped their other lucrative activities, they did regroup for a week of Lollapalooza dates in 1996 and 1997, considering it taking a week vacation to play rock stars.

DISC.: *Q: Are We Not Men? A: We Are Devo* (1978); *Duty Now for the Future* (1979); *Freedom of Choice* (1980); *New Traditionalists* (1981); *Oh, No! It's Devo* (1982); *Shout* (1984); *EZ Listening Disc* (1987); *Total Devo* (1988); *Now It Can Be Told* (compact disc video; 1988); *The Men Who Make the Music* (video; 1990); *Greatest Hits* (1990); *Hardcore, Vol. 1 (The Evolution of Devolution)* (1990); *Smooth Noodle Maps* (1990); *Hardcore, Vol. 2 (1974–77)* (1991); *Live: The Mongoloid Years* (compact disc video; 1992); *The Complete Truth About De-Evolution* (video; 1993); *Adventures of the Smart Patrol* (1996); *Greatest* (1998).—**HB**

De Vocht, Lodewijk, Belgian conductor, teacher, and composer; b. Antwerp, Sept. 21, 1887; d. 's Gravenzel, near Antwerp, March 27, 1977. He spent his entire career in Antwerp, where he was a student of Gilson and Mortelmans at the Royal Flemish Cons. He became a violinist in the orch. of the Société des Concerts Nouveaux in 1903, serving as its conductor from 1921; he also was choirmaster at the Cathedral (1912–50) and founder-conductor of the Chorale Caecilia (1915–68). From 1921 to 1953 he taught at the Royal Flemish Cons., and also was conductor of its concerts (1935–53). De Vocht's works were composed in a Romantic vein.

WORKS: ORCH.: 3 syms.; Violin Concerto (1944); Cello Concerto (1955); Recorder Concerto (1957); symphonic poems. **CHAMBER:** Wind Trio (1955); *Suite champêtre* for Guitar (1971–73); 2 piano sonatas; organ preludes and fugues. **VOCAL:** *Primavera* for Soprano, Tenor, Chorus, and Orch. (1963–65); *Scaldis aeterna,* cantata (1966); choruses; songs. —**NS/LK/DM**

Devol, Luana, American soprano; b. San Francisco, Nov. 30, 1942. She studied at the Univ. of San Diego, in London with Vera Rozsa, and with Jess Thomas. In 1983 she made her operatic debut as Strauss's Ariadne in San Francisco, and that same year made her European operatic debut in Stuttgart as Beethoven's Leonore. In 1986 she appeared for the first time in Berlin at both the State Opera and the Deutsche Oper. From 1987 to 1991 she was a member of the Mannheim National Theater. In 1989 she appeared as Irene in *Rienzi* at the Hamburg State Opera and as Eva in Schreker's *Irrelohe* in Vienna. Her debut at the Bayreuth Festival followed in 1990 as Brünnhilde, the same year she sang Leonore in a concert perf. in London. In 1991 she sang Wagner's Gutrune in a concert perf. In Rome. She appeared as Andromache in Reimann's *Troades* in Frankfurt am Main in 1992. After singing Strauss's Empress in Munich in 1993, she reprised that role in Paris in 1994. Among her other admired roles were Donna Anna, Agathe, Euryanthe, Amelia, Isolde, Elisabeth in *Tannhäuser,* and Elisabeth de Valois.—**NS/LK/DM**

DeVoto, Mark (Bernard), American composer, teacher, writer on music, pianist, and conductor; b. Cambridge, Mass., Jan. 11, 1940. His father was the American novelist, journalist, historian, and critic Bernard (Augustine) DeVoto. He studied at the Longy School of Music (1946–56), then with Thompson, Piston, Pirrotta, and Ward at Harvard Univ. (B.A., 1961), with Foss at the Berkshire Music Center in Tanglewood (summer 1959), and with Sessions, Kim, Babbitt, and Cone at Princeton Univ. (M.F.A., 1963; Ph.D., 1967, with the diss. *Alban Berg's Picture-Postcard Songs*). He taught at Reed Coll. (1964–68), Portland State Univ. (1968), the Univ. of N.H. (1968–81), and Tufts Univ. (from 1981), where he was director of its sym. orch. He was founding ed. of the International Alban Berg Soc. newsletter (1968–75). DeVoto also rev. and aug. Walter Piston's *Harmony* (4th ed., 1978; 5th ed., 1987) and publ. a vol. of essays on Debussy (2000).

WORKS: ORCH.: 4 piano concertos: No. 1 (1956), No. 2 (1965–66), No. 3, *The Distinguished Thing* (1968), and No. 4 with Symphonic Wind Ensemble, Women's Voices, and Viola obbligato (1983); *Night Songs and Distant Dances* (1962); *3 Little Pieces* (1964); *Interior Dialogue* (1991). **CHAMBER:** 2 Etudes for Piano, Left Hand (1970); Quartet for Flute, Clarinet, Guitar, and Harp (1987); *Lux benigna* for Euphonium, Violin, Organ, and Piano (1988); *Zvon* for Flute, Violin, and Piano (1992); String Quartet No. 2 (1993); *Pavane and Zortzico* for Piano (1997); *Cloud Piece* for 2 Pianos, 8-Hands (1999). **VOCAL:** *Planh* for 6 Solo Voices and 5 Instruments (1960); *3 Edgar Allan Poe Songs* for Soprano, Concertina, Guitar, Harpsichord, and 8 Flutes (1967; rev. 1970); *Fever-Dream Vocalise* for Soprano, Flute, Cello, Piano, and Percussion (1968); *Ornières* for Soprano, Piano, Organ, and Percussion Ensemble (1974); *The Caucasian Chalk Circle* for Voices and 9 Instruments (1979–80); *H* for Reciter and Flute Choir (1981); *Psalm 98* for Chorus, 2 Trumpets, and 2 Trombones (1983); *Herbstlieder,* 6 songs for Mezzo-soprano and Piano (1986); *Hodayot* for Chorus and Orch. (1989–90). **OTHER:** Orch. and band arrangements.—**NS/LK/DM**

Devreese, Frédéric, Belgian conductor and composer, son of **Godefroid Devreese;** b. Amsterdam, June 2, 1929. He studied first at the Mechelen Cons., and then took courses in composition from Poot and conducting from Defossez at the Brussels Cons. He subsequently studied with Pizzetti at the Accademia di Santa Cecilia in Rome (1952–55). Returning to Belgium, he became associated with the Flemish TV as program director.

WORKS: DRAMATIC: Opera: *Willem van Saeftinghe* (Brussels TV, Sept. 28, 1964; 1st stage perf., Antwerp, Nov. 21, 1964); *De vreemde ruiter* (1966). **Ballet:** *Mascarade* (1955; Aix-les-Bains, France, 1956); *L'Amour de Don Juan* (1973). **ORCH.:** 4 piano concertos (1949; 1952; 1955–56; 1983); Violin Concerto (1951); Sym. (1953); *Mouvement lent* for Strings (1953); *Recitativo et Allegro* for Trumpet and Orch. (1959); *Mouvement vif* for Strings (1963); *Evocation*, suite (1967); *Divertimento* for Strings (1970); *Prelude* (1981); Suite for Brass Band (1985); *Gemini, bewegingen* (1986); *L'Oeuvre au noir*, suite (1988). **CHAMBER:** *Complainte* for Cello or Oboe, and Piano (1951); Quintet for Flute, Clarinet, Bassoon, Piano, and Percussion (1957); *Ensorbeelden*, suite for Brass Quintet (1972); Suite No. 2 for Brass Quintet (1981); *5 Divertimenti* for 4 Saxophones (1985); piano pieces. **VOCAL:** Choruses.—NS/LK/DM

Devreese, Godefroid, Belgian conductor, teacher, and composer, father of **Frédéric Devreese;** b. Kortrijk, Jan. 22, 1893; d. Brussels, June 4, 1972. He studied at the Brussels Cons. with Ysaÿe and César Thomson (violin) and Rasse and Gilson (composition). He was a conductor of the Antwerp Opera (1919–20). He also was a violinist with the Concertgebouw Orch. in Amsterdam (1925–30) and director of the Mechelin Cons. (1930–58), concurrently giving courses at the Brussels Cons. (1944–59).

WORKS: DRAMATIC: Ballet: *Tombelène* (1927). **ORCH.:** *Poème héroïque* (1923); *Symphonic Variations on a Popular Scottish Theme* (1923); Concertino for Cello and Chamber Orch. (1926); *In memoriam* (1928); 2 violin concertos (1936, 1970); Piano Concerto (1938); 4 syms.: No. 1, *Gothique* (1944), No. 2, *Goethe*, for Chorus and Orch. (1952), No. 3, *Sinfonietta* (1962), and No. 4 (1965–66); *Rhapsodie* for Clarinet and Orch. (1948); *Allegro* for Trumpet and Orch. (1950); Suite (1953); *Sinfonietta* for Strings (1962); *6 Variations on a Popular Theme* for Strings (1963); *Capriccio* for Violin and Strings (1963). **CHAMBER:** Violin Sonata (1924); Cello Sonata (1926); String Quartet (1937); Piano Trio (1950). **Piano:** *Scherzo de concert* (1921); *Danse lente* (1924); 7 sonatinas (1944–45); Sonata (1945). **VOCAL:** *Stabat mater* for Soprano, Chorus, and Orch. (1965); *Te Deum* for Chorus and Orch. (1967; Brussels, March 30, 1973); songs. —NS/LK/DM

Devrient, Eduard (Philipp), German baritone, librettist, and writer on music; b. Berlin, Aug. 11, 1801; d. Karlsruhe, Oct. 4, 1877. He studied singing and thorough-bass with Zelter in Berlin, giving his first public performance there in 1819. He then joined the Royal Opera, but after the loss of his voice (1834) he went over to the spoken drama, without losing his interest in music. He sang the role of Christ in the famous performance of Bach's *St. Matthew Passion* under Mendelssohn on March 11, 1829. He was chief producer and actor at the Dresden Court Theater (1844–46) and director at the Karlsruhe Court Theater (1852–70); also the author of the text to Marschner's *Hans Heiling*, and created the title role (1833). His chief work is *Geschichte der deutschen Schauspielkunst* (5 vols., 1848–74); his works concerning music are *Briefe aus Paris* (1840; about Cherubini) and *Meine Erinnerungen an Felix*

Mendelssohn-Bartholdy und seine Briefe an mich (Leipzig, 1869). Within weeks after publication of the latter, Wagner issued a polemical pamphlet entitled *Herr Eduard Devrient und sein Styl* (Munich, 1869) under the pseudonym Wilhelm Drach, violently attacking Devrient for his literary style. Devrient's book was publ. in Eng. (London, 1869; 3rd ed., 1891).

BIBL.: J. Bab, *Die D.s* (Berlin, 1932).—NS/LK/DM

Devroye, Théodore-Joseph, Belgian music scholar; b. Villers-la-Ville, Brabant, Aug. 19, 1804; d. Liège, July 19, 1873. He trained for the priesthood at the seminaries in Mechelen and Liège, and was ordained in Münster in 1828. He was active at the church of St. Christophe in Liège (1830–35), then was canon at Liège Cathedral and precentor for the Liège diocese. He advocated the restoration of churches, the building of organs, and the revitalization of church music; he also promoted the reform of plainsong melodies in Catholic liturgy.

WRITINGS (all publ. in Liège unless otherwise given): *Traité de plainchant à l'usage des séminaires* (1831; 2nd ed., 1839); *Vesperale romanum sive Antiphonale romanum abreviatum cum Psalterio* (1842; 3rd ed., 1860); *Manuale cantorum ad laudes et parvas horas, juxta Breviarum romanum, cum psalmis capitulis et orationibus* (1849); *Processionale romanum continens responsoria, hymnos, antiphonas psalmos in processionibus dicenda additis laudibus vespertinis de SS. Sacramento de S. Cruce de Beata M.V. et suppleneto ex pontificali romano* (1849); *Graduale romanum juxta missale et officia nomvissme auctoritate Apostolica pro universali ecclesia approbata* (1851; 3rd ed., 1869); *Manuale cantorum officia propria Sanctorum ecclesiae cathedralis civitatis et diocesis Leodiensis* (1858); *Concours de musiques religieuses* (Brussels, 1867); *Sur la peinture chrétienne* (Antwerp, 1871).—NS/LK/DM

Dew, John, English opera producer and administrator; b. Santiago di Cuba, June 1, 1944. He received training in opera production in Germany from Walter Felsenstein and Wieland Wagner. In 1971 he began his career with a staging of *The Rake's Progress* in Ulm, and then attracted notice with his Mozart and Wagner productions in Krefeld. He was named head of production with the Bielefeld Theater in 1981, where he staged Schreker's *Irrelohe*, Brand's *Maschinist Hopkins*, Hindemith's *Neues von Tage*, and Krenek's *Der Sprung über den Schatten*. As a guest producer, he staged Neikrug's *Las Alamos* at the Berlin Deutsche Oper (1988), *Les Huguenots* at London's Covent Garden (1991), *Aida* at the Hamburg State Opera (1993), and *I Puritani* at the Vienna State Opera (1994). In 1995 he returned to Hamburg to stage the premiere of Schnittke's *Historia von D. Johann Fausten*. From 1995 he was Generalintendant of the Dortmund Theater.—NS/LK/DM

De Waart, Edo
See **Waart, Edo de**

Dexter, John, English opera director; b. Derby, Aug. 2, 1925; d. London, March 23, 1990. He worked in London in the theater and in films; from 1957 to 1972 he was associated with the English Stage Company, and also was assoc. director of the National Theatre from 1963. In 1966 he staged his first opera, *Benvenuto Cellini*, at London's Covent Garden. After staging operas in Hamburg (1969–72) and Paris (1973), he was director of production at the Metropolitan Opera in N.Y. (1974–81), where his memorable achievements included *Les Dialogues des Carmélites* and *Lulu* (1977), *Billy Budd* (1978), *Aufstieg und Fall der Stadt Mahagonny* (1979), and the triple bill of Satie's *Parade*, Poulenc's *Les Mamelles de Tirésias*, and Ravel's *L'Enfant et les sortilèges* (1981). From 1981 to 1984 he served as production advisor at the Metropolitan.—NS/LK/DM

Deyo, Felix, American composer and pianist, second cousin of **Ruth Lynda Deyo;** b. Poughkeepsie, N.Y., April 21, 1888; d. Baldwin, N.Y., June 21, 1959. He studied piano with his mother, Mary Forster Deyo (1857–1947), then at the Brooklyn Cons. of Music; after graduation, he taught there (1911–39). In 1939 he became director of the Baldwin (Long Island) Cons. of Music. He wrote 3 syms.—*A Lyric Symphony* (Babylon, Long Island, Dec. 8, 1949), *An Ancient Symphony*, and *A Primeval Symphony*—as well as 2 piano sonatas, a Violin Sonata, and numerous piano pieces of a programmatic nature (*Flight of the Dodo Bird*, etc.). His wife, Asta Nygren Deyo (1898–1953), was a piano teacher. —NS/LK/DM

Deyo, Ruth Lynda, American pianist and composer, second cousin of **Felix Deyo;** b. Poughkeepsie, N.Y., April 20, 1884; d. Cairo, March 4, 1960. She studied piano with William Mason and Teresa Carreño and composition with MacDowell. She made her debut at the age of 9 at the World's Columbian Exposition in Chicago (1893); made her concert debut in Berlin (March 23, 1904); subsequently played with major orchs. in the U.S. and in Europe; appeared in recitals with Kreisler and Casals. In 1925 she settled in Egypt and devoted herself mainly to composition. In 1930 she completed the full score of an opera on Egyptian themes, *The Diadem of Stars*, to a libretto by her husband, Charles Dalton; its *Prelude* was perf. by Stokowski and the Philadelphia Orch. (April 4, 1931).—NS/LK/DM

Dezède, Nicolas, composer; b. c. 1742; d. Paris, Sept. 11, 1792. He is believed to have been of noble birth. After initial training in the fundamentals of music and the harp, he settled in Paris and studied composition. He subsequently launched a successful career as a composer for the theater, scoring a major triumph with his opéra-comique *Blaise et Babet, ou La Suite des trois fermiers* (Versailles, April 4, 1783) and finding a patron in Duke Maximilian of Zweibrücken in 1785. Dezède's liaison with Mme. Belcour of the Comédie- Française resulted in a daughter, Florine (b. c. 1766; d. c. 1792), who wrote the comedy *Lucette et Lucas, ou La Paysanne curieuse* (Paris, 1781). Mozart used the air "Lison dormait dans un bocage" from Dezède's opéra comique *Julie* as the theme for his 9 variations for piano, K. 264. Dezède is believed to have composed the air "Ah, vous dirais-je, Maman?," celebrated in English as "Twinkle, Twinkle, Little Star."

WORKS: DRAMATIC (all first perf. in Paris unless otherwise given): *Julie*, opéra-comique (Sept. 28, 1772); *L'erreur d'un moment, ou La Suite de Julie*, opéra- comique (June 14, 1773); *Le Stratagème découvert*, comédie (Oct. 4, 1773); *Les Trois Fermiers*, comédie (May 24, 1777); *Fatmé, ou Le Langage des fleurs*, comédie-ballet (Fontainebleau, Oct. 30, 1777); *Zulima ou L'Art et la nature, ou La Nature et l'art*, opéra-comique (May 9, 1778); *Le Porteur de chaise*, opéra-comique (Dec. 10, 1778; rev. as *Jerôme et Champagne*, Jan. 11, 1781); *Cécile*, opéra-comique (Versailles, Feb. 24, 1780); *A trompeur, trompeur et demi, ou Les Torts du sentiment*, opéra-comique (May 3, 1780; also known as *Fin contre fin*); *Blaise et Babet, ou La Suite des trois fermiers*, opéra- comique (Versailles, April 4, 1783); *Péronne sauvée*, opera (May 27, 1783); *Alexis et Justine*, opéra-comique (Versailles, Jan. 14, 1785); *Alcindor*, opéra-féerie (April 17, 1787); *Auguste et Théodore, ou Les Deux Pages*, opéra-comique (March 6, 1789); *Les Trois Noces*, pièce champêtre (Feb. 23, 1790); *Ferdinand, ou La Suite des Deux Pages*, comédie (June 19, 1790); *Adèle et Didier*, opéra-comique (Nov. 5, 1790); *Paulin et Clairette, ou Les Deux Espiègles*, prose comédie (Jan. 5, 1792); *Mélite*, opéra-comique (March 19, 1792); *La Fête de la cinquantaine*, opera (Jan. 9, 1796).—NS/LK/DM

D'Haene, Rafaël, Belgian composer and teacher; b. Gullegem, Sept. 29, 1943. He studied piano with E. del Pueyo in Brussels and composition with Dutilleux in Paris (Licence de Composition, 1968) and Legley at the Chapelle Musicale Reine Elisabeth in Brussels. In 1970 he became prof. of counterpoint and fugue at the Brussels Cons. and prof. of musical analysis at the Chapelle Musicale Reine Elisabeth.

WORKS: *9 Stukken* for Piano (1967–68); *Werk uit Roemenie*, lieder cycle for Baritone (1969); *Miroir des vanités* for Chorus (1970); Trumpet Sonata (1970); String Quartet (1971); *Klage der Ariadne*, cantata for Soloists, Chorus, and Orch. (1971–72); *Capriccio* for Orch. (1972); *5 Orchestral Lieder* (1972); *Praeludia* for Orch. (1974); *Impressions*, lieder cycle for Mezzo- soprano (1980); *Canzone* for Piano (1983); *Lettres persanes* for Orch. (1986); *Cassazione*, piano trio (1986); *Sonette an Orpheus*, 3 lieder for Soprano and Orch. (1987).—NS/LK/DM

D'Hoedt, Henri-Georges, Belgian composer; b. Ghent, June 28, 1885; d. Brussels, May 14, 1936. He was a student of Emile Mathieu and Leo Moeremans. He became director of the Louvain Cons. in 1924, serving until his death. He was one of the first Belgian composers to depart from late 19th-century Romanticism and come under the influence of French Impressionism.

WORKS: *Klaas au Pays de Cocagne*, opera (Antwerp, 1926); *Les Brèves Chroniques de la vie bourgeoise*, satirical symphonic study (1934); *Narcisse* for Orch.; *L'Ile de Cythère* for Chorus and Orch.; *La Vocation de Siddartha*, symphonic trilogy; *Dionysos*, symphonic poem; *Poème pantagruélique* for Orch.; chamber music.—NS/LK/DM

Dhomont, Francis, French composer; b. Paris, Nov. 2, 1926. He studied in France with Ginette Waldmeier, Charles Koechlin, and Nadia Boulanger. In the early decade of his career as a composer, he wrote works for acoustic instruments, but by the early 1960s was composing exclusively with and for electroacoustic media. He is a five-time winner of the Bourges International Electroacoutic Music Competition in Paris (1976,

1979, 1981, 1984, 1988), where he was also awarded the Magisterium Prize in 1998. He received second prize at the Prix Ars Electronica (1992) and numerous other international distinctions and awards, including the Stockholm Electronic Arts Award (1991, 1992) and first prize in both Prague's Musica Nova competition (1999) and in Italy's Prix Pierre Schaeffer (1999). In 1999 he also won first prizes in both São Paulo's CIMESP and Budapest's EAR competitions. He is the author of various theoretical texts and essays. He ed. "L'espace du son," a series of special issues of the journal *Lien*, Belgium, as well as the issue of *Circuit*, "Électroacoustique- Québec: L'essor," publ. by Les Presses de l'Université de Montréal. He has produced radio programs for Radio France in Paris and, with Diane Maheux, the series "Voyage au bout de l'inouï" for Radio Canada in Montreal. Dhomont is currently an assoc. composer of the Canadian Music Centre and a founding and honorary member of the Canadian Electroacoustic Community (CEC). His *Frankenstein Symphony* (1997) is an unusual electroacoustic adventure, containing parts from works by 21 composers in addition to portions of earlier works by Dhomont himself. A hybrid, 4-movement work, it is made up of recycled snippets of works that are juxtaposed into surprising new configurations and relationships.

WORKS (all for Tape unless otherwise noted): *Cité du dedans* (1972); *Assemblages* (1972); *Syntagmes* (1975); *Puzzle* (1975); *Asie* (1975); *La liberté ou la mort*, incidental music (1976); *Espaces sonores pour des textes de Jean Tortel* (1976); *Mais laisserons-nous mourir Arianna?* (1976); *Métonymie ou Le corps impossible* (1977); *A cordes perdues* for Double Bass and Tape (1977); *Sous le regard d'un soleil noir* (1981); *Points de fuite* (1982); *Transits élémentaires* (1983); *...mourir un peu* (1984); *Drôles d'oiseaux* (1985); *Signé Dionysos* (1986–90); *Les traces du rêve*, soundtrack for film (1986); *Chiaroscuro* (1987); *Poe-Debussy/Autour de la Maison Usher*, incidental music (1988); *Chroniques de la lumière* (1989); *Novars* (1989); *Espace/Escape* (1989); *Qui est là?*, electro-clip (1990); *L'électro*, electro-clip (1990); *Simulacres: un autoportrait*, radiophonic work (1990–91); *Figures de la nuit/Faces of the night*, radiophonic work (1991); *Studio de nuit*, electro-clip (1992); *Previews*, electro- clip (1994); *Convulsive*, electro-clip (1995); *Lettre de Sarajevo* (1995–96); *Nocturne à Combray* (1995–96); *Objets retrouvés*, "In Memoriam Pierre Schaeffer" (1996); *Forêt profonde* (1996); *CPH Pendler Music* (1997); *Frankenstein Symphony* (1997; a collective work); *L'air du large* (1997–98); *Ricercare*, an 8-track piece (1998); *En cuerdas* (1998); *AvatArsSon* (1998); *Les moirures du temps* (1999); *Je te salue, vieil océan!* (1998–99); *Vol d'arondes* (1999).—**LK/DM**

D'Hooghe, Clement (Vital Ferdinand), noted Belgian organist, pedagogue, and composer; b. Temse, April 21, 1899; d. Wilrijk, near Antwerp, April 1, 1951. He studied classics at the Episcopal Coll. of St. Niklaas (1913–17). After training in organ with Paepen, harmony and composition with Wambach, De Boeck, and Mortelmans, and orchestration with Gilson at the Antwerp Cons. (1918–27), he studied organ improvisation with Dupré in Paris. From 1926 until his death, D'Hooghe was organist at St. Paul's in Antwerp. As a recitalist, he acquired an outstanding reputation as a virtuoso. From 1942 he also was a prof. at the Antwerp Cons.

WORKS: *Preludium* for Orch. (1928); *Variations on a Swedish Song* for Orch. (1936); Piano Concerto (1949); Piano Quartet (1939); String Quartet (1944); Cello Sonata (1945); choral works; songs; children's pieces.—**NS/LK/DM**

Diabelli, Anton, Austrian composer and publisher; b. Mattsee, near Salzburg, Sept. 5, 1781; d. Vienna, April 8, 1858. He was a choirboy in the monastery at Michaelbeurn, and at Salzburg Cathedral. He studied for the priesthood at the Munich Latin School, but continued his musical work, submitting his compositions to Michael Haydn, who encouraged him. On the secularization of the Bavarian monasteries, Diabelli, who had already entered that at Raichenhaslach, embraced the career of a musician, went to Vienna (where Joseph Haydn received him kindly), taught piano and guitar for a living, and in 1818 became a partner of Cappi, the music publisher, assuming control of the firm (Diabelli & Co.) in 1824. He publ. much of Schubert's music, but underpaid the composer, and complained that he wrote too much. In 1852 he sold his firm to C.A. Spina. A facile composer, Diabelli produced an opera, *Adam in der Klemme* (Vienna, 1809; 1 perf.), masses, cantatas, chamber music, etc., which were consigned to oblivion; however, his sonatinas are still used for beginners. His name was immortalized through Beethoven's set of 33 variations (op.120) on a waltz theme by Diabelli.

BIBL.: A. Weinmann, *Verlagsverzeichnis A. D. & Co., 1824 bis 1840* (Vienna, 1985).—**NS/LK/DM**

Diaghilev, Sergei (Pavlovich), famous Russian impresario; b. Gruzino, Novgorod district, March 31, 1872; d. Venice, Aug. 19, 1929. He was associated with progressive artistic organizations in St. Petersburg, but his main field of activity was in western Europe. He established the Ballets Russes in Paris in 1909; he commissioned Stravinsky to write the ballets *The Firebird, Petrouchka,* and *Le Sacre du printemps*; also commissioned Prokofiev, Milhaud, Poulenc, Auric, and other composers of the younger generation. Ravel and Falla also wrote works for him. The great importance of Diaghilev's choreographic ideas lies in the complete abandonment of the classical tradition; in this respect he was the true originator of the modern dance.

BIBL.: A. Haskell, *D.: His Artistic and Private Life* (London, 1935); V. Kamenev, *Russian Ballet through Russian Eyes* (London, 1936); S. Lifar, *S. D.: His Life, His Work, His Legend* (London, 1940); S. Grigoriev, *The D. Ballet* (London, 1953); B. Kochno, *D. and the Ballets Russes* (N.Y., 1970); R. Buckle, *D.* (N.Y., 1979). —**NS/LK/DM**

Diamond, David (Leo), eminent American composer; b. Rochester, N.Y., July 9, 1915. After attending the Cleveland Inst. of Music (1927–29), he was a student of Rogers at the Eastman School of Music in Rochester, N.Y. (1930–34). He then studied at the New Music School and the Dalcroze Inst. in N.Y. (1934–36) with Boepple and Sessions. In 1936 he went to Paris to pursue studies with Boulanger, and during the summers of 1937 and 1938 he attended the American Cons. in Fontainebleau; he also studied with Ribaupierre and

Scherchen. While in Paris, he became associated with the most important musicians and writers of his time, including Stravinsky, Ravel, Roussel, and Milhaud. His *Psalm* for Orch. (1936) won the Juilliard Publication Award in 1937 and brought him wide recognition. In 1941 he received the Prix du Rome and in 1942 the American Academy in Rome Award. With his *Rounds for Strings* (1944), he established himself as one of America's most important composers. This highly successful score won the N.Y. Music Critics' Circle Award in 1944. In subsequent years, Diamond received various commissions and had his works performed by major conductors. After serving as the Fulbright Prof. at the Univ. of Rome (1951–52), he settled in Florence. In 1961 and 1963 he was the Slee Prof. at the State Univ. of N.Y. at Buffalo. In 1965 he removed to the U.S. and taught at the Manhattan School of Music in N.Y. until 1968, serving as chairman of its music dept. in 1967–68. In 1970 he was a visiting prof. at the Univ. of Colo. in Boulder. In 1971–72 he was composer-in-residence at the American Academy in Rome. He then was prof. of composition and lecturer in graduate studies at the Juilliard School in N.Y. from 1973. In 1983 he also was a visting prof. at the Univ. of Denver. From 1991 to 1994 he was composer-in-residence at the Tisch Center for the Arts in N.Y. In 1938, 1941, and 1958 he held Guggenheim fellowships. In 1966 he was elected to membership in the National Inst. of Arts and Letters. In 1985 he received the William Schuman Lifetime Achievement Award and in 1991 the Edward MacDowell Gold Medal. In 1995 he received the Medal of Arts from President Bill Clinton. As a composer, Diamond developed an original and recognizable style of harmonic and contrapuntal writing with the clearest sense of tonality. The element of pitch, often inspired by natural folklike patterns, is strong in all of his music. He later adopted a modified dodecaphonic method, while keeping free of doctrinaire serialism. His orch., chamber, and vocal output constitutes a significant contribution to 20th-century American music.

WORKS: DRAMATIC: O p e r a : *The Noblest Game* (1971–75). **M u s i c a l C o m e d y :** *Mirandolina* (1958). **M u s i c a l F o l k P l a y :** *The Golden Slippers* (N.Y., Dec. 5, 1965). **D a n c e D r a m a :** *Icaro* (1937). **B a l l e t :** *A Myriologue* (1935); *Formal Dance* (N.Y., Nov. 10, 1935); *Dance of Liberation* (1936; N.Y., Jan. 23, 1938); *Tom* (1936); *Duet* (1937); *Prelude* (1937); *The Dream of Audubon* (1941); *Labyrinth* (N.Y., April 5, 1946). **I n c i d e n t a l M u s i c T o :** Shakespeare's *The Tempest* (1944; N.Y., Jan. 25, 1945; rev. 1946 and 1968) and *Romeo and Juliet* (1947; rev. 1950; N.Y., March 10, 1951); Williams's *The Rose Tattoo* (1950–51; N.Y., Feb. 3, 1951). **F i l m :** *A Place to Live* (1941); *Dreams that Money can Buy* (1943); *Strange Victory* (1948); *Anna Lucasta* (1949); *Lippold's the Sun* (1965); *Life in the Balance* (1966). **R a d i o :** *Hear it Now* (1942); *The Man Behind the Gun* (1942).

ORCH.: *Divertimento* for Piano and Small Orch. (1935); *Threnody* (1935); *Variations on a Theme by Erik Satie* (1935–36); *Psalm* (Rochester, N.Y., Dec. 10, 1936); Suite No. 1 from the ballet *Tom* (1936); 3 violin concertos: No. 1 (1936; N.Y., March 24, 1937), No. 2 (1947; Vancouver, Feb. 29, 1948), and No. 3 (1967–68; N.Y., April 1, 1976); *Aria and Hymn* (1937); *Variations on an Original Theme* for Chamber Orch. (1937; Rochester, N.Y., April 23, 1940); *Overture* (1937); Cello Concerto (1938; Roches-

ter, N.Y., April 30, 1942); *Heroic Piece* for Chamber Orch. (Zürich, July 29, 1938); *Elegy in Memory of Maurice Ravel* for Brass, Harp, and Percussion (Rochester, N.Y., April 28, 1938; rev. for Strings and Percussion, 1938–39); *Music for Double Strings, Brass, and Timpani* (1938–39; rev. 1968); *Concert Piece* (1939; N.Y., May 16, 1940); Concerto for Chamber Orch. (Yaddo, N.Y., Sept. 7, 1940); 11 syms.: No. 1 (1940–41; N.Y., Dec. 21, 1941), No. 2 (1942; Boston, Oct. 13, 1944), No. 3 (1945; Boston, Nov. 3, 1951), No. 4 (1945; Boston, Jan. 23, 1948), No. 5 (1951; rev. 1964; N.Y., April 26, 1966), No. 6 (1951–54; Boston, March 8, 1957), No. 7 (1959; N.Y., Jan. 26, 1962), No. 8 (1960; N.Y., Oct. 26, 1961), No. 9 for Baritone and Orch. (N.Y., Nov. 17, 1985), No. 10 (in progress), and No. 11 (N.Y., Dec. 3, 1992); *Ballade* for Chamber Orch. (1935); *Rounds* for Strings (Minneapolis, Nov. 24, 1944); *The Enormous Room* (1948; Cincinnati, Nov. 19, 1949); *Timon of Athens*, symphonic portrait (Louisville, 1949); Piano Concerto (1949–50; N.Y., April 28, 1966); *Ceremonial Fanfare* for Brass and Percussion (1950); *Sinfonia Concertante* (1954–56; Rochester, N.Y., March 7, 1957); *Diaphony* for Organ, Brass, 2 Pianos, and Timpani (1955; N.Y., Feb. 22, 1956; rev. for Organ and Orch., 1968); *The World of Paul Klee* (1957; Portland, Ore., Feb. 15, 1958); *Elegies* for Flute, English Horn, and Strings (1962–63); Piano Concertino (1964–65); *Music* for Chamber Orch. (1969–70); *A Buoyant Music*, overture No. 2 (1970); *Sinfonietta* (1989; Koger, July 20, 1990); *Kaddish* for Cello and Orch. (1989; Seattle, April 9, 1990).

CHAMBER: *6 Pieces* for String Quartet (1935); *Partita* for Oboe, Bassoon, and Piano (1935); Chamber Sym. for Clarinet, Bassoon, Trumpet, Viola, and Piano (1935–36); *Chamber Music for Young People* for Violin and Piano (1936); Cello Sonata (1936; rev. 1938); Concerto for String Quartet (1936); Quintet for Flute and Piano Quartet (1937); String Trio (1937); Violin Sonatina (1937); 2 piano quartets (1938, 1972); 9 string quartets (1940; 1943–44; 1946; 1951; 1960; 1962; 1963–64; 1964; 1966); 2 violin sonatas (1943–46; 1981); *Canticle* for Violin and Piano (1946); *Perpetual Motion* for Violin and Piano (1946); *Chaconne* for Violin and Piano (1948); Quintet for Clarinet, 2 Violas, and 2 Cellos (1950); Piano Trio (1951); Sonata for Solo Violin (1954–59); Sonata for Solo Cello (1956–59); Wind Quintet (1958); *Night Music* for Accordion and String Quartet (1961); Nonet for 3 Violins, 3 Violas, and 3 Cellos (1961–62); Accordion Sonata (1963); *Introduction and Dance* for Accordion (1966). **P i a n o :** *4 Gymnopedies* (1937); Concerto for 2 Pianos (1942); *The Tomb of Melville* (1944–49); Sonata (1947); *A Private World* (1954–59); *Then and Now* (1962); *Alone at the Piano* (1967); *Prelude, Fantasy, and Fugue* (1983).

VOCAL: *2 Elegies* for Voice and String Quartet (1935); *This Is the Garden* for Chorus (1935); *4 Ladies*, song cycle (1935; rev. 1962); *Vocalise* for Voice and Viola (1935); *Paris this April Sunset* for Women's Chorus, Cello, and Double Bass (1937); *3 Madrigals*, after James Joyce, for Chorus (1937); *The Mad Maid's Song* for Voice, Flute, and Harpsichord (1937; rev. 1953); *Somewhere I Have Never Travelled* for Voice and Orch. (1938); *3 Epitaphs*, song cycle (1938); *5 Songs from The Tempest* (1944); *Young Joseph*, after Thomas Mann, for Women's Chorus and String Orch. (1944); *L'Ame de Claude*, song cycle setting extracts from Debussy's letters to Jacques Durand (1949); *The Martyr* for Men's Chorus and Optional Orch. (1950; rev. 1964); *Mizmor L'David*, sacred service for Tenor, Chorus, and Organ (1951); *The Midnight Meditation*, song cycle (1951); *Ahavah*, symphonic eulogy for Male Narrator and Orch. (1954); *2 Anthems* for Chorus (1955); *Prayer for Peace* for Chorus (1960); *This Sacred Ground* for Baritone, Chorus, Children's Chorus, and Orch. (1962); *We Two*, song cycle (1964); *To Music*, choral sym. for Tenor, Bass-baritone, Chorus, and Orch. (1967); *A Secular Cantata* for Tenor, Baritone, Chorus, and Small Orch. (1976; N.Y., Feb. 5, 1977); *A Song for Hope* for 8 Solo Voices and Orch. (1978).

BIBL.: V. Kimberling, *D. D.: A Bio-bibliography* (Metuchen, N.J., 1987); C. Shore, ed., *D. D.: A Musical Celebration* (Stuyvesant, N.Y., 1995).—**NS/LK/DM**

Diamond, Jody, American composer, scholar, performer, publisher, and teacher; b. Pasadena, Calif., April 23, 1953. After attending courses at the Calif. Inst. of the Arts (1970–72) and the Univ. of Calif. at Los Angeles (1972–73), she studied at the Univ. of Calif. at Berkeley (B.A. in music, communication, and culture, 1977) and San Francisco State Univ. (M.A. in education and music, 1979), and received a Senior Fulbright Research Fellowship in 1988. She also was trained in Indonesian music, performance, and theory at the Center for World Music in Berkeley (1971–75), attended summer workshops in Indonesian music and culture at the Univ. of Washington in Seattle (1973, 1976), and earned a level one certificate in Orff-Schulwerk technique in San Francisco (1979), and had private training with numerous Javanese and Balinese master artists in both Indonesia and the U.S., including K. R. T. Wasitodiningrat, Nyai Bei Mardusari, and Nyi Supadmi (from 1971). In 1981 Diamond founded the American Gamelan Inst., which publishes scores and monographs on the Indonesian percussion ensemble known as gamelan. She is also the editor of *Balungan*, a journal of Indonesian performing arts. She has become an expert in Indonesian culture, with special expertise in contemporary music and practices. She has contributed innumerable articles to scholarly journals, and has given lectures, presentations, and workshops the world over. Two particularly noteworthy articles are "There Is No They There: Global Values in Cross-cultural Research" (*Musicworks*, No. 37, June 1990), on the ethics of cross-cultural interaction and research, and "Out of Indonesia: Global Gamelan" (*Ethnomusicology*, Vol. 42, No. 1, Winter 1998), an extensive review of gamelan outside of Indonesia. She has held teaching positions at John F. Kennedy Univ. in Orinda, Calif. (1980), the Univ. of Calif at Berkeley (1976–88), Mills Coll. (1981–89), Dartmouth Coll. (1990–92), Goddard Coll. (1993–97), and Monash Univ. in Clayton, Australia (1996). From 1999 she returned to Dartmouth Coll. as a Visiting Scholar in Asian Studies and a visiting asst. prof. of music. She also has appeared widely as a performer. She is married to **Larry Polansky**, which whom she founded and directs Frog Peak Music (A Composers' Collective).

WORKS: GAMELAN: *In That Bright World* (1981); *Sabbath Bride* (1982); *Gending Chelsea* (1982; in collaboration with Virgil Thomson); *Dance Music I, II,* and *III* (1983); *Bubaran Bill* (1984); *Pangkur GMT* (1987); *Pangkur/Ricik-ricik* (1987); *Pangkur N.Z.* (New Zealand; 1992); *Kenong* (1990); also numerous arrangements. **CHORUS AND JAVANESE GAMELAN:** *"Kabe baud..."* for Chorus and Javanese Gamelan (1982; in collaboration with Ki Mantle Hood). **GAMELAN AND OTHER INSTRUMENTS:** *Oh Little Mother* for Gamelan, Flute, Banjo, Guitar, and Voices (1982); *Maggie in Two Modes* for Cello and Gamelan (1983); *Hard Times* for Gamelan, Mandocello, and Chorus (1984); *Lagu Didalam Kotak/The Melody Within the Box* for Gamelan and Computer-controlled Matrix Switcher

(1986); *Pieces of Eight* for 8 Tapes of Indonesian Music and Computer-controlled Matrix Switcher (1986); *Prelude: Anyone Can Play* for Audience and Gamelan (1987); *UK 789* for Gamelan and Tape (1989); *"We taste the spices of Arabia, yet we cannot feel the scorching sun that brings them forth"* for Guitar, Piano, French Horn, Singers, and Readers, after Goenawan Mohamad (1997). **OTHER:** *Deep Blue Sea* for Chorus (1982); *Pangkur Tunggal* for Singer and Real-time Multi-tracked Tape (1992); *We Need More Time* for 2 Performers (1997); *the betrayal of the wedhatama* for Voices, Percussion, and Shadow Puppets (2000).—**LK/DM**

Diamond, Neil (Leslie), popular songwriter nicknamed "the Jewish Elvis"; b. Brooklyn, Jan. 24, 1941. An army brat, Neil Diamond never stayed in one school for very long. One summer, Diamond spent the season at Surprise Lake Camp in Cold Springs, N.Y. Legendary folk singer Pete Seeger lived close by and played for the campers. Some of the campers played their own songs for Seeger. The idea of songwriting intrigued Diamond. When he turned 16, someone gave him a guitar for his birthday. While he continued to study at Erasmus Hall High, and work with the fencing team, he took lessons and started writing songs. He continued to write songs while studying for a pre-med degree at N.Y.U. on a fencing scholarship. After the fall semester of his senior year, however, he quit school to take a $50 a week job as a contract songwriter with a N.Y. publishing company.

Within a few years, Diamond rented his own office, actually little more than a closet over the famous jazz club, Birdland, and started his own publishing company. He was marginally successful, cutting some records as a performer in the early 1960s, as well. One of his demos came into the hands of Jeff Barry and Ellie Greenwich, who went to see him perform at a club in Greenwich Village. They had started a new label called Bang, and quickly signed the young songwriter.

In 1966, Diamond recorded his first sides for Bang, including "Solitary Man," "Cherry Cherry," and "I Got the Feeling (Oh No, No)." "Cherry Cherry" hit #6 on the charts, one of Bang's first hits. "I Got the Feeling (Oh No, No)" rose to #16, and Diamond's career as a performer was underway. Ironically, at the same time, Diamond landed one of his first major hits as a writer with "I'm a Believer" a song that Barry had produced for the Monkees. It topped the charts for seven weeks.

Diamond hit a run of success, landing four more hits as a performer with Bang over the course of the next year: "You Got to Me" hit #18, "Girl, You'll Be a Woman Soon" hit #10, "I Thank the Lord for the Night Time" rose to #13, and "Kentucky Woman" went to #22. Additionally, performers including Jay and the Americans, Lulu, and Deep Purple recorded Diamond songs.

In 1969, Diamond moved on to UNI records. Here, he started to experiment a little. He recorded an album that fused pop and gospel themes. The first hit, the title track from *Brother Love's Travelling Salvation Show*, only reached #22. However, the second single, "Sweet Caroline," was Diamond's biggest single to date, going platinum and hitting #4. His next album, *Touching You Touching Me* produced another platinum single, "Holly

Holy," which rose to #6. The album hit #30 and went gold.

Bang Records, hoping to cash in on the sudden success of Diamond, re-released his 1968 single "Shilo" which hit #24. This was better than the next single UNI put out, "Soolaimon (African Trilogy)," the product of Diamond experimenting with African rhythms on his *Taproot Manifesto* album. The album yielded one more hit, however, a song based on a story a shaman once told Diamond about a tribe with more men than women. The men-without-women would take a bottle of wine to be their woman for the weekend. This led to the platinum-selling "Cracklin' Rosie," Diamond's first chart topper as a performer. It took the album to #13 and platinum. As "Cracklin' Rosie" was climbing the charts, Bang re-released an almost hit from 1967, "Solitary Man," which went to #21. Similarly, Diamond's cover of "He Ain't Heavy, He's My Brother" for UNI, which hit #20, was dogged by a reissue of "Do It," a Bang tune that hit #36.

Diamond had moved to L.A. shortly after signing to UNI, and once again all those Army brat emotions of not fitting in surfaced. They became the subject of a song that took him close to a year to write. That tune, "I Am I Said" rose to #4 in 1971, launching the album *Stones* to #11 and gold sales. The title track from the album hit #14.

Diamond topped the charts again with "Song Sung Blue" in 1972. The single went gold. Along with the #11 single "Play Me" and the #17 "Walk On Water," the album *Moods* went platinum, hitting #5, Diamond's highest-charting album to that point. It also won a Grammy for Best Engineering.

Along with having success as a recording artist, Diamond became a major live attraction. His next project was a double-live album recorded at L.A.'s Greek Theater. *Hot August Night* also rose to #5, selling double platinum, despite the lone hit from the album, a live version of "Cherry Cherry", stalling at #31. When the tour that spawned the album arrived in N.Y., Diamond played 20 sold-out shows at Broadway's Winter Garden Theater, the first rock-era star to headline on Broadway. After these shows, Diamond announced a hiatus from performing live, which lasted for nearly four years

He didn't stop recording, however. His next album was the soundtrack to the movie based on the best-selling book *Jonathan Livingston Seagull*. While the movie was a stiff, the album did surprisingly well, hitting #2 on the charts and selling double platinum. It was doubly surprising because the only semi-hit from the album, "Be," stalled at #34. The album won the Grammy for Best Original Score Written for a Motion Picture.

Diamond returned to the top reaches of the pop charts with his next single, "Longfellow Serenade." The song hit #5 pop, topping the Adult Contemporary charts. The album *Serenade* went platinum and hit #3.

Former Band guitarist Robbie Robertson worked with Diamond on his next project, the sprawling *Beautiful Noise*. This album also went platinum, peaking at #4, propelled in part by the hit "If You Know What I Mean," which went as high as #11 and topped the Adult Contemporary chart. Diamond's association with Robertson would lead him to appear at the famous Last Waltz concert.

In 1976, Diamond once again recorded an album live at the Greek Theater. *Love at the Greek* was a double platinum, #8 album, and also a television special. Diamond was becoming such a phenomenon that his albums didn't need Top 40 airplay to sell by the end of the 1970s. *I'm Glad You're Here with Me Tonight* went double platinum and hit #6 on the charts even though the single, "Desiree," peaked at #16.

Diamond's next hit was something of a fluke. He wrote and recorded a song called "You Don't Bring Me Flowers." Around the same time, Barbra Streisand covered the record. Individually, their versions garnered some airplay. One astute DJ noticed that the songs were in the same key. He started alternating lines. The effect was galvanic. The request lines lit up, first with people who wanted to hear it, then with retailers who wanted to sell it. Both artists recorded for the same company, so they were put into the studio and cut the tune as a duet. The song went to the top of the charts. Along with the #20 hit "Forever in Blue Jeans," it propelled Diamond's *You Don't Bring Me Flowers* to #4 and double platinum. He followed this with the platinum, #10 *September Morn*. The title track hit #17.

In 1980, Diamond attempted a film career. He chose as his vehicle a remake the first talkie, *The Jazz Singer*, taking the Jolson role of the cantor's son who wants to be a pop star. In addition to doing decent box office, the soundtrack went quintuple platinum. The album spawned some of Diamond's biggest, highest-charting hits, including the #2 "Love on the Rocks," the #6 hit "Hello Again," and the Adult Contemporary chart topper (#8 pop) "America," a swirling oratorio about the immigrant experience.

The early 1980s were golden for Diamond. In the wake of his film success, *On the Way to the Sky* went platinum and reached #17. It also spun off another Adult Contemporary chart topper in "Yesterday's Songs" (#11 pop) and the #35 "Be Mine Tonight." *Heartlight*, inspired by the movie *ET*, went platinum and hit #9 based on the #5 title track and the #35 "I'm Alive." The *Primitive* album went gold and hit #20 with no Top 40 play at all, as did the #20 album *Headed for the Future*.

As the 1980s went on, Diamond was heard less and less on Top 40 radio. His albums, however, generally continued to sell. While the 1988 redux of *Hot August Night*, imaginatively called *Hot August Night II*, stalled at #59, it managed to go gold. *Headed for the Future*, an album that included songs by contemporary soul legends Stevie Wonder and Maurice White, sold gold and went to #20 despite no hit singles. Indeed, while Diamond put out a spate of albums, he didn't experience much in the way of high profile hits, though the #44 *Lovescape* managed to quietly go platinum. Ironically, this nice Jewish boy from Brooklyn cut a 1992 Christmas Album that hit #8 and went platinum.

Diamond's next album was an exercise in nostalgia, of sorts. *Up on the Roof: Songs from the Brill Building* captured the essence of Diamond's early years, with songs from the era when he just got started. The album entered the charts at its peak of #28. He continued to be a major draw live, and was the top concert attraction in the U.S. for the first half of 1992. He holds the record for consecutive sold-out shows at both N.Y.'s Madison Square Garden and the Los Angeles Forum.

In the 1990s, Diamond's recording activity slowed. In 1996, for his first new recording in five years, Diamond chose to make a country record. *Tennessee Moon* did well, both on the country album charts, where it hit #3, and the pop album charts where it topped out at #14. The album was gold within six months of its release. Two years later, Diamond cut an album of movie chestnuts. *As Time Goes By* presented Diamond's versions of songs from films ranging from *Casablanca* to *Hard Day's Night*. It peaked in its first week at #31 on the album charts and didn't go gold.

At the turn of the 21st century, Diamond has achieved near-legendary status. With over 90 million records sold, his middle-of-the-road pop has served "billions and billions" of customers—like the fast food of McDonalds. Just like Frank Sinatra, he will probably go on recording and performing on the lounge circuit for decades to come.

Disc.: *The Feel of Neil Diamond, Just for You* (1967); *Velvet Gloves & Spit* (1968); *Sweet Caroline: Brother Love's Traveling...* (1969); *Brother Love's Traveling Salvation Show* (1969); *Touching You, Touching Me* (1969); *Neil Diamond* (1970); *Shilo* (1970); *Tap Root Manuscript* (1970); *Do It!* (1971); *Stones* (1971); *Moods* (1972); *Hot August Night* (live; 1972); *Rainbow* (1973); *Jonathan Livingston Seagull* (1973); *Serenade* (1974); *Focus on Neil Diamond* (1975); *And the Singer Sings His Song* (1976); *Beautiful Noise* (1976); *I'm Glad You're Here with Me Tonight* (1977); *Love at the Greek* (live; 1977); *Carmelita's Eyes* (1978); *You Don't Bring Me Flowers* (1978); *September Morn* (1979); *The Jazz Singer* (1980); *Diamonds* (1981); *Solitary Man* (1981); *Love Songs* (1981); *On the Way to the Sky* (1981); *Song Sung Blue* (1982); *Live Diamond* (1982); *Heartlight* (1982); *Primitive* (1984); *Headed for the Future* (1986); *Hot August Night 2* (live; 1987); *Red Red Wine* (1988); *The Best Years of Our Lives* (1988); *Lovescape* (1991); *The Christmas Album* (1992); *Up on the Roof: Songs from the Brill Building* (1993); *The Christmas Album, Vol. 2* (1994); *Live in America* (1995); *I Knew Love* (1996); *Tennessee Moon* (1996); *Live in Concert Reader's* (1997); *The Movie Album: As Time Goes By* (1998); *This Time*—**HB**

Dianda, Hilda,

Argentine composer; b. Córdoba, April 13, 1925. She studied in Europe with Scherchen and Malipiero, and from 1958 to 1962 she worked at Radiodiffusion Française in Paris. Upon returning to Argentina, she devoted herself to composition and organization of concerts of ultramodern music.

Works: 3 string quartets (1947, 1960, 1962); Concertante for Cello and Chamber Orch. (1952); Trio for Flute, Oboe, and Bassoon (1953); Wind Quintet (1957); *Díptico* for 16 Instruments (1962); *Núcleos* for String Orch., 2 Pianos, and Percussion (1964); works for various ensembles under the generic titles *Resonancias* and *Ludus* (1964–69).—**NS/LK/DM**

Díaz, Justino,

noted Puerto Rican bass; b. San Juan, Jan. 29, 1940. He studied at the Univ. of Puerto Rico (1958–59) and at the New England Cons. of Music in Boston (1959–62); he also received training from Frederick Jagel. In 1957 he made his operatic debut as Ben in Menotti's *The Telephone* in San German, Puerto Rico, and in 1961 appeared with the New England Opera Theater in Boston. After winning the Metropolitan Opera Auditions of the Air, he made his debut with the company in N.Y. as Monterone on Oct. 23, 1963; was chosen to create the role of Antony in Barber's *Antony and Cleopatra* at the opening of the new Metropolitan Opera house at Lincoln Center on Sept. 16, 1966. He made guest appearances in Salzburg, Hamburg, Vienna, Munich, Milan, and other European music centers. On Sept. 10, 1971, he appeared in the premiere of Ginastera's *Beatrix Cenci*, which inaugurated the opera house at the Kennedy Center in Washington, D.C. On March 4, 1973, he made his N.Y.C. Opera debut as Francesco in the same opera. In 1976 he made his first appearance at London's Covent Garden as Escamillo. In 1987 he sang Iago in Zeffirelli's film version of *Othello*. In 1990 he made his debut with the Cincinnati Opera as Amonasro. —**NS/LK/DM**

Diaz (de la Peña), Eugène (-Emile),

French composer; son of the celebrated painter; b. Paris, Feb. 27, 1837; d. Coleville, Sept. 12, 1901. He was a pupil at the Paris Cons., studying with Halévy and Reber. He produced the comic opera *Le Roi Candaule* (Paris, 1865) and won the government prize for the opera *La Coupe du roi de Thulé* (Paris, Jan. 10, 1873), which, however, proved a complete failure.—**NS/LK/DM**

Dibdin, Charles,

English composer; b. Dibdin, near Southampton (baptized), March 15, 1745; d. London, July 25, 1814. From 1756 to 1759 he was a chorister at Winchester Cathedral. He took lessons there from Kent and Fussell, but was chiefly self-taught in composition. At age 15, he went to London. He was engaged at Covent Garden as a singing actor, and soon began to write for the stage. His first piece, *The Shepherd's Artifice*, was produced at his benefit performance at Covent Garden on May 21, 1764. He was engaged at Birmingham from 1763 to 1765, and at Covent Garden again until 1768, when he went over to Drury Lane. During this period, he wrote his most successful theater scores, among them the comic operas *Lionel and Clarissa* (Covent Garden, Feb. 25, 1768), *The Padlock* (Drury Lane, Oct. 3, 1769), and *The Ephesian Matron* (Ranelagh House, May 12, 1769), the afterpiece *The Waterman, or The First of August* (His Majesty's Theatre, Aug. 8, 1774), and the opera *The Quaker* (Drury Lane, May 3, 1775). Falling out with Garrick, he went to France in 1776 to avoid imprisonment for debt, remaining there until 1778, when he was appointed composer to Covent Garden, having up to that time brought out 8 operas. From 1782 to 1784, he was manager of the newly erected Royal Circus (later the Surrey Theatre). After the failure of certain theatrical enterprises, and a projected journey to India, he commenced a series of monodramatic "table-entertainments," of which song was a principal feature, and which were extremely popular from 1789 to 1805; in these Dibdin appeared as author, composer, narrator, singer, and accompanist. He then built and managed a small theater of his own, which opened in 1796; he retired in 1805 on a pension, which was withdrawn for a time, but subsequently restored. Dibdin also composed numerous sea songs which were very popular at the time. He publ. *The Musical Tour of Mr. Dibdin* (1788), *History of the Stage* (5 vols., 1795), *The Professional Life of Mr. Dibdin* (4 vols., 1803), and various novels. His grandson, Henry Edward Dibdin (b. London, Sept. 8, 1813; d. Edinburgh, May 6, 1866), was an organist, harpist, and teacher who compiled the collection *The Standard Psalm Tune Book* (1851).

BIBL.: E. Dibdin, *A C. D. Bibliography* (Liverpool, 1937); E. Holmes, *C. D.* (diss., Univ. of Southampton, 1974). —NS/LK/DM

di Bonaventura, Anthony
See **Bonaventura, Anthony di**

di Bonaventura, Mario
See **Bonaventura, Mario di**

Di Capua, Eduardo, Italian composer of Neapolitan ballads; b. Naples, 1864; d. there, 1917. He earned his living by playing in small theaters and cafes in and around Naples, and later in the cinemas; also gave piano lessons. His most famous song was *O sole mio* (1898); its popularity was immense, and never abated. Other celebrated songs were *Maria Mari* (1899), *Torna maggio* (1900); *Canzona bella*, etc. Di Capua sold these songs to publishers outright, and so did not benefit by their popularity. He died in extreme poverty. —NS/LK/DM

Dichter, Misha, talented American pianist; b. Shanghai (of Polish-Jewish refugees), Sept. 27, 1945. He was reared in Los Angeles; at the age of 15, he won a contest of the Music Educators National Conference, Western Division. While attending the Univ. of Calif. at Los Angeles, he enrolled in a master class conducted by Rosina Lhévinne; later joined her class at the Juilliard School of Music in N.Y. In 1966 he entered the Tchaikovsky Competition in Moscow and won second prize, scoring popular acclaim among Russian audiences. Returning to the U.S., he made his Boston Sym. Orch. debut as soloist at the Tanglewood Festival in 1966; numerous appearances with major American and European orchs. followed; he also gave recitals. His wife, Cipa (b. Rio de Janeiro, May 20, 1944), is also a fine pianist with whom he often appeared in duo recitals. Dichter's natural predilections lie in the Romantic repertoire; his playing possesses a high emotional appeal; but he also can render full justice to Classical masterpieces.—NS/LK/DM

Dick, Marcel, Hungarian-American violist, conductor, pedagogue, and composer, b. Miskolcz, Aug. 28, 1898; d. Cleveland Heights, Ohio, Dec. 13, 1991. He was a pupil of Joseph Bloch (violin) and Kodály (composition) at the Royal Academy of Music in Budapest. After playing violin in the Budapest Phil., he was first violist in the Vienna Sym. Orch. (1924–27); he also played in

the Kolisch and Rosé Quartets. In 1934 he settled in the U.S.; after serving as second violist in the Detroit Sym. Orch., he held that position with the Cleveland Orch. (1943–49). In 1946 he joined the faculty of the Cleveland Inst. of Music, where he was head of the theory dept. from 1948 until his retirement in 1973. As a composer, he was influenced by the 12-tone system of his friend Schoenberg. Among his works were a Sym. (Cleveland, Dec. 14, 1950), a Sym. for 2 String Orchs. (1964), chamber music, and vocal pieces. His great-uncle was **Eduard Reményi.**—NS/LK/DM

Dickerson, Carroll, jazz violinist, and noted band leader; b. 1895; d. Chicago, Ill., Oct. 1957. There is little information on his early family life or training. He was only a mediocre violinist, but a talented bandleader. He led bands in Chicago from 1920, working at Entertainers' Cafe (1921), and then a long residency at Sunset Cafe (1922–24). In late 1924, he formed a new band for a 48-week tour on Pantages Circuit (after touring with Dickerson, most of the band personnel then worked as Lottie Hightower's Nighthawks). Dickerson returned to Chicago; in April of 1926 he reformed own band for Sunset Cafe residency, which featured Louis Armstrong until February 1927. Subsequently, he led the group at the Savoy Dance Hall (1927–29; with Armstrong from March 1928). Among the musicians who worked for him were Johnny Dunn, Tommy Ladnier, Zutty Singleton, Buster Bailey, Earl Hines, and Jimmy Mundy. Armstrong drew on some of these players for his Hot Five recordings in 1928. The band left Chicago in spring of 1929 with Armstrong. After gigging in N.Y. under Louis Armstrong's name, with Dickerson as conductor, the band began residency at Harlem's Connie's Inn (without Armstrong) until spring of 1930, when they disbanded. Dickerson remained in N.Y. and worked briefly with the Mills Blue Rhythm Band, then toured with King Oliver. He returned to Chicago in the early 1930s and resumed leading his own band. After a residency at Chicago's Swingland club in 1937, he temporarily left full-time music, but made a comeback early in 1939 and continued leading own bands during the 1940s, including a long residency at the Rhumboogie club. Dickerson's band style probably influenced Armstrong's recording "Beau Koo Jack" (1928; its arranger, Alex Hill, also worked for Dickerson).

DISC.: *Ain't Misbehavin'* (1929).—JC/LP

Dickerson, Walt(er Roland), jazz vibraphonist; b. Philadelphia, Pa., April 16, 1928. He was raised in a musical family. He graduated from Morgan State Coll. in Baltimore. He performed around Philadelphia with Jimmy Heath and others, including a ballroom dance with Heath's big band on May 16, 1947 in Millsboro, Del. After spending two years in the army, he sold real estate in Calif. In 1960 he moved to N.Y.C., where he worked and recorded with Andrew Hill, H. Grimes, and A. Cyrille. Between 1961 and 1965 he recorded four albums under his own name, including *To My Queen*, dedicated to his wife Elizabeth, whose picture graces the cover. A *Down Beat* "New Star" winner in 1962, Dickerson later teamed with Sun Ra on the 1965 recording *Impressions of a Patch of Blue*, based on an arrangement Dickerson had made for the music of a Jerry Goldsmith film of the same name. He developed a very individualistic sound, in part because he hardened his sticks with a special solution. He ceased playing abruptly in 1965. After a 10-year hiatus, Dickerson returned working mainly in Europe. In the 1990s, he has lived in Willow Grove, Pa., and though he receives very few offers to play, performs periodically in Philadelphia and gives solo concerts in Europe and Japan; his wife travels with him.

DISC.: *This Is Walt Dickerson!* (1961); *A Sense of Direction* (1961); *Relativity* (1962); *Jazz Impressions of "Lawrence of Arabia"* (1963) *To My Queen* (1963); *Unity* (1964); *Impressions of a Patch of Blue* (1965); *Peace* (1975); *Tell Us Only Beautiful Things* (1975); *Serendipity* (1976); *Tenderness* (1977); *Divine Gemini* (1977); *To My Queen Revisited* (1978); *Visions* (1978); *To My Son* (1978); *Shades of Love* (1978); *Landscape with Open Door* (1978); *I Hear You John* (1978); *Life Rays* (1982). **SUN RA:** *Visions* (1978); *P. Dorge: Open Door* (1978).—**LP**

Dickie, Murray, Scottish tenor; b. Bishopton, April 3, 1924. After studies in Glasgow, he pursued training with Dino Borgioli in London, Stefan Pollmann in Vienna, and Guido Farinelli in Milan. In 1947 he made his operatic debut as Count Almaviva in London, where he appeared at the Cambridge Theatre (1947–49) and at Covent Garden (1949–52). He sang at the Glyndebourne Festivals (1950–54), the Vienna State Opera (from 1951), and the Salzburg Festivals (from 1955). On Oct. 18, 1962, he made his Metropolitan Opera debut in N.Y. as David in *Die Meistersinger von Nürnberg*, remaining on the roster until 1965; he was again on its roster (1966–67; 1970–72). He became well known for his buffo roles. —**NS/LK/DM**

Dickinson, Clarence, distinguished American organist, pedagogue, and composer; b. Lafayette, Ind., May 7, 1873; d. N.Y., Aug. 2, 1969. After training at Miami Univ in Oxford, Ohio, and at Northwestern Univ. in Chicago, he studied in Berlin and Paris, his principal mentors being Moszkowski (piano), Guilmant (organ), and Pierné (composition). He was organist at St. James's Episcopal Church in Chicago before settling in N.Y. in 1909 as organist at the Brick (Presbyterian) Church; in 1912 he became prof. of church music at the Union Theological Seminary, where he founded its School of Sacred Music in 1928 and served as its director until 1945. With his wife, the writer Helen Adell Dickinson, he publ. the book *Excursions in Musical History* (1917) and ed. a valuable collection of Moravian anthems (1954). He ed. the influential series *Historical Recitals for Organ* (50 numbers) and a hymnal for the Presbyterian Church (1933), and publ. *Technique and Art of Organ Playing* (1922). Among his compositions were the operas *The Medicine Man* and *Priscilla*, the *Storm King Symphony* for Organ and Orch. (1921), much sacred music, including various anthems, and many organ pieces. —**NS/LK/DM**

Dickinson, Meriel, English mezzo-soprano, sister of **Peter Dickinson;** b. Lytham St. Annes, Lancashire,

April 8, 1940. She studied piano and voice in England, and also attended the Vienna Academy of Music. After making her London debut in 1964, she devoted herself mainly to the performance of modern music; her brother toured with her as accompanist, and also composed a number of works for her. In 1986 she made her N.Y. debut in Berio's *Laborintus*.—**NS/LK/DM**

Dickinson, Peter, English composer, pianist, and teacher, brother of **Meriel Dickinson;** b. Lytham St. Annes, Lancashire, Nov. 15, 1934. He was educated at Queen's Coll., Cambridge (B.A., 1956; M.A., 1960), and also studied with Wagenaar at the Juilliard School of Music in N.Y. (1958–59). After lecturing at the Coll. of St. Mark and St. John in London (1962–66), he was a staff tutor in music in the extramural dept. (1966–70) and a lecturer in music on the faculty (1970–74) of the Univ. of Birmingham. In 1974 he became the first prof. of music at the Univ. of Keele, where he set up the new dept. with its Centre for American Music. In 1984 he was made emeritus prof. and returned to London for considerable freelance activity. From 1991 to 1997 he was a prof. at Goldsmiths' Coll., Univ. of London, and then became prof. emeritus. He then became head of music at the Inst. of United States Studies at the Univ. of London. He toured widely as accompanist to his sister, for whom he has composed various works. As a composer, Dickinson has been particularly influenced by Satie, Ives, ragtime, blues, and jazz. He has developed what he describes as "style modulation," a layering of serious and popular styles. His interest in literature has facilitated his preparation of deft settings of vocal texts. In addition to his books, he has contributed chapters to many books and articles to many publications.

WRITINGS: Ed. *Twenty British Composers* (London, 1975); *The Music of Lennox Berkeley* (London, 1988); *Marigold: The Music of Billy Mayerl* (Oxford, 1999).

WORKS: ORCH.: *Monologue* for Strings (1959); *5 Diversions* (1969); *Transformations* (Cheltenham, July 3, 1970); Organ Concerto (Gloucester, Aug. 22, 1971); Piano Concerto (1978–84; Cheltenham, July 22, 1984); Violin Concerto (1986; Leeds, Jan. 31, 1987]; *Jigsaws* (1988); *Merseyside Echoes* (1988). **CHAMBER:** 2 string quartets: No. 1 (1958; rev. 1974) and No. 2 with Tape or Piano (1975); *Juilliard Dances* for 8 Instruments (1959); Violin Sonata (1961); *Music for Oboe and Chamber Organ* (1962); 4 *Duos* for Flute or Oboe and Cello (1962; rev. 1978); *Fanfares and Elegies* for 3 Trumpets, 3 Trombones, and Organ (1967); *Translations* for Recorder, Viola da Gamba, and Harpsichord (1971); *Recorder Music* for Recorder and Tape or 2 Recorders (1973); *Solo for Baryton* with Tape and Viola da Gamba or 2nd Baryton (1976); *Aria* for Horn, Oboe, Clarinet, and Bassoon (1977); *American Trio* for Violin, Clarinet, and Piano (1985); *London Rags* for 2 Trumpets, Horn, Trombone, and Tuba (1986); *Cellars Clough Duo* for 2 Guitars (1988); *Auden Studies* for Oboe and Piano (1988); *Swansongs* for Cello and Piano (1993). **Piano:** *Piano Variations* (1957; renamed *Vitalitas Variations*); *Paraphase II* (1967); *Rags, Blues, and Parodies* (1970–86); *Sonatas* for Piano and Tape (1987). **VOCAL: Choral:** 4 *Hopkins Poems*, with Soprano, Baritone, and Organ (1960–64); *Martin of Tours*, with Tenor, Baritone, Chamber Organ, and Piano Duet (1966); *The Dry Heart* (1967); *Outcry*, with Contralto and Orch. (1969); *Late Afternoon in November* for 16 Solo Voices (1975); *Tianamen 1989* for Double Chorus and Tubular Bells (1990). **Sacred:** *Jesus Christ Is*

Risen Today for Chorus (1955); 2 motets (1963); *Magnificat and Nunc Dimittis* for Voices and Organ (1963); *Mass* (1965); *A Mass of the Apocalypse* for Chorus, Speaker, Percussion, and Piano (London, July 15, 1984). **O t h e r V o c a l :** *Four W.H. Auden Songs* for Soprano and Piano (1956); *A Dylan Thomas Song Cycle* for Baritone and Piano (1959); *Three Comic Songs* for Tenor and Piano, after Auden (1960); *An E. E. Cummings Song Cycle* for Mezzo-soprano and Piano (1965); *Elegy* for Countertenor, Cello, and Harpsichord (1966); *Extravaganzas* for Mezzo-soprano and Piano, after Gregory Corso (1969); *Winter Afternoons*, cantata for 6 Solo Voices and Double Bass (1970); *Surrealist Landscape* for High Voice, Piano, and Tape (1973); *Lust* for Voices and Optional Tape (1974); *A Memory of David Munrow* for 2 Countertenors, 2 Recorders, Viola da Gamba, and Harpsichord (1977); *Reminiscences* for Mezzo-soprano, Saxophone, and Piano (1978); *The Unicorns* for Soprano and Brass Band (1982); *Larkin's Jazz* for Speaker-Singer and Chamber Group (1989); *Summoned by Mother* for Mezzo- soprano and Harp, after Betjeman (1991). —NS/LK/DM

Dickman, Stephen, American composer and librettist; b. Chicago, March 2, 1943. He studied at Bard Coll. (B.A., 1965) and Brandeis Univ. (M.A., 1968), and also attended courses at the Berkshire Music Center in Tanglewood (summer 1968) and on a Fulbright fellowship at the Academia di Santa Cecilia in Rome (1971–72). His mentors have included Petrassi, Krenek, Shapero, Berger, and Druckman. He also studied cello (1964–72) with Louis Garcia-Renard, Peter Rosenfeld, and Giuseppe Selmi, and sarangi with Pandit Ram Narayan in London and Bombay (1972–74) and in San Francisco (1978). Among his numerous awards are BMI Student Composer's Awards (1968, 1969), grants from Meet the Composer (1990, 1995, 1996), a grant from the NEA (1995), and a commission from the American Composers Forum for a work to celebrate the 350th anniversary of East Hampton, N.Y. (1998). Dickman's music has been critically lauded as lovely, rich, haunting, and strikingly original, garnering his greatest success in his works involving voice. He currently is working on a musical, *The Violin Maker*, to his own story and libretto, as well as a setting of *The Epic of Gilgamesh* for Baritone, Mezzo-soprano, Violin, Cello, Flute, and Percussion, on a commission from N.Y.'s Mutable Music and scheduled for a 2002 premiere.

WORKS: DRAMATIC: O p e r a : *Real Magic in New York*, a cappella opera, to a libretto by Richard Foreman (1971); *Tibetan Dreams* (1987–90). **ORCH.:** *The Wheels of Ezekiel* for Chamber Orch. (1985). **CHAMBER:** 2 string quartets (1967, 1978); *Damsel* for 16 Instruments and 2 Conductors (1968); String Trio (1970–71). **P i a n o :** *Trees and Other Inclinations* (1983). **VOCAL:** Song Cycle 3 Sopranos and 3 Violins (1975–77); *Orchestra by the Sea* for 4 Sopranos and Orch. (1983); *Maximus Song Cycle*, 5 pieces for Soprano and Ensemble, after Charles Olson (1987); *Duets* for 2 a cappella Singers, after Jelaluddin Rumi (1992–98); *Rabbi Nathan's Prayer* for Soprano and Violin, after Rabbi Nathan of Bratslav (1995); *Four for Tom* [Buckner] for Baritone and Piano, after Jelaluddin Rumi and Milarepa (1997); *The Music of Eric Zann* for Baritone Solo, after H.P. Lovecraft (1998). **OTHER:** *Musical Journeys* for Unspecified Instruments (1972–76).—LK/DM

Diddley, Bo (originally, **McDaniel, Ellas**), best remembered for his percussive "shave-and-a-haircut" guitar-playing style that influenced The Yardbirds and The Rolling Stones. Bo Diddley was one of rock 'n' roll's first electric guitarist-singers; b. Ellas Bates, McComb, Miss., Dec. 30, 1928 (soon adopted by the McDaniel family).

Ellas McDaniel moved to Chicago with his adopted family in 1934. Nicknamed Bo Diddley as a child, he began 12 years of violin studies upon arrival and took up guitar as a teenager. He manned a washboard trio to play the streets and rent parties from 1946 to 1951, when he debuted at the 708 Club. Diddley began playing with maraca player Jerome Green, and eventually signed with Chess Records in 1955, recording on the sister label, Checker. His first single, "Bo Diddley/I'm a Man," became a top R&B hit, and Muddy Waters soon recorded his own smash hit version of "I'm a Man" as "Manish Boy." Subsequent R&B Diddley hits included "Diddley Daddy" and "Pretty Thing," but classics such as "Who Do You Love" and "Mona" failed to chart. He broke through into the pop field in 1959 with "Say Man," on which he traded insults with Green. In the early 1960s he also hit with "Road Runner" and "You Can't Judge a Book by the Cover." Diddley toured throughout the 1960s with Green and his half-sister guitarist- vocalist, simply known as "The Duchess."

Bo Diddley first toured Great Britain in 1963. His influence on 1960s British groups became apparent when The Yardbirds hit with "I'm a Man" and The Rolling Stones recorded "Mona." During the 1960s Diddley teamed with Chuck Berry for *Two Great Guitars*, Muddy Waters and Little Walter for *Super Blues*, and Muddy Waters and Howlin' Wolf for *Super, Super Blues Band*. Diddley worked the rock 'n' roll revival circuit from 1969–74, appearing in the 1973 film *Let the Good Times Roll*. After leaving Chess in 1974, he recorded an album for RCA. In 1979 he opened for The Clash on their debut tour of the United States.

Inducted into the Rock and Roll Hall of Fame in 1987, Bo Diddley toured with Ron Wood in 1988 and returned to recording with *Breaking through the B.S.* on Triple X Records in 1989. In 1992 Rhino Records issued the tribute set Bo Diddley Beats, assembling recordings by Buddy Holly, Dee Clark, The Miracles and others. In the mid 1990s Bo Diddley recorded for MCA and Atlantic Records.

DISC.: *Bo Diddley* (1958; reissued as *Boss Man*, 1968); *Go Bo Diddley* (1959); *Bo Diddley/Go Bo Diddley* (recorded 1955–58); *Have Guitar, Will Travel* (1960); *In the Spotlight* (1960); *Bo Diddley Is a Gunslinger* (1960); *Bo Diddley Is a Lover* (1961); *Bo Diddley's a Twister* (1962; reissued as *Roadrunner*, 1968); *Bo Diddley* (1962); *Hey Bo Diddley* (1963); *Bo Diddley and Company* (1963); *Surfin' with Bo Diddley* (1963); *Bo Diddley's Beach Party* (1963); *16 All-Time Greatest Hits* (1964); *Hey Good Lookin'* (1965); *500% More Man* (1966); *The Originator* (1967); *Black Gladiator* (1969); *Another Dimension* (1971); *Where It All Began* (1972); *Got My Own Bag of Tricks* (1972); *The London Bo Diddley Sessions* (1973); *Big Bad Bo* (1974); *20th Anniversary of Rock 'n' Roll* (1976); *Toronto Rock 'n' Roll Revival, Vol. 5* (1982); *Give Me a Break* (1988); *Breaking through the B.S.* (1989); *His Greatest Sides, Vol. I*; *The Chess Box* (1990); *Rare and Well Done* (1991); *Bo's Blues* (1993); *Bo Knows Bo* (1995); *A Man amongst Men* (1996); *Mona* (1996); *His Best* (1997).

BO DIDDLEY AND CHUCK BERRY: *Two Great Guitars* (1964). BO DIDDLEY, MUDDY WATERS, AND LITTLE WATER: *Super Blues* (1967). BO DIDDLEY, MUDDY WATERS, AND HOWLIN' WOLF: *The Super Super Blues Band* (1968).—BH

Diderot, Denis, illustrious French man of letters and philosopher; b. Langres, Oct. 5, 1713; d. Paris, July 30, 1784. In his work *Mémoirs sur différents sujets de mathématiques* (The Hague, 1748) are the essays "Des principes d'acoustique" and "Projet d'un nouvel orgue," the latter being an impracticable idea for a new kind of barrel organ. For his writings on music, see B. Durand- Sendrail, ed., *D. D.: Écrits sur la musique* (Paris, 1987).—NS/LK/DM

Didkovsky, Nick (actually, **Nicholas Russel**), American composer, performer, and programmer; b. Bronxville, N.Y., Nov. 22, 1958. He studied at Dartmouth Coll. (1976–78), Brown Univ. (B.A. in mathematics, 1980), and at N.Y.U. (M.M. in computer music, 1991), numbering among his composition teachers Christian Wolff, Paul Nelson, Vincent Martucci, and Gerald Shapiro. After college, he worked for a time at The Kitchen and the Experimental Intermedia Foundation in N.Y., then moved to Woodstock, N.Y., where his concept for the "avant metal/mutant jazz/thrash combo" Doctor Nerve was born. The group was formally banded after his return to N.Y. in 1985, with its personnel largely unchanged to date: in addition to Didkovsky, Greg Anderson, Yves Duboin, Michael Lytle, Leo Ciesa, and Rob Henke, and Marc Wagnon. Divkovsky writes his own software and his works, variously described as raw, raspy, cogent, and extraordinarily musical, are often computer-composed.

WORKS: ORCH.: *Their Eyes Bulged with Sparkling Pockets* for Chamber Orch. (N.Y., March 25, 1995). CHAMBER: Guitar Quartet: *Black Iris* (1989); *Black Irish Deconstruction* (1991); *Four Gestures* for Ebow and Slide (1992); *Antaeus* (1994); *Just A Voice That Bothered Him* (1994); *She Closes Her Sister with Heavy Bones* (1994); *To Laugh Uncleanly at the Nurse* (1994); *Egil the Skald* (1996); *Out to Bomb Fresh Kings* (1996); *We'll Ask the Questions Around Here, Parts 1 and 2* (1996; also for Guitar and 2 Percussionists); *No Meat No Belfry* (N.Y., May 5, 1999). Other: *Beta 14 ok* for Guitar, Trumpet, and Saxophone (1991); *In His Feet Were Burned Because of Many Waters* for Guitar, Vibraphone, Bass, and Drum Set (1991); *They Were As If They Also Which Pierced Him* for Guitar, Bass, and Drum Set (1991); *Three Curiously Insubstantial Duets* for Guitar and Saxophone (1991); *Recursive Systems, Part 1: Towers of Hanoi* for Drum Set (1992) and *Part 2: Pascal's Triangle* (1992; also for 2 Trumpets); *The Ballad of Dean Mellberg* for Guitar, Saxophone, and Drum Set (1993); *Eyes Bigger Than Her Forehead* for Guitar, Saxophone, and Drum Set (1993); *Amalia's Secret* for Piano, Drum Set, Guitar, Bass, and Cello (N.Y., May 8, 1994); *Did Sprinting Die?* for Guitar and Bass (1994); *Ironwood* for Drum Set (1995); *I Kick My Hand* for Guitar, Bass, and Drums (1996; also for 2 Guitars and for Solo Guitar); *We'll Ask the Questions Around Here* (1996; also for Guitar Quartet); *Caught By The Sky With Wire* for Cello and Percussion (N.Y., April 14, 1997); *Ereia* for String Quartet, Guitar, Bass, Drum Set, Piano, Soprano Saxophone, Flute, Trumpet, and Bass Clarinet (Victoriaville, Quebec, May 19, 1997); *Overlife* for Guitar and Percussion (San

Diego, Jan. 16, 1999); *One Wooden Leg, Stuffed* for Guitar and Drum Set (Vandoeuvre, France, May 22, 1999); *The Corpse Was Born Half As Long As Life* for Guitar and Drum Set (Vandoeuvre, France, May 22, 1999); *The Round Nose of Some Twenty Years* for Guitar and Drum Set (Vandoeuvre, France, May 22, 1999); *Two Languages Take Twice As Long* for Guitar and Drum Set (Vandoeuvre, France, May 22, 1999); *The Man Who Hated Pets* for Guitar and Drum Set (Grenoble, France, March 21, 2000). Piano: "*Schubert's Impromptu in Eb Maj, Opus 90 (arr. Minsky Popolov)*" for MIDI-controlled Piano (1991; N.Y., Sept. 12, 1997); *Our Soldiers Are Soft Pianos* for Any Number of Pianos (1995). GAMELAN: *Phase 10* (1985); *Don't Be A Hog* (1986); *Phoneme Music* for Gamelan, Voices, and Computer (1990). COMPUTER AND LIVE PERFORMER(S): *MetaMusic/MetaText* for 5 Instrumental Performers, Voice, Computer Voice Synthesis, and MIDI Piano (1989); *Fourier Music* for Solo Performer with MIDI Instrument and Computer (1990); *Lottery* for Any Number of Performers and Computer Network (Oakland, Calif., April 1, 1990); *Rainy Day Markov Chains* for 2 Performers, one with MIDI Instrument (1990); *Fast Fourier Fugue*, computer solo (1991); *Slippers of Steel* for 2 Instrumental Performers and 2 Networked Computers (1991); *Yudishthira's Quartet*, computer solo (1999); *MandelMusic...*, solo computer (1999); *A Loop's A Loop's A Loop's A...*, computer solo (1999); *What Sheet Herd* for Erh Hu (Chinese fiddle), Voice, and Computer (Warwick, N.Y., Feb. 26, 2000). OTHER: Various works for Doctor Nerve (Guitar, Bass, Drums, Vibraphone/Keyboard, Trumpet, Soprano Saxophone, Bass Clarinet, and MIDI Vibraphone; 1981–94), including *Don't Be Hog* (1984), *Nerveware No. 2* (1989), *Armed Observation* (1991), *Trash* (1991), *Preaching to the Converted* (1993), *Plague* (1994), and *Take Your Ears As The Bones Of Their Queen* (1994).—LK/DM

Di Domenica, Robert (Anthony), American composer, flutist, and teacher; b. N.Y., March 4, 1927. He studied music education at N.Y.U. (B.S., 1951), composition with Riegger and Josef Schmid, and flute with Harold Bennett (1949–55). He was a flutist with various orchs. and ensembles, and also taught flute. In 1969 he joined the faculty of the New England Cons. of Music in Boston, where he was an assoc. dean (1973–76) and dean (1976–78), and then a teacher of theory and composition (from 1978). In 1972 he held a Guggenheim fellowship. In 1994 the Robert Di Domenica Collection was accepted by the Library of Congress in Washington, D.C. In his works, he follows a serial course while utilizing such diverse elements as classical music, jazz, and American popular music.

WORKS: DRAMATIC: Opera: *The Balcony* (1972; Boston, June 16, 1990); *The Scarlet Letter* (1986); operatic trilogy: *Francesco Cenci* (1996), *Beatrice Cenci* (1993), and *The Cenci* (1995). ORCH.: Sym. (1961; Boston, Nov. 15, 1972); Concerto for Violin and Chamber Orch. (1962; N.Y., April 15, 1965); 2 piano concertos (1963, 1982); Concerto for Wind Quintet, Strings, and Timpani (1964; Boston, May 7, 1981); *Music for Flute and Strings* (1967; Boston, Nov. 16, 1980); *Variations on a Theme by Gunther Schuller* for Chamber Orch. (1983; Boston, Dec. 11, 1984); *Dream Journeys* (1984; Plymouth, Mass., Oct. 5, 1985); *Variations and Soliloquies* (1988); *Gone Are the Rivers and Eagles* (1992). CHAMBER: Flute Sonata (1957); Quartet for Flute, Violin, Horn, and Piano (1959); Quartet for Flute, Violin, Viola, and Cello (1960); *Variations on a Tonal Theme* for Flute (1961); Wind Quintet with Soprano Voice (1963); Quintet for Clarinet and String Quartet (1965); Violin Sonata (1966); *Saecu-*

lum aureum for Flute, Piano, and Tape (1967); Alto Saxophone Sonata (1968); *Music for Stanzs* for Flute, Clarinet, Bassoon, Horn, and Tape (1981). **P i a n o :** Sonatina (1958); *4 Movements* (1959); *11 Short Pieces* (1973); *Improvisations* (1974); *The Art of the Row* (1989; Boston, Dec. 12, 1990). **V O C A L:** *The First Kiss of Love* for Soprano and Piano (1960); *4 Short Songs* for Soprano and 6 Instruments (1975); *Black Poems* for Baritone, Piano, and Tape (1976); *Sonata after Essays for Piano* for Soprano, Baritone, Piano, Flute, and Tape (1977; also as *Concord Revisited* for Soprano, Baritone, Piano, Chamber Orch., and Tape, 1978); *Arrangements* for Soprano, 6 Instruments, and Tape (1979); *The Holy Colophon* for Soprano, Tenor, Chorus, and Orch. (1980; Boston, Oct. 11, 1983); *Hebrew Melodies* for Soprano, Violin, and Piano (1983).—**NS/LK/DM**

Didur, Adamo, famous Polish bass; b. Wola Sekowa, near Sanok, Galicia, Dec. 24, 1874; d. Katowice, Jan. 7, 1946. He studied with Wysocki in Lemberg and Emmerich in Milan, where he made his concert debut in 1894; later that year he made his operatic debut as Méphistophélès in Rio de Janeiro. He sang at the Warsaw Opera (1899–1903), Milan's La Scala (1903–06), London's Covent Garden (1905), and Buenos Aires's Teatro Colón (1905–08). On Nov. 4, 1907, he made an auspicious N.Y. debut as Alvise at the Manhattan Opera. His Metropolitan Opera debut followed as Ramfis on Nov. 16, 1908, and he remained on its roster as one of its leading artists until 1932. He then returned to Poland. His appointment as director of the Warsaw Opera in 1939 was aborted by the outbreak of World War II. He later settled in Katowice as a voice teacher, founding an opera company (1945) and becoming director of the Cons. His portrayals of Leporello and Boris Godunov were particularly memorable.—**NS/LK/DM**

Didymus, Chalcenterus (Of the Brazen Guts), Greek scholar and grammarian of Alexandria who flourished from c.80 to 10 B.C. He earned the nickname of Chalcenterus for his large output of books, which is said to have numbered about 3,500 vols. He wrote a tract on music, now known only by an epitome of Porphyry's, and some quotations by Ptolemy. In his system the octave of the diatonic genus is formed by 2 precisely similar tetrachords, and in all 3 species of tetrachord (diatonic, chromatic, enharmonic) the ratio for the interval of the major third is 4:5. He also recognized the difference between the major and minor whole tone; this difference (9/8:10/9 = 81:80) is, therefore, rightly termed the "comma of Didymus." Salinas and Doni have written on his musical system. —**NS/LK/DM**

Diemer, Emma Lou, American composer, keyboard player, and teacher; b. Kansas City, Mo., Nov. 24, 1927. She was a pupil of Donovan and Hindemith at Yale Univ. (B.M., 1949; M.M., 1950), of Toch and Sessions at the Berkshire Music Center in Tanglewood (summers 1954, 1955), and of Rogers, Hanson, and Craighead at the Eastman School of Music in Rochester, N.Y. (Ph.D., 1960). She was composer-in-residence for the Ford Foundation Young Composers Project in Arlington, Va. (1959–61) and also on the faculties of the Univ. of Md.

(1965–70) and the Univ. of Calif. at Santa Barbara (1971–91). From 1990 to 1992 she was composer-in-residence of the Santa Barbara Sym. Orch. In 1992 she won a Kennedy Center Friedheim Award. She was Composer of the Year of the American Guild of Organists in 1995. In 1999 she received an honorary doctorate of letters from Central Mo. State Univ. Her works are included in several anthologies and many have been recorded. Several doctoral dissertations have been written on her music.

WORKS: O R C H .: 4 syms. (1953; 1955; *On American Indian Themes*, 1959; *Symphonie antique*, 1961); 2 piano concertos (1953, 1991); Concerto for Harpsichord and Chamber Orch. (1958); *Pavane* for Strings (1959); *Youth Overture* (1959); *Rondo Concertante* (1960); *Festival Overture* (1961); Flute Concerto (1963); *Fairfax Festival Overture* (1967); *Concert Piece* for Organ and Orch. (1977); *Winter Day* (1982); Trumpet Concerto (1983; rev. as a violin concerto, 1983); *Suite of Homages* (1985); *Serenade* for Strings (1988); Marimba Concerto (1990); Concerto in One Movement for Organ and Chamber Orch., *Alaska* (1995; Fairbanks, Jan. 1996, composer soloist); *Santa Barbara Overture* (Santa Barbara, March 1996). **CHAMBER:** Violin Sonata (1949); Piano Quartet (1954); Flute Sonata (1958); Woodwind Quintet No. 1 (1960); Sextet for Piano and Woodwind Quintet (1962); Toccata for Flute Chorus (1968); *Music for Woodwind Quartet* (1972); Trio for Flute, Oboe, Harpsichord, and Tape (1973); *Pianoharpsichordorgan* for 1 or 3 Performers (1974); *Movement* for Flute, Oboe, Clarinet, and Piano (1976); *Quadralogue* for Flute Quartet (1978); *Summer of 82* for Cello and Piano (1982); String Quartet No. 1 (1987); *Catch-A-Turian* for Violin and Piano (1988; also for Flute and Piano, 1994); *Laudate* for Trumpet and Organ (1990); *A Quiet, Lovely Piece* for Clarinet and Piano (1991); Sextet for Flute, Oboe, Clarinet, Violin, Cello, and Piano (1992); *Psalms* for Flute and Organ or Piano (1998); *Psalm 121* for Organ, Brass, and Percussion (1998); *Psalm 122* for Bass Trombone or Tuba and Organ (1998); *Psalms* for Organ and Percussion (1998). **O r g a n :** *Four Biblical Settings* (1993); *Variations on Rendez a Dieu* (1999). **V O C A L:** *Kyrie* for Chorus, 2 Pianos, and Percussion (1993); *Gloria* for Chorus, 2 Pianos, and Percussion (1996; orchestrated 1998); *O Viridissima Virga* for Women's Chorus, Organ, and Percussion (1998).—**NS/LK/DM**

Diemer, Louis (Joseph), distinguished French pianist and pedagogue; b. Paris, Feb. 14, 1843; d. there, Dec. 21, 1919. He was a pupil of Marmontel at the Paris Cons., where he took the premier prix in piano (1856). He also studied with Thomas and Bazin (composition), taking premiers prix in solfège (1855), harmony and accompaniment (1859), and counterpoint and fugue (1861); he likewise took a second prix in organ (1861). He played with great success at the Alard, Pasdeloup, and Paris Cons. concerts; succeeded Marmontel (1887) as prof. of piano at the Cons. The immense success of his series of historical recitals, in 1889, made him resolve to specialize in early music, and led to his establishing the Societe des Anciens Instruments. Widor, Saint-Saëns, Lalo, and others wrote pieces for him. He ed. a number of early French keyboard pieces; his collection *Clavecinistes français* was publ. posth. in 1928. In 1889 he was made a Chevalier de la Légion d'honneur.—**NS/LK/DM**

Diepenbrock, Alphons (Johannes Maria), eminent Dutch composer; b. Amsterdam, Sept. 2, 1862; d. there, April 5, 1921. He learned to play violin and piano in his childhood. In 1880 he entered the Univ. of Amsterdam, where he studied classical philology and received his Ph.D. in 1888. He taught academic subjects at the grammar school at 's-Hertogenbosch (1888–94), then abandoned his pedagogical activities and devoted himself primarily to music. He studied works of the Flemish School of the Renaissance, and later perused the scores of Berlioz, Wagner, and Debussy. Despite this belated study, he succeeded in developing a rather striking individual style of composition, in which Wagnerian elements curiously intertwine with impressionistic modalities. However, he had difficulty in putting the results into definite shape, and he left more than 100 incomplete MSS at his death. His Catholic upbringing led him to concentrate mainly on the composition of sacred choral music; he wrote no syms., concertos, or instrumental sonatas. A collection of Diepenbrock's writings, *Verzamelde geschriften*, ed. by E. Reeser, was publ. in Utrecht (1950). A catalog of his works was issued in Amsterdam in 1962. E. Reeser brought out his *Brieven en documenten* (Letters and Documents; 2 vols., Amsterdam, 1962–67). He also wrote "Some Melodic Patterns in the Music of Alphons Diepenbrock," *Composers' Voice*, 3 (1976/1).

WORKS: *Stabat Mater* for Men's Chorus; *Missa in die festo* for Tenor, Men's Chorus, and Organ (1890–91); *Les Elfes* for Soprano, Baritone, Women's Chorus, and Orch. (1896); *Te Deum* for Soloists, Double Chorus, and Orch. (1897); 2 *Hymnen an die Nacht*, after Novalis, 1 each for Soprano and Contralto, with Orch. (1899); *Vondel's vaart naar Agrippine* (Vondel's Journey to Agrippina) for Baritone and Orch. (1902–3); *Im grossen Schweigen*, after Nietzsche, for Baritone and Orch. (Amsterdam, May 20, 1906); *Hymne aan Rembrandt* for Soprano, Women's Chorus, and Orch. (1906); incidental music to Verhagen's mythical comedy *Marsyas of De betooverde bron* (Marsyas or The Enchanted Well; 1909–10); *Die Nacht*, after Hölderlin, for Mezzo-soprano and Orch. (1910–11); *Lydische Nacht* for Baritone and Orch. (1913); incidental music to Aristophanes' *The Birds* (1917); incidental music to Goethe's *Faust* (1918); incidental music to Sophocles' *Electra* (1920); numerous choruses and songs.—NS/LK/DM

Dieren, Bernard van, Dutch-English composer and writer; b. Rotterdam, Dec. 27, 1887; d. London, April 24, 1936. He began playing the violin at an early age but later pursued his enthusiasm for literature and science. As a composer, he was self-taught. In 1909 he settled in England, where he devoted much time to writing criticism for continental newspapers and magazines. Among his writings were a study of the sculptor Jacob Epstein (London, 1920) and an interesting collection of essays, *Down Among the Dead Men* (London, 1935). As a composer, he developed a highly personal style of harmonic and contrapuntal complexity.

WORKS: DRAMATIC: O p e r a : *The Tailor* (1917). **ORCH.:** *Elegy* for Cello and Orch. (1908); *Beatrice Cenci* (1909); Overture (1916); *Serenade* for Small Orch. (c. 1923); *Anjou*, overture (1935); Sym. (unfinished). **CHAMBER:** *Canzonetta* for Violin and Piano (c. 1907); *Impromptu Fantasiestück* for Violin (1909); 6 string quartets (1912, 1917, 1918, 1923, 1927, 1928); *Sonata tyroica* for Violin and Piano (1913); Sonata for Solo Cello (1929); *Duettino* for 2 Violins (1933); Sonata for Solo Violin (1935). **P i a n o :** *6 Sketches* (1911); *Toccata* (1912); *12 Netherlands*

Melodies (1918); *Tema con variazione* (1928). **VOCAL:** *Balsazar* for Chorus and Orch. (1908); *Chinese Symphony* for 5 Soli, Chorus, and Orch. (1914); *Diaphonia* for Baritone and Chamber Orch. (1916); *2 Poems* for Speaker and String Quartet (1917); *2 Songs* for Baritone and String Quartet (1917); *Les propous des beuveurs* for Chorus and Orch. (1921); *Sonetto VII of Edmund Spenser's Amoretti* for Tenor and Chamber Orch. (1921); various other songs.

BIBL.: A. Chisolm, *B. v. D.: An Introduction* (London, 1984). —NS/LK/DM

Diet, Edmond-Marie, French composer; b. Paris, Sept. 25, 1854; d. there, Oct. 30, 1924. He was a pupil of César Franck and Guiraud.

WORKS: DRAMATIC: O p e r a : *Stratonice* (1887); *Le Cousin Placide* (1887); *Fleur de vertu* (1894); *Gentil Crampon*, operetta (Paris, 1897); *La Revanche d'Iris* (1905). **B a l l e t a n d P a n t o m i m e s :** *Scientia* (1889); *La Grève; Masque rose; M. Ruy-Blas* (1894); *La Belle et la bête* (1895); *L'Araignée d'or* (1896); *Rêve de Noël* (1896); *Watteau* (1900; in collaboration with Pujet). **OTHER:** Songs; church music.—NS/LK/DM

Dietrich, Albert (Hermann), German conductor and composer; b. Forsthaus Golk, near Meissen, Aug. 28, 1829; d. Berlin, Nov. 19, 1908. He was a pupil of J. Otto in Dresden (1842–47) and of Moscheles and Rietz at Leipzig (1847–51). He also studied with Schumann (was one of Schumann's best pupils) at Düsseldorf (1851–54). From 1855 to 1861 he was a concert conductor, and from 1859 municipal music director, at Bonn. From 1861 he was at Oldenburg. After his retirement in 1890 he lived in Berlin, where he was made Royal Prof. in 1899. He wrote *Erinnerungen an Johannes Brahms in Briefen, besonders aus seiner Jugendzeit* (Leipzig, 1898; Eng. tr., 1899).

WORKS: DRAMATIC: O p e r a : *Robin Hood* (Frankfurt am Main, 1879); *Das Sonntagskind* (Bremen, 1886). **OTHER:** Incidental music; orch. works, chamber music, including the 1st movement of the *F-A-E* Sonata for Violin (other movements by Brahms and Schumann); songs.—NS/LK/DM

Dietrich or **Dieterich, Sixtus,** important German composer; b. Augsburg, c. 1493; d. St. Gallen, Switzerland, Oct. 21, 1548. He was a chorister in Constance (1504–08), then studied in Freiburg. After returning to Constance (1517), he became informator choralium at the Cathedral chapter; was made altar prebend and then became a priest (1522), remaining there after the Catholic clergy left as a result of the Reformation (1527). He was also a guest lecturer at the Univ. of Wittenberg (1540–41). He was a significant composer of early Protestant sacred music.

WORKS: *Epicedion Thomae Sporeri* (Strasbourg, 1534); *Magnificat octo tonorum...liber primus* (Strasbourg, 1535); *Novum ac insigne opus musicum 36 antiphonarum* (Wittenberg, 1541; ed. by W. Buszin, Kassel and St. Louis, 1964); *Novum opus musicum tres tomos* [122] *sacrorum hymnorum* (Wittenberg, 1545; ed. by H. Zenck and W. Gurlitt in Das Erbe Deutscher Musik, 1st series, XXIII, 1942–60); *Laudate Dominum* for 4 Voices (Augsburg, 1547); various other works publ. in contemporary collections.

BIBL.: H. Zenck, *S. D.: Ein Beitrag zur Musik und Musikanschauung im Zeitalter der Reformation* (Leipzig, 1928); A. Grauer, *The Vocal Style of S. D. and Johann Eccard and Their Contributions to Lutheran Church Music* (diss., Univ. of Rochester, 1960). —NS/LK/DM

Dietsch, (Pierre-)Louis(-Philippe), French conductor and composer; b. Dijon, March 17, 1808; d. Paris, Feb. 20, 1865. He studied at Choron's Institution Royale de Musique Classique et Religieuse in Paris, then with A. Reicha (counterpoint) and M. P. Chenie (double bass) at the Paris Cons., winning a premier prix for the latter (1830). He played double bass in the orchs. of the Théâtre-Italien and the Paris Opéra. He was also maître de chapelle at St. Eustache (1830–39) and at the Madeleine (from 1849), as well as chorus master at the Opera (from 1840). With Paul Foucher and Henri Revoil as librettists, he wrote the opera *Le Vaisseau fantôme* (Opera, Nov. 9, 1842), a subject also treated by Wagner in his opera *Der fliegende Holländer*. Dietsch's opera received only 11 hearings and then was totally forgotten. He became conductor of the Paris Opéra in 1860, where he led the 3 notorious performances of the Paris version of Wagner's *Tannhäuser* in 1861. After an argument with Verdi, he resigned his post in 1863. He also wrote many masses and other sacred works. —NS/LK/DM

Dietz, Howard, charming American lyricist, librettist, and film-company executive; b. N.Y., Sept. 8, 1896; d. there, July 30, 1983. Like such contemporaries as E. Y. Harburg and Ira Gershwin, Dietz wrote lyrics to hundreds of songs used in Broadway shows and Hollywood films during the middle decades of the 20th century; unlike them, he did so while maintaining a full-time job in a different if related field. While handling advertising and publicity for a major film studio, he found time, especially in the late 1920s and 1930s, to write for a series of successful Broadway revues, usually working with Arthur Schwartz, though his other collaborators included Jerome Kern, George Gershwin, Walter Donaldson, Jimmy McHugh, Vernon Duke, and Sammy Fain. Because his successes came exclusively with revues, he is best remembered for individual songs; among his most popular: "I Guess I'll Have to Change My Plan," "Dancing in the Dark," and "That's Entertainment."

Dietz's father, a Russian immigrant, was a jeweler. Dietz attended the Columbia Univ. School of Journalism starting in the fall of 1913, and while a student worked as a newspaper stringer, also contributing light verse to such columns as Franklin P. Adams's *The Conning Tower*. In his junior year he won $500 in a contest to provide advertising copy for a cigarette manufacturer, which led him to a copywriting job for an advertising agency. One of the agency's clients was the Goldwyn Pictures Corporation, for which Dietz created the corporate logo, a roaring lion dubbed "Leo," and the company slogan, in mangled Latin, "Ars Gratia Artis." (It means "Art for art's sake," but the correct form would be "Ars Artis Gratia.")

In 1917, Dietz married Elizabeth Bigelow Hall (they later divorced). With the American entry into World War I, he enlisted in the navy. After the war he was hired by Goldwyn as a publicist. When the company was merged into Metro-Goldwyn-Mayer in 1924, Dietz became director of publicity and advertising.

Meanwhile, Dietz was beginning to find outlets for his lyrics. His first song to be used in a revue came with "Power of Light" (music by Morrie Ryskind) from *The '49ers* (N.Y. Nov. 7, 1922), for which he also contributed sketch material alongside many of the famous Algonquin Roundtable group of writers such as Robert Benchley, George S. Kaufman, Ring Lardner, and Dorothy Parker. Dietz's first song to be published was "Alibi Baby" (music by Arthur Samuels), which was used in the musical *Poppy* (N.Y., Sept. 3, 1923), which starred W. C. Fields. Dietz then teamed with Kern and they wrote the songs for the unsuccessful 1924 musical *Dear Sir*. Dietz was brought in to assist the ailing Ira Gershwin on *Oh, Kay!* (N.Y., Nov. 8, 1926), collaborating with the Gershwin brothers on several songs.

Dietz's next attempt to write lyrics for a musical was an embarrassing failure. *Hoop-La!*, with music by Jay Gorney, closed during a tryout in Stamford, Conn., on April 25, 1927, after only one act had been performed. Dietz was back only a month later with *Merry-Go-Round*, for which he co-wrote the lyrics and the libretto with Ryskind; it ran 135 performances. Later that year Dietz had his first song to be associated with a motion picture, "That Melody of Love" (music by Donaldson), written to promote the silent film *Love*. It was also his first hit, in a recording by Fred Waring's Pennsylvanians, in June.

Dietz's first real stage success came with the revue *The Little Show*, for which he wrote the sketches as well as the lyrics to songs mostly by Arthur Schwartz. It ran 321 performances and generated a hit for Libby Holman, who appeared onstage, with "Moanin' Low" (music by Ralph Rainger) in September 1929. Ultimately, however, the biggest hit from the score turned out to be "I Guess I'll Have to Change My Plan" (music by Schwartz), which finally took off when it was recorded by Rudy Vallée in August 1932. "(When I Am) Housekeeping for You" (music by Gorney) was not a hit, but it is notable as the first Dietz lyric to be heard in a sound film, Paramount's *The Battle of Paris* (1929), and it is the first song Dietz wrote under the pseudonym Dick Howard, a name he apparently used to hide his identity when working for studios other than MGM.

Dietz and Schwartz were retained for *The Second Little Show*, but the principal performers from the earlier edition—Holman, Fred Allen, and Clifton Webb—were not, and the new revue ran only 63 performers. A month later, however, the songwriters were reunited with the trio of actors in the aptly named revue *Three's a Crowd*, resulting in a 271-performance run and another record hit by Holman, "Something to Remember You By," at the end of 1930. (Dietz also contributed sketch material to the show.)

The Band Wagon (1931) did not have Holman, Allen, and Webb in its cast, but it did boast the dancing team of Fred and Adele Astaire in their final stage appearance before Adele married and retired and her brother headed to Hollywood. The show ran 260 performances and produced four hits for Dietz and Schwartz. Fred Waring had a popular record combining "Dancing in the Dark" (with which Bing Crosby had equal success) and "High and Low" (lyrics also by Desmond Carter), while Leo Reisman and His Orch. combined "I Love Louisa" and "New Sun in the Sky" on one disc, both songs sung by Fred Astaire. Dietz shared credit for the sketches with George S. Kaufman.

Dietz directed *Flying Colors* in addition to writing some of the sketches and penning the lyrics to Schwartz's melodies. Opening at a low point of the Depression, the revue ran a barely successful 188 performances, but it contained three songs that became hits in the fall of 1932: "Alone Together" and "Louisiana Hayride," both recorded by Leo Reisman, the latter with Schwartz as vocalist; and "A Shine on Your Shoes," recorded by Roger Wolfe Kahn and His Orch.

Having written five revues in three-and-a-half years, Dietz and Schwartz branched out after 1932. Schwartz wrote music (with lyrics by Dietz) for the 1934 radio series *The Gibson Family*, while Dietz co-produced and co-wrote the screenplay for the MGM movie musical *Hollywood Party* (1934), also cowriting the song "Feelin' High" with Walter Donaldson for the film. Dietz and Schwartz teamed up to write "Born to Be Kissed" for the Jean Harlow film *The Girl from Missouri* (1934), which became a hit in July 1934 in a recording by Freddy Martin and His Orch. But Dietz and Schwartz's main project for 1934 was their first book musical, *Revenge with Music*, for which Dietz co-wrote the libretto and which he co-directed. At 158 performances, the show missed making a profit, but it contained two songs that became hits in early 1935: "You and the Night and the Music," recorded by Libby Holman, and "If There Is Someone Lovelier Than You," recorded by Enric Madriguera and His Orch.

Dietz and Schwartz returned to the revue format in 1935 for *At Home Abroad*, for which Dietz again wrote some of the sketches; it ran 198 performances. The 1936 British revue *Follow the Sun*, for which Dietz wrote lyrics with Desmond Carter to Schwartz's music, was drawn largely from earlier American efforts; it had a run of 204 performances. Later in 1936, Dietz and Schwartz contributed songs to the 20th Century–Fox feature *Under Your Spell* and the Broadway revue *The Show Is On* (N.Y., Dec. 25, 1936). In 1937, after his first marriage ended, Dietz married British heiress Tanis Guinness. They had a daughter.

Between the Devil (1937), for which Dietz wrote the libretto as well as the lyrics, was his and Schwartz's second attempt at a book musical. It flopped, running only 93 performances, but produced a song hit in "I See Your Face before Me," which was in the hit parade in March 1938 in a recording by Guy Lombardo and His Royal Canadians. Dietz and Schwartz had several songs in the British revue *Happy Returns* (London, April 19, 1938), but the failure of *Between the Devil* marked the end of their partnership for the time being.

When Al Dubin became ill, Dietz contributed lyrics to several songs with music by Jimmy McHugh for the musical *Keep off the Grass* (N.Y., May 23, 1940). Artie Shaw and His Orch. reached the Top Ten in March 1941

with an instrumental revival of "Dancing in the Dark." "Somebody Else Is Taking My Place" (music and lyrics by "Dick Howard," Bob Ellsworth, and Russ Morgan) was featured in the Universal film *Strictly in the Groove* (1942) and generated hit recordings by Morgan and His Orch. and Benny Goodman and His Orch. Dietz also had songs in the MGM films *Crossroads* and *Cairo* in 1942, both with music by Schwartz. By this time he had become a vice president of the movie company.

Dietz teamed with Vernon Duke in 1943. Their initial musical effort, *Dancing in the Streets* (Boston, March 23, 1943), closed during tryouts without reaching Broadway. *Jackpot*, their second show, made it to N.Y. for a run of 69 performances; *Sadie Thompson*, their third, managed only 60. During this period, Dietz was serving in the Coast Guard, and he and Duke also wrote *Tars and Spars*, a musical service revue that ran on Broadway and toured naval bases. With Schwartz, Dietz wrote the USO camp show *At Ease*.

Dietz's next songwriting credit came in 1948 with "The Dickey-Bird Song" (music by Sammy Fain), written for the MGM film *Three Daring Daughters*, which became a Top Ten hit for Freddy Martin in the spring. Dietz reunited with Schwartz for their most successful revue, *Inside U.S.A.*, which ran 399 performances and provided a chart record to Perry Como in June with "Haunted Heart."

In the early 1950s, Dietz did two new English translations for the Metropolitan Opera, *Die Fledermaus* and *La Bohème*. He married for the third time, to costume designer Lucinda Ballard. He and Schwartz had songs in two 1953 MGM films. *The Band Wagon* came to the screen 21 years after its Broadway production as a backstage movie musical starring Fred Astaire. The score was a virtual Dietz-Schwartz anthology, featuring songs from *The Little Show*, *Three's a Crowd*, *Flying Colors*, *Revenge with Music*, *At Home Abroad*, and *Between the Devil* as well as the original production of *The Band Wagon*. Dietz and Schwartz also wrote a new song, "That's Entertainment," an anthem to show business that later became the title song for a series of MGM compilation films. They also wrote "Two-Faced Woman" for *The Band Wagon*, though it was used in the Joan Crawford film *Torch Song*.

Dietz began to suffer from Parkinson's disease in 1954 and retired from MGM in 1957. He and Schwartz mounted two musicals in the early 1960s, *The Gay Life* and *Jennie*, but neither was successful. Dietz was largely inactive for the last 20 years of his life, though he did complete an entertaining autobiography, *Dancing in the Dark, Words by Howard Dietz* (N.Y., 1974).

WORKS (only works for which Dietz was a primary, credited lyricist are listed): **MUSICALS/REVUES** (dates refer to N.Y. opening unless otherwise noted): *Dear Sir* (Sept. 23, 1924); *Merry-Go-Round* (May 31, 1927); *The Little Show* (April 30, 1929); *The Second Little Show* (Sept. 2, 1930); *Three's a Crowd* (Oct. 15, 1930); *The Band Wagon* (June 3, 1931); *Flying Colors* (Sept. 15, 1932); *Revenge with Music* (Nov. 28, 1934); *At Home Abroad* (Sept. 19, 1935); *Follow the Sun* (London, Feb. 4, 1936); *Between the Devil* (Dec. 22, 1937); *Jackpot* (Jan. 13, 1944); *Tars and Spars* (May 5, 1944); *Sadie Thompson* (Nov. 16, 1944); *Inside U.S.A.* (April 30, 1948); *The Gay Life* (Nov. 18, 1961); *Jennie* (Oct. 17, 1963).

FILMS: *Under Your Spell* (1936); *The Band Wagon* (1953). OP-ERAS: *Die Fledermaus* (1950); *La Bohème* (1952). RADIO: *The Gibson Family* (1934). TELEVISION: *A Bell for Adano* (June 2, 1956).—WR

Dieupart, Charles François, French violinist, harpsichordist, and composer; b. c. 1670; d. London, c. 1740. He went to London in 1700, where he was maestro al cembalo for several years of Handel's operas; died almost destitute. He publ. *6 Suites de clavecin...composées et mises en concert pour un violon et une flûte, avec basse de viole et un archiluth.* Bach copied 2 of Dieupart's clavecin suites, and used various themes in his own *English Suites.* The Lyrebird Press of Paris publ. 2 vols. of Dieupart's works, ed. by P. Brunold (1934; Vol. I, *6 suites pour clavecin*; Vol. II, *Airs et Chansons*).—NS/LK/DM

Di Giuseppe, Enrico, American tenor; b. Philadelphia, Oct. 14, 1932. He was a pupil of Richard Bonelli at the Curtis Inst. of Music in Philadelphia and of Hans Heinz at the Juilliard School of Music in N.Y. In 1959 he made his operatic debut as Massenet's Des Grieux in New Orleans; then toured with the Metropolitan Opera National Co. On March 18, 1965, he made his first appearance at the N.Y.C. Opera as Michele in Menotti's *The Saint of Bleecker Street*; he then sang there regularly from 1967 to 1981. He made his Metropolitan Opera debut in N.Y. as Turiddu on June 20, 1970, where he later sang many Italian and French roles. He also sang opera in other major U.S. operatic centers and toured as a concert artist. Among his finest portrayals were Mozart's Ferrando and Almaviva, Bellini's Pollione, Verdi's Alfredo, Massenet's Werther, and Puccini's Pinkerton.—NS/LK/DM

Dijk, Jan van, Dutch pianist, teacher, and composer; b. Oostzaan, June 4, 1918. He studied composition with Pijper in Rotterdam (1936–46). He taught at the Brabant Cons. in Tilburg from its founding in 1955, and at the Royal Cons. of Music in The Hague from 1961. A prolific composer, he wrote hundreds of works. He also produced music in the 31-tone system devised by the Dutch physicist Adriaan Fokker.

WORKS: DRAMATIC: Opera: *Flying Dutchman* (1953); *Protesilaus and Laodamia* (1968). ORCH.: Concertino for Flute, Piano, Percussion, and Strings (1938); 3 sinfoniettas (1940, 1952, 1956); *Cassatio* for Strings and Piano obbligato (1943); 9 syms. (1944–95); *Capriccio* for Viola and Orch. (1946); 4 piano concertinos (1948–49; 1953; 1966; 1966); Concertino for 2 Pianos and String or Wind Orch. (1949); *Suite pastorale* for Oboe, English Horn, and Small Orch. (1953); *3 Suites da Sonar* (1954, 1955, 1958); *Cortège en Rondeau* (1955); Saxophone Concertino (1956); *Toccata* for Strings (1957); Concertino for Recorder and Chamber Orch. (1958); *Serenade* for Winds, Percussion, and Piano (1959); *4 Bagatelles* (1960); Concertino for Accordion and Strings (1960); Dance Suite for Orch. and Jazz Combo (1961); *17 Projections* (1962); Double Bass Concerto (1962); *Salon symphonique* (1963); Concerto for Piano, 4-Hands, and Small Orch. (1963); *Contrasts* for Orch. and Jazz Combo (1964); *Décorations et décompositions* (1964); *Duetto accompagnato* for Saxophone, Trombone, and Strings (1964); 2 serenades for Small Orch. (1966, 1970); *Jardin public* for Flute and Orch. (1967); Triple Concerto

for Flute, Recorder, Harpsichord, and Orch. (1968); *Makedonski* for Chamber Orch. (1969); 2 *Résumés* for Piano and Small Orch. (1970); *Touch after Finish* for Trumpet, Organ, Piano, and Strings (1971); *Fantaisie* for Double Bass and Orch. (1972); *About* (1973); *Kleine Concertante* for 2 Flutes and Chamber Orch. (1974); *Affiche pour la réouverture du magasin* (1974); *Accomplishement* for Small Orch. (1975); *Sinfonia e Fughetta* (1976); *Parties sur l'amitié* (1977); Pianola Concerto (1978); *5 Miniatures* (1986–91); *Concerto da camera* for Clarinet and Strings (1990); *Flirt aux fleurs* for Piano and Orch. (1991); Overture (1992); *Cinco noticias* (1993); *Andante* for Strings and Organ (1994); *Sévérac* (1994); *Nocturne* for Piano and Orch. (1995); Violin Concerto (1995); *Drie choralen* (1996); *Concertino '97* for Flute and Strings (1997); *Qui se repete* (1998). CHAMBER: 6 string quartets (1940, 1941, 1942, 1965, 1974, 1994); *Divertimento* for Clarinet, Viola, and Cello (1941); Septet (1949–50); Piano Trio (1950); *Divertimento* for 2 Violins and Cello (1951); Duo for Cello and Piano (1953); Saxophone Sonata (1953); *Serenade* for Trumpet and Horn (1955); Suite for 2 Flutes and Piano (1957); 2 sonatas for Solo Flute (1961, 1966); *Musica sacra I* for 2 Violins, Viola, and Organ (1966), *II* for Flute, Cello, and Piano (1968), and *III* for Clarinet, Violin, and Piano (1975); *Musique à trois* for Flute, Recorder, and Harpsichord (1967); Sonata for Solo Violin (1968); *Quintetto* for Mandolin, Bass Clarinet, Percussion, Organ, and Piano (1969); 4 *Caprices* for Accordion (1969); *Pet* for Flute, Saxophone, Trumpet, Violin, and Double Bass (1973); *Concertino à 3* for Flute, Violin and Viola (1975); Quartet for Flute, 2 Clarinets, and Trumpet (1997). Piano: Sonata (1942); 18 sonatinas (1944–74); Rondino (1955); Sonatina for Piano, 4-Hands (1956); 2 *Kantieks* (1964, 1976); *Couple* (1969); *Something* for 2 Piano Players (1969); *Partita piccola* (1970); *Alba Communis* (1973); 3 *Inventions* (1976); *Regardez les oiseaux...* (1996). 31-tone Pieces: 7 *Pieces* for Organ (1948); *Musica per organo trentunisono I* for 31-tone Organ (1950–51) and *II*, 7 pieces for 31-tone Organ (1957); Concertino for Trombone, Violin, and Cello (1961). VOCAL: *Jaergetijde* for Chorus and Orch. (1944); *Het masker van den Rooden Dood* for Narrator and Chamber Orch. (1952); *Zwartbaard* for Men's Chorus and Orch. (1953); *De Kommandeur* for Soloists, Narrator, Boys' Chorus, and String Quartet or String Orch. (1958); *Heer en Knecht*, cantata (1963); *Coornhert*, cantata (1964); *Quodlibet* for Chorus and Orch. (1967); *Pros romaious*, cantata (1968); *Ars vivendi* for Chorus and Orch. (1977); *Onbeduidende polka en twee wiegeliedjes* for Chorus and Orch. (1985); *Nijmegen, Nijmegen* for Chorus and Orch. (1985); *Cantatelle* for Soprano, Clarinet, and Piano (1994).—NS/LK/DM

Diller, Angela, American pianist and pedagogue; b. Brooklyn, Aug. 1, 1877; d. Stamford, Conn., April 30, 1968. She studied music at Columbia Univ. with MacDowell and Goetschius, and also with Johannes Schreyer in Dresden. From 1899 to 1916 she was head of the theory dept. of the Music School Settlement in N.Y. From 1916 to 1921 she was an administrator at the David Mannes School in N.Y., and then director of the Diller-Quaile School of Music in N.Y. (1921–41); also was on the faculty of the Univ. of Southern Calif. in Los Angeles (1932), Mills Coll. in Oakland, Calif. (1935), and the New England Cons. of Music in Boston (1936–37). She was co-founder, with Margarethe Dessoff, of the Adesdi Chorus and A Cappella Singers of N.Y. With E. Quaile, K. Stearns Page, and Harold Bauer, she ed. many educational music works. In 1953 she received a

Guggenheim fellowship. She publ. *First Theory Book* (1921), *Keyboard Harmony Course* (4 vols., 1936, 1937, 1943, 1949), and *The Splendor of Music* (1957). —NS/LK/DM

Dilling, Mildred, noted American harpist and teacher; b. Marion, Ind., Feb. 23, 1894; d. N.Y., Dec. 30, 1982. She studied with Louise Schellschmidt-Koehne and later, in Paris, with Henriette Renie. After her concert debut in Paris (1911), she played in N.Y. (1913) with the Madrigal Singers of the MacDowell Chorus; appeared in joint recitals in Europe with de Reszkes and Yvette Guilbert, and in the U.S. with Alma Gluck and Frances Alda; toured the U.S. and Great Britain many times; also made concert tours in South America, the Middle East, and the Orient. She had numerous private pupils who became well-known harp players; her most famous student was the comedian Harpo Marx. She cultivated calluses on her fingers to achieve sonority. Dilling was the owner of a large collection of harps that she acquired in different parts of the world. She publ. *Old Tunes for New Harpists* (1934) and *30 Little Classics for the Harp* (1938).—NS/LK/DM

Dillon, Henri, French composer; b. Angers, Oct. 9, 1912; d. in combat in Indochina on July 9, 1954. He studied at the Military School in St.-Cyr, and served in the army during World War II. He was largely self-taught in music, and adopted a classical style of composition, derived mainly from the melodic patterns of French folk songs.

WORKS: ORCH.: Cello Concerto (1949); Violin Concerto (1949); *Arlequin*, divertimento for Strings (1949); Viola Concerto (1952); Concerto for 2 Trumpets and Orch. (1953). CHAMBER: Saxophone Sonata (1949); Violin Sonata (1952); Concerto for 2 Pianos (Paris, Dec. 15, 1952); *Cassation* for 12 Wind Instruments (1953); various works for piano, including a Sonata (1953). —NS/LK/DM

Dillon, James, Scottish composer; b. Glasgow, Oct. 29, 1950. He attended the Glasgow School of Art (1967–68) and the Polytechnic of Central London (1972–73), then studied acoustics, music, and linguistics at the Polytechnic of North London (1973–76). He was active at the summer courses in new music in Darmstadt (1982, 1984, 1986, 1988). In 1986 he pursued research in computer music at IRCAM in Paris and was a visiting lecturer at the State Univ. of N.Y. in Stony Brook. In 1986–87 he was a lecturer at Goldsmith's Coll., Univ. of London. As a composer, Dillon was largely autodidact. In his music, he pursued a course marked by diversity and complexity.

WORKS: ORCH.: *Windows and Canopies* (1985); *Überschreiten* (1986); *helle Nacht* (1986–87); *La femme invisible* for Chamber Orch. (1989); *Introitus* for 12 Strings, Tape, and Live Electronics (1989–90); *L'oeuvre au noir* for Chamber Orch. and Live Electronics (1990); *ignis noster* (1991–92); *Vernal Showers* for Violin and Chamber Orch. (1992); *Blitzschlag* for Flute and Orch. (1994). CHAMBER: *Crossing Over* for Clarinet (1978); *Ti re-Ti ke-Dha* for Drummer (1979); *...Once Upon a Time* for 8 Instruments (1980); *Who do you love* for Flute, Clarinet, Woman's Voice, Percussion, Violin, and Cello (1980–81); *Parjanya-Vata* for

Cello (1981); *Come live with me* for Flute, Oboe, Mezzo-soprano, Piano, and Percussion (1981); *East 11th St. N.Y. 10003* for 6 Percussionists (1982); 2 string quartets (1983, 1991); *Zone (...de azul)* for 8 Instruments (1983); *Le Rivage* for Flute, Oboe, Clarinet, Horn, and Bassoon (1984); *Sgothan* for Flute (1984); *Diffraction* for Piccolo (1984); *Shrouded Mirrors* for Guitar (1988); *Del Cuatro Elemento* for Violin (1988): *L'ECRAN parfum* for 6 Violins and 3 Percussionists (1988); *éileadh sguaibe* for 9 Instrumentalists and Live Electronics (1990); Trio for Violin, Viola, and Cello (1990–91); *Siorram* for Viola (1992); *Lumen naturae* for Violin, Viola, and Cello (1992). P i a n o : *Dillug-Kefitsab* (1976); *Spleen* (1980). VOCAL: *Evening Rain* for Voice (1981); *A Roaring Flame* for Woman's Voice and Double Bass (1981–82); *(Time Lag Zerø)* for Woman's Voice and Viola (1982); *L'évolution du vol* for Woman's Voice, Clarinet, 2 Percussionists, Piano, and Double Bass (1993); *Viriditas* for 16 Solo Voices (1993); *Oceanos* for 16 Voices, Orch., and Electronics (1994).—NS/LK/DM

Dima, Gheorghe, Rumanian composer; b. Brasov, Oct. 10, 1847; d. Cluj, June 4, 1925. He was a pupil of Giehne in Karlsruhe, of Uffmann in Vienna, of Thieriot in Graz, and of Richter, Jadassohn, and Reinecke at the Leipzig Cons. He directed musical societies and church choirs in Sibiu and Brasov, and also taught music in those cities. Among his works were *La Mère d'Etienne le Grand*, oratorio, *Voilà la hora qui tourne* for Chorus and Orch., *Salvum fac regem* for Voices and Orch., etc. —NS/LK/DM

Dimas de Melo Pimenta, Emanuel, Brazilian-born Portuguese composer, architect, and urban planner; b. São Paulo, June 3, 1957. He studied at the Braz Cubas Univ. in São Paulo (degree in architecture and urbanism, 1985); also studied semiotics with Decio Pignatari and Roti Nielba Turin. In 1986 he settled in Lisbon, where he began and quickly aborted postgraduate studies in art history at the Universidade Nova; also studied Zen techniques of composition, gagaku, rāgas, and occidental music with Koellreutter, and learned to play alto and soprano flutes. In 1993 he completed an M.B.A. degree at the European Univ. His compositions, in particular the tape works, represent an eclectic incorporation of unusual source materials and utilization of novel compositional methods. From the 1970s he applied computer technologies and from the mid-1980s both Virtual Reality and Cyperspace technologies to both music and architecture. His career has spanned the arts to include graphic and urban design, photography, and creative writing. He publ. three highly creative theoretical treatises, *Tapas: Architecture and the Unconscious* (São Paulo, 1985), *Virtual Architecture* (London, 1991), and *Teleanthropos* (Lisbon, 1999). Exhibits of his graphic scores using virtual environments have been shown at the São Paulo Cultural Centre (1984), the Calouste Gulbenkian Foundation in Lisbon (1987), the Bibliotèque Nationale de Paris (1993), the Computer Art Museum in Seattle (1993), and the National Gallery of Budapest (1994). Several of his musical scores were commissioned by the Merce Cunningham Dance Company, including *Microcosmos* (1993–95). His catalog numbers some 300 works, almost all prerecorded.

WORKS: ACOUSTIC: *Spheres* for Large Ensemble (1981); *Cantos* for Ensemble (1982); *Quartet 1* for Bass Clarinet,

Tenor Saxophone, Clarinet, and Flute (1984) and 2 for Piano, Flute, Clarinet, and Cello (1984); *Concert for 2 Musicians and 1 Piano* (1985); *La Mer* for Large Ensemble (1985; also for electronics); *Constellation* for 4 Marimbas (1991); *Pulsar* for Percussion (1991); *Through the Looking Glass* for Ensemble (1992); *Olivestone* for Soprano and Alto Transverse Flutes (1999); *Voglio Vedere Le Mie Montagne* for Large Ensemble (1999); *Interior Folds* for Viola (1999). **ELECTROACOUSTIC:** *Spheres III* for Ensemble and Tape (1981–82); *Vazio* for Chorus, Percussion, Keyboards, and Tape (1982); *Frankenstern*, opera for 20 TV Sets, Soprano, 2 Mezzo-sopranos, Baritone, Piano, and Tape (1984); *20 TV Sets and a Priest* for 20 TV Sets and Tape (1984); *A Bao a Qu* for Ensemble, Synthesizers, Video Score, and Tape (1985); *Concert for Frogs and Crickets*, with Brazilian forest sounds (1985); *Factory* for 2 Tenors and Tape, based on a fragment from Mozart's *Don Giovanni* (1986–87); *Intra-Uterine Sounds* for Doppler and Electronics (1992); *Microcosmos* for Percussion and Tape, based on nanotechnology principles (1993–95); *Voglio Veere Le Mie Montagne 2* for Tape and Electronics (1999). **MAGNETIC TAPE:** *Emiedrico* (1981); *Airports* (1984); *Short-Waves 1985*, utilizing radio emissions (1985), and *SBb(r)* (1986), both for the Merce Cunningham Dance Co.; *On Bartók*, based on the 1st movement of Bartók's *Music for Strings, Percussion, and Celesta* (1986); *Stones*, using indigenous Brazilian instruments (1988). **DIGITAL TAPE:** *Music from 144 Voices* (1987); *Webern Variation* (1987); *Sun*, using the structure of the sound waves from the sun (1987); *Plan*, using sound particles of medieval instruments from 8th- to 11th-century Islamic music from Andalusia, structured on patterns first used by Palestrina (1987); *Twilight*, based on gagaku music (1987); *wHALLtz*, using 32 loudspeakers from 3 structural fragments of J. Strauss Jr.'s *Kaiserwalzer* (1987); *Crossing Over* (1988); *Beethoven Quartet*, based on a fragment from Beethoven's Quartet, op.130 (1988); *Strange Loopings*, following Kurt Gödel's theorem (1988); *Musak*, "kitsch music" for supermarkets, elevators, shopping centers, postal centers, etc. (1988); *Dipak*, based on an ancient North Indian evening rāga (1989); *Finnegans* for Voice and Computer (1989); *Music for Nothing*, "constructed from a graphical complex drawn from the frontiers of chaos" (1989); *Gravitational Sounds*, using strange mathematical attractors (1991; for the Merce Cunningham Dance Company); *Area* (1996); *Andromeda* (1997); *Book One*, using digital voices (1997). **OTHER:** *Difesa Della Natura*, soundtrack to a film on Joseph Beuys (1998).—NS/LK/DM

Di Meola, Al, jazz guitarist; b. Jersey City, N.J., July 22, 1954. He began playing guitar at age nine, then at 15 picked up the steel-string guitar. Inspired to play fusion by hearing Miles Davis and Chick Corea, he attended Berklee in Boston in the mid-1970s and joined Corea's Return to Forever band in 1974. He remained with the group until it broke up in 1976, and then formed his own electric group that consistently won musicians' polls for outstanding albums but achieved only limited commercial success. In 1980, he joined John McLaughlin and Paco De Lucia in an acoustic trio, which toured and recorded together several times, including in 1983 and 1996. Later albums were recorded as The Al Di Meola Project featuring percussionist Airto, Phil Markowitz on keyboards, Danny Gottlieb on drums, and bassist Chip Jackson, and included Di Meola on guitar synthesizer.

DISC.: *Land of the Midnight Sun* (1976); *Elegant Gypsy* (1977); *Casino* (1978); *Endido Hotel* (1980); *Electric Rendezvous* (1981); *Tour De Force: Live* (1982); *Scenario* (1983); *Cielo E Terra* (1985); *Soaring Through a Dream* (1985); *Kiss My Axe* (1988); *Tirami Su* (1990); *World Sinfonia* (1990); *Heart of the Immigrants* (1993); *Di Meola Plays Piazzolla* (1996). *Friday Night in San Francisco* (1981); *Passion, Grace & Fire* (1983); *The Guitar Trio* (1996); *Anthology* (2000).

WRITINGS: *Artist Transcriptions, Guitar: Music, Words, Pictures* (Milwaukee, Wisc., 1983).—MM/LP

Dimitrova, Ghena, Bulgarian soprano; b. Beglj, May 6, 1941. She studied with Christo Brumbarov at the Bulgarian State Cons. in Sofia; then sang with the Sofia Opera. After winning 1st prize in the Sofia Competition in 1970, she scored a major success as Amelia in *Un ballo in maschera* in Parma (1972); subsequently held engagements in France, Spain, South America, Moscow, Vienna, and Rome. In 1983 she made her London debut in a concert performance of *La Gioconda*; later that year she appeared as Turandot at Milan's La Scala. In 1984 she sang at N.Y.'s Carnegie Hall and at the Salzburg Festival; later operatic roles included Turandot at London's Covent Garden (1985) and Leonora in *Il Trovatore* at the San Francisco Opera (1986). On Dec. 14, 1987, she made her Metropolitan Opera debut in N.Y. as Turandot. In 1992 she appeared as Leonora in *La forza del destino* in Naples. She sang Lady Macbeth in Athens in 1997. Among her other roles were Aida, Norma, Santuzza, and Tosca.—NS/LK/DM

D'Indy, (Paul-Marie-Théodore-) Vincent *See* Indy, (Paul-Marie-Théodore-) Vincent d'

Dinerstein, Norman (Myron), American music educator and composer; b. Springfield, Mass., Sept. 18, 1937; d. Cincinnati, Dec. 23, 1982. He studied at Boston Univ. (B.M., 1960), the Hartt Coll. of Music in Hartford, Conn. (M.M., 1963), and Princeton Univ. (Ph.D., 1974); also took courses at the Berlin Hochschule für Musik (1962–63), the Berkshire Music Center in Tanglewood (summers, 1962, 1963), and in Darmstadt (1964). He was then on the faculties of Princeton Univ. (1965–66), the New England Cons. of Music in Boston (1968–69; 1970–71), Hartt Coll. (1971–76), and the Univ. of Cincinnati Coll.-Cons. of Music (1976–81), where he was dean (1981–82).

WORKS: *4 Movements* for 3 Woodwind Instruments (1961); *Terzetto* for Brass Trio (1961); *Cassation* for Orch. (1963); *Serenade* for Oboe, Clarinet, Harp, Violin, and Cello (1963); *Schir ha Schirim* for Chorus and Orch. (1963); *Intermezzo* for Orch. (1964); *Pezzi piccoli* for Flute and Viola (1966); *Contrasto* for Orch. (1968); *Sequoia* for Jazz Ensemble (1969); *Refrains* for Orch. (1971); *The Answered Question* for Wind Ensemble (1972); *Songs of Remembrance* for Soprano and Strings (1976–79); *Tubajubalee* for Tuba Ensemble (1978); *Golden Bells* for Chorus and Orch. (1980–82; completed by M. Schelle); also choral music; song cycles; piano pieces.—NS/LK/DM

Dinescu, Violeta, Romanian-born German composer, teacher, and writer on music; b. Bucharest, July 13, 1953. She studied at the Bucharest Cons. (B.A. in composition, piano, and pedagogy, 1977; M.A. in composition, 1978). After teaching at the George Enescu Music School in Bucharest (1978–82), she settled in West Germany and in 1989 became a naturalized German citizen. From 1986 to 1991 she taught at the Heidelberg Cons. for Church Music, and from 1989 to 1991 at the Frankfurt am Main Cons. From 1990 to 1994 she taught at the Bayreuth Academy of Music. In 1996 she became prof. of applied composition at the Univ. of Oldenburg. She contributed articles on music to publs. in Europe and the U.S. In her compositions, melodic and rhythmic elements are complemented by a concern for mathematical exactitude, the exploration of sound potentials, and the utilization of electronic instruments.

WORKS: DRAMATIC: Opera: *Hunger and Thirst*, chamber opera (1985; Freiburg-im-Breisgau, Feb. 1, 1986); *Der 35. Mai*, children's opera (Mannheim, Nov. 30, 1986); *Eréndira*, chamber opera (1992); *Schachnovelle*, chamber opera (1994). Ballet: *Der Kreisel* (Ulm, May 26, 1985); *Effi Briest* (Magdeburg, July 9, 1998). Film: *Tabu*, music for the F. Murnau film of 1931 (Frankfurt am Main, April 5, 1988). ORCH.: *Transformation* (1978); *Anna Perenna* (1979); *Memories* for Strings (1980); *Akrostichon* (1983); *Map 67* for Chamber Orch. (1987); *Kybalion* for Strings (1991); *Fresco* for Youth Orch. (1992); *Vortex-Wolken I–III* for Small Orch. (1998). CHAMBER: Sonata for Violin and Piano (1973); *Satya I* for Violin (1981), *II* for Bassoon (1981), *III* for Double Bass (1981), and *IV* for Clarinet (1981); *Echoes I* for Flute, *II* for Piano and Percussion, and *III* for Organ (all 1980); *Alternances* for Wind Quintet (1982); *Nakris* for Saxophone Quartet (1985); *Melismen* for Recorder Quintet (1985); *Quasaar Paal 2* for Mutabor (Computer Organ) and Cello (1985); *New Rochelle* for DX7 Synthesizer (1987); *Trio d'Anches* for Oboe, Clarinet, and Bassoon (1987); *Loc Maria* for Organ and Percussion (1987); *Ostrov I* for Viola Quartet (1987) and *II* for Clarinet Quartet (1988); *Din Terra Lonhdana* for String Quartet (1987); *Terra Lohndana* for Chamber Ensemble (1988); *Kata* for Flute and Piano (1989); *...wenn der freude thränen flessen...* for Cello and Piano (1990); *Lichtwellen* for Clarinet (1991); *Trautropfen* for Clarinet and Piano (1992); String Quartet (1993); *Kathargos* for Zither (1996); *Les Cymbales du Soleil* for Oboe and 2 Percussion (1996). VOCAL: *Bewitch Me Into a Silver Bird!* for Chorus and Orch. (1975); *Mondnacht* for Voice and Organ (1985); *Zebaoth* for Baritone and 2 Organs (1986); Concertino for Voice and Orch. (1986; Ulm, March 5, 1987); *Mondnächte* for Voice, Saxophone, and Percussion (1986); *Dona nobis pacem* for Voice, Cello, and Percussion (1987); Concertino for Voice and Orch. (Baden-Baden, Aug. 26, 1988); also various choruses and solo songs.—NS/LK/DM

Dinicu, Grigoraş, Romanian violinist and composer; b. Bucharest, April 3, 1889; d. there, March 28, 1949. He was of a family of musicians. In 1902 he studied violin with Flesch, who taught at the Bucharest Cons. At his graduation in 1906, Dinicu played a violin piece of his own based on popular Romanian rhythms, *Hora staccato*; Jascha Heifetz made a virtuoso arrangement of it in 1932. Subsequently Dinicu played in hotels, restaurants, nightclubs, and cafés in Bucharest and in western Europe. He also composed numerous other pieces of light music in the gypsy and Romanian manner.—NS/LK/DM

Dion, Celine, Canadian pop-balladeer who has scored Titanic-sized hits; b. Charlemagne, Quebec,

Canada, March 16, 1968. The youngest of 14 French Canadian children, some of Celine Dion's earliest memories were of performing. Her parents owned a small bar and, on the weekends, the family provided the entertainment. When Celine was 12, she made a demo tape of a song written by her mother and an older brother. Manager Rene Angelil heard the tape and, recognizing the star quality in the girl's voice, signed her, mortgaging his home to pay for her first recording.

Dion's French recording career immediately took off among French-speaking people around the world. Her albums regularly went platinum in Canada. In 1983, she became the first Canadian singer to score a gold record in France. She also won the Eurovision Song Contest in 1988.

With these worlds conquered, Dion set about the Herculean task of conquering the English-speaking world in the early 1990s. Both she and Angelil recognized that this could not be done on her terms (i.e., in French), so Dion took a crash course in English, discovering a facility for language. Within a year she was ready to record her first English album, *Unison*. The album spun off the #35 hit "(If There Was) Any Other Way" and the #4 "Where Does My Heart Beat Now." The album hit #74 and would eventually go platinum, but it took seven years.

Her voice impressed the Disney people, and they chose Dion to duet with Peabo Bryson on the closing track of their 1991 animated feature *Beauty and the Beast*. The song went platinum, won a Best Pop Vocal by a Duo or Group Grammy, Song of the Year Oscar, rose to #9, and established Dion as a vocalist to be reckoned with. She kept the momentum going with her eponymous 1992 album. The album produced three more big hits, the adult contemporary chart-toppers "If You Asked Me" (#4 pop) and "Nothing Broken but My Heart" (#29 pop), as well as "Love Can Move Mountains" which hit #36. The album peaked at #34 and eventually went double platinum.

Dion's 1993 album *Color of My Love* proved to be a major commercial breakout, powered by the platinum single "The Power of Love," which spent four weeks atop the pop charts. The album also included her version of "When I Fall in Love" from the soundtrack to the hit film *Sleepless in Seattle*, which hit #27, and "Misled" which rose to #23. The album hit #4 and sold quadruple platinum.

In 1994, Dion went back to her roots and recorded an album in French. She also released a live album. Neither of these sold spectacularly well in the U.S. That year, Dion married her manager, despite a 26-year age difference.

While her 1994 albums didn't sell exceptionally well or make many waves on the pop scene, Dion's next major release, *Falling into You* did. Her first chart-topping album, it contained the theme from the film *Up Close and Personal*, "Because You Loved Me," a massive platinum #1 hit and one of the most popular adult contemporary hits of all time. Its uplifting sentiments, powered by Dion's heartfelt, lung-stretching vocals, set the pattern for her following hits. The album also produced the #2 single "It's All Coming Back to Me

Now," and the Eric Carmen-penned #4 hit "All by Myself." The album won Album of the Year and Pop Album of the Year at the Grammys, and became one of the first Diamond Award–winning albums, signifying sales of over 10 million copies in the U.S. It topped the charts in 11 countries and sold in excess of 25 million copies worldwide.

People wondered how Dion could top that, but she managed with *Let's Talk about Love*. Dion found herself at the core of a phenomenon, singing the main theme from one of the most popular movies of all time, *Titanic*. This song, "My Heart Will Go On," topped the charts and went gold, winning best female Pop Performance and Record of the Year at the Grammys. The album sold nine times platinum. Dion's performance on the Grammy award show raised eyebrows due to an unintentionally revealing gown, made more translucent by the use of dramatic back-lighting.

Even putting out a holiday album, as Dion did in 1998, she could do no wrong. *These Are Special Times* hit #2 on the pop charts, going triple platinum. It produced the chart-topping duet with R. Kelly, "I'm Your Angel." The following spring, she got her due sharing a stage with Gloria Estefan, Aretha Franklin, Shania Twain, and Mariah Carey for the first VH-1 *Divas Live* concert. The album of the show topped the charts.

Dion sums up her life simply by saying, "I have a perfect life and a perfect career."

DISC.: *Unison* (1990); *Celine Dion* (1992); *The Colour of My Love* (1993); *Dion Chante Plamondon* (1994); *Premieres Années* (1993); *The French Album* (1995); *Power of Love* (1995); *Des Mots Qui Sonnent* (1995); *Falling into You* (1996); *Live in Paris* (1996); *Let's Talk about Love* (1997); *A l'Olympia* (live; 1998); *Chansons en Or* (1998); *Ne Partez Pas Sans* (1998); *Ne Partez Pas Sans Moi* (1998); *D'Eux* (1998); *Celine Dion, Vol. 2* (1998); *S'Il Suffisait d'Aimer* (If Only Love Was Enough; 1998); *These Are Special Times* (1998); *Celine Au Coeur Du Stade* (1999); *All The Way.. A Decade of Song* (1999); *Celine Dion/Unison* (1999); *Let's Talk About Love (Australian Bonus CD)* (1999); *Amour* (1999); *Let Talk About Love (Canada Bonus Tracks)* (1999); "Treat Her Like a Lady"(1999); "To Love You More" (1999); "That's the Way It Is" (Germany CD single; 1999); *These Are Special Times* (2000); "That's the Way It Is Pt. 1" (import CD single; 1999); "First Time Ever I Saw, Pt. 1" (2000); "First Time Ever I Saw, Pt. 2" (2000); "That's The Way It Is" (2000); "Ne Partez Pas Sans Moi" (2000); "If You Asked Me To" (2000).—**HB**

Dion (Di Mucci) and The Belmonts, the most successful white doo-wop vocal group, emerging from the N.Y. a cappella street corner scene of the 1950s.

MEMBERSHIP: Dion DiMucci, lead voc. (b. Bronx, N.Y., July 18, 1939); Angelo D'Aleo, 1st ten. (b. Bronx, N.Y., Feb. 3, 1940); Fred Milano, 2nd ten. (b. Bronx, N.Y., Aug. 22, 1939); Carlo Mastrangelo, bass voc. (b. Bronx, N.Y., Oct. 5, 1938).

Dion DiMucci started singing at the age of five and began making public appearances playing acoustic guitar around the age of 11. In 1957 he joined The Timberlanes to record "The Chosen Few" for Mohawk Records, and formed Dion and The Belmonts in 1958. Signing with the newly formed Laurie Records label, the group soon hit with "I Wonder Why" and "No One Knows."

D'Aleo served in the Navy in 1959 while the group scored smash hits with Doc Pomus and Mort Shuman's "A Teenager in Love" and the Rodgers and Hart's classic "Where or When."

Dion left the group to pursue a solo career in the fall of 1960. Dion quickly hit with "Lonely Teenager," followed in 1961 by the top pop/smash R&B hit "Runaround Sue," backed by The Del Satins and cowritten with Ernie Maresca. (Maresca later scored a smash pop/major R&B hit with "Shout! Shout! Knock Yourself Out" in 1962.) Dion also appeared in the 1961 film *Teenage Millionaire*. In the meantime, Angelo D'Aleo rejoined The Belmonts and Carlo Mastrangelo switched to lead, and the group recorded for their own Sabina label. They achieved moderate hits with "Tell Me Why" and "Come On, Little Angel," but Mastrangelo left in 1962, to be replaced by Frank Lyndon. The Belmonts moved to United Artists in 1964, reuniting with Dion for 1967's *Together Again* on ABC and the live Warner Brothers set *Reunion*, recorded June 2, 1972, at Madison Square Garden. The Belmonts later recorded for Dot, Buddah, and Strawberry, eventually scoring a minor hit in 1981 with "Let's Put the Fun Back in Rock 'n' Roll," recorded with Freddy Cannon.

Continuing to be backed by The Del Satins, Dion scored smash hits on Laurie with "The Wanderer" (written by Maresca), "Lovers Who Wander" (cowritten with Maresca), and his own "Little Diane," as well as the major hits "Love Came to Me" and "Sandy." Moving to Columbia and retaining The Del Satins, Dion scored smash pop hits with "Ruby Baby" (an R&B hit) and "Drip Drop," both previously recorded by The Drifters, and "Donna the Prima Donna" (cowritten with Maresca). In the mid 1960s Dion began exploring blues material, with little commercial success.

In 1968 Dion moved to Fla., kicked a heroin habit that dated back to his early teens, and returned to Laurie Records. *Dion*, regarded as his most fully realized album, contained songs by contemporary artists such as Bob Dylan, Leonard Cohen, Fred Neil, and Joni Mitchell, and yielded a smash pop hit with Dick Holler's ode to assassinated leaders, Lincoln, King, and Kennedy, "Abraham, Martin and John." Dion subsequently toured the college- and coffeehouse circuit playing acoustic guitar, and switched to Warner Bros. in 1970, with little success. He recorded *Born to Be with You* under producer-extraordinaire Phil Spector in 1974; however, the album was released only in England.

For much of The 1980s Dion recorded modern Christian music. He returned to rock 'n' roll in June 1987 with a series of sold-out concerts at Radio City Music Hall. He published his autobiography, *The Wanderer*, in 1988 and was inducted into the Rock and Roll Hall of Fame in 1989. Also that year, with the assistance of Paul Simon, Lou Reed, and k.d. lang, Dion recorded *Yo Frankie* under producer Dave Edmunds, managing a minor hit with "And the Night Stood Still." In 1990 Dion toured with Edmunds, Graham Parker, and Kim Wilson of The Fabulous Thunderbirds. By the mid 1990s Dion had moved back to N.Y. and formed the group Little Kings with guitarist Scott Kempner of The Dictators and The Del Lords, bassist Mike Mesaros of The Smithereens, and drummer Frank Funaro of The Del Lords for engagements on the East Coast.

DISC.: DION AND THE BELMONTS: *Presenting* (1959); *When You Wish upon a Star* (1960); *Together Again* (1967); *Reunion: Live at Madison Square Garden, 1972* (1973). **THE BELMONTS:** *Carnival of Hits* (1962); *Summer Love* (1969); *Cigars, Accapella, Candy* (1973); *Cheek to Cheek* (1978). **DION (DIMUCCI):** *Alone with Dion* (1960); *Runaround Sue* (1961); *Lovers Who Wander* (1962); *Sings His Greatest Hits* (1962); *Love Came to Me* (1963); *Dion Sings to Sandy* (1963); *Ruby Baby* (1963); *Donna, The Prima Donna* (1963); *Bronx Blues: The Columbia Recordings* (recorded 1962–65; 1991); *Wonder Where I'm Bound* (1965); *Dion* (1968); *Sit Down Old Friend* (1970); *You're Not Alone* (1971); *Sanctuary* (1971); *Suite for Late Summer* (1972); *Streetheart* (1976); *The Return of the Wanderer* (1978); *Inside Job* (1980); *I Put Away My Idols* (1983); *Seasons* (1985); *Kingdom in the Streets* (1985); *Velvet and Steel* (1987); *Yo Frankie* (1989).

WRITINGS: Dion with Davin Seay, *The Wanderer: Dion's Story* (N.Y., 1988).—**BH**

Dippel, (Johann) Andreas, German-American tenor and operatic impresario; b. Kassel, Nov. 30, 1866; d. Los Angeles, May 12, 1932. He studied with Nina Zottmayr in Kassel, Julius Hey in Berlin, Alberto Leoni in Milan, and Johannes Ress in Vienna. In 1887 he made his operatic debut as Lionel in *Martha* in Bremen, where he sang until 1892; he also appeared at the Bayreuth Festival in 1889. On November 26, 1890, he made his Metropolitan Opera debut in N.Y. as Asrael, returning on its roster from 1898 to 1902 and from 1903 to 1910; he also sang in Breslau (1892–93), at the Vienna Court Opera (1893), and at London's Covent Garden (1897–1900). With Gatti-Casazza, he shared administrative duties at the Metropolitan Opera (1908–10), then was manager of the Chicago Grand Opera (1910–13). After managing his own light opera company, he settled in Los Angeles as a vocal coach. His repertoire included almost 150 roles; he was particularly successful in operas by Wagner.—**NS/LK/DM**

Diruta, Girolamo, celebrated Italian organist, teacher, and music theorist; b. Deruta, near Perugia, c. 1554; d. after 1610. He was a pupil of Zarlino, Costanzo Porta, and Claudio Merulo, the last of whom mentions the fact with pride in the preface of Diruta's *Il Transilvano.* In 1574 Diruta was in the Franciscan monastery at Correggio. He then was church organist in Venice (1582–93), at the Cathedral of Chioggia (1593–1603), and at Agobbio (Gubbio) Cathedral (1609–10). His *Il Transilvano* is a valuable treatise on organ playing, the first work to treat the organ and its playing technique as distinct and separate from the clavier. It is in two parts, in dialogue form: *Dialogo sopra il vero modo di sonar organi e istromenti da penna* (Venice, 1593; further eds., 1597, 1609, 1612, 1625) and *Dialogo diviso in quattro libri... il vero modo e la vera regola d'intavolare ciascun canto* (Venice, 1609; 2nd ed., 1622). In his *Musical Ornamentation,* Dannreuther gives a thorough analysis of Diruta's system of ornamentation. Vol. III of L. Torchi's *L'arte musicale in Italia* contains a Ricercare and two toccatas for organ by Diruta.—**NS/LK/DM**

Disley, Diz (actually, William Charles), noted Canadian-born, British jazz guitarist (bjo., singer); b. Winnipeg, Manitoba, Canada, May 27, 1931. His parents were British, and the family moved back to Wales when Diz was four, then on to Yorkshire five years later. He played banjo in local jazz-flavored bands including the Rotherham. Jazz Hounds and the Vernon Street Ramblers, while studying at the Leeds Coll. of Art. He joined the Yorkshire Jazz Band in 1949, but left to enlist in the Army a year later. After two years of service, he moved to London, worked with Jeremy French (late 1953), and began specializing on guitar. He worked with a number of trad-jazz ensembles through the 1950s; towards the end of the decade, he also became involved with the skiffle/folk-revival movement, and accompanied popular folk-styled singers like Nancy Whiskey. From 1958–60, he appeared regularly with own Soho String Quintet, modeled after the famous "Hot Club" ensemble led by Django Reinhardt in the 1930s. He played folk and jazz gigs throughout the 1960s and early 1970s, and led his own quintet and band. He began a long working association with Stephane Grappelli in 1973 (interrupted by Diz breaking his wrist in 1979), continuing through late 1982. He reformed his Soho String Quintet in 1983. Disley lived in Spain for part of the 1970s and 1980s, and opened jazz club (with clarinetist Bernie Holden) in Almeria in 1988. He returned to Britain in the early 1990s, and has led his own String Quintet and regularly guested with Dick Laurie's Elastic Band (including bookings in Hong Kong). Disley freelanced in Europe and in the U.S.A. during the mid- 1990s.

DISC.: *Zing Went the Strings* (1986); *At the White Bear* (1995); *With Stephane Grappelli: I Got Rhythm* (1973); *Violinspiration* (1976); *With Martin Carthy & Dave Swarbrick: Rags, Reels, and Airs* (1967).—**JC-B/LP**

Di Stefano, Giuseppe, noted Italian tenor; b. Motta Santa Anastasia, near Catania, July 24, 1921. He was a pupil of Adriano Torchi and Luigi Montesanto in Milan. During World War II, he was conscripted into the Italian army but in 1943 he went AWOL to Switzerland, where he was interned as a refugee. After making appearances on Swiss radio and in concert in 1944, he returned to Italy and made his operatic debut in 1946 as Massenet's Des Grieux in Reggio Emilia, a role he also chose for his first appearance at Milan's La Scala the following year. He made his Metropolitan Opera debut in N.Y. on February 25, 1948, as the Duke of Mantua; he remained on its roster until 1952, appearing as Rossini's Almaviva, as well as Faust, Nemorino, Rinuccio in *Gianni Schicchi,* Alfredo, Rodolfo, and Pinkerton; he returned for the 1955–56 and 1964–65 seasons. From 1948 to 1952 he appeared in Mexico City. In 1950 he made his San Francisco Opera debut as Rodolfo. From 1952 to 1961 he was a principal member at La Scala, where he appeared as Radames, Canio, and Turiddu, and where he created the role of Giuliano in Pizzetti's *Calzare d'Argento* in 1961. In 1954 he made his first appearance at the Lyric Theatre of Chicago as Edgardo. His British debut followed in 1957 as Nemorino at the Edinburgh Festival. In 1961 he made his debut at London's Covent Garden as Cavaradossi. He also sang at the Vienna State Opera, the Berlin State Opera, the Paris Opéra, and the Teatro Colón in Buenos Aires. In 1973–74 he made a concert tour of the world with Maria Callas.—NS/LK/DM

Distler, Hugo, distinguished German composer, organist, choral conductor, and pedagogue; b. Nuremberg, June 24, 1908; d. (suicide) Berlin, Nov. 1, 1942. He was a student of Martienssen (piano), Ramin (organ), and Grabner (harmony) at the Leipzig Cons. (1927–31). In 1931 he became organist at St. Jakobi in Lübeck. In 1937 he became a lecturer at the Württemberg Hochschule für Musik in Stuttgart, where he also conducted its two choirs. In 1940 he was called to Berlin as prof. at the Hochschule für Musik, where he also conducted its choir from 1941. In 1942 he was also named conductor of the State and Cathedral Choir. Despite the prominence Distler achieved as a performing musician and teacher, the Nazi disdain for his work led him to take his own life. He is now recognized as one of the most significant German composers of his generation. While his works remain tonally anchored, they reveal an innovative harmonic sense.

WORKS: ORCH.: Concerto for Harpsichord and Strings (1935; Hamburg, April 29, 1936); *Konzertstück* for Piano and Orch. (1937; Oldenburg, Feb. 11, 1955). **CHAMBER:** *Kammermusik* for 6 Instruments (1927); *Sonata über alte deutsche Volkslieder* for 2 Violins and Piano (1938); String Quartet (1939). **KEYBOARD: Piano:** *Kleine Sonate* (1927); *Konzertante Sonate* for 2 Pianos (1931); *Elf kleine Klavierstücke für die Jugend* (1936); *Konzertstück* for 2 Pianos (1940). **Organ:** 2 partitas (1932, 1935); *Sieben kleine Orgelchoralbearbeitungen* (1938); Sonata (1938–39). **VOCAL: Sacred:** *Deutsches Choralmesse* (1932); *Der Jahrkreis* for Chorus (1932–33); *Choralpassion* for Soloists and Chorus (Berlin, March 29, 1933); *Die Weihnachtsgeschichte* for Soloists and Chorus (1933); *Liturgische Sätze* for Chorus (1933–35); *Wo Gott zum Haus nit gibt sein Gunst,* cantata for Chorus, 2 Oboes, Strings, and Harpsichord (1934); *Geistliche Chormusik,* 9 motets for Chorus (1934–41); *Drei geistliche Konzerte* for Soprano and Organ or Harpsichord (1938); *Nun danket all und bringet Ehr,* cantata for Soloists, Chorus, Strings, and Organ (1941); many other works. **Secular:** *An die Natur,* cantata for Soprano, Chorus, Piano or Harpsichord, and Strings (Pyrmont, Aug. 16, 1933); *Das Lied von der Glocke* for Baritone, Chorus, and Orch. (1933); *Neues Chorliederbuch* for Chorus (1936–38); *Mörike-Chorliederbuch* for Chorus (1938–39; Graz, June 26, 1939); *Lied am Herde,* cantata for Bass or Baritone and Chamber Orch. (1941; Berlin, Feb. 3, 1942; also for Baritone or Alto and Piano); *Kleine Sommerkantate* for 2 Sopranos and String Quartet (1942); various other works.

BIBL.: U. von Rauchhaupt, *Die vokale Kirchenmusik H. D.s* (Gütersloh, 1963); L. Palmer, *H. D. and His Church Music* (St. Louis, 1967); U. Herrmann, *H. D.—Rufer und Mahner* (Berlin, 1972); A Sievers, *Der Kompositionsstil H. D.s dargestellt an Beispielen aus dem Mörike-Chorliederbuch* (Wiesbaden, 1989); H. Grabner et al., *H. D.* (Tutzing, 1990); D. Lemmermann, *Studien zum weltlichen Vokalwerk H. D.s* (Frankfurt am Main, 1996); S. Hanheide, ed., *H. D. im Dritten Reich* (Osnabrück, 1997). —NS/LK/DM

Ditson, Oliver, American music publisher, founder of the firm of **Oliver Ditson & Co.;** b. Boston, Oct. 20, 1811; d. there, Dec. 21, 1888. He established himself as a music seller and publisher in Boston in 1835. He became a partner of G. H. Parker, his employer, under the firm name of Parker & Ditson. He carried on the business in his own name (1842–57), but when J. C. Haynes joined the firm, Ditson changed its name to O. Ditson & Co. His eldest son, Charles, took charge of the N.Y. branch (Ch. H. Ditson & Co.) in 1867, the business being continued until his death. A Philadelphia branch, opened in 1875 by J. Edward Ditson as J. E. D. & Co., was in existence until 1910. A branch for the importation and sale of instruments, etc., was established at Boston in 1860 as John C. Haynes & Co. On Oliver Ditson's death, the firm of Oliver Ditson & Co. was reorganized as a corporation, with J. C. Haynes as president (d. May 3, 1907); from 1907 until his death, on May 14, 1929, Charles H. Ditson managed the business; he was succeeded by H. H. Porter. In 1931 Theo. Presser Co. of Philadelphia took over the management of the firm. Its catalog embraced about 52,000 titles, and it also publ. the *Musical Record* (a monthly periodical) from 1878 to 1903, the *Musician* from 1896 to 1918, and several library series. The music house Lyon & Healy was founded by Oliver Ditson in Chicago in 1864 as a western branch. —NS/LK/DM

Dittersdorf, Karl Ditters von (original name, **Karl Ditters**), eminent Austrian composer and violinist; b. Vienna, Nov. 2, 1739; d. Schloss Rothlhotta, Neuhof, Bohemia, Oct. 24, 1799. He played violin as a child, then studied with König and Ziegler. The Prince of Sachsen- Hildburghausen made it possible for him to take private violin lessons with Trani and to study composition with Bonno; he played in the Prince's orch. from 1751 to 1761. In 1761 he went to Vienna, where he was engaged as a member of the Court Theater Orch. (until 1764). He was befriended by Gluck, who took him along on his Italian journey, where he had an occasion to appear in public as a violinist. In 1765 he assumed the post of Kapellmeister to the Bishop of Grosswardein in Hungary, where he remained until 1769. His career as a composer began in earnest at this time; he wrote an oratorio, *Isacco, figura del redentore,* several cantatas, and many pieces of orch. and chamber music. In 1770 he became Kapellmeister to the Prince-Bishop of Breslau, Count von Schaffgotsch, at Johannisberg in Silesia. There he wrote mostly for the stage, bringing out 12 works between 1771 and 1776. However, he wrote his most important dramatic works in Vienna for the ducal theater in Oels. He gained fame with his first singspiel, *Doctor und Apotheker,* produced in Vienna on July 11, 1786; it was followed by other successful stage works, *Betrug durch Aberglauben, Die Liebe im Narrenhause, Das rote Käppchen,* and *Hieronymus Knicker.* He received several honors during his lifetime: in 1770 the Pope bestowed upon him the Order of the Golden Spur; in 1773 he was ennobled by the Emperor as von Dittersdorf. Upon the death of the Prince-Bishop in 1795, he was granted a small pension, and found himself in straitened circumstances until a friend, Baron von Stillfried, took him into his castle, Rothlhotta, where he remained until his death. Dittersdorf was an important figure in the Viennese Classical school of composition, although he lacked the genius of Haydn and

Mozart. He was able to fuse the common folk-song elements of the period with brilliant ensembles characteristic of opera buffa. His singspiels reveal a jovial humor, melodic charm, and rhythmic vitality. His syms. and concertos are also of interest as characteristic specimens of the period.

WORKS: DRAMATIC: *Il viaggiatore americano in Joannesberg*, farce (Johannisberg, May 1, 1771; not extant); *L'amore disprezzato (Pancratio; Amore in musica)*, operetta buffa (Johannisberg, 1771); *Il finto pazzo per amore*, operetta giocosa (Johannisberg, June 3, 1772); *Il tutore e la pupilla*, dramma giocoso (Johannisberg, May 1, 1773); *Lo sposo burlato*, operetta giocosa (Johannisberg, 1773 or 1775; another version as *Der gefoppte Bräutigam*); *Il tribunale di Giove*, serenade with prologue (Johannisberg, 1774); *Il maniscalco*, operetta giocosa (Johannisberg, May 1, 1775); *La contadina fedele*, opera giocosa (Johannisberg, 1776); *La moda ossia Gli scompigli domestici*, dramma giocoso (Johannisberg, June 3, 1776); *L'Arcifanfano, re de' matti*, opera giocosa (Johannisberg, 1776); *Il barone di Rocca Antica*, operetta giocosa (Johannisberg, 1776); *I visionari* (Johannisberg, 1776; not extant); *Doctor und Apotheker (Der Apotheker und der Doctor)*, Singspiel (Vienna, July 11, 1786); *Betrug durch Aberglauben oder Die Schatzgräber (Der glückliche Betrug; Die dienstbaren Geister)*, Singspiel (Vienna, Oct. 3, 1786); *Democrito corretto*, opera giocosa (Vienna, Jan. 24, 1787; performed under various titles); *Die Liebe im Narrenhause*, Singspiel (Vienna, April 12, 1787); *Das rote Käppchen oder Hilft's nicht so schadt's nicht (Die rote Kappe; Das Rotkäppchen)*, comic operetta (Vienna, 1788); *Im Dunkeln ist nicht gut munkeln oder Irrung über Irrung (25,000 Gulden)*, comic opera (Vienna, Feb. 1789); *Hieronymus Knicker (Lucius Knicker; Chrisostomus Knicker; Hokus Pokus oder Die Lebensessenz)*, Singspiel (Vienna, July 7, 1789); *Die Hochzeit des Figaro*, Singspiel (Brunn, 1789?; music not extant); *Der Schiffspatron oder Der neue Gutsherr*, Singspiel (Vienna, 1789); *Hokus-Pokus oder Der Gaukelspiel*, comic opera (Vienna, 1790); *Der Teufel ein Hydraulikus*, comedy (Gratz, 1790); *Der Fürst und sein Volk*, pasticcio (Leipzig, March 5?, 1791; music not extant; in collaboration with F. Piterlin and F. Bertoni); *Das Gespenst mit der Trommel (Geisterbanner)*, Singspiel (Oels, Aug. 16, 1794); *Don Quixote der Zweyte (Don Chisciotto)*, Singspiel (Oels, Feb. 4, 1795); *Gott Mars und der Hauptmann von Bärenzahn (Gott Mars oder Der eiserne Mann)*, Singspiel (Oels, May 30, 1795); *Der Durchmarsch*, an arrangement of J. Paneck's *Die christliche Judenbraut* (Oels, Aug. 29, 1795); *Der Schach von Schiras*, Singspiel (Oels, Sept. 15, 1795); *Die befreyten Gwelfen (Die Guelfen)*, prologue (Oels, Oct. 29, 1795); *Ugolino*, serious Singspiel (Oels, June 11, 1796); *Die lustigen Weiber von Windsor*, Singspiel (Oels, June 25, 1796); *Der schöne Herbsttag*, dialogue (Oels, Oct. 29, 1796); *Der Ternengewinnst oder Der gedemütigte Stolz (Terno secco)*, Singspiel (Oels, Feb. 11, 1797); *Der Mädchenmark*, singspiel (Oels, April 18, 1797); *Die Opera buffa*, comic opera (Vienna, 1798); *Don Coribaldi ossia L'usurpata prepotenza*, drama (Dresden, 1798?); *Ein Stück mit kleinen Liedern*, opera based on *Frau Sybilla trinkt keinen Wein* and *Das Reich der Toten*; comic opera version based on *Amore in musica* (Grosswardein, 1767?; not extant); etc. ORCH.: A great number of syms. have been attributed to Dittersdorf, with over 100 being most likely by him. Most famous are the 12 syms. on Ovid's *Metamorphoses*; only Nos. 1–6 are extant, although Nos. 7–12 have survived in arrangements for Piano, 4-Hands, by Dittersdorf. He also composed many concertos, including 18 for violin, 3 for 2 violins, 1 for cello, 5 for viola, 4 for oboe, 5 for harpsichord, and 1 for flute. CHAMBER: 15 divertimentos, including *Il combattimento dell'umane passioni*; 4 string serenades

(with 2 horns); numerous string quartets; many sonatas for 4-Hands; preludes; etc. VOCAL: O r a t o r i o s : *Isacco, figura del redentore* (Grosswardein, 1766); *Il Davide nella Valle di Terebintho (Davidde penitente)* (Johannisberg, 1771); *L'Esther ossia La Liberatrice del popolo giudaico nella Persia* (Vienna, Dec. 19, 1773); *Giobbe (Hiob)* (Vienna, April 8–9, 1786). O t h e r : Several cantatas, both sacred and secular; masses; offertories; graduals; motets; etc.

WRITINGS: "Briefe über Behandlung italienischer Texte bei der Composition," *Allgemeine musikalische Zeitung* (Leipzig, 1799); an autobiography publ. as *K. v. D.s Lebensbeschreibung, Seinem Sohne in die Feder diktiert* (Leipzig, 1801; Eng. tr., London, 1896; new ed. by N. Miller, Munich, 1967).

BIBL.: C. Krebs, *D.iana* (Berlin, 1900); K. Holl, *Carl D. v. D.s Opern für das wiederhergestellte Johannisberger Theater* (diss., Univ. of Bonn, 1913); H. Kralik, *Carl D. v. D.s Symphonien und Konzerte* (diss., Univ. of Vienna, 1913); M. Grave, *D.'s First-movement Form as a Measure of His Symphonic Development* (diss., N.Y.U., 1977); H. Unverricht, *Carl D. v.D. 1739–1799: Der Schlesische Opernkomponist* (Würzburg, 1991); H. Unverricht, ed., *C. D. v. D.: Leben, Umwelt, Werk* (Tutzing, 1997).—NS/LK/DM

Dittrich, Paul-Heinz, German composer and teacher; b. Gornsdorf, Dec. 4, 1930. He studied composition at the Leipzig Hochschule für Musik (1951–56; diploma, 1958), and then attended Wagner-Régeny's master classes at the Academy of Arts in East Berlin (1958–60). From 1960 to 1976 he taught at the Hanns Eisler Hochschule für Musik in East Berlin, returning there as a prof. of composition in 1990. In 1991 he founded the Bandenburgische Colloquium für Neue Musik in Zeuthen. In 1976 he won the UNESCO Rostrum of Composers Prize, in 1978 the Hanns Eisler Prize of Berlin, and in 1990 the Berlin Music Critics Prize. He received the Artist's Prize in 1981 and the National Prize in 1988 of the German Democratic Republic. In 1983 he became a member of the Academy of Arts in East Berlin, and in 1998 of the Academy of Arts "Saxonia" in Dresden. His works astutely utilize modern forms and technical idioms while observing and preserving the pragmatic elements of instrumental and vocal writing.

WORKS: CHAMBER O p e r a : *Zerbrochene Bilder* (1998). ORCH.: *Passacaglia* (1955); *Divertimento* for Chamber Orch. (1959); *9 Pieces* (1960); Cello Concerto (1974–75; Berlin, Feb. 24, 1976); *Cantus I* (1975; Hamburg, Dec. 20, 1977); *Illuminations* (1976; Royan, April 3, 1977); *Concert avec plusieurs instruments* No. 2 for Viola, Cello, and 2 Orch. Groups (1977–78; Metz, Nov. 18, 1978), No. 3 for Flute, Oboe, Orch., and Live Electronics (1978–79; Dresden, May 31, 1979), No. 4 for Piano and Orch. (1983; Warsaw, Sept. 25, 1984), No. 6 for Oboe and Chamber Orch. (1985; Berlin, Nov. 15, 1991), and No. 8 for Cello and Chamber Orch. (1992); *Etym* (1981–82; Leipzig, Oct. 2, 1984). CHAMBER: Violin Sonata (1954); 4 string quartets (1958–59; 1982; 1987; 1991–92); *Kammermusik I* for Flute, Oboe, Clarinet, Bassoon, Piano, and Tape (1970), *II* for Oboe, Cello, Piano, and Tape (1973), *V* for Wind Quintet and Live Electronics (1976–77), *VI* for Oboe, Engish Horn, Trombone, Viola, Cello, Double Bass, Piano, and Percussion (1980), *VIII* for Oboe, Cello, and Piano (1988), *IX* for Flute, Clarinet, Cello, Harpsichord, Speaker, and Tape (1988), *X* for Flute, Bass Clarinet, and Piano (1989), *XII* for Flute, Cello, and Piano (1997), and *XIII* for Oboe, Cello, and Piano (1997); *Concert avec plusieurs instruments* No. 1 for Harpsichord and 7 Instruments (1976) and No. 5 for Flute and 7 Cellos (1984); String Trio (Berlin, Dec. 3, 1995); *Pierre de*

Coeur for Chamber Ensemble (1997; Dresden, Oct. 2, 1998). VOCAL: *Memento vitae* for Baritone, 12 Vocalists, 4 Choral Groups, and Percussion (1971–73); *Vokalblätter* for Soprano and 12 Vocalists (1972–73); *Areae Sonantes* for 3 Vocal Groups and Orch. (1972–73); *Kammermusik III* for Baritone and Wind Quintet (1974), *IV* for Soprano, 7 Instruments, and Live Electronics (1977), *VII* for 5 Speakers, Wind Quintet, and Harpsichord (1985), and *XI* for Soprano, Cello, Piano, and Wind Quintet (1990); *Laudatio Pacis* for Reciter, 4 Soloists, Chorus, and Vocal Ensemble (1975; Berlin, Oct. 3, 1993; in collaboration with S. Gubaidulina and M. Kopelent); *Cantus II* for Soprano, Cello, Orch., Tape, and Live Electronics (1977); *Engfürung* for 6 Vocalists, 6 Instrumentalists, Orch., Live Electronics, and Tape (Donaueschingen, Oct. 16, 1981); *Memento mori* for Baritone, Double Chorus, and Percussion (1985; Stuttgart, March 15, 1988); *Spiel* for 3 Speakers, 3 Singers, 11 Instrumentalists, and Live Electronics (1986–87; Berlin, Nov. 17, 1987); *Hymnischer Entwurf* for Speaker and Orch. (1987; Dresden, June 10, 1989); *Concert avec plusieurs instruments* No. 7 for Oboe, Trombone, Cello, 2 Pianos, 4 Speakers, 4 Percussion, and Chamber Orch. (1989); *Menetekel* for Soprano, Tenor, Speaker, 8 Vocalists, and 6 Instruments (Berlin, Nov. 4, 1993); *Dies irae* for Soloist, Chorus, and Orch. (1994–95; Stuttgart, Aug. 16, 1995); *Fahlstimmig* for Soprano, 3 Women's Voices, and Chamber Ensemble (Berlin, Dec. 3, 1995); *Der Glücklose Engel* for Soprano and Ensemble (N.Y., Nov. 21, 1997).—**NS/LK/DM**

Divitis (de Ryche, le Riche), Antonius (Antoine), celebrated Flemish composer; b. Louvain, c. 1475; d. after 1526. He was a singer and choirmaster at St. Donatien in Bruges (Brugge) from 1501 to 1504. In 1504–05 he was choirmaster at St. Rombaut in Malines, and then was in the service of Philippe le Beau in Brussels. From 1506 to 1515 he was a chapel singer to Louis XII.

WORKS: Motets and chansons are scattered in collections, e.g., *Motetti de la corona* (1514), and others printed by Rhaw, Attaignant, etc. At Cambrai is a mass in MS; at Munich, 2 credos and a Salve Regina a 5; at Rome, *Quem dicunt homines* for 4 Voices.

BIBL.: W. Nugent, *The Life and Works of A. D.* (diss., North Tex. State Univ., 1970).—**NS/LK/DM**

Dixon, Bill (actually, **William Robert**), jazz trumpeter, composer; b. Nantucket, Mass., Oct. 5, 1925. He studied painting at Boston Univ. In 1959, while leading his own band in N.Y.C., he met Cecil Taylor and the two worked together for a few months. In 1960 he started to restrict himself to performing his own compositions; he worked intermittently with Archie Shepp in 1962–63. He formed the New York Contemporary Five with Shepp, John Tchicai, D. Moore, and J. C. Moses; Don Cherry later took Dixon's place. He became the artistic director in charge of the jazz catalogue for Savoy and gave opportunities to many younger artists. In 1964 Dixon promoted and presented a series of concerts at the Cellar Cafe in N.Y. that gave forums to then largely unknown players such as Roswell Rudd, Milford Graves, Paul Bley, and his own group, and to those who were always in need of exposure like Sun Ra. He formed the Jazz Composers Guild in late 1964 or 1965, which was a collective that intended to support musicians independently of clubs and booking agents.

Though the idea had widespread support and members including Taylor, Mike Mantler, Rudd, Tchicai, Sun Ra, and both Carla and Paul Bley, it didn't last. Dixon began a ten-year collaboration with dancer Judith Dunn in 1965; they presented multi-media events including free jazz and dance concerts at the 1966 Newport Jazz Festival. In 1967 while teaching art history elsewhere, he started a music education program at N.Y.'s "University of the Streets," the first neighborhood project of its kind. He has been a full-time teacher since 1968, at Univ. of Wisc. at Madison, then Bennington Coll., Vt., where Dixon helped found a department of black music. He left Bennington in 1996, and has since taught as a guest professor at various universities. He went to Paris in 1976 for a week of concerts. In 1984, he was the recipient of a BMI "Jazz Pioneer" award. His compositions have since been presented at jazz festivals internationally. He has also continued to paint, with his artworks gracing many of his album covers, while he has also completed commissioned works and been an artist-in-residence worldwide.

DISC.: *Bill Dixon's 7-Tette* (1962); *Archie Shepp- Bill Dixon Quartet* (1962); *Jazz Artistry of Bill Dixon* (1966); *Collection* (1970); *In Italy, Vol. 1, 2* (1980); *November 1981* (1982); *Thoughts* (1985); *Sons of Sisyphus* (1988); *Vade Mecum* (1994).

BIBL.: Bill Dixon, *L' Opera: A Collection of Letters, Writings, Musical Scores, Drawings, and Photographs 1967–1986* (North Bennington, Vt., 1986); Ben Young, *Dixonia: A Bio-discography of Bill Dixon* (Westport, Conn., 1998).—**LP**

Dixon, (Charles) Dean, African American conductor; b. N.Y., Jan. 10, 1915; d. Zug, near Zürich, Nov. 3, 1976. He showed a musical talent as a child and began to take violin lessons. At the age of 17, he organized at his high school in the Bronx a group called the Dean Dixon Sym. Soc. He studied violin at the Juilliard School of Music in N.Y. (1932–36); on a conducting fellowship, he took lessons with Albert Stoessel at the Juilliard Graduate School (1936–39); also enrolled in academic classes at Columbia Univ. Teachers Coll., receiving an M.A. in 1939. On May 7, 1938, he made his professional conducting debut at N.Y.'s Town Hall; that same year, he also founded the N.Y. Chamber Orch. Eleanor Roosevelt became interested in his career, and helped him to obtain some conducting engagements, including an appearance with the N.Y. Phil. at the Lewisohn Stadium on August 10, 1941, making him the first of his race to conduct this orchestra. In 1944 Dixon organized the American Youth Orch., which had a limited success. In 1949 he went to Europe in the hopes of securing wider opportunities. These hopes were fully realized; he was engaged as music director of the Göteborg Sym. Orch. (1953–60), the Hessian Radio Sym. Orch. in Frankfurt am Main (1961–70), and the Sydney (Australia) Sym. Orch. (1964–67). Returning briefly to the U.S. in 1970, he was guest conductor for a series of N.Y. Phil. summer concerts in Central Park, then returned to Europe and settled in Switzerland in 1974. His career was cut short when he underwent open-heart surgery in 1975.—**NS/LK/DM**

Dixon, James, American conductor; b. Estherville, Iowa, April 26, 1928. He studied at the Univ. of Iowa

(B.M., 1952; M.M., 1956). He was conductor of the U.S. 7th Army Sym. Orch. in Germany (1951–54), the Univ. of Iowa Sym. Orch. in Iowa City (1954–59), and the New England Cons. of Music in Boston (1959–61). In 1962 he returned to the Univ. of Iowa Sym. Orch. as conductor; from 1965 he also served as conductor of the Tri-City Sym. Orch. in Davenport, Iowa, and Rock Island, Ill. In addition, he was assoc. conductor of the Minneapolis Sym. Orch. (1961–62). He was the recipient of the Gustav Mahler Medal in 1963.—NS/LK/DM

Dixon, Willie (James), American blues songwriter, bass player, and singer; b. Vicksburg, Miss., July 1, 1915; d. L.A., Jan. 29, 1992. Primarily known as a songwriter, Dixon helped to shape the recordings of a host of notable blues musicians, among them Muddy Waters and Howlin' Wolf, not only by writing the songs they sang but also by producing, arranging, and playing bass on their sessions for Chess Records and other labels. Nevertheless, it was Dixon's catalog of blues songs, including "I'm Your Hoochie Coochie Man," "The Seventh Son," and "Wang Dang Doodle," that became a basic repertoire for blues-based rock 'n' roll performers and made him a major influence on popular music from the 1950s on.

Dixon was the illegitimate son of Daisy McKenzie Dixon and, probably, Anderson "A. D." Bell. Between the ages of about 11 to 21, he wandered around the country, working at manual labor. He also wrote songs, and he became the bass singer in the Union Jubilee Singers, a gospel group that performed on local radio in Vicksburg in the early 1930s. He moved to Chicago in 1936 and was a professional boxer for a time. Around 1939 he learned to play bass and became a member of the group the Five Breezes, with whom he made his recording debut for Bluebird Records in November 1940. After Pearl Harbor he refused induction into the military, claiming conscientious-objector status, and spent a year dealing with the resulting legal complications. Around 1942 he formed The Four Jumps of Joy, who recorded for Mercury Records in 1945. In 1946 he formed The Big Three Trio, which also featured Leonard "Baby Doo" Caston on piano and Bernardo Dennis (later replaced by Ollie Crawford) on guitar. This group began recording for Columbia Records in 1947 and scored a Top Ten R&B hit in April 1948 with "You Sure Look Good to Me" (music and lyrics by Art Tatum and Joe Turner).

Dixon began working as a sideman on recording sessions during the second half of the 1940s. In November 1948 he played his first session for Aristocrat Records, which became Chess Records in 1950. By the end of the 1940s he had entered into a common-law marriage with Elenora Franklin, who bore him seven children. The Big Three Trio broke up after its final recording session in December 1952, and Dixon went to work at Chess as a salaried employee. He scored his first major success as a writer with Eddie Boyd's recording of "Third Degree" (music and lyrics also by Boyd), a Top Ten R&B hit in July 1953. Muddy Waters enjoyed the biggest hit of his career with Dixon's "I'm Your Hoochie Coochie Man," which reached the R&B Top Ten in

March 1954, followed into the Top Ten by Waters recordings of "Just Make Love to Me" (aka "I Just Want to Make Love to You") in June and "I'm Ready" in October. Dixon also began to write for Howlin' Wolf, penning "Evil," which the singer first recorded in May.

Dixon's most successful composition of 1955 was "My Babe," recorded by Little Walter and His Jukes (including Dixon on bass), which topped the R&B charts in April 1955. Though Dixon's own recording career was generally neglected during this period, his recording of his own "Walking the Blues" made the R&B Top Ten in September, along with an equally successful version by Jack Dupree and Mr. Bear. Another notable Dixon composition in 1955 was "The Seventh Son," initially recorded by Willie Mabon. In the mid-1950s, Dixon separated from his first common-law wife and began living with a second, Marie Booker, with whom he had five children.

Bo Diddley hit the R&B Top Ten in January 1956 with Dixon's "Pretty Thing"; Muddy Waters reached the R&B Top Ten in September with his "Don't Go No Farther." Dixon moved from Chess to Cobra Records, where he scored a Top Ten R&B hit with Otis Rush's recording of his "I Can't Quit You, Baby" in October. Starting in the late 1950s, Dixon's songs began to be recorded by rock 'n' roll performers. Elvis Presley cut "Doncha' Think It's Time" (music and lyrics also by Clyde Otis) for a Top Ten R&B hit and a Top 40 pop hit in May 1958, and Ricky Nelson revived "My Babe" on his Top Ten *Ricky Nelson* album in July 1958. In October, Muddy Waters had a Top Ten R&B hit back at Chess with Dixon's "Close to You."

Upon the demise of Cobra Records, Dixon formed a duo with blues pianist and singer Memphis Slim. They toured together and recorded a series of albums: *Willie's Blues* (1959) for Prestige/Bluesville; *Memphis Slim and Willie Dixon* (1959) and *At the Village Gate* (1960) for Folkways; and *The Blues Every Which Way* (1960) for Verve. Dixon went back to work at Chess, where he had a series of memorable songs recorded by Howlin' Wolf: "Back Door Man," "Spoonful," and "Wang Dang Doodle" in 1960; and "I Ain't Superstitious," "Little Red Rooster," and "You'll Be Mine" in 1961. "Spoonful" was also recorded at Chess by Etta (James) and Harvey (Fuqua), and their version reached the Top 40 of the R&B charts and was a pop chart entry in December 1960. Bo Diddley entered the pop charts and the Top 40 of the R&B charts with Dixon's "You Can't Judge a Book by the Cover" in August 1962, and the same year Muddy Waters recorded the notable Dixon compositions "You Need Love" and "You Shook Me" (music and lyrics also by J. B. Lenoir).

Dixon participated in the annual American Folk Blues Festival tours of Europe from 1962 to 1964, helping to spread the popularity of blues music. From this point on, both in the U.S. and the U.K., popular musicians began to revive Dixon's songs in earnest. Peter, Paul, and Mary reached the pop charts in December 1962 with "Big Boat," a Dixon composition recorded by the Big Three Trio in 1951 as "Tell That Woman." In January 1963, Sonny Boy Williamson recorded Dixon's "Bring It on Home." The Righteous Brothers revived

"My Babe" for a pop chart entry in September 1963, and in November Sam Cooke revived "Little Red Rooster" for a Top Ten R&B hit and a Top 40 pop hit. Dion revived "I'm Your Hoochie Coochie Man" for a pop chart entry in February 1964, and The Rolling Stones revived two Dixon songs: "I Just Want to Make Love to You" appeared on their gold-selling U.S. debut album, *England's Newest Hit Makers* in May (the chart-topping British equivalent, *The Rolling Stones*, had been released in April); and "Little Red Rooster" became a #1 hit in the U.K. in December, later appearing on the gold, Top Ten U.S. album *The Rolling Stones, Now!* in February 1965.

Johnny Rivers reached the pop Top Ten in June 1965 with a revival of "The Seventh Son." Dixon produced and sang backup vocals on Koko Taylor's revival of "Wang Dang Doodle" on the Chess subsidiary Checker Records; it reached the R&B Top Ten and the pop Top 40 in the spring of 1966. That August, Jimmy Smith reached the R&B and pop charts with his revival of "I'm Your Hoochie Coochie Man." The Doors' self-titled debut album, a multiplatinum Top Ten hit released in January 1967, featured their rendition of "Back Door Man." "I'm Your Hoochie Coochie Man" turned up on the gold, Top Ten self-titled debut album by Steppenwolf in February 1968, and in June, Cream put "Spoonful" on its chart-topping gold album *Wheels of Fire*.

Two Dixon compositions, "I Can't Quit You, Baby" and "You Shook Me," were on the Top Ten, multiplatinum self-titled debut album by Led Zeppelin, released in January 1969. Howlin' Wolf's revival of "Evil" made the R&B charts in April. Jose Feliciano put "Little Red Rooster" on his gold *Feliciano/10 to 23* album, released in June. The multiplatinum, chart-topping *Led Zeppelin II*, released in October, featured "Bring It on Home" and "Whole Lotta Love," which bore a similarity to Dixon's "You Need Love"; the latter also became a Top Ten gold single. Neither song was credited to Dixon, however, and legal action, leading to financial settlements, followed. Also in October, Willie Mitchell revived "My Babe" for an R&B Top 40 hit, and the following month Elvis Presley covered the same song on his gold *From Memphis to Vegas/From Vegas to Memphis* album.

Chess Records was sold to the tape manufacturer GRT in January 1969, after which Dixon's involvement with the label ended. He formed a touring group, the Chicago Blues All-Stars, and recorded an album of his best-known songs, *I Am the Blues*, released in 1970. He also started his own record label, Yambo, which released his next album, *Peace*, in 1971. He then cut *Maestro Willie Dixon and His Chicago Blues Band* for Spivey Records and *Catalyst* for Ovation, both of which were released in 1973; the latter earned him a Grammy nomination for Best Ethnic or Traditional Recording.

Meanwhile, Dixon's songs continued to attract popular covers. Humble Pie put "I'm Ready" on their gold *Performance—Rockin' the Fillmore* album, released in October 1971, and Foghat reached the charts with a revival of "I Just Want to Make Love to You" in October 1972. The Pointer Sisters scored a Top 40 R&B hit and a pop chart entry with their revival of "Wang Dang Doodle" in December 1973.

Dixon released a second album on Ovation, *What's Happened to My Blues?*, in 1976, and it earned him a second Grammy nomination for Best Ethnic or Traditional Recording. During 1977 he was hospitalized, suffering from diabetes, and one of his legs was amputated. Foghat reached the Top 40 in October with a live version of "I Just Want to Make Love to You."

Dixon returned to performing, and his appearance at Chicagofest in 1981 brought him a third Grammy nomination for Best Ethnic or Traditional Recording for the various-artists album *Blues Deluxe*. In 1983 he performed at the Montreux Jazz Festival, and the show was recorded by Pausa Records for the 1985 album *Live! Backstage Access*, which was a Grammy nominee for Best Traditional Blues Recording. The label had also released his April 1984 album *Mighty Earthquake and Hurricane*. Meanwhile, other musicians, from purveyors of country to heavy metal, continued to mine Dixon's catalog: Stevie Ray Vaughan and Double Trouble covered "You'll Be Mine" on their platinum *Soul to Soul* album in September 1985 and "Let Me Love You Baby" (originally recorded by Koko Taylor) on their multiplatinum *In Step* lbum in June 1989 (Buddy Guy also put the latter on his gold *Damn Right, I've Got the Blues* album in October 1991); Hank Williams Jr. sang "You Can't Judge a Book by the Cover" on his *Montana Café* album in July 1986; "I Ain't Superstitious" was on Megadeath's platinum *Peace Sells... But Who's Buying?* George Thorogood performed "I'm Ready" on his gold *Born to be Bad* album in January 1988.

Dixon signed to the Capitol Records subsidiary Bug and released *Hidden Charms* in September 1988; it won the Grammy Award for Best Traditional Blues Recording. He was nominated for the same award the following year for his final album, the soundtrack to the film *Ginger Ale Afternoon*, released by Varèse Sarabande. He died at 76 in 1992 of heart failure. But his songs continued to be influential: in September 1994, Eric Clapton put three Dixon songs—"I'm Your Hoochie Coochie Man," "Third Degree," and "Groaning the Blues"—on his all-blues album *From the Cradle*, which topped the charts and went multiplatinum.

WRITINGS: With D. Snowden, *I Am the Blues: The W. D. Story* (London, 1989).—**WR**

Dizi, François-Joseph, famous French harpist; b. Namur, Jan. 14, 1780; d. Paris, Nov. 1847. He set out for London when he was only 16. He lost his harp on the way but went on without it, and introduced himself to Érard, who gave him a harp and obtained pupils for him. Besides winning fame as a concert player and as a harpist at the principal theaters, he invented the "perpendicular harp" (which was unsuccessful), and composed sonatas, romances, variations, studies, etc., for his instrument. He also publ. *Ecole de Harpe, Being a Complete Treatise on the Harp* (London, 1827). In 1830 he went to Paris, and established a harp factory with Pleyel, which did not do well. There he was appointed harp teacher to the royal princesses.—**NS/LK/DM**

DJ Jazzy Jeff and the Fresh Prince, the duo that made hip-hop safe for middle-class pop fans.

MEMBERSHIP: Jeffery Townes, DJ (b. Philadelphia, Jan. 22, 1965); Willard C. Smith Jr., rapper (b. Philadelphia, Sept. 25, 1968).

Like Run-DMC, Will Smith and Jeffery Townes were raised in comfortable middle-class circumstances. Smith's dad was a refrigeration engineer and his mother worked for the school board. One of Smith's high school teachers dubbed him "the prince" for his ability to talk his way out of every situation.

Smith started rapping at around 12 years old, rhyming about what he knew on jams like "Girls Ain't Nothin' But Trouble." This minor hit helped propel their debut album, *Rock the House*, to gold status.

Their first major hit, "Parents Just Don't Understand" dealt with Smith going shopping for clothes with his mom. Middle-class kids could identify, and this safe-as-milk rap got the good housekeeping seal from those good housekeepers that took the time to listen. The single went gold, hitting #12 on the charts despite only rising to #19 in pop airplay. It also became the first rap record to win a Grammy Award, taking the first Best Rap Performance by a Duo or Group. The follow-up "Nightmare on My Street" went to #15. The following album, *He's the DJ, I'm the Rapper*, sold triple platinum and peaked at #4.

Their next album, *In This Corner*, had the minor hit "I Think I Can Beat Mike Tyson." While the single failed to chart pop, the album still went gold. *Homebase*, an album released in 1991, brought them back to the pop charts with the platinum "Summertime," which took them to the top of the R&B charts, hit #4 on the pop charts, and won them their second Grammy. The follow-up single, "Ring My Bell" went gold, hitting #20 despite getting virtually no airplay. *Homebase* also went platinum, hitting #4.

The group's biggest moneymaker, however, was their 900 phone number. Its success amazed even Smith, who noted that they made more from the 900 number in nine months than they did in five years as recording artists and performers.

Smith, who had a bit part in the 1986 film *The Image Maker*, had started acting in earnest by 1990. He was tapped to star in the television show *The Fresh Prince of Bel-Air*, which became a major hit; Townes made occasional appearances on the show, as well. However, Smith was already becoming a solo sensation. He had supporting roles in several other films, breaking through in the serious 1993 drama *Six Degrees of Separation*. He became big box office with the films *Bad Boys* (1995), *Independence Day* (1996), and *Men in Black* (1997). It is estimated his films have earned in excess of $1 billion. Smith contributed music to several of the films, including the title song for *Men in Black*, which won him a Grammy for Best Rap Solo Performance despite not hitting the pop charts. His rap for the 1999 film *The Wild Wild West*, which featured Dru Hill and Kool Mo Dee, did considerably better than the film, rising in the charts and going gold.

After six years without an album, Smith went into the studio under his own name and cut *Big Willie Style* in 1997. The album hit #8 on the charts and went sextuple platinum, powered by the hits "Miami" and the monster, chart-topping single "Gettin' Jiggy wit It," which went gold, and earned Smith yet another Best Rap Solo Performance at the Grammys. Clearly, Smith is an artist who can ply his talents in any number of directions.

DISC.: *Rock the House* (1987); *He's the D.J., I'm the Rapper* (1988); *And in This Corner...* (1989); *Homebase* (1991); *Code Red* (1993). **WILL SMITH:** *Big Willie Style* (1997); *Willennium* (1999).—**HB**

Dlabacž, Gottfried Johann (actually, Bohumír Jan Dlabač),

Bohemian music scholar; b. Cerhenice, near Český Brod, July 17, 1758; d. Prague, Feb. 4, 1820. He was librarian and choirmaster of the Premonstratensian monastery in Prague. He publ. a valuable reference work, *Allgemeines historisches Künstlerlexikon für Böhmen...* (three vols., 1815–18), and contributed articles to Riegger's *Materialien zur alten und neuen Statistik von Böhmen.*—**NS/LK/DM**

Dlugoszewski, Lucia,

innovative American composer, performer, teacher, and inventor; b. Detroit, June 16, 1931; d. N.Y., April 11, 2000. She studied piano with Agelageth Morrison at the Detroit Cons. (1940–46); after courses in physics at Wayne State Univ. in Detroit (1946–49), she went to N.Y. and studied analysis with Salzer at the Mannes Coll. of Music (1950–53); she also had lessons in piano with Grete Sultan and in composition with Varèse. The latter greatly influenced her, as did the N.Y. School of painters and poets. In an effort to expand her compositional parameters, she invented several instruments. Her most noteworthy creation was the so-called timbre piano (c. 1951), a revamped conventional piano activated by striking the strings with mallets, or having the strings bowed and picked. She became especially successful as a composer for the dance, and was closely associated with the Erick Hawkins Dance Co. From 1960 she was also with the Foundation for Modern Dance. In 1966 she received the National Inst. of Arts and Letters Award and in 1977 she became the first woman to receive the Koussevitzky International Recording Award for her *Fire Fragile Flight*.

WORKS: DRAMATIC: O p e r a : *Tiny Opera* (1953); *The Heidi Songs* (1970). **D a n c e :** *Openings of the Eye* (1952); *Here and Now with Watchers* (1954–57); *8 Clear Places* (1958–60); *Cantilever* (1964); *To Everyone Out There* (1964); *Geography of Noon* (1964); *Lords of Persia* No. 1 (1965), No. 2 (1968), and No. 3 (1971); *Dazzle on a Knife's Edge* (1966); *Tight Rope* (1968); *Agathlon Algebra* (1968); *Black Lake* (1969); *Of Love... Or He Is a Cry, She Is His Ear* (1971); *Angels of the Inmost Heaven* (1972); *Avanti* (1983); *The Woman Deunde Amor* (1984–85). Also incidental music and film scores. **ORCH.:** *Orchestra Structure for the Poetry of Everyday Sounds* (1952); *Orchestral Radiant Ground* (1955); *Arithmetic Points* (1955); *Flower Music for Left Ear in a Small Room* (1956); *Instants in Form and Movements* for Timbre Piano and Chamber Orch. (1957); *Suchness Concerto* for Orch. of Invented Percussion (1958–60); *4 Attention Spans* (1964); *Beauty Music 3* for Timbre Piano and Chamber Orch. (1965); *Quick Dichotomies* for 2 Trumpets, Clarinet, and Orch. of Invented Percussion (1965); *Naked Flight Nageire* for Chamber Orch. (1966); *Hanging Bridges* (1968; also for String Quartet); *Kitetail*

Beauty Music for Violin, Timbre Piano, and Orch. of Invented Percussion (1968); *Naked Swift Music* for Violin, Timbre Piano, and Orch. of Invented Percussion (1968); *Skylark Concert: An Evening of Music* for Chamber Orch. (1969–70); *Kireji: Spring and Tender Speed* (1972); *Tender Theatre Flight Nageire* for Brass Quintet and Percussion Orch. (1972–79); *Abyss and Caress* for Trumpet and Small Orch. (1975); *Amor New Tilting Night* for Chamber Orch. (1978); *Startle Transparent Terrible Freedom* (1981); *Quidditas Sorrow Terrible Freedom* (1983–84); *Duenda Amor* (1983–84). **CHAMBER:** Flute Sonata (1950); *Transparencies No. 1* for Harp (1952), *No. 2* for Flute (1952), *No. 3* for Harp and Violin (1952), and *No. 4* for String Quartet (1952); *Naked Wabin* for 6 Instruments (1956); *Flower Music* for String Quartet (1959); *Rates of Speed in Space* for Ladder Harp and Quintet (1959); *Delicate Accidents in Space* for Unsheltered Rattle Quintet (1959); *Concert of Man Rooms and Moving Space* for Flute, Clarinet, Timbre Piano, and 4 Unsheltered Rattles (1960); *Archaic Aggregates* for Timbre Piano, Ladder Harps, Tangent and Unsheltered Rattles, and Gongs (1961); *Beauty Music* for Clarinet, Percussion, and Timbre Piano (1965); *Suchness with Radiant Ground* for Clarinet and Percussion (1965); *Balance Naked Flung* for 5 Instrumentaliss (1966); *Naked Quintet* for Brass (1967); *Leap and Fall, Quick Structures* for 2 Trumpets, Clarinet, 2 Violins, and Percussion (1968); *Space Is a Diamond* for Trumpet (1970); *Swift Diamond* for Timbre Piano, Trumpet, and Invented Percussion (1970); *Velocity Shells* for Timbre Piano, Trumpet, and Invented Percussion (1970); *pure Flight Air* for String Quartet (1970); *Amor Elusive Empty August* for Woodwind Quintet (1979); *Cicada Terrible Freedom* for Flute, String Quintet, and Bass Trombone (1980–81); *Wilderness Elegant Tilt* for 11 Instruments (1981–84); *Quidditas* for String Quartet (1984–85). **VOCAL:** *Fire Fragile Flight* for Voice and Orch. (1973).—**NS/LK/DM**

Doane, William H(oward),
American hymn writer; b. Preston, Conn., Feb. 3, 1832; d. South Orange, N.J., Dec. 24, 1915. He served as a clerk and later entered the manufacturing business. He composed more than 2,000 gospel songs and a Christmas cantata, *Santa Claus*. His hymn *Pass Me Not* was popular.—**NS/LK/DM**

Döbber, Johannes,
German composer; b. Berlin, March 28, 1866; d. there, Jan. 26, 1921. He was a pupil, in the Stern Cons. in Berlin, of R. Radecke, L. Bussler (composition), and C. Agghazy (piano). He taught the first piano class in the Kullak Cons. in Berlin. After serving as Kapellmeister at Darmstadt, he was at Coburg-Gotha as tutor in music to Princess Beatrice. He was a teacher and music critic of the Volkszeitung in Berlin (1908).

WORKS: DRAMATIC: Opera: *Die Strassensängerin* (Gotha, 1890); *Der Schmied von Gretna-Green* (Berlin, 1893); *Dolcetta* (Brandenburg, 1894); *Die Rose von Genzano* (Gotha, 1895); *Die Grille* (Leipzig, 1897); *Die drei Rosen* (Coburg, 1902); *Der Zauberlehrling* (Braunschweig, 1907); *Die Franzosenzeit* (Berlin, 1913). **Operetta:** *Die Millionenbraut* (Magdeburg, 1913); *Des Kaisers Rock* (Berlin, 1915). **Song-play:** *Fahrende Musikanten* (Magdeburg, 1917). **OTHER:** Sym.; piano pieces; over 60 songs; quartets, duets, etc.—**NS/LK/DM**

Dobbs, Mattiwilda,
black American soprano and teacher; b. Atlanta, July 11, 1925. She was educated at Spelman Coll. in Atlanta (B.A., 1946) and at Columbia Univ. (M.A., 1948); pursued vocal training with Lotte Leonard in N.Y. (1946–50) and Bernac in Paris (1950–52). In 1948 she won the Marian Anderson scholarship contest and made her debut as a concert artist; in 1951 she won 1st prize in singing in the Geneva Competition. After appearing in opera and recitals in Holland (1952), she sang at Milan's La Scala, the Glyndebourne Festival, and London's Covent Garden (1953). In 1955 she appeared at the San Francisco Opera; on Nov. 9, 1956, she made her Metropolitan Opera debut in N.Y. as Gilda. In 1957 she made her first appearance at the Royal Swedish Opera in Stockholm; also sang at the Hamburg State Opera (1961–63; 1967). In addition to her operatic and concert engagements in the U.S. and Europe, she toured in Australia, New Zealand, and Israel. She was a visiting prof. at the Univ. of Tex. in Austin (1973–74), then was a prof. at the Univ. of Ill. (1975–76), the Univ. of Ga. (1976–77), and Howard Univ. in Washington, D.C. (from 1977).—**NS/LK/DM**

Dobiáš, Václav,
Czech composer; b. Radčice, near Semily, Sept. 22, 1909; d. Prague, May 18, 1978. He studied violin and composition at the Prague Cons., where he also took courses in microtonal music with A. Hába, and wrote a *Lento* for three Harps (1940) and a Violin Concerto (1941) making use of quarter tones. After 1945 he became involved in the political problems of musical education; in conformity with the ideology of the Communist Party, he began to write music for the masses in the manner of socialist realism; in 1958 he was elected to the Central Committee of the Communist Party and was a member of the National Assembly from 1960 to 1969.

WORKS: ORCH.: Chamber Sym. (1939); 2 numbered syms. (1943, 1956–57); Sinfonietta (1946–47; rev. 1962); Sonata for Piano, Wind Quintet, Strings, and Timpani (1947); *The Grand Procession*, symphonic poem (1948). **CHAMBER:** 4 string quartets (1931, 1936, 1938, 1942); Violin Sonata (1936); Cello Sonata (1939); *Říkadla* (Rhymes) for 9 Instruments (1938); *Pastoral Wind Quintet* (1943); *4 Nocturnes* for Cello and Piano (1944); *Quartettino* for String Quartet (1944); *Dance Fantasy* for 9 Instruments (1948). **Piano:** 2 sonatas (1931, 1940). **VOCAL:** Cantatas; mass choruses; songs.

BIBL.: J. Štilec, *V. D.* (Prague, 1985).—**NS/LK/DM**

Dobos, Kálmán,
Hungarian composer and pianist; b. Szolnok, July 22, 1931. Although he became blind in 1945, he began his training in music that same year. He studied composition with Viski at the Budapest Academy of Music (graduated, 1957). From 1958 he made tours as a pianist, and also worked in the music dept. of the Hungarian Radio.

WORKS: DRAMATIC: Incidental music to radio plays and films. **ORCH.:** Sym. (1957); *3 Hungarian Dances* (1964); *Hangjelenségek* (Sound Phenomena; 1968). **CHAMBER:** Cello Sonata (1956); *Adagio and Fugue* for String Quartet (1959); *2 Movements* for Violin, Cello, and Piano (1960); *Musica da camera* for Violin and Piano (1962); String Trio (1963); *Megnyilatkozások* (Manifestations) for String Quartet, Piano, and Percussion (1969); *Belső mozdulatok* (Inner Movements) for Clarinet, Piano, and Percussion (1970); *Vetületek* (Projections) for 4 Percussionists (1975); Sonatina for 2 Horns (1976); *Összefüggések* (Connections) for Cello, Piano, and Percussion (1985); Chamber Concerto for Cello and Ensemble (1993); *Passacaglia* for Trumpet and Organ (1996). **KEYBOARD: P i a n o :** Sonata (1957); *Meditation* (1964); *Variations on a Hungarian Folk Song* (1972); *Ringató* (Rocking; 1972). **O r g a n :** *Variations and Fugue* (1974); *Variáciok Szent István emlékére* (Variations in Memory of St. Stephen; 1988); *Introduction, Variations, and Fugue on a Melody of the Geneva-Psalm No. 103* (1990). **VOCAL:** *Emlékezés* (Remembrance) for Voice and Orch. (1959); *Villanások* (Flashes) for Soprano, Violin, Cello, and Piano (1963); *Hungarian Folk Songs from Moldavia* for Mezzo-soprano and Chamber Ensemble (1974); *Whitsun Variations*, cantata (1984); *Mysterium*, cantata for Baritone and Percussion (1995); sacred and secular choral works; songs.—NS/LK/DM

Döbricht, Johanna Elisabeth, German soprano; b. Weissenfels, Sept. 16, 1692; d. Darmstadt, Feb. 23, 1786. Her parents were the singers Daniel Döbricht (1650–94) and Katharina Elisabeth Grosse. She studied in Weimar with Christoph Alt. After singing at the Leipzig Opera, she became a court and church singer in Darmstadt. She also made tours as a concert artist. In 1740 she was granted a pension by the Darmstadt court, but she continued to appear in public for many years thereafter. In 1713 she married **Ernst Christian Hesse.** —NS/LK/DM

Dobronić, Antun, Croatian composer and teacher; b. Jelsa, island of Hvar, April 2, 1878; d. Zagreb, Dec. 12, 1955. He studied music with Novák in Prague, then returned to Yugoslavia, and in 1921 was appointed a prof. at the Zagreb Cons. He wrote many stage works, among them the operas *Ragusean Diptych, The Man of God, Mara, Dubrovnički triptihon* (1925), *Udovica Rozlinka* (1934), *Rkac* (1938), and *Goran* (1944). He also wrote a ballet, *The Giant Horse,* 8 syms., 2 symphonic poems: *Au long de l'Adriatique* (1948) and *Les Noces* (1949), chamber music in the national style, including a Piano Quintet, subtitled *Bosnian Rhapsody,* and 5 string quartets, choruses, and songs.—NS/LK/DM

Dobrowen, Issay (Alexandrovich) (real name, Ishok Israelevich Barabeichik), distinguished Russian conductor; b. Nizhny- Novgorod, Feb. 27, 1891; d. Oslo, Dec. 9, 1953. His orphaned mother was adopted by Israil Dobrovel; Issay Dobrowen changed his legal name, Dobrovel, to Dobrowein, and later to Dobrowen. He studied at the Nizhny-Novgorod Cons. as a small child (1896–1900), then entered the Moscow Cons. and studied with Igumnov (piano) and Taneyev (composition). Dubrowen went to Vienna for additional training with Godowsky (piano). Returning to Moscow, he made his conducting debut at the Kommisarzhevsky Theater in 1919; he then conducted at the Bolshoi Theater (1921–22). In 1922 he led the Dresden State Opera in the German premiere of Mussorgsky's opera *Boris Godunov;* he subsequently conducted at the Berlin Volksoper (1924–25) and the Sofia Opera (1927–28). In 1931 he made his American debut conducting the San Francisco Sym. Orch. And was guest conductor with the Minneapolis Sym. Orch., the Philadelphia Orch., and the N.Y. Phil. He was a regular conductor of the Budapest Opera from 1936 to 1939; at

the outbreak of World War II he went to Sweden, where he won his greatest successes as conductor and producer at the Stockholm Royal Theater (1941–45). From 1948 he conducted at La Scala in Milan. In 1952 he conducted at London's Covent Garden. He was a prolific composer, writing several piano concertos and pieces for piano solo in a Romantic vein as well as an orch. fairy tale, *1,001 Nights* (Moscow, May 27, 1922). —NS/LK/DM

Dobrowolski, Andrzej, Polish composer and teacher; b. Lwów, Sept. 9, 1921; d. Graz, Aug. 8, 1990. He studied organ, clarinet, and voice at the Warsaw Cons., then composition with Malawski and theory with Lobaczewska at the Kraków State Coll. of Music (1947–51). He taught at the Warsaw State Coll. of Music (1954–75), then was a prof. of composition at the Graz Hochschule für Musik (from 1976), serving as head of its faculty of composition, theory, and conducting (from 1980). His music is a paradigm of modern structuralism and textural abstraction.

WORKS: ORCH.: *Symphonic Variations* (1949); *Overture* (1950); Bassoon Concerto (1953); Sym. No. 1 (1955); *Music for Strings and 4 Groups of Wind Instruments* (1964); *Music for Strings, 2 Groups of Wind Instruments, and 2 Loudspeakers* (1967); *Music 1* (1968), *2: Amar* (1970), *3* (1972–73), *4: A-La* (1974), *5: Passacaglia* (1978–79), and *6* (1981–82); *Music for Chamber Orch.* (1982–83); *Music for Orch. and Oboe* (1984–85); *Flütchen* for Chamber Ensemble and Reciter (1986). **OTHER:** Trio for Oboe, Clarinet, and Bassoon (1956); Studies for Oboe, Trumpet, Bassoon, and Double Bass (1959); *Passacaglia from 40 to 5,* electronic music (1959); *Music for Tape No. 1* (1962); *Music for Tape and Oboe* (1965); *Krabogapa* for 4 Instruments (1969); *Music for Tape and Piano* (1971); *Music for Chorus, 2 Groups of Winds, Double Basses, and Percussion* (1975); *Music for Tape and Double Bass* (1977); *Music for 3 Accordions, Mouth Harmonicas, and Percussion* (1977); *Music for Tape and Clarinet* (1980); *Musik für Grazer Bläserkreis* for 8 Trumpets, 8 Horns, 8 Trombones, and Percussion (1984).—NS/LK/DM

Dobrzynski, Ignacy Felix, Polish pianist and composer; b. Romanov, Volhynia, Feb. 15, 1807; d. Warsaw, Oct. 10, 1867. The son of composer Ignacy Dobrzynski (b. Warsaw, Feb. 2, 1779; d. there, Aug. 16, 1841), he was taught by his father, then, being a fellow pupil and close friend of Chopin, by Chopin's teacher Elsner. On subsequent pianistic tours to Leipzig, Dresden, and Berlin (1845–47), he had great success. For a time he directed opera in Warsaw, where he finally settled. He wrote an opera, *Monbar or The Filibuster* (1838; Warsaw, Jan. 10, 1863); *Symphonie caractéristique;* String Sextet; two string quintets; three string quartets; Piano Trio; Violin Sonata; a nocturne for Violin and Piano, *Les Larmes;* mazurkas for piano; songs. His son Bronislaw Dobrzynski publ. a monograph on him (Warsaw, 1893).—NS/LK/DM

Doche, Joseph-Denis, French organist, conductor, and composer; b. Paris, Aug. 22, 1766; d. Soissons, July 20, 1825. He was a chorister at the Cathedral of Meaux, then organist at Coutances in Normandy. He played string instruments in a theater orch. in Paris from 1794 until 1810, then became a conductor, retiring in 1823. He wrote numerous successful vaudevilles, as well as the operas *Point de bruit, ou Le Contrat simulé* (Paris, Oct. 25, 1802) and *Les Deux Sentinelles* (Paris, Sept. 27, 1803).—NS/LK/DM

Dodds, Baby (actually, **Warren**), famed New Orleans jazz drummer, brother of Johnny Dodds; b. New Orleans, La., Dec. 24, 1898; d. Chicago, Ill., Feb. 14, 1959. He gained his nickname through being the youngest of six children. While doing day work in a sack-making factory (1912), he took first drum lessons from Dave Perkins and later studied with Walter Brundy and Louis Cottrell Sr. He did occasional parade work with Bunk Johnson, but had his first regular gigs with Willie Hightower's American Stars. Played for a while at Fewclothes Cabaret, then did a spell with Manuel Manetta at The Casino before returning to Fewclothes. He worked with Frankie Dusen's Eagle Band, then with Papa Celestin, before joining Fate Marable on the S.S. Sydney in the autumn of 1918. He remained with Marable until September 1921, then returned to New Orleans. King Oliver—then in San Francisco—sent for the young musician, and he joined the band on the road. Dodds moved to Chicago with Oliver in 1922, but left the band by late 1923. Early in 1924, he worked in Honore Dutrey's Band at Dreamland, then played at Kelly's Stables with Freddie Keppard and Johnny Dodds. During the period 1925–30 played for various leaders in Chicago including: Willie Hightower, Lil Armstrong, Ralph Brown, Charlie Elgar, Hugh Swift, etc. He worked regularly at Kelly's Stables with Johnny Dodds from 1927–29 and also did extensive freelance recordings, including sessions with Louis Armstrong, Jelly Roll Morton, and many others. He performed briefly with Dave Peyton at Club Baghdad (December l927 to January l928). Throughout the 1930s he played many residencies in Chicago with small groups led by Johnny Dodds, and also helped his brother Bill run a taxi service. From 1936 to 1939 he worked on and off as house drummer at The Three Deuces, Chicago. In January 1940 played at 9750 Club with his brother Johnny's band. Trouble with his teeth forced Johnny to leave, and Baby became the band's leader until the end of the residency in March 1940. He continued to work in Chicago through the mid-1940s, working with various musicians. He recorded with Bunk Johnson in 1944, and worked with Bunk the following year, including his first visit to N.Y. in September 1945. After briefly returning to Chicago, he was back in N.Y. working with Art Hodes in 1946–47, and was regularly featured on Rudi Blesh's *This Is Jazz* radio series. Dodds traveled to Europe in February 1948 to play at the Nice Festival with Mezz Mezlrow, did a brief tour, then returned to the U.S. He returned to working with Art Hodes in N.Y. (April–September 1948), but then returned to Chicago to work at Beehive Club with Miff Mole from late 1948 to March 1949. While visiting N.Y. in spring 1949, he suffered a stroke; while recuperating he played occasionally with a band led by trombonist Conrad Janis. He had a second stroke in spring 1950, but resumed playing the following year. He worked with Natty Dominique in 1951 and 1952 (sharing drum duties with Jasper Taylor), and also

visited N.Y. in 1951 and 1952. He played at Ryan's, N.Y., in December 1952, but was again taken ill and returned to Chicago to convalesce. In late 1954 he played again in N.Y. with the Dor Frye Trio at Ryan's, then returned to Chicago. By this time Baby was suffering from partial paralysis. He played occasionally until 1957, but was then forced to quit. He directly influenced Dave Tough and Gene Krupa.

DISC.: *Baby Dodds Drum Method: Trio* (1944); *Baby Dodds Drum Method: Band* (1945); *Footnotes to Jazz, Vol. 1* (1946); *Baby Dodds Drum Method: Solo* (1951).

BIBL.: Warren Dodds and Larry Gara, *The Baby Dodds Story* (Los Angeles, 1959).—JC/LP

Dodds, Johnny (actually, **John M.**), legendary New Orleans jazz clarinetist, sometime alto saxophonist, brother of Baby Dodds; b. New Orleans, La., April 12, 1892; d. Chicago, Ill., Aug. 8, 1940. One of six children, Johnny started on clarinet at 17; he was mainly self-taught but took lessons from Lorenzo Tio Jr, and Charlie McCurdy. He did day work until joining Kid Ory's band at the Come Clean club in Gretna (1911); he worked on and off with Ory until 1917, while also doing occasional parade work with Jack Carey and various other marching bands. He played for a short spell with Fate Marable on the S.S. *Capitol* riverboat, then left New Orleans to tour with Billy and Mary Mack's Merrymakers Show (1917–18). In 1919, he returned to New Orleans and briefly rejoined Kid Ory, then went to Chicago to join King Oliver. He was with King Oliver in Calif. and Chicago, then worked with Honore Dutrey at Dreamland cafe, Chicago (early 1924). He joined Freddie Keppard at Bert Kelly's Stables, Chicago (spring 1924), was later appointed leader at this venue, and played a residency there for almost six years (Keppard frequently returned to front the band). Dodds made prolific freelance recordings from 1924, including Louis Armstrong's Hot Fives and Hot Sevens, King Oliver, Jelly Roll Morton, and blues singers Ida Cox and Lovie Austin. He led his own small band at Chicago clubs throughout the 1930s. In January 1938 Dodds made his only trip to N.Y., to take part in a recording session. He quickly returned to Chicago to play residencies at Three Deuces, Club 29 (1938), and the Hayes Hotel. He suffered a severe heart attack in May 1939 but was back in action by Jan. 20, 1940 to begin a residency with his own quartet at the 9750 Club. However, soon afterwards he was again forced to quit playing because of trouble with his teeth. Within a few weeks he was equipped with new teeth and returned to play weekend dates at the same venue with Baby Dodds' Quartet until the residency ended in March 1940. From then until his death that August he played occasional gigs and made one recording session, but concentrated his energies on supervising the apartment block that he owned in Chicago.

DISC.: *Wild Man Blues* (1927); *Alligator Crawl* (1927); *S.O.L. Blues* (1927); *Johnny Dodds' Washboard Band* (1928); *Chicago Mess Around*; "*After You've Gone*" (1927); *Blue Clarinet Stomp* (1928); *Weary City* (1928); *Bull Fiddle Blues* (1928); *High Society Rag* (1928).—JC/LP

Dodge, Charles (Malcolm), American composer and teacher; b. Ames, Iowa, June 5, 1942. He studied composition with Hervig and Bezanson at the Univ. of Iowa (B.A., 1964), Milhaud at the Aspen (Colo.) Music School (summer, 1961), and Schuller at the Berkshire Music Center in Tanglewood (summer, 1964), where he also attended seminars given by Berger and Foss. He then studied composition with Chou Wenchung and Luening, electronic music with Ussachevsky, and theory with William J. Mitchell at Columbia Univ. (M.A., 1966; D.M.A., 1970). He was a teacher at Columbia Univ. (1967–69; 1970–77) and Princeton Univ. (1969–70); was assoc. prof. (1977–80) and prof. (1980–95) of music at Brooklyn Coll. and the graduate center of the City Univ. of N.Y. In 1993–94 and again from 1995 he served as a visiting prof. of music at Dartmouth Coll. He was president of the American Composers Alliance (1971–75) and the American Music Center (1979–82). In 1972 and 1975 he held Guggenheim fellowships. In 1974, 1976, 1987, and 1991 he held NEA composer fellowships. With T. Jerse, he publ. *Computer Music: Synthesis, Composition, and Performance* (N.Y., 1985).

WORKS: *Composition in 5 Parts* for Cello and Piano (1964); *Solos and Combinations* for Flute, Clarinet, and Oboe (1964); *Folia* for Chamber Orch. (1965); *Rota* for Orch. (1966); *Changes* for Computer Synthesis (1970); *Earth's Magnetic Field* for Computer Synthesis (1970); *Speech Songs* for Computer-Synthesized Voice (1972); *Extensions* for Trumpet and Computer Synthesis (1973); *The Story of Our Lives* for Computer-Synthesized Voice (1974; also for Videotape, 1975); *In Celebration* for Computer-Synthesized Voice (1975); *Palinode* for Orch. and Computer Synthesis (1976); *Cascando*, radio play by Samuel Beckett (1978); *Any Resemblance Is Purely Coincidental* for Piano and Computer-Synthesized "Caruso Voice" (1980); *Han motte henne i parken*, radio play by Richard Kostelanetz (1981); *He Met Her in the Park*, radio play by Richard Kostelanetz (1982); *Distribution, Redistribution* for Violin, Cello, and Piano (1983); *Mingo's Song* for Computer-Synthesized Voice (1983); *The Waves* for Soprano and Computer Synthesis (1984); *Profile* for Computer Synthesis (1984); *Roundelay* for Chorus and Computer Synthesis (1985); *A Postcard from the Volcano* for Soprano and Computer Synthesis (1986); *Song without Words* for Computer Synthesis (1986); *A Fractal for Wiley* for Computer Synthesis (1987); *Viola Elegy* for Viola and Computer Synthesis (1987); *Clarinet Elegy* for Bass Clarinet and Computer Synthesis (1988); *Wedding Music* for Violin and Computer Synthesis (1988); *Allemande* for Computer Synthesis (1988); *The Voice of Binky* for Computer Synthesis (1989); *Imaginary Narrative* for Computer Synthesis (1989); *Hoy (In His Memory)* for Voice and Computer Synthesis (1990); *The Village Child*, puppet theater (1992); *The One and the Other* for Chamber Orch. (1993; Los Angeles, April 11, 1994); *Concert Études* for Violin and Computer Synthesis (N.Y., April 12, 1994). —NS/LK/DM

Dodgson, Stephen (Cuthbert Vivian), English composer; b. London, March 17, 1924. He studied with R.O. Morris at the Royal Coll. of Music in London, where he subsequently taught (1965–82). He was also active as a broadcaster.

WORKS: DRAMATIC: O p e r a : *Margaret Catchpole* (1979). **ORCH.:** 2 concertos for Guitar and Chamber Orch. (1959, 1972); Bassoon Concerto (1969); Wind Sym. (1974); 7 *Essays* (1980–92); Clarinet Concerto (1983); *Capriccio Concertante: All Hallows' Eve* for Clarinet and Large Symphonic Wind Ensemble (1984); Trombone Concerto (1986); *Sinfonia: Troia-Nova* for Chamber Orch. (1989); Duo Concerto for Violin, Guitar, and Orch. (1990); *Flowers of London Town* for Symphonic Wind Ensemble (1990); *Marchrider* for Symphonic wind Ensemble (1990); Flute Concerto (1991); *Bandwagon* for Symphonic Wind Ensemble (1991); *The Rising of Job* for Chamber Orch. (1995); Concertino for 2 Guitars and Orch. (1998); *St. Elmo's Fire* for Symphonic Wind Ensemble (1998). **CHAMBER:** 2 string trios (1951, 1964); Suite for Wind Quintet (1965); 2 piano quintets (1966, 1999); 2 piano trios (1967, 1973); Cello Sonata (1968); Quintet for Guitar and String Quartet (1973); Trio for Oboe, Bassoon, and Piano (1973); 5 string quartets (1985, 1987, 1989, 1993, 1998); *Partita* for 10 Winds (1994); String Sextet (1996); *Pieces of Eight* for Wind Octet (1997); numerous solo works, including 6 piano sonatas (1959, 1975, 1983, 1988, 1992, 1994). **VOCAL:** *Cadilly* for 4 Singers and Wind Quintet (1968); *Te Deum* for Chorus (1972); *Magnificat* for Soloists and Orch. (1975); *The Innocents*, motet for Chorus (1975); *In Wilde America*, cantata for Soloists, Chorus, and 8 Instrumentalists (1977); *Epigrams from a Garden* for Contralto and Clarinet Choir (1977); *Sir John*, cantata for Chorus and Horn Trio (1980); *'tis Almost One*, sequence of anthems for Chorus and Organ (1984); *The Country Wedding* for Men's Chorus and Violin (1987); *Four Poems of Mary Coleridge* for Chorus and Flute (1987); *Missa Brevis* for Chorus (1991); *Lines from Hal Summers* for Chorus (1997); songs.—NS/LK/DM

Doebler, Curt, German organist, teacher, and composer; b. Kottbus, Jan. 15, 1896; d. Berlin, June 19, 1970. He studied organ with A. Dreyer. From 1919 to 1932 he was organist and choirmaster at the Catholic church in Charlottenburg; after occupying various positions as an organist and a teacher elsewhere, he returned to Charlottenburg (1950). In his music, Doebler attempted to establish a modern style based on Palestrina's polyphony. His numerous choruses enjoyed success in Germany in their day.—NS/LK/DM

Doese, Helena, Swedish soprano; b. Göteborg, Aug. 13, 1946. She received training in Göteborg and from Luigi Ricci in Rome and Erik Werba and Gerald Moore in Vienna. Following her operatic debut in 1971 as Aida in Göteborg, she sang with the Bern Opera. In 1974 she made her first appearance at the Glyndebourne Festival as Mozart's Countess and made her debut at London's Covent Garden as Mimi. From 1975 she made regular appearances at the Royal Opera in Stockholm, where her roles included Eva, Liù, Mimi, and Kát'a Kabanová. She made her U.S. debut in 1982 at the San Francisco Opera as Countess Almaviva. In 1987 she portrayed Agathe at the Berlin Deutsche Oper. In 1992 she was engaged as Ariadne in Stuttgart. She appeared as Chrysothemis in Frankfurt am Main in 1994. Among her other roles were Fiordiligi, Amelia Boccanegra, Sieglinde, the Marschallin, and Jenůfa.—NS/LK/DM

Doggett, Bill (actually, **William Ballard**), jazz/R&B pianist, organist, arranger; b. Philadelphia, Pa., Feb. 16, 1916; d. N.Y., Nov. 13, 1996. He played with the Jimmy Gorham Band from the mid-1930s. In 1938 he formed his own band with several of his colleagues; Lucky Millinder fronted the band for a 1938 tour (Doggett reputedly traded the entire outfit to Millinder for a soda). He played with Lucky Millinder until joining Jimmy Mundy in late 1939; in 1940 he returned to Millinder's band, and remained there until 1942. From the summer of 1942, he spent two years as pianist-arranger with The Ink Spots, and also arranged for Lionel Hampton, Count Basie, and the Louis Armstrong Big Band, among others. He was with Willie Bryant (1946) and with Louis Jordan from 1948. From 1951 he specialized on organ, leading his own small combo with great success throughout the 1950s and 1960s. His R&B combo signed with King in Cincinnati around 1953, churning out a slew of sizzling instrumentals, including one of the biggest-sellers of all time in 1956: the two-part "Honky Tonk," with Clifford Scott on tenor sax, guitar by Billy Butler linking choruses, and Doggett playing a boogie woogie-like slow shuffle on the organ. It was in the Top Ten in the U.S. for 14 weeks, and hit #1 on the R&B chart. Other hits were "Ram-Bunk-Shush" in 1957 and "Leaps and Bounds" in 1958 and the often-covered "Hold It." He scored seven Hot 100 hits until 1960, including "Slow Walk" (Sil Austin also had an R&B hit with this number). He arranged and conducted the album *Rhythm Is Our Business* for Ella Fitzgerald on Verve in 1963. That same year he toured France. He continued to tour and record through the 1970s, 1980s, and 1990s.

DISC.: *His Organ and Combo* (1955); *His Organ and Combo, Vol. 2* (1955); *Everybody Dance to the Honky Tonk* (1956); *Hot Doggett* (1957); *Salute to Ellington* (1958); *On Tour* (1959); *Bill Doggett Swings* (1962); *Impressions* (1963); *Honky Tonk Ala Mode* (1966); *Hampton, Lionel, Presents B.D.* (1977); *Mr. Honky Tonk* (1985).—JC/MM/LP

Döhl, Friedhelm, German composer and teacher; b. Göttingen, July 7, 1936. He was a pupil of Fortner at the Freiburg im Breisgau Hochschule für Musik (1956–64) and pursued his academic studies at the Univ. of Göttingen (Ph.D., 1966, with the diss. *Weberns Beitrag zur Stilwende der neuen Musik*; publ. in Munich, 1976). After lecturing at the Düsseldorf Hochschule für Musik (1965–68), he was principal lecturer (1969–72) and prof. (1972–74) at the Musicological Inst. of the Free Univ. in Berlin; then was founder-director of the studio for electronic music, for music and theater, and for non-European music at the Basel Academy of Music (1974–82). He served as a prof. of composition at the Lübeck Hochschule für Musik from 1983, and as its director from 1991. Döhl's earliest creative efforts were heavily influenced by Webern and Schoenberg; he later developed an innovative style notable for both exploration of color and experimental instrumentation.

WORKS: DRAMATIC: O p e r a : *Medea* (1987–90). B a l l e t : *Ikaros* (1977–78); *Fiesta* (1982). ORCH.: *Zorch*, concerto for 3 Open Pianos and Big Band (1972); Sym. for Cello and Orch. (1980–81); *Tombeau: Metamorphose* (1982–83); *Passion* (1984); *Winterreise* for Strings (1986; also for String Quintet, 1985); Sym. (Lübeck, April 26, 1998). CHAMBER: Duo for Violin and Piano (1961); *Varianti*, octet for Flute, Oboe, Clarinet, Bassoon, and String Quartet (1961); *Klangfiguren* for Wind Quintet (1962); *Canto W* for Flute (1962); *Oculapis: Reflexe* for Flute and Piano (1962); *Albumblatter* for 1 to 10 Flutes (1963); *Julianische Minuten* for Flute and Piano (1963); Toccata for Flute, Trumpet, Harpsichord, and Piano (1964); *Tappeto: Impressionen* for Cello and Harp (1967); *Pas de deux* for Violin and Guitar (1968); *Klang-Szene I* for 2 Electric Organs, Live Electronics, 4 Groups of Loudspeakers, Props, and Lights (1970) and *II* for 5 Ensembles, Live Electronics, Props, and Lights (1971); *Textur I* for Flute (1971); String Quartet (1971–72); *Sotto voce* for Flute, Cello, and Piano (1973); *Der Abend/Die Nacht* for Flute and Cello (1979); *Conductus* for 4 Percussion (1980); *5 Pieces* for Flute (1980); *2 Songs of Palamidi* for Flute and Guitar (1980); *Nachklänge* for Guitar (1981); *Ballet mécanique (Hommage à la laveuse inconnue)* for 2 Flutes, 2 Clarinets, Cello, Piano, and Percussion (1984); *Nachtfahrt* for Open Piano (Tape ad libitum) and Percussion (1984); *Winterreise*, string quintet (1985; also for String Orch., 1986); *Kadenz* for Cello (1986–87); *Missa (Medea- Interpolation)* for 2 Trombones and 3 Percussion (1989); *Posaunen im Raum (Medea-Material I)* for Trombone Ensemble (1990); *Flöten im Raum (Medea-Material II)* for Flute Ensemble (1990); *Medeas Lied* for Chamber Ensemble (1991); *Moin moin* for 7 Percussion and 4 Trombones (1993). KEYBOARD: P i a n o : 4 sonatas (1959, 1960, 1961, 1962); *Klangmodell I* and *II* (1971); *Textur II* (1971); *Cadenza* for 1 to 3 Open Pianos (1972); *Odradek* for 2 Open Pianos (1976); *8 Porträts* (1977–78); *3 Traumstücke* (1978); *7 Haiku* (1979); *Bruchstücke zur Winterreise* (1985); "*Und wenn die Stimme...*" (1986); *4 Bagatellen* (1989). O r g a n : *Improvisation I* (1962): *Fragment (Kyrie eleison)* (1980); *Gloria: Fragment II* (1986). VOCAL: *Hälfte des Lebens* for Chorus and Instruments (1959); *7 Haiku* for Soprano, Flute, and Piano (1963); *Fragment: Sybille* for Baritone, Flute, Viola, Cello, and Piano (1963); *Epitaph: Tich Yuang Tuc* for Soprano, Clarinet, and Chamber Ensemble (1963); *Melancolia: Magische Quadrate* for Soprano, Chorus, and Orch. (1967–68); "*...wenn aber...*": *9 Fragmente* for Baritone and Piano (1969); *Süll: Mikrodrama I* for Speaker, Flute, and Props (1972); *A & O (Textur III): Mikrodrama II* for Speaker, Microphone, Loudspeaker, Props, and Tape ad libitum (1973); *Anna K. Informationen über einen Leichenfund: Mikrodrama III* for Speaker, Tape, Bass Drum, and Cello (1974); *Szene über einen kleinen Tod* for Woman's Voice, Flute, and Cello, and Cymbal and Tape ad libitum (1975); *Unterwegs: 7 Stationen* for Soprano and Piano (1978); *Auf schmalem Grat*, Requiem for 6 Voices and Tam-tam (1978); *Itke-Songs* for Voice and Accordion, or Guitar, or Piano (1978); *Medea: Monolog* for Soprano and Chamber Orch. (1979–80).—NS/LK/DM

Döhler, Theodor (von), Austrian pianist and composer; b. Naples, April 20, 1814; d. Florence, Feb. 21, 1856. He was a pupil of Julius Benedict at Naples and of Czerny (piano) and Sechter (composition) at Vienna. In 1831 he became pianist to the Duke of Lucca; lived for a time in Naples; made brilliant pianistic tours from 1836 to 1846 in Germany, Italy, France, the Netherlands, and England; in 1843 went to Copenhagen, and then to Russia, and in 1846 to Paris; settled in Florence in 1848. In 1846 the Duke, his patron, ennobled him, and he married a Russian countess. He wrote an opera, *Tancreda*, which was performed posthumously in Florence in 1880, as well as many piano pieces, nocturnes, tarantellas, *12 études de concert, 50 études de salon*, variations, fantasias, and transcriptions.—NS/LK/DM

Dohnányi, Christoph von, eminent German conductor of Hungarian descent, grandson of **Ernst (Ernő) von Dohnányi**; b. Berlin, Sept. 8, 1929. He began to study the piano as a child; his musical training was interrupted by World War II. His father, Hans von Dohnányi, a jurist, and his uncle, Dietrich Bonhoeffer, the Protestant theologian and author, were executed by the Nazis for their involvement in the July 20, 1944, attempt on Hitler's life. After the war, he studied jurisprudence at the Univ. of Munich; in 1948 he enrolled at the Hochschule für Musik in Munich, and won the Richard Strauss Prize for composition and conducting. Making his way to the U.S., he continued his studies with his grandfather at Fla. State Univ. at Tallahassee; also attended sessions at the Berkshire Music Center at Tanglewood. Returning to Germany, he received a job as a coach and conductor at the Frankfurt am Main Opera (1952–57). Progressing rapidly, he served as Generalmusikdirektor in Lübeck (1957–63) and Kassel (1963–66), chief conductor of the Cologne Radio Sym. Orch. (1964–70), and director of the Frankfurt am Main Opera (1968–77). From 1977 to 1984 he was Staatsopernintendant of the Hamburg State Opera. In 1984 he assumed the position of music director of the Cleveland Orch., having been appointed music director designate in 1982, succeeding Lorin Maazel. In the meantime, he had engagements as a guest conductor of the Vienna State Opera, Covent Garden in London, La Scala in Milan, the Metropolitan Opera in N.Y., the Berlin Phil., the Vienna Phil., and the Concertgebouw Orch. in Amsterdam. In 1992 the Cleveland Orch., under Dohnányi's direction, became the resident orch. of the Salzburg Festival, the first time this honor was bestowed upon an American orch. On Dec. 12, 1993, he conducted Beethoven's 9th Sym. in a gala concert at Cleveland's Public Auditorium marking the 75th[th] anniversary of the founding of the Cleveland Orch. He also was principal guest conductor (1994–97) and principal conductor (from 1997) of the Philharmonia Orch. in London. From 1998 to 2000 he also was principal guest conductor and artistic director of the Orchestre de Paris. On Jan. 8, 2000, he conducted the Cleveland Orch. in the Gala Celebration Concert opening the refurbished Severance Hall, the ensemble's home. He concluded his tenure with the Cleveland Orch. in 2002. As both a sym. and opera conductor, Dohnányi has proved himself a master technician and a versatile musician capable of notably distinguished interpretations of all types of music, from Baroque to the avant-garde. He married **Anja Silja.—NS/LK/DM**

Dohnányi, Ernst (Ernő) von, eminent Hungarian pianist, composer, conductor, and pedagogue, grandfather of **Christoph von Dohnányi;** b. Pressburg, July 27, 1877; d. N.Y., Feb. 9, 1960. He began his musical studies with his father, an amateur cellist; then studied piano and theory with Károly Forstner. In 1894 he entered the Royal Academy of Music in Budapest, where he took courses in piano with Thomán and in composition with Koessler. In 1896 he received the Hungarian Millennium Prize, established to commemorate the thousand years of existence of Hungary, for his sym. He graduated from the Academy of Music in 1897, and then went to Berlin for additional piano studies with d'Albert. He made his debut in a recital in Berlin on Oct. 1, 1897; on Oct. 24, 1898, he played Beethoven's 4th Piano Concerto in London; then followed a series of successful concerts in the U.S. Returning to Europe, he served as prof. of piano at the Hochschule für Musik in

Berlin (1908–15). He then returned to Budapest, where he taught piano at the Royal Academy of Music; served briefly as its director in 1919, when he was appointed chief conductor of the Budapest Phil. In 1928 he became head of the piano classes at the Academy of Music; in 1934 he became its director. In 1931 he assumed the post of music director of the Hungarian Radio. As Hungary became embroiled in the events of World War II and partisan politics that invaded even the arts, Dohnányi resigned his directorship in 1941, and in 1944 he also resigned his post as chief conductor of the Budapest Phil. Personal tragedy also made it impossible for him to continue his work as a musician and teacher: both of his sons lost their lives; one of them, the German jurist Hans von Dohnányi, was executed for his role in the abortive attempt on Hitler's life; the other son was killed in combat. Late in 1944 he moved to Austria. At the war's end, rumors were rife that Dohnányi used his influence with the Nazi overlords in Budapest to undermine the position of Bartók and other liberals, and that he acquiesced in anti-Semitic measures. But in 1945 the Allied occupation authorities exonerated him of all blame; even some prominent Jewish-Hungarian musicians testified in his favor. In 1947–48 he made a tour of England as a pianist; determined to emigrate to America, he accepted the position of piano teacher at Tucuman, Argentina; in 1949 he became composer-in-residence at Fla. State Univ. in Tallahassee.

Dohnányi was a true virtuoso of the keyboard, and was greatly esteemed as a teacher; among his pupils were Solti, Anda, and Vázsonyi. His music represented the terminal flowering of European Romanticism, marked by passionate eloquence of expression while keeping within the framework of Classical forms. Brahms praised his early efforts. In retrospect, Dohnányi appears as a noble epigone of the past era, but pianists, particularly Hungarian pianists, often put his brilliant compositions on their programs. His most popular work with orch. is *Variations on a Nursery Song;* also frequently played is his Orch. Suite in F-sharp minor. Dohnányi himself presented his philosophy of life in a poignant pamphlet under the title *Message to Posterity* (Jacksonville, Fla., 1960).

WORKS: DRAMATIC: *Der Schleier der Pierrette,* pantomime (1908–09; Dresden, Jan. 22, 1910); *Tante Simona,* comic opera (1911–12; Dresden, Jan. 10, 1913); *A vajda tornya* (The Tower of the Voivod), opera (1915–22; Budapest, March 19, 1922); *Der Tenor,* comic opera (1920–27; Budapest, Feb. 9, 1929). **ORCH.:** 1 unnumbered sym. (1896; Budapest, June 3, 1897); 2 numbered syms.: No. 1 (1900–1901; Manchester, Jan. 30, 1902) and No. 2 (1943–44; London, Nov. 23, 1948; rev. 1953–56; Minneapolis, March 15, 1957); *Zrinyi,* overture (1896; Budapest, June 3, 1897); 2 piano concertos: No. 1 (1897–98; Budapest, Jan. 11, 1899) and No. 2 (1946–47; Sheffield, England, Dec. 3, 1947); *Konzertstück* for Cello and Orch. (1903–04; Budapest, March 7, 1906); Suite (1908–09; Budapest, Feb. 21, 1910); *Variationen über ein Kinderlied* for Piano and Orch. (1913; Berlin, Feb. 17, 1914, composer soloist); 2 violin concertos: No. 1 (1914–15, Copenhagen, March 5, 1919) and No. 2 (1949–50; San Antonio, Jan. 26, 1952); *Unnepi nyitány* (Festival Overture; 1923); *Ruralia hungarica* (Budapest, Nov. 17, 1924, composer conducting); *Szimfonikus percek* (Symphonic Minutes; 1933); *Suite en valse* (1942–43); Concertino for Harp and Chamber Orch. (1952);

American Rhapsody (1953; Athens, Ohio, Feb. 21, 1954, composer conducting). **CHAMBER:** 2 piano quintets (1895, 1914); 3 string quartets (1899, 1906, 1926); Cello Sonata (1899); *Serenade for String Trio* (1902); Violin Sonata (1912); Sextet for Piano, Clarinet, Horn, and String Trio (1935); *Aria* for Flute and Piano (1958); *Passacaglia* for Flute (1959). **Piano:** 4 Pieces (1896–97); Waltz for Piano, 4-Hands (1897); *Variations and Fugue on a Theme of E(mma) G(ruber)* (1897); *Gavotte and Musette* (1898); *Passacaglia* (1899); 4 rhapsodies (1902–03); *Winterreigen*, 10 bagatelles (1905); *Humoresken in Form einer Suite* (1907); 3 Pieces (1912); Fugue for Piano, Left-Hand or 2-Hands (1913); *Suite im alten Stil* (1913); 6 Concert Etudes (1916); *Variations on a Hungarian Folk Song* (1917); *Pastorale*, Hungarian Christmas song (1920); *Suite en valse* for 2 Pianos (1945); 6 Pieces (1945); *3 Singular Pieces* (1951); didactic pieces. **VOCAL:** *Magyar hiszekegy* (Hungarian Credo) for Tenor, Chorus, and Orch. (1920); *Missa in Dedicatione Ecclesiae* (Mass of Szeged) for Soloist, Chorus, Organ, and Orch., for the consecration of Szeged Cathedral (Szeged, Oct. 25, 1930); *Cantus vitae*, symphonic cantata (1939–41); *Stabat Mater* for 3 Soloists, Children's Chorus, and Orch. (1952–53; Wichita Falls, Tex., Jan. 16, 1956); songs.

BIBL.: V. Papp, *D. E.* (Budapest, 1927); M. Reuth, *The Tallahassee Years of E. v.D.* (diss., Fla. State Univ., 1962); B. Vázsonyi, *D. E.* (Budapest, 1971).—**NS/LK/DM**

Dohnányi, Oliver von, Czech conductor; b. Trencin, March 2, 1955. He received training in violin, conducting, and composition at the Bratislava Cons., and in conducting at the Prague Academy of Music and the Vienna Hochschule für Musik. From 1979 to 1986 he conducted the Slovak Radio Sym. Orch. in Bratislava, where he also served as principal conductor of the Slovak National Opera. He was music director of the National Theater in Prague from 1993 to 1996. He appeared as a guest conductor with many of the major European opera companies and orchs.—**NS/LK/DM**

Doire, René, French composer; b. Evreux, June 13, 1879; d. Paris, July 9, 1959. He studied in Rouen and later in Paris with Widor and d'Indy; he then was engaged as a bandleader in the casinos of various French spas. He composed an opera, *Morituri* (1903), *Vision d'Espagne* for Violin and Orch. (1916), *Dramatico* for Piano and Orch. (1923), Violin Sonata (1918), *Reflets de jeunesse*, song cycle for Voice and Piano or Orch. (1902), and solo songs.—**NS/LK/DM**

Dokshitcher, Timofei, Russian trumpeter and pedagogue; b. Nezhin, Dec. 13, 1921. He was a student in Moscow of Vassilenki and at the Gnessin Inst. of Vasilevski and Tabakov; he later studied conducting with Ginzburg at the Moscow Cons. (1952–57). From 1945 to 1983 he was principal trumpet in the orch. of the Bolshoi Theater in Moscow; he also pursued a solo career, and from 1971 served as a prof. at the Moscow Cons. In addition to championing the works of contemporary Russian composers, he also prepared transcriptions for his instrument.—**NS/LK/DM**

Doktor, Paul (Karl), distinguished Austrian-born American violist and pedagogue; b. Vienna, March 28, 1919; d. N.Y., June 21, 1989. He studied with his father,

Karl Doktor, violist of the renowned Busch Quartet. He graduated as a violinist at the Academy of Music in Vienna in 1938, but subsequently changed to viola, and in 1942 received the 1st prize at the Geneva Competition. From 1939 to 1947 he was solo violist of the Lucerne Orch. He emigrated to the U.S. in 1947, and in 1948 he made his U.S. debut at the Library of Congress in Washington, D.C. In 1952 he became a naturalized American citizen. In 1953 he was appointed to the faculty of the Mannes Coll. of Music in N.Y.; taught at the Philadelphia Musical Academy from 1970 and the Juilliard School from 1971. He commissioned several composers to write works for his instrument, including Walter Piston and Quincy Porter. He also prepared various transcriptions for viola and ed. a number of viola pieces by other composers.—**NS/LK/DM**

Doles, Johann Friedrich, German composer; b. Steinbach, April 23, 1715; d. Leipzig, Feb. 8, 1797. He studied theology in Leipzig, then became a pupil of Bach (1740–44), who recommended him for the post of cantor in Salzwedel. He instead became cantor in Freiberg, Saxony, in 1744. In 1743–44 he conducted a series of concerts in Leipzig that proved to be the precursor to the famous concerts of the Gewandhaus Orch. In 1756 he became cantor at the St. Thomas School in Leipzig. He was also director of the St. Thomas Church until 1789, when he resigned. He wrote a great number of sacred works.

BIBL.: H. Banning, *J.F. D.: Leben und Werke* (Leipzig, 1939).—**NS/LK/DM**

Dolin, Samuel (Joseph), Canadian composer and teacher; b. Montreal, Aug. 22, 1917. He received training in piano and theory in Montreal, and then pursued his education at the Univ. of Toronto (B.Mus., 1942). In 1945 he joined the staff of the Toronto Cons. of Music, where he studied composition with Weinzweig. He also studied piano and had lessons in composition with Krenek before completing his education at the Univ. of Toronto (D.Mus., 1958). Dolin continued to serve on the staff at the Cons. as a teacher for 50 years, founding its electronic music studio in 1966, and teaching composition in the Glenn Gould Professional School. He served as vice-president (1967–68) and president (1969–73) of the Canadian League of Composers, and also as chairman (1970–74) of the Canadian section of the ISCM. From 1972 to 1975 he was vice-president of the ISCM. In 1984 he was founding artistic director of the Canadian Contemporary Music Workshop. Dolin's music ranges widely in scope, from the traditional in manner to multimedia scores.

WORKS: DRAMATIC: *Casino (Greed)*, opera (1966–67); *Drakkar*, entertainment for Narrator, Mezzo-soprano, 2 Baritones, 2 Dancers, Chamber Ensemble, 2 Synthesizers, and Amplifiers (1972; Toronto, Feb. 17, 1973); *Golden Section: The Biography of a Woman* for Soprano, Dancer, Slides, Narrator, Lighting, and Orch. (1981); *Hero of Our Time* for Baritone, Men's Chorus, Dancers, and Orch. (1985). **ORCH.:** *Sinfonietta* (1950); *Serenade* for Strings (1951); 3 syms. (1956, 1957, 1976); *Isometric Variables (Bassooneries in Free Variations)* for Bassoon and Strings (1957); Sonata for Strings (1962); *Fantasy* for Piano and Chamber

Orch. (1967); Piano Concerto (1974); Accordion Concerto (1984); Concerto for Oboe, Cello, and Orch. (1989). **CHAMBER:** Violin Sonata (1960); *Portrait* for String Quartet (1961); *Georgian Bay*, concerto grosso for Percussion, Accordion, and Tape (1970); Sonata for Solo Accordion (1970); Sonata for Violin and Tape (1973); Sonata for Flute and Tape (1973); Sonata for Cello and Tape (1973); *Adikia* for 1 to 5 Accordions and Tape (1975); *Prelude, Interlude, and Fantasy* for Cello (1976); Duo Concertante for Free Bass Accordion and Guitar (1977); Cello Sonata (1978); Trio for Violin, Cello, and Piano (1980); *Blago's Trio* for Flute, Clarinet, and Bassoon (1980); *Sonata Fantasia* for Baroque Flute and Fortepiano (1980); Brass Quintet (1981); *Psalmody* for Oboe (1982); *2 Vocalises* for 2 Cellos (1990); *Variables* for Cello and Piano (1994). **P i a n o :** *4 Miniatures* (1943); *3 Preludes* (1949); Sonata (1950); *Little Suite* (1954); *Little Toccata* (1959); Sonatina (1959); *Slightly Square Round Dance* (1966); *If* (1972); *Prelude for John Weinzweig* (1973); *Queekhoven and A. J.* (1975); *Y Not* (1995). **V O C A L :** 3 song sets (1951); *Chloris* for Voice and Piano (1951); *The Hills of Hebron* for Chorus and Piano (1954; also for Men's Chorus and Piano, 1999); *Marchbankantata* for Baritone, Chorus, Piano, and Synthesizer (1971); *Mass* for 6 Voices, Congregation, and Organ (1972); *Deuteronomy XXXII* for Voice and Flute (1977).—**NS/LK/DM**

Dolmetsch, Carl Frederick, French recorder player, instrument maker, and scholar, son of **(Eugène) Arnold Dolmetsch;** b. Fontenay-sous-Bois, near Paris, Aug. 23, 1911. He received a thorough musical education from his father. He was only seven when he made his first public appearance, and only eight when he made his first tour. In 1937 he became director of the Society of Recorder Players. In 1940 he succeed his father as director of the Haslemere Festivals. From 1940 to 1976 he served as chairman of the firm Arnold Dolmetsch, Ltd. In 1971 he became director of the Dolmetsch International Summer School. He was chairman of Dolmetsch Musical Instruments from 1982. As a recorder player, he made regular tours of Europe and North and South America. He also commissioned scores for his instrument and prepared many recorder editions. He was the author of *Recorder and German Flute during the 17th and 18th Centuries* (London, 1960). In 1954 he was made a Commander of the Order of the British Empire.—**NS/LK/DM**

Dolmetsch, (Eugène) Arnold, eminent French-born English music scholar and instrumentalist, father of **Carl Frederick Dolmetsch;** b. Le Mans, Sarthe, Feb. 24, 1858; d. Haslemere, Surrey, Feb. 28, 1940. His father and maternal grandfather maintained an organ and piano workshop in Le Mans in which he was apprenticed in the construction and repair of instruments. He received piano lessons at age four, then took violin lessons from an itinerant violinist, and later from his uncle. After his father's death in 1874, he carried on the family business. In 1878, however, he eloped to Nancy with Marie Morel, a widow ten years his senior; following the birth of their daughter, they proceeded to London, where they were married (May 28, 1878). In 1879 he went to Brussels to study violin with Vieuxtemps; he then came under the influence of Gevaert at the Brussels Cons., where he also studied harmony and counterpoint with Kufferath and piano with de Greef

(1881–83); also learned to play the viola d'amore. Upon his return to London, he took courses in violin with Henry Holmes, in harmony and counterpoint with Frederick Bridge, and in composition with Parry at the Royal Coll. of Music (1883–85). From 1885 to 1889 he was an asst. violin teacher at Dulwich Coll.; he also spent much time researching and copying early MSS in the Royal Coll. of Music library, and later in the British Library. He began collecting old books on early music, and proceeded to collect and restore viols; he also taught his wife, daughter, and selected pupils to play the instruments, and presented concerts of Elizabethan music. Expanding his activities still more widely, he set about restoring a variety of keyboard instruments, and later learned to build the instruments himself. At the invitation of Bridge, he performed the music of Byrd, Bull, Purcell, Locke, Lawes, Jenkins, and Simpson at Bridge's lecture at Gresham Coll. on Nov. 21, 1890; this was the first time the music of these early composers had been played on original instruments in modern times. On April 27, 1891, he gave a notable "Concert of Ancient Music of the XVI and XVII Centuries" in London, playing works on the viols, lute, and harpsichord, assisted by two vocal soloists. He worked industriously to establish himself as an authority on early music and instruments, a distinguished performer, and a skilled craftsman; his cause was championed by George Bernard Shaw. Dolmetsch and his wife separated in 1893 and were divorced in 1899. From 1895 he lived with his divorced sister-in-law, Elodie, a fine keyboard player; in 1899 they were married. Dolmetsch, his wife, and Mabel Johnston, a player on the viola da gamba and the violone, made their U.S. debut in N.Y. on Jan. 6, 1903. Dolmetsch and his 2nd wife were divorced later that year, at which time he married Johnston; with Kathleen Salmon, his pupil and a harpsichordist, they made an extensive U.S. tour in 1904–05. He was hired by Chickering & Sons of Boston in 1905 to oversee the manufacture of early keyboard instruments, viols, and lutes. From 1906 to 1911 he lived in Cambridge, Mass.; he also continued to give concerts. In 1911 he began working at the Gaveau factory in Fontenay-sous-Bois, near Paris. In 1914 he returned to England and settled in Haslemere in 1917, where he maintained a workshop and built the first modern recorder (1918). In 1925 he organized the Haslemere Festivals, where he and his family presented annual concerts. In 1927 the Dolmetsch Foundation was organized by his pupils and friends with the goal of furthering his work. Its journal, *The Consort*, began publication in 1929. Dolmetsch was awarded the cross of the Légion d'honneur of France (1938) and an honorary doctorate in music from the Univ. of Durham (1939). He prepared eds. of early music, including *Select English Songs and Dialogues of the 16th and 17th Centuries* (2 vols., London, 1898, 1912), *English Tunes of the 16th and 17th Centuries for Treble Recorder in F and Pieces for 2, 3 and 4 Recorders* (Haslemere, 1930), *Select French Songs from the 12th to the 18thth Century* (London, 1938), and *The Dolmetsch Collection of English Consorts* (ed. by P. Grainger; N.Y., 1944). He also contributed articles to journals and publ. the book *The Interpretation of the Music of the XVII and XVIII Centuries* (London, 1915; 2nd ed., 1946). U. Supper ed. *A Catalogue of the Dolmetsch Library* (Haslemere, 1967).

BIBL.: R. Donington, *The Work and Ideas of A. D.* (Haslemere, 1932); M. Dolmetsch, *Personal Recollections of A. D.* (London, 1958); M. Campbell, *D.: The Man and His Work* (London and Seattle, 1975).—**NS/LK/DM**

Dolphy, Eric (Allan), jazz alto saxophonist, bass clarinetist, flutist; b. Los Angeles, Calif., June 20, 1928; d. Berlin, Germany, June 29, 1964. Dolphy's parents were Panamian immigrants who settled in Los Angeles. He took up the clarinet around 1937 and was clearly devoted to music; his grades from junior and senior high school are average except for those from Orchestra and Band. He studied music at Los Angeles City Coll. He apprenticed with an R&B band, Roy Porter's big band (recording eight titles in 1949), and navy bands, and had numerous opportunities to try out his ideas in jam sessions with many prominent Los Angeles progressive musicians. His father built a small music studio for him in 1955. After playing in the Chico Hamilton quintet, he moved to N.Y., where in 1960 he worked with Charles Mingus in various groups, usually with Ted Curson and Danny Richmond (including a concert in Antibes, France with Booker Ervin in the group and Bud Powell sitting in). The following year he led his own quintet at the Five Spot with Booker Little, Mal Waldron, Ed Blackwell, and Richard Davis and worked with George Russell. The first albums he made for Prestige had surrealistic cover portraits created by "Prophet" (a legendary artist among L.A. musicians) and had titles such as *Out There, Where?* (led by Ron Carter), and *Far Cry.* He played with John Coltrane from 1961 until around February 1962, including a European tour in November 1961, and again on Dec. 31, 1963, at Lincoln Center. By this time he owned a Selmer alto, a Buffet soprano clarinet, a Selmer bass clarinet, a Buffet bass clarinet, a Powell flute, and a piccolo. He led a group with Freddie Hubbard in 1962, and also toured with only a rhythm section (at times including Herbie Hancock and Richard Davis); in 1963 he worked in John Lewis's Orch. U.S.A. and appeared in a Leonard Bernstein Young People's Concert television program on "jazz and the concert hall" (reissued on video). He also recorded with Oliver Nelson, George Russell, Ornette Coleman, and Gunther Schuller. His repertoire included several avant-garde classical pieces, such as Edgard Varèse's *Density 21.5* for solo flute. He toured Europe with Mingus in April 1964, from which many concert recordings survive. During the tour he decided he would remain in Europe rather than return to the U.S. with Mingus at the end of April. He performed and recorded with a number of French musicians and resident African- Americans such as Donald Byrd. He died of complications from untreated diabetes. At the time of his death he was working on a string quartet entitled *Love Suite.* Composer Hale Smith, a mentor to Dolphy in his classical interests, wrote Dolphy's parents indicating that he was sending the scores to "Love Suite" and to "Red Planet" (raising the possibility that the latter, also known as "Miles' Mode" and credited to John Coltrane, could have been a Dolphy composition or perhaps a collaboration), but neither exists. Gunther Schuller, another classical mentor, has some unfinished Dolphy scores. After his parents died around 1988, one Joe O'Con bought their house and was using it as a sort of museum/community center. Unfortunately, in the spring of 1992 the house was trashed during the violence that erupted in L.A. and much was lost, but the house still includes a bass clarinet Dolphy used in the 1950s, the Wurlitzer electric piano he used for composing, stacks of sheet music, exercise books, tons of paperwork, and many photos.

DISC.: *Candid Dolphy* (1960); *Far Cry* (1960); *Fire Waltz* (1960); *Looking Ahead* (1960); *Other Aspects* (1960); *Out There* (1960); *Outward Bound* (1960); *Status* (1960); *Berlin Concerts* (1961); *Copenhagen Concert* (1961); *Eric Dolphy and Booker Little* (1961); *Eric Dolphy in Europe, Vol. 1–3* (1961); *Great Concert of Eric Dolphy* (1961); *Latin Jazz Quintet* (1961); *Live! at the Five Spot, Vol. 1, 2* (1961); *Quartet 1961* (1961); *Stockholm Sessions* (1961); *Iron Man* (1963); *Jitterbug Waltz* (1963); *Last Date* (1964); *Out to Lunch* (1964).

BIBL.: Raymond Horricks, *The Importance of Being E.D.* (Tunbridge Wells, 1989); V. Simosko and B. Tepperman, *E.D.: A Musical Biography and Discography* (N.Y., 1996).—**LP**

Dolukhanova, Zara, Russian mezzo-soprano of Armenian descent; b. Moscow, March 5, 1918. She studied with private teachers. She joined the Moscow Radio staff in 1944. A lyric singer, she excelled in the Romantic Russian repertoire. In 1959 she made her first American tour, enjoying great acclaim; she toured America again in 1970. In 1966 she was awarded the Lenin Prize.—**NS/LK/DM**

Domanínská (real name, Klobásková), Libuše, Czech soprano; b. Brno, July 4, 1924. She was a student at the Brno Cons. of Hana Pírková and Bohuslav Sobeský. In 1945 she made her operatic debut as Blaženka in Smetana's *Tajemství,* and continued to sing there until 1955. In 1955 she became a member of the Prague National Theater, where she was a principal artist until 1985. She also was a member of the Vienna State Opera (1958–68) and a guest artist with other European opera companies. She likewise pursued an active concert career. In 1966 she was made an Artist of Merit and in 1974 a National Artist by the Czech government. In addition to her roles in operas by Mozart, Verdi, and Puccini, she won particular praise for her portrayals in operas by Czech and Russian masters.—**NS/LK/DM**

Domanský, Hanuš, Slovak composer; b. Nový Hrozenkov, March 1, 1944. He studied composition with Ján Duchaň and piano with Jaroslav Sháněl at the Brno Cons. (1962–65) and composition with Dezider Kardoš at the Bratislava Academy of Music and Drama (1965–70). In 1975 he became deputy senior editor of the music dept. of the Slovak Radio in Bratislava, where he became senior editor in its dept. of symphonic, operatic, and chamber music in 1990. From 1975 to 1983 he was chairman of the composers' section of the Union of Slovak Composers. In 1976 he won the Ján Levoslav Bella Award. He was honored with the Union of Slovak Composers Award in 1984. His music combines the Czech tradition of Janáček with techniques of Berg and

Stravinsky.

WORKS: ORCH.: *Concerto piccolo* (1970); 2 syms. (1979, 1983); Piano Concerto (1986); *Homage to the Land*, overture (1987); *Music from the Hont Region* for Small Orch. (1987); *Under the Makyta* for Chamber Orch. (1988); *Doma ste, doma* for Small Orch. (1990). **CHAMBER:** *Music* for Trumpet, Flute, and Bass Clarinet (1966); 2 string quartets (1968, 1977); *Musica giocosa* for Violin and Piano (1971); *Dianoia* for Violin (1976); *Ad libitum* for Clarinet, Vibraphone, Percussion, and Piano (1987). **KEYBOARD: P i a n o :** *Passacaglia* (1966); Sonata (1967); *Fragment of a Sonata* (1977); *Bagatelles* (1978); *Dithyrambs* (1980); *Miniatures* (1985); *XX Fantasies* (1993); *Fantasy* (1997). **O r g a n :** *Inno* (1973). **VOCAL:** *6 Songs* for Soprano and Piano (1964); *Of Winter*, cantata for Speaker, Children's Chorus, and Orch. (1968); *Son et lumière* for Soprano and Piano (1969); *Fiat lux*, oratorio for Speaker, Soprano, Chorus, and Orch. (1970); *Lullabies from the Liptov Region* for Woman's Voice and Small Orch. (1984); *Liptov Imphorsions* for Soprano, Women's Chorus, and Orch. (1985); *Žiale, moje žiale* for Soprano and Orch. (1986); *Elegiac Suite* for Soprano and Piano (1987); *Christmas Mystery Play* for Soloists, Chorus, and Orch. (1992). **TAPE:** *Homage to Life* (1989); *Music for Piano* (1992).—NS/LK/DM

Domgraf-Fassbänder, Willi, German baritone, father of **Brigitte Fassbänder**; b. Aachen, Feb. 9, 1897; d. Nuremberg, Feb. 13, 1978. He first studied in Aachen, where he made his operatic debut (1922), then with Jacques Stückgold and Paul Bruns in Berlin and with Giuseppe Borgatti in Milan. He sang in Berlin, Düsseldorf, and Stuttgart, and was a leading member of the Berlin State Opera from 1928 until the end of World War II; he also appeared at the Glyndebourne Festivals (1934–35; 1937). After the war, he sang in Hannover, Vienna, Munich, and Nuremberg, serving as chief producer at the latter opera house (1953–62). He also taught at the Nuremberg Cons. (from 1954). Among his finest roles were Figaro, Papageno, and Guglielmo. —NS/LK/DM

Domingo, Plácido, famous Spanish tenor and able conductor; b. Madrid, Jan. 21, 1941. His parents were zarzuela singers; after a tour of Mexico, they settled there and gave performances with their own company. Plácido joined his parents in Mexico at the age of seven and began appearing with them in various productions while still a child; he also studied piano with Manuel Barajas in Mexico City and voice with Carlo Morelli at the National Cons. there (1955–57). Originally a baritone, he made his operatic debut in the tenor role of Borsa in *Rigoletto* with the National Opera in Mexico City in 1959. His first major role was as Alfredo in *La Traviata* in Monterrey in 1961; that same year he made his U.S. debut as Arturo in *Lucia di Lammermoor* with the Dallas Civic Opera; then was a member of the Hebrew National Opera in Tel Aviv (1962–64). He made his first appearance with the N.Y.C. Opera as Pinkerton in *Madama Butterfly* on Oct. 17, 1965. On Aug. 9, 1966, he made his Metropolitan Opera debut as Turiddu in a concert performance of *Cavalleria rusticana* at N.Y.'s Lewisohn Stadium; his formal debut on the stage of the Metropolitan followed on Sept. 28, 1968, when he essayed the role of Maurice de Saxe in *Adriana Lecouvreur*, establishing himself as one of its principal

members. He also sang regularly at the Vienna State Opera (from 1967), Milan's La Scala (from 1969), and London's Covent Garden (from 1971). His travels took him to all the major operatic centers of the world, and he also sang for recordings, films, and television. He also pursued conducting. He made his formal debut as an opera conductor with *La Traviata* at the N.Y.C. Opera on Oct. 7, 1973, and on Oct. 25, 1984, he appeared at the Metropolitan Opera, conducting *La Bohème*. He commissioned Menotti's opera *Goya* and sang the title role at its premiere in Washington, D.C., on Nov. 15, 1986. In 1987 he sang Otello at the 100th anniversary performances at La Scala. On New Year's Eve 1988 he appeared as a soloist with Zubin Mehta and the N.Y. Phil in a gala concert televised live to millions, during which he also conducted the orch. in the overture to *Die Fledermaus*. On July 7, 1990, he participated in a celebrated concert with fellow tenors José Carreras and Luciano Pavarotti in Rome, with Mehta conducting. The concert was telecast live to the world and subsequently became a best-selling video and compact disc. Thereafter the "three tenors" toured the globe. In 1993 he sang Parsifal at the Bayreuth Festival with extraordinary success. Domingo celebrated his 25th anniversary with the Metropolitan Opera singing Siegmund in Act 1 of *Die Walküre* in a performance broadcast live on radio throughout the world on Sept. 27, 1993. In 1994 Domingo was named principal guest conductor of the Los Angeles Opera, where he sang the title role in Verdi's *Stiffelio* (1995). In 1996 he assumed the position of artistic director of the Washington (D.C.) Opera. In 1996 he also appeared as Siegfried at the Metropolitan Opera, where he returned in a remarkable portrayal of Siegmund in 1997. He sang Samson there in 1998. Domingo sang excerpts from *Die Walküre* and *Fidelio* with Deborah Polaski at the reopening gala of the refurbished Royal Opera House at Covent Garden on Dec. 1, 1999. On Jan. 26, 2000, he made his belated U.S. recital debut in Chicago, followed by his N.Y. recital debut at Carnegie Hall on Jan. 30, 2000. From 2000 he was artistic director of the Los Angeles Opera while retaining his position in Washington, D.C. One of the best-known lyric tenors of his era, Domingo has gained international renown for his portrayals of such roles as Cavaradossi, Des Grieux, Radames, Don Carlo, Otello, Don José, Hoffmann, Canio, and Samson. He publ. an autobiography, *Plácido Domingo: My First Forty Years* (N.Y., 1983).

BIBL.: D. Snowman, *The World of P. D.* (London, 1985); L. Fayer, *Von Don Carlos bis Parsifal: P. D., 25 Jahre an der Wiener Staatsoper* (Vienna, 1992); R. Stefoff, *P. D.* (N.Y., 1992); M. Lewis, *The Private Lives of the Three Tenors: Behind the Scenes With P. D., Luciano Pavarotti, and José Carreras* (N.Y., 1996); C. Schnauber, *P. D.* (Boston, 1997).—NS/LK/DM

Dominguez, Oralia, Mexican contralto; b. San Luis Potosí, Oct. 15, 1927. She studied at the National Cons. in Mexico City, during which time she made her first appearance as a singer in Debussy's *La Damoiselle élue*. After making her stage debut at the Mexico City Opera in 1950, she made her European debut at a concert at London's Wigmore Hall in 1953, and then toured in France, Spain, Germany, and the Netherlands; that same year she appeared as Princess de Bouillon in

Adrienne Lecouvreur at Milan's La Scala. She then sang opera in Naples, Brussels, Vienna, and Paris. In 1955 she created the role of Sosostris in Tippett's *A Midsummer Marriage* at London's Covent Garden, and then appeared regularly at the Glyndebourne Festivals from 1955 to 1964. She was a member of the Deutsche Oper am Rhein in Düsseldorf from 1960. She also appeared as soloist with major orchs. and as a recitalist.—**NS/LK/DM**

Dominiceti, Cesare, Italian composer; b. Desenzano, July 12, 1821; d. Sesto di Monza, June 20, 1888. He studied in Milan, where all his operas were brought out. He lived for a long time in Bolivia, where he made a fortune. In 1881 he was appointed prof. of composition at the Milan Cons. He wrote the operas *Due mogli in una* (June 30, 1853), *La maschera* (March 2, 1854), *Morovico* (Dec. 4, 1873), *Il lago delle fate* (May 18, 1878), and *L'Ereditiera* (Feb. 14, 1881).—**NS/LK/DM**

Domino, Fats (actually, **Antoine**), b. New Orleans, Feb. 26, 1928. The second (to Elvis) most successful of the 1950s rock 'n' rollers, selling more than 65 million records, Fats Domino made the transition from R&B to rock 'n' roll with his pleasant, upbeat songs and gentle, engaging piano style. An established R&B artist when he broke through into the pop field with "Ain't That a Shame" in 1955, Fats Domino would become the most famous musician from New Orleans since Louis Armstrong. Far less frantic and threatening than many of his contemporaries, Domino co-wrote virtually all of his hits with bandleader Dave Bartholomew, who, along with tenor saxophonists Herb Hardesty and Alvin "Red" Tyler and drummer Earl Palmer, helped produce his characteristic sound. Fats Domino helped focus attention on the music of New Orleans and inspired other Southern black singers such as Little Richard and Lloyd Price.

"Fats" Domino learned piano as a child, debuting professionally around the age of ten. By 14 he had dropped out of school to perform in local nightclubs, including The Hideaway Club, where he was discovered by bandleader David Bartholomew in 1949. Joining Bartholomew's band, Domino signed with Lew Chudd's Imperial label. He began a string of ten years of smash hits recorded with cowriter-arranger-producer Bartholomew and tenor saxophonist Herb Hardesty in 1950 with "The Fat Man." Domino formed his own touring band in the early 1950s and produced smash R&B hits with "Every Night about This Time," "Goin' Home," "Goin' to the River," "Please Don't Leave Me," "Something's Wrong," and "Don't You Know."

Fats Domino broke through into the pop market in the spring of 1955 with "Ain't That a Shame." He appeared in the early rock 'n' roll movies *Shake, Rattle and Roll* and *The Girl Can't Help It* from 1956 and *Jamboree* and *The Big Beat* from 1957. In addition to the standard "Blue Monday" and Bobby Charles's "Walking to New Orleans," Domino scored smash pop and R&B hits with "I'm in Love Again," "I'm Walkin'," "It's You I Love," "Whole Lotta Loving," "I Want to Walk You Home," and "Be My Guest" through 1960. Major pop hits of the era included the standard "My Blue Heaven," "Valley of Tears," "I'm Ready," "I'm Gonna Be a Wheel Someday," and "My Girl Josephine," an early example of reggae rhythm.

Beginning in 1961 Fats Domino began performing frequently in Las Vegas, managing major hits on Imperial with "What a Price," "It Keeps Rainin'," "Let the Four Winds Blow," and "What a Party," and the Hank Williams classics "Jambalaya" and "You Win Again," through 1962. In 1963 he signed with ABC-Paramount Records, recording in Nashville, and subsequently switched to Mercury in 1965. He toured Great Britain in 1967 and moved to Reprise Records for his final pop hit with The Beatles' "Lady Madonna" in 1968. Domino appeared in the rock 'n' roll revival film *Let the Good Times Roll* in 1973 and toured six months out of every year until the mid 1970s, after which he performed primarily in Las Vegas. He achieved a modest country hit with "Whiskey Heaven" from the movie *Any Which Way You Can* in 1980 and was inducted into the Rock and Roll Hall of Fame in its inaugural year, 1986. In 1993, Fats Domino recorded his first new album in over 20 years, *Christmas Is a Special Day*, and, in 1996, EMI issued the tribute album *That's Fats*, which featured covers of Domino's songs by Ricky Nelson, The Band, Dr. John, Cheap Trick, and others.

DISC.: *Rock and Rollin' with Fats Domino* (1956); *Rock and Rollin'* (1956); *Here Stands Fats Domino* (1957); *This Is Fats* (1957); *The Fabulous Mr. D* (1958); *Fats Domino Swings/12,000,000 Records* (1959); *Let's Play Fats Domino* (1959); *Sings Million Record Hits* (1960); *A Lot of Dominos* (1961); *I Miss You So* (1961); *Let the Four Winds Blow* (1961); *What a Party* (1961); *Twistin' the Stomp* (1962); *Million Sellers by Fats* (1962); *Just Domino* (1962); *Here Comes Fats Domino* (1963); *Walking to New Orleans* (1963); *Let's Dance with Domino* (1963); *Here He Comes Again* (1963); *Fats on Fire* (1964); *Getaway with Fats Domino* (1965); *'65* (1965); *Fats Is Back* (1968); *Fats* (1971); *Legendary Masters* (1972); *Superpak-Cookin' with Fats* (1973); *Live in Montreaux* (recorded 1973; 1974; 1987); *Very Best* (1974); *Play It Again, Fats—The Very Best* (1974); *Best* (1987); *My Blue Heaven: The Best of Fats Domino; They Call Me the Fat Man: The Legendary Imperial Recordings* (1991); *The Fat Man: 25 Classic Performances* (1996).—**BH**

Dömling, Wolfgang, German musicologist; b. Munich, Dec. 20, 1938. He was educated at the Univ. of Munich, where he took his Ph.D. with the diss. *Der mehrstimmigen Balladen, Rondeaux und Virelais von Guillaume de Machaut* (publ. in the *Münchner Veröffentlichung zur Musikgeschichte*, XVI, Tutzing, 1970). From 1977 he was a prof. at the Univ. of Hamburg. Dömling has pursued studies in music of the Middle Ages, of the 19th century, and of the early 20th century. In addition to his articles in journals, he wrote *Hector Berlioz: Die symphonisch-dramatischen Werke* (Stuttgart, 1979), *Igor Strawinsky: Studien zu Ästhetik und Kompositionstechnik* (with T. Hirsbrunner; Laaber, 1985), and "Kunstwerk der Zukunft—Gegenwart der Moderne: Über einige Aspekte der französisch Wagner-Rezeption" in the Floros Festschrift (Wiesbaden, 1990).—**NS/LK/DM**

Donahue, Sam(uel) (Koontz), tenor saxophonist, leader, trumpeter, arranger; b. Detroit, Mich., March 18, 1918; d. Reno, Nev., March 22, 1974. He began on clarinet at age nine and later played in the Redford H.S. Band. After playing local jobs in Mich., he led his own band. He was with Gene Krupa (1938–40), briefly with Harry James and Benny Goodman (October 1940), and then led his own band prior to joining the U.S. Navy in 1942. He led a navy big band that played in Europe during World War II and recorded. He led his own band from 1946, which had a dozen hits in the late 1940s; during this time he also taught until re-entering the U.S. Navy for several months in 1952. He played with Tommy Dorsey, then fronted Billy May's orch. for the Ray Anthony organization on tour in 1956. He led his own band in the late 1950s, worked with Stan Kenton from 1960–61, and then fronted Tommy Dorsey's "Memorial" Band from 1961 to 1965, when they stopped using Dorsey's name. A year later the group was cut down to an octet (and eventually became the Frank Sinatra Jr. show band). In the late 1960s he led his own band and became musical director for N.Y.'s Playboy Club; then in 1969 led his own band in Reno, Nev., until he was stricken with cancer.

Disc.: *For Young Moderns in Love* (1954).—**LP**

Donalda (real name, Lightstone), Pauline,

Canadian soprano; b. Montreal, March 5, 1882; d. there, Oct. 22, 1970. The original family name was Lichtenstein, which her father changed to Lightstone when he became a British subject. She received her first musical training at Royal Victoria Coll. in Montreal, and then was a private pupil of Duvernoy in Paris. She made her operatic debut as Massenet's Manon in Nice, Dec. 30, 1904; the next year she appeared at the Théâtre Royal de la Monnaie in Brussels and at Covent Garden in London; in 1906–07 she appeared at the Manhattan Opera House in N.Y., and in London and Paris, mainly in oratorios and concerts. From the time of her retirement in 1922 until 1937 she had a singing school in Paris; in 1937 she returned to Montreal. In 1938 she presented her valuable music library (MSS, autographs, and music) to McGill Univ. In 1942 she founded the Opera Guild in Montreal, serving as its president until it ceased operations in 1969. In 1967 she was made an Officer of the Order of Canada. Her stage name was taken in honor of Sir Donald Smith (later Lord Strathcona), who endowed the Royal Victoria Coll. and was her patron.

Bibl.: C. Brotman, *P. D.* (Montreal, 1975).—**NS/LK/DM**

Donaldson, Walter J., American song composer and lyricist; b. N.Y., Feb. 15, 1893; d. Santa Monica, Calif., July 15, 1947. Though he was the primary composer for two Broadway shows and six movie musicals and contributed to dozens more, Donaldson primarily worked in Tin Pan Alley, writing pop songs for performance in vaudeville and on records. He was consistently successful as this. Between 1918 and 1936 not a year went by without the emergence of at least one hit song by him. Sometimes writing his own lyrics (notably "At Sundown," "Little White Lies," and "You're Driving Me Crazy! [What Did I Do?]"), he collaborated most often with Gus Kahn; the two wrote "My Buddy," "Carolina in the Morning," "Yes Sir, That's My Baby," "Love Me or Leave Me," and "Makin' Whoopee." Early

in his career Donaldson collaborated frequently with the team of Sam M. Lewis and Joe Young, resulting in such hits as "How Ya Gonna Keep 'em Down On the Farm (after They've Seen Paree)?" and "My Mammy," but he also wrote with many other lyricists, and his biggest hit, "My Blue Heaven," was his sole composition with George Whiting.

Donaldson's father was a shoe cutter and his mother was a music teacher, but he took little interest in her piano lessons until he was in high school, when he taught himself in order to write songs for student shows. After graduation, he worked at a Wall Street brokerage, then became a staff pianist for a music publisher. Though "On the Good Ship Whipoorwill" (lyrics by Coleman Goetz) was used in the show *Down in Bom-Bom Bay* in 1915, he had his first song publication with "Just Try to Picture Me Back Home in Tennessee" (lyrics by William Jerome), which had its title shortened to "Back Home in Tennessee" when Prince's Orch. made an instrumental recording that became a hit at the start of 1916. It was the first of many songs alluding to southern locales written by a composer who rarely if ever visited the South. He followed it immediately with "You'd Never Know That Old Home Town of Mine" (lyrics by Howard Johnson), which became a hit for Arthur Collins and Byron Harlan in February 1916. "I've Got the Sweetest Girl in Maryland" is notable as the first song with Donaldson's own lyrics to gain attention; it was used in the show *So Long, Letty* (N.Y., Oct. 23, 1916).

Donaldson was inducted into the army during World War I and stationed at Camp Upton on Long Island, where he encountered Irving Berlin. Upon his discharge he took a job with Berlin's publishing company that he held until he cofounded his own company, Donaldson, Douglas, and Gumble, in 1928. Even before the Armistice he had another hit, "The Daughter of Rosie O'Grady" (lyrics by Monty C. Brice), that was turned into a popular recording by Lewis James in September 1918. His biggest early hit came with a song that reflected the postwar mood, "How Ya Gonna Keep 'Em Down on the Farm (after They've Seen Paree)?"; it inaugurated his work with Lewis and Young (Nora Bayes's was the most successful of several recordings, in March 1919). He had several songs interpolated into *Ed Wynn Carnival* (N.Y., April 5, 1920) and wrote for other shows, but he continued to find his greatest success in Tin Pan Alley. "My Little Bimbo Down on the Bamboo Isle" (lyrics by Grant Clarke) was a hit for Frank Crumit in November 1920.

At the end of January 1921, Al Jolson interpolated "My Mammy" into the touring production of *Sinbad*; though the song would be forever associated with him, the biggest hit recording initially was the instrumental version by Paul Whiteman and His Orch. that became a best-seller in June 1921. Jolson interpolated a pair of Donaldson songs into his next show, *Bombo* (N.Y., Oct. 6, 1921), both with lyrics by B. G. De Sylva: "Down South" and "Give Me My Mammy"; the latter became a record hit for him in April 1922. That same month Donaldson extended the southern tone of his songs with "Seven or Eleven, My Dixie Pair o' Dice" (lyrics by Lew Brown), which was interpolated into the Eddie Cantor stage vehicle *Make It Snappy* (N.Y., April 13, 1922), and "On the 'Gin 'Gin 'Ginny Shore" (lyrics by Edgar Leslie), a record hit for Ray Miller and His Orch. "Georgia" (lyrics by Howard Johnson) was given its most successful recording by Whiteman in July. Donaldson then moved north, writing his own lyrics for "Sweet Indiana Home," which became a hit for Aileen Stanley in September.

Donaldson seems to have first collaborated with Kahn on "Little Rover (Don't Forget to Come Back Home)," an unused song intended for *Make It Snappy*. "Carolina in the Morning" was interpolated into *The Passing Show of 1922* (N.Y., Sept. 20, 1922). Henry Burr's recording of the sentimental ballad "My Buddy" (written for Donaldson's fiancée, who had died) became a best-seller in November. The team's "Dixie Highway" was a hit for Stanley in December. Van and Schenck's recording of "Carolina in the Morning" became the most successful of many in March 1923. In July, Marion Harris's recording of "Beside a Babbling Brook" gave the songwriters their fourth hit. Donaldson had a rare nonvocal success when the hot jazz band the California Ramblers made a popular recording of "Roamin' to Wyomin'" in April 1924.

Donaldson continued to write his own lyrics, notably for "Chiquita," interpolated into *Round the Town* (N.Y., May 21, 1924) and the Jolson hit "My Papa Doesn't Two-Time No More" in June, but his biggest success of the year came with another Kahn collaboration, "Mindin' My Business," the most popular rendition by Crumit in May.

In 1925 he scored hits with various writers, coming up with his own lyrics for "My Best Girl," which had equally successful recordings by Isham Jones and His Orch., in an instrumental treatment, and Nick Lucas, with a vocal; teaming with Billy Rose for "Swanee Butterfly," another instrumental hit for Jones; and returning to his favorite geographical theme with "Let It Rain! Let It Pour! (I'll Be in Virginia in the Morning)" (lyrics by Cliff Friend), with the most popular recording by Gene Austin. But again, it was the team of Donaldson and Kahn that proved most successful, as "Yes Sir, That's My Baby" became one of the biggest hits of the year in September, with Austin's recording again leading the way. The team also scored the same month with Georgie Price's recording of "Isn't She the Sweetest Thing? (Oh Maw, Oh Paw)."

Donaldson wrote his first full Broadway score (albeit with many interpolations by others) in *Sweetheart Time* (N.Y., Jan. 19, 1926), a collaboration with Ballard Macdonald. The show was moderately successful, running 145 performances. But it produced no hits, even though Donaldson continued to turn out popular songs outside the theater: "I Wonder Where My Baby Is Tonight" (lyrics by Kahn), the only record duet by Burr and Billy Murray, in March; "That Certain Party" (lyrics by Kahn), by Ted Lewis and His Band, among others, in April; "Let's Talk about My Sweetie" (lyrics by Kahn), by Ruth Etting in June; "But I Do, You Know I Do" (lyrics by Kahn), by Etting in August; "Where'd You Get Those Eyes?" (lyrics by Donaldson), by Lewis in September; and "That's Why I Love You" (lyrics by Paul

Ash), by Johnny Hamp and His Orch. in November.

Donaldson's most successful year yet for scoring song hits was 1927. In January, "Just a Bird's Eye View of My Old Kentucky Home" (lyrics by Kahn) had a successful recording by Abe Lyman and His Orch.; Fred Waring's Pennsylvanians had a hit with "It Made You Happy When You Made Me Cry" (lyrics by Donaldson); and "Whispering" Jack Smith hit with "There Ain't No 'Maybe' in My Baby's Eyes" (lyrics by Kahn and Raymond B. Egan). In February, Etting had the most popular version of "(I've Grown So Lonesome) Thinking of You" (lyrics by Paul Ash). Austin had a hit in April with "I've Got the Girl" (lyrics by Donaldson), and Lewis scored with "If You See Sally" (lyrics by Kahn and Egan). George Olsen and His Orch. had the best-selling recording of "At Sundown" (lyrics by Donaldson) in May, the same month that "Sam, the Old Accordion Man" (lyrics by Donaldson) became a hit for Etting. And in June, "Don't Be Angry with Me" (lyrics by Donaldson) became an instrumental hit for Jean Goldkette and His Orch.

Donaldson had written the tune for "My Blue Heaven" years before; given a lyric by vaudeville entertainer George Whiting, it was interpolated into the *Ziegfeld Follies of 1927* (N.Y., Aug. 16, 1927) and performed by Cantor. The most successful of many recordings was Austin's, which sold a million copies, though it was also a best-seller for Whiteman, and in all its versions "My Blue Heaven" became the most popular song on record in history, a title it held for 15 years until the release of "White Christmas" in 1942. The last Donaldson hit of the year was "Just Once Again" (lyrics by Ash) in a recording by Whiteman in September.

Jolson sang "My Mammy" and other songs in *The Jazz Singer*, the first film with synchronized sound, in October 1927. The film's success helped make Jolson's recording of the song a hit in June 1928. Donaldson wrote his first song for the cinema with "That Melody of Love" (lyrics by Howard Dietz) in *Love*, released before the end of 1927, though it was a promotional song; *Love* was a silent movie. Donaldson continued to score hits in 1928 as "Changes" (lyrics by Donaldson) had a popular recording by Whiteman in February and yet another state was added to his song list with "My Ohio Home" (lyrics by Kahn), recorded by Lucas in March.

Inevitably, Donaldson began to contribute to the new sound films, placing "Out of the Dawn" (lyrics by Donaldson) in *Warming Up* and "You're in Love and I'm in Love" (lyrics by Donaldson) in *Hit of the Show* during the summer. His other hits of the year, all with his own lyrics, were "Just Like a Melody Out of the Sky," for Austin in August, "Because My Baby Don't Mean 'Maybe' Now," for Etting in August, and "Anything You Say!," for Cliff Edwards in September.

Donaldson's greatest success on Broadway came with *Whoopee* (N.Y., Dec. 4, 1928), with lyrics by Kahn and starring Cantor and Etting; it ran 407 performances and featured three hits: "Makin' Whoopee," recorded by Cantor, and "Love Me or Leave Me" and "I'm Bringing a Red, Red Rose," both recorded by Etting. Before the end of the year, Whiteman had scored a hit with the independent song "Out-o'-Town Gal" (lyrics by Donaldson).

After contributing "Reminiscing" (lyrics by Leslie) to the first 1929 edition of the *Ziegfeld Midnight Frolic* (N.Y., Jan. 7, 1929), Donaldson earned his first film credit as a composer, writing the songs for Fox's *Hot for Paris* (1929) with Harold Adamson. His work was also featured in two Paramount films, *The Dance of Life* and *Glorifying the American Girl*, but he wrote nothing new for them. Early in 1930, he and Leslie wrote the songs for 20th Century–Fox's *Cameo Kirby* and contributed "A Cottage in the Country (That's the Thing)" (lyrics by Donaldson) to the Richard Rodgers–Lorenz Hart musical *Simple Simon* (N.Y., Feb. 18, 1930). His next hit song was "Lazy Lou'siana Moon" (lyrics by Donaldson), recorded by Guy Lombardo and His Royal Canadians in March. "Little White Lies," the biggest hit for which he wrote his own lyrics, was a best-seller for Waring, against many competing versions, in August.

When it appeared in the fall, United Artists' film version of *Whoopee!* added an exclamation mark and a new Donaldson-Kahn composition, "My Baby Just Cares for Me," which became a hit for Ted Weems and His Orch. Donaldson closed the year with two more hits that he wrote alone, "Sweet Jennie Lee!," recorded by Jones in November, and "You're Driving Me Crazy! (What Did I Do?)," the best-selling version of which was by Lombardo.

The early years of the Depression saw declines in record sales and in Broadway and Hollywood productions, and Donaldson's song successes became less frequent. Nevertheless, he had a hit with Wayne King and His Orch.'s recording of "Hello, Beautiful!" (lyrics by Donaldson) in March 1931; he placed "I'm with You" (lyrics by Donaldson) in the *Ziegfeld Follies of 1931* (N.Y., July 1, 1931); and "Without That Gal" (lyrics by Donaldson) was a hit for Lombardo in July. "Goodnight, Moon" (lyrics by Donaldson) became a hit for Ben Selvin and His Orch. in January 1932, and "My Mom" (lyrics by Donaldson) was a hit for Kate Smith in April. With the success of *42nd Street* in 1933, the movie studios returned to extensive production of film musicals, and Donaldson signed to MGM. His first effort, "You've Got Everything" (lyrics by Kahn) for *The Prizefighter and the Lady*, was used only instrumentally in the film but became a hit for Jan Garber and His Orch. in November.

The busiest year of Donaldson's career in terms of film work was 1934. In addition to being the credited songwriter with Kahn on two films, *Operator 13* and United Artists' Cantor vehicle *Kid Millions*, he also wrote songs for at least another five films. But his first hit of the year was a revival, Benny Goodman and His Orch.'s instrumental treatment of "Love Me or Leave Me," in February. In March, Rudy Vallée and His Connecticut Yankees had a hit with "Dancing in the Moonlight" (lyrics by Kahn), and Don Bestor and His Orch. scored with "A Thousand Goodnights" (lyrics by Donaldson). Donaldson and Kahn's "Riptide" was used only instrumentally in the film of that name, but it became a hit for Lombardo in May. That same month Eddy Duchin and His Orch. had a hit with "I've Had My Moments" (lyrics by Dietz), which was featured in *Hollywood Party*. The hit from *Operator 13* in June was

"Sleepy Head," recorded by the Mills Brothers, who appeared in the film. The hits from *Kid Millions*, released in November, were "An Earful of Music," sung on screen and on records by Ethel Merman, and "Okay, Toots" by Cantor.

On Oct. 6, 1934, Donaldson married actress Walda (real name Dorothy) Mansfield; the couple had two daughters and were later divorced. After such a busy year, Donaldson was surprisingly inactive in 1935, gaining only one new hit song, "Clouds" (lyrics by Kahn), recorded by Ray Noble and His Orch. in February, and contributing only one new song to a movie, "Tender Is the Night" (lyrics by Donaldson), in *Here Comes the Band*, in September. (Kay Kyser and His Orch. revived "[I've Grown So Lonesome] Thinking of You" in June for their first hit. Kyser then used it as his theme song.)

The year 1936 was another productive one in which Donaldson was the credited songwriter with Adamson on one film, *The Great Ziegfeld*, and wrote songs for five more, all MGM productions, as well as writing independent hits. Goodman's recording of "It's Been So Long" (lyrics by Adamson) was in the hit parade starting in February, outdistancing other versions: "You," from *The Great Ziegfeld*, topped the hit parade in May for Tommy Dorsey and His Orch.; and "Did I Remember?" (lyrics by Adamson), featured in the Jean Harlow film *Suzy*, was at the top of the hit parade for Shep Fields and His Rippling Rhythm Orch. in August and September. It became an Academy Award nominee for Best Song. In October, Goodman had an even bigger hit than he had two years before with a second instrumental recording of "Love Me or Leave Me."

By the end of 1936, Donaldson had begun collaborating with the lyric-writing team of Robert Wright and George Forrest. The team had songs in five MGM films over the next year, most prominently the final Harlow film, *Saratoga*. None of their songs became record hits, however, and 1938 went by without a Donaldson song in the theaters or the hit parade. In January 1939, Sammy Kaye and His Orch. had a hit revival of "My Blue Heaven." "Could Be" (lyrics by Johnny Mercer) was a hit for Johnny Messner and His Orch. in February. In March, Kyser had a double-sided hit with "Cuckoo in the Clock" and "Gotta Get Some Shut-Eye" (both lyrics by Mercer). "Time Changes Everything but Love" (lyrics by Kahn) was used in the film *Broadway Serenade* in April. And in November "I'm Fit to Be Tied" (lyrics by Donaldson) was in the Kyser film *That's Right—You're Wrong*.

Donaldson's output diminished in the 1940s. He wrote music for *Two Girls on Broadway*, released in the spring of 1940, and enjoyed a modest hit with an instrumental revival of "(What Can I Say) after I Say I'm Sorry?" by Will Bradley and His Orch. in May. "Mister Meadowlark," a collaboration with Mercer, was recorded by Bing Crosby and Mercer in April. Donaldson had songs in the MGM features *Ziegfeld Girl* (1941) and *Panama Hattie* (1942), then worked for Universal on the Andrews Sisters' films *Give Out, Sisters* (1942) and *Follow the Boys* (1944), and for Columbia on *What's Buzzin' Cousin?* (1943) and *Beautiful but Broke* (1944). He retired in 1946.

Two previously unheard Donaldson songs turned up in the 1952 film *Everything I Have Is Yours*, and his work was also prominently featured in the Kahn film biography *I'll See You in My Dreams* (1952), *The Eddie Cantor Story* (1953), and the Etting film biography *Love Me or Leave Me* (1955). His songs also enjoyed regular chart revivals. "Little White Lies" was revived for a gold-selling record by Dick Haymes in April 1948, and Benny Strong and His Orch. had a Top Ten revival of "That Certain Party" the same year. Sammy Davis Jr. and Lena Horne each enjoyed Top 40 revivals of "Love Me or Leave Me" in the wake of the Etting film in 1955. "My Blue Heaven" was given a rock 'n' roll treatment for a Top 40 hit by Fats Domino in 1959, and Duane Eddy recorded it as a guitar instrumental for a chart record in 1961, the same year that the Temperance Seven topped the U.K. charts with "You're Driving Me Crazy." The Happenings had a Top 40 hit with "My Mammy" in 1967.

In 1985, Donaldson's "Riptide" was the title track of a multimillion-selling album by Robert Palmer. Nina Simone scored a belated Top Ten U.K. hit in 1987 with her 1959 recording of "My Baby Just Cares for Me." —WR

Donath, Helen (née **Erwin**), American soprano; b. Corpus Christi, Tex., July 10, 1940. After attending Del Mar Coll. in Corpus Christi, she studied voice with Paola Novikova and Maria Berini. She then joined the Cologne Opera studio, where she made her formal operatic debut as Inez in *Il Trovatore* in 1960. From 1963 to 1967 she sang at the Hannover Opera, and then joined the Bavarian State Opera in Munich in 1967, where she quickly rose to prominence. In 1971 she made her U.S. operatic debut as Sophie at the San Francisco Opera. In 1979 she made her first appearance at London's Covent Garden as Anne Trulove. She also appeared as a guest artist in Salzburg, Vienna, Hamburg, Berlin, Bayreuth, Milan, and Zürich. In 1990 she was made a Bavarian Kammersängerin. Among her many roles were Susanna, Zerlina, Ilia in *Idomeneo*, Marcelline in *Fidelio*, Ännchen in *Der Freischütz*, Micaëla, Mélisande, and Mimi.—NS/LK/DM

Donati or **Donato, Baldassare**, famous Italian composer; b. Venice, c. 1527; d. there, c. June 1603. He became a chorister at San Marco in Venice in 1550, where he also became a singing teacher to the choirboys in 1562. He was director of the cappella piccola there from 1564 until it was disbanded by Zarlino when he became maestro di cappella in 1565. Donati then resumed his place as a chorister at San Marco. He was appointed maestro of the singers at the Scuola Grande di San Rocco in 1577, but again resumed his place at San Marco in 1578. He was made maestro di canto to the Seminario Gregoriano di San Marco in 1580, and in 1588 was named vice-maestro di cappella at San Marco, succeeding Zarlino as its maestro di cappella in 1590. He was a particularly notable composer of secular works in a lighter vein.

WORKS (all publ. in Venice): *Le napollitane et alcuni madrigali* for 4 Voices (1550); *Il primo libro di madrigali* for 5 to 6 Voices *con 3 dialoghi* for 7 Voices (1553); *Il secondo libro de madrigali* for 4 Voices (1558); *Il primo libro de motetti* for 5 to 6 and 8 Voices (1599); various other works in contemporary collections. —NS/LK/DM

Donati, Ignazio, Italian composer; b. Casalmaggiore, near Parma, c. 1575; d. Milan, Jan. 21, 1638. He served as maestro di cappella at Urbino Cathedral (1596–98; 1612–15), Pesaro (1600), Fano (1601–05), the Accademia dello Spirito Santa in Ferrara (1616), Casalmaggiore (1618–23), Novara Cathedral (1623–29), Lodi Cathedral (1629–30), and Milan Cathedral (1631–38).

WORKS (all publ. in Venice): *Sacri concentus* for 1 to 5 Voices and Organ (1612); *Motetti* for 5 Voices, in concerto con due sorti di letanie della beata vergine et nel fine alcuni canoni (1616); *Concerti ecclesiastici* for 2 to 5 Voices and Basso Continuo (organ), op.4 (1618); *Concerti ecclesiastici* for 1 to 4 Voices and Basso Continuo (organ), op.5 (1618); *Motetti concertati* for 5 to 6 Voices, con dialoghi, salmi e letanie della beata vergine and Basso Continuo (organ), op.6 (1618); *Il primo libro de motetti* for Voice and Basso Continuo, op.7 (1619; 2nd ed., 1634); *Messe* for 4 to 6 Voices, parte da cappella e da concerto and Basso Continuo (organ; 1622); *Salmi boscarecci concertati* for 6 Voices and 6 Voices ad libitum ...con una messa... and Basso Continuo (organ), op.9 (1623); *Madre de quatordeci figli...il secondo libro de motetti, in concerto...fatti sopra il basso generale Perfecta sunt in te* for 5 Voices (1629); *Le fanfalughe* for 2 to 5 Voices (1630); *Il secondo libro delle messe da cappella* for 4 to 5 Voices, op.12 (1633); *Li vecchiarelli et perregrini concerti* for 2 to 4 Voices, con una messa for 3 to 4 Voices concertata, op.13 (1636); *Il secondo libro de motetti* for Voice and Basso Continuo, op.14 (1636); various other works in contemporary collections.

BIBL.: H. McElrath, *A Study of the Motets of I. D. (ca. 1575–1638)* (diss., Univ. of Rochester, 1967).—NS/LK/DM

Donati, Pino, Italian opera director, administrator, and composer; b. Verona, May 9, 1907; d. Rome, Feb. 24, 1975. After studying violin, he received instruction in composition from Paribeni. He was an opera director at the Verona Arena (1936–43), in Lisbon (1946–50), and in Bologna (1950–56). In 1958 he became artistic director of the Chicago Lyric Opera; from 1964 until his death he served as its co-artistic director with Bruno Bartoletti; from 1968 he also was director of the Florence Opera. In 1939 he married **Maria Caniglia**. Among his works were the operas *Corradino lo Svevo* (Verona, April 4, 1931) and *Lancillotto del lago* (Bergamo, Oct. 2, 1938), and chamber music.—NS/LK/DM

Donato, Anthony, American violinist, conductor, teacher, and composer; b. Prague, Nebr., March 8, 1909. He studied violin with Gustave Tinlot, conducting with Goossens, and composition with Hanson, Royce, and Rogers at the Eastman School of Music in Rochester, N.Y. (B.M., 1931; M.M., 1937; Ph.D., 1947). After playing violin in the Rochester Phil. (1927–31) and the Hochstein Quartet (1929–31), he served as head of the violin depts. at Drake Univ. (1931–37), Iowa State Teachers Coll. (1937–39), and the Univ. of Tex. (1939–46); he then was prof. of theory and composition at Northwestern Univ. (1947–76), where he also conducted its chamber orch. (1947–58). He publ. a valuable textbook on notational techniques, *Preparing Music Manuscripts* (Englewood Cliffs, N.J., 1963). As a composer, Donato was particularly successful writing choral works and piano pieces.

WORKS: DRAMATIC: Opera: *The Walker through Walls* (1964; Evanston, Ill., Feb. 26, 1965). **ORCH.:** 2 sinfoniettas (1936, 1959); *Elegy* for Strings (1938); 2 syms. (1944, 1945); *Mission San José de Aguaya* (1945); *Prairie Schooner*, overture (1947); Suite for Strings (1948); *The Plains* (1953); *Episode* (1954); *Solitude in the City* for Narrator and Orch. (1954); Serenade for Small Orch. (1962); *Centennial Ode* (Omaha, Dec. 11, 1967; for Nebraska's centennial); *Improvisation* (1968); *Discourse* for Flute and Strings (1969; also for Flute and Piano). **CHAMBER:** 2 violin sonatas (1938, 1949); 4 string quartets (1941, 1947, 1951, 1975); *Drag and Run* for Clarinet, 2 Violins, and Cello (1946); *Pastorale and Dance* for 4 Clarinets (1947); Sonatine for 3 Trumpets (1949); Horn Sonata (1950); Wind Quintet (1955); *Prelude and Allegro* for Trumpet and Piano (1957); Piano Trio (1959); Clarinet Sonata (1966); *Discourse I* for Flute and Piano (1969; also for Flute and Strings) and *II* for Saxophone and Piano (1974); many piano pieces. **VOCAL:** *March of the Hungry Mountains* for Tenor, Chorus, and Small Orch. (1949); *Last Supper* for Baritone and Chorus (1952); *The Congo* for Soprano, Chorus, and Orch. (1957); *Prelude and Choral Fantasy* for Men's Voices, 2 Trumpets, 2 Trombones, Percussion, and Organ (1961); *Blessed is the Man* for Chorus, Brass Quartet, and Organ (1970); many songs.—NS/LK/DM

Donatoni, Franco, noted Italian composer and pedagogue; b. Verona, June 9, 1927. He commenced his musical training with Piero Bottagisio at the Verona Liceo Musicale. After further studies in composition with Desderi at the Milan Cons. (1946–48), he was a student of Liviabella at the Bologna Cons., where he took diplomas in composition and band orchestration (1949), choral music (1950), and composition (1951). He pursued advanced composition studies with Pizzetti at the Accademia di Santa Cecilia in Rome (graduated, 1953), and then attended the summer courses in new music in Darmstadt (1954, 1956, 1958, 1961). He taught at the Bologna Cons. (1953–55), the Turin Cons. (1956–69), and the Milan Cons. (1969–78) before holding the chair in advanced composition at the Accademia di Santa Cecilia. He also taught advanced composition at the Accademia Musicale Chigiana in Siena (from 1970), and was concurrently on the faculty of the Univ. of Bologna (1971–85). In addition, he taught at the Civica Scuola in Milan, the Perosi Academy in Biella, and the Forlanini Academy in Brescia; also gave master classes. He publ. the vols. *Questo* (1970), *Antecedente X* (1980), *Il sigaro di Armando* (1982), and *In-oltre* (1988). In addition to his memberships in the Accademia Nazionale di Santa Cecilia and the Accademia Filarmonica of Rome, the French government honored him as a Commandeur of l'Order des Arts et des Lettres in 1985. As a composer, Donatoni was deeply influenced by Schoenberg, Boulez, and Stockhausen, particularly in his mature aleatoric style. His gifts as a master of his craft are most fully revealed in his orch. works and chamber music, which are notable for their imaginative manipulation of sonorities and colors.

WORKS: DRAMATIC: Opera: *Atem* (1983–84; Milan, Feb. 16, 1985). **Ballet:** *La lampara* (1957). **ORCH.:** Concertino for Brass, Timpani, and Strings (1952); Concerto for Bassoon and Strings (1952); Overture for Chamber Orch. (1953); Sinfonia for Strings (1953); *Divertimento I* for Violin and Chamber Orch. (1954) and *II* for Strings (Venice, Sept. 10, 1965); *Musica* for Chamber Orch. (1955); *Strophes* (1959; RAI, Jan. 30, 1960); *Sezioni* (1960; North German Radio, Hamburg, May 14, 1962); *Puppenspiel I* (1961; Palermo, Oct. 8, 1962) and *II* for Flute and Orch. (Valdagno, Sept. 17, 1966); *Per orchestra* (1962; Warsaw, Sept. 24, 1963); *Black and White* for Strings (1964; Palermo, Sept. 6, 1965); *Doubles II* (1970; Venice, Jan. 15, 1971); *To Earle I* for Chamber Orch. (1970; Bolzano, Feb. 2, 1971) and *II* (1971–72; Kiel, Sept. 2, 1972); *Voci* (1972–73; Rome, Feb. 3, 1974); *Espressivo* for Oboe and Orch. (1974; Royan, March 24, 1975); *Duo per Bruno* (1974–75; West German Radio, Cologne, Sept. 19, 1975); *Portrait* for Harpsichord and Orch. (1976–77; Radio France, Paris, Oct. 6, 1977); *Le ruisseau sur l'escalier* for Cello and Chamber Orch. (1980; Paris, April 30, 1981); *Sinfonia Op.63 "Anton Webern"* (Naples, May 13, 1983); *Diario '83* for 4 Trumpets, 4 Trombones, and Orch. (1983–84; Milan, Feb. 16, 1985); *Eco* for Chamber Orch. (1985–86); Concerto grosso for Orch. and Electronics (Bologna, June 5, 1992). **CHAMBER:** *Quartetto I* (1950), *II* (1958; Florence, March 23, 1962), and *IV* (Palermo, Oct. 5, 1963) for String Quartet; Viola Sonata (1952); Harp Sonata (1953); *Movimento* for Harpsichord, Piano, and 9 Instruments (Milan, Nov. 30, 1959); *For Grilly* for 7 Instrumentalists (Rome, May 24, 1960); *Asar* for 10 Strings (1964); *Etwas ruhiger im Ausdruck* for Flute, Clarinet, Violin, Cello, and Piano (1967; Rome, Feb. 1, 1968); *Souvenir I:* Chamber Sym. for 15 Instruments (Venice, Sept. 12, 1967) and *II: Orts* for 14 Instruments and Speaker ad libitum (Paris, March 21, 1969); *Solo* for 10 Strings (1969); *Estratto I* for Piano (1969; Trieste, Feb. 19, 1970), *II* for Piano, Harpsichord, and Harp (Brescia, June 9, 1970), *IV* for 8 Instruments (Rome, Feb. 3, 1974), and *III* for Piano and Wind Octet (1975; Milan, Feb. 12, 1976); *Lied* for 13 Instruments (1972; Siena, Sept. 3, 1973); *Jeux pour deux* for Harpsichord and Organ (1973; Royan, March 28, 1975); *Duetto* for Harpsichord (Brescia, June 5, 1975); *Lumen* for 6 Instruments (Siena, Aug. 27, 1975); *Ash* for 8 Instruments (Siena, Aug. 27, 1976); *Musette per Lothar* for Musette (Siena, Aug. 27, 1976); *Toy* for 2 Violins, Viola, and Harpsichord (Turin, June 23, 1977); *Algo* for Guitar (Milan, Nov. 2, 1977); *Ali* for Viola (Paris, June 26, 1978); *Spiri* for 10 Instruments (Rome, June 18, 1978); *About...* for Violin, Viola, and Guitar (Siena, Aug. 25, 1979); *Argot* for Violin (Siena, Aug. 25, 1979); *Nidi I* for Piccolo (Venice, Sept. 26, 1979) and *II* for Baroque Tenor Flute (1992); *Marches I* for Harp (Berkeley, Nov. 25, 1979) and *II* for Harp, 3 Women's Voices ad libitum, and Chamber Ensemble (Alessandria, Sept. 18, 1990); *Clair* for Clarinet (Siena, Aug. 26, 1980); *Tema* for Chamber Ensemble (1981; Paris, Feb. 8, 1982); *Small* for Piccolo, Clarinet, and Harp (Siena, Aug. 25, 1981); *The Heart's Eye* for String Quartet (Venice, Oct. 7, 1981); *Fili* for Flute and Piano (Venice, Oct. 7, 1981); *Lame* for Cello (Siena, Aug. 26, 1982); *Feria I* for 5 Flutes, 5 Trumpets, and Organ (Bologna, Sept. 24, 1982) and *II* for Organ (Milan, June 17, 1992); (28) *François Variationen* for Piano (1983–89); *Rima* for Piano (Cortona, July 9, 1983); *Alamari* for Cello, Double Bass, and Piano (Siena, Aug. 29, 1983); *Ala* for Cello and Double Bass (1983; Siena, Aug. 23, 1985); *Ronda* for Violin, Viola, Cello, and Piano (La Rochelle, June 24, 1984); *Lem* for Double Bass (Sesto San Giovanni, March 31, 1984); *Ombra* for Bass Clarinet (Certaldo, July 26, 1984); *Darkness* for 6 Percussionists (Strasbourg, Sept, 18, 1984); *Cadeau* for 11 Instruments (Turin, July 7, 1985); Septet for 2 Violins, 2 Violas, and 2 Cellos (Cremona, Sept. 22, 1985); *Omar* for Vibraphone (Siena, Aug. 23, 1985); *Refrain I* for 8 Instruments (Amsterdam, July 7, 1986) and *II* for Chamber Ensemble (Melbourne, Sept. 29, 1991); *Arpège* for 6

Instruments (1986; Paris, March 30, 1987); *Flag* for 13 Instruments (Milan, May 9, 1987); *Ave* for Piccolo, Glockenspiel, and Celesta (Strasbourg, Oct. 3, 1987); *Short* for Trumpet (Cosenza, May 9, 1988); *La souris sans sourire* for String Quartet (1988; Paris, Dec. 18, 1989); *Cloche I* for 2 Pianos, 8 Winds, and 2 Percussion (1988–89; Strasbourg, Sept. 19, 1989), *II* for 2 Pianos (Rome, Oct. 1, 1990), and *III* for Chamber Ensemble (Ravenna, July 21, 1991); *Frain* for 8 Instruments (1989); *Soft* for Bass Clarinet (Fermo, July 31, 1989); *Midi* for Flute (Turin, Sept. 27, 1989); *Hot* for Soprano or Tenor Saxophone and Chamber Ensemble (Metz, Nov. 17, 1989); *Blow* for Wind Quintet (1989; Milan, Feb. 11, 1990); *Caglio* for Violin (Milan, Nov. 28, 1989); *Chantal* for Harp, Flute, Clarinet, and String Quartet (Geneva, July 12, 1990); *Het* for Flute, Bass Clarinet, and Piano (Siena, Aug. 22, 1990); *Rasch* for Saxophone Quartet (Graz, Oct. 6, 1990); *Spice* for Violin, Clarinet, Cello, and Piano (1990; London, Feb. 19, 1991); *Holly* for Chamber Ensemble (1990; Toronto, March 22, 1991); *Bok* for Bass Clarinet and Marimba (1990; Rome, April 8, 1991); *Sweet* for Flute (1992); *Sincronie* for Piano and Cello (Huddersfield, Nov. 28, 1992). **VOCAL:** *Il libro dei sette sigilli* for Soloists, Chorus, and Orch. (1951); *Serenata* for Woman's Voice and 16 Instruments (Milan, April 11, 1959); *Madrigale* for Chorus and Percussion Quartet (1968); *Arie* for Voice and Orch. (1978; RAI, Rome, March 15, 1980); *...ed insieme bussarono* for Woman's Voice and Piano (Strasbourg, Nov. 7, 1978); *De Pres* for Woman's Voice, 2 Piccolos, and 3 Violins (Radio France, Paris, Feb. 9, 1980); *L'ultima sera* for Woman's Voice and 5 Instruments (1980; Radio France, Paris, June 18, 1981); *Abyss* for Woman's Voice, Flute, and Instruments (Metz, Nov. 18, 1983); *In cauda* for Chorus and Orch. (1983; Cologne, Dec. 6, 1991); *She* for 3 Sopranos and 6 Instruments (Rome, Sept. 24, 1983); *Still* for High Soprano and 6 Instruments (Milan, April 21, 1985); *O si ride* for 12 Vocalists (1987; Paris, May 19, 1988); *Cinis* for Woman's Voice and Piano (Strasbourg, Sept. 21, 1988); *Åse: Algo II* for Woman's Voice and Guitar (1990); *Aahiel* for Soprano or Mezzo- soprano, Clarinet, Vibraphone or Marimba, and Piano (1992). **TAPE:** *Quartetto III* (1961; Venice, April 15, 1962).

BIBL.: G. Mazzola Nangeroni, *F. D.* (Milan, 1989).
—**NS/LK/DM**

Donaudy, Stefano, composer; b. Palermo (of a French father and an Italian mother), Feb. 21, 1879; d. Naples, May 30, 1925. He was a pupil at the Palermo Cons. of G. Zuelli from 1896 to 1900. He wrote the operas *Folchetto* (Palermo, 1892), *Scampagnata* (Palermo, 1898), *Theodor Körner* (Hamburg, Nov. 27, 1902), *Sperduti nel buio* (Palermo, April 27, 1907), *Ramuntcho* (Milan, March 19, 1921), and *La Fiamminga* (Naples, April 25, 1922), as well as a symphonic poem, *Le Rêve de Polysende*, 12 *airs de style ancien* for Voice and Piano, and numerous piano pieces.—**NS/LK/DM**

Dönch, Karl, German bass-baritone; b. Hagen, Jan. 8, 1915; d. Vienna, Sept. 16, 1994. He studied at the Dresden Cons., then made his operatic debut in Görlitz (1936). He sang in Reichenberg, Bonn, and Salzburg, later becoming a member of the Vienna State Opera (1947) and making regular appearances at the Salzburg Festivals (from 1951). He was a guest artist at the Berlin Städtische Oper, the Deutsche Oper am Rhein in Düsseldorf, Milan's La Scala, and the Teatro Colón in Buenos Aires. On Jan. 22, 1959, he made his Metropoli-

tan Opera debut in N.Y. as Beckmesser; was on its roster from 1962 to 1965 and again from 1966 to 1969. From 1973 to 1986 he was director of the Vienna Volksoper. In addition to the standard Austro-German repertoire, Dönch sang in several contemporary works, including Liebermann's *Penelope* (1954) and Frank Martin's *Tempest* (1956).—**NS/LK/DM**

Donegan, Lonnie (actually, **Anthony James**), Scottish pop singer, guitarist, and banjoist; b. Glasgow, April 29, 1931. Donegan's popularizing of skiffle music—a British hybrid of American folk, blues, country, and jazz that was exemplified in his signature hit, "Rock Island Line," influenced a generation of British musicians to take up guitars, helping to lead to the wave of internationally successful British rock groups of the 1960s. In the U.K. he was a major star of the late 1950s and early 1960s. He had dozens of chart records, most of them, like "Rock Island Line"— adaptations of American folk music.

Donegan was the son of a violinist with the National Scottish Orch. He began playing drums at 13 and guitar at 17. At 18 he was drafted into the army for two years, playing drums in a jazz band and learning banjo during his service. Upon his discharge in 1951 he moved to London and joined a jazz band led by Ken Colyer as guitarist/banjoist; his specialty within the group was to play and sing American folk and blues material. In 1952 he adopted the first name "Lonnie" in tribute to American blues performer Lonnie Johnson.

Many of Colyer's backup musicians, including Donegan, split from him in January 1954 and formed the Chris Barber Jazz Band. The group signed to Decca Records and in 1955 recorded the album *New Orleans Joys*, on which Donegan sang "Rock Island Line," learned from a Lead Belly record. Decca released a single of the song under Donegan's name, and it entered the charts in January 1956, peaking in the Top Ten the following month. Surprisingly, the record also succeeded in the U.S., peaking in the Top Ten in April. Donegan signed a solo recording contract with Pye Nixa Records and toured Britain and the U.S.

Donegan's next single, "Lost John"/"Stewball," reached the charts briefly in the U.S., but in the U.K. it was another Top Ten hit in June. Skiffle became a national craze, with thousands of young people taking up stringed instruments, among them the future members of The Beatles. Donegan had a third British Top Ten single in September with "Bring a Little Water Sylvie"/"Dead or Alive." He was even more successful in 1957, scoring four Top Ten records, among them the chart-toppers "Cumberland Gap" and "Gamblin' Man"/"Putting on the Style."

Donegan's five chart entries in 1958 included Top Ten renditions of Woody Guthrie's "Grand Coolie Dam" and his version of The Kingston Trio's "Tom Dooley." Another five chart entries in 1959 included Top Tens with the novelty "Does Your Chewing Gum Lose Its Flavour on the Bedpost Over Night?" (an adaptation of the 1924 song "Does the Spearmint Lose Its Flavor on the Bedpost Over Night?"; music by Ernest Breuer, lyrics by Billy Rose and Marty Bloom) and "Battle of

New Orleans" (music and lyrics by Jimmy Driftwood), an American hit for Johnny Horton. (Released in the U.S., "Does Your Chewing Gum Lose Its Flavour on the Bedpost Over Night?" suddenly caught on two years later, reaching the American Top Ten in September 1961.)

Donegan topped the British charts in March 1960 with the comic song "My Old Man's a Dustman," the first of another five chart entries that year. He continued to reach the charts in 1961 and 1962, but his string of hits ended with the onset of The Beatles and the rock groups that followed. Nevertheless, Donegan had established himself as a cabaret entertainer, and he was able to perform successfully in Britain and the U.S. from then on.

Donegan returned to the British charts in February 1978 with the album *Putting on the Style*, on which he rerecorded his hits with an all-star backing band consisting of well-known rock musicians he had influenced, among them Elton John, Ringo Starr of The Beatles, and Ron Wood of The Rolling Stones. Despite a series of heart attacks, he continued to perform during the 1990s. —WR

Dong, Kui, innovative Chinese composer; b. Beijing, Feb. 14, 1967. She began piano lessons at the age of 4 with her mother, a coloratura soprano with the Chamber Orch. of the Central Philharmonic Soc. in Beijing. She studied composition and theory with Mingxin Du and Zuqing Wu at the Central Cons. of Music in Beijing (B.A., 1987; M.A., 1989); in 1991 she entered the doctoral program in composition and computer music composition at Stanford Univ., where her principal mentors were John Chowning, Chris Chafe, Leland Smith, and Wayne Peterson. Her compositions have won numerous awards, including the 1st prize National Music Award for Music and Dance in Beijing (1990), 1st prize in Boston's Alea III International Competition (1994), ASCAP (1995), Meet the Composer (1997–98), and The Mary Flagler Cary Charitable Trust (1999–2000); in 1995 she held the Gerald Oshita Stipend for Composers in the Artists in Residence Program at the Djerassi Foundation in Woodside, Calif. In 1995 she received a Young Composers Award. Her music video, *The Horizon* (1993), was funded by a research grant from the Asia-Pacific National Fund. Dong is currently an asst. prof. at Dartmouth Coll.

WORKS: *Piano Suite* (Beijing, Sept. 4, 1984); *Sigui* for Sanxian, Bamboo Flute, and Chinese Percussion (Beijing, Sept. 4, 1984); *Chen* for Piano Duet (1986); *Imperial Concubine Yang* for Orch. (1988–89; Beijing, Feb. 9, 1989); *Zhang Jing Tang* for Orch. (Beijing, Dec. 14, 1989); *Four Image Songs* (1990); *Eclipse I*, computer- generated tape music installation (1992; San Jose, Calif., Nov. 13, 1993); *Prelude, Fugue, and Postlude* for Piano (Stanford, Calif., Dec. 14, 1992); *The Horizon*, music video (1993); *The Blue Melody* for Violin, Cello, Flute, Clarinet, and Piano (Stanford, Calif., May 12, 1993); *Invisible Scenes I* for String Orch. (Windsor, Canada, Nov. 4, 1994); *Flying Apples*, computer algorithmic composition for quadraphonic tape (Stanford, Calif., July 12, 1994); *Cycle of Light* for 12 Musicians (1995); Clarinet Concert (1995–96).—NS/LK/DM

Doni, Antonio Francesco or **Antonfrancesco,** Italian writer; b. Florence, May 16, 1513; d. Monselice, near Padua, Sept. 1574. For several years he was a member of the Servite fraternity in Florence; after leaving it in 1539, he led a wandering life as a lay priest. He publ., besides various non-musical treatises, a *Dialogo della musica* (Venice, 1544; includes a list of 17 composers living in Venice at the time, with works of each) and *La libraria* (two vols., Venice, 1550–51), containing a description of all publ. and unpubl. musical books in Italian known to him at the time, as well as a list of the music academies then in existence and details of their foundation.—NS/LK/DM

Doni, Giovanni Battista, Italian music theorist; b. 1594; d. Florence, Dec. 1, 1647. He studied literature and philosophy at Bologna and Rome, and from 1613 to 1618 was a law student at Bourges, France. He took his degree at Pisa. In 1621 he accompanied Cardinal Corsini to Paris, where he zealously pursued his literary and antiquarian studies. He went to Rome in 1622 at the invitation of Cardinal Barberini, who was passionately fond of music, and with whom he traveled. In the intervals of his profound study of ancient music, he found time to construct the "Lira Barberina," or "Amphichord," a species of double lyre that he dedicated to Pope Urban VIII. Recalled to Florence in 1640 by deaths in his family, he settled there, married the next year, and accepted a professorship of elocution offered him by the Grand Duke. His criticism and discussions of the earliest operas are very valuable, and were publ. for the first time by A. Solerti in *Origini del melodramma. Testimonianze dei contemporanei* (Turin, 1903).

WRITINGS: *Compendio del trattato de' generi e de' modi della musica* (Rome, 1635); *Annotazioni* on the above (Rome, 1640); *De praestantia musicae veteris libri tres* (Florence, 1647).

BIBL.: A. Blandini, *Commentarium de vita et scriptis G.B. D.* (Florence, 1755); F. Vatielli, *La lira barberina di G.B. D.* (Pesaro, 1909).—NS/LK/DM

Donington, Robert, distinguished English musicologist; b. Leeds, May 4, 1907; d. Firle, Sussex, Jan. 20, 1990. He studied at Queen's Coll., Oxford (B.A., 1930; B. Litt., 1946), and also took a course in composition with Wellesz at Oxford. He became associated with Arnold Dolmetsch in his workshop in Haslemere and studied the technique of early instruments; contributed to the revival of Elizabethan instruments and music. He was a member of the English Consort of Viols (1935–39); then played with the London Consort (1950–60); in 1956 he founded the Donington Consort, and led it until 1961. He lectured extensively in the U.S. He was made a Commander of the Order of the British Empire in 1979.

WRITINGS: *The Work and Ideas of Arnold Dolmetsch* (Haslemere, 1932); with E. Hunt, *A Practical Method for the Recorder* (2 vols., London, 1935); *The Instruments of Music* (London, 1949; 4th ed., rev., 1982, as *Music and Its Instruments*); *Music for Fun* (London, 1960); *Tempo and Rhythm in Bach's Organ Music* (London, 1960); *The Interpretation of Early Music* (N.Y., 1963; 3rd ed., rev., 1974; corrected ed., 1989); *Wagner's "Ring" and Its Symbols* (London, 1963; 3rd ed., rev. and enl., 1974); *A Performer's Guide to Baroque Music* (London, 1973); *String-playing in Baroque*

Music (London, 1977); *The Opera* (London, 1978); *The Rise of Opera* (London, 1981); *Baroque Music: Style and Performance: A Handbook* (London, 1982); *Opera and Its Symbols: The Unity of Words, Music, and Singing* (London, 1991).—NS/LK/DM

Donizetti, (Domenico) Gaetano (Maria),

famous Italian composer, brother of Giuseppe Donizetti; b. Bergamo, Nov. 29, 1797; d. there, April 1, 1848. His father was from a poor family of artisans who obtained the position of caretaker in the local pawnshop. At the age of nine, Gaetano entered the Lezioni Caritatevoli di Musica, a charity institution that served as the training school for the choristers of S. Maria Maggiore; he studied singing and harpsichord there, later studying harmony and counterpoint with J.S. Mayr. With the encouragement and assistance of Mayr, he enrolled in the Liceo Filarmonico Comunale in Bologna in 1815, where he studied counterpoint with Pilotti; later, he studied counterpoint and fugue with Padre Mattei. His first opera, *Il Pigmalione* (1816), appears never to have been performed in his lifetime. He composed two more operas in quick succession, but they were not performed. Leaving the Liceo in 1817, he was determined to have an opera produced. His next work, *Enrico di Borgogna*, was performed in Venice in 1818, but it evoked little interest. He finally achieved popular success with his opera buffa *Il Falegname di Livonia, o Pietro il grande, czar delle Russie* (Venice, Dec. 26, 1819). In Dec. 1820 he was exempted from military service when a woman of means paid the sum necessary to secure his uninterrupted work at composition. His opera seria *Zoraide de Granata* (Rome, Jan. 28, 1822) proved a major success. During the next nine years, Donizetti composed 25 operas, none of which remain in the active repertoire today; however, the great success of his *L'Ajo nell'imbarazzo* (Rome, Feb. 4, 1824) brought him renown at the time. In 1825–26 he served as musical director of the Teatro Carolino in Palermo. From 1829 to 1838 he was musical director of the royal theaters in Naples. With *Anna Bolena* (Milan, Dec. 26, 1830), Donizetti established himself as a master of the Italian operatic theater. Composed for Pasta and Rubini, the opera was an overwhelming success. Within a few years it was produced in several major Italian theaters, and was also heard in London, Paris, Dresden, and other cities. His next enduring work was the charming comic opera *L'elisir d'amore* (Milan, May 12, 1832). The tragic *Lucrezia Borgia* (Milan, Dec. 26, 1833), although not entirely successful at its premiere, soon found acceptance and made the rounds of the major opera houses. In 1834 Donizetti was appointed prof. of counterpoint and composition at the Conservatorio di San Pietro a Majella in Naples. His *Maria Stuarda* (Oct. 18, 1834) was given its first performance as *Buondelmonte* in Naples after the Queen objected to details in the libretto. He then went to Paris, where his *Marino Faliero* had a successful premiere at the Théâtre-Italien on March 12, 1835. Returning to Italy, he produced his tragic masterpiece *Lucia di Lammermoor* (Naples, Sept. 26, 1835). Upon the death of Zingarelli in 1837, Donizetti was named director pro tempore of the Conservatorio in Naples. On July 30, 1837, he suffered a grievous loss when his wife died following the 3rd stillbirth of a child after nine years of

marriage. On Oct. 29, 1837, *Roberto Devereux* garnered acclaim at its first performance in Naples. In 1838 Donizetti resigned his positions at the Conservatorio when his post as director was not made a permanent appointment. When the censor's veto prevented the production of *Poliuto* due to its sacred subject (it was written for Nourrit after Corneille's *Polyeucte*), he decided to return to Paris. He produced the highly successful *La Fille du régiment* there on Feb. 11, 1840. It was followed by *Les Martyrs* (April 10, 1840), a revision of the censored *Poliuto*, which proved successful. His *La Favorite* (Dec. 2, 1840) made little impression at its first performance, but it soon became one of his most popular operas. He spent 1841–42 in Italy, and then went to Vienna. His *Linda di Chamounix* received an enthusiastic reception at its premiere there on May 19, 1842. The Emperor appointed Donizetti Maestro di Cappella e di Camera e Compositore di Corte. In 1843 he once more went to Paris, where he brought out his great comic masterpiece *Don Pasquale*. With such famous singers as Grisi, Mario, Tamburini, and Lablache in the cast, its premiere on Jan. 3, 1843, was a triumph. He then returned to Vienna, where he conducted the successful premiere of *Maria di Rohan* on June 5, 1843. Back again in Paris, he produced *Dom Sébastien* (Nov. 11, 1843). The audience approved the work enthusiastically, but the critics were not pleased. Considering the opera to be his masterpiece, Donizetti had to wait until the Vienna premiere (in German) of 1845 before the work was universally acclaimed. The last opera produced in his lifetime was *Caterina Cornaro* (Naples, Jan. 12, 1844). By this time Donizetti began to age quickly; in 1845 his mental and physical condition progressively deteriorated as the ravages of syphilis reduced him to the state of an insane invalid. In 1846 he was placed in a mental clinic at Ivry, just outside Paris; in 1847 he was released into the care of his nephew, and was taken to his birthplace to await his end. Donizetti was a prolific composer of operas whose fecundity of production was not always equaled by his inspiration or craftsmanship. Many of his operas are hampered by the poor librettos he was forced to use on so many occasions. Nevertheless, his genius is reflected in many of his operas. Indeed, his finest works serve as the major link in the development of Italian opera between the period of Rossini and that of Verdi. Such operas as *Anna Bolena, L'elisir d'amore, Lucia di Lammermoor, Roberto Devereux, La Favorite, La Fille du régiment,* and *Don Pasquale* continue to hold a place in the repertoire.

WORKS: DRAMATIC: O p e r a : *Il Pigmalione,* scena drammatica (1816; Teatro Donizetti, Bergamo, Oct. 13, 1960); *L'ira d'Achille* (1817; not perf.); *L'Olimpiade* (1817; not perf.); *Enrico di Borgogna,* opera semiseria (1818; Teatro San Luca, Venice, Nov. 14, 1818); *Una follia (di Carnevale),* farsa (1818; Teatro San Luca, Venice, Dec. 15, 1818); *Piccioli Virtuosi ambulanti* (also known as *Piccoli Virtuosi di musica ambulanti*), opera buffa (1819; Bergamo, 1819); *Il Falegname di Livonia, o Pietro il grande, czar delle Russie,* opera buffa (1819; Teatro San Samuele, Venice, Dec. 26, 1819); *Le nozze in villa,* opera buffa (1820; Teatro Vecchio, Mantua, 1820 or 1821); *Zoraide di Granata,* opera seria (1822; Teatro Argentina, Rome, Jan. 28, 1822); *La Zingara,* opera seria (1822; Teatro Nuovo, Naples, May 12, 1822); *La lettera anonima,* farsa (1822; Teatro del Fondo, Naples, June 29, 1822);

Chiara e Serafina, o I Pirati, opera semiseria (1822; Teatro alla Scala, Milan, Oct. 26, 1822); *Alfredo il grande*, opera seria (1823; Teatro San Carlo, Naples, July 2, 1823); *Il Fortunato inganno*, opera buffa (1823; Teatro Nuovo, Naples, Sept. 3, 1823); *L'Ajo nell'imbarazzo, o Don Gregorio*, opera buffa (1823–24; Teatro Valle, Rome, Feb. 4, 1824); *Emilia di Liverpool* (also known as *Emilia* or *L'eremitaggio di Liverpool*), opera semiseria (1824; Teatro Nuovo, Naples, July 28, 1824); *Alahor di Granata*, opera seria (1825; Teatro Carolino, Palermo, Jan. 7, 1826); *Il castello degli invalidi*, farsa (1825–26?; 1st perf. may have taken place at the Teatro Carolino, Palermo, 1826); *Elvida*, opera seria (1826; Teatro San Carlo, Naples, July 6, 1826); *Gabriella di Vergy*, opera seria (1826; Teatro San Carlo, Naples, Nov. 22, 1869; 2nd version, 1838?; Whitla Hall, Belfast, Nov. 7, 1978); *La bella prigioniera*, farsa (1826; not perf.); *Olivo e Pasquale*, opera buffa (1826; Teatro Valle, Rome, Jan. 7, 1827); *Otto Mesi in due ore, ossia Gli Esiliati in Siberia*, opera romantica (1827; Teatro Nuovo, Naples, May 13, 1827); *Il Borgomastro di Saardam*, opera buffa (1827; Teatro Nuovo, Naples, Aug. 19, 1827); *Le convenienze ed inconvenienze teatrali*, farsa (1827; Teatro Nuovo, Naples, Nov. 21, 1827); *L'Esule di Roma, ossia Il Proscritto* (also known as *Settimio il proscritto*), opera seria (1827; Teatro San Carlo, Naples, Jan. 1, 1828); *Alina, regina di Golconda* (also known as *La Regina di Golconda*), opera buffa (1828; Teatro Carlo Felice, Genoa, May 12, 1828); *Gianni di Calais*, opera semiseria (1828; Teatro del Fondo, Naples, Aug. 2, 1828); *Il Giovedì grasso, o Il nuovo Pourceaugnac*, farsa (1828; Teatro del Fondo, Naples, 1828); *Il Paria*, opera seria (1828; Teatro San Carlo, Naples, Jan. 12, 1829); *Elisabetta al castello di Kenilworth* (also known as *Il castello di Kenilworth*), opera seria (1829; Teatro San Carlo, Naples, July 6, 1829); *I Pazzi per progetto*, farsa (1830; Teatro del Fondo, Naples, Feb. 7, 1830); *Il diluvio universale*, azione tragico-sacra (1830; Teatro San Carlo, Naples, Feb. 28, 1830); *Imelda de' Lambertazzi*, opera seria (1830; Teatro San Carlo, Naples, Aug. 23, 1830); *Anna Bolena*, opera seria (1830; Teatro Carcano, Milan, Dec. 26, 1830); *Francesca di Foix*, opera semiseria (1831; Teatro San Carlo, Naples, May 30, 1831); *La Romanziera e l'uomo nero*, opera buffa (1831; Teatro del Fondo, Naples, June 18, 1831); *Gianni di Parigi*, opera comica (1831; Teatro alla Scala, Milan, Sept. 10, 1839); *Fausta*, opera seria (1831; Teatro San Carlo, Naples, Jan. 12, 1832); *Ugo, conte di Parigi*, opera seria (1832; Teatro alla Scala, Milan, March 13, 1832); *L'elisir d'amore*, opera comica (1832; Teatro della Canobbiana, Milan, May 12, 1832); *Sancia di Castiglia*, opera seria (1832; Teatro San Carlo, Naples, Nov. 4, 1832); *Il Furioso all'isola di San Domingo*, opera semiseria (1832; Teatro Valle, Rome, Jan. 2, 1833); *Parisina*, opera seria (1833; Teatro della Pergola, Florence, March 17, 1833), *Torquato Tasso* (also known as *Sordello il trovatore* or *Sordello*), opera seria (1833; Teatro Valle, Rome, Sept. 9, 1833); *Lucrezia Borgia*, opera seria (1833; Teatro alla Scala, Milan, Dec. 26, 1833); *Rosmonda d'Inghilterra*, opera seria (1834; Teatro della Pergola, Florence, Feb. 27, 1834); *Maria Stuarda*, opera seria (1834; 1st perf. as *Buondelmonte* at the Teatro San Carlo, Naples, Oct. 18, 1834; 1st perf. as *Maria Stuarda* at the Teatro alla Scala, Milan, Dec. 30, 1835); *Gemma di Vergy*, opera seria (1834; Teatro alla Scala, Milan, Dec. 26, 1834); *Adelaide*, opera comica (1834?; not completed); *Marino* (or *Marin*) *Faliero*, opera seria (1835; Théâtre-Italien, Paris, March 12, 1835); *Lucia di Lammermoor*, opera seria (1835; Teatro San Carlo, Naples, Sept. 26, 1835); *Belisario*, opera seria (1835–36; Teatro La Fenice, Venice, Feb. 4, 1836); *Il campanello (di notte* or *dello speziale)*, farsa (1836; Teatro Nuovo, Naples, June 1, 1836); *Betly* (or *Bettly), ossia La Capanna svizzera*, opera giocosa (1836; Teatro San Carlo, Naples, Aug. 24, 1836); *L'assedio di Calais*, opera seria (1836; Teatro San Carlo, Naples,

Nov. 19, 1836); *Pia de' Tolomei*, opera seria (1836–37; Teatro Apollo, Venice, Feb. 18, 1837); *Roberto Devereux, ossia Il Conte di Essex*, opera seria (1837; Teatro San Carlo, Naples, Oct. 29, 1837); *Maria di Rudenz*, opera seria (1837; Teatro La Fenice, Venice, Jan. 30, 1838); *Poliuto*, opera seria, 1839; 1st perf. as *Les Martyrs* at the Opéra, Paris, April 10, 1840; 1st perf. as *Poliuto* at the Teatro San Carlo, Naples, Nov. 30, 1848); *L'Ange de Nisida* (incomplete opera; transformed into *La Favorite* [1840]); *Le Duc d'Albe* (1839 and later; not completed; finished by Matteo Salvi and tr. into Italian by Angelo Zanardini as *Il Duca d'Alba*, Teatro Apollo, Rome, March 22, 1882); *La Fille du régiment*, opéra- comique (1839–40; Opéra-Comique, Paris, Feb. 11, 1840); *Les Martyrs*, grand opera (1840; rev. version of *Poliuto* [1839]; Opéra, Paris, April 10, 1840); *La Favorite*, grand opera (1840; rev. version of *L'Ange de Nisida* [1839]; Opéra, Paris, Dec. 2, 1840); *Adelia, o La Figlia dell'arciere*, opera seria (1840–41; Teatro Apollo, Rome, Feb. 11, 1841); *Rita, ou Le Mari battu* (also known as *Deux hommes et une femme*), opéra-comique (1841; Opéra-Comique, Paris, May 7, 1860); *Maria Padilla*, opera seria (1841; Teatro alla Scala, Milan, Dec. 26, 1841); *Linda di Chamounix*, opera semiseria (1842; Kärnthnertortheater, Vienna, May 19, 1842); *Don Pasquale*, opera buffa (1842; Théâtre-Italien, Paris, Jan. 3, 1843); *Maria di Rohan*, opera seria (1843; Kärnthnertortheater, Vienna, June 5, 1843); *Dom Sébastien, roi de Portugal*, grand opera (1843; Opéra, Paris, Nov. 11, 1843); *Caterina Cornaro*, opera seria (1842–43; Teatro San Carlo, Naples, Jan. 12, 1844). **OTHER:** His other vocal music includes 28 cantatas, several masses, vespers, Psalms, motets, many songs, ariettas, duets, and conzonets. His instrumental music includes many sinfonias, marches, 19 string quartets, and quintets.

BIBL.: F. Regli, *G. D. e le sue opere* (Turin, 1850); F. Cicconetti, *Vita di G. D.* (Rome, 1864); A. Bellotti, *D. e i suoi contemporanei* (Bergamo, 1866); F. Alborghetti and M. Galli, *G. D. e G. Simone mayr, Notizie e doumenti* (Bergamo, 1875); B. Zendrini, *D. e Simone Mayr* (Bergamo, 1875); F. Marchetti and A. Parisotti, eds., *Lettere inedite di G. D.* (Rome, 1892); E. Verzino, *Contributo ad una biografia di G. D.* (Bergamo, 1896); P. Bettòli, ed., *G. D.: Numero Unico nel Primo Centenario della sua nascita, 1797–1897* (Bergamo, n.d.); A. Calzado, *D. e l'opera italiana in Spagna* (Paris, 1897); C. Malherbe, *Centenaire de G. D.: Catalogue bibliographique de la Section Française à l'exposition de Bergame* (Paris, 1897); I. Valetta, *D.* (Rome, 1897); E. Verzino, *Le opere di G. D.: Contributo alla loro storia* (Bergamo and Milan, 1897); A. Gabrielli, *G. D.* (Rome and Turin, 1904); A. Cametti, *D. a Roma* (Milan, Turin, and Rome, 1907); N. Bennati, *Quattro lettere inedite di G. D. e una lettera di Giacomo Meyerbeer* (Ferrara, 1907); C. Caversazzi, *G. D.: La casa dove nacque, La famiglia, L'inizio della malattia* (Bergamo, 1924); G. Donati-Pettèni, *L'Istituto musicale G. D. La Cappella musicale di Santa Maria Maggiore. Il Museo D.ano* (Bergamo, 1928); idem, *Studi e documenti D.ani* (Bergamo, 1929); idem, *D.* (Milan, 1930; 3rd ed., 1940); G. Morazzoni, *Lettere inedite* (Milan, 1930); G. Zavadini, *Museo D.ano di Bergamo: Catalogo generale* (Bergamo, 1936); G. Gavazzeni, *D.: Vita e musiche* (Milan, 1937); A. Geddo, *D.* (Bergamo, 1938); G. Monaldi, *G. D.* (Turin, 1938); G. Zavadini, *G. D.: Vicende della sua vita artistica* (Bergamo, 1941); G. Pinetti, *Le opere di D. nei teatri di Bergamo* (Bergamo, 1942); G. Barblan, *L'opera di D. nell'eta romantica* (Bergamo, 1948); A. and G. Rizzi, *G. D. nel primo centenario della morte* (Bergamo, n.d.); G. Zavadini, *D.: Vita—Musiche—Epistolario* (Bergamo, 1948); L. Bossi, *D.* (Brescia, 1956); A. Geddo, *D. (L'uomo—le musiche)* (Bergamo, 1956); H. Weinstock, *D. and the World of Opera in Italy, Paris, and Vienna in the First Half of the Nineteenth Century* (N.Y., 1963); W. Ashbrook, *D.* (London, 1965); V. Sacchiero et al., *Il Museo D.ano* di Bergamo (Bergamo, 1970); F. Speranze, ed., *Studi D.ani*, II (1972); J. Allitt, *D. and the Tradition of Romantic Love: A Collection of Essays on a Theme* (London, 1975); W. Ashbrook, *D. and His Operas* (Cambridge, 1982); G. Barblan and B. Zanolini, *G. D.: Vita e opera di un musicista romantico* (Bergamo, 1983); P. Gossett, *Anna Bolena and the Artistic Maturity of G. D.* (Oxford, 1985); C. Osborne, *The Bel Canto Operas of Rossini, D., and Bellini* (Portland, Ore., 1994); S. Fayad, *Vita di D.* (Milan, 1995); F. Mancini and S. Ragni, eds., *D. e i treatri napoletani nell'Ottocento* (Naples, 1997); L. Kantner, ed., *D. in Wien* (Vienna, 1998); J. Cassaro, *G. D.: A Guide to Research* (N.Y., 2000).—**NS/LK/DM**

Donizetti, Giuseppe, Italian bandmaster and composer, brother of **(Domenico) Gaetano (Maria) Donizetti;** b. Bergamo, Nov. 9, 1788; d. Constantinople, Feb. 10, 1856. In 1832 he was summoned by the sultan of Turkey to take charge of Turkish military bands. He accepted, and successfully accomplished the task of introducing Western instruments and modernizing the repertoire. The sultan richly rewarded him with honors and money, and Donizetti remained in Constantinople to the end of his life.—**NS/LK/DM**

Donohoe, Peter (Howard), English pianist and conductor; b. Manchester, June 18, 1953. He began piano study at the age of four and later attended Chetham's School of Music in Manchester (1964–71); at age 12, he made his debut as soloist in Beethoven's 3rd Piano Concerto in Manchester. After attending the Univ. of Leeds (1971–72), he studied at the Royal Manchester Coll. of Music (1972–73) and the Royal Northern Coll. of Music (1973–76) before completing his training with Loriod at the Paris Cons. (1976–77). In 1979 he made his first appearance at the London Promenade Concerts. After winning joint 2nd-prize in the Tchaikovsky Competition in Moscow in 1982, he pursued a global career as a soloist with orchs., a recitalist, and a chamber music player. As a conductor, he served as artistic director of the Northern Chamber Orch. (1984–87) and as founder-conductor of the Manchester Sinfonietta (from 1986). As a piano virtuoso, Donohoe has won accolades for both his fine performances of the standard repertoire and for his championship of an extensive modern repertoire, ranging from Stravinsky and Prokofiev to Messiaen and Muldowney.—**NS/LK/DM**

Donostia, José Antonio de (real name, **José Gonzalo Zulaica y Arregui),** Spanish organist, musicologist, and composer; b. San Sebastián, Jan. 10, 1886; d. Lecároz, Navarre, Aug. 30, 1956. He studied with Echazarra at the Lecároz Franciscan Coll., Esquerrá in Barcelona, Gaviola in San Sebastián, and Cools and Roussel in Paris. He worked in Toulouse (1936), Paris (1939–40), and Bayonne (1941–43) as an organist and choirmaster, then became head of the folklore dept. of Barcelona's Spanish Inst. of Musicology (1943), where he brought out monographs and eds. of Basque folk song.

WORKS: CHAMBER: 12 romanzas for Violin and Piano (1905–10); String Quartet (1906); *3 piezas* for Cello and Piano (1906); *La Quête héroïque de Graal* for 4 Ondes Martenot and Piano (1938); *Página romántica* for Violin and Piano (1941); piano pieces; organ music. **VOCAL:** *Les Trois Miracles de Ste. Cécile* for Chorus and Orch. (1920); *La Vie profonde de St. François d'Assise* for Chorus and Orch. (1926); *Le Noël de Greecio* for Chorus and Orch. (1936); *Poema de la Pasión* for 2 Sopranos, Chorus, and English Horn (1937); *Missa pro defunctis* for Chorus and Organ (1945).

WRITINGS: *La música popular vasca* (Bilbao, 1918); *Euskel eres-sorta* (Bilbao, 1922); *Essai d'une bibliographie musicale populaire basque* (Bayonne, 1932); *Música y músicos en el pais vasco* (San Sebastián, 1951); *El "Moto proprio" y la canción popular religiosa* (San Sebastián, 1954); *Euskal-erriko otoitzak* (San Sebastián, 1956).

BIBL.: J. de Riezu, *J.A. d.D.* (Pamplona, 1956). —**NS/LK/DM**

Donovan (Leitch), b. Glasgow, Scotland, May 10, 1946. Initially appearing in the mid-1960s as an English (actually Scottish) folk artist strongly resembling America's Bob Dylan, Donovan later embraced beneficent psychedelia and naive spiritualism for a series of self-penned hit singles and best-selling albums during the late 1960s.

Donovan moved to the London area at the age of ten, taking up guitar as a teenager. Becoming a regular on BBC-TV's *Ready, Steady, Go* in early 1965, he signed with Pye Records (Hickory Records in the U.S.), hitting with the title cut to his first album *Catch the Wind. Fairy Tale* produced hits with "Colours" and Buffy Sainte-Marie's "Universal Soldier," and included "Sunny Goodge Street," recorded by Judy Collins for her *In My Life* album. Donovan made his American debut at the Newport Folk Festival in 1965 but subsequently abandoned the Dylan-like image and switched to Epic Records under producer Mickie Most for a number of psychedelic, quasi-mystical hits through the late 1960s. His debut Epic album, *Sunshine Superman,* yielded a top American and smash British hit with the title cut (featuring guitarist Jimmy Page) and included perhaps his finest composition, the ominous "Season of the Witch," with Steve Stills as lead guitarist.

Donovan's *Mellow Yellow* produced a smash hit with the title song and included the haunting "Young Girl Blues." After the subdued hits "Epistle to Dippy," "There Is a Mountain," and "Wear Your Love Like Heaven," *Hurdy Gurdy Man* produced one mellow hit, "Jennifer Juniper," and one hard-driving hit with the title cut. *Barabajagal* yielded three hits with "Barabajagal" (recorded with The Jeff Beck Group), "To Susan on the West Coast Waiting," and the inane "Atlantis."

By the middle of 1970, Donovan had split from Mickie Most and formed his own band, but he soon retreated to Ireland. He reemerged in 1974 and continued to record for Epic until 1976, with little success. In virtual retirement from the mid-1970s to the early 1980s, Donovan toured again in the late 1980s and eventually recorded for American Records in 1995. By the 1990s, he was perhaps better known as the father of actress Ione Skye and model-actor-singer Donovan Leitch Jr. than as a musician in his own right. The glitter rock group Nancy Boy, with lead singer Donovan Leitch Jr. and guitarist Jason Nesmith (son of Michael Nesmith), released their major label debut album in 1996.

DONOVAN: *Catch the Wind* (1965); *Fairy Tale* (1965); *The Real Donovan* (1966); *Like It Is, Was and Evermore Shall Be* (1967); *Best* (1969); *Donovan P. Leitch* (1970); *History of British Pop* (1976); *History of British Pop, Vol. 2* (1976); *The Early Years; Sunshine Superman* (1966); *Mellow Yellow* (1967); *A Gift from a Flower to a Garden* (1967); *Wear Your Love Like Heaven* (1967); *For Little Ones* (1967); *In Concert* (1968); *Sunshine Superman/In Concert* (1967); *Hurdy Gurdy Man* (1968/86); *Greatest Hits* (1969); *Barabajagal* (1969/87); *Open Road* (1970); *World—Physical/Spiritual* (1972); *Cosmic Wheels* (1973); *Essence to Essence* (1974); *7-Tease* (1974); *Barabajagal/Hurdy Gurdy Man* (1975); *Slow Down World* (1976); *Troubadour: The Definitive Collection 1964–1976* (1992); *Donovan* (1977); *Lady of the Stars* (1987); *The Classics Live* (1991); *Donovan* (1996); *Sunshine Superman—20 Songs of Love and Freedom* (1996); *Sutras* (1996). **NANCY BOY:** *Sire* (1996).

WRITINGS: *Dry Songs and Scribbles* (1971).

Donovan, Richard Frank, American organist, conductor, teacher, and composer; b. New Haven, Conn., Nov. 29, 1891; d. Middletown, Conn., Aug. 22, 1970. He studied music at Yale Univ. and at the Inst. of Musical Art in N.Y. (M.B., 1922); also took lessons in organ with Widor in Paris. Returning to America, he served as organist in several N.Y. churches; from 1923 to 1928 he was on the faculty of Smith Coll.; in 1928 he was appointed to the School of Music at Yale Univ., where he later was a prof. of theory (1947–60). From 1936 to 1951 he conducted the New Haven Sym. Orch.; was also organist and choirmaster of Christ Church in New Haven. As a composer, Donovan adopted a modern polyphonic style in his choral works, while his instrumental scores often reveal impressionistic traits.

WORKS: ORCH.: *Smoke and Steel*, symphonic poem (1932); Sym. for Chamber Orch. (1936); *New England Chronicle*, overture (1947); *Passacaglia on Vermont Folk Tunes* (1949); Sym. (1956); *Epos* (1963). **CHAMBER:** *Wood-Notes* for Flute, Harp, and Strings (1925); Sextet for Wind Instruments and Piano (1932); 2 piano trios (1937, 1963); Serenade for Oboe, Violin, Viola, and Cello (1939); *Terzetto* for 2 Violins and Viola (1950); Woodwind Quartet (1953); *Soundings* for Trumpet, Bassoon, and Percussion (1953); *Music for 6* (1961). **KEYBOARD:** 2 suites for piano (1932, 1953); much organ music. **CHORAL:** *Fantasy on American Folk Ballads* for Men's Voices and Piano (1940); *Mass* for Unison Voices, Organ, 3 Trumpets, and Timpani (1955); *Forever, O Lord* for Chorus (1965).—**NS/LK/DM**

Dont, Jakob, Austrian violinist, teacher, and composer; b. Vienna, March 2, 1815; d. there, Nov. 17, 1888. He was the son of the cellist Joseph Valentin Dont (b. Georgenthal, Bohemia, April 15, 1776; d. Vienna, Dec. 14, 1833). He was a pupil of Bohm and Hellmesberger (Sr.) at the Vienna Cons., and then joined the orch. of the Hofburgtheater in 1831, and the court orch. in 1834. He taught in the Akademie der Tonkunst and the Seminary at St. Anna; Leopold Auer was his pupil. From 1873 he was a prof. at the Vienna Cons. His book of violin studies, *Gradus ad Parnassum*, is widely known. Altogether he publ. some 50 works.—**NS/LK/DM**

Donzelli, Domenico, Italian tenor; b. Bergamo, Feb. 2, 1790; d. Bologna, March 31, 1873. He was a student of Branchi in Bergamo, where he made his operatic debut in Mayr's *Elisa* in 1808. He then continued his training in Naples with Viganoni and Crivelli. After appearing throughout his homeland, he made his Paris debut as Rossini's Otello in 1825. In 1829 he sang at the King's Theatre in London. On Dec. 26, 1831, he created the role of Pollione in Bellini's *Norma* at Milan's La Scala. He continued to sing widely until his retirement in 1844.—**NS/LK/DM**

Dooley, William (Edward), American baritone; b. Modesto, Calif., Sept. 9, 1932. He was a pupil of Lucy Lee Call at the Eastman School of Music in Rochester, N.Y., and of Viktoria Prestel and Hedwig Fichtmüller in Munich. In 1957 he made his operatic debut as Rodrigo in *Don Carlos* in Heidelberg; after singing at the Bielefeld Stadttheater (1959–62), he was a member of the Berlin Deutsche Oper (from 1962), where he sang in the premieres of Sessions's *Montezuma* (1964), Reimann's *Gespenstersonate* (1984), and Rihm's *Oedipus* (1987). In 1964 he appeared at the Salzburg Festival, returning there in 1966 to sing in the premiere of Henze's *The Bassarids*. On Feb. 15, 1964, he made his Metropolitan Opera debut in N.Y. as Eugene Onegin, remaining on its roster until 1977. His engagements as a concert artist took him to many of the principal North American and European music centers. Among his prominent roles were Pizarro, Kothner, Escamillo, Macbeth, Amonasro, Telramund, Mandryka, Nick Shadow, and Wozzeck.—**NS/LK/DM**

Door, Anton, noted Austrian pianist and pedagogue; b. Vienna, June 20, 1833; d. there, Nov. 7, 1919. He was a pupil of Czerny (piano) and Sechter (composition) in Vienna. He gave successful concerts in Germany. After a tour in Sweden (1856–57), he went to Russia and taught at the Moscow Cons. (1864). In 1869 he returned to Vienna and was prof. of the advanced piano class at the Cons. (1869–1901).—**NS/LK/DM**

Doors, The, hugely influential rock group of the 1960s. **MEMBERSHIP:** Jim Morrison, lead voc. (b. Melbourne, Fla., Dec. 8, 1943; d. Paris, France, July 3, 1971); Ray Manzarek, kybd., voc. (b. Chicago, Feb. 12, 1935); Robby Krieger, gtr. (b. Los Angeles, Jan. 8, 1946); John Densmore, drm. (b. Los Angeles, Dec. 1, 1945).

Jim Morrison was born into a naval family and eventually enrolled in the theater arts department of UCLA in 1964, majoring in film. In 1965, he met classically trained keyboardist Ray Manzarek while attending film classes at UCLA The two quickly contacted jazz drummer John Densmore about forming a music group, and The Doors' lineup was completed with the addition of Densmore's acquaintance Robbie Krieger. After several months of rehearsal, The Doors were hired to play at L.A.'s Whiskey-A-Go-Go for four months. Recommended to Jac Holzman of Elektra Records by Love's Arthur Lee, the group signed with the label and recorded their debut album in 1966. A stunning blend of rock and aural theater, *The Doors* was an instant success through widespread FM radio airplay, thus becoming one of the first rock albums popularized by the "alternative" media. The album contained Morrison's psychosexual epic "The End" and sported a number of hard-driving rock songs such as "Break on Through," "Take It as It Comes" and Krieger's "Light My Fire." Shortened from its original seven-minute length for release as a single, "Light My Fire" became a top hit in 1967 and broadened The Doors' base of popularity beyond the underground. The album remained on the album charts for more than two years.

Exhibiting more sophisticated musical arrangements, *Strange Days* contained another extended Morrison piece, the 11-minute "When the Music's Over," the potent rock song "My Eyes Have Seen You," and the haunting ballads "Strange Days" and "Unhappy Girl." "People Are Strange" and "Love Me Two Times" became the hits from the album. *Waiting for the Sun* included the printed words to the epic Morrison poem "The Celebration of the Lizard," and featured "Not to Touch the Earth," Krieger's puerile top hit "Hello, I Love You," and the moderate hit "Unknown Soldier." Morrison's anarchistic "Five to One" bore stark contrast to the album's otherwise shallow ballads.

In the meantime, given Morrison's penchant for drama in performance, The Doors became an enormous concert attraction by the end of 1968. As audiences grew larger, Morrison increased the theatricality, but his performances became erratic in 1969, culminating in his arrest for indecent exposure in Miami that March. Many subsequent concerts turned into outrageous fiascos due to Morrison's antics.

The Soft Parade was dominated by Krieger's juvenile lyrics and produced one major hit with "Touch Me." The Doors returned to rock with "Roadhouse Blues" and "You Make Me Real" from *Morrison Hotel*. Following the album's release, The Doors completed a successful tour largely free of untoward incidents. *L.A. Woman*, The Doors' final album with Jim Morrison, included the excellent title song and yielded two hits with "Love Her Madly" and "Riders on the Storm."

In March 1971, a disillusioned and weary Jim Morrison, beset by legal problems and years of alcohol and drug abuse, moved to Paris, France, for rest and recuperation, intent on devoting himself to his poetry. He died under mysterious circumstances on July 3, 1971, and was buried in Pere Lachaise cemetery without an autopsy. News of his death was withheld until after his burial, and speculation began that he died of a heroin overdose, although the cause of death was listed as a heart attack. The three remaining Doors persevered for two albums before disbanding at the end of 1972.

Ray Manzarek recorded two obscure albums for Mercury before forming Nite City with vocalist Noah James for one album on 20th Century. Manzarek subsequently produced the first four albums by the L.A. band X. Robbie Krieger and John Densmore formed The Butts Band for two albums on Blue Thumb. Krieger later recorded the jazz-rock album *Robbie Krieger and Friends* before working with X, Iggy Pop, and Phillip Glass. In 1989, he recorded the all-instrumental album *No Habla* for the I.R.S. label and toured with Eric Burdon in 1990. Beginning in the late 1980s, Manzarek collaborated with poet Michael McClure, resulting in the poetry and music set *Love Lion* in 1993. By the mid-1990s Manzarek

was involved in a variety of film projects.

In 1978, Robbie Krieger, Ray Manzarek, and John Densmore edited over 20 hours of Jim Morrison's recited poetry for *An American Prayer*, for which they provided the musical backdrop. The opening sequence to Francis Ford Coppola's epic 1979 Vietnam War film *Apocalypse Now* used The Doors' "The End." Interest in the career of Jim Morrison and The Doors was fully revived in 1980 with the publication of longtime Doors associate Danny Sugerman's Morrison biography *No One Here Gets Out Alive* (with Jerry Hopkins) and the release of *Greatest Hits*, which stayed on the album charts for nearly two years. Volumes of Jim Morrison's poetry were published in 1988 and 1990, and another surge of interest in the group took place with the release of the Oliver Stone movie *The Doors* in 1991.

One of the first groups to achieve "underground" popularity by means of extensive FM radio airplay, The Doors were one of the first rock groups to have an extended album cut edited down for release as a single ("Light My Fire"). An excellent improvisatory group, The Doors' sound was grounded in the keyboard playing of Ray Manzarek, who became one of the few rock keyboardists to be recognized for his individual style. Fronted by vocalist Jim Morrison, who contributed powerful pieces of surreal poetry often preoccupied with sex and death, The Doors explored the dark and forbidding side of life years before heavy-metal and punk artists did. In acting out Morrison's poetry with carefully orchestrated performances in concert, The Doors became perhaps the first rock group to consciously inject serious and often compelling theatrics into their act. Furthermore, like Bob Dylan and John Lennon, Morrison was able to use his musical success as a springboard for recognition as a literary poet. As Morrison's latter-day performances turned into self-indulgent spectacle, he set the stage for the mythologizing of his persona that occurred after his unexpected death in 1971. The Doors were inducted into the Rock and Roll Hall of Fame in 1993.

DISC.: THE DOORS: *The Doors* (1967); *Strange Days* (1967); *Waiting for the Sun* (1968); *The Soft Parade* (1969); *Morrison Hotel* (1970); *Absolutely Live* (1970); *13* (1970); *L.A. Woman* (1971); *Strange Days/L.A. Woman; Other Voices* (1971); *Weird Scenes inside the Gold Mine* (1971); *Full Circle* (1972); *Best* (1973); *An American Prayer* (1978); *Greatest Hits* (1980/91); *Alive She Cried* (1983/84); *Classics* (1985); *Best* (1987); *Live at the Hollywood Bowl* (1987; recorded July 5, 1968); *The Doors* (music from the soundtrack; 1991); *In Concert* (1991); *Live in Europe 1968* (1991); *Vision* (1991); *Elektra* (1995); *The Doors Box Set* (1997). **THE BUTTS BAND:** *The Butts Band* (1974); *Hear and Now* (1975); *The Complete Recordings* (1995). **ROBBIE KRIEGER:** *Robbie Krieger and Friends* (1977); *World Pacific* (1991); *Door Jams* (1989; recorded 1977–85); *No Habla* (1989); *RKO Live* (1995). **RAY MANZAREK:** *The Golden Scarab* (1973); *The Whole Thing Started with Rock and Roll* (1975); *Carmina Burina* (1983). **NITE CITY:** *Nite City* (1977). **MICHAEL MCCLURE/RAY MANZAREK:** *Love Lion* (1993).

WRITINGS: J. Morrison, *Wilderness: The Lost Writings of J. M.* (1988; 1989); J. Morrison, *The American Night: The Writings of J. M.* (1990); J. Densmore, *Riders on the Storm: My Life with J. M. and The Doors* (1990).

BIBL.: M. Jahn, *J. M. and The Doors* (1969); J. Hopkins and D. Sugerman, *No One Here Gets Out Alive* (1980); D. Sugerman *The Doors: An Illustrated History* (1983); *The Lord and the New Creatures* (1970; 1987); J. Tobler and A. Doe, *The Doors: In Their Own Words* (1988; 1991); D. Dalton, *Mr. Mojo Risin': J. M., The Last Holy Fool* (1991); F. Lisciandro, *Morrison: A Feast of Friends* (1991); J. Morrison, J. Riordan, J. Prochnicky, *Break on Through: The Life and Death of J. M.* (1991); J. Hopkins, *The Lizard King: The Essential J. M.* (1992); R. Clarke, *The Doors: Dance on Fire* (1993); F. Lisciandro, *J. M., An Hour of Magic* (1996); J. M. Rocco (ed.), *The Doors Companion: Four Decades of Commentary* (1997); P. Butler, *Angels Dance and Angels Die: The Tragic Romance of Pamela and Jim Morrison* (1998).—BH

Doorslaer, Georges van, Belgian music scholar; b. Mechelen, Sept. 27, 1864; d. there, Jan. 16, 1940. He studied medicine; music was his avocation. In association with Charles van den Borren, he began a detailed study of early Belgian music, becoming particularly interested in the history of the carillon. He wrote numerous articles on Philippe de Monte, and ed. his works with van den Borren (31 vols., Bruges, 1927–39; reprint 1965).

WRITINGS: *La vie et les oeuvres de Philippe de Monte* (Brussels, 1921); *Le Carillon de la Tour de Saint-Rombaut à Malines* (Mechelen, 1926); *De Beiaard van Aalst* (Mechelen, 1926); *La corporation et les ouvrages des orfèvres malinois* (Antwerp, 1935).—NS/LK/DM

Dopper, Cornelis, Dutch conductor and composer; b. Stadskanaal, near Groningen, Feb. 7, 1870; d. Amsterdam, Sept. 18, 1939. He was a student of Jadassohn and Reinecke at the Leipzig Cons. (1887–90). After serving as a coach and conductor with the Netherlands Opera in Amsterdam (1896–1903), he was conductor of the Savage Opera Co., with which he toured North America. From 1908 to 1931 he held the post of 2nd conductor under Mengelberg with the Concertgebouw Orch. in Amsterdam. He introduced youth concerts to the Netherlands. His well-crafted scores were composed in a late Romantic vein.

WORKS: DRAMATIC: O p e r a : *Het blinde meisje von Castel Cuillé* (1892; The Hague, Dec. 17, 1894); *Frithof* (1895); *William Ratcliff* (1896–1901; Weimar, Oct. 19, 1909); *Het eerekruis* (1902; Amsterdam, Jan. 9, 1903); *Don Quichotte* (unfinished). B a l l e t : *Meidevorn.* ORCH.: 7 syms.: No. 1, *Diana* (1896), No. 2 (1903), No. 3, *Rembrandt* (1892), No. 4, *Symphonietta* (1906), No. 5, *Symphonia epica* (1914), No. 6, *Amsterdam* (1912), and No. 7, *Zuiderzee* (1919); *Ciaconna gotica* (Amsterdam, Oct. 24, 1920); overtures; concertos; suites. OTHER: Chamber music; piano pieces; choral works; songs.—NS/LK/DM

Doppler, (Albert) Franz (Ferenc), Austrian flutist, composer, and conductor, brother of **Karl (Károly) Doppler;** b. Lemberg, Oct. 16, 1821; d. Baden, near Vienna, July 27, 1883. He studied music with his father, then played 1st flute in the Pest Opera Orch. In 1858 settled in Vienna as ballet conductor at the court opera, and also taught flute at the Cons. from 1865. His first opera, *Benjowsky,* was well received in Pest (Sept. 29, 1847) and had several revivals under the title *Afanasia.* The following operas were also produced in Pest:

Ilka (Dec. 29, 1849), *Wanda* (Dec. 20, 1850), and *A két huszár* (March 12, 1853). His last opera, *Judith,* was produced in Vienna (Dec. 30, 1870). He also wrote 15 ballets, various orch. works, choral music, etc.—NS/LK/DM

Doppler, Árpád, Austrian pianist and composer, son of **Karl (Károly) Doppler;** b. Pest, June 5, 1857; d. Stuttgart, Aug. 13, 1927. He went to Stuttgart as a young man and studied there. He was engaged to teach in N.Y. and spent three years there (1880–83). He later returned to Stuttgart and taught at the Cons. He publ. a number of salon pieces for piano, and also wrote two operas, *Halixula* (Caligula; Stuttgart, 1891) and *Much Ado about Nothing.*—NS/LK/DM

Doppler, Karl (Károly), Austrian flutist, composer, and conductor, brother of **(Albert) Franz (Ferenc) Doppler;** b. Lemberg, Sept. 12, 1825; d. Stuttgart, March 10, 1900. Like his father and his brother, he became an excellent flute player and gave concerts in all the major cities of Europe. He was then appointed as court Kapellmeister in Stuttgart, and held this position for 33 years (1865–98). He wrote an opera, *A gránátos tábór* (The Grenadier Camp; Pest, 1853), and pieces for the flute.—NS/LK/DM

Doran, Matt (Higgins), American composer, teacher, and flutist; b. Covington, Ky., Sept. 1, 1921. He studied flute, attended Los Angeles City Coll., and pursued training in composition at the Univ. of Southern Calif. in Los Angeles (B.M., 1947; D.M.A., 1953). He taught at Del Mar Coll. in Corpus Christi (1953–55) and at Ball State Coll. in Muncie, Ind. (1956–57). In 1957 he became an instructor at Mount St. Mary Coll. in Los Angeles, where he served as a prof. from 1966 to 1986. While his output includes works in most of the major genres, he has composed many scores for flute.

WORKS: DRAMATIC: 10 operas, including *The Committee* (1954–55; Corpus Christi, May 25, 1955) and *Marriage Counselor* (Los Angeles, March 12, 1977). ORCH.: 3 syms. (1946, c. 1960, 1977); *Essay* (1955); *Youth Overture* (1964); Piano Concerto (1970; rev. 1973); Double Concerto for Flute, Guitar, and Strings (1975); Cello Concerto (1976); 2 chamber syms. (1979, 1984); Concertino for Marimba and Chamber Orch. (1986); Double Concerto for Piano, Flute, and Strings (1991). CHAMBER: *7 Short Pieces* for Clarinet (1966); Clarinet Sonata (1967); Sonatina for Flute and Cello (1968); Quartet for 4 Cellos (1976); Trio for Flute, Clarinet, and Piano (1979); Sonatina for Oboe and Piano (1982); Flute Sextet (1987); Octet for Flutes (1989); *Faces of Jazz* for Flute and Piano (1990); Flute Sonata (1993); Trio for Flute, Viola, and Harp (1998). P i a n o : 4 sonatas (1960; 1981–82; 1993; 1994). VOCAL: *Song of Mercy and Judgment,* oratorio (1953); *Eskaton,* oratorio (1976); *To the Moon* for Soprano, Horn, and Piano (1979).—NS/LK/DM

Doráti, Antal, distinguished Hungarian-born American conductor and composer; b. Budapest, April 9, 1906; d. Gerzensee, near Bern, Nov. 13, 1988. He studied with Leo Weiner, both privately and at the Franz Liszt Academy of Music in Budapest, where he also received instruction in composition from Kodály

(1920–24). He was on the staff of the Budapest Opera (1924–28); after conducting at the Dresden State Opera (1928–29), he was Generalmusikdirektor in Münster (1929–32). In 1933 he went to France, where he conducted the Ballets Russes de Monte Carlo, which he took on a tour of Australia (1938). He made his U.S. debut as guest conductor with the National Sym. Orch. in Washington, D.C., in 1937. In 1940 he settled in the U.S., becoming a naturalized citizen in 1947. He began his American career as music director of the American Ballet Theatre in N.Y. (1941–44); after serving as conductor of the Dallas Sym. Orch. (1945–49), he was music director of the Minneapolis Sym. Orch. (1949–60). From 1963 to 1966 he was chief conductor of the BBC Sym. Orch. in London; then of the Stockholm Phil. (1966–70). He was music director of the National Sym. Orch. in Washington, D.C. (1970–77), and of the Detroit Sym. Orch. (1977–81); was also principal conductor of the Royal Phil. in London (1975–79). He made numerous guest conducting appearances in Europe and North America, earning a well- deserved reputation as an orch. builder. His prolific recording output made him one of the best-known conductors of his time. His recordings of Haydn operas and all the Haydn syms. were particularly commendable. In 1984 he was made an honorary Knight Commander of the Order of the British Empire. In 1969 he married **Ilse von Alpenheim**, who often appeared as a soloist under his direction. His autobiography was publ. as *Notes of Seven Decades* (London, 1979).

Works: *Divertimento* for Orch.; *Graduation Ball*, ballet, arranged from the waltzes of Johann Strauss; *The Way of the Cross*, dramatic cantata (Minneapolis, April 19, 1957); 2 syms.: No. 1 (Minneapolis, March 18, 1960) and No. 2, *Querela pacis* (Detroit, April 24, 1986); *7 Pieces* for Orch. (1961; perf. as a ballet, *Maddalena*); Piano Concerto (1974; Washington, D.C., Oct. 28, 1975); Cello Concerto (Louisville, Oct. 1, 1976); chamber music. **—NS/LK/DM**

Doret, Gustave, Swiss composer and conductor; b. Aigle, Sept. 20, 1866; d. Lausanne, April 19, 1943. He received his first instruction at Lausanne; studied violin with Joachim in Berlin (1885–87); then entered the Paris Cons. as a pupil of Marsick (violin) and Dubois and Massenet (composition). He was conductor of the Concerts d'Harcourt and of the Société Nationale de Musique in Paris (1893–95); at the Opéra-Comique (1907–09); also appeared as a visiting conductor in Rome, London, and Amsterdam. In his music, Doret cultivated the spirit of Swiss folk songs; his vocal writing is distinguished by its natural flow of melody. He publ. *Musique et musiciens* (1915), *Lettres à ma nièce sur la musique en Suisse* (1919), *Pour notre indépendance musicale* (1920), and *Temps et contretemps* (1942).

Works: DRAMATIC: O p e r a : *Maedeli* (1901); *Les Armaillis* (Paris, Oct. 23, 1906; rev. version, Paris, May 5, 1930); *Le Nain du Hasli* (Geneva, Feb. 6, 1908); *Loÿs*, dramatic legend (Vevey, 1912); *La Tisseuse d'Orties* (Paris, 1926); incidental music. **OTHER:** *Voix de la Patrie*, cantata (1891); *Les Sept Paroles du Christ*, oratorio (1895); *La Fête des vignerons* (1905); String Quartet; Piano Quintet; about 150 songs.

Bibl.: J. Dupérier, *G. D.* (Paris, 1932).**—NS/LK/DM**

Dorfmann, Ania, Russian-American pianist and teacher; b. Odessa, July 9, 1899; d. N.Y., April 21, 1984. As a very young child in Russia, she teamed up with Jascha Heifetz in duo recitals; then was accepted at the age of 12 at the Paris Cons., where her teacher was Isidor Philipp. She returned to Russia just before the Revolution, but was able to leave again in 1920; she toured in Europe as a concert pianist; in 1936 she emigrated to America, giving her first American recital in N.Y. on Nov. 27, 1936. On Dec. 2, 1939 and Nov. 12, 1944 she appeared as a soloist with Toscanini and the NBC Sym. Orch. in N.Y. She later devoted herself mainly to teaching and was on the faculty of the Juilliard School of Music in N.Y. from 1966.**—NS/LK/DM**

Doria, Clara
See **Rogers, Clara Kathleen (née Barnett)**

Dorian, Frederick (real name, **Friedrich Deutsch**), eminent Austrian-born American music scholar; b. Vienna, July 1, 1902; d. Pittsburgh, Jan. 24, 1991. He studied musicology with Adler at the Univ. of Vienna (Ph.D., 1925, with the diss. *Die Fugenarbeit in den Werken Beethovens*; publ. in *Studien zur Musikwissenschaft*, XIV, 1927); also took piano lessons with Steuermann and studied composition privately with Webern. He was also closely associated with Schoenberg; Dorian's family apartment housed the headquarters of the famous Soc. for Private Musical Performances, organized by Schoenberg, Berg, and Webern. He also took courses in conducting, achieving a high degree of professionalism. He served as music critic of the *Berliner Morgenpost* (1930–33), the *Frankfurter Zeitung* (1934), and the *Neues Wiener Journal* (1935–36). In 1936 he emigrated to the U.S., becoming a naturalized citizen in 1941. From 1936 to 1954 he was a member of the Carnegie-Mellon Univ. (formerly Carnegie Inst. of Technology) in Pittsburgh; there he organized an opera dept., and conducted its inaugural performance; from 1971 to 1975 he served as Andrew Mellon Lecturer there. From 1975 to 1977 he was visiting lecturer on music history at the Curtis Inst. of Music in Philadelphia. In 1978 he gave lectures on musicology at the Hebrew Univ. in Jerusalem. He also served, from 1945, as program annotator for the Pittsburgh Sym. Orch. program magazine.

Writings: *Hausmusik alter Meister* (3 vols., Berlin, 1933); *The History of Music in Performance* (N.Y., 1942; 2nd ed., 1966); *The Musical Workshop* (N.Y., 1947); *Commitment to Culture* (Pittsburgh, 1964).**—NS/LK/DM**

Dorn, Alexander (Julius Paul), German pianist, conductor, and composer, son of **Heinrich (Ludwig Egmont) Dorn;** b. Riga, June 8, 1833; d. Berlin, Nov. 27, 1901. He studied with his father, and then traveled as a pianist and choral conductor. He was in Egypt (1855–65) and then settled in Berlin, where he taught piano at the Hochschule für Musik. He wrote more than 400 compositions, including masses, operettas, and a number of salon pieces for piano.**—NS/LK/DM**

Dorn, Heinrich (Ludwig Egmont), noted German conductor, pedagogue, and composer, father of

Alexander (Julius Paul) Dorn; b. Königsberg, Nov. 14, 1800; d. Berlin, Jan. 10, 1892. He was a law student at Königsberg in 1823, but studied music diligently, continuing in Berlin under L. Berger (piano), Zelter, and B. Klein. After teaching in Frankfurt am Main, he became Kapellmeister of the Königsberg Theater in 1828. In 1829 he became music director of the Leipzig Theater. In 1830 Schumann became his pupil. In 1832 he went to the Hamburg Theater, and was concurrently music director at St. Peter's Cathedral in Riga. Wagner conducted the premiere of his opera *Der Schöffe von Paris* in Riga in 1838. After Wagner lost his post at the Riga Theater in 1839, Dorn was named his successor. The two subsequently became bitter enemies. Dorn next went to Cologne, where he served as Kapellmeister at the theater and of the concerts of the Singverein and Musikalischen Gesellschaft (1843–44). He then was conductor of the Lower Rhenish Music Festivals (1844–47). In 1845 he founded the Rheinische Musikschule, which became the Cologne Cons. under Hiller's directorship in 1850. For his services to music in Cologne, he was accorded the title of Royal Musikdirektor in 1847. In 1849 he succeeded Nicolai as court Kapellmeister of the Royal Opera in Berlin. In 1854 he anticipated Wagner by bringing out his opera *Die Nibelungen*; although initially successful, it was eventually supplanted by Wagner's masterful *Ring* cycle. Dorn was pensioned with the title of Royal Prof. in 1869. He subsequently busied himself with teaching and writing music criticism. He publ. an autobiography, *Aus meinem Leben* (7 vols., Berlin, 1870–86; includes various essays).

WORKS: DRAMATIC: Opera: *Die Rolandsknappen* (Berlin, 1826); *Der Zauberer und das Ungethüm* (Berlin, 1827); *Die Bettlerin* (Königsberg, 1827); *Abu Kara* (Leipzig, 1831); *Das Schwärmermädchen* (Leipzig, 1832); *Der Schöffe von Paris* (Riga, Sept. 27, 1838); *Das Banner von England* (Riga, 1841); *Die Musiker von Aix-la-Chapelle* (1848); *Artaxerxes* (Berlin, 1850); *Die Nibelungen* (Berlin, March 27, 1854); *Ein Tag in Russland* (Berlin, 1856); *Der Botenläufer von Pirna* (Mannheim, March 15, 1865); *Gewitter bei Sonnenschein* (Dresden, 1865). **Ballet:** *Amors Macht* (Leipzig, 1830). **OTHER:** Orch. music; choral pieces; songs; piano music.

BIBL.: A. Rauh, *H. D. als Opernkomponist* (diss., Univ. of Munich, 1939).—NS/LK/DM

Dorough, Bob (actually, Robert),

jazz pianist, singer, writer; b. Cherry Hill, Ark., Dec. 12, 1923. Dorough studied composition and piano at North Tex. State Teachers' Coll., the first American school with a jazz curriculum. He moved to N.Y. in 1949, studying at Columbia Univ. through 1952. During the early 1950s, Dorough accompanied boxer Sugar Ray Robinson's musical revue, then performed in Paris with Blossom Dearie and her Blue Stars. He returned to N.Y. in 1955, and recorded his first session as a leader a year later, featuring his vocal tribute to Charlie Parker, "Yardbird Suite." He got his next big break in 1962 when Miles Davis asked him to write some songs for his band, resulting in the decidedly unsentimental Christmas Tune "Blue Xmas" as well as "Nothing Like You"; the latter did not appear on disc until Davis's 1967 album *Sorcerer*. He wrote and performed many of the songs, such as "Multiplication Rock," for the popular children's educational cartoon series *Schoolhouse Rock* in the 1970s; Rhino Records released a four-CD box set of these much-loved tunes in 1996. He continues to tour on the jazz circuit, and released his first "new" album in a decade on a major label in 1997. He lives in the Delaware Water Gap area of Pa.

DISC.: *Devil May Care* (1956, 1982); *Yardbird Suite* (1956); *Oliver (Songs from the Hit Show)* (1963); *Just About Everything* (1966); *Beginning to See the Light* (1976); *That's the Way I Feel Now: A Tribute to Thelonious Monk* (1984); *Memorial to Charlie Parker* (with Phil Woods; 1985); *Skabadabba* (1987); *Schoolhouse Rock!* (1996); *Right on My Way* (1997).—LP

Dorsey, Jimmy (actually, James Francis),

American bandleader, saxophonist, and clarinet player; b. Shenandoah, Pa., Feb. 29, 1904; d. N.Y., June 12, 1957. Dorsey's was one of the top orchestras of the Swing Era. He reached his commercial peak during the first half of the 1940s, when he scored such Latin-tinged hits as "Amapola," "Besame Mucho," and "Tangerine," but his notable work as an instrumentalist dates back to the 1920s.

Dorsey was the first son of Thomas Francis and Theresa Langton Dorsey. His father, a music teacher and the director of the Elmore marching band, gave him early music instruction, and he was playing cornet in his father's band from the age of seven. He made his professional debut in September 1913 when he appeared with J. Carson McGee's King Trumpeters in N.Y. By 1915 he had switched to reed instruments, playing alto saxophone and clarinet.

Dorsey and his younger brother, trombonist **Tommy Dorsey**, formed Dorsey's Novelty Six in 1920, later renamed Dorsey's Wild Canaries when the group played an extended engagement at a Baltimore amusement park and became one of the first bands to appear on local radio. Dorsey left to join the Scranton Sirens. He moved to the N.Y.–based California Ramblers about September 1924; in 1925 he played with the Jean Goldkette Orch., and in 1926 he joined Paul Whiteman, the leading bandleader of the day.

Dorsey married Jane Porter on Nov. 5, 1927. They had a daughter, then separated in 1949. By 1928, Dorsey was living in N.Y. and working as a session musician. He and his brother assembled a studio group that recorded as the Dorsey Brothers Orch., scoring their first hit with "Coquette" (music by Carmen Lombardo and John Green, lyrics by Gus Kahn) in June 1928. The Dorseys also played in radio orchestras and in the pit bands of the Broadway musicals *Girl Crazy* (Oct. 14, 1930) and *Everybody's Welcome* (Oct. 13, 1931).

The Dorseys launched a full-fledged performing band in April 1934. They topped the hit parade in May 1935 with "Lullaby of Broadway" (music by Harry Warren, lyrics by Al Dubin). That same month they had a falling-out, and Tommy Dorsey left the band to form his own orchestra. "Chasing Shadows" (music by Abner Silver, lyrics by Benny Davis), recorded prior to the split, reached the top of the hit parade in June.

Dorsey and his band backed Bing Crosby on the weekly radio series *Kraft Music Hall* from December 1935 to July 1937. In June 1936, Dorsey scored his first chart-topping record on the hit parade under his own name with "Is It True What They Say about Dixie?" (music by Gerald Marks, lyrics by Irving Caesar and Sammy Lerner). His version of "Change Partners" (music and lyrics by Irving Berlin) shared #1 honors on the hit parade with Fred Astaire's in the fall of 1938.

Dorsey became one of the most successful recording artists of the first half of the 1940s by releasing a series of songs with a Spanish or South American feel, arranged for him by Tutti Camerata and prominently featuring vocalists Bob Eberly (originally, Eberle) and Helen O'Connell. The first of these was "The Breeze and I" (music by Ernesto Lecuona, English lyrics by Al Stillman), adapted from Lecuona's "Andalucia, Suite Española" for solo piano, which went to #1 in September 1940.

In 1941, a year in which Dorsey ranked second only to Glenn Miller as the most popular recording artist in the U.S., he scored five #1 hits: "Amapola (Pretty Little Poppy)" (music by Joseph M. Lacalle, English lyrics by Albert Gamse), the biggest hit of the year and his first million-seller; "My Sister and I" (music and lyrics by Hy Zaret, Joan Whitney, and Alex Kramer); "Maria-Elena" (music by Lorenzo Barcelata, English lyrics by Bob Russell), another million-seller; "Green Eyes (Aquellos Ojo Verdes)" (music by Nilo Menendez, English lyrics by Eddie Woods), a third million-seller; and "Blue Champagne" (music and lyrics by Jimmy Eaton, Grady Watts, and Frank Ryerson).

Dorsey's success stirred the interest of Hollywood, and he began to appear in motion pictures with *Lady, Be Good*, released in September 1941. *The Fleet's In*, released in March 1942, contained his next #1 hit, "Tangerine" (music by Victor Schertzinger, lyrics by Johnny Mercer).

The recording ban launched on Aug. 1, 1942, slowed Dorsey's momentum, but after Decca, his record label, settled with the musicians' union in the fall of 1943, he launched a series of hits, the most successful of which was "Bésame Mucho (Kiss Me Much)" (music by Consuelo Velazquez, English lyrics by Sunny Skylar), which went to #1 in March 1944 and became his fourth million-seller.

Dorsey continued to score hits through 1950 while appearing in a series of films. He and his brother appeared as themselves in the fictionalized screen biography *The Fabulous Dorseys*, released in May 1947. But with the decline of the Swing Era he was forced to disband, and in 1953 he rejoined his brother in a reconstituted Dorsey Brothers Orch. The two hosted a musical variety series on television from 1954 to 1956; in January 1956 they gave Elvis Presley his TV debut.

Dorsey contracted throat cancer in 1956. He took over the leadership of the orchestra following Tommy Dorsey's death in November 1956 but was forced to relinquish it to Lee Castle when he was hospitalized in March 1957. He had recorded a final session, however, and, as he lay dying, his revival of the 1937 song "So Rare" (music by Jack Sharpe, lyrics by Jerry Herst) reached the Top Ten, becoming his fifth million-seller.

DISC.: *Plays His Greatest Hits* (1987); *Dorsey, Then & Now—Fabulous New Jimmy Dorsey* (1988); *Jazz Collector's Edition* (1991); *Pennies from Heaven* (1992); *Best of Jimmy Dorsey & His Orchestra* (1992); *Giants of the Big Band Era: Jimmy Dorsey* (1992); *Contrasts* (1993); *1939–1940* (1993); *Uncollected Jimmy Dorsey* (1993); *22 Original Recordings* (1994); *Perfidia* (1994); *At the 400 Restaurant 1946* (1994); *Don't Be That Way* (1995); *Jimmy Dorsey* (1995); *Tangerine* (1995); *Frolic Club, Miami 7/16/44* (1995); *America Swings—The Great Jimmy Dorsey* (1996); *Mood Hollywood* (1996); *So Rare: Jimmy Dorsey's Boogie Woogie* (1996); *Jimmy Dorsey & His Orchestra: 1940–1950* (1998). **THE DORSEY BROTHERS:** *I'm Getting Sentimental Over You* (1990); *The Dorsey Brothers: Best of the Big Bands* (1992); *Harlem Lullaby* (1994); *Live in the Big Apple* (1994); *NBC Bandstand 8/2/56* (1995); *Live in the Meadowbrook* (1995); *Mood Hollywood* (1996); *Opus No. 1* (1996); *Dorsey-itis* (1996); *Stage Show* (1996); *The Dorsey Brothers, Vol. 1—New York 1928* (1997); *The Dorsey Brothers, Vol. 2—New York 1929–1930* (1997); *1954–1956* (1997); *Tommy & Jimmy Dorsey: Swingin' in Hollywood* (1998).

BIBL.: E. Edwards Jr., G. Hall, and B. Korst, *J. D. and His Orchestra: A Complete Discography* (1966); H. Sanford, *Tommy and J.: The D. Years* (1972); C. Garrod, *J. D. and His Orchestra* (1980). **—WR**

Dorsey, Tommy (actually, Thomas Francis Jr.), American bandleader and trombonist; b. Shenandoah, Pa., Nov. 19, 1905; d. Greenwich, Conn., Nov. 26, 1956.

Dorsey was the most popular bandleader of the Swing Era, consistently placing among the top recording and performing artists from 1935 to 1945. His accomplished trombone playing set the tone for his band's sound, but he maintained his popularity by straddling the sweet and hot styles of swing, balancing ballads and novelty numbers sung by such notable vocalists as Frank Sinatra, Dick Haymes, and Jo Stafford with inventive jazz arrangements by Sy Oliver, Bill Finegan, and others. His record label, RCA Victor, claimed sales of 37 million copies between 1935 and 1950, his biggest hits being "Marie," "I'll Never Smile Again," and "There Are Such Things."

Dorsey was the second son of Thomas Francis and Theresa Langton Dorsey; his older brother **Jimmy Dorsey** was trained by their father, a music teacher and band director, in reed instruments, while Tommy Dorsey received instruction in brass instruments, concentrating primarily on the slide trombone, though he also played trumpet professionally, especially early in his career. The Dorsey brothers played in local bands in Pa. before forming their first group, Dorsey's Novelty Six, in 1920. The group was renamed Dorsey's Wild Canaries when they played an extended engagement at an amusement park in Baltimore in 1922 and made their debut on local radio there.

Over the next several years the brothers played in a succession of bands, including The Scranton Sirens, The California Ramblers, and the orchestras of Jean Goldkette and Paul Whiteman. By the late 1920s they had settled in N.Y., where they worked as session musicians. They made their first recordings with the Dorsey Brothers Orch. in 1927, though this was a studio-only group. Their first hit came with "Coquette" (music by Carmen Lombardo and John Green, lyrics by Gus Kahn) in June 1928.

In 1934 the Dorseys organized a permanent touring band featuring Glenn Miller as arranger and Bob

Crosby as vocalist. The group broke through to popular success in the spring of 1935, first topping the hit parade with "Lullabye of Broadway" (music by Harry Warren, lyrics by Al Dubin) in May. Unfortunately, the brothers feuded, and Tommy Dorsey left to organize his own orchestra. In the meantime, "Chasing Shadows" (music by Abner Silver, lyrics by Benny Davis), recorded before the split, topped the hit parade in June, and "Every Little Movement" and "Every Single Tingle of My Heart" were also in the chart during the summer.

Dorsey began his solo bandleading career successfully; his initial single, "On Treasure Island" (music by Joe Burke, lyrics by Edgar Leslie), with a vocal by Edythe Wright, went to #1 in December, by which time "Don't Give up the Ship" (music by Harry Warren, lyrics by Al Dubin) and "Take Me Back to My Boots and Saddle" (music and lyrics by Walter G. Samuels, Leonard Whitcup, and Teddy Powell) had also reached the hit parade. "Alone" (music by Arthur Freed, lyrics by Nacio Herb Brown) entered the chart at the end of the year and went to #1 in February 1936, but it was preceded by "The Music Goes 'Round and 'Round" (music by Edward Farley and Michael Riley, lyrics by Red Hodgson), featuring the Dorsey small group the Clambake Seven, which entered the chart the first week of January and topped it the second. "Rhythm in My Nursery Rhymes" (music by Jimmie Lunceford and Saul Chaplin, lyrics by Sammy Cahn and Don Raye) was also in the hit parade in January, followed by "Little Rendezvous in Honolulu" (the first Dorsey hit to feature vocalist Jack Leonard) in February and "Lovely Lady" (music by Jimmy McHugh, lyrics by Ted Koehler) in March.

April 1936 saw two more Dorsey-recorded songs in the hit parade, "You Started Me Dreaming" (music by J. Fred Coots, lyrics by Benny Davis) and a fourth chart-topper, "You" (music by Walter Donaldson, lyrics by Harold Adamson). The second half of the year was not quite as successful for Dorsey, but he did have chart entries with "No Regrets" (music by Roy Ingraham, lyrics by Harry Tobias) in July, "Close to Me" (music by Peter De Rose, lyrics by Sam M. Lewis) in October, and "I'm in a Dancing Mood" (music and lyrics by Al Hoffman, Al Goodhart, and Maurice Sigler) in November.

On Jan. 29, 1937, Dorsey recorded an unusual arrangement of Irving Berlin's 1928 song "Marie" in which Jack Leonard's vocal was undercut by interjections from the band. Though the song did not place in the hit parade, the record sold a million copies. (Its B-side, the instrumental "Song of India," based on Rimsky-Korsakov's "Chanson Indoue" from his opera *Sadko*, was also popular.) "Marie" became one of Dorsey's signature songs, and Leonard became one of the most popular band singers. With his success Dorsey gained a sponsored weekly radio program that ran for nearly three years.

Dorsey returned to the hit parade with three songs in August 1937: the instrumental "Satan Takes a Holiday" (music by Larry Clinton); "My Cabin of Dreams" (music and lyrics by Nick Madison, Al Frazzini, Charles Kenny, and Nick Kenny); and "Stardust on the Moon" (music

and lyrics by Emery Deutsch and Jimmy Rogan). "Have You Got Any Castles, Baby?" (music by Richard A. Whiting, lyrics by Johnny Mercer) was in the chart in September, and in November Dorsey had two listings: "If It's the Last Thing I Do" (music by Saul Chaplin, lyrics by Sammy Cahn) and "Once in a While" (music by Michael Edwards, lyrics by Bud Green), which became his fifth #1 hit.

Dorsey had 11 songs in the hit parade in 1938: "The Dipsy Doodle" (music and lyrics by Larry Clinton); "In the Still of the Night" (music and lyrics by Cole Porter); "I Can Dream, Can't I?" (music by Sammy Fain, lyrics by Irving Kahal); "You Couldn't Be Cuter" (music by Jerome Kern, lyrics by Dorothy Fields); "Bewildered" (music and lyrics by Leonard Whitcup and Teddy Powell); "You Leave Me Breathless" (music by Frederick Hollander, lyrics by Ralph Freed); his sixth #1, "Music, Maestro, Please" (music by Allie Wrubel, lyrics by Herb Magidson); "Now It Can Be Told" (music and lyrics by Irving Berlin); "Stop Beating 'Round the Mulberry Bush" (music by Clay Boland, lyrics by Bickley Reichner); "My Own" (music by Jimmy McHugh, lyrics by Harold Adamson); and "You Got Me." On Sept. 16, 1938, he cut the best-selling record of his career, an instrumental treatment of "Boogie Woogie" (music by Clarence "Pinetop" Smith) that sold a reported four million copies in its initial release and subsequent reissues.

Dorsey scored another 11 hit parade entries in 1939: "This Is It" (music by Arthur Schwartz, lyrics by Dorothy Fields); his seventh chart-topper, "Our Love" (music and lyrics by Larry Clinton, Buddy Bernier, and Bob Emmerich); "A New Moon and an Old Serenade" (music by Nacio Herb Brown, lyrics by Arthur Freed); "All I Remember Is You" (music by James Van Heusen, lyrics by Eddie DeLange); "In the Middle of a Dream"; "This Is No Dream" (music by Ted Shapiro and Tommy Dorsey, lyrics by Benny Davis); "The Lamp Is Low" (music by Peter De Rose and Bert Shefter, lyrics by Mitchell Parish); "To You" (music by Ted Shapiro and Tommy Dorsey, lyrics by Benny Davis); "Oh, You Crazy Moon" (music by James Van Heusen, lyrics by Johnny Burke); "Are You Having Any Fun?" (music by Sammy Fain, lyrics by Jack Yellen); and his eighth chart-topper, "All the Things You Are" (music by Jerome Kern, lyrics by Oscar Hammerstein II). All but one of these records had lead vocals by Jack Leonard, who left Dorsey in November.

Dorsey's first two chart entries of 1940, "Indian Summer" (music by Victor Herbert, lyrics by Al Dubin—his ninth #1 hit) and "To You, Sweetheart, Aloha" (music and lyrics by Harry Owens), also had Leonard vocals, offering a considerable challenge to his replacement. Alan DeWitt was Dorsey's first choice, and he sang on "I've Got My Eyes on You" (music and lyrics by Cole Porter), which was in the hit parade in March. But by that time Dorsey had dismissed him and hired away the male singer in Harry James's band, Frank Sinatra.

Sinatra's first hit parade entry with Dorsey came in June 1940 with "You're Lonely and I'm Lonely" (music and lyrics by Irving Berlin), but he really made his mark with "I'll Never Smile Again" (music and lyrics by Ruth Lowe), on which he was accompanied by Dorsey's vocal group, the Pied Pipers, whose female member was Jo Stafford; it topped the charts in July. Also in July, "Imagination" (music by James Van Heusen, lyrics by Johnny Burke) was in the Top Ten for Dorsey and Sinatra. Alan Storr sang lead on "Only Forever" (music by James V. Monaco, lyrics by Johnny Burke), a Top Ten hit for Dorsey in October, but Sinatra was back on vocals on Dorsey's three remaining Top Ten hits of the year, "Trade Winds" (music by Cliff Friend, lyrics by Charles Tobias), "Our Love Affair" (music by Roger Edens, lyrics by Arthur Freed), and "We Three (My Echo, My Shadow and Me)" (music and lyrics by Nelson Cogane, Sammy Mysels, and Dick Robertson).

Dorsey had nine Top Ten hits in 1941, and Sinatra sang on eight of them. On "Everything Happens to Me" (music by Matt Dennis, lyrics by Tom Adair),"This Love of Mine" (music by Sol Parker and Hank Sanicola, lyrics by Sinatra), and "Two in Love" (music and lyrics by Meredith Willson), Sinatra had the microphone to himself. On "Star Dust" (music by Hoagy Carmichael, lyrics by Mitchell Parish), "Do I Worry?" (music and lyrics by Stanley Cowan and Bobby Worth), and "Dolores" (music by Louis Alter, lyrics by Frank Loesser), he was accompanied by the Pied Pipers. (The last was featured in the Dorsey Orch.'s first film appearance, *Las Vegas Nights*, in March.) "Oh! Look at Me Now" (music by Joe Bushkin, lyrics by John De Vries) and "Let's Get Away from It All" (music by Matt Dennis, lyrics by Tom Adair) found female vocalist Connie Haines joining in with Sinatra and the Pied Pipers. "Yes Indeed!," the sole Dorsey Top Ten hit without Sinatra in 1941, featured vocals by its songwriter, Sy Oliver, and Jo Stafford.

The first full year of World War II in the U.S., 1942, was a difficult one for the recording industry in general and Dorsey in particular. His troupe appeared in a second motion picture, *Ship Ahoy*, in June. At the start of August the musicians' union instituted a recording ban that kept Dorsey out of the studio for more than two years. Sinatra's departure for a solo career was announced that same month. (He was replaced by Dick Haymes, who was unable to record with Dorsey due to the recording ban.) Nevertheless, Dorsey managed three Top Ten hits during the year, "Just as Though You Were Here" (music by John Benson Brooks, lyrics by Eddie DeLange), "Take Me" (music by Rube Bloom, lyrics by Mack David), and "Daybreak" (music by Ferde Grofé, lyrics by Harold Adamson); the first was sung by Sinatra and the Pied Pipers, the other two by Sinatra alone.

In anticipation of the recording ban, Dorsey had stockpiled recordings, and after they were exhausted his record label began reissuing earlier recordings, resulting in a stream of hits over the next two years. "There Are Such Things" (music and lyrics by Stanley Adams, Abel Baer, and George W. Meyer), with vocals by Sinatra and the Pied Pipers, topped the charts in January 1943 and sold a million copies. "It Started All Over Again" (music by Carl Fischer, lyrics by Bill Carey), also with vocals by Sinatra and the Pied Pipers, reached the Top Ten in March. "It's Always You" (music by James Van Heusen,

lyrics by Johnny Burke), with a Sinatra vocal, was originally released in 1941; reissued, it hit the Top Ten in July. "In the Blue of Evening" (music by Alred A. D'Artega, lyrics by Tom Adair), another feature for Sinatra, first appeared in 1942; it went to #1 in August 1943.

Dorsey's 1938 recording of "Boogie Woogie" hit the Top Ten in January 1944. "I'll Be Seeing You" (music by Sammy Fain, lyrics by Irving Kahal), a Sinatra vocal recorded in February 1940, was in the Top Ten in July 1944. Meanwhile, Dorsey continued to perform, and he appeared in a number of MGM movie musicals during the war years: *Presenting Lily Mars* starring Judy Garland in April 1943; *DuBarry Was a Lady* with Red Skelton in August 1943; *Girl Crazy* with Garland and Mickey Rooney in December 1943; and *Broadway Rhythm* with George Murphy in April 1944. He also ended his first marriage to Mildred Kroft, which had produced two children, and married actress Pat Dane on April 8, 1943. This marriage, too, would end in divorce and be followed by a third.

Dorsey's record label settled with the musicians' union in the fall of 1944, and he returned to the studio, resulting in six newly recorded Top Ten hits in 1945. "I Dream of You (More Than You Dream I Do)" (music and lyrics by Marjorie Goetschius and Edna Osser), with a vocal by Freddy Stewart, was popular in January; its flip side, the instrumental "Opus No. 1" (music by Sy Oliver), peaked in March and remained a standard of the Swing Era. "More and More" (music by Jerome Kern, lyrics by E. Y. Harburg), with Bonnie Lou Williams on vocals, hit in April; "A Friend of Yours" (music by James Van Heusen, lyrics by Johnny Burke), vocal by Stuart Foster, in July; "On the Atchison, Topeka & and the Santa Fe" (music by Harry Warren, lyrics by Johnny Mercer), sung by Dorsey's vocal group The Sentimentalists, in August; and "Hong Kong Blues" (music and lyrics by Hoagy Carmichael) with "Skeets" Herfurt on vocals, in October. ("Boogie Woogie," reissued a second time, also reached the Top Ten for a second time in September.) Dorsey appeared in a last MGM feature, *Thrill of a Romance*, starring Esther Williams, in May.

Dorsey also began to score on the album charts in 1945, with his *Getting Sentimental* making the Top Ten in March. His album of songs from *Show Boat* was in the Top Ten in February 1946. Like other bandleaders, however, he suffered from the decline in popularity of swing music, and he disbanded his group in December 1946. He reorganized in 1947 and continued to score on the record charts. His *All-Time Hits* album was in the Top Ten in February 1947, and "How Are Things in Glocca Morra?" (music by Burton Lane, lyrics by E. Y. Harburg) with Stuart Foster on vocals was a Top Ten single for him in March. In May he and his brother starred in their own film biography, *The Fabulous Dorseys*, though it was largely fictionalized.

A second recording ban in 1948 kept Dorsey out of the charts for most of the year, but *Clambake Seven* was a Top Ten hit in October and "Until" (music and lyrics by Jack Fulton and Bob Crosby) featuring the Clark Sisters and the Town Criers reached the Top Ten in November. Dorsey appeared in the Danny Kaye film *A*

Song Is Born in October. He scored his last Top Ten singles hits with both sides of a disc released in the spring of 1949, "The Huckle-Buck" (music by Andy Gibson, lyrics by Roy Alfred), vocal by trumpeter Charlie Shavers, and "Again" (music by Lionel Newman, lyrics by Dorcas Cochran), sung by Marcy Lutes. He continued to enjoy album hits for another year, reaching the Top Ten in September 1949 with *And the Band Sings Too* and in April 1950 with *Tommy Dorsey Plays Cole Porter*. He made his final film appearance in *Disc Jockey* in September 1951.

Dorsey and his brother reunited in May 1953; Jimmy Dorsey broke up his band and joined his brother's unit as a featured attraction. The brothers appeared at the Statler Hilton Hotel in N.Y. and launched a television program, *Stage Show*, as a summer replacement for Jackie Gleason's show in the summer of 1954. The show ran occasionally during the 1954–55 season, then regularly during the 1955–56 season. Starting on Jan. 28, 1956, it presented Elvis Presley in his first network television appearances on six consecutive programs. The show went off the air in September 1956. Two months later, Dorsey accidentally choked to death in his sleep after eating a heavy meal and taking sleeping pills. Following Jimmy Dorsey's death in 1957, the Tommy Dorsey orchestra was led by various people. Under the direction of Warren Covington, it scored a million-selling Top Ten hit with "Tea for Two Cha Cha" (music by Vincent Youmans, lyrics by Irving Caesar) in November 1958.

DISC.: *The One and Only Tommy Dorsey* (1988); *All-Time Greatest Hits, Vol. 1* (with Frank Sinatra; 1988); *All-Time Greatest Hits, Vol. 2* (with Frank Sinatra; 1988); *All-Time Greatest Hits, Vol. 3* (with Frank Sinatra; 1989); *Well Get It! The TD CD* (1989); *Best of Tommy Dorsey* (1989); *Sentimental* (1989); *The 17 Number Ones* (1990); *Oh! Look at Me Now & Other Big Band Hits* (with Frank Sinatra; 1990); *The Great Tommy Dorsey* (1991); *Jazz Collector's Edition, Vol. 1* (1991); *Jazz Collector's Edition, Vol. 2* (1991); *Best of Tommy Dorsey & His Orchestra* (1991); *Yes, Indeed!* (1991); *1942 War Bond Broadcasts* (1992); *Boogie Woogie* (1992); *Radio Days* (1992); *Live in Hi-Fi at Casino Gardens* (1992); *One Night Stand with Tommy Dorsey* (1992); *Stardust* (with Frank Sinatra; 1992); *Best of Tommy Dorsey* (1992); *The Post War Era* (1993); *Stop, Look & Listen* (1993); *Tommy Dorsey and His Greatest Band* (1994); *At the Fat Man's 1946–48* (1994); *The Carnegie Hall V-Disc Session—April 1944* (1994); *All Time Hit Parade Rehearsals 1944* (1994); *1936–1938* (1994); *The Song Is You* (with Frank Sinatra; 1994); *I'll Be Seeing You* (with Frank Sinatra; 1994); *24 Gems* (1994); *Sheik of Swing* (1995); *1935–1936* (1995); *His Best Recordings 1928–1942* (1996); *1936* (1996); *Irish American Trombone* (1996); *Dance with Dorsey* (1996); *Greatest Hits* (1996); *The Sentimental Gentleman of Swing* (1996); *Tommy Dorsey/Frank Sinatra: Greatest Hits* (with Frank Sinatra; 1996); *Tommy Dorsey* (1997); *Tommy Dorsey: Members Edition* (1997); *1936–1937* (1997); *Best of Tommy Dorsey & The Clambake Seven 1936–38* (with The Clambake Seven; 1997); *1937* (1997); *1936–41 Broadcasts* (1997); *1938–1939 in Hi-Fi Broadcasts* (1997); *Golden Hits* (1997). **THE DORSEY BROTHERS:** *I'm Getting Sentimental Over You* (1990); *The Dorsey Brothers: Best of the Big Bands* (1992); *Harlem Lullaby* (1994); *Live in the Big Apple* (1994); *NBC Bandstand 8/2/56* (1995); *Live in the Meadowbrook* (1995); *Mood Hollywood* (1996); *Opus No. 1* (1996); *Dorsey-itis* (1996); *Stage Show* (1996); *The Dorsey Brothers, Vol. 1—New York 1928* (1997); *The Dorsey Brothers, Vol. 2—New York 1929–1930* (1997); *1954–1956* (1997); *Tommy & Jimmy Dorsey: Swingin' in Hollywood* (1998).

WRITINGS: *The Modern Trombonist* (1944); *Love in Swingtime* (novel).

BIBL.: H. Sanford, *T. and Jimmy: The D. Years* (1972); C. Garrod, W. Scott, and F. Green, *T. D. and His Orchestra* (discography in two volumes; 1980–82; rev. ed. 1988); R. Stockdale, *T. D.: On the Side* (1995).—**WR**

Dorus-Gras, Julie (-Aimée-Josephe née Van Steenkiste),

South Netherlands soprano; b. Valenciennes, Sept. 7, 1805; d. Paris, Feb. 6, 1896. After training at the Paris Cons., she made her operatic debut at the Théâtre Royal de la Monnaie in Brussels in 1825. On Feb. 12, 1829, she sang in the first Brussels staging of Auber's *La muette de Portici*. She later sang in the famous staging of the score there on Aug. 25, 1830, which set the spark of the Belgian revolution. In 1831 she joined the Paris Opéra, where she created roles in many operas, among them Alice in *Robert le diable* (Nov. 21, 1831), Eudoxie in *La juive* (Feb. 23, 1835), Marguerite de Valois in *Les Huguenots* (Feb. 29, 1836), and Teresa in *Benvenuto Cellini* (Sept. 3, 1838). She continued to sing in Paris until 1846. In 1839 she appeared as a concert artist in London, returning there to sing Lucia at Drury Lane in 1847 and Elvira in *La muette de Portici* at Covent Garden in 1849.—**NS/LK/DM**

Doss, Adolf von,

German composer and priest; b. Pfarrkirchen, Sept. 10, 1823; d. Rome, Aug. 13, 1886. He attended the Dutch Inst. in Munich (1835–43) before going to Switzerland to enter the Jesuit Order in Brig in 1843; he later pursued studies in Fribourg, Vals-les-Bains, Namur, Maastricht, Cologne, and Louvain. After his ordination as a priest in 1855, he served his church in Münster (1855–62), Bonn (1862–66), and Mainz (1866–73). From 1873 to 1884 he was a prof. at St. Servais Jesuit Coll. in Liège, and then was father confessor at the Collegio Germanico in Rome. His entire output was sacred in nature, including his operas and other stage works.

WORKS (all 1st perf. in Liège unless otherwise given): **DRAMATIC: Opera:** *Jean-sans-terre* (Aug. 12, 1875); *Maurice et la légion thébaine* (Aug. 10, 1876); *Robert Bruce* (Aug. 13, 1878); *Witikind, ou La conversion des Saxons* (Aug. 11, 1880); *Un vaut dix* (1881; not perf.); *Percival* (March 1883); also incidental music. **SACRED: Oratorios:** *Oratorio pour la béatification du vénérable Pierre Claver* (Namur, 1852); *La fosse aux lions* (Dec. 29, 1875); *L'hymne de la nuit* (Dec. 27, 1876); *Le festin de Balthazar* (Nov. 27, 1879); *Héliodore* (1881; not perf.); *Ste. Cécile* (Sept. 28, 1883); also 11 masses, numerous motets, and many sacred songs.

BIBL.: O. Pfülf, *Erinnerungen an P. A.v. D., S.J., einen Freund der Jugend* (Freiburg, 1887); J. Ilias, *Un jésuite musicien: Le Père de D.* (Liège, 1938).—**LK/DM**

Dostal, Nico(laus Josef Michäel),

Austrian composer; b. Korneuburg, Nov. 25, 1895; d. Vienna, Oct. 27, 1981. He was the nephew of Hermann Dostal (1874–1930), a composer of operettas and military marches. After studies in Linz and Vienna, he was active at the Innsbruck City Theater; then conducted in St.

Pölten, Romania, and Salzburg. In 1924 he went to Berlin and was active as an arranger and orchestrator of operettas, and as a composer of songs for the theater and films. In 1927 he became a conductor at the Theater am Nollendorfplatz, where he scored a fine success with his first operetta *Clivia* (Dec. 23, 1933). It was followed by the successful operettas *Die Vielgeliebt* (March 5, 1935), *Monika* (Stuttgart, Oct. 3, 1937), *Die ungarische Hochzeit* (Stuttgart, Feb. 4, 1939), and *Manina* (Berlin, Nov. 28, 1942). Among his well-received postwar scores was *Doktor Eisenbart* (Nuremberg, March 29, 1952). His autobiography was publ. as *Ans Ende deiner Träume kommst du nie: Berichte, Bekenntniss, Betrachtungen* (Innsbruck, 1982).

WORKS: DRAMATIC: M u s i c   T h e a t e r : *Clivia* (Berlin, Dec. 23, 1933); *Die Vielgeliebte* (Berlin, March 5, 1935); *Prinzessin Nofretete* (Cologne, Sept. 12, 1936); *Extrablätter* (Bremen, Feb. 17, 1937); *Monika* (Stuttgart, Oct. 3, 1937); *Die ungarische Hochzeit* (Stuttgart, Feb. 4, 1939); *Die Flucht ins Glück* (Stuttgart, Dec. 23, 1940); *Die grosse Tänzerin* (Chemnitz, Feb. 15, 1942); *Eva im Abendkleid* (Chemnitz, Nov. 21, 1942); *Manina* (Berlin, Nov. 28, 1942); *Süsse kleine Freundin* (Wuppertal, Dec. 31, 1949); *Zirkusblut* (Leipzig, March 3, 1950); *Der Kurier der Königin* (Hamburg, March 2, 1950); *Doktor Eisenbart* (Nuremberg, March 29, 1952); *Der dritte Wunsch* (Nuremberg, Feb. 20, 1954); *Liebesbriefe* (Vienna, Nov. 25, 1955); *So macht man Karriere* (Nuremberg, April 29, 1961); *Rhapsodie der Liebe* (Nuremberg, Nov. 9, 1963).—**NS/LK/DM**

Dotzauer, (Justus Johann) Friedrich, famous German cellist; b. Haselrieth, near Hildburghausen, Jan. 20, 1783; d. Dresden, March 6, 1860. He studied piano and violin with Heuschkel and Gleichmann, cello with Hessner, and composition with Ruttinger in Hildburghausen. He made his debut as a cellist at a court concert (1798) and then completed his cello studies with Kriegck in Meiningen (1799). He was a member of the Meiningen Court Orch. (1801–5) and the Leipzig Gewandhaus Orch. (1805–11) before joining the Dresden Court Orch. (1811), where he served as 1st cellist (1821–50). He prepared several valuable teaching manuals. He wrote an opera, *Graziosa* (Dresden, 1841), syms., overtures, cello concertos and other works for cello, sonatas, masses, etc., but these works are conventional and undistinguished. Among his pupils were Carl Schuberth, Friedrich Kummer, and his own son, Karl Ludwig Dotzauer (b. Dresden, Dec. 7, 1811; d. Kassel, July 1, 1897), who was cellist in the Kassel Court Orch. (1830–97).—**NS/LK/DM**

Doubrava, Jaroslav, Czech composer; b. Chrudim, April 25, 1909; d. Prague, Oct. 2, 1960. He was a student of Otakar Jeremiáš (1931–37). During the German occupation of his homeland, he was active in the partisan movement. After the liberation in 1945, he joined the staff of the Czech Radio in Prague, where he served as head of music (1950–55). Among his compositions are particularly well-crafted works for the theater.

WORKS: DRAMATIC: O p e r a : *Sen noci svatojanské* (A Midsummer Night's Dream; 1942–49; Opava, Dec. 21, 1969); *Křest svatého Vladimíra* (The Conversion of St. Vladimir; 1949–50; unfinsihed); *Líný Honza* (Lazy Honza; 1952; unfin-

ished); *Balada o lásce* (Ballad of Love) or *Láska čarovana* (Love Bewitched), opera-ballad (1960; orchestrated by J. Hanuš; Prague, June 21, 1962). **B a l l e t :** *Král Lávra* (King Lavra; 1951); *Don Quijote* (1955). **ORCH.:** 3 syms.: No. 1, *Chorální* (1938–40), No. 2, *Stalingradská* (1943–44), and No. 3, *Tragická* (1956–58); *Partisan March* (1945); *Festive March* (1945); *Autumn Pastorale* (1960; arranged from his unfinished 4th Sym. by O. Macha). **CHAMBER:** 2 violin sonatas (1942, 1958); Sonata for Solo Violin (1942). **P i a n o :** Suite (1937); Sonatina (1938); Sonata (1948–49); children's pieces. **VOCAL:** *Poselstvi* (The Message), oratorio (1939–40); *Bala o krásné smrti* (Ballad of a Beautiful Death), cantata (1941); song cycles.—**NS/LK/DM**

Dougherty, Celius (Hudson), American pianist and composer; b. Glenwood, Minn., May 27, 1902; d. Effort, Pa., Dec. 22, 1986. After training in piano and composition with Ferguson at the Univ. of Minn., he was a piano scholarship student of J. Lhévinne and Goldmark at the Juilliard School of Music in N.Y. He toured as an accompanist to noted singers of the day, several of whom championed his songs; he also toured in duo-piano recitals with Vincent Ruzicka, giving first performances of works by Stravinsky, Schoenberg, Berg, Hindemith et al. Among his compositions were *Many Moons*, opera (Poughkeepsie, N.Y., Dec. 6, 1962), Piano Concerto (1922), String Quartet (1938), Violin Sonata (1928), 2 pianos sonatas (1925, 1934), *Music from Seas and Ships*, sonata for 2 Pianos (1942–43), and more than 100 songs.

BIBL.: J. Bender, *The Songs of C. D.* (thesis, Univ. of Minn., 1981).—**NS/LK/DM**

Douglas, Barry, Irish pianist and conductor; b. Belfast, April 23, 1960. He studied clarinet, cello, and organ, and also received piano lessons from Felicitas Lewinter; he then attended the Belfast School of Music, winning a scholarship to continue training with John Barstow at the Royal Coll. of Music in London, and with Maria Curcio. In 1981 he made his London debut, subsequently winning the Silver Medal at the Arthur Rubinstein Competition in Israel (1983), the Bronze Medal at the Van Cliburn Competition in Fort Worth (1985), and the Gold Medal at the Tchaikovsky Competition in Moscow (1986). In 1988 he made his N.Y. recital debut at Carnegie Hall. During the 1988–89 season, he toured in the U.S., concluding his engagements with an appearance as soloist with the St. Louis Sym. Orch. at N.Y.'s Lincoln Center. He subsequently toured throughout the world. In later years, he also became active as a conductor. In 1999 he founded and became conductor of the Camerata Ireland.—**NS/LK/DM**

Douglas, Clive (Martin), Australian conductor and composer; b. Rushworth, Victoria, July 27, 1903; d. Melbourne, April 29, 1977. He received lessons in violin, piano, orchestration, and conducting before pursuing training with Nickson and Heinze at the Univ. of Melbourne Conservatorium of Music (Mus.B., 1934). In 1936 he joined the conducting staff of the Australian Broadcasting Commission, appearing as a conductor with its orchs. in Hobart (1936–41) and Brisbane (1941–47), and then as assoc. conductor in Sydney

(1947–53) and assoc. and resident conductor in Melbourne (1953–66). In 1953 he received the Coronation Medal, in 1958 he was awarded a Doctor of Music degree from the Univ. of Melbourne, and in 1963 he was made a Life Fellow of the International Inst. of Arts and Letters. In many of his scores, Douglas made use of aboriginal melorhythmic patterns.

WORKS: DRAMATIC: *The Scarlet Letter*, opera (1925–29; unfinished); *Ashmadai*, operetta (1929; 1934–35; 1st public perf. in a radio broadcast, Melbourne, Aug. 17, 1936); *Kaditcha* or *A Bush Legend*, operetta (1937–38; ABC, Tasmania, June 22, 1938; rev. 1956); *Corroboree*, ballet from the operetta *Kaditcha* (1939); *Eleanor*, *Maid Rosamond*, and *Henry of Anjou*, opera trilogy (1941–43); documentary film scores; music for radio and television. ORCH.: *Symphonic Fantasy* (1938); *Carwoola* (1939); *Meet the Orchestra*, educational suite (1944); 3 syms. (*Jubilee*, 1950; *Namatjira*, 1956; 1963); *Sturt 1829* (1952); *Essay* for Strings (1952); *Wangadilla Suite* (1954); *Festival in Natal* (1954); *Greet the Orchestra*, educational suite (1955); *Olympic Overture* (1956); *Coolawidgee*, miniature suite for Small Orch. (1957); *Sinfonietta: Festival of Perth* (1961); *Variations Symphoniques* (1961); *Fanfare Overture* (1961); *Divertimento II* for 2 Pianos and Small Orch. (1962; rev. 1967); *4 Light Orchestra Pieces* (1964); *3 Frescoes* (1969); *Movement in C Major on a Theme of Alfred Hill* (1969); *Pastoral* (1970); *Carnival* (1970); *Discourse* for Strings (1971). CHAMBER: *Divertimento I* for Woodwind Quintet (1962–65). VOCAL: *The Hound of Heaven* for Baritone, Chorus, and Orch. (1933; rev. 1938); *5 Pastels* for Soprano, Celesta, and Strings (1952); *The Lakes of Tasmania* for Voice and Orch. (1954); *Song Landscape* for Soprano or Tenor and String Orch. (1955); *Terra Australis* for Narrator, Soprano, Chorus, and Orch. (1959).—NS/LK/DM

Douglas, Dave (actually, David Dewel),

jazz/world-music trumpeter, composer; b. East Orange, N.J., March 24, 1963. He is an innovative musician often featured at the Knitting Factory in Manhattan with a variety of groups. As a youth he was exposed to many different types of music. He began playing improvised music while attending a year abroad in Barcelona, Spain, as part of a special program offered through his high school. He went on to study composition and performance in Boston for two years at the Berklee Coll. of Music and the New England Cons. Moving to N.Y. in 1984, he completed a Bachelor of Arts degree at N.Y.U.'s Gallatin Division; also during this time he performed in the streets of N.Y.C. with other young musicians. His education continued on the bandstand with Horace Silver's ensemble, touring internationally for three months in 1987. His experiences with Eastern European music began in the late 1980s in an experimental Dance/Music/Theater group in Switzerland, which was using Romanian folk music as the basis of a show. He began transcribing tapes of various different traditional music from that part of the world. In 1990 he began playing klezmer music with Don Byron, and soon began writing his own music in these various traditions. He has recorded tribute albums to Booker Little, Wayne Shorter, and Joni Mitchell. He is perhaps best known as a member of John Zorn's Masada. He also appears on recordings by pianists Myra Melford, Uri Caine, Steve Beresford, Fred Hersch; bassists Michael Formanek, Mark Dresser, Greg Cohen, Mario Pavone, and John

Lindberg; clarinetists Don Byron, Ned Rothenberg, and Francoise Houle, and saxophonist Larry Ochs. He has repeatedly appeared in the *Down Beat* Critics' Poll as TDWR (Talent Deserving Wider Recognition). He leads his String Group with Mark Feldman (violin), Erik Friedlander (cello), Drew Gress (bass), and Michael Sarin (drums); a group called Sanctuary; one called Charms of the Night Sky; and the Tiny Bell Trio. He plays in the group Satya with Myra Melford on harmonium, Samir Chatterjee (or Badal Roy) on tabla, and Sanghamitra Chatterjee (tamboura and voice); they played at the Jazz Yatra Festival in Bombay in 1998, and planned more concerts for 1999. He also briefly worked in the Naguib Mahfousz (named after the writer) electronic music project (with Ikue Mori—sampler, Jamie Saft—keyboards, Kenny Wolleson—drums). His "In Twilight Found," a concerto for improvising trio (trumpet, cello, drums) and orchestra, was completed in August 1996. As yet, no premiere has been scheduled. His Tiny Bell Trio went on a three-week tour of Europe in April–May 1999. On June 14, 1999 he received four awards at the Jazz Awards in N.Y.

DISC.: *Parallel Worlds* (1993); *In Our Lifetime* (1994); *Five* (1995); *Sanctuary* (1997); *Stargazer* (1997); *Moving Portrait* (1998); *Charms of the Night Sky* (1998); *Magic Triangle* (1998); *Convergence* (1999); *Live at Birdland* (1999); *Soul on Soul* (2000); *Leap of Faith* (2000).—LP

Douglass, Bill, jazz bassist, bamboo flutist; b. San

Francisco, 1945. He was greatly influenced by John Coltrane, who played in San Francisco in 1965; too young to be admitted, Douglass stood outside the window of the club where the master was playing. He did, however, spend a substantial amount of time with Coltrane's friend Donald Rafael Garrett, who became a major influence and sparked his interest in the bamboo flutes. Performing in the San Francisco Bay Area since 1965, Douglass has played with Marion McPartland, Bobby McFerrin (at Davies Symphony Hall, San Francisco), Mose Allison, composer Terry Riley, Art Lande and Mark Isham (Rubisa Patrol), and Bobby Bradford. His bamboo flute playing is featured on numerous film soundtracks, including *The Black Stallion*, *Never Cry Wolf*, and *Dim Sum*, as well as in television programs for National Geographic Specials and a children's series produced by Rabbit Ears Productions. He has taught at the Cazadero/Aptos Jazz Camp through a Marin County Arts Grant, in the public school music program, 1993–94; at Vocal Workshops with Madeline Eastman, and is presently on the faculty of The Jazzschool in Berkeley, Calif.—LP

Dounias, Minos, Greek violinist, musicologist,

and music critic; b. Cetate, Romania, Sept. 26, 1900; d. Athens, Oct. 20, 1962. He studied at Robert Coll. in Constantinople, where he received instruction in violin, and with Moser and Kulenkampff at the Berlin Hochschule für Musik (1921–26); then studied musicology with Abert and Schering at the Univ. of Berlin (Ph.D., 1932, with the diss. *Die Violinkonzerte Giuseppe Tartinis*; publ. in Wolfenbüttel, 1935; 2nd ed., 1966). He settled in

Athens in 1936, where he taught at Pierce Coll., wrote music criticism, and made appearances as a violinist. He was particularly active in the promotion of early music. —NS/LK/DM

Dounis, Demetrius Constantine, Greek-American violinist and teacher; b. Athens, Dec. 7, 1886; d. Los Angeles, Aug. 13, 1954. He studied violin with Ondricek in Vienna and simultaneously enrolled as a medical student at the Univ. of Vienna; made several tours as a violinist in Europe. After World War I, he was appointed prof. at the Salonika Cons. He then lived in England and eventually settled in America; established his N.Y. studio in 1939; went to Los Angeles in 1954. He originated the technique of the "brush stroke," in which the bow is handled naturally and effortlessly. He wrote numerous manuals.

BIBL.: V. Leland, *D. Principles of Violin Playing* (London, 1949); C. Costantakos, *D.C. D.: His Method in Teaching the Violin* (N.Y., 1988).—NS/LK/DM

Dourlen, Victor(-Charles-Paul), French pedagogue and composer; b. Dunkerque, Nov. 3, 1780; d. Batignolles, near Paris, Jan. 8, 1864. He studied with Gossec and F.A. Boieldieu at the Paris Cons. (1799–1805), sharing the Prix de Rome in 1805 for his cantata *Cupidon pleurant Psyché*. He subsequently taught there (1812–42). Of his nine operas, eight were produced at the Opéra-Comique: *Philoclès* (Oct. 4, 1806), *Linnée, ou La Mine de Suéde* (Sept. 10, 1808), *La Dupe de son art* (Sept. 9, 1809), *Cagliostro, ou Les Illuminés* (with A. Reicha; Nov. 27, 1810), *Plus heureux que sage* (May 25, 1816), *Le Frère Philippe* (Jan. 20, 1818), *Marini, ou Le Muet de Venise* (June 12, 1819), *La Vente après décès* (Théâtre du Gymnase-Dramatique; Aug. 1, 1821), and *Le Petit Souper* (Feb. 22, 1822). He also wrote a Piano Concerto, chamber music, and songs. He publ. three harmony textbooks based upon the methods of C.S. Catel.—NS/LK/DM

Dowland, John, great English composer and famous lutenist, father of **Robert Dowland;** b. probably in London, 1563; d. there (buried), Feb. 20, 1626. In 1580 he went to Paris in the service of Sir Henry Cobham, but by 1584 he was back in England, where he eventually married. On July 8, 1588, he was admitted to his Mus.B. from Christ Church, Oxford, and in 1592 he played before the Queen. Unsuccessful in his effort to secure a position as one of the Queen's musicians, he set out in 1594 for Germany, where he received the patronage of the Duke of Braunschweig in Wolfenbuttel and the Landgrave of Hesse in Kassel. He then went to Italy and visited Venice, Padua, Genoa, Ferrara, and Florence; in Florence he played before Ferdinando I, the Grand Duke of Tuscany. He then made his way home, returning to England in 1595. In 1598 he was appointed lutenist to King Christian IV of Denmark, remaining in his service until 1606. He then returned to England, where he became lutenist to Lord Howard de Walden. In 1612 he became one of the lutenists to King Charles I. Dowland was a foremost representative of the English school of lutenist-composers. He was also noted for his songs, in which he made use of novel chromatic devel-

opments; he treated the accompanying parts as separate entities, thereby obtaining harmonic effects quite advanced for his time.

WORKS: *The 1ˢᵗ Booke of Songes or Ayres of fowre partes with Tableture for the Lute...* (London, 1597); *The 2ⁿᵈ Booke of Songs or Ayres, of 2. 4. and 5. parts; With Tableture for the Lute or Orpherian...* (London, 1600); *The 3ʳᵈ and Last Booke of Songs or Aires...* (London, 1603); *Lachrimae, or 7 Teares Figvred in Seaven Passionate Pauans,....set forth for the Lute, Viols, or Violons, in fiue parts* (London, 1604); songs in *A Mvsicall Banquet* (London, 1612) and *A Pilgrimes Solace. Wherein is contained Musicall Harmonie of 3. 4. and 5. parts, to be sung and plaid with the Lute and Viols* (London, 1612).

WRITINGS: Dowland tr. into Eng. *The Micrologus of Ornithoparcus* (Andreas Vogelsang; London, 1609; modern ed. in Eng. and Latin, ed. by G. Reese and S. Ledbetter, N.Y., 1973); also with his son Robert, the *Necessarie Observations Belonging to the Lute, and Lvte playing, by John Baptisto Besardo [Jean-Baptiste Besard] of Visconti: with choise varietie of Lvte-lessons...* (includes compositions by John Dowland; London, 1610). **EDITIONS:** These include E. Fellowes's eds. of *The 1ˢᵗ Book of Songs* (London, 1920; rev. ed., 1965, by T. Dart), *The 2ⁿᵈ Book of Songs* (London, 1922; rev. ed., 1969, by T. Dart), *The 3ʳᵈ and Last Book of Songs* (London, 1923; rev. ed., 1970, by T. Dart), *A Pilgrimes Solace* (London, 1924; rev. ed., 1969, by T. Dart), and *7 Hymn Tunes...Lamentatio Henrici Noel* (London, 1934); P. Warlock, *Lachrimae or 7 Tears...Transcribed from the original edition of 1605* (without tablature; London, 1927); T. Dart and N. Fortune, eds., *Ayres for 4 Voices,* in Musica Britannica (Vol. 6, London, 1953; 2ⁿᵈ ed., rev., 1963); D. Poulton and B. Lam, eds., *The Collected Lute Music of J. D.* (London, 1974).

BIBL.: E. D. Poulton, *J. D.: His Life and Works* (Berkeley and Los Angeles, 1972; 2ⁿᵈ ed., rev., 1982); M. Pilkington, *Campion, D. and the Lutenist Songwriters* (London, 1989).—NS/LK/DM

Dowland, Robert, English lutenist and composer, son of **John Dowland;** b. probably in London, c. 1591; d. there, Nov. 28, 1641. He remained in London after his father went abroad; in 1626, succeeded his father as lutenist to Charles I. He ed. the anthologies *Varietie of Lute Lessons* (London, 1610) and *A Musicall Banquett* (London, 1610), a collection of English, French, Spanish, and Italian airs (ed. in *The English Lute Songs,* vol. 20). —NS/LK/DM

Downes, Edward O(lin) D(avenport), American music historian, son of **(Edwin) Olin Downes;** b. Boston, Aug. 12, 1911. He was educated at Columbia Univ. (1929–30), the Univ. of Paris (1932–33), the Univ. of Munich (1934–36; 1938), and Harvard Univ. (Ph.D., 1958, with the diss. *The Operas of Johann Christian Bach as a Reflection of the Dominant Trends in Opera seria, 1750–1780*). He was a music critic for the *N.Y. Post* (1935–38), the *Boston Transcript* (1939–41), and the *N.Y. Times* (1955–58). After serving as a lecturer in music history at Wellesley Coll. (1948–49) and Harvard Univ. (1949–50), he was prof. of music history at the Univ. of Minn. (1950–55), Queens Coll. of the City Univ. of N.Y. (1966–81), N.Y.U. (1981–86), and the Juilliard School in N.Y. (1986–94). From 1958 to 1996 he was quizmaster of the Metropolitan Opera radio broadcasts, from 1959 to 1965 musicologist-in-residence at the Bayreuth master classes, and from 1960 to 1974 program annotator of the N.Y. Phil.

WRITINGS: *Verdi: The Man in His Letters* (N.Y., 1942); *Adventures in Symphonic Music* (N.Y., 1943); ed. with B. Brook and S. van Solkema, *Perspectives in Musicology* (N.Y., 1972); *The New York Philharmonic Guide to the Symphony* (N.Y., 1976; 2nd ed., 1981, as *Guide to Symphonic Music*).—**NS/LK/DM**

Downes, (Edwin) Olin, eminent American music critic, father of **Edward O(lin) D(avenport) Downes;** b. Evanston, Ill., Jan. 27, 1886; d. N.Y., Aug. 22, 1955. He studied piano at the National Cons. of Music of N.Y. and was a pupil in Boston of Louis Kelterborn (history and analysis), Carl Baermann (piano), Homer Norris and Clifford Heilman (theory), and John Marshall (music criticism). After establishing himself as a music critic of the *Boston Post* (1906–24), he was the influential music critic of the *N.Y. Times* from 1924 until his death. He was also active as a lecturer and served as quizmaster of the Metropolitan Opera broadcasts. His valuable collection of letters (about 50,000) to and from the most celebrated names in 20th-century music history is housed at the Univ. of Ga. Downes did much to advance the cause of Strauss, Stravinsky, Sibelius, Prokofiev, and Shostakovich in the U.S. In 1937 he received the order Commander of the White Rose of Finland and in 1939 an honorary Mus.Doc. from the Cincinnati Cons. of Music.

WRITINGS (all publ. in N.Y.): *The Lure of Music* (1918); ed. *Select Songs of Russian Composers* (1922); *Symphonic Broadcasts* (1931); *Symphonic Masterpieces* (1935); ed. *Ten Operatic Masterpieces, From Mozart to Prokofiev* (1952); *Sibelius the Symphonist* (1956); I. Downes, ed., *Olin Downes on Music* (1957).

BIBL.: G. Goss, *Jean Sibelius and O. D.: Music, Friendship, Criticism* (Boston, 1995).—**NS/LK/DM**

Downes, Ralph (William), English organist, organ designer, and teacher; b. Derby, Aug. 16, 1904; d. London, Dec. 24, 1993. He studied at the Royal Coll. of Music in London (1922–25), and then was an organ scholar at Keble Coll., Oxford. Making his way to the U.S., he was music director and organist at Princeton Univ. (1928–36). He then returned to London, where he became organist of Brompton Oratory and in 1948 resident organist of the London Phil. He was appointed a prof. at the Royal Coll. of Music in 1954. He designed many notable organs, including the instrument for London's Royal Festival Hall. He publ. the vol. *Baroque Tricks: Adventures with the Organ Builders* (Oxford, 1983). In 1969 he was made a Commander of the Order of the British Empire.—**NS/LK/DM**

Downes, Sir Edward (Thomas), respected English conductor; b. Birmingham, June 17, 1924. After studies at the Univ. of Birmingham (M.A., 1944), he took courses in horn and composition at the Royal Coll. of Music in London (1944–46). In 1948 he received the Carnegie Scholarship and pursued training in conducting with Scherchen. He was an asst. conductor with the Carl Rosa Opera (1950–52); he then was on the conducting staff at London's Covent Garden (1952–69), where he led an extensive repertoire of standard and modern scores, including his own translation of Shostakovich's *Katerina Ismailova* (1963); he also conducted Wagner's *Ring* cycle there (1967). In 1972 he became musical director of the Australian Opera in Sydney, inaugurating the new Sydney Opera House in 1973 with his own translation of Prokofiev's *War and Peace.* In 1976 he left this post, and in 1980 became principal conductor of the BBC Northern Sym. Orch. in Manchester, a post he retained in 1983 when it was renamed the BBC Phil. In 1992 he left this post, having been appointed assoc. music director and principal conductor at Covent Garden in 1991. In 1986 he was made a Commander of the Order of the British Empire, and in 1991 he was knighted.—**NS/LK/DM**

Downey, John (Wilham), American composer and teacher; b. Chicago, Oct. 5, 1927. He was a pupil of Tarnovsky (piano) and Stein (composition) at De Paul Univ. in Chicago (B.M., 1949) and of Ganz, Rieti, Krenek, and Tcherepnin at the Chicago Musical Coll. (M.M., 1951). He then went to Paris, where he studied with Milhaud, Boulanger, and Messiaen at the Cons. (1952) and with Chailley and Jankélévitch at the Sorbonne (docteur dès lettres, 1957). After teaching at De Paul Univ., Chicago City Coll., and Roosevelt Univ., he was prof. of composition and composer-in-residence at the Univ. of Wisc. in Milwaukee (from 1964). He publ. the study *La musique populaire dans l'oeuvre de Béla Bartók* (1966). In 1980 he was made a Chevalier de l'Ordre des Arts et Lettres of France. In 1999 a festival featuring 28 of his orchestral and chamber works was held in London. In his music, Downey adopted modified serial techniques and also utilized electronic and computer-generated sounds.

WORKS: DRAMATIC: *Ageistics,* ballet (1967); incidental music to Shakespeare's *Twelfth Night* (1971). **ORCH.:** *La Joie de la paix* (1956); *Chant to Michelangelo* (1958); Concerto for Harp and Chamber Orch. (1964); *Jingalodeon* (1968); *Prospectations III-II-I* for 3 Orchs. (1970); *Symphonic Modules 5* (1972); *Tooter's Suite* for Youth Orch. (1973); *The Edge of Space* for Bassoon and Orch. (1978; also for Bassoon and Piano); *Discourse* for Oboe, Harpsichord, and Strings (1984; N.Y., Jan. 15, 1987); Double Bass Concerto (1985; Sydney, Sept. 1987); *Declamations* (Albany, N.Y., Dec. 6, 1985); *Call for Freedom* for Symphonic Winds (1989); *Ode to Freedom* (Milwaukee, Oct. 1992); Sym. No. 1 (1992; Palatine, Ill., Feb. 14, 1993); *Yad Vashem: An Impression* for Chamber Orch. (Milwaukee, June 8, 1994). **CHAMBER:** String Trio (1953); Violin Sonata (1954); Wind Octet (1954); 2 string quartets (1964, 1975); Cello Sonata (1966); *Eartheatrics* for 8 Percussionists (1967); *Agort* for Woodwind Quintet (1967); *Almost 12* for Wind Quintet, String Quintet, and Percussion (1970); *Ambivalences I* for Any Chamber Combination (1972); *Crescendo* for Percussion Ensemble (1977); *High Clouds and Soft Rain* for 24 Flutes (1977); Duo for Oboe and Harpsichord (1981); *Portrait* No. 2 for Clarinet and Bassoon (1983) and No. 3 for Flute and Piano (1984); Piano Trio (1984); *Prayer* for Violin, Viola, and Cello (1984); *Recombinance* for Double Bass and Piano (1985); *Rough Road* for Flute and Guitar (1994; WFMT-FM, Chicago, Jan. 15, 1995); *Angel Talk* for 8 Cellos (1995); *Ghosts* for 8 Violins (1995); *Soliloquy* for English Horn (1997); *Irish Sonata* for Violin and Piano (1999). **Piano:** 2 sonatas (1949, 1951); *Adagio lyrico* for 2 Pianos (1953); *Eastlake Terrace* (1959); *Edges* (1960); *Pyramids* (1961); *Ambivalences II* (1973); *Portrait* No. 1 (1982); *Memories* (1991); *Mountains and Valleys* (1999–2000). **VOCAL:** *Lake Isle of Innisfree* for High Voice and Piano (1963);

What If? for Chorus, Timpani, and 8 Brass (1973); *A Dolphin* for High Voice, Alto Flute, Viola, Piano, and Percussion (1974); *Tangents*, jazz oratorio for Soprano, Chorus, String Quintet, Electric Guitar, and Percussion (1981); *Psalm 100* for Chorus (1989); *Meni Odnakovo* for Bass and Orch. (1990); *Psalm 90* for Soprano, Chorus, Organ, Brass, and Timpani (1990). —NS/LK/DM

Doyen, Albert, French composer and choral conductor; b. Vendresse, Ardennes, April 3, 1882; d. Paris, Oct. 22, 1935. He studied composition with Widor at the Paris Cons. In 1917 he established the choral society Fêtes du Peuple. Among his works are a Sym., an ode in memory of Emile Zola, String Quartet, Piano Trio, Violin Sonata, and numerous choral compositions. —NS/LK/DM

Doyle, Arthur, free-jazz tenor saxophonist, bass-clarinetist, flutist; b. Birmingham, Ala., June 26, 1944. He began playing music at the age of 13. After attending Parker H.S., in Birmingham, he went to Tenn. State Univ. in Nashville, where he studied composition with Dr. T. J. Anderson. He played local engagements with former Sun Ra trumpeter Walter Miller, and with trumpeter Louis Smith in Nashville. In 1967 he moved to N.Y and worked with N. Howard, B. Dixon, D. Burrell, and M. Graves. He continued to play and record sporadically until the early 1990s when Thurston Moore, guitarist with the rock band Sonic Youth, befriended him. This led to several albums on Moore's label and new attention directed to Doyle. He currently lives and teaches in Binghamton, N.Y. Most of his playing is in a free-jazz style, emphasizing offbeat instrumental sounds (often combined with vocalizations) and unplanned improvisations.

DISC.: *Plays More Alabama Feeling* (1990); *The Songwriter* (1994); *Plays and Sings from the Songbook, Vol. I* (1995); *Live at the Cooler* (1995).—LP

D'Oyly Carte, Richard
See **Carte, Richard D'Oyly**

Draeseke, Felix (August Bernhard), distinguished German composer and pedagogue; b. Coburg, Oct. 7, 1835; d. Dresden, Feb. 26, 1913. At age 17, he became a student at the Leipzig Cons., where he studied with Rietz. His advanced proclivities met with opposition, so in 1855 he left the Cons. to continue private training with Rietz. His first opera, *König Sigurd* (1856–58), won the highest praise from Liszt, who planned to stage it in Weimar. However, Liszt's resignation in 1858 led to the cancellation of the production. In 1861 Draeseke met Wagner, who also praised his creative talents. The failure of several of his works, however, led him to Vevey in 1862 to teach piano. From 1864 to 1868 he taught at the Lausanne Cons. After serving as director of the Munich Cons. (1868–69), he again taught at the Lausanne Cons. (1869–74). In the meantime, Draeseke was afflicted with a deterioration in his hearing (from 1865) and a lack of appreciation of his compositions. In 1876 he returned to Germany, and in 1884 he became a teacher of composition at the Dresden

Cons. On Nov. 5, 1885, his opera *Gudrun* was premiered in Hannover, the first of his operas to be staged. His opera *Herrat* was first performed in Dresden on March 10, 1892. That same year Draeseke was officially named prof. of composition at the Dresden Cons. In 1898 he was elevated to the title of Hofrat. His most ambitious work was his *Christus* (1897–99), which he called a mysterium consisting of a prelude and oratorio trilogy. In effect, it was his homage to Wagner's *Ring* cycle. Draeseke's early progressive inclinations were soon moderated by his adherence to classical precepts. His works reveal a notable command of contrapuntal writing. In his last years, he became an ardent upholder of conservative musical values. His article, "Die Konfusion in der Musik," *Neue Stuttgarter Musikzeitung*, XXVIII (1906), attacked the modern trends evident in the early years of the 20th century. Although Draeseke's music remains generally unknown outside Germany, an International Draeseke Soc. was founded in Coburg in 1986 to further its propagation. The Soc. commenced publishing a critical ed. of his works in 1987.

WRITINGS: *Anweisung zum kunstgerechten Moduliren* (Freienwalde, 1876); *Die Beseitigung des Tritons* (Leipzig, 1880); *Die Lehre von der Harmonia in lustige Reimlein gebracht* (Leipzig, 1883; 2nd ed., enl., 1887); *Der gebundene Styl: Lehrbuch für Kontrapunkt und Fuge* (Hannover, 1902); "Die Konfusion in der Musik," *Neue Stuttgarter Musikzeitung*, XXVIII (1906; also publ. separately).

WORKS: DRAMATIC: Opera: *König Sigurd* (1856–58); *Dietrich von Bern* (1877); *Herrat* (1879; Dresden, March 10, 1892); *Gudrun* (1879; 1882–84; Hannover, Nov. 5, 1884); *Bertram de Born* (1893); *Fischer und Kalif* (1894–95; Prague, April 15, 1905); *Merlin* (1900; 1903–05; Gotha, April 18, 1913). **Incidental Music To:** Kleist's *Hermannsschlacht* (1860; rev. 1897–98; Dresden, March 3, 1905). **ORCH.:** 3 symphonic poems: *Frithjof* (1859–65), *Julius Caesar* (1860; rev. 1861 and 1865), and *Der Thuner See* (1903; Bonn, March 27, 1913); *Germania-Marsch* (c. 1860); *Ouvertüre zum Namenstag des Fürsten Constantin zu Hohenzollern-Hechingen* (1862); 4 syms.: No. 1 (1868–69; 1871–72; Dresden, Jan. 31, 1873), No. 2 (1876; Dresden, Feb. 15, 1878), No. 3, *Symphonia tragica* (1866; Dresden, Jan. 13, 1888), and No. 4, *Symphonia comica* (1912); *Symphonische Andante* for Cello and Orch. (1876); Violin Concerto (1881; Leipzig, April 11, 1886); Piano Concerto (Sondershausen, June 4, 1886); *Jubiläums-festmarsch* (1886); *Serenade* (1888; Dresden, Oct. 21, 1889); 3 symphonic preludes: *Das Leben ein Traum* (1888; Dresden, Jan. 25, 1889), *Penthesilea* (1888; Eisenbach, June 19, 1890), and *Der Traum ein Leben* (1904; Dresden, Oct. 13, 1905); *Akademische Festouvertüre* (Dresden, Dec. 19, 1890); *Jubel-Ouvertüre* (Dresden, April 19, 1898); *Trauermarsch* (1906); *Feenzauber* for Horn and Orch. (1910). **CHAMBER:** *Ballade* for Piano and Cello (c. 1867); *Barcarole* for Cello and Piano (1872); 3 string quartets: No. 1 (1880; Dresden, March 28, 1887), No. 2 (Dresden, Oct. 8, 1886), and No. 3 (1895; Dresden, Dec. 28, 1896); *Adagio* for Horn and Piano (1885); *Romanze* for Horn and Piano (1885); Clarinet Sonata (1887); Quintet for Piano, Violin, Viola, Cello, and Horn (1888; Dresden, March 18, 1889); Cello Sonata (1890; Dresden, Oct. 10, 1892); 2 viola sonatas (1892, 1902); *Stelzner-Quintett* for 2 Violins, Viola, Violetta, and Cello (Dresden, Dec. 6, 1897); *Szene* for Violin and Piano (1899); Quintet for 2 Violins, Viola, and 2 Cellos (1900–01; Basel, June 13, 1903); Suite for 2 Violins (1911); *Kleine Suite* for English Horn or Oboe and Piano (1911); many piano works, including a Sonata (1862–67), concert waltzes, and fantasies. **VOCAL**: *Germania an ihre Kinder*, ode for Soprano, Men's Chorus, and Orch. (1859; Altenburg, May 1876); *Germania- Kantate* for Men's Chorus and Orch. (1859; Weimar, Aug. 4–7, 1861); *Schur im Rütli* for Soprano, Men's Chorus, and Orch. (1862–68); *Osterszene nach Goethes Faust* for Baritone, Chorus, and Orch. (1863–65; 1886–87; Dresden, Dec. 9, 1889); *Adventlied* for 4 Soloists, Chorus, and Orch. (1875; Dresden, Nov. 22, 1878); 2 Requiems: No. 1 for 4 Soloists, Chorus, and Orch. (1877–80; Dresden, Oct. 26, 1881) and No. 2 for 5 Voices (1909–10; Chemnitz, Oct. 30, 1913); *Columbus*, cantata for Soprano, Baritone, Men's Chorus, and Orch. (1889; Leipzig, Feb. 16, 1891); 2 *Grosse Messe*: No. 1 for Soloists, Chorus, and Orch. (1890–91; Leipzig, Nov. 18, 1892) and No. 2 for Chorus (1908–09; Chemnitz, Oct. 17, 1909); *Sachsen-Hymne* for Men's Chorus and Orch. (1893); *Christus*, mysterium consisting of a *Vorspiel: Die Geburt des Herrn* and an oratorio trilogy *Christi Weihe, Christus der Prophet*, and *Tod und Sieg der Herrn* (1896–99; 1st complete perf., Berlin, Feb. 6, 13, and 20, 1912); *Faust in Schlauf Gesungen* for Chorus and Orch. (1907); *Psalms*; choruses; lieder.

BIBL.: H. Platzbecker, *F. D.* (Leipzig, 1900); O zur Nedden, *F. D.'s Opern und Oratorien* (diss., Univ. of Marburg, 1925); E. Roeder, *F. D.* (2 vols., Dresden, 1932 and Berlin, 1937); A. Krueck, *The Symphonies of F. D.* (diss., Univ. of Zürich, 1967); M. Gutiérrez-Denhoff, *F. D.: Chronik seines Lebens* (Bonn, 1989). **—NS/LK/DM**

Dräger, Hans-Heinz, German-born American musicologist; b. Stralsund, Dec. 6, 1909; d. Austin, Tex., Nov. 9, 1968. He studied musicology with Blume, Schering, Hornbostel, Schünemann, and Sachs at the Univ. of Berlin (Ph.D., 1937, with the diss. *Die Entwicklung des Streichbogens und seine Anwendung in Europa*; publ. in Kassel, 1937), completing his Habilitation at the Univ. of Kiel in 1946 with his *Prinzip einer Systematik der Musikinstrumente* (publ. in Kassel, 1948). While in Berlin, he was active with the State Inst. for German Music Research (1937–38) and at the State Museum of Musical Instruments (1938–39); also was lecturer in organology at the Hochschule für Musik (1939). He was prof. of musicology at the univs. of Greifswald (1947–49) and Rostock (1948–49), at Humboldt Univ. in East Berlin (1949–53), and at the Free Univ. in West Berlin (1953–61). In 1955 he was a visiting prof. at Stanford Univ. He settled in the U.S. in 1961, becoming a naturalized citizen in 1966; he was on the musicology faculty at the Univ. of Austin (1961–66).**—NS/LK/DM**

Draghi, Antonio, noted Italian-born Austrian composer; b. Rimini, c. 1634; d. Vienna, Jan. 16, 1700. He received musical training in his homeland and was active as a bass singer in Venice by 1657. He settled in Vienna in 1658, where he was asst. Kapellmeister (1668–69) and then Kapellmeister (1669–82) to the dowager empress Eleonora. He was appointed director of dramatic music at the Imperial court in 1673 and then its Kapellmeister in 1682. Draghi was a leading representative of the Venetian school of composition at Vienna's Imperial court, being a prolific composer of operas, oratorios, and other dramatic works. From 1666 to 1700 he composed over 100 operas, prologues, and intermezzi, some 13 oratorios, 29 Sepolcri, vocal chamber works, and other sacred works. Much of his music is not extant.

BIBL.: R. Schnitzler, *The Sacred-Dramatic Music of A. D.* (diss., Univ. of N.C., 1971); N. Hiltl, *Die Oper am Hofe Kaiser Leopolds I. mit besonderer Berücksichtigung der Tätigkeit von Minato und D.* (diss., Univ. of Vienna, 1974); H. Seifert, *Neues zu A. D.s weltlichen Werken* (Vienna, 1978).**—NS/LK/DM**

Draghi, Giovanni Battista, Italian organist, harpsichordist, and composer; b. c. 1640; d. London, 1708. He was in London by 1667, where he became chief organist at the Queen's Catholic Chapel in 1673. In 1687 he was made organist at King James II's private chapel. He also was music teacher to the princesses Mary and Anne. He wrote the music to Dryden's ode *From Harmony, from Heavenly Harmony for the Song for St. Cecilia's Day* (1687) and (with Locke) to Shadwell's *Psyche* (1675) and d'Urfey's *The Wonders in the Sun, or The Kingdom of Birds* (1706); also many songs, and instructive harpsichord lessons.**—NS/LK/DM**

Drăgoi, Sabin V(asile), eminent Romanian composer, folklorist, and pedagogue; b. Selişte, June 18, 1894; d. Bucharest, Dec. 31, 1968. He studied harmony with Zirra in Iaşi (1918–19), theory with Bena and counterpoint with Klee in Cluj (1919–20), and composition with Novák, conducting with Ostrčil, and music history with Krupka in Prague (1920–22). After teaching music in Deva (1922–24), he was director of the Timişoara Cons. (1925–43) and then a teacher at the Cluj Cons. (1943–45). He served as prof. of folklore at the Cons. (1950–52) and as director of the Folklore Inst. (1950–64) in Bucharest. He received the Enesco prize 3 times (1922, 1923, 1928) and the Romanian Academy prize (1933). His extensive folklore research in the Banat and in Transylvania is often reflected in his compositions.

WORKS: DRAMATIC: *Năpasta* (Disaster), opera (1927; Bucharest, May 30, 1928; rev. 1958; Bucharest, Dec. 23, 1961); *Constantin Brîncoveanu*, scenic oratorio (1929; Bucharest, Oct. 25, 1935); *Kir Ianulea*, comic-fantastic opera (1930–38; Cluj-Napoca, Dec. 22, 1939); *Horia*, historical opera (1945; rev. 1959); *Păcală*, comic opera (1954–56; Brasov, May 6, 1962); film music. **ORCH.:** 3 *Tablouri simfonice* (1921); *Memento mori—La groapa lui Scărlătescu* (1923); *Divertisment rustic* (1928); *Divertisment sacru* for Chamber Orch. (1933); Piano Concerto (1940–41; Bucharest, Feb. 14, 1943); *Rapsodia din Belint* (1942; Bucharest, Dec. 12, 1943); 2 *Dansuri pe tempe populare mureşene* (1942); *Petrecere populară*, suite (1950); *La Mislea—La moartea unei tovarăşe căzute în ilegalitate*, symphonic poem (1951); *Mitrea Cocor*, suite (1953); *Suită făgărăşană* (1954); *Suită de 7 dansuri populare* (1960); *Suită tătară* (1961); *Suită lipoveana* (1962). **CHAMBER:** 2 string quartets (1920, 1922); Violin Sonata (1949); *Dixtour* for Winds, Strings, and Piano (1955). **Piano:** *Suită de dansuri populare* (1923); 8 *Miniaturi* (1923); *Mica suită: In memoriam Béla Bartók* (1955); 30 *Colinde* (1958); 10 *Miniaturi* (1960); 12 *Miniaturi* (1966). **VOCAL:** *Povestea neamului* for Chorus and Orch. (1936; Bucharest, Nov. 10, 1938); *Balada celor patru mineri* for Soli, Chorus, and Orch. (1950); *Mai multă lumina*, cantata for Chorus and Orch. (1951); *Povestea bradului*, oratorio for Soli, Chorus, and Orch. (1952); *Cunună—Serbarea secerişului*, cantata for Soli, Chorus, and Orch. (1959).

BIBL.: N. Rădulescu, *S.V. D.* (Bucharest, 1971). **—NS/LK/DM**

Dragon, Carmen, American conductor, composer, and arranger; b. Antioch, Calif., July 28, 1914; d. Santa Monica, Calif., March 28, 1984. He learned to play piano and other instruments; after studies at San Jose State Coll., he found his niche as a successful conductor, composer, and arranger for films, radio, and recordings; he also conducted pop concerts and served as conductor of the Glendale (Calif.) Sym. Orch. (from 1963). His son, Daryl Dragon (b. Los Angeles, Aug. 27, 1942), was one-half of the popular music team of Captain and Tennille.—**NS/LK/DM**

Dragonetti, Domenico (Carlo Maria), famous Italian double bass player; b. Venice, April 7, 1763; d. London, April 16, 1846. He received a few lessons from Berini, the double bass player at San Marco in Venice, but he was mainly autodidact. After playing in theater orchs. in Venice, he succeeded Berini at San Marco when he was 18. In 1794 he settled in London, where he was engaged as an orch. player. He also appeared in recitals with Robert Lindley throughout England. During visits to Vienna, he was befriended by Haydn and Beethoven. Dragonetti played in the orch. for the premiere of Beethoven's 9th Sym. under the composer's direction in Vienna (May 7, 1824). At the age of 82, he led the double bass section in the performance of Beethoven's 9th Sym. at the unveiling of the Beethoven monument in Bonn in 1845. Dragonetti's virtuosity garnered him the title of the Paganini of the double bass. He composed a number of works for his instrument. He left a remarkable collection of scores, engravings, and old instruments to the British Museum.

BIBL.: F. Caffi, *Biografia di D. D.* (Venice, 1846); F. Palmer, *D. D. in England (1794–1846): The Career of a Double Bass Virtuoso* (Oxford, 1997).—**NS/LK/DM**

Drake, Alfred (real name, **Alfredo Capurro**), esteemed American baritone, actor, and director; b. N.Y., Oct. 7, 1914; d. there, July 25, 1992. He sang in a Brooklyn church choir and then in the glee club at Brooklyn Coll., from which he graduated in 1935. He began his career as a chorus singer. His rich baritone voice caught the attention of Rodgers and Hart, who cast him in a supporting role in their Broadway musical *Babes in Arms* (1937). After further stage appearances, he was chosen by Rodgers and Hammerstein to create the role of Curly in the award-winning musical *Oklahoma!* in 1943, which made Drake a star on Broadway and also winner of the Drama Critics' Circle Award. Following appearances on stage in *Sing Out, Sweet Land* (1944), *The Beggar's Holiday* (1946), and *The Cradle Will Rock*, and in the film *Tars and Spars* (1946), he again won critical accolades when he created the role of Fred Graham in Cole Porter's Broadway musical *Kiss Me, Kate* in 1948. In 1953 he scored another Broadway triumph when he created the role of Haji in the musical *Kismet*, for which he won a second Drama Critics' Circle Award as well as a Tony Award. In later years, he pursued a career mainly as a fine dramatic actor and director. In 1973 he again won accolades as Honore

Lachalles in the revival of *Gigi*. In 1981 he was inducted into the Theatre Hall of Fame. In 1990 he was awarded the Tony Honor of Excellence for his contributions to the American theater.—**NS/LK/DM**

Drake, Earl R(oss), American violinist and composer; b. Aurora, Ill., Nov. 26, 1865; d. Chicago, May 6, 1916. He studied violin in Chicago, and later with Joachim in Berlin. He was head of the violin dept. at the Gottschalk Lyric School in Chicago (1893–97). In 1900 he organized his own school of music in Chicago.

WORKS: *The Blind Girl of Castel-Cuille*, opera and ballet (Chicago, Feb. 19, 1914); *The Mite and the Mighty*, light opera (Chicago, 1915); *Dramatic Prologue* for Orch.; *Ballet* for Orch.; *Gypsy Scenes* for Violin and Orch.; pieces for violin and piano (*Polish Dance, Mazurka, An Alpine Farewell*, etc.).—**NS/LK/DM**

Dranishnikov, Vladimir, Russian conductor and composer; b. St. Petersburg, June 10, 1893; d. Kiev, Feb. 6, 1939. He studied at the St. Petersburg Cons. with Essipova (piano), Steinberg, Liadov, and Wihtol (composition), and Nikolai Tcherepnin (conducting). He was employed as a rehearsal pianist at the St. Petersburg Imperial Opera (1914–18); in 1918, became conductor there, earning great esteem for his skill in both the classical and the modern repertoire; he conducted the first Soviet performance of Berg's *Wozzeck*, and of numerous Soviet operas. In 1930 he was appointed conductor of the Kiev Opera. He wrote symphonic works and choruses.—**NS/LK/DM**

Draper, Charles, English clarinetist and pedagogue; b. Odcombe, Somerset, Oct. 23, 1869; d. Surbiton, Oct. 21, 1952. He studied with his brother and with Henry Lazarus, and then was a scholarship student at the Royal Coll. of Music in London. He was active in London, where he joined the Crystal Palace Orch. in 1895; he also played in the orch. of the Phil. Soc. and in 1905 became a founding member of the New Sym. Orch.; from 1895 to 1940 he taught at the Guildhall School of Music. Through his appearances as a soloist and chamber music player, he played a decisive role in establishing the clarinet as a worthy solo instrument. His nephew, Haydn (Paul) Draper (b. Penarth, Glamorganshire, Wales, Jan. 21, 1889; d. London, Nov. 1, 1934), was also a clarinetist and pedagogue. After training with his father, he entered the Royal Coll. of Music in London on a scholarship in 1908 and studied with his uncle and with Julian Egerton. He played principal clarinet in the Queen's Hall Orch. in London, and later was a member of the London Wind Quintet; from 1923 he was a teacher at the Royal Academy of Music in London, where he was mentor to Reginald Kell. —**NS/LK/DM**

Drdla, Franz (actually, **František Alois**), Bohemian violinist and composer; b. Saar, Moravia, Nov. 28, 1868; d. Badgastein, Sept. 3, 1944. After training with Bennewitz (violin) and Foerster (composition) at the Prague Cons. (1880–82), he studied at the Vienna Cons. (1882–88) with J. Hellmesberger Jr. (violin) and Krenn and Bruckner (composition), winning 1st prize

for violin and the medal of the Gesellschaft der Musikfreunde. He was a violinist in the orch. of the Vienna
Court Opera (1890–93); after serving as concertmaster of
the orch. of the Theater an der Wien (1894–99), he made
successful tours as a violinist in Europe (1899–1905) and
the U.S. (1923–25). His lighter pieces for violin and
piano won enormous popularity in their day, especially
his *Serenade No. 1* (1901), *Souvenir* (1904), and *Vision*. He
also wrote the operettas *Zlatá sít* (1st perf. as *Das goldene
Netz*, Leipzig, 1916; rev. as *Bohyně lásky* [The Goddess of
Love], Brno, 1941) and *Komtesa z prodejny* (1st perf. as *Die
Ladenkomtesse*, Brünn, 1917), and a Violin Concerto
(1931).

BIBL.: J. Květ, *F. D.* (Ždár nad Sázavou, 1968).
—NS/LK/DM

Dr. Dre (originally, Young, Andre), one of
the architects of gangsta rap, and the producer who
brought a sense of melody back to rap—not to be
confused with radio DJ, MTV personality, and film star
Doctor Dre.; b. South Central, Los Angeles, Calif., Feb.
18, 1965.

Called Dr. Dre as a parody of/homage to basketball
star Julius "Dr. J." Irving, the 6' 4" Andre Young was
pretty good at hoops, but was bestknown for his
excellent musical taste. By his teens, Young was spinning records at Eve after Dark in L.A. In addition to the
turntables that he used in the club to spin everything
from Martha and the Vandellas to P-Funk, the club had
a small four-track studio in the back room. There, with
friends like Lonzo Williams and Antoine Carraby (aka
McRen and DJ Yella), he started cutting demos. The trio
became the heart of the World Class Wreckin' Cru,
which Dre formed at 17. They had minor hits with
"Turn off the Lights" and "Lay Your Body Down."

The trio hooked up with O'Shea Jackson and Eric
Wright, better known as Ice Cube and Eazy-E. The latter
ran Ruthless records, and the quintet started recording
as NWA (Niggaz with Attitude). NWA's second album,
Straight Outta Compton, went double platinum and rose
to #37 on the album charts with virtually no airplay.
The controversy over the song "F*** tha Police" helped
promote the album, although it made the group less
than a favorite among law enforcement agents. Main
lyricist Ice Cube went solo after that album. The rest
continued, releasing the broader *100 Miles and Running*,
which sold platinum and hit #27. With their 1991 album
Efil4zaggin, they achieved the unprecedented for a "hard
core" rap band, topping the album charts.

Dre and Eazy-E fought over money, so Dre formed a
label with Vanilla Ice's former music publicist, Marion
"Suge" Knight. With Knight taking care of the business
and Dre taking care of the music, their label, Death Row
Records, was soon earning $100 million a year. One of
their first major hits was Dre's solo debut, *The Chronic*.
The album generated three hit singles. "Nuthin' but a
'G' Thang" which hit #2 on the pop charts, topped the
R&B charts, and sold platinum. "Dre Day" went gold
and hit #8 on the pop charts. Part of the charm of the
first two singles was the laconic rapping of Dre's new
sidekick, a rapper named Calvin Broadus, though he
became better known as Snoop Doggy Dogg (later

Shoop Dogg). "Let Me Ride" only hit #34, but was
notable for including George Clinton from P-Funk; Dre
frequently sampled Clinton's band. The album sold
triple platinum, hitting #3 on the charts.

Although Dre was successful as an artist, with the
track "Keep Their Heads Ringing" off of the soundtrack
from the film *Friday* hitting #10 and going gold he was
even more triumphant as a producer. He produced
Doggystyle, the debut album by Snoop Doggy Dog, as
well as hit albums by Warren G and Black Street. He
also orchestrated soundtracks for the film *Above the Rim*.
Ice Cube and Dre reunited for the tune "Natural Born
Killaz." While his own albums, after the successful *The
Chronic*, were not especially great sellers, by 1996 Dre
had produced records that had generated a quarter of a
billion dollars in sales.

Also by 1996, Dre saw the end coming for both
gangsta rap and Death Row records. Two years earlier,
Warner Bros. dropped their distribution deal with
Death Row after stockholders complained about the
violent and sexist nature of most of the label's material.
Dre left the label in the summer of 1996; before the
summer was over, the label's star rap artist Tupac
Shakur had been murdered and label kingpin Suge
Knight was fighting off racketeering charges that would
send him to prison a year later.

Dre formed Aftermath records, releasing *Dr. Dre
Presents the Aftermath*. The hit from the album was his
own "Been There, Done That," a farewell to the G
Thang. In the late 1990s, Dre expanded his horizons into
writing orchestral music and directing films. He has
also mentored the successful white rap artist Eminem,
whit whom Dre and Snoop Dogg toured in 2000.

DISC.: *The Chronic* (1992); *Concrete Roots* (1994); *First Round
Knockout* (1996); *Back 'n the Day* (1996); *Da Chronic 2000* (1999).
—BH

Drechsler, Joseph, Bohemian-born Austrian composer; b. Wallisch-Birken, May 26, 1782; d. Vienna, Feb.
27, 1852. He was a pupil of the organist Grotius at
Florenbach. He was asst. Kapellmeister (1812) at the
Vienna Court Opera, then conductor in the theaters at
Baden (near Vienna) and Pressburg. Returning to Vienna, he became organist of the Servite church. In 1816
precentor at St. Ann's, in 1823 Kapellmeister at the Univ.
church and the Hofpfarrkirche, and from 1824 to 1830
Kapellmeister at the Leopoldstadt Theater. Among his
works are 6 operas, including *Die Feldmühle*, Singspiel
(Vienna, Sept. 29, 1812) and *Pauline* (Vienna, Feb. 23,
1821), about 30 operettas, vaudevilles, and pantomimes,
a Requiem, 16 masses, three cantatas, offertories, etc.,
string quartets, organ fugues, piano sonatas, other piano
music, and songs. He also publ. a method for organ, and
a treatise on harmony.

BIBL.: C. Preiss, *J. D.* (Graz, 1910).—NS/LK/DM

Drechsler, Karl, German cellist and teacher; b.
Kamenz, May 27, 1800; d. Dresden, Dec. 1, 1873. He
studied in Dresden with F. Dotzauer (1824–26) and was
a cellist in the Dessau Court Orch. (1820–71). Among his
distinguished pupils were B. Cossmann, F. Grutzma-
cher, A. Lindner, and C. Schroder.—NS/LK/DM

Dreier, Per, Norwegian conductor; b. Trondheim, Dec. 25, 1929. He studied conducting with Paul van Kempen and Willem van Otterloo at the Royal Cons. of Music in The Hague. He made his debut with the Trondheim Sym. Orch. in 1953. He then was a conductor at the Württemberg State Theater at Stuttgart (1953–57) and chief conductor and artistic director of the Århus Sym. Orch. (1957–73); also served as chief conductor of the Jutland Opera (1957–71). Dreier has done much to promote contemporary Norwegian music.—NS/LK/DM

Drejsl, Radim, Czech composer; b. Dobruska, April 29, 1923; d. (suicide) Prague, April 20, 1953. He studied piano at the Prague Cons. and composition with Bořkovec at the Prague Academy of Musical Arts (1946–50). From 1949 until his death he was music director of the Vít Nejedlý Army Artistic Ensemble.

WORKS: 2 piano suites (1945, 1946); 2 piano sonatas (1946, 1947); Flute Sonatina (1947); Bassoon Sonatina (1948); *Spring* for Wind Quintet (1948); Sym. for Strings (1948); Piano Concerto (1948–49); *Dožínková Suite* (Harvest Home Suite) for Oboe or English Horn and Piano (1949–50); military marches; choruses; songs.—NS/LK/DM

Dresden, Sem, notable Dutch composer and pedagogue; b. Amsterdam, April 20, 1881; d. The Hague, July 30, 1957. He studied composition with Zweers at the Amsterdam Cons., and then composition and conducting with Pfitzner at the Stern Cons. in Berlin (1903–05). Returning to Amsterdam, he was conductor of the Motet and Madrigal Soc. (1914–26); he also taught composition at (1919–24) and was director (1924–37) of the Cons. In 1937 he became director of the Royal Cons. of Music in The Hague, but was removed from his position by the Nazi occupation authorities in 1940; upon the liberation in 1945, he was restored to his position, which he held until 1949. He publ. *Het Muziekleven in Nederlands sinds 1880* (Amsterdam, 1923) and *Stromingen en Tegenstromingen in de Muziek* (Haarlem, 1953); he also rev. Worp's *Algemeene Muziekleer* (Groningen, 1931; 9th ed., 1956). His compositions reveal both German and French influences with a distinctive Dutch strain.

WORKS: DRAMATIC: O p e r a : *François Villon* (1956–57; orchestrated by J. Mul; Amsterdam, June 15, 1958). O p e r e t t a : *Toto* (1945). ORCH.: *Theme and Variations* (Amsterdam, March 29, 1914); 2 violin concertos (1936, 1942); Symphonietta for Clarinet and Orch. (1938); Oboe Concerto (1939); Piano Concerto (1942–46); Flute Concerto (1949); *Dansflitsen* (Dance Flashes; The Hague, Oct. 20, 1951); Organ Concerto (1952–53). C H A M B E R : 2 piano trios (1902, 1942); Violin Sonata (1905); Trio for 2 Oboes and English Horn (1912); 2 cello sonatas (1916, 1942); Sonata for Flute and Harp (1918); String Quartet (1924); Sonata for Solo Violin (1943); Suite for Cello (1943–47); piano pieces; organ music. V O C A L : *Chorus tragicus* for Chorus, 5 Trumpets, 2 Bugles, and Percussion (1927); *4 Vocalises* for Mezzo-soprano and 7 Instruments (1935); *O Kerstnacht* for Chorus and Strings (1939); *Chorus symphonicus* for Soprano, Tenor, Chorus, and Orch. (1943–44; rev. 1955); *Psalm 99* for Chorus, Organ, and 4 Trombones (1950); *St. Antoine,* oratorio (1953); *Psalm 84* for Soprano, Tenor, Chorus, and Orch. (1954); *Carnival Cantata* for Soprano, Men's Chorus, and Orch. (1954); *De wijnen van Bourgondië* (The Wines of Burgundy) for

Chorus and Orch. (1954); *St. Joris,* oratorio (1955); *Catena musicale* for Soprano, Woodwind Quartet, String Trio, and Orch. (1956); *Rembrandt's "Saul and David"* for Soprano and Orch. (1956); choruses; songs.—NS/LK/DM

Dresher, Paul (Joseph), American composer and performer; b. Los Angeles, Jan. 8, 1951. He studied music at the Univ. of Calif. at Berkeley (B.A., 1977) and composition with Erickson, Reynolds, and Oliveros at the Univ. of Calif. at San Diego (M.A., 1979). He also received training in Ghanaian drumming, Javanese and Balinese gamelan, and North Indian classical music. In 1985 he founded the Paul Dresher Ensemble, and in 1993 the Paul Dresher Ensemble's Electro-Acoustic Band. The latter ensemble has commissioned and/or performed significant new works by such composers as John Adams, David Lang, Eve Beglarian, and Terry Riley. In 1997 it began an ongoing program to commission concerti from noted soloists. The first pair of works (1998) were by Alvin Curran and Dresher, both featuring noted violinist David Abel, and the second (2000) were by Anthony Davis and Dresher, both featuring noted cellist Joan Jeanrenaud, formerly of the Kronos Quartet. In 1998 the ensemble also commissioned and produced *Ravenshead,* an opera by Steve Mackey to a libretto by Rinde Eckert. After touring this work throughout the U.S. in 1999–2000, the ensemble embarked on the production of Erling Wold's *A Little Girl Dreams of Taking the Veil,* a chamber opera based on Dorothea Tanning's translation of Max Ernst's 1930 surrealist collage novel.

Dresher's awards include an NEA grant (1979), the Goddard Lieberson fellowship of the American Academy and Inst. of Arts and Letters (1982), and a Fulbright fellowship (1984). In 1996–97 he was a fellow in the Asia Pacific Performance Exchange at the Univ. of Calif. at Los Angeles. In addition to orch. and chamber works, he has written experimental operatic and theater pieces, as well as various electroacoustic taped scores for use in theater, dance, video, radio, and film. As a composer, he is perhaps best known for his collaborations with writer/performer Rinde Eckert on "American Trilogy," a set of experimental operatic works comprised of *Slow Fire* (1985–88), *Power Failure* (1988–89), and *Pioneer* (1989–90).

WORKS: Guitar Quartet (1975); *Z* for Soprano, 6 Percussion, and Tape (1978); *Liquid and Stellar Music,* live perf. solo piece (1981); *The Way of How,* music theater (1981); *Dark Blue Circumstance,* live perf. solo piece for Electric Guitar and Electronics (1982); *Casa Vecchia* for String Quartet (1982); *Are Are,* music theater (1983); *Seehear,* music theater (1984); *re:act:Ion* for Orch. (1984); *Was Are/Will Be,* staged concert piece (1985); *Freesound* (1985–88); *Slow Fire,* music theater/opera (1985–88); *Figaro Gets a Divorce,* theater score (1986); *The Tempest,* theater score (1987); *Shelflife,* live perf. dance piece (1987); *Rhythmia,* tape piece for Dance (1987); *Loose the Thread,* dance piece for Violin, Piano, and Percussion (1988); *Power Failure,* music theater/opera (1988–89); *Pioneers,* music theater/opera (1989–90; Spoleto Festival, May 26, 1990); *Awed Behavior,* music theater (1992–93; Los Angeles, May 1, 1993); *The Gates,* music theater (Lee, Mass., July 23, 1993; in collaboration with Margaret Jenkins); *The Myth of the Hero,* opera/dance theater piece (1996–97; in collaboration with Chen Shi-Zheng).—NS/LK/DM

Dressel, Erwin, German pianist, conductor, and composer; b. Berlin, June 10, 1909; d. there, Dec. 17, 1972. He studied in Berlin with Klatte at the Stern Cons. and with Juon at the Hochschule für Musik. He was active in Berlin as a pianist, theater conductor, arranger, and composer.

WORKS: DRAMATIC: O p e r a : *Der arme Columbus* (Kassel, Feb. 19, 1928); *Der Kuchentanz* (Kassel, May 18, 1929); *Der Rosenbusch der Maria* (Leipzig, June 23, 1930); *Die Zwillingsesel* (Dresden, April 29, 1932); *Jery und Bätely* (Berlin, 1932); *Die Laune der Verliebten* (Hamburg and Leipzig, 1949); *Der Bar* (Bern, 1963). ORCH.: 4 syms. (1927, 1929, 1932, 1948); Concerto for Oboe, Clarinet, Bassoon, and Orch. (1951); Clarinet Concerto (1961); *Cassation* (1961); *Variationen-Serenade* for Piano and Orch. (1962); *Caprice fantastique* (1963); Saxophone Concerto (1965); Viola Concerto (1969). CHAMBER: 2 string quartets; String Trio; piano pieces. VOCAL: Choral music; songs. —NS/LK/DM

Dressler, Gallus, important German composer and music theorist; b. Nebra, Thuringia, Oct. 16, 1533; d. Zerbst, Anhalt, c. 1584. He entered the Jena Academy (later Univ.) in 1557, and the following year he was made Kantor at the Magdeburg grammar school. In 1570 he received his master's degree at the Univ. of Wittenberg, then went to Zerbst as a deacon (1575). He is of historical significance for his contributions to the development of the German-language motet and to modal theory.

WORKS: *Aliquot psalmi latini et germanici* for 4 to 6 Voices (1560); *Zehen deutscher Psalmen* for 4 to 5 Voices (Jena, 1562); *XVII cantiones sacrae* for 4 to 5 Voices (Wittenberg, 1565; ed. in Publikationen älterer praktischer und theoretischer Musikwerke, XXIV, 1903); *Epitaphium piissimae et honestissimae matronae Magdalenae conjugis...Christophori Petzelii* (Wittenberg, 1566); *XVIII cantiones* for 4 or more Voices (Magdeburg, 1567); *XVII cantiones sacrae* for 4 to 5 Voices (Wittenberg, 1568); *Das schöne Gebet, Herr Jesu Christ* for 4 Voices (Magdeburg, 1569); *XIX cantiones* for 4 to 5 Voices (Magdeburg, 1569); *XC cantiones* for 4 or more Voices (Magdeburg, 1570); *XVI Geseng* for 4 or more Voices (Magdeburg, 1570); *Opus sacrarum cantionum, nunc denuo recognitum, et multo quam antea correctius* for 4 or more Voices (Nuremberg, 1570); *Magnificat octo tonorum* for 4 Voices (Magdeburg, 1571); *Ausserlesene teutsche Lieder* for 4 to 5 Voices and Instruments (Nuremberg, 1575).

WRITINGS: *Practica modorum explicatio* (Jena, 1561); *Praecepta musicae poeticae* (MS, 1563; ed. by B. Engelke in *Geschichtsblätter für Stadt und Land Magdeburg*, XLIX-1, 1914–15); *Musicae practicae elementa in usum scholae Magdeburgensis edita* (Magdeburg, 1571; 4th ed., 1601).

BIBL.: W. Luther, *G. D.: Ein Beitrag zur Geschichte des Schulkantorats im 16. Jahrhundert* (Kassel, 1941).—NS/LK/DM

Dreves, Guido Maria, German music historian and priest; b. Hamburg, Oct. 27, 1854; d. Mitwitz, near Kronach, June 1, 1909. He entered the Jesuit order, and lived in Vienna and Würzburg. For distinguished service to the cause of hymnology and medieval music, the Univ. of Munich made him a Ph.D. (*honoris causa*).

WRITINGS: Co-ed., with C. Blume and H. Bannister, *Analecta hymnica medii aevi* (55 vols., 1886–1922); *Cantiones bohemicae*

(1886); *Die Hymnen des Johannes von Jenstein* (1886); *Aurelius Ambrosius, der Vater des Kirchengesanges* (1893); *Psalteria rhythmica* (1901); *Die Kirche der Lateiner in ihren Liedern* (1908). —NS/LK/DM

Drew, James, multifaceted American composer, playwright, pianist, and teacher; b. St. Paul, Minn., Feb. 9, 1929. He studied at the N.Y. School of Music (1954–56), with Varèse (1956), and with Riegger (1956–59). Following further training at Tulane Univ. (M.A., 1964), he pursued postgraduate studies at Washington Univ. in St. Louis (1964–65). In 1972–73 he held a Guggenheim fellowship. He taught at Northwestern Univ. (1965–67), Yale Univ. (1967–73), the Berkshire Music Center at Tanglewood (summer, 1973), La. State Univ. (1973–76), Calif. State Univ. at Fullerton (1976–77), and the Univ. of Calif. at Los Angeles (1977–78). As a composer and playwright, Drew has pursued an active career outside of academia. Except for master classes and lectures, he has worked since 1980 on independent projects for the theater, concert stage, and film. His Grey Wolf Atelier International, which is devoted to the arts education of children, parents, and teachers, was founded in 1993. With his colleague, the educator Mary Gae George, the Atelier operates in Florica, Utah, Ind., and the Netherlands. He also is composer/director of the Nighttown Opera Theatre.

WORKS: DRAMATIC: *Toward Yellow*, ballet (1970); *Mysterium*, television opera (1974–75); *Crucifixus Domini Christi* (1975); *Suspense Opera* (1975); *Dr. Cincinnati* (1977); *5 O'Clock Ladies* (1981); *Himself, the Devil* (1982); *Whisper*, video piece (1982); *Becket: The Final Moments*, automated drama (1984); *One Last Dance*, theater and/or video piece (1985); *Blue in Atlantis*, audio-theater piece (1986); *"Live" from the Black Eagle* (1987–88); *Rat's Teeth* (1989); *Surprise Operas* (1989); *Theater of Phantom Sounds* (1993); *The Voice* (1995); *Club Berlin is Closed: Hello?*, theater piece (1995); *Survivors in Pale Light* (1996); *Cantolobosolo*, monodrama- audiotheater (1997); *Powder Songs of the Lady Magicians* (1997–98); *The Ringing Hour*, miracle play (1998–99); *The Clown's Evening* (1999). ORCH.: *Passacaglia* (1957); *Contrappunto* (1965); 3 syms.: No. 1 for Chamber Orch. (1968), No. 2 for Chorus and Orch. (Norfolk, Va., Aug. 20, 1971), and No. 3 (1977; Providence, R.I., April 6, 1991); *Symphonies* for Orch., Chorus, and 3 Conductors (1969); 2 violino grande concertos (1969, 1993); *October Lights* (New Haven, Conn., Oct. 18, 1969); 2 viola concertos (1973; *Cellar-Lise's Alleluias*, 1996–97); *Metal Concerto* for Percussion (N.Y., Feb. 2, 1971); Percussion Concerto (1972–73; N.Y., March 21, 1973); *West Indian Lights* (Tanglewood, Aug. 9, 1973); *Metal Assemblage* for Wind Orch. (1976); Violin Concerto (1977); Sinfonia for Strings (1980); Concerto for 2 Violins and Orch. (1981); *St. Mark Triple Concerto* for Violin, Cello, Piano, and Brass or Winds (1981); *Open/Closed Forms* for Chamber Orch. (1983); *Courtyard Music* for Chamber Orch. and Kinisones (1983); *Faustus: An Epilogue* for 2 Pianos, Viola, and Chamber Orch. (1984); *Donaldsonville: Steeples, Whistles, Fog* (1988); Piano Concerto, *The Celestial Cabaret* (1991); *Inaudible Answers* (1992); Concerto for Cello and Chamber Orch. (1994); *Walden Songs* for Chamber Orch. (1994); Contrabass Concerto, *Jacopo's Sub-Harmonic Hymns* (1999). CHAMBER: *Indigo Suite* for Piano, Double Bass, and Percussion (1959); *Divisiones* for 6 Percussion (1962); Piano Trio (1962); *Polifonica I* for Flute, Clarinet, Oboe, String Quartet, and Piano (1963) and *II* for Flute and Percussion (1966); *Almost Stationary* for Piano Trio (1971); *Gothic Lights* for Brass (1972); 3 string quartets (1972–75; 1977;

1989); *Epitaphium pour Stravinsky* for 3 Trombones, Horn, Tuba, and Piano (1973); *Trio for the Fiery Messengers* for Piano Trio (1979); Violin Sonata (1979); Cello Sonata (1980); Sonata for Solo Viola (1983); *American Elegy* for Brass Quintet (1983); *Chartres Street Processional* for Brass (1986); *The Bejesus Redemption Psalter* for Percussion (1987); *Lincoln Center Blues* for Any Instrument or Piano (1987); *Some Sad Songs and Marches* for Brass (1988); *Antitangoes* for Flute and Contrabass (1992); *Book of Lights* for Clarinet, Cello, Viola, and Piano (1993); *Elephants Coming* for String Quartet (1994); *Sonata Appassionata* for Cello and Piano (1994); *Sacred Dances of the Tunnel Saints* for 2 Pianos and 2 Percussionists (1995); *Hypothetical Structures* for 2 Pianists (1996); *Submerged Choruses* for 2 or More Pianists (1998); *Snow Under Candlelight* for Piano (1999); *Winter Coloraturas* for 1 or 2 Pianists (2000). **VOCAL:** *The Lute in the Attic* for Voice, Flute, Clarinet, Cello, and 3 Gongs (1963); *The Fading of the Visible World*, oratorio for Soprano, Tenor, Bass, Chorus, and Orch. (1975); *The Orangethorpe Aria* for Soprano, Piano Trio, and Clarinet (1978); *Trinity* for Soprano and Chamber Ensemble (1983); *Dublin Dream Songs* for Soprano and Percussionist (1992); *Many Moons, Many Winters* for Soprano and String Orch. (1994).—**NS/LK/DM**

Drew, Kenny (actually, Kenneth Sidney),

jazz pianist; b. N.Y., Aug. 28, 1928; d. Copenhagen, Denmark, Aug. 4, 1993. Drew was one of the most widely recorded sidemen of the hard bop era. He was perhaps more famous for his adaptability and consistency than for the depth of his musical insights. However, he displayed a polished technique and a peerless sense of swing, and sessions usually were better for his presence at the keyboard. His recording debut was on a Howard McGhee session in 1949, followed by a Sonny Stitt date a few months later. Although he led sessions for Riverside, Norgran, and Blue Note from 1953 until 1960, his most significant work during this period was as a sideman. He recorded with Sonny Rollins and John Coltrane in the late 1950s, during crucial phases in the development of both of those artists. He also had strong outings on Blue Note in support of Kenny Dorham, Tina Brooks, and Jackie McLean. In the early 1960s, Drew left the American jazz scene and moved to Europe, where he was to remain for the rest of his life. Dexter Gordon's early 1960s albums with him were a high point in the careers of both artists, and the two of them would reunite several times over the next ten years. He led the house band at the Jazzhaus Montmarte in Copenhagen into the 1970s, performing with many prominent expatriate jazzmen. Here he began a productive musical partnership with Scandinavian bassist Niels-Henning Orsted Pederson which would last into the 1970s. Although he made some solid recordings as a leader throughout his career, Drew is heard to best advantage supporting other artists of stronger musical personality. His recordings with Ben Webster, Johnny Griffin, Jackie McLean, Dexter Gordon, Sonny Rollins, and John Coltrane were high points in the careers of those artists. Few pianists of his generation could claim such a distinguished résumé. His son, Kenny Drew Jr. (b. N.Y., 1958), is also a jazz pianist who has performed with Mingus Dynasty, among other groups.

DISC.: *Introducing the Kenny Drew Trio* (1953); *Modernity of Kenny Drew* (1953); *New Sounds, New Faces* (1953); *Progressive*

Piano (1954); *Trio-Quartet-Quintet* (1956); *This Is New* (1957); *Undercurrent* (1960); *Duo, Vol. 1* (1973); *Everything I Love* (1973); *Duo, Vol. 2* (1974); *If You Could See Me Now* (1974); *In Concert* (1977); *Ruby My Dear* (1977); *Duo Live in Concert* (1978); *Home Is Where the Soul Is* (1978); *Live in Concert* (1978); *It Might As Well Be Spring* (1981); *Your Soft Eyes* (1981); *And Far Away* (1983); *Recollections* (1989).—**WB**

Dreyer, Johann Melchior,

German organist and composer; b. Röttingen, Württemberg, June 24, 1747; d. Ellwangen, March 22, 1824. He studied in Ellwangen, where he became a church organist. He wrote chiefly church music. Among his publ. works are *18 Missae breves* (1790–1802), *24 Hymni brevissimi ad vesperas* (1791), *Te Deum* (1800), and organ music.—**NS/LK/DM**

Dreyfus, George (actually, Georg),

German-born Australian bassoonist, conductor, and composer; b. Wuppertal, July 22, 1928. He and his family fled Nazi Germany in 1939, and settled in Australia. He received training in clarinet, and in 1946 studied bassoon with Fred Morgan at the Univ. of Melbourne Conservatorium. In 1955–56 he studied at the Vienna Academy of Music. He was a bassoonist in the orch. of Her Majesty's Theatre (1948–52) and in the Victorian Sym. Orch. (1953–64) in Melbourne. In 1958 he founded the New Music Ensemble in Melbourne, which became the George Dreyfus Chamber Orch. in 1970. He held a creative arts fellowship from the Australian National Univ. in Canberra in 1967, the Prix de Rome of the German Academy in Rome in 1976, and the Don Banks fellowship of the Australian Council in 1991. In 1992 he received the Order of Australia. He publ. an autobiography, *The Last Frivolous Book* (Sydney, 1984). The vol. *Being George... and liking it: Reflections on the Life and Work of George Dreyfus on his 70th birthday* (Richmond, Va., 1998), includes essays by the composer and others. Dreyfus has composed works in all major genres, ranging from opera to music for television.

WORKS: DRAMATIC: *Garni Sands*, opera (1965–66; Sydney, Aug. 12, 1972); *The Takeover*, school musical (1969); *The Gilt- Edged Kid*, opera (1970; Melbourne, April 11, 1976); *The Lamentable Reign of Charles the Last*, "pantopera" (1975; Adelaide, March 23, 1976); *Smash Hit!*, musical (1980); *The Sentimental Bloke*, musical (Melbourne, Dec. 12, 1985); *Rathenau*, opera (1991–92; Kassel, June 19, 1993); *The Marx Sisters*, opera (1994–95; Bielefeld, April 20, 1996); incidental music; over 35 film scores; television music, including *Rush* (1974). **ORCH.:** 2 syms. (1967, 1976); *Jingles* (1968); *...and more Jingles* (1972); *A Steam Train Passes* (1974); *Hallelujah for Handel* (1976); *Symphonie Concertante* for Bassoon, Violin, Viola, Cello, and Strings (1978); *Mary Gilmore Goes to Paraguay* for Strings, Brass, and Percussion (1979); *Dimboola Water Music and Waltz* (1979); *Grand Ridge Road*, suite for Small Orch. (1980); *Folk Music with Large Orchestra* (1982); *German Teddy* for Mandolin Orch. (1984); *Great Expectations* (1986); *Larino, Safe Haven* for Flute or Oboe and Strings (1990); *Sound Sculptures from Rathenau* (1991); *Lighthouse* for Strings (1993); *Love Your Animal* (1996); *You're remembr'd well, Clive Douglas!*, overture for Concert Band (1998); *Mr. Lewis Comes to Wuppertal* for Didjeridu and Orch. (1998). **CHAMBER:** Trio for Flute, Clarinet, and Bassoon (1956); *The Seasons* for Flute, Viola, and Percussion (1963); 2 wind quintets (1965, 1968); Sextet for Didjeridu and Winds (1971); *Old Melbourne* for

935

Bassoon and Guitar (1973); *In Memoriam Raoul Wallenberg* for Clarinet and Piano (1984); *Song and Dance for Gabor* for Clarinet, Taganing, and Double Bass (1988); *for four Bassoons*, quartet (1988); Sonata for Violin and Viola (1989); *There is Something of Don Quixote in All of Us* for Guitar (1990); *Odyssey for a Lone Bassoon* (1990); *Homage à Victor Bruns* for Bassoon Quartet (1994). VOCAL: *Galgenlieder* for Baritone, Flute, Clarinet, Violin, and Bassoon (1957); *Songs Comic and Curious* for Baritone, Flute, Oboe, Clarinet, Horn, and Bassoon (1959); *The Adventures of Sebastian the Fox* for Narrator and Orch. (1963); *Song of the Maypole*, cantata for Children's Choruses and Orch. (1968); *Reflections in a Glass-house: An Image of Captain James Cook* for Speaker, Children's Chorus, and Orch. (1969); *Mo* for Baritone, String Orch., and Continuo (1972); *Ein Kaffeekonzert* for Soprano, Violin, Cello, and Piano (1977); *An Australian Folk Mass* for Chorus (1979); *Celebration* for Women's Voices, Piano, and Orch. (1981); *Psalms 100 & 150* for Chorus and Orch. (1981); *Visions* for Chorus and Orch. (1983); *Charles Rasp* for Men's Chorus, Children's Chorus, Pop Singer, and Concert Band (1984); *The Box Hill Gloria*, cantata for Mixed Chorus, Children's Chorus, Pop Singer, Brass Band, Concert Band, Pipe Band, and Strings (1985); *The Song of Brother Sun* for Chorus and Harp or Keyboard (1988); *Auscapes* for Chorus (1990); *Else* for Countertenor or Contralto, Boy's Chorus, and Men's Chorus (1993); *Song of the Republic* for Chorus and Orch. (1998).—NS/LK/DM

Dreyfus, Huguett (Pauline), French harpsichordist; b. Mulhouse Nov. 30, 1928. She studied in Paris at the École Normale de Musique and with Dufourcq at the Cons. (graduated, 1950) before pursuing advanced training with Gerlin at the Accademia Musicale Chigiana in Siena (1953). After winning the 1st medal in harpsichord at the Geneva competition in 1958, she toured internationally; also was a prof. at the Paris Schola Cantorum (from 1967). While she has concentrated on the music of Bach, Couperin, Scarlatti, and Rameau, her repertory also includes adventuresome scores by contemporary composers.—NS/LK/DM

Dreyschock, Alexander, brilliant Bohemian pianist, teacher, and composer, brother of **Raimund Dreyschock;** b. Zack, Oct. 15, 1818; d. Venice, April 1, 1869. A student of Tomaschek, he acquired a virtuoso technique and was regarded as a worthy rival of Liszt in technical dexterity. At eight he was able to play in public. He toured North Germany (1838), spent two years in Russia (1840–42), and visited Brussels, Paris, and London, then the Netherlands and Austria. In 1862 he was called to St. Petersburg as a prof. at the newly founded Cons. In 1868 he went to Italy. His astounding facility in playing octaves, double sixths, and thirds, and performing solos with the left hand alone cast a glamour about his performance. Among his compositions are the opera *Florette, oder Die erste Liebe Heinrichs des IV.,* an Overture for Orch., Rondo for Orch., String Quartet, and 140 piano pieces of the salon type.—NS/LK/DM

Dreyschock, Felix, German pianist, son of **Raimund Dreyschock;** b. Leipzig, Dec. 27, 1860; d. Berlin, Aug. 1, 1906. He studied under Grabau, Ehrlich, Taubert, and Kiel. He gave successful concerts, and was a prof. at the Stern Cons. in Berlin. His piano pieces are well written and effective. He also publ. a Violin Sonata and songs.—NS/LK/DM

Dreyschock, Raimund, Bohemian violinist, brother of **Alexander Dreyschock** and father of **Felix Dreyschock;** b. Zack, Aug. 20, 1824; d. Leipzig, Feb. 6, 1869. He was a pupil of Pixis in Prague. He was concertmaster at the Gewandhaus concerts (1850–69) and a violin teacher in the Cons. at Leipzig. His wife, Elizabeth (née Nose, b. Cologne, 1832; d. there, July, 1911), was a contralto singer who founded and managed a vocal academy in Berlin.—NS/LK/DM

Drieberg, Friedrich von, German music historian and composer; b. Charlottenburg, Dec. 10, 1780; d. there, May 21, 1856. He served in the Prussian army until 1804, when he went to Paris to study composition with Spontini; also traveled to Vienna. He produced two operas, *Don Cocagno* (Berlin, 1812) and *Der Sänger und der Schneider* (Berlin, Nov. 23, 1814), but became known mainly through his speculative publications concerning Greek music, promulgating theories and conclusions that were utterly unfounded. However, they were publ. and seriously discussed, if only in refutation. These are *Die mathematische Intervallenlehre der Griechen* (1818), *Aufschlüsse über die Musik der Griechen* (1819), *Die praktische Musik der Griechen* (1821), *Die pneumatischen Erfindungen der Griechen* (1822), *Wörterbuch der griech. Musik* (1835), *Die griechische Musik, auf ihre Grundgesetze zurückgeführt* (1841), and *Die Kunst der musikalischen Composition... nach griechischen Grundsätzen bearbeitet* (1858). —NS/LK/DM

Driessler, Johannes, German composer and pedagogue; b. Friedrichsthal, Jan. 26, 1921. He received training in organ, choral conducting, and theory from Karl Rahner at the Saarbrücken Cons. and in composition from William Maler at the Cologne Cons. In 1946 he became a teacher of church music at the North West German Music Academy in Detmold, where he was a prof. of composition (from 1958) and deputy director (1960–83). He was especially adept at composing choral works in an acceptable tonal idiom.

WORKS: DRAMATIC: Opera: *Claudia amata* (1952); *Prinzessin Hochmut* (1952); *Der Umfried,* youth opera (1957); *Doktor Luzifer Trux* (1958). ORCH.: Piano Concerto (1953); Cello Concerto (1954); *Ikarus,* sym. for 2 Soloists, Chorus, and Orch. (1960); 3 numbered syms.: No. 1, *Dum spiro spero* (1964), No. 2, *Dum ludo laudo* (1966), and No. 3, *Amo dum vivo,* for Strings and Percussion (1969); Concerto for String Trio and Orch. (1963). ORGAN: *20 Choralsonaten* (1954–55). VOCAL: Oratorios: *Dein Reich komme* (1949); *Gaudia mundana* (1951); *De profundis* for Soloists, 2 Choruses, Winds, Timpani, and Piano (1950–52); *Darum seid getrost* (1954); *Der Lebendige* (1956); *Der grosse Lobgesang* for Mezzo-soprano, Chorus, Winds, and Brass (1959). Other: *Denn dein Reich komme,* cantata for Soloists, 2 Choruses, and Instruments (1947); *Sinfonia sacra* for Chorus (1948); *Christe eleison,* Passion motet (1948); *Triptychon,* cantata for Chorus and Small Orch. (1950); *12 Spruchmotetten und 10 Spruchkanons* for Chorus (1950); *Balduin Brummsel,* cantata for Soloists and Orch. (1952); *Altenberger Messe* for Chorus and Winds (1955); *Markus-Passion* for Chorus (1955); *2 Concerti sacri* for Soloist and Organ (1961).—NS/LK/DM

Drigo, Riccardo, Italian composer and conductor; b. Padua, June 30, 1846; d. there, Oct. 1, 1930. He studied music in Padua and Venice, then conducted opera in Venice and Milan. In 1879 he was engaged to conduct the Italian opera in St. Petersburg; in 1886 became permanent ballet conductor of the Imperial Theater there. He conducted first performances of Tchaikovsky's ballets *The Sleeping Beauty* and *The Nutcracker*. After Tchaikovsky's death, Drigo ed. the score of the ballet *Swan Lake* and orchestrated a number of Tchaikovsky's piano pieces. Drigo's own ballets, melodious and easy to listen to, also enjoyed excellent success in Russia. Particularly popular was his ballet *Les Millions d'Arlequin*, which includes the famous *Serenade* for a soulful cello solo and the ingratiating *Valse bluette*. Drigo conducted the first performance of this ballet in St. Petersburg on Feb. 10, 1900. From 1914 to 1916 he was in Italy, from 1916 to 1920 again in St. Petersburg, finally returning to Italy.

BIBL.: S. Travaglia, *R. D., L'uomo e l'artista* (Padua, 1929). —NS/LK/DM

Dring, Madeleine, English violinist, pianist, singer, and composer; b. Hornsey, Sept. 7, 1923; d. London, March 26, 1977. She studied violin at the Junior Dept. of the Royal Coll. of Music in London, and also acquired professional skill as a pianist, singer, and actress. She took courses in composition at the Royal Coll. of Music with Howells and Vaughan Williams. She developed a knack for writing attractively brief pieces. She also wrote a short opera, *Cupboard Love*, several trios, a suite for Harmonica and Piano, and incidental music for radio and television.—NS/LK/DM

Drinker, Henry S(andwith, Jr.), American music scholar and translator; b. Philadelphia, Sept. 15, 1880; d. Merion, Pa., March 9, 1965. He was a lawyer by profession, but devoted much time to musical pursuits. He founded the Accademia dei Dilettanti di Musica in his home in 1930, which gave performances of choral music ranging from the 17th to the 20th centuries until it was disbanded in 1960. He also founded the Drinker Library of Choral Music, which he later donated to the Free Library of Philadelphia. He tr. the texts of 212 cantatas by Bach, as well as the *St. Matthew Passion*, the *St. John Passion*, the *Christmas Oratorio*, the *Easter Oratorio*, and the *Magnificat*; also all of Mozart's choral music, all of Schumann's songs, all of the solo songs of Schubert and Wolf, and the complete vocal works of Brahms. His wife, Sophie (Lewis) (née Hutchinson) Drinker (b. Philadelphia, Aug. 24, 1888; d. Chestnut Hill, Pa., Sept. 6, 1967) was a champion of women in music; she publ. *Music and Women* (1948) and *Brahms and His Women's Choruses* (1952).

WRITINGS: *The Chamber Music of Johannes Brahms* (Philadelphia, 1932); *Bach's Use of Slurs in Recitativo Secco* (Merion, Pa., 1946); *Drinker Library of Choral Music: Catalogue* (Philadelphia, 1957); *Accademia dei Dilettanti di Musica, 1930–1960* (Merion, Pa., 1960).—NS/LK/DM

D'Rivera, Paquito, leading Latin American bop alto saxophonist, clarinetist, b. Havana, Cuba, June 4. 1948. If there is a singular musician carrying on the legacy of Dizzy Gillespie, it is bandleader and reed player Paquito D'Rivera. Inspired at a young age by the music of John Coltrane, Charlie Parker, and Lee Konitz, he added rhythms from his native Cuba and melded them into bopped-up, romantic, salty, and sensuous sounds. In Cuba he was influenced by his father, a classical saxophonist who introduced his son to the recordings of Charlie Parker. D'Rivera was a prodigy who was playing professionally by his mid-teens. He entered the Havana Cons. in 1960 to pursue classical studies, joined the Orquesta Cubana de Música Moderna in 1967, and, with some of the members of the Orquesta, formed Irakere, an 11-member band that played a sizzling mixture of jazz, rock, classical, and traditional Cuban music from 1973–80. Irakere performed in the United States during 1978 at the Newport Jazz Festival as well as at others worldwide, causing a sensation that resulted in an historic March 1979 concert in Cuba featuring an array of American pop artists who performed along with the best musicians of the contemporary Cuban music scene. The event was documented on two albums, *Havana Jam* and *Havana Jam II*. Albums with his group Irakere followed in 1979 and 1980.

While on tour in Spain with Irakere in 1980, he defected. He eventually settled in N.Y. and within three years was playing in the most prestigious clubs and concert halls and touring Europe with Dizzy Gillespie. Throughout the 1980s D'Rivera continued performing, recording, and touring globally with his own groups. After performing regularly in Gillespie's United Nation Orch. (UNO), which Gillespie founded in 1988, D'Rivera took over leadership of the band following its leader death in 1993. His first albums as leader, *Paquito Blowin'* in 1981 and *Mariel* in 1982, solidified his reputation in the United States, and numerous albums as leader and sideman have followed. As well as recording as sideman with McCoy Tyner, Hendrik Meurkens, Claudio Roditi, Arturo Sandoval, Bobby Sanabria, Richie Cole, the Caribbean Jazz Project, and many others, he has chalked up a significant number of richly diverse albums for Columbia, Chesky, Messidor, Candid, and TropiJazz. His broad-based performances and recordings brilliantly continue to straddle the fence between modern American music and his native Cuban rhythms.

DISC.: *Blowin'* (1981); *Mariel* (1982); *Live at Keystone Korner* (1983); *Why Not* (1984); *Explosion* (1985); *Manhattan Burn* (1985); *Havana Café* (1991); *Reunion* (1991); *Who's Smoking?!* (1991); *40 Years of Cuban Jam Session* (1993); *Night in Englewood* (1994). —NAL

Drogin, Barry (Jay), American composer and electrical engineer; b. Oyster Bay, N.Y., May 2, 1960. After taking theater and music courses at Emerson Coll. (1977–79), he was trained as an electrical engineer, earning degrees from The Cooper Union in N.Y. (B.E., 1983; M.E., 1986). He also also attended music classes there, and studied privately (1977–83) with Mark Kroll and Scott Wheeler in Boston, Elie Siegmeister in Great Neck, N.Y., and Gil Robbins and Laurie Spiegel in N.Y. His awards and commissions include a grant from Meet the Composer for his *The Clean Platter* for Chorus, String Quartet, and Piano (1983). In 1988 he founded the self-publishing co., Not Nice Music, which sponsored a competition, "The Lullaby Project," in 1997. For his Jewish compositions, Drogin uses the pseudonym **Baruch Skeer.**

WORKS: DRAMATIC: O p e r a : *Love and Idols/A Jewish Opera* for 4 Voices and Grand Piano (1984). I n c i d e n t a l M u s i c : *Working All Day* for Voice and Piano, incidental music to the composer's play *Fast Food* (1977); *Twelfth Night,* songs and incidental music for Voice and Piano to Shakespeare's play (1978); *The Good Doctor* for Piano, incidental music to Neil Simon's play (1979); *Fornication Makes the World Go Round* for Piano, incidental music for Brett Somers's play *Anterooms* (1983); *Peter Had a Plan* for 5 Voices and Piano (1983). D a n c e : *Butterfly Dream* for Chamber Orch. (1981); *Typhoid Mary* for Alto and Piano (1988). CHAMBER: Piano Variations (1980); *Chamber Music,* "little concerto for amateur ensemble" (1982); Duet for Flute and Bass Clarinet (1982; originally for Flute and Trombone); *Perceptions* for Electric Keyboard (1983); *J.J. Comes to Cooper,* oboe sonatina (1989). VOCAL: *Shma* for Tenor, Chorus, and Organ (1978); *Fugitive Configurations* for Chorus (1981); *To A Lady Passing Time Better Left Unpassed* for Chorus (1981); *The Clean Platter* for Chorus, String Quartet, and Piano, after Ogden Nash (1983); *Love Poems from the Hebrew* for Soprano and Piano (1985); *Alamo!* for Solo Voice (1995; rev. 1998); *Yisroayl B'Mitzroyim (Israel in Egypt),* oratorio for Soloists and Chorus (1999).—LK/DM

Drouet, Louis François-Philippe, famous French flutist and composer; b. Amsterdam, April 14, 1792; d. Bern, Sept. 30, 1873. He studied composition at the Paris Cons. At the age of 16, he was appointed solo flutist to King Louis of the Netherlands, and at 19 became solo flutist to Napoleon. After Napoleon's defeat, he played the flute with fine impartiality for King Louis XVIII. In 1817 he went to London, and subsequently made concert tours across Europe. In 1840 he was appointed Kapellmeister at Coburg. In 1854 he visited America for a few months, then lived in Gotha and Frankfurt am Main before going to Switzerland. He composed mainly for the flute, numbering among his works ten flute concertos, two fantasias for flute and piano, three trios for three flutes, and numerous sonatas and variations for flute and assorted instruments. —NS/LK/DM

Druckman, Jacob (Raphael), outstanding American composer and teacher; b. Philadelphia, June 26, 1928; d. New Haven, Conn., May 24, 1996. He received lessons in theory, composition, and violin from Gessensway (1938–40) and in solfège and score reading from Longy (1945). During the summers of 1949 and 1950, Druckman attended the composition course of Aaron Copland at the Berkshire Music Center at Tanglewood. He pursued his studies with Persichetti, Mennin, and Wagenaar at the Juilliard School of Music in N.Y. (B.S., 1954; M.S., 1956), and with Aubin at the École Normale de Musique in Paris on a Fulbright fellowship (1954–55). Later he did research in electronic music at the Columbia-Princeton Electronic Music Center (1965–66) and at the ORTF in Paris (1968). From 1957 to 1972 he taught at the Juilliard School of Music. He also taught at Bard Coll. (1961–67) and was an assoc. director of the Columbia-Princeton Electronic Music Center (1967). In 1971–72 he was director of the electronic

music studio at the Yale Univ. School of Music. After serving as assoc. prof. of composition at Brooklyn Coll. of the City Univ. of N.Y. (1972–76), he was chairman of the music dept. of the Yale Univ. School of Music (from 1976), where he again was director of the electronic music studio (from 1976). He was president of the Koussevitzky Music Foundation from 1981. In 1982 he was in residence at the American Academy in Rome. From 1982 to 1986 he was composer-in-residence of the N.Y. Phil. He was president of the Aaron Copland Music Fund for Music from 1991. He was appointed the Charles Ives Memorial Composer Laureate of the State of Conn. in 1993. In 1957 and 1968 he held Guggenheim fellowships. In 1972 he won the Pulitzer Prize in Music for his *Windows* for Orch. He received the Brandeis Univ. Creative Arts Award in 1975. In 1978 he was elected to membership in the Inst. of the American Academy and Inst. of Arts and Letters. In his distinguished body of works, Druckman demonstrated an assured handling of various contemporary means of expression, ranging from 12-tone procedures and electronics to traditional and new Romantic elements. His mastery of orchestration was particularly notable.

WORKS: DRAMATIC: *Spell,* ballet (1951); *Interlude,* ballet (1953); *Suite,* ballet (1953); *Performance,* ballet (1960); *Measure for Measure,* incidental music to Shakespeare's play (1964); *Look Park,* film score (1970); *Traite du rossignol,* film score (1970). ORCH.: *Music for the Dance* (1949); Concerto for Strings (1951); *Volpone Overture* (1953); Concerto for Violin and Small Orch. (1956); *Odds and Evens: A Game* for Children's Orch. (1966); *Windows* (Chicago, March 16, 1972); *Incenters* for Trumpet, Horn, Trombone, and Orch. (Minneapolis, Nov. 23, 1973; also for Chamber Ensemble, 1968); *Mirage* (St. Louis, March 4, 1976); *Chiaroscuro* (1976; Cleveland, March 14, 1977); Viola Concerto (N.Y., Nov. 2, 1978); *Aureole* (N.Y., June 6, 1979); *Prism* (Baltimore, May 21, 1980); *A Birthday Bouquet* (N.Y., April 26, 1986); *Athanor* (N.Y., May 8, 1986); *Paean* (1986; Houston, Jan. 3, 1987); *In Memoriam Vincent Persichetti* (N.Y., Dec. 6, 1987); *Variation on Bernstein's "New York, New York"* (Tanglewood, Aug. 28, 1988); *Brangle* (Chicago, March 28, 1989); *Nor Spell Nor Charm* for Chamber Orch. (Los Angeles, March 2, 1990); *Shog* (Paris, Feb. 21, 1991); *Summer Lightning* (Tanglewood, July 19, 1991); *Seraphic Games* (Costa Mesa, Calif., April 25, 1992); *Demos* (Brussels, Dec. 31, 1992); *With Bells On,* fanfare for Symphonic Winds and Percussion (Los Angeles, March 31, 1994); Piano Concerto (New Haven, Oct. 17, 1996). CHAMBER: 3 string quartets: No. 1 (1948), No. 2 (N.Y., Dec. 13, 1966), and No. 3 (Milwaukee, Nov. 17, 1981); Duo for Violin and Piano (1949; Tanglewood, Aug. 1950); *Divertimento* for Clarinet, Horn, Harp, Violin, Viola, and Cello (1950; N.Y., March 1953); *Animus I* for Trombone and Tape (Annandale-on- Hudson, N.Y., May 23, 1966) and *III* for Clarinet and Tape (Paris, Oct. 23, 1969); *Incenters* for Chamber Ensemble (New Brunswick, N.J., May 7, 1968; also for Trumpet, Horn, Trombone, and Orch., 1973); *Valentine* for Double Bass (N.Y., Nov. 19, 1969); *Orison* for Organ and Tape (1969; N.Y., Jan. 19, 1970); *Delizie contente che l'alme beate* for Wind Quintet and Tape (N.Y., Dec. 13, 1973); *Other Voices* for Brass Quintet (Aspen, Colo., July 20, 1976); *Tromba Marina* for 4 Double Basses (N.Y., Dec. 29, 1981); *Reflections on the Nature of War* for Marimba (Washington, D.C., Nov. 7, 1986); *Dance With Shadows* for Brass Quintet (1989); *Come Round* for Chamber Ensemble (Santa Fe, N.Mex., Aug. 16, 1992); Duo for Violin and Cello (Charonne, France, June 17, 1994); *Glint* for

Clarinet, Violin, and Piano (N.Y., Oct. 17, 1995). V O C A L : *Laude* for Baritone, Flute, Viola, and Cello (1952); *The Simple Gifts* for Chorus and Piano (1954); *4 Madrigals* for Chorus (1958; N.Y., March 6, 1959); *Dark Upon the Harp* for Mezzo-soprano, Brass Quintet, and Percussion (1962); *Antiphonies I, II,* and *III* for 2 Choruses (1963; I and II, N.Y., Feb. 28, 1964; *III*, Tanglewood, July 30, 1976); *The Sound of Time* for Soprano and Piano (N.Y., Dec. 3, 1964; also for Soprano and Orch., Provincetown, Mass., July 25, 1965); *Dance of the Maidens* for Chorus, Organ, and Percussion (1965); *Hymnus referamus* for Chorus, Organ, and Percussion (1965); *Psalm 89* for Chorus, Organ, and Percussion (1965); *Shir Shel Yakov: Sabbath Eve Service* for Tenor, Chorus, and Organ (N.Y., April 21, 1967); *Animus II* for Soprano, 2 Percussionists, and Tape (1968; Paris, Feb. 2, 1970) and *IV* for Tenor, Instrumental Ensemble, and Tape (Paris, Sept. 29, 1977); *Lamia* for Soprano and Orch. (Albany, N.Y., April 20, 1974; rev. version, N.Y., Oct. 17, 1975; also for Soprano and Small Orch., St. Paul, Minn., Nov. 7, 1986); *Bō* for 3 Women's Voices, Marimba, Harp, and Bass Clarinet (N.Y., March 3, 1979); *Vox Humana* for Soprano, Mezzo-soprano, Tenor, Bass, Chorus, and Orch. (1982–83; Washington, D.C., Oct. 25, 1983); *Nor Spell* for Mezzo-soprano and English Horn (Aspen, Colo., July 19, 1990); *Counterpoise* for Soprano and Orch. (Philadelphia, April 28, 1994).—NS/LK/DM

Drummond, Billy,

drummer; b. Newport News, Va., 1959. He began to play drums at the age of four, influenced by his father, who was also a drummer. His love for jazz was sparked by his father's record collection, which included many of the classic recordings of Miles Davis, Art Blakey, Max Roach, and so on. During his youth, Drummond played in various school and local bands, and studied many styles of music. He then went on to college, taking a degree in Music Performance. In early 1988, Billy arrived in N.Y. His first major break on the circuit was to join the young band "Out of the Blue" (OTB), with which he played on the group's final recording for Blue Note. Soon after, he joined Horace Silver's Sextet and toured with them extensively. During the 1990s he performed and recorded with Sonny Rollins, J.J. Johnson (1992–95), Joe Henderson, Nat Adderley, Bobby Hutcherson, James Moody, Steve Kuhn, Freddie Hubbard, and Buster Williams. He and Renee Rosnes met and married while they were in J.J. Johnson's band. He has also worked with Vincent Herring, Christian McBride, and Javon Jackson and is a member of the cooperative band Native Colours with Ralph Moore, Rosnes, and bassist Larry Grenadier. Peter Watrous, jazz critic for the *New York Times*, named Drummond's *Dubai* as the top jazz recording for 1996.

DISC.: *Native Colours* (1992); *The Gift* (1994); *Native Colours: One World* (1994); *Dubai* (1996).—LP

Drummond, Dean,

American composer, conductor, instrumentalist, and inventor of musical instruments; b. Los Angeles, Jan. 22, 1949. He was educated at the Univ. of Southern Calif. in Los Angeles (B.M. in composition, 1971) and the Calif. Inst. of the Arts in Valencia (M.F.A. in composition, 1973), where he studied composition with Leonard Stein; while a student, he also worked closely with Harry Partch, whose instruments and works he later championed. In 1977 he co-founded Newband with the flutist Stefanie Starin,

whom he subsequently married; in 1990 he became director of the Harry Partch Instrumentarium, which in 1993 moved to the State Univ. of N.Y. at Purchase, where Drummond was also composer-in-residence. In 1999 he joined the faculty at Montclair State Univ. in N.J. as a visiting specialist. Drummond's compositions frequently feature newly invented instruments (including his own zoomoozophone and juststrokerods), synthesizers, microtones, new techniques for winds and strings, and large ensembles of specialized percussion. He also made three arrangements: *Two Studies on Ancient Greek Scales* for Flute and Zoomoozophone, after Harry Partch (1978); *'Round Midnight* for Cello and Zoomoozophone (three players), after Thelonius Monk (1990; rev. 1993), and *Najma* for Alto Flute, Chromelodeon, Harmonic Canon, Kithara, and Zoomoozophone (two players), after John Coltrane (1994). Among his awards are a Guggenheim fellowship (1995–96), awards from the Koussevitzky Foundation (1992), Fromm Foundation (1993), and the Cary Trust Commission (1993), NEA fellowships (1988–89; 1995–96), a N.Y. Foundation for the Arts fellowship (1989), and 2nd prize in the John F. Kennedy Friedheim Award for Chamber Music for his *Dance of the Seven Veils* (1993); in 1995–96 he also received a Meet the Composer/Reader's Digest commission for his live film score, *Der Lezte Mann* (The Last Laugh). He invented two instruments: the zoomoozophone (1978) and the juststrokerods (1988), which have been utilized by numerous contemporary composers, including John Cage, Ezra Sims, and Muhal Richard Abrams.

WORKS: *Suite* for Clarinet (1970; Los Angeles, May 24, 1971); *Bertrans de Born* for Bass-baritone, Flute, Clarinet, Bass Clarinet, Bassoon, Horn, Piano/Celeste, String Quartet, and Double Bass (Los Angeles, May 24, 1971); *Ni Kioku* for Flute, Celeste, Harp, 2 Percussionists, Violin, and Cello (Los Angeles, May 24, 1971); *Organ Toccata* for Pipe Organ (1971); *Dedication* for Oboe, Harp, 3 Percussionists, String Quartet, and Double Bass (Valencia, Calif., May 11, 1972); *Fission* for Flute, Oboe, Clarinet, Bassoon, Horn, Trumpet, Trombone, Harp, Vibraphone, Violine, Viola, and Cello (1972); *Ghost Tangents* for Prepared Piano and 3 Percussionists (Portland, Ore., March 11, 1973; rev. 1975); *Cloud Garden I* for Flute, Piano, and 4 Percussionists (Santa Monica, Calif., March 1, 1974) and *II* for Piano, Celeste, and Almglocken (1 player) (KPFK Radio, Los Angeles, Oct. 12, 1974); *Zurrjir* for Flute, Clarinet, Piano/Celeste, and 3 Percussionists (Ventura, Calif., Jan. 20, 1976); *Dirty Ferdie* for 4 Percussionists (1976; N.Y., Feb. 18, 1982; also for 8 Percussionists, 1982; Baltimore, April 22, 1986); *Post Rigabop Mix* for Flute (N.Y., Nov. 3, 1977); *Copegoro* for Zoomoozophonist (1978; Stony Brook, N.Y., March 12, 1979); *Little Columbus* for 2 Zoomoozophonists (N.Y., May 29, 1979); *Columbus* for Flute and 3 Zoomoozophonists (1980; N.Y., Feb. 22, 1981); *Mysteries* for 4 Zoomoozophonists and Percussionist (N.Y., May 15, 1983; also for Flute, Bass Trombone, 4 Zoomoozophonists, and Percussionist, 1983, N.Y., April 5, 1984, and for Flute, Violin, Cello, 4 Zoomoozophonists, and Percussionists, 1982; rev. 1986); *Then or Never* for Flute, Viola, Double Bass, and 3 Zoomoozophonists (1984; N.Y., March 3, 1985); *Columbus Fullmoon* for Zoomoozophone (1979; rev. 1985; N.Y., Jan. 20, 1987); *Ruby Half Moon* for 2 Trumpets, Trombone, Bass Trombone, and 4 Zoomoozophonists/Percussionists (Croton Falls, N.Y., June 14, 1987); *Incredible Time (to live and die)* for Amplified Flute, Yamaha

DX7IID, and 3 Percussionists (Zoomoozophone, Percussion, and Korg DDD1 Digital Drums) (San Antonio, June 10, 1988); *Different Drums for Different Strokes* for Korg DDD1 Digital Drums, Yamaha DX7IID, Stroke Rods, and Percussion (1 player) (N.Y., Nov. 18, 1988); *Dance of the Seven Veils* for 6 Players (N.Y., Nov. 13, 1992); *The Day the Sun Stood Still* for 9 Players (N.Y., Nov. 8, 1994); *Before the Last Laugh* for 7 Players (Minneapolis, Oct. 14, 1995); *The Last Laugh (Der Lezte Mann)*, live film score, for Chamber Ensemble, for F.W. Munau's 1924 silent film of the same name (Columbus, Ohio, Sept. 28, 1996); *Four Miniatures*: *Syncopation in Glass* and *Talking Bowls* for Cloud Chamber Bowls (solo) and *Bow, Chords, and Zoom* and *Three Dream Fragments* for Zoomoozophone (duet; 1997); *It Must Be Time* for Soprano and Microtonally programmed Synthesizer (1997); *Mars Face* for Violin and Microtonally programmed Synthesizer (Washington, D.C., March 11, 1997); *My Data's Gone* for Bass and Microtonally programmed Synthesizer (1997); *Precious Metals* for Flute (1997); *Two Short Zoomoozophone Duos* (1997); *Two Short Solos for Cloud Chamber Bowls* (1997); *For the Last Laugh*, suite from the film score for 10 Players (1998); *Congressional Record* for Baritone and 8 Players (N.Y., June 4, 1999); *Café Buffé*, chamber opera for 5 Singers, 9 Instrumentalists, and 4 Dancers, after Charles Bernstein (1997–2000).—**NS/LK/DM**

Drummond, Ray, bassist; b. Brookline, Mass., Nov. 23, 1946. His father was in the U.S. Army and his family frequently moved around the United States and Europe. In 1954 he began playing brass instruments; he took up bass in 1961. He graduated from Nuremberg American H.S. in Nuremberg, Germany (1964); that fall he entered Claremont Men's Coll. near L.A., graduating in June 1968 with a B.A. in Political Science; then he went to Stanford Business School M.B.A. program, 1970–71. He lived in San Francisco from 1971–74 and actively freelanced there; from 1974 to 1977 he lived on the Monterey Peninsula; in November 1977 he moved to N.Y. He began working with Thad Jones, the Mel Lewis Orch., and Betty Carter. He has since played with numerous bands on over 200 recordings. He has worked as a leader and composer as well, producing a few excellent recordings.

DISC.: *Susanita* (1986); *Camera in a Bag* (1989); *One to One I and II* (with Bill Mays; 1990, 1991); *The Essence* (1990); *Excursion* (1993); *Continuum* (1994); *Vignettes* (1996).—**LP**

Drury, Stephen, American pianist; b. Spokane, Wash., April 13, 1955. His mother taught him piano; he then went to Harvard Univ., where he worked at the Electronic Music Studio. In 1977 he continued his piano studies in N.Y. with William Masselos, then returned to Harvard and organized an Experimental Music Festival, during which he gave a complete performance of Satie's *Vexations*. He also played the piano sonatas of Ives and piano pieces by Cage. While preoccupied with avant-garde music, Drury also took occasional lessons in classical piano with Arrau in N.Y. On the musical far-out frontier, he became a member of a conceptual team called Beaux Eaux Duo.—**NS/LK/DM**

Drysdale, (George John) Learmont, Scottish composer; b. Edinburgh, Oct. 3, 1866; d. there, June 18, 1909. He was a pupil at the Royal Academy of Music in London, and winner of the Lucas prize for composition (1890). He composed the orch. overtures *Tam O'Shanter* (1890; awarded a prize by the Glasgow Soc. of Musicians) and *Herondean* (1893), as well as two operas, *The Red Spider* (1898) and *Fionn and Tera* (1909), and some choral works.—**NS/LK/DM**

Drzewiecki, Zbigniew, distinguished Polish pianist and pedagogue; b. Warsaw, April 8, 1890; d. there, April 11, 1971. After preliminary training in Warsaw, he studied with C. Prohaska at the Vienna Academy of Music (1909–11) and privately with Maria Prentner (1911–15). He had a few private lessons with Paderewski (1928). In 1916 he made his debut as a soloist with the Warsaw Phil.; he taught at the Warsaw Academy of Music (1916–44; 1945–68) and at the Lvov Cons. (1930–40); in 1945 he founded the Kraków Cons., where he was rector (1945–50) and teacher (until 1968). His fame as a pedagogue reached beyond his homeland; his students included Roger Woodward from Australia and Fou Ts'ong from China. He was active in ISCM activities in Poland and served as a jurist for the Chopin Piano Competition, in which 1st prizes were captured by his students Halina Czerny- Stefanska (1949) and Adam Harasiweicz (1955).

BIBL.: S. Kisielewski, *Z. D.* (Kraków, 1973).—**NS/LK/DM**

Dubensky, Arcady, Russian-American violinist and composer; b. Viatka, Oct. 15, 1890; d. Tenafly, N.J., Oct. 14, 1966. He learned to play the violin in his youth, and then was a student of Hřímalý (violin), Ilyinsky (composition), and Arends (conducting) at the Moscow Cons. (1904–09; diploma, 1909). After playing 1st violin in the Moscow Imperial Opera orch. (1910–19), he settled in N.Y. in 1921 and was a violinist in the N.Y. Sym. Orch. (1922–28) and the N.Y. Phil. (1928–53). While he composed in a conservative idiom, he made adroit use of unusual instrumental combinations.

WORKS: DRAMATIC: O p e r a : *Romance with Double Bass* (1916; N.Y., Oct. 31, 1936); *Downtown* (1930); *On the Highway* (1936); *2 Yankees in Italy* (1944). **I n c i d e n t a l M u s i c T o :** Tarkington's *Mowgli* (1940). **ORCH.:** Sym. (1916); *Russian Bells*, symphonic poem (N.Y., Dec. 29, 1927); *Intermezzo and Complement* (1927); *From Old Russia* (1927); *Gossips* for Strings (Philadelphia, Nov. 24, 1928); *Caprice* for Piccolo and Orch. (1930); *The Raven* for Narrator and Orch. (1931); *Prelude and Fugue* (1932; Boston, April 12, 1943); *Fugue* for 18 Violins (Philadelphia, April 1, 1932); *Tom Sawyer*, overture (Philadelphia, Nov. 29, 1935); *Political Suite: Russian Monarchy, Nazi and Fascist, Communist* (radio broadcast, N.Y., Sept. 17, 1936); *Serenade* (1936); *Rondo and Gigue* for Strings (1937); *Fantasy on a Negro Theme* for Tuba and Orch. (1938); *Stephen Foster: Theme, Variations, Finale* (1940; Indianapolis, Jan. 31, 1941); *Orientale* (1945); *Fugue* for 34 Violins (1948); *Concerto grosso* for 3 Trombones, Tuba, and Orch. (1949); *Trumpet Overture* for 18 Toy Trumpets and 2 Bass Drums (N.Y., Dec. 10, 1949); Trombone Concerto (1953). **CHAMBER:** 2 string quartets (1932, 1954); *Variations* for 8 Clarinets (1932); *Theme and Variations* for 4 Horns (1932); String Sextet (1933); *Prelude and Fugue* for 4 Double Basses (1934); Suite for 4 Trumpets (1935); Suite for 9 Flutes (1935); *Song of November* for Oboe and Piano (1950). —**NS/LK/DM**

Dubin, Al(exander), Swiss-born American lyricist; b. Zurich, June 10, 1891; d. N.Y., Feb. 11, 1945. He was the first lyricist to work for a major film studio. Though he found success in Tin Pan Alley and on Broadway before and after his sojourn in Hollywood, Dubin did his best and most popular work writing for a series of early movie musicals in collaboration with either Joseph A. Burke or Harry Warren. Among his biggest hits are "Tip Toe through the Tulips with Me," "Dancing with Tears in My Eyes," "You're Getting to Be a Habit with Me," "I'll String Along with You," "Lullaby of Broadway," "I Only Have Eyes for You," and "September in the Rain."

Dubin's parents were Russian émigrés. His father, Simon, was a doctor; his mother, Minna, a chemist. The family immigrated to the U.S. in 1896, settling in Philadelphia. By his teens, Dubin was traveling to N.Y. to place his lyrics in Tin Pan Alley and vaudeville. "Prairie Rose" (music by Morris Siltmitzer) and "Sunray" (music by Charles P. Shisler) were his first songs to be published, in 1909. He attended Perkiomen Seminary from 1909 to 1911, after which he worked as a singing waiter in a restaurant in Philadelphia. But soon he moved to N.Y. and went to work in music publishing.

Dubin's first song to be placed in a Broadway show was "'Twas Only an Irishman's Dream" (lyrics also by John O'Brien, music by Rennie Cormack), used in *Broadway and Buttermilk* (N.Y., Aug. 15, 1916). He had his first major song hit with "All the World Will Be Jealous of Me" (music by Ernest R. Ball), which enjoyed a popular recording by Charles Harrison in August 1917.

Dubin was drafted into the Army after the U.S. entry into World War I and saw action in France in 1918. He married vaudeville entertainer Helen McClay in 1919; they had a son, who died shortly after birth, and a daughter. "Crooning" (music by William F. Caesar) became a hit in September 1921 for the Benson Orch. of Chicago, albeit in an instrumental rendition. Henry Burr had a popular record with "Just a Girl That Men Forget" (lyrics also by Fred Rath, music by Joe Garren) in November 1923. "A Cup of Coffee, a Sandwich, and You" (lyrics also by Billy Rose, music by Joseph Meyer) was interpolated into the British *Charlot Revue of 1926* (N.Y., Nov. 10, 1925), sung by Gertrude Lawrence and Jack Buchanan, who made a hit recording of it.

"The Lonesomest Girl in Town" (music by Jimmy McHugh and, supposedly, Irving Mills) was a modest hit for Morton Downey in January 1926. Dubin wrote the songs for the musical *White Lights* (N.Y., Oct. 11, 1927) with composer J. Fred Coots, but the show lasted only 31 performances. "Memories of France" (music by J. Russel Robinson) was given a hit recording by Gene Austin in September 1928, and Lou Gold and His Orch. had a minor hit with "I Must Be Dreaming" (lyrics and music by Dubin and Al Sherman) in October. (Dubin's biographer claims he wrote the lyrics to "Among My Souvenirs" [music by Lawrence Wright] and sold them to the credited lyricist, Edgar Leslie. The song became a best-seller for Paul Whiteman and His Orch. in March 1928 and was revived as a gold-selling Top Ten hit by Connie Francis in December 1959.)

Dubin earned his first screen credit as lyricist for Paramount's *The First Kiss* in 1928; in 1929 he found himself under contract with Warner Bros. when the studio bought his music publisher. That year he moved to Hollywood and was the credited lyricist on two films while writing songs for at least another five. *Gold Diggers of Broadway* drew his most successful efforts, both with Burke: "Tip Toe through the Tulips with Me" became the biggest record hit of 1929 for Nick Lucas, who appeared in the film. Lucas also had a hit with "Painting the Clouds with Sunshine."

Dubin wrote the lyrics for four more films in 1930 and contributed to several others. His most successful film song of the year was "The Kiss Waltz" (music by Burke) from *Dancing Sweeties*, a hit for George Olsen and His Orch. But his biggest hit of the year was a song cut from *Dancing Sweeties*, "Dancing with Tears in My Eyes," which became a best-seller for Nat Shilkret and the Victor Orch. in June.

Hollywood's early enthusiasm for film musicals waned in 1931 after several of them flopped at the box office, and Dubin had only one major screen credit during the year, for *Her Majesty Love*, which he wrote with composer Walter Jurmann. But he and Burke had an independent hit in August with "Many Happy Returns of the Day," recorded by Bing Crosby. The drought continued into 1932, during which Dubin had no major screen credits, though "Too Many Tears," which he wrote with Warren, became a best-selling record for Guy Lombardo and His Royal Canadians in March, and "Three's a Crowd," also composed by Warren, was used in the film *The Crooner* and became a hit for Tom Gerun in September.

The dearth of film musicals ended for Dubin and for Hollywood in general with the release of *42nd Street* in March 1933. The box office smash featured four Dubin-Warren hits: "You're Getting to Be a Habit with Me" was a best-seller for Crosby, backed by Lombardo; also a best-seller was "Forty-Second Street" in a recording by Don Bestor and His Orch.; Bestor and Hal Kemp and His Orch. had equally successful recordings of "Shuffle Off to Buffalo"; and Crosby and Lombardo's recording of "Young and Healthy" was also popular. Within months, Dubin and Warren were back in theaters with *Gold Diggers of 1933*, which boasted the hits "Shadow Waltz," a best-seller for Crosby, "We're in the Money" (also known as "The Gold Diggers' Song"), recorded most successfully by Ted Lewis and His Band, and "I've Got to Sing a Torch Song," another hit for Crosby. By the end of the year they had also worked on *Footlight Parade*, featuring "Honeymoon Hotel," a hit for Leo Reisman and His Orch. Dubin had been loaned to United Artists for the Eddie Cantor vehicle *Roman Scandals*, which contained "Keep Young and Beautiful," a hit for Abe Lyman and His California Orch.

Dubin and Warren had four film musicals in release in 1934, each of which added to their catalog of song hits. *Moulin Rouge* (also for United Artists), released in February, included "The Boulevard of Broken Dreams," a hit for Jan Garber and His Orch.; "Coffee in the Morning (Kisses at Night)," recorded by the Boswell Sisters, who appeared in the film; and "Song of Surrender," recorded by Wayne King and His Orch. *Wonder Bar*, the film adaptation of Al Jolson's stage success, featured the interpolations "Why Do I Dream Those Dreams?" by Eddy Duchin and His Orch., and "Wonder Bar," recorded by Emil Coleman and His Palais Royal Orch. *Twenty Million Frenchmen* had Dubin and Warren's biggest hit of the year, the best-seller "I'll String Along with You," recorded by Ted Fiorito and His Orch., as well as "Fair and Warmer" by the film's star, Dick Powell. And *Dames* introduced one of the duo's most frequently revived songs, "I Only Have Eyes for You," initially a hit for Ben Selvin and His Orch.; the film's title song was also a hit for Duchin.

Dubin was the credited lyricist on six Warner Bros. films released in 1935, and he contributed lyrics to several more, resulting in 15 song hits during the year. For *Gold Diggers of 1935*, he and Warren wrote "Lullaby of Broadway," which topped the hit parade in a recording by the Dorsey Brothers Orch. in May and went on to win an Academy Award. Little Jack Little and His Orch. had a minor hit with "I'm Goin' Shoppin' with You," also from the film. Dubin and Warren's title song from the Rudy Vallée film *Sweet Music* became a hit for Victor Young and His Orch. Ozzie Nelson's Orch. had the most successful recording of "About a Quarter to Nine," from the Jolson–Ruby Keeler vehicle *Go into Your Dance*, which also featured "The Little Things You Used to Do" and the title song, both hits for Johnny Green and His Orch., and "She's a Latin from Manhattan," another hit for Young.

In the summer of 1935, *Broadway Gondolier* introduced "Lulu's Back in Town," with which Fats Waller scored a hit, and "The Rose in Her Hair," a hit for Russ Morgan and His Orch. Kemp's recording of Dubin and Warren's title song for *Page Miss Glory* was in the hit parade in August. The team's major films for the fall were *Shipmates Forever* and *Stars over Broadway*. The former included the hits "I'd Love to Take Orders from You" (for Phil Harris), "I'd Rather Listen to Your Eyes" (for Jacques Renard and His Orch.), and "Don't Give Up the Ship" (for Tommy Dorsey and His Orch.), adopted as the official song of the Naval Academy. The latter featured the hits "Where Am I? (Am I in Heaven?)" (for Little) and "You Let Me Down" (for Teddy Wilson and His Orch., with vocal by Billie Holiday).

Dubin and Warren wrote the songs for three Warners musicals released in 1936 and contributed to other films, their most successful efforts being "I'll Sing You a Thousand Love Songs" in *Cain and Mabel* (which topped the hit parade for Duchin in December), "My Kingdom for a Kiss" in *Hearts Divided* (recorded by Powell, the film's star), and "With Plenty of Money and You" (another hit parade chart-topper for Henry Busse and His Orch. in February 1937). The team worked on another half-dozen films released in 1937, resulting in the hits "Summer Night" from *Sing Me a Love Song* (recorded by Enoch Light and His Light Brigade), "How Could You?" from *San Quentin* (recorded by Anson Weeks and His Orch.), "September in the Rain" from *Melody for Two* (which topped the hit parade in May and June for Lombardo), "Remember Me?" from *Mr. Dodd Takes the Air* (at the top of the hit parade in November

for Crosby and an Academy Award nominee), and, from *The Singing Marine*, "I Know Now" (recorded by Lombardo) and "'Cause My Baby Says It's So" (recorded by Kay Kyser and His Orch.).

Warner Bros. brought in Johnny Mercer to work on *The Singing Marine* after Dubin became undependable in the wake of an operation that led to an addiction to morphine. Mercer also contributed to the two films Dubin worked on in 1938, *Gold Diggers in Paris* and *Garden of the Moon*, the latter producing hits in the title song (for Red Norvo and His Orch.) and "The Girl Friend of the Whirling Dervish" (for Lombardo). Dubin then obtained his release from Warner Bros. and moved back to N.Y. to work on Broadway.

Dubin wrote lyrics to McHugh's music for *The Streets of Paris* (N.Y., June 19, 1939), which ran 274 performances and generated the hits "Rendezvous Time in Paree" (for Dorsey), "South American Way" (for Lombardo), and "Is It Possible?" (for Ray Noble and His Orch.). Dubin set lyrics to a 1919 piano piece by Victor Herbert to create "Indian Summer," which Dorsey took to the top of the hit parade in February 1940. Dubin's next musical, *Keep Off the Grass* (N.Y., May 23, 1940), lasted only 44 performances, but he was back in the hit parade in June with Charlie Barnet and His Orch.'s recording of "Where Was I?" (music by W. Franke Harling) from the film *'Til We Meet Again*. "Along the Santa Fe Trail" (music by Will Grosz) was written for the December 1940 film *Santa Fe Trail*; though it was not used, it was published, and Crosby scored a chart hit with it in February 1941.

Dubin's last major film credit came with the songs he and composer James V. Monaco wrote for the film *Stage Door Canteen* (1943), including the Oscar-nominated "We Mustn't Say Goodbye." In the last year of his life Dubin worked on the shows *Laffing Room Only* (N.Y., Dec. 23, 1944), apparently contributing only the title to the song "Feudin' and Fightin'" (music by Burton Lane), the lyrics for which were written by Lane and/or Frank Loesser, and *She Had to Say Yes* with composer Sammy Fain, which closed out of town. Dubin died of barbiturate poisoning.

Dubin's songs continued to become hits after his death. "Feudin' and Fightin'" was held back from recording for years by a dispute between the Shubert Organization and ASCAP; Dorothy Shay scored a Top Ten hit with it in September 1947. "September in the Rain" enjoyed a chart revival in a recording by Sam Donohue and His Orch. in December 1948, followed by a Top 40 revival by Dinah Washington in November 1961. Dubin and Burke's early 1930s composition "For You" belatedly made the hit parade for Glen Gray and the Casa Loma Orch., also in December 1948, and the song was revived by Rick Nelson for a Top Ten hit in January 1964. An instrumental version of "Dancing with Tears in My Eyes" by Mantovani and His Orch. was in the charts in April 1952. The Flamingos took "I Only Have Eyes for You" into the Top Ten in July 1959, followed by chart revivals in June 1966 (the Lettermen) and May 1972 (Jerry Butler), and a Top 40 revival in September 1975 by Art Garfunkel that topped the charts in the U.K. in October.

Ukulele-strumming novelty performer Tiny Tim took "Tip Toe Through the Tulips with Me" into the Top 40 in June 1968. The show *42nd Street* opened on Broadway as a stage musical on Aug. 25, 1980, its film score augmented by songs from other Dubin-Warren movie musicals of the 1930s. The show ran 3,486 performances, one of the longest runs in Broadway history.

BIBL.: P. McGuire (his daughter), *Lullaby of Broadway: Life and Times of A. D.* (1983).—**WR**

Dubois, (François-Clément) Théodore, eminent French organist, pedagogue, and composer; b. Rosnay, Marne, Aug. 24, 1837; d. Paris, June 11, 1924. He began his training with the Rheims Cathedral choirmaster, Louis Fanart, and then pursued studies at the Paris Cons. with Marmontel (piano), Benoist (organ), Bazin (harmony), and Thomas (fugue and counterpoint), where he won several 1st prizes and later the Grand Prix de Rome in 1861 with his cantata *Atala*. During his stay in Rome, he was befriended by Liszt. Returning to Paris, he served as maître de chapelle at Ste. Clotilde (1867–69) and at the Madeline (1869–77), where he subsequently was organist. In 1871 he became prof. of harmony and in 1891 prof. of composition at the Paris Cons., becoming its director in 1896; he was compelled to resign his directorship in 1905 in the wake of the scandal caused by Ravel's failure to be awarded the Grand Prix de Rome. In 1894 he was elected to membership in the French Academy. Dubois distinguished himself as a composer in the French classical tradition, most notably in his works for the church and in his concert scores. However, he was especially important as a pedagogue, and publ. the books *Notes et études d'harmonie pour servir de supplément au traité de H. Reber* (1889), *87 leçons d'harmonie* (1891), *Traité de contrepoint et de fugue* (1901), *Leçons de solfège* (1905), and *Traité d'harmonie théorique et pratique* (1921).

WORKS: DRAMATIC: *La prova di un'opera seria* (1863); *La Guzla de l'Emir*, opéra-comique (Paris, April 30, 1873); *Le pain bis, ou La Lilloise*, opéra-comique (Paris, Feb. 26, 1879); *La Farandole*, ballet (Paris, Dec. 14, 1883); *Aben-Hamet*, opera (Paris, Dec. 16, 1884); *Xavière*, idylle dramatique (Paris, Nov. 26, 1895). **ORCH.:** 3 overtures (1865, 1879, 1881); 2 suites (1874, 1877); *Concerto-Capriccioso* for Piano and Orch. (1876); *2 suites d'orchestre sur la farandole* (1884, 1889); *Deuxième concerto* for Piano and Orch. (1897); *Adonis*, symphonic poem (1907); 3 syms. (1908, 1913, 1924); Violin Concerto; *Fantasie-Stück* for Cello and Orch. **CHAMBER:** 2 string quartets (1908, 1924); *Dixtuor* for String Quintet and Wind Quintet (1909); *Nonetto* for Flute, Oboe, Clarinet, Bassoon, and String Quintet (1926); piano pieces, including a Sonata (1908); many organ pieces. **VOCAL:** *Atala*, cantata (1861); 5 oratorios, including *Les sept paroles du Christ* (1867), *Le paradis perdu* (1879), and *Notre-Dame de la mer* (1897); *Messe de Requiem* (n.d.); *Messe solennelle de Saint-Remi* (1900); *Messe de la Délivrance* (1919); some 70 motets; over 70 songs.

BIBL.: M. Widor, *Notice sur la vie et les travaux de T. D.* (Paris, 1924).—**NS/LK/DM**

Dubois, Léon, Belgian conductor and composer; b. Brussels, Jan. 9, 1859; d. Boitsfort, Nov. 19, 1935. He won the Prix de Rome at the Brussels Cons. in 1885. He conducted opera at the Théâtre de la Monnaie in Brussels (1890–97), was director of the Louvain Music School (1899–1912), and then director of the Brussels Cons. (1912–26). He wrote the operas *Son Excellence ma femme* (1884), *La Revanche de Sganarelle* (1886), *Édénie* (Antwerp, March 7, 1912), and *Vers la gloire* (Brussels, March 28, 1919), as well as a ballet, *Smylis* (Brussels, 1891), the mimodrama *La Mort* (Brussels, 1894), and chamber music.—**NS/LK/DM**

Dubois, Pierre-Max, French composer; b. Graulhet, Tarn, March 1, 1930; d. Rocquencourt, Aug. 29, 1995. He studied at the Tours Cons., obtaining a prize in piano at the age of 15; later studied composition with Milhaud at the Paris Cons. In 1955 he won the Grand Prix de Rome and the music prize of the City of Paris.

WORKS: DRAMATIC: *Impressions foraines*, ballet (1951); *Le Docteur OX*, ballet-bouffe, after Jules Verne (Lyons, Feb. 23, 1964); *Cover Girls*, choreographic spectacle (1965); *Comment causer*, "opéra pouf" (1970); *Les Suisses*, opera (1972); *Hommage à Hoffnung*, ballet (1980). **ORCH.:** *Impressions foraines* (1949); *Divertissement* for Saxophone and Orch. (1952); *Sérénades* for Bassoon and Orch. (1953); *Capriccio* for Violin and Orch. (1954); 2 violin concertos: No. 1 (1955; Strasbourg, June 20, 1957) and No. 2 (1964); Cello Concerto (1958); Concerto for Saxophone and Strings (1959); 2 syms.: No. 1, *Drame pour Epidaure* (1960) and No. 2, *Symphonie-Sérénade* for Strings (1964); *Concerto italien* for 2 Pianos and Orch. (1962); Concerto for Violin, Piano, and Orch. (Besançon, Sept. 15, 1963); *Musique pour un Western* (1964); *Concerto ironico* for Bassoon and Orch. (1968); Concertino for 4 Saxophones and Orch. (1969); *Beaujency concerto* for Clarinet and Orch. (1969); *Sinfonia militare* (1969); *Beaugency-Concerto* for Clarinet and Orch. (1969); Bass Clarinet Concerto (1978); *Suite concertante* for Wind Quintet and Orch. (1980); *Hommage à Rabelais*, overture (1981). **CHAMBER:** *Concertstück* for Saxophone and Piano (1955); Quartet for 4 Horns (1961); Quartet for 4 Flutes (1961); Quartet for 4 Trombones (1961); Quartet for 4 Clarinets (1962); *Pop Variations* for Flute and Piano (1971); *Le cinéma muet* for Horn, Trumpet, Trombone, and Tuba (1972); *Coïncidence* for Clarinet and Piano (1977); *Les Nouvelles Saisons* for Double Wind Quintet and Piano (1982). —**NS/LK/DM**

Dubrovay, László, Hungarian composer; b. Budapest, March 23, 1943. He studied at the Bartók Cons. and the Academy of Music in Budapest (graduated, 1966), his principal mentors being István Szelényi, Ferenc Szabó, and Imre Vincze; then continued his training in West Germany on a scholarship from the Deutscher Akademischer Austauschdienst, receiving instruction in composition from Stockhausen and in electronic music from Hans-Ulrich Rumpert (1972–74). Returning to Budapest, he taught theory at the Academy of Music (from 1976); was awarded the Erkel Prize (1985). In some of his works, he utilizes electronic and computer resources.

WORKS: DRAMATIC: *Il ricatto*, opera (1991); *The Sculptor*, dance-play (1993); *Faust, the Damned*, ballet (1995). **ORCH.:** *Verificazione* (1970); *Succession* (1974); Concerto for 11 Strings (1979); Concerto for Flute and 45 Strings (1981); Concerto for Trumpet and 15 Strings (1981); Concerto for Piano, Orch., and Synthesizer (1982); Piano Concerto (1984); *Variations on an Oscillating Line* (1987); *Deserts* for Brass Orch. (1987); Triple Concerto for Tuba, Trombone, Trumpet, and Orch. (1989);

March for Winds (1990); Violin Concerto (1991); Concerto for Cimbalom and Strings (1994); *Psychographic* for Brass Band (1994); Triple Concerto for Trumpet, Trombone, and Winds (1994); *Hungarian Symphony* for Winds (1997); *Timbre Symphony* (1998). C H A M B E R : *Cinque pezzi* for Bassoon and Piano (1967); *Sei duo* for Violin and Percussion (1969); 2 brass quintets (1971, 1980); 2 wind quintets (1972, 1983); *Magic Squares* for Violin and Cimbalom (1975); *Matuziáda* Nos. 1 to 5 for 4 Flutes (1975–76); *Geometrum II*: String Quartet No. 2 (1976); *Number-play No. 1* for 20 Players (1976); *Interferences No. 1* for 2 Cimbaloms (1976); *Music* for 2 Cimbaloms (1977); *Solo* Nos. 1–3, each for a Different Solo Instrument (1978–98); Brass Septet for 3 Trumpets, Horn, 2 Trombones, and Tuba (1980); String Quartet No. 3 (1983); Octet for Clarinet, Bassoon, Horn, and String Quartet (1985–87); *Scherzo* for Bassoon (1995); *Waltz and Scherzo* for Trumpet and Piano (1997). O T H E R : Pieces for chorus, live electronics, computer, and tape.—**NS/LK/DM**

Dubuque, Alexander, Russian pianist, composer, and teacher; b. Moscow, March 3, 1812; d. there, Jan. 8, 1898. He was a pupil of John Field, about whom he publ. a vol. of memoirs. He was a prof. at the Moscow Cons. (1866–72). He wrote piano pieces, songs, and a work on piano technique (1866).—**NS/LK/DM**

Du Cange, Charles Du Fresne, Sieur, eminent French scholar; b. Amiens, Dec. 18, 1610; d. Paris, Oct. 23, 1688. He was educated at the Jesuit Coll. in Amiens and studied law at the Univ. of Orléans. An erudite scholar in many disciplines, he is best known for his historical approach to language, which anticipated the development of modern linguistic criticism. He is important to musicology because he included definitions of Latin musical terms in his lexicographies. The most valuable of his many works are the *Glossarium ad scriptores mediae et infimae latinitatis* (3 vols., Paris, 1678) and the *Glossarium ad scriptores mediae et infimae graecitatis* (Lyons, 1688).

BIBL.: H. Hardouin, *Essai sur la vie et sur les ouvrages de D. C.* (Amiens, 1849).—**NS/LK/DM**

Du Caurroy, François-Eustache, Sieur de St.- Frémin, French composer; b. Beauvais (baptized), Feb. 4, 1549; d. Paris, Aug. 7, 1609. He was a member of the French nobility; his father was "procureur du roi." He entered the Royal Chapel as a singer in 1569, and in 1575 received a prize for a chanson, *Beaux yeux.* In 1578 he was "sous-maître," and in 1599 he became superintendent of "la musique du roi." Influenced by Le Jeune, he began to compose "musique mesurée." He advanced in the favor of the court, and received honors and awards. He held the ecclesiastical titles of canon at the Ste. Chapelle of Dijon, Ste. Croix of Orleans, and other provincial posts. His greatest work was the collection *Meslanges de la musique,* containing Psalms, "chansons mesurées," noëls, in 4, 5, and 6 Voices (Paris, 1610; some specimens reprinted in Expert's *Maîtres musiciens,* Vol. XIII). Other works include *Preces ecclesiasticae* for 4 to 7 Voices (Paris, 1609), instrumental *Fantaisies* for 3 and 6 parts (Paris, 1610; several publ. separately by Expert), and *Missa pro defunctis* for 5 Voices (Paris, 1636).—**NS/LK/DM**

Duchâble, François-René, French pianist; b. Paris, April 22, 1952. He was a pupil of Joseph Benvenutti and Madeleine Giraudeau-Basset at the Paris Cons. At age 16, he received 11th prize at the Queen Elisabeth of Belgium competition in Brussels, and in 1973 won the Prix de la Fondation Sacha Schneider, which led to his first major engagement in Paris at the Salle Gaveau. In 1980 he won critical accolades as soloist in Bartók's 3rd Piano Concerto with Karajan and the Berlin Phil., and thereafter pursued an international career as a virtuoso.—**NS/LK/DM**

Ducis, Benedictus, distinguished composer; b. probably near Constance, c. 1490; d. Schalckstetten, near Ulm, 1544. He may or may not be identical with Benedictus de Opitiis, who was organist at the Antwerp Cathedral (1514–16) and at the Chapel Royal in London (1516–22). It is known for a certainty that Benedictus Ducis was in Vienna c. 1515; he probably studied there; in 1532 he applied for a pastorate at Ulm (under the name Benedict Duch), but failed to obtain it. In 1533 he succeeded in receiving a pastorate at Stubersheim, near Geislingen; in 1535 he became pastor at Schalckstetten. Benedictus Ducis has been confused by many writers with Benedictus Appenzeller. A few of his works have been publ. in modern editions.

BIBL.: D. Bartha, *B. D. und Appenzeller* (Wolfenbüttel, 1930).—**NS/LK/DM**

Duckles, Vincent H(arris), American musicologist; b. Boston, Sept. 21, 1913; d. Berkeley, Calif., July 1, 1985. He began his training at the Univ. of Calif., Berkeley (A.B., 1936). After studies at Columbia Univ. (M.A. in music education, 1937; Ed.D., 1941), he pursued training once more at the Univ. of Calif., Berkeley (B.L.S., 1949; Ph.D., 1953, with the diss. *John Gamble's Commonplace Book*). He also held Fulbright senior research scholarships at the Univ. of Cambridge (1950–51) and at the Univ. of Göttingen (1957–58), and a grant-in-aid from the American Council of Learned Societies for research in Europe (1964–65). He was a music librarian (1949–57), assoc. prof. (1957–60), and prof. (1960–81) at the Univ. of Calif., Berkeley. In 1982 he was made an honorary member of the American Musicological Soc. He specialized in 17th-century English song literature, music bibliography, and the history of musical scholarship. He publ. the valuable and enduring source *Music Reference and Research Materials: An Annotated Bibliography* (N.Y., 1964; 5th ed., rev., 1997 by I. Reed).

BIBL.: P. Elliott and M. Roosa, "V. D. (1913–1985): A Bibliography of His Publications," *Notes* (Dec. 1987). —**NS/LK/DM**

Duckworth, William (Ervin), versatile American composer, pianist, teacher, and writer on music; b. Morganton, N.C., Jan. 13, 1943. He studied with Mailman (composition) at East Carolina Univ. (B.M., 1965) and with Johnston (composition), Robert Gray (trombone), and Charles Leonhard (education) at the Univ. of Ill. (M.S., 1966; D.M.Ed., 1972, with the diss. *Expanding Notational Parameters in the Music of John Cage*). He was founder-director of the Assn. of Independent Composers and Performers (1969–72) and president of the Media Press (1969–72). From 1973 he taught at Bucknell Univ. He was also active as a pianist. In his highly diversified output as a composer, Duckworth has imaginatively utilized pop, jazz, minimalist, and other elements to forge a remarkable personal style of expression. His *The Time Curve Preludes* for Piano (1977–78) marked the beginning of postminimalism. In his *Gathering Together/Revolution* for Mallet Percussion, Drums, and Keyboards (1992–93), he created the first chance-determined postminimalist "moment form." His *Cathedral*, a work especially created for the Internet, went on line on June 10, 1997, and incorporates acoustic and computer music, live webcasts, and newly created virtual instruments. This five-year work is planned for completion in 2001 in a live and online 48-hour concert with sounds incorporated into the piece from sites around the globe.

WORKS: *An Unseen Action* for Flute, Prepared Piano, and 4 Percussion (1966; Cleveland, May 17, 1968); *Gambit* for Percussion and Tape (1967); *Non-ticking Tenuous Tintinnabule Time* for 4 Electric Metronomes and Percussion Quartet (Hamilton, N.Y., Oct. 15, 1968); *Introjection* for Guitar (1968); *A Peace for 20 Voices* (1968); *A Ballad in Time and Space* for Tenor Saxophone and Piano (1968); *Knight to King's Bishop 4* for Dancer and Gong (1968); *The Sleepy Hollow Elementary School Band* for 20 to 60 Instrumentalists (1968); *Pitch City* for Any 4 Wind Players (1969); *Western Exit* for Movie, Slides, Announcer, and Chamber Ensemble (1969); *Memories of You...* for Any Instrumentation (1969); *When in Eternal Lines to Time Thou Grow'st* for Orch. (1970; Philadelphia, June 22, 1974); *Walden* for Any Number of Instruments, Dancers, Readers, Slides, and Movies and/or Lights (1971; Hartford, Dec. 10, 1972); *Walden Variations* for Any Number of Instruments, Dancers, Readers, Slides, Movies and/or Lights (1971; Urbana, March 14, 1972); *Sound World I* for 3 or More Instrumentalists (1972; Chapel Hill, N.C., Sept. 27, 1973); *A Mass for These Forgotten Times* for Chorus (1973); *Gymel* for 4 Mallet Percussionists or Keyboards (1973); *7 Shades of Blue* for Flute, Clarinet, Violin, Cello, and Piano (Brunswick, Maine, April 29, 1974); *A Summer Madrigal* for Flute, Violin, Piano, 2 Percussion, and Rock Singer (1976); *Silent Signals* for Percussion Quartet (1976); *A Book of Hours* for Flute, Violin, Clarinet, Cello, and Piano (Brunswick, Maine, Oct. 17, 1976); *The Last Nocturn* for Piano (1976); *The Time Curve Preludes* (1977–78; Middletown, Conn., Feb. 6, 1979); *Year* for Amplified Prepared Piano and Slides (1979); *Music in 7 Regions* for Amplified Piano or Synthesizer (1979; Philadelphia, June 17, 1983); *Southern Harmony* for Chorus (1980–81; 1st complete perf., Lewisburg, Pa., Feb. 28, 1992); *Simple Songs About Sex and War* for Voice and Piano (1983–84; Huddersfield, England, Nov. 29, 1987); *Songs of the Pale Horseman* for Chorus and Live Electronics (1984; rev. 1985 and 1990); *Tango Voices* for Piano (Oslo, Aug. 19, 1984); *Imaginary Dances* for Piano (1985; rev. 1988); *31 Days* for Any Solo Woodwind (1986); *Music in the Combat Zone* for Soprano and Chamber Ensemble (Philadelphia, Nov. 1, 1986); *Polking Around* for Accordion (1986; arranged for Ensemble by G. Klucevsek, 1988); *12 Words* for Solo Instrument or Voice and 4 Similar Instruments (1989–90; N.Y., March 24, 1990); *Slow Dancing in Yugoslavia* for Accordion (WNYC-FM, N.Y., March 21, 1990); *Blue Rhythm* for Violin/Flute, Cello, and Piano (1990; Philadelphia, Feb. 3, 1991); *Their Song* for Baritone and Piano (1991; N.Y., May 13, 1993); *Gathering Together* for 2 Keyboards and 2 Mallet Percussion (Rome, Sept. 21, 1992); *Revolution* for 2 Pianos and 4 Percussion, amplified (1992–93; N.Y., March 25, 1993); *Proces-*

sional for String Orch. (1994); *Mysterious Numbers* for Flute, Clarinet, Violin, Cello, Piano, and Percussion (Orlando, Fla., June 21, 1996; also for Orch., Cleveland, April 14, 1997); *Nostradamus*, computer-generated piece for the Internet (Oct. 5, 1997); *Cathedral*, piece for the Internet (1997–2001); *Ghost Dance* for Orch. (Charleston, S.C., May 29, 1998); *Dreaming Dances, Round and Square* for Chamber Ensemble (Philadelphia, Oct. 2, 1998).

WRITINGS: With E. Brown, *Theoretical Foundations of Music* (1978); *A Creative Approach to Music Fundamentals* (1981; 5th ed., 1994); ed. with R. Fleming, *John Cage at Seventy-Five* (1989); *Talking Music: Conversations with 5 Generations of American Experimental Composers* (1995); *Sound and Light: La Monte Young and Marian Zazeela* (1996).—**NS/LK/DM**

Ducloux, Walter (Ernest), Swiss-born American conductor and teacher; b. Kriens, April 17, 1913. He was educated at the Univ. of Munich (Ph.D., 1935) and studied conducting at the Vienna Academy of Music (diploma, 1937). After conducting in Lucerne (1937–39), he emigrated to the U.S. and became a naturalized citizen in 1943. He appeared as a conductor in the U.S. and Europe; also served on the faculties of the Univ. of Southern Calif. in Los Angeles (1953–68) and the Univ. of Tex. in Austin (from 1968). He was music director of the Austin (Tex.) Sym. Orch. (1973–75) and the Austin (Tex.) Lyric Opera (from 1986).—**NS/LK/DM**

Dudarova, Veronika, Russian conductor; b. Baku, Dec. 5, 1916. After training in Baku, she attended the Leningrad Cons. and studied conducting with Anosov and Ginzburg at the Moscow Cons. (graduated, 1947). She then was a conductor with the State Sym. Orch. of the U.S.S.R. in Moscow. In 1960 she became its chief conductor, the first woman in Russia to attain such a position. She conducted the orchestra both throughout the country and abroad. After conducting in Istanbul (from 1989), she returned to Moscow and was founder-conductor (from 1991) of the Sym. Orch. of Russia. In 1960 she was made a People's Artist of the U.S.S.R. in recognition of her pioneering career as a woman conductor in Russia.—**NS/LK/DM**

Duesing, Dale, American baritone; b. Milwaukee, Sept. 26, 1947. He studied voice at Lawrence Univ. in Appleton, Wisc. Following appearances in Bremen (1972) and Düsseldorf (1974–75), he sang in the premiere of Imbrie's *Angle of Repose* in San Francisco in 1976; that same year, he made his first appearance at the Glyndebourne Festival as Strauss's Olivier. On Feb. 22, 1979, he made his Metropolitan Opera debut in N.Y. as Strauss's Harlekin, returning there in later seasons as Rossini's Figaro, as Pelléas, and as Billy Budd; also sang opera in Seattle, Santa Fe, Chicago, Houston, Brussels, Barcelona, Salzburg, and Milan. Duesing won critical acclaim when he created the tasking role of I in the premiere of Schnittke's *Zhizn s Idiotom* (Life with an Idiot) in Amsterdam in 1992. Among his other operatic roles are Guglielmo, Eugene Onegin, Belcore, Wolfram, and Janáček's Goryanshikov.—**NS/LK/DM**

Dufallo, Richard (John), American conductor; b. East Chicago, Ind., Jan. 30, 1933; d. Denton, Tex., June

16, 2000. He played clarinet as a youngster; then enrolled at the American Cons. of Music in Chicago. He subsequently studied composition with Foss at the Univ. of Calif., Los Angeles; in 1957 he joined the Improvisation Chamber Ensemble organized by Foss, and showed an exceptional talent for controlled improvisation in the ultramodern manner. He then joined Foss as his assoc. conductor with the Buffalo Phil. (1962–67); also served on the faculty of the State Univ. of N.Y. at Buffalo (1963–67), where he directed its Center of Creative and Performing Arts. He attended a conducting seminar with William Steinberg in N.Y. (1965); Boulez gave him additional instruction in Basel (1969). In 1967 he went to Japan and other Asian countries as asst. tour conductor with the N.Y. Phil. In 1971 he made his European conducting debut in Paris. He served as conductor of the "Mini- Met," an adjunct to the Metropolitan Opera in N.Y. (1972–74), and was director of the series of new music sponsored by the Juilliard School in N.Y. (1972–79). From 1970 to 1985 he was artistic director of the Aspen Music Festival's Conference on Contemporary Music. From 1980 to 1982 he also served as artistic adviser of Het Gelders Orkest in Arnhem, the Netherlands. In 1984–85 he was acting director of the Aspen Inst. Italia in Rome. He appeared as a guest conductor with many orchs. in the U.S. and Europe, securing a reputation as an advocate of contemporary music. He publ. the book *Trackings: Composers Speak with Richard Dufallo* (N.Y. and Oxford, 1989).—**NS/LK/DM**

Du Fay, Guillaume (real name, **Willem Du Fayt**), great French composer; b. in or near Brussels, Aug. 5, 1397; d. Cambrai, Nov. 27, 1474. He was the illegitimate son of a priest, and thus took his mother's name. By 1408 he was in Cambrai, where he received training from Jehan Rogier de Hesdin, one of the chaplains at Notre Dame. From 1409 to 1413 he was a chorister at Cambrai Cathedral, where he most likely continued his training under its magister puerorum, Richard de Loqueville. By 1414 he held a chaplaincy at the altar of the Salve at St. Géry. He was in Constance by 1415. By 1417 he was again at St. Géry, where he became a subdeacon in 1418. From 1420 to 1423 he was in Italy, where he most likely was in the service of the branch of the Malatesta family in Rimini. From about 1424 to 1426 he was a singer at Laon Cathedral. In 1426 he returned to Italy, where he was in the service of Louis Aleman, the governor of Bologna. He was in Rome as a singer in the papal choir (Dec. 1428–Aug. 1433), during which period he consolidated his reputation as one of the most significant musicians of his day. His motet *Ecclesie militantis* may have been composed for the consecration of Pope Eugene IV in 1431. He found a patron in Niccolò III, Marquis of Ferrara, in 1433, and made a visit to his court in May 1437. He also found a patron in Louis, Duke of Savoy. On Feb. 8, 1434, he served as maître de chappelle for the marriage of Louis and Anne of Cyprus at the Savoy court. After a visit to Cambrai in Aug. 1434, he returned to Savoy. He was again a singer in the papal choir (June 1435–June 1437), which was maintained at this time in Florence until 1436, and then in Bologna. It was about this time that he received a degree in canon law from the Univ. of Turin. In 1436 he was made canon of Cambrai Cathedral. After again serving the Savoy court (1437–39), he returned to Cambrai in 1440 to assume his duties as canon. In 1446 he was also made canon of Ste. Waudru in Mons. In 1450 he returned to Italy. He visited Turin from May to July of that year and then was subsequently active in Savoy from 1451 to 1458, serving once more as maitre de chappelle at the court (May 1, 1455–May 1, 1456). In 1458 he returned to Cambrai, where he lived and worked in comfort for the rest of his life. He was held in the highest esteem in his lifetime by the church authorities and his fellow musicians; Compère described him as "the moon of all music, and the light of all singers." He was the foremost representative of the Burgundian school of composition. He proved himself a master of both sacred and secular music, producing masses, motets, and chansons of extraordinary beauty and distinction. His contributions to the development of faux-bourdon and the cyclic mass are particularly noteworthy. A list of his works, including MS sources and approximate dates of composition, is found in C. Hamm's *A Chronology of the Works of Guillaume Dufay Based on a Study of Mensural Practice* (Princeton, N.J., 1964). The *Opera omnia*, ed. by G. de Van and H. Besseler in the Corpus Mensurabilis Musicae series, i/1–6 (1947–49; 1951–66), also contains valuable commentary. A compilation of the papers read at the Dufay Quincentennial Conference held at Brooklyn Coll. on Dec. 6–7, 1974, was ed. by A. Atlas and publ. in 1976.

BIBL.: C. van den Borren, *G. D.: Son importance dans l'évolution de la musique au XVᵉ siècle* (Brussels, 1925); R. Bockholdt, *Die frühen Messenkompositionen von G. D.* (Tutzing, 1960); S. Brown, *The Motets of Ciconia, Dunstable, and D.* (diss., Ind. Univ., 1962); C. Hamm, *A Chronology of the Works of G. D. Based on a Study of Mensural Practice* (Princeton, N.J., 1964); W. Nitschke, *Studien zu den Cantus-Firmus-Messen G. D.s* (Berlin, 1968); A. Atlas, ed., *Papers Read at the D. Quincentenary Conference, Brooklyn Coll., December 6–7, 1974* (Brooklyn, 1976); D. Fallows, *D.* (London, 1982; rev. ed., 1987); S. Monge, ed., *G. D.* (Turin, 1997).—**NS/LK/DM**

Duffy, John, noted American music administrator and composer; b. N.Y., June 23, 1926. He received training in composition from Aaron Copland, Henry Cowell, Dallapiccola, Solomon Rosowsky, and Herbert Zipper. From 1953 to 1963 he was active as composer and music director of Shakespeare Under the Stars and the Ohio Shakespeare Festival, and from 1963 to 1974 of the American Shakespeare Festival, the Guthrie Theater, the Long Wharf Theater, and the Vivian Beaumont Theater in N.Y. In 1974 Duffy founded and became president of the innovative Meet the Composers organization, which he led until 1995. Under his leadership, it became a vital force in American music via the creation, performance, and recording of American music. For his own compositions, Duffy received Emmy Awards in 1984 and 1986. In 1987 he received the N.Y. State Governor's Art Award and in 1991 the N.Y.C. Mayor's Award for Arts and Culture. In addition to his many scores for the theater, film, and television, he has composed a number of works for the concert hall and opera house. Among the latter are *Heritage*, suite for Narrator and Orch. (1986; Washington, D.C., May 14,

1988; based on his score for the PBS-TV series *Heritage: Civilization and the Jews*), Sym. No. 1, *Utah* (N.Y., Nov. 29, 1989), *Freedom Overture* (Leipzig, Nov. 8, 1990), *A Time for Remembrance*, peace cantata for Soprano, Speaker, and Orch., in commemoration of the 50th anniversary of the attack on Pearl Harbor (Honolulu, Dec. 7, 1991; rev. 1993), *Black Water*, opera after Joyce Carol Oates (Philadelphia, May 1, 1995), *Unity* for Chorus and Orch. (Toledo, April 1997), and *Testament* for Chorus and Band (Skowhegan, Maine, Jan. 1998).—**LK/DM**

Dufourcq, Norbert, distinguished French music historian and organist; b. St. Jean-de-Braye, Loiret, Sept. 21, 1904; d. Paris, Dec. 19, 1990. He was educated at the Sorbonne, where he studied history and geography, then at the École Nationale des Chartes (1924–28), graduating as an archivist-palaeographer. He also studied piano and music history with Gastoué (1913–20), organ with Marchal (1920–40), and harmony, counterpoint, and fugue with Marie-Rose Hublé. He took his Ph.D. at the Univ. of Paris in 1935 with the diss. *Esquisse d'une histoire de l'orgue en France: XIII^ee-XVIIIe siècles* (publ. in Paris, 1935). He was a teacher of history at the Collège Stanislas in Paris (1935–46); also prof. of music history and musicology at the Paris Cons. (1941–76). In addition to other teaching positions, he appeared as an organist. He ed. performing and scholarly eds. of works for the organ and harpsichord of 17th- and 18th- century French composers.

WRITINGS (all publ. in Paris): *Documents inédits pour servir à l'histoire de l'orgue* (1935); *Les Clicquot, facteurs d'orgues du Roy* (1942; 2nd ed., 1990); ed. *La Musique des origines à nos jours* (1946); *Jean-Sebastien Bach: génie allemand, génie latin?* (1947; 2nd ed., 1949); *Jean-Sébastien Bach, le maître de l'orgue* (1948; 2nd ed., 1973); *L'Orgue* (1948; 5th ed., 1976); *Cesar Franck* (1949); *La Musique française* (1949; 2nd ed., aug., 1970); *Le Clavecin* (1949; 2nd ed., 1967); *Autour de Coquard, César Franck et Vincent d'Indy* (1952); *Nicolas Lebègue, organiste de la Chapelle Royale* (1954); ed. with F. Raugel and A. Machabey, *Larousse de la musique* (1957); *Jean-Baptiste Boesset, surintendant de la Musique du Roi* (1963); ed *La Musique: Les hommes, les instruments, les hommes* (1965); *Le livre de l'orgue français, 1589–1789* (6 vols., 1969–82); with M. Benoit and B. Gagnepain, *Les Grandes Dates de l'histoire de la musique* (1969; 2nd ed., 1975).—**NS/LK/DM**

Dufourt, Hugues, French composer and teacher; b. Lyons, Sept. 28, 1943. He was a student of Louis Hiltbrand (piano, 1961–68) and of Jacques Guyonnet (composition, 1965–70) at the Geneva Cons., and also studied at the Univ. Jean Moulin in Lyons (philosophy, 1968–73). From 1975 to 1981 he was co-director of the Itinéraire ensemble. With Alain Bancquart and Tristan Murail, he founded the Collectif de Recherche Instrumentale de Synthèse Sonore (CRISS) in 1977. He later served as director of research at the CNRS and as a teacher at the École des Hautes études en Sciences Sociales in Paris. In 1975 he won the Grand Prix de Musique de Chambre of the SACEM, in 1985 the Koussevitzky Prize, and in 1994 the composer's prize of the SACEM.

WORKS: *Brisants* for Piano and 16 Instrumentalists (Geneva, Nov. 30, 1968); *Mura della cita di dite* for 17 Instruments (Geneva, Oct. 19, 1969); *Down to a Sunless Sea* for 16 Strings (Geneva, Aug. 20, 1970); *Dusk Light* for Soprano, Mezzo-soprano, Tenor, Baritone, and 16 Instrumentalists (Geneva, Oct. 10, 1971); *Erewhon* for 6 Percussionists (1972–76; Royan, April 4, 1977); *La Tempesta* for Instrumental Ensemble (1976–77; Royan, April 2, 1977); *Antiphysis* for Flute and Chamber Orch. (La Rochelle, July 7, 1978); *Sombre Journée* for 6 Percussionists (Paris, March 30, 1979); *Saturne* for Electronic Instruments, 6 Percussionists, and Instrumental Ensemble (Paris, Dec. 3, 1979); *Surgir* for Orch. (1980–84; Paris, Feb. 13, 1985); *La nuit face au ciel* for 6 Percussionists (Aix en Provence, July 3, 1984); *L'heure des traces* for 20 Instruments (Milan, May 19, 1986); *La mort de Procris* for Chorus, after Shakespeare (Strasbourg, Sept. 26, 1986); *Hommage à Charles Nègre* for 6 Instruments (Paris, Dec. 2, 1986); Saxophone Quartet (1993); *The Watery Star* for 8 Instruments (1993); *An Schwager Kronos* for Piano (1994); *Dédale*, opera (1995); *L'espace aux ombres* for 16 Instruments (1995); *Euclidean Abyss* for 8 Instruments (1996); *La Maison du Sourd* for Flute and Orch. (1996–97).—**LK/DM**

Dufranne, Hector (Robert), Belgian bass-baritone; b. Mons, Oct. 25, 1870; d. Paris, May 3, 1951. He studied in Brussels, making his operatic debut there at the Théâtre Royal de la Monnaie as Valentine in *Faust* (Sept. 9, 1896). He then went to Paris as a member of the Opéra-Comique (1899–1909) and the Opéra (from 1909). He also sang at the Manhattan Opera in N.Y. (1908–10), the Chicago Grand Opera (1910–22), and London's Covent Garden (1914); he retired from the stage in 1939. He created roles in several French operas, including Golaud in Debussy's *Pelléas et Mélisande* (1902). —**NS/LK/DM**

Dugan, Franjo, Croatian organist, teacher, and composer; b. Krapinica, Sept. 11, 1874; d. Zagreb, Dec. 12, 1948. After studies with Bruch in Berlin, he was cathedral organist (1912–48) and a teacher at the Cons. in Zagreb. He publ. manuals on orchestration and musical form. His compositions included choral works and chamber music.—**NS/LK/DM**

Duhamel, Antoine, French composer; b. Valmondois, July 30, 1925. He was the son of the writer Georges Duhamel and the comedienne Blanche Albane. In 1944–45 he studied with Messiaen and Leibowitz, and concurrently took courses at the Sorbonne in Paris. In 1977 he was awarded the Georges Enesco Prize of the SACEM, and in 1997 he received its Grand Prize. While Duhamel has composed numerous dramatic works, he has also written various orch. and chamber pieces, most notably the monumental *Villeurbanne Symphonie* (1990) for 550 performers.

WORKS: DRAMATIC: *Opéra radiophonique* (1951); *L'Ivrogne*, opera after Baudelaire (1952–53; rev. version as *Le Seieur de long*, Tours, March 9, 1984); *Gala de Cirque*, opéra-ballet (1965); *Le Rital*, renamed *Lundi, Monsieur, vous serez riche*, music theater (1968); *L'Opéra des Oiseaux*, opera after Aristophanes (Lyons, May 18, 1971); *Ubu à l'Opéra*, spectacle after Alfred Jarry (Avignon, July 16, 1974); *Gambara*, opera after Balzac (Lyons, June 2, 1978); *Les Traveaux d'Hercule*, children's opera (Vaise, June 25, 1981); *Le Transsibérien*, opera (Paris, Nov. 29, 1983); *Quatrevingt- treize*, opera after Hugo (Fourvière, July 10, 1989); *Les Adventures de Sinbad le marin*, opera (Colmar, Feb. 12, 1991); *Carmenmania*, ballet (1994); over 50 film scores (1962–96); incidental music; television music. ORCH.: Piano Concerto (1957–58); *Diamètres*, concerto for Organ, Strings, and Piano (1962); *Territoires* for Strings (1974); *Animus-Anima* (1975); *Le Tombeau de Philippe d'Orléans* for Strings (Chambéry, Nov. 1978); *Sérénade à la quinte* for Violin, Cello, and Orch. (1984); *Ballade au vibraphone* for Vibraphone and Small Orch. (Chambéry, Nov. 22, 1992); *Valse d'Hiver* (1993; Paris, Jan. 1994); *Lamento mémoire* for Viola and Chamber Orch. (Fresnes, March 31, 1996); *Carmenmania*, suite after the ballet (Lyons, April 1996). CHAMBER: String Quartet (1950–52); 2 violin sonatas (1954, 1957); *Silence de la Nuit* for Clarinet and Piano (1969); *Hommage à Mingus* for Saxophone Quintet (1970); *Madrigal à Quatre* for String Quartet (1973); *Les Cinq Si*, quintet for Flute, Oboe, Clarinet, Horn, and Bassoon (1981); *Flûte, flûte, flûte, ô my Lord* for 3 Flutes (1985); *Prélude et Fugue* for Trumpet and Organ (1985); *Dialogue des Anges* for Solo Tuba and 3 Tubas (1985); Cello Sonata (1986); *Divertissement à la Bulgare* for Clarinet and Marimba (1987); *Contrebasse oblige*, trio for Double Bass, Violin, and Piano (1991); *24 Images de mon Cinéma* for Clarinet, Accordion, Double Bass, Piano, Vibraphone, Guitar, and Voice (1998). KEYBOARD: P i a n o : *Variations sur l'Opus 19, No. 6, de Schoenberg* (1947); *Impromptu* (1955); *Petite Suite de Noël* for Piano, 2-, 4-, and 6-Hands (1978); *Pénélope* (1984). O r g a n : *Fantaisie* (1952). VOCAL: *4 Mélodies* for Bass and Orch., after Eluard (1947); *La Maison des Morts*, oratorio for Soprano, Alto, Tenor, Bass, Chorus, and Orch. (1954–57); *Lectures de Michaux* for Voice and Small Ensemble (1970–73); *Nel Giro* for Soprano and Orch. (1977–96); *L'Impossible Chanson des Matelots* for Voice and String Quartet (1979); *Le Concile Féerique*, cantata for Mezzo-soprano, Baritone, 2 Choruses, and Orch. (1982); *Music to hear*, small cantata for Soprano, Mezzo-soprano, Baritone, Reciter, and 5 Instruments (1984); *Le Jardin de Daubigny* for Baritone and Winds (1986); *Villeurbanne Symphonie*, cantata for Soloists, Chorus, Orch., Big Band, Jazz Ensemble, and Rock Group (Villeurbanne, Dec. 20, 1990); *Requiem de Jean Cocteau* for Baritone, Dancers, Reciters, and Orch. (Fresnes, March 30, 1993); *L'Eté 14* for Voice and Piano (1993); *Trois Fables de notre Jardin*, cantata for Reciters, Soloists, Choruses, and Orch. (Oise, June 21, 1995); *Révérance parler* for Baritone and Piano (1995); *Dixit Farouche* for Soloists, Chorus, and Chamber Orch. (d'Ambronay, Sept. 7, 1999).—NS/LK/DM

Duiffoprugcar (real name, Tieffenbrucker), Gaspar, German-born French viol maker; b. Tieffenbruck, Bavaria, 1514; d. Lyons, Dec. 16, 1571. He was long reputed to be the first maker of violins, but Vidal, in his *Les Instruments à archet*, states that all the so-called Duiffoprugcar violins are spurious, having been made by Vuillaume, who in 1827 conceived the idea of making violins after the pattern of a viola da gamba by Duiffoprugcar. Apparently, the latter learned his trade in Italy; the usual spellings of his name show it to be Italianized rather than gallicized. He settled in Lyons in 1553, and was naturalized in 1558.

BIBL.: H. Coutagne, *G. D. et les luthiers lyonnais du XVIe siècle* (Paris, 1893).—NS/LK/DM

Dukas, Paul, famous French composer and teacher; b. Paris, Oct. 1, 1865; d. there, May 17, 1935. From 1882 to 1888 he was a student at the Paris Cons., studying under Mathias (piano), Dubois (harmony), and Guiraud (composition). He won 1st prize for counterpoint and fugue in 1886, and the 2nd Prix de Rome with a cantata,

Velléda (1888). He began writing music reviews in 1892, and was music critic of the *Revue Hebdomadaire* and *Gazette des Beaux-Arts*. In 1906 he was made a Chevalier of the Légion d'honneur. From 1910 to 1913, and again from 1928 to 1935, he was prof. of the orch. class at the Cons. In 1918 he was elected Debussy's successor as a member of the *Conseil de l'enseignement supérieur* there; also taught at the École Normale de Musique. Although he was not a prolific composer, Dukas wrote a masterpiece in his orch. scherzo *L'Apprenti Sorcier*; his opera *Ariane et Barbe-Bleue* is one of the finest French operas in the impressionist style. Among his other notable works are the Sym. in C major and the ballet *La Péri*. Shortly before his death, he destroyed several MSS of his unfinished compositions.

WORKS: DRAMATIC: O p e r a : *Ariane et Barbe- Bleue* (1899–1906; Paris, May 10, 1907). B a l l e t : *La Péri* (1911–12; Paris, April 22, 1912). ORCH.: 3 overtures: *King Lear* (1883), *Götz von Berlichingen* (1884), and *Polyeucte* (1891); Sym. in C major (1896; Paris, Jan. 3, 1897); *L'Apprenti Sorcier*, scherzo (Paris, May 18, 1897). OTHER: *Villanelle* for Horn and Piano (1906); piano music, including a Sonata (1899–1901), *Variations, Interlude et Finale (sur un thème de Rameau)* (1903), *Prélude élégiaque* (1908), and *La Plainte au loin du faune* (1920); *Sonnet de Ronsard* for Voice (1924). With Saint-Saëns, he completed Guiraud's opera *Frédégonde*.

BIBL.: G. Samazeuilh, *P. D.* (Paris, 1913; 2nd ed., 1936); V. d'Indy, *Emmanuel Chabrier et P. D.* (Paris, 1920); G. Samazeuilh, *P. D., musicien français* (Paris, 1936); G. Favre, *P. D.: Sa vie, son oeuvre* (Paris, 1948); N. Demuth, *P. D.* (London, 1949); G. Favre, *L'Oeuvre de P. D.* (Paris, 1969); idem, ed., *Correspondance de P. D.* (Paris, 1971); W. Moore, *The Significance of Late Nineteenth-Century French Wagnérisme in the Relationship of P. D. and Edouard Dujardin: A Study of Their Correspondence, Essays on Wagner, and D.'s Opera Ariane et Barbe-Bleue* (diss., Univ. of Tex., 1986). —NS/LK/DM

Duke, Doug(las) (originally, Ovidio Fernandez), Argentine-born jazz organist; b. Buenos Aires, Argentina, 1920; d. Rochester, N.Y., Nov. 10, 1973. His family moved to Rochester, N.Y. when he was a youth. He began classical piano lessons at the age of six and at ten began pipe organ lessons. By age 15 he was playing piano in local jazz clubs. After graduating from high school, he toured with Shep Fields and later with Mal Hallet, Jan Savitt, Mitch Ayres, Dick Stabile, and as the only white musician in one of Lionel Hampton's bands (appearing at the Apollo in 1948). In the 1950s he toured primarily as an organist with his own groups, appearing at the Meadowbrook in N.J., the Hickory House in Manhattan, and on Steve Allen's TV show. From the late 1950s through the mid-1960s, he made several trips to Europe, performing on his own and with other jazz artists, and may have lived in Denmark for a period in 1965. In 1966 he played for three months in Rochester at John Amalfi's Hi-Fi 400 club, and on Nov. 16, 1966 he opened a small music room, Doug Duke's, in the Charlotte suburb of Rochester. Until his death, he accompanied guest artists including Coleman Hawkins, Roy Eldridge, Lionel Hampton, Clark Terry, Moe Koffman (1967), Marian McPartland (Nov. 15–16, 1968; piano and organ), and Teddy Wilson (piano and organ) at Doug Duke's. The room was also used as a recording studio. Duke was a man of many interests; he flew airplanes, constructed two 22-foot cabin cruiser boats, and built a combined piano and organ that he called a "Dukeatron," which he only used at home.

DISC.: *Jazz Organist Doug Duke Playing* (1953); *Douglas Duke, Vol. 2* (1954); *Sounds Impossible* (1956); *The Music Room* (1960).—**LP**

Duke, John (Woods), American pianist, pedagogue, and composer; b. Cumberland, Md., July 30, 1899; d. Northampton, Mass., Oct. 26, 1984. He studied piano with Harold Randolph and composition with Gustav Strube at the Peabody Cons. of Music in Baltimore (1915–18), then studied piano with Franklin Cannon and composition with Howard Brockway and Bernard Wagenaar in N.Y.; later received instruction in piano from Schnabel in Berlin and in composition from Boulanger in Paris (1929). He was asst. prof. (1923–38) and prof. (1938–67) of music at Smith Coll. in Northampton, Mass., becoming prof. emeritus at his retirement. He composed over 200 songs, some of which are outstanding contributions to the genre.

WORKS: DRAMATIC: *Captain Lovelock*, opera (Hudson Falls, N.Y., Aug. 18, 1953); *The Sire de Maledroit*, opera (Schroon Lake, N.Y., Aug. 15, 1958); *The Yankee Pedlar*, operetta (Schroon Lake, N.Y., Aug. 17, 1962). **ORCH.:** Concerto for Piano and Strings (1938); *Carnival Overture* (1940). **CHAMBER:** Suite for Solo Viola (1933); *Fantasy* for Violin and Piano (1936); String Trio (1937); 2 string quartets (1941, 1967); Piano Trio (1943). **VOCAL:** Choral works; more than 200 songs, including major cycles to poems of Emily Brontë and Emily Dickinson. —**NS/LK/DM**

Duke, Vernon (originally, **Dukelsky, Vladimir**), Russian-born American classical and popular composer; b. Parfianovka, Oct. 10, 1903; d. Santa Monica, Calif., Jan. 16, 1969. Even more than his friend George Gershwin, Duke had one foot in classical music, having gained formal music training as a child and retaining his real name for his instrumental works until 1955. As theatrical composer Vernon Duke, however, he enjoyed his greatest success with such songs as "April in Paris," "I Can't Get Started," and "Taking a Chance on Love," as well as the musical *Cabin in the Sky*.

Duke's parents were Alexander and Anna Kopyloff Dukelsky; his father was a civil engineer. Duke began to study music at seven and wrote a ballet score at eight. Admitted to the Kiev Cons. of Music at 13, he studied composition with Reinhold Glière and piano with Marian Dombrovsky. In 1920 his family was forced to flee Russia in the wake of the revolution; they lived in Turkey for two years, then moved to Paris.

Duke visited the U.S. in 1921, where he met Gershwin, who encouraged him to write popular music and suggested his pseudonym. He returned to Paris where in 1924 he wrote a piano concerto that led Ballet Russe director Sergei Diaghilev to commission him to write music for the ballet *Zéphyr et Flore* (Paris, Jan. 31, 1925). His first work for the musical theater was to write interpolations for an Austrian musical, *Katja, the Dancer*, which opened in London in 1925 and in N.Y. the

following year. *Yvonne* (1926), for which he wrote half the score, was another Austrian import to the U.K.; it ran 280 performances. He wrote his first complete score for *The Yellow Mask* (1928), which ran 218 performances.

In 1929, Duke wrote a final British show, *Open Your Eyes*, which closed during tryouts but finally opened in London for 24 performances the following year. He moved to the U.S. permanently in June, later becoming an American citizen. Initially he worked for Paramount Pictures, and his music was used in the 1930 features *The Sap from Syracuse, Follow Thru, Laughter,* and *Follow the Leader*. His first work for the American musical theater came with several song interpolations to the third edition of the revue *The Garrick Gaieties* (N.Y., June 4, 1930), among them "I Am Only Human After All" (lyrics by Ira Gershwin and E. Y. Harburg), which became a hit for the Colonial Club Orch. in July 1930.

The revue *Walk a Little Faster* (1932) marked Duke's first complete American score. It ran 121 performances and is remembered for "April in Paris" (lyrics by Harburg), which became a hit for Freddy Martin and His Orch. in December 1933, long after the show closed. Meanwhile, Ben Bernie and His Orch. scored a hit with Duke's independently published song "This Is Romance" (lyrics by Edward Heyman) in October 1933.

Duke was hired to write the songs for a new edition of the *Ziegfeld Follies*, mounted by the Shuberts after Florenz Ziegfeld's death, which opened at the start of 1934. It ran 182 performances and produced a song hit in "What Is There to Say?" (lyrics by Harburg) for Emil Coleman and His Orch. Duke wrote his own lyrics for a follow-up to "April in Paris," "Autumn in New York," which was featured in *Thumbs Up!* (N.Y., Dec. 27, 1934) and became a standard without ever becoming a hit.

Duke teamed with Ira Gershwin to write the songs for the *Ziegfeld Follies of 1936*; the show ran 115 performances, and its most memorable song was "I Can't Get Started," which became associated with Bunny Berigan and His Orch. Berigan's second recording of the song in 1937 was inducted into the Grammy Hall of Fame in 1975.

Duke wrote most of the score for the revue *The Show Is On* (N.Y., Dec. 25, 1936), though much of it was cut and replaced by interpolations before its Broadway opening. After the death of George Gershwin on July 11, 1937, Duke was brought in to complete the music for the film *The Goldwyn Follies*, which was released in February 1938.

Duke scored his greatest success with a book musical with *Cabin in the Sky*, starring Ethel Waters, in 1940. The show ran 156 performances; it was made into a successful film released in April 1943 that retained only three of Duke's songs, one of which was "Taking a Chance on Love" (lyrics by John Latouche and Ted Fetter). The appearance of the film sparked a revival of a 1940 recording of the song by Benny Goodman and His Orch. that went to #1 in June 1943, becoming one of the biggest hits of the year.

In 1941, Duke wrote the songs for *Banjo Eyes*, a stage vehicle for Eddie Cantor, which ran 126 performances. With the onset of World War II, Duke enlisted in the

Coast Guard in August 1942 and led a service band. In 1943 he teamed with Howard Dietz to write songs for the musical *Dancing in the Streets,* starring Mary Martin, which closed out of town, but two more shows with Dietz, *Jackpot* and *Sadie Thompson,* reached Broadway for brief runs in 1944. During that year Duke also wrote a service musical, *Tars and Spars,* which played on Broadway and then toured the war zones.

Duke returned to live in Paris for two years, 1947–48, and upon returning to the U.S. had trouble getting productions for his stage musicals. He wrote songs for two movie musicals released in 1952: *April in Paris,* starring Doris Day, and *She's Working Her Way through College,* both with lyrics by Sammy Cahn. He then managed to get a revue, *Two's Company,* on Broadway with Bette Davis as star. The show ran 91 performances.

Count Basie and His Orch. revived "April in Paris" in early 1956 with a recording that made the R&B Top Ten and was inducted into the Grammy Hall of Fame in 1985. In the spring of 1956, Duke had an Off-Broadway show, *The Littlest Revue,* which ran 32 performances.

Duke married singer Kay McCracken on Oct. 30, 1957. His final appearance on Broadway came less than two weeks later with the two songs and incidental music he wrote for the play *Time Remembered,* which ran 247 performances. He continued to try to mount Broadway musicals during the last decade of his life, including two shows that closed during tryouts and one that went unproduced. He died of lung cancer at 65 in 1969.

WORKS (only works for which Duke was a primary, credited composer are listed): MUSICALS/REVUES (dates refer to N.Y. openings unless otherwise noted): *Yvonne* (London, May 22, 1926); *The Yellow Mask* (London, Feb. 8, 1928); *Open Your Eyes* (London, Sept. 8, 1930); *Walk a Little Faster* (Dec. 7, 1932); *Ziegfeld Follies* (Jan. 4, 1934); *Ziegfeld Follies of 1936* (Jan. 30, 1936); *Cabin in the Sky* (Oct. 25, 1940); *Banjo Eyes* (Dec. 25, 1941); *The Lady Comes Across* (Jan. 19, 1942); *Jackpot* (Jan. 13, 1944); *Tars and Spars* (May 5, 1944); *Sadie Thompson* (Nov. 16, 1944); *Two's Company* (Dec. 15, 1952); *The Littlest Revue* (May 22, 1956); *Time Remembered* (Nov. 12, 1957). FILMS: *She's Working Her Way through College* (1952); *April in Paris* (1952).

WRITINGS: *Passport to Paris* (1955); *Listen Here! A Critical Essay on Music Depreciation* (1963).

Dukelsky, Vladimir (Alexandrovich),

versatile Russian- born American composer who used the name **Vernon Duke**; b. Parfianovka, Oct. 10, 1903; d. Santa Monica, Calif., Jan. 16, 1969. He was a student of Glière (1916–19) and Dombrovsky (1917–19) at the Kiev Cons. After living in Constantinople (1920–21), he went to N.Y. in 1922 and to Paris in 1924, where Diaghilev commissioned him to write the ballet *Zéphyr et Flore* (Monte Carlo, April 28, 1925); he also found a champion in Koussevitzky, who conducted his works in Paris and later in Boston. After composing for the London stage (1926–29), he returned to N.Y. and studied orchestration with Schillinger (1934–35). In 1936 he became a naturalized American citizen. Upon settling in the U.S., Dukelsky pursued a dual career as a composer of both serious and popular music. At George Gershwin's suggestion, he adopted the name Vernon Duke for his popular scores, and in 1955 he dropped his real name entirely.

He scored his greatest success with the Broadway musical *Cabin in the Sky* (Oct. 25, 1940), which was also made into a film (1943). His amusing autobiography was publ. as *Passport to Paris* (Boston, 1955); he also wrote the polemical book *Listen Here! A Critical Essay on Music Depreciation* (N.Y., 1963).

WORKS: DRAMATIC (all 1st perf. in N.Y. unless otherwise given): **R e v u e s :** *Walk a Little Faster* (Dec. 7, 1932); *Ziegfeld Follies of 1934* (Jan. 4, 1934); *Ziegfeld Follies of 1936* (Jan. 30, 1936); *The Show is On* (Dec. 25, 1936); *Dancing in the Streets* (Boston, 1943); *Sweet Bye and Bye* (New Haven, Conn., Oct. 10, 1946); *Two's Company* (Dec. 15, 1952). **O p e r e t t a :** *Yvonne* (London, May 22, 1926; in collaboration with J. Gilbert). **M u s i c a l C o m e d y :** *The Yellow Mask* (London, Feb. 8, 1928). **M u s i c a l s :** *Cabin in the Sky* (Oct. 25, 1940; film version in collaboration with H. Arlen, 1943); *Banjo Eyes* (Dec. 25, 1941); *The Lady Comes Across* (Jan. 9, 1942); *Jackpot* (Jan. 13, 1944); *Sadie Thompson* (Nov. 16, 1944). **O p e r a :** *Mistress into Maid* (Santa Barbara, Calif., 1958); *Zenda* (San Francisco, Aug. 1963). **I n c i d e n t a l M u s i c :** *Time Remembered* (1957). **B a l l e t :** *Zéphyr et Flore* (Monte Carlo, April 28, 1925); *Public Gardens* (Chicago, March 8, 1935); *Le bal des blanchisseuses* (Paris, Dec. 19, 1946); *Emperor Norton* (San Francisco, 1957); *Lady Blue* (1961). **F i l m :** *April in Paris* (1952); *She's Working Her Way Through College* (1952); also completed G. Gershwin's *The Goldwyn Follies* (1938). **ORCH.:** Piano Concerto (1924); 3 syms.: No. 1 (1927–28; Paris, June 14, 1928), No. 2 (1928–30; Boston, April 25, 1930), and No. 3 (Brussels Radio, Oct. 10, 1947); *Ballade* for Piano and Chamber Orch. (1931); Violin Concerto (Boston, March 19, 1943); *Ode to the Milky Way* (1945; N.Y., Nov. 18, 1946); Cello Concerto (1945; Boston, Jan. 4, 1946); *Variations on an Old Russian Chant* for Oboe and Strings (1958). **CHAMBER:** Trio (Variations) for Flute, Bassoon, and Piano (1930); *Capriccio mexicano* for Violin and Piano (1939); *Etude* for Violin and Bassoon (1939); *3 Pieces* for Flute, Oboe, Clarinet, Bassoon, and Piano (1946); *Nocturne* for 6 Wind Instruments and Piano (1947); 2 violin sonatas (1948, 1960); String Quartet (1956). **P i a n o :** Sonata (1928); *2 pièces* (1930); *Printemps* (1931); *N.Y. Nocturne* (1939); *Surrealist Suite* (1940); *Vieux carré* (1940); *Homage to Boston* (1943); *3 Caprices* (1944); *Music for Moderns* for 6 Players (1944); *Parisian Suite* (1955); *Souvenir de Venise* (1955); *Serenade to San Francisco* (1956). **VOCAL:** *Dushenka* for Women's Voices and Orch. (1927); *Epitaph* for Soprano, Chorus, and Orch. (Boston, April 15, 1932); *Dédicaces* for Soprano, Piano, and Orch. (1934; Boston, Dec. 16, 1938); *The End of St. Petersburg,* oratorio (1937; N.Y., Jan. 12, 1938); *Moulin-Rouge* for Soprano, 6 Voices, and Piano (1944); *Paris aller et retour,* cantata for Chorus and Piano (1948). **S o n g s :** *Triolets for the North,* song cycle (1922); (8) *Poésies de Hyppolite Bogdanovitch* (1927–30); *5 poésies* (1930); *I'm Only Human After All* (1930); *Autumn in N.Y.* (1935); *3 Chinese Songs* (1937); *5 Victorian Songs* (1942); *5 Victorian Street Ballads* (1944); *Ogden Nash's Musical Zoo,* 20 songs (1947); *La bohème et mon coeur,* 7 songs (1949); *A Shropshire Lad,* 6 songs (1949); 4 songs (1955).—**NS/LK/DM**

Dulcken, Ferdinand Quentin,

German pianist and composer, son of **Luise (née David) Dulcken** and nephew of **Ferdinand David;** b. London, June 1, 1837; d. Astoria, N.Y., Dec. 10, 1901. He was a pupil of Moscheles and Gade at the Leipzig Cons., and also received encouragement from Mendelssohn. He subsequently taught at the Warsaw Cons., and also at Moscow and St. Petersburg. He also made many concert tours in Europe as a pianist with Wieniawski, Vieuxtemps, and others.

In 1876 he emigrated to America and gave concerts with Remenyi, then settled in N.Y. as a teacher and composer. He publ. nearly 400 piano pieces of the salon type and also some vocal works.—NS/LK/DM

Dulcken, Luise (née **David**), German pianist, sister of **Ferdinand David** and mother of **Ferdinand Quentin Dulcken;** b. Hamburg, March 29, 1811; d. London, April 12, 1850. She was taught by C. F. G. Schwencke and Wilhelm Grund and played in public in Germany when she was 11 years of age. She married in 1828 and went to London, where she met with brilliant success as a pianist and teacher. Queen Victoria was one of her many pupils.—NS/LK/DM

Dulichius, Philipp, esteemed German composer; b. Chemnitz, Dec. 18, 1562; d. Stettin, March 24, 1631. He studied at the Univ. of Leipzig (1579). He became cantor at the Stettin ducal Gymnasium (1587) and at the Marienkirche and director of music at the Pomeranian court. Dulichius was deputized as cantor at Danzig's Marienkirche in 1604–05 and then returned to his positions in Stettin. He retired in 1630. He was highly regarded as a composer of sacred music, and was called the "Pomeranian Lassus." His works, all publ. in Stettin, comprise 12 vols. of liturgical music (1589–1630), including some 250 motets.—NS/LK/DM

Dülon, Friedrich Ludwig, notable German flutist and composer; b. Oranienburg, near Berlin, Aug. 14, 1769; d. Würzburg, July 7, 1825. When he was nine, he heard the blind flutist Joseph Winter, whose example inspired Dülon to pursue his love of music. He studied flute with his father; his phenomenal memory enabled him not only to master solo pieces quickly, but also chamber works and even concertos. He also received training in keyboard playing and composition. In his tenth year he began to play in public, and on Oct. 9, 1781, he made his Berlin recital debut. In 1783–84 he made his first extensive tour of Germany. While visiting Potsdam in 1783, he furthered his training in composition with Karl Benda. In 1785–86 he toured abroad, visiting Amsterdam and Rotterdam. On March 26, 1786, he played before King George III in London. On April 5, 1786, he made his first public appearance there to much praise. In 1790 he was a participant in the coronation festivities for Leopold III in Frankfurt am Main as Holy Roman Emperor. He appeared in Vienna in 1791. In 1793 he went to St. Petersburg, where he entered the service of Grand Duke Alexander, remaining with that patron until 1795. Returning to Germany, he made only occasional appearances there from 1798. In addition to his success as a flute virtuoso, he also composed a number of effective works for his instrument. His output included a Flute Concerto, nine duets for Flute and Violin, three duets for Flute and Viola, three duets for two Flutes, Theme and Variations for Flute and Violin, and 11 caprices for Flute and three caprices for two Flutes. C. Wieland ed. his autobiography as *Dülons des blinden Flötenspielers Leben und Meynungen von ihm selbst bearbeitet* (2 vols., Zürich, 1807–08).—NS/LK/DM

Dumitrescu, Gheorghe, Romanian composer and pedagogue, brother of **Ion Dumitrescu;** b. Oteşani, Dec. 27, 1914; d. Bucharest, Feb. 20, 1996. He studied at the Bucharest Cons. (1934–41), where he served as a prof. of harmony from 1951 until 1979.

WORKS (all 1st perf. in Bucharest unless otherwise given): **DRAMATIC**: *Miorița,* ballet-oratorio (1947; March 16, 1978); *Tarsița si Rosiorul,* operetta (1949; Dec. 12, 1950; in collaboration with Viorel Dobos); *Ion Vodă del Cumplit,* musical drama (1955; April 12, 1956); *Decebal,* opera (1957; Oct. 4, 1969); *Răscoala,* musical drama (Aug. 18, 1959); *Fata cu garoafe,* opera (May 6, 1961); *Meşterul Manole,* opera (1969–70; Oct. 4, 1971); *Geniu pustiu,* opera (1973; Cluj-Napoca, March 11, 1977); *Vlad Tepes,* musical drama (1974; Feb. 6, 1975); *Orfeu,* opera (1977–78; May 22, 1980); *Luceafărul,* ballet-opera (1979; Dec. 29, 1981); *Marea iubire,* opera (Dec. 13, 1982); *Ivan Turbincă,* opera (1983); *Prometheu,* opera (1985; Oct. 15, 1987); *Mihai Viteazul,* opera (1986); *Avram Iancu,* musical drama (1986); *Voievodul Gelu,* opera (1987); *Mesia-Jertfa supremă,* opera-oratorio (1988); *Osiris,* sacred opera (1991); *Făt-Frumos,* opera (1992). **ORCH.:** *Poem psaltic* (1940; May 8, 1941); *Poem rustic* (1940); *Poem trist* (1941); *Poem vesel* (1941; Oct. 28, 1943); *Poemul amurgului* (1941; May 23, 1945); *Uvertură eroică* (1942); 4 suites (1942, 1943, 1944, 1965); 11 syms.: No. 1 (1945; May 16, 1948), No. 2 (1962), No. 3 (1965; June 20, 1966), No. 4 (1968; Sibiu, May 18, 1971), No. 5 (1983; March 1, 1984), No. 6 (1990), No. 7 (1990), No. 8 (1990), No. 9 (1990), No. 10 (1990), and No. 11 (1993); Cello Concerto (1947). **OTHER:** Numerous chamber pieces, oratorios, cantatas, songs, etc.—NS/LK/DM

Dumitrescu, Ion, Romanian composer and pedagogue, brother of **Gheorghe Dumitrescu;** b. Oteşani, June 1, 1913; d. Bucharest, Sept. 6, 1996. He studied at the Bucharest Cons. (1933–40), where he was a prof. from 1944 to 1979. From 1963 to 1977 he also was chairman of the Union of Composers and Musicologists of Romania.

WORKS (all 1st perf. in Bucharest):**DRAMATIC:** Incidental music; film scores. **ORCH.:** 3 suites: No. 1 (Dec. 20, 1938), No. 2 (1940), and No. 3 (1944; May 23, 1945); 2 Pieces (May 9, 1940); *Poem* for Cello and Orch. (1940); Sym. (1948; May 8, 1949); Symphonic Prelude (Feb. 3, 1952); Concerto for Strings (1956); *Muntele Retezat,* suite (1956; new version, May 29, 1982); *Simfonietta* (Oct. 19, 1957). **CHAMBER:** *Suită în stil vechi* for Viola and Piano (1939); String Quartet (1949). **Piano:** Sonata (1938); Sonatina (1940); 2 Pieces (1942). **VOCAL:** Choral pieces; songs.—NS/LK/DM

Du Mont or **Dumont** (real name, **de Thier**), **Henri** or **Henry,** eminent Belgian-born French organist, harpsichordist, and composer; b. Villers-L'Evêque, near Liège, 1610; d. Paris, May 8, 1684. He entered the choir school of Maastricht Cathedral in 1621 and, after serving as its organist (1630–32), studied with Léonard de Hodemont in Liège. In 1638 he settled in Paris, where he was organist at St. Paul's Church (1643–84); he also served as organist and harpsichordist to the Duke of Anjou, brother of the King (c. 1652–60), and harpsichordist to Queen Marie-Thérèse (from 1660). In 1663 he was made sous-maitre of the royal chapel, sharing his duties with Gobert, and later with Expilly and Robert. After Gobert and Expilly retired in 1669, Du Mont and Robert shared the title of compositeur de musique de la Chapelle Royale (1672–83). Du Mont was also maître de la musique de la Reine from 1673 to 1681.

He was a significant composer of sacred music; his *Cinq messes en plain-chant* (Paris, 1669) were widely esteemed. He also greatly distinguished himself as a composer of grands motets. For his output, see A. Gastoué, ed., *Les messes royales de Henry Du Mont:Étude historique avec transcriptions faites sur les originaux des messes des 1er, 2e et 6e tons* (Paris, 1909), H. Expert and C. Pineau, eds., *Musique d'église des XVIIᵉ et XVIIIᵉ siècles* (Paris, 1913–14), F. Raugel, ed., *Les maîtres français de l'orgue aux XVIIᵉ et XVIIIᵉ siècles* (Paris, 1951), and D. Launay, ed., *Anthologie du motet latin polyphonique* (Paris, 1963).

BIBL.: H. Quittard, *Un musicien en France au XVIIIᵉ siècle: H.D. M.* (Paris, 1906); A. Gastoué, *Les Messes Royales de H.D. M.* (Paris, 1912).—**NS/LK/DM**

Dunbar, Ted (actually, **Earl Theodore Dunbar Jr.**), jazz guitarist, educator; b. Port Arthur, Tex., Jan. 17, 1937; d. New Brunswick, N.J., May 29, 1998.

In 1946 he started studying trumpet and teaching himself guitar. He attended local Lincoln H.S. playing trumpet in the Concert Band, Marching Band, and Jazz Band. He also sang in the boys quartet, choir, and Glee Club. He graduated with honors from Lincoln High in 1955, and, honoring his parents' wishes, enrolled that fall in Tex. Southern Univ.'s School of Pharmacy in Houston. He graduated with honors in 1959. He passed the Tex. Pharmacy Board and received a license to practice pharmacy in Tex. (he was also eventually licensed in N.Y., Ind., and N.J.). While in college, he played jazz in Houston with Arnett Cobb (1956–58), Don Wilkerson (1957–59), singer Joe Turner (1958), Perry Deal, Jual Curtis, and others. He then moved back to Port Arthur to practice pharmacy with his mother and father at their family drugstore. In 1957, he met Wes Montgomery in Indianapolis, Ind., on a pharmacy field trip. Around 1961 he traveled to Indianapolis to look into a job with a drugstore chain called Hook's; he decided to move to Indianapolis and take the position. He found it was across the street from where Montgomery was playing at the Ebony Missile Room. During his two-year stay, Dunbar played with Montgomery and substituted for him at Primo's Club when Montgomery was on tour. He also played with David Baker and studied George Russell's Lydian Concept of Tonal Organization with Baker as well. In 1965, he moved to Dallas and worked for Skillern's drug chain and also played with "Fathead" Newman, James Clay, Red Garland, Billy Harper, Roger Boykins, and others.

He moved to N.Y. in 1966 and performed and recorded with Gil Evans from 1970–73 (including a film soundtrack), Tony Williams's group Lifetime (1971–72), and Frank Foster (1973–79); he also played with Sonny Rollins, Ron Carter, Billy Harper, Roy Haynes, Seldon Powell, pianist Billy Taylor (on the Jazzmobile), McCoy Tyner, the New Jazz Repertory Co., and the National Jazz Ensemble. He began teaching in the late 1960s at Jazz-in-the-School concerts on Long Island, N.Y., with Seldon Powell, Billy Mitchell, and opera singer Andrew Frierson, and in schools in St. Thomas, St. Croix, and St. John in the Caribbean. He was the advanced guitar teacher at Jazzmobile Workshop for over 20 years and taught at the Jazz Interactions Workshop. He joined the faculty of music at Livingston Coll., Rutgers, in 1972 and remained there as it became incorporated into the Mason Gross School of the Arts at Rutgers, where he taught until late 1997 as a full professor. He was closely associated with his Rutgers colleague Kenny Barron, with whom he recorded several albums. Though he performed less often he became well-respected as an educator. He also conducted workshops and clinics all over the world. Among his students were Kevin Eubanks, Rodney Jones, Ed Cherry, Nile Rodgers, singer Regina Belle, and saxophonist Thomas Chapin. His four guitar method books, which build in his own way on Russell's approach, have been influential with many guitarists. At the time of his death, he was at work on several other books. He recorded movie soundtracks, including *Fortune and Men's Eyes* making several with Galt McDermott. He appeared on-camera in the 1996 movie *The Preacher's Wife* playing behind Whitney Houston. In the 1990s he occasionally led a quartet with Earl May on bass, Brandon McCune at piano, and David Jones on drums in N.Y. at the Rainbow Room, Smalls, and the Blue Note. He was also a numerologist and remained a practicing pharmacist. He had a history of heart and kidney problems. In 1997, he suffered a heart attack. He subsequently died of a massive stroke.

DISC.: *In Tandem* (1975); *Opening Remarks* (1978); *Secundum Artem* (1980); *Jazz Guitarist* (1982); *Gentle Time Alone* (1992). M. Tyner: *Asante* (1970). K. Barron: *Peruvian Blue* (1974). D. Newman: *House of David* (1967).—**LP**

Dunbar, W. Rudolph, black flutist, conductor, teacher, and writer; b. Nabaclis, British Guiana, April 5, 1907; d. London, June 10, 1988.

He was clarinetist in the British Guiana Militia Band (1916–19), then went to the U.S., where he studied clarinet, piano, and composition at the Inst. of Musical Art in N.Y. (graduated, 1924). He pursued further training in Paris with Louis Cahuzac, Gaubert, and Vidal, and in Vienna with Weingartner. In 1931 he settled in London, becoming the first black musician to conduct a band on the BBC (1934) and with the London Phil. (April 26, 1942). While working as a newspaper correspondent with the Allies in France, he appeared as conductor with the Pasdeloup Orch. in Paris (Nov. 18, 1944); in 1945 he conducted the Berlin Phil. He subsequently devoted himself mainly to the cause of racial justice and wrote extensively on international affairs. In 1964 he became the first black musician to conduct in the Soviet Union.—**NS/LK/DM**

Duncan, (Robert) Todd, black American baritone; b. Danville, Ky., Feb. 12, 1903; d. Washington, D.C., Feb. 28, 1998.

He was educated at Butler Univ. in Indianapolis (B.A., 1925) and at Columbia Univ. Teachers Coll. (M.A., 1930); then taught voice at Harvard Univ. in Washington, D.C. (until 1945). In 1934 he made his operatic debut with the Aeolian Opera in N.Y. as Alfio in *Cavalleria rusticana*. On Oct. 10, 1935, he created the role of Porgy in Gershwin's *Porgy and Bess* in N.Y., and subsequently sang in revivals of the score. He was the first black American to become a member of a major opera company when he made his first appearance at the N.Y. Opera City on Sept. 28, 1945, as Tonio. He appeared as Stephen Kumalo in Weill's *Lost in the Stars* (1949–50), winning both the Donaldson and N.Y. Drama Critics' Circle awards in 1950.—NS/LK/DM

Dunhill, Thomas (Frederick), English composer, teacher, and writer on music; b. London, Feb. 1, 1877; d. Scunthorpe, Lincolnshire, March 13, 1946. He entered the Royal Coll. of Music in London in 1893, and studied with Franklin Taylor (piano) and Stanford (theory); in 1905 he was appointed a prof. there. In 1907 he founded the Concerts of British Chamber-Music, which he oversaw until 1916. He publ. *Chamber Music* (1912), *Mozart's String Quartets* (two vols., 1927), *Sullivan's Comic Operas* (1928), and *Sir Edward Elgar* (1938).

WORKS: DRAMATIC: O p e r a : *The Enchanted Garden* (London, March 1928); *Tantivy Towers* (London, Jan. 16, 1931); *Happy Families* (Guildford, Nov. 1, 1933). B a l l e t : *Gallimaufry* (Hamburg, Dec. 11, 1937); *Dick Whittington* (n.d.). CHAMBER: *Phantasy* for String Quartet; Piano Quintet; Quintet for Violin, Cello, Clarinet, Horn, and Piano; Quintet for Horn and String Quartet; Piano Quartet; Viola Sonata; 2 violin sonatas; violin pieces; cello pieces. VOCAL: *The Wind among the Reeds*, song cycle for Tenor and Orch.—NS/LK/DM

Duni, Egidio (Romualdo), noted Italian composer; b. Matera, Feb. 9, 1709; d. Paris, June 11, 1775. Nothing definitive is known about his musical training. He may have studied at the Loreto Cons. in Naples. His first opera, *Nerone*, was successfully premiered in Rome on May 21, 1735. He visited London in 1737; produced his opera *Demofoonte* at the King's Theatre there on May 24, 1737. Making his way to Holland, he studied at the Univ. of Leiden (1738). He returned to Italy in 1739; was appointed maestro di cappella of S. Nicola di Bari in Naples in 1743, and took up the same post at the court of the Duke of Parma about 1748, where he also served as music teacher to the Duke's daughter. His opéra-comique *Le Peintre amoureux de son modèle* was premiered in his presence in Paris on July 26, 1757. Following its success, he settled in Paris. From 1761 to 1768 he was music director of the Comédie-Italienne, where he brought out such successful works as *Mazet* (1761), *Les Deux Chasseurs et la laitière* (1763), *L'École de la jeunesse* (1765), *La Clochette* (1766), and *Les Moissonneurs* (1768). Duni was a significant contributor to the opéra-comique genre. By fusing Italian and French strains in his work, he was instrumental in developing the comédie melée d'ariettes.—NS/LK/DM

Dunlap, Arlene, American pianist and teacher; b. Seattle, Nov. 22, 1937. She studied at the Univ. of Wash. (B.A., 1960). After moving to Santa Barbara, Calif., in 1969, she became active as a teacher. She also performed widely, specializing in new music; composers who have written works for her include Daniel Lentz, Gary Eister, Michael John Fink, and Harold Budd; from the 1970s she was particularly active in performance ensembles organized by Lentz. She has recorded extensively as a keyboardist, vocalist, and conductor, both in ensembles and as a soloist; also has given numerous lecture-recitals. She composed music for film, video, and dance, as well as collected pedagogical pieces for beginning piano students. She is married to **Richard Dunlap**. —NS/LK/DM

Dunlap, Richard, American pianist, composer, and performer; b. Seattle, Dec. 7, 1939. He studied with Spencer Moseley and Alden Mason at the Univ. of Wash. (B.F.A., 1966; M.F.A., 1968). After moving to Santa Barbara, Calif., in 1969, he became active as a performer; he also was lecturer (1969–72) and asst. prof. (1972–77) at the Univ. of Calif. at Santa Barbara, and a visiting artist at the Univ. of Nev., Las Vegas (1973), the Univ. of Hawaii, Hilo (1974), Ohio State Univ. (1979), Ariz. State Univ. West in Phoenix (1994) et al. Dunlap has performed widely in solo and group performances ("Soundworks" [1978] and "Soundworks 2" [1992], "Intersphere" [1981], and "History of Animals" [1992]), as well as in exhibitions of his own design ("Three for Icarus" [1975], "Of This Time, Of This Place" [1983], "Constructures: New Perimetrics in Abstract Painting" [1985], "V. Forest '94" [1992], and "In the Spirit of FLUXUS" [1994]). He is married to **Arlene Dunlap**. —NS/LK/DM

Dunn, James Philip, American organist, teacher, and composer; b. N.Y., Jan. 10, 1884; d. Jersey City, N.J., July 24, 1936. He studied at the Coll. of the City of N.Y. (B.A., 1903) and with MacDowell, Leonard McWhood, and Rybner at Columbia Univ. (M.A., 1905). He was active as an organist in Catholic churches in N.Y. and Jersey City, and also devoted time to teaching and writing on music.

WORKS: DRAMATIC: *The Galleon* (1918); *Lyric Scenes* (n.d.). ORCH.: *Lovesight*, symphonic poem (1919); *The Confessions of St. Augustine* (1925); *Overture on Negro Themes* (1925); *We*, tone poem commemorating Lindbergh's transatlantic flight (N.Y., Aug. 27, 1927); Sym. (1929); *The Barber's Six Brothers: Passacaglia and Theme Fugatum* (1930); *Choral* (1930). CHAMBER: Piano Quintet (1910); Violin Sonata (1912); Piano Trio (1913); 2 string quartets (1913); *Variations* for Violin and Piano (1915); much piano and organ music. VOCAL: *Annabel Lee* for Voice and Orch. (1913); *The Phantom Drum*, cantata for Soloists, Women's Voices, and Orch. (1918); *It was a lover and his lass* for Women's Chorus and Orch. (1918); *The Music of Spring* for Women's Voices and Piano or Orch. (1918); *Marquesan Isle* for Women's Voices and Piano (1923; also for Voices and Orch. or Jazz Band, 1924); *Song of the Night* for Chorus (1923); *Salve Regina* for Women's Chorus (1924); part songs; solo songs.

BIBL.: J. Howard, *Studies of Contemporary American Composers: J.P. D.* (N.Y., 1925).—NS/LK/DM

Dunn, Johnny, early jazz trumpeter, leader; b. Memphis, Tenn., Feb. 19, 1897; d. Paris, France, Aug. 20, 1937. He attended Fisk Univ. in Nashville. He began working as a solo act at the Metropolitan Theatre, Memphis (1916), and then was signed by W. C. Handy and worked with Handy until 1920. During the early 1920s, he worked as an accompanist to Mamie Smith and Edith Wilson; appeared in several N.Y.–based revues including *Dixie to Broadway* and the *Put & Take* show (1921); regularly recorded with Perry Bradford;

and played a long stint with Will Vodery's Plantation Orch. He joined Vodery in February 1922, traveling with the band in 1923 to Europe, and continuing to work with them through the mid-1920s, while also leading his own small groups. The second half of the decade was made up of similar activities; a trip to Europe with the revue *Blackbirds of 1926*; several extended N.Y. engagements leading his own band; a residency in Chicago in March 1928; and a return to Paris in fall 1928 to work with Noble Sissle and bassist John Ricks' Band. In the early 1930s, he formed his own New Yorkers Band for work in Europe, and also worked with Joe Baker's Orch. at the Casino de Paris. For the last few years of his life, he worked mainly in Holland and Denmark (1935). He returned to Paris in 1937, and died in the American Hospital there. Dunn was one of the most influential jazz trumpeters before Armstrong. His use of the mute to produce a wa-wa effect, exemplified on "Dunn's Cornet Blues," influenced Bubber Miley (who replaced him in Mamie Smith's band).

DISC.: *Dunn's Cornet Blues* (1924); *Sergeant Dunn's Bugle Call Blues* (1928); *You Need Some Lovin'* (1928). E. Wilson: *What Do You Care* (1922).—JC/LP

Dunn, Mignon, American mezzo-soprano; b. Memphis, Tenn., June 17, 1931. She attended Southwestern Univ. in Memphis and the Univ. of Lausanne; at 17 she was awarded a Metropolitan Opera scholarship and pursued vocal training in N.Y. with Karin Branzell and Beverley Johnson. In 1955 she made her operatic debut as Carmen in New Orleans, and then appeared as Maddalena in Chicago later that year; on March 28, 1956, she made her N.Y.C. Opera debut as the 4th Lady in Walton's *Troilus and Cressida*. She remained on the City Opera's roster until 1957 and sang there again in 1972 and 1975. On Oct. 29, 1958, she made her Metropolitan Opera debut in N.Y. as the Nurse in *Boris Godunov*; in subsequent seasons she appeared in more than 50 roles there, including Amneris, Azucena, Fricka, Herodias, Marina, and Ortrud. She also made guest appearances in San Francisco, London, Paris, Berlin, Hamburg, Milan, and Vienna. In 1972 she married the conductor Kurt Klippstatter.—NS/LK/DM

Dunn, Susan, American soprano; b. Malvern, Ark., July 23, 1954. She was educated at Hendrix Coll. in Ark. and at Ind. Univ. in Bloomington. In 1982 she made her operatic debut as Aida in Peoria. After winning the Richard Tucker Award in 1983, she attracted favorable notice as Sieglinde in a concert performance of Act I of *Die Walküre* at N.Y.'s Carnegie Hall in 1985. She subsequently appeared with the Chicago Lyric Opera, the Washington (D.C.) Opera, the Houston Grand Opera, and the San Francisco Opera. In 1986 she made her European operatic debut in Bologna as Hélène in *Les Vêpres siciliennes*; also sang Aida at Milan's La Scala and appeared at the Vienna State Opera. On Feb. 5, 1990, she made her debut at the Metropolitan Opera in N.Y. as Leonora in *Il Trovatore*.—NS/LK/DM

Dunn, Thomas (Burt), American conductor; b. Aberdeen, S.Dak., Dec. 21, 1925. He studied at the Peabody Cons. of Music, Johns Hopkins and Harvard Univs., and the Amsterdam Cons.; his teachers included Fox and Biggs (organ) and Shaw (choral conducting) in the U.S., and Leonhardt (harpsichord) and Anton van der Horst (conducting) in the Netherlands. He began his career as a church music director in Baltimore and Philadelphia; in 1959 he was appointed director of the Cantata Singers in N.Y.; also organized the Festival Orch. there, which he led from 1959 to 1969. From 1967 to 1986 he was music director of the Handel and Haydn Soc. of Boston. He taught at the Ind. Univ. School of Music in Bloomington from 1990.—NS/LK/DM

Dunstable or **Dunstaple, John,** great English composer; b. c. 1390; d. London, Dec. 24, 1453. Almost nothing is known about his life with any certainty. He may have been the John Dunstaple who was in the service of the Duke of Bedford; if he was the same man, he may have accompanied his patron to France. He appears to have been well versed in astronomy and mathematics. The J. Dunstaple buried in the church of St. Stephen, Walbrook (destroyed in the Great Fire of 1666), was undoubtedly the composer. The Old Hall Manuscript and other MSS reveal the existence of a highly developed art in England in the early 15th century, antedating the full flowering of the Burgundian school of Dufay, Binchois, and other masters. Dunstable's style appears to be a direct outgrowth of the English school. He was the most important figure in English music in his time. His works were widely known on the Continent as well as in his homeland. Most of his known compositions are preserved in manuscripts on the Continent, although discoveries have recently been made in England. Some works formerly attributed to him are now known to be by Power, Benet, Binchois, and others. Other works remain doubtful. The styles of Dunstable and Power are so comparable that it has not always been possible to separate their works. Undoubtedly, some of Dunstable's works are in anonymous collections and await verification. M. Bukofzer ed. *John Dunstable: Complete Works* in Musica Britannica, VIII (London, 1953; 2nd ed., rev., 1970 by M. and I. Bent and B. Trowell); the rev. ed. includes 73 works, several of which are now considered doubtful.

BIBL.: M. Bent, *Dunstaple* (London, 1981).—NS/LK/DM

Duparc (real name, **Fouques-Duparc**), **(Marie-Eugène-)Henri,** remarkable French composer of songs; b. Paris, Jan. 21, 1848; d. Mont-de-Marsan, Feb. 12, 1933. He was a student of Franck at the Jesuit Coll. of Vaugirad. Between 1868 to 1885 he composed a series of innovative songs, distinguished by exquisitely phrased melodies in fluid modal harmonies. He subsequently was stricken with a neurasthenic malady and went blind, a condition that brought an early end to his compositional career.

WORKS: ORCH.: *Danse lente* (n.d.); 2 symphonic poems: *Aux Étoiles* (Paris, April 11, 1874) and *Lénore* (1875). **CHAMBER:** Cello Sonata (1867); *Feuilles volantes*, suite of 6 piano pieces. **VOCAL: S o n g s :** *Chanson triste* (1868; orchestrated); *Lamento* (1868); *Au Pays ou l'on fait la guerre* (1870;

orchestrated); *L'Invitation au voyage* (1870; orchestrated); *Soupir* (1870); *La Vague et la cloche* (1871; orchestrated); *Estase* (1872; orchestrated); *Élégie* (1874); *La Manoir de Rosamonde* (1879); *Sérénade florentine* (1880; orchestrated); *Phidyle* (1882; orchestrated); *Testament* (1883; orchestrated); *La Vie antérieure* (1884; orchestrated); also the motet *Benedicat vobis Dominus*.

BIBL.: G. Ferchault, *H. D.* (Paris, 1944); S. Northcote, *The Songs of H. D.* (London, 1949); N. Van Der Elst, *H. D.: L'Homme et son oeuvre* (Lille, 1972); S. Stricker, *Les mélodies de D.: Essai* (Arles, 1996).—NS/LK/DM

Dupin, Paul, French composer; b. Roubaix, Aug. 14, 1865; d. Paris, March 6, 1949. He worked in a factory, then was a menial clerk, but turned to music against all odds. He took some lessons with Emile Durand and then proceeded to compose with fanatic compulsion; somehow he managed to have more than 200 works actually publ. Of these, the most original were about 500 canons for 3–12 voices, and 40 string quartets titled *Poèmes*. He wrote much other chamber music, some pretty piano pieces with fanciful titles, such as *Esquisse fuguées* and *Dentelles*, and even a grand opera, *Marcelle*, which he later hopefully renamed *Lyszelle* for exotic effect. He was much admired in Paris for his determination to succeed, but his works were rarely performed.

BIBL.: P. Ladmirault, *Les Choeurs en canon de P. D.: Notice biographique et analytique* (Paris, 1925).—NS/LK/DM

Dupont, Gabriel, French composer; b. Caen, March 1, 1878; d. Vesinet, Aug. 2, 1914. He was a pupil of his father, the organist at the Cathedral, of Gédalge, and later of Massenet and Widor at the Paris Cons. He won the 2nd Prix de Rome in 1901. In a contest conducted in 1903 by Sonzogno, the publishing house in Milan, his opera *La Cabrera* was selected, along with two others, to be performed and judged by the public (237 works were submitted); it was produced at Milan on May 17, 1904, with great success, thereby winning for Dupont the prize of 50,000 lire. He wrote other operas: *La Glu* (Nice, Jan. 24, 1910), *La Farce du cuvier* (Brussels, March 21, 1912), and *Antar* (1913; Paris Opéra, March 14, 1921), as well as *Les Heures dolentes* for Orch., four pieces from a suite of 14 compositions for Piano (1903–5), *Poèmes d'automne* for Piano, two symphonic poems: *Hymne à Aphrodite* and *Le Chant de la destinée*, *Poème* for Piano Quintet and many other piano pieces, and songs. —NS/LK/DM

Dupont, Pierre, French songwriter; b. Rochetaillée, near Lyons, April 23, 1821; d. St. Etienne, July 25, 1870. The son of a laborer, and himself uneducated, he attracted attention by his political and rustic ditties. He wrote the words, and then sang the airs to Reyer, who put them into shape. His political songs (*Le Pain*, *Le Chant des ouvriers*, etc.) created such disturbances that he was banished in 1851, but in 1852 he was pardoned. His song *Les Boeufs* enjoyed some popularity.—NS/LK/DM

Duport, Jean-Louis, famous French cellist, brother of **Jean-Pierre Duport;** b. Paris, Oct. 4, 1749; d. there, Sept. 7, 1819. He made his public debut at a Concert Spirituel (1768). He joined his brother in Berlin at the outbreak of the Revolution. Returning in 1806, he became musician to Charles IV, the ex-king of Spain, at Marseilles. In 1812 he returned to Paris, where he taught at the Cons. (1813–15). He wrote six cello concertos, sonatas, duos, airs variées, nine nocturnes (for harp and cello), etc. His *Essai sur le doigté du violoncelle et la conduite de l'archet, avec une suite d'exercices* was for decades a standard textbook, and practically laid the foundations of modern cello virtuosity.—NS/LK/DM

Duport, Jean-Pierre, eminent French cellist, brother of **Jean-Louis Duport;** b. Paris, Nov. 27, 1741; d. Berlin, Dec. 31, 1818. He studied with Berteau. He made his debut at a Concert Spirituel in Paris (1761), where he subsequently gave concerts regularly; was also in the service of the Prince of Conti. In 1773 he settled in Berlin as 1st cellist in the orch. of the Royal Chapel, continuing to play there until 1811; was also director of the court concerts (1787–1806). In addition to his brother, he taught Prince Friedrich Wilhelm II. He composed a number of works for his instrument, including a concerto and many sonatas. Beethoven composed his two cello sonatas, op.5, for Duport; Beethoven played these works with him during his visit to the Berlin court in 1796.—NS/LK/DM

Duprato, Jules-Laurent, French composer; b. Nimes, Aug. 20, 1827; d. Paris, May 20, 1892. He studied with Leborne at the Paris Cons., and in 1848 won the Prix de Rome. He composed operettas, cantatas, songs, etc., as well as recitatives for Hérold's *L'Illusion* and Balfe's *The Bohemian Girl*.

BIBL.: F. Clauzel, *J. D.* (1896).—NS/LK/DM

DuPré, Jacqueline, renowned English cellist; b. Oxford, Jan. 26, 1945; d. London, Oct. 19, 1987. She entered the London Cello School at the age of five. While still a child, she began studies with her principal mentor, William Pleeth, making her first public appearance on British television when she was 12. She was awarded a gold medal upon graduation from the Guildhall School of Music in London (1960); also studied with Casals in Zermatt, Switzerland, with Tortelier at Dartington Hall and in Paris, and with Rostropovich in Moscow. After winning the Queen's Prize (1960), she made her formal debut in a recital at London's Wigmore Hall on March 1, 1961. She made her North American debut at N.Y.'s Carnegie Hall as soloist in Elgar's Cello Concerto with Dorati and the BBC Sym. Orch. on May 14, 1965, an appearance that electrified the audience and elicited rapturous critical reviews. On June 15, 1967, she married **Daniel Barenboim** in Jerusalem, with whom she subsequently performed. In 1973 she was diagnosed as having multiple sclerosis, at which time she abandoned her career. She later gave master classes as her health permitted. In 1976 she was made an Officer of the Order of the British Empire, and in 1979 was awarded an honorary doctorate in music by the Univ. of London. The Jacqueline DuPré Research Fund was founded to assist in the fight against multiple sclerosis. Her life was the subject of a Broadway play, *Duet for One* (1981), and a film, *Hillary and Jackie* (1998).

BIBL.: W. Wordsworth, ed., *J. d. P.: Impressions* (N.Y., 1983; 2nd ed., 1989); C. Easton, *J. d.P.: A Biography* (London, 1989); E. Wilson, *J. D. P.* (London, 1997).—NS/LK/DM

Dupré, Marcel, celebrated French organist, pedagogue, and composer; b. Rouen, May 3, 1886; d. Meudon, near Paris, May 30, 1971. At age seven, he began his musical studies with his father, Albert Dupré, a church organist. At 12 he became organist at St. Vivien in Rouen and also began private organ lessons with Guilmant in Paris. In 1902 he entered the Paris Cons., where he studied piano with Diémer (premier prix, 1905), organ with Guilmant and Vierne (premier prix, 1907), and fugue with Widor (premier prix, 1909); he also received training in composition from Widor, winning the Grand Prix de Rome in 1914 with his cantata *Psyché*. He was interim organist at Notre-Dame in 1916; in 1920 he gave a cycle of ten recitals of Bach's complete organ works at the Paris Cons., playing from memory; that same year, he became asst. organist under Widor at St. Sulpice. On Nov. 18, 1921, he made his U.S. debut in N.Y., followed by a transcontinental tour, performing 94 recitals in 85 American cities; a 2nd U.S. tour in 1923 included 110 concerts; he made his 10th tour of the U.S. in 1948. In 1939 he gave 40 concerts in Australia on his world tour. He had, meanwhile, been appointed prof. of organ at the Paris Cons. in 1926; in 1934 he succeeded Widor as organist at St. Sulpice, continuing there until his death at the age of 85. He became general director of the American Cons. in Fontainebleau in 1947 and was appointed director of the Paris Cons., in succession to Delvincourt, in 1954 (until 1956). Dupré wrote his first work, the oratorio *La Vision de Jacob*, at the age of 14; it was performed on his 15th birthday at his father's house in Rouen, in a domestic production assisted by a local choral society. Most of his organ works are products of original improvisations. Thus *Symphonie-Passion*, first improvised at the Wanamaker organ in Philadelphia (Dec. 8, 1921), was written down much later and performed in its final version at Westminster Cathedral in London (Oct. 9, 1924). Similarly, *Le Chemin de la Croix* was improvised in Brussels (Feb. 13, 1931) and performed in a definitive version in Paris the following year (March 18, 1932). Among precomposed works were two syms. for Organ: No. 1 (Glasgow, Jan. 3, 1929) and No. 2 (1946); Concerto for Organ and Orch. (Groningen, April 27, 1938, composer soloist); *Psalm XVIII* (1949); 76 chorales and several a cappella choruses; also numerous "verset- préludes." He was the author of *Traité d'improvisation à l'orgue* (Paris, 1925), *Méthode d'orgue* (Paris, 1927), and *Manuel d'accompagnement du plainchant gregorien* (Paris, 1937). R. Kneeream ed. and tr. his autobiography as *Recollections* (Melville, N.Y., 1975).

BIBL.: R. Delestre, *L'Oeuvre de M. D.* (Paris, 1952); B. Gavoty and R. Hauert, *M. D.* (Geneva, 1955); M. Murray, *M. D.: The Work of a Master* (Boston, 1985); C. Colleney, *M. D., 1886–1971, ou, Le cause de l'orgue* (Bordeaux, 1987). —NS/LK/DM

Duprez, Gilbert(-Louis), French tenor and pedagogue; b. Paris, Dec. 6, 1806; d. there, Sept. 23, 1896. He began his training in Paris at Choron's Inst. de Musique Classique et Religieuse, then continued his studies with Rogat at the Cons. He made his operatic debut as Count Almaviva at Paris's Odéon (1825); dissatisfied with his performance, he pursued further vocal training in Italy, where he became notably successful in Italian roles (1829–35); Donizetti chose him to create the role of Edgardo in *Lucia di Lammermoor* (Naples, 1835). Returning to France, he was a principal member of the Paris Opéra (1837–49), where he created a number of roles, including Berlioz's Benvenuto Cellini (1838), Donizetti's Polyeucte in *Les Martyrs* (1840), and Fernando in *La Favorite* (1840); retired from the stage in 1855. He taught at the Paris Cons. (1842–50) and founded his own vocal school (1853). His most famous pupil was Emma Albani. He wrote several operas and other works. He also publ. the methods *L'Art du chant* (Paris, 1845) and *La Mélodie, études complémentaires vocales et dramatiques de l'Art du chant* (Paris, 1846); he also publ. *Souvenirs d'un chanteur* (Paris, 1880) and *Récréations de mon grand âge* (Paris, 1888). His wife, Alexandrine (née Duperron) (b. Nantes, 1808; d. Brussels, Feb. 27, 1872), and daughter, Caroline (b. Florence, April 10, 1832; d. Pau, April 17, 1875), were also singers.

BIBL.: A. Elwart, *D.: Sa vie artistique* (Paris, 1838). —NS/LK/DM

Dupuis, Albert, eminent Belgian composer; b. Verviers, March 1, 1877; d. Brussels, Sept. 19, 1967. He studied piano, violin, and flute at the Verviers Cons. before pursuing training with d'Indy and others at the Paris Schola Cantorum (1897–99). Returning to his homeland, he won the Belgian Prix de Rome in 1903 with his cantata *La chanson d'Halewyn*, which was premiered in Brussels on Nov. 25 of that year; it later was rev. as the opera of the same title and premiered in Antwerp on Feb. 14, 1914. In 1907 he became director of the Verviers Cons., which post he held until 1947. He distinguished himself as a composer for the theater, in a style reflecting his French training.

WORKS: DRAMATIC: O p e r a : *Idylle* (Verviers, March 5, 1895); *Bilitis* (Verviers, Dec. 21, 1899); *Jean- Michel* (1901–02; Brussels, March 5, 1903); *Martille* (1904; Brussels, March 3, 1905); *Fidélaine* (Liège, March 30, 1910); *Le château de la Bretêche* (Nice, March 28, 1913); *La chanson d'Halewyn* (Antwerp, Feb. 14, 1914; based on the cantata of the same title, 1903); *La passion* (Monte Carlo, April 2, 1916); *La délivrance* (Verviers, Dec. 19, 1918); *La barrière* (Verviers, Feb. 26, 1920); *La victoire* (Brussels, March 28, 1923); *Un drame sous Philippe II* (Liège, Dec. 29, 1926); *Hassan* (Antwerp, Nov. 5, 1931); *Ce n'était qu'un rêve* (Antwerp, Jan. 26, 1932). **ORCH.:** 2 syms. (1904; 1922–23); *Fantaisie rhapsodique* for Violin and Orch. (1906); *Poème oriental* for Cello and Orch. (1924); Cello Concerto (1926); *Epitaphe* (1929); *Aria* for Viola and Orch. (1933); Piano Concerto (1940); *Caprice rhapsodique* (1941); Violin Concerto (1944). **CHAMBER:** Violin Sonata; String Quartet; 2 piano trios; Piano Quartet; many piano pieces. **VOCAL:** Oratorios; cantatas; choruses; songs.

BIBL.: J. Dor, *A. D.* (Liège, 1935); R. Michel, *Un grand musicien belge méconnu: A. D.* (Verviers, 1967).—NS/LK/DM

Dupuis, Sylvain, Belgian conductor and composer; b. Liège, Oct. 9, 1856; d. Bruges, Sept. 28, 1931. He was a pupil at the Liège Cons., winning the Prix de

Rome in 1881. He became a teacher of counterpoint there, and was also conductor of the singing society La Légia. In 1888 he established the Nouveaux Concerts Symphoniques. He was appointed 1st conductor at the Théâtre Royal de la Monnaie in Brussels in 1900, and conductor of the Concerts Populaires. From 1911 until 1926, he was director of the Cons. at Liège.

WORKS: DRAMATIC: O p e r a : *Coûr d'Oignon; Moina.* CANTATAS: *La Cloche de Roland; Camoëns; Le Chant de la Création.* ORCH.: *Macbeth,* symphonic poem; Concertino for Oboe and Orch.; 2 suites. OTHER: Pieces for violin; choruses. —NS/LK/DM

Durand, Emile, French composer and teacher; b. St.- Brieuc, Feb. 16, 1830; d. Neuilly, May 6, 1903. In 1850, while still a student at the Paris Cons., he was appointed teacher of an elementary singing class; in 1871 he became prof. of harmony there. He publ. *Traité d'harmonie* and *Traité de composition musicale,* and also wrote several light operas.—NS/LK/DM

Durand, Marie-Auguste, French organist and music publisher; b. Paris, July 18, 1830; d. there, May 31, 1909. He studied organ with Benoist, and in 1849 was organist at St. Ambroise; then at Ste.- Geneviève, St.-Roch, and (1862–74) St. Vincent de Paul. He also occupied himself with music criticism and composition (his *Chaconne* and *Valse* for piano were especially popular). In 1870 he entered into partnership with Schönewerk (acquiring Flaxland's music publishing business), the firm then being known as Durand & Schönewerk. When his son, Jacques (b. Paris, Feb. 22, 1865; d. Bel-Ebat, Aug. 22, 1928), replaced Schönewerk in 1891, the title became Durand & Fils. The house is now known as Durand & Cie., and has made a specialty of publishing works of the outstanding French composers. It also brought out French eds. of Wagner, as well as several eds. of early masters, including a complete critical ed. of Rameau. Jacques Durand publ. *Cours professionel à l'usage des employés du commerce de* musique (two vols., 1923), *Quelques souvenirs d'un éditeur de musique* (two vols., 1924–25), and *Lettres de Cl. Debussy à son éditeur* (Paris, 1927).—NS/LK/DM

Duran Duran, one of MTV's original great success stories; formed 1978, Birmingham, England. MEMBERSHIP: Nick Rhodes (real name, Nicholas Bates), kybd. (b. Birmingham, England, June 8, 1962); John Taylor, bs., gtr. (b. Birmingham, England, June 20, 1960); Andy Taylor, gtr. (b. Dolver-Hampton, England, Feb. 16, 1961); Roger Taylor, drm. (b. Birmingham, England, April 26, 1960); Simon LeBon, voc. (b. Bushey, England, Oct. 27, 1958). (Note: none of the Taylors are related.)

Nick Rhodes and John Taylor were both huge fans of David Bowie and Roxy Music. Beginning under the aegis of the post-punk "New Romantic" movement, they started playing together with several other musicians. Landing a steady gig at a Birmingham Club called Barbarellas, the group took on the name of the villain in the Roger Vadim film for which the club was named. Eventually, the lineup shook out to the three Taylors, Rhodes, and LeBon. They gigged steadily, landing a slot

at the Edinburgh festival, which in turn landed them a contract with EMI.

The band became an instant success in England. Their first single, "Planet Earth," landing at #12 in the U.K. charts. With their next single, "Girls on Film," the band started to capitalize on the newest medium for promoting records in 1980, music video. The provocative "Girls on Film" clip featured attractive, scantily clad women. Ironically the clip appealed most strongly to their female fans, who watched the clip to see a bunch of good-looking boys. The song went Top Ten in the U.K. in advance of their debut album, which hit #3 in the U.K. out of the box.

It took the release of their second album *Rio* before the U.S. caught on. The album entered the U.K. charts at #2 fueled by the hits "Hungry Like the Wolf" and "Save a Prayer." When MTV got onto the Sri Lanka–lensed video for "Hungry Like the Wolf," fans in the U.S. finally caught on. The single rose to #3 and went gold. The video for their follow-up single, the album's title track, was filmed in the Caribbean. "Rio" hit #14 and *Rio* rose to #6 and sold double- platinum.

Duran-mania was now planet-wide, overwhelming even the band. They likely made as much money from posters and other merchandise as they did from music. The band's debut album returned to the charts, reaching #10 about six months after *Rio* peaked, selling platinum. Six months after that, they released *Seven and the Ragged Tiger.* It contained the hits "Is There Something I Should Know," which topped the U.K. charts and hit #4 in the U.S.; "Union of the Snake" which went to #3 in the U.S., "New Moon on Monday" which hit #10, and their transatlantic chart-topping gold record "The Reflex." This album went double-platinum.

The band next released a live album, *Arena.* They appended an English non-LP single to the U.S. version of the album. That tune, "The Wild Boys," reached #2 on both sides of the Atlantic, selling gold in the U.S. The *Arena* album sold double-platinum.

The hunger for Duran Duran music was still great. They finally released the single "Save a Prayer" in the U.S. The three-year-old English hit rose to #16. The fevered pitch of releases was capped by the theme to the James Bond film *A View to a Kill,* which topped the U.S. charts, the first James Bond theme to do so.

In what some saw as the demise of the group, they split off in two directions. Andy and John Taylor, the more rock-oriented members of the group, hooked up with vocalist Robert Palmer and Chic drummer Tony Thompson to form The Power Station (named after the studio where the band recorded). The new album produced three hits. They took a cover of T-Rex's "Bang a Gong" to #9; "Some Like It Hot" topped out at #6; and "Communication" charted at #34. Indeed, the group's success (the album went platinum) might have spelled the end of Duran Duran had Palmer not wanted to return to his solo career. In Power Station concerts, Michael Des Barres, who was not nearly as impressive, replaced him.

Meanwhile, the remaining three Duranites went into the studio for their own project, under the new name of

Arcadia. The album *So Red the Rose* was a more ethereal affair than Duran Duran and far less rocking than The Power Station. It did, however, go platinum and reach #23 on the charts with the singles "Election Day" (featuring vocalist Grace Jones) rising to #6 and "Goodbye Is Forever" topping out at #33.

The hiatus did change Duran Duran. Both Roger Taylor and Andy Taylor left the band. Duran Duran recorded *Notorious* as a trio in 1986, thinking in terms of making a white funk album. It was produced by Nile Rogers, who had helped remix "The Reflex." The title track hit #2, and the tune "Skin Trade" nicked the Top 40 at #39. The album rose to #12 and went platinum. However, Duranmania had peaked, and now they were just another group of musicians—a situation they claimed they enjoyed.

The trio recorded *Big Thing* in 1988 as Duranduran. Despite the #4 single "I Don't Want Your Love" and the #22 "All She Wants," the album stalled at #24, and only sold gold. Their 1989 greatest hits package took three years to sell that much, eventually going platinum. Their next album, *Liberty*, didn't even manage that, peaking at #46. The band needed new blood and added former Frank Zappa and Missing Persons guitarist Warren Cuccurullo to the lineup. The group released *Duran Duran* (also called *The Wedding Album*) in 1993, reaching out to the adult fans who had been their core audience a decade before. The strategy worked. They scored two huge hits with the gold #3 "Ordinary World" and the #7 "Come Undone." The album went platinum and peaked at #7.

However, their next effort, an eclectic album of covers called *Thank You* with songs by groups as diverse as Public Enemy, Led Zepelin, and Lou Reed only sold gold, peaking at #19. John Taylor left the band, making Duran Duran a trio once more. Their 1997 opus *Medazzaland* didn't reap any heavy sales, though it did generate the #56 hitlet "Electric Barbarella." The album peaked at #58 in its first week on the charts.

By the turn of the millenium, Duran Duran were still around and still recording. They had parted ways with their label Capitol after nearly 20 years. At the time of this writing, they released *Pop Trash*, a sign that they maintained both their dignity and also their sense of humor.

DISC.: *Duran Duran* (1981); *Rio* (1982); *Seven and the Ragged Tiger* (1983); *Arena* (live; 1984); *Notorious* (1986); *Master Mixes* (1987); *Big Thing* (1988); *Liberty* (1990); *Duran Duran (The Wedding Album)* (1993); *In Conversation* (1994); *Thank* (1995); *Medazzaland* (1997); *Pop Trash* (2000).—**HB**

Durante, Francesco, celebrated Italian composer and pedagogue; b. Frattamaggiore, March 31, 1684; d. Naples, Sept. 30, 1755. His uncle, Don Angelo Durante, was a priest and composer. Francesco most likely received his early training at home from his uncle. He then continued his studies with him at the Conservatorio S. Onofrio a Capuana in Naples (1702–5) and with the violinist Gaetano Francone there; he may have subsequently studied with Pasquini and Pitoni in Rome. He taught at the Conservatorio S. Onofrio a Capuana (1710–11) and was maestro of the Congregatione and Accademia di Santa Cecilia in Rome (1718). Little else is known about him until he was appointed primo maestro of the Conservatorio Poveri di Gesu Cristo in Naples in 1728, which position he held until 1739. In 1742 he became primo maestro there of the Conservatorio S. Maria di Loreto, and also of the Conservatorio S. Onofrio a Capuana in 1745; he retained both positions until his death. With his fellow Neapolitans Porpora, Leo, Feo, and Vinci, Durante ranks among the most important composers of his era. Although the former were renowned as composers of opera, Durante was a particularly significant composer of sacred music, his output being notable for its resourcefulness of styles and practices as well as for originality. He was greatly renowned as a teacher, numbering among his pupils Pergolesi, Abos, Anfossi, Traetta, Sacchini, Piccini, and Paisiello.

WORKS: SACRED DRAMAS: *Prodigii della divina misericordia verso i devoti del gloriosa S. Antonio di Padova* (scherzo drammatico; Naples, June 13, 1705; music not extant); *La cerva assetata ovvero L'anima nelle fiamme della gloria* (Naples, Feb. 18, 1719; not extant); *Abigaile* (Rome, Nov. 22, 1736; music not extant); *S. Antonio di Padova* (Venice, 1754); 5 choruses for *Flavio Valente*, a tragedy by Duke Annibale Marchese (publ. in *Tragedie cristiane*, Naples, 1729). **Other Sacred Music:** 19 masses; 3 Mass cycles, including *Missa in Palestrina* (1739; ed. by V. Dufaut, Paris, 1921); 3 Requiem masses, including one in G minor (1738; ed. in *Periodico di musica sacra*, Rome, 1880); Mass movements; 30 Psalms; 14 motets, including *Nascere, nascere dive puellule* (ed. by R. Ewerhart in *Cantico sacro geistliche Solokantaten*, II, Cologne, 1954); antiphons; hymns; sequences; cantatas; arias; duets; terzettos; *XII duetti* (madrigali; canzoni) *da camera*, based on recitatives from solo cantatas of A. Scarlatti (ed. by M. Ivanoff-Boretsky, Moscow, 1931); etc. **INSTRUMENTAL:** *8 concerti per quartetto* (Nos. 1, 2, and 4 ed. by E. Doflein, Mainz, 1966); Harpsichord Concerto (c. 1750; ed. by F. Degrada, Milan, 1968); *6 sonate per cembalo divisi in studii e divertimenti* (Naples, c. 1732; ed. by B. Paumgartner, Kassel, 1949); 7 harpsichord sonatas; other keyboard works; pedagogical pieces.

BIBL.: V. de Rubertis, *Dos Bajetes de F. D., erroneamente interpretados por Fetis y de Nardis* (Buenos Aires, 1947); J. Auerbach, *Die Messen des F. D.* (diss., Univ. of Munich, 1954); G. Brungardt, *Some Selected Motets of F. D.* (diss., Univ. of Ill., 1967). —**NS/LK/DM**

Durey, Louis (Edmond), French composer; b. Paris, May 27, 1888; d. St. Tropez, July 3, 1979. He received training in solfège, harmony, counterpoint, and fugue from Léon Saint-Requier at the Paris Schola Cantorum (1910–14); he was self-taught in orchestration. In 1936 he joined the French Communist Party. During the German occupation (1940–44), he was a member of the Résistance. He was secretary-general of the Fédération Musicale Populaire (1937–56) and of the Assn. Française des Musiciens Progressistes (from 1948); he also wrote music criticism for the Paris Communist newspaper *L'Humanité* (from 1950). In 1961 he received the Grand Prix de la Musique Française. Although Durey was one of Les Six, he early on adopted a distinct path as a composer. His works owe much to the examples of Satie and Stravinsky. He was at his best writing chamber and vocal works.

WORKS: DRAMATIC: *Judith,* monodrama for Voice and Piano (1918); *L'occasion,* comic opera (1923–25; Strasbourg Radio, May 22–25, 1974); *L'intruse,* puppet play (1936); *Feu la mère de madame,* radio score (1945); *Chant des partisans coréens,* incidental music (1952); film scores. **ORCH.:** *Carillons* (1919; orchestration of a piano duet, 1916); *Neige* (1919; orchestration of a piano duet, 1918); *Pastorale* (1920); *Fantasie concertante* for Cello and Orch. (1947); *Ile-de-France,* overture (1955); Concertino for Piano, 16 Winds, Double Bass, and Timpani (1956); *Mouvement symphonique* for Piano and Strings (1963); Sinfonietta for Strings (1966); *Dilection* for Strings (1967); *Obsession* (1970; orchestration of a piano piece, 1968). **CHAMBER:** 3 string quartets (1917, 1922, 1928); String Trio (1919); Sonatine for Flute and Piano (1929); *Trio-sérénade* for Violin, Viola, and Cello (1955); *Les soirées de Valfère* for Wind Quintet (1963); *Octophonies* for 8 Strings (1965); *Divertissement* for 3 Winds (1966); *Nicolios et la flûte* for Flute and Harp (1968). **Piano:** *Carillons* for Piano Duet (1916; orchestrated 1919); *Neige* for Piano Duet (1918; orchestrated 1919); *Romance sans paroles* (1919); *3 Préludes* (1920); 3 sonatines (1926); *Nocturne* (1928); *10 Inventions* (1928); *De l'automne 53* (1953); *Auto-portraits* (1967); *Obsession* (1968; orchestrated 1970). **VOCAL:** *Eloges* for Soprano, Alto, Tenor, Bass, and Chamber Orch. (1917–62; also for Soli, Chorus, and Orch.); *Le printemps au fond de la mer* for Voice and 10 Winds (1920); *Cantate de la prison* for Voice and Piano or Orch. (1923); *3 chansons musicales* for Chorus (1948); *La guerre et la paix* for Tenor, Bass, Chorus, and 8 Instruments (1949); *La longue marche* for Tenor, Chorus, and Orch. (1949); *Paix aux hommes par millions* for Soprano, Chorus, and Orch. (1949); *Cantate à Ben-Ali* for Tenor, Chorus, and Piano or Chamber Orch. (1952); *3 poèmes* for Baritone and Piano or Orch. (1953); *10 choeurs de métiers* for Chorus and 6 Instruments ad libitum (1957); *Cantate de la rose et de l'amour* for Soprano and Piano or String Orch. (1965); many other vocal pieces.

BIBL.: F. Robert, *L. D.: L'aîné des Six* (Paris, 1968); J. Roy, *Le groupe des six: Poulenc: Poulenc, Milhaud, Honegger, Auric, Tailleferre, D.* (Paris, 1994).—**NS/LK/DM**

Durham, Eddie, jazz trombonist, guitarist, arranger; b. San Marcos, Tex., Aug. 19, 1906; d. Brooklyn N.Y., March 6, 1987. The entire Durham family was musical; Eddie's brothers included Joe (bass), Allen (trombone), Roosevelt (violin/piano/guitar), Earl (piano) Clyde (bass), and Sylvester (piano/organ). He received initial training from a brother, later attending the Chicago Cons. He first played guitar in the Durham Brothers Orch., then began doubling on trombone. He toured (on trombone) with the 101 Ranch Circus Band until 1926, then worked with Edgar Battle's Dixie Ramblers. During the late 1920s he played in the Midwest with Eugene Coy, Jesse Stone, Terrence Holder, and Walter Page's Blue Devils. He briefly played with Elmer Payne's Ten Royal Americans (1929), then joined Bennie Moten (1929), remaining with the Moten band until 1933. After working with a few other bands briefly, he joined Jimmie Lunceford early in 1935 as trombonist-arranger. He was also featured as solo guitarist, and was one of the pioneers of amplified guitar work. He joined Count Basie in 1937, principally as arranger, but also featured on trombone and guitar. He left in 1938 to concentrate on full-time arranging, and scored for most of the popular big bands. He formed his own big band in June 1940, and later that year was musical director for Eon Eon (Tunnell) and His Buddies. From 1941–43, he

toured as musical director for the all-girl International Sweethearts of Rhythm, and later he directed his own all-girl band. During 1947 he toured with the Cavalcade of Jazz, and in 1952–53 led a small touring band accompanying vocalists Wynonie Harris and Larry Darnell. He continued regular arranging throughout the 1950s and 1960s, including scoring for and playing with Swingers Inc. From 1957 through the 1960s has led his own small band for residencies on Long Island. In October 1969, he joined Buddy Tate on trombone (doubling guitar). He performed with The Harlem Blues and Jazz Band (from 1977).

A prolific composer; his joint composition (with Edgar Battle) of "Topsy" was made into an international hit by Cozy Cole's Band, and he was also part-composer of "Don't Want to Set the World on Fire." With Buster Smith, he wrote the standard "One O'Clock Jump" for Basie. Durham was also a creative player somewhat ahead of his time. His first trombone solos with the Moten band have the surprising leaps characteristic of Miff Mole and his circle. His first electric guitar solos (with Lester Young and The Kansas City Six in September 1938) are also jagged and full of jumps from high to low strings, a far cry from the smooth flow and long lines of Charlie Christian, who nevertheless probably knew these recordings.

DISC.: Lunceford: *Hittin' the Bottle* (1935). Kansas City Six: *Kansas City* (1983).—**JC/LP**

Durkó, Zsolt, prominent Hungarian composer; b. Szeged, April 10, 1934. He was a student of Farkas at the Budapest Academy of Music (1955–60) and of Petrassi at the Accademia di Santa Cecilia in Rome (1961–63). After teaching at the Budapest Academy of Music (1971–77), he was active with the Hungarian Radio (from 1982). In 1978 he won the Kossuth Prize, and in 1983 the Bartók-Pasztory Award. He was made a Merited Artist in 1983 and an Outstanding Artist in 1987 by the Hungarian government. His varied output reveals an assured craftsmanship and imaginative use of traditional forms in a contemporary style.

WORKS: DRAMATIC: Opera: *Mózes* (1972–77; Budapest, May 15, 1977). **ORCH.:** *Episodi sul tema B-A-C-H* (1962–63); *Organismi* for Violin and Orch. (1964); *Una rapsodia ungherese* for 2 Clarinets and Orch. (1964–65); *Cantilene* for Piano and Orch. (1968); *Concerto for Orchestra* (1970); *Ballad* for Youth Orch. (1970); *Fantázia és utójáték* (Fantasy and Postlude) for Youth Orch. (1979); *Quattro dialoghi* for 2 Percussion Soloists and Orch. (1979); *Refrains* for Violin and Chamber Orch. (1979); Piano Concerto (1980); *Ornamenti 1* (1984) and *2* (1985); Violin Concerto (1992–93). **CHAMBER ENSEMBLE:** *Colloides* for Flute and Chamber Ensemble (1969); *Iconography No. 2* for Horn and Chamber Ensemble (1971); *Chamber Music* for 2 Pianos and 11 Strings (1972–73); *Turner Illustrations* for Violin and 14 Instruments (1976); *Impromptus* for Flute and Chamber Ensemble (1983); *Téli zene* (Winter Music) for Horn and Chamber Ensemble (1984). **CHAMBER:** *11 pezzi per quartetto d'archi* (1962); *Improvvisazioni* for Wind Quintet (1965); 2 string quartets (1966, 1969); *Symbols* for Horn and Piano (1968–69); *Quartetto d'ottoni* (1970); *Iconography No. 1* for 2 Bass Viols or Cellos and Harpsichord (1971); *Fire Music* for Flute, Clarinet, Piano, and String Trio (1971); *Serenata* for 4 Harps (1973); *Varianti* for Viola and Piano (1974); 8 Duos for 2 Horns (1977); 5 Pieces for Tuba and Piano (1978); *Movements* for Tuba and Piano (1980); *3 Essays* for Clarinet and Piano (1983); Sinfonietta for 10 Brass Instruments (1983); *Clair- obscure* for Organ and Trumpet (1984); Sextet for 5 Clarinets and Piano (1987); Woodwind Octet (1988); also piano pieces and organ music. **VOCAL:** *Fioriture* for Chamber Chorus and Orch. (1966); *Altamira* for Chamber Chorus and Orch. (1967–68); *Halotti beszed* (Burial Prayer), oratorio for Tenor, Baritone, Chorus, and Orch. (1967–72); *Hat tanulmáńy* (6 Studies) for Chorus and Piano (1970–72); *Cantata No. 1* for Baritone, Chorus, and Orch. (1971) and *No. 2* for Chorus and Orch. (1972); *Hét dallamrajz* for Chorus and Piano (1972); *Széchenyi Oratorio* for Baritone, Chorus, and Orch. (1981–82); *Pillanatképek a Kalevalából* for Chorus (1986); *Ilmarinen* for Chorus (1986); *3 English Verses* for Mezzo-soprano and 12 Instruments (1991).—**NS/LK/DM**

Durlet, Emmanuel, Belgian pianist, teacher, and composer; b. Antwerp, Oct. 11, 1893; d. there, Feb. 7, 1977. He studied piano with Frans Lenaerts, and also took a course in Vienna with Godowsky (1912–14). Returning to Belgium, he developed a brilliant career as a pianist; gave a cycle of all 32 sonatas by Beethoven. He held the post of prof. of advanced piano playing at the Antwerp Cons. (1920–59). Among his works are a Piano Concerto, a Violin Concerto, a Violin Sonata, and numerous teaching pieces for piano in a Romantic vein, as well as songs.—**NS/LK/DM**

Durme, Jef van
See **Van Durme, Jef**

Dürr, Alfred, distinguished German musicologist and editor; b. Berlin, March 3, 1918. He was educated at the Univ. of Göttingen (Ph.D., 1950, with the diss. *Studien über die frühen Kantaten Johann Sebastian Bachs*; publ. in Leipzig, 1951). In 1951 he became a research assistant at the Johann-Sebastian-Bach-Inst. in Göttingen. From 1962 to 1981 he served as its director, and continued to be associated with it until 1983. He was a member of the Akademie der Wissenschaften in Göttingen from 1976. He was an ed. of the *Bach-Jahrbuch* and also ed. works for the Bach *Neue Ausgabe sämtlicher Werke*. With Y. Kobayashi, he ed. the *Kleine Ausgabe* of Schmieder's *Bach-Werke-Verzeichnis* (Wiesbaden, 1998). In 1988 he was elected a corresponding member of the American Musicological Soc.

WRITINGS: *Johann Sebastian Bach, Weihnachts oratorium* (Munich, 1967); *Die Kantaten von Johann Sebastian Bach* (Kassel and Munich, 1971; 5th ed., rev., 1985); *Johann Sebastian Bach: Seine Handschrift-Abbild seines Schaffens* (Wiesbaden, 1984); *Im Mittelpunkt Bach: Ausgewählte Aufsätze und Vorträge* (Kassel, 1988); *Die Johannes-Passion von Johann Sebastian Bach: Entstehung, Überlieferung, Werkeinführung* (Kassel and Munich, 1988); *Bachs Werk vom Einfall bis zur Drucklegung* (Wiesbaden, 1989).

BIBL.: W. Rehm, ed., *Bachiana et alia musicologica: Festschrift A. D. zum 65. Geburtstag am 3. März 1983* (Kasse, 1983).
—**NS/LK/DM**

Dürr, Walther, German musicologist; b. Berlin, April 27, 1932. He was educated at the Univ. of Tübingen, where he took his Ph.D. in 1956 with the diss. *Studien zu Rhythmus und Metrum im italienischen Madri-*

gal, insbesondere bei Luca Marenzio. From 1964 he was one of the editors of the new and exhaustive critical ed. of the works of Schubert. He also was a prof. at the Univ. of Tübingen from 1977. W. Aderhold and W. Litschauer ed. the vol. *Zeichen-Setzung: Aufsätze zur musikalisch Poetik* (Kassel, 1992) in honor of his 60th birthday.

WRITINGS: *Franz Schuberts Werke in Abschriften: Liederalben und Sammlungen* (Kassel, 1975); *Das deutsche Sololied im 19. Jahrhundert* (Wilhelmshaven, 1984); with A. Feil and W. Litschauer, *Reclams Musikführer "Franz Schuberts"* (Stuttgart, 1991); *Sprache und Musik: Geschichte, Gattungen, Analysemodelle* (Kassel, 1994); with A. Krause, *Schubert Handbuch* (Kassel and Stuttgart, 1997).—**NS/LK/DM**

Dürrner, Ruprecht Johannes Julius, German conductor and composer; b. Ansbach, Bavaria, July 15, 1810; d. Edinburgh, June 10, 1859. He was a pupil of Friedrich Schneider at Dessau. From 1831 to 1842 he was a cantor at Ansbach, then studied under Mendelssohn and Hauptmann at Leipzig, and settled in Edinburgh as a conductor and vocal teacher. His choruses and quartets for men's voices won great favor. —**NS/LK/DM**

Duruflé, Marie-Madeleine (née **Chevalier**), distinguished French organist and teacher; b. Marseilles, May 8, 1921; d. Paris, Oct. 5, 1999. She displayed remarkable musical talent at an early age and was made organist at the Cathedral of St. Véran de Cavaillon when she was only 11. At the age of 12, she became a student at the Avignon Cons. In 1946 she entered the Paris Cons. as a student of Dupré, where she won the premier prix in organ. In 1953 she was awarded the Grand Prix International Charles-Marie Widor. Following her marriage to **Maurice Duruflé** in 1953, she served as co-organist with him at the church of St. Étienne-du-Mont in Paris. They also toured widely as duo organ recitalists, making their first tour of the U.S. in 1964. She and her husband were severely injured in southeastern France in 1975 when their car was hit by a speeding car. Neither ever fully recovered from this tragic experience, although, after a long and painful recuperation, she appeared in public as a recitalist in 1989 when she played at the Duruflé Festival in N.Y. She played for the last time in public at the Church of the Ascension in N.Y. in 1993. In addition to her authoritative interpretations of her husband's works, she also excelled as an interpreter of Widor, Vierne, Dupré, and Langlais. She also was greatly admired for her masterful improvisations.—**LK/DM**

Duruflé, Maurice, eminent French organist, pedagogue, and composer; b. Louviers, Jan. 11, 1902; d. Paris, June 16, 1986. He attended the maîtrise at Rouen Cathedral and received training in piano and organ. In 1919 he settled in Paris and pursued his studies in organ with Tournemire, Guilmant, and Vierne. In 1920 he entered the Cons., where he was a student of Gigout (premier prix in organ, 1922), Jean Gallon (premier prix in harmony, 1924), Caussade (premier prix in fugue, 1924), and Dukas (composition, 1928). In 1930 he became organist at the church of St. Étienne-du-Mont. He also was a prof. at the Cons. from 1943 until 1969. In 1953 he married **Marie-Madeleine Duruflé** (née **Chevalier**), who subsequently served as co-organist with him at St. Étienne-du-Mont. They also toured extensively as duo organ recitalists. In 1964 they made their first tour of the U.S. In 1975 Duruflé and his wife sustained severe injuries in southeastern France when their car was hit by a speeding car, and neither Duruflé nor his wife ever fully recovered. He was honored with the Grand Prix for music of the département of the Seine in 1956. While his output was not large, he made a notable contribution to the repertoire in his outstanding organ and sacred vocal works. He pursued a conservative course as a composer, producing works notable for their remarkable craftsmanship and beauty. His outstanding Requiem (1947) stands as one of the most important and performed liturgical scores of the 20th century.

WORKS: ORCH.: *Trois Danses* (1932); *Andante et scherzo* (1940). **CHAMBER:** *Prélude, récitatif et variations* for Flute, Viola, and Piano (1928). **KEYBOARD: P i a n o :** *Triptyque* (1927). **O r g a n :** *Scherzo* (1926); *Prélude, adagio et choral varié sur le thème du "Veni Creator"* (1930); *Suite* (1933); *Prélude et fugue sur le nom d'Alain* (1942). **VOCAL:** Requiem for Mezzo-soprano, Baritone, Chorus, and Orch. (1947); *Quatre Motets sur des thèmes grégoriens* for Chorus (1960); *Messe "cum jubilo"* for Baritone, Men's Chorus, and Orch. (1966).—**NS/LK/DM**

Dusapin, Pascal, French composer; b. Nancy, May 29, 1955. He went to Paris, where he studied organ with Jean Langlais at the Schola Cantorum and pursued academic studies at the Sorbonne. From 1974 to 1978 he studied with Xenakis, and later was in residence at the Villa Medici in Rome from 1981 to 1983. He served as composer-in-residence of the Orchestre National de Lyon in 1993–94. In 1979 he was awarded the Prix Hervé Dujardin of the SACEM, and in 1994 its Prix symphonique. He won the prize of the Académie des Beaux Arts in 1983. In 1992 he was made a Chevalier de l'Ordre des Arts et des Lettres. He was awarded the Grand prix National de la Musique in 1995.

WORKS: DRAMATIC: *Niobé (ou le Rocher de Sypile)* (1982; Radio France, Paris, June 16, 1984); *Roméo & Juliette*, opera (1985–88; Montpellier, July 10, 1989); *Medeamaterial*, opera (1991; Brussels, March 11, 1992); *La Melancholia*, operatorio (1991; Paris, March 17, 1992); *To be sung*, chamber opera (1992–93; Paris, Nov. 17, 1994). **ORCH.:** *Souvenir du silence* for 13 Strings (1976); *Timée* (1978); *Le Bal* (1978); *La Rivière* (Metz, Nov. 1979; rev. 1980); *L'Aven* for Flute and Orch. (1980–81; Metz, Nov. 1983); *Tre Scalini* (1981–82; Paris, April 27, 1983); *Assaï* (Venice, Sept. 22, 1985); *Haro* (Lyons, Sept. 20, 1986); *Aria*, concerto for Clarinet and Small Orch. (1991; Salzburg, Feb. 4, 1992); *Go* (1992); *Khôra* for 60 Strings (1993; Paris, Feb. 18, 1994; also for 30 Strings, Strasbourg, Sept. 28, 1997); *Extenso* (1993–94; Lyons, Oct. 13, 1994); *Watt* for Trombone and Orch. (1994; Las Vegas, June 1, 1995); *Apex* (1995; Lyons, Jan. 11, 1996); *Quad—In memoriam Gilles Deluze*, concerto for Violin and Small Orch. (1996; Paris, March 12, 1997); *Celo*, cello concerto (1996; Caen, March 18, 1997). **CHAMBER:** String Trio No. 1, *Musique fugitive* (Aix-en-Provence, June 1980); *Musique captive* for 9 Winds (1981; La Rochelle, July 1981); *Inside* for Viola (1980; La Rochelle, July 1981); *Fist* for 8 Players (1982; Paris, March 1983); *Incisa* for Cello (1982; Siena, Aug. 1984); 4 string quartets: No. 1 (1983; rev. 1992–96; Strasbourg, Oct. 1, 1996), No. 2, *Time zones*

(1989; 1st complete perf., Paris, Oct. 19, 1990), No. 3 (Paris, Nov. 3, 1993), and No 4 (Fontainebleau, Dec. 13, 1997); *Hop'* for 12 Players (Nice, Feb. 1983); *If* for Clarinet (La Rochelle, July 1984); *Item* for Cello (London, June 21, 1985); *Itou* for Bass Clarinet (Strasbourg, Sept. 26, 1985); *Ici* for Flute (Orléans, Jan. 22, 1986); *Indeed* for Trombone (1987; Bordeaux, May 18, 1988); *Iti* for Violin (Montpellier, Aug. 12, 1987); *Laps* for Clarinet and Double Bass (1987; Bordeaux, May 18, 1988); *In & Out* for Double Bass (Paris, May 10, 1989); *I Pesci* for Flute (1989); *Stanze* for Wind Quintet (Rome, July 1991); *Attacca* for 2 Trumpets and Timpani (1991; Brussels, Jan. 12, 1992); *Coda* for 13 Players (Donaueschingen, Oct. 18, 1992); *Invece* for Cello (Arcs, Dec. 25, 1992); *Ohimé* for Violin and Viola (Paris, June 16, 1992); *Ipso* for Clarinet (1994; Caen, March 23, 1997); *Loop* for 8 Cellos (1995; Beauvais, May 7, 1996); *Ohé* for Clarinet and Cello (1996); *Immer* for Cello (1996; Metz, Feb. 5, 1997); Trio No. 1 for Piano, Violin, and Cello (St. Jean-de-Luz, Sept. 15, 1997); *Cascando* for 8 Players (Klosteneuburg, Nov. 22, 1997). **VOCAL:** *Igitur* for Woman's Voice and 13 Players (1977); *Lumen* for Woman's Voice and 6 Players (1977); *L'Homme aux liens* for 2 Sopranos and 3 Violins (1978; Radio France, Paris, March 1980); *Shin'gyo* for Soprano and Piccolo (1981; Paris, March 1982); *Semino* for 6 Voices (1985; Royaumont, Sept. 6, 1992); *To God* for Soprano and Clarinet or Soprano Saxophone (1985; Strasbourg, Sept. 30, 1997); *Mimi* for 2 Women's Voices, Oboe, Bass Clarinet, and Trombone (Paris, Nov. 1987); *Il-li-ko* for Soprano (Royaumont, May 29, 1987); *Aks* for Mezzo-soprano and 7 Players (Paris, Nov. 13, 1987); *Anacoluthe* for Woman's Voice, Double Bass, and Double Bass (1987; Bordeaux, May 18, 1988); *For O.* for 2 Women's Voices and 2 Bass Clarinets (1988; Strasbourg, Sept. 17, 1989); *So full of shapes is fancy* for Soprano and Bass Clarinet (Paris, Sept. 25, 1990); *Comoedia* for Soprano and 6 Players (Toulouse, April 1, 1993); *Canto* for Soprano, Clarinet, and Cello (Villeneuve-les-Avignon, July 14, 1994); *Two Walking* for 2 Women's Voices (1994; Caen, March 22, 1997).—**LK/DM**

Duschek, Franz Xaver (real name, **František Xaver Dušek**), Bohemian pianist and composer; b. Chotěborky, Dec. 8, 1731; d. Prague, Feb. 12, 1799. He studied in Prague with F. Habermann and in Vienna with Wagenseil. He settled in Prague in 1763, as a teacher and performer; was a close friend of Mozart. He wrote several keyboard sonatas and concertos, syms., quartets, and trios.

BIBL.: V. Sýkora, *František Xaver Dušek: Žzivot a dilo* (Life and Works; Prague, 1958; contains a thematic catalog of his works).—**NS/LK/DM**

Dushkin, Samuel, Polish-American violinist; b. Suwalki, Dec. 13, 1891; d. N.Y., June 24, 1976. He was taken to America as a child and was adopted by the composer Blair Fairchild, who gave him his primary musical education. He then received training in violin from Remy and in composition from Ganaye at the Paris Cons. He studied violin with Auer in N.Y. and later took several lessons with Kreisler. He made his European debut as a violinist in 1918, and subsequently toured widely in Europe and America. In 1928 he became associated with Stravinsky and helped him to solve the technical problems in the violin part of his Violin Concerto; was the soloist in the first performance of this work in Berlin on Oct. 23, 1931, with Stravinsky conducting. He also gave the first performance of Stravinsky's *Duo concertant* for Violin and Piano, with Stravinsky playing the piano part (Berlin, Oct. 28, 1932). He recounted the details of these collaborations in his article "Working with Stravinsky," publ. in the Merle Armitage collection *Stravinsky* (N.Y., 1936). He publ. teaching manuals for violin, and also ed. works for violin ranging from the Baroque to the Classical periods (several "ed." works were later discovered to be by Dushkin).—NS/LK/DM

Dussek, Johann Ladislaus (real name, Jan Ladislav Dusík), outstanding Bohemian pianist and composer; b. Tschaslau, Feb. 12, 1760; d. St.-Germain-en-Laye, March 20, 1812. He studied piano at age five and organ at age nine, and then became a chorister at the Iglau Minorite church and a pupil at the Jesuit Gymnasium. After further studies at the Kuttenberg Jesuit Gymnasium, he continued his studies at Prague's New City Gymnasium (1776–77) and at the Univ. of Prague (1778). He found a patron in Count Manner, with whose assistance he was able to go to Malines in 1779, where he became active as a piano teacher. Dussek made his public debut there as a pianist on Dec. 16, 1779, and then set out on a highly successful tour, visiting Bergen op Zoom, Amsterdam, and The Hague. He then went to Hamburg, where he gave a concert on July 12, 1782, and also met C. P. E. Bach, with whom he may have studied. In 1783 he played at the St. Petersburg court. After spending about a year in the service of Prince Karl Radziwill as Kapellmeister in Lithuania, he made a major tour of Germany in 1784, winning notable acclaim in Berlin, Mainz, Kassel, and Frankfurt am Main as a piano and glass harmonica virtuoso. In 1786 he went to Paris, where he performed at the court for Marie Antoinette; except for a brief trip to Milan and Bohemia, he remained in Paris until the outbreak of the French Revolution in 1789 compelled him to flee to London. On June 1, 1789, he made his London debut at the Hanover Square Rooms. He soon became successful as a pianist and teacher in the British capital, appearing regularly at Salomon's concerts and being an active participant in these concerts during Haydn's two visits. In 1792 Dussek married the singer, pianist, and harpist Sophia Corri. With his father-in-law, Domenico Corri, he became active as a music publisher. Both men were ill suited for such a venture, however, and Dussek's love for the good life further contributed to the failure of the business. Dussek fled to Hamburg in 1799, leaving his father-in-law to serve a jail sentence for debt. Dussek apparently never saw his wife or daughter again. He seems to have spent about two years in Hamburg, where he was active as a performer and teacher. In 1802 he played in his birthplace, and then in Prague. From 1804 to 1806 he served as Kapellmeister to Prince Louis Ferdinand of Prussia. After the latter's death at the battle of Saalfeld (Oct. 10, 1806), Dussek composed a piano sonata in his memory, the *Elégie harmonique sur la mort du Prince Louis Ferdinand de Prusse*, op.61. He then was briefly in the service of Prince Isenburg. In 1807 he settled in Paris, where he served Prince Talleyrand, gave concerts, and taught. His health began to fail due to excessive drinking, and he was compelled to abandon his career. Dussek was a remarkable composer for the piano, proving himself a master craftsman capable of producing the most brilliant works for the instrument. In his later works he presaged the development of the Romantic school, anticipating such composers as Chopin, Mendelssohn, Schumann, and even Brahms. As a celebrated virtuoso of the keyboard, he shares with Clementi the honor of having introduced the "singing touch." He publ. *Instructions on the Art of Playing the Piano Forte or Harpsichord* (London, 1796; numerous later eds.; Fr. tr. as *Methode pour le piano forte*, Paris, 1799; Ger. tr. as *Pianoforte-Schule*, Leipzig, 1802). A complete ed. of his works was publ. by Breitkopf & Härtel (12 vols., Leipzig, 1813–17; reprint, 6 vols., N.Y., 1976). A number of his works have appeared in modern eds. in the Musiqua Antiqua Bohemica series. See also H. Craw, ed., *J.L. D.: Selected Piano Works* (Madison, Wisc., 1977).

WORKS: *The Captive of Spilberg*, musical drama (London, Nov. 14, 1798); incidental music to Sheridan's melodrama *Pizarro* (London, Jan. 19, 1799); *Auszug aus einer Oster-Cantate* (1786); Mass (1807); 15 piano concertos (1 not extant; 4 arranged for Harp); Concerto for 2 Pianos and Orch.; Harp Concerto (not extant); 34 piano sonatas (several arranged for other instruments); 9 sonatas for Piano, 4-Hands (several arranged for other instruments); 68 sonatas for Piano and Violin (several arranged for Piano and Flute); 16 sonatas for Piano, Violin, and Cello (6 not extant); 2 sonatas for Piano, Violin, and Double Bass; many solo piano pieces, including *The Sufferings of the Queen of France* (1793); Piano Quartet; Piano Quintet; 3 string quartets; numerous other chamber works, including the Sonata for Piano, Violin, Cello, and Percussion entitled *The Naval Battle and Total Defeat of the Dutch by Admiral Duncan* (London, Oct. 11, 1797).

BIBL.: F. Schiffer, *J.L. D.: Seine Sonaten und seine Konzerte* (Leipzig, 1914); H. Craw, *A Biography and Thematic Catalog of the Works of J.L. D. (1760–1812)* (diss., Univ. of Southern Calif., 1964); O. Grossman, *The Piano Sonatas of J.L. D. (1760–1812)* (diss., Yale Univ., 1975); L. Richter, *An Analytic Study of Selected Piano Concertos of J.L. D.* (diss., N.Y.U., 1985); L. Palazzolo, *Il tocco cantante: J.L. D., compositore e virtuoso tra Mozart e Clementi* (Bologna, 1992).—NS/LK/DM

Dutilleux, Henri, distinguished French composer and teacher; b. Angers, Jan. 22, 1916. He was a student at the Paris Cons. (1933–38) of J. and N. Gallon (harmony and counterpoint), Büsser (composition), and Emmanuel (music history), winning the Grand Prix de Rome in 1938. He pursued his career in Paris, where he worked for the French Radio (1944–63) and was a prof. of composition at the École Normale de Musique (1961–70). In 1970–71 he was a guest prof. at the Paris Cons. In 1967 he was awarded the Grand Prix National de la Musique. In 1987 he received the Prix Maurice Ravel for his complete works. He was awarded the Praemium Imperial of Japan in 1994. In 1995 he was composer-in-residence at the Tanglewood Festival of Contemporary Music. Dutilleux developed a thoroughly individualistic contemporary style of composition, marked by a meticulous craftsmanship.

WORKS: DRAMATIC: *L'anneau du roi*, lyric scene (1938); *Les Hauts de Hurle-vent*, incidental music (1945; orch. suite, 1945); *La Princesse d'Élide*, incidental music (1946); *Monsieur de Pourceaugnac*, incidental music (1948); *Hernani*, incidental music (1952); *Le Loup*, ballet (Paris, March 18, 1953); film scores. **ORCH.**: *Sarabande* (1941); *Danse fantastique* (1943); 2 syms.: No. 1 (Paris, June 7, 1951) and No. 2, *Le Double* (1957–59; Boston, Dec. 11, 1959); *Métaboles* (1962–64; Cleveland, Jan. 14, 1965); *Tout un monde lointain...*, cello concerto (1967–70; Aix-en-Provence, July 25, 1970); *Timbres, espace, mouvement ou "La nuit étoilée"* (1977–78; Washington, D.C., Jan. 10, 1978); *L'Arbre des songes*, violin concerto (1980–85; Paris, Nov. 5, 1985); *Mystère de l'insant* for 24 Strings, Cimbalom, and Percussion (1986–89); *The Shadows of Time* (Boston, Oct. 9, 1997). **CHAMBER**: *Sarabande et cortège* for Bassoon and Piano (1942); Flute Sonatine (1943); Oboe Sonata (1947); *Choral, cadence et fugato* for Trombone and Piano (1950: *Ainsi la nuit*, string quartet (1974–76); *Trois strophes sur le nom de SACHER* for Cello (1982); *Les Citations*, diptyque for Oboe, Harpsichord, Double Bass, and Percussion (1991). **Piano**: Sonata (1946–48); *Blackbird* (1950); *Tous les chemins* (1961); *Résonances* (1965); *Figures de Résonances* for 2 Pianos (1970); *Deux Preludes* (1973–88); *Petit air à dormir debout* (1983); *Le jeu des contraires* (1988). **VOCAL**: *Gisèle*, cantata for Soprano, Tenor, Bass, and Orch. (1936); *Quatre mélodies* for Medium Voice and Piano (1942; also for Medium Voice and Orch., 1954); *La Geôle* for Medium Voice and Piano or Orch. (1944); *Deux Sonnets* for Medium Voice and Piano (1944–50); *Chanson de la déportée* for Voice and Piano (1945); (2) *Chansons de bord* for Children's Chorus (1950); *San Francisco Night* for Soprano and Piano (1963).

BIBL.: P. Mari, *H. D.* (Paris, 1973; 2nd ed., 1988); R. Jacobs, *H. D.* (Paris, 1974); D. Humbert, *H. D.: L'oeuvre et le style musical* (Paris, 1985); C. Glayman, *H. D.: Mystère et memoire des sons* (Paris, 1993; 2nd ed., rev., 1997); C. Potter, *H. D.: His Life and Works* (Aldershot, 1997).—**NS/LK/DM**

Dutoit, Charles (Edouard), outstanding Swiss conductor; b. Lausanne, Oct. 7, 1936. He took courses in violin, piano, and conducting at the Lausanne Cons., graduating at age 17. He then pursued training in conducting with Baud-Bovy at the Geneva Cons. (1st prize, 1958), with Galliera at the Accademia Musicale Chigiana in Siena (diploma, 1958), and with Munch at the Berkshire Music Center in Tanglewood (summer, 1959). He was a choral conductor at the Univ. of Lausanne (1959–63), and then conducted the Lausanne Bach Choir. After appearing as a guest conductor with the Bern Sym. Orch. in 1963, he served as its 2nd conductor (1964–66) and music director (1966–78). He also was chief conductor of the Zürich Radio Orch. (1964–66), assoc. conductor of the Zürich Tonhalle Orch. (1966–71), and conductor of the National Sym. Orch. in Mexico City (1973–75) and the Göteborg Sym. Orch. (1976–79). On Aug. 31, 1972, he made his U.S. debut conducting at the Hollywood Bowl. In subsequent years, he made extensive guest conducting tours of Europe, North and South America, Australia, Japan, and Israel. In 1977 he became music director of the Orchestre Symphonique de Montréal, which gained international recognition under his guidance. He also was principal guest conductor of the Minn. Orch. in Minneapolis (from 1983). On Dec. 21, 1987, he made his Metropolitan Opera debut in N.Y. conducting *Les Contes d'Hoffmann*. While retaining his position in Montreal, he also served as chief conductor of the Orchestre National de France in Paris (1990–2001). He likewise was chief conductor of the NHK (Japan Broadcasting Corp.) Sym. Orch. in Tokyo (from 1996). Dutoit's extensive repertoire embraces works from the Baroque era to modern scores, but he has won a particularly notable reputation as a consummate interpreter of French music. He was married three times, his 2nd wife being **Martha Argerich**.

BIBL.: G. Nicholson, *C.D.: Le Maître de l'orchestre* (Lausanne, 1986).—**NS/LK/DM**

Dutrey, Honore, pioneering jazz trombonist; b. New Orleans, La., Oct. 1887; d. Chicago, Ill., July 21, 1935. Dutrey had two older brothers who were musicians, Pete (violin) and Sam (alto/tenor/clarinet). He worked in the Melrose Brass Band (1910), then with various bands including Buddie Petit- Jimmie Noone Band and John Robichaux's Orch. He was regularly with the Silver Leaf Orch. from 1913 until joining the U.S. Navy in 1917. During his service career he was involved in an accident that permanently damaged his lungs; it is reported that he suffered carbide poisoning while working in the torpedo room of his ship. After his release he moved to Chicago, worked with King Oliver from January 1920 until 1921, and again from mid-1922 until early 1924, then led his own band at the Lincoln Gardens, Chicago, until June 1924. He then toured with Carroll Dickerson and later worked with Dickerson at the Sunset Cafe, Chicago. In the late 1920s, he played in Johnny Dodds' Band at Kelly's and also worked in Louis Armstrong's Stompers at the Sunset Cafe. Dutrey retired from music around 1930.—**JC/LP**

Duval, Denise, French soprano; b. Paris, Oct. 23, 1921. She studied at the Bordeaux Cons. In 1941 she made her operatic debut as Lola at the Bordeaux Grand Théâtre. In 1944 she joined the Folies Bergères in Paris, where she won notice; in 1947 she was chosen to create Thérèse in Poulenc's *Les Mamelles de Tirésias* at the Paris Opéra-Comique, where she also created Elle in his *La Voix Humaine* in 1959; she also appeared regularly at the Paris Opéra. In 1953 she sang in N.Y., in 1960 at the Edinburgh Festival (as Elle), and in 1962 at the Glyndebourne Festival (as Mélisande); she also made guest appearances in Milan, Cologne, Brussels, Amsterdam, Geneva, and Buenos Aires. After retiring in 1965, she taught voice in Paris. Among her other roles were Massenet's Salomé, Ravel's Concepción, and Poulenc's Blanche.—**NS/LK/DM**

Duvernoy, Charles, French clarinetist, teacher, and composer, father of **Henri-Louis-Charles Duvernoy**; b. Montbéliard, 1776; d. Paris, Feb. 28, 1845. He went to Paris in 1810, and was 1st clarinet at the Théâtre de Monsieur and the Feydeau, retiring in 1824. Until 1802 he was also a prof. at the Cons. He wrote several clarinet sonatas and clarinet duets.—**NS/LK/DM**

Duvernoy, Frédéric Nicolas, outstanding French horn player and teacher; b. Montbéliard, Oct. 16, 1765; d. Paris, July 19, 1838. He was self-taught. Having settled in Paris, he became a member of the orch. of the Comédie-Italienne (1788) and also appeared at the Concert Spirituel. He was made 2nd horn in the orch. of the Opéra-Comique (1790). He joined the orch. of the Opéra (1796), serving as its principal horn (1799–1817), and also served as 1st horn in the Imperial Chapel under Napoleon, and, later, under Louis XVIII and Charles X. He was on the faculty of the Cons. (1795–1816). In 1815 he became a Chevalier of the Légion d'honneur. He developed the cor mixte technique of horn playing, specializing in the middle register. He wrote a *Méthode pour le cor* (1802), and also composed horn concertos and chamber music.—NS/LK/DM

Duvernoy, Henri-Louis-Charles, French composer and teacher, son of **Charles Duvernoy;** b. Paris, Nov. 16, 1820; d. there, Jan. 1906. He was a pupil of Halévy and Zimmerman at the Paris Cons. where, in 1848, he was appointed a prof. He publ. (with Kuhn) *Nouveaux choix de psaumes et de cantiques* (1848), *Solfège des chanteurs* (1855), *Solfège à changements de clefs* (1857), and *Solfège artistique* (1860); also some 100 light piano pieces.—NS/LK/DM

Duvernoy, Victor-Alphonse, French pianist and composer; b. Paris, Aug. 30, 1842; d. there, March 7, 1907. He was a pupil of Bazin and Marmontel at the Paris Cons., taking the 1st prize for piano (1855). Together with Léonard, Stiehle, Trombetta, and Jacquard, he founded a series of chamber music concerts in 1869. He devoted his time otherwise to composing and teaching, and held a professorship at the Cons. For some 11 years, he was music critic of the *République Française*. He was made a Chevalier of the Légion of Honor, and was an officer of public instruction. As a dramatic composer, he produced the opera *Sardanapale* (concert perf., Paris, 1882), the "scene lyrique" *Cléopâtre*, and the opera *Hellé* (Paris, 1896). His symphonic poem *La Tempête* won the City of Paris prize in 1880. He also wrote a ballet, *Bacchus* (1902), an overture, *Hernani*, and much piano music.—NS/LK/DM

Duvosel, Lieven, Belgian composer; b. Ghent, Dec. 14, 1877; d. Sint-Martens-Latem, April 20, 1956. He studied in Antwerp and Paris, then lived in Berlin (where Nikisch and R. Strauss performed his works), later in The Hague and Haarlem. His most representative work is the symphonic cycle in 5 parts *Leie*: 1. *De Morgen*, 2. *De Leie*, 3. *De Liefde aan de Leie*, 4. *Kerstnacht (Christmas)*, and 5. *Het Leieland*. Other compositions include 3 syms., *Den Avond* (Evening), symphonic poem, *Wereldwee* (World's Grief), many cantatas, choruses, and songs.

BIBL.: F. van Durme, *L. D.* (Antwerp, 1943); E. Collumbien, *Lijst der werken van D.* (Ghent, 1950).—NS/LK/DM

Dux, Claire, German-American soprano; b. Witkowicz, Aug. 2, 1885; d. Chicago, Oct. 8, 1967. She was a student of Maria Schwadtke, Adolf Deppe, and Teresa Arkel in Berlin before completing her training in Milan. In 1906 she made her operatic debut as Pamina in Cologne, singing there until 1911. From 1911 to 1918 she was a member of the Berlin Royal Opera; she also sang in London, where she was the first British Sophie at Covent Garden (1913) and appeared as Pamina at Drury Lane (1914). After singing at Stockholm's Royal Theater

(1918–21), she was a member of the Chicago Grand (later Civic) Opera (1921–22; 1923–24); she also toured the U.S. with the German Opera Co. In 1926 she married her 3rd husband, the wealthy Chicagoan Charles H. Swift, and retired from the operatic stage. She then sang in concerts until making her farewell in Berlin in 1932. —NS/LK/DM

Dvarionas, Balis, Lithuanian composer, conductor, and teacher; b. Leipaia, June 19, 1904; d. Vilnius, Aug. 23, 1972. He studied at the Leipzig Cons. with Teichmüller (piano) and Karg-Elert (composition), and also received training in piano from Petri at the Berlin Hochschule für Musik and in conducting from Abendroth. In 1926 he went to Kaunas and taught piano there until 1940; in 1947 he became a prof. at the Lithuanian Cons. in Vilnius; also conducted the Lithuanian Phil. there (1940–41; 1958–61). Among his works are a Sym. (1947); Violin Concerto (1948; received a State Prize), two piano concertos (1958, 1962); opera, *Dalia* (1959); and many choral works. He wrote the music for the national anthem of the Lithuanian Soviet Socialist Republic (1950).

BIBL.: Y. Gaudrimas, *B. D.* (Moscow, 1960).—NS/LK/DM

Dvořáček, Jiří, Czech composer and pedagogue; b. Vamberk, June 8, 1928. He studied organ at the Prague Cons. (1943–47) and composition with Řídký and Dobiáš at the Prague Academy of Music (1949–53), where he subsequently taught (from 1953), later serving as a prof. of composition and chairman of the composition dept. (1979–90). In 1983 he was made an Artist of Merit by the Czech government. From 1987 to 1989 he was president of the Union of Czech Composers and Concert Artists. His works represent a median course of Central European modernism.

WORKS: DRAMATIC: O p e r a : *Ostrov Afrodity* (Aphrodite's Island; 1967; Dresden, Feb. 13, 1971). **ORCH.:** 2 syms. (1953, 1985); *Symphonic Suite* (1958); *Overture* (1958); *Concertante Suite* (1962); *Ex post*, symphonic movement for Piano and Orch. (1963); *Quattro episodi*, symfonietta (1971); *Žiji a zpívám* (I Am Living and Singing), cantata for Soloists, Chorus, Reciter, Children's Chorus, and Orch. (1978); *Giubilo* (1983); Violin Concerto (1989). **CHAMBER:** *Sonata Capricciosa* for Violin and Piano (1956); *Invention* for Trombone and Piano or Small Orch. (1961); *Meditations* for Clarinet and Percussion (1964); *Music* for Harp (1970); *Due per duo*, 2 rondos for Horn and Piano (1970); Brass Quintet (1973); Trumpet Sonata (1977); Organ Sonata (1979); Accordion Sonata (1979); *Tema con Variazioni per trombone e pianoforte* (1980); *Prague Transformations* for Wind Quintet (1981); *Partita* for Oboe and Bassoon (1986); *Partita piccola* for Violin, Guitar, and Harmonica (1987); *3 Movements* for String Quartet (1990); Trio for Clarinet, Violin, and Piano (1994).—NS/LK/DM

Dvořák, Antonín (Leopold), famous Czech composer; b. Mühlhausen, Sept. 8, 1841; d. Prague, May 1, 1904. His father ran a village inn and butcher shop and intended Antonín to learn his trade. However, when he showed his musical inclinations, his father let him study piano and violin with a local musician. He also received financial help from an uncle. Later, Dvořák went to Prague, where he studied with the director of a church music school, Karel Pitsch, and his successor, Josef Krejcí. Dvořák also began to compose assiduously, including two operas. His first public appearance as a composer took place in Prague on March 9, 1873, with a perf. of his cantata *The Heirs of the White Mountain (Hymnus)*. An important event in his career occurred in Prague on March 29, 1874, when Smetana conducted his Sym. in E-flat major, op.10. Dvořák then entered several of his works in a competition for the Austrian State Prize, adjudicated by a distinguished committee that included Herbeck, Hanslick, and Brahms. He won the prize in 1875 and twice in 1877. Brahms, in particular, appreciated Dvořák's talent and recommended him to Simrock for publication of his *Moravian Duets* and the highly popular *Slavonic Dances*. His *Stabat Mater* (Prague, Dec. 23, 1880) and Sym. in D major, op.60 (Prague, March 25, 1881), followed in close succession, securing for him a leading position among Czech composers.

At the invitation of the Phil. Soc. of London, Dvořák visited England in 1884 and conducted several of his works. He then was commissioned to compose a new sym. for the Phil. Soc.; this was his Sym. in D minor, op.70, which he conducted in London on April 22, 1885. His cantata *The Spectre's Bride*, composed for the Birmingham Festival, was accorded an excellent reception when he conducted the English performance there on Aug. 27, 1885. On his 3rd visit to England, he conducted the premiere of his oratorio *St. Ludmila*, at the Leeds Festival on Oct. 15, 1886. In 1890 he appeared as a conductor of his own works in Russia. On Feb. 2, 1890, he conducted in Prague the first performance of his Sym. in G major, op.88, which became one of his most popular works. In 1891 Dvořák was appointed prof. of composition at the Prague Cons.; he then received honorary degrees from the Charles Univ. in Prague (Ph.D.) and the Univ. of Cambridge (D.Mus.). There followed his brilliant *Carnival Overture* of 1891.

In 1892 Dvořák accepted the position of director of the National Cons. of Music of America in N.Y. He composed his *Te Deum* for his first U.S. appearance as a conductor (N.Y., Oct. 21, 1892); he also conducted a concert of his music at the 1892 World Columbian Exposition in Chicago. It was in the U.S. that he composed his most celebrated work, the Sym. in E minor, op.95, *From the New World*, which received its premiere performance on Dec. 15, 1893, with Anton Seidl conducting the N.Y. Phil. The sym. is essentially a Czech work from the old world; nevertheless, by appearing as a proponent of the use of Negro-influenced themes in symphonic music, Dvořák had a significant impact on American musical nationalism. He discussed the idea in an article, "Music in America" (*Harper's New Monthly Magazine*, Feb. 1895). Dvořák also composed his great Cello Concerto during his American sojourn, and conducted its first performance in London on March 19, 1896. Resigning his N.Y. position in 1895, he returned home to resume his duties at the Prague Cons.; he became its director in 1901. During the last years of his life, Dvořák devoted much of his creative efforts to opera; *Rusalka* (1900) remains best known outside Czechoslovakia. He made his last appearance as a conductor on April 4, 1900, leading a concert of the Czech Phil. in Prague. He was made a member of the Austrian House of Lords in 1901, the first Czech musician to be so honored. Czechs celebrated his 60th birthday with special performances of his music in Prague.

Dvořák's musical style was eclectic. His earliest works reflect the influence of Beethoven and Schubert, then Wagner, culminating in the Classicism of Brahms. After mastering his art, he proved himself to be a composer of great versatility and fecundity. A diligent and meticulous craftsman, he brought to his finest works a seemingly inexhaustible and spontaneous melodic invention, rhythmic variety, judicious employment of national folk tunes, and contrapuntal and harmonic skill. Many of his last works have become staples of the repertoire.

WORKS (the B. numbers are those established by J. Burghauser in *A. D.: Thematic Catalogue, Bibliography, and Survey of Life and Work* [Prague, 1960; 2nd ed., 1997]): **DRAMATIC: Opera**: *Alfred*, B.16 (1870; Czech Theater, Olomouc, Dec. 10, 1938); *Kraál a uhlíř* (King and Charcoal Burner), B.21 (1st version, 1871; National Theater, Prague, May 28, 1929; 2nd version, 1874, with music recomposed, op.14, B.42; Provisional Theater, Prague, Nov. 24, 1874; rev. 1887 and listed as B.151; National Theater, Prague, June 15, 1887); *Tvrdé palice* (The Stubborn Lovers), op.17, B.46 (1874; New Czech Theater, Prague, Oct. 2, 1881); *Vanda*, op.25, B.55 (1875; Provisional Theater, Prague, April 17, 1876; rev. 1879 and 1883); *Šelma sedlák* (The Cunning Peasant), op.37, B.67 (1877; Provisional Theater, Prague, Jan. 27, 1878); *Dmitrij*, op.64, B.127 (1881–82; New Czech Theater, Prague, Oct. 8, 1882; rev. 1883, 1885, and 1894–95; the latter is listed as B.186; National Theater, Prague, Nov. 7, 1894); *Jakobín* (The Jacobin), op.84, B.159 (1887–88; National Theater, Prague, Feb. 12, 1889; rev. 1897 and listed as B.200; National Theater, Prague, June 19, 1898): *Čert a Káča* (The Devil and Kate), op.112, B.201 (1898–99; National Theater, Prague, Nov. 23, 1899); *Rusalka*, op.114, B.203 (1900; National Theater, Prague, March 31, 1901); *Armida*, op.115, B.206 (1902–03; National Theater, Prague, March 25, 1904). Also the overture *Domov můj* (My Home), B.125a, and the incidental music to F. Samberk's drama *Josef Kajetán Tyl*, op.62, B.125 (1881–82; Provisional Theater, Prague, Feb. 3, 1882). **ORCH.**: Syms.: No. 1 in C minor, *Zlonické zvony* (The Bells of Zlonice), B.9 (1865; score lost until 1923; Brno, Oct. 4, 1936); No. 2 in B-flat major, op.4, B.12 (1865; rev. 1887; Prague, March 11, 1888); No. 3 in E-flat major, op.10, B.34 (1873; Prague, March 29, 1874, Smetana conducting); No. 4 in D minor, op.13, B.41 (scherzo only perf. in Prague, May 25, 1874, Smetana conducting; 1st complete perf. in Prague, April 6, 1892, composer conducting); No. 5 (old No. 3, op.24) in F major, op.76, B.54 (1875; Prague, March 25, 1879; rev. 1887); No. 6 (old No. 1, op.58) in D major, op.60, B.112 (1880; Prague, March 25, 1881); No. 7 (old No. 2) in D minor, op.70, B.141 (1884–85; London, April 22, 1885, composer conducting; rev. 1885); No. 8 (old No. 4) in G major, op.88, B.163 (1889; Prague, Feb. 2, 1890, composer conducting); No. 9 (old No. 5) in E minor, *Z nového světa* (From the New World), op.95, B.178 (N.Y., Dec. 15 [public rehearsal], Dec. 16 [official premiere], 1893, Anton Seidl conducting); Cello Concerto in A major, B.10 (1865; left unorchestrated; unidiomatic ed. by G. Raphael, 1929; later ed. by J. Burghauser, 1977); Piano Concerto in G minor, op.33, B.63 (1876; Prague, March 24, 1878; rev. 1883); Violin Concerto in A minor, op.53, B.96 and 108 (1879–80; rev. 1882; Prague, Oct. 14, 1883); Cello Concerto in B minor, op.104, B.191 (1894–95; rev. 1895; London, March 19, 1896, Leo Stern soloist, composer conducting). **Overtures**: *Tragic Overture* (*Dramatic Over-*

ture), B.16a (1870; overture from the opera *Alfred*); Concert Overture in F major, B.21a (1871; overture from the 1st version of the opera *Král a uhlíř*; Prague, April 14, 1872, Smetana conducting); *Romeo and Juliet*, B.35 (not extant); *Husitská* (Hussite), op.67, B.132 (Prague, Nov. 18, 1883); Triple Overture or *Příroda, Život a láska* (Nature, Life, and Love), op.91, Nos. 1–3 (1891–92; Prague, April 28, 1892, composer conducting; later listed as *V přírodě* (In Nature's Realm), op.91, B.168, *Karneval* (Carnival), op.92, B.169, and *Othello*, op.93, B.174). **S y m -p h o n i c   P o e m s :** *Vodník* (The Watersprite), op.107, B.195 (London, Nov. 14, 1896, Henry J. Wood conducting); *Polednice* (The Noonday Witch), op.108, B.196 (London, Nov. 21, 1896, Wood conducting); *Zlatý kolovrat* (The Golden Spinning Wheel), op.109, B.197 (London, Oct. 26, 1896, Hans Richter conducting); *Holoubek* (The Wild Dove), op.110, B.198 (1896; Brünn, March 20, 1898, Leos Janáček conducting); *Píseň bohatýrská* (Heroic Song), op.111, B.199 (1897; Vienna, Dec. 4, 1898, Gustav Mahler conducting). **OTHER:** Romance in F minor for Violin and Orch., op.11, B.39 (1873–79; a transcription of the andante con moto of the String Quartet in F minor, op.9, B.37); Symphonic Poem or Rhapsody in A minor, op.14, B.44 (1874); Nocturne in B major for String Orch., op.40, B.47 (1875?; from the String Quartet in E minor, B.19, and the String Quintet in G major, B.49; rev. 1882–83); Serenade in E major for Strings, op.22, B.52 (1875; Prague, Dec. 10, 1876); Symphonic Variations on a theme from the men's chorus *Já jsem huslař* (I Am a Fiddler), op.78 (old 28), B.70 (Prague, Dec. 2, 1877); Serenade in D minor for Wind Instruments, op.44, B.77 (Prague, Nov. 17, 1878); *3 Slavonic Rhapsodies*, op.45, B.86 (Nos. 1 and 2, Prague, Nov. 17, 1878, composer conducting; No. 3, 1878); *8 Slavonic Dances*, op.46, B.83 (1878); *Czech Suite* in D major, op.39, B.93 (Prague, May 16, 1879); *Mazurek* for Violin and Orch., op.49, B.90 (1879); *10 Legendy* (Legends), op.59, B.122 (1881; orchestrated from a piano duet version); *Scherzo capriccioso*, op.66, B.131 (Prague, May 16, 1883); *8 Slavonic Dances*, op.72, B.147 (1886–87); Rondo in G minor for Cello and Orch., op.94, B.181 (1893); *Klid* (Silent Woods) for Cello and Orch., op.68/5, B.182 (1893); Suite in A major, op.98b, B.190 (1895–96). **CHAMBER: S t r i n g   Q u a r t e t s :** A major, op.2, B.8 (1862; rev. 1887); B-flat major, B.17 (1869–70); D major, B.18 (1869–70); E minor, B.19 (1870); F minor, op.9, B.37 (1873; original version not extant; publ. version by G. Raphael, 1929); A minor, op.12, B.40 (1873, unfinished; completed by J. Burghauser and publ. in the complete ed. of Dvořák's works in 1979); A minor, op.16, B.45 (1874); E major, op.80 (originally op.27), B.57 (1876; rev. 1888); D minor, op.34, B.75 (1877; rev. 1879); E-flat major, op.51, B.92 (1878–79); C major, op.61, B.121 (1881); F major, *The American*, op.96, B.179 (1893); G major, op.106, B.192 (1895); A-flat major, op.105, B.193 (1895). **S t r i n g   Q u i n t e t s :** A minor for 2 Violins, 2 Violas, and Cello, op.1, B.7 (1861; rev. 1887); G major for 2 Violins, Viola, Cello, and Double Bass, op.77 (originally op.18), B.49 (1875; rev. 1888); E-flat major for 2 Violins, 2 Violas, and Cello, *The American*, op.97, B.180 (1893); also a Sextet in A major for 2 Violins, 2 Violas, and 2 Cellos, op.48, B.80 (1878). **P i a n o   T r i o s :** Op.13/1, B.25 (1871–72; not extant); op.13/2, B.26 (1871–72; not extant); B-flat major, op.21, B.51 (1875); G minor, op.26, B.56 (1876); F minor, op.65, B.130 (1883); *Dumkas* (Dumky) Trio, op.90, B.166 (1890–91). **Q u i n t e t s :** A major, op.5, B.28 (1872); A major, op.81, B.155 (1887). **Q u a r -t e t s :** D major, op.23, B.53 (1875); E-flat major, op.87, B.162 (1889). **O t h e r :** Sonata in F minor for Cello and Piano, B.20 (1870–71; not extant); Sonata in A minor for Violin and Piano, B.33 (1873; not extant); Sonata in F major for Violin and Piano, op.57, B.106 (1880); also many solo keyboard pieces, duets, etc.

VOCAL: C h o r a l : Mass in B-flat major, B.2 (1857–59; not extant); *Dědicové bílé hory* (The Heirs of the White Mountain) or *Hymnus* for Chorus and Orch., op.30, B.27 (1872; Prague, March 9, 1873; rev. 1880 and listed as B.102; rev. 1884 and perf. in London, May 13, 1885, composer conducting); *Stabat Mater* for Soprano, Alto, Tenor, Bass, Chorus, and Orch., op.58, B.71 (1876–77; Prague, Dec. 23, 1880); *149th Psalm*, op.79, B.91 (1st version for Men's Chorus and Orch., 1879; Prague, March 16, 1879; 2nd version for Mixed Chorus and Orch., 1887, and listed as B.154; Boston, Feb. 27, 1890); *Svatební košile* (The Spectre's Bride), cantata for Soprano, Tenor, Bass, Chorus, and Orch., op.69, B.135 (1884; Pilsen, March 28, 1885, composer conducting); *St. Ludmila*, oratorio for Soprano, Alto, Tenor, Bass, Chorus, and Orch., op.71, B.144 (1885–86; Leeds Festival, Oct. 15, 1886, composer conducting; with added recitative, 1901, and listed as B.205; this version 1st perf. as *Svatá Ludmila* in Prague, Oct. 30, 1901); Mass in D major for Soprano, Alto, Tenor, Bass (or Semi-Chorus), Chorus, and Organ, op.86, B.153 (1st perf. privately, Luzany, Sept. 11, 1887; rev. version for orch., 1892, and listed as B.175; London, March 11, 1893); Requiem Mass for Soprano, Alto, Tenor, Bass, Chorus, and Orch., op.89, B.165 (1890; Birmingham Festival, Oct. 9, 1891, composer conducting); *Te Deum* for Soprano, Bass, Chorus, and Orch., op.103, B.176 (N.Y., Oct. 21, 1892, composer conducting); *Americky prapor* (The American Flag), cantata for Alto, Tenor, Bass, Chorus, and Orch., op.102, B.177 (1892–93; N.Y., May 4, 1895); *Slavnostní zpěv* (Festival Song) or *Ode* for Chorus and Orch., op.113, B.202 (1st perf. privately, Prague, May 29, 1900). **O t h e r   V o c a l :** Numerous songs, including *Cypřiše* (Cypresses), B.11 (18 songs, 1865); *Biblické písné* (Biblical Songs), op.99, B.185 (10 songs, 1894); also the *Moravské dvojzpěvy* (Moravian Duets), 3 sets: for Soprano or Contralto and Tenor, op.20, B.50 (1875), for Soprano and Contralto, op.32, B.60 and 62 (1876), and for Soprano and Contralto, op.38, B.69 (1877).

BIBL.: O. Šourek inaugurated a complete ed. of D.'s works, which commenced publ. in Prague in 1955. The standard thematic catalog was compiled by J. Burghauser as *A. D.: Thematic Catalogue, Bibliography, and Survey of Life and Work* (in Czech, Ger., and Eng.; Prague, 1960; 2nd ed., 1997). See also the following: J. Bartoš, *A. D.* (Prague, 1913); O. Šourek, *Život a dílo A.a D.a* (The Life and Work of A. D.; 4 vols., Prague, 1916–33; Vols. I-II, 3rd ed., 1955–56; Vols. III-IV, 2nd ed., 1957–58; in an abr. Ger. tr. by P. Stefan as *D.: Leben und Werk*, 1 vol., Vienna, 1935; in Eng. tr. by Y. Vance as *A. D.*, N.Y., 1941); idem, *D.'s Werke: Ein vollständiges Verzeichnis in chronologischer, thematischer und systematischer Anordnung* (Berlin, 1917; rev. Czech ed., Prague, 1960); idem, *D.ovy symfonie* (Prague, 1922; 3rd ed., 1948; abr. Ger. ed. in *A. D. Werkanalysen I, Orchesterwerke*, Prague, 1954, and in Eng. in *The Orchestral Works of A. D.*, Prague, 1956); K. Hoffmeister, *A. D.* (Prague, 1924; Eng. tr. by R. Newmarch, London, 1928); O. Šourek, *A. D.* (Prague, 1929; 4th ed., 1947; Eng. tr. as *A. D.: His Life and Work*, Prague, 1952); idem, *D.ve vzpomínkach a dopisech* (Prague, 1938; 9th ed., 1951; Eng. tr. as *D.: Letters and Reminiscences*, Prague, 1954); H. Sirp, *A. D.* (Potsdam, 1939); O. Šourek, *D.ovy skladby komorni* (Prague, 1943; 2nd ed., 1949; abr. ed. in Ger. in *A. D. Werkanalysen II, Kammermusik*, Prague, 1954, and in Eng. in *The Chamber Music of A. D.*, Prague, 1956); idem, *D.ovy skladby orchestralní* (2 vols., Prague, 1944 and 1946; abr. ed. in Ger. in *A. D. Werkanalysen I, Orchesterwerke*, Prague, 1954, and in Eng. in *The Orchestral Works of A. D.*, Prague, 1956); A. Robertson, *D.* (London, 1945; 2nd ed., 1964); H. Kull, *D.s Kammermusik* (Bern, 1948); H. Boese, *Zwei Urmusikanten: Smetana, D.* (Zürich, 1955); A. Hořejš, *A. D.: The Composer's Life and Work in Pictures* (Prague, 1955); R. Smetana, *A.*

D.: O místo a význam skladatelského díla v českém hudebním vývoji (A. D.: The Place and Meaning of D.'s Compositions in the Development of Czech Music; Prague, 1956); A. Sychra, *Estetika D.ovy symfonické tvorby* (The Aesthetics of D.'s Symphonic Work; Prague, 1959; in Ger. as *A. D.: Zur Ästhetik seines sinfonischen Schaffens*, Leipzig, 1973); M. Aborn, *The Influence on American Musical Culture of D.'s Sojourn in America* (Ann Arbor, 1966); J. Burghauser, *A. D.* (Prague, 1966; in Ger. and Eng., 1967); J. Clapham, *A. D.: Musician and Craftsman* (London and N.Y., 1966); E. Herzog, *A. D. v obrazech* (A. D. in Pictures; Prague, 1966); G. Hughes, *D.: His Life and Music* (N.Y., 1967); J. Berkovec, *A. D.* (Prague, 1969); K. Honolka, *A. D. in Selbstzeugnissen und Bilddokumenten* (Reinbek, 1974); R. Layton, *D. Symphonies and Concertos* (London, 1978); J. Clapham, *D.* (London and N.Y., 1979); N. Butterworth, *D.: His Life and Times* (Tunbridge Wells, 1980); H.-H. Schönzeler, *D.* (London, 1984); K. Döge and P. Jost, eds., *D.-Studien* (Mainz and N.Y., 1994); D. Beveridge, ed., *Rethinking D.: Views from Five Countries* (Oxford, 1996); M. Irrgang, *A. D.: Untersuchungen zur Formentwicklung in den drei ersten Symphonien* (Frankfurt am Main, 1997). —NS/LK/DM

Dvořáková, Ludmila, Czech soprano; b. Kolin, July 11, 1923. She was a pupil of Jarmila Vavrdova at the Prague Cons. (1942–49). In 1949 she made her operatic debut as Kát'a Kabanová in Ostrava, and then appeared in Bratislava and at the Smetana Theater in Prague from 1952; was a member of the Prague National Theater (1954–57). In 1956 she made her first appearance at the Vienna State Opera, and from 1960 she sang at the Berlin State Opera; she also sang at the Bayreuth Festivals (1965–71) and at London's Covent Garden (1966–71). On Jan. 12, 1966, she made her Metropolitan Opera debut in N.Y. as Beethoven's Leonore, remaining on its roster until 1968. In addition to her roles in Czech operas, she was admired for her Wagner, Verdi, and Strauss. —NS/LK/DM

Dvorský, Peter (actually, **Petr**), esteemed Czech tenor; b. Partizánske, Sept. 25, 1951. He studied at the Bratislava Cons. and with Gina Cigna in Palermo. In 1972 he made his operatic debut as Lensky at the Slovak National Theater in Bratislava. In 1974 he took 5th prize in the Tchaikovsky Competition in Moscow, and then 1st prize in the Geneva Competition in 1975. From 1975 he sang at the Vienna State Opera, where he was made a Kammersänger in 1986. On Nov. 15, 1977, he made his Metropolitan Opera debut in N.Y. as Alfredo, where he sang Rodolfo in 1987. He made his first appearance at London's Covent Garden as the Duke of Mantua in 1978, returning there as Alfredo in 1986 and as Lensky in 1988. In 1981 he sang Rodolfo at Milan's La Scala. In 1986 he toured Japan with the Vienna State Opera. After portraying Cavaradossi at the Salzburg Festival in 1989, he appeared as Massenet's Des Grieux in Barcelona in 1990. He sang Don Alvaro at the Maggio Musicale di Fiorentino in 1992. In 1997 he appeared again in Japan. While Dvorský has won particular praise for his roles in operas by Smetana, Dvořák, and Janáček, he has also been admired for his various Verdi and Puccini portrayals.

BIBL.: D. Štilichová, *P. D.* (Bratislava, 1991).—NS/LK/DM

Dwight, John Sullivan, American music critic and editor; b. Boston, May 13, 1813; d. there, Sept. 5, 1893. He graduated from Harvard in 1832, and was one of the founders and most active members of the Harvard Musical Assn. After studying for the ministry, in 1840 he took charge of the Unitarian Church at Northampton, Mass. His literary and socialistic proclivities, however, gained the mastery; he gave up his pastorate, and entered the ill-starred Brook Farm Community as a teacher of German music and the classics. Returning to Boston in 1848, after the failure of the socialistic experiment, he devoted himself to literature, founded *Dwight's Music Journal* in 1852, and remained its ed. in chief until its discontinuance in 1881. A prominent feature in this periodical was the valuable historical essays of A.W. Thayer. The entire journal is available in reprint (N.Y., 1968). Dwight also publ. *Translations of Select Minor Poems from the German of Goethe and Schiller, with Notes.*

BIBL.: G. Cooke, *J. S. D., Brook-Farmer, Editor, and Critic of Music* (Boston, 1898).—NS/LK/DM

Dyer-Bennet, Richard, English-born American singer; b. Leicester, Oct. 6, 1913; d. Monterey, Mass., Dec. 14, 1991. He emigrated to the U.S. in 1925 and became a naturalized citizen in 1935. He studied voice with Cornelius Reid and guitar with José Rey De La Torre. He made his concert debut in N.Y. in 1944; also sang in nightclubs. In 1970 he joined the State Univ. of N.Y. at Stony Brook as an instructor in the theater arts dept. He acquired popularity mainly as a singer of English and American ballads, but he was also praised for his performance of Schubert song cycles, especially *Die schöne Müllerin* in his own tr., under the title "The Lovely Milleress."—NS/LK/DM

Dykema, Peter (William), American music pedagogue; b. Grand Rapids, Mich., Nov. 25, 1873; d. Hastings-on-Hudson, N.Y., May 13, 1951. He studied law at the Univ. of Mich. (B.S., 1895; M.L., 1896), and then took lessons in voice and in theory at the Inst. of Musical Art in N.Y. (1903–05) and studied with Edgar Stillman Kelley in Berlin (1911–12). He was music supervisor at the N.Y. Ethnical Culture School (1903–13). From 1913 to 1924 he was prof. of music and chairman of the public school music dept. at the Univ. of Wisc., and from 1924 to 1939 he was a prof. of music education at Teachers Coll., Columbia Univ. He publ. a number of music handbooks for schools, among them *Twice 55 Community Songs* (6 vols., 1919–27); *School Music Handbook* (1931; rev. ed., 1955, by H. Cundiff), *Singing Youth* (1935), *Golden Key Orchestral Series* (1937), with N. Church, *Modern Band Training Series* (1938), and with K. Gehrkens, *The Teaching and Administration of High School Music* (1941).

BIBL.: H. Eisenkramer, *P. W. D.: His Life and Contribution to Music Education* (diss., Univ. of Mich., 1963); H. Dengler, *Music for All: A Biography of P.W. D.* (Baltimore, 1994).—NS/LK/DM

Dykes, John Bacchus, English composer of hymn tunes; b. Kingston-upon-Hull, March 10, 1823; d. Ticehurst, Sussex, Jan. 22, 1876. He was educated at

Cambridge, and was ordained a minor canon and precentor at Durham Cathedral in 1849. In 1862 he became vicar of St. Oswald, Durham. He composed numerous anthems and part-songs.

BIBL.: J. Fowler, *Life and Letters of J. B. D.* (London, 1897). —NS/LK/DM

Dylan, Bob (originally, Zimmerman, Robert),

the single most important figure in contemporary music during the 1960s, comparable in impact to Elvis Presley in the 1950s. Bob Dylan was the first and most significant singer-songwriter to emerge from the folk music scene, inspiring a whole generation of folk (and later rock) artists to explore the vast potential of songwriting in matters socially conscious, personal, spiritual, philosophical and intellectual; b. Duluth, Minn., May 24, 1941.

Robert Zimmerman moved with his family to Hibbing, Minn., when he was six. Taking up guitar and harmonica at the age of 12, he later formed several rock bands, including The Golden Chords, while still in high school. After graduation, he attended the Univ. of Minn. for several months, dropping out to concentrate on his music. Adopting the name Bob Dylan, he traveled to N.Y. at the beginning of 1961 to visit his early idol Woody Guthrie, who was hospitalized with Huntington's disease. Dylan debuted that April in the Greenwich Village folk club Gerde's Folk City, where he first met Joan Baez, who would become one of the first artists to record his songs. Playing harmonica on recording sessions for Harry Belafonte and Carolyn Hester, Dylan received his first public recognition from *N.Y. Times* critic Robert Shelton that September. Signed to Columbia Records by John Hammond in October, Dylan's first album featured traditional folk and blues songs such as "Man of Constant Sorrow" and "House of the Rising Sun," as well as Eric Von Schmidt's "Baby, Let Me Follow You Down" and his own "Song to Woody." His first single, the rock 'n' roll–styled "Mixed Up Confusion," backed with "Corrina, Corrina," failed to sell.

Dylan's second album, *The Freewheelin' Bob Dylan*, was dominated by his own material and effectively established him as a leader in the burgeoning folk singer-songwriter and youth protest movements. Displaying an astonishing range of material, the album included a number of potent protest songs such as "Masters of War," "A Hard Rain's A-Gonna Fall," and "Blowin' in the Wind," as well as "Girl from the North Country" and "Don't Think Twice, It's Alright." His triumphant appearance at the 1963 Newport Folk Festival with Joan Baez and the subsequent success of his "Blowin' in the Wind" (a major British hit) and "Don't Think Twice, It's All Right" as performed by Peter, Paul and Mary, launched him into international prominence.

The Times They Are A-Changin' featured the powerful protest songs "The Lonesome Death of Hattie Carroll," "Only a Pawn in Their Game," and "With God on Our Side," and the anthemic title song, as well as the gentler "One Too Many Mornings" and "Boots of Spanish Leather." The more personal *Another Side of Bob Dylan*, his last entirely acoustic album, included a number of

songs later recorded by others in the folk-rock style: "It Ain't Me Babe" (The Turtles), "All I Really Want to Do" (The Byrds and Cher), and "Chimes of Freedom" and "My Back Pages" (The Byrds).

Bob Dylan left the folk and protest movements behind with 1965's *Bringing It All Back Home* album. Half acoustic and half electric, the album contained a number of songs written in a stream-of-consciousness style, pervaded with incisive, evocative, and surreal images, such as "Gates of Eden" and "Subterranean Homesick Blues," his first, albeit moderate, American hit and a near-smash British hit. Other inclusions were the provocative "It's Alright Ma (I'm Only Bleeding)" and "It's All Over Now, Baby Blue," the caustic "Maggie's Farm," the underrated love songs "She Belongs to Me" and "Love Minus Zero/No Limit," and "Mr. Tambourine Man." The Byrds soon recorded "Mr. Tambourine Man," a top American and British hit, as the first folk-rock song. Dylan's brief May 1965 tour of Great Britain was documented by filmmaker D. A. Pennebaker and released as the film *Don't Look Back* in May 1967. By now an international celebrity, Dylan was being hailed by critics as the spokesman of his disillusioned and alienated generation.

Already dismayed by the electric rock sound of "Subterranean Homesick Blues," folk fans and critics were positively outraged by the *Highway 61 Revisited* album; "Like a Rolling Stone," a smash American and British hit single; and Dylan's performance at the Newport Folk Festival in June 1965 backed by keyboardist Al Kooper and members of the electrified Paul Butterfield Blues Band. The album, recorded with Kooper and electric guitarist Mike Bloomfield, showcased an unmistakable sound and featured some of Dylan's most startling songwriting efforts. Filled with surreal images, stimulating existential observations, and evocative song-poetry, the album contained a number of classics of 1960s songwriting: "Ballad of a Thin Man," "Queen Jane Approximately," and the masterpiece "Desolation Row." Indeed, the album was remarkably consistent in its high level of songwriting and performance, and effectively made the entire album the unit of Dylan's expression. The quintessential "Like a Rolling Stone," arguably his finest composition, became Dylan's first smash American (as well as British) hit single and established his credibility with a new rock audience. "Positively 4th Street" soon became a smash American and British hit, followed by the minor hit "Please Crawl Out Your Window."

During the summer of 1965, Bob Dylan contacted a Canadian group known as Levon and The Hawks, then touring the United States' East Coast. Between the fall of 1965 and the summer of 1966, the group (Robbie Robertson, Richard Manuel, Rick Danko, Garth Hudson, and Levon Helm), later known simply as The Band, toured internationally with Dylan, although Helm left mid-tour. Dylan's infamous "Royal Albert Hall" concert, actually recorded in Manchester, England, on May 17, 1966, became perhaps the most famous bootleg record of all time and was eventually released in its entirety by Columbia in 1998.

In the summer of 1966, Columbia issued Dylan's *Blonde on Blonde* as one of the first non-anthology double-record sets in rock history. Another masterpiece, the album was recorded with outstanding Nashville sessions musicians such as Wayne Moss, Charlie McCoy, Kenny Buttrey, and Hargus "Pig" Robbins, as well as Al Kooper and The Band's Robbie Robertson. An immensely wide-ranging album in terms of the songwriting, *Blonde on Blonde* yielded four hits with "Rainy Day Women #12 & 35" (a smash American and British hit), "I Want You," "Just Like a Woman," and "Leopard-Skin Pill-Box Hat." Another strikingly consistent set in terms of musical performance and lyrical invention, the album included "Just Like Tom Thumb's Blues," the desolate "Visions of Joanna," the vituperative "Most Likely You'll Go Your Way and I'll Go Mine," and the side-long "Sad Eyed Lady of the Lowlands," ostensibly composed in the studio as the musicians waited.

In late July 1966, Bob Dylan was seriously injured in a motorcycle accident. He subsequently retreated to recuperate amidst a variety of wild and irresponsible rumors. He summoned the members of The Band and rehearsed and recorded with them during his public absence. The recordings, made between June and September of 1967, were somehow pirated and released on so-called "bootleg" albums, most notably *Great White Wonder*, one of the first such records to sell in significant quantities. The material included a number of previously unrecorded Dylan songs such as "Million Dollar Bash," "Lo and Behold!" and "Please, Mrs. Henry." Several of the songs were later recorded by other groups: "Too Much of Nothing" by Peter, Paul and Mary; "The Mighty Quinn" by Manfred Mann; "Million Dollar Bash" by Fairport Convention; and "You Ain't Goin' Nowhere" and "Nothing Was Delivered" by The Byrds on their landmark *Sweetheart of the Rodeo* album. The Band's debut album featured "Tears of Rage," written with Richard Manuel, and "This Wheel's on Fire," written with Rick Danko. The recordings were eventually released in 1975 as *The Basement Tapes*.

Bob Dylan reemerged in January 1968 with an appearance at the Woody Guthrie memorial concert at Carnegie Hall and the release of *John Wesley Harding*, yet another album that befuddled many of his fans. The harsh strident voice was replaced by one that was mellow and pleasing, and the songs contained little of the vituperation and anger of his previous albums. Instead, the songs were concerned with resignation, regeneration, and resurrection, and an almost religious wariness. Moreover, the songs exhibited little of the rock 'n' roll raunch evident earlier. Recorded with Charlie McCoy on bass, Kenny Buttrey on drums, and the assistance of steel guitarist Pete Drake, the album yielded no hit singles, yet featured a number of profoundly moving existential pieces, including "Dear Landlord," "Drifter's Escape," "The Wicked Messenger," and "All Along the Watchtower," later recorded in its definitive version by Jimi Hendrix. The album's final two songs, "Down Along the Cove" and "I'll Be Your Baby Tonight," introduced another stylistic shift fully realized with 1969's *Nashville Skyline*—a decisive move toward country music.

Recorded with the same basic personnel as used earlier (Buttrey, McCoy, and Drake as well as Charlie Daniels), *Nashville Skyline* once again turned critics and fans' heads in confused dismay. Attacked as sentimental and simplistic, the album included a duet with Johnny Cash on "Girl from the North Country" and a number of songs written in a country-pop style. "Lay Lady Lay" became a near-smash American and British hit from the album, which also contained ""I Threw It All Away," "To Be Alone with You," and "Tonight I'll Be Staying Here with You." In June, Dylan appeared in an ABC-TV special recorded at the Grand Ole Opry in Nashville with Johnny Cash. Foregoing the Woodstock Festival, he and The Band headlined late August's Isle of Wight Festival.

The disjointed *Self Portrait* contained a variety of different material, including live recordings from the Isle of Wight with The Band ("Like a Rolling Stone" and "The Mighty Quinn") and cover versions of songs by Paul Simon and Gordon Lightfoot. Universally panned, the album was hastily followed by *New Morning*, which contained ditties such as "If Dogs Run Free," "Time Passes Slowly" and "If Not for You." For several years after *New Morning*, Dylan was largely out of the public eye. Macmillan published his novel *Tarantula* in late 1970, and he appeared at George Harrison's August 1971 Concert for Bangladesh. His only recordings of the period were five songs for *Greatest Hits, Vol. II* and the singles "Watching the River Flow" and "George Jackson," both moderate hits. In 1973, he appeared in a minor role in the Sam Peckinpah–directed film *Pat Garrett and Billy the Kid*, for which he wrote and performed the soundtrack music. The album yielded a major hit with the plaintive "Knockin' on Heaven's Door," but his next album, *Dylan*, consisted of outtakes from the *Self Portrait* sessions such as Jerry Jeff Walker's "Mr. Bojangles" and Joni Mitchell's "Big Yellow Taxi."

After his Columbia contract expired in September 1973, Bob Dylan signed with Asylum Records in November. Bob Dylan was soon back, first with *Planet Waves*, recorded with The Band. Again, Dylan received a critical drubbing, although some of the songs, such as "Going, Going, Gone," "Something There Is about You," and "Forever Young," were finely crafted. In January and February 1974, he toured for the first time in eight years, again with The Band. The tour was an instant sell-out and yielded the double-record set *Before the Flood*.

Resigning with Columbia in August 1974, Bob Dylan convincingly reestablished himself as a powerful songwriter with *Blood on the Tracks*. The album included diverse material, from the vituperative "Idiot Wind" to moving songs such as "Tangled Up in Blue," "Simple Twist of Fate," and "Shelter from the Storm," as well as the epic Western tale "Lily, Rosemary and the Jack of Hearts." In an effort to reestablish himself as a performer, Dylan assembled the Rolling Thunder Revue for engagements in the Northeast in late 1975. Participants varied greatly, with appearances by Roger McGuinn, Joan Baez, Ramblin' Jack Elliott, Ronnie Hawkins, Mick Ronson, and others. The tour culminated in the Dec. 8, 1975, benefit performance at Madison Square Garden for ex-boxer Rubin "Hurricane" Carter, who was alleged to have been unjustly convicted of three N.J. murders in 1974. The companion single, "Hurricane," became a moderate hit, and the tour resumed in the spring of 1976, yielding *Hard Rain*.

Recorded with the assistance of harmony vocalist Emmylou Harris and violinist Scarlet Rivera, Bob Dylan's next album, *Desire*, largely a collaborative effort with Jacques Levy, featured "Romance in Durango" and "Black Diamond Bay." Dylan appeared at The Band's "Last Waltz" at San Francisco's Winterland in November 1976 and released the three-hour, 52-minute movie *Renaldo and Clara*, shot during the Rolling Thunder Revue tour, in early 1978. Written, produced, directed, and coedited by Dylan, the film assembled 56 songs from the tour within a series of confusing and widely careening parables revolving around Renaldo (Dylan), Clara (then-wife Sara), The Woman in White (Joan Baez) and Dylan (Ronnie Hawkins). Greeted by disparaging reviews, the film was later withdrawn for reediting.

Beginning in February 1978, Bob Dylan made his first appearances outside the U.S. in more than 11 years at concerts in Japan, Australia, New Zealand, and Europe. The tour produced *Bob Dylan at Budokan*, recorded in March. At mid-year, the erratic *Street Legal*, with "Changing of the Guard" and "Is Your Love in Vain," was issued to mixed reviews and his subsequent three-month North American tour was the subject of negative criticism.

Bob Dylan next recorded three overtly religious albums that reflected his conversion to Christianity. The best-selling *Slow Train Coming*, recorded with Dire Straits guitarist Mark Knopfler, yielded a major hit with "Gotta Serve Somebody" while containing "When You Gonna Wake Up," "Gonna Change My Way of Thinking," and "When He Returns." *Saved* sold less well, but included two intriguing secular songs, "What Can I Do for You" and "Solid Rock." *Shot of Love* featured "Every Grain of Sand."

Bob Dylan did not record for two years. *Infidels*, released in 1983, was greeted by mixed reviews, hailed by some as a powerful comeback and his best album since *Blood on the Tracks*. Coproduced by Dylan and Mark Knopfler, the album included pointed songs such as "Man of Peace" and "Neighborhood Bully," as well as the gentle "Don't Fall Apart on Me" and the rousing "Sweetheart Like You," his last, albeit minor, hit. His 1984 European tour with Santana yielded *Real Live*. During 1985, he appeared at the Live Aid and inaugural Farm Aid benefits and joined in the recording of the benefit singles "We Are the World" and "Sun City." *Empire Burlesque*, recorded with members of Tom Petty's Heartbreakers, was received equivocally, again acclaimed by some as his strongest album since *Blood on the Tracks*. The album included the ballad "Dark Eyes" and "Emotionally Yours," covered by The O'Jays in 1991. The retrospective boxed-set *Biograph* was greeted enthusiastically, especially by Dylan collectors. The album contained 53 songs recorded between 1962 and 1981, including 18 previously unreleased tracks and three hard-to-find singles, plus a fascinating 36-page booklet written by Cameron Crowe.

In 1986, Dylan conducted his first major American tour in seven years, backed by Tom Petty and The Heartbreakers, the most skilled band he had played with since The Band. Petty and The Heartbreakers also helped record his *Knocked Out Loaded* album, which contained a number of collaborative efforts, including "Got My Mind Made Up" (with Petty), "Under Your Spell" (with Carole Bayer Sager), and "Brownsville Girl" (with playwright Sam Shepard). In the later part of the year, Dylan acted in the movie *Hearts of Fire*, but the film was released in Europe only in 1987 and panned upon U.S. release in 1990. During June 1987, he played six stadium shows with The Grateful Dead that yielded *Dylan and The Dead* in 1989. His 1988 tour was neither well attended nor well received, and *Down in the Groove* failed to sell, despite the assistance of Eric Clapton, Mark Knopfler, and Jerry Garcia and the inclusion of two songs cowritten by Grateful Dead lyricist Robert Hunter.

Bob Dylan contributed to *Folkways: A Vision Shared—A Tribute to Woody Guthrie and Leadbelly* and was inducted into the Rock and Roll Hall of Fame in 1988. He also recorded with George Harrison, Jeff Lynne, Tom Petty, and Roy Orbison as The Traveling Wilburys, contributing "Tweeter and the Monkey Man" and "Congratulations." A second Traveling Wilburys set, without Orbison, was released in 1990. His well-received *Oh Mercy* album, produced by Daniel Lanois and recorded in New Orleans with backing by the Neville Brothers, included "Shooting Star" and "Most of the Time." Lanois also produced 1990's disappointing *Under the Red Sky*, recorded with David Crosby, George Harrison, Al Kooper, and the Vaughan Brothers.

In an effort to thwart long-active bootleggers, Columbia issued *The Bootleg Series—Vols. 1–3* in 1991. The three-CD set contained 58 songs never before officially released, including "Quit Your Lowdown Ways," "She's Your Lover Now," and "Seven Days." Later in the year, Rhino released *I Shall Be Unreleased: The Songs of Bob Dylan*, with selections by Rod Stewart, Joan Baez, Rick Nelson, and Roger McGuinn, among others. In October 1992, "Columbia Records Celebrates the Music of Bob Dylan" was staged at N.Y.'s Madison Square Garden. Musicians who played one or more Dylan songs included Neil Young, George Harrison, Eric Clapton, Tom Petty, Willie Nelson, and Tracy Chapman.

Bob Dylan next recorded two albums of folk and blues material performed solo and acoustically, *Good as I Been to You* and *World Gone Wrong*. He appeared at the Woodstock II concert-festival in Saugerties, N.Y., in August 1994, and recorded a performance with his current band—guitarist John Jackson, multi-instrumentalist Bucky Baxter, bassist Tony Garnier, and drummer Winston Watson—for the MTV cable network series *Unplugged* aired in December. Recordings from the show were released as an album in 1995. In February 1995, Bob Dylan was the subject of the CD-ROM *Bob Dylan: Highway 61 Interactive*, which included several rare early recordings and a brief clip from his 1965 Newport Folk Festival performance.

By late 1995, Bob Dylan was enjoying an amazing revitilization of his career owing, in part, to performing more than 100 engagements a year with his exceptional band. He formed his own record label, Egyptian Records, in 1996 and played before 200,000 fans and Pope John Paul II in Bologna, Italy, in September 1997. That same month, Columbia issued Dylan's *Time Out of Mind*, recorded with Baxter, Garnier, Winston, organist Augie Meyer, blues guitarist Duke Robillard, and guitarist-producer Daniel Lanois. Unequivocally his most engaging work since *Blood on the Tracks*, the album featured a number of incisive, intense, and demanding reflections on the limits of faith, love, and patience in face of life's inevitable failures and disappointments. Outstanding songs included "Standing in the Doorway," "Tryin' to Get to Heaven," "'Til I Fell in Love with You," and "Not Dark Yet." After more than 35 years of recording, including at least four classic albums, Dylan finally won his first Grammy Award for the album. Winner of awards and honors too numerous to list, Dylan was inducted into the Rock and Roll Hall of Fame in 1995 and was a Kennedy Center Honoree in December 1997.

WRITINGS: *Tarantula* (1971); *Writings and Drawings* (1973); *Lyrics, 1962–1985* (1985).

DISC.: BOB DYLAN: *B. D.* (1962); *The Freewheelin' B. D.* (1963); *The Times They Are A-Changin'* (1964); *Another Side of B. D.* (1964); *Bringing It All Back Home* (1965); *Highway 61 Revisited* (1965); *Blonde on Blonde* (1966); *Greatest Hits* (1967); *John Wesley Harding* (1968); *Nashville Skyline* (1969); *Self Portrait* (1970); *New Morning* (1970); *Greatest Hits, Vol. 2* (1971); *Pat Garrett and Billy the Kid* (soundtrack; 1973); *Dylan* (1973); *Blood on the Tracks* (1975) *Desire* (1976); *Hard Rain* (1976); *Street Legal* (1978); *B. D. at Budokan* (1979); *Slow Train Coming* (1979); *Saved* (1980); *Shot of Love* (1981); *Infidels* (1983); *Real Live* (1984) *Empire Burlesque* (1985); *Biograph (1961–1981)* (1985); *B. D./The Times They Are a Changin'* (1986); *Knocked Out Loaded* (1986); *Hearts of Fire* (soundtrack; 1987); *Down in the Groove* (1988); *Oh, Mercy!* (1989); *Under the Red Sky* (1990); *The Bootleg Series, Vols. 1–3 (Rare and Unreleased) 1961–1991* (1991); *Good as I Been to You* (1992); *World Gone Wrong* (1993); *Greatest Hits, Vol. 3* (1994); *MTV Unplugged* (1995); *Highway 61 Interactive* (1995); *Time Out of Mind* (1997); *The Bootleg Series, Vol. 4: Live 1966 The "Royal Albert Hall" Concert* (1998). **BOB DYLAN AND THE BAND:** *The Basement Tapes* (recorded 1967; 1975); *Planet Waves* (1974); *Before the Flood* (1974). **BOB DYLAN AND THE GRATEFUL DEAD:** *Dylan and The Dead* (recorded 1987; 1989). **THE TRAVELING WILBURYS:** *Volume One* (1988); *Volume Three* (1990).

BIBL.: D. Kramer, *B. D.* (1967); D. A. Pennebaker, *B. D.: Don't Look Back* (1968); S. Pickering (ed.), *Dylan: A Commemoration* (1971); A. Scaduto, *B. D.: An Intimate Biography* (1971); T. Thompson, *Positively Main Street: An Unorthodox View of B. D.* (1971); M. Gray, *Song and Dance Man: The Art of Bob Dylan* (1972); C. McGregor, *B. D.: A Retrospective* (1972); *Rolling Stone, Knockin' on Dylan's Door: On the Road in 1974* (1974); S. Pickering, *B. D. Approximately* (1975); S. Shepard, *Rolling Thunder Logbook* (1977); P. Cable, *B. D.: His Unreleased Works* (1978); P. Marchbank (ed.), *B. D. in His Own Words* (1978); A. Rinzler, *B. D.: An Illustrated Record* (1978); L. Sloman, *On the Road with B. D.* (1978); B. Bowden, *Performed Literature: Words and Music by B. D.* (1982); T. Dowley and B. Dunnage, *B. D.: From a Hard Rain to a Slow Train* (1982); J. Herdman, *Voice without Restraint: A Study of B. D.'s Lyrics and Their Background* (1982); J. Cott, *Dylan* (1984); W. Mellers, *A Darker Shade of Pale: A Backdrop to B. D.* (1984); D.

Williams, *B. D.: The Man, the Music, the Message* (1985); W. Hampton, *Guerilla Minstrels: John Lennon, Joe Hill, Woody Guthrie, and B. D.* (1986); R. Shelton *No Direction Home: The Life and Music of B. D.* (1986); B. Spitz, *Dylan: A Biography* (1989); E. M. Thompson and D. Gurman, *The Dylan Companion* (1990); J. Bauldie (ed.), *Wanted Man: In Search of B. D.* (1991); C. Heylin, *Dylan—Behind the Shades: A Biography* (1991); P. Humphries, *Oh No! Not Another Dylan Book* (1991); T. Riley, *Hard Rain: A Dylan Commentary* (1992); P. Williams, *B. D.: Performing Artist: The Middle Years, 1974–1986* (1992); W. McKeen, *B. D.: A Bio-Bibliography* (1993); C. Heylin, *B. D.: The Recording Sessions (1960–1994)* (1996); C. Heylin, *B. D.: A Life in Stolen Moments: Day by Day 1941–1995* (1996); G. Marcus, *Invisible Republic: B. D.'s Basement Tapes* (1997); C. Benson (ed.), *The B. D. Companion* (1998).—**BH**

Dyson, Sir George, English composer and pedagogue; b. Halifax, Yorkshire, May 28, 1883; d. Winchester, Sept. 28, 1964. He was a scholarship student in organ and composition at the Royal Coll. of Music in London (1900–04), and then continued his training in Italy and Germany (1904–08). After serving as music master at Osborne, Marlborough, Rugby, and Wellington, he was director of music at Winchester Coll. (1924–37); he subsequently was director of the Royal Coll. of Music (1938–52). In 1941 he was knighted and in 1953 he was made a Knight Commander of the Royal Victorian Order. He publ. *The New Music* (1924), *The Progress of Music* (1932), and the candid autobiography *Fiddling While Rome Burns: A Musician's Apology* (1954). C. Palmer ed. *Dyson's Delight: An Anthology of Sir George Dyson's Writings and Talks on Music* (London, 1989).

WORKS: Sym. (1937); Violin Concerto (1943); 2 concerti for Strings (1949); chamber music; piano pieces; cantatas: *In Honour of the City* (1928), *The Canterbury Pilgrims* (1931; overture perf. as *At the Tabard Inn*, 1946), *St. Paul's Voyage to Melita* (1933), and *Quo Vadis?* (1939); songs; pedagogical pieces.

BIBL.: C. Palmer, *G. D.: A Centenary Appreciation* (Borough Green, 1984).—**NS/LK/DM**

Dyson, Willard, jazz drummer; b. Berkeley, Calif., July 22, 1962. He has been playing the drums since receiving his first set in fifth grade. He sang in the church choir throughout junior and senior high school and received a scholarship to participate in the Young Musicians Program at the Univ. of Calif. at Berkeley. He took a B.A. in Percussion Performance from Calif. State Hayward Univ. and a M.M. in Jazz and Commercial Music from the Manhattan School of Music in N.Y.C., where he moved in 1986. He has worked with Regina Belle, with whom he toured the U.S., Japan, and Europe, as well as appearing on the Tonight Show, Soul Train, The Arsenio Hall Show, Good Morning America, and BET. He has performed at the New Zealand, JVC, Playboy, and Essence Music festivals. He has also worked with Grady Tate, Jimmy Scott, The New York Voices, Dakota Staton, and Cassandra Wilson. He toured the U.S. and Europe with Charlie Hunter's group Pound for Pound in 1998 (which recorded one title on the CD *Blue Note Salutes Motown*). He is also very active in the jazz clubs of N.Y.C., and plays in various Broadway and Off-Broadway shows.—**LP**

Dzegelenok, Alexander (Mikhailovich),
Russian composer; b. Moscow, Aug. 24, 1891; d. there,
Jan. 31, 1969. He studied piano (diploma, 1914) and
composition (with Koreshchenko, 1918) at the Music
and Drama School of the Moscow Phil. Soc. In 1919 he
organized the Moscow People's Cons., serving as its
director (1920–21). He then taught piano at the Moscow
Technical School of Music (1926–34).

WORKS: DRAMATIC: *Niyazgyul,* opera (1941); film
scores. **ORCH.:** *Egipet* (Egypt; 1921); 2 cello concertos (1929,
1936); *Chapayev,* march-ballad (1933; also for Band, 1938); *Na
golubom ozere* (On the Blue Sea; 1936); Sinfonia (1944); *Vostoch-
naya syuita* (Eastern Suite, 1951). **B a n d :** *Geroicheskaya syuita*
(1948); *Prazdnichnaya uvertyura* (Festival Overture; 1948); *Stal-
ingradskaya bitva* (The Battle of Stalingrad; 1950); *Muzhestvo*
(Courage), sym. (1972); many other pieces; arrangements.
CHAMBER: Piano Trio (1926); *2 Pieces* for Violin and Piano
(1933); *Poeme-paysage* for Violin and Piano (1953). **P i a n o :**
March-Humoresque (1924); *Humoresque* (1925); *Poem* (1925); *Mazurka* (1925). **VOCAL:** Songs.—NS/LK/DM

Dzerzhinsky, Ivan (Ivanovich), Russian composer; b. Tambov, April 9, 1909; d. Leningrad, Jan. 18,
1978. He went to Moscow and studied piano with
Yavorsky at the First Music School (1925–29) and composition with Gnessin at the Gnessin Music School
(1929–30). He then went to Leningrad to pursue training
in composition with Popov and Riazanov at the Central
Music School (1930–32) and with Asafiev at the Cons.
(1932–34). While still a student, he composed his first
opera, *Tikhiy Don* (Quiet Flows the Don). After its failure
in an opera competition, he sought the assistance of
Shostakovich, who helped him to revamp the score. It
received its premiere in Leningrad on Oct. 22, 1935.
After Stalin attended a performance of the work in
Moscow on Jan. 17, 1936, the Soviet propaganda machine was set in motion to proclaim it a model for the
development of the so-called "song opera" in the socialist realist manner. Dzerzhinsky's limited compositional
gifts frustrated him in repeating this signal success,
although he continued to compose a large catalog of
music. He held various administrative positions with
the Union of Soviet Composers from 1936, serving on its
central committee from 1948.

WORKS: DRAMATIC: O p e r a : *Tikhiy Don* (Quiet
Flows the Don; 1932–34; Leningrad, Oct. 22, 1935; rev. version,
Leningrad, Nov. 7, 1947); *Podnyataya tselina* (Virgin Soil Up-
turned; Moscow, Oct. 23, 1937; rev. version, Perm, May 30,
1964); *Volochayevskiye dni* (Volochayev Days; 1939); *Groza* (The
Storm; 1940–55; concert perf., Moscow, April 17, 1956); *Krov
naroda* (The Blood of the People; 1941; Orenburg, Jan. 21, 1942);
Nadezhda Svetlova (1942; Orenburg, Sept. 8, 1943); *Metel (v
zimnyuyu noch)* (The Blizzard [on a Winter's Night]), comic
opera (Leningrad, Nov. 24, 1946); *Knyaz-ozero* (The Prince Lake),
folk opera (Leningrad, Oct. 26, 1947); *Daleko ot Moskvï* (Far from
Moscow; Leningrad, July 19, 1954; rev. version, Leningrad, Nov.
8, 1954); *Sudba cheloveka* (The fate of a Man; 1959; Moscow and
Leningrad, Oct. 17, 1961); *Grigori Melekhov* (Leningrad, Nov. 4,
1967). **OTHER:** Incidental music; film scores. **ORCH.:** 3 piano concertos (1932, 1934, 1945); *Povest o partizane* (Tale About
a Partisan), symphonic poem (1934); *Ermak,* symphonic poem
(1949). **OTHER:** Many vocal works; piano pieces.

BIBL.: O. Tompakova, *Ocherk o zhizni i tvorchestve I.I. D.*
(Study of the Life and Work of I.I. D.; Leningrad, 1964); S.
Aksyuk, ed., *I. D.: Stati, vospominaniya* (I. D.: Articles, Reminis-
cences; Moscow, 1988).—NS/LK/DM

Eaglen, Jane, remarkable English soprano; b. Lincoln, April 4, 1960. She was a student of Joseph Ward at the Royal Northern College of Music in Manchester (1978–83). In 1984 she made her debut at the English National Opera in London as Lady Ella in *Patience*, where she served as principal soprano until 1991. She made her first appearance at London's Covent Garden as Berta in *La Barbiere di Siviglia* in 1986. After singing Mimi at the Scottish Opera in Glasgow in 1988, she returned there to sing Brünnhilde in *Die Walküre* in 1991. She first appeared at the London Promenade Concerts as Sieglinde in Act III of *Die Walküre* in 1989. Following her debut at the Vienna State Opera in 1993 as Donna Anna, she made first appearances at Milan's La Scala as Brünnhilde in *Die Walküre*, the Seattle Opera as Norma, and the Opéra de la Bastille in Paris as Amelia in 1994. In 1995 she sang Brünnhilde in *Die Walküre* at the San Francisco Opera. She made her Metropolitan Opera debut in N.Y. as Donna Anna on Jan. 18, 1996, and appeared that same season at the Lyric Opera in Chicago as Brünnhilde in its mounting of the *Ring* cycle and at the Seattle Opera as Turandot. She made her first appearance with the N.Y. Phil. on May 22, 1997, singing the Liebestod from *Tristan und Isolde* under Masur's direction. That same year she returned to the Metropolitan Opera as Turandot. Her return to the Seattle Opera to sing Isolde on Aug. 1, 1998, proved a triumph. In 1999 she returned to the San Francisco Opera and won further acclaim for her portrayal of Bünnhilde in the *Ring* cycle. Eaglen's outstanding vocal gifts have rendered her one of the leading Wagnerian interpreters of her era.—NS/LK/DM

Eagles, The, the most popular American rock band of the 1970s, the group used rock instrumentation to create a distinctive country sound based on easily identifiable melodies, strong vocal harmonies, and engaging lyrics. **Membership:** Glenn Frey, gtr., kybd., voc. (b. Detroit, Mich., Nov. 6, 1948); Don Henley, drm., voc. (b. Gilmer, Tex., July 22, 1947); Bernie Leadon, gtr.,

bjo., mdln., slide and steel gtrs., voc. (b. Minneapolis, Minn., July 19, 1947); Randy Meisner, bs., voc. (b. Scottsbluff, Neb., March 8, 1946). In January 1974 the group added Don Felder, gtr., bjo., pedal steel gtr. (b. Gainesville, Fla., Sept. 21, 1947). Bernie Leadon left in December 1975, to be replaced by Joe Walsh, voc., gtr. (b. Wichita, Kan., Nov. 20, 1947). Randy Meisner left in September 1977, to be replaced by Timothy B. Schmit (b. Sacramento, Calif., Oct. 30, 1947).

As a singles band the Eagles approached the consistency of Creedence Clearwater Revival; as an album band they featured the incisive and affecting songwriting of Don Henley and Glenn Frey, proclaimed as the most successful and prolific rock songwriting pair of the 1970s. Their second album, *Desperado*, had a certain conceptual consistency with its theme of outlaws of the old and new West, yet the group benefited greatly when joined by guitarist Joe Walsh, who added much-needed instrumental punch to their otherwise tame sound. *Hotel California* became the group's masterpiece, with its tough sound, gutsy singing, and powerful lyrics exploring existential and social concerns. However, the album was so successful that the group began disintegrating while attempting to record an equally significant and moving follow-up.

All former members of the Eagles recorded solo albums following the dissolution of the group, but only Don Henley was able to establish a distinctive musical identity. With *Building the Perfect Beast* and *The End of the Innocence*, his songwriting became more mature, provocative, and profound. The Eagles reunited in 1994 for their *Hell Freezes Over* tour and album.

Glenn Frey took piano lessons as a child and played Detroit clubs with his first band, the Subterraneans, often with Bob Seger. He relocated to Calif., and along with Detroit-born singer-songwriter J. D. Souther formed the duo Longbranch-Pennywhistle, recording an album for Amos Records in Los Angeles. Don Henley grew up in Linden, Tex., and played in bands during and after high school. He attended four years of college, but did not graduate, electing to move to Los Angeles with his band Shiloh, who also recorded an album for Amos. Randy Meisner had been an original member of Poco before playing in Rick Nelson's Stone Canyon Band from 1969 to 1971. Bernie Leadon had recorded single albums with Hearts and Flowers and Dillard and Clark before recording two albums with the Flying Burrito Brothers. Frey, Henley, Meisner, and Leadon worked as Linda Ronstadt's backing band in 1970 before forming the Eagles a year later.

Signed to Asylum Records, the Eagles recorded their first album in London. "Take It Easy," written by Frey and Jackson Browne, was the group's first big hit, followed by Henley and Leadon's "Witchy Woman" and Jack Tempchin's "Peaceful Easy Feeling." The debut album also contained "Train Leaves Here This Morning," written by Leadon and Gene Clark, originally included on the first Dillard and Clark album. *Desperado*, also recorded in London, was somewhat of a concept album, based on the theme of the rock band as old-and new- West outlaws. The album yielded only two minor hits with Henley and Frey's classic "Desperado" and David Blue's "Outlaw Man." During 1973 the Eagles successfully toured the United States, but they displayed little instrumental punch.

While recording *On the Border* in early 1974 the Eagles added session musician Don Felder to fill out their sound. Felder had recorded one album with the jazz band Flow. *On the Border* contained three songs written by outside writers—Paul Craft's "Midnight Flyer," Tom Waits's "Ol' 55," and Jack Tempchin's "Already Gone" (a moderate hit)—and included the Eagles' first top hit, the tender and delicate "Best of My Love."

The Eagles' popularity was established with 1975's *One of These Nights*. The album produced the top hit title song and the smash "Lyin' Eyes" (both written by Henley and Frey), and the smash "Take It to the Limit" (written by Meisner, Henley, and Frey). During that year the band toured internationally in support of the album, but by year's end Leadon had departed. Guitarist-vocalist Joe Walsh, formerly with the James Gang and also a solo recording artist, was added to provide a more dynamic, rough-edged quality to the group's sound.

Joe Walsh's contribution was immediately evident on the group's masterwork *Hotel California*. The album's first (top) hit, "New Kid in Town" (by Henley, Frey, and J. D. Souther) resembled the group's earlier hits, but the top hit "Hotel California" (by Felder, Henley, and Frey) and the major hit "Life in the Fast Lane" (by Henley, Frey, and Walsh) exhibited the verve of Walsh's lead-guitar playing. The album also revealed the growing maturity of Henley and Frey's songwriting with "Wasted Time" and "The Last Resort," the latter expressing a deep if pessimistic concern with the environment.

During 1977 the Eagles successfully toured the United States, Great Britain, and Europe. In September Randy Meisner left the group, to be replaced by former Poco bassist-vocalist Tim Schmit. In late 1978 the Eagles scored a major hit with "Please Come Home for Christ-

mas" as they struggled to complete work on the follow-up to *Hotel California*. Finally issued in late 1979, *The Long Run* yielded the top hit "Heartache Tonight" (by Henley, Frey, J. D. Souther, and Bob Seger) and the near-smashes "The Long Run" (by Henley and Frey) and "I Can't Tell You Why" (by Schmit, Henley, and Frey), the latter with lead vocals by Schmit. In September 1980 Glenn Frey informed Don Henley that he was making a solo album, essentially ending the group, although no official announcement was ever made. They managed to put together the double-record set *Eagles Live*, which produced a major hit with Steve Young's "Seven Bridges Road."

Bernie Leadon was the first former Eagle to record an album away from the group. *Natural Progressions*, recorded with guitarist-vocalist Michael Georgiades, was issued in 1977. In 1987 Leadon was a member of the Nitty Gritty Dirt Band. Randy Meisner recorded three albums through 1982, scoring major hits with "Deep Inside My Heart" and "Hearts on Fire" from *One More Song*, and "Never Been in Love." Don Felder managed a moderate hit in 1981 with "Heavy Metal (Takin' a Ride)" from the animated movie *Heavy Metal*, contributed "Never Surrender" to the soundtrack for the 1982 movie *Fast Times at Ridgemont High*, and recorded a solo album in 1983. Timothy Schmit achieved a minor hit with "So Much in Love" (also from *Fast Times at Ridgemont High*) and a major hit with "Boys Night Out" in 1987; he recorded three albums, including 1990's *Tell Me the Truth*. During the 1980s Joe Walsh recorded four albums, hitting with "A Life of Illusion" in 1981 and "Space Age Whiz Kids" in 1983. In 1991 Pyramid Records issued his *Ordinary Average Guy*.

The two principal songwriters of the Eagles, Glenn Frey and Don Henley, were the most active of the former members during the 1980s. Frey collaborated with Jack Tempchin on six songs for his album *No Fun Aloud*, which yielded major to moderate hits with "I Found Somebody," "The One You Love," and "All Those Lies." The album also included "Partytown" and Bob Seger's "That Girl." *The Allnighter* produced a major hit with "Sexy Girl." In 1985 Frey scored a smash hit with "The Heat Is On" from the movie *Beverly Hills Cop*, and a major hit with "Smuggler's Blues" and smash hit with "You Belong to the City," both from the television show *Miami Vice*. He made his acting debut in *Miami Vice* and later appeared in seven episodes of *Wiseguy*. He hit again with "True Love" in 1988 and "Part of Me, Part of You" (from the movie *Thelma and Louise*) in 1991. In 1993 Frey starred in the short-lived CBS private detective series *South of Sunset*; it was canceled after only one episode!

Commercially and artistically, Don Henley was the most successful of the former Eagles in the 1980s. In late 1981 he scored a smash hit with Stevie Nicks on "Leather and Lace" from her *Bella Donna* album. Henley's 1982 *I Can't Stand Still*, was recorded with former James Taylor and Jackson Browne guitarist Danny "Kootch" Kortchmar, who cowrote the smash hit "Dirty Laundry." The album also included "Johnny Can't Read" and "I Can't Stand Still" (minor hits), and "Nobody's Business" and "You Better Hang Up." With the mature and finely crafted *Building the Perfect Beast*, Henley established his own musical identity and broke through commercially. The album yielded four hits with the nostalgic smash "The Boys of Summer," the near-smash "All She Wants to Do Is Dance," and the major hits "Not Enough Love in the World" and "Sunset Grill." "Drivin' with Your Eyes Closed" and "You're Not Drinking Enough" were also on the album.

Don Henley's 1989 album *The End of the Innocence* remained on the charts for nearly three years and produced five hit singles in a year and a half: the moving title ballad, cowritten with Bruce Hornsby; the major hits "The Last Worthless Evening" and, perhaps his finest composition since "Desperado," "The Heart of the Matter"; and the minor hits "How Bad Do You Want It?" and "New York Minute." Touring in 1989 and 1990, Henley scored another smash in 1992 with "Sometimes Love Just Ain't Enough" with Patty Smyth, the lead singer of Scandal. Henley issued a greatest-hits package in 1995, *Actual Miles*, including a new song, "In the Garden of Allah."

In late 1993 Giant Records issued the Eagles tribute album *Common Thread*, with contemporary country artists such as Travis Tritt and Alan Jackson covering Eagles songs. The album proved enormously successful and encouraged the Eagles to reunite. In April 1994 Don Henley, Glenn Frey, Don Felder, Timothy Schmit, and Joe Walsh taped an MTV reunion special backed by a 30-piece orchestra that yielded *Hell Freezes Over* late in the year. In addition to the live cuts, the album included four new songs recorded in the studio, including Henley and Frey's acerbic "Get Over It," a moderate pop hit, and Schmit and Paul Carrack's "Love Will Keep Us Alive," a top easy-listening hit. The Eagles began touring again in May 1994, but the tour was interrupted in October by Frey's surgery for intestinal problems before it resumed in January 1995.

DISC.: LONGBRANCH/PENNYWHISTLE (WITH GLENN FREY): *Longbranch/Pennywhistle* (1969). **SHILOH (WITH DON HENLEY):** *Shiloh* (1970). **HEARTS AND FLOWERS (WITH BERNIE LEADON):** *Of Horses, Kids and Forgotten Women* (1968). **FLOW (WITH DON FELDER):** *Flow* (1970). **THE EAGLES:** *The Eagles* (1972); *Desperado* (1973); *On the Border* (1974); *One of These Nights* (1975); *Greatest Hits, 1971–1975* (1976); *Hotel California* (1976); *The Long Run* (1979); *Eagles Live* (1980); *Greatest Hits, Vol. 2* (1982); *Hell Freezes Over* (1994). **TRIBUTE ALBUM:** *Common Thread: The Songs of the Eagles* (1993). **THE BERNIE LEADON--MICHAEL GEORGIADES BAND:** *Natural Progressions* (1977). **RANDY MEISNER:** *Randy Meisner* (1978); *One More Song* (1980). **GLENN FREY:** *No Fun Aloud* (1982); *The Allnighter* (1984); *Soul Searchin'* (1988); *Strange Weather* (1992); *Glenn Frey Live* (1993); *Solo Collection* (1995). **DON HENLEY:** *I Can't Stand Still* (1982); *Building the Perfect Beast* (1984); *The End of Innocence* (1989); *Actual Miles: Don Henley's Greatest Hits* (1995). **TIMOTHY B. SCHMIT:** *Tell Me the Truth* (1990).

BIBL.: J. Swenson, *The E.* (N.Y., 1981).—BH

Eames, Emma (Hayden), famous American soprano; b. Shanghai, China, Aug. 13, 1865; d. N.Y., June 13, 1952. Her mother, who was her first teacher, took her to America as a child; she then studied with Clara Munger in Boston and with Marchesi in Paris. She made her operatic debut at the Paris Opéra on March 13, 1889, as Juliette in Gounod's *Roméo et Juliette*, singing there until 1891. On April 7, 1891, she made her first appearance at London's Covent Garden as Marguerite, and continued to sing there until 1901. On Nov. 9, 1891, she made her first appearance with the Metropolitan Opera as Elsa in *Lohengrin* during its visit to Chicago. On Dec. 14, 1891, she made her formal debut with the company as Juliette in N.Y. She remained with the Metropolitan until 1909, appearing as Marguerite in *Faust*, Desdemona in *Othello*, Elisabeth in *Tannhäuser*, Aida, Tosca, and Donna Anna in *Don Giovanni*. In 1911–12 she was a member of the Boston Opera, and then retired from the operatic stage. She received the Jubilee Medal from Queen Victoria, and was decorated by the French Academy with the order of Les Palmes Académiques. Her emotional life was turbulent; she married the painter Julian Story in 1891, but they were separated in the midst of a widely publicized scandal; in 1911 she married **Emilio de Gogorza,** but left him too. She publ. an autobiography, *Some Memories and Reflections* (N.Y., 1927).—NS/LK/DM

Earhart, Will, American music educator; b. Franklin, Ohio, April 1, 1871; d. Los Angeles, April 23, 1960. From 1900 to 1912 he was a school supervisor in various localities in Ohio and Ind. In 1912 he went to Pittsburgh, where he was director of music in the public schools (1912–40). He was also founder and head of public school music at the Univ. of Pittsburgh (1913) and a lecturer on music education at the Carnegie Inst. of Technology. He publ. a number of books on musical education, among them *Music in the Public Schools* (1914); with O. McConathy, *Music in Secondary Schools* (1917); *Music to the Listening Ear* (1932); *The Meaning and Teaching of Music* (1935); and with C. Boyd, *Elements of Music Theory* (2 vols., 1938); ed. *Art Songs for High Schools* (1910); and *The School Credit Piano Course* (1918).

BIBL.: F. McKernan, *W. E.: His Life and Contributions to Music Education* (diss., Univ. of Southern Calif., Los Angeles, 1956).—NS/LK/DM

Earth, Wind and Fire, the most successful black crossover band of the 1970s, the group enjoyed extensive popularity beginning with their 1975 album *That's the Way of the World*. **MEMBERSHIP:** Maurice White, drm., voc. (b. Memphis, Tenn., Dec. 19, 1941); Verdine White, bs., voc. (b. Chicago, Ill., July 25, 1951); Philip Bailey, voc., perc. (b. Denver, Colo., May 8, 1951); Andrew Woolfolk, horns (b. Oct. 11, 1950); Ralph Johnson, perc. (b. July 4, 1951). Larry Dunn (born Lawrence Dunhill), kybd. (b. June 19, 1953); Al McKay, gtr., perc. (b. Los Angeles, Feb. 2, 1948), were added by 1974.

Earth, Wind and Fire featured the songwriting of leader-producer-vocalist Maurice White and the stunning falsetto of co-lead vocalist Philip Bailey surrounded by punchy horn playing and exquisite vocal harmonies. Purveyors of dance tunes and gentle ballads, Earth, Wind and Fire promoted spiritual brotherhood through music. Disbanded from 1984 to 1987 for solo projects by White and Bailey, the group did not approach the level of their early success upon reuniting.

Originally conceived as a cooperative musical ensemble by Maurice White in Los Angeles, Earth, Wind and Fire recorded two albums for Warner Bros. before switching to Columbia in 1972. Maurice White had been raised in Chicago and served as a session drummer at Chess Records for three years. Beginning in 1967 he toured with popular jazz pianist Ramsey Lewis for three years before forming the Salty Peppers with his brother, bassist Verdine White. With the core of the White brothers plus percussionist-vocalist Philip Bailey, Earth, Wind and Fire added horn player Andrew Woolfolk and percussionist Ralph Johnson after their Columbia debut. Their third Columbia album, 1974's *Open Our Eyes*, yielded smash R&B hits with "Kalimba Story" and "Mighty Mighty," also a major pop hit, as was "Devotion."

Earth, Wind and Fire began establishing themselves as a major crossover act with 1975's *That's the Way of the World*. The album included the top R&B and pop hit "Shining Star," and the title song, a smash hit in both fields. Their next three, best-selling albums conveyed a sense of spiritual brotherhood through lyrics and music while producing a number of crossover hits. *Gratitude* was comprised mostly of live material and yielded a top R&B and smash pop hit with the studio-recorded "Sing a Song." *Spirit* contained the major pop and smash R&B hits "Getaway" and "Saturday Night," while *All 'n All* included the major hits "Serpentine Fire" (a top R&B hit) and "Fantasy." In 1978 Earth, Wind and Fire scored a smash crossover hit with the Beatles' "Got to Get You into My Life" from the *Sgt. Pepper* movie. They continued the pattern through 1981 with "September," "Boogie Wonderland" (with the Emotions), the classic "After the Love Has Gone," and "Let's Groove." "Fall in Love with Me" and "Magnetic" became the hits from *Electric Universe*, but in 1984 Earth, Wind and Fire disbanded.

During the 1980s Maurice White produced albums for Ramsey Lewis, Jennifer Holliday, Deniece Williams, and Barbra Streisand (*Emotion*) and recorded his debut solo album. Philip Bailey recorded both religious and pop albums, scoring a smash pop and R&B hit in 1984–1985 with "Easy Lover," in duet with Phil Collins.

In 1987 Earth, Wind and Fire reunited with Maurice and Verdine White, Philip Bailey, Andrew Woolfolk, and Ralph Johnson. However, *Touch the World* yielded only minor pop hits with "System of Survival" and "Thinking of You," although both were smash R&B hits. In 1993 the group scored a moderate pop hit with "Sunday Morning" on Reprise. By 1995 only Philip Bailey and Verdine White remained from the original members for touring, although Maurice White continued to record with the group in the studio.

DISC.: *Earth, Wind and Fire* (1971); *The Need of Love* (1971); *Another Time* (1974); *Last Days and Times* (1972); *Head to the Sky* (1973); *Open Our Eyes* (1974); *That's the Way of the World* (1975); *Gratitude* (1975); *Spirit* (1976); *All 'n All* (1977); *Best, Vol. 1* (1978); *I Am* (1979); *Faces* (1980); *Raise!* (1981); *Electric Universe* (1983); *Powerlight* (1983); *Touch the World* (1987); *Best, Vol. 2* (1988); *Heritage* (1990); *The Eternal Dance* (1992); *Millennium* (1993). **PHILIP BAILEY:** *Continuation* (1983); *Chinese Wall* (1984);

Inside Out (1986); *Philip Bailey* (1994). **RELIGIOUS ALBUMS BY PHILIP BAILEY:** *The Wonders of His Love* (1984); *Triumph* (1986); *Family Affair* (1991); *The Best of Philip Bailey: A Gospel Collection* (1991). **MAURICE WHITE:** *Maurice White* (1985).—BH

Easdale, Brian, English composer; b. Manchester, Aug. 10, 1909; d. Oct. 30, 1995. He studied at the Royal Coll. of Music in London (1925- 33). He became interested in theatrical music; wrote 3 operas, *Rapunzel* (1927), *The Corn King* (1935), and *The Sleeping Children* (1951); incidental music to Shakespeare's plays; also several film scores, of which the most successful was *The Red Shoes* (1948). Other works include a Piano Concerto (1938) and several orch. pieces of a descriptive nature (*Dead March*; *The Phoenix*; *Bengal River*; etc.), *Cavatina* for Brass Ensemble (1961), *Missa coventrensis* (1962) for the consecration of Coventry Cathedral, and songs.—NS/LK/DM

East, Michael, English composer; b. c. 1580; d. Lichfield, 1648. He was educated at Cambridge (B.Mus., 1606), and then was a lay clerk at Ely Cathedral (1609–14). By 1618 he was Master of the Choristers at Lichfield Cathedral. He publ. seven vols. of works (1604–38), including anthems, madrigals, consort songs, and fancies for viols, and was a contributor to *The Triumphes of Oriana* (1601).—LK/DM

East, Thomas, English music printer and publisher of Elizabethan madrigals; b. London, c. 1535; d. there, Jan. 1608. He received his license as a printer in 1565; his first musical publication was Byrd's collection *Psalmes, Sonets and Songs of Sadnes and Pietie* (1588); he was also the assignee of Byrd's patent for printing music paper and musical compositions. In 1592 he brought out *The Whole Booke of Psalmes, with their wonted tunes as they are sung in Churches*, composed in 4 parts, containing harmonizations by Allison, Blancks, Cavendish, Cobbold, Dowland, Farmer, Farnaby, Hooper, Johnson, and Kirbye (repub. 1594 and 1604; reprinted in score by the Musical Antiquarian Soc., 1844). This collection is of historic significance, for it was the first to be printed in score rather than in separate partbooks; also for the first time, the tunes were designated by specific names, such as "Kentish" and "Cheshire." Other works printed by East were Yonge's *Musica Transalpina* (1588 and 1597), Byrd's *Songs of Sundrie Natures* (1589), Watson's *Madrigals* (1590), Byrd's *Cantiones Sacrae* (2 books, 1589, 1591), Morley's *Canzonets* (1593), Mundy's *Songs and Psalmes* (1594), Kirbye's *Madrigals* (1596), Wilbye's *Madrigals* (1598), Dowland's *Ayres* (1600), Bateson's *Madrigals* (1603), Michael East's *Madrigals* (1604), Pilkington's *Songs or Ayres* (1605), Byrd's *Gradualia* (1605), and Youll's *Canzonets* (1607).—NS/LK/DM

Eastman, George, prominent American industrialist and philanthropist; b. Waterville, N.Y., July 12, 1854; d. (suicide) Rochester, N.Y., March 14, 1932. He perfected a process for making dry plates for photocopy (1880) and in 1884 founded the Eastman Dry Plate and Film Co., which in 1892 became the Eastman Kodak Co., subsequently one of the leading companies of its kind in the world. A munificent philanthropist, he gave away more than $75 million to various scientific, educational, and cultural organizations. He founded the Eastman School of Music of the Univ. of Rochester (1921), and also endowed the Eastman Theatre. He took his own life after learning that he had cancer.—NS/LK/DM

Easton, Florence (Gertrude), English soprano; b. South Bank, Yorkshire, Oct. 25, 1882; d. N.Y., Aug. 13, 1955. She studied with Agnes Larkcom at the Royal Academy of Music in London and with Elliott Haslam in Paris; in 1903 she made her operatic debut as the Shepherd in *Tannhäuser* with the Moody-Manners Co. in Newcastle upon Tyne; toured the U.S. with Savage's opera company in 1904–05 and 1906–07. She was a member of the Berlin Royal Opera (1907–13) and the Hamburg Opera (1912–16); after singing with the Chicago Grand Opera (1915–17), she made her Metropolitan Opera debut in N.Y. as Santuzza on Dec. 7, 1917, remaining on its roster until 1929; she created the role of Lauretta in *Gianni Schicchi* there in 1918. In 1927 and 1932 she sang at London's Covent Garden and in 1934 appeared at Sadler's Wells Opera in London. She then returned to the Metropolitan Opera in 1936 as Brünnhilde in *Die Walküre* before retiring from the stage. —NS/LK/DM

Easton, Sheena (originally, **Orr, S. Shirley**), petite Scottish pop singer; b. Bellshill, Scotland, April 27, 1959. Sheena Orr was the youngest of six children. Her father worked in a steel mill, and when he died in 1969, her mother worked as a laborer to support the family. She studied to be a speech and drama teacher at the Royal Scottish Academy of Music and Dance and worked in a band evenings to help pay her tuition. She briefly married Sandi Easton, and kept his name.

Shortly after graduation in 1980, the 21-year-old performer became the subject in the BBC documentary series *The Big Time*. The crew followed her on her quest to become a pop star, capturing an audition for EMI and the recording of her debut single. The song, "Modern Girl," was released just before her episode, but topped out only at #56 on the U.K. charts. Her next single, "9 to 5," a pleasant paean about waiting for her baby to come home from work, did considerably better, hitting #3 on the U.K. charts. "Modern Girl" made a comeback in the wake of this success, zooming to #8 and making Easton the first artist since the 1950s to have two simultaneous U.K. Top Ten singles.

The single "9 to 5" came out in the U.S. in 1981, but to avoid confusion with the Dolly Parton hit of the same name, the record company retitled the tune "Morning Train." The single sold a million copies and topped both the pop and adult charts. The U.S. release of "Modern Girl" hit #18. Her eponymous debut album went gold and hit #24. In the wake of this phenomenal start, Easton performed the theme to the James Bond movie *For Your Eyes Only*, which hit #4.

Her sophomore effort *You Could Have Been with Me* came out shortly after her debut. Although the title track reached #15, and the follow-up, "When He

Shines," hit #30, the album did not sell nearly as well as her debut, despite being in release when Easton won the 1981 Best New Artist Grammy. Her next album, *Madness, Money and Music*, did even worse. However, when it looked like Easton was destined to succumb to the Best New Artist curse and flash in the pan, her duet with Kenny Rogers on "We've Got Tonight" topped the country charts and brought her to #6 in the pop charts. Building on this, Easton took her next singles, "Telefone (Long Distance Love Affair)," to #9 and "Almost Over You" to #25, propelling the *Best Kept Secret Album* to a respectable #33. Still, there was a problem with Easton, and that was her wholesome image. People perceived songs like "Morning Train" and "We've Got Tonight" as music for women who subscribed to Phyllis Shafaly. The sweetness in this music was almost painful.

Easton took a step back during 1984 and recorded an album of her greatest hits in Spanish, along with a few other Spanish tunes. Ironically, the album earned her a second Grammy Award for Best Mexican American Performance for a duet with Luis Miguel.

After reassessing her English career, Easton replaced the sweetness with sass and sexuality. The platinum *A Private Heaven* featured the funky tune "Strut," which went to #7 on the charts, and the even funkier "Sugar Walls," a tune written and produced by Prince (as "Alexander Nevermind"). The song was so risqué it earned the ire of the Parents Music Resource Council (PMRC), then at the height of its power trying to get record companies to label recordings based on their content. Needless to say, the song rose high on the charts, reaching #9. The album topped out at #15.

Easton's next album didn't fare nearly so well. *Do You* did reach #40 on the chart and produced one single, the #29 hit "Do You." In 1987, EMI was sold. Easton did not like the new management and managed to get out of her contract. Despite review copies of her next album, *No Sound but a Heart*, being sent out to the press, it never came out in the U.S. Instead, she worked again with Prince, recording "U Got the Look," with him. That tune went to #2. She became part of his entourage, appearing in the tour documentary *Sign o' the Times*. She also returned to acting, working on the hit TV series *Miami Vice*.

In 1989, Easton surfaced again musically with the soulful *The Lover in Me*. The title track, an early production of Kenneth "Babyface" Edmonds, went to #2 pop, topping the R&B charts. Another collaboration with Prince, "101," didn't do well on the pop charts, but hit #2 R&B. She recorded "Arms of Orion" with Prince later in the year for the soundtrack to the movie *Batman*, and the tune hit #36 pop. In 1991, she released *What Comes Naturally*. The title track went to #19. Recognizing her fortunes slipping as a recording artist, Easton took to the stage, touring in a revival of *Man of LaMancha*. By 1992, the play had hit Broadway.

In the 1990s, Easton kept active as a recording artist, cutting a track for the film *Fern Gully* and making an album of standards called *No Strings*, but acting became her mainstay. While she remains a very popular singer in Japan (and continues to release records in that market), her acting and voiceover work in commercials became her mainstays through the 1990s.

DISC.: *Take My Time* (1981); *Sheena Easton* (1981); *You Could Have Been with Me* (1982); *Madness, Money and Music* (1982); *Best Kept Secret* (1983); *A Private Heaven* (1984); *Do You* (1985); *No Sound but a Heart* (1987); *For Your Eyes Only* (1989); *The Lover in Me* (1989); *What Comes Naturally* (1991); *Sheena!* (1992); *No Strings* (1993); *Body and Soul* (1997).—**HB**

Eaton, John (Charles), American composer and teacher; b. Bryn Mawr, Pa., March 30, 1935. He studied composition with Babbitt, Cone, and Sessions at Princeton Univ. (1953–59; B.A., M.F.A.). He also received training in piano from Steuermann, Erich Kahn, and Frank Sheridan. In 1959, 1960, and 1962 he held American Prix de Rome prizes. In 1962 and 1965 he held Guggenheim fellowships. In 1970 he became composer-in-residence at the Ind. Univ. School of Music in Bloomington, where he was assoc. prof. (1971–73) and prof. (1973–91). In 1976–77 he was composer-in-residence at the American Academy in Rome. In 1990 he received the MacArthur Award. He was a prof. at the Univ. of Chicago from 1991. He publ. the book *Involvement with Music: New Music since 1950* (1976). Eaton has made use of various modern resources in his compositions, including electronics. In some pieces, he has employed the Syn-Ket, a synthesizer invented by Paolo Ketoff.

WORKS: DRAMATIC: *Ma Barker*, opera (1957); *Heracles*, opera (1964; Turin, Oct. 10, 1968); *Myshkin*, television opera (1971; Bloomington, Ind., April 23, 1973); *The 3 Graces*, theater piece (1972); *The Lion and Androcles*, children's opera (1973; Indianapolis, May 1, 1974); *Danton and Robespierre*, opera (Bloomington, Ind., April 21, 1978); *The Cry of Clytaemnestra*, opera (1979; Bloomington, Ind., March 1, 1980); *The Tempest*, opera (1983–85; Santa Fe, July 27, 1985); *The Reverend Jim Jones*, opera (1988); *Peer Gynt*, theater piece (1990; Chicago, May 29, 1992); *Let's Get This Show on the Road: An Alternative View of Genesis*, opera (Chicago, Dec. 8, 1993); *Don Quixote*, theater piece (1994). **ORCH.:** *Tertullian Overture* (1958); *Concert Piece for Syn-Ket and Orch.* (1966); Sym. No. 2 (1980–81); *Remembering Rome*, sinfonietta for Strings (Bloomington, Ind., March 1, 1987). **CHAMBER:** String Quartet (1958); *Encore Piece* for Flute and Piano (1959); Trumpet Sonata (1959); *Adagio and Allegro* for Flute, Oboe, and Strings (1960); *Concert Piece 1* for Clarinet and Piano (1960) and *2* for Syn-Ket (1966); *Epigrams* for Clarinet and Piano (1960); *Concert Music* for Clarinet (1961); *Variations* for Flute (1964); *Vibrations* for Flute, 2 Oboes, and 2 Clarinets (1967); *Thoughts for Sonny* for Trumpet (1968); *Sonority Movement* for Flute and 9 Harps (1971); Piano Trio, *In Memoriam Mario Cristini* (1971); *Burlesca* for Tuba and Piano (1981); *Fantasy Romance* for Cello and Piano (1989); *2 Plaudits for Ralph Shapey* for Flute, Oboe, and Cello (1991); *Salome's Flea Circus* for Clarinet and Piano (1994). **Piano:** *Variations* (1957); *Microtonal Fantasy* for 2 Pianos (1965). **VOCAL:** *Song Cycle* for Voice and Piano, after Donne (1956); *Songs for R.P.B.* for Voice, Piano, and Synthesizer (1964); *Thoughts on Rilke* for Soprano, 2 Syn-Kets, Syn-Mill, and Reverberation Plate (1966); *Blind Man's Cry* for Soprano, Syn- Ket, Moog Synthesizer, Syn-Mill, and 2 Tapes (1968); Mass for Soprano, Clarinet, and Synthesizers (1969); *Ajax* for Baritone and Orch. (1972); *Guillen Songs* for Voice and Piano (1974); *Oro* for Voice and Synthesizers (1974); *Land of Lampedusa* for Mezzo-soprano, Soprano, Piano, and Synthesizers (1974); *Lullaby for Estela* for Voice and Piano (1975); Duo for Chorus (1977); *A Greek Vision* for Soprano, Flute, and Electronics (1982); *El Divino Narciso*, cantata for Soprano, Mezzo-soprano,

Tenor, Flute, 2 Percussionists, Cello, and Optional Electronics (1989); *A Packet for Emily and Bill* for Mezzo-soprano or Soprano, Clarinet, and Electronics or Piano (1991); *Notes on Moonlight* for Soprano, Mezzo-soprano, and Chamber Ensemble (1991); *Trumpet Voluntary* for Soprano and Brass Quintet (1991); *Songs of Desperation and Comfort* for Mezzo-soprano and Chamber Orch. (1993; Cleveland, May 9, 1994); *Lettere* for Mezzo-soprano, Flute, Harp, and String Quartet (1994; Chicago, April 21, 1995). **OTHER:** *Soliloquy* for Synthesizer (1967); Duet for Syn-Ket and Synthesizer (1968); *Genesis* for Eaton-Moog Multiple-Touch-Sensitive Keyboard (1992).—**NS/LK/DM**

Ebel, Arnold, German composer, organist, and choral conductor; b. Heide, Holstein, Aug. 15, 1883; d. Berlin, March 4, 1963. He studied at the Univ. of Berlin, and also took private lessons with Max Bruch. From 1909 he was active in Berlin as an organist, choral conductor, and teacher. He served as president of the German Composers' Assn. (1920–33, and again from 1949). He wrote numerous piano pieces and songs, as well as a *Sinfonietta giocosa* for Orch.—**NS/LK/DM**

Ebeling, Johann Georg, German composer; b. Lüneburg, July 8, 1637; d. Stettin, Dec. 4, 1676. He was a pupil of Michael Jacobi, Kantor of the St. Johannis Gymnasium in Lüneburg, and then pursued theological studies at the Univ. of Helmstedt. After serving in the Hamburg collegium musicum (1660–62), he was Kantor of St. Nicolai in Berlin (1662–67). He then was the principal music teacher at the Gymnasium Carolinum in Stettin from 1667 until his death. He collected the hymns of the poet Paul Gerhardt as *Pauli Gerhardi geistliche Andachten* (Berlin, 1666–67; ed. by K. Ameln, Kassel, 1934), consisting of 120 works for domestic devotions, of which 112 were set to his melodies as harmonized in four parts with two optional parts for instruments. The most celebrated work from the collection was *Gib dich zufrieden und sei stille*. He also wrote one of the earliest histories of music, *Archaiologia Orphicae/i.e. Antiquitates musicae* (Stettin, 1675).—**LK/DM**

Eben, Petr, Czech composer, teacher, organist, and pianist; b. Žamberk, Jan. 22, 1929. He studied piano, cello and organ in Český Krumlov, and was active as an organist at St. Vitus Church there while still young. Although his family had embraced the Catholic faith, his father's Jewish heritage prompted the Nazis occupiers of his homeland to expel Eben from school in 1943 and to send him and his family to the Buchenwald concentration camp. After his liberation in 1945, Eben was determined to follow his intention to become a musician. In 1948 he entered the Prague Academy of Music as a piano student of František Rauch. In 1950 he entered the composition class of Pavel Bořkovec there, from which he graduated in 1954. In 1955 he became a lecturer in music history at the Charles Univ. in Prague. Eben's refusal to join the Communist Party and his open espousal of Christianity made his life difficult throughout the long and suffocating years of the Communist regime. He was, however, allowed to serve as a visiting prof. at the Royal Northern Coll. of Music in Manchester in 1978–79. After the Communist regime collapsed in the face of the "velvet revolution" in 1989, Eben finally won recognition as one of his homeland's most important musicians. In 1989 he was made a senior lecturer at the Charles Univ. He became senior lecturer in composition at the Prague Academy of Music in 1990, and in 1991 he was made a prof. there. Eben was named a Chevalier de l'Ordre des Arts et des Lettres of France in 1991, and in 1994 he was awarded an honorary doctorate by the Charles Univ. His 70th birthday in 1999 was the occasion for many tributes to him in his homeland and abroad. As a performing artist, Eben has demonstrated a mastery of organ improvisation. His mastery, in all the major genres, is also found in his compositions. In addition to his outstanding works for organ, he has also composed compelling choral works of a liturgical nature.

WORKS: DRAMATIC: *Faust*, incidental music to Goethe's play (1976); *Hamlet*, incidental music to Shakespeare's play (1977); *Curses and Blessings*, ballet (1983); *Jeremias*, church opera after Stefan Zweig (1996-97). **ORCH.:** 2 organ concertos: No. 1, *Symphonia gregoriana* (1954) and No. 2 (1982); Piano Concerto (1962); *Vox clamantis* for 3 Trumpets and Orch. (1969); *Night Hours*, concertante sym. (1975); *Prague Nocturne: Hommage à W.A. Mozart* (1983); *Improperia* (1995). **CHAMBER:** Oboe Sonata (1950); *Suita balladica* for Cello and Piano (1955); *Sonatina semplice* for Violin or Flute and Piano (1955); *Duetti per due trombe* (1956); *Duettinos* for Soprano Instrument and Piano (1963); *Ordo modalis* for Oboe and Harp (1964); *Quintettto per stromenti a fiato*, wind quintet (1965); *Fantasia vespertina* for Trumpet and Piano (1967); *Variations on Chorale*, brass quintet (1968-69); *Music* for Oboe, Bassoon, and Piano (1970); *Windows* for Trumpet and Organ (1976); *"Wood and Wind"*, sonata for Flute and Marimba (1978); *Tabulatura nova* for Guitar (1979); *Mutationes* for Organ and Piccolo (l980); String Quartet (1981); *Fantasia* for Viola and Organ (l982); *Landscapes of Patmos* for Organ and Percussion (1984); *Opponents* for Clarinet, Piano, and Percussion (1985); Piano Trio (1986); *Risonanza* for Harp (1986); *Tres iubilationes* for 4 Brass Instruments and Organ (1987); Harpsichord Sonata (1988); Nonet (1988); *2 Movements* for Trombone and Organ (1988); Piano Quintet (1991-92); *Apello* for Oboe and Piano (1995). **KEYBOARD: Organ:** *Sunday Music* (1957-59); *Laudes* (1964); 10 chorale overtures (1971); 2 chorale fantasias (1972); *Faust*, 9-part cycle (1979- 80); *Versetti* (1982); *Hommage à Dietrich Buxtehude* (1987); *Job*, 8-part cycle (1987); *Biblical Dances* (1990-91); *2 Festive Preludes* (1992); *Momenti d'organo* (1994); *Versio ritmica* (1995). **Piano:** Sonata (1951); *Differences and Contrasts*, 11 "motion" études (1969); *Letters to Milena* (1990). **VOCAL:** *6 Love Songs* for Medium Voice and Piano (1951); *Missa adventus et quadragesimae* for Men's Chorus and Organ (1952); *The Lover's Magic Spell* for Woman's Voice and Chorus (1957); *Love and Death* for Chorus (1957-58); *6 Songs on Rainer Maria Rilke* for Low Voice and Piano (1961); *Unkind Songs* for Alto and Viola (1963); *Apologia Socratus* for Alto, Baritone, Chorus, Children's Chorus, and Orch. (1967); *Trouvere Mass* for Chorus, Guitar, and Recorders (1968-69); *Cantica Comeniana* for Mixed or Women's Chorus (1970); *Pragensia* for Chamber Chorus and Renaissance Instruments (1972); *Salve Regina* for Chorus (1973); *Greek Dictionary* for Women's Chorus and Harp (1974); *Honor to Charles IV* for Men's Chorus and Orch. (1978); *Missa cum populo* for Chorus, Congregation, 4 Brass Instruments, and Organ (1981-82); *Cantico delle creature* for Chorus (1987); *Prague Te Deum* for Chorus and Brass Instruments or Organ (1990); *Verba sapientiae* for Chorus (1991); *Holy Signs* for Chorus, Wind Ensemble, and Organ (1992–93); *Anno Domini*, oratorio (1998–99).

BIBL.: K. Vondrovicová, *P. E.* (Prague, 1993; 2nd ed., 1995). —NS/LK/DM

Eberhard, Dennis, American composer; b. Cleveland, Dec. 9, 1943. He contracted polio at an early age but persevered in his determination to adapt to his disability. He studied composition at Kent State Univ. (B.M., 1967) and at the Univ. of Ill. at Urbana-Champaign (M.M., 1969; D.M.A., 1973), where he studied with Martirano, Mumma, and Brün and worked with Cage and Hiller, before pursuing postdoctoral studies at the Warsaw Cons. (1973–75) on a Fulbright fellowship. In 1972–73 he was a lecturer at the Univ. of Ill. After serving as an asst. prof. at Western Ill. Univ. (1976–77), he was a visiting prof. at the Univ. of Nebr. (1980). From 1983 to 1987 he was a lecturer at Cleveland State Univ., where he returned as a prof. of music in 1993 and as an adjunct prof. in 1996. In 1991 he was a visiting assoc. prof. at the Oberlin (Ohio) Coll. Cons. of Music. From 1996 to 1998 he was a prof. of music at Kent State Univ. In 1998 he became director of transitional education of Services for Independent Living in Euclid, Ohio, where he works to empower people with disabilities. In 1978 he won the Prix de Rome and held a residency at the American Academy in Rome. He held MacDowell Colony residencies in 1980, 1988, and 1989. In 1982 and 1987 he received NEA grants. He was awarded the Cleveland Arts Prize in 1984, and in 1994 he held the Ore. Bach Festival/Composer's Symposium Fellowship.

WORKS: ORCH.: *Marginals* for Antiphonal Trombone Quartet and 3 String Orch. Groups (1976; Hilversum, Sept. 10, 1977); *Janus Music* for 3 Orchs. (1978; Rome, June 27, 1981); *Ephrata* for 4 Solo Percussion and Orch. (1981; São Paulo, May 17, 1982); *Voix Célestes* for Prepared Organ and Strings (Cleveland, Nov. 14, 1983); *Night Tides* (1983; Cleveland, Feb. 24, 1984); *Elegies* (Cleveland, Nov. 3, 1985); *Lucifer Rising* for Cello and Orch. (1985); *The Bells of Elsinore* (1988; Cleveland, March 9, 1989); *To the End of Dreamtime* for Harp and Orch. (1988–91); *Berceuse* for Clarinet, Harp, and Strings (Shaker Heights, Ohio, April 16, 1989); *The Bird of Four Hundred Voices* for Violin and Orch. (1993; Cleveland, Jan. 23, 1995); *For the Musicians of the Queen: Fanfare and Fugues* (1994; Cleveland, Jan. 12, 1996); *Crooked River Oracle* (Cleveland, May 9, 1996); *Prometheus Wept (August 6, August 9, 1945)* for Strings (Shaker Heights, Ohio, Aug. 4, 1998). **Band:** *Anamorphoses* (Kent, Ohio, June 7, 1967); *Morphos* (Champaign, Ill., May 25, 1973). **CHAMBER:** *Paraphrases* for Woodwind Quintet (Urbana, Ill., Nov. 3, 1968); *Two Poems* for Clarinet and Piano (1970–71; Urbana, Ill., March 4, 1972); *Chamber Music* for 2 Percussion (1971; Urbana, Ill., Nov. 3, 1972); *Verse varied* for Slightly Amplified String Quartet (1971; Urbana, Ill., Nov. 3, 1972); *Dialogues I* for Clarinet, Bass Trombone, Cello, Piano, and Lighting Effects (1973–74; Warsaw, April 8, 1975); *Labyrinth* for Trombone and Piano or Trombone Alone or Piano Alone (1974; Warsaw, April 8, 1975); *Epodie* for Violin, Viola, Cello, Percussion, and Piano (Cleveland, March 19, 1982); *"Especially..."* for Harp (Cleveland, Oct. 14, 1983); *Returning* for Guitar (1987; Cleveland, April 24, 1988); *Endgame* for Clarinet, Bassoon, Horn, 2 Violins, Viola, Cello, and Contrabass (1987; Cleveland, May 9, 1988); *Encontros (Cadenzas & Interludes)* for Harp, Violin, and Cello (Cleveland, May 13, 1990); Suite for Cello (Cleveland, July 15, 1992); *On Celestial Wings* for Violin,

Contrabass, and Piano (1997; Akron, May 8, 1998); *Phantom Dancer* for Viola (1998). **VOCAL:** *Parody* for Soprano and Chamber Ensemble (1972; Urbana, Ill., April 14, 1973); *Veillées* for Mezzo-soprano, Multiple Choirs, and Chamber Ensemble (1974); *Visions of the Moon* for Soprano and Chamber Ensemble (Rome, June 6, 1978); *De Profundis* for Chorus, 16 Flutes, 8 Horns, Organ, and Percussion (1983; Berea, Ohio, Jan. 17, 1987); *Let the Heavens be Glad*, cantata for Chorus, Organ, and Digital Tape (Cleveland, May 17, 1986); *O Sing a New Song to God* for Chorus, Boys' Choir, 3 Trumpets, Harp, Organ, and Percussion (Cleveland, June 19, 1989); *To Catch the Light: Songs of Grieving Children* for Mezzo-soprano, Boy Soprano, Boys' Choir, and Orch. (1995). **T a p e :** *Mariner* (1969–70; Urbana, Ill., March 29, 1971); *Dialogues II* (Warsaw, April 8, 1975); *Ikona* (1975). **—LK/DM**

Eberhardt, Siegfried, German violin pedagogue; b. Frankfurt am Main, March 19, 1883; d. Zwickau, June 29, 1960. He studied violin with Dessau at the Stern Cons. in Berlin, and then with Serato. He was a teacher of violin at the Stern Cons. (1908–33), and then its director (1933–35); then lived in Halle and Lübeck. In 1945 he founded the Hochschule für Theater und Musik in Halle and the Zwickau Academy.

WRITINGS: With C. Flesch, *Der beseelte Violinton* (1910); *Absolute Treffsicherheit auf der Violine* (1911); *Virtuose Violin-Technik* (1921); *Paganinis Geigenhaltung* (1921); *Die Lehre der organischen Geigenhaltung* (1922); with G. Eberhardt, *Der natürliche Weg zur höchsten Virtuosität* (1923–24); *Der Körper in Form und Hemmung* (1926); *Hemmung und Herrschaft auf dem Griffbrett* (1931); *Wiederaufstieg oder Untergang der Kunst der Geigen* (1956).

BIBL.: K. Schröter, *Flesch-E., Naturwidrige oder natürliche Violintechnik?* (Leipzig, 1924).**—NS/LK/DM**

Eberl, Anton (Franz Josef), Austrian pianist and composer; b. Vienna, June 13, 1765; d. there, March 11, 1807. On Feb. 27, 1787, he produced in Vienna the Singspiel *La Marchande des modes*. This was followed by several other stage works, including *Die Zigeuner* (Vienna, 1793). His syms. and piano music were praised by Mozart and Gluck. He made a concert tour with Mozart's widow in 1795. From 1796 to 1799 he lived in St. Petersburg, visiting Russia in 1801, where he gave concerts on Dec. 8, 15, and 28, 1801, presenting the first performances in Russia of Haydn's *The Creation.* He returned to Vienna early in 1802; traveled through Germany in 1806. Besides 4 more stage works, he wrote 2 cantatas, syms., piano concertos, much chamber music, many piano works (especially sonatas), songs, etc.

BIBL.: F. Ewens, *A. E.: Ein Beitrag zur Musikgeschichte in Wien um 1800* (Dresden, 1927; with thematic catalog); A. White, *The Piano Works of A. E. (1765–1807)* (diss., Univ. of Wisc., 1971). **—NS/LK/DM**

Eberlin, Daniel, German violinist and composer; b. Nuremberg (baptized), Dec. 4, 1647; d. probably in Kassel, between Dec. 1713 and July 5, 1715. He was a treble in the Gotha Hofkapelle. After studies with Adam Drese in Jena, he was in the service of Duke Johann Georg of Saxe-Eisenach. Following a sojourn in Rome, he was active as a violinist and composer in Eisenach (1671–73), returning there as Kapellmeister of the

Hofkapelle (1675–78). After serving as Kapellmeister of the Kassel Hofkapelle (from 1678), he resumed his post as Kapellmeister of the Eisenach Hofkapelle about 1685. In 1691–92 he served as master of the mint. By 1705 he was in Kassel as captain of the militia. Eberlin was held in high esteem as both a violinist and composer. Only a few of his vocal works are extant. His son-in-law was **Georg Phillipp Telemann.—LK/DM**

Eberlin (Eberle), Johann Ernst, German composer; b. Jettingen, Bavaria, March 27, 1702; d. Salzburg, June 19, 1762. He settled in Salzburg, where he studied at the Benedictine Univ. (1721–23). He was fourth organist (1726–29) and principal organist and choirmaster (1727–49) at the Cathedral, then court and cathedral Kapellmeister (1749–62). **Anton Adlgasser** was his pupil and son-in-law. Among his compositions are a pastoral play, *Daphne* (1758), 61 school plays, intermezzos, 3 syms., much keyboard music (especially for organ), and much sacred music, including 21 oratorios and about 70 masses.

BIBL.: M. Cuvay-Schneider, *Die Instrumentalwerke J.E. E.s* (diss., Univ. of Salzburg, 1975).**—NS/LK/DM**

Ebert, (Anton) Carl, noted German opera producer and administrator; b. Berlin, Feb. 20, 1887; d. Santa Monica, Calif., May 14, 1980. He studied acting with Max Reinhardt; then appeared in theaters in Berlin and Frankfurt am Main. In 1927 he became general administrator of the State Theater in Darmstadt and began to produce operas there. He then held a similar post at the Berlin City Opera (1931–33); he left Germany when the Nazis came to power. Ebert was one of the founders of the Glyndebourne Festival (1934), serving as its artistic director until 1939; in 1936 he organized the Turkish National School for Opera and Drama in Ankara, serving as its director until 1947; then was again artistic director at Glyndebourne (1947–59). He was also a prof. and head of the opera dept. at the Univ. of Southern Calif., Los Angeles (1948–54). He subsequently was administrator of the Berlin Städtische Opera (1956–61). As a producer, he gave much importance to the fusion of the music with the dramatic action on stage.**—NS/LK/DM**

Eberwein, (Franz) Carl (Adalbert), German violinist and composer, brother of **Traugott (Maximilian) Eberwein;** b. Weimar, Nov. 10, 1786; d. there, March 2, 1868. He received training in music from his father in Weimar, where he was a flutist and then a violinist (from 1803) in the ducal orch. In 1807 he was made music director of Goethe's household. After further studies with Zelter in Berlin (1808–09), he returned to Weimar and served as a chamber musician in the ducal orch. and at the Stadtkirche (1810–18). He then was director of music at the Cathedral (1818–26), and subsequently ducal music director and director of the Court Theater (1826–29). He composed stage works and songs to texts by his friend Goethe. Among his works were the Singspiels *Die Heerschau, Der Gras zu Gleichen,* and *Der Teppichhändler,* cantatas, and chamber music. His autobiographical sketch is included in W. Bode, *Goethes Schauspieler und Musiker* (Berlin, 1912).**—NS/LK/DM**

Eberwein, Traugott (Maximilian), German violinist and composer, brother of **(Franz) Carl (Adalbert) Eberwein;** b. Weimar, Oct. 27, 1775; d. Rudolstadt, Dec. 2, 1831. He studied violin with his father in Weimar, where he joined the ducal orch. as a youth. He then studied theory with Kenzen in Frankfurt am Main, violin with Schick in Mainz, and counterpoint with Kittel in Erfurt. In 1793–94 he gave concerts in Germany, France, and Italy, and also studied theory in Naples with Fenaroli. He then became court musician to Prince Ludwig Friedrich von Schwarzburg-Rudolstadt, later becoming one of his chamber musicians (1810) and eventually his Kapellmeister (1817). He wrote the Singspiels *Claudine von Villa Bella* (1815) and *Der Jahrmarkt zu Plundersweilen* (1818), to texts by his friend Goethe, orch. pieces, and sacred works.—NS/LK/DM

Ebner, Wolfgang, German organist and composer; b. Augsburg, 1612; d. Vienna, Feb. 11 or 12, 1665. He settled in Vienna, where he was made organist at St. Stephen's Cathedral in 1634. From 1637 he was active at the imperial court, serving first as organist of the Kapelle and then as Cathedral Kapellmeister (from 1663). He also was court ballet composer. With Froberger, he was influential in establishing the Viennese keyboard style of his day, notable for its fusion of German, French, and English styles. His most celebrated work was a set of 36 harpsichord variations (Prague, 1648), based on a theme by Ferdinand III. He also prepared 15 rules of thoroughbass realization, which were included in a German tr. by J. Herbst in his *Arte prattica & poëtica* (Frankfurt am Main, 1653). The greater portion of his output was destroyed during World War II.—LK/DM

Eccard, Johannes, eminent German composer; b. Mühlhausen, 1553; d. Berlin, 1611. He studied at the Mühlhausen Lateinschule. He was a chorister at the Weimar court Kapelle (1567–71) and the Bavarian Hofkapelle in Munich (1571–73), where he studied with Lassus. He was in the service of Jakob Frugger in Augsburg (1577–78), then became a member of the Hofkapelle of Margrave Georg Friedrich of Brandenburg-Ansbach in Königsberg, where he later was made Vice-Kapellmeister (1579) and Kapellmeister (1604); subsequently was Kapellmeister to the Elector of Berlin (from 1608). Eccard was one of the most significant Protestant composers of chorale motets of his day.

WORKS (all publ. in Mühlhausen unless otherwise given): *20 neue christliche Gesäng Ludovici Helmboldi...artlich und lieblich zu singen, und auff allerley Instrumenten der Musik zu spielen* for 4 Voices (1574); *Neue deutsche Lieder* for 4 to 5 Voices, *gantz lieblich zu singen, und auff allerley musicalischen Instrumenten zu gebrauchen* (1578); *Neue Lieder* for 4 to 5 Voices, *gantz lieblich zu singen und auff allerley Instrumenten zu gebrauchen* (Königsberg, 1589); *20 odae sacrae Ludovici Helmboldi I. Harmonicis numeris pro scansione versuum, ornatae et compositae* for 4 Voices (1596); *Der erste Teil geistlicher Lieder auff den Choral oder gemeine Kirchenmelodey durchauss gerichtet* for 5 Voices (Königsberg, 1597); *Der ander Teil geistlicher Lieder auf den Choral oder gemeine Kirchenmelodey durchauss gerichtet* for 5 Voices (Königsberg, 1597); also publications with Joachim à Burck.

BIBL.: G. Reichmann, *J. E.s weltliche Werke* (diss., Univ. of Heidelberg, 1923); A. Grauer, *The Vocal Style of Sixt Dietrich and Johann E. and Their Contributions to Lutheran Church Music* (diss., Univ. of Rochester, 1960).—NS/LK/DM

Eccles, English family of musicians.

(1) Eccles (Eagles), Solomon, English virginalist, violist, and teacher; b. c. 1617; d. London, Jan. 2, 1682. He was born into a musical family. He was active as a musician and teacher until becoming a Quaker about 1660. He then publicly burned his music and instruments and thereafter preached against the evils of music. He wrote a tract entitled *A Musick-lector* (1667).

(2) Eccles (Eagles), Solomon, English bass violinist and composer; b. between 1640 and 1650; d. Guildford (buried), Dec. 1, 1710. He was a member of the King's Private Musick from Aug. 31, 1685, to Aug. 6, 1710. He composed music for a number of plays.

(3) Eccles (Eagles), Henry, English musician, father of **John Eccles**; b. between 1640 and 1650; d. London (buried), March 31, 1711. He became a member of the King's Private Musick on July 17, 1689.

(4) Eccles, Henry, English violinist and composer; b. between 1675 and 1685; d. between 1735 and 1745. He is first mentioned in a concert notice in London in 1705, and later was in the service of the Duke d'Aumont, the French ambassador to London; subsequently he served the Duke in Paris. He publ. under his own name 12 violin sonatas in Paris in 1720; 18 movements were adapted from Valentini's *Allettamenti per camera*, op. 8, and 1 movement from Bonporti's *Invenzioni*, op. 10. He also brought out there several more violin sonatas and 2 flute sonatas in 1723.

(5) Eccles, John, English composer, son of **(3) Henry Eccles (Eagles);** b. probably in London, c. 1668; d. Hampton Wick, Jan. 12, 1735. He became a composer for the United Companies at the Drury Lane Theatre in 1693, and was also a musician-in-ordinary without pay in the King's band. In 1695 he was made music director of the theater company at Lincoln's Inn Fields. He composed numerous songs and other music for plays presented there until his retirement in 1706. He was made one of the King's 24 musicians-in-ordinary in 1696, and was named Master of Musick in 1700. Eccles excelled as a composer of songs for the theater. He composed several important masques and other dramatic works, and also numerous court odes. In addition to his compositions, he also publ. *Theatre Musick, Being a Collection of the Newest Aires for Violin* (London, 1698), *A Collection of Lessons and Aires for the Harpsichord or Spinnett Composed by Mr. J. Eccles, Mr. D. Purcell and Others* (London, 1702), *A Sett of Airs Made for the Queen's Coronation* (London, 1702), and *A Collection of Songs for One, Two and Three Voices* (London, 1704).

WORKS: MASQUES AND OTHER DRAMATIC PIECES (all 1st perf. in London): *Macbeth*, after Shakespeare (Dorset Garden, 1694); *The Rape of Europa* (1694?); *The Loves of Mars and Venus*, after Motteux (perf. in Ravenscroft's *The Anatomist*, Lincoln's Inn Fields, Nov. 1696; with G. Finger); *A Musical Entertainment: Joy to the Youthful Pair* (perf. in Ravenscroft's *The Italian Husband*, Lincoln's Inn Fields, Nov. 1697); *Ixion*, after Ravenscroft (perf. in Ravenscroft's *The Italian Hus-*

band, Lincoln's Inn Fields, Nov. 1697); *Europe's Revels for the Peace*, written for the *Peace of Ryswick*, after Motteux (Lincoln's Inn Fields, Nov. 1697); *Hercules*, after Motteux (perf. in Motteux's *The Novelty*, Lincoln's Inn Fields, June 1698); *Rinaldo and Armida*, after J. Dennis (Lincoln's Inn Fields, Nov. 1698); *Acis and Galatea*, after Motteux (perf. in Motteux's *The Mad Lover*, Lincoln's Inn Fields, Dec.[?] 1700); *The Judgment of Paris, or The Prize of Music*, after Congreve (Dorset Garden, March 1701); *The British Enchanters, or No Magick Like Love*, an adaptation of Lully's *Amadis* (Haymarket, Feb. 1706; with W. Corbett; only 2 songs extant); *Semele*, after Congreve (1707; not perf.). INCIDENTAL MUSIC TO: More than 60 plays, including Dryden's *Troilus and Cressida, or Truth Found Too Late* (1694?), Dryden's *Aureng-Zebe* (1694), and Congreve's *The Way of the World* (Lincoln's Inn Fields, March 1700). OTHER: His odes number about 40, but many have been lost.

BIBL.: J. Jeffreys, *The E. Family* (Enfield, 1951); S. Lincoln, *J. E.: The Last of a Tradition* (diss., Oxford Univ., 1963). **—NS/LK/DM**

Eck, Friedrich Johann (Gerhard), German violinist and composer; b. Schwetzingen, May 25, 1767; d. there, Feb. 22, 1838. He studied violin with Christian Danner. In 1778 he became a supernumerary violinist in the Mannheim Orch., and that same year he removed with the court to Munich to study composition with Peter Winter. He won distinction as a violinist there, serving later as Konzertmeister (1788–1800). Among his works are several violin concertos, a *Première concertante* for 2 Violins and Orch., and a *Concertante* for 2 Violins. His brother, Franz Eck (b. Mannheim, 1774; d. probably in Strasbourg, 1804), was a violinist in the Munich Orch. before pursuing a solo career. In 1803 he went to St. Petersburg, where he served as soloist of the court orch. until his career was derailed by mental illness. Spohr was his pupil.**—LK/DM**

Eckard (Eckardt, Eckart), Johann Gottfried, German pianist and composer; b. Augsburg, Jan. 21, 1735; d. Paris, July 24, 1809. He was a copper engraver by profession and learned music in his spare time. In 1758 he was taken to Paris by the piano manufacturer J. A. Stein, and remained there. He acquired a great facility as a pianist, and gave successful concerts in Paris. In the preface to his album of 6 sonatas he states that his task was to compose music suitable for any keyboard instrument, but the indications of dynamics in the MS show that he had mainly the then-novel piano in view. Mozart admired Eckard's works, and there are traits in Mozart's keyboard music of the Paris period that may be traced to Eckard's usages. A complete ed. of Eckard's works for piano, ed. by E. Reeser and annotated by J. Ligtelijn, was publ. (Amsterdam, 1956).

BIBL.: E. Reeser, *Ein Augsburger Musiker in Paris: J.G. E. (1735-1809)* (Augsburg, 1984).**—NS/LK/DM**

Eckardt, Hans, distinguished German musicologist; b. Magdeburg, Oct. 9, 1905; d. Berlin, Feb. 26, 1969. He studied philology in Leipzig, took courses in musicology with Sachs, Hornbostel, and Schünemann at the Univ. of Berlin, and received his Ph.D. in 1932 at the Univ. of Heidelberg with the diss. *Die Musikanschauung der französischen Romantik* (publ. in Kassel, 1935). He then went to Japan, where he taught at the Imperial Univ. in Fukuoka (1932–35); after studies at the Univ. of Tokyo (1936–37), he served as director of the Japanese-German Research Inst. of Cultural History in Kyoto (1938–45) and was a teacher at St. Thomas's Philosophical Coll. there (1946–47). Upon his return to Germany, he completed his Habilitation in 1954 at the Free Univ. of Berlin with his *Das Kokonchomonshû des Tachibana Narisve als musikgeschichtliche Quelle* (publ. in Wiesbaden, 1956), joining its faculty as a lecturer in 1958 and as a prof. in 1964. He was an authority on Japanese music, and contributed many articles to both Japanese and German publications.**—NS/LK/DM**

Eckelt, Johann Valentin, German organist, music theorist, and composer; b. Werningshausen, near Erfurt (baptized), May 8, 1673; d. Sondershausen, Dec. 18, 1732. He was a pupil of Johann Pachelbel in Erfurt. In 1697 he became organist in Wernigrode, and about 1701 in Sondershausen. He amassed a valuable library, which was acquired by Gerber. Eckelt's writings, as well as a Passion, sacred arias, and instrumental pieces, are not extant.**—NS/LK/DM**

Eckerberg, (Axel) Sixten (Lennart), Swedish conductor, pianist, and composer; b. Hjältevad, Sept. 5, 1909; d. Göteborg, April 9, 1991. After training at the Stockholm Cons. (1927-32), he studied conducting with Weingartner in Basel (1932–34) and piano with Sauer in Vienna and Philipp in Paris. From 1937 to 1969 he was chief conductor of the Göteborg Radio Orch. His autobiography was publ. as *Musiken och mitt lif* (Stockholm, 1970). In his compositions, his contrapuntal writing tended toward the austere with occasional impressionist elements.

WORKS: DRAMATIC: *Ånger*, musical (1972; Swedish Radio, July 22, 1975); *Det stora bankränet*, opera (1975); *Uppståndelse*, opera (1975-76). **ORCH.:** *Melodi* for Piano and Strings (1935); 3 syms. (1941; 1943–45; 1966); *Sommarmusik* (1941); *Sub luna* (1942); 3 piano concertos (1943, 1949, 1971); *Visione* (1961); Piano Concertino (1962); *La danza della vita* (1970); *Promenade Suite* for Winds and Percussion (1971); *Sagan om asarna* (1971); *Serenade* (1972); *Skogssuset* (1973); Cello Concerto (1974). **OTHER:** *Nocturne* for Alto and Orch. (1970–71); chamber music; piano pieces.**—NS/LK/DM**

Eckert, Karl (Anton Florian), German composer and conductor; b. Potsdam, Dec. 7, 1820; d. Berlin, Oct. 14, 1879. At the age of 6 he was considered a prodigy. The poet F. Förster became interested in him and sent him to the best teachers. He studied piano with Rechenberg and Greulich, violin with Botticher and Ries, and composition with Rungenhagen in Berlin. At the age of 10 he wrote an opera, *Das Fischermädchen* and at 13, an oratorio, *Ruth*. After completing his training with Mendelssohn in Leipzig, he began his career as a conductor at the Berlin Royal Opera, where his opera *Das Käthchen von Nürnberg* was premiered in 1837. With the outbreak of revolution in 1848, he went to the Netherlands and Belgium. He then conducted at the

Théâtre-Italien in Paris (1851–53), and also toured the U.S. as an accompanist to Henriette Sontag (1852). He was conductor of the Vienna Court Opera (1853–60) and of the Vienna Phil. (1854–60). After serving as conductor of the Stuttgart Court Opera (1860–67), he was called to Berlin in 1869 to succeed Heinrich Dorn as conductor of the Royal Opera. Unlike Dorn, Eckert was a friend and champion of Wagner. Although he composed several ambitious works, his music met with little success. His songs, however, proved popular; of these, the "Swiss Echo Song" is best known.

WORKS: DRAMATIC Opera: *Das Fischermädchen* (1830); *Das Käthchen von Nürnberg* (Berlin, 1837); *Der Laborant im Riesengebirge* (1838); *Scharlatan* (Königsberg and Berlin, 1840); *Wilhelm von Oranien* (Berlin, 1846). **OTHER:** Oratorios; Cello Concerto; songs.—**NS/LK/DM**

Eckert, Rinde, American avant-garde vocalist, librettist, and composer; b. Mankato, Minn., Sept. 20, 1951. He studied at the Univ. of Iowa (B.M., 1973) and Yale Univ. (M.M., 1975), then was on the faculty of the Cornish Inst. (1980–82) and resident stage director of the Cornish Opera Theater. Since 1980 he has worked primarily with the composer Paul Dresher, and is principal performer and collaborator on their American opera trilogy (*Slow Fire* [1985–88], *Power Failure* [1989], and *Pioneers*). He was also principal performer and collaborator on the *How Trilogy* with George Coates Performance Works (*The Way of How* [1981], *are are* [1983], and *Seehear* [1984]; music by Dresher). Other works with Dresher include *Was Are/Will Be* (1983–85), *Shelf Life* (1987, with choreographer Margaret Jenkins), and *Secret House* (1990, with the Oberlin Dance Collective). His intense vocal style indicates both classical and rock training; his libretti are complex explorations, drenched with verbal paradox, of the pressure and instability of contemporary life. Among his own musical compositions are a radio opera, *Shoot the Moving Things* (1987), *Shorebirds Atlantic* for Voice, Harmonica, and Tape (1987), and *Dry Land Divine* for Voice, Accordion, Harmonica, and Electronics (1988).—**NS/LK/DM**

Eckhard, Jacob, German-American organist and composer; b. Eschwege, Hesse, Nov. 24, 1757; d. Charleston, S.C., Nov. 10, 1833. He went to the U.S. in 1776 and settled in Richmond, Va. In 1786 he was organist of St. John's Lutheran Church in Charleston; in 1809 received the post of organist at St. Michael's Episcopal Church. He publ. a hymn book (Boston, 1816), and also wrote 2 patriotic naval songs, *The Pillar of Glory* and *Rise, Columbia, Brave and Free.*—**NS/LK/DM**

Eckhardt-Gramatté, S(ophie)-C(armen) "Sonia," Russian-born Canadian violinist, pianist, teacher, and composer; b. Moscow, Jan. 6, 1899; d. in a traffic accident in Stuttgart, Dec. 2, 1974. Her mother, a former pupil of Anton and Nikolai Rubinstein, gave her piano lessons in Paris (1906–08). She then studied violin with Alfred Brun and Guillaume Rémy, piano with S. Chenée, and chamber music with d'Indy and Chevillard at the Paris Cons. (1909–13); while still a student, she gave concerts in Paris, Geneva, and Berlin, appearing as

both a violinist and a pianist; she later received additional violin training from Huberman. In 1920 she married the painter Walter Gramatté; they lived in Barcelona (1924–26), but spent most of their time in Germany, where she toured as a duo pianist with Edwin Fischer in 1925. Her husband died in 1929. During the 1929–30 season, she toured the U.S., settling again in Germany in 1934, where she married the art critic Ferdinand Eckhardt; she assumed the name Eckhardt-Gramatté in 1939. She took additional courses in composition from Max Trapp at Berlin's Preussische Akademie (from 1936). The couple went to Vienna in 1939 and to Winnipeg in 1953. In 1958 she became a naturalized Canadian citizen. Her works are marked by an impressive craftsmanship.

WORKS: ORCH.: 3 piano concertos (1925, 1946, 1967); 2 syms. (1939; Manitoba, 1969–70); *Capriccio concertante* (1940); *Markantes Stück* for 2 Pianos and Orch. (1946–50); Concertino for Strings (1947); Triple Concerto for Trumpet, Clarinet, Bassoon, Strings, and Timpani (1949); Bassoon Concerto (1950); 2 violin concertos (1951, 1952); *Concerto for Orchestra* (1953–54); *Symphony-Concerto* for Piano and Orch. (1966–67). **CHAMBER:** 4 suites for Violin (1922–68); 6 piano suites (1923–52); *10 Caprices* for Violin (1924–34); Concerto for Violin (1925); *6 Caprices* for Piano (1934–36); 3 string quartets (1938; 1943; 1962–64); 2 duos for 2 Violins (1944); Duo for Viola and Cello (1944); Duo for 2 Cellos (1944); Wind Quartet (1946); 2 string trios (1947); *Ruck-Ruck Sonata* for Clarinet and Piano (1947; rev. 1962); Wind Trio (1947); 2 violin sonatas (1950, 1951); *Duo concertante* for Flute and Violin (1956); *Duo concertante* for Cello and Piano (1959); Wind Quintet (1962–63); Nonet (1966); Piano Trio (1967); Woodwind Trio (1967); Concertino for Viola da Gamba and Harpsichord (1971); *Fanfare* for 8 Brasses (1971).

BIBL.: F. Eckhardt, *Music from Within: A Biography of the Composer S. C. E.-G.* (Manitoba, 1985).—**NS/LK/DM**

Eckstein, Pavel, Czech musicologist; b. Opava, April 27, 1911. He studied jurisprudence at Charles Univ. in Prague, graduating in 1935; received his musical education there. During the German occupation (1941–45), he was in a concentration camp in Łódź but survived and returned to Prague, where he became active as an organizer of music festivals, an ed., and a writer on music. From 1969 to 1992 he was artistic advisor of the Prague National Theater, and subsequently was chief dramaturg there from 1992. Among his books are *Czechoslovak Opera* (Prague, 1964) and *The Czechoslovak Contemporary Opera—Die tschechoslowakische zeitgenössische Oper* (Prague, 1967).—**NS/LK/DM**

Eckstine, Billy (actually, **William Clarence Eckstein**), American singer and bandleader; b. Pittsburgh, July 8, 1914; d. there, March 8, 1993. With his rich bass-baritone voice and impeccable enunciation, Eckstine drew upon the influence of such crooners as Bing Crosby and Russ Columbo while taking a more jazz-oriented approach. In jazz circles he is remembered for having led a big band that contributed to the development of bebop, but he achieved his greatest popularity as a ballad singer from the mid-1940s to the early 1950s, when he recorded such hits as "My Foolish Heart," "I

Wanna Be Loved," and "I Apologize."

Eckstine grew up in Pittsburgh and Washington, D.C., and left college to work as a singer. By 1937 he was in Chicago, where he was invited to join the orchestra led by pianist Earl Hines. He stayed with Hines until 1943, recording such popular songs as "Jelly, Jelly" (music and lyrics by Earl Hines and Billy Eckstine) and "Stormy Monday Blues" (music and lyrics by Earl Hines, Billy Eckstine, and Robert Crowder); the latter hit #1 on the R&B charts in November 1942. He left Hines in 1943 and initially worked as a solo act, then in the spring of 1944 organized his own big band, which featured bebop progenitors Dizzy Gillespie and Charlie Parker as well as singer Sarah Vaughan. He signed to DeLuxe Records and released "I Stay in the Mood for You," which entered the R&B charts in September 1944 to become the first of his 12 R&B Top Ten hits through 1952.

In 1945, Eckstine switched to the National Records label, for which he mostly recorded pop ballads, in contrast to the bebop arrangements favored in his band. A revival of the 1930 song "A Cottage for Sale" (music by Willard Robison, lyrics by Larry Conley) became his first pop Top Ten hit in October 1945. He revived "Prisoner of Love" (music by Russ Columbo and Clarence Gaskill, lyrics by Leo Robin), which had been introduced by Russ Columbo in 1931, for a pop Top Ten hit in May 1946.

By 1947, Eckstine was forced to break up his big band, and he signed to newly formed MGM Records as a solo singer. He reached the pop charts with seven singles in 1949 but did not score another major hit until his album *Songs by Billy Eckstine* charted in February 1950, reaching the Top Ten. In June his recording of the movie title song "My Foolish Heart" (music by Victor Young, lyrics by Ned Washington) hit #1 and became a million-seller. It was the first of four straight Top Ten hits for him, the others being a revival of the 1933 song "I Wanna Be Loved" (music by John Green, lyrics by Edward Heyman and Billy Rose) in July 1950; a revival of the 1934 English song "If" (music by Tolchard Evans, lyrics by Robert Hargreaves and Stanley Damerell) in March 1951; and a revival of the 1931 Bing Crosby hit "I Apologize" (music and lyrics by Al Hoffman, Al Goodhart, and Ed Nelson) in May 1951, which became his second million-seller.

Eckstine appeared as himself in the movie musical *Skirts Ahoy!* in May 1952, but he made only one other screen appearance, a minor role in *Let's Do It Again* in 1975. In 1953, after having divorced his first wife, June, and fathered an illegitimate child, he married model and actress Carol Drake, with whom he had four children. They divorced in 1978.

Eckstine's record sales declined after the early 1950s, although he continued to record and to perform successfully in nightclubs and, increasingly, at hotels in Las Vegas. He reached the pop charts in March 1956 with "The Bitter with the Sweet" on RCA; with "Passing Strangers" (music and lyrics by Rita Mann and Mel Mitchell) a duet with Sarah Vaughan, in July 1957; and with "Gigi" (music by Frederick Loewe, lyrics by Alan Jay Lerner) in March 1958, the last two on Mercury

Records.

Eckstine made three albums for Roulette Records in 1959, then returned to Mercury, for which he recorded the album *Don't Worry 'bout Me*, which charted in November 1962. He recorded less frequently after the 1960s, though he maintained a busy touring schedule. His album *Billy Eckstine Sings with Benny Carter* was nominated for a 1987 Grammy Award for Best Jazz Vocal Performance, Male. He continued to perform until he suffered a stroke in 1992. He died of cardiac arrest at 78 in 1993.

DISC.: "I Want to Talk About You" (1944); "Duke, the Blues and Me" (1945); "My Deep Blue Dream" (1945); "Prisoner of Love" (1945); "You Call It Madness" (1945); *Billy Eckstine Sings* (1950); "Tenderly" (1952); "Blues for Sale" (1954); "Mister B with a Beat" (1955); *Basie and Eckstine, Inc.* (1959); *Billy and Sarah* (1959); *At Basin St. East* (1961); *Billy Eckstine and Quincy Jones* (1961); *Billy Eckstine Sings with Benny Carter* (1986).

BIBL.: L. G. Feather, *The Pleasures of Jazz* (N.Y., 1976); L. Gourse, *Louis' Children* (1984); M. Jones, *Talking Jazz* (Basingstoke, England, 1987); G. Simon, *The Big Bands* (N.Y., 1978); D. Travis, *Autobiography of Black Jazz* (Chicago, Ill., 1983).—**WR**

Écorcheville, Jules (Armand Joseph), French writer on music; b. Paris, July 17, 1872; d. in a battle in Perthes-lès-Hurlus, Feb. 19, 1915. He was a pupil of Franck (1887–90), then studied literature and art history at the Sorbonne (bachelier ès lettres, 1891; licencié ès lettres, 1894; Ph.D., 1906, with the diss. *Vingt suites d'orchestre du XVIIᵉ siècle français*; publ. in Paris and Berlin, 1906; suppl. diss., 1906, *De Lulli à Rameau, 1690–1730: L'Esthétique musicale*; publ. in Paris, 1906); he also studied musicology with Riemann at the Univ. of Leipzig (1905). He was active as a writer on the history and aesthetics of music. He was ed. of the *Mercure musical et bulletin français de la S.I.M.* (and its successors) from 1907, he ed. *Actes d'État-civil de musiciens insinués au Chatelet de Paris* (1539–1650) (Paris, 1907), and also prepared a *Catalogue du fonds de musique ancienne de la Bibliothèque Nationale* (some 10,000 items projected in 10 vols., of which only 8 were publ.).

BIBL.: L. Laloy, L. de la Laurencie, and E. Vuillermoz, *Le Tombeau de J. É.: Suivi de lettres inédites* (Paris, 1916). —**NS/LK/DM**

Eda-Pierre, Christiane, esteemed French soprano; b. Fort-de-France, Martinique, March 24, 1932. She studied at the Paris Cons., graduating with 3 premiers prix in 1957. In 1958 she made her operatic debut in Nice as Leila in *Les Pêcheurs de perles*; after singing Pamina at the Aix-en-Provence Festival (1959), she went to Paris and made debuts at the Opéra-Comique (as Lakmé, 1961) and the Opéra (as Lucia di Lammermoor, 1962). In 1966 she made her first appearance at London's Covent Garden as Teresa in *Benvenuto Cellini*. She appeared as Mozart's Countess with the Paris Opéra during its visit to N.Y. in 1976. On April 3, 1980, she made her Metropolitan Opera debut in N.Y. as Mozart's Constanze, and returned there for the 1981–82 season. In 1983 she created the role of the Angel in Messiaen's *St. François d'Assise* in Paris. She also served as a prof. of voice at the Paris Cons. (from 1977). Among her other admired roles were Rameau's Dardanus, the Queen of the Night, Berlioz's Hero, Zerbinetta, Gilda, and Milhaud's Médée.—NS/LK/DM

Eddy, Duane, rock 'n' roll's best-selling instrumentalist, inventor of the "twangy" guitar style; b. Corning, N.Y., April 26, 1938. Duane Eddy started playing guitar at age five and moved with his family to the Phoenix, Ariz., area at 13. At 16 he left high school and obtained a Chet Atkins-model Gretsch guitar, performing locally and meeting multi-instrumentalist Al Casey in 1955. While performing with Casey's group, Eddy devised the technique of playing lead on his guitar's bass strings to produce a low, reverberant "twangy" sound. In 1957 he met disc jockey Lee Hazlewood, who also wrote songs, published music, produced records and ran a recording studio. Eddy recorded "Movin' and Groovin'", a song co-written with Hazlewood, with studio musicians dubbed The Rebels. Forwarded to Dick Clark, the song won Eddy a recording contract with Jamie Records.

The smash instrumental hit "Rebel Rouser," written by Eddy and Hazlewood, launched Duane Eddy's popular recording career. Recording with studio aces such as Al Casey; pianist Larry Knechtel; and saxophonists Plas Johnson, Jim Horn, and Steve Douglas, he scored a series of major pop instrumental hits on Jamie with "Ramrod," "Cannonball," "The Lonely One," the classic "Forty Miles of Bad Road," and "Peter Gunn." In 1960 Eddy toured Great Britain and made a cameo appearance in the film *Because They're Young,* scoring a smash hit with the title song, which featured one of the first uses of horns and strings on an instrumental rock single.

By 1962 Duane Eddy had left Lee Hazlewood and switched to RCA Records, where he achieved a moderate hit with an instrumental version of "The Ballad of Paladin," the theme for the CBS-television western *Have Gun, Will Travel,* in which he appeared. He also managed hits with two songs recorded with the intrusive female chorus dubbed The Rebelettes (actually Darlene Love and The Blossoms), "(Dance with The) Guitar Man" and "Boss Guitar." Eddy continued to record for RCA, Colpix and Reprise through the 1960s with little success. He appeared in a straight dramatic role in the 1968 motorcycle movie *The Savage Seven* and later moved to Calif. He backed B. J. Thomas's 1972 hit "Rock and Roll Lullaby" and produced Phil Everly's 1973 album *Star Spangled Springer.* He moved to Lake Tahoe in 1976 and scored a British-only hit with "Play Me Like You Play Your Guitar" in 1975 and a country-only hit in 1977 with "You Are My Sunshine," backed by Waylon Jennings and Willie Nelson.

Duane Eddy returned to live performance in 1983, backed by Ry Cooder and Steve Douglas. He moved to Nashville in 1985, and the following year managed a moderate hit with "Peter Gunn," recorded with the British band The Art of Noise. During 1987 he recorded *Duane Eddy* for Capitol with George Harrison, Paul McCartney, John Fogerty, Jeff Lynne, and sessions guitarists Steve Cropper, David Lindley, James Burton, and

Ry Cooder, but the album was quickly deleted. Duane Eddy was inducted into the Roll and Roll Hall of Fame in 1994.

DISC.: DUANE EDDY AND THE REBELS: *Have Twangy Guitar, Will Travel* (1958); *Especially for You* (1959); *The Twang's the Thang* (1960); *Plays Songs of Our Heritage* (1960); *$1,000,000 Worth of Twang* (1960); *Have Twangy Guitar, Will Travel* (1959); *Girls! Girls! Girls!* (1961); *$1,000,000 Worth of Twang, Vol. 2* (1962); *Twisting with Duane Eddy* (1962); *Surfin' with Duane Eddy* (1963); *Duane Eddy with The Rebels in Person* (1963); *16 Greatest Hits* (1964). **DUANE EDDY AND THE RE-BELETTES:** *Twangy Guitar-Silky Strings* (1962); *Dance with the Guitar Man* (1963); *Duane Eddy Guitar Man* (1975). **DUANE EDDY:** *Twistin' 'n' Twangin'* (1962); *"Twangs" A Country Song* (1963); *Twangin' Up a Storm* (1963); *Lonely Guitar* (1964); *Water Skiing* (1964); *A- Go-Go* (1965); *Goes Bob Dylan* (1965); *The Biggest Twang of All* (1966); *The Roaring Twangies* (1967); *Duane Eddy* (1987).—BH

Eddy, (Hiram) Clarence, distinguished American organist; b. Greenfield, Mass., June 23, 1851; d. Winnetka, Ill., Jan. 10, 1937. He studied with Dudley Buck in N.Y., and in 1871 went to Berlin to study piano with Loschhorn. He made frequent tours in America and Europe; appeared at the Vienna Exposition of 1873; at the Philadelphia Centennial in 1876; gave a series of 100 organ recitals in Chicago (1879) with completely different programs; appeared at the Chicago Columbian Exposition in 1893, etc. He wrote many pieces for organ. He publ. *The Church and Concert Organist* (2 vols., 1882–85), *The Organ in Church* (1887), and *A Method for Pipe Organ* (1917).—NS/LK/DM

Edel, Yitzhak, Polish-born Israeli composer, choral conductor, and teacher; b. Warsaw, Jan. 1, 1896; d. Tel Aviv, Dec. 14, 1973. He learned to play the violin as a youth, and later pursued training in theory and composition with Rytel and Statkowsky at the Warsaw Cons. (graduated, 1928). Emigrating to Palestine in 1929, he taught and was choir director at the Lewinsky Teacher's Seminary until 1965. His output was profoundly influenced by Jewish folk and liturgical music. Among his works were the orch. pieces *Capriccio* (1948), *Israeli Dance* (1950), and *Sinfonietta rusticana* (1969), chamber music, piano pieces, and various choral works, including the folk cantata *Lamitnadvim ba'am* (To the People's Volunteers) for Tenor, Chorus, and Orch. (1957), songs, and folk song arrangements.—NS/LK/DM

Edelmann, Jean-Frédéric, famous Alsatian harpsichordist, pianist, composer, and teacher; b. Strasbourg, May 5, 1749; d. (executed by guillotine) Paris, July 17, 1794. He studied law at the Univ. of Strasbourg (matriculated 1770). He went to Paris about 1774, where he gained distinction as a performer, teacher, and composer. His students included Jean- Louis Adam and Méhul. His life took a tempestuous and ultimately tragic turn after he joined the Jacobin cause. Returning to Strasbourg in 1789, he was appointed administrator of the Lower Rhine. However, he soon fell out with his former friend Philippe-Frédéric Dietrich, the mayor of Strasbourg. Edelmann assisted in bringing about his arrest, trial, and execution in 1793. After further Jacobin intrigues, Edelmann himself became a victim of the Reign of Terror and was executed by guillotine. Through his teaching and compositions, Edelmann helped to make the piano a fashionable instrument in Paris. Many of his keyboard works were publ. in his lifetime. Ironically, his lyric drama *Arianne dans l'isle de Naxos* (1782) was dedicated to Joseph Ignace Guillotin. See R. Benton, "The Instrumental Music of Jean-Frederich Edelmann: A Thematic Catalogue and List of Early Editions," *Fontes Artis Musicae*, XI/2 (1964).

WORKS: DRAMATIC: *La Bergère des Alpes*, scène lyrique (Paris, July 20, 1781); *Ariane dans l'isle de Naxos*, drame lyrique (Opéra, Paris, Sept. 24, 1782); *Diane et l'amour*, opera-ballet (Paris, 1802); *Feu*, ballet (Opéra, Paris, Sept. 24, 1782). **INSTRUMENTAL:** *Six sonates pour le clavecin* and Violin ad libitum, op.1 (Paris, 1775); *Six sonates pour le clavecin* and Violin ad libitum, op.2 (Paris, 1776); *2 divertissements pour le clavecin* and Violin ad libitum, op.3 (Paris, 1776); *Sinfonie pour le clavecin*, accompanied by 2 Violins, 2 Horns, and Cello ad libitum, op.4 (Paris, 1776); 4 *sonates* for Clavecin with Violin ad libitum, op.5 (Paris, 1777); 3 *sonates* for Clavecin with Violin ad libitum, op.6 (Paris, 1778); 2 *sonates* for Clavecin with Violin ad libitum, op.7 (Paris, 1779); 3 *sonates* for Clavecin with Violin ad libitum, op.8 (Paris, 1779; No. 2 composed by Edelmann's sister); 4 *quatuor* for Clavecin, 2 Violins, and Viola, op.9 (Paris, 1781); 4 *sonates* for Clavecin with Violin ad libitum, op.10 (Paris, 1782); Concerto for Clavecin, 2 Violins, 2 Oboes, 2 Horns, and Bass ad libitum, op.12 (Paris, 1782); 4 *sonates en quatuor* for Clavecin, accompanied by 2 Violins with Bass ad libitum, op.13 (Paris, 1784); 3 concerts for Clavecin, 2 Violins, and Viola, op.14 (Paris, 1785); 4 *divertissements* for Clavecin, 2 Violins, and Viola, op.15 (Paris, 1786); *Airs pour clavecin ou le forte piano*, op.16 (Paris, 1788). **ORATORIO:** *Esther* (Concert Spirituel, Paris, April 8, 1781; not extant).—NS/LK/DM

Edelmann, Otto (Karl), noted Austrian bass-baritone; b. Brünn am Gebirge, near Vienna, Feb. 5, 1917. He studied with Lierhammer and Graarud at the Vienna Academy of Music, making his operatic debut as Mozart's Figaro in Gera in 1937; he then sang in Nuremberg (1938–40). After military service during World War II, he resumed his career as a leading member of the Vienna State Opera from 1947. He also sang at the Bayreuth Festival, the Salzburg Festival, La Scala in Milan, the Hamburg State Opera, the Edinburgh Festival, and other major operatic centers. On Nov. 11, 1954, he made his Metropolitan Opera debut in N.Y. as Hans Sachs, a role in which he particularly excelled; he continued to sing there regularly until 1976. His most famous role was that of Baron Ochs in *Der Rosenkavalier*.

BIBL.: S. M. Schlinke, *O. E.: Ein Meistersinger aus Wien* (Vienna, 1987).—NS/LK/DM

Edelmann, Sergei, remarkable Russian-born pianist; b. Lwow, July 22, 1960. He trained with his father, the head of the piano dept. at the Lwow Cons., then made his public debut at the age of 10 as soloist in Beethoven's 1st Piano Concerto with the Lwow Phil. After emigrating to the U.S. in 1979, he continued his studies with Firkušný at the Juilliard School in N.Y., and

with Claude Frank at the Aspen School of Music. Blessed with an extraordinary virtuoso technique, he is esteemed for his performances of the Romantic repertoire.—NS/LK/DM

Eder, Helmut, Austrian composer and pedagogue; b. Linz, Dec. 26, 1916. He studied at the Linz teacher training inst. (diploma, 1937). In 1938 he entered the Austrian Army. During his service in World War II, he was taken prisoner of war. After his release, he studied with Hindemith in Salzburg (1947, 1950), Orff in Munich (1953–54), and J. N. David in Stuttgart (1954). From 1950 to 1967 he was prof. of theory at the Linz Cons. He subsequently was prof. of composition at the Salzburg Mozarteum from 1967. In 1962 he was awarded the Austrian State Prize. In 1963 he received the Theodor Körner Prize for music. He was awarded the Würdigungspreis in 1972. In 1986 he was made an honorary member of the Austrian Composers Guild.

WORKS: DRAMATIC: Opera: *Ödipus* (1958); *Der Kardinal* (1962); *Die weisse Frau* (1968); *Konjugationen 3*, television opera (1969); *Der Aufstand* (1975); *Georges Dandin oder Der betrogene Ehemann* (1978–79); *Mozart in New York* (1989–90; Salzburg, Aug. 15, 1991). **Ballet:** *Moderner Traum* (Linz, Sept. 29, 1957); *Anamorphose* (1963; Linz, June 22, 1966); *Die Irrfahrten des Odysseus* (1964–65). **ORCH.:** *Präludium und Ricercar* for Strings (1949; Linz, May 16, 1950); 5 syms.: No. 1 (1950), No. 2 (Vienna, Jan. 31, 1962), No. 3 for Strings (1959), No. 4, *Choral* (1973–75; Vienna, Oct. 15, 1977), and No. 5, *Organ* (1979–80; Salzburg, Aug. 13, 1980); *Musica semplice* for Flute, Harpsichord, and Strings (1953); *Tanzreihen*, ballet suite (1954; Linz, Jan. 24, 1956); *Musik* for 2 Trumpets and Strings (1955); Concerto for Piano, 15 Winds, Double Basses, and Percussion (1956); *Pezzo sereno* (1958); *Concerto semiserio* for 2 Pianos and Orch. (1960); Oboe Concerto (1962); 3 violin concertos: No. 1 (1963; Vienna, Feb. 10, 1964), No. 2 for Violin and Strings (1964; Linz, Jan. 31, 1967), and No. 3 (1981–82; Munich, Jan. 21, 1983); *Danza a solatio* (1963; Linz, Jan. 27, 1964); *Concerto a dodici per* [12] *archi* (Vienna, Oct. 22, 1963); *Nil admirari* (1966; Linz, Oct. 2, 1967); *Syntagma* (Vienna, Oct. 6, 1967); Concerto for Bassoon and Chamber Orch. (Vienna, June 4, 1968); *L'Homme armé*, organ concerto (1968-69; Nuremberg, July 5, 1969); *Metamorphosen* for Flute, Oboe, String Quartet, and Orch. (1970; Salzburg, Jan. 31, 1971); *Memento* for Positive Organ, String Quartet, and String Orch. (1970; Bayreuth, May 22, 1971); *Melodia-ritmica* for Strings (Linz, Dec. 13, 1973); *Pastorale* for Strings (Linz, Nov. 30, 1974); *Jubilatio* (Linz, Dec. 26, 1976); *Serenade* for 6 Horns and 46 Strings (1977); Double Concerto for Cello, Double Bass, and Orch. (1977–78; Saarbrücken, May 21, 1979); Cello Concerto (Linz, Sept. 5, 1981); *Concerto A. B.* for Chamber Orch. (1982; Linz, March 17, 1983; also for Orch., 1983; Vienna, March 14, 1984); *Notturni...von Tänzern, Träumen und allerlei Vogelsang* for Flute, Oboe, and Strings (Munich, Sept. 29, 1983); *Haffner Concerto* for Flute and Orch. (1983–84; Salzburg, Jan. 31, 1985); Concertino for Classical Orch. (1984; Graz, April 14, 1986); *Pièce de concert* for Strings (1984); *Schwanengesang* for Cello and Chamber Orch. (Linz, Nov. 22, 1987); *Stracci II*, chamber sym. (Vienna, May 14, 1993). **CHAMBER:** Trio for Violin, Viola, and Cello (Vienna, Jan. 8, 1957); 3 wind quintets: No. 1 (1958; Linz, May 6, 1959), No. 2, *Septuagesima instrumentalis* (1968–69; Mannheim, June 11, 1969), and No. 3, *Begegnung* (1987–88; Berlin, Sept. 29, 1989); *Ottetto breve* for Flute, Oboe, Clarinet, Bassoon, 2 Violins, Viola, and Cello (1960; Vienna, Feb. 12, 1961); *Impressioni* for String Quartet (Linz, Oct. 4, 1966);

Wind Septet, *Hommage à Johannes Kepler* (1970; ORF, Linz, April 16, 1971); Piano Trio (Salzburg, May 24, 1971); *So-no-ro I* for Clarinet, Viola, Piano or Celesta, and Organ (1974; Salzburg, April 23, 1975) and *II* for Clarinet, Bass Clarinet, Cello, Double Bass, Guitar, and Piano (Hamburg, Dec. 1, 1977); *Litzlberg Serenade* for 2 Clarinets, Trumpet, Horn, and Bassoon (1976; Litzlberg, July 29, 1986); *Suite mit intermezzi* for 11 Winds (1979; London, May 29, 1981); 4 Pieces for 2 Violins (1980; Linz, June 14, 1981); 6 Bagatelles for 3 Violins (1980); Clarinet Quintet (1982; Berlin, Feb. 18, 1984); Quartet for Flute and String Trio (1983; Vienna, Jan. 9, 1984); String Quartet (1985); *Aulodie* for Flute, Bassoon or Cello, Double Bass, and Percussion (Cardiff, Nov. 21, 1986); *Gedanken* for Horn, Violin, and Piano (Vienna, April 26, 1993); piano pieces; organ music. **VOCAL:** *Drei Tierlieder* for High Voice and Orch. (1966); *Cadunt umbrae* for Alto, 8 Women's Voices, Orch., and Tape (1973–74; Salzburg, May 22, 1974); *Non sum qualis eram*, oratorio for Soprano, Baritone, Bass, Chorus and Orch. (1975; Salzburg, Dec. 10, 1976); *Divertimento* for Soprano and 2 Orch. Groups (Salzburg, Aug. 14, 1976); *... Missa est* for 3 Soloists, 2 Choruses, and 3 Orch. Groups (Salzburg, Aug. 23, 1986); *Dir, Seele des Weltalls*, cantata for 2 Tenors, Bass, Men's Chorus, and Orch. (Vienna, June 7, 1991); *Gebet und Verzweiflung* for Chorus and Orch. (1992–93); *Herbstgesänge* for Chamber Chorus and 7 Instruments (Vienna, Nov. 25, 1993). **BIBL.:** G. Gruber and G. Kraus, *H. E.* (Vienna, 1988). —NS/LK/DM

Edison, Harry Sweets, blues-flavored jazz trumpeter; b. Columbus, Ohio, Oct. 10, 1915; d. July 27, 1999. His intensely bluesy muted work is a trademark. He was nicknamed "Sweets" by Lester Young while they were working with Count Basie between 1938–50. He began playing trumpet at age 12. As a teenager, he gigged with local bands, then toured with Alphonse Irent's Band (at that time temporarily led by guitarist Anderson Lacy), and also worked with Eddie Johnson's Crackerjacks. In the summer of 1933, he joined Jeter-Pillars' Band in Cleveland and for the next three years toured major Midwest towns with this band. In February 1937, he joined Lucky Millinder, and then from June 1938 until February 1950 worked with Count Basie, except for a stint in an Army band. He provided the vocals on Basie's #1 pop hit, the R&B novelty "Open the Door, Richard" in 1947. After leaving Basie, Edison played in a small group led by Jimmy Rushing before regular tours with J.A.T.P, from September 1950. He joined Buddy Rich's Band early in 1951 and for the next two years worked on and off with Rich including work in Calif. accompanying the *Josephine Baker Revue* in 1953. Remaining on the West Coast, Edison did studio work through most of the 1950s including many sessions with the Nelson Riddle Orch., starting with Frank Sinatra's *Wee Hours* album. He also did club work in the area with his own small ensemble. In September 1958, he moved back to N.Y. where he led his own group during the late 1950s and early 1960s working the jazz club scene, while continuing freelance session work. He worked with George Auld's Band in spring 1964, and later that year toured Europe with J.A.T.P. From the mid- 1960s through Basie's death, he again worked with the Count, occasionally rejoining the band for brief spells (including a 1970 European tour). During the late 1960s, Edison returned to Calif., mainly leading his own small group at Memory Lane, Los Angeles, from 1966–70, while also continuing to freelance with various big bands. He was featured in the film *Jammin' the Blues*. He visited Europe with Count Basie (1970), and undertook several tours of Europe in the late 1970s, some with Eddie "Lockjaw" Davis. Beginning in the 1980s, Edison began to lose some of his facility on the trumpet, leading him to pare back his solo work; still he continued to record and perform through the 1990s.

DISC.: *Harry Edison Quartet* (1953); *Inventive Harry Edison* (1953); *Sweets at the Haig* (1953); *Harry Edison Swings Buck Clayton* (1958); *Swinger* (1958); *Jawbreakers* (1962); *Ben Webster and Sweets Edison* (1962); *Home with Sweets* (1964); *When Lights Are Low* (1965); *Oscar Peterson and Harry Edison* (1974); *Just Friends* (1975); *Edison's Lights* (1976); *Opus Funk* (1976); *Blues for Basie* (1977); *Simply Sweets* (1977); *Swing Summit* (1990); *Swinging for the Count* (1995).—JC/LP

Edlund, Lars, Swedish organist, conductor, teacher, and composer; b. Karlstad, Nov. 6, 1922. He studied in Arvika and at the Stockholm Musikhögskolan (1942–47). After serving as an organist in Tranås and Södertälje (1948–60), he taught aural training at the Stockholm Musikhögskolan until 1971; then devoted himself to performing and composing. He publ. 2 influential books, *Modus novus: Lärobok i fritonal melodiläsning* (New method: Textbook in atonal melody reading: 1963) and *Modus vetus: Gehörstudier i dur/moll-tonalitet* (Old method: Ear training in major/minor tonalities; 1967), which have guided his path as a composer. He won particular distinction for his choral music. Among his works are a chamber opera, *Flickan i ögat* (1979); chamber music, including 2 string quartets (1980–81; 1993); piano pieces; organ music; *Elegi* for Chorus (1971); *Missa Sancti Nicolai* for Soloists, Chorus, and Percussion (Stockholm, July 10, 1979); *Adonai* for Baritone, Chorus, Organ, and Percussion (1983). His son, Mikael Edlund (b. Tranås, Jan. 19, 1950), is also a composer.—NS/LK/DM

Edmonds, Kenneth ("Babyface"), phenomenally successful writer, producer, and singer, and one of the most successful music makers of the 1990s; b. Indianapolis, April 10, 1959. The youngest of six boys, Ken Edmonds picked up a guitar at the age of ten and within a year was playing with two of his brothers at high school dances. By the age of 18, he was recording with the band Manchild and was featured on their hit "Especially for You." He also worked with P-Funk bassist Bootsy Collins, who offhandedly called the young guitarist "Babyface," and the name stuck. In the early 1980s, he started working with the lite-funk band The Deele. He observed that during his featured tune in concert, the nights that he was introduced as Kenny Edmonds, the response was so-so, but the nights he was introduced as Babyface, people screamed. It became his professional moniker from then on.

The drummer in The Deele was Mark "L. A." Reid Rooney (son of Herb Rooney and Brenda Reid of The Exciters). He and Edmonds started collaborating in the studio on projects with other artists (as well as on Babyface's less-than-successful solo debut) in 1987.

They produced The Whispers' biggest hit, "Rock Steady," Sheena Easton's "For the Lover in Me," as well as hits for After 7, a group that featured Reid's cousin and two of Edmonds's brothers. They also wrote the tune "Two Occasions" for The Deele's *Eyes of a Stranger* album. It became the band's only pop hit, reaching #10. Shortly after that, the band broke up.

Reid and Edmonds continued working together, however. They helped engineer the phenomenal early success of Bobby Brown, Whitney Houston, and Pebbles (Reid's wife). With a successful career as a producer well underway, Edmonds went back into the studio for himself. The result, *Tender Love*, became a double-platinum hit. The title track topped the R&B charts (#14 pop), as did "It's No Crime" (#7 pop). "My Kinda Girl" only hit #3 R&B and #30 pop, but the successful producer and songwriter had taken the step to becoming a successful performer in his own right.

The next world to conquer was running a record company. Reid and Edmonds founded LaFace records in 1989. The company became the home to such successful artists as Toni Braxton and TLC.

But Edmonds's primary passion continued to be writing and producing. In 1992, he had a #29 hit with Toni Braxton on the duet "Give You My Heart" from the Eddie Murphy movie *Boomerang*. He set records with work he did with Boys II Men. The Edmonds-written and produced "End of the Road" became one of the biggest singles ever, surpassing Elvis Presley's record of 13 weeks at #1 for "Heartbreak Hotel." The next single, "I'll Make Love to You," surpassed that. The former earned Edmonds, Reid, and their partner Darryl Simmons the Producer of the Year Grammy; the latter earned Edmonds the Grammy for Best R&B Song.

Edmonds returned to the studio for his own new album, releasing it in 1993. *The Cool in You* surpassed *Tender Love*, selling triple platinum (though it only hit #16 on the album charts). He further established his smooth, romantic style of R&B with the #4 gold record "When Can I See You," as well as "Never Keeping Secrets" (#15) and "And Our Feelings" (#21).

In 1995, Edmonds took on the ultimate diva project, producing and writing the bulk of the songs for the soundtrack to the film *Waiting to Exhale*, which included Whitney Houston, Toni Braxton, Aretha Franklin, Mary J. Blige, and Patti LaBelle. The soundtrack topped the album pop charts for five weeks, and the R&B album charts for ten. Nearly every song on the album became a hit, including Brandy's "Sittin' Up in My Room" and "Not Goin' Cry" by Mary J. Blige. Whitney Houston's title track "Exhale (Shoop Shoop)," topped the pop and R&B charts and went platinum. It also won him a Best R&B Song Grammy, one of a dozen for which he was nominated in 1995. As coproducer of Eric Clapton's "Change My World" he earned Record of the Year honors. With 15 separate Grammy nominated recordings to his credit, he also took home Producer of the Year honors.

In 1996, Edmonds stopped working with Reid in the studio, under circumstances neither has yet discussed for publication. Although their creative partnership ended, they continued to run LaFace together.

After all the production work for other artists, he created his next solo album, *The Day*. It entered the charts at #6, sold double-platinum and generated two #6 hits. "Every Time I Close My Eyes," a duet with sax player Kenny G that featured Mariah Carey. His remake of Shalamar's "This Is for the Lover in You" included all the original members of the group and a rap break by L. L. Cool J. He followed that album fairly quickly with his episode of MTV *Unplugged*, with guest appearances by Clapton and Stevie Wonder. That album went gold, but topped out at #106.

In 1997, Edmonds expanded his horizons to film, co-producing the film *Soul Food* and doing the soundtrack. He continues to be one of the most in-demand producers and songwriters in the music industry.

DISC.: *Lovers* (1989); *Tender Lover* (1989); *A Closer Look* (1991); *For the Cool in You* (1993); *Day* (1996); *Kenny "Babyface" Edmonds & Manchild* (1997); *MTV Unplugged NYC 1997* (live; 1997); *Christmas with Babyface* (1998). **K. E. WITH THE DEELE:** *Street Beat* (1984); *Material Thangz* (1985); *Eyes of a Stranger* (1988).—HB

Edmunds, John (actually, **Charles Sterling**), American composer and music scholar; b. San Francisco, June 10, 1913; d. Berkeley, Dec. 9, 1986. He studied with Scalero at the Curtis Inst. of Music in Philadelphia, Piston at Harvard Univ. (M.A., 1941), Harris at Cornell Univ., Luening at Columbia Univ., and Goldsbrough and Dart in England. He taught at Syracuse Univ. (1946–47), and was co-founder of the Campion Soc. in San Francisco (1946–53), notable for its annual Festival of Unfamiliar Music. After serving as head of the Americana collection at the N.Y. Public Library (1957–61), he taught at the Univ. of Calif. at Berkeley (1965–66). In 1951 he held a Fulbright scholarship and in 1969 a Guggenheim fellowship. As a music scholar, Edmunds devoted much time to preparing *The Major Epoch of English Song: The 17th-Century from Dowland to Purcell* (12 vols., 1940–76), an unpublished collection of more than 300 songs arranged for voice and piano as realized from lute tablatures and figured basses. He also publ. *The Garden of the Muses* (N.Y., 1985). As a composer, he was especially successful as a songwriter. Among his other works were masques, ballets, and choral music.—NS/LK/DM

Edson, Lewis, American composer; b. Bridgewater, Mass., Jan. 22, 1748; d. Woodstock, N.Y., 1820. Originally a blacksmith by trade, he became very active as a music teacher. He went to N.Y. in 1776, and in 1817 he moved to Woodstock. With Thomas Seymour he compiled *The New York Collection of Sacred Music*. Among his compositions were the hymn tunes *Bridgewater, Lenox,* and *Greenfield*.—NS/LK/DM

Edvaldsdóttir, Sigrún, Icelandic violinist; b. Reykjavík, Jan. 13, 1967. She commenced violin training when she was 5. She undertook formal studies with Gudný Gudmundsdóttir at the Reykjavík Coll. of Music, graduating at 17 as the youngest person ever with a soloist diploma. She then went to the U.S. to study with

Roland and Almita Amos, and then with Jascha Brodsky and Jaime Laredo at the Curtis Inst. of Music in Philadelphia (B.M., 1988). In 1987 she took second prize in the Leopold Mozart competition in Augsburg; in 1988 she won fifth prize in the Carl Nielsen competition in Denmark; in 1990 she captured the Bronze Medal at the Sibelius Competition in Helsinki. In 1988 she became first violinist of the newly-founded Miami (Fla.) String Quartet. She also pursued a career as a soloist and as a recitalist.—NS/LK/DM

Edwards, Bass (Henry), jazz tuba player, bassist; b. Atlanta, Ga., Feb. 22, 1889; d. N.Y., Aug. 22, 1965. At 14, he began playing in local Odd Fellows' Band, and subsequently studied music at Morris Brown Coll. and Morehouse Coll. in Atlanta. During World War I, Edwards played in U.S. Army Bands, including a spell with Lt. J. Tim Brymn's 350th F.A. Band. From 1919, he played in Philadelphia with various concert orchestras and with the Madarn I. O. Keene Dance Orch. (1919–20). From 1921–25, he played with several dance bands in the Philadelphia-Atlantic City area. In mid-1925, Edwards joined Duke Ellington, but only remained with the band until spring 1926. Edwards then joined Leon Abbey in N.Y. and on a tour of South America during the spring 1927. When he returned to N.Y., he joined the Allie Ross Orch., which played for the *Blackbirds* shows. In May 1929, he joined Noble Sissle's band on brass bass, and sailed to Europe with Sissle. On his return to N.Y., he worked with Fats Waller, James P. Johnson, and Eubie Blake, before rejoining Allie Ross for the *Rhapsody in Black* show. His last major jazz position was with the Charlie Matson Orch. during 1933. He then worked mainly on string bass with various light and classical orchestras, including N.Y. Sym. Band, W.N.Y.C. Sym. Orch., and many others. "Bass" Edwards has often been confused with the N.Y. string bass/tuba player Sumner Leslie "King" Edwards. "King," who worked in Europe with Louis Mitchell, Sam Wooding, etc., was the brother of trumpeter Maceo Edwards.—JC/LP

Edwards, Cliff (actually, **Clifton A.; Ukulele Ike**), American singer and actor; b. Hannibal, Mo., June 14, 1895; d. Hollywood, July 17, 1971. Edwards was a major star in vaudeville and on records in the 1920s. In the late 1920s he moved into film acting, frequently playing character parts through the 1940s. He introduced the songs "Fascinating Rhythm," "Toot, Toot, Tootsie! (Goo'bye)," "Singin' in the Rain," "It's Only a Paper Moon," and "When You Wish upon a Star," the last in the Walt Disney animated film *Pinocchio*. In his later years he was employed primarily by Disney.

Edwards took up playing the ukulele as a newspaper boy to attract and entertain his customers. He went to St. Louis as a teenager and began performing in saloons, then in carnivals, before finally breaking into vaudeville. In Chicago in 1918, working with songwriter/pianist Bob Carleton, he introduced the hit novelty song "Ja-Da." It was there he acquired his nickname, Ukulele Ike, from a waiter who couldn't remember his name. He was part of an act with

singer/dancer Pierce Keegan called "Jazz as Is" and went to N.Y. as part of comedian Joe Frisco's troupe in 1920. His first appearance in the legitimate theater came in *The Mimic World of 1921* (N.Y., Aug. 15, 1921), which ran for 27 performances. In 1922 he introduced "Toot, Toot, Tootsie! (Goo'bye)" in vaudeville, though the song became identified with Al Jolson after Jolson interpolated it into his show *Bombo*.

Edwards reached the pinnacle of success in vaudeville by headlining at the Palace in N.Y. in April 1924. He began recording, scoring his first hit with "Where the Lazy Daisies Grow" in June 1924. He was a featured performer in the George Gershwin musical *Lady, Be Good!* (N.Y., Dec. 1, 1924), in which he closed the first act performing "Fascinating Rhythm." He scored record hits with that and the title song in the spring of 1925. During the course of the show's 330-performance run, he interpolated his own "Insufficient Sweetie" into the score. He then appeared in the Jerome Kern musical *Sunny* (N.Y., Sept. 23, 1925), performing "I'm Moving Away," which he wrote with Irving Caesar; the show ran 517 performances.

Edwards scored one of the biggest hits of his career with his recording of "I Can't Give You Anything but Love," which was a best-seller in October 1928. He was appearing at the Orpheum in L.A. when he signed a four-year film contract with MGM, making his movie debut in *Hollywood Revue of 1929*, in which he performed "Singin' in the Rain," which he recorded for a best-seller in August 1929. He worked frequently in films over the next few years, notably interpolating songs of his own into *Doughboys* (1930) and *Laughing Sinners* (1931).

Cutting down on his film work after his MGM contract expired in 1932, Edwards returned to vaudeville, once again performing at the Palace in August, and launched his first radio show, *Cliff Edwards, Ukulele Ike*, on NBC. Undeniably, however, his career went into decline in the early 1930s, as vaudeville became defunct and the record business shrank dramatically during the Depression. At the same time Edwards's lifestyle—which included profligate spending, an addiction to morphine, and alcoholism—contributed to his difficulties; he filed for bankruptcy for the first of three times during his life in March 1933.

The Paramount feature *Take a Chance*, released in the fall of 1933, featured Edwards singing "It's Only a Paper Moon," which became his first hit record in four years and helped reestablish his career. He was also notable in the Fox feature *George White's 1935 Scandals*, released in the spring of 1935, and at the end of the year he returned to Broadway in the latest stage edition of the revue *George White's Scandals* (N.Y., Dec. 25, 1935), which had a run of 110 performances.

Edwards was back at MGM by 1937, playing supporting parts in many of the company's films, including *Gone with the Wind* (1939). In 1940 he gave voice to Jiminy Cricket in the animated Disney classic *Pinocchio*, singing "When You Wish upon a Star," which won an Academy Award for Best Song. Edwards formed a permanent association with Disney, also lending his voice to *Dumbo* (1941). But in the early 1940s most of his many film appearances came in supporting roles in

Western B movies made by the Columbia and RKO studios. In RKO's *The Avenging Rider* (1942) he got to sing one of his own songs, "Minnie My Mountain Moocher."

Edwards returned to radio in the late 1940s, appearing frequently on Rudy Vallée's show. At the dawn of television he became a regular on CBS's *The 54th Street Revue*, a variety show, in May 1949, and the same month the network also launched the 15-minute live program *The Cliff Edwards Show*, which ran through the summer.

Edwards worked for Walt Disney Productions in the 1950s, especially on the *Disneyland* and *Mickey Mouse Club* television shows. His final film credit came when his voice was used in the cartoon Western *The Man from Button Willow* in 1965. In his last years Edwards continued to be supported by the Disney organization, which paid for his stay in the nursing home where he died at the age of 76.

Selling a reported 74 million records in his career and appearing in as many as 100 films, Edwards had an extensive and successful career. Historically, his casual, folksy style exerted an important influence on the soft-voiced radio crooners who followed him, especially Bing Crosby.—**WR**

Edwards, Eddie (actually **Edwin Branford; Daddy**), early jazz trombonist, violinist; b. New Orleans, May 22, 1891; d. N.Y., April 9, 1963. He began playing violin at 10, then took up trombone at 15, but did his first gigs on violin in a local theatre orchestra in 1910. He played trombone with Papa Laine's Reliance bands in 1912, and worked regularly with Ernest Giardina's Orch. from 1914. He also played semi-professional baseball in and around New Orleans. On March 1, 1916, he traveled to Chicago with a band led by drummer Johnny Stein (real name: Hountha) called Stein's Dixie Jazz Band. He left Stein in late May 1916 and, with Nick LaRocca, became founder- member of The Original Dixieland Jazz Band. He played with the band in N.Y. until serving briefly in the U.S. Army (July 1918 to March 1919). On his return, he formed his own band and played in a band led by Jimmy "Schnozzle" Durante, then rejoined O.D.J.B., and remained until the group broke up early in 1925. During the later 1920s, he led his own band at various N.Y.-area clubs. Around the end of the decade, Edwards left full-time music, had his own newspaper stand, and also worked for several years as a part-time sports coach. He returned to regular playing to join the reformed O.D.J.B. in autumn 1936, working with LaRocca until February 1938, then continued gigging with Larry Shields, Tony Spargo, etc., until 1940. He did part-time playing in N.Y. during the early 1940s, then in 1943–44 toured with the Katherine Dunham Revue. He continued occasional playing in and around N.Y. until shortly before his death. He co-composed "Tiger Rag," "Fidgety Feet," and other Chicago-jazz standards.

DISC.: *Eddie Edwards and His Original Dixieland Jazz Band* (1949).—**JC/LP**

Edwards, Julian, English-born American conductor and composer; b. Manchester, Dec. 11, 1855; d. Yonkers, N.Y., Sept. 5, 1910. He was a student of Oakeley in Edinburgh and of Macfarren in London. While still young, he wrote several short operettas (1873–77) for the small theater company run by his sister Fanny. He then was active as a theater conductor and composer. After working as a conductor with the Carl Rosa Opera Co., he went to the U.S. in 1888 and became a naturalized American citizen in 1900. He centered his activities in N.Y., where he was a theater conductor and composer. Although his opera *King Rene's Daughter* (Nov. 22, 1893) enjoyed favor, it was as a composer of lighter scores that he was successful. Of these, the most popular were *Madeleine, or The Magic Kiss* (Feb. 25, 1895), *Princess Chic* (Feb. 12, 1900), *Dolly Varden* (Jan. 27, 1902), *When Johnny Comes Marching Home* (Dec. 26, 1902), and *The Girl and the Wizard* (Sept. 27, 1909).

WORKS: DRAMATIC: O p e r a : *Corinna* (1880); *Victorian, the Spanish Student* (Sheffield, March 6, 1883); *King Rene's Daughter* (N.Y., Nov. 22, 1893); *Brian Boru* (N.Y., Oct. 19, 1896); *The Patriot* (1907; N.Y., Nov. 23, 1908). **M u s i c a l T h e a t e r** (all 1st perf. in N.Y. unless otherwise given): *Dorothy* (London, Sept. 24, 1877); *Jupiter, or the Cobbler and the King* (May 2, 1892); *Friend Fritz* (Jan. 20, 1893); *Madeleine, or The Magic Kiss* (Feb. 25, 1895); *The Goddess of Truth* (Feb. 26, 1896); *The Wedding Day* (April 8, 1897); *The Jolly Musketeer* (Nov. 14, 1898); *Princess Chic* (Feb. 12, 1900); *Dolly Varden* (Jan. 27, 1902), *When Johnny Comes Marching Home* (Dec. 26, 1902); *Love's Lottery* (Oct. 3, 1904); *The Pink Hussars*, later retitled *His Honor the Mayor* (Chicago, Oct. 23, 1905); *The Belle of London Town* (Jan. 28, 1907); *The Girl and the Governor* (Feb. 4, 1907); *The Gay Musician* (May 18, 1908); *The Motor Girl* (June 15, 1909; rev. version as *2 Men and a Girl* or *The Aero Girl*, Detroit, Feb. 13, 1911); *The Girl and the Wizard* (Sept. 27, 1909); *Molly May* (April 8, 1910). **O T H E R :** 4 sacred cantatas, including *Lazarus* for Soloists, Chorus, and Orch. (1907); 2 secular cantatas; numerous songs.—**NS/LK/DM**

Edwards, Richard, English poet, dramatist, and composer; b. Somerset, 1524; d. London, Oct. 31, 1566. He was educated at Corpus Christi Coll., Oxford, and at Christ Church, Oxford (M.A., 1547). He became a member of the Chapel Royal in London, where he was made Master of the Children in 1561. With the choirboys there, he presented his play with his own songs, *Damon and Pithias* (Lincoln's Inn, 1564). His most celebrated musical work was the partsong *In goinge to my naked bedde*, written to his own text, and included in his collection of verse *The Paradyse of Daynty Devises* (1576; ed. by E. Fellowes in *The English Madrigal School*, XXXVI).

BIBL.: L. Bradner, *The Life and Poems of R. E.* (New Haven, Conn., and London, 1927).—**NS/LK/DM**

Edwards, Ross, Australian composer; b. Sydney, Dec. 23, 1943. He studied at the New South Wales State Conservatorium of Music in Sydney (1959–62), the Univ. of Sydney (1963), and the Univ. of Adelaide (B.Mus., 1968; M.Mus., 1971), his principal mentors being Meale and Sculthorpe. A Commonwealth postgraduate scholarship enabled him to pursue studies in London with Maxwell Davies. He also studied with Veress. After serving as senior tutor (1973–76) and lecturer (1976–80) in composition at the New South Wales State Conservatorium of Music, he was composer-in-residence at the

Univ. of Wollongong (1983). In 1989 he was made the Australia Council's Don Banks fellow. In 1990 he received the D.Mus. degree from the Univ. of Sydney. He held 2 Australian Creative Artists fellowships. Edwards has developed a highly imaginative style of composition. In his works, designated as his "sacred series," an austere meditative aura prevails. In other scores he has been much influenced by the sounds of the natural world, including those of insects and birds.

WORKS: DRAMATIC: *Christina's World*, chamber opera (1983; rev. 1989); *Sensing*, television dance score (1993). **ORCH.:** *Mountain Village in a Clearing Mist* (1973); Piano Concerto (1982); Violin Concerto, *Maninyas* (Sydney, Aug. 9, 1988); *Yarrageh: Nocturne* for Solo Percussion and Orch. (Sydney, July 19, 1989); *Aria and Transcendental Dance* for Horn and Strings (1990); 2 syms.: No. 1, *Da Pacem Domine* (1991; Perth, Aug. 7, 1992) and No. 2 (1997–98); Concerto for Guitar and Strings (Darwin, July 8, 1995). **CHAMBER:** *Monos I* for Cello (1970) and *II* for Piano (1970); *Shadow D- Zone* for Flute, Clarinet, Piano, Percussion, Violin, and Cello (1977); *The Tower of Remoteness* for Clarinet and Piano (Sydney, Dec. 15, 1978); *Laikan* for Flute, Clarinet, Piano, Percussion, Violin, and Cello (1979); *10 Little Duets* for Recorder Duet (1982); *Marimba Dances* for Marimba (1982); *Maninya II* for String Quartet (1982), *III* for Wind Quintet (1985), and *IV* for Clarinet, Trombone, and Marimba (1985); *Reflections* for Piano and 3 Percussion (1985); *Ecstatic Dances* for 2 Flutes (1990); *Booroora* for Clarinet, Percussion, and Double Bass (1990); *Prelude and Dragonfly Dance* for Percussion Quartet (1991); *Black Mountain Duos* for 2 Cellos (1992); *Veni Creator Spiritus* for String Octet (Perth, Nov. 2, 1993); *Ulpirra* for Recorder (1993); *Laughing Rock* for Cello (1993–94); *Enyato I* for String Quartet (1994) and *II* for Viola (1994). **VOCAL:** *5 Carols from Quem Quaeritis* for Women's Chorus (1967); *Antifon* for Chorus, Brass Sextet, Organ, and 2 Tam-tams (1973); *The Hermit of Green Light*, song cycle for Countertenor and Piano (1979); *Ab Estasias Foribus* for Chorus (1980–87); *Maninya I* for Countertenor and Cello (1981–86) and *V* for Countertenor and Piano (1986); *Flower Songs* for Chorus and 2 Percussion (1987); *Dance Mantra* for 6 voices and Drum (1992). **—NS/LK/DM**

Edwards, Sian, English conductor; b. Sussex, May 27, 1959. She studied horn before entering the Royal Northern Coll. of Music in Manchester, where she turned to conducting; following studies with Sir Charles Groves and Norman Del Mar, and in the Netherlands with Neeme Järvi, she pursued diligent training with Ilya Musin at the Leningrad Cons. (1983–85). In 1984 she won the Leeds Competition and subsequently appeared as a guest conductor with principal British orchs. In 1986 she made her first appearance as an operatic conductor at Glasgow's Scottish Opera with Weill's *Mahogonny*. In 1987 she conducted *La Traviata* at the Glyndebourne Festival. She became the first woman ever to conduct at London's Covent Garden when she led a performance of Tippett's *The Knot Garden* in 1988; that same year she conducted the premiere of Turnage's *Greek* at the Munich Biennale. In 1989 she made her U.S. debut as a guest conductor with the St. Paul (Minn.) Chamber Orch.; she continued to conduct at Covent Garden, leading performances of *Rigoletto* (1989), *Il Trovatore* (1990), and *Carmen* (1991). From 1993 to 1995 she was music director of the English National Opera in London.—NS/LK/DM

Eeden, Jean-Baptiste van den, Belgian composer; b. Ghent, Dec. 26, 1842; d. Mons, April 4, 1917. He was a pupil in the conservatories at Ghent and Brussels, winning at the latter the first prize for composition (1869) with the cantata *Faust's laatste nacht*. In 1878, he was appointed director of the Mons Cons., succeeding Huberti.

WORKS: DRAMATIC: Opera: *Numance* (Antwerp, Feb. 2, 1897); *Rhena* (Brussels, Feb. 15, 1912). **Other:** *Judith*, dramatic scene for 3 Voices **ORCH.:** *La Lutte au XVIᵉ siècle*, symphonic poem; *Marche des esclaves*; etc. **VOCAL: Oratorios:** *Brutus; Jacqueline de Bavière; Jacob van Artevelde; Le Jugement dernier.* **Cantatas:** *Het Woud; De Wind.* **Other:** choruses; songs.

BIBL.: M. Delsaux, *J. v.d.E. et son oeuvre* (Mons, 1925). **—NS/LK/DM**

Effinger, Cecil, American composer; b. Colorado Springs, July 22, 1914; d. Boulder, Colo., Dec. 22, 1990. He took courses in mathematics at Colo. Coll. (B.A., 1935), then studied harmony and counterpoint with Frederick Boothroyd in Colorado Springs (1934–36). He then studied composition with Wagenaar in N.Y. (1938) and Boulanger in Fontainebleau (1939), where he was awarded the Stoval composition prize. He was oboist in the Colorado Springs Sym. Orch. (1932–41) and the Denver Sym. Orch. (1937–41); taught at Colo. Coll. (1936–41) and the Colo. School for the Blind (1939–41). During World War II, he conducted the 506th Army Band (1942–45), then taught at the American Univ. in Biarritz, France (1945–46). After teaching at Colo. Coll. (1946–48), he was music ed. of the *Denver Post* (1947–48); then was head of the composition dept. (1948–81) and composer-in-residence (1981–84) at the Univ. of Colo. in Boulder. In 1954 he patented a practical music typewriter as the "Musicwriter." In his music he maintained a median modern style, making use of polytonal and atonal procedures, without abandoning the basic sense of tonality.

WORKS: DRAMATIC: *Pandora's Box*, children's opera (1961); *Cyrano de Bergerac*, opera (Boulder, July 21, 1965); *The Gentleman Desperado*, music theater (1976); incidental music. **ORCH.:** *Concerto Grosso* (1940); *Western Overture* (1942); Concertino for Organ and Small Orch. (1945); 2 Little Syms. (1945, 1958); Suite for Cello and Chamber Orch. (1945); 5 syms. (1946–58); Piano Concerto (1946); *Lyric Overture* (1949); *Pastorale* for Oboe and Strings (1949); Sym. Concertante for Harp, Piano, and Orch. (1954); *Tone Poem on the Square Dance* (1955); Trio Concertante for Trumpet, Trombone, Horn, and Chamber Orch. (1964; also for 2 Pianos, 1968); *Landscape I* for Brass and Strings (1966) and *II* (1984); Violin Concerto (1972); *Toccata* for Chamber Orch. (1980); band pieces. **CHAMBER:** 6 string quartets (1943, 1944, 1948, 1963, 1985; No. 2, n.d., unfinished); Viola Sonata (1944); 3 piano sonatas (1946, 1949, 1968); Piano Trio (1973); *Intrada* for Brass Quintet (1982); Flute Sonata (1985); also band music. **VOCAL: Oratorios:** *The Invisible Fire* for Soloists, Chorus, and Orch. (1957); *Paul of Tarsus* for Chorus, Strings, and Organ (1968). **Cantatas:** *Cantata for Easter* for

Chorus and Organ (1971); *Cantata Opus 111: From Ancient Prophets* for Chorus, Wind, Cello, and Double Bass (1983); other vocal works.

BIBL.: L. Worster, *C. E.: A Colorado Composer* (Lanham, Md., 1997).—NS/LK/DM

Egenolff, Christian, German music publisher; b. Hadamar, July 26, 1502; d. Frankfurt am Main, Feb. 9, 1555. He was educated at the Univ. of Mainz. He then went to Strasbourg, where he began to publish music in 1528. In 1530 he settled in Frankfurt am Main and continued to publish music until his death. His widow carried on the business until 1572, and the Egenolff name continued to be used until 1605. Egenolff publ. a series of partbooks, but few are extant. He publ. two collections of 4-part songs as *Gassenhawerlin* and *Reutterlieden* in 1535, which were issued in a combined edition about the same time. H. Moser prepared a facsimile edition using the three extant partbooks of the individual collections and the discant of the combined edition (Augsburg and Cologne, 1927).

BIBL.: H. Grotefend, *C. E., der erste ständige Buchdrucker zu Frankfurt am Main und seine Vorläufer* (Frankfurt am Main, 1881); H. Müller, *Die Liederdrucke C. E.s* (diss., Univ. of Kiel, 1964). —NS/LK/DM

Egge, Klaus, prominent Norwegian composer; b. Gransherad, Telemark, July 19, 1906; d. Oslo, March 7, 1979. He was a student of Larsen (piano), Sandvold (organ), and Valen (composition) in Oslo, and later of Gmeindl (composition) at the Berlin Hochschule für Music (1937-38). From 1945 to 1972 he was president of the Soc. of Norwegian Composers. In 1949 he was awarded a government life pension. His works were conditioned by Scandinavian modalities, within a framework of euphonious and resonantly modernistic harmonies. He liked to sign his scores with the notes E-g-g-e, a motto which also occasionally served as a basic theme.

WORKS: BALLET: *Fanitullen* (Devil's Dance; 1950). **ORCH.:** 3 piano concertos: No. 1 (Oslo, Nov. 14, 1938), No. 2 (Oslo, Dec. 9, 1946), and No. 3 (Bergen, April 25, 1974); 5 syms.: No. 1, *Lagnadstonar* (Sounds of Destiny; Oslo, Oct. 4, 1945), No. 2, *Sinfonia giocosa* (Oslo, Dec. 9, 1949), No. 3, *Louisville Symphony* (Louisville, Ky., March 4, 1959), No. 4, *Sinfonia seriale sopra B.A.C.H.-E.G.G.E.* (Detroit, March 28, 1968), and No. 5, *Sinfonia dolce quasi passacaglia* (Oslo, Sept. 27, 1969); *Tårn over Oslo,* overture (1950); Violin Concerto (Oslo, Nov. 5, 1953); Cello Concerto (Oslo, Sept. 9, 1966). **CHAMBER:** Violin Sonata (1932); String Quartet (1933; rev. 1963); 2 piano sonatas: No. 1, *Draumkvede* (Dream Vision; 1933) and No. 2, *Patética* (1955); 3 *Fantasies* for Piano (1939); 2 wind quintets (1939, 1976); Piano Trio (1941); Duo concertante for Violin and Viola (1950); Harp Sonatina (1974). **VOCAL:** *Sveinung Vreim* for Soli, Chorus, and Orch. (Oslo, Dec. 1, 1941); *Elskhugskvaede* (Love Song) for Voice and Strings (1942); *Draumar i stjernesno* (Starsnow Dreams), 3 songs for Soprano and Orch. (1943); *Fjell-Norig* (Mountainous Norway) for Voice and Orch. (Oslo, Oct. 1, 1945); *Noreg-songer* (The Norway Song) for Chorus and Orch. (Oslo, May 2, 1952); choruses; other songs.—NS/LK/DM

Eggebrecht, Hans Heinrich, eminent German musicologist and editor; b. Dresden, Jan. 5, 1919; d.

Freiburg im Breisgau, Aug. 30, 1990. He attended the Gymnasium in Schleusingen, of which his father was superintendent. Eggebrecht was drafted into the army during World War II, and was severely wounded. He then studied music education in Berlin and Weimar, and received his teacher's certificate in 1948. He subsequently studied musicology with H. J. Moser, R. Münnich, and M. Schneider, and received his Ph.D. in 1949 from the Univ. of Jena with the diss. *Melchior Vulpius.* He was asst. lecturer under Vetter in music history at the Univ. of Berlin from 1949 to 1951, then conducted lexicographical work in Freiburg and taught musicology at the Univ. there (1953–55). He completed his Habilitation there in 1955 with his *Studien zur musikalischen Terminologie* (publ. in Mainz, 1955; 2nd ed., 1968). He was Privatdozent at the Univ. of Erlangen (1955–56) and taught musicology at the Univ. of Heidelberg (1956–57). From 1961 to 1988 he was prof. of musicology at the Univ. of Freiburg im Breisgau. In 1964 he became ed. of the *Archiv für Musikwissenschaft.* One of his major musicological contributions was his publication of the vol. on musical terms and historical subjects (*Sachteil*) for the 12th ed. of the *Riemann Musik-Lexikon* (Mainz, 1967), in which he settles many debatable points of musical terminology. Equally important has been his editorship of the *Handwörterbuch der musikalischen Terminologie* from 1972. He also was an ed. of the *Brockhaus-Riemann Musik-Lexikon* with Carl Dahlhaus (2 vols., Wiesbaden and Mainz, 1978–79; suppl., 1989) and of Meyers *Taschenlexikon Musik* (3 vols., Mannheim, 1984).

WRITINGS: *Heinrich Schütz: Musicus poeticus* (Göttingen, 1959); *Ordnung und Ausdruck im Werk von Heinrich Schütz* (Kassel, 1961); *Die Orgelbewegung* (Stuttgart, 1967); *Schütz und Gottesdienst* (Stuttgart, 1969); *Versuch über die Wiener Klassik: Die Tanzszene in Mozarts Don Giovanni* (Wiesbaden, 1972); *Zur Geschichte der Beethoven-Rezeption: Beethoven 1970* (Wiesbaden, 1972); *Musikalische Denken: Aufsätze zur Theorie und Ästhetik der Musik* (Wilhelmshaven, 1977); *Die Musik Gustav Mahlers* (Munich, 1982); *Bachs Kunst der Fuge: Erscheinung und Deutung* (Munich, 1984; 4th ed., 1998; Eng. tr., 1993); *Die mittelalterliche Lehre von der Mehrstimmigkeit* (Darmstadt, 1984); *Musik im Abendland: Prozesse und Stationen vom Mittelalter bis zur Gegenwart* (Munich, 1991); *Orgelbau und Orgelmusik in Russland* (Kleinblittersdorf, 1991); *Zur Geschichte der Beethoven-Rezeption* (Laaber, 1994); *Musik verstehen* (Munich, 1995); *Die Musik und das Schöne* (Munich, 1997); *Texte über Musik: Bach, Beethoven, Schubert, Mahler* (Essen, 1997).

BIBL.: W. Breig, R. Brinkmann, and E. Budde, eds., *Analysen: Beiträge zu einer Problemgeschichte des Komponierens. Festschrift für H. H. E. zum 65. Geburtstag* (Stuttgart, 1984). —NS/LK/DM

Eggen, Arne, Norwegian organist and composer, brother of **Erik Eggen;** b. Trondheim, Aug. 28, 1881; d. Baerum, near Oslo, Oct. 26, 1955. He studied at the Christiania Cons. (1903–05) and then with Straube (organ) and Krehl (composition) at the Leipzig Cons. (1906–07). He toured Norway and Sweden giving organ recitals; from 1927 to 1945 he was president of the Soc. of Norwegian Composers. In 1934 he received a government life pension.

WORKS: DRAMATIC: O p e r a : *Olav Liljekrans* (1931–40; Oslo, 1940); *Cymbeline* (1943–48; Oslo, Dec. 7, 1951).

ORCH.: Sym. (Christiania, March 4, 1920); *Chaconne* for Orch. or Organ (1917). **CHAMBER:** 2 violin sonatas; Piano Trio; Cello Sonata; Suite for Violin and Piano; organ music; piano pieces. **VOCAL:** *King Olav*, oratorio (Oslo, March 30, 1933); many songs.—**NS/LK/DM**

Eggen, Erik, Norwegian music scholar and composer, brother of **Arne Eggen;** b. Trondheim, Nov. 17, 1877; d. Ringsaker, June 7, 1957. He studied theory with Hilde (1895), and later pursued his education at the Univ. of Oslo (Ph.D., 1925). He was a school teacher (1898–1939); was also ed. of *Norsk toneblad* (1910–17) and devoted much time to the study of folk music. His writings include *Edvard Grieg* (Christiania, 1911) and *Norsk musikksoge* (Christiania, 1923). Among his compositions are *Norsk Rapsodi* for Orch., a cantata, and choral pieces.—**NS/LK/DM**

Eggert, Joachim (Georg) Nicolas, German violinist, conductor, pedagogue, and composer; b. Gingst, Rügen, Feb. 22, 1779; d. Thomestorp, Östergötland, April 14, 1813. He received training in violin, piano, and harp from J. F. Dammas in Gingst, in violin and composition from F. G. Kahlow in Stralsund, and in theory from Ferdinand Fischer. After serving as music director of the court theater of the Duke of Mecklenburg-Schwerin in 1802, he went to Stockholm in 1803 and joined the Swedish Royal Orch. as a violinist; he later was its conductor (1808–10). In 1807 he was elected to membership in the Swedish Royal Academy of Music. His works follow in the Viennese classical tradition, which he introduced to Sweden in his capacity as a conductor. He wrote five syms., coronation music for King Karl XIII of Sweden (1809), chamber music, including nine string quartets and a Piano Quartet, and five cantatas and other vocal pieces.—**LK/DM**

Eggerth, Martha (real name, **Márta Eggert**), Hungarian soprano; b. Budapest, April 17, 1912. She was only 12 when she began appearing in juvenile roles in light theater performances in Budapest. In 1930 she attracted favorable notice in the title role of *Das Veilchen vom Montmartre* in Vienna, and in subsequent years had a notably successful career both on stage and in films. Her theater engagements took her all over Europe and to N.Y., where she was notably successful in *The Merry Widow* with her husband, **Jan Kiepura.** She pursued her career to an advanced age, appearing in her 80th year in Stolz's *Servus Du* in Vienna.—**NS/LK/DM**

Egk (real name, **Mayer**), **Werner,** significant German composer; b. Auchsesheim, May 17, 1901; d. Inning am Ammersee, July 10, 1983. He studied piano with Anna Hirzel-Langenhan and composition with Carl Orff in Munich. His early success as a composer began with his scores for the puppet theater and radio, and he soon began to acquire distinction with his operas and ballets. In 1936 he wrote music for the Berlin Olympic Games, for which he was awarded a Gold Medal and the approbation of the Nazi regime. However, the satirical bent of his opera *Peer Gynt* (Berlin, Nov. 24, 1938) was not met with favor by the regime.

Still, he served as head of the Union of German Composers from 1941 to 1945. The apparent favor in which he had been held by the Nazi regime made it necessary for him to stand trial before the Allied Denazification Tribunal for Artists in 1947, but he was absolved from all political taint. From 1950 to 1953 he served as director of the Berlin Hochschule für Musik. While Egk gained particular renown as a master of dramatic composition, he also wrote a number of orch., chamber, and vocal pieces of distinction. His compositions display a mastery of extended tonality. He was also a fine writer who seasoned his output with a philosophical sarcasm. He not only wrote the librettos for his dramatic compositions, but also critical essays, poetry, plays, etc. He publ. a vol. of essays as *Musik, Wort, Bild* (Munich, 1960).

WORKS: DRAMATIC: Opera: *Columbus*, radio opera (1932; Bavarian Radio, Munich, July 13, 1933, composer conducting; first stage perf., Frankfurt am Main, Jan. 13, 1942); *Die Zaubergeige* (Frankfurt am Main, May 19, 1935; new version, Stuttgart, May 2, 1954); *Peer Gynt* (Berlin, Nov. 24, 1938, composer conducting); *Circe*, semibuffa opera, after Calderon (1945; Berlin, Dec. 18, 1948; new version as *Siebzehn Tage und vier Minuten*, Stuttgart, June 2, 1966); *Irische Legende*, after Yeats (Salzburg, Aug. 17, 1955; new version, 1970); *Der Revisor*, comic opera, after Gogol (1956; Schwetzingen, May 9, 1957, composer conducting); *Die Verlobung in San Domingo*, after Kleist (Munich, Nov. 27, 1963, composer conducting). **Singspiels:** *Der Löwe und die Maus* (1931); *Der Fuchs und der Rabe* (1932); *Die Historie vom Ritter Don Juan aus Barcelona* (1932). **Ballet:** *Joan von Zarissa* (1939; Berlin, Jan. 20, 1940, composer conducting); *Abraxas* (Munich, June 6, 1948, composer conducting); *Ein Sommertag* (Berlin, June 11, 1950); *Die chinesische Nachtigall* (Munich, May 20, 1953, composer conducting); *Französische Suite nach Rameau* (Hamburg, Feb. 1, 1952); *Danza* (Munich, Feb. 16, 1960, composer conducting); *Casanova in London* (1968; Munich, Nov. 23, 1969, composer conducting). **ORCH.:** *Musik for Strings* (1923); *Musik* for Small Orch. (1925-26); *Kleine Symphonie* (1926); *Blasmusik* for Wind Orch. (1931); *Georgica* (N.Y., Nov. 14, 1934); *Geigenmusik* for Violin and Orch. (Baden-Baden, April 3, 1936, composer conducting); *Olympische Festmusik* (Berlin, Aug. 1, 1936); *Triptychon aus Joan von Zarissa* (1940); *Abraxas*, suite from the ballet (1948); 2 sonatas: No. 1 (Darmstadt, April 11, 1948, composer conducting) and No. 2 (Ludwigshafen, Sept. 14, 1969); *Französische Suite* (1949; Munich, Jan. 27, 1950); *Allegria* (Baden-Baden, April 25, 1952, composer conducting); *Variationen über ein karibisches Thema* (1959; Freiburg im Breisgau, Jan. 18, 1960, composer conducting); *Englische Suite*, after the ballet *Casanova in London* (1968; Baden-Baden, Feb. 14, 1969, composer conducting); *Moira* (1972; Nuremberg, Jan. 12, 1973); *Spiegelzeit* (Landau, Sept. 14, 1979); *Ouvertüre* (1979–80; Recklinghausen, Sept. 14, 1980); *Der Revisor*, suite for Trumpet and Orch., after the comic opera (1980; Schwetzingen, May 1981); *Canzone* for Cello and Orch. (1981; Salzburg, Jan. 16, 1982); *Nachtanz* (1983; Augsburg, April 15, 1985). **CHAMBER:** Piano Trio (1922); String Quartet (1924); String Quintet (1924); Piano Sonata (1947; Berlin, Feb. 22, 1948); *Divertissement* for 10 Wind Instruments (1973–74; Schwetzingen, May 8, 1974); *5 Stücke* for Wind Quintet (1974; Porto, Jan. 30, 1975); *Polonaise, Adagio und Finale* for 9 Instruments (1975–76; 1st complete perf., Munich, Sept. 30, 1976); *Ouvertüre* for the opera *Die Zaubergeige* for 10 Wind Instruments (1980; Kloster Eberbach, June 14, 1981); *Die Nachtigall*, divertimento for String Quartet, after the ballet *Die chinesische Nachtigall*

(1981; Donauwörth, Oct. 24, 1982). V O C A L : *Furchtlosigkeit und Wohlwollen* for Tenor, Chorus, and Orch. (1931–32; Baden-Baden, April 3, 1936; new version, Vienna, July 5, 1959, composer conducting); *Quattro Canzoni* for High Voice and Orch. (1932; new version, 1956; Aachen, April 23, 1958, composer conducting); *Natur—Liebe—Tod*, cantata for Bass and Chamber Orch. (Göttingen, June 26, 1937, composer conducting); *Mein Vaterland*, hymn for Chorus and Orch. or Organ (Göttingen, June 26, 1937, composer conducting); *Variationen über ein altes Wiener Strophenlied* for Soprano and Orch. (1937; Berlin, Sept. 16, 1938); *La Tentation de Saint Antoine* for Alto, String Quartet, and String Orch. (1947; Südwestfunk, Baden-Baden, May 18, 1947, composer conducting; also for Alto and String Quartet; also for Chorus and Orch., Munich, May 17, 1978); *Chanson et Romance* for Soprano and Orch. (Aix-en-Provence, July 19, 1953); *Nachgefühl*, cantata for Soprano and Orch. (1975; Munich, Sept. 30, 1976). O T H E R : Arrangement of Mozart's Sinfonia concertante, K.297b, for 8 Wind Instruments and Double Bass (1982–83; Donauwörth, Oct. 8, 1986).

BIBL.: B. Kohl and E. Nölle, eds., *W. E.: Das Bühnenwerk* (Munich, 1971); E. Krause, *W. E.: Oper und Ballet* (Wilhelshaven, 1971); A. Böswald et al., *W. E.* (Tutzing, 1997).—**NS/LK/DM**

Egli, Johann Heinrich, Swiss composer, violinist, and teacher; b. Seegräben, near Zürich, March 4, 1742; d. Zürich, Dec. 19, 1810. He studied voice, violin, piano, and composition, his principal mentor being Johannes Schmidlin. He also perused the theoretical works of Kirnberger, C. P. E. Bach, and F. W. Marpurg. He was active in Zürich as a violinist and as a teacher of voice and piano. Egli composed choral works, cantatas, and numerous songs. More than 400 of his songs were publ. in various collections (1775–1816), and he also publ. arrangements of Swiss folk songs in *Schweizerlieder* (Zürich, 1787).—**NS/LK/DM**

Egmond, Max (Rudolf) van, admired Dutch bass-baritone; b. Semarang, Java, Feb. 1, 1936. He studied with Tine van Willingen-de Lorme and took prizes in the 's-Hertogenbosch (1959), Brussels (1962), and Munich (1964) competitions. He then pursued a distinguished career as a concert and oratorio artist, touring extensively in Europe and North America. From 1973 he also taught singing at the Amsterdam Musieklyceum. He was particularly associated with Baroque music, excelling in the works of Bach.

BIBL.: J. Müller, *M. v. E., toonaangevend kunstenaar* (Zutphen, 1984).—**NS/LK/DM**

Egorov, Youri, Russian pianist; b. Kazan, May 28, 1954; d. Amsterdam, April 15, 1988. He learned to play the piano as a child in Kazan, and later was a pupil of Zak at the Moscow Cons. In 1971 he won 4th prize in the Long-Thibaud competition in Paris, and in 1974 third prize in the Tchaikovsky competition in Moscow. In 1976 he left his homeland and settled in the Netherlands. He made his N.Y. debut in 1978 and appeared for the first time in England in 1980. In subsequent years, he appeared with many of the principal orchs. of the world and as a recitalist. His career was cut tragically short by AIDS. He was particularly admired for his performances of the Romantic repertory.—**NS/LK/DM**

Egüés, Manuel de, Spanish composer; b. San Martín del Río, June 3, 1657; d. Burgos, April 11, 1729. After serving as choirmaster at Lérida Cathedral, he held that title in Burgos (1685–91) and Saragossa (1691–92) before returning to Burgos. He was one of the principal Spanish composers of his era, producing 181 villancicos, 14 Salves en romance, eight motets, and seven Psalms.—**LK/DM**

Ehlers, Alice (Pauly), Austrian-born American harpsichordist and teacher; b. Vienna, April 16, 1887; d. Los Angeles, March 1, 1981. She studied piano with Leschetizky in Vienna, and, during World War I, she took lessons in harpsichord with Landowska in Berlin. In 1936 she emigrated to the U.S. and became a naturalized citizen in 1943. From 1941 to 1967 she taught harpsichord at the Univ. of Southern Calif. in Los Angeles; she also gave courses at the Juilliard School of Music in N.Y. and the Univ. of Calif. in Berkeley. She continued to appear in concert as a harpsichordist and gave occasional performances even as a nonagenarian.

BIBL.: K. and A. Bergel, trs. and eds., *Albert Schweitzer and A. E.: A Friendship in Letters* (Lanham, Md., 1991).—**NS/LK/DM**

Ehlert, Louis, German composer and teacher; b. Königsberg, Jan. 13, 1825; d. Wiesbaden, Jan. 4, 1884. He was a pupil of Mendelssohn and Schumann at the Leipzig Cons., and later studied in Vienna and Berlin. He taught piano at Tausig's school in Berlin (1869–71), and later in Meiningen and Wiesbaden. Among his works were a *Frühlingssinfonie*, a *Requiem für ein Kind*, and many piano pieces. He publ. *Briefe über Musik an eine Freundin* (Berlin, 1859; Eng. tr., 1870, as *Letters on Music, to a Lady*) and a collection of essays, *Aus der Tonwelt* (Berlin, 1877; Eng. tr., 1885, as *From the Tone World*).—**NS/LK/DM**

Ehmann, Wilhelm, German musicologist; b. Freistatt, Dec. 5, 1904; d. Freiburg im Breisgau, April 16, 1989. He studied musicology at the univs. of Freiburg and Leipzig; received his Ph.D. in 1934 with the diss. *Adam von Fulda als Vertreter der ersten deutschen Komponisten-Generation* (publ. in Berlin, 1936) from the Univ. of Freiburg; completed his Habilitation there with his *Der Thibaut-Behaghel-Kreis* in 1937. From 1934 to 1940 he was on the faculty of the Univ. of Freiburg; from 1940 to 1945 he taught at the Univ. of Innsbruck. In 1948 he founded and became director of the church-music school in Westphalia (later named the Hochschule für Kirchenmusik); he retired in 1972. He also taught at the Univ. of Munster (1948–54).

WRITINGS: *Die Chorführung* (2 vols., Kassel, 1949; 3rd ed., 1956; vol. II, in Eng., Minneapolis, 1936); *Tibilustrium: Das geistliche Blasen, Formen und Reformen* (Kassel, 1950); *Erziehung zur Kirchenmusik* (Gütersloh, 1951); *Erbe und Auftrag musikalischer Erneuerung: Entromantisierung der Singbewegung* (Kassel, 1951); *J. S. Bach in unserem Leben* (Wolfenbüttel, 1952); *Das Chorwesen in der Kulturkrise* (Regensburg, 1953); *Kirchenmusik, Vermächtnis und Aufgabe* (Darmstadt, 1958); *Alte Musik in der neuen Welt* (Darmstadt, 1961); *Der Bläserchor: Besinnung und Aufgabe* (Kassel, 1969).—**NS/LK/DM**

Ehrenberg, Carl (Emil Theodor), German conductor, teacher, and composer; b. Dresden, April 6,

1878; d. Munich, Feb. 26, 1962. He studied with Draeseke at the Dresden Cons. (1894–98). From 1898 he was engaged as a conductor in Germany; from 1909 to 1914 he conducted concerts in Lausanne, and from 1915 to 1918 he was first conductor at the Augsburg Opera; then conducted at the Berlin State Opera (1922–24). Subsequently he was a prof. at the Cologne Hochschule für Musik (1924–35) and at the Akademie der Tonkunst in Munich (1935–45).

WORKS: DRAMATIC: O p e r a : *Und selig sind* (1904); *Anneliese* (1922). **ORCH.:** Several overtures; 2 syms.; *Sinfonietta*; Cello Concerto. **CHAMBER:** 4 string quartets; Piano Trio; Wind Quartet; String Trio; Violin Sonata; piano pieces. **VOCAL:** Many choruses; songs.—**NS/LK/DM**

Ehrlich, Abel, German-born Israeli composer and teacher; b. Cranz, Sept. 3, 1915. He began violin lessons at the age of 6, and later was a student at the Zagreb Academy of Music (1934–38). After emigrating to Palestine, he studied composition with Rosowsky at the Jerusalem Academy of Music (1939–44). Ehrlich later attended the Darmstadt summer courses in new music under Stockhausen, Nono et al. (1959, 1961, 1963, 1967). He taught composition in various Israeli academies, conservatories, and teacher training colleges. From 1966 to 1982 he was on the faculty of the Univ. of Tel Aviv. He received many awards and prizes for his works. In 1989 he was awarded the Israeli government prize. In 1994 he was awarded the prize of the Soc. of Authors, Composers, and Music Publishers (ACUM) for his life's work. He received the Israel Prize in Music in 1997. Ehrlich's prolific output includes scores in every conceivable field. In his early works, he adhered to a Romantic line with infusions of Middle Eastern themes. Later he adopted an advanced idiom marked by a personal amalgam of traditional Jewish cantillation and serialism.

WORKS: DRAMATIC: *Immanuel Haromi*, musical spectacle (1971); *Dead Souls*, opera bouffa (1978); *Geburtstag einer Bank*, Singspiel after Kafka (1995); *The Jubilee*, chamber opera (1997). **ORCH.:** *A Game of Chess* for Jazz Orch. (1957); *And Though Thou Set Thy Nest Among the Stars* (1969); *Evolution* (1970); *Deliver Them That Are Drawn Unto Death* for Strings (1970); *7 Minutes* for Strings and Percussion (1971); *Divertimento* for Oboe, Clarinet, 2 Horns, and Strings (1971); *Carolus-Music* (1975); *Azamer Bishvahin*, 5 pieces for Small Orch. (1977); *Music for Symphony Orchestra* (1990); *Our Modest Friend Avraham* for Chamber Orch. (1992); *Das Buch des Zeichens* for Strings (1992). **CHAMBER:** 6 string quartets (1947, 1947, 1952, 1962, 1967, 1969); *Testimony* for 2 Flutes (1961); *Riv* for Violin (1962); *Secrets* for Flute (1963); 4 wind quintets (1966–70); *Music for Cello* (1970); *Improvisations with a Game in Hell* for String Trio (1970); Trio for Horn, Cello, and Percussion (1970); Trio for Violin, Flute, and Bassoon (1971); Trio for Horn, Violin, and Piano (1972); *Djerba Dance Song* for Oboe (1973); *Music* for Violin, Cello, Piano, and 2 Tape Recorders (1974); *The Beauty from Marseilles* for Harp (1977); *The Legend of Oof and Whoof* for Clarinet, Violin, and Piano (1992); *Flee to the Mountains Like a Bird* for Chamber Ensemble (1993); *Wishful Thinking* for String Quartet (1994); *And the Doors of the Pit Will Shut*, octet (1995); *Crossed Over the City Like a Giant Bird* for Guitar and String Quartet (1995); *Jeremia und Spinoza* for Violin (1997). **KEY-BOARD: P i a n o :** *Reincarnations* (1965); *Sonata* (1973); *Mu-*

sic (1980); *Signature* (1982); *Mystery of Trees* (1990). **O r g a n :** *Freundschaft in K* for Organ, 4-Hands (1994). **VOCAL:** *The Towers and the Shadows* for Narrator, Singers, and Instruments (1960); *The Writing of Hezekiah* for Soprano, Violin, Oboe, and Bassoon (1962; also for Soprano and Chamber Orch.); *Echa* for Chorus and Chamber Orch. (1970); *The Unicorn* for 12 Singers, 3 Percussionists, and 3 Oboes (1971); *Job 7, 11–16* for Baritone, Chorus, and Orch. (1971); *Ne subito...* for Chorus and Orch. (1971); *arpmusic* for Baritone, Mime, 8 Instruments, and Electroacoustics (1971); *For the Memory of Them is Forgotten* for Chorus and 5 Instruments (1973); *A Vision of God* for 8 Groups, each consisting of Soprano, Alto, Violin, and Viola (1975); *Let Us Proclaim*, oratorio for Soloists, Chorus, and Orch. (1982); *Giordano Bruno*, semi-oratorio (1986); *Because You Are My Kinsman* for Soprano, Cello, and Piano (1989).—**NS/LK/DM**

Ehrlich, (Karl) Heinrich (Alfred), Austrian pianist, pedagogue, and writer; b. Vienna, Oct. 5, 1822; d. Berlin, Dec. 30, 1899. He studied piano with Henselt, Thalberg, and Bocklet, and composition with Sechter. He served as court pianist in Hannover (1852–55), and eventually settled in Berlin in 1862, where he taught piano at the Stern Cons. (1864–72; 1886–89) and was music critic of the *Berliner Tageblatt* (1878–98). In addition to many pedagogical books, he also wrote novels. —**NS/LK/DM**

Ehrlich, Marty, contemporary jazz reeds player, composer, arranger; b. St. Paul, Minn., May 31, 1955. Ehrlich grew up in Louisville, Ky., and started on clarinet in a summer band program at age seven. When he was 10 his social-worker parents moved to the St. Louis, Mo., suburb of University City. He picked up the sax in junior high and played in the band. At a weekend arts program he met dramatist Malinke Elliott, who was a founder of the Black Artists Group (BAG). Elliott gave him records by Ornette Coleman and Albert Ayler and Ehrlich's sister brought home Eric Dolphy's *Alone Together*. His mentors were Oliver Lake and especially Julius Hemphill; Ehrlich also worked with J.D. Parran. Erhlich jammed regularly with BAG members, sat in playing standards at clubs, and made his first record in high school. Rejected by the jazz program at the New England Cons. of Music, he entered the classical department as a clarinetist, but the next fall got into the jazz department, where Fred Hersch and Anthony Coleman were classmates. He had private lessons with Joe Allard. By his third year, he was in both George Russell's and Jaki Byard's big bands, as well as Gunther Schuller and Ran Blake's third stream department. He also worked locally with Stan Strickland and recorded with guitarist Michael Gregory Jackson. At Christmas 1978, about six months after graduating with honors (he received the Outstanding Alumni Award in 1992), he moved to N.Y. to live with Tim Berne, a fellow protégé of Hemphill. His first N.Y. gig was with Hemphill and John Hicks for "family day" at Hicks's father's church in Harlem. He worked with Chico Hamilton and George Russell, including many dates at the Village Vanguard. In 1978 he toured Europe for the first time with Braxton's big band. With Charles "Bobo" Shaw's Human Arts Ensemble, he opened the Antibes Jazz Festival for Cecil Taylor and Ornette Coleman. He has played with leading modern jazz performer/composers, including Hemphill, Lake, Anthony Davis (including the N.Y.C. Opera premiere of *X* in fall 1986), Leroy Jenkins, John Lindberg, Muhal Richard Abrams, Wayne Horvitz, Bobby Previte, John Carter, Roscoe Mitchell, Jack DeJohnette, George Gruntz, and John Zorn. In the 1980s he settled in N.Y.'s East Village and became active in the so-called downtown scene around the Knitting Factory. His own trio in the 1980s consisted of Pheeroan Aklaff and Anthony Cox. Later he formed a quartet with Bobby Previte, Lindsay Horner, and Stan Strickland. In 1995, he toured Europe with Don Grolnick and the Brecker Brothers and played at the Knitting Factory in a quartet led by Braxton on piano. A new trio Relativity with Mike Formanek and Peter Erskine recorded in February 1998. As a composer, he has been commissioned by the N.Y. Composer's Orch. (who recorded his "After All"), the Boston Jazz Composer's Alliance, and the N.Y. String Trio. His mid-1990s premieres include String Quartet No. 1, commissioned by the Lydian String Quartet and "Bright Canto," commissioned by pianist Ursula Oppens. He has received commissioning grants from the N.Y. Foundation for the Arts, the National Endowment for the Arts, and Meet the Composer.

Disc.: *Welcome* (1984); *Eight Bold Souls* (1986); *Pliant Plaint* (1987); *Falling Man* (1989); *Traveller's Tale* (1989); *Emergency Peace* (1990); *Side by Side* (1991); *Can You Hear a Motion?* (1993); *Just Before Dawn* (1995); *New York Child* (1996); *Open Air Meeting* (1997); *Light at the Crossroads* (1997); *At Dr. King's Table* (1997). —LP

Ehrling, (Evert) Sixten, noted Swedish conductor; b. Malmö, April 3, 1918. He studied piano, organ, composition, and conducting at the Royal Academy of Music's Cons. in Stockholm. After a brief career as a concert pianist, he joined the staff of the Royal Opera in Stockholm as a rehearsal pianist, and made his conducting debut there in 1940. He then took conducting lessons with Karl Böhm in Dresden (1941) and, after the end of World War II, with Albert Wolff in Paris. In 1942 he was appointed conductor in Göteborg; in 1944 he became a conductor at the Royal Opera in Stockholm, where he served as chief conductor from 1953 to 1960. From 1963 to 1973 he was music director of the Detroit Sym. Orch.; then headed the orch. conducting class at the Juilliard School in N.Y. In 1978 he became music adviser and principal guest conductor of the Denver Sym. Orch., and from 1979 to 1985, he was its principal guest conductor; he was also artistic adviser to the San Antonio Sym. Orch. (1985–88). He was chief conductor and musical advisor of the orchs. at the Manhattan School of Music in N.Y. from 1993.

Bibl.: L. Aare, *Maestro: S. E., en dirigent och hans epok* (Stockholm, 1995).—NS/LK/DM

Eichberg, Julius, German-American violinist, teacher, and composer; b. Düsseldorf, June 13, 1824; d. Boston, Jan. 19, 1893. He studied with his father, Eichler in Mainz, Fröhlich in Würzburg, Rietz in Düsseldorf, and Meerts and Bériot at the Brussels Cons. (1843–45). After serving as prof. of violin at the Geneva Cons. (1845–56), he emigrated to N.Y. in 1857. In 1859 he

settled in Boston and was director of the Museum Concerts until 1866. In 1867 he helped to found the Boston Cons., where he oversaw its violin dept. He also was superintendent of music in the public schools, for which he publ. singing books and music collections. Eichberg's light stage work *The Doctor of Alcantara* (Boston, April 7, 1862) was the most successful score of its kind in America in its day. It was subsequently performed in various American cities and in Great Britain and Australia.

Works: Operettas (all first perf. in Boston): *The Doctor of Alcantara* (April 7, 1862); *A Night in Rome* (Nov. 26, 1864); *The 2 Cadis* (March 5, 1866); *The Rose of Tyrol* (April 6, 1868). **Other:** Chamber music; many studies, duets, and characteristic pieces for Violin; vocal music, including *To Thee, O Country Great and Free* for Chorus (1872).—NS/LK/DM

Eichborn, Hermann, German composer, writer on music, and inventor; b. Breslau, Oct. 30, 1847; d. Gries, near Bozen, April 15, 1918. He studied jurisprudence, then became interested in music and took organ lessons with the organist of the Breslau Cathedral. His income from a wine-brewing business in Gries enabled him to devote himself to writing and the invention of instruments. He also supported a local orch. that performed several of his works. In 1882 he patented his invention of the soprano horn in F, which he called Oktav Waldhorn, and which was adopted in many Silesian bands.

Works: Sonata for Waldhorn and Piano; *Rondo brillant* for Waldhorn and Orch.; *Trompeters Berglied,* "echo piece" for 2 Trumpets; *Trompeter blas! Nur ein Spass!* for 2 Trumpets and Orch.; several operettas.

Writings: *Die Trompete in alter und neuer Zeit* (Leipzig, 1881; new ed., Wiesbaden, 1968); *Das alte Clarinblasen auf Trompeten* (Leipzig, 1894); *Die Dampfung beim Horn* (Leipzig, 1897); *Militarismus und Musik* (Leipzig, 1909).—NS/LK/DM

Eichheim, Henry, American composer and violinist; b. Chicago, Jan. 3, 1870; d. Montecito, near Santa Barbara, Calif., Aug. 22, 1942. He received elementary musical training from his father, Meinhard Eichheim, a cellist in the Theodore Thomas Orch., then studied with Becker, L. Lichtenberg, and S. Jacobson at the Chicago Musical Coll. After a season as a violinist in the Thomas Orch. in Chicago, he was a member of the Boston Sym. Orch. (1890–1912). He then devoted himself to concert work and composition. He made 5 trips to the Orient (1915, 1919, 1922, 1928, mid-1930s) and collected indigenous instruments, which he subsequently used in his orch. music. All of his works are based on oriental subjects, with their harmonic idiom derived from Debussy and Scriabin.

Works: Dramatic: *The Rivals,* ballet (1924; Chicago, Jan. 1, 1925; rev. as *Chinese Legend* for Orch., Boston, April 3, 1925); *A Burmese pwé,* incidental music (N.Y., March 16, 1926). **Orch.:** *Oriental Impressions* or *The Story of the Bell* (1919–22; Boston, March 24, 1922; rev. of a piano piece, 1918–22); *Malay Mosaic* (1924; N.Y., March 1, 1925); *Impressions of Peking* and *Korean Sketch* for Chamber Orch. (Venice, Sept. 3, 1925); *Java* (Philadelphia, Nov. 8, 1929); *Bali* (Philadelphia, April 20, 1933). **Chamber:** 2 violin sonatas (1892–95; 1934); String Quartet

(1895); violin music; piano pieces. **VOCAL**: *The Moon, My Shadow, and I* for Soprano and Orch. (1926); songs. —**NS/LK/DM**

Eichhorn, Kurt (Peter), German conductor; b. Munich, Aug. 4, 1908; d. Murnau am Staffelsee, June 29, 1994. He studied with Hermann Zilcher. He made his professional debut at the Bielefeld Opera in 1932. In 1941 he conducted at the Dresden State Opera. After World War II, he returned to Munich as a conductor at the Gärtnerplatz Theater; also conducted at the Bavarian State Opera. From 1967 to 1975 he served as chief conductor of the Munich Radio Orch.—**NS/LK/DM**

Eichner, Ernst (Dieterich Adolph), German bassoonist and composer; b. Arolsen, Hesse (baptized), Feb. 15, 1740; d. Potsdam, 1777. He joined the orch. of Duke Christian IV of Pfalz-Zeibrücken in 1762, serving as its concertmaster (1769–72). He also made tours as a concert artist from 1767, visiting Paris in 1770 and London in 1773. He then was in the service of the Prussian court.

WORKS: 31 syms.; keyboard concertos; quintets for Flute and String Quartet; quartets for Flute, Violin, Viola, and Cello; piano trios; duets for Violin and Viola; piano sonatas.

BIBL.: A. Volk, *E. E.: Sein Leben und seine Bedeutung für die Kammermusik und das Solokonzert* (diss., Univ. of Cologne, 1943); M. Reissinger, *Die Sinfonien E. E.s (1740–1777)* (diss., Univ. of Frankfurt am Main, 1970).—**NS/LK/DM**

Eilers, Albert, German bass; b. Cothen, Dec. 21, 1830; d. Darmstadt, Sept. 4, 1896. He studied at the Milan Cons., making his opera debut in Dresden (1854). He sang at the German Theater in Prague (1858–65). In 1876 Wagner selected him to sing the part of the giant Fasolt at Bayreuth. In 1882 he became a member of the Darmstadt Opera. He wrote a fairly successful comic opera, *Die Johannisnacht* (Koblenz, 1889).—**NS/LK/DM**

Eimert, (Eugen Otto) Herbert, German musicologist and composer; b. Bad Kreuznach, April 8, 1897; d. Cologne, Dec. 15, 1972. He took courses with Abendroth, Bölsche, and Othegraven at the Cologne Cons. (1919–24) and studied musicology with Bücken, Kahl, and Kinsky at the Univ. of Cologne (Ph.D., 1931, with the diss. *Musikalische Formstrukturen im 17. und 18. Jahrhundert*; publ. in Augsburg, 1932). He worked for the Cologne Radio from 1927 until the advent of the Nazis in 1933; after the fall of the Third Reich in 1945, he resumed his activities (until 1965); was founder-director of its electronic music studio (1951–62). He served as a prof. at the Cologne Hochschule für Musik (1965–71). He composed a number of electronic works. His important writings include *Atonale Musiklehre* (Leipzig, 1924), *Lehrbuch der Zwölftontechnik* (Wiesbaden, 1950; 6th ed., 1966), and *Grundlagen der musikalischen Reihentechnik* (Vienna, 1963). With H. Humpert, he ed. *Das Lexikon der elektronischen Musik* (Regensburg, 1973).—**NS/LK/DM**

Einem, Gottfried von, outstanding Austrian composer; b. Bern, Switzerland, Jan. 24, 1918. He was

taken to Germany as a child and pursued academic studies in Plön and Ratzeburg. In 1938 he was arrested and briefly imprisoned by the Gestapo, but that same year he became a coach at the Bayreuth Festival and at the Berlin State Opera. After studying composition with Blacher in Berlin (1941–42), he went to the Dresden State Opera in 1944 as resident composer and musical advisor. Later that year he settled in Austria, where he studied counterpoint with J.N. David. From 1963 to 1972 he taught at the Vienna Hochschule für Musik. He also served as president of the Austrian Soc. of Authors, Composers, and Music Publishers (1965–70). Einem publ. the books *Das musikalische Selbstporträt von Komponisten, Dirigenten, Sängerinnen und Sänger unserer Zeit* (Hamburg, 1963) and *Komponist und Gesellschaft* (Karlsruhe, 1967). Einem achieved an original mode of expression within tonal parameters which allowed him to explore a remarkable range of dynamic, rhythmic, and harmonic effects. He especially excelled as a composer of dramatic scores, but he also revealed himself as a distinguished composer of instrumental music.

WORKS: **DRAMATIC**: **O p e r a**: *Dantons Tod* (1944–46; Salzburg, Aug. 6, 1948); *Der Prozess* (1950–52; Salzburg, Aug. 17, 1953); *Der Zerrissene* (1961–64; Hamburg, Sept. 17, 1964); *Der Besuch der alten Dame* (1970; Vienna, May 23, 1971); *Kabale und Liebe* (1975; Vienna, Dec. 17, 1976); *Jesu Hochzeit* (Vienna, May 18, 1980); *Tulifant* (1989-90; Vienna, Oct. 30, 1990). **B a l l e t**: *Prinzessin Turandot* (1942–43; Dresden, Feb. 5, 1944); *Rondo von goldenen Kalb* (1950; Hamburg, Feb. 1, 1952); *Pas de coeur* (Munich, July 22, 1952); *Glück, Tod und Traum* (1953; Alpbach, Aug. 23, 1954); *Medusa* (Vienna, Jan. 16, 1957; rev. 1971). **ORCH.**: *Capriccio* (1942–43; Berlin, March 3, 1943); *Concerto for Orchestra* (1943; Berlin, April 3, 1944); *Orchestermusik* (Vienna, June 21, 1948); *Serenade* for Double String Orch. (1949; Berlin, Jan. 30, 1950); *Meditations* (Louisville, Nov. 6, 1954); Piano Concerto (1955; Berlin, Oct. 6, 1956); *Wandlungen* (1956); *Symphonic Scenes* (1956; Boston, Oct. 11, 1957); *Ballade* (1957; Cleveland, March 20, 1958); *Tanz-Rondo* (Munich, Nov. 13, 1959); 4 syms.: No. 1, *Philadelphia Symphony* (1960; Vienna, Nov. 11, 1961), No. 2, *Wiener Symphonie* (1976; Minneapolis, Nov. 16, 1977), No. 3, *Münchner Sinfonie* (1985), and No. 4 (1988); *Nachstück* (1960; Kassel, Nov. 16, 1962); Violin Concerto (1966–67; Vienna, May 31, 1970); *Hexameron* (1969; Los Angeles, Feb. 19, 1970); *Bruckner Dialog* (1971; Linz, March 23, 1974); *Arietten* for Piano and Orch. (1977; Berlin, Feb. 20, 1978); *Ludi Leopoldini*, variations on a theme of Emperor Leopold I (Berlin, Oct. 12, 1980); Organ Concerto (1981; Linz, Feb. 1, 1983); *Fraktale*, "Concerto Philharmonico" for the 150th anniversary of the Vienna Phil. (Vienna, Oct. 18, 1992). **CHAMBER**: Violin Sonata (1947); 5 string quartets (1975; 1977; 1980; 1981; 1989–91); Sonata for Solo Violin (1975); Wind Quintet (1976); Sonata for Solo Viola (1980); *Steinbeis Serenade*, octet (1981); Sonata for Solo Double Bass (1982); String Trio (1985); Cello Sonata (1987); *Sonata enigmatica* for Double Bass (1988); Flute Quartet (1988); Trio for Violin, Clarinet, and Piano (1992); *Jeux d'amour* for Horn and Piano (1993); *Karl-Hartwig Kaltners Malerei* for 4 Brass Instruments (1993). **VOCAL**: *Hymnus* for Alto, Chorus, and Orch. (1949; Vienna, March 31, 1951); *Das Stundenlied* for Chorus and Orch. (1958; Hamburg, March 1, 1959); *Von der Lieb* for Soprano or Tenor and Orch. (Vienna, June 18, 1961); *Kammergesänge* for Mezzo-soprano, Baritone, and Small Orch. (1965); *Geistliche Sonata* for Soprano, Trumpet, and Organ (1971–73); *Rosa mystica* for Baritone and Orch. (1972; Vienna, June 4, 1973); *An die Machgebornen* for Alto, Baritone, Chorus, and Orch. (1973–75; N.Y., Oct. 24, 1975); *Gute Ratschläge*, cantata for Soloists, Chorus, and Guitar (1982); *Missa Claravallensis* for Chorus, Winds, and Percussion (1987–88); *Alchemistenspiegel* for Baritone and Orch. (Bregenz, July 30, 1990); song cycles; solo songs.

BIBL.: D. Hartmann, *G. v. E.* (Vienna, 1967); H. Hopf and B. Sonntag, eds., *G. v. E.: Ein Komponist unseres Jahrhunderts* (Münster, 1989); K. Lezak, *Das Opernschaffen G.u. E.s* (Vienna, 1990); T. Eickhoff, *Politische Dimensionen einer Komponistien-Biographie im 20. Jahrhundert—G. v. E.* (Stuttgart, 1998). —NS/LK/DM

Einstein, Alfred, eminent German-born American musicologist; b. Munich, Dec. 30, 1880; d. El Cerrito, Calif., Feb. 13, 1952. He studied law before pursuing training in composition with Beer-Walbrunn at the Munich Akademie der Tonkunst and in musicology with Sandberger at the Univ. of Munich (Ph.D., 1903, with the diss. *Zur deutschen Literatur für Viola da Gamba in 16. und 17. Jahrhundert;* publ. in Leipzig, 1905). He greatly distinguished himself as the first ed. of the *Zeitschrift für Musikwissenschaft* (1918–33); he also was the music critic of the *Münchner Post* (until 1927) and of the *Berliner Tageblatt* (1927–33). After Hitler came to power in 1933, he went to England. Following an Italian sojourn, he emigrated to the U.S. in 1939 and became a naturalized American citizen in 1945. From 1939 to 1950 he was prof. of music history at Smith Coll. in Northampton, Mass. Einstein was an outstanding music scholar, ed., and critic. Although some of his writings have been superseded by later scholarship, they remain brilliant in style, vivid and richly metaphorical, and capable of conveying to the reader an intimate understanding of music of different eras. His study *The Italian Madrigal* (1949) was a particularly notable achievement. Einstein was the ed. of the rev. editions of Riemann's *Musik Lexikon* (Berlin, 9th ed., 1919; 10th ed., 1922; 11th ed., aug., 1929); he also ed. Riemann's *Handbuch der Musikgeschichte* (Leipzig, 2nd ed., rev., 1929) and prepared an augmented German tr. of Eaglefield-Hull's *Dictionary of Modern Music* (1924) as *Das neue Musiklexikon* (Berlin, 1926). His rev. of Kochel's *Chronologisch-thematisches Verzeichnis sämtlicher Tonwerke Wolfgang Amade Mozarts* (Leipzig, 3rd ed., 1937; reprint, with suppl., Ann Arbor, 1947) was valuable in its day. He contributed many scholarly articles to learned journals, Jahrbücher, Festschrifte et al. He likewise ed. works by Marenzio, Gluck, Antico, and Mozart, as well as *The Golden Age of the Madrigal* (N.Y., 1942).

WRITINGS: *Geschichte der Musik* (Leipzig, 1917; 6th ed., rev., 1953; Eng. tr., 1936; 5th ed., 1948, as *A Short History of Music*); *Heinrich Schütz* (Kassel, 1928); *Gluck* (London, 1936; Ger. ed., 1954); *Greatness in Music* (N.Y., 1941; Ger. ed., 1951, as *Grösse in der Musik*); *Mozart: His Character, His Work* (N.Y., 1945; 4th ed., 1959; Ger. ed., 1947; 2nd ed., rev., 1953); *Music in the Romantic Era* (N.Y., 1947; 2nd ed., 1949; Ger. ed., 1950, as *Die Romantik in der Musik*); *The Italian Madrigal* (Princeton, N.J., 1949); *Schubert: A Musical Portrait* (N.Y., 1951; Ger. ed., 1952); P. Lang, ed., *Essays on Music* (N.Y., 1956; 2nd ed., rev., 1958); *Von Schütz bis Hindemith* (Zürich and Stuttgart, 1957); *Nationale und Universale Musik* (Zürich and Stuttgart, 1958); C. Dower, ed., *Alfred Einstein on Music: Selected Music Criticisms* (N.Y. 1991).—NS/LK/DM

Eiríksdóttir, Karólína, Icelandic composer; b. Reykjavík, Jan. 10, 1951. She studied composition with Thorkell Sigurbjornsson at the Reykjavík Coll. of Music and with George Wilson and William Albright at the Univ. of Mich. (M.M., 1978); taught at the Kopavogur School of Music and the Reykjavík Coll. of Music. In 1985 she received an Icelandic Artists' Grant. Her music is stark and austere, laden with northern Romanticism.

WORKS: DRAMATIC: *Someone I Have Seen*, chamber opera (1988); *Madur Lifandi*, chamber opera (1999). **ORCH.:** *Notes* (1978; Ann Arbor, Mich., March 1, 1979); *Sónans* (Reykjavík, Oct. 15, 1981); *5 Pieces* for Chamber Orch. (Reykjavík, April 30, 1983); *Sinfonietta* (Reykjavík, Nov. 3, 1985); *Rhapsody* for Chamber Orch. (1990); *Klifur* (1991); Clarinet Concerto (1994). **CHAMBER:** *IVP* for Flute, Violin, and Cello (1977); *Nabulations* for 2 Flutes, 2 Trumpets, 2 Trombones, 2 Percussion, Violin, and Double Bass (1978); *Fragments* for Flute, Oboe, Clarinet, Horn, Harp, Percussion, Violin, Viola, and Cello (1979); *In vultus solis* for Violin (1980); *Ylir* for Bassoon, Horn, Trumpet, Trombone, 2 Violins, Viola, Cello, and Harpsichord (1981); *The Blue Maid* for Clarinet, Violin, and Piano (1983); *6 Movements* for String Quartet (1983); Trio for Violin, Cello, and Piano (1987); *Hringhenda* for Clarinet (1989); *Whence This Calm?* for Guitar (1990); *Mutanza* for Wind Quintet and Harpsichord (1991); *Spring Verse* for Harpsichord (1991); *Spil* for 2 Flutists (1993); *Hugleiding* for Violin (1996); *Miniatures* for Clarinet, Violin, and Cello (1999). **Piano:** *A Kind of Rondo* (1984); *Finger Travels* (1986); *Rhapsody* (1986). **VOCAL:** *6 Poems from the Japanese* for Mezzo-soprano, Flute, and Cello (1977); *Some Days* for Soprano, Flute, Clarinet, Cello, and Piano (1982; also for Soprano, Flute, Clarinet, Cello, Guitar, and Harpsichord, 1991); *2 Miniatures* for Chorus (1983); *Land Possessed by Poems* for Baritone and Piano (1987); *Ungadei* for Chorus (1991); *Winter* for Chorus (1991); *Sumir Dagar* for Soprano and 5 Instruments (1991); *Na Carenza* for Mezzo-soprano and Oboe (1993); *Sjávarsteinn* for Baritone and Piano (1996); *Tjaldurinn* for Soprano and Piano (1997).—NS/LK/DM

Eisenberg, Maurice, outstanding German-born American cellist and pedagogue; b. Königsberg, Feb. 24, 1900; d. while teaching a cello class at the Juilliard School of Music in N.Y., Dec. 13, 1972. He was taken to the U.S. as a child. He studied violin, then, at the age of 12, he took up the cello. He played as a youth in café orchs., and studied at the Peabody Cons. of Music in Baltimore. He was a cellist of the Philadelphia Orch. (1917- 19); then joined the N.Y. Sym. Orch. He went to Europe in 1927 and studied in Berlin with Hugo Becker; in Leipzig with Julius Klengel; in Paris with Alexanian, where he also took lessons in harmony and counterpoint with Boulanger; and in Spain with Casals. He then taught at the École Normale de Musique in Paris (1929–39); then appeared with major sym. orchs. and taught at various colleges. With M. Stanfield, he publ. *Cello Playing of Today* (1957).—NS/LK/DM

Eisfeld, Theodor(e), German conductor and composer; b. Wolfenbüttel, April 11, 1816; d. Wiesbaden, Sept. 2, 1882. He was a pupil of Karl Müller (violin) in Braunschweig and of Reissiger (composition) in Dresden, and later had some lessons with Rossini in Bologna. After conducting at the Wiesbaden court theater (1839–43), he went to Paris. In 1848 he went to N.Y. and in 1849 he made his first appearance with the N.Y. Phil., with which he was active until 1852 when he was made its sole conductor. From 1854 to 1865 he shared the conductorship with Carl Bergmann. He also was active in sponsoring chamber music in N.Y. from 1851, and was founder-conductor of the Brooklyn Phil. in 1857. In 1866 he returned to Germany.—NS/LK/DM

Eisler, Hanns (Johannes), remarkable German composer; b. Leipzig, July 6, 1898; d. Berlin, Sept. 6, 1962. He began to study music on his own while still a youth, then studied with Weigl at the New Vienna Cons. and later privately with Schoenberg (1919–23); he also worked with Webern. In 1924 he won the Vienna Arts Prize. He went to Berlin in 1925 and taught at the Klindworth-Scharwenka Cons. In 1926 he joined the German Communist Party; after the Nazis came to power in 1933, he left Germany; made visits to the U.S. and was active in Austria, France, England, and other European countries. He taught at the New School for Social Research in N.Y. (1935–36; 1937–42) and at the Univ. of Calif. in Los Angeles (1942–48); then left the U.S. under the terms of "voluntary deportation" on account of his Communist sympathies. In 1949 he settled in East Berlin and became a prof. at the Hochschule für Musik and a member of the German Academy of the Arts. Under Schoenberg's influence, Eisler adopted the 12-tone method of composition for most of his symphonic works. However, he demonstrated a notable capacity for writing music in an accessible style. His long association with Bertolt Brecht resulted in several fine scores for the theater; he also worked with Charlie Chaplin in Hollywood (1942–47). His songs and choral works became popular in East Germany. He composed the music for the East German national anthem, *Auferstanden aus Ruinen*, which was adopted in 1949. His writings include *Composing for the Films* (with T. Adorno; N.Y., 1947), *Reden und Aufsätze* (Berlin, 1959), and *Materialen zu einer Dialektik der Musik* (Berlin, 1973). G. Mayer ed. his *Musik und Politik* (2 vols., Berlin, 1973 and Leipzig, 1982). A collected ed. of his compositions and writings was undertaken by the German Academy of the Arts in East Berlin in association with the Hanns Eisler Archive.

WORKS: DRAMATIC: *Johannes Faustus*, opera (Berlin, March 11, 1953); some 38 scores of incidental music, to works by Brecht (*Rote Revue*, 1932; *Die Rundköpfe und die Spitzköpfe*, 1934-36; *Furcht und Elend des dritten Reiches*, 1945; *Galileo Galilei*, 1947; *Tage der Kommune*, 1950; *Die Gesichte der Simone Machard*, 1957; *Schweyk im zweiten Weltkrieg*, 1943-59), by Feuchtwanger (*Kalkutta, 4.Mai*, 1928), by Ernst Toller (*Feuer aus den Kesseln*, 1934; *Peace on Earth*, 1934), by Ben Jonson (*Volpone*, 1953), by Aristophanes (*Lysistrata*, 1954), by Shakespeare (*Hamlet*, 1954), by Schiller (*Wilhelm Tell*, 1961), etc.; some 42 film scores (*None but the Lonely Heart*, 1944; *Woman on the Beach*, 1947; *Der Rat der Götter*, 1950; *Fidelio*, 1956; *The Witches of Salem*, 1957; *Trübe Wasser*, 1959; etc.). ORCH: 6 orch. suites drawn from films (1930–33); other orch. works drawn from films and stage pieces, including 5 *Orchesterstücke* (1938); *Kammersinfonie* (1940). CHAMBER: 3 piano sonatas (1923, 1924, 1943); *Divertimento* for Wind Quintet (1923); Duo for Violin and Cello (1924); Piano Sonatine (1934); *Präludium und Fuge über BACH* for String Trio (1934); Sonata for Flute, Oboe, and Harp (1935); Violin Sonata

(1937); String Quartet (1938); 2 nonets (1939, 1941); 2 septets (1940, 1947); *14 Arten, den Regen zu beschreiben* for Flute, Clarinet, Violin, Cello, and Piano (1940); piano albums for children, etc. VOCAL: Chorus and Orch.: *Tempe der Zeit*, cantata (1929); *Die Massnahme* (1930); *Die Mutter* (1931); *Kalifornische Ballade*, cantata (1934; based on a radio score); *Deutsche Sinfonie* for Soloists, 2 Speakers, Chorus, and Orch. (Paris, June 25, 1937); *Lenin*, Requiem (1936-37); *Mitte des Jahrhunderts*, cantata (1950); *Bilder aus der "Kriegsfibel"* (1957). Voice and Orch.: *Glückliche Fahrt* for Soprano and Orch. (1946); *Rhapsodie* for Soprano and Orch. (1949); *Die Teppichweber von Kujan-Bulak*, cantata for Soprano and Orch. (1957); *Es lächelt der See* for Soprano, Tenor, and Orch. (1961); *Ernste Gesänge*, 7 songs for Baritone and Strings (1936–62). OTHER: Works for Voice and Smaller Ensembles, including 9 works entitled *Kammerkantate* (1937); many songs with piano.

BIBL.: H. Brockhaus, *H. E.* (Leipzig, 1961); N. Notowicz, *H. E.: Quellennachweise* (Leipzig, 1966); H. Bunge, *Fragen Sie mehr über Brecht: H. E. im Gespräch* (Munich, 1970); E. Klemm, *H. E.: Für Sie porträtiert* (Leipzig, 1973); A. Betz, *H. E.: Musik einer Zeit* (Munich, 1976; Eng. tr., 1982, as *H. E.: Political Musician*); M. Grabs, *H. E.: Kompositionen, Schriften, Literatur: Ein Handbuch* (Leipzig, 1984); D. Blake, *H. E.: A Miscellany* (London, 1995); J. Schebera, *H. E.: Eine Biographie in Texten, Bildern und Dokumenten* (Mainz, 1998).—NS/LK/DM

Eisler, Paul, Austrian pianist, conductor, and composer; b. Vienna, Sept. 9, 1875; d. N.Y., Oct. 16, 1951. He was a pupil of Bruckner at the Vienna Cons. He conducted in Riga, Vienna, and at the Metropolitan Opera in N.Y. (1916–17; 1920–29), and also made numerous tours as an accompanist to Caruso, Ysaÿe, and others. He composed several operettas, including *Spring Brides*, *The Sentinel*, *The Little Missus*, and *In the Year 1814*. —NS/LK/DM

Eisma, Will (Leendert), Dutch violinist and composer; b. Sungailiat, Dutch East Indies, May 13, 1929. He received violin lessons from his father, and then studied violin and counterpoint at the Rotterdam Cons. (1948–53). He also had private composition lessons with Kees van Baaren, and later studied violin with André Gertler and composition with Goffredo Petrassi at the Accademia di Santa Cecilia in Rome (1959–61), and took a course in electronic music in Utrecht. Eisma was a violinist in the Rotterdam Phil. (1953–59), the Società Corelli Chamber Orch. (1960–61), and the Hilversum Radio Chamber Orch. (1961–89). He also organized his own electronic music studio in 1973. His output is in an uncompromisingly modern idiom.

WORKS: ORCH.: 3 concertos (1958, 1959, 1960); Concerto for 2 Violins and Orch. (1961); *Taurus* (1963); *Volumina* (1964); *Diaphora* (1964); *Vanbridge Concerto* for Horn and Orch. (1970); *Little Lane*, oboe concerto (1973); *Le Choix du costume est libre* for String Trio and Chamber Orch. (1974); *Metselwerk* for Percussion and Orch. (1979); *Indian Summer*, English horn concerto (1981); *Suara-suara pada waktu fajar* (Voices at Daybreak) for Gamelan-Slendro and Orch. (1985); *Silver Plated Bronze* for Double Bass and Orch. (1986); *Passo del diavolo* (1988; rev. 1990). CHAMBER: Septet (1959); String Quintet (1961); *Archipel* for String Quartet (1964); *Fontemara* for Wind Quintet (1965); *La Sonorité suspendue* for String Trio (1970); *Concert a vapeur* for Violin, Tape, and Synthesizer (1974); *Mandi* for Brass

Ensemble (1981); *Adventures of a Shawl* for 9 Instruments (1984); *Kalos* for String Quartet and Piano (1987); *Reflections* for Oboe, Clarinet, and Bassoon (1989); *Cairngorm* for 4 Clarinets (1990); *Roestbruin* for 4 Trombones (1991); *Mawar jiwa* for Gamelan and Electronics (1992); *Tjempaka* for String Quartet (1996); *Venezia* for 2 Discant Gambas and Bass Gamba (1998). **VOCAL:** *Orchestral Music with Voice* for Soloists, Chorus, and Orch. (1969); *Le Gibet* for Baritone, 7 Instruments, and Live Electronics (1971); *Le Cheval mort* for Mezzo-soprano, Bass Clarinet, Piano, Percussion, 2 Synthesizers, and Tape (1976); *Du Dehors—Du Dedans* for Mezzo-soprano and Orch. (1983).—**NS/LK/DM**

Eitler, Esteban, Austrian-Chilean composer; b. Bolzano, Tirol, June 25, 1913; d. Sao Paulo, Brazil, June 25, 1960. He studied at the Univ. of Budapest. Leaving Europe in 1936, he went to Buenos Aires, where he was associated with modernist music groups. In 1945 he settled in Santiago, Chile.

WORKS: ORCH.: *Microsinfonia politonal* (1943); *Policromia* for Strings (1950); *Serie boliviana* for Flute and String Orch. (1941); *Microsinfonia atonal* (1956). **CHAMBER:** Concertino for Piano and 11 Instruments (1947); Concertino for Horn and 11 Instruments (1949); Wind Quintet (1945); Quartet for Piccolo, Flute, Trumpet, and Saxophone (1945); Quartet for Flute, Violin, Viola, and Cello (1950).—**NS/LK/DM**

Eitner, Robert, eminent German music scholar; b. Breslau, Oct. 22, 1832; d. Templin, Feb. 2, 1905. He studied in Breslau with Brosig. In 1853 he settled in Berlin, where he taught. In 1868 he founded the Gesellschaft für Musikgeschichte, serving as ed. of its journal, the *Monatschefte für Musikgeschichte*, from 1869; he also ed. the Publikationen älter praktischer und theoretischer Musikwerke from 1873. In 1902 he was granted the honorary title of prof. His major contribution to musical scholarship was his *Biographisch-bibliograsphisches Quellen-Lexikon der Musiker und Musikgelehrten der Christlichen Zeitrechnung bis zur Mitte des neunzehten Jahrhunderts* (10 vols., Leipzig, 1900–04; additions and corrections ed. by H. Springer, M. Schneider, and W. Wolffheim as *Miscellanea Musicae Bio-bibliographica*, 4 vols., 1912–16; 2nd ed., rev. and aug., 1959–60). This invaluable source gives information on publ. and MS music in more than 200 libraries in Europe. He also publ. *Verzeichnis neuer Ausgaben alter Musikwerke aus der frühesten Zeit bis zum Jahre 1800* (Berlin, 1871); with F. Haberl, A. Lagerberg, and C. Pohl, *Bibliographie der Musik-Sämmelwerke des XVI. und XVII. Jahrhunderts* (Berlin, 1877); *Die Oper von ihren ersten Anfängen bis 1750* (3 vols., Berlin, 1881–85); *Bücherverzeichnis der Musik-Literatur aus den Jahren 1839 bis 1846 im Anschluss an Becker und Büchtig* (Berlin, 1885); *Quellen- und Hilfswerke beim Studium der Musikgeschichte* (Leipzig, 1891); *Buch- und Musikalienhandler, Buch- und Musikaliendrucker nebst Notenstecher, nur die Musik betreffend* (Leipzig, 1904). He also composed the biblical opera *Judith*, an overture, a piano fantasia on themes from *Tristan und Isolde*, and songs.—**NS/LK/DM**

Eitz, Carl (Andreas), German music theorist; b. Wehrstedt, near Halberstadt, June 25, 1848; d. Eisleben, April 18, 1924. He originated a new system of solmisa-

tion ("Tonwortmethode"), somewhat similar to the English tonic sol-fa system. He also proposed a new unit of musical interval ("Millioktav"), a division of the octave into 1,000 equal parts, which was not adopted.

WRITINGS: *Das mathematisch-reine Tonsystem* (1891); *100 geistliche Liedweisen in Tonsilben gesetzt* (1893); *Deutsche Singfibel* (1899); *Tonwort-Wandtafel* (1907); *Bausteine zum Schulgesangunterricht im Sinne der Tonwortmethode* (Leipzig, 1911; 2nd ed., ed. by F. Bennedik, 1928).

BIBL.: G. Borchers, *C. E.* (1908); O. Messmer, *Die Tonwortmethode von C. E.* (Würzburg, 1911); F. Bennedik, *Historische und psychologisch-musikalische Untersuchungen über die Tonwortmethode von E.* (Langensalza, 1914); M. Koch, *Kurzgefasste Einführung in das Esche Tonwort* (Würzburg, 1925); F. Bennedik and A. Strube, *Handbuch für den Tonwortunterricht* (Leipzig, 1926; 5th ed., 1932); W. Stolte, *C. E. in seiner Bedeutung für Wissenschaft und Schule* (Detmold, 1951).—**NS/LK/DM**

Ek, (Fritz) Gunnar (Rudolf), Swedish cellist, organist, and composer; b. Åsarum, June 21, 1900; d. Lund, June 21, 1981. After training in Lund, he studied with Gustaf Hägg and Otto Olsson (cello and organ) and Ernst Ellberg (composition) at the Stockholm Cons. (1920–26). He was a cellist in the orch. of the Swedish film industry (1928–37); after serving as organist in Ostra Eneby, near Norrköping (1938–42), he was organist and director of music at All Saint's Church in Lund; he also was cellist in the Skåne Quartet. His output reveals a sure hand at contrapuntal writing.

WORKS: ORCH.: 3 syms.: No. 1 (1922–24; rev. 1940), No. 2 (1928–30), and No. 3 (1931–32); *Svensk fantasi* (1935); *Fantasi* for Violin and Orch. (1936); *Koralsvit* (1936); *Fantasy and Fugue* for Strings (1939–40; rev., 1963, as *Fantasy, Fugue, and Coda*); Concert Overture (1940); Piano Concerto (1944); *Dorisk Suite* for Strings and 5 Winds (1966; rev. 1968–69); *Variations on a Chorale Theme* for Strings (1969); Concertino for Strings (1971). **CHAMBER:** Wind Octet (1970); Organ Suite (1966); organ pieces. **VOCAL:** *Doomsday Cantata* (1946); *Dig vare lov och pris, O Krist*, choral fantasy with organ and strings (1950; Malmö, Dec. 13, 1964); songs.—**NS/LK/DM**

Ekier, Jan (Stanisław), Polish pianist, pedagogue, editor, and composer; b. Kraków, Aug. 29, 1913. He studied musicology with Zdzisław Jachimecki at the Jagiellonian Univ. in Kraków (1932–34), and then was a student at the Warsaw Cons. (1934–39) of Zbigniew Drzewiecki (piano) and Kazimierz Sikorski (composition). In 1940–41 he pursued training in organ with Bronisław Rutkowski. After winning eighth prize in the Chopin Competition in Warsaw in 1937, he toured as a pianist in Europe, South America, and Japan. In 1946–47 he taught at the State Secondary Music School in Lublin, and then was rector of the State Higher School of Music in Sopot in 1947–48. He became a prof. at the State Higher School of music (later the Academy of Music) in Warsaw, where he held the piano chair from 1964 to 1972 and again from 1974. He also gave masterclasses around the world. In 1959 he became ed.-in-chief of the "National Edition" of Chopin's complete works. From 1985 he also served as president of the jury of the Chopin Competition in Warsaw. In 1964 and 1974 he received the Minister of Culture and Arts Award, First Class.

WORKS: DRAMATIC: *Straszak*, children's ballet (1933); *Émierć Fauna* (A Faun's Death), stage piece (1933); *Tempo dnia* (The Pace of Day), ballet (1934). **ORCH.:** *Suita góralska* (Highlander's Suite) for Chamber Orch. (1935; also for Orch., 1937); Piano Concerto (1949). **CHAMBER:** *Variations and Fugue for String Quartet* (1937). **Piano:** 2 Preludes (1932); *Humoreska* (1933); 2 Mazurkas (1933); *Kołysanka* (Lullaby; 1933); *Toccata* (1935); *Mazurka* (1935); *Krakowiak* (1936); *Taniec góralski* (A Highlander Dance; 1938); *Kolorowe melodie* (Colorful Melodies; 1949). **VOCAL:** *Kolorowe melodie* (Colorful Melodies) for Chorus and Orch. (1951).—**NS/LK/DM**

Eklund, Hans, prominent Swedish composer and teacher; b. Sandviken, July 1, 1927; d. Stockholm, March 8, 1999. He studied at the Stockholm Musikhogskolan with Åke Uddén and Lars-Erik Larsson (1947–52) and with Ernst Pepping in Berlin (1954) before completing his training in Rome (1957). He was prof. of harmony and counterpoint at the Stockholm Musikhögskolan (from 1964). In 1975 he was elected a member of the Royal Swedish Academy of Music. In 1985 he was awarded the degree of Litteris et Artibus from the King of Sweden. Edlund's large output was notable for its imaginative handling of traditional forms.

WORKS: Radio Opera: *Moder Svea* (Mother Svea; Swedish Radio, Oct. 7, 1972). **ORCH.:** *Variations for Strings* (1952); *Symphonic Dances* (1954); *Musica da camera*: No. 1 for Cello and Chamber Orch. (1955), No. 2, *Art Tatum in Memoriam*, for Trumpet, Piano, Percussion, and Strings (1956), No. 3 for Violin and Chamber Orch. (1957). No. 4 for Piano and Orch. (1959), No. 5, *Fantasia*, for Cello and Strings (1970), and No. 6 for Oboe and Chamber Orch. (1970); 12 syms.: No. 1, *Sinfonia seria* (1958), No. 2, *Sinfonia breve* (1964), No. 3, *Sinfonia rustica* (1967–68), No. 4, *Hjalmar Branting in Memoriam*, for Narrator and Orch. (1973–74), No. 5, *Quadri* (1978), No. 6, *Sinfonia senza speranza* (1983), No. 7, *La Serenata* (1984), No. 8, *Sinfonia grave* (1985), No. 9, *Sinfonia introvertita* (1992- 93), No. 10, *sine nomine* (1994), No. 11, *Sinfonia piccola* (1995), and No. 12, *Sinfonia freschi* (1996); *Introduzione-Versioni e Finale* for Strings (1962–63); *Facce* (1964); *Toccata* (1966); *Interludio* (1967); *Primavera* for Strings (1967); *Pezzo elegiaco* for Cello, Percussion, and Strings (1969); *Introduction and Allegro* for Harpsichord and Strings (1972); Concerto for Trombone, Winds, and Percussion (1972); *Variazioni pastorali* for Strings (1974); Chamber Concerto for Violin and Strings (1977); Horn Concerto (1979); Concerto for Clarinet and Strings (1980); Concerto for Tuba and Brass Orch. (1980); Concerto for Clarinet, Cello, and Orch. (1983); *Fantasie breve* (1986); *Divertimento* (1986); *L'estate* for Strings (1986); *Concerto Grosso* for String Quartet and String Orch. (1987); *Due pezzi* (1988); *Mesto per archi* (1989); *Apertura* (1991). **CHAMBER:** 4 string quartets (withdrawn, 1954, 1960, 1964); 2 sonatas for Solo Violin (1956, 1982); *Improvisata* for Wind Quintet (1958); Piano Trio (1963); *4 Temperamenti* for 4 Clarinets (1963); *Sommarparafras* for Wind Quintet (1968); *Serenade* for Mixed Quintet (1978); *Omaggio à San Michele* for 4 Saxophones (1981); *5 Pieces for Clarinet* (1983), Oboe (1983), Bassoon (1983), and Double Bass (1984); *Serenade* for 10 Brass Instruments (1986); *Serenata* for Flute and Piano (1990); piano pieces; organ music. **VOCAL:** *Den fula ankungen* for Soloists, Children's Chorus, and Orch. (1976); *Requiem* for 2 Soloists, Chorus, and Orch. (1978; Stockholm, Nov. 24, 1979); *Homofoni* for Chorus (1987); *3 Sea Poems* for Chorus (1988).—**NS/LK/DM**

Ekman, Karl, Finnish pianist and conductor; b. Kaarina, near Åbo, Dec. 18, 1869; d. Helsinki, Feb. 4, 1947. He studied in Helsinki (1889–92), and from 1892 to 1895 was a pupil of H. Barth in Berlin and A. Grünfeld in Vienna. In 1895 he became a piano teacher at the Helsinki Cons., and from 1907 to 1911 he was director there; from 1912 to 1920 he was conductor of the orch. at Åbo. He arranged Swedish and Finnish folk songs, and ed. a piano method; publ. a biography of Sibelius (Stockholm, 1935; Eng. tr., 1936). His wife, Ida (b. Helsinki, April 22, 1875; d. there, April 14, 1942), was a concert singer. She studied in Helsinki, Paris, and Veinna, being later distinguished for her performances of Sibelius's songs.—**NS/LK/DM**

El-Dabh, Halim (Abdul Messieh), Egyptian-born American composer; b. Cairo, March 4, 1921. He studied piano and Western music at the Sulcz Cons. in Cairo (1941–44), then went to the U.S. in 1950 on a Fulbright fellowship, studying with Aaron Copland and Irving Fine at the Berkshire Music Center at Tanglewood and taking graduate degrees from the New England Cons. of Music and Brandeis Univ. In 1961 he became a naturalized American citizen. He taught at Haile Selassie Univ. in Ethiopia (1962–64), Howard Univ. (1966–69), and Kent State Univ. (from 1969), where he later also was co-director of its Center for the Study of World Musics (from 1979). His compositions reveal Afro-Arab influences, especially in their rhythmic structures and their incorporation of unusual percussive devices. He publ. *The Derabucca: Hand Techniques in the Art of Drumming* (1965).

WORKS: DRAMATIC: *Clytemnestra*, epic dance drama (for Martha Graham; 1958); *The Egyptian Series: Lament of the Pharaohs, Pyramid Rock to the Sky, Gloria Aton*, and *Prayer to the Sphinx* for Solo Voices, Chorus, and Orch. (1960); *The Islamic Series: Allahu Akbar, Al- khaeera, Ya Leiyly, Saladin and the Citadel*, and *The Nile* for Voices ad libitum and Orch. (1960); *Theodora in Byzantium* (1965); *Black Epic*, opera-pageant (1968); *Opera Flies* (1971); *Ptahmose and the Magic Spell*, opera trilogy: *The Osiris Ritual, Aton, the Ankh, and the World*, and *The 12 Hours Trip* (1972–73); *Drink of Eternity*, opera-pageant (1981). **ORCH.:** 3 syms. (1950, 1952, 1956); Concerto for Darabukka or Timpani and Strings (1954); *Fantasia-Tahmeel* for Darabukka or Timpani and Strings (1954); *Bacchanalia* (1958); *Tahmeela* for Flute and Chamber Orch. (1958–59); *Nomadic Waves* for Double Wind Orch. and Percussion; *Unity at the Cross Road*; Concerto for Darabukka, Clarinet, and Strings (1981); *Rhapsodia egyptiabrasileira* (1985). **OTHER:** Chamber music; piano pieces; choruses.—**NS/LK/DM**

Elder, Mark (Philip), prominent English conductor; b. Hexham, June 2, 1947. He studied in Bryanston and played bassoon in the National Youth Orch. before pursuing his education at the Univ. of Cambridge (B.A., M.A.). In 1969–70 he was on the music staff of the Wexford Festival. In 1970 he became an asst. conductor at the Glyndebourne Festival, serving as chorus master until 1972. From 1972 to 1974 he was a staff conductor at the Australian Opera in Sydney. In 1974 he became a conductor at the English National Opera in London. He made his debut at London's Covent Garden in 1976 conducting *Rigoletto*. In 1977 he became assoc. conductor at the English National Opera, and subsequently served as its music director from 1979 to 1993. During his tenure there, Elder conducted the British premieres of several operas by masters of the past as well as the world premieres of operas by contemporary composers. From 1980 to 1983 he was principal guest conductor of the London Mozart Players, and, from 1982 to 1985, of the BBC Sym. Orch. in London. In 1981 he made his first appearance at the Bayreuth Festival conducting *Die Meistersinger von Nürnberg*. He made his U.S. debut as a guest conductor of the Chicago Sym. Orch. in 1983. In 1988 he conducted *Le Nozze di Figaro* at the Metropolitan Opera in N.Y. From 1989 to 1994 he was music director of the Rochester (N.Y.) Phil. From 1992 to 1995 he was principal guest conductor of the City of Birmingham Sym. Orch. In 1999 he became music director of the Hallé Orch. in Manchester. In 1989 he was made a Commander of the Order of the British Empire. —NS/LK/DM

Eldridge, (David) Roy (aka Little Jazz),

noted jazz trumpeter, flugelhornist, singer, drummer, pianist; b. Pittsburgh, Jan. 30, 1911; d. Valley Stream, L.I., N.Y., Feb. 26, 1989. Eldridge was a brilliant, hair-raising daredevil of an improvisor, especially on his recordings of 1936–41. He was the primary influence on young Dizzy Gillespie, Joe Guy, and numerous other trumpeters. Trombonist Otto Hardwick gave him his nickname of "Little Jazz."

Eldridge played drums at the age of six, then the bugle before graduating to trumpet taught by P. M. Williams and his brother Joe (b. Pittsburgh, 1908; d. March 5, 1952), who was an alto saxophonist and violinist. Roy also picked up some ability on piano. As a youngster, Eldridge played throughout the Midwest with traveling shows and territory bands. He moved to N.Y. in November 1930, working with Elmer Snowden, Charlie Johnson, and Teddy Hill before touring with the *Hot Chocolates Show*. In 1933, he founded his first band with his brother Joe in Pittsburgh, then worked with McKinney's Band in Baltimore. In 1935, he returned to N.Y. to rejoin Teddy Hill at the Savoy Ballroom. After a spell with Fletcher Henderson (1935–36), Eldridge formed his own band (again with Joe) for a long residency at Sam Beer's Three Deuces Club in Chicago (in autumn 1937, Eldridge took a brief break to recover from pneumonia). The band toured in 1938, making its N.Y. debut at the Savoy Ballroom in August 1938. Soon after, Eldridge briefly left full-time music to study radio engineering, but by November, he had reformed his own band playing N.Y.–area clubs through October 1940, when the group disbanded.

Eldridge then returned to Chicago, leading his own small group for residency at Capitol Lounge. He joined Gene Krupa as featured soloist in April 1941, being the first black musician to join an otherwise white band not just as a featured attraction or singer, but as a regular member of the section. He remained until the band broke up in the spring of 1943 (he occasionally played drums while Krupa fronted the band). From June 1943 to early 1944, he again led his own band, playing in N.Y., Toronto, and Chicago. He then worked as a single and in pickup bands, until joining Artie Shaw, playing

with the band from October 1944–September 1945. By February 1946, he was back in the leader's chair, playing residencies in Chicago, N.Y., and Calif. This band lasted until February 1949, when he rejoined Gene Krupa; Eldridge left in September 1949 to feature in first national J.A.T.P. tour. He went to Europe with Benny Goodman in April 1950; when Goodman returned home in June, Roy toured Europe as a single. After a long stay in Paris, he returned to N.Y. in 1951. Through the 1950s, Roy lead small groups, made many guest star appearances, and was regularly featured with Norman Granz's J.A.T.P. tours (including many trips to Europe). Beginning in 1952, he did regular club and concert dates in quintet co-led with Coleman Hawkins, together they did several overseas tours for Norman Granz, and also appeared at many jazz festivals in the U.S. During the 1950s he also recorded on drums and piano; Garvin Bushell says he gave Eldridge some lessons on saxophone during this period as well. In the late 1950s and early 1960s, Eldridge played many dates with clarinetist Sol Yaged. While still leading his own small groups, Eldridge worked with Ella Fitzgerald from late 1963–March 1965, and then briefly with Count Basie from July 1–Sept. 17, 1966. He toured Europe with the "Jazz from a Swinging Era" package in the spring of 1967. Eldridge continued to work as a soloist and group leader through the 1970s, including an appearance at the first New Orleans Jazz Festival (1969). He was featured at President Jimmy Carter's White House Jazz Party in June 1978. Although plagued by ill health after a 1980 heart attack, he made occasional appearances as a singer, drummer, and pianist until his death. A party was thrown for him at St. Peter's Church in Manhattan around the time of his 75th birthday in January 1986. He died three years later.

DISC.: *After You've Gone* (1936); *Live at the Three Deuces* (1937); *Arcadia Shuffle* (1939); *At Jerry Newman's* (1940); *All the Cats Join In* (1943); *I Remember Harlem* (1950); *Roy Eldridge in Paris* (1950); *Roy Eldridge in Sweden* (1951); *Dale's Wail* (1952); *Roy Eldridge with Zoot Sims* (1954); *Roy and Diz, Vols. 1, 2* (1954); *Tour De Force* (1955); *1957 Live* (1957); *And Benny Carter* (1957); *At the Opera House* (1957); *Little Jazz Live in 1957* (1957); *Swing Goes Dixie* (1957); *Just You Just Me, Live in 1959* (1959); *Nifty Cat Strikes West* (1966); *Jazz Maturity...Where It's Coming From* (1975); *Little Jazz & The Jimmy Ryan All Stars* (1975); *Trumpet Kings at Montreux* (1975); *What It's All About* (1976); *Montreux* (1977); *Roy Eldridge Four* (1977).

BIBL.: J. Evensmo, *The Trumpet of R. E. 1929–1944* (Hosle, Norway, 1979); *The Artistry of Roy Eldridge* (trans. by Thomas W. Stewart Jr.; Denton, Tex.,1989).—JC/LP

Electric Light Orchestra (ELO),

an enigmatic and controversial 1960s British singles band; formed in 1971 by Roy Wood, Jeff Lynne, and Bev Bevan. **MEMBERSHIP:** Roy Wood, gtr., voc. (b. Birmingham, England, Nov. 8, 1946); Jeff Lynne, gtr., voc. (b. Birmingham, England, Dec. 30, 1947); Bev Bevan, drm. (b. Birmingham, England, Nov. 25, 1945). Roy Wood left after the first album and Richard Tandy, kybd. (b. Birmingham, England, March 26, 1948) was added.

Formed out of the Move, the Electric Light Orchestra realized Roy Wood's conception of an electric rock band augmented by a classical string section. Ironically, Wood left after only one album, ceding leadership of the group to Jeff Lynne. Despite the fact that the string section produced little more than gratuitous four- and eight-bar introductions and a lush orchestral sound, the Electric Light Orchestra was hailed as one of the most successful progressive- rock groups of the 1970s. Certainly one of the world's top concert attractions by the late 1970s, the Electric Light Orchestra toured America in 1978 with a massive stage structure and laser light show, a testament to technology and the public's apparent demand for extravagant stage presentation. After the group's demise, during the late 1980s Jeff Lynne established himself as a producer and member of the supergroup the Traveling Wilburys.

Formed in late 1965 by a number of musicians from the Birmingham area, the Move quickly drew the attention of the London underground with their dramatic and often violent stage presentations. Roy Wood had previously manned Gerry Levene and the Avengers with Graeme Edge (later with the Moody Blues) and Mike Sheridan and the Nightriders. Trevor Burton had played guitar with Danny King and the Mayfair Set, while Bev Bevan had drummed with Denny Laine and the Diplomats and Carl Wayne and the Vikings, which included vocalist Wayne and bassist Ace Kefford. With Wood composing virtually all the Move's material, the band scored a series of British hits with "Night of Fear,""I Can Hear the Grass Grow," "Flowers in the Rain," "Fire Brigade," and "Blackberry Way." Gaining notoriety for smashing TV sets and pianos on stage, the Move remained virtually unknown in the United States for years. Personnel changes started in 1968, and by 1970 guitarist-vocalist Jeff Lynne was brought in for the avowed reason of forming an outfit that would combine classical strings and rock instrumentation. Lynne had played with the Idle Race for four years, recording one album with the group. By the time of the Move's first (minor) American hit, Lynne's "Do Ya," the group had disbanded.

The newly-formed Electric Light Orchestra signed with United Artists and recorded the critically acclaimed *No Answer*, which yielded a British hit with Lynne's "10538 Overture." However, by 1972 Wood had lost interest in the project and left the group to form Wizzard with onetime Move bassist Rick Price. During the 1970s Wood recorded two albums with Wizzard and three solo albums.

The true beginning of the Electric Light Orchestra came with the album *ELO II*. Jeff Lynne assumed the role of producer, arranger, composer, lead vocalist, and lead guitarist, and added keyboardist Richard Tandy, a bassist, and three former members of the London Symphony Orchestra (two cellists and a violinist). *ELO II* secured the band's position at the forefront of progressive rock and yielded their first albeit minor American hit with a remake of Chuck Berry's "Roll Over, Beethoven." The band completed its first American tour in the summer of 1973, in support of their next album, *On the Third Day*, which produced two minor American hits, "Showdown" and "Daybreaker." *Eldorado* yielded a near-smash hit with the Bee Gees—sounding "Can't Get It Out of My Head."

When their next album, *Face the Music*, was released in 1975, the Electric Light Orchestra's lineup had stabilized with Lynne, Tandy, Bevan, bassist-vocalist Kelly Groucutt, cellists Hugh McDowell and Melvyn Gale, and violinist Mik Kaminski. The album featured the major hits "Evil Woman" and "Strange Magic," whereas 1976's *A New World Record* produced the hits "Livin' Thing," "Telephone Line," and a remake of the Move's "Do Ya." *Out of the Blue* contained Lynne's first extended piece since *Eldorado*, the side-long "Concerto for a Rainy Day," and the hits "Turn to Stone" and "Sweet Talkin' Woman."

For their 1978 American tour the Electric Light Orchestra assembled one of the most spectacular and grandiose stage presentations in the history of rock music. For approximately half of the tour's shows, the band utilized a 5-ton, 60-foot-wide fiberglass structure resembling a spaceship. The top half of the structure ascended to reveal the band inside. Complete with synchronized lasers, the production stood as a remarkable tribute to technology and showmanship.

In 1978 the Electric Light Orchestra switched to Columbia Records, with all previous and subsequent albums through 1983 released on the Jet subsidiary. Their Jet debut, *Discovery*, was recorded with a 42-piece German Orchestra and a 30-voice all-male choir, yielding two smash hits, "Shine a Little Love" and "Don't Bring Me Down," and two moderate hits, "Confusion" and "Last Train to London." In 1980 the group recorded most of the music for the movie *Xanadu*, starring Gene Kelly and Olivia Newton-John. The soundtrack album produced two Electric Light Orchestra hits with "I'm Alive" and "All Over the World," and a near-smash hit with the title song, recorded with Newton- John. Adopting the moniker ELO for a time, the group scored major hits with the rockabilly-style "Hold on Tight" in 1981 and "Rock 'n' Roll Is King" in 1983, but then the band dissolved.

Jeff Lynne managed a minor solo hit with "Video" from the 1984 movie *Electric Dreams*. The Electric Light Orchestra (Lynne, Tandy, and Bevan) reemerged in 1986 with *Balance of Power* and the hit "Calling America" on CBS Associated. During the late 1980s Lynne produced albums for George Harrison (*Cloud Nine*) and Tom Petty (*Full Moon Fever*) and worked on albums by Duane Eddy, Del Shannon, and Roy Orbison. In 1988 and again in 1990 he recorded with the supergroup the Traveling Wilburys. A playful exercise, the group's members all took fictitious names, such as Nelson (George Harrison), Lucky (Bob Dylan), Lefty (Roy Orbison), Charlie T. Jr. (Tom Petty), and Otis (Lynne); for *Volume 3* the Wilburys were Spike (Harrison), Boo (Dylan), Muddy (Petty), and Clayton (Lynne). In the 1990s Lynne recorded *Armchair Theatre* for Reprise, which disappeared on the charts, and produced Tom Petty and the Heartbreakers' *Into the Great Wide Open*. In 1991 Bev Bevan formed Electric Light Orchestra Part Two; one year later they enlisted the aid of the Moscow Symphony Orchestra to stage a live show of their greatest hits, subsequently released on record.

DISC.: THE IDLE RACE (WITH JEFF LYNNE): *The Birthday Party* (1969). **THE MOVE:** *Shazam* (1970); *Looking On* (1971); *Message from the Country* (1971); *Split Ends* (1973); *Best* (1974); *Best* (1994). **ROY WOOD:** *Wizzard's Brew* (1973); *Boulders* (1973); *Introducing Eddy and the Falcons* (1974); *Mustard* (1976); *Super Active Wizzo* (1977); *On the Road* (1981); *One Man Band* (1981). **THE ELECTRIC LIGHT ORCHESTRA:** *No Answer* (1972); *ELO II* (1973); *On the Third Day* (1973); *Eldorado* (1974); *Face the Music* (1975); *Olé ELO* (1976); *A New World Record* (1976); *Out of the Blue* (1977); *Discovery* (1979); *Greatest Hits* (1979); *A Box of Their Best* (1980); *Time* (1981); *Secret Messages* (1983); *Balance of Power* (1986); *Afterglow* (1990); *Moment of Truth* (1995). **ELO AND OLIVIA NEWTON-JOHN:** *Xanadu* (soundtrack; 1980). **THE TRAVELING WILBURYS (WITH JEFF LYNNE):** *Volume One* (1988); *Volume 3* (1990). **JEFF LYNNE:** *Armchair Theatre* (1990). **ELECTRIC LIGHT ORCHESTRA PART TWO:** *ELO Part Two* (1991); *ELO's Greatest Hits Live* (1992).—**BH**

Eler, André-Frédéric, French composer and pedagogue; b. Alsace, 1764; d. Paris, April 21, 1821. He settled in Paris, where he was a librarian (1795–97) and then a teacher (1797–1821) at the Cons.

WORKS: DRAMATIC: *Le chant des vengeances* (Paris, May 7, 1798); *Apelle et Campaspe*, opera (Paris, July 12, 1798); *L'habit de la Duchesse de Grammont*, opéra-comique (Paris, Jan. 8, 1801); *L'habit du Chevalier de Grammont*, opéra comique (Paris, Dec. 6, 1803); *La forêt de Brama*, opera (not perf.). **ORCH.:** Symphonie concertante for Flute, Clarinet, Horn, Bassoon, and Orch.; Symphonie concertante for Flute, Horn, Bassoon, and Orch.; Ouverture; Ouverture for Wind Band; 2 horn concertos; Oboe Concerto. **CHAMBER:** 21 quartets: 3 for Horn, Violin, Viola, and Bass; 3 for 2 Violins, Viola, and Bass; 3 for Flute, Clarinet, Horn, and Bassoon; 3 for Flute, Violin, Viola, and Bass; 3 for 2 Clarinets, Horn, and Bassoon; 3 for Flute, Clarinet, Horn, and Bassoon; 3 for Flute, Violin, Viola, and Bass; 6 trios: 3 for 2 Violins and Cello; 3 for Flute, Clarinet, and Bassoon; 3 sonatas for Piano and Violin ad libitum. **VOCAL:** *Scène française* (Paris, Aug. 15, 1789); *Ode sur la situation de la République en prairial, an VII* for Voice, 2 Clarinets, 2 Horns, and 2 Bassoons (1799); various canons.—**LK/DM**

Elf, Mark, bebop-flavored guitarist, composer, arranger, educator; b. Queens, N.Y., Dec. 13, 1949. He studied from 1969 to 1971 at Berklee Coll. of Music, and studied privately with Barry Galbraith and Chuck Wayne. He then moved to N.Y. where he worked as a freelance musician. He has performed with many leading names in the bop field, both from the first and second generations of players. He has also accompanied jazz and pop vocalists, including Etta James, Ruth Brown, and Liza Minelli. His educational activities began in 1974–75 with an International Art of Jazz Concert Series in the Nassau County Schools, N.Y. He has subsequently taught at S.U.N.Y., Stonybrook, the New School, and at various summer clinics and other colleges. From 1997, he has been on the faculty at Aaron Copland School of Music, Queens Coll., N.Y. Two of his CDs, *A Minor Scramble* and *Trickynometry*, reached the top of the Gavin Jazz Chart, indicating that they were widely played on radio stations. He operates his own record label to release his works.

DISC.: *Mark Elf Trio, Vol. I* (1986); *Eternal Triangle* (1988); *Mark Elf Trio* (1993); *A Minor Scramble* (1997); *New York Cats* (1998); *Trickynometry* (1998).—**LP**

Elfman, Danny, noted composer of film soundtracks; b. Amarillo, Tex., May 29, 1953. Danny Elfman comes by his creativity honestly. His mother, Blossom Elfman, wrote a number of popular novels and won an Emmy for a TV movie. He was raised in L.A., but by their late teens, he and his brother Richard had relocated to France where Danny became a member of a theatrical group. He then spent some time in Africa, but a severe case of malaria sent him home to the U.S. His brother, in the meanwhile, had made a film called *The Forbidden Zone.* He asked Danny to create the score. Danny assembled a group for this purpose, which he called "The Mystic Knights of Oingo Boingo." After the soundtrack was complete, the group took on a life of its own. Led by Elfman, they became a new-wave band with horns, performing often strange and macabre tunes. They earned a massive following in Calif. but not much interest elsewhere. While it didn't earn the band hits, they did land songs in many movies, including *Fast Times at Ridgemont High.*

However, one of the Californians who liked the band was Tim Burton. He asked Elfman to create a score for his film *Pee-Wee's Big Adventure.* This led to a long and fruitful relationship that found Elfman scoring the Burton films *Beetlejuice, Batman, Edward Scissorhands,* and *Mars Attacks. Batman* won him a Grammy Award in 1990 for Best Instrumental Composition. More of a collaboration, Burton's animated *The Nightmare Before Christmas* featured Elfman, scoring, writing songs, and performing the singing voice of the film's main character. When not working with Burton, he created the scores for *Darkman, Dick Tracy, Good Will Hunting, Mission Impossible,* and *Men in Black,* among many others. He scored his friend Francis Delia's film *Freeway,* charging $1 for the service. He also wrote the theme music to the TV show *The Simpsons,* and his themes from *Beetlejuice* and *Batman* were used as themes for the subsequent cartoons based on them.

By 1995, his workload in Hollywood made continuing with the band untenable, and Oingo Boingo (by then further shortened to just Boingo) broke up. He continues to work with the band's guitarist, Steve Bartek, who does most of Elfman's orchestrations.

DISC.: *So Lo* (1984); *Midnight Run* (1988); *Beetlejuice* (1988); *Big Top Pee Wee* (1988); *Batman* (1989); (composer of original motion picture score) *Nightbreed* (1990); *The Story of Edward Scissorhands* (1990); *Dick Tracy* (score; 1990); *Darkman* (1990); *Edward Scissorhands* (original soundtrack; 1990); *Article 99* (1992); *Batman Returns* (1992); *Dolores Claiborne* (1995); *Mission Impossible* (score; 1996).—**HB**

Elgar, Sir Edward (William), great English composer; b. Broadheath, near Worcester, June 2, 1857; d. Worcester, Feb. 23, 1934. He received his earliest music education from his father, who owned a music shop and was organist for the St. George's Roman Catholic Church in Worcester, and then took violin lessons from a local musician. He rapidly acquired the fundamentals of theory and served as arranger with the Worcester Glee Club, becoming its conductor at the age of 22. He accepted a rather unusual position for a young aspiring musician with the County of Worcester Lunatic Asylum at Powick, where he was for several years in charge of the institution's concert band. He was also engaged in various other musical affairs. In 1885 he succeeded his father as organist at St. George's. He married in 1889 and moved to Malvern, where he stayed from 1891 to 1904. During these years, he conducted the Worcestershire Phil. (1898–1904). In 1905 he accepted the position of Peyton Prof. of Music at the Univ. of Birmingham, and in 1911–12 served as conductor of the London Sym. Orch. He then settled in Hampstead. His wife died in 1920, at which time he returned to Worcester.

Elgar's first major success was with the concert overture *Froissart* (Worcester, Sept. 9, 1890). His cantata *The Black Knight* was premiered at the Worcester Festival (April 18, 1893) and was also heard in London at the Crystal Palace (Oct. 23, 1897). The first performance of his cantata *Scenes from the Saga of King Olaf* at the North Staffordshire Music Festival (Oct. 30, 1896) attracted considerable attention. He gained further recognition with his *Imperial March* (1897), composed for the Diamond Jubilee of Queen Victoria. From then on, Elgar's name became familiar to the musical public. There followed the cantata *Caractacus* (Leeds Festival, Oct. 5, 1898) and Elgar's great masterpiece, the oratorio *The Dream of Gerontius* (Birmingham Festival, Oct. 14, 1900). He began to give more and more attention to orch. music. On June 19, 1899, Hans Richter presented the first performance of Elgar's *Variations on an Original Theme* (generally known as the *Enigma Variations*) in London. This work consists of 14 sections, each marked by initials of fancied names of Elgar's friends; in later years, Elgar issued cryptic hints as to the identities of these persons, which were finally revealed. He also stated that the theme itself was a counterpoint to a familiar tune, but the concealed subject was never revealed by the composer. The success of the *Enigma Variations* was followed (1901–30) by the composition of Elgar's *Pomp and Circumstance* marches, the first of which became his most famous piece through a setting to words by Arthur Christopher Benson, used by Elgar in the *Coronation Ode* (1902) as *Land of Hope and Glory*; another successful orch. work was the *Cockaigne Overture* (London, June 20, 1901). Elgar's 2 syms., written between 1903 and 1910, became staples in the English orch. repertoire. His Violin Concerto, first performed by Fritz Kreisler (London, Nov. 10, 1910), won notable success; there was also a remarkable Cello Concerto (London, Oct. 26, 1919, Felix Salmond soloist, composer conducting). About 1909 Elgar began sketching a piano concerto, but the score was never finished. Some measures were used in the finale of his uncompleted 3rd Sym. In the 1950s a pianist uncovered what was purported to be the full sketch of the concerto's slow movement. In the 1990s Robert Walker converted Elgar's sketches, with added material of his own, into a piece for piano and orch. he titled Fragments of Elgar, which was premiered in Dartington in 1997. Elgar's

sketches for his 3rd Sym. (1933) were realized by Anthony Payne in 1998.

The emergence of Elgar as a major composer about 1900 was all the more remarkable since he had no formal academic training. Yet he developed a masterly technique of instrumental and vocal writing. His style of composition may be described as functional Romanticism; his harmonic procedures remain firmly within the 19th century tradition; the formal element is always strong, and the thematic development logical and precise. Elgar had a melodic gift, which asserted itself in his earliest works, such as the popular *Salut d'amour*; his oratorios, particularly *The Apostles*, were the product of his fervent religious faith (he was a Roman Catholic). He avoided archaic usages of Gregorian chant; rather, he presented the sacred subjects in a communicative style of secular drama. Elgar was the recipient of many honors. He was knighted in 1904. He received honorary degrees of Mus.Doc. from Cambridge (1900), Oxford (1905), and Aberdeen (1906), and also an LL.D. from Leeds (1904). During his first visit to the U.S., in 1905, he received a D.Mus. degree from Yale Univ.; in 1907 he was granted the same degree from the Univ. of Western Pa. (now the Univ. of Pittsburgh). He received the Order of Merit in 1911, and was made a Knight Commander of the Royal Victorian Order in 1928 and a baronet in 1931. Elgar was appointed Master of the King's Musick in 1924. He was not a proficient conductor, but appeared on various occasions with orchs. in his own works; during the 3rd of his 4 visits to the U.S. (1905, 1906, 1907, 1911), he conducted his oratorio *The Apostles* (N.Y., 1907); also led the mass chorus at the opening of the British Empire Exhibition in 1924. His link with America was secured when the hymnlike section from his first *Pomp and Circumstance* march became a popular recession march for American high school graduation exercises.

WORKS: DRAMATIC: Opera: *The Spanish Lady*, op.89 (unfinished; sketches date from 1878; 15 excerpts orchestrated by Percy M. Young; BBC, London, Dec. 4, 1969). **INCIDENTAL MUSIC TO:** *Grania and Diarmid*, op.42 (Yeats and Moore; Dublin, Oct. 1901); *The Starlight Express*, op.78 (Blackwood and Pearn; London, Dec. 29, 1915); *King Arthur* (Binyon; London, March 12, 1923); *Beau Brummel* (Matthews; Birmingham, Nov. 5, 1928, composer conducting). **MASQUE:** *The Crown of India*, op.66 (1902-12; London, March 11, 1912; as a suite for Orch., Hereford Festival, Sept. 11, 1912, composer conducting). **Ballet:** *The Sanguine Fan*, op.81 (London, March 20, 1917). **ORCH.:** *Introductory Overture for Christy Minstrels* (Worcester, June 12, 1878, composer conducting); *Minuet-grazioso* (Worcester, Jan. 23, 1879); Suite in D major for Small Orch. (1882; 1st complete perf., Birmingham, March 1, 1888; rev. as 3 Characteristic Pieces, op.10 [1899]: No. 1, *Mazurka*, No. 2, *Serenade mauresque*, and No. 3, *Contrasts: The Gavotte A.D. 1700 and 1900*); *Sevillana*, op.7 (Worcester, May 1, 1884; rev. 1889); *Salut d'amour (Liebesgruss)*, op.12 (1888; London, Nov. 11, 1889); *Froissart*, concert overture, op.19 (Worcester, Sept. 9, 1890, composer conducting); *Serenade* in E minor for Strings, op.20 (1892; 1st complete perf., Antwerp, July 23, 1896); *Sursum corda* for Strings, Brass, and Organ, op.11 (Worcester, April 9, 1894); *Minuet* for Small Orch., op.21 (orig. for Piano, 1897; orchestrated 1899; New Brighton, July 16, 1899); *Chanson de matin*, op.15, No. 1, and *Chanson de nuit*, op.15, No. 2 (orig. for Violin and Piano, c. 1889–90; orchestrated 1901; London, Sept. 14, 1901); *Imperial March*, op.32 (London, April 19, 1897, A. Manns conducting; for Queen Victoria's Diamond Jubilee); *Variations on an Original Theme (Enigma Variations)*, op.36 (1898–99; London, June 19, 1899, Richter conducting); *Serenade lyrique* for Small Orch. (London, Nov. 27, 1900); *Pomp and Circumstance*, 5 marches for Sym. Orch., op.39: No. 1, in D major (1901), No. 2, in A minor (1901; Liverpool, Oct. 19, 1901, A. Rodewald conducting), No. 3, in C minor (1904; London, March 8, 1905, composer conducting), No. 4, in G major (London, Aug. 24, 1907, H. Wood conducting), and No. 5, in C major (London, Sept. 20, 1930, H. Wood conducting); *Cockaigne (In London Town)*, concert overture, op.40 (London, June 20, 1901, composer conducting); *Dream Children*, 2 pieces for Small Orch., op.43 (London, Sept. 4, 1902; also for Piano); *In the South (Alassio)*, concert overture, op.50 (1903–04; London, March 16, 1904, composer conducting); *Introduction and Allegro* for String Quartet and String Orch., op.47 (1904–05; London, March 8, 1905, composer conducting); *The Wand of Youth*, 2 suites for Orch., comprising the last revision of his music for a children's play composed c. 1867: Suite No. 1, op.1A (London, Dec. 14, 1907, H. Wood conducting) and Suite No. 2, op.1B (Worcester, Sept. 9, 1908, composer conducting); Sym. No. 1, in A-flat major, op.55 (1907–08; Manchester, Dec. 3, 1908, Richter conducting); *Elegy* for Strings, op.58 (London, July 13, 1909); Concerto in B minor for Violin and Orch., op.61 (1909–10; London, Nov. 10, 1910, Fritz Kreisler soloist, composer conducting); *Romance* for Bassoon and Orch., op.62 (1910; Herefordshire Orch. Soc., Feb. 16, 1911); Sym. No. 2, in E-flat major, op.63 (1903–10; London, May 24, 1911, composer conducting); *Coronation March*, op.65 (Westminster Abbey, London, June 22, 1911; for the coronation of King George V); Carissima for Small Orch. (1913; 1st public perf., London, Feb. 15, 1914); *Falstaff*, symphonic study in C minor with 2 interludes, op.68 (1902–13; Leeds Festival, Oct. 1, 1913, composer conducting); *Sospiri* for Strings, Harp, and Organ, op.70 (London, Aug. 15, 1914, H. Wood conducting); *Carillon*, recitation with Orch., op.75 (London, Dec. 7, 1914, composer conducting); *Polonia*, symphonic prelude, op.76 (London, July 6, 1915, composer conducting); *Une Voix dans le desert*, recitation with Orch., op.77 (1915; London, Jan. 29, 1916, composer conducting); *Le Drapeau belge*, recitation with Orch., op.79 (London, April 14, 1917, H. Harty conducting); Concerto in E minor for Cello and Orch., op.85 (London, Oct. 26, 1919, Felix Salmond soloist, composer conducting; later arranged as a viola concerto by Lionel Tertis; Hereford Festival, Sept. 6, 1933, Tertis soloist, composer conducting); *Empire March* (Wembley, April 23, 1924, composer conducting); *Severn Suite* for Brass Band, op.87 (London, Sept. 27, 1930; also for Orch., 1932; 1st public perf., Worcester, Sept. 7, 1932, composer conducting); *Nursery Suite* (London, Aug. 20, 1931, composer conducting; also arranged as a ballet, *Ninette de Valois*, by C. Lambert; London, March 21, 1932, Lambert conducting); *Mina* for Small Orch. (1933); Sym. No. 3 (unfinished; sketches, 1933; realization by Anthony Payne, 1998). **CHAMBER:** *Promenades* for Wind Quintet (1878); *Romance* for Violin and Piano, op.1 (1878; Worcester, Oct. 20, 1885); *Harmony Music* for Wind Quintet (1879); String Quartet, op.8 (1887; MS destroyed); Violin Sonata, op.9 (1887; MS destroyed); *Allegretto on GEDGE* for Violin and Piano (1888); *Liebesahnung* for Violin and Piano (1889); *La Capricieuse* for Violin and Piano, op.17 (1891); *Very Melodious Exercises in the 1st Position* for Violin, op.22 (1892); *Études caractéristiques pour violon seul*, op.24 (1882–92); Sonata in E minor for Violin and Piano, op.82 (1918; 1st public perf., London, March 21, 1919); String Quartet in E minor, op.83

(1918; 1st public perf., London, May 21, 1919); Quintet in A minor for Strings and Piano, op.84 (1918–19; 1st public perf., London, May 21, 1919).

KEYBOARD: P i a n o : *Rosemary* (1882); *May Song* (1901); *Concert Allegro*, op.46 (London, Dec. 2, 1901); *Skizze* (1903); *In Smyrna* (1905); Sonatina (1932); *Adieu* (1932); *Serenade* (1932). **O r g a n :** *11 Vesper Voluntaries*, op.14 (1889); Sonata in G major, op.28 (Worcester Cathedral, July 8, 1895).

VOCAL: O r a t o r i o s : *The Light of Life (Lux Christi)*, op.29 (Worcester Festival, Sept. 10, 1896, composer conducting); *The Dream of Gerontius*, op.38 (1899–1900; Birmingham Festival, Oct. 3, 1900, Richter conducting; although commonly listed as an oratorio, Elgar did not designate it as such); *The Apostles*, op.49 (Birmingham Festival, Oct. 14, 1903, composer conducting); *The Kingdom*, op.51 (1901–06; Birmingham Festival, Oct. 3, 1906, composer conducting). **C a n t a t a s :** *The Black Knight*, op.25 (Worcester Festival, April 18, 1893, composer conducting); *Scenes from the Saga of King Olaf*, op.30 (1894–96; North Staffordshire Music Festival, Hanley, Oct. 30, 1896, composer conducting); *Caractacus*, op.35 (Leeds Festival, Oct. 5, 1898, composer conducting). **OTHER VOCAL:** *Salve Regina* (1878); *Domine salvan fac* (1878); *Tantum ergo* (1878); *O salutaris hostia* for Chorus (1880); *Credo*, in E minor (1880); *4 Litanies for the Blessed Virgin Mary* for Chorus (1882); *Ave, Verum Corpus (Jesu, Word of God Incarnate)*, op.2, No. 1 (1887); *Ave Maria (Jesu, Lord of Life and Glory)*, op.2, No. 2 (1887); *Ave Maris Stella (Jesu, Meek and Lowly)*, op.2, No. 3 (1887); *Ecce sacerdos magnus* for Chorus and Organ (Worcester, Oct. 9, 1888); *My Love Dwelt in a Northern Land*, part-song for Mixed Voices (Tenbury Musical Soc., Nov. 13, 1890); *Spanish Serenade (Stars of the Summer Night)* for Mixed Voices, op.23 (1891; with orch. accompaniment, 1892; Herefordshire Phil. Soc., April 7, 1893); *Scenes from the Bavarian Highlands*, 6 choral songs with Piano or Orch., op.27 (piano version, 1895; orch. version, 1896; Worcester Festival, April 21, 1896, composer conducting); *The Banner of St. George*, ballad for Chorus and Orch., op.33 (London, March 14, 1895; 2nd version, London, May 18, 1897); *Te Deum and Benedictus* for Chorus and Organ, op.34 (Hereford Festival, Sept. 12, 1897); *Sea-Pictures*, song cycle for Contralto or Mezzo-soprano and Orch., op.37 (1897–99; Norwich Festival, Oct. 5, 1899, Clara Butt soloist, composer conducting); *To Her Beneath Whose Steadfast Star*, part-song for Mixed Voices (Windsor Castle, May 24, 1899; dedicated to Queen Victoria); *Weary Wind of the West*, part-song for Mixed Voices (1902; Morecambe Festival, May 2, 1903); *Coronation Ode* for Soloists, Chorus, and Orch., op.44 (Sheffield Festival, Oct. 2, 1902, composer conducting); *5 Part-Songs from the Greek Anthology* for Men's Voices, op.45 (1902; London, April 25, 1904); *Evening Scene*, part-song for Mixed Voices (1905; Morecambe Festival, May 12, 1906); *4 Part-Songs* for Mixed Voices, op.53 (1907); *The Reveille* for Men's Voices, op.54 (1907; Blackpool Music Festival, Oct. 17, 1908); *Angelus (Tuscany)*, part-song for Mixed Voices, op.56 (1909; London, Dec. 8, 1910); *Go, Song of Mine* for Chorus, op.57 (Hereford Festival, Sept. 9, 1909); song cycle with Orch., op.59, Nos. 3, 5, and 6 (Nos. 1, 2, and 4 not composed; 1909-10; London, Jan. 24, 1910, Muriel Foster soloist, composer conducting); *O hearken thou, offertory* for Chorus and Orch., op.64 (Westminster Abbey, London, June 22, 1911; for the coronation of King George V); *Great Is the Lord (Psalm 48)*, anthem for Mixed Voices, op.67 (1910–12; Westminster Abbey, London, July 16, 1912); *The Music Makers*, ode for Soloists, Chorus, and Orch., op.69 (1902–12; Birmingham Festival, Oct. 1, 1912, composer conducting); *Give unto the Lord (Psalm 29)*, anthem for Mixed Voices, Organ, and Orch., op.74 (St. Paul's Cathedral, London, April 30, 1914); *2 choral songs for Mixed*

Voices, op.71 (1914); *Death on the Hills,* choral song for Mixed Voices, op.72 (1914); 2 choral songs for Mixed Voices, op.73 (1914); *The Spirit of England* for Soloists, Chorus, and Orch., op.80 (1915–17; 1st complete perf., London, Nov. 24, 1917, composer conducting); *The Wanderer* for Men's Voices (1923); *Zut, zut, zut* for Men's Voices (1923); also many solo songs.

A collected ed. of his works, *The Elgar Complete Edition,* ed. by Jerrold Northrop Moore and Christopher Kent, commenced publication in 1981.

BIBL.: R. Buckley, *Sir E. E.* (London, 1904; new ed., 1925); E. Newman, *E.* (London, 1906); J. Porte, *Sir E. E.* (London, 1921); J. Shera, *E.'s Instrumental Works* (London, 1931); B. Maine, *E., His Life and Works* (2 vols., London, 1933); J. Porte, *E. and His Music* (London, 1933); A. Sheldon, *E. E.* (London, 1933); W. Reed, *E. as I Knew Him* (London, 1936; new ed., 1973); Mrs. R. Powell, *E. E.: Memories of a Variation* (London, 1937; 2nd ed., 1947; rev. ed., 1994, by C. Powell); W. Reed, *E.* (London, 1939); W. Anderson, *Introduction to the Music of E.* (London, 1949); D. McVeagh, *E. E., His Life and Music* (London, 1955); P. Young, *E., O.M.* (London, 1955; new ed., 1973); idem, ed., *Letters of E. E. and Other Writings* (London, 1956); idem, ed., *Letters to Nimrod from E. E.* (London, 1965); M. Kennedy, *Portrait of E.* (London, 1968; 2nd ed., rev., 1982); M. Hurd, *E.* (London, 1969); I. Parrott, *E.* (London, 1971); C. Kent, *E. E.: A Composer at Work: A Study of His Creative Processes as Seen through His Sketches and Proof Corrections* (diss., King's Coll., Univ. of London, 1978); S. Mundy, *E.: His Life and Times* (Tunbridge Wells, 1980); G. Hodgkins, *Providence and Art: A Study of E.'s Religious Beliefs* (London, 1982); M. De-la-Noy, *E. the Man* (London, 1983); C. Redwood, ed., *An E. Companion* (Ashbourne, 1983); D. Bury, *E. and the Two Mezzos* (London, 1984); J. Northrop Moore, *E. E.: A Creative Life* (Oxford, 1984); idem, *Spirit of England: E. E. and His World* (London, 1984); J. Moore, ed., *E. E.: The Windflower Letters: Correspondence with Alice Caroline Stuart Wortley and Her Family* (Oxford, 1989); C. Weaver, *The Thirteenth Enigma? The Story of E. E.'s Early Love* (London, 1989); R. Anderson, *E. in Manuscript* (London, 1990); R. Monk, ed., *E. Studies* (Aldershot, 1990); J. Northrop Moore, *E. E.: Letters of a Lifetime* (Oxford, 1990); C. Kent, *E. E.: A Guide to Research* (N.Y., 1993); R. Monk, ed., *E. E.: Music and Literature* (Aldershot, 1993); J. Allison, *E. E.: Sacred Music* (Bridgend, 1994); S. Craggs, *E. E.: A Source Book* (Aldershot, 1995); P. Young, *E., Newman and the Dream of Gerontius: In the Tradition of English Catholicism* (Brookfield, Vt., 1995); A. Payne, *E.'s Third Symphony: The Story of the Reconstruction* (London, 1998); J. Rushton, *E.: Enigma Variations* (Cambridge, 1999).—NS/LK/DM

Elías, Alfonso de, Mexican pianist, conductor, pedagogue, and composer, father of **Manuel Jorge de Elías;** b. Cuernavaca, Aug. 30, 1902; d. Mexico City, Aug. 19, 1984. He was a student of José Velasquez (piano), Gustavo Campa (orchestration), and Rafael Tello (composition) at the National Cons. in Mexico City (1915–27). He was active as a pianist and conductor, and also taught in Mexico City at the Universidad Autónoma (from 1958) and at the National Cons. (from 1963). His works were in a thoroughly Romantic style.

WORKS: B a l l e t : *Las Biniguendas de plata* (1933). **ORCH.:** *El jardín encantado,* symphonic triptych (1924); 3 syms. (1926, 1934, 1968); *Variaciones sobre un tema mexicano* (1927); 2 symphonic poems: *Leyenda mística del Callejón del Ave María* (1930) and *Cacahuamilpa* (1940); *Rúbrica* (1944); *Marcha en sol* for Organ and Strings (1958); Violin Concertino (1967). **CHAMBER:** 2 string quartets (1930, 1961); Violin Sonata (1932); 4 Pieces for Cello and Piano (1966); 8 Pieces for String Quartet (1971); *Reverie* for String Quartet (1980); *Allegro* for String Quartet (1980). **O r g a n :** Sonata (1963). **VOCAL:** Various works, including masses and motets.—NS/LK/DM

Elias, Eliane, jazz keyboard player, pianist; b. Sao Paulo, Brazil, March 19, 1960. Her mother played classical piano, her mother's Italian grandparents sang opera, and her maternal grandmother played the guitar and wrote chorinhos and other kinds of Brazilian songs. She first became interested in the piano at age seven, and by 12 wanted to be a professional musician. Her mother collected jazz records, and Elias listened to them and began transcribing the work of a diverse range of jazz pianists from Art Tatum to Keith Jarrett. She also played and studied classical piano, and was influenced by the Brazilian pop-jazz of Antonio Carlos Jobim. By age 15 she was gigging and teaching master classes at Sao Paulo's Free Center of Music Apprenticeship jazz program, where she studied for six years. Her formal career as a professional musician began in 1978, working in a bossa nova group with Jobim's co-writer Vinicius de Moraes in the show *Ten Years with Toquinho and Vinicius.* She met Jobim before the show ended in 1980 when Moraes died. The following year she moved to N.Y. In 1983, she was offered a job with Steps Ahead. She remained with the group for one year and appears on the band's self-titled debut for Elektra Records. She married Randy Brecker during this time. In 1986, she made her first recording as a leader, and has subsequently continued to record and tour, leading her own trio. She teaches at the Manhattan School of Music, and is IAJE's International Interest Chair for piano.

DISC.: *Illusions* (1986); *Cross Currents* (1987); *Eliane Elias Plays Jobim* (1989); *So Far So Close* (1989); *A Long Story* (1991); *Fantasia* (1992); *Paulistana* (1993); *On the Classical Side* (1993); *Solos and Duets* (1995); *The Three Americas* (1997).—LP

Elías, Manuel Jorge de, Mexican composer, son of **Alfonso de Elías;** b. Mexico City, June 5, 1939. He received his early musical training from his father. He pursued his training at the Autonomous National Univ. of Mexico and the National Cons. in Mexico City, where he studied piano, organ, flute, violin, and cello (1959–62), and later attended a class in electronic music at Columbia Univ. in N.Y. (1974). Returning to Mexico, he founded in 1976 the Inst. of Music of the Univ. of Veracruz. In 1991 he became director of the Música de Bellas Artes. His music is hedonistically pragmatic and structurally precise, but allows interpolation of aleatory passages.

WORKS: *Suite romantica,* 10 pieces for Piano (1954–56); *Pequeños corales* for Chorus (1954–57); *Suite de miniaturas* for Wind Quartet (1957); *Sonata breve* for Piano (1958); Sinfonietta (1958–61); *Estampas infantiles* for Strings (1959); *Vitral No. 1* for Chamber Orch. (1962), *No. 2* for Chamber Orch. and Tape (1967), and *No. 3* for Orch. (Mexico City, Nov. 7, 1969); *Divertimento* for Percussion (1963); *Aforismo No. 1, Pájaros perdidos* for Chorus (1963) and *No. 2* for Flute and Tape (1968); *Guanajuato,* overture-divertimento for Orch. (1964); *Jabel,* ballet for 2 Pianos (1964); *Impresiones sobre una estampa colonial,* divertimento for Orch. (1965); *Ciclos elementarios* for Wind Quartet (1965); *Speculamen* for 2 Violins, 2 Violas, 3 Cellos, and Double Bass (1967);

Elegía heroica, symphonic poem (1967); *Memento* for Recorder, Chorus, Strings, and Narrator (1967); String Quartet No. 1 (1967); *Música nupcial* for Contralto and Brass or Strings (1967); *Pro pax* for Tape (1968); 2 sonatas for Solo Violin (1968, 1969); *3 Quimeras* for 2 Pianos (1969, 1973, 1974); *3 Kaleidoscopios* for Organ (1969, 1973, 1974); *Sonante No. 1* for Piano (1971), *No. 2* for Clarinet (1970), *No. 3* for Trumpet, Trombone, and Horn (1970; also for Orch., 1974), *No. 4* for Orch. (Mexico City, March 26, 1971), *No. 5* for Orch. (Mexico City, Nov. 24, 1972), *No. 6, Homenaje a Neruda*, for Strings (1973), *No. 7* for Orch. (Brussels, Dec. 1974), *No. 8* for Orch. (1977), *No. 9* for Orch. (1978), *No. 10* (1978), and *No. 11, Bosquejos para una ofrenda* (1995); *Parametros I* for Synthesizer (1971); *Ludus* for 3 Choruses (1972–73); *Concertante No. 1* for Violin and Orch. (1973) and *No. 2* for Piano and Orch. (1975); *Música domestica* for Recorder and Percussion (1973); *Sine nomine* for String Quartet and Piano (1975); *Jeux* for Horn, Trumpet, and Bassoon (1975); *Obertura-Poema* for Soloists, Chorus, Organ, and Wind Orch. (1975); *Balada Concertante* for Trombone and Orch. (1983); *Lírica breve* for String Orch., Piano, and Timbales (1984); *Mictlán-Tlatelolco* for Strings (1986); *Cartas de primavera* for Strings (1986); *Canciones del ocaso* for Mezzo-soprano and Orch. (1988); *Poema* for String Orch. (1988); Cello Concerto (1990); *Fax Music* for Winds (1990); *Tri-Neos* for Clarinet, Bassoon, and Piano (1991); *Concierto da cámera* for Viola, Strings, and Percussion (1992); *Canción de cuna* for Guitar and Strings (1994).—NS/LK/DM

Elias, Rosalind, American mezzo-soprano; b. Lowell, Mass., March 13, 1930. She began her training at the New England Cons. of Music in Boston, and during her student days there, she sang Poppaea in *L'incoronazione di Poppea* and appeared with the Boston Sym. Orch. She then studied at the Berkshire Music Center in Tanglewood. After singing with the New England Opera Co. (1948–52), she completed her training in Italy with Luigi Ricci and Nazareno de Angelis. Following engagements at Milan's La Scala and Naples's Teatro San Carlos, she made her Metropolitan Opera debut in N.Y. as Grimgerde in *Die Walküre* on Feb. 23, 1954; she created roles there in Barber's *Vanessa* (Erika, 1958) and *Antony and Cleopatra* (Charmian, 1966), remaining on its roster for over 30 years. She also made guest appearances in Europe and toured as a concert artist. Among her other roles were Dorabella, Rosina, Cherubino, Giordano's Bersi, Carmen, and Octavian. —NS/LK/DM

Elias Salomon or **Salomonis,** French monk and music theorist who flourished in the second half of the 13th century. He was active at Sainte-Astere, Perigord. He was the author of a treatise on improvised counterpoint, *Scientia artis musicae* (1274).—NS/LK/DM

Elizalde, Federico, Spanish conductor and composer; b. Manila, Philippines (of Spanish parents), Dec. 12, 1908; d. there, Jan. 16, 1979. He studied piano at the Madrid Cons. (First prize, 1923), law at Stanford Univ., and composition with Ernest Bloch. In 1930 he became conductor of the Manila Sym. Orch. and in 1948 president of the Manila Radio. His works include *Paul Gauguin*, opera (1948), *Sinfonia Concertante* (Barcelona, April 23, 1936), Violin Concerto (1943), Piano Concerto (1947), and chamber music.—NS/LK/DM

Elizza, Elise (real name, **Elisabeth Letztergroschen**), Austrian soprano; b. Vienna, Jan. 6, 1870; d. there, June 3, 1926. She studied in Vienna with Adolf Limley, making her debut there at the Carl Theater in 1892 in Weinberger's operetta *Lachenden Erben*. She then made her operatic debut in 1894 in Olmütz. After further studies with Materna, she joined the Vienna Court Opera in 1895, where she sang until 1919. She retired in 1923. She was admired for her coloratura roles but she also had success as a Wagnerian.—NS/LK/DM

Elkus, Albert (Israel), American composer and teacher, father of **Jonathan (Britton) Elkus;** b. Sacramento, April 30, 1884; d. Oakland, Feb. 19, 1962. He studied at the Univ. of Calif. (M.Lit., 1907). He also studied piano with Hugo Mansfeldt and Oscar Weil in San Francisco, and later with Harold Bauer and Josef Lhévinne. He went to Vienna, where he took lessons in conducting with Franz Schalk and counterpoint with Karl Prohaska, and then took courses with Robert Fuchs and Georg Schumann in Berlin. Returning to the U.S., he taught at Dominican Coll. in San Rafael, Calif. (1924–31); was on the faculty of the San Francisco Cons. (1923–25; 1933–37), serving as its director (1951–57); he also taught at Mills Coll. in Oakland (1929–44) and at the Univ. of Calif. at Berkeley (1935–51). Among his compositions are *Concertino on Lezione III of Ariosto* for Cello and Strings (1917); *Impressions from a Greek Tragedy* for Orch. (San Francisco, Feb. 27, 1921); *I Am the Reaper*, chorus for Men's Voices (1921).—NS/LK/DM

Elkus, Jonathan (Britton), American conductor, pedagogue, and composer, son of **Albert (Israel) Elkus;** b. San Francisco, Aug. 8, 1931. He studied composition with Cushing and Denny at the Univ. of Calif. in Berkeley (B.A., 1953), Ernst Bacon and L. Ratner at Stanford Univ. (M.A., 1954), and Milhaud at Mills Coll. in Oakland, Calif. (1957). He was asst. director of bands at Stanford Univ. (1955–57), and then taught at Lehigh Univ. in Bethlehem, Pa. (1957–73), and also conducted its bands. After serving as director of music (1979–85) and chairman of the humanities dept. (1985–89) at Cape Cod Academy in Osterville, he was chairman of the history dept. at Stuart Hall School in Staunton (from 1989). He established the publishing firms of J. B. Elkus & Son and Laureate Music Press in 1984, and of East Bay Books in 1985. He publ. *Charles Ives and the American Band Tradition: A Centennial Tribute* (Exeter, England, 1974) and the critical edition of Ives's *Thanksgiving and Forefathers' Day* (N.Y., 1991).

WORKS: DRAMATIC: Opera: *The Outcasts of Poker Flat* (1959; Bethlehem, Pa., April 16, 1960); *Medea* (1963; Milwaukee, Nov. 13, 1970); *The Mandarin* (N.Y., Oct. 26, 1967); *Helen in Egypt* (Milwaukee, Nov. 13, 1970). **Musicals:** *Tom Sawyer* (San Francisco, May 22, 1953); *Treasure Island* (1961); *A Little Princess* (1980); *Act Your Age!* (Osterville, May 31, 1983). Also incidental music. **Band:** *Camino Real* (1955); *Serenade* for Horn, Baritone Horn, and Band (1957); *CC Rag* (1974); *The Apocalypse*, rag (1974); *Pipers on Parade* (1976); *Chiaroscuro*, suite (1977); *Cal Band March* (1978); transcriptions and arrangements for the Goldman, New Sousa, and U.S. Marine bands. **CHAMBER:** *3 Sketches* for 2 Clarinets and Bassoon (1954); *The Charmer*, rag for Clarinet, Trombone, and Piano (1972); piano rags; organ music. **VOCAL:** Choruses.—NS/LK/DM

Ella, John, English violinist, conductor, and writer on music; b. Leicester, Dec. 19, 1802; d. London, Oct. 2, 1888. He studied violin in London, and then enrolled as a harmony student at the Royal Academy of Music there. In 1827 he went to Paris to study with Fétis. Returning to London, he played in theater orchs. He was director of Lord Saltoun's musical society until 1846, and in 1845 he established the Musical Union, presenting morning concerts of chamber music. He was its director until 1880. In 1850 he opened a series of "Music Winter Evenings" which continued until 1859. For these organizations he wrote analytical program notes, of excellent quality for the time. He was a contributor of reviews and music articles to the *Morning Post*, the *Musical World*, and the *Athenaeum*.

WRITINGS: *Lectures on Dramatic Music Abroad and at Home* (1872); *Musical Sketches Abroad and at Home* (3 eds., 1861, 1869, 1878); *Record of the Musical Union* (1845–80); *Personal Memoir of Meyerbeer* (1868).—**NS/LK/DM**

Ellberg, Ernst (Henrik), Swedish composer and pedagogue; b. Söderhamm, Dec. 11, 1868; d. Stockholm, June 14, 1948. He studied with J. Lindberg (violin) and J. Dente (composition) at the Stockholm Cons. (1886–92), and then held a state composer's fellowship (1894–96). From 1887 to 1905 he was a violist in the Royal Orch. in Stockholm; he taught composition, counterpoint, and orchestration at the Stockholm Cons. (1904–33), and then taught military musicians there until 1943. In 1912 he was made a member of the Swedish Royal Academy of Music, and in 1916 he was granted the title of prof. Ellberg was an influential teacher. His music is steeped in the Romantic tradition. Among his compositions are the operas *Den röda liljan* (The Red Lily) and *Rassa*; ballets; *Introduction and Fugue* for Strings (1891); a Sym. (1896); also overtures; chamber music; songs for Men's Chorus.—**NS/LK/DM**

Eller, Heino, noted Estonian composer and pedagogue; b. Yuryev, March 7, 1887; d. Tallinn, June 16, 1970. He studied law at the Univ. of St. Petersburg (1908–12). Following service in the army during World War I, he studied violin and composition (with Kalafati) at the Petrograd Cons. (graduated, 1920). After teaching theory and composition at the Tartu Higher Music School (1920–40), he was prof. of composition at the Tallinn Cons. (1940–70). In 1957 he was honored with the title of People's Artist of the Estonian S.S.R. In 1965 he was awarded the prize of the Estonian Republic. Eller was one of the principal founders of the modern Estonian national school of music. Many of his students became prominent figures in the musical life of Estonia. Eller's works adhered to Classical precepts but explored modern harmonic and timbral usages.

WORKS: ORCH.: *Fantasy* for Violin and Orch. (1916; rev. 1963); 6 symphonic poems: *Twilight* (1918); *Dawn* (1918); *Nocturnal Sounds* (1920); *Apparitions* (1924); *The Eagle's Flight* (1949); *The Singing Fields* (1951); *Symphonic Scherzo* (1921); Violin Concerto (1933; rev. 1965); 3 syms. (1936, 1947, 1961); *White Night*, symphonic suite (1939); *Dance Suite* (1942); *5 Pieces* for Strings (1953); Sinfonietta for Strings (1965); *Episode from Revolutionary Times* (n.d.). **CHAMBER:** 2 violin sonatas (1922, 1946); 5 string quartets (1925, 1930, 1945, 1954, 1959); many violin pieces; pieces for Cello and Harp. **P i a n o :** 4 sonatas (1920, 1938, 1944, 1958); about 200 other pieces.

BIBL.: H. Sepp, *H. E. i klaverilooming* (Tallinn, 1958); idem, ed., *H. E. sonas ja pildis* (H. E. in Words and Pictures; Tallinn, 1967).—**NS/LK/DM**

Eller, Louis, Austrian violinist; b. Graz, June 9, 1820; d. Pau, July 12, 1862. He studied with Hysel. From 1836 he made tours in central Europe; traveled to Spain and Portugal with Gottschalk. He wrote several effective pieces for the violin, including *Valse diabolique* and *Menuet sentimental*.—**NS/LK/DM**

Ellerton, John Lodge (real name, **John Lodge**), English poet and composer; b. Chester, Jan. 11, 1801; d. London, Jan. 3, 1873. He was educated at Brasenose Coll., Oxford (B.A., 1821; M.A., 1828) and also studied counterpoint under Pietro Terriani in Rome, where he composed 7 Italian operas. He lived for some time in Germany, where he wrote 2 German operas. Besides his operas, he wrote an oratorio, *Paradise Lost* (1856), 6 syms., 4 concert overtures, 4 string quintets, 50 string quartets, 3 string trios, 8 trios for various instruments, 13 sonatas, 61 glees, 83 vocal duets, and songs.—**NS/LK/DM**

Elleviou, (Pierre-) Jean (-Baptiste-François), notable French tenor; b. Rennes, June 14, 1769; d. Paris, May 5, 1842. He made his operatic debut as a baritone in Monsigny's *Le Déserteur* at the Comédie-Italienne in Paris in 1790. Turning to tenor roles, he made his first appearance there in Dalayrac's *Philippe et Georgette* in 1791. During the French Revolution, he was compelled to leave its roster but was able to return in 1797. In 1801 he became a leading member of the Paris Opéra-Comique, where he won distinction in roles created especially for him by Grétry. He also created roles in operas by various other composers, including Méhul's *Joseph* (1807) and Boieldieu's *Jean de Paris* (1812). In 1813 he retired from the operatic stage. He wrote the libretto for Berton's *Délia et Verdikan* (1805).

BIBL.: E. H. P. de Curzon, *J. E.* (Paris, 1930).—**NS/LK/DM**

Elling, Catharinus, Norwegian organist, composer, and writer on music; b. Christiania, Sept. 13, 1858; d. there (Oslo), Jan. 8, 1942. He studied in Christiania, Leipzig (1877–78), and with Herzogenberg at the Berlin Hochschule für Musik (1886–87). Returning to Christiania in 1896, he taught counterpoint and composition at the Cons. until 1908; he was also active as a choral conductor (1897–1901) and as a church organist (1909–26). In 1898 he received a government subvention to study Norwegian folk songs, which resulted in essays and books. He also wrote biographies of Bull, Grieg, Svendsen, and Kjerulf.

WORKS: *Kosakkerne* (The Cossacks), opera (1890–94); 2 syms. (1890, 1897); *Norwegian Suite* for Orch. (1904); Violin Concerto (1919); *Den forlorne søn* (The Prodigal Son), oratorio (1895–96); incidental music to plays; chamber music; songs.

BIBL.: Ø. Gaukstad, *Melodi- og tekstregister til C. E.s opptegnelser av folkemusikk* (Oslo, 1963).—**NS/LK/DM**

Ellington, Duke (actually, **Edward Kennedy**), elegant American jazz composer, bandleader, and pianist; b. Washington, D.C., April 29, 1899; d. N.Y., May 24, 1974. Ellington was the most important composer in the history of jazz, writing a variety of works, from songs to extended suites, that were tailored to the talents of the musicians in the band he led for nearly 50 years, many of whom stayed with him for lengthy tenures. He wrote for the stage and the screen on occasion, and many of his instrumental works were turned into popular songs with the addition of lyrics, the resulting royalties helping to keep his organization solvent especially after the 1940s, when his style of big band jazz diverged from popular taste. But the bulk of his work consisted of pieces intended to showcase the many jazz soloists who played with him night after night, decade after decade. Critical opinion and audience appreciation for the more ambitious works that occupied him especially in his later decades remain divided. But the songs that helped him to achieve widespread recognition and popularity during his life continue to be performed and recorded, among them "Sophisticated Lady," "Don't Get Around Much Anymore," and "I'm Beginning to See the Light."

Ellington was born into a relatively comfortable African-American family—his father, James Edward Ellington, was a White House butler who later became a blueprint maker for the Navy. Ellington showed an early interest in music, beginning piano lessons at age seven. He was writing music as early as 1914, and he dropped out of high school in his junior year in 1917 to become a professional musician. On July 2, 1918, he married Edna Thompson. The couple had one child, Mercer Ellington (1919–96), who became a composer and later led his father's band. They separated in the late 1920s but never divorced.

Ellington's group, the five-piece Washingtonians, moved permanently to N.Y. in September 1923, establishing a residency at the Hollywood Club (later the Kentucky Club) in the Times Square district. The Washingtonians made their first recordings in November 1924, working for various record companies under various names over the next several years. As the ten-piece Duke Ellington and His Kentucky Club Orch., they first recorded Ellington's theme song, "East St. Louis Toodle-oo," for Vocalion in November 1926; it became their first hit after they rerecorded it for Columbia in March 1927 as Duke Ellington and His Washingtonians. The tune was cowritten by trumpeter James "Bubber" Miley, whose muted "growling" style of playing defined the group's "jungle" sound. (Unless otherwise noted, all compositions are by Ellington.)

On Dec. 4, 1927, Ellington began a residency at the Cotton Club in Harlem that lasted more than three years. The band was given increased exposure through radio broadcasts from the club. Ellington's next hit was the two-sided "Black and Tan Fantasy" (music also by Miley)/"Creole Love Call" on Victor in the spring of 1928. In the fall, "The Harlem Footwarmers" had a two-sided hit on Okeh with songs from the Broadway revue *Blackbirds of 1928*, "Diga Diga Doo"/"Doin' the New Low Down" (music by Jimmy McHugh, lyrics by Dorothy Fields). Ellington's own name was on the

OKeh recording of "The Mooche," a hit at the end of the year.

In the summer of 1929, Ellington's orchestra appeared in the Broadway musical *Show Girl*, which had songs by George and Ira Gershwin and Gus Kahn and also starred Ruby Keeler with an impromptu cameo by her husband, Al Jolson; the show ran 111 performances. The band traveled to the West Coast in the summer of 1930 to appear in the film *Check and Double Check*; from its score came another two-sided hit on Victor, "Three Little Words" (music by Harry Ruby, lyrics by Bert Kalmar), with vocals by the Rhythm Boys, a trio including Bing Crosby, which became a best-seller in November, and "Ring Dem Bells" (music and lyrics by Ellington and, supposedly, his publisher/manager Irving Mills, who was frequently "cut in" on songwriting royalties until the two split up in 1939).

Ellington left his regular job at the Cotton Club (though he would return periodically) for a national tour in February 1931. His popular recordings of the year included an instrumental treatment of "Mood Indigo" (music and lyrics credited to Mills, clarinetist Barney Bigard, and Ellington, though the lyrics were actually by Mitchell Parish) and his first extended composition, "Creole Rhapsody," which took up two sides of a 78-rpm disc and was credited to the Jungle Band.

Ellington scored a major vocal hit in February 1932 with "It Don't Mean a Thing (If It Ain't Got That Swing)" (lyrics by Mills), sung by Ivie Anderson, which also became his first hit cover song in September when the Mills Brothers released their version. Ellington introduced another standard in the spring of 1933 with "Sophisticated Lady" (lyrics by Parish and Mills). The composer's own version was backed by a popular recording of "Stormy Weather" (music by Harold Arlen, lyrics by Ted Koehler); Glen Gray and the Casa Loma Orch. also recorded it successfully.

In the spring of 1934, Ellington again went west to appear in the film *Murder at the Vanities*. His recording of "Cocktails for Two" (music and lyrics by Arthur Johnston and Sam Coslow) from the film became a best-seller in May. Ellington's other big hit of the year was the two-sided disc of "Moon Glow" (lyrics and music by Will Hudson, Eddie DeLange, and Mills) and his own "Solitude" (lyrics by DeLange and Mills) in October. While in Hollywood the Ellington Orch. also appeared in *Belle of the Nineties* and performed music for *Many Happy Returns* that was mimed on screen by Guy Lombardo and His Royal Canadians.

Ellington was in the hit parade in September 1935 with the title song from the motion picture *Accent on Youth* (music by Vee Lawnhurst, lyrics by Tot Seymour). That same month he doubled the length of his previous long work, "Creole Rhapsody," with "Reminiscing in Tempo," recorded on both sides of two records. In the spring of 1936 he was back in the hit parade with "Love Is Like a Cigarette" (music and lyrics by Jerome Jerome, Richard Byron, and Walter Kent). In late 1936 and early 1937 the band was in Hollywood, recording material for such films as *A Day at the Races* and *Hit Parade of 1937*. Among Ellington's notable works of the period were the swing standard "Caravan" (music also by trombonist Juan Tizol, lyrics by Mills), "Diminuendo in Blue," and "Crescendo in Blue." He scored one of the biggest hits of his career in the spring and summer of 1938 with "I Let a Song Go Out of My Heart" (lyrics by Henry Nemo, John Redmond, and Mills), which topped the hit parade in July.

Ellington entered a particularly accomplished period of his career at the end of the 1930s, aided by the addition of certain key associates. Composer, lyricist, arranger, and pianist Billy Strayhorn joined the Ellington organization in the early months of 1939; in time, his collaboration with Ellington would become so close as to be indistinguishable. Bassist Jimmy Blanton joined the group in September and tenor saxophonist Ben Webster in December, their contributions so crucial that this edition of the Ellington Orch. would become known informally as the Blanton-Webster band.

Ellington scored a hit in June 1941 with "Flamingo" (music by Ted Grouya, lyrics by Edmund Anderson), which featured a vocal by Herb Jeffries. The following month, the orchestra had a hit with Strayhorn's first major contribution, the big band standard "Take the 'A' Train," which became their theme song. Meanwhile, they were in L.A., appearing in the musical revue *Jump for Joy* (July 10, 1941), which ran 101 performances but closed without moving east. Nevertheless, it featured a hit song in "I Got It Bad (And That Ain't Good)," recorded by both Ellington and Dinah Shore.

Ellington's career was slowed by the U.S. entry into World War II in December 1941 and the musicians' union recording ban that began in August 1942. So he turned to the concert stage, beginning an annual series of appearances at Carnegie Hall on Jan. 23, 1943, with the premiere of the lengthy composition "Black, Brown and Beige." He also returned to Hollywood for appearances in *Cabin in the Sky* and *Reveille with Beverly*. And despite the recording ban, he scored surprise hits with two recordings made in 1940. Lyricist Bob Russell set words to "Never No Lament" to create "Don't Get Around Much Anymore." The Ink Spots had a giant hit with it in early 1943, bringing Ellington's original instrumental into the Top Ten as well. Russell then turned Ellington's "Concerto for Cootie" into "Do Nothin' Till You Hear from Me."

The Top Ten recordings by the orchestras of Woody Herman and Stan Kenton had vocals, but the biggest hit came with Ellington's original instrumental version. At the same time Ellington topped the black-oriented charts with a series of recordings made just before the start of the ban: "A Slip of the Lip (Can Sink a Ship)," "Sentimental Lady," and "Main Stem." Ellington's biggest pop hit of the period was "I'm Beginning to See the Light" (music and lyrics by Ellington, Don George, Harry James, and saxophonist Johnny Hodges), which topped the charts for James in April 1945 and was also a hit for Ellington and for Ella Fitzgerald and the Ink Spots. (Ellington also scored Top Ten hits in the "race" charts in 1945 with "Don't You Know I Care [Or Don't You Care to Know]" [lyrics by Mack David] and "I Ain't Got Nothin' but the Blues" [lyrics by George].)

Ellington's most successful theatrical work during his lifetime was the Broadway musical *Beggar's Holiday* (based on *Beggar's Opera*) (N.Y., Dec. 26, 1946), with lyrics by John Latouche, which ran for 108 performances. Though he scored a couple of minor hits—"Come to Baby, Do!" (music and lyrics by Inez James and Sidney Miller) on the pop charts in 1946 and "Don't Be So Mean to Baby ('Cause Baby's So Good to You)" (music and lyrics by Peggy Lee and Dave Barbour) on the R&B charts in 1948—Ellington focused more on his extended compositions as popular music became less jazz-oriented in the late 1940s. He wrote his first film score for *The Asphalt Jungle* in 1950.

The early 1950s was a period of struggle for the Ellington Orch., which was hit by an unusually large number of personnel changes. But Ellington made a notable comeback with a triumphant appearance at the Newport Jazz Festival on July 7, 1956, when saxophonist Paul Gonsalves turned in a memorable solo during "Diminuendo and Crescendo in Blue." *Ellington at Newport* became the band's first album to appear in the pop charts the following year. It was the best-selling album of Ellington's career.

Though Ellington had occasionally performed overseas, the 50-day concert tour of Europe he undertook in October and November 1958 marked the beginning of extensive international appearances that continued until the end of his life. Between tours Ellington continued to write and record substantial instrumental works. He scored and appeared in the film *Anatomy of a Murder* in 1959, its soundtrack album earning him his first three Grammys, for Best Performance by a Dance Band, Best Musical Composition of the Year, and Best Soundtrack. His score for *Paris Blues* (1961) earned him an Academy Award nomination. In August 1963 his musical theater work *My People*, a celebration of African-American history, was performed at the Century of Negro Progress Exposition in Chicago.

Ellington's musical efforts in the last decade of his life were varied. Having signed to Frank Sinatra's Reprise label, he recorded *Ellington '65*, a collection of instrumental versions of contemporary pop hits, which reached the pop charts in late 1964 though it was scorned by jazz fans. Inaugurating the major effort of his last years, he mounted his first sacred concert at Grace Cathedral in San Francisco on Sept. 16, 1965. He made another try at a Broadway musical with an adaptation of the film *The Blue Angel*, *Pousse-Café* (N.Y., March 18, 1966), but it lasted only three performances. His collaboration with Arthur Fiedler and the Boston Pops, *The Duke at Tanglewood*, was a chart album in May. In June the Sinatra film *Assault on a Queen*, with Ellington's score, opened. He won the 1966 Grammy Award for Best Original Jazz Composition for his sacred work "In the Beginning, God." His fifth Grammy came for Best Instrumental Jazz Performance for the 1967 album *Far East Suite*. *Francis A. & Edward K.*, a collaboration with Sinatra, reached the pop charts in 1968, and Ellington's other album of the year, *And His Mother Called Him Bill*, a tribute to Strayhorn, who had died the previous year, won him a sixth Grammy Award for Best Instrumental Jazz Performance in 1969. That same year he scored the film *Change of Mind*.

Ellington won 1971 and 1972 Grammys for Best Jazz Performance by a big band for his compositions "New Orleans Suite" and "Togo Brava Suite." He published his autobiography, *Music Is My Mistress* (1973), and continued to perform regularly with his orchestra until shortly before his death from lung cancer and pneumonia at the age of 75. Previously unreleased studio and concert recordings continued to be issued, and he won another Grammy Award for Best Jazz Performance by a Big Band for the 1976 album *The Ellington Suites*. A Broadway revue based on his music, *Sophisticated Ladies* (N.Y., March 1, 1981), was a major hit, running 767 performances.

DISC.: *Piano Duets: Great Times with Billy Strayhorn* (1950); *The 1952 Seattle Concert* (1954); *D. E. Presents...* (1956); *E. at Newport* (1956); *Such Sweet Thunder* (1957); *All Star Road Band Vol. II* (1957); *E. Jazz Party* (1959); *Anatomy of a Murder* (soundtrack; 1959); *Money Jungle* (with Charles Mingus and Max Roach; 1962); *The Great Paris Concert* (1963); *Back to Back: D. E. and Johnny Hodges Play the Blues* (1963); *Ella at D.'s Place* (with Ella Fitzgerald; 1965); *This One's for Blanton—Duets* (with Ray Brown; 1972); *D.'s Big Four* (1973); *The Ellington Suites* (1976); *D. E.: The Blanton-Webster Band, 1939–1942* (1986); *D. E. Meets Coleman Hawkins* (1986); *Side by Side* (with Johnny Hodges; 1986); *First Time: The Count Meets the D.–1961* (with Count Basie; 1987); *Uptown—Early 1950s* (1987); *Compact Jazz: And Friends* (1987); *The Blanton-Webster Years* (1987); *Walkman Jazz/Compact Jazz* (1988); *Black, Brown & Beige 1944–46* (1988); *Blues in Orbit—1960* (1988); *D. E. & John Coltrane* (1988); *The Piano Album* (1989); *Braggin' in Brass: The Immortal 1938 Year* (1989); *E. Indigos: Sept.–Oct. 1957* (1989); *The Private Collection, Vols. I–IV* (1989); *The Private Collection, Vol. V: "The Suites" 1968* (1989); *The Private Collection, Vols. VI–X: Dance Dates, California, 1958* (1989); *The Best of D. E.* (1989); *New Mood Indigo* (1989); *Solos, Duets, and Trios* (1990); *The Jungle Band: The Brunswick Era, Vol. II—1929–31* (1990); *The Intimacy of the Blues: 1967 & 1970* (1991); *1924–1927* (1991); *Compact Jazz: D. E. and Friends* (1991); *Up in D.'s Workshop—1969–72* (1991); *The Essence of D. E.: I Like Jazz* (1991); *D. E.'s My People* (1992); *D. E. & His Orchestra: Jazz Cocktail: 1928–31* (1992); *Live at the Blue Note—1952* (1992); *D. E. Vol. IV: 1928* (1992); *The Pianist: 1966, 1970* (1992); *1937* (with Chick Webb; 1993); *Original Hits, Vol. I: 1927–31* (1993); *Original Hits, Vol. II: 1931–38* (1993); *The Great London Concerts—1964* (1993); *D. E. & His Orchestra—1938, Vol. II* (1993); *D. E. & His Orchestra—1938, Vol. III* (1993); *In the 20s—Jazz Archives No. 63* (1993); *Things Ain't What They Used to Be* (1993); *Things Ain't What They Used to Be/S.R.O.* (1993); *Live at the Rainbow Grill* (1993); *Mood Indigo* (1994); *Live at the Blue Note* (1994); *Black, Brown, and Beige—Mastersound Series* (1994); *D. E., 1938–1939* (1994); *D. E., Vol. II: Swing 1930–38* (1994); *D. E. & His Orchestra Live at Newport—1958* (1994); *16 Most Requested Songs* (1994); *Uptown Downbeat with His Orchestra: Cotton Club, Jungle Band 1927–40* (1995); *Satin Doll, 1958–59* (1995); *D. E., 1924–30* (1995); *From the Blue Note—Chicago 1952* (1995); *In a Mellotone—1940–44* (1995); *70th Birthday Concert—Nov. 1969* (1995); *Live at the Whitney: April 10, 1972* (1995); *The Cornell University Concert—December 1948* (1995); *New York Concert: In Performance at Columbia University—1964* (1995); *D. E. & His Great Vocalists* (1995); *The Best of D. E.* (1995); *D. E. & John Coltrane with Jimmy Garrison, Aaron Bell etc., Recorded September 1962* (1995); *D. E.: Greatest Hits* (1996); *E.ia* (1996); *This Is Jazz* (1996); *Vol. IV: The Mooche, 1928* (1996); *Vol. V: Harlemania, 1928–29* (1996); *Vol. VI: Cotton Club Stomp* (1996); *Vol. IX: Mood Indigo, 1930* (1996); *Vol. X: Rockin' in Rhythm, 1930–31* (1996); *Sophisticated Lady—1941–49* (1996); *E. at Basin Street East: The Complete Concert of 14 January 1964* (1996); *Rockin' in Rhythm, 1958–59* (1996); *Best of Early E.* (1996); *D. E. & His Famous Orchestra: Fargo, North Dakota, Nov. 7, 1940* (1996); *The Great D. E.* (1996); *Cornell University Concert* (1996); *Cornell University: Second Set* (1997); *D. E.'s Greatest Hits* (1997); *Jazz Profile* (1997); *Revue Collection* (1997); *Priceless Jazz* (1998); *This Is Jazz: D. E. Plays Standards* (1998); *The Centennial Edition: The Complete RCA-Victor Recordings* (1999); *The Best of the D. E. Centennial Edition* (1999); *Blues and Ballads* (2000); *The Great Summit: The Complete Sessions* (with Louis Armstrong; 2000); *The D.: The Essential Collection, 1927–1962* (2000).

WRITINGS: *Music Is My Mistress* (1973).

BIBL.: D. Preston, *Mood Indigo* (1946); B. Ulanov, *D. E.* (1946); P. Gammond, ed., *D. E.: His Life and Music* (1958); G. Lambert, *D. E.* (1959); S. Dance, *The World of D. E.* (1970); D. Jewell, *Duke: A Portrait of D. E.* (1977); Mercer Ellington (his son) with S. Dance, *D. E. in Person: An Intimate Memoir* (1978); W. Timner, *Ellingtonia: The Recorded Music of D. E. and His Sidemen* (1979, 4th rev. ed., 1996); D. George, *Sweet Man: The Real D. E.* (1981); J. Collier, *D. E.* (1987); P. Gammond, *D. E.* (1987); M. Tucker, *Ellington: The Early Years* (1991); Tucker, ed., *The D. E. Reader* (1993); K. Rattenbury, *D. E.: Jazz Composer* (1990); J. Hasse, *Beyond Category: The Life and Genius of D. E.* (1993).—**WR**

Ellinwood, Leonard (Webster), American musicologist; b. Thomaston, Conn., Feb. 13, 1905; d. Washington, D.C., July 8, 1994. He studied at Aurora (Ill.) Coll. (B.A., 1926) and with Charles Warren Fox at the Eastman School of Music in Rochester, N.Y. (M.Mus., 1934; Ph.D., 1936, with the diss. *The Works of Francesco Landini*). He taught at Mich. State Coll. (1936–39); then was a cataloguer at the Library of Congress in Washington, D.C., where he later was head of its humanities division (1970–75). He publ. *Musica Hermanni Contracti* (Rochester, N.Y., 1936), *Bio-bibliographical Index of Musicians in the U.S.A. Since Colonial Times* (Washington, D.C., 1941; 2nd ed., 1956), and *The History of American Church Music* (N.Y., 1953); he also ed. Landini's works (Cambridge, Mass., 1939) and Tallis's English sacred music in the Early English Church Music series, XII-XIII (1971–72).—**NS/LK/DM**

Elliott, Missy "Misdemeanor" (actually, Melissa Arnette), one of the most formidable personalities in hip-hop, both behind the scenes and in the grooves; b. Portsmouth, Va., c. 1972. As a young child, Missy Elliott used to stand on overturned trash cans in front of her house and sing Motown songs for the passing cars. Daughter of a former marine and a dispatcher for a Va. utility company, her mother left her father early in Elliott's teen years. Raised by a strong woman, she learned to take care of herself. Always interested in music, she learned everything there was to know about it. In high school, she formed the vocal group Fay Z, which became the R&B group Sista. She also started writing songs with her friend Tim Mosely. After graduation, she and the group went professional—much to the consternation of her mother, who wanted her to go to college or join the military and get a trade.

With a brashness that would serve her well through the years, she auditioned for Devante Swing of Jodeci, who took Sista to N.Y. and arranged for a contract for them with Elektra Records. Their record never came out, however, and the group broke up. A couple of songs that Elliott wrote, "Want Some More" and "Sweaty," appeared on Jodeci's *Diary of a Mad Band*. Using them as an entree, she and Mosely—renamed Timbaland—started selling songs. They wrote songs for Ginuwine, 702, Craig Mack, Levert, and Aaron Hall. Aaliyah's #1 hit "If Your Girl Only Knew" (and most of the rest of her *One in a Million* album) was written by the duo, which opened the floodgates for them as songwriters and producers.

Elliott also started rapping on other people's records, using the laid-back but assertive style that would become her trademark. She appeared on tunes by Levert, 702, and L'il Kim. On the strength of these projects, Elektra reapproached her, offering her a custom label. The day that Elliott established Gold Mind records, she signed Nicole Ray; Nicole's debut album went gold. Finally setting to work on her own project, she and Timbaland finished *Supa Dupa Fly* in less than two weeks.

The album debuted at #3 powered by "The Rain" and its accompanying video by Hype Williams. Elliott earned three Grammy nominations. It also set in motion Missy Mania, with Elliott becoming the first hip-hop artist to play the Lilith festival, moving her further into the pop mainstream. She was featured in commercials for Sprite and The Gap. Professionally, Elliot produced the soundtrack for the film *Why Do Fools Fall in Love*, as well as tracks for projects by Whitney Houston. She cowrote the tune "Babydoll" for Mariah Carey and remixed records for Janet Jackson and Paula Cole.

A line of lipstick called "Misdemeanor" came out the same day as Elliott's sophomore release *Da Real World* (a portion of the cosmetic's profits go to Break the Cycle, an organization dedicated to the end of domestic abuse). The new album generated raves, led by the single "She's a Bitch." Songs on *Da Real World* featured a who's who of hip-hop, from the great white hope Eminem, to the leading lady of Jamaican dancehall, Lady Saw.

One of the smartest people in the music business, Elliott has a tremendous future.

DISC.: *Supa Dupa Fly* (1997); *Da Real World* (1999).—HB

Elliott, Paul, English tenor; b. Macclesfield, Cheshire, March 19, 1950. He was a choral scholar at Magdalen Coll., Oxford (1969–72), later pursuing his education at the Univ. of Oxford (B.A., 1973; M.A., 1977). His principal vocal teachers were David Johnston and Peter Pears. He served as vicar choral at St. Paul's Cathedral (1972–75) and sang with various choral and early music groups, including the John Alldis Choir (1972–76), the Deller Consort (1973–82), the Monteverdi Choir (1973–78), and the Academy of Ancient Music (from 1973); also was a founding member of the Hilliard Ensemble (1974–84) and the London Early Music Group (1976–79). From 1984 to 1989 he sang with the Newberry Consort in Chicago. He toured widely as a solo concert artist, and also sang in opera, scoring success as Han-

del's *Acis* in St. Gallen (1984) and as Mozart's Belmonte in Chicago (1988). In 1987 he joined the faculty of the Ind. Univ. School of Music in Bloomington, but continued to make appearances as a singer.—NS/LK/DM

Ellis (real name, **Sharpe**), **Alexander J(ohn),** English philologist, mathematician, and writer on music; b. Hoxton, June 14, 1814; d. Kensington, Oct. 28, 1890. He studied philology and mathematics at Trinity Coll., Cambridge (graduated, 1837). He also studied music. In 1864 he was elected a Fellow of the Royal Soc., contributing articles on musical science to its journal, as well as to others. Among his books were *On the Basis of Music* (1877), *On the Measurement and Settlement of Musical Pitch* (1877), and *Speech in Song* (1878).—NS/LK/DM

Ellis, Brent, American baritone; b. Kansas City, Mo., June 20, 1946. He studied with Edna Forsythe (1962–65), Marian Freschl (1965–71), and Daniel Ferro in N.Y. (from 1971), where he also attended classes at the Juilliard School of Music (1965–67; 1970–72). In 1965 he made his first appearance at the Santa Fe Opera, where he later sang regularly (1972–82); also appeared at the Houston Grand Opera (1972–81). In 1973 he won both the WGN Radio Auditions of the Air and the Montreal International Competition, and on April 28, 1974, made his N.Y.C. Opera debut as Ottone in *L'incoronazione di Poppea*; then sang with the Chicago Lyric Opera (1974), the San Francisco Opera (1974–78), the Boston Opera (1975–83), the Glyndebourne Festival (1977–78), the Hamburg State Opera (1977–79), and the Vienna State Opera (1977–79). On Oct. 25, 1979, he made his Metropolitan Opera debut in N.Y. as Silvio in *Pagliacci*. From 1984 he sang at the Cologne Opera. In 1989 he made his first appearance at London's Covent Garden as Rigoletto. He sang Amonasro in Seattle in 1992. In 1996 he portrayed Dandini in *La Cenerentola* in Toronto.—NS/LK/DM

Ellis, Don(ald Johnson), innovative jazz trumpeter, composer, leader, also trombonist; b. Los Angeles, July 25, 1934; d. Hollywood, Dec. 17, 1978. He led groups from an early age. He studied composition at Boston Univ. with Gardner Read, earning a B.M. He worked with Herb Pomeroy and was influenced by Jaki Byard, who often worked with Pomeroy. He took trumpet lessons in Boston, N.Y., and Los Angeles. He studied composition at the Univ. of Calif., Los Angeles, with John Vincent. He worked in Army bands. At various times he played with Jesse Smith, the Glenn Miller Orch. (under Ray McKinley), Charlie Barnet, Sam Donahue, Claude Thornhill, Maynard Ferguson (touring in 1958–59, Byard also was a member), Woody Herman, and Lionel Hampton. He recorded with Mingus in 1959; led a trio at the Village and elsewhere in the summer of 1960; then attended the Lenox School of Jazz in August 1960, where he met composer Don Heckman and studied with George Russell. He returned to N.Y. and Heckman introduced him to composer John Benson Brooks, who instructed him in applications of 12-tone rows. He used a 12-tone row when he recorded his first album as a leader that October, with Byard. He played with a quartet at Wells's in Harlem, performed and recorded with Russell in 1961–62. He played at the Warsaw Jazz Jamboree in 1962 with a Polish trio and in Scandinavia in 1963. On Feb. 10, 1963 his Improvisational Workshop made its début at the Five Spot in Manhattan, using methods associated with John Cage, such as choosing random cards from a deck to structure the music; they also improvised in response to a painter in action. This group performed at other clubs and on TV. He performed with Eric Dolphy and others on April 18, 1963, at Carnegie Hall as part of the Twentieth-Century Innovations series organized by Gunther Schuller (recorded by Schuller and partly issued). He was a trumpet soloist in Larry Austin's "Improvisations for Orch. and Jazz Soloists" performed by the N.Y. Philharmonic in January 1964, including a TV special with the conductor Leonard Bernstein. After that, Ellis returned to L.A. and began graduate studies at UCLA. While there, he studied tabla drumming with Hari Har Rao, and later in 1964 founded the Hindustani Jazz Sextet, with Rao, to apply his interests in Indian music, and he and Rao wrote about their concepts. (Ellis was the author of a number of articles and short monographs.) The group performed in Hollywood Clubs, in a joint appearance with Stan Kenton in 1966, and on July 14, 1966, at the Fillmore, on a bill with the Grateful Dead and Big Brother & the Holding Co. He also became interested in quartertones in early 1965; learning that a Soviet-bloc composer had written a piece for a trumpet with a special fourth valve that produced reliable quartertones; he persuaded the Holton company to build him such a trumpet, which he used exclusively from September 1965. Meanwhile he began leading his own big band, incorporating influences of Indian music and unusual meters, first at a rehearsal group in 1964 and then in 1965 working one night a week at a club. By 1966 the group was appearing regularly at Bonesville in Hollywood. Most of the charts were written and arranged by Ellis, but several band members and Hank Levy also contributed pieces. The group developed a following and had a very successful appearance at the Monterey festival in September 1966 (released on LP). Ellis was a talented crowd-pleaser and promoted the group by using such tactics as distributing bumper stickers that asked "Where is Don Ellis?" The band appeared at the jazz festival in West Berlin in late 1967. Rock and blues artist Al Kooper was such a fan that in 1968 he used the band on a cut of one of his albums and produced the band's LP *Autumn*. From June 18–21, 1970, the band performed at the Fillmore, where they recorded live. Ellis also wrote large classical works, including *Contrasts* for two orchs. and trumpet, which was performed by the L.A. Philharmonic under Zubin Mehta (composed 1965; premiered around Thanksgiving 1967) and his Music for Big Band and Symphony Orch. (1966). He did studio work and played on film soundtracks; he won a Grammy Award in 1972 for his arrangement of the theme to *The French Connection*, which appeared on his album *Connection*. From 1971 on his groups usually included an amplified string quartet. In the early 1970s he regularly presented clinics at high schools and colleges. He had a serious heart attack in

1975. He took up the Superbone (combined slide/valve trombone) in 1976 and formed a new 21-member band named Survival. He appeared on a Shirley MacLaine TV special around 1976, demonstrating his echoplex and other electronic effects. In the summer of 1977 he appeared at Montreux as part of an Atlantic Records showcase and returned there in 1978 with his big band (released on his last LP). A second heart attack on the evening of Dec. 17 took his life. The Don Ellis Memorial Library in Mesquite, Tex., at Eastfield Coll. houses his works and memorabilia, and distributes Ellis sheet music and videos. He played on soundtracks for numerous TV shows and movies; some listeners have noted that the trumpet solos heard on the *Klute* soundtrack bear Ellis's style.

DISC.: *How Time Passes* (1960; with Byard); *New Ideas* (1961); *Out of Nowhere* (1961); *Essence* (1962); *Don Ellis and the Karolak Trio* (1962); *Don Ellis at Monterey* (1966); *Live in 3 2/3 4; Time* (1966); *Electric Bath* (1967); *Autumn* (1968); *Shock Treatment* (1968); *New Don Ellis Band Goes Underground* (1969); *Don Ellis at Fillmore* (1970); *Tears of Joy* (1971); *Connection* (1972); *Haiku* (1973); *Soaring* (1974); *Live at Montreux* (1977); *Music from Other Galaxies and Planets* (1977). *Music for Big Band and Symphony Orchestra.* Charles Mingus: *Nostalgia in Times Square* (1959; uncut version of "Mingus Dynasty" including an Ellis trumpet solo). Maynard Ferguson: *A Message from Birdland* (1959); *MF Plays Jazz for Dancing* (1959); *Newport Suite* (1960). George Russell: *Ezz-thetics* (1961); *The Stratus Seekers* (1962); *The Outer View* (1962). Eric Dolphy: *Vintage Dolphy* (1963). Frank Zappa/Mothers of Invention: *Absolutely Free* (1967; Ellis on one track). Al Kooper: *I Stand Alone* (1968; features the Don Ellis Orch. on "Coloured Rain"). Leonard Bernstein: *Conducts Music for Our Time* (includes Larry Austin "Improvisations for Orch. and Jazz Soloists" with Ellis, recorded on Jan. 13, 1964 in Philharmonic Hall, now Avery Fisher Hall, Lincoln Center, N.Y.C.). Red Mitchell: "Where's Don Ellis Now?" on *Simple Isn't Easy* is a spoof of Ellis's style.

WRITINGS: With Milcho Leviev, Dave McDaniel, and Ralph Humphrey, *The New Rhythm Book* (North Hollywood, Calif., 1972); *Quarter Tones: A Text with Musical Examples, Exercises, and Etudes* (Plainview, Long Island, N.Y.: c. 1975).

BIBL.: A. Agostinelli, *D. E.: A Man for Our Time* (Providence, R.I., 1984).—LP

Ellis, Osian (Gwynn),

Welsh harpist and teacher; b. Fynnongroew, Feb. 8, 1928. He received training at the Royal Academy of Music in London. He played in the Melos Ensemble and was solo harpist with the London Sym. Orch.; acquired a fine reputation as a concert artist via engagements as a soloist with the foremost orchs. and as a recitalist around the globe. From 1959 to 1989 he was also prof. of harp at the Royal Academy of Music. In 1971 he was made a Commander of the Order of the British Empire. In addition to the standard harp literature, Ellis commissioned works for his instrument from Britten, Hoddinott, Mathias, Menotti, Schuman, and others. He publ. *The Story of the Harp in Wales* (1991).—NS/LK/DM

Elman, Mischa (actually, Mikhail Saulovich),

remarkable Russian-born American violinist; b. Talnoy, Jan. 20, 1891; d. N.Y., April 5, 1967. At the age of 6, he was taken by his father to Odessa, where he became a violin student of Fidelmann and a pupil of Brodsky. His progress was extraordinary, and when Leopold Auer heard him play in 1902, he immediately accepted him in his class at the St. Petersburg Cons. In 1904 he made his debut in St. Petersburg with sensational acclaim; on Oct. 14, 1904, he made a brilliant Berlin debut; on March 21, 1905, he made his first appearance in London to great acclaim. On Dec. 10, 1908, he made his U.S. debut as soloist in an extraordinary performance of the Tchaikovsky concerto with Altschuler and the Russian Sym. Orch. in N.Y., and was hailed as one of the greatest virtuosos of the time; he played with every important sym. orch. in the U.S. In the following years, he played all over the world, and, with Jascha Heifetz, became a synonym for violinistic prowess. His playing was the quintessence of Romantic interpretation; his tone was mellifluous but resonant; he excelled particularly in the concertos of Mendelssohn, Tchaikovsky, and Wieniawski; but he could also give impressive performances of Beethoven and Mozart. He publ. several violin arrangements of Classical and Romantic pieces, and he also composed some playable short compositions for his instrument. His father publ. a sentimental book, *Memoirs of Mischa Elman's Father* (N.Y., 1933). In 1923 Elman became a naturalized American citizen.

BIBL.: A. Kozinn, *M. E. and the Romantic Style* (Chur and N.Y., 1990).—**NS/LK/DM**

Elman, Ziggy (originally, **Finkelman, Harry**), jazz trumpeter, also multi-instrumentalist; b. Philadelphia, May 26, 1914; d. Van Nuys, Calif., June 26, 1968. His brash, exciting style was featured with Benny Goodman's band on the Jewish, klezmer styled solos in the middle of "And the Angels Sing" and "Bei Mir Bist Du Schön." Elman lived in Atlantic City from early childhood, playing local gigs on many instruments from early teens. He became a resident musician at Steel Pier, Atlantic City, during the early 1930s, originally working on trombone with Alex Bartha's band (with which he recorded in 1932). In September 1936, he left Bartha to join Benny Goodman, remaining with Goodman through July 1940. After a month in Joe Venuti's Band, Elman joined Tommy Dorsey in August 1940, remaining with him until 1943 when he was drafted into the Army. After the war, he rejoined Tommy Dorsey in February 1946, briefly playing baritone sax, then rejoined the trumpet section (and occasionally doubled on trombone while Tommy Dorsey played trumpet). Except for a brief period from January–May 1947 when he had his own band, he worked with Dorsey until July 1948. After again reviving his own band from August–December 1948, Elman began working on soundtracks for films and television, which occupied him for the balance of his professional career. He appeared in the film *The Benny Goodman Story* but through illness was unable to play (the version of his feature "And the Angels Sing" was soundtracked by Manny Klein). He semi-retired from studio work in 1957, and also ran his own music store. He died of a liver ailment in 1968. Throughout his career, Ziggy occasionally did section work on instruments other than trumpet, i.e, clarinet, baritone sax, and trombone.

DISC.: *Dancing with Zig* (1952); *Sentimental Trumpet* (1956). B. Goodman: *And the Angels Sing; Bei Mir Bist Du Schön.*—**JC/LP**

Elmendorff, Karl (Eduard Maria), eminent German conductor; b. Düsseldorf, Oct. 25, 1891; d. Hofheim am Taunus, Oct. 21, 1962. He was a student of Steinbach and Abendroth at the Cologne Hochschule für Musik. After conducting opera in Düsseldorf, Mainz, Hagen, and Aachen, he held the post of first conductor at the Berlin State Opera and the Bavarian State Opera in Munich (from 1925). He won distinction as a conductor at the Bayreuth Festivals (1927–42); he also was Generalmusikdirektor in Kassel and Wiesbaden (1932–35), and then conducted in Mannheim (1935–42), at the Berlin State Opera (1937–45), and at the Dresden State Opera (1942–45); he subsequently was Generalmusikdirektor in Kassel (1948–51) and Wiesbaden (1951–56). Elmendorff was greatly esteemed as a Wagnerian.—**NS/LK/DM**

Elming, Poul, Danish tenor; b. Ålborg, July 21, 1949. He studied at the Ålborg Cons. and the Århus Cons., and was a student in Wiesbaden of Paul Lohmann. In 1979 he joined the Jutland Opera in Århus, where he began his career singing baritone roles. He became a member of the Royal Opera in Copenhagen in 1984. Following further training with Susanna Eken in Copenhagen and Oren Brown in N.Y., he returned to the Royal Opera in 1989 to make his tenor debut as Parsifal. In 1990 he made his first appearance at the Bayreuth Festival as Siegmund, which role he then sang at London's Covent Garden in 1991. He sang Parsifal at the Berlin State Opera in 1992, and returned there in 1993 as Lohengrin and in 1995 as Parsifal. As a guest artist, he sang with many European opera houses. He also was active as a recitalist and concert artist. Among his other roles were Erik in *Der fliegende Holländer* and Max in *Der Freischütz.*—**NS/LK/DM**

Elmo, Cloe, Italian mezzo-soprano; b. Lecce, April 9, 1910; d. Ankara, May 24, 1962. She was a pupil of Chibaudo at the Accademia di Santa Cecilia in Rome; after winning the Vienna singing competition (1932), she pursued training with Rinolfi and Pedrini. In 1934 she made her operatic debut as Santuzza in Cagliara, and then was a valued member of Milan's La Scala (1936–43). On Nov. 14, 1947, she made her Metropolitan Opera debut in N.Y. as Azucena, remaining on its roster until 1949. From 1951 to 1954 she again sang at La Scala, and then taught voice at the Ankara Cons. Her repertoire included both standard and contemporary roles in Italian operas.—**NS/LK/DM**

Elmore, Robert Hall, American organist, teacher, and composer; b. Ramapatnam, India (of American parents), Jan. 2, 1913; d. Ardmore, Pa., Sept. 22, 1985. He studied with Pietro Yon (organ) and Harl McDonald (composition), at the Royal Academy of Music in London (licentiate, 1933), and at the Univ. of Pa. (B.Mus., 1937). He taught organ at Philadelphia's Clarke Cons. of Music (1936–53) and Musical Academy (from 1939), and composition at the Univ. of Pa. (from 1940); he also was organist at various churches. His *It Began at Breakfast* was the first televised opera by an American composer.

WORKS: *It Began at Breakfast*, opera (Philadelphia, Feb. 8, 1941); 2 tone poems: *Valley Forge* (Philadelphia, April 9, 1937) and *Prelude to Unrest*; 2 orch. suites: *3 Colors* and *Legend of Sleepy Hollow*; Organ Concerto, String Quartet; organ pieces; sacred music; songs.—NS/LK/DM

Eloy, Jean-Claude, French composer; b. Mont-Saint-Aignan, Seine-Maritime, June 15, 1938. He studied in Paris at the Schola Cantorum, and then at the Cons. with Lucette Descaves and Nat (premier prix in piano, 1957), Février (premier prix in chamber music, 1958), N. Gallon (premier prix in counterpoint, 1959), Martenot (premier prix in Ondes Martenot, 1960), and Milhaud (2nd prix in composition, 1961). He also attended the summer courses in new music in Darmstadt (1957, 1960, 1961), where he workd with Stockhausen, Messiaen, Pousseur, and Scherchen. From 1961 to 1963 he studied with Boulez in Basel. In 1972–73 he worked at the Cologne electronic music studio under Stockhausen. From 1971 to 1987 he was a producer for Radio-France in Paris. In 1963 he won the Prix de la Biennale of Paris and in 1981 the Prix national de la musique. In 1983 he was made a Chevalier dans l'Ordre des Arts et Lettres. He held a Deutscher Akademischer Austauschdienst fellowship in Berlin in 1991–92. From his earliest works, he adopted the advanced techniques of serialism, being particularly influenced by Boulez, Varèse, and Webern.

WORKS: ORCH.: *Étude III* (1962); *Équivalences* for 18 Instruments (1963); *Polychronies I* and *II* (1964); *Macles* for 6 Instrumental Groups (1967); *Faisceaux- Diffractions* for 28 Instruments (1978); *Fluctuante-Immuable* (1977; Paris, May 5, 1978). **VOCAL:** *Cantate* for Soprano and Instruments (1961); *Chants pour une ombre* for Soprano and 9 Instruments (1961); *Kâmakalâ* for 5 Choruses and 3 Orch. Ensembles, and 3 Conductors (1971); *Kshara-Akshara* for Soprano Chorus, 3 Orch. Ensembles, and 3 Conductors (1974); *A l'approche du feu méditant...* for 2 Buddhist Monk Choruses and Gagaku Ensemble (Tokyo, Sept. 30, 1983); *Anâhata* for 2 Soloists, 3 Gagaku Instruments, Percussion, Electronics, and Concrete Sounds (1984–86; Paris, Nov. 19, 1986); *Sappho Hikètis* for 2 Women's Voices and Electronics (Paris, Oct. 24, 1989); *Butsumyôe* for 2 Women's Voices (Paris, Oct. 24, 1989); *Erkos* for Woman's Voice, Percussion, and Electro-acoustic Environment (1990–91); *Rosa, Sonia...* for 2 Women's Voices (1991); *Gaia* for Soprano and Electroacoustic Environment (1991–92). **ELECTRONIC:** *Shanti* (Royan, March 23, 1974); *Gaku-no-Michi* for Electronics and Concrete Sounds (1977–78); *Poème-Picasso* (1978); *Étude IV: Points-lignes-paysages* (1978–80); *Yo- In* (1980); *...d'une étoile oubliée* for Electronics and Percussion (1986).—NS/LK/DM

Elschek, Oskár, Slovak ethnomusicologist; b. Bratislava, June 16, 1931. He studied musicology and aesthetics at the Univ. of Bratislava (degree, 1954), then became a member of the Musicology Inst. of the Slovak Academy of Sciences. In 1963 he was appointed ed.-in-chief of *Slovenská Hudba*, and in 1967 he co-ed. the *Annual Bibliography of European Ethnomusicology*. His publications include studies of Slovak and European folk music, organology, and the sociology of music. With his wife Alica Elscheková (b. Bratislava, Nov. 21, 1930), he wrote books on Slovak folk music (1956, 1962)

and ed. the 1st vol. of Bartók's folk songs (1959). He publ., with A. Elschekova, *Úvod do štúdia slovenskej l'udovej hudby* (Introduction to the Study of Slovak Folk Music; Bratislava, 1962). He also publ. *Slovenské l'udové píst'aly a d'alšie aerofóny* (Bratislava, 1991) and *Die Musikforschung der Gegenwart: Ihre Systematik, Theorie und Entwicklung* (2 vols., Vienna, 1992).—NS/LK/DM

Elsner, Joseph (Anton Franciskus) (Józef Antoni Franciszek), noted Polish pedagogue and composer of German descent; b. Grottkau, Silesia, June 1, 1769; d. Warsaw, April 18, 1854. After singing in the local church choir, he studied at the Breslau Jesuit Gymnasium (1781–88), concurrently singing in the opera chorus, playing violin in chamber music concerts, and beginning to compose. After studying theology and medicine at the Univ. of Breslau and the Univ. of Vienna (1789), he turned decisively to music. He was concertmaster of the Brünn Opera orch. (1791–92) and Kapellmeister in Lemberg (1792–99), then settled in Warsaw, where he served as director of the Opera for 25 years. He was also active as a teacher (Chopin was his most famous student) and founded several music schools, one of which later became the Warsaw Cons. In 1823 he was awarded the Order of St. Stanislaw. His compositions presage the development of the Polish national school.

WRITINGS: *Początki muzyki a szczególniej épiewania* (The Beginnings of Music, Especially of Singing; Warsaw, 1818–21); *Szkola épiewu* (School of Singing; Warsaw, 1834; 2nd ed., Leipzig, 1855); *Sumarius moich utworów z objaénieniami o czynnoéciach i dzialaniach moich jako artysty muzycznego* (Summary of My Works with Explanations of My Functions and Activities as a Musician; 1840–49; Kraków, 1957).

WORKS (all 1st perf. in Warsaw unless otherwise given): **O p e r a :** *Amazonki czyli Herminia* (The Amazons, or Herminia; Lemberg, July 26, 1797); *Sultan Wampum czyli Nieroztropne zyczenie* (Sultan Vampum, or The Rash Wish; 1800); *Siedem razy jeden* (7 Times 1; Dec. 14, 1804); *Stary trzpiot i mlody mędrzec* (The Old Dolt and the Young Sage; Feb. 15, 1805); *Wieszczka Urzella czyli To co się damom podoba* (The Soothsayer Urzella, or What Pleases the Ladies; March 7, 1806); *Andromeda* (Jan. 14, 1807); *Chimère et réalité or Urojenie i rzeczywistoéć* (April 22, 1808); *Leszek Bialy czyli Czarownica z-Lysej Góry* (Leszek the White or The Witch of the Bald Mountain; Dec. 2, 1809); *Wawozy Sierra Modena* (The Ravines of the Sierra Modena; Jan. 31, 1812); *Kabalista* (The Cabalist; Jan. 29, 1813); *Król Lokietek czyli Wiéliczanki* (King Lokietek, or The Women of Wislica; April 3, 1818); *Jagiello w Tenczynie* (Jagiello in Tenczyn; Jan. 1, 1820). **OTHER:** Melodramas; duodramas; ballets; 8 syms.; 6 string quartets; Piano Quartet; String Quintet; Septet; 3 violin sonatas; 24 Latin masses; 9 Polish masses; 4 oratorios; offertories; hymns; 55 secular cantatas; some 100 songs.

BIBL.: J. Reiss, *Élązak Józef E.: Nauczyciel Chopina* (Silesian J. E.: Chopin's Teacher; Katowice, 1936); A. Nowak- Romanowicz, *Józef E.* (Krakow, 1957).—NS/LK/DM

Elson, Arthur, American writer on music, son of **Louis (Charles) Elson;** b. Boston, Nov. 18, 1873; d. N.Y., Feb. 24, 1940. After training from his father, he studied at the New England Cons. of Music in Boston, Harvard Univ. (graduated, 1895), and the Mass. Inst. of Technology (graduated, 1897). He served as music critic of the *Boston Advertiser* (from 1920).

WRITINGS: *A Critical History of the Opera* (1901; new ed., 1926, as *A History of Opera*); *Orchestral Instruments and Their Use* (1902; new ed., 1930); *Woman's Work in Music* (1903; new ed., 1931); *Modern Composers of Europe* (1905; new ed., 1922); *Music Club Programs from All Nations* (1906; new ed., 1928); *The Musician's Guide* (1913); *The Book of Musical Knowledge* (1915; new ed., 1934); *Pioneer School Music Course* (1917).—**NS/LK/DM**

Elson, Louis (Charles), American music historian, father of **Arthur Elson;** b. Boston, April 17, 1848; d. there, Feb. 14, 1920. He studied voice with Kreissmann at Boston and theory with Karl Gloggner Castelli in Leipzig. Returning to Boston, he was music ed. of the *Boston Advertiser* (1886–1920); was a teacher (from 1880) and head of the theory dept. (from 1881) at the New England Cons. of Music. He was ed.-in-chief of the *University Encyclopedia of Music* (10 vols., 1912). In his music criticism, he attacked the modernists with vicious eloquence, reserving the choicest invective for Debussy; he called *La Mer* "Le Mal de Mer," and said that the faun of *L'Après-midi d'un faune* needed a veterinary surgeon. His widow endowed a memorial fund for the presentation of lectures on music at the Library of Congress in Washington, D.C., in 1945.

WRITINGS: *Curiosities of Music* (1880); *The History of German Song* (1888); *The Theory of Music* (1890; rev. by F. Converse, 1935); *European Reminiscences, Musical and Otherwise* (1891; new ed., 1914); *The Realm of Music* (1892); *Great Composers and Their Work* (1898); *The National Music of America and Its Sources* (1899; new ed., rev. by A. Elson, 1924); with P. Hale, *Famous Composers and Their Works* (1900); *Shakespeare in Music* (1901); *The History of American Music* (1904; 2nd ed., 1915; rev. by A. Elson, 1925); *Elson's Music Dictionary* (1905); *Elson's Pocket Music Dictionary* (1909); *Mistakes and Disputed Points in Music* (1910); *Women in Music* (1918); *Children in Music* (1918).

BIBL.: *Lectures on the History and Art of Music: The L.C. E. Memorial Lectures at the Library of Congress, 1946–1963* (Washington, D.C., 1969).—**NS/LK/DM**

Elston, Arnold, American composer; b. N.Y., Sept. 30, 1907; d. Vienna, June 6, 1971. He studied harmony and counterpoint with Goldmark in N.Y. and took courses at City Coll. (B.A., 1930) and Columbia Univ. (M.A., 1932); after composition studies with Webern in Vienna (1932–35), he continued his training at Harvard Univ. (Ph.D., 1939), while concurrently studying conducting with Fiedler in Boston (1939). He taught at the Longy School of Music in Cambridge, Mass. (1939–40), the Univ. of Ore. (1941–58), and the Univ. of Calif. at Berkeley (1958–71). He wrote the books *Music and Medicine* (1948) and *A Modern Guide to Symphonic Music* (1966).

WORKS: DRAMATIC: Opera: *Sweeney Agonistes,* chamber opera (1948–50); *The Love of Don Perlimplin* (1957–58). **ORCH.:** *Suite* (1931); *Prelude, Paean and Furioso* for Orch. (1967–71). **CHAMBER:** 2 string quartets (1932, 1961); *Variations* for String Quartet (1934); Piano trio (1967); piano music. **VOCAL:** *Chorus for Survival,* chamber cantata for Soprano, Baritone, Chorus, and 7 Instruments (1954–55); *Great Age, Behold Us,* cantata for Chorus and Orch. (1965–66). —**NS/LK/DM**

El-tour, Anna, Russian soprano; b. Odessa, June 4, 1886; d. Amsterdam, May 30, 1954. She studied at the St. Petersburg Cons. (voice with Mme. von Hecke; piano with Essipova). From 1913 to 1920, she taught in Moscow. Leaving Russia, from 1922 to 1925 she was in Berlin, and from 1925 to 1948 she taught at the Cons. International de Paris. After 1948, she was a prof. of singing at the Amsterdam Cons. She traveled widely in the Far East; gave recitals in Israel in 1953.—**NS/LK/DM**

Elvey, Sir George (Job), English organist and composer, brother of **Stephen Elvey;** b. Canterbury, March 27, 1816; d. Windlesham, Surrey, Dec. 9, 1893. He studied with Skeats at Canterbury Cathedral, and with Potter and Crotch at the Royal Academy of Music in London. From 1835 until 1882 he served as organist and master of the boys at St. George's Chapel, Windsor; received a Mus.Bac. (1838) and a Mus.Doc. (1840) from Oxford; was knighted in 1871. His widow publ. a memoir, *Life and Reminiscences of George J. Elvey* (London, 1894). His works included 2 oratorios, *The Resurrection and Ascension* (London, Dec. 2, 1840) and *Mount Carmel* (London, June 30, 1886), as well as many pieces of church music, glees, part-songs, and organ pieces. —**NS/LK/DM**

Elvey, Stephen, English organist and composer, brother of **Sir George (Job) Elvey;** b. Canterbury, June 27, 1805; d. Oxford, Oct. 6, 1860. He was a chorister of Canterbury Cathedral, and a pupil of Skeats there. In 1830 he became organist of New Coll., Oxford. He received a Mus.Bac. (1831) and a Mus.Doc. (1838) from the Univ. of Oxford, where he was Choragus from 1840 until his death. He wrote mostly church music, and publ. a successful handbook, *The Psalter, or Canticles and Psalms, Pointed for Chanting, upon a New Principle* (London; 6 eds. to 1866).—**NS/LK/DM**

Elvira, Pablo, Puerto Rican baritone; b. Santurce, Sept. 24, 1937; d. Bozeman, Mont., Feb. 5, 2000. He studied voice at the Puerto Rico Cons., becoming a finalist in the Metropolitan Opera auditions in 1966. He taught at the Ind. Univ. School of Music in Bloomington (1966-74), where he made his formal debut as Rigoletto (1968). On Feb. 23, 1974, he made his first appearance at the N.Y.C. Opera as Germont, where he sang regularly in subsequent seasons. His final appearance there was as Rigoletto in 1989. He made his Metropolitan Opera debut in N.Y. as Rigoletto on March 22, 1978. He sang Figaro at his last appearance there in 1990. In addition to his operatic engagements, he also sang frequently in concert. Among his finest roles were Don Carlo, Renato, Leoncavallo's Tonio, and Puccini's Lescaut.—**NS/LK/DM**

Elwart, Antoine (-Amable-Élie), French writer on music, pedagogue, and composer; b. Paris, Nov. 18, 1808; d. there, Oct. 14, 1877. He entered the Paris Cons. in 1825, where he studied counterpoint and fugue with Fétis and composition with Le Sueur. In 1831 he won the second Prix for composition, and then served as asst. prof. to Reicha there (1832–34). In 1834 he won the Grand Prix de Rome. After returning from

Rome, he was again asst. prof. at the Paris Cons. (1836–40) before serving there as prof. of harmony (1840–71).

WORKS: 3 operas: *Les Catalans* (Rouen, Jan. 1840), *La Reine de Saba*, and *Les chercheurs d'or*; incidental music; *Noé, ou le déluge universel*, oratorio-sym. (Paris, 1845); *Ruth et Booz*, vocal sym. (1850); *La Naissance d'Éve*, oratorio (Paris, 1846); *Les Noces de Cana*, mystery for Soloists, Chorus, and Orch. (1853); masses; Te Deum; cantatas; chamber music.

WRITINGS (all publ. in Paris): *Théorie musicale, solfège progressif...* (1830); *Duprez, sa vie artistique, avec une biographie authentique de son maître Alexandre Choron* (1838); with others, *Études élémentaires de Musique...* (1838–45); *Le Contrepoint et la Fugue...* (1840); *Petit manuel d'Harmonie...* (1841; 5th ed., 1870); *Feuille harmonique...* (1841); *L'Art de jouer impromptu de l'alto-viola...* (1844); *Le chanteur-accompagnateur...* (1844); *L'harmonie musicale* (4 vols., 1853); *Histoire de la Société des Concerts du Conservatoire* (1860); *Histoire des Concerts Populaires de musique classique...* (1864); *Petit Traité d'instrumentation à l'usage des jeunes compositeurs* (1864; 10th ed., 1903); *Lutrin et Orphéon ou le plain chant et la Musique appris en chantant des choeurs, Grammaire pratique* (1865); *Essair sur la composition chorale* (1867). —NS/LK/DM

Elwell, Herbert, American composer, teacher, and music critic; b. Minneapolis, May 10, 1898; d. Cleveland, April 17, 1974. He studied at the Univ. of Minn.; then took courses with Bloch in N.Y. (1919–21) and Boulanger in Paris (1921–24). He received a Prix de Rome in 1923, and from 1924 to 1927 he held a fellowship at the American Academy in Rome. Returning to the U.S., he held a post as teacher of composition at the Cleveland Inst. of Music (1928–45). From 1932 to 1964 he served as music critic for the *Cleveland Plain Dealer*.

WORKS: B a l l e t : *The Happy Hypocrite* (1925; orch. suite, Rome, May 21, 1927). **ORCH.:** *The Centaur* (1924); *Orchestral Sketches* (1937); *Introduction and Allegro* (N.Y., July 12, 1942); *Ode* (1950); *Concert Suite* for Violin and Orch. (1957). **CHAMBER:** Piano Quintet (1923); Violin Sonata (1927); 2 string quartets (1929, 1937); *Variations* for Violin and Piano (1951); piano pieces, including a Sonata (1926). **VOCAL:** *I Was with Him*, cantata for Tenor, Men's Chorus, and 2 Pianos (1937; Cleveland, Nov. 30, 1942); *Blue Symphony* for Voice and String Quartet (1944; Cleveland, Feb. 2, 1945); *Lincoln: Requiem Aeternam* for Baritone, Chorus, and Orch. (1946; Oberlin, Feb. 16, 1947); *Pastorale* for Voice and Orch. (1947; Cleveland, March 25, 1948); *Watch America* for Chorus (1951); *The Forever Young* for Voice and Orch. (Cleveland, Oct. 29, 1953); songs.—NS/LK/DM

Elwes, Gervase (Cary), noted English tenor; b. Billing Hall, near Northampton, Nov. 15, 1866; d. when hit by a train in the railroad station in Boston, Jan. 12, 1921. He was educated at Christ Church, Oxford, and then entered the diplomatic service. While stationed in Vienna (1891–95), he studied singing, and then took voice lessons in Brussels with Demest, in London with Henry Russell and Victor Beigel, and in Paris with Bouhy. In 1903 he made his professional debut at the Westmoreland Festival, and that same year his first London appearance in concert. Thereafter he distinguished himself as a concert and oratorio singer in England. In 1909 he toured the U.S., and again in 1920–21, at which time he lost his life. After his death, a special fund was organized in his memory, which became the Musicians' Benevolent Fund of London. He was especially esteemed as the Evangelist in Bach's *St. Matthew Passion*, as Elgar's Gerontius, and as an interpreter of Brahms's lieder.

BIBL.: W. and R. Elwes, *G. E.: The Story of His Life* (London, 1935).—NS/LK/DM

Emerson, Lake and Palmer, one of the first supergroups to effectively introduce the synthesizer into rock music; the band debuted at the 1970 Isle of Wight Festival, disbanded in 1979, and eventually reunited in 1992. **MEMBERSHIP:** Keith Emerson, kybd. (b. Todmorden, England, Nov. 2, 1944); Greg Lake, bs., gtr., voc. (b. Bournemouth, Dorset, England, Nov. 10, 1948); Carl Palmer, drm. (b. Birmingham, England, March 20, 1947).

One of the first British rock bands to provide classical music within the rock format during the late 1960s was the Nice. After their debut album, they were perhaps the first rock group to explore the trio format utilizing keyboards rather than electric guitar as the primary musical focus. Disbanding by 1970, the Nice were superseded by Emerson, Lake and Palmer. The group continued the progressive, keyboard-based power-trio format, and became one of the biggest American concert attractions by the mid-1970s. Emerson, Lake and Palmer were one of the first rock bands to tour with a truly quadraphonic sound system (in 1974) and perhaps the first to attempt to tour with a full symphony orchestra (in 1977).

Originally formed to back soul singer Pat Arnold, the Nice began touring on their own in October 1967. Signed to Andrew Oldham's Immediate label, the Nice's debut album featured Emerson's rousing "Rondo." With the departure of David O'List (b. Chiswick, London, England, Dec. 13, 1948), the group's primary singer and songwriter, Emerson became the musical and visual focus of the Nice. His flamboyant stage act, which included stabbing and assaulting his electric organ, brought the group widespread notoriety in Great Britain and Europe. As a keyboard-based power trio—Emerson; Lee Jackson (b. Newcastle upon Tyne, England, Jan. 8, 1943) on bass, guitar, and vocals; and Brian "Blinky" Davison (b. Leicester, England, May 25, 1942) on drums—the group recorded *Ars Longa Vita Brevis*, which showcased the title composition performed in four movements with coda. By 1970 the group was on the verge of an American breakthrough but elected to disband. Ironically, the Nice soon entered the American album charts with *Five Bridges Suite*, perhaps their finest work.

In late 1969 in San Francisco, Keith Emerson, still with the Nice, met guitarist-bassist-vocalist Greg Lake, a founding member of King Crimson. With the demise of the Nice, they formed Emerson, Lake and Palmer with drummer Carl Palmer, a former member of the Crazy World of Arthur Brown (1968's smash "Fire") and Atomic Rooster. With Emerson exploring the sound of the synthesizer, the group garnered a reputation for their furious stage act and virtuoso abilities. Their first two albums were best-sellers, with the debut yielding a minor hit, the somber ballad "Lucky Man." Their third album was an ambitious live recording based on Modest Mussorgsky's classical composition *Pictures at an Exhibition*. The follow-up, *Trilogy*, contained Aaron Copland's "Hoedown," Maurice Ravel's "Bolero," and the subtle and intricate "In the Beginning," a moderate hit.

In 1974 Emerson, Lake and Palmer recorded *Brain Salad Surgery* for their own Manticore label. To support the album, they completed a spectacular American tour, transporting 36 tons of equipment. Emerson played six Moog synthesizers, two organs, a Steinway, and an electric piano. Each of Palmer's drums had its own synthesizer, and his equipment included two timpani, two gongs, chimes, and a large church bell. In addition, the tour used the first truly quadraphonic sound system. The live set *Welcome Back, My Friends, to the Show That Never Ends* was issued following the tour.

The group took a two-year hiatus following the tour, eventually releasing the double-record set *Works, Vol. 1*, in 1977. Each member used one side for a solo effort, with all three playing together on the final side. The haunting "C'est La Vie," composed by Lake, became a minor hit from the album. That May the group embarked on a comeback tour of America with a 57-piece orchestra and six-person vocal choir. The cost proved prohibitive and the orchestra was dismissed after 15 concerts. Late 1978's *Love Beach* was greeted hastily and in 1979 Emerson, Lake and Palmer disbanded.

In the early 1980s Keith Emerson recorded the soundtrack to the movie *Nighthawks* and Greg Lake recorded solo albums. In spring 1981 Carl Palmer joined in the formation of the supergroup Asia with guitarist Steve Howe (Yes), keyboardist Geoff Downes (Yes), and bassist-vocalist John Wetton (King Crimson). They recorded two best-selling albums, scoring a smash hit with "Heat of the Moment" and major hits with "Only Time Will Tell" and "Don't Cry." In 1986 Emerson and Lake recruited drummer Cozy Powell (Jeff Beck Group, Rainbow, Whitesnake) for touring and the album *Emerson, Lake and Powell*. Palmer left Asia around 1986 and formed 3 with Emerson and Calif. session musician Robert Berry in 1988. Emerson, Lake and Palmer ultimately reunited in 1992 for *Black Moon* and another round of touring.

DISC.: THE NICE: *The Thoughts of Emerlist Davjack* (1968); *Ars Longa Vita Brevis* (1969); *The Nice* (1969); *Five Bridges Suite* (1970); *Elegy* (1971); *Keith Emerson with the Nice* (1972); *Autumn to Spring* (1973); *Immediate Story, Vol. 1* (1976); *Elegy/Five Bridges Suite* (highlights; 1987). **EMERSON, LAKE AND PALMER:** *Emerson, Lake and Palmer* (1971); *Tarkus* (1971); *Pictures at an Exhibition* (1972); *Trilogy* (1972); *Brain Salad Surgery* (1973); *Welcome Back, My Friends ...* (1974); *Works, Vol. 1* (1977); *Works, Vol. 2* (1977); *Love Beach* (1978); *In Concert* (1979); *Best* (1980); *The Atlantic Years* (1992); *Black Moon* (1992); *Live at Royal Albert Hall by Appointment* (1993); *The Return of the Manticore* (1993); *Works Live* (1993); *In the Hot Seat* (1994). **KEITH EMERSON:** *Nighthawks* (soundtrack; 1981). **GREG LAKE:** *Greg Lake* (1981); *Manoeuvres* (1983). **ASIA (WITH CARL PALMER):** *Asia* (1982); *Alpha* (1983); *Astra* (1985); *Then and Now* (1990); *Asia Live in Moscow* (1992); *Aqua* (1994). **EMERSON, LAKE AND POWELL:** *Emerson, Lake and Powell* (1986); *...To the Power of Three* (1988).—**BH**

Emerson, Luther Orlando, American composer, conductor, and music editor; b. Parsonfield, Maine, Aug. 3, 1820; d. Hyde Park, Mass., Sept. 29, 1915. He learned to play cello from his father. After attending the singing- schools of Benjamin F. Butler and George F. Root (1841–43), he studied with Isaac B. Woodbury in Boston. He was active as a church musician in Salem, Mass., Boston, and Greenfield, Mass. before concentrating on conducting, composing, and music editing. Among his works were masses, anthems, vocal quartets, songs, and piano pieces, but he became best known for his numerous collections of church and school music. He also publ. pedagogical methods.—**NS/LK/DM**

Emery, Stephen Albert, American music teacher, writer, and composer; b. Paris, Maine, Oct. 4, 1841; d. Boston, April 15, 1891. His first teacher was H. S. Edwards, of Portland, Maine, and in 1862 he went to Leipzig, where he studied with Plaidy, Papperitz, Richter, and Hauptmann. He returned to Portland in 1864, and in 1866 he went to Boston, where he taught at the New England Cons. from 1867. He publ. 2 textbooks, *Foundation Studies in Pianoforte Playing* (1882) and *Elements of Harmony* (1880; 2nd ed., 1907).—**NS/LK/DM**

Emery, Walter (Henry James), English organist and writer; b. Tilshead, Wiltshire, June 14, 1909; d. Salisbury, June 24, 1974. He studied organ at the Royal Academy of Music in London, and then was engaged as a church organist. From 1937 to 1969 he was an associate at Novello & Co. in the editorial dept. He publ. *The St. Matthew Passion: Its Preparation and Performance* (with Sir Adrian Boult; London, 1949); *Bach's Ornaments* (London, 1953); *Editing Early Music: Notes on the Preparation of Printer's Copy* (with T. Dart and C. Morris; London, 1963); commentaries on Bach's organ works; etc. —**NS/LK/DM**

Emmanuel, (Marie François) Maurice, eminent French music scholar; b. Bar-sur-Aube, May 2, 1862; d. Paris, Dec. 14, 1938. He received his primary education in Dijon. He sang in the church choir in Beaune, and then studied at the Paris Cons. (1880–87) with Savard, Dubois, Delibes, and Bourgault-Ducoudray. He then specialized in the musical history of antiquity under Gevaert in Brussels, and also studied ancient languages at the Sorbonne, becoming a licencié ès lettres (1887) and a docteur ès lettres (1895) with the theses *De saltationis disciplina apud Graecos* (publ. in Latin, Paris, 1895) and *La Danse grecque antique d'après les monuments figurés* (Paris, 1896; Eng. tr. as *The Antique Greek Dance after Sculptured and Painted Figures*, N.Y., 1916). He was a prof. of art history at the Lycée Racine and Lycée Lamartine (1898–1905), maître de chapelle at Ste.-Clotilde (1904–07), and in 1909 succeeded Bourgault-Ducoudray as prof. of music history at the Paris Cons., holding this post until 1936. He ed. vols. 17 and 18 of the complete works of Rameau, as well as Bach's works in Durand's ed. of the classical masters.

WRITINGS: *Histoire de la langue musicale* (2 vols., Paris, 1911; new ed., 1928); *Traité de l'accompagnement modal des psaumes* (Lyons, 1912); with R. Moissenet, *La Polyphonie sacrée*

(Dijon, 1923); *Pelléas et Mélisande de Claude Debussy* (Paris, 1926; 2nd ed., 1950); *César Franck* (Paris, 1930); *Anton Reicha* (Paris, 1936).

WORKS: DRAMATIC: *Salamine*, opera (1921-23; 1927-28; Paris, June 28, 1929); *Amphitryon*, opéra-bouffe (1936; Paris, Feb. 20, 1937). **OTHER:** 2 syms. (1919, 1931); 2 string quartets and other chamber music; 6 piano sonatinas; vocal music.
—NS/LK/DM

Emmett, Daniel Decatur, American composer of popular songs and minstrel performer; b. Mt. Vernon, Ohio, Oct. 29, 1815; d. there, June 28, 1904. After teaching himself to play the fiddle, he was a drummer and fifer in the U.S. Army (1834–35). He then appeared as a blackface banjoist and singer with circus troupes until going to N.Y. in 1842, where he formed a duo with Frank Brower. Emmett played the fiddle and Brower bones. With William Whitlock on banjo and Richard Pelham on tambourine, they formed the Virginia Minstrels in 1843 and toured extensively. After disbanding the group, Emmett performed with Brant's Minstrels (1858–66). In 1859 he wrote the lyrics and music to the song "I Wish I Was in Dixie's Land," which was first heard in N.Y. on April 4th of that year. After its publication, its popularity spread widely as it became known simply as "Dixie"; it was adopted as a Southern fighting song during the Civil War. Emmett lived in Chicago (1867–70; 1871–88). Following the loss of his voice, he resorted to playing the fiddle in saloons. In 1888 he returned to his birthplace and lived out the remainder of his life in straitened circumstances. Although he wrote many songs and tunes, they were all eclipsed by the success of the ubiquitous "Dixie."

BIBL.: C. Galbreath, *D. D. E., Author of Dixie* (Columbus, Ohio, 1904); H. Wintermute, *D. D. E.* (Mt. Vernon, Ohio, 1955); H. Nathan, *D. E. and the Rise of Early Negro Minstrelsy* (Norman, Okla., 1962).—NS/LK/DM

Emsheimer, Ernst, German-born Swedish ethno-musicologist; b. Frankfurt am Main, Jan. 15, 1905; d. Stockholm, June 12, 1989. He studied musicology with Adler and Fischer at the Univ. of Vienna (1924) and the Univ. of Freiburg im Breisgau (Ph.D., 1927). He was musicological consultant in Leningrad at the National Academy for the History of Art, the Hermitage Collection, and the Museum of Ethnography (1932–36), where he led a field recording expedition into the northern Caucasus (1936). Emsheimer settled in Stockholm in 1937, becoming musicological adviser to the Museum of Ethnography. From 1949 to 1973 he was director of the Museum of Music History in Stockholm. Under his direction, it became an important center of Swedish musical and musicological activity. He was co-founder of the *Handbücher der Europäischen Volksmusikinstrumente*. He publ. *Studia ethnomusicologica eurasiatica* (Stockholm, 1964 et seq.; collected writings).
—NS/LK/DM

Enacovici, George, Romanian composer, teacher, and violinist; b. Focşani, May 4, 1891; d. Bucharest, Jan. 26, 1965. He studied at the Bucharest Cons. with Kiriac and Castaldi (1905–12); studied composition with

d'Indy, and violin at the Schola Cantorum in Paris (1914–18). He taught violin at the Bucharest Cons. (1919–54) and was concertmaster of the Bucharest Phil. (1920–21) and the Bucharest Radio Orch. (1928–33).

WORKS: *Intermezzo* for String Orch. and Harp (1912); *Poem* for Violin and Orch. (1920); *Suite in a Romanian Style* for Orch. (1928); *Symphonic Episode* (1933); *Rapsodie romana* for Orch. (1934); *Amfitrita*, symphonic poem (1940); *Arlequinada*, capriccio for 2 Violins and Chamber Orch. (1941); Sym. (1954); Violin Concerto (1956); 3 string quartets; Violin Sonata; Piano Sonata; minor pieces in various genres.—NS/LK/DM

Encina, Juan del, Spanish poet, dramatist, and composer; b. Salamanca, July 12, 1468; d. León, late 1529 or 1530. He was the son of a shoemaker of Salamanca named Juan de Fermoselle. He became a chorister at Salamanca Cathedral, and studied music under his elder brother, Diego de Fermoselle, and under Fernando de Torrijos. He took his degree in law at Salamanca Univ., where he enjoyed the favor of the chancellor, Don Gutiérrez de Toledo. In 1492 he entered the household of the 2nd Duke of Alba, for whom he wrote a series of pastoral eclogues that form the foundation of the Spanish secular drama. These eclogues included "villancicos," or rustic songs, for which Encina composed the music. He went to Rome in 1500, and on May 12, 1500 he was appointed canon at the Cathedral of Salamanca. From Feb. 2, 1510 until 1512 he was archdeacon and canon of Málaga. On May 2, 1512, he again went to Rome, where his *Farsa de Plácida e Vittoriano* was performed in the presence of Pope Julius II on Jan. 11, 1513. In 1517, he was "subcollector of revenues to the Apostolic Chamber." In 1519 he was appointed prior of León, and that same year made a pilgrimage to Jerusalem, where he was ordained a priest. He described his sacred pilgrimage in *Tribagia o Via Sacra de Hierusalem* (Rome, 1521). After the death of Pope Leo X in 1521, Encina returned to Spain and spent his last years as prior at León. Besides being a leading figure in the development of the Spanish drama, Encina was the most important Spanish composer of the reign of Ferdinand and Isabella. He cultivated with notable artistry a type of part-song akin to the Italian "frottola," setting his own poems to music. Some 62 works are found in H. Anglès, ed., *La música en la corte de los Reyes Catolicos: Cancionero de Palacio*, in Monumentos de la Música Española, V, X, and XIV (1947–65). Another modern ed. was publ. by C. Terni, *Juan del Encina: L'opera musicale* (Florence, 1974 et seq.).—NS/LK/DM

Enesco, Georges (real name, **George Enescu**), famous Romanian violinist, conductor, teacher, and composer; b. Liveni-Virnav, Aug. 19, 1881; d. Paris, May 4, 1955. He began to play the piano when he was 4, taking lessons with a Gypsy violinist, Nicolas Chioru, and began composing when he was 5; then studied with Caudella in Iaşi. On Aug. 5, 1889, he made his formal debut as a violinist in Slánic, Moldavia. In the meantime, he had enrolled in the Cons. of the Gesellschaft der Musikfreunde in Vienna (1888), where he studied violin with S. Bachrich, J. Grün, and J. Hellmesberger Jr.; piano with L. Ernst; harmony, counterpoint, and composition with R. Fuchs; chamber music with J. Hellmesberger Sr.; and music history with A. Prosnitz, winning 1st prizes in violin and harmony (1892). After his graduation (1894), he entered the Paris Cons., where he studied violin with Marsick and J. White, harmony with Dubois and Thomas, counterpoint with Gédalge, composition with Fauré and Massenet, and early music with Diémer, winning 2nd accessit for counterpoint and fugue (1897) and graduating with the premier prix for violin (1899). At the same time, he also studied cello, organ, and piano, attaining more than ordinary proficiency on each. On June 11, 1897, he presented in Paris a concert of his works, which attracted the attention of Colonne, who brought out the youthful composer's op.1, *Poème roumain*, the next year. Enesco also launched his conducting career in Bucharest in 1898. In 1902 he first appeared as a violinist in Berlin and also organized a piano trio; in 1904 he formed a quartet. On March 8, 1903, he conducted the premiere of his 2 *Romanian Rhapsodies* in Bucharest, the first of which was to become his most celebrated work. He soon was appointed court violinist to the Queen of Romania. In 1912 he established an annual prize for Romanian composers, which was subsequently won by Jora, Enacovici, Golestan, Otescu, and others. In 1917 he founded the George Enescu sym. concerts in Iaşi. After the end of World War I, he made major tours as a violinist and conductor; he also taught violin in Paris, where his pupils included Menuhin, Grumiaux, Gitlis, and Ferras. He made his U.S. debut in the triple role of conductor, violinist, and composer with the Philadelphia Orch. in N.Y. on Jan. 2, 1923; he returned to conduct the N.Y. Phil. on Jan. 28, 1937. He led several subsequent concerts with it with remarkable success; led it in 14 concerts in 1938, and also appeared twice as a violinist; he conducted 2 concerts at the N.Y. World's Fair in 1939. The outbreak of World War II found him in Romania, where he lived on his farm in Sinaia, near Bucharest. He visited N.Y. again in 1946 as a teacher. On Jan. 21, 1950, during the 60th anniversary season of his debut as a violinist, he gave a farewell concert with the N.Y. Phil. in the multiple capacity of violinist, pianist, conductor, and composer, in a program comprising Bach's Double Concerto (with Menuhin), a violin sonata (playing the piano part with Menuhin), and his 1st *Romanian Rhapsody* (conducting the orch.). He then returned to Paris, where his last years were marked by near poverty and poor health. In July 1954 he suffered a stroke and remained an invalid for his remaining days.

Although Enesco severed relations with his Communist homeland, the Romanian government paid homage to him for his varied accomplishments. His native village, a street in Bucharest, and the State Phil. of Bucharest were named in his honor. Periodical Enesco festivals and international performing competitions were established in Bucharest in 1958. Enesco had an extraordinary range of musical interests. His compositions include artistic stylizations of Romanian folk strains; while his style was neo-Romantic, he made occasional use of experimental devices, such as quarter tones in his opera, *Oedipe*. He possessed a fabulous memory and was able to perform innumerable works without scores. He not only distinguished himself as a violinist and conductor, but he was also a fine pianist and a gifted teacher.

WORKS: DRAMATIC Opera: *OEdipe*, op.23 (1921–31; Paris, March 10, 1936). **ORCH.:** 3 unnumbered syms. (1895, 1896, 1898); 5 numbered syms.: No. 1, op.13 (1905; Paris, Jan. 21, 1906), No. 2, op.17 (1912–14; Bucharest, March 28, 1915), No. 3, op.21, for Chorus and Orch. (1916–18; Bucharest, May 25, 1919; rev. 1921), No. 4 (1934; unfinished), and No. 5 for Tenor, Women's Chorus, and Orch. (1941; unfinished); *Uvertura tragica* (1895); *Ballade* for Violin and Orch. (1896); *Uvertura triumfală* (1896); Violin Concerto (Paris, March 26, 1896); *Fantaisie* for Piano and Orch. (1896; Bucharest, March 26, 1900); Piano Concerto (1897; unfinished); 2 *Suites roumaines*: No. 1 (1896; unfinished) and No. 2 (1897); *Poème roumain*, op.1, for Wordless Chorus and Orch. (1897; Paris, Feb. 9, 1898); *Pastorale* for Small Orch. (Paris, Feb. 19, 1899); *Symphonie concertante* for Cello and Orch., op.8 (1901; Paris, March 14, 1909); 2 *Rhapsodies roumaines*, op.11 (1901; Bucharest, March 8, 1903); 2 *Intermezzi* for Strings, op.12 (1902- 03); Suite No. 1, op.9 (1903; Paris, Dec. 11, 1904); *Suite châtelaine*, op.17 (1911; unfinished); Suite No. 2, op.20 (1915; Bucharest, March 27, 1916); Suite No. 3, op.27, *Villageoise* (1938; N.Y., Feb. 2, 1939); *Concert Overture*, op.32, "sur des thèmes dans le caractère populaire roumain" (1948; Washington, D.C., Jan. 23, 1949); *Symphonie de chambre* for 12 Instruments, op.33 (1954; Paris, Jan. 23, 1955); *Vox maris*, symphonic poem, op.31 (c. 1929–55; Bucharest, Sept. 10, 1964). **CHAMBER:** 2 piano quintets: No. 1 (1895) and No. 2, op.29 (1940); 3 numbered sonatas for Violin and Piano: No. 1, op.2 (1897), No. 2, op.6 (1899), and No. 3, "dans le caractère populaire roumain" (1926); 2 cello sonatas: No. 1, op.26 (1898) and No. 2, op.26 (1935); 2 piano trios (1897, 1916); *Aubade* for String Trio (1899); Octet for 4 Violins, 2 Violas, and 2 Cellos, op.7 (1900); *Dixtuor* for Wind Instruments, op.14 (1906); *Au soir*, nocturne for 4 Trumpets (1906); *Konzertstück* for Viola and Piano (1906); 2 piano quartets: No. 1, op.16 (1909) and No. 2, op.30 (1943–44); 2 string quartets: No. 1, op.22 (1916–20) and No. 2, op.22 (1950–53); other chamber works. **Piano:** *Introduzione* (1894); *Ballade* (1894); *Praeludium* (1896); *Scherzo* (1896); 3 suites: No. 1, op.3, "dans le style ancien" (1897), No. 2, op.10 (1901–03), and No. 3, op.18, *Pièces impromptues* (1913–16); *Variations on an Original Theme* for 2 Pianos, op.5 (1898); *Impromptu* (1900); *Pièce sur le nom de Fauré* (1922); 2 sonatas: No. 1, op.24 (1924) and No. 2, op.24 (1933–35; incorrectly publ. as "No. 3"). **VOCAL:** *La Vision de Saul*, cantata (1895); *Ahasverus*, cantata (1895); *L'Aurore*, cantata (1897–98); *Waldgesang* for Chorus (1898); Cantata for Soprano and Orch. (1899); about 25 songs, many to words by the Queen of Romania, who wrote poetry in German under the pen name Carmen Sylva.

BIBL. (all publ. in Bucharest unless otherwise given): M. Costin, *G. E.* (1938); V. Cheorghiu, *Un muzician genial: G. E.* (1944); F. Brulez, *G. E.* (1947); B. Gavoty, *Yehudi Menuhin–G. E.* (Geneva, 1955); A. Tudor, *E.* (1956); L. Voiculescu, *G. E. i opera şa Oedip* (1956); A. Tudor, *G. E.: Viaţă in imagini* (1959; Fr. tr., 1961); *G. E. on the 80th Anniversary of His Birth* (1961); G. Bălan, *G. E.: Mesajul--estetica* (1962); idem, *E.* (1963; Ger. tr., 1964); F. Foni, N. Missir, M. Voicana, and E. Zottoviceanu, *G. E.* (1964); B. Kotlyarov, *G. E.* (Moscow, 1965); E. Ciomac, *E.* (1968); M. Voicana et al., eds., *G. E.: Monografie* (2 vols., 1971); R. Draghici, *G. E.* (Bacau, 1973); M. Voicana, ed., *Enesciana*, I (1976; in Fr., Ger., and Eng.); A Cosmovici, *G. E. în lumea muzicii şi în familie* (1990); N. Malcolm, *G. E.: His Life and Music* (London, 1990); V. Cosma, *G.E.: Cronica unei vieţi zbuciumstei* (1991); M. Brediceanu et al., *Celebrating G. E.: A Symposium* (Washington, D.C., 1997). —NS/LK/DM

Engel, Carl, German-English music scholar; b. Thiedewiese, near Hannover, July 6, 1818; d. (suicide) London, Nov. 17, 1882. He studied organ with Enckhausen at Hannover and piano with Hummel at Weimar. After residing in Hamburg, Warsaw, and Berlin, he went to Manchester, England, in 1844, and in 1850 to London. There he became an influential writer, and an authority on musical history and musical instruments.

WRITINGS: *Reflections on Church Music* (1856); *The Music of the Most Ancient Nations, Particularly of the Assyrians, Egyptians, and Hebrews* (1864); *An Introduction to the Study of National Music* (1866); *Musical Instruments of All Countries* (1869); *Musical Myths and Facts* (1876); *The Literature of National Music* (1879); *Researches into the Early History of the Violin Family* (1883). —NS/LK/DM

Engel, Carl, distinguished American musicologist of German descent; b. Paris, July 21, 1883; d. N.Y., May 6, 1944. He was educated at the univs. of Strasbourg and Munich, and also was a composition pupil of Thuille in Munich. In 1905 he emigrated to the U.S. and in 1917 became a naturalized American citizen. He was music ed. for the Boston Music Co. (1909–22), head of the music division of the Library of Congress in Washington, D.C. (1922–34), and president of G. Schirmer, Inc., in N.Y. (1929–32; 1934–44). From 1922 he contributed to the *Musical Quarterly,* serving as its eminent ed. from 1929 to 1942. In 1937–38 he was president of the American Musicological Soc. A writer of brilliance and wide learning, he publ. the essay collections *Alla Breve, from Bach to Debussy* (N.Y., 1921) and *Discords Mingled* (N.Y., 1931). He also was a composer, producing chamber music, piano pieces, and songs.

BIBL.: G. Reese, ed., *A Birthday Offering to C. E.* (N.Y., 1943). —NS/LK/DM

Engel, Hans, eminent German musicologist; b. Cairo, Egypt, Dec. 20, 1894; d. Marburg, May 15, 1970. He studied at the Akademie der Tonkunst in Munich with Klose and at the Univ. of Munich with Sandberger (Ph.D., 1925, with the diss. *Die Entwicklung des deutschen Klavierkonzertes von Mozart bis Liszt;* publ. in Leipzig, 1927); completed his Habilitation at the Univ. of Greifswald in 1926; then taught there (1926–35). He was on the faculty of the Univ. of Königsberg (1935–46) and the Univ. of Marburg (1946–63).

WRITINGS: *Carl Loewe* (Greifswald, 1934); *Franz Liszt* (Potsdam, 1936); *Deutschland und Italien in ihren musikgeschichtlichen Beziehungen* (Regensburg, 1944); *Johann Sebastian Bach* (Berlin, 1950); *Musik der Völker und Zeiten* (Hannover, 1952; rev. ed., 1968); *Luca Marenzio* (Florence, 1956); *Musik in Thuringen* (Cologne and Graz, 1966).—NS/LK/DM

Engel, Joel, Russian writer on music and composer; b. Berdiansk, April 16, 1868; d. Tel Aviv, Feb. 2, 1927. He studied law at the Univ. of Kharkov, and then was a pupil at the Moscow Cons. of Taneyev and Ippolitov-Ivanov (1893–97). He subsequently was active as a music critic and writer on music, and also was a publisher, bringing out a collection of Jewish folk songs (3 vols., Moscow, 1900 and 1909, and Berlin, 1923). In 1924 he settled in Tel Aviv. Among his works were the opera *Esther* (1894) and incidental music.—NS/LK/DM

Engel, Karl (Rudolf), esteemed Swiss pianist and pedagogue; b. Basel, June 1, 1923. He was a student of Baumgartner at the Basel Cons. (1942–45) and of Cortot at the École Normale de Musique in Paris (1947–48). After winning second prize in the Queen Elisabeth of Belgium Competition in Brussels in 1952, he toured internationally as a soloist with orchs., a recitalist, and a chamber music performer. He became especially known for his complete cycles of the Mozart piano sonatas and concertos, and the Beethoven piano sonatas. He also distinguished himself as an accompanist, often appearing in lieder recitals with Dietrich Fischer-Dieskau, Hermann Prey, and Peter Schreier. From 1959 to 1986 he was prof. of piano at the Hannover Hochschule für Musik.—NS/LK/DM

Engel, Lehman, American conductor, composer, and writer on music; b. Jackson, Miss., Sept. 14, 1910; d. N.Y., Aug. 29, 1982. He attended the Univ. of Cincinnati and studied composition at the Cincinnati Cons. of Music (1927–29) before completing his training in N.Y. with Goldmark at the Juilliard Graduate School (1930–34) and with Sessions (1931–37). After conducting his own Lehman Engel Singers and the Madrigal Singers (1935–39), he concentrated on conducting and composing for the serious and popular N.Y. theater.

WORKS: DRAMATIC: Opera: *The Pierrot of the Minuet* (1927; Cincinnati, April 3, 1928); *Malady of Love* (N.Y., May 27, 1954); *The Soldier* (1955; concert perf., N.Y., Nov. 25, 1956). **Musical Comedies:** *Golden Ladder* (Cleveland, May 28, 1953); *Serena* (1956). **Ballet:** *Ceremonials* (1932; N.Y., May 13, 1933); *Phobias* (N.Y., Nov. 18, 1932); *Ekstasis* (1933); *Transitions* (N.Y., Feb. 19, 1934); *Imperial Gesture* (1935); *Marching Song* (1935); *Traditions* (1938); *The Shoe Bird* (1967; Jackson, Miss., April 20, 1968). Also incidental music to over 50 plays and some film scores. **ORCH.:** 2 syms. (1939, 1945); *Overture for the End of the World* (1945); Viola Concerto (1945); *Jackson,* overture (Jackson, Miss., Feb. 13, 1961). **CHAMBER:** String Quartet (1933); Cello Sonata (1945); Violin Sonata (1953). **VOCAL:** *The Chinese Nightingale,* cantata (1928); *The Creation* for Narrator and Orch. (1945); choruses.

WRITINGS (all publ. in N.Y.): *This Bright Day* (autobiography; 1956; 2nd ed., rev., 1974); *Planning and Producing the Musical Show* (1957; 2nd ed., rev., 1966); *The American Musical Theatre: A Consideration* (1967; 2nd ed., rev., 1975); *The Musical Book* (1971); *Words with Music* (1972); *Getting Started in the Theater* (1973); *Their Words are Music: The Great Lyricists and Their Lyrics* (1975); *The Critics* (1976); *The Making of a Musical* (1977); *Getting the Show On: The Complete Guidebook for Producing a Musical in Your Theatre* (1983).—NS/LK/DM

Engelmann, Georg, German organist and composer; b. Mansfeld, near Eisleben, c. 1575; d. Leipzig (buried), Nov. 11, 1632. He went to Leipzig, where he matriculated at the Univ. in 1593. About 1596 he was made organist at St. Pauli, the Univ. church, and later was its music director. From 1625 he also served as organist at the Thomaskirche. He excelled as a composer of dances, mainly pavans and galliards, which he publ. in three vols. (Leipzig, 1616, 1617, 1622). His motets are also of interest. His son, also named Georg Engelmann (b. Leipzig, c. 1602; d. there, Sept. 1, 1663), was an organist and composer. After matriculating at the Univ. of Leipzig (1618), he succeeded his father as organist at the Thomaskirche in 1632. In 1659 he was removed from his post for excessive drinking, and spent his last days in poverty.—LK/DM

Engelmann, Hans Ulrich, German composer and pedagogue; b. Darmstadt, Sept. 8, 1921. He received training in architecture (1945–47), studied composition with Hermann Heiss, and attended the first summer course in new music at Kranichstein/Darmstadt in 1946. In 1947 he entered the Univ. of Frankfurt am Main, where he pursued studies in German literature and art history, in philosophy with Adorno, and in musicology with Gennrich and Osthoff (Ph.D., 1951, with the diss. *Béla Bartóks Mikrokosmos: Versuch einer Typologie "Neuer Musik"*; publ. in Würzburg, 1953). He also studied with Leibowitz (1948) and Krenek (1951) in Darmstadt. From 1954 to 1961 he was active at the Hessisches Landestheater in Darmstadt. In 1960, 1967, and 1983 he held fellowships at the Villa Massimo in Rome. He taught in Darmstadt from 1960 to 1968, and was a dramaturgical associate at the Mannheim National Theater from 1961 to 1969. In 1969 he became a lecturer at the Frankfurt am Main Hochschule für Musik, where he was prof. of composition from 1973 until 1986. In 1972-73 he was artistic advisor of the Bonn City Theater. He was a visiting prof. at the Univ. of Ghent (1977), the Univ. of Frankfurt am Main (1978–79), the Hochschule für Gestaltung in Offenbach (1979–84), and at the Univ. of Tel Aviv and the Rubin Academy of Music in Jerusalem (1983), and also gave courses in composition in Moscow and Vilnius (1985) and at Columbia Univ. (1995). Engelmann was awarded the Goethe Gold Medal of the state of Hesse in 1986, the Bundesverdienstkreuz of the Federal Republic of Germany in 1991, and the Verdienstorden of the state of Hesse in 1997. In his large oeuvre, he has explored the potentialities of various compositional methods, ranging from aleatory to collage with 12-tone procedures serving as the foundation of his craft.

WORKS: DRAMATIC: *Ballett Coloré* (1948); *Doctor Faust's Höllenfahrt*, burlesque chamber opera (1949–50; Hamburg, Jan. 11, 1951; rev. 1962); *Magog*, music drama (1955–56); *Noche de Luna*, pantomime (1958); *Operetta*, music theater (1959); *Verlorener Schatten*, lyric opera (1960); *Serpentina*, ballet (1962–63); *Der Fall van Damm*, opera (1966–67; Cologne, June 7, 1968); *Ophelia*, multimedia theater piece (Hannover, Feb. 1, 1969); *Revue*, music theater piece (1972–73; Bonn, Oct. 24, 1973); incidental music to over 20 plays; 6 film scores. **ORCH.:** *Kaleidoskop*, suite for Chamber Orch. (1941); Concerto for Cello and Strings (1948); *Musik* for Strings, Brass, and Percussion (1948); *Prelude* for Jazz Band (1949); *Leopoldskron*, divertimento for Chamber Orch. (1949); *Impromptu* (1949); 2 syms.: No. 1, *Orchester- Fantasie* (1951; rev. 1963) and No. 2, *Sinfonies* (1968); *Partita* for Strings, Percussion, and 3 Trumpets (1953); *Strukturen* for Chamber Orch. (1954); *Vier Orchesterstücke* (1956); *Polifonica* for Chamber Orch. (1957); *Nocturnos* for Chamber Orch. and Soprano (1958); *Ezra Pound Music* (1959); *Trias* for Piano, Orch., and Tape (1962); *Shadows* (1964); *Sonate* for Jazz Orch. (1967–95); *Capricciosi* (1967); *Modelle I oder "I love you Bäbi"* (1969) and *II* (1970); *Sinfonia da camera* (1981). **CHAMBER:** *Klangstück* for Violin and Piano (1947); Cello Sonata (1948); String Quartet (1952); *Komposition in vier Teilen* for Soprano,

Flute, Piano, Timpani, and Percussion (1953); *Integrale* for Saxophone and Piano (1954); *Permutazioni* for Flute, Oboe, Clarinet, and Bassoon (1959); *Variante* for Flute (1959); *Timbres* for Harp, Celesta, Piano, Percussion, and Tape (1963); *Divertimento* for Flute, Oboe, Clarinet, and Bassoon (1966); *Mobile II* for Clarinet and Piano (1968); *mini-music to siegfried palm* for Cello (1970); *Mobili* for Oboe (1971); *Epitaph für einem imaginaren Freund* for Trumpet and Piano (1983); *Assonanzen* for 2 Cellos (1983); *Inter-Lineas* for Alto Saxophone and Percussion (1985; also for Alto Saxophone, Clarinet, and Percussion); *Dialoge* for Piano and Percussion (1985–90); *Clarinota* for Clarinet (1991); *Modus* for Bassoon (1993); *Ciacona* for Flute, Clarinet, Violin, Viola, Cello, Vibraphone, and Piano (1993); *Black Invocations* for Jazz Sextet (1994); *per Luigi* for Flute, Clarinet, Cello, Vibraphone, Percussion, and Tape (1996). **KEYBOARD: P i a n o :** *Jazz-Sonatine* (1945); 2 sonatinas (1945); *Toccata* (1948); 2 suites (1948, 1952); 2 pieces (1950); *Cadenza* for Piano and Tape ad libitum (1961); *Duplum* for 2 Pianos (1965); *Mobile I, "Fragmente"* for Piano and Synthesizer ad libitum (1967–71); *Klangstück* (1972); *Divertimento* for 2 Pianos (1980); *Tastenstück* (1991–93). **O r g a n :** *Essay* (1992). **H a r p s i c h o r d :** *99 Takte* (1951–52). **VOCAL:** *Elegia e Canto* for Soprano, Piano, and String Orch. (1952); *Cansolationes* for Chorus and String Orch. ad libitum (1952); *Die Mauer*, cantata for Soloists, Chorus, and Orch. (1954; rev. 1983); *Atlantische Ballade* for Alto, Baritone, String Orch., and Percussion (1955); *Die Freiheit*, cantata for Chorus and Orch. (1957); *Metall*, cantata for Soloists, Chorus, and Orch. (1958); *Incanto* for Soprano, Soprano Saxophone, and 5 Percussionists (1959); *Eidophonie* for Chorus and 3 to 4 Percussionists (1962); *Manifest vom Menschen*, oratorio for Soloists, Chorus, and Orch. (1966); *Commedia humana*, revue for Double Chorus, Speaker, Electronically Modulated Cello, and Tape (1972); *Missa Popularis* for Soloists, Chorus, Brass, and Percussion (1980; rev. 1983); *Les Chansons* for Singer/Speaker, Flute, Clarinet, Viola, Cello, and Piano (1982); *Stele für Büchner*, canto sinfonico for Soloists, Chorus, and Orch. (1986–87).

BIBL.: *Commedia humana: H. U. E. und sein Werk* (Wiesbaden, 1985).—NS/LK/DM

Engerer, Brigitte, French pianist; b. Tunis, Oct. 27, 1952. She was taken to Paris at an early age, where at 6 she became a pupil of Lucette Descaves and made her public debut. After further training at the Paris Cons., she completed her studies with Stanislav Neuhaus at the Moscow Cons. (graduated, 1975). She won prizes at the Long-Thibaud Competition in Paris (sixth, 1969), the Tchaikovsky Competition in Moscow (6th, 1974), and the Queen Elisabeth of Belgium Competition in Brussels (third, 1978). Engerer appeared as a soloist with the world's leading orchs. and gave recitals in the major music centers.—NS/LK/DM

Engländer, Ludwig, Austrian-American composer, arranger, and conductor; b. Vienna, c. 1851; d. Far Rockaway, N.Y., Sept. 13, 1914. After training in Vienna, he went to Paris and in 1882 to N.Y., where he became a conductor at the Thalia Theater. His operetta *Der Prinz Gemahl* was successfully premiered there (April 11, 1883). It was first given in Eng. as *The Prince Consort* at Wallack's Theater (June 4, 1883). Success continued with his *1776* or *Adjutant James* (Feb. 26, 1884), which was first performed in a rev. Eng. version as *A Daughter of the Revolution* (May 27, 1895). After bringing out *Madelaine*

or *Die Rose der Champagne* (Hamburg, June 26, 1888), he became conductor at N.Y.'s Casino Theater. His greatest success came with the revue *The Passing Show* (N.Y., May 12, 1894). He then gave up conducting to devote himself fully to composing Broadway musicals and revues. Among his most successful subsequent scores were *The Little Corporal* (Sept. 19, 1898), *The Man in the Moon* (April 24, 1899; in collaboration with G. Kerker and R. De Koven), *The Rounders* (July 12, 1899), *The Casino Girl* (March 19, 1900), *The Strollers* (June 24, 1901), and *Miss Innocence* (Nov. 30, 1908). His *Vielliebchen* was premiered in Vienna (May 5, 1911), and then given in various European venues.—**LK/DM**

English, Granville, American composer; b. Louisville, Jan. 27, 1895; d. N.Y., Sept. 1, 1968. He studied with Borowski, Reuter, and Gunn at the Chicago Musical Coll. (B.M., 1915), and with Boulanger, Haubiel, Riegger, and Serly. He taught in Chicago and N.Y., and in 1961 was composer-in-residence at Baylor Univ.

WORKS: DRAMATIC: F o l k O p e r a : *Wide, Wide River.* **B a l l e t :** *Sea Drift.* **ORCH.:** *The Ugly Duckling* (1924); *Ballet Fantasy* (1937); *Among the Hills* (Oklahoma City, March 9, 1952); *Mood Tropicale* (Baltimore, Feb. 5, 1955); *Evenings by the Sea* (Port Washington, N.Y., Jan. 20, 1956). **OTHER:** Chamber music, choral works, and songs.—**NS/LK/DM**

Englund, (Sven) Einar, outstanding Finnish composer; b. Ljugarn, Gotland, Sweden, June 17, 1916; d. Helsinki, June 27, 1999. He began to play the piano in his youth. When he was 17, he entered the Sibelius Academy in Helsinki, where he studied piano with Martti Paavola and Ernst Linko, composition with Bengt Carlson and Selim Palmgren, and orchestration with Leo Funtek. Following his graduation in 1941, he was drafted into the Finnish army and saw service during World War II. His harrowing military experience, which almost cost him his life and resulted in permanent damage to his left hand, found release in his Sym. No. 1 (1946). This remarkable neo-Classical score, which soon became known as *The War Symphony*, was hailed at its premiere in Helsinki on Jan. 17, 1947. It was soon followed by his Sym. No. 2, *The Blackbird Symphony*, which was first performed in Helsinki on Oct. 8, 1948, and which became one of Englund's most celebrated works. With a recommendation from Sibelius and a stipend, he attended the Berkshire Music Center in Tanglewood in the summer of 1949, where he worked with Copland. Returning to Finland, he pursued an active career as a composer until the rising tide of total serialism led him to cease composing in the late 1950s. From 1956 to 1976 Englund was music critic of Helsinki's Swedish-language newspaper *Hufvudstadsbladet*. He also was a lecturer in composition and theory at the Sibelius Academy from 1957 to 1981, being named an honorary prof. in 1976. With his Sym. No. 3, *Barbarossa* (1969–71), Englund resumed composition in earnest. While continuing along the path of neo-Classicism, his works revealed a mastery of concentrated power, invention, and lyricism which placed him among the foremost composers of Finland. In 1978 he was elected to membership in the Royal Swedish Academy of Music in Stockholm.

WORKS (all first perf. in Helsinki unless otherwise given): **DRAMATIC:** *The Great Wall of China*, incidental music to Max Frisch's play (1949; concert suite, Oct. 21, 1949); *Valkoinen peura* (The White Reindeer), film score (1952; concert suite, 1954; March 14, 1955); *Sinuhe*, ballet (1953; orch. version, Sept. 9, 1965); *Odysseus*, ballet (Worcester, Mass., Sept. 30, 1959; concert suite, Nov. 18, 1959; orch. version, March 2, 1960). **ORCH.:** 7 syms.: No. 1, *Sotasinfonia* (The War Symphony; 1946; Jan. 17, 1947), No. 2, *Mustarastassinfonia* (The Blackbird Symphony; 1947; Oct. 8, 1948), No. 3, *Barbarossa* (1969–71; May 12, 1972), No. 4, *Nostalginen* (The Nostalgic), chamber sym. for Strings and Percussion (Oct. 26, 1976), No. 5, *Fennica* (Dec. 6, 1977), No. 6, *Aforismeja* (Aphorisms) for Chorus and Orch. (1984; March 12, 1986), and No. 7 (1988; Tampere, Jan. 10, 1991); *Epinikia*, symphonic poem (July 2, 1947); *Valsuralia*, concert waltz for Chekov's play *The Cherry Orchard* (Feb. 7, 1951); *Neljä tanssi-impressiota* (Four dance-impressions), suite from the ballet *Sinuhe* (Feb. 16, 1954); Cello Concerto (1954; May 17, 1955); 2 piano concertos: No. 1 (1955; March 2, 1956, composer soloist) and No. 2 (1974; Feb. 4, 1975, composer soloist); Concerto for 12 Cellos (1980-81; April 3, 1981); Violin Concerto (1981; Tampere, March 26, 1982); *Serenade* for Strings (1983; Kaustinen, Feb. 15, 1984); Flute Concerto (1985; Sept. 16, 1986); *Lahti-fanfaari* (Lahti, Aug. 28, 1986); *Juhlasoitto "1917"* (1986; Turku, Nov. 12, 1987); *Odéion*, festival overture (1987; Mikkeli, Nov. 18, 1988); *Opening Brass* (Stockholm, Oct. 7, 1988); *Vivat academia*, fanfare (1989; March 26, 1990); *Ciacona: Hommage à Sibelius* (Sept. 13, 1990); Clarinet Concerto (1990–91; Sept. 5, 1991). **CHAMBER:** Piano Quintet (May 1941); *Introduzione e capriccio* for Violin and Piano (1970; Sept. 17, 1973); *Panorama* for Trombone (1976); *Divertimento Upsaliensis* for Wind Quintet, String Quintet, and Piano (1978; Uppsala, Dec. 9, 1979); Violin Sonata (1979; May 5, 1980); *Arioso Interrotto* for Violin (1979; Nov. 1980); *Serenata elegiaco* for Violin (1979); *De profundis* for 14 Brass Instruments (Lieksa, July 12, 1980); Cello Sonata (Sept. 4, 1982); Trio for Piano, Violin, and Cello (1982; Kuhmo, July 17, 1983); *Pavane* for Violin and Piano (1983); String Quartet (1985; Jyväskylä, June 27, 1986); Suite for Cello, *Viimeinen saari* (The Last Island; 1986; Finnish TV 2, Tampere, May 26, 1987); *Intermezzo* for Oboe (1987, Uusikaupunki, July 27, 1988); Wind Quintet (1989; Sept. 8, 1990). **KEYBOARD: P i a n o :** *Humoresque* (1935); *Introduzione e Toccata* (Nov. 29, 1950); 2 sonatinas: No. 1 (1960; Finnish TV 1, Dec. 18, 1967, composer pianist) and No. 2, *Pariisilainen* (The Parisian; 1984; Oct. 11, 1987); *Notturno* (1967); Sonata No. 1 (Reykjavík, Oct. 21, 1978, composer pianist); *Pavane e Toccata* (Nov. 11, 1983); *Preludium & Fughetta* (1986; June 17, 1996). **O r g a n :** *Passacaglia* (1971; Feb. 9, 1973); *Marcia Funerale* (July 1, 1976, composer organist). **VOCAL:** *Chaconne* for Chorus (1969; also for Chorus, Trombone, and Double Bass); *Hymnus Sepulcralis* for Chorus, after Prudentius (London, Sept. 27, 1975); *Med herrarna i hagen* (Down the meadow with gentlemen) for Women's Chorus (March 20, 1977); *Rukkaset* (Refused Proposal) for Women's Chorus (March 20, 1977); *Valvokaa* (Watch) for Chorus, after the Bible (Nov. 16, 1980); *Merkkituli* (The Traffic Light) for Men's Chorus (1983; Espoo, April 14, 1984); *Kanteletar-sarja* (Kanteletar Suite) for Women's Chorus (1984; Joensuu, June 18, 1985).—**NS/LK/DM**

Enna, August (Emil), eminent Danish composer; b. Nakskov, May 13, 1859; d. Copenhagen, Aug. 3, 1939. He was partly of German and Italian blood; his grandfather, an Italian soldier in Napoleon's army, married a German girl, and settled in Denmark. Enna was taken to Copenhagen as a child, and learned to play piano and violin. He had sporadic instruction in theory, and later became a member of a traveling orch. and played with it in Finland (1880). Upon his return to Copenhagen, he taught piano and played for dancers. In 1883 he became music director of Werner's Theatrical Soc. and wrote his first stage work, *A Village Tale*, which he produced the same year. After these practical experiences, he began to study seriously. He took lessons with Schjorring (violin), Matthesson (organ), and Rasmussen (composition) and soon publ. a number of piano pieces, which attracted the attention of Niels Gade, who used his influence to obtain a traveling fellowship for Enna. This made it possible for Enna to study in Germany (1888–89) and acquire a complete mastery of instrumental and vocal writing. He followed the German Romantic school, being influenced mainly by Weber's type of opera, and by Grieg and Gade in the use of local color. The first product of this period was his most successful work, the opera *Heksen* (The Witch), produced in Copenhagen (Jan. 24, 1892), then in Germany.

WORKS: DRAMATIC: O p e r a : *Agleia* (1884); *Heksen* (Copenhagen, Jan. 24, 1892); *Cleopatra* (Copenhagen, Feb. 7, 1894); *Aucassin and Nicolette* (Copenhagen, Feb. 2, 1896); *The Match Girl*, after Andersen (Copenhagen, Nov. 13, 1897); *Lamia* (Antwerp, Oct. 3, 1899); *Ung Elskov* (1st produced in Weimar, under the title *Heisse Liebe*, Dec. 6, 1904); *Princess on the Pea*, after Andersen (Arhus, Sept. 15, 1900); *The Nightingale*, after Andersen (Copenhagen, Nov. 10, 1912); *Gloria Arsena* (Copenhagen, April 15, 1917); *Comedians*, after Victor Hugo's *L'Homme qui rit* (Copenhagen, April 8, 1920); *Don Juan Manara* (Copenhagen, April 17, 1925). **B a l l e t :** *The Shepherdess and the Chimney Sweep* (Copenhagen, Oct. 6, 1901); *St. Cecilia's Golden Shoe* (Copenhagen, Dec. 26, 1904); *The Kiss* (Copenhagen, Oct. 19, 1927). **OTHER:** Violin Concerto (1897); 2 syms. (1886, 1908); an overture, *Hans Christian Andersen* (1905); choral pieces. **—NS/LK/DM**

Eno, Brian (Peter George St. John le Baptiste de la Salle),

English composer, musician, and producer; b. Woodbridge, Suffolk, May 15, 1948. Although interested in tape recorders and recorded music at an early age, he received no formal music training, studying art at Ipswich and Winchester art schools (1964–69). He then became involved in avant-garde experiments, performing works by LaMonte Young and Cornelius Cardew. He helped found the art- rock band Roxy Music in 1971, leaving it 2 years later for a solo career that resulted in 4 modestly successful progressive-rock albums during the mid-1970s. In 1975, while confined to bed after being struck by a London taxi, he was also struck by the pleasures of minimalism, shifting his style to what he has termed "ambient," a sort of high-art Muzak. He has collaborated with David Bowie, Talking Heads, U2, and Harold Budd. In 1979 he became interested in video, subsequently producing "video paintings" and "video sculptures" used as ambient music in galleries, museums, airport terminals, and private homes. In the late 1990s he began experimenting with combinatorial composition which resulted in a series of works which change characteristics in playback. His music has significantly influenced both New Wave and New Age genres. With R. Mills, he publ. *More Dark than Shark* (London, 1986). Among his works

are *Another Green World* (1975), *Discreet Music* (1975), *Before and after Science* (1977), *Music for Airports* (1978), *The Plateaux of Mirror* (with H. Budd; 1980), and *On Land* (1984).

BIBL.: E. Tamm, *B. E.: His Music and the Vertical Color of Sound* (Boston, 1989).—**NS/LK/DM**

Enríquez, Manuel,

significant Mexican composer, violinist, and teacher; b. Ocotlan, June 17, 1926; d. Mexico City, April 26, 1994. He was 6 when he began violin lessons with his father, and 5 years later he started composing. He studied violin with Ignacio Camarena at the Guadalajara Cons. (1935–45) and composition with Bernal Jiménez in Morelia (1952–55). From 1949 to 1955 he was concertmaster of the Guadalajara Sym. Orch. He then continued his training with Mennin (composition) and Galamian (violin) at the Juilliard School of Music in N.Y. (1955–57), and also had private theory lessons with Wolpe (1957). Later he pursued research at the Columbia-Princeton Electronic Music Center (1971). Enríquez was asst. concertmaster of the National Sym. Orch. of Mexico (1958–65) and concertmaster of the National Sym. Chamber Orch. (from 1965). He also taught violin and composition at the National Cons. in Mexico City (1964–75), where he served as director (1972–74). From 1977 to 1988 he was director of CENIDIM (the National Searching and Information Music Center). After serving as music director of the National Inst. of Fine Arts (1988–92), he taught at the Univ. of Calif. at Los Angeles (1992–94). Enríquez was a leading composer of the post-Chávez generation in Mexico. His early works show the influences of Hindemith, Bartók, and jazz. After his U.S. studies, his music progressed into the vanguard of severe constructivism, employing dodecaphony, serialism, sonorism, indeterminacy, and graphic notation.

WORKS: DRAMATIC: *Mixteria* for Actress, 4 Musicians, and Tape (1970); *Trauma* for Actress/Dancer, Musicians, Dancers, and Tape (1974); *La Casa del Sol* for Musicians, Dancers, Actors, and Tape (1976). **ORCH.:** *Música Incidental* (1952); 2 violin concertos (1955, 1966); Suite for Strings (1957); 2 syms. (1957, 1962); *Preámbulo* (1961); *Obertura Lírica* (1963); *Transición* (1965); *Poema* for Cello and Strings (1966); *Trayectorias* (1967); *Si Lebet* (1968); *Ixamatl* (Donaueschingen, Oct. 19, 1969); Piano Concerto (1970; Mexico City, March 19, 1971); *El y...ellos* for Violin and Orch. Ensemble (1971); *Encuentros* for Strings and 4 Percussionists (1972); *Ritual* (1973); *Corriente Alterna* (1977); *Raíces* (1977); *Fases* (1978); *Concierto Barroco* for 2 Violins, Strings, and Harpsichord (1978); *Interminado sueño* (1981); *Manantial de soles* (1984); Cello Concerto (1990); Concerto for 2 Guitars and Orch. (1992). **CHAMBER:** Suite for Violin and Piano (1949); 5 string quartets (1959; 1967; 1974; 1984; *Xopan cuicatl*, 1988); *Divertimento* for Flute, Clarinet, and Bassoon (1962); 4 Pieces for Viola and Piano (1962); *Pentamúsica* for Wind Quintet (1963); *3 Formas Concertantes* for Violin, Cello, Clarinet, Bassoon, Horn, Piano, and Percussion (1964); Violin Sonata (1964); *Ambivalencia* for Violin and Cello (1967); *Concierto para 8* for 7 Musicians and Conductor (1968); *Diptico I* for Flute and Piano (1969) and *II* for Violin and Piano (1971); *Móvil II* for Violin With or Without Tape (1969); *3 x Bach* for Violin and Tape (1970); *Monólogo* for Trombone (1971); *á...2* for Violin and Piano (1972); Piano Trio (1974); *Tlachtli* for Violin, Cello, Flute, Clarinet, Horn, Trombone, and Piano (1976); *Conuro* for Double Bass and Tape (1976); *Tzicuri* for Cello, Clarinet, Trombone, and Piano (1976); *Oboemia* for Oboe (1982); *Poliptico* for 6 Percussionists (1983); *Interecos* for Percussion and Electronic Sound (1984); *Vivencias líricas* for Wind Ensemble (1986); *Quasi libero* for Flute and String Quartet (1989); *Tercia* for Clarinet, Bassoon, and Piano (1990); *Fantasía concertante* for Cello and Piano (1991); *Diálogo* for Cello (1992). **KEYBOARD: P i a n o :** *A Lapiz* (1965); *Módulos* for 2 Pianos (1965); *Móvil I* (1968–69); *Para Alicia* (1970); *1 x 4* for Piano, 4-Hands (1975); *Hoy de ayer* (1981). **O r g a n :** *Imaginario* (1973). **VOCAL:** *Ego*, cantata for Woman's Voice, Flute, Cello, Piano, and Percussion (1966); *Contravox* for Chorus, 2 Percussionists, and Tape (1977); *Manantial de soles* for Soprano, Actor, and Chamber Orch. (1984); *Cantata a Juárez* for Baritone, Chorus, and Orch. (1984); *Rapsodia latinoamericana* for Orch. and Optional Chorus (1987); *Piedras del viento* for Narrator, Chorus, and Orch. (1991); *Visión de los vencidos* for Mezzo-soprano, Chorus, and Orch. (1993). **ELECTRONIC:** *La Reunión de los Saurios* (1971); *Láser I* (1972); *Música para Federico Silva* (1974); *Cantos de los Volcanos* (1977); *Interecos* (1984).—**NS/LK/DM**

Enriquez de Valderrabano, Enrique, 16th-century Spanish lutenist. He was a native of Peñaranda de Duero. He wrote the tablature book *Libro de música de vihuela, intitulado Silva de Sirenas* (Valladolid, 1547), containing transcriptions for vihuela (large 6- stringed guitar) of sacred and secular vocal works (some arranged for 2 vihuelas), and also some original pieces.—**NS/LK/DM**

Enthoven, (Henri) Emile, Dutch composer; b. Amsterdam, Oct. 18, 1903; d. N.Y., Dec. 26, 1950. He studied composition with Wagenaar at the Royal Cons. of Music in The Hague and with Schreker in Berlin. At the age of 14, he wrote an adolescent but well-crafted sym., which Mengelberg performed with the Concertgebouw Orch. in Amsterdam (1918). But this precocious success was not a manifestation of enduring talent; his later works lacked originality. Soon he abandoned composition altogether and took up jurisprudence; in 1939 he emigrated to N.Y. Among his works are 3 syms. (1917, 1924, 1931) and a Violin Concerto (1920).—**NS/LK/DM**

Entremont, Philippe, eminent French pianist and conductor; b. Rheims, June 6, 1934. He began his training with his parents, both of whom were musicians. After piano lessons with Rose Aye and Marguerite Long (1944–46), he entered the Paris Cons. as a pupil of Jean Doyen, winning the premier prix for solfège at 12, for chamber music at 14, and for piano at 15. At 17, he made his formal debut as a pianist in Barcelona. In 1951 he won 5th prize and in 1953 the joint second prize in the Long-Thibaud Competition in Paris, and in 1952 he also was a finalist in the Queen Elisabeth of Belgium Competition in Brussels. In 1953 he won accolades for his first engagements in the U.S. and thereafter toured with notable success as a virtuoso around the world. From 1967 he also pursued a career as a conductor. From 1976 to 1991 he was chief conductor of the Vienna Chamber Orch., and thereafter its lifetime honorary conductor. He also served as music adviser and princi-

pal conductor (1980–81) and as music director (1981–86) of the New Orleans Phil. He then was principal conductor (1986-87), music director-designate (1987–88), and music director (1988–89) of the Denver Sym. Orch. From 1988 to 1990 he was music director of the Colonne Orch. in Paris. He also was principal guest conductor of the Netherlands Chamber Orch. in Amsterdam from 1993. His performances, both as a pianist and conductor, reveal a discriminating Gallic sensibility.—**NS/LK/DM**

En Vogue, female vocalists that updated the girl group for the 1990s, with new jack swing and Motown style (July 18, 1988, San Francisco). **MEMBERSHIP:** Dawn Robinson (b. New London, Conn., Nov. 28, 1968); Cindy Herron (b. San Francisco, Sept. 26, 1965); Maxine Jones (b. Paterson, N.J., Jan. 16, 1966); Terry Ellis (b. Houston, Tex., Sept. 5, 1966).

Assembled via audition by producers Denzil Foster and Thomas McElroy, the guiding lights behind Club Nouveau, Tony! Toni! Toné!, and the Timex Social Club, the four young women selected to form this group had never met before. What each brought to the group was a large measure of pulchritude (Herron was a former Miss Black California), a sense of style, and the vocal goods, which they demonstrated by singing a cappella at any opportunity. All of the women shared the spotlight on stage, no one personality allowed to eclipse the others.

They debuted as Vogue on two tracks of Foster and McElroy's *FM2*. They followed this with their own 1990 album, *Born to Sing*, becoming En Vogue when another group claimed the name Vogue. Their first single, "Hold On," hit #2 on the charts and sold platinum. Their follow-up, "Lies," topped the R&B chart, but only hit #38 pop. The album hit #21 and followed the first single to platinum.

As auspicious as their debut was, their sophomore effort, *Funky Divas*, proved that these women were not a novelty. The album kicked off with another #2 single, "My Lovin' (You're Never Gonna Get It)," which also topped the R&B charts and went gold. The bouncy, gold selling "Giving Him Something He Can Feel" also topped the R&B charts, rising to #6 pop. Both songs were aided by clever videos, emphasizing the women's natural allure. Yet another gold single, "Free Your Mind" got to #8 pop and earned three MTV Video awards. The #15 "Give It Up, Turn It Loose" was something of a turntable hit, rising to #12 in airplay but a disappointing #43 in sales. Similarly, "Love Don't Love You" charted at #36 overall, even with a #28 ranking in airplay. The album sold over three million copies.

Suddenly, En Vogue reached iconic status. They appeared on magazine covers from *Vogue* to *Rolling Stone*. They appeared on the late night talk shows and even made a Diet Coke commercial with director Spike Lee. They put out an EP, *Runaway Love*, with a new title track, four remixes from *Funky Divas*, and the group's duet with rappers Salt 'n' Pepa "Whatta Man." "Whatta Man" went platinum, hitting #3 pop. The EP rose to #49.

The next few years were relatively quiet for the group. Jones and Herron started families. Ellis recorded a solo album, *Southern Girl*. They got back together to cut a track for the 1996 film *Set It Off*. The song, "Don't Let Go (Love)" rose to #2 on the pop charts. As they started work on their third album, Robinson decided to leave the group and pursue a solo career. The trio continued working together, releasing *EV3* in 1997. The single "Whatever" hit #16 pop (#8 R&B) and went gold. The Diane Warren penned "Too Gone Too Long" rose to #33 pop, #25 R&B. The sales and overall impact of this third effort were disappointing, and it was unclear whether the group could regain the momentum it had just a few years earlier.

During the summer of 1999, the group released a greatest hits collection. They claimed it would be their first of many.

DISC.: *Born to Sing* (1990); *Remix to Sing* (1991); *Funky Divas* (1992); *Runaway Love* (1993); *EV3* (1997).—**HB**

Enya (actually, Eithne Ni Bhraonain), Irish

vocalist, one of the biggest stars of "new-age" music; b. Gweedore, Donegal, May 17, 1961. When Enya was seven years old, her siblings Cioaran and Po and her uncles Padraig and Noel O Dugain formed a folk group An Clann As Dobhar. Her sister Maire (aka Marie Brennan) joined several years later and the group became known as Clannad. Enya joined the family business in 1980, playing keyboards and doing some backing vocals. When the group severed relations with producer Nicky Ryan, Enya went to work with Ryan and his wife Roma.

She started getting work on soundtracks, contributing to David Puttnam's 1984 film *The Frog Prince* and the BBC television series *The Celts* in 1986. Although she left Clannad partly due to a disagreement about modernizing their sound, her own music leaned heavily on atmospheric synthesizers.

The Celts caught the attention of Warner Music U.K. Signed to the label, she recorded *Watermark*, which became an international hit, reaching #25 and going quadruple-platinum in the U.S., largely on the success of the single "Orinoco Flow," which topped off at #24 pop, but was very successful on the new wave format radio stations. Her follow-up, 1991's *Shepherd Moons*, was even more successful, hitting #17 on the charts and eventually selling quintuple-platinum without benefit of a hit single, and won her a Best New Age Album Grammy Award. This led to more sales of her U.S. debut as well.

Her 1995 album *Memory of Trees* also took home a Best New Age Grammy. It entered the U.S. charts at #9 and quickly went double platinum. The re- release of *The Celts*, now on her label, also went platinum. Her 1998 best of album went platinum out of the box. Enya remains one of the most popular artists in the new age bins, easily outselling the bulk of the artists with whom she shares shelf space.

DISC.: *Enya (The Celts)* (1987); *Watermark* (1988); *Shepherd Moons* (1991); *Memory of Trees* (1995); *Frogprince* (1995); *On My Way Home* (1996); *Storms in Africa* (1989).—**HB**

Eötvös, Peter, Hungarian conductor, composer,

and pedagogue; b. Székelyudvarhely, Jan. 2, 1944. He received training in composition at the Franz Liszt Academy of Music in Budapest (1958–65) and in conducting at the Cologne Hochschule für Musik (1966–68). From 1966 he worked closely with Stockhausen, and was also associated with the electronic music studio of the WDR in Cologne from 1971 to 1979. He appeared as a guest conductor in contemporary programs with major European orchs. from 1974. From 1979 to 1992 he was music director of the Ensemble InterContemporain in Paris, and also was principal guest conductor of the BBC Sym. Orch. in London from 1985 to 1988. In 1991 he founded the International Eötvös Inst. and Foundation for young conductors and composers. From 1992 to 1995 he held the position of first guest conductor of the Budapest Festival Orch. He was a prof. at the Karlsruhe Hochschule für Musik from 1992 to 1998, and at the Cologne Hochschule für Musik from 1998. In 1994 he also became co-chief conductor of the Netherlands Radio Chamber Orch. in Hilversum. He was named a Chevalier de l'Ordre des Arts et des Lettres of France in 1988 and was awarded the Bartók-Pásztory Prize of Hungary in 1997. In 1997 he also became a member of the Akademie der Künste in Berlin and of the Szechenyi Academy of Art in Budapest. His opera *Three Sisters* (1996–97) was awarded the Prix Claude-Rostand, Grand Prix de la Critique 1997–98 and the Victoires de la Musique Classique et du Jazz 1999 in France. Eötvös's compositions have been performed throughout the world and are regularly featured at European music festivals.

WORKS: DRAMATIC: *Harakiri*, sound-play (1973); *Radames*, chamber opera (1975); *Three Sisters*, opera (1996–97); *As I Crossed a Bridge of Dreams*, sound-theater (1999); film music. **ORCH.:** *Pierre Idyll* (1984-90); *Chinese Opera* (1986); *Triangel* for 1 Creative Percussionist and 27 Musicians (1993); *Psychokosmos* for Cimbalom and Traditional Orch. (1993); *Shadows* for Flute, Amplified Clarinet, and Chamber Orch. or Ensemble (1996); *Replica* for Viola and Orch. (1997-98). **CHAMBER: Ensemble:** *"Now, Miss!"* for Violin and Electric Organ or Synthesizer (1972); *Windsequenzen* for Flute and Ensemble (1975-87); *Intervalles-Intérieurs* for Tape and Ensemble (1981); *Steine* for Ensemble (1985-90); *Brass: The Metal Space* for Brass and Percussion (1990); *Korrespondenz* for String Quartet (1992); *Countdown* for 4 Timpani (1996); *Psy* for Flute, Cello, and Cimbalom or Piano, or Harp, or Marimba (1996). **Solo:** *Kosmos* for Piano (1961); *Il maestro* for Pianist and 2 Steinway Pianos (1974); *Psalm 151: "In memoriam Frank Zappa"* for Solo or 4 Percussion (1993); *Thunder* for Bass Timpanist (1994); *Two Poems to Polly* for Speaking Cellist (1998). **VOCAL:** *Moro Lasso* for Vocal Ensemble (1963–72); *Hochzeitsmadrigal* for Vocal Ensemble (1963–76); *Insetti galanti* for Vocal Ensemble (1970–90); *Endless Eight I* (1981) and *II: Apeiron musikon* (1988–89) for Vocal Ensemble; *Atlantis* for Baritone, Boy Soprano, Cimbalom, and Orch. (1995); *Two Monologues* for Baritone and Orch. (1998). **OTHER:** *Mese (Märchen/Tales)*, Sprachkomposition on tape (1968); *Cricketmusic*, organized nature sounds on tape (1970); *Elektrochronik*, stereophonic tape (1974); *Der Blick*, multimedia piece on video and tape (1997).—**NS/LK/DM**

Ephrikian, Angelo, Italian conductor and music

scholar of Armenian descent; b. Treviso, Oct. 20, 1913; d. Rome, Oct. 30, 1982. He received training in violin and composition, making his conducting debut in Venice in 1945. His diligent study of the vast output of Vivaldi led him to organize the Instituto Italiano Antonio Vivaldi in Venice with Malipiero in 1947. He subsequently conducted the chamber orch. of the Scuola Veneziana, with which he championed Vivaldi's music. With Malipiero et al., he also prepared a complete edition of Vivaldi's works (Rome, 1947–72). From 1959 to 1973 he was artistic director of the recording firm Arcophon. In 1971 he became director of the Bologna Phil. He served as conductor of the Angelicum Chamber Orch. in Milan from 1978. Ephrikian also did much to advance the cause of Monteverdi, Marcello, Alessandro and Domenico Scarlatti, Boccherini, and other Italian masters of the past.—LK/DM

Eppert, Carl, American composer and conductor; b. Carbon, Ind., Nov. 5, 1882; d. Milwaukee, Oct. 1, 1961. He studied with Harris and Wells at the American Cons. in Chicago, and then with Kaun, Nikisch, and Kunwald in Berlin (1907–14). After conducting the Seattle Grand Opera, he led the Milwaukee Civic Orch. (1921–26) and was head of the theory and composition dept. at the Wisc. Cons. in Milwaukee (1921–23).

WORKS: DRAMATIC: O p e r a : *Kaintuckee* (1915). ORCH.: *Arabian Suite* (1915); *Serenade* for Strings (1917); 4 symphonic poems: *The Pioneer* (1925), *Traffic* (NBC, May 8, 1932; later used as the 1st movement of the Sym. No. 1), *City Shadows*, and *Speed* (both Rochester, N.Y., Oct. 30, 1935); *Concert Waltz* (1930); 7 syms. (1934–45); *Escapade* (1937; Indianapolis, Jan. 3, 1941); *Ballet of the Vitamins* (1937–38); Concerto grosso for Flute, Oboe, Clarinet, Bassoon, and Strings (1940); *2 Symphonic Impressions* (Chicago, Feb. 13, 1941); also band pieces. CHAMBER: Violin Sonata (1912); 2 string quartets (1927, 1935); 3 woodwind quintets (1935, 1935, 1936); Woodwind Quartet (1937). VOCAL: Choral music.—NS/LK/DM

Epstein, David M(ayer), American composer, conductor, and writer on music; b. N.Y., Oct. 3, 1930. He learned to play the piano and clarinet and took part in jazz bands. He studied at Antioch Coll. (A.B., 1952), and then took courses with Carl McKinley and Francis Judd Cooke at the New England Cons. of Music (M.M., 1953), with Irving Fine, Shapero, and Berger at Brandeis Univ. (M.F.A., 1954), and with Babbitt and Sessions at Princeton Univ. (M.F.A., 1956; Ph.D., 1968, with the diss. *Schoenberg's Grundgestalt and Total Serialism: Their Relevance to Homophonic Analysis*). In 1955–56 he took lessons in composition with Milhaud in Aspen. In conducting, his mentors were Max Rudolf, Izler Solomon, and Szell. He taught at Antioch Coll. (1957–62), and became an assoc. prof. of music at the Mass. Inst. of Technology in 1965, being named a prof. there in 1971. He has also served as music director of the M.I.T. Sym. Orch. from 1965. In addition, he was music director of the Harrisburg (Pa.) Sym. Orch. (1974–78). In 1983 he was appointed conductor of the New Orch. of Boston. From 1983 to 1988 he was a member of the Herbert von Karajan Musikgesprache in Vienna and at the Salzburg Easter Festival. He publ. *Beyond Orpheus: Studies in Musical Structure* (Cambridge, Mass., 1979). In his music, he follows a serial method, cleansed of impurities and reduced to a euphonious, albeit contrapuntally dissonant, idiom.

WORKS: ORCH.: *Movement* (1953); Sym. (1958); *Sonority-Variations* (1968); *Ventures*, 3 Pieces for Symphonic Wind Ensemble (Rochester, N.Y., Dec. 11, 1970); Cello Concerto (1979). CHAMBER: Piano Trio (1953); String Trio (1964); String Quartet (1971). VOCAL: *Excerpts from a Diary*, song cycle (1953); *The Seasons*, song cycle to poems by Emily Dickinson (1956); *Night Voices* for Narrator, Children's Chorus, and Orch. (1974); *The Concord Psalter* for Chorus (1979); *The Lament of Job* for Chorus (1982). OTHER: *Piano Variations* (1961); film music. —NS/LK/DM

Epstein, Julius, Austrian pianist and pedagogue, father of **Richard Epstein;** b. Agram, Croatia, Aug. 7, 1832; d. Vienna, March 1, 1926. He was a pupil at Agram of Ignaz Lichtenegger, and at Vienna of Anton Halm (piano) and Johann Rufinatscha (composition). From 1867 to 1901 he was a prof. of piano at the Vienna Cons. Among his pupils were Gustav Mahler and Ignaz Brüll.

BIBL.: H. Schuster, *J. E.: Ein tonkünstlerisches Charakterbild zu seinem 70. Geburts-Feste* (Vienna, 1902).—NS/LK/DM

Epstein, Richard, Austrian pianist, son of **Julius Epstein;** b. Vienna, Jan. 26, 1869; d. N.Y., Aug. 1, 1919. He was a pupil at the Vienna Cons. of his father and R. Fuchs (composition). He was a prof. of piano at the Vienna Cons., then lived in London (1904–14) and later in N.Y. He excelled as an accompanist, in which capacity he was frequently heard with such artists as Sembrich, Fremstad, Culp, Gerhardt, Destinn, Elman, and Kreisler; and as assisting artist with famous chamber music organizations, including the Joachim, Rosé, and Bohemian Quartets.—NS/LK/DM

Equiluz, Kurt, esteemed Austrian tenor and teacher; b. Vienna, June 13, 1929. He received instruction in piano and violin as a child, and was a member of the Vienna Boys Choir (from 1939). In 1944 he entered the Vienna Academy of Music, where he studied with Hubert Jelinek (harp), Adolf Vogel (voice), and Ferdinand Grossmann (choral conducting). He then was a member of the Vienna Academy Chamber Choir (1946–51), and in 1949 won the Vienna Mozart Competition. In 1950 he joined the Vienna State Opera chorus, making his debut as a solo artist in 1957 and subsequently singing roles in operas by Mozart, Beethoven, and Strauss. However, it was as an oratorio and lieder artist that he acquired an international reputation, excelling particularly in the works of Bach. In 1980 he was made an Austrian Kammersänger. In 1964 he joined the faculty of the Graz Hochschule für Musik, and in 1981 the faculty of the Vienna Hochschule für Musik. —NS/LK/DM

Érard, Sébastien, famous Alsatian piano and harp maker; b. Strasbourg, April 5, 1752; d. La Muette, near Paris, Aug. 5, 1831. His family name was originally Erhard. His father was a cabinetmaker by trade, and Sébastien worked in his shop until he was 16, when his father died. He was then engaged by a Paris harpsichord maker, who dismissed him "for wanting to know everything." Under a second employer his ingenuity made a stir in the musical world, and the invention of a "clavecin mécanique" (described by Abbé Roussier,

1776) made him famous. The Duchess of Villeroy became his patroness, and fitted up in her home a workshop for Érard in which (1777) he finished the first pianoforte made in France. In the meantime, his brother, Jean-Baptiste, joined him, and they founded an instrument factory in the Rue Bourbon. Their growing success led to a conflict with the fan-makers' guild (to which the brothers did not belong), which tried to prevent them from working. But the Érards obtained a special "brevet" from Louis XVI for the manufacture of "fortépianos" and this enabled them to continue their trade unmolested. In the following years, Érard invented the "piano organisé" with 2 keyboards, one for piano and the other for a small organ. He also became interested in the harp, and invented the ingenious double- action mechanism, perfected in 1811. From 1786 to 1796 he was in London. Returning to Paris, he made his first grand piano, and employed the English action until his invention, in 1809, of the repetition action, which is regarded as his supreme achievement. An "orgue expressif," built for the Tuileries, was his last important work. His nephew, Pierre Érard (1794–1865), succeeded him. He publ. *The Harp in its present improved state compared with the original Pedal Harp* (1821), and *Perfectionnements apportés dans le mécanisme du piano par les Érards depuis l'origine de cet instrument jusqu'à l'exposition de 1834* (1834). Pierre's successor was his wife's nephew, Pierre Schäffer (d. 1878). The firm merged with Gaveau in 1859.

BIBL.: F. Fétis, *Notice biographique sur Sébastien Érard* (Paris, 1831).—NS/LK/DM

Eratosthenes, Greek philosopher; b. Cyprene, c.276 B.C.; d. Alexandria, Egypt, c. 194 B.C. He wrote on numerous subjects, chiefly mathematics, and was custodian of the Alexandria library. The *Catasterismi*, attributed to Eratosthenes, contain scattered notes on Greek music and instruments, especially the "lyra" (Ger. tr. by Schaubach, 1795; Bernhardy publ. in 1822 an ed. of the original text). His work on music is lost; Ptolemy quotes his division of the tetrachord.—NS/LK/DM

Erb, Donald (James), significant American composer and teacher; b. Youngstown, Ohio, Jan. 17, 1927. He studied composition with Harold Miles and Kenneth Gaburo and received training in trumpet at Kent State Univ. (B.S., 1950). He pursued training in composition with Marcel Dick at the Cleveland Inst. of Music (M.M., 1953), and also studied with Nadia Boulanger in Paris (1952). His studies in composition were completed under Bernhard Heiden at Ind. Univ. (D.M., 1964). From 1953 to 1961 he taught at the Cleveland Inst. of Music. In 1964–65 he was an asst. prof. of composition at Bowling Green (Ohio) State Univ. He was a visiting asst. prof. for research in electronic music at Case Inst. of Technology in Cleveland from 1965 to 1967. From 1966 to 1981 he was composer-in-residence at the Cleveland Inst. of Music, which position he also held with the Dallas Sym. Orch. in 1968–69. He served as a staff composer at the Bennington (Vt.) Composers Conference from 1969 to 1974. He was the Meadows Prof. of Composition at Southern Methodist Univ. from 1981 to 1984, and also

was president of the American Music Center from 1982 to 1986. From 1984 to 1987 he was a prof. of music at Ind. Univ. In 1987 he became prof. of composition at the Cleveland Inst. of Music, from which he retired in 1996. He also held a Meet the Composer Residency with the St. Louis Sym. Orch. (1988–91), was resident composer at the American Academy in Rome (1991), was composer-in-residence at the Aspen (Colo.) Music Festival (summer, 1993) and the Schweitzer Inst. (1994, 1995), and was artist-in-residence at the Atlantic Center for the Arts (1995). Erb held a Guggenheim fellowship in 1965, was awarded the Cleveland Arts Prize in 1966, and received an American Academy and Inst. of Arts and Letters award in 1985.

As a composer, Erb is exceptionally liberal in experimenting in all useful types of composition, from simple folklike monody to the strict dodecaphonic structures; as a former trumpeter in jazz bands, he also makes use of the jazz idiom as freely as of neo-Classical pandiatonic techniques. His most popular composition, *The 7th Trumpet* for Orch. (Dallas, April 5, 1969), is an epitome of his varied styles. He furthermore applies electronic sound in several of his works. In his band compositions, he achieves an extraordinary degree of pure sonorism, in which melody, harmony, and counterpoint are subordinated to the purely aural effect. He also cleverly introduces strange-looking and unusual-sounding musical and unmusical and antimusical instruments, such as euphonious goblets, to be rubbed on the rim, and telephone bells. Thanks to the engaging manner of Erb's music, even when ultradissonant, his works safely traverse their premieres and endure through repeated performances.

WORKS: ORCH.: Chamber Concerto for Piano and Strings (1958; Chicago, Feb. 12, 1961); *Symphony of Overtures* (1964; Bloomington, Ind., Feb. 11, 1965); Concerto for Solo Percussion and Orch. (Detroit, Dec. 29, 1966); *Christmasmusic* (Cleveland, Dec. 21, 1967); *The 7th Trumpet* (Dallas, April 5, 1969); *Klangfarbenfunk I* for Orch., Rock Band, and Electronic Sounds (Detroit, Oct. 1, 1970); *Autumnmusic* for Orch. and Electronic Sounds (New Haven, Conn., Oct. 20, 1973); *Treasures of the Snow* (1973; Bergen, N.J., June 8, 1974); *Music for a Festive Occasion* for Orch. and Electronic Sounds (1975; Cleveland, Jan. 11, 1976); Cello Concerto (1975; Rochester, N.Y., Nov. 4, 1976); Trombone Concerto (St. Louis, March 11, 1976); Concerto for Keyboards and Orch. (1978; Akron, Ohio, March 23, 1981); Trumpet Concerto (1980; Baltimore, April 29, 1981); *Sonneries* (1981; Rochester, N.Y., March 18, 1982); *Prismatic Variations* (1983; St. Louis, Jan. 28, 1984); Contrabassoon Concerto (1984; Houston, March 15, 1985); Clarinet Concerto (1984); *Concerto for Orchestra* (Atlanta, Sept. 12, 1985); Concerto for Brass and Orch. (1986; Chicago, April 16, 1987); *Solstice* for Chamber Orch. (Cleveland, June 3, 1988); Sym. for Winds (1989; Elmhurst, Ill., May 11, 1990); *Ritual Observances* (St. Louis, April 30, 1991); Violin Concerto (1992; Grand Rapids, Mich., April 16, 1993); *Evensong* (1993; Cleveland, May 5, 1994).

CHAMBER: 3 string quartets (1960, 1989, 1995); Quartet for Flute, Oboe, Alto Saxophone, and Double Bass (1961); Sonata for Harpsichord and String Quartet (1961); *Dance Pieces* for Violin, Piano, Trumpet, and Percussion (1963); *Hexagon* for Flute, Alto Saxophone, Trumpet, Trombone, Cello, and Piano (1963); *Antipodes* for String Quartet and Percussion Quartet (1963); *Phantasma* for Flute, Oboe, Double Bass, and Harpsichord (1965); *Diversion for 2 (other than sex)* for Trumpet and Percussion (1966); *Andante* for Piccolo, Flute, and Alto Flute (1966); Trio for Violin, Electric Guitar, and Cello (1966); *Reconnaissance* for Violin, Double Bass, Piano, Percussion, and 2 Electronic Setups (1967); *Trio for 2* for Alto Flute or Percussion, and Double Bass (1968); *Harold's Trip* to the Sky for Viola, Piano, and Percussion (1972); Quintet for Violin, Cello, Flute, Clarinet, and Piano (1976); Trio for Violin, Percussion, and Piano (1977); Sonata for Clarinet and Percussion (1980); *3 Pieces* for Harp and Percussion (1981); *Déjà vu*, 6 études for Double Bass (1981); *The St. Valentine's Day Brass Quintet* (1981); *Aura* for String Quintet (1981); *The Last Quintet* for Woodwinds (1982); *The Devil's Quickstep* for Flute, Clarinet, Violin, Cello, Percussion, Keyboards, and Harp (1982); *Fantasy for Cellist and Friends* (1982); *Adieu* for Bass Clarinet and 2 Percussionists (1984); *The Rainbow Snake* for Trombone, 2 Percussion, Keyboards, and Tape (1985); *Views of Space and Time* for Violin, Keyboards, Harp, 2 Percussion, and Amplification (1987); *A Book of Fanfares* for Brass Quintet (1987); *The Watchman Fantasy* for Amplified Piano with Digital Delay, Violin, and Synthesizer (1988); *Woody* for Clarinet (1988); *4 Timbre Pieces* for Cello and Double Bass (1989); *5 Red Hot Duets* for 2 Contrabassoons (1989); *Celebration Fanfare* for 13 Instruments (1990); *Drawing Dawn the Moon* for Piccolo and Percussion (1991); *Illwarra Music* for Bassoon and Piano (1992); Sonata for Solo Violin (1994); *Remembrances* for 2 Trumpets (1994); *Changes* for Clarinet and Piano (1994); Harp Sonata (1995); *Sunlit Peaks and Dark Valleys* for Violin, Clarinet, and Piano (1995); *Dance, You Monster, to My Soft Song* for Trumpet (1998).

VOCAL: *Cummings Cycle* for Chorus and Orch. (1963); *Fallout?* for Narrator, Chorus, String Quartet, and Piano (1964); *God Love You Now* for Chorus, Hand Percussion, and Harmonicas (1971); *New England's Prospect* for Choruses, Narrator, and Orch. (Cincinnati, May 17, 1974).

ELECTRONIC: *Reticulation* for Symphonic Band and Electronic Tape (1965); *Stargazing* for Band and Electronic Tape (1966); *Fission* for Electronic Tape, Soprano Saxophone, Piano, Dancers, and Lights (1968); *In No Strange Land* for Tape, Trombone, and Double Bass (1968); *Basspiece* for Double Bass and 4 tracks of prerecorded Double Bass (1969); *Souvenir* for Tape, Instruments, Lights, etc. (1970); *Z milosci do Warszawy* for Piano, Clarinet, Cello, Trombone, and Electronic Sound (1971); *The Purple-roofed Ethical Suicide Parlor* for Wind Ensemble and Electronic Sound (1972); *The Towers of Silence* for Electronic Quintet (1974); *Suddenly It's Evening* for Electronic Cello (1998).
—NS/LK/DM

Erb, Karl, noted German tenor; b. Ravensburg, July 13, 1877; d. there, July 13, 1958. He was self-taught. He made his debut in Stuttgart in 1907; then sang in Lübeck (1908–10), Stuttgart (1910–13), and Munich (1913–25); later embarked on a series of appearances as a concert and oratorio singer. He was best known for his portrayal of roles in the works of Mozart; he created the title role in Pfitzner's *Palestrina* (1917). From 1921 to 1932 he was married to **Maria Ivogün.**—NS/LK/DM

Erb, Marie Joseph, Alsatian composer and organist; b. Strasbourg, Oct. 23, 1858; d. Andlau, July 9, 1944. He studied at first in Strasbourg, then (1875–80) in Paris, under Saint-Saëns, Gigout, and Loret, at the École de Musique Classique. Returning to Strasbourg, he was teacher of piano and organ, and organist in the Johan-

niskirche (Roman Catholic) and at the Synagogue.

WORKS: DRAMATIC: O p e r a (all first perf. in Strasbourg, unless otherwise noted): *Der letzte Ruf* (1895); *Der glückliche Taugenichts* (1897); *Abendglocken* (1900); *Eifersüchtig* (Leipzig, 1901); *Der Riese Schletto* (1901); *Der Zaubermantel* (1901); *Die Vogesentanne* (1904); *Der Heimweg*, ballet-opera (1907); *Prinzessin Flunkerli* (1912). OTHER: Sym. in G; 3 violin sonatas; Cello Sonata; 2 string quartets; String Trio; Octet for Wind and Strings; *Sonata liturgica* (1919); *Suite liturgique; Danses et pièces alsaciennes* (1924, 1925); 8 masses; organ pieces; pieces for piano (2- and 4-hands); songs; 2 vols. of Alsatian folk songs.

BIBL.: P. de Bréville, *M. J. E., Sa vie et son oeuvre* (Strasbourg, 1948).—NS/LK/DM

Erbach, Christian, noted German organist, teacher, and composer; b. Gaualgesheim, near Mainz, c. 1568; d. Augsburg, summer 1635. He went to Augsburg and entered the service of Marcus Fugger, then became organist at the church of St. Moritz, as well as town organist and head of the Stadtpfeifer in 1602. He was made asst. organist at the Cathedral in 1614, and then chief organist in 1625; he also taught organ and composition at the Catholic choir school. Although a Catholic, he was allowed to retain his position at the Cathedral after Swedish troops took control of the town in 1632 during the 30 Years' War; however, he was dismissed on June 9, 1635, when funds could no longer be found to pay him. His music reflects the influence of the Italian masters of his day. See A. Grotton, ed., *Christian Erbach: Ausgewahlte geistliche Chorwerke* (Mainz, 1943), and C. Raynor, ed., *Christian Erbach (c. 1570–1635): Collected Keyboard Compositions* in Corpus of Early Keyboard Music, XXXVI (1971 et seq.).

WORKS: VOCAL: *Modi sacri sive cantus musici, ad ecclesiae catholicae usum* for 4 to 10 Voices...*liber primus* (Augsburg, 1600); *Mele sive cantiones sacrae ad modum canzonette ut vocant* for 4 to 6 Voices (Augsburg, 1603); *Modorum sacrorum sive cantionum* for 4 to 9 Voices...*Lib. secundus* (Augsburg, 1603–04); *Modorum sacrorum tripertitorum* for 5 Voices...*pars prima* (Dillingen, 1604); *Modorum sacrorum tripertitorum* for 5 Voices...*pars altera* (Dillingen, 1606); *Modorum sacrorum tripertitorum* for 5 Voices...*pars tertia* (Dillingen, 1606); *Sacrarum cantionem* for 4 to 5 Voices...*liber tertius* (Augsburg, 1611); also *Acht underschiedtliche geistliche teutsche Lieder* for 4 Voices (Augsburg, n.d.); other works in various anthologies of the day. INSTRUMENTAL: Many keyboard works, including 35 toccatas, 32 ricercari, 22 canzonas, 11 introits, and 4 fantasias.

BIBL.: S. Sharpe, *An Introduction to the Keyboard Works of C. E. (1573–1635)* (diss., Ind. Univ., 1961); W. Haldeman, *The Vocal Compositions of C. E. (c. 1570–1635)* (diss., Univ. of Rochester, 1962).—NS/LK/DM

Erben, (Johann) Balthasar, German composer; b. Danzig, 1626; d. there (buried), Oct. 3, 1686. After travels in Germany, the Netherlands, England, France, and Italy (from 1653), he returned to Danzig in 1658 as city Kapellmeister, a position he retained for the remainder of his life. He was admired as a composer of sacred concertos.—LK/DM

Erbse, Heimo, German-born Austrian composer; b. Rudolstadt, Feb. 27, 1924. He received training in piano and composition at the Weimar Hochschule für Musik (1941–42; 1945–47) and studied composition with Blacher at the Berlin Hochschule für Musik (1950–52). He was an opera producer in Jena and Sondershausen (1947–50), and then devoted himself fully to composition. In 1957 he settled in Austria and in 1964 became a naturalized Austrian citizen. Erbse received the Würdigungspreis für Musik in 1973, and in 1985 the Austrian president bestowed on him the title of Prof. His music is constructed upon classical principles with an infusion of chromatic harmonies.

WORKS: DRAMATIC: *Fabel in C*, chamber opera (1952); *Julietta*, opera semi-seria after Kleist (1957; Salzburg, Aug. 17, 1959); *Ruth*, ballet (1958); *Der Herr in Grau*, comic opera (1965–66); *Der deserteur*, opera (1983). ORCH.: *6 Miniatures* for Small String Orch., Piano, and Percussion (1951); *Capriccio* for Piano, Strings, and Percussion (1952); *Impression* (1954); *Praeludium* (1954); *Dialog* for Piano and Orch. (1955); *Sinfonietta giocosa* (1955); *Tango-Variationen* (1958); *Pavimento* (1960); 2 piano concertos (1962, 1991); 5 syms. (1963–64; 1969–70; 1990; 1992; 1993); *7 Skizzen in Form einer alten Suite* for Violin and Chamber Orch. (1974–75; also for Cello and Piano, 1976); Triple Concerto for Violin, Cello, Piano, and Orch. (1975); Chamber Concerto (1978); Concerto for 2 Pianos and Small Orch. (1996). CHAMBER: 2 string quartets (1951, 1987); Piano Trio (1953); *12 Aphorismen* for Flute, Violin, and Piano (1954); Quartet for Flute, Oboe, Clarinet, and Bassoon (1961); Flute Sonata (1966); *For String and Wind Players* for Nonet (1971); *7 Skizzen in Form einer alten Suite* for Cello and Piano (1976; also for Violin and Chamber Orch., 1974–75); Trio for Oboe, Clarinet, and Bassoon (1977); Trio for Violin, Clarinet, and Piano (1978); *Divertimento* for String Trio (1987–88); Trumpet Sonata (1991); *3 Pieces* for Trombone and Piano (1991); Sextet for Wind Quintet and Piano (1991); Clarinet Sonata (1993); Concerto for Violin and String Quintet (1996). PIANO: Sonata for 2 Pianos (1951); Sonata (1952); *Ekstato* (1953); *4 Rhapsodies* (1979); *Scherzo* for 2 Pianos (1996). VOCAL: *Das hohe Lied Salomos* for Soprano, Baritone, Piano, and Orch. (1968; also for Soprano, Baritone, and Piano); *5 Orchestergesänge nach Georg Trakl* for Baritone and Orch. (1969); *3 Chöre nach Texten von Nelly Sachs* for Chorus (1971); *4 Gesänge aus den "Anakreontischen Liedern"* for High Voice, Flute, and Harpsichord (1976).—NS/LK/DM

Erdélyi, Miklós, Hungarian conductor; b. Budapest, Feb. 9, 1928; d. there, Sept. 2, 1993. He studied at the Franz Liszt Academy of Music in Budapest (1946–50) with Ferencsik (conducting), Zalánfy (organ), and Kókai (composition). After making his conducting debut in Budapest in 1947, he was music director of the Hungarian Radio Choir there (1950–52). In 1951 he became a répétiteur at the Hungarian State Opera in Budapest, where he was a conductor from 1959. He also appeared as a guest conductor in various European music centers, and in 1972 made his U.S. debut as a guest conductor with the San Antonio Sym. Orch. He was the author of *Schubert* (Budapest, 1963; 2nd ed., 1979).—NS/LK/DM

Erdmannsdörfer, Max von, German conductor; b. Nuremberg, June 14, 1848; d. Munich, Feb. 14, 1905. He studied at the Leipzig Cons. (1863–67), and in Dresden (1868–69). From 1871 to 1880 he was court conductor at Sondershausen, and then was active in Vienna, Leipzig, and Nuremberg. In 1882 he was engaged as conductor of the Imperial Musical Soc. in Moscow; in 1885, became prof. at the Moscow Cons. His sym. concerts in Moscow were of great importance to Russian music. He introduced many new works by Russian composers, and his influence was considerable in Moscow musical circles, despite the mediocrity of his conducting. Returning to Germany, he became conductor of the Bremen Phil. Concerts (until 1895). In 1897 he settled in Munich.—NS/LK/DM

Erede, Alberto, Italian conductor; b. Genoa, Nov. 8, 1908. After training in Genoa and at the Milan Cons., he studied conducting with Weingartner in Basel (1929–31) and Busch in Dresden (1930). In 1930 he made his debut at the Accademia di Santa Cecilia in Rome; then was on the staff of the Glyndebourne Festival (1934–39); he also conducted the Salzburg Opera Guild (1935–38). In 1937 he made his U.S. debut with the NBC Sym. Orch. in N.Y. After serving as chief conductor of the RAI Orch. in Turin (1945–46), he was music director of the New London Opera Co. (1946–48). On Nov. 11, 1950, he made his Metropolitan Opera debut in N.Y. conducting *La Traviata*, remaining on its roster until 1955; he conducted there again in 1974. He was Generalmusikdirektor of the Deutsche Oper am Rhein in Düsseldorf (1958–62). In 1968 he conducted *Lohengrin* at the Bayreuth Festival. He subsequently was active as a guest conductor in Europe, and in 1975 became artistic director of the Paganini Competition in Genoa. —NS/LK/DM

Erić, Zoran, Serbian composer and teacher; b. Belgrade, Oct. 1950. He studied with Rajičič at the Belgrade Academy of Music, took specialized courses at the Orff Inst. in Salzburg, and attended Lutosławski's master's course in Groznian. Erić became a prof. of composition and orchestration at the Univ. of the Arts in Belgrade, where he was vice dean from 1992 to 1998. His compositions explore music's acoustic properties.

WORKS: *Behind the Sun's Gate* for Orch. (1971); *Concerto for Orchestra with Soloists* (1975); *Mirage* for Piano, Synthesizer, Electronic Piano, and Orch. (1979); *Banovic Strahinja*, ballet (1981); *Scenario* for 2 Cellos (1981); *Off* for Double Bass and Strings (1982); *Cartoon* for Strings and Harpsichord (1984); *Subito* for 2 Double Basses, Women's Chorus, and Tape (1984); *Elizabeth, Princess of Montenegro*, ballet (1985); *Artes Liberales* for Chorus, Timpani, and Gong (1986); *Talea Konzertstück* for Violin and Strings (1989); *Images of Chaos*, cycle of 5 pieces: *The Great Red Spot of Jupiter* for Amplified Harpsichord, Percussion, and Live Electronics (1990), *The Abnormal Beats of Dogon* for Bass Clarinet, Piano, Harmonica, Percussion, and Live Electronics (1990–91), *Helium in a Small Box* for Strings (1991), *I Have Not Spoken* for Saxophone, Bass Harmonica, Actor- Narrator, and Chorus (1995), and *Oberon Concerto* for Flute and Instrumental Ensemble (Belgrade, Oct. 7, 1997); much stage and film music. —LK/DM

Erickson, Robert, American composer and teacher; b. Marquette, Mich., March 7, 1917; d. Encinitas, Calif., April 24, 1997. He studied with Wesley La Violette at the Chicago Cons. and with Krenek at Hamline Univ. in St. Paul (B.A., 1943; M.A., 1947). In 1950 he attended a seminar in composition under Sessions at the Univ. of Calif. at Berkeley. In 1966 he held a Guggenheim fellowship. He taught at the Coll. of St. Catherine in St. Paul, Minn. (1947–53), at San Francisco State Coll. (1953–54), at the Univ. of Calif. at Berkeley (1956–58), and at the San Francisco Cons. of Music (1957–66). From 1967 to 1987 he was a prof. of composition at the Univ. of Calif. at San Diego. In his early works, he utilized serial techniques. After exploring electronic music, he resumed non-electronic means of expression. He publ. *The Structure of Music: A Listener's Guide to Melody and Counterpoint* (1955) and *Sound Structure in Music* (1975).

WORKS: ORCH.: *Introduction and Allegro* (Minneapolis, March 11, 1949); *Divertimento* for Flute, Clarinet, and Strings (1953); *Fantasy* for Cello and Orch. (1953); *Variations* (1957); Chamber Concerto (1960); *Sirens and Other Flyers* (1965); *Rainbow Rising* (1974); *East of the Beach* for Small Orch. (1980); *Auroras* (1982). **CHAMBER**: 2 string quartets (1953, 1956); Piano Trio (1953); Duo for Violin and Piano (1959); Concerto for Piano and 7 Instruments (1963); *Ricercar a 5* for Trombone and Tape (1966); *Scapes*, a "contest for 2 groups" (1966); *Birdland* for Electronic Tape (1967); *Ricercar a 3* for Double Bass and Electronic Tape (1967); *Pacific Sirens* for Instruments and Tape (1969); *Taffytime* for Large Ensemble (1983); *Solstice* for String Quartet (1984-85). **P i a n o** : Sonata (1948). **VOCAL**: *Cardenitas*, dramatic aria for Singer, Mime, Conductor, 7 Musicians, and Stereophonic Prerecorded Tape (1968); *The Idea of Order at Key West* for Voice and Instruments (1979); *Mountain* for Mezzo-soprano and Chamber Orch. (1983); *Sierra* for Tenor or Baritone and Chamber Orch. (1984).

BIBL.: J. MacKay, *Music of Many Means: Sketches and Essays on the Music of R. E.* (Lanham, Md., 1995); C. Shere, *Thinking Sound Music: The Life and Work of R. E.* (Berkeley, 1995).—**NS/LK/DM**

Ericson, Eric, distinguished Swedish choral conductor, organist, and pedagogue; b. Borås, Oct. 26, 1918. He studied at the Stockholm Musikhögskolan (1941–43) and at the Basel Schola Cantorum (1943–49). He served as an organist and choirmaster in Stockholm churches, including the Jakobskirche from 1949. In 1945 he became conductor of the Swedish Radio Chamber Choir in Stockholm, which he subsequently conducted as the expanded Swedish Radio Choir from 1951 to 1984. He also was conductor of the noted men's choir Orphei Dränger in Uppsala from 1951 to 1985. In 1952 he became a teacher and in 1968 a prof. at the Stockholm Musikhögskolan. In 1995 he received the Nordic Council Music Prize. Ericson was an inspirational choral conductor and influential pedagogue.

BIBL.: L. Reimers and B. Wallner, eds., *Choral Music Perspectives: Dedicated to E. E.* (Stockholm, 1993).—**NS/LK/DM**

Erigena, John Scotus, Irish philosopher, theologian, and translator; b. Ireland, c.810; d. probably in England, c.877. He went to Gaul about 845, where he was a teacher of grammar and dialectic in Charles the Bald's palace school. His *De divisione naturae or Perifiseon* (c.866) contains references to music.

BIBL.: M. Cappuyns, *Jean Scot Erigene* (Louvain, 1933); E. Waltner, *Organicum melos: Zur Musikanschauung der Iohannes Scottus* (Munich, 1977).—**NS/LK/DM**

Erk, Ludwig (Christian), German conductor, music scholar, and pedagogue; b. Wetzlar, Jan. 6, 1807; d. Berlin, Nov. 25, 1883. He studied with his father, Adam Wilhelm Erk (1779–1820), the Wetzlar cantor, cathedral organist, and teacher. He then was a pupil of Rinck (organ), Reinwald (violin), and André (composition) at Spiess's educational inst. in Offenbach (1820–24), where he subsequently taught. In 1826 he became a prof. at the teacher's seminary in Mörs, and he also founded and conducted the Lower Rhine music festivals. In 1835 he settled in Berlin, teaching liturgical singing at the Royal Seminary until 1840. From 1836 he was conductor of the Royal Cathedral Choir, and he also was a member of the Singakademie (1836–47). In 1843 he founded his own men's choral union and in 1852 his own mixed chorus. He was honored with the titles of Royal Music Director (1857) and Prof. (1876). He compiled a vast collection of folk song materials, authentic as well as non-authentic. His major work was the *Deutscher Liederhort* (Vol. I, Berlin, 1856; completed by F. Böhme, 3 vols., Leipzig, 1893–94). Among his other useful collections were *Die deutschen Volkslieder mit ihren Singweisen* (Berlin, 1838–45) and *Deutscher Liederschatz* (Berlin, 1859–72). His valuable library is housed in the Deutsche Staatsbibliothek in Berlin.

BIBL.: A. Birlinger and W. Crescelius, *Deutsche Lieder: Festgruss an L. E.* (Heilbronn, 1876); K. Schultze, *L. E.: Eine biographische Skizze* (Berlin, 1876); H. Schmeel, *L. E.: Ein Lebensbild* (Giessen, 1908).—**NS/LK/DM**

Erkel, Franz (actually, Ferenc), distinguished Hungarian pianist, conductor, composer, and pedagogue; b. Gyula, Nov. 7, 1810; d. Budapest, June 15, 1893. He studied in Pozsony at the Benedictine Gymnasium (1822–25) and with Heinrich Klein. He then went to Koloszvár, where he began his career as a pianist and became conductor of the Kaschau opera troupe (1834), with which he traveled to Buda (1835). He became conductor of the German Municipal Theater in Pest in 1836. In 1838 he was made music director of the newly founded National Theater, an influential post he held until 1874, was conductor at the Opera House from 1884, and also founded the Phil. concerts (1853), which he conducted until 1871. He was the first prof. of piano and instrumentation at the Academy of Music, and was its director from 1875 to 1888. He gave his farewell performance as a pianist in 1890 and as a conductor in 1892. Erkel was one of the most significant Hungarian musicians of his era. After the premiere of his opera *Báthory Mária* (1840), he gained lasting fame in his homeland with the opera *Hunyady László* (1844), which is recognized as the first truly national Hungarian work for the theater. He composed the Hungarian national anthem in 1844. He later achieved extraordinary success with the opera *Bánk-Bán* (1861), written in collaboration with his sons Gyula (b. Pest, July 4, 1842; d. Ujpest, March 22, 1909) and Sandor (b. Pest, Jan. 2, 1846; d. Békéscsaba, Oct. 14, 1900). He also collaborated with his other sons, Elek (b. Pest, Nov. 2, 1843; d. Budapest, June 10, 1893) and László (b. Pest, April 9, 1844; d. Pozsonyi, Dec. 3, 1896), who were successful musicians. A catalog of the works of Franz Erkel was publ. by E. Major (Budapest, 1947; 2nd ed., rev., 1967).

WORKS: D R A M A T I C : O p e r a : *Báthory Mária* (Pest, Aug. 8, 1840); *Hunyady László* (Pest, Jan. 27, 1844); *Erzsébet* (Pest, May 6, 1857; in collaboration with Franz and Karl Doppler); *Bánk-Bán* (Pest, March 9, 1861; orchestrated with Gyula and Sandor Erkel); *Sarolta*, comic opera (Pest, June 26, 1862; mainly orchestrated by Gyula Erkel); *Dózsa György* (Pest, April 6, 1867; in collaboration with Gyula and Sandor Erkel); *Brankovics György* (Budapest, May 20, 1874; in collaboration with Gyula and Sandor Erkel); *Névtelen hösök* (Budapest, Nov. 30, 1880; in collaboration with Gyula, Sandor, Elek, and László Erkel); *István király* (Budapest, March 14, 1885; generally believed to be principally the work of Gyula Erkel). **B a l l e t :** *Sakk-játék* (Pest, Feb. 2, 1853; not extant). **OTHER DRAMATIC:** Incidental music. **OTHER:** Choral music; chamber works; piano pieces; songs. *The Festival Overture* for Orch. (1887) may be mainly the work of Gyula Erkel.

BIBL.: K. Abrányi, *Erkel Franz* (Budapest, 1895); F. Scherer, *Erkel Franz* (Gyula, 1944); A. Németh, *Erkel Ferenc* (Budapest, 1967); D. Legány, *Erkel Ferenc művei* (Works of Ferenc E.; Budapest, 1974).—NS/LK/DM

Erkin, Ulvi Cemal,

Turkish composer and teacher; b. Constantinople, March 14, 1906; d. Ankara, Sept. 15, 1972. He studied piano with Philipp in Paris and composition with Boulanger in Fontainebleau. Returning to Turkey, he became a piano instructor at the Ankara Cons. His works include *Bayram*, tone poem (Ankara, May 11, 1934), 2 syms. (Ankara, April 20, 1946; 1948–51), Violin Concerto (Ankara, April 2, 1948), chamber music, and piano pieces.—NS/LK/DM

d'Erlanger, Baron François Rodolphe,

French ethnomusicologist; b. Boulonge-sur-Seine, June 7, 1872; d. Sidi bou Said, Tunisia, Oct. 29, 1932. He settled in Tunis in 1910 and, from 1924, assisted by Arab scholars and musicians, he made intensive study of Arabic music, translating many major theoretical treatises. His most important work, the source collection *La Musique arabe* (6 vols., Paris, 1930–59), was intended to spark a Renaissance of Arab music and its study. The first 4 vols. contain translations of writings from the 10th to 16th centuries, and the last two vols. codify contemporary theory. Most of his books were publ. after his death. They became primary sources on Arab music, as they include trs., transcriptions, and extended analytic studies. His own compositions were written according to Arab theoretical principles.

WRITINGS: *La Musique arabe* (6 vols., Paris, 1930-59); *Chants populaires de l'Afrique du nord* (Paris, 1931); *Mélodies tunisiennes, hispano-arabes, arabo-berbères, juives, nègres* (Paris, 1937).—NS/LK/DM

d'Erlanger, Baron Frédéric,

French-born English composer; b. Paris, May 29, 1868; d. London, April 23, 1943. He was born into the family of French bankers. He studied music with Ehmant in Paris, and then settled in London, where he was active as a banker and a composer. In 1897 he assumed the pseudonym Regnal, formed by reading backward the last 6 letters of his name.

WORKS: D R A M A T I C O p e r a : *Jehan de Saintre* (Aix-les-Bains, Aug. 1, 1893); *Inez Mendo* (London, July 10, 1897, under the pseudonym Regnal); *Tess*, after Thomas Hardy (Naples, April 10, 1906); *Noël* (Paris, Dec. 28, 1910). **OTHER:** Piano Quintet; String Quartet; Violin Concerto (London, March 12, 1903; Kreisler, soloist); Violin Sonata; Andante for Cello and Orch.—NS/LK/DM

Erlanger, Camille,

French composer; b. Paris, May 25, 1863; d. there, April 24, 1919. He was a pupil of the Paris Cons. under Delibes, Durand, and Matthias. In 1888 he took the Grand Prix de Rome for his cantata *Velléda*. He earned fame with his opera *Le Juif polonais* (Paris, April 11, 1900). His other operas are *Kermaria* (Paris, Feb. 8, 1897), *Le Fils de l'étoile* (Paris, April 20, 1904), *Aphrodite* (Paris, March 27, 1906), *Bacchus triomphant* (Bordeaux, Sept. 11, 1909), *L'Aube rouge* (Rouen, Dec. 29, 1911), *La Sorcière* (Paris, Dec. 18, 1912), *Le Barbier de Deauville* (1917), and *Forfaiture* (Paris, 1921). He also wrote several symphonic poems (*Maître et serveteur*, after Tolstoy, etc.) and a French Requiem.—NS/LK/DM

Erlebach, Philipp Heinrich,

important German composer; b. Esens, East Frisia, July 25, 1657; d. Rudolstadt, April 17, 1714. He was in the service of the Rudolstadt court by the winter of 1678–79, where he was Hofkapellmeister from 1681. He was a significant composer of sacred music, especially cantatas. All of his oratorios and most of his cantatas are lost. His surviving cantatas reveal the influence of Heinrich Schütz. He also composed 4 operas, but only a few arias from 2 of these are extant. His instrumental works number about 120 in all, but only 6 overtures, 6 trio sonatas, and a march are extant. His suites reveal the influence of Lully, while his sonatas follow Italian precepts.

WORKS: 6 overtures (Nuremberg, 1693; 2 in *Organum*, III/15–16, Leipzig, 1926); sonatas for Violin, Viola da Gamba, and Basso Continuo (Nuremberg, 1694; 1 in *Organum*, III/5, Leipzig, 1924, and 2 in Hortus Musicus, CXVII–CXVIII, 1954); a number of secular songs, including *Harmonische Freude musicalischer Freunde* (2 vols., Nuremberg, 1697, 1710; ed. in Denkmäler Deutscher Tonkunst, 46/47, 1914); *Gott-geheiligte Sing-Stunde*, 12 cantatas (Rudolstadt, 1704).

BIBL.: B. Baselt, *Der Rudolstädter Hofkapellmeister P. H. E.* (diss., Univ. of Halle, 1963); K. H. Wiechers, *P. H. E.* (Aurich, 1964).—NS/LK/DM

Ermatinger, Erhart,

Swiss composer; b. Winterthur, Feb. 16, 1900; d. Arnhem, July 14, 1966. He studied at the Zürich Cons. with Jarnach, then at the Berlin Hochschule für Musik. In 1922–23 he was chorus master at the Zürich Opera; later a private teacher there; in 1925–26, was a teacher of theory at Freiburg Univ.; lived in Berlin, then in the Netherlands. He wrote an opera, *Gijsbrecht van Amstel* (1947), 3 syms., 2 string quartets, and songs. He publ. a book, *Bildhafte Musik: Entwurf einer Lehre von der musikalischen Darstellungskunst* (Tübingen, 1928).—NS/LK/DM

Ermler, Mark,

Russian conductor; b. Leningrad, May 5, 1932. He studied with Khaiken and Rabinovich at the Leningrad Cons., graduating in 1956. In 1952 he made his debut with the Leningrad Phil., and in 1953 his debut as an opera conductor with *Die Entführung aus dem Serail* in Leningrad. From 1956 he was on the conducting staff of the Bolshoi Theater in Moscow, where he led a vast operatic and ballet repertoire; also appeared with the company on its tours to Montreal (1967), Paris and Tokyo (1970), Milan (1974), N.Y. and Washington, D.C. (1975), Berlin (1980), and other major music centers. As a guest conductor, he appeared throughout Europe, North America, and Japan. —NS/LK/DM

Ernesaks, Gustav (Gustavovich), Estonian composer and conductor; b. Chariu, Dec. 12, 1908; d. Tallinn, Jan. 24, 1993. He was a pupil of A. Kapp at the Tallinn Cons. He subsequently was active as a composer and conductor. Among his works were several operas, music for films and plays, choruses, and songs. —NS/LK/DM

Ernst, Alfred, French writer on music, son of **Heinrich Wilhelm Ernst;** b. Périgueux, April 9, 1860; d. Paris, May 15, 1898. A pupil of the École Polytechnique, he abandoned science for art. He was a passionate admirer and defender of Wagner. Besides many contributions to musical journals, he publ. *L'OEuvre dramatique de Berlioz* (1884), *Richard Wagner et le drame contemporain* (1887), *L'Art de Richard Wagner, L'OEuvre poétique* (1893; a projected 2nd vol. on *L'OEuvre musicale* remained unfinished), and *Étude sur "Tannhäuser,"* analysis and thematic guide (1895; with E. Poirée). He also tr. *Die Meistersinger* and *Der Ring des Nibelungen* into French.—NS/LK/DM

Ernst, Heinrich Wilhelm, famous Moravian violinist and composer, father of **Alfred Ernst;** b. Brünn, May 6, 1814; d. Nice, Oct. 8, 1865. He made his first public appearance at age 9. He became a student of Bohm at the Vienna Cons. (1825), and also studied composition with Seyfried; later continued his training with Mayseder. After Paganini visited Vienna in 1828, Ernst decided to follow in the footsteps of the legendary Italian virtuoso. He launched his career in 1829. He made his Paris debut in 1831, and then toured throughout Europe with enormous success. On July 18, 1843, he made his London debut, and thereafter made regular visits to the British capital before settling there in 1855. He subsequently participated in a series of celebrated quartet performances with Joachim, Wieniawski, and Piatti. Ernst was also a distinguished violist, and played Berlioz's *Harold in Italy* under the composer's direction in Brussels (1842), St. Petersburg (1847), and London (1855). Stricken with tuberculosis, he was compelled to abandon his brilliant career in 1859. He spent his last years in Nice. After the death of Paganini in 1840, Ernst was duly acknowledged as the greatest violin virtuoso of his time. Unlike Paganini, he did not restrict himself to virtuoso showpieces. He was also a composer of brilliant works for the violin. Among his approximately 30 compositions are the celebrated *Élégie,* op.10 (Vienna, 1840), the *Othello Fantasy* on themes of Rossini, op.11, *Le Carnaval de Venise* (Leipzig, 1844), and the *Concerto pathétique* in F-sharp minor (1st perf. by Ernst in Vienna, 1846; publ. in Leipzig, 1851). He also wrote 6 *Polyphonic*

Studies for Solo Violin, as well as a transcription of Schubert's *Erlkönig,* pieces of fiendish difficulty for even the most gifted executant.

BIBL.: A. Heller, *H. W. E. im Urteile seiner Zeitgenossen* (Brünn, 1904; Eng. tr., 1986, as *H. W. E. as Seen by His Contemporaries*).—NS/LK/DM

Ernster, Desző, Hungarian bass; b. Pécs, Nov. 23, 1898; d. Zürich, Feb. 15, 1981. He studied in Budapest and Vienna, and then sang in Plauen, Gera, and Düsseldorf. In 1929 he appeared at the Berlin State Opera, in 1931 at the Bayreuth Festival, and in 1933 at the Vienna State Opera. He then was a member of the Graz City Theater (1935–36). He made his first visit to the U.S. during the 1938-39 season, when he sang in N.Y. with the Salzburg Opera Guild. During World War II, he was interned in a concentration camp. On Nov. 20, 1946, he made his Metropolitan Opera debut in N.Y. as Marke in *Tristan und Isolde;* remained on its roster until 1964; was also a member of the Deutsche Oper am Rhein in Düsseldorf (1950–67).

BIBL.: J. Fábián, *E.* (Budapest, 1969).—NS/LK/DM

Erpf, Hermann (Robert), German musicologist and composer; b. Pforzheim, April 23, 1891; d. Stuttgart, Oct. 17, 1969. He studied with Wolfrem in Heidelberg (1909–11) and with Riemann at the Univ. of Leipzig (Ph.D., 1913, with the diss. *Der Begriff der musikalischen Form;* publ. in Stuttgart, 1914). He taught at Pforzheim (1919–23) and at the Univ. of Freiburg am Breisgau (1923–25); was asst. director at the Academy of Speech and Music in Münster (1925–27); was in charge of the Folkwangschule in Essen (1927–43). From 1943 to 1945, and again from 1952 to 1956, he was director of the Hochschule für Musik in Stuttgart. He composed choral pieces, chamber music, and songs.

WRITINGS: *Entwicklungszuge in der zeitgenössischen Musik* (Karlsruhe, 1922); *Studien zur Harmonie- und Klangtechnik der neueren Musik* (Leipzig, 1927; 2nd ed., 1969); *Harmonielehre in der Schule* (Leipzig, 1930); *Vom Wesen der neuen Musik* (Stuttgart, 1949); *Neue Wege der Musikerziehung* (Stuttgart, 1953); *Gegenwartskunde der Musik* (Stuttgart, 1954); *Form und Struktur in der Musik* (Mainz, 1967).—NS/LK/DM

Errani, Achille, Italian tenor and vocal pedagogue; b. Faenza, Aug. 1823; d. N.Y., Jan. 6, 1897. He was trained by Vaccai at the Milan Cons. After appearances throughout Italy, Spain, and Greece, he joined Maretzek's Italian Opera Co. in Havana in 1858. In 1860 he made his U.S. debut as Verdi's Alfredo in Philadelphia, and toured widely with Maretzek's company until the end of the Civil War, when he settled in N.Y. as a teacher. Among his many students were Emma Abbott, Minnie Hauk, Clara Louise Kellogg, and Emma Thursby. His death from a heart attack followed a suicide-murder attempt involving a domestic in his household and her lover.—NS/LK/DM

Ershov, Ivan (Vasilievich), celebrated Russian tenor; b. Maly Nesvetai, near Novocherkassk, Nov. 20, 1867; d. Tashkent, Nov. 21, 1943. He studied voice in

Moscow with Alexandrova-Kochetova and in St. Petersburg with Gabel and Paleček. In 1893 he made his operatic debut at the Maryinsky Theater in St. Petersburg as Faust, which became one of his most popular roles; then went to Italy and took voice lessons with Rossi in Milan; appeared in Turin as Don José in *Carmen*. He returned to Russia in 1894 and joined the Kharkov Opera; in 1895 he became a member of the Maryinsky Opera Theater in St. Petersburg, and served with it until 1929. He achieved fabulous success as the greatest performer of the tenor roles in the Russian repertoire, and he also was regarded by music critics and audiences as the finest interpreter of the Wagnerian operas; he sang Siegfried, Tannhäuser, Lohengrin, and Tristan with extraordinary lyric and dramatic penetration; as an opera tenor in his time, he had no rivals on the Russian stage. In 1929, at the age of 62, he sang Verdi's Otello; he also appeared in oratorio and solo recitals. From 1916 to 1941 he taught voice at the Petrograd (Leningrad) Cons. At the beginning of the siege of Leningrad in 1941, Ershov was evacuated with the entire personnel of the Cons. to Tashkent in Central Asia, where he died shortly afterward.

BIBL.: V. Bogdanov-Berezovsky, *I. E.* (Leningrad, 1951).—NS/LK/DM

Ertel, (Jean) Paul, German pianist and composer; b. Posen, Jan. 22, 1865; d. Berlin, Feb. 11, 1933. He studied with L. Brassin (piano) and later took lessons with Liszt; also studied law. He was music critic of the *Berliner Lokal Anzeiger* and ed. of *Deutscher Musikerzeitung* (1897–1905). He wrote several symphonic poems in a general Lisztian vein (*Der Mensch, Die nachtliche Heerschau*, etc.), many ballads for voice and instruments, and a Violin Sonata and other chamber music.—NS/LK/DM

Ertmann, (Catharina) Dorothea von (née **Grautmann**), German pianist, niece of **Mathilde Marchesi de Castrone**; b. Offenbach am Main, May 3, 1768; d. Vienna, March 16, 1849. While still a youth, she earned a fine reputation as a pianist. In 1798 she married an infantry officer, Stephan von Ertmann, and settled with him in Vienna. In 1804 she met Beethoven, who subsequently became her mentor and good friend. In return, Ertmann championed his piano music. Beethoven's Piano Sonata, op.101, was dedicated to her. In 1820 her husband was stationed in Milan, where she lived until his death in 1835, when she returned to Vienna.—LK/DM

Erwin, Pee Wee (actually, **George**), jazz trumpeter; b. Falls City, Nebr., May 30, 1913; d. Teaneck, N.J., June 20, 1981. Raised in Kansas City; his father, James O. Erwin (d. 1938), was a professional trumpeter. Erwin began playing trumpet at age four, and made his first radio broadcast at eight. He spent the 1930s playing in a variety of big bands, including a stint with Isham Jones in N.Y. (1932–34), Freddie Martin (1934), Benny Goodman (November 1934–May 1935 and again February–September 1936; briefly late 1942), Ray Noble (June 1935–January 1936 and again October 1936–January 1939), and Tommy Dorsey (February–July 1939). Erwin worked in Fla. for a while, then worked in a few minor bands before turning to studio work until 1949, along with several unsuccessful attempts to start his own band. In the 1950s, he switched to leading a Dixieland styled ensemble at Nick's in N.Y.; he also worked with Tony Parenti in 1957, and continued studio work. During the 1960s, Erwin was active as a studio musician, and also ran a trumpet school with Chris Griffin. During the 1970s, he played regularly with the N.Y. Jazz Repertory Company. He also toured Europe with Warren Covington and his own group the Kings of Jazz. He played three weeks before his death at the Sarasota (Fla.) Jazz Festival, and the same week flew to Amsterdam, Holland, for his last appearance, at a jazz festival there. He died after a long illness.

DISC.: *Land of Dixie* (1953); *Accent on Dixieland* (1955); *Dixieland at Grandview Inn* (1956); *Oh, Play That Thing!* (1958); *Down by the Riverside* (1960); *Pee Wee in Hollywood* (1980); *Pee Wee in N.Y.* (1980).

WRITINGS: With Warren W. Vaché Sr., *Pee Wee Erwin: This Horn for Hire* (Metuchen, N.J, and London, 1987).—JC/LP

Eschenbach (real name, **Ringmann**), **Christoph,** remarkably talented German pianist and conductor; b. Breslau, Feb. 20, 1940. His mother died in childbirth; his father, the musicologist Heribert Ringmann, lost his life in battle soon thereafter; his grandmother died while attempting to remove him from the advancing Allied armies. Placed in a refugee camp, Eschenbach was rescued by his mother's cousin, who adopted him in 1946. He began studying piano at age 8 with his foster mother. His formal piano training commenced at the same age with Eliza Hansen in Hamburg, and continued with her at the Hochschule für Musik there; he also studied piano with Hans-Otto Schmidt in Cologne, and received instruction in conducting from Brückner-Ruggeberg at the Hamburg Hochschule für Musik. In 1952 he won first prize in the Steinway Piano Competition; after winning second prize in the Munich International Competition in 1962, he gained wide recognition by capturing first prize in the first Clara Haskil Competition in Montreux (1965). In 1966 he made his London debut; following studies with Szell (1967–69), the latter invited him to make his debut as soloist in Mozart's Piano Concerto in F major, K. 459, with the Cleveland Orch. on Jan. 16, 1969. In subsequent years, he made numerous tours as a pianist, appearing in all of the major music centers of the world. He also gave duo concerts with the pianist Justus Frantz. In 1972 he began to make appearances as a conductor; made his debut as an opera conductor in Darmstadt with *La Traviata* in 1978. He pursued a successful career as both a pianist and a conductor, sometimes conducting from the keyboard. After serving as Generalmusikdirektor of the Rheinland-Pfalz State Phil. (1979–81), he was first permanent guest conductor of the Zürich Tonhalle Orch. (1981–82); then was its chief conductor (1982–85). In 1988 he became music director of the Houston Sym. Orch. He also served as music director of the Ravinia Festival in Chicago from 1995. Eschenbach maintains a varied repertoire, as both a pianist and a conductor; his sympathies range from the standard literature to the cosmopolitan avant-garde.

BIBL.: W. Erk, ed., *Für C. E. zum 20. Februar 1990: Eine Festgabe* (Stuttgart, 1990).—**NS/LK/DM**

Escher, Rudolf (George), noted Dutch composer; b. Amsterdam, Jan. 8, 1912; d. De Koog, March 17, 1980. He studied harmony, violin, and piano at the Toonkunst Cons. in Rotterdam (1931–37), and was a student in composition of Pijper (1934). He worked in the electronic music studios in Delft (1959–60) and in Utrecht (1961). He taught at the Amsterdam Cons. (1960–61) and at the Inst. for Musical Science at the Univ. of Utrecht (1964–75). In 1977 he was awarded the Johan Wagenaar Prize for his compositions. Escher's music was very much influenced by the modern French school.

WORKS: ORCH.: *Sinfonia in memoriam Maurice Ravel* (1940); *Musique pour l'esprit en deuil* (1941–43; Amsterdam, Jan. 19, 1947); *Passacaglia* (1945; withdrawn); Concerto for Strings (1947–48; withdrawn); *Hymne de Grand Meaulnes* (1950–51); 2 syms. (1953–54; 1958; rev. 1964 and 1971); *Summer Rites at Noon* for 2 facing Orchs. (1962–68); orchestration of Debussy's *6 épigraphes antiques* for Piano Duet (1976–77; Hilversum Radio, July 6, 1978). **CHAMBER:** *Sonata concertante* for Cello and Piano (1943); Sonata for 2 Flutes (1944); Sonata for Solo Cello (1945); Trio for Oboe, Clarinet, and Bassoon (1946); Sonata for Solo Flute (1949); Violin Sonata (1950); *Le Tombeau de Ravel* for Flute, Oboe, Violin, Viola, Cello, and Harpsichord (1952); *Air pour charmer un lezard* for Flute (1953); Trio for Violin, Viola, and Cello (1959); Wind Quintet (1966–67); *Monologue* for Flute (1969); Sonata for Solo Clarinet (1973); *Sinfonia* for 10 Instruments (1976); Flute Sonata (1975–77); Trio for Clarinet, Viola, and Piano (1978). **Piano:** Sonata No. 1 (1935); *Arcana musae dona,* suite (1944); *Habanera* (1945); *Due voci* (1949); *Non troppo,* 10 easy pieces (1949); Sonatina (1951). **VOCAL:** *Nostalgies* for Tenor and Orch. (1951; rev. 1961); *Le Vrai Visage de la paix* for Chorus (1953; rev. 1957); *Song of Love and Eternity* for Chorus (1955); *Ciel, air et vents* for Chorus (1957); *Univers de Rimbaud* for Tenor and Orch. (1970).—**NS/LK/DM**

Escobar, Luis Antonio, Colombian composer; b. Villapinzón, near Bogotá, July 14, 1925. He studied at the Bogotá Cons., then took courses with Nicolas Nabokov at the Peabody Cons. in Baltimore and with Boris Blacher in Berlin. He returned to Bogotá in 1953, and received the post of prof. at the Cons., which he held until 1962. His style is brisk and terse in the modern manner; but there is in his music also a melo-rhythmic pattern of Spanish-American dances.

WORKS: Flute Concertino (1951); *Avirama,* ballet (1955); *Sinfonía Cero* (1955); *Sinfonía X* (1955); Harpsichord Concertino (1958); Piano Concerto (1959); *Los hampones,* opera for Soloists, Chorus, and Percussion (1961); *Juramento a Bolívar* for Men's Chorus and Orch. (1964); *Little Symphony* (Washington, D.C., May 7, 1965); 2 string quartets; 2 violin sonatas; 5 piano sonatinas (1950–59); etc.—**NS/LK/DM**

Escobar, Roberto, Chilean composer and musicologist; b. Santiago, May 11, 1926. He studied at the Escuela Moderna de Música in Santiago and at the Manhattan School of Music in N.Y. In 1972 he was a senior Fulbright scholar at Columbia Univ., and in 1976–77 at the Univ. of Mo. From 1974 he held chairmanships at the Univ. of Chile in Santiago, where he became a Distinguished Prof. in 1981; he also was made a prof. extraordinary at the Catholic Univ. in Valparaiso that same year. He served as president of the Asociación Nacional de Compositores (1974–77) and the Sociedad Chilena de Filosofía (1985–88). Among his books are *Músicos sin pasado* (Barcelona, 1971), *Filosofía en Chile* (Santiago, 1976), *Teoria de Chileno* (Santiago, 1981), and *Creadores Musicales Chilenos* (Santiago, 1997).

WORKS: ORCH.: 4 syms.: No. 1 (1962), No. 2 (1992), No. 3 (Santiago, Oct. 9, 1993), and No. 4 (1995); *Tsunami* (1993). **CHAMBER:** *Cuarteto Estructural* for String Quartet (1966); *Ceremonia de Percusion,* Mass for Percussion and Guitar (1974); *Cuarteto Funcional* for String Quartet (1979); *The Tower of the Winds* for String Quartet (1992); pieces for Solo Instruments. **VOCAL:** *Laberinto* for 4 Voices, 16 Instruments, and Percussion (1971).—**NS/LK/DM**

Escobedo, Bartolomé de, Spanish singer and composer; b. Zamora province, c. 1500; d. between March 21 and Aug. 11, 1563. From 1536 to 1541, and again from 1545 to 1554, he was a singer in the Papal Choir at Rome. He was a judge in the famous dispute between Nicola Vicentino and Vincento Lusitano (1551) over the qualities of Greek modes. He composed 2 masses and a number of motets.—**LK/DM**

Escot, Pozzi, American composer, teacher, music theorist, and writer; b. Lima, Peru (of French-Morrocan parents), Oct. 1, 1933. She began her training in Lima, where she studied with Andrés Sás at the Sás-Rosay Academy of Music (1949–53) and took courses in mathematics at San Marcos Univ. (1950–52). In 1953 she emigrated to the U.S. and shortly thereafter became a naturalized American citizen. After studies at Reed Coll. in Portland, Ore., she pursued training with Bergsma at the Juilliard School of Music in N.Y. (B.S., 1956; M.S., 1957). In 1957 she went to Germany on a Deutscher Akademischer Austauchdienst fellowship and pursued studies with Jarnach at the Hamburg Hochschule für Musik until 1961. In 1964 she joined the faculty of the New England Cons. of Music in Boston, and concurrently taught at Wheaton Coll. in Norton, Mass., from 1972. She held Harvard-Radcliffe Bunting Inst. fellowships (1969–71) and a residency at the Rockefeller Foundation Center for Scholars in Bellagio (1995). In 1980 she became ed. of the journal *Sonus*. She became president of the International Soc. of Hildegard von Bingen Studies in 1993. Escot has lectured widely in the U.S. and abroad on various interdisciplinary aspects of music. She has described her compositions as "pure arithmetic and geometry," in which "every dimension of the sonic design is structured accordingly." Her works have received many performances and recordings.

WRITINGS: With R. Cogan, *Sonic Design: The Nature of Sound and Music* (1976); with R. Cogan, *Sonic Design: Practice and Problems* (1981); *The Poetics of Simple Mathematics in Music* (1999).

WORKS: ORCH.: 6 syms.: No. 1, *Little* (1954), No. 2 (1955), No. 3 (1957), No. 5, *Sands* (1965), and No. 6, *Naye-e Sin* (1999); Piano Concerto (1982). **CHAMBER:** *Metamorphosis*, ballet for Chamber Ensemble (1952); 5 string quartets: No. 1 (1953), No. 2 (1956), and No. 5, *Jubilation* (1991); Concertino for 9 Instruments (1956); *Three Movements* for Violin and Piano (1960); *Trilogy* No. 2, *Christos*, for 3 Violins, Alto Flute or Flute, Contrabassoon or Bassoon, and Percussion (1963); *Interra I* for Piano, Tape, Spot Lights, and Film or Piano (1968); *Neyrac Lux* for 3 Guitars, 1 Performer (1978); *Eure Pax* for Violin (1980); *Pluies* for Alto Saxophone and Tape (1981); *In Memoriam Solrac* for Violin, Cello, and Piano (1984); *Mirabilis I* for Viola and Tape (1990) and *II* for Clarinet or Saxophone or Trumpet, Piano, and Percussion (1991); *Sarabande* for 5 Flutes, 2 Cellos, and 2 Snare Drums (1999). **KEYBOARD: Piano:** *Six Portraits* (1949); 4 sonatinas (1951, 1951, 1951, 1992); *Differences* (2 groups, 1961, 1963); *Interra II* for Piano Left Hand or Both Hands and Tape or Without Tape (1980). **Organ:** *Are* (1975). **VOCAL:** *Two Lamentations* for Soprano and Piano (1951); Four Songs for Soprano and Piano (1955); *Songs of Wisdom* for Soprano and Piano (1956); String Quartet No. 3, *Credo*, with Soprano (1958), and No. 4, *Three Poems of Rilke*, with Reciter (1959); Sym. No. 4, *Cantata Roots*, for Alto, Chorus, and Orch. (1958); *Trilogy* No. 1, *Lamentus*, for Soprano, 2 Violins, 2 Cellos, Piano, and 3 Percussion (1962) and No. 3, *Visions*, for Flute, Piccolo, Alto Flute, Alto Saxophone, Soprano, Contrabassoon, and Percussion (1964); *Ainu I* for Chorus (1970) and *II* for Voice (1978); *Fergus Missa Triste* for Chorus, Women, and Any 3 Instruments (1981); *Visione 87* for Voice and Piano or Tape (1987); *Your Kindled Valors Bend* for Voice, Clarinet, and Piano (1989); *Mirabilis III* for Voice, 3 Flutes, and 3 Violins (1995); *Bels Dous Amics* for Voice, Oboe, and Viola (1993); *Vollkommen ist den wessen* for Voice, Flute, Drum, and Bell (1994); *Visione 97* for 8 Solo Voices or Chorus (1997); *Aria* for Voice, Flute, Clarinet, and Saxophone (1998). **—NS/LK/DM**

Escovedo, Pete, American percussionist; b. Pittsburg, Calif., July 13, 1935. Percussionist Pete Escovedo has been an active force in Latin jazz since the 1960s as both a session player and a solo recording artist; his credits include work with Carlos Santana, Herbie Hancock, Mongo Santamaria, Angela Bofill, Barry White, Cal Tjader, Tito Puente, Woody Herman, Billy Cobham, Anita Baker, Stephen Stills, Bobby McFerrin, Chris Isaak, Boz Scaggs, and George Duke. He has released a number of fine contemporary jazz-pop albums as a leader on the Concord label; although the "jazz-pop" categorization might be somewhat deceiving. His trademark sound combines equal parts jazz, salsa, funk, Brazilian, pop, and rock influences with traditional Afro-Cuban sounds and odd meters to create a very listenable, cohesive whole. He has also made musical history as co-leader (with brother Coke) of the groundbreaking Latin/fusion big-band Azteca. The Escovedo musical dynasty in the San Francisco Bay area is similar to that which the Marsalis family has achieved in New Orleans. Pete is not only the brother of Coke (deceased) and Phil Escovedo—both performing musicians and former members of the Escovedo Brothers Band—but also the father of Sheila "E" Escovedo—L.A. studio percussionist and former pop-singing Prince-protege—and musician/producer/arranger and studio engineer Peter Michael Escovedo. Pete Escovedo continues to perform and record as a leader, with various

members of his family, and in support of some of the world's most famous jazz and pop acts.

DISC.: *Yesterday's Memories—Tomorrow's Dreams* (1987); *Mister E* (1988); *Azteca* (1972); *Pyramid of the Moon* (1973); *Flying South* (1996); *E Street* (1997).**—GJ**

Escudier, Léon, French music journalist; b. Castelnaudary, Aude, Sept. 17, 1816; d. Paris, June 22, 1881. He was a brother and partner of Marie (-Pierre-Yves) Escudier (b. Castelnaudary, June 29, 1809; d. Paris, April 18, 1880). In 1837, the brothers began publishing the periodical *La France Musicale* and soon afterward established a music shop. Industrious writers, they issued jointly the following works: *Études biographiques sur les chanteurs contemporains* (1840), *Dictionnaire de musique d'après les théoriciens, historiens et critiques les plus célèbres* (2 vols., 1844; reprinted in 1854 as *Dictionnaire de musique, théorique et historique;* 5th ed., 1872), *Rossini, Sa vie et ses oeuvres* (1854), and *Vie et aventures des cantatrices célèbres, précédées des musiciens de l'Empire, et suivies de la vie anecdotique de Paganini* (1856). Léon broke up partnership with his brother in 1860, retaining the music business. He established a new journal, *L'Art Musical*, which continued to appear until Sept. 27, 1894. Marie retained the publishing and editorial rights to *La France Musicale*, which ceased publication in 1870.**—NS/LK/DM**

Esham, Faith, American soprano; b. Vanceburg, Ky., Aug. 6, 1948. Following training with Vasile Venettozzi in Ky., she pursued vocal studies at the Juilliard School of Music in N.Y. with Adele Addison, Beverly Johnson, and Jennie Tourel. She made her formal operatic debut in 1977 as Cherubino at the N.Y.C. Opera, and then her European operatic debut in 1980 as Nedda in Nancy. In 1981 she won the Concours International de Chant in Paris, and sang Cherubino at the Glyndebourne Festival. After appearing in the same role at Milan's La Scala in 1982, she sang Micaëla at the Vienna State Opera and Mélisande at the Geneva Opera in 1984. On Dec. 27, 1986, she made her Metropolitan Opera debut in N.Y. as Marzelline. She appeared as Desdemona at the Welsh National Opera in Cardiff in 1990, and then as Musetta at the Cologne Opera and as Pamina at the Washington (D.C.) Opera. In 1992 she sang Micaëla at the Cincinnati Opera, Cio-Cio-San at the Opera Theatre of St. Louis, and Cherubino at the Dallas Opera. She also pursued an active concert career and sang with major American orchs.**—NS/LK/DM**

Eshpai, Andrei (Yakovlevich), Russian composer and pianist, son of **Yakov (Andreievich) Eshpai;** b. Kozmodemiansk, May 15, 1925. He studied piano with Safranitsky and composition with Miaskovsky and Golubev (1948–53) at the Moscow Cons., where he completed his training in composition with Khatchaturian (1953–56). From 1965 to 1970 he was on its faculty. He made tours as a pianist throughout Russia and abroad. In 1986 he received the Lenin Prize. His output, which includes both serious and light scores, is written in an accessible style. He has made use of folk motifs of the Mari nation from which he descended.

WORKS: DRAMATIC: Operettas; musicals; ballets, including *The Circle* (1980; Kuibishev, Feb. 23, 1981); incidental music to plays; many film scores. ORCH.: *Symphonic Dances* (1951); *Hungarian Melodies* for Violin and Orch. (1952); 2 piano concertos (1954, 1972); 7 syms. (1959; 1962; 1964; 1982; 1985–86; 1988–89; 1991); *Concerto for Orchestra* (1967); *Festival Overture* for Chorus and Orch. (1970); Oboe Concerto (1982); Concerto for Saxophone, Soprano, and Orch. (1986); Viola Concerto (1988); Cello Concerto (1989); Violin Concerto No. 3 (1990); Concerto for Double Bass and String Orch. (1994–95); Concerto for Solo Horn, Strings, and 4 Horns (1995); Concerto for Trumpet, Trombone, and Orch. (1995). CHAMBER: 2 violin sonatas (1966, 1970); String Quartet (1992).—NS/LK/DM

Eshpai, Yakov, Russian composer of Mari extraction, father of **Andrei Eshpai**; b. near Zvenigorodsk, Oct. 30, 1890; d. Moscow, Feb. 20, 1963. He studied violin and singing in Kazan, and later at the Moscow Cons. He publ. important collections of national songs of the Ural region, particularly of the Mari ethnic group. He also composed vocal and instrumental music on native themes.—NS/LK/DM

Eslava (y Elizondo), (Miguel) Hilarión, Spanish pedagogue and composer; b. Burlada, Navarra, Oct. 21, 1807; d. Madrid, July 23, 1878. He studied piano, organ, and violin with Julián Prieto and composition with Francisco Secanilla in Calahorra. In 1827 he was made maestro de capilla at Burgo de Osma Cathedral. After taking holy orders, he held that title in Seville (1832–44) and at the Royal Chapel in Madrid (from 1844). In 1854 he became a prof. of composition and in 1866 director of music at the Madrid Cons. He publ. a valuable anthology of Spanish sacred music from the 16th to the 19th centuries as *Lira sacro-hispana* (10 vols., Madrid, 1869). He also publ. *Método completo de solfeo sin accompañamiento* (Madrid, 1846) and *Escuela de armonía y composición* (Madrid, 1851). Among his compositions were the operas *Il Solitario del Monte Selvaggio* (Cádiz, June 1841), *La tregua di Ptolemaide* (Cádiz, May 24, 1842), and *Pietro el crudele* (Seville, 1843), and sacred works. —NS/LK/DM

Esplá (y Triay), Oscar, Spanish music educator and composer; b. Alicante, Aug. 5, 1886; d. Madrid, Jan. 6, 1976. He began his musical studies in Alicante, and then pursued training in engineering and philosophy at the Univ. of Barcelona (1903–11); subsequently he studied with Reger in Meiningen and Munich (1912) and Saint-Saëns in Paris (1913). In 1930 he became a prof. at the Madrid Cons., serving as its director (1936–39); was also president of the Junta Nacional de Música y Teatros Líricos (1931–34). He became director of the Laboratoire Musical Scientifique in Brussels in 1946; returning to Spain, he became director of his own cons. in Alicante (1958). He publ. *El arte y la musicalidad* (Alicante, 1912), *Fundamento estético de las actividades del espíritu* (Munich, 1915), and *Función musical y música contemporánea* (Madrid, 1955). A. Iglesias ed. *Escritos de Oscar Esplà* (3 vols., 1977–86). His compositions show the influence of Spanish folk music; he utilized his own Levantine scale in his works.

WORKS: DRAMATIC: Opera: *La bella durmiente* (Vienna, 1909); *La balteira* (N.Y., 1935); *Plumes au vent* (1941); *El* *pirata cautivo* (Madrid, 1974); *Calixto y Melibea* (1974–76). Scenic Cantata: *Nochebuena del diablo* for Soprano, Chorus, and Orch. (1923). Ballet: *Ciclopes de Ifach* (1920?); *El contrabandista* (Paris, 1928); *Fiesta* (1931; unfinished). ORCH.: *El sueño de Eros*, symphonic poem (1904); *Suite levantina* (1911; rev. as *Poema de miños*, 1914); *Don Quijote velando las armas*, symphonic episode (1924); *Schubertiana* (1928); *El ámbito de la danza* (1929–34); 2 *suites folklóricas* for Chamber Orch. (1932, 1934); *Concierto de cámara* (1937); *Sonata del sur* for Piano and Orch. (1943–45); *Sinfonía aitana* (Madrid, Oct. 31, 1964); *Sinfonia de retaguardia* (1969–76). CHAMBER: Violin Sonata (1915); Piano Trio (1917); 2 string quartets (1920, 1943); *Sonata concertante* (1939); *Lírica española* for Piano and Instruments (1952-54); organ music. VOCAL: Choral pieces; cantatas.

BIBL.: E. García Alcázar, *O. E.y.T.: (Alicante, 5–8–1886–Madrid, 6–1–1976): Estudio monográfico documental* (Alicante, 1993).—NS/LK/DM

Esposito, Michele, Italian composer, pianist, and conductor; b. Castellammare di Stabia, near Naples, Sept. 29, 1855; d. Florence, Nov. 23, 1929. He studied at the Cons. San Pietro e Majella at Naples with Cesi (piano) and Serrao (theory). For a time he gave piano concerts in Italy. From 1878 to 1882 he was in Paris, and in 1882 he was engaged as a piano teacher at the Royal Irish Academy of Music in Dublin. He organized the Dublin Orch. Soc. in 1899 and conducted it until 1914, and again in 1927. He held the honorary degree of Mus.Doc. of Trinity Coll., Dublin. He composed several works on Irish subjects, including the Irish operetta, *The Post Bag* (London, Jan. 27, 1902), incidental music for *The Tinker and the Fairy* (Dublin, 1910), *Suite of Irish Dances* for Orch., 2 Irish rhapsodies, and several arrangements of Irish melodies. He received 1st prizes for his cantata *Deirdre* (Irish Festival, Dublin, 1897) and *Irish Symphony* (Irish Festival, Dublin, 1902). His other works include 2 string quartets, 2 violin sonatas, cello sonatas, etc. —NS/LK/DM

Esquivel Barahona, Juan (de), significant Spanish composer; b. Ciudad Rodrigo, c. 1563; d. probably there, after 1613. He received training from Juan Navarro, the maestro de capilla at Ciudad Rodrigo Cathedral, whom he succeeded in that position in 1608. He was one of the leading Spanish composers of his era, and publ. a vol. of masses for 4 to 6 Voices (Salamanca, 1608) and 2 vols. of motets for 4 to 6 and 8 Voices (Salamanca, 1608, 1613).

BIBL.: R. Snow, *The 1613 Print of J. E. B.* (Detroit, 1979). —LK/DM

Esser, Heinrich, German conductor and composer; b. Mannheim, July 15, 1818; d. Salzburg, June 3, 1872. He was a student of Jakob Heinefetter (violin), Carl Eschborn (harmony), and Lachner in Mannheim, continuing his training with the latter in Munich. He completed his studies with Sechter in Vienna (1839–40). After serving as Konzertmeister of the Mannheim National Theater (1838–41), he went to Mainz as conductor of the Liedertafel (1841) and as Kapellmeister of the city (1845). He then was conductor of the Vienna Court Opera (1847–69).

WORKS: DRAMATIC Opera: *Sitas* (Mannheim, Dec. 26, 1840); *Thomas Riquiqui oder Die politische Heirath* (Frankfurt am Main, March 8, 1843); *Die zwei Prinzen* (Munich, April 10, 1845). **OTHER:** 5 syms.; 2 orch. suites; String Quartet; many vocal pieces.

BIBL.: M. Wöss, *H. E.: Eine Darstellung seines Lebens und Wirkens als Dirigent unter besonderer Berücksichtigungseiner Beziehung zu Richard Wagner* (diss., Univ. of Vienna, 1947); K. J. Müller, *H. E. als Komponist* (diss., Univ. of Mainz, 1969). —NS/LK/DM

Essipoff (Essipova), Anna, famous Russian pianist and pedagogue; b. St. Petersburg, Feb. 13, 1851; d. there, Aug. 18, 1914. She was a pupil of Leschetizky, whom she married in 1880 and divorced in 1892. She made her debut in St. Petersburg, and subsequently made long concert tours throughout Europe and in America. Her distinguishing artistic quality was a singing piano tone and "pearly" passage work. From 1870 to 1885 she gave 669 concerts. In 1893 she was engaged as a prof. of piano at the St. Petersburg Cons., where she taught until 1908. Many famous pianists and composers, Prokofiev among them, were her students. —NS/LK/DM

Esswood, Paul (Lawrence Vincent), English countertenor; b. West Bridgford, June 2, 1942. He studied with Gordon Clinton at the Royal Coll. of Music in London (1961-64), and then was a lay vicar at Westminster Abbey until 1971. In 1965 he made his formal debut as a countertenor in a BBC performance of Handel's *Messiah*; his operatic debut followed in Cavalli's *Erismena* in Berkeley, Calif., in 1968. In 1967 he co-founded the Pro Cantione Antiqua, an a cappella male vocal group, but he also continued to pursue his solo career, appearing at many major European festivals. He also was a prof. at the Royal Coll. of Music (1977–80) and at the Royal Academy of Music (from 1985). While he was best known for his performances of such early masters as Monteverdi, Cavalli, Purcell, Bach, and Handel, he also appeared in modern works, including the premieres of Penderecki's *Paradise Lost* (Chicago, Nov. 29, 1978) and Glass's *Akhnaten* (Stuttgart, March 24, 1984). —NS/LK/DM

Estefan, Gloria (Maria nee **Fajardo),** petite powerhouse Cuban expatriate who went from singing watered-down pop music in Spanish to become one of the most versatile and durable pop singers of the 1980s and 1990s; b. Havana, Cuba, Sept. 1, 1957. Jose Fajardo, a former Olympic wrestler, was a bodyguard for Samoza in the pre-revolutionary Cuban government. Like so many loyal Cuban expatriates, he couldn't give up his motherland without a fight. He was involved in the ill-fated Bay of Pigs invasion and became a "guest" of the Castro government for the next two years. Upon his release from a Cuban prison, he relocated to Miami and went to war for his new country, fighting in Vietnam. He spent the 12 years after his return dying from exposure to Agent Orange.

Gloria showed early talents as both a singer and songwriter. She entered the musical arena after she met Emilio Estefan, a member of a local Miami group, The Miami Latin Boys. Gloria's mother urged her to sing a couple of songs with the band. When she did, the band hired her. Because they were no longer "boys," the group changed its name to the Miami Sound Machine. They made an album in 1978, spending $2,000 of their own money, which led to a contract with CBS International. For the label, they made four albums of mainstream, middle-of-the-road pop sung in Spanish. During the course of this time, Gloria and Emilio got married.

Emilio urged the record company to let him record at least a couple of tracks in English, believing the band had crossover potential. Emilio hooked up with three aspiring songwriter/producers, Joe Galdo, Lawrence Dermer, and Rafael Virgil, who were working on a project called *Salsasize*. Estefan liked one of their songs, which he felt could be that crossover hit: "Dr. Beat," a nifty fusion of upbeat Afro-Cuban swing and mainstream dance rhythms. Ironically, while the Sound Machine's Spanish language hits were largely MOR pop, the songs that set them on fire among mainstream (read: English-speaking) audiences around the world were distinctive for their Latin beat. "Dr. Beat" was a European hit in 1984 and even got some dance play in the U.S., but the album *The Eyes of Innocence* didn't chart.

The success of "Dr. Beat" led to a tour of Europe. At one show, after they ran through their repertoire, the audience still wouldn't let them off stage, so the group drew on their wedding background and played a Conga. The crowd went nuts. So, with the trio of Galdo, Dermer, and Virgil, now redubbed The Jerks, they wrote a high-tech dance song incorporating these rhythms: "Conga." The song launched the band into the U.S. Top Ten and sold gold. Suddenly, there was no stopping them. The next single, a similarly Latinesque dance track called "Bad Boys," also went gold, peaking at #8. The ballad "Words Get in The Way" did even better, rising to #5. "Falling in Love (Uh Oh)" only hit #25, but their 1986 album *Primitive Love* rose to #21 and triple-platinum.

Capitalizing on the newfound status as hit makers and Gloria's dynamic presence as a frontperson, in 1988 the band became Gloria Estefan and the Miami Sound Machine on their next release, *Let It Loose*. Musically, they picked up where they left off with the drum intensive "Rhythm Is Gonna Get You," which peaked at #5. The video for the song underlined the group's "exotic" Latin heritage, with Gloria adopting an almost tribal look in her dress and makeup. They followed this with the #36 "Betcha Say That." The ballad "Can't Stay Away from You" landed at #6, topping the adult contemporary chart. Cleverly, the B-side of this single was the same song, sung in Spanish, which topped the Latin charts. In this way, the Estefans kept both of their audiences happy, the traditional Spanish market and the new-found pop one. The song's success built up to the chart-topping ballad "Anything for You," which went gold. The fifth hit from the album, the bouncy "1-2-3," also topped the adult contemporary charts, while rising to #3 pop. *Let It Loose* wound up rising to #6 on the charts, staying in the Top 40 for nearly a year and equaling *Primitive Love*'s triple platinum status.

The Jerks left the fold after *Primitive Love*, striking out on their own (and landing a production deal with Island). People wondered who would take the reins, and Gloria and Emilio answered in several ways. Gloria wrote or cowrote most of the songs on the next album, 1989's *Cuts Both Ways*. Additionally, the pretense of a band was abandoned: The album was billed solely as a Gloria Estefan project. Many solo singers cannot equal the success they had when fronting a band; Estefan defied the odds by achieving enormous success with this first "solo" outing. Her first single, the dramatic ballad "Don't Wanna Lose You," went to #1 and sold gold. Again, it had a Spanish version on the B-side. The danceable concert opener, "Get on Your Feet," rose to #11. Another ballad, "Here We Are," rose to #6 and topped the adult contemporary charts for six weeks. *Cuts Both Ways* also went triple platinum, peaking at #8.

While touring to support the album, a serious accident nearly derailed Gloria's career. On their way to a concert in upstate N.Y., the group's tour bus was involved in an accident. Both Gloria and her 11-year-old son were badly hurt. For a while her doctors worried if she would walk again. Eventually, she had two metal rods surgically implanted in her back to support her spine. Thus began a long, painful process of recovery.

Gloria returned to performing in 1991 with the aptly titled ballad "Coming Out of the Dark" from her new album *Into the Light*. The single topped the charts for two weeks, and also was successful in a Spanish version. The spritely "Live for Loving You" only reached #22, despite a clever video clip featuring Estefan and her dog in various settings (and with various hairdos). The album sold double-platinum, hitting #5. She followed with a world tour in 1992. One of the shows, a benefit for the victims of Hurricane Andrew, which devastated her home turf in Fla., raised $4 million.

Well-situated in the pop market and an international star, Gloria once again went back to her roots, recording *Mi Tierra* in 1993, a tribute to Cuban music of the 1940s. The album sold platinum in America, rising to #27 on the charts, an unprecedented success for a Spanish language album. It also won Gloria her first Grammy Award, taking home the statuette for Best Tropical Album. In Spain, the album became the best-selling recording in the country's history.

In 1994, Gloria became pregnant again. With her health already precarious due to the accident, she had to take the year very slowly. She recorded an album of covers, *Hold Me, Thrill Me, Kiss Me*. Her version of the 1970s disco hit "Turn the Beat Around," also featured in the movie *The Specialist*, sold gold and hit #13. Because of Estefan's large size, her role in the video was taken by several (male) Gloria interpreters, gently mocking the convention of using a star's visual appeal to sell records. Her cover of "Everlasting Love" rose to #27. The album peaked at #9 and sold double-platinum. Not long after the album came out, so did Gloria and Emilio's daughter, Emily.

Gloria's next recording was another Spanish album, *Abriendo Puertas* (Open Doors). A more diversified al-

bum covering Spanish music of much of Latin America, it too won a Grammy for Best Tropical Album, reaching #67 and selling gold.

For the 1996 Olympics, Gloria and Diane Warren wrote the song "Reach." While it didn't crack the Top 40, stalling at 42, it was heard in billions of households around the world. Part of Gloria's *Destiny* album, it was one of the few songs not infused with a heavy dose of Latin rhythms. Its only hit, "I'm Never Giving You Up," fared only a little better than "Reach," topping out at #40. The album sold platinum and peaked at #23. Despite these lackluster sales, Gloria was named *Billboard's* #1 dance artist of 1996.

In 1998, Gloria went back to her roots again, only this time not her Latin roots. Instead, she took on dance music. What was originally slated to be an album of remixes became a set of steaming dance music, including "Heaven's What I Feel," which peaked at #23. The album did the same, in its first week on the charts, selling gold. She also made her film-acting debut, co-starring with Meryl Streep and Angela Bassett in Wes Craven's 1999 *Music of the Heart*.

Despite a slight slowing of her career in the mid-1990s, Estefan's strong talent—as vocalist, songwriter, and producer—plus her winning personality ensure that she will be a major star for years to come. That she has been able to achieve this without denying her Latino heritage in primarily whitebread America is a testimony to her determination and her capabilities.

DISC.: *Rio* (1978); *Eyes of Innocence* (1984); *Primitive Love* (1986); *A Toda Maquina* (1986); *Anything for You* (1988); *Let It Loose* (1988); *Cuts Both Ways* (1989); *Into the Light* (1991); *Mi Tierra* (1993); *Hold Me, Thrill Me, Kiss Me* (1994); *Christmas through Your Eyes* (1995); *Abriendo Puertas* (1995); *Destiny* (1996); *Gloria!* (1998); *Otra Vez* (1982).—**HB**

Estes, Simon (Lamont),

noted black American bass-baritone; b. Centerville, Iowa, Feb. 2, 1938. He sang in a local Baptist church choir as a child, then studied voice with Charles Kellis at the Univ. of Iowa and on scholarship at N.Y.'s Juilliard School of Music. He made his operatic debut as Ramfis at the Berlin Deutsche Oper (1965); after winning a silver medal at the Tchaikovsky Competition in Moscow (1966), he appeared with the San Francisco Opera and the Chicago Lyric Opera, but was mainly active as a concert artist. On June 10, 1976, he made his first appearance with the Metropolitan Opera as Oroveso in *Norma* during the company's visit to the Wolf Trap Farm Park in Vienna, Va. However, it was not until he sang the Dutchman at the Bayreuth Festival in 1978 that his remarkable vocal gifts began to be widely appreciated. He subsequently appeared as the Dutchman throughout Europe to notable acclaim. In 1980 he made his U.S. recital debut at N.Y.'s Carnegie Hall, and in 1981 returned to the Metropolitan Opera roster, singing Wotan opposite Birgit Nilsson's Brünnhilde in a concert performance of Act III of *Die Walküre* in N.Y. He finally made his formal stage debut with the company there as the Landgrave on Jan. 4, 1982. In 1985 he returned to sing Porgy in *Porgy and Bess*. He sang Wotan in the *Ring* cycle at the Metropolitan Opera from 1986 to 1988. He made his debut at the London Promenade Concerts in 1989. In 1990 he appeared in the title role of the musical *King* in London. In 1992 he appeared as Macbeth in Miami and as Wotan in Bonn. He portrayed Zaccaria at the Orange Festival in 1994. After singing Porgy in Cape Town in 1996, he appeared as Jochanaan in Toronto in 1998. His comprehensive operatic and concert repertoire ranges from Handel to spirituals.—NS/LK/DM

Esteve (Estebe) y Grimau, Pablo, Catalonian composer; b. probably in Barcelona, c. 1730; d. Madrid, June 4, 1794. He went to Madrid about 1760, and was maestro di cappella to the Duke of Osuna. In 1778 was appointed official composer for the municipal theaters of Madrid. He composed over 400 tonadillas, and some zarzuelas. His song *El jilguerito con pico de oro* was arranged for soprano and orch. by Joaquín Nin. —NS/LK/DM

Estévez, Antonio, Venezuelan composer; b. Calabozo, Jan. 3, 1916; d. Caracas, Nov. 26, 1988. He studied composition with Sojo and oboe at the Caracas Escuela de Música y Declamación (1934–44), composition with Copland at the Berkshire Music Center in Tanglewood, and electronic music in Paris. Among his works were *Suite Llanera* for Orch. (1942); *Concerto for Orchestra* (1949–50); choruses; piano pieces; *Cosmovibrafonía,* electronic pieces (1968).—NS/LK/DM

Estrada, Carlos, Uruguayan conductor, music educator, and composer; b. Montevideo, Sept. 15, 1909; d. there, May 7, 1970. He was a student in Montevideo of Adelina Pérez Montero (piano), Carlos Correa Luna (violin), and Manuel Fernández Espiro (harmony, counterpoint, and composition), and at the Paris Cons. of Roger-Ducasse and Büsser (composition), N. Gallon (counterpoint and fugue), and Paray, Wolff, and Gaubert (conducting). He was active in Montevideo as a conductor, and also was director of the National Cons. (1954-68). Among his works were *L'Annonce faite à Marie,* opera (1943), 2 syms. (1951, 1967), *Daniel,* oratorio (1942), chamber music, and piano pieces.—NS/LK/DM

Estrada, Julio, Mexican composer, theoretician, historian, and pedagogue; b. Mexico City (of exiled Spanish parents), April 10, 1943. He studied in Mexico with del Castillo, de Elías, de Tercero, and Julian Orbón (1955–63), in Germany with Gerhard Muench (1963–65), and in Paris (1965–69) with Boulanger, Barraine, Raffi Ourgandjian, Messiaen, Jean E. Marie, Pousseur, and Xenakis; then returned briefly to Germany, where he studied with Stockhausen at the Kölner Kurse für Neue Musik and with Ligeti at the Darmstadter Musikferienkurse. Upon his return to Mexico in 1970, he worked at Radio Universidad. He created several new-music ensembles, including Pro-Música Nueva and Compañía Musical de Repertorio Nuevo, introducing to Mexico the works of Cage, Ligeti, Oliveros, Riley, Stockhausen, and others. From 1973 he taught in the Escuela Nacional de Mñsica at the Universidad Nacional Autónoma de México. He was the first full-time music researcher at the Instituto de Investigaciones Estéticas (from 1976)

and the first music scholar to be appointed by the Mexican Education Ministry as Investigador Nacional (1984–87; 1987–90). He was general ed. of *La música de Mexico* (10 vols., 1984); he also publ. a collection of essays on new Latin American and Mexican music, *Reunión entre tiemps* (1990). His work with Jorge Gil in the Finite Group's Theory and Boolean Algebra Applications in Music (resulting in *Música y teoriá de Grupos Finitos, 3 variables booleanas* [1984]) was the first instance in Mexico in which musicians used computers as both a theoretical and a precompositional tool. Estrada also posited his general theory of intervallic cycles as a hierarchical system applied to musical systems based on scales in his *El espectro interválico, una teoría general de la interválica y sus aplicaciones al estudio precomposicional y al análisis musical del gregoriano a la música actual* (1990). He conceives of musical composition as a field where new solutions can be obtained from an objective order and organization according to its inner characteristics of discontinuity or continuity; his own compositions demand the invention of new technical and theoretical models coming out of "the primordial needs of fantasy." Profoundly political, Estrada identifies the act of composition with the act of liberation, with "the permissiveness of musical ideas becoming at the same time the powerful exigency of a true, almost phonographic representation of each detail belonging to sounds already internally experienced."

WORKS: *Persona* (1969); *Solo* (1970); *Memorias, para teclado* (1971); *Melódica* (1973); *Canto mnémico, fuga en 4 dimensiones* (1973; rev. 1983); *Canto tejido* for Piano (1974); *Canto naciente* for 3 Trumpets, 2 Cornets, 2 Trombones, and Tuba (1975–78); *Canto oculto* for Violin (1977); *Canto alterno* for Cello (1978); *Diario* for 15 Stringed Instruments (1980); *eua'on I* for Tape (1981) and *II* for Orch. (1983); *eolo'oolin* for 6 Percussionists (1981–82); *yuunohui'yei* for Cello (1983); *ishini'ioni* for String Quartet (1984–90); *yuunohui'nahui* for Double Bass (1985); *yuunohui'ce* for Violin (1990); *yuunohui'ome* for Viola (1990).—NS/LK/DM

Etcheverry, Henri-Bertrand, French bass-baritone; b. Bordeaux, March 29, 1900; d. Paris, Nov. 14, 1960. He studied in Paris, where he made his operatic debut as Ceprano in *Rigoletto* at the Opéra in 1932; from 1937 he was a member of the Paris Opéra-Comique, and he also sang at London's Covent Garden (1937, 1949). He was greatly admired for his portrayal of Golaud; among his other notable roles were Don Giovanni, Wotan, Boris Godunov, and Gounod's Méphistophélès and Friar Lawrence.—NS/LK/DM

Etcheverry, Jésus, French conductor of Basque descent; b. Bordeaux, Nov. 14, 1911; d. Paris, Jan. 12, 1988. As a violin prodigy, he appeared as a soloist at an early age with the Casablanca orch. He later served as concertmaster of the Opéra orch. there, where he began his conducting career in 1944. After conducting opera in Nancy (1947–57), Tunis (1949–53), and Luxembourg (1948–57), he was chief conductor of the Paris Opéra-Comique (1957–72); he also conducted at the Paris Opéra (1966–72). He then was music director of the Nantes Opéra (1972–77) before conducting at the Nancy Théâtre (1977–79). As a guest conductor, he appeared in Germany, Switzerland, Italy, Spain, and England. —LK/DM

Etheridge, Melissa, bluesy rocker, a cross between Janis Joplin and Bruce Springsteen, b. Leavenworth, Kans, May 29, 1961. Melissa Etheridge's career broke just as the early 1980s album rock wave crested. She was the right artist at the right time with the right song, a bluesy rocker, "Bring Me Some Water." While the tune didn't hit the pop charts, it started Etheridge on the road to stardom.

Etheridge was born and raised in Leavenworth, Kans., a place she claimed instilled her with big dreams and small-town sensibility. She attended the Berklee Coll. of music in Boston, leaving after two years for L.A. By 1984, she had attracted a good-sized following. A&M hired her as a songwriter. She worked with Nick Nolte, teaching him how to sing for the film *Weeds*. She also contributed to the soundtrack. She played clubs around L.A., and Island Records founder Chris Blackwell caught her one night in Long Beach and signed her.

Etheridge went to work on her debut, but the overblown album she left the studio with didn't thrill her or Blackwell. Blackwell sent her back and she re-recorded a stripped-down version of the album in four days. The album produced the rock hit "Bring Me Some Water," which she performed on the Grammys. The album went platinum and topped out at #22.

Etheridge spent much of the next two years on the road, although she did take time to record a track for the 1990 film *Welcome Home Roxy Carmichael*, probably a leftover from the sessions she was doing for her next album, 1989's *Brave and Crazy*. The album lacked a "power track" like "Bring Me Some Water," but had star power with guest artists like U2's Bono. The album also went platinum and topped out at #22. After another two years on the road, Etheridge put out her third album, *Never Enough*. It peaked at #21 and went gold, but after three albums, Etheridge was beginning to get respect. She appeared on both the *Tonight Show* and *Late Night with David Letterman*.

Always an outspoken advocate for women's rights and other causes, Etheridge attended the Triangle Ball, a gay and lesbian party celebrating the Clinton inauguration in 1992. At the urging of her friend k.d. Lang, Etheridge publicly announced that she was a lesbian. Although this might have seemed like a public relations disaster, it seemed to help in Etheridge's case. Less than two months later, she took home a Grammy Award for Best Rock Vocal Performance, Female. She appeared in the film *Theresa's Tattoo*, contributing two songs to the soundtrack.

Less than a year after coming out, she released the Hugh Padgham produced *Yes, I Am*. It entered the charts at its peak of #16, but stayed on the charts for two years. It took nearly a year for the first single, "Come to My Window," to reach the singles charts. While the archetypal power ballad only hit #25, it stayed on the chart for nearly a year. Where it took her earlier albums several years to go platinum, *Yes, I Am* was double platinum in less than a year. In 1995, she was asked to perform "Piece of my Heart" at the Rock and Roll Hall of Fame induction of Janis Joplin. She performed "Come to My Window" at the 1995 Grammy Awards and took home a little gold gramophone statu-ette for Best Female Rock Vocal Performance.

Ironically, her biggest hit, "I'm the Only One," was climbing the charts at this time. A sinuous piece of pop, it would hit #8 and top the Adult Contemporary Chart. The final single from the album to chart, "If I Wanted To," hit #16. All in all, the album went quintuple platinum.

Her next Padgham produced album, *Your Little Secret*, came out in December of 1995 and instantly hit #6 on the charts, and certified platinum in a little over a month. With Etheridge fronting a hard-rocking, stripped-down, four-piece band, the album featured more electric guitar, but the standout track was the ballad, "Nowhere to Go." She won the ASCAP award for co-songwriter of the year.

Etheridge continued to perform extensively and appear for causes ranging from gay rights to animal rights. Her sixth album, *Breakdown*, came out shortly after this was written.

DISC.: *Melissa Etheridge* (1988); *Brave and Crazy* (1989); *Never Enough* (1992); *Yes I Am* (1993); *Your Little Secret* (1995); *Breakdown* (1999).—**HB**

Etler, Alvin (Derald), American oboist, teacher, and composer; b. Battle Creek, Iowa, Feb. 19, 1913; d. Northampton, Mass., June 13, 1973. He studied at the Univ. of Ill., with Shepherd at Case Western Reserve Univ., and with Hindemith at Yale Univ. (M.B., 1944), where he also taught (1942–46). He later taught at Cornell Univ. (1946–47), the Univ. of Ill. (1947–49), and Smith Coll. (1949–73). He held 2 Guggenheim fellowships (1940, 1941). He was the author of *Making Music: An Introduction to Theory* (N.Y., 1974). His music is marked by stately formality of design.

WORKS: ORCH.: *Music* for Chamber Orch. (1938); 2 sinfoniettas (1940, 1941); *Passacaglia and Fugue* (1947); Concerto for String Quartet and Strings (1948); Sym. (1951); *Dramatic Overture* (1956); *Concerto for Orchestra* (1957); *Elegy* for Small Orch. (1959); Concerto for Wind Quintet and Orch. (1960; Tokyo, Oct. 18, 1962); *Triptych* (1961); Concerto for Clarinet and Chamber Ensemble (1962; N.Y., Dec. 20, 1965); Concerto for Brass Quintet, Strings, and Percussion (1967); Concerto for String Quartet and Orch. (Milwaukee, June 13, 1968); *Convivialities* (1968); Concerto for Cello and Chamber Group (N.Y., March 2, 1971). **CHAMBER:** Suite for Oboe, Violin, Viola, and Cello (1936); Sonata for Oboe, Clarinet, and Viola (1944); Bassoon Sonata (1951); 2 clarinet sonatas (1952, 1969); Oboe Sonata (1952); 2 wind quintets (1955, 1957); Cello Sonata (1956); Concerto for Violin and Wind Quintet (1958); Sonata for Viola and Harpsichord (1959); 2 string quartets (1963, 1965); Brass Quintet (1963); *Sonic Sequence* for Brass Quintet (1967). **VOCAL:** *Onomatopoesis* for Men's Chorus, Winds, Brass, and Percussion (1965).

BIBL.: P. Shelden, *A. E. (1913–1973); His Career and His Two Sonatas for Clarinet* (diss., Univ. of Md., 1978).—**NS/LK/DM**

Eto, Toshiya, Japanese violinist and teacher; b. Tokyo, Nov. 9, 1927. He was a student of Suzuki in Japan and of Zimbalist at the Curtis Inst. of Music in Philadelphia, where he taught (1953–61) before joining the Toho School of Music in Tokyo. In 1951 he made his U.S. debut at N.Y.'s Carnegie Hall and in 1968 his British debut in London.—**NS/LK/DM**

Ett, Kaspar, German organist and composer; b. Eresing, Jan. 5, 1788; d. Munich, May 16, 1847. From 1816, he was court organist at St. Michael's Church in Munich. He was active in reviving the church music of the 16th and 17th centuries; his own sacred compositions (of which but a few graduals and cantica sacra were printed) follow these early works in style. He composed 273 separate works. A complete enumeration is given in F. Bierling, *Kaspar Ett* (1906).—**NS/LK/DM**

Ettinger, Max (Markus Wolf), German conductor and composer; b. Lemberg, Dec. 27, 1874; d. Basel, July 19, 1951. He studied with Herzogenberg in Berlin and with Thuille and Rheinberger at the Munich Akademie der Tonkunst. After conducting in Munich (1900–1920), Leipzig (1920–29), and Berlin (1929–33), he settled in Switzerland in 1938.

WORKS: DRAMATIC: O p e r a : *Judith* (Nuremberg, Nov. 24, 1921); *Der eifersüchtige Trinker* (Nuremberg, Feb. 7, 1925); *Juana* (Nuremberg, Feb. 7, 1925); *Clavigo* (Leipzig, Oct. 19, 1926); *Frühlings Erwachen* (Leipzig, April 14, 1928); *Dolores* (1930–31). V O C A L : *Weisheit des Orients,* oratorio for 4 Soloists, Chorus, and Orch. (1924); *Das Lied von Moses* for 4 Soloists, Chorus, and Orch. (1934–35); *Königen Esther* for Chorus (1940–41); *Jiddisch Leben* for Chorus (1942); *Jewish Requiem* (1947). O T H E R : Chamber music and songs.—**NS/LK/DM**

Eubanks, Robin, jazz trombonist; brother of Kevin Eubanks; b. Philadelphia, Oct. 25, 1955. At the age of eight, he began playing the trombone and then through high school and college studied theory, harmony, and arranging. After graduating cum laude from the Univ. of the Arts in Philadelphia, he moved to N.Y. From there he was Music Director for Art Blakey and the Jazz Messengers, and did composing and performing for McCoy Tyner's Big Band, and Slide Hampton's Jazz Masters. He toured and recorded with the Rolling Stones, Talking Heads, and Barbara Streisand (on her 1994 tour). He has performed on several television shows and specials, including *The Tonight Show,* featuring Jay Leno, *Saturday Night Live,* the *Grammy Awards,* and *Motown at the Apollo,* and has worked on several projects for Broadway and film. He is currently a member of Dave Holland's Quintet. He also leads his own groups, which have toured Europe and Japan. He toured the European Festivals for the month of July 1999 as a member of the Elvin Jones Jazz Machine. He was appointed Assistant Professor of Jazz Trombone at the Oberlin Coll. Cons. of Music (in 1997). He is also on the faculty at the Manhattan School of Music and adjunct faculty at the Univ. of the Arts in Philadelphia. He teaches privately in N.Y. and has taught and delivered seminars at universities and colleges throughout the world, and is a national clinician for Yamaha Musical Instruments. He is a chief proponent in developing the sound and utilization of the electric trombone.

DISC.: *Different Perspectives* (1988); *Dedication* (1989); *Karma* (1990); *Mental Images* (1994); *Wake Up Call* (1997); *J. J. Johnson: Brass Orch.* (1997).—**LP**

Euclid, famous Greek mathematician who flourished in Alexandria c.300 B.C. Among the works attributed to him is a vol. on the elements of music, which most likely contains some material not by Euclid. See his writings as ed. by J. Heiberg (8 vols. and suppl., 1916). —**NS/LK/DM**

Eulenburg, Ernst (Emil Alexander), German music publisher, father of **Kurt Eulenburg;** b. Berlin, Nov. 30, 1847; d. Leipzig, Sept. 11, 1926. He studied at the Leipzig Cons. In 1874 he established in Leipzig the publishing house bearing his name, and after his acquisition of Payne's *Kleine Partitur-Ausgabe* (1891), he enormously increased the scope of that publication so that large orch. scores could be included. Upon his death the firm was taken over by his son.—**NS/LK/DM**

Eulenburg, Kurt, German music publisher, son of **Ernst (Emil Alexander) Eulenburg;** b. Berlin, Feb. 22, 1879; d. London, April 10, 1982 (at the age of 103!). Apprenticed by his father, he joined the Eulenburg firm in 1911, and upon his father's death in 1926 became its sole owner. He extended the dept. of miniature scores and also publ. the original text ("Urtext") of many of Mozart's works, ed. by Alfred Einstein, Blume, Kroyer, and others. During World War II, he lived in Switzerland. He settled in London in 1945 and took over the management of the London branch of his publishing business. He retired in 1968.—**NS/LK/DM**

Euler, Leonard, great Swiss mathematician, scientist, and philosopher; b. Basel, April 15, 1707; d. St. Petersburg, Sept. 18, 1783. He studied with Johann Bernoulli at the Univ. of Basel. In 1727 he went to Russia, where he became a member of the St. Petersburg Academy of Sciences; in 1733 he succeeded Daniel Bernoulli in the chair of mathematics there. In 1741 he was called to Berlin by Friedrich the Great, where he was a member of the Academy until being invited to St. Petersburg by Catherine the Great in 1766. Although he became totally blind shortly thereafter, he continued to pursue his work until his death. In addition to his enormous output of writings on non-musical subjects, he wrote several valuable works on music theory and acoustics, the most important being *Tentamen novae theoriae musicae, ex certissimis harmoniae principiis dilucidae expositae* (St. Petersburg, 1739). He was the first to employ logarithms to explain differences in pitch. An *Opera omnia* began publication in 1911.

BIBL.: C. Smith, *L. E.'s Tentamen noviae theoriae musicae* (diss., Ind. Univ., 1960); H. Busch, *L. E.s Beitrag zur Musiktheorie* (diss., Univ. of Cologne, 1970).—**NS/LK/DM**

Europe, James Reese, famed pre-jazz bandleader, pianist, violinist; b. Mobile, Ala., Feb. 22, 1881; d. Boston, May 10, 1919. One of the most celebrated musicians of his day, he recorded arrangements of ragtime and dance numbers between 1913 and 1919, with perhaps a bit of improvisation, that provide an important picture of the music that was around while jazz was developing. His family moved to Washington, D.C., when he was 10. He studied music there, and first went to N.Y. in 1904. He toured as musical director for traveling shows, then organized the New Amsterdam Musical Association in N.Y. (1906), and subsequently formed the Clef Club Orch. Through the 1910s he led his own "Society Orch." which accompanied dancers Vernon and Irene Castle in "Watch Your Step" (1912). Then, as a lieutenant in the U.S. Army he directed the 369th infantry Regiment Band, known as The Hell-Fighters, which toured Europe during World War I. The band returned to the U.S.A. in February 1919 and began a triumphant tour of American cities. During a performance in Boston, Europe was stabbed while in his dressing-room by a snare-drummer in the band, Private Herbert Wright. He died shortly afterwards.

DISC.: *Featuring Noble Sissle* (1919); *James Reese Europe's 369th U.S. Infantry Regiment Band* (1919).

BIBL.: R. Badger, *A Life in Ragtime; The Biography of James Reese Europe* (N.Y., 1995).—JC/LP

Eurythmics, dynamic English duo that turned creative tension into great pop music. **MEMBERSHIP:** Annie Lennox, voc., kybd., flt. (b. Aberdeen, Scotland, Dec. 25, 1954); David Stewart, kybd., gtr., synth. (b. Aug. 9, 1952).

Dave Stewart met Annie Lennox while she was studying at the Royal Academy of Music and supporting herself as a waitress. Stewart was between bands and working on songs with guitarist Peet Coombes. One night Lennox served Stewart and Coombes dinner, and Stewart proposed to her on the spot. Lennox and Stewart became lovers and, together with Coombes, became the nucleus of a group called the Tourists. The band released three records in the two years they were together, creating an updated version of the Byrds's sound with Lennox's imposing personality and voice up front. They met with middling success in England and were widely ignored in the U.S.

Stewart and Lennox discovered they were such opposites they really couldn't go on seeing each other personally. Around the same time, the Tourists broke up. Ironically, now that they weren't together romantically, Stewart and Lennox discovered that they could write together. They decided to continue performing together, taking the name Eurythmics from the famous early 20th century movement analyst, Emile Jaques-Dalcroze. They recorded their debut, *In the Garden*, in Germany with members of the progressive synthesizer-based band Can, along with Blondie drummer Clem Burke. It didn't sell well on either side of the Atlantic.

Deciding to give it one more shot, Stewart set up a home studio and he and Lennox recorded *Sweet Dreams (Are Made of This)*, continuing in the electro-pop vein. Although the initial single, "Love Is a Stranger" didn't make much noise when released in advance of the album, the title track exploded on both sides of the Atlantic, largely thanks to its slightly gender-bending video. (In one sequence, Lennox appeared with close-cropped, bright orange-dyed hair, in a man's suit, and holding a riding crop.) The single topped the U.S. charts and went gold. The re-released "Love Is a Stranger" was also successful, reaching #23. The album also went gold.

Fueled by this success, they recorded *Touch*. The album spun off the hits "Here Comes the Rain Again," which rose to #4. "Who's That Girl" rose to #21 and "Right By Your Side" charted at #29. The album went platinum and topped out at #7. They also cut the music for the soundtrack to the film *1984*. However, the director opted instead for more traditional movie music by Dominic Muldowny and used only their song "Sexcrime." The film stiffed, as did the duo's soundtrack album. Too many radio stations in the States found the song "Sexcrime" objectionable, but it did hit #10 in England.

The band rebounded with 1985's *Be Yourself Tonight*. Lennox duetted soulfully with Aretha Franklin on "Sisters Are Doin' It for Themselves," which hit #18. "Would I Lie to You" hit #5 and "There Must Be an Angel (Playing with My Heart)" rose to #22. The album went platinum and went to #9.

If nothing else, the follow-up, 1986's *Revenge*, followed the soul path even harder. However, the single "Missionary Man" only reached #14, and the album topped out at #14, going gold. With the group starting to lose commercial steam, Stewart took the production chops he'd honed with the Eurythmics and the Tourists and plied them for Mick Jagger and Bob Dylan, among others. Lennox tried some acting in the film *Revolution* and the TV movie *The Room*.

While they remained popular at home, their next album, 1987's *Savage*, only reached #41 on the U.S. charts, with no singles reaching the Top 40. Lennox, however, had a #9 hit duetting with Al Green on "Put a Little Love in Your Heart" on the soundtrack to the film *Scrooged*. Their 1989 album, *We Too Are One* reached #34 and spawned their first single in three years, "Don't Ask Me Why," which spent a disappointing week at #40, despite the album topping the charts in England.

While Eurythmics never officially disbanded, Lennox went on to record two double-platinum solo albums, *Diva* and *Medusa*. *Diva* offered the #34 hit "Why" and the #14 "Walking on Broken Glass" in 1992. The song was propelled by a nifty video in which Lennox appeared in full Renaissance regalia. The album rose to #27 in the U.S., and topped the English charts. Her 1995 *Medusa*, an album of covers, rose to #11 in the U.S., again topping the English charts on the strength of the single "No More I Love You's" and the overall quality of the songs. Stewart released several projects that didn't generate a great deal of excitement, including his Spiritual Cowboys band, which recorded a pair of records in 1990 and 1991. He did however continue as an in-demand producer, working with artists ranging from lite-jazz sax player Candy Dulfer to hard-pop artist Jon Bon Jovi. His *Sly-Fi* album was initially issued solely on the Internet in the U.S., taking advantage of the then-nascent form of music distribution. He also got into filmmaking, directing the movie *Honest*.

In the summer of 1999, the band announced they would return with an album and a tour. All proceeds from the tour were to go to Greenpeace and Amnesty International.

DISC.: *In the Garden* (1981), *Sweet Dreams (Are Made of This)*

(1983), *Touch* (1983), *Touch Dance* (1984), *1984 (For the Love of Big Brother)* (1984), *Be Yourself Tonight* (1985), *Revenge* (1986), *Savage* (1987), *We Too Are One* (1989), *Live 1983–1989* (1993), *Greatest Hits* (1998).—HB

Evangelisti, Franco, Italian composer; b. Rome, Jan 21, 1926; d. there, Jan. 28, 1980. He studied with Daniele Paris in Rome (1948–53) and Harald Genzmer at the Freiburg-im-Breisgau Hoschschule für Musik (1953–56). He also attended the Darmstadt summer courses in new music with Eimert and Stockhausen, and worked at the electronic music studios in Cologne and Warsaw. He was active in new music circles in Rome, where he became president of Nuova Consonanza in 1961. He taught there at the Accademia di Santa Cecilia (1968–72), the Conservatorio dell'Aquila (1969–75), and the Conservatorio Santa Cecilia (1974–80). Evangelisti was the author of the book *Dal silenzio ad una nuova musica* (Palermo, 1967).

WORKS: DRAMATIC: *Die Schachtel* (1963). ORCH.: *Variazioni* (1955); *Ordini* (1955); *Random or not Random* (1962); *Condensazioni* (1962); *3 strutture* (1963). CHAMBER: *4! for Violin and Piano* (1955); *Proiezioni sonore* for Piano (1956); *Proporzioni* for Flute (1958); *Aleatorio* for String Quartet (1960); *Spazio a 5* for Percussion, Voices, and Electronics (1961). ELECTRONIC: *Incontri di fasce sonore* (1957); *Campi integrati* (1959). —NS/LK/DM

Evans, Anne, esteemed English soprano; b. London, Aug. 20, 1941. She was a student of Ruth Packer at the Royal Coll. of Music in London and of Maria Carpi, Herbert Graf, and Lofti Mansouri at the Geneva Cons. After singing secondary roles at the Geneva Grand Théâtre, she returned to London in 1968 to join the Sadler's Wells Opera (later the English National Opera), where she was notably successful in such roles as Mimi, Tosca, Elsa, the Marschallin, and Sieglinde; she also appeared with the Welsh National Opera in Cardiff as Senta, Chrysothemis, the Empress, Donna Anna, and Brünnhilde (1985). Her Brünnhilde elicited critical acclaim when the company visited London's Covent Garden in 1986, which role she also sang at the Bayreuth Festival for the first time in 1989. On Feb. 6, 1992, she made her Metropolitan Opera debut in N.Y. as Elisabeth in *Tannhäuser*. In 1993 she appeared as Isolde with the Welsh National Opera in Cardiff, and then with the company at London's Covent Garden. She appeared as the Marschallin at the English National Opera in 1994. In 1996 she sang Brünnhilde at Covent Garden. She portrayed Isolde at the Semper Opera in Dresden in 1997.—NS/LK/DM

Evans, David (Emlyn), Welsh writer on music and composer; b. near Newcastle, Emlyn, Sept. 21, 1843; d. London, April 19, 1913. He was a student of John Roberts (1858). He won many prizes in the Eisteddfodau (Welsh music festivals), and also served as ed. of *Y Gerddorfa* (from 1872), *Cronicl y Cerddor* (1880-83), and *Y Cerddor* (from 1889). He publ. a collection of 500 Welsh airs as *Alawon Fy Ngwlad* (2 vols., 1896), cantatas, anthems, glees, and part songs.—NS/LK/DM

Evans, Edwin, Jr., English writer on music, son of **Edwin Evans Sr.**; b. London, Sept. 1, 1874; d. there,

March 3, 1945. He studied for a business career, and then was engaged in telegraphy, railroads, and finance from 1889 to 1913. He then devoted himself exclusively to musical pursuits. He was music critic of the *Pall Mall Gazette* (1912–23) and the *Daily Mail* (1933–45), as well as one of the founders of the ISCM (1922). In 1938 he was elected its president, retaining this post until his death. He wrote *Tchaikovsky* (London, 1906; 3rd ed., rev., 1966), *The Margin of Music* (London, 1924), and *Music and the Dance* (London, 1948).—NS/LK/DM

Evans, Edwin, Sr., English writer on music, father of **Edwin Evans Jr.**; b. London, 1844; d. there, Dec. 21, 1923. His most important writings were *Beethoven's Nine Symphonies, fully described and analyzed* (2 vols., London, 1923–24) and *Historical, Descriptive and Analytical Account of the Entire Works of Johannes Brahms* (4 vols., London, 1912, 1933, 1935, and 1936).—NS/LK/DM

Evans, Gil (originally, **Green, Ian Ernest Gilmore**), influential jazz arranger, composer, pianist, leader; famous for his collaborations with Miles Davis; b. Toronto, Canada, May 13, 1912; d. Cuernavaca, Mexico, March 20, 1988. He is considered among musicians and critics to have been one of the finest jazz composers, influencing Herbie Hancock, Maria Schneider (a personal protégé), and many others. He had a lower public profile than his reputation would suggest; this was due to his quiet personality, infrequent tours leading his own bands, his work behind the scenes and on soundtracks, and because he was a perfectionist with little regard for record company rehearsal budgets and thus did not work as much as he might have. Though his writing is known for its moody and evocative colors and voicings, it was various and his brass parts would often be fiendishly high and loud. As a result much rehearsal was needed; for example, hours of rehearsal for *Sketches of Spain* were recorded (some bits of the rehearsal are issued) and a complete take was never achieved, so the issued result is spliced from successful sections.

He lived in British Columbia, and Spokane, Wash., before settling in Calif. Mostly self-taught, he played in high school bands, and co-led the Briggs-Evans Orch. in 1933; this band formed the nucleus of the band that Evans led at Balboa Beach from 1936 until 1939, when vocalist Skinnay Ennis took the band over, with Evans remaining as staff-arranger for almost two years. In 1941 he moved to N.Y., where he joined Claude Thornhill as staff-arranger until serving in the U.S. Army in 1942. After his release, he re-joined Claude Thornhill. His basement flat was a meeting place for George Russell, Charlie Parker, Gerry Mulligan, and others. This led to several 1948 broadcasts and a series of recordings with Miles Davis, which won international acclaim. In 1959 Evans requested from George Avakian, who was then a producer at Columbia, the LPs in the "Columbia World Library of Folk and Primitive Music" (field recordings) in order to get ideas for an album of "international music." The album never came off as planned, but became *Sketches of Spain*. From the LP *Spanish Folk Music, Vol. XIV* of the Columbia series, he and Davis took "Saeta" (complete with the marching band at the beginning and end) and "The Pan Piper" (using almost the same album notes). Coltrane said he had spoken with Evans before his 1961 Africa/Brass date, but for unknown reasons Evans was not involved.

Later Evans led his own band, and did widespread freelance writing during the 1960s. On some sessions he played quiet but effective piano parts. He wrote for Peggy Lee, Tony Bennett, and Benny Goodman, among others. After a less active period as a bandleader, Evans again led his own big band in the U.S. and Europe during the 1970s, including a concert tour in 1978. He became more consistently visible and was able to keep fairly stable personnel together for long stretches of time; musicians wanted to work with him even when jobs and money were little. Evans experimented with electronics and free-jazz improvisatory principles. He admired Jimi Hendrix and arranged some of his pieces with plans for the guitarist to record with Evans's orchestra. When Hendrix died the pieces were eventually recorded with John Abercrombie and Ryo Kawasaki. In the last years of his life he did some film scoring (*The Color of Money*; *Absolute Beginners*), was reunited with Miles in the studios, and visited Brazil. In early 1988, he went to Cuernavaca to recuperate from prostate surgery, taking his synthesizer to work on new compositions. He died there of peritonitis resulting from the surgery.

DISC.: *Gil Evans and Ten* (1957); *Cannonball Adderley and Gil Evans* (1958); *Pacific Standard Time* (1958); *Great Jazz Standards* (1959); *Out of the Cool* (1960); *America's #1 Arranger* (1961); *Into the Hot* (1961); *Individualism of Gil Evans* (1963); *Guitar forms* (1964) *Blues in Orbit* (1969); *Gil Evans* (1969); *Where Flamingos Fly* (1971); *Svengali* (1973); *Gil Evans's Orchestra Plays the Music of Jimi Hendrix* (1974); *There Comes a Time* (1975); *Live '76* (1976); *Tokyo Concert* (1976); *Priestess* (1977); *Little Wing* (1978); *Live at the Royal Festival Hall* (1978); *Parabola* (1978); *Anti- Heroes* (1980); *Heroes* (1980); *British Orchestra* (1983); *Live at Sweet Basil, Vols. 1 & 2* (1984); *Bud & Bird* (1986); *Farewell* (1986); *Paris Blues* (1987); *Rhythm-A-Ning* (1987); *Collaboration* (1989).

BIBL.: Tetsuva Tajiri, *Gil Evans Discography, 1941–1982* (Tokyo, 1983); R. Horricks, *Svengali, or, The Orchestra Called G. E.* (N.Y., 1984); G. Evans, *The Gil Evans Collection: 15 Study and Sketch Scores from Gil's Manuscripts* (Milwaukee, 1997).—**LP**

Evans, Herschel, tenor saxophonist, clarinetist; b. Denton, Tex., 1909; d. N.Y., Feb. 9, 1939. He did early work in "T.N.T." (Alphonse Trent's Number Two) Band in Tex. (1926), then worked in The St. Louis Merrymakers (a Tex. band). He had brief spells with Edgar Battle, Terrence Holder, and with Sammy Holmes in Tex. before joining Troy Floyd's Band in Tex. (1929). He left Troy Floyd in 1931, and had stints with Grant Moore's Band, then worked with Benny Moten (February 1933–35), worked in Kansas City with Hot Lips Page's Band, moved on to Chicago, played briefly in Dave Peyton's Band (autumn 1935), then settled in Los Angeles. He played in Charlie Echols's Band in Los Angeles, also worked with Lionel Hampton's Band at the Paradise Cafe and with Buck Clayton's Band in the *Brownskin Revue*. He joined Count Basie (with Buck Clayton) in autumn 1936 and remained with Basie until

fatal illness. He had been unwell for some months and collapsed while working with Count Basie at the Crystal Ballroom in Hartford, Conn. He was admitted to the Wadsworth Hospital in N.Y. where he succumbed to a cardiac condition. Lester Young claimed in his last interview that "I was there when he died—paid his doctor bills and everything!" His burial took place in Los Angeles.—**JC/LP**

Evans, Richard (Joseph) Bunger, American composer and pianist; b. Allentown, Pa., June 1, 1942. During the first phase of his career, Evans used his adopted surname Bunger. From 1982 he has used his birth surname, Evans. He studied at Oberlin (Ohio) Coll. Cons. of Music (B.Mus., 1964), where he began composing seriously, and at the Univ. of Ill. (M.Mus., 1966). In 1968–69 he taught music theory at Oberlin Cons. He played jazz professionally in Los Angeles in 1969–70, and in 1970 was appointed to the faculty of Calif. State Univ., Dominguez Hills. From 1968 to 1982 he was the first concert pianist and lecturer to tour through the U.S. and Europe exclusively performing and advocating piano music by 20th century American composers. His interest in the new resources provided by the prepared piano especially led to his publ. of an illustrated vol., *The Well-Prepared Piano* (1973; rev. 1980), with a foreword by John Cage; it was also published in Japanese. Evans also evolved and published a comprehensive notational system called "Musicglyph," which incorporates standard musical notation and musical graphics indicating special instrumental techniques. He is the inventor of the "Bungerack," a flexible music holder for the piano, particularly convenient for pianists playing on the inside of the instrument with fingers, mallets, etc. His published compositions from this period include *Three Bolts Out of the Blues, Money Music,* and *Pianography* for Piano and Electronics, which he recorded for the BBC. He also unearthed, edited, and recorded numerous "lost" early works by Cage. In 1982 he was named "Outstanding Professor of the Year" by the State of Calif., and retired the same year from both music and teaching. For 10 years he worked as a real estate broker and developer in Calif., then returned to music full time in 1992. Since that time he has fulfilled numerous commissions for art songs with Irish and Italian texts, including *Yeats Song* and *Canzoni d',* numerous choral works, including *Music for a Medieval Christmas Feast* and a setting for band and chorus of the *Pledge of Allegiance,* chamber music in the "Celtic" style, including his well-known *Celtic Air (Kilmainham Goal),* commissioned and recorded by the Irish government, *The Rising,* oratorio with texts from the Irish Celtic Renaissance, and several complete works for music theater, including *Middas & Marigold, The Golden Touch, Tyburn Fair,* and *Treasure Island.* He currently divides his time between the West Coast and N.Y. Evans has 3 musical children: Berklee, a dancer (b.1977), Blake (b.1981), and Beka (b.1984). His other compositions include *Suite for Piano; 3 Songs on Poems of e.e. cummings; Three French Songs,* after Hugo; *Syzgy;* Music for *The Good Woman of Setzuan;* Music for *Love's Labors Lost* for Electronic Tape; *Five for Two* for Violin and Cello; Music for *Oedipus Rex* for Electronic Tape; *Sherwood Estates* (in collaboration with R. Dehmel); *Adirondack Air* for Violin and Piano or Orch.; songs with texts by R. Ruggiero and F. Pascale for 1 or 2 Voices and Piano or Orch., including *Al Tramonto, Che Bella Sera, Fiamme Mattutine,* and *Onde d'Amore; Musical Portraits,* suite for 2 Violins and Piano or Orch., based on tunes by John Sheahan; *The McDermott Roes,* suite for Strings and Optional Solo Instruments, based on tunes by Turlough O'Carolan; *Two Celtic Graces,* after R. Burns; *The Town Rat & The City Cat,* after Maureen Charlton, for 2 Singers and Piano, 4-Hands; *Moon on the Ruined Castle; Three Moore Songs,* after Thomas Moore; *Two Burns Songs,* after Robert Burns; *Renunciation,* after P. Pearse; *The Funeral of O'Donovan Rossa,* after P. Pearse; *The Famine Queen,* after Maude Gonne; *Lament for Thomas MacDonagh,* after F. Ledwidge; *Two Wexford Carols; Songs for Fathers,* after Christopher Weiss, including *Daffodils Sometimes, Still, Mother Says a Glacier,* and *This Poem is for You; An Inventory,* after John Winstanley; *I'll Always be Home on Christmas Morning,* after Evans & Schwartz; *Über allen Gipfellen ist Rüh,* after T. MacDonagh; *Christmas is Begun!; Festival Anthem on a French Carol;* numerous settings of poems by W.B. Yeats, including *When You Are Old and Grey, Fiddler of Dooney, A Toast: To Love, Song of the Wandering Aengus, Ghost of Roger Casement, Cradle Song,* and *He Wishes for the Cloths of Heaven.*—**NS/LK/DM**

Evans, Sir Geraint (Llewellyn),

distinguished Welsh baritone; b. Pontypridd, South Wales, Feb. 16, 1922; d. Aberystwyth, Sept. 19, 1992. He began to study voice in Cardiff when he was 17, and, after serving in the RAF during World War II, resumed his vocal studies in Hamburg with Theo Hermann; then studied with Fernando Carpi in Geneva and Walter Hyde at the Guildhall School of Music in London. He made his operatic debut as the Nightwatchman in *Die Meistersinger von Nürnberg* at London's Covent Garden (1948); thereafter was a leading member of the company. He also sang at the Glyndebourne Festivals (1949–61). In 1959 he made his U.S. debut with the San Francisco Opera; first appearances followed at Milan's La Scala (1960), the Vienna State Opera (1961), the Salzburg Festival (1962), N.Y.'s Metropolitan Opera (debut as Falstaff, March 25, 1964), and the Paris Opéra (1975). In 1984 he made his farewell operatic appearance as Dulcamara at Covent Garden. He was also active as an opera producer. In 1959 he was made a Commander of the Order of the British Empire and was knighted in 1969. With N. Goodwin, he publ. an entertaining autobiography, *Sir Geraint Evans: A Knight at the Opera* (London, 1984). His finest roles included Figaro, Leporello, Papageno, Beckmesser, Falstaff, Don Pasquale, and Wozzeck.—**NS/LK/DM**

Everding, August,

German opera director and administrator; b. Bottrop, Oct. 31, 1928; d. Munich, Jan. 27, 1999. He received training in piano and also took courses in Germanic studies, philosophy, theology, and dramaturgy at the univs. of Bonn and Munich. From 1959 he worked regularly at the Munich Kammerspiele, later serving as its Intendant (1963–73). From 1973 to 1977 he was Intendant at the Hamburg State Opera, and from 1977 to 1982 at the Bavarian State Opera in Munich, where he subsequently was Generalintendant of the Bavarian State Theater (1982–93). In 1993 he became founder-president of the Bavarian Theater Academy. In addition to staging operas during his tenures in Hamburg and Munich, he worked as a guest opera director at the Bayreuth Festival, the Savonlinna Festival, London's Covent Garden, N.Y.'s Metropolitan Opera, and other music centers. He publ. *Mir ist die Ehre widerfahren: An-Reden, Mit-Reden, Aus-Reden, Zu-Reden* (Munich, 1985), *Wenn für Romeo der letzte Vorhang fällt: Theater, Musik, Musiktheater: Zur aktuellen Kulturszene* (Munich, 1993), and, with A. Kluge, *Der Mann der 1000 Opern: Gespräche und Bilder* (Hamburg, 1998).

BIBL.: K. Seidel, *Die ganze Welt ist Bühne: A. E.* (Munich, 1988).—**NS/LK/DM**

Everly Brothers, The

the most popular vocal duo from the rock 'n' roll 1950s. **MEMBERSHIP:** Don Everly (b. Brownie, Ky., Feb. 1, 1937); Phil Everly (b. Brownie, Ky., Jan. 19, 1939, although some say Chicago). Don and Phil Everly were taught the guitar at an early age. Their parents, Ike and Margaret, were touring musicians and began hosting a weekly radio show on KMA in Shenandoah, Ia., in 1945. The brothers began appearing on *The Everly Family Show* when Don was eight and Phil six. During summers they toured the country circuit with their parents. In 1954, with the help of family friend Chet Atkins, Don was signed to a songwriting contract with Acuff-Rose Publishing, providing Kitty Wells with the major country hit "Thou Shalt Not Steal." A year later the brothers moved to Nashville, recording briefly for Columbia Records in late 1955. Early the following year, Wesley Rose became their manager, introducing them to the songwriting team of Felice and Boudleaux Bryant in 1957.

Signed to Cadence Records, the Everly Brothers scored their first hit in 1957 with "Bye Bye Love," written by the Bryants. The song, like many that followed, became a three-way hit, making the pop, R&B and country-western charts. "Wake Up Little Susie," written by the Bryants, topped all three charts, as did Boudleaux's "All I Have to Do Is Dream." The Bryants' "Problems" was both a pop smash and major country hit, and Boudleaux's "Bird Dog" was a top pop/country/R&B hit. They debuted at the Grande Ole Opry in May and appeared on CBS Television's *Ed Sullivan Show* in August. Their major hits through 1958 included Ray Charles's "This Little Girl of Mine" Roy Orbison's "Claudette," and Boudleaux's "Devoted to You." The Everly Brothers briefly visited Great Britain in early 1959 and continued their string of pop hits with "Take a Message to Mary" backed with "Poor Jenny" (both by the Bryants). Don's "('Til) I Kissed You," recorded with the Crickets, was a pop/country/R&B hit. The tender ballad "Let It Be Me" (their first recording with strings) and Phil's "When Will I Be Loved" became near-smashes on the pop charts.

In 1960 the Everly Brothers were the first artists signed to the newly formed Warner Brothers label, for a reported $1,000,000. They toured Great Britain in the spring of 1960 and moved to Hollywood in early 1961.

Without the services of producer Atkins, they scored a top pop/R&B hit with their own "Cathy's Clown," ultimately their biggest selling record. "So Sad" was a near-smash pop/R&B hit, "Walk Right Back" (by Sonny Curtis) a near-smash pop hit, and "Ebony Eyes" (by John D. Loudermilk) a near-smash pop/major country/major R&B hit. Parting company with Wesley Rose in the summer of 1961, the duo's last major pop hits came in 1962 with "Crying in the Rain" (written by Carole King and Howie Greenfield) and "That's Old Fashioned." The brothers joined the Marine Corps Reserve in late 1961, serving six months of active duty. They reunited with the Bryants for *Gone, Gone, Gone*, which yielded a moderate hit with their own title song, and recorded *Two Yanks in England* in London with the assistance of Jimmy Page plus Graham Nash, Allan Clarke and Tony Hicks of the Hollies. The brothers scored a British smash with "The Price of Love" in 1965, and a moderate American pop hit with "Bowling Green" in 1967.

The Everly Brothers' 1968 *Roots* was acclaimed as one of the finest early country-rock albums, and in 1970 they hosted *The Everly Brothers Show*, a summer replacement for *The Johnny Cash Show*, on ABC-TV. By the early 1970s they had switched to RCA Records, touring and recording the excellent 1972 set *Stories We Could Tell* with guitarist-keyboardist Warren Zevon and guitarist Waddy Wachtel. However, despite the inclusion of John Sebastian's title song, Rod Stewart's "Mandolin Wind," Jesse Winchester's "Brand New Tennessee Waltz" and Don's ironic "I'm Tired of Singing My Songs in Las Vegas," the album failed to sell, as did *Pass the Chicken and Listen*, recorded in Nashville with producer Chet Atkins.

On July 14, 1973, Phil Everly smashed his guitar and stormed off stage at Knotts Berry Farm in Buena Park, Calif., effectively ending the brothers' 28-year career. Both pursued solo careers and recorded solo albums. Don recorded *Sunset Towers* with British guitarist Albert Lee and scored his biggest solo hit in the country field with "Yesterday Just Passed My Way Again" in 1976. Phil performed on albums by John Sebastian, Dion, Warren Zevon (his debut), and J. D. Souther during the 1970s. In 1978 Phil made a cameo appearance in the Clint Eastwood film *Every Which Way But Loose*, performing "Don't Say You Don't Love Me No More" with co-star Sandra Locke. In 1983 Phil managed a moderate country hit with "Who's Gonna Keep Me Warm" and a major British hit with "She Means Nothing to Me," recorded with Cliff Richard.

Don and Phil ended their bitter separation in September 1983 with concerts at London's Royal Albert Hall. The following year they recorded *EB '84* with producer Dave Edmunds, guitarist Albert Lee and keyboardist Pete Wingfield (1975's "Eighteen with a Bullet"). The album produced a country/pop hit with Paul McCartney's "On the Wings of a Nightingale."

They toured with Lee and Wingfield in 1984 and 1986 and recorded *Born Yesterday* with Edmunds producing. The Everly Brothers were inducted into the Rock and Roll Hall of Fame in its inaugural year, 1986, and recorded *Some Hearts* with Brian and Dennis Wilson

of the Beach Boys in 1988. Don's daughter Erin was briefly married to Axl Rose of Guns N' Roses in 1990. In 1992 Don's son Edan recorded *Dead Flowers* with his band Edan for Hollywood Records. Despite a distinguished career, the Everly Brothers were without a record label by the mid 1990s.

The Everly Brothers introduced country harmonies into rock music, with Don usually singing tenor lead and Phil supplying high harmony. Their precise, assured harmonies influenced a whole generation of rock singers, from the Beatles to the Hollies, the Beach Boys to the Byrds, from Simon and Garfunkel to the Eagles. Aided immeasurably by the songwriting team of Felice and Boudleaux Bryant and the guitar playing and production of Chet Atkins, the Everly Brothers recorded songs on topics of concern to teenagers such as parents, school, and young love.

DISC.: *The Everly Brothers* (1958); *Songs Our Daddy Taught Us* (1958); *Best* (1959); *The Fabulous Style of the Everly Brothers* (1960); *It's Everly Time* (1960); *A Date with the Everly Brothers* (1960); *Both Sides of an Evening* (1961); *Folk Songs* (1962); *Instant Party* (1962); *Golden Hits* (1962); *Christmas with the Everly Brothers* (1962); *Sing Great Country Hits* (1963); *Very Best* (1964); *Rock 'n' Soul* (1965); *Gone, Gone, Gone* (1965); *Beat 'n' Soul* (1965); *In Our Image* (1965); *Two Yanks in England* (1966); *Hit Sound* (1967); *The Everly Brothers Sing* (1967); *Roots* (1968); *The Everly Brothers Show* (1970); *Stories We Could Tell* (1972); *Pass the Chicken and Listen* (1972); *Home Again* (1985); *The Reunion Concert* (1984); *EB '84* (1984); *Born Yesterday* (1985); *Some Hearts* (1985).

BIBL.: Phyllis Karpp, *Ike's Boys: The Story of the Everly Brothers* (Ann Arbor, Mich., 1988); Consuelo Dodge, *The Everly Brothers: Ladies Love Outlaws* (Starke, Fla., 1991).—**BH**

Evett, Robert, American composer and writer on music; b. Loveland, Colo., Nov. 30, 1922; d. Takoma Park, Md., Feb. 3, 1975. He studied with Roy Harris in Colorado Springs (1941–47) and with Persichetti at the Juilliard School of Music in N. Y. (1951–52). He was chairman of the music dept. of the Washington (D.C.) Inst. of Contemporary Arts (1947–50), and then was book ed. and music critic for the *New Republic* (1952–68). He was also a contributing critic on books and music for the *Washington Star* (1961–75), and then its book ed. (1970–75). His compositions were basically neo-Classical in nature, with an infusion of dissonant harmonic writing.

WORKS: ORCH.: Concertino (1952); Concerto for Small Orch. (1952); Cello Concerto (1954); *Variations* for Clarinet and Orch. (1955); Piano Concerto (1957); 3 syms.: No. 1 (1960), No. 2, *Billy Ascends*, for Voices and Orch. (Washington, D.C., May 7, 1965), and No. 3 (Washington, D.C., June 6, 1965); Harpsichord Concerto (Washington, D.C., April 25, 1961); *Anniversary Concerto 75* (Washington, D.C., Oct. 19, 1963); *The Windhover* for Bassoon and Orch. (Washington, D.C., May 20, 1971); *Monadnock*, dance music (1975). **CHAMBER:** Clarinet Sonata (1948); Piano Quintet (1954); Duo for Violin and Piano (1955); Cello Sonata (1955); Viola Sonata (1958); 2 violin sonatas (1960; 1975, unfinished); Piano Quartet (1961); Oboe Sonata (1964); *Fantasia on a Theme by Handel* for Piano, Violin, and Cello (1966). **KEYBOARD: P i a n o :** 5 *Capriccios* (1943–49); 4 sonatas (1945, 1952, 1953, 1956); *Chaconne* (1950); *Toccata* for 2 Pianos (1959); *Ricercare* for 2 Pianos (1961); 6 *Études* (1961). **O r g a n :** Trio Sonata (1953). **H a r p s i c h o r d :** Sonata (1961). **VO-**

CAL: *The Mask of Cain* for 2 Baritones, Soprano, and Harpsichord (1949); *Mass* for Voices and Organ (1950); *Billy in the Darbies* for Baritone, Clarinet, String Quartet, and Piano (1958); *The 5 Books of Life* for 2 Baritones, Soprano, and Harpsichord (1960); *Requiem* for Chorus (1973); choruses; songs. —NS/LK/DM

Evseyev, Sergei, Russian composer and pedagogue; b. Moscow, Jan. 24, 1893; d. there, March 16, 1956. He studied piano with Medtner as a youth, then entered the Moscow Cons., where he continued to study piano with Goldenweiser and also attended classes in composition with Taneyev; upon graduation, he devoted himself to teaching theory at the Moscow Cons. His compositions included 3 syms. (1925, 1933, 1943), 2 piano concertos (1932), Clarinet Concerto (1943), 2 string quartets (1935, 1945), Dramatic Sonata for Cello and Piano (1941), and many piano pieces.—NS/LK/DM

Evstatieva, Stefka, Bulgarian soprano; b. Rousse, May 7, 1947. She was a pupil of Elena Kiselova at the Bulgarian State Cons. in Sofia. In 1971 she made her operatic debut as Amelia at the Rousse Opera, where she was a member until 1979. She was also a member of the Bulgarian State Opera in Sofia from 1978. In 1980 she made her first appearance with the Royal Opera, Covent Garden, London as Desdemona during its visit to Manchester; in 1981 she sang with the company in London as Donna Elvira. After engagements in Berlin and Vienna in 1982, and in Milan and Paris in 1983, she made her Metropolitan Opera debut in N.Y. as Elisabeth in *Don Carlos* on April 9, 1984. In 1984 she appeared with the San Francisco Opera as Aida, which role she portrayed at the Savonlinna Festival in 1990. In 1992 she sang Tosca at the Teatro Colón in Buenos Aires, returning there as Maddalena in 1996. She was engaged as Elisabeth in *Don Carlos* in Montreal in 1998. She also toured as a concert artist. Among her other roles were Donna Elvira, Leonora, Mimi, Suor Angelica, Madeleine de Coigny, and Lisa in *The Queen of Spades.*—NS/LK/DM

Ewart, Douglas, Jamaican musician; b. Kingston, Jamaica, Sept. 13, 1946. As a child in Jamaica, the story goes, he was always building things, from go-carts, to kites, to musical instruments, fashioning drums and shakers, and even then seizing on the possibilities of flutes made from bamboo. When his family moved to Chicago in 1963, he attended vocational school where he studied tailoring. Music entered his life forcefully, though, through his association with the Association for the Advancement of Creative Musicians, which as part of its activist outreach, ran a music school where he studied with founding members Muhal Richard Abrams, Roscoe Mitchell, and Joseph Jarman. He has since blossomed both as a maker of music and musical instruments, particularly bamboo instruments. He has performed on flutes, saxophones, and electronics with many of his fellow Chicagoans, including recording sessions with pianist Abrams; saxophonists Chico Freeman, Henry Threadgill, and Anthony Braxton; and trombonist George Lewis, with whom he shared the eponymous duets project, *George Lewis/Douglas Ewart.*

He is also a sculptor and educator. He has been chairman of the AACM and participant in panels for the National Endowment for the Arts and other arts organizations. Under an NEA fellowship, he studied the crafting and playing of shakuhachi flutes in Japan for a year.

DISC.: *George Lewis/Douglas Ewart* (1979); *The Bamboo Forest* (1990); *Bamboo Meditations at Banff* (1994).—WKH

Ewen, David, Polish-born American writer on music; b. Lemberg, Nov. 26, 1907; d. Miami Beach, Dec. 28, 1985. He was taken to the U.S. in 1912 and pursued his training in N.Y. at City Coll. and Columbia Univ.; also studied theory with Max Persin. He was music ed. of *Reflex Magazine* (1928–29), *The American Hebrew* (1935), and *Cue* (1937–38), and then was active with the publ. firm of Allen, Towne, and Heath (1946–49). In 1965 he joined the faculty of the Univ. of Miami, which awarded him an honorary D.Mus. in 1974. In 1985 he received the ASCAP Award for Lifetime Achievement in Music. Ewen publ. more than 80 books during a career of some 50 years, including *The Book of Modern Composers* (1942; 3rd ed., 1961, as *The New Book of Modern Composers*), *Encyclopedia of the Opera* (1955; 2nd ed., rev., 1971 as *New Encyclopedia of the Opera*), *Panorama of American Popular Music* (1957), *Complete Book of the American Musical Theater* (1958; 3rd ed., rev., 1976 as *New Complete Book of the American Musical Theater*), *Encyclopedia of Concert Music* (1959), *The Story of America's Musical Theater* (1961; 2nd ed., rev., 1968), *Popular American Composers: From Revolutionary Times to the Present* (1962; suppl., 1972), *The Complete Book of Classical Music* (1963), *The Life and Death of Tin Pan Alley* (1964), *American Popular Songs: From the Revolutionary War to the Present* (1966), *Great Composers: 1300–1900* (1966), *Composers Since 1900* (1969; suppl., 1981), *Great Men of American Popular Song* (1970; 2nd ed., rev., 1972), *Mainstreams of Music* (4 vols., 1972–75), *All the Years of American Popular Music* (1977), *Musicians Since 1900* (1978), and *American Composers: A Biographical Dictionary* (1982).—NS/LK/DM

Ewing, Maria (Louise), noted American mezzo-soprano and soprano; b. Detroit, March 27, 1950. She commenced vocal training with Marjorie Gordon, continuing her studies with Steber at the Cleveland Inst. of Music (1968–70), and later with Tourel and O. Marzolla. In 1973 she made her professional debut at the Ravinia Festival with the Chicago Sym. Orch., and subsequently was engaged to appear with various U.S. opera houses and orchs.; she also appeared as a recitalist. On Oct. 14, 1976, she made her Metropolitan Opera debut in N.Y. as Cherubino, and returned there to sing such roles as Rosina, Dorabella, Mélisande, Blanche in *Les Dialogues des Carmélites*, and Carmen. In 1976 she made her first appearance at Milan's La Scala as Mélisande; in 1978 she made her Glyndebourne Festival debut as Dorabella, and returned there as a periodic guest. In 1986 she sang Salome in Los Angeles and appeared in *The Merry Widow* in Chicago in 1987. In 1988 she sang Salome at London's Covent Garden, a role she sang to enormous critical acclaim in Chicago that same year; she returned there as Tosca in 1989 and Susanna in 1991. After a dispute over artistic matters at the Metropolitan Opera in 1987, she refused to sing there until 1993 when she returned as Dido. After singing Katerina Ismailova there in 1994, she was engaged as Tosca at Covent Garden in 1995. In 1997 she returned to the Metropolitan Opera as Berg's Marie. She was married for a time to **Sir Peter Hall.—NS/LK/DM**

Exaudet, André-Joseph, French violinist and composer; b. Rouen, c. 1710; d. Paris, 1762. After serving as first violinist of the Académie de Musique in Rouen, he settled in Paris and played in the orchs. of the Opéra (1749–62) and the Concert Spirituel (1751–62). He was a fine violinist and an accomplished composer for his instrument; a minuet from his Trio Sonata No. 1, op.2, became quite popular.

WORKS: 6 sonatas for Violin, op.1 (Paris, 1744); 6 sonatas en trio for 2 Violins and Basso Continuo, op.2 (Paris, 1751); 6 sonatas for Violin and Basso Continuo, op.3 (c. 1766).—**LK/DM**

Excestre, William, English singer and composer who flourished c. 1390–1410. He was clerk of the Chapel Royal in 1393, and received a prebend in St. Stephen's, Westminster, in 1394. He was one of the composers whose music is contained in the Old Hall Manuscript. A Gloria, a Credo, and a Sanctus (all for 3 Voices) are extant.—**NS/LK/DM**

Exile, one of the longest-running bands in popular music, successfully making the switch from pop to country. Formed in 1963 in Lexington, Ky. **MEMBERSHIP:** The band has had over 25 members over the last 35 years, but the core band is J.P. (James Preston) Pennington, gtr., voc. (b. Berea, Ky., Jan. 22, 1949); Les Taylor, gtr., voc. (b. Oneida, Ky., Dec. 27, 1948); Buzz Cornelison, kybd; Jimmy Stokely, voc. (b. c. 1944, d. Aug. 12, 1985); Steve Goetzman, drm. (b. Louisville, Ky., Sept. 1, 1950); Sonny Lemaire, bs. (b. Fort Lee, Va., Sept. 16, 1946).

Formed while Stokely, Pennington, and Cornelison were in high school, by 1965, the Exiles (as they were then known) were touring with Dick Clark's Caravan of Stars, backing artists such as Tommy Roe. They lost the "s" in their name, and cut several records in the 1960s and early 1970s, although nothing caught fire. In the late 1970s, one of their demos fell into the hands of producer Mike Chapman, who had a string of successful English hits with Suzy Quatro and Gary Glitter. He produced two albums with the band, the second of which, *Mixed Emotions,* produced the monster hit "Kiss You All Over." The middle-of-the-road song with light funk underpinnings and a borderline dirty lyric stormed to #1, going gold in the U.S. and selling over five million copies worldwide. When they couldn't follow it up with anything nearly as successful from either *Mixed Emotions* (which hit #14 and went gold as well) or the follow-up albums, the group went back to Ky. to regroup.

Although Chapman and his partner Nicky Chinn wrote the hit, several of the band's own compositions were covered by country stars Alabama, Jane Fricke, Dave and Sugar, and Kenny Rogers. With that in mind,

the band started playing every night in the lounge at a bowling alley near their homes in Lexington, taking home $200 a week each. Stokely couldn't handle this and left the band. After about a year of perfecting their country sound, they came back as a country band in the mold of Alabama. Over the course of the next decade, the band put together a string of 10 country chart-toppers. By 1989, Pennington decided that 26 years on the road was enough and left the group. Taylor followed in favor of a solo career. The band came back again in the early 1990s, earning some country Top Tens, but the thrill was gone and they called it quits in 1994. By 1997, Pennington and Taylor were back on the road using the Exile name, with Goetzman as their manager.

DISC.: *Mixed Emotions* (1978), *All There Is* (1979), *Stage Pass* (1979), *Don't Leave Me This Way* (1980), *Heart & Soul* (1981), *Kentucky Hearts* (1984), *Hang On to Your Heart* (1985), *Shelter from the Night* (1987), *I Love Country* (1988), *Keeping It Country* (1990), *Still Standing* (1990), *Justice* (1991), *Latest & Greatest* (1995).—**HB**

Eximeno (y Pujades), Antonio, important Spanish writer on music; b. Valencia, Sept. 26, 1729; d. Rome, June 9, 1808. He entered the Soc. of Jesus at the age of 16. He became a prof. of rhetoric at the Univ. of Valencia, and in 1764 was appointed prof. of mathematics at the military academy in Segovia. When the Jesuits were expelled from Spain in 1767, he went to Rome, and in 1768 began to study music. In 1774 he publ. *Dell' origine e delle regole della musica colla storia del suo progresso, decadenza e rinnovazione* (Rome; Sp. tr. by Gutierrez, 3 vols., 1776), in which he protested against pedantic rules and argued that music should be based on the natural rules of prosody. His theories were strongly controverted, especially by Padre Martini. In answer to the latter, Eximeno publ. *Dubbio di Antonio Eximeno sopra il Saggio fondamentale, pratico di contrappunto del reverendissimo Padre Maestro Giambattista Martini* (Rome, 1775). His dictum that the national song should serve as a basis for the art-music of each country was taken up by Pedrell and led to the nationalist movement in modern Spanish music. Eximeno also wrote a satirical musical novel, *Don Lazarillo Vizcardi,* directed against the theories of Pietro Cerone (publ. by Barbieri, 2 vols., 1872–73).

BIBL.: F. Pedrell, *Padre A. E.* (Madrid, 1920).—**NS/LK/DM**

Expert, (Isidore-Norbert-) Henry, eminent French music librarian and editor; b. Bordeaux, May 12, 1863; d. Tourettes-sur-Loup, Alpes-Maritimes, Aug. 18, 1952. He settled in Paris in 1881 and studied with Franck and Gigout. He taught at the École Nationale de Musique Classique (1902–05) and at the École des Hautes Sociales. In 1909 he became deputy librarian and in 1921 chief librarian at the Paris Cons., retiring in 1933. He ed. the valuable collections *Les maîtres musiciens de la renaissance française* (23 vols., Paris, 1894–1908) and *Monuments de la musique française au temps de la renaissance* (10 vols., Paris, 1924–29; new ed. by B. Loth and J. Chailley, 1958 et seq.). The Assn. des Amis d'Henry Expert et de la Musique Française Ancienne was founded after his death and sponsored the publ. of his MS transcriptions as *Maîtres anciens de la musique française* (Paris, 1966 et seq.).—**NS/LK/DM**

Eybler, Joseph Leopold, Edler von, Austrian composer; b. Schwechat, near Vienna, Feb. 8, 1765; d. Schönbrunn, July 24, 1846. He began his musical training with his father. Settling in Vienna, he continued his studies at St. Stephen's choir school and also received instruction from Albrechtsberger (1776–79). Haydn became his friend and mentor, and he was also befriended by Mozart. From 1794 to 1824 he was choirmaster of the Schottenkloster. He also became music teacher at the court (1801) and was named deputy Hofkapellmeister under Salieri (1804), succeeding him as Hofkapellmeister (1824). In 1833 he suffered a stroke while conducting Mozart's *Requiem* and was compelled to retire. He was ennobled by the Emperor in 1835.

WORKS: DRAMATIC Opera: *Das Zauberschwert*. Oratorios: *Die Hirten bei der Krippe* (1794); *Die vier letzten Dirge* (1810). OTHER: Cantatas; 32 masses; Mass sections; *Requiem* (1825); 7 *Te Deums*; 33 offertories; 40 graduals; 15 hymns; 2 syms.; Clarinet Concerto (1798); chamber music; piano pieces; songs.

BIBL.: F. Oelsinger, *Die Kirchenmusikwerke J. E.s* (diss., Univ. of Vienna, 1932); R. Ricks, *The Published Works of J. E.* (diss., Catholic Univ. of America, 1967); H. Herrmann, *Thematische Verzeichnis der Werke von J. E.* (Munich and Salzburg, 1976). —NS/LK/DM

Eyck, Jacob van, Dutch carillonist, recorder player, teacher, and composer; b. c. 1589; d. Utrecht, March 26, 1657. He became carillonist in Utrecht in 1625. Eyck was the first to demonstrate that a bell's purity of sound is a direct consequence of its shape. He publ. the recorder collections *Euterpe oft Speel-goddine* (Amsterdam, 1644; 2nd ed., aug., 1649, as *Der fluyten lust-hof*, I) and *Der fluyten lust-hof*, II (Amsterdam, 1646), both of which were ed. by G. Vellekeep (Amsterdam, 1957–58).

BIBL.: R. van Baak Griggioen, *J. v. E.'s "Der Fluyten Lusthof" (1644–c. 1655)* (Utrecht, 1991).—LK/DM

Eyken (Eijken), Jan Albert van, Dutch organist, teacher, and composer; b. Amersfoort, April 26, 1823; d. Elberfeld, Sept. 24, 1868. He studied at the Leipzig Cons., and afterward at Dresden with Schneider. In 1848, he became organist of the Remonstrantenkerk in Amsterdam; in 1853, of the Zuyderkerk, and teacher at the music school in Rotterdam; in 1854, he became organist at Elberfeld. His organ pieces (150 chorales with introductions, 25 preludes, a toccata and fugue on B-A-C-H, 3 sonatas, variations, transcriptions, etc.) are well and favorably known.—NS/LK/DM

Eyser, Eberhard, German violist and composer; b. Kwidzyn, Poland, Aug. 1, 1932. He studied composition at the Hannover Hochschule für Musik (1952–57); his principal mentor was Fritz von Bloh, but he also attended the Salzburg Mozarteum, the Accademia Musicale Chigiana in Siena, and seminars with Xenakis, Maderna, and Scherchen. He was a violist in the Hannover Opera orch. (1956–57), the Stuttgart Radio Sym. Orch. (1957–61), and the Royal Theater orch. in Stockholm (from 1961).

WORKS: DRAMATIC: Opera: *Molonne*, chamber opera (Stockholm, Oct. 27, 1970); *Abu Said, Kalifens son* (1970–76;

Stockholm, March 10, 1976); *Sista resan*, chamber opera (1972–73; Vadstena, July 24, 1974); *Carmen 36*, chamber opera (1972–77); *Det djupa vattnet*, lyric scene (1979); *Sensommardag*, chamber opera (1979); *Sista dagen på jorden*, chamber opera (1979); *Altaret* (1980); *Bermuda-Triangeln* (1981); *Der letzte Tag auf Erden* (1979–82); *Rid i natt* (1982–91); *Destination Mars*, chamber opera (1983); *Das gläserne Wand*, chamber opera (1985); *Herr Karls likvaka*, madrigal-opera (1985–88); *The Picture of Dorian Gray* (1986); *Intimate Letters*, chamber opera (1989). Ballet: *Golgata* (1983). ORCH.: *Metastrophy* (1965); *Symphonie orientale* for Chamber Orch. (1974); Piano Concerto (1974–77); *Sima*, symphonic variations (1977); 3 sinfoniettas (1977, 1979, 1993); *Burloni* for Wind Orch. (1985); *Aneio noma* (1988); *Itabol* (1989); *Giuochi dodecafonici* for Wind Orch. (1990); *Stoccata* (1992); *Alba* for Strings (1995); *Ardogini* (1996); *Gatto nero*, "sinfonia confuziana" (1997). CHAMBER: *Podema* for String Quartet (1969); Sonata for Bass Clarinet, Cymbal, and Piano (1972); Sonata for Solo Bassoon (1973); *Ottoletto* for 8 Clarinets (1975); 5 saxophone quartets (1976–89); *Submarine Music* for Bass Clarinet and Tape (1979); *Umoett* for Guitar, 2 Violins, Viola, and Cello (1983); *Tonadas* for Horn, Violin, 2 Violas, and Cello (1986); *Quintette à la mode dodecaphonique* for Saxophones (1988); *Trio a la mode dodecaphonique* for Oboe, Alto Saxophone, and Cello (1989); Violin Sonata (1989); *Panteod* for String Quartet (1990); *Igomantra*, viola sonata (1992); *Litalò: Hommage à Arvo Pärt* for String Quartet (1992); *Espièglerie* for String Quartet (1994); *Pres* for Brass Quintet (1995); *L'usignuolo nel mio giardino* for String Quartet (1996); *Salmini* for String Quartet (1998); *Saronette* for Baritone Saxophone and Piano (1998); *Settimetto d'archi* for 2 Violins, 2 Violas, 2 Cellos, and 2 Double Basses (1999). VOCAL: *The Vineyard*, scenic cantata for Soloists and Orch. (1993); *Minimali* for Soprano, Cello, Piano, and String Orch. (1995). —NS/LK/DM

Eysler (actually, Eisler), Edmund, noted Austrian composer; b. Vienna, March 12, 1874; d. there, Oct. 4, 1949. He was a student of Door (piano), R. Fuchs (harmony and counterpoint), and J. N. Fuchs (composition) at the Vienna Cons. He made Vienna the center of his activities, beginning with the premiere of his operetta *Bruder Straubinger* (Feb. 20, 1903). Its waltz song *Kussen ist keine Sund* became celebrated. Success continued with *Pufferl* (Feb. 10, 1905), *Die Schützenliesel* (Oct. 7, 1905), *Künstlerblut* (Oct. 20, 1906), and *Vera Violetta* (Nov. 30, 1907). Further success attended his *Der unsterbliche Lump* (Oct. 14, 1910), *Der Natursänger* (Dec. 22, 1911), *Der Frauenfresser* (Dec. 23, 1911), *Der lachende Ehemann* (March 19, 1913), and *Ein Tag im Paradies* (Dec. 23, 1913). Even during World War I, his works were produced unabated: *Die--oder keine* (Oct. 9, 1915), *Wenn zwei sich lieben* (Oct. 29, 1915), *Warum geht's denn jetzt?* (July 5, 1916), *Hanni geht's tanzen* (Nov. 7, 1916), and *Graf Toni* (March 2, 1917). After the War, Eysler brought out a steady stream of additional scores. His greatest postwar success came with *Die goldene Meisterin* (Sept. 13, 1927), which was acclaimed as one of his finest scores. His last major success came with *Ihr erster Ball* (Nov. 21, 1929). As a Jew, Eysler was compelled to go into hiding during World War II. After the War, his status was restored as one of Vienna's master melodists of the operetta genre.

WORKS: DRAMATIC: Musical Theater (all first perf. in Vienna unless otherwise given): *Das Gastmahl des Lucullus* (Nov. 23, 1901); *Bruder Straubinger* (Feb. 20, 1903); *Pufferl* (Feb. 10, 1905); *Die Schützenliesel* (Oct. 7, 1905); *Phryne*

(Oct. 6, 1906); *Künstlerblut* (Oct. 20, 1906); *Vera Violetta* (Nov. 30, 1907); *Ein Tag auf dem Mars* (Jan. 17, 1908); *Das Glücksschweinchen* (June 26, 1908); *Johann der Zweite* (Oct. 3, 1908); *Der junge Papa* (Feb. 3, 1909); *Lumpus und Pumpus* (Jan. 21, 1910); *Der unsterbliche Lump* (Oct. 14, 1910); *Der Zirkuskind* (Feb. 18, 1911); *Der Natursänger* (Dec. 22, 1911); *Der Frauenfresser* (Dec. 23, 1911); *Der lachende Ehemann* (March 19, 1913); *Ein Tag im Paradies* (Dec. 23, 1913); *Komm, deutscher Brüder* (Oct. 4, 1914); *Der Kriegsberichterstatter* (Oct. 9, 1914; in collaboration with others); *Frühling am Rhein* (Oct. 10, 1914); *Der Durchgang der Venus* (Nov. 28, 1914); *Die—oder keine* (Oct. 9, 1915); *Wenn zwei sich lieben* (Oct. 29, 1915); *Das Zimmer der Pompadour* (Dec. 1, 1915); *Warum geht's denn jetzt?* (July 5, 1916); *Hanni geht's tanzen* (Nov. 7, 1916); *Der berühmte Gabriel* (Nov. 8, 1916); *Graf Toni* (March 2, 1917); *Der Aushilfsgatte* (Nov. 7, 1917); *Leute von heute* (June 22, 1918; in collaboration with R. Stolz and A. Werau); *Der dunkel Schatz* (Nov. 14, 1918); *Der fidele Geiger* (Jan. 17, 1919); *Rund um die Bühne* (March 1, 1920); *Der König heiratet* (April 1920); *Wer hat's gemacht* (Oct. 1, 1920); *La bella Mammina* (Rome, April 9, 1921; German version as *Die schöne Mama*, Vienna, Sept. 17, 1921); *Die fromme Helene* (Dec. 22, 1921); *Die Parliamentskathi* (April 15, 1922); *Fräulein Sopherl, die schöne vom Markt* (May 19, 1922); *Schummel macht alles* (July 1, 1922); *Drei auf einmal* (March 29, 1923); *Der ledige Schwiegersohn* (April 20, 1923); *Vierzehn Tage (im) Arrest* (June 16, 1923); *Lumpenlieschen* (May 21, 1923); *Das Land der Liebe* (Aug. 27, 1926); *Die goldene Meisterin* (Sept. 13, 1927); *Ihr erster Ball* (Nov. 21, 1929); *Das Strumpfband der Pompadour* (Augsburg, March 16, 1930); *Durchlaucht Mizzi* (Dec. 23, 1930); *Die schlimme Paulette* (Augsburg, March 1, 1931); *Zwei alte Wiener* (Feb. 12, 1932); *Die Rakete* (Innsbruck, Dec. 23, 1932); *Donauliebchen* (Dec. 25, 1932); *Das ist der erste Liebe(lei)* (Dec. 23, 1934); *Wiener Musik* (Dec. 22, 1947). **O p e r a :** *Der Hexenspiegel* (1900); *Hochzeitspräludium* (1946). **B a l l e t :** *Schlaraffenland* (1899). **O t h e r   D r a m a t i c :** Dances. **OTHER:** Piano pieces; songs.

BIBL.: K. Ewald, *E. E.: Ein Musiker aus Wien* (Vienna, 1934); R. Prosl, *E. E.* (Vienna, 1947).—**NS/LK/DM**

Ezaki, Kenjiro, Formosan-born Japanese composer; b. Tainan, Oct. 27, 1926. He studied at the Nihon Univ. in Tokyo (1953–57), at the Univ. of Ill. Experimental Music Studio, and with Ussachevsky at the Columbia- Princeton Electronic Music Center. Returning to Japan, he operated his own electronic music studio in Tokyo. In 1971 he was appointed to the faculty of the Univ. of Tokyo. He uses electronic sound in many of his works.

WORKS: *Discretion* for Woman's Voice (1961); *Concretion* for String Trio (1962); *Dim Light* for Chorus and 6 Instruments (1962); *Contention* for Soprano and Guitar (1963); *Presage* for Orch., in mobile configuration (1964); *Omen* for Modified Orch. (1964); Piano Trio (1964); *Pharos No. 1* and *No. 2* for Chorus, Flute, Clarinet, Oboe, and Piano (1965); *Music I* and *II* for Guitar and Tape (1967, 1971); *Ensemble* for Piano and 2 Playback Devices (1967); *Composition 5* for Flute, 2 Guitars, Cello, Percussion, and Soprano (1968); *Musicronics No. 1* for Piano, Percussion, and Tape (1968); *Zamuzara*, ballet music for Tape (1968); *Requiem 1970* for Soprano and Tape (1969); *Computer Music No. 1* (1969; composed on the FACOM 270–30 computer); *Liaison* for 12-channel Tape (1971).—**NS/LK/DM**

F

Fabbri, Inez (real name, **Agnes Schmidt**), Austrian- American soprano and operatic impresario; b. Vienna, Jan. 26, 1831; d. San Francisco, Aug. 30, 1909. She was trained in Vienna and made her operatic debut as Abigail in *Lucrezia Borgia* in Kaschau on Oct. 5, 1847. In 1857 she sang at the Hamburg Opera and then joined the traveling opera company of Richard Mulder (b. Amsterdam, Dec. 31, 1822; d. San Francisco, Dec. 22, 1874). She toured throughout North and South America with his company, eventually becoming his wife and adopting the professional name of Inez Fabbri. In 1860 she attracted much notice when she appeared at N.Y.'s Winter Gardens as a rival to Adelina Patti. After singing at the Frankfurt am Main Stadttheater (1864–70), she and her husband teamed up with the Theodore Habelmann-Karl Formes troupe in N.Y. in 1872, but that same year they went to San Francisco to produce operas until Mulder's death. In 1877 she married the German tenor Jacob Müller (1845–1901), and remained active as a singer until 1880. After teaching voice in Los Angeles (1892–99), she settled in San Francisco.—NS/LK/DM

Faber, Heinrich, German music theorist, teacher, and composer, known as **Magister Henricus Faber**; b. Lichtenfels, c. 1500; d. Ölsnitz, Saxony, Feb. 26, 1552. He was a teacher at the Benedictine monastery of St. George near Hamburg from 1538, and then entered the Univ. of Wittenberg in 1542, receiving the degree of Master of Liberal Arts in 1545. He was rector of the Cathedral School in Naumburg from 1544, and in 1551 he was appointed lecturer at Wittenberg Univ. He then was rector at Ölsnitz.

WRITINGS: *Compendiolum musicae pro incipientibus* (Braunschweig, 1548; reprinted many times and also issued in Ger. tr. as *Musica, Kurtzer Inhalt der Singkunst*, 1572; ed. by A. Gumpelzhaimer and publ. as *Compendium musicae pro illius artis tironibus*, 1591); *Ad musicam practicam introductio* (Nuremberg, 1550). *Musica poetica* (manuscript).—NS/LK/DM

Fabian (actually, **Forte, Fabiano**), one of the first teen idols of the rock and roll era, b. Philadelphia,

Feb. 6, 1943. One of a gaggle of cute pop singers, Fabian proved only slightly less durable than his Philadelphia neighbor, Frankie Avalon. Avalon was already recording for an upstart Philly label called Chancellor. The label's owners, Pete DeAngelis and Bob Marcucci, turned Avalon into a teen idol and wanted someone else on whom to work their magic. Avalon introduced them to his 15-year-old friend Fabiano Forte. Despite the fact that Forte had failed chorus, they decided to work with him. They went into the studio, and after a few failures, they came up with "I'm a Man." They poured their new artist into a sweater, tight chinos, and white bucks, and brought him to a Dick Clark sock hop where he proceeded to leave a trail of swooning teen-aged girls. The teen and movie magazines picked up on the good-looking singer with articles like "I Blew a Fuse over Fabian." The song became a modest (#31) hit in 1959. His next single, "Turn Me Loose" went to #9, boosted by appearances on Clark's *American Bandstand*. Two months later, "Tiger" surged to #3.

Music critics hated the teen pop trend and Fabian in particular. One described the singer as "an off-key, depraved cub scout." Yet, through 1959, Fabian could do no wrong. He signed a contract as an actor, appearing in the film *Hound Dog Man*, for which he also performed the title track, which rose to #9, and the #12 hit "This Friendly World." Through 1959 and 1960, he had three more minor hits including "Come and Get Me" (#29), "About This Thing Called Love" (#31), and "String Along" (#39). After that, the hits stopped coming. Fabian managed to continue acting, however, starring in the TV series *Bus Stop* and making a slew of films, including a handful of beach blanket movies and the John Wayne vehicle *North to Alaska*. Fabian continues to perform occasionally on the oldies circuit, and records from time to time.

WORKS: FILMS: *High Time* (1960); *North to Alaska* (1960); *Love in a Goldfish Bowl* (1961); *Five Weeks in a Balloon* (1962); *Mr. Hobbs Takes a Vacation* (1962); *Ride the Wild Surf* (1964); *Ten Little Indians* (1965); *Dear Brigitte* (1965); *Fireball 500* (1966); *Dr.*

Goldfoot and The Girl Bombs (1966); *Thunder Alley* (1967); *Maryjane* (1968); *The Wild Racers* (1968); *The Devil's Eight* (1969); *Little Laura and Big John* (1973); *Soul Hustler* (1976); *Getting Married* (1978); *Katie: Portrait of a Centerfold* (1978); *Disco Fever* (1978); *America's Music: Rock 'N' Roll V. 1* (1985); *America's Music: Rock 'N' Roll V. 2*; *Good Time Rock 'n Roll* (1985); *Kiss Daddy Goodbye* (1988); *Revenge of the Zombie* (1988).

DISC.: *Fabulous Fabian* (1959); *Hold That Tiger* (1959); *Good Old Summertime* (1960); *Facade Young & Wonderful* (1960); *The Hit Makers* (1960); *Rockin' Hot* (1961); *Fabian* (1974); *Fabulously Grateful* (1987); *The Tiger* (1987); *Schöne Lieder* (1997).—**HB**

Fabini, (Felix) Eduardo, Uruguayan violinist and composer; b. Solís del Mataojo, May 18, 1882; d. Montevideo, May 17, 1950. He studied violin at the Cons. la Lira in Montevideo, and later as a student of César Thomson (violin) and Auguste de Boeck (composition) at the Brussels Cons. (1900–03), winning 1st prize for violin. He then gave concerts as a violinist in South America and in the U.S. (1926). He eventually returned to Montevideo, where he was active as a composer and educator. His music is inspired entirely by South American folklore. The idiom is mildly modernistic, with lavish use of whole-tone scales and other external devices of Impressionism.

WORKS (all 1st perf. in Montevideo): **DRAMATIC: Ballet:** *Mburucuyá* (April 15, 1933); *Mañana de Reyes* (July 31, 1937). **ORCH.:** *Campo*, symphonic poem (April 29, 1922); *La isla de los Ceibos*, overture (Sept. 14, 1926); *Melga sinfónica* (Oct. 11, 1931); *Fantasia* for Violin and Orch. (Aug. 22, 1929). **OTHER:** Piano pieces; choral works; songs.

BIBL.: R. Lagarmilla, *E. F.* (Montevideo, 1954); G. Paraskevaídis, *E. F.: La obra sinfónica* (Montevideo, 1992). —**NS/LK/DM**

Fabri, Annibale Pio, famous Italian tenor, known as "Il Bolognese" and "Il Balino"; b. Bologna, 1697; d. Lisbon, Aug. 12, 1760. He studied with Pistocchi. While in the service of Prince Ruspoli in Rome, he sang female roles in operas by Caldara (1711); then made his public debut in Bologna in 1716. He quickly gained renown for his performances throughout Italy (1716–28); then was engaged by Handel for the King's Theatre in London, making his debut there in Handel's *Lotario* on Dec. 2, 1729, creating the role of Berengario. During his 2 seasons in London, he also created the roles of Handel's Emilio in *Partenope* (1730) and Alexander in *Poro* (1731). He subsequently appeared throughout Italy again, and then retired in Lisbon as a member of the royal chapel. He was also a composer; was elected to membership in the Accademia Filarmonica in Bologna in 1719 and from 1725 to 1750 served intermittently as its president. —**NS/LK/DM**

Fabricius, Johann Albert, eminent German bibliographer, son of **Werner Fabricius**; b. Leipzig, Nov. 11, 1668; d. Hamburg, April 30, 1736. A learned man, he was a prof. of elocution. He publ. important reference books, valuable to musicology for the information they contain on musical topics.

WRITINGS: *Thesaurus antiquitatum hebraicarum* (7 vols., 1713); *Bibliotheca latina mediae et infimae aetatis* (6 vols., 1712–22; 2nd ed., 1734); *Bibliotheca graeca sive notitia scriptorum veterum graecorum* (14 vols., 1705–28).—**NS/LK/DM**

Fabricius, Werner, German organist and composer, father of **Johann Albert Fabricius;** b. Itzehoe, April 10, 1633; d. Leipzig, Jan. 9, 1679. He began his musical studies with Paul Moth in Flensburg, and at age 12 went to Hamburg to continue his training with Thomas Selle and Heinrich Scheidemann. He then studied law, philosophy, and mathematics at the Univ. of Leipzig. He became organist and director of music at the Paulinerkirche of the Univ. there in 1656, and also was made organist of the city's Nicolaikirche in 1658. He publ. a treatise on organ building, *Unterricht wie man ein neu Orgelwerk in- und auswendig examiniren, und so viel wie möglich probiren soll* (Frankfurt am Main and Leipzig, 1656), and well as an instruction manual, *Manuductio zum General Bass bestehend aus lauter Excempeln* (Leipzig, 1675).

WORKS: SACRED: 100 melodies in *E.C. Homburgs geistlicher Lieder erster Theil* for 2 Voices and Basso Continuo (Jena, 1659); *Geistliche Arien, Dialogen, und Concerten...* for 4 to 6 Voices, Basso Continuo, and Instruments (Leipzig, 1662); other works in contemporary collections; also German and Latin motets in MS. **INSTRUMENTAL:** *Deliciae harmonicae oder Musikalische Ergötzung, von allerhand Paduaenen, Alemanden, Couranten, Balletten, Sarabanden von 5 Stimmen*, Basso Continuo, Viols or Other Instruments (Leipzig, 1656).

BIBL.: R. Mayer, *The Keyboard Tablature by W. F.* (diss., Roosevelt Univ., 1972).—**NS/LK/DM**

Fabrizi, Vincenzo, Italian composer; b. Naples, 1764; d. after 1812. After bringing out operas in Naples and Bologna, he went to Rome and was elected maestro di cappella at the Univ. in 1786. From then until 1788 he was musical director of Rome's Teatro Capranica, where he won particular success with his comic operas *La sposa invisibile* (Feb. 20, 1786) and *Il convitato di pietra*, also known as *Don Giovanni Tenorio ossia Il convitato di pietra* (Carnival 1787). The latter was performed throughout Europe with fine success.—**NS/LK/DM**

Faccio, Franco (Francesco Antonio), Italian composer and conductor; b. Verona, March 8, 1840; d. near Monza, July 21, 1891. His first teacher was G. Bernasconi. From 1855 to 1864 he studied at the Milan Cons. Arrigo Boito was his fellow pupil and friend, and together they wrote a vocal misterio, *Le Sorelle d'Italia*, which was produced by the students. The two served together under Garibaldi in 1866. Faccio's first opera was *I profughi fiamminghi* (La Scala, Milan, Nov. 11, 1863). This was followed by the Shakespearean opera *Amleto*, for which Boito wrote the libretto (Genoa, May 30, 1865). From 1866 to 1868 Faccio made a tour in Scandinavia as a sym. conductor. In 1868 he became a prof. at the Milan Cons., and in 1871 succeeded Terziani as conductor at La Scala. On April 25, 1886, he conducted for the 1,000th time there. His performances of Verdi's operas were regarded as most authentic; he gave the world premiere of *Otello* at La Scala (1887).

BIBL.: R. de Rensis, *F. F. e Verdi* (Milan, 1934).—**NS/LK/DM**

Fachiri, Adila, Hungarian violinist, grandniece of Joseph Joachim and sister of **Jelly d'Arányi;** b. Budapest, Feb. 26, 1886; d. Florence, Dec. 15, 1962. She studied with Joachim, and received from him a Stradivarius violin. In 1909 she settled in London, where she married Alexander Fachiri, a lawyer (1915). She appeared many times with her sister in duets. On April 3, 1930, they gave in London the first performance of Holst's Concerto for 2 Violins, written especially for them.

BIBL.: J. Macleod, *The Sisters d'Aranyi* (London, 1969). —NS/LK/DM

Faerber, Jörg, German conductor; b. Stuttgart, June 18, 1929. He studied at the Stuttgart Hochschule für Musik. He then began his career in Stuttgart as a theater conductor. In 1960 he founded the Württemberg Chamber Orch. in Heilbronn, and subsequently established it as one of the finest ensembles of its kind in Europe. He was especially distinguished as an interpreter of the Baroque repertoire.—NS/LK/DM

Fagan, Chris, jazz alto saxophonist; b. Seattle, Wash., July 11, 1962. After a number of moves throughout the U.S. and Europe, Fagan's family settled in Bloomington, Ind., where he grew up and began the saxophone. He attended Pomona Coll. in Claremont, Calif., in the early 1980s, and while there studied with John Carter, and came under the wings of Bobby Bradford and Charlie Shoemaker. Fagan made his professional debut with Dick Berk at The Becket Jazz Festival in 1984. In 1986, he traveled to N.Y. on an N.E.A. grant to study with David Murray. He pursued jazz in N.Y. until 1991, working with small groups as well as big bands at Visiones and Zanzibar with Jack McDuff, Dave Douglas, and Bill Warfield. He also made regular appearances at Greenwich Village's Blue Willow club with his own quartet. In 1991, he moved to Amsterdam to become guest saxophone instructor at the Sweelinck Cons. He returned to N.Y. in 1992, then to Seattle in 1995.

DISC.: *Lost Bohemia* (1992); *Signs of Life* (1997).—LP

Fagan, Gideon, South African conductor and composer; b. Somerset West, Cape Province, Nov. 3, 1904; d. Cape Town, March 21, 1980. He studied at the South African Coll. of Music in Cape Town with W.H. Bell (1916–22) and later in London at the Royal Coll. of Music (1922–26), where his teachers were Boult and Sargent (conducting) and Vaughan Williams (composition). Fagan established residence in London, where he led theatrical companies, arranged light music for broadcasts and films, and acted as guest conductor with the BBC and other orchs. In 1949 he returned to South Africa, where he became active as arranger and conductor at the Johannesburg Radio (SABC); later was its head of music (1963–66). He also taught composition and conducting at the Univ. of Cape Town (1967–73). In 1979 he received the Medal of Honor of the South African Academy for Science and Art.

WORKS: ORCH.: *Ilala,* symphonic poem (1941); *South African Folk-tune Suite* (1942); *5 Orchestral Pieces* (1948–49); *Concert Overture* (1954); *Heuwelkruin* (Hill Crest), suite for Piano and Orch. (1954); *Albany,* overture (1970); *Ex unitate vires,* symphonic sketch (1970); *Suite for Strings* (1974); *Karoosimfonie*

(1976–77). **CHAMBER:** *Nocturne* for Woodwinds and Strings (1926); Nonet (1958); *Quintics* for 5 Brasses (1975); piano pieces. **VOCAL:** *Tears,* symphonic poem for Soloist, Chorus, and Orch. (1954); *My Lewe,* 6 poems for Baritone, Flute, Clarinet, Piano, and String Quartet (1969); *Een vaderland,* oratorio (1977–78); songs.—NS/LK/DM

Fago, (Francesco) Nicola, esteemed Italian composer and pedagogue, known as **Il Tarantino**; b. Taranto, Feb. 26, 1677; d. Naples, Feb. 18, 1745. After initial training in Taranto, he settled in Naples and studied with Provenzale at the Cons. della Pietà dei Turchini (1693–95). He was primo maestro at the Cons. di Sant' Onofrio (1704–08) and at the Cons. della Pietà dei Turchini (1705–40), as well as maestro di cappella at the Tesoro de San Gennaro of the Cathedral (1709–31) and at the San Giacomo degli Spagnuoli Church (1736–45). His son, Lorenzo Fago (b. Naples, Aug. 13, 1704; d. there, April 30, 1793), an organist and composer, was also known as Il Tarantino. He studied with his father and then was organist of the primo coro of the chapel of the Tesoro di San Gennaro, where he was maestro di cappella (1731–66; 1771–81). He also was secondo (1747–44) and primo (1744–93) maestro at the Cons. della Pietà dei Turchini. Among his works were sacred pieces and cantatas. His son, Pasquale Fago (b. c. 1740; d. before 1795), was a composer of operas and maestro di cappella at the Tesoro di San Gennaro (1766–71).

WORKS: DRAMATIC: Opera: *Radamisto* (Piedimonte, 1707); *Astarto* (Naples, Dec. 24, 1709); *La Cassandra indovina* (Piedimonte, Oct. 26, 1711); *Lo Masiello* (Naples, 1712; Act 2 by M. Falco). **VOCAL: Oratorios:** *Faraone sommerso* (n.d.); *Il monte fiorito* (Naples, 1707); *Il sogno avventurato ovvero Il trionfo della Providenza* (Naples, 1711). **OTHER:** Requiem; 7 Magnificats; Masses; Stabat mater; 19 Psalms; 2 motets; secular cantatas and arias.

BIBL.: E. Faustini-Fasini, *N. F., "Il Tarantino" e la sua famiglia* (Taranto, 1931).—NS/LK/DM

Fahrbach, Philipp, Austrian conductor and composer; b. Vienna, Oct. 26, 1815; d. there, March 31, 1885. He joined the orch. of Johann Strauss Sr., when he was 10. At age 20, he organized his own orch., which proved popular until it was overshadowed by the orch. of Johann Strauss Jr. In later years, Fahrbach conducted a military band. He publ. about 400 dances and marches, many of which were popular in his day. M. Singer ed. his memoirs as *Alt-Wiener Erinnerungen* (Vienna, 1935). His son, Philipp Fahrbach (b. Vienna, Dec. 16, 1843; d. there, Feb. 15, 1894), was also a conductor and composer. He studied violin with Jakob Dont. After conducting his father's orch., he became a successful conductor and composer in his own right. He publ. some 350 dances and marches.—NS/LK/DM

Faignient, Noë, Flemish composer; b. c. 1540; d. Antwerp, c. 1595. He settled in Antwerp, where he was made a citizen in 1561 and was active as a music teacher. He publ. *Chansons, madrigales et motetz* for 4 to 6 voices (Antwerp, 1568). Other works were publ. in contemporary collections, and some have appeared in modern eds.—NS/LK/DM

Failoni, Sergio, Italian conductor; b. Verona, Dec. 18, 1890; d. Sopron, July 25, 1948. He received his musical education in Verona and Milan. He conducted opera throughout Italy, from 1932 making appearances at La Scala in Milan. From 1928 to 1947 he was chief conductor of the State Opera in Budapest. In 1947 he was invited to make his debut at the Metropolitan Opera in N.Y.; however, he suffered a stroke and died the following year. He was regarded as one of the leading interpreters of the Italian repertoire. —NS/LK/DM

Fain, Sammy (originally, **Samuel Feinberg**), durable American composer; b. N.Y., June 17, 1902; d. Los Angeles, Dec. 6, 1989. In a professional career lasting more than 50 years, Fain was rivaled only by Harry Warren as the most productive songwriter in Hollywood; his songs were used in more than a hundred features between the dawn of the sound era and the mid- 1970s. These efforts brought him 10 Academy Award nominations and two Oscars, for "Secret Love" and "Love Is a Many-Splendored Thing." Though he had less success on Broadway, he wrote the songs for the longest- running show up to its time, *Hellzapoppin*, and unlike many of his peers he did not abandon the theater for film. Many of his songs became record hits, and five sold over a million copies, including his two Oscar winners, "I Can Dream, Can't I?," "Dear Hearts and Gentle People," and "April Love." In addition, his "I'll Be Seeing You" was one of the most popular songs of the World War II era. His primary lyric collaborators were Irving Kahal and Paul Francis Webster, but he also worked with many of the major lyricists of his time, including Alan and Marilyn Bergman, Sammy Cahn, Howard Dietz, Al Dubin, Mack Gordon, E. Y. Harburg, and Ted Koehler.

The son of a cantor, Fain was a self-taught musician. After graduating from high school he found a job as a song plugger for a music publishing company, then launched a vaudeville and radio performing duo with Artie Dunn while trying to establish himself as a songwriter. "Hay-Long" (lyrics by comedians Eugene and Willie Howard) may have given him his first placement in a Broadway revue, *The Passing Show of 1921* (N.Y., Dec. 29, 1920), though it's not certain the song was performed onstage. The first definite interpolation Fain achieved was "In a Little French Café" (lyrics by Mitchell Parish), used in the revue *Chauve Souris* (N.Y., Feb. 1, 1922). His first published song came in 1924 with "Nobody Knows What a Red Headed Mama Can Do" (lyrics by Irving Mills and Al Dubin).

Fain met Kahal, a fellow vaudevillian, in 1927 and they formed a regular though not exclusive songwriting partnership. Their first successful collaboration was "Let a Smile Be Your Umbrella" (lyrics also by Francis Wheeler), which the still-active team of Fain and Dunn introduced in vaudeville and which was recorded for a hit in April 1928 by Roger Wolfe Kahn and His Orch. They broke into the movies with "Judy" (music and lyrics by Fain, Kahal, and Pierre Norman Connor), which was used in the film *Romance of the Underworld*, released at the end of 1928. In May, Gene Austin scored a hit with Fain and Kahal's "Wedding Bells Are Breaking Up That Old Gang of Mine" (lyrics also by Willie Raskin). Fain, meanwhile, had not yet given up the idea of a performing career, and in November he scored a minor hit with his recording of Joe Burke and Al Dubin's "Painting the Clouds with Sunshine."

Fain and Kahal signed to the Paramount film studio and contributed music to six movies released in 1930. Their most substantial work was for *Young Man of Manhattan*, released in April and starring Ginger Rogers; they wrote four of the songs (all cocomposed by Pierre Norman Connor). Their most successful effort for the year was "You Brought a New Kind of Love to Me" (music also by Connor), which Maurice Chevalier sang in *The Big Pond*, released in May. Chevalier also scored a hit recording of the song, although the most popular version was by Paul Whiteman and His Orch. with vocals by Bing Crosby.

Hollywood temporarily lost interest in movie musicals after 1930, and Fain and Kahal returned to Tin Pan Alley and Broadway in 1931. "When I Take My Sugar to Tea" (music and lyrics by Fain, Kahal, and Connor) became the Boswell Sisters' first hit in April, and Fain and Kahal wrote their first Broadway musical with *Everybody's Welcome* in the fall. Though no hits emerged from the show, it ran 139 performances.

Working apart from Kahal, Fain had two hits in the first half of 1932, "Was That the Human Thing to Do?" (lyrics by Joe Young), recorded most successfully by Bert Lown and His Orch., in February, and "Hummin' to Myself" (lyrics by Herb Magidson and Monty Siegel), the most popular version of which was by Johnny Hamp and His Orch., in May. He then signed a film contract with Warner Bros., and he and Young contributed two songs to *Crooner*, both of which became hits prior to the movie's release in August: "Now You've Got Me Worryin' for You," for Eddy Duchin and His Orch., and "Banking on the Weather," for Ted Black and His Orch.

The reestablished team of Fain and Kahal provided the songs for two Warner Bros. movie musicals in the fall of 1933, *Footlight Parade* and *College Coach*, and the former brought them a hit with "By a Waterfall," recorded with equal success by Guy Lombardo and His Royal Canadians and Leo Reisman and His Orch.

Hollywood's renewed enthusiasm for musicals was reflected in Fain and Kahal's busy schedule in 1934. They contributed to at least ten movies released during the year, Fain being the primary composer for four. *Mandalay*, released in February, contained "When Tomorrow Comes," recorded for a hit by Freddy Martin and His Orch. Among the five songs the team contributed to *Harold Teen* was a hit for Guy Lombardo in May, "How Do I Know It's Sunday?" The Mills Brothers had a hit with "Money in My Pockets" in June, though when they sang it in RKO's *Strictly Dynamite* the following month, it was called "Money in My Clothes." Fain added acting to his credits in August when he turned up in *Dames* playing a songwriter.

Fain and Kahal's last major screen effort for Warner Bros. was *Sweet Music* starring Rudy Vallée, released in February 1935, from which Victor Young and His Orch.

found a hit with "Ev'ry Day." They then moved to Paramount for the troubled production of Mae West's *Goin' to Town*, released in May.

After a relatively inactive 1936, Fain signed to RKO in 1937 and, with Lew Brown, wrote songs for *New Faces of 1937*, released in July. But his greatest success for the year was "That Old Feeling" (lyrics by Brown), featured in United Artists' *Vogues of 1938*, which despite its title was released in August 1937. Shep Fields and His Orch. took the song to the top of the hit parade in October, and it earned Fain his first Academy Award nomination.

Fain and Kahal reunited and returned to Broadway at the start of 1938 for the musical *Right This Way*. It ran only 15 performances, but two of its songs would be among Fain's most successful. "I Can Dream, Can't I?" was taken into the hit parade by Tommy Dorsey and His Orch. in February, after the show had closed, while "I'll Be Seeing You" would wait years for recognition.

The 1,404-performance run of the revue *Hellzapoppin*, which opened in the fall of 1938, generally is ascribed not to Fain and lyricist Charles Tobias's songs, but to the antics of the comedy team of (Ole) Olsen and (Chic) Johnson; in any case, it was the most successful Broadway musical in history until *Oklahoma!* came along.

Fain stayed in N.Y. to appear in the brief run of *Blackbirds of 1939* (N.Y., Feb. 11, 1939), to which he contributed a few songs with lyrics by Mitchell Parish. Parish was also the lyricist for "The Moon Is a Silver Dollar," which reached the hit parade in a recording by the Lawrence Welk orchestra in April. Fain was then hired to contribute the songs for what turned out to be the final edition of *George White's Scandals*, among them "Are You Havin' Any Fun?" (lyrics by Jack Yellen), actually used earlier in the second edition of the *Ziegfeld Follies of 1936* and taken into the hit parade in October by Tommy Dorsey. The show ran 120 performances.

Fain worked on two stage shows for the fall of 1940: the revue *Boys and Girls Together* starring comedian Ed Wynn, who was responsible for its run of 191 performances, and *She Had to Say Yes*, a musical on which Fain collaborated with Al Dubin that closed during previews in Philadelphia.

Fain married Sally Fox on June 18, 1941. They had one son and divorced in 1954. In the fall Fain collaborated with Jack Yellen on *Sons o' Fun*, a sequel to *Hellzapoppin* starring Olsen and Johnson; it ran 742 performances and featured some of the last lyrics written by Irving Kahal, who died Feb. 7, 1942.

Fain returned to Hollywood in 1943 and signed to MGM, getting his first credit for the Red Skelton film *I Dood It*, released in November, even though most of his songs were cut. Working with lyricist Ralph Freed, he had songs in five MGM features released in 1944, although the scores contained many interpolations. His big hit of the year was a surprise: spurred by the poignant separations necessitated by the war, "I'll Be Seeing You" enjoyed a massive revival, with Bing Crosby's recording hitting the top of the charts in July, beating out the reissue of an earlier recording by Tommy Dorsey featuring Frank Sinatra.

In 1945, Fain contributed to another three MGM features and to a film version of *George White's Scandals*

at RKO. He had songs in four MGM films in 1946, after which he briefly returned to Broadway for the 60-performance flop *Toplitzky of Notre Dame*. As a result he was less active on the MGM lot, contributing to only one 1947 feature, *This Time for Keeps*, released in December. He concluded his MGM contract by contributing "The Dickey-Bird Song" (lyrics by Howard Dietz) to the February 1948 release *Three Daring Daughters*; in May it became a Top Ten hit for Freddy Martin.

At the end of 1949, Fain enjoyed two major hits simultaneously. The Andrews Sisters revived "I Can Dream, Can't I?"; their recording topped the charts in January 1950, selling a million copies. Meanwhile, the newly written "Dear Hearts and Gentle People" (lyrics by Bob Hilliard, based on a note found in Stephen Foster's pocket at the time of his death) drew numerous recordings, the most popular of which were those by Bing Crosby (another million-seller) and Dinah Shore.

Fain wrote songs in 1950 for a couple of Broadway revues, notably *Alive and Kicking* (N.Y., Jan. 17, 1950), which represented his first work with Paul Francis Webster, who would become his lyric partner for much of the rest of his career. He also wrote songs for the Jimmy Durante feature *The Milkman* at Universal. In 1951 he had three very different works in release with three different lyricists. *Call Me Mister*, to which he contributed three songs with lyrics by Mack Gordon, opened in January, a typical service comedy starring Betty Grable. The politically oriented stage musical *Flahooley*, with lyrics by E. Y. Harburg, was a satire on the toy industry; it ran only 40 performances. Next, Fain teamed with Hilliard for the Walt Disney animated film *Alice in Wonderland*, which opened in July.

The long production periods required for animated films meant that Fain's next Disney project, *Peter Pan*, on which he collaborated with Sammy Cahn, was not released until February 1953. In the meantime he signed to Warner Bros. and wrote songs for a remake of *The Jazz Singer* with Jerry Seelen; it was released in January 1953. He had two Warner Bros. musicals for the fall: *Three Sailors and a Girl*, another collaboration with Cahn, in November; and, released two weeks earlier, *Calamity Jane*, starring Doris Day, his first major collaboration with Paul Francis Webster. "Secret Love," recorded by Day, became a #1 hit in February 1954, sold a million copies, and won the Academy Award for Best Song. (It also became a Top Ten country hit for Slim Whitman.)

Not surprisingly, Fain and Webster were assigned to the next Doris Day film for Warner Bros., *Lucky Me*, released in April 1954. They responded with a score that included "I Speak to the Stars," which Day recorded for a hit. In May the Four Aces revived "Wedding Bells Are Breaking Up That Old Gang of Mine" for a chart entry. The newly divorced Fain married Jane Fischer on Sept. 11, 1954; they divorced on May 22, 1957.

Fain completed his Warner Bros. contract with another Doris Day film, *Young at Heart*, released in January 1955, after which he worked for the studios on a freelance basis. Returning to Broadway, he collaborated with Dan Shapiro on the musical *Ankles Aweigh*, which failed to turn a profit despite a run of 176 performances. He and Webster wrote the title song for the film *Love Is a Many-Splendored Thing*, released in August; the Four Aces' recording topped the charts in October, selling a million copies, and the song won Fain his second Academy Award.

Fain and Webster contributed "If You Wanna See Mamie Tonight" to the May 1956 release *The Revolt of Mamie Stover*, resulting in a chart record for the Ames Brothers, and wrote the songs for the Dean Martin-Jerry Lewis comedy *Hollywood or Bust*, released in December. Their major assignment for 1957 was to write the songs for the Pat Boone movie *April Love*, released in November. Boone's recording of the title song went to #1 in December and sold a million copies; the soundtrack album spent three months in the charts; and "April Love" brought Fain his fourth Oscar nomination.

Fain and Webster wrote the songs for Boone's next film, *Mardi Gras*, released in November 1958, and Boone made a Top 40 hit out of "I'll Remember Tonight." Their other assignments for the year were for single songs for nonmusical films, rather than full scores. For *Marjorie Morningstar* they wrote "A Very Precious Love," taken into the Top 40 by the Ames Brothers, and the title song "A Certain Smile" became a Top 40 hit for Johnny Mathis; both songs were nominated for the 1958 Academy Award.

Fain did extensive work on the Disney animated film *Sleeping Beauty*, but most of it was cut from the final film, released in February 1959. Though opportunities for movie songwriting had become more sporadic by the end of the 1950s, Fain and Webster wrote songs for *Big Circus*, released in July, and for a television musical, *A Diamond for Carla*. In 1960 they returned to Broadway for the musical *Christine*, but it ran only 12 performances. A stage adaptation of *Calamity Jane* (St. Louis, June 5, 1961) was given a tryout by the St. Louis Municipal Opera but did not move to N.Y. The following year the St. Louis Municipal Opera staged Fain and lyricist Harold Adamson's version of *Around the World in Eighty Days* (St. Louis, June 11, 1962), which retained much of the Victor Young score from the 1956 film version. The show was mounted by Guy Lombardo at the Jones Beach Marine Theatre on Long Island during the summer of 1963, but it never ran on Broadway.

Fain's final theatrical work, directed by Jule Styne, was *Something More!* with lyrics by Alan and Marilyn Bergman. It reached Broadway in 1964 but ran for only 15 performances.

Meanwhile, Fain continued to place songs in films occasionally. His title song for *Tender Is the Night* (1962) with lyrics by Webster earned his seventh Oscar nomination. He wrote songs for two Warner Bros. films with Adamson: *Island of Love*, released in June 1963, and *The Incredible Mr. Limpet*, released in March 1964, after which he worked less frequently. But he earned an eighth Oscar nomination for "Strange Are the Ways of Love" (lyrics by Webster) from the 1972 film *The Stepmother*, a ninth for "A World That Never Was" (lyrics by Webster) from the 1976 film *Half a House*, and, at the age of 75, a tenth for "Someone's Waiting for You" (lyrics by Carol Connors and Ayn Robbins) from the animated Disney film *The Rescuers* (1977). Meanwhile, in 1975, Freddie Fender revived "Secret Love" for a #1 country and Top 40 pop hit. Fain died of a heart attack at the age of 87.

WORKS (only works for which Fain was a primary, credited composer are listed): **MUSICALS/REVUES** (all dates refer to N.Y. openings): *Everybody's Welcome* (Oct. 13, 1931); *Right This Way* (Jan. 4, 1938); *Hellzapoppin* (Sept. 22, 1938); *George White's Scandals* (Aug. 28, 1939); *Boys and Girls Together* (Oct. 1, 1940); *Sons o' Fun* (Dec. 1, 1941); *Toplitzky of Notre Dame* (Dec. 26, 1946); *Flahooley* (May 14, 1951); *Ankles Aweigh* (April 18, 1955); *Christine* (April 28, 1960); *Something More!* (Nov. 10, 1964). **FILMS:** *Young Man of Manhattan* (1930); *Footlight Parade* (1933); *College Coach* (1933); *Fashions of 1934* (1934); *Harold Teen* (1934); *Gentlemen Are Born* (1934); *Sweet Music* (1935); *Goin' to Town* (1935); *New Faces of 1937* (1937); *I Dood It* (1943); *Swing Fever* (1944); *Meet the People* (1944); *Maisie Goes to Reno* (1944); *George White's Scandals* (1945); *Two Sisters from Boston* (1946); *No Leave, No Love* (1946); *The Milkman* (1950); *Alice in Wonderland* (1951); *The Jazz Singer* (1953); *Peter Pan* (1953); *Calamity Jane* (1953); *Three Sailors and a Girl* (1953); *Lucky Me* (1954); *Hollywood or Bust* (1956); *April Love* (1957); *Mardi Gras* (1958); *The Big Circus* (1959); *Island of Love* (1963); *The Incredible Mr. Limpet* (1964). **TELEVISION:** *A Diamond for Carla* (1959).—**WR**

Fairchild, Blair, American composer; b. Belmont, Mass., June 23, 1877; d. Paris, April 23, 1933. He studied composition with J.K. Paine and Walter Spalding at Harvard Univ. (B.A., 1899), and then took courses with Giuseppe Buonamici in Florence. From 1901 until 1903 he was an attaché in the American embassies in Turkey and Persia. From 1905 he lived mostly in Paris, where he continued his musical studies with Charles Widor. Influenced by his travels in the Orient, and fascinated by the resources of exotic melos and rhythm, he wrote a number of pieces for orch. and for piano, and many songs in a pseudo-oriental manner; despite the imitative qualities of his music, Fairchild must be regarded as one of the few Americans who tried to transplant exotic folkways, both in subject matter and in melodic turns.

WORKS: *East and West*, tone poem (1908); *Légende* for Violin and Orch. (1911); *Tamineh*, symphonic poem after a Persian legend (1913); *6 chants nègres* for Piano (also orchestrated, Boston, Dec. 6, 1929); 2 violin sonatas (1908, 1919); 5 sets of *Stornelli Toscani* for Voice and Piano; song cycles. —**NS/LK/DM**

Fairlamb, James Remington, American organist and composer; b. Philadelphia, Jan. 23, 1838; d. Ingleside, N.Y., April 16, 1908. As a youth he played the organ in several Philadelphia churches. In 1858 he went to Paris, where he studied with Marmontel. While in Europe, he was appointed by President Lincoln as American Consul at Zürich (1861), where he stayed until 1865, when he returned to the U.S. He organized an amateur opera company with which he brought out his 4-act grand opera *Valerie, or Treasured Tokens* (Philadelphia, Dec. 15, 1869). From 1872 to 1898 he was church organist in Philadelphia, Jersey City, and N.Y. He wrote another grand opera, *Lionello*, and 2 light operas: *Love's Stratagem* and *The Interrupted Marriage*; some 50 of his choral works and nearly 150 songs and organ pieces were publ. He was one of the founders of the American Guild of Organists.—**NS/LK/DM**

Fairport Convention, seminal British folk-rock group. **MEMBERSHIP:** Richard Thompson, gtr. voc.

(Totteridge, London, April 3, 1949); Simon Nicol, gtr., bjo., dul., bs., vla., voc. (b. Muswell Hill, London, Oct. 13, 1950); Ashley "Tyger" Hutchings, bs., gtr., voc. (b. Southgate, Middlesex, England, Jan. 26, 1945); Judy Dyble, pno., voc. (b. London, Feb. 13, 1949); Martin Lamble, drm. (b. St. Johns Wood, London, Aug. 28, 1949; d. in a car accident in Warwickshire, England, May 14, 1969); Ian Matthews, gtr., voc. (b. Iain Matthews Mac-Donald, Scunthorpe, Lincolnshire, England, June 16, 1946) joined in 1967 and left in 1969. Dyble left in May 1968, to be replaced by Sandy Denny, gtr., kybd., alto voc. (b. Alexandra, Wimbledon, London, England, Jan. 6, 1947; d. London, April 21, 1978).

Later members included Dave Swarbrick, vln. (b. New Malden, Surrey, England, April 5, 1941); Dave Mattacks, kybd., drm. (b. Edgware, Middlesex, England, March 1948); Dave Pegg, bs. (b. Birmingham, West Midlands, England, Nov. 2, 1947); Trevor Lucas, gtr., voc. (b. Bungaree, Victoria, Australia, Dec. 25, 1943; d. Sydney, Australia, Feb. 4, 1989); Jerry Donahue, gtr., voc. (b. N.Y.C., Sept. 24, 1946); Bruce Rowland, drm. (b. Melbourne, Australia).

Officially formed in 1967, Fairport Convention's initial lineup was Richard Thompson, Simon Nicol, and Ashley "Tyger" Hutchings. Richard Thompson had taken up guitar by age 11, turned professional by 14, and turned to folk and traditional British music by his late teens. Around 1965, he began playing with Nicol and Hutchings. Soon augmented by Judy Dyble, Ian Matthews, and Martin Lamble, Fairport Convention played their first major engagement in January 1968 and recorded one album before the departure of Dyble in May. Dyble was replaced by Sandy Denny, who had worked London folk clubs and been a member of The Strawbs for six months. Fairport Convention's next album, *Fairport Convention* (*What We Did on Our Holidays* in Great Britain), came to be regarded as the first British folk-rock album. It featured Denny's stunning contralto voice and included her "Fotheringay," Thompson's "Meet on the Ledge," and a moving version of Bob Dylan's "I'll Keep It with Mine," as well as the obscure Joni Mitchell song "Eastern Rain." Ian Matthews left the group in February 1969 and Martin Lamble died on May 14, 1969, from injuries received in a wreck of the group's van. For *Unhalfbricking*, Fairport Convention was assisted by virtuoso violinist Dave Swarbrick. The album contained Thompson's "Genesis Hall" and an 11-minute version of the traditional folk song "A Sailor's Life," as well as Denny's best known composition, "Who Knows Where the Time Goes," and their first major British hit, Bob Dylan's "If You Gotta Go, Go Now," sung by Denny in French. Swarbrick, who had previously toured and recorded with Martin Carthy and Simon Nicol, joined Fairport Convention on a permanent basis in September, as did drummer-keyboardist Dave Mattacks.

Liege & Lief won Fairport Convention its first substantial recognition and became their best-remembered album. It included the traditional "Matty Groves" and "Tam Lin" as well as Denny and Hutchings's "Come All Ye" and Thompson's "Farewell, Farewell." However, Hutchings, who favored the traditional English music

rather than original material, left in November, as did Denny in December. Bassist Dave Pegg was brought in for Fairport Convention's *Full House*, which included Thompson's "Sloth." Personnel changes continued to plague the group, as Richard Thompson quit the band in January 1971 to work with Matthews and Denny and later record solo. Nicol, Swarbrick, Pegg, and Mattacks recorded two more albums as Fairport Convention.

In the meantime, Ian Matthews recorded *Matthews' Southern Comfort* and subsequently formed the namesake group for recordings in a country-rock vein, eventually scoring a major American and top British hit with a thinly sung version of Joni Mitchell's "Woodstock." He left the group abruptly in late 1970 and recorded two solo albums for Vertigo before forming Plainsong with singer-guitarist Andy Roberts. At the end of 1972, Matthews moved to Los Angeles to work with ex-Monkee Michael Nesmith, who produced his *Valley Hi* album. He subsequently switched to Columbia Records for two albums before moving to Seattle for six years, hitting with "Shake It" on Mushroom Records in 1978. During the 1980s, Matthews worked as an artists-and-repertoire representative for Island, then Windham Hill Music. He reemerged in 1988 with the first all-vocal album on the new age Windham Hill label, *Walking a Changing Line*, comprising songs written by Jules Shear, the author of Cyndi Lauper's smash 1984 hit "All Through the Night." Matthews relocated to Austin, Tex., in 1989 and reverted to the Gaelic spelling of his first name, Iain. He reunited with Andy Roberts for *Dark Side of the Room* as Plainsong and later recorded solo albums for Mesa and Watermelon. In 1995, he joined Michael Fracasso and Mark Hamilton in Hamilton Pool.

Ashley Hutchings became a mainstay of traditional English folk music performed by a rock band. He formed Steeleye Span in 1969 with multi-instrumentalist Tim Hart, vocalist Maddy Prior, and, later, Martin Carthy and John Kirkpatrick. After three albums with the group (released in the United States in 1976), Hutchings left to form The Albion Country Band in 1971. He recorded *No Roses* with his then-wife Shirley Collins and, along with Richard Thompson, provided rock instrumentation to the folk dance form known as Morris dancing on *Morris On*. The Albion Country Band's *Battle of the Field* was recorded in 1973 but not released until 1976. With Hutchings as the mainstay, the group became The Albion Dance Band, then simply The Albion Band for British recordings throughout the 1970s and 1980s. Recent recordings by The Albion Band were issued on Magnum America and M.I.L. Multimedia. Two 1996 sets, *The Guv'nor* and *The Guv'nor, Vol. 2* anthologized Hutchings's long career from Fairport Convention on.

Sandy Denny formed the short-lived Fotheringay in March 1970 with American guitarist Jerry Donahue and two former members of Eclection, guitarist Trevor Lucas and drummer Gerry Conway. Their sole album for A&M featured the excellent Denny-Lucas composition "Peace in the End." Denny subsequently recorded two outstanding solo albums for A&M and assembled The Bunch with Lucas, Conway, Richard Thompson, Ashley Hutchings, and Dave Mattacks for *Rock On*, an album of rock 'n' roll oldies that showcased Denny's duet with Linda Peters on "When Will I Be Loved." She married Lucas in 1973 and switched to Island Records for the excellent *Like an Old Fashioned Waltz* and *Rendezvous*.

In the autumn of 1972, Fairport Convention regrouped with Dave Swarbrick, Jerry Donahue, Trevor Lucas, Dave Mattacks, and Dave Pegg. Augmented by Richard Thompson and Sandy Denny, the group recorded *Rosie*. Denny rejoined Fairport Convention for their late 1973 world tour and stayed until December 1975, recording two more albums with the group. By the end of 1976, the group comprised Simon Nicol, Dave Swarbrick, Dave Pegg, and drummer Bruce Rowland.

On April 21, 1978, Sandy Denny died of a cerebral hemorrhage after suffering a fall. Lucas subsequently returned to Australia and worked as a producer, dying in Sydney on February 4, 1989, of a suspected heart attack. In August 1979, Fairport Convention disbanded. Pegg next joined Jethro Tull as bassist, while Swarbrick formed Whippersnapper.

Beginning in 1980, Dave Pegg organized a Fairport Convention reunion concert every summer. The first reunion featured Richard and Linda Thompson and the second Judy Dyble. Fairport Convention once more reassembled in 1983 with Simon Nicol, Dave Pegg, and Dave Mattacks, who recorded *Gladys's Leap*. The group added violinist Ric Sanders in 1985 and multi-instrumentalist Martin Allcock joined for the all-instrumental album *Expletive Delighted!* Oddly enough, this later-day Fairport lineup was the most stable of all the Fairports that had come and gone, with its membership remaining the same until 1996, when first Martin Allcock and then Dave Mattacks left. They were replaced by fiddler/mandolin player Chris Leslie and drummer Gerry Conway.

Although sorely neglected in the United States, Fairport Convention was perhaps the first British group to combine traditional British folk music, compelling original songs, and rock instrumentation to emerge as the first British folk-rock group. An immensely seminal group with one of rock's most complicated histories, Fairport Convention introduced Ian Matthews, Ashley Hutchings, Sandy Denny, and Richard Thompson to a wider audience. During her tenure with Fairport Convention, Sandy Denny became established as one of the top British female vocalists and won recognition as an outstanding songwriter, primarily on the strength of "Who Knows Where the Time Goes," popularized by Judy Collins. Ian Matthews later pursued a remarkably diverse career, while Ashley Hutchings proved an important purveyor of traditional English folk music set to rock music. Mainstay Dave Swarbrick was one of the first musicians to play violin as a lead instrument within the rock format. After his stint with Fairport Convention, Richard Thompson emerged as a cult figure, recognized by critics and his devoted following as an excellent songwriter and compellingly innovative guitarist (some claim he is one of only a handful of original and creative guitarists working in rock today). Acclaimed for his recordings with one-time wife Linda (particularly *Shoot Out the Lights*) and subsequent solo recordings, Richard Thompson eventually began receiving wider recognition during the 1980s and 1990s.

DISC.: *Fairport Convention* (1968); *What We Did on Our Holidays* (1969); *Unhalfbricking* (1970); *Liege & Lief* (1970); *Full House* (1970); *Angel Delight* (1971); *Babbacombe Lee* (1972); *Rosie* (1973); *Nine* (1974); *A Movable Feast* (1974); *Rising for the Moon* (1975); *Gottle O'Geer* (1976); *Bonny Bunch of Roses* (1977); *Tippler's Tales* (1978); *Adieu Adieu* (1979); *Moat on the Ledge* (1982); *Gladys's Leap* (1986); *Expletive Delighted!* (1987); *In Real Time* (1988); *Red and Gold* (1993); *Jewel in the Crown* (1995); *Old New Borrowed Blue* (1996); *Who Knows Where the Time Goes?* (1998); *The Wood and the Wire* (2000).—**BH**

Faisst, Immanuel (Gottlob Friedrich), German organist, choral conductor, pedagogue, and composer; b. Esslingen, Oct. 13, 1823; d. Stuttgart, June 5, 1894. He studied theology in Schönthal (1836–40) and Tübingen (1840–44). After lessons with Mendelssohn, he was a pupil in Berlin of Dehn (theory) and Haupt (organ). In 1846 he settled in Stuttgart, where he was founder-director of the Verein für Klassische Kirchenmusik (1847–91) and the Schwäbischer Sängerband (from 1849). In 1857 he helped to organize the Cons., where he became director in 1859. In 1865 he was named organist and choirmaster of the Stiftskirche. For his essay "Beiträge zur Geschichte der Claviersonate," *Cacilia*, XXV (1846), he was awarded a Ph.D. from the Univ. of Tübingen in 1849. He ed. didactic vols. and composed much vocal music.—**NS/LK/DM**

Faith, Percy, Canadian-born American popular bandleader, arranger, and conductor; b. Toronto, April 7, 1908; d. Los Angeles, Feb. 9, 1976. Faith was a major arranger and orchestra leader of the 1950s and 1960s, charting with over 30 albums and scoring #1 hits with "Delicado," "The Song from *Moulin Rouge* (Where Is Your Heart)," and "The Theme from *A Summer Place*." He arranged and conducted recordings for some of the top singers of the era, including Tony Bennett, Doris Day, and Johnny Mathis, and he wrote the musical scores for a half dozen films.

Faith began studying the violin at seven but switched to piano. He attended the Toronto Cons., studying with Louis Waizman and Frank Wellman, and made his debut as a pianist at Massey Hall in Toronto at the age of 15. His career as a concert pianist was curtailed by an accident: His three-year-old sister caught fire, and he beat out the flames, severely burning his hands. Thereafter, he turned to studying composition and arranging.

By 1931, Faith was conducting his own string ensemble on the radio in Toronto. From 1933 to 1940 he had his own show, *Music by Faith*, on the CBC, the Canadian national radio network. In 1940 he moved to the U.S., eventually becoming a naturalized citizen. During the 1940s he conducted on a series of network radio shows, including *The Carnation Contented Hour*, *The Coca-Cola Show*, and *The Woolworth Hour*.

In 1950, Faith went to work for Columbia Records as an arranger/conductor and recording artist. He had his first singles chart entry with "I Cross My Fingers" (music and lyrics by Walter Kent and Walter Farrar) in June. "All My Love" (music by Paul Durand, English lyrics by Mitchell Parish) peaked in the Top Ten in

October. He made his mark as a songwriter with "My Heart Cries for You" (music and lyrics by Faith and Carl Sigman, based on the French folk song "Chanson de Marie Antoinette"), which was a million-selling Top Ten hit for Guy Mitchell in January 1951. "On Top of Old Smoky" (music and lyrics adapted by Pete Seeger from a traditional folk song), credited to Percy Faith with Burl Ives, reached the Top Ten in May. Faith's instrumental recording of "Delicado" (music by Waldyr Azevedo, lyrics by Jack Lawrence) reached #1 in July 1952. He returned to the top of the singles chart in May 1953 with the million-seller "The Song from *Moulin Rouge* (Where Is Your Heart)" (music by Georges Auric, lyrics by William Engvick). His first chart album was the Top Ten hit *Music from Hollywood* in July 1953, his second *Music of Christmas* in December 1954.

Faith wrote his first film score for *Love Me or Leave Me*, released in May 1955; it earned an Academy Award nomination. His version of the music from the Broadway musical *My Fair Lady* was a Top Ten hit in May 1957. In December, Columbia released *Viva—The Music of Mexico*, which eventually went gold.

The movie *A Summer Place*, starring Troy Donahue and Sandra Dee, was released in October 1959. Faith's single recording of composer Max Steiner's instrumental theme from the movie became a massive hit, topping the charts in February 1960, and, at sales of two million copies, becoming the best-selling single of the year. It was also the Grammy winner for Record of the Year and earned Grammy nominations for Best Arrangement and Best Orchestral Performance.

Faith had a gold-selling Top Ten LP in 1960 with *Bouquet*, which he followed with two Top Ten albums in 1961, *Jealousy* and *Camelot*. He had his last gold-selling album with *Themes for Young Lovers* in the spring of 1963; it earned him another Grammy nomination for Best Orchestral Performance. Meanwhile, he wrote a series of film scores during the mid-1960s and continued to chart with two or more albums a year, usually devoted to orchestral versions of movie themes or popular songs, through 1972. He last reached the easy-listening charts in November 1975 with a disco version of "The Theme from *A Summer Place*." He died of cancer in 1976 at 67.

WORKS: FILMS: *Love Me or Leave Me* (1955); *Tammy Tell Me True* (1961); *I'd Rather Be Rich* (1964); *The Third Day* (1965); *The Oscar* (1966).—**WR**

Faithfull, Marianne,

one of the toughest and most durable women in popular music; b. London, England, Dec. 29, 1946. Marianne Faithfull's parents might have been one of the classic mismatches of the century. Her mother, Baroness Ava Sacher-Masoch—unlike her great uncle Leopold who set the standards for Victorian era literary debauchery—disliked sex. Her father Glynn Faithfull was a sexologist, inventor of the Frigidity Machine designed to "unblock primal libidinal energy." It apparently didn't work on his wife and he ran off with an exotic dancer. His daughter Marianne wound up in convent school despite his arguments that it would give her problems with sex. He was right, and interesting problems they were.

While still attending convent school in 1964, she met Andrew Loog Oldham, producer and manager of the Rolling Stones. Without even hearing her voice, he signed her to a recording agreement. "He thought he could sell me," she told England's *Record Mirror* in 1964, "not my voice."

As it turned out, her voice was nearly as angelic as her looks. Oldham set her up with as yet unrecorded Jagger/Richards composition, "As Tears Go By," loading his production with a full complement of weeping strings. It became a substantial hit on both sides of the Atlantic, hitting #22 in the U.S. Over the next year, she landed three more hits, taking Jackie DeShannon's "Come and Stay with Me" to #26, "This Little Bird" to #32, and "Summer Nights" to #24. Her albums featured music by Donovan and Tim Hardin, but anything she attempted artistically in the 1960s—and she performed on stage and film as well as recording—was overshadowed by her other passions.

Her liaisons became far more notorious. Faithfull got plugged into the whole Rolling Stones orbit, sleeping by her own admission with Richards and Brian Jones before settling into a four-year affair with Mick Jagger. She inspired such Stones classics as "Let's Spend the Night Together," "Wild Horses," and "You Can't Always Get What You Want," and even wrote the lyrics to "Sister Morphine." Indeed, she says she left Jagger after four years for her greater love of drugs. She was the subject of the infamous 1967 drug bust that put both her and Jagger in the pokey, with the London papers reporting "Scantily Clad Woman at Drug Party."

The 1970s were mostly a lost decade for Faithfull. After a post-Jagger suicide attempt, she dropped out of the public eye and her life was mostly informed by her drug abuse. She recorded a country album with Joe Cocker's Grease Band in 1976, but it was her stunning 1979 rock record *Broken English* that thrust her back into the public eye, and caused a reappraisal of her artistry. Her virginal voice and good looks had been ravaged by all the years of abuse, but the undeniable power of the music turned the album into a cult hit, partly fueled by an appearance on *Saturday Night Live*. Her songs like the title track, "Why'd You Do It?," and "Time Square" were edgier than anything the Stones had recorded in years, edgier even than much of the punk and new wave music with which she competed. While her next albums, *Dangerous Acquaintances* and *A Child's Adventure* were good, they lacked the raw power and surprise of *Broken English*.

In 1985, Faithfull checked into the Hazelden clinic to go through detox, cleaning up her act physically. Her music continued to grow. *Strange Weather*, a powerful collection of dark standards and originals, recorded in the wake of a boyfriend's suicide was described as "music to slit your wrists by." The live album, *Blazing Away*, attempted to recapture her past in the context of her present. She recorded *A Secret Life*, a moody atmospheric album, with *Twin Peaks* composer Angelo Badalamente. In the mid- and late 1990s, she turned toward cabaret songs and covers. Her live album *20th Century Blues*, included a cover of "Falling in Love Again." She continued to emphasize her German sensibilities when she tackled Kurt Weill's *Seven Deadly Sins* in 1998.

DISC.: *Marianne Faithfull* (1965); *Go Away from My World* (1965); *Come My Way* (1965); *Faithful Forever* (1966); *North Country Maid* (1966); *Love in a Mist* (1967); *The World of Marianne Faithfull* (1969); *Dreaming My Dreams* (1977); *Faithless Sony* (1978); *Broken English* (1979); *Dangerous Acquaintances* (1981); *As Tears Go By* (1981); *A Child's Adventure* (1983); *Summer Nights* (1984); *Music for the Millions* (1985); *Strange Weather* (1987); *Rich Kid Blues* (1988); *Blazing Away* (live; 1990); *A Secret Life* (1995); *20th Century Blues* (1997); *The Seven Deadly Sins* (1998); *Vagabond Ways* (1999).

WRITINGS: M. F. with David Dalton, *Faithfull, An Autobiography* (Boston, c. 1994).—**HB**

Falabella (Correa), Roberto, Chilean composer; b. Santiago, Feb. 13, 1926; d. there, Dec. 15, 1958. He was paralyzed by polio as a child. He pursued his studies with Lucila Césped (1945–46), Alfonso Letelier (1949–50), Gustavo Becerra (1952), and Miguel Aguilar and Esteban Eitler (1956–57). His music was Classical in form, Romantic in content, and modernistic in technique.

WORKS: DRAMATIC: *Epitafios fúnebres,* chamber opera (1952); *Del diario morir,* miniature opera (1954); *El peine de oro,* ballet (1954); *Andacollo,* ballet (1957). **ORCH.:** Sym. (1955); *2 divertimenti* for Strings (1955); *Emotional Studies* (1957; also for Piano). **CHAMBER:** *Dueto* for Flute and Violin (1952); Violin Sonata (1954); Cello Sonata (1954); String Quartet (1957). **KEYBOARD: P i a n o :** 2 sonatas (1951, 1954); *Preludios episódicos* (1953); *Impresiones* (1955); *Retratos* (1957). **VOCAL:** *Palimpsestos* for Contralto, Bassoon, Horn, and Percussion (1954); *La Lámpara en la tierra,* cantata for Baritone and Orch. (1958).—**NS/LK/DM**

Falchi, Stanislao, Italian composer; b. Terni, Jan. 29, 1851; d. Rome, Nov. 14, 1922. He studied in Rome with C. Maggi and S. Meluzzi. In 1877 he became a teacher at the Accademia di Santa Cecilia there; from 1902 till 1915, he was its director. Among his pupils were A. Bonaventura, A. Bustini, V. Gui, B. Molinari, L. Refice, and F. Santoliquido. He wrote the operas *Lorhelia* (Rome, Dec. 4, 1877), *Giuditta* (Rome, March 12, 1887), and *Il Trillo del diavolo* (Rome, Jan. 29, 1899), as well as a Requiem for the funeral of Victor Emmanuel II (Jan. 17, 1883).—**NS/LK/DM**

Falcinelli, Rolande, French organist, pedagogue, and composer; b. Paris, Feb. 18, 1920. She entered the Paris Cons. in 1932, where she was a student of Samuel-Rousseau, Plé-Caussade, Büsser, and Dupré, taking premiers prix in harmony and piano accompaniment (1938), fugue (1939), and organ (1942), and the 2nd Prix de Rome (1942). In 1945 she became organist at the basilica of Sacré-Couer de Montmarte in Paris. As a recitalist, she made tours of Europe and North America. She was prof. of organ at the American Cons. in Fontainebleau (1948–55), The École Normale de Musique in Paris (1951–55), and the Paris Cons. (1955–86).

WORKS: DRAMATIC: O p e r a : *Pygmalion délivré* (1942); *Icare* (1943); *Louise de la Miséricorde* (1944). **B a l l e t :** *Cecca, la Bohémienne ensorcelée* (1943–45). **ORCH.:** *Polska* for Piano and Orch. (1940); *Choral et variation sur le Kyrie de la messe "Orbis Factor"* for Organ and Orch. (1942); *Mausolée* for Organ

and Orch. (1971–72); *Marana Tha* (1989). **CHAMBER:** String Quartet (1940); *Berceuse* for Bassoon or Cello and Piano (1955); *Chant de peine et de lutte* for Violin and Organ (1974); *Chant d'ombre et de clarté* for Cello (1975); *Aphorismes* for Piano and Organ (1979); *Kénose* for Cello and Organ (1983); *Tzinomio* for Oboe and English Horn (1988). **KEYBOARD:** Numerous organ pieces; many piano works. **VOCAL:** *La Messiade,* oratorio for Soloists, Chorus, and Orch. (1941); *Cavalier* for Chorus and Orch. (1942); *Messe de Saint-Dominique* for Chorus (1947); *Quatrains d'Omar Khayyam* for Voice and String Quartet (1973); *Psautier* for Soprano and Orch. (1980).—**NS/LK/DM**

Falckenhagen, Adam, German lutenist and composer; b. Grossdalzig, near Leipzig, April 26, 1697; d. Bayreuth, 1761. He studied harpsichord and lute in Knauthain. After further lute training from Johann Jacob Frag in Merseburg, he attended the Univ. of Leipzig (1719–20). He taught lute in Wiessenfels (1720–27), and also was a chamber musician and lutenist to Duke Christian there. After further lute studies with Weiss in Dresden, he was active in Jena (1727–29) before serving Duke Ernst August of Sachsen-Weimar (1729–32). He then settled in Bayreuth, where he was in the service of the court by 1734. Falckenhagen was one of the last important composers of lute music. Among his publ. works were 6 lute sonatas (1740), 6 lute partitas (c. 1742), and 6 concerti for flute, oboe or violin, cello, and Opera Nuova (c. 1743).—**LK/DM**

Falco, Michele, Italian composer; b. Naples, c. 1688; d. after 1732. He was trained at the Cons. di S. Onofrio in Naples, where he became a member of the Reale Congregazione e Monte dei Musici in 1712. He served as maestro di cappella and organist at the church of S. Geronimo in Naples, and also as maestro di cappella in Pollena, near Naples. Falco was one of the most important exponents of opera buffa, composing the following scores for Naples: *Lo Lollo pisciaportelle* (1700), *Lo Masiello* (1712; Acts 1 and 3 by N. Fago), *Lo Imbruoglio d'ammore* (Dec. 27, 1717), *Armida abbandonata* (Oct. 1, 1719), *Lo castiello saccheiato* (Oct. 1720), and *Le pazzie d'ammore* (April 1723). He also wrote oratorios and cantatas.—**NS/LK/DM**

Falcon, (Marie-) Cornélie, renowned French soprano; b. Paris, Jan. 28, 1814; d. there, Feb. 25, 1897. She studied with Henri, Pelegrini, Bordogni, and Nourrit at the Paris Cons. (1827–31), taking premiers prix in singing and lyric declamation. On July 20, 1832, she made her operatic debut as Alice in *Robert le diable* at the Paris Opéra, where she subsequently sang with such brilliant success that she was chosen to create the roles of Rachel in *La Juive* (Feb. 23, 1835) and Valentine in *Les Huguenots* (Feb. 29, 1836). In the spring of 1837 she suffered a vocal collapse, but soon managed to resume her career at the Opéra and sang there until her final performance in *Les Huguenots* on Jan. 15, 1838. She made many attempts to regain her vocal prowess, resorting to various quack remedies and bogus treatments, all to no avail. On March 14, 1840, she made an unsuccessful return to the Opéra in a special benefit performance, but her attempt proved disastrous and she retired to her villa near Paris. Despite the brevity of her remarkable career, her portrayals of Donna Anna, Giulia in *Vestale*, and the heroines in all 4 Rossini French operas, as well as those already noted, brought her great fame. Indeed, so much fame, that the description "Falcon type" subsequently was given to those singers who excelled in her chosen repertory.

BIBL.: C. Bouvet, *C. F.* (Paris, 1927).—**NS/LK/DM**

Falcon, Ruth, American soprano; b. New Orleans, Nov. 2, 1946. She studied in New Orleans before pursuing training in N.Y. and with Tito Gobbi and Luigi Ricci in Italy. In 1968 she sang Frasquita in New Orleans. In 1974 she made her first appearance at the N.Y. City Opera as Micaëla, and in 1975 her European debut in the title role of Mayr's *Medea in Corinto* in Bern. She made her first appearance at the Bavarian State Opera in Munich in 1976 as Leonora, and continued to appear there until 1980. Her debut at the Paris Opéra followed in 1981 as Donna Anna. In 1983 she was engaged as Leonora at the Vienna State Opera. After singing Anna Bolena in Nice in 1985, she portrayed Leonora at London's Covent Garden in 1987. On Nov. 13, 1989, she made her Metropolitan Opera debut in N.Y. as Strauss's Empress. In 1990 she sang Norma in New Orleans. After appearing as Turandot at the Teatro Colón in Buenos Aires in 1993, she returned to New Orleans as Chrysothemis in 1994 and as Leonora in 1997.
—**NS/LK/DM**

Falcone, Achille, Italian composer; b. Cosenza, c. 1573; d. there, Nov. 9, 1600. He was educated under his father, the composer Antonio Falcone. He became maestro di cappella in Caltagirone in Sicily, and also was a member of the Accademia in Cosenza. In 1600 he was challenged to a musical competition by the Spanish composer Sebastián Raval, which he won. Raval appealed the decision of the adjudicator to the viceroy and demanded a new examination. Raval won the 2nd competition, probably as a result of Spanish favoritism. Falcone then appealed to Nanino and Soriano for a 3rd competition in Rome, but died before it could be held. Falcone's father publ. Achille's 5-part madrigals (Venice, 1603), which also contains an account of his competitions with Raval, along with the competition pieces.
—**LK/DM**

Falconieri, Andrea, Italian lutenist and composer; b. Naples, 1585 or 1586; d. there, July 19 or 29, 1656. He may have been a student of Giovanni de Marque in Naples and of Santino Garsi in Parma, where he became a lutenist in 1604 and where he succeeded Garsi as court lutenist in 1610. In 1615 he was in Florence and in 1616 he may have visited Rome. In 1619 he was again in Florence, and then was at the Modena court in 1620–21. After travels in Spain and France, he was once more in Florence in 1628 and then in Parma (1629–32). From 1632 until about 1637 he was a music teacher at the Collegia S. Brigida in Genoa. In 1642 he was again in Modena. In 1647 he became maestro di cappella at the Naples court, remaining there until his death from the plague. He was an adept composer of both vocal and instrumental works.

WORKS: *Libro primo di Villanelle...con l'alfabeto per la chitarra spagnola* for 1 to 3 Voices (Rome, 1616); *Il quinto libro delle musiche* for 1 to 3 Voices (Florence, 1619); *Musiche...libro sexto, con l'alfabbetto della chitarra spagnuola* for 1 to 3 Voices (Venice, 1619); *Sacrae modulationes* for 5 to 6 Voices (Venice, 1619); *Il primo libro di canzone, sinfonie, fantasie, capricci, brandi, correnti, gagliarde, alemane, volte* for 1 to 3 Violins, Viola or Other Instruments, and Basso Continuo (Naples, 1650).—**NS/LK/DM**

Falik, Yuri, greatly talented Russian cellist and composer; b. Odessa, July 30, 1936. He composed music from adolescence. In 1955 he enrolled in the composition class of Boris Arapov at the Leningrad Cons., graduating in 1964. He also studied cello there with A. Strimer and in 1962 won 1st prize in the Helsinki Competition. He subsequently joined the staff of the Leningrad Cons., teaching both cello and composition. In his music, Falik reveals a quasi-Romantic quality, making use of tantalizingly ambiguous melodic passages approaching the last ramparts of euphonious dissonance. His angular rhythms, with their frequently startling pauses, suggest a theatrical concept.

WORKS: DRAMATIC: *Till Eulenspiegel*, "mystery ballet" (1967); *Oresteia*, choreographic tragedy (1968); *Les Fourberies de Scapin*, opéra bouffe (Tartu, Dec. 22, 1984). **ORCH.:** Concertino for Oboe and Chamber Orch. (1961); Sym. for Strings and Percussion (1963); 2 concertos for Orch. (1967; *Symphonic Études*, 1977); *Music for Strings* (1968); 2 syms.: No. 1, *Easy Symphony* (1971) and No. 2, *Kaddish* (1993); Violin Concerto (1971); *Elegiac Music in Memoriam Igor Stravinsky* for Chamber Orch. (1975). **CHAMBER:** 7 string quartets (1955–93); Trio for Oboe, Cello, and Piano (1959); Wind Quintet (1964); *The Tumblers* for 4 Woodwinds, 2 Brasses, and 19 Percussion Instruments (1966); *Inventions* for Vibraphone, Marimba, and 5 Tam-tams (1972); *English Divertimento* for Flute, Clarinet, and Bassoon (1978). **VOCAL:** *Solemn Song*, cantata (1968); *Winter Songs* for Chorus (1975); 3 concertos for Chorus (1979, 1987, 1988); *Russian Orthodox Liturgical Songs* for Soloists and Chorus (1990–92); Mass for Soloists, Chorus, and Chamber Orch. (1996); songs.
—**NS/LK/DM**

Falkner, Sir (Donald) Keith, English bass-baritone and pedagogue; b. Sawston, Cambridgeshire, March 1, 1900; d. Bungay, Suffolk, May 17, 1994. He studied at New Coll., Oxford, and with Plunkett Greene in London, Lierhammer in Vienna, Grenzebach in Berlin, and Dossert in Paris. From 1923 to 1946 he was active mainly as a concert singer, appearing principally in oratorios. After serving as visiting prof. (1950–51), assoc. prof. (1951–56), and prof. (1956–60) at Cornell Univ., he was director of the Royal Coll. of Music in London (1960–74). He was joint artistic director of the Kings Lynn Festival (1981–83). In 1974 he was knighted.
—**NS/LK/DM**

Fall, Leo(pold), notable Austrian composer; b. Olmütz, Feb. 2, 1873; d. Vienna, Sept. 16, 1925. He began his musical training with his father, Moritz Fall (1840–1922), a military bandmaster and composer. At 14, he enrolled at the Vienna Cons. to study violin and piano, and also had courses in harmony and counterpoint with J.N. Fuchs and R. Fuchs. He was active as a theater conductor in Berlin (1894–96), and then was conductor of the Centralhallen-Theater in Hamburg (1896–98). Returning to Berlin, he conducted in theaters before becoming music director of the Intimes-Theater, a cabaret. There he brought out his comic opera *Paroli* (Oct. 4, 1902). After the failure of his grand opera *Irrlicht* (Mannheim, 1905), Fall concentrated his efforts on lighter stage works. Although his first operetta *Der Rebell* (Vienna, Nov. 28, 1905) was a failure at its premiere, its rev. version as *Der liebe Augustin* (Berlin, Feb. 3, 1912) was a resounding success. In the meantime, Fall scored his first unqualified success with *Der fidele Bauer* (Mannheim, July 25, 1907). With *Die Dollarprinzessin* (Vienna, Nov. 2, 1907), Fall also was acclaimed in Great Britain and America, establishing him as one of the principal operetta composers of his time. His *Die geschiedene Frau* (Vienna, Dec. 23, 1908) was so successful that it was heard around the world. His success continued with *Das Puppenmädel* (Vienna, Nov. 4, 1910), *Die shöne Risette* (Vienna, Nov. 19, 1910), *Die Sirene* (Vienna, Jan. 5, 1911), and *The Eternal Waltz* (London, Dec. 22, 1911). During World War I, Fall continued to compose, producing the outstanding *Die Kaiserin* or *Fürstenliebe* (Berlin, Oct. 16, 1916) and the popular *Die Rose von Stambul* (Vienna, Dec. 2, 1916). With the war over, Fall turned out the notable scores *Der goldene Vogel* (Dresden, May 21, 1920), *Die spanische Nachtigall* (Berlin, Nov. 18, 1920), and *Die Strassensängerin* (Berlin, Sept. 24, 1921). His greatest postwar success came with his *Madame Pompadour* (Berlin, Sept. 9, 1922), which became an international favorite. His brother, Richard Fall (b. Gewitsch, April 3, 1882; d. in the concentration camp in Auschwitz about Nov. 20, 1943), was also a composer. He wrote operettas, revues, and film scores. Among his best known stage works were *Der Wiener Fratz* (Vienna, Jan. 1, 1912), *Der Weltenbummler* (Berlin, Nov. 18, 1915), *Die Puppenbaronessen* (Vienna, Sept. 1, 1917), and *Grossstadtmärchen* (Vienna, Jan. 10, 1920).

WORKS: DRAMATIC: Music Theater: *Lustige Blätter* (Hamburg, July 25, 1896); *1842* or *Der grosse Brand* (Hamburg, Aug. 1, 1897); *Der Brandstifter* (Berlin, Jan. 1, 1899); *Die Jagd nach dem Glück* (Berlin, Feb. 1, 1900); *'ne feine Nummer* (Berlin, Feb. 16, 1901; in collaboration with V. Hollander); *Paroli* or *Frau Denise* (Vienna, Oct. 4, 1902); *Der Rebell* (Vienna, Nov. 28, 1905; rev. version as *Der liebe Augustin*, Berlin, Feb. 3, 1912); *Der Fuss* (Chemnitz, Sept. 18, 1906); *Der fidele Bauer* (Mannheim, July 25, 1907); *Die Dollarprinzessin* (Vienna, Nov. 2, 1907); *Die geschiedene Frau* (Vienna, Dec. 23, 1908); *Brüderlein fein* (Berlin, Dec. 31, 1908); *Die Schrei nach der Ohrfeige* (1909); *Brüderlein fein* (Vienna, Dec. 1, 1909); *Das Puppenmädel* (Vienna, Nov. 4, 1910); *Die schöne Risette* (Vienna, Nov. 19, 1910); *Die Sirene* (Vienna, Jan. 5, 1911); *The Eternal Waltz* (London, Dec. 11, 1911); *Die Studentengräfin* (Berlin, Jan. 18, 1913); *Der Nachtschnellzug* (Vienna, Dec. 18, 1913); *Jung England* (Berlin, Feb. 14, 1914; rev. version as *Frau Ministerpräsident*, Dresden, Feb. 3, 1920); *Der künstliche Mensch* (Berlin, Oct. 2, 1915); *Die Kaiserin* or *Fürstenliebe* (Berlin, Oct. 16, 1915); *Tantalus im Dachstüberl* (Würzburg, March 26, 1916); *Seemansliebchen* (Berlin, Sept. 4, 1916; in collaboration with F. Warnke); *Die Rose von Stambul* (Vienna, Dec. 2, 1916); *Der goldene Vogel* (Dresden, May 21, 1920); *Die spanische Nachtigall* (Berlin, Nov. 18, 1920); *Die Strassensängerin*

(Berlin, Sept. 24, 1921); *Der heilige Ambrosius* (Berlin, Nov. 3, 1921); *Madame Pompadour* (Berlin, Sept. 9, 1922); *Der süsse Kavalier* (Vienna, Dec. 11, 1923); *Jugen in Mai* (Dresden, Oct. 22, 1926); *Rosen aus Florida* (Vienna, Feb. 22, 1929; arranged by E. Korngold). **OTHER:** Waltzes; songs.

BIBL.: W. Zimmerli, *L. F.* (Zürich, 1957).—NS/LK/DM

Falla (y Matheu), Manuel (Maria) de,

great Spanish composer; b. Cadíz, Nov. 23, 1876; d. Alta Gracia, Córdoba province, Argentina, Nov. 14, 1946. He studied piano with his mother; after further instruction from Eloisa Galluzo, he studied harmony, counterpoint, and composition with Alejandro Odero and Enrique Broca; then went to Madrid, where he studied piano with José Tragó and composition with Felipe Pedrell at the Cons. He wrote several zarzuelas, but only *Los amores de la Inés* was performed (Madrid, April 12, 1902). His opera *La vida breve* won the prize of the Real Academia de Bellas Artes in Madrid in 1905, but it was not premiered until 8 years later. In 1905 he also won the Ortiz y Cussó Prize for pianists. In 1907 he went to Paris, where he became friendly with Debussy, Dukas, and Ravel, who aided and encouraged him as a composer. Under their influence, he adopted the principles of Impressionism without, however, giving up his personal and national style. He returned to Spain in 1914 and produced his tremendously effective ballet *El amor brujo* (Madrid, April 2, 1915). It was followed by the evocative *Noches en los jardines de España* for piano and orch. (Madrid, April 9, 1916). In 1919 he made his home in Granada, where he completed work on his celebrated ballet *El sombrero de tres picos* (London, July 22, 1919). Falla's art was rooted in both the folk songs of Spain and the purest historical traditions of Spanish music. Until 1919 his works were cast chiefly in the Andalusian idiom, and his instrumental technique was often conditioned by effects peculiar to Spain's national instrument, the guitar. In his puppet opera *El retablo de maese Pedro* (1919–22), he turned to the classical tradition of Spanish (especially Castilian) music. The keyboard style of his Harpsichord Concerto (1923–26), written at the suggestion of Wanda Landowska, reveals in the classical lucidity of its writing a certain kinship with Domenico Scarlatti, who lived in Spain for many years. Falla became president of the Instituto de Espana in 1938. When the Spanish Civil War broke out, and General Franco overcame the Loyalist government with the aid of Hitler and Mussolini, Falla left Spain and went to South America, never to return to his homeland. He went to Buenos Aires, where he conducted concerts of his music. He then withdrew to the small locality of Alta Gracia, where he lived the last years of his life in seclusion, working on his large scenic cantata *Atlántida*. It remained unfinished at his death and was later completed by his former pupil, Ernesto Halffter.

WORKS: DRAMATIC: *La vida breve*, opera (1904–05; Nice, April 1, 1913); *El amor brujo*, ballet (1914–15; Madrid, April 2, 1915; concert version, 1916); *El corregidor y la molinera*, farsa mimica (1916–17; Madrid, April 7, 1917; rev. and expanded as *El sombrero de tres picos*); *El sombrero de tres picos*, ballet (rev. and expanded from *El corregidor y la molinera*; 1918–19; 2 orch. suites, 1919; London, July 22, 1919); *El retablo de maese Pedro*, puppet opera (1919–22; concert perf., Seville, March 23, 1923; private stage perf. in the salon of Princess de Poligna, Paris, June 25, 1923; public stage perf., Paris, Nov. 13, 1923); *Atlántida*, cantata escenica (1925–46; unfinished; completed by E. Halffter; Milan, June 18, 1962; rev. and perf. in concert form, Lucerne, Sept. 9, 1976); also several zarzuelas, including *Los amores de la Inés* (Madrid, April 12, 1902); incidental music, and a comic opera, *Fuego fatuo* (1918–19). **O R C H . :** *Noches en los jardines de España* for Piano and Orch. (1909–15; Madrid, April 9, 1916); Concerto for Harpsichord or Piano, Flute, Oboe, Clarinet, Violin, and Cello (1923–26; Barcelona, Nov. 4, 1926); *Homenajes*, 4 pieces: 1, *à Cl. Debussy* (orig. for Guitar as *Le Tombeau de Claude Debussy*, 1920); 2, *Fanfare sobre el nombre de E.F. Arbós* (1933); 3, *à Paul Dukas* (orig. for Piano as *Pour le tombeau de Paul Dukas*, 1935); 4, *Pedrelliana* (1924–39; 1st perf. of entire suite, Buenos Aires, Nov. 18, 1939). **C H A M B E R :** *Melodía* for Cello and Piano (1897–99); *Mireya* for Flute and Piano Quartet (1899); Piano Quartet (1899); *Romanza* for Cello and Piano (1899); *Serenata andaluza* for Violin and Piano (1899; not extant); *Fanfare pour une fête* (1921). **K E Y B O A R D : P i a n o :** *Nocturno* (1899); *Serenata andaluza* (1899); *Canción* (1900); *Vals-capricho* (1900); *Cortejo de gnomos* (1901); *Suite fantástica* (1901; not extant); *Hoja de album* (1902); *Pièces espagnoles: Aragonesa, Cubana, Montanesa,* and *Andaluza* (1902–8); *Allegro de concierto* (1903); *Fantasía bética* (1919); *Canto de los remeros del Volga* (1922); *Pour le tombeau de Paul Dukas* (1935; orch. version as *Homenajes*). **G u i t a r :** *Homenaje "Le Tombeau de Claude Debussy"* (1920; orch. version as *Homenajes*). **V O C A L :** *Dos rimas* (1899–1900); *Preludios* (1900); *Tus ojillo negros* (1902); *Trois mélodies* (1909); *Siete canciones populares españolas* (1914–15); *Oracion de las madres que tienen a sus hijos en brazos* (1914); *El pan de ronda* (1915); *Psyché* for Voice, Flute, Harp, and String Trio (1924); *Soneto a Córdoba* for Voice and Harp or Piano (1927).

WRITINGS: *Escritos sobre música y músicos* (ed. by F. Sopeña; Madrid, 1950; 3rd ed., 1972; Eng. tr., 1979, as *On Music and Musicians*); *Cartas a Segismondo Romero* (ed. by P. Recuero; Granada, 1976); *Correspondencia de Manuel de Falla* (ed. by E. Franco; Madrid, 1978).

BIBL.: J. Trend, *M. d.F. and Spanish Music* (N.Y., 1929; new ed., 1934); Roland-Manuel, *M. d.F.* (Paris, 1930); A. Sagardia, *M. d.F.* (Madrid, 1946); J. Thomas, *M. d.F. en la Isla* (Palma, 1947); J. Jaenisch, *M. d.F. und die spanische Musik* (Zürich and Freiburg im Breisgau, 1952); L. Campodonico, *F.* (Paris, 1959); R. Arizaga, *M. d.F.* (Buenos Aires, 1961); E. Molina Fajardo, *M. d.F. y el "cante jondo"* (Granada, 1962); J. Viniegra, *M. d.F.: Su vida intima* (Cádiz, 1966); A. Saeardia, *Vida y Obra de M. d.F.* (Madrid, 1967); J. Grunfeld, *M. d.F.: Spanien und die neue Musik* (Zürich, 1968); M. Orozco, *M. d.F.: Biografia illustrada* (Barcelona, 1968); A. Campoamor Gonzalez, *M. d.F., 1876–1946* (Madrid, 1976); R. Crichton, *M. d.F.: Descriptive Catalogue of His Works* (London, 1976); B. James, *M. d.F. and the Spanish Musical Renaissance* (London, 1979); R. Crichton, *F.* (London, 1982); G. Chase and A. Budwig, *M. d.F.: A Bibliography and Research Guide* (N.Y., 1986); J. de Persia, *Los últimos años de M. d.F.* (Madrid, 1989); T. Garms, *Der Flamenco und der spanische Folklore in M. d.F.s Werken* (Wiesbaden, 1990); K. Pahlen, *M. d.F. und der Musik in Spanien* (Mainz, 1993); A. Ruiz-Pipó, *Catalogo de l'oeuvre de M. d. F.* (Paris, 1993); N. Harper, *M. d.F.: A Bio-Bibliography* (Westport, Conn., 1998).—**NS/LK/DM**

Falletta, JoAnn, American conductor; b. N.Y., Feb. 27, 1954. She began classical guitar and piano lessons at age 7. In 1972 she entered the Mannes Coll. of Music in N.Y. to continue her guitar studies but the next year became a conducting student of Sung Kwak (B.M., 1976; M.A., 1978). In 1982 she entered the Juilliard School in N.Y. on a conducting scholarship, completing her advanced training with Mester and Ehrling (M.M. 1983; D.M.A., 1989). From 1978 to 1990 she was music director of the Queens (N.Y.) Phil., and was also music director of the Denver Chamber Orch. (1983–92) and assoc. conductor of the Milwaukee Sym. Orch. (1985–88). In 1985 she won both the Stokowski and Toscanini conducting awards. From 1986 to 1995 she was music director of the Bay Area Women's Phil. in San Francisco, with which she presented works by women composers of all eras. She concurrently served as music director of the Long Beach (Calif.) Sym. Orch. (1989–2000) and the Va. Sym. Orch. in Norfolk (from 1991). In 1998 she became music director of the Buffalo Phil. As a guest conductor, she appeared with orchs. in the U.S. and abroad.—**NS/LK/DM**

Fallows, David (Nicholas), English musicologist; b. Suxton, Dec. 20, 1945. He was educated at Jesus Coll., Cambridge (B.A., 1967), King's Coll., Univ. of London (M.Mus., 1968), and the Univ. of Calif. at Berkeley (Ph.D., 1973). In 1973–74 he was a lecturer in music at the Univ. of Wisc. at Madison. In 1976 he became a lecturer, in 1982 a senior lecturer, and in 1992 a reader in music at the Univ. of Manchester. In 1982–83 he also was a visiting assoc. prof. at the Univ. of N.C. at Chapel Hill. He was awarded the Dent Medal in 1982 and in 1994 he was made a Chevalier de l'Ordre des Arts et des Lettres of France. In 1999 he was made a corresponding member of the American Musicological Soc. Fallows has contributed articles to various journals and reference works on early music. He also publ. the study *Dufay* (London, 1982; rev. 1987), *Songs and Musicians in the Fifteenth Century* (Brookfield, Vt., 1996), and *Catalogue of Polyphonic Songs, 1415–1480* (1999).—**LK/DM**

Fame, Georgie (originally, **Powell, Clive**), pop-jazz piano/organ/vocals/composer; b. Leigh, Lancashire, England, June 26, 1943. His father gigged in local dance bands. He began playing piano at age of seven, and played with a local group, The Dominoes, from 1957. In 1958, he spent a season at Butlin's, Pwllheli, Wales, with Rory Blackwell. Fame then went to London with Blackwell in early 1959. Signed by famed pop agent Larry Parnes, he played various gigs, then became accompanist for pop-rocker Billy Fury (1960–61). Fame worked briefly with Earl Watson then formed his own Blue Flames (July 1962), and began specializing on Hammond organ in December 1962. He played a long residency at Flamingo Club, London, and produced hit records through the mid-1960s that popularized R&B and ska rhythms. He temporarily disbanded Blue Flames in 1966 to work with Harry South's Big Band, and then played solo cabaret dates (1967–68), and was also featured with Count Basie's Band (1967 and 1968). He led his own band again then worked in duo with ex- Animals singer-keyboard player Alan Price (1971–73). Fame has been featured with his own band through the 1980s and 1990s, toured Australia, guested in Scandinavia, also toured in shows devised by Keith Smith, including *Stardust Road*, a tribute to Hoagy

Carmichael. Georgie has two sons; Tristram (b. 1971) plays guitar, and James (b. 1975) plays drums.

DISC.: *Rhythm and Blues at the Flamingo* (1963); *Fame at Last* (1964); *Yeh Yeh* (1965); *Sweet Things* (1966); *Sound Adventure* (1966); *Get Away* (1966); *Two Faces of Fame* (1967); *Hall of Fame* (1967); *The Ballad of Bonnie and Clyde* (1968); *Third Face of Fame* (1968); *Seventh Son* (1969); *Georgie Does His Thing with Strings* (1970); *Going Home* (1971); *Fame and Price: Together* (1971); *All Me Own Work* (1972); *Georgie Fame* (1974); *That's What Friends Are For* (1979); *Right Now* (1979); *Closing the Gap* (1980); *Hoagland* (1981); *In Goodman's Land* (1983); *My Favorite Songs* (1984); *No Worries* (1988); *Cool Cat Blues* (1990); *And the Danish Radio Big Band* (1993); *The Blues and Me* (1994).—**JC-B/LP**

Famintsyn, Alexander (Sergeievich),
Russian music critic and composer; b. Kaluga, Nov. 5, 1841; d. Ligovo, July 6, 1896. He studied with Vogt in St. Petersburg and attended the Univ. there. After further training with Santis, he studied with Hauptmann, Richter, and Riedel at the Leipzig Cons. (1862–64) and with Seifriz in Löwenberg. He was prof. of music history and aesthetics at the St. Petersburg Cons. (1865–72), and then devoted himself principally to music criticism in which he acquired a reputation as a trenchant polemicist against the Russian nationalist school of composition. Famintsyn wrote the operas *Sardanapal* (St. Petersburg, Dec. 5, 1875) and *Uriel Acosta* (1883), a piano quintet, a string quartet, and songs.—**NS/LK/DM**

Fancelli, Giuseppe,
admired Italian tenor; b. Florence, Nov. 24, 1833; d. there, Dec. 23, 1887. He had no formal musical instruction and never learned to read music. However, his natural vocal gifts were discovered and he made his operatic debut as the Fisherman in *Guglielmo Tell* at Milan's La Scala in 1860. After singing in Ancona, Rome, and Trieste, he appeared at London's Covent Garden (1866–68; 1870–72), where he excelled as Edgardo, Alfredo, Raoul, and Pollione. In 1872 he sang Radames in the first Italian staging of *Aida* at La Scala. Fancelli's marvelous high C endeared him to a generation of opera aficionados.—**NS/LK/DM**

Fanciulli, Francesco,
Italian-American conductor and composer; b. Porto San Stefano, July 17, 1850; d. N.Y., July 17, 1915. He studied in Florence. After some years as an opera conductor in Italy, he went to America (1876) and earned his living as an organist and theatrical conductor. In 1893 he succeeded Sousa as conductor of the Marine Band in Washington, D.C., and then was bandmaster of the 71st Regiment in N.Y. (1898–1904); after that, he conducted his own band. He wrote 5 operas, including *Priscilla* (Norfolk, Va., Nov. 1, 1901), as well as a number of marches and other pieces for band, orch. music, choral works, chamber music, songs, and piano pieces.—**NS/LK/DM**

Fanelli, Ernest,
French composer; b. Paris, June 29, 1860; d. there, Nov. 24, 1917. He played drums in orchs. as a small boy, and entered the Paris Cons. in 1876, in the class of Delibes. He worked as a copyist and music engraver for many years. In 1912 he applied to Gabriel Pierné for work, submitting the score of his symphonic poem *Thèbes* as a specimen of his handwriting. This score, composed by Fanelli as early as 1883, seemed to anticipate the instrumental and harmonic usages of Debussy and other composers of impressionist music, and Pierné decided to perform it as a curiosity. He conducted it at a Colonne concert in Paris (March 17, 1912), and the novelty created a mild sensation in French musical circles. Other works by Fanelli (*Impressions pastorales*; *L'Effroi du Soleil*; *Suite rabelaisienne*; etc.), all written before 1893, were also found interesting. However, the sensation proved of brief duration, and the extravagant claims for Fanelli's talent collapsed. —**NS/LK/DM**

Fano, (Aronne) Guido Alberto,
Italian composer, teacher, and writer on music; b. Padua, May 18, 1875; d. Tauriano di Spilimbergo, Friuli, Aug. 14, 1961. He was a pupil of Orefice and Pollini in Padua, then of Martucci at the Bologna Liceo Musicale (composition diploma, 1897); received a law degree from the Univ. of Bologna (1901). He taught piano at the Bologna Liceo Musicale (1900–1905), and then was director of the conservatories in Parma (1905–12), Naples (1912–16), and Palermo (1916–22);. He subsequently taught piano at the Milan Cons. (1922–38; 1945–47).

WORKS: DRAMATIC: *Astraea*, poema drammatico; *Juturna*, dramma musicale. **ORCH.:** *La tentazione di Gesù*, symphonic poem; overture (1912); *Andante e allegro con fuoco* for Piano and Orch. (1936); *Impressioni sinfoniche da Napoleone* (1949). **OTHER:** Chamber music, piano pieces, and songs.

WRITINGS: *Pensieri sulla musica* (Bologna, 1903); *Nella vita del ritmo* (Naples, 1916); *Lo studio del pianoforte* (3 vols., Milan, 1923–24).—**NS/LK/DM**

Farberman, Harold,
American conductor and composer; b. N.Y., Nov. 2, 1929. He was educated at the Juilliard School of Music in N.Y. (diploma, 1951) and the New England Cons. of Music in Boston (B.S., 1956; M.S., 1957). He was a percussionist in the Boston Sym. Orch. (1951–63) and conductor of the New Arts Orch. in Boston (1955–63); then was conductor of the Colorado Springs (Colo.) Phil. (1967–68) and the Oakland (Calif.) Sym. Orch. (1971–79); subsequently was principal guest conductor of the Bournemouth Sinfonietta (from 1986). In 1975 he became founder-president of the Conductors' Guild. In 1980 he organized the Conductors' Inst. at the Univ. of W.Va., which removed to the Univ. of S.C. in 1987.

WORKS: DRAMATIC: *Medea*, chamber opera (1960–61; Boston, March 26, 1961); *If Music Be*, mixed media piece (1965); *The Losers*, opera (N.Y., March 26, 1971); ballets; film scores. **ORCH.:** Concerto for Bassoon and Strings (1956); Sym. (1956–57); Timpani Concerto (1958); *Impressions* for Oboe, Strings, and Percussion (1959–60); Concerto for Alto Saxophone and Strings (1965); *Elegy, Fanfare, and March* (1965); Violin Concerto (1976); *The You Name it March* (1981); *Shapings* for English Horn, Strings, and Percussion (1984); *A Summer's Day in Central Park* (1987; N.Y., Jan. 21, 1988). **CHAMBER:** *Variations* for Percussion and Piano (1954); *Variations on a Familiar Theme* for Percussion (1955); *Music Inn Suite* for 6 Percussion (1958); String Quartet (1960); *Progressions* for Flute and Percussion (1961); *Quintessence* for Woodwind Quintet (1962); Trio for Violin, Piano, and Percussion (1963); *For Eric and Nick* for

Chamber Group (1964); *Images for Brass* for 2 Trumpets, Horn, Trombone, and Tuba (1964); *The Preacher* for Electric Trumpet and 4 Percussion (1969); *Alea* for 6 Percussion (1976); Duo for English Horn and Percussion (1981). **VOCAL:** *Evolution* for Soprano, Horn, and 7 Percussion (1954); *Greek Scene* for Mezzo-soprano, Piano, and Percussion (1957; also for Mezzo-soprano and Orch.); *August 30, 1964-N.Y. Times* for Mezzo-soprano, Piano, and Percussion (1964); *War Cry on a Prayer Feather* for Soprano, Baritone, and Orch. (1976).—**NS/LK/DM**

Farina, Carlo, significant Italian violinist and composer; b. Mantua, c. 1600; d. c. 1640. He was a violinist at the Mantuan court, where he acquired a notable reputation. In 1625 he was called to Dresden as Konzertmeister of the court, a position he held for some four years. In 1637 he was active in Danzig, and then most likely returned to his homeland. Farina was one of the leading violin virtuosos of his era. As a composer, he profoundly influenced the development of the sonata form in Germany. Among his publ. works were sinfonias, sonatas, dances, canzonas, and programmatic pieces. The latter call upon the violin to imitate other instruments and even animals.

WORKS (all publ. in Dresden): *Libro delle pavane, gagliarde, brand: mascherata, aria franzesa, volte, balletti, sonate, canzone* a 2–4 and Basso Continuo (1626); *Ander Theil neuer Paduanen, Gagliarden, Couranten, französischen Arien...Quodlibet von allerhand seltzamen Inventionen...etlichen teutschen Täntzen* a 4 (1627); *Il terzo libro delle pavane, gagliarde, brand: mascherata, arie franzese, volte, corrente, sinfonie* a 3, 4, and Basso Continuo (1627); *Il quarto libro delle pavane, gagliarde, balletti, volte, passamezi, sonate, canson* a 2–4 and Basso Continuo (1628); *Fünffter Theil neuer Pavanen, Brand: Mascheraden, Balletten, Sonaten* a 2–4 and Basso Continuo (1628).—**LK/DM**

Fariñas, Carlos, Cuban composer and teacher; b. Cienfuegos, Nov. 28, 1934. He was a student of Ardévol and Gramatges at the Havana Cons., of Copland at the Berkshire Music Center at Tanglewood (summer, 1956), and of Pirumov and Rogal-Levitski at the Moscow Cons. (1961–63); later he worked in Berlin on a grant from the Deutscher Akademischer Austauschdienst (1975–77). After serving as director of the Conservatorio Alejandro García Caturla in Havana (1963–67), he was head of the music dept. of the Biblioteca Nacional de Cuba there (1967–77). In 1978 he joined the faculty of music at the Instituto Superior de Arte de Cuba in Havana, where he was founder-director of the Estudio de Música Electroacustica y por Computadoras (from 1989). His works are generally cast along avant-garde lines. While he used Afro-Cuban folk sources for inspiration in some of his works, he eventually embraced the most technologically advanced means of expression, including electronic and computer-processed scores.

WORKS: DRAMATIC: Opera: *Escenas* (1990). **Ballet:** *Despertar* (1959–60); *Yagruma* (1975). **ORCH.:** *Música* for Strings (1957); *Relieves* for 5 Orch. Groups (1969); *Muros rejas y vitrales* (1969–71); *El bosque ha echado a andar* (1976); *Punto y tonadas* for Strings (1981); *Nocturno de enero* (1989); *En tres partes* for Cuban Lute and Strings (1990). **CHAMBER:** Sonata for Violin and Cello (1961); String Quartet (1962–63); *Tiento I* for Clarinet, Guitar, Piano, and Percussion (1966) and *II* for 2 Pianos and Percussion (1969); *In rerum natura* for Clarinet,

Violin, Cello, and Harp (1972); *Tatomaitee* for String Quartet and Percussion (1972); Concerto for Violin and 2 Percussion (1976); *Impronta* for Piano, 4 Percussion, and Tape (1985); guitar pieces. **KEYBOARD: Piano:** (6) *Preludios* (1953–64); *6 Sones sencillos* (1956–64); *Atanos* (1972); *Alta gracia* (1984); *Sonero* (1992); *Conjuro: John Cage in memoriam* (1993). **OTHER:** Choral pieces; multimedia music; tape pieces.—**NS/LK/DM**

Farinelli (real name, **Finco**), **Giuseppe (Francesco),** Italian composer; b. Este, May 7, 1769; d. Trieste, Dec. 12, 1836. After initial training in Este, he studied in Venice with Antonio Martinelli. He adopted the name Farinelli when he was befriended by the celebrated castrato soprano. He was a pupil of La Barbiera (voice), Fago (harmony), Sala (counterpoint), and Tritto (composition) at the Cons. della Pietà dei Turchini in Naples. After his first opera was premiered at the Cons. in 1792, he went on to compose some 20 opere serie and 38 comic operas. A number of his operas were popular until being eclipsed by the masterpieces of Rossini. From 1817 until his death he was maestro al cembalo at the Teatro Grande in Trieste, and was also organist and maestro di cappella at the cathedral of S. Giusto there from 1819. Among his other works were 3 oratorios, 5 Masses, 2 Te Deums, and 11 cantatas.—**NS/LK/DM**

Farjeon, Harry, English composer; b. Hohokus, N.J. (of English parents), May 6, 1878; d. London, Dec. 29, 1948. He was a son of the English novelist B.L. Farjeon, and grandson of the famous actor Joseph Jefferson. He was educated in England, taking music lessons with Landon Ronald and John Storer. He then studied composition with Corder at the Royal Academy of Music in London, winning the Lucas Medal and other prizes. In 1903 he became an instructor at the Royal Academy of Music.

WORKS: *Floretta*, opera (1899); *The Registry Office*, operetta (1900); *A Gentleman of the Road*, operetta (1902); Piano Concerto (1903); *Hans Andersen Suite* for Small Orch. (1905); *Summer Vision*, symphonic poem (not extant); 2 song cycles: *Vagrant Songs* and *The Lute of Jade*.—**NS/LK/DM**

Farkas, Edmund Ödön, Hungarian conductor, pedagogue, and composer; b. Pusztamonostor, Jan. 27, 1851; d. Klausenburg, Sept. 11, 1912. He studied engineering at the Univ. (1870–75) and was a student of Erkel, Ábrányi, and Volkmann at the Royal Academy of Music (graduated, 1878) in Budapest. In 1879 he settled in Klausenburg as a teacher at the Cons., where he was its director from 1880 until his death. He also conducted at the National Theater (1881–82), organized his own orch., founded a music journal, and promoted the cause of national Hungarian music. As a composer, he was adept at writing songs.

WORKS: DRAMATIC (all are operas unless otherwise given): *Radó és Ilonka* (Conrad and Helen), operetta (1872); *Bajadér* (Budapest, Aug. 23, 1876); *A vezeklők* (The Penitents; 1884; Klausenburg, 1893); *Tündérforrás* (Fairy Fountain; Klausenburg, 1893); *Balassa Bálint*, comic opera (1895; Budapest, Jan. 16, 1896); *Tetemrehívás* (Ordeal of the Bier; Budapest, Oct. 5, 1900); *Kurucvilág* (The World of the Kurucs), occasional piece

(Budapest, Oct. 28, 1906). **OTHER**: Sym. (1898); *Rákóczy Symphony* (1903); Violin Concerto (1903); symphonic poems; sacred music; 5 string quartets; piano pieces.—**NS/LK/DM**

Farkas, Ferenc, prominent Hungarian composer and teacher; b. Nagykanizsa, Dec. 15, 1905. He began to study piano as a child. He took courses with Leo Weiner and Albert Siklos at the Academy of Music in Budapest (1922–27); a state scholarship enabled him to study with Respighi at the Accademia di Santa Cecilia in Rome (1929–31). Returning to Hungary, he was a music teacher at the municipal school in Budapest (1935–41). From 1941 to 1944 he taught at the Cluj Cons., and from 1946 to 1948 he was director of the music school in Székesfehérvár; from 1949 to 1975 he was a prof. of composition at the Academy of Music in Budapest. In 1950 and 1991 he was awarded the Kossuth Prize and in 1960 the Erkel Prize; was made Merited Artist (1965) and Honored Artist (1970) of the Hungarian People's Republic. He also received the Herder Prize of Hamburg (1979) and was made a Cavaliere dell'Ordine della Repubblica Italiana (1985).

WORKS: DRAMATIC: *The Magic Cupboard*, comic opera (1938–42; Budapest, April 22, 1942; also a separate overture, 1952); *The Sly Students*, ballet (1949); *Csinom Palkó*, musical play (1950; rev. 1960); *Vidróczki*, radio ballad (1959; rev. as an opera, 1964); *Piroschka*, musical comedy (1967); *Story of Noszty Junior with Mari Tóth*, musical comedy (1971); *Panegyricus*, ballet (1972); *A Gentleman from Venice*, opera (1980). Also incidental music and film scores. **ORCH.**: *Fantasy* for Piano and Orch. (1929); *Divertimento* (1930); Harp Concertino (1937; rev. 1956); *Dinner Music* for Chamber Orch. (1938); *Rhapsodia carpathiana* (1940); *Marionette's Dance Suite* (1940–41); *Musica pentatonica* for Strings (1945); *Musica dodecatonica*, later renamed *Prelude and Fugue* (1947); Piano Concertino (1947–49); *Lavotta*, suite (1951); Sym. (1951–52); *Scherzo sinfonico* (1952); *Symphonic Overture* (1952); *Sketches from the Bukk* (1955); *Piccola musica di concerto* for Strings (1961); *Trittico concertato* for Cello and Strings (1964); *Gyász és vígasz* (Planctus et Consolationes; 1965); *Concerto all'Antica* for Baryton or Viola da Gamba, and Strings (1965); *Serenata concertante* for Flute and Strings (1967); *Festive Overture* (1972); *Variazioni classiche* (1975–76); *Ouverture philharmonique* (1977–78); *Musica serena* for Strings (1982); *Musica giocosa*, suite (1982); Concertino for Trumpet and Strings (1984). **CHAMBER**: 3 violin sonatinas (1930, 1931, 1959); *Alla danza ungherese* for Cello or Violin and Piano (1934); *Scherzino and Intermezzo* for Recorder and Piano (1940); *Serenade* for Wind Quintet (1951); *Antiche danze ungheresi* for Wind Quintet (1953); *Sonata a due* for Viola and Cello (1961); Serenade for Flute and 2 Violins (1965); String Quartet (1970–72); *Tower Music of Nyirbátor* for 3 Trumpets, 4 Horns, 3 Trombones, and Tuba (1974); Trio for Violin, Cello, and Piano (1979); 10 Studies for 2 Violins (1982); *Trigon* for Flute, Bassoon, and Piano (1988). **VOCAL**: *Cantata lirica* for Chorus and Orch. (1945); *Cantus Pannonicus* for Soprano, Chorus, and Orch. (Budapest, April 3, 1959); *Flying Flags* for Soprano, Baritone, Men's Chorus, and Orch. (1972–73); *Aspirationes principis* for Tenor, Baritone, and Orch. (1974–75); *Vita poetae* for Men's Trio, Chorus, and Instruments (1976); *Ad Musicam* for Chorus (1981); songs.

BIBL.: J. Ujfalussy, *F. F.* (Budapest, 1969).—**NS/LK/DM**

Farkas, Philip (Francis), American horn player and teacher; b. Chicago, March 5, 1914; d. Bloomington,

Ind., Dec. 21, 1992. After study with Louis Defrasne in Chicago, he was 1st horn player in the Kansas City Phil. (1933–36), the Chicago Sym. Orch. (1936–41; 1947–60), the Cleveland Orch. (1941–45; 1946–47), and the Boston Sym. Orch. (1945–46). He taught at the Ind. Univ. School of Music in Bloomington (1960–82) and founded his own publishing company, Wind Music, Inc. He also authored *The Art of French Horn Playing* (1956), *The Art of Brass Playing* (1962), and *A Photographic Study of 40 Virtuoso Horn Players' Embouchures* (1970).

BIBL.: M. Stewart, ed., *P.: The Legacy of a Master* (Northfield, Ill., 1990); N. Fako, *P. F. & His Horn: A Happy, Worthwhile Life* (Elmhurst, Ill., 1998).—**NS/LK/DM**

Farley, Carole Ann, talented American soprano; b. Le Mars, Iowa, Nov. 29, 1946. She studied at the Ind. Univ. School of Music (Mus.B., 1968), with Reid in N.Y., and on a Fulbright scholarship with Schech at the Munich Hochschule für Musik (1968–69). In 1969 she made her debut at the Linz Landestheater and also her U.S. debut at N.Y.'s Town Hall; subsequently appeared as a soloist with major orchs. of the U.S. and Europe, and sang with the Welsh National Opera (1971–72), the Cologne Opera (1972–75), the Strasbourg Opera (1975), the N.Y. City Opera (1976), and the Lyons Opera (1976–77). She made her formal Metropolitan Opera debut in N.Y. as Lulu on March 18, 1977, and continued to sing there in later seasons; she also sang at the Zürich Opera (1979), the Deutsche Oper am Rhein in Düsseldorf (1980–81; 1984), the Chicago Lyric Opera (1981), the Florence Maggio Musicale (1985), and at the Teatro Colón in Buenos Aires (1989). In addition to her esteemed portrayal of Lulu, which she essayed over 80 times in various operatic centers, she also sang Poppea, Donna Anna, Violetta, Massenet's Manon, Mimi, and various roles in Richard Strauss's operas. She married **José Serebrier** in 1969.—**NS/LK/DM**

Farmer, Henry George, eminent Irish musicologist; b. Birr, Jan. 17, 1882; d. Law, Scotland, Dec. 30, 1965. He studied piano and violin, and as a boy joined the Royal Artillery Orch. in London, playing the violin and clarinet at its concerts. He then studied philosophy and languages at Glasgow Univ. An extremely prolific writer, he publ. a number of original works, dealing with such varied subjects as military music and Arabic musical theories. He was the founder and conductor of the Glasgow Sym. Orch. (1919–43). Among his compositions were a ballet and other works for the theater, several overtures, and some chamber music.

WRITINGS: *Memoirs of the Royal Artillery Band* (1904); *The Rise and Development of Military Music* (1912); *The Arabian Influence on Musical Theory* (1925); *Byzantine Musical Instruments in the 9th Century* (1925); *The Arabic Musical MSS. in the Bodleian Library* (1925); *A History of Arabian Music to the 13th Century* (1929); *Music in Medieval Scotland* (1931); *Historical Facts for the Arabian Musical Influence* (1930); *The Organ of the Ancients from Eastern Sources, Hebrew, Syriac and Arabic* (1931); *Studies in Oriental Musical Instruments* (1931); *An Old Moorish Lute Tutor* (1933); *Al-Farabi's Arabic- Latin Writings on Music* (1934); *Turkish*

Instruments of Music in the 17th Century (1937); *A History of Music in Scotland* (1947); *Music Making in the Olden Days* (1950); *Oriental Studies, Mainly Musical* (1953); *The History of the Royal Artillery Band* (1954); *British Bands in Battle* (1965).—**NS/LK/DM**

Farmer, John, English organist and composer; b. c. 1570; d. after 1601. He was organist and Master of the Children at Christ Church Cathedral in Dublin in 1595, where he was made vicar-choral in 1596. In 1599 he went to London. He publ. *Divers and Sundry Waies of Two Parts in One, to the number of Fortie, uppon One Playn Song* (London, 1591) and *The First Set of English Madrigals: To Foure Voices* (London, 1599; ed. by E. Fellowes, *The English Madrigal School*, VIII, 1914), which includes the celebrated madrigal *Faire Phyllis I saw sitting all alone.* He contributed canticles and hymns to Thomas East's *The Whole Booke of Psalmes* (1592) and a madrigal to *The Triumphes of Oriana* (1603).—**NS/LK/DM**

Farnaby, Giles, significant English composer; b. c. 1563; d. London (buried), Nov. 25, 1640. He was a joiner by trade. After taking his B.M. at the Univ. of Oxford in 1592, he spent most of his life in London. He excelled as a composer of keyboard music. More than 50 of his virginal pieces were included in the *Fitzwilliam Virginal Book* (c. 1612–19; 54 pieces [1 doubtful] were ed. in Musica Britannica, XXIV, 1965). He publ. 20 *Canzonets to Foure Voyces with a Song of Eight Parts* (London, 1598; ed. in The English Madrigalists, XX, 2nd ed., 1962). Other vocal works, including madrigals and Psalms, appeared in various collections of his day. His son, Richard Farnaby (b. London, c. 1594; d. place and date unknown), was also a composer. Some 52 of his keyboard pieces were included in the *Fitzwilliam Virginal Book.*

BIBL.: R. Marlow, *The Life and Music of G. F.* (diss., Univ. of Cambridge, 1966).—**NS/LK/DM**

Farnadi, Edith, Hungarian pianist and teacher; b. Budapest, Sept. 25, 1921; d. Graz, Dec. 14, 1973. She entered the Budapest Academy of Music at the age of 9, and studied with Bartók and Weiner. She made her debut at age 12, and was granted her diploma at 16. She made appearances with the violinists Hubay and Huberman. She taught at the Budapest Academy of Music, and then became a teacher in Graz.—**NS/LK/DM**

Farnam, (Walter) Lynnwood, outstanding Canadian organist and pedagogue; b. Sutton, Quebec, Jan. 13, 1885; d. N.Y., Nov. 23, 1930. He studied piano in Dunham, and then held the Lord Strathcona Scholarship to the Royal Coll. of Music in London (1900–1904), where he was a student of Franklin Taylor (piano) and Parratt and W.S. Hoyte (organ). He was organist in Montreal at St. James' Methodist Church (1904–05) and at the Church of St. James the Apostle (1905–08), and then organist-choirmaster at Christ Church Cathedral (1908–13); he also was active as a recitalist and in 1912–13 taught at the McGill Cons. After serving as organist at Boston's Emmanuel Church (1913–18), he went to N.Y. as organist at the Fifth Ave. Presbyterian Church (1919–20) and then at the Church of the Holy Communion (1920–30). His recital tours took him all over North America, England, and France. In addition to teaching in N.Y., he was on the faculty of the Curtis Inst. of Music in Philadelphia (1927–30). Farnam's recital repertoire was extraordinary, ranging from the pre-Bach masters to his own era. He played the complete works of Bach, and also of many Romantic composers, among them Franck and Brahms. Louis Vierne's 6th Organ Sym. (1931) is dedicated to Farnam's memory.—**NS/LK/DM**

Farncombe, Charles (Frederick), English conductor; b. London, July 29, 1919. He first studied engineering at the Univ. of London (B.S., 1940). After military service in World War II, he enrolled at the Royal School of Church Music, Canterbury, and the Royal Academy of Music, London. In 1955 he organized the Handel Opera Soc., serving as its music director and conductor. From 1970 to 1979 he was chief conductor of the Drottningholm Court Theater in Stockholm, and then music director of the London Chamber Opera (from 1983) and the Malcolm Sargent Festival Choir (from 1986). In 1977 he was made a Commander of the Order of the British Empire.—**NS/LK/DM**

Farquhar, David (Andross), New Zealand composer and teacher; b. Cambridge, New Zealand, April 5, 1928. He studied with Douglas Lilburn, at Canterbury Coll., and at Victoria Coll. (B.A., B.M., 1948), and then went to England and took his M.A. at Emmanuel Coll., Cambridge (1951), completing his training with Benjamin Frankel at the Guildhall School of Music in London (1951–52). Returning to New Zealand, he was a lecturer (1953–76) and prof. of music (1976–93) at Victoria Univ. of Wellington. In 1974 he was founding president of the Composers Assn. of New Zealand. His music is contrapuntal in structure and neo-Romantic in mood.

WORKS: DRAMATIC: *A Unicorn for Christmas,* opera (1962); *Oh Captain Cook!,* musical (1969); *Shadow,* opera (1970; Wellington, Sept. 19, 1988); *Fives* for 5 Dancers and 5 Instruments (1971); *The Uses of Adversity,* chamber opera (1996); *Enchanted Island,* opera (1997). **ORCH.:** *Ring Round the Moon,* suite (1953–57); *Epithalamion Overture* for Strings (1954); *Harlequin Overture* (1959); 2 syms.: No. 1 (1959; Wellington, Aug. 13, 1960) and No. 2 (1982; Wellington, Nov. 5, 1983); *Elegy* for Strings (1961); *Anniversary Suite No. 1* (1961) and *No. 2* (1965); *Echoes and Reflections* for Strings (1974); *Evocation* for Orch. of Violins (1975); *March* for Clarinet and Strings (1984); *Scherzo* (1992); Concerto for Guitar and Small Orch. (1992); *Serenade* for Strings (1993); *Auras* for Piano and Orch. (1994). **CHAMBER:** *5 Canons* for 2 Clarinets (1951); *Divertimento* for Brass (1960); *Anniversary Duos* for 2 Guitars (1961–69); Concerto for Wind Quintet (1966); Suite for Guitar (1966); *3 Pieces* for Violin and Piano (1967); *5 Scenes* for Guitar (1971); *Inside-Out* for Piano Duet and 2 Percussionists (1972); *Scenes and Memories* for Violin, Piano, and Percussion (1972); *3 Pieces* for Double Bass (1976); *Exchanges* for Guitar Quartet (1979); *Homage to Stravinsky* for Brass Quintet or Wind Octet (1986); *Concerto for Six* for Flute, Clarinet, Violin, Cello, Vibraphone, and Piano (1987); 4 string quartets (1989, 1995, 1998, 1998); *Equali* for 2 Cellos (1991); *Bachiana* for Wind Quintet (1994); *Three for Two* for Clarinet and Guitar (1995); *Obsessions* for Treble Recorder (1997); various piano pieces. **VOCAL:** *8 Blake Songs* for Baritone or Mezzo-soprano and Piano (1947–49; rev. 1955); *6 Songs of Women* for

Soprano and Piano (1957); *In Despite of Death* for Baritone and Piano (1958); *3 Scots Ballads* for Baritone and Piano (1958); *Three of a Kind* for Chorus (1967); *Play-Sing the Music*, 14 songs for Young People (1969); *Bells in Their Seasons* for Double Chorus and Orch. (1974); *Magpies and Other Birds* for Vocal Quartet (1976); *Waiata Maori* for Chorus (1985); *3 Cilla McQueen Songs* for Mezzo-soprano or Baritone and Piano (1987); *Remembrance of Things Past* for High Voice and Piano (1995).—NS/LK/DM

Farrant, John, English organist and composer who was active in the 16th century. He served as lay clerk (1571–78) and subsequently as organist at the Salisbury Cathedral (1587–92); he was briefly organist at Hereford (1593). Contemporary records testify to his intractable temper, which resulted in physical clashes with the dean of the Salisbury Cathedral, and led to his expulsion. As a composer, Farrant is chiefly distinguished for his Service in D minor (misattributed in a 19th-century ed. to Richard Farrant). His son, also named John Farrant (baptized in Salisbury, Sept. 28, 1575; d. there, 1618), was a chorister at the Salisbury Cathedral in 1585, and organist there from 1598 until his death. Another John Farrant, possibly related to the preceding, was organist at Christ Church, Newgate, London. He was the author of a Magnificat, which, sometimes referred to as "Farrant in G minor," is often confused with Richard Farrant's Cathedral Service in A minor.—NS/LK/DM

Farrant, Richard, English organist and composer; b. c. 1527; d. London, Nov. 30, 1580. He was a Gentleman of the Chapel Royal. In 1564 he became master of the choristers at St. George's Chapel, Windsor, where he also was a lay clerk and organist. From 1567 he presented a play annually with the Windsor boys before Queen Elisabeth I. In 1569 he became master of the choristers of the Chapel Royal while retaining his Windsor position. In 1577 he combined the boys with the Chapel Royal choristers to form the Windsor-Chapel Royal Co. His Service in A minor for 4 voices is often confused with John Farrant's Magnificat, sometimes designated as "Farrant in G minor." Among other extant works are the anthems *Hide Not Thou Thy Face* and *Call to Remembrance*, both for 4 voices, and the verse anthem *When as We Sat in Babylon* for 1 to 4 voices.—NS/LK/DM

Farrar, Ernest (Bristow), English organist and composer; b. London, July 7, 1885; d. in the battle of the Somme, France, Sept. 18, 1918. He studied at the Royal Coll. of Music in London with Stanford and Parratt. He served as organist of the English Church in Dresden (1909), and then at various churches in England (1910–14). His orch. suite English *Pastoral Impression* won the Carnegie Award. He further wrote the orch. pieces *The Open Road, Lavengro, The Forsaken Merman,* and *Heroic Elegy, 3 Spiritual Studies* for strings, variations on an old English sea song for piano and orch., the cantatas *The Blessed Damozel* and *Out of Doors,* chamber music, organ preludes, songs, etc.—NS/LK/DM

Farrar, Geraldine, celebrated American soprano; b. Melrose, Mass., Feb. 28, 1882; d. Ridgefield, Conn., March 11, 1967. She studied music with Mrs. J.H. Long

of Boston; took lessons with Emma Thursby in N.Y., Trabadello in Paris, and Graziani in Berlin. She made a successful debut at the Berlin Royal Opera on Oct. 15, 1901, as Marguerite, under the direction of Karl Muck, and then studied with Lilli Lehmann. She sang at the Monte Carlo Opera (1903–06). Her career in Europe was well established before her American debut as Juliette at the Metropolitan Opera in N.Y. (Nov. 26, 1906); she remained on the roster for 16 years; made her farewell appearance in *Zaza* on April 22, 1922, but continued to sing in concert; gave her last public performance at Carnegie Hall in N.Y. in 1931 and then retired to Ridgefield, Conn. Her greatest success was Cio-Cio-San, which she sang opposite Caruso's Pinkerton in *Madama Butterfly* at its American premiere at the Metropolitan on Feb. 11, 1907; she subsequently sang this part in America more than 100 times. Her interpretation of Carmen was no less remarkable. She also appeared in silent films between 1915 and 1919; her film version of *Carmen* aroused considerable interest. On Feb. 8, 1916, she married the actor Lou Tellegen, from whom she was subsequently divorced. She made adaptations of pieces by Kreisler, Rachmaninoff, and others, for which she publ. the lyrics. She wrote an autobiography, *Such Sweet Compulsion* (N.Y., 1938), which had been preceded in 1916 by *Geraldine Farrar: The Story of an American Singer.*

BIBL.: E. Wagenknecht, *G. F.: An Authorized Record of Her Career* (Seattle, 1929); E. Nash, *Always First Class: The Career of G. F.* (Washington, D.C., 1982); A. Truxall, ed., *All Good Greetings, G. F.: Letters of G. F. to Ilka Marie Stolker, 1946–1958* (Pittsburgh, 1991).—NS/LK/DM

Farrell, Eileen, brilliant American soprano; b. Willimantic, Conn., Feb. 13, 1920. Her parents were vaudeville singers. She received her early vocal training with Merle Alcock in N.Y., and later studied with Eleanor McLellan. In 1940 she sang on the radio. In 1947–48 she made a U.S. tour as a concert singer, and then toured South America in 1949. Her song recital in N.Y. on Oct. 24, 1950, was enthusiastically acclaimed and secured for her immediate recognition. She was soloist in Beethoven's 9th Sym. with Toscanini and the NBC Sym. Orch. She also appeared many times with the N.Y. Phil. She made her operatic debut as Santuzza with the San Carlo Opera in Tampa, Fla., in 1956. In 1958 she joined the San Francisco Opera and in 1957 became a member of the Lyric Opera of Chicago. On Dec. 6, 1960, she made a successful debut with the Metropolitan Opera in N.Y. as Gluck's Alcestis; she remained on its roster until 1964; then returned in 1965–66. She was a Distinguished Prof. of Music at the Ind. Univ. School of Music in Bloomington from 1971 to 1980, and then held that title at the Univ. of Maine in Orono from 1983 to 1985. With B. Kellow, she publ. the autobiography *Can't Help Singing: The Life of Eileen Farrell* (1999).—NS/LK/DM

Farrell, Joe, American saxophonist; b. Chicago Heights, Ill., Dec. 16, 1937; d. Los Angeles, Calif., Jan. 10, 1986. He began studying tenor saxophone at 16 and moved to N.Y. after receiving a degree in music education from the Univ. of Ill. He began working with Maynard Ferguson and also worked and/or recorded with Charles Mingus, Slide Hampton, Dizzy Reece, Jaki

Byard, and others in the early 1960s. Farrell quickly rose to prominence in the late 1960s for his creations as a founding member of the Thad Jones–Mel Lewis Orch. and as a featured soloist with Elvin Jones. In the early 1970s, Farrell's saxophone and flute solos reached wider audiences through his stints with two of the three versions of Chick Corea's Return of Forever. During that same period, he recorded several albums for Creed Taylor's CTI label, which showed him to be one of the finest voices of that period on tenor and soprano saxophones and flute, playing all with equal finesse.

Although he was at home in a variety of contexts, Farrell's modal and hard bop work was most exceptional. Unfortunately, he was extremely underrated and he did not become the huge name that many had expected. For the latter part of the 1970s he worked with Flora Purim and Airto, among others, and in jazz-rock contexts before he joined the Mingus Dynasty band in 1979. The 1980s found him back in a mainstream jazz direction and he recorded albums for Xanadu, Timeless and Contemporary and toured with Joanne Brackeen before his untimely passing in 1986.

DISC.: *Outback* (1971); *Darn That Dream* (1982); *Vim 'N Vigor* (1983); *Joe Farrell Quartet* (1987); *Moon Germs* (1987); *Sonic Text* (1990).—**BW**

Farrenc, (Jacques Hippolyte) Aristide,

French flutist and music editor; b. Marseilles, April 9, 1794; d. Paris, Jan. 31, 1865. He studied flute, and went to Paris in 1815, where he studied at the Cons.; at the same time was engaged as 2nd flutist at the Théâtre-Italien. In 1821 he established a music shop and printing press. He publ. French eds. of Beethoven, and also composed music for the flute. He married **(Jeanne-) Louise (née Dumont) Farrenc**. He diligently collected material for the rectification of existing biographies, but generously turned it over to Fétis for use in the 2nd ed. of his great work, of which Farrenc also read proofs. Jointly with Fétis's son, Édouard, he began the publication of *Le Trésor des pianistes* (23 vols., 1861–74; reprinted N.Y., 1977, foreword by Bea Friedland), a collection of piano music from the 16th century to Mendelssohn, with historical notes; it was continued after his death by his wife. From 1854 he contributed articles to *La France Musicale* and other journals.—**NS/LK/DM**

Farrenc, (Jeanne-) Louise (née Dumont),

French pianist and composer; b. Paris, May 31, 1804; d. there, Sept. 15, 1875. She studied music with Reicha. In 1821 she married **(Jacques Hippolyte) Aristide Farrenc,** but was not entirely eclipsed by his acknowledged eminence. Her 3 syms. had respectable performances: No. 1 in Brussels (Feb. 23, 1845), No. 2 in Paris (May 3, 1846), and No. 3 in Paris (April 22, 1849); the last received an accolade in the prestigious, and definitely male-oriented, *Gazette Musicale*, which conceded that "she revealed, alone among her sex in musical Europe, genuine learning, united with grace and taste." She also wrote a piano concerto, 30 études in all major and minor keys for piano, 2 piano trios, cello sonata, 2 violin sonatas, 2 piano quintets, and a sextet and a nonet for winds and strings. One of her overtures (1840) was reviewed by Berlioz, who remarked that it was orchestrated "with a talent rare among women." She was a brilliant pianist, and taught piano at the Paris Cons. from 1842 until 1872, the only woman ever to hold a permanent position as an instrumentalist there in the 19th century. Her daughter Victorine (b. Paris, Feb. 23, 1826; d. there, Jan. 3, 1859) was also a talented pianist whose promising career was cut short by an early death. After the death of her husband in 1865, Louise Farrenc assumed the editorship of his monumental collection *Le Trésor des pianistes*.—**NS/LK/DM**

Farrow, Norman D.,

Canadian baritone; b. Regina, May 6, 1916; d. Greensboro, N.C., Sept. 22, 1984. He studied at the Juilliard School of Music and at N.Y. Univ., and took voice lessons with Mack Harrell and others. He was one of the organizers of the Bach Aria Group. He toured as soloist with choral ensembles, and in 1960 was engaged as artist-in-residence at Southern Methodist Univ. in Dallas.—**NS/LK/DM**

Farwell, Arthur (George),

American composer and music educator; b. St. Paul, Minn., April 23, 1872; d. N.Y., Jan. 20, 1952. He studied at the Mass. Inst. of Technology, graduating in 1893, and then music with Homer Norris and George Chadwick in Boston, Humperdinck and Pfitzner in Berlin (1897–99), and Guilmant in Paris. He was a lecturer on music at Cornell Univ. (1899–1901). From 1909 to 1914 he was on the editorial staff of *Musical America*, and also directed municipal concerts in N.Y. City (1910–13); then was director of the Settlement Music School in N.Y. (1915–18). He was acting head of the music dept. at the Univ. of Calif., Berkeley (1918–19). In 1919 he founded the Santa Barbara Community Chorus, which he conducted until 1921. He later taught theory at Mich. State Coll. in East Lansing (1927–39). Farwell was a pioneer in new American music, and tirelessly promoted national ideas in art. He contributed to various ethnological publications. From 1901 to 1911 he operated the Wa-Wan Press (Newton, Mass.), a periodical (quarterly, 1901–07; monthly, 1907–11) that printed piano and vocal music of "progressive" American composers of the period, the emphasis being on works that utilized indigenous (black, Indian, and cowboy) musical materials. Disillusioned about commercial opportunities for American music, including his own, he established at East Lansing, in 1936, his own lithographic handpress, with which he printed his music, handling the entire process of reproduction, including the cover designs, by himself.

WRITINGS: *A Letter to American Composers* (N.Y., 1903); with W. Dermot Darby, *Music in America in The Art of Music, IV* (N.Y., 1915).

WORKS: ORCH.: *The Death of Virginia*, symphonic poem (1894); *Academic Overture: Cornell* (1900); *Dawn*, fantasy on Indian themes (1904; orig. for Piano); *The Domain of Hurakan* (1910; orig. for Piano); *Symbolistic Study No. 3*, after Whitman's *Once I Passed Through a Populous City* (1905; rev. 1921; Philadelphia, March 30, 1928); *Symphonic Poem on March! March!* for Orch. and Chorus ad libitum (1921); *The Gods of the Mountain*, suite from the incidental music to Dunsany's play (1928;

Minneapolis, Dec. 13, 1929); Concerto for 2 Pianos and Strings (1931; CBS, May 28, 1939; orig. *Symbolistic Study No. 6: Mountain Vision* for Piano); *Rudolph Gott Symphony* (1932–34); *Navao Dance No. 1* (1944; orig. for Piano); *The Heroic Breed, in memoriam General Patton* (1946). CHAMBER: *Fugue Fantasy* for String Quartet (1914); String Quartet, *The Hako* (1922); Violin Sonata (1927; rev. 1935); Piano Quintet (1937); Suite for Flute and Piano (1949); Cello Sonata; many piano pieces. VOCAL: Many pieces for Chorus and Orch., school choruses, and songs; music for pageants and masques, including *Caliban* for MacKaye's Shakespeare tercentenary masque (1915) and incidental music to C.W. Stevenson's *The Pilgrimage Way* (1920–21). OTHER: Collections of American Indian melodies and folk songs of the South and West; arrangements of American Indian melodies.

BIBL.: E. Kirk, *Toward American Music: A Study of the Life and Music of A.G. F.* (diss., Univ. of Rochester, 1958); B. Farwell et al., *Guide to the Music of A. F. and to the Microfilm Collection of His Work* (Briarcliff Manor, N.Y., 1971); E. Culbertson, *He Heard America Singing: A. F., Composer and Crusading Music Educator* (Metuchen, N.J., 1992).—NS/LK/DM

Fasano, Renato, Italian conductor; b. Naples, Aug. 21, 1902; d. Rome, Aug. 3, 1979. He studied piano and composition at Naples, specializing in Renaissance music. In 1941 he founded the Collegium Musicum Italicum of Rome and in 1947 he organized the distinguished chamber group I Virtuosi di Roma, leading its performances on European tours. In 1957 he also founded the Piccolo Teatro Musicale Italiano; in 1960 he was named director of the Accademia di Santa Cecilia in Rome. Fasano was greatly esteemed for his effort to revive a proper appreciation of Italian music of the Renaissance period.—NS/LK/DM

Fasch, Johann Friedrich, important German composer, father of **Karl Friedrich Christian Fasch;** b. Buttelstädt, near Weimar, April 15, 1688; d. Zerbst, Dec. 5, 1758. At age 13 he entered the Leipzig Thomasschule, where he came under the tutelage of Kuhnau, and later studied at the Univ. of Leipzig and with Graupner and Grunewald in Darmstadt (1713). He was active as a violinist and organist, then was Kapellmeister to Count Václav Morzin in Prague (1721–22) and court Kapellmeister in Zerbst (from 1722). Although none of his music was publ. in his lifetime, his church cantatas and festival pieces for the Zerbst court were performed in many German cities. His friend Telemann gave performances of his church music in Hamburg, and J.S. Bach prepared several transcriptions of his overtures for performances with the Leipzig Collegium Musicum. Fasch's innovative orch. writing foreshadowed the Classical style of Haydn and Mozart. Although much of his vocal output is not extant, many of his orch. works have survived. He composed 4 operas, 12 cantata cycles, 16 masses and mass movements, 5 Psalms, 19 syms., some 90 overtures (suites), about 70 concertos, 18 trio sonatas, etc. See R. Pfeiffer, ed., *Verzeichnis der Werke von Johann Friedrich Fasch (FWV): Kleine Ausgabe* (Magdeburg, 1988). His autobiography appeared in vol. III of F.W. Marpurg's *Historisch-kritische Beyträge zur Aufnahme der Musik* (Berlin, 1757).

BIBL.: P. Tryphon, *Die Symphonien von J.F. F.* (diss., Free Univ. of Berlin, 1954); G. Küntzel, *Die Instrumentalkonzerte von J.F. F.* (diss., Univ. of Frankfurt am Main, 1965); D. Sheldon, *The Chamber Music of J.F. F.* (diss., Ind. Univ., 1968); E. Thom, ed., *J.F. F. (1688–1758): Bericht über die wissenschaftliche Konferenz in Zerbst am 16. und 17. April 1988 aus Anlass des 300. Geburtstages* (Michaelstein, 1989); R. Dittrich, *Die Messen von J.F. F., 1688–1758* (Frankfurt am Main, 1992); R. Pfeiffer, *J.F. F., 1688–1758: Leben und Werk* (Wilhelmshaven, 1992); K. Musketa and B. Reul, eds., *J.F. F. und sein Wirken für Zerbst* (Dessau, 1997).—NS/LK/DM

Fasch, Karl Friedrich Christian (baptized **Christian Friedrich Carl**), noted German harpsichordist, choral conductor, and composer, son of **Johann Friedrich Fasch;** b. Zerbst, Nov. 18, 1736; d. Berlin, Aug. 3, 1800. He studied keyboard playing and theory with his father, then violin with Karl Höckh, concertmaster of the Zerbst Court Orch. From the age of 14 he received a thorough music education from Johann Wilhelm Hertel in Strelitz. While in Strelitz, he impressed the violinist Franz Benda, who recommended him to the court of Friedrich the Great in Berlin as 2nd harpsichordist (1756). He was also active as a teacher and composer in Berlin. When C.P.E. Bach left the Berlin court for Hamburg in 1767, Fasch was named his successor as principal harpsichordist. He also served as conductor of the Royal Opera (1774–76). In later years his work at the court was greatly diminished, and he devoted himself to teaching, conducting, and composing. In 1789 he organized his own choral soc., which soon became known as the Singakademie. He composed a great amount of sacred vocal music, much of which he discarded. A supposedly complete ed. of his works was publ. by the Singakademie (7 vols., Berlin, 1839).

BIBL.: K. Zelter, *K.F.C. F.* (Berlin, 1801); C. von Winterfeld, *Über K.F.C. F.'s geistliche Gesangwerke* (Berlin, 1829).—NS/LK/DM

Fassbänder, Brigitte, noted German mezzo-soprano, opera producer, and Intendant, daughter of **Willi Domgraf-Fassbänder;** b. Berlin, July 3, 1939. She studied with her father and attended the Nuremberg Cons. (1952–61). In 1961 she made her operatic debut as Nicklausse in *Les Contes d'Hoffman* at the Bavarian State Opera in Munich, where she became one of its most esteemed members. In 1970 she was honored as a Bavarian Kammersängerin. She appeared as Carmen at the San Francisco Opera in 1970, as Octavian at London's Covent Garden in 1971, and as Brangäne at the Paris Opéra in 1972. From 1972 to 1978 she appeared regularly at the Salzburg Festivals. On Feb. 16, 1974, she made her Metropolitan Opera debut in N.Y. as Octavian, returning there as Fricka in *Die Walküre* in 1986. In 1989 she sang Clytemnestra at the Salzburg Festival, returning in 1990 as Clairon in *Capriccio*. On Jan. 9, 1994, she made her N.Y. recital debut at Alice Tully Hall. In 1995 she retired from singing. From 1999 she was the Intendant of the Innsbruck Opera. While her operatic repertoire ranged from Gluck to contemporary scores, she won special distinction for her roles in operas by Mozart and Strauss. She also pursued a distinguished concert career.—NS/LK/DM

Fassbender, Zdenka, Bohemian soprano; b. Děčín, Dec. 12, 1879; d. Munich, March 14, 1954. She studied voice in Prague with Sophie Löwe-Destinn; made her operatic debut in Karlsruhe in 1899; from 1906 to 1919 she was one of the principal singers at the Munich Opera; she also sang at Covent Garden in London (1910, 1913). **Felix Mottl** married her on his deathbed to sanction their long- standing alliance. —NS/LK/DM

Fattorini, Gabriele, Italian composer; b. Faenza in the latter part of the 16th century; d. place and date unknown. He was maestro di cappella at Faenza, and possibly in Venice. His compositions include *Sacri concerti a due voci* (Venice, 1600; further eds., 1602, 1608), *Completorium romanum* (Venice, 1602), motets, madrigals, etc. Several of his works appeared in contemporaneous collections between 1605 and 1622 (Bodenschatz, Donfried, Diruta, etc.). Two of his ricercari for organ are in vol. III of Torchi's *L'arte musicale in Italia*. Banchieri mentions Fattorini in his *Conclusioni del suono dell'Organo* (Lucca, 1591; Bologna, 1609).—NS/LK/DM

Fauchet, Paul Robert, French composer; b. Paris, June 27, 1881; d. there, Nov. 12, 1937. He studied at the Paris Cons., where he later taught harmony. He also was maître de chapelle of St.-Pierre de Chaillot in Paris. He wrote a number of sacred works, but is remembered mainly for his *Symphonie* for band, the earliest example of a classical sym. written for the medium (1936); its *Scherzo* is profusely enmeshed with whole-tone scales. —NS/LK/DM

Faulk, Dan, jazz tenor/soprano saxophonist, composer, educator; b. Philadelphia, Pa., Nov. 22, 1969. He was raised mainly in Prescott, Ariz. At the age of eight, he began playing the alto saxophone, but at 14, switched to the tenor. Shortly after, he began to work and perform throughout Ariz. in various musical settings. In 1987, he attended Boston's Berklee Coll. of Music and studied with Billy Pierce. A year and a half later, he transferred to William Paterson Coll. (N.J.) and continued his musical studies with Rufus Reid, Joe Lovano, Harold Mabern, Steve Turré, Norman Simmons, and guest artist Benny Golson, as well as private studies with Barry Harris. In 1991, he finished his studies at William Paterson and received a Bachelor's Degree of Music, and has remained in the N.Y. area since that time. Soon after graduation, he was hired by WPC's Director of Jazz Studies and Performance—bassist Rufus Reid—to join the TanaReid quintet. He was a member of this ensemble for three years and recorded two albums with the group. For nearly two years, Dan toured with the J.J. Johnson Quintet until Johnson retired from performing in December 1997. He recorded on two albums with Johnson for Verve Records. Since July 1997, Dan has freelanced and has regularly been a featured soloist with Steve Turré and the Sanctified Shells. He has also performed with the Smithsonian Jazz Orch., The Mingus Dynasty, Valarie Ponomarov, and James Spaulding, and has recorded with Jimmy Heath, Louis Hayes, Richard Davis, and Spaulding. He also has toured with

his own ensembles as well as with the collaborative group Quintet X. He has written over 75 compositions, 10 of which have been recorded. He was a part-time faculty member at Rutgers–Newark from September 1997, teaching courses until completing his M.A. in Jazz History and Research in May 1999 there, where he studied with Lewis Porter. In September 1999, he began as a full-time faculty member at SUNY at Stonybrook, while he continues to be active as a freelance performer.

DISC.: *Focusing In* (1994; with Barry Harris, Rufus Reid, Carl Allen). J.J. Johnson: *The Brass Orchestra* (1996). James Spaulding: *Blues Nexus* (1993). TanaReid: *Blue Motion* (1992); *Passing Thoughts* (1992).—LP

Faull, Ellen, American soprano and teacher; b. Pittsburgh, Oct. 14, 1918. She studied at the Curtis Inst. of Music in Philadelphia and at Columbia Univ. She made her debut as Donna Anna in *Don Giovanni* with the N.Y. City Opera on Oct. 23, 1947, establishing herself as one of its principals, singing there regularly until 1979. She also appeared in San Francisco, Boston, and Chicago, and as a soloist with many U.S. orchs. Faull taught at N.Y.'s Manhattan School of Music (from 1971) and the Juilliard School (from 1981). She was particularly noted for her roles in Italian operas.—NS/LK/DM

Fauré, Gabriel (-Urbain), great French composer and pedagogue; b. Pamiers, Ariège, May 12, 1845; d. Paris, Nov. 4, 1924. His father was a provincial inspector of primary schools; noticing the musical instinct of his son, he took him to Paris to study with Louis Niedermeyer; after Niedermeyer's death in 1861, Fauré studied with Saint-Saëns, from whom he received thorough training in composition. In 1866 he went to Rennes as organist at the church of St.-Sauveur; returned to Paris on the eve of the Franco-Prussian War in 1870, and volunteered in the light infantry. He was organist at Notre Dame de Clignancourt (1870), St.-Honoré d'Elyau (1871), and St.-Sulpice (1871–74). He then was named deputy organist (to Saint-Saëns, 1874), choirmaster (1877), and chief organist (1896) at the Madeleine. In 1896 he was appointed prof. of composition at the Paris Cons. He was an illustrious teacher; among his students were Ravel, Enesco, Koechlin, Roger-Ducasse, Florent Schmitt, and Nadia Boulanger. In 1905 he succeeded Théodore Dubois as director and served until 1920. Then, quite unexpectedly, he developed ear trouble, resulting in gradual loss of hearing. Distressed, he made an effort to conceal it but was eventually forced to abandon his teaching position. From 1903 to 1921 he wrote occasional music reviews in *Le Figaro* (a selection was publ. as *Opinions musicales*, Paris, 1930). He was elected a member of the Académie des Beaux Arts in 1909, and in 1910 was made a Commander of the Legion d'honneur. Fauré's stature as a composer is undiminished by the passage of time. He developed a musical idiom all his own; by subtle application of old modes, he evoked the aura of eternally fresh art; by using unresolved mild discords and special coloristic effects, he anticipated procedures of Impressionism; in his piano works, he shunned virtuosity in favor of the Classical lucidity of the French masters of the clavecin; the precisely articulated melodic line of his songs is in the finest tradition of French vocal music. His great *Requiem* and his *Élégie* for Cello and Piano have entered the general repertoire.

WORKS: DRAMATIC: *Barnabé*, opéra-comique (1879; unfinished; not perf.); *Caligula*, op.52, incidental music to a play by A. Dumas père (Paris, Nov. 8, 1888); *Shylock*, incidental music to a play by E. de Haraucourt, after Shakespeare, op.57 (Paris, Dec. 17, 1889); *La Passion*, incidental music to a play by Haraucourt (Paris, April 21, 1890); *Le Bourgeois Gentilhomme*, incidental music to a play by Molière (1893); *Pelléas et Mélisande*, incidental music to a play by Maeterlinck, op.80 (London, June 21, 1898); *Prométhée*, tragédie lyrique, op.82 (Béziers, Aug. 27, 1900); *Le Voile du bonheur*, incidental music to a play by Clémenceau, op.88 (Paris, Nov. 4, 1901); *Pénélope*, drame lyrique (Monte Carlo, March 4, 1913); *Masques et bergamasques*, comédie musicale, op.112 (Monte Carlo, April 10, 1919). **ORCH.:** *Suite d'orchestre*, op.20 (1865–74; 1st movement publ. in 1895 as *Allegro symphonique*, op.68, in an arrangement for Piano, 4-Hands, by L. Boëllmann); Violin Concerto, op.14 (1878–79; 2nd movement destroyed); *Berceuse* for Violin and Orch., op.16 (1880; original version for Violin and Piano, 1879); *Ballade* for Piano and Orch., op.19 (Paris, April 23, 1881; original version for Solo Piano, 1877–79); *Romance* for Violin and Orch., op.28 (1882; original version for Violin and Piano, 1877); Sym. in D minor, op.40 (1884; Paris, March 15, 1885); *Pavane* for Orch. and Chorus ad libitum, op.50 (1887; Paris, March 28, 1888); *Shylock*, suite from the incidental music, op.57 (1890); *Menuet* in F major (1893); *Élégie* for Cello and Orch., op.24 (1896?; original version for Cello and Piano, 1880); *Pelléas et Mélisande*, suite from the incidental music, op.80 (1898); *Jules César*, suite after *Caligula*, op.52 (1905); *Dolly*, suite, op.56 (an orchestration by H. Rabaud [1906] of the pieces for Piano, 4-Hands, 1894–97); *Fantaisie* for Piano and Orch., op.111 (1918–19; Paris, March 14, 1919); *Masques et bergamasques*, suite from the comédie musicale, op.112 (1919); *Chant funéraire* (1921). **CHAMBER** (all 1st perf. in Paris unless otherwise given): 2 violin sonatas: No. 1, op.13 (1875–76; Jan. 27, 1877) and No. 2, op.108 (1916–17; Nov. 10, 1917); 2 piano quartets: No. 1, op.15 (1876–79; Feb. 14, 1880; rev. 1883) and No. 2, op.45 (1885–86; Jan. 22, 1887); *Romance* for Violin and Piano, op.28 (1877; Feb. 3, 1883; 2nd version for Violin and Orch., 1882); *Berceuse* for Violin and Piano, op.16 (1879; Feb. 14, 1880; 2nd version for Violin and Orch., 1880); *Élégie* for Cello and Piano, op.24 (1880; Dec. 15, 1883; 2nd version for Cello and Orch., 1896?); *Papillon* for Cello and Piano, op.77 (1884?); *Petite pièce* for Cello, op.49 (1887?); 2 piano quintets: No. 1, op.89 (1887–95; 1903–5; Brussels, March 23, 1906) and No. 2, op.115 (1919–21; May 21, 1921); *Romance* for Cello and Piano, op.69 (1894); *Andante* for Violin and Piano, op.75 (1897; Jan. 22, 1898); *Sicilienne* for Cello or Violin and Piano, op.78 (1898); *Fantaisie* for Flute and Piano, op.79 (July 28, 1898; orchestrated by L. Aubert, 1957); *Sérénade* for Cello and Piano, op.98 (1908); 2 cello sonatas: No. 1, op.109 (1917; Jan. 19, 1918) and No. 2, op.117 (1921; May 13, 1922); Piano Trio, op.120 (1922–23; May 12, 1923); String Quartet, op.121 (1923–24; June 12, 1925). **KEYBOARD: P i a n o** (all for Solo Piano unless otherwise given): *3 romances sans paroles*, op.17 (1863); *Intermède symphonique* for Piano, 4-Hands (1869; included as the Ouverture in *Masques et bergamasques*, op.112); *Gavotte* (1869; also in the Sym., op.20, and *Masques et bergamasques*, op.112); *Prélude et fugue* (1869; fugue the same as op.84, no. 6); *8 pièces brèves*, op.84 (1869–1902); *Nocturne* No. 1, op.33, no. 1 (1875), No. 2, op.33, no. 2 (1880), No. 3, op.33, no. 3 (1882), No. 4, op.36 (1884), No. 5, op.37 (1884), No. 6, op.63 (1894), No. 7, op.74 (1898), No. 9,

op.97 (1908), No. 10, op.99 (1908), No. 11, op.104, no. 1 (1913), No. 12, op.107 (1915), and No. 13, op.119 (1921); *Ballade*, op.19 (1877–79; 2nd version for Piano and Orch., 1881); *Mazurka*, op.32 (1878); *Barcarolle* No. 1, op.26 (1880), No. 2, op.41 (1885), No. 3, op.42 (1885), No. 4, op.44 (1886), No. 5, op.66 (1894), No. 6, op.70 (1896), No. 7, op.90 (1905), No. 8, op.96 (1906), No. 9, op.101 (1909), No. 10, op.104, no. 2 (1913), No. 11, op.105 (1913), No. 12, op.106bis (1915), and No. 13, op.116 (1921); *Impromptu* No. 1, op.25 (1881), No. 2, op.31 (1883), No. 3, op.34 (1883), No. 4, op.91 (1905–06), and No. 5, op.102 (1909); *Valse-caprice* No. 1, op.30 (1882), No. 2, op.38 (1884), No. 3, op.59 (1887–93), and No. 4, op.62 (1893–94); *Souvenirs de Bayreuth: Fantaisie en forme de quadrille sur les thèmes favoris de l'Anneau de Nibelung* for Piano, 4-Hands, op. posth. (with Messager; 1888); *Dolly*, pieces for Piano, 4-Hands, op.56 (1894–97; orchestrated by H. Rabaud, 1906); *Allegro symphonique* for Piano, 4-Hands, op.68 (an arrangement by L. Boëllmann [1895] of the 1st movement of the *Suite d'orchestre*, op.20 [c. 1865]); *Thème et variations*, op.73 (1895; orchestrated by Inghelbrecht, 1955); *9 préludes*, op.103 (1909–10). **VOCAL: C h o r a l : S a c r e d :** *Super flumina* for Chorus and Orch. (1863); *Cantique de Jean Racine* for Chorus and Organ, op.11 (1865; rev. version for Chorus, Harmonium, and String Quintet, 1866); *Cantique à St. Vincent de Paul* (1868; not extant); *Tu es Petrus* for Baritone, Chorus, and Organ (1872?); *Messe basse* for Soloists, Women's Chorus, Harmonium, and Violin (1881); *Messe de Requiem* (1886–87; orig. in 5 movements for Soprano, Chorus, Organ, String Ensemble, and Timpani; Madeleine, Paris, Jan. 16, 1888; expanded to 7 movements, adding a Baritone Solo, Horns, and Trumpets, c. 1889; full orch. version, c. 1900); *Tantum ergo* in E major for Chorus, 3 Children's Voices, Solo Voices, and Organ, op.65, no. 2 (1894); *Sancta mater* for Tenor, Chorus, and Organ (1894); *Tantum ergo* in F major for Soprano, Chorus, and Organ (1904). **S e c u l a r :** *Les Djinns* for Chorus and Orch., op.12 (1875?); *La Naissance de Vénus* for Soloists, Chorus, and Orch., op.29 (1882; Paris, April 3, 1886); etc. **S o n g s :** *Le Papillon et la fleur*, op.1, no. 1 (V. Hugo; 1861); *Mai*, op.1, no. 2 (Hugo; 1862); *Rêve d'amour*, op.5, no. 2 (Hugo; 1862); *L'Aube naît* (Hugo; 1862); *Puisque j'ai mis lèvre* (Hugo; 1862); *Tristesse d'Olympio* (Hugo; 1865); *Dans les ruines d'une abbaye*, op.2, no. 1 (Hugo; 1866); *Les Matelots*, op.2, no. 2 (T. Gautier; 1870); *Lydia*, op.4, no. 2 (Leconte de Lisle; 1870); *Hymne*, op.7, no. 2 (C. Baudelaire; 1870); *Seule!*, op.3, no. 1 (Gautier; 1871); *L'Absent*, op.5, no. 3 (Hugo; 1871); *L'Aurore* (Hugo; 1871); *La Rançon*, op.8, no. 2 (Baudelaire; 1871); *Chant d'automne*, op.5, no. 1 (Baudelaire; 1871); *La Chanson de pêcheur*, op.4, no. 1 (Gautier; 1872); *Aubade*, op.6, no. 1 (L. Pomey; 1873); *Tristesse*, op.6, no. 2 (Gautier; 1873); *Barcarolle*, op.7, no. 3 (M. Monnier; 1873); *Ici-bas!*, op.8, no. 3 (S. Prudhomme; 1874); *Au bord de l'eau*, op.8, no. 1 (Prudhomme; 1875); *Sérénade toscane*, op.3, no. 2 (1878); *Après un rêve*, op.7, no. 1 (1878); *Sylvie*, op.6, no. 3 (P. de Choudens; 1878); *Nell*, op.18, no. 1 (Leconte de Lisle; 1878); *Le Voyageur*, op.18, no. 2 (A. Silvestre; 1878); *Automne*, op.18, no. 3 (Silvestre; 1878); *Poème d'un jour*, op.21 (C. Grandmougin; 1878); *Les Berceaux*, op.23, no. 1 (Prudhomme; 1879); *Notre amour*, op.23, no. 2 (Silvestre; 1879); *Le Secret*, op.23, no. 3 (Silvestre; 1880–81); *Chanson d'amour*, op.27, no. 1 (Silvestre; 1882); *La Fée aux chansons*, op.27, no. 2 (Silvestre; 1882); *Aurore*, op.39, no. 1 (Silvestre; 1884); *Fleur jetée*, op.39, no. 2 (Silvestre; 1884); *Le Pays des rêves*, op.39, no. 3 (Silvestre; 1884); *Les Roses d'Ispahan*, op.39, no. 4 (Leconte de Lisle; 1884); *Noël*, op.43, no. 1 (V. Wilder; 1886); *Nocturne*, op.43, no. 2 (Villiers de l'Isle Adam; 1886); *Les Présents*, op.46, no. 1 (Villiers de l'Isle Adam; 1887); *Clair de lune*, op.46, no. 2 (P. Verlaine, 1887); *Larmes*, op.51, no. 1 (J. Richepin; 1888); *Au cimetière*, op.51, no. 2 (Richepin;

1888); *Spleen*, op.51, no. 3 (Verlaine; 1888); *La Rose*, op.51, no. 4 (Leconte de Lisle; 1890); *Chanson and Madrigal*, op.57 (Haraucourt; 1889); *En prière* (S. Bordèse; 1889); *Cinq mélodies "de Venise,"* op.58 (Verlaine): *Mandoline; En sourdine; Green; À Clymène; C'est l'extase* (1891); *Sérénade du Bourgeois gentilhomme*, op.posth. (Molière; 1893); *La Bonne Chanson*, op.61 (Verlaine): *Une Sainte en son auréole; Puisque l'aube grandit; La Lune blanche luit dans les bois; J'allais par des chemins perfides; J'ai presque peur, en vérité; Avant que tu ne t'en ailles; Donc, ce sera par un clair jour d'été; N'est-ce pas?; L'Hiver a cessé* (1892–94); *Prison*, op.83, no. 1 (Verlaine; 1894); *Soir*, op.83, no. 2 (A. Samain; 1894); *Le Parfum inpérissable*, op.76, no. 1 (Leconte de Lisle; 1897); *Arpège*, op.76, no. 2 (Samain; 1897); *Mélisande's Song*, op.posth. (Maeterlinck; tr. by Mackail; 1898); *Dans la forêt de septembre*, op.85, no. 1 (C. Mendès; 1902); *La Fleur qui va sur l'eau*, op.85, no. 2 (Mendès; 1902); *Accompagnement*, op.85, no. 3 (Samain; 1902); *Le Plus Doux Chemin*, op.87, no. 1 (Silvestre; 1904); *Le Ramier*, op.87, no. 2 (Silvestre; 1904); *Le Don silencieux*, op.92 (J. Dominique; 1906); *Chanson*, op.94 (H. de Regnier; 1906); *Vocalise-étude* (1907); *La Chanson d'Ève*, op.95 (C. Van Lerberghe; 1906–10); *Le Jardin clos*, op.106 (Van Lerberghe; 1914); *Mirage*, op.113 (Baronne A. de Brimont; 1919); *C'est la paix*, op.114 (G. Debladis; 1919); *L'Horizon chimérique*, op.118 (J. de la Ville de Mirmont; 1921).

BIBL.: L. Vuillemin, *G. F. et son oeuvre* (Paris, 1914); L. Aguettant, *La Génie de G. F.* (Lyons, 1924); A. Bruneau, *La Vie et les oeuvres de G. F.* (Paris, 1925); C. Koechlin, *G. F.* (Paris, 1927; Eng. tr., 1945; 2nd ed., 1949); P. Fauré-Fremiet, *G. F.* (Paris, 1929; 2nd ed., aug., 1957); G. Servières, *G. F.* (Paris, 1930); V. Jankélévitch, *G. F. et ses mélodies* (Paris, 1938; 3rd ed., aug., 1974, as *G. F. et l'inexprimable*); G. Faure, *G. F.* (Paris, 1945); C. Rostand, *L'Oeuvre de G. F.* (Paris, 1945); N. Suckling, *F.* (London, 1946); M. Favre, *G. F.s Kammermusik* (Zürich, 1949); V. Jankélévitch, *Le Nocturne: F., Chopin et la nuit, Satie et le matin* (Paris, 1957); E. Vuillermoz, *G. F.* (Paris, 1960; Eng. tr., 1969); M. Long, *Au piano avec G. F.* (Paris, 1963); J.-M. Nectoux, *F.* (Paris, 1972; 3rd ed., aug., 1995); idem, *Phonographie de G. F.* (Paris, 1979); R. Orledge, *G. F.* (London, 1979); J.-M. Nectoux, ed., *G. F.: Correspondance* (Paris, 1980); idem, *G. F.: His Life through His Letters* (London, 1984); J. Barrie Jones, tr. and ed., *G. F.: A Life in Letters* (London, 1989); R. Tait, *The Musical Language of G. F.* (N.Y. and London, 1989); J. Nectoux, *G. F.: Le voix du clair-obscur* (Paris, 1990; Eng. tr., 1991, as *G. F.: A Musical Life*); C. Breitfeld, *Form und Struktur in der Kammermusik von G. F.* (Kassel, 1992); P. Jost, ed., *G. F., Werk und Rezeption: Mit Werkverzeichnis und Bibliographie* (Kassel, 1996); E. Phillips, *G. F.: A Guide to Research* (N.Y., 1999).—NS/LK/DM

Faure, Jean-Baptiste, famous French baritone; b. Moulins, Jan. 15, 1830; d. Paris, Nov. 9, 1914. He was a choirboy in Paris, then entered the Paris Cons. in 1851. On Oct. 20, 1852, he made his operatic debut at the Opéra-Comique as Pygmalion in Massé's *Galathée*. He subsequently created the roles of Malipieri in Auber's *Haydée* (July 5, 1853) and Hoël in Meyerbeer's *Dinorah, ou Le Pardon de Ploërmel* (April 4, 1859) there. It was as Hoël that he made his Covent Garden debut in London on April 10, 1860; he continued to sing there, as well as at Drury Lane and Her Majesty's Theatre, until 1877. He made his debut at the Paris Oéra as Julien in Poniatowsky's *Pierre de Médicis* on Oct. 14, 1861; he continued to sing there until 1869, and then again from 1872 to 1876 and in 1878. Among the roles he created at the Opéra were Nelusko in Meyerbeer's *L'Africaine* (April 28, 1865), Posa in Verdi's *Don Carlos* (March 11, 1867),

and Hamlet in Thomas's opera (March 9, 1868). In later years he appeared in concerts, garnering notable acclaim in Vienna and London. He excelled in dramatic roles in French and Italian operas, and was particularly renowned for his portrayals of Don Giovanni, Méphistophélès, and Guillaume Tell. He publ. 2 books on singing, and also taught at the Paris Cons. (1857–60). He was married to the singer Constance Caroline Lefèbvre (1828–1905).—NS/LK/DM

Favart, Charles-Simon, French librettist and impresario; b. Paris, Nov. 13, 1710; d. Belleville, near Paris, March 12, 1792. He publ. satirical plays as a youth. After a successful performance of one of his vaudevilles at the Opéra-Comique in Paris, he was appointed stage manager there and in 1758 became its director, a post he retained until 1769; its theater was named in his honor in 1781. In 1745 he married **Marie Favart**. He wrote about 150 librettos, and also was the author of *Les Amours de Bastien et Bastienne* (1753), which was used by Mozart in a German version for his early Singspiel *Bastien und Bastienne* (1768).—NS/LK/DM

Favart, Marie (née -Justine-Benoîte Duronceray), French soprano, actress, and dramatist; b. Avignon, June 15, 1727; d. Paris, April 21, 1772. Her father was André- Réné Duronceray, a musician in the Chapel Royal under Louis XV. In 1744 she bean her career under the name Mlle. de Chantilly in Charles-Simon Favart's *Les Fêtes publiques* at the Paris Opéra-Comique, becoming his wife in 1745. They subsequently were active in Flanders until the unwanted advances of her patron, the Maréchal de Saxe, caused them to flee in 1747. In 1749 she appeared at the Paris Comédie-Italienne, and then was notably successful in soubrette roles at the Théâtre-Italien there from 1751 to 1771. Her most famous role was Serpina in *La Serva padrona*. She also collaborated with her husband on several works, and often appeared in many of the works he wrote. Her career was marked by various theatrical intrigues, leading Offenbach to compose the operetta *Mme. Favart* (1878).

BIBL.: A. Pougin, *Madame F.* (Paris, 1912).—NS/LK/DM

Favero, Mafalda, Italian soprano; b. Portamaggiore, near Ferrara, Jan. 6, 1903; d. Milan, Sept. 3, 1981. She studied at the Bologna Cons. with Alessandro Vezzani. Under the stage name of Maria Bianchi, she made her operatic debut in 1926 in Cremona as Lola; in 1927 she made her formal operatic debut at Liù in Parma. In 1928 she made her first appearance at Milan's La Scala as Eva in *Die Meistersinger von Nürnberg*, and subsequently sang there regularly until 1943, then again from 1945 to 1950. In 1937 and 1939 she appeared at London's Covent Garden. On Nov. 24, 1938, she made her Metropolitan Opera debut in N.Y. as Mimi, remaining on its roster for a season. Among her finest roles were Mimi, Adriana Lecouvreur, Manon, and Thaïs.

BIBL.: I. Buscaglia, *M. F. nella vita e nell'arte* (1946).—NS/LK/DM

Fay, Amy (Amelia Muller), American pianist, teacher, and writer on music; b. Bayou Goula, La., May

21, 1844; d. Watertown, Mass., Feb. 28, 1928. She studied in Berlin with Tausig and Kullak, then became a pupil of Liszt in Weimar. After gaining recognition as a pianist in Boston (1875–78), she went to Chicago, where she was active as a lecturer, writer on music, and teacher, as well as a pianist. She promoted the cause of women in American music, and served as president of the N.Y. Women's Phil. Soc. (1903–14). She publ. a vivid book of impressions, *Music-Study in Germany* (1880), which went through more than 25 printings and was tr. into French and German.—**NS/LK/DM**

Fay, Maude, American soprano; b. San Francisco, April 18, 1878; d. there, Oct. 7, 1964. She studied in Dresden, and became a member of the Munich Opera (1906–14). She also appeared at Covent Garden in London in 1910, and with the Beecham Opera Co. in 1914. After the outbreak of World War I, she returned to America. She sang with the Metropolitan Opera in 1916, and also appeared with the Chicago Opera Co. She was particularly distinguished in Wagnerian roles. —**NS/LK/DM**

Fayer, Yuri, Russian conductor; b. Kiev, Jan. 17, 1890; d. Moscow, Aug. 3, 1971. After attending the Kiev Cons., he studied violin and composition at the Moscow Cons. He played in various orchs. before conducting opera in Riga (1909–10). In 1916 he joined the orch. of the Bolshoi Theater in Moscow, where he was asst. conductor (1919–23) and chief conductor (1923–63) of its ballet. He toured with it in Europe, the U.S., and China. His memoirs were publ. in 1970.—**NS/LK/DM**

Fayolle, François (-Joseph-Marie), French writer on music; b. Paris, Aug. 15, 1774; d. there, Dec. 2, 1852. He was educated in Paris at the École Polytechnique (mathematics) and the Collège Mazarin, and also studied with Perne (voice and harmony) and Barny (cello). He lived in London (1815–29), where he contributed to *The Harmonicon*, and then settled in Paris. With A.-E. Choron, he publ. the *Dictionnaire historique des musiciens, artistes, amateurs, morts ou vivants* (2 vols., Paris, 1810–11); he also publ. *Notices sur Corelli, Tartini, Gaviniès, Pugnani et Viotti* (Paris, 1810) and *Paganini et Bériot* (Paris, 1830).—**NS/LK/DM**

Fayrfax, Robert, English composer; b. Deeping Gate, Lincolnshire (baptized), April 23, 1464; d. St. Alban, Hertfordshire, Oct. 24, 1521. He was a Gentleman of the Chapel Royal in 1496, and organist at St. Alban's Abbey and at King's Chapel (1497–98). He received a B.M. (1501) and a D.M.A. (1504) from the Univ. of Cambridge and a D.M.A. from the Univ. of Oxford (1511; with his Mass *O quam glorifica*). In 1520 he led the Royal Singers accompanying King Henry VIII to the Field of the Cloth of Gold in France. Of his works, 29 are extant: 6 masses (4 are in the Oxford Museum School Collection), 2 Magnificats, 10 motets, 8 part-songs, and 3 instrumental pieces. His sacred and secular vocal works are in the *Fayrfax Book* (British Library MS Add. 5465); lute arrangements of several sacred compositions and an instrumental piece for 3 parts are in the British Library. E. Warren ed. *Robert Fayrfax: Collected Works*, in Corpus Mensurabilis Musicae, XVII/1–3 (1959–66). —**NS/LK/DM**

Feather, (Billie Jane Lee) Lorraine, jazz singer; daughter of Leonard Feather; b. N.Y., Sept. 10, 1948. She was named after her godmother Billie Holiday, her mother Jane (formerly a singer), her mother's ex-roommate Peggy Lee, and the song "Sweet Lorraine." The Feathers moved to L.A. when Lorraine was 12; at 18, after two years as a theater arts major at L.A.C.C., she returned to N.Y. to pursue an acting career. Some touring, regional theater, Off-Broadway work and the concert and Broadway versions of *Jesus Christ Superstar* followed, interspersed with many waitressing jobs. She turned to singing with jazz and Top 40 bands in N.Y., N.J. and Pa., sang backup for Petula Clark and Grand Funk Railroad, and then put her own act together, performing in cabarets, then moving back to L.A. Jake Hanna saw her at Donte's and recommended her to Concord Jazz head Carl Jefferson, leading to a recording. Soon after, she joined producer Richard Perry's vocal trio Full Swing and spent the 1980s with them, which included the Monterey, Playboy and Kool Jazz Festivals, travels to Japan and Brazil and backing Bette Midler. She wrote lyrics for 23 songs on the group's releases, some for classic pieces like Duke Ellington's "Rockin' in Rhythm," the Yellowjackets' "Ballad of the Whale" and Horace Henderson's "Big John's Special" (later heard in the movie *Swing Shift*). Full Swing was featured on Barry Manilow's *Swing Street* album and TV special. Their recording of Feather's song "2 Good 2 Be 4gotten," written with Morgan Ames and Russ Freeman, became a Top 40 Adult Contemporary single. When Full Swing dissolved, she focused on writing. Songs with her lyrics were recorded by Patti Austin, Phyllis Hyman, Djavan, Diane Schuur, Maria Muldaur, Kenny Rankin, Cleo Laine (three versions of Ellington instrumentals released in 1995), and others. She wrote or co-wrote (and sometimes performed) TV soundtrack songs for *Beverly Hills 90210*, *Family Matters*, *Days of Our Lives*, *Santa Barbara* (Emmy nominations in 1992 and 1993), Disney's *Dinosaurs* (the TV show and album), the animated film *Babes in Toyland* (1997); numerous songs for the TV series *All Dogs Go to Heaven* and the show's theme, which earned her a third Emmy nomination in 1997. In early 1996, she wrote the lyrics (music by Mark Watters) to "Faster, Higher, Stronger," the finale for the opening ceremony of the Summer Olympics.

DISC.: *The Body Remembers* (1997); *Sweet Lorraine* (1978); *In Full Swing* (1988); *End of the Sky.*—**LP**

Feather, Leonard (Geoffrey Feder), jazz author, composer, arranger, pianist, also vibraphonist; father of Lorraine Feather; b. London, England, Sept. 13, 1914; d. Encino, Calif., Sept. 22, 1994. Of Jewish ancestry, he studied at St. Paul School in London; in the late 1930s, he went to the U.S., and was naturalized in 1948. He held various jobs as an arranger, lyricist, adviser for jazz festivals, radio commentator, and lecturer; he specialized in the field of jazz and folk music. Like all critics, he had his detractors, but he was one of the few who was highly trained musically, and he was an innovator, pioneering in writing a jazz waltz in 1938, in writing a 12-tone jazz tune, in organizing all women jazz groups (1945 and after, led by Mary Lou Williams and others), and in organizing international jazz groups for recordings. He gave Dinah Washington her first shot as a solo artist and wrote her hit "Evil Gal Blues" (1945). He wrote the sophisticated altered blues "I Remember Bird" (recorded in 1960). He produced a vocal group called the Sound of Feeling (1970). As a writer, his many accomplishments include establishing the *Esquire* magazine jazz poll in the 1940s, originating the Blindfold test in *Down Beat*, writing a syndicated column in the *Los Angeles Times*, and penning encyclopedias of jazz. His encyclopedias were probably the first to be based on information submitted by the musicians (as opposed to being based on secondary sources) and he deserves great credit for conducting that research; however the musicians' material often had errors and he did not do additional research to catch such problems. In 1964, he won the first Grammy ever awarded for journalism by the National Academy of Recording Arts and Sciences. He died of pneumonia at Encino Tarzana Medical Center.

DISC.: *Leonard Feather's Swingin' Swedes* (1951); *Cats vs. Chicks* (1954); *Winter Sequence* (1954); *Dixieland vs. Birdland* (1954); *Swingin' on the Vibories* (1956); *West Coast Vs. East Coast* (1956); *Hi-Fi Suite* (1957); *Oh, Captain!* (1958); *Swingin' Seasons* (1958); *All- Stars* (1971); *Night Blooming Jazzmen* (1971).

WRITINGS: *Inside Be-bop* (N.Y., 1949); *The Encyclopedia of Jazz* (N.Y., 1984); *The Encyclopedia of Jazz in the 60's* (1986); *The Encyclopedia of Jazz in the 1970s* (N.Y., 1987); *The Jazz Years: Earwitness to an Era* (N.Y.,1987); *The Passion for Jazz* (N.Y., 1990). —LP

Fedeli, family of Italian musicians:

(1) Carlo Fedeli, instrumentalist and composer; b. Venice, c. 1622; d. there, Dec. 19, 1685. He was a string player at the basilica of San Marco in Venice from 1643, where he was maestro de concerti of its orch. (1661–85). He also played in theater orchs. and was maestro di strumenti at the orphanage of the Mendicanti (1662–72). He publ. a set of 12 sonatas for 2 to 4 Instruments (Venice, 1685). His two sons were also musicians:

(2) Ruggiero Fedeli, singer, instrumentalist, and composer; b. Venice, c. 1655; d. Kassel, Jan. 1722. He was a violist in theater orchs. in Venice, and then at the basilica of San Marco (1669–74), where he subsequently was a bass in its choir (1674–77). He then settled in Germany and was active in many court and theater establishments. In 1691 he was a composer at the Berlin court chapel. He became Kapellmeister in Kassel in 1700, a post he held until 1702. In 1708 he was named court composer and conductor in Berlin, but in 1709 he returned to Kassel as Kapellmeister. His deft handling of vocal writing in his opera *Almira* (Braunschweig), his cantatas, and his sacred works helped to shape the course of German composition.

(3) Giuseppe Fedeli, instrumentalist and composer; b. Venice, date unknown; d. probably in Paris, c. 1733. He became a trombonist at the basilica of San Marco in 1680, but eventually settled in Paris. He wrote an opera, *The Temple of Love* (London, March 1706), chamber music, and vocal works.—LK/DM

Fedeli, Vito, Italian composer; b. Fogligno, June 19, 1866; d. Novara, June 23, 1933. He was a pupil of Terziani in Rome. He was director of the Novara Cons. from 1904. He contributed valuable historical articles to the *Rivista Musicale Italiana* and the *Zeitschrift der Internationalen Musik-Gesellschaft*. He also wrote a book, *Giacomo e Gaudenzio Battistini* (1932). Among his compositions are the operas *La Vergine della Montagna* (Reggio-Calabria, Sept. 6, 1897) and *Varsovia* (Rome, Dec. 15, 1900), several a cappella masses, and pieces for Orch.

BIBL.: G. Bustico, *Bibliografia di un musico novarese, V. F.* (1925).—NS/LK/DM

Feder, (Franz) Georg, distinguished German musicologist; b. Bochum, Nov. 30, 1927. After studies at the univs. of Tübingen and Göttingen, he completed his education at the Univ. of Kiel (Ph.D., 1955, with the diss. *Bachs Werke in ihren Bearbeitungen 1750–1950, I: Die Vokalwerke*). In 1957 he became asst. to Jens Peter Larsen at the Joseph- Haydn-Inst. in Cologne, whom he succeeded as director in 1960, and as chief ed. of the complete ed. of Haydn's works. In 1965 he also became ed. of the publication *Haydn-Studien*. Feder retired from these positions in 1990, but continued to work at the Joseph-Haydn-Inst. until 1992.

WRITINGS: *Musikphilologie: Eine Einführung in die musikalische Textkritik, Hermeneutik und Editionstechnik* (Darmstadt, 1987); *Haydn's Streichquartette* (Munich, 1998); *Joseph Haydn, Die Schöpfung: Werkeinführung* (Kassel, 1999). —NS/LK/DM

Federhofer, Hellmut, eminent Austrian musicologist; b. Graz, Aug. 6, 1911. He studied piano and theory in Graz, and then continued his studies at the Vienna Academy of Music with Stöhr and Kabasta, graduating in 1936 with a diploma in conducting. He also took private lessons in composition with Berg, Sauer, and Jonas. He took courses in musicology with Orel and Lach at the Univ. of Vienna, receiving his Ph.D. in 1936 with the diss. *Akkordik und Harmonik in frühen Motetten der Trienter Codices*. From 1937 to 1944 he was State Librarian. He completed his Habilitation in 1944 at the Univ. of Graz with his *Musikalische Form als Ganzheit* (publ. as *Beiträge zur musikalischen Gestaltanalyse*, Graz, 1950). He became Privatdozent at the Univ. of Graz in 1945, and in 1951 prof. of musicology. In 1962 he became director of the Musicological Inst. at the Johannes Gutenberg Univ. in Mainz. That same year he became ed. of *Acta Musicologica*. In 1986 he became editorial director of the new critical ed. of the works of Fux. His books include *Musikpflege und Musiker am Grazer Habsburgerhof der Erzherzöge Karl und Ferdinand von Innerösterreich* (1564–1619; Mainz, 1967), *Neue Musik: Ein Literaturbericht* (Tutzing, 1977), *Akkord und Stimmführung in den Musiktheoretischen Systemen von Hugo Riemann, Ernst Kurth und Heinrich Schenker* (Vienna, 1981), *Musikwissen-*

schaft und Musikpraxis (Vienna, 1985), and Motivtechnik von Johannes Brahms und Arnold Schönbergs Dodekaphonie (Vienna, 1989). He also ed. Heinrich Schenker als Essayist und Kritiker: Gesammelte Aufsätze, Rezensionen und kleine Berichte aus den Jahren 1891–1901 (Hildesheim, 1990).

BIBL.: C.-H. Mahling, ed., Florilegium Musicologicum: H. F. zum 75. Geburtstag (Tutzing, 1988).—**NS/LK/DM**

Federici, Vincenzo, Italian composer; b. Pesaro, 1764; d. Milan, Sept. 26, 1826. He studied harpsichord and was autodidact as a composer. In 1790 he became maestro al cembalo at the Italian Opera in London, and later that year at the King's Theatre. In 1802 he returned to Italy and in 1808 he became a harmony teacher at the Milan Cons.

WORKS: DRAMATIC: O p e r a : L'Olimpiade (Turin, Dec. 26, 1789); L'usurpator innocente (London, April 6, 1790); Castore e Polluce (Milan, Jan. 1803); Oreste in Tauride (Milan, Jan. 27, 1804); Sofonisba (Turin, Carnival 1805); Idomeneo (Milan, Jan. 31, 1806); La conquista delle Indie orientali (Turin, Carnival 1808); Ifigenia in Aulide (Milan, Jan. 28, 1809).—**NS/LK/DM**

Fedorov, Vladimir (Mikhailovich), Russian-born French music librarian, scholar, and composer; b. near Chernigov, Aug. 18, 1901; d. Paris, April 9, 1979. After training at the Univ. of Rostov, he settled in Paris and studied with Gédalge (counterpoint and fugue) and Vidal (composition) at the Cons. (1921–30), and with Pirro (musicology) at the Sorbonne (1921–32). He was librarian at the Sorbonne (1933–39), and then was head of the music division of the Bibliothèque Nationale (1946–66); he also was librarian at the Cons. (1958–64). In 1951 he founded the International Assn. of Music Libraries (IAML), serving as its vice president (1955–62) and president (1962–65), and as ed. of its journal, Fontes Artis Musicae (1954–75). He publ. a biography of Mussorgsky (Paris, 1935) and was one of the eds. of the Encyclopédie de la Musique (3 vols., Paris, 1958–61). Among his compositions were chamber music and piano pieces.—**NS/LK/DM**

Fedoseyev, Vladimir (Ivanovich), prominent Russian conductor; b. Leningrad, Aug. 5, 1932. He studied with N. Reznikov at the Gnesin Inst. in Moscow (graduated, 1957) and with L. Ginzburg at the Moscow Cons. (graduated, 1971). He conducted an orch. of native instruments (1959–74) and was principal conductor of the Grand Orch. of the All-Union Radio and Television in Moscow (from 1974). He is distinguished for his interpretations of 19th-century Russian music as well as for his work with indigenous music. In 1970 he was awarded the Glinka Prize, and in 1973 was made a National Artist of the Russian S.F.S.R.—**NS/LK/DM**

Feghali, José, Brazilian pianist; b. Rio de Janeiro, March 28, 1961. He began piano lessons as a child, appearing for the first time in public when he was only 5. At age 8 he was a soloist with the Brazilian Sym. orch. in Rio de Janeiro. In 1976 he went to London to study with Maria Curcio, and then pursued training with Christopher Elton on scholarship at the Royal Academy of Music. After capturing 1st prize in the Van Cliburn

Competition in Ft. Worth in 1985, he was engaged as a soloist with the world's principal orchs. and as a recitalist. He also served as artist-in-residence at Tex. Christian Univ. in Ft. Worth.—**NS/LK/DM**

Fehr, Max, Swiss musicologist; b. Bulach, near Zürich, June 17, 1887; d. Winterthur, April 27, 1963. He studied at the Univ. of Zürich with Eduard Bernoulli (Ph.D., 1912). In 1917 he became librarian, and in 1923 president, of the Allgemeine Musikgesellschaft of Zürich; he retired as librarian in 1957. In addition to his scholarly works on music, he wrote a satirical novelette, Die Meistersinger von Zürich (Zürich, 1916).

WRITINGS: Spielleute im alten Zürich (Zürich, 1916); Unter Wagners Taktstock (Winterthur, 1922); Geschichte des Musikkollegiums Winterthur, I. Teil:1629–1830 (Winterthur, 1929); Richard Wagners Schweizer Zeit (2 vols., Aarau, 1934, 1953); Die Familie Mozart in Zürich (Zürich, 1942); Die wandernden Theatertruppen in der Schweiz: Verzeichnis der Truppen, Auffuhrungen und Spieldaten für das 17. und 18. Jahrhundert (Einsiedeln, 1949); with L. Caflisch, Der junge Mozart in Zürich (Zürich, 1952); Musikalische Jagd (Zürich, 1954).

BIBL.: E. Nievergelt, M. F. (Zürich, 1968).—**NS/LK/DM**

Feicht, Hieronim, Polish musicologist; b. Mogilno, near Poznań, Sept. 22, 1894; d. Warsaw, March 31, 1967. He studied theology, then composition in Kraków, and musicology with Chybiński at the Univ. of Lwów (Ph.D., 1925); later completed his Habilitation at the Univ. of Poznań (1946). He taught at the Kraków Cons. from 1927 to 1930 and again from 1935 to 1939; in the interim he was a prof. at the State Coll. of Music in Warsaw (1930–32). From 1946 to 1952 he was chairman of the musicology dept. at the Univ. of Wroclaw; was rector of the State Coll. of Music in Wroclaw (1948–52), and a prof. of music history at the Univ. of Warsaw (1952–64). He publ. important essays on Polish music: Musik-historische Bemerkungen uber die Lemberger Handschriften des Bogarodzica-Liedes (Poznań, 1925); Wojciech Debolecki, Ein polnischer Kirchenkomponist aus der 1. Halfte des 17. Jahrhunderts (Lwów, 1926); Polifonia renesansu (Kraków, 1957); also ed. works by Polish composers. A Festschrift was publ. in honor of his 70th birthday in 1964.—**NS/LK/DM**

Feinberg, Samuel, eminent Russian pianist, pedagogue, and composer; b. Odessa, May 26, 1890; d. Moscow, Oct. 22, 1962. He moved to Moscow in 1894, where he studied piano with Goldenweisser at the Cons.; also took theory lessons with Zhilayev; graduated in 1911. In 1922 he was appointed prof. of piano at the Cons., holding this post until his death. He also gave piano recitals in Russia in programs emphasizing new Russian music; he performed all of Beethoven's sonatas and the complete set of Bach's Wohl-temperiertes Clavier, as well as Chopin and Schumann. As a composer, he limited himself almost exclusively to piano music, which was influenced mainly by Chopin and Scriabin in its fluidity and enhanced tonality.

WORKS: ORCH.: 3 piano concertos (1931; 1944; 1947, rev. 1951). **KEYBOARD: P i a n o :** 12 sonatas (1915, 1916, 1917, 1918, 1921, 1923, 1924, 1933, 1939, 1940, 1954, 1960); 2 fantasias

(1916–17; 1924); 4 preludes (1922); 3 preludes (1923); 2 suites (1926, 1936). **VOCAL:** Various songs.

BIBL.: V. Belayev, *S. F.* (Moscow, 1927; in Russian and German).—**NS/LK/DM**

Feinhals, Fritz, distinguished German baritone; b. Cologne, Dec. 4, 1869; d. Munich, Aug. 30, 1940. He studied in Milan and Padua. He made his operatic debut in Essen in 1895 as Silvio, and in 1898 he joined the Munich Court (later State) Opera, where he remained until his retirement in 1927. On Nov. 18, 1908, he made his debut at the Metropolitan Opera in N.Y. as Wotan in *Die Walküre*, but was on its roster for only the 1908–09 season. He also made appearances in London, Paris, and Vienna. He was a Wagnerian singer par excellence. His portrayal of Wotan was imperious in its power, and he was also successful in the role of Hans Sachs. He also excelled in operas by Mozart and Verdi. —**NS/LK/DM**

Feinstein, Michael, archivist and avatar of the American standard popular song, b. Columbus, Ohio, Sept. 7, 1956. As a child, Michael Feinstein didn't like what the other kids liked. When they were busy listening to the Beatles and the Stones, he was more apt to be listening to the Gershwins and Cole Porter. He came by this honestly enough; his mother was a professional tap dancer, and his father—a salesman for Sara Lee—had a marked fondness for show music and other light classics. By the time he was five, Feinstein was playing the piano by ear. During his teen years, he collected old 78s (he had over 6,000 of them), show albums, and sheet music. He learned not only the standards, but also more obscure tunes from the standards era.

When his parents moved to the Los Angeles area, he followed them and got a job selling pianos. He continued haunting old record stores in search of old tunes. While trying to find an old recording by Oscar Levant, he stumbled onto some rare Levant acetates. He bought them and called Levant's widow about them. She asked him over to her home, where he captivated her, not only with the recordings but by his ability to sit at her piano and play her husband's compositions; renowned for playing Gershwin's music, Levant's own songs suffered by comparison. Mrs. Levant became the first of Feinstein's sponsors, making Ira Gershwin aware of this young man who knew all the old songs.

Gershwin hired Feinstein to work as his archivist. From 1977 until just after Gershwin's death in 1983, Feinstein sifted through the piles of manuscripts generated by the Gershwin brothers and their collaborators. During this time, he accompanied Gershwin to Hollywood parties, and when the hired pianist took a break, Feinstein would play. At one party, he stumbled over the lyrics to "Lorelei" and a woman in the audience fed them to him. That woman, Liza Minelli, became his next sponsor, helping him put together a cabaret act after Gershwin's passing.

While Feinstein does not have the range of a Mandy Patinkin, his purist interpretations of the songs in his pleasantly nasal voice went over well with fans of cabaret and standards. He also presented the songs with background information about the composers that appealed strongly to the music's fans. He earned months-long engagements at the Mondrian in L.A., The Plush Room in San Francisco, and the Oak Room in N.Y. He started recording, first for companies that specialized in cabaret performers and later for more mainstream labels.

By the time he transcended the cabaret rooms and was opening on Broadway in 1988, Feinstein had signed to Elektra records. As a performer, his archivist tendencies often come through—he is apt to include verses of songs that never made the "hit version" and fell by the wayside of history. His version of "Lydia the Tattooed Lady," for example, includes a verse Yip Harburg wrote referring to Hitler that Groucho Marx would sing in concert but didn't make it to the movie *At the Circus*. His album of Burton Lane songs featured the composer on the piano. He frequently brought his interpretations to the TV talk shows and his own PBS specials.

DISC.: *Live at the Algonquin* (1986); *Pure Gershwin* (1987); *Remember: M. F. Sings Irving...* (1987); *Isn't It Romantic* (1988); *The M.G.M. Album* (1989); *M. F. Sings the Burton Lane...* (1990); *M. F. Sings the Jule Styne...* (1991); *M. F. Sings the Burton Lane...* (1992); *Pure Imagination* (1992); *Forever* (1993); *The M. F. Sings the Jerry Herman...* (1993); *Such Sweet Sorrow* (1995); *The M. F. Sings the Hugh Martin...* (1995); *Nice Work If You Can Get It* (1996); *Michael & George: Feinstein Sings Gershwin* (1998); *Nobody But You* (1998).

WRITINGS: *Nice Work If You Can Get It: My Life in Rhythm and Rhyme* (N.Y., 1996).—**HB**

Fel, Marie, famous French soprano; b. Bordeaux, Oct. 24, 1713; d. Paris, Feb. 2, 1794. She studied with Christina VanLoo in Paris, making her debut as Venus in the prologue to La Coste's *Philomèle* at the Opéra on Oct. 29, 1734; she subsequently sang with notable success there, and also at court and at the Concert Spirituel. She retired from the operatic stage in 1758. She was renowned for her performances of roles in French operas. Sophie Arnould was one of her pupils. Her brother, Antoine Fel (b. Bordeaux, 1694; d. Bicêtre, June 27, 1771), was a singer at the Paris Opéra as well as a composer.—**NS/LK/DM**

Felciano, Richard, American composer; b. Santa Rosa, Calif., Dec. 7, 1930. He studied with Milhaud at Mills Coll. in Oakland, Calif. (1952) and subsequently at the Paris Cons. (1953–55). As a student living in San Francisco, he supported himself by singing in a liturgical choir of men and boys, during which time he twice sang the complete liturgical year in Dominican chant and from neumatic notation. This experience had a profound effect on his style, even in orchestral and electronic music, and it was reinforced by several residencies at the Abbey of Solesmes while he was a student in Paris. After a period of service in the U.S. Army, he studied privately with Dallapiccola in Florence. While there, he met and married Rita Baumgartner, a native of Zürich, who later, as Rita Felciano, became a recognized American dance critic. In 1959 he took his Ph.D. at the Univ. of Iowa. In 1964 he received a Ford Foundation fellowship to serve as composer-in-residence to Cass Technical H.S. in Detroit, during which time he composed a number of works for student ensembles, some of which employed aleatory techniques and graphic notation. Returning to San Francisco in 1965, he received a series of commissions for the Roman Catholic liturgy in the wake of the liberalizing directives of the 2nd Vatican Council (1964). One of these commissions, *Pentecost Sunday*, introduced electronic sound into liturgical music and assumed a permanent place in its repertory. In 1967 he was appointed resident composer to the National Center for Experiments in Television in San Francisco, a pioneering effort by the Rockefeller Foundation to explore television as a non-documentary, non-narrative medium. As a participant in this project, he created *Linearity*, a television piece for harp and live electronics, the first musical work using the technical properties of a television system as an instrumental component. In the same year, he joined the music faculty of the Univ. of Calif. at Berkeley. In 1968 he received a Guggenheim fellowship and in 1971 a 2-year fellowship from the Ford Foundation as composer-in-residence to the City of Boston. During that residency, he created a 14-channel electronic environment with light sculptures of his own design for Boston City Hall and *Galactic Rounds* (1972), an orchestral work whose climax deploys rotating trumpets and trombones to create Doppler shifts, an early indication of his interest in acoustics which was to become pronounced in later decades. In 1974 he received an award from the American Academy of Arts and Letters and in 1975 was a resident fellow at the Rockefeller Foundation's International Study and Conference Center in Bellagio. From 1974 to 1978 he served as a panelist for the NEA and from 1976 to 1980 was an Art Commissioner for the City of San Francisco. In 1976 he was commissioned to compose a work joining an Eastern with a Western instrument for the 12th World Congress of the International Musicological Soc. at Berkeley, a pioneering forum in the growth of East-West studies in music. The result was *In Celebration of Golden Rain* (1977) for Indonesian gamelan and pipe organ, a work which addressed the conflicting scales, design, and intent of the instruments of these 2 cultures as a problem of symbiosis rather than one of fusion, making a philosophical as well as a musical statement. Many subsequent works show the influence of non-Western cultures. In 1982–83 he was active at IRCAM in Paris, where his encounter with the new field of cognitive psychology in its musical applications gave a scientific articulation to a lifelong interest in acoustics. He returned to Berkeley and in 1987 founded the Center for New Music and Audio Technologies (CNMAT), an interdisciplinary facility linking music, cognitive psychology, linguistics, computer science, and architecture. His interest in the latter is reflected in his musical analysis and commentary in M. Treib, *Space Calculated in Seconds: The Philips Pavilion, Le Corbusier, Varèse* (Princeton, N.J., 1996). In 1999 he received a Library of Congress Koussevitzky commission. His music reflects an acute interest in acoustics and sonority, and an attempt to cast them in ritual, architectural, or dramatic forms.

WORKS: DRAMATIC: O p e r a : *Sir Gawain and the Green Knight* (San Francisco, April 4, 1964). **ORCH.:** *Mutations* (1966); *Galactic Rounds* (1972); *Orchestra* (San Francisco, Sept. 24,

1980); Organ Concerto (1986); *Camp Songs* for Chamber Orch. (1992); Sym. for Strings (1993); *Overture Concertante* for Clarinet and Orch. (1995). **CHAMBER:** *Evolutions* for Clarinet and Piano (1962); *Contractions,* mobile for Woodwind Quintet (1965); *Aubade* for String Trio, Harp, and Piano (1966); *Spectra* for Double Bass and Flutes (1967); *In Celebration of Golden Rain* for Indonesian Gamelan and Western Pipe Organ (1977); *from and to, with* for Violin and Piano (1980); *Crystal* for String Quartet (1981); *Of Things Remembered* for Harp, Flute, and Viola (1981); *Salvador Allende* for String Quartet, Clarinet, and Percussion (1983); *Volkan* for 5 Flutes (1 Player) (1983); *Pieces of Eight* for Double Bass and Organ (1984); *Dark Landscape* for English Horn (1985); *Lontano* for Harp and Piano (1986); *Constellations* for Multiple Brass Quintets and Horn Choir (1987); *Shadows* for 6 Players (1987); *Masks* for Flute and Trumpet (1989); *Palladio* for Violin, Piano, and Percussion (1989); *Primal Balance* for Contrabass and Flute (1991); *Cante jondo* for Bassoon, Clarinet, and Piano (1993); String Quartet (1995); Woodwind Quintet (1999). **KEYBOARD: P i a n o :** *Gravities* for Piano, 4-Hands (1965); *5 Short Piano Pieces* (1986); Prelude (1997; rev. 1998). **O r g a n :** *On the Heart of the Earth* (1976). **VOCAL:** *The Eyes of All* for Voices (1955); *Communion Service* for 2 Equal Voices and Organ (1961); *A Christmas Madrigal* for Chorus and Brass Ensemble (1964); *4 Poems from the Japanese* for Women's Voices, 5 Harps, and Percussion (1964); *The Captives* for Chorus and Orch. (1965); *Give Thanks to the Lord*, anthem for Small Chorus (1966); *Short Unison Mass* for Voices and Organ (1966); *Pentecost Sunday: Double Alleluia* for Unison Chorus, Organ, and Electronic Sounds (1967); *Glossolalia* for Baritone, Organ, Percussion, and Electronic Sounds (1967); *Songs of Darkness and Light* for Chorus and Organ (1970); *Te Deum* for Soloists, 3 Boy Sopranos, Chorus, Marimba, and Organ (1974); *Alleluia to the Heart of (the) Matter* for 2 Equal Voices and Organ (1976); *The Seasons* for Chorus (1978); *The Tuning of the Sky* for Voices (1978); *Lumen* for Soprano and Organ (1980); *Mass for Catherine of Siena* for Chorus and Organ (1981); *Furies* for 3 Sopranos and 3 Flutes (1988); *Mad With Love* for Unison and Mixed Chorus and Handbells (1993); *Streaming/Dreaming* for Soprano (1994); *Vac* for Woman's Voice, Clarinet, Violin, Cello, and Piano (1995); *Walden* for Soprano and Organ or String Quartet (1998). **ELECTRONIC: S o u n d :** *Words of St. Peter* for Chorus, Organ, and Electronic Sounds (1965); *Crasis* for Flute, Clarinet, Violin, Cello, Piano, Harp, Percussion, and Electronic Sounds (1967); *Noösphere I* for Alto Flute and Electronic Tape (1967); *Background Music*, theater piece for Harp and Live Electronics (1969); *6 Electronic Dances* (1969); *The Architect and the Emperor of Assyria*, electronic score for Arrabal's play (1969); *Quintet, "Frames and Gestures"* for String Quartet, Piano, and Electronic Sounds (1970); *Lamentations for Jani Christou* for 12 Instruments and Electronic Sounds (1970); *Sic Transit* for Equal or Mixed Voices, Organ, Electronic Sounds, and Light Sources (1970); *Litany* for Organ and Electronic Tape (1971); *Signs* for Chorus, Electronic Sounds, and 3 Slide Projectors (1971); *Out of Sight* for Chorus, Organ, and Electronic Sounds (1971); *God of the Expanding Universe* for Organ and Electronic Sounds (1971); *Ekagrata* for Organ, 2 Drummers, and Electronic Sounds (1972); *I Make My Own Soul From All the Elements of the Earth* for Organ and Electronic Sounds (1972); *Stops* for Organ and Electronic Sounds (1972); *The Angels of Turtle Island* for Soprano, Flute, Violin, Percussion, and Live Electronics (1972); *2 Public Pieces* for Unison Voices and Electronic Sounds (1972); *The Passing of Enkidu* for Chorus, Piano, Percussion, and Electronic Sounds (1973); *Hymn of the Universe* for Chorus and Electronic Sounds (1973); *Susani* for Chorus, Organ, Bell-tree, and Electronic Sounds (1974); *Chöd* for

Violin, Cello, Contrabass, 2 Percussion, Piano, and Live Electronics (1975); *And From the Abyss* for Tuba and Electronic Sounds (1975); *Windows in the Sky* for Unison Chorus, Organ, and Electronic Sounds (1976); *Alleluia to the Heart of Stone* for Reverberated Recorder (1984); *The Hollow Woods* for 2 Recorders and Live Electronics (1989); *Responsory* for Man's Voice and Interactive Live Electronics (1991); *A Japanese Songbook* for Soprano and Electronic Sounds (1992). OTHER: Video: *Instruments of Violence* (1967); *Linearity* for Harp and Live Electronics (1968); *Mother Goose: A Parable of Man* (1970); *Point of Inflection* (1971); *The Place for No Story* (1972); also *Trio for Speaker, Screen, and Viewer*, interactive piece for broadcast television (1968); *Islands of Sound*, environmental music for 14 Carillons (1975); *Berlin Feuerwerkmusik* for 3 Mobile Carillons at Berlin's Tempelhof Airfield (1987).—NS/LK/DM

Feld, Jindřich, Czech composer; b. Prague, Feb. 19, 1925. He studied violin and viola with his father, a prof. of violin at the Prague Cons., and then took courses in composition there with Hlobil (1945–48) and with Řídký at the Prague Academy of Music (1948–52). He also studied musicology, aesthetics, and philosophy at the Charles Univ. in Prague (Ph.D., 1952). His 4th string quartet was awarded the State Prize in 1968. In 1968–69 he was a visiting prof. at the Univ. of Adelaide. During this time, he composed his *Dramatic Fantasy: The Days of August*, an orch. score in protest to the Soviet invasion of his homeland. From 1972 to 1986 he was a prof. of composition at the Prague Cons. He subsequently was head of the music dept. of the Czech Radio from 1990. After composing works reflective of the Czech tradition, he developed a distinctive voice utilizing a variety of modern compositional methods.

WORKS: DRAMATIC: *Poštácká pohádka* (The Postman's Tale), children's opera (1956). ORCH.: 2 divertimentos: No. 1 for Strings (1950) and No. 2 for Wind Band (1997); *Furiant* (1950); *Concerto for Orchestra* (1951; rewritten 1957); *Comedy Overture* (1953); Flute Concerto (1954); *Rhapsody* for Violin and Wind Orch. (1956); Concerto for Chamber Orch. (1957); Sonata for Flute and Strings (1957–65); Cello Concerto (1958); Bassoon Concerto (1959); *May 1945*, dramatic overture (1960); Suite for Chamber Strings (1961); *Thuringian Overture* (1961); *3 Frescoes* (1963); *Concert Music* for Oboe, Bassoon, and Orch. (1964); *Concert Piece* for Horn and Orch. (1966); *Serenata giocosa* for Chamber Orch. (1966); 3 syms.: No. 1 (1967), No. 2 (1983), and No. 3, *Fin de siècle* (1994–98); *Dramatic Fantasy: The Days of August* (1968–69); Oboe Concerto (1970); Chamber Sinfonietta for Strings (1971); *Concert Suite* for Bass Clarinet, Piano, Strings, and Percussion (1972); Piano Concerto (1973); Trombone Concerto (1975); Accordion Concerto (1975); *Partita piccola* for Accordion Orch. (1976); Violin Concerto (1977); *Evocations* for Accordion Orch. and Percussion (1978); *Serenade* for Chamber Strings (1979); *Concert Fantasy* for Flute, Strings, and Percussion (1980); Saxophone Concerto (1980); Harp Concerto (1982); *H.C. Andersen's Fairy Tales* for Accordion Orch. (1984); *Fresco* for Symphonic Wind Band (1985); Concertino for Flute, Piano, and Orch. (1991); *Elegy and Burlesque* for Cello and Orch. (1992); *Joyful Overture* for Symphonic Band (1996); Concertino for Cello and String Chamber Orch. (1999). CHAMBER: 6 string quartets (1949, 1952, 1962, 1965, 1979, 1993); 2 wind quintets (1949, 1968); Suite for Clarinet and Piano (1949); Sonatina for 2 Violins (1953); *4 Pieces* for Flute (1954); *Elegy and Burlesque* for Cello and Piano (1954–55); Viola Sonata (1955); *Rhapsody* for Violin and Piano (1956); Flute Sonata (1957); Chamber Suite for Nonet

(1960); Trio for Violin, Viola, and Cello (1961); Duo for Flute and Bassoon or Bass Clarinet (1962); Trio for Flute, Violin, and Cello (1963); *Caprices* for Wind Quartet and Guitar (1964); Suite for Accordion (1965); Bassoon Sonatina (1969); Brass Quintet (1970); Clarinet Sonatina (1970); Trio for Violin or Flute, Cello, and Piano (1972); Cello Sonata (1972); *5 Stylistic Studies* for String Quartet, Flute, and Harp (1974); Guitar Sonata (1974); *Suite Rhapsodica* for Clarinet (1976); *Toccata and Passacaglia* for Harp (1976); *Partita canonica* for 3 Trumpets and 3 Trombones (1977); *Epigrams* for Piccolo Flute, Tuba, and Harp (1977); *Serenade* for 4 Horns (1978); *Music* for 2 Accordions (1979); *Cassation* for 9 Flutes (1980); Concert Duo for 2 Flutes (1981); Saxophone Quartet (1981); *Elegy* for Soprano Saxophone or Oboe and Piano (1981); Oboe or Soprano Saxophone Sonata (1982); *Introduction and Allegro* for Accordion and Percussion (1983); *Concert Music* for Viola and Piano (1983; also for Quinton and Piano, 1988); Quartettino for Recorder Quartet (1985); Violin Sonata (1985); Sonatina for Flute and Harp (1986); *Concerto da camera* for 2 String Quartets (1987); Trio for Oboe, Clarinet, and Bassoon (1987); Duo for Violin and Cello or Viola (1989); Horn Sonatina (1989); Alto Saxophone Sonata (1989–90); *Partita concertante* for Cello (1990); *Introduzione, toccata e fuga* for Flute (1991); *Suite Rapsodica* for Alto Saxophone (1992); Concerto for Saxophone, 2 Pianos, and 2 Percussionists (1992); *Cassation* for 8 Horns (1993); *Trio giocoso* for Clarinet or Alto Saxophone, Bassoon, and Piano (1994); *American Sonatina* for Flute and Piano (1995); *Quintetto capriccioso* for Flute, Violin, Viola, Cello, and Harp (1995); *Divertimento* for Flute and Guitar (1996); *Musica capricciosa* for Alto Saxophone and Piano (1998); Quintet for Saxophone or Clarinet and String Quartet (1999). KEYBOARD: Piano: *Prelude and Toccata* (1958–59); Sonata (1972). Organ: *Rhapsody* (1963). VOCAL: *Nonsense Rhymes* for Women's Chorus and Small Instrumental Ensemble (1973); *Laus Cantus* for Soprano and String Quartet (1985); *COSMAE CHRONICA BOEMORUM*, oratorio-cantata for Soloists, Chorus, and Orch. (1988); choruses; songs. OTHER: Small instruction pieces, etc.—NS/LK/DM

Feldbrill, Victor, Canadian conductor; b. Toronto, April 4, 1924. He received training in violin from Sigmund Steinberg (1936–43) and in theory from Weinzweig (1939) before studying conducting at the Toronto Cons. of Music with Mazzoleni (1942–43), during which time he was conductor of the Univ. of Toronto Sym. Orch. Following training in harmony and composition with Howells at the Royal Coll. of Music and in conducting with Ernest Read at the Royal Academy of Music in London, he was concertmaster and asst. conductor of the Royal Cons. of Music of Toronto Sym. Orch. and Opera Co. (1946–49). He studied violin with Kathleen Parlow (1945–49), took his artist diploma from the Univ. of Toronto (1949), was a conducting student at the Berkshire Music Center in Tanglewood (summer, 1947), of Monteux in Hancock, Maine (summers, 1949–50), and of Otterloo and Zallinger in Salzburg (summer, 1956). He played 1st violin in the Toronto Sym. Orch. (1949–56) and the CBC Sym. Orch. (1952–56). In 1952 he became founder-conductor of the Canadian Chamber Players. In 1956–57 he was asst. conductor of the Toronto Sym. Orch. From 1958 to 1968 he was music director of the Winnipeg Sym. Orch. He served on the staff of the Univ. of Toronto from 1968 to 1982. He also was director of the youth programming of the Toronto Sym. (1968–78); from 1973 to 1977 he was likewise the resident conductor of the Toronto Sym. He was founder-conductor of the Toronto Sym. Youth Orch. (1973–78). From 1979 to 1981 he was acting music director of the London (Ontario) Sym. Orch. He was a prof. at the Tokyo National Univ. of Art and Music from 1981 to 1987. He served as interim music advisor (1990–91), as music director (1991–93), and as principal guest conductor (from 1993) of the Hamilton (Ontario) Phil. In appreciation for his yeoman service in the cause of promoting contemporary Canadian music, he was made an Officer of the Order of Canada in 1985. —NS/LK/DM

Feldbusch, Eric, Belgian cellist, music educator, and composer; b. Grivegnée, March 2, 1922. He studied cello at the Liège Cons. (1934–39), and later took courses in composition with Quinet and Legley (1947–48). He was director of the Mons Cons. (1963–72) and of the Brussels Cons. (1974–87).

WORKS: DRAMATIC: *Orestes,* opera (1969); *El Diablo Cojuelo,* ballet (1972). **ORCH.:** *Variations sur un air connu* (1955); *Contrastes* (1956); *Les Moineaux de Baltimore,* suite (1958); *Adagio* for Strings (1958); *Adagio* for 3 Cellos and String Orch. (1960); *Mosaïque* for Strings (1961); *Overture* for Strings (1961); *Shema Israël* for Strings (1962); *Ode à des enfants morts* (1965–66); Violin Concerto (1967); *Fantaisie- Divertissement* (1967); *Piccola musica* for Strings (1971); *Pointes Sèches* (1977); *Triade* for Chamber Orch. (1977); *Itinéraire* (1982); *Dichroisme II* (1983); *Concertante* for 2 Pianos and Orch. (1986); Cello Concerto (1988). **CHAMBER:** *Aquarelles* for Wind Quintet (1947); 4 string quartets (1955, 1958, 1963, 1971); Sonata for Violin and Cello (1955); *Cadence and Allegro* for Cello and Piano (1956); Violin Sonata (1957); Piano Trio (1958); *Variations extra- formelles* for Cello and Piano (1959); Trio for Flute, Violin, and Cello (1961); Duo for Flute and Viola (1963); Septet for Soprano, 2 Violins, Double Bass, Flute, Trumpet, and Percussion (1969); piano pieces. **OTHER:** Vocal works.—NS/LK/DM

Felderhof, Jan (Reindert Adriaan), Dutch composer and pedagogue; b. Bussum, near Amsterdam, Sept. 25, 1907. He studied violin with Felice Togni and Hendrik Rynbergen (diploma, 1931) and theory and composition with Sem Dresden (diploma, 1933) at the Amsterdam Cons., and he later studied with Chris Bos at the Utrecht Cons. (diploma, 1958). He taught at the Amsterdam Cons. (1934–54; 1958–68), where he was adjunct director (1968–73). He also taught at the Bussum music school (1944–54), served as director of the Rotterdam Cons. (1954–55), and taught at the Utrecht Cons. (1956–67). In 1970 he was made a Knight of the Order of Oranje Nassau by the Dutch government. His works have an agreeable veneer of simple musicality, and all are excellently written.

WORKS: DRAMATIC: O p e r a : *Vliegvuur* (Wildfire; 1959–64; Dutch Radio, Nov. 10, 1965). **ORCH.:** *Music for 15 Winds and Percussion* (1930); *5 Dance Sketches* (1930); 2 sinfoniettas (1932, 1962); Suite for Flute and Small Orch. (1933); *Rhapsodie* for Oboe and Small Orch. (1937); Sym. (1949); *Ouverture* (1955); Concerto for Flute, Strings, and Percussion (1955); *Omaggio* (1974); *Complimento* for Strings (1975); *Introduction and Rondo* (1980); *Chanterelle* (1985); *Nostalgic Suite* (1989). **CHAMBER:** 3 violin sonatas (1932, 1939, 1965); 5 string quartets (1932, 1936, 1938, 1957, 1990); Suite for Flute and Piano (1933);

String Trio (1934); Cello Sonata (1935); Piano Trio (1936); *Divertimento* for Brass Quartet (1950); Violin Sonatina (1953); *Rondo* for Oboe, Clarinet, and Bassoon (1960); Trio for 3 Different Clarinets (1968); Suite for Flute, Oboe, and Piano (1974); Sonata for 2 Violins and Piano (1977); *Andante* for Flute, Oboe, and Harp (1983); Sonatine for Flute, Oboe, and Harp (1988); *Improvisatie* for Viola and Piano (1991); *Impuls* for 4 Saxophones (1992); *Ringraziamento* for Alto Saxophone (1995; also for Viola); piano pieces, including 5 sonatinas (1933–62); organ music. **VOCAL:** *Tot wien zullen wij henengaan* (To Whom Shall We Make Our Way), cantata (1935; rev. 1941); *Groen is de gong* for Chorus and Orch. (1977); *Composite* for Women's Chorus, Flute, and Harp (1984); songs.—NS/LK/DM

Feldhoff, Gerd, German baritone; b. Radervormwald, near Cologne, Oct. 29, 1931. He studied at the North West Music Academy in Detmold. He made his operatic debut in Essen in 1959 as Figaro in *Le nozze di Figaro;* then sang at the Städtische Oper in Berlin, the Hamburg State Opera, and the Frankfurt am Main Opera. From 1968 to 1978 he appeared at the Bayreuth Festivals. He made his Metropolitan Opera debut in N.Y. as Kaspar in *Der Freischütz* on Sept. 28, 1971. He was especially noted as a dramatic baritone; he also made tours as a concert artist.—NS/LK/DM

Feldman, Jill, esteemed American soprano; b. Los Angeles, April 21, 1952. She studied with Michael Ingham at the Univ. of Calif. at Santa Barbara (B.A. in musicology, 1975), Lillian Loran in San Francisco (1975–95), Andrea von Ramm in Basel (1980–81), and Nicole Fallien (1987–91) and Anna Maria Bondi (1992–93) in Paris. In 1977 she made her recital debut in Berkeley, returning there in 1978 to make her first appearance as a soloist with the Univ. of Calif. Orch. In 1979 she made her operatic debut in the role of La Musica in *Orfeo* in Berkeley, and then made her European operatic debut in 1980 as Clerio in Cavalli's *Erismena* in Spoleto. In 1981 she became a leading member of William Christie's Les Arts Florissants in Paris, where she won acclaim in the title role of Charpentier's *Medée* at the Salle Playel in 1983. In 1986 she made her first appearance with the Philharmonia Baroque Orch. under Nicholas McGegan's direction. She appeared in recital at London's Wigmore Hall in 1987, and returned to England in 1988 to sing with the Taverner Players under Andrew Parrott's direction at the Bath Festival. In 1990 she was engaged as a soloist in Haydn's *Die Schöpfung* under Frans Bruggen's direction at the Flanders Festival and the Utrecht Festival. She gave solo recitals in Boston, Geneva, and Paris in 1995. Feldman's superb vocal gifts are complemented by her expert knowledge of early music performance practice. Her repertoire ranges from the medieval to Romantic periods, and includes works by Hildegard von Bingen, Monteverdi, Charpentier, Cavalli, Purcell, Cesti, Handel, Campra, Rameau, Mozart, and Meyerbeer. —NS/LK/DM

Feldman, Ludovic, Romanian composer and violinist; b. Galaţi, June 6, 1893; d. Bucharest, Sept. 11, 1987. He studied violin in Galaţi, with Klenck at the Bucharest

Cons. (1910–11), and with Ondříček at the New Vienna Cons. (1911–13). He was a violinist in the Phil. and in the orch. of the State Opera in Bucharest (1926–40). Following training in composition with Jora in Bucharest (1941–42), he devoted himself fully to composing.

WORKS: ORCH.: 5 suites (1948; 1949; 1951–52; 1960; 1960); *Fantezie concertantă* for Cello and Orch. (1949); *Poem concertant* for Violin and Orch. (1950–51); Concerto for Flute and Chamber Orch. (1953); Concerto for 2 String Orchs., Celesta, Piano, and Percussion (Brasov, Oct. 15, 1958); 5 Symphonic Pieces (1960–61); *Sonată concertantă* for Violin and Chamber Orch. (1964); *Variațiuni simfonice* (1966; Bucharest, June 14, 1967); *Simfonie concertantă* for Chamber Orch. (1971; Paris, Jan. 11, 1973); *Simfonie omagială* (1978; Bucharest, June 6, 1983); *Poem simfonie* (1981). **CHAMBER:** 2 suites for Violin and Piano (1947, 1948); Flute Sonata (1952); 2 viola sonatas (1953, 1965); String Trio (1955); String Quartet (1957); 2 quintets (1956–57; 1977); Violin Sonata (1962–63); Cello Sonata (1963–64); *Improvizație*, trio for Violin, Cello, and Piano (1979); piano pieces.

BIBL.: D. Dediu, *Episoade și viziuni: L. F.* (Bucharest, 1991). —NS/LK/DM

Feldman, Morton, significant American composer and pedagogue; b. N.Y., Jan. 12, 1926; d. Buffalo, Sept. 3, 1987. At 12, he began piano lessons with Vera Maurina-Press. In 1942 he commenced composition lessons with Riegger, and in 1944 with Wolpe. In 1950 he was befriended by Cage, and soon moved in the circles of such musicians as Brown, Wolff, and Tudor, and such abstract expressionist painters as Rothko, Guston, Kline, Pollock, and Rauschenberg. The influence of these musicians and painters was pronounced, but Feldman pursued his own path as a composer. In his *Projections* series (1950–51), he first utilized graph notation. In 1953 he abandoned it, only to resort to it again from time to time between 1958 and 1967. In his *Durations* series (1960–61), he utilized what he described as "race-course" notation in which exact notation for each instrumental part still allows for relative freedom in durations and vertical coordination. About 1979 he began to compose works of extended duration, producing in his 2nd String Quartet (1983) a score which can run for almost 6 hours. In 1966 Feldman held a Guggenheim followship. He received awards from the National Inst. of Arts and Letters in 1970 and from the Koussevitzky Foundation in 1975. From 1973 until his death he was the Edgard Varèse Prof. at the State Univ. of N.Y. at Buffalo, where he was a major influence as both a composer and a teacher. Collections of his writings were ed. by W. Zimmermann as *Morton Feldman Essays* (Kerpen, 1985), by J.-Y. Bousseur as *Morton Feldman, Ecrits et Paroles* (Paris, 1998), and by B.H. Friedman as *Morton Feldman: Give My Regards to Eighth Street: Essays & Lectures* (Boston, 1999).

WORKS: *Journey to the End of Night* for Soprano or Tenor, Flute, Clarinet, Bass Clarinet, and Bassoon (1947); *Only* for Voice (1947); *Illusions* for Piano (1949); *Piece* for Violin and Piano (1950); *2 Intermissions* for Piano (1950); *Projection I* for Cello (1950), *II* for Flute, Trumpet, Piano, Violin, and Cello (1951), *III* for 2 Pianos (1951), *IV* for Violin and Piano (1951), and *V* for 3 Flutes, Trumpet, 2 Pianos, and 3 Cellos (1951); *4 Songs to e.e. cummings* for Soprano, Piano, and Cello (1951); *Jackson Pollock*, film score (1951); *Marginal Intersection* for Orch. (1951); *Structures* for String Quartet (1951); *Extensions I* for Violin and Piano (1951), *II* (withdrawn), *III* for Piano (1952), and *IV* for 3 Pianos (1952–53); *Intersection I* for Orch. (1951), *II* for Piano (1951), *III* for Piano (1953), and *IV* for Cello (1953); *Intermission V* for Piano (1952) and *VI* for Piano or 2 Pianos (1953); *Piano Piece* (1952, 1955, 1956a, 1956b, 1963, 1964); *11 Instruments* for Flute, Alto Flute, Horn, Trumpet, Bass Trumpet, Trombone, Tuba, Vibraphone, Piano, Violin, and Cello (1953); *Intersection* for Tape (1953); *3 Pieces* for Piano (1954); *2 Pieces* for 2 Pianos (1954); *3 Pieces* for String Quartet (1954, 1954, 1956); *2 Pieces for 6 Instruments* for Flute, Alto Flute, Horn, Trumpet, Violin, and Cello (1956); *Piano (3 Hands)* (1957); *Piece for 4 Pianos* (1957); *2 Pianos* (1957); *Ixion* for 10 Instruments (1958; N.Y., April 14, 1966); *Out of "Last Pieces"* for Orch. (1958); *Piano 4 Hands* (1958); *2 Instruments* for Horn and Cello (1958); *Atlantis* for 17 Instruments (1959; also for 10 Instruments); *Last Pieces* for Piano (1959); *The Swallows of Salangan* for Chorus and 23 Instruments (1960); *Durations I* for Alto Flute, Piano, Violin, and Cello (1960), *II* for Cello and Piano (1960), *III* for Tuba, Piano, and Violin (1961), *IV* for Violin, Cello, and Vibraphone (1961), and *V* for Horn, Celesta, Piano, Harp, Vibraphone, Violin, and Cello (1961); *Structures* for Orch. (1960–62); *Intervals* for Bass-baritone, Trombone, Cello, Vibraphone, and Percussion (1961); *The Straits of Magellan* for Flute, Horn, Trumpet, Piano, Amplified Guitar, Harp, and Double Bass (1961); *2 Pieces* for Clarinet and String Quartet (1961); *For Franz Kline* for Soprano, Horn, Piano, Tubular Bells, Violin, and Cello (1962); *The O'Hara Songs* for Bass-baritone, Tubular Bells, Piano, Violin, Viola, and Cello (1962); *Christian Wolff in Cambridge* for Chorus (1963); *De Kooning* for Horn, Percussion, Piano, Violin, and Cello (1963); *Rabbi Akiba* for Soprano and 10 Instruments (1963); *Vertical Thoughts I* for 2 Pianos (1963), *II* for Violin and Piano (1963), *III* for Soprano, Flute, Horn, Trumpet, Trombone, Tuba, 2 Percussion, Piano, Celesta, Violin, Cello, and Double Bass (1963), *IV* for Piano (1963), and *V* for Soprano, Tuba, Percussion, Celesta, and Violin (1963); *Chorus and Instruments I* for Chorus, Horn, Tuba, Percussion, Piano, Celesta, Violin, Cello, and Double Bass (1963) and *II* for Chorus, Tuba, and Tubular Bells (1967); *The King of Denmark* for Percussion (1964); *Numbers* for Flute, Horn, Trombone, Tuba, Percussion, Piano, Celesta, Violin, Cello, and Double Bass (1964); *4 Instruments* for Tubular Bells, Piano, Violin, and Cello (1965); *2 Pieces* for 3 Pianos (1966); *First Principles I* (1966) and *II* (1966–67) for 19 Instruments; *In Search of an Orchestration* for Orch. (1967); *False Relationships and the Extended Ending* for Trombone, Tubular Bells, 3 Pianos, Violin, and Cello (1968); *Between Categories* for 2 Tubular Bells, 2 Pianos, 2 Violins, and 2 Cellos (1969); *On Time and the Instrumental Factor* for Orch. (1969; Dallas, April 24, 1971); *Madame Press Died Last Week at Ninety* for 12 Instruments (1970); *The Viola in My Life I* for Viola, Flute, Percussion, Piano, Violin, and Cello (London, Sept. 19, 1970), *II* for Viola, Flute, Clarinet, Percussion, Celesta, Violin, and Cello (1970), *III* for Viola and Piano (1970), and *IV* for Viola and Orch. (Venice, Sept. 16, 1971); *I Met Heine in the Rue Fürstenberg* for Mezzo-soprano, Flute, Clarinet, Percussion, Piano, Violin, and Cello (1971); *Rothko Chapel* for Soprano, Alto, Chorus, Percussion, Celesta, and Viola (1971; Houston, April 1972); *3 Clarinets, Cello, and Piano* (1971; BBC, London, March 1972); *Chorus and Orchestra I* (1971; Cologne, March 1973); and *II* for Soprano, Chorus, and Orch. (1972; London, Jan. 5, 1973); *Cello and Orchestra* (1972); *Pianos and Voices II*, renamed *Pianos and Voices* for 5 Pianos and 5 Women's Voices (1972); *Voices and Instruments I* for Chorus, 2 Flutes, English Horn, Clarinet, Bassoon, Horn, Timpani, Piano, and Double Bass (Dartington, Aug. 11, 1972) and *II* for 3

Women's Voices, Flute, 2 Cellos, and Double Bass (1972); *Voice and Instruments I* for Soprano and Orch. (1972; Berlin, March 14, 1973) and *II* for Woman's Voice, Clarinet, Cello, and Double Bass (1974); *For Frank O'Hara* for Flute, Clarinet, 2 Percussion, Piano, Violin, and Cello (1973); *String Quartet and Orchestra* (1973); *Voices and Cello* for 2 High Voices and Cello (1973); *Instruments I* for Alto Flute, Piccolo, Oboe, English Horn, Trombone, Percussion, and Cello (1974), *II* for Flute, Piccolo, Alto Flute, Oboe, English Horn, Clarinet, Bass Clarinet, Trumpet, Trombone, Tuba, Percussion, Harp, Piano, and Double Bass (1974), *III* for Flute, Oboe, and Percussion (1977), and *IV: Why Patterns?* for Violin, Piano, and Percussion (1978; also for Flute, Alto Flute, Percussion, and Piano (1979); *4 Instruments* for Violin, Viola, Cello, and Piano (1975); *Piano and Orchestra* (1975); *Elemental Procedures* for Soprano, Chorus, and Orch. (1976; West German Radio, Cologne, Jan. 22, 1977); *Oboe and Orchestra* (1976); *Orchestra* (Glasgow, Sept. 18, 1976); *Routine Investigations* for Oboe, Trumpet, Piano, Viola, Cello, and Double Bass (1976); *Voice, Violin, and Piano* (Holland Festival, June 2, 1976); *Neither*, monodrama for Soprano and Orch. (Rome, May 13, 1977); *Piano* (1977); *Flute and Orchestra* (1977–78); *Spring of Chosroes* for Violin and Piano (1978); 2 string quartets: No. 1 (1979; N.Y., May 4, 1980) and No. 2 (Toronto, Dec. 4, 1983); *Violin and Orchestra* (1979; Hessian Radio, Frankfurt am Main, April 12, 1984); *Principal Sound* for Organ (1980); *The Turfan Fragments* for Chamber Orch. (1980; Swiss- Italian Radio, Lugano, March 26, 1981); Trio for Violin, Viola, and Piano (1980); *Bass, Clarinet, and Percussion* for Clarinet, Percussion, and Double Bass (1981; Middelburg, July 1, 1982); *Triadic Memories* for Piano (London, Oct. 5, 1981); *Untitled Composition*, later named *Patterns in a Chromatic Field* for Cello and Piano (1981; Middelburg, July 1982); *For John Cage* for Violin and Piano (N.Y., March 1982); *3 Voices* for 3 Sopranos or 3 Solo Voices and Tape (1982; Valencia, Calif., March 1983); *Clarinet and String Quartet* (Newcastle upon Tyne, Oct. 9, 1983); *Crippled Symmetry* for Flute, Bass Flute, Vibraphone, Glockenspiel, Piano, and Celesta (1983; Berlin, March 1984); *For Philip Guston* for Flute, Alto Flute, Percussion, Piano, and Celesta (1984; Buffalo, April 21, 1985); *For Bunita Marcus* for Piano (Middelburg, June 1985); *Violin and String Quartet* (1985); *Piano and String Quartet* (Los Angeles, Nov. 2, 1985); *Coptic Light* for Orch. (N.Y., May 30, 1986); *For Christian Wolff* for Flute, Piano, and Celesta (Darmstadt, July 1986); *For Stefan Wolpe* for Chorus and 2 Vibraphones (1986; River Falls, Wisc., April 30, 1987); *Palais de Mari* for Piano (N.Y., Nov. 20, 1986); *Samuel Beckett, Words and Music* for a radio play for 2 Flutes, Vibraphone, Piano, Violin, Viola, and Cello (N.Y., March 1987); *Piano, Violin, Viola, Cello* (Middelburg, July 4, 1987).

BIBL.: K. Potter, *An Introduction to the Music of M. F.* (diss., Univ. of Wales, Cardiff, 1973); T. DeLio, *Circumscribing the Open Universe: Essays on Cage, F., Wolff, Ashley and Lucier* (Washington, D.C., 1984; 2nd ed., 1996); S. Josek, *The New York School: Earle Brown, John Cage, M. F., Christian Wolff* (Saarbrücken, 1998); C. Sebastian, *Neither: Die Musik M. F.* (Hofheim, 1999).—NS/LK/DM

Feliciano, José, Latin pop guitarist/vocalist; b. Lares, P.R., Sept. 10, 1945. Blind at birth from congenital glaucoma, Feliciano became a pop sensation in the late 1960s. Moving easily between flamenco, soul, jazz, and softer pop, between English-language and Spanish-language recording, Feliciano has been a notable performer for more than three decades. Born in P.R., Feliciano came with his family to Spanish Harlem in the early 1950s. His first "instrument" was a tin cracker can,

which he used to back up his also-musical uncle. A prodigy, Feliciano taught himself to play the concertina at age six and effortlessly moved on to accordion and guitar soon afterward. When he first heard rock 'n' roll, he was inspired to add singing to his talents. To help support the family, Feliciano quit school at age 17 and spent the remainder of his teenage years busking at the same Greenwich Village coffeehouses that produced Bob Dylan. After an appearance at the Newport Jazz Festival, he released a pair of albums that showcased his supple vocals and flamenco-influenced fretwork—*The Voice and Guitar of José Feliciano* and *The Fantastic Feliciano*—and then a set of Spanish- language LPs. But Feliciano's name first loomed truly large in 1968, when his cover of The Doors' "Light My Fire" hit #1, and his stylized version of the national anthem at the World Series in Detroit stirred controversy. The following year, his "Light My Fire" seemed to be everywhere, and Feliciano was everywhere else, releasing three new albums, charting with a cover of Tommy Tucker's "Hi Heeled Sneakers," and netting a Grammy for Best New Artist.

Continuing to release English- and Spanish-language albums, Feliciano recorded the holiday standard "Feliz Navidad," hit the charts occasionally (most notably with the theme song to the Freddie Prinze sitcom *Chico and the Man*), and guested on records by performers as diverse as Michael Nesmith, Joni Mitchell, Minnie Riperton, and John Lennon. Then, in 1998, Feliciano enjoyed an echo of his heyday, seeing his album *Señor Bolero* go platinum and its first single, "Me Has Echado Al Olvido," hit #1 in N.Y. An overdue resurgence in a career that's far from over, these honors merely contributed to the stats on Feliciano's 40+ gold and platinum records, 16 Grammy nominations, six Grammy wins, and five-time placement as *Guitar Player* magazine's annual Best Pop Guitarist. A Grammy winner in two languages, Feliciano is an icon to culture-crossing successors like Ricky Martin.

DISC.: *El Sentimiento, La Voz Y La Guitarra* (1967); *Feliciano!* (1968); *Souled* (1969); *The Christmas Album* (1970); *Escenas De Amor* (1982); *Tu Inmenso Amor* (1987); *All Time Greatest Hits* (1988); *Light My Fire* (1992); *Mis Mejores Canciones—17 Super Exitos* (1993); *Americano* (1996); *Exitos Y Recuerdos* (1996); *...On Second Thought* (1996); *Passion of Feliciano* (1997); *Señor Bolero* (1998); *El Amor De Mi Vida—Masterpieces* (1998); *The Very Best of Josée Feliciano* (1999); *Noches De Bohemia* (2000).

Felix, Hugo, Austrian composer; b. Vienna, Nov. 19, 1866; d. Los Angeles, Aug. 14, 1934. Although he earned a Ph.D. in science from the Univ. of Vienna, he opted to pursue a career as a composer of light theater scores. His first operetta, *Die Kätzchen*, was successfully premiered in Lemberg in Jan. 23, 1890. His first Vienna success came with his fourth operetta, *Rhodope* (Feb. 1, 1900). He then had a substantial hit with *Madame Sherry* (Berlin, Nov. 1, 1902), which subsequently was played throughout Europe. His *Les Merveilleuses* or *The Lady Dances* was first performed in London on Oct. 27, 1906). After the premiere of *Tantalizing Tommy* (N.Y., Oct. 2, 1912), he brought out the successful score *The Pearl Girl*

(London, Sept. 25, 1913). His subsequent theater scores were composed for N.Y., among them *Pom-Pom* (Feb. 28, 1916), *Lassie* (April 6, 1920), *The Sweetheart Shop* (Aug. 31, 1920), and *Marjolaine* (Jan. 24, 1922).—NS/LK/DM

Felix, Václav, prominent Czech composer and pedagogue; b. Prague, March 29, 1928. He studied composition with Bořkovec and Dobiáš at the Prague Academy of Music (graduated, 1953), then did postgraduate study in theory with Janeček (1953–56). He completed his education at the Charles Univ. in Prague (Ph.D. in philosophy, 1957; Candidatus scientiarum, 1961). He was ed. of *Hudební Rozhledy* in Prague (1959–61). In 1960 he joined the faculty of the Prague Academy of Music, where he was head of the theory and music history dept. (1979–85), dean of the music faculty (1985–90), and a prof. (1985–92). From 1978 to 1989 he was vice president of the central committee of the Union of Czech Composers and Concert Artists. He received the prize of the Czech Minister of Culture (1976), was made an Artist of Merit (1978), and received the prize of the Union of Czech Composers and Concert Artists (1980) and the National Prize (1986). His music follows the golden mean of agreeable Central European modernism.

Works (all 1st perf. in Prague unless otherwise given): DRAMATIC: O p e r a : *Nesmělý Kasanova aneb Čím zrají muži* (Shy Casanova or What Makes Men Ripe; 1966; Dec. 13, 1967); *Inzerát* (The Advertisement; Brno, April 25, 1975); *Mariana* (1982; Brno, April 11, 1985). ORCH.: *Concerto romantico* for Violin, Clarinet or Viola, Harp, and Strings (Oct. 19, 1953); *Fantasy* for Clarinet and Orch. (1959; March 30, 1960); *Concertant Variations* (1962; Feb. 17, 1963); Suite for Strings (1969); *Joyful Overture* (1971; March 8, 1972); *Concert Waltz* (1973); 6 syms.: No. 1 for Woman's Voice and Orch. (1974; May 25, 1975), No. 2 for Small Orch. (1981; Karlovy Vary, March 19, 1982), No. 3 for Chorus and Orch. (1986; March 10, 1988), No. 4 (Nov. 12, 1987), No. 5 for Chamber Orch. (1987), and No. 6 for Large Wind Orch. (1990); Concertino for Flute and Strings (1976; Jan. 18, 1977); *Labor Victorious*, gala overture for Large Wind Orch. (1977; March 8, 1978); Double Concerto for Cello or Bass Clarinet, Piano, and Strings (1978; March 17, 1979); *Symphonic Variations on a Czech Recruit Song* for Large Wind Orch. (1979; March 23, 1980); *Summer Day Romance* for Clarinet and Orch. (1979; Teplice, July 3, 1980); Trumpet Concerto (1984; Poděbrady, May 20, 1986); Cello Concerto (1990). CHAMBER: 3 piano trios (1955, 1956, 1962); Cello Sonata (1960); String Trio (1961); *The Story of Snow White*, quintet for Harp and String Quartet (1963); *Sonata a tre* for Violin, Viola, and Harp (1967); *Sonata da Requiem* for Horn or Bass Clarinet and Piano (1969); Wind Quintet (1972); Brass Quintet (1972); Trio for Violin, Horn, and Piano (1973); Trio for Clarinet, Cello, and Piano (1977); *Sonata Lirica* for Oboe and Piano (1978); *Quartetto amoroso* for 2 Violins, Viola, and Cello (1979); *Sonata Capricciosa* for Flute and Piano (1981); *We Have a Baby at Home*, suite for Flute, Violin, and Piano (1984); *A Small Afternoon Music* for Flute, Viola, and Cello (1985); *Sonata concertante* for Viola and Piano (1989); piano pieces, including 3 sonatinas (1969) and *Sonata poetica* (1988). VOCAL: 3 cantatas: *The Celebration* (1963), *Where Do the Months Come From?* (1965), and *Always Generous* (1980; Olomouc, Sept. 3, 1981); *Sententiae Nasonis* for Chorus (1995); numerous other vocal pieces. —NS/LK/DM

Fellegara, Vittorio, Italian composer and teacher; b. Milan, Nov. 4, 1927. He received training in physics and mathematics at the Univ. (1945–50) and in theory from Chailly at the Verdi Cons. (graduated, 1951) in Milan. Thereafter he was active as a composer and teacher.

Works: DRAMATIC: B a l l e t : *Mutazioni* (1962; Milan, Jan. 27, 1965; as 4 symphonic fragments, Copenhagen, May 28, 1964). ORCH.: *Concerto for Orchestra* (1952; RAI, Feb. 28, 1957); *Concerto breve* for Chamber Orch. (Milan, Dec. 15, 1956); *Sinfonia 1957* (1957; Rome, June 28, 1958); *Serenata* for Chamber Orch. (Rome, May 24, 1960; also for 9 Instruments); *Frammenti I* for Chamber Orch. (1960; Palermo, May 21, 1961) and *II: Variazioni* for Chamber Orch. (Milan, April 17, 1961); *Studi in forma di variazioni* for Chamber Orch. (Piacenza, May 23, 1978); *Trauermusik* for Strings (1978; Bergamo, April 6, 1982); *You Wind of March* for Flute and Orch. (1979; Verona, May 21, 1988); *Berceuse* for Flute and Chamber Orch. (1982; also for Flute and Piano, 1980); *Primo vere* for Piano and Chamber Orch. (1988; Ancona, Jan. 26, 1991; also for Piano and Small Orch., Frankfurt am Main, Feb. 25, 1992). CHAMBER: *Ottetto* for Winds (1953; Donaueschingen, Oct. 15, 1955); *Serenata* for 9 Instruments (1960; also for Chamber Orch.); *Berceuse* for Flute and Piano (1980; also for Flute and Chamber Orch., 1982); *Wiegenlied* for Clarinet and Piano (Siena, Aug. 25, 1981; also for Clarinet Concertante and 8 Winds, 1982; Bergamo, March 30, 1985); *Contrasti* for Chamber Ensemble (1982; Bergamo, March 26, 1983); *Wintermusic* for Violin, Cello, and Piano (1983; Bergamo, March 17, 1984); *Eisblumen* for Guitar (1985); *Der Musensohn* for Oboe (1985); *Herbstmusik: Omaggio a Mahler* for String Quartet (1986; Bergamo, April 11, 1987); *Stille Nacht* for Organ and 9 Winds (Bergamo, Oct. 6, 1990); *Arabeschi* for Harp (1991); *Pampas Flash* for Chamber Ensemble (1992); *Winterzeit* for Guitar Quartet (1992). KEYBOARD: P i a n o : *Invenzioni* (1949); *Ricercare fantasia* (1951; Milan, May 30, 1952); *Preludio, fuga e postludio* (1952–53; Bayreuth, Aug. 4, 1953); *Omaggio a Bach* (Brescia, June 7, 1975). VOCAL: *Requiem di Madrid* for Chorus and Orch. (1958; RAI, Turin, Oct. 17, 1959); *Dies irae* for Chorus and Instruments (1959; RAI, Milan, April 11, 1973); *Epitaphe* for 2 Sopranos and 5 Instrumentalists (Venice, Sept. 12, 1964); Cantata for 2 Women's Voices and Orch. (Donaueschingen, Oct. 23, 1966); *Madrigale* for Vocal Quintet and Instruments (Milan, Nov. 25, 1969; also for Small Chorus and Chamber Orch.); *Notturno* for Soprano, Contralto, Men's Chorus, and Orch. (1971; RAI-TV, Nov. 29, 1975); *Chanson* for Soprano and Chamber Orch. (1974; RAI, Milan, Oct. 1, 1975); *Zwei Lieder* for Women's Chorus (1974); *Shakespearian Sonnet* for Chorus and Timpani ad libitum (1985).—NS/LK/DM

Fellerer, Karl Gustav, eminent German musicologist and editor; b. Freising, July 7, 1902; d. Munich, Jan. 7, 1984. He studied at the Regensburg School of Church Music and took courses in composition with Heinrich Schmid and Joseph Haas in Munich. He then studied musicology at the Univ. of Munich with Sandberger and at the Univ. of Berlin with Hornbostel, Abert, Wolf, and Sachs, and received his Ph.D. in 1925 from the Univ. of Munich with the diss. *Beiträge zur Musikgeschichte Freisings von den ältesten christlichen Zeiten bis zur Auflösung des Hofes 1803* (Freising, 1926). He completed his Habilitation in 1927 at the Univ. of Munster with his *Der Palestrina stil und seine Bedeutung in der vokalen Kirchenmusik des 18. Jahrhunderts* (Augsburg, 1929). In 1927 he became a lecturer at the Univ. of Munster, in

1931 a prof. at the Univ. of Fribourg in Switzerland, in 1934 head of the dept. of musicology at the Univ. of Munster, and in 1939 prof. of music history at the Univ. of Cologne, retiring in 1970. Fellerer distinguished himself as an outstanding authority on the history of music of the Roman Catholic church. He contributed valuable studies on the music of the Middle Ages, the Renaissance, and the 19th century, and also served as ed. of several important music journals and other publications. His 60th birthday was honored by the publication of 3 Festschrifts, and another Festschrift was publ. in honor of his 70th birthday.

WRITINGS: *Die Deklamationsrhythmik in der vokalen Polyphonie des 16. Jahrhunderts* (Düsseldorf, 1928); *Orgel und Orgelmusik: Ihre Geschichte* (Augsburg, 1929); *Palestrina* (Regensburg, 1930; 2nd ed., rev., 1960); *Studien zur Orgelmusik des ausgehenden 18. und frühen 19. Jahrhunderts* (Kassel, 1932); *Beiträge zur Choralbegleitung und Choralverarbeitung in der Orgelmusik des ausgehenden 18. und beginnenden 19. Jahrhunderts* (Leipzig, 1932); *Die Aufführung der katholischen Kirchenmusik in Vergangenheit und Gegenwart* (Einsiedeln, 1933); *Mittelalterliches Musikleben der Stadt Freiburg im Uechtland* (Regensburg, 1935); *Der gregorianische Choral im Wandel der Jahrhunderte* (Regensburg, 1936); *Giacomo Puccini* (Potsdam, 1937); *Geschichte der katholischen Kirchenmusik* (Düsseldorf, 1939); *Deutsche Gregorianik im Frankenreich* (Regensburg, 1941); *Edvard Grieg* (Potsdam, 1942); *Einführung in die Musikwissenschaft* (Berlin, 1942; 2nd ed., rev., 1953); *Georg Friedrich Händel: Leben und Werk* (Hamburg, 1953); *Mozarts Kirchenmusik* (Salzburg, 1955); *Soziologie der Kirchenmusik* (Cologne, 1963); *Bearbeitung und Elektronik als musikalisches Problem in Urheberrecht* (Berlin and Frankfurt am Main, 1965); *Klang und Struktur in der abendländischen Musik* (Cologne, 1967); *Das Problem Neue Musik* (Krefeld, 1967); *Monodie und Polyphonie in der Musik des 16. Jahrhunderts* (Brussels, 1972); *Der Stilwandel in der abendländischen Musik um 1600* (Cologne, 1972); *Geschichte der katholischen Kirchenmusik* (Kassel, 1972–76); *Max Bruch* (Cologne, 1974); *Der Akademismus in der deutschen Musik des 19. Jahrhunderts* (Opladen, 1976); *Die Kirchenmusik W.A. Mozarts* (Laaber, 1985).—**NS/LK/DM**

Fellowes, E(dmund) H(orace), eminent English musicologist and editor; b. London, Nov. 11, 1870; d. Windsor, Dec. 20, 1951. He was educated at Winchester Coll. and Oriel Coll., Oxford (B.M. and M.A., 1896), his teachers in music being P. Buck, Fletcher, and L. Straus. He was ordained in 1894, and then served as asst. curate in Wandsworth, London (until 1897). After serving as minor canon and precentor of Bristol Cathedral (1897–1900), he became minor canon at St. George's Chapel, Windsor Castle, a position he held until his death; he was also choirmaster there (1924–27). He was honorary librarian of St. Michael's Coll., Tenbury Wells (1918–48), and also a lecturer at various English univs. His importance rests upon his valuable writings on and eds. of early English music. He received honorary Mus.D. degrees from the univs. of Dublin (1917), Oxford (1939), and Cambridge (1950). He was made a Companion of Honour by King George VI in 1944.

WORKS: EDITIONS: The English Madrigal School (36 vols., 1913–24; 2nd ed., rev., 1956, by T. Dart as The English Madrigalists); The English School of Lutenist Song Writers (32 vols., 1920–32; 2nd ed., partly rev., 1959–66, by T. Dart as The English Lutesongs; 3rd ed., rev., 1959 et seq.); with P. Buck, A. Ramsbotham, and S. Warner, Tudor Church Music (10 vols., 1922–29; appendix, 1948, by Fellowes); The Collected Works of William Byrd (20 vols., London, 1937–50; 2nd ed., rev., 1962 et seq., by T. Dart, P. Brett, and K. Elliott).

WRITINGS: *English Madrigal Verse, 1588–1632* (Oxford, 1920; 3rd ed., rev. and enl., 1967); *The English Madrigal Composers* (Oxford, 1921; 2nd ed., 1948); *William Byrd: A Short Account of His Life and Work* (Oxford, 1923; 2nd ed., 1928); *The English Madrigal School: A Guide to Its Practical Use* (London, 1924); *Orlando Gibbons: A Short Account of His Life and Work* (Oxford, 1925; 2nd ed., 1951, as *Orlando Gibbons and His Family*); *The English Madrigal* (Oxford, 1925); *The Catalogue of Manuscripts in the Library of St Michael's Coll., Tenbury* (Paris, 1934); *William Byrd* (a larger study than the 1923 monograph; Oxford, 1936; 2nd ed., 1948); *Organists and Masters of the Choristers of St George's Chapel in Windsor Castle* (London and Windsor, 1939); *English Cathedral Music from Edward VI to Edward VII* (London, 1941; 5th ed., rev., 1969); with E. Pine, *The Tenbury Letters* (London, 1942); *Memoirs of an Amateur Musician* (London, 1946).—**NS/LK/DM**

Felsenstein, Walter, influential Austrian opera producer; b. Vienna, May 30, 1901; d. East Berlin, Oct. 8, 1975. He studied at a Graz technical college; then went to Vienna, where he enrolled in drama courses at the Burgtheater. In 1923 he appeared as an actor in Lübeck. In 1925 he became dramatic adviser and producer in Beuthen, Silesia; in 1927 he was called to Basel to become chief opera and drama producer at the Stadttheater; in 1929 he went to Freiburg im Breisgau as both actor and dramatic adviser and producer. He served as chief producer at the Cologne Opera in 1932 and at the Frankfurt am Main Opera in 1934. Despite his differences with the policies of the Nazi authorities, he was able to continue producing operas and dramas. From 1938 to 1940 he produced plays in Zürich; he then served as producer in Berlin (1940–44); he was drafted by the military despite his age, and served for a year. From 1947 until his death he was director of the Komische Oper in East Berlin. During his tenure, the Komische Oper established itself as one of the best opera houses of Europe; his productions of *Die Fledermaus, Carmen, Le nozze di Figaro, Otello, Les Contes d'Hoffmann,* and *Die Zauberflöte* were artistically of the first rank. He also made operatic films and gave courses on theater arts. Among his students were the opera producers Götz Friedrich and Joachim Herz. With S. Melchinger, he compiled *Musiktheater* (Bremen, 1961); with G. Friedrich and J. Herz, he publ. *Musiktheater: Beiträge zur Methodik und zu Inszenierungs- Konzeptionen* (Leipzig, 1970).

BIBL.: R. Münz, *Untersuchungen zum realistischen Musiktheater W. Fs* (diss., Humboldt Univ., Berlin, 1964); G. Friedrich, *W. F.: Weg und Werk* (Berlin, 1967); P. Fuchs, ed. and tr., *The Music Theater of W. F.: Collected Articles, Speeches and Interviews by F. and Others* (N.Y., 1975); I. Kobán, ed., *W. F.: Theater: Gespräche, Briefe, Dokumente* (Berlin, 1991).—**NS/LK/DM**

Felsztyna (Felsztyn, Felstin, Felstinensis, Felsztyński), Sebastian z (von), noted Polish music theorist and composer; b. Felsztyn, Galicia, c. 1490; d. c. 1543. He studied at the Univ. of Kraków (1507–09), and also studied theology. He was made a priest in Felsztyn c. 1528, and he most likely served in that capacity in Przemysl. He then became parish priest in Sanok c. 1536. He wrote the first Polish treatise on mensural theory, *Opusculum musice mensuralis* (Kraków, 1517), and a compendium on Gregorian chant, *Opusculum musice compilatum noviter* (Kraków, 1517; 3rd ed., aug., 1534, as *Opusculum musices noviter congestum*). His manual for church singing, *Directiones musicae ad cathedralis ecclesiae Premisliensis usum* (Kraków, 1543), is not extant. He also publ. a vol. of hymns, *Aliquot hymni ecclesiastici vario melodiarum genere editi* (Kraków, 1522; not extant). His significance as a composer lies in the fact that he was the first Polish musician to employ consistent 4-part writing; 3 sacred motets are extant: *Prosa ad Rorate tempore paschali virgini Mariae laudes* in Surzynski's *Monumenta musices sacrae in Polonia*, vol. II (1887), *Alleluia ad Rorate cum prosa Ave Maria* in Szweykoski's *Muzyka w dawnym Krakowie* (Kraków, 1964), and *Alleluia, Felix es sacro virgo Maria* in Feicht's *Muzyka staropolska* (Kraków, 1966).—NS/LK/DM

Felton, William, English organist, harpsichordist, composer, and clergyman; b. Drayton, Shropshire, 1715; d. Hereford, Dec. 6, 1769. He was educated at St. John's Coll., Cambridge (B.A., 1738; M.A., 1743). In 1742 he was ordained a priest. In 1743 he became vicar-choral and sub-chanter at Hereford Cathedral; in 1760 he was made a minor canon. His mastery as a keyboard artist is revealed in his 32 keyboard concertos (London, 1744–60) and his 16 harpsichord suites (2 vols., London, 1750, 1758).—LK/DM

Feltsman, Vladimir, prominent Russian-born American pianist; b. Moscow, Jan. 8, 1952. He was born into a musical family; his father, Oskar Feltsman, was a composer of popular music. He began taking piano lessons at the age of 6 from his mother, and then enrolled at Moscow's Central Music School, completing his training with Yakov Flier at the Moscow Cons. At age 11, he made his debut as a soloist with the Moscow Phil., and at 15 he won 1st prize in the Prague Concertino Competition. After capturing joint 1st prize in the Long-Thibaud Competition in Paris in 1971, he pursued a successful career as a soloist with major Soviet and Eastern European orchs.; he made particularly successful appearances in works in the Romantic repertoire, his specialty, in Japan (1977) and France (1978). His auspicious career was interrupted by the Soviet authorities when, in 1979, he applied for a visa to emigrate to Israel with his wife. His application was denied and he subsequently was allowed to give concerts only in remote outposts of the Soviet Union. With the support of the U.S. ambassador, he gave several private concerts at the ambassador's official residence in Moscow; in 1984 one of these was surreptitiously recorded and later released by CBS Masterworks. When his plight became a cause célèbre in the West, Feltsman was allowed to give his first Moscow recital in almost a decade (April 21, 1987). In June 1987 he was granted permission to emigrate, and in Aug. 1987 went to the U.S., where he accepted an appointment at the State Univ. of N.Y. at New Paltz. On Sept. 27, 1987, he gave a special concert at the White House for President Reagan, and on Nov. 11, 1987, gave his first N.Y. recital in Carnegie Hall. He subsequently appeared as a soloist with various orchs. and as a recitalist. In 1995 he became a naturalized American citizen.—NS/LK/DM

Felumb, Svend Christian, Danish oboist and conductor; b. Copenhagen, Dec. 25, 1898; d. there, Dec. 16, 1972. He studied in Copenhagen with L. Nielsen and Bruce, and in Paris with Blenzel and Vidal. From 1924 until 1947 he was an oboist in the Danish Royal Orch. in Copenhagen. From 1947 to 1962 he conducted the Tivoli Orch. in Copenhagen. He was the founder of the Ny Musik soc. in Copenhagen and a leader of the movement for modern national Danish music.—NS/LK/DM

Fenaroli, Fedele, Italian composer and pedagogue; b. Lanciano, April 25, 1730; d. Naples, Jan. 1, 1818. After studies with his father, a church organist, he settled in Naples and continued his training with Durante and Gallo at the Cons. of S. Maria di Loreto. In 1762 he was made its 2nd maestro di cappella, and in 1777 its maestro di cappella. After it was merged with the Turchini Cons. in 1807 to form the Cons. of S. Pietro a Majella, he became a teacher of counterpoint there. He was held in great esteem as a teacher, and was the mentor of Cimarosa, Mercadante, and Zingarelli. He publ. *Regole musicali per i principianti di cembalo nel sonar coi numeri* (Naples, 1775), *Partimento ossia Basso numerato* (Rome, 1800), and *Studio del contrappunto* (Rome, 1800). He composed the operas *I due sediarii* (Naples, 1759; not extant) and *La disfatta degli Amaleciti* (Chieti, 1780), as well as much sacred music.

BIBL.: T. Consalvo, *La teoria musicale del F.* (Naples, 1826). —NS/LK/DM

Fenby, Eric (William), English composer; b. Scarborough, April 22, 1906. He studied piano and organ; after a few years as an organist in London, he went (1928) to Grez-sur-Loing, France, as amanuensis for Frederick Delius, taking down his dictation note by note, until Delius's death in 1934. He publ. his experiences in a book entitled *Delius as I Knew Him* (London, 1936; 4th ed., N.Y., 1981). He was director of music of the North Riding Training School (1948–62); from 1964, was a prof. of composition at the Royal Academy of Music in London. In 1964 he was made an Officer of the Order of the British Empire. Because of the beneficent work he undertook, he neglected his own compositions; however, he wrote some pleasant music for strings. He also publ. the books *Menuhin's House of Music* (London, 1969) and *Delius* (London, 1971).

BIBL.: C. Redwood, ed., *A Delius Companion: A 70th Birthday Tribute to E. F.* (London, 1976).—NS/LK/DM

Fender, Freddy (originally, **Huerta, Baldemar**), country- pop star of Hispanic heritage, b. San Benito, Tex., June 4, 1937. Baldemar Huerta's family were migrant workers, picking crops from Tex. to Ind. Baldemar started playing the guitar early in childhood, learning Tejano wedding music by watching other musicians and learned the blues from the black migrant workers with whom he worked. By the age of ten, he was performing on the radio and winning talent shows. At 16, he left school and joined the Marines. After a three-year hitch, he started playing bars and honky-tonks. Starting in 1956, he began recording both Tejano music and Spanish versions of American hits, including "Don't Be Cruel" and "Jamaica Farewell." These sides were popular with listeners in Tex. and Mexico.

In 1959, Huerta decided to make the move to the mainstream. He injected a bit more rockabilly into his sound and adopted the name Freddy Fender, taking his last name from the popular electric guitar maker. Fender signed to Imperial records, home of Fats Domino and other major late 1950s stars. His song, "Wasted Days and Wasted Nights" started to become a hit in some regions. However, before the song could catch fire, Fender was arrested for possession of two marijuana joints and sentenced to five years in La.'s legendary Angola prison. He was paroled after serving three years of the sentence on the condition that he stay away from the "corruptive influence" of the music business.

Fender returned to Tex., took college courses toward a degree in sociology, and supported himself as an auto mechanic. After his probation was over, he started playing music in bars again. It wasn't until 1974, over ten years after his release from Angola, that he recorded again. Legendary producer Huey Meaux who signed Fender to his own Crazy Cajun records revived his career. Meaux convinced Fender to channel his Tejano and rockabilly tendencies into a more country direction. Meaux produced a single of a Fender ballad, "Before the Next Teardrop Falls." Unable to license it, Meaux released it himself and it started to climb the charts until Dot records finally bought it. They took the record to the top of both the pop and country charts, and the single went gold. He re-recorded his 1950s song, "Wasted Days and Wasted Nights," and it also topped the country charts, rising to #8 and going gold. Those two hits were both on the *Before the Next Teardrop Falls* LP, which also went gold, rising to #20, Fender's only Top 40 album.

He next cut a version of the old Doris Day #1 hit, "Secret Love" which Fender took to the top of the country charts and #20 on the pop charts. His last pop hit, "You'll Lose a Good Thing," reached #20 during the spring of 1976 and also topped the country charts. Fender followed that with a spate of country hits that lasted for the next seven years before his chart success began to ebb. Fortunately his face, etched with his years of tribulation, put him in demand as a character actor, most notably in the 1988 film *The Milagro Beanfield War*.

Fender's music career revived in 1990 when he joined up with fellow Texans Doug Sahm, Augie Meyers, and Flaco Jimenez in a "supergroup" called the Texas Tornados. The band took a 1990 Grammy Award for Best Mexican American Performance. He alternated touring with the Tornados and as a solo act with a backup band that featured Meyers and Charlie Rich Jr. The Tornados did the song "A Little Is Better Than Nada" for the film *Tin Cup*.

When the Tornados broke up, after three albums, Fender went back to touring as a solo act. In 1998, he reunited with Jimenez and hooked up with Los Lobos member Rick Trevino in the group Los Super Seven. They took home another Grammy Award in 1999.

DISC.: *Are You Ready for Freddy?* (1975); *Since I Met You Baby* (1975); *Before the Next Teardrop Falls* (1975); *Rock 'n' Country* (1976); *If You're Ever in Texas* (1976); *Swamp Gold* (1978); *Christmas Time in the Valley* (1991); *In Concert* (live; 1995); *Live at Gilley's* (1999).—**HB**

Fénelon, Philippe, French composer; b. Suèvres, Nov. 23, 1952. He studied at the Orléans Cons. and with Messiaen at the Paris Cons. (premier prix in composition, 1977). From 1981 to 1983 he was in residence at the Casa Velasquez in Spain. In 1984 he received the Prix Hervé Dugardin from the SACEM. He was in Berlin in 1988 under the auspices of the Deutscher Akademischer Austauschdienst. In 1991 he was a laureate of the external Prix Villa Médicis.

WORKS: DRAMATIC: O p e r a : *Salammbô*, after Flaubert (1992–93; Paris, May 28, 1998). **ORCH.:** *Diagonal* (1983); *Éclipses* (1983); *Midtown*, concerto for 2 Trumpets and Orch. (1994); Piano Concerto (1996). **CHAMBER:** *L'Oeil du rêve* for Clarinet (1976; rev. 1995); *Caprice* for Viola (1977; rev. 1982); *Dédicace* for Cello (1982); *Maipú 994* for 8 Players (1983; also for 5 Instruments); *Paral.lel* for Bassoon (1984); *Les Combats nocturnes* for Piano and Percussion (1986–87); *Orion* for Clarinet, Trombone, Viola, and Harp (1988–89); *La Colère d'Achille* for Flute, English Horn, Horn, and Violin (1989–90); *Trait* for Flute (1989–90); *Impromptu* for Clarinet (1990); *Omaggio* for Violin (1990); *Ulysse* for Flute, Clarinet, Horn, Violin, and Cello (1990); String Quartet No. 3 (1991); *Nit* for Viola (1994); *Zabak* for Percussion (1994); *Die Nacht* for Accordion (1997); *Fragment I* for Violin and Cello (1997). **KEYBOARD: P i a n o :** *Épilogue* (1980); *Melody of Spring 1947* (1984). **H a r p s i c h o r d :** *Hélios* (1989). **VOCAL:** *Pré-Texte* for Woman's Voice (1982); *Du blanc le jour son espace* for Baritone and 15 Instruments (1984); *Notti* for Voice and Double Bass Obbligato (1990); *Le Jardin d'Hiver*, cantata for Tenor, Chorus, and 12 Instruments (1991); *Dix-Huit Madrigaux* for 6 Voices, String Trio, and Theorbo (1996).—**NS/LK/DM**

Fennell, Frederick, noted American conductor and teacher; b. Cleveland, July 2, 1914. He first began conducting at the National Music Camp in Interlochen, Mich. (summers, 1931–33), and then studied at the Eastman School of Music in Rochester, N.Y. (B.M., 1937; M.M., 1939), where he subsequently conducted various ensembles (1939–65). He also was founder-conductor of the Eastman Wind Ensemble (from 1952), which he developed into one of the premier groups of its kind. After serving as conductor-in-residence at the Univ. of Miami School of Music in Coral Gables (1965–80), he was conductor of the Kosei Wind Orch. in Tokyo from 1984 to 1989, and thereafter was its conductor emeritus. He publ. *Time and the Winds* (Kenosha, Wisc., 1954) and *The Drummer's Heritage* (Rochester, N.Y., 1956).

BIBL.: R. Rickson, *Fortissimo: A Bio-Discography of F. F.: The First Forty Years, 1953 to 1993* (Cleveland, 1993).—**NS/LK/DM**

Fennelly, Brian, American composer and teacher; b. Kingston, N.Y., Aug. 14, 1937. After attending Union

Coll. in Schenectady, N.Y. (B.M.E. in mechanical engineering, 1958; B.A., 1963), he was a student of Mel Powell, Gunther Schuller, and Allen Forte at Yale Univ. (M.M., 1965; Ph.D., 1968, with the diss. *A Descriptive Notation for Electronic Music*). From 1968 to 1997 he was a prof. of music at N.Y. Univ., where he then became prof. emeritus. In 1975, 1977, and 1980 he received grants from the Martha Baird Rockefeller Fund. He held NEA Composer fellowships in 1977, 1979, and 1985. In 1980 he received a Guggenheim fellowship. In 1983 and 1999 he received Koussevitzky Foundation commissions. He was honored with a lifetime achievement award from the American Academy of Arts and Letters in 1997. In his music, Fennelly follows the American traditions set by Sessions and Carter, while often reflecting the influence of jazz and the inspiration of nature. He strives for maximum expressivity and structural rigor, extending from the virtuosic possibilities of a solo instrument to the coloristic potential of the full orch.

WORKS: ORCH.: *In Wildness is the Preservation of the World*, Thoreau fantasy (1975); *Thoreau Fantasy No. 2* (1984–85); Concert Piece for Trumpet and Orch. (1976); *Quintuplo* for Brass Quintet and Orch. (1977–78); *Scintilla Prisca* for Cello and Orch. (1980); *Tropes and Echoes* for Clarinet and Orch. (1981); Concerto for Saxophone and Strings (1983–84); *Fantasy Variations* (1984–85); *Lunar Halos: Paraselenae* (1990); *A Thoreau Symphony* (1992–97); *Reflections/Metamorphoses* (1995). **CHAMBER:** Suite for Double Bass (1963; rev. 1981); Duo for Violin and Piano (1964); *For Solo Flute* (1964; rev. 1976); *2 Movements* for Oboe, Clarinet, Trumpet, and Trombone (1965); *Divisions* for Violin (1968; rev. 1981); Wind Quintet (1967); *Evanescences* for Alto Flute, Clarinet, Violin, Cello, and Tape (1969); String Quartet (1971); *Tesserae I* for Harpsichord (1971), *II* for Cello (1972), *III* for Viola (1976), *IV* for Contrabass Trombone (1976), *V* for Tuba (1980), *VI* for Trumpet (1976), *VII* for Clarinet (1979), *VIII* for Alto Saxophone (1980), and *IX* for Percussion (1981); *Prelude and Elegy* for Brass Quintet (1973); *Consort I* for Trombone Quintet (1976); *Empirical Rag* for Brass Quintet (1977; also for other instruments); *Canzona and Dance* for Clarinet, Violin, Viola, Cello, and Piano (1982–83); *3 Intermezzi* for Bass Clarinet and Marimba (1983); *Triple Play* for Violin, Cello, and Piano (1984); *Corollary I: Coralita* for Horn and Piano (1986), *II* for Alto Saxophone and Piano (1987–88), and *III* for Trumpet and Piano (1989); Trio No. 2 for Violin, Cello, and Piano or Harpsichord (1986–87); 3 brass quintets: No. 1 (1987), No. 2, *Locking Horns* (1993), and No. 3, *Velvet and Spice* (1999); *Reflected Arc* for Oboe and Piano (1991); *Skyscapes I* for Saxophone and String Quartet (1995) and *II* for Trumpet and String Quartet (1999). **KEYBOARD: P i a n o :** 2 sonatas (*Seria*, 1976; *Serena*, 1997); *Paraphrasis* (1991). **VOCAL:** *Songs with Improvisation* for Mezzo-soprano, Clarinet, and Piano (1964; rev. 1969); *Psalm XIII* for Chorus and Brass (1965); *Festive Psalm* for Chorus, Narrator, Organ, and Tape (1972); *Praise Yah!* for Chorus and Organ (1974); *Winterkill* for Chorus and Piano (1981); *2 Poems of Shelley* for Chorus (1982); *Keats on Love* for Chorus and Piano (1989); *Proud Music* for Chorus, Organ, 2 Trumpets, and 2 Trombones (1994); *Soon Shall the Winter's Foil* for Chorus (1994). **ELECTRONIC:** *SUNYATA* (1970).—**NS/LK/DM**

Feo, Francesco, celebrated Italian composer and pedagogue; b. Naples, 1691; d. there, Jan. 18, 1761. He studied with Andrea Basso and Nicola Fago at the Cons. S. Maria della Pietà dei Turchini (1704–12), subsequently serving as maestro (with Ignazio Prota) at the Cons. S.

Onofrio (1723–39) and as primo maestro at the Cons. dei Poveri di Gesù Cristo (1739–43). His most famous pupil was Nicolò Jommelli, who studied with him at the Cons. S. Onofrio. He composed over 150 works, including much sacred music.

WORKS: D R A M A T I C : O p e r a : *L'amor tirannico, ossia Zenobia* (Naples, Jan. 18, 1713); *La forza della virtù* (Naples, Jan. 22, 1719); *Teuzzone* (Naples, Jan. 20, 1720); *Siface, re di Numidia* (Naples, Nov. 4, 1720); *Ipermestra* (Rome, Jan. 1728); *Arianna* (Turin, Carnival 1728); *Tamase* (Naples, 1729); *Andromaca* (Rome, Feb. 5, 1730); *L'Issipile* (Turin, 1733?); *Arsace* (Turin, Dec. 26, 1740). **I n t e r m e z z o s :** *Morano e Rosina* (Naples, 1723), *Don Chisciotte della Mancia* (Rome, Carnival 1726); *Coriando lo speciale* (Rome, Carnival 1726); *Il vedovo* (Naples, 1729). **S e r e n a t a s :** *Oreste* (Madrid, Jan. 20, 1738); *Polinice* (Madrid, June 19, 1738).—**NS/LK/DM**

Ferand, Ernst (Thomas), Hungarian musicologist; b. Budapest, March 5, 1887; d. Basel, May 29, 1972. He studied composition at the Royal Academy of Music in Budapest (diploma, 1911), and then was a student of Jaques- Dalcroze in Hellerau, near Dresden (1913–14). He also took courses in music history, psychology, and philosophy at the Univ. of Budapest, and later in musicology and psychology at the Univ. of Vienna (Ph.D., 1937, with the diss. *Die Improvisationspraxis in der Musik*; publ. as *Die Improvisation in der Musik*, Zürich, 1938). After teaching at the Fodor Cons. of Music in Budapest (1912–19), he was director of the Dalcroze School in Hellerau (1920–25) and of the Hellerau-Laxenburg Coll., near Vienna (1925–38); he then taught at the New School for Social Research in N.Y. (1939–65). In addition to valuable articles in journals, he publ. a harmony textbook (Budapest, 1914) and *Die Improvisation in Beispielen aus neun Jahrhunderten abendländischer Musik* (Cologne, 1956; 2nd ed., rev., 1961; Eng. tr., 1961, in Das Musikwerk, XII).—**NS/LK/DM**

Ferchault, Guy, French musicologist; b. Mer, Loire-et-Cher, Aug. 16, 1904; d. Paris, Nov. 14, 1980. He studied with C. Lalo, Pirro, and Masson at the Cons. and philosophy at the Sorbonne (graduated, 1942) in Paris. He held teaching positions in music education in Paris, Orléans (1941), Poitiers (1942–49), Tours (1948–51), and Roubaix (from 1952). From 1943 to 1967 he was also a prof. of music history at the Cons. Régional de Musique in Versailles, and then at St. Maur.

WRITINGS: *Henri Duparc, Une Amitié mystique, d'après ses lettres à Francis Jammes* (Paris, 1944); *Les Créatures du drame musical: De Monteverdi à Wagner* (Paris, 1944); *Introduction à l'esthétique de la mélodie* (Gap, 1946); *Claude Debussy, musicien français* (Paris, 1948); *Faust, J.-S. Bach et l'esthétique de son temps* (Zürich, 1950).—**NS/LK/DM**

Fere, Vladimir, Russian composer and ethnomusicologist; b. Kamyshin, May 20, 1902; d. Moscow, Sept. 2, 1971. He studied piano with Goldenweiser and composition with Glière and Miaskovsky at the Moscow Cons. (1921–29). In 1936 he went to Frunze, Kirghizia, where he composed, in collaboration with Vlasov, a number of operas based on native folk motifs, all first premiered there: *Golden Girl* (May 1, 1937); *Not Death but Life*

(March 26, 1938); *Moon Beauty* (April 15, 1939); *For People's Happiness* (May 1, 1941); *Patriots* (Nov. 6, 1941); *Son of the People* (Nov. 8, 1947); *On the Shores of Issyk-Kul* (Feb. 1, 1951); *Toktogul* (July 6, 1958); *The Witch* (1965); *One Hour before Dawn* (1969). He also wrote several symphonic pieces on Kirghiz themes, numerous choruses, and chamber music.—NS/LK/DM

Ferencsik, János, noted Hungarian conductor; b. Budapest, Jan. 18, 1907; d. there, June 12, 1984. He studied organ and theory at the Budapest Cons. He became répétiteur at the Hungarian State Opera (1927), and subsequently conductor there (from 1930). He was also an assistant at the Bayreuth Festivals (1930, 1931). He was chief conductor of the Hungarian Radio and Television Sym. Orch. (1945–52), the Hungarian State Sym. Orch. (1952–84), and the Budapest Phil. (1953–76); also appeared as a guest conductor in Europe and North America. He was awarded the Kossuth Prize (1951, 1961), and the Order of the Banner was bestowed upon him by the Hungarian government on his 70th birthday. He was a persuasive interpreter of the Hungarian repertoire.—NS/LK/DM

Ferenczy, Oto, Slovak composer and teacher; b. Brezovica nad Torysou, March 30, 1921. He went to Bratislava and studied musicology and psychology at the Comenius Univ. (Ph.D., 1945). From 1945 to 1951 he was head of the music dept. of the Univ. Library. In 1951 he became a lecturer, in 1953 a senior lecturer, and in 1966 a prof. at the Academy of Music and Drama, where he also was pro-rector (1956–62) and rector (1962–66) before retiring in 1989. He was head of the Union of Slovak Composers (1970–72; 1982–86).

WORKS: DRAMATIC: O p e r a : *An Uncommon Humoresque* (1967). ORCH.: *Merrymaking* (1951); *Hurbanovská*, overture (1952); *Serenade* (1955); *Elegy* (1958); *Finale* (1958); *Partita* for Chamber Orch. (1964); *Symphonic Prologue* (1974); *Concertino* (1975); *Overture* (1977); *Piano Concerto* (1978). CHAMBER: *Music for 4 Strings* (1947); *String Quartet* (1962); *Violin Sonata* (1964). KEYBOARD: P i a n o : *Intermezzo* (1943; rev. 1957). O r g a n : *Fantasia* (1943; rev. 1957). VOCAL: *3 Highwayman's Songs* for Baritone and Orch. (1952); *My Country*, cantata for Men's Chorus and Piano (1959; also for Chorus and Orch.); *The Star of the North*, cantata for Baritone, Chorus, and Orch. (1960); *The Bouquet of Forest Flowers*, song cycle for Baritone and Piano (1961); *3 Sonnets from Shakespeare* for Baritone and Piano (1965); *2 Nocturnes* for Chorus (1972). —NS/LK/DM

Ferguson, Donald (Nivison), American music educator; b. Waupun, Wisc., June 30, 1882; d. Minneapolis, May 11, 1985. He studied at the Univ. of Wisc. (B.A., 1904), then went to London, where he studied composition with Josef Holbrooke and piano with Michael Hambourg (1905–08). He later studied at the Univ. of Minn. (M.A., 1922) and at the Univ. of Vienna (1929–30). In 1913 he joined the faculty of the Univ. of Minn., where he was named full prof. in 1927. He retired in 1950, but returned to teach as prof. emeritus there from 1953 to 1956. Concurrently he was head of the music dept. at Macalester Coll. in St. Paul (1950–59). From 1930

to 1960 he served as program annotator for the Minneapolis Sym. Orch.

WRITINGS: *A History of Musical Thought* (N.Y., 1935; 3rd ed., rev., 1959); *A Short History of Music* (N.Y., 1943); *Piano Music of 6 Great Composers* (N.Y., 1947); *Masterworks of the Orchestral Repertoire* (Minneapolis, 1954); *Music as Metaphor; The Elements of Expression* (Minneapolis, 1960); *Image and Structure in Chamber Music* (Minneapolis, 1964); *The Why of Music* (Minneapolis, 1969).—NS/LK/DM

Ferguson, Howard, Irish pianist, musicologist, and composer; b. Belfast, Oct. 21, 1908; d. Cambridge, Nov. 1, 1999. He studied piano with Harold Samuel, and also took courses in composition with R.O. Morris and in conducting with Sargent at the Royal Coll. of Music in London (1924–28). From 1948 to 1963 he was a prof. of composition at the Royal Academy of Music in London. His music is neo-Classical in its idiom; in some of his compositions he made use of English, Scottish, and Irish folk songs.

WORKS: EDITIONS: *W. Tisdall: Complete Keyboard Works* (London, 1958); *Style and Interpretation: An Anthology: Early Keyboard Music: England and France; Early Keyboard Music: Germany and Italy; Classical Piano Music; Romantic Piano Music; Keyboard Duets* (2 vols., London, 1963–71); *Style and Interpretation: Sequels: Early French Keyboard Music, I, II; Early Italian Keyboard Music, I, II; Early German Keyboard Music, I, II; Early English Keyboard Music, I, II* (8 vols., London, 1966–71); with C. Hogwood, *W. Croft: Complete Harpsichord Works* (2 vols., London, 1974); *Anne Cromwell's Virginal Book, 1638* (London, 1974); *F. Schubert, Piano Sonatas* (London, 1979); *Keyboard Works of C.P.E. Bach* (4 vols., London, 1983). DRAMATIC: B a l l e t : *Chauntecleer* (1948). ORCH.: *Partita* (1935–36; also for 2 Pianos); *4 Diversions on Ulster Airs* (1939–42); *Overture for an Occasion* (1952–53); Concerto for Piano and Strings (1950–51; London, May 29, 1952, Myra Hess soloist). CHAMBER: *5 Irish Folktunes* for Cello or Viola and Piano (1927); 2 violin sonatas (1931, 1946); *4 Short Pieces* for Clarinet or Viola and Piano (1932–36); *3 Sketches* for Flute and Piano (1932–52); Octet for Clarinet, Bassoon, Horn, String Quartet, and Double Bass (1933); *5 Pipe Pieces* for 3 Bamboo Pipes (1934–35); *Flute Sonata* (1938–40); *2 Fanfares* for 4 Trumpets and 3 Trombones (1952). KEYBOARD: P i a n o : *5 Bagatelles* (1944). VOCAL: *2 Ballads* for Baritone, Chorus, and Orch. (1928–32); *3 Medieval Carols* for Voice and Piano (1932–33); *Discovery* for Voice and Piano (1951); *5 Irish Folksongs* for Voice and Piano (1954); *Amore langueo* for Tenor, Chorus, and Orch. (1955–56); *The Dream of the Rood* for Soprano or Tenor, Chorus, and Orch. (1958–59).

BIBL.: A. Ridout, ed., *The Music of H. F., a Symposium* (London, 1989).—NS/LK/DM

Ferguson, Maynard, trumpeter best known for the burning intensity of his upper register, b. Montreal, Quebec, Canada, May 4, 1928. Ferguson's talents were evident at a young age. Growing up in Montreal, he was playing piano and violin before discovering the trumpet at age nine. He won a scholarship to the French Cons. of Music, where he received formal training. At age 13 Ferguson soloed with the Canadian Broadcasting Co. Orch. and two years later began to gain the attention of leaders of the big band era. He played in a 14-musician local band that opened for touring big band acts. While still a teenager, Ferguson moved to the U.S., and he has since established himself far beyond his abilities as a trumpet player and composer.

Ferguson came to the U.S. to join Stan Kenton's Orch. When Kenton took a one-year hiatus, Ferguson pursued stints with bands led by Boyd Rayburn, Charlie Barnet, and Jimmy Dorsey before joining Kenton for three years. Leaving Kenton in 1953, Ferguson worked extensively as a Los Angeles studio musician and performed with Leonard Bernstein and the New York Philharmonic in a performance of William Russo's "Symphony No. 2 in C ('Titans')." In 1956 Ferguson formed an all-star jazz band, featuring pianist Hank Jones, saxophonist Budd Johnson, bassist Milt Hinton, and others, for an extended run at the famous N.Y. club, Birdland. Over the next decade, Ferguson recorded in big band and sextet settings and toured the college circuit before living and touring in Spain, England, and India in the late 1960s and early 1970s.

He returned to the U.S. in 1974 and signed with Columbia, for which he produced some now out-of-print jazz-fusion albums (*M.F. Horn, Vol. 1, M.F. Horn, Vol. 2,* and two more volumes in that series, of which *M.F. Horn, 4 & 5* is considered a best example of his jazz playing during the 1970s). He also released the Columbia albums *Chameleon* (1974) and *Conquistador* (1977), a gold album that cracked the pop charts with its featured theme from the *Rocky* soundtrack ("Gonna Fly Now"). After leaving Columbia, Ferguson recorded two lackluster albums with his funk-fusion combo, High Voltage.

In the late 1980s Ferguson returned to the bop-oriented roots of his earlier years and created what has proved to be one of his most successful bands, Big Bop Nouveau, a 10-musician ensemble of shifting young players with whom he has released four CDs to date, two on the Jazz Alliance label and two more after joining the Concord Jazz roster in 1995. Ferguson has recorded on about 200 albums as sideman and leader, not all of which are available or reissued on CD. He has designed instruments, produced recordings, served as an educator/clinician, and been a consistent jazz poll winner. Ferguson now resides in Ojai, Calif., about 90 miles north of Los Angeles. With his Big Bop Nouveau band, he tours regularly (and intensely), maintaining a somewhat grueling schedule that probably accounts for the personnel turnover. A musician first, educator second, Ferguson also tours internationally, instructing students at universities around the world.

DISC.: *Jam Session Featuring Maynard Ferguson* (1953); *Stratospheric* (1954); *Dimensions* (1954); *Maynard Ferguson's Hollywood Party* (1954); *Maynard Ferguson Octet* (1955); *Around the Horn* (1955); *The Birdland Dream Band, Vol. 1* (1956); *Maynard Ferguson and His Original Dreamband* (live; 1956); *Boys with Lots of Brass* (1957); *The Birdland Dream Band, Vol. 2* (1957); *The Complete Roulette Recordings of the Maynard Ferguson Orchestra* (1958; reissued 1996); *A Message from Newport* (1958); *Swingin' My Way through College* (1958); *Jazz for Dancing* (1959); *Newport Suite* (1960); *Maynard 1961* (1960); *Two's Company* (1960); *Let's Face the Music and Dance* (1960); *"Straightaway" Jazz Themes* (1961); *Maynard 1962* (1962); *Message from Maynard* (1962); *Maynard 1963* (1962); *Come Blow Your Horn* (1964); *Color Him Wild* (1964); *Blues Roar* (1964); *The New Sound of Maynard Ferguson* (1964); *The World of Maynard Ferguson* (1965); *Maynard*

Ferguson Sextet (1965); *Six by Six: Maynard Ferguson and Sextet* (1965); *Ridin' High* (1966); *Sextet 1967* (live; 1967); *Orchestra 1967* (live; 1967); *Trumpet Rhapsody* (1967); *Maynard Ferguson's Horn, Vol. 1* (1970); *Magnitude* (1971); *Maynard Ferguson's Horn, Vol. 2* (1972); *Maynard Ferguson's Horn, Vol. 3* (1973); *Maynard Ferguson's Horn, Vol. 4&5* (1973); *Chameleon* (1974); *Primal Scream* (1976); *Conquistador* (1977); *Carnival* (1978); *Storm* (1982); *Hollywood* (1982); *Live from San Francisco* (1983); *Body and Soul* (1986); *High Voltage* (1987); *Big Bop Nouveau* (1988); *Footpath Cafe* (1992); *The Essence of Maynard Ferguson* (1993); *Live from London* (1993); *Live at Peacock Lane Hollywood* (1994); *These Cats Can Swing!* (1995); *One More Trip to Birdland* (1996); *Verve Jazz Masters, Vol. 52* (1996); *Brass Attitude* (1998).—**NAL/SH**

Fernándes, Armando José, Portuguese composer and teacher; b. Lisbon, July 26, 1906; d. there, May 3, 1983. He studied piano with Rey Colaço and Varela Cid, composition with A. da Costa Ferreira, and musicology with Freitas Branco at the Lisbon Cons. After training in piano with Cortot and in composition with Boulanger in Paris (1933–36), he taught composition at the Lisbon Cons.

WORKS: *O homem do cravo,* ballet (1941); *Fantasia sobre temas populares portugueses* for Piano and Orch. (1945); Violin Concerto (1948); Concerto for Piano and String Orch. (1951); *O terramoto de Lisboa,* symphonic poem (1962); *Suite Concertante* for Harpsichord and Chamber Orch. (1967); Violin Sonata (1946); piano pieces.—**NS/LK/DM**

Fernández, Oscar Lorenzo
See **Lorenzo Fernández, Oscar**

Fernandez, Wilhelmina, black American soprano; b. Philadelphia, Jan. 5, 1949. Following training in Philadelphia (1969–73), she completed her studies at the Juilliard School in N.Y. She made her debut as Gershwin's Bess at the Houston Grand Opera in 1977, and then toured the U.S. and Europe in that role. After appearing as Musetta at the Paris Opéra in 1979, she sang with the N.Y. City Opera, and in Boston, Toulouse, Strasbourg, and Liège. She sang Bess at the Theater des Westens in Berlin in 1988, and then Aida in Bonn in 1989. In 1991 she scored a great success as Carmen Jones in London. During the 1994–95 season, she sang Aida at the Deutsche Oper in Berlin. She also appeared widely as a concert artist and recitalist. Among her other roles were Purcell's Dido, Mozart's Countess, Donna Anna, Marguerite, and Luisa Miller.—**NS/LK/DM**

Fernández Arbós, Enrique
See **Arbós, Enrique Fernández**

Fernández Bordas, Antonio, Spanish violinist; b. Orense, Jan. 12, 1870; d. Madrid, Feb. 18, 1950. He studied at the Madrid Cons. with Jesús de Monasterio, and, at the age of 11, won 1st prize for violin. After giving concerts in England, France, and other European countries, he returned to Spain and became a prof. of violin at the Madrid Cons. In 1921 he was elected director.—**NS/LK/DM**

Ferneyhough, Brian (John Peter), English composer and teacher; b. Coventry, Jan. 16, 1943. He studied at the Birmingham School of Music (1961–63), then took courses with Lennox Berkeley and Maurice Miles at the Royal Academy of Music in London (1966–67); furthermore, received instruction in advanced composition with Ton de Leeuw in Amsterdam and Klaus Huber in Basel (1969–73). From 1971 to 1986 he was on the faculty at the Hochschule für Musik in Freiburg im Breisgau. He then taught at the Royal Cons. of Music at The Hague (from 1986) and at the Univ. of Calif. at San Diego (from 1987). His output is marked by an uncompromising complexity.

WORKS: 4 *Miniatures* for Flute and Piano (1965); *Coloratura* for Oboe and Piano (1966); Sonata for 2 Pianos (1966); *Prometheus* for Wind Sextet (1967); 4 string quartets (1967; 1980; 1986–87; 1990); *Epicycle* for 20 Strings (Hilversum, Sept. 7, 1969); *Firecycle Beta* for Orch. and 5 Conductors (1969–71); *Funèrailles I* for String Sextet, Double Bass, and Harp (1969–77) and *II* for 7 Strings and Harp (1980); *Missa brevis* for 12 Solo Voices (1971); *7 Sterne* for Organ (1971); *Time and Motion Study I* for Bass Clarinet (1971–77), *II* for Cello and Electronics (1973–75), and *III* for 16 Solo Voices and Percussion (1974); *Transit* for 6 Amplified Voices and Chamber Orch. (1972–75; Royan, France, March 25, 1975); *Perspectivae corporum irregularum* for Oboe, Viola, and Piano (1975); *Unity Capsule* for Flute (1975–76); *La Terre est un homme* for Orch. (1976–79); *Lemma-Icon-Epigram* for Piano (1981); *Superscriptio* for Piccolo (1981); *Carceri d'invenzione I* for 16 Instruments (1981–82), *II* for Flute and Chamber Orch. (1984), and *III* for 15 Wind Instruments and 3 Percussionists (1986); *Adagissimo* for String Quartet (1983); *Études transcendantales* for Mezzo-soprano, Flute, Oboe, Cello, and Harpsichord (1982–85); *Allgebrah* for Oboe and String Orch. (1990); *Bone Alphabet* for Percussion (1991); *Terrain* for Violin and Ensemble (1992).—**NS/LK/DM**

Ferni-Giraldoni, Carolina, Italian soprano, mother of **Eugenio Giraldoni;** b. Como, Aug. 20, 1839; d. Milan, June 4, 1926. She studied violin in Paris and Brussels, and later took voice lessons with Pasta. She made her debut as Leonora in *La Favorite* in Turin in 1862, then sang at La Scala in Milan (1866–68). She retired in 1883 and taught voice, numbering Caruso as one of her pupils. She was married to **Leone Giraldoni.** —**NS/LK/DM**

Fernström, John (Axel), Swedish violinist, conductor, teacher, and composer; b. Ichang, China (of Swedish parents), Dec. 6, 1897; d. Lund, Oct. 19, 1961. He was the son of a Swedish missionary in China. After settling in Sweden, he studied violin at the Malmö Cons. (1913–15); also with Max Schlüter in Copenhagen (1917–21; 1923–24), and with Issay Barmas in Berlin (1921–22). He also studied composition with Peder Gram in Copenhagen (1923–30) and pursued composition and conducting studies at the Sonderhausen Cons. (1930). After playing violin in the Hälsingborg Sym. Orch. (1916–39), he was director of the Malmö Radio (1939–41). He then settled in Lund, where he was director of the municipal music school (1948–61); he also was conductor of the Orch. Soc. and founder-conductor of the Nordic Youth Orch. In 1953 he was made a member of the Royal Academy of Music in Stockholm. In addition to his writings on music theory, he was the author of the interesting autobiography *Jubals son och*

blodsarvinge (1967). Fernström was an adept composer of instrumental music. In his works, he pursued a median course between traditional idioms and avant-garde styles; he wrote both tonal and atonal scores with fine results.

WORKS: DRAMATIC: O p e r a : *Achnaton* (1931); *I-sissystarnas bröllop* (1942); *Livet en dröm* (1946). **ORCH.:** 12 syms. (1920; 1924; *Exotica*, 1928; 1930; 1932; 1938; *Sinfonietta in forma di sonata de chiesa*, 1941; *Amore studiorum*, 1942; *Sinfonia breve*, 1943; *Sinfonia discrète*, 1944; *Utan mask*, 1945; 1951); *Symphonic Variations* (1930); *Chaconne* for Cello and Orch. (1936); Clarinet Concerto (1936); Viola Concerto (1937); 2 violin concertos (1938, 1952); Concertino for Flute, Women's Chorus, and Small Orch. (1941); Bassoon Concerto (1946); Cello Concertino (1949); *Ostinato* for Strings (1952). **CHAMBER:** 8 string quartets (1920, 1925, 1931, 1942, 1945, 1947, 1950, 1952). **VOCAL:** Mass for Soli, Chorus, and Orch. (1931); *Stabat Mater* for Soli, Chorus, and Strings (1943); *Den mödosamma vä gen*, profane oratorio (1947); choral pieces; songs.—**NS/LK/DM**

Ferrabosco, Alfonso, the Elder, Italian composer, son of **Domenico Maria Ferrabosco** and father of **Alfonso Ferrabosco, the Younger;** b. Bologna (baptized), Jan. 18, 1543; d. there, Aug. 12, 1588. From 1562 to 1564 he was in the service of Queen Elizabeth I in England; was again in England from 1572 to 1578. He entered the service of the Duke of Savoy in Turin (1582), accompanying him to Spain; he died while on a visit to his native city. His influence on the English court as a representative of the Italian style was considerable. Of his sacred works, 79 compositions are extant; many are housed in MS collections in English and American libraries. They include 110 Italian madrigals, 73 motets, 4 Lamentations, an anthem, 5 French chansons, 3 English songs, 2 secular Latin songs, 17 pieces for solo lute, 2 fantasias for keyboard, and a pavan for a mixed consort. A number of his madrigals were publ. in anthologies of his time. R. Charteris ed. *Alfonso Ferrabosco the Elder (1543–1588): Opera omnia* in Corpus Mensurabilis Musicae, XCVI/1–9 (1984–88).

BIBL.: J. Cockshoot, *The Sacred Music of A. F., Father (1543–88), with Critical Commentary* (diss., Oxford Univ., 1963); R. Charteris, *A. F. the Elder (1543–1588): A Thematic Catalogue of His Music with a Biographical Calendar* (N.Y., 1984).—**NS/LK/DM**

Ferrabosco, Alfonso, the Younger, Italian-English composer, illegitimate son of **Alfonso Ferrabosco, the Elder;** b. probably in Greenwich, England, c. 1575; d. there (buried), March 11, 1628. He was reared by a musician at the English court. He received an annuity from 1592 to 1601, and then entered the service of King James I. He became teacher to the Prince of Wales in 1604. He was granted an annual pension in 1605, and continued as an active musician in the royal service. In 1626 he was named Composer of Music in ordinary and Composer of Music to the King. Ferrabosco was a friend of the dramatist Ben Jonson, for whom he wrote music for several masques produced at the court. He publ. a book of *Ayres* (dedicated to Prince Henry; London, 1609) and a book of *Lessons for 1, 2 and 3 Viols* (London, 1609). His works for viol demonstrate extraordinary ability in contrapuntal writing while preserving the rhythmic quality of the dance forms and the free ornamental style of the fantasies.

BIBL.: J. Duffy, *The Songs and Motets of A. G., the Younger (1575–1628)* (Ann Arbor, Mich., 1980).—NS/LK/DM

Ferrabosco, Domenico Maria, Italian composer, father of **Alfonso Ferrabosco, the Elder;** b. Bologna, Feb. 14, 1513; d. there, Feb. 1574. He was active in Bologna as director of the public performances of the palace musicians (from 1540) and as a singer at S. Petronio. After serving as magister puerorum at the Cappella Giulia at the Vatican in Rome (1546–47), he returned to Bologna and became maestro di cappella at S. Petronio in 1548. From 1551 to 1555 he was again at the Vatican as a singer at the papal chapel, and eventually returned to Bologna. He publ. two vols. of madrigals (1542, 1557) and a vol. of motets (1554). R. Charteris ed. his works in Corpus Mensurabilis Musicae, CII (1992).—NS/LK/DM

Ferrandini, Giovanni Battista (actually, **Zaneto**), Italian composer; b. Venice, c. 1710; d. Munich, Sept. 25, 1791. He studied at the Cons. dei Mendicanti in Venice with Antonio Biffi. While still a boy, he went to Munich and in 1722 he became an oboist in the service of Duke Ferdinand of Bavaria. He remained in his service until 1726, although about 1723 he also entered the service of the elector, becoming his chamber composer in 1732. In 1737 he was made kurfurtstlicher Rat and director of chamber music to the elector. His opera *Catone in Utica* inaugurated the new residence theater in Munich on Oct. 12, 1753. When he was stricken with ill health in 1755, the elector awarded him the title of Truchsess (Lord High Steward), granted him a pension, and gave him permission to settle in Padua, where he continued to write operas for the Munich court. During the young Mozart's visit to Padua in 1771, he demonstrated his skill as a harpsichordist before Ferrandini. About 1790 Ferrandini returned to Munich. As a teacher, he numbered the Elector Maximilian III Joseph and Anton Raaff among his students. His daughter, Maria Anne Elisabeth, became a singer. Ferrandini's operas were held in high esteem in Munich, and they also were given successfully in other operatic centers.

WORKS: DRAMATIC (all are operas 1st perf. in Munich unless otherwise given): *Gordio* (Oct. 22, 1727); *Il sacrificio invalido* (Nymphenburg, July 10, 1729); *Colloquio pastorale,* serenata (Nymphenburg, Aug. 6, 1729); *Berencie* (Feb. 5, 1730); *Scipio nelle Spagna* (1732); *Adriano in Siria* (Carnival 1737); *Demofoonte* (Oct. 22, 1737); *Componimento dramatico per l'incoronatione di Carlo VII* (1742); *Catone in Utica* (Oct. 12, 1753); *Diana placata,* serenata (Aug. 17, 1755; rev. 1758); *Demetrio* (c. 1757); *Talestri* (n.d.); *Nice e Tirsi,* cantata (c. 1777); *L'amor prigionero* (1781). **OTHER:** 6 syms.; chamber music; some 75 cantatas; about 60 arias.—LK/DM

Ferrani (real name, **Zanaggio**), **Cesira,** admired Italian soprano; b. Turin, May 8, 1863; d. Pollone, May 4, 1943. She studied with Antonietta Fricci in Turin, where she made her operatic debut in 1887 at the Teatro Carignano as Gilda. She then sang at the Teatro Regio there, where she created the roles of Manon Lescaut (Feb. 1, 1893) and Mimi (Feb. 1, 1896). From 1894 to 1909 she was a principal singer at Milan's La Scala. Among her other notable roles were Elsa, Eva, and Mélisande. —NS/LK/DM

Ferrante (Arthur) and (Louis) Teicher, American easy-listening piano duo. Ferrante (b. N.Y., Sept. 7, 1921) and Teicher (b. Wilkes-Barre, Pa., Aug. 24, 1924) perfected a twin-piano style that brought them four Top Ten hits and 30 chart albums between 1960 and 1972.

The pair met as children at the Juilliard School of Music, where they studied with Carl Friedberg. They both graduated from Juilliard as piano majors and taught at the school from 1944 to 1947, after which they turned to performing full-time, making their first recordings for Columbia Records in 1953. In 1960 they signed to United Artists Records and released the single "Theme from *The Apartment*" (music by Charles Williams), actually a 1949 tune called "Jealous Love" that was featured in the newly released film *The Apartment*; the record reached the Top Ten in September. The pianists followed it with an even more successful movie theme, "Exodus" (music by Ernest Gold), which reached the Top Ten in December and went gold.

These hits set a pattern for Ferrante and Teicher, who went on to record a string of singles and albums mostly employing music from motion pictures. "Love Theme from *One Eyed Jacks*" (music by Hugh Friedhofer) reached the Top 40 in April 1961. "Tonight" (music by Leonard Bernstein, lyrics by Stephen Sondheim) from the musical *West Side Story*, made current by the release of the film version, became a Top Ten hit in December 1961, and the album it was on, *West Side Story & Other Motion Picture & Broadway Hits*, also hit the Top Ten, remaining in the charts 11 months.

Ferrante and Teicher's singles sales eventually fell off, but they began to place many albums in the charts, averaging about three per year into the early 1970s. In September 1969 they released a compilation, *10th Anniversary/Golden Piano Hits*, that went gold. The following month came their version of the title song from the film *Midnight Cowboy* (music by John Berry), which hit the Top Ten and earned them a Grammy nomination for Best Instrumental Arrangement.

DISC.: *West Side Story & Other Motion Picture and Broadway Hits* (1961); *Love Themes* (1961); *Golden Piano Hits* (1962); *Tonight* (1962); *Golden Themes from Motion Pictures* (1962); *Pianos in Paradise* (1962); *Snowboard* (1962); *Love Themes from "Cleopatra"* (1963); *Concert for Lovers* (1963); *50 Fabulous Piano Favourites* (1964); *The Enchanted World of Ferrante and Tiecher* (1964); *My Fair Lady* (1964); *The People's Choice* (1964); *Springtime* (1965); *By Popular Demand* (1965); *Only the Best* (1965); *Music to Read James Bond By* (1965); *The Ferrante and Teicher Concert* (1965); *For Lovers of All Ages* (1966); *You Asked for It!* (1966); *"A Man and a Woman" & Other Motion Pictures Themes* (1968); *Our Golden Favourites* (1967); *A Bouquet of Hits* (1968); *Midnight Cowboy* (1969); *Getting Together* (1970); *Love Is a Soft Touch* (1970); *The Music Lovers* (1971); *It's Too Late* (1971); *Fiddler on the Roof* (1972); *Fill the World with Love* (1976); *Nostalgic Hits* (1977); *The Twin Pianos of Ferrante and Teicher* (1984).—WR

Ferrara, Franco, Italian conductor and pedagogue; b. Palermo, July 4, 1911; d. Florence, Sept. 6, 1985. He studied piano, violin, organ, and composition at the conservatories of Palermo and Bologna. He made his debut as a conductor in Florence in 1938. From 1958 poor health prompted him to devote himself to teaching.—NS/LK/DM

Ferraresi del Bene, Adriana (née **Gabrieli**), Italian soprano, known as **La Ferrarese**; b. Ferrara, c. 1755; d. Venice, after 1799. She was trained at Venice's Ospedaletto. After marrying Luigi del Bene in 1783, she was generally known as Ferraresi del Bene or La Ferrarese. In 1785 she appeared in Cherubini's *Demetrio* at His Majesty's Theatre in London and then created the role of Epponina in his *Giulio Sabbino* at Milan's La Scala in 1787. In 1788 she made her debut in Vienna in Martín y Soler's *L'arbore di Diana* and then sang there in operas by Salieri, Guglielmi, and Paisiello. As the mistress of Da Ponte, she became acquainted with Mozart, who wrote the role of Fiordiligi for her in his *Così fan tutte* (Jan. 26, 1790). All the same, Mozart thought little of her vocal abilities. Indeed, her quarrels with singers and her scandalous conduct in general led to her dismissal from the Viennese court in 1792.—NS/LK/DM

Ferrari, Benedetto, Italian librettist and composer, called "Dalla Tiorba" for his proficiency on the theorbo; b. Reggio Emilia, c. 1603; d. Modena, Oct. 22, 1681. He studied music in Rome, then served as a choirboy at the Collegio Germanico in Rome (1617–18). He subsequently was a musician at the Farnese court in Parma (1619–23). In 1637 he proceeded to Venice, where he wrote the libretto for Manelli's opera *L'Andromeda*; it was produced at the Teatro di San Cassiano in 1637, the first Venetian opera performed in a theater open to the public. He then wrote librettos for *La Maga fulminata* by Manelli (1638), *L'inganno d'Amore* by Bertali (Regensburg, 1653), *La Licasta* by Manelli (Parma, 1664), and 4 of his own operas, all produced in Venice: *L'Armida* (Feb. 1639), *Il Pastor regio* (Jan. 23, 1640), *La Ninfa avara* (1641), and *Il Principe giardiniero* (Dec. 30, 1643). From 1651 to 1653 he was in Vienna. From 1653 to 1662 he served as court choirmaster in Modena; after a hiatus of employment, he was reinstated in 1674, remaining in this post until his death. In Modena he produced the opera *L'Erosilda* (1658). Six of Ferrari's librettos were publ. in Milan in 1644 under the title *Poesie drammatiche*. —NS/LK/DM

Ferrari, Carlotta, Italian composer; b. Lodi, Jan. 27, 1837; d. Bologna, Nov. 23, 1907. She studied with Strepponi and Mazzucato at the Milan Cons., and then devoted herself to the composition of operas to her own librettos. The following operas were produced: *Ego* (Milan, 1857), *Sofia* (Lodi, 1866), and *Eleanora d'Armorea* (Cagliari, 1871).—NS/LK/DM

Ferrari, Domenico, famous Italian composer and violinist; b. Piacenza, c. 1722; d. Paris, 1780. He studied with Tartini, and traveled as a concert violinist, obtaining great success. In 1753 he joined the orch. of the Duke of Württemberg in Stuttgart. In 1754 he went to Paris, where he became extremely successful. Ferrari excelled as a virtuoso; his employment of passages in octaves,

and particularly of harmonics, was an innovation at the time. He publ. 36 sonatas for Violin and Bass, opp. 1 to 6 (Paris, 1758–62), 6 trio sonatas for 2 Violins, or Flute and Basso Continuo (London, c. 1758–65), and 6 sonatas or duets for 2 Violins (London, c. 1765; 1st 2 sonatas by Nardini).

BIBL.: V. Kock, *The Works of D. F., 1722–1780* (diss., Tulane Univ., 1969).—NS/LK/DM

Ferrari, Gabrielle, French pianist and composer; b. Paris, Sept. 14, 1851; d. there, July 4, 1921. She studied at the Milan Cons. and later in Paris, where she had lessons with Gounod. She wrote a number of effective piano pieces (*Rapsodie espagnole, Le Ruisseau, Hirondelle*, etc.) and songs (*Larmes en songe, Chant d'exil, Chant d'amour*, etc.). She composed the operas *Le Dernier Amour* (Paris, June 11, 1895), *Sous le masque* (Vichy, 1898), *Le Tartare* (Paris, 1906), and *Le Cobzar*, which proved to be her most successful (Monte Carlo, Feb. 16, 1909). —NS/LK/DM

Ferrari, Giacomo Gotifredo, Italian composer; b. Rovereto, Tirol (baptized), April 2, 1763; d. London, Dec. 1842. He studied harpsichord and voice with Marcolla and Borsaro in Verona, counterpoint and theory with Stecher at the Marienberg monastery in Switzerland, and counterpoint with Latilla in Naples. In 1787 he became a court musician at the Tuileries in Paris, and was active as accompanist to the queen, voice teacher to the nobility, and maestro al cembalo at the Théâtre de Monsieur. After the French Revolution, he settled in London in 1792 and pursued his career as a composer and voice teacher; among his students was the Prince of Wales. He publ. *Breve tratto di canto italiano* (London, 1818; Eng. tr., 1818, by W. Shield as *Concise Treatise on Italian Singing*), *Studio di musica teorica pratica* (London, 1830), and *Anedotti piacevoli e interessanti occorsi nella vita Giacomo Gotifredo Ferrari da Rovereto* (London, 1830).

WORKS: DRAMATIC: Opera (all 1st perf. in London): *I due Svizzeri* (May 14, 1799); *Il Rinaldo d'Asti* (March 16, 1802); *L'eroina di Raab* (April 8, 1813); *Lo Sbaglio fortunato* (May 8, 1817). **OTHER:** 2 ballets; 2 piano concertos; trios; about 40 sonatas for Piano with violin or flute accompaniment; 12 piano sonatas; etc.

BIBL.: E. Zaniboni, *G.G. F. musicista e viaggiatore* (Trent, 1907); D. Fino, *G.G. F., musicista roveretano* (Trent, 1928). —NS/LK/DM

Ferrari, Gustave, Swiss pianist, singer, conductor, and composer; b. Geneva, Sept. 28, 1872; d. there, July 29, 1948. He studied at the Geneva Cons. and in Paris. After a period as an operetta conductor, he toured as accompanist to Yvette Guilbert; later toured on his own as a singer-pianist in the folk song repertoire. He wrote some dramatic music.—NS/LK/DM

Ferrari-Fontana, Edoardo, Italian tenor; b. Rome, July 8, 1878; d. Toronto, July 4, 1936. He studied voice and gained experience singing in operetta in Argentina and Milan before making an impressive operatic debut as Tristan in Turin on Dec. 23, 1909. He sang at Milan's La Scala (1912–14), where he created the role of Avito in *L'amore dei tre re* on April 10, 1913. It was as Avito that he made his Metropolitan Opera debut in N.Y. on Jan. 2, 1914, remaining on its roster until 1915. He also sang with the Boston Opera Co. (1913–14) and the Chicago Grand Opera Co. (1915–16). In 1926 he settled in Toronto as a voice teacher. He was married for a time to **Margarete Matzenauer**. In addition to the Italian repertory, he was esteemed for his portrayals of Siegfried, Siegmund, and Tannhäuser.—**NS/LK/DM**

Ferrari-Trecate, Luigi, Italian composer; b. Alessandria, Piedmont, Aug. 25, 1884; d. Rome, April 17, 1964. He studied with Antonio Cicognani at the Pesaro Cons., and also with Mascagni. Subsequently he was engaged as a church organist. He was prof. of organ at the Liceo Musicale in Bologna (1928–31), and from 1929 to 1955 director of the Parma Cons. He wrote several operas which had considerable success: *Pierozzo* (Alessandria, Sept. 15, 1922), *La Bella e il mostro* (Milan, March 20, 1926), *Le astuzie di Bertoldo* (Genoa, Jan. 10, 1934), *Ghirlino* (Milan, Feb. 4, 1940), *Buricchio* (Bologna, Nov. 5, 1948), *L'Orso Re* (Milan, Feb. 8, 1950), *La capanna dello Zio Tom* (Parma, Jan. 17, 1953), *La fantasia tragica*, and *Lo spaventapasseri* (1963). He also composed music for a marionette play, *Ciottolino* (Rome, Feb. 8, 1922), *In hora calvarii*, sacred cantata (1956), and *Contemplazioni* for Orch. (1950).—**NS/LK/DM**

Ferras, Christian, outstanding French violinist and pedagogue; b. Touquet, June 17, 1933; d. Paris, Sept. 14, 1982. He was a remarkably gifted child who began to study at a very early age with Charles Bistesi at the Nice Cons. In 1942 he made his public debut as soloist with an orch. in Nice. He then continued his training at the Paris Cons. with René Benedetti (violin) and Joseph Calvet (chamber music), taking premiers prix in both subjects in 1946, the year he made his Paris debut. In 1949 he had further lessons with Enesco and captured 2nd prize in the Long-Thibaud competition in Paris. Thereafter, he pursued a distinguished career as a soloist with orchs. and as a recitalist. In 1975 he became a prof. at the Paris Cons. His interpretations were notable for their stylistic fidelity to the score and virtuoso execution.—**NS/LK/DM**

Ferrell, Rachelle, American singer; b. Berwyn, Pa., 1961. A professional singer since the age of 13, Ferrell has an unusual, two-label recording contract. She records R&B for Capitol and jazz for Blue Note, and no matter what she's singing, her multi-octave vocals are a joy to listen to. She attended Boston's Berklee Coll. of Music with Branford Marsalis and later taught music for the N.J. State Council of the Arts with Dizzy Gillespie. In fact, it was Gillespie who once told her parents that she would be a "major force" in the music industry. For such a prolific composer, she records relatively infrequently.

DISC.: *Rachelle Ferrell* (1992); *First Instrument* (1995); *Individuality (Can I Be Me?)* (2000).—**DDD**

Ferrer, Mateo, famous Spanish organist, teacher, and composer; b. Barcelona, Feb. 25, 1788; d. there, Jan.

4, 1864. He studied with Francisco Queralt and Carlos Baguer, then became organist (1808) and maestro de capilla (1830) at the Barcelona Cathedral, where he was active until his death. In addition, he became director of the Teatro de la Cruz in 1827, holding that post for some 30 years. He was renowned for his improvisations on the organ, and was also esteemed as a teacher. He composed a large body of music for the church and the theater, but many works are lost. His Piano Sonata (1814), publ. by J. Nin in his collection *Seize sonates anciennes d'auteurs espagnols* (Paris, 1925), shows a certain affinity with early Beethoven.—**NS/LK/DM**

Ferrer, Rafael, Spanish conductor; b. St.-Celoni, near Barcelona, May 22, 1911. He studied with Luis Millet and Enrique Morera (composition) and Eduardo Toldrá (violin). He played the violin in various orchs. in Spain; then devoted himself mainly to conducting. He specialized in Spanish music, and revived many little-known works of Granados, Turina, and other Spanish composers.—**NS/LK/DM**

Ferrero, Lorenzo, Italian composer; b. Turin, Nov. 17, 1951. He was basically self-taught in music, but received some training from Bruni and Zaffiri. He also attended the Milan Cons. and studied aesthetics with Battimo at the Univ. of Turin (graduated, 1974, with a study of the writings of John Cage). In 1974 he began working with the group Musik-Dia-Licht-Film-Galerie in Munich. In 1980–81 he was assistant to Bussotti at the Puccini Festival in Torre del Lago, where he was artistic director in 1984. In 1981 he became a prof. at the Milan Cons. In 1982–83 he worked at IRCAM in Paris. He was artistic director of the Unione Musicale concert series in Turin from 1982 to 1988, and of the Verona Arena from 1991 to 1994. In his music, Ferrero bridges the gap between traditional opera and rock and popular music.

WORKS: DRAMATIC: *Rimbaud ou Le fils de soleil*, melodrama (1978); *Marilyn*, theater piece (1980); *La figlia del mago*, children's opera (1981); *Mare nostro*, comic opera (1985); *Salvatore Giuliano*, opera (1986); *Carlotta Corday*, opera (1988). **ORCH.:** *Siglied* for Chamber Orch. (1975); *Arioso* (1977; rev. 1981); *Balletto* (1981); *Thema 44* for Small Orch. (1982); *Dance Music* (1985); *My Rock* for Small Orch. (1986). **CHAMBER:** *My Rock, My Rag, My Blues* for Piano (1984); *Ostinato* for 6 Cellos (1987). **VOCAL:** *Canzoni d'amore* for Voices and 9 Instruments (1985); *Non parto, non resto* for Chorus (1987).—**NS/LK/DM**

Ferrero, Willy, American-born Italian conductor and composer; b. Portland, Maine, May 21, 1906; d. Rome, March 24, 1954. He appeared as a conductor at the Teatro Costanzi in Rome at 6, and then conducted with great success throughout Europe at 8. After studies at the Vienna Academy of Music (graduated, 1924), he resumed his career but never fulfilled his early promise. He wrote a symphonic poem, *Il mistero dell' aurora*, and some chamber music.—**NS/LK/DM**

Ferretti, Dom Paolo, eminent Italian musicologist; b. Subiaco, Dec. 3, 1866; d. Bologna, May 23, 1938. He studied theology at the Benedictine Coll. of S. Anselmo in Rome, taking his vows as a Benedictine monk in 1884 and being ordained a priest in 1890. From 1900 to 1919 he was abbot of the Benedictine monastery of S. Giovanni in Parma; in 1922 he was made director of the Scuola Pontificia by Pope Piux XI, which became the Pontificio Istituo di Musica Sacra in 1931. He was an authority on Gregorian chant.

WRITINGS: *Princippi teorici e pratici di canto gregoriano* (Rome, 1905); *El Cursus Metrico e il ritmo delle melodie del Canto Gregoriano* (Rome, 1913); *Estetica gregoriana ossia Trattato delle forme musicali del canto gregoriano* (Rome, 1934); P. Ernetti, ed., *Estetica gregoriana dei recitativi liturgici* (Venice, 1964). —NS/LK/DM

Ferretti, Giovanni, Italian composer; b. c. 1540; d. after 1609. He was maestro di cappella at Ancona Cathedral (1575–79), the Santa Casa, Loreto (1580–82), in Gemona (1586–88), in Cividale del Friuli (1589), and once more at the Santa Casa, Loreta (1596–1603). He publ. seven vols. of napolitane (Venice, 1567–85), some of the early ones being so popular that they carried his name as far as England, where they proved influential in the development of the English madrigal style. —LK/DM

Ferri, Baldassare, celebrated Italian castrato soprano; b. Perugia, Dec. 9, 1610; d. there, Nov. 18, 1680. He was a choirboy in Orvieto, where he entered the service of Cardinal Crescenzio in 1622. He then studied in Naples and with Vincenzo Ugolini in Rome. He entered the service of Prince Wladyslaw of Poland in Warsaw in 1625 and continued in his employ when he became King Wladyslaw IV Vasa in 1632. In 1655 he went to Vienna, where he served the emperors Ferdinand III and Leopold I until about 1665; he then returned to Italy. He gained public renown with his appearances in major music centers, his travels taking him as far as London. According to contemporary accounts, he possessed a phenomenal voice and accumulated a great fortune.—NS/LK/DM

Ferrier, Kathleen (Mary), remarkable English contralto; b. Higher Walton, Lancashire, April 22, 1912; d. London, Oct. 8, 1953. She grew up in Blackburn, where she studied piano and began voice lessons with Thomas Duerden. In 1937 she won 1st prizes for piano and singing at the Carlisle Competition; she then decided on a career as a singer, and subsequently studied voice with J.E. Hutchinson in Newcastle upon Tyne and with Roy Henderson in London. After an engagement as a soloist in *Messiah* at Westminster Abbey in 1943, she began her professional career in full earnest. Britten chose her to create the title role in his *Rape of Lucretia* (Glyndebourne, July 12, 1946); she also sang Orfeo in Gluck's *Orfeo ed Euridice* there in 1947 and at Covent Garden in 1953. She made her American debut with the N.Y. Phil. on Jan. 15, 1948, singing *Das Lied von der Erde*, with Bruno Walter conducting. She made her American recital debut in N.Y. on March 29, 1949. Toward the end of her brief career, she acquired in England an almost legendary reputation for vocal excellence and impeccable taste, so that her untimely death (from cancer) was greatly mourned. In 1953 she was made a Commander of the Order of the British Empire and received the Gold Medal of the Royal Phil. Soc.

BIBL.: N. Cardus, ed., *K. F., A Memoir* (London, 1955; 2nd ed., rev., 1969); W. Ferrier, *The Life of K. F.* (London, 1955); C. Rigby, *K. F.* (London, 1955); W. Ferrier, *K. F., Her Life* (London, 1959); P. Lethbridge, *K. F.* (London, 1959); M. Leonard, *K.: The Life of K. F.: 1912–1953* (London, 1988); J. Spycket, *K. F.* (Lausanne, 1990); P. Campion, *F.: A Career Recorded* (London, 1992); B. Mailliet Le Penven, *La voix de K. F.: Essai* (Paris, 1997). —NS/LK/DM

Ferris, Glenn, American trombonist; b. Los Angeles, Calif., June 27, 1950. He discovered the trombone at eight years old, studied classically, and later studied theory and improvisation with Don Ellis (1964–66). He joined Don Ellis's innovative big band when he was 16, touring and performing until 1970. His warm, mellow sound was inspiring and admired, and he worked around Los Angeles in the 1970s with Frank Zappa, Harry James, Billy Cobham, Bobby Bradford, and also played in a number of classical, pop, rock, and R&B groups. He formed a duo with Milcho Leviev and organized his own 10-piece band, Celebration, in the late 1970s. During the 1980s, he recorded with Tony Scott and toured Europe with Jack Walrath's quintet. Since settling in Europe in 1980, he's played and recorded with Steve Lacy, Barry Altschul, Chris McGregor, Louis Sclavis, Franco D'Andrea, Peter Schärli, Enrico Rava, Michel Portal, Joachim Kuhn, Aldo Romano, and Henri Texier.

DISC.: *That's Nice* (1985); *Tomorrow* (1992); *Flesh & Stone* (1994); *Face Lift* (1995).—TP

Ferris, William (Edward), American composer, choral conductor, and organist; b. Chicago, Feb. 26, 1937; d. there of a heart attack while rehearsing Verdi's *Requiem*, May 16, 2000. He studied composition with Alexander Tcherepnin at the De Paul Univ. School of Music (1955–60) and privately with Leo Sowerby (1957–62) in Chicago. In 1960 he founded the William Ferris Chorale, specializing in the works of 20th century composers and often bringing them to Chicago for festival concerts of their music. He served as organist of Holy Name Cathedral in Chicago (1954–58; 1962–64), and as director of music at Sacred Heart Cathedral in Rochester, N.Y., for Bishop Fulton J. Sheen (1966–71). From 1973 to 1983 he was on the faculty of the American Cons. of Music in Chicago, and thereafter served as composer-in-residence and director of music at Our Lady of Mt. Carmel Church in Chicago. In 1992 Northwestern Univ. established the William Ferris Archive, which contains his musical compositions, preliminary sketches, correspondence, and memorabilia.

WORKS: DRAMATIC: *Little Moon of Alban*, opera (1974); *The Diva*, opera (1979; Chicago, June 13, 1987; rev. version, Evanston, Ill., June 5, 1998); *Angels*, miracle play (Chicago, June 5, 1998). **ORCH.:** *October-November*, symphonic movement (1962; Rochester, N.Y., Nov. 6, 1968); *Concert-Piece* for Organ and Strings (1963; Worcester, Mass., Nov. 19, 1967); *Acclamations* for Organ and Orch. (1981–82; Chicago, Jan. 27, 1983). **CHAMBER:** Flute Sonata (1983; Chicago, May 13, 1984); *Parables* for Harp (Rome, May 29, 1988). **KEYBOARD:**

P i a n o : Sonata (Washington, D.C., April 5, 1976). **VOCAL :** *De profundis* (N.Y., Nov. 22, 1964); *Ed e subito sera* for Tenor and Strings (1965; Chicago, March 10, 1989); *Make We Joy*, cantata (Chicago, Dec. 12, 1976); *A Song of Light*, cantata (Chicago, Oct. 11, 1977); *Snowcarols*, cantata (Chicago, Dec. 7, 1980); *Beat! Beat! Drums* (Chicago, May 5, 1984); *3 Spirituals* for Tenor, Harp, and Double Bass (Geneva, July 8, 1990); *Gloria* for Soloists, Chorus, and Orch. (Chicago, May 15, 1992); *Corridors of Light* for Baritone, Oboe, Strings, and Percussion (1994; Chicago, May 19, 1995); liturgical works; numerous works for chorus and organ; a cappella choruses; songs.—**NS/LK/DM**

Ferro, Gabriele, Italian conductor; b. Pescara, Nov. 15, 1937. He studied with Franco Ferrara at the Cons. di Santa Cecilia in Rome. In 1967 he founded the Bari Sym. Orch., and from 1974 he conducted sym. concerts with the La Scala Orch. in Milan. He made his U.S. debut as a guest conductor with the Cleveland Orch. in 1978. He was music director of the Orch. Sinfonica Siciliana in Palermo, and, from 1988, served as chief conductor of the RAI Orch. in Rome. From 1992 to 1997 he was Generalmusikdirektor of the Stuttgart Opera. —**NS/LK/DM**

Ferroud, Pierre-Octave, French composer and music critic; b. Chasselay, near Lyons, Jan. 6, 1900; d. in an automobile accident near Debrecen, Hungary, Aug. 17, 1936. He studied harmony with Commette in Lyons and attended the Univ. there, and then pursued his training with Ropartz in Strasbourg (1920–22) and Schmitt in Lyons. In 1923 he settled in Paris as a composer and music critic. His output was influenced by Schmitt and Bartók. He publ. *Autour de Florent Schmitt* (Paris, 1927).

WORKS: DRAMATIC : O p e r a t i c S k e t c h : *Chirurgie* (Monte Carlo, March 20, 1928). **B a l l e t :** *Le Porcher* (Paris, Nov. 15, 1924); *Jeunesse* (1931; Paris, April 29, 1933); *Vénus ou L'Équipée planétaire* (1935). **ORCH.:** *Foules*, symphonic poem (1922–24; Paris, March 21, 1926); *Sérénade* (1929); Sym. (1930; Paris, March 8, 1931). **CHAMBER:** Violin Sonata (1928–29); Cello Sonata (1932); Trio for Oboe, Clarinet, and Bassoon (1933); String Quartet (1934); piano pieces. **VOCAL :** Song cycles.

BIBL.: C. Rostand, *L'oeuvre de P.-O. F.* (Paris, 1958); R. Melkis Bihler, *P.-O. F. (1900–1936): Ein Beitrag zur Geshichte der Musik in Frankreich* (Frankfurt am Main, 1995).—**NS/LK/DM**

Fesca, Alexander (Ernst), German pianist and composer, son of **Friedrich (Ernst) Fesca;** b. Karlsruhe, May 22, 1820; d. Braunschweig, Feb. 22, 1849. He began training with his father in Karlsruhe, where he made his debut as a pianist at age 11. When he was 14, he went to Berlin to study with Taubert (piano), Rungenhagen and A.W. Bach (composition and harmony), and Schneider (instrumentation) at the Royal Academy of Arts. From 1839 he made highly successful tours as a pianist. He served as chamber musician to Prince Fürstenberg (1841–42) before settling in Braunschweig.

WORKS: DRAMATIC : O p e r a : *Mariette* (Karlsruhe, 1838); *Die Franzosen in Spanien* (Karlsruhe, 1841); *Der Troubadour* (Braunschweig, July 25, 1847); *Ulrich von Hutten* (Karlsruhe, 1849). **OTHER:** Chamber music; piano pieces; songs.

BIBL.: M. Frei-Hauenscild, *F.E. F. (1789–1826): Studien zu Biographie und Streichquartettschaffen* (Göttingen, 1998). —**NS/LK/DM**

Fesca, Friedrich (Ernst), German violinist and composer, father of **Alexander (Ernst) Fesca;** b. Magdeburg, Feb. 15, 1789; d. Karlsruhe, May 24, 1826. He studied piano and at age 9 began violin lessons with Lohse, making his debut in Magdeburg at 11; he also studied with Zacharia (theory) and Pitterlin (composition). He then went to Leipzig as a pupil of A. Müller (composition) and Matthai (violin), where he played in the Gewandhaus Orch. (1805–06). After playing in the orch. of the Duke of Oldenburg (1806–08), he served at the court of Jérôme Buonaparte in Kassel (1808–13). In 1814 he became a member of the chapel orch. of the Grand Duke of Baden in Karlsruhe. In 1821 he was stricken with tuberculosis.

WORKS: DRAMATIC : O p e r a : *Cantemire* (Karlsruhe, April 27, 1820); *Omar und Leila* (Karlsruhe, Feb. 26, 1824). **OTHER :** 3 syms.; overtures; Violin Concerto (1805); 16 string quartets; 4 string quintets; 4 flute quintets; Flute Quintet; choral works.—**NS/LK/DM**

Festa, Costanzo, important Italian composer; b. c. 1480; d. Rome, April 10, 1545. He was a singer in the Pontifical Chapel from 1517. He was a composer of much importance, being regarded as a forerunner of Palestrina, whose works were strongly influenced by those of Festa. He was the first important Italian musician who successfully fused the Flemish and Italian styles, melodically and harmonically. His madrigals were widely known through various publ. collections (1530–49). Among his extant works are 4 masses, mass movements, about 60 motets, and 30 vesper hymns. A. Main ed. *Costanzo Festa, Opera omnia*, in Corpus Mensurabilis Musicae, XXV (1962–68).

BIBL.: H. Musch, *C. F. als Madrigalistkomponist* (Baden-Baden, 1977).—**NS/LK/DM**

Festing, Michael Christian, esteemed English violinist and composer; b. London, c. 1680; d. there, July 24, 1752. He received training from Richard Jones and Geminiani. In 1724 he made his first public appearance as a violinist in London, where he played in the orch. of the King's Theatre (from 1727), and served as director of the orchs. of the Italian Opera (from 1737) and at Ranelagh Gardens (from 1742); he also was active as a chamber musician. In 1735 he was named Master of the King's Musick. With Maurice Greene et al., he founded the Soc. of Musicians, a charitable organization, in 1738. His instrumental works were composed in the virtuoso manner of Geminiani.

WORKS: INSTRUMENTAL (all publ. in London): 12 solos for Violin and Basso Continuo (1730); 12 sonatas for 1 or 2 Recorders and Violin or Bass (1731); 12 concerti grossi (1734); 8 solos for Violin and Basso Continuo (1736); 8 concerti grossi (1739); 6 sonatas for 2 Violins and Bass (1742); 6 solos for Violin and Basso Continuo (1747); 6 solos for Violin and Basso Continuo (c. 1750); 6 concerti grossi (1756). **VOCAL:** Cantatas and songs.—**NS/LK/DM**

Fétis, Adolphe (-Louis-Eugène), Belgian-French pianist, teacher, and composer, son of **François-**

Joseph and brother of **Édouard (-Louis-François) Fétis**; b. Paris, Aug. 20, 1820; d. there, March 20, 1873. He studied music with his father and then at the Brussels Cons.; subsequently studied piano with Herz and composition with Halévy in Paris. After living in Brussels and Antwerp, he settled in Paris in 1856 as a music teacher and composer. He wrote several comic operas and music for the piano.—NS/LK/DM

Fétis, Edouard (-Louis-François), Belgian writer on music and librarian, son of **François-Joseph** and brother of **Adolphe (-Louis-Eugene) Fétis**; b. Bouvignes, near Dinant, May 16, 1812; d. Brussels, Jan. 31, 1909. After editing his father's *La Revue Musicale* (1833–35), he was a librarian at the Royal Library in Brussels from 1836. He publ. in Brussels *Description des richesses artistiques de Bruxelles* (1847), *Les Musiciens belges* (1848; 2nd ed., 1854), *Les Artistes belges à l'étranger* (1857–65), and *L'art dans la société et dans l'état* (1872). —NS/LK/DM

Fétis, François-Joseph, erudite Belgian music theorist, historian, and critic, father of **Édouard (-Louis-François)** and **Adolphe (-Louis-Eugène) Fétis**; b. Mons, March 25, 1784; d. Brussels, March 26, 1871. He received primary instruction from his father, an organist at the Mons Cathedral. He learned to play the violin, piano, and organ when very young, and in his 9th year wrote a Concerto for Violin, with Orch. As a youth, he was organist to the Noble Chapter of Ste.-Waudru. In 1800 he entered the Paris Cons., where he studied harmony with Rey and piano with Boieldieu and Pradher. In 1803 he visited Vienna, where he studied counterpoint, fugue, and masterworks of German music. Several of his compositions (a Sym., an overture, sonatas and caprices for Piano) were publ. at that time. In 1806 he began the revision of the plainsong and entire ritual of the Roman Church, a vast undertaking, completed, with many interruptions, after 30 years of patient research. A wealthy marriage in the same year, 1806, enabled him to pursue his studies at ease for a time; but the fortune was lost in 1811, and he retired to the Ardennes, where he occupied himself with composition and philosophical researches into the theory of harmony; in 1813 he was appointed organist for the collegiate church of St.-Pierre at Douai. In 1818 he settled in Paris; in 1821 became a prof. of composition at the Paris Cons. In 1824 his *Traité du contrepoint et de la fugue* was publ. and accepted as a regular manual at the Cons. In 1827 he became librarian of the Cons., and in the same year founded his unique journal *La Revue Musicale*, which he ed. alone until 1832 (his son Édouard ed. it from 1833 until 1835, when its publication ceased). He also wrote articles on music for *Le National* and *Le Temps*. In 1828 he competed for the prize of the Netherlands Royal Inst. with the treatise *Quels ont été les mérites des Neerlandais dans la musique, principalement aux XIVᵉ-XVIᵉ siècles...*; Kiesewetter's essay on the same subject won, but Fétis's paper was also printed by the Inst. In 1832 he inaugurated his famous series of historical lectures and concerts. In 1833 he was called to Brussels as maître de chapelle to King Leopold I, and director of the Cons.; during his long tenure in the latter position, nearly 40 years, the Cons. flourished as never before. He also conducted the concerts of the Academy, which elected him a member in 1845. He was a confirmed believer in the possibility of explaining music history and music theory scientifically; in his scholarly writings he attempted a thorough systematization of all fields of the art; he was opinionated and dogmatic, but it cannot be denied that he was a pioneer in musicology. He publ. the fist book on music appreciation, *La Musique mise à la portée de tout le monde* (Paris, 1830; numerous reprints and trs. into Eng., Ger., It., Sp., Russ.); further pedagogical writings are *Solfèges progressifs* (Paris, 1837) and *Traité complet de la théorie et de la pratique de l'harmonie* (Brussels, 1844). As early as 1806 Fétis began collecting materials for his great *Biographie universelle des musiciens et bibliographie générale de la musique* in 8 vols. (Paris, 1833–44; 2nd ed., 1860–65; suppl. of 2 vols., 1878–80; ed. by A. Pougin). This work of musical biography was unprecedented in its scope; entries on composers and performers whom he knew personally still remain prime sources of information. On the negative side are the many fanciful accounts of composers' lives taken from unreliable sources; in this respect Fétis exercised a harmful influence on subsequent lexicographers for a whole century. His *Histoire générale de la musique*, in 5 vols., goes only as far as the 15th century (Paris, 1869–76; reprint, Hildesheim, 1983); this work exhibits Fétis as a profound scholar, but also as a dogmatic philosopher of music propounding opinions without convincing evidence to support them. Of interest are his *Esquisse de l'histoire de l'harmonie considerée comme art et comme science systématique* (Paris, 1840), *Notice biographique de Nicolo Paganini* (Paris, 1851; with a short history of the violin), *Antoine Stradivari* (Paris, 1856; with a commentary on bowed instruments), reports on musical instruments at the Paris Expositions of 1855 and 1867; etc. He was also a composer. Between 1820 and 1832 he wrote 7 operas, serious and light, for the Opéra-Comique; composed church music, 3 string quartets, 3 string quintets, 2 syms., and a Flute Concerto. His valuable library of 7,325 vols. was acquired after his death by the Bibliothèque Royale of Brussels; a catalog was publ. in 1877.

BIBL.: K. Gollmick, *Herr F., Vorstand des Brüsseler Conservatoriums als Mensch, Kritiker, Theoretiker und Componist* (Leipzig and Brussels, 1852); L. Alvin, *Notice sur F.-J. F.* (Brussels, 1874); R. Wangermée, *F.-J. F.: Musicologue et compositeur* (Brussels, 1951); B. Huys et al., *F.-J. F. et la vie musicale de son temps: 1784–1871* (Brussels, 1972).—NS/LK/DM

Fetler, Paul, American composer and teacher; b. Philadelphia, Feb. 17, 1920. His family moved to Europe when he was a child, and he had early music studies in Latvia, the Netherlands, Sweden, and Switzerland. He composed 2 dozen small works and part of a sym. that were later discarded. In 1939 he returned to the U.S. and studied briefly at the Chicago Cons. of Music. He then studied composition with David Van Vactor at Northwestern Univ. (graduated, 1943). Drafted into military service, he was sent at the end of World War II to Berlin as a liaison officer and Russian interpreter assigned to the Allied Control Council. It was during this time that he became a student of Celibidache, who arranged the premiere of his *Prelude* for Orch. with the Berlin Phil. (July 13, 1946, composer conducting). In 1946 he returned to the U.S. to study with Porter and Hindemith at Yale Univ. (M.M., 1948). In 1948 he was appointed to the music faculty of the Univ. of Minn., which became his permanent position and where he earned his Ph.D. degree in 1956. He retired in 1990. He returned to Berlin in 1953 to study with Blacher on a Guggenheim fellowship. His 2nd Guggenheim fellowship (1960) took him to Kreuth, Bavaria, where he composed his *Soundings* for Orch. (Minneapolis, Oct. 12, 1962). One of his most successful scores, *Contrasts* for Orch. (Minneapolis, Nov. 7, 1958), was widely performed. He received 3 NEA grants (1975, 1977, 1980).

WORKS: DRAMATIC: *Sturge Maclean*, opera for youth (St. Paul, Minn., Oct. 11, 1965); incidental music to plays; film scores. **ORCH.:** *Symphonic Fantasia* (1941); *Passacaglia* (1942); *Dramatic Overture* (1943); *Berlin Scherzo* (1945); *Prelude* (Berlin, July 13, 1946); 4 syms.: No. 1 (1948), No. 2 (Rochester, N.Y., Nov. 5, 1951), No. 3 (1954; Minneapolis, Nov. 25, 1955), and No. 4 (Minneapolis, May 1, 1968); *Orchestral Sketch* (Minneapolis, Aug. 15, 1949); *A Comedy Overture* (Minneapolis, March 2, 1952); *Gothic Variations*, on a theme of Machaut (Minneapolis, Nov. 13, 1953); *Contrasts* (Minneapolis, Nov. 7, 1958); *Soundings* (Minneapolis, Oct. 12, 1962); *Cantus tristis*, in memory of President John F. Kennedy (Minneapolis, Nov. 20, 1964); 2 violin concertos: No. 1 (St. Paul, Minn., March 27, 1971) and No. 2 (1980; Minneapolis, March 18, 1981); *Celebration* (1976; Indianapolis, Dec. 16, 1977); *3 Impressions* for Guitar and Orch. (1977; Minneapolis, May 31, 1978); *Serenade* (Minneapolis, July 26, 1981; rev. 1982); Piano Concerto (Minneapolis, Oct. 4, 1984); *Capriccio* for Flute, Winds, and Strings (Minneapolis, June 6, 1985); *3 Excursions*, concerto for Percussion, Piano, and Orch. (1987; Buffalo, Dec. 10, 1988); *Divertimento* for Flute and Strings (Rochester, N.Y., May 15, 1994). **CHAMBER:** Sextet for String Quartet, Clarinet, and Horn (1942); 2 string quartets (1947, 1989); 2nd Violin Sonata (Minneapolis, March 6, 1952); *Cycles* for Percussion and Piano (Washington, D.C., May 31, 1970); *Dialogue* for Flute and Guitar (1973); *Pastoral Suite* for Piano Trio (St. Paul, Minn., April 11, 1976); *Rhapsody* for Violin and Piano (1985; rev. 1987); *6 Pieces* for Flute and Guitar (1985; rev. 1987); *12 Hymn Settings* for Organ and Instruments (1994); Suite for Oboe, Clarinet, and Bassoon (1995); *Saraband Variations* for Guitar (1999). **VOCAL:** 3 cantatas: *Of Earth's Image* for Soprano, Chorus, and Orch. (1958), *This Was the Way* for Chorus and Orch. (St. Paul, Minn., May 7, 1969), and *The Hour Has Come* for 2 Choruses, Organ, and Brass (1981); *Lamentations* for Chorus, Narrator, Organ, and Flute (1974); *The Poems of Walt Whitman* for Narrator and Orch. (1976); *Missa de Angelis* for 3 Choruses, Organ, and Handbells (1980); *The Garden of Love* for Voice and Chamber Orch. (1983); *December Stillness* for Voices, Flutes, and Harp (Minneapolis, Dec. 3, 1994); *Up the Dome of Heaven*, 3 pieces for Mixed Voices and Flute (1996).—**NS/LK/DM**

Feuermann, Emanuel, greatly gifted Austrian-born American cellist; b. Kolomea, Galicia, Nov. 22, 1902; d. N.Y., May 25, 1942. As a child he was taken to Vienna, where he first studied cello with his father; subsequently studied cello with Friedrich Buxbaum and Anton Walter. He made his debut in Vienna in 1913 in a recital. He went to Leipzig in 1917 to continue his studies with Julius Klengel. His progress was so great that he was appointed to the faculty of the Gurzenich Cons. in Cologne by Abendroth at the age of 16; he also

was 1st cellist in the Gurzenich Orch. and was a member of the Bram Eldering Quartet. In 1929 he was appointed prof. at the Hochschule für Musik in Berlin; as a Jew, he was forced to leave Germany after the advent of the Nazis to power; he then embarked on a world tour (1934–35). He made his American debut on Dec. 6, 1934, with the Chicago Sym. Orch., and then appeared as soloist with leading American orchs. He also played chamber music with Schnabel and Huberman, and later with Rubinstein and Heifetz.

BIBL.: S. Itzkoff, *E. F., Virtuoso: A Biography* (Univ., Ala., 1979).—**NS/LK/DM**

Févin Antoine de, French composer; b. probably in Arras, c. 1470; d. Blois, 1511 or 1512. He was greatly admired as a composer of sacred music by contemporaries via works publ. in various collections. His extant output includes 9 Masses, 3 Magnificats, 3 Lamentations, motets, and chansons. **Robert de Févin** may have been his brother.

BIBL.: E. Clinkscale, *The Complete Works of A. d.F.* (diss., N.Y. Univ., 1965).—**NS/LK/DM**

Févin, Robert de, French composer who flourished in the early 16th century. He served as maître de chapelle to the dukes of Savoy in Cambrai. Among his works were several Masses, including *La Sol mi fa mi re*. He may have been the brother of **Antoine de Févin**. —**NS/LK/DM**

Février, Henri, French composer; b. Paris, Oct. 2, 1875; d. there, July 6, 1957. He studied at the Paris Cons. with Fauré, Leroux, Pugno, and Massenet, and also privately with Messager. He publ. a monograph on the latter (Paris, 1948).

WORKS: DRAMATIC: Opera: *Le Roi aveugle* (Paris, May 8, 1906); *Monna Vanna* (Paris, Jan. 13, 1909); *Gismonda* (Chicago, Jan. 14, 1919; Paris, Oct. 15, 1919); *La Damnation de Blanche- Fleur* (Monte Carlo, March 13, 1920); *La Femme nue* (Monte Carlo, March 23, 1929). **Operetta:** *Agnés, dame galante* (1912); *Carmosine* (1913); *Ile désenchantée* (Paris, Nov. 21, 1925). **OTHER:** Chamber music; piano pieces; choral works; songs.—**NS/LK/DM**

Fewkes, Jesse Walter, pioneering American ethnologist; b. Newton, Mass., Nov. 14, 1850; d. Forest Glen, Md., May 31, 1930. He studied biology at Harvard Univ. (Ph.D., 1877), then did postgraduate work at Leipzig and at the Univ. of Ariz. He was field director of the Hemenway Southwestern Archaeological Expedition (1889–94), on which he used a phonograph to preserve songs of the Passamaquoddy Indians of Maine (1890). These were followed by Zuni (1890) and Hopi (1891) Pueblo Indian recordings, which were analyzed by Benjamin Gilman. From 1895 he was an ethnologist at the Bureau of American Ethnology in Washington, D.C.; he became chief in 1918, retiring in 1928. He is important to ethnomusicology as the first researcher to record non-Western music for scientific study. His studies of the Pueblo Indians of Ariz., which include extensive observation of music along with relevant ritual, folklore, and language considerations, are still of value. He did extensive field work in ethnology, archeology, and zoology, and authored some 228 articles and publications. Among them are "On the Use of the Phonograph in the Study of Languages of American Indians," *Science*, XV (1890), "Additional Studies of Zuni Songs and Rituals with the Phonograph," *American Naturalist*, XXIV (1890), and "Tusayan Flute and Snake Ceremonies," *Annual Report of the Bureau of American Ethnology*, XIX (1900).—NS/LK/DM

Ffrangcon-Davies, David (Thomas) (real name, **David Thomas Davis,** prominent Welsh baritone; b. Bethesda, Caernarvon, Dec. 11, 1855; d. London, April 13, 1918. (The surname Ffrangcon was taken from the Nant- Ffrangcon mountain range near his birthplace.) He was ordained a priest in 1884, but later left the church to take up a musical career. He studied singing with Richard Latter, Shakespeare, and Randegger in London, and made his concert debut in Manchester (Jan. 6, 1890) and his stage debut at Drury Lane Theatre in London (April 26, 1890). From 1896 to 1898, he sang in festivals throughout the U.S. and Canada, then lived in Berlin (1898–1901). From 1903 he was a prof. of singing at the Royal Coll. of Music in London. After a nervous breakdown in 1907, he gave up public singing. His book, *The Singing of the Future* (London, 1905), was republ. by his daughter, Marjorie Ffrangcon-Davies, as Part II of *David Ffrangcon-Davies, His Life and Book* (London, 1938).—NS/LK/DM

Fiala, George (Joseph), Russian-born Canadian composer, pianist, organist, and teacher; b. Kiev, March 31, 1922. As the son of pianists, he began his own piano lessons at 7. At 12, he became a piano student of Mikhailov, and also had training in theory and composition. Following composition studies with Groudine, Revutsky, Liatoshinsky, and Olkhovsky at the Kiev Cons. (1939–41), he went to Berlin to study composition (with Dombrowski), conducting (with Furtwängler) and musicology at the Hochschule für Musik (Ph.D., 1945); he then completed his training with L. Jongen in Brussels. In 1949 he emigrated to Canada and in 1955 became a naturalized Canadian citizen. In addition to his activities as a performer, teacher, and composer, he produced programs for the Russian section of Radio Canada International (1967–87). He composed in a tonal style until the early 1960s, and then began to utilize some serial procedures in his works while retaining traditional forms.

WORKS: ORCH.: Piano Concerto (1946); *Autumn Music* (1949); 5 syms., including Sym. in E minor (1950), No. 4, *Ukrainian* (1973; Toronto, Nov. 21, 1982), and No. 5, *Sinfonia breve* (1981); Concertino for Piano, Trumpet, Timpani, and Strings (1950); *Suite concertante* for Oboe and Strings (1956); *Introduction and Fugato* for English Horn and Strings (1961); *Capriccio* for Piano and Orch. (1962); *Shadows of Our Forgotten Ancestors* (1962); *Divertimento concertante* for Violin and Orch. (1965); *Eulogy: In Memory of President J.F. Kennedy* (1965; rev. 1985); *Montreal* (1967); *Musique concertante* for Piano and Orch. (1968); *Serenade concertante* for Cello and Strings (1968); *Sinfonietta concertata* for Accordion, Harpsichord, and Strings (1971);

Ouverture burlesque (1972); Violin Concerto (1973); *Overtura buffa* (1981); *The Kurelek Suite* (1982); *Festive Ouverture* (1983); *Music for Strings No. 1* (1985) and No. 2 (1989); *Overture and out* (1989); *Divertimento capriccioso* for Flute and Strings (1990). CHAMBER: *Chamber Music for 5 Wind Instruments* for Flute, Oboe, Clarinet, Horn, and Bassoon (1948); *Ukrainian Suite* for Cello and Piano (1948); Trio for Oboe, Cello, and Piano (1948); Wind Octet (1948); 3 saxophone quartets (1955, 1961, 1983); String Quartet (1956); Piano Quartet (1957); *3 Movements* for Violin, Viola, Cello, and Piano (1957); *Pastorale and Allegretto* for 4 Recorders (1963); 3 cello sonatas (1969, 1971, 1982); Violin Sonata (1969); Saxophone Sonata (1970); *Duo Sonata* for Violin and Harp (1971); *Sonata for 2* for Soprano Saxophone and Accordion (1971); *Concertino canadese* for 4 Harps (1972); *Sonata breve* for Clarinet and Harp (1972); *Partita da camera* for 2 Violins (1977); *Duettino concertante* for Clarinet and Harp (1981); *Terzetto concertante* for Clarinet, Cello, and Harp (1981); *Partita concertata* for Violin and Cello (1982); Piano Quintet (1982); *2 Movements* for Oboe and Piano (1984); Flute Sonata (1986); Trio Sonata for Violin, Cello, and Piano (1987); Viola Sonata (1989). KEYBOARD: Piano: *Children's Suite* (1941; rev. 1975); 8 sonatas (n.d.–1970); *10 Postludes* (1947; rev. 1968); *Australian Suite* (1963); *3 Bagatelles* (1968); 3 sonatas for 2 Pianos (1970, 1983, 1989); *Piano Music Nos. 1–3* (1976–89); *Concerto da camera* for Piano, 4-Hands (1978); *Concerto breve* for 2 Pianos (1979); *Ukrainian Dance* for 2 Pianos (1979); *Canadian Sketches* (1989). VOCAL: *Cantilena and Rondo* for Soprano, Recorder, and Piano (1963); *Canadian Credo* for Chorus and Orch. (1966); *5 Ukrainian Songs* for Soprano and Orch. (1973); *Concerto Cantata* for Chorus, Piano, and Chimes Obbligato (1984); *The Millennium Liturgy* for Chorus (1986); other songs.—NS/LK/DM

Fiala, Joseph, Bohemian oboist, cellist, viola da gambist, and composer; b. Lochovice, Feb. 3, 1748; d. Donaueschingen, July 31, 1816. He studied oboe with Stiastny and cello with Werner. After playing oboe in the band of Prince Kraft Ernst in Oettingen-Wallerstein (1774–77), he was in the service of the Elector Maxmilian Joseph in Munich, where he became a friend of Mozart. From 1778 to 1785 he was a member of the orch. of the archbishop of Salzburg. Following a sojourn in Vienna (1785–86), he was in the service of Catherine the Great in St. Petersburg. In 1790 he returned to Germany and was active as a viola da gambist in Breslau and Berlin. In 1792 he settled in Donaueschingen as Kapellmeister to Prince Fürstenberg. Among his works were orch. pieces, music for wind band, a Mass, chamber music, and keyboard works.—LK/DM

Fialkowska, Janina, Canadian pianist; b. Montreal, May 7, 1951. She was born of a Polish father and a Canadian mother. At age 5, she commenced piano lessons with her mother. Later she was a pupil of Yvonne Hubert at the École Vincent-d'Indy in Montreal (B.M., 1968; M.Mus., 1968). After studies with Yvonne Lefébure in Paris (1968), she attended Sascha Gorodnitzki's classes at the Juilliard School in N.Y. (1969). She continued to work with him until 1976, and then served as his assistant (1979–84). After taking one of the 3rd prizes at the 1st Artur Rubinstein competition in Israel in 1974, she appeared as a soloist with leading orchs. and as a recitalist in North and South America and Europe. Her fluent technique and beauty of expression have suited her well in the Romantic repertoire. She has played the complete works of Chopin and on May 3, 1990, she was soloist with the Chicago Sym. Orch. in the first performance of the newly discovered Liszt E-flat major Concerto.—NS/LK/DM

Fibich, Zdeněk (Antonín Václav), important Czech composer; b. Všebořice, Dec. 21, 1850; d. Prague, Oct. 15, 1900. He studied piano with Moscheles and theory with E.F. Richter at the Leipzig Cons. (1865–66), then composition privately with Jadassohn (1866–67) and in Mannheim with V. Lachner (1869–70). Upon his return to Prague (1871), he was deputy conductor and chorus master at the Provisional Theater (1875–78) and director of the Russian Orthodox Church Choir (1878–81). He was a fine craftsman and facile melodist, and one of the leading representatives of the Czech Romantic movement in music. His extensive output reveals the pronounced influence of Weber, Schumann, and especially Wagner. His operas *Nevěsta mesinská* (The Bride of Messina) and *Pád Arkuna* (The Fall of Arkun) are recognized as significant achievements, although they have not gained a place in the standard repertoire. He remains best known for his effective music for piano. A critical ed. of his works was publ. in Prague (1950–67).

WORKS (all 1st perf. in Prague unless otherwise given): **DRAMATIC: O p e r a :** *Bukovín* (1870–71; April 16, 1874); *Blaník* (1874–77; Nov. 25, 1881); *Nevěsta mesinská* (The Bride of Messina, after Schiller; 1882–83; March 28, 1884); *Bouře* (The Tempest, after Shakespeare; 1893–94; March 1, 1895); *Hedy*, after Byron's Don Juan (1894–95; Feb. 12, 1896); *Šárka* (1896–97; Dec. 28, 1897); *Pád Arkuna* (The Fall of Arkun; 1898–99; Nov. 9, 1900). **S t a g e M e l o d r a m a T r i l o g y :** *Hippodamie (Hippodamia)*, after Sophocles and Euripides: *Námluvy Pelopovy* (The Courtship of Pelops; 1888–89; Feb. 21, 1890), *Smir Tantaluv* (The Atonement of Tantalus; 1890; June 2, 1891), and *Smrt Hippodamie* (Hippodamia's Death; Nov. 8, 1891). **C o n c e r t M e l o d r a m a s F o r R e c i t e r a n d P i a n o :** *Štědrý den* (Christmas Day; 1875; orchestrated 1899); *Pomsta květin* (The Revenge of the Flowers; 1877); *Věčnost* (Eternity; 1878); *Královna Ema* (Queen Emma; 1883). **F o r R e c i t e r a n d O r c h . :** *Vodník* (The Water Goblin; 1883); *Hakon* (1888). **ORCH.:** 7 syms. including No. 1 (1877–83), No. 2 (1892–93; Prague, April 9, 1893), and No. 3 (1898; Prague, March 7, 1899); 7 symphonic poems (1873–1900; 6 extant); 4 overtures (1873–98). **VOCAL: S a c r e d C h o r a l :** *Meluzina* for Soloists, Chorus, and Orch. (1872–74); *Svatební scéna* (Wedding Scene) for 7 Soloists, Chorus, and Orch. (1872–74); *Jarní romance* (A Springtime Tale) for Soprano, Bass, Chorus, and Orch. (1880–81); *Missa brevis* for Chorus and Organ (1885). **O t h e r :** Secular choral music; part-songs; songs. **CHAMBER:** Piano Trio (1872); Piano Quartet (1874); 2 string quartets (1874, 1878); 2 violin sonatas (1874, 1875); Piano Quintet (1893); etc. **KEYBOARD: P i a n o :** Many works, including 376 pieces publ. as *Nálady, dojmy a upomínky* (Moods, Impressions, and Reminiscences; 1892–99).

BIBL.: J. Bartoš, *Z. F.* (Prague, 1914); J. Plavec, *Z. F., mistr české balady* (Z. F., Master of the Czech Ballad; Prague, 1940); K. Jirák, *Z. F.* (Prague, 1947).—NS/LK/DM

Ficher, Jacobo, Russian-Argentine composer; b. Odessa, Jan. 15, 1896; d. Buenos Aires, Sept. 9, 1978. He studied violin with Stolarsky and Korguev in Odessa and composition with Kalafati and Steinberg at the St. Petersburg Cons., graduating in 1917. In 1923 he emigrated to Argentina. In 1956 he was appointed prof. of composition at the National Cons. of Music in Buenos Aires. His music is characterized by a rhapsodic fluency of development and a rich harmonic consistency. He particularly excelled in chamber music.

WORKS: DRAMATIC: O p e r a : *El oso* (1952); *Pedido de mano* (1955). **B a l l e t :** *Colombina de Hoy* (1933); *Los Invitados* (1933); *Melchor* (1938–39); *Golondrina* (1942). **ORCH.:** *Poema heroico* (1927; rev. 1934); *Sulamita*, tone poem (1927; Buenos Aires, July 20, 1929; rev. 1960); *Obertura patética* (1928; Buenos Aires, May 17, 1930; rev. as *Exodus*, 1960); 8 syms. (1932; 1933; 1938–40; 1947; 1948; 1956; 1958–59; 1965); Violin Concerto (1942); 3 piano concertos (1945, 1954, 1960); Harp Concerto (1956); Flute Concerto (1965). **CHAMBER:** 4 string quartets (1927, 1936, 1943, 1952); 3 violin sonatas (1929, 1945, 1959); *Suite en estilo antiguo* for Woodwind Quintet (1930); Sonata for Viola, Flute, and Piano (1931); Sonatina for Saxophone, Trumpet, and Piano (1932); Piano Trio (1935); Flute Sonata (1935); Clarinet Sonata (1937); Oboe Sonata (1940); Cello Sonata (1943); Sonata for Flute and Clarinet (1949); Sonata for Flute, Oboe, and Bassoon (1950); Viola Sonata (1953); Piano Quintet (1961); Wind Quintet (1967). **KEYBOARD: P i a n o :** 8 sonatas; several sets of pieces (including 2 groups of effective "fables," descriptive of animals). **VOCAL:** 3 cantatas: *Salmo de alegria* (1949), *Mi aldea* (1958), and *Kadisch* (1969).

BIBL.: B. Zipman, *J. F.* (Buenos Aires, 1966).—NS/LK/DM

Fickénscher, Arthur, American pianist, teacher, and composer; b. Aurora, Ill., March 9, 1871; d. San Francisco, April 15, 1954. He studied at the Munich Cons. with Rheinberger and Thuille, graduating in 1898. He toured the U.S. as accompanist to famous singers, among them Bispham and Schumann-Heink. From 1920 to 1941 he was head of the music dept. of the Univ. of Va., Charlottesville. In 1947 he settled in San Francisco. An inquisitive musician, he elaborated a system of pure intonation; contrived the "Polytone," an instrument designed to play music in which the octave is subdivided into 60 tones. He publ. an article, "The Polytone and the Potentialities of a Purer Intonation," *Musical Quarterly* (July 1941). His major work was the *Evolutionary Quintet*, evolved from a violin sonata and an orch. scherzo written in the 1890s; the MSS were burned in the San Francisco earthquake and fire of 1906; the musical material was then used from memory for a Quintet for Piano and Strings, in 2 movements; the 2nd movement, entitled *The 7th Realm*, became an independent work. He also wrote *Willowwave and Wellowway* for Orch. (1925), *The Day of Judgment* for Orch. (1927; Grand Rapids, Feb. 10, 1934), *Dies irae* for Chamber Orch. (1927), *Out of the Gay Nineties* for Orch. (Richmond, Va., Dec. 4, 1934, composer conducting), *Variations on a Theme in Medieval Style* for Strings (1937), *The Chamber Blue*, mimodrama (1907–09; rev. 1935; Charlottesville, Va., April 5, 1938), *The Land East of the Sun* for chorus and orch. (unfinished), and piano quintet (1939).

BIBL.: W. Jones, *Life and Works of A. F., American Composer (1871–1954)* (Memphis, Tenn., 1992).—NS/LK/DM

Ficker, Rudolf von, distinguished German musicologist; b. Munich, June 11, 1886; d. Igls, near Innsbruck, Aug. 2, 1954. From 1905 to 1912 he studied at the Univ. of Vienna with Adler (musicology), and in Munich with Thuille and Courvoisier (composition). He received his Ph.D. from the Univ. of Vienna in 1913 with the diss. *Die Chromatik im italienischen Madrigal des 16. Jahrhunderts.* He taught at the Univ. of Innsbruck from 1920, becoming a prof. in 1923. He then taught at the Univ. of Vienna in 1927, and in 1931 at the Univ. of Munich. He was a specialist in medieval music. In addition to articles for music journals, he also left unfinished a book entitled *Die Grundlagen der abendländischen Mehrstimmigkeit.*—NS/LK/DM

Fiedler, Arthur, highly popular American conductor; b. Boston, Dec. 17, 1894; d. Brookline, Mass., July 10, 1979. Of a musical family, he studied violin with his father, Emanuel Fiedler, a member of the Boston Sym. Orch. In 1909 he was taken by his father to Berlin, where he studied violin with Willy Hess, and attended a class on chamber music with Dohnányi; he also had some instruction in conducting with Kleffel and Krasselt. In 1913 he formed the Fiedler Trio with 2 other Fiedlers. In 1915 he returned to America, and joined the 2nd violin section of the Boston Sym. Orch.; later he moved to the viola section; he also doubled on the celesta, when required. In 1924 he organized the Arthur Fiedler Sinfonietta, a professional ensemble of members of the Boston Sym. Orch. In 1929 he started a series of free open-air summer concerts at the Esplanade on the banks of the Charles River in Boston, presenting programs of popular American music intermingled with classical nos. The series became a feature in Boston's musical life, attracting audiences of many thousands each summer. In 1930 Fiedler was engaged as conductor of the Boston Pops, which he led for nearly half a century. Adroitly combining pieces of popular appeal with classical works and occasional modern selections, he built an eager following, eventually elevating the Boston Pops to the status of a national institution via numerous tours, recordings, radio broadcasts, and television concerts. In 1977 President Gerald Ford bestowed upon him the Medal of Freedom.

BIBL.: R. Moore, *F., The Colorful Mr. Pops* (Boston, 1968); C. Wilson, *A. F., Music for the Millions* (N.Y., 1968); J. Holland, *Mr. Pops* (N.Y., 1972); H. Dickson, *A. F. and the Boston Pops* (Boston, 1981).—NS/LK/DM

Fiedler, (August) Max, German conductor and composer; b. Zittau, Dec. 31, 1859; d. Stockholm, Dec. 1, 1939. He studied with his father (piano), with G. Albrecht (organ and theory), and at the Leipzig Cons. (1877–80). He then was a teacher (from 1882) and director (from 1903) of the Hamburg Cons., and was also conductor of the Hamburg Phil. (1904–08). Subsequently he was conductor of the Boston Sym. Orch. (1908–12) and music director in Essen (1916–33). Among his compositions were a Sym., *Lustpiel,* overture, piano quintet, string quartet, and piano pieces; songs.

BIBL.: G. Dejmek, *M. F.: Werden und Werken* (Essen, 1940). —NS/LK/DM

Field, Helen, Welsh soprano; b. Awyn, May 14, 1951. She was educated at the Royal Northern Coll. of Music in Manchester and at the Royal Coll. of Music in London. In 1976 she made her operatic debut as Offenbach's Eurydice at the Welsh National Opera in Cardiff, where she returned in subsequent years in such roles as Desdemona, Tatiana, Marzelline, Micaëla, the Vixen, and Jenůfa. Following her debut at London's Covent Garden as Emma in *Khovanshchina* in 1982, she sang at the English National Opera in London from 1983, where she was particularly admired for her portrayals of Pamina, Gilda, Marguerite, and Violetta. In 1987 she sang the title role in the British premiere of Strauss's *Daphne* with Opera North in Leeds. She created the role of JoAnn in Tippett's *New Year* in Houston in 1989, a role she reprised at her Glyndebourne Festival debut in 1990. In 1994 she returned to Glyndebourne to create the role of Pearl in Birtwistle's *The Second Mrs. Kong.* She created the title role in MacMillan's *Inés de Castro* at the Edinburgh Festival in 1996. In 1997 she sang Salome at Covent Garden, and then was engaged for that role in Los Angeles in 1998. As a concert artist, she appeared with leading British and European orchs.—NS/LK/DM

Field, John, remarkable Irish pianist and composer; b. Dublin, July 26, 1782; d. Moscow, Jan. 23, 1837. His father was a violinist, and his grandfather was an organist. It was from his grandfather that he received his first instruction in music. At the age of 9 he began study with Tommaso Giordani, making his debut in Dublin on March 24, 1792. He went to London in 1793, and gave his first concert there that same year. He then had lessons with Clementi, and was also employed in the salesrooms of Clementi's music establishment. He began his concert career in earnest with a notable series of successful appearances in London in 1800–01. He then accompanied Clementi on his major tour of the Continent, beginning in 1802. After visiting Paris in 1802, they proceeded to St. Petersburg in 1803; there Field settled as a performer and teacher, giving his debut performance in 1804. He made many concert tours in Russia. Stricken with cancer of the rectum, he returned to London in 1831 for medical treatment. He performed his piano concerto in E-flat major at a Phil. Soc. concert there on Feb. 27, 1832. Later that year he played in Paris, and then subsequently toured various cities in France, Belgium, Switzerland, and Italy until his health compelled him to abandon his active career. He eventually returned to Moscow, where he died. Field's historical position as a composer is of importance, even though his music does not reveal a great original talent. He developed the free fantasias and piano recitative, while following the basic precepts of Classical music; he was also the originator of keyboard nocturnes. He composed 7 concertos (1799, 1814, 1816, 1816, 1817, 1819 [rev. 1820], 1822), 4 sonatas (1801, 1801, 1801, 1813), about 30 nocturnes (1812–36?), polonaises, etc., as well as a quintet for piano and strings (1816) and 2 divertimenti for piano, strings, and flute (c. 1810–11).

BIBL.: F. Liszt, *Über J. F.s Nocturnes* (Hamburg, 1859; also in Vol. IV of *Liszt's Gesammelte Schriften,* Leipzig, 1882); H. Dessauer, *J. F., Sein Leben und seine Werke* (Langensalza, 1912); W. Grattan Flood, *J. F. of Dublin* (Dublin, 1920); A. Nikolaev, *J. F.* (Moscow, 1960; Eng. tr., 1973); C. Hopkinson, *A Bibliographical Thematic Catalogue of the Works of J. F.* (London, 1961); G.

Southall, *J. F.'s Piano Concertos: An Analytical and Historical Study* (diss., Univ. of Iowa, 1966); D. Branson, *J. F. and Chopin* (London, 1972); P. Piggott, *The Life and Music of J. F.* (London, 1973; 2nd ed., 1984).—**NS/LK/DM**

Fielder, Alvin Jr., jazz drummer, percussionist; brother of William Fielder; b. Nov. 23, 1935, Meridian, Miss. His father, Alvin Sr., studied cornet, his mother played piano and violin, his grandmother piano, and his mother's brother clarinet. At 13, he began musical studies by joining the Harris Senior High Band in Meridian, under "Duke" Otis, with whom he was gigging three years later. He continued studies with Ed Blackwell and met Earl Palmer while in New Orleans studying to be a pharmacist at Xavier Univ. in 1952–53. After transferring to Tex. Southern Univ. in Houston, he continued musical study with Herb Brockstein. He had private lessons with George "Dude" Brown (Gene Ammons's drummer from Washington, D.C.) and Clarence Johnston (James Moody's drummer from Boston, Mass.) whenever they came through Houston working. From 1954–56, he worked with the "Pluma" Davis Sextet (with Don Wilkerson, Richard "Dicky Boy" Lillie, John Browning, Carl Lott Sr., and other Houston jazz luminaries). The sextet played for two years at the Eldorado in Houston, backing Big Joe Turner, Ivory Joe Hunter, Amos Milburn, Lowell Fulsom, and other R&B artists with extended engagements. Pluma Davis introduced Fielder to Bobby Bland, and the drummer did occasional live gigs with Bland, and also did several studio dates for Duke Records backing gospel and blues artists. Through late 1958, Fielder was active on the Houston jazz scene with Jimmy Harrison Quintet, John Browning Quintet, and Eddie "Cleanhead" Vinson sextet (1955).

Fielder arrived in Chicago in December 1958, joined Sun Ra from early 1959 until early 1961; then played with Muhal Richard Abrams in 1962–63. During 1962, he spent some time in Denver and N.Y. He returned to Chicago in early 1963, and performed in the area with Roscoe Mitchell (1963–66), Eddie Harris (1964), co-op group with Anthony Braxton, Charles Clark, Leroy Jenkins and Kalaparusha (1965), co-op trio with Fred Anderson and Lester Lashley (1967–68). In between, he worked with John Stubblefield, Jack DeJohnette, "Scotty" Holt, Joseph Jarman, and other Chicago jazz musicians. He was a charter member of Association for the Advancement of Creative Music (AACM) in 1965. He moved back to Miss. around August 1968 to take over the family-owned pharmacy and later acquired two more pharmacies. In 1971, Fielder joined the Black Arts Music Society in Jackson, Miss., which helped bring progressive jazz musicians to the area to lead workshops. In the early 1970s, he met Edward "Kidd" Jordan in New Orleans with whom the Improvisational Arts Quintet was founded with bassist London Branch, Clyde Kerr, Alvin Thomas (tenor saxophone; died before 1983). This was the first new music group based on the idea of the AACM in the southeastern U.S. Other important associates in New Orleans have been Elton Herron and Darrell Levine. Fielder joined the La. Jazz Federation, New Orleans, in 1981. His first European tour in 1982 was to the Netherlands and Moers festival in Germany; he returned to the Netherlands in 1984 (Northsea festival) and 1988, and later made tours of France and Austria. In 1986, he met Dennis Gonzalez, and worked with him for three years and recorded. He formed the Southeastern Jazz All Stars, featuring from time to time James Clay, Charles Davis, Joe Jennings, and Jothan Callins for southeast festivals and college dates from 1990–94. He met Joel Futterman and formed a trio along with "Kidd" Jordan in 1994. He conducted performances with trio and guest bassists William Parker, Barry Guy and Elton Herron at festivals in U.S. and Europe in late 1990s.

DISC.: *Sound* (1967); *No Compromise!* (1983); *Namesake* (1987); *The New New Orleans Music* (1988); *Debenge-Debenge* (1988); *New Desert Wind* (1993); *Nickelsdorf Konfrontation* (1996); *New Orleans Rising* (1997).—**LP**

Fielder, William (Butler), jazz trumpeter, educator; brother of **Alvin Fielder Jr.;** b. July 2, 1938, Meridian, Miss. He grew up in Meridian until age 16. He started playing piano in seventh grade, then four months later his father's cornet. His mother played piano and violin. The cornet was considered therapy for his lungs, which were weakened by asthma. Harry James was an early influence, then Dizzy Gillespie and Stan Kenton. Like his brother, Fielder studied with Duke Otis, a former classmate of Teddy Edwards who directed the school bands, and played alto sax and taught all instruments. Fielder later played French horn in the school band. He began studying with George Frank Sims, a trumpeter influenced by Armstrong. He practiced day and night (once a neighbor called the police who came and took the trumpet away). In ninth grade, he began studies with William "Hillbilly" Davis, who had played in Cab Calloway's band and was band director at Jackson State Coll. Davis used Fielder in demonstrations in front of his college students and had him play first trumpet in the Jackson State Coll. band while in tenth grade. Fielder transferred from Meridian H.S. to Tougaloo Coll. Prep School, where he studied physics and chemistry for two years. Although his parents wanted him to become a doctor, his heart was set on music. When he graduated, he accepted a music scholarship at Tenn. State. Hank Crawford, Les Spann, Phineas Newborn, Leon Thomas and Cleveland Eaton were involved in the band program there. Crawford formed a band in 1955 to play jazz. Although Fielder was a strong technician he needed work on playing changes. In 1956, the Dizzy Gillespie big band played Tenn. State and Fielder asked Dizzy for advice on improvising. Gillespie introduced him to Lee Morgan who played duets with him and told him to contact Booker Little, who had left Tenn. for Chicago.

In 1957, after a year and a half at Tenn. State, Fielder left for Chicago. His parents were furious and his father cut off his financial support. Booker Little advised him to take lessons from a symphony player and when he went to Orch. Hall with his trumpet case in the winter of 1957, he was asked by chance to audition for Adolph Herseth, the principal trumpeter of the Chicago Sym. Orch. He played the Haydn trumpet concerto from memory and was placed in the Chicago Civic Sym., playing first trumpet, side by side with Charlie Geyer (now at Eastman School of Music), and trombonist Jay

Friedman (who along with Herseth remained in the Chicago Sym.). He studied with Vincent Cichowicz, the second trumpeter in the CSO where he was introduced to the airflow and breathing principles that have become such an important part of his playing and teaching.

Between mid 1958 and early 1959, Fielder was rehearsing every day with Sun Ra. The Arkestra only played a few engagements (including a 1958 road trip to Indianapolis where Wes Montgomery sat in with the band at the YMCA), so many of its members also worked the Chicago theaters such as the Tivoli and the Regal, making up to $800 a week. Fielder played such gigs with Ray Charles and B.B. King, and behind Dinah Washington, Abbey Lincoln, Redd Foxx and Diahann Carroll as a member of Morris Ellis's band at Robert's Show Club (with Art Hoyle, tenor saxophonist John Neely, trombonist John Avant and drummer Harold Jones). He also played with Captain Walter Dyett's working band at the Parkway Ballroom. In late 1958, he dropped out of the American Cons. of Music and toured with B.B. King, playing across the U.S. and Canada. Although offered the straw boss job in this band, he turned it down and returned to Chicago. There he joined Slide Hampton's group, which included George Coleman and Hobart Dotson. Fielder played on the premiere performance of Hampton's "Cloister Suite" at the Cloister Inn in Chicago. The Hampton band played engagements in Philadelphia and Pittsburgh and also made short trips to other locations such as Montreal.

In late 1960, Fielder returned to Miss. for a few months, then moved to N.Y.C. Around this time, he subbed in the Duke Ellington Orch., spent time back in Slide Hampton's group, subbing for Freddie Hubbard, and played in Danny Small's band which frequently played gigs on Long Island with Philly Joe Jones, Norris Turney, Donald Byrd, Herbie Hancock, Marcus Belgrave, and others. In 1961, Fielder moved back to Chicago, auditioned at the C & C Lounge for a gig with Gene Ammons and spent three years there with the band (co-led by tenor saxophonist Eddie Williams). He also worked with Eddie Harris at the Old East End club. In 1964, Lee Morgan offered Fielder the trumpet chair with Art Blakey and James Spaulding encouraged him to move back to N.Y., but Fielder refused to leave Chicago. He had resumed his studies with Herseth and Cichowicz and received his Bachelor's and Master's degrees from the American Cons. of Music.

Fielder began his career as an educator at Ala. State Univ. (1965–72), where he taught trumpet, directed the brass ensemble and was assistant band director, and played in the Birmingham Symphony. He attended an international trumpet symposium in Denver in 1970, where he met and worked with Maurice Andre (an early idol), Louis Davidson, William Vacchiano, and Harry Glantz. He began suffering from glaucoma shortly after this and stopped playing entirely for six months. In 1972, Fielder accepted the head band director position at Tenn. State and worked with the Nashville Symphony under music director Dr. Thor Johnson. In late 1974, he left TSU and worked for a semester at the Univ. of Okla. In 1975, he moved back to Miss., teaching at several

schools. At Miss. Valley State Coll. in Greenwood, Miss. he met Mulgrew Miller and recorded informally with him. Miller played these tapes while on tour with the Duke Ellington Orch. and Mercer Ellington offered Fielder the featured trumpet position. Due to his teaching responsibilities, Fielder could not accept, although he did work with the Ellington Orch. in the N.C. area. An offer to join the Count Basie Orch. as lead trumpeter for a world tour was similarly declined. Fielder also led a group in Memphis, which included his brother Alvin, Bill Easley, Phineas Newborn or Donald Brown and bassist London Branch. It was during this period that Ellis Marsalis asked Fielder to teach trumpet to his son, Wynton. He also worked with Kidd Jordan's son Kent and Wynton's brother Branford. From 1977 to 1979, Fielder worked in N.C., as director of the jazz studies program at Shaw Univ. In 1979 he accepted a position at Rutgers Univ., where he has remained. During this time he played Jazzmobile concerts with Frank Foster, David Newman, Charlie Rouse and Kenny Barron, who was also a member of the Jazz Professors group, which toured the country. In 1981, Fielder gigged in Brooklyn with Mulgrew Miller, Kenny Garrett and David Eubanks, but cut back on his performing engagements to concentrate on running the Rutgers jazz program. Since the mid- 1980s, he has played very rarely in public, an exception being an all-star brass concert featuring Slide Hampton and Jimmy Heath arrangements. He is a legendary instructor whose students include Michael Mossman, Terence Blanchard, Terrell Stafford, Riley Mullins, George Shaw, Frank Lacy, and others. He can be seen coaching Wynton Marsalis in the televised classical video *Baroque Duet*.

DISC.: Chicago Symphony Orchestra/Fritz Reiner: *Pines of Rome* (1959); *Love Progression* (1984).—**MF**

Fields, prominent American family associated with the musical theater:

(1) **Lew Fields** (real name, **Lewis Maurice Schanfield**), actor, singer, producer, and director; b. N.Y., Jan. 1, 1867; d. Beverly Hills, July 20, 1941. He was only 10 when he made his first stage appearance with the young Joe Weber. They subsequently toured for some 20 years as the comedy duo of Weber and Fields. In 1896 they opened Weber and Field's Broadway Music Hall in N.Y., where their burlesque productions and variety musicals became celebrated. Although they went their separate ways in 1904, they did make a few reunion appearances in subsequent years. Fields pursued his solo career by appearing in and producing musicals. His last appearance on the N.Y. musical stage was in Jimmy McHugh's *Hello Daddy* (1928), to a text by Field's son Herbert and daughter Dorothy. Field's children, whose entries follow, were also closely associated with the musical theater.

BIBL.: F. Inman, *Weber and F.* (N.Y., 1924).

(2) **Joseph (Albert) Fields**, playwright and librettist; b. N.Y., Feb. 21, 1895; d. Beverly Hills, March 3, 1966. Although mainly known as a playwright, he also collaborated on the librettos of four musicals: Styne's *Gentlemen Prefer Blondes* (1949; with Anita Loos), Bernstein's *Wonderful Town* (1953; with Jerome Chodorov),

Romberg's *The Girl in Pink Tights* (1956; with Chodorov), and Rodgers's *Flower Drum Song* (1958; with Oscar Hammerstein, II).

(3) Herbert Fields, librettist; b. N.Y., July 26, 1897; d. there, March 24, 1958. He was educated at Columbia Univ., where he first collaborated with Rodgers and Hart. Between 1925 and 1928 he wrote the librettos for seven of their Broadway shows, including *Dearest Enemy* (1925), *The Girl Friend* (1926), and *A Connecticut Yankee* (1927). He also wrote the libretto for Youmans's *Hit the Deck* (1927). For Porter, he wrote the librettos for *50 Million Frenchmen* (1929), *The New Yorkers* (1930), *Dubarry Was a Lady* (1939), and *Panama Hattie* (1940). In collaboration with his sister Dorothy, he wrote the librettos for Porter's *Let's Face It* (1941), *Something for the Boys* (1943), and *Mexican Hayride* (1944), Romberg's *Up in Central Park* (1945), Berlin's *Annie Get Your Gun* (1946), Gould's *Arms and the Girl* (1950), Schwartz's *By the Beautiful Sea* (1954), and Hague's *Redhead* (1959).

(4) Dorothy Fields, lyricist and librettist; b. Allenhurst, N.J., July 15, 1904; d. N.Y., March 28, 1974. She had her first success as a lyricist working with Jimmy McHugh. Their hits included "I Can't Give You Anything But Love" from the revue *Blackbirds of 1928* and "On the Sunny Side of the Street" from the *International Revue* (1930). They subsequently worked on Hollywood films. She also collaborated with Kern on his film versions of *Roberta* (1935) and *Swing Time* (1936). Thereafter she pursued a notably successful career working as a librettist on Broadway shows. She collaborated with her brother Herbert on Porter's *Let's Face It* (1941), *Something for the Boys* (1943), and *Mexican Hayride* (1944), Romberg's *Up in Central Park* (1945), Berlin's *Annie Get Your Gun* (1946), Gould's *Arms and the Girl* (1950), Schwartz's *By the Beautiful Sea* (1954), and Hague's *Redhead* (1959). She was also the librettist for Schwartz's *A Tree Grows in Brooklyn* (1951) and for Coleman's *Sweet Charity* (1966) and *Seesaw* (1973).—**LK/DM**

Fields, Dorothy,

affectionate American lyricist and librettist; b. Allenhurst, N.J., July 15, 1904; d. N.Y., March 28, 1974. Fields was the most successful female theater lyricist of the 20th century. With her primary collaborators, Jimmy McHugh, Jerome Kern, and Cy Coleman, she contributed extensively to Broadway shows and Hollywood films over a period of nearly 50 years, including the musical *Sweet Charity* and the film *Swing Time*. Her most popular songs were some of her earliest, notably "I Can't Give You Anything but Love," "On the Sunny Side of the Street," and "I'm in the Mood for Love." In addition to her main partners, she also worked on at least one project each with Arthur Schwartz, Sigmund Romberg, Harold Arlen, Harry Warren, and Burton Lane, among others, bringing a distinctively female perspective to lyrics that were warm, humorous, and sophisticated, their frequent earthiness tempered by an insouciant tone. She was also an accomplished librettist and screenwriter.

Fields was the daughter of Rose Harris and Lew M. Fields (real name, Moses Schoenfeld). Her father was a vaudeville comedian whose successful partnership with Joe Weber broke shortly before her birth; he then continued alone and became a theatrical producer. Fields's two older brothers, Herbert and Joseph, became playwrights and librettists, and she worked with each of them. In fact, her earliest connection with the theater came with a series of amateur shows written by her brother Herbert with aspiring songwriters Richard Rodgers and Lorenz Hart in which she appeared in the early 1920s, two of them at the Benjamin School for Girls, which she attended. After graduating she became the school's drama teacher. In 1925 she married Dr. Jack J. Weiner, a surgeon, but despite remaining married for a decade, the couple separated shortly after their marriage.

After publishing light verse in magazines, Fields came to the attention of composer J. Fred Coots, with whom she wrote song lyrics. Coots introduced her to Jimmy McHugh, who was writing music for revues at the Cotton Club. Together they wrote the songs for the 11th edition of the *Cotton Club Revue*, which opened Dec. 4, 1927, starring Duke Ellington and His Orch. This led to their being hired by producer Lew Leslie for the all-black Broadway revue *Blackbirds of 1928*. The show was an enormous success, running 519 performances. The biggest hit to emerge from it was "I Can't Give You Anything but Love," which earned many recordings, the most popular of them a best-seller for Cliff Edwards in October 1928. (It has long been speculated that the song was actually written by Fats Waller and Andy Razaf and purchased by McHugh.) Three other songs from the show also became hits: "I Must Have That Man" for Ben Selvin and His Orch., and "Diga Diga Doo" and "Doin' the New Low-Down" for Duke Ellington.

Lew Fields hired his daughter and McHugh to write songs for his next musical, *Hello, Daddy!*, for which he served as producer and star, with book by Herbert Fields. The family show ran 197 performances and produced a hit for Annette Hanshaw with "In a Great Big Way."

Fields and McHugh continued to write for various nightclub revues and in 1929 placed their first song in a motion picture with "Collegiana," used in *The Time, the Place, and the Girl*, which opened in July. They returned to Broadway in February 1930 with Lew Leslie's *The International Revue*, which ran only 95 performances but contained two hits: "On the Sunny Side of the Street," recorded by Ted Lewis and His Band, and "Exactly Like You," recorded by Ruth Etting, among others.

Fields and McHugh signed to MGM and went to Hollywood in 1930. They wrote songs for one film, *Love in the Rough*, released in September, and one of them, "Go Home and Tell Your Mother," became a hit for Gus Arnheim and His Orch. But as the movie studios temporarily lost interest in musicals, the team shuttled back to N.Y. where they wrote songs for *The Vanderbilt Revue*, codirected and coproduced by Fields's father. The score included "Blue Again," a hit for Red Nichols and His Five Pennies in February 1931; but the success came too late for the show, which ran a mere 13 performances in November 1930.

Fields and McHugh provided song interpolations for several shows in the first half of 1931, then wrote songs for two films released at the end of the year: a movie version of the De Sylva, Brown, and Henderson musical *Flying High*, and a vehicle for opera singer Lawrence Tibbett, *The Cuban Love Song*. Jacques Renard and His Orch. scored a hit with their recording of the latter's title song, which was cocomposed by Herbert Stothart.

The year 1932 was less active for the team, although they scored a rare independent hit in April with "Goodbye Blues" (music and lyrics by McHugh, Fields, and Arnold Johnson), recorded by the Mills Brothers and adopted as their theme song. In 1933 they were involved in a Lew Leslie revue, *Clowns in Clover*, that never made it to Broadway, although their song "Don't Blame Me" became a hit for Ethel Waters in August. Back at MGM, the pair wrote a promotional title song for the nonmusical film *Dinner at Eight*, which opened in August, and Ben Selvin recorded it for a hit in October.

Fields and McHugh continued to score stray hits in 1934. "Thank You for a Lovely Evening," written for Phil Harris to perform at the Palais Royale nightclub, became a hit for Don Bestor and His Orch. in July; "Lost in a Fog," written for the Dorsey Brothers Orch., became an even bigger hit for Rudy Vallée and His Connecticut Yankees in September; and the team provided lyrics to Reginald Forsythe and His Orch.'s November instrumental hit, "Serenade for a Wealthy Widow."

Fields and McHugh went to RKO, where Fields was asked to revise and add lyrics for songs to the studio's adaptation of Jerome Kern's musical *Roberta* into a vehicle for Fred Astaire and Ginger Rogers. She developed "Lovely to Look At" out of a musical fragment and replaced the Oscar Hammerstein II lyrics to "I Won't Dance," a song from Kern's 1934 London musical *Three Sisters*. The film was released in March 1935 and both songs became major hits for Eddy Duchin and His Orch., with "Lovely to Look At" topping the hit parade in April and earning an Academy Award nomination. Not surprisingly, Kern wanted to work with Fields again, and this proved to be the beginning of the end of her partnership with McHugh.

Fields and McHugh had two projects in the works, however, and they contained more successful songs. *Hooray for Love*, released in July 1935, featured "I'm Living in a Great Big Way," which Louis Prima and His Orch. took into the hit parade. And *Every Night at Eight*, which opened in August, included "I'm in the Mood for Love," given its initial hit recording by Little Jack Little, which topped the hit parade and went on to become one of the team's most popular songs, with hundreds of recordings and millions of copies of sheet music sold.

Notwithstanding this success, the team split up: McHugh signed to 20th Century–Fox, while Fields returned to RKO. Fields teamed with Kern for the November 1935 release *I Dream Too Much*, a vehicle for opera singer Lily Pons. Neither this nor a couple of other films she worked on during this period produced hits, but she and Kern had much better luck writing the next Astaire-Rogers picture, *Swing Time*. Released in August 1936, the film featured "The Way You Look Tonight," which topped the hit parade for Astaire and won the Academy Award for Best Song, and "A Fine Romance," also a hit parade entry for Astaire.

Fields and Kern contributed a couple of songs to the February 1937 release *When You're in Love*, but their next full-scale project, *Joy of Living*, was delayed when Kern became ill. Finally released in May 1938, it produced a hit in "You Couldn't Be Cuter," which was recorded by Tommy Dorsey and His Orch.

Fields married for the second time to clothing manufacturer Eli D. Lahm (the couple had two children) and moved back to N.Y., where she teamed with Arthur Schwartz on the songs for the Broadway musical *Stars in Your Eyes*, starring Ethel Merman and Jimmy Durante. It ran 127 performances and gave Tommy Dorsey a hit parade entry with "This Is It" in March 1939.

In the early 1940s, Fields eschewed songwriting in favor of writing scripts and librettos with her brother Herbert. They first teamed on the screenplay for the comedy *Father Takes a Wife*, which was released in September 1941. Then they wrote the books for three straight hit musicals with songs by Cole Porter, *Let's Face It!* (Oct. 29, 1941), *Something for the Boys* (Jan. 7, 1943), and *Mexican Hayride* (Jan. 28, 1944). They also wrote the book for the 1945 musical *Up in Central Park*, but this time Fields also wrote the songs with Sigmund Romberg. The show ran 504 performances, and Benny Goodman and His Orch. scored a hit with "Close as Pages in a Book" in May 1945. In July, Jo Stafford revived "On the Sunny Side of the Street" for a hit. Fields enjoyed another song revival in early 1946 when "I'm in the Mood for Love" was featured in the motion picture *People Are Funny* and recorded for a hit by Billy Eckstine.

Fields was set to write the book for a musical about sharpshooter Annie Oakley with her brother Herbert and the songs with Jerome Kern, but Irving Berlin was enlisted as songwriter when Kern died, and so Fields was only credited as colibrettist for *Annie Get Your Gun* (May 16, 1946). It was her last credit for nearly four years, until the Broadway opening of *Arms and the Girl* (1950), for which she cowrote the book with Herbert Fields and director Rouben Mamoulian and the songs with Morton Gould. Featuring Pearl Bailey, the musical ran 134 performances. Fields only wrote the songs for the musical *A Tree Grows in Brooklyn* (1951), her second collaboration with Arthur Schwartz. It ran 270 performances and the cast album was a Top Ten hit.

Fields signed to MGM and returned to movie work, writing three films released during 1951: in June came *Excuse My Dust*, a collaboration with Schwartz; in October, *Texas Carnival* with Harry Warren; and, also in October, *Mr. Imperium* with Harold Arlen. In 1952 she revised the score of *Roberta* for a remake called *Lovely to Look At*. The film was released in May, and its soundtrack LP reached the Top Ten. She concluded her stay in Hollywood again collaborating with Arlen on *The Farmer Takes a Wife*, released in June 1953.

Fields returned to N.Y. and to working with Arthur Schwartz for the songs and her brother Herbert for the book of the 1954 musical *By the Beautiful Sea*, which ran 270 performances. More than three and a half years later she collaborated with Burton Lane on songs for *Junior Miss*, a television musical based on a play written by her brother Joseph and Jerome Chodorov that was broadcast during the 1957 Christmas season.

Fields was widowed in 1958, and she also lost her brother Herbert during preparations for their next musical, *Redhead* (1959). The show, which had music by Albert Hague and a book coauthored by Fields, Herbert Fields, Sidney Sheldon, and David Shaw, ran 452 performances and won the Tony Award for Best Musical. The cast album reached the charts and won the Grammy Award for Best Show Album.

In 1961, Fields enjoyed Top 40 revivals of "Don't Blame Me," by the Everly Brothers, and "The Way You Look Tonight," by the Lettermen, but she remained inactive until the mid-1960s, when she reteamed with Gwen Verdon and Bob Fosse, the star and director of *Redhead*, for *Sweet Charity*, which had music by Cy Coleman. It became the longest running show of her songwriting career during her lifetime at 608 performances. The cast album spent several months in the charts, and the score contained four songs that were covered for hits on the easy-listening charts: "Where Am I Going?" by Barbra Streisand; "Big Spender" by Peggy Lee; "Baby, Dream Your Dream" by Tony Bennett; and "There's Gotta Be Something Better than This" by Sylvia Sims. (The show's best-known song, "If My Friends Could See Me Now," did not produce a chart single until it was revived by Linda Clifford in 1978.)

Fields and Coleman wrote some new material for the 1969 film version of *Sweet Charity*; its soundtrack album spent nearly five months in the charts. They next worked on a musical based on the life of Eleanor Roosevelt that was never produced, but in 1973 they got to Broadway with *Seesaw*, which ran 296 performances. A year later Fields died of a heart attack at 69. In 1979 many of her songs with Jimmy McHugh were featured in the Broadway revue *Sugar Babies*, which ran 1,208 performances.

WORKS (only works for which Fields was a primary credited lyricist are listed): **MUSICALS/REVUES** (dates refer to N.Y. openings): *Blackbirds of 1928* (May 9, 1928); *Hello, Daddy!* (Dec. 26, 1928); *Ziegfeld Midnight Frolic* (Feb. 6, 1929); *Ziegfeld Midnight Frolic* (second edition) (1929); *The International Revue* (Feb. 25, 1930); *The Vanderbilt Revue* (Nov. 5, 1930); *Singin' the Blues* (Sept. 16, 1931); *Stars in Your Eyes* (Feb. 9, 1939); *Up in Central Park* (Jan. 27, 1945); *Arms and the Girl* (Feb. 2, 1950); *A Tree Grows in Brooklyn* (April 19, 1951); *By the Beautiful Sea* (April 8, 1954); *Redhead* (Feb. 5, 1959); *Sweet Charity* (Jan. 30, 1966); *Seesaw* (March 18, 1973); *Sugar Babies* (Oct. 9, 1979). **FILMS:** *Love in the Rough* (1930); *The Cuban Love Song* (1931); *Flying High* (1931); *Meet the Baron* (1933); *Hooray for Love* (1935); *Every Night at Eight* (1935); *I Dream Too Much* (1935); *In Person* (1935); *The King Steps Out* (1936); *Swing Time* (1936); *When You're in Love* (1937); *Joy of Living* (1938); *One Night in the Tropics* (1940); *Up in Central Park* (1948); *Excuse My Dust* (1951); *Texas Carnival* (1951); *Mr. Imperium* (1951); *The Farmer Takes a Wife* (1953); *Sweet Charity* (1969). **TELEVISION:** *Junior Miss* (CBS, Dec. 20, 1957).

BIBL.: D. Winer, *On the Sunny Side of the Street: The Life and Lyrics of D. F.* (N.Y., 1997).—**WR**

Fiévet, Paul, French composer; b. Valenciennes, Dec. 11, 1892; d. Paris, March 15, 1980. His father, Claude Fiévet (1865–1938), was a composer. Paul Fiévet studied piano and music theory at the Paris Cons., where he was a student of Xavier Leroux, Caussade, and Widor, obtaining 1st prize in harmony in 1913, and

1st prize in composition in 1917, 1918, and 1919. He received the Grand Prix International in Ostende in 1931 and the Grand Prix of Paris in 1932. Among his works are an operetta, *Le Joli Jeu* (Lyons, 1933), and several symphonic suites of the type of "landscape music," e.g., *Les Horizons dorés* (Paris, 1932), *Puerta del Sol* (Paris, 1933), *Images de France* (Paris, 1964), *Orient* (Paris, 1929), and *En hiver*. He also wrote several string quartets (one of which he whimsically entitled *Sputnik*), a Brass Sextet, and numerous choruses and piano pieces. —**NS/LK/DM**

Fifth Dimension, The, one of the more popular black vocal groups of the late 1960s and early 1970s. **MEMBERSHIP:** Lamonte McLemore (b. St. Louis, Mo., Sept. 17, 1939); Marilyn McCoo (b. Jersey City, N.J., Sept. 30, 1943); Billy Davis Jr. (b. St. Louis, Mo., June 26, 1940); Florence LaRue (b. Philadelphia, Feb. 4, 1944); Ron Townson (b. St. Louis, Mo., Jan. 20, 1941).

Lamonte McLemore formed the vocal group The Hi-Fi's in Los Angeles during the mid-1960s with Marilyn McCoo, Floyd Butler, and Harry Elston. They toured with the Ray Charles Revue for six months and when they broke up, two new groups were formed. Butler and Elston eventually formed The Friends of Distinction, who scored smash pop and rhythm-and-blues hits with a vocal version of Hugh Masakela's "Grazing in the Grass" and "Love or Let Me Be Lonely," in 1969 and 1970, respectively. McLemore and McCoo formed The Versatiles with Florence LaRue, Ron Townson, and McLemore's cousin, Billy Davis Jr. Davis had formed his first group while still in high school and later served with The Emeralds and The St. Louis Gospel Singers. Signed to Johnny Rivers's Soul City Records in 1966, they soon changed their name to The Fifth Dimension.

The Fifth Dimension's debut album yielded a major pop hit with John Phillips's "Go Where You Wanna Go" and a near-smash with Jimmy Webb's "Up, Up and Away," a tame recording somehow identified with psychedelic music. Their second album consisted almost entirely of Jimmy Webb songs. During 1968, the group scored a smash pop and rhythm-and-blues hit with Laura Nyro's "Stoned Soul Picnic" and major pop hits with Nyro's "Sweet Blindness" and Nicholas Ashford and Valerie Simpson's "California Soul." The following year, they had top pop hits with the medley "Aquarius/Let the Sun Shine In" (a smash R&B hit) from the Broadway musical *Hair* and Nyro's "Wedding Bell Blues," and major pop hits with "Blowing Away" and Neil Sedaka's "Workin' on a Groovy Thing."

In 1970, The Fifth Dimension switched to Bell Records, managing a major hit with Nyro's "Save the Country" and a pop and rhythm-and-blues smash with "One Less Bell to Answer," written by Burt Bacharach and Hal David. By the early 1970s, The Fifth Dimension were established on the supper club circuit. They achieved their final (near-smash) hits with "(Last Night) I Didn't Get to Sleep at All" and "If I Could Reach You" in 1972. With McLemore, Townson, and LaRue as mainstays, The Fifth Dimension moved to ABC, then Motown, while continuing to tour the supper club circuit. In 1995, the group recorded their first album in 16 years.

Married in 1969, Marilyn McCoo and Billy Davis Jr., left The Fifth Dimension in November 1975. They scored a top pop and rhythm-and-blues hit with "You Don't Have to Be a Star (To Be in My Show)" and a near-smash hit in both fields with "Your Love." They hosted their own summer CBS-TV variety show in 1977, yet McCoo went solo in 1978, launching her own supper club career while hosting the television show Solid Gold from 1981 to 1984. She later appeared in the soap opera Days of Our Lives and, in 1991, recorded an album of contemporary gospel music, The Me Nobody Knows.

DISC.: The F. D.: Up, Up and Away (1967); The Magic Garden (1967); Stoned Soul Picnic (1968); The Age of Aquarius (1969); Greatest Hits (1970); The July 5th Album (1970); Portrait (1970); Love's Lines, Angles and Rhymes (1971); Live! (1971); Reflections (1971); Individually and Collectively (1972); Living Together, Growing Together (1973); Soul and Inspiration (1975); Earthbound (1975); Star Dancing (1978); High on Sunshine (1979); The F. D. Is in the House (1995). **MARILYN MCCOO AND BILLY DAVIS JR.:** I Hope We Get to Love in Time (1976); Two of Us (1977); Marilyn and Billy (1978). **MARILYN MCCOO:** The Me Nobody Knows (1991).—**BH**

Figner, Medea, famous Italian-Russian mezzo-soprano, later soprano; b. Florence, April 3, 1858; d. Paris, July 8, 1952. She studied voice with Bianchi, Carozzi-Zucchi, and Panofka in Florence. She made her debut as Azucena in Sinalunga, near Florence, in 1875; then sang in the opera theaters of Florence. From 1877 to 1887 she toured in Italy, Spain, and South America; she met **Nikolai (Nikolaievich) Figner** during her travels, and followed him to Russia; after their marriage in 1889, she appeared under the name Medea Mei-Figner; they were divorced in 1903. She became extremely successful on the Russian operatic stage, and was a member of the Maryinsky Imperial Opera Theater in St. Petersburg from 1887 until 1912. She then devoted herself mainly to voice teaching. Her voice was described by critics as engagingly soft, rich, "velvety," and "succulent." She could sing soprano roles as impressively as those in the mezzo-soprano range. She was fortunate in having been coached by Tchaikovsky in the role of Liza in his opera The Queen of Spades, which she sang at its premiere in St. Petersburg (Dec. 19, 1890); her husband sang the role of her lover in the same opera. Her other successful roles were Tosca, Mimi, Donna Anna, Elsa, Brünnhilde, Marguerite, Desdemona, Aida, Amneris, and Carmen. She publ. a book of memoirs (St. Petersburg, 1912). —**NS/LK/DM**

Figner, Nikolai (Nikolaievich), celebrated Russian tenor; b. Nikiforovka, Feb. 21, 1857; d. Kiev, Dec. 13, 1918. He was a lieutenant in the Russian navy before deciding upon a career in music, then studied voice with Prianishnikov and Everardi in St. Petersburg (1881–82), and with De Roxas in Naples, where he made his operatic debut at the Teatro Sannazaro in Gounod's Philémon et Baucis in 1882. After singing in various Italian cities and in Latin America, he was a leading member of the Maryinsky Imperial Opera Theater in St. Petersburg (1887–1907). He made his debut at Covent Garden in London on May 26, 1887, as the Duke in Rigoletto. After singing in private Russian theaters

(1907–10), he served as director of the Narodny Dom in St. Petersburg (1910–15). He was married to **Medea Figner** (1889–1903), who described their careers in her memoirs (St. Petersburg, 1912). He was the favorite tenor of Tchaikovsky and was selected to create the roles of Hermann in The Queen of Spades (Dec. 19, 1890) and Count Vaudemont in Yolanta (Dec. 18, 1892) at their St. Petersburg premieres. His other roles included Lensky, Otello, Don José, Faust, Radames, Werther, Lohengrin, and Roméo.

BIBL.: L. Kutateladse, N. F.: Recollections, Letters, Materials (Leningrad, 1968).—**NS/LK/DM**

Figulus (real name, **Töpfer**), **Wolfgang,** German composer and writer on music; b. Naumburg an der Saale, c. 1525; d. Meissen, Sept. 1589. He was cantor in Lübben, Lower Austria (1545–46) before pursuing his education at the univs. of Frankfurt an der Oder (1547) and Leipzig (1548). From 1549 to 1551 he was cantor at the Leipzig Thomaskirche, and he also taught music at the Univ. of Leipzig. He then was cantor and teacher at the Fürstenschule and at the church of St. Afra in Meissen from 1551 to 1588.

WRITINGS: Elementa musica (1555; aug. ed., Nuremberg, 1565 as Libri primi musicae practicae elementa brevissima); Deutsche Musica und Gesängbuchlein (Nuremberg, 1560; aug. ed. of M. Agricola's Ein Sangbuchlein aller Sontags Evangelein, 1541); De musica practica liber primus (Nuremberg, 1565).

WORKS: Precationes aliquot musicis numeris for 3 Voices (Leipzig, 1553); Tricinia sacra ad voces pueriles for 3 Voices (Nuremberg, 1559); Cantionum sacrarum...primi toni decas prima for 4 to 6 and 8 Voices (Frankfurt an der Oder, 1575); Vetera nova carmina sacra et selecta de natali Domini...a diversis musicis composita for 4 Voices (Frankfurt an der Oder, 1575); Hymni sacri et scholastici cum melodiis (c. 1580; aug. ed., Leipzig, 1594; new ed., 1604).—**NS/LK/DM**

Figuš-Bystrý, Viliam, Slovak composer; b. Banská Bystrica, Feb. 28, 1875; d. there, May 11, 1937. He spent many years collecting Slovak folk melodies, which he publ. in 5 vols. (1906–15) for voice and piano; he also publ. a collection of 1,000 arranged for piano only (1925–31). He further wrote an opera, Detvan (1924; Bratislava, Aug. 1, 1928), a cantata, Slovenská Piesen (1913), an orch. suite, From My Youth, piano quartet, piano trio, 3 violin sonatines, other violin pieces, piano works, choruses, and songs.—**NS/LK/DM**

Filiasi, Lorenzo, Italian composer; b. Naples, March 25, 1878; d. Rome, July 30, 1963. He studied at the Conservatorio di S. Pietro a Majella in Naples with Nicola d'Arienzo. His first success came with the opera Manuel Menendez (Milan, May 15, 1904), which won the Sonzogno Competition Prize in 1902. His other operas included Fior di Neve (Milan, April 1, 1911) and Messidoro (1912). He also wrote a pantomime, Pierrot e Bluette (1895), La preghiera del marinaio italiano for Chorus and Orch., Visioni romantiche for Orch., violin pieces, and many songs.—**NS/LK/DM**

Filippi, Filippo, Italian writer on music and composer; b. Vicenza, Jan. 13, 1830; d. Milan, June 24, 1887.

He studied law at Padua, taking his degree in 1853. In 1851 he began his career as a music critic with a warm defense of Verdi's *Rigoletto*. From 1859 until 1862 he was ed. of the *Gazzetta Musicale*, and from 1859 to 1862 music critic of the newly founded *Perseveranza* and then its ed. (1862–87). He publ. a collection of essays on great musicians, *Musica e musicisti* (Milan, 1876). As a zealous Wagnerite, he wrote a pamphlet, *Riccardo Wagner* (in German, as *Richard Wagner: Eine musikalische Reise in das Reich der Zukunft*, 1876); also publ. a monograph, *Della vita e delle opere di Adolfo Fumagalli* (Milan, 1857). Among his compositions were a String Quintet, 9 string quartets, piano trio, piano pieces, and songs.—NS/LK/DM

Filleul, Henry, French composer; b. Laval, May 11, 1877; d. Saint-Omer, May 1, 1959. He studied at the Paris Cons. with Lavignac and Casadesus. In 1908 he became director of the École Nationale de Musique at St. Omer.

WORKS: *Le Jugement de Triboulet*, comic opera (1923); 5 oratorios: *Le Christ vainqueur* (1925), *Le Miracle de Lourdes* (1927), *Les Doulces Joyes de Nostre Dame* (1928), *Jeanne d'Arc* (1929), and *Eva* (1931); *Variations symphoniques sur un thème languedocien* (1939); *Fantaisie concertante* for Piano and Orch. (1950); Cello Concerto; violin pieces, with organ; motets; men's choruses.

BIBL.: *Hommage à Henri F.* (St. Omer, 1952).—NS/LK/DM

Fillmore, (James) Henry (Jr.), American bandmaster and composer; b. Cincinnati, Feb. 3, 1881; d. Miami, Fla., Dec. 7, 1956. His paternal grandfather was August Damerin Fillmore (2nd cousin of President Millard Fillmore); his father, James Henry Fillmore, and his uncles Fred A. and Charles M. Fillmore were the founders of the Cincinnati music publishing firm of Fillmore Bros. Co. Henry Fillmore was educated at the Miami (Ohio) Military Inst., and later at the Cincinnati Coll. of Music. As a bandmaster, he led the Syrian Shrine Band of Cincinnati to national prominence in the period from 1920 to 1926, making several transcontinental tours. In 1915 he founded the Fillmore Band, which was one of the earliest bands to make regular radio broadcasts (1927–34). In 1938 he moved to Miami, Fla., where he conducted bands at the Orange Bowl. He is best known, however, as the composer of numerous popular marches (*Americans We, Men of Ohio, His Honor* et al.), second only to Sousa's in their tuneful liveliness. He was also the leading proponent of the "trombone smear," a humorous effect of the trombone glissando. He used numerous pseudonyms in his publ. pieces (**Al Hayes, Harry Hartley, Ray Hall, Gus Beans, Henrietta Moore,** and **Harold Bennett,** under which name he publ. the popular *Military Escort March*). He was also a compiler of sacred songs and tune books. In 1956 he received an honorary D.M.A. degree from the Univ. of Miami (Fla.).

BIBL.: P. Bierley, *Hallelujah Trombone: The Story of H. F.* (Columbus, Ohio, 1982); idem, *The Music of H. F. and Will Huff* (Columbus, Ohio, 1982).—NS/LK/DM

Fillmore, John Comfort, American music educator; b. Franklin, Conn., Feb. 4, 1843; d. Norwich, Conn., Aug. 14, 1898. He was a pupil of G.W. Steele at Oberlin Coll. in Ohio, then at the Leipzig Cons.

(1865–67). He was director of the music dept. at Oberlin Coll. (1867–68), Ripon Coll. in Wisc. (1868–78), and Milwaukee Coll. for Women (1878–84). In 1844 he founded the Milwaukee School of Music, of which he was director until 1895, when he took charge of the School of Music of Pomona Coll. in Claremont, Calif.

WRITINGS: *Pianoforte Music: Its History, with Biographical Sketches and Critical Estimates of Its Greatest Masters* (Chicago, 1883); *New Lessons in Harmony* (Philadelphia, 1887); *Lessons in Music History* (Philadelphia, 1888); *A Study of Omaha Indian Music* (with Alice C. Fletcher and F. La Flesche, 1893). —NS/LK/DM

Filtsch, Karl (actually, **Károly**), precocious Hungarian pianist and composer; b. Mühlbach, May 28, 1830; d. Venice, May 11, 1845. He studied with his father and made his first public appearance at the age of 5 in Koloszvár. After further studies in Vienna, he gave concerts there and in Budapest in 1841 before completing his training in Paris with Chopin and Liszt (1841–43). Chopin considered Filtsch to be a talent of great promise, and the young virtuoso championed the music of his mentor. He played in Paris and in London in 1843, then in Vienna in 1843–44 before the ravages of tuberculosis overcame him. Some of his piano pieces were publ.—LK/DM

Filtz, (Johann) Anton, German cellist and composer; b. Eichstätt (baptized), Sept. 22, 1733; d. Mannheim (buried), March 14, 1760. He studied with J. Stamitz in Mannheim. In 1754 he became 2nd cellist in the orch. of the Palatine court. His extensive output included about 60 syms., concertos for various instruments, and a large body of chamber music.—NS/LK/DM

Finazzi, Filippo, Italian castrato soprano and composer; b. Bergamo, c. 1706; d. Jersbeck, near Hamburg, April 21, 1776. After singing in Venice in 1726, he was a member of the Italian Opera in Breslau (1728–30). By 1732 he was again in Venice and by 1739 he was in the service of the Duke of Modena. In 1743 he joined Pietro Mingotti's opera company in Linz, and then was active with it in Hamburg in 1743–44. Thereafter he worked with the company mainly as a composer, giving his last public appearance as a singer in his own opera *Temistocle* (Hamburg, Feb. 16, 1746). After a decade of teaching, he retired to his country estate in Jersbeck. In 1762 a special decree of the Hamburg Senate allowed him to marry his housekeeper. Among his publ. works were 6 Sinfonien (Hamburg, 1754).—NS/LK/DM

Finck, Heinrich, German composer, great-uncle of **Hermann Finck;** b. probably in Bamberg, 1444 or 1445; d. Vienna, June 9, 1527. He grew up in Poland. He was educated at the Univ. of Leipzig (matriculated in 1482). He was in the service of Prince Alexander of Vilnius, Lithuania, as Kapellmeister by 1498, and continued in his service when Alexander became king of Poland in 1501, being active at the court in Krakow until at least 1505. He left Poland in 1510, and then was Singemeister at the ducal Kapelle in Stuttgart until 1514; he subsequently served the court in Augsburg until being appointed composer of the cathedral chapter in Salzburg in 1519. On Jan. 1, 1527, he formally assumed the position of Hofkapellmeister to the court in Vienna. A large portion of his output has not survived; 113 pieces are known to be by him, some incomplete. Among his works are 7 masses, 40 motets, motet cycles for the Proper of the Mass, 28 hymns, 38 songs, and instrumental pieces. See L. Hoffmann-Erbrecht, ed., *Heinrich Finck: Ausgewählte Werke*, I, in Das Erbe Deutscher Musik (1962).

BIBL.: L. Hoffmann-Erbrecht, *Henricus F., musicus excellentissimus (1445–1527)* (Cologne, 1982).—**NS/LK/DM**

Finck, Henry T(heophilus),

prominent American music critic and editor; b. Bethel, Mo., Sept. 22, 1854; d. Rumford Falls, Maine, Oct. 1, 1926. He was brought up in Ore., then entered Harvard Univ., where he studied with J.K. Paine. After graduation in 1876 he went to Germany. He studied comparative psychology in Berlin and Vienna, and publ. a book, *Romantic Love and Personal Beauty* (1887), propounding a theory that romantic love was unknown to the ancient nations. He was music critic of the *N.Y. Evening Post* and the *Nation* from 1881 to 1924, and occasionally wrote for other journals. Finck was a brilliant journalist. In his books on music he stressed the personal and psychological elements. He married the pianist Abbie Cushman in 1890; a fine literary stylist, she succeeded in copying her husband's style and even wrote music reviews for him.

WRITINGS: *Chopin, and Other Musical Essays* (1889); *Wagner and His Works* (2 vols., 1893; reprinted 1968); with others, *Anton Seidl: A Memorial by His Friends* (1899); *Songs and Song Writers* (1900); *Edvard Grieg* (1906); *Grieg and His Music* (1909); *Success in Music and How It Is Won* (1909); *Massenet and His Operas* (1910); *Richard Strauss* (1917); *Musical Progress* (1923).—**NS/LK/DM**

Finck, Hermann,

German organist, music theorist, and composer, great-nephew of **Heinrich Finck**; b. Pirna, Saxony, March 21, 1527; d. Wittenberg, Dec. 28, 1558. He was educated at the court chapel of King Ferdinand I of Hungary and Bohemia, and also studied at Wittenberg Univ. (1545), where he then taught music (1554). He was appointed town organist in 1557. His major work is the treatise *Practica musica* (1556).

BIBL.: P. Matzdorf, *Die Practica musica H. Fs* (Frankfurt am Main, 1957); F. Kirby, *H. F.'s Practica musica: A Comparative Study in 16th Century German Musical Theory* (diss., Yale Univ., 1957).—**NS/LK/DM**

Findeisen, Nikolai (Fyodorovich),

Russian music historian and editor; b. St. Petersburg, July 23, 1868; d. there (Leningrad), Sept. 20, 1928. He studied with Nicolai Sokolov. In 1893 he founded the *Russian Musical Gazette* and remained its ed. until it ceased publication in 1917. His writings include monographs on Verstovsky (1890), Serov (1900; 2nd ed., aug., 1904), Dargomyzhsky (1902), Anton Rubinstein (1905), and Rimsky-Korsakov (1908). He also publ. a series of brochures and books on Glinka: the first vol. of a projected large biography, *Glinka in Spain*, appeared in 1896; a catalog of Glinka's MSS, letters, and portraits was publ. in 1898; and he also ed. Glinka's correspondence (2 vols., 1907–08). Findeisen's major achievement was the extensive history of Russian music up to the year 1800, publ. in 2 vols. (partly posth.) in Leningrad (1928–29), under the title *Sketches of Music in Russia from the Most Ancient Times until the End of the 18th Century.*—**NS/LK/DM**

Fine, Irving (Gifford),

remarkable American composer and teacher; b. Boston, Dec. 3, 1914; d. there, Aug. 23, 1962. He studied piano with Frances Glover in Boston (1924–35) ad pursued training in composition with Hill and Piston at Harvard Univ. (B.A., 1937; M.A., 1938) and with Boulanger in Cambridge, Mass., and Paris (1938–39). From 1939 to 1945 he was asst. conductor of the Harvard Glee Club. He taught in the music dept. at Harvard Univ. from 1939 to 1950, and also taught composition at the Berkshire Music Center at Tanglewood (summers, 1946–57). From 1950 util his death he taught theory and composition at Brandeis Univ., where he was the Walter W. Naumburg Prof. of Music and chairman of the School of Creative Arts. In 1949 he won the N.Y. Music Critics' Circle Award for his *Partita* for Wind Quintet. In 1949–50 he was in Paris on a Fulbright research fellowship. He held Guggenheim fellowships in 1951–52 and 1958–59. O Aug. 12, 1962, he conducted a performance of his *Symphony 1962* with the Boston Sym. Orch. at the Berkshire Music Center. He succumbed to a heart attack just 11 days later. Fine was at first influenced by the music of Stravinsky and Hindemith, which led him to adopt a cosmopolitan style of composition in which contrapuntal elaboration and energetic rhythms were his main concern. He later developed a distinctive personal style, marked by a lyrical flow of cohesive melody supported by lucid polyphony.

WORKS: ORCH.: *Toccata Concertante* (1947; Boston, Oct. 22, 1948); *Notturno* for Strings and Harp (1950–51; Boston, March 28, 1951); *Serious Song: A Lament* for Strings (Louisville, Nov. 16, 1955); *Blue Towers* (1959; Boston, May 31, 1960); *Diversions* (1959–60; Boston, Nov. 5, 1960); *Symphony 1962* (Boston, March 23, 1962). **CHAMBER:** Violin Sonata (1946; N.Y., Feb. 9, 1947); *Partita* for Wind Quintet (1948; N.Y., Feb. 19, 1949); String Quartet (1952; N.Y., Feb. 18, 1953); *Fantasia* for String Trio (1959); *Romanza* for Wind Quintet (1959; Washingto, D.C., Feb. 1, 1963); *One, Two, Buckle My Shoe* for Oboe, Clarinet, Violin, and Cello (WGBH-TV, Boston, Nov. 3, 1959). **KEYBOARD: Piano:** *Music* (1947; Boston, Nov. 19, 1948); didactic pieces: *Victory March of the Elephants* (1956), *Lullaby for a Baby Panda* (1956), and *Homage à Mozart* (1956). **VOCAL:** 3 *Choruses from Alice in Wonderland* for Chorus and Piano (1942; Cambridge, Mass., March 4, 1943; also for Chorus and Orch., Worcester, Mass., Oct. 1949); *The Choral New Yorker* for Chorus and Piano Obbligato (1944; Cambridge, Mass., Jan. 25, 1945); *A Short Alleluia* for Women's Voices (1945); *Hymn "In Grato Jubilo"* for Women's Voices and Small Orch. (Boston, May 2, 1949); *The Hour-Glass* for Chorus (1949; Boston, May 1, 1952); *Mutability*, 6 songs for Mezzo-soprano and Piano (N.Y., Nov. 28, 1952); *An Old Song* for Chorus (1953; Cambridge, Mass., March 1954); 3 *Choruses from Alice in Wonderland* for Women's Voices and Piano (1953; Bradford, Mass., April 1954); *Childhood Fables for Grown-ups* for Medium Voice and Piano (set 1, 1954, N.Y., Feb. 20, 1956; set 2, 1955); *McCord's Menagerie* for Men's Voices (1957; Cambridge, Mass., June 9, 1958).—**NS/LK/DM**

Fine, Vivian, American composer, teacher, and pianist; b. Chicago, Sept. 28, 1913; d. Bennington, Vt., March 20, 2000. She became a scholarship student in piano at the age of 5 at the Chicago Musical Coll.; she studied piano with Djane Lavoie-Herz, harmony and composition with Ruth Crawford and Adolf Weidig, and composition with Cowell; in 1931 she went to N.Y., where she studied piano with Whiteside, composition with Sessions, and orchestration with Szell; she also appeared as a pianist. She held teaching positions at N.Y. Univ. (1945–48), the Juilliard School of Music in N.Y. (1948), the State Univ. of N.Y. at Potsdam (1951), the Conn. Coll. School of Dance (1963–64), and Bennington (Vt.) Coll. (1964–87). In 1980 she received a Guggenheim fellowship and was elected to the American Academy and Inst. of Arts and Letters. She was particularly adept at writing vocal and instrumental works in a dissonant but acceptable style. In 1935 she married the sculptor Benjamin Karp.

WORKS: DRAMATIC: T h e a t e r : *The Race of Life* (1937; N.Y., Jan. 23, 1938); *Opus 51* (Bennington, Vt., Aug. 6, 1938); *Tragic Exodus* (N.Y., Feb. 16, 1939); *They Too Are Exiles* (1939; N.Y., Jan. 7, 1940); *Alcestis* (N.Y., April 29, 1960); *My Son, My Enemy* (New London, Conn., Aug. 15, 1965). O p e r a : *The Women in the Garden* (1977; San Francisco, Feb. 12, 1978). ORCH.: *Elegiac Song* for Strings (1937; Lenox, Mass., Aug. 8, 1971); *Concertante* for Piano and Orch. (1944); *Romantic Ode* for Violin, Viola, Cello, and String Orch. (Bennington, Vt., Aug. 28, 1976); *Drama for Orchestra* (1982; San Francisco, Jan. 5, 1983); *Poetic Fires* for Piano and Orch. (1984; N.Y., Feb. 21, 1985, composer soloist); *Dancing Winds* (1987); *After the Tradition* for Chamber Orch. (1988). CHAMBER: String Trio (1930); *Prelude* for String Quartet (1937); *Capriccio* for Oboe and String Trio (1946); Violin Sonata (1952); String Quartet (1957); *3 Pieces* for Flute, Bassoon, and Harp (1961); *Dreamscape* for 3 Flutes, Cello, Piano, and Percussion Ensemble (1964); Chamber Concerto for Solo Cello, Oboe, Violin, Viola, Cello, Double Bass, and Piano (1966); Quintet for String Trio, Trumpet, and Harp (1967); Brass Quintet (1978); Piano Trio (1980); Quintet for Oboe, Clarinet, Violin, Cello, and Piano (1984); Cello Sonata (1986); also piano pieces; other works for solo instruments. VOCAL: *The Great Wall of China* for Medium Voice, 2 Violins, Viola, and Cello (1947); *Psalm 13* for Baritone, Women's Chorus, and Piano or Organ (1953); *Valedictions* for Soprano, Tenor, Chorus, and 10 Instruments (1959); *Epitaph* for Chorus and Orch. (1967; Bennington, Vt., Nov. 5, 1983); *Sounds of the Nightingale* for Soprano, Women's Chorus, and Nonet (1971); *Meeting for Equal Rights, 1866* for Soprano, Baritone, Narrator, Chorus, and Orch. (N.Y., April 23, 1976); *3 Sonnets* for Baritone and Orch. (Bennington, Vt., Dec. 12, 1976); *Ode to Purcell* for Medium Voice and String Quartet (1984).

BIBL.: H. Von Gunden, *The Music of V. F.* (Lanham, Md., 1999).—NS/LK/DM

Finger, Gottfried, Moravian composer; b. probably in Olomouc, c. 1660; d. Mannheim (buried), Aug. 31, 1730. After traveling in Italy, he made his way to England, where he was an instrumentalist in the Roman Catholic chapel of King James II (1687–88). He subsequently was active as a composer of incidental music for the London stage, and also wrote operas. He left England in 1704, in 1706 entering the service of Duke Karl Philipp of Neuburg in Breslau, where he remained until 1723.

WORKS: DRAMATIC: O p e r a : *The Rival Queens, or The Death of Alexander* (also known as *Alexander the Great*; London, 1696 or 1703; with D. Purcell); *The Virgin Prophetess, or The Fate of Troy* (London, May 15, 1701); *Der Sieg der Schönheit über die Helden* (Berlin, 1706; in collaboration with Greber and Stricker; not extant). I n c i d e n t a l M u s i c : To plays by Congreve, Dryden, Shakespeare, Cibber, and others; masques, odes, and serenades. OTHER: Much instrumental music, including numerous sonatas.—NS/LK/DM

Fink, Christian, German organist and composer; b. Dettingen, Aug. 9, 1822; d. Esslingen, near Stuttgart, Sept. 5, 1911. He studied at the Leipzig Cons., where he became organist (1856–60). In 1863 was appointed church organist at Esslingen. He publ. numerous organ works. Fink was greatly esteemed in Germany, where his choral works and organ pieces were often performed.—NS/LK/DM

Fink, (Christian) Gottfried Wilhelm, German writer on music, editor, and theologian; b. Sulza, Thuringia, March 8, 1783; d. Leipzig, Aug. 27, 1846. He studied theology (later took holy orders) and history in Leipzig. In 1808 he became a contributor to the *Allgemeine Musikalische Zeitung*, serving as its ed. (1828–41). He also taught at the Leipzig Cons. (1838–43), where he was director in 1842. In his music criticism, he opposed the Romantic inclinations of Schumann and his contemporaries. He contributed many articles to various German reference works, and also left unfinished a history of music.

BIBL.: K.-E. Eicke, *Der Streit zwischen A.B. Marx und G.W. F. um die Kompositionslehre* (Regensburg, 1966).—NS/LK/DM

Fink, Michael Jon, American composer, performer, and teacher; b. Los Angeles, Dec. 7, 1954. He studied composition at the Calif. Inst. of the Arts with Budd, Kraft, Childs, and Powell (B.F.A., 1976; M.F.A., 1980). He performed with the Negative Band and Stillife. In 1982 he joined the faculty of the Calif. Inst. of the Arts. In 1985 he was composer-in-residence at Northern Mich. Univ. His music is unusually spare and quiet and meticulously crafted, achieving a graceful sense of timelessness. Among his compositions are *2 Pieces* for piano (1983), an untitled work for small orch. (1986), *Living to Be Hunted by the Moon* for clarinet, bass clarinet, and electronics (1987), *A Temperament for Angels* for computer-controlled electronics and 3 electronic keyboards (1989), *Sound Shroud Garden*, sound installation (with Jim Fox; 1989), *Epitaph* for bass clarinet (1990), *Thread of Summer* for clarinet and string quartet (1990), *Spring Steps Into Darkness* for bass clarinet and orch. (1992), *Mind of Winter* for soprano saxophone and orch. (1994), and *Temptation to Flower* for 18 players (1995). He publ. *Inside the Music Business: Music in Contemporary Life* (N.Y., 1989).—NS/LK/DM

Fink, Myron S(amuel), American composer; b. Chicago, April 19, 1932. He received training from Borowski and Castelnuovo-Tedesco, and studied at the Juilliard School of Music in N.Y. with Wagenaar and at the Univ. of Ill. with Burrill Phillips. He was awarded a

Woodrow Wilson Memorial Fellowship and studied with Robert Palmer at Cornell Univ. (1954–55) before completing his training on a Fulbright Scholarship in Vienna (1955–56). Fink subsequently taught at Alma Coll., Hunter Coll., the Curtis Inst. of Music in Philadelphia, the State Univ. of N.Y. at Purchase, and the City Univ. of N.Y. Graduate Center. He wrote the operas *The Boor* (St. Louis, Feb. 14, 1955), *Susanna and the Elders* (1955), *Jeremiah* (Binghamton, N.Y., May 25, 1962), *Judith and Holofernes* (concert perf., Purchase, N.Y., Feb. 4, 1978), *Chinchilla* (Binghamton, N.Y., Jan. 18, 1986), *The Island of Tomorrow* (N.Y., June 19, 1986), and *The Conquistador* (San Diego, March 1, 1997).—NS/LK/DM

Finke, Fidelio F(ritz or Friedrich), German composer and pedagogue; b. Josefsthal, near Gablonz, Bohemia, Oct. 22, 1891; d. Dresden, June 12, 1968. He studied with his father and with his uncle, Romeo Finke, director of the German Academy of Music in Prague, and then attended Novák's master classes in composition at the Prague Cons. (1908–11). He joined its faculty as a teacher of theory and piano in 1915, becoming a prof. in 1926; he also was national inspector of the German music schools in Czechoslovakia (1920–38) and head of the master classes in composition at the German Academy of Music in Prague (1927–45). After serving as director and as a teacher of a master class in composition at the Dresden Akademie für Musik und Theater (1946–51), he was a prof. of composition at the Leipzig Hochschule für Musik (1951–59). His works evolved from German classicism to the exploration of the Second Viennese School and neo-Classicism before embracing a readily accessible style.

WORKS: DRAMATIC: O p e r a : *Die versunkene Glocke* (1915–18); *Die Jakobsfahrt* (Prague, Oct. 17, 1936); *Der schlagfertige Liebhaber* (1950–54); *Der Zauberfisch* (Dresden, June 3, 1960). **D a n c e P a n t o m i m e :** *Lied der Zeit* (1946). **ORCH.:** *Eine Schauspiel-Ouvertüre* (1908); 8 suites: No. 1 for Strings (1911), No. 2 (1948), No. 3 (1949), No. 4 for 16 Winds and Percussion (1953), No. 5 for Winds (1955), No. 6 (1956), No. 7 (1961), and No. 8 for 5 Winds, 2 Pianos, and Strings (1961); *Pan*, sym. (1919); Piano Concerto (1930); *Concerto for Orchestra* (1931); *Divertimento* for Chamber Orch. (1964); *Festliche Musik* (1965). **C H A M B E R :** Piano Quintet (1911); 5 string quartets (1914–64); Piano Trio (1923); Violin Sonata (1924); Sonata for Solo Cello (1926); Flute Sonata (1927); Sonata for 4 Recorders (1936); *100 Stücke* for Recorder (1936); Sonata for Solo Harp (1945); Horn Sonata (1946); Clarinet Sonata (1949); Viola Sonata (1954); Wind Quintet (1955); piano pieces; organ music. **VOCAL:** *Deutsche Kantate* for Soprano, Bass, Chorus, Boy's Chorus, Organ, and Orch. (1940); *Eros*, cantata for Soprano, Tenor, and Orch. (1966); songs.

BIBL.: D. Härtwig, *F.F. F.: Leben und Werk* (Habilitationsschrift, Univ. of Leipzig, 1970).—NS/LK/DM

Finko, David, Russian-born American composer and teacher; b. Leningrad, May 15, 1936. He received training in piano and violin at the Rimsky-Korsakov School of Performing Arts in Leningrad (1950–55; 1956–58). After graduating from the Leningrad Inst. of Naval Architecture (1959), he studied composition and theory (1960–65) and conducting (with Musin, 1970–79) at the Leningrad Cons. He then emigrated to the U.S.

and became a naturalized American citizen in 1986. After lecturing at the Univ. of Pa. in Philadelphia (1980–84), he was an adjunct prof. of music there (1986–92). He also was composer-in-residence at the Univ. of Tex. in El Paso (1981–84) and a faculty member of the Combs Coll. of Music in Philadelphia (1984–90), Swarthmore Coll. (1987), Gratz Coll. (1990–91), and Yale Univ. (1991–92). In 1981 he founded Dako Publishers in Philadelphia. He frequently appeared as a pianist, violinist, and conductor of his own works. His music reflects his Jewish heritage and is set in a modern style but not without melodic overtones.

WORKS: DRAMATIC: O p e r a : *Polinka* (1965); *That Song* (1970; rev. 1991); *The Enchanted Tailor* (1983–93); *The Klezmers* (1989); *The Kabbalists* (1990); *Abraham and Hanna* (1993); *The Woman is a Devil* (1993; Philadelphia, July 15, 1995); *At the Ocean Bottom* (1999). **ORCH.:** *The Holocaust*, tone poem (1965; rev. 1985); 2 syms. (1969, 1972); Piano Concerto (1971); Viola Concerto (1971); Concerto for Violin, Viola, and Orch. (1973); *Russia*, tone poem (1974; rev. 1990); Concerto for Viola, Double Bass, and Orch. (1975); Harp Concerto (1976); Concerto for Viola d'Amore, Guitar, and Orch. (1977); *The Wailing Wall*, tone poem (1983); Concerto for 3 Violins and Orch. (1984); Violin Concerto (1988); Concerto Grosso for Flute, Oboe, Bassoon, Percussion, and Strings (1994). **C H A M B E R :** *Mourning Music* for Violin, Viola, and Cello (1968); *Lamentations of Jeremiah* for Violin (1969); *Dithyramb* for Viola and Organ (1974); *Fromm Septet* for Oboe, Clarinet, Bass Clarinet, Violin, Cello, Double Bass, and Percussion (1981); *Triptych for Three* for Violin, Marimba, and Piano (1999). **KEYBOARD: P i a n o :** *Fantasia on a Medieval Russian Theme* (1961); 2 sonatas (1964, 1998); *B–88* (1973). **VOCAL:** *Hear, O Israel*, Sabbath Eve service for 2 Singers, Chorus, and Orch. (1986); *A Symphony of Celebration* for Mixed, Children's, and Community Choruses and Orch. (1997). —NS/LK/DM

Finney, Ross Lee, distinguished American composer and teacher, brother of **Theodore M(itchell) Finney;** b. Wells, Minn., Dec. 23, 1906. He studied at the Univ. of Minn. with Donald Ferguson and received a B.A. in 1927 from Carleton Coll. In 1927 he went to Paris, where he took lessons with Boulanger. Returning to America, he enrolled at Harvard Univ., where he studied with Edward Burlingame Hill (1928–29); in 1935 he had instructive sessions with Sessions. From 1929 to 1949 he was on the faculty of Smith Coll. He concurrently he taught at Mt. Holyoke Coll. (1938–40). In 1931–32 he was in Vienna, where he took private lessons with Berg; in 1937 he studied with Malipiero in Asolo. He then taught composition at the Hartt School of Music in Hartford, Conn. (1941–42), and at Amherst Coll. (1946–47). His professional career was facilitated by 2 Guggenheim fellowships (1937, 1947) and a Pulitzer traveling fellowship (1937). In 1948–49 he was a visiting lecturer at the Univ. of Mich. in Ann Arbor; from 1949 to 1973 he was a prof. there, and also served as chairman of the dept. of composition; furthermore, he established there an electronic music laboratory. He was the author of *Profile of a Lifetime: A Musical Autobiography* (N.Y., 1992). In 1962 he was elected a member of the National Inst. of Arts and Letters. F. Goossen ed. *Thinking About Music: The Collected Writings of Ross Lee Finney* (Tuscaloosa, 1990). Because of the wide diversification of his stylistic propensities, Finney's works represent a veritable encyclopedic inventory of styles and idioms, from innocently pure modalities to highly sophisticated serialistic formations. About 1950 he devised a sui generis dodecaphonic method of composition which he called "complementarity." In it a 12-tone row is formed by 2 mutually exclusive hexachords, often mirror images of each other; tonal oases make their welcome appearances; a curious air of euphony of theoretically dissonant combinations is created by the contrapuntal superposition of such heterophonic ingredients, and his harmonies begin to sound seductively acceptable despite their modernity.

WORKS: DRAMATIC: O p e r a : *Weep Torn Land* (1984); *Computer Marriage* (1987). **D a n c e :** *Heyoka* (N.Y., Sept. 14, 1981); *The Joshua Tree* (N.Y., Oct. 10, 1984); *Ahab* (1985). **ORCH.:** 2 violin concertos: No. 1 (1933; rev. 1952) and No. 2 (1973; Dallas, March 31, 1976; rev. 1977); *Barbershop Ballad* (CBS, Feb. 6, 1940); *Overture for a Drama* (1940; Rochester, N.Y., Oct. 28, 1941); *Slow Piece* for Strings (1940; Minneapolis, April 4, 1941); 4 syms.: No. 1, *Communiqué 1943* (1942; Louisville, Dec. 8, 1964), No. 2 (1958; Philadelphia, Nov. 13, 1959), No. 3 (1960; Philadelphia, March 6, 1964), and No. 4 (1972; Baltimore, March 31, 1973); *Hymn, Fuguing, and Holiday*, based on a hymn tune of William Billings (1943; Los Angeles, May 17, 1947); 2 piano concertos: No. 1 (1948) and No. 2 (968; Ann Arbor, Mich., Nov. 1, 1972); *Variations* (1957; Minneapolis, Dec. 30, 1965); *3 Pieces* for Chamber Orch. and Tape (1962; Toledo, Ohio, Feb. 23, 1963); Concerto for Percussion and Orch. (1965; Northfield, Minn., Nov. 17, 1966); *Symphonie Concertante* (1967; Kansas City, Mo., Feb. 27, 1968); *Summer in Valley City* for Band (1969; Ann Arbor, Mich., April 1, 1971); *Landscapes Remembered* (1971; Ithaca, N.Y., Nov. 5, 1972); *Spaces* (1971; Fargo, N.Dak., May 26, 1972); Concerto for Alto Saxophone and Wind Orch. (1974; Ann Arbor, Mich., April 17, 1975); *Narrative* for Cello and 14 Instruments (1976; Urbana, Ill., March 5, 1977); Concerto for Strings (N.Y., Dec. 5, 1977); *Skating on the Sheyenne* for Band (1977; N.Y., May 20, 1978). **CHAMBER:** 3 violin sonatas (1934, 1951, 1955); 8 string quartets (1935–60); 2 viola sonatas (1937, 1953); 2 piano trios (1938, 1954); Piano Quartet (1948); Cello Sonata No. 2 (1950); 2 piano quintets (1953, 1961); *Chromatic Fantasy* for Cello (1957); String Quintet (1958); *Fantasy in 2 Movements* for Violin (Brussels, June 1, 1958); *Divertissement* for Piano, Clarinet, Violin, and Cello (1964); *3 Studies in 4* for 4 Percussionists (1965); *2 Acts for 3 Players* for Clarinet, Percussion, and Piano (1970); *2 Ballades* for Flute and Piano (1973); *Tubes I* for 1 to 5 Trombones (1974); Quartet for Oboe, Cello, Percussion, and Piano (1979); *2 Studies* for Saxophones and Piano (1981); solo pieces. **KEYBOARD: P i a n o :** 5 sonatas (1933–61); *Fantasy* (1939); *Nostalgic Waltzes* (1947); *Variations on a Theme by Alban Berg* (1952); *Sonata quasi una fantasia* (1961); *Waltz* (1977); *Lost Whale Calf* (1980); *Youth's Companion* (1980); *Narrative in Retrospect* (1983). **VOCAL:** *Pilgrim Psalms* for Chorus (1945); *Spherical Madrigals* for Chorus (1947); *Immortal Autumn* for Tenor and Chorus (1952); *Edge of Shadow* for Chorus and Orch. (1959); *Earthrise: A Trilogy Concerned with the Human Dilemma:1, Still Are New Worlds* for Baritone, Chorus, Tape, and Orch. (1962; Ann Arbor, Mich., May 10, 1963), *2, The Martyr's Elegy* for High Voice, Chorus, and Orch. (Ann Arbor, Mich., April 23, 1967), and *3, Earthrise* for Soloists, Chorus, and Orch. (1978; Ann Arbor, Mich., Dec. 11, 1979); *The Remorseless Rush of Time* for Chorus and Orch. (1969; River Falls, Wisc., April 23, 1970).

BIBL.: D. Amman, *The Choral Music of R.L. F.* (diss., Univ. of Cincinnati, 1972); E. Borroff, *Three American Composers* (1986); S. Hitchens, *F.L. F.: A Bio-Bibliography* (Westport, Conn., 1996). **—NS/LK/DM**

Finney, Theodore M(itchell), American music educator, brother of **Ross Lee Finney;** b. Fayette, Iowa, March 14, 1902; d. Pittsburgh, May 19, 1978. He studied with Donald Ferguson at the Univ. of Minn. (B.A., 1924), at the American Cons. in Fontainbleau (1926), at the Stern Cons. and the Univ. of Berlin (1927–28), and at the Univ. of Pittsburgh (Litt.M., 1938). After serving as a violist in the Minneapolis Sym. Orch. (1923–25), he was an asst. prof. of music at Carleton Coll. (1925–32) and a lecturer at the Smith Coll. Summer School (1930–32); subsequently he was a prof. and chairman of the music dept. at the Univ. of Pittsburgh (1936–68).

WRITINGS: *A History of Music* (N.Y., 1935; 2nd ed., rev., 1947); *Hearing Music: A Guide to Music* (N.Y., 1941); *We Have Made Music* (Pittsburgh, 1955); *A Union Catalogue of Music and Books on Music Printed before 1801 in Pittsburgh Libraries* (Pittsburgh, 1959; 2nd ed., 1963; suppl., 1964).**—NS/LK/DM**

Finnie, Linda, Scottish mezzo-soprano; b. Paisley, May 9, 1952. She was a student of Winifred Busfield at the Royal Scottish Academy of Music in Glasgow. In 1976 she made her operatic debut with Glasgow's Scottish Opera. In 1977 she won the Kathleen Ferrier Prize at the Hertogenbosch Competition in the Netherlands, and then pursued successful engagements in both opera and concert. In 1979 she became a member of the Welsh National Opera in Cardiff; also appeared as a guest artist in London with the English National Opera and at Covent Garden. In 1986 she was a soloist in Mahler's 8th Sym. at the London Promenade Concerts and in Verdi's *Requiem* in Chicago; in 1988, made her first appearance at the Bayreuth Festival. In 1995 she sang in the *Ring* cycle at the Vienna State Opera. Among her prominent operatic roles are Amneris, Eboli, Ortrud, Brangäne, Fricka, and Waltraute. Her concert repertoire extends from Handel to Prokofiev.**—NS/LK/DM**

Finnilä, Birgit, Swedish contralto; b. Falkenberg, Jan. 20, 1931. She studied with I. Linden in Göteborg and with Roy Henderson at the Royal Academy of Music in London. In 1963 she made her formal concert debut in Göteborg, and then sang regularly in her homeland. After making her London debut in 1966, she sang in Germany. In 1967 she made her operatic debut as Gluck's Orfeo in Göteborg. In 1968 she toured North America, and then appeared in many of the major European music centers. She was active principally as a concert artist, appearing as a soloist with the major orchs. and as a recitalist.**—NS/LK/DM**

Finnissy, Michael (Peter), English composer; b. London, March 17, 1946. He studied composition with Bernard Stevens and Humphrey Searle at the Royal Coll. of Music in London (1964–66) and with Roman Vlad in Rome. In 1969 he organized the music dept. of the London School of Contemporary Dance, where he taught until 1974; later he taught at Winchester Coll.

(from 1987). He served as president of the ISCM from 1991.

WORKS: DRAMATIC: Music Theater: *Mysteries*, in 8 parts, for Vocal and Instrumental Forces, some with Dancers and Mimes: 1, *The Parting of Darkness from Light*; 2, *The Earthly Paradise*; 3, *The Great Flood*; 4, *The Prophecy of Daniel*; 5, *The Parliament of Heaven*; 6, *The Annunciation*; 7, *The Betrayal and Crucifixion of Jesus of Nazareth*; 8, *The Deliverance of Souls* (1972–79); *Circle, Chorus, and Formal Act* for Baritone, Women's Chorus, Percussion, Chorus, 6 Sword Dancers, 4 Mimes, and Small Ensemble (1973); *Mr. Punch* for Speaker, 5 Instruments, and Percussion (1976–77); *Vaudeville* for Mezzo-soprano, Baritone, 2 Mimes, 6 Instruments, and Percussion (1983); *The Undivine Comedy*, opera for 5 Singers and 9 Instruments (1988). **ORCH.:** *Song II* and *IV* (1963–69); *Song X* (1968–75); piano concertos: No. 1 (1975; rev. 1983–84), No. 2 (1975–76; Saintes, France, July 15, 1977), No. 3 (1978), and No. 7 (1981); *Offshore* (1975–76); *Pathways of Sun and Stars* (London, Nov. 15, 1976); *Alongside* for Small Orch. (1979); *Sea and Sky* (1979–80); *Red Earth* (London, Aug. 2, 1988); *Eph-Phatha* (1988–89; Northampton, May 2, 1989). **Instrumental Ensemble:** *As when upon a tranced summer night* for 3 Cellos, 2 Pianos, and 2 Percussion (1966–68); *Transformations of the Vampire* for Clarinet, Violin, Viola, and 3 Percussion (1968–71); *Evening* for 6 Instruments and Percussion (1974); *Long Distance* for Piano and 14 Instruments (1977–78); *Keroiylu* for Oboe, Bassoon, and Piano (1981); *Banumbirr* for Flute, Clarinet, Violin, Cello, and Piano (1982); *Australian Sea Shanties II* for Recorder Consort (1983); *Cātana* for 8 Instruments and Percussion (1984); String Quartet (1984); String Trio (1986); *Obrecht Motetten I* for 9 Instruments (1988), *II* for 3 Instruments (1989), and *IV* for Brass Quintet (1990). **VOCAL:** *From the Revelations of St. John the Divine* for Soprano, Flute, and String Sextet (1965–70); *Jeanne d'Arc* for Soprano, Tenor, Cello, and Small Orch. (1967–71); *World* for 2 Sopranos, Contralto, Tenor, Baritone, Bass, and Orch. (1968–74); Piano Concerto No. 5 for Piano, Mezzo-soprano, and Ensemble (1980); *Ngano* for Mezzo-soprano, Tenor, Chorus, Flute, and 2 Percussion (1983–84; London, June 12, 1984); *Celi* for 2 Sopranos, Flute, Oboe, Bass Trombone, and Double Bass (1984); *Haiyim* for Chorus and 2 Cellos (1984; London, March 15, 1985); *The Battle of Malden* for Baritone, Chorus, and Small Ensemble (1990–91).

BIBL.: H. Brougham, C. Fox, and I. Pace, eds., *Uncommon Ground: The Music of M. F.* (Aldershot, 1997).—**NS/LK/DM**

Finscher, Ludwig,

eminent German musicologist and lexicographer; b. Kassel, March 14, 1930. He was a student of Gerber at the Univ. of Göttingen (Ph.D., 1954, with the diss. *Die Messen und Motetten Loyset Compères*; publ. as *Loyset Compère (c. 1450–1518): Life and Works* in Musicological Studies and Documents, XII, 1964), completing his Habilitation at the Univ. of Saarbrücken in 1967 with his *Das klassische Streichquartett und seine Grundlegung durch Joseph Haydn* (publ. as *Studien zur Geschichte des Streichquartetts: I, Die Entstehung des klassischen Streichquartetts: Von den Vorformen zur Grundlegung durch Joseph Haydn*, Kassel, 1974). He was asst. lecturer at the inst. of musicology at the Univ. of Kiel (1960–65), and then at the Univ. of Saarbrücken (1965–68). After serving as prof. of musicology at the Univ. of Frankfurt am Main (1968–81), he held that position at the Univ. of Heidelberg (from 1981). He was ed. (1961–68) and co-ed. (1968–74) of *Die Musikforschung*. Finscher served as president of the Gesellschaft für Musikforschung (1974–77), and also was vice president (1972–77) and president (1977–82) of the International Musicological Soc. He ed. 2 vols. of the complete musical works of Gaffurius in the Corpus Mensurabilis Musicae series (1955, 1967; not continued), and a collected ed. of the works of Compère in the same series (15 vols., 1958–72). With K. von Fischer, he ed. the complete works of Hindemith (Mainz, 1976 et seq.). He also ed. (with F. Blume et al.) *Geschichte der Evangelischen Kirchenmusik* (Kassel, 2nd ed., 1965; Eng. tr., aug., 1974 as *Protestant Church Music: A History*), *Quellenstudien zu Musik der Renaissance* (2 vols., Munich, 1981, Wiesbaden, 1983), *Ludwig van Beethoven* (Darmstadt, 1983), *Die Musik des 15. und 16. Jahrhunderts* (Laaber, 1989 et seq.), and *Die Mannheimer Hofkapelle im Zeitalter Carl Theodors* (Mannheim, 1992). Finscher holds the prestigious position of ed. of the exhaustive revision of *Die Musik in Geschichte und Gegenwart*, which commenced publication in 1994. That same year he was made a member of the order Pour le mérite. In 1997 he received the Great Order of Merit of the Federal Republic of Germany.

BIBL.: A. Laubenthal, ed., *Studien zur Musikgeschichte: Eine Festschrift für L. F.* (Kassel, 1995).—**NS/LK/DM**

Finzi, Gerald (Raphael),

gifted English composer; b. London, July 14, 1901; d. Oxford, Sept. 27, 1956. After training with Ernest Farrar in Harrogate (1914–16) and Edward Bairstow in York (1917–22), he studied counterpoint with R.O. Morris in London (1925). From 1930 to 1933 he taught composition at the Royal Academy of Music in London. In 1940 he founded the Newbury String Players, which he conducted in varied programs, including music of 18th century English composers. During World War II, he worked in the Ministry of War Transport (1941–45). He also made his home a haven for German and Czech refugees. In 1951 he was stricken with Hodgkin's disease, but he continued to pursue his activities until his death. While the influence of Parry, Elgar, and Vaughan Williams may be discerned in some of his works, he found a distinctive style which is reflected in a fine body of orch. and vocal scores. Among his most notable works are the Concerto for Clarinet and Strings, the Cello Concerto, the cantata *Dies Natalis*, the *Intimations of Immortality* for Tenor, Chorus, and Orch., and *For St. Cecilia* for Tenor, Chorus, and Orch.

WORKS: DRAMATIC: *Love's Labours Lost*, incidental music to Shakespeare's play (BBC, Dec. 16, 1946; orch. suite, 1952, 1955; 1st complete perf., BBC, July 26, 1955). **ORCH.:** *Prelude* for Strings (1920s; Stockcross, Berks, April 27, 1957); *A Severn Rhapsody* for Chamber Orch. (1923; Bournemouth, June 4, 1924); *Introit* for Violin and Small Orch. (1925; 1st perf. as the 2nd movement of a Violin Concerto, later withdrawn, London, May 4, 1927; 1st perf. as a separate work, London, Jan. 31, 1933; rev. 1942); *New Year Music (Nocturne)* (1926; Bournemouth, March 16, 1932; rev. 1940s); *Eclogue* for Piano and Strings (late 1920s; rev. late 1940s; London, Jan. 27, 1957); *Fantasia* for Piano and Orch. (c. 1928; rev. version as *Grand Fantasia and Toccata*, Newbury, Dec. 9, 1953); *The Fall of the Leaf (Elegy)* (1929; rev. 1939–41; orchestration completed by H. Ferguson; Manchester, Dec. 11, 1957); *Interlude* for Oboe and Strings (1932–36; also for Oboe and String Quartet); Concerto for Clarinet and Strings (1948–49; Hereford, Sept. 9, 1949); Cello Concerto (1951–52,

1954–55; Cheltenham, July 19, 1955) CHAMBER: *Interlude* for Oboe and String Quartet (1932–36; London, March 24, 1936; also for Oboe and String Orch.); *Prelude and Fugue* for String Trio (1938; Birmingham, May 13, 1941); *5 Bagatelles* for Clarinet and Piano (1938–43; London, Jan. 15, 1943; arranged for Symphonic Wind Band by B. Wiggins, 1984, and for Clarinet and String Orch. by L. Ashmore, 1992); *Elegy* for Violin and Piano (1940; London, Dec. 1954). VOCAL: (10) *Children's Songs* for Chorus and Piano (1920–21); *By Footpath and Stile*, song-cycle for Baritone and String Quartet (1921–22; London, Oct. 14, 1923; rev. 1941); *To a Poet*, 6 songs for Low Voice and Piano (1920s–56; London, Feb. 20, 1959); *Oh Fair to See*, 7 songs for High Voice and Piano (1921–56; London, Nov. 8, 1965); *Requiem da camera* for Baritone, Chorus, and Orch. (1924; London, June 7, 1990); *Farewell to Arms* for Voice and Small Orch. or Strings (c. 1925, 1944; Manchester, March 30, 1945); *2 Sonnets* for Tenor or Soprano and Small Orch. (c. 1925; London, Feb. 6, 1936); *Dies natalis*, cantata for Tenor or Soprano and Strings (c. 1925, 1938–39; London, Jan. 26, 1940); *3 Short Elegies* for Chorus (1926; BBC, March 23, 1936); *A Young Man's Exhortation*, 10 songs for Tenor and Piano (1926–29; London, Dec. 5, 1933); *Till Earth Outwears*, 7 songs for High Voice and Piano (1927–56; London, Feb. 21, 1958); *Earth and Air and Rain*, 10 songs for Baritone and Piano (1928–32; London, July 2, 1945); *I Said to Love*, 6 songs for Baritone and Piano (1928–56; London, Jan. 27, 1957); *Let Us Garlands Bring*, 5 songs for Baritone and Piano (1929–42; London, Oct. 12, 1942; also for Baritone and Strings, BBC, Oct. 18, 1942); *Before and After Summer*, 10 songs for Baritone and Piano (1932–49); *7 Unaccompanied Part Songs* (1934–37; BBC, Dec. 29, 1938); *Intimations of Immortality*, ode for Tenor, Chorus, and Orch. (c. 1938, 1949–50; Gloucester, Sept. 5, 1950); *Lo, the full, final sacrifice*, festival anthem for Chorus and Organ (Northampton, Sept. 21, 1946; also for Chorus and Orch., Gloucester, Sept. 12, 1947); *For St. Cecilia*, ceremonial ode for Tenor, Chorus, and Orch. (1946–47; London, Nov. 22, 1947); *My lovely one*, anthem for Chorus and Orch. (1947); *Muses and Graces* for Soprano or Treble Voices and Piano or Strings (Northamptonshire, June 10, 1950); *God is gone up*, anthem for Chorus and Organ (Holborn Viaduct, Nov. 22, 1951; arranged for Chorus, Organ, and Strings by W. Godfree, London, May 20, 1952); *Thou didst delight my eyes* for Men's Chorus (1951); *All this night*, motet for Chorus (London, Dec. 6, 1951); *Let us now praise famous men* for Tenors or Sopranos, Basses or Contraltos, and Strings (1951; also with piano, 1952); *Magnificat* for Chorus and Organ (Northampton, Mass., Dec. 12, 1952; also for Soloists ad libitum, Chorus, and Orch., Bromley, May 12, 1956); *White-flowering days* for Chorus (1952–53; London, June 2, 1953); *Welcome sweet and sacred feast*, anthem for Chorus and Organ (BBC, Oct. 11, 1953); *In terra pax*, Christmas scene for Soprano, Baritone, Chorus, and Orch. (1954; BBC, Feb. 27, 1955; rev. version, Gloucester, Sept. 6, 1956).

BIBL.: J. Dressler, *F. F.: A Bio-Bibliography* (Westport, Conn., 1997).—NS/LK/DM

Finzi, Graciane, French composer and teacher; b. Casablanca, Morocco, July 10, 1945. She entered the Paris Cons. in 1955 and studied with Joseph Benvenuti (piano) and Barraine and Aubin (theory), taking premiers prix in harmony (1962), counterpoint and fugue (1964), and composition (1969). From 1975 to 1979 she served as director of music of the Festival de la Defense. In 1979 she became a teacher at the Paris Cons. She was awarded prizes from the SACEM in 1982 and 1989, and her opera *Pauvre Assassin* was awarded the SACD Prize in 1992.

WORKS: DRAMATIC: *Songs* for 3 Dancers and Instruments (1975); *Avis de recherche*, music theater (1981); *3 Opéras drôles* (1984); *Pauvre Assassin*, opera (1987; Strasbourg, Jan. 1992). ORCH.: *Édifice*, violin concerto (1976); *De la terre à la vie* for Clarinet and Strings (1979); *Il était tant de fois*, cello concerto (1979); *Trames* for 26 Instruments (1981); Concerto for 2 Violins and Orch. (1981); *Soleil vert* (1984); *Cadenza*, bassoon concerto (1987); Concerto for Flute, Harp, and Orch. (1989); *Univers de lumière*, symphonic poem for Reciter and Orch. (1990–91; Seville, Sept. 30, 1992); *Sud* (1992); *Terre, mer, soleil* (1993). CHAMBER: *Toujours plus* for Organ and Harpsichord (1975); *4 Études* for String Quartet (1976); Saxophone Quartet (1982); *Free-Quartet* for Piano Quartet (1984) and II for Oboe, English Horn, Bassoon, and Harpsichord (1988); *Phobie* for Violin (1990); *Ainsi la vie* for Viola (1991); *Engrenage* for Brass Quintet (1992); *Interférences* for String Sextet (1992); *9'30* for Bass Clarinet and Cello (1994). VOCAL: *Processus I* for Soprano, Flute, Cello, and Piano (1972) and II for Voice and Double Bass (1986); *Quand les étoiles* for 6 Voices (1990); *La robe de l'univers* for Bass-baritone and Piano (1994).—NS/LK/DM

Fiocco, Jean-Joseph, Belgian organist and composer, 2nd son of **Pietro Antonio Fiocco** (of his 1st marriage); b. Brussels (baptized), Dec. 15, 1686; d. there, March 30, 1746. He succeeded his father as music master at the ducal chapel (1714–44). He composed 5 oratorios, 8 Psalms, 9 repons de mort, motets, etc. He publ. *Sacri concentus* for 4 voices and 3 instruments.

BIBL.: C. Stellfeld, *Les F.: Une Famille de musiciens belges aux XVIIe et XVIIIe siècles* (Brussels, 1941).—NS/LK/DM

Fiocco, Joseph-Hector, Belgian organist, harpsichordist, and composer, 8th child of **Pietro Antonio Fiocco** (of his 2nd marriage); b. Brussels, Jan. 20, 1703; d. there, June 22, 1741. He was sous-maître at the royal chapel from c. 1729 to 1731, and from 1731 to 1737 he was maître de chapelle at the Antwerp Cathedral. He was master of the collegiate church of SS. Michel and Gudule in Brussels until his death. He wrote numerous sacred works, publ. in *Monumenta Musicae Belgicae* (vol. III). He also wrote *Pièces de clavecin* (2 suites of 12 pieces each).

BIBL.: C. Stellfeld, *Les F.: Une Famille de musiciens belges aux XVIIe et XVIIIe siècles* (Brussels, 1941).—NS/LK/DM

Fiocco, Pietro Antonio, Italian-born Belgian composer, father of **Jean-Joseph** and **Joseph-Hector Fiocco**; b. Venice, c. 1650; d. Brussels, Sept. 3, 1714. After settling in Brussels, he married a Belgian woman in 1682; following her death in 1691, he remarried in 1692. In 1687 he became master of the ducal chapel. With Giovanni Paolo Bombarda, he was co-director of the Opéra du Quai du Forn (1694–98). By 1696 he was lieutenant de la chapelle at the electoral court chapel, being named maître de chapelle in 1706; he also served as maître de musique at the Church of Notre Dame du Sablon from 1703. He composed music for the court and publ. a vol. of *Sacri concerti* for 1 and 2 voices (Antwerp, 1691). Among his extant instrumental works are a symphonia and a flute sonata. He also prepared special prologues for Lully's operas.

BIBL.: C. Stellfeld, *Les F.: Une famille de musiciens belges aux XVIIe et XVIIIe siècles* (Brussels, 1941).—NS/LK/DM

Fioravanti, Valentino, Italian composer, father of **Vincenzo Fioravanti;** b. Rome, Sept. 11, 1764; d. Capua, June 16, 1837. He was a pupil of Toscanelli and Jannacconi in Rome, and then of Sala in Naples (1779–81). His first notable success as a composer for the theater came with his opera buffa *Gl'inganni fortunati* (Naples, 1788). His most enduring score was the opera buffa *Le Cantatrici villane* (Naples, 1799), which was rev. as *Le Virtuose redicole* (Venice, Dec. 28, 1801) and performed throughout Europe. The success of *Camilla* (Lisbon, 1801) garnered for him the directorship of the Teatro San Carlo there (1801–06). In 1816 he was named maestro di cappella at St. Peter's in Rome, and subsequently wrote much sacred music. In all, he composed 77 operas (1784–1824). While he was at his best in opera buffa, he also wrote serious operas, the most significant being *Adelaide e Comingio* (Naples, 1817). G. Roberti ed. his autobiographical sketch in *Gazzetta musicale di Milano,* I (1895).—NS/LK/DM

Fioravanti, Vincenzo, Italian composer, son of **Valentino Fioravanti;** b. Rome, April 5, 1799; d. Naples, March 28, 1877. His father wanted him to study medicine but he pursued musical raining with Jannacconi without his father's knowledge. He later studied with his father, and subsequently received advice from Donizetti. As a composer of operas, he gained his greatest success with *Il ritorno di Pulcinella degli studi di Padova, ossia Il pazzo per amore* (Naples, Dec. 28, 1837). From 1839 to 1843 he was maestro di cappella at Lanciano Cathedral, but he continued to turn out operas until 1856. From 1867 to 1872 he was director of the music school of the Albergo dei Poveri in Naples. He wrote some 35 operas, several of them in the Neapolitan dialect. He also wrote sacred pieces, including two oratorios.—NS/LK/DM

Fiorè, Andrea Stefano, Italian composer; b. Milan, 1686; d. Turin, Oct. 6, 1732. He was the precocious child of the cellist and composer Angelo Maria Fiorè (b. c. 1660; d. Turin, June 4, 1723), who served as a cellist in the Franese court in Parma (1688–95) and in the ducal court in Turin (1697–1723). When he was 11, he joined his father as a member of the Accademia dei Filarmonici in Bologna. His *Sinfinie da chiesa* were publ. when he was 13 (Modena, 1699), during which time he was musico di camera of the Duke of Savoy. His patron made it possible for him to study with G.B. Somis in Rome. Upon resuming his duties with the Duke of Savoy, he served as his maestro di cappella from 1707 until his death. He composed some 21 operas (1707–29), several solo cantatas, and sacred works.—LK/DM

Fiore, John, American conductor; b. N.Y., Aug. 18, 1960. He began music studies with his father, a pianist and choral director, and his mother, a pianist. He pursued training in piano and string instruments in Seattle, and worked as an asst. at the Seattle Opera (1975–80). He completed his piano studies with Frank Glazer and David Burge at the Eastman School of Music in N.Y. (B.A., 1982), and also had private instruction with Earl Wild. From 1981 to 1985 he was an asst.

conductor at the Santa Fe Opera, from 1983 to 1988 at the San Francisco Opera, where he made his professional conducting debut with *Faust* in 1986, from 1983 to 1988 at the Lyric Opera in Chicago, where he conducted *Faust* in 1988, and from 1984 to 1989 at the Metropolitan Opera in N.Y. In 1985 he was a guest conductor with the Seattle Sym. Orch. He appeared as a guest conductor with the Boston Sym. Orch. and the Minn. Orch. in Minneapolis in 1990, and also conducted *Manon Lescaut* at the Cologne Opera. In 1991 he made his Metropolitan Opera debut conducting *La Traviata*, and also conducted *Turandot* at the Australian Opera. He conducted *Rigoletto* at the Bordeaux Opera in 1992. In 1993 he conducted the first mounting of *Rusalka* at the Metropolitan Opera, and also conducted *La Traviata* at the Semper Opera in Dresden and was a guest conductor with the Gürzenich Orch. in Cologne. In 1994 he conducted the first staging of *Les Troyens* by the Australian Opera, and also conducted *Der fliegende Holländer* at the Bavarian State Opera in Munich and was a guest conductor with the Dresden State Orch. He was a guest conductor with the Los Angeles Phil. in 1996, and also conducted *La Bohème* at the Genoa Opera. In 1999 he was a guest conductor with the NHK Sym. Orch. in Tokyo. He became Generalmusikdirektor of the Deutsche Oper-am-Rhein in Düsseldorf in 1999, and also of the Düsseldorf Sym. Orch. in 2000. Fiore has won critical accolades for his interpretations of German and Italian operas, particularly of works by Wagner, Strauss, Verdi, and Puccini. He has also won success as a conductor of operas by Dvořák, Debussy, and Janáček.—NS/LK/DM

Fiorillo, Federigo, Italian violinist and composer, son of **Ignazio Fiorillo;** b. Braunschweig (baptized), June 1, 1755; d. after 1823. He was taught by his father, then traveled as a violinist and conductor. He appeared as a violinist in St. Petersburg in 1777, then in Poland (1780–81), and also conducted in Riga (1782–84). In 1785 he went to Paris, where he participated in the Concert Spirituel. In 1788 he was in London, where he played the viola in Salomon's quartet. He probably remained in London until c. 1815, then was in Amsterdam and again in Paris. He was a prolific composer for violin and various combinations of string instruments. Fiorillo is known chiefly through his useful collection *Études de violon,* comprising 36 caprices, which was frequently reprinted.—NS/LK/DM

Fiorillo, Ignazio, Italian composer, father of **Federigo Fiorillo;** b. Naples, May 11, 1715; d. Fritzlar, near Kassel, June 1787. He studied with Durante and Leo in Naples, and composed his first opera, *Mandane,* at the age of 20 (Venice, 1736). Other operas were *Artimene* (Milan, 1738), *Partenope nell' Adria* (Venice, 1738), and *Il Vincitor di se stesso* (Venice, 1741). He traveled as a theater conductor. He was appointed court conductor at Braunschweig (1754), and in 1762 he received a similar post at Kassel, retiring in 1780. He wrote a number of German operas in Braunschweig and 3 Italian operas in Kassel. An oratorio, *Isacco,* a Requiem, and other church works are also noteworthy.—NS/LK/DM

Fioroni, Giovanni Andrea, Italian composer; b. Pavia, c. 1704; d. Milan, Dec. 14 or 19, 1778. After studies with Leonardo Leo in Naples, he was active as maestro di cappella in various churches in Milan, particularly at the Cathedral from 1747 until his death; he also taught. His extensive output included operas and oratorios, as well as some 300 sacred vocal works. Of the latter, his choral works for 8 voices, and his 15 solo motets and 37 motets for 2 voices are particularly noteworthy.—**LK/DM**

Firkušný, Rudolf, eminent Czech-born American pianist and pedagogue; b. Napajedla, Feb. 11, 1912; d. Staatsburg, N.Y., July 19, 1994. He studied composition privately with Janáček in 1919 and piano with Růžena Kurzová at the Brno Cons. (1920–27), and also attended the Univ. of Brno. His further instructors were Vilém Kurz and Rudolf Karel (theory) at the Prague Cons., Suk (composition; 1929–30), and Artur Schnabel in N.Y. (1932). He made his debut as a child pianist in Prague on June 14, 1920, playing a Mozart piano concerto. He first performed in London in 1933, and on Jan. 13, 1938, he made his U.S. debut in N.Y., where he settled in 1940 and became a naturalized citizen. In 1943–44 he made a tour of Latin America and in 1946 participated in the Prague Festival; in subsequent years he also toured Europe, Israel, and Australia. After an absence of 44 years, he again played in Prague in 1990 as soloist in Martinů's 2nd piano concerto. His interpretations of the standard piano literature were greatly esteemed. Firkušný was a champion of the music of Janáček; he also gave the first performances of Martin's 3rd (Dallas, Nov. 20, 1949) and 4th (N.Y., Oct. 4, 1956) piano concertos. He likewise gave the first performances of piano concertos of Menotti (No. 1; Boston, Nov. 2, 1945) and Howard Hanson (Boston, Dec. 31, 1948). His technical equipment was of the highest caliber; his lyrical talent enhanced his virtuosity. He was also a composer; he wrote a piano concerto, a string quartet, and a number of attractive piano études and miniatures. In 1979 he began publication, with the violinist Rafael Druian, of a complete ed. of the Mozart violin sonatas. An excellent teacher, Firkušný gave master classes at the Juilliard School of Music in N.Y. and at the Aspen Music School in Colo.

BIBL.: J. Šafařík, *R. F.* (Brno, 1994).—**NS/LK/DM**

Firsova, Elena (Olegovna), Russian composer and teacher; b. Leningrad, March 21, 1950. She was a student of Pirumov (composition) and Kholopov (analysis) at the Moscow Cons. (1970–75), and also profited from further studies with Denisov. From 1979 her works were heard abroad. In 1993 she became a prof. and composer-in-residence at the Univ. of Keele in England. In 1972 she married **Dmitri Smirnov**. In her works, she has developed an intimate style notable for its poetic handling of both harmony and melody.

WORKS: DRAMATIC: O p e r a : *Feast in Plague Time,* chamber opera (1972); *The Nightingale and the Rose* (1991). ORCH.: *5 Pieces* (1971); *Chamber Music* for Strings (1973); 2 cello concertos: No. 1 (1973; Moscow, June 10, 1975) and No. 2, as *Chamber Concerto No. 2* (Moscow, Oct. 17, 1982); *Stanzas* (1975); 2 violin concertos (1976, 1983); *Postlude* for Harp and Orch. (1977; Moscow, Feb. 22, 1978); *Chamber Concerto No. 1* for Flute and Strings (1978; Moscow, March 10, 1980), *No. 3* for

Piano and Orch. (1985), *No. 4* (1988), *No. 5* (n.d.), and *No. 6* (1997); *Autumn Music* for Chamber Orch. (1988); *Nostalgia* (1989); *Cassandra* (1992). **CHAMBER:** *Scherzo* for Flute, Oboe, Clarinet, Bassoon, and Piano (1967); 10 string quartets (1970, 1974, 1980, 1989, 1992, 1994, 1995, 1996, 1997, 1999); Cello Sonata (1971); Piano Trio (1972); *Capriccio* for Flute and Saxophone Quartet (1976); Sonata for Solo Clarinet (1976); *3 Pieces* for Xylophone (1978); *Sphinx* for Harp (1982); *Spring Sonata* for Flute and Piano (1982); *Mysteria* for Organ and 4 Percussion (1984); *Music for 12* (1986); *Monologue* for Bassoon (1989); *Odyssey* for 7 Players (1990); *Verdehr-Terzett* for Violin, Clarinet, and Piano (1990); *Far Away* for Saxophone Quartet (1991); *Meditation in the Japanese Garden* for Flute, Viola, and Piano (1992); *You and I* for Cello and Piano (1992); *Starry Flute* for Flute (1992); *Vigilia* for Violin and Piano (1992); *Otzuki* for Flute and Guitar (1992); *Phantom* for 4 Viols (1993); *Monologue* for Alto Saxophone (1994). **VOCAL:** *3 Poems by Osip Mandelstam* for Chorus (1970); *Petrarca's Sonnets* for Voice and 8 Instruments (1976); *The Bell* for Chorus (1976; in collaboration with D. Smirnov); *Night* for Voice and Saxophone Quartet (1978); *Tristia* for Voice and Chamber Orch. (1979); *Shakespeare's Sonnets* for Voice and Organ (1981); *The Stone* for Voice and Orch. (1983); *Earthly Life* for Soprano and 10 Instruments (1986); *Augury* for Chorus and Orch. (1988); *Stygian Song* for Soprano and Ensemble (1989); *7 Haiku* for Voice and Lyre (1991); *Sea Shell* for Voice and Ensemble (1991); *Whirlpool* for Voice, Flute, and Percussion (1991); *Silentium* for Voice and String Quartet (1991); *Secret Way* for Voice and Orch. (1992); *Distance* for Voice and Ensemble (1992).—**NS/LK/DM**

Fischer, Ádám, Hungarian conductor, brother of **Iván Fischer;** b. Budapest, Sept. 9, 1949. He studied at the Béla Bartók Cons. in Budapest, and then took conducting courses with Swarowsky at the Vienna Academy of Music and with Ferrara in Venice and Siena (1970–71). In 1971–72 he was an asst. conductor in Graz. In 1972–73 he was chief conductor in St. Pölten. He won 1st prize in the Cantelli Competition in Milan in 1973. After serving as an asst. conductor at the Vienna State Opera (1973–74), he was a conductor at the Finnish National Opera in Helsinki from 1974 to 1977. From 1977 to 1979 he held the position of 1st conductor at the Karlsruhe Opera. In 1980 he made his first appearance at the Salzburg Festival, and in 1981 he made his U.S. debut at the San Francisco Opera conducting *Don Giovanni.* From 1981 to 1984 he was Generalmusikdirektor in Freiburg im Breisgau. In 1984 he conducted *Der Rosenkavalier* at his first appearance at the Paris Opéra, and in 1986 he made his debut at Milan's La Scala conducting *Die Zauberflöte.* From 1987 to 1992 he was Generalmusikdirektor in Kassel. He also founded the Austro-Hungarian Haydn Festival in Eisenstadt, and served as music director of the Austro-Hungarian Haydn Orch. In 1989 he made his debut at London's Covent Garden conducting *Die Fledermaus.* He returned to London in 1991 to make his first appearance at the English National Opera with *Bluebeard's Castle.* On April 14, 1994, he made his debut at the Metropolitan Opera in N.Y. conducting *Otello.* He also appeared as a guest conductor with major orchs. on both sides of the Atlantic.—**NS/LK/DM**

Fischer, Annie (actually, **Anny**), distinguished Hungarian pianist; b. Budapest, July 5, 1914; d.

there, April 11, 1995. She attended the Franz Liszt Academy of Music in Budapest and also was a pupil of Székely and Dohnányi. At the age of 8, she made her first public appearance in Budapest as soloist in Beethoven's 1st piano concerto. Her formal debut followed in Zürich in 1926. After winning 1st prize in the Liszt Competition in Budapest in 1933, she performed throughout Europe until World War II forced her to seek refuge in Sweden. After the War, she pursued an international career as a soloist with orchs. and as a recitalist. She was widely admired for her patrician interpretations of Mozart, Beethoven, and Schubert. In 1937 she married **Aladár Tóth.**—NS/LK/DM

Fischer, Betty, Austrian operetta singer; b. Vienna, Oct. 27, 1887; d. there, Jan. 19, 1969. She centered her career in Vienna, where she sang in variety productions and operetta at a young age. After establishing herself as a valuable member of the Raimundtheater (1900–1903), she was prima donna at the Theater an der Wien (1903–28). In 1928 she starred at the Johann Strauss-Theater. She also made guest appearances at other theaters in Vienna and other music centers. In later years, she appeared in character roles at the Raimundtheater and taught at the Vienna Cons. Fischer was an outstanding operetta singer in her day, excelling in both traditional and contemporary roles.—NS/LK/DM

Fischer, Carl, German-American music publisher; b. Buttstadt, Thuringia, Dec. 7, 1849; d. N.Y., Feb. 14, 1923. He studied music in Gotha. He entered a partnership in an instrument manufacturing business with his brother August Emil Fischer in Bremen. In 1872 he went to N.Y. and opened a music store at 79 East 4th St. In 1923 the store was moved to 62 Cooper Square. He secured the rights for republishing orch. scores and parts by German composers, eventually creating one of the most important of American music publishing firms. From 1907 to 1931 the firm publ. a monthly periodical, the *Musical Observer*, ed. by Gustav Sänger; in 1923 the business was incorporated and Carl Fischer's son Walter S. Fischer (b. N.Y., April 18, 1882; d. there, April 26, 1946) became president; after his death, Frank H. Connor (1903–77) was elected president; upon his death he was succeeded by his son. In 1909 the firm established a branch in Boston, which was expanded in 1960 through the purchase of the Charles Homeyer Music Co. of Boston; in 1935 a branch was also opened in Los Angeles, and in 1969 one in San Francisco. In 1947 the firm occupied a new building in N.Y. at 165 West 57th St., which also housed a concert hall. The catalog of the firm is representative of all genres of musical composition; early acquisitions were works by composers living in America, including Rachmaninoff and Ernest Bloch. In the last quarter of the century, the firm publ. a number of instrumental and vocal works by composers of the avant-garde, including some in graphic notation.—NS/LK/DM

Fischer, Edwin, eminent Swiss pianist, conductor, and pedagogue; b. Basel, Oct. 6, 1886; d. Zürich, Jan. 24, 1960. He was a pupil of Hans Huber at the Basel Cons.

(1896–1904) before pursuing his studies with Martin Krause at the Stern Cons. in Berlin (1904–05), where he subsequently was a faculty member (1905–14). He was conductor of the Lübeck Musikverein (1926–28) and the Munich Bachverein (1928–32) before founding his own chamber orch. in Berlin, which he regularly conducted from the keyboard; he also taught at the Hochschule für Musik there (from 1931). In 1942 he returned to his homeland, where he played in a noted trio with Kulenkampff (later succeeded by Schneiderhan) and Mainardi. From 1945 to 1958 he gave master classes in Lucerne. Although his interpretations were securely rooted in the Romantic tradition, he eschewed the role of the virtuoso in order to probe the intellectual content of the score at hand. He ed. works by Bach, Mozart, and Beethoven, composers he championed. Among his books were *J.S. Bach* (Potsdam, 1945), *Musikalische Betrachtungen* (Wiesbaden, 1949; Eng. tr., 1951, as *Reflections on Music*), *Ludwig van Beethovens Klaviersonaten* (Wiesbaden, 1956; Eng. tr., 1959), and *Von den Aufgaben des Musikers* (Wiesbaden, 1960).

BIBL.: B. Gavoty and R. Hauert, *E. F.* (Geneva and Monaco, 1954); H. Haid, ed., *Dank an E. F.* (Wiesbaden, 1962). —NS/LK/DM

Fischer, Emil (Friedrich August), distinguished German bass; b. Braunschweig, June 13, 1838; d. Hamburg, Aug. 11, 1914. He received his vocal training entirely from his parents, who were opera singers. He made his debut in Graz in 1857, then was with the Danzig Opera (1863–70), in Rotterdam (1875–80), and with the Dresden Opera (1880–85). He made his debut with the Metropolitan Opera in N.Y. on Nov. 23, 1885, as King Heinrich, and remained on the staff for 5 years; then sang with the Damrosch Opera Co. (1894–98). He lived mostly in N.Y. as a vocal teacher, returning to Germany shortly before his death. On March 15, 1907, a testimonial performance was held in his honor at the Metropolitan Opera, at which he sang one of his greatest roles: that of Hans Sachs (Act 3, Scene 1). He was particularly famous for his Wagnerian roles. —NS/LK/DM

Fischer, György, Hungarian-born Austrian conductor and pianist; b. Budapest, Aug. 12, 1935. He received training at the Franz Liszt Academy of Music in Budapest and at the Salzburg Mozarteum. After working as an assistant to Karajan at the Vienna State Opera, where he conducted works by Mozart, he was active as a conductor at the Cologne Opera (from 1973). In 1973 he made his British debut conducting *Die Zauberflöte* with the Welsh National Opera in Cardiff; made his London debut conducting *Mitridate* in 1979. From 1980 he appeared as a conductor with the English Chamber Orch. in London; also conducted widely in other European music centers, as well as in North and South America, and in Australia. As a piano accompanist, he toured the world with many outstanding artists. For a time he was married to **Lucia Popp.**—NS/LK/DM

Fischer, Irwin, American composer, teacher, and conductor; b. Iowa City, July 5, 1903; d. Wilmette, Ill.,

May 7, 1977. He graduated in 1924 from the Univ. of Chicago; studied organ with Middelschulte, piano with Robyn, and composition with Weidig at the American Cons. in Chicago (M.M., 1930). He later studied composition briefly with Boulanger in Paris (1931) and Kodály in Budapest (1936), and took lessons in conducting with Paumgartner and Malko at the Salzburg Mozarteum (1937). In 1928 he joined the faculty of the American Cons. in Chicago, becoming its dean in 1974; he also conducted several community orchs. As a composer, Fischer held fast to tonal techniques. In the 1930s he developed a polytonal technique, which he described as biplanal, and from 1960 he utilized serialism.

WORKS: ORCH.: *Rhapsody of French Folk Tunes* (1933); Piano Concerto (1935; Chicago, Feb. 23, 1936); *Marco Polo*, fantasy overture (1937); *Hungarian Set* (1938); *Lament* for Cello and Orch. (1938); *Chorale Fantasy* for Organ and Orch. (1940); Sym. No. 1 (1943); *Variations on an Original Theme* (1950); *Legend* (1956); *Poem* for Violin and Orch. (1959); *Passacaglia and Fugue* (1961); *Overture on an Exuberant Tone Row* (1964–65); *Short Symphony* (1970–71; Hinsdale, April 16, 1972; orchestration of Piano Sonata); *Concerto giocoso* for Clarinet and Orch. (1971; Hinsdale, Jan. 21, 1973). **CHAMBER:** *Divertimento* for Flute, Clarinet, Bassoon, Horn, Trumpet, Violin, Cello, and Double Bass (1963); *Fanfare* for Brass and Percussion (1976). **KEYBOARD: Piano:** *Introduction and Triple Fugue* (1929); *Rhapsody* (1940); Sonata (1960). **VOCAL:** *5 Symphonic Psalms* for Soprano, Chorus, and Orch. (1967); *Orchestral Adventures of a Little Tune* for Narrator and Orch. (1974; Chicago, Nov. 16, 1974); *Statement 1976* for Soprano, Chorus, Brass, Strings, and Percussion (New Haven, April 25, 1976); choruses; songs.

BIBL.: E. Borroff, *Three American Composers* (1986). —NS/LK/DM

Fischer, Iván, Hungarian conductor, brother of **Ádám Fischer;** b. Budapest, Jan. 20, 1951. He studied cello and composition at the Béla Bartók Cons. in Budapest (1965–70); then took lessons in conducting with Swarowsky at the Vienna Academy of Music and with Harnoncourt in Salzburg. During the 1975–76 season, he conducted concerts in Milan, Florence, Vienna, and Budapest; beginning in 1976, he filled engagements with the BBC Sym. Orch. in London and the BBC regional orchs. From 1979 to 1982 he was co-conductor of the Northern Sinfonia Orch. in Newcastle upon Tyne. In 1983 he became music director of the Budapest Festival Orch. Also in 1983 he made his first appearance in the U.S. as a guest conductor with the Los Angeles Phil. He was music director of the Kent Opera (1984–88), and then its artistic director. From 1989 to 1995 he was principal guest conductor of the Cincinnati Sym. Orch.—NS/LK/DM

Fischer, Jan (Frank), Czech composer; b. Louny, Sept. 15, 1921. He studied at the Prague Cons. (1940–45) and took lessons in composition from Řídký at the master class there (1945–48). He also attended the Charles Univ. in Prague (1945–48), where he later received his Ph.D. (1990). He won prizes from the city of Prague (1966) and the Guild of Composers (1986). His music occupies the safe ground of Central European Romanticism, not without some audacious exploits in euphonious dissonance.

WORKS: DRAMATIC: Opera: *Ženichové* (Bridegrooms; 1956; Brno, Oct. 13, 1957); *Romeo, Julie a tma* (Romeo, Juliet, and Darkness; 1959–61; Brno, Sept. 14, 1962); *Oh, Mr. Fogg*, comic chamber opera after Jules Verne's *Around the World in 80 Days* (1967–70; Saarbrücken, June 27, 1971); *Miracle Theater*, radio opera (1970); *Decamerone*, chamber opera (1975–76); *Copernicus* (1981); *Rites* (1990). **Ballet:** *Eufrosyne* (1951); *Le Marionnettists* (1978); *Battalion* (1996). **ORCH.:** *Pastoral Sinfonietta* (1944); Viola Concerto (1946); *Essay* for Piano and Jazz Orch. (1947); *Popular Suite* for Piano and Wind Orch. (1950); *Dance Suite* (1957); *Fantasia* for Piano and Orch. (1953); Sym. No. 1, *Monothematic* (1959); Clarinet Concerto (1965); *Obrazy* (Pictures) *I* (1970), *II* (1973), and *III* (1977); Harp Concerto (1972); *Tryzna* (Commemoration; 1973); *Večerní hudba* (Night Music) for Strings (1973); *Concerto for Orchestra* (1980); *Partita* for Strings (1982). **CHAMBER:** Flute Sonata (1944); Suite for Wind Sextet (1944); Suite for English Horn and Piano (1945); *Ballada* for String Quartet and Clarinet (1949); Piano Quintet (1949); *Ut stellae* for Soprano, 2 Pianos, Flute, Bass Clarinet, Percussion, and Tape (1966); *Amoroso* for Clarinet and Piano (1970); Wind Quintet (1971); *4 Studies* for Harp (1971); *Conversation with Harp*, quintet for Flute, Violin, Viola, Cello, and Harp (1979); *A Fairy Tale* for Harp and Flute (1979); Brass Quintet (1983); *Prague Preludes* for 5 Harps (1983); Duet for 2 Harps (1986); *Lyric Rhapsody* for Viola and Piano (1987); *Hommage à Bohuslav Martinů*, suite for Flute and Harp (1988); *Monologues* for Harp (1991); *Cante Hondo* for Flute and Guitar (1992); *Due pezzi per amici* for Bass Clarinet and Piano (1992); *Armoioso* for Violin and Piano (1998); *Vzpomínka na Romea* (She Remembers Romeo) for Oboe, Clarinet, Bassoon, and Piano (1998).—NS/LK/DM

Fischer, Johann, German violinist and composer; b. Augsburg, Sept. 25, 1646; d. Schwedt, Pomerania, 1716 or 1717. After studies with Tobias Kiregsdorfer in Augsburg, and then with Samuel Capricornus in Stuttgart (1661–65), he worked as a copyist for Lully in Paris. From 1674 to 1683 he was a church musician in Augsburg, and then a violinist at the Ansbach court chapel (1683–86) and the Mitau court (1690–97). After extensive travels, he was made Konzertmeister at the Schwerin court in 1701. He spent his last years as Kapellmeister to the Margrave of Brandenburg-Schwedt. Fischer was one of the earliest advocates of scordatura tunings. He was an especially fine composer of chamber music, in which he championed the French style.—LK/DM

Fischer, Johann Caspar Ferdinand, significant German composer; b. c. 1665; d. Rastatt, Aug. 27, 1746. He was in the service of the Margrave of Baden (1696–1716), and continued when the court moved to Rastatt in 1716. He adopted Lully's style in his compositions, and thereby influenced other German composers. His *Ariadne musica neo-organoedum* (1702), a collection of 20 organ preludes and fugues in 20 different keys, foreshadowed Bach's *Well-Tempered Clavier*. All of the works listed below were ed. by E. von Werra (Leipzig, 1901). Fischer also publ. several of his vocal works.

WORKS: *Le Journal du printemps*, 8 suites for 5 Strings and 2 Trumpets ad libitum, op. 1 (Augsburg, 1695; ed. in Denkmäler Deutscher Tonkunst, X, 1902); *Les Pièces de clavessin*, 8 suites for

Keyboard, op. 2 (Schlackenworth, 1696; reprinted as *Musikalisches Blumen- Büschlein*, 1698); *Ariadne musica neo-organoedum*, 20 preludes and fugues in 20 different keys for Organ, op. 4 (Schlackenworth, 1702); *Blumen Strauss...in 8 Tonos Ecclesiasticos eingetheilet* for Organ (Augsburg, 1732); *Musicalischer Parnassus*, 9 suites for Keyboard (Augsburg, 1738).—NS/LK/DM

Fischer, Johann Christian, German oboist and composer; b. Freiburg, 1733; d. London (buried), May 3, 1800. He studied oboe in Turin with Alessandro Besozzi. After playing in the Dresden Court Orch. and at the court of Friedrich the Great in Potsdam, he toured extensively. In 1768 he settled in London, where he often played in the Bach-Abel Concerts until 1782. After a Viennese sojourn (1787–90?), he returned to London. He was fatally stricken with a stroke while performing before the royal family. His publ. works include 10 concertos for oboe or flute (London, c. 1768–95) and 10 flute sonatas (London, c. 1780). A minuet from his first oboe concerto proved highly popular, so much so that Mozart wrote a set of keyboard variations on it. —LK/DM

Fischer, (Johann Ignaz) Ludwig, renowned German bass; b. Mainz, Aug. 18, 1745; d. Berlin, July 10, 1825. He studied voice with Anton Raaff in Mannheim, then obtained the post of virtuoso da camera at the Mannheim court (1772); also taught voice at the Mannheim Seminario Musico from 1775, continuing in the court's service when it moved to Munich in 1778. He then proceeded to Vienna (1780), where he first gained recognition as a leading opera singer. He became a friend of Mozart, who wrote the role of Osmin in his *Die Entführung aus dem Serail* (July 16, 1782) for him. In 1783 he went to Paris, where he was notably successful at the Concert Spirituel; subsequently toured Italy, and then sang in Vienna, Prague, and Dresden (1785). After serving the Prince of Thurn und Taxis in Regensburg (1785–89), he received an appointment for life in Berlin. He continued to make guest appearances in other cities, including London (1794, 1798), giving his last public performance in Berlin in 1812; he was pensioned in 1815. The MS of his autobiography, which covers his life to 1790, is in the Berlin Staatsbibliothek.—NS/LK/DM

Fischer, Kurt von, distinguished Swiss musicologist; b. Bern, April 25, 1913. He studied piano with Hirt and Marek at the Bern Cons. and musicology with Kurth and Gurlitt at the Univ. of Bern (Ph.D., 1938, with the diss. *Griegs Harmonik und die nordländische Folklore*; publ. in Bern, 1938; Habilitationsschrift, 1948, *Die Beziehungen von Form und Motiv in Beethovens Instrumentalwerken*; publ. in Strasbourg, 1948; 2nd ed., 1972). After teaching piano at the Bern Cons. (1939–57) and musicology at the Univ. of Bern (1948–57), he was prof. of musicology at the Univ. of Zürich (1957–79). In 1965 he became co-ed. of the *Archiv für Musikwissenschaft*. From 1967 to 1972 he was president of the International Musicological Soc. He was general ed. of the series Polyphonic Music of the 14th Century from 1977 to 1992. From 1979 to 1987 he was president of the commission of the Répertoire International des Sources

Musicales. He was honored with Feschriften on his 60th (1973), 70th (1983), and 80th (1993) birthdays. In 1980 he was made a corresponding member of the American Musicological Soc.

WRITINGS: *Die Variation* (Cologne, 1956; Eng. tr., 1962); *Studien zur italienischen Musik des Trecento und frühen Quattrocento* (Bern, 1956); *Der Begriff des "Neuens" in der Musik von der Ars nova bis zur Gegenwart* (N.Y., 1961); *Die Passion von ihren Anfangen bis ins 16. Jahrhundert* (Bern and Munich, 1973); *Arthur Honegger* (Zürich, 1977); T. Evans, ed., and C. Skoggard, tr., *Essays in Musicology* (N.Y., 1989); E. Schmid (Zürich, 1992); *Die Passion: Musik zwischen Kunst und Kirche* (Kassel, 1997). —NS/LK/DM

Fischer, Michael Gottard, German organist and composer; b. Alach, near Erfurt, June 3, 1773; d. Erfurt, Jan. 12, 1829. He studied organ and counterpoint with Kittel in Erfurt, where he settled. He was organist of the Barfüsserkirche and director of the city concerts. In 1809 he succeeded Kittel as organist of the Predigerkirche. From 1816 he also taught at the teacher's seminary. He became best known as a composer of organ music, but he also wrote syms., concertos, chamber music, and vocal pieces.

BIBL.: K. Plesse, *M.G. F. und die Musik in Erfurt um 1800* (diss., Univ. of Jena, 1945).—NS/LK/DM

Fischer, Res (actually, **Maria Theresia**), German contralto; b. Berlin, Nov. 8, 1896; d. Stuttgart, Oct. 4, 1974. She studied in Stuttgart and Prague; then took lessons in Berlin with Lilli Lehmann. She made her debut in 1927 in Basel, where she sang until 1935; then appeared with the Frankfurt am Main Opera (1935–41); in 1941 she joined the Stuttgart Opera, remaining on its roster until 1961; was made its honorary member in 1965. She also sang at the festivals of Salzburg and Bayreuth, and with the state operas in Vienna, Hamburg, and Munich. She created the title role in Orff's *Antigonae* (Salzburg, 1949) and sang in the first performance of Wagner- Régeny's *Bergwerk von Falun* (Salzburg, 1961).—NS/LK/DM

Fischer, Wilhelm (Robert), eminent Austrian musicologist; b. Vienna, April 19, 1886; d. Innsbruck, Feb. 26, 1962. He studied with Guido Adler at the Univ. of Vienna, where he received his Ph.D. with the diss. *Matthias Georg Monn als Instrumentalkomponist* in 1912; he completed his Habilitation there with his *Zur Entwicklungsgeschichte des Wiener klassischen Stils* in 1915. He joined the faculty of the Univ. of Vienna in 1919, and subsequently was lecturer in musicology at the Univ. of Innsbruck from 1928 until the Anschluss of 1938, when he was conscripted as a forced laborer. After World War II, he was restored to the faculty of the Univ. of Innsbruck as a prof., serving there from 1948 until his retirement in 1961. In 1951 he was elected president of the Central Inst. of Mozart Research at the Mozarteum in Salzburg. He publ. numerous essays on Mozart and other Classical composers; wrote the valuable study "Geschichte der Instrumentalmusik 1450 bis 1880" for Adler's *Handbuch der Musikgeschichte* (Frankfurt am Main, 1924; 2nd ed., rev., 1930).—NS/LK/DM

Fischer-Dieskau, (Albert) Dietrich, great

German baritone; b. Berlin, May 28, 1925. The original surname of the family was Fischer. His father, Albert Fischer (1865–1937), a classical scholar, headmaster of a secondary school, and composer, legally conjoined his mother's maiden surname to his in 1934. Dietrich began to study piano when he was 9. At age 16, he became a student of voice of Georg Walter in Berlin. On Jan. 31, 1942, he gave his first public recital in Zehlendorf. He then pursued vocal training with Hermann Weissenborn at the Berlin Hochschule für Musik. Following his graduation in 1943, he was drafted into the German army. On May 5, 1945, he was captured by U.S. forces in Italy's Po Valley, and was held as a prisoner of war until 1947. Upon returning to Berlin, he completed his vocal studies with Weissenborn. His performances of Schubert's *Winterreise* in a RIAS radio broadcast in Berlin in Dec. 1947 won fine critical notices, and in 1948 he began to give public lieder recitals. On May 6, 1948, he made his operatic debut in the bass role of Colas in a RIAS broadcast in Berlin of Mozart's *Bastien und Bastienne*. His operatic stage debut followed on Nov. 18, 1948, when he sang Verdi's Rodrigo, Marquis of Posa, at the Berlin Städtische Oper. He soon established himself as an invaluable member of the company, appearing there and with its successor, the Deutsche Oper, for 35 years. In 1949 he sang Schubert's *Die schöne Müllerin* in Berlin to great effect, and also appeared as Wolfram for the first time at the Städtische Oper. His appearance as a soloist in the Brahms Requiem under Furtwängler's baton in Vienna in 1951 prompted Furtwängler to engage him for the Salzburg Festival that same year, where he won extraordinary acclaim for his performance of Mahler's *Lieder eines fahrenden Gesellen.* On June 7, 1951, he made his London debut as a soloist in Delius's *A Mass of Life* with Beecham conducting. That same year, he sang Wolfram at his debut at the Bavarian State Opera in Munich and portrayed Mozart's Count Almaviva at the Städtische Oper. In 1952 he made his first appearance at the Edinburgh Festival and sang Jochanaan at the Städtische Oper, where he returned as Don Giovanni in 1953. His notable debut at the Bayreuth Festival followed in 1954 as Wolfram.

Fischer-Dieskau made his U.S. debut on April 5, 1955, as a soloist in the Brahms Requiem with the Cincinnati Sym. Orch. conducted by Thor Johnson. His U.S. recital debut then followed at N.Y.'s Town Hall on May 2, 1955. In 1957 he sang Falstaff for the first time at the Städtische Oper, and also sang that composer's Renato at the Hamburg State Opera. He portrayed Hindemith's Mathis der Maler at the Städtische Oper in 1959, and returned there as Berg's Wozzeck in 1960. On May 20, 1961, he created the role of Gregor Mittenhofer in Henze's *Elegie für junge Liebende* in Schwetzingen. He was engaged as Don Giovanni for the opening of the new Deutsche Oper in Berlin in 1961. On May 30, 1962, he was a soloist in the premiere of Britten's *War Requiem* at Coventry Cathedral under the composer's direction. In 1963 he made his first highly acclaimed tour of Japan, and then sang Barak at the opening of the renovated National Theater of the Bavarian State Opera. In 1964 he was engaged as Macbeth at the Salzburg Festival. He appeared as Mandryka at London's Covent Garden and

as Hindemith's Cardillac at the Bavarian State Opera in 1965. His notable Falstaff was portrayed at the Vienna State Opera in 1966, and then at Covent Garden in 1967. In 1968 he sang Berg's Dr. Schön in Berlin and Wotan in *Das Rheingold* at the Salzburg Festival. He returned to Berlin in 1969 as Iago. In 1971 he made his first tour of Israel with enormous success. His long-standing interest in conducting led to his engagement to record with the New Philharmonia Orch. of London in Feb. 1973. In Oct. of that year he made his public conducting debut with the Camerata Academica of Salzburg. He made his U.S. conducting debut with the Los Angeles Phil. in 1974.

In 1976, toward the close of his operatic career, Fischer-Dieskau won critical accolades for his outstanding characterization of Hans Sachs at the Deutsche Oper. He also won critical approbation for his portrayal of the title role in Reimann's *Lear* at its premiere at the Bavarian State Opera on July 9, 1978, which role he chose for his final operatic performance, on Aug. 3, 1982, at the Munich Opera Festival. In 1983 he became prof. of voice at the Berlin Hochschule für Künste, but continued to pursue a concert and lieder career until his farewell public appearance as a singer at the Bavarian State Opera on Dec. 31, 1992. Thereafter he gave increasing attention to teaching and writing while making occasional appearances as a conductor. Few singers of the 20th century ever attained and none ever surpassed Fischer-Dieskau in his dedication to and exposition of the vocal art. Whether in opera, concert, or lieder, he was acknowledged as a master recreative artist. While he will also be considered a foremost interpreter of the Romantic repertoire, his important contribution to the music of his own era must also be recognized via his performances of works ranging from Schoenberg to Matthus. Still, his name will be forever linked with Schubert, Schumann, Brahms, and Wolf as the peerless concert and lieder baritone of the age. His collaboration with the pianist Gerald Moore in an exhaustive survey of almost every Schubert lieder setting for the male voice stands as one of the great landmarks in the history of recording. Among Fischer-Dieskau's numerous awards and honors are the Arts Prize of Berlin (1950), membership in the Berlin Akademie der Künste (1956), Kammersänger of Bavaria (1959), the Mozart Medal of Vienna (1962), Kammersänger of Berlin (1963), honorary doctorates from Yale Univ. (1977), the Univ. of Oxford (1978), the Sorbonne in Paris (1980), the Royal Coll. of Music in London (1997), and the Univ. of Heidelberg (1998), the Grand Cross of Merit of the Federal Republic of Germany (1978), and the Gold Medal of the Royal Phil. Soc. of London (1988). In 1977 he married his 4th wife, **Julia Varady.**

WRITINGS: *Texte deutscher Lieder: Ein Handbuch* (Munich, 1968; 7th ed., 1986; Eng. tr., 1976, as *The Fischer-Dieskau Book of Lieder*); *Auf den Spuren der Schubert-Lieder: Werden-Wesen-Wirkung* (Wiesbaden, 1971; Eng. tr., 1976, as *Schubert: A Biographical Study of His Songs*); *Wagner und Nietzsche: Der Mystagoge und sein Abtrünniger* (Stuttgart, 1974; Eng. tr., 1976, as *Wagner and Nietzsche*); *Robert Schumann, Wort und Musik: Das Vokalwerk* (Stuttgart, 1981; Eng. tr., 1988, as *Robert Schumann, Words and Music: The Vocal Compositions*); *Töne sprechen, Worte klingen: Zur Geschichte und Interpretation des Gesangs* (Stuttgart and Munich, 1985); *Nachklang: Ansichten und Erinnerungen* (Stuttgart, 1988; Eng. tr., 1989, as *Echoes of a Lifetime*); *Wenn Musik der Liebe Nahrung ist: Künstler-Schicksale im 19. Jahrhundert* (Stuttgart, 1990); *Weil nicht alle Blütenträume reiften: Johann Friedrich Reichardt, Hofkapellmeister dreier Preussenkönige* (Stuttgart, 1992); *Fern die Klage des Fauns: Claude Debussy und seine Welt* (Stuttgart, 1993); *Schubert und seine Lieder* (Stuttgart, 1996); *Carl Friedrich Zelter und das Berliner Musikleben seiner Zeit: Eine Biographie* (Berlin, 1997).

BIBL.: K. Whitton, *D. F.-D.—Mastersinger: A Documented Study* (London and N.Y., 1981); W.-E. von Lewinski, *D. F.-D.* (Munich and Mainz, 1988); H. Neunzig, *D. F.-D.: Eine Biographie* (Stuttgart, 1995; Eng. tr., 1998, as *D. F.-D.: A Biography*). —**NS/LK/DM**

Fischhof, Joseph, Austrian pianist, pedagogue, and composer; b. Butschowitz, Moravia, April 4, 1804; d. Vienna, June 28, 1857. He settled in Vienna and studied with Halm (piano) and Seyfried (composition). In 1833 he joined the faculty of the cons. of the Gesellschaft der Musikfreunde. His valuable collection of rare musical MSS is housed in the Berlin Staatsbibliothek. He publ. *Versuch einer Geschichte des Klavier-Baus* (Vienna, 1853) and composed many piano pieces.

BIBL.: H. Kleinlercher, *J. F.* (diss., Univ. of Vienna, 1948). —**NS/LK/DM**

Fischietti, Domenico, Italian composer; b. Naples, c. 1725; d. probably in Salzburg, c. 1810. He was the son of the organist, teacher, and composer Giovanni Fischietti (1692–1743). He was a student at the S. Onofrio Cons. in Naples of Leo and Durante. After beginning his career as an opera composer in Naples, he went to Venice to collaborate with Goldoni on 4 highly successful comic operas: *Lo speziale* (Carnival 1754; Act 1 by V. Pallavicini), *La ritornata di Londra* (Feb. 1756), *Il mercato di Malmantile* (Dec. 26, 1757), and *Il Signor dottore* (1758). He then was active in Prague and Dresden, serving as court Kapellmeister in the latter city (1765–72). Upon settling in Salzburg, he was Kapellmeister to the Archbishop (1772–75) and a teacher at the Institut der Domsängerknaben (1779–83). In all, he wrote some 20 operas, the oratorio *La morte d'Abele* (1767), a Magnificat, masses, Psalms, and motets.—**NS/LK/DM**

Fišer, Luboš, Czech composer; b. Prague, Sept. 30, 1935; d. there, June 28, 1999. He studied composition with Hlobil at the Prague Cons. (1952–56) and with Bořkovec at the Prague Academy of Music, graduating in 1960. His music is often associated with paintings, archeology, and human history; his style of composition employs effective technical devices without adhering to any particular doctrine. His *15 Prints after Dürer's Apocalypse* for Orch. (1964–65), his most successful work, received the UNESCO prize in Paris in 1967.

WORKS: DRAMATIC: *Lancelot*, chamber opera (1959–60; Prague, May 19, 1961); *Dobrý voják Švejk* (The Good Soldier Schweik), musical (Prague, 1962); *Changing Game*, ballet (1971); *Faust Eternal*, television opera (1986). **ORCH.:** Suite (1954); 2 syms. (1956; 1958–60); *Symphonic Fresco* (1962–63); *Chamber Concerto* for Piano and Orch. (1964; rev. 1970); *15 Prints after Dürer's Apocalypse* (1964–65; Prague, May 15, 1966); *Pietà* for

Chamber Ensemble (1967); *Riff* (1968); *Double* (1969); *Report* for Wind Instruments (1971); *Kreutzer Étude* for Chamber Orch. (1974); *Labyrinth* (1977); *Serenade for Salzburg* for Chamber Orch. (1978); *Albert Einstein*, portrait for Organ and Orch. (1979); Piano Concerto (1980); *Meridian* (1980); *Romance* for Violin and Orch. (1980); *Centaures* (1983); Concerto for 2 Pianos and Orch. (1986); Sonata (1998; Prague, Feb. 18, 1999). **CHAMBER:** 4 *Compositions* for Violin and Piano (1955); String Quartet (1955); Sextet for Wind Quintet and Piano (1956); *Ruce* (Hands), violin sonata (1961); *Crux* for Violin, Kettledrums, and Bells (1970); Cello Sonata (1975); *Variations on an Unknown Theme* for String Quartet (1976); Piano Trio (1978); Sonata for 2 Cellos and Piano (1979); *Testis* for String Quartet (1980); Sonata for Solo Violin (1981). **KEYBOARD: Piano:** 8 sonatas (1955–96). **VOCAL:** *Caprichos* for Vocalists and Chorus (1966); Requiem for Soprano, Baritone, 2 Choruses, and Orch. (Prague, Nov. 19, 1968); *Lament over the Destruction of the City of Ur* for Soprano, Baritone, 3 Narrators, Chorus, Children's and Adult's Speaking Choruses, 7 Timpani, and 7 Bells (1969; as a ballet, 1978); *Ave Imperator* for Cello, Men's Chorus, 4 Trombones, and Percussion (1977); *The Rose* for Chorus (1977); *Per Vittoria Colona* for Cello and Women's Chorus (1979); *Istanu*, melodrama for Narrator, Alto Flute, and 4 Percussionists (1980); *Znameni* (The Sign) for Soloists, Chorus, and Orch. (1981); *Address to Music*, melodrama for Narrator and String Quartet (1982).—**NS/LK/DM**

Fisher, Avery (Robert), American pioneer in audio equipment and munificent music patron; b. N.Y., March 4, 1906; d. New Milford, Conn., Feb. 26, 1994. He was educated at N.Y. Univ. (B.S., 1929); then worked for the publishing house of Dodd, Mead as a graphics designer (1933–43). In 1937 he founded the Phil. Radio firm, later known as Fisher Radio. It became one of the foremost manufacturers of audio equipment in the world, producing high-fidelity and stereophonic components. Having amassed a substantial fortune, he sold the firm in 1969. In 1973 he gave the N.Y. Phil. $10 million to renovate the interior of Phil. Hall; in 1976 it was inaugurated at a gala concert in which it was officially renamed Avery Fisher Hall in his honor. He also created the Avery Fisher Prize, which is awarded to outstanding musicians of the day.—**NS/LK/DM**

Fisher, John Abraham, English violinist and composer; b. Dunstable or London, 1744; d. probably in London, 1806. After training with Thomas Pinto, he was a violinist in various theater orchs. in London. From about 1769 to 1778 he was concertmaster at Covent Garden, where he had success as a composer for the stage. In 1777 he received his B.M. and D.M.A. degrees from the Univ. of Oxford. During the next few years, he made successful tours of Europe as a violinist. While in Vienna in 1783, he took **Nancy Storace** as his 2nd wife, but his poor treatment of her led the Emperor to expel him the following year and his marriage collapsed. After a sojourn in Ireland (1786–88), he settled in London.

WORKS: DRAMATIC (all 1st perf. at Covent Garden, London): *The Court of Alexander*, burlesque opera (Jan. 5, 1770); *The Golden Pippin*, burletta (Feb. 5, 1773); *The Beggar's Opera*, ballad opera after John Gay (Sept. 27?, 1776); *The Tempest*, dramatic opera after Shakespeare (Dec. 27, 1776); *Love Find the Way*, comic opera (Nov. 18, 1777); also pantomimes, masques, and incidental music. **OTHER**: *Providence*, oratorio (Oxford, July 2, 1777); *6 Simphonies* (London, c. 1775); Concerto for Violin, 2 Violins, Viola, and Basso Continuo (Berlin, c. 1782); chamber music; cantatas; songs.—**NS/LK/DM**

Fisher, Sylvia (Gwendoline Victoria), admired Australian soprano; b. Melbourne, April 18, 1910. She was a student of Adolf Spivakovsky at the Melbourne Cons. In 1932 she made her operatic debut as Hermione in Lully's *Cadmus et Hermione* in Melbourne. After settling in London, she made her first appearance at Covent Garden as Beethoven's Leonore in 1949; subsequently she was a leading dramatic soprano there until 1958, excelling particularly as Sieglinde, the Marschallin, and Kostelnička in *Jenůfa*. In 1958 she sang at the Chicago Lyric Opera. She was a member of the English Opera Group in London (1963–71), and also sang there with the Sadler's Wells (later the English National) Opera. She created the role of Miss Wingrave in Britten's *Owen Wingrave* (BBC-TV, London, May 16, 1971), and was notably successful as Elizabeth I in his *Gloriana*.—**NS/LK/DM**

Fisher, William Arms, American music editor and publisher; b. San Francisco, April 27, 1861; d. Boston, Dec. 18, 1948. He studied theory with Horatio Parker and singing with William Shakespeare in London. When Dvořák went to N.Y. in 1892, Fisher became his pupil. In 1897 he settled in Boston as ed. and director of music publication for O. Ditson & Co.; was its vice president (1926–37). He ed. several vocal albums, among them *60 Irish Folksongs* (Boston, 1915) and *Ye Olde New England Psalm Tunes* (Boston, 1930). He wrote the words of the song "Goin' Home" to the melody of the slow movement of Dvořák's *New World Symphony*, a setting that became enormously popular.

WRITINGS: *Notes on Music in Old Boston* (1918); *The Music That Washington Knew* (1931); *One Hundred and Fifty Years of Music Publishing in the U.S.* (1933); *Music Festivals in the U.S.* (1934).—**NS/LK/DM**

Fisk, Eliot (Hamilton), outstanding American guitarist; b. Philadelphia, Aug. 10, 1954. He studied with Oscar Ghiglia at the Aspen School of Music (1970–76); also studied with Ralph Kirkpatrick and Albert Fuller at Yale Univ. (B.A., 1972; M.M., 1977). In 1976 he made his recital debut at N.Y.'s Alice Tully Hall. After winning the Gargano classical guitar competition in Italy in 1980, he appeared as a soloist with orchs., as a recitalist, and as a chamber music artist. He was on the faculty at the Aspen (Colo.) School of Music (1973–82), Yale Univ. (1977–82), and the Mannes Coll. of Music in N.Y. (1978–82); in 1982 he became a prof. at the Cologne Hochschule für Musik. He has expanded the repertoire of his instrument by preparing his own brilliant transcriptions of works by Bach, Scarlatti, Mozart, Paganini et al.—**NS/LK/DM**

Fiske, Roger (Elwyn), English musicologist; b. Surbiton, Sept. 11, 1910; d. London, July 22, 1987. He attended Wadham Coll., Oxford (B.A. in English, 1932), then received instruction in composition from Herbert

Howells at the Royal Coll. of Music in London before completing his education at the Univ. of Oxford (D.M.A., 1937). He was active as a BBC broadcaster (1939–59), and served as general ed. of the Eulenburg miniature scores (1968–75).

WRITINGS (all publ. in London): *Beethoven's Last Quartets* (1940); *Listening to Music* (1952); *Ballet Music* (1958); *Score Reading* (1958–65); *Chamber Music* (1969); *Beethoven's Concertos and Overtures* (1970); *English Theatre Music in the Eighteenth Century* (1973; 2nd ed., 1986); *Scotland in Music* (1983).—**NS/LK/DM**

Fistoulari, Anatole, Russian-born English conductor; b. Kiev, Aug. 20, 1907; d. London, Aug. 21, 1995. He studied with his father, Gregory Fistoulari, an opera conductor. He was only 7 when he conducted Tchaikovsky's 6th Sym. in Kiev, and he subsequently conducted throughout Russia. At 12, he made his first conducting tour of Europe. In 1931 he appeared as conductor with the Grand Opera Russe in Paris, and later conducted the Ballets Russes de Monte Carlo on tours of Europe and in 1937 on a tour of the U.S. In 1939 he joined the French Army; after its defeat in 1940, he made his way to London. In 1942 he appeared as a guest conductor with the London Sym. Orch., and then served as principal conductor of the London Phil. (1943–44). He subsequently appeared as a conductor of sym. concerts and opera in England, becoming a naturalized British subject in 1948. In 1956 he toured the Soviet Union with the London Phil. In 1942 he married Mahler's daughter Anna, but their union was dissolved in 1956.—**NS/LK/DM**

Fitelberg, Grzegorz, eminent Latvian-born Polish conductor and composer, father of **Jerzy Fitelberg**; b. Dvinsk, Oct. 18, 1879; d. Katowice, June 10, 1953. He was a student of Barcewicz (violin) and Noskowski (composition) at the Warsaw Cons. With his friend Szymanowski, he helped to found the Assn. of Young Polish Composers in Berlin in 1905. He began his career as a violinist in the Warsaw Phil., eventually serving as its concertmaster before being named its conductor in 1908. He then was a conductor at the Vienna Court Opera (1911–14) in Russia, and with Diaghilev's Ballets Russes in Paris (1921–23). After again conducting the Warsaw Phil. (1923–34), he was founder-conductor of the Polish Radio Sym. Orch. in Warsaw (1934–39). At the outbreak of World War II, he fled Europe and eventually reached Buenos Aires in 1940, later residing in the U.S. (1942–45). In 1945–46 he was a guest conductor with the London Phil. In 1947 he became conductor of the Polish Radio Sym. Orch. in Katowice. Fitelberg was a distinguished champion of Polish music. The Polish government awarded him a state prize in 1951. He composed 2 syms. (1903, 1906); Violin Concerto (1901); 2 Polish rhapsodies for Orch. (1913, 1914); *In der Meerestiefe*, symphonic poem (1913); Violin Sonata (Paderewski prize, 1896) and other chamber works.—**NS/LK/DM**

Fitelberg, Jerzy, talented Polish composer, son of **Grzegorz Fitelberg**; b. Warsaw, May 20, 1903; d. N.Y., April 25, 1951. He studied with his father before pursuing his training with Schreker at the Berlin Hochschule für Musik (1922–26). After living in Paris (1933–39), he settled in N.Y. in 1940. His works were performed at various festivals, including those at the ISCM (1932, 1937). In 1936 he was awarded the Elizabeth Sprague Coolidge price for his 4th String Quartet and in 1945 received a prize from the American Academy of Arts and Letters. His works were notable for their energetic rhythm and strong contrapuntal texture. A rather unconventional neo-Classical style later admitted elements of Polish melos.

WORKS: ORCH.: 3 suites (1925, 1928, 1930); 2 violin concertos: No. 1 (1928; Vienna, June 20, 1932; rev. 1947) and No. 2 (1935; Paris, June 22, 1937); 2 piano concertos (1929, 1934); *Prometeusz źle spętany* (The Badly Hobbled Prometheus), ballet suite (1929); Concerto for Strings (1930); String Quartet Concerto (1931); Cello Concerto (1931); *3 Mazurkas* (1932); *4 Studies* (1932); Suite for Violin and Orch. (1932); *Divertimento* (1934); *Konzertstück* (1937); *Złoty róg* (Golden Horn) for Strings (1942); *Epitafium* for Violin and Orch. (1942); *Nocturne* (1944; N.Y., March 28, 1946); Sinfonietta (1946); *Obrazy polskie* (Polish Pictures; 1946); Sym. for Strings (1946); Concerto for Trombone, Piano, and Strings (1947); Clarinet Concerto (1948). **CHAMBER**: Wind Octet (1925); 5 string quartets (1926, 1928, 1936, 1936, 1945); *Serenade* for 9 Instruments (1926); Wind Quintet (1929; rev. as *Capriccio*, 1947); *Divertimento* for Winds (1929); Piano Trio (1937); Violin Sonata (1938); Sonata for 2 Violins and Piano (1938); Sonata for Solo Cello (1945); piano pieces, including 3 sonatas (1926, 1929, 1936).—**NS/LK/DM**

Fitzenhagen, (Karl Friedrich) Wilhelm,

eminent German cellist and pedagogue; b. Seesen, Sept. 15, 1848; d. Moscow, Feb. 14, 1890. He studied piano, violin, and cello in his youth, and then cello with Plock and Theodore Müller, and finally with Grützmacher in Dresden (1867–68). He subsequently was a member of the Hofkapelle there. In 1870 he went to Moscow, where he became prof. of cello at the Imperial Cons.; thereafter gained great renown as a virtuoso and teacher. Tchaikovsky composed his *Variations on a Rococo Theme* for cello and orch. for him.—**NS/LK/DM**

Fitzgerald, Ella (Jane),

celebrated American jazz singer; b. Newport News, Va., April 25, 1917; d. Los Angeles, June 15, 1996. In a career lasting from the 1930s to the 1990s, Fitzgerald was hailed as the most accomplished female jazz singer of her time. She had a multioctave range and precise intonation and was noted for her imaginative improvisations. Getting her start as a big band singer in the 1930s, she scored an early hit with "A- Tisket, A-Tasket." Going solo in the 1940s, she paired with various other performers, including the Ink Spots, with whom she recorded the hits "Into Each Life Some Rain Must Fall" and "I'm Making Believe." She also developed a facility for scat singing apparent in her frequent performances of "Flying Home," "How High the Moon," and "Oh, Lady Be Good." She gave concerts around the world into the 1990s while continuing to make records that brought her 13 Grammy Awards.

Fitzgerald was the illegitimate daughter of William Fitzgerald and Temperance Williams. Her parents separated when she was a child, and she and her mother

moved to Yonkers, N.Y. Her mother died when she was 14, and she at first lived with an aunt in Harlem, then was placed in a reformatory, and for a time lived on the streets. On Nov. 21, 1934, she won an amateur contest at the Apollo Theatre, after which she performed in other amateur contests and began attracting attention as a singer. She made her professional debut at the Harlem Opera House the week beginning Feb. 15, 1935, an engagement that led to her being hired to sing with Chick Webb and His Orch.

Webb performed primarily at the Savoy Ballroom in N.Y. He also recorded for Decca Records, and Fitzgerald made her recording debut with him on June 12, 1935, singing "Love and Kisses" (music by J. C. Johnson, lyrics by George Whiting and Nat Schwartz). In November 1936 she did a session with Benny Goodman and His Orch., resulting in her first hit, "Goodnight, My Love" (music by Harry Revel, lyrics by Mack Gordon), which topped the hit parade in February 1937. With Webb, she returned to the top of the hit parade in August 1938 with the million-selling "A-Tisket, A-Tasket" (music and lyrics by Fitzgerald and Al Feldman, based on a traditional nursery rhyme); the recording was inducted into the Grammy Hall of Fame in 1986. Her recording with Webb of "F. D. R. Jones" (music and lyrics by Harold Rome) spent four weeks in the hit parade starting in January 1939.

Webb died on June 16, 1939, after which his band was fronted by Fitzgerald. From August to September she had a 15-minute weekly network radio show. She and the orchestra scored a Top Ten hit in January 1941 with "Five O'Clock Whistle" (music and lyrics by Josef Myrow, Kim Gannon, and Gene Irwin). She married Benjamin Kornegay on Dec. 26, 1941, but they soon separated and the marriage was annulled. In March 1942 she made her film debut in the Abbott and Costello comedy *Ride 'Em Cowboy*.

Fitzgerald's orchestra continued to perform until July 1942, after which the singer appeared with a vocal-instrumental group, The Four Keys. They had a network radio program twice a week from August to November, and Fitzgerald then hosted her own weekly show from December to June 1943. She was teamed with the Ink Spots for a recording of "Cow-Cow Boogie (Cuma-Ti-Yi-Yi-Ay)" (music and lyrics by Don Raye, Gene DePaul, and Benny Carter), which reached the Top Ten in April 1944, and they recorded together again for the million-selling hits "Into Each Life Some Rain Must Fall" (music by Doris Fisher, lyrics by Allan Roberts) and "I'm Making Believe" (music by James V. Monaco, lyrics by Mack Gordon), both of which went to #1 in December.

For her next Top Ten hit, "And Her Tears Flowed Like Wine" (music by Stan Kenton and Charles Lawrence, lyrics by Joe Greene) in January 1945, Fitzgerald was billed as a solo performer, though she was backed by the vocal group the Song Spinners and the Johnny Long Orch. She was again backed by the Song Spinners on "My Happiness" (music by Borney Bergantine, lyrics by Betty Peterson), a Top Ten hit in October 1948.

The rest of her Top Ten hits of the next five years found her paired with other performers: "I'm Beginning to See the Light" (music and lyrics by Don George, Johnny Hodges, Duke Ellington, and Harry James) with the Ink Spots in May 1945; "It's Only a Paper Moon" (music by Harold Arlen, lyrics by Billy Rose and E. Y. Harburg) with the Delta Rhythm Boys in September 1945; "You Won't Be Satisfied (Until You Break My Heart)" (music and lyrics by Teddy Powell and Larry Stock) with Louis Armstrong in April 1946; "Stone Cold Dead in the Market (He Had It Coming)" (music and lyrics by Wilmoth Houdini) with Louis Jordan and His Tympany Five in August 1946 (#1 on the R&B charts); "(I Love You) For Sentimental Reasons" (music by William Best, lyrics by Deek Watson) with the Delta Rhythm Boys in February 1947; and "Baby, It's Cold Outside" (music and lyrics by Frank Loesser) with Jordan in July 1949.

In addition to scoring pop hits, Fitzgerald consolidated her status as a major jazz singer with such performances as her October 1945 recording of "Flying Home" (music by Lionel Hampton and Benny Goodman, lyrics by Sid Robin), her March 1947 recording of "Oh, Lady Be Good" (music by George Gershwin, lyrics by Ira Gershwin), and her December 1947 recording of "How High the Moon" (music by Morgan Lewis, lyrics by Nancy Hamilton), which featured her scat singing; and with her appearances, starting in February 1949, with the all-star Jazz at the Philharmonic touring troupe, organized by impresario Norman Granz.

On Dec. 10, 1947, Fitzgerald married jazz bass player Ray Brown. They adopted a son, Ray Brown Jr., who became a drummer, and were divorced on Aug. 28, 1953. Fitzgerald made her second movie appearance in *Pete Kelly's Blues*, released in August 1955. Peggy Lee also appeared in it, and the singers' album of music from the film became a Top Ten hit.

As early as 1951, on *Ella Fitzgerald Sings Gershwin Songs*, Fitzgerald had explored the idea of recording songbooks devoted to popular song composers, but it was not until she moved from Decca Records to Norman Granz's newly formed Verve label at the start of 1956 that she turned to such recordings in earnest, beginning with the double LP *Ella Fitzgerald Sings the Cole Porter Song Book*, which reached the charts in June 1956 and was followed by collections devoted to the work of Richard Rodgers and Lorenz Hart (a chart entry in February 1957), Duke Ellington (a 1958 Grammy winner for Best Jazz Performance, Individual), Irving Berlin (a 1958 Grammy winner for Best Vocal Performance, Female, and nominee for Album of the Year), George and Ira Gershwin (a five-LP box set that made the charts and included "But Not for Me," a 1959 Grammy winner for Best Vocal Performance, Female), Harold Arlen, Jerome Kern, and Johnny Mercer. In addition, during the second half of the 1950s she recorded three duet albums with Louis Armstrong, including two, *Ella and Louis* (1956) and *Porgy and Bess* (1959), that reached the charts, as well as the LP *Ella Swing Lightly*, a 1959 Grammy winner for Best Jazz Performance, Soloist.

Fitzgerald performed extensively, at prestigious clubs like the Copacabana in N.Y. and such concert venues as the Hollywood Bowl and Carnegie Hall. She also made another movie appearance, in the W. C. Handy film biography *St. Louis Blues* in April 1958, as well as occasionally working on television. She also toured internationally, and on Feb. 13, 1960, her concert in Berlin was recorded for the album *Mack the Knife—Ella in Berlin*. The title track was released as a single, made the Top 40 in May 1960, and earned a Grammy for Best Vocal Performance, Single Record or Track, Female, and a nomination for Record of the Year; the album remained in the charts for a year and won a Grammy for Best Vocal Performance, Album, Female.

Fitzgerald made her final film appearance in November 1960 in *Let No Man Write My Epitaph*. In October 1961 she released another live album, *Ella in Hollywood*, preceded by a single version of one of her showcase songs, "Mr. Paganini (You'll Have to Swing It)" (music and lyrics by Sam Coslow), which made the easy-listening charts in August and was nominated for a Grammy for Best Solo Vocal Performance, Female. The album spent more than seven months in the charts. Her 1962 album accompanied by Nelson Riddle, *Ella Swings Brightly with Nelson*, won the year's Grammy for Best Solo Vocal Performance, Female. She reached the charts with her 1963 collaboration with Count Basie, *Ella and Basie!*, and with her 1964 collection, *Hello, Dolly!* She toured with Duke Ellington in 1965–66 and released a collaboration with him, *Ella at Duke's Place*, which earned her another Grammy nomination for Best Vocal Performance, Female.

In 1967, Fitzgerald moved to Capitol Records and recorded an album of religious songs, *Brighten the Corner*, that reached the charts in August. She also reached the charts in October 1969 with *Ella*, an album of contemporary pop songs, on Reprise. In 1972 she returned to jazz-oriented music on Norman Granz's new label, Pablo, with which she stayed for the rest of her life. Eye trouble caused her to reduce her performance schedule from 1970 to 1973, but she launched a series of appearances with symphony orchestras with a performance accompanied by the Boston Pops Orch. in 1973. She also continued to tour the U.S. and internationally.

In 1976 a Grammy for Best Jazz Vocal Performance was introduced, and Fitzgerald frequently won it, starting with the 1976 award for *Fitzgerald & Pass... Again*, an album on which she was accompanied by guitarist Joe Pass. She won the 1979 award for the album *Fine and Mellow*, the 1980 award for *A Perfect Match* (recorded with Count Basie at the 1979 Montreux Jazz Festival), and the 1981 award for her two songs on *Digital III at Montreux* (also from the 1979 Montreux Jazz Festival). She was nominated for the 1982 award for *A Classy Pair* (with Count Basie) and won the 1983 award for *The Best Is Yet to Come*.

In the summer of 1986, Fitzgerald collapsed from congestive heart failure and underwent open-heart surgery. But she recovered and went back to performing and recording. She was nominated for a 1987 Grammy for Best Jazz Vocal Performance, Female, for *Easy Living*, another album with Joe Pass, and won her 13th Grammy in the same category for her final album, *All That Jazz*, released in 1990. She retired from performing in 1992 and died from complications of diabetes in 1996 at 79.

DISC.: *Ella and Ray* (1948); *The Ella Fitzgerald Set* (1949); *Souvenir Album* (1950); *Ella Fitzgerald Sings Gershwin Songs* (1950); *Songs in a Mellow Mood* (1954); *Lullabies of Birdland* (1955); *Sweet and Hot* (1954); *Ella Fitzgerald Sings the Cole Porter Songbook* (1956); *Ella Fitzgerald Sings the Rodgers and Hart Songbook* (1956). *Porgy and Bess* (1956); *Like Someone in Love* (1957); *Ella Fitzgerald Sings the Duke Ellington Songbook* (1957); *Ella Fitzgerald Sings the Gershwin Songbook* (1957); *Ella Sings Gershwin* (1957); *Ella and Her Fellas* (1957); *Ella Fitzgerald at the Opera House* (1958); *Ella Fitzgerald Sings the Irving Berlin Songbook* (1958); *First Lady of Song* (1958); *Miss Ella Fitzgerald and Mr. Nelson Riddle Invite You to Listen and Relax* (1958); *Ella Fitzgerald and Billie Holiday at Newport* (1958); *For Sentimental Reasons* (1958); *Ella Fitzgerald Sings the George and Ira Gershwin Songbook* (1959); *Ella Swings Lightly* (1959); *Ella Sings Sweet Songs for Swingers* (1959); *Hello Love* (1959); *Get Happy!* (1959); *Mack the Knife—Ella in Berlin* (1960); *Ella Wishes You a Swinging Christmas* (1960); *The Intimate Ella* (1960); *Golden Favorites* (1961); *Ella Returns to Berlin* (1961); *Ella Sings the Harold Arlen Songbook* (1961); *Clap Hands, Here Comes Charlie!* (1962); *Ella Swings Brightly with Nelson* (1962); *Ella Swings Gently with Nelson* (1962); *Rhythm Is My Business* (1962); *Ella Fitzgerald Sings the Jerome Kern Songbook* (1963); *These Are the Blues* (1963); *Ella Sings Broadway* (1963); *Ella and Basie!* (1963); *Ella at Juan-Les-Pins* (1964); *Hello, Dolly!* (1964); *Stairway to the Stars* (1964); *Early Ella* (1964); *A Tribute to Cole Porter* (1964); *Ella Fitzgerald Sings the Johnny Mercer Songbook* (1965); *Ella in Hamburg* (1966); *The World of Ella Fitzgerald* (1966); *Whisper Not* (1966); *Brighten the Corner* (1967); *Misty Blue* (1968); *Ella 'Live* (1968); *30 by Ella* (1968); *Sunshine of Your Love/Watch What Happens* (1969); *Ella* (1969); *Things Ain't What They Used to Be* (1970); *Ella at Nice* (1971); *Ella Fitzgerald at Carnegie Hall* (1973); *Ella in London* (1974); *Fine and Mellow* (1974); *Ella—At the Montreux Jazz Festival, 1975* (1975); *Lady Time* (1978); *Dream Dancing* (1978); *Digital III at Montreux* (1980); *Ella Fitzgerald Sings the Antonio Carlos Jobim Songbook* (1981); *The Best Is Yet to Come* (1982); *Speak Love* (1983); *Nice Work If You Can Get It* (1983); *Easy Living* (1986); *All That Jazz* (1990); *A 75th Birthday Tribute* (1993). Count Basie and Joe Williams: *One O' Clock Jump* (1956). Louis Armstrong: *Ella and Louis* (1956); *Ella and Louis Again* (1956). Duke Ellington: *Ella at Duke's Place* (1966); *The Stockholm Concert* (1966); *Ella and Duke at the Cote D'Azure* (1966). Joe Pass: *Take Love Easy* (1974); *Fitzgerald and Pass Again* (1976). Oscar Peterson: *Ella and Oscar* (1975). Tommy Flanagan: *Ella Fitzgerald with the Tommy Flanagan Trio* (1977). Count Basie: *A Classy Pair* (1979); *A Perfect Match: Basie and Ella* (1979).

BIBL.: S. Colin, *E. The Life and Times of E. F.* (London, 1986); B. Kliment, *E. F.* (N.Y., 1988); J. Haskins, *E. F.: A Life Through Jazz* (London, 1991); S. Nicholson, *E. F.* (London, 1993); C. Wyman, *E. F.: Jazz Singer Supreme* (N.Y., 1993); G. Fidelman, *First Lady of Song: E. F. for the Record* (N.Y., 1994); L. Gourse, ed., *The E. F. Companion* (N.Y., 1998).—**WR**

Fitzwilliam, Viscount Richard, wealthy English collector of paintings, engravings, books, and musical MSS; b. Richmond, Surrey, Aug. 1745; d. London, Feb. 4, 1816. He bequeathed his library to Cambridge Univ. The musical MSS include especially valuable works: the immensely important *Fitzwilliam Virginal Book* (often wrongly termed *Virginal Booke of Queen Elizabeth*), anthems in Purcell's hand, sketches by Handel, and many early Italian compositions. Vincent Novello ed. and publ. 5 vols. of the Italian sacred music as *The Fitzwilliam Music* (London, 1825); J.A. Fuller Maitland and A.H. Mann made a complete catalog of it (1893). The entire contents of the *Fitzwilliam Virginal Book* were ed. and publ. by J.A. Fuller Maitland and William Barclay Squire (2 vols., Leipzig and London, 1894–99; facsimile reprint, N.Y., 1954).

BIBL.: E. Naylor, *An Elizabethan Virginal Book* (London, 1905).—**NS/LK/DM**

Fiume, Orazio, Italian composer and teacher; b. Monopoli, Jan. 16, 1908; d. Trieste, Dec. 21, 1976. He studied piano and theory in Palermo and Naples, and was later a student of Pizzetti (composition) and Molinari (conducting) in Rome. He taught harmony at the Parma Cons. (1941–51), in Milan (1951–59), and in Pesaro (1959–60); was director of the Trieste Cons. (from 1961). His music followed the tradition of expansive Italian Romanticism. He wrote *3 Pieces* for Chamber Orch. (1937), *Ajace*, cantata (1940), 2 concertos for Orch. (1945, 1956), Sym. (1956), *Il tamburo di panno*, opera (Rome, April 12, 1962), and songs.—**NS/LK/DM**

Five Satins, The, a pioneering doo-wop group, founded in New Haven, Conn., 1955. Leader Fred Parris (b. New Haven, Conn., March 26, 1936) and several other members over the course of 45 years.

While on guard duty one night during his tour in the army, Freddie Parris wrote one of the all-time vocal group classics, "In the Still of the Nite." Parris had led several vocal groups at home in New Haven, recording several singles with The Scarletts. The Scarletts were called to the service pretty much en masse and stationed all over the world. After writing this tune, Paris returned to New Haven on leave, assembled several singers and a band. He arranged for space in the basement of St. Bernadette's church and cut the tune. Because it was a new group, he didn't feel right using the Scarletts's name, so the new group became the Five Satins. The song's nonsense syllable backing track is often credited with giving the doo-wop genre its name. The song rose to #24 pop, #3 R&B. Anxious to follow up the hit, the group cut another track, "To the Aisle," despite Parris being stationed in Japan at the time (Bill Baker sang lead).

"In the Still of the Nite" proved incredibly durable, charting again in both 1960 and 1961. After spending much of the 1960s on the sidelines of pop, Parris reformed the group in 1969 as the only original member. They hit the oldies circuit with great success, and continue to be a draw on revival tours. They also tried some fresh music. As Black Satin they released the 1976 top 50 R&B hit "Everybody Stand Up and Clap Your Hands (For the Entertainer)." In 1982, they hit #71 on the pop charts with a medley of doo-wop hits called "Memories of Days Gone By." Parris contends that "In the Still of the Nite" has sold over ten million copies, yet he has not even received a gold record for it. He continues to take quintets on tour as the Five Satins, still singing that tune he wrote on guard duty those many years ago.

DISC.: *F. S. Sing* (1957); *Encore, Vol. 2* (1960); *The F. S.* (1981); *In the Still of the Night* (1990); *Lost Treasures* (1995).—**HB**

Fizdale, Robert, American pianist; b. Chicago, April 12, 1920; d. N.Y., Dec. 6, 1995. He studied with Ernest Hutcheson at the Juilliard School of Music in N.Y. He formed a piano duo with Arthur Gold, and they made their professional debut at N.Y.'s New School for Social Research in 1944 in a program devoted entirely to John Cage's music for prepared pianos. They toured widely in the U.S., Europe, and South America; works were written specially for them by Barber, Milhaud, Poulenc, Auric, Thomson, Dello Joio, and Rorem. With Gold, Fizdale publ. a successful book, *Misia* (N.Y., 1979), on the life of Maria Godebska, a literary and musical figure in Paris early in the century. He retired in 1982. —**NS/LK/DM**

Fjeldstad, Øivin, Norwegian conductor; b. Christiania, May 2, 1903; d. there (Oslo), Oct. 16, 1983. He was a pupil of Lange at the Christiania Cons., Davisson at the Leipzig Cons., and Krauss at the Berlin Cons. He began his career as a violinist in 1921, and then was a member of the Christiania (later Oslo) Phil. (1924–45). In 1931 he made his conducting debut with the Oslo Phil. He served as chief conductor of the Norwegian State Broadcasting Orch. in Oslo (1945–62), the Oslo Opera (1958–59), and the Oslo Phil. (1962–69). He was a persuasive advocate of Scandinavian music. —**NS/LK/DM**

Flackton, William, English organist and composer; b. Canterbury (baptized), March 1709; d. there, Jan. 5, 1798. He was a bookseller and stationer by trade, but he also served as organist at Faversham (1735–52). He composed 6 sonatas for 2 violins and cello or harpsichord (1758), 6 solos for cello or viola and cello or harpsichord (1770), 6 overtures adapted for harpsichord or piano (1771), 2 solos, 1 for cello and 1 for viola (1776), church music, etc.—**NS/LK/DM**

Flagello, Ezio (Domenico), American bass, brother of **Nicolas (Oreste) Flagello;** b. N.Y., Jan. 28, 1931. He was a pupil of Schorr and Brownlee at the Manhattan School of Music in N.Y. In 1952 he made his debut in a concert perf. of *Boris Godunov* at N.Y.'s Carnegie Hall, followed in 1955 by his stage debut as Dulcamara at the Empire State Festival in Ellenville, N.Y. He then pursued his training in Rome on a Fulbright scholarship with Luigi Rossi, appearing as Dulcamara with the Opera there in 1956. In 1957 he won the Metropolitan Opera Auditions of the Air, which led to his debut with the company in N.Y. as the Jailer in *Tosca* on Nov. 9 of that year. He subsequently sang regularly there until 1987. In 1966 he created the role of Enobarbus in Barber's *Antony and Cleopatra* at the opening of the new Metropolitan Opera house. He also was a guest artist in Vienna, Berlin, and Milan. He was particularly known for his buffo roles, excelling in operas by Mozart and Rossini. He also was successful in operas by Verdi and Wagner.—**NS/LK/DM**

Flagello, Nicolas (Oreste), American composer and conductor, brother of **Ezio (Domenico) Flagello;** b. N.Y., March 15, 1928; d. New Rochelle, N.Y., March 16, 1994. He began piano lessons at the incredible age of 3, and played in public at 5. At 6, he began taking violin lessons with Francesco di Giacomo. He also learned to play the oboe, and was a member of the school band, performing on these instruments according to demand. In 1945–46 he played the violin in Stokowski's All-American Youth Orch. in N.Y. In 1946 he entered the Manhattan School of Music (B.M., 1949; M.M., 1950), studying with a variety of teachers in multifarious subjects (Harold Bauer, Hugo Kortschak, Hugh Ross, and Vittorio Giannini). He also took conducting lessons with Mitropoulos. It was with Giannini that he had his most important training in composition (1935–50), and it was Giannini who influenced him most in his style of composition—melodious, harmonious, euphonious, singingly Italianate, but also dramatically modern. After obtaining his master's degree, Flagello took lessons with Pizzetti at the Accademia di Santa Cecilia in Rome (Mus.D., 1956). He taught composition and conducting at the Manhattan School of Music from 1950 to 1977. He also appeared as a guest conductor with the Chicago Lyric Opera and the N.Y. City Opera, and toured as accompanist to Tito Schipa, Richard Tucker, and other singers.

WORKS: DRAMATIC: O p e r a : *Mirra* (1953); *The Wig* (1953); *Rip Van Winkle* (1957); *The Sisters* (1958; N.Y., Feb. 23, 1961); *The Judgment of St. Francis* (1959; N.Y., March 18, 1966); *The Piper of Hamelin* (1970); *Beyond the Horizon* (1983). **ORCH.:** *Beowulf* (1949); 4 piano concertos (1950, 1956, 1962, 1975); *Symphonic Aria* (1951); *Overture giocosa* (1952); Flute Concerto (1956); *Missa sinfonica* (1957); Concerto for Strings (1959); *Capriccio* for Cello and Orch. (1962); *Lautrec* (1965); 2 syms. (1968, 1970); *Serenata* (1968); *Credendum* for Violin and Orch. (1974); *Odyssey* for Band (1981); *Concerto sinfonico* for Saxophone Quartet and Orch. (1985). **CHAMBER:** *Divertimento* for Piano and Percussion (1960); Harp Sonata (1961); *Burlesca* for Flute and Guitar (1961); Piano Sonata (1962); Concertino for Piano, Brass, and Timpani (1963); Violin Sonata (1963); Suite for Harp and String Trio (1965); *Electra* for Piano and Percussion (1966); *Declamation* for Violin and Piano (1967); *Ricercare* for Brass and Percussion (1971); *Prisma* for 7 Horns (1974); *Diptych* for 2 Trumpets and Trombone (1979). **VOCAL:** *The Land* for Bass-baritone and Orch. (1954); 5 songs for Soprano and Orch. (1955); *Tristis est anima mea* for Chorus and Orch. (1959); *Dante's Farewell* for Soprano and Orch. (1962); *Contemplazioni* for Soprano and Orch. (1964); *Te Deum for All Mankind* for Chorus and Orch. (1967); *Passion of Martin Luther King*, oratorio for Bass-baritone, Chorus, and Orch. (1968); *Remembrance* for Soprano, Flute, and String Quartet (1971); *Canto* for Soprano and Orch. (1978); *Quattro amori* for Mezzo-soprano and Piano (1983). —**NS/LK/DM**

Flagg, Josiah, American bandmaster; b. Woburn, Mass., May 28, 1737; d. probably in Boston, Jan. 2, 1795(?). He organized and drilled the first regular militia band of Boston (most probably the first group of that nature in America). On June 29, 1769, he presented its first concert, and on Oct. 28, 1773, he gave a "final Grand Concert" at Faneuil Hall with about 50 players. Subsequently he settled in Providence and served there as lieutenant colonel during the Revolution. Little is known of his other activities. He publ. *A Collection of the best Psalm Tunes in 2, 3 and 4 parts...To which is added some Hymns and Anthems, the Greater part of them never before printed in America* (1764; introduced the anthem to the English colonies; engraved by Paul Revere) and *Sixteen Anthems...To which is added a few Psalm Tunes* (1766). Flagg was the first in America to establish a connection between sacred and secular music. That he was an educated practical musician and was acquainted with European music is evidenced by the type of programs he conducted.—NS/LK/DM

Flagstad, Kirsten (Malfrid),

famous Norwegian soprano; b. Hamar, July 12, 1895; d. Oslo, Dec. 7, 1962. She studied voice with her mother and with Ellen Schytte-Jacobsen in Christiania, then made her operatic debut there as Nuri in d'Albert's *Tiefland* (Dec. 12, 1913). During the next 2 decades, she sang throughout Scandinavia, appearing in operas and operettas, and in concert. In 1933 she sang a number of minor roles at Bayreuth, and then scored her first major success there in 1934 when she appeared as Sieglinde. She made an auspicious Metropolitan Opera debut in N.Y. in that same role on Feb. 2, 1935, and was soon hailed as the foremost Wagnerian soprano of her time. On May 18, 1936, she made her first appearance at London's Covent Garden as Isolde. While continuing to sing at the Metropolitan Opera, she made guest appearances at the San Francisco Opera (1935–38) and the Chicago Opera (1937), and also gave concerts with major U.S. orchs. She returned to her Nazi-occupied homeland in 1941 to be with her husband, a decision that alienated many of her admirers. Nevertheless, after World War II, she resumed her career with notable success at Covent Garden. In 1951 she also returned to the Metropolitan Opera, where she sang Isolde and Leonore; made her farewell appearance there in Gluck's *Alceste* on April 1, 1952. She retired from the operatic stage in 1954, but continued to make recordings. From 1958 to 1960 she was director of the Norwegian Opera in Oslo. Among her other celebrated roles were Brünnhilde, Elisabeth, Elsa, and Kundry. She narrated an autobiography to L. Biancolli, which was publ. as *The Flagstad Manuscript* (N.Y., 1952).

BIBL.: E. McArthur, *F.: A Personal Memoir* (N.Y., 1965); T. Gunnarson, *Sannheten om K. F.: En dokumentarbiografi* (Oslo, 1985); H. Vogt, *F.* (London, 1987); E. Østby, ed., *K. F.: Århundrets stemme: The Voice of a Century* (Hamar, 1994).—NS/LK/DM

Flament, Édouard,

French bassoonist, conductor, and composer; b. Douai, Aug. 27, 1880; d. Bois-Colombes, Seine, Dec. 27, 1958. He studied at the Paris Cons. with Bourdeau (bassoon), Lavignac, Caussade, and Lenepveu (composition). After graduation (1898), he played the bassoon in the Lamoureux Orch. (1898–1907) and in the Société des Instruments à Vent (1898–1923) in Paris; conducted opera and concerts in Paris (1907–12), Algiers (1912–14), and Marseilles (1919–20), and summer concerts at Fontainebleau (1920–22); then with the Diaghilev ballet in Monte Carlo, Berlin, London, and Spain (1923–29). In 1930 he became conductor at the Paris Radio.

WORKS: DRAMATIC: Opera: *La Fontaine de Castalie*; *Le Coeur de la rose*; *Lydéric et Rosèle*. **ORCH.:** 8 syms.; *Oceano Nox*, symphonic poem; *Variations radio-phoniques*; 5 piano concertos; *Concertstück* for Bassoon and Orch. **CHAMBER:** *Divertimento* for 6 Bassoons; Quintet for 5 Bassoons; Quartet for 4 Bassoons; 3 string quartets; Violin Sonata; Viola Sonata; 2 cello sonatas.—NS/LK/DM

Flamingos, The,

seminal, and perhaps the best, vocal group of the doo-wop era. **MEMBERSHIP:** Zeke Carey (b. Bluefield, Va., Jan. 24, 1933); Jake Carey (b. Pulaski, Va., Sept. 9, 1926); Johnny Carter (b. Chicago, June 2, 1934); Sollie McElroy (b. Gulfport, Mass., July 16, 1933; d. Jan. 14, 1995); Paul Wilson (b. Chicago, Jan. 6, 1935; d. May 1988).

The Flamingos were unique among vocal harmony groups of the 1950s because of their emphasis on harmony. Jake and Zeke Carey, cousins from Va., moved to Chicago in 1950. They met Paul Wilson and Johnny Carter while singing in the church choir. The group honed their sound singing at rent parties, sometimes doing as many as four or five on a Saturday night. They had some minor local hits in the early 1950s with songs that have become treasures among vocal group aficionados: "If I Can't Have You," "That's My Desire," and "Golden Teardrops" showcased the group's complex, sweet and sour harmonies. When lead singer McElroy left in the mid 1950s, replaced by Nate Nelson (b. Chicago, April 10, 1932; d. April 10, 1984), the group started enjoying some chart success, landing a #5 R&B hit early in 1956 with "I'll Be Home." Pat Boone recorded the song at nearly the same time. His version went gold and hit #4 on the pop charts.

After this small success, the group broke up temporarily when several members were drafted. They re-formed a year later. In 1958, they recorded an updated version of a 1930s chestnut that had been a #2 hit in 1934. The song, "I Only Have Eyes for You" rose to #11 and has become one of the standards for oldies radio. The group didn't see royalties for the record, however, until 1991. Over the next several years, the group was intensely prolific, cutting several albums and landing R&B hits with "I Was Such a Fool" and "Time Was." In 1960, they took Sam Cooke's "Nobody Loves Me Like You" to #30 on the pop charts. The group remained active, touring regularly. They tried to remain relevant and even landed several hits with the #22 R&B flavored "Boogaloo Party" in 1966 and the #28 "Buffalo Soldier" in 1970. By the mid-1970s, they were relegated to the oldies circuit. Into the late 1990s, Jake and Zeke Carey continued to tour with various Flamingos.

DISC.: *The F. Meet the Moonglows on the Dusty Road of Hits* (1953); *The F.* (1959); *Flamingo Serenade* (1959); *Flamingo Favorites* (1960); *Requestfully Yours* (1960); *The Sound of the F.* (1962); *Collectors Showcase* (1964); *The F.* (1965); *Today* (1972); *The Fabulous Flamingos* (1992).—HB

Flanagan, Tommy (Lee),

jazz pianist; b. Detroit, March 16, 1930. Flanagan's father was Irish, and his mother African-American. He commenced clarinet studies at six and piano training at 11, working throughout his adolescence in local jazz haunts with various senior musicians, including Milt Jackson, Thad Jones, and Elvin Jones. He made his pro debut with Dexter Gordon in 1945. In 1956 he went to N.Y., where he performed and recorded with Oscar Pettiford, J.J. Johnson, Miles Davis, and others. He admired Coltrane, employed him on his album *The Cats,* and although the two never performed together in public Coltrane in turn employed Flanagan for the album *Giant Steps* (1959). He explained his famously cautious solo on this difficult piece by reporting that Coltrane had casually shown him the chords at the piano before the session but had not indicated that it was to be played fast! He subsequently was pianist for Coleman Hawkins, and music director for Ella Fitzgerald (1962 to 1965 and again 1968–78) and accompanied Tony Bennett. Since 1978, he has toured primarily with a trio. He won the Danish Jazzpar Award in 1992 and the NEA Jazzmasters award in 1996.

DISC.: *Overseas* (1957); *Cats* (1957); *Moodsville* (1960); *Trinity* (1975); *Montreux 1977* (1977); *Eclypso* (1977); *Confirmation* (1977); *Alone Too Long* (1977); *Together with Kenny Barron* (1978); *Our Delights* (1978); *More Delights with Hank Jones* (1978); *Magnificent Tommy Flanagan* (1981); *Thelonica* (1982); *Giant Steps* (1982); *Blues in the Closet* (1983); *Jazz Poet* (1989); *Little Pleasure* (1990); *Beyond the Blue Bird* (1990); *Lady Be Good...For Ella* (1994). —LP

Flanagan, William (Jr.), American composer and music critic; b. Detroit, Aug. 14, 1923; d. of an overdose of barbituates in N.Y., Aug. 31, 1969. He studied composition at the Eastman School of Music in Rochester, N.Y., with Phillips and Rogers; then at the Berkshire Music Center in Tanglewood with Honegger, Berger, and Copland; also, in N.Y., with Diamond. Concurrently, he became engaged in musical journalism; was a reviewer for the *N.Y. Herald Tribune* (1957–60) and later wrote for *Stereo Review.* His style of composition was characterized by an intense pursuit of an expressive melodic line, projected on polycentric but firmly tonal harmonies.

WORKS: DRAMATIC: Opera: *Bartleby* (1952–57; N.Y., Jan. 24, 1961); *The Ice Age* (1967; unfinished); incidental music to E. Albee's plays *The Sandbox* (1961), *The Ballad of Bessie Smith* (1961), *The Ballad of the Sad Cafe* (1963), and *Malcolm* (1966). **CHAMBER:** *Divertimento* for String Quartet (1947); *Chaconne* for Violin and Piano (1948). **KEYBOARD: Piano:** *Passacaglia* (1947); Sonata (1950). **VOCAL:** *The Waters of Babylon* for Voices and String Quartet (1947); *Billy in the Darbies* for Chorus and Piano or Orch. (1949); *A Woman of Valor* for Chorus (1949); *The Weeping Pleiades* for Baritone and 5 Instruments (1953); *The Lady of Tearful Regret* for Soprano, Baritone, Flute, Clarinet, String Quartet, and Piano (1959); *King Midas* for Soloists and Orch. (c. 1961); *Chapter from Ecclesiastes* for Chorus and String Quintet (1962); *Another August* for Soprano, Piano, Harpsichord, and Small Orch. (1966); various songs. **OTHER:** 2 films scores. **ORCH.:** *A Concert Overture* (1948; N.Y., Dec. 4, 1959); *Divertimento* (1948; Toledo, Ohio, Jan. 9, 1960); *A Concert Ode* (1951; Detroit, Jan. 14, 1960); *Notations* (1960); *Narrative* (1964; Detroit, March 25, 1965).**—NS/LK/DM**

Flatt and Scruggs, American bluegrass duo. Lester Raymond Flatt, voc., gtr. (b. Overton County, Tenn., June 28, 1914; d. Nashville, May 11, 1979) and

Earl Eugene Scruggs, bjo. (b. Cleveland County, N.C., Jan. 6, 1924), along with their group, the Foggy Mountain Boys, were, after Bill Monroe, the primary performers of bluegrass music from the 1940s to the 1960s. Scruggs was a virtuoso banjo player who revolutionized the approach to the instrument, notably on such self-written hits as "Foggy Mountain Breakdown." The duo popularized bluegrass music and made inroads into folk and pop during the 1960s with such hits as "The Ballad of Jed Clampett."

Flatt and Scruggs first played together as members of Bill Monroe's backup group, the Bluegrass Boys, from December 1945, when Scruggs joined the band, to January 1948, when both musicians resigned. Forming the Foggy Mountain Boys, they began a series of jobs at local radio stations around the South. They signed to Mercury Records and made their first recordings for the label in October 1948. At their third recording session on Dec. 11, 1949, they recorded Scrugg's fast-paced instrumental "Foggy Mountain Breakdown." In 1950 they switched to Columbia Records, with which they remained for the rest of their career.

Flatt and Scruggs reached the Top Ten of the country charts in February 1952 with "'Tis Sweet to Be Remembered" (music and lyrics by Foggy Mountain Boys guitarist and singer Mac Wiseman). In June 1953 they began to perform on WSM, the Nashville radio station that sponsors the *Grand Ole Opry.* They joined the *Grand Ole Opry* in 1955.

Flatt and Scruggs scored their second Top Ten country hit with "Cabin in the Hills" (music and lyrics by Cal DeVoll) in 1959. Their career was buoyed by the folk music revival of the late 1950s. Scruggs appeared at the first Newport Folk Festival in 1959, and the group performed at the second in 1960. They made their network television debut in July 1960 on the special *Folk Sound, U.S.A.* They hit the Top Ten of the country charts for the third time in 1961 with "Go Home" (music and lyrics by Onie Wheeler). In September 1962 the situation comedy *The Beverly Hillbillies* began a nine-year run on television, using as its themesong the duo's recording of "The Ballad of Jed Clampett" (music and lyrics by Paul Henning). Their single of the song entered the pop and country charts in December 1962, becoming a #1 country hit in January 1963. It was nominated for the 1962 Grammy Award for Best Folk Recording.

The success of "The Ballad of Jed Clampett" expanded Flatt and Scruggs's popularity. On Dec. 8, 1962, they performed at Carnegie Hall in N.Y., recording the show for an album that made the Top Ten of the country charts and crossed over to the pop charts; it also was nominated for a 1963 Grammy Award for Best Country & Western Recording. In the spring of 1963 they returned to the Top Ten of the country singles charts with "Pearl Pearl Pearl" (music and lyrics by Paul Henning), another song featured on *The Beverly Hillbillies.*

Flatt and Scruggs placed two more albums, *Recorded Live at Vanderbilt University* and *The Fabulous Sound of Lester Flatt & Earl Scruggs* in the Top Ten of the country charts in 1964 and continued to reach the country charts consistently for the next few years. Their career took another upswing when their 1949 recording of "Foggy

1129

Mountain Breakdown" was used in the film *Bonnie & Clyde* in 1967. They rerecorded the song for Columbia, and Mercury rereleased the original, under the title "Theme from *Bonnie & Clyde*"; both made the pop singles charts in March 1968. There were also three competing LPs: Columbia's *Changin' Times Featuring Foggy Mountain Breakdown* reached the country Top Ten and crossed over to the pop charts and its *The Story of Bonnie & Clyde* reached both charts, as did Mercury's *Original Theme from "Bonnie & Clyde"*. The Columbia rerecording of "Foggy Mountain Breakdown" won Flatt and Scruggs their only Grammy Award, for Best Country Performance, Duo or Group, Vocal or Instrumental.

Despite their success, Flatt and Scruggs disagreed over musical direction. Scruggs favored a more eclectic approach, while Flatt preferred to play in a traditional style. As a result, they broke up in March 1969. Flatt formed the Nashville Grass to play in a similar manner to the early Flatt and Scruggs. Scruggs formed the Earl Scruggs Revue, which featured his sons and played in more of a country-rock style. Flatt died of a heart attack at 64 in 1979.

WRITINGS: E. Scruggs, *Earl Scruggs and the 5-String Banjo* (N.Y., 1968).

BIBL.: J. Lambert and C. Seckler, *The Good Things Outweigh the Bad: A Biography of Lester Flatt* (Hendersonville, Tenn., 1982). —WR

Flecha, Mateo, Spanish composer; b. Prades, Tarragona, c. 1530; d. Solsona, Lerida, Feb. 20, 1604. He received his musical education from his uncle, also named Mateo Flecha (1481–1553); was boy chorister in the court chapel at Arevalo. In 1564 he entered the imperial chapel in Vienna; by 1579 was in Prague with the Emperor; Philip III made it possible for him to return to Spain as abbot of Portella in 1599. He publ. a book of madrigals in Venice (1568), and the collection *Las ensaladas* (Prague, 1581), containing "ensaladas" (quodlibets, comic songs) by his uncle, and some by himself. This collection was brought out in a modern ed. by Higinio Angles, with an introductory essay on the Flechas (Barcelona, 1954).—NS/LK/DM

Fleck, Bela, bluegrass/jazz banjo player, b. N.Y.C., July, 10, 1958. He has played traditional bluegrass, newgrass (with the New Grass Revival), and his own innovative material with his band the Flecktones. He has been in high demand as a session player. Bela Fleck was given his first banjo by his grandfather in 1973, when he was 15 years old. He attended N.Y.C.'s H.S. of Music and Art. Early influences were Flatt and Scruggs, Chick Corea and Charlie Parker. Especially inspired by a Corea performance, Fleck moved to Boston in 1976 where he joined Tasty Licks. In 1979 he moved to Ky. and founded Spectrum. Two years later, he joined the New Grass Revival and moved to Nashville. He stayed with them through the 1980s and also released solo albums including the Grammy-nominated *Drive*, had a jazz band called Banjo Jazz, and produced the Nashville Bluegrass Band, and Maura O'Connell. In 1989 New Grass Revival gave its farewell concert and he founded the Flecktones. After appearances on *The Tonight Show*

and *The Today Show* as well as two Grammy nominations, the band released 1991's *Flight of the Cosmic Hippo*, an album that hit #1 on the jazz charts.

DISC.: *Crossing the Tracks* (1979); *Natural Bridge* (1982); *Deviation* (1984); *Double Time* (1984); *Inroads* (1986); *60 Plus Series* (1987); *Day Break* (1988); *Drive* (1988); *Places* (1988); *Bela Fleck & The Flecktones* (1990); *Flight of the Cosmic Hippo* (1991); *Ufo Tofu* (1992); *Three Flew over the Cuckoo's Nest* (1993); *Tales from the Acoustic Planet* (1995); *Live Art* (1996).—LP

Fleetwood Mac, one-time blues band that grew into a monstrously popular rock ensemble and traveling soap opera. **MEMBERSHIP:** Mick Fleetwood, drm. (b. London, June 24, 1942); John McVie, bs. (b. London, Nov. 26, 1945); Peter Green, gtr., voc. (b. Bethnal Greenbaum, London, Oct. 29, 1946); Jeremy Spencer, gtr., voc. (b. West Hartlepool, Lancashire, England, July 4, 1948); Danny Kirwan, gtr. voc. (b. London, May 13, 1950) was added in August 1968. Green departed in May 1970. Christine McVie, kybd., voc. (b. Perfect, Birmingham, England, July 12, 1943), joined in August 1970. Spencer left in February 1971. Bob Welch, lead gtr., voc. (b. Los Angeles, July 31, 1946), joined in April 1971 and left at the end of 1974. In January 1975, Lindsey Buckingham, gtr., voc. (b. Palo Alto, Calif., Oct. 3, 1947) and Stephanie "Stevie" Nicks, voc. (b. Phoenix, Ariz., May 26, 1948) joined. Later members included guitarist-vocalists Billy Burnette (b. Memphis, Tenn., May 8, 1953); Rick Vito (b. Darby, Pa., Oct. 13, 1949); Dave Mason (b. Worcester, England, May 10, 1946), and singer Bekka Bramlett.

Undergoing numerous personnel and stylistic changes for over 25 years, Fleetwood Mac was one of the longest lived of the British groups of the 1960s, surpassed in terms of longevity by only The Rolling Stones. Formed by two former members of John Mayall's Bluesbreakers in 1967, Fleetwood Mac initially pursued a successful British career as a blues band during the late 1960s blues revival. For a time sporting a three-guitar front line of Peter Green, Jeremy Spencer, and Danny Kirwan, the band gradually left the blues behind with the departure of cofounder Green in 1969. At the time of his exit, Peter Green was considered one of Great Britain's premier blues-based guitarists, rivaled by only Eric Clapton in terms of aptitude and stature. Breaking through in the United States with 1970's *Kiln House*, Fleetwood Mac subsequently added singer-keyboardist-songwriter Christine McVie and singer-songwriter Bob Welch, eventually transforming into a British-Calif. soft-rock band with the addition of Californians "Stevie" Nicks and Lindsey Buckingham in 1975. Achieving massive sales with 1975's *Fleetwood Mac* and 1977's *Rumours*, one of the biggest-selling albums of all time, Fleetwood Mac endured into the 1990s with Mick Fleetwood and John McVie as the mainstays.

Fleetwood Mac was formed in July 1967 by two former members of John Mayall's Bluesbreakers, Peter Green and Mick Fleetwood, with Jeremy Spencer and Bob Brunning. Green had joined Mayall following Eric Clapton's departure to form Cream in mid-1966 and appeared on Mayall's *A Hard Road* album. Green had previously been a member of Peter B's Looners and Shotgun Express, as had Mick Fleetwood. Fleetwood, a drummer since the age of 13, worked with Mayall's group in 1967. Bassist John McVie, a member of The Bluesbreakers since 1963, replaced Brunning in September.

Originally known as Peter Green's Fleetwood Mac, the group debuted at the British National Jazz and Blues Festival on Aug. 12, 1967, and soon signed with Mike Vernon's Blue Horizon label. Issued on Epic in the United States, their debut album included songs by Elmore James, Howlin' Wolf, and Sonny Boy Williamson, as well as blues-based originals by Green and Spencer. Only marginally successful in the United States, the album proved immensely popular in Great Britain and helped spark the British blues explosion of the late 1960s. The group soon scored their first (top) British-only hit with Green's instrumental "Albatross." In August 1968, Green brought in a third guitarist-vocalist, Danny Kirwan, and Fleetwood Mac's second American album, *English Rose*, contained songs by all three guitarists, including Green's "Black Magic Woman," popularized by Santana in 1970. Green's "Man of the World" became a smash British hit in 1969, the year Fleetwood Mac recorded two albums in Chicago with blues greats such as Otis Spann and Willie Dixon.

Switching to Reprise Records, Fleetwood Mac next recorded *Then Play On*. One of the most diverse recordings by the group, the album featured a number of pop-style songs by Green. His "Oh Well" became a smash British and minor American hit, but, unexpectedly, he announced his departure from the group, playing his last engagement with them in May 1970. He subsequently recorded an album for Reprise, only to drop out of sight for many years. Green eventually reemerged in the late 1970s on Sail Records, only to abandon music once again.

Fleetwood Mac's first album without Peter Green, *Kiln House*, confirmed the group's move toward a softer, more harmonic, and pop-oriented sound. Containing widely divergent material, the album included Spencer's Western parody "Blood on the Floor," Kirwan's rousing "Tell Me All the Things You Do," and "Station Man" and "Jewel-Eyed Judy," both featuring lead vocals by Kirwan. The album became the group's first substantial success in the United States and expanded their popularity beyond the cult following that had attended their American tours since 1968. For the album, Fleetwood Mac was assisted by John McVie's wife Christine. Married in August 1968, the former Christine Perfect had been a member of Chicken Shack from April 1967 to August 1969, playing piano and singing on the group's British-only 1969 hit "I'd Rather Go Blind." She also recorded a solo album in 1970 that was reissued in 1976 as *The Legendary Christine Perfect Album*. She officially joined Fleetwood Mac in August 1970, shortly before the release of *Kiln House*. However, in February 1971, during Christine's first American tour with Fleetwood Mac, Jeremy Spencer abruptly left the group while in Los Angeles.

Fleetwood Mac, now comprising Kirwan, Fleetwood, and the McVies, held auditions for Spencer's replacement, eventually choosing lead guitarist- singer-songwriter Bob Welch, who joined in April 1971. Welch, a veteran of both the Los Angeles and Las Vegas club scenes, had been a member of the rhythm-and- blues band The Seven Sons. With the departures of original guitarists Peter Green and Jeremy Spencer, Fleetwood Mac switched to ballads and softer-rock songs with *Future Games*, Christine McVie and Bob Welch's debut recording with the group. The follow-up, *Bare Trees*, included Kirwan's "Dust" and "Bare Trees," Christine's "Spare Me a Little," and Welch's "Sentimental Lady." In August 1972, Danny Kirwan was asked to leave Fleetwood Mac. He eventually recorded three albums for DJM Records.

Experiencing several personnel changes over the next few years, Fleetwood Mac recorded *Penguin* and *Mystery to Me*, which sold surprisingly well in the United States. *Heroes Are Hard to Find*, regarded as Fleetwood Mac's first album as a transplanted Los Angeles band, yielded an underground hit with Welch's "Bermuda Triangle." A protracted series of legal and financial problems beset Fleetwood Mac, as their manager, claiming control of the group name, assembled a group of unknowns to tour America as Fleetwood Mac. The matter was litigated as the real Fleetwood Mac moved to Los Angeles and Mick Fleetwood assumed the group's management. Eventually vindicated by the courts, the real Fleetwood Mac suffered the departure of Bob Welch at the end of 1974.

Reduced to a trio, Fleetwood Mac recruited Stephanie "Stevie" Nicks and Lindsey Buckingham. Nicks had been raised in Calif. and ended up in the San Francisco Bay Area after dropping out of San Jose State Coll. In 1968, she joined a band named Fritz, whose bassist and second vocalist was Buckingham. The two persevered with the group until 1971, later moving to Los Angeles, where they recorded a duet album for Polydor Records. The two had come to the attention of Fleetwood Mac through producer Keith Olsen before Welch's departure. With Buckingham and Nicks joining the group in January 1975, the new lineup recorded *Fleetwood Mac* in Los Angeles. Once again featuring three independent singer-songwriters, Fleetwood Mac had become the quintessential British-Calif. rock band. The album stayed on the charts for nearly three years and yielded three major hits with Christine's "Over My Head" and "Say You Love Me" and Nicks's "Rhiannon," while containing Christine's "Warm Ways" and Nicks's "Landslide." Spurred by the visual and musical focus provided by Christine McVie and Stevie Nicks, the subsequent six-month tour made Fleetwood Mac a massively popular concert attraction and established the group as one of the prime purveyors of pop-oriented, harmonically rich, and extravagantly produced music.

The self-produced follow-up to *Fleetwood Mac*, *Rumours*, capitalized on the group's burgeoning popularity as the two couples, John and Christine McVie and Lindsey Buckingham and Stevie Nicks, were splitting up. The album produced four hits, Buckingham's "Go Your Own Way," Nicks's top hit "Dreams," and Christine's "Don't Stop" and "You Make Loving Fun." It remained on the American album charts for more than two years and eventually sold more than 25 million copies worldwide. Their popularity as a concert attraction was enhanced by a ten-month, ten-country world tour in support of *Rumours*.

Fleetwood Mac's *Tusk*, recorded over a two-year period at the cost of over $1 million, was issued in late 1979. Overlong and disjointed, the highly experimental album marked the creative ascendancy of Lindsey Buckingham, whose odd, near-smash hit title cut was recorded with the U.S.C. Trojan Marching Band. *Tusk* also yielded a near-smash hit with Nicks's "Sara" and a major hit with "Think About Me." The group completed an exhaustive American tour in late 1979 and a nine-month world tour in 1980. They did not return to the studio until 1982.

During 1981, Stevie Nicks and Lindsey Buckingham each launched solo recording careers. Following 1982's *Mirage* (and its hits "Hold Me," "Love in Store" and "Gypsy") and subsequent tour, Fleetwood Mac were generally inactive as a group. Christine McVie's 1984 album produced hits with "Got a Hold on Me" and "Love Will Show Us How," cowritten by guitarist Todd Sharp. She remarried in 1986. The group reassembled for 1987's *Tango in the Night*, which produced smash hits with "Big Love" and "Little Lies" and major hits with "Seven Wonders" and "Everywhere." On the eve of the tour in support of the album, Lindsey Buckingham abruptly quit the group. Guitarist-vocalist Billy Burnette (Dorsey Burnette's son), a member of Mick Fleetwood's side band The Zoo for many years, was added for the tour, as was guitarist-vocalist Rick Vito, a veteran of the touring bands of Jackson Browne and Bob Seger. As full-fledged members, the two recorded *Behind the Mask* with Fleetwood Mac and performed on their subsequent tour. The album failed to produce any major hits and, with their final performance in Los Angeles on Dec. 7, 1990, Christine McVie and Stevie Nicks vowed to never tour with the group again. The two did record several new songs for 1992's *25 Years—The Chain*, but by then Rick Vito had also left the group.

In 1993, the *Rumours* edition of Fleetwood Mac reunited to perform at President Bill Clinton's inauguration. By 1994, Fleetwood Mac (Mick Fleetwood, John and Christine McVie, and Billy Burnette) had recruited Dave Mason, a former member of Traffic, and Bekka Bramlett, the daughter of Bonnie and Delaney Bramlett. In 1997, the *Rumours* edition of Fleetwood Mac reunited yet again for an MTV concert that produced a live album and subsequent support tour. The enormous popularity of *Rumours* resulted in the 1998 release of *Legacy: A Tribute to Fleetwood Mac's Rumours*, recorded by Jewel, Elton John, Shawn Colvin, and The Goo Goo Dolls, among others.

DISC.: Fleetwood Mac (1967); English Rose (1969); Blues Jam in Chicago, Vol. 1 (1969); Blues Jam in Chicago, Vol. 2 (1969); Jumping at Shadows (recorded 1969, rel. 1986); Then Play On (1969); Kiln House (1970); Future Games (1971); The Original Fleetwood Mac (1971); Bare Trees (1972); Penguin (recorded 1973); Mystery to Me (1973); Heroes Are Hard to Find (recorded 1974); Fleetwood Mac (1975); Rumours (1977); Tusk (1979); Live (1980); Mirage (recorded 1982, rel. 1984); Tango in the Night (1987); Greatest Hits (1988); Behind the Mask (1989); The Blues Collection (1989); 25 Years—The Chain (1992); Early Treasures (1992); The Early Years (1993); Time (1995); London Live '68 (1995); The Dance (1997). CHICKEN SHACK: 40 Blue Fingers Freshly Packed and Ready to Serve (1969); O.K. Ken? (1969). CHRISTINE MCVIE: The Legendary Christine Perfect Album (1976); Christine McVie (1984). PETER GREEN: End of the Game (1971); In the Skies (1979); Little Dreamer (1980). GREEN & GUITAR: The Best of Peter Green, 1977–1981 (1996). JEREMY SPENCER: Jeremy Spencer and the Children of God (1972); Flee (1979). DANNY KIRWAN: Second Chapter (1975); Danny Kirwan (1977); Hello There, Big Boy (1979). LINDSEY BUCKINGHAM AND STEVIE NICKS: Buckingham/Nicks (1973). STEVIE NICKS: Bella Donna (1981); The Wild Heart (1983); Rock a Little (1985); The Other Side of the Mirror (1989); Timespace: The Best of Stevie Nicks (1991); Street Angel (1994). LINDSEY BUCKINGHAM: Law and Order (1981/1984); Go Insane (1984); Out of the Cradle (1992). MICK FLEETWOOD: The Visitor (1981); I'm Not Me (1983). JOHN MCVIE: John McVie's "Gotta Band" (1992).

WRITINGS: M. Fleetwood with S. Davis, *Fleetwood: My Life and Adventures in Fleetwood Mac* (N.Y., 1990).

BIBL.: R. Carr and S. Clarke, *Fleetwood Mac: Rumours 'n' Fax* (N.Y., 1978); S. Graham, *Fleetwood Mac: The Authorized History* (N.Y., 1978).—BH

Fleischer, Oskar, eminent German musicologist; b. Zorbig, Nov. 2, 1856; d. Berlin, Feb. 8, 1933. He studied philology at Halle (1878–83), then musicology in Berlin under Spitta. In 1892 he became Privatdozent at the Univ. of Berlin, and in 1895 he was promoted to prof. He was a founder and the first president of the Internationale Musik-Gesellschaft (1899). With Johannes Wolf he ed. its publications, *Zeitschrift and Sammelbande*, until 1904.

WRITINGS: *Führer durch die königliche Sammlung alter Musikinstrumente* (Berlin, 1892); *Musikinstrumente aus deutscher Urzeit* (1893); *W.A. Mozart* (1899); *Führer durch die Bachausstellung im Festsaale des Berliner Rathauses* (Berlin, 1901); *Neumen-Studien* (4 vols.:1895; 1897; 1904, with facsimiles of late Byzantine notation; 1923, *Die germanischen Neumen als Schlüssel zum altchristlichen und gregorianischen Gesang*).—NS/LK/DM

Fleischer-Edel, Katharina, German soprano; b. Mühlheim an der Ruhr, Sept. 27, 1873; d. Dresden, July 18, 1928. She was a pupil of August Iffert at the Dresden Don. In 1893 she made her debut in a concert in Dresden, and then was a member of the Court Opera there (1894–97). From 1899 to 1914 she was a principal member of the Hamburg Opera. She also made guest appearances at the Bayreuth Festivals (1904–08), at London's Covent Garden (1905–07), and at the Metropolitan Opera in N.Y. (debut as Elisabeth in *Tannhäuser*, Nov. 30, 1906). She was principally known for her Wagnerian roles.—LK/DM

Fleischmann, Ernest (Martin), German-born English music administrator; b. Frankfurt am Main, Dec. 7, 1924. His family moved to Johannesburg, where he studied accounting at the Univ. of the Witwatersrand. He then devoted himself to music studies, obtaining a B.M. at the Univ. of Cape Town (1954). He was ambitious and took lessons in conducting with

Coates; also acted as an organizer of musical events, including the Van Riebeeck Festival in Cape Town (1952). Furthermore, he served as director of music and drama for the Johannesburg Festival (1956). In the process he learned Afrikaans, and acquired a literary fluency in English. Seeking ever wider fields of endeavor, he went to London, becoming a naturalized British subject in 1959. Fleischmann was general manager of the London Sym. Orch. until 1967 and also made a number of conducting appearances in England. He finally emigrated to the U.S., which became the main center of his activities. From 1969 to 1997 he was executive director of the Los Angeles Phil. as well as general manager of the Hollywood Bowl. Ever sure of his direction, he was a powerful promoter of the orch. he headed, so that the Los Angeles Phil. became actively involved in extensive national and international tours, garnering profitable recording contracts in addition to television and radio broadcasts, youth programs, and special festivals. In 1998 he became artistic director of the Ojai Festival. Well-educated and fluent in several European languages, Fleischmann acquired an international reputation as a highly successful entrepreneur. —NS/LK/DM

Fleisher, Edwin A(dler), American music patron; b. Philadelphia, July 11, 1877; d. there, Jan. 9, 1959. He studied at Harvard Univ. (B.A., 1899). He founded a Sym. Club in Philadelphia (1909) and engaged conductors to rehearse an amateur orch. there. At the same time he began collecting orch. scores and complete sets of parts, which became the nucleus of the great Edwin A. Fleisher Collection, presented by him to the Free Library of Philadelphia. A cumulative catalog covering the period from 1929 to 1977 was publ. in Boston in 1979. —NS/LK/DM

Fleisher, Leon, distinguished American pianist, conductor, and teacher; b. San Francisco, July 23, 1928. His mother was a singing teacher. He received the rudiments of music from his mother; then studied piano with Lev Shorr. He played in public at the age of 6. He then was sent to Europe for studies with Schnabel at Lake Como, Italy; continued his studies with him in N.Y. At the age of 14, he appeared as soloist in the Liszt A major piano concerto with the San Francisco Sym. Orch. (April 16, 1943); at 16, he was soloist with the N.Y. Phil. (Nov. 4, 1944); in 1952 he became the first American to win 1st prize at the Queen Elisabeth of Belgium International Competition in Brussels; this catapulted him into a brilliant career. He made several European tours; also gave highly successful recitals in South America. In 1964 he was stricken with repetitive stress syndrome of the right hand. Disabled, Fleisher turned to piano works written for left hand alone (Ravel, Prokofiev, and others). He also began to conduct. He had studied conducting with Monteux in San Francisco and at the conducting school established by Monteux in Hancock, Maine; he also profited from advice from Szell. In 1968 he became artistic director of the Theater Chamber Players in Washington, D.C.; in 1970 he became music director of the Annapolis Sym. Orch. as well. From 1973 to 1977 he was assoc. conductor of the

Baltimore Sym. Orch.; then was its resident conductor in 1977–78. He also made guest conducting appearances with major U.S. orchs. A treatment with cortisone injections and even acupuncture and the fashionable biofeedback to control the electrophysiological motor system did not help. In 1981 he decided to undergo surgery; it was momentarily successful, and on Sept. 16, 1982, he made a spectacular comeback as a bimanual pianist, playing the *Symphonic Variations* by Franck with Comissiona and the Baltimore Sym. Orch. In 1985 he became artistic director-designate of the Berkshire Music Center at Tanglewood, and fully assumed his duties as artistic director in 1986. In 1993 he marked the 50th anniversary of his professional career with a gala concert at the San Francisco Cons. of Music. On July 23, 1994, he was soloist in the premiere of Foss's Piano Concerto for Left Hand and Orch. with Ozawa and the Boston Sym. Orch. at Tanglewood. Fleisher devoted much time to teaching; he joined the faculty of the Peabody Cons. of Music in Baltimore in 1959, and subsequently was named to the Andrew W. Mellon Chair in Piano. Among his brilliant pupils were André Watts and Lorin Hollander.—NS/LK/DM

Fleming, Renée, gifted American soprano; b. Indiana, Pa., Feb. 14, 1959. She received vocal training in N.Y. After winning a Metropolitan Opera Audition in 1988, she made her debut at London's Covent Garden as Dircé in Cherubini's *Médée* in 1989. In 1990 she received the Richard Tucker Award, and also took the Grand Prix in the Belgian singing competition. Following engagements as Dvořák's Rusalka at the Houston Grand Opera and the Seattle Opera, she made her Metropolitan Opera debut in N.Y. as Mozart's Countess on March 16, 1991, which role she also sang at the Teatro Colón in Buenos Aires. On Dec. 19, 1991, she appeared as Rosina in the premiere of Corigliano's *The Ghosts of Versailles* at the Metropolitan Opera, returning in subsequent seasons to sing Mozart's Countess and Pamina, and Desdemona. In 1992 she returned to Covent Garden as Rossini's Mme. de Folleville, sang Mozart's Donna Elvira at Milan's La Scala and his Fiordiligi at the Geneva Opera and the Glyndebourne Festival, and appeared as Mimi at the opening of the new Bath and Wessex Opera. She made her N.Y. recital debut at Alice Tully Hall on March 29, 1993. In Aug. 1993 she was the soloist in Barber's *Knoxville: Summer of 1915* at the opening of the new concert hall in Aspen, Colo. In Oct. 1993 she sang the title role in the revival of Floyd's *Susannah* at the Chicago Lyric Opera. She appeared as Mozart's Countess at the opening of the new opera theater at the Glyndebourne Festival on May 28, 1994. On Sept. 10, 1994, she sang Mme. de Tourvel in the premiere of Susa's *The Dangerous Liaisons* at the San Francisco Opera. In 1995 she appeared as Rusalka at the San Diego Opera and at the San Francisco Opera, and sang Desdemona at the Metropolitan Opera. She returned to the Metropolitan Opera in 1997 as Gounod's Marguerite and as Manon, the latter role being one she also portrayed that year in Paris at the Opéra de la Bastille. After singing Arabella in Houston and Lucrezia Borgia at La Scala in 1998, she created Previn's Blanche in *A Streetcar Named Desire* in San Francisco (Sept. 19,

1998). She appeared in recital at N.Y.'s Carnegie Hall in 1999. As a concert and oratorio artist, Fleming had many engagements in North America and Europe. Among her other outstanding operatic roles are Rossini's Armida, Tatiana, the Marschallin, Salome, Jenůfa, and Ellen in *Peter Grimes*.—NS/LK/DM

Fleming, Robert (James Berkeley), Canadian composer, pianist, organist, choirmaster, and teacher; b. Prince Albert, Saskatchewan, Nov. 12, 1921; d. Ottawa, Nov. 28, 1976. He was a student of Benjamin (piano) and Howells (composition) at the Royal Coll. of Music in London (1937–39); he then studied piano with Lyell Gustin (1941–42) and attended the Toronto Cons. of Music (1941, 1945) as a student of Norman Wilks (piano), Frederick Silvester and John Weatherseed (organ), Mazzoleni (conducting), and Willan (composition). In 1945–46 he taught piano at Upper Canada Coll., and then was a staff composer (1946–58) and music director (1958–70) with the National Film Board; he also served as organist-choirmaster at Glebe United Church (1954–56) and at St. George's Anglican Church of Ste-Anne-de-Bellevue (1959–70) in Quebec. Settling in Ottawa, he joined the faculty of Carleton Univ. in 1970 and in 1972 he became organist-choirmaster at St. Matthias' Church. In his extensive catalogue of works, Fleming adhered to a generally tonal path.

WORKS: DRAMATIC: B a l l e t : *Chapter 13* (1948); *Shadow on the Prairie* (1951); *Romance* (1954). **OTHER:** 3 puppet plays; more than 250 film scores. **ORCH.:** 5 suites (1942–63); *Rondo* (1942); *6 Variations on a Liturgical Theme* for Strings (1946); *Red River Country* (1953); *Seaboard Sketches* (1953); *Recollections* for Violin and Strings (1954); *Ballet Introduction* (1960); *Concerto 64* for Piano and Orch. (1964); *Tuba Concerto* (1966); *4 Fantasias on Canadian Folk Themes* (1966); *Hexad* (1972); band pieces. **CHAMBER:** Violin Sonata (1944); *A Musician in the Family* for Trombone and Piano (1952); *A 2 Piece Suite* for 2 Clarinets and Bass Clarinet (1958); *Colours of the Rainbow* for Wind Quartet, String Quartet, and Harp (1962); *Maritime Suite* for Wind Quartet, String Quartet, and Harp (1962); *3 Miniatures* for Brass Quintet (1962); *Go for Baroque* for Flute, Oboe, and Harpsichord (1963); *3 Dialogues* for Flute or Oboe and Piano or Harpsichord (1964); Brass Quintet (1965); String Quartet (1969); *Almost Waltz* for Flute and Piano (1970); *Divertimento* for Organ, 2 Oboes, 2 Violins, Viola, Cello, and Double Bass (1970); *Explorations* for Accordion (1970); *Threo* for Soprano Saxophone and Piano (1972); many piano pieces; organ music. **VOCAL:** Choral works and songs.—NS/LK/DM

Fleming, Shirley (Moragne), American music critic and editor; b. N.Y., Dec. 2, 1931. She was educated at Smith Coll. in Northampton, Mass. (B.A., 1952; M.A., 1954). She was asst. music ed. of *Hi-fi Music at Home* (1958–60) and of *High Fidelity* (1960–64); then was ed. of *Musical America* (1964–91), and subsequently of the valuable "Music in Concert" section of the expanded *American Record Guide* (from 1992). She also wrote for other periodicals.—NS/LK/DM

Flesch, Carl (actually, **Károly**), celebrated Hungarian violinist and pedagogue; b. Moson, Oct. 9, 1873; d. Lucerne, Nov. 14, 1944. He began to study the violin at the age of 6 in Moson, then continued his training with Jakob Grün at the Vienna Cons. (1886–90), and with Sauzay (1890–92) and Marsick (1892–94) at the Paris Cons., graduating with the premier prix. While still a student, he played in the Lamoureux Orch. in Paris and made his formal debut in Vienna (1895); went to Bucharest (1897), where he was active as a performer and as a prof. at the Cons. until 1902; he subsequently went to Amsterdam, where he taught at the Cons. (1903–08). In 1908 he made his home in Berlin, where he engaged in private teaching when not engaged on extensive tours. In 1913 he made his N.Y. debut; then served as head of the violin dept. at the Curtis Inst. of Music in Philadelphia (1924–28). Returning to Berlin in 1928, he joined the faculty of the Hochschule für Musik. With the advent of Hitler, he went to London (1934). He was in the Netherlands when World War II erupted in 1939, and lived there until the Nazi invasion in 1940; then made his way to Hungary, finally settling in Lucerne in 1943 as a teacher at the Cons. He acquired an outstanding reputation as an interpreter of the German repertoire. However, his greatest legacy remains his work as a pedagogue. His *Die Kunst des Violin-Spiels* is an exhaustive treatise on violin technique and interpretation, and is duly recognized as the standard work of its kind. He also prepared eds. of the violin concertos of Beethoven, Mendelssohn, and Brahms, the violin sonatas of Mozart (with A. Schnabel), 20 études of Paganini, and the études of Kreutzer. In 1945 the Flesch Competition was organized in London to honor his memory; it later became part of the City of London International Competition for Violin and Viola, which awards the Flesch Medal.

WRITINGS: *Urstudien* (Berlin, 1911); *Die Kunst des Violin-Spiels* (vol. I, Berlin, 1923; 2nd ed., 1929; Eng. tr., Boston, 1924; vol. II, Berlin, 1928; Eng. tr., Boston, 1934); *Das Klangproblem im Geigenspiel* (Berlin, 1931; Eng. tr., N.Y., 1934); H. Keller and C.F. Flesch, eds., *The Memoirs of Carl Flesch* (London, 1957; 3rd ed., 1974; Ger. ed. as *Erinnerungen eines Geigers*, Freiburg im Breisgau, 1960); *Die hohe Schule des Fingersetzes auf der Geige* (MS; 1st publ. in Italian as *Alta scuola di diteggiature violinistica*, Milan, 1960; Eng. tr., 1966, as *Violin Fingering: Its Theory and Practice*).

BIBL.: W. Brederode, *C. F.* (Haarlem, 1938); C.F. Flesch, *Und spielste Die auch Geige?* (Zürich, 1990).—NS/LK/DM

Fleta, Miguel, Spanish tenor, father of **Pierre Fleta;** b. Albalate, Dec. 28, 1893; d. La Coruña, May 30, 1938. He studied at the Barcelona and Madrid conservatories; also took vocal lessons in Italy with Louisa Pierrick, who became his wife. He made his debut in Trieste on Nov. 14, 1919 as Paolo in Zandonai's *Francesca da Rimini*. After several busy tours in Europe, Mexico, and South America, he made his debut at the Metropolitan Opera in N.Y. on Nov. 8, 1923, as Cavaradossi; remained on its roster until 1925. From 1923 to 1926 he sang at La Scala in Milan, where he created the role of Prince Calaf in *Turandot* (April 25, 1926). In 1926 he returned to Spain.

BIBL.: A. Sáliz Valdivielso, *M. F.: Memoria de una voz* (Bilbao, 1997).—NS/LK/DM

Fleta, Pierre, French tenor of Spanish descent, son of **Miguel Fleta;** b. Villefranche-sur-Mer, July 4, 1925.

He studied with his mother, Luisa Pierrick. In 1949 he made his operatic debut in Barcelona, and then sang in Nice (1949–51) and at the Théâtre Royal de la Monnaie in Brussels (from 1952); he also toured as a concert artist. —NS/LK/DM

Fletcher, Alice Cunningham, American ethnologist; b. Cuba (of American parents), March 16, 1838; d. Washington, D.C., April 6, 1923. She devoted her life to the study of North American Indians, among whom she lived for a number of years, becoming president of the American Anthropological Soc. (1903) and the American Folk Lore Soc. (1905). She was the author of *Indian Story and Song from North America* (1900), *A Study of Omaha Indian Music* (1903), and *Indian Games and Dances* (1915), as well as numerous articles in the *Journal of American Folk Lore*; etc.—NS/LK/DM

Fletcher, (Horace) Grant, American composer and teacher; b. Hartsburg, Ill., Oct. 25, 1913. He studied composition with William Kritch, theory with Bessie Louise Smith, and conducting with Henry Lamont at Ill. Wesleyan Univ. (1932–35). He also took a course in conducting with Thor Johnson, and for 3 summers (1937–39) attended composition classes with Krenek at the Univ. of Mich. He then took classes with Willan in Toronto, and later studied at the Eastman School of Music in Rochester, N.Y., where his teachers were Rogers and Hanson (1947–49; Ph.D., 1951). He also had private lessons with Elwell in Cleveland. From 1945 to 1948 he was conductor of the Akron (Ohio) Sym. Orch., and from 1952 to 1956 of the Chicago Sinfonietta; from 1949 to 1951 he was on the faculty of the Chicago Musical Coll.; later taught at Ariz. State Univ. at Tempe (1956–78). In his music, Fletcher follows the median line of modern techniques.

WORKS: DRAMATIC: *The Carrion Crow,* buffa fantasy opera (1948); *Lomotawi,* ballet-pantomime (1957); *The Sack of Calabasas,* opera (1964–66); *Cinco de Mayo,* ballet (1973); incidental music. **ORCH.:** *Rhapsody* for Flute and Strings (1935; withdrawn); *A Rhapsody of Dances* for Chamber Orch. (1935; for Wind Instruments, 1970; for Full Orch., 1972); *Nocturne* (1938); *Song of Honor,* on Yugoslav themes (1944; 1st perf. as *A Song for Warriors,* Rochester, N.Y., Oct. 25, 1945); *An American Overture* (1945; Duluth, April 23, 1948); *Panels from a Theater Wall* (Rochester, N.Y., April 27, 1949); 2 syms.: No. 1 (1950; Rochester, N.Y., April 24, 1951) and No. 2 (1982–83); *The Pocket Encyclopedia of Orchestral Instruments,* with optional Narrator (1953; also perf. as *Dictionary of Musical Instruments*); 4 concertos: No. 1 for Piano and Orch. (1953), No. 2, *Regency Concerto,* for Piano and Strings (1966), No. 3, Concerto for Winds (1969), and No. 4, Multiple Concerto for 5 Solo Winds, for 1 Soloist playing on 5 different Wind Instruments, with Wind Ensemble (1970); *Sumare and Wintare* (1956); *7 Cities of Cibola* (1961); *Retrospection (Rhapsody III)* for Flute, 9 Strings, and Tape (1965; revision of *Rhapsody* of 1935); *Dances from the Southwest* for Strings and Piano (1966); *Glyphs* for Band (1970); *Diversion III* for Strings (1971); *The 5th of May,* ballet suite (1972); *Aubade* for Wind Instruments (1974); *Celebration of Times Past* (1976); *A More Proper Burial Music for Wolfgang* for Wind Instruments (1977); *Saxson II* for Saxophone and Strings (1977); *Serenade* (1979); *Symphonic Suite* (1980); *Partita* for Chamber Orch. (1985). **CHAMBER:** *Musicke for Christening:* No. 1 for Cello and Piano (1945), No. 2 for Saxophone and Piano (1979), and No. 3

for Clarinet and Piano (1979); *Heralds* for Brass and Timpani (1949); *Tower Music* for Brass (1957); 5 sonatas: No. 1 for Clarinet and Piano (1958), No. 2, *Sōn,* for Cello and Piano (1972), No. 3 for Saxophone and Piano (1974), No. 4 for Solo Viola (1977), and No. 5 for Solo Violin (1983); *Prognosis Nos. 1–3* for Brass Quintet (1965–67); *Uroboros* for Percussion (1967); *Octocelli* for 8 Solo Cellos or their multiples (1971); Trio for Flute, Guitar, and Piano (1973); *Toccata II* for Marimba (1979); *Quadra* for Percussion (1975); String Quartet (1975; 4 earlier quartets were withdrawn); *Zortzicos No. 2* for Double Bass and Piano (1977), *No. 3* for Bassoon and Piano (1979), *No. 4* for Cello and Piano (1979), *No. 5* for Clarinet and Piano (1980), and *No. 6* for Viola and Piano (1980; *Zortzicos No. 1* is the last movement of the piano piece *Izquierdas*); *Saxsōn I* for Saxophone (1977); *Trio Bulgarico* for Flute, Oboe, and Bassoon (1980); *Palimpsest* for Flute Choir (1980); *Madrigals* for Clarinet Choir (1981). **KEYBOARD: Piano:** *2 Books of Nocturnes* (1935); *4 American Dance Pieces* (1944); *Openend Triptych* (1957); *Izquierdas* for Piano, Left Hand (1967); *Diversion I* and *II* (1971); *Toccata I* (1974). **Organ:** *Dodecachordon* (1967). **VOCAL:** *The Crisis* for Chorus and Orch. (1945; Walla Walla, Wash., Feb. 22, 1976); *House Made of Dawn* for Alto, Piano, Flute, Indian Drum, and Rattle (1957); 4 sacred cantatas: No. 1, *O Childe Swete* (1965), No. 2 (1967), No. 3, *The Branch* (1970), and No. 4, *Judas* (1978); *Who Is Sylvia?* for Baritone, Flute, Oboe, Bassoon, and Guitar (1969); *Psalm I* for Chorus and Organ (1979); choruses; songs.

WRITINGS: *Fundamental Principles of Counterpoint* (Rock Hill, S.C., 1942); *Syllabus for Advanced Integrated Theory* (Tempe, Ariz., 1962; 4th ed., rev., 1976); *Rhythm: Notation and Production* (Tempe, 1967).—NS/LK/DM

Fletcher, Percy (Eastman), English conductor and composer; b. Derby, Dec. 12, 1879; d. London, Sept. 10, 1932. He went to London in 1899 as a conductor at various theaters there. He composed many works in a light, melodious style, including the orch. pieces *Woodland Pictures, Sylvan Scenes, Parisian Sketches, 3 Frivolities,* and the overture *Vanity Fair.* He also composed a short sacred cantata, *Passion of Christ.*—NS/LK/DM

Fletchtenmacher, Alexandru (Adolf), Romanian violinist, conductor, pedagogue, and composer; b. Iaşi, Jan. 4, 1824; d. Bucharest, Feb. 9, 1898. He learned to play the violin in his youth, and then studied in Vienna with J. Böhm and Mayseder. Upon his return to Iaşi, he conducted and composed for the National Theater. He then settled in Bucharest, where he founded the Craiova Phil. Soc. and the Cons. in 1864, serving as director and prof. of violin of the latter. Flechtenmacher was one of the most influence Romanian musicians of his day. His works include the operetta *Baba- Hîrca* (The Witch Hîrca, 1848; Iaşi, Jan. 8, 1849), the overture *Moldova,* choruses, songs, and piano pieces.

BIBL.: R. Oana-Pop, *A. F.: Viţa în imagini* (Bucharest, 1964). —LK/DM

Fleury, André (Edouard Antoine Marie), French organist, pedagogue, and composer; b. Neuilly-sur-Seine, July 25, 1903; d. Le Vésinet, Aug. 6, 1995. After training with his father, he studied with Gigout and Dupré at the Paris Cons., taking a premier prix in improvisation in 1926; he also was a private student in organ of Marchal and Vierne and in composition of Vidal. He was active in Paris as organist at St. Augustin (from 1930) and as a prof. of organ at the École Normale de Musique (from 1943). After serving as organist at the Cathedral and as a prof. at the Cons. in Dijon (1949–71), he returned to Paris as co-organist at St. Éustache and as a prof. at the Schola Cantorum. He wrote 2 organ syms. (1947, 1949) and many other organ works.—NS/LK/DM

Fleury, Louis (François), eminent French flutist; b. Lyons, May 24, 1878; d. Paris, June 11, 1926. He studied at the Paris Cons. From 1905 until his death he was head of the famous Société Moderne d'Instruments à Vent; also (from 1906) of the Société des Concerts d'Autrefois, with which he gave concerts in England; made appearances with Melba and Calve. Debussy composed *Syrinx* for Unaccompanied Flute for him. He ed. much early flute music, including sonatas and other pieces by Blavet, Naudet, Purcell, J. Stanley et al., and contributed to French and English periodicals. —NS/LK/DM

Flier, Yakov (Vladimirovich), Russian pianist and pedagogue; b. Orekhovo-Zuyevo, Oct. 21, 1912; d. Moscow, Dec. 18, 1977. He was a pupil at the Moscow Cons. of Kozlovsky and Igumnov. From 1935 he made tours in Russia, and later appeared abroad. From 1937 he also taught at the Moscow Cons., numbering among his notable students Bella Davidovich and Viktoria Postnikova.—NS/LK/DM

Flipse, Eduard, Dutch conductor; b. Wissekerke, Feb. 26, 1896; d. Etten-Leur, Sept. 11, 1973. He studied piano and composition in Rotterdam and conducting in Utrecht. In 1930 he became chief conductor of the Rotterdam Phil., a post he retained until 1965. In 1952 he became chief conductor of the Holland Festival, and was later chief conductor of the Antwerp Phil. (1961–70). During his long tenure in Rotterdam, he introduced works of numerous contemporary composers. He was also a passionate propagandist of the music of Mahler.—NS/LK/DM

Flodin, Karl (Theodor), Finnish composer; b. Vaasa, July 10, 1858; d. Helsinki, Nov. 30, 1925. He studied music with Faltin in Helsinki (1877–83), and with Jadassohn at the Leipzig Cons. (1890–92). In 1908 he went to Buenos Aires as music critic for a German paper there. He returned to Finland in 1921. He publ. numerous essays on Finnish music (in Finnish and German) and wrote a biography of Martin Wegelius (1922). He composed a *Cortège* for Horn and Orch., incidental music to various plays, and publ. some 80 piano pieces. He was married to the singer Adée Leander (1873–1935).—NS/LK/DM

Flood, W(illiam) H(enry) Grattan, Irish organist and music historian; b. Lismore, Nov. 1, 1859; d. Enniscorthy, Aug. 6, 1928. He served as a church organist in Dublin, and achieved recognition as a writer on Irish music and musicians. He publ. *History of Irish Music* (1895; 4th ed., 1927), *The Story of the Harp* (1905), *The Story of the Bagpipe* (1911), *William Vincent Wallace, A Memoir* (1912), *John Field of Dublin* (Dublin, 1920), *Introductory Sketch of Irish Musical History* (1921), *Early Tudor Composers* (1925), and *Late Tudor Composers* (1929). He was the ed. of *Songs and Airs of O'Carolan, Moore's Irish Melodies, Armagh Hymnal,* and *The Spirit of the Nation.* —NS/LK/DM

Floquet, Étienne Joseph, French composer; b. Aix-en-Provence, Nov. 23, 1748; d. Paris, May 10, 1785. After studying in his native town, he went to Paris, where he wrote the opéra-ballet *L'Union de l'amour et des arts,* which was produced with great success at the Académie Royale de Musique (Sept. 7, 1773). His second opera, *Azolan, ou Le Serment indiscret* (Nov. 22, 1774, also at the Académie), was a fiasco. Floquet then went to Italy, where he perfected his knowledge by studying with Sala in Naples and with Martini in Bologna. Returning to Paris, he had 2 operas performed at the Académie: *Hellé* (Jan. 5, 1779) and *Le Seigneur bien-faisant* (Dec. 14, 1780). He also wrote a comic opera, *La Nouvelle Omphale* (Comédie-Italienne, Nov. 22, 1782). In an attempt to challenge Gluck's superiority, Floquet wrote the opera *Alceste* on the same subject as Gluck's famous work, but it was never produced.

BIBL.: A. Pougin, *É.-J. F.* (Paris, 1863); F. Huot, *Étude biographique sur É.-J. F.* (Aix, 1903).—NS/LK/DM

Flor, Claus Peter, German conductor; b. Leipzig, March 16, 1953. He entered the Zwickau Cons. at 10 to study violin and clarinet, and then continued his training at the Weimar Hochschule für Musik. He completed his study of the violin at the Leipzig Hochschule für Musik, and also received training in conducting with Reuter and Masur. Flor later continued his conducting studies with Kubelik and Kurt Sanderling. In 1979 he won the Mendelssohn-Stipendium of the Ministry of Culture and captured 1st prize in the Fitelberg Competition in Katowice, and subsequently took prizes in the Kubelik Competition in Lucerne (1982) and in the Malko Competition in Copenhagen (1983). From 1981 to 1984 he was chief conductor of the Suhler Phil. In 1984–85 he was chief conductor of the (East) Berlin Sym. Orch., and then was made its Generalmusikdirektor in 1985. That same year, he made his U.S. debut at the Hollywood Bowl. In 1988 he took the Berlin Sym. Orch. on a world tour. In 1991 he left his Berlin post to serve as principal guest conductor of the Philharmonia Orch. in London and as principal guest conductor and artistic advisor of the Tonhalle Orch. in Zürich. He concluded his London tenure in 1994 and his Zürich tenure in 1995. As a guest conductor, he has appeared with many of the world's major orchs. He has also appeared as an opera conductor.—NS/LK/DM

Florence, Bob, American musician, arranger; b. Los Angeles, Calif., May 20, 1932. He has sporadically maintained an orchestra to play his charts since 1958, though his Limited Edition band has worked steadily since the late 1970s. Strongly influenced by Bill Holman, he studied arranging at Los Angeles City Coll. and played weekend gigs with saxophonists Lanny Morgan and Herb Geller in the mid-1950s. His career took off when his arrangement of "Up the Lazy River" became a hit in 1960 for Si Zentner's band, with whom he worked as pianist and arranger from 1959–64. A mainstay on the L.A. studio scene, he also served as Julie Andrews's music director for years.

Though he made a number of obscure albums in the late 1950s and 1960s, he came into his own as a band leader in 1978, when he began a series of big-band sessions featuring top LA jazz and studio players. Though his writing is solidly in the modern, mainstream, big-band tradition, his idiosyncratic and sometimes brilliant charts demonstrate just how much room there is for individuality within that tradition. Since the late 1970s he has recorded for Trend, USA, Discovery, and Bosco, though in the 1990s he's done work for the MAMA Foundation label.

DISC.: *State of the Art* (1988); *Funupmanship* (1993); *Treasure Chest* (1994); *With All the Bells and Whistles* (1995); *Earth* (1997). —AG

Floridia, Pietro, Italian composer; b. Modica, Sicily, May 5, 1860; d. N.Y., Aug. 16, 1932. He studied in Naples with Cesi (piano) and Lauro Rossi (composition), and while at the Naples Cons. publ. several piano pieces which became quite popular. On May 7, 1882, he brought out in Naples a comic opera, *Carlotta Clepier*. From 1888 to 1892 he taught at the Palermo Cons., and then lived in Milan. In 1904 he emigrated to the U.S. He taught at the Cincinnati Coll. of Music (1906–08), and in 1908 settled in N.Y. where in 1913 he organized and conducted an Italian Sym. Orch. there. His music (mostly for the stage) is written in a competent manner, in the style of the Italian verismo. Floridia ed. a valuable collection in 2 vols., *Early Italian Songs and Airs* (Philadelphia, 1923). His other operas included *Maruzza* (Venice, Aug. 23, 1894), *La colonia libera* (Rome, May 7, 1899), and *Paoletta* (Cincinnati, Aug. 29, 1910), as well as *The Scarlet Letter* (1902; not produced) and *Malia* (completed in 1932; not produced).—NS/LK/DM

Florimo, Francesco, Italian music historian; b. S. Giorgio Morgeto, Calabria, Oct. 12, 1800; d. Naples, Dec. 18, 1888. In 1817 he entered the Collegio di Musica at Naples, numbering Furno, Elia, Zingarelli, and Tritto among his teachers. From 1826 to 1851 he was librarian there. He was Bellini's closest friend, and in 1876 escorted the latter's remains from Paris to Catania. He publ. the pamphlet "Trasporto delle ceneri di Bellini a Catania." He composed *Sinfonia funebre per la morte di Bellini,* and also founded the Bellini Prize, a competition open to Italian composers not over 30. His chief work is *Cenno storico sulla scuola musicale di Napoli* (2 vols., Naples, 1869–71; republ. 1880–84, in 4 vols., as *La scuola musicale di Napoli e i suoi Conservatori*), a complete musical history of Naples and its conservatories, their teachers and pupils, etc. Despite numerous errors, it remains an extremely valuable guide. He also wrote *Riccardo Wagner ed i Wagneristi* (Naples, 1876), *Bellini, Memorie e lettere* (Florence, 1882), *Album Bellini* (Naples, 1886), which contains opinions by many eminent musicians on Bellini's works, and *Metodo di canto*, which was adopted by the Paris Cons. and described as "magistrale" by Rossini. Florimo was also an excellent singing teacher.

BIBL.: G. Megali del Giudice, *F. F.* (Naples, 1901). —NS/LK/DM

Florio, Caril (real name, **William James Robjohn**), English-American composer; b. Tavistock, Devon, Nov. 2, 1843; d. Morganton, N.C., Nov. 21, 1920. He was taken to N.Y. when he was 14 and held various posts as a church organist and choirmaster. In 1862 he took up acting and toured throughout the North. In 1868 he returned to N.Y. and was active as a pianist, conductor, teacher, critic, and music ed. In response to his family's opposition to a career in music, he adopted the pseudonym Caryl Florio in 1870. From 1896 to 1901 he was head of the musical establishment at the Vanderbilt estate near Asheville, N.C. In 1903 he settled in Asheville as a teacher and choral conductor. He publ. *A Textbook of Practical Harmony* (1892). His works reveal a British-German derivation, but are not without interest.

WORKS: DRAMATIC: *Le tours de Mercure*, operetta (1869); *Inferno*, burlesque (1870); *Gulda* (1879; unfinished); *Suzanne*, operetta (1879; unfinished); *Uncle Tom's Cabin*, opera (1881–82; Philadelphia, 1882); incidental music. **ORCH.:** *Marche des fées* (1870); *Reverie and Scherzo* for 2 Clarinets, Violin, Cello, and Strings (1872); Piano Concerto (1875–86; rev. 1915); *Marche triomphale* (1878); *Introduction, Theme, and Variations* for Alto Saxophone and Orch. (1879; unfinished); 2 syms. (No. 2 based on the 1st String Quartet); 2 overtures. **CHAMBER:** Piano Trio (1866); *Aspiration*, romanza for String Quartet (1872); 3 string quartets (1877, rev. 1887; 1878, rev. 1893; 1886, unfinished); Horn Quartet (1877); Saxophone Quartet (1879); Quintet for Piano and Saxophones (n.d.); Violin Sonatine (1902–03); 2 violin sonatas; piano pieces, including 2 sonatas and *Abraham Lincoln's Funeral March* (1865); organ music. **VOCAL:** *The Song of the Elements*, cantata (1872); *The Crown of the Year*, cantata (1887); *Christmas Past and Present* (1889); *The Night at Bethlehem* (1891); anthems; part songs; solo songs.—NS/LK/DM

Floros, Constantin, distinguished Greek musicologist; b. Thessalonika, Jan. 4, 1930. He studied composition with Uhl and conducting with Swarowsky and Kassowitz at the Vienna Academy of Music, graduating in 1953. He concurrently studied musicology with Schenck at the Univ. of Vienna (Ph.D., 1955, with the diss. *C.A. Campioni als Instrumentalkomponist*) and then continued his training with Husmann at the Univ. of Hamburg, where he completed his Habilitation in 1961. In 1967 he became ausserplanmässiger prof. and in 1972 prof. of musicology there. P. Petersen ed. a Festschrift in honor of his 60th birthday (Wiesbaden, 1990).

WRITINGS: *Universale Neumenkunde* (3 vols., Kassel, 1970); *Gustav Mahler* (3 vols., Wiesbaden, 1977–85); *Beethovens Eroica und Prometheus-Musik: Sujet Studien* (Wilhelmshaven, 1978); *Mozart-Studien I: Zu Mozarts Sinfonik, Opern- und Kirchenmusik* (Wiesbaden, 1979); *Brahms und Bruckner: Studien zur musikalischen Exegetik* (Wiesbaden, 1980); *Einführung in die Neumenkunde* (Wilhelmshaven, 1980); *Musik als Botschaft* (Wiesbaden, 1989);

Alban Berg: Musik als Autobiographie (Wiesbaden, 1992); *Gustav Mahler: The Symphonies* (Portland, Ore., 1993); *György Ligeti: Jenseits von Avantgarde und Postmoderne* (Vienna, 1996); *Johannes Brahms, "frei aber einsam:" Eine Leben für eine poetische Musik* (Zürich, 1997).—NS/LK/DM

Flosman, Oldřich, Czech composer; b. Plzeň, April 5, 1925. He studied composition with K. Janeček at the Prague Cons. (1944–46), and with Bořkovec at the Prague Academy of Music, graduating in 1950. In his music, he follows the neo-Romantic tradition of the Czech school of composition, with strong formal design and an animating rhythmic pulse; the influence of Prokofiev's lyrical dynamism is much in evidence.

WORKS: DRAMATIC: Ballet: *Pierrot and Columbine* (1957); *The Woman Partisan* (1959); *The Taming of the Shrew* (1960); *The Salted Fairy-Tale* (1982). **ORCH.:** Double Concerto for Harp, Clarinet, and Orch. (1950); Clarinet Concerto (1954); Bassoon Concertino (1956); 2 violin concertos (1958, 1972); *Dances* for Harp and String Quartet or String Orch. (1961); *Cuban Overture* (1962); 3 syms. (1964, 1974, 1984); *3 Studies* for Piano and Strings (1965); *Concertant Music* for Wind Quintet and Chamber Orch. (1965); Flute Concerto (1969); Horn Concerto (1970); Fugues for Strings (1970); *Fires on the Hills,* overture (1973); *Visions of Michelangelo* for Viola and Orch. (1979); *Rural Partita* for Chamber Orch. (1976); *Symphonic Fugue* (1977); Sym.- Concerto for Piano and Orch. (1979); *Philharmonic Variations* (1980); *Symphonic Plays* for Bass Clarinet, Piano, and Orch. (1983); *Nuptial Dances of Charles IV* for Piano and Chamber Orch. (1984). **CHAMBER:** 2 wind quintets (1948, 1962); *Bagatelles* for Winds and Piano (1950); Clarinet Sonatina (1952); *Jesenik Suite* for Viola and Piano (1956); 3 string quartets (1956, 1963, 1966); *Dreaming about a Violin* for Violin and Piano (1962); *Romance and Scherzo* for Flute and Harp (1962); Nonet No. 2 (1967); Sonata for Wind Quintet and Piano (1970); *Chamber Music* for Flute, Oboe, Violin, Viola, and Cello (1971); Sonata for Violin, Cello, and Piano (1971); *Music* for Double Bass and String Quartet (1980); Serenade for Brass Quintet (1981); *Music* for Flute and Piano or Guitar (1984); piano pieces, including *Motýli zde nežijí* (Butterflies Don't Live Here Any Longer), sonata inspired by the film about children's drawings from a Nazi concentration camp (1961). **VOCAL:** Sonata for Soprano and Strings (1967); choral pieces; songs.—NS/LK/DM

Flothuis, Marius (Hendrikus), Dutch composer and musicologist; b. Amsterdam, Oct. 30, 1914. He received his rudimentary musical education at home from his uncle, who taught him piano. He then had piano lessons with Arend Koole and studied piano, harpsichord, and theory with Hans Brandts-Buys. After studying classical philology at the Univ. of Amsterdam (1932–36) and musicology at the Univ. of Utrecht (1932–34), he returned to the Univ. of Amsterdam to study musicology (1934–37). Flothuis was awarded his doctorate in 1969 for his diss. *Mozarts Bearbeitungen eigener und fremder Werke* (publ. in Kassel, 1969). He served as asst. manager of the Concertgebouw Orch. Amsterdam. After the occupation of the Netherlands by the Germans in 1940, he was dismissed from his job (his wife was half Jewish). On Sept. 18, 1943, he was arrested by the Nazis on the charge of hiding Jews, and transported to the concentration camp in Vught, the Netherlands, and a year later to a German labor camp. His liberation came on May 4, 1945, in a forest near Schw-erin. He returned to Amsterdam and was reinstated at his managerial job at the Concertgebouw Orch. in 1953. From 1955 to 1974 he was artistic director of the Concertgebouw Orch. In 1974 he was appointed prof. of musicology at the Univ. of Utrecht. In his compositions, Flothuis adopted the motivic method of melodic writing and its concomitant form of variations in freely dissonant counterpoint and largely neo- Classical format. Dissatisfied with his youthful works, he destroyed his MSS dating before 1934.

WORKS: ORCH.: Concertino for Small Orch. (1940); *Small Overture* for Soprano and Orch. (1942); *Dramatic Overture* (1943–46); Flute Concerto (Utrecht, Dec. 19, 1945); Concerto for Horn and Small Orch. (1945); *Valses sentimentales* for Small Orch. (1946; also for Piano, 4-Hands); Concerto for Piano and Small Orch. (1946–48); *Capriccio* for Wind Orch. (1949); *Capriccio* for String Orch. (1949); Concerto for Violin and Small Orch. (1950; Utrecht, Jan. 14, 1952); *Fantasia* for Harp and Small Orch. (1953; Amsterdam, May 26, 1955); *Sinfonietta concertante* for Clarinet, Saxophone, and Small Orch. (1954–55; Amsterdam, June 2, 1955); Concert Overture (1955); *Rondo festoso* (Amsterdam, July 7, 1956); Clarinet Concerto (1957); *Symphonic Music* (1957); *Spes patriae,* sinfonietta for Small Orch. (1962); *Espressioni cordiali,* 7 bagatelles for Strings (1963); *Canti e Giouchi* (Songs and Games) for Wind Quintet and Strings (1964); Concertino for Oboe and Small Orch. (1968); *Per Sonare ed Ascoltare,* 5 canzonas for Flute and Orch. (1971); *Nocturne* (1977); *Cantus amoris* for Strings (1979); *Adagio* for String Orch. and Speaking Voice (1997). **CHAMBER:** Sonata for Solo Cello (1937–38); *Nocturne* for Flute, Oboe, and Clarinet (1941); Quintet for Flute, Oboe, Clarinet, Bass Clarinet, and Bassoon (1941–42); *Sonata da camera* for Flute and Piano (1943); *Aria* for Trumpet and Piano (1944); *3 Pieces* for 2 Horns (1945); *Ronde champêtre* for Flute and Harpsichord (1945); Sonata for Solo Violin (1945); *Partita* for Violin and Piano (1950); *Pour le tombeau d'Orphée* for Harp (1950); *Trio serio* for Viola, Cello, and Piano (1950–51); *Sonata da camera* for Flute and Harp (1951); *Small Suite* for 12 Harps (1951; in collaboration with L. van Delden); String Quartet (1951–52); *Small Suite* for Oboe, Trumpet, Clarinet or Saxophone, and Piano (1952); *Divertimento* for Clarinet, Bassoon, Horn, Violin, Viola, and Double Bass (1952); *4 invenzioni* for 4 Horns (1963); Partita for 2 Violins (1966); Concertino for Oboe, Violin, Viola, and Cello (1967); *Allegro vivace* for 2 Harps (1969); *Caprices roumains* for Oboe and Piano (1975); *Adagio* for Piano, 4-Hands, and Percussion (1975); *Romeo's Lament* for Horn (1975); *Canzone* for 2 Clarinets, Basset Horn, and Bass Clarinet (1978); *Capriccio* for 4 Saxophones (1985–86); Sonata for Oboe, Horn, and Harpsichord (1986); *Preludio e Fughetta* for 3 Trumpets (1986); Quartet for 2 Violins, Viola, and Cello (1991–92); Quintet for Harp, Flute, Violin, Viola, and Cello (1995); piano pieces. **VOCAL:** *Hymnus* for Soprano and Orch. (1965); *Santa Espina* for Mezzo-soprano and Orch. (1985–86); numerous other pieces, including choral works and songs.—NS/LK/DM

Flotow, Friedrich (Adolf Ferdinand) von, famous German opera composer; b. Teutendorf, April 27, 1813; d. Darmstadt, Jan. 24, 1883. He was a scion of an old family of nobility. He received his first music lessons from his mother, then was a chorister in Güstrow. At the age of 16 he went to Paris, where he entered the Cons. to study piano with J.P. Pixis and composition with Reicha. After the revolution of 1830, he returned home, where he completed his first opera, *Pierre et Cathérine,* set to a French libretto; it was premiered in a German tr. in Ludwigslust in 1835. Returning to Paris, he collaborated with the Belgian composer Albert Grisar on the operas *Lady Melvil* (1838) and *L'Eau merveilleuse* (1839). With the composer Auguste Pilati, he composed the opera *Le Naufrage de la Méduse* (Paris, May 31, 1839; perf. in a Ger. tr. as *Die Matrosen*, Hamburg, Dec. 23, 1845). He scored a decisive acclaim with his romantic opera *Alessandro Stradella*, based on the legendary accounts of the life of the Italian composer; it was first performed in Hamburg on Dec. 30, 1844, and had numerous subsequent productions in Germany. He achieved an even greater success with his romantic opera *Martha, oder Der Markt zu Richmond* (Vienna, Nov. 25, 1847); in it he demonstrated his ability to combine the German sentimental spirit with Italian lyricism and Parisian elegance. The libretto was based on a ballet, *Lady Henriette, ou La Servante de Greenwich* (1844), for which Flotow had composed the music for Act I; the ballet in turn was based on a vaudeville, *La Comtesse d'Egmont*; the authentic Irish melody *The Last Rose of Summer* was incorporated into the opera by Flotow, lending a certain nostalgic charm to the whole work. Flotow's aristocratic predilections made it difficult for him to remain in Paris after the revolution of 1848. He accepted the post of Intendant at the grand ducal court theater in Schwerin (1855–63), then moved to Austria; he returned to Germany in 1873, settling in Darmstadt in 1880.

WORKS: DRAMATIC: O p e r a : *Pierre et Cathérine* (1st perf. in a German version, Ludwigslust, 1835); *Die Bergknappen; Alfred der Grosse; Rob-Roy* (Royaumont, Sept. 1836); *Sérafine* (Royaumont, Oct. 30, 1836); *Alice* (Paris, April 8, 1837); *La Lettre du préfet* (Paris, 1837; rev. 1868); *Le Comte de Saint-Mégrin* (Royaumont, June 10, 1838; rev. as *Le Duc de Guise*, Paris, April 3, 1840; in German, Schwerin, Feb. 24, 1841); *Lady Melvil* (with Albert Grisar; Paris, Nov. 15, 1838); *L'Eau merveilleuse* (with Grisar; Paris, Jan. 30, 1839); *Le Naufrage de la Méduse* (with Auguste Pilati; Paris, May 31, 1839; in German as *Die Matrosen*, Hamburg, Dec. 23, 1845); *L'Esclave de Camoëns* (Paris, Dec. 1, 1843; subsequent revisions under different titles); *Alessandro Stradella* (Hamburg, Dec. 30, 1844); *L'Âme en peine* (Der Förster; Paris, June 29, 1846); *Martha, oder Der Markt zu Richmond* (Vienna, Nov. 25, 1847); *Sophie Katharina, oder Die Grossfürstin* (Berlin, Nov. 19, 1850); *Rübezahl* (private perf., Retzien, Aug. 13, 1852; public perf., Frankfurt am Main, Nov. 26, 1853); *Albin, oder Der Pflegesohn* (Vienna, Feb. 12, 1856; rev. as *Der Müller von Meran*, Königsberg, 1859); *Herzog Johann Albrecht von Mecklenburg, oder Andreas Mylius* (Schwerin, May 27, 1857); *Pianella* (Schwerin, Dec. 27, 1857); *La Veuve Grapin* (Paris, Sept. 21, 1859; in German, Vienna, June 1, 1861); *La Châtelaine* (Der Märchensucher, 1865); *Naida* (St. Petersburg, Dec. 11, 1865); *Zilda, ou La Nuit des dupes* (Paris, May 28, 1866); *Am Runenstein* (Prague, April 13, 1868); *L'Ombre* (Paris, July 7, 1870; in German as *Sein Schatten*, Vienna, Nov. 10, 1871); *Die Musikanten, or La Jeunesse de Mozart* (Mannheim, June 19, 1887). **B a l l e t :** *Lady Henriette, ou La Servante de Greenwich* (Act II by R. Burgmüller and Act III by E. Deldevez; Paris, Feb. 21, 1844); *Die Libelle, or La Demoiselle, ou Le Papillon ou Dolores* (Schwerin, Aug. 8, 1856); *Die Gruppe der Thetis* (Schwerin, Aug. 18, 1858); *Der Tannkönig* (Schwerin, Dec. 22, 1861); *Der Königsschuss* (Schwerin, May 22, 1864). **ORCH.:** Sym. (1833; not extant); 2 piano concertos (1830, 1831); *Jubel-Ouverture* (1857). **CHAMBER:** *Trio de salon* for Violin, Piano, and Cello (1845); Violin Sonata (1861). **VOCAL:** Songs.

BIBL.: G. von Flotow, *Beiträge zur Geschichte der Familie von F.* (Dresden, 1844); A. Bussensius, *F. v.F.: Eine Biographie* (Kassel, 1855); B. Bardi-Poswiansky, *F. als Opernkomponist* (diss., Univ. of Königsberg, 1924); J. Weissmann, *F.* (London, 1950). —NS/LK/DM

Flower, Sir (Walter) Newman, noted English publisher and writer on music; b. Fontmell Magna, Dorset, July 8, 1879; d. Blandford, Dorset, March 12, 1964. He joined the firm of Cassel & Co. in 1906 and purchased it in 1927. He became deeply interested in music; publ. an extensive biography, *George Frideric Handel: His Personality and His Times* (London, 1923; 2nd ed., rev., 1947); also *Sir Arthur Sullivan: His Life, Letters and Diaries* (London, 1927; 2nd ed., rev., 1950); *Franz Schubert: The Man and His Circle* (London, 1928; 2nd ed., rev., 1949); also prepared a *Catalogue of a Handel Collection Formed by Newman Flower* (Sevenoaks, 1921); publ. a vol. of memoirs, *Just As It Happened* (London, 1950). He was knighted in 1938.

BIBL.: A. Walker, *George Frideric Handel: The N. F. Collection* (Manchester, 1972).—NS/LK/DM

Floyd, Carlisle (Sessions, Jr.), esteemed American composer; b. Latta, S.C., June 11, 1926. He was a student of Ernst Bacon at Syracuse Univ. (Mus.B., 1946; Mus.M, 1949), and also received private instruction in piano from Rudolf Firkušny and Sydney Foster. After teaching at Fla. State Univ. in Tallahassee (from 1947), he became prof. of music at the Univ. of Houston in 1976. Floyd's opera *Susannah* (1953–54; Tallahassee, Feb. 24, 1955) established his reputation as a composer of dramatic works, and in 1956 it won the N.Y. Music Critics Circle Award. In subsequent years, it became one of the most widely performed American operas at home and abroad. Floyd also won critical acclaim for his opera *Of Mice and Men*, after Steinbeck (1969; Seattle, Jan. 22, 1970). His other stage works included the musical play *Slow Dusk* (1948–49; Syracuse, May 1949) and the operas *Wuthering Heights* (Santa Fe, July 16, 1958), *The Passion of Jonathan Wade* (N.Y., Oct. 11, 1962; rev. 1989; Houston, Jan. 18, 1991), *Markheim* (New Orleans, March 31, 1966), *Bilby's Doll* (Houston, Feb. 28, 1976), *The Sojourner and Mollie Sinclair* (Raleigh, N.C., Dec. 2, 1976), *Willie Stark* (Houston, April 24, 1981), and *Cold Sassy Tree* (Houston, April 14, 2000). He also wrote some instrumental and vocal pieces, but it is as a composer for the theater that Floyd has secured his place in American music. His stage works, all written to his own libretti, reveal a mastery of dramatic writing in an accessible style.—NS/LK/DM

Flummerfelt, Joseph, American conductor; b. Vincennes, Ind., Feb. 24, 1937. He studied at DePauw Univ. (B.M., 1958), the Philadelphia Cons. of Music (M.Mus., 1962), and the Univ. of Ill. (D.M.A., 1971), and also privately with Julius Herford, Nadia Boulanger, and Elaine Brown. From 1964 to 1968 he was director of choral activities at DePauw Univ., and then at Fla. State Univ. from 1968 to 1971. In 1971 he was appointed director of choral activities at Westminster Choir Coll., where he became artistic director and principal conductor in 1982. He also serves as an artistic director of the Spoleto Festival U.S.A. and, from 1971 to 1993, was maestro del coro of the Spoleto Festival in Italy. He likewise was founder-music director of the N.Y. Choral Artists and choral director of the N.Y. Phil. From 1994 to 1999 he was music director of Singing City of Philadelphia.—NS/LK/DM

Flury, Richard, Swiss composer, conductor and teacher; b. Biberist, March 26, 1896; d. there, Dec. 23, 1967. He studied musicology in Basel, Bern, and Geneva, then theory and composition with Kurth, Hubert, Lauber, and Marx. He conducted orchs. and choral societies in Switzerland; taught at the Solothurn Canton School. He wrote an autobiography, *Lebenserinnerungen* (1950; with a list of works).

WORKS: DRAMATIC: O p e r a : *Eine florentinische Tragödie* (1926); *Die helle Nacht* (1932); *Casanova e l'Albertolli* (1937). B a l l e t : *Die alte Truhe* (1945). ORCH.: 7 syms.: No. 1 (1923), *Fastnachts-Symphonie* (1928), *Tessiner Symphonie* (No. 2, 1936), *Waldsymphonie* (1942), *Bucheggbergische Symphonie* (No. 3, 1946), *Liechtensteinische Symphonie* (No. 4, 1951), and No. 5 (1955–56); 6 symphonic overtures; 2 piano concertos (1927, 1943); 4 violin concertos (1933, 1940, 1944, 1965); *Caprice* for Violin and Orch. (1967). CHAMBER: Oboe Sonata (1926); 7 string quartets (1926, 1929, 1938, 1940, 1955, 1958, 1964); 3 cello sonatas (1937, 1941, 1966); Piano Quintet (1948); 11 violin sonatas (Nos. 5–11, 1940–61). KEYBOARD: P i a n o : Sonata (1920); *50 romantische Stücke*; 24 preludes. OTHER: 15 military marches and other music for Band; choruses; about 150 songs.—NS/LK/DM

Flying Burrito Brothers, The, legendary folk-rock band led by the quixotic Gram Parsons. MEMBERSHIP: Gram Parsons (real name, Cecil Connor III), gtr., kybd., voc. (b. Winter Haven, Fla., Nov. 5, 1946; d. Joshua Tree, Calif., Sept. 19, 1973); Chris Hillman, gtr., mdln., voc. (b. Los Angeles, Dec. 4, 1942); "Sneaky" Pete Kleinow, pedal steel gtr. (b. South Bend, Ind., c. 1934); Chris Ethridge, bs., pno. Later members included Bernie Leadon, gtr., voc. (b. Minneapolis, July 19, 1947); Michael Clarke, drm. (b. N.Y., June 3, 1944; d. Treasure Island, Fla., Dec. 19, 1993); Al Perkins, pedal steel gtr. Gram Parsons left in 1970, to be replaced by Rick Roberts, gtr., voc. (b. Clearwater, Fla. Aug. 31, 1949).

Gram Parsons grew up in Waycross, Ga., where he learned to play piano and later took up guitar. After playing with several Ga. bands, he formed the folk-style quartet the Shilos, with whom he performed in the first half of the 1960s. After briefly studying theology at Harvard Univ., Parsons formed perhaps the first country-rock band, the International Submarine Band, in 1965 in the Cambridge area. The group recorded two obscure singles before relocating to L.A. in 1966 and realigning with a new bassist and drummer for *Safe at Home*, recorded for Lee Hazlewood's LHI label. The album included four Parsons originals, including "Luxury Liner."

In 1968, Parsons joined the Byrds for their celebrated *Sweetheart of the Rodeo* album. Hailed as the first country-rock record, the album included two Parsons songs, "Hickory Wind" and "One Hundred Years from Now." Leaving the Byrds after only three months as the group was preparing for a tour of South Africa, Parsons was soon followed by Chris Hillman.

In late 1968, Parsons and Hillman formed the Flying Burrito Brothers with "Sneaky" Pete Kleinow and Chris Ethridge. Signed to A&M Records, their debut album, *The Gilded Palace of Sin*, pictured the members in elaborate country western–style Nudie suits (Parsons's suit prominently featured marijuana leaves). The album contained some of Parsons's finest songwriting efforts, including "Sin City" and "Juanita" (coauthored by Hillman) and "Hot Burrito #1" (coauthored by Ethridge), with lead vocals by Parsons. In September 1969, Ethridge exited for sessions work and was replaced by future Eagle Bernie Leadon, formerly with Dillard and Clark, with Hillman switching to bass. Ex-Byrd Michael Clarke became the group's drummer that year. *Burrito Deluxe* featured a fine countrified version of Mick Jagger and Keith Richards's "Wild Horses," as well as a number of songs written or cowritten by Parsons, including "High Fashion Queen" and "Lazy Days."

Parsons left the Flying Burrito Brothers in April 1970, shortly before the release of *Burrito Deluxe*. He was replaced by Rick Roberts, who led the group through a variety of incarnations until 1972. *The Flying Burrito Brothers* included Roberts's "Colorado" and Gene Clark's "Tried So Hard," but both Kleinow and Leadon departed in 1971. By October, the group was reconstituted with Roberts, Hillman, Clarke, pedal steel guitarist Al Perkins, and three members of Country Gazette. This grouping recorded the live *Last of the Red Hot Burritos*, but, before a late 1971 tour undertaken as the Hot Burrito Revue with Country Gazette, Hillman, Perkins, and Clarke dropped out. By June 1972, the Burritos had dissolved, although Roberts assembled a new group for a 1973 European tour.

Spending two years in Europe, often in the company of Keith Richards, Parsons eventually returned to recording in 1972. For his two solo albums, Parsons enlisted vocalist Emmylou Harris, fiddler Byron Berline, steel guitarist Al Perkins, bassist Rick Grech (a former member of Blind Faith), and guitarist extraordinaire James Burton. The debut album *GP* included Parsons's "Kiss the Children," cowritten with Grech, and "She," cowritten with Chris Ethridge. In the spring of 1973, Parsons toured with the Fallen Angels (including Harris) and recordings from the tour eventually surfaced on Sierra Records in 1982. Harris stepped to the fore as harmony vocalist for *Grievous Angel*, as evidenced by "Love Hurts" and "Hearts on Fire." The album also contained "In My Hour of Darkness," cowritten by Parsons and Harris, another Parsons-Grech collaboration, "Las Vegas," and the Parsons originals "Return of the Grievous Angel" and "Brass Buttons." However, several months before the release of the album, Parsons died from apparent multiple drug use at the age of 26 on Sept. 19, 1973, at Joshua Tree, Calif. Parsons subsequently found life in the work of Harris, whose popularity, ironically, was primarily in the country field.

A burgeoning interest in Parsons soon developed and A&M Records scoured their vaults for additional recordings by the group. The 1974 album *Close Up the Honky Tonks* included five out-takes recorded by the Parsons edition of the Flying Burrito Brothers. The 1976 album *Sleepless Nights* contained out-takes recorded by Parsons in 1973, as well as Flying Burrito Brothers out-takes from 1970.

In 1975, the Flying Burrito Brothers re-formed with Kleinow, Ethridge, La. fiddler Floyd "Gib" Guilbeau, bassist Joel Scott Hill, and drummer Gene Parsons. After one album, *Flying Again*, Ethridge departed and Skip Battin came on board for the release of the 1976 album *Airborne*.

With guitarist Greg Harris, the group scored a minor country hit in 1980 with "White Line Fever." As the Burrito Brothers, the group released two albums, *Hearts on the Line* and *Sunset Sundown* for Curb Records. After the release of *Sunset Sundown* in 1982, Pete Kleinov left the band to pursue other interests and Gib Guilbeau and John Beland carried on. This edition of the Flying Burrito Brothers disbanded in 1985, but mainstay Guilbeau assembled yet another group that endured until 1988, touring America and Europe. Since then, occasional reunions have resulted in tours and recordings, including 1999's *Sons of the Golden West*.

DISC.: *The Gilded Palace of Sin* (1969); *Burrito Deluxe* (1970); *The Flying Burrito Brothers* (1971); *Last of the Red Hot Burritos* (1972); *Hot Burrito* (1975); *Close Up the Honky Tonks* (1974); *Flying Again* (1975); *Airborne* (1976); *Sin City* (rec. 1976, rel. 1992); *Live from Tokyo* (1978); *Cabin Fever* (1985); *Live from Amsterdam* (1985); *Live from Europe* (1986); *Farther Along: The Best of The Flying Burrito Brothers* (1988); *Encounters from the West* (reissue of *Live from Tokyo*, 1991); *Eye of a Hurricane* (1994); *Relix's Best of the Flying Burrito Brothers* (1995). The Shilos: *Gram Parsons: The Early Years* (1979). The International Submarine Band: *Safe at Home* (1968). Gram Parsons/The Flying Burrito Brothers: *Sleepless Nights* (1976). The Burrito Brothers (with Gib Guilbeau): *Double Barrel* (1995); *Back to the Sweetheart of the Rodeo* (1996). Swampwater and The Flying Burrito Brothers (with Gib Guilbeau and Sneaky Pete Kleinow): *Live at the Cannary* (1996). Gram Parsons: *GP* (1973); *Grievous Angel* (1974); *Cosmic American Music: The Rehearsal Tapes 1972* (1995). Gram Parsons and the Fallen Angels: *Live 1973* (1973); *Live 1973—Original Unedited Broadcast Recording* (1997).

BIBL.: Ben Fong-Torres, *Hickory Wind: The Life and Times of Gram Parsons* (N.Y., 1991).

Flynn, George (William), American composer and teacher; b. Miles City, Mont., Jan. 21, 1937. He studied with Ussachevsky, Beeson, and Luening at Columbia Univ. (D.M.A., 1972). After serving on its faculty (1966–73), he taught at City Coll. of the City Univ. of N.Y. (1973–76). In 1977 he became chair of the musicianship and composition dept. at DePaul Univ. in Chicago. In 1988 he founded New Music DePaul, a professional new music perf. series, which he subsequently led as director. His music is of a quaquaversal nature, disdaining nothing and absorbing anything of modernistic applicability.

WORKS: DRAMATIC: B a l l e t : *Mrs. Brown* (1965). **ORCH.:** 2 syms.: No. 1, *Music for Orchestra* (1966) and No. 2 (Chicago, May 19, 1981); *Lammy* for Strings (1973); *Javeh* (1973); *Meditations, Praises* (Chicago, June 20, 1981); *Lost and Found* for

Youth Orch. (1984); *A Reign of Love* for Orch. and Narrator (1992); *The Density of Memory* for Clarinet Trio and Orch. (Chicago, April 16, 1997); *American City* for Piano and Wind Ensemble (Chicago, Nov. 7, 1998); *Winter Dusk* for Strings (1999); *Rita's Dance* (2000). **CHAMBER:** Piano Quartet (1963); *Solo and Duos* for Violin and Piano (1964); Wind Quintet (1965; rev. 1983); *4 Pieces* for Violin and Piano (1965); *Duo* for Clarinet and Piano (1966); *Duo* for Trumpet and Piano (1974); *Duo* for Viola and Piano (1974); *American Rest* for Clarinet, Viola, Cello, and Piano (1975; rev. 1982); *American Festivals and Dreams* for String Quartet (1976); *Winter Landscape*, duo for Cello and Piano (1977; rev. 1998); *Celebration* for Violin and Piano (1980); Saxophone Quartet (1980); *4 Fantasy-Etudes* for Violin (1981); *Diversion* for Flute, Clarinet, Violin, Cello, and Piano (1984); *American Summer* for Piano Trio (1986); *'Til Death* for Violin and Piano (1988); *Who Shall Inherit the Earth?* for Clarinet, Violin, and 2 Pianos (1989); *Forms of Flight* for Clarinet (1991); *The Streets Are Empty* for Saxophone Quartet (1992). **KEYBOARD: P i a n o :** *Fuguing* (1962); *4 Preludes* (1965); *Fantasy No. 1* (1966) and *No. 2* (1980–82); *Music* for Piano, 4-Hands (1966); *Trinity*, cycle (*Wound*, 1968, *Kanal*, 1976, and *Salvage*, 1993); *Pieces of Night (American Nocturnes)* (1986–89); *American Icon* (1988); *Toward the Light* (1991); *Derus Simples* (1995). **H a r p s i c h o r d :** *Drive* (1973). **VOCAL:** *Tirades and Dreams* for Actress, Soprano, and Chamber Orch. (1972); *Songs of Destruction* for Soprano and Piano (1973–74); (6) *American Songs* for Chorus, Horn, and Piano (1983–84); *St. Vincent' Words* for Chorus, 8 Brasses, and 2 String Basses (1995); choruses. **OTHER:** Electronic pieces.—**NS/LK/DM**

Foch (real name, Fock), Dirk, Dutch composer and conductor; b. Batavia, Java (where his father was governor general of the Dutch East Indies), June 18, 1886; d. Locarno, Switzerland, May 24, 1973. He studied in the Netherlands and Germany, then began his career in Sweden. He conducted the Goteborg Sym. Orch. (1913–15); and was guest conductor of the Concertgebouw Orch. in Amsterdam and of the orch. at The Hague (1917–19). He made his American debut as conductor with a specially assembled orch. at Carnegie Hall in N.Y., April 12, 1920; also conducted orch. groups elsewhere in the U.S., and in Vienna.

WORKS: *Ein hohes Lied*, 5 fragments from the Bible for Recitation and Orch. (Amsterdam, 1931); a musical pageant in the style of the medieval mystery plays, *From Aeon to Aeon*; 3 ballades for Piano (1913); a cycle of songs from the Chinese (1921); *Java Sketches* for Piano (1948).—**NS/LK/DM**

Fodi, John, Hungarian-born Canadian composer; b. Nagyteval, March 22, 1944. He emigrated to Canada from Germany with his family in 1951, becoming a naturalized Canadian citizen in 1961. He studied theory and composition with Betts in Hamilton (1964–66), composition with Weinzweig and Beckwith and electronic music with Ciamaga at the Univ. of Toronto (B.M., 1970), and composition with Anhalt and electronic music with Pedersen at McGill Univ. in Montreal (1970–71). He then returned to the Univ. of Toronto to complete his training in composition with Weinzweig (M.Mus., 1972). He subsequently had some lessons with Davidovsky at Johnson State Coll. (1973) and later took his M.L.S. degree at the Univ. of Toronto (1990). In 1967 he founded the Contemporary Music Group at the Univ.

of Toronto, serving as its artistic director until 1970. While at McGill Univ., he was co-founder of the New Music Group and in 1971 helped to organize ARRAY, a contemporary music group, later serving as its president and artistic director (1976–79). In 1974 he joined the staff of the Edward Johnson Music Library at the Univ. of Toronto, where he worked as a technical librarian and sound recordings cataloguer. He ed. a viola discography (2000). His compositions partake of multifarious techniques of ultramodern music, with an evident preoccupation with abstract textures and mathematical processes.

WORKS: DRAMATIC: *Music Bockxd* for 3 Actors or Dancers, 7 Music Boxes, and Tape (1969). **ORCH.:** 2 syms.: No. 1 (1964–66) and No. 2 (1987–); *Symparanekromenoi* (1969–71; Toronto, July 25, 1974); Concerto for Viola and 2 Wind Ensembles (1972); *Dragon Day* (1976); *Adagio* for Strings (1980); Concertino for Bassoon and Chamber Orch. (1983); Concerto Grosso for Chamber Ensemble (1984); *Kootenay* for Chamber Orch. (1986); Suite for Junior String Orch. (1988–89); 2 Pieces:1, *Within hours...* and 2, *Rose crowned into darkness* (1991–93); Violin Concerto (1992–96). **CHAMBER:** 7 string quartets: No. 1 (1963), No. 2, *Short* (1963), No. 3 (1965), No. 4, *Fantasia* (1967), No. 5, *Concerto a quattro* (1973), No. 6, *Aus tiefer Not* (1981), and No. 7, *Without the spring, no wild geese* (1987–89; rev. 1998); Piano Sonata (1964–66); Chamber Sym. for Flute, Horn, Piano, and String Quartet (1967); *Tettares* for Percussion Quartet (1968); Harpsichord Sonata (1968); *4 for 4* for Clarinet Quartet (1968); *Signals* for Soprano Saxophone, Tenor Saxophone, Trombone, Percussion, and Piano (1969); *Ch'ien* for String Quartet (1969); *Elements* for 1 to 5 Melody Instruments (1972); *Variations II* for Woodwind Quintet (1975); *In campo aperto* for Flute, Oboe, Percussion, 2 Pianos, and Cello (1976); Trio for Flute, Viola, and Harpsichord (1977); *Concerto in 4 Parts* for Accordion (1978); *Dum transisset, "sonata for 5 instruments"* for Flute, Trombone, Piano, Viola, and Cello (1978–); *Birds*, 4 pieces for Various Instruments (1978–79); *Time's fell hand defac'd* for Flute, English Horn or Clarinet, Percussion, Piano, and Cello (1978–89); *Western Wynde, "serenata for 7 instruments"* for Flute, Clarinet, Brass Instrument, Piano, Violin, Viola, and Cello (1979; rev. 1986); Wind Octet for 2 Oboes, 2 Clarinets, 2 Bassoons, and 2 Horns (1980–81); Partita for Brass Quintet (1981–82); Sonata for Double Wind Quintet (1982–83); Tuba Quartet for 2 Euphoniums and 2 Tubas (1984); *Rhapsody* for Bass Clarinet and Piano (1985); *The Green Goads* for Flute, Clarinet, Harp, and String Quintet (1992); 3 Pieces for Violin and Piano (1993); *Distant Music Like Murmuring Rain* for Flute, Harp, and 2 Percussion (1995); *Of Siren Tears* for Clarinet, Violin, and Marimba (1995); *Against Black Woods Long Streaks of Rain* for Viola (1997); *Distant Roads* for Flute, Clarinet, Harp, Marimba, and String Quintet (1997). **VOCAL:** Choruses; songs.—NS/LK/DM

Fodor, Eugene (Nicholas, Jr.), American violinist; b. Turkey Creek, Colo., March 5, 1950. His great-great-grandfather founded the Fodor Cons. in Hungary. He studied violin with Harold Wippler in Denver. In 1967 he went to N.Y. and studied with Galamian, and then with Gingold at the Ind. Univ. School of Music in Bloomington (diploma, 1970); later took lessons in the master class of Heifetz at the Univ. of Southern Calif. in Los Angeles (1970–71). In 1972 he won the Paganini Competition in Genoa, Italy. In 1974 he shared 2nd prize with 2 Soviet violinists (no 1st prize was awarded) at the Tchaikovsky Competition in Moscow. Returning to America, he was given the honors of the state of Colo., and on Sept. 12, 1974, played at a state dinner at the White House in Washington, D.C., for the premier of Israel, Rabin. In subsequent years, he appeared as a soloist with a number of major orchs., and also was active as a recitalist. His seemingly successful career took a bizarre twist in 1989 when he was arrested and jailed for cocaine and heroin possession, cocaine trafficking, and breaking-and-entering on Martha's Vineyard in Mass. However, he was able to overcome this setback and resumed his career.—NS/LK/DM

Fodor-Mainvielle, Joséphine, famous French soprano; b. Paris, Oct. 13, 1789; d. Saint-Génis, near Lyons, Aug. 14, 1870. She made her debut in 1808 in St. Petersburg in Fioravanti's *Le Cantatrici villane.* She gained renown for her performances in the operas of Mozart and Rossini at the King's Theatre in London (1816–18); was likewise successful in her many engagements in Paris, Naples, and Vienna. During a performance of the title role of *Sémiramide* in Paris on Dec. 9, 1825, she suddenly lost her voice and was eventually compelled to quit the stage. She went to Naples in the hopes of recovery under the warm sun, but her attempts to renew her career in 1828 and 1831 failed, and she spent the rest of her long life in retirement.—NS/LK/DM

Foerster, Josef Bohuslav, eminent Czech composer and teacher, son of **Josef Förster;** b. Prague, Dec. 30, 1859; d. Nový Vestec, near Stará Boleslav, May 29, 1951. He studied at the Prague Organ School (1879–82), then was organist at St. Vojtěch (1882–88) and choirmaster of Panna Marie Sněžná (1889–94). He married the Czech soprano **Berta Foerstrová-Lautererová;** (b. Prague, Jan. 11, 1869; d. there, April 9, 1936) in 1888; when she became a member of the Hamburg Opera in 1893, he settled there as a music critic and later became a prof. of piano at the Cons. in 1901. After his wife became a member of the Vienna Court Opera in 1903, he became a prof. of composition at the New Vienna Cons. He returned to Prague in 1918; then taught composition at the Cons. (1919–22), at its master school (1922–31), and at the Univ. of Prague (1920–36). He served as president of the Czech Academy of Sciences and Art (1931–39), and was awarded the honorary title of National Artist of the Czech government in 1945. He continued to teach privately and to compose during the last years of his long life. He taught many distinguished Czech composers of the 20th century. He publ. a detailed autobiography (Prague, 1929–47), as well as several vols. of essays and articles. Of his numerous compositions, the most important are his operas, instrumental music, and choral pieces written before World War I. His works from this period are suffused with lyric melos, and reveal characteristic national traits in Foerster's treatment of melodic and rhythmic material; his harmonic idiom represents the general style of Central European Romanticism.

WORKS: DRAMATIC: Opera (all 1st perf. in Prague): *Debora* (1890–91; Jan. 27, 1893); *Eva* (1895–97; Jan. 1, 1899); *Jessika* (1902–04; April 16, 1905); *Nepřemoženi* (Invincibilities; 1917; Dec. 19, 1918); *Srdce* (Hearts; 1921–22; Nov. 15, 1923);

Bloud (The Fool; 1935–36; Feb. 28, 1936). **CHAMBER:** 3 piano trios (1883; 1894; 1919–21); String Quintet (1886); 5 string quartets (1888; 1893; 1907–13; 1944; 1951); 2 cello sonatas (1898, 1926); Wind Quintet (1909); Piano Quintet (1928); Nonet (1931); Violin Sonata (1925); *Sonata quasi fantasia* for Solo Violin (1943); piano pieces. **VOCAL:** Choral works; songs. **OTHER:** Incidental music for various plays. **ORCH.:** 5 syms.: No. 1 (1887–88), No. 2 (1892–93), No. 3 (1894), No. 4 (1905), and No. 5 (1929); *Mé mládí* (My Youth), symphonic poem (1900); *Cyrano de Bergerac*, suite (1903); *Ze Shakespeara* (From Shakespeare), suite (1908–09); *Legenda o štěstí* (Legend of Happiness), symphonic poem (1909); 2 violin concertos (1910–11; 1925–26); *Jaro a touha* (Spring and Longing), symphonic poem (1912); *Jičínská suita* (1923); Cello Concerto (1930); Capriccio for Flute and Small Orch. (1945–46).

BIBL.: Z. Nejedlý, *J.B. F.* (Prague, 1910); J. Bartoš, *J.B. F.* (Prague, 1923); J. Bartoš, P. Pražák, and J. Plavec, eds., *J.B. F.: Jeho životní pout a tvorba:1859–1949* (Prague, 1949); F. Pala, *J.B. F.* (Prague, 1962).—**NS/LK/DM**

Foerstrová-Lautererová, Berta, Czech soprano; b. Prague, Jan. 11, 1869; d. there, April 9, 1936. She studied in Prague, and made her debut as Agathe in *Der Freischütz* at the Prague National Theater in 1887. During her tenure there, she created roles in Dvořák's operas *Jakobin* and *Dimitrij*. She was a member of the Hamburg Opera (1893–1901), and then sang with the Vienna Court Opera (1901–13), appearing under the name of **Foerster-Lauterer**; she retired in 1914. Her husband was **Josef Bohuslav Foerster.—NS/LK/DM**

Fogelberg, Dan, mellow pop singer/songwriter; b. Peoria, Ill., Aug. 13, 1951. His father was a musician, a fact that he celebrated in one of his biggest hits, 1981's "Leader of the Band"; his mother was an opera singer. Initially, Fogelberg wanted to be a painter. He played in several bands while in high school, including a Beatles cover band and a group called the Coachmen that recorded two singles before Fogelberg turned 16, but his future plans were to study art. He went to the Univ. of Ill. to pursue painting, but the lure of performing was too much for him. Fogelberg started playing solo acoustic guitar at local coffeehouses, developing a strong following. Within two years, he became so successful, he left school to perform full time.

By 1972, Fogelberg was in L.A., affiliated with Eagles and REO Speedwagon manager (and future record company president) Irving Azoff. Azoff hooked Fogelberg up with Columbia Records for his debut, *Home Free*, which did not do especially well. He moved to Full Moon/Epic and scored a hit with the album *Souvenirs*, with the help of Eagles guitarist Joe Walsh who produced and played guitar. The success of *Souvenirs* was due in part to the popularity of the song "Part of the Plan" which achieved #31 on the pop charts, but was a bigger hit on album rock radio with its catchy Walsh guitar hook. The album went double platinum and hit #17.

Over the next two years, Fogelberg released *Captured Angel* and *Netherlands*. Both projects went platinum without benefit of a hit single (the former peaking at #23, the latter #17), although they did get considerable play on album rock radio during this mellow period in the rock spectrum. Fogelberg's next hit, ironically, came with a project for which he didn't hold out much commercial hope. *Twin Sons of Different Mothers* paired him with flautist Tim Weisberg. While most of the album sported fusion-lite instrumentals, the tune "The Power of Gold" with Eagle Don Henley on backing vocals became a substantial hit, reaching #24, and propelling the album to #8. *Twin Sons of Different Mothers* was Fogelberg's fourth consecutive platinum album.

Phoenix, featured the massive hit "Longer," destined to become a major hit at weddings and in elevators around the world. The song topped the adult contemporary chart and hit #2 on the pop charts. The other single from the album, "Heart Hotels" didn't do as well, despite a solo by jazz-fusion sax player Tom Scott. It only hit #21. The album rose to #3 and went platinum.

It was his double album *The Innocent Age* that secured Fogelberg's place in the pop pantheon. A musing on turning 30, the album spoke to baby boomers in a powerful way for such a laid-back record. It spawned three Top Ten hits: the bittersweet New Year's ballad, "Same Old Lang Syne" (#9), "Hard to Say" (#7), and his tribute to his father, "Leader of the Band" (#1 adult contemporary, #9 pop). Another hit, the ode to the Kentucky Derby, "Run for the Roses," hit #18. The album went platinum and peaked at #6.

Fogelberg built a studio on his ranch in Colo. (he also has a home in Maine). While he tackled this, Epic released a greatest hits package. With the new hit "Missing You," which reached #23, the album hit #15 and went platinum. It was his last platinum record to date.

From his own studios, Fogelberg released more unusual, experimental albums. His next album, *Windows and Walls* produced the #1 adult contemporary song "Make Love Stay" (#29 pop) and the #13 hit "The Language of Love." The album went gold and hit #15. He followed that with an album as whimsically experimental as his project with Weisberg. *High Country Snow* found Fogelberg working with bluegrass heavyweights like Ricky Skaggs, David Grisman, former Byrd Chris Hillman, Jerry Douglas, and Doc Watson on an album of quasi-bluegrass music. This album also went gold, reaching #30. It was his last major hit to date.

As his career fell into a lower gear, his marriage fell apart. *Exiles* chronicled this on an album that was his most rock-oriented since his work with Joe Walsh. *The Wild Places* dealt with his environmental concerns. *River of Souls* set his lyrics to a modified world beat. His 20-years-later reunion with Tim Weisberg, *No Resemblance Whatsoever*, didn't have the commercial resonance of their first outing, but had a good, light jazz feel. In 1998, Legacy released a four CD, 25-year retrospective box. *First Christmas Morning* found him performing Medieval Christmas carols in time for the holidays. While his hits have stopped coming, he claims to be happier with his more streamlined career.

DISC.: *Home Free* (1973); *Souvenirs* (1974); *Captured Angel* (1975); *Netherlands* (1977); *Twin Sons of Different Mothers* (1978); *Phoenix* (1980); *The Innocent Age* (1981); *Windows and Walls*

(1984); *High Country Snow* (1985); *Exiles* (1987); *The Wild Places* (1990); *Dan Fogelberg Live: Greetings from the West* (1991); *River of Souls* (1993); *No Resemblance Whatsoever* (1995); *Love Songs* (1995); *First Christmas Morning* (1999).—**HB**

Fogg, (Charles William) Eric, English organist and composer; b. Manchester, Feb. 21, 1903; d. London, Dec. 19, 1939. He studied organ with his father and composition with Granville Bantock. He was active as an organist in Manchester, then was on the staff of the BBC. He wrote an overture to the *Comedy of Errors* (1922), *Poem* for cello and piano, suite for violin, cello, and harp, songs (*Love and Life, The Little Folk,* etc.), piano pieces, choral works, etc.—**NS/LK/DM**

Foggia, Francesco, Italian composer; b. Rome, 1604; d. there, Jan. 8, 1688. He was a pupil of A. Cifra and P. Agostini;. After serving at several German courts, he returned to Rome, where he maestro di cappella at the Lateran (1636–61), at S. Lorenzo in Damaso (1661), and, from 1677, at S. Maria Maggiore. A prolific and masterly composer, he continued the traditions of the Roman School. He wrote the oratorios *David fugiens a facie Saul* and *San Giovanni Battista* (1670), numerous masses a cappella (also a few with organ), litanies, motets, etc.—**NS/LK/DM**

Fogliani (Fogliano), Giacomo, Italian organist and composer, brother of **Ludovico Fogliani;** b. Modena, 1468; d. there, April 10, 1548. He was organist at Modena Cathedral from 1479 to at least 1497. By 1504 he was again organist there, later serving as its choirmaster.—**NS/LK/DM**

Fogliani (Fogliano), Ludovico, Italian music theorist, brother of **Giacomo Fogliani (Fogliano);** b. Modena, 2nd half of the 15th century; d. there, 1538. He was famous for his book *Musica theorica...* (Venice, 1529; modern facsimile ed., Bologna, 1970), in which he preceded Zarlino in declaring the correct proportion of the major third to be 4:5, and in distinguishing between the major and minor (greater and lesser) semitones. In Petrucci's *Frottole* (1504–08) are some specimens of his compositions.—**NS/LK/DM**

Foignet, Charles Gabriel, French singer and composer; b. Lyons, 1750; d. Paris, 1823. He settled in Paris in 1779, where he taught harpsichord, harp, and singing. After publishing keyboard pieces and songs, he devoted himself to composing for the stage from 1791. With his son, François Foignet (b. Paris, Feb. 17, 1782; d. Strasbourg, July 22, 1845), who was also a singer and composer, he was active with his own Théâtre des Jeunes-Artistes from 1798 to 1807. François scored his most celebrated success there when he sang in his own *La naissance d'Arlequin, ou Arlequin dans un oeuf* (July 15, 1803). After 1807, François pursued his singing career in Liège, Bruges, Nantes, Lille, Ghent, and Rouen. Charles had another son, Gabriel Foignet, who was a harpist and composer.—**NS/LK/DM**

Foldes (actually, **Földes**), **Andor,** admired Hungarian-born American pianist; b. Budapest, Dec. 21,

1913; d. Herrliberg, Switzerland, Feb. 9, 1992. He began piano lessons at an early age with his mother, and was only 8 when he appeared as soloist in Mozart's 15th Piano Concerto, K.450, with the Budapest Phil. In 1922 he entered the Royal Academy of Music in Budapest and studied with Dohnányi (piano), Weiner (composition), and Ernst Unger (conducting). Upon graduating and winning the Liszt Prize in 1933, he made his first tour of Europe. In 1939 he went to N.Y., where he made his U.S. debut as an orch. soloist in a radio concert in 1940. In 1941 he made his U.S. recital debut at N.Y.'s Town Hall. He became a naturalized American citizen in 1948, but pursued a global concert career. From 1957 to 1965 he also gave master classes at the Saarbrücken Hochschule für Musik. In 1961 he settled in Switzerland. While he continued to devote himself mainly to his career as a piano virtuoso, he occasionally appeared as a conductor and was active as a composer, primarily of piano pieces. Foldes was esteemed for his performances of the Classical and early Romantic masters, but he also displayed a special affinity for the music of Bartók. With his wife Lili Foldes, he publ. *Two on a Continent* (N.Y., 1947). He also publ. *Keys to the Keyboard* (N.Y., 1948) and *Gibt es einen zeitgenössischen Beethoven-Stil? und andere Aufsätze* (Wiesbaden, 1963). His *Erinnerungen* appeared posthumously (Frankfurt am Main, 1993).

BIBL.: W.-E. von Lewinski, *A. F.* (Berlin, 1970). —**NS/LK/DM**

Foley, Red (Clyde Julian), American country singer and radio and television host; b. Blue Lick, Ky., June 17, 1910; d. Fort Wayne, Ind., Sept. 19, 1968. One of the major country music singers of the 1940s and 1950s, Foley helped popularize country music through extensive radio and television appearances, notably on *The National Barn Dance* and the *Grand Ole Opry* on radio and *Ozark Jubilee* on television. Among the 56 Top Ten country hits he scored between 1944 and 1956, the most popular were "Chattanoogie Shoe Shine Boy," "Smoke on the Water," and "Birmingham Bounce."

Foley was the son of Ben and Kate Foley; his father played the fiddle. When he was a child, the family moved to Berea, Ky., where his father ran a general store. His father gave him a guitar when he was six, and he also learned to play harmonica. But he showed particular talent as a singer, winning a contest sponsored by the Kent-Atwater radio manufacturing company when he was 17, after which he began taking singing lessons. He graduated from high school in 1930 and earned a voice scholarship to Georgetown Coll. in Georgetown, Ky., but during his first semester he accepted a job performing with the Cumberland Ridge Runners on the *WLS Barn Dance* radio show in Chicago. He recorded with the group on the Conqueror Records label between 1933 and 1936.

Foley's first wife, Pauline Cox, died giving birth to his first daughter, Betty, on Feb. 3, 1933. Betty Foley grew up to be a country singer and performed with her father. He remarried, to Eva Overstake, a singer on the *Barn Dance* who performed under the name Judy Martin. They had three daughters, including Shirley Lee, who later married Pat Boone; in turn, their daughter Debby Boone also became a successful singer.

On Sept. 23, 1933, a one-hour segment of the *Barn Dance* was picked up for national broadcast, becoming *The National Barn Dance*. In October 1937, Foley, along with other employees of the show, left to set up the *Renfro Valley Barn Dance*, which also gained network distribution. During 1938 he also appeared on the *Plantation Party* series, and from October 1938 to July 1939 on *Avalon Variety Time*, a comedy-variety series that starred comedian Red Skelton starting in January 1939.

Foley returned to Chicago and *The National Barn Dance* in 1940. In 1941 he signed to Decca Records and, in June, appeared in the film *The Pioneers*. He first reached the country charts with "Smoke on the Water" (music and lyrics by Earl Nunn and Zeke Clements), which went to #1 in September 1944 and also made the Top Ten of the pop charts. "Shame on You" (music and lyrics by Spade Cooley) was Foley's second country #1 in November 1945; the record was credited to Lawrence Welk and His Orch. with Red Foley.

On April 13, 1946, Foley joined the Nashville-based Grand Ole Opry as the star of its *Prince Albert Show* segment, the portion of the program that was broadcast nationally; he replaced Roy Acuff. He continued to score country hits, topping the charts with "New Jolie Blonde (New Pretty Blonde)" (music and lyrics by Lew Wayne and Moon Mullican) in May 1947 and "Tennessee Saturday Night" (music and lyrics by Billy Hughes) in March 1949. In early 1950 he enjoyed his biggest hit, "Chattanoogie Shoe Shine Boy" (music and lyrics by Harry Stone and Jack Stapp), which topped the country charts in January and the pop charts in February, selling a million copies. "Birmingham Bounce" (music and lyrics by Sid "Hardrock" Gunter) went to #1 in the country charts in May, as did "Mississippi" (music and lyrics by Curley Williams and Billy Simmons) in July. Foley and Ernest Tubb's recording of "Goodnight Irene" (music and lyrics by Lead Belly) topped the country charts in August and made the pop Top Ten. In September, Foley peaked in the pop Top Ten with "Cincinnati Dancing Pig" (music by Guy Wood, lyrics by Al Lewis).

Foley's 1951 recording of Thomas A. Dorsey's gospel song "(There'll Be) Peace in the Valley (For Me)" became his second million-seller. The same year, his wife committed suicide in the wake of revelations about his affair with radio singer Sally Sweet; he married Sweet in 1954. His recording of "Midnight" (music and lyrics by Boudleaux Bryant and Chet Atkins) topped the country charts in January 1953; that year he left the Grand Ole Opry and moved to Springfield, Mo., where he joined the radio show *Ozark Jubilee*. "One By One" (music by Johnnie Wright, Jack Anglin, and Jim Anglin), a duet between Foley and Kitty Wells, topped the country charts in July 1954.

Foley launched a network television version of *Ozark Jubilee* in January 1955 that ran until November 1961. During the 1962–63 television season, he had a feature role on the situation comedy *Mr. Smith Goes to Washington*. In the last five years of his life he toured extensively. He was elected to the Country Music Hall of Fame in 1967 and was nominated for a 1967 Grammy Award for Best Sacred Performance for the album *Songs of the Soul*. He died of a heart attack in 1968 at age 58 while on tour.

DISC.: *Hot Today* (1941); *Just a Closer Walk with Thee* (1950); *John Edwards Memorial Collection, ca. 1950s* (1959); *Lift Up Your Voice* (1951); *Hillbilly Fever in the Ozarks* (1954); *Red and Ernie* (1956); *Souvenir Album* (1958); *He Walks with Thee* (1958); *My Keepsake Album* (1958); *Beyond the Sunset* (1958); *Let's All Sing to Him* (1959); *Let's All Sing with Red Foley* (1959); *Company's Comin'* (1961); *Songs of Devotion* (1961); *Red Foley's Golden Favorites* (1961); *Dear Hearts and Gentle People* (1962); *The Red Foley Show* (1963); *The Red Foley Story* (1964); *Songs Everybody Knows* (1965); *I'm Bound for the Kingdom* (1965); *Red Foley* (1966); *Songs for the Soul* (1967); *Red Foley's Greatest Hits 1937—39, Vol. 1* (1968); *Gospel Favorites* (1976); *Country and Western Memory Lane, Vol. 3* (1985); *Country Music Hall of Fame* (1991). Patsy Cline: *Live, Vol. 2* (1989). Rex Griffin: *Last Letter* (1996). Hank Snow: *Singing Ranger* (1959). Ernest Tubb: *Let's Say Goodbye Like We Said Hello* (1959). Kitty Wells: *Queen of Country*. Various Artists: *Heroes of Country Music, Vol. 2*; *Heroes of Country Music, Vol. 3*.—**WR**

Foli (real name, **Foley**), **A(llan) J(ames)**, Irish bass; b. Cahir, Tipperary, Aug. 7, 1835; d. Southport, Oct. 20, 1899. He was a pupil of Bisaccia in Naples. Following a widespread fashion among aspiring English opera singers, he changed his name to an Italian-sounding homonym, Foli, and made a career as "Signor Foli." He made his professional debut as Elmiro in Rossini's *Otello* in Catania in 1862, then sang throughout Italy. He appeared in London at Her Majesty's Theatre in 1865, and later at Covent Garden and Drury Lane. He toured the U.S. with Mapleson's opera company (1878–79), and also traveled in South Africa, Australia, and Russia.—**NS/LK/DM**

Folville, Eugénie-Émilie Juliette, Belgian pianist and composer; b. Liège, Jan. 5, 1870; d. Dourgne, France, Oct. 28, 1946. She studied piano with her father and violin with César Thomson; she also took lessons in composition with Radoux at the Liège Cons. She was only 17 when her *Chant de Noël* was performed at the Liège Cathedral. In 1898 she was appointed prof. at the Liège Cons. After the outbreak of World War I in 1914 she lived in Bournemouth, England; later returned to the Continent. She wrote an opera, *Atala* (Lille, 1892), a violin concerto, a piano concerto, piano pieces, and songs.—**NS/LK/DM**

Fomin, Evstignei, Russian composer; b. St. Petersburg, Aug. 16, 1761; d. there, April 27, 1800. He was sent to Bologna to study with Padre Martini. Returning to St. Petersburg in 1785, he became a singing teacher and operatic coach at the theatrical school there. He composed about 10 operas, including *Novgorod Hero Vassily Boyeslavich* (St. Petersburg, Dec. 8, 1786), *Yamshchiki* (Coachmen; St. Petersburg, Jan. 13, 1787), *Orpheus and Eurydice* (St. Petersburg, Jan. 13, 1792), and *The Americans* (St. Petersburg, Feb. 19, 1800; the title refers to the Russians in Alaska; vocal score publ. in 1893; the opera was revived in a perf. at Moscow, Jan. 17, 1947). A number of other operas were erroneously attributed to

Fomin, among them the popular *Miller, Wizard, Cheat, and Marriage-Broker*, produced in Moscow on Jan. 31, 1779, the music of which was actually written by an obscure violinist named Sokolovsky.

BIBL.: B. Dobrokhotov, *E. F.* (Moscow, 1949; 2nd ed., 1968). —**NS/LK/DM**

Fongaard, Björn, Norwegian composer and guitarist; b. Christiania, March 2, 1919; d. there (Oslo), Oct. 26, 1980. He took up the guitar at an early age before pursuing his musical training at the Oslo Cons. with Per Steenberg, Bjarne Brustad, and Karl Andersen. He appeared as a guitarist and also taught guitar at the Oslo Cons. His interest in the potentialities of fractional intervals led him to devise special guitars for playing microtonal music with the aid of electronic techniques which he described as "orchestra microtonalis." He composed a prolific corpus of works in every conceivable genre.

WORKS: DRAMATIC: *Skapelse II* (Creation II), church opera (1972); *Andromeda*, ballet music (1972); *Dimensions*, ballet music (1974). **ORCH.:** 2 sinfoniettas (1951, 1968); Sonata Concertante for Guitar and Orch. (1963); 12 symphonic poems (1963–71); *Orchestral Antiphonalis* (1968); *Symphony of Space I-III* (1969); *Sinfonia Geo-Paleontologica I-V* (1970); *Relativity: Symphony I-III* (1970); 23 piano concertos (1973–76); 3 flute concertos (1973–76); 7 violin concertos (1973–77); 3 horn concertos (1973–77); 2 oboe concertos (1976); 2 clarinet concertos (1976); 2 trumpet concertos (1977); 5 organ concertos (1977–78); many other concertos; 7 syms. for Strings (1980). **CHAMBER:** 2 guitar sonatas (1947, 1963); 2 microtonal guitar sonatas (1965, 1975); 2 sonatas for Solo Oboe (1967, 1968); Sonata for Electronically Metamorphosed Tam-tam (1968); Sonata for Saxophone and Microtonal Guitar (1970); Sonata for Solo Bassoon (1972); Trio for Flute, Viola, and Harp (1971); 21 string quartets (1973); 9 wind quintets (1974); 9 wind trios (1975); 6 wind quartets (1975); 12 string trios (1975); numerous other works, including 57 solo sonatas. Additional works include a vast amount of piano music, organ pieces, vocal music, and tape pieces. —**NS/LK/DM**

Fonseca, Julio, Costa Rican composer; b. San José, May 22, 1885; d. there, June 22, 1950. He received elementary musical training at home from his father, a military band musician. A government grant enabled him to pursue serious study at the Milan Cons. and in Brussels. Returning to Costa Rica, he became active as a teacher at music schools in San Jose and as a church organist. His works consist mostly of pleasant salon music for piano and effective band pieces, much of it based on native folk rhythms.—**NS/LK/DM**

Fontana, Giovanni Battista, Italian composer and violinist; b. Brescia, date unknown; d. Padua, c. 1630. He pursued his career in Brescia, Rome, Venice, and Padua. Fontana was one of the principle figures in the development of the sonata, mostly notable of the solo sonata. A posthumous set of his sonatas, including 6 for Violin or Cornett and Bass, and 12 for 2 Violins and Bass, was publ. in Venice in 1641.—**LK/DM**

Fontanelli, Alfonso, eminent Italian composer; b. Reggio Emilia, Feb. 15, 1557; d. Rome, Feb. 11, 1622. He

entered the service of Cesare d'Este, a nephew of Duke Alfonso II d'Este in Ferrara, in 1586, then was in the service of the latter (1588–97). In 1598 re-entered the service of Cesare d'Este, who had become the Duke of Modena in the interim. He remained in his service until Nov. 1601, when he was found guilty of murdering a man, punished, and banned from the ducal states; was pardoned in 1602. He then was in the service of Cardinal Alessandro in Rome (1602–8), and subsequently active at the court in Florence (1608–10). He later was an emissary for Duke Cesare (1611–14), traveling as far as Spain. He returned to Rome in 1620 and took Holy Orders. He was greatly esteemed as a composer of madrigals. He publ. *Primo libro de' madrigali senza nome* for 5 voices (Ferrara, 1595; reprint, Venice, 1603) and *Secondo libro de' madrigali senza nome* for 5 voices (Venice, 1604; reprints 1609 and 1619).—**NS/LK/DM**

Fontei, Nicolò, Italian composer and organist; b. Orciano di Pesaro, March, date unknown; d. probably in Verona, c. 1647. He was active in Venice as a church organist before settling in Verona in 1645 as choirmaster at the Cathedral and teacher of the acolytes. In both his secular and sacred works, he acquired mastery of the Venetian triple-time bel canto aria. In his secular works, he also pioneered in the use of rondo or refrain structures. Among his secular works were 3 vols. of *Bizzarrie poetiche poste in musica* for 1 to 3 voices (Venice, 1635, 1636, 1639) and the opera *Sidonio e Dorisbe* (Venice, 1642). His sacred output included a Mass for 1 to 8 voices and instruments and other polyvocal works, as well as solo vocal pieces.—**LK/DM**

Fontyn, Jacqueline, Belgian composer and teacher; b. Antwerp, Dec. 27, 1930. She studied piano with Ignace Bolotine in her native city, and later with Marcel Maas; took theory, orchestration, and composition lessons with Marcel Quinet in Brussels and Max Deutsch in Paris; then completed her study of composition at the Chapelle Musicale Reine Elisabeth in Brussels (graduated, 1959). She taught at the Royal Flemish Cons. in Antwerp (1963–70); then was a prof. of composition at the Brussels Cons. (1970–90). Fontyn won many prizes for her compositions, including the Koopal Prize of the Belgian Ministry of Culture (1961, 1979), the Camille Huismans Prize of Antwerp (1974), and the Arthur Honegger Prize of Paris (1987). In 1961 she married **Camille Schmitt**.

WORKS: DRAMATIC: Ballet: *Piedigrotta* (1958). **ORCH.:** *Petite suite* (1951); *Divertimento* for Strings (1953); *Danceries* (1956); *Prelude and Allegro* (1957); *Mouvements concertants* for 2 Pianos and Strings (1957); *Deux estampies* (1961); *Digressions* for Cello and Chamber Orch. (1962); *Six ébauches* (1963); *Digressions* for Chamber Orch. (1964); *Galaxie* for Chamber Orch. (1965); Piano Concerto (1967); *Colloque* for Wind Quintet and Strings (1970); *Pour 11 archets* (1971); *Evoluon* (1972); *Per archi* for Strings (1973); Violin Concerto (1975); *Frises I* (1975) and *II* (1976); *Halo* for Harp and 16 Instruments or Chamber Orch. (1978); *Creneaux* (1982); *Arachne* (1985); *In the Green Shade* (1988); *Reverie and Turbulence*, piano concerto (1989); *A l'orée du Songe*, viola concerto (1990); *Colinda*, cello concerto (1991). **CHAMBER:** Wind Quintet (1954); Trio for Violin, Cello, and Piano (1956); String Quartet (1958); *Musica a quattro* for Violin,

Clarinet, Cello, and Piano (1966); Nonet (1969); *Strophes* for Violin and Piano (1970); *Six climats* for Violin and Piano (1972); *Horizons* for String Quartet (1977); *Zones* for Flute, Clarinet, Cello, Percussion, and Piano (1979); *Rhumbs* for 2 Trumpets, Horn, Trombone, and Tuba (1980); *Analecta* for 2 Violins (1981); *Controverse* for Bass Clarinet or Tenor Saxophone and Percussion (1983); *Either...or entweder...oder* for String Quintet or Clarinet and String Quartet (1984); *Cheminement* for 9 Instrumentalists (1986); *La Deviniére* for Violin and Piano (1988); *Scurochiatro* for 7 Instrumentalists (1989); *Compagnon de la nuit* for Oboe and Piano (1989). **KEYBOARD: Piano Solo:** 2 *Impromptus* (1950); *Capriccio* (1954); *Ballade* (1964); *Mosaici* (1964); *Le Gong* (1980); *Bulles* (1980); *Aura* (1982). **Piano:** 2 *Spirales* (1971). **Harpsichord:** *Shadows* (1973). **VOCAL:** *La Trapéziste qui a perdu son coeur* for Mezzo- soprano and Chamber Orch. (1953); *Deux rondels de Charles d'Orléans* for Soprano and Piano (1956); *Psalmus Tertius* for Baritone, Chorus, and Orch. (1959); *Ephémères* for Mezzo-soprano and 11 Instruments (1979); *Alba* for Soprano and 4 Instruments (1981); *Pro & Antiverbe(e)s* for Soprano and Cello (1984).

BIBL.: B. Brand, *J. F.* (Berlin, 1991).—**NS/LK/DM**

Foote, Arthur (William), distinguished American composer; b. Salem, Mass., March 5, 1853; d. Boston, April 8, 1937. He studied harmony with Emery at the New England Cons. of Music in Boston (1867–70) and took courses in counterpoint and fugue with Paine at Harvard Coll. (1870–74), where he received the first M.A. degree in music granted by an American univ. (1875). He also studied organ and piano with B.J. Lang, and later with Stephen Heller in France (1883). Returning to the U.S., he taught piano, organ, and composition in Boston; was organist at Boston's Church of the Disciples (1876–78) and at the 1st Unitarian Church (1878–1910); also frequently appeared as a pianist with the Kneisel Quartet (1890–1910), performing several of his own works. He was a founding member and president (1909–12) of the American Guild of Organists. He taught piano at the New England Cons. of Music (1921–37). Foote was elected a member of the National Inst. of Arts and Letters (1898). His music, a product of the Romantic tradition, is notable for its fine lyrical élan. His Suite in E major for Strings (1907) enjoyed numerous performances and became a standard of American orch. music. He publ. *Modern Harmony in Its Theory and Practice* (with W.R. Spalding; 1905; rev. ed., 1959; republ. as *Harmony*, 1969), *Some Practical Things in Piano- Playing* (1909), and *Modulation and Related Harmonic Questions* (1919). His autobiography was privately printed (Norwood, Mass., 1946) by his daughter, Katharine Foote Raffy.

WORKS: ORCH.: *In the Mountains*, overture (1886; Boston, Feb. 5, 1887; rev. 1910); Cello Concerto (1887–93); *Francesca da Rimini*, symphonic prologue (1890; Boston, Jan. 24, 1891); *Serenade* for Strings (1891; based on the earlier Suites, opp. 12 and 21); Suite in D minor, op.36 (1894–95; Boston, March 7, 1896); *4 Character Pieces* after the *Rubáiyát* of Omar Khayyam (1900; based on a set of piano pieces); Suite in E major for Strings, op.63 (1907; rev. 1908; Boston, April 16, 1909); *A Night Piece* for Flute and Strings (1922; derived from the *Nocturne and Scherzo* for Flute and String Quartet, 1918). **CHAMBER:** 2 piano trios (1882; rev. 1883; 1907–08); 3 string quartets (1883; 1893; 1907–11); Violin Sonata (1889); *Romance and Scherzo* for

Cello and Piano (1890); Piano Quartet (1890); Piano Quintet (1897); Sonata for Cello or Viola and Piano (n.d.); *Nocturne and Scherzo* for Flute and String Quartet (1918; also as *A Night Piece* for Flute and Strings, 1922); also various piano pieces; organ music. **VOCAL:** *The Farewell of Hiawatha* for Men's Chorus and Orch. (1885); *The Wreck of the Hesperus* for Chorus and Orch. (1887–88); *The Skeleton in Armor* for Chorus and Orch. (1891); *O Fear the Immortals, Ye Children of Men* for Mezzo-soprano and Orch. (1900); *Lygeia* for Women's Chorus and Orch. (1906); some 100 songs, 52 part songs, and 35 anthems.

BIBL.: F. Kopp, *A. F.: American Composer and Theorist* (diss., Univ. of Rochester, 1957); D. Alviani, *The Choral Church Music of A.W. F.* (diss., Union Theological Seminary, 1962); D. Moore, *The Cello Music of A. F., 1853–1937* (diss., Catholic Univ. of America, 1977); W. Cipolla, *A Catalog of the Works of A. F. (1853–1937)* (Detroit, 1980); N. Tawa, *A. F.: A Musician in the Frame of Time and Place* (Lanham, Md., 1997).—**NS/LK/DM**

Foote, George (Luther), American composer; b. Cannes, France (of American parents), Feb. 19, 1886; d. Boston, March 25, 1956. He studied with E.B. Hill at Harvard Univ., and then in Berlin with Koch and Klatte. Upon his return to the U.S., he was a member of the staff in the music dept. of Harvard Univ. (1921–23) and president of the South End Music School in Boston (until 1943).

WORKS: *98th Psalm* for Chorus and Organ (1934); *Variations on a Pious Theme* for Orch. (Boston, Feb. 11, 1935); *In Praise of Winter*, symphonic suite (Boston, Jan. 5, 1940); *We Go Forward*, sacred pantomime (1943); Trio for Flute, Harp, and Violin; other chamber music; piano pieces.—**NS/LK/DM**

Forbes, Elliot, American choral conductor and musicologist; b. Cambridge, Mass., Aug. 30, 1917. He was educated at Harvard Univ. (B.A., 1941; M.A., 1947) and also attended the Salzburg Mozarteum (1937). From 1947 to 1958 he was a member of the music dept. at Princeton Univ. He was a prof. at Harvard Univ. from 1958 to 1984, and also was conductor of the Harvard Glee Club and Radcliffe Choral Soc. from 1958 to 1970. He conducted the Harvard Glee Club on a world tour in 1961, and the Harvard-Radcliffe Chorus on a North American tour in 1964 and a world tour in 1967. From 1959 to 1970 he was general ed. of the Harvard-Radcliffe Choral Music Series. He ed. the revision of *Thayer's Life of Beethoven* (Princeton, 1964; 2nd ed., rev., 1967) and the *Harvard Song Book* (Boston, 1965). He publ. *A History of Music at Harvard to 1972* (Cambridge, Mass., 1988) and *A Report of Music at Harvard 1972–1990* (Cambridge, Mass., 1993).

BIBL.: L. Lockwood and P. Benjamin, eds., *Beethoven Essays: Studies in Honor of E. F.* (Cambridge, Mass., 1984).—**NS/LK/DM**

Forbes, Henry, English organist and composer; b. London, 1804; d. there, Nov. 24, 1859. He studied with George Smart in London, and with Moscheles and Hummel in Germany. He was engaged as a church organist, and publ. a collection of Psalm tunes, *National Psalmody* (1843). His opera *The Fairy Oak* was produced in London (Oct. 18, 1845) with considerable success.—**NS/LK/DM**

Forbes, Sebastian, English organist, choral conductor, and composer; b. Amersham, Buckingham, May 22, 1941. He studied with Ferguson at the Royal Academy of Music in London (1958–60) and with Radcliffe and Dart at King's Coll., Cambridge (1960–64). He subsequently held positions as conductor of the Aeolian Singers (1965–69), Seiriol Singers (1969–72), and Horniman Singers (1981–90), and was a univ. lecturer at Bangor (1968–72) and Surrey (from 1972).

WORKS: *Pageant of St. Paul*, suite for Orch. (1964); Piano Trio (1964); *Antiphony* for Violin and Piano (1965); *Partita* for Clarinet, Cello, and Piano (1966); *Chaconne* for Orch. (1967); *Sequence of Carols* for Chorus (1967); *2nd Sequence of Carols* for Men's Chorus, String Orch., and Organ (London, May 1, 1968); String Quartet (1969); *Essay* for Clarinet and Orch. (London, July 28, 1970); *3rd Sequence of Carols* for Chorus (1971); 3 syms. (1972, 1978, 1990); *Fantasy* for Cello (1974); Sonata for 8 Instruments (1978); String Quartet No. 3 (1982).—**NS/LK/DM**

Ford, Bruce (Edwin), American tenor; b. Lubbock, Tex., Aug. 15, 1956. He studied at West Tex. A. & M. Univ., Tex. Tech Univ., and the Houston Opera Studio, where he appeared in student productions. In 1981 he sang in the premiere of Floyd's *Willie Stark* at the Houston Grand Opera. From 1983 to 1985 he was a member of the Wuppertal Opera. In 1985 he sang Count Almaviva in Bordeaux and Tamino at the Minn. Opera. He was a member of the Mannheim National Theatre from 1985 to 1987. In 1986 he appeared as Rossini's Argirio at the Wexford Festival. After singing that composer's Agorante in Pesaro in 1990, he made his debut at London's Covent Garden as Count Almaviva in 1991. In 1992 he appeared as Rossini's Uberto at Milan's La Scala and as his Rodrigo at the San Francisco Opera in 1994. He sang Ernesto in *Don Pasquale* at the Lyric Opera in Chicago in 1995. His Metropolitan Opera debut in N.Y. followed as Count Almaviva on Oct. 22, 1997. In 1998 he was engaged as Lindoro in Paris. He portrayed Don Ottavio in Geneva in 1999.—**NS/LK/DM**

Ford, Ricky (actually, Richard Allen), jazz tenor saxophonist; b. Boston, March 4, 1954. As a 20-year-old (student at NEC), he made his debut with Gunther Schuller and worked with Jaki Byard and Ran Blake. His style, which blended swing-era volume, bop discipline, and harmonic knowledge, matured with the Charles Mingus group in the late 1970s. During the 1980s, he penned charts for Lionel Hampton and the Mingus Dynasty, toured and recorded as a leader, and was part of a wonderful Afro-jazz group led by Abdullah Ibrahim. He has directed the Brandeis Univ. Jazz Ensemble since the mid-1980s.

DISC.: *Loxodonta Africana* (1977); *Manhattan Plaza* (1978); *Flying Colors* (1980); *Tenor for the Times* (1981); *Interpretations* (1982); *Future's Gold* (1983); *Shorter Ideas* (1984); *Saxotic Stomp* (1987); *Manhattan Blues* (1989); *Hard Groovin'* (1989); *Ebony Rhapsody* (1990); *Hot Brass* (1991); *American-African Blues* (1991); *Tenor Madness Too* (1995).—**LP**

Ford, Robben, jazz-rock guitarist; b. Woodlake, Calif., Dec. 16, 1951. His father, Charles, was an amateur county musician on guitar and harmonica; Robben began playing sax at age 11, and then two years later took up guitar. In 1970, he moved to San Francisco, forming The Charles Ford Blues Band with his brother Pat; another brother, Mark, joined the band in time for their first album. From 1972–73, Robben toured with Jimmy Witherspoon and then in 1974 worked with Tom Scott's L.A. Express, accompanying singer/songwriter Joni Mitchell; he also backed up George Harrison on his "Dark Horse" tour that year. He was a founding member of The Yellowjackets in 1978 along with Russel Ferrante (keyboards and primary composer) and Jimmy Haslip (bass). Primarily a blues and fusion player, he achieved some recognition in jazz circles during his tenure with Miles Davis (1985–86) with whom he appeared in a televised benefit for Amnesty International. After working with Davis, Ford has primarily recorded and toured with his own group, playing blues-based jazz; in the 1990s, he turned to more commercial pop-vocal music.

DISC.: *Schizophonic* (1976); *Inside Story* (1979); *Yellowjackets* (1981); *Samurai Samba* (1984); *Mirage a Trois* (1985); *Politics* (1988); *Words and Music* (1988); *Talk to Your Daughter* (1988); *Robben Ford* (1988); *Robben Ford & The Blue Line* (1992); *Blues and Beyond* (1992); *Mystic Mile* (1993); *Dreamland* (1995); *Handful of Blues* (1995).—**LP**

Ford, Tennessee Ernie (actually, Ernest Jennings), finger-snappin', pencil-moustached TV star and country-pop singer; b. Bristol, Tenn., Feb. 13, 1919; d. Reston, Va., Oct. 17, 1991. Ford is best-remembered for his (melo)dramatic rendition of Merle Travis's "Sixteen Tons," a mid-1950s hit. Ford was as much a personality as a country singer, and became a well-recognized icon of 1950s and 1960s TV variety shows.

Ford did not have a particularly rural upbringing; he was raised in Bristol, a Southern mill town, where he sang in the high school choir and played in the school band. When he was 18, he got his first job as an announcer at a local radio station, and then enrolled in the Cincinnati Cons. of Music for classical music training. After serving in World War II, he returned to radio work in Pasadena, Calif., and began working as a vocalist with West-Coast area cowboy-styled bands, most notably that of Cliffie Stone, a prominent West Coast musician/bandleader/promoter who quickly took Ford under his wing. As an executive of the newly formed Capitol Records, Stone got Ford his recording contract, and went on to manage his lengthy career.

Signed to Capitol in 1948, Ford had a number of hits with pseudo-Western numbers, beginning with 1949's "Mule Train," "Smokey Mountain Boogie," and "Anticipation Blues," jazz-flavored renderings of pop songs written in the style of country blues and cowboy numbers. A year later, he scored big with his own composition, "Shotgun Boogie," which lead to his own network radio show.

In 1955, Ford covered Merle Travis's "Sixteen Tons," a song about the life of a coal miner that Travis had written in the folk style. Ford's rendition became a massive hit, decked out with its crooning chorus and popish instrumental arrangement. Following the success of "Sixteen Tons" on pop and country charts, Ford hosted his own TV variety show on NBC until 1961. Added to his regular appearances on a number of other shows, Ford was a familiar face in American households.

In the early 1960s, Ford turned to more conservative material. *Hymns*, the first in a series of all-religious recordings, released in 1963, was country music's first million-selling album. Balancing this with remakes of patriotic material like "America the Beautiful," Ford became a leading conservative voice in the country hierarchy. His smooth-voiced, non-threatening renditions of mostly time-worn material cemented his 1960s popularity. Although he had a chart hit in 1971 with "Happy Songs of Love," Ford's career had pretty much ended by that time. He performed live into the 1980s however.

In 1990, he was inducted into the Country Music Hall of Fame. A year later, he collapsed at a White House dinner, and died of liver disease soon after.

DISC.: *This Lusty Land!* (1956); *Tennessee Ernie Ford Hymns* (1956); *Spirituals* (1957); *Ford Favorites* (1957); *Ol' Rockin' Ern'* (1957); *The Star Carol* (1958); *Nearer the Cross* (1958); *Gather 'Round* (1959); *A Friend We Have* (with the Jordanaires; 1959); *Sing a Hymn with Me* (1960); *Sixteen Tons* (1960); *Sing-a-Spiritual-with-Me* (1960); *Come to the Fair* (1960); *Ernie Looks at Love* (1961); *Civil War Songs of the North* (1961); *Civil War Songs of the South* (1961); *Hymns at Home* (1961); *Here Comes the Mississippi Showboat* (1962); *I Love to Tell the Story* (1962); *Book of Favorite Hymns* (1962); *Long, Long Ago* (1963); *We Gather Together* (with The San Quentin Prison Choir; 1963); *The Story of Christmas* (with The Roger Wagner Chorale and Orchestra; 1963); *Great Gospel Songs* (with The Jordanaires; 1964); *Country Hits—Feelin' Blue* (with Billy Strange and John Mosher; 1964); *Tennessee Ernie Ford Sings the World's Best Loved Hymns* (1965); *Let Me Walk with Thee—Tennessee Ernie Ford Sings Songs for Quiet Worship* (1965); *Sing We Now of Christmas* (1965); *My Favorite Things* (1966); *Wonderful Peace* (1966); *God Lives* (1966); *Aloha from Tennessee Ernie Ford* (1967); *Faith of our Fathers* (1967); *Our Garden of Hymns—Tennessee Ernie Ford and Marilyn Horne* (1968); *Tennessee Ernie Ford's World of Pop and Country Hits* (1968); *The Best of Tennessee Ernie Ford's Hymns* (1968); *O Come All Ye Faithful* (1968); *A Treasury of Inspirational Songs* (1968); *The Tennessee Ernie Ford Deluxe Set* (1968); *Songs I Like to Sing* (1969); *The New Wave* (1969); *Holy, Holy, Holy* (1969); *America the Beautiful* (1970); *Sweet Hour of Prayer/Let Me Walk with Thee* (1970); *Everything Is Beautiful* (1970); *A Tennessee Ernie Ford Christmas Special* (1970); *Abide with Me* (1971); *C-H-R-I-S-T-M-A-S* (1971); *The Folk Album* (1971); *Mr. Words and Music* (1971); *It's Tennessee Ernie Ford!* (1972); *Country Morning* (1973); *Ernie Ford Sings about Jesus* (1973); *Make a Joyful Noise* (1974); *Yesterday—Today—25th Anniversary* (1974); *Gospel—Hymns—25th Anniversary* (1974); *Precious Memories* (1975); *Ernie Sings & Glen Picks* (1975); *Sing His Great Love* (1976); *For the 83rd Time* (1976); *He Touched Me* (1977); *Swing Wide Your Golden Gate* (1978); *Tell Me the Old, Old Story* (1981); *Sings 22 Favorite Hymns* (1983); *Sings Songs of the Civil War* (1991); *Red, White & Blue* (1991); *The Heart of Christmas* (1991); *My Christmas Favorites* (1992); *What a Friend We Have in Jesus* (1995); *Christmas* (1995); *Christmas with Tennessee Ernie Ford & Wayne Newton* (1995); *Favorite Songs of Christmas* (1995); *The Real Thing* (2000); *16 Tons of Boogie: The Best of Tennessee Ernie Ford* (1990); *All-Time Greatest Hymns* (1990); *Country Gospel Classics, Vol. 1* (1991); *Country Gospel Classics, Vol. 2* (1991); *Capitol's Collector's Series* (1991); *Best-Loved Hymns* (1992); *Best*

Sacred Memories (1993); *Greatest Hits* (1993); *Masters 1949—1976* (1994); *His Greatest Hymns* (1995); *Vintage Collections Series* (1997); *The Ultimate Collection (1949—1965)* (1997); *Amazing Grace: 25 Treasured Hymns* (1997); *Greatest Hymns* (1997); *How Great Thou Art* (1998); *The Best of Tennessee Ernie Ford* (1998); *Amazing Grace: 40 Treasured Hymns* (1998); *Sings from His Book of Favorite Hymns* (2000); *Country Music Hall of Fame: 1990* (2000); *Best of Best Gospel* (2000). Rosemary Clooney: *Come on a My House* (1997). Kay Starr: *Greatest Hits* (1948). Merle Travis: *Unissued Radio Shows, 1944—1948* (1995). Speedy West & Jimmy Bryant: *Flamin' Guitars* (1997). Various Artists: *Great Records of the Decades: 40's Hits Country, Vol. 1* (1990); *Great Records of the Decades: 50's Hits Country, Vol. 1* (1990); *Christmas All-Time Greatest Records* (1990); *Golden Jukebox Favorites* (1991); *Best of Christmas (Capitol; 1991)*; *Country Christmas Classics* (Capitol; 1991); *Smithsonian Collection of Country Music, Vol. 2* (1991); *Legends of the West Coast* (1996); *Cliffie Stone's Radio Transcriptions 1945–49.*—**RC**

Ford, Thomas, English lutenist and composer; b. c. 1580; d. London (buried), Nov. 17, 1648. He was appointed musician to Prince Henry in 1611, and to Charles I in 1626. He was especially successful in the "ayre," a type of composition developed by Dowland, in which melodic prominence is given to the upper voice. These "ayres" appear in alternative settings, either as solo songs with lute accompaniment or as 4-part a cappella songs. He wrote *Musicke of Sundrie Kindes* (1607; the 1st part contains 11 ayres), 2 anthems in Leighton's *Teares*, canons in Hilton's *Catch that catch can*, and the famous madrigal *Since first I saw your face*. His MSS are at Christ Church, Oxford, and at the British Library.—**NS/LK/DM**

Fordell, Erik, Finnish composer; b. Kokkola, July 2, 1917; d. Kaarlela, Dec. 21, 1981. He studied in Helsinki at the Sibelius Academy and the Inst. of Church Music. Fordell's output was enormous.

WORKS: 45 syms. (1949–81); 2 violin concertos (1955, 1959); Horn Concerto (1956); 4 piano concertos (1961–62); 8 string suites; 4 wind quintets; 7 string quartets; Violin Sonata; Flute Sonata; piano pieces; choral music; songs.—**NS/LK/DM**

Forkel, Johann Nikolaus, erudite German music historian; b. Meeder, near Coburg, Feb. 22, 1749; d. Göttingen, March 20, 1818. He was a chorister at Lüneburg (1762–66) and Schwerin (1766). In 1769 he began the study of law at the Univ. of Göttingen, where he became its organist in 1770 and its music director in 1779. Forkel remains best known for his classic biography of Bach. His publ. compositions include piano sonatas and songs; in MS are the oratorio *Hiskias*; 2 cantatas: *Die Macht des Gesangs* and *Die Hirten an der Krippe zu Bethlehem*; syms., trios, choruses, etc.

WRITINGS: *Über die Theorie der Musik, sofern sie Liebhabern und Kennern derselben nothwendig und nützlich ist* (1774); *Musikalischkritische Bibliothek* (3 vols., Gotha, 1778–79); *Über die beste Einrichtung öffentlicher Concerte* (1779); *Genauere Bestimmung einiger musikalischer Begriffe* (1780); *Musikalischer Almanach für Deutschland* (1782, 1783, 1784, and 1789); *Allgemeine Geschichte der Musik* (2 vols., Leipzig, 1788, 1801); *Allgemeine Literatur der Musik, oder Anleitung zur Kenntniss musikalischer*

Bücher (1792); *Über Johann Sebastian Bachs Leben, Kunst und Kunstwerke* (Leipzig, 1802; Eng. tr., 1820; new Eng. tr., 1920, by C. Terry).

BIBL.: H. Edelhoff, *J.N. F.: Ein Beitrag zur Geschichte der Musikwissenschaft* (Göttingen, 1935); G. Stauffer and A. Mendel, *The F.-Hoffmeister & Kühnel Correspondence: A document of the early 19th-century Bach revival* (annotated Ger.-Eng. ed., N.Y., 1990).—NS/LK/DM

Formé, Nicolas, French countertenor and composer; b. Paris, April 26, 1567; d. there, May 27, 1638. He entered the priesthood and by 1592 he was a singer at the Royal Chapel, where he served as sous-maître and composer from 1609 until his death. An accomplished composer of sacred music, he wrote *Aeterane Henrici magni...missam hanc duobus choris* for 4/5 voices (Paris, 1638) and 8 Magnificat settings on the 8 church modes. —LK/DM

Formes, Karl Johann, German bass, brother of **Theodor Formes;** b. Mülheim, Aug. 7, 1815; d. San Francisco, Dec. 15, 1889. He was a pupil of Basodowa in Vienna. After making his operatic debut as Sarastro in Cologne (Jan. 6, 1842), he sang in Mannheim before appearing in Vienna (1843–49). In 1849 he made his London debut at Drury Lane. On March 16, 1850, he made his first appearance at London's Covent Garden as Caspar in *Der Freischütz*, returning there regularly until 1868. He also sang at London's Royal Italian Opera (1852–57). In 1857 he made his N.Y. debut as Bertram in *Robert le diable* at the Academy of Music, where he sang for some 20 years. After his retirement, he settled in San Francisco as a voice teacher. He publ. a *Method of Singing* (3 vols., 1865; 2nd ed., 1885) and an autobiography, *Aus meinem Kunst- und Bühnenleben: Erinnerungen des Bassisten* (Cologne, 1888; Eng. tr., 1891, as *My Memoirs*). Among his best known roles were Leporello, Rocco, Nicolai's Falstaff, and Flotow's Plunkett.—NS/LK/DM

Formes, Theodor, German tenor, brother of **Karl Johann Formes;** b. Mülheim, June 24, 1826; d. Endenich, near Bonn, Oct. 15, 1874. He made his debut at Ofen (1846); then sang in Vienna (1848) and Berlin (1851–66); made a tour in America with his brother. He lost his voice temporarily. After returning to the stage for a few years, he suffered a setback, became insane, and died in an asylum.—NS/LK/DM

Formichi, Cesare, Italian baritone; b. Rome, April 15, 1883; d. there, July 21, 1949. He studied in Rome. He made his debut at the Teatro Lirico in Milan in 1911; then sang at the Teatro Colón in Buenos Aires, in Madrid, in Barcelona, and at the Paris Opéra; appeared with the Chicago Opera Co. (1922–32); sang at Covent Garden in London (1924). He was particularly effective in dramatic roles, such as Rigoletto, Iago, and Scarpia. —NS/LK/DM

Fornerod, Alöys, Swiss violinist, music critic, educator, and composer; b. Montet-Cudrefin, Nov. 16, 1890; d. Fribourg, Jan. 8, 1965. He studied violin and theory at the Lausanne Cons. and at the Schola Cantorum in Paris. He was a member of the Lausanne Sym. Orch., and in 1954 was appointed director of the Fribourg Cons. As a composer, he followed the French modern style, in the spirit of fin-de-siècle Impressionism. He publ. *Les Tendances de la musique moderne* (Lausanne, 1924). He was for 40 years a critic for *La Tribune de Lausanne*.

WORKS: DRAMATIC: Comic Opera: *Geneviève* (Lausanne, May 20, 1954). **ORCH.:** *Le Voyage de printemps*, suite (1943); Piano Concerto (1944). **CHAMBER:** Violin Sonata (1925); Concerto for 2 Violins and Piano (1927); Cello Sonata (1934). **VOCAL:** Te Deum for Soloists, Chorus, and Orch. (1955); *Hymne à la Très Sainte Trinité* for Chorus and Brass (1961); choruses; songs.

BIBL.: J. Viret, *A. F., ou, Le Musicien et le pays* (Lausanne, 1982).—NS/LK/DM

Fornia-Labey, Rita (née **Regina Newman**), American soprano, later mezzo-soprano; b. San Francisco, July 17, 1878; d. Paris, Oct. 27, 1922. She adopted the name Fornia after Calif.; following her marriage to J.P. Labey in 1910, she used the name Fornia-Labey. She studied with Emil Fischer and Sofia Scalchi in N.Y. and Selma Nicklass-Kempner in Berlin. After making her operatic debut in Hamburg in 1901, she completed her training with Jean de Reszke in Paris. In 1903 she made her N.Y. debut as Siebel in *Faust* at the Brooklyn Academy of Music, and then toured with H.W. Savage's Opera Co. On Dec. 6, 1907, she made her Metropolitan Opera debut in N.Y. as the Geisha in Mascagni's *Iris*, remaining on its roster for the rest of her life. —NS/LK/DM

Foroni, Jacopo, Italian conductor and composer; b. Verona, July 25, 1825; d. Stockholm, Sept. 8, 1858 (of cholera). He settled in Stockholm in 1849, and became court conductor there, becoming very successful at his public concerts and as a composer. He wrote several operas, among them *I Gladiatori* (Milan, Oct. 7, 1851) and *Advokaten Patelin* (perf. posth., Stockholm, Dec. 4, 1858).—NS/LK/DM

Forrest, Hamilton, American composer; b. Chicago, Jan. 8, 1901; d. London, Dec. 26, 1963. He was a student of Weidig at the American Cons. of Music in Chicago (M.M., 1926). His opera *Yzdra* (1925) received the Bispham Memorial Medal, and his opera *Camille*, with Mary Garden in the title role, was highly praised at its premiere (Chicago, Dec. 10, 1930). He prepared settings of 33 Kentucky mountain melodies and Negro folk songs, including *He's Got the Whole World in His Hands*, which were championed by Marian Anderson.

WORKS: DRAMATIC: Opera: *Yzdra* (1925); *Camille* (Chicago, Dec. 10, 1930); *Marie Odile* (n.d.); *Don Fortunio* (Interlochen, Mich., July 22, 1952); *Daelia* (Interlochen, July 21, 1954); *Galatea* (1957). **Ballet:** *The Yellow Wind* and *Le Paus des Revenants*. Also incidental music. **OTHER:** 2 piano concertos; *Panorama* for Piano and Orch.; *Watercolors* for 14 Wind Instruments and Harp; piano pieces; songs.—NS/LK/DM

Forrester, Maureen (Kathleen Stewart), outstanding Canadian contralto; b. Montreal, July 25, 1930. She studied piano and sang in Montreal church choirs. At 16, she began vocal training with Sally Martin in Montreal; at 19, she became a student of Frank Rowe; at 20, she found a mentor in Bernard Diamant, with whom she continued to work for over a decade; she also had lessons with Michael Raucheisen in Berlin in 1955. On Dec. 8, 1951, she made her professional debut in Elgar's *The Music Makers* with the Montreal Elgar Choir. Her recital debut followed in Montreal on March 29, 1953. On Feb. 14, 1955, she made her European debut in a recital at the Salle Gaveau in Paris, and then toured throughout Europe. She made her N.Y. debut at Town Hall on Nov. 12, 1956. Her extraordinary success as a soloist in Mahler's 2nd Sym. with Bruno Walter and the N.Y. Phil. on Feb. 17, 1957, set the course of a brilliant international career as a concert artist. In subsequent years, she appeared as a soloist with most of the principal conductors and orchs. of the world, and also gave numerous recitals. From 1965 to 1974 she was a member of the Bach Aria Group in N.Y., and also served as chairman of the voice dept. at the Philadelphia Musical Academy (1966–71). She also began to give increasing attention to opera. On May 28, 1962, she made her Toronto stage debut as Gluck's Orfeo. In 1963 she appeared as Brangäne at the Teatro Colón in Buenos Aires. She made her U.S. stage debut as Cornelia in Handel's *Julius Caesar* at the N.Y. City Opera on Sept. 27, 1966. On Feb. 10, 1975, she made her Metropolitan Opera debut in N.Y. as Erda in *Das Rheingold*. In 1982 she appeared as Madame de la Haltière in Massenet's *Cendrillon* at the San Francisco Opera. In 1990 she made her debut at Milan's La Scala as the Countess in *The Queen of Spades*. From 1983 to 1988 she was chairperson of the Canada Council, and from 1986 to 1990 she was chancellor of Wilfrid Laurier Univ. She received over 30 honorary doctorates. In 1967 she was made a Companion of the Order of Canada and in 1990 received the Order of Ontario. With M. MacDonald, she wrote *Out of Character: A Memoir* (Toronto, 1986). In spite of her later success in opera, Forrester's reputation was first and foremost that of a remarkable interpreter of solo works with orch., oratorio, and Lieder.—NS/LK/DM

Forsell, John (actually, **Carl Johan Jacob**), famous Swedish baritone and pedagogue; b. Stockholm, Nov. 6, 1868; d. there, May 30, 1941. He served as an officer in the Swedish Army before pursuing vocal training in Stockholm. On Feb. 26, 1896, he made his operatic debut as Figaro in *Il Barbiere di Siviglia* at the Royal Opera in Stockholm, where he was a member until 1901, and again from 1903 to 1909. On June 26, 1909, he made his debut at London's Covent Garden as Don Giovanni, his most celebrated role. He made his Metropolitan Opera debut in N.Y. on Nov. 20, 1909, as Telramund, but remained on its roster for only that season before pursuing his career in Europe. He made guest appearances in Berlin, Vienna, Bayreuth, and other music centers. In 1938 he appeared as Don Giovanni for the last time in Copenhagen. From 1923 to 1939 he was director of the Royal Opera in Stockholm, and he also was prof. of voice at the Stockholm Cons. from 1924 to 1931. His notable students included Jussi Björling, Set Svanholm, and Aksel Schiøtz. The beauty of his voice was ably seconded by his assured vocal

technique. Among his other roles were Hans Sachs, Beckmesser, Amfortas, Eugene Onegin, Germont, and Scarpia.

BIBL.: E. Ljungberger, *J. F.* (Stockholm, 1916); *Boken om J. F.* (Stockholm, 1938); K. Liliedahl, *J. F.: A Discography* (Trelleborg, 1972).—NS/LK/DM

Förster, Christoph (Heinrich), German composer; b. Bibra, Thuringia, Nov. 30, 1693; d. Rudolstadt, Dec. 5 or 6, 1745. He was a student in Bibra of the organist Pitzler before taking lessons in thoroughbass and composition in Weissenfels with Heinichen and in Merseburg with G.F. Kauffmann. In 1717 he became a violinist in the Merseburg court orch., serving there later as its Konzertmeister. In 1743 he was named Vice-Kapellmeister in Rudolstadt, being promoted to Kapellmeister a few weeks before his death. His considerable output included stage music, sinfonias, orch. suites, concertos, chamber music, and sacred works, including more than 25 cantatas.—LK/DM

Förster, Josef, Bohemian organist, teacher, and composer, father of **Josef Bohuslav Foerster;** b. Osojnitz, Feb. 22, 1833; d. Prague, Jan. 3, 1907. He was organist in several churches in Prague, and a prof. of theory at the Prague Cons. He wrote organ pieces, church music, and a treatise on harmony.—NS/LK/DM

Förster, Kaspar, German composer; b. Danzig (baptized), Feb. 28, 1616; d. Oliva, near Danzig, Feb. 2, 1673. He began his training with his father, the Kapellmeister of the Danzig Marienkirche, and then studied composition with Carissimi in Rome (1633–36). He was a bass singer and choral conductor at the Polish court in Warsaw (c. 1638–43), during which time he also studied with Marco Scacchi. From 1652 to 1655 he was Kapellmeister to King Frederik II of Denmark in Copenhagen. After serving as his father's successor at the Danzig Marienkirche (1655–57), he resumed his Danish post, retiring in 1667. Förster introduced the Italian style of composition to Danzig and Copenhagen. Among his extant works are 3 oratorios, several sacred vocal concertos, and 6 trio sonatas.

BIBL.: J. Babb, *The Sacred Latin Works of K. F. (1616–73)* (diss., Univ. of N.C., 1970).—LK/DM

Forsyth, Cecil, English composer and writer on music; b. Greenwich, Nov. 30, 1870; d. N.Y., Dec. 7, 1941. He received his general education at the Univ. of Edinburgh; then studied at the Royal Coll. of Music in London with Stanford and Parry. He joined the viola section in the Queen's Hall Orch. He also was connected with the Savoy Theatre, where he produced 2 of his comic operas, *Westward Ho!* and *Cinderella*. After the outbreak of World War I, he went to N.Y., where he remained for the rest of his life. He composed a Viola Concerto and *Chant celtique* for Viola and Orch.; also songs, sacred music, and instrumental pieces. He was the author of a comprehensive manual, *Orchestration* (N.Y., 1914; 2nd ed., 1935; reprinted 1948); *Choral Orchestration* (London, 1920); also a treatise on English opera, *Music and Nationalism* (London, 1911). He publ. (in collaboration with Stanford) *A History of Music* (London, 1916) and a collection of essays, *Clashpans* (N.Y., 1933).—NS/LK/DM

Forsyth, Malcolm (Denis), South African-born Canadian composer, trombonist, conductor, and teacher; b. Pietermaritzburg, Dec. 8, 1936. He was educated at the Univ. of Cape Town (M.Mus., 1966; D.M.A., 1972), numbering among his mentors Stefans Grove, Mátyás Seiber, and Gideon Fagan (composition), George Hurst and Georg Tintner (conducting), and Hans Grin (trombone). He was co-principal trombonist in the Cape Town Municipal Orch. (1961–67) before settling in Canada; in 1974 he became a naturalized Canadian citizen. He played in the Edmonton Sym. Orch. (from 1968), serving as its principal trombone (1973–80); also was a member of the Univ. of Alberta Brass Quintet (1975–83), and founder-leader of the Malcolm Forsyth Trombone Ensemble (1976–83). He served as conductor of the St. Cecilia Orch. in Edmonton (1977–86). In 1968 he joined the faculty of the Univ. of Alberta, becoming artistic director of its music dept. in 1986. As a composer, he successfully applied both African and North American folk elements.

WORKS: ORCH.: *Erewhon*, overture (1962); *Jubilee Overture* (Cape Town, May 5, 1964; rev. 1966); *Essay for Orchestra '67* (Cape Town, Dec. 15, 1967); 3 syms.: No. 1 (1968–72; Cape Town, Sept. 5, 1972), No. 2, *...a host of nomads...* (1976; Edmonton, March 11, 1977), and No. 3, *African Ode* (1980–87; Edmonton, Jan. 30, 1987); *Sketches from Natal* (CBC, March 23, 1970); Piano Concerto (1973–75; Edmonton, March 30, 1979); 3 concerti grossi: No. 1, *Sagittarius* (Banff, Aug. 16, 1975), No. 2, *Quinquefid* (1976–77; Edmonton, April 6, 1977), and No. 3, *The Salpinx* (1981; Edmonton, Feb. 5, 1982); *Images of Night* (1982); *Rhapsody for 14 Strings* (1982; Edmonton, April 18, 1983); *Ukuzalwa* (1983); *Springtide* (Banff, April 3, 1984); *Atayoskewin*, suite (Edmonton, Nov. 16, 1984); *Serenade* for Strings (1985–86; Toronto, May 12, 1986); Trumpet Concerto (1987; Montreal, Jan. 11, 1988); *Songs from the Qu'appelle Valley* for Brass Band (1987); *Little Suite* for Strings (1988); *Valley of a Thousand Hills* (1989). **CHAMBER:** *Quartet '61* for Brass (1961); *Pastorale and Rondo* for Flute, Clarinet, Horn, Bassoon, and Piano (1968–69); *Quartet '74* for Brass (1974); *6 Episodes after Keats* for Violin, Viola, and Piano (1979–81); *Music for Wit and Science* for Recorder, Lute, and Viola da Gamba, or for Flute, Guitar, and Cello (1982); Wind Quintet (1986); *Soliloquy, Epitaph, and Allegro* for Trombone and Organ (1988); *Zephyrus* for Brass (1989).—NS/LK/DM

Forte, Allen, significant American music theorist; b. Portland, Ore., Dec. 23, 1926. He was educated at Columbia Univ. (B.A., 1950; M.A., 1952), where he served on the faculty of its Teachers Coll. (1953–59). After teaching at the Manhattan School of Music (1957) and the Mannes Coll. of Music (1957–59) in N.Y., he joined the faculty of Yale Univ., where he was an instructor (1959–61), asst. prof. (1961–64), assoc. prof. (1964), prof. (1968–91), and the Battell Prof. of the Theory of Music (from 1991). He served as ed. of the *Journal of Music Theory* (1960–67) and general ed. of the *Composers of the Twentieth Century* (from 1980). From 1977 to 1982 he was president of the Soc. for Music Theory. In 1981 he held a Guggenheim fellowship. He

was elected a fellow of the American Academy of Arts and Sciences in 1995. The vol. *Music Theory in Concept and Practice* (1997), ed. by D. Beach, J. Bernard, and J. Baker, is dedicated to him. Forte's most important contribution to music theory is an analytic method designed for the explication of atonal music. His *Tonal Harmony in Concept and Practice* (1962; 3rd ed., 1979) represents an original and sophisticated approach to traditional harmony. In addition to his other books, he has also contributed many articles to scholarly vols. and journals.

WRITINGS: *Contemporary Tone-Structure* (1955); *The Compositional Matrix* (1961); *Tonal Harmony in Concept and Practice* (1962; 3rd ed., 1979); *The Structure of Atonal Music* (1973); *The Harmonic Organization of The Rite of Spring* (1978); with S. Gilbert, *Introduction to Schenkerian Analysis* (1982); *The American Popular Ballad of the Golden Era 1924–1950* (1995); *The Atonal Music of Anton Webern* (1998); *Listening to Classic American Popular Songs* (2000).—NS/LK/DM

Forti, Anton, famous Austrian tenor and baritone; b. Vienna, June 8, 1790; d. there, June 16, 1859. He first sang in Esterháza (1807–11), then went to Vienna, where he appeared at the Theater an der Wien (1811–13). In 1813 he joined the Court Theater, singing both tenor and baritone roles; also sang in Prague, Hamburg, and Berlin, continuing to sing until late in his life. He was particularly esteemed for his performances in the roles of Figaro and Don Giovanni.—NS/LK/DM

Fortner, Wolfgang, important German composer and pedagogue; b. Leipzig, Oct. 12, 1907; d. Heidelberg, Sept. 5, 1987. He studied in Leipzig, where he was a student of Grabner (composition) and Straube (organ) at the Cons., and of Kroyer (musicology) and Korff (literature) at the Univ. (1927–31). In 1931 he passed the state examinations as a teacher and joined the faculty of the Inst. of Church Music in Heidelberg, where he taught composition and theory until 1954. From 1946 he taught at the summer course in new music in Darmstadt. He was active with the Musica-viva-Konzerte in Heidelberg from 1947, and became director of the Musica-viva-Konzerte in Munich in 1964. From 1954 to 1957 he was prof. of composition at the North West German Music Academy in Detmold, and from 1957 to 1973 at the Freiburg im Breisgau Staatliche Hochschule für Musik. In 1955 he was made a member of the Akademie der Künste in West Berlin, and in 1956 of the Bayerischen (Bavarian) Akademie der Schönen Künste in Munich. His music was marked by exceptional contrapuntal skills, with the basic tonality clearly present even when harmonic density reached its utmost; in some of his works from 1947, Fortner gave a dodecaphonic treatment to melodic procedures; in his textures, he often employed a "rhythmic cell" device. He was equally adept in his works for the musical theater and purely instrumental compositions; the German tradition is maintained throughout, both in the mechanics of strong polyphony and in rational innovations.

WORKS: DRAMATIC: Opera: *Bluthochzeit*, after García Lorca (1956; Cologne, June 8, 1957; rev. 1963; a reworking of a dramatic scene, *Der Wald* for Voices, Speaker, and Orch.,

Frankfurt am Main, June 25, 1953); *Corinna*, opera buffa (Berlin, Oct. 3, 1958); *In seinem Garten liebt Don Perlimplín Belisa*, after García Lorca (1961–62; Schwetzingen, May 10, 1962); *Elisabeth Tudor* (1968–71; Berlin, Oct. 23, 1972); *That Time*, after Samuel Beckett (Baden-Baden, April 24, 1977). **B a l l e t :** *Die weisse Rose* (1949; concert perf., Baden-Baden, March 5, 1950; stage perf., Berlin, April 28, 1951); *Die Witwe von Ephesus* (Berlin, Sept. 17, 1952); *Mouvements* (1953; Essen, Feb. 26, 1960; also as *Mouvements* for Piano and Orch., Baden- Baden, Feb. 5, 1954); *Ballett blanc* (1958; Wuppertal, Dec. 30, 1959; also for 2 Solo Violins and Strings, Zürich, Dec. 5, 1958); *Triplum* (1965–66; also for Orch. and Piano Obbligato, Basel, Dec. 15, 1966); *Carmen*, after Bizet (1970; Stuttgart, Feb. 28, 1971). **I n c i d e n t a l M u s i c T o :** Aristophanes's *Lysistrata* (1945). **ORCH.:** Suite, after Sweelinck (Wuppertal, Oct. 10, 1930); Concerto for Organ and Strings (Frankfurt am Main, April 27, 1932; also for Harpsichord and Strings, Basel, Oct. 2, 1935); Concerto for Strings (Basel, Dec. 8, 1933); Concertino for Viola and Small Orch. (1934); *Capriccio und Finale* (1939; Mannheim, Oct. 29, 1940); *Ernste Musik* (1940); Piano Concerto (1942); *Streichermusik II* for Strings (1944; Basel, Feb. 1945); Violin Concerto (1946; Baden-Baden, Feb. 16, 1947); Sym. (1947; Baden-Baden, May 2, 1948); *Die weisse Rose*, suite after the ballet (1949; Heidelberg, Oct. 8, 1951); *Phantasie über die Tonfolge b-a-c-h* for 2 Pianos, 9 Solo Instruments, and Orch. (Donaueschingen, Sept. 10, 1950); Cello Concerto (Cologne, Dec. 17, 1951); *Mouvements* for Piano and Orch. (1953; Baden-Baden, Feb. 6, 1954; as a ballet, Essen, Feb. 26, 1960); *La Cecchina*, overture after Piccini (Braunschweig, Nov. 12, 1954); *Impromptus* (Donaueschingen, Oct. 20, 1957); *Ballet blanc* for 2 Solo Violins and Strings (Zürich, Dec. 5, 1958); also as a ballet, Wuppertal, Dec. 30, 1959); *Aulodie* for Oboe and Orch. (Cologne, June 16, 1960; new version, Baden-Baden, May 27, 1966); *Triplum* for Orch. and Piano Obbligato (1965–66; Basel, Dec. 15, 1966; also as a ballet); *Immagini* for Large String Orch. (1966–67; Baden- Baden, Sept. 1970; also for Small String Orch., Zagreb, May 13, 1967); *Marginalien* (1969; Kiel, Jan. 12, 1970); *Zyklus* for Cello, Winds, Harp, and Percussion (1969; Graz, Oct. 26, 1970; also for Cello and Piano, Düsseldorf, Nov. 10, 1964); *Prolegomena*, suite after the opera *Elisabeth Tudor* (1973; Nuremberg, April 19, 1974); *Prismen* for Flute, Oboe, Clarinet, Harp, Percussion, and Orch. (1974; Basel, Feb. 13, 1975); *Triptychon* (1976–77; Düsseldorf, April 6, 1978); *Variationen* for Large Chamber Orch. (1979; Basel, March 27, 1980); *Klangvariation* for 4 Violins and Orch. (1981; Stuttgart, June 6, 1982). **C H A M B E R :** 4 string quartets: No. 1 (1929), No 2 (1938), No. 3 (1948), and No. 4 (1975; Saarbrücken, Oct. 14, 1977); Suite for Cello (1932); Violin Sonata (1945); *Serenade* for Flute, Oboe, and Bassoon (1945); Flute Sonata (1947); Cello Sonata (1948); Trio for Violin, Viola, and Cello (1952); *New-Delhi-Musik* for Flute, Violin, Cello, and Harpsichord (Donaueschingen, Oct. 18, 1959); *5 Bagatellen* for Flute, Oboe, Clarinet, Horn, and Bassoon (Donaueschingen, Oct. 15, 1960); *Zyklus* for Cello and Piano (Düsseldorf, Nov. 10, 1964; also for Cello, Winds, Harp, and Percussion, 1969; Graz, Oct. 26, 1970); *Thema und Variationen* for Cello (1975; Zürich, May 2, 1976); *9 Inventionen und ein Anhang* for 2 Flutes (1976); Trio for Violin, Cello, and Piano (Freiburg im Breisgau, Nov. 28, 1978); *Capricen* for Flute, Oboe, and Bassoon (1979; Freiburg im Breisgau, Dec. 29, 1980). **KEYBOARD: P i a n o :** Sonatina (1935); *Kammermusik* (1944); *7 Elegien* (1950); *Epigramme* (1964); *6 späte Stücke* (Cologne, Oct. 24, 1982). **O r g a n :** *Toccata und Fugue* (1928); *Preambel und Fuge* (1932); *Intermezzi* (1962); *4 Preludes* (1980; Tholey, April 12, 1981). **VOCAL:** *Fragment Maria*, chamber cantata for Soprano and 8 Instruments (Königsberg, Dec. 12, 1929); *Grenzen der Menschheit*, cantata for Bari-

tone, Chorus, and Orch., after Goethe (1930; Heidelberg, June 9, 1931); *4 Gesänge* for Voice and Piano, after Hölderlin (1933); *3 geistliche Gesänge* for Chorus (Dresden, June 24, 1934); *Eine deutsche Liedmesse* for Chorus (1934); *Nuptiae Catulli* for Tenor, Chamber Chorus, and Chamber Orch. (1937; Basel, April 5, 1939); *Herr, bliebe bei uns* for Voice, Chorus (Violin, Cello, and Double Bass ad libitum), and Organ or Harpsichord (1945); *Shakespeare-Songs* for Middle Voice and Piano (1946; Darmstadt, July 25, 1947); *An die Nachgeborenen*, cantata for Speaker, Tenor, Chorus, and Orch., after Brecht (1947; Baden-Baden, April 4, 1948); *2 Exerzitien* for Soprano, Mezzo-soprano, Alto, and Chamber Orch., after Brecht (1948; Heidelberg, May 6, 1949); *Mitte des Lebens*, cantata for Soprano and 5 Instruments, after Hölderlin (1951; Basel, May 7, 1952); *Isaaks Opferung*, oratorio-scene for Alto, Tenor, Bass, and 40 Instruments (Donaueschingen, Oct. 12, 1952); *The Creation* for Middle Voice and Orch., after James Weldon Johnson (1954; Basel, Feb. 18, 1955); *Chant de naissance* for Soprano, Violin, and String Orch. (1958; Hamburg, April 12, 1959; also for Soprano and 7 Players, 1975; Hamburg, June 15, 1976); *Prélude und Elegie*, parergon to the *Impromptus* for Soprano and Orch., after Hölderlin (Donaueschingen, Oct. 18, 1959); *Die Pfingstgeschichte* for Tenor, Chorus, and 11 Instrumentalists or Chamber Orch. and Organ (1962–63; Düsseldorf, May 7, 1964); *Der 100. Psalm* for Chorus, 3 Horns, 2 Trumpets, and 2 Trombones (Hamburg, Nov. 1963); *Terzinen* for Man's Voice and Piano, after Hofmannsthal (1965; Berlin, Oct. 5, 1970); *Versuch eines Agon um...?* for 7 Singers and Orch. (Hannover, Nov. 8, 1973); *Gladbacher Te Deum* for Bass-baritone, Chorus, Tape, and Orch. (1973; Mönchengladbach, June 6, 1974); *Machaut- Balladen* for Voice and Orch. (1973; Saarbrücken, Jan. 19, 1975); *Petrarca-Sonette* for Chorus (1979; Schwetzingen, May 13, 1980); *Farewell* for Middle Voice, 2 Flutes, Cello, and Piano (1981); *Widmungen* for Tenor and Piano, after Shakespeare (1981).

BIBL.: B. Weber, *Die Opernkompositionen von W. F.* (diss., Univ. of Hannover, 1992).—**NS/LK/DM**

Förtsch, Johann Philipp, German composer and physician; b. Wertheim am Main (baptized), May 14, 1652; d. Eutin, near Lübeck, Dec. 14, 1732. He received training in music at the Frankfurt am Main Gymnasium, in philosophy and medicine in Jena, and in jurisprudence in Erfurt. In 1678 he went to Hamburg, where he was the principal composer at the Opera from 1684 to 1690; he also served as director of the Gottorf Hofkapelle (from 1680). In 1681 he took his doctorate in medicine at the Univ. of Kiel, and then practiced in Schleswig (1690–92) and Eutin (from 1692). He composed some 12 operas and a large body of sacred music.

BIBL.: C. Weidemann, *Leben und Wirken des J.P. F.* (Kassel, 1955).—**LK/DM**

Fortunato, D'Anna, American mezzo-soprano; b. Pittsburgh, Feb. 21, 1945. She studied with Frederick Jagel, Gladys Miller, and John Moriarty at the New England Cons. of Music in Boston (1965–72) and with Phyllis Curtin at the Berkshire Music Center in Tanglewood (1971, 1972). She made her European opera debut with the Boston Camerata as Dido in Purcell's *Dido and Aeneas* in Paris in 1980, and her U.S. opera debut at the N.Y. City Opera as Ruggiero in Handel's *Alcina* in 1983.

From 1974 to 1982 she taught at the Longy School of Music in Cambridge, Mass. Her operatic and concert repertoire is extensive, ranging from early music to contemporary works.—NS/LK/DM

Fortune, Nigel (Cameron), English musicologist; b. Birmingham, Dec. 5, 1924. He was educated at the Univ. of Birmingham (B.A., 1950) and at Gonville and Caius Coll., Cambridge (Ph.D., 1954, with the diss. *Italian Secular Song from 1600 to 1635: The Origins and Development of Accompanied Monody*). After serving as music librarian at the Univ. of London (1956–59), he was a lecturer (1959–69) and a reader (1969–85) in music at the Univ. of Birmingham. He was co-ed. of several Purcell Soc. vols. (1959–67) and a senior consulting ed. of *The New Grove Dictionary of Music and Musicians* (1980). In 1981 he became joint ed. of *Music & Letters.*

WRITINGS: Ed. with D. Arnold, *The Monteverdi Companion* (London, 1968; 2nd ed., rev., 1985, as *The New Monteverdi Companion*); ed. with D. Arnold, *The Beethoven Companion* (London, 1971); ed. *Music and Theatre: Essays in Honour of Winton Dean* (Cambridge, 1987).—NS/LK/DM

Fortune, Sonny, American saxophonist and composer; b. Philadelphia, Pa., May 19, 1939. A highly underrated alto saxophonist, he is also a fine composer and many of his best recordings are versions of his own material. A hard-bop player who is equally at home on alto and soprano saxes and flute, he has a passionate, unmistakable style which often sounds as though he's either laughing or crying through his instrument.

After moving to N.Y. in 1967, he began working with Elvin Jones, an association that continues sporadically today, and he also performed and recorded with Mongo Santamaria, McCoy Tyner, and Miles Davis. He recorded albums as a leader for Strata-East, A&M Horizon, and Atlantic in the mid- to late 1970s, becoming a bit more commercial with each release. However, his live shows were far from commercial, with Fortune taking solos of 30 minutes or more with the right audience. Fortune recorded for the Konnex label and toured and recorded in the 1980s with Nat Adderley (with whom his style fit perfectly). Working with Elvin Jones in the early 1990s, Fortune, by Jones's request, has played tenor. He signed with Blue Note Records as a leader in 1993.

DISC.: *Long Before Our Mothers Cried* (1974); *Awakening* (1975); *In Waves of Dreams* (1976); *Serengeti Minstrel* (1977); *Infinity Is* (1978); *With Sound Reason* (1979); *It Ain't What It Was* (1991); *Four in One* (1994); *A Better Understanding* (1995); *Monk's Mood* (1995); *From Now On* (1996); *Sonny Fortune & Eddie Vinson* (1997); *In the Spirit of John Coltrane* (2000).—BW

Foss (real name, **Fuchs**), **Lukas,** brilliant German-born American pianist, conductor, and composer; b. Berlin, Aug. 15, 1922. He was a scion of a cultural family; his father was a prof. of philosophy and his mother was a talented painter. He studied piano and theory with Julius Goldstein-Herford in Berlin. When the dark shadow of the Nazi dominion descended upon Germany in 1933, the family prudently moved to Paris; there Foss studied piano with Lazare Lévy, composition

with Noël Gallon, and orchestration with Felix Wolfes. He also took flute lessons with Louis Moÿse. In 1937 he went to the U.S. and enrolled at the Curtis Inst. of Music in Philadelphia, where he studied piano with Vengerova, composition with Scalero, and conducting with Reiner; in 1939–40 he took a course in advanced composition with Hindemith at Yale Univ., and also studied conducting with Koussevitzky at the Berkshire Music Center in Tanglewood (summers, 1939–43). He became a naturalized American citizen in 1942. He was awarded a Guggenheim fellowship in 1945; in 1960 he received his 2nd Guggenheim fellowship. His first public career was that of a concert pianist, and he elicited high praise for his appearances as soloist with the N.Y. Phil. and other orchs. He made his conducting debut with the Pittsburgh Sym. Orch. in 1939. From 1944 to 1950 he was pianist of the Boston Sym. Orch.; then traveled to Rome on a Fulbright fellowship (1950–52). From 1953 to 1962 he taught composition at the Univ. of Calif. at Los Angeles, where he also established the Improvisation Chamber Ensemble to perform music of "controlled improvisation." In 1963 he was appointed music director of the Buffalo Phil.; during his tenure, he introduced ultramodern works, much to the annoyance of some regular subscribers; he resigned his position in 1970. In 1971 he became principal conductor of the Brooklyn Philharmonia; also established the series "Meet the Moderns" there. From 1972 to 1975 he conducted the Jerusalem Sym. Orch. He became music director of the Milwaukee Sym. Orch. in 1981; relinquished his position in 1986 after a tour of Europe, and was made its conductor laureate; continued to hold his Brooklyn post until 1990. In 1986 he was the Mellon Lecturer at the National Gallery of Art in Washington, D.C. In 1962 he was elected a member of the National Inst. of Arts and Letters. He was elected a member of the American Academy and Inst. of Arts and Letters in 1983. Throughout the years, he evolved an astounding activity as conductor, composer, and lately college instructor, offering novel ideas in education and performance. As a composer, he traversed a protean succession of changing styles, idioms, and techniques. His early compositions were marked by the spirit of Romantic lyricism, adumbrating the musical language of Mahler; some other works reflected the neo-Classical formulas of Hindemith; still others suggested the hedonistic vivacity and sophisticated stylization typical of Stravinsky's productions. But the intrinsic impetus of his music was its "pulse," which evolves the essential thematic content into the substance of original projection. His earliest piano pieces were publ. when he was 15 years old; there followed an uninterrupted flow of compositions in various genres. Foss was fortunate in being a particular protégé of Koussevitzky, who conducted many of his works with the Boston Sym. Orch.; and he had no difficulty in finding other performers. As a virtuoso pianist, he often played the piano part in his chamber music, and he conducted a number of his symphonic and choral works.

WORKS: DRAMATIC: O p e r a : *The Jumping Frog of Calaveras County* (1949; Bloomington, Ind., May 18, 1950); *Griffelkin* (1953–55; NBC-TV, Nov. 6, 1955); *Introductions and*

Goodbyes (1959; N.Y., May 7, 1960). **B a l l e t :** *The Heart Remembers* (1944); *Within These Walls* (1944); *Gift of the Magi* (1944; Boston, Oct. 5, 1945). **I n c i d e n t a l   M u s i c   T o :** Shakespeare's *The Tempest* (1939–40; N.Y., March 31, 1940). **ORCH.:** *2 Symphonic Pieces* (1939–40; not extant); *2 Pieces* (1941); 2 clarinet concertos: No. 1 (1941; rev. as Piano Concerto No. 1, 1943) and No. 2 (1988); 2 piano concertos: No. 1 (1943) and No. 2 (1949–51; Venice, Oct. 7, 1951; rev. version, Los Angeles, June 16, 1953); *The Prairie,* symphonic suite after the cantata (Boston, Oct. 15, 1943); 3 syms.: No. 1 (1944; Pittsburgh, Feb. 4, 1945), No. 2, *Symphony of Chorales* (1955–58; Pittsburgh, Oct. 24, 1958), and No. 3, *Symphony of Sorrows* (1991; Chicago, Feb. 19, 1992); *Ode* (1944; N.Y., March 15, 1945; rev. version, Philadelphia, Oct. 17, 1958); *Pantomime,* suite after *Gift of the Magi* (1945); *Recordare* (Boston, Dec. 31, 1948); *Elegy* for Clarinet and Orch. (1949); Concerto for Improvising Instruments and Orch. (Philadelphia, Oct. 7, 1960); *Elytres* for Chamber Orch. (Los Angeles, Dec. 8, 1964); *Stillscape,* renamed *For 24 Winds* for Wind Orch. (Caracas, May 11, 1966); *Cello Concert* for Cello and Orch. (N.Y., March 5, 1967); *Baroque Variations* (Chicago, July 7, 1967); *Geod* (1969); *Orpheus* (1972; Ojai, Calif., June 2, 1973; rev. as *Orpheus and Euridice* for 2 Violins, Chamber Orch., and Tape, 1983); *Fanfare* (Istanbul, June 28, 1973); Concerto for Solo Percussion and Orch. (1974; Camden, N.J., April 9, 1975); *Folksong* (1975–76; Baltimore, Jan. 21, 1976; rev. 1978); *Salomon Rossi Suite* (1974); *Quintets* (Cleveland, April 30, 1979); *Night Music for John Lennon* for Brass Quintet and Orch. (1980–81; N.Y., April 1, 1981); *Dissertation* (Bloomington, Ind., July 2, 1981; new version as *Exeunt,* 1982); *Renaissance Concerto* for Flute and Orch. (1985–86; Buffalo, May 9, 1986); *Griffelkin Suite,* after the opera (Oshkosh, May 3, 1986); *For Lenny (Variation on N.Y., N.Y.)* for Piano Obbligato and Orch. (1988); *Elegy for Anne Frank* for Piano Obbligato and Orch. (N.Y., June 12, 1989); Guitar Concerto, *American Landscapes* (N.Y., Nov. 29, 1989); *Celebration,* renamed *American Fanfare,* for the 50th anniversary of the Berkshire Music Center at Tanglewood (July 6, 1990); Concerto for Piano, Left-hand, and Orch. (1993; Tanglewood, July 23, 1994). **C H A M B E R :** *4 Preludes* for Flute, Clarinet, and Bassoon (1940); Duo (Fantasia) for Cello and Piano (1941); *3 Pieces* for Violin and Piano (N.Y., Nov. 13, 1944; arranged as *3 Early Pieces* for Flute and Piano, 1986); 4 string quartets: No. 1 (1947), No. 2, *Divertissement pour Mica* (1973), No. 3 (1975; N.Y., March 15, 1976), and No. 4 (Buffalo, Oct. 6, 1998); *Capriccio* for Cello and Piano (1948); *Studies in Improvisation* for Clarinet, Horn, Cello, Percussion, and Piano (1959; N.Y., March 11, 1962); *Echoi* for 4 Players (1961–63; N.Y., Nov. 11, 1963); *Non- Improvisation* for Clarinet, Cello, Piano or Electric Organ, and Percussion (N.Y., Nov. 7, 1967); *Paradigm* for Percussionist-Conductor (N.Y., Oct. 31, 1968; rev. version, Buffalo, Nov. 8, 1969); *Waves* for Instruments (Hempstead, N.Y., Jan. 17, 1969); *MAP (Musicians at Play),* musical game for 5 Players (St. Paul de Vence, July 16, 1970; rev. version for 4 Players, Buffalo, June 14, 1977); *The Cave of Winds (La Grotte des Vents)* for Flute, Oboe, Clarinet, Bassoon, and Horn (N.Y., Dec. 14, 1972); *Ni Bruit Ni Vitesse* for 2 Pianos and 2 Percussion (Buffalo, Feb. 13, 1972); *Chamber Music* for Percussion and Electronics (Buffalo, March 22, 1975; in collaboration with J. Chadabe); *Quartet Plus* for 2 String Quartets, Narrator, and Video (N.Y., April 29, 1977; based on String Quartet No. 3); *Music for 6* for 6 Treble Clef Instruments (1977; rev. 1978); *Curriculum Vitae* for Accordion (N.Y., Nov. 1, 1977); Brass Quintet (1978); *Round a Common Center* for Piano Quartet or Quintet (1979; Lake Placid, N.Y., Jan. 30, 1980); *Percussion Quartet* (Rochester, N.Y., Nov. 5, 1983); Horn Trio (1983); Saxophone Quartet (Buffalo, Sept. 22, 1985); *Embros* for 3 Winds, 3

Brass, Percussion, Strings, and Electric Instruments (1985; N.Y., Feb. 25, 1986); *Tashi* for Clarinet, 2 Violins, Viola, Cello, and Piano (1986; Washington, D.C., Feb. 17, 1987); *Central Park Reel* for Violin and Piano (Singapore, June 17, 1987); *Chaconne* for Guitar (N.Y., Nov. 8, 1987). **K E Y B O A R D : P i a n o :** *Fantasy Rondo* (1944); *Prelude* (1949); *Scherzo Ricercato* (1953); *Solo* (1981; Paris, March 24, 1982; new version as *Solo Observed* for Piano and 3 Instruments, Miami, June 7, 1982). **O r g a n :** *Etudes* (Mount Vernon, Iowa, Nov. 14, 1967). **VOCAL:** *Melodrama and Dramatic Song for Michelangelo* for Voice and Orch. (1940); *We Sing,* cantata for Children's Chorus and Piano (1941); *The Prairie* for Soprano, Alto, Tenor, Bass, Chorus, and Orch. (1943; N.Y., May 15, 1944); *Song of Anguish* for Baritone or Bass and Orch. (1945; Boston, March 10, 1950); *Song of Songs* for Soprano or Mezzo-soprano and Orch. (1946; Boston, March 7, 1947); *Adon Olom: A Prayer* for Cantor or Tenor, Chorus, and Organ (1948); *Behold! I Build an House* for Chorus and Organ (Boston, March 14, 1950); *A Parable of Death* for Narrator, Tenor, Chorus, and Orch. (1952; Louisville, March 11, 1953); *Psalms* for Chorus and Orch. (1955–56; N.Y., May 9, 1957); *Time Cycle* for Soprano and Orch. (1959–60; N.Y., Oct. 20, 1960; also for Soprano and Chamber Group, Tanglewood, July 10, 1961); *Fragments of Archilochos* for Countertenor, Male Speaker, Female Speaker, 4 Small Choruses, Optional Large Chorus, and Orch. (Potsdam, N.Y., May 1965); *3 Airs for Frank O'Hara's Angel* for Male Speaker, Soprano, Women's Chorus, and Instruments (N.Y., April 26, 1972); *Lamdeni (Teach Me)* for Chorus and 6 Instruments (1973); *American Cantata* for Soprano, Tenor, Speakers, Chorus, and Orch. (Interlochen, Mich., July 24, 1976; rev. version, N.Y., Dec. 1, 1977); *Then the Rocks on the Mountain Begin to Shout* for Chorus (1978; N.Y., Nov. 9, 1985); *13 Ways of Looking at a Blackbird* for Soprano or Mezzo-soprano, Instruments, and Tape (1978); *Measure for Measure* for Tenor and Chamber Orch. (1980); *De Profundis* for Chorus (1983); *With Music Strong* for Chorus and Orch. (1988; Milwaukee, April 15, 1989). **O T H E R :** *For 200 Cellos (A Celebration)* (Coll. Park, Md., June 4, 1982).

BIBL.: K. Perone, *L. F.: A Bio-Bibliography* (N.Y., 1991).
—NS/LK/DM

Foss, Hubert J(ames), English writer on music and composer; b. Croydon, May 2, 1899; d. London, May 27, 1953. He attended Bradfield Coll. In 1921 he became a member of the educational dept. of the Oxford Univ. Press, and in 1924 founded the music dept., which he headed until 1941. He composed *7 Poems by Thomas Hardy* for baritone, men's chorus, and piano; instrumental pieces; songs. He was the author of *Music in My Time* (1933); *The Concertgoer's Handbook* (London, 1946); *Ralph Vaughan Williams* (London, 1950); also collected and ed. *The Heritage of Music, Essays...* (2 vols., London, 1927–34). His book *London Symphony: Portrait of an Orchestra* remained unfinished at his death, and was completed by Noel Goodwin (London, 1954).
—NS/LK/DM

Foster, Frank, American saxophonist, arranger; b. Cincinnati, Ohio, Sept. 23, 1928. He proved to be musically adept from an early age, and by the time he entered high school, he was writing and arranging for his own 12-piece band. While studying music at Wilberforce Univ. (now Central State Univ.), he composed, arranged, and played alto and tenor saxophones with the Wilberforce Collegians, a 20-piece band. Following his college years, he joined the "Snooky" Young band in Detroit as an alto saxophonist, and worked as a freelance artist with Milt Jackson and Wardell Gray. After returning from the Far East in 1953, where he served with the 7th Army Infantry Division Band, he joined the Count Basie Band as a tenor saxophonist. In addition to performing, he made significant contributions to the band with his compositions and arrangements, which included "Down for the Count," "Blues Backstage," "Shiny Stockings," and "Four-Five-Six," among others. Foster remained with the Basie Band until 1964. In addition to touring and recording with his own groups, he has worked with Clark Terry, Elvin Jones, the Johnny Richards Orch., Dexter Gordon, the Thad Jones-Mel Lewis Orch., and Benny Goodman.

In 1980 he was commissioned by Jazzmobile to write a suite for the Winter Olympics. The resulting *Lake Placid Suite* was performed at the Olympics by a 20-piece orchestra, under his direction. In 1986, Foster took over the leadership of the Count Basie Orch., writing and arranging for the band until he resigned in 1995. During these years, his arrangements helped to earn the band numerous Grammy nominations, two of which resulted in Grammy awards. His Loud Minority Big Band, which he formed during the early 1980s, has reunited and is still performing today.

DISC.: *The Loud Minority* (1983); *Two for the Blues* (1983); *Frankly Speaking* (1984).—**SKB**

Foster, Gary, American jazz musician; b. Leavenworth, Kans., May 25, 1936. He studied clarinet at the Univ. of Kans. but plays flute and soprano, tenor, and alto saxophone. He moved to Los Angeles in 1961, where he began a long association with pianist-composer Clare Fischer in 1965 and was a busy studio musician. Admired for his cool-tone, straight-ahead approach, he continued his jazz work as a sideman in the big bands of Louie Bellson, Mike Barone, and Toshiko Akiyoshi (1970s), as well as with small groups led by Dennis Budmir, Jimmy Rowles, Warne Marsh, and Laurindo Almeida. Foster has recorded with Cal Tjader, Poncho Sanchez, and Mel Tormé. He continues to be active in studio work, primarily because of his flute and clarinet abilities.

DISC.: *Make Your Own Fun* (1994); *Concord Duo Series, Vol. Four* (1995).—**BM**

Foster, Lawrence (Thomas), noted American conductor; b. Los Angeles, Oct. 23, 1941. He studied conducting with F. Zweig in Los Angeles. He made his first conducting appearance with the Young Musicians Foundation Debut Orch. in Los Angeles in 1960. At the age of 24, he was appointed asst. conductor of the Los Angeles Phil., which post he held until 1968; in 1966, received the Koussevitzky Memorial Conducting Prize at the Berkshire Music Center at Tanglewood. From 1969 to 1974 he was chief guest conductor of the Royal Phil. in London. From 1971 to 1978 he was conductor-in-chief of the Houston Sym. Orch. From 1979 to 1990 he was chief conductor of the Opera and the Orchestre National de Monte Carlo (called Orchestre Philharmonique de Monte Carlo from 1980). He also became

Generalmusikdirektor in the city of Duisburg in 1981, remaining in that position until 1988. From 1990 to 1998 he was music director of the Aspen (Colo.) Music Festival. In 1992 he resumed the position of chief conductor of the Orchestre Philharmonique in Monte Carlo. He was also music director of the Lausanne Chamber Orch. (1985–90) and the Jerusalem Sym. Orch. (1988–92). In 1996 he became music director of the Barcelona Sym. Orch. Foster is particularly notable for his dynamic interpretations of modern works, but has also been acclaimed for his precise and intelligent presentations of the Classical and Romantic repertoire. —**NS/LK/DM**

Foster, Pops (actually, **George Murphy**), pioneering jazz bassist; b. on a plantation in McCall, La., May 18, 1892; d. San Francisco, Oct. 30, 1969. His family moved to New Orleans when "Pops" was 10; he played cello for three years, then switched to string bass. From 1906–the teens, played with local brass bands, and various dance bands, including those led by Kid Ory and King Oliver. Foster worked briefly with Fate Marable in 1917, and then joined him regularly on riverboats in summer 1918, playing both tuba and bass, remaining with him until 1921. After a stint in St. Louis, Foster went to Los Angeles to join Kid Ory (1923), remaining there until 1925. After another period in St. Louis, he came to N.Y. in 1928, and joined Luis Russell a year later, working with Luis Russell and Louis Armstrong throughout the 1930s (with a brief absence from the band in late 1937). Foster left Louis Armstrong in spring 1940 due to illness, and was hospitalized until that September. Next he worked briefly with Teddy Wilson and Happy Caldwell before forming a duo with guitarist Norman "Isadore" Langlois in 1941. From 1942–45, Foster worked in the N.Y. subways, but continued to do regular gigs. After playing with Sidney Bechet (1945) and Art Hodes (1945–46), Foster went to Europe in February 1948, played at Nice Jazz Festival with Mezz Mezzrow's Band, and did a brief tour of France with Mezzrow. He returned to play in Bob Wilber's Band in Boston, which subsequently became Jimmy Archey's Band (1950). Foster toured Europe with Archey in late 1952. After working in N.Y. and New Orleans briefly, Forster returned to Europe with Sam Price's Bluesicians (December 1955 to May 1956), then moved to San Francisco. He was with Earl Hines's Small Band during the late 1950s and early 1960s, and then freelanced from 1962. He toured Europe as a member of the New Orleans All Stars (early 1966). He remained based in Calif., but did widespread touring in the U.S. and Canada through the late 1960s. He recovered from serious illness in 1968 and briefly resumed playing before his death. His brother, Willie (William; b. McCall, La., Dec. 27, 1888; d. Baton Rouge, La., Aug. 1969), was a violinist, banjo player, and guitarist.

WRITINGS: With Tom Stoddard, *Pops Foster: The Autobiography of a New Orleans Jazzman* (Berkeley, Calif., 1971, 1973). —**JC/LP**

Foster, Sidney, esteemed American pianist and pedagogue; b. Florence, S.C., May 23, 1917; d. Boston,

Feb. 7, 1977. He began piano training as a child with Walter Goldstein in New Orleans, and at the age of 10 was admitted to the Curtis Inst. of Music in Philadelphia, where he studied with Vengerova and Saperton and took his diploma in 1938. In 1940 he won the 1st Leventritt Foundation Award, which entitled him to an appearance as soloist with the N.Y. Phil. in Beethoven's 3rd Piano Concerto on March 16, 1941. This was the beginning of a fine international career. In 1964 he played 16 concerts in Russia. He taught piano at Fla. State Univ. (1949–51); from 1952 to 1977 he was on the piano faculty of Ind. Univ. at Bloomington.—**NS/LK/DM**

Foster, Stephen C(ollins), premier American songwriter; b. Lawrenceville, Pa., July 4, 1826; d. N.Y., Jan. 13, 1864. Foster is the best-remembered and most influential American songwriter of the 19th century, composing both minstrel songs (including "Oh! Susanna," "Old Folks at Home," "My Old Kentucky Home," and "De Camptown Races") and romantic ballads ("I Dream of Jeanie with the Light Brown Hair" and "Beautiful Dreamer"). During his lifetime, his songs were among the most popular in the world. Long after Foster's death his songs have maintained their popularity, achieving the status of folk songs: everyone knows them, though only some people know who wrote them. His mix of European melodic styles with African-American rhythms into a peculiarly American form has proven to be the dominant characteristic of American popular music from his time forward. As such, his influence is incalculable.

Foster was the ninth of ten children of William Barclay Foster (b. Berkeley County, Va., Sept. 7, 1779; d. Allegheny, Pa., July 27, 1855), a businessman and minor political figure who established the town in which his son was born, and Eliza Clayland Tomlinson (b. Wilmington, Del., Jan. 21, 1788; d. Pittsburgh, Jan. 18, 1855), whom he had married Nov. 14, 1807. His paternal ancestors were Irish; his great-grandfather, Alexander Foster, emigrated from Londonderry about 1728, and his grandfather, James Foster, fought in the Revolutionary War. His mother's family had come to Md. from England in the 17th century.

Foster showed an early interest in music, picking out harmonies on a guitar at the age of two, playing the drum at five, and playing the flageolet (a kind of flute) at seven. In January 1840 he left home to attend Athens Academy at Tioga Point, where he wrote his first musical composition, "Tioga Waltz." He also briefly attended the Towanda Academy. On July 20, 1841, he began to attend Jefferson Coll. in Canonsburg, Pa., but stayed only a week before dropping out and returning home. In addition, he may have studied music privately with a German-born teacher named Henry Kleber.

Though an indifferent student and largely self-taught, Foster showed what his father called "a strange talent" for music. One of the strange elements of that talent, revealed as early as the age of nine, was an affinity for "Ethiopian" songs, i.e., the songs of African-Americans and similar material performed by blackface minstrels. (Elements of Irish melodies, German songs, and Italian operas also have been identified in his

music.) His first published song was "Open Thy Lattice, Love" (December 1844), with lyrics from a poem by journalist George P. Morris (also lyricist of "Woodman, Spare That Tree") that had appeared in a supplement to the *New York Mirror* and previously set to music by Joseph Philip Knight.

In 1845, Foster became a member of an informal men's club for which he began to write songs in the style of those he had heard in minstrel shows. Enormously popular at the time, the minstrel shows can be viewed as having a double-edged impact on race relations: On the one hand, by portraying African-Americans in a sympathetic light they helped promote abolitionist sentiment in the North; on the other, by portraying them as inferior they tended to reinforce established prejudices. For his part Foster was genuinely engaged by the black-based music, and though he wrote songs in Southern Negro dialect at first, his later minstrel songs eliminated such demeaning elements. The minstrel songs he composed for the men's club may have included "Lou'siana Belle," "Old Uncle Ned," and "Oh! Susanna." He also tried to interest traveling minstrel groups in performing his songs when they appeared locally.

Foster moved to Cincinnati in late 1846 or early 1847 and took a job as a bookkeeper for his brother Dunning. Meanwhile, a few minstrel performers began featuring Foster's work and often submitted his songs under their own names for copyright (a common practice of the day); this created some confusion in chronicling his early songwriting efforts, particularly "Oh! Susanna," which was copyrighted and published more than 20 times between Feb. 25, 1848, and Feb. 14, 1851. During that time the song, with its jaunty melody and clever, contradictory nonsense lyrics ("It rained all night the day I left / The weather it was dry / The sun so hot I froze to death / Susanna, don't you cry"), became a substantial success and was adopted by the forty-niners as the unofficial anthem of the 1849 Calif. Gold Rush.

The popularity of "Oh! Susanna" and other songs led publishers Firth, Pond & Co. of N.Y. in 1849 to offer Foster royalty payments of two cents per copy of sheet music for his future compositions, which at the time was an unusually generous form of compensation. Foster may have made a similar arrangement with F. D. Benteen publishers of Baltimore, which also began to issue his copyrights in 1850. As a result, he gave up his bookkeeping job in early 1850 and returned home to his family (now living in Allegheny, Pa.) to pursue a career as a full-time songwriter.

Many of Foster's songs were popularized by the most successful minstrel group of the day, the Christy Minstrels, founded by Edwin P. Christy. On Feb. 23, 1850, Foster sent Christy the nonsense song "De Camptown Races" (which had been published four days earlier by Benteen), and when the group began to perform it, it became an enormous popular success. By 1851, Foster was giving Christy first look at all his newly written minstrel songs, and Christy was paying $10 for the right to premiere each of them.

On July 22, 1850, Foster married Jane Denny McDowell; the union produced a daughter on April 18,

1851. But the marriage proved tumultuous, marked by separations and reconciliations. What part Foster's economic situation may have played in the couple's difficulties cannot easily be said.

In 1851, Foster sent Christy the sentimental minstrel song "Old Folks at Home," also known as "Swanee River" (deliberately truncated; it referred to the Suwanee River in Fla., which Foster's brother Morrison found listed in an atlas). Christy introduced the song and initially claimed authorship of it with Foster's permission, in exchange for a financial consideration (probably $5). Foster had decided to remove his name from his minstrel songs and to associate himself with more socially acceptable romantic ballads. Within a year, however, he tried, unsuccessfully, to reclaim title to "Old Folks at Home," which had become an overwhelming success. By November 1854 it was reported to have sold more than 130,000 copies of sheet music. It eventually topped 20 million, making it Foster's most popular composition and arguably the most successful song ever published. Despite lacking the songwriting credit, Foster was paid his usual royalty. When the copyright was renewed in 1879, his name was restored to the song. In 1935, "Old Folks at Home" became the official state song of Fla.

Christy also introduced Foster's "Massa's in de Cold Ground" (1852), reported to have sold 74,000 copies by November 1854, and "My Old Kentucky Home" (1853), which sold almost 90,000 copies by the same time. In 1928, "My Old Kentucky Home" was named the official state song of Ky.

By July 1853, Foster, separated from his wife, was living in N.Y. to be closer to Firth, Pond & Co., by then his exclusive publisher. On Jan. 26, 1854, the company published *The Social Orchestra*, a music book compiled by Foster containing arrangements of previously published songs, new instrumental pieces, and works by others. Foster and his wife reconciled in the spring of 1854 and lived in Hoboken, N.J. "Jeanie with the Light Brown Hair," the best known of the songs he wrote for his wife, was composed there and published in June. By October the Fosters had returned to Allegheny.

In the late 1850s, Foster's songwriting output diminished. As his finances became precarious, he sold his earlier songs to his publishers outright and drew advances on yet-to-be-written ones. In 1860 he moved back to N.Y. and concentrated on sentimental ballads rather than minstrel songs. He spent his last years as a penniless alcoholic in the city's skid-row district, the Bowery, selling his songs cheaply. He was unusually prolific during this period but produced little of lasting value. Of his posthumously published songs, the most successful was "Beautiful Dreamer," composed at least six months before his death. In poor health, he died after falling down and suffering a severe cut to his neck.

Foster's songs maintained their popularity into the age of recording. "Old Folks at Home" and "My Old Kentucky Home" repeatedly became pop hits for recording artists from the 1890s through the 1930s. As late as 1957, Ray Charles hit the Top 40 with "Swanee River Rock (Talkin' 'Bout That River)," and the Osborne Brothers and Johnny Cash reached the country charts

with versions of "My Old Kentucky Home" in the 1970s. Several of Foster's other songs also became perennial hits. In 1911, Billy Murray successfully recorded what he called "The Camptown Races (Gwine to Run All Night)." In 1922, Lambert Murphy scored with "I Dream of Jeannie [sic] with the Light Brown Hair." In 1924, Wendell Hall and the Shannon Four had a hit with "Oh! Susanna," and there was even a novelty version by the Singing Dogs (a recording of dogs barking) that made the Top 40 in 1955. George Gershwin and Irving Caesar's "Swanee," a 1920 hit for Al Jolson, who interpolated it into the Broadway show *Sinbad*, was, of course, inspired by "Old Folks at Home."

In 1939, 20th Century–Fox released *Swanee River*, a film biography of Foster starring Don Ameche, with Jolson portraying Christy and Andrea Leeds as Mrs. Foster. In 1940, Foster became the first popular composer to be elected to the Hall of Fame for Great Americans at N.Y.U. In 1941, when all ASCAP songs were banned from airplay in a dispute between the song licensing organization and radio stations, Foster's songs, by then in the public domain, were played frequently. A second film biography, *I Dream of Jeanie*, starring Ray Middleton and Muriel Lawrence, was released by Republic Pictures in 1952.

Various institutions have been established to honor and memorialize Foster, including the Stephen Foster Memorial at the Univ. of Pittsburgh, Federal Hill in Bardstown, Ky, an exhibit at the Henry Ford Museum in Dearborn, Mich., and the Stephen Foster Museum in White Springs, Fla.

BIBL.: M. Foster (his brother), *Biography, Songs and Musical Compositions of S. C. F.* (Pittsburgh, 1896); W. R. Wittlesey and O. G. Sonneck, *Catalogue of First Editions of S. C. F.* (Washington, D.C., 1915); H. V. Milligan, *S. C. F., A Biography* (N.Y., 1920); D. J. Rice, *Two S. C. F. Songs* (N.Y., 1931); J. T. Howard, *S. F., America's Troubadour* (N.Y., 1934; 3rd ed., 1962); Howard, *Newly Discovered F.iana* (N.Y., 1935); R. Walters, *S. F.: Youth's Golden Dream* (Princeton, N.J., 1936); E. Foster Mornewick, *Chronicles of S. F.'s Family* (2 vols.; Pittsburgh, 1944); J. T. Howard, ed., *A Treasury of S. F.* (N.Y., 1946); H. Gaul, *The Minstrel of the Alleghenies* (Pittsburgh, 1952); J. J. Fuld, *A Pictorial Bibliography of the First Editions of S. C. F.* (Philadelphia, 1957); G. Chase, "America's Minstrel," *America's Music* (N.Y., 1955; 2nd ed., rev., 1966); R. Jackson, ed., *S. F. Song Book* (N.Y., 1974); W. W. Austin, *"Susanna," "Jeanie," and "The Old Folks at Home": The Songs of S. C. F. from His Time to Ours* (N.Y., 1975); E. List, ed., *S. F.: Complete Piano Music* (N.Y., 1984); C. Elliker, *S. C. F.: A Guide to Research* (N.Y., 1988); K. Emerson, *Doo-Dah! S. F. and the Rise of American Popular Culture* (N.Y., 1997).—**WR**

Fotek, Jan, Polish composer; b. Czerwińsk-on-the-Vistula, Nov. 28, 1928. He studied composition with Stanisław Wiechowicz at the State Higher School of Music in Kraków (1952–53), and then with Tadeusz Szeligowski at the State Higher School of Music in Warsaw (graduated, 1958). In 1973 he received the Prime Minister's Award for his children's and young people's works, and in 1977 the Friar Albert's Award for his sacred music.

WORKS: DRAMATIC: *Morze jedności odnalezionej* (The Sea of Recovered Unity), radio opera (1967); *Galileusz* (Galileo), musical drama (1969); *Vir sapiens dominabitur astris*, radio opera

(1973); *Łyżki i księżyc* (Spoons on the Moon), opera (1976); *Leśna Królewna* (A Forest King's Daughter), opera-ballet (1977); *Każdy* (Anyone), opera-mystery (1983). **ORCH.:** 2 syms. (1958, 1959); *Kategorie* for Strings, Harp, Celesta, and Percussion (1963); *Epitasis* (1967; Warsaw, Sept. 24, 1971); *Partita* for 12 Bassoons and 3 Double Basses (1968); *Opus concertante II* (1968); *Fantazja na temat "Prząśniczki" S. Moniuszki* (Fantasy on the Theme of "The Spinner" from S. Moniuszko; 1974); *Musica cromatica* for Chamber String Orch. (1982; Warsaw, Sept. 23, 1984); *Melodia Lubuska* (The Lubusz Melody) for Instrumental Ensemble (1983); *Passacaglia* (1985); *Suita czarnoleska* (Czarnolas Suite) for Flute, Harpsichord, and Chamber String Orch. (1986); *Canzona from Jasna Góra* (1993). **CHAMBER:** Trio for Clarinet, Violin, and Piano (1955); *Opus concertante I* for Organ, Piano, and Percussion (1959); Trio for Violin, Viola, and Cello (1961); *Trimorphie* for 3 Flutes, Harpsichord, and Prepared Piano (1966); 2 string quartets (1967, 1978); *Trzy scherza* (Three Scherzos) for Bassoon and Piano (1979); *Musiquette* for 3 Saxophones (1982); *Variations* for Saxophone and Piano (1984); *Sonata romantica* for Tuba and Piano (1985); *Szkice* (Sketches) for Violin and Piano (1985). **KEYBOARD: Piano:** 7 Preludes (1973). **Organ:** *Partita concertante* (1964); *Quattri impressioni* (1983). **Harpsichord:** Sonata (1979). **VOCAL:** *Poesia con musica—Niobe* for Reciters, Chorus, and Orch. (1960); 3 Laudi for Chorus (1963); *Hymn gregoriański* (Gregorian Hymn) for Chorus and Orch. (1963); *Cykl wierszy* (A Cycle of Verses) for Children's Chorus and Orch. (1963; also as *Sny dziecięce* [Children's Dreams] for Children's Chorus, 2 Pianos, and Percussion, 1974); *Oda* (Ode) for Solo Voices, Chorus, and Orch. (1965); *Apostrofy* (Apostrophes) for Baritone and 2 Pianos (1966); *Verbum* for Chorus, Organ, 2 Pianos, and Percussion (1967); *Nokturny* (Nocturnes) for Soprano and Chamber Orch., after Sappho (1968); *Hymne de Sainte Brigitte* for Mezzo-soprano and 7 Instruments (1970; Warsaw, Sept. 17, 1972); *Ostatnia wojna* (The Last War) for Reciter, Chorus, and Orch. (1971); *Pieśni taneczne* (Dance Songs) for Woman's Voice and Piano (1971; also for Woman's Voice and Orch., 1979); *Wariacje na zaday temat* (Variations on a Given Theme) for Children's Chorus (1971); *Heroikon* for Mezzo-soprano, Baritone, Reciter, Chorus, and Orch. (1974; Warsaw, Oct. 30, 1999); *Msza ku czci NMP Matki Kościoła* (Mass in Praise of St. Mary, Mother of the Church) for Mezzo-soprano, Chorus, and Orch. (1976); *Pieśni sponad wód* (Songs Upon the Water) for Chorus or Men's Chorus (1976); Chorale for Baritone, Chorus, and Orch. (1978); *Fraszki* (Epigrams) for Chorus (1979); *Ecloga* (Eclogue) for Countertenor and Period Instrumental Ensemble (1987); Mass for Men's Chorus (1993).—**NS/LK/DM**

Fou Ts'ong, Chinese pianist; b. Shanghai, March 10, 1934. He studied piano in his native city; then won 3rd prizes in the Bucharest Piano Competition (1953) and the Warsaw International Chopin Competition (1955); continued his studies at the Warsaw Cons. In 1958 he decided to make his home in London. He subsequently appeared with many of the major orchs. of Europe and the U.S., and also gave many recitals. He was particularly noted for his expressive playing of works by Chopin and Debussy.—**NS/LK/DM**

Foucquet, Pierre-Claude, French organist and composer; b. Paris, c. 1694; d. there, Feb. 13, 1772. He was born into a family of organists. After serving at St. Honoré, the Abbey of St. Victor, and St. Eustache, he became organist of the Royal Chapel in 1758. He also was one of the four organists at Notre Dame from 1761. He publ. 3 vols. of harpsichord music (Paris, 1749–51). —**LK/DM**

Fougstedt, Nils-Eric, Finnish conductor and composer; b. Raisio, near Turku, May 24, 1910; d. Helsinki, April 12, 1961. He studied composition in Helsinki with Furuhjelm, in Italy with Carlo Felice Boghen, and in Berlin with Max Trapp. Upon returning to Finland in 1932, he lectured in theory at the Music Inst. in Helsinki. He was also active as a conductor, and led the Finnish Radio Orch. from 1951 until his death.

WORKS: Piano Trio (1933); Suite for Orch. (1936); *Divertimento* for Wind Quintt (1936); Violin Concertino (1937); Violin Sonata (1937); 2 syms. (1938, 1949); String Quartet (1940); Cello Concerto (1942); Piano Concerto (1944); *Tulukset* (The Tinderbox), cantata after Hans Christian Andersen (1950); *Trittico sinfonico* (1958); many choruses and songs.—**NS/LK/DM**

Foulds, John (Herbert), significant English composer and music theorist; b. Manchester, Nov. 2, 1880; d. Calcutta, April 24, 1939. He was precocious and began to compose at a single-digit age. He learned to play cello, and earned a living by playing in theater orchs. In 1900 he joined the Hallé Orch. in Manchester; then moved to London in 1910, where he served as music director for the Central YMCA (1918–23); also conducted the Univ. of London Music Soc. (1921–26). In 1935 he went to India and undertook a thorough study of Indian folk music. He served as director of European music for the All-India Radio at Delhi and Calcutta (1937–39) and also formed an experimental "Indo-European" orch., which included both European and Asian instruments. He was the first English composer to experiment with quarter tones, and as early as 1898 wrote a string quartet with fractional intervals; he also composed semi-classical pieces using traditional Indian instruments. Unfortunately, many of his MSS are lost.

WORKS: DRAMATIC: *The Vision of Dante*, concert opera (1905–08); *Cleopatra*, miniature opera (1909; not extant); *The Tell-Tale Heart*, melodrama (1910); *Avatara*, opera (1919–30; not extant); music for the ritual play *Veils* (1926; unfinished). **ORCH.:** *Undine Suite* (c. 1899); *Epithalamium* (London, Oct. 9, 1906); *Lento e scherzetto* for Cello and Orch. (c. 1906); 2 cello concertos: No. 1 (1908–09; Manchester, March 16, 1911) and No. 2 (c. 1910; not extant); *Apotheosis* for Violin and Orch. (1908–09); *Mirage*, symphonic poem (1910); *Suite française* (1910); *Keltic Suite* (1911); *Music Pictures (Group III)*, suite (London, Sept. 4, 1912); *Hellas* for Double String Orch., Harp, and Percussion (1915–32); *Miniature Suite* (1915); *Peace and War*, meditation (1919); *3 Mantras* (1919–30); *Le Cabaret*, overture to a French comedy (1921); *Suite fantastique* (1922); *Music Pictures (Group IV)* for Strings (c. 1922); *Saint Joan Suite* (1924–25); *Henry VIII Suite* (1925–26); *April-England*, tone poem (1926–32); *Dynamic Triptych* for Piano and Orch. (1929; Edinburgh, Oct. 15, 1931); *Keltic Overture* (1930); *Indian Suite* (1932–35); *Pasquinades symphoniques*, sym. in 3 movements (1935; finale left unfinished); *Deva-Music* (1935–36; only fragments extant); *Chinese Suite* (1935); 3 *Pasquinades* (c. 1936); *Symphony of East and West* for European and Indian Instruments (1937–38; not extant); *Symphonic Studies* (1938; not extant). **CHAMBER:** 10 string quartets: Nos. 1–3 (before 1899; not extant), No. 4 (1899), No. 5 (not extant), No. 6,

Quartetto romantico (1903), No. 7 (not extant), No. 8 (1907–10), No. 9, *Quartetto intimo* (1931–32), and No. 10, *Quartetto geniale* (1935; only the 3rd movement, *Lento quieto*, extant); Cello Sonata (1905; rev. 1927); *Impromptu on a Theme of Beethoven* for 4 Cellos (1905); *Music Pictures (Group I)* for Piano Trio (1910; not extant); *Ritornello con variazioni* for String Trio (1911); *Aquarelles (Music Pictures—Group II)* for String Quartet (c. 1914); *Sonia* for Violin and Piano (1925). **KEYBOARD: P i a n o :** *Dichterliebe*, suite (1897–98); *Essays in the Modes*, 6 studies (1920–27); *Egotistic*, modal essay (1927); *2 Landscapes* (c. 1928); *Scherzo chromatico* (1927; not extant). **VOCAL:** *The Song of Honor* for Speaker, Chamber Orch., and Women's Chorus ad libitum (1918); *A World Requiem* for 4 Soloists, Small Boy's Chorus, Mixed Chorus, and Orch. (1919–21; London, Nov. 11, 1923); choruses; songs.

WRITINGS: *Music To-Day: Its Heritage from the Past, and Legacy to the Future* (London, 1934).

BIBL.: M. MacDonald, *J. F.: His Life in Music* (London, 1975); idem, *J. F., A centenary brochure from Musica Viva* (1979); idem, *J. F. and His Music* (N.Y. and London, 1990).—**NS/LK/DM**

Fountain, Pete, American clarinetist; b. New Orleans, La., July 3, 1930. He identifies strongly with New Orleans; he was born there, learned to play there, and continues to perform there in a nightclub in the Hilton hotel, complete with red velvet on the walls, that bears his iconic name. Although he borrowed a great deal from Benny Goodman, his most enduring influence on clarinet was his teacher and early mentor, Irving Fazola. By 1950, after playing with various New Orleans–based Dixieland combos, Fountain made his recording debut with Phil Zito's International Dixieland band. In the 1950s, he led his own combo, and toured Chicago with the Dukes of Dixieland. From 1957 to 1959, he achieved widespread popularity during a stint with *The Lawrence Welk Show*, on which he played Dixieland numbers. After leaving Welk, he returned to New Orleans, purchased his first nightclub, and began a productive association with the Decca subsidiary Coral Records. Little else has changed since then—Fountain is still a New Orleans monument, he still plays with the same warm tone and Dixieland style, and he still wanders into the studio every now and then.

DISC.: *Pete Fountain's New Orleans* (1959); *The Blues* (1959); *Pete Fountain Day* (1960); *At the Bateau Lounge* (1960); *Salutes the Great Clarinetists* (1960); *Music from Dixie* (1961); *New Orleans at Midnight* (1961); *Pete Fountain's French Quarter* (1961); *Mr. New Orleans* (1961); *Plenty of Pete* (1962); *South Rampart Street Parade* (1963); *Pete's Place* (1964); *Standing Room Only* (1965); *Those Were the Days* (1968); *Pete Fountain's Crescent City* (1973); *Alive in New Orleans* (1977); *Jazz Reunion* (1981); *Basin Street Blues* (1985); *Dixieland* (1987); *Swingin' Blues* (1990); *Something Misty* (1991); *Live at the Ryman* (1992); *High Society* (1992); *Pete's Beat* (1992); *Cheek to Cheek* (1993); *Country* (1994); *A Touch of Class* (1995); *Do You Know What It Means to Miss New Orleans?* (1996); *The Best of Pete Fountain* (1996); *New Orleans All Stars* (1997); *I Got Rhythm* (1997); *Basin Street Blues* (1997).—**DK**

Fourestier, Louis (Félix André), French conductor, pedagogue, and composer; b. Montpellier, May 31, 1892; d. Boulogne- Billancourt, Sept. 30, 1976. He was a student of Gédalge and Leroux at the Paris Cons., winning the Grand Prix de Rome with his cantata *La*

Mort d'Adonis in 1925. After conducting in the French provinces, he returned to Paris and conducted at the Opéra-Comique (1927–32) and the Opéra (1938–45). On Nov. 11, 1946, he made his Metropolitan Opera debut in N.Y. conducting *Lakmé*, and remained on its roster until 1948. From 1945 to 1963 he was a prof. at the Paris Cons. He wrote mainly orch. works and chamber music. —**NS/LK/DM**

Fouret, Maurice, French composer; b. St.-Quentin, Nov. 28, 1888; d. Paris, Jan. 22, 1962. He studied with Ravel, Charpentier, and Büsser. He composed several symphonic poems on exotic subjects, among them *Al-addin* (Paris, Nov. 28, 1920) and *Danse de Sita* (1922), as well as the ballets *Le Rustre imprudent* (1931) and *La Jeune Fille aux joues roses* (1934), a group of symphonic suites inspired by Alsatian folklore, and songs. —**NS/LK/DM**

Fournet, Jean, distinguished French conductor and pedagogue; b. Rouen, April 14, 1913. He received training in flute from M. Moyse (premier prix, 1932) and in conducting from Gaubert (1930–36) at the Paris Cons. In 1936 he made his conducting debut in Rouen, where he was active until 1940. After conducting in Marseilles (1940–44), he returned to Paris and served as music director of the Opéra-Comique (1944–57) and as a teacher of conducting at the École Normale de Musique (1944–62). From 1961 to 1968 he was principal guest conductor of the Hilversum Radio Orch. in the Netherlands, where he was also engaged in teaching conducting. In 1965 he made his debut with the Chicago Lyric Opera. After serving as music director of the Rotterdam Phil. (1968–73) and l'Orchestre de l'Ile-de-France (1973–82), he was active as a guest conductor. He made his belated Metropolitan Opera debut in N.Y. on March 28, 1987, conducting *Samson et Dalila*. Fournet was especially esteemed for his idiomatic interpretations of scores from the French symphonic and operatic repertory.—**NS/LK/DM**

Fournier, Pierre (Léon Marie), famous French cellist; b. Paris, June 24, 1906; d. Geneva, Jan. 8, 1986. He first studied piano with his mother. Stricken by polio at age 9, he turned to the cello, studying with Paul Bazelaire and André Hekking at the Paris Cons., and at the École Normale de Musique. He made his debut in 1925 and subsequently appeared both as a soloist with orchs. and as a chamber music artist; taught at the Paris Cons. (1941–49). After World War II, he made major tours throughout the world; he appeared regularly in the U.S. from 1948. He was made a Chevalier of the Legion of Honor in 1953, and in 1963 was promoted to Officier. In 1970 he settled in Switzerland, where he gave master classes. He was renowned for his elegant tone and impeccable musicianship; his repertoire was comprehensive, ranging from Bach to contemporary music. Several composers wrote works for him; he gave first performances of works by Roussel, Martin, Poulenc, and Martinů.

BIBL.: B. Gavoty, *P. F.* (Geneva, 1957); A. Hughes, *P. F.: Cellist in a Landscape With Figures* (Aldershot, 1998). —**NS/LK/DM**

Fournier, Pierre-Simon, French cutter and founder of music type; b. Paris, Sept. 15, 1712; d. there, Oct. 8, 1768. Instead of the lozenge- shaped types in the style of Hautin's (1525), Fournier introduced round-headed notes, described in his *Essai d'un nouveau caractère de fonte...* (1756). He also publ. a *Traité historique sur l'origine et le progrès des caractères de fonte pour l'impression de la musique* (Paris, 1765).—NS/LK/DM

Four Seasons, The, one of longest-lived and most successful white doo-wop groups of the 1960s, led by high-note warbler Frankie Valli. **MEMBERSHIP:** Frankie Valli (real name, Francis Castelluccio), voc. (b. Newark, N.J., May 3, 1937); Bob Gaudio, voc. (b. Bronx, N.Y., Nov. 17, 1942); Tommy DeVito, voc. (b. Bellville, N.J., June 19, 1935); Nick Massi (real name, Nicholas Macioci), voc. (b. Newark, N.J., Sept. 19, 1935).

The Four Seasons scored a series of smash hit singles between 1962 and 1967 featuring the piercing falsetto lead voice of Frankie Valli. One of the few American white groups other than The Beach Boys to challenge The Beatles for chart supremacy, The Four Seasons became so popular that they were able to launch Valli on a successful simultaneous solo recording career in 1965. The Four Seasons and Frankie Valli enjoyed renewed success in the mid-1970s, but have since been relegated to the oldies revival circuit. They were inducted into the Rock and Roll Hall of Fame in 1990.

Frankie Valli started out as a solo singer in 1952 and formed The Varietones with guitarist brothers Nick and Tommy DeVito and bassist Hank Majewski around 1954. Changing their name to The Four Lovers in 1956, the group signed with RCA Victor Records and scored a minor hit with "You Are the Apple of My Eye." They subsequently languished on the lounge circuit for several years. In the meantime, another N.J. group, originally formed in 1957, achieved a major hit as The Royal Teens with the novelty song "Short Shorts" in early 1958. Among the members were songwriter-keyboardist Bob Gaudio and, for a brief time in 1959, Al Kooper.

By 1960, Gaudio and Nick Massi had replaced DeVito and Majewski in The Four Lovers. With a name change to The Four Seasons around 1961, the group recorded the unsuccessful single "Bermuda" for George Goldner's Gone label before signing with Vee Jay Records with the help of writer-producer Bob Crewe. With Gaudio and Crewe acting as principal songwriters, The Four Seasons scored a top pop and rhythm-and-blues hit with Gaudio's "Sherry" in the late summer of 1962. "Big Girls Don't Cry" and "Walk Like a Man," written by Crewe and Gaudio, became top pop and smash rhythm-and-blues hits, followed by the pop-only hits "Candy Girl" (a smash), "Stay," and "Alone." Near the end of 1964, Vee Jay assembled early recordings by The Beatles and hits by The Four Seasons as *The Beatles Versus The Four Seasons,* today one of the most valuable of all rock collectors' items.

By 1964, The Four Seasons had switched to Philips Records, where the smash hits continued with Crewe and Gaudio's "Ronnie," "Save It for Me," and the classic top hit "Rag Doll," as well as "Dawn (Go Away)," "Let's Hang On," and "Working My Way Back to You." The

Four Seasons's sound was so popular that the group was able to score a major hit as The Wonder Who with a dreadful version of Bob Dylan's "Don't Think Twice." They also recorded the album *The Four Seasons Sing Big Hits by Burt Bacharach...Hal David...Bob Dylan,* certainly one of the worst albums of the 1960s—bad enough to make even the most casual Dylan fan cringe.

In 1965, Massi left The Four Seasons, yet the group continued to achieve hits with "I've Got You Under My Skin," "Tell It to the Rain," and "C'mon Marianne." During this time Valli initiated his solo recording career with the smash hit "Can't Take My Eyes Off You." In 1968, The Four Seasons attempted to be progressive and socially conscious with *The Genuine Imitation Life Gazette,* but the album sold poorly. Tommy DeVito retired around 1971 and Bob Gaudio ceased performing with the group in the early 1970s, taking over for Crewe as producer.

With Frankie Valli as the mainstay, The Four Seasons recorded for Mowest and Warner Brothers in the early 1970s, while Valli recorded for Motown and Private Stock. Between 1974 and 1976, Valli scored smash hits with "My Eyes Adored You" and "Swearin' to God" on Private Stock, while The Four Seasons achieved smashes with "Who Loves You" and "December, 1963 (Oh, What a Night)" on Warner/Curb. The Four Seasons had no more major hits and Frankie Valli scored his last major hit with the title song to the 1978 movie *Grease.* Valli and Bob Gaudio re-formed The Four Seasons in 1980 and formed FBI Records in 1984. The Four Seasons were inducted into the Rock and Roll Hall of Fame in 1990.

DISC.: The Four Lovers: *Joyride* (1956). The Royal Teens: *Short Shorts: Golden Classics* (1958). The Four Seasons: *Sherry and 11 Others* (1962); *Four Seasons' Greetings* (1963); *Big Girls Don't Cry and Twelve Others* (1963); *Ain't That a Shame and 11 Others* (1963); *Golden Hits* (1963); *Stay and Other Great Hits* (reissued as *Folk-Nanny;* 1964); *More Golden Hits* (1964); *Dawn (Go Away) and 11 Other Great Songs* (1964); *Born to Wander* (1964); *Rag Doll* (1964); *The Four Seasons Entertain You* (1965); *Sing Big Hits by Burt Bacharach...Hal David...Bob Dylan* (1965); *Gold Vault of Hits* (1965); *Girls, Girls, Girls, We Love Girls* (1965); *Recorded Live on Stage* (1965); *Working My Way Back to You* (1966); *Second Vault of Golden Hits* (1966); *Lookin' Back* (1966); *The Four Seasons' Christmas Album* (1966); *New Gold Hits* (1967); *Edizione D'Oro (Gold Edition)—29 Golden Hits* (1968); *The Genuine Imitation Life Gazette* (1968); *Half and Half* (1970); *Brotherhood of Man* (1970); *Chameleon* (1972); *Who Loves You* (1975); *The Four Seasons Story* (1975); *Fallen Angel* (1975); *Helicon* (1977); *In Resonance* (1982); *24 Original Classics* (1984); *Streetfighter* (1985); *25th Anniversary Collection* (1987); *Anthology* (1988); *Rarities, Vol. 1* (1990); *Rarities, Vol. 2* (1990); *Greatest Hits, Vol. 1* (1991); *Greatest Hits, Vol. 2* (1991); *20 Greatest Hits: Live* (1990); *Greatest Hits* (1991); *Hope + Glory* (1992); *The Dance Album* (1993); *Oh What a Night* (1994); *Christmas Album/Born to Wander* (1995); *Original Classics Vol. 1: Sherry and 11 Other Hits* (1995); *Original Classics Vol. 2: Big Girls Don't Cry and 12 Other Hits* (1995); *Original Classics Vol. 3: Ain't That a Shame and 11 Other Hits* (1995); *Original Classics Vol. 4: Dawn (Go Away) and 11 Other Hits* (1995); *Original Classics Vol. 5: Rag Doll and 10 Other Hits* (1995); *Original Classics Vol. 6: Let's Hang On and 11 Others Hits* (1995); *Original Classics Vol. 7: New Gold Hits* (1995); *Original Classics Vol. 8: Who Loves You* (1995). The Four Seasons and the Beatles: *The Beatles Versus the Four Seasons*

1161

(1964). Frankie Valli and The Four Seasons: *Reunited Live* (1981). Frankie Valli: *Solo* (1967); *Timeless* (1968); *Inside You* (1975); *Closeup* (1975); *Gold* (1975); *Our Day Will Come* (1975); *Valli* (1977); *Lady Put the Light Out* (1978); *Hits* (1978); *Frankie Valli...Is the Word* (1978); *Very Best* (1979); *Heaven Above Me* (1980); *Motown Superstar Series, Vol. 4* (1981); *Greatest Hits* (1996).—**BH**

Four Tops, The, Motown chart-toppers of the 1960s. **MEMBERSHIP:** Levi Stubbs (Stubbles), lead voc. (b. Detroit, June 6, 1936); Abdul "Duke" Fakir, voc. (b. Detroit, Dec. 26, 1935); Renaldo "Obie" Benson, voc. (b. Detroit, c. 1937); Lawrence Payton Jr., voc. (b. Detroit, c. 1938; d. Southfield, Mich., June 20, 1997).

Performing with their original members for over 40 years, The Four Tops were the most stable and consistent vocal group to emerge from Motown Records in the 1960s. Scoring a series of major pop and smash R&B hits between 1964 and 1967, almost all written by the songwriting-production team of Brian Holland, Lamont Dozier, and Eddie Holland, The Four Tops featured the gruff pleading voice of lead vocalist Levi Stubbs. Acclaimed for their polished close-harmony singing, precise choreography, and complex stage routines, The Four Tops were the most popular Motown act in Great Britain, yet they were overshadowed by The Supremes in the United States. Persevering despite the departure of Holland-Dozier-Holland from Motown in 1967, the group recorded for a number of different labels beginning in 1972 while maintaining their status as a popular supper club act. The Four Tops were inducted into the Rock and Roll Hall of Fame in 1990.

Born and raised in Detroit, the members of The Four Tops began singing together as high school students and later performed in local nightclubs. Known as The Four Aims since their formation in 1953, the group changed their name to The Four Tops upon signing with Chess Records in 1956. Their sole single for the label failed to sell, and they subsequently recorded for Red Top, Riverside, and Columbia. Performing at top nightclubs since the 1950s, The Four Tops toured with the Billy Eckstine revue in the early 1960s. Signing with the infant Motown Records aggregation in March 1963, The Four Tops initially recorded for the company's short-lived jazz-oriented Workshop label, but their debut album was never released.

Switching to the parent label Motown and assigned to the songwriting-production team of Holland-Dozier-Holland, The Four Tops scored major R&B and pop hits with H-D-H's "Baby I Need Your Loving" and William Stevenson's "Ask the Lonely" from their eponymous debut album. Their *Second Album* yielded a top pop and R&B hit with the classic "I Can't Help Myself (Sugar Pie, Honey Bunch)" and smash R&B and pop hits with "It's the Same Old Song" and "Something about You," all written by H-D-H. "Shake Me, Wake Me (When It's Over)" became a major R&B and pop hit and "Reach Out, I'll Be There" proved a top pop and R&B hit, as well as a top British hit. The Four Tops subsequently achieved crossover hits with "Standing in the Shadows of Love" and "Bernadette," and hits with "Seven Rooms of Gloom" and "You Keep Running Away."

H-D-H left Motown in late 1967, and by 1968, The Four Tops were covering The Left Banke's "Walk Away Renee" and Tim Hardin's "If I Were a Carpenter." They did not achieve another major pop hit until 1970, when they scored with a remake of "It's All in the Game" and Smokey Robinson and Frank Wilson's "Still Water (Love)." In the early 1970s, The Four Tops recorded three albums with The Supremes, scoring a major pop and R&B hit with them on a remake of "River Deep–Mountain High."

Renaldo "Obie" Benson coauthored Marvin Gaye's smash "What's Going On" and The Four Tops managed a R&B near-hit with "(It's the Way) Nature Planned It" in 1972. However, when Berry Gordy moved the Motown organization to Los Angeles in 1972, they declined to go. They signed with ABC–Dunhill Records, where they worked with Dennis Lambert and Brian Potter and achieved major pop and R&B hits with "Keeper of the Castle," "Ain't No Woman (Like the One I've Got)," and "Are You Man Enough" from the movie *Shaft in Africa*. Subsequent R&B successes through 1976 included "Sweet Understanding Love," "One Chain Don't Make No Prison," and "Midnight Flower" for Dunhill and "Catfish" for ABC.

The Four Tops scored another top hit with "When She Was My Girl" in 1981 on Casablanca. Levi Stubbs was the voice of the voracious plant Audrey II in the 1986 musical movie *Little Shop of Horrors*. Following their sensational appearance with The Temptations at the 25th anniversary celebration of Motown Records in 1983, The Four Tops re-signed with their old label and toured with The Temptations. However, their next moderate hit did not come until "Indestructible" in 1988 on Arista Records. They recorded a Christmas album for 1995 release, but, on June 20, 1997, Lawrence Payton died of liver cancer at his home in the Detroit suburb of Southfield. He was 59 years old.

DISC.: *The Four Tops* (1965); *Second Album* (1965); *On Top* (1966); *Live!* (1966); *On Broadway* (1967); *Reach Out* (1967); *Yesterday's Dream* (1968); *Now* (1969); *Soul Spin* (1969); *Still Waters Run Deep* (1970); *Changing Times* (1970); *Nature Planned It* (1972); *Keeper of the Castle* (1972); *Main Street People* (1973); *Meeting of the Minds* (1974); *Live and in Concert* (1974); *Night Lights Harmony* (1975); *Catfish* (1976); *The Show Must Go On* (1977); *At the Top* (1978); *Tonight* (1981); *One More Mountain* (1982); *Back Where I Belong* (1983); *Magic Motown* (1985); *Indestructible* (1988); *Christmas Here with You* (1995). The Four Tops and The Supremes: *The Magnificent Seven* (1970); *The Return of the Magnificent Seven* (1971); *Dynamite* (1972); *The Best of the Supremes and The Four Tops* (1991).—**BH**

Fowler, Jennifer, Australian composer; b. Bunbury, Western Australia, April 14, 1939. She studied at the Univ. of Western Australia, graduating in arts (1961) and music (1968). After working at the electronic music studio at the Univ. of Utrecht on a Dutch scholarship (1968–69), she settled in London to pursue her career as a composer. In 1971 she was joint winner of England's Radcliffe Award. In 1975 she won 1st prize in the International Competition for Women Composers in Mannheim.

WORKS: ORCH.: *Sculpture in 4 Dimensions* (1969); *Look on This Oedipus* (1973); *Chant with Garlands* (1974); *Ring Out the Changes* for Strings and Bells (1978); *Plainsong* for Strings (1992).

CHAMBER: String Quartet (1967); *Ravelation* for 2 Violins, Viola, and 2 Cellos (1971); *Chimes, Fractured* for 2 Flutes, 2 Oboes, 2 Clarinets, 2 Bassoons, Organ, Bagpipes, and Percussions (1971); *The Arrows of Saint Sebastian II* for Bass Clarinet, Cello, and Tape (1981); *The Invocation to the Veiled Mysteries* for Flute, Clarinet, Bassoon, Violin, Cello, and Piano (1982); *Line Spun With Stars* for Violin or Flute, Cello, and Piano (1982); *Echoes from an Antique Land* for 5 Percussion Players (1983; also for Flute, Clarinet, Piano, and Bass, 1983, or for 5 or 10 Instruments, 1986); *Threaded Stars* for Harp (1983); *Blow Flute: Answer Echoes in Antique Lands Dying* for Flute (1983); *Between Silence and the Word* for Wind Quintet (1987); *Lament* for Baroque Oboe and Bass Viol or Cello (1987); *We Call to You, Brother* for Flute, English Horn, Cello, Percussion, 2 Trombones, and Didjeridoo (1988); *Restless Dust* for Viola, Cello, and Double Bass (1988; also for Cello and Piano); *Reeds, Reflections...Ripples Re-sound Resound* for Oboe, Violin, Viola, and Cello (1990); *Lament for Mr. Henry Purcell* for Alto Flute, Viola, Harp or Violin, Clarinet, and Marimba (1995; also for 2 or 3 Instruments, 1996). KEYBOARD: P i a n o : *Piece for an Opera House* for 2 Pianos or Piano and Tape or Solo Piano (1973); *Music for Piano: Ascending and Descending* (1981); *Piece for E.L.* (1981). VOCAL: *Hours of the Day* for 4 Mezzo-sopranos, 2 Oboes, and 2 Clarinets (1968); *Veni Sancte Spiritus: Veni Creator* for Chamber Chorus or 12 Solo Singers (1971); *Voice of the Shades* for Soprano, Oboe or Clarinet, and Violin or Flute (1977; also for Soprano, 2 Trumpets, and Oboe or Clarinet, and for Soprano, Clarinet, Oboe, and Violin or Flute); *Tell Out, My Soul: Magnificat* for Soprano, Cello, and Piano (1980; rev. 1984); *When David Heard...* for Chorus and Piano (1982); *Letter from Haworth* for Mezzo-soprano, Clarinet, Cello, and Piano (1984); *And Ever Shall Be*, 4 songs for Mezzo-soprano and Chamber Ensemble (1989); *Australia Sends Greetings to Alaska* for Soprano, Alto, and Optional Piano (1992); *Let's Stop Work!* for 2 Equal Treble Parts, 3rd Treble Part, and Optional Piano (1992); *Singing the Lost Places* for Soprano and Large Ensemble or Chamber Orch. (1996); *Lament for Dunblane* for 2 Sopranos, Tenor, and Bass or Chorus (1996). —NS/LK/DM

Fox, Charles Warren, American musicologist; b. Gloversville, N.Y., July 24, 1904; d. there, Oct. 15, 1983. He took courses in psychology at Cornell Univ. (B.A., 1926; Ph.D., 1933), and also studied musicology there with Kinkeldey. In 1932 he became a part-time instructor in psychology at the Eastman School of Music in Rochester, N.Y. In 1933 he began giving courses in music history and musicology, retiring in 1970. From 1952 to 1959 he was ed. of the *Journal of the American Musicological Society*. From 1954 to 1956 he served as president of the Music Library Assn.—NS/LK/DM

Fox, Donal, jazz composer, pianist; b. July 17, 1952, Boston, Mass. His mother studied violin and sang in choruses in her native Panama; his father played both classical and jazz clarinet in high school and college and studied composition at Boston Univ. before majoring in physics. When Donal was eight years old, he began piano lessons privately and began to improvise with his father, then studied piano at the New England Cons. until he was 19. At the age of 22, Fox and Reginald Hubbard initiated a concert series featuring Fox's early compositions. Under the direction of pianist Vivian Taylor, the chamber group Videmus performed Fox's

music and a two-piano work, "Dialectics," was commissioned by Ms. Taylor. Other chamber groups followed suit. He was awarded a two-year residency with the St. Louis Symphony (1991–93), was special guest of the Library of Congress (1993–94 season), a visiting artist at Harvard Univ. (1993–94), and was awarded the Guggenheim Fellowship in Music Composition (l997). He has performed and recorded duets with jazz artists Oliver Lake, John Stubblefield, David Murray, Billy Pierce, and with poet Quincy Troupe. He has also broadcast on the National Public Radio program *JazzSet*, and two 1993 programs of the PBS television show *Say, Brother*: "Donal Fox and David Murray in Session" and "The Fox/Troupe Duo in Performance and Rehearsal." In 1998 he performed at the Regattabar in Cambridge, Mass. with John Stubblefield, Kenny Davis, and Pheeroan Aklaff.

DISC.: *Variants on a Theme by Monk* (l990); *Etched in Stone* (1993); *Ugly Beauty* (1993); *Gone City* (1994).—LP

Fox, Frederick (Alfred), American composer and teacher; b. Detroit, Jan. 17, 1931. He received training in saxophone from Laurence Teal and in theory and arranging from Ray McConnell. He then pursued studies in composition with Ruth Shaw Wylie at Wayne State Univ. in Detroit (B.M., 1953), Ross Lee Finney at the Univ. of Mich. in Ann Arbor (1953–54), and Bernhard Heiden at Ind. Univ. in Bloomington (M.M., 1957; D.M.A., 1959). After teaching at Franklin (Ind.) Coll. (1959–61) and Sam Houston State Univ. in Huntsville, Tex. (1961–62), he was composer-in-residence of the Minneapolis Public Schools (1962–63). In 1964 he joined the faculty of Calif. State Univ. at Hayward, where he was chairman of the music dept. (1970–72) and prof. of composition (1972–74). In 1974–75 he was a visiting prof. of composition at Ind. Univ, and in 1975 became prof. of composition there. He also was founder-director of its New Music Ensemble and from 1981 to 1994 was chairman of its composition dept. Fox's music reflects his interest in jazz, improvisation, and serialism.

WORKS: ORCH.: Violin Concerto (1971); *Ternion* for Oboe and Orch. (1972); *Variables 5* (1974); *Beyond Winterlock* (1977); *Night Ceremonies* (1979); *Tracings* (1981); *Januaries* (1984); Fanfare for Wind and Percussion Orch. (1984); *Now and Then* for Chamber Orch. (1985); *In the Elsewhere* (1986); *Polarities* for Symphonic Band (1987); *Mystic Dances* for Chamber Orch. (1990); *Dark Moons/Bright Shadows* (1991); *Echo Blues* (1992); *3 Epigrams* for Concert Band (1993); Concerto for Symphonic Band (1994). CHAMBER: *Quantic* for Woodwind Quintet (1969); *Variations* for Violin, Cello, and Piano (1970); *Ad Rem* for Guitar (1970); *Matrix* for Cello, Strings, and Percussion (1972); *Variables 1* for Violin and Piano (1972), *2* for Flute (1973), *3* for Flute, Clarinet, Horn, Violin, Cello, and Piano (1973), *4* for Clarinet (1973), and *6* for Flute, Clarinet, Violin, Cello, and Percussion (1975); Quartet for Violin, Piano, and Percussion (1974); *Connex* for Brass Ensemble (1974); *Tria* for Flute, Piano, and Percussion (1975); *Ambient Shadows* for 8 Instrumentalists (1978); *S.A.X.* for Alto Saxophone and Saxophone Quartet (1979); *Annexus* for Alto Saxophone and Piano (1980); *Sonaspheres 1* for 10 Instrumentalists (1980), *2: Nexus* for Flute, Viola, Cello, and Piano (1983), *3: Ensphere* for 6 Instrumentalists (1983), *4: Tromper* for Trumpet, Trombone, and Percussion (1983), and *5* for 10 Instrumentalists (1983); *Bren* for Brass Ensemble (1982);

Gaber! for 6 Percussionists (1982); *Visitations* for 2 Saxophones (1982); *Dawnen Grey* for String Quartet (1984); *Fanfare '84* for 5 Trumpets, 4 Horns, 4 Trombones, and Tuba (1984); *Vis-a-vis* for Horn and String Quartet (1985); *Shaking the Pumpkin* for Saxophone, Piano, and 2 Percussionists (1986); *3 Diversions* for Saxophone Quartet (1987); *Silver Skeins* for 9 Flutes (1987); *Upon the Reedy Stream* for Oboe and String Quartet (1987); *Nightscenes* for Strings, Harp, Piano or Celesta, and 5 Percussionists (1988); *Time Messages* for Brass Quintet (1988); *Flight of Fantasy* for Cello and Piano (1988); *Auras* for Flute, Clarinet, Cello, Piano, and Percussion (1988); *The Avenging Spirit* for Saxophone Quartet (1989); *Fantasy* for Woodwind Quintet and Piano (1989); *Devil's Tramping Ground* for 7 Instrumentalists (1991); *Hear Again in Memory* for Saxophone (1991); *Sing Down the Moon* for Clarinet and Piano (1992); *Echoes and Shadows* for Violin and Piano (1993); *Fantasy* for Viola and Piano (1993); *Time Weaving* for Clarinet Trio (1993); *Kokopelli* for Flute and Piano (1994); *Dreamcatcher* for 13 Instrumentalists for the 175th anniversary of the founding of Ind. Univ. (1994). **VOCAL:** *A Stone, a Leaf, and Unfound Door* for Soprano, Chorus, Clarinet, and Percussion (1966–68); *The Descent* for Chorus, Piano, and 2 Percussionists (1969); *Time Excursions* for Soprano, Speaker, and 7 Instrumentalists (1976); *Nilrem's Odyssey* for Baritone/Speaker and Chorus (1980); *A Threat* for Soprano and Viola (1981).—**NS/LK/DM**

Fox, Virgil (Keel), famous American organist; b. Princeton, Ill., May 3, 1912; d. West Palm Beach, Fla., Oct. 25, 1980. He studied piano as a child, but soon turned to the organ as his favorite instrument. He played the organ at the First Presbyterian Church in his hometown at the age of 10, and gave his first public recital in Cincinnati at 14. He then enrolled in the Peabody Cons. of Music in Baltimore, graduating in 1932. To perfect his playing he went to Paris, where he took lessons with Dupré at St. Sulpice and Vierne at Notre Dame. He returned to the U.S. in 1938 and became head of the organ dept. at the Peabody Cons. of Music. From 1946 to 1965 he was organist at the Riverside Church in N.Y., where he played on a 5-manual, 10,561-pipe organ specially designed for him. He then launched a remarkable career as an organ soloist. He was the first American to play at the Thomaskirche in Leipzig, and also played at Westminster Abbey in London. As a solo artist, he evolved an idiosyncratic type of performance in which he embellished Baroque music with Romantic extravaganza; he also took to apostrophizing his audiences in a whimsical mixture of lofty sentiment and disarming self-deprecation. This type of personalized art endeared him to the impatient, emancipated musical youth of America, and he became one of the few organists who could fill a concert hall. He also displayed a robust taste for modern music; he often played the ear-stopping, discordant arrangement of America by Charles Ives. Wracked by cancer, he gave his last concert in Dallas on Sept. 26, 1980.—**NS/LK/DM**

Fox Strangways, A(rthur) H(enry), noted English writer on music and editor; b. Norwich, Sept. 14, 1859; d. Dinton, near Salisbury, May 2, 1948. He studied at Wellington Coll., London; received his M.A. in 1882 from Balliol Coll., Oxford, and then was a schoolmaster at Dulwich Coll. (1884–86) and Wellington Coll. (1887–1910). From 1911 to 1925 he wrote music criticism for the *Times* of London, and in 1925 he became music critic of the *Observer*. In 1920 he founded the quarterly journal *Music & Letters*, which he ed. until 1937. He was a specialist on Indian music and wrote several books on the subject, including *The Music of Hindostan* (Oxford, 1914); he also publ. a collection of essays, *Music Observed* (London, 1936), and a biography of Cecil Sharp (with M. Karpeles; London, 1933; 2nd ed., 1955). He contributed the article "Folk-Song" to the introductory vol. of *The Oxford History of Music* (London, 1929).—**NS/LK/DM**

Frackenpohl, Arthur (Roland), American composer and teacher; b. Irvington, N.J., April 23, 1924. He studied with Rogers at the Eastman School of Music in Rochester, N.Y. (B.A., 1947; M.A., 1949), took courses with Milhaud at the Berkshire Music Center in Tanglewood (summer, 1948) and with Boulanger in Fontainebleau (1950), and then completed his studies at McGill Univ. in Montreal (D.M.A., 1957). He became a teacher at the Crane School of Music at the State Univ. of N.Y. at Potsdam (1949); was a prof. there (1961–85). He publ. *Harmonization at the Piano* (1962; 6th ed., 1990).

WORKS: CHAMBER Opera: *Domestic Relations* ("To Beat or Not to Beat"), after O. Henry (1964). **ORCH.:** *Allegro giocoso* for Band (1956); *A Jubilant Overture* (1957); *Allegro scherzando* (1957); *Overture* (1957); Sym. for Strings (1960); *Largo and Allegro* for Horn and Strings (1962); *Short Overture* (1965); Concertino for Tuba and Strings (1967); Suite for Trumpet and Strings (1970); *American Folk Song Suite* for Band (1973); *Flute Waltz* for 3 Flutes and Orch. (1979); Concerto for Brass Quintet and Strings (1986). **CHAMBER:** Brass Quartet (1950); 2 brass quintets (1963, 1972); Trombone Quartet (1967); Brass Trio (1967); String Quartet (1971); *Breviates* for Brass Ensemble (1973); Trio for Oboe, Horn, and Bassoon (1982); Tuba Sonata (1983); piano pieces. **VOCAL:** *The Natural Superiority of Men,* cantata for Women's Voices and Piano (1962); (7) *Essays on Women,* cantata for Soloists, Chorus, and Piano (1967); *Meet Job,* 3 litanies for 4 Voices and Winds (1978); *A Child This Day,* cantata for Soloists, Chorus, Narrator, Brass Quartet, and Organ (1980); Mass for Chorus and Orch. (1990); song cycles. —**NS/LK/DM**

Fraenkel, Wolfgang, German composer; b. Berlin, Oct. 10, 1897; d. Los Angeles, March 8, 1983. He studied violin, piano, and theory at the Klindworth-Scharwenka Cons. in Berlin; at the same time, he took courses in jurisprudence and was a judge in Berlin until the advent of the Nazi regime in 1933. He was interned in the Sachsenhausen concentration camp, but as a 50 percent Jew (his mother was an Aryan, as was his wife), he was released in 1939, and went to China, where he enjoyed the protection of Chiang Kai-shek, who asked him to organize music education in Nanking and Shanghai. In 1947 he emigrated to the U.S. and settled in Los Angeles. He earned a living by composing background music for documentary films in Hollywood, supplementing his income by copying music (he had a calligraphic handwriting). Fraenkel's music was evolved from the standard German traditions, but at a later period he began to experiment with serial methods of composition. His 3rd string quartet (1960) won the

Queen Elisabeth of Belgium Prize and his *Symphonische Aphorismen* (1965) won 1st prize at the International Competition of the City of Milan. His works, both publ. and in MS, were deposited in the Moldenhauer Archive in Spokane, Wash.

WORKS: DRAMATIC: Opera: *Der brennende Dornbusch* (1924–27). **ORCH.:** Flute Concerto (1930); *Frescobaldi*, transcription for Orch. of 5 organ pieces by Frescobaldi (1957); *Symphonische Aphorismen* (1965). **CHAMBER:** 3 string quartets (1924, 1949, 1960); Cello Sonata (1934); Violin Sonata (1935); Sonata for Solo Violin (1954); *Variations and a Fantasy on a Theme by Schoenberg* for Piano (1954); Viola Sonata (1963); *Klavierstück* for Tape and Piano (1964); String Quintet (1976). **VOCAL:** *Der Wegweiser*, cantata (1931); *Filippo* for Speaker and Orch. (1948); *Joseph* for Baritone and Orch., to a text by Thomas Mann (1968); *Missa aphoristica* for Chorus and Orch. (1973).—**NS/LK/DM**

Frager, Malcolm (Monroe), outstanding American pianist; b. St. Louis, Jan. 15, 1935; d. Pittsfield, Mass., June 20, 1991. He commenced piano lessons at a very early age and made his recital debut in St. Louis when he was only 6. He continued his training there with Carl Madlinger (1942–49). At 10, he appeared as soloist in Mozart's 17th Piano Concerto, K.453, with Golschmann and the St. Louis Sym. Orch. He subsequently pursued his studies with Carl Friedberg in N.Y. (1949–55), and attended the American Cons. in Fontainebleau (1951–52), where he won the Prix d'Excellence; he also majored in Russian at Columbia Univ., taking his B.A. in 1957. After capturing the highest honors at the Geneva (1955), Leventritt (N.Y., 1959), and Queen Elisabeth of Belgium (Brussels, 1960) competitions, he toured throughout the world with enormous success. Frager was an extraordinary virtuoso who tempered his brilliant technique with a profound sensitivity. His repertory ranged from Haydn to the moderns, and included such rare works as the original versions of the Schumann Piano Concerto and Tchaikovsky's 1st Piano Concerto.—**NS/LK/DM**

Framery, Nicolas Étienne, French composer, writer on music, and poet; b. Rouen, March 25, 1745; d. Paris, Nov. 26, 1810. He composed the text and music for the comic opera *La Sorcière par hasard* (1768); its performance at Villeroy earned him the position of superintendent of music with the Count of Artois. The opera was performed at the Comédie-Italienne (Paris, Sept. 3, 1783), but suffered a fiasco because of the antagonism against Italian opera generated by the adherents of Gluck. He also wrote librettos for Sacchini, Salieri, Paisiello, Anfossi, and other Italian composers; ed. the *Journal de Musique* (1770–78) and *Calendrier Musical Universel* (1788–89) in Paris. He compiled, together with Ginguené and Feytou, the musical part of vol. I of *Encyclopédie méthodique* (1791; vol. II by Momigny, 1818); besides smaller studies, he wrote *De la nécessité du rythme et de la césure dans les hymnes ou odes destinées à la musique* (1796); tr. into French *Azopardi's Musico prattico*, as *Le Musicien pratique* (2 vols., 1786).

BIBL.: J. Carlez, *F.: Littérateur-musicien* (Caen, 1893). —**NS/LK/DM**

Frampton, Peter, guitarist who gained initial recognition in the late 1960s with the British band The Herd, and was introduced to American audiences during his membership in Humble Pie; b. Beckenham, Kent, England, April 22, 1950. Acknowledged as an early hard-rock romanticist for his early-1970s recordings, Frampton broke through with the totally unexpected success of 1976's *Frampton Comes Alive!*, which prominently featured his use of the voice-box, a synthesizer-type device that seemed to make words emanate from his guitar. The album became both the best-selling live album and the best-selling double-record set in music history, eventually selling more than 15 million copies worldwide. However, his career faded quickly after the followup album, due perhaps to his unfortunate appearance in the inane *Sgt. Pepper's Lonely Hearts Club Band* movie with the Bee Gees, and a serious automobile accident in 1978.

Peter Frampton got his first guitar at age eight and debuted professionally at 12. By 16 he was a member of The Herd, who scored several British hits and recorded one album for Fontana Records. In late 1968 Frampton left The Herd to form Humble Pie with ex—Small Face guitarist-vocalist Steve Marriott, ex—Spooky Tooth bassist Greg Ridley, and drummer Jerry Shirley. After two albums for Andrew Oldham's Immediate label, Humble Pie began displaying a harder and louder sound at A&M Records, thus thwarting Frampton's gentler, more romantic style. He quit the group before their breakthrough with the live set *Rockin' at the Fillmore*.

Peter Frampton then pursued session work, assisting in the recording of George Harrison's *All Things Must Pass* and Harry Nilsson's *Son of Schmilsson*. He recorded his debut solo album in 1972, and formed Frampton's Camel for one album and an American tour before disbanding the group in 1974. His first album to sell in significant quantities in the U.S., 1975's *Frampton*, contained the unsuccessful singles "Show Me the Way" and "Baby, I Love Your Way."

Peter Frampton finally broke through in the U.S. with the live double-record set *Frampton Comes Alive!*, recorded at San Francisco's Winterland on June 14, 1975. Compiling much of his earlier material, the album yielded the smash hit "Show Me the Way" and the near-smashes "Baby, I Love Your Way" and "Do You Feel Like We Do" and included "All I Want to Be (Is by Your Side)." "Do You Feel Like We Do" featured Frampton using a so-called voice-box, a device which sent the electric guitar signal through a tube in his mouth, making the guitar "sing" synthesized words. The album took critics totally by surprise and stayed on the album charts for nearly two years, eventually selling 15 million copies. Frampton instantly (if temporarily) became a superstar, playing to stadium audiences throughout the summer of 1976 and into 1977.

Peter Frampton's follow-up album, *I'm in You*, produced a smash hit with the title song, but subsequent singles fared progressively less well. During 1977 and 1978 he worked on the $12 million Robert Stigwood film production of *Sgt. Pepper's Lonely Hearts Club Band*. Costarring with the Bee Gees, Frampton filled the role of Billy Shears in this abysmal fairytale-like musical featuring 29 Beatles songs. Poorly received by critics and the public alike, the movie was quickly relegated to the cheap-movie-house circuit. To add injury to insult, Frampton was severely hurt in an automobile accident on June 29, 1978, in the Bahamas that necessitated an extended period of recuperation.

Peter Frampton's career never regained its momentum. Albums sold progressively less well and he played small venues rather than baseball stadiums on tour. After a four-year hiatus he returned in 1986 with another album and a tour opening for Stevie Nicks. He performed as guest guitarist on David Bowie's 1987 *Never Let Me Down* album and the following Glass Spider tour. In 1989 he recorded another unsuccessful album. Frampton began collaborating again with Steve Marriott, in 1991, but Marriott died in a house fire that April 20th. Peter Frampton toured again in 1992 and 1995.

DISC.: THE HERD: *Lookin' Through You* (1968); *The Herd Featuring P. F.* (1994). **PETER FRAMPTON:** *Wind of Change* (1972); *Frampton's Camel* (1973); *Somethin's Happening* (1974); *Frampton* (1975); *Frampton Comes Alive!* (1976); *I'm in You* (1977); *Where Should I Be* (1979); *Breaking All the Rules* (1981); *The Art of Control* (1982); *Premonition* (1986); *When All the Pieces Fit* (1989); *P. F.*; *Shine On: A Collection* (1992).

BIBL.: Marsha Daly, *P. F.* (N.Y., 1978); Irene Adler, *P. F.* (N.Y., 1979).—BH

Françaix, Jean, significant French composer; b. Le Mans, May 23, 1912; d. Paris, Sept. 25, 1997. He was born into a musical family. His father was a composer and pianist who served as director of the Le Mans Cons., and his mother taught voice. He settled in Paris, where he studied at the Cons., taking the premier prix in 1930. His mentor in composition was Nadia Boulanger. Although he made some appearances as a pianist, principally as a exponent of his own works, he devoted himself mainly to composition. In his large output, he demonstrated his remarkable craftsmanship in writing scores with Gallic refinement and wit.

WORKS: DRAMATIC: Opera: *Le diable boîteux,* comic chamber opera (1937; Paris, June 30, 1938); *L'Apostrophe,* musical comedy after Balzac (1940; Amsterdam, July 1, 1951); *La main gloire* (1945; Bordeaux, May 18, 1951); *Paris à nous deux (ou Le Nouveau Rastignac),* comic opera (Fontainebleau, Aug. 7, 1954); *La princesse de Clèves* (1961–65; Rouen, Dec. 11, 1965). **Ballet:** *Beach* (Monte Carlo, April 18, 1933); *Scuola di Ballo* (Monte Carlo, April 25, 1933); *Le roi nu* (1935; Paris, June 15, 1936); *Les malheurs de Sophie* (1935; Paris, Feb. 25, 1948); *La lutherie enchantée* (Antwerp, March 21, 1936); *Le jugement d'un fou* (1937; London, Feb. 6, 1938); *Verreries de Venise* (1938; Paris, June 22, 1939); *Les demoiselles de la nuit* (Paris, May 20, 1948); *Die Kamelien* (Wiesbaden, Oct. 15, 1950); *A la Française* (N.Y., Sept. 11, 1951); *Le Roi Midas* (1952); *La dame dans la lune* (1957–58; Paris, Feb. 18, 1958); *Adages et Variations* (Paris, Dec. 10, 1965); *Le Croupier amoureux* (1967); *Pierrot ou Les Secrets de la nuit* (1980; Salzburg, March 27, 1988). **ORCH.:** 2 syms.: No. 1 (Paris, Nov. 6, 1932) and No. 2 (La Jolla, Calif., Aug. 9, 1953); Piano Concertino (1932; Paris, Feb. 13, 1934); *Sérénade* for Small Orch. (1934); Suite for Violin and Orch. (1934; Paris, Nov. 27, 1937); *Fantaisie* for Cello and Orch. (Paris, May 23, 1935; new version, 1951); *Divertissement* for Violin, Viola, Cello, and Orch. (Paris, Dec. 22, 1935); Quadruple Concerto for Flute, Oboe, Clarinet, Bassoon, and Orch. (1935; Paris, Jan. 22, 1936); Piano Concerto

(Berlin, Nov. 3, 1936); *Musique de cour,* duo concertante for Flute, Violin, and Orch. (Paris, Dec. 2, 1937); *Divertissement* for Bassoon and Strings (1942; Schwetzingen, May 5, 1968; also for Bassoon and String Quintet); *Rhapsodie* for Viola and Small Orch. (1945; London, Jan. 1946); *La douce France* (Paris, Nov. 21, 1946); *Les bosquets de Cythère,* 7 waltzes (1946; Paris, July 8, 1947); *L'heure du berger* for Piano and Strings (1947); *Symphonie d'archets* for Strings (BBC, London, Nov. 1948); *Les zigues de mars* (Paris, Feb. 19, 1950); *Variations de Concert* for Cello and Strings (1950; 1st perf. in a recording, Paris, Sept. 15, 1952); *Scuola de ballo,* suite after the ballet (1950; Clichy-la-Garenne, Feb. 25, 1968); *Si Versailles m'était conté* (Paris, May 5, 1954); *Sérénade BEA* for Strings (1955; Paris, Feb. 23, 1966); *Au musée Grévin,* suite (Paris, March 1, 1956); *Six grandes marches* (Paris, June 25, 1957; also for Piano); Harpsichord Concerto (1959; Paris, Feb. 7, 1960); *L'Horloge de flore* for Oboe and Orch. (1959; Philadelphia, March 31, 1961); *Divertimento* for Horn and Orch. (1959; Paris, March 13, 1968; also for Horn and Piano, Paris, March 15, 1968); *Le dialogue des carmélites,* symphonic suite (1960; Paris, April 4, 1969); *Sei preludi* for Small String Orch. (1963; Lucerne, Sept. 3, 1964); Concerto for 2 Pianos and Orch. (Maastricht, Nov. 26, 1965); Flute Concerto (1966; Schwetzingen, May 13, 1967); Clarinet Concerto (1967; Nice, July 30, 1968); 2 violin concertos: No. 1 (1968; Quebec, Jan. 26, 1970; rev. version, Paris, Nov. 22, 1970) and No. 2 for Violin and Chamber Orch. (Braunschweig, Nov. 30, 1979); *Jeu poétique en six mouvements* for Harp and Orch. (1969; Dresden, Oct. 12, 1972); *Thème et variations* (1971; Bochum, Dec. 12, 1974); *15 Portraits d'enfants d'Auguste Renoir* for Strings (Paris, May 25, 1972; also for Piano, 4-Hands, 1971); *La ville mystérieuse* (1973; Nuremberg, March 15, 1974); Double Bass Concerto (Frankfurt am Main, Nov. 1, 1974); *Divertimento* for Flute and Chamber Orch. (Braunschweig, Nov. 29, 1974); *Le gay Paris* for Trumpet and Winds (1974; Wiesbaden, April 27, 1975); *Cassazione* for 3 Orchs. (Salzburg, Aug. 12, 1975); *Prélude, Sarabande et Gigue* for Trumpet and Orch. (1975–86; also for Trumpet and Piano); Concerto grosso for Flute, Oboe, Clarinet, Bassoon, Horn, String Quintet, and Orch. (1976; Mainz, Feb. 6, 1977); *Tema con variazioni* for Clarinet and Strings (Florence, Sept. 14, 1978); Concerto for 2 Harps and 11 Strings (1978; Schwetzingen, May 11, 1979); *Ouverture anacréontique* (1978; Recklinghausen, Feb. 22, 1981); Concerto for Bassoon and 11 Strings (1979; Frankfurt am Main, May 20, 1980; also for Bassoon and Piano); Concerto for Guitar and Strings (1982–83; Schwetzingen, May 25, 1984); Concerto for Trombone and 10 Winds (1983); *Impromptu* for Flute and Strings (Paris, Sept. 8, 1983); *Ode à la Liberté* for Wind Orch., Timpani, Percussion, Celesta, and Harp (1985); *Pavane pour un génie vivant* (Montpellier, July 23, 1987); Concerto for 15 Soloists, Timpani, and Strings or Orch., *Suivi d'une surprise* (1988; Vienna, May 16, 1990); *85 mesures et un Da capo* for Small Orch. (1991); Double Concerto for Flute, Clarinet, and Orch. (1991; Schwetzingen, June 8, 1992); Accordion Concerto (1993; Montreux, Nov. 18, 1994). **CHAMBER:** Trio for Violin, Viola, and Cello (1933); Septet for Flute, Oboe, Bassoon, 2 Violins, Cello, and Piano (Paris, June 20, 1933); Quartet for Flute, Oboe, Clarinet, and Bassoon (1933; Paris, April 26, 1936); 2 quintets for Flute, Violin, Viola, Cello, and Harp: No. 1 (1934; Paris, May 24, 1935) and No. 2 (1989; Berlin, Oct. 15, 1992); Sonatine for Piano and Violin (1934; Paris, Feb. 17, 1936); *Petit Quatuor* for 4 Saxophones (1935; also for 2 Clarinets, Basset Horn, and Bass Clarinet, 1992; Itzehoe, July 23, 1993); Quartet for 2 Violins, Viola, and Cello (1938); *Divertissement* for Bassoon and String Quintet (1942; also for Bassoon and String Orch., Schwetzingen, May 5, 1968); *Divertissement* for Oboe, Clarinet, and Bassoon (1946; Paris, Jan.

26, 1947); 2 quintets for Flute, Oboe, Clarinet, Bassoon, and Horn: No. 1 (1948; Paris, Dec. 2, 1954) and No. 2 (Neumünster, July 18, 1987); *Les vacances* for 2 Violins, Cello and Piano (Paris, Dec. 1953); *Divertimento* for Flute and Piano (1953; Paris, Jan. 12, 1955); *Divertimento* for Horn and Piano (1959; Paris, March 15, 1968; also for Horn and Orch., Paris, March 13, 1968); *Scuola di cello* for 10 Cellos (1960); *Cinq danses exotiques* for Alto Saxophone and Piano (1961; Paris, Feb. 21, 1967); Suite for Flute (Paris, May 5, 1962); Quartet for English Horn, Violin, Viola, and Cello (1970; London, March 21, 1971); Trio for Flute, Harp, and Cello (1971); Octet for Clarinet, Horn, Bassoon, 2 Violins, Viola, Cello, and Double Bass (Vienna, Nov. 7, 1972); *9 Pièces caractéristiques* for 2 Flutes, 2 Oboes, 2 Clarinets, 2 Bassoons, and 2 Horns (1973; Schwetzingen, May 8, 1974); *Tema con variazioni* for Clarinet and Piano (Paris, May 31, 1974); *Aubade* for 12 Cellos (1974; Berlin, Sept. 30, 1975); *Cinque piccoli duetti* for Harp and Flute (1975); *Prélude, Sarabande et Gigue* for Trumpet and Piano (1975–86; also for Trumpet and Orch.); *Thème varié* for Double Bass (Paris, June 17, 1976); *Variations sur un thème plaisant* for Piano and Wind Ensemble (1976; Mainz, May 9, 1977); *Chaconne* for Harp and 11 Strings (1976; Gargilesse, Sept. 1, 1977); Quintet for Clarinet, 2 Violins, Viola, and Cello (1977; Munich, June 18, 1978); *Sept impromptus* for Flute and Bassoon (1977; Seattle, Oct. 12, 1978); Suite for Harp (1978); *Serenata* for Guitar (1978; Florence, Nov. 19, 1986); *Les petits Paganini* for Solo Violin and 4 Violins (1979); *Petite valse européenne* for Tuba and Double Wind Quintet (1979; Schwetzingen, May 14, 1980); *Tema con 8 variazioni* for Violin (1980; Paris, March 19, 1981); *Duo baroque* for Double Bass and Harp (1980; Frankfurt am Main, Aug. 11, 1982); *8 Bagatelles* for String Quartet and Piano (1980; Montreal, Jan. 16, 1983); *Danses Exotiques* for 11 Winds and Percussion (1981; Landau, Oct. 29, 1982); *Mozart new-look* for Double Bass and Winds (1981; Kloster Eberbach, June 5, 1983); *Onze Variations* for 9 Winds and Double Bass (Kloster Eberbach, June 6, 1982); Sonata for Recorder and Guitar (1984; Paris, Oct. 23, 1986); *Hommage à l'ami Papageno* for Piano and Wind Ensemble, after Mozart (1984; Wiesbaden, Oct. 11, 1987); *Passacaille* for Guitar (Geneva, March 1, 1985); Trio for Violin, Cello, and Piano (1986; Cheltenham, July 11, 1987); *Noël nouvelet"—et "Il est ne, le Devin Enfant* for 12 Cellos (1987); *Dixtour*, double quintet for Winds and Strings (Kissingen, July 8, 1987); *Notturno* for 4 Horns (Mainz, May 21, 1987); Quintet for Recorder, 2 Violins, Cello, and Harpsichord (London, April 12, 1988); *Le Colloque des deux perruches* for Flute and Alto Flute (1989); Trio for Clarinet, Viola, and Piano (1990); Suite for 4 Saxophones (Boutigny-sur-Essone, Oct. 20, 1990); *Elégie* for Wind Ensemble (1990; Schwetzingen, May 18, 1991); Wind Sextet (1991; Neumünster, July 3, 1992); *Pour remercier l'Auditoire* for Flute, Clarinet, Horn, Violin, Cello, and Piano (1994; Tokyo, Jan. 21, 1995); Quartet for Clarinet, Basset Horn, Bass Clarinet, and Piano (1994; Husum, July 1, 1995); Trio for Oboe, Bassoon, and Piano (1994; Rotterdam, Aug. 29, 1995); Trio for Flute, Cello, and Piano (1995; Fautenbach, Sept. 26, 1998); *Deux pièces* for Bassoon and Piano (Paris, May 8, 1996); Flute Sonata (1996; Chicago, Aug. 15, 1997); *Celestes Schubertiades* for 2 Flutes, 2 Oboes, 2 Clarinets, 2 Bassoon, and 2 Horns, after Schubert (1996; Meran, April 4, 1997). **KEYBOARD: P i a n o :** *Scherzo* (Paris, March 5, 1932); *Cinq portraits de jeunes filles* (1936; Mans, Oct. 26, 1938); *Éloge de la danse* (1947; Montreux, Sept. 15, 1954); *Si Versailles m'était conté...* (1953); *Napoléon* for Piano, 4-Hands (1954; Paris, April 23, 1955); *Six grandes marches* (1957; also for Orch., Paris, June 25, 1957); *Huit danses exotiques* for 2 Pianos (Paris, Nov. 15, 1957); *Danse des trois arlequins* (1958); Sonata (1960); *Cinq "Bis"* (1965; Schwetzingen, May 16, 1986); *Scuola de Ballo*, after the ballet (1966); *15 Portraits d'enfants d'Auguste Renoir* for Piano, 4-Hands (1971; also for String Orch., Paris, May 25, 1972); *Zehn Stücke für Kinder zum Spielen und Träumen* (1975); *Acht Variationen über den Namen Johannes Gutenberg* (Mainz, Dec. 2, 1982); *La Promenade d'un Musicologue Eclectique* (1987; Rouen, May 2, 1990); *Nocturne* (Paris, June 30, 1994). **O r g a n :** *Marche solennelle* (1956); *Suite carmelite* (1960); *Suite profane* (1984); *Messe de Mariage* (Oberalm, Aug. 5, 1988). **H a r p s i c h o r d :** *L'Insectarium* (1953; Royaumont, July 14, 1957); *Deux pièces* (1977). **VOCAL:** *Cinq chansons pour les enfants* for Children's Chorus and Orch. (1932); *Trois épigrammes* for Chorus and String Quintet or String Orch. (Nantes, Nov. 30, 1938; also for Soprano or Tenor and Piano); *L'Apocalypse selon St. Jean*, fantastic oratorio for 4 Soloists, Chorus, and 2 Orchs. (1939; Paris, June 11, 1942); *L'Adolescene clémentine* for Voice and Piano (1941); *Cinq poèmes de Charles d'Orléans* for Voice and Piano (1946); *Invocation à la volupté* for Baritone and Orch. (1946); *Juvenalia* for Soprano, Alto, Tenor, Bass, and Piano, 4-Hands (1947); *Prière du soir—Chanson* for Voice and Guitar or Piano (1947); *Huit anecdotes de Chamfort* for Low Voice and Piano (Royaumont, June 26, 1949); *Scherzo impromptu* for Voice and Piano (N.Y., Nov. 6, 1949); *La cantate de Méphisto* for Bass and String Orch. (1952; N.Y., Jan. 25, 1953); *Deploration de tonton*, humorous cantata for Mezzo-soprano and String Orch. (1956); *La chatte blanche* for Tenor and Piano (Aix-en- Provence, July 27, 1957); *Le grenouille qui veut se faire aussi grosse que le boef* for Soprano or Tenor and Piano (1963); *Le coq et le renard* for Men's Chorus or Men's Vocal Quartet and Piano (1963); *Les inestimables chroniques du bon geant Gargantua* for Speaker and String Orch. (Paris, May 17, 1971); *La promenade à Versailles*, cantata for 4 Men's Voices and 11 Strings (1976); *La Cantate des Vieillards* for Tenor, Bass, and Strings (1978); *Psyché* for Speaker and Orch. (1981; Radio Geneva, Sept. 3, 1982); *Trois Poèmes de Paul Valéry* for Chorus (1982; Darmstadt, June 29, 1984); *Triade de toujours* for Soprano, Baritone, Wind Quintet, String Quintet, and Harp (1991; Bad Urach, Sept. 28, 1992); *Neuf Historiettes* for Baritone, Tenor Saxophone, and Piano (Paris, May 25, 1997). **OTHER:** Film scores.

BIBL.: M. Lanjean, *J. F.* (Paris, 1961).—NS/LK/DM

Francescatti, Zino (actually, René-Charles),

eminent French violinist; b. Marseilles, Aug. 9, 1902; d. La Ciotat, Sept. 17, 1991. He studied with his father René, a violinist and cellist, and with his mother Erneste, a violinist. When he was only 5, he made his public debut in a recital. At age 10, he appeared as soloist in the Beethoven Violin Concerto. After making his Paris debut in 1925, he toured England in duo recitals with Ravel in 1926. He soon established himself as a virtuoso via tours of Europe and South America. On Nov. 18, 1939, he made his U.S. debut as soloist in Paganini's 1st Violin Concerto with Barbirolli and the N.Y. Phil. After the close of World War II in 1945, he pursued an outstanding international career until his retirement in 1976. He then sold his celebrated "Hart" Stradivarius of 1727 and established the Zino Francescatti Foundation in La Ciotat to assist young violinists. In 1987 an international violin competition was organized in his honor in Aix-en-Provence. Francescatti's playing was marked by a seemingly effortless technique, warmth of expression, and tonal elegance. —NS/LK/DM

Francesch, Homero, Uruguayan pianist; b. Montevideo, Dec. 6, 1947. He studied piano with Santiago Baranda Reyes, then took piano lessons in Munich with Maria Hindemith-Landes and Steurer. Following concerts in West Germany, he began an international career. He appeared as soloist with the Berlin Phil., London Sym., Vienna Sym., Orchestre National de France of Paris, and other leading orchs.—NS/LK/DM

Franceschini, Petronio, Italian composer; b. Bologna, c. 1650; d. Venice, Dec. 18?, 1680. His brother was the painter M.A. Franceschini. After studies with Lorenzo Perti, he completed his training with Giuseppe Corsi in Rome. He was one of the first members of the Accademia Filarmonica in Bologna, and was its principe in 1673. He served as a cellist at the Cathedral (1675–80) and as maestro di cappella at the Arciconfraternità di S. Maria della Morte (1679–80) in Bologna.

> **WORKS: DRAMATIC: O p e r a :** *Le gare di Sdegno, d'Amore e di Gelosia* (Bologna, 1674); *L'Oronte di Menfi* (Bologna, Jan. 10, 1676); *Arsinoe* (Bologna, Dec. 26, 1676); *Apollo in Tessaglia* (Bologna, May 27, 1679); *Dionisio, overo La virtù trionfante del vitio* (Venice, Jan. 12, 1681; Act 1 by Franceschini; completed by G. Partenio). **S a c r e d :** 2 oratorios: *La vittima generosa* (Bologna, March 6, 1679) and *Gefte* (Ferrara, 1679); masses; Magnificat; motets; Psalms. **CHAMBER:** Sonata for 2 Violins and Basso Continuo (1680); Sonata a 7 for 2 Trumpets, Strings, Trombone, Organ, and Theorbo (ed. by E. Tarr, London, 1968).—LK/DM

Francesco Canova de Milano, Italian lutenist, viol player, and composer; b. Monza, Aug. 18, 1497; d. Milan, April 15, 1543. He was a pupil of Giovanni Testagrossa. For periods between 1516 and 1539 he was active in Rome as a lutenist and viol player to the papacy, and he also served Ippolito de' Medici and Cardinal Alessandro Farnese. His lute music—ricercares, fantasias, and arrangements of vocal pieces—comprises more than 40 tablatures (publ. 1536–1603) and 25 MSS. See A. Ness, ed., *The Lute Music of Francesco Canova da Milano (1497–1543)*, Harvard Publications in Music, III-IV (1970), and R. Chiesa, ed., *Francesco da Milano: Opere complete per liuto* (Milan, 1971).—LK/DM

Francés de Iribarren, Juan, Spanish organist and composer; b. Sangüessa, Navarre, 1698; d. Málaga, Sept. 2, 1767. He became organist at Salamanca Cathedral in 1717, serving as its asst. maestro de capilla (1732–33) and titular maestro (1733–66). He was a notable composer of villancicos, of which he wrote some 500.—LK/DM

Franchetti, Alberto, Italian composer; b. Turin, Sept. 18, 1860; d. Viareggio, Aug. 4, 1942. He studied in Turin with Niccolo Coccon and Fortunato Magi, then with Rheinberger in Munich and with Draeseke in Dresden. He devoted his entire life to composition, with the exception of a brief tenure as director of the Cherubini Cons. in Florence (1926–28). His most successful opera was *Germania* (Milan, March 11, 1902).

> **WORKS: DRAMATIC: O p e r a :** *Asrael* (Reggio Emilia, Feb. 11, 1888); *Cristoforo Colombo* (Genoa, Oct. 6, 1892); *Fior d'Alpe* (Milan, March 15, 1894); *Il Signor di Pourceaugnac* (Milan, April 10, 1897); *Germania* (Milan, March 11, 1902); *La Figlia di Jorio* (Milan, March 29, 1906); *Notte di leggenda* (Milan, Jan. 14, 1915); *Giove a Pompei* (Rome, June 5, 1921; in collaboration with Umberto Giordano); *Glauco* (Naples, April 8, 1922);. **OTHER:** Sym. (1886); symphonic poems: *Loreley* and *Nella selva nera*; *Inno* for Soli, Chorus, and Orch. (for the 800th anniversary of the Univ. of Bologna); several pieces of chamber music and songs.—NS/LK/DM

Franchomme, Auguste (-Joseph), famous French cellist; b. Lille, April 10, 1808; d. Paris, Jan. 21, 1884. He studied at the Lille Cons., then with Levasseur and Norblin at the Paris Cons. He then played cello in various opera houses, and in 1828 became solo cellist of the Royal Chapel and was a founding member of the Société des Concerts du Conservatoire. In 1846 he was appointed prof. at the Paris Cons. He was an intimate friend of Chopin, and with Hallé and Alard, established evenings of chamber music in Paris. He wrote cello pieces, mostly in variation form, and operatic potpourris.—NS/LK/DM

Franci, Benvenuto, Italian baritone, father of **Carlo Franci;** b. Pienza, near Siena, July 1, 1891; d. Rome, Feb. 27, 1985. He was a student of Cotogni and Rosati in Rome. In 1918 he made his operatic debut at Rome's Teatro Costanzi as Giannetto in Mascagni's *Lodoletta*, where he later sang in the premiere of that composer's *Il piccolo Marat* in 1921. In 1923 he sang Amonasro at Milan's La Scala, where he returned to sing in the premieres of Giordano's *Cena delle Beffe* in 1924 and Zandonai's *Cavalieri di Ekebù* in 1925. From 1928 to 1949 he was a principal member of the Rome Opera. He also made guest appearances at London's Covent Garden in 1925, 1931, and 1946. In 1955 he made his farewell appearance in Trieste. Among his other roles were Rigoletto, Macbeth, Gerard, Telramund, Barnaba, Barak, and Scarpia.—NS/LK/DM

Franci, Carlo, Italian conductor and composer, son of **Benvenuto Franci;** b. Buenos Aires, July 18, 1927. He went to Rome and studied composition with Turchi and Petrassi at the Cons. and conducting with Previtali at the Accademia di Santa Cecilia. After conducting the Radio Eireann Sym. Orch. in Dublin (1955–57) and the RAI in Rome (1961–63), he appeared with the Rome Opera. In 1968 he conducted the Rome Opera production of Rossini's *Otello* during its visit to the Metropolitan Opera in N.Y. On Feb. 1, 1969, he made his debut at the Metropolitan Opera conducting *Lucia di Lammermoor*, and remained on its roster until 1972. As a guest conductor, he appeared with opera houses in Milan, Berlin, Budapest, Munich, Madrid, Paris, Hamburg, Zürich et al. In 1988 he appeared as a guest conductor with the PACT (Performing Arts Council, Transvaal) Opera in Pretoria, where he subsequently served as principal conductor of the Transvaal Phil. Among his compositions are *4 Studies* for Orch. (1993) and the *African Oratorio* (1994).—NS/LK/DM

Francis, Connie (actually, **Concetta Franconero**), America's top-selling female recording artist of the late 1950s and early 1960s; b. Newark, N.J.,

Dec. 12, 1938. Connie Francis recorded popular up-tempo songs and heart-rending ballads during a time dominated by male acts. Rivaled at the time by only Brenda Lee, Francis charted more than 50 singles, a record eventually broken by Aretha Franklin. Moving firmly into the pop field in the 1960s, Connie Francis proved herself a survivor, eventually returning to touring and recording in the late 1980s after years of psychological problems brought on by her rape after a performance in 1974.

Concetta Franconero began accordion lessons at age three and sang at local functions as a child. In 1950 she won first place on the national television show *Talent Scouts*, hosted by Arthur Godfrey, who suggested that she change her name to Connie Francis. From 1950 to 1954 she performed weekly on the TV variety program *Startime*. Signed to MGM Records in 1955, Francis recorded 10 unsuccessful singles for the label before breaking through with the smash hit "Who's Sorry Now" in 1958. Originally popularized in 1923, the song was followed by the major hit "Stupid Cupid," written by Neil Sedaka and Howard Greenfield. Through 1964 she scored hits with standards such as "My Happiness," "Among My Souvenirs," "Mama," and "Together" and softly rocking contemporary songs such as "Lipstick on Your Collar," "Everybody's Somebody's Fool," and "My Heart Has a Mind of Its Own" (both top hits) and "Vacation." She also achieved hits with tearful ballads such as "Many Tears Ago," "Breakin' in a Brand New Broken Heart," "Don't Break the Heart that Loves You," and "Second Hand Love." During the first half of the 1960s she worked in four films, including *Where the Boys Are* and *Follow the Boys*, which featured her hit title songs.

Since 1960 Connie Francis had recorded albums of Italian, Spanish, Latin, and Jewish favorites that endeared her to the easy-listening audience. She turned to those fans to sustain her career as she faded from the charts after the advent of the Beatles. Francis recorded albums throughout the 1960s (including folk and country albums, even an album with Hank Williams Jr.) and toured into the 1970s.

However, after a performance at the Westbury Music Fair in N.Y. on Nov. 8, 1974, Francis was raped. She performed sporadically thereafter, enduring psychiatric treatment and confinement, a temporarily damaged voice, and the Mafia-style slaying of her brother. She made a much-publicized return appearance at Westbury in 1981, but her father had her committed, against her will, to a psychiatric hospital in 1983. Francis published her memoirs, *Who's Sorry Now*, in 1984, and eventually she regained her health. She returned to performing in 1989, adopting as her theme song the poignant "If I Never Sing Another Song." In 1992 Connie Francis's *Tourist in Paradise* was released on Liberty Records. The German label Bear Family issued a comprehensive box of her early recordings in 1993.

DISC.: CONNIE FRANCIS: *Who's Sorry Now* (1958); *Exciting C. F.* (1959); *My Thanks to You* (1959); *Italian Favorites* (1959); *Christmas in My Heart* (1959); *Greatest Hits* (1959); *Rock 'n' Roll Million Sellers* (1959); *Country and Western Golden Hits* (1960); *Spanish and Latin American Favorites* (1960); *Jewish Favor-ites* (1960); *More Italian Favorites* (1960); *Songs to a Swingin' Band* (1961); *At the Copa* (1961); *More Greatest Hits* (1961); *Never on Sunday* (1961); *Folk Song Favorites* (1961); *Irish Favorites* (1962); *Do the Twist* (1962); *Fun Songs* (1962); *Award Winning Motion Picture Hits* (1962); *C. F. Sings* (1962); *Country Music Connie Style* (1962); *More Italian Hits* (1963); *Follow the Boys* (1963); *Greatest American Waltzes* (1963); *Mala Femmena (Evil Woman)* (1963); *Very Best* (1963); *German Favorites* (1964); *In the Summer of His Years* (1964); *Looking for Love* (1964); *A New Kind of Connie* (1964); *Rocksides (1957–1964)* (1988); *Sings for Mama* (1965); *All-Time International Hits* (1965); *C. F.* (1965); *Folk Favorites* (1965); *When the Boys Meet the Girls* (1966); *Jealous Heart* (1966); *At the Sahara in Las Vegas* (1967); *Love Italian Style* (1967); *Happiness* (1967); *My Heart Cries for You* (1967); *Incomparable* (1967); *Hawaii* (1968); *Connie and Clyde* (1968); *Sings Burt Bacharach/Hal David* (1968); *Wedding Cake* (1969); *Songs of Les Reed* (1970); *Greatest Golden Groovie Goodies* (1970); *Spanish and Latin American Favorites* (1971); *I'm Me Again* (1981); *Tourist in Paradise* (1992). **CONNIE FRANCIS AND HANK WILLIAMS JR.:** *Great Country Favorites* (1965). **ANTHOLOGIES:** *Very Best, Vol. II* (1988); *Greatest Hits* (1994); *De Coleccion* (1995); *White Sox, Pink Lipsticks... and Stupid Cupid* (1993).—**BH**

Francis, Panama (actually, **David Albert**), jazz drummer; b. Miami, Dec. 21, 1918. He learned his craft playing in his church in Miami at revivals. He got his nickname from wearing a Panama hat. He worked in Fla. with George Kelly's Cavaliers from 1934, and later joined the Florida Collegians, He moved to N.Y. in the summer of 1938, joined Tab Smith, had a brief spell with Billy Hicks's Sizzling Six, then joined Roy Eldridge in mid-1939. He played with Lucky Millinder (1940–46), often at the Savoy, then Cab Calloway (early 1947 until late 1952). He freelanced in N.Y., played regularly at Central Plaza sessions, and also led his own band in Montevideo (1954). For some years he had a lucrative studio career as an R&B session player. He had regular studio work in Calif. (1971), played with the Teddy Wilson Trio (spring 1971), and toured Japan with Sam "The Man" Taylor (1970–71). He moved back to N.Y. (1973), toured Europe with Warren Covington (1974), and was featured at many international jazz festivals during the 1970s. He periodically re-forms various editions of his Savoy Sultans.

DISC.: *All-Stars 1949* (1949); *Explosive Drums* (1959); *Battle of Jericho* (1962); *Gettin' in the Groove* (1979); *Francis & The Savoy Sultans* (1979).—**JC/LP**

Franck, César (-Auguste-Jean-Guillaume-Hubert), great Belgian composer and organist, brother of **Joseph Franck;** b. Liege, Dec. 10, 1822; d. Paris, Nov. 8, 1890. He studied first at the Royal Cons. of Liège with Daussoigne and others. At the age of 9 he won 1st prize for singing, and at 12 1st prize for piano. As a child prodigy, he gave concerts in Belgium. In 1835 his family moved to Paris, where he studied privately with Anton Reicha. In 1837 he entered the Paris Cons., studying with Zimmerman (piano), Benoist (organ), and Leborne (theory). A few months after his entrance examinations he received a special award of "grand prix d'honneur" for playing a fugue a third lower at sight; in 1838 he received the 1st prize for piano, in 1839, a 2nd prize for counterpoint, in 1840, 1st prize for fugue, and in 1841, 2nd prize for organ. In 1842 he was back in Belgium, but in 1843 he returned to Paris, where he settled for the rest of his life. On March 17, 1843, he presented there a concert of his chamber music. On Jan. 4, 1846, his first major work, the oratorio *Ruth*, was given at the Paris Cons. On Feb. 22, 1848, in the midst of the Paris revolution, he married. In 1851 he became organist of the church of St.-Jean-St.-François, in 1853, maître de chapelle, and, in 1858, organist at Ste.-Clotilde, which position he held until his death. In 1872 he succeeded his former teacher Benoist as prof. of organ at the Paris Cons. Franck's organ classes became the training school for a whole generation of French composers; among his pupils were d'Indy, Chausson, Bréville, Bordes, Duparc, Ropartz, Pierné, Vidal, Chapuis, Vierne, and a host of others, who eventually formed a school of modern French instrumental music. Until the appearance of Franck in Paris, operatic art dominated the entire musical life of the nation, and the course of instruction at the Paris Cons. was influenced by this tendency. By his emphasis on organ music, based on the contrapuntal art of Bach, Franck swayed the new generation of French musicians toward the ideal of absolute music. The foundation of the famous Schola Cantorum by d'Indy, Bordes, and others in 1894 realized Franck's teachings. After the death of d'Indy in 1931, several members withdrew from the Schola Cantorum and organized the École César Franck (1938).

Franck was not a prolific composer, but his creative powers rose rather than diminished with advancing age. His only sym. was completed when he was 66, his remarkable Violin Sonata was written at the age of 63, and his String Quartet was composed in the last year of his life. Lucidity of contrapuntal design and fullness of harmony are the distinguishing traits of Franck's music; in melodic writing he balanced the diatonic and chromatic elements in fine equilibrium. Although he did not pursue innovation for its own sake, he was not averse to using unorthodox procedures. The novelty of introducing an English horn into the score of his Sym. aroused some criticism among academic musicians of the time. Franck was quite alien to the Wagner-Liszt school of composition, which attracted many of his own pupils; the chromatic procedures in Franck's music derive from Bach rather than from Wagner.

WORKS: DRAMATIC: O p e r a : *Le Valet de Ferme* (1851–53); *Hulda* (1882–85; Monte Carlo, March 8, 1894); *Ghisèle* (unfinished; orchestration completed by d'Indy, Chausson, Bréville, Rousseau, and Coquard; Monte Carlo, March 30, 1896). **O r a t o r i o s :** *Ruth* (1843–46; Paris, Jan. 4, 1846; rev. 1871); *La Tour de Babel* (1865); *Les Béatitudes* (1869–79; Dijon, June 15, 1891); *Rédemption* (1st version, Paris, April 10, 1873; final version, Paris, March 15, 1875); *Rébecca* (Paris, March 15, 1881; produced as a 1-act sacred opera at the Paris Opéra, May 25, 1918). **ORCH.: S y m p h o n i c P o e m s :** *Les Éolides* (Paris, May 13, 1877); *Le Chasseur maudit* (Paris, March 31, 1883); *Les Djinns* (Paris, March 15, 1885); *Psyché* (Paris, March 10, 1888). **O T H E R :** *Variations symphoniques* for Piano and Orch. (Paris, May 1, 1886); Sym. in D minor (Paris, Feb. 17, 1889). **CHAMBER:** 4 piano trios (early works; 1841–42); *Andante quietoso* for Piano and Violin (1843); *Duo pour piano et violon concertants*, on themes from Dalayrac's *Gulistan* (1844); Quintet in F minor for Piano and Strings (1879); Violin Sonata (1886);

String Quartet (1889). **KEYBOARD: P i a n o :** 4 *fantaisies; Prélude, Choral et Fugue; Prélude, Aria et Final; 3 petits riens; Danse lente;* etc. **O r g a n :** 6 *pièces* (*Fantaisie; Grande pièce symphonique; Prélude, Fugue, et Variations; Pastorale; Prière; Finale*); 3 *pieces* (*Fantaisie; Cantabile; Piece heroique*); *Andantino;* 3 *chorales;* an album of 44 *Petites pièces;* an album of 55 pieces, entitled *L'Organiste;* etc. **SACRED VOCAL:** *Messe solennelle* (1858); *Messe a 3 voix* (1860); *Panis angelicus* for Tenor, Organ, Harp, Cello, and Double Bass; offertories, motets, etc.; 16 songs, among them *La Procession* (also arranged for Voice and Orch.).

BIBL.: A. Coquard, *C. F.* (Paris, 1890; new ed., 1904); E. Destranges, *L'OEuvre lyrique de C. F.* (Paris, 1896); G. Derepas, *C. F.:Étude sur sa vie, son enseignement, son oeuvre* (Paris, 1897); A. Meyer, *Les Critiques de C. F.* (Orléans, 1898); P. Garnier, *L'Héroïsme de C. F.: Psychologie musicale* (Paris, 1900); F. Baldensperger, *C. F., L'Artiste et son oeuvre* (Paris, 1901); R. Canudo, *C. F. e la giovane scuola musicale francesa* (Rome, 1905); C. Van den Borren, *L'OEuvre dramatique de C. F.* (Brussels, 1906); V. d'Indy, *C. F.* (Paris, 1906; Eng. tr., London, 1910); J. Hinton, *C. F., Some Personal Reminiscences* (London, 1912); M. de Rudder, *C. F.* (Paris, 1920); E. Closson, *C. F.* (Charleroi, 1923); R. Jardillier, *La Musique de chambre de C. F.* (Paris, 1929); M. Emmanuel, *C. F.* (Paris, 1930); C. Tournemire, *C. F.* (Paris, 1931); T. Lynn, *C. F.: A Bio-bibliography* (N.Y., 1934); H. Haag, *C. F. als Orgelkomponist* (Kassel, 1936); P. Kreutzer, *Die sinfonische Form C. F.s* (Düsseldorf, 1938); M. Kunel, *La Vie de C. F.* (Paris, 1947); J. Horton, *C. F.* (London, 1948); N. Demuth, *C. F.* (London, 1949); N. Dufourcq, *C. F.: Le Milieu, l'oeuvre, l'art* (Paris, 1949); L. Vallas, *La Véritable Histoire de C. F.* (Paris, 1950; Eng. tr., London, 1951); C. Taube, *C. F. und wir: Eine Biographie* (Berlin, 1951); E. Buenzod, *C.A. F.* (Paris, 1966); W. Mohr, *C. F.* (Tutzing, 1969); L. Davies, *C. F. and His Circle* (Boston, 1970); R. Smith, *Toward an Authentic Interpretation of the Organ Works of C. F.* (N.Y., 1983); K. Bungert, *C. F.—Die Musik und das Denken: Das Gesamtwerk, neubetrachtet für Hörer, Wissenschaftler und ausübende Musiker* (Frankfurt am Main, 1996); R. Smith, *Playing the Organ Works of C. F.* (Stuyvesant, N.Y., 1997).—**NS/LK/DM**

Franck, Eduard, German pianist, pedagogue, and composer, father of **Richard Franck;** b. Breslau, Oct. 5, 1817; d. Berlin, Dec. 1, 1893. At the age of 17 he studied with Mendelssohn, and later he met Schumann and became his friend. These assns. were the formative factor in the development of his career. He wrote piano pieces and songs in a Romantic vein, closely adhering to the style of Mendelssohn and, to some extent, of Schumann. As a piano teacher, he enjoyed great renown. He taught in Cologne (1851–58), Bern (1859–67), and Berlin (1867–92). Among his works are 2 piano concertos, 2 violin concertos, much chamber music, and numerous collections of piano pieces.

BIBL.: P. and A. Feuchte, *Die Komponisten E. F. und Richard Franck: Leben und Werk, Dokumente, Quellen* (Stuttgart, 1993). —**NS/LK/DM**

Franck, Johann Wolfgang, German composer; b. Unterschwaningen (baptized), June 17, 1644; d. c. 1710. He was brought up in Ansbach, and served there as court musician from 1665 until 1679. He composed 3 operas for the Ansbach court: *Die unvergleichliche Andromeda* (1675), *Der verliebte Föbus* (1678), and *Die drei Töchter Cecrops* (1679). On Jan. 17, 1679, in a fit of jealousy, he allegedly killed the court musician Ulbrecht, and was forced to flee. He found refuge in Hamburg with his wife, Anna Susanna Wilbel (whom he had married in 1666), and gained a prominent position at the Hamburg Opera. Between 1679 and 1686 he wrote and produced 17 operas, the most important of which was *Diokletian* (1682). His private life continued to be stormy; he deserted his wife and their 10 children, and went to London, where he remained from 1690 to about 1702. The exact place and date of his death are unknown. In London he organized (with Robert King) a series of Concerts of Vocal and Instrumental Music. He publ. *Geistliche Lieder* (Hamburg, 1681, 1685, 1687, 1700; republ. in 1856 by D.H. Engel, with new words by Osterwald; newly ed. by W. Krabbe and J. Kromolicki in vol. 45 of Denkmäler Deutscher Tonkunst), *Remedium melancholiae* (25 secular solo songs with Basso Continuo; London, 1690), arias, etc.

BIBL.: F. Zelle, *J.W. F., Ein Beitrag zur Geschichte der ältesten deutschen Oper* (Berlin, 1889); R. Klages, *J.W. F., Untersuchungen zu seiner Lebensgeschichte und zu seinen geistlichen Kompositionen* (Hamburg, 1937).—**NS/LK/DM**

Franck, Joseph, Belgian-French organist and composer, brother of **César (-Auguste-Jean-Guillaume-Hubert) Franck;** b. Liège, Oct. 31, 1825; d. Issy, near Paris, Nov. 20, 1891. He studied organ with Benoist at the Paris Cons., obtaining the 1st prize (1852), then was organist at the church of St. Thomas d'Aquin in Paris. He composed sacred music and piano works, and publ. several manuals on harmony, piano technique, and other pedagogical subjects.—**NS/LK/DM**

Franck, Melchior, significant German composer; b. Zittau, c. 1579; d. Coburg, June 1, 1639. He served as a church chorister in Augsburg about 1600 before going to Nuremberg in 1601, where he was active at St. Egidien's Church. About 1602 he settled in Coburg as court Kapellmeister, where he pursued a distinguished career until the Thirty Years War wreaked havoc on the court musical establishment in the last years of his life. Franck was primarily influenced by H.L. Hassler in his formative years. He became one of the principal German Protestant composers, publishing over 40 vols. of motets (more than 600 such works, 1601–36), and composing 30 Magnificats. mong his many secular works were quodlibets, songs, and dances. A number of his works have appeared in modern eds.

BIBL.: A. Obrist, *M. F.: Ein Beitrag zur Geschichte der weltlichen Composition in Deutschland* (Berlin, 1892).—**NS/LK/DM**

Franck, Richard, German pianist, son of **Eduard Franck;** b. Cologne, Jan. 3, 1858; d. Heidelberg, Jan. 22, 1938. He studied with his father in Berlin and also attended the Leipzig Cons. (1878–80). He was in Basel from 1880 to 1883 and again from 1887 until 1900, and was active there as a pianist and teacher. He later lived in Kassel, and finally in Heidelberg. He was highly regarded as an interpreter of Beethoven's sonatas. He publ. a book of memoirs, *Musikalische und unmusikalische Erinnerungen* (Heidelberg, 1928).

BIBL.: P. and A. Feuchte, *Die Komponisten Eduard Franck und R. F.: Leben und Werk, Dokumente, Quellen* (Stuttgart, 1993).—**NS/LK/DM**

Franckenstein, Clemens von, German composer; b. Wiesentheid, July 14, 1875; d. Hechendorf, Aug. 19, 1942. He spent his youth in Vienna, then went to Munich, where he studied with Thuille. He later took courses with Knorr at the Hoch Cons. in Frankfurt am Main. He traveled with an opera company in the U.S. in 1901, then was a theater conductor in London (1902–07). From 1912 to 1918 and from 1924 to 1934 he was Intendant at the Munich Opera. He wrote several operas, the most successful of which was *Des Kaisers Dichter* (on the life of the Chinese poet Li-Tai Po), performed in Hamburg (Nov. 2, 1920). Other operas are *Griselda* (Troppau, 1898), *Fortunatus* (Budapest, 1909), and *Rahab* (Hamburg, March 25, 1911). He also wrote several orch. works.—**NS/LK/DM**

Franco, Guilherme, jazz percussionist, drummer; b. Sao Paulo, Brazil, Nov. 25, 1946. He had begun dabbling with the piano when, as a 13-year-old, he became inspired to study with a drummer he saw at a party during Carnival. Practicing 14 hours a day, he managed to squeeze in time for club dates, television performances, studio recordings, and even appearances with the national symphony orchestra. In 1971, answering an invitation from some musician friends, he moved to N.Y. and within a week, he had been asked to join Keith Jarrett's ensemble. After a year with Jarrett, he began a seven-year affiliation with McCoy Tyner. In 1978, Guilherme Franco was ranked second overall jazz percussionist in both the *Down Beat* Reader's and Critic's polls, and in 1979, the "New York Jazz Award" named him as the Best Jazz Percussionist in the tri-state area. In 1981 he formed Pe De Boi (literally in Portuguese "foot of ox," but meaning as steady as an ox), comprised of seven drummers and two dancers. It was the featured band at the opening night in 1982 of S.O.B.'s (Sounds of Brazil). In 1996 he co-founded Nova Bossa Nova with Brazilian bassist Alberto Beserra, who lives in Japan and whom he met there while with Tyner in 1975.

DISC.: *Jazz Influence* (1987); *Pe De Boi* (1989).—**LP**

Franco, Johan (Henri Gustav), Dutch-born American composer; b. Zaandam, July 12, 1908; d. Virginia Beach, Va., April 14, 1988. After studies at the Amsterdam Cons. (1929–34), he emigrated to the U.S. and in 1942 became a naturalized American citizen.

WORKS: ORCH.: 5 syms. (1933, 1939, 1940, 1950, 1958); 5 "concertos liricos": No. 1 for Violin and Chamber Orch. (1937), No. 2 for Cello and Orch. (1962), No. 3 for Piano and Chamber Orch. (1967), No. 4 for Percussion and Chamber Orch. (1970), and No. 5 for Guitar and Chamber Orch. (1973); Violin Concerto (Brussels, Dec. 6, 1939); *Serenata concertante* for Piano and Chamber Orch. (N.Y., March 11, 1940); *Fantasy* for Cello and Orch. (1951). **CHAMBER:** 6 string quartets (1931–60); Violin Sonata (1965); piano pieces; numerous carillon pieces. **OTHER:** Many vocal works; incidental music.—**NS/LK/DM**

Francoeur, François, French composer and violinist, uncle of **Louis-Joseph Francoeur;** b. Paris, Sept. 8, 1698; d. there, Aug. 5, 1787. He was a musician in the royal service, being compositeur de la chambre du roi

(1727–56) and surintendant de la musique de la chambre (1744–46). He was also active at the Paris Opéra, where he became maître de musique in 1739. With his close friend Rebel, he was inspecteur adjoint de l'Opéra (1743–53) and joint director (1757–67). With Rebel, he collaborated on 20 successful stage pieces. He also wrote orch. music and 2 sets of violin sonatas. —NS/LK/DM

Francoeur, Louis-Joseph, French violinist, conductor, and composer, nephew of **François Francoeur;** b. Paris, Oct. 8, 1738; d. there, March 10, 1804. He became a violinist in the orch. of the Paris Opéra when he was 14. After serving as its asst. (1764–67) and 1st (1767–79) maître de musique, he was its director (1779–81). During the French Revolution, he was imprisoned until 1794 when he was made administrator of the Paris Opéra. He retired in 1799. His output included stage and other vocal pieces. He also publ. the treatise *Diapason général de tous les instruments à vent* (1772). —NS/LK/DM

François, Samson, admired French pianist; b. Frankfurt am Main (son of the French consul there), May 18, 1924; d. Paris, Oct. 22, 1970. He began piano studies at a very early age and was only 6 when he played a Mozart concerto under Mascagni in Italy. While still a youth, he obtained 1st prizes at the Belgrade Cons. and the Nice Cons. He continued his training in Paris with Cortot at the École Normale de Musique and then with Long at the Cons. (premier prix, 1940). In 1943 he won 1st prize at the first Long-Thibaud Competition in Paris. From 1945 he toured regularly in Europe, and in 1947 he made his first appearances in the U.S. He subsequently played all over the globe, including Communist China in 1964. In addition to his notable performances of works by such French masters as Fauré, Debussy, and Ravel, he was equally notable in his performances of Chopin and Schumann.

BIBL.: J. Roy, *S. F.: Le poete du piano* (Paris, 1997). —NS/LK/DM

Franco of Cologne, German music theorist of the 13th century. His identity is conjectural; there was a learned man known as Magister Franco of Cologne who flourished as early as the 11th century; several reputable scholars regard him as identical with the music theorist Franco; against this identification is the improbability of the emergence of theories and usages found in Franco's writings at such an early date. The generally accepted period for his activities is 1250 to about 1280. The work on which the reputation of Franco of Cologne rests is the famous treatise *Ars cantus mensurabilis.* Its principal significance is not so much the establishment of a new method of mensural notation as the systematization of rules that had been inadequately or vaguely explained by Franco's predecessors. The treatise is valuable also for the explanation of usages governing the employment of concords and discords. It was reprinted from different MSS, in Gerbert's *Scriptores* (vol. III) and in Coussemaker's *Scriptores* (vol. I). Gerbert attributes it to a Franco of Paris, a shadowy figure who may have been

the author of a treatise and 3 summaries, all beginning with the words "Gaudent brevitate moderni." The *Ars cantus mensurabilis* is reproduced in English in O. Strunk's *Source Readings in Music History* (N.Y., 1950).

BIBL.: F. Gennrich, F. von Koln, *Ars cantus mensurabilis* (Darmstadt, 1955).—NS/LK/DM

Frandsen, John, respected Danish conductor; b. Copenhagen, July 10, 1918. He was educated at the Royal Danish Cons. of Music in Copenhagen. He then was organist at the Domkirke there (1938–53), and also made appearances as a conductor. After serving as conductor with the Danish Radio Sym. Orch. in Copenhagen (1945–46), he became a conductor at the Royal Danish Theater there; also made appearances with the Royal Danish Orch. in Copenhagen. In 1958 he toured the U.S. with the Danish Radio Sym. Orch. He was also active as a teacher, at both the Royal Danish Cons. of Music and the Opera School of the Royal Danish Theater. In 1980 he was named orch. counselor of the Danish Radio. He was particularly noted for his outstanding performances of Danish music.—NS/LK/DM

Frank, Alan (Clifford), English music scholar; b. London, Oct. 10, 1910; d. July 9, 1994. He studied the clarinet, conducting, and composition. At the age of 17, he joined the staff of the Oxford Univ. Press; during World War II, he was in the Royal Air Force. In 1947 he was appointed music ed. of the Oxford Univ. Press; in 1954 he became head of its music dept.; retired in 1975. In 1935 he married **Phyllis Tate**. He publ. *The Playing of Chamber Music* (with G. Stratton; London, 1935; 2nd ed., 1951) and *Modern British Composers* (London, 1953); he was also co-author (with F. Thurston) of *A Comprehensive Tutor for the Boehm Clarinet* (London, 1939). —NS/LK/DM

Frank, Claude, esteemed German-born American pianist and pedagogue, father of **Pamela Frank;** b. Nuremberg, Dec. 24, 1925. After the consolidation of power by the Nazis, he went with his family to Paris in 1937; from there they fled to Lisbon and finally reached safety in the U.S. in 1940. In 1944 he became a naturalized American citizen. Following training with A. Schnabel (piano) and Dessau (theory and composition) in N.Y. (1941–44), he pursued composition studies with Lockwood (1946–48) and attended Koussevitzky's conducting course at the Berkshire Music Center in Tanglewood (summer, 1947); he also attended Columbia Univ. In 1947 he made his N.Y. recital debut. After appearing as a soloist with the NBC Sym. Orch. in 1948, he toured as a soloist with various other orchs., as a recitalist, and as a chamber music player. He also devoted time to teaching. In 1959 he married **Lilian Kallir**, with whom he appeared as a duo pianist. He also appeared in duo concerts with his daughter. Frank is highly admired for his insightful performances of the classics.—NS/LK/DM

Frank, Ernst, German conductor and composer; b. Munich, Feb. 7, 1847; d. Oberdöbling, near Vienna, Aug. 17, 1889. He was a student of M. de Fontaine (piano) and F. Lachner (composition). After conducting in

Würzburg (1868), he was 2nd chorus master at the Vienna Court Opera (from 1869); he also served as chorus master of the Gesellschaft der Musikfreunde in Vienna (1870–71). He was court Kapellmeister in Mannheim (1872–78), conductor at the Frankfurt am Main Stadttheater (1878–79), and court Kapellmeister in Hannover (1879–87). In 1887 he was committed to a mental asylum. He wrote the operas *Adam de la Halle* (Karlsruhe, April 9, 1880), *Hero* (Berlin, Nov. 26, 1884), and *Der Sturm* (Hannover, Oct. 14, 1887); also completed Goetz's opera *Francesca da Rimini* (Mannheim, Sept. 30, 1877).—**NS/LK/DM**

Frank, Pamela, American violinist and teacher, daughter of **Claude Frank** and **Lilian Kallir**; b. N.Y., June 20, 1967. She began violin lessons at the age of 5. Following studies with Shirley Givens, she pursued training with Szymon Goldberg and Jaime Laredo, graduating from the Curtis Inst. of Music in Philadelphia in 1989. In 1985 she made her formal debut as soloist with Alexander Schneider and the N.Y. String Orch. at N.Y.'s Carnegie Hall. In 1988 she was awarded the Avery Fisher Career Grant, and in 1999 the Avery Fisher Prize. In addition to engagements as a soloist with major American orchs., she is active as a recitalist and chamber music player. She frequently appears in concert with her parents, as well as with other artists, including Peter Serkin and Yo-Yo Ma.—**NS/LK/DM**

Frankel, Benjamin, English composer; b. London, Jan. 31, 1906; d. there, Feb. 12, 1973. He worked as an apprentice watchmaker in his youth, then went to Germany to study music. Returning to London, he earned his living by playing piano or violin in restaurants. It was only then that he began studying composition seriously. In the interim, he made arrangements, played in jazz bands, and wrote music for films; some of his film scores, such as that for *The Man in the White Suit*, are notable for their finesse in musical characterization. In 1946 he was appointed to the faculty of the Guildhall School of Music and Drama in London. Frankel also took great interest in political affairs; was for many years a member of the British Communist Party and followed the tenets of socialist realism in some of his compositions.

WORKS: DRAMATIC: O p e r a : *Marching Son* (1972–73). O R C H .: Violin Concerto (1951; Stockholm, June 10, 1956); 8 syms.: No. 1 (1952), No. 2 (Cheltenham, July 13, 1962), No. 3 (1964), No. 4 (London, Dec. 18, 1966), No. 5 (1967), No. 6 (London, March 23, 1969), No. 7 (1969; London, June 4, 1970), and No. 8 (1971); *Concertante Lirico* for Strings (1953); *Serenata concertante* for Piano Trio and Orch. (1961); Viola Concerto (1966); *A Catalogue of Incidents* for Chamber Orch. (1966); *Overture for a Ceremony* (1970); *Pezzi melodici* (Stroud Festival, Oct. 19, 1972). C H A M B E R : 5 string quartets (1944, 1945, 1947, 1948, 1965); String Trio (1944); 2 sonatas for Solo Violin (1944, 1962); *3 Poems* for Cello and Piano (1950); Quintet for Clarinet and Strings (1953); Piano Quartet (1953); *Bagatelles* for 11 Instruments (1959); *Pezzi pianissimi* for Clarinet, Cello, and Piano (1964). VOCAL: *The Aftermath* for Tenor, Trumpet, Harp, and Strings (1947); *8 Songs* for Medium Voice and Piano (1959).—**NS/LK/DM**

Frankie Lymon and The Teenagers, tremendously popular 1950s vocal group that introduced teen vocalist Frankie Lymon. MEMBERSHIP: Frankie Lymon, lead voc. (b. N.Y., Sept. 30, 1942; d. N.Y., Feb. 28, 1968); Herman Santiago, ten. (b. N.Y., Feb. 18, 1941); Jimmy Merchant, 2nd ten. (b. N.Y., Feb. 10, 1940); Joe Negroni, bar. (b. N.Y., Sept. 9, 1940; d. N.Y., Sept. 5, 1978); Sherman Garnes, bs. voc. (b. N.Y., June 8, 1940; d. N.Y., Feb. 26, 1977).

After forming several short-term vocal groups, two black students from Edward D. Stitt Junior H.S. in the Washington Heights section of N.Y., Jimmy Merchant and Sherman Garnes, recruited neighborhood Puerto Ricans Herman Santiago and Joe Negroni for another group. Ultimately becoming The Premiers, with Santiago as lead singer, the group was joined by Frankie Lymon in 1955. Lymon had grown up harmonizing with his brothers Lewis and Howie in The Harlemaire Juniors. The Premiers were discovered by Richard Barrett, talent scout and lead singer of The Valentines, and signed to George Goldner's Gee Records. They recorded a song ostensibly written by Merchant and Santiago, "Why Do Fools Fall in Love," released at the beginning of 1956 under the name The Teenagers Featuring Frankie Lymon. With Lymon on boyish soprano lead, the song became a top R&B / smash pop hit, as well the first top British hit by an American vocal group. The song was subsequently covered by The Diamonds and Gale Storm, but, unlike most songs re-recorded by white artists, the original proved the biggest hit.

Sporting a clean-cut, wholesome image and benefiting from dance instructions provided by noted choreographer Cholly Atkins, the group began touring extensively. They soon scored a smash R&B / major pop hit with "I Want You to Be My Girl," followed by the near-smash R&B hits ""I Promise to Remember"/"Who Can Explain?" and "The ABC's of Love," all included on their debut album. They also appeared in the 1956 film *Rock, Rock, Rock*, performing "I Am Not a Juvenile Delinquent."

In the meantime, Frankie Lymon's youngest brother, Lewis, formed The Teenchords in 1956. Signed to Richard Robinson's newly formed Fury label, the group became popular on the East Coast, despite achieving no hits. They appeared in the 1957 film *Jamboree* and later recorded for End and Juanita, breaking up in 1958.

In 1957 Frankie Lymon and The Teenagers toured Great Britain, appeared in the film *Mister Rock and Roll*, and scored their last major R&B hit with the ballad "Out in the Cold Again." In the summer of 1957 Lymon scored a pop hit with "Goody Goody," recorded solo in London, and, by year's end, he had left the group to record solo for Roulette. The Teenagers persevered for a time without Lymon, recording for Roulette, Columbia and End through 1961. Lymon did not achieve another hit until 1960's remake of "Little Bitty Pretty One." Deprived of his youthful soprano voice, he was unable to make a convincing comeback. Having experimented with narcotics since 1958, Lymon entered a drug rehabilitation program in Manhattan in 1961; nonetheless, in 1964 he was convicted of narcotics possession. The Teenagers briefly reunited with Lymon in 1965, but on

Feb. 28, 1968, his body was found in a N.Y. aparment, the victim of a heroin overdose at the age of 25.

Sherman Garnes died of a heart attack on Feb. 26, 1977, and Joe Negroni died on Sept. 5, 1978, after suffering a cerebral hemorrhage. In the early 1980s, surviving members Herman Santiago and Jimmy Merchant reformed The Teenagers with Pearl McKinnon of The Kodaks. In 1981 Diana Ross scored a near-smash pop and R&B hit with "Why Do Fools Fall in Love." Frankie Lymon and The Teenagers were inducted into the Rock and Roll Hall of Fame in 1993.

In 1984 Lymon's widow, Emira, filed for renewal of the copyright to "Why Do Fools Fall in Love," only to discover that it was the property of Morris Levy, who had acquired George Goldner's catalog. Merchant and Santiago pressed their own legal case, and, in 1992 a federal court proclaimed them and Lymon the authors, awarding them royalties back to 1969.

DISC.: THE TEENAGERS: *The Teenagers Featuring Frankie* (1957); *Rock and Roll* (1958); *Jerry Blavatt Presents The Teenagers* (1964). FRANKIE LYMON: *Frankie Lymon at the London Palladium* (1957); *Rock and Roll with Frankie Lymon* (1958). FRANKIE LYMON AND THE TEENAGERS: *Why Do Fools Fall in Love* (1991); *The Best of Frankie Lymon and The Teenagers* (1989); *Why Do Fools Fall in Love?* (1996); *Singing Their Hits.*—BH

Frankl, Peter, notable Hungarian-born English pianist; b. Budapest, Oct. 2, 1935. He was a student of Kodály, Weiner, and Hernadi at the Franz Liszt Academy of Music in Budapest. In 1957 he won 1st prize in both the Long-Thibaud (Paris) and Munich competitions, and in 1959 he captured 1st prize in the Rio de Janeiro competition. Following his successful London debut in 1962, he returned there in 1963 as soloist in Beethoven's *Emperor Concerto* with Kertesz and the London Sym. Orch. In 1965 he made his U.S. debut in a recital in Dallas. He became a naturalized British subject in 1967. That same year, he made his first tour of Australia, was soloist in Mozart's E-flat major Concerto, K.482, with Szell and the Cleveland Orch. in Cleveland and on tour in N.Y., and played Mozart's B- flat major Concerto, K.450, with Martinon and the Chicago Sym. Orch. In 1969 he made his debut with the Berlin Phil. as soloist in Mozart's G major Concerto, K.453, under Barbirolli's direction. With the violinist György Pauk and the cellist Ralph Kirshbaum, he founded a trio in 1972 with which he subsequently toured widely. The trio celebrated its 25th anniversary in 1997. In 1975 he made his debut with Maazel and the Israel Phil. as soloist in Mozart's C minor Concerto, K.491, the same year that he made his first tour of New Zealand. He made his first appearance in Tokyo as soloist in Beethoven's 4th Concerto under Masur's direction in 1976. In 1977 he played Mozart's D major Concerto, K.451, at his debut with Haitink and the Concertgebouw Orch. in Amsterdam. In subsequent years, Frankl's engagements as a soloist with orchs. and as a recitalist took him all over the globe. In 1987 he became a visiting prof. at the Yale Univ. School of Music. He received the Order of Merit from the president of Hungary in 1995.—NS/LK/DM

Franklin, Aretha, the most exciting, inspiring, and influential female soul singer of the 1960s; b. Memphis, Tenn., March 25, 1942. Aretha Franklin started her career as a gospel singer touring with her father C. L. Franklin's evangelistic troupe as a teenager. Her secular career, launched in 1960, languished for a number of years at Columbia Records, where her undeniably powerful and emotive vocal style was constricted by inappropriate material, production, and arrangements. She ultimately found sympathetic treatment in the late 1960s under veteran producer Jerry Wexler at Atlantic Records, where she recorded a series of classic pop and R&B hits and best- selling albums, including *I Never Loved a Man the Way I Love You* and *Lady Soul.* Acclaimed at that time as the most popular female artist in rock music, Franklin endured a fallow period before coming back in the early 1970s with the astonishing *Live at Fillmore West* and gospel *Amazing Grace* albums. Subsequently recording a number of uneven albums under a variety of producers, she reemerged in the mid-1980s with the rocking *Who's Zoomin' Who?* album. Aretha Franklin was inducted into the Rock and Roll Hall of Fame in 1987.

Born the daughter of well-known evangelist preacher Cecil "C. L." Franklin, Aretha Franklin was raised in Buffalo and Detroit, where she began singing in her father's New Bethel Baptist Church Choir with sisters Carolyn and Erma at the age of eight. By 14, she was a featured vocalist on his evangelistic tour, performing on the gospel circuit for four years and recording *The Gospel Sound of Aretha Franklin* (now *Aretha Gospel*) for the Checker subsidiary of Chess Records.

In 1960, with the encouragement of her father and Teddy Wilson bassist Major "Mule" Holly, Aretha Franklin auditioned for Columbia Records' John Hammond, who immediately signed her to a five-year contract. She toured the upper echelon of the so-called "chitlin circuit" as Hammond guided her in the direction of classic jazz and blues singers such as Bessie Smith and Billie Holiday. She managed major R&B hits with "Today I Sing the Blues" and "Won't Be Long" from her debut album and "Operation Heartbreak," and a moderate pop hit with "Rock-A- Bye Your Baby with a Dixie Melody," but subsequent recordings of Tin Pan Alley- –style material using glossy pop arrangements met with little success. Of her Columbia albums, her tribute to Dinah Washington, *Unforgettable,* was perhaps her best.

In November 1966, Aretha Franklin switched to Atlantic Records, where she was personally supervised by veteran producer Jerry Wexler. Her first Atlantic single, "I Never Loved a Man (The Way I Love You)," recorded in Muscle Shoals, Ala., with Franklin on piano and King Curtis on saxophone, became a top R&B and near-smash pop hit. Her debut album also contained favorites such as "Do Right Woman–Do Right Man" and "Dr. Feelgood," and yielded the pop and R&B classic "Respect," written by Otis Redding. *Lady Soul,* perhaps her finest album ever, produced four crossover hits: "(You Make Me Feel Like) A Natural Woman" (by Carole King and Gerry Goffin), "Chain of Fools" (by Don Covay), "(Sweet, Sweet Baby) Since You've Been Gone" (coauthored by Franklin), and the major hit "Ain't No Way," written by sister Carolyn Franklin.

In the late 1960s, Aretha Franklin's sisters Carolyn and Erma inaugurated their own recording careers. Carolyn had written "Baby Baby Baby" (a minor R&B hit for Anna King and Bobby Byrd in 1964) and "Don't Wait Too Long" (a major R&B hit for Bettye Swann in 1965). She managed two moderate R&B hits in 1969 and 1970. Erma scored an R&B hit in 1967 with "Piece of My Heart," arranged by Carolyn. The song was later popularized by Janis Joplin.

Aretha Franklin achieved four crossover smashes from *Aretha Now* with her own "Think," "The House That Jack Built," Burt Bacharach and Hal David's "I Say a Little Prayer," and Don Covay and Steve Cropper's "See Saw," but she subsequently experienced personal and marital problems. In 1969, she had major hits with Robbie Robertson's "The Weight," "I Can't See Myself Leaving You," Lennon and McCartney's "Eleanor Rigby," and "Call Me." In 1970, she hit with "Spirit in the Dark" and Ben E. King's "Don't Play That Song," disbanding her 16-piece band that fall in favor of a tighter combo of sessions players directed by saxophonist King Curtis. This unit recorded the astounding *Live at Fillmore West* album, which featured a surprise appearance by Ray Charles and yielded a smash crossover hit with Simon and Garfunkel's "Bridge Over Troubled Water." Following the successful "Spanish Harlem," Franklin registered four hits from *Young, Gifted and Black*, including "Rock Steady" and "Day Dreaming."

In early 1972, Aretha Franklin returned to her gospel roots, recording the double-record set *Amazing Grace* at the New Temple Missionary Baptist Church in Watts, Calif., with perennial gospel favorite Reverend James Cleveland and his Southern Calif. Community Choir. The album was a surprise success, becoming possibly the best-selling gospel album of all time. Major R&B hits for Franklin continued with "All the King's Horses," "Master of Eyes," Carolyn Franklin's "Angel," Stevie Wonder's "Until You Come Back to Me," "I'm in Love," "Ain't Nothing Like the Real Thing," and "Without Love," but only "Until You Come Back to Me" crossed over to the top of the pop charts as well.

In 1976, Aretha Franklin worked with songwriter-producer Curtis Mayfield on the soundtrack to the movie *Sparkle*, which produced a top R&B and pop hit with "Something He Can Feel" and the R&B near-smash "Look into Your Heart." However, subsequent albums for Atlantic sold less well. In 1980, she appeared in *The Blues Brothers* film and switched to Arista Records for the R&B hits "United Together" and "Love All the Hurt Away," the latter recorded with George Benson. In the early 1980s, she scored a major hit with "Jump to It," written and produced by Luther Vandross.

Aretha Franklin reestablished her popularity with the pop audience with 1985's *Who's Zoomin' Who?* album. It yielded the crossover smashes "Freeway of Love" and "Who's Zoomin' Who" and the major pop hits "Sisters Are Doin' It for Themselves" (recorded with The Eurythmics) and "Another Night." Major pop hits continued in 1986 with "Jumpin' Jack Flash" and "Jimmy Lee," with 1987's duet with George Michael on "I Knew You Were Waiting (For Me)" becoming a top pop and R&B hit. Another gospel album, *One Lord, One Faith, One Baptism*, failed to match the success of *Amazing Grace*. Franklin scored pop hits with "Through the Storm," recorded with Elton John, and "It Isn't, It Wasn't, It Ain't Never Gonna Be," recorded with Whitney Houston, in 1989. She ceased touring in the 1990s, yet continued to record and appear on television. In 1994, Aretha Franklin created a major R&B hit with "Willing to Forgive." She subsequently formed her own record labels, World Class Records and Alf Records, in 1995 and 1996, respectively.

DISC.: Ray Bryant Trio: *Aretha* (1961). *Electrifying* (1962); *Tender, Moving, Swinging* (1962); *Laughing on the Outside* (1963); *The Gospel Sound of Aretha Franklin* (1964); *Unforgettable* (1964); *Runnin' Out of Fools* (1964); *Yeah!!!* (1965); *Soul Sister* (1966); *Take It Like You Give It* (1967); *Take a Look* (1967); *I Never Loved a Man the Way I Loved You* (1967); *Aretha Arrives* (1967); *Aretha Franklin* (1968); *Lady Soul* (1968); *Queen of Soul* (1968); *Aretha Now* (1968); *Aretha in Paris* (1968); *Soft and Beautiful* (1969); *Once in a Lifetime* (1969); *Soul '69* (1969); *Today I Sing the Blues* (1970); *2 Sides of Love* (1970); *This Girl's in Love with You* (1970); *Spirit in the Dark* (1970); *Live at Fillmore West* (1971); *Young, Gifted and Black* (1972); *Amazing Grace* (1972); *Hey, Now, Hey (The Other Side of the Sky)* (1973); *Let Me in Your Life* (1974); *With Everything I Feel in Me* (1974); *You* (1975); *Sparkle* (1976); *Sweet Passion* (1977); *Almighty Fire* (1978); *La Diva* (1979); *Aretha* (1979); *Love All the Hurt Away* (1981); *The Legendary Queen of Soul* (1981); *Jump to It* (1982); *Sweet Bitter Love* (1982); *Get It Right* (1983); *Who's Zoomin' Who?* (1985); *Aretha Franklin* (1986); *One Lord, One Faith, One Baptism* (1987); *Through the Storm* (1989); *What You See Is What You Get* (1991); *Jazz to Soul* (1992); *Queen of Soul* (1997); *A Rose Is Still a Rose* (1998).

BIBL.: Mark Bego, *Aretha Franklin: The Queen of Soul* (N.Y., 1989).—BH

Franklin, Benjamin, great American statesman; b. Boston, Jan. 17, 1706; d. Philadelphia, April 17, 1790. An amateur musician, he invented (1762) the "armonica," an instrument consisting of a row of glass discs of different sizes, set in vibration by light pressure. A string quartet mistakenly attributed to him came to light in Paris in 1945, and was publ. there (1946); the parts are arranged in an ingenious "scordatura"; only open strings are used, so that the quartet can be played by rank amateurs. Franklin wrote entertainingly on musical subjects; his letters on Scottish music are found in vol. VI of his collected works.—NS/LK/DM

Franko, Nahan, American violinist and conductor, brother of **Sam Franko;** b. New Orleans, July 23, 1861; d. Amityville, N.Y., June 7, 1930. As a child prodigy, he toured with Adelina Patti. He then studied in Berlin with Joachim and Wilhelmj. Returning to America, he joined the orch. of the Metropolitan Opera, which he served as concertmaster from 1883 to 1905. He made his debut there as a conductor on April 1, 1900, to be the first native-born American to be so engaged (1904–07).—NS/LK/DM

Franko, Sam, American violinist, brother of **Nahan Franko;** b. New Orleans, Jan. 20, 1857; d. N.Y., May 6, 1937 (from a skull fracture resulting from a fall). He studied in Berlin with Joachim, Heinrich de Ahna, and

Eduard Rappoldi. Returning to the U.S. in 1880, he joined the Theodore Thomas Orch. in N.Y., and was its concertmaster from 1884 to 1891. In 1883 he toured the U.S. and Canada as a soloist with the Mendelssohn Quintette Club of Boston. In order to prove that prejudice against native orch. players was unfounded, he organized in 1894 the American Sym. Orch., using 65 American-born performers; this orch. was later used for his Concerts of Old Music (1900–1909). In 1910 he went to Berlin and taught at the Stern Cons. He then returned to N.Y. in 1915, where he remained for the rest of his life. He publ. various works for piano, including *Album Leaf* (1889) and *Viennese Silhouettes* (6 waltzes, 1928), as well as several violin pieces and practical arrangements for violin and piano. His memoirs were publ. posth. under the title *Chords and Discords* (N.Y., 1938).—NS/LK/DM

Franks, Rebecca Coupe, trumpet player; b. Nov. 27, 1961. She has gained considerable recognition playing trumpet and flugelhorn with great technical skill. From an early age, she wanted to play the trumpet; her brother played the instrument and she loved hearing the sound. Beginning in the fifth grade, she began taking private lessons, and in ninth grade, she began playing with the nearby college band. By the time she was in high school, she was performing nightly in a local restaurant with much older players. Finishing high school, she then moved to San Francisco, where she joined the band Chevere and met Virginia Mayhew. Moving on to N.Y., she co-led a group with Mayhew, playing Monday nights at the Blue Note. She has performed or recorded with Milt Hinton, Lou Donaldson, and other players.

DISC.: *Suit of Armor* (1991); *All of a Sudden* (1992).—SKB

Frantz, Ferdinand, German bass-baritone; b. Kassel, Feb. 8, 1906; d. Munich, May 26, 1959. He made his debut at the opera in Kassel in 1927 as Ortel in *Die Meistersinger von Nürnberg*; then sang in Halle (1930–32) and Chemnitz (1932–37). He was a leading member of the Hamburg State Opera (1937–43) and the Bavarian State Opera in Munich (1943–59). He made a fine impression at his Metropolitan Opera debut in N.Y. on Dec. 12, 1949, as Wotan in *Die Walküre*; sang there until 1951 and again in 1953–54; he also appeared at Covent Garden in London in 1953–54. He was primarily known as an effective Wagnerian bass and baritone. —NS/LK/DM

Frantz, Justus, German pianist, conductor, and teacher; b. Hohensalza, May 18, 1944. He studied piano with Eliza Hansen at the Hamburg Hochschule für Musik, and later took private courses with Kempff. After winning a prize in the Munich Competition in 1967, he began appearing with leading European orchs. He made his U.S. debut with the N.Y. Phil. in 1975; subsequently appeared with many other American orchs. He also toured with Christoph Eschenbach in duo-piano concerts. In 1986 he founded the Schleswig-Holstein Music Festival, with which he was associated until 1994. He was a prof. at the Hamburg Hochschule für Musik from 1986. In 1990 he launched a career as a conductor.—NS/LK/DM

Franz (originally, **Knauth**), **Robert,** famous German song composer; b. Halle, June 28, 1815; d. there, Oct. 24, 1892. His father, Christoph Franz Knauth, legally adopted the name Franz in 1847. The parents did not favor music as a profession, but Franz learned to play the organ and participated as an accompanist in performances in his native city. In 1835 he went to Dessau, where he studied with Friedrich Schneider; in 1837 he returned to Halle. He publ. his first set of songs in 1843, which attracted immediate attention and were warmly praised by Schumann. In 1841 he received an appointment as organist at the Ulrichskirche in Halle, and also as conductor of the Singakademie there in 1842; later he received the post of music director at Halle Univ. (1851–67), which conferred on him the title of Mus.D. in 1861. The successful development of his career as a musician was interrupted by a variety of nervous disorders and growing deafness, which forced him to abandon his musical activities in 1867. Liszt, Joachim, and others organized a concert for his benefit, collecting a large sum of money (about $25,000); admirers in America (Otto Dresel, S.B. Schlesinger, B.J. Lang) also contributed funds for his support. He publ. *Mitteilungen über J.S. Bachs Magnificat* (Leipzig, 1863) and *Offener Brief an Ed. Hanslick über Bearbeitungen alterer Tonwerke, namentlich Bachscher und Handelscher Vokalwerke* (Leipzig, 1871), both of which were reprinted by R. Bethge as *Gesammelte Schriften uber die Wiederbelebung Bachscher und Händelscher Werke* (Leipzig, 1910). Franz was undoubtedly one of the finest masters of the German lied. He publ. about 350 songs, of which the best known were *Schlummerlied, Die Lotosblume, Die Widmung,* and *Wonne der Wehmuth.*

BIBL.: F. Liszt, *R. F.* (Leipzig, 1855; reprinted in *Gesammelte Schriften,* vol. IV, Leipzig, 1882); H. Schuster, *R. F.* (Leipzig, 1874); La Mara, *R. F.,* in vol. III of *Musikalische Studienköpfe* (Leipzig, 1868–82; publ. separately, 1911); R. Prochazka, *R. F.* (Leipzig, 1894); W. Golther, *R. F. und Arnold Freiherr Senfft von Pilsach: Ein Briefwechsel 1861–89* (Berlin, 1907); R. Bethge, *R. F.: Ein Lebensbild* (Halle, 1908); S. Barbak, *Die Lieder von R. F.* (Vienna, 1922); H. von der Pfordten, *R. F.* (Leipzig, 1923); J. Boonin, *An Index to the Solo Songs of R. F.* (Hackensack, N.J., 1970).—NS/LK/DM

Franz, Paul (real name, **François Gautier**), French tenor; b. Paris, Nov. 30, 1876; d. there, April 20, 1950. After private voice studies with Louis Delaquerrière, he made his debut at the Paris Opéra in 1909 as Lohengrin. He remained on its roster until 1938, and also appeared at London's Covent Garden (1910–14). From 1937 he taught voice at the Paris Cons. —NS/LK/DM

Fränzl, Ferdinand (**Ignaz Joseph**), German violinist, conductor, and composer, son of **Ignaz** (**Franz Joseph**) **Fränzl**; b. Schwetzingen, May 25, 1767; d. Mannheim, Oct. 27, 1833. After training from his father, he studied composition with F.X. Richter and Pleyel in Strasbourg and with Mattei in Bologna. He began his career as a violinist on concert tours with his father. In 1789 he became royal concertmaster in Munich, and then music director of the National Theater in Frankfurt am Main in 1792. After conducting the Kammerkapelle in Offenbach (1795–99), he gave concerts as a violin virtuoso in London, Hamburg, Vienna, and Russia. In 1806 he became music director at the Munich court, where he was made Kapellmeister in 1823.

WORKS: DRAMATIC: *Die Luftbälle, oder Der Liebhaber à la Montgolfier*, Singspiel (Mannheim, April 15, 1787); *Adolf und Clara*, operetta (Frankfurt am Main, 1800); *Der beiden Gefangenen*, opera (Mannheim, 1802); *Carlo Fioras, oder Die Stumme in der Sierra Morena*, opera (Munich, Oct. 16, 1810); *Hadrian Barbarossa*, opera (Munich, March 1815); *Die Weihe*, Festspiel (Munich, Oct. 12, 1818); *Der Fassbinder*, Singspiel (Munich, Dec. 21, 1824); *Der Bandit*, Singspiel (Mannheim, Dec. 1835); *Der Einsiedler*, Singspiel (n.d.). **OTHER:** Syms.; overtures; 9 violin concertos; Double Concerto for 2 Violins and Orch.; chamber music; songs.—**NS/LK/DM**

Franzl, Ignaz (Franz Joseph), German violinist, conductor, and composer, father of **Ferdinand (Ignaz Joseph) Franzl**; b. Mannheim, June 3, 1736; d. there, Sept. 3, 1811. He entered the Mannheim Court Orch. as a boy of 11. He became co-concertmaster in 1774, and was conductor from 1790 to 1803. He made several concert tours with his son; composed syms. and music for the violin, and also wrote for the stage. His Singspiel *Die Luftbälle* was produced in Mannheim with excellent success (April 15, 1787). He also wrote music for Shakespeare's plays.

BIBL.: R. Wurtz, *I. F.* (Mainz, 1970).—**NS/LK/DM**

Fraschini, Gaetano, noted Italian tenor; b. Pavia, Feb. 16, 1816; d. Naples, May 23, 1887. He studied with F. Moretti, making his debut in Pavia in 1837. He subsequently sang in Milan, Venice, Trieste, Rome, and other Italian cities, and also appeared in London at Her Majesty's Theatre (1847) and Drury Lane (1868). He created the role of Genaro in Donizetti's *Caterina Cornaro*. Much esteemed by Verdi, he sang in the premieres of *Attila, Il Corsaro, La battaglia di Legnano, Alzira, Stiffelio,* and *Un ballo in maschera*. The opera house in Pavia is named for him.—**NS/LK/DM**

Fraser, Norman, Chilean-born English pianist and composer; b. Valparaiso, Nov. 26, 1904. He pursued his musical studies in Chile, and in 1917 went to England, where he attended classes at the Royal Academy of Music in London. He then took piano lessons with Isidor Philipp in Paris. He subsequently made several tours in South America as a representative of various British organizations. From 1954 to 1971 he was engaged as European music supervisor at the BBC. He gave numerous joint recitals with his wife, Janet Fraser, the English mezzo-soprano (b. Kirkealdy, May 22, 1911). In 1973 he settled at Seaford, England. He composed a number of attractive piano pieces and some chamber music.—**NS/LK/DM**

Frauenlob (actually, Heinrich von Meissen), famous German Minnesinger; b. in or near Meissen, c. 1255; d. Mainz, Nov. 29, 1318. He became renowned as a poet and singer via his travels throughout northern and eastern Germany. Frauenlob (his name

most likely refers to his songs in honor of the Virgin) was one of the most significant masters of late courtly Spruch poetry. The Meistersingers revered him as one of their alte Meisters. For his works, see L. Ettmüller, ed., *Heinrichs von Meissen des Frauenlobs Leiche, Sprüche, Streitgedichte und Lieder* (Quedlinburg, 1843) and H. Rietsch, ed., *Gesänge von Frauenlob*, Denkmäler der Tonkunst in Österreich, XLI, Jg. XX/2 (1913).

BIBL.: W. Kirsch, *F.s Kreuzleich* (Dillingen, 1930); H. Kretschmann, *Der Stil F.s* (Jena, 1933); H. Thomas, *Untersuchungen zur Überlieferung der Spruchdichtung F.s* (Leipzig, 1939); R. Krayer, *F. und die Natur-Allegorese* (Heidelberg, 1960).—**LK/DM**

Frazzi, Vito, Italian composer and teacher; b. San Secondo Parmense, Aug. 1, 1888; d. Florence, July 8, 1975. He studied organ at the Parma Cons., and also took courses in piano and theory. From 1912 to 1958 he taught at the Florence Cons.; also taught at the Accademia Chigiana in Siena (1932–63). He wrote a music drama, *Re Lear*, after Shakespeare (Florence, 1939), an opera, *Don Quixote* (Florence, April 27, 1952), several symphonic poems, and chamber music. He also orchestrated Monteverdi's stage works.—**NS/LK/DM**

Freccia, Massimo, Italian conductor; b. Florence, Sept. 19, 1906. He studied at the Florence Cons. and later in Vienna with Franz Schalk. From 1933 to 1935 he conducted the Budapest Sym. Orch. He was guest conductor at the Lewisohn Stadium in N.Y. (1938–40), and then conductor of the Havana Phil. (1939–43), the New Orleans Sym. Orch. (1944–52), and the Baltimore Sym. Orch. (1952–59). He returned to Italy in 1959, and conducted the Rome Radio Orch. until 1963. —**NS/LK/DM**

Frederick II (Fredrick the Great), King of Prussia; b. Berlin, Jan. 24, 1712; d. Potsdam, Aug. 17, 1786. He was an enlightened patron of music, a flute player of considerable skill, and an amateur composer. He studied flute with Quantz. In 1740, when he ascended to the throne, he established a Court Orch. and an opera house; Bach's son Carl Philipp Emanuel was his harpsichordist until 1767. In 1747 J.S. Bach was invited to Potsdam. The fruit of this visit was Bach's *Musical Offering*, written on a theme by Frederick II. A collection of 25 flute sonatas and 4 concertos by Frederick was publ. by Spitta (3 vols., Leipzig, 1889; reprinted, N.Y., 1967); other works were publ. in vol. XX of *Die Musik am preussischen Hofe*. Besides instrumental works, Frederick contributed arias to several operas: *Demofoonte* by Graun (1746), *Il Re pastore* (1747; in collaboration with Quantz and others), *Galatea ed Acide* (1748; in collaboration with Hasse, Graun, Quantz, and Nichelmann), and *Il trionfo della fedeltà* (1753; in collaboration with Hasse and others).

BIBL.: K. Müller, *Friedrich der Grosse als Kenner und Dilettant auf dem Gebiete der Tonkunst* (Potsdam, 1847); W. Kothe, *Friedrich der Grosse als Musiker* (Leipzig, 1869); G. Thouret, *Friedrichs des Grossen Verhältniss zur Musik* (Berlin, 1895); idem, *Friedrich der Grosse als Musikfreund und Musiker* (Leipzig, 1898); K. von Forstner, *Friedrich der Grosse, Künstler und König* (Berlin, 1932); G. Müller, *Friedrich der Grosse, Seine Flöten und sein Flötenspiel* (Berlin, 1932); E. Helm, *Music of the Court of F. the Great* (Norman, Okla., 1960).—**NS/LK/DM**

Freed, Isadore, Russian-born American composer and teacher; b. Brest-Litovsk, March 26, 1900; d. Rockville Centre, N.Y., Nov. 10, 1960. He went to the U.S. at an early age. He graduated from the Univ. of Pa. in 1918 (Mus.B.), then studied with Bloch and with d'Indy in Paris. He returned to the U.S. in 1934, where he held various teaching positions. In 1944 he was appointed head of the music dept. at the Hartt Coll. of Music in Hartford, Conn.

WORKS: DRAMATIC: O p e r a : *Homo Sum* (1930); *The Princess and the Vagabond* (Hartford, May 13, 1948). B a l - l e t : *Vibrations* (Philadelphia, 1928). ORCH.: *Jeux de timbres* (Paris, 1933); 2 syms.: No. 1 (1941) and No. 2 for Brass (San Francisco, Feb. 8, 1951); *Appalachian Symphonic Sketches* (Chautauqua, N.Y., July 31, 1946); *Festival Overture* (San Francisco, Nov. 14, 1946); *Rhapsody* for Trombone and Orch. (radio premiere, N.Y., Jan. 7, 1951); Violin Concerto (N.Y., Nov. 13, 1951); Cello Concerto (1952); Concertino for English Horn and Orch. (1953). CHAMBER: 3 string quartets (1931, 1932, 1937); Trio for Flute, Viola, and Harp (1940); *Triptych* for Violin, Viola, Cello, and Piano (1943); *Passacaglia* for Cello and Piano (1947); Quintet for Woodwinds and Horn (1949); Oboe Sonatina (1954); piano pieces; organ music. OTHER: Vocal music.

BIBL.: E. Steinhauer, *A Jewish Composer by Choice, I. F.: His Life and Work* (N.Y., 1961).—NS/LK/DM

Freed, Richard (Donald), distinguished American music critic, annotator, and broadcaster; b. Chicago, Dec. 27, 1928. He was educated at the Univ. of Chicago (graduated, 1947). After working for various newspapers, he was a contributor to the *Saturday Review* (1959–71) and a critic for the *N.Y. Times* (1965–66). He served as assistant to the director of the Eastman School of Music in Rochester, N.Y. (1966–70). He was a contributing ed. to *Stereo Review* (1973–99) and a record critic for the *Washington Star* (1972–75), the *Washington Post* (1976–84), and radio station WETA-FM in Washington, D.C. (from 1985). He likewise was program annotator for the St. Louis Sym. Orch. (1973–96), the Philadelphia Orch. (1974–84), the Houston Sym. Orch. (1977–80), the National Sym. Orch. in Washington, D.C. (from 1977), the Baltimore Sym. Orch. (1984–92), and the Flint (Mich.) Sym. Orch. (from 1992). From 1974 to 1990 he was executive director of the Music Critics Assn., and was named consultant to the music director of the National Sym. Orch. in 1981. He received the ASCAP-Deems Taylor Award in 1984 for his erudite and engagingly indited program annotations, and again in 1986 for his equally stylish record annotations. In 1995 he received a Grammy Award for his perspicacious liner notes. He occasionally wrote under the names Paul Turner, Gregor Philipp, and Priam Clay.—NS/LK/DM

Freedman, Harry, Polish-born Canadian composer; b. ód, April 5, 1922. He was taken to Canada as a child and became a naturalized Canadian citizen in 1931. At 13, he became a student at the Winnipeg School of Art to study painting. At 18, he took up the clarinet, and then studied oboe with Perry Bauman and composition with John Weinzweig at the Royal Cons. of Music of Toronto (1945–51). He also attended Messiaen's class in composition at the Berkshire Music Center in Tanglewood (summer, 1949). Freedman began his career performing with and composing for dance bands and jazz ensembles. He played English horn in the Toronto Sym. Orch. (1946–70), then served as its composer-in-residence (1970–71) and was a founder and president (1975–78) of the Canadian League of Composers. In 1985 he was made an Officer of the Order of Canada. In his works, he reveals a fine command of writing in various idioms, ranging from symphonic to jazz scores.

WORKS: DRAMATIC: O p e r a : *Abracadabra* (1979). M u s i c a l : *Fragments of Alice* (1988). B a l l e t : *Rose Latulippe* (Stratford, Aug. 16, 1966); *5 over 13* (1969); *The Shining People of Leonard Cohen* (1970); *Star Cross'd* (1973; rev. 1975; retitled *Romeo and Juliet*); *Oiseaux exotiques* (1984–85); *Heroes of Our Time* (1986); *Breaks* (1987). ORCH.: *Nocturne I* (1949) and *II* (1975); *Matinee Suite* (1951–55); *Images*, symphonic suite (1957–58); 3 syms.: No. 1 (1954–60; Washington, D.C., April 23, 1961), No. 2, *A Little Symphony* (1966), and No. 3 (1983; rev. 1985); *Chaconne* (1964); *Tangents*, symphonic variations (Montreal, July 21, 1967); *Klee Wyck* (The Laughing One [Indian name of the artist Emily Carr]; 1970); *Graphic I (Out of Silence...)* for Orch. and Tape (Toronto, Oct. 26, 1971); *Preludes* (1971; orchestrated from Debussy); *Tapestry* for Small Orch. (1973); *Tsolum Summer* for Flute, Percussion, and Strings (1976); *Royal Flush*, concerto grosso for Brass Quintet and Orch. (1981); *Chalumeau* for Clarinet and String Orch. or String Quartet (1981); *Concerto for Orchestra* (1982); *The Sax Chronicles* for Saxophone and Orch. (1984); *Passacaglia* for Jazz Band and Orch. (1984); *Graphic VI (Town)*, after the paintings of Harold Town (1986); *A Dance on the Earth* (1988); Sonata for Symphonic Winds (1988); *Marigold* for Viola and Orch. (1999). CHAMBER: Wind Quintet (1962); *The Tokaido* for Chorus and Wind Quintet (1964); *Variations* for Oboe, Flute, and Harpsichord (1965); *5 Rings* for Brass Quintet (1976); *Monday Gig* for Woodwind Quintet (1978); *Opus Pocus* for Flute, Violin, Viola, and Cello (1979); *Blue* for String Quartet (1980); *Little Girl Blew* for Bass Clarinet (1988); other chamber works. VOCAL: *3 poèmes de Jacques Prevert* for Soprano and String Orch. (1962); *2 Sonnets of Love and Age* for Soprano, Baritone, Woodwind Quintet, and Brass Quintet (1975); *Fragments of Alice* for Soprano, Alto, Baritone, and Chamber Orch. (1976); *Nocturne III* for Chorus and Orch. (1980); *A Time Is Coming* for Voices (1982); *Rhymes from the Nursery* for Children's Chorus (1986); *Borealis* for 4 Choruses and Orch. (1997); *Voices* for Chorus (1999); other vocal works. OTHER: Incidental music; film and television scores.—NS/LK/DM

Freelon, Nnenna, American jazz vocalist; b. Cambridge, Miss. After graduating from Simmons Coll., she worked in the health services field in Durham, N.C. Making the decision to pursue a career as a jazz vocalist, she worked diligently learning her craft and, as good fortune sometimes prevails, she took part in a key jam session in Atlanta that became a very important turning point in her career. While there, she made an indelible impression on fellow performer Ellis Marsalis, who brought her to the attention of Dr. George Butler at Columbia Records. Signed by Columbia, she recorded her self-title debut CD in 1992. Through her recordings, she has begun to stretch, proving an individual talent. After releasing three Columbia albums, Freelon recently switched to Concord.

DISC.: *Nnenna Freelon* (1992); *Heritage* (1994); *Listen* (1994); *Shaking Free* (1997).—SKB

Freeman, Betty (née **Wishnick**), American music patron, photographer, and record producer; b. Chicago, June 2, 1921. She studied music, piano, and English literature at Wellesley Coll. (B.A., 1942); later took piano lessons with Johanna Harris at the Juilliard School of Music in N.Y. and at the New England Cons. of Music in Boston. She also studied privately in N.Y. with Erich Itor Kahn (harmony) and Beveridge Webster (piano) and in Los Angeles with Victoria Front and Joanna Graudan. After moving to Los Angeles in 1950, she began collecting American avant-garde art. In 1960 she became a founding member of the Contemporary Art Council of the Los Angeles County Museum of Art. In the 1960s she completed books on Clyfford Still and Sam Francis. From 1964 to 1973 she was one of the leaders of the music program "Encounters" at the Pasadena Art Museum. During this time, she became the patron and promoter of the uniquely original composer Harry Partch, who became the subject of her prize- winning documentary film *The Dreamer That Remains* (1972). She also began still photography, studying with Ansel Adams, Cole Weston, Fred Picker and others, her subjects being largely the American composers and performing artists who were also her beneficiaries. Her premiere photo exhibit took place at the Otis-Parsons Gallery in Los Angeles in 1985; other shows followed in Milan (1987), the Los Angeles Phil. (1988), the Brooklyn Academy of Music (1988), the Univ. of Calif. at Irvine (1989), the Berlin Phil. (1990), four locations throughout Japan (1990), the Cologne Phil. (1991, 1997), Ace Gallery in Los Angeles (1991), Ferrara, Italy (1991), the Eastman School of Music (1991), the Univ. of Calif. at San Diego (1992, 1999), the Salzburg Festival (1992), the Théâtre Royal de la Monnaie in Brussels (1993), the Ojai Festival (1993), Budapest (1993), Museum of Contemporary Art, Los Angeles (1993–95), the Univ. of Calif. at San Diego (1995), La Fenice Theatre, Venice (1995), Royal Festival Hall in London (1996), N.Y.'s Lincoln Center (1996, 1997), Helsinki (1996), the Univ. of Calif. at Berkeley (1996), Cité de la musique in Paris (1997), the Frankfurt am Main Oper (1997), the Deutsche Oper, Berlin (1998), London's Barbican Centre (1998), Dartington International Summer School (1999), the Hollywood Bowl (1999), the Ojai Music Festival (2000), and the Nord Deutsche Rundfunk in Hamburg (2000). From 1981 to 1991 she presented monthly musicales of contemporary composers at her home in Beverly Hills with the music critic Alan Rich. From the 1960s she was an active supporter of West Coast composers, including Robert Erickson, Paul Dresher, Morton Subotnick, Terry Riley, Lou Harrison, Dane Rudhyar, Peter Garland, Daniel Lentz, and John Adams. In addition, she supported the work of Steve Reich, Philip Glass, La Monte Young, John Cage, Virgil Thomson, Conlon Nancarrow, Christopher Rouse, and Steven Mackey. Later her support extended to Europe, particularly to the composers Birtwistle, Lutosławski, George Benjamin, György Ligeti, and György Kurtag, and to the Salzburg Festival. She served twice on the Inter-Arts Panel of the NEA (1983–84), and received the Cunningham Dance Foundation award for "distinguished support of the arts" (1984). She further received an award from the American Music Center (1986) and the Gold Baton from the American Sym. Orch. League (1987). She has great admirers in the artists she supports; she was the dedicatee of John Cage's *Freeman Etudes* (1977) and John Adams's *Nixon in China* (1987). From 1989 to 1994 she served on the board of directors of the Los Angeles Phil. She was married to Stanley Freeman with whom she busily produced 4 children in 6 years. Divorced in 1971, she married the Italian artist Franco Assetto, with whom she divided her time between Turin and Los Angeles until his death. Her belief in and support of contemporary music resulted from her firm belief that "music written since 1950 is infinitely more compelling and convincing than anything written during the 19th century with, of course, the exceptions of Beethoven and Schubert."—NS/LK/DM

Freeman, Bud (Lawrence), tenor saxophonist, clarinetist, composer; b. Chicago, April 13, 1906; d. there, March 15, 1991. Freeman started on "C" melody sax in 1923, taking a few lessons from Jimmy McPartland's father, then studied for six months with Duke Real. He was an early cohort of the Austin High Gang, playing regularly with Jimmy (cornet) and Dick (guitar) McPartland, and Frank Teschmacher (reed player) in The Blue Friars. From April 1925, he played the tenor sax. The Blue Friars worked under Husk O'Hare's management as The Red Dragons and began broadcasting on radio station WHT; when the original Wolverines disbanded. During 1926, the group worked as Husk O'Hare's Wolverines, played at White City Ballroom, Chicago, and in other local venues. Later that year, Bud joined Herb Carlin, then toured with Art Kassel. On his return to Chicago, he played for various leaders, and recorded with the McKenzie and Condon Chicagoans, as well as leading his own recording band. In late 1927, he joined Ben Pollack and moved with the band to N.Y. in February 1928. He had left Pollack by summer of 1928, briefly accompanied Bea Palmer (left after a week), and then sailed to Europe for a two-week date playing aboard the Ile de France. He returned to N.Y. and then worked through mid-1934 with Red Nichols, Zez Confrey, and other jazz-pop bands. From 1934 on, he worked primarily with big bands, including Joe Haymes from (spring 1934), Ray Noble's Orch. (opening at Rainbow Room, Radio City, N.Y., 1935), Tommy Dorsey (April 1936–March 1938), and Benny Goodman (March–November 1938). In April 1939, he took his own Summa Cum Laude Band into Kelly's, N.Y. The band played many residencies, as well as for the short-lived musical *Swingin' the Dream* (a version of *A Midsummer Night's Dream* with Louis Armstrong and Maxine Sullivan) in November 1939. They disbanded in July 1940, and Bud toured with his own big band before joining Joe Marsala in October 1940. He returned to Chicago, and then led his own big band (soon reduced to a small group) for club work. He served in the U.S. Army from June 1943 until 1945, and led a service band at Fort George, Md., then led a big band in the Aleutians. After the war, he worked stints in Chicago and N.Y., leading his own small bands, and continuing prolific freelance recording activities, including regular sessions with Eddie Condon. He continued leading small groups throughout the 1950s and 1960s, regularly featured at major jazz festivals throughout the U.S. He was temporarily out of action for six months (late 1967 to spring 1968) after an automobile accident. In 1969, he was a founding member of the World's Greatest Jazz Band, with co-leaders Bob Haggart and Yank Lawson, remaining with it until 1971. He moved to London in 1974, continuing to perform and tour. In 1978, he returned to Chicago. He worked club jobs and toured through the remainder of his life, and also authored three books. He died of cancer just short of his 85th birthday. Critics mistakenly listed him as a source of Lester Young's style, based on Young's comment that he liked Bud Freeman's playing with Benny Goodman in 1938; too late for either of them to influence each other. In any case Freeman's earliest recordings are in a heavy style quite unlike Young's, or his own bubbling later work.

DISC.: *Midnight at Eddie Condon's* (1945); *Comes Jazz* (1950); *Bud Freeman* (1955); *Newport News* (1956); *And His Summa Cum Laude Trio* (1958); *Midnight Session* (1959); *All Stars with Shorty Baker* (1960); *Something Tender* (1963); *Compleat Bud Freeman* (1969); *Joy of Sax* (1974); *Song of the Tenor* (1975); *Jazz Meeting in Holland* (1975); *Bucky and Bud* (1976); *Live in Harlem* (1978); *Real Bud Freeman* (1983).

WRITINGS: *You Don't Look Like a Musician* (Detroit, 1974), *If You Know a Better Life, Please Tell Me* (Dublin, 1976); *Crazeology: The Autobiography of a Chicago Jazzman* (Oxford, 1989).—**JC/LP**

Freeman, David, Australian opera producer; b. Sydney, May 1, 1952. He was educated at the Univ. of Sydney (1971–74). In 1973 he founded the Opera Factory in Sydney, in 1976 the Opera Factory Zürich, and in 1981 the Opera Factory London. In 1985 he oversaw the British premiere in London of Glass's *Akhnaten*. In 1986 he was producer of the premieres of Osborne's *Hell's Angels* and Birtwistle's *The Mask of Orpheus* and *Yan Tan Tethera* in London. He produced the British premieres of Ligeti's *Aventures & Nouvelles aventures* in 1988 and Reimann's *Die Gespenstersonate* in 1989. Freeman founded Opera Factory Films in 1991. In 1992 he produced Prokofiev's *The Fiery Angel* in St. Petersburg, at London's Covent Garden, and at the Metropolitan Opera in N.Y. His production of *Die Zauberflöte* was mounted in London in 1996. He married **Marie Angel** in 1985, the same year he was made a Chevalier of l'Ordre des arts et lettres of France.—**NS/LK/DM**

Freeman, George, American jazz musician; b. Chicago, Ill., April 10, 1927. Another talented member of the musical Freeman family of Chicago, he is a soulful but somewhat idiosyncratic player whose recordings have been infrequent. He was inspired to play guitar after witnessing a performance by T-Bone Walker at a Chicago club in the 1940s and by guitarists Charlie Christian, Oscar Moore, and Wes Montgomery, his strongest influences came from non-guitarists—Charlie Parker, Art Tatum, and his saxophonist brother, Von. Freeman was first recorded while backing Parker on a live date released on Savoy. From the late 1940s through the 1950s he backed a series of R&B stars, including Joe Morris, Sil Austin, and Jackie Wilson, before hooking up with "Groove" Holmes in the 1960s. He has since been most often heard in soul-jazz settings, working exten-

sively with Gene Ammons in the late 1960s (Freeman appeared on a few of Ammons's late 1960s Prestige LPs) and with Jimmy McGriff in the early 1970s. He recorded his debut as a leader for Delmark in 1969, an LP for Sonny Lester's Groove Merchant label in 1974 called *New Improved Funk*, and finally resurfaced on CD in the 1990s with a session for Chicago's Southport label. A unique player who has kept his ears wide open to post-bop developments, Freeman exhibits a unique penchant for sprawling rapid-fire lines of notes with unexpected turns.

DISC.: *The Groover* (1968); *Birth Sign* (1972); *Rebellion* (1995); *Funkiest Little Band in the Land* (1996).—**DB**

Freeman, Harry Lawrence, African-American composer, conductor, and teacher; b. Cleveland, Oct. 9, 1869; d. N.Y., March 24, 1954. He studied theory with J.H. Beck and piano with E. Schonert and Carlos Sobrino. He taught at Wilberforce Univ. (1902–04) and the Salem School of Music (1910–13). He organized and directed the Freeman School of Music (1911–22) and the Freeman School of Grand Opera (from 1923); also conducted various theater orchs. and opera companies. In 1920 he organized the Negro Opera Co., and in 1934 he conducted a pageant, *O Sing a New Song*, at the Chicago World's Fair. He was the first black composer to conduct a sym. orch. in his own work (Minneapolis, 1907), and the first of his race to write large operatic compositions. All of his music is written in folk-song style, his settings in simple harmonies; his operas, all on Negro, oriental, and Indian themes, are constructed of songs and choruses in simple concatenation of separate nos.

WORKS: DRAMATIC: O p e r a : *The Martyr* (Denver, 1893); *Zuluki* (1898); *African Kraal* (Chicago, June 30, 1903; rev. 1934); *The Octoroon* (1904); *Valdo* (Cleveland, May 1906); *The Tryst* (N.Y., May 1911); *The Prophecy* (N.Y., 1912); *The Plantation* (1914); *Athalia* (1916); *Vendetta* (N.Y., Nov. 12, 1923); *American Romance*, jazz opera (1927); *Voodoo* (N.Y., Sept. 10, 1928); *Leah Kleschna* (1930); *Uzziah* (1931); *Zululand*, tetralogy of music dramas: *Nada, The Lily* (1941–44), *Allah* (1947), and *The Zulu King* (1934). **B a l l e t :** *The Slave* for Choral Ensemble and Orch. (N.Y., Sept. 22, 1932). **OTHER:** Songs.—**NS/LK/DM**

Freeman, Paul (Douglas), African-American conductor; b. Richmond, Va., Jan. 2, 1936. He studied piano, clarinet, and cello in his youth, then continued his musical training at the Eastman School of Music in Rochester, N.Y. (B.M., 1956; M.M., 1957; Ph.D., 1963); also took courses at the Berlin Hochschule für Musik (1957–59). Returning to the U.S., he took conducting lessons with Richard Lert and Pierre Monteux. He subsequently held the post of conductor with the Opera Theater of Rochester (1961–66), the San Francisco Cons. Orch. (1966–67), and the San Francisco Little Sym. Orch. (1967–68); then was assoc. conductor of the Dallas Sym. Orch. (1968–70) and resident conductor of the Detroit Sym. Orch. (1970–79); also served as principal guest conductor of the Helsinki Phil. (1974–76). From 1979 to 1988 he was music director of the Victoria (B.C.) Sym. Orch. In 1987 he became music director of the Chicago Sinfonietta.—**NS/LK/DM**

Freeman, Robert (Schofield), American musicologist, pianist, and educator; b. Rochester, N.Y., Aug. 26, 1935. He received training in piano from Gregory Tucker, Artur Balsam, and Rudolf Serkin, and pursued his academic studies at Harvard Coll. (A.B., *summa cum laude*, 1957) and at Princeton Univ. (M.F.A., 1960; Ph.D., 1967, with the diss. *Opera without Drama: Currents of Change in Italian Opera, 1675–1725*; publ. in Ann Arbor, 1981). Freeman also studied at the Univ. of Vienna on a Fulbright fellowship (1960–62). He taught at Princeton Univ. (1963–68) and at the Mass. Inst. of Technology (1968–73), and also was a visiting assoc. prof. at Harvard Univ. (1972). In 1972 he became director and prof. of musicology at the Eastman School of Music in Rochester, N.Y., where he revitalized its administration and oversaw an extensive renovation of its facilities. From 1996 to 1999 he was president of the New England Cons. of Music in Boston. In 1999 he became dean of the Coll. of Fine Arts at the Univ. of Tex. at Austin. As a musicologist and educator, Freeman has contributed many articles to journals, as well as to *The New Grove Dictionary of Music and Musicians* (1980).—**NS/LK/DM**

Freer, Eleanor (née Everest), American composer; b. Philadelphia, May 14, 1864; d. Chicago, Dec. 13, 1942. She studied singing in Paris (1883–86) with Mathilde Marchesi, then took a course in composition with Benjamin Godard. Upon her return to the U.S., she taught singing at the National Cons. of Music of America in N.Y. (1889–91). She then settled in Chicago, where she studied theory with Bernhard Ziehn (1902–07). She publ. some light pieces under the name Everest while still a young girl, but most of her larger works were written after 1919. She also wrote an autobiography, *Recollections and Reflections of an American Composer* (Chicago, 1929). Among her works were 9 operas, of which the following were performed: *The Legend of the Piper* (South Bend, Ind., Feb. 28, 1924), *The Court Jester* (Lincoln, Nebr., 1926), *A Christmas Tale* (Houston, Dec. 27, 1929), *Frithiof* (concert perf., Chicago, Feb. 1, 1931), and *A Legend of Spain* (concert perf., Milwaukee, June 19, 1931). She also composed *Sonnets from the Portuguese*, song cycle, about 150 songs, and piano pieces.

BIBL.: A. Foster, *E. F. and Her Colleagues* (Chicago, 1927). —**NS/LK/DM**

Frege, Livia (née Gerhard), German soprano; b. Gera, June 13, 1818; d. Leipzig, Aug. 22, 1891. She studied with Pholenz. In 1832 she made her concert debut in Leipzig, where her operatic debut followed in 1833 as Spohr's Jessonda. After singing at the Berlin Royal Opera (1835–36), she pursued a concert career. She organized her own orch. and choir in Leipzig, and became a close friend and admired interpreter of Mendelssohn.—**LK/DM**

Freire (actually, **Pinto Freire**), **Nelson (José),** Brazilian pianist; b. Boa Esperanza, Oct. 18, 1944. He began to play the piano at a very early age and made his public debut when he was only 5. After winning the Rio de Janeiro competition at 13, he went to

Vienna to study with Bruno Seidlhofer; in 1964 he won the Vianna da Motta Prize in Lisbon. After making a major tour of Europe in 1968, he made his U.S. debut in N.Y. in 1969. He subsequently appeared in all the major music centers, winning particular praise for his refulgent performances of the Romantic repertory. —**NS/LK/DM**

Freisslich, Johann Balthasar Christian, German composer; b. Immelborn, near Bad Salzungen (baptized), March 30, 1687; d. Danzig, 1764. He was director of the Hofkapelle in Sondershausen in 1719–20. Upon the detah of his half-brother, the composer Maximilian Dietrich Freisslich (b. Immelborn [baptized], Feb. 6, 1673; d. Danzig, April 10, 1731), he succeeded him as Kapellmeister at St. Mary's in Danzig, which position he retained for the rest of his life. His vast output included Passions, cantatas, and choruses.—**LK/DM**

Freitas (Branco), Frederico (Guedes) de, Portuguese conductor and composer; b. Lisbon, Nov. 15, 1902; d. there, Jan. 12, 1980. He studied piano with Aroldo Silva, composition with A.E. da Costa Ferreira, musicology with Luis de Freitas Branco, and violin at the National Cons. in Lisbon (1919–24). He won the National Composition prize (1926). He conducted the Lisbon Emissora National Orch. (from 1934), the Lisbon Choral Soc. (1940–47), the Oporto Sym. Orch. (1949–53), and the Orquesta de Concierto (from 1955). In his Violin Sonata (1923) he made the first known use of linear polyphony by a Portuguese composer.

WORKS: DRAMATIC: O p e r a : *O eremita* (1952); *A igreja do mar*, radio opera (1957; Lisbon, Feb. 5, 1960); *Don João e a máscara*, radio opera (1960). **B a l l e t :** *Muro do derrete* (1940); *A dança da Menina Tonta* (1941); *Imagens da terra e do mar* (1943); *Nazaré* (1948). **ORCH.:** *A lenda dos bailarins*, symphonic poem (1926); *Quarteto concertante* for 2 Violins, 2 Cellos, and String Orch. (1945); Flute Concerto (1954); *Suite Medieval* (1958); *Os Jerónimos*, sym. (1962). **CHAMBER:** *Nocturno* for Cello and Piano (1926); Violin Sonata (1946); String Quartet (1946); Wind Quintet (1950); *3 Peças sem importância* for Violin and Piano (1959). **KEYBOARD: P i a n o :** *Dança* (1923); *Ingenuidades* (1924); Sonata (1944); *Ciranda* (1944); *6 Pieces* (1946); *Bagatelles* (1953); *Variations* (1954). **O r g a n :** Sonata (1963). **VOCAL:** *Missa solene* for 4 Soloists, Chorus, and Orch. (1940); *As sete palavras de Nossa Senhora*, cantata (1946); songs.—**NS/LK/DM**

Freitas Branco, Luís de, eminent Portuguese composer, pedagogue, musicologist, and music critic; b. Lisbon, Oct. 12, 1890; d. there, Nov. 27, 1955. He was a student of Tomás Borba, Désiré Pâque, Augusto Machado, and Luigi Mancinelli in Lisbon, of Humperdinck in Berlin, and of Grovlez in Paris. He taught at the National Cons. in Lisbon from 1916, and also was active as a musicologist and music critic. He also held government positions, but lost these in 1939 for his outspoken criticism of the treatment of musicians in Germany and Italy; it was not until 1947 that these positions again became available to him. Freitas Branco was one of the most significant figures in Portuguese musical life. As a composer, he introduced impressionism and expressionism to Portugal.

WORKS: ORCH.: *Manfredo*, dramatic sym. for Soli, Chorus, and Orch. (1905); 5 symphonic poems: *Antero do Quental* (1908); *Os paraisos artificias* (1910); *Vathek* (1913); *Viriato* (1916); *Solemnia verba* (1952); Violin Concerto (1916); *Balada* for Piano and Orch. (1917); *Cena lirica* for Cello and Orch. (1917); *Suite alentejana* No. 1 (1919) and No. 2 (1927); 4 syms. (1924, 1926, 1943, 1952); *Variaçoes e fuga tríplice sobre um tema original* for Organ and Strings (1947); *Homenagem a Chopin: Polaca sobre um tema de Chopin* (1949). **CHAMBER:** 2 violin sonatas (1907, 1928); String Quartet (1911); Cello Sonata (1913); piano pieces; organ music. **VOCAL:** Sacred choral works; songs. **—NS/LK/DM**

Freithoff, Johan Henrik, Norwegian violinist and composer; b. Christiansand, 1713; d. Copenhagen, June 24, 1767. He received training from his father. Following extensive travels, he settled in Copenhagen in 1742, where he was made violinist extraordinary to the Danish court in 1744 and secretary to the Danish chancellery in 1745. He was an accomplished composer of chamber music. B. Kortsen ed. a complete collection of his output (Bergen, 1974).

BIBL.: B. Korsten, *J.H. F. (1713–1767): Man and Music* (Bergen, 1974).**—LK/DM**

Frémaux, Louis, French conductor; b. Aire-sur-la-Lys, Aug. 13, 1921. He attended the Valenciennes Cons., but his education was interrupted by World War II. He served in the Résistance during the Nazi occupation. After the war, he studied conducting at the Paris Cons. with Fourestier, graduating in 1952 with the premier prix. From 1956 to 1965 he was chief conductor of the Orchestre National de Monte Carlo, and then music director of the Orchestre Philharmonique Rhône-Alpes in Lyons (1968–71). From 1969 to 1978 he was music director of the City of Birmingham Sym. Orch. From 1979 to 1982 he was chief conductor of the Sydney (Australia) Sym. Orch.**—NS/LK/DM**

Fremstad, Olive, famous Swedish-born American soprano; b. Stockholm, March 14, 1871 (entered into the parish register as the daughter of an unmarried woman, Anna Peterson); d. Irvington-on-Hudson, N.Y., April 21, 1951. She was adopted by an American couple of Scandinavian origin, who took her to Minn.; she studied piano in Minneapolis; went to N.Y. in 1890 and took singing lessons with E.F. Bristol. She then held several church positions; in 1892 she sang for the first time with an orch. (under C. Zerrahn) in Boston. In 1893 she went to Berlin to study with Lilli Lehmann; made her operatic debut in Cologne as Azucena (1895); sang contralto parts. at the Bayreuth Festival in 1896; in 1897 she made her London debut; also sang in Cologne, Vienna, Amsterdam, and Antwerp. From 1900 to 1903 she was at the Munich Court Opera. She made her American debut as Sieglinde at the Metropolitan Opera in N.Y. on Nov. 25, 1903. Subsequently she sang soprano parts in Wagnerian operas; at first she was criticized in the press for her lack of true soprano tones; however, she soon triumphed over these difficulties, and became known as a soprano singer to the exclusion of contralto parts. She sang Carmen with great success at the Metropolitan

(March 5, 1906) with Caruso; her performance of Isolde under Mahler (Jan. 1, 1908) produced a deep impression; until 1915 she was one of the brightest stars of the Metropolitan, specializing in Wagnerian roles, but she was also successful in *Tosca* and other Italian operas. She sang Salome at the first American performance of the Strauss opera (N.Y., Jan. 22, 1907) and in Paris (May 8, 1907). After her retirement from the Metropolitan, she appeared with the Manhattan Opera, the Boston Opera, and the Chicago Opera, and in concerts; presented her last song recital in N.Y. on Jan. 19, 1920. In 1906 she married Edson Sutphen of N.Y. (divorced in 1911); in 1916 she married her accompanist, Harry Lewis Brainard (divorced in 1925). In Willa Cather's novel *The Song of the Lark*, the principal character was modeled after Fremstad.**—NS/LK/DM**

French, Jacob, American composer of Psalm tunes; b. Stoughton, Mass., July 15, 1754; d. Simsbury, Conn., May 1817. He was co-founder, with William Billings, of the Stoughton Music Soc. in 1774. He fought at the battle of Bunker Hill in the Revolutionary War, and was one of the few survivors of the Cherry Valley Massacre. After the war he became a singing teacher, retiring in 1814. He publ. *New American Melody* (1789), *Psalmodist's Companion* (1793), and *Harmony of Harmony* (1802).

BIBL.: M. Genuchi, *The Life and Music of J. F. (1754–1817), Colonial American Composer* (diss., Univ. of Iowa, 1964). **—NS/LK/DM**

Freni (real name, **Fregni**), **Mirella,** noted Italian soprano; b. Modena, Feb. 27, 1935. She studied voice with her uncle, Dante Arcelli, making her first public appearance at the age of 11. Her accompanist was a child pianist named Leone Magiera, whom she married in 1955. She later studied voice with Ettore Campogalliani. Freni made her operatic debut in Modena on Feb. 3, 1955, as Micaëla, and then sang in provincial Italian opera houses. In 1957 she took 1st prize in the Viotti Competition in Vercelli. In 1959 she sang with the Amsterdam Opera at the Holland Festival; then at the Glyndebourne Festival (1960), Covent Garden in London (1961), and La Scala in Milan (1962). She gained acclaim as Mimi in the film version of *La Bohème*, produced at La Scala in 1963 under Karajan's direction. When La Scala toured Russia in 1964, Freni joined the company and sang Mimi at the Bolshoi Theater in Moscow. She also chose the role of Mimi for her U.S. debut with the Metropolitan Opera in N.Y. on Sept. 29, 1965. She subsequently sang with the Vienna State Opera, the Bavarian State Opera in Munich, the Teatro San Carlo in Naples, and the Rome Opera. In 1976 she traveled with the Paris Opéra during its first U.S. tour. In addition to Mimi, she sang the roles of Susanna, Zerlina, Violetta, Amelia in *Simon Boccanegra*, and Manon. She won acclaim for her vivid portrayal of Tatiana, which she sang with many major opera companies, including the Metropolitan Opera in 1989. In 1990 she celebrated the 35th anniversary of her debut in Modena by returning there as Manon Lescaut. In 1992 she sang Alice Ford at the Metropolitan Opera, and that year also appeared as Mimi in Barcelona and Rome. She was engaged in 1994 as Fedora at La Scala, at the Lyric Opera in Chicago, and at Covent Garden, and then sang that role at the Metropolitan Opera in 1997. In 1998 she portrayed Fedora at the Washington (D.C.) Opera and at the Teatro Colón in Buenos Aires.—NS/LK/DM

Freschi, (Giovanni) Domenico, Italian composer; b. Bassano del Grappa, c. 1630; d. Vicenza, July 2, 1710. He was a singer and priest at Vicenza Cathedral, where he received a canonry in 1650 and was made maestro di cappella in 1656. He wrote 15 operas, some for Venice and others for the private theater in Piazzola sul Brenta, near Padua. His other works included the oratorios *Clotilde, Giuditta,* and *Il Miracolo del mago,* dramatic cantatas, masses, hymns, etc.—NS/LK/DM

Frescobaldi, Girolamo, great Italian organist and composer; b. Ferrara (baptized), Sept. 9, 1583; d. Rome, March 1, 1643. He studied with Luzzasco Luzzaschi in Ferrara; by the age of 14, he was organist at the Accademia della Morte there. In 1604 he was elected to membership in the Accademia di Santa Cecilia in Rome. In early 1607 he became organist of S. Maria in Trastevere; then, in June 1607, traveled to Brussels in the retinue of the Papal Nuncio. He publ. his first work, a collection of 5-part madrigals, in Antwerp in 1608, printed by Phalèse. Returning to Rome in the same year, he was appointed organist at St. Peter's on July 21 and assumed his duties on Oct. 31. He retained this all-important post until his death, with the exception of the years 1628 to 1634, when he was court organist in Florence. A significant indication of Frescobaldi's importance among musicians of his time was that Froberger, who was court organist in Vienna, came to Rome especially to study with him (1637–41). Fresco baldi's place in music history is very great; particularly as a keyboard composer, he exercised a decisive influence on the style of the early Baroque; he enl. the expressive resources of keyboard music so as to include daring chromatic progressions and acrid passing dissonances, "durezze" (literally, "harshnesses"); in Frescobaldi's terminology "toccata di durezza" signified a work using dissonances; he used similar procedures in organ variations on chorale themes, "fiori musicali" ("musical flowers"). His ingenious employment of variations greatly influenced the entire development of Baroque music. O. Mischiati and L. Tagliavini ed. Frescobaldi's complete works (Milan, 1974 et seq.)

WORKS: INSTRUMENTAL: 3 canzonas a 4, 5, and 8 (1608); *Il primo libro delle* [12] *fantasie a 4* (Milan, 1608); (12) *Toccate e* [3] *partite d'intavolatura di cembalo...libro primo* (Rome, 1615; 2nd ed., rev. and aug., 1616; 3rd ed., c. 1617–26; 4th ed., 1628, as *Il primo libro d'intavolatura di toccate di cimbalo*); (10) *Ricercari, et* [5] *canzoni franzese fatte sopra diverse oblighi in partitura...libro primo* (Rome, 1615); *Il primo libro di* [12] *capricci fatti sopra diversi soggetti et arie in partitura* (Rome, 1624); *Il secondo libro di* [11] *toccate,* [6] *canzone,* [4] *versi d'hinni,* [3] *Magnificat,* [5] *gagliarde,* [6] *correnti et altre* [4] *partite d'intavolatura di cimbalo et organo* (Rome, 1627); *Il primo libro delle* [35] *canzoni a 1 to 4, basso continuo, accomodate per sonare con ogni sorte de stromenti* (Rome, 1628); *In partitura, il primo libro delle* [38] *canzoni a 1 to 4, basso continuo per sonare con ogni sorte di stromenti, con 2 toccate in fine* (Rome, 1628); (40) *Canzoni da sonare, a 1 to 4, basso continuo,...li-*

bro primo (Venice, 1635); *Fiori musicali, di diverse compositioni, toccate, kyrie, canzoni, capricci, e ricercari, in partitura a 4* (Venice, 1635); (12) *Toccate d'intavolatura di cimbalo et organo, partite di diverse arie, e correnti, balletti, ciaconne, passacagli...libro primo* (Rome, 1637); (11) *Canzoni alla francese in partitura...libro quarto a 4* (Venice, 1645). **VOCAL: Sacred:** *Liber secundus diversarum modulationum* for 1 to Voices (Rome, 1627); *Missa sopra l'aria della monica* for 8 Voices and Basso Continuo (n.d.); *Missa sopra l'aria di Fiorenza* for 8 Voices and Basso Continuo (n.d.). **Secular:** *Il primo libro de'* [19] *madrigali* for 5 Voices (Antwerp, 1608); *Primo libro d'arie musicali per cantarsi* for 1 to 3 Voices, Theorbo, and Harpsichord (Florence, 1630); *Secondo libro d'arie musicale per cantarsi* for 1 to 3 Voices, Theorbo, and Harpsichord (Florence, 1630).

BIBL.: N. Bennati, ed., *Ferrara a G. F.* (Ferrara, 1908); L. Ronga, *G. F.* (Turin, 1930); F. Morel, *G. F., organista di S. Pietro di Roma* (Winterthur, 1945); A. Machabey, *G. F.: La Vie, l'oeuvre* (Paris, 1952); F. Hammond, *G. F.* (Cambridge, Mass., 1983); C. Gallico, *G. F.: L'affetto, l'ordito, le meta morfosi* (Florence, 1986); A. Silbiger, ed., *F. Studies* (Durham, N.C., 1987); F. Hammond, *G. F.: A Guide to Research* (N.Y., 1988); H. Klein, *Die Toccaten G. F.s* (Mainz, 1989).—NS/LK/DM

Frešo, Tibor, Slovak conductor and composer; b. Spišský, Nov. 20, 1918; d. Bratislava, July 7, 1987. He studied composition with A. Moyzes and conducting with J. Vincourek at the Bratislava Cons., graduating in 1938; then studied with Pizzetti at the Accademia di Santa Cecilia in Rome (1939–42). Returning to Czechoslovakia, he served as conductor of the Slovak National Theater in Bratislava (1942–49) and the Košice Opera (1949–52). In 1953 he was appointed chief opera conductor of the Slovak National Opera.

WORKS: DRAMATIC: Opera: *Martin and the Sun,* children's opera (Bratislava, Jan. 25, 1975); *Poor Francois* (1982–84). **ORCH.:** *Little Suite* (1938); *Concert Overture* (1940); *Symphonic Prolog* (1943); symphonic poems: *A New Morning* (1950) and *Liberation* (1955); *Little Concerto* for Piano and Orch. (1976). **CHAMBER:** Wind Quintet (1983). **VOCAL:** 3 cantatas: *Stabat Mater* (1940), *Mother* (1959), and *Hymn to the Fatherland* (1961); *Meditation* for Soprano and Orch. (1942); *Song about Woman* for Alto, Narrator, Children's and Mixed Choruses, and Orch. (1975).—NS/LK/DM

Freund, John Christian, English-American music journalist; b. London, Nov. 22, 1848; d. Mt. Vernon, N.Y., June 3, 1924. He studied music in London and Oxford. In 1871 went to N.Y., where he became ed. of the *Musical and Dramatic Times;* in 1890 began publishing a commercial magazine, *Music Trades.* In 1898 he founded the weekly magazine *Musical America* and was its ed. until his death. In his editorials he fulminated against the rival magazine *Musical Courier,* and also wrote sharp polemical articles denouncing composers and music critics who disagreed with his viewpoint. In this respect he was a typical representative of the personal type of musical journalism of the time. —NS/LK/DM

Freund, Marya, German soprano; b. Breslau, Dec. 12, 1876; d. Paris, May 21, 1966. She was a student of Sarasate (violin) and Stockhausen (voice). After making her debut in 1909, she appeared as a soloist with orchs. and as a recitalist in Europe and the U.S., gaining distinction as a champion of contemporary music. She settled in Paris and taught voice during the last 30 years of her life.—NS/LK/DM

Freundt, Cornelius, German organist and composer; b. Plauen, c. 1535; d. Zwickau (buried), Aug. 26, 1591. After serving as a cantor in Borna, he went to Zwickau and became cantor of St. Marien in 1565. He also was active as an organist and teacher. He wrote music for church and school use.

BIBL.: G. Göhler, *C. F.* (Leipzig, 1896).—NS/LK/DM

Frey, Emil, eminent Swiss pianist, teacher, and composer, brother of **Walter Frey**; b. Baden, April 8, 1889; d. Zürich, May 20, 1946. He studied with Otto Barblan at the Geneva Cons.; at the age of 15, he was accepted as a student of Diemer in piano and Widor in composition; in 1907 he went to Berlin, and later to Bucharest, where he became a court pianist. In 1910 he won the Anton Rubinstein prize for his Piano Trio in St. Petersburg; on the strength of this success, he was engaged to teach at the Moscow Cons. (1912–17). Returning to Switzerland after the Russian Revolution, he joined the faculty of the Zürich Cons.; he continued his concert career throughout Europe and also in South America. He wrote 2 syms. (the 1st with a choral finale), piano concerto, violin concerto, cello concerto, *Swiss Festival Overture*, piano quintet, string quartet, piano trio, violin sonata, cello sonata, several piano sonatas, piano suites, and sets of piano variations. He publ. a piano instruction manual, *Bewusst gewordenes Klavierspiel und seine technischen Grundlagen* (Zürich, 1933).—NS/LK/DM

Frey, Paul, Canadian tenor; b. Heidelberg, Ontario, April 20, 1941. He received vocal instruction from Douglas Campbell and Victor Martens, and then studied at the Univ. of Toronto Opera School with Louis Quilico and at the Royal Cons. of Music in Toronto. In 1976 he made his debut as Werther with Opera in Concert. He joined the Basel Opera in 1978, where he made his debut in that same role. In 1985 he sang Lohengrin in Karlsruhe, and then portrayed that role with great success in Mannheim in 1986. In 1987 he appeared in that role at his Bayreuth Festival debut. On Sept. 23, 1987, he made his Metropolitan Opera debut in N.Y. as Strauss's Bacchus. He sang Lohengrin at his first appearance at London's Covent Garden in 1988. After appearing as Huon in *Oberon* at Milan's La Scala in 1989, he was engaged as Siegmund at the Cologne Opera for the 1990–91 season. In 1994 he created the title role in Jost Meier's *Dreyfus—Die Affäre* at the Deutsche Oper in Berlin. He appeared as Schoeck's Venus in Geneva in 1997. Among his other roles were Mozart's Titus and Don Ottavio, Florestan, Max, Parsifal, and Strauss's Flamand and Emperor.—NS/LK/DM

Frey, Walter, Swiss pianist and teacher, brother of **Emil Frey**; b. Basel, Jan. 26, 1898; d. Zürich, May 28, 1985. He studied piano with F. Niggli and theory with

Andreae. From 1925 to 1958 he was an instructor in piano at the Zürich Cons. He concurrently evolved an active concert career in Germany and Scandinavia. He specialized in modern piano music and gave first performances of several piano concertos by contemporary composers; later he became well known for his championship of the keyboard works of Bach. He publ. (with W. Schuh) a collection, *Schweizerische Klaviermusik aus der Zeit der Klassik und Romantik* (Zürich, 1937). —NS/LK/DM

Freyer, August, German-born Polish organist, pedagogue, and composer; b. Mulda, near Dresden, Dec. 15, 1803; d. Pilica, near Warsaw, May 28, 1883. He studied with F. Schneider and C. Pohlenz in Leipzig, and completed his training in Warsaw with Lenz (figured bass and organ) and Elsner (composition). In 1837 he became organist of the Evangelical Church in Warsaw, which post he held for more than four decades. He also toured Europe as an organ virtuoso. In 1831 he founded his own free school for organ instruction, and in 1858 he became a teacher of organ, harmony, and counterpoint at the Warsaw Music Inst. His most famous pupil was Moniuszko. Freyer's virtuoso organ works made a notable addition to the repertory. —LK/DM

Frezzolini, Erminia, Italian soprano; b. Orvieto, March 27, 1818; d. Paris, Nov. 5, 1884. She studied with her father, the bass Giuseppe Frezzolini, and with Nencini, Ronconi, Manuel García, and Tacchinardi. In 1838 she made her operatic debut in *Beatrice di Tenda* in Florence, and then appeared in London in 1842. On Feb. 11, 1843, she created the role of Viclinda in *I Lombardi* in Milan, returning there to create the title role in *Giovanna d'Arco* on Feb. 15, 1845. In 1850 she again sang in London, and in 1855 she appeared in N.Y., where she was the first Gilda. She also sang in Vienna, St. Petersburg, Madrid, and Paris. In 1860 she retired from the stage, but resumed her career in 1863. In 1868 she retired for good.—NS/LK/DM

Fribec, Krešimir, Croatian composer; b. Daruvar, May 24, 1908. He studied with Zlatko Grgošević in Zagreb, and later was active as music ed. of the Zagreb Radio (1943–64). He also served as director of the Croatian Music Soc. Most of his large output was composed in an accessible style.

WORKS: DRAMATIC: O p e r a : *Sluga Jernej* (1951); *Krvava svadba* (Blood Wedding; 1958); *Prometej* (1960); *Jerma* (1960); *Maljiva* (1962); *Čehovljev humoristicon* (1962); *Nova Eva* (1963); *Juduška Golovljiev* (1964); *Adagio melancolico* (1965); *Dolazi revisor* (The Government Inspector; 1965); *Dunja u kovčegu* (1966); *Veliki val* (The Large Wave; 1966); *Heretik* (1971); *Ujak Vanja* (Uncle Vanya; 1972). O t h e r : Many ballets. ORCH.: *Ritmi drammatici* for Chamber Orch. (1960); *Accenti tragici* (1961); *Kosmička kretanja* (Cosmic Movements; 1961); Piano Concerto (1964); *Canto* for Strings (1965); *Ekstaza*, symphonic suite (1965); *Simfonija* (1965); *Lamento* for Strings (1967); *Koncertantna muzika* for Violin and Orch. (1970); Cello Concerto (1971);

Covjek, sym. (1972). **CHAMBER:** 7 string quartets (1962–72); *Musica aleatorica* for Flute, Cello, Vibraphone, and Piano (1961); Sonata for Cello (1966); Violin Sonata (1967); *Divertimento* for Viola and Percussion (1970); *Alterations*, piano trio (1971). —**NS/LK/DM**

Fricci (real name, **Frietsche**), **Antonietta,** Austrian soprano; b. Vienna, Jan. 8, 1840; d. Turin, Sept. 7, 1912. She studied with Marchesi in Vienna, making her debut in 1858 in Pisa as Violetta. She was a principal singer at La Scala in Milan (1865–73). After her retirement in 1878, he taught voice in Florence and Turin. —**NS/LK/DM**

Frick, Gottlob, German bass; b. Olbronn, Württemberg, July 28, 1906; d. Mühlacker, near Pforzheim, Aug. 18, 1994. He studied at the Stuttgart Cons. and also took vocal lessons with Neudörfer-Opitz. After singing in the Stuttgart Opera chorus, he made his operatic debut as Daland in *Der fliegende Holländer* in Coburg (1934); then sang in Freiburg im Breisgau and Königsberg, and subsequently was a leading member of the Dresden State Opera (1941–52). He appeared at the Städtische Oper in West Berlin (from 1950), the Bavarian State Opera in Munich (from 1953), and the Vienna State Opera (from 1953); made his debut at London's Covent Garden (1951), and later sang there regularly (1957–67). On Dec. 27, 1961, he made his Metropolitan Opera debut in N.Y. as Fafner in *Das Rheingold*; also sang at Bayreuth, Milan's La Scala, and Salzburg. He gave his farewell performance in 1970, but continued to make a few stage appearances in later years. A fine Wagnerian, he excelled as Gurnemanz and Hagen; was also admired for his portrayal of Rocco in *Fidelio.*—**NS/LK/DM**

Fricke, Heinz, German conductor; b. Halberstadt, Feb. 11, 1927. He studied in Halberstadt and with Abendroth in Weimar (1948–50). From 1950 to 1960 he was conductor at the Leipzig City Theater. In 1960–61 he was Generalmusikdirektor in Schwerin, and then held that title with the Berlin State Opera from 1961 to 1992. He also appeared as a guest conductor with many opera houses in Europe and South America. In 1992 he conducted *Parsifal* at the reopening of the Chemnitz Opera House. In 1993 he became music director of the Washington (D.C.) Opera.—**NS/LK/DM**

Fricker, Herbert (Austin), English organist and composer; b. Canterbury, Feb. 12, 1868; d. Toronto, Nov. 11, 1943. He studied organ with W.H. Longhurst, and composition with Sir Frederick Bridge and Edwin Lemare. After filling posts as organist in Canterbury, Folkstone, and Leeds, he moved to Toronto in 1917, and conducted the Mendelssohn Choir there until 1942. He composed sacred and secular choruses and organ pieces.—**NS/LK/DM**

Fricker, Peter Racine, distinguished English composer and pedagogue; b. London, Sept. 5, 1920; d. Santa Barbara, Calif., Feb. 1, 1990. He studied theory and composition with R.O. Morris at the Royal Coll. of Music in London, and, following service in the Royal Air Force (1941–46), he completed his training with Mátyás Seiber (1946–48). He was director of music at Morley Coll. in London (from 1952) and a prof. of composition at the Royal Coll. of Music (from 1955). In 1964 he was a visiting prof. at the Univ. of Calif. at Santa Barbara, where he then was a full prof. (from 1965); he also was chairman of its music dept. (1970–74). In his works, Fricker utilized various techniques. His output revealed a fascination for the development of small cells, either melodically, harmonically, or rhythmically.

WORKS: DRAMATIC: Opera: *The Death of Vivien* (1956). **Ballet:** *Canterbury Prologue* (1951). **ORCH.:** *Rondo scherzoso* (1948); 5 syms.: No. 1 (1949; Cheltenham, July 5, 1950), No. 2 (1950–51; Liverpool, July 26, 1951), No. 3 (London, Nov. 8, 1960), No. 4, "in memoriam Mátyás Seiber" (1966; Cheltenham, Feb. 14, 1967), and No. 5 (1975–76); *Prelude, Elegy, and Finale* for Strings (1949); 2 violin concertos: No. 1 (1949–50) and No. 2, *Rapsodia Concertante* (1952–54; Cheltenham, July 15, 1954); Concerto for English Horn and Strings (1950); *Concertante* for 3 Pianos, Strings, and Timpani (1951; London, Aug. 10, 1956); Viola Concerto (1952; Edinburgh, Sept. 3, 1953); Piano Concerto (1952–54; London, March 21, 1954); *Litany* for Double String Orch. (1955); *Comedy Overture* (1958); *Toccata* for Piano and Orch. (1959); *3 Scenes* (1966; Santa Barbara, Calif., Feb. 26, 1967); *7 Counterpoints* (Pasadena, Calif., Oct. 21, 1967); *Nocturne* for Chamber Orch. (1971); *Introitus* (Canterbury, June 24, 1972); *Sinfonia in memoriam Benjamin Britten* for 17 Wind Instruments (1976–77); *Laudi Concertati* for Organ and Orch. (1979); *Rondeaux* for Horn and Orch. (1982); *Concerto for Orchestra* (1986); *Walk by Quiet Waters* (1989). **CHAMBER:** Wind Quintet (1947); 3 string quartets (1947; 1952–53; 1975); 2 violin sonatas (1950, 1988); Horn Sonata (1955); Cello Sonata (1956); Octet for Wind and String Instruments (1957–58); *Serenade* No. 1 for 6 Instruments (1959), No. 2 for Flute, Oboe, and Piano (1959), and No. 3 for Saxophone Quartet (1969); *4 Dialogues* for Oboe and Piano (1965); *Fantasy* for Viola and Piano (1966); *Concertante* No. 5 for Piano and String Quartet (1971); *Spirit Puck* for Clarinet and Percussion (1974); *Aspects of Evening* for Cello and Piano (1985). **KEYBOARD: Piano:** *Variations* (1957–58); *12 Studies* (1961); *Episodes I* (1967–68) and *II* (1969); *Anniversary* (1978); Sonata for 2 Pianos (1978). **Organ:** Sonata (1947); *Choral* (1956); *Ricercare* (1965); *6 Pieces* (1968); *Toccata* (1968); *Praeludium* (1970); Trio-Sonata (1974). **VOCAL:** *Madrigals* for Chorus (1947); *Night Landscape* for Soprano and String Trio (1947); *3 Sonnets by Cecco Angiolieri* for Tenor, Wind Quintet, Cello, and Double Bass (1947); *Musick's Empire* for Chorus and Small Orch. (1955); *Tomb of St. Eulalia* for Countertenor, Viola da Gamba, and Harpsichord (1955); *The Vision of Judgement*, oratorio for Soprano, Tenor, Chorus, and Orch. (1957–58; Leeds, Oct. 13, 1958); Cantata for Tenor and Chamber Orch. (1962); *O Longs désirs*, 5 songs for Soprano and Orch. (1963); *The Day and the Spirits* for Soprano and Harp (1966–67); *Ave Maris Stella* for Chorus (1967); *Magnificat* for Soloists, Chorus, and Orch. (Santa Barbara, May 27, 1968); *Some Superior Nonsense* for Tenor, Flute, Oboe, and Harpsichord (1968); *The Roofs* for Coloratura Soprano and Percussion (1970); *Come, sleep* for Contralto, Alto Flute, and Bass Clarinet (1972); *6 Melodies de Francis Jammes* for Tenor and Piano Trio (1980); *Whispers at These Curtains*, oratorio for Baritone, Chorus, Boy's Chorus, and Orch. (1984). —**NS/LK/DM**

Fricsay, Ferenc, distinguished Hungarian-born Austrian conductor; b. Budapest, Aug. 9, 1914; d. Basel, Feb. 20, 1963. He received his initial musical training from his father, a military bandmaster, and then was a pupil of Bartók (piano) and Kodály (composition) at the Budapest Academy of Music; he learned to play almost every orchestral instrument. He was conductor in Szeged (1933–44), and also held the post of 1st conductor at the Budapest Opera (1939–45). In 1945 he became music director of the Hungarian State Opera in Budapest. On Aug. 6, 1947, he made an impressive debut at the Salzburg Festival conducting the premiere of Gottfried von Einem's opera *Dantons Tod*, which led to engagements in Europe and South America. In 1948 he became a conductor at the Städtische Oper in West Berlin; in 1951–52 he was its artistic director but resigned after a conflict over artistic policies. In 1949 he became chief conductor of the RIAS (Radio in the American Sector) Sym. Orch. in Berlin, an esteemed position he retained until 1954. After it became the Radio Sym. Orch. of Berlin in 1955, he appeared with it regularly until 1961. On Nov. 13, 1953, he made his U.S. debut as a guest conductor of the Boston Sym. Orch. In 1954 he was engaged as conductor of the Houston Sym. Orch., but he resigned his position soon afterward following a disagreement with its management over musical policies. From 1956 to 1958 he was Generalmusikdirektor of the Bavarian State Opera in Munich. In 1959 he became a naturalized Austrian citizen. In 1961 he was invited to conduct *Don Giovanni* at the opening of the Deutsche Oper in West Berlin. Soon thereafter leukemia compelled him to abandon his career. Fricsay excelled as an interpreter of the Romantic repertory but he also displayed a special affinity for the masterworks of the 20th century. He was the author of the book *Über Mozart und Bartók* (Frankfurt am Main, 1962).

BIBL.: F. Herzfeld, *E. F.: Ein Gedenkbuch* (Berlin, 1964). —NS/LK/DM

Frid, Géza, Hungarian-born Dutch composer; b. Máramarossziget, Jan. 25, 1904; d. Beverwijk, Sept. 13, 1989. He studied composition with Kodály and piano with Bartók at the Budapest Academy of Music (1912–24). He settled in Amsterdam in 1929, becoming a naturalized Dutch citizen in 1948. He later taught at the Utrecht Cons. (1964–69).

WORKS: DRAMATIC: Opera: *De zwarte bruid* (1959). **Ballet:** *Luctor et Emergo* (1953); *Euridice* (1961). **ORCH.:** *Podium-Suite* for Violin and Orch. (1928); Violin Concerto (1930); *Tempesta d'orchestra* (1931); *Divertimento* for String Orch. or String Quintet (1932); Sym. (1933); *Romance and Allegro* for Cello and Orch. (1935); *Abel et Cain*, symphonic tableau for Low Voice and Orch. (1938); *Nocturnes* for Flute, Harp, and String Orch. or String Quintet (1946); *Paradou*, symphonic fantasy (1948); *Fête champêtre*, suite of dances for Strings and Percussion (1951); Concerto for 2 Violins and Orch. (1952); *Caecilia Ouverture* (1953); *Études symphoniques* (1954); *South African Rhapsody* for Orch. or Wind Orch. (1954); Serenade for Chamber Orch. (1956); Concerto for 2 Pianos and Orch. (1957); Concertino for Violin, Cello, Piano, and Orch. (1961); *Sinfonietta* for Strings (1963); *7 pauken en een koperorkest*, concerto for 7 Percussionists and Brass Orch. (1964); Concerto for 3 Violins and Orch. (The Hague, July 4, 1970); Concerto for 4 different Clarinets (1 Soloist) and Strings (1972); *Olifant-variaties*, double bass concerto (1977). **CHAMBER:** 5 string quartets (1926, 1939, 1949, 1956, 1984); String Trio (1926); *Serenade* for Wind Instruments (1928); Cello Sonata (1931); Sonata for Solo Violin (1936); Piano Trio (1947); Violin Sonata (1955); *12 Metamorphoses* for 2 Flutes and Percussion (1957); *Fuga* for 3 Harps (1961); Sextet for Wind Quintet and Piano (1965); *Dubbeltrio* for Wind Instruments (1967); *Chemins divers* for Flute, Bassoon, and Piano (1968; also for 2 Violins and Piano); *Paganini Variations* for 2 Violins (1969); *Caprices roumains* for Oboe and Piano (1975); *Sons roumains* for Flute, Viola, Harp, and Percussion (1975); *Music for 2 Violins and Viola* (1977); *Vice Versa* for Alto Saxophone and Marimba (1982); piano pieces. **VOCAL:** Various works. —NS/LK/DM

Friderici, Daniel, German composer and music theorist; b. Klein-Eichstedt, near Querfurt, 1584; d. Rostock, Sept. 23, 1638. He pursued his musical training in various German cities, his principal mentors in composition being Friedrich Weissensee in Magdeburg and Valentin Haussmann in Gerbstedt; he also attended the Univ. of Rostock (1612). He was in the service of Count Anton Gunther of Oldenburg (1614–18) before settling in Rostock as cantor at the Marienkirche, a post he held until his death from the plague; he also was Kapellmeister of all of the churches there from 1623. In 1618 he was in charge of the musical celebrations for the 200th anniversary of the Univ. of Rostock, which awarded him an M.A. degree in 1619. Friderici composed a large body of sacred and secular music. E. Schenk and W. Voll ed. his sacred music in Das Erbe Deutscher Musik, 2nd series (1942). His important treatise *Musica figuralis oder newe...Unterweisung des Singe Kunst* (Rostock, 1618; 7 subsequent eds.) placed special significance on singing and the use of modes.

BIBL.: W. Voll, *D. F.: Sein Leben und seine geistlichen Werke* (Kassel and Hannover, 1936).—NS/LK/DM

Friderici-Jakowicka, Teodozja, Polish soprano; b. Kielce, 1836; d. Warsaw, Nov. 4, 1889. She studied piano with J. Drobrzyński and voice with Ovattrini and J. Dobrski in Warsaw, completing her voice training in Milan with Lamperti. In 1865 she made her operatic debut in *La sonnambula* in Warsaw, and then was engaged in opera houses throughout Europe and in N.Y. before retiring in 1885. Her best roles were in operas by Bellini, Donizetti, Meyerbeer, and Verdi. —LK/DM

Friebert, (Johann) Joseph, Austrian tenor and composer; b. Gnadendorf, Lower Austria (baptized), Dec. 5, 1724; d. Passau, Aug. 6, 1799. After vocal studies with Bonno, he entered the service of the Prince of Saxe-Hildburgshausen in Vienna. In 1755 he became a member of the Vienna Court Theater, and then was Kapellmeister to the Prince-Bishop of Passau from 1763 until his death. He was a composer of Singspiels, Italian operas, oratorios, and cantatas. His brother, Karl Friebert (b. Wullersdorf, Lower Austria, June 7, 1736; d. Vienna, Aug. 6, 1816), was also a tenor and composer. After singing in Eisenstadt (1759–76), he settled in Vienna as Kapellmeister to the two Jesuit churches and the Minorite Church.—NS/LK/DM

Fried, Alexej, Czech composer; b. Brno, Oct. 13, 1922. He studied piano and composition at the Brno

Cons., and then composition with Hlobil and Bořkovec at the Prague Academy of Music (graduated, 1953). He also led his own orchs., lectured, and composed. Many of his works are in the "3rd-stream" manner, fusing jazz with Classical styles.

WORKS: ORCH.: Triple Concerto for Flute, Clarinet, Horn, and Orch. (1971); Concerto (1974); Concerto No. 2 for Clarinet and Orch. (1976); Concerto for Horn and Chamber Orch. (1977); *Concerto di Freiberg* for Chamber Orch. (1977; rewritten 1982 as *Gothic Concerto*); Triple Concertino for Oboe, Clarinet, Bassoon, 2 Percussion, and Strings (1981); *Bread and Games*, musical picture for Flute, Soprano Saxophone, Horn, and Orch. (1982); *Cassation* for Chamber Orch. (1985). **CHAMBER:** *Sonatina drammatica* for Violin and Piano (1975); *Moravian Trio* for Flute, Marimba, and Harp (1978); *Guernica*, quintet for Soprano Saxophone and String Quartet (1978); Quintet for Flute, Violin, Viola, Cello, and Piano (1979); *Tympanum*, trio for Violin, Soprano Saxophone, and Piano (1982); Sextet for Flute, Clarinet, Bass Clarinet, Piano, Double Bass, and Percussion (1984); Sonata for Saxophone Quartet (1987); *3 Characteristic Études* for Horn (1990); Concertino for Flute, Guitar, String Quartet, and 2 Percussion (1992); *Paraphrases and Variations on Themes from West Side Story* for Violin, Cello, Clarinet, and Piano (1996). **Jazzworks For Big Band:** *The Act* for Trumpet, Flute, and Big Band (1968); Jazz Concerto for Clarinet and Big Band (1970); *Souvenir* (1970); *Jazz Ballet Études* for Clarinet and Big Band (1970); *Sidonia* for Trumpet and Big Band (1971); *Moravian Wedding*, sinfonietta (1972); *The Solstice*, concerto for 2 Big Bands (1973); Concertino for Clarinet and Big Band (1974); *Dialogue* for 2 Alto Saxophones and Big Band (1974); *Paraphrases to Motives of Blue Skies* for Soprano Saxophone and Big Band (1975); Concerto (1976); *Jazz Composition* for Trombone and Big Band (1977); *Polyphone* (1978); *Song* for Trumpet and Big Band (1979); *Plays* for Percussion, Tenor Saxophone, and Big Band (1980); *Silhouettes* for Baritone Saxophone and Big Band (1983); *A Picture Postcard from Moravia* for Baritone Saxophone and Big Band (1985); *The Nude* for Trumpet, Flute, and Big Band (1986); *Salute* for Soprano Saxophone, Flute, and Big Band (1987).—**NS/LK/DM**

Fried, Miriam, Romanian-born Israeli violinist and teacher; b. Satu Mare, Sept. 9, 1946. She was taken to Israel at age 2. After studies at the Rubin Academy of Music in Tel Aviv, she pursued her training with Gingold at the Ind. Univ. School of Music in Bloomington (1966–67) and Galamian at the Juilliard School of Music in N.Y. (1967–69). In 1968 she won 1st prize in the Paganini Competition in Genoa, and in 1971 won 1st prize in the Queen Elisabeth of Belgium Competition in Brussels. Following her N.Y. debut in 1969 and her British debut at Windsor Castle in 1971, she appeared as a soloist with many of the principal world orchs., as a recitalist, and as a chamber music artist. She also was a prof. at the Ind. Univ. School of Music from 1986. —**NS/LK/DM**

Fried, Oskar, German-born Russian conductor and composer; b. Berlin, Aug. 10, 1871; d. Moscow, July 5, 1941. He studied with Humperdinck in Frankfurt am Main and P. Scharwenka in Berlin. He played the horn in various orchs. until the performance of his choral work with orch. *Das trunkene Lied*, given by Muck in Berlin (April 15, 1904), attracted much favorable atten-

tion; he continued to compose prolifically. At the same time, he began his career as a conductor, achieving considerable renown in Europe; he was conductor of the Stern Choral Soc. in Berlin (from 1904), of the Gesellschaft der Musikfreunde in Berlin (1907–10), and of the Berlin Sym. Orch. (1925–26). He left Berlin in 1934 and went to Russia; became a naturalized Russian citizen in 1940. For several years he was conductor of the Tbilisi Opera; later was chief conductor of the All-Union Radio Orch. in Moscow.

BIBL.: P. Bekker, *O. F.* (Berlin, 1907); P. Stefan, *O. F.* (Berlin, 1911); D. Rabinovitz, *O. F.* (Moscow, 1971).—**NS/LK/DM**

Friedberg, Carl, noted German pianist and teacher; b. Bingen, Sept. 18, 1872; d. Merano, Italy, Sept. 8, 1955. He studied piano at the Frankfurt am Main Cons. with Kwast, Knorr, and Clara Schumann; also took a course in composition with Humperdinck. He subsequently taught piano at the Frankfurt am Main Cons. (1893–1904) and at the Cologne Cons. (1904–14). In 1914 he made his first American tour, with excellent success. He taught piano at the Inst. of Musical Art in N.Y.; was a member of the faculty of the Juilliard School of Music in N.Y. Among his pupils were Percy Grainger, Ethel Leginska, Elly Ney, and other celebrated pianists.

BIBL.: J. Smith, *Master Pianist: The Career and Teaching of C. F.* (N.Y., 1963).—**NS/LK/DM**

Friedheim, Arthur, German pianist; b. St. Petersburg (of German parents), Oct. 26, 1859; d. N.Y., Oct. 19, 1932. He was a pupil of Anton Rubinstein and Liszt, and became particularly known as an interpreter of Liszt's works. He made his first American tour in 1891. He taught at the Chicago Musical Coll. in 1897, and then traveled. He lived in London, Munich, and (after 1915) N.Y. as a teacher and pianist. Among his compositions were a piano concerto, many pieces for solo piano, and an opera, *Die Tänzerin* (Karlsruhe, 1897). His memoirs, *Life and Liszt: The Recollections of a Concert Pianist*, were publ. posth. (N.Y., 1961).—**NS/LK/DM**

Friedhofer, Hugo (William), American composer of film music; b. San Francisco, May 3, 1901; d. Los Angeles, May 17, 1981. He studied composition with Domenico Brescia. In 1929 he went to Hollywood, where he worked as an arranger and composer for early sound films. In 1935 he was engaged as an orchestrator for Warner Brothers, and received valuable instruction from Korngold and Steiner. In Los Angeles he attended Schoenberg's seminars and took additional lessons in composition with Toch and Kanitz; he also had some instruction with Boulanger during her sojourn in Calif. He wrote his first complete film score for *The Adventures of Marco Polo* in 1938, and in the following years composed music for about 70 films. His film music for *The Best Years of Our Lives* won the Academy Award in 1946. His other distinguished film scores included *Broken Arrow* (1950), *Vera Cruz* (1954), *The Rains of Ranchipur* (1955), *The Sun Also Rises* (1957), and *The Young Lions* (1958). Friedhofer was highly esteemed for his ability to create a congenial musical background, alternatively lyrical and dramatic, for the action on the screen, never sacrificing the purely musical quality for the sake of external effect.

BIBL.: I. Atkins, *H. F.* (Los Angeles, 1974).—**NS/LK/DM**

Friedlaender, Max, eminent German musicologist; b. Brieg, Silesia, Oct. 12, 1852; d. Berlin, May 2, 1934. He was first a bass, and studied voice with Manuel Garcia in London and Julius Stockhausen in Frankfurt am Main. He appeared at the London Monday Popular Concerts in 1880. He returned to Germany in 1881 and took a course at Berlin Univ. with Spitta, obtaining the degree of Ph.D. at Rostock with the diss. *Beiträge zur Biographie Franz Schuberts* (1887; publ. in Berlin, 1887). He then was Privatdozent at Berlin Univ. in 1894, and a prof. and director of music there from 1903. He was exchange prof. at Harvard Univ. in 1911. He lectured at many American univs. and received the degree of LL.D. from the Univ. of Wisc.; retired in 1932. He discovered the MSS of more than 100 lost songs by Schubert and publ. them in his complete ed. (7 vols.) of Schubert's songs. Together with Johann Bolte and Johann Meier, he searched for years in every corner of the German Empire in quest of folk songs still to be found among the people. Some of these he publ. in a vol. under the title *100 deutsche Volkslieder in Goethe Jahrbuch* (1885). He was ed. of *Volksliederbuch für gemischten Chor* (1912) and edited songs of Mozart, Schumann, and Mendelssohn, Beethoven's "Scotch Songs," the first version of Brahms's *Deutsche Volkslieder* (1926), *Volksliederbuch für die deutsche Jugend* (1928), etc. He publ. *Das Deutsche Lied im 18. Jahrhundert* (2 vols., 1902), *Brahms Lieder* (1922; Eng. tr., London, 1928), and *Franz Schubert, Skizze seines Lebens und Wirkens* (1928).—**NS/LK/DM**

Friedman, Erick, remarkable American violinist, conductor, and teacher; b. Newark, N.J., Aug. 16, 1939. He began his studies with his father. After lessons from Samuel Applebaum, he enrolled at age 10 as a pupil of Galamian at the Juilliard School of Music in N.Y. He also received lessons from Milstein, and then from Heifetz (1956–58). In 1953 he won the Music Education League Competition and made his formal debut as a soloist with the Little Orch. Soc. of N.Y. After making his recital debut at N.Y.'s Carnegie Hall in 1956, he toured widely as a recitalist. He also appeared as a soloist with many of the foremost orchs. in North America and overseas, and performed at various festivals. In 1983 he was soloist in the Bartók Violin Concerto on A & E TV. Turning his attention to conducting, he became music director of the Garrett Lakes (Md.) Summer Festival Orch. in 1988. He also taught at the Yale Univ. School of Music from 1989. In 1993 he likewise resumed his career as a stunning virtuoso violinist. In 1998 he received extraordinary critical acclaim for the mastery he displayed in London. In addition to his outstanding interpretations of the standard violin repertoire, Friedman has had works written for and/or dedicated to him by such composers as Mario Castelnuovo-Tedesco, Isadore Freed, Ezra Laderman, and Laurent Petitgirard. —**NS/LK/DM**

Friedman, Ignaz, famous Polish pianist and composer; b. Podgorze, near Kraków, Feb. 14, 1882; d.

Sydney, Australia, Jan. 26, 1948. He studied theory with Riemann in Leipzig and piano with Leschetizky in Vienna. In 1904 he launched an extensive career as a concert pianist; gave about 2,800 concerts in Europe, America, Australia, Japan, China, and South Africa. In 1941 he settled in Sydney. He was renowned as an interpreter of Chopin; prepared an annotated ed. of Chopin's works in 12 vols.; also edited piano compositions of Schumann and Liszt. Among his compositions were a hundred or so pieces for piano in an effective salon manner, among them a group of *Fantasiestücke*. —**NS/LK/DM**

Friedman, Ken, American composer; b. New London, Conn., Sept. 19, 1939. He became associated with Richard Maxfield, who initiated him into the arcana of modern music. Friedman developed feverish activities in avant-garde intellectual and musical fields. Most of his works are verbal exhortations to existentialist actions, e.g., *Scrub Piece* (scrubbing a statue in a public square), *Riverboat Brawl* (starting a brawl in a riverboat at Disneyland), *Goff Street* (a "theft event," transplanting a street sign), *Come Ze Revolution* (chanting pseudo-Greek songs), and *Watermelon* (splitting a watermelon with a karate blow). He also composed a *Quiet Sonata* (1969) for 75 Truncated Guitar Fingerboards with no strings attached and realized for Nam June Paik his alleged *Young Penis Symphony* for 10 ditto, and had it performed at a hidden retreat in San Francisco. —**NS/LK/DM**

Friedman, Richard, American composer; b. N.Y., Jan. 6, 1944. He received training in electronics. After working with Morton Subotnick at the Intermedia Electronic Music Studio at N.Y. Univ. (1966–68), he joined the music dept. of KPFA radio in Berkeley. His output reflected his interest in avant-garde pursuits with a special emphasis on the application of electronics. —**NS/LK/DM**

Friedrich II (der Grosse)
See **Frederick II (Frederick the Great)**

Friedrich, Götz, notable German opera producer and administrator; b. Naumburg, Aug. 4, 1930. He was educated at the Deutsches Theaterinstitut in Weimar (1949–53). In 1953 he became an assistant to Walter Felsenstein at the Komische Oper in Berlin, where he was a producer from 1959 to 1968, and then its chief producer from 1968 to 1972. In 1972 he gained wide notoriety with his highly controversial staging of *Tannhäuser* at the Bayreuth Festival, and then returned there to produce *Lohengrin* in 1978 and *Parsifal* in 1982. In 1973 he became Oberspielleiter at the Hamburg State Opera, and then was its Chefregisseur from 1977 to 1981. His first *Ring* cycle was staged at London's Covent Garden from 1974 to 1976, and from 1977 to 1981 he served as director of productions there. In 1981 he staged the 3-act version of *Lulu* there. In 1981 he became Generalintendant of the Deutsche Oper in Berlin, where he produced the *Ring* cycle in 1984–85, a staging later seen in many opera houses. In 1982 he staged *Wozzeck* at the Houston

Grand Opera. He produced the premiere of Berio's *Un re in ascolto* in Salzburg in 1984. From 1984 to 1993 he was artistic director of the Theater des Westens in Berlin while retaining his position at the Deutsche Oper. After staging *Otello* in Los Angeles in 1986, he returned there to produce *Kát'a Kabanová* in 1988. In 1987 he oversaw the premiere of Rihm's *Oedipus* in Berlin. He produced the premiere of Matthus's *Desdemona und ihre Schwestern* at the Schwetzingen Festival in 1992. After staging *Faust* at the Zürich Opera in 1997, he produced *Samson et Dalila* at the New Israeli Opera in Tel Aviv in 1998. In 2000 he retired from his position with the Deutsche Oper.

Friedrich's productions reflect his humanistic ideals and commitment to the Left. His writings include *Die humanistische Idee der Zauberflöte* (Berlin, 1954), *Die Zauberflöte in der Inszenierung Walter Felsensteins an der Komischen Oper Berlin* (Berlin, 1958), *Walter Felsenstein: Weg und Werk* (Berlin, 1961), *Musiktheater: Beiträge zur Methodik und zu Inszenierungs-Konzeptionen* (Leipzig, 1970; 2nd ed., 1978), *Wagner-Regie* (Zürich, 1983), and *Musiktheater: Ansichten, Einsichten, Konzepte, Versuche, Erfahrungen* (Frankfurt am Main, 1986). He married **Karan Armstrong**.

BIBL.: D. Kranz, *Der Regisseur G. F.* (Berlin, 1972); P. Barz, *G. F.: Abenteur Musiktheater* (Bonn, 1978); N. Ely, *Richard Wagner: Der Ring des Nibelungen in der Inszenierung von G. F.: Deutsche Oper Berlin* (Vienna, 1987); *Zeit für Oper: G. F.s Musiktheater, 1958–90* (Frankfurt am Main, 1991); J. Krogoll and D. Steinbeck, eds., *Musik, Musiktheater, Musiktheater-Regie: Festschrift anlässlich des 60. Geburtstages von G. F. sowie des zwanzigjährigen Bestehen des Studienganges Musiktheater-Regie der Universität Hamburg und der Hochschule für Musik und Theater* (Frankfurt am Main, 1994). —NS/LK/DM

Friedrichs (real name, **Christofes**), **Fritz,** German baritone; b. Braunschweig, Jan. 13, 1849; d. Königslutter, May 15, 1918. He joined the chorus of the Braunschweig Opera in 1869, where he soon appeared in minor operatic roles. After singing in provincial opera centers, he was a member of the operas in Nuremberg (from 1883) and Bremen (from 1886), where he acquired distinction as a Wagnerian. From 1888 to 1902 he sang at the Bayreuth Festivals, most notably as Alberich, Beckmesser, and Klingsor. His guest engagements took him to Berlin, Vienna, London, Hamburg, and N.Y.'s Metropolitan Opera (debut as Beckmesser, Jan. 24, 1900).—NS/LK/DM

Friemann, Witold, Polish composer and teacher; b. Konin, Aug. 20, 1889; d. Laski, near Warsaw, March 22, 1977. He was a student of Noskowski (composition) and Michalowski (piano) at the Warsaw Cons. (graduated, 1910), and of Reger in Leipzig. After teaching at the Lwów Cons. (1921–29) and the Katowice Military School of Music (1929–33), he was head of the music division of the Polish Radio (1934–39); he later taught at a school for the blind in Laski.

WORKS: DRAMATIC: Opera: *Giewont* (1934); *Polski misterium narodowe* (1946); *Kain* (1952); *Bazyliszek* (1958). **ORCH.:** 3 syms.: No. 1, *Slavonic* (1948), No. 2, *Mazovian* (1950), and No. 3 (1953); also concertos:5 for Piano (1911, 1951, 1952,

1956, 1960), 3 for Trombone (1969, 1969, 1970), 2 for Viola (1952, 1968), 2 for Clarinet (1954, 1964), and 1 for Cello (1950), Violin (1953–54), 2 Pianos (1960), Oboe (1961), Flute (1963), Bassoon (1965–67), Horn (1966–68), Trumpet (1967), and 2 Bassoons (1968). **OTHER:** Much chamber music and vocal pieces. —NS/LK/DM

Fries, Wulf (Christian Julius), German-American cellist and teacher; b. Garbeck, Jan. 10, 1825; d. Roxbury, Mass., April 29, 1902. He was mainly autodidact. After playing in the Bergen (Norway) theater orch. (from 1842) and at Old Bull's concerts, he settled in Boston in 1847, where he was a founder-member of the Mendelssohn Quintette Club (1849–72). In 1873 he became a founder-member of the Beethoven Quartet and was a member of the Boston Sym. Orch. in 1881–82. He became a teacher at the New England Cons. of Music (1869), Carlyle Petersilea's Music School (1871), and the Boston Cons. of Music (1889). —NS/LK/DM

Frigel, Pehr, Swedish composer; b. Kalmar, Sept. 2, 1750; d. Stockholm, Nov. 24, 1842. He was educated at the Univ. of Uppsala and studied composition with J.G. Naumann and J.M. Kraus. He made his living as a civil servant. In 1778 he was elected to the Swedish Royal Academy of Music; in 1796 he became its secretary, a position he retained for 45 years. He also taught theory there (1813–30). Among his works were syms., overtures, the oratorio *Försonaren på Oljebergt* (The Redeemer on the Mount of Olives; 1815), and cantatas.

BIBL.: B. von Beskow, *P. F.* (Stockholm, 1843; 3rd ed., 1923). —LK/DM

Frijsh, Povla (real name, **Paula Frisch**), Danish- American soprano; b. Århus, Aug. 3, 1881; d. Blue Hill, Maine, July 10, 1960. She studied piano and theory in Copenhagen with O. Christensen, later voice in Paris with Jean Périer. She made her debut in Paris at the age of 19; appeared in concert and recital in Paris and briefly in opera in Copenhagen; made her American debut in 1915. She gave many first performances of modern vocal music and made a specialty of the modern international song literature.—NS/LK/DM

Friml (actually, **Frimel**), **(Charles) Rudolf,** famous Bohemian-American operetta composer; b. Prague, Dec. 2, 1879; d. Los Angeles, Nov. 12, 1972. He was a pupil at the Prague Cons. of Juranek (piano) and Foerster (theory and composition). He toured Austria, England, Germany, and Russia as accompanist to Kubelik, the violinist, going with him to the U.S. in 1900 and again in 1906. He remained in the U.S. after the 2nd tour, gave numerous recitals, appeared as soloist with several orchs. (played his piano concerto with the N.Y. Sym. Orch.), and composed assiduously. He then lived in N.Y. and Hollywood, composing for motion pictures. In 1937 M-G-M made a film of his operetta *The Firefly* (Syracuse, Oct. 14, 1912), the popular *Donkey Serenade* being added to the original score.

WORKS: DRAMATIC Operetta: *The Firefly* (Syracuse, Oct. 14, 1912); *High Jinks* (Syracuse, Nov. 3, 1913); *Katinka*

(Morristown, N.Y., Dec. 2, 1915); *You're in Love*, musical comedy (Stamford, Conn., 1916); *Glorianna* (1918); *Tumble In* (1919); *Sometime* (1919); *Rose Marie* (N.Y., Sept. 2, 1924; very popular); *Vagabond King* (N.Y., Sept. 21, 1925; highly successful). OTHER: A great number of piano pieces in a light vein. —NS/LK/DM

Frimmel, Theodor von, Austrian writer on music; b. Amstetten, Dec. 15, 1853; d. Vienna, Dec. 25, 1928. He first studied medicine in Vienna, then became interested in art and maintained an art gallery. He taught the history of art at the Athenaum in Vienna and served as asst. curator of the Hofmuseum (1884–93). In music his main research concentrated on Beethoven.

WRITINGS: *Beethoven und Goethe: Eine Studie* (Vienna, 1883); *Neue Beethoveniana* (Vienna, 1888; 2nd ed., 1890); *Beethovens Wohnungen in Wien* (Vienna, 1894); "Beethoven," in *Berühmte Musiker* (Berlin, 1901; 6th ed., 1922); *Beethoven Studien* (Vol. I, *Beethovens äussere Erscheinung*, and Vol. II, *Bausteine zu einer Lebensgeschichte des Meisters*; Munich and Leipzig, 1905–06); *Beethoven-Forschung, Lose Blätter* (10 issues, Vienna and Mödling, 1911–25); *Beethoven im zeitgenössischen Bildnis* (Vienna, 1923); *Beethoven-Handbuch* (2 vols., Leipzig, 1926).—NS/LK/DM

Frischenschlager, Friedrich, Austrian composer and teacher; b. Gross Sankt Florian, Styria, Sept. 7, 1885; d. Salzburg, July 15, 1970. He studied music in Graz. In 1909 he went to Berlin, where he studied musicology with J. Wolf and Kretzschmar, and also attended Humperdinck's master classes in composition. In 1918 he was engaged as a music teacher at the Mozarteum in Salzburg, and remained there until 1945; also ed. its bulletin. An industrious composer, Fritschenschlager wrote the fairy tale operas *Der Schweinehirt*, after Hans Christian Andersen (Berlin, May 31, 1913), *Die Prinzessin und der Zwerg* (Salzburg, May 12, 1927), and *Der Kaiser und die Nachtigall*, after Andersen (Salzburg, March 27, 1937). Other works include *Symphonische Aphorismen* for Orch., choral works, and teaching materials for voice.—NS/LK/DM

Frishberg, David, American lyricist and pianist; b. St. Paul, Minn., March 23, 1933. He has written dozens of humorous, sophisticated tunes that have been recorded by numerous singers. After studying journalism at the Univ. of Minn. and spending a couple of years in the U.S. Air Force, he moved to N.Y. in 1957. A fine swing pianist, he manned the rhythm sections of notables such as Al Cohn, Zoot Sims, and Gene Krupa. In addition, he accompanied a very diverse group of singers, including Carmen McRae, Jimmy Rushing, and Anita O'Day. He began writing songs during the 1960s, and continues today. After moving to Los Angeles in 1971, he began writing for both television and motion pictures. Since starting to perform his own material regularly during the late 1970s, he has performed around the world. His classic, very "hip" tunes, include "The Underdog," "Peel Me a Grape," "Sweet Kentucky Ham," "My Attorney Bernie," "Van Lingo Mungo," "I'm Hip," "Z's," and "Quality Time," among many others. His remarkably quirky lyrics put a stamp on Frishberg as a unique musical voice in the jazz world.

DISC.: *Getting Some Fun out of Life* (1977); *Classics* (1983); *Live at Vine Street* (1984); *Can't Take You Nowhere* (1986); *Let's Eat Home* (1989); *Double Play* (1992); *Quality Time* (1993); *Not a Care in the World* (1995).—SKB

Friskin, James, Scottish-American pianist and composer; b. Glasgow, March 3, 1886; d. N.Y., March 16, 1967. He studied with E. Dannreuther (piano) and Stanford (composition) at the Royal Coll. of Music in London, then taught at the Royal Normal Coll. for the Blind (1909–14). In 1914 he went to the U.S. In 1934 he gave 2 recitals in N.Y. consisting of the complete *Wohltemperierte Clavier* of Bach. In 1944 he married **Rebecca Clarke**. Among his works were *Phantasie* for string quartet, *Phantasie* for piano trio, *Phantasy* for piano, 2 violins, viola, and cello (1912), quintet for piano and strings, and violin sonata. He publ. *The Principles of Pianoforte Practice* (London, 1921; new ed., N.Y., 1937) and (with I. Freundlich) *Music for the Piano* (N.Y., 1954). —NS/LK/DM

Frith, Fred, English composer, improvisational performer, instrumentalist, and teacher; b. Heathfield, Sussex, Feb. 17, 1949. He studied English literature at the Univ. of Cambridge (B.A., 1970; M.A., 1974), and was largely autodidact as a musician. From 1954 to 1964 he studied violin and taught himself piano, and from 1967 to 1970 he played guitar and bass in various bands. He co-founded the British underground band Henry Cow (1968–78), which played both improvised and composed material incorporating an eclectic range of genres and influences. He went to N.Y. in 1978, returning in 1979 and entering into enduring collaborative relationships with a number of American composers, including John Zorn, Zeena Parkins, and Bob Ostertag. Subsequent bands he formed and with which he performed include Massacre, Skeleton Crew, and Keep the Dog, the last a sextet performing an extensive repertoire of his own work. In the 1980s he began to compose for dance, film, and theater, and for such ensembles as the Rova Sax Quartet, Ensemble Modern, the Asko Ensemble, and his own critically acclaimed Guitar Quartet (from 1992). As a performer, Frith is best known as an improviser, but he has also performed in other contexts, i.e. bass in Zorn's Naked City, violin in Lars Hollmer's Looping Home Orch., and guitar on recordings ranging from The Residents and René Lussier to Brian Eno and Amy Denio. Throughout the 1990s he gave improvising workshops for musicians and non-musicians alike in Argentina, Australia, Chile, France, Germany, Israel, Italy, Canada, Mexico, and the U.S., and in 1999 he became the Marchant Prof. of Composition at Mills Coll. Frith is the subject of the award- winning documentary by Nicolas Humbert and Werner Penzel, *Step Across the Border* (1990).

WORKS: *Jigsaw*, music for dance (1987); *Propaganda*, incidental music (1987); *Technology of Tears*, music for dance (1987); *Disinformation Polka* for Accordion (1988); *Long on Logic* for Saxophone Quartet (1988); *Allies*, dance piece (1989); *In Memory* for 12 Musicians and Animated Film (by Pierre Hébert, with text by Sara Miles; 1989); *The As Usual Dance Towards the Other Flight to What Is Not* for 4 Guitars (1989); *The Top of His Head*, soundtrack for the film by Peter Mettler (1989); *Dropéra*, petite operetta mystérieuse (1990; in collaboration with Ferdinand Richard); *Helter Skelter*, opera (1990; in collaboration with François-Michel Pesenti); *Lelekovice* for String Quartet (1991); *Stone, Brick, Glass, Wood, Wire*, graphic scores for up to 21 Musicians (1992); *Elegy for Elias* for Piano, Violin, and Marimba (1993); *Endurance* for Double Bass (1993); *Freedom in Fragments* for Saxophone Quartet (1993); *The Previous Evening I (Hommage to John Cage)* for 4 Clarinets, 2 Guitars, Bass, Keyboard, Gravel, Whirled Instruments, Rice, Tapes, and Voice (1993), *Part II (Hommage to Morton Feldman)* for 3 Pianos, Clarinet, and Percussion (1996), and *Part III (Hommage to Earle Brown)* for Chamber Ensemble (1996); *22, Rue Lacépède* for Free-bass Accordion (1993); *Goongerah & Motormouth*, 2 pieces for Electric Guitar Quartet (1994); *Nous Sommes les Vaincus*, dance piece (1994; in collaboration with choreographer François Verret and instrument builder/inventor Claudine Brahem); *Pacifica*, a "meditation" for 21 Musicians (1994); *Portraits d'Inconnus*, installation with painter Béatrice Turquand d'Auzay (1994); *A Somewhat Circular Suite* for Chamber Ensemble (1995); *Hocket Etude* for Recorder Ensemble (1995); Music for *Middle of the Moment*, soundtrack (1995); *On the Red/No Mopin'/Belle de Mai*, 3 pieces for Jazz Group (1995); *Seven Circles* for Piano (1995); *Impur* for 100 Musicians, Large Building, and Mobile Audience (1996); *Doppelganger* for Oboe (1996); *Rogue Tool*, dance piece (1996); *Shortened Suite* for Marimba, Oboe, Trumpet, and Cello (1996); *Tense Serenity* for Trombone and String Trio (1996); *Traffic Continues* for 15 Musicians (1996); *Back to Life* for Marimba, Oboe, Trumpet, and Cello (1997); *Meister Leonhardt*, Hörspiel (1997; in collaboration with Alexander Schuhmacher); *Pop Mechanics* for Disklavier (1997); *Traffic in Trouble*, Hörspiel (1997; in collaboration with A. Schuhmacher); *Brecht Zap 98*, Hörspiel (1998; in collaboration with A. Schuhmacher and Nathalie Singer); *Centre Moving Out* for Chamber Ensemble (1998); *Question and Other Pieces* for Chamber Ensemble (1998); *Traffic Continues II (Gusto)* for Electronic Percussion, Harp/Electric Harp, and Chamber Ensemble (1998); *Final* for Orch. (1999); *Mickey la Torche*, Hörspiel (1999; in collaboration with A. Schuhmacher); *Raumschiff Titanic*, Hörspiel (1999; in collaboration with A. Schuhmacher); *Weatherwise or Otherwise* for Chamber Ensemble (1999); *The Big Picture* for 2 Unspecified Soloists and Saxophone Quartet (2000).—**LK/DM**

Fritz, Gaspard, Swiss violinist, teacher, and composer; b. Geneva, Feb. 18, 1716; d. there, March 23, 1783. He was a student in Turin of G.B. Somis, and then won distinction as a violin virtuoso in Geneva and Paris; he also engaged in teaching. His worthy output in the early Classical manner includes 6 syms. (c. 1770–71) and some 30 cantatas.—**LK/DM**

Froberger, Johann Jakob, famous German organist and composer; b. Stuttgart, May 18, 1616; d. Héricourt, Haute-Saône, May 7, 1667. About 1634 he went to Vienna, where he entered the Inst. of Singer oder Canthoreyknaben; there it was the custom to allow the choirboys, when their voices had changed and when they had attained a certain degree of musical scholarship, to serve as apprentices to famous masters of the time on stipends given by Emperor Ferdinand II. Froberger, however, did not apply for the subvention until late 1636, when it was refused him; thereupon, he held the position of 3rd organist at the court from Jan. 1 to Oct. 30, 1637. He then again applied, with success, and was granted a stipend of 200 gulden; in Oct. of that year

he left to study under Frescobaldi in Rome. In 1641 he returned to Vienna, where he again was organist (1641–45; 1653–58). He also visited Florence, Mantua, Brussels, and Paris, as well as Germany, Holland, and England between 1645 and 1653. His harpsichord suites were presented to the Emperor in 2 autograph vols. (1649, 1656). He spent his last years in the service of Princess Sybille of Württemberg at her chateau near Héricourt. Although 2 collections of toccatas, canzoni, and partitas were publ. long after his death (1693 and 1696), there is internal evidence that the majority of these works were written before 1650. Among his organ works are 25 toccatas, 15 ricercari, 8 fantasias, 6 canzonas, and 17 capriccios. Publications of his works followed after his death: *Diverse ingegnosissime, rarissime, et non maj più viste curiose partite di toccate, canzoni, ricercari, capricci*, etc. (1693; reprinted at Mainz, 1695) and *Diverse curiose e rare partite musicali*, etc. (1696). His works were ed. by G. Adler in Denkmäler der Tonkunst in Österreich (vols. 8, 13, 21; formerly vols. 4.i, 6.ii, 10.ii; 1897–1903). See also H. Schott, *A Critical Edition of the Works of J.J. F. with Commentary* (diss., Univ. of Oxford, 1978).

BIBL.: K. Seidler, *Untersuchungen über Biographie und Klavierstil J.J. F.s* (diss., Univ. of Königsberg, 1930); A. Somer, *The Keyboard Music of J.J. F.* (diss., Univ. of Mich., 1963); D. Starke, *F.s Suiten tänze* (Darmstadt, 1972); H. Siedentop, *J.J. F.: Leben und Werk* (Stuttgart, 1977).—**NS/LK/DM**

Fröhlich, Friedrich Theodor, Swiss composer; b. Brugg, Feb. 20, 1803; d. (suicide) Aarau, Oct. 16, 1836. He studied composition before going to Berlin in 1826 as a student of Zelter and B. Klein. In 1830 he settled in Aarau as a prof. of music at the cantonal school; he also was an instructor at the teachers's college and director of the Singakademie. The lack of recognition of his considerable talent led Fröhlich to take his own life during a fit of depression. His choral works and songs, all in a Romantic vein, are particularly noteworthy. He also composed 2 syms., overtures, much chamber music, and piano pieces.

BIBL.: E. Regardt, *T. F., ein schweitzer Musiker der Romantik* (Basel, 1947).—**LK/DM**

Frøhlich, Johannes Frederik, Danish violinist, conductor, and composer; b. Copenhagen, Aug. 21, 1806; d. there, May 21, 1860. He spent his entire life in Copenhagen, where he first studied piano, violin, and flute with his brother-in-law, C.F. Kittler. He then was a violinist in the Royal Theater Orch., during which time he completed his training with its Kapellmeister, Claus Schall. In 1827 he became chorus master of the Royal Theater, and then was a conductor there from 1834 to 1844; he also was director of the Musikforening (1836–41). Among his works were a Sym. (1830), overtures, 4 violin concertos (1825; 1825; 1829; 1829–30), ballets, string quartets, and other chamber pieces.
—**LK/DM**

Froidebise, Pierre (Jean Marie), eminent Belgian composer, musicologist, and organist; b. Ohey, May 15, 1914; d. Liège, Oct. 28, 1962. Following training

1191

in harmony and organ with Camille Jacquemin (1932–35), he studied with Barbier at the Namur Cons. He then was a student of Moulaert (composition), J. Jongen (fugue), Malengreau (premier prix in organ, 1939), and Absil (composition) at the Brussels Cons. He also studied composition with Gilson, and then went to Paris to complete his training in organ with Tournemire. Returning to Belgium, he won the 2nd Prix de Rome with his cantata *La navigation d'Ulysse* in 1943. In 1947 he became prof. of harmony at the Liège Cons. In 1949 he organized his so-called "Variation" group for young performers and composers, which sought to champion a broad expanse of music, ranging from the 13th to the 20th centuries. Froidebise was especially known for his championship of early organ music, and was ed. of the monumental *Anthologie de la musique d'orgue des primitifs à la renaissance* (Paris, 1958). In his own compositions, he favored an advanced idiom utilizing aleatoric and serial procedures.

WORKS: DRAMATIC: Radio Opera: *La lune amère* (1956); *L'aube* (n.d.); *La bergère et le ramoneur* (n.d.). Ballet: *Le bal chez le voisin* (c. 1953). Incidental Music To: Sophocles' *Antigone* (1936) and *Oedipe roi* (c. 1946); A. Curvers' *Ce vieil Oedipe* (c. 1946); M. Lambilliotte's *Jan van Nude* (1951); Aeschylus' *Les choéphores* (1954); Euripides' *Hippolyte* (n.d.); Calderón's *La maison a deux portes* (n.d.); etc. Film Scores: *Visite à Picasso* (1951; in collaboration with A. Souris); *Lumière des hommes* (1954). ORCH.: *De l'aube à la nuit* (1934–37); *La légende de St. Julien l'Hospitalier* (1941). CHAMBER: Violin Sonata (1938); *Petite suite monodique* for Flute or Clarinet (n.d.); *Petite suite* for Wind Quintet (n.d.). KEYBOARD: Piano: *7 croquis brefs* (1934); *Hommage à Chopin* (1947). Organ: *Suite brève* (1935); *Diptyque* (1936); *Prélude et Fugue* (1936); *Sonatine* (1939); *Prélude et fughetta* (n.d.); *Livre de noëls belges* (n.d.); *3 pièces* (n.d.); *Hommage à J.S. Bach* (n.d.). VOCAL: *La lumière endormie*, cantata (1941); *3 poèmes japonais* for Soprano or Tenor and Orch. (1942); *La navigation d'Ulysse*, cantata (1943); *5 comptines* for Soprano or Tenor and 11 Instruments (1947); *Amercoeur* for Soprano and 7 Instruments (1948); *La cloche engloutie*, cantata (1956); *Stèle pour sei Shonagon* for Soprano and 19 Instruments (1958).—NS/LK/DM

Froment, Louis (Georges François) de, French conductor; b. Toulouse, Dec. 5, 21; d. Cannes, Aug. 19, 1994. He received training in violin, flute, and harmony at the Toulouse Cons., and then was a student of Fourestier, Bigot, and Cluytens at the Paris Cons. (premier prix in conducting, 1948). He was active as a conductor with the French Radio in Paris, and also was music director of the casinos in Cannes and Deauville (1950–56), and in Vichy (1953–69). In 1958–59 he was conductor of the Nice Radio Chamber Orch. From 1958 to 1980 he was chief conductor of the Luxembourg Radio Sym. Orch.—NS/LK/DM

Fromm, Andreas, German composer; b. Planitz, near Wusterhausen, 1621; d. Prague, Oct. 16, 1683. A son of a Lutheran pastor, he studied theology and in 1649 became a cantor in Stettin. He was subsequently in Rostock (1651), Wittenberg (1668), and Prague, where he turned to the Roman Catholic Church. His principal musical work was an "actus musicus," *Die Parabel von dem reichen Mann und dem armen Lazarus* (1649). The opinion that it was the first German oratorio (cf. R. Schwartz, "Das erste deutsche Oratorium," *Jahrbuch der Musikbibliothek Peters 1899*) is discounted by later analysts.—NS/LK/DM

Fromm, Herbert, German-born American organist, conductor, and composer; b. Kitzingen, Feb. 23, 1905; d. Brookline, Mass., March 10, 1995. He studied piano, organ, conducting, and composition at the Munich Academy of Music (M.A.). He was conductor of the theaters in Bielefeld (1930) and Würzburg (1931–33). In 1937 the Nazis forced him out of Germany and he emigrated to the U.S. He served as organist and choirmaster at Temple Beth Zion in Buffalo (1937–41) and at Temple Israel in Boston (1941–73). In addition to his articles and essays in various journals and newspapers, he wrote the books *The Key of See: Travel Journey of a Composer*, *Seven Pockets*, and *On Jewish Music: A Composer's View*. He composed an extensive body of music for the synagogue, and also a number of secular works. —NS/LK/DM

Fromm, Paul, prominent German-born American music patron; b. Kitzingen, Sept. 28, 1906; d. Chicago, July 4, 1987. He was born into a family of vintners. He emigrated to the U.S. in 1938, becoming a naturalized American citizen in 1944. He founded the Great Lakes Wine Co. in Chicago in 1940, subsequently organizing the Fromm Music Foundation (1952), which assumed a leading role in commissioning and sponsoring performances of contemporary music, including those at the Berkshire Music Center in Tanglewood (from 1956), the annual Festival of Contemporary Music there (1964–83), and the Aspen (Colo.) Music Festival (from 1985). —NS/LK/DM

Frontini, Francesco Paolo, Italian composer; b. Catania, Aug. 6, 1860; d. there, July 26, 1939. He was a pupil of his father, Martino Frontini, who was also an opera composer, and of Lauro Rossi at Naples. He was director of the Catania Cons. until 1923. Ricordi publ. his collection of Sicilian songs, *Eco di Sicilia* (1883), and of Sicilian dances, *Antiche danze di Sicilia* (3 vols., 1936).

WORKS: DRAMATIC: Opera: *Nella* (Catania, March 30, 1881); *Malia* (Bologna, May 30, 1893); *Il Falconiere* (Catania, Sept. 15, 1899). VOCAL: *Sansone e Dalila*, oratorio (Catania, Aug. 23, 1882); numerous choral pieces and songs.

BIBL.: G. Balbo, *Note critico-biografiche su F.P. F.* (Catania, 1905).—NS/LK/DM

Froschauer, Johann, German printer who flourished at the end of the 15th century. He was long thought to have been the first to print music with movable type, in Michael Keinspeck's *Lilium musicae planae* (1498). However, it is now known that wood blocks were employed for the music illustrations in that work and it also appears fairly certain that music printing with movable type preceded Froschauer's work.—NS/LK/DM

Frotscher, Gotthold, German musicologist; b. Ossa, near Leipzig, Dec. 6, 1897; d. Berlin, Sept. 30, 1967.

He studied in Bonn and Leipzig, receiving his Ph.D. from the Univ. of Leipzig in 1922 with the diss. *Die Ästhetik des Berliner Liedes*. He completed his Habilitation at the Technische Hochschule in Danzig with his *Hauptprobleme der Musikästhetik im 18. Jahrhundert* (1924; publ. in Danzig, 1924). He taught at the Univ. of Danzig (1924–32) and then was a prof. at the Univ. of Berlin (1935–45); from 1950 he taught at the Pedagögische Hochschule in Berlin. He wrote the valuable *Geschichte des Orgelspiels und der Orgelkomposition* (2 vols., Berlin, 1935; 3rd ed., rev., 1966); also publ. *Aufführungspraxis alter Musik* (Wilhelmshaven, 1963; 4th ed., 1977) and *Orgeln* (Karlsruhe, 1968).—NS/LK/DM

Frugoni, Orazio, Italian pianist and pedagogue; b. Davos, Switzerland, Jan. 28, 1921; d. April 1997. After graduating as a student of Scuderi at the Milan Cons. in 1939, he attended the master classes of Casella at the Accademia Musicale Chigiana in Siena and of Lipatti at the Geneva Cons., where he was awarded the prix de virtuosité in 1945. From 1939 he played in Italy. After making his U.S. debut at N.Y.'s Town Hall in 1947, he performed throughout the U.S. He also taught at the Eastman School of Music in Rochester, N.Y. (1951–67), and then was director of the Graduate School of Fine Arts at Villa Schifanoia in Florence (1967–75). He taught at the Cherubini Cons. in Florence (from 1972). —NS/LK/DM

Frühbeck de Burgos (originally, **Frühbeck**), **Rafael,** eminent Spanish conductor; b. Burgos, Sept. 15, 1933. His father was German, his mother Spanish. He studied violin before pursuing musical training at the Bilbao Cons. and the Madrid Cons. (1950–53), and then received instruction in conducting from Eichhorn at the Munich Hochschule für Musik (1956–58). He was conductor of the Bilbao Municipal Orch. (1958–62), chief conductor of the Orquesta Nacional de España in Madrid (1962–77), Generalmusikdirektor of the Düsseldorf Sym. Orch. (1966–71), and music director of the Orchestre Symphonique de Montréal (1975–76). He appeared as a guest conductor with major European and North American orchs. He served as principal guest conductor of the National Sym. Orch. in Washington, D.C. (1980–89) and of the Yomiuri Nippon Sym. Orch. in Tokyo (1980–93). He was chief conductor of the Vienna Sym. Orch. (1991–96), Generalmusikdirektor of the Deutsche Oper in Berlin (1992–97), and chief conductor of the Radio Sym. Orch. in Berlin (from 1993). His idiomatic performances of Spanish music have won him many accolades; he has also demonstrated expertise as an interpreter of the standard orch. repertoire. —NS/LK/DM

Frumerie, (Per) Gunnar (Fredrik) de, esteemed Swedish composer, pianist, and teacher; b. Nacka, near Stockholm, July 20, 1908; d. Mörby, Sept. 9, 1987. He was a student of Lundberg (piano) and Ellberg (composition) at the Stockholm Cons. (1923–29). After pursuing his training with Sauer (piano) and Stein (composition) on a Jenny Lind Foundation stipend in Vienna (1929–31), he completed his studies with Cortot (piano) and Sabaneyev (composition) in Paris. He was active as a concert pianist in Sweden, and also taught piano at the Stockholm Musikhögskolan (1945–74). In 1943 he was made a member of the Royal Swedish Academy of Music. His music reflected the influence of Scandinavian Romanticism, crafted along traditional lines with a respect for folk elements.

WORKS: DRAMATIC: *En Moder*, melodrama (1932); *Singoalla*, opera (1937–40; Stockholm, March 16, 1940); *Johannesnatten*, ballet (1947). ORCH: 2 piano concertos (1929, 1932); *Suite in an Anciet Style* for Chamber Orch. (1930); *Variations and Fugue* for Piano and Orch. (1932); Violin Concerto (1936; rev. 1976); *Partita* for Strings (1937); *Pastoral Suite* for Flute, Harp, and Strings (1941; also for Flute and Piano, 1933); Symphonic Variations (1941); *Symphonie Ballad* for Piano and Orch. (1943–44); *Divertimento* (1951); Concerto for 2 Pianos and Orch. (1953); Concerto for Clarinet, Harp, Percussion, and Strings (1958); Trumpet Concerto (1959); Concertino for Oboe, Harp, Percussion, and Strings (1960); Flute Concerto (1969); Horn Concerto (1971–72); *Ballad* (1975); Violin Concerto (1976); Concertino for Piano and Strings (1977); Cello Concerto (1984; orchestration of the 2nd Cello Sonata, 1949; also orchestrated as a Trombone Concerto, 1986). CHAMBER: 2 piano trios (1932, 1952); 2 violin sonatas (1934, 1944); 2 piano quartets (1941, 1963); *Elegiac Suite* for Cello and Piano (1946); Suite for Wind Quintet (1973); String Quintet (1974); *Musica per nove*, octet (1976); piano pieces, including 2 sonatas (1968). VOCAL: *Fader var*, cantata (1945); 8 Psalms for Chorus and Orch. (1953–55); a cappella choruses; songs.—NS/LK/DM

Fry, William Henry, American composer and journalist; b. Philadelphia, Aug. 10, 1813; d. Santa Cruz, West Indies, Dec. 21, 1864. He was one of the most vociferous champions of American music, and particularly of opera on American subjects in the English language. Ironically, his own opera *Leonora* (Philadelphia, June 4, 1845), for which he claimed the distinction of being the first grand opera by a native American composer, was a feeble imitation of Italian vocal formulas in the manner of Bellini, with a libretto fashioned from a novel by Bulwer-Lytton, *The Lady of Lyons*. *Leonora* ran for 16 performances before closing; a revival of some numbers in concert form was attempted in N.Y. on Feb. 27, 1929, but was met with puzzled derision. Fry continued his campaign in favor of American opera in English, and composed 3 more operas, 1 of which, *Notre Dame de Paris*, after Victor Hugo, was produced in Philadelphia on May 3, 1864; 2 other operas, *The Bridal of Dunure* and *Aurelia the Vestal*, were not performed. He also wrote several syms., including *The Breaking Heart* (1852; not extant), *Santa Claus (Christmas Symphony)* (N.Y., Dec. 24, 1853), *A Day in the Country* (1853?; not extant), and *Childe Harold* (N.Y., May 31, 1854; not extant), as well as a symphonic poem, *Niagara* (N.Y., May 4, 1854). Fry's various proclamations, manifestos, and prefaces to publ. eds. of his works are interesting as illustrations of the patriotic bombast and humbug that agitated American musicians in the mid-19th century.

BIBL.: W. Upton, *The Musical Works of W.H. F.* (Philadelphia, 1946); idem, *W.H. F., American Journalist and Composer-Critic* (N.Y., 1954).—NS/LK/DM

Frye, Walter, English composer who flourished in the 15th century. Nothing is known regarding his life, but from indirect indications, it appears that he was attached to the court of Burgundy. Of his 3 masses (in MS at the Royal Library in Brussels), 2 are without a Kyrie, a lack characteristic of the English school; his *Ave Regina* is an early example of the "song motet." His works have been ed. by S. Kenney in *Walter Frye: Collected Works*, in Corpus Mensurabilis Musicae, XIX (1960).—NS/LK/DM

Fryer, George Herbert, English pianist, pedagogue, and composer; b. London, May 21, 1877; d. there, Feb. 7, 1957. He studied in London with Beringer at the Royal Academy of Music (1893–95) and with Franklin Taylor at the Royal Coll. of Music (1895–98). After further studies with Busoni in Weimar (1898), he made his London debut on Nov. 17, 1898, and subsequently toured in Europe; in 1914 he made his first tour of North America. He taught at the Royal Academy of Music (1905–14), and, after teaching in N.Y. (1915–17), he was on the faculty of the Royal Coll. of Music (1917–47). He continued to tour in Europe, and also played in Canada and the Far East. He publ. *Hints on Pianoforte Practice* (N.Y., 1914) and composed piano pieces and songs. —NS/LK/DM

Fryklöf, Harald (Leonard), Swedish organist, teacher, and composer; b. Uppsala, Sept. 14, 1882; d. Stockholm, March 11, 1919. He studied organ at the Stockholm Cons. (diploma, 1903), where he also had lessons in composition and counterpoint with Lindegren (1902–05); he likewise studied piano with Richard Andersson (1904–10), and went to Berlin to study orchestration with P. Scharwenka (1905). In 1904 he became a teacher at Andersson's music school; in 1908 he was made organist at the Cathedral and a teacher at the Cons. in Stockholm. He was elected to membership in the Swedish Royal Academy of Music in 1915. Fryklöf publ. the book *Harmonisering av koraler i dur och moll jämte kyrkotonarterna* (1916). With H. Palm, O. Sandberg, and A. Hellerström, he ed. *Musica sacra: Körsånger för kyrkan och skolan* (Stockholm, 1915). His music reflected German and French tendencies.

WORKS: Concert Overture (1908); *Sonata alla leggenda* for Violin and Piano (1919); organ music, including a Fugue (1909), Doppel-Canon (1910), and Passacaglia (n.d.); piano pieces; Psalm 98 for Chorus; songs.—NS/LK/DM

Fryklund, (Lars Axel) Daniel, Swedish musicologist; b. Vasterås, May 4, 1879; d. Hälsingborg, Aug. 25, 1965. He studied Romanic philology at the Univ. of Uppsala (Ph.D., 1907). He taught at the Univ. of Hälsingborg (1921–44). He was a specialist in the history and etymology of musical instruments; publ. many articles and books, and also amassed a collection of over 800 musical instruments and 10,000 MSS.—NS/LK/DM

Fuchs, Carl (Dorius Johannes), distinguished German organist and writer on music; b. Potsdam, Oct. 22, 1838; d. Danzig, Aug. 27, 1922. He studied piano with Bülow, thoroughbass with Weitzmann, and com-

position with Kiel. He took his Ph.D. in Greifswald, with the diss. *Präliminarien zu einer Kritik der Tonkunst* (1871). In 1868 he became a teacher at the Kullak Academy in Berlin; then gave piano concerts in Germany. In 1874 he went to Hirschberg, and in 1879, to Danzig, where he was organist at the Petrikirche and music critic of the *Danziger Zeitung* (1887–1920). He was also organist for many years at the Synagogue in Danzig. His letters were publ. by his son, Hans Fuchs, in *Ostdeutsche Monatshefte* (Sept. 1923).

WRITINGS: *Betrachtungen mit und gegen Arthur Schopenhauer* (1868); *Ungleiche Verwandte unter den Neudeutschen* (1868); *Virtuos und Dilettant* (Leipzig, 1871); *Die Zukunft des musikalischen Vortrags* (Danzig, 1884); *Die Freiheit des musikalischen Vortrags* (Danzig, 1885); with H. Riemann, *Praktische Anleitung zum Phrasieren* (Berlin, 1886; Eng. tr., N.Y., 1892); *Künstler und Kritiker* (1898); *Takt und Rhythmus im Choral* (Berlin, 1911); *Der taktgerechte Choral, Nachweisung seiner 6 Typen* (Berlin, 1923). —NS/LK/DM

Fuchs, Johann Nepomuk, Austrian conductor and composer, brother of **Robert Fuchs;** b. Frauenthal, Styria, May 5, 1842; d. Vöslau, near Vienna, Oct. 5, 1899. He studied with Sechter at Vienna. He conducted the Pressburg Opera in 1864, and also held similar positions at Brünn, Kassel, Cologne, Hamburg, Leipzig, and (from 1880) the Vienna Court Opera. In 1894 he succeeded Hellmesberger as director of the Vienna Cons. He produced the opera *Zingara* (Brünn, 1892) and several others.—NS/LK/DM

Fuchs, Joseph (Philip), American violinist and teacher, brother of **Lillian Fuchs;** b. N.Y., April 26, 1900. He studied violin with Kneisel at the Inst. of Musical Art in N.Y. He was concertmaster of the Cleveland Orch. (1926–40), making his N.Y. debut in 1943. He joined the faculty of the Juilliard School of Music in N.Y. in 1946. He toured Europe in 1954, South America in 1957, and Russia in 1965.—NS/LK/DM

Fuchs, (Leonard Johann Heinrich) Albert, German composer and pedagogue; b. Basel, Aug. 6, 1858; d. Dresden, Feb. 15, 1910. He studied with Selmar Bagge in Basel, and later at the Leipzig Cons. with Reinecke and Jadassohn (1876–79). He conducted in Trier (1880–83), then was director of the Wiesbaden Cons. (1889–98). In 1898 he joined the staff of the Dresden Cons.; was also conductor at the Schumann Singakademie (from 1901). He was a prolific composer, and publ. a number of choral works and songs. His works include 2 oratorios, *Selig sind, die in dem Herrn sterben* (1906) and *Das tausendjähriges Reich* (1908), and several instrumental concertos. He publ. *Taxe der Streichinstrumente* (1907; many reprints).

BIBL.: F. Geissler, *A. F.,* in Vol. III of *Monographien moderner Musiker* (Leipzig, 1909).—NS/LK/DM

Fuchs, Lillian, American violist, teacher, and composer, sister of **Joseph (Philip) Fuchs;** b. N.Y., Nov. 18, 1903; d. Englewood, N.J., Oct. 6, 1995. After taking up the piano at an early age, she studied violin with her father. She then was a student of violin of Svecenski and

Kneisel and of composition of Goetschius at the Inst. of Musical Art in N.Y. (graduated, 1924). In 1926 she made her N.Y. debut as a violinist, but soon concentrated her career on the viola. She made appearances as a soloist with major American orchs. and played in various chamber music ensembles. She also appeared in concerns with her brothers, Joseph and Harry. Fuchs was the first violist to play and record Bach's 6 suites for solo cello. She taught at the Manhattan School of Music in N.Y. (1963–91), the Aspen (Colo.) Music School (1964–90), and the Juilliard School in N.Y. (1971–93). Her compositions were mainly for the viola.

BIBL.: A. Williams, *L. F.: First Lady of the Viola* (Lewiston, 1994).—NS/LK/DM

Fuchs, Marta, admired German soprano; b. Stuttgart, Jan. 1, 1898; d. there, Sept. 22, 1974. She was trained in Stuttgart, Munich, and Milan. In 1928 she made her operatic debut in Aachen as a mezzo-soprano, singing there until 1930. She then was a prominent member of the Dresden State Opera (1930–45); she also was a guest artist at the Berlin State Opera, the Bayreuth Festival, and the Vienna State Opera, and toured as a concert singer. Among her notable roles were Brünnhilde, Isolde, Kundry, Donna Anna, the Marschallin, and Ariadne.—NS/LK/DM

Fuchs, Robert, renowned Austrian composer and pedagogue, brother of **Johann Nepomuk Fuchs;** b. Frauenthal, Styria, Feb. 15, 1847; d. Vienna, Feb. 19, 1927. He studied at the Vienna Cons., where, from 1875 to 1912, he was a prof. of harmony, establishing himself as a teacher of historical importance; among his students were Gustav Mahler, Hugo Wolf, and Schreker. His own compositions are, however, of no consequence, and there is no evidence that he influenced his famous pupils stylistically or even technically. The only pieces that were at all successful were his 5 serenades for string orch. He also wrote 2 operas, 5 syms., piano concerto, 2 piano trios, 3 string quartets, 2 piano quartets, piano quintet, and numerous pieces for piano solo and for piano, 4-hands.

BIBL.: A. Mayr, *Erinnerungen an R. F.* (Graz, 1934); A. Grote, *R. F.: Studien zu Person und Werk des Wiener Komponisten und Theorielehrers* (Munich, 1994).—NS/LK/DM

Fučik, Julius (Arnošt Vilém), Bohemian bandmaster and composer; b. Prague, July 18, 1872; d. Leitmeritz, Sept. 25, 1916. He studied composition with Dvořák at the Prague Cons., where he also received instruction in violin and bassoon (1885–91). After playing in regimental bands and theater orchs., he was bandmaster of the 86th Austro-Hungarian Regiment in Sarajevo (1897–1900), and later in Budapest, and then was bandmaster of the 92nd Regiment in Theresienstadt (1910–13). He composed many dances and marches for band, including the enormously popular march *Entrance of the Gladiators.*—NS/LK/DM

Fuenllana, Miguel de, blind Spanish vihuela virtuoso and composer; b. Navalcarnero, Madrid, early in the 16th century; d. place and date unknown. He was chamber musician to the Marquesa de Tarifa, and later at the court of Philip II, to whom he dedicated his *Libro de música para vihuela, intitulado Orphenica Lyra* (1554; modern ed. by C. Jacobs, London, 1979). From 1562 to 1568 he was chamber musician to Queen Isabel de Valois, 3rd wife of Philip II. The *Libro* gives evidence of a high state of musical art in Spain during the 16th century; besides fantasias and other compositions for vihuela by Fuenllana and old Spanish ballads (such as the famous *Ay de mi, Alhama*), it contains arrangements for vihuela of works by Vásquez, Morales, P. and F. Guerrero, Flecha, Bernal, and several Flemish masters. —NS/LK/DM

Fuerstner, Carl, German-born American pianist, conductor, teacher, and composer; b. Strasbourg, June 16, 1912; d. Bloomington, Ind., Dec. 5, 1994. He studied composition and conducting at the Cologne Hochschule für Musik (1930–34), where his teachers were Abendroth, Braunfels, Jarnach, and Klussmann. While still a student, he composed incidental music for theatrical plays. In 1939 he went to the U.S. as asst. conductor of the San Francisco Opera; he became a naturalized American citizen in 1945. From 1945 to 1950 he was head of the opera dept. at the Eastman School of Music in Rochester, N.Y.; then served on the faculty of Brigham Young Univ. in Provo, Utah (1951–61), where he was resident pianist, opera conductor, principal piano teacher, and head of the composition dept. (1955–61); also toured widely as a piano accompanist to many celebrated artists of the day and conducted an impressive repertoire of standard and modern operas in the U.S. and Europe. From 1963 to 1982 he was principal opera coach at the Ind. Univ. School of Music in Bloomington, where he also conducted operas. He also was on the faculty of the Summer Academy of the Salzburg Mozarteum (1973–82); then was active with the American Inst. of Musical Studies in Graz (1983–85); concurrently was associated with the "Festa Musica Pro" in Assisi, Italy. From 1981 to 1989 he was music director of the Bloomington (Ind.) Sym. Orch.

WORKS: *Concerto rapsodico* for Cello and Orch. (Rochester, N.Y., May 11, 1947); *Metamorphoses on a Chorale Theme* for 20 Trombones, 2 Tubas, and Percussion (Rochester, N.Y., April 5, 1949); *Symphorama* for Orch. (1960); *Overture* (1954), *Allegro ritmico* (1958), and many other pieces for Concert Band, as well as band transcriptions of Classical and Romantic works; *Divertimento* for String Quartet (1950); Clarinet Sonata (1950); *Allegro concertante* for Trombone and 10 Instruments (1966); Sonata for Bass Clarinet and Piano or Cello (1977); *Conjurations* for Soprano Saxophone and Piano (1985); piano pieces; choral works, including the *46th Psalm* for Chorus, 4 Trumpets, 4 Trombones, and Organ (1983).—NS/LK/DM

Fuga, Sandro, Italian pianist, teacher, and composer; b. Mogliano Veneto, Nov. 26, 1906; d. Turin, March 1, 1994. He studied piano, organ, and composition at the Turin Cons. He was a concert pianist until 1940, then became a lecturer at the Turin Cons. in 1933. In 1966 he became its director, which post he held until 1977.

WORKS: DRAMATIC: *La croce deserta* (Bergamo, 1950); *Otto Schnaffs* (Turin, 1950); *Confessione* (RAI Radio, 1962). **ORCH.:** *Ode in memoria* (1945; Turin, March 5, 1948); *Passacaglia* (1950); Toccata for Piano and Orch. (1952); Trumpet Concertino (1953); *Concerto sacro III* (1954); Cello Concerto (1955); Violin Concerto (1959); Concerto for Strings and Percussion (1963); Oboe Concertino (1964); Sym. (1967); Piano Concerto (Rome, Jan. 14, 1970). **CHAMBER:** Piano Trio (1943); 4 string quartets (1943, 1945, 1948, 1965); Violin Sonata (1951); piano pieces, including 2 sonatas (1957, 1978). **VOCAL:** *Concerto sacro I* for Chorus and Orch. (1938; Turin, Feb. 3, 1939), *II* for Baritone, Men's Chorus, and Orch. (1951), and *IV* for Tenor and Double Chorus (1956).—**NS/LK/DM**

Fugère, Lucien, remarkable French baritone; b. Paris, July 22, 1848; d. there, Jan. 15, 1935. He was a student at the Paris Cons. of Ragueneau and Batiste. In 1870 he began his career singing at the Café- Concert, Ba-ta-can. In 1874 he joined the Bouffes-Parisiens. He made his debut at the Paris Opéra-Comique in 1877 as Jean in Masse's *Les noces de Jeannette*, and remained on its roster until 1910. He appeared in over 100 roles there, including the premieres of Chabrier's *Le roi malgré lui* (1887), Messager's *La Basoche* (1890), Saint-Saëns' *Phryné* (1893), Massenet's *Cendrillon* (1899), and Charpentier's *Louise* (1900). In 1897 he sang at London's Covent Garden. After appearing at the Gaîté-Lyrique in Paris (1910–19), he returned to the Opéra-Comique, where he celebrated his 50th anniversary as a singer on March 5, 1920. He continued to make appearances until he was 80, singing his farewell performance in *La Basoche* in Le Touquet in 1928, the year he was awarded the Légion d'honneur. He was particularly celebrated for his portrayals of Leporello, Papageno, Figaro, and Bartolo. Mary Garden was among his students.

BIBL.: R. Duhamel, *L. F.* (Paris, 1929).—**NS/LK/DM**

Fugs, The, archetypical N.Y. downtown proto-punk band of the 1960s. **MEMBERSHIP:** Ed Sanders, gtr., voc. (b. Kansas City, Mo., Aug. 17, 1939); Naphtali "Tuli" Kupferberg, voc. (b. N.Y., Sept. 28, 1928); Ken Weaver, voc., drm. (b. Galveston, Tex., Aug. 23, 1940).

Organized by two Beat-generation poets, The Fugs sought to stir 1960s audiences with outrageous and iconoclastic poetry, satire, and outright obscenity in their songs concerned with sex, drugs, and politics. One of the earliest rock satire groups and certainly the first "underground" group, The Fugs' pioneering efforts paved the way for the premeditated offensiveness of Frank Zappa's Mothers of Invention, Iggy Pop and The Stooges, Alice Cooper, and the late 1970s "punk-rockers," as well as the silliness of Flo & Eddie and Cheech & Chong.

Conceived by poets Ed Sanders and Tuli Kupferberg near the end of 1964, The Fugs also included poet-drummer Ken Weaver and a host of guitarists, bassists, keyboard players, and other musicians. Sanders, a former classical languages major at N.Y.U., had published *Poem from Jail* in 1963 and served as editor of *Fuck You* and as owner-manager of the Peace Eye Bookstore in N.Y.'s Lower East Side. Kupferberg, an avowed anarchist, had published *Snow Job: Poems: 1946–1959* in 1959.

Debuting at Greenwich Village's Folklore Center, the ever-changing Fugs later occupied the Players Theater on MacDougal Street, logging some 900 consecutive performances there. Aided by multi-instrumentalist Peter Stampfel and guitarist Steve Weber of The Holy Modal Rounders (best known for "If You Want to Be a Bird" from the 1969 soundtrack *Easy Rider*), The Fugs' debut album was recorded for the small Broadside label. It included songs such as "Slum Goddess," "I Couldn't Get High," "Boobs a Lot," and "Nothing." Their second album, recorded for the avant-garde jazz label ESP, contained Sanders's "Group Grope" and "Dirty Old Man," Kupferberg's antiwar "Kill for Peace," and the uncommonly lyrical "Morning, Morning," composed by Kupferberg and recorded by Richie Havens on his *Mixed Bag* album. *The Virgin Fugs* sported Fugs classics such as "Caca Rock," "Coca Cola Douche," and "New Amphetamine Shriek."

Along with the MC5, The Fugs were one of the most politically active rock groups, appearing at demonstrations at the Pentagon and Democratic National Convention in 1968. Seemingly on the verge of a major breakthrough with their signing to the major label Reprise, The Fugs managed only modest sales. Their second album for the label featured "Johnny Pissoff Meets the Red Angel," "Burial Waltz," and "National Haiku Contest." By late 1969, The Fugs had disbanded. Ken Weaver returned to the Southwest, whereas Sanders recorded two obscure country albums for Reprise. Tuli Kupferberg recorded one album before compiling the book *Listen to the Mockingbird: Satiric Songs to Tunes You Know*, published in 1973. Ed Sanders returned to writing with 1971's *The Family*, chronicling the story of the Charlie Manson commune, and *Tales of Beatnik Glory*, published in 1975. Moving to Woodstock, N.Y., where he involved himself in various social causes, he presented the irreverent two-hour "Karen Silkwood Cantata" locally in 1979. Sanders continued to write poetry in the 1980s and 1990s, and he and Kupferberg reformed The Fugs in the mid-1980s, recording for the New Rose and Gazell labels. In 1994, the two reunited to undermine the Woodstock II Festival at an alternative site in upstate N.Y. with Country Joe McDonald and Alan Ginsberg.

DISC.: *Ballads of Contemporary Protest, Point of Views, and General Dissatisfaction* (1966); *The Fugs* (1966); *The Virgin Fugs: For Adult Minds Only* (1967); *Tenderness Junction* (1968); *It Crawled Into My Hand, Honest* (1968); *Belle of Avenue A* (1969); *Golden Fifth* (1970); *Fugs Four, Rounder's Score* (1975); *Refuse to Be Burnt Out* (1985); *Songs from a Portable Forest* (1991); *The Fugs* (1993); *Fugs* (1995); *The Real Woodstock Festival* (1996). **TULI KUPFERBERG:** *No Deposit, No Return* (1967); *Tuli and Friends* (1989). **ED SANDERS:** *Sanders' Truckstop* (1970); *Beer Cans on the Moon Reprise* (1972); *Songs in Ancient Greek* (1992).

WRITINGS: Tuli Kupferberg: *Snow Job: Poems: 1946–1959* (N.Y., 1959); *First Glance: Childhood Creations of the Famous* (Maplewood, N.J., 1978); with Robert Bashlow, *1001 Ways to Beat the Draft* (N.Y., 1965); with Sylvia Topp, *As They Were: Celebrated People's Pictures* (N.Y., 1973). Ed Sanders: *Poem from Jail* (San Francisco, 1963); *Peace Eye* (Buffalo, 1965); *Shards of God* (N.Y., 1970); *The Family: The Story of Charles Manson's Dune Buggy Attack Battalion* (N.Y., 1971); *Tales of Beatnik Glory* (N.Y., 1975); *Investigative Poetry* (San Francisco, 1976); *20,000 A.D.*

(Plainfield, Vt., 1976); *Fame and Love in New York* (Berkeley, Calif., 1980); *The Z-D Generation* (Barrytown, N.Y., 1981); *Thirsting for Peace in a Raging Century: Selected Poems, 1960–985* (Minneapolis, 1987); *The Family: The Manson Group and Its Aftermath* (N.Y., 1989); *Hymn to the Rebel Cafe* (Santa Rosa, 1993). —**BH**

Führer, Robert (Johann Nepomuk), Bohemian composer and organist; b. Prague, June 2, 1807; d. Vienna, Nov. 28, 1861. He studied with Johann Vitásek, and was an organist in provincial towns before succeeding his teacher as Kapellmeister at the Prague Cathedral in 1839. He became involved in fraudulent transactions and was dismissed from his post in 1845. He then held various positions as an organist and choral conductor in Vienna, Salzburg, Munich, Augsburg, and Gmunden. A series of embezzlements and other criminal offenses perpetrated by him resulted in his dismissal from several of his positions, but he continued to compose and perform. In 1856 he was Bruckner's competitor for the post of organist in Linz, arousing great admiration for his skill, even though Bruckner was selected. He served a prison term in 1859, but was given full freedom to write music. He publ. numerous sacred works and many organ pieces as well as handbooks on harmony and organ playing. Despite his notoriously dishonest acts and professional untrustworthiness (he publ. one of Schubert's masses under his own name), he enjoyed a fine reputation for his musicianship.—**NS/LK/DM**

Fujiie, Keiko, Japanese composer; b. Tokyo, July 22, 1963. She received training at the Tokyo National Univ. of Fine Arts and Music (graduated, 1987). She was awarded the Asian Cultural Counsel fund and lived in N.Y. in 1992–93.

WORKS: ORCH.: *Malposition* (Tokyo, June 6, 1985); *Panorama* (1986); Clarinet Concerto (1986; rev. 1993); *Intermezzo* for String Ensemble (1986); *Jade Sea Panorama* (1992; Amsterdam, Sept. 11, 1993); *Beber* for Chamber Orch. (1994); Guitar Concerto (1997); *Kyoto- Reverberation* for Guitar, Double Bass, and Orch. (1997). **CHAMBER:** *Reunion* for Flute, Violin, Cello, Piano, and 2 Percussionists (1984); 3 Pieces for Clarinet (1985); *Pas de Deux I and II* for Piano (1987–89); String Trio (1988–92); *Midday Island* for 6 Players (1991); *Flower Garden* for 5 Percussionists (1992); *Bodrum Sea* for Guitar (1992); *Samsara* for Wind Quintet (1993); *Yellow Cow* for Oboe, Accordion, and Double Bass (1993); Suite for Violin (1996); *Be It Dream or Reality* for Cello and Piano (1997); *The Day Spring Returned* for Violin, Double Bass, and String Quartet (1998); *Sun and Moon* for Guitar and Double Bass (1998). **VOCAL:** *Love Song* for Soprano, Flute, Harp, Double Bass, and Percussion (1987); *Nobody, Not Even the Rain, Has Such Small Hands* for Mezzo-soprano, Prepared Piano, 4-Hands, and Tape (1990); *Fountains for Paradise* for Chorus, Guitar, and Violin (1995); *Niña de Cera* for Mezzo-soprano, Guitar, Piano, and String Quartet (1995); *In Their Shoes* for Voice, Violin, Cello, Guitar, and Piano (1998).—**NS/LK/DM**

Fujikawa, Mayumi, Japanese violinist; b. Asahigawa, July 27, 1946. She studied at the Toho School of Music in Tokyo and at the Antwerp Cons., and later took lessons with Leonid Kogan in Nice. In 1970 she won 2nd prize in the Tchaikovsky Competition in Moscow and 1st prize in the Vieuxtemps Competition in Verviers, Belgium. She then appeared as soloist with major orchs. in Europe and America and was active as a recitalist and chamber music player.—**NS/LK/DM**

Fukai, Shiro, Japanese composer; b. Akita-City, April 4, 1907; d. Kyoto, July 2, 1959. He studied composition in Tokyo with Sugawara. Perhaps his most notable score is a large choral work, *Prayer for Peace* (Tokyo, Aug. 15, 1949). His other works are the ballets *A City* (Tokyo, June 18, 1936) and *Ocean* (Tokyo, Jan. 30, 1938), and several symphonic suites of "landscape music."—**NS/LK/DM**

Fuleihan, Anis, Cypriot-born American pianist, conductor, and composer; b. Kyrenia, April 2, 1900; d. Palo Alto, Calif., Oct. 11, 1970. He studied at the English School in Kyrenia; went to the U.S. in 1915 and continued his study of the piano in N.Y. with Alberto Jonás. He toured the U.S. and the Near East from 1919 to 1925, then lived in Cairo, returning to the U.S. in 1928. He was on the staff of G. Schirmer, Inc. in N.Y. (1932–39). In 1947 he became a prof. at Ind. Univ. in Bloomington, and, in 1953, director of the Beirut Cons. in Lebanon. In 1962 he went to Tunis under the auspices of the State Dept. and in 1963 organized the Orch. Classique de Tunis, remaining there until 1965.

WORKS: DRAMATIC: O p e r a : *Vasco* (1960). **ORCH.:** *Mediterranean Suite* (1930; Cincinnati, March 15, 1935); *Preface to a Child's Story Book* (1932); 2 syms.: No. 1 (N.Y., Dec. 31, 1936) and No. 2 (N.Y., Feb. 16, 1967); 3 piano concertos: No. 1 (Saratoga Springs, N.Y., Sept. 11, 1937), No. 2 (1938), and No. 3 (1963); *Fantasy* for Viola and Orch. (1938); 3 violin concertos (1930, 1965, 1967); *Fiesta* (Indianapolis, Dec. 1, 1939); *Symphonie concertante* for String Quartet and Orch. (N.Y., April 25, 1940); Concerto for 2 Pianos and Orch. (Hempstead, N.Y., Jan. 10, 1941); *Epithalamium* for Piano and Strings (Philadelphia, Feb. 7, 1941); Concerto for Theremin and Orch. (N.Y., Feb. 26, 1945); *Invocation to Isis* (Indianapolis, Feb. 28, 1941); Concerto for Violin, Piano, and Orch. (1943); Ondes Martenot Concerto (1944); *3 Cyprus Serenades* (Philadelphia, Dec. 13, 1946); *Rhapsody* for Cello and Strings (Saratoga Springs, Sept. 12, 1946); *The Pyramids of Giza*, symphonic poem (1952); *Toccata* for Piano and Orch. (1960); *Islands*, symphonic suite (1961); Flute Concerto (1962); Cello Concerto (1963); Viola Concerto (1963); *Le Cor anglais s'amuse* for English Horn and Strings (1969). **CHAMBER:** 5 string quartets (1940–67); 14 piano sonatas (1940–68); *Overture* for 5 Winds (N.Y., May 17, 1947); Horn Quintet (1959); Piano Quintet (1967); Piano Trio (1969); Clarinet Quintet; Violin Sonata; Viola Sonata; Cello Sonata. **VOCAL:** Choral pieces; songs.—**NS/LK/DM**

Fulkerson, Gregory (Locke), American violinist; b. Iowa City, May 9, 1950. He received lessons from Paul Kling in Louisville (1961–66), and then studied mathematics at Oberlin (Ohio) Coll. (B.A., 1971), where he also was a student at its Cons. of David Cerone, Richard Kapuszinski, and Robert Fountain (B.M., 1971). Following studies with Peter Marsh at the State Univ. of N.Y. in Binghamton (1974–75), he completed his education at the Juilliard School in N.Y. (M.M., 1977; D.M.A., 1987), where his mentors included Ivan Galamian, Felix

Galimir, Robert Mann, and Dorothy DeLay. From 1971 to 1974 he played in the Cleveland Orch. He made his recital debut at Cleveland's Music School Settlement House in 1973, and in 1974 he founded the Audubon String Quartet. From 1979 to 1981 he was concertmaster of the Honolulu Sym. Orch., with which he made his debut as a soloist in the Dvořák Concerto under Donald Johanos's direction in 1979. In 1980 he won 1st prize in the International American Music Competition in Washington, D.C. His N.Y. recital debut followed at the 92nd St. YMHA in 1981. He returned to N.Y. in 1982 as soloist in the Barber Concerto with the American Sym. Orch. conducted by David Ramadanoff. In 1983 he made debut appearances in London, Paris, Hannover, and Rome, and in 1991 in Santiago. In 1992 he appeared as Einstein in Glass's *Einstein on the Beach* with the Philip Glass Ensemble at the Brooklyn Academy of Music. Fulkerson's enormous repertoire includes some 50 concertos. Among composers he has frequently played are Bach, Beethoven, Brahms, Schoenberg, Berg, Weill, and Barber. Several composers have written works for him, including Erb, Wernick, and Daugherty. Fulkerson also gave posthumous premieres of the concertos of John J. Becker (Cahttanooga, Jan. 18, 1983) and Roy Harris (Wilmington, N.C., March 21, 1984).—**NS/LK/DM**

Fulkerson, James (Orville), American composer and trombonist; b. Streator, Ill., July 2, 1945. He studied composition with Wilbur Ogdon and Abram Plum and trombone with John Silver at Ill. Wesleyan Univ. (B.A., 1966) and composition with Maritirano, Gaburo, Hiller, and Brun at the Univ. of Ill. (M.M., 1969). He was a creative assoc. of the Center for the Creative and Performing Arts at the State Univ. of N.Y. in Buffalo (1969–72), then composer-in-residence at the Deutscher Akademischer Austauschdienst in Berlin (1973), the Victorian Coll. of the Arts in Melbourne (1977–79), and Dartington Coll. in Devon, England (from 1981). Fulkerson is a virtuoso on the trombone, and he makes a specialty of playing the most fantastically difficult modern pieces. His own compositions are no less advanced.

WORKS: DRAMATIC: *Raucasity and the Cisco Kid...or, I Skate in the Sun* (1977–78); *Vicarious Thrills* (1978–79); *Cheap Imitations II: Madwomen* (1980); *Force Fields and Spaces* (1981); *Cheap Imitations IV* (1982); *Put Your Foot Charlie* (1982); *Rats Tale* (1983); *Studs,* ballet music (1992). **ORCH.:** *Globs* for Small Orch., Live Electronics, and Tape (1968); *About Time* (1969); *Something about Mobiles* (1969); *Planes* for 4 Orch. Groups (1969); *Behind Closed Doors* for Violin and Orch. (1971); *Patterns IX* (1972); *To See a Thing Clearly* (1972); *For We Don't See Anything Clearly* (1972); Guitar Concerto (1972); Trombone Concerto, with Tape (1973); *Orchestra Piece* (1974); *Stations, Regions, and Clouds* for Bass Trombone and Orch. (1977); Concerto for Amplified Cello and Large Ensemble (1978); Sym. (1980); Concerto *(...fierce and coming from far away)* (1981); *Pessoa I* for Large Ensemble (1992); Concerto for Electric Violin and Large Ensemble (1992). **CHAMBER:** *Co-ordinative Systems* Nos. 1–10 (1972–76); *Music for Brass Instruments* Nos. 1–6 (1975–78); Suite for Amplified Cello (1978–79).—**NS/LK/DM**

Fuller, Albert, American harpsichordist and teacher; b. Washington, D.C., July 21, 1926. He studied organ with Paul Callaway at the National Cathedral in Washington, D.C., then attended classes at the Peabody Cons. of Music and at Georgetown and Johns Hopkins Univs. He studied harpsichord with Kirkpatrick at Yale Univ. and also theory there with Hindemith, graduating with a M.M. in 1954. He then went to Paris on a Ditson fellowship; upon his return to the U.S., he made his N.Y. recital debut in 1957; his European debut followed in 1959. In 1964 he became a prof. of harpsichord at the Juilliard School of Music in N.Y. He also was on the faculty of Yale Univ. from 1976 to 1979. From 1972 to 1983 he was founder-artistic director of the Aston Magna Foundation.—**NS/LK/DM**

Fuller, Curtis, American trombonist; b. Detroit, Mich., Dec. 15, 1934. Along with J.J. Johnson, he presents the quintessence of modern trombone playing, with a technical command and fluid sound that set him apart from the swing players that came before him. Picking up the horn at the age of 16, he had the choice opportunity to be part of a fertile Detroit jazz scene that found Donald Byrd, Louis Hayes, Kenny Burrell, Pepper Adams, Tommy Flanagan, and many others, among his peers. His first important gig was with Yusef Lateef's group, which brought him to N.Y. in the Spring of 1957. Very soon, he became a hot commodity on the scene. Within an eight-month span he recorded six albums as a leader (two on Prestige, the rest on Blue Note) and appeared as sideman on 15 others. Following a brief stay with the Jazztet (which also featured Art Farmer and Benny Golson), he would work with Art Blakey's Jazz Messengers from 1961–65. Since the 1970s, he has toured with the Count Basie Band, the Timeless All-Stars, Benny Golson, and numerous groups of his own. Indeed, he remains one of the music's most valuable and legendary practitioners of the jazz trombone.

DISC.: *Curtis Fuller with Red Garland* (1957); *New Trombone* (1957); *Sliding Easy* (1959); *Blues-Ette* (1959); *The Curtis Fuller Jazztet with Benny Golson* (1959); *Imagination* (1960); *Images of Curtis Fuller* (1960); *Four on the Outside* (1978); *Blues-Ette, Part 2* (1993); *The Complete Blue Note/United Artists Curtis Fuller Sessions* (1996).—**CH**

Fuller, Jeff, jazz bassist; b. Nov. 30, 1945, Southbridge, Mass. Fuller has toured worldwide and recorded with Lou Donaldson since 1979, and he was also a member of Paquito D'Rivera's New York/Havana Quintet, with whom he recorded four albums. He has appeared with Dizzy Gillespie, Mose Allison, Scott Hamilton, Jo Jones, Gerry Mulligan, Clark Terry and "Big Nick" Nicholas and recorded with Herman Foster, Don Lanphere and others. He is an expert in Latin music and has toured with the Hilton Ruiz group, Daniel Ponce's Jazzbatá, Mario Rivera's Refugiados de Salsa, and Puerto Rican singer Roy Brown. He composes and arranges for the salsa group, Irazú, whose four albums have featured Arturo Sandoval and Tata Güines. He has lived in the New Haven area for many years, holds a master's degree in composition from Yale Univ., and is a teacher and clinician. He has taught at the university level and commissions and grants to write original music.—**LP**

Fuller Maitland, J(ohn) A(lexander), eminent English music scholar; b. London, April 7, 1856; d. Carnforth, Lancashire, March 30, 1936. He studied at Westminster School and Trinity Coll. in Cambridge (M.A., 1882), then took piano lessons with Dannreuther and W.S. Rockstro. He was music critic of the *Pall Mall Gazette* (1882–84) and of the *Manchester Guardian* (1884–89). He also lectured extensively on the history of English music, and appeared as a pianist with the Bach Choir and as a performer on the harpsichord in historical concerts. He contributed to the first ed. of *Grove's Dictionary of Music and Musicians* and edited the Appendix; was editor-in-chief of the 2nd ed. (1904–10). He was also ed. of various other works, including the *Fitzwilliam Virginal Book* (1899; with W. Barclay Squire).

WRITINGS: *Schumann* (1884); *Masters of German Music* (1894); *The Musician's Pilgrimage* (1899); *English Music in the 19th Century* (1902); *The Age of Bach and Handel* (Vol. IV of *The Oxford History of Music*, 1902; new ed., 1931); *Joseph Joachim* (1905); *Brahms* (1911; Ger. tr., 1912); *The Concert of Music* (1915); *The "48"—Bach's Wohltemperiertes Clavier* (2 vols., 1925); *The Keyboard Suites of J.S. Bach* (1925); *The Spell of Music* (1926); *A Door-Keeper of Music* (1929); *Bach's Brandenburg Concertos* (1929); *Schumann's Concerted Chamber Music* (1929); *The Music of Parry and Stanford* (1934).—NS/LK/DM

Fulton, (Robert) Norman, English composer and teacher; b. London, Jan. 23, 1909; d. Birmingham, Aug. 5, 1980. He studied harmony and composition with Demuth at the Royal Academy of Music in London (1929–33). After serving on the staff of the BBC (1936–60), he was prof. of harmony and composition at the Royal Academy of Music (from 1966).

WORKS: DRAMATIC: *Augury*, ballet (1960); radio and film music. ORCH.: *Serenade* for Strings (1944); *5 Entertainments* for Small Orch. (1946); *Overture* (1950); 3 syms.: No. 1, *Sinfonia pastorale* (1950), No. 2 (1955), and No. 3, *Mary Stuart* (1971–73); *Curtain Wells Sketches* for Small Orch. (1959); *Waltz Rhapsody* for Piano and Orch. (1961); *Symphonic Dances* (1965). CHAMBER: *Sonata da camera* for Viola and Piano (1946); *Introduction, Air, and Reel* for Viola and Piano (1950); *Piano Trio* (1950); *3 Movements* for Clarinet and Piano (1951); *Scottish Suite* for Recorder and Piano or Harpsichord (1954); *Oboe Sonatina* (1962); *Night Music* for Flute and Piano (1969). KEYBOARD: Piano: *Sonatina* (1945); *Waltz, Air, and Polka* for 2 Pianos (1947); *Prelude, Elegy, and Toccata* (1954); *Fantasy on a Ground* (1969); *3 Pieces* (1970). VOCAL: Choral music; songs. —NS/LK/DM

Fulton, Thomas, American conductor; b. Memphis, Sept. 18, 1949; d. Milan, Aug. 4, 1994. He studied at the Curtis Inst. of Music in Philadelphia, where his conducting mentors were Max Rudolf and Eugene Ormandy. He began his career as a staff conductor at the San Francisco Opera and the Hamburg State Opera. In 1978 he joined the conducting staff of the Metropolitan Opera in N.Y., where he made his house debut with *Manon Lescaut* on April 4, 1981. He also made guest appearances with various opera companies, including the Paris Opéra (1979), the Rome Opera (1986), the Berlin Deutsche Oper (1986), and the Greater Miami Opera (1989).—NS/LK/DM

Fumagalli, family of Italian musicians, all brothers:

(1) Disma Fumagalli, b. Sept. 8, 1826; d. Milan, March 9, 1893. He was a pupil at, and from 1857 a prof. of, the Milan Cons. He was a prolific composer of piano music (over 250 numbers).

(2) Adolfo Fumagalli, b. Oct. 19, 1828; d. Florence, May 3, 1856. He was a pianist, pupil of Gaetano Medaglia, and later of Angeleri and Ray at the Milan Cons. He then undertook tours throughout Italy, France, and Belgium, earning the sobriquet "the Paganini of the pianoforte." During his brief lifetime he publ. about 100 elegant and effective piano pieces, which obtained an extraordinary vogue. Filippo Filippi wrote a sketch, *Della vita e delle opere di Adolfo Fumagalli* (Milan, 1857).

(3) Polibio Fumagalli, b. Oct. 26, 1830; d. Milan, June 21, 1900. He was a pianist and a composer for piano and for organ.

(4) Luca Fumagalli, b. May 29, 1837; d. Milan, June 5, 1908. He was a pupil at the Milan Cons. He played with great success in Paris (1860), and publ. salon music for piano. He also composed an opera, *Luigi XI* (Florence, 1875).—NS/LK/DM

Fumet, Dynam-Victor, French organist and composer; b. Toulouse, May 4, 1867; d. Paris, Jan. 2, 1949. He studied with Franck and Guiraud at the Paris Cons. At an early age he became involved in the political activities of French anarchists and was forced to leave school. For a time he earned his living as a piano player in Paris nightclubs; in 1910 became organist of St. Anne's Church in Paris. His music follows the precepts of French Wagnerism, but the influence of Franck is also noticeable. He wrote several orch. works on mystic themes, among them *Magnetisme céleste* for cello and orch. (1903), *Trois âmes* (1915), *Transsubstantiation* (1930), and *Notre mirage, notre douleur* (1930). During the German occupation he wrote *La Prison glorifiée* (1943). —NS/LK/DM

Funcke, Friedrich, German composer and clergyman; b. Nossen, Saxony, 1642; d. Römstedt, near Lüneburg, Oct. 20, 1699. After training in theology in Wittenberg (1660–61), he was cantor at St. Johannis in Lüneburg (1664–94) and then pastor in Römstedt. A *St. Matthew Passion* (2 versions, c. 1668–74; ed. in *Das Chorwerk*, LXXVIII-IX, 1961) attributed to him is historically significant in the development of the Passion oratorio. He publ. *Danck- und Denck-Mahl* for 8 voices, 5 instruments, and basso continuo (Hamburg, 1666), and also composed a cantata for New Year 1684.—LK/DM

Furlanetto, Bonaventura, Italian composer; b. Venice, May 27, 1738; d. there, April 6, 1817. He received training from his uncle, Nicolò Formenti, an amateur organist, and from Giacopo Bolla, a priest. In 1768 he was made maestro at S. Maria della Visitazione (the Pietà) in Venice. From 1781 he also was associated with San Marco in Venice, where he became primo maestro about 1808. He acquired a distinguished reputation in Venice as a composer of sacred music, including about 25 oratorios, masses, cantatas, and motets.

BIBL.: F. Caffi, *Della vita e del comporre di B. F. detto Musin* (Venice, 1820).—**LK/DM**

Furlanetto, Ferruccio, Italian bass; b. Pordenone, Sicily, May 16, 1949. He was a student of Campogaliahi and Casagrande. After making his operatic debut as Sparafucile in Vicenza in 1974, he held engagements in Turin, Trieste, Bologna, Venice, Parma, and Aix-en-Provence. In 1978 he made his U.S. debut as Zaccaria with the New Orleans Opera. He first appeared at the San Francisco Opera as Alvise in 1979. On Feb. 26, 1980, he made his Metropolitan Opera debut in N.Y. as the Grand Inquisitor. He also appeared at the Glyndebourne Festival (1980), the San Diego Opera (1985), the Paris Opéra (1985), the Salzburg Festival (1986), the Royal Opera, Covent Garden, London (1988), the Rome Opera (1998), and the Seville Opera (1999). In addition to such Mozart roles as Figaro, Don Alfonso, Leporello, and Don Giovanni, he has sung in many operas by Rossini and Verdi.—**NS/LK/DM**

Furno, Giovanni, Italian composer and pedagogue; b. Capua, Jan. 1, 1748; d. Naples, June 20, 1837. He studied at the Cons. di S. Onofrio in Naples, and in 1775 became a teacher of theory of composition there; retired in 1835. Among his pupils were Bellini and Mercadante. He wrote 2 operas, sacred choral music, and some instrumental pieces.—**NS/LK/DM**

Furrer, Beat, Swiss-born Austrian composer, conductor, and teacher; b. Schaffhausen, Dec. 6, 1954. He received training in piano at the Schaffhausen Cons. In 1975 he emigrated to Austria and studied composition (with Haubenstock-Ramati) and conducting at the Vienna Hochschule für Musik, graduating in 1983. In 1985 he co-founded and became director of Klangforum Wien, and from 1992 he also taught at the Graz Hochschule für Musik. He has made appearances as a guest conductor throughout Austria and Germany. In 1996 Furrer was the featured composer at both the Salzburg and Lucerne festivals.

WORKS: DRAMATIC: *Die Blinden*, music theater after Maeterlinck (Vienna, Nov. 25, 1989); *Narcissus*, opera (1992–94; Graz, Oct. 1, 1994). **ORCH.:** *Tsunamis* (1983–86; Wuppertal, Jan. 22, 1987); *Sinfonia* for Strings (1984); *Tiro mis tristes reder* (1984; Hannover, Nov. 10, 1986); *Risonanze* for 3 Orch. Groups (1988); *Studie—Übermalung* (1989–90); *Face de la chaleur* for Flute, Clarinet, Piano, and 4 Orch. Groups (Lucerne, Aug. 30, 1991); *Madrigal* (1992); *Nuun* for 2 Pianos and Orch. (Salzburg, Aug. 16, 1996). **CHAMBER:** *Frau Nachtigall* for Cello (1982); *Ensemble* for 8 Instruments (1983); 2 string quartets (1984, 1988); Duo for 2 Cellos (1985); Trio for Flute, Oboe or Saxophone, and Clarinet (1985); *Wie diese Stimmen* for 2 Cellos (1985–86); *Retour an dich*, piano trio (1986); *In der Stille des hauses wohnt ein Ton* for Chamber Ensemble (1987); *Epilog* for 3 Cellos (1988); *Gaspra* for Ensemble (1988); *A un moment de terre perdu* for Ensemble (1990); *Aer*, trio for Piano, Clarinet, and Cello (1991); *Time Out I* for 10 Instruments (1995) and *II* for 8 Instruments (1995–96); Quartet for 4 Percussionists (1995); *a due* for Viola and Piano (1997); Piano Quintet (1997–98). **KEYBOARD: P i a n o :** *Irgendwo fern* for 2 Pianos (1984); *Voicelessness: The Snow Has No Voice* (1986). **VOCAL:** *Illuminations* for Soprano and Chamber Ensemble (1985); *Dort ist das Meer—Nachts steig' ich hinab* for Chorus and Orch., after Neruda (1985–86); *Ultimi cori* for Chorus and 3 Percussion Groups (1987–88); *Stimmen/Quartett* for Chorus and 4 Percussionists (1995–96; rev. 1998); *Aria* for Soprano and Instruments (1998–99).—**LK/DM**

Fürsch-Madi(er), Emma or **Emmy,** French soprano; b. Bayonne, 1847; d. Warrenville, N.J., Sept. 19, 1894. She studied at the Paris Cons., making her operatic debut as Marguerite in Paris (1868). She then sang with the French Opera Co. in New Orleans (1873–74), making her first appearance at London's Covent Garden as Valentine in *Les Huguenots* (May 9, 1881). After adopting the name Fürsch-Madi (1882), she sang there again (1883–88). She made her Metropolitan Opera debut in N.Y. as Ortrud on Nov. 7, 1883, appearing again on its roster in 1893–94. She was particularly noted for her portrayals of Donna Anna, Lucrezia Borgia, and Aida.—**NS/LK/DM**

Fürst, Janos, Hungarian conductor; b. Budapest, Aug. 8, 1935. He received training in violin at the Franz Liszt Academy of Music in Budapest. In the aftermath of the failed Hungarian Revolution of 1956, he fled his homeland and pursued violin studies at the Brussels Cons., where he won the premier prix. He went to Dublin and was a violinist in the Irish Radio Orch. (1958–63). In 1963 he became founder-conductor of the Irish Chamber Orch. In 1968 he was made resident conductor of the Ulster Orch. in Belfast. Following his London debut with the Royal Phil. in 1972, he appeared as a guest conductor with principal British orchs. and with various orchs. on the Continent. From 1974 to 1978 he was music director of the Malmö Sym. Orch., then music director of the Ålborg Sym. Orch. (1980–83). From 1981 to 1989 he was music director of the Opera and Phil. in Marseilles; was also principal conductor of the RTE (Radio Telefís Eireann) Orch. in Dublin (1983–89). On April 12, 1990, he made his U.S. debut as a guest conductor of the Indianapolis Sym. Orch. From 1990 to 1995 he was music director of the Winterthur Stadtorchester.—**NS/LK/DM**

Fürstenau, Moritz, German writer on music and flutist; b. Dresden, July 26, 1824; d. there, March 25, 1889. He was a member of the Dresden Court Orch. from 1842, and from 1852 librarian of the music section of the Royal Library. From 1856 he was a flute teacher at the Cons.

WRITINGS: *Beiträge zur Geschichte der königlich-sächs. musikalischen Kapelle* (1849); *Zur Geschichte der Musik und des Theaters am Hofe zu Dresden* (2 vols., 1861–62; suppl. by H. van Brescius, *Die königliche sächs. musikalische Kapelle von Reissiger bis Schuch*, 1826–98, Dresden, 1898); with T. Berthold, *Die Fabrikation musikalischer Instrumente im königlich sächsischen Vogtland* (1876); also essays and articles in musical journals.—**NS/LK/DM**

Furtwängler, (Gustav Heinrich Ernst Martin) Wilhelm, great German conductor; b. Berlin, Jan. 25, 1886; d. Ebersteinburg, Nov. 30, 1954. His father, Adolf Furtwängler, was a distinguished archaeologist and director of the Berlin Museum of Antiquities, and his mother, Adelheid (née Wendt) Furtwängler, was a painter. A precocious child, he received instruction in piano at a very early age from his mother and his aunt; by the time he was 7, he had begun to compose. After his father was called to the Univ. of Munich as prof. of archaeology in 1894, he was tutored at home by the archaeologist Ludwig Curtius, the art historian and musicologist Walter Riezler, and the sculptor Adolf Hildebrand. He commenced formal training in composition with Beer-Walbrunn, and then pursued the study of advanced counterpoint with Rheinberger (1900–1901); he subsequently completed his studies with Schillings. After working as répétiteur at the Breslau Opera (1905–06), he became 3rd conductor at the Zürich Opera in 1906; that same year he scored a notable success conducting Bruckner's 9th Sym. in Munich with the Kaim Orch. From 1907 to 1909 he was an asst. conductor under Mottl at the Munich Court Opera. He then was 3rd conductor under Pfitzner at the Strasbourg Municipal Opera from 1909 to 1911. In 1911 he was appointed music director in Lübeck, a position he held until 1915 when he was called to Mannheim as Generalmusikdirektor. It was during this period that Furtwängler began to secure his reputation as a conductor of great promise. In 1915 he made his first appearance in Vienna conducting the Konzertvereinsorchester. He scored a notable success at his debut with the Berlin Phil. on Dec. 14, 1917. In 1920 he resigned his position in Mannheim to serve as Strauss's successor as music director of the Berlin State Opera orch. concerts, remaining there until 1922; concurrently he served as Mengelberg's successor as music director of the Frankfurt am Main Museumgesellschaft concerts. On Aug. 30, 1921, he made his debut with the Leipzig Gewandhaus Orch. to critical acclaim. Upon the death of Nikisch in 1922, Furtwängler was appointed his successor as music director of both the Berlin Phil. and the Leipzig Gewandhaus Orch., retaining the latter position until 1928. On March 27, 1922, he made his debut with the Vienna Phil. He made his first appearance in Milan in 1923 when he conducted the La Scala Orch. On Jan. 24, 1924, Furtwängler made his British debut with the Royal Phil. Soc. in London. His auspicious U.S. debut followed on Jan. 3, 1925, with the N.Y. Phil.; he returned to conduct there again in 1926 and 1927. Upon Weingartner's resignation as regular conductor of the Vienna Phil. in 1927, Furtwängler was elected his successor. He made his debut at the Vienna State Opera conducting *Das Rheingold* on Oct. 17, 1928. That same year he was awarded an honorary doctorate by the Univ. of Heidelberg. His debut as an opera conductor in Berlin took place on June 13, 1929, when he conducted *Le nozze di Figaro* at the Berlin Festival. In 1929 the German government awarded him the medal Pour le Mérite in recognition of his outstanding contributions to German musical culture. In 1930 he resigned his position with the Vienna Phil., having been named Generalmusikdirektor of Berlin. In 1930 he was made music director of the Bayreuth Festival. He made his first appearance there conducting *Tristan und Isolde* on July 23, 1931, but resigned his position at the close of the season. He then made his debut at the Berlin State Opera on Nov. 12, 1931, conducting the local premiere of Pfitzner's *Das*

Herz, and in 1932 was appointed its music director.

After the Nazis came to power in 1933, they moved quickly to appropriate Furtwängler's stature as Germany's greatest conductor for their own propaganda purposes. He was made vice president of the newly organized Reichsmusikkammer and then was appointed one of the newly created Prussian State Councilors, an honorary lifetime title which Furtwängler refused to use. He also refused to join the Nazi party. Early on, he began to encounter difficulties with the authorities over personal and artistic matters. He opposed the regime's policies against the Jews and others, and did all he could to assist those who sought him out, both musicians and non-musicians alike, often at great personal risk. For the 1933–34 season of the Berlin State Opera, Furtwängler scheduled the premiere of Hindemith's *Mathis der Maler*, even though the Nazis had branded the composer a "cultural Bolshevist" and a "spiritual non-Aryan" (his wife was half Jewish). The Nazis compelled Furtwängler to withdraw the work, but he attempted to defy them by conducting a symphonic version of the score with the Berlin Phil. on March 11, 1934. It elicited a prolonged ovation from the audience, but drew condemnation from the Nazi press as a contemptible example of "degenerate" music. The ensuing polemical campaign against Furtwängler led him to resign all of his positions on Dec. 4, 1934. (As a propaganda ploy, the Nazis would not accept his resignation as a Prussian State Councilor since this was a lifetime "honor" granted by the regime.) Furtwängler's devotion to what he considered to be the true (non-Nazi) Germany and his belief that it was his duty to preserve its great musical heritage compelled him to make an uneasy peace with the regime. On April 25, 1935, he returned as a conductor with the Berlin Phil. Although he appeared regularly with it in succeeding years, he refused an official position with it so as not to be beholden to the Nazis. In 1936 he was offered the position of conductor of the N.Y. Phil. in succession to Toscanini, but he declined the offer in the face of accusations in the American press that he was a Nazi collaborator. In 1937 he was invited to London to participate in the musical celebrations in honor of the coronation of King George VI, where he conducted the *Ring* cycle at Covent Garden and Beethoven's 9th Sym. On Aug. 27, 1937, he made his first appearance at the Salzburg Festival conducting Beethoven's 9th Sym. In 1939 he was honored by the French government as a Commandeur of the Légion d'honneur. After the outbreak of World War II on Sept. 1, 1939, Furtwängler confined his activities almost exclusively to Germany and Austria, principally with the Berlin Phil. and the Vienna Phil. In 1944, after learning that Himmler had placed him on the Nazi's liquidation list, Furtwängler sent his family to Switzerland for safety, while he remained behind to keep his conducting engagements for the 1944–45 season. However, after conducting the Vienna Phil. in Jan. 1945, he too fled to Switzerland. His decision to pursue his career in his homeland during the Third Reich left him open to charges by the Allies after the war of being a Nazi collaborator. Although the Vienna denazification commission cleared him on March 9, 1946, as a German citizen he was ordered to stand trial in Berlin before the Allied Denazification Tribunal for Artists. Following his trial on Dec. 11 and 17, 1946, he was acquitted of all charges; it was not until March 1947, however, that he was formally "normalized." On May 25, 1947, he conducted the Berlin Phil. for the first time since the close of World War II, leading an all- Beethoven concert to extraordinary approbation. On Aug. 10, 1947, he also resumed his association with the Vienna Phil. when he conducted it at the Salzburg Festival. He made his first postwar appearance at the Berlin State Opera on Oct. 3, 1947, conducting *Tristan und Isolde*. In Feb. 1948 he returned to England for the first time in more than a decade to conduct a series of concerts with the London Phil. He also became active as a conductor with the Philharmonia Orch. of London. When the management of the Chicago Sym. Orch. announced Furtwängler's engagement as a guest conductor for the 1949–50 season, a campaign against him as a Nazi collaborator compelled him to cancel his engagements. However, in Western Europe his appearances on tours with the Berlin Phil. and the Vienna Phil. were acclaimed. In 1950 he made his debut at Milan's La Scala conducting the *Ring* cycle. With Flagstad as soloist, he conducted the premiere of Strauss's *Vier letzte Lieder* in London on May 22, 1950. On July 29, 1951, he reopened the Bayreuth Festival conducting Beethoven's 9th Sym. In 1952 he resumed his position of music director of the Berlin Phil., but increasing ill health and growing deafness clouded his remaining days. He was scheduled to conduct the Berlin Phil. on its first tour of the U.S. in the spring of 1955, but his health further declined, leading to his death in the fall of 1954; Herbert von Karajan was elected his successor.

Furtwängler was the perfect embodiment of all that was revered in the Austro-German tradition of the art of conducting. As its foremost exponent, he devined and made manifest the spiritual essence of the great masterworks of the symphonic and operatic repertory. His often refulgent and always-inspired interpretations of Mozart, Beethoven, Schubert, Schumann, Brahms, Wagner, and Bruckner, many of which have been preserved on recordings, attest to his greatness as a recreative artist of the highest order. Furtwängler was also a creative artist who composed in an expansive Romantic style. Sketches for an early sym. (1903) were utilized in a mature sym. (1937–41), premiered in Marl kreis Recklinghausen on April 27, 1991, Alfred Walter conducting. Another sym. (1943–47) had 3 of its movements premiered in Berlin on Jan. 26, 1956, Joseph Keilberth conducting. Among his other works were a *Te Deum* (1910); Piano Quintet (1935); Symphonie Concertante for Piano and Orch. (1937); 2 violin sonatas (1937, 1940).

WRITINGS: *Johannes Brahms und Anton Bruckner* (Leipzig, 1941; 2nd ed., 1952); W. Abendroth, ed., *Gespräche über Musik* (Zürich, 1948; 7th ed., 1958; Eng. tr., 1953, as *Concerning Music*); *Ton und Wort* (Wiesbaden, 1954; 8th ed., 1958); M. Hürlimann, ed., *Der Musiker und sein Publikum* (Zürich, 1955); S. Brockhaus, ed., *Vermächtnis* (Wiesbaden, 1956; 4th ed., 1958); F. Thiess, ed., *Briefe* (Wiesbaden, 1964); E. Furtwängler and G. Birkner, *Wilhelm Furtwängler Aufzeichnungen 1924–54* (Mainz, 1980; Eng. tr., 1989); R. Taylor, tr. and ed., *Furtwängler on Music: Essays and Addresses* (Aldershot and Brookfield, Vt., 1991).

BIBL.: R. Specht, *W. F.* (Vienna, 1922); O. Schrenck, *W. F.* (Berlin, 1940); F. Herzfeld, *W. F.: Weg und Wesen* (Leipzig, 1941; 3rd ed., rev., 1950); B. Geissmar, *Two Worlds of Music* (N.Y., 1946); W. Siebert, *F.: Mensch und Künstler* (Buenos Aires, 1950); C. Riess, *F.: Musik und Politik* (Bern, 1953; abridged Eng. tr., 1955); B. Gavoty and R. Hauert, *W. F.* (Geneva, 1954); M. Hürlimann, ed., *W. F.: Im Urteil seiner Zeit* (Zürich, 1955); D. Gillis, ed., *F. Recalled* (Tuckahoe, N.Y., 1966); idem, *F. and America* (Woodhaven, N.Y., 1970); E. Furtwängler, *Über W. F.* (Wiesbaden, 1979; Eng. tr., 1993); K. Hoecker, *Die nie vergessenen Klänge: Erinnerungen an W. F.* (Berlin, 1979); P. Pirie, *F. and the Art of Conducting* (London, 1980); J. Hunt, *The F. Sound* (London, 1985; 3rd ed., 1989); J. Squire and J. Hunt, *F. and Great Britain* (London, 1985); B. Wessling, *W. F.: Eine kritische Biographie* (Stuttgart, 1985); G. Gefen, *F.: Une Biographie par le Disque* (Paris, 1986); J. Matzner, *F.: Analyse, Dokument, Protokoll* (Zürich, 1986); F. Prieberg, *Kraftprobe: W. F. im Dritten Reich* (Wiesbaden, 1986; Eng. tr., 1991); H.-H. Schönzeler, *F.* (London, 1990); S. Shirakawa, *The Devil's Music Master: The Controversial Life and Career of W. F.* (Oxford, 1992).—NS/LK/DM

Furuhjelm, Erik Gustaf, Finnish composer; b. Helsinki, July 6, 1883; d. there, June 13, 1964. He studied violin, then took lessons in composition with Sibelius and Wegelius. He continued his studies in Vienna with Robert Fuchs. From 1909 to 1935 he lectured on theory at the Helsinki School of Music, and from 1920 to 1935 served as asst. director there. He founded the magazine *Finsk Musikrevy*, and in 1916 wrote the first book-length biography of Sibelius.

WORKS: ORCH.: 2 syms. (1906–11; 1925–26); *Romantic Overture* (1910); *Konzertstück* for Piano and Orch. (1911); *Intermezzo and Pastorale* (1920–24); *Fem bilder* (1924–25); *Phantasy* for Violin and Orch. (1925–26); *Folklig svit* (1939); *Solitude* (1940). **OTHER:** Chamber music.—NS/LK/DM

Fussan, Werner, German composer and teacher; b. Plauen, Dec. 25, 1912; d. Mainz, Aug. 16, 1986. He was a pupil of Gmeindl and Höffer at the Berlin Hochschule für Musik (1937–40). After teaching at the Wiesbaden Cons. (1945–48), he joined the faculty of the Mainz Hochschule für Musik, where he later was prof. of music education (1966–78).

WORKS: ORCH.: *Musik* for Strings (1943); *Musik* (1947); *Prelude* (1947); *Capriccio* (1949); *Musik* for Strings, Piano, Timpani, and Percussion (1950); Suite for Strings (1951); Concertino for Flute and Strings (1957); *Little Suite* for Strings (1958); Concertino for Clarinet, Strings, and Trumpet (1966). **CHAMBER:** Piano Sonata (1946); *Musik* for Flute and Piano (1947); *Musik* for Violin and Piano (1949); String Trio (1953). **VOCAL:** *Heiteres Aquarium* for Chorus (1967); *Tanzlieder-Kantate* for Soloists, Choruses, and Orch. (1970); *Feier-Kantate* for Choruses and Small Orch. (1972); *Swing and Sing* for Chorus and Rhythm Group (1972). **OTHER:** Numerous educational pieces. —NS/LK/DM

Fussell, Charles C(lement), American composer and conductor; b. Winston-Salem, N.C., Feb. 14, 1938. He received lessons in piano from Clemens Sandresky in Winston-Salem, and in 1956 enrolled in the Eastman School of Music in Rochester, N.Y., where he studied composition (B.M., 1960) with Thomas Canning, Wayne Barlow, and Bernard Rogers, piano with José Echaniz, and conducting with Herman Genhart. In 1962 he received a Fulbright grant and studied with Blacher at the Berlin Hochschule für Musik. He attended Friedelind Wagner's Bayreuth Festival Master Class in opera production and conducting in 1963, and then completed his training in composition at the Eastman School of Music (M.M., 1964). In 1966 he joined the faculty of the Univ. of Mass. in Amherst, where he founded its Group for New Music in 1974 (later renamed Pro Musica Moderna). He taught composition at the N.C. School of the Arts in Winston-Salem (1976–77) and at Boston Univ. (1981). In 1981–82 he conducted the Longy School Chamber Orch. in Cambridge, Mass. In his music, he adopts a prudent modernistic idiom and favors neo-Romantic but never overladen sonorities, without doctrinaire techniques.

Works: Dramatic: Opera: *Caligula* (1962). **Orch.:** 4 syms.: No. 1, *Symphony in 1 Movement* (1963), No. 2 for Soprano and Orch. (1964–67), No. 3, *Landscapes,* for Chorus and Orch. (1978–81), and No. 4, *Wilde,* for Baritone and Orch. (1989); *3 Processionals* (1972–73; Springfield, Mass., April 25, 1974); *Northern Lights,* 2 portraits for Chamber Orch., portraying Leoš Janáček and Edvard Munch (1977–79); *Virgil Thomson Sleeping,* portrait for Chamber Orch. (1981); *4 Fairy Tales,* after Oscar Wilde (1980–81); *Maurice Grosser Cooking,* portrait No. 2 for Chamber Orch. (1982–83); *Jack Larson,* portrait No. 3 for Chamber Orch. (1986). **Chamber:** Trio for Violin, Cello, and Piano (1962); *Dance Suite* for Flute, Trumpet, Viola, and 2 Percussionists (1963); *Ballades* for Cello and Piano (1968; rev. 1976); *Greenwood Sketches: Music for String Quartet* (1976); *Free Fall* for 7 Players (N.Y., May 9, 1988); *Last Trombones* for 6 Trombones, 5 Percussion, and 2 Pianos (1990). **Vocal:** *Saint Stephen and Herod,* drama for Speaker, Chorus, and Winds (1964); *Poems* for Voices and Chamber Orch. (1965); *Julian,* drama for Soprano, Tenor, Chorus, and Orch. (1969–71; Winston-Salem, N.C., April 15, 1972); *Voyages* for Soprano, Tenor, Women's Chorus, Piano, Winds, and Recorded Speaker (Amherst, Mass., May 4, 1970); *Eurydice* for Soprano and Chamber Ensemble (1973–75; Winston-Salem, N.C., Jan. 30, 1976); *Résumé,* cycle of 9 songs for Soprano, Clarinet, String Bass, and Piano (1975–76); *Cymbeline,* romance for Soprano, Tenor, Narrator, and Chamber Ensemble (Boston, April 2, 1984); *The Gift* for Soprano and Chorus (1986; Boston, Dec. 24, 1987); *5 Goethe Lieder* for Soprano or Tenor and Piano (1987; also for Soprano or Tenor and Orch., 1991); *A Song of Return* for Chorus and Orch. (1989); *Wilde,* 2 monologues for Baritone and Orch. (1989–90); other vocal works.—NS/LK/DM

Füssl, Karl Heinz, Austrian composer, musicologist, publisher, and music critic; b. Jablonec, Czechoslovakia, March 21, 1924; d. Eisenstadt, Sept. 4, 1992. He went to Berlin and began his formal training at 15 with Konrad Friedrich Noetel (composition), Gerd Otto (piano), and Hugo Distler (choral conducting). Following World War II, he settled in Vienna and completed his studies with Alfred Uhl (composition), Erwin Ratz (analysis), and Hans Swarowsky (conducting). He was active as a music critic and served as head of production for Universal Edition. In addition to overseeing its Urtext Editions, he was associated with the publication of the works of Haydn, Mozart, Johann Strauss, and Mahler. In 1974 he became a teacher of form analysis at the Vienna Academy of Music, where he served as a prof. from 1985. In his music, Füssl demonstrated an adept handling of dodecaphonic procedures.

Works: Dramatic: *Die Maske,* ballet (1954); *Dybuk,* opera (1958–70; Karlsruhe, Sept. 26, 1970); *Celestina,* opera (1973–75); *Kain,* religious play (1984–85); *Resurrexit,* musical play (1991–92); incidental music. **Orch.:** *Divertimento* (1952); *Szenen* for Strings (1954); *Epitaph und Antistrophe* (1956; rev. 1971); *Refrains* for Piano and Orch. (1972); *Sonate: Arkadenhof-Serenade* (1983; rev. 1988); *Moments Musicaux,* 8 pieces (1988); *7 Haikai* for Strings and Percussion (1991). **Chamber:** *Kleine Kammermusik* for Flute, Oboe, Clarinet, Horn, and Bassoon (1940); *Duo* for Cello and Piano (1948–53; rev. 1983); Concertino I (1948) and II (1952) for Clarinet and Piano, 4-Hands; *Triptychon* for Cello and Organ (1976); *2 Stücke* for Clarinet and Piano (1977); *Ragtime* for Guitar and Piano (1977); *Nachtmusik* for String Trio (1977; rev. 1988); *Improvisation* for String Quartet (1979); *Les Rondeaux,* 3 duets for 2 Violins (1980; 2nd version, 1981); *Aphorismen über Rhythmische Modelle* for Clarinet and Piano (1980); *Perpetuum Mobile* for Oboe or Trumpet and Piano (1987); *Ekloge* for Cello and Piano (1987); *Konzert zu Viert* for Clarinet and Saxophone (1989); *1 Minute* for String Quartet (1991); *Cantus I* and *II* for String Quartet (both 1991); *Ricercare* for String Quartet (1992). **Keyboard:** *Fünf Töne-Fünf Finger,* 6 little pieces for Piano (1941; rev. 1959); *Motetus Victimae Pascali Laudes* for Organ and Voice(s) ad libitum (1976; rev. 1988); *Fantasia for Organ* (1978–79); Concertino for Organ (1980); *Esercizi: Hommage à Domenico Scarlatti* for Harpsichord or Piano (1992). **Vocal:** *Dialogue in Praise of the Owl and the Cuckoo* for Tenor and 7 Instruments (1947–48; rev. 1961; also for Bass and 4 Instruments, 1968); *Görög Ilona* for Chorus (1948; rev. 1971); *Concerto Rapsodico* for Alto or Mezzo-soprano and Chamber Orch. (1957); *Miorita* for High Voice, Women's Chorus ad libitum, and 5 Instruments (1963); *Missa* for Chorus and Organ (1966; 2nd version, 1986); *A Medieval Passion* for Alto, Bass, Chorus, and Orch. (1967); *Cantiunculae Amoris* for Tenor and String Quartet or String Orch. (1976); *Bilder der Jahreszeit* for High Voice and String Orch. (1981); *Suspirium ad Amorem,* 2 cantatas for Medium Voice(s), Chorus, and Chamber Orch. (1986); *3 Mediaeval Songs* for Alto or Baritone and Chamber Orch. (1987); *10 Lieder nach Hölderlin* for Medium Voice and Chamber Orch. (1987); *4 Lieder nach Hölderlin* for High Voice and Chamber Orch. (1989); *2 Kommentare zu Hölderlin* for High Voice and String Orch. (1989); various other choral works and song cycles.—NS/LK/DM

Fusz, János, Hungarian composer; b. Tolna, Dec. 16, 1777; d. Buda, March 9, 1819. He began his training in Baja. After teaching piano in Pressburg, he went to Vienna to study with Albrechtsberger, where he was befriended by Haydn; in 1817 he settled in Buda. He composed an opera, *Watwort,* music for Schiller's *Die Braut von Messina* (1811), chamber music, piano pieces, and lieder.—LK/DM

Futterer, Carl, Swiss composer; b. Basel, Feb. 21, 1873; d. Ludwigshafen, Nov. 5, 1927. He studied to be a lawyer; then began taking lessons in composition with Hans Huber. He wrote operas and other works but kept them hidden until late in life. His comic opera *Don Gil mit den grünen Hosen* (1915) was produced in Freiburg im Breisgau in 1922, and another opera, *Der Geiger von Gmünd* (1917), was produced in Basel in 1921. He further wrote a *Sinfonietta* (1917), octet (1921), quartet for oboe, clarinet, horn, and bassoon (1921), trio for clarinet, cello, and piano (1924), piano trio (1927), violin sonata (1927), and piano concerto (1927).—**NS/LK/DM**

Futterman, Joel, jazz pianist, soprano saxophonist, Indian flutist; b. April 30, 1946 in Chicago. He studied privately in Chicago, then at age 17 or 18 he met Gene (Clarence) Shaw, with whom he played and studied. He earned his B.S. at the Univ. of Ill. in Chicago and his M.S.Ed. at Northwestern Univ. He left Chicago in 1972 and relocated to Virginia Beach, Va., and studied at Old Dominion Univ., Norfolk, Va. He independently produced albums with Jimmy Lyons, Richard Davis, and others, usually with drummer Robert Adkins; he frequently performed at European festivals and recorded. He joined with Edward Kidd Jordan and Alvin Fielder in 1994 to form a performing trio. He has also played with Jimmy Garrison, Rahsaan Roland Kirk, Jimmy Lyons, Joseph Jarman, Nina Simone, Frank Foster, and Ira Sullivan.

DISC.: *Cafeteria* (1980); *Moments* (1981); *The End Is the Beginning* (1981); *In-Between Positions* (1982); *Inneraction* (1984); *Vision in Time* (1990); *Inner Conversations* (1990); *Moments* (1990); *Passage* (1991); *Berlin Images* (1992); *Naked Colours* (1994); *Silhouettes* (1995); *Nickelsdorf Konfrontation* (1996); *New Orleans Rising* (1997).—**LP**

Fux, Johann Joseph, renowned Austrian organist, music theorist, pedagogue, and composer; b. Hirtenfeld, near St. Marein, Styria, 1660; d. Vienna, Feb. 13, 1741. He was born into a peasant family. Fux enrolled in the Jesuit Univ. in Graz as a "grammatista" in 1680, then in 1681 he entered the Ferdinandeum there, a Jesuit residential school made up mostly of musically gifted students. He also studied at the Jesuit Univ. of Ingolstadt, being listed as logica studiosus in 1683. He served as organist at St. Moritz there until 1688. By 1696 he was in Vienna, where he was organist at the Schottenkirche until 1702. Fux was made court composer by the Emperor in 1698; about 1700 the latter is believed to have sent him to Rome, where he studied composition. He became vice Kapellmeister at St. Stephen's Cathedral in Vienna in 1705, and was then its principal Kapellmeister from 1712 to 1715. He became vice Kapellmeister to the court in 1713. Fux was named Ziani's successor as principal Kapellmeister to the court in 1715. Among his noted students were Gottlieb Muffat, G.C. Wagenseil, and J.D. Zelenka. Fux was the last representative of the Baroque tradition in composition and music theory in Austria. As a composer, he was an outstanding contrapuntist. He found inspiration in the a cappella polyphonic mastery of Palestrina, which led to his adoption of 2 contrasting styles in his sacred music: the stylus a cappella (without instruments) and the stylus mixtus (with instruments). In his solo motets, operas, and oratorios, he prepared the way for the Viennese Classicists. More than 200 works have been added to the original 405 cataloged by Köchel. As a music theorist, he produced the classic treatise on counterpoint, *Gradus ad Parnassum* (1725). It had a profound influence on his successors, and remains an invaluable textbook.

WORKS: DRAMATIC: O p e r a (all 1st perf. at the Hoftheater, Vienna, unless otherwise given): *Il fato monarchico*, festa teatrale (Feb. 18, 1700; music not extant); *Neo- exoriens phosphorus, id est neo-electus et infulatus praesul Mellicensis*, Latin school opera (1701; music not extant); *L'offendere per amare ovvero La Telesilla*, dramma per musica (June 25, 1702; music not extant); *La clemenza d'Augusto*, poemetto drammatico (Nov. 15, 1702; music not extant); *Julo Ascanio, rè d'Alba*, poemetto drammatico (March 19, 1708); *Pulcheria*, poemetto drammatico (June 21, 1708); *Il mese di Marzo, consecrato a Marte*, componimento per musica (March 19, 1709); *Gli ossequi della notte*, componimento per musica (July 15, 1709); *La decima fatica d'Ercole, ovvero La Sconfitta di Gerione in Spagna*, componimento pastorale-eroico (Oct. 1, 1710); *Dafne in Lauro*, componimento per camera (Oct. 1, 1714); *Orfeo ed Euridice*, componimento da camera per musica (Oct. 1, 1715); *Angelica vincitrice di Alcina*, festa teatrale (Sept. 14, 1716); *Diana placata*, componimento da camera (Nov. 19, 1717); *Elisa*, festa teatrale per musica (Laxenburg, Aug. 28, 1719); *Psiche*, componimento da camera per musica (Nov. 19, 1720); *Le nozze di Aurora*, festa teatrale per musica (Oct. 6, 1722); *Costanza e Fortezza*, festa teatrale (Prague, Aug. 28, 1723); *Giunone placata*, festa teatrale per musica (Nov. 19, 1725); *La corona d'Arianna*, festa teatrale (Aug. 28, 1726); *Enea negli Elisi, ovvero Il tempio dell'Eternità*, festa teatrale (Aug. 28, 1731). **O r a t o r i o s :** *Die Heilige Dimpna, Infantin von Irland* (1702; only part 2 extant); *La fede sacrilega nella morte del Precursor S. Giovanni Battista* (1714); *La donna forte nelle madre de' sette Maccabei* (1715); *Il trionfo della fede* (1716); *Il disfacimento di Sisara* (1717); *Cristo nell'orto* (1718); *Gesù Cristo negato da Pietro* (1719); *Santa Geltrude* (1719); *La cena del Signore* (1720); *Ismaele* (1721); *Il testamento di nostro Signor Gesù Cristo sul calvario* (1726); *Oratorium germanicum de passione Domini* (1731; music not extant). **OTHER SACRED:** *Il fonte della salute, aperto dalla grazia nel calvario*, componimento sacro (1716); *La deposizione dalla croce di Gesù Cristo Salvator Nostro*, componimento sacro per musica al SS. Sepolcro (1728); about 80 masses; Te Deum for Double Choir (1706); motets; vespers and Psalms; antiphons; offertories; hymns; etc. **INSTRUMENTAL:** About 50 church sonatas; some 80 partitas and overtures; *Concentus musico-instrumentalis* (1701); keyboard works.

WRITINGS: *Gradus ad Parnassum* (Vienna, 1725; partial Eng. tr. as *Steps to Parnassus: The Study of Counterpoint*, N.Y., 1943; 2nd ed., rev., 1965, as *The Study of Counterpoint*); *Singfundament* (Vienna, c. 1832); *Exempla dissonantiarum ligatarum et non ligatarum* (publ. in H. Federhofer, "Drei handscriftliche Quellen zur Musiktheorie in Österreich um 1700," *Musa—mens—musici: Im Gedenken an Walther Vetter* [Leipzig, 1969]). A complete ed. of his works, ed. by H. Federhofer and O. Wessely under the auspices of the J.J. Fux-Gesellschaft, began publication in 1959.

BIBL.: L. von Köchel, *J.J. F.* (Vienna, 1872; includes thematic catalog and list of works); A. Liess, *Die Triosonaten von J.J. F.* (Berlin, 1940); idem, *F.iana* (Vienna, 1958); J. van der Meer, *J.J. F. als Opernkomponist* (3 vols., Bilthoven, 1961); E. Wellesz, *F.* (London, 1965; new ed., 1991, as *J.J. F.*); C. Rutherford, *The Instrumental Music of J.J. F.* (diss., Colo. State Univ., 1967); R. Flotzinger, *F. Studien* (Graz, 1985); B. Habla, ed., *J.J. F. und die barocke Bläsertradition* (Tutzing, 1987); R. Flotzinger, ed., *J.J. F.-Symposium Graz '91* (Graz, 1992); H. White, ed., *J.J. F. and the Music of the Austro-Italian Baroque* (Aldershot, 1992); A. Edler and F. Riedel, eds., *J.J. F. und seine Zeit: Kultur, Kunst und Musik im Spätbarock* (Laaber, 1996).—**NS/LK/DM**

G

Gabriel, Charles H(utchinson), American composer and music editor; b. Wilton, Iowa, Aug. 18, 1856; d. Los Angeles, Sept. 14, 1932. He went to Chicago in 1892 and became active as a composer of gospel hymns for various evangelists. He then worked for Homer A. Rodeheaver's publishing company (1912–32), and ed. the journal *Gospel Choir* (1915–23), for which he wrote his memoirs (IV, 1918), 35 gospel songbooks, 19 anthem collections, and 8 vols. of Sunday-school songs. He also authored the book *Gospel Songs and Their Writers* (Chicago, 1915). He was a prolific composer, and included in his more than 8,000 works are gospel hymns, Christmas cantatas, sacred cantatas, children's cantatas, and secular operettas.—**NS/LK/DM**

Gabriel, Mary Ann Virginia, English composer; b. Banstead, Surrey, Feb. 7, 1825; d. London, Aug. 7, 1877. She studied with Pixis, Dohler, Thalberg, and Molique. She married George E. March (1874), who wrote most of her librettos.

WORKS: DRAMATIC: O p e r e t t a : *Widows Bewitched* (London, Nov. 13, 1867); *Grass Widows*; *Shepherd of Cornouailles*; *Who's the Heir?*; *Follies of a Night*; *A Rainy Day*. C a n t a t a s : *Evangeline* (Brighton Festival, Feb. 13, 1873); *Dreamland*; *Graziella*. OTHER: Piano pieces.—**NS/LK/DM**

Gabriel, Peter, the genesis and genius of all that's good in progressive music (b. Surrey England, May 13, 1950). By going with his best creative instincts, Peter Gabriel stayed on the cutting edge of popular music, modern but always accessible, from the 1960s with the group Genesis to his interest in world-music artists in the 1990s. Enamored of soul stars like Otis Redding and James Brown, in 1966, Gabriel started writing songs with pianist Tony Banks and drummer Chris Stewart at the Charterhouse School. After graduation, they added guitarists Mike Rutherford and Anthony Phillips and started playing around England as Genesis. Their show featured Gabriel's increasingly Byzantine theatrics and

musical development from near-Celtic to more complex, orchestrally textured pomp rock.

After the success of the 1974 album *The Lamb Lies Down on Broadway*, Gabriel left Genesis. His early solo recordings were more direct, less portentous, and more humorous than his previous work with the art-rock group. Two years in the making, the first *Peter Gabriel* album (his first four albums were self-titled), his solo debut, featured "Solisbury Hill" (#68) and even an extended musical joke, "Excuse Me," with its jug-band-meets-barbershop-quartet sound. Even "Down the Dolce Vita," featuring a tasteful part performed by the London Symphony Orch., avoided getting bogged down in its own pretensions.

The second edition of *Peter Gabriel* (#48) came out in 1978 at the height of the British punk movement. Following the punk aesthetic, the album made a direct reference to the "do-it-yourself" punk ethic on the underground hit "DIY." Using a core band of Tony Levin on bass, Robert Fripp on guitar, Jerry Marotta on drums, Roy Bittan on piano, and Larry Fast on synths, *PG2* is lean, but lacked the loud, snotty edge of 1978-era punk. Instead it channeled the energy of punk and started turning it into new wave.

These proto-new wave influences combined with a new infatuation with music from developing nations on the third edition of *Peter Gabriel*. With its striking Hipgnosis-designed cover of his melting face, the album sported some heavyweight songs. "Games without Frontiers" became a Top Five English hit. "I Don't Remember" and "Biko" (the first known recording to combine Surdo drums with bagpipes) helped make *PG3* one of the most cutting-edge slices of rock released in 1980 (maybe ever). Add to this the advent and rise of MTV, which offered Gabriel's visual histrionics a new outlet. He created memorable clips for "Games..." and "I Don't Remember." The album rose to #22 in the U.S. and topped the English charts.

The fourth and final edition of *Peter Gabriel* (which his American record company called *Security*, without his sanction) was not as accessible as *PG3*. His densest aural testament since Genesis's *The Lamb,* the album reflected Gabriel's growing interest in non- Western music. Ethiopian pipes ran through "The Family and the Fishing Net." The Ekome Dance Company added intense African drumming to the climax of "Rhythm of the Heat." "Shock the Monkey" garnered Gabriel his first Top 40 U.S. hit (#29) with its striking video.

The 1982 tour brought all of Gabriel's solo repertoire to the stage and was recorded for the *Plays Live* double-album set. The record works on several levels, as a greatest hits collection and as a document of Gabriel's live sound (although he does admit to tinkering with it in the studio after the fact). That same year Gabriel's fascination with non- Western music spawned the World of Music and Dance (WOMAD) festival with performers from all over the world. Like much of what Gabriel does, WOMAD was ahead of its time, attracting lots of critical praise and very few paying customers.

Still, in the three years between the live album and his next rock project, Gabriel released but one album, the soundtrack for the film *Birdy.* This recording uses many of the same musicians from *Security,* including Fast, Levin, Marotta, and the Ekome Drummers, as well as the music from previously released (he calls them "recycled") tracks. The alternately ambient and aggressive new material complements the recycled work.

Nearly five years after the release of *Security* came the follow-up, *So.* What *Security* accomplished critically, *So* attained popularly, garnering Gabriel something that longtime fans would have thought impossible: a chart-topping single, "Sledgehammer." Even more accessible than *PG3*, the hits, especially, hark back to Gabriel's affection for American soul. Both "Sledgehammer" and the other Top Ten hit, "Big Time," were downright funky, while "In Your Eyes" became a standard at hip weddings. In lieu of theatricality, Gabriel put together one of the most challenging and funny music videos ever, a claymation epic, for "Sledgehammer." The video took home Best Video and eight other MTV video awards. The album peaked at #2 on the charts, and went triple platinum.

So also expanded on Gabriel's interest in pan-global music, featuring international performers of note that were largely unknown to western audiences like Youssou N'Dour, Manu Katche, and L. Shankar. After *So,* Gabriel spent much of his time with these artists. He started his own state-of-the-art studios, Real World, and a label of the same name to go with it. He brought artists like N'Dour and Nusrat Fateh Ali Khan to ears around the world, making stars of both. His work on the soundtrack to *The Last Temptation of Christ,* released as *Passion,* featured Vatche Houseprian and Antrianik Askarian playing Armenian doudouk, alongside the double Indian violin of Shankar, and vocals by Malian star Baaba Maal as well as N'Dour. This music represents Gabriel's most thorough fusion of electronic and acoustic elements and is remarkable for the fusion of North African and Asian musics with Western ideas. The album won Gabriel a Best New Age Grammy and peaked at #60.

Capitalizing on the success of *So,* a compilation of "the best" of Gabriel's first three albums—*Shaking the Tree*—came out, went gold, and peaked at #48.

Meanwhile, Gabriel's personal life suffered as his popularity peaked. His marriage to childhood sweetheart Jill Moore (daughter of the Queen's private secretary) fell apart. He chronicled this on his next album, *Us.* In terms of sales, it picked up where *So* left off, entering the charts at #2. In the eight years since *So,* however, a lot had changed. Despite more remarkable videos, the single "Digging in the Dirt" didn't break the Top 40, and "Steam," a lukewarm rehash of "Sledgehammer," peaked at #32.

Since then, Gabriel has kept busy on a variety of projects. He released a live album, put out several multimedia endeavors, and recorded non-Western artists extensively for his Real World label. He created music for Britain's Millenium Dome and worked with his old school chums from Genesis on a track for a greatest hits record. The turn of the millennium finds Gabriel releasing his first new album in eight years, entitled *OVO: Millennium Show.*

DISC.: *Peter Gabriel* (1977); *Peter Gabriel* (1978); *Peter Gabriel* (1980); *Peter Gabriel* (aka *Security;* 1982); *Plays Live* (1983); *Birdy* (soundtrack; 1985); *So* (1986); *Passion: Music for the Last Temptation of Christ* (soundtrack; 1989); *Shaking the Tree: 16 Golden Greats* (1990); *Revisited* (1992); *Us* (1992); *Secret World Live* (1994); *OVO: Millennium Show* (2000).

WRITINGS: *P.G.: In His Own Words* (N.Y., 1994).

BIBL. R. Star, *Peter Gabriel* (1988); Spencer Bright, *Peter Gabriel: An Authorized Biography* (London, 1988); C. Welch, *The Secret Life of Peter Gabriel* (N.Y., 1998).—**HB**

Gabrieli, Andrea (also known as **Andrea di Cannaregio**), eminent Italian organist and composer, uncle of **Giovanni Gabrieli;** b. Venice, c. 1510; d. there, 1586. He may have been a pupil of Adrian Willaert at S. Marco while serving as a chorister there (1536). He was organist at S. Geremia in Cannaregio in 1557–58. He was in Frankfurt am Main for the coronation of Maximilian II as court organist of Duke Albrecht V of Bavaria in 1562. In 1566 he returned to Venice and was appointed 2nd organist at S. Marco; became 1st organist on Jan. 1, 1585, succeeding Merulo. He enjoyed a great reputation as an organist (his concerts with Merulo, on 2 organs, were featured attractions). Among his pupils were his nephew and Hans Leo Hassler. A prolific composer, he wrote a large number of works of varied description, many of which were publ. posth., ed. by his nephew. His versatility is attested by the fact that he was equally adept in sacred music of the loftiest spirit and in instrumental music, as well as in madrigals, often of a comic nature.

WORKS: VOCAL: S a c r e d : *Sacrae cantiones vulgo motecta appellatae, liber primus* for 5 Voices and Instruments (Venice, 1565); *Primus liber missarum* for 6 Voices (Venice, 1572); *Ecclesiasticarum cantionum omnibus sanctorum solemnitatibus deservientium liber primus* for 4 Voices (1576); *Psalmi Davidici, qui poenitentiales nuncupantur* for 6 Voices and Instruments (1583); *Concerti...continenti musica di chiesa, madrigali, & altro...liber primo et secondo* for 6 to 8, 10, 12, and 16 Voices and Instruments (1587). **M a d r i g a l s :** *Il primo libro di madrigali* for 5 Voices (1566); *Il secondo libro di madrigali* for 5 and 6 Voices, & uno dialogo for 8 Voices (1570; 3rd ed., Aug., 1588); *Greghesche et iustiniane...libro primo* for 3 Voices (1571); *Il primo libro de madrigali* for 6 Voices (1574); *Libro primo di madrigali* for 3 Voices (1575); *Il secondo libro de madrigali* for 6 Voices (1580); *Il terzo libro de madrigali* for 5 Voices (1589); *Madrigali e ricercari* for 4 Voices (1589); also *Chori in musica...sopra li chori della tragedia di Edippo Tiranno* (1588) and *Mascherate* for 3 to 6 and 8 Voices (1601). I n s t r u m e n t a l : *Canzoni alla francese per sonar sopra stromenti da tasti* (1571; not extant); *Madrigali et ricercari* for 4 Voices (1589); *Intonationi d'organo...libro primo* (1593); *Ricercari...composti et tabulati per ogni sorte di stromenti da tasti...libro secondo* (1595); *Il terzo libro de ricercari* for Keyboard (1596); *Canzoni alla francese per sonar sopra instrumenti da tasti...libro sesto* (1605); 3 organ masses and other pieces.

BIBL.: I. Zerr-Becking, *Studien zu A. G.* (Prague, 1933); F. Degrada, *A. G. e il suo tempo* (Florence, 1988).—**NS/LK/DM**

Gabrieli, Giovanni,

celebrated Italian organist, composer, and teacher, nephew of **Andrea Gabrieli;** b. Venice, c. 1555; d. there, Aug. 12, 1612. He received training from his uncle. He lived in Munich from 1575 to 1579. On Nov. 1, 1584, he was engaged to substitute for Merulo as 1st organist at S. Marco in Venice. On Jan. 1, 1585, he was permanently appointed as 2nd organist (his uncle meanwhile took charge of the 1st organ), and retained this post until his death. As a composer, he stands at the head of the Venetian school; he was probably the first to write vocal works with parts for instrumental groups in various combinations, partly specified, partly left to the conductor, used as accompaniment as well as interspersed instrumental sinfonie (*Sacrae symphoniae*). His role as a composer and teacher is epoch-making; through his innovations and his development of procedures and devices invented by others (free handling of several choirs in the many-voiced vocal works, "concerted" solo parts and duets in the few-voiced vocal works, trio-sonata texture, novel dissonance treatment, speech rhythm, root progressions in fifths, use of tonal and range levels for structural purposes, coloristic effects) and through his numerous German pupils (particularly Schutz) and other transalpine followers, he gave a new direction to the development of music. His instrumental music helped to spark the composition of German instrumental ensemble music, which reached its apex in the symphonic and chamber music works of the Classical masters. Of interest also is the fact that one of his ricercari, a 4-part work in the 10th tone (1595), is an early example of the "fugue with episodes." Many of his works also appeared in various collections of the period. The *Opera Omnia* began publication in 1956 in the *Corpus Mensurabilis Musicae* series.

WORKS: VOCAL: S a c r e d : *Concerti...continenti musica di chiesa, madrigali, & altro...libro primo et secondo* for 6 to 8, 10, 12, and 16 Voices, and Instruments (Venice, 1587); *Sacrae symphoniae* for 6 to 8, 10, 12, and 14 to 16 Voices, and Instruments (Venice, 1597); *Symphoniae sacrae...liber secundus* for 7, 8, 10 to 17, and 19 Voices, and Instruments (Venice, 1615). **S e c u - l a r :** *Concerti...continenti musica di chiesa, madrigali, & altro...primo et secondo* for 6 to 8, 10, 12, and 16 Voices, and Instruments (Venice, 1587). **INSTRUMENTAL:** *Sacrae symphoniae* for 6 to 8, 10, 12, and 14 to 16 Voices, and Instruments (Venice, 1597); *Intonationi d'organo...libro primo* (Venice, 1593);

Canzoni et sonate for 3, 5 to 8, 10, 12, 14, 15, and 22 Instruments, with Basso Continuo (organ) (Venice, 1615).

BIBL.: J. Flower, *G. G.'s Sacrae Symphoniae* (1597) (diss., Univ. of Mich., 1955); S. Kunze, *Die Instrumentalmusik G. G.s* (Tutzing, 1963); E. Kenton, *Life and Works of G. G.*, Musicological Studies and Documents, XVI (1967); D. Arnold, *G. G.* (London, 1974); W.Müller-Blattau, *Tonsatz und Klanggestaltung bei G. G.* (Kassel, 1975); D. Arnold, *G. G. and the Music of the Venetian High Renaissance* (Oxford, 1979); P. Manzini, *G. G.: Il suo linguaggio musicale* (Genoa, 1984); R. Charteris, *G. G. (ca. 1555–1612): A Thematic Catalog of his Music with A Guide to the Source Materials, and Translations of his Vocal Texts* (N.Y., 1996).—**NS/LK/DM**

Gabrielli, Caterina,

famous Italian soprano; b. Rome, Nov. 12, 1730; d. there, Feb. 16, 1796. Her father served as a cook to Prince Gabrielli, and the prince made it possible for her to pursue vocal training. She thus took his name in appreciation; her nickname "La Coghetta" ("Little Cook") derives from her father's position. She most likely studied with Porpora in Venice (1744–47), then sang throughout Italy with notable success. She subsequently went to Vienna, where she made her concert debut at the Burgtheater on Feb. 16, 1755. She found a friend and mentor in Metastasio, and quickly established herself as one of the leading singers of the day. In 1758 she went to Milan, where she found another mentor in the castrato Gaetano Guadagni. That same year she was in Padua and Lucca, and later appeared in Parma (1759–60). She then returned to Vienna, where she created the title roles in Gluck's *Tetide* (Oct. 8, 1760) and Traetta's *Armide* (Jan. 3, 1761). Following further appearances in Italy, she sang in St. Petersburg (1772–75) and in London (1775–76); she then returned to Italy, singing in Naples, Venice, Lucca, and Milan until her 1780 retirement. Her reputed beauty and scandalous liaisons made her a legendary figure in operatic lore.

BIBL.: H. de Koch, *La G.* (Paris, 1878).—**NS/LK/DM**

Gabrielli, Domenico,

renowned Italian cellist and composer, called the "Menghino dal violoncello" ("Mignàn dal viulunzaal" in Bolognese dialect), the first part of his nickname being the diminutive of Domenico; b. Bologna, April 15, 1651; d. there, July 10, 1690. He studied composition with Legrenzi in Venice and cello with Petronio Franceschini in Bologna. He was elected a member of the Accademia Filarmonica in Bologna in 1676, and became its president in 1683. He became cellist at S. Petronio in Bologna in 1676. His fame as a virtuoso led him to travel often, a circumstance that resulted in his dismissal in 1687; however, he was restored to his post in 1688. He was one of the first great masters of the cello, both as a performer and as a composer for the instrument, and also a distinguished composer of vocal music, both sacred and secular. —**NS/LK/DM**

Gabrielli, Nicolò,

Italian composer; b. Naples, Feb. 21, 1814; d. Paris, June 14, 1891. He was a pupil of Buonamici, Conti, Donizetti, and Zingarelli at the Naples Cons. From 1854 he lived in Paris. He wrote about 20 operas and 60 ballets, produced at Naples, Paris, and Vienna.—**NS/LK/DM**

Gabrilowitsch, Ossip (Salomonovich),

notable Russian-American pianist and conductor; b. St. Petersburg, Feb. 7, 1878; d. Detroit, Sept. 14, 1936. From 1888 to 1894 he was a pupil at the St. Petersburg Cons., studying piano with A. Rubinstein and composition with Navratil, Liadov, and Glazunov. He graduated as winner of the Rubinstein Prize, and then completed his piano training in Vienna with Leschetizky (1894–96). He subsequently toured Germany, Austria, Russia, France, and England. His first American tour (debut Carnegie Hall, N.Y., Nov. 12, 1900) was eminently successful, as were his 7 subsequent visits (1901–16). During the 1912–13 season, he gave in Europe a series of 6 historical concerts illustrating the development of the piano concerto from Bach to the present day; on his American tour in 1914–15, he repeated the entire series in several of the larger cities, meeting with an enthusiastic reception. On Oct. 6, 1909, he married the contralto Clara Clemens (daughter of Mark Twain), with whom he frequently appeared in joint recitals. He conducted his first N.Y. concert on Dec. 13, 1916; was appointed conductor of the Detroit Sym. Orch. in 1918. From 1928 he also conducted the Philadelphia Orch., sharing the baton with Leopold Stokowski, while retaining his Detroit position.

BIBL.: C. Clemens, *My Husband G.* (N.Y., 1938). —NS/LK/DM

Gaburo, Kenneth (Louis),

American composer and teacher; b. Somerville, N.J., July 5, 1926; d. Iowa City, Jan. 26, 1993. He studied composition, piano, and theory at the Eastman School of Music in Rochester, N.Y. (B.M., 1944; M.M., 1949), composition and conducting at the Cons. di Santa Cecilia in Rome (1954–55), and composition, theater, and linguistics at the Univ. of Ill., Urbana (D.M.A., 1962); he also studied composition at the Berkshire Music Center at Tanglewood (summer, 1956), and attended the Princeton Seminar in Advanced Musical Studies (summer, 1959). After teaching at Kent State Univ. (1950), he was assoc. prof. at McNeese State Univ. (1950–54). He then was a prof. at the Univ. of Ill. (1955–67) and at the Univ. of Calif. at San Diego (1967–75), founder-director of the Studio for Cognitive Studies in San Diego (1975–83), and a prof. at the Univ. of Iowa (from 1983). He was the recipient of a Fulbright fellowship (1954), ASCAP awards (from 1960), a Guggenheim fellowship (1967), and an NEA award (1975); in 1985 he received the Milhaud Chair fellowship at Mills Coll. in Oakland, Calif. His music was quaquaversal.

WORKS: DRAMATIC Opera: *The Snow Queen* (Lake Charles, La., May 5, 1952); *Blur* (Urbana, Ill., Nov. 7, 1956); *The Widow* (Urbana, Ill., Feb. 26, 1961). **ORCH.:** *3 Interludes for Strings* (Rochester, N.Y., May 27, 1948); *Concertante* for Piano and Orch. (Rochester, N.Y., April 29, 1949); *On a Quiet Theme* (1950; N.Y., Feb. 26, 1955); *Elegy* for Small Orch. (1956; N.Y., April 3, 1959); *Shapes and Sounds* (1960); *Antiphony IX (—a dot is no mere thing—)* for Orch., Children, and Tape (1984–85; Kansas City, Mo., Oct. 13, 1985). **CHAMBER:** *Music for 5 Instruments* for Flute, Clarinet, Trumpet, Trombone, and Piano (1954); *Ideas and Transformations No. 1* for Violin and Viola, *No. 2* for Violin and Cello, *No. 3* for Viola and Cello, and *No. 4* for Violin, Viola, and Cello (all 1955); String Quartet (1956); *Line Studies* for Flute, Clarinet, Viola, and Trombone (N.Y., Dec. 15, 1957). **ELECTRONIC AND TAPE:** *Antiphony I (Voices)* for 3 String Groups and Tape (1958), *II (Variations on a Poem of Cavafy)* for Soprano, Chorus, and Tape (1962), *III (Pearl-White Moments)* for Chamber Chorus and Tape (1963), *IV (Poised)* for Piccolo, Trombone, Double Bass, and Tape (1967), *V* for Piano and Tape (1968–89), *VI (Cogito)* for String Quartet, Slides, and 2- and 4-channel Tape (1971), *VII (—And)* for 4 Video Systems and 4-channel Tape (1974–89), *VIII (Revolution)* for Percussionist and Tape (1983–84), and *X (Winded)* for Organ and Tape (1985–89); numerous other works involving tape, actors, slides, film, lighting, and various acoustic instruments. **OTHER:** Vocal pieces.—NS/LK/DM

Gabussi, Giulio Cesare,

Italian composer; b. Bologna, 1555; d. Milan, Sept. 12, 1611. He was a pupil of Costanzo Porta. In 1582 he was called to Milan as singer and composer at the Cathedral, and remained in that post until his death, with the exception of a brief stay in Poland in the service of Sigismund III (1601–2). He publ. 2 books of madrigals for 5 Voices (Venice, 1580, 1598), motets for 5 and 6 Voices (Venice, 1586), *Te Deum* for 4 Voices (Milan, 1589); etc. He was one of the first composers whose works in the Ambrosian ritual (litanies, etc.) appeared in print.—NS/LK/DM

Gade, Axel Willy,

Danish violinist, son of **Niels Gade;** b. Copenhagen, May 28, 1860; d. there, Nov. 9, 1921. He studied with his father and with Joachim, then was active in Copenhagen as a theater conductor and teacher. He wrote a Violin Concerto and an opera, *Venezias Nat* (Copenhagen, Jan. 18, 1919).—NS/LK/DM

Gade, Jacob,

Danish conductor and composer; b. Vejle, Nov. 29, 1879; d. Copenhagen, Feb. 21, 1963. He studied violin. He was a member of the N.Y. Sym. Orch. (1919–21), then returned to Copenhagen, where he was active as a conductor. Among his light compositions, *Jalousie* (1925) attained great popularity. He also wrote several symphonic poems (*Den sidste Viking, Leda and the Swan,* etc.).

BIBL.: K. Bjarnjof, *Tango Jalousie* (Copenhagen, 1969); J. Gram Christensen, *J. G., et evntyr I musik: Biografi og vaerkfortegnelse* (Vejle, 1996).—NS/LK/DM

Gade, Niels (Wilhelm),

greatly significant Danish composer, conductor, and pedagogue, father of **Axel Willy Gade;** b. Copenhagen, Feb. 22, 1817; d. there, Dec. 21, 1890. The son of a maker of instruments, he studied violin with F.T. Wexschall and theory and composition with A.P. Berggreen. After making his debut as a violinist in 1833, he joined the Royal Orch. in Copenhagen in 1834. He first came to prominence as a composer with his concert overture *Efterklange af Ossian* (1840), which won the prize of the Copenhagen Musical Soc. This popular score was followed by his outstanding 1st Sym. (1841–42), which Mendelssohn conducted in its premiere performance in Leipzig at a Gewandhaus concert on March 2, 1843, with extraordinary success. Gade was appointed asst. conductor to Mendelssohn and the Gewandhaus Orch. He also joined the faculty of the Leipzig Cons. Upon Mendelssohn's death in 1847,

Gade was named Gewandhaus Kapellmeister. However, with the outbreak of the Schleswig-Holstein War in 1848, he returned to Copenhagen and quickly assumed a preeminent place in the musical life of his homeland. He reorganized the Copenhagen Musical Soc. And became its chief conductor in 1850, leading its orch. and choir in distinguished performances of his own music as well as that of other composers. In 1866 he helped to organize the Copenhagen Cons., and thereafter served as one of its directors; also taught composition and music history there. In 1876 the Danish government awarded him a life pension. Gade was an ardent admirer of Mendelssohn and Schumann and thus adopted the prevalent German Romantic style in his own works; his influence was nonetheless great in Denmark. His activities as a conductor and teacher were also extremely important. In 1990 the Danish Musicological Soc. organized a foundation for the purpose of publishing a critical edition of Gade's works, which subsequently appeared in 12 vols. (Copenhagen, 1994–2000).

WORKS: DRAMATIC: S i n g s p i e l : *Mariotta* (1848–49). B a l l e t : *Faedrelandets muser* (The Muses of Our Fatherland; 1840); *Napoli* (1842; Act 2 only); *Et folkesagn* (1853–54; Act 2 by J.P.E. Hartmann). OTHER: Incidental music. ORCH.: 8 syms.: No. 1, "Paa Sjolunds fagre sletter" (1841–42; Leipzig, March 2, 1843), No. 2 (1843; Leipzig, Jan. 18, 1844), No. 3 (1846; Leipzig, Dec. 9, 1847), No. 4 (Copenhagen, Nov. 16, 1850), No. 5 (Copenhagen, Dec. 11, 1852), No. 6 (Copenhagen, March 17, 1857), No. 7 (Leipzig, March 2, 1865), and No. 8 (Copenhagen, Dec. 7, 1871); *Efterklange af Ossian* (Echoes from Ossian), overture (1840; Copenhagen, Nov. 19, 1841); *I højlandene* (In the Highlands), overture (1844); *Nordisk soeterrejse* (A Mountain Trip in the North), overture (1850); *Festmarsch ved Kong Christian IX.'s regjerings-jubilaeum* (1850); *Hamlet*, overture (1861); *Michel Angelo*, overture (1861); *Sørgemarsch ved Kong Frederik d. 7des* (Funeral March for King Frederik VII; 1863); 2 *Novelletter*: No. 1 for Strings (1874) and No. 2 (1883; rev. 1886); *Capriccio* for Violin and Orch. (1878); *En sommerdag paa landet* (A Summer's Day in the Country), 5 pieces (1879); Violin Concerto (1880); *Holbergiana*, suite (1884); *Ulysses-marsch: Forspil til Holberg's Ulysses von Ithaca* (1888–90). CHAMBER: 3 violin sonatas (1842, 1849, 1885); 2 string quartets (n.d., 1889); 2 string quintets (1845, 1851); Octet (1848); String Sextet (1863); *Fantasiestücke* for Clarinet and Piano (1864); *Folkesdanse* for Violin and Piano (1888); etc. P i a n o : Sonata (1840; rev. 1854); *Foraarstoner* (Spring Flowers; 1841); *Akvareller* (1850); *Albumsblade* (1850); *Arabeske* (1854); *Folkedanse* (1855); *Idyller* (1857); also organ pieces. VOCAL: C a n t a t a s : *Comala* (1846); *Mindekantate over Fru Anna Nielsen* (Cantata in Memory of Fru Anna Nielsen; 1856); *Baldurs drøn* (Baldur's Dream; 1858); *Frühlings-Botschaft* (1858); *Mindekantate over Overhofmarschal Chamberlain Levetzau* (Cantata in Memory of Count Chamberlain Levetzau; 1859); *Mindekantate over skuespiller Nielsen* (Cantata in Memory of the Actor Nielsen; 1860); *Die heilige Nacht* (1862); *Ved solnedgang* (At Sunset; 1863); *Korsfarerne* (The Crusader; 1865–66); *Kalanus* (1869); *Gefion* (1869); *Zion* (1874); *Den bjergtagne* (The Mountain Thrall; 1873); *Psyche* (1881–82); *Der Strom* (1889). O t h e r V o c a l : *Frühlings-Fantasie* for Solo Voices and Orch. (1852); *Elverskud* (Elf-King's Daughter) for Solo Voices, Chorus, and Orch. (1853); etc.; songs.

BIBL.: R. Henriques, *N. W. G.* (Copenhagen, 1891); D. Gade, *N. W. G.: Optegnelser og breve* (Copenhagen, 1892; Ger. tr.,

1894); C. Kjerulf, *N. W. G.* (Copenhagen, 1917); W. Behrend, *Minder om N. W. G.* (Copenhagen, 1930); J. Gade, *Omkring N. W. G.: Breve fra fader og son* (Copenhagen, 1967); *N. W. G.—Katalog* (Copenhagen, 1986); S. Oechsle, *Symphonik nach Beethoven: Studien zu Schubert, Schumann, Mendelssohn, und G.* (Kassel, 1992).—NS/LK/DM

Gadski, Johanna (Emilia Agnes), celebrated German soprano; b. Anklam, June 15, 1872; d. as a result of an automobile accident, Berlin, Feb. 22, 1932. She studied with Schroeder-Chaloupka in Stettin, making her operatic debut as Lortzing's Undine at Berlin's Kroll Opera (1889). She continued to appear there until 1893, and also sang in Mainz, Stettin, and Bremen. On March 1, 1895, she made her U.S. debut as Elsa in *Lohengrin* with the Damrosch Opera Co. in N.Y.; continued to sing with it until 1898, appearing in such roles as Elisabeth, Eva, and Sieglinde. She made her first appearance at London's Covent Garden as Elisabeth on May 15, 1899, and sang there until 1901; also appeared as Eva in Bayreuth (1899). On Jan. 6, 1900, she made her Metropolitan Opera debut in N.Y. as Senta, and quickly established herself there as an outstanding interpreter of such compelling roles as Brünnhilde and Isolde. She made 2 transcontinental concert tours of the U.S. (1904–6), then returned to the Metropolitan Opera (1907), making her farewell performance there as Isolde on April 13, 1917. Having married Lt. Hans Tauscher on Nov. 11, 1892, she returned to Germany in 1917 when her husband was deported as an enemy alien. She sang opera again in the U.S. with a touring German company from 1929 to 1931.—NS/LK/DM

Gadzhibekov, Sultan, Azerbaijani conductor, pedagogue, and composer; b. Shusha, May 8, 1919; d. Baku, Sept. 19, 1974. He studied composition with B. Zeidman at the Baku Cons. (graduated, 1946), where he then taught instrumentation and composition, later becoming a prof. (1965) and rector (1966); also conducted the Azerbaijan Phil. (1955–62). He received state prizes for his ballet *Gulshen* (1952) and his *Concerto for Orchestra* (1970). He was named a People's Artist of the Azerbaijan S.S.R. (1960).

WORKS: DRAMATIC: S t a g e : *The Red Rose*, musical comedy (1940); *Iskender and the Shepherd*, children's opera (1947); *Gulshen*, ballet (1950). ORCH.: *Variations* (1941); 2 syms. (1944, 1946); *Caravan*, symphonic picture (1945); Violin Concerto (1945); Overture (1956); Concerto (1964); 3 suites: *Gulshen* (1953), *Bulgarian* (1957), and *Indian* (1970). CHAMBER: String Quartet (1943); 2 scherzos (1949). P i a n o : Sonata (1940); 6 *Preludes* (1941). OTHER: Vocal works.

BIBL.: D. Danilov, *S. G.* (Baku, 1956); E. Abasova, *S. G.* (Baku, 1965); A. Tagizade, *S. G.* (Baku, 1967).—NS/LK/DM

Gadzhibekov, Uzeir, Azerbaijani composer; b. Agdzhabedy, near Shusha, Sept. 17, 1885; d. Baku, Nov. 23, 1948. He studied in Shusha, and then lived in Baku, where he produced his first opera on a native subject, *Leyly and Medzhnun* (Jan. 25, 1908). His comic opera *Arshin Mal Alan* (Baku, Nov. 27, 1913) had numerous performances; another opera, *Kyor-Oglu* (A Blind Man's Son), was premiered at the Azerbaijan Festival in Moscow (April 30, 1937).—NS/LK/DM

Gadzhiev, (Akhmed) Jevdet, Azerbaijani composer; b. Nukha, June 18, 1917. He studied with M. Rudolf and U. Gadzhibekov at the Baku Cons. (1936–38), and with Anatoli Alexandrov, S. Vasilenko, and Shostakovich at the Moscow Cons. (1938–41; graduated, 1947). He then taught composition at the Baku Cons., where he later was a prof. (from 1963) and rector (until 1969). He received state prizes for his opera *Veten* (1946) and the symphonic poem *For Peace* (1952). He was made a People's Artist of the Azerbaijan S.S.R. (1960).

WORKS: DRAMATIC: O p e r a : *Veten* (1945; in collaboration with K. Karayev); *Ghazal My Flower* (1956); *The Maiden Gathering Apples* (1957). ORCH.: 3 symphonic poems: *Azerbaijan* (1936), *Epistle to Siberia* (1937), and *For Peace* (1951); *Sinfonietta* (1938); *Azerbaijan Suite* (1941); 5 syms. (1944; 1946; 1947; *In Memory of Lenin*, 1956; *Man, Earth, Universe*, 1971). CHAMBER: *Fugue* (1940); *3 Fugues* (1941); String Quartet (1941); *Quartet Poem* (1961). P i a n o : *24 Preludes* (1935); *Ballade* (1950); Sonata (1956); *Scherzo* (1957); *Children's Corner Suite* (1962). OTHER: Vocal works.

BIBL.: E. Muradova, *J. G.* (Baku, 1962); K. Abezgauz, *J. G.* (Baku, 1965); E. Abasova, *J. G.* (Baku, 1967).—NS/LK/DM

Gaffurius (also **Gafurius, Gaffurio, Gafori,** etc.), **Franchinus** (also **Franchino**), important Italian music theorist and composer; b. Lodi, Jan. 14, 1451; d. Milan, June 25, 1522. He entered the Benedictine monastery of St. Peter in his youth, and also was a singer at Lodi Cathedral, where he studied mensural music with Johannes Bonadies (also known as Godendach). In 1474 he was ordained a secular priest. After living in Mantua and Verona, he was called by the Doge Prospero Adorno of Genoa in 1477 to work as a music teacher and composer. The two became friends, and following a major uprising in 1478, they fled together to the court in Naples, where Gaffurius was befriended by Tinctoris, Ycart, and Guarnerius. In 1480 he returned to Lodi as a teacher of the singers at the castle of Monticelli d' Ongina. After serving as director of music at Bergamo Cathedral (1483–84), he was made maestro di cappella at Milan Cathedral in 1484, a position he held with great distinction until his death. He also was active at the court of Duke Lodovico Sforza, and taught music at the ducal school from 1492. In addition to his cathedral and court duties, Gaffurius composed and wrote his most significant treatises. His last years were marked by a controversy with Spataro. His sacred music, mainly masses and motets, display a mastery of the Franco-Netherlands and Italian styles. The MSS of these works, as well as those by other composers, are extant and are known as the Gaffurius Codices. His works have been ed. by A. Bortone, F. Fano, and L. Migliavacca in the *Archivium musices metropolitantum mediolanense* series (5 vols., Milan, 1958–60).

WRITINGS: PUBL.: *Theoricum opus* (Naples, 1480); *Theorica musica* (Milan, 1492; Eng. tr., 1993); *Practica musicae* (Milan, 1496; rev. ed., 1508, as *Angelicum ac divinum opus musicae*; Eng. tr., 1968); *De harmonia musicorum instrumentorum opus* (Milan, 1518); *Apologia adversum Ioannem Spatarium* (Turin, 1520); *Epistula prima in solutiones obiectorum Io. Vaginarii Bononien.* (Milan, 1521); *Epistula secunda apologetica* (Milan, 1521). MSS: *Extractus*

parvus musicae (c. 1474; ed. by F. Gallo, Bologna, 1969); *Tractatus brevis cantus plani* (c. 1474); *Theoriae musicae tractatus* (c. 1479); *Micrologus vulgaris cantus plani* (c. 1482).

BIBL.: A. Cretta, L. Cremascoli, and L. Salamina, *Francino Gaffurio* (Lodi, 1951).—NS/LK/DM

Gage, Irwin, American pianist and teacher; b. Cleveland, Sept. 4, 1939. He studied with Eugene Bossart at the Univ. of Mich., with Ward Davenny at Yale Univ., and with Erik Werba, Hilde Langer-Rühl, Kurt Schmidek, and Klaus Vokurka at the Vienna Academy of Music. He subsequently acquired a fine reputation as an accompanist to the leading singers of the day, with whom he appeared in all the principal music centers of the globe. He also was a prof. at the Zürich Cons. and gave master classes around the world. —NS/LK/DM

Gagliano, famous family of violin makers in Naples. **Alessandro Gagliano,** who worked from 1695 to 1725, was a pupil of Stradivari, and he, as well as his sons **Nicola Gagliano** (1695–1758) and **Gennaro Gagliano** (1700–1788), followed largely the Stradivari model. The instruments of **Ferdinando Gagliano** (c. 1724–81), a son of Nicola, exhibit less skillful workmanship than those of the older members of the family.—NS/LK/DM

Gagliano, Giovanni Battista da, Italian singer, instrumentalist, and composer, brother of **Marco da Gagliano;** b. Florence, Dec. 20, 1594; d. there, Jan. 8, 1651. He pursued his career in Florence, where he carried out the duties of maestro di cappella at the court and cathedral from 1643. He was a composer of sacred music.—LK/DM

Gagliano, Marco da, significant Italian composer, brother of **Giovanni Battista da Gagliano;** b. Florence, May 1, 1582; d. there, Feb. 25, 1643. He studied with Luca Bati, and became his assistant at S. Lorenzo in 1602; concurrently studied with the Compagnia dell' Arcangelo Raffaello, serving as maestro di cappella in 1607 and 1609. He also took Holy Orders. In 1607 he went to Mantua, where his opera *La Dafne* was given with great success in 1608. After returning to Florence, he succeeded Bati as maestro di cappella at the Cathedral in 1608; was later in the service of the Medici court. He was made canon in 1610 and Apostolic Protonotary in 1615, and founded the Accademia degli Elevati in 1607. With Jacopo Peri, he wrote the opera *Lo sposalizio di Medoro e Angelica,* which was performed in honor of the election of Emperor Ferdinand III at the Palazzo Pitti on Sept. 25, 1619. He also composed the opera *La Flora,* for which Peri wrote the role of Clori; it was performed in honor of the wedding of Margherita de' Medici and Duke Odoardo Farnese of Parma at the Palazzo Pitti on Oct. 14, 1628. Gagliano was one of the earliest composers to write in the *stile rappresentativo,* which he developed further by ornamentation.

WORKS: DRAMATIC O p e r a : *La Dafne* (Mantua, 1608); *Lo sposalizio di Medoro e Angelica* (Palazzo Pitti, Florence, Sept. 25, 1619; in collaboration with J. Peri); *La Flora, overo Il* natal di Fiori (Palazzo Pitti, Florence, Oct. 14, 1628; major portion by Gagliano, with the role of Clori by Peri). Another dramatic work, *La liberazione di Tirreno e d'Arnea* (Florence, Feb. 6, 1617), may be by Gagliano; he may have collaborated with Peri on the score, or it may be entirely the work of Peri. **VOCAL:** Secular: Books of madrigals for 5, 6, 7, and 8 Voices (1602–17); *Musiche* for 1 to 3 and 5 Voices (1615). Sacred: *Officium defunctorum* for 4 to 8 Voices (Venice, 1607–08); *Missae et sacrarum cantionum* for 6 Voices (Florence, 1614); *Sacrarum cantionum...liber secundus* for 1 to 4 and 6 Voices (1622); *Responsoria maioris hebdomadae* for 4 Voices (1630–31).

BIBL.: D. Butchart, *I Madrigali di M. d.G.* (Florence, 1982). —NS/LK/DM

Gagnebin, Henri, Swiss music educator and composer; b. Liège (of Swiss parents), March 13, 1886; d. Geneva, June 2, 1977. He studied organ with Vierne and composition with d'Indy at the Paris Cons. He was organist in Paris (1910–16) and in Lausanne (1916–25). From 1925 to 1957 he was director of the Geneva Cons. In 1938 he founded the Geneva International Competition, which he served as president until 1959. He was the author of *Entretiens sur la musique* (Geneva, 1943), *Musique, mon beau souci* (Paris, 1968), and *Orgue, musette et bourbon* (Neuchâtel, 1975).

WORKS: ORCH.: 4 syms. (1911; 1918–21; 1955; 1970); Suite (1936); *3 Tableaux symphoniques d'après F. Hodler* (1942); *Suite d'orchestre sur des psaumes huguenots* (1950); Piano Concerto (1951); Clarinet Concerto (1971); Concerto for Oboe, Bassoon, and Strings (1972). **CHAMBER:** Violin Sonata (1915); 3 string quartets (1916–17; 1924; 1927); Cello Sonata (1922); Suite for Cello (1932); Trio for Piano, Flute, and Cello (1941); Quartet for Piano, Flute, Violin, and Cello (1961); String Trio (1968); Wind Octet (1970); Brass Quintet (1970); Wind Sextet (1971). **KEYBOARD: Piano:** Suite (1936). **Organ:** *100 Pièces sur des psaumes huguenots* (1940–64). **VOCAL:** Choruses; songs. —NS/LK/DM

Gaigerova, Varvara, Russian pianist and composer; b. Oryekhovo-Zuyevo, Oct. 17, 1903; d. Moscow, April 6, 1944. She studied piano at the Moscow Cons. with Neuhaus and composition with Miaskovsky. In most of her compositions, she cultivated folk materials of the constituent republics of the U.S.S.R., including those of the Mongol populations of Siberia and Central Asia.

WORKS: ORCH.: 3 syms. (1928, 1934, 1937); 3 suites for Domra Ensembles (1932, 1934, 1935). **CHAMBER:** 2 string quartets (1927, 1947); piano pieces. **VOCAL:** *The Sun of Socialism*, cantata (1932); some 150 songs.—NS/LK/DM

Gailhard, Pierre, noted French bass and opera manager; b. Toulouse, Aug. 1, 1848; d. Paris, Oct. 12, 1918. He began his vocal studies in his native city, and entered the Paris Cons. in 1866. After a year of study under Revial, he graduated in 1867, winning 3 1st prizes. He made his debut at the Opéra-Comique (Dec. 4, 1867) as Falstaff in Thomas's *Songe d'une nuit d'été*; on Nov. 3, 1871, he made his debut at the Opéra as Méphistophélès in Gounod's *Faust*. At the height of his powers and success he gave up the stage when, in 1884, he accepted, jointly with M. Ritt, the management of the

famous institution; on the appointment of M. Bertrand as successor to Ritt, in 1892, he retired, but joined Bertrand the following year as co-director; after the latter's death, in 1899, he remained sole director until 1908. His administration was remarkably successful, considering both the novelties produced and the engagement of new singers (Melba, Eames, Bréval, Caron, Ackté, Alvarez, Saléza, Renaud, the 2 de Reszkes, et al.). Against violent opposition he introduced, and maintained in the repertoire, *Lohengrin* (1895), *Die Walküre* (1893), *Tannhäuser* (1895; the 1st perf. after the notorious fiasco of 1861), *Meistersinger* (1897), and *Siegfried* (1902). His son, André Gailhard (b. Paris, June 29, 1885; d. Ermont, Val d'Oise, July 3, 1966), composed the operas *Amaryllis* (Toulouse, 1906), *Le Sortilège* (Paris, 1913), and *La Bataille* (Paris, 1931).—NS/LK/DM

Gaillard, Marius-François, French composer and conductor; b. Paris, Oct. 13, 1900; d. Evecquemont, Yvelines, July 23, 1973. He studied with Diémer and Leroux at the Paris Cons. He began his career as a pianist, then conducted concerts in Paris (1928–49). He traveled all over the world, collecting examples of primitive music. His compositions follow a neo-impressionist trend.

WORKS: ORCH: 3 syms.; *Guyanes*, symphonic suite (1925); *Images d'Epinal* for Piano and Orch. (1929); *Concerto classique* for Cello and Orch. (1950); *Tombeau romantique* for Piano and Orch. (1954); *Concerto leggero* for Violin and Orch. (1954); *Concerto agreste* for Viola and Orch. (1957); Harp Concerto (1960). **Ballet:** *La Danse pendant le festin* (1924); *Détresse* (1932). **CHAMBER:** Violin Sonata (1923); String Trio (1935); *Sonate baroque* for Violin and Piano (1950); piano pieces. **VOCAL:** Many songs.—NS/LK/DM

Gaillard, Slim (Bulee), jazz singer, guitarist, pianist, vibraphonist, and saxophonist; b. Santa Clara, Cuba, Jan. 1, 1916; d. London, England, Feb. 26, 1991. His father was a steward on a liner; Gaillard traveled with him during holidays and was once accidentally left behind on Crete, remaining there for six months. He entered show business in the early 1930s as a solo variety act, simultaneously playing guitar and tap-dancing. Moving to N.Y. in 1937, he formed a duo with Slam Stewart, in which he sang and played guitar. Slim and Slam had a long-running radio program on WNEW-AM, N.Y., and a number of hits in the late 1930s, notably "Flat Foot Floogie," covered by Fats Waller, Benny Goodman and others. By 1940 he was leading his own quintet in Chicago, although the duo performed occasionally before he joined the Army in 1943. Discharged the following year, he led a trio at clubs in L.A., including Billy Berg's and the Swing Club. Among his postwar hits was "Cement Mixer (Put-ti, Put-ti)" in 1946. During the 1950s and 1960s he performed solo as a vocalist, master of ceremonies, and comedian. After managing a motel in San Diego, he held residencies in N.Y. and San Jose, Calif. (1963). He briefly reunited with Stewart at the 1970 Monterey Festival, and worked in L.A. (1970–71). He recorded with Bucky Pizzarelli and Major Holley, did sessions on his own, and made many club and festival appearances. From the early 1980s he lived in London's Chelsea district and was the subject of a BBC television documentary in the late 1980s. He performed at jazz clubs and festivals in Britain and France until diagnosed with cancer in 1991. He appeared in many films, including *Star Spangled Rhythm, Hellzapoppin', Almost Married, Go Man Go,* and *Two Joes from Brooklyn,* as well as the television mini-series *Roots—The Next Generation.* He invented the Vout Oreenie jive language.

DISC.: *S.G. Cavorts* (1952); *S.G. Mish Mash* (1953); *Wherever They May Be* (1954); *Dot Sessions* (1958); *S.G. Rides Again* (1959); *Anytime, Anyplace, Anywhere* (1982). **SLIM AND SLAM:** *Flat Foot Floogie* (1938).—**NS/LP**

Gaito, Constantino, Argentine composer; b. Buenos Aires, Aug. 3, 1878; d. there, Dec. 14, 1945. He studied in Naples with Platania, then lived in Buenos Aires as a teacher. He wrote the operas (all produced in Buenos Aires) *Shafras* (1907), *I Doria* (1915), *I paggi di Sua Maestà* (1918), *Caio Petronio* (Sept. 2, 1919), *Flor de nieve* (Aug. 3, 1922), *Ollantay* (July 23, 1926), *Lázaro* (1929), and *La sangre de las guitarras* (Aug. 17, 1932). Other works include the ballet *La flor del Irupé* (Buenos Aires, July 17, 1929), the oratorio *San Francisco Solano* (1940), the symphonic poem *El ombu* (1924), songs, and piano pieces. —**NS/LK/DM**

Gál, Hans, Austrian musicologist and composer; b. Brunn, near Vienna, Aug. 5, 1890; d. Edinburgh, Oct. 3, 1987. He studied with Mandyczewski and Adler at at the Univ. of Vienna, where he lectured (1919–29), and then was director of the Mainz Cons. (1929–33). He returned to Vienna in 1933. After the Anschluss, he was compelled to leave Vienna in 1938, and settled in Edinburgh, where he lectured on music at the Univ. (1945–65) while continuing to compose.

WRITINGS: *Anleitung zum Partiturlesen* (Vienna, 1923; Eng. tr., 1924, as *Directions for Score-Reading*); *The Golden Age of Vienna* (London, 1948); *Johannes Brahms* (Frankfurt am Main, 1961; Eng. tr., 1964); *Richard Wagner* (Frankfurt am Main, 1963); *The Musician's World: Great Composers in Their Letters* (London, 1965; Ger. tr., 1966); *Franz Schubert, oder Die Melodie* (Frankfurt am Main, 1970; Eng. tr., 1974); *Giuseppe Verdi und die Oper* (Frankfurt am Main, 1982).

WORKS: DRAMATIC: Opera: *Der Arzt der Sobeide* (Breslau, 1919); *Die heilige Ente* (Düsseldorf, April 29, 1923); *Das Lied der Nacht* (Breslau, April 24, 1926); *Der Zauberspiegel* (Breslau, 1930; also as an orch. suite); *Die beiden Klaas* (1933). **ORCH.:** 4 syms. (1928, 1949, 1952, 1975); Violin Concerto (1931); *A Pickwickian Overture* (1939); Cello Concerto (1944); Piano Concerto (1947); Concertino for Organ and Strings (1948); Concertino for Cello and Strings (1965); *Idyllikon* for Small Orch. (1969); *Triptych* (1970). **CHAMBER:** Piano Quartet (1915); 4 string quartets (1916, 1929, 1969, 1971); Violin Sonata (1921); String Trio (1931); Piano Trio (1948). **VOCAL:** Numerous sacred and secular choral works.

BIBL.: W. Waldstein, *H. G.* (Vienna, 1965); *H. G. zum 100. Geburtstag* (Mainz, 1990).—**NS/LK/DM**

Galajikian, Florence Grandland, American pianist and composer; b. Maywood, Ill., July 29, 1900; d. River Forest, Ill., Nov. 16, 1970. She studied at Northwestern Univ. and Chicago Musical Coll., her teachers being Oldberg, Lutkin, Rubin Goldmark, Carl Beecher, and Noelte. She toured as a pianist. She composed a number of songs that enjoyed favor among sopranos, as well as orch. pieces. Her *Symphonic Intermezzo* was awarded NBC's 4th prize, and was performed by the NBC Sym. Orch. on May 8, 1932.—**NS/LK/DM**

Galamian, Ivan (Alexander), eminent Armenian-born American violinist and pedagogue; b. Tabriz, Persia (of Armenian parents), Feb. 5, 1903; d. N.Y., April 14, 1981. He studied with Konstantin Mostras at the school of Moscow's Phil. Soc. (1916–22), then attended Lucien Capet's master course in Paris (1922–23), where he made his formal debut (1924). He taught at the Russian Cons. (1925–39) and at the École Normale de Musique (1936–39) there. He settled in N.Y. (1939), becoming a teacher at the Henry St. Settlement School (1941). He was later named to the faculty of the Curtis Inst. of Music in Philadelphia (1944) and of the Juilliard School of Music in N.Y. (1946), and also founder of the Meadowmount School for string players in Westport, N.Y. (1944). Among his numerous students were Itzhak Perlman, Michael Rabin, Kyung-Wha Chung, Erick Friedman, Miriam Fried, Pinchas Zuckerman, Young-Uck Kim, and Jaime Laredo. He publ. *Principles of Violin Playing and Teaching* (with E. Green; Englewood Cliffs, N.J., 1962; 2nd ed., rev., 1985) and *Contemporary Violin Technique* (with F. Neumann; 2 vols., N.Y., 1966, 1977).

BIBL.: E. Green et al., *Miraculous Teacher: I. G. and the Meadowmount Experience* (Ann Arbor, 1993).—**NS/LK/DM**

Galas, Diamanda (Dimitria Angeliki Elena), remarkable American avant-garde composer and vocalist of Greek descent; b. San Diego, Aug. 29, 1955. She studied biochemistry, psychology, music, and experimental performance at the Univ. of Calif. at San Diego (1974–79); she also took private vocal lessons. In her scientific studies, she and a group of medical students began investigating extreme mental states, using themselves as subjects in a series of bizarre mind-altering experiments; her resultant understanding of psychopathology (notably schizophrenia and psychosis) became an underlying subject in most of her work. After some success as a jazz pianist, she began a vocal career, in which her remarkable precision and advanced technique attracted attention. Although she has performed such demanding works as Xenakis's microtonal *N'Shima* (Brooklyn, Jan. 15, 1981) and Globokar's *Misère* (Cologne, 1980), she is best known for her theatrical performances of her own solo vocal works, given at venues ranging from the Donaueschingen Festival to the N.Y. rock club Danceteria. Her compositions, most of which employ live electronics and/or tape, are improvised according to rigorous, complex "navigation(s) through specified mental states." Her performances have stringent requirements for lighting and sound and possess a shattering intensity. Her brother, Philip Dimitri Galas, a playwright whose works were as violent as is his sister's music, died of AIDS in the late 1980s; her increasing emotional and political involvement in what she regards as this "modern plague" led to her 4-part work *Masque of the Red Death* (1986–). She publ. an aesthetic statement as "Intravenal Song" in *Perspectives of New Music*, XX (1981).

WORKS: VOCAL: *Medea tarantula* for Voice (1977); *Les Yeux sans sang* for Voice and Electronics (1978); *Tragouthia apo to aima exoun fonos* (Song from the Blood of Those Murdered) for Voice and Tape (1981); *Wild Women with Steak Knives* for Tape and Live Electronics (1981–83); *Litanies of Satan* for Voice, Tape, and Live Electronics (1982); *Panoptikon* for Voice, Tape, and Live Electronics (1982–83); *Masque of the Red Death* for Voice, Electronics, and Instrument (*The Divine Punishment, Saint of the Pit, You Must Be Certain of the Devil*, and a 4th work in progress; 1986 et seq.).—**NS/LK/DM**

Galeazzi, Francesco, Italian violinist, music theorist, and composer; b. Turin, 1758; d. Rome, Jan. 1819. Following his studies in Turin, he settled in Rome as a violin teacher, music director of the Teatro Valle, and composer. His treatise *Elementi teorico-pratici di musica* (2 vols., Rome, 1791, 1796; annotated Eng. tr. of Vol. 1 by A. Frascarelli, diss., Univ. of Rochester, 1969) is an important exposition on the Classical style.—**LK/DM**

Galeffi, Carlo, esteemed Italian baritone; b. Malamocco, near Venice, June 4, 1882; d. Rome, Sept. 22, 1961. He was a student of Sbrigilia in Paris and of Cotogni in Rome. In 1903 he made his operatic debut in Rome as Enrico, and then won success in Naples as Amonasro and Rigoletto. On Nov. 29, 1910, he made his only appearancce at the Metropolitan Opera in N.Y. as Germont. In 1911 he sang in the premiere of Mascagni's *Isabeau* in Buenos Aires. From 1912 to 1938 he was a leading member of Milan's La Scala, winning particular distinction in such roles as Tell, Rigoletto, Boccanegra, Nabucco, Luna, and Germont; he also created the roles of Manfredo in Montemezzi's *L'amore dei tre Re* (1913) and Fanuel in Boito's *Nerone* (1924). His operatic farewell performance took place in 1954.

BIBL.: A. Marchetti, *C.G.: Una vita per el canto* (Rome, 1973). —**NS/LK/DM**

Galeotti, Cesare, Italian composer; b. Pietrasanta, June 5, 1872; d. Paris, Feb. 19, 1929. He studied piano with Sgambati and composition with Guiraud at the Paris Cons. Several of his symphonic works were performed in Paris, and his opera *Anton* was staged at La Scala, Milan (Feb. 17, 1900). Another opera, *Dorisse*, was first given in Brussels (April 18, 1910).—**NS/LK/DM**

Gales, Weston, American organist and conductor; b. Elizabeth, N.J., Nov. 5, 1877; d. Portsmouth, N.H., Oct. 21, 1939. He studied composition with Horatio Parker at Yale Univ. and organ with Gaston-Marie Dethier in N.Y. He held various posts as church organist in Boston, then took additional instruction with Widor and Vierne in Paris. Returning to America, he was active as a choral conductor. In 1914 he organized the Detroit Sym. Orch., which he conducted until 1918. In 1924 he became assoc. conductor of the N.Y. State Sym. Orch. In 1928 he was made répétiteur at the Bayreuth Festivals, returning to the U.S. in 1933.—**NS/LK/DM**

Galilei, Vincenzo, celebrated Italian lutenist, composer, and music theorist; b. S. Maria a Monte, near Florence, c. 1520; d. Florence (buried), July 2, 1591. He was the father of the great astronomer Galileo Galilei. A skillful lutenist and violinist, and a student of ancient Greek theory, Vincenzo was a prominent member of the artistic circle meeting at Count Bardi's house known as the Florentine Camerata. His compositions for solo voice with lute accompaniment may be regarded as the starting point of the monody successfully cultivated by Peri, Caccini, etc., the founders of the "opera in musica." A zealous advocate of Grecian simplicity, in contrast with contrapuntal complexity, he publ. a *Dialogo...della musica antica et della moderna* (Florence, 1581; to the 2nd ed. [1602] is appended a polemical *Discorso...intorno all' opere di messer Gioseffo Zarlino da Chioggia*, which had appeared separately in 1589) and *Fronimo. Dialogo...* (in 2 parts:Venice, 1568 and 1569; new ed., 1584), all of considerable historical interest. Vol. IV of *Istituzioni e Monumenti dell' Arte Musicale Italiana* (Milan, 1934), ed. by F. Fano, is devoted entirely to Galilei; it contains a large selection of music reprints from his *Fronimo. Dialogo...* (lute transcriptions by Galilei and original compositions), *Libro d'intavolatura di liuto* (1584), *Il secondo libro de madrigali a 4 et a 5 voci* (1587), and a 4-part *Cantilena*, together with biographical details, list of works, notes about extant MSS, reprints, transcriptions, etc. His *Contrapunti a due voci* (1584) was ed. by Louise Read (Smith Coll. Music Archives, Vol. VIII, 1947).

BIBL.: O. Fleissner, *Die Madrigale V. G.s und sein Dialogo della musica antica e moderna* (Munich, 1922).—**NS/LK/DM**

Galimir, Felix, Austrian-born American violinist and pedagogue; b. Vienna, May 12, 1910; d. N.Y., Nov. 10, 1999. He studied with Adolf Bak at the Vienna Cons. (diploma, 1928) and with Carl Flesch in Berlin and Baden-Baden (1929–30). In 1929 he founded the Galimir String Quartet in Vienna. Emigrating to the U.S. in 1938, he made his debut at N.Y.'s Town Hall, and also organized a new Galimir String Quartet, which subsequently acquired a fine reputation for its performances of contemporary music. Galimir remained active with it until 1993. He became a naturalized American citizen in 1944. He was 1st violinist of the NBC Sym. Orch. in N.Y. (1939–54), concertmaster of the Sym. of the Air in N.Y. (1954–56), and a performer and teacher at the Marlboro (Vt.) Festival and Music School (from 1954). He held teaching positions at the Juilliard School of Music in N.Y. (from 1962), the Curtis Inst. of Music in Philadelphia (from 1972), and the Mannes Coll. of Music in N.Y. (from 1977), where his quartet was in residence. —**NS/LK/DM**

Galin, Pierre, French music pedagogue; b. Samatan, Gers, 1786; d. Bordeaux, Aug. 31, 1821. He was a mathematics teacher at the Lycée in Bordeaux, and conceived the idea of simplifying music instruction by a method which he termed the "Méloplaste" and explained in his work *Exposition d'une nouvelle méthode pour l'enseignement de la musique* (1818; 3rd ed., 1831). The method attracted attention, and was energetically promoted by Chevé.—**NS/LK/DM**

Galindo (Dimas), Blas, noted Mexican composer and pedagogue; b. San Gabriel, Jalisco, Feb. 3,

1910; d. Mexico City, April 19, 1993. He was 7 when he began his musical training with Antonio Velasco. In 1931 he entered the Conservatorio Nacional de Música de México in Mexico City, where he studied with José Rolón (harmony, counterpoint, and fugue), Candelario Huizar (analysis and orchestration), César Chávez (composition), and Rodríguez Vizcarra (piano), and graduated with highest honors in 1944; he also attended Copland's composition classes at the Berkshire Music Center in Tanglewood (summers, 1941, 1942). With Daniel Ayala, Salvador Contreras, and José Pablo Moncayo, he was a founder-member of the contemporary music group El Grupo de los Cuatro (1935–40). In 1944 he became a teacher at the Conservatorio Nacional de Música de México, where he later was its director (1947–61). In 1966 he became a founder-member of the Mexican National Academy of the Arts. The Mexican government honored him with the National Award of Arts and Sciences in 1964. In his extensive output, he displayed a genuine respect for traditional forms. The folkloric element of his early works gave way to a sophisticated use of dissonance without abandoning accessibility.

WORKS: ORCH.: *Obra para orquesta mexicana* (1938); *Sones de mariachi* for Small Orch. (1940; also for Large Orch., 1941); 2 piano concertos: No. 1 (Mexico City, July 24, 1942) and No. 2 (1961; Mexico City, Aug. 17, 1962); *Nocturno* (1945); *Arrullo* for Strings (1945); *Don Quijote* (1947); *Homenaje a Cervantes*, suite (1947); *Poema de Neruda* for Strings (1948); *Pequeñas variaciones* (1951); 3 syms.: No. 1, *Sinfonía breve* or *Pequeña sinfonía* for Strings (Mexico City, Aug. 22, 1952), No. 2 (Caracas, March 19, 1957), and No. 3 (Washington, D.C., April 30, 1961); *Obertura mexicana* No. 1 (1953), No. 2 (1981), and No. 3 (1982); 2 flute concertos: No. 1 with Orch. (1960, New Orleans, April 3, 1965) and No. 2 with Symphonic Band (1979); *4 Pieces* (1961; Mexico City, Nov. 15, 1963); Violin Concerto (1962; Mexico City, Sept. 13, 1970); *3 Pieces* for Clarinet and Orch. (1962); Overture for Organ and Strings (1963); *3 Pieces* for Horn and Orch. (1963); Concertino for Electric Guitar and Orch. (1973; Mexico City, June 12, 1977); *Tríptico* for Strings (1974); Concertino for Violin and Strings (1978); *Homenaje a Juan Rulfo* (1980); Cello Concerto (1984); Suite for Chamber Orch. (1985); Concerto for Guitar and Symphonic Band (1988); *Homenaje a Rodolfo Halffter* (1989). **DRAMATIC: B a l l e t :** *Entre sombras anda el fuego* (Mexico City, March 23, 1940); *Danza de las fuerzas nuevas* (1940); *El zánate* (Mexico City, Dec. 6, 1947); *La manda* (Mexico City, March 31, 1951); *El sueño y la presencia* (Mexico City, Nov. 24, 1951); *La hija del yori* (1952); *El maleficio* (Mexico City, Oct. 28, 1954). **T h e - a t e r :** *Astucia* (1948); *Los signos del zodiaco* (1951). **O t h e r :** Incidental music. **CHAMBER:** Suite for Violin and Cello (1933); Quartet for Cellos (1936); *Bosquejos* for Oboe, Clarinet, Horn, and Bassoon (1937); *Dos preludios* for Oboe, English Horn, and Piano (1938); *Sexteto de alientos* for Flute, Clarinet, Bassoon, Horn, Trumpet, and Trombone (1941); Violin Sonata (1945); Cello Sonata (1948); Suite for Violin and Piano (1957); Quintet for Bow Instruments and Piano (1957); *Tres sonsonetes* for Wind Quintet and Tape (1967); Quartet for Bow Instruments (1970); *Titoco-tico* for Native Percussion (1971); *Invenciones* for Brass Quintet (1977); *3 Pieces* for Percussion (1980); Sonata for Solo Cello (1981); Wind Quintet (1982); Duo for Violin and Cello (1984). Also many piano pieces, including a Sonata (1976); organ music. **VOCAL:** *Primavera* for Children's Chorus and Band or Piano (1944); *Arrullo* for Voices and Orch. (1945); *A la patria* for Chorus and Orch. (1946); *Homenaje a Juárez* for Soprano, Tenor, Bass, Reciter, Chorus, and Orch. (1957); *A la independencia* for Soprano, Alto, Tenor, Bass, Chorus, and Strings (1960); *Tríptico Teotihuacan* for Soprano, Baritone, Chorus, Band, and Native Instruments (1964); *Letanía erótica para La Paz* for Narrator, Alto, Tenor, Bass, Chorus, Organ, and Orch. (1965); *Homenaje a Ruben Darío* for Reciter and String Orch. (1966); *Popocatepetl*, symphonic poem for Soprano, Tenor, and Orch. (1990); *Homenaje a Rufino Tamayo* for Tenor and Orch. (1987).

BIBL.: X. Ortiz, *B. G.: Biografía, antología de textos y catálogo* (Mexico City, 1994).—**NS/LK/DM**

Galkin, Elliott W(ashington), American conductor, music critic, and educator; b. N.Y., Feb. 22, 1921; d. Baltimore, May 24, 1990. He studied at Brooklyn Coll. (B.A., 1943), then served with the U.S. Air Force (1943–46). While stationed in France, he received conducting diplomas from the Paris Cons. (1948) and the École Normale de Musique (1948). Returning to the U.S., he studied at Cornell Univ. (M.A., 1950; Ph.D., 1960, with the diss. *The Theory and Practice of Orchestral Conducting from 1752*). During 1955–56, he was an apprentice conductor with the Vienna State Opera. In 1956 he joined the faculty of Goucher Coll. in Towson, Md., where he served as chairman of the music dept. (1960–77) and as a prof. (1964–77). In 1957 he joined the faculty of the Peabody Cons. of Music in Baltimore as a conductor. He was chairman of its music history and literature dept. (1964–77), and also director of musical activities and a prof. at Johns Hopkins Univ. (from 1968). From 1977 to 1982 he served as director of the Peabody Cons. of Music, and subsequently was director of its graduate program in music criticism. He also was active as conductor of the Baltimore Chamber Orch. (from 1960) and served as music ed. and critic of the *Baltimore Sun* (1962–77). In 1972 and 1975 he received ASCAP-Deems Taylor Awards, and in 1982 was awarded the George Foster Peabody Medal for outstanding contributions to music. He publ. the valuable study *A History of Orchestral Conducting* (Stuyvesant, N.Y., 1988).—**NS/LK/DM**

Gall (real name, **Galle**), **Yvonne,** French soprano; b. Paris, March 6, 1885; d. there, Aug. 21, 1972. She studied at the Paris Cons. She made her operatic debut at the Paris Opéra in 1908 as Mathilde, and remained on its roster until 1935; also sang at the Opéra-Comique in Paris (1921–34). From 1918 to 1921 she was a member of the Chicago Grand Opera, then sang in San Francisco (1931). After her retirement, she taught voice at the Paris Cons. She was highly successful in the French and Italian operatic repertoire. In 1958 she married **Henri Büsser**, who, although much older, outlived her and reached the age of 101.—**NS/LK/DM**

Gall, Jeffrey (Charles), American countertenor; b. Cleveland, Sept. 19, 1950. He was educated at Princeton Univ. (B.A., 1972) and Yale Univ. (M.Phil., 1976), and received vocal instruction from Blake Stern (1972–75) and Arthur Burrows (1976–80). After singing with the Waverly Consort (1974–78), he made his debut in Cavalli's *Erismena* at the Brooklyn Academy of Music in 1980. He sang at Milan's La Scala (1981), the Edinburgh Festival (1982), the Lyric Opera in Chicago (1986), and the Santa Fe Opera (1986). On Sept. 27, 1988, he made his Metropolitan Opera debut in N.Y. as Tolomeo in *Giulio Cesare*. He appeared as Britten's Oberon in Los Angeles in 1992. Following an engagement as Monteverdi's Ottone in Cologne in 1993, he returned to the Metropolitan Opera in 1994 in Britten's *Death in Venice*. In 1996 he sang Ottone at the Dallas Opera. He also appeared in roles in operas by Cesti, Purcell, Lully, Jommelli, Pergolesi, Scarlatti, and Mozart.—NS/LK/DM

Galla-Rini, Anthony, American accordionist, composer, and arranger; b. Manchester, Conn., Jan. 18, 1904. He began his musical training with his father, a bandmaster, and from the age of 6 played the accordion and other instruments on tours of the U.S. and Canada. He studied harmony with John Van Broekhaven in N.Y. (1918) and theory and conducting with Gaston Usigli at the San Francisco Cons. (1933). As a champion of the accordion as a classical instrument, he was the first to give accordion recitals in the major music centers. He was also the first accordionist to appear as a soloist with a sym. orch. when he gave the premiere of his own 1st Accordion Concerto in Oklahoma City on Nov. 15, 1941. He made many technical improvements for his instrument. Among his books were a *Method for Accordion* (1931), an *Accordion Course* (1955–56), the *Galla-Rini Accordion Primer* (1958), and *A Collection of Lectures* (1981). He composed 2 accordion concertos (1941, 1976), an Accordion Sonata (1981), and solo accordion pieces; he also prepared numerous transcriptions for the accordion.

BIBL.: O. Hahn, *A. G.-R.* (Stockholm, 1986).—NS/LK/DM

Gallenberg, (Wenzel) Robert, Graf von, Austrian composer; b. Vienna, Dec. 28, 1783; d. Rome, March 13, 1839. He studied under Albrechtsberger in Vienna. In 1803 he married Countess Giulietta Guicciardi (to whom Beethoven dedicated his Sonata No. 2, op.27, the *Moonlight*). In Naples shortly thereafter, he made the acquaintance of the impresario Barbaja; wrote numerous successful ballets for him, and in 1822–23 was his partner in various operatic enterprises in Vienna. He attempted the management of Vienna's Kärnthnertortheater (1828–30) but failed, and was obliged to return to Italy, rejoining Barbaja. He wrote about 50 ballets; also a Sonata, marches, fantasies, and other works for piano. Beethoven wrote a set of variations on one of his themes.—NS/LK/DM

Gallès, José, Catalan organist and composer; b. Casteltersol, 1761; d. Vich, 1836. He was organist of the Vich Cathedral. He was ordained a priest. J. Nin publ. his Piano Sonata (1800) in the collection *17 sonates et pièces anciennes d'auteurs espagnols* (Paris, 1929). —NS/LK/DM

Galli, Amintore, Italian composer, music critic, and teacher; b. Talamello, near Rimini, Oct. 12, 1845; d. Rimini, Dec. 8, 1919. He was a pupil of Mazzucato at the Milan Cons. (1862–67). He was music editor for the publisher Sonzogno, and critic of *Il Secolo* (1873–1904). He later ed. *Il Teatro Illustrato* (1881–92) and *Musica Popolare* (1882–85). From 1878 to 1903 he taught at the Milan Cons. He publ. *Musica e musicisti dal secolo X sino ai nostri giorni* (1871), *Estetica della musica* (1900), *Storia e teoria del sistema musicale* (1901), and *Piccolo lessico di musica* (1902). His compositions include the operas *Il corno d'oro* (Turin, Aug. 30, 1876) and *David* (Milan, Nov. 12, 1904), the oratorios *Espiazione* (after Moore's Paradise and Peri) and *Cristo al Golgota, Totentanz* (after Goethe) for Baritone Solo and Orch., and a String Quintet.—NS/LK/DM

Galli, Caterina, Italian mezzo-soprano; b. c. 1723; d. Chelsea, 1804. She went to London and sang for the first time at the King's Theatre in 1742. She then became a favorite of Handel, who engaged her to sing in his oratorios (1747–54) and for whom he wrote several parts. About 1754 she left England to pursue her career in Genoa, Naples, Venice, and Mantua. In 1773 she returned to England and sang in opera, oratorios, and concerts until 1797.—NS/LK/DM

Galli, Filippo, celebrated Italian bass; b. Rome, 1783; d. Paris, June 3, 1853. He made his operatic debut as a tenor in Naples in 1801, and continued to sing tenor roles until an illness interrupted his career in 1811. He soon returned to the stage as a bass singing in a performance of Rossini's *La Cambiale di matrimonio* in Padua in 1811. Galli created roles in several of Rossini's operas, including Fernando in *La gazza ladra* (Milan, May 31, 1817) and the title role in *Maometto II* (Naples, Dec. 3, 1820). In 1823 he made his first appearance in Paris. From 1827 to 1833, he was a leading singer at the King's Theatre in London. On Dec. 26, 1830, Galli created the role of King Henry VIII in Donizetti's *Anna Bolena* in Milan. His voice began to decline about 1840, after which he was active as a chorus master in Lisbon and Madrid. From 1842 to 1848 he taught voice at the Paris Cons.—NS/LK/DM

Galliard, Johann Ernst, German oboist, organist, and composer; b. Celle, c. 1680; d. London, 1749. He was a pupil of A. Steffani in Hannover. A skillful oboist, he went to London (1706) as chamber musician to Prince George of Denmark. He succeeded Draghi as organist at Somerset House, and in 1713 played in the Queen's Theatre orch. From 1717 to 1736 he engaged in writing music for the stage productions at Covent Garden and Lincoln's Inn Fields. He last appeared as an oboist probably in 1722. Besides the music to numerous plays, masques, and pantomimes, he wrote several operas, including *Calypso and Telemachus* (London, Queen's Theatre, May 17, 1712), *Circe* (London, Lincoln's Inn Fields, April 11, 1719; 3 songs extant), and *The Happy Captive* (London, Little Theatre in the Haymarket, April 16, 1741; music not extant). He also composed cantatas, a Te Deum, a Jubilate, anthems, soli for Flute and Cello, etc., and set to music the *Morning Hymn of Adam and Eve*, from Milton's *Paradise Lost*.—NS/LK/DM

Gallico, Paolo, Italian-American composer and pianist; b. Trieste, May 13, 1868; d. N.Y., July 6, 1955. At the age of 15, he gave a recital at Trieste, then studied at the Vienna Cons. under Julius Epstein, graduating at 18 with highest honors. After successful concerts in Italy, Austria, Russia, Germany, etc., he settled in N.Y. in 1892 as a concert pianist and teacher. He also toured the U.S. frequently as pianist in recitals and as a soloist with the principal orchs. He won the prize of the National Federation of Music Clubs in 1921 with his dramatic oratorio *The Apocalypse* (N.Y., Nov. 22, 1922). His symphonic episode, *Euphorion*, was performed in Los Angeles (April 6, 1923), N.Y., and Detroit; his Sextet was performed by the Soc. of the Friends of Music in N.Y. He also wrote an opera, *Harlekin* (1926), piano pieces, and songs. His son, Paul Gallico, was a well-known writer. —NS/LK/DM

Galliculus, Johannes, German music theorist and composer who was known as **Johannes Alectorius** and **Johannes Hähnel**; b. probably in Dresden, 1490; d. probably in Leipzig, 1550. He received training from Isaac, and settled in Leipzig as a teacher and composer. He publ. a treatise on counterpoint, *Isagoge de compositione cantus* (Leipzig, 1520; Eng. tr. by A. Moorefield, 1992), and composed sacred music, including a *St Mark Passion*, 3 Magnificats, and 9 motets. Several of his works were publ. by his friend, Georg Rhau. A. Moorefield ed. his complete works (Brooklyn, 1975 et seq.).

BIBL.: A. Moorefield, *An Introduction to J. G.* (Brooklyn, 1969).—LK/DM

Galli-Curci, Amelita, brilliant Italian soprano; b. Milan, Nov. 18, 1882; d. La Jolla, Calif., Nov. 26, 1963. She studied in Milan and intended to be a pianist; graduated in 1903 from the Milan Cons., winning 1st prize. She then had a few voice lessons with Carignani and Dufes, and received advice from Mascagni and William Thorner. She made her operatic debut in Trani as Gilda (Dec. 26, 1906), then sang in various opera houses in Italy and in South America (1910). She continued her successful career as an opera singer in Europe until 1915; then made a sensationally successful U.S. debut with the Chicago Opera Co. as Gilda (Nov. 18, 1916); made her first appearance with the Metropolitan Opera in N.Y. as Violetta (Nov. 14, 1921); remained as a member of the Metropolitan until 1930, and then toured as a recitalist. She was married to the painter Luigi Curci (1910; divorced 1920) and to Homer Samuels, her accompanist.

BIBL.: C. LeMassena, *G.-C.'s Life of Song* (N.Y., 1945). —NS/LK/DM

Galliera, Alceo, Italian conductor and composer; b. Milan, May 3, 1910; d. Brescia, April 20, 1996. He studied piano, organ, and composition at the Milan Cons., and then was on its faculty. After World War II, he appeared as a conductor throughout Europe and South America; was music director of the Victorian Sym. Orch. in Melbourne (1950–51), at the Teatro Carlo Felice in Genoa (1957–60), and of the Strasbourg Phil. (1964–71).—NS/LK/DM

Gallignani, Giuseppe, Italian composer and writer on music; b. Faenza, Jan. 9, 1851; d. (suicide)

Milan, Dec. 14, 1923. He studied at the Milan Cons., and then was choir leader at the Milan Cathedral. He ed. the periodical *Musica Sacra* (1886–94). He was director of the Parma Cons. (1891–97), and, from 1897, director of the Milan Cons. He produced the operas *Il Grillo del focolare* (Genoa, Jan. 27, 1873), *Atala* (Milan, March 30, 1876), and *Nestorio* (Milan, March 31, 1888), which were unsuccessful, but his church music was greatly appreciated (particularly his Requiem for King Umberto I). —NS/LK/DM

Galli-Marié, Célestine (Laurence née **Marié de l'Isle),** French mezzo-soprano; b. Paris, Nov. 1840; d. Vence, near Nice, Sept. 22, 1905. Her father, an opera singer, was her only teacher. She made her debut at Strasbourg (1859), then sang in Toulouse (1860) and in Lisbon (1861). She sang *La Bohème* at Rouen (1862) with such success that she was immediately engaged for the Paris Opéra-Comique; made her debut there (1862) as Serpina in *La Serva padrona*. She created the roles of Mignon (1866) and Carmen (1875).—NS/LK/DM

Gallmeyer, Josefine, (real name, **Josefina Tomaselli**) German soprano; b. Leipzig, Feb. 27, 1838; d. Vienna, Feb. 2, 1884. She began her stage career at 15. After appearing in Brünn, Budapest, Hermannstadt, and Temesvár, she became a star soubrette artist at Vienna's Theater an der Wien in 1865. She was bested in a rivalry there with Marie Geistinger, and in 1867 went to Berlin. Upon returning to Vienna, she became one of the principal singers at the Carltheater. She later was active at the Strampfertheater and the Theater an der Wien. After her final appearance at the Carltheater in 1882, she went to N.Y. for engagements at the Thalia Theater. Her N.Y. appearances were bedeviled by illness, and she died shortly after returning to Vienna. Gallmeyer was affectionately known as Pepi. Her roles in the lighter scores of the Viennese musical theater were memorable. Her career was the subject of a Volksstuck (1905) and a Singspiel by Paul Knepler (1921).

BIBL.: M. Waldstein, *Erinnerungen an J. G.* (Berlin, 1885). —NS/LK/DM

Gallo, Fortune, Italian-American impresario; b. Torremaggiore, May 9, 1878; d. N.Y., March 28, 1970. After piano studies, he emigrated to the U.S. in 1895. In 1909 he founded the San Carlo Opera Co., which toured throughout the U.S. until it disbanded in 1955. In 1926 he built the Gallo Theater in N.Y. He was a pioneering figure in the production of operatic sound films, *Pagliacci* being the first such effort in 1928.—NS/LK/DM

Gallois-Montbrun, Raymond, French violinist, music educator, and composer; b. Saigon, Aug. 15, 1918; d. Paris, Aug. 13, 1994. He studied at the Paris Cons. (1929–39) with Firmin Touche (violin), Büsser (composition), and Jean and Noël Gallon (theory). In 1944 he won the Prix de Rome with his cantata *Louise de la miséricorde*. He made concert tours in Europe, and also played in Japan and Africa. He served as director of the Versailles Cons. (1957–62), and then of the Paris Cons.

(1962–83). In 1980 he was made a member of the Académie des Beaux-Arts.

WORKS: DRAMATIC: O p e r a : *Le Rossignol et l'Empereur*, chamber opera (1959); *Stella ou le Piège de sable* (1964). **ORCH.:** *Symphonie concertante* for Violin and Orch. (1949); *Symphonie japonaise* (1951); Violin Concerto (1957); *Le Port de Delft*, symphonic poem (1960); Cello Concerto (1961); *Les Ménines*, symphonic poem (1961); Piano Concerto (1964). **OTHER:** *Louise de la miséricorde*, cantata for 3 Soloists and Orch. (1944); *Tableaux indochinois* for String Quartet (1946) and other chamber pieces.—NS/LK/DM

Gallon, Jean, French composer and pedagogue, brother of **Noël Gallon;** b. Paris, June 25, 1878; d. there, June 23, 1959. He studied piano with Diémer and theory with Lavignac and Lenepveu at the Paris Cons. He was chorus master of the Paris Société des Concerts du Conservatoire (1906–14) and at the Paris Opéra (1909–14). From 1919 to 1949 he taught harmony at the Paris Cons. Among his pupils were Robert Casadesus, Marcel Delannoy, Henri Dutilleux, Olivier Messiaen, and Jean Rivier. He publ. harmony exercises for use at the Cons.; with his brother, he composed several pieces of theater music, among them a ballet, *Hansli le Bossu* (1914); also composed some chamber music and songs. —NS/LK/DM

Gallon, Noël, French composer and pedagogue, brother of **Jean Gallon;** b. Paris, Sept. 11, 1891; d. there, Dec. 26, 1966. He studied piano with Philipp and Risler, and theory with Caussade, Lenepveu, and Tabaud at the Paris Cons. In 1910 he received the 1st Prix de Rome. From 1920 he was on the faculty of the Paris Cons. as an instructor in solfège, counterpoint, and fugue. As a composer, he was influenced by his brother, his first tutor in music, with whom he wrote a ballet, *Hansli le Bossu* (1914). His own works comprise a few symphonic pieces, Suite for Flute and Piano (1921), Quintet for Horn and Strings (1953), and teaching pieces. —NS/LK/DM

Gallus, Johannes (Jean le Cocq, Maître Jean, Mestre Jhan), Flemish composer; d. c. 1543. He was maestro di cappella to Duke Ercole of Ferrara in 1534 and 1541. Many of his pieces were publ. In collections and in a vol. of motets printed by Scotto (1543). He was long confused with Jhan Gero. —NS/LK/DM

Gallus (Petelin), Jacobus, important Slovenian composer; b. Carniola (probably in Ribnica), between April 15 and July 31, 1550; d. Prague, July 24, 1591. His Slovenian name was Petelin (which means "cockerel"); its Germanic equivalent was **Handl,** or **Hähnel** (diminutive of Hahn, "rooster"); he publ. most of his works under the corresponding Latin name Gallus ("rooster"). As a master of polychoral counterpoint, Gallus was highly regarded in his time. He held several important positions as an organist and music director. He was Kapellmeister to the Bishop of Olmütz (1579–85), and later was employed at the church of St. Johannes in Vado in Prague. A number of his works

were publ. during his lifetime. Of these there are several masses: *Selectiores quaedam Missae* (Prague, 1580), containing 4 books of 16 masses, from 4 to 8 Voices; a modern ed. by P. Pisk was publ. in Denkmäler der Tonkunst in Osterreich (Vienna, 1935; reprinted in 1959, 1967, and 1969); 4 books of motets were publ. in Prague between 1586 and 1591 under the title *Opus musicum*: 1st part (1586) from 4 to 8 Voices (exact title, *Tomus primus musici operas harmonium quatuor, quinque, sex, octo et pluribus vocum*); 2nd and 3rd were publ. in 1587, and 4th in 1591; 5 additional motets were printed individually from 1579 to 1614. *Opus musicum* was reprinted in a modern ed. by E. Bezecny and J. Mantuani in Denkmäler der Tonkunst in Osterreich (Vienna, 1899, 1905, 1908, 1913, 1917, 1919; all reprinted again in 1959); *Moralia 5, 6 et 8 vocibus concinnata*, orig. publ. in 1596, was reprinted in a modern ed. by D. Cvetko (Ljubljana, 1968) and A. Skei (Madison, Wisc., 1970). His secular works include *Harmoniae morales* (Prague, 1589–90; modern ed. by D. Cvetko, Ljubljana, 1966) and *Moralia* (Prague, 1596). A motet by Gallus, *Ecce quomodo moritur justus*, was borrowed by Handel for his *Funeral Anthem*.

BIBL.: D. Cvetko, *J. G., Sein Leben und Werk* (Munich, 1972). —NS/LK/DM

Galper, Hal (actually, **Harold**), jazz pianist; b. Salem, Mass., April 18, 1938. He studied with Margaret Chaloff and Ray Santisi; his primary influences were McCoy Tyner and Oscar Peterson. He became house pianist at such Boston venues as Herb Pomeroy's club, the Stables, and Connelly's, playing with Johnny Hodges, Roy Eldridge, James Moody, Art Blakey, Sam Rivers, and the Bobby Hutcherson-Harold Land Quintet. He considered himself a free-jazz performer, and moved to Paris in 1960, hoping to find more success. After two discouraging months, he returned to Boston and gave up performing for two years. He sat in with Chet Baker at the Jazz Workshop in Boston and was hired to tour and record. During a residency in N.Y., he left Baker and returned to New England (1966) to play in the house band at Lenny's on the Turnpike; Phil Woods was a guest soloist there. In 1967, Galper went back to N.Y., playing with Woods, Donald Byrd, Stan Getz, Chuck Mangione, Joe Henderson, and Al Cohn and Zoot Sims; he recorded three albums as a leader. In 1973, he replaced George Duke in Cannonball Adderley's group, touring almost continuously until he left in 1975. Having decided to concentrate on acoustic piano, he wheeled his Fender Rhodes to a dock on N.Y.'s Hudson River and threw it in. For the next year and a half, he played in a quintet with Randy and Michael Brecker, Wayne Dockery, and Billy Hart, culminating in an appearance at the 1978 Berlin Jazz Festival. He returned to work as a sideman, with Lee Konitz, Nat Adderley, John Scofield, and Slide Hampton. After sitting in with the Phil Woods Quartet in N.Y. (September 1979), he began a 10-year stint with Woods as pianist, composer, and arranger. He left Woods in August 1990 to tour and record with his own trio. He spends six months out of a year on the road; his trio in the late 1990s included drummer Steve Ellington and bassist Jeff Johnson. He has taught at N.Y.'s New School for Social Research and various jazz camps, and has been a guest lecturer and clinician at over 100 colleges and universities and at IAJE conferences in 1990–91, 1994, and 1996. His recordings have won several awards; he has over 100 compositions recorded, and has received numerous grants from public and private endowments.

DISC.: *Wild Bird* (1971); *Guerilla Band* (1972); *Inner Journey* (1973); *Reach Out* (1976); *Now Hear This* (1977); *Redux 1978* (1978); *Speak with a Single Voice* (1978); *Portrait* (1989); *Invitation to a Concert* (1990); *Live at Maybeck Recital Hall* (1990); *H. G. Quartet* (1992); *Tippin'* (1992); *Just Us* (1993); *Rebop* (1995).—**LP**

Galpin, Francis W(illiam), English writer on music; b. Dorchester, Dorset, Dec. 25, 1858; d. Richmond, Surrey, Dec. 30, 1945. He graduated with classical honors from Trinity Coll., Cambridge (B.A., 1882; M.A., 1885), and received his music education from Garrett and Sterndale Bennett. He held various posts as vicar and canon (1891–1921). He wrote many articles on early instruments for *Music & Letters* and *Monthly Musical Record* (1930–33). A Galpin Soc. was formed in London in 1946 with the object of bringing together all those interested in the history of European instruments and to commemorate the pioneer work of Galpin; it publishes the *Galpin Society Journal* (1948 et seq.). In addition to his numerous monographs, Galpin was the editor of the revised and augmented ed. of Stainer's *Music of the Bible* (1913).

WRITINGS: *Descriptive Catalogue of the European Instruments in the Metropolitan Museum of Art, N.Y.* (1902); *The Musical Instruments of the American Indians of the North West Coast* (1903); *Notes on the Roman Hydraulus* (1904); *The Evolution of the Sackbut* (1907); *Old English Instruments of Music* (1910; 4th ed., rev., 1965, by T. Dart); *A Textbook of European Musical Instruments* (1937); *The Music of the Sumerians, Babylonians and Assyrians* (1937); *The Music of Electricity* (1938).—**NS/LK/DM**

Galston, Gottfried, Austrian-American pianist; b. Vienna, Aug. 31, 1879; d. St. Louis, April 2, 1950. He was a pupil of Leschetizky in Vienna, and of Jadassohn and Reinecke at the Leipzig Cons., and from 1903 to 1907 he taught at the Stern Cons. in Berlin. On his extended concert tours, he proved himself a player of keen analytical powers and intellectual grasp. In 1902 he toured Australia, and then Germany, France, and Russia. In 1912–13 he toured America, and also toured Russia 11 times (last, in 1926). He returned to the U.S. in 1927 and settled in St. Louis. He publ. a *Studienbuch* (1909; 3rd ed., Munich, 1920) and analytical notes to a series of 5 historical recitals.—**NS/LK/DM**

Galuppi, Baldassare, celebrated Italian composer, called "Il Buranello" after his birthplace; b. on the island of Burano, near Venice, Oct. 18, 1706; d. Venice, Jan. 3, 1785. He began his musical training with his father, a barber and violinist, writing his first opera, *La fede nell'incostanza ossia gli amici rivali*, when he was 16. It failed at its premiere in Vicenza in 1722, so he pursued a thorough course of instruction in composition and keyboard playing with Antonio Lotti. He garnered his first unqualified success as a composer with the opera *Dorinda* (Venice, June 9, 1729), written in collaboration

with G.B. Pescetti, and subsequently wrote numerous operas for the leading Italian opera houses. From 1740 to 1751 he was maestro di musica of the Ospedale dei Mendicanti in Venice. He was active as a composer in London at the King's Theatre at the Haymarket (1741–43), and also visited Vienna in 1748. He was named vice- maestro of the cappella ducale of S. Marco in Venice in 1748, and in 1762 was made Venice's maestro di cappella. Turning to the new form of opera buffa, he established himself as a master of the genre with his *L'Arcadia in Brenta* (Venice, May 14, 1749), sealing his fame with his *Il Filosofo di campagna* (Venice, Oct. 26, 1754), which was performed with great acclaim all over Europe. He was called to Russia in 1765 to serve as music director of the court chapel of Catherine the Great in St. Petersburg; his opera seria *Ifigenia in Tauride* was given at the court on May 2, 1768. He returned to Venice in 1768, and resumed his post at S. Marco; that same year, he also became maestro di coro of the Ospedale degli Incurabili. Galuppi was a pivotal figure in the development and refinement of opera buffa. His effective vocal and orch. writing, combined with Goldoni's innovative librettos, ensured popular success. He was also a distinguished composer for the keyboard; his sonatas confirm his contemporary renown as a harpsichord virtuoso.

WORKS: DRAMATIC: O p e r a (all 1st perf. in Venice unless otherwise given): *Gl'odj delusi dal sangue* (Feb. 4, 1728; in collaboration with G.B. Pescetti); *L'odio placato* (Dec. 27, 1729); *Argenide* (Jan. 15, 1733); *L'ambizione depressa* (1733); *Tamiri* (Nov. 17, 1734); *Elisa regina di Tiro* (Jan. 27, 1736); *Ergilda* (Nov. 12, 1736); *L'Alvilda* (May 29, 1737); *Issipile* (Turin, Dec. 26, 1737); *Alessandronelle Indie* (Mantua, Carnival 1738); *Adriano in Siria* (Turin, Jan. 1740); *Gustavo primo re di Svezia* (May 25, 1740); *Oronte re de' Sciti* (Dec. 26, 1740); *Berenice* (Jan. 27, 1741); *Didone abbandonata* (Modena, Carnival 1741); *Penelope* (London, Dec. 23, 1741); *Scipione in Cartagine* (London, March 13, 1742); *Enrico* (London, Jan. 12, 1743); *Sirbace* (London, April 20, 1743); *Ricimero* (Milan, Dec. 26, 1744); *Antigono* (London, May 24, 1746); *Scipione nelle Spagne* (Nov. 1746); *Evergete* (Rome, Jan. 2, 1747); *L'Arminio* (Nov. 26, 1747); *L'Olimpiade* (Milan, Dec. 26, 1747); *Vologeso* (Rome, Feb. 13?, 1748); *Demetrio* (Vienna, Oct. 16?, 1748); *Clotilde* (Nov. 1748); *Semiramide riconosciuta* (Milan, Jan. 25, 1749); *Artaserse* (Vienna, Jan. 27, 1749); *Demofoonte* (Madrid, Dec. 18, 1749); *Olimpia* (Naples, Dec. 18?, 1749); *Alcimena principessa dell'Isole Fortunate, ossia L'amore fortunato ne' suoi disprezzj* (Dec. 26, 1749); *Antigona* (Rome, Jan. 9, 1751); *Dario* (Turin, Carnival 1751); *Lucio Papirio* (Reggio Emilia, 1751); *Artaserse* (Padua, June 11, 1751); *Sofonisba* (Rome, Feb. 24?, 1753); *L'eroe cinese* (Naples, July 10, 1753); *Siroe* (Rome, Feb. 10, 1754); *Attalo* (Padua, June 11, 1755); *Idomeneo* (Rome, Jan. 7, 1756); *Ezio* (Milan, Jan. 22, 1757); *Sesostri* (Nov. 26, 1757); *Ipermestra* (Milan, Jan. 14, 1758); *Adriano in Siria* (Livorno, 1758); *Meilite riconosciuto* (Rome, Jan. 13, 1759); *La clemenza di Tito* (1760); *Solimano* (Padua, 1760); *Antigono* (Carnival 1762); *Il re pastore* (Parma, 1762); *Siface*, later known as *Viriate* (May 19, 1762); *Il Muzio Scevola* (Padua, June 1762); *Adrianna e Teseo* (Padua, June 12, 1763); *Sonofisba* (Turin, Carnival 1764); *Cajo Mario* (May 31, 1764); *Ifigenia in Tauride* (St. Petersburg, May 2, 1768); *Montezuma* (May 27, 1772). D r a m m a s G i o - c o s o : *La forza d'amore* (Jan. 30, 1745); *L'Arcadia in Brenta* (May 14, 1749); *Il conte Caramella* (Verona, Dec. 18, 1749?); *Arcifanfano re dei matti* (Dec. 27, 1749); *Il paese della Cuccagna* (May 7, 1750);

Il mondo alla roversa, ossia Le Donne che comandano (Nov. 14, 1750); *La mascherata* (Dec. 26?, 1750); *Le virtuose ridicole* (Carnival 1752); *La calamità de' cuori* (Dec. 26, 1752); *I bagni d'Abano* (Feb. 10, 1753; in collabortion with Bertoni); *Il filosofo di campagna* (Oct. 26, 1754); *Il povero superbo* (Feb. 1755); *Le nozze* (Bologna, Sept. 14, 1755); *La diavolessa* (Nov. 1755); *L'amante di tutte* (Nov. 15, 1760); *Li tre amanti ridicoli* (Jan. 18, 1761); *Il caffè di campagna* (Nov. 18, 1761); *Il marchese villano* (Feb. 2, 1762); *L'uomo femmina* (Dec. 26, 1762); *Il puntiglio amoroso* (Dec. 26, 1762); *Il re alla caccia* (1763); *La donna di governo* (Rome, 1761; rev. version, Prague, 1763); *La partenza il ritorno de' marinari* (Dec. 26, 1764); *La cameriera spiritosa* (Milan, Oct. 4, 1766); *Il villano geloso* (Nov. 1769); *Amor lunatico* (Jan. 1770); *L'inimico delle donne* (1771); *Gl'intrighi amorosi* (Jan. 1772); *La serva per amore* (1773; Act 1 unfinished). **OTHER:** Several other dramatic works, including farsettas, pastorales, intermezzos, serenatas, and cantatas. His sacred works include oratorios, masses, Requiems, Magnificats, motets, and a number of pieces for the Russian Orthodox church. Among his instrumental works are numerous sonatas, toccatas, divertimenti, and other pieces for keyboard.

BIBL.: F. Raabe, *G. als Instrumentalkomponist* (diss., Univ. of Munich, 1926); W. Bollert, *Die Buffoopern B. G.s* (diss., Univ. of Berlin, 1935); A. Chiuminatto, *The Liturgical Works of B. G.* (diss., Northwestern Univ., 1959); D. Pullmann, *A Catalogue of the Keyboard Sonatas of B. G. (1706–1785)* (diss., American Univ., 1972); R. Holmes, *A Critical Edition of Selected Keyboard Sonatas by B. G. (1706–1785)* (diss., Tex. Tech. Univ., 1976); R. Wiesend, *Studien zur Opera Seria von B. G.* (2 vols., Tutzing, 1984). —NS/LK/DM

Galvani, Giacomo, noted Italian tenor; b. Bologna, Nov. 1, 1825; d. Venice, May 7, 1889. He studied in Bologna with Gamberini and Zamboni, making his debut in *I Masnadieri* in Spoleto in 1849. He subsequently sang in Bologna, Milan, London, Barcelona, and other cities with great success. After his retirement, he taught voice in Venice and at the Moscow Cons. (1869–87). He was acclaimed for his performances in the operas of Rossini and Donizetti.—NS/LK/DM

Galway, James, famous Irish flutist; b. Belfast, Dec. 8, 1939. He took up the tin whistle at 7 and began playing the flute in a neighborhood flute band when he was 9. He then went to London on a scholarship, where he studied with John Francis at the Royal Coll. of Music (1956–59) and with Geoffrey Gilbert at the Guildhall School of Music and Drama (1959–60); a 2nd scholarship allowed him to proceed to Paris to continue his training with Gaston Crunelle at the Cons. and privately with Marcel Moyse and Jean-Pierre Rampal. He was a flutist in the orchs. of the Sadler's Wells Opera (1961–66) and the Royal Opera, Covent Garden (1965), in London; after playing in the London Sym. Orch. (1966–67) and the Royal Phil. of London (1967–69), he was a member of the Berlin Phil. (1969–75). Thereafter he pursued a brilliant career as a flute virtuoso, making highly successful tours all over the world. In later years, he also took up conducting. He publ. *James Galway: An Autobiography* (London, 1978) and *Flute* (London, 1982). In 1977 he was made an Officer of the Order of the British Empire and in 1987 an Officier des Arts et Lettres of

France. Galway's repertory ranges over a vast expanse of music, including not only the classics and contemporary scores, but traditional Irish music and popular fare. —NS/LK/DM

Gamba, Piero, (actually, **Pierino**) Italian conductor; b. Rome, Sept. 16, 1936. From a musical family (his father was a professional violinist), he was trained at home; his precocity was so remarkable that he was reportedly able to read an orch. score at the age of 8, and at 9 conducted a regular sym. concert in Rome. He also composed. Unlike the talent of so many child musicians, his gift did not evaporate with puberty; he became a professional artist. According to ecstatic press reports, he conducted in 40 countries and 300 cities, so that his name became familiar to uncounted multitudes (including a billion people in China). From 1970 to 1981 he served as music director of the Winnipeg Sym. Orch.; from 1982 to 1987 he was principal conductor of the Adelaide (Australia) Sym. Orch.—NS/LK/DM

Gamble, Kenny, and **Huff, Leon,** the producers who gave Philadelphia soul and a sound in the 1970s. **MEMBERSHIP:** Kenny Gamble (real name, Kenneth) (b. Philadelphia, Aug. 11, 1943); Leon Huff (b. Camden, N.J., April 8, 1942). These two Philadelphia natives first joined forces during the 1950s in a vocal group called The Romeos, which also featured a young man named Thom Bell. A pianist, Leon Huff had already worked with Phil Spector and done extensive session work in N.Y., including the Danny and the Juniors hit "Let's Go to the Hop." Going back to Philadelphia, he did sessions for local label Cameo, already successful with Chubby Checker and Bobby Rydell. Fellow Romeo Kenny Gamble co-wrote a song for Candy and the Kisses that Huff played on. They started working together, finally hitting the charts with the Soul Survivors' "Expressway to Your Heart." They continued working as independent producers with acts like Archie Bell and the Drells and Jerry Butler. They also had their own Neptune Label (through Chess) and Gamble records.

Their success led them to CBS. CBS had little success in the R&B market in the early 1970s. Gamble and Huff offered to provide it, and thus Philadelphia International Records was born. CBS gave the pair $75,000 in seed money for 15 singles. Within a year of signing, Gamble and Huff had sold over ten million records with artists like Billy Paul, Harold Melvin and the Blue Notes, and The O'Jays. Their signature sound incorporated sophisticated touches like strings, horn sections, and an always-insistent groove. A precursor to disco, when the clubs started playing an important role in the music business, Philadelphia International helped shape the direction with hits like 1974's "TSOP," the R&B, adult contemporary and pop chart–topping tune that became the theme to the TV show *Soul Train*.

In 1975, however, the pair fell victim to a payola scandal, charged with offering bribes for radio play. Gamble was fined $2500, Huff was exonerated, but the proceedings killed their momentum. They continued to have hits, most notably with former Howard Melvin and the Blue Notes drummer and vocalist Teddy Pendergrass. They also released McFadden and Whitehead's platinum R&B chart topper "Ain't No Stopping Us Now." In 1995, they were inducted into the Songwriter's Hall of Fame.—BH

Ganassi dal Fontego, Sylvestro di, Italian writer on music; b. Fontego, near Venice, 1492; d. place and date unknown. He was active as an instrumentalist in Venice. He publ. important treatises on the recorder, *Opera initulata Fontegara* (Venice, 1535; Eng. tr., 1959), and on the viola da gamba, *Regola rubertina* (Venice, 1542) and *Lettione seconda* (Venice, 1543).—LK/DM

Ganche, Edouard, French physician and writer on music; b. Baulon, Ille-et-Vilaine, Oct. 13, 1880; d. Lyons, May 31, 1945. He was trained in medicine but also received instruction in music in Paris from Imbert and Expert. Although a practicing physician, he devoted much time to the study of Chopin, and was ed. of the Oxford edition of Chopin's works (3 vols., 1928–32).

WRITINGS (all publ. in Paris): *La Vie de Frédéric Chopin dans son oeuvre: Sa liaison avec George Sand* (1909); *Frédéric Chopin: Sa vie et ses oeuvres, 1810–1849* (1909; 3rd ed., 1949); *La Pologne et Frédéric Chopin* (1921); *Dans le souvenir de Frédéric Chopin* (1925); *Souffrances de Frédéric Chopin: Essai de medicine et de psychologie* (1934; 2nd ed., 1935); *Voyages avec Frédéric Chopin* (1934). —NS/LK/DM

Gandini, Gerardo, Argentine composer, pianist, and teacher; b. Buenos Aires, Oct. 16, 1932. He studied with Pia Sebastini, Roberto Caamaño, and Ginastera in Buenos Aires (1956–59), then completed studies in Rome with Petrassi (1966–67). He taught in Buenos Aires and N.Y. As a pianist, he specialized in contemporary music.

WORKS: DRAMATIC: O p e r a : *La Pasión de Buster Keaton* (1978). ORCH.: *Variations* (1962); *Música nocturna II* for Chamber Orch. (1965); *Cadencias I* for Violin and Chamber Orch. (1966) and *II* for Chamber Orch. (1967); *Mutantes I* for Chamber Orch. (1966); *Fuggevole* for Chamber Orch. (1967); *Contrastes* for 2 Pianos and Orch. (1968); *Fases* for Clarinet and Orch. (1969); *Fantasie-Impromptu,* "imaginary portrait of Chopin" for Piano and Orch. (1970); Guitar Concerto (1975; Washington, D.C., May 18, 1976); Piano Concerto (Washington, D.C., April 25, 1980); *Soria Moria II* for Strings (1981); Concerto for Flute, Guitar, and Orch. (1986). CHAMBER: *Concertino I* for Clarinet, String Trio, and Percussion, *II* for Flute and Instruments, and *III* for Harpsichord and Instruments (1962–63); *Musica nocturna I* for Flute, Piano, and String Trio (1964); *L'Adieu* for Piano, Vibraphone, 3 Percussionists, and Conductor (1967); *A Cow in a Mondrian Painting* for Flute and Instruments (1967); *Soria Moria* for Variable Instrumental Ensemble (1968); *Play* for Piano and an Instrument (1969); *Piange e sospira* for Flute, Violin, Clarinet, and Piano (1970); *Il concertino* for Flute and Instruments (1971); *Lunario sentimental* for Violin, Cello, and Piano (1989).—NS/LK/DM

Gandolfi, Riccardo (Cristoforo Daniele Diomede), Italian composer; b. Voghera, Piedmont, Feb. 16, 1839; d. Florence, Feb. 5, 1920. He was a pupil of Carlo Conti at the Naples Cons., then of Mabellini in Florence. He was appointed inspector of studies at the Real Istituto di Musica in Florence (1869), and chief librarian in 1889. In 1912 he was pensioned. He began as a dramatic composer, then turned to the larger instrumental and vocal forms, and finally abandoned composition altogether, devoting himself to historical studies, which won him distinction.

WORKS: DRAMATIC: O p e r a : *Aldina* (Milan, 1863); *Il Paggio* (Turin, 1865); *Il Conte di Monreale* (Genoa, 1872); *Caterina di Guisa* (Catania, 1872). OTHER: *Messa da Requiem*; cantata, *Il Battesimo di S. Cecilia*; several overtures; chamber music.

WRITINGS: *Sulla relazione della poesia colla musica melodrammatica* (1868); *Una riparazione a proposito di Francesco Landino* (1888); *Commemorazioni di W.A. Mozart* (1891); *Illustrazioni di alcuni cimeli concernanti l'arte musicale in Firenze* (1892); *Appunti di storia musicale* (1893); *Onoranze Fiorentine a G. Rossini* (1902). —NS/LK/DM

Ganelin, Viacheslav, Russian pianist and composer; b. Kraskovo, 1944. He graduated from the Lithuanian State Cons. in Vilnius and was music director of the Russian Dramatic Theater. He wrote much theater music, film scores, an opera, *The Red-Haired Liar and the Soldier,* and a rock musical, *The Devilish Bride.* When he met the percussionist Vladimir Tarasov (b. Archangelsk, 1947) in Vilnius, the two formed what was to be the basis of the Ganelin Trio; after playing at the Jazz Club in Sverdlovsk in the early 1960s, they were joined by Chaksin (b. Sverdlovsk, 1947), a graduate of the Sverdlovsk Cons. The Ganelin Trio has an eclectic and ironic style, synthesizing strong formal structural ideas with improvisation and stressing constant innovation and Ganelin's conviction that the 2 most important elements of jazz are "swing and improvisation." Ganelin himself plays the piano and basset horn, providing harmony and bassline; Tarasov, on percussion, states the rhythms; Chaksin controls the melodic line, strongly influenced by Ornette Coleman and John Coltrane, on an assortment of reeds, flute, trombone, and violin. In time, the trio was widely acclaimed on its visits to European jazz festivals.—NS/LK/DM

Gange, Fraser, distinguished Scottish-American baritone and pedagogue; b. Dundee, June 17, 1886; d. Baltimore, July 1, 1962. He studied with his father in Dundee and with Amy Sherwin in London. After making his debut at 16, he toured in England, Scotland, Australia, and New Zealand. On Jan. 18, 1924, he made his U.S. debut in N.Y., and subsequently toured as an oratorio and lieder artist. He also taught at the Peabody Cons. of Music in Baltimore (1931–57) and at the Juilliard School of Music in N.Y. (summers, 1932–46). —NS/LK/DM

Gann, Kyle (Eugene), American music critic and composer; b. Dallas, Nov. 21, 1955. His mother was a piano teacher and his first teacher. He studied formally with Randolph Coleman at the Oberlin (Ohio) Coll. Cons. of Music (B.Mus., 1977) and with Peter Gena at Northwestern Univ. (M.Mus., 1981; D.Mus., 1983); also privately with Ben Johnston and Morton Feldman. He began writing freelance music criticism for a variety of Chicago newspapers, and in 1986 joined the staff of the *Village Voice* in N.Y., where he became especially well known as a provocative and insightful reviewer of contemporary music. In 1997 he joined the faculty at Bard Coll. His compositions are written in a postminimalist style, although with a complex rhythmic idiom derived from his study of Hopi and Zuni musics. In the 1990s he turned to synthesizers and computers in order to explore just intonation pitch systems of up to 31 and more pitches per octave; the pitch, rhythm, and ethnomusicological interests collided in a one-man electronic opera, *Custer and Sitting Bull* (1998–99), based on historical texts. Acoustic works such as *Astrological Studies* (1994) and *Time Does Not Exist* (2000) draw on his interests in Renaissance occultism and Jungian psychology. Several interviews in Mexico City with the reclusive expatriate composer Conlon Nancarrow resulted in the publication of his *The Music of Conlon Nancarrow* (Cambridge, 1995). He also published an extremely useful history, *American Music in the Twentieth Century* (N.Y., 1997), as well as a collection of his reviews from the *Village Voice* (Los Angeles and Berkeley, 2001).

WORKS: ORCH.: *The Disappearance of All Holy Things From This Once So Promising World* for Orch. (1998). **CHAMBER:** *Long Night* for 3 Pianos (1981); *Mountain Spirit* for 2 Flutes, Synthesizer, and 2 Drums (1982–83); *Baptism* for 2 Flutes, Synthesizer, and 2 Drums (1983); *The Black Hills Belong to the Sioux* for Trumpet or Saxophone, Accordion or Synthesizer, Flute, and Drum (1984); *L'itoi Variations* for 2 Pianos (1985); *Cyclic Aphorisms* for Violin and Piano (1986–88); *Chicago Spiral* for Octet (1991); *Snake Dance No. 1* (1991) and *No. 2* (1995) for Percussion Quartet; *Astrological Studies* for Octet (1994); *"Last Chance" Sonata* for Clarinet and Piano (1999). **Piano:** *Windows to Infinity (A Meditation on Nietzsche)* for Piano (1987); *Paris Intermezzo* for Toy Piano (1989); *The Convent at Tepoztlan (Homage to Nancarrow)* for Piano and Tape or 2 Pianos (1989); *Desert Sonata* for Piano (1994–95); *Time Does Not Exist* for Piano (2000). **ELECTRONIC:** *Superparticular Woman* for Synthesizer (1992); *Ghost Town* for Synthesizer and Sampler (1994); *So Many Little Dyings* for Keyboard Sampler (1994); *Homage to Cowell* for Keyboard Sampler (1994); *Fractured Paradise* for Synthesizer and Tape (1995); *How Miraculous Things Happen* for Synthesizer and Tape (1997); *Despotic Waltz* for Computerized Piano (1997); *The Waiting* for Computerized Piano (1997); *Arcana XVI: Homage to Joan Tower* for 3 Synthesizers (1998); *Custer and Sitting Bull* for Narrator and Computer Electronics (1998–99); *Nude Rolling Down an Escalator* for Computerized Piano (1999); *Folk Dance for Henry Cowell* for Computerized Piano (1999).—**NS/LK/DM**

Ganne, (Gustave) Louis, French conductor and composer; b. Buxières-les-Mines, Allier, April 15, 1862; d. Paris, July 13, 1923. He studied at the Paris Cons. with Dubois, Massenet, and Franck. He was a conductor for the Bals de l'Opéra in Paris and in various spa towns. In 1905 he organized his own Concerts Louis Ganne series in Monte Carlo. As a composer, Ganne wrote many light scores. His circus musical *Les Saltimbanques* (Paris, Dec. 30, 1899) was popular, but he scored his greatest success with the operetta *Hans, le joueur de flûte* (Monte Carlo, April 14, 1906). He also composed the popular *La Marche Lorraine* and the march *Le Père de la Victoire*.

WORKS: DRAMATIC: Musical Theater (all 1st perf. in Paris unless otherwise given): *Tout Paris* (June 16, 1891); *Rabelais* (Oct. 24, 1892); *Les Colles des femmes* (Sept. 29, 1893); *Les Saltimbanques* (Dec. 30, 1899); *Hans, le joueur de flûte* (Monte Carlo, April 14, 1906); *Rhodope* (Monte Carlo, Dec. 13, 1910); *Cocorico* (Nov. 29, 1913); *L'Archiduc des Folies- Bergère* (Oct. 7, 1916); *La Belle de Paris* (Oct. 22, 1921); vaudevilles; ballet music. **OTHER:** Dances; marches, including *La Marche Lorraine* and *La Père de la Victoire*; many piano pieces; songs. —**NS/LK/DM**

Gänsbacher, Johann (Baptist), Austrian composer; b. Sterzing, Tirol, May 8, 1778; d. Vienna, July 13, 1844. He studied with Abbé Vogler (1803–04) and Albrechtsberger in Vienna (1806), and then continued his study under Vogler, at Darmstadt (Weber and Meyerbeer were his fellow pupils). He served in the war of 1813, led a roving life for several years, and finally settled in Vienna as Kapellmeister of the Cathedral in 1823. He wrote masses, Requiems, orch. works, piano pieces, songs, etc.

BIBL.: C. Fischnaler, *J. G.* (Innsbruck, 1878); J. Woerz, *J. G.* (Innsbruck, 1894).—**NS/LK/DM**

Ganz, Rudolph, distinguished Swiss-American pianist, conductor, and pedagogue; b. Zürich, Feb. 24, 1877; d. Chicago, Aug. 2, 1972. He studied music assiduously, first as a cellist (with Friedrich Hegar), then as a pianist (with Robert Freund) in Zürich; also took composition lessons with Charles Blanchet at the Lausanne Cons. In 1897–98 he studied piano with F. Blumer in Strasbourg, and in 1899 took a course in advanced piano playing with Busoni in Berlin. He made his first public appearance at the age of 12 as a cellist, and at 16 as a pianist. In 1899 he was the soloist in Beethoven's *Emperor Concerto* and Chopin's E-minor Concerto with the Berlin Phil., and in May 1900 the Berlin Phil. performed his 1st Sym. In 1901 he went to the U.S. and was engaged as a prof. of piano at the Chicago Musical Coll.; between 1905 and 1908 he made several tours of the U.S. and Canada, and from 1908 to 1911 toured Europe. After 1912 he toured in both Europe and America. From 1921 to 1927 he was music director of the St. Louis Sym. Orch.; from 1938 to 1949 he conducted a highly successful series of Young People's Concerts with the N.Y. Phil.; concurrently (1929–54) he served as director of the Chicago Musical Coll. He played first performances of many important works, including those of Busoni, Ravel, and Bartók. He was a highly successful pedagogue, and continued to teach almost to the time of his death, at the age of 95. Besides the early sym., he wrote a lively suite of 20 pieces for Orch., *Animal Pictures* (Detroit, Jan. 19, 1933, composer conducting), a Piano Concerto (Chicago, Feb. 20, 1941, composer soloist), *Laughter—Yet Love, Overture to an Unwritten Comedy* (1950), solo piano pieces, and about 200 songs to German, French, English, Swiss, and Alsatian texts. He publ. *Rudolph Ganz Evaluates Modern Piano Music* (N.Y., 1968).

BIBL.: J. Collester, *R. G.: A Musical Pioneer* (Metuchen, N.J., 1995).—**NS/LK/DM**

Ganz, Wilhelm, German-born English pianist, violinist, and conductor; b. Mainz, Nov. 6, 1833; d. London,

Sept. 12, 1914. He studied piano and conducting with his father, Adolf Ganz (b. Mainz, Oct. 14, 1796; d. London, Jan. 11, 1870), and with Karl Anschütz. He settled in England in 1850. He was active as an accompanist to Jenny Lind and other musicians, and was also a violinist in Henry Wylde's New Phil. Orch. in London (from 1852). He was then joint conductor with Wylde (1874–79) and subsequently sole conductor, organizing his own "Mr. Ganz's Orchestral Concerts" in 1880. After their discontinuance in 1883, he taught voice at the Guildhall School of Music. He publ. *Memories of a Musician* (London, 1913).—NS/LK/DM

Ganzarolli, Wladimiro, Italian bass-baritone; b. Venice, Jan. 9, 1936. He received his training at the Venice Cons. In 1958 he made his operatic debut as Méphistophélès in *Faust* at Milan's Teatro Nuovo, and from 1959 was a member of Milan's La Scala; from 1964 he also sang at the Vienna State Opera. In 1965 he made his debut at London's Covent Garden as Figaro. His guest engagements in the U.S. took him to San Francisco, Chicago, Dallas, and N.Y. In addition to his roles in Italian operas, he was especially admired for his roles in Mozart's operas.—NS/LK/DM

Garaguly, Carl von, Hungarian-born Swedish violinist and conductor; b. Budapest, Dec. 28, 1900; d. Stockholm, Oct. 8, 1984. He studied violin with Hubay at the Royal Academy of Music in Budapest (1907–09) and with Marteau at the Berlin Hochschule für Musik (1911–16). After playing in the Berlin Phil. (1917–18), he pursued violin studies with Kresz at the Stern Cons. in Berlin and privately with Marteau (1920–23). He then settled in Sweden, becoming a naturalized Swedish citizen in 1930. He was concertmaster of the Göteborg Sym. Orch. (1923–30) and the Stockholm Concert Soc. Orch. (1930–40), subsequently serving as conductor of the latter (1941–53). From 1940 he also appeared with his own string quartet. He was music director of the Bergen Phil. (1953–58), Arnhem's Het Gelders Orch. (1959–70), and the Sønderborg Sym. Orch. (1965–80).
—NS/LK/DM

Garant, (Albert Antonio) Serge, Canadian composer, conductor, pianist, and teacher; b. Quebec City, Sept. 22, 1929; d. Sherbrooke, Quebec, Nov. 1, 1986. He learned to play the clarinet and saxophone, and then played in the Sherbrooke Sym. Orch. and in jazz groups. He also studied piano and harmony in Sherbrooke (1946–50), and was a student of Yvonne Hubert (piano) and Champagne (composition) in Montreal (1948–50) before pursuing his training in Paris with Messiaen (musical analysis) and Vaurabourg-Honegger (counterpoint) in 1951–52; later he had lessons in conducting with Boulez in Basel (summer, 1969). He was actively engaged in contemporary music circles in Montreal. In 1966 he helped found the Société de musique contemporaine du Québec there, for which he served as conductor for the rest of his life. From 1967 he also taught at the Univ. of Montreal. In 1980 he was made a member of the Order of Canada. His output charted a thoroughly contemporary course in which serial tech-

niques were relieved by an infusion of lyricism. His *Nucléogame* (1955) was the first score by a Canadian composer to combine the use of tape and instruments.

WORKS: ORCH.: *Musique pour la mort d'un poète* for Piano and Strings (1954); *Ennéade* (1963); *Ouranos* (1963); *Amuya* (1968); *Phrases II* (1968); *Offrande I* (1969) and *II* (1970); *Circuits III* (1973); *Plages* (1981). **CHAMBER:** *Nucléogame: In Memoriam Anton Webern* for Flute, Oboe, Clarinet, Trumpet, Trombone, Piano, and Tape (1955); *Canon VI* for 10 Performers (1957); *Pièces pour quatuor* for String Quartet (1958–59); *Asymétries No. 2* for Clarinet and Piano (1959); *Jeu à quatre* for 4 Instrumental Groups (1968); *Offrande III* for 3 Cellos, 2 Harps, Piano, and 2 Percussion (1971); *Circuits I* for 6 Percussionists (1972) and *II* for 14 Performers (1972); Quintet for Flute, Oboe, Cello, Piano, and Percussion (1978). **Piano:** *Pièce No. 1* (1953; rev. 1959) and *No. 2* (1962); *Musique rituelle* (1954); *Variations* (1954); *Asymétries No. 1* (1958). **VOCAL:** *Anerca* for Soprano and 8 Performers (1961); *Cage d'oiseau* for Soprano and Piano (1962); *Phrases I* for Mezzo-soprano, Piano, Celesta, and Percussion (1967); *...chant d'amours* for Soprano, Contralto, Baritone, and 13 Performers (1975); *Rivages* for Baritone and 8 Performers (1976). **OTHER:** Film and television scores.

BIBL.: M.-T. Lefebvre, *S. G. et la révolution musicale au Québec* (Montreal, 1986).—NS/LK/DM

Garat, (Dominique) Pierre (Jean), famous French singer and teacher; b. Ustaritz, Bas-Pyrénées, April 25, 1762; d. Paris, March 1, 1823. His talent was discovered early, and he studied theory and singing with Franz Beck in Bordeaux. His father wished him to become a lawyer, and sent him to the Univ. of Paris in 1782. However, he neglected his legal studies, and, aided by the Count d'Artois, he was introduced to Marie Antoinette, whose special favor he enjoyed up to the Revolution. He earned his livelihood as a concert singer; accompanied Rode, in 1792, to Rouen, where he gave numerous concerts before being arrested as a suspect during the Terror; subsequently he went to Hamburg. He returned to Paris in 1794, and sang (1795) at the Feydeau Concerts, where his triumphs speedily procured him a professorship of singing in the newly established Cons. For 20 years longer, his fine tenor-baritone voice, trained to perfection, made him the foremost singer on the French concert stage. Nourrit, Levasseur, and Ponchard were his pupils.

BIBL.: P. Lafond, *G.* (Paris, 1899); B. Miall, *P. G., Singer and Exquisite: His Life and His World* (London, 1913); I. de Fagoaga, *P. G., le chanteur* (Bayonne, 1944).—NS/LK/DM

Garaudé, Alexis (Adélaide-Gabriel) de, French singer and composer; b. Nancy, March 21, 1779; d. Paris, March 23, 1852. He studied theory under Cambini and Reicha, and singing under Crescentini and Garat. He was a singer in the royal choir (1808–30) and prof. of singing at the Cons. (1816–41). He publ. 3 string quintets, many ensemble pieces for violin, flute, clarinet, and cello, sonatas and variations for piano, a solemn Mass, and various vocal works, including vocalises, arias, duets, and songs. He also publ. a *Méthode de chant* (1809, op.25; rev. ed. As *Méthode complète de chant*, op.40), *Solfège, ou Méthode de musique, Méthode complète de piano,* and *L'Harmonie rendue facile, ou Théorie pratique de cette science* (1835).—NS/LK/DM

Garbin, Edoardo, Italian tenor; b. Padua, March 12, 1865; d. Brescia, April 12, 1943. He studied with Alberto Selva and Vittorio Orefice in Milan. In 1891 he made his operatic debut in Vicenza as Alvaro in *La forza del destino*; also sang in Milan (Teatro dal Verme), Naples, and Genoa. On Feb. 9, 1893, he created the role of Fenton in Verdi's *Falstaff* at La Scala in Milan. Garbin made guest appearances in Rome, Vienna, Berlin, London, Russia, and South America. He married **Adelina Stehle.** He was particularly distinguished in *verismo* roles.—NS/LK/DM

Garbousova, Raya, greatly admired Russian-born American cellist and pedagogue; b. Tiflis, Sept. 25, 1906. She began to study piano as a very small child, and then took up playing a small cello when she was 6. When she was 7, she entered the Tiflis Cons. as a pupil of Konstantin Miniar, and soon thereafter made her first public appearance in Tiflis. After giving concerts in Moscow and Leningrad in 1924, she went to Berlin to pursue her training with Heinz Becker. Following successful concerts in Berlin in 1926 and in Paris in 1927, she had further instruction with Diran Alexanian. She appeared as a soloist with U.S. orchs., and then made her N.Y. recital debut at Town Hall in 1934. In subsequent years, she appeared with orchs. on both sides of the Atlantic and as a recitalist. She lived in Paris until her husband, a Frenchman in the Résistance, was killed in 1943. She eventually made her way to the U.S., where she married the cardiologist Kurt Biss in 1946 and became a naturalized citizen. Garbousova resumed her international career, but she also devoted increasing attention to teaching. In addition to giving masterclasses around the world, she taught at the Hartt School of Music at the Univ. of Hartford (1970–89) and then at Northern Ill. Univ. in DeKalb. She distinguished herself as an interpreter not only of the standard repertory, but also of contemporary music. She gave the premieres of a number of major scores, including the cello concertos of Barber (1946) and Rieti (1956).—NS/LK/DM

García, Eugénie, French soprano and teacher; b. Paris, 1815; d. there, Aug. 12, 1880. She was a pupil of **Manuel (Patricio Rodríguez) García,** who became her husband. After singing in Italy, she appeared at the Paris Opéra-Comique (1840) and in London (1842). Upon separating from her husband, she settled in Paris to teach voice.—NS/LK/DM

García, Manuel (del Popolo Vicente Rodríguez), famous Spanish tenor, singing teacher, and composer, father of **Manuel Patricio Rodríguez García;** b. Seville, Jan. 21, 1775; d. Paris, June 9, 1832. A chorister in the Seville Cathedral at 6, he was taught by Ripa and Almarcha, and at 17 was already well known as a singer, composer, and conductor. After singing in Cadiz, Madrid, and Málaga, he proceeded (1807) to Paris, and sang to enthusiastic audiences at the Théâtre-Italien. In 1809, at his benefit, he sang his own monodrama *El poeta calculista* with extraordinary success. From 1811 to 1816 he was in Italy. On his return to Paris, his disgust at the machinations of Catalani, the manageress of the Théâtre-Italien, caused him to break his engagement and go to London (1817), where his triumphs were repeated. From 1819 to 1824 he was again the idol of the Parisians at the Théâtre-Italien; sang as 1st tenor at the Royal Opera in London (1824) and in 1825 embarked for N.Y. with his wife, his son Manuel, and his daughter Maria (Malibran), and the distinguished artists Crivelli *fils*, Angrisani, Barbieri, and de Rosich; from Nov. 29, 1825, to Sept. 30, 1826, they gave 79 performances at the Park and Bowery theaters in N.Y.; the troupe then spent 18 months in Mexico. García returned to Paris, and devoted himself to teaching and composition. His operas, all forgotten, comprise 17 in Spanish, 18 in Italian, and 8 in French, besides a number never performed, and numerous ballets. He was a preeminently successful teacher, numbering his 2 daughters, **María Malibran** and **Pauline Viardot-García,** and Nourrit, Rimbault, and Favelli among his best pupils.

BIBL.: G. Malvern, *The Great G.s* (N.Y., 1958).—NS/LK/DM

García, Manuel Patricio Rodríguez, distinguished Spanish vocal teacher, son of **Manuel (del Popolo Vicente Rodríguez) García;** b. Madrid, March 17, 1805; d. London, July 1, 1906. He was intended to be a stage singer; in 1825 went to N.Y. with his father, but in 1829 adopted the vocation of a singing teacher (in Paris), with conspicuous success. An exponent of his father's method, he carefully investigated the functions of the vocal organs; in 1855 he invented the laryngoscope, for which the Univ. of Königsberg made him a Dr.Phil. In 1840 he sent to the Academy a *Mémoire sur la voix humaine*, a statement of the conclusions arrived at by various investigators, with his own comments. He was appointed prof. at the Paris Cons. in 1847, but resigned in 1848 to accept a similar position at the London Royal Academy of Music, where he taught uninterruptedly until 1895. Among García's pupils were his first wife, **Eugénie García,** Jenny Lind, Henriette Nissen, and Stockhausen. His *Traité complet de l'art du chant* was publ. in 1847 (Eng. ed., 1870; rev. ed. by García's grandson Albert García as *García's Treatise on the Art of Singing*, London, 1924). He also publ. (in Eng.) *Hints on Singing* (London, 1894).

BIBL.: M. Sterling Mackinlay, *G.: The Centenarian, and His Time* (Edinburgh, 1908); J. Levien, *The G. Family* (London, 1932); G. Malvern, *The Great G.s* (N.Y., 1958).—NS/LK/DM

García Fajer, Francisco Javier, Spanish composer; b. Nalda, 1730; d. Saragossa, Feb. 26, 1809. He lived for some years in Rome as a student and singing teacher, and in 1756 he was appointed maestro at Saragossa Cathedral. His works show a marked contrast to the fugal style prevailing before, being more natural and simple. He wrote the componimento sacro *Il Tobia* (Rome, 1752), and the operas *La finta schiava* (Rome, 1754), *Pompeo Magno in Armenia* (Rome, 1755), *La Pupilla* (Rome, 1755), and *Lo Scultore deluso* (Rome, 1756). He also composed masses and motets, chiefly in 8 parts.

BIBL.: J. Carreras López, *La musica en las catedrales durante el siglo XVIII: F. J. G. "El Españoleto" (1730–1809)* (Saragossa, 1983).—NS/LK/DM

García Mansilla, Eduardo, American-born French- Argentine composer; b. Washington, D.C., March 7, 1870; d. Paris, May 9, 1930. He studied composition with Massenet, Saint-Saëns, and d'Indy in Paris and with Rimsky-Korsakov in St. Petersburg. His opera *Ivan* was produced in St. Petersburg in 1905, and another opera, *La angelica Manuelite*, in Buenos Aires in 1917. He also wrote choruses.—NS/LK/DM

García Navarro, (Luis Antonio)
See **Navarra, (Luis Antonio) García**

Gardano (also **Gardane**), **Antonio,** Italian music publisher and composer; b. 1509; d. Venice, Oct. 28, 1569. He was active as a music publisher in Venice from 1538, where he utilized Attaingnant's single-impression printing method. His output included works by leading Italian composers of his era, including vols. of lute tablatures (from 1546) and keyboard pieces (from 1551). He also publ. his own works, among them *Motetti del frutto* (1538) and *Canzoni franzese* (1539). Following his death, his sons Alessandro (c. 1539-c. 1591) and Angelo (1540–1611) Gardano carried on the business in partnership until 1575. Angelo continued the business in Venice until his death, and his heirs continued publishing under his name until 1677. Alessandro was active as a music publisher in Rome from 1582 until his death.

BIBL.: M. Lewis, *A. G., Venetian Music Printer, 1538–1569: A Descriptive Bibliography and Historical Study* (2 vols., N.Y., 1988, 1997); R. Agee, *The G. Music Printing Firms, 1569–1611* (Rochester, N.Y., 1998).—NS/LK/DM

Gardelli, Lamberto, distinguished Italian conductor; b. Venice, Nov. 8, 1915; d. Munich, July 17, 1998. He studied piano and composition at the Liceo Musicale Rossini in Pesaro, and then completed his training in Rome with Zanella, Ariani, Petrassi, and Bustini. He was an assistant to Serafin in Rome, where he made his conducting debut at the Opera with *La Traviata* in 1944; then he conducted at the Royal Opera in Stockholm (1946–55). From 1955 to 1961 he was conductor of the Danish Radio Sym. Orch., and then conducted at the Hungarian State Opera in Budapest (1961–65) and at the Glyndebourne Festivals (1964–65; 1968). In 1964 he made his first appearance in the U.S. conducting *I Capuleti e i Montecchi* at N.Y.'s Carnegie Hall. On Jan. 30, 1966, he made his Metropolitan Opera debut in N.Y. conducting *Andrea Chénier*; he remained on its roster until 1968. He made his first appearance at London's Covent Garden in 1969 conducting *Otello*, and returned for the 1970–71, 1975–76, and 1979–80 seasons. From 1970 to 1975 he was music director of the Bern City Theater. From 1973 he also conducted at the Royal Opera in Copenhagen. He later was chief conductor of the Munich Radio Orch. (1983–88) and of the Danish Radio Sym. Orch. in Copenhagen (1986–89). Gardelli acquired a notable reputation as an interpreter of the Italian operatic repertory. He himself composed 4 operas.

BIBL.: P. Csák, *A mi L. G.nk* (Budapest, 1996).—NS/LK/DM

Garden, Mary, celebrated Scottish soprano; b. Aberdeen, Feb. 20, 1874; d. Inverurie, Jan. 3, 1967. She went to the U.S. as a child; studied violin and piano; in 1893 she began the study of singing with Mrs. Robinson Duff in Chicago; in 1895 she went to Paris, where she studied with Sbriglia, Bouhy, Trabadello, Mathilde Marchesi, and Lucien Fugere. Her funds, provided by a wealthy patron, were soon depleted, and Sybyl Sanderson introduced her to Albert Carré, director of the Opéra-Comique. Her operatic debut was made under dramatic circumstances on April 10, 1900, when the singer who performed the title role of Charpentier's *Louise* at the Opéra-Comique was taken ill during the performance, and Garden took her place. She revealed herself not only as a singer of exceptional ability, but also as a skillful actress. She subsequently sang in several operas of the general repertoire; also created the role of Diane in Pierné's *La Fille de Tabarin* (Opéra-Comique, Feb. 20, 1901). A historic turning point in her career was reached when she was selected to sing Mélisande in the premiere of Debussy's *Pelléas et Mélisande* (Opéra-Comique, April 30, 1902); she became the center of a raging controversy when Maurice Maeterlinck, the author of the drama, voiced his violent objection to her assignment (his choice for the role was Georgette Leblanc, his common-law wife) and pointedly refused to have anything to do with the production. Garden won warm praise from the critics for her musicianship, despite the handicap of her American-accented French. She remained a member of the Opéra-Comique; also sang at the Grand Opéra, and at Monte Carlo. She made her U.S. debut as Thaïs at the Manhattan Opera House, N.Y. (Nov. 25, 1907), and sang Mélisande there the first U.S. performance of *Pelléas et Mélisande* (Feb. 19, 1908). In 1910 she joined the Chicago Opera Co.; she was its general director for the 1921–22 season, during which the losses mounted to about $1,000,000. She continued to sing at the Chicago Opera until 1931, and then made sporadic operatic and concert appearances until giving her farewell performance at the Paris Opéra-Comique in 1934. In 1939 she settled in Scotland. With L. Biancolli, she publ. *Mary Garden's Story* (N.Y., 1951).

BIBL.: M. Turnbull, *M. G.* (Portland, Ore., 1997). —NS/LK/DM

Gardiner, H(enry) Balfour, English composer, great-uncle of **Sir John Eliot Gardiner;** b. London, Nov. 7, 1877; d. Salisbury, June 28, 1950. He was a pupil of Iwan Knorr in Frankfurt am Main. He taught singing for a short time in Winchester, but then devoted himself to composition. He was also an ardent collector of English folk songs, and his compositions reflect the authentic modalities of the English countryside. He wrote a *Fantasy* for Orch. (1908; not extant), *English Dance* (1904), Sym. in D major (1908; not extant), *News from Wydah* for Soloists, Chorus, and Orch. (1912), piano pieces, and songs. His most successful piece was *Shepherd Fennel's Dance* for Orch. (1911).

BIBL.: S. Lloyd, *H. B. G.* (Cambridge, 1984).—NS/LK/DM

Gardiner, Sir John Eliot, outstanding English conductor, great-nephew of **H(enry) Balfour Gardiner;** b. Fontmell Magna, Dorset, April 20, 1943. As a child, he attended the Bryanston Summer School of Music and later played in the National Youth Orch. He studied history at King's Coll., Cambridge (M.A., 1965) and pursued advanced training in music with Dart at King's Coll., London (1966); a French government scholarship enabled him to study with Boulanger in Paris and Fontainebleau (1966–68). In 1964 he founded the Monteverdi Choir, followed by its complement, the Monteverdi Orch., in 1968. In the latter year, he conducted his own performing edition of Monteverdi's *Vespers* at the London Promanade Concerts. He made his first appearance at the Sadler's Wells Opera in London in 1969 conducting *Die Zauberflöte*. In 1971 he discovered in Paris the MS of Rameau's opera *Abaris, ou Les Boréades*, which he conducted in its concert premiere in London on April 19, 1975, and in its stage premiere at the Aix-en-Provence Festival on July 21, 1982. In 1973 he made his debut at London's Covent Garden conducting Gluck's *Iphigénie en Tauride*. He founded the English Baroque Soloists in 1977, which he conducted in performances utilizing original instruments of the Baroque era. From 1980 to 1983 he was principal conductor of the CBC Orch. in Vancouver. He served as artistic director of the Göttingen Handel Festivals from 1981 to 1990. From 1983 to 1988 he was music director of the Lyons Opera. In 1990 he organized the Orchestre Révolutionaire et romantique, an orch. devoted to performing scores on instruments of the period. He conducted it in Beethoven's 9th Sym. at its U.S. debut in N.Y. in 1996. From 1991 to 1994 he was chief conductor of the North German Radio Sym. Orch. in Hamburg. As a guest conductor, Gardiner has appeared in many of the principal music centers of the world. To commemorate the 250th anniversary of the death of Bach, Gardiner conducted his English Baroque Soloists and Monteverdi Choir on a major tour of Europe in 2000, during which he made various broadcasts and recordings. In 1990 he was made a Commander of the Order of the British Empire. In 1998 he was knighted. His repertoire is immense, ranging from the pre-Baroque to modern eras. His interpretations reflect his penchant for meticulous scholarship while maintaining stimulating performance standards.—**NS/LK/DM**

Gardiner, William, English writer on music; b. Leicester, March 15, 1770; d. there, Nov. 16, 1853. His father, a hosiery manufacturer, was an amateur musician from whom he acquired the rudiments of music. During his travels on the Continent on his father's business he gathered materials for a collection, *Sacred Melodies* (1812–38), adapted to English words from works by Mozart, Haydn, and Beethoven. His book *The Music of Nature* (London, 1832) enjoyed a certain vogue. He also publ. memoirs, *Music and Friends, or Pleasant Recollections of a Dilettante* (3 vols.; I-II, London, 1838; III, 1853) and *Sights in Italy, with some Account of the Present State of Music and the Sister Arts in that Country* (London, 1847).

BIBL.: J. Wilshire, *W. G. of Leicester, 1770–1853* (London, 1970).—**NS/LK/DM**

Gardner, John (Linton), English composer and teacher; b. Manchester, March 2, 1917. He studied with Sir Hugh Allen, Ernest Walker, Thomas Armstrong, and R.O. Morris at Exeter Coll., Oxford (Mus.B., 1939). He pursued his career in London, where he was a répétiteur at Covent Garden, and a tutor (1952–76) and director of music (1965–69) at Morley Coll. He also taught at the Royal Academy of Music (1956–86) and was director of music at St. Paul's Girls' School (1962–75). In 1976 he was made a Commander of the Order of the British Empire. His extensive catalogue of works reveals a fine craftsmanship in an eclectic style ranging from dodecaphony to popular modes of expression.

WORKS: DRAMATIC: Opera: *A Nativity Opera* (1950); *The Moon and Sixpence* (1956; London, May 24, 1957); *The Visitors* (1971; Aldeburgh, June 10, 1972); *Bel and the Dragon* (1973); *Tobermory* (1976). **Musical:** *Vile Bodies* (1960). **Masque:** *The Entertainment of the Senses* (1973; London, Feb. 2, 1974). **Ballet:** *Reflection* (1952); *Dress Rehearsal* (1958). Also incidental music. **ORCH.:** 3 syms.: No. 1 (1950; Cheltenham, July 5, 1951), No. 2 (1985), and No. 3 (1989); *A Scots Overture* (London, Aug. 16, 1954); Piano Concerto No. 1 (1957); *Suite of 5 Rhythms* (1960); *Sinfonia piccola* for Strings (1960); Concerto for Trumpet and Strings (1963); *Occasional Suite* (1968); *An English Ballad* (1969); *3 Ridings Suite* (1970); Sonatina for Strings (1974); *English Suite* for Concert Band (1977); Oboe Concerto (1990). **CHAMBER:** 3 string quartets (1938, 1979, 1986); 2 oboe sonatas (1953, 1986); *Concerto da camera* for Recorder, Violin, Cello, and Harpsichord (1967); Chamber Concerto for Organ and 11 Instruments (1969); *Sonata secolare* for Organ and Brass Quintet (1973); *Sonata da chiesa* for 2 Trumpets and Organ (1977); *Sonatina lirica* for Brass Quintet (1983); Saxophone Quartet (1985); *Pentad* for Recorder Octet (1986); *French Suite* for Saxophone Quartet (1986); *Chanson triste* for Oboe and Piano (1989). Also piano pieces and organ music. **VOCAL:** *Cantiones Sacrae* for Soprano, Chorus, and Orch. (1952); *Jubilate Deo* for Chorus (1957); *The Ballad of the White Horse* for Chorus and Orch. (1958); *Herrick Cantata* for Tenor, Chorus, and Orch. (1960); *A Latter Day Athenian Speaks* for Chorus (1961); *The Noble Heart* for Soprano, Bass, Chorus, and Orch. (1964); *Mass* for Chorus (1965); *Mass* for Mezzo-soprano, Chorus, and Orch. (1983); *A Burns Sequence* for Chorus and Orch. (1993); numerous choral pieces; many songs. —**NS/LK/DM**

Gardner, Samuel, Russian-American violinist and composer; b. Elizavetgrad, Aug. 25, 1891; d. N.Y., Jan. 23, 1984. He went early to the U.S. and studied violin with Felix Winternitz and Franz Kneisel; also studied composition with Goetschius, and later with Loeffler in Boston. He was a member of the Kneisel String Quartet (1914–15), and also played in American orchs. From 1924 to 1941 he taught violin at the Inst. of Musical Art in N.Y. Among his works were a tone poem, *Broadway* (Boston, April 18, 1930), and *Country Moods* for String Orch. (N.Y., Dec. 10, 1946). He publ. *Essays for Advanced Solo Violin* (1960).—**NS/LK/DM**

Garland, Ed Montudi(e) (actually, **Edward Bertram**), bassist; b. New Orleans, La., Jan. 9, 1885; d. Jan. 22, 1980. He worked in parade marching bands, first as a drummer, then on tuba and mellophone. He added double bass to his repertoire and worked with the Imperial Orch. and with John Robichaux in that capacity, while continuing on brass bass in parade work with the Eagle, Security, Excelsior, and Superior bands. He moved to Chicago in 1914. He led his own band on the Orpheum Circuit accompanying Mabel Lee Lane, then returned to Chicago, working with Manuel Perez, Lawrence Duhe, and Freddie Keppard. He joined King Oliver in Chicago and moved to the West Coast with the band (1921); remaining in Calif., he joined Kid Ory, with whom he would play at subsequent intervals over the years (1921–23, 1924–25, 1944–55). He worked with the Black and Tan Orch. (1923–24) and with Mutt Carey (1925–27). From c. 1927 he led his own band in a lengthy residency at the 111 Dance Hall, L.A. He gigged with Jelly Roll Morton in one of the pianist's last performances (1940). Garland continued leading his own groups until rejoining Ory in 1944. He abruptly left to join Andrew Blakeney (1955), then played with Earl Hines in San Francisco (1955–56). He worked with Turk Murphy and Joe Darensbourg, freelanced in Los Angeles (from 1960), and appeared regularly with Blakeney in the mid-1960s. He appeared in the films *Hotel* (1966) and *Young Men of New Orleans* (1969). He continued to play regularly during the 1970s, touring internationally with the Legends of Jazz.—JC/LP

Garland, Judy (originally, **Gumm, Frances Ethel**), vibrant American singer and actress; b. Grand Rapids, Minn., June 10, 1922; d. London, June 22, 1969. Garland was an outstanding star of movie musicals who also enjoyed an extensive career as a concert singer. Her vitality and showmanship were apparent in the 32 feature films in which she appeared between 1936 and 1963, most of them musicals, notably *The Wizard of Oz* (in which she sang "Over the Rainbow") and *A Star Is Born* (in which she sang "The Man That Got Away"). She was the recipient of an Academy Award for her film work, a Tony Award for her stage work, two Grammy Awards for her chart-topping, gold-selling album *Judy at Carnegie Hall*, and several Emmy nominations for her television work, which included her own series.

Garland's parents, Frank Avent Gumm and Ethel Marion Milne Gumm, were former vaudevillians who were running a theater at the time of her birth. She made her stage debut at the age of two on Dec. 26, 1924, in her parents' theater, and thereafter was part of an act with her two older sisters. In the fall of 1926 the family moved to southern Calif., where Garland and her sisters performed locally and on radio. They studied at the Meglin School of Dance starting in 1927, and in 1929 made their first film appearance in the short *The Meglin Kiddie Revue*. In the summer of 1934 they toured the Midwest.

In 1935 one of Garland's older sisters got married, breaking up the act, and Garland successfully auditioned for the MGM film studio, signing a contract on Sept. 27, 1935. There, songwriter/producer Roger Edens became her vocal coach. She performed on the network radio series *The Shell Chateau Hour* on October 26, the first of nearly 200 radio appearances over the next 20 years, though she never had time to host her own show. In November she did a test recording session for Decca Records, but the label did not sign her to her first recording contract until the following year. Her first

contracted recording session came on June 12, 1936; it consisted of "Stompin' at the Savoy" (music by Benny Goodman, Chick Webb, and Edgar Sampson, lyrics by Andy Razaf) and "Swing Mister Charlie" (music and lyrics by J. Russel Robinson, Irving Taylor, and Harry Brooks), which were released on either side of Decca 848 in July.

Garland was loaned out to 20th Century–Fox for her first film, making her feature debut in *Pigskin Parade* in November 1936. She appeared for 16 consecutive weeks on the radio series *Jack Oakie's College* from March to June 1937 while filming her first MGM feature, *Broadway Melody of 1938*, in which she sang a version of "You Made Me Love You (I Didn't Want to Do It)" (music by James V. Monaco, lyrics by Joseph McCarthy) with special lyrics by Roger Edens concerning MGM star Clark Gable. The film began to establish her as a juvenile star upon its release in August. In November she had top billing in *Thoroughbreds Don't Cry*, in which she was paired for the first time with juvenile star Mickey Rooney.

Garland appeared in three films released in 1938 while also continuing to record and to make appearances on such radio shows as *Good News of 1938*. But it was not until the release of her seventh feature, *The Wizard of Oz*, on Aug. 17, 1939, that she achieved major stardom. The film itself was not a commercial success at first, but Garland's Decca recording of "Over the Rainbow" (music by Harold Arlen, lyrics by E. Y. Harburg) competed with Glenn Miller's as the song topped the hit parade in September; it became her signature song, and her initial recording of it was inducted into the Grammy Hall of Fame in 1981. Her stardom was consolidated by the release of *Babes in Arms*, in which she co-starred with Mickey Rooney, in October; in February 1940 she was given a special Academy Award "for her outstanding performance as a screen juvenile during the past year."

The first of the three MGM films in which Garland appeared during 1940 was *Andy Hardy Meets Debutante*, released in July, in which she sang the 1921 song "I'm Nobody's Baby" (music and lyrics by Benny Davis, Milton Ager, and Lester Sandy); her Decca recording of the song peaked in the Top Ten in September. She appeared in another three MGM films in 1941, along with her radio and recording activities. On July 28, 1941, she married composer, arranger, and orchestra leader David Rose, from whom she was divorced in June 1945. She was in only one MGM feature in 1942, the October release *For Me and My Gal*, in which she co-starred with Gene Kelly. Kelly joined her on a Decca recording of the 1917 song "For Me and My Gal" (music by George W. Meyer, lyrics by Edgar Leslie and E. Ray Goetz), and it peaked in the Top Ten in April 1943.

Garland appeared in three more films during 1943 but thereafter tended to star in only one each year. In 1944 that one was the November release *Meet Me in St. Louis*, in which she sang "The Trolley Song" (music and lyrics by Hugh Martin and Ralph Blane); her Decca recording of the song peaked in the Top Ten in December, and Decca's album of songs from the film, in which she was featured, also became a Top Ten hit.

Meet Me in St. Louis was directed by Vincente Minnelli, as was *The Clock,* released in May 1945, in which Garland appeared in a non-singing dramatic role for the first time. On June 15, 1945, Garland married Minnelli. In June she scored a rare hit with a song not featured in one of her films when her duet with Bing Crosby, "Yah-Ta-Ta Yah-Ta-Ta (Talk, Talk, Talk)" (music by James Van Heusen, lyrics by Johnny Burke) reached the Top Ten. She returned to the Top Ten in September with "On the Atchison, Topeka and the Santa Fe" (music by Harry Warren, lyrics by Johnny Mercer), from her forthcoming film *The Harvey Girls,* which was released in January 1946.

Garland gave birth to a daughter, future entertainer Liza May Minnelli, on March 12, 1946. Then she was a guest star in the film biography of Jerome Kern, *Till the Clouds Roll By,* released in December, performing two songs. MGM launched its own record label by releasing a soundtrack album from the film, and it became a Top Ten hit. Garland remained nominally contracted to Decca until 1951, but she did not record for the label after 1947, more frequently being represented by MGM soundtracks of her film performances.

Garland appeared in three MGM films released in 1948, starring in *The Pirate,* with songs by Cole Porter, in May, and in *Easter Parade,* with songs by Irving Berlin, in June, and making a guest appearance in the Richard Rodgers–Lorenz Hart film biography *Words and Music,* released in December, her two songs turning up on the MGM soundtrack album that hit #1 in February 1949. She completed two more films at MGM, *In the Good Old Summertime,* released in August 1949, and *Summer Stock,* released in August 1950 and featuring a Top Ten soundtrack album. But she had become increasingly unreliable due to illness, and she was released from her MGM contract on Sept. 29, 1950. On March 22, 1951, she and Vincente Minnelli divorced.

Garland turned to concert performing with a month-long engagement at the London Palladium beginning April 9, 1951. On Oct. 16, 1951, she reopened the premiere American vaudeville theater, the Palace in N.Y., playing there for 19 weeks, an achievement that earned her a special Tony Award "for an important contribution to the revival of vaudeville." On June 2, 1952, she married Sid (Michael Sidney) Luft, a film producer who had become her manager; their daughter Lorna Luft was born on Nov. 21, 1952, and grew up to become a professional singer.

Garland's triumph as a concert singer led to renewed interest from record and film companies. In 1953 she signed to Columbia Records and began filming a musical remake of *A Star Is Born* at Warner Bros. Released in September 1954, the film had one of the highest grosses of the year; Columbia's *A Star Is Born* album reached the Top Ten; and Garland was nominated for the Academy Award for Best Actress. On March 29, 1955, Garland gave birth to a son, Joey Luft. She toured the western United States and western Canada in July. She signed to Capitol Records and recorded her debut album for the label, *Miss Show Business,* in late August and early September. On Sept. 24 she made her television debut with the live 90-minute special *Ford Star Jubilee,* per-

forming many of the songs from *Miss Show Business,* which was released two days later and became a Top Ten hit. The show earned her an Emmy nomination for Best Female Singer.

Garland repeated many of her recent accomplishments in 1956. She starred in a television special, *The Judy Garland Show,* in April, played in Las Vegas in July, opened an eight-week return engagement at the Palace on Sept. 26, and released a second Capitol album, *Judy,* arranged and conducted by Nelson Riddle, that made the charts in November. In February 1957 she recorded her third Capitol LP, *Alone,* a concept album in the tradition of Frank Sinatra's thematic records, devoted to ballads and arranged and conducted by Gordon Jenkins. Released in May, it made the charts, and she toured around the country for the rest of the year. She continued to record and perform through 1958 and 1959 until November 1959, when she was hospitalized with hepatitis. After a period of convalescence she returned to performing, touring Europe in the last quarter of 1960 and undertaking an extensive American tour that took up all of 1961.

Garland appeared at Carnegie Hall on April 23, 1961, and her performance was recorded for an album, *Judy at Carnegie Hall.* The two-LP set, released in June, hit #1 in September and went gold. It won the Grammy for Album of the Year, and Garland won the Grammy for Best Solo Vocal Performance, Female. In December 1961 she made her first film appearance in seven years in a non-singing role in the film *Judgment at Nuremberg* and was nominated for an Academy Award for Best Supporting Actress.

In 1962, in addition to performing and recording, Garland taped another television special, *The Judy Garland Show,* which was broadcast on Feb. 25 and earned Emmy nominations for the Program of the Year and for Outstanding Program Achievement in the Field of Variety. She starred in two films released in 1963, the drama *A Child Is Waiting,* released in February, and *I Could Go on Singing,* released in May, in which she portrayed a concert singer. Another television special, *Judy Garland,* broadcast on March 19, 1963, earned an Emmy nomination for Outstanding Program Achievement in the Field of Music and led CBS to offer her a musical variety series. The weekly hour-long program, *The Judy Garland Show,* ran on Sunday nights for 26 weeks from Sept. 29, 1963, to March 30, 1964, and earned her an Emmy nomination for Outstanding Performance in a Variety or Musical Program or Series.

Garland returned to concert work after the demise of her television series, touring Australia in May 1964, returning to the London Palladium in November, and spending 1965 on the road in the U.S. On May 20, 1965, she divorced Sid Luft, and on Nov. 14 she married actor Mark Herron. They divorced on April 11, 1967. She did relatively little performing in 1966 but returned to frequent appearances in June 1967. On July 31 she opened a month-long engagement at the Palace recorded by ABC Records for the chart album *Judy Garland at Home at the Palace—Opening Night,* and she continued to tour the U.S. extensively through December and from February to July 1968. She opened an engagement at the Talk of the Town club in London on Dec. 30, 1968. On March 15, 1969, she married Mickey Deans, a nightclub manager. She gave her final performances during a Scandinavian tour in March. She died at 47 in June 1969 of an accidental overdose of barbiturates.

DISC.: *Easter Parade* (1950); *Summer Stock* (1950); *Till the Clouds Roll By* (1950); *Words and Music* (soundtrack; 1950); *Pirate/Summer Stock* (1951); *Judy at the Palace* (1952); *Girl Crazy* (1953); *If You Feel Like Singing, Sing* (1955); *In the Good Old Summertime* (1955); *Miss Show Business* (1955); *Judy* (1956); *Judy Garland with the MGM Orchestra* (1956); *The Wizard of Oz* (soundtrack; 1956); *Alone* (1957); *Harvey Girls* (1957); *Meet Me in St. Louis* (1957); *In Love* (1958); *Garland at the Grove* (1958); *A Star is Born* (1958); *The Letter* (1959); *Judy! That's Entertainment* (1960); *The Magic of Judy Garland* (1961); *Judy at Carnegie Hall* (1961); *The Garland Touch* (1962); *Gay Purr-ee* (1962); *I Could Go on Singing* (1963); *Our Love Letter* (1963); *Just for Openers* (1964); *Live at the London Palladium* (1965); *At Home at the Palace* (1967); *Deluxe Set* (1967).

BIBL.: J. Morella and E. Epstein, *Judy: The Films and Career of Judy Garland* (Secaucus, N.J., 1969); M. Tormé, *The Other Side of the Rainbow with Judy Garland and the Dawn Patrol* (N.Y., 1970); M. Deans and A. Pinchot, *Weep No More, My Lady: Judy Garland by Her Last Husband* (London, 1972); D. Melton, *Judy: A Remembrance* (Hollywood, 1972); A. DiOrio Jr., *Little Girl Lost: The Life and Hard Times of Judy Garland* (New Rochelle, N.Y., 1973); B. Baxter, *The Films of Judy Garland* (Bembridge, Iowa, 1974); A. Edwards, *Judy Garland: A Mortgaged Life* (N.Y., 1974); J. Juneau, *Judy Garland* (1974); D. Dahl and B. Kehoe, *Young J.* (N.Y., 1975); C. Finch, *Rainbow: The Stormy Life of Judy Garland* (N.Y., 1975); G. Frank, *J.* (N.Y., 1975); H. Harnne, ed., *The Judy Garland Souvenir Songbook* (N.Y., 1975); L. Smith, *J., with Love: The Story of Miss Show Business* (London, 1975); J. Meyer, *Heartbreaker: Two Months with Judy Garland* (Garden City, N.Y., 1983); J. Spada with K. Swenson, *Judy and Liza* (Garden City, N.Y., 1983); T. Watson and B. Chapman, *Judy, Portrait of an American Legend* (N.Y., 1986); L. Smith, *My Life over the Rainbow* (1983); E. Coleman, *The Complete Judy Garland* (1990); C. Sanders, *Rainbow's End: The Judy Garland Show* (N.Y., 1990); J. Fricke, *Judy Garland: World's Greatest Entertainer: A Pictorial History of Her Career* (N.Y., 1992); D. Shipman, *Judy Garland: The Secret Life of an American Legend* (N.Y., 1992); B. Nestor, *J.: A Life in Pictures* (1997); L. Luft (her daughter), *Me and My Shadows: A Family Memoir* (N.Y., 1998); R. Piro, *Zing: The Early Life and Career of Judy Garland: A Loving Scrapbook* (1998); E. Vare, ed., *Rainbow: A Star-Studded Tribute to Judy Garland* (1998).—**WR**

Garland, Peter, American composer, publisher, and writer on music; b. Portland, Maine, Jan. 27, 1952. He studied music with James Tenney and Harold Budd, performance art and video with the visual artist Wolfgang Stoerchie, and American literature with the poet Clayton Eshleman at the Calif. Inst. of the Arts (B.F.A., 1972). From 1971 to 1991 he edited and published Soundings Press, which published articles and music by over 120 composers and writers, as well as *Collected Studies* (6 vols.) of Conlon Nancarrow and the *Selected Songs* of Paul Bowles. During the 1970s and the 1990s he was a resident of Mexico, living first in a Zapotec village in Oaxaca, then a Purepecha village in Michoacan, and conducting fieldwork among the Nahua Indians in the Sierra of Puebla and Veracruz. From 1980 to 1991 he lived in Santa Fe, N.Mex., where he directed his own performing ensemble in addition to studying Hispanic and Indian musical traditions in the U.S. Southwest. From late 1991 to 1995 he made an around-the-world journey that took him to 12 countries on 5 continents, resulting in his third book of (yet-unpublished) essays, *Gone Walkabout: Essays 1991–1995*. From 1997 he has lived in Mexico, most currently in southern Veracruz, where in addition to composing, he is working on his fourth book of essays and studying Jarocho music and culture. As a composer, Garland is influenced by native American and Mexican cultures and since the late 1980s has maintained a close working relationship with both New York's Essential Music and the Japanese pianist Aki Takahashi. His works are highly original—spare and lyrical—and often incorporate exotic instruments. In 1991 Essential Music presented a 20-year retrospective concert of his music in N.Y. In addition to editing nearly 30 vols. of contemporary music scores and critical articles through Soundings Press, and innumerable articles for a wide variety of journals, he publ. *Americas: Essays on American Music and Culture 1973–80* (Santa Fe, 1982) and *In Search of Silvestre Revueltas: Essays 1978–1990* (Santa Fe, 1991).

WORKS: CHAMBER: *Apple Blossom* for 2 to 4 Marimbas (1972); Piano, Bass Drum, and Bullroarer (1972–73); *Three Songs of Mad Coyote* for 8 Tom-toms, 2 Bass Drums, 2 Pianos, 2 Bullroarers, and Lion's Roar (1973); *Obstacles of Sleep* for 2 Sirens, Amplified Ratchet, Piccolo, Lion's Roar, and 2 Pianos (1973); *Hummingbird Songs 1–10* for Cupped Bands, Voices, Handclaps, Rasps, Dijeridu, Whistling, and 3 Log Drums(1974–76); *Matachin Dances* for 2 Violins and Gourd Rattles (1980–81); *Three Valentines* for Violin (1983); *Monkey* for 2 Pianos and Vibraphone (1983–84); *Sones de Flor* for Violin, Piano, Vibraphone, and 3 Tuned Drums (1984–85); *Cantares de la Frontera* for Harp (1986); String Quartet No. 1, "In Praise of Poor Scholars" (1986) and No. 2, "Crazy Cloud" (1994); *The Club Nada Polka* for Accordion (1987–88; also for Violin, Cello, and Accordion); *Old Men of the Fiesta—4 Dances* for Violin, Harp, and 3 Percussionists (1989); *Nana & Victorio* for Percussion (1991); *Where Beautiful Feathers Abound* for Piano, Violin, Viola, and Cello (1991–92); *I Have Had to Learn the Simplest Things Last* for Piano and 3 Percussionists (1993); *Love Songs* for Violin, Piano, Marimbula, and Rattles (1993); *Another Sunrise* for 2 Pianos and 4 Percussionists (1995); *Dancing on Water* for Chiapan Marimba and Clarinet (1999); *Palm Trees—Pine Trees* for Flute, Cello, Piano, and 2 Percussionists (1999). **Piano:** *Four Short Pieces* For Piano (1971–76); *A Song* For Piano (1971); *The Days Run Away* For Piano (1971); *Three Dawns* For Piano (1981–82); *Jornada Del Muerto* For Piano (1987); *Goddess of Liberty—"you've Got to Hide Your Love Away"* For Piano (1989); *Walk in Beauty* For Piano (1989); *Bush Radio Calling* For Piano (1992); *Bright Angel—hermetic Bird* For Piano (1996). **VOCAL:** *Dreaming of Immortality in a Thatched Cottage* For 3 Voices, Angklung, Marimba, Harpsichord, Wooden Clappers, and Log Drum (1977); *Romance (After Anne Waldman)* For Narrator, Muted Trumpet, Piano, and Percussion (1985); *A Season in the Congo* For Chorus, Trumpet, Bass Clarinet, Harp, Bass, Piano, Rattles, and Double Bells (1986–87); *The Rogue Dalton Songs* For Tenor, Trumpet, Bass Clarinet, 2 Violins, Harp, Piano, and 4 Percussionists (1988); *Drinking Wine* For Mezzo-soprano and Piano (1989); *A Green Pine* For Soprano and Accordion (1990); *Three Folksongs For Makiko* For Woman's Voice and Piano (1994–96); (7) *Songs of Exile and Wine* For Soprano and Piano

(1999). **M I X E D M e d i a :** *The Conquest of Mexico,* shadow play for Dancers, Shadow Puppets, Soloists, Recorder, Harp, Harpsichord, and Percussion (1977–80). **O T H E R :** Numerous improvisational works, both solo and in collaboration with others, including *Monkey Saves the World From Nuclear Destruction* (1982), *The Bone Show* for Solo Performers, Poet, and Puppeteer (1987), *Dead Sheldons* (1991), and *Calling All Tengu* (2000).—**NS/LK/DM**

Garlandia, Johannes de, significant music theorist who flourished in the 13th century. He was on the faculty of the Univ. of Paris. His treatise *De plana musica* is a study on plainchant. In his important treatise *De musica mensurabili positio* (ed. by E. Reimer, 2 vols., Wiesbaden, 1972), he discusses mensural music, making it the first such work to explore in detail rhythm and notation. Through his theoretical treatment of rhythmic modes and Notre Dame polyphonic writing, he made possible the development of the mensural system and the late medieval polyphonic style.

BIBL.: R. Rasch, *I. d.G. en de ontwikkeling van de voor-Franconsiche notatie* (Brooklyn, 1969; with summaries in Eng. and Ger.).—**NS/LK/DM**

Garner, Erroll, "The Elf" (Louis), pop-jazz pianist and composer; b. Pittsburgh, June 15, 1921; d. Los Angeles, Jan. 2, 1977. He played piano regularly over KDKA, Pittsburgh, at age 7 with the Candy Kids; as an adolescent, he played on riverboats cruising the Allegheny River. He became a featured pianist in night-clubs and restaurants. Moving to N.Y. in 1944, he formed a trio there in 1946. In 1948, he made his first trip to Paris. His *Concert by the Sea,* recorded live in Carmel, Calif. in 1955, became one of jazz's best-selling records of all time. He made his first European tour in 1957–58, and would make many more appearances there through the 1960s. In the 1950s and 1960s, he regularly appeared on television. Although less popular in the 1970s, he still was very active, touring South America (1970) and the Far East (1973). He made some appearances with symph. orchs. through the U.S. in 1974–75, but then contracted pneumonia in early 1975, which two years later led to his death.

Garner was self-taught and unable to read music, hiring others to write down his compositions. His irrepressible humor, melodic gift, and swing—with a pronounced lag between hands—contributed to his great popularity. He sat high at the piano so that his fingers pointed down at the keys. He often began pieces with elaborate and suspenseful introductions, one of several ways in which the influence of Earl Hines was evident. His trademark whimsical style appealed particularly to French jazz critics, who called him the "Picasso of the Piano" and, alluding to his digital dexterity, the "Man with 40 Fingers." "Misty" (1954) has been repeatedly honored by ASCAP as one of the most played standards over the decades, and played a narrative role in the film *Play Misty for Me,* directed by Clint Eastwood (1972). Garner's recording of the song was voted into the NARAS Hall of Fame in 1991. In 1971 the Republic of Mali issued a postage stamp in his honor. Among his other 200 songs are "Dreamy," "Solitaire,"

and "That's My Kick." Garner's brother, Linton (b. Greensboro, N.C., March 25, 1915), is also a jazz pianist, although he plays in a totally different style than Erroll; he has mostly been active in Canada since the mid-1970s.

DISC.: *Overture to Dawn, Vols. 1–5* (1944); *Yesterdays* (1944); *Passport to Fame* (1944); *Serendade in Blue* (1944); *Separate Keyboards* (1945); *Erroll Garner and Billy Taylor* (1945); *The Elf* (1945); *Savoy Sessions* (1945); *Serenade to Laura* (1945); *Gone with Garner* (1945); *Jazz Round Midnight: Erroll Garner* (1945); *Cocktail Time* (1947); *Penthouse Serenade* (1949); *Rhapsody* (1949); *Garnering* (1949); *Long Ago and Far Away* (1950); *Gone-Garner-Gonest* (1951); *Gems* (1951); *Garnerland* (1951); *Solo Flight* (1952); *E. G. Plays "Misty"* (1954); *Mambo Moves Garner* (1954); *Erroll!* (1954); *Solo* (1955); *Solitaire* (1955); *Concert by the Sea* (1955); *Afternoon of an Elf* (1955); *He's Here! He's Gone! He's Garner* (1956); *Most Happy Piano* (1956); *Other Voices* (1956); *Soliloquy* (1957); *Another Voice* (1957); *Paris Impressions, Vol. 1, 2* (1958); *Erroll Garner Plays Gershwin and Kern* (1958); *Dreamstreet* (1959); *The One and Only Erroll Garner* (1960); *Dancing on the Ceiling* (1961); *Easy to Love* (1961); *One World Concert* (1963); *Campus Concert* (1964); *A Night at the Movies* (1964); *That's My Kick* (1966); *Now Playing* (1966); *Seeing Is Believing* (1967); *Up in Erroll's Room* (1968); *Gemini* (1971); *Feeling Is Believing* (1971); *Magician* (1974).—**NS/MM**

Garreta, Julio, Catalan composer; b. San Feliu, March 12, 1875; d. there, Dec. 2, 1925. Entirely self-taught, he learned piano and composition. He wrote a great number of "sardanas" (the Catalan national dance). A friendship with Casals stimulated several larger works, including his *Impressions symphoniques* for String Orch., which was performed in Barcelona on Oct. 29, 1907. His *Suite Empordanesa* for Orch. received 1st prize at the Catalan Festival in 1920. He also wrote a Cello Sonata, a Piano Sonata, and a Piano Quartet. —**NS/LK/DM**

Garrett, Donald (Rafael), avant-garde jazz bassist, clarinetist, and flutist; b. El Dorado, Ark., Feb. 28, 1932; d. Champaign, Ill., Aug. 14, 1989. While studying at Du Sable H.S., Chicago, he met Sun Ra, Richard Abrams, Johnny Griffin, Roland Kirk, Eddie Harris, and John Gilmore. He was performing professionally in 1955 when he met John Coltrane while the latter was touring with Miles Davis. The two performed together; Garrett played recordings of Indian music for Coltrane that influenced the latter. He played with Ira Sullivan during the early 1960s, and recorded with Sullivan, Kirk, and Harris (1960–62). With Abrams he co-founded the Experimental Band (1961), forerunner of AACM. Moving to San Francisco (1964), he organized concerts, made instruments, and taught; one protégé was bassist and flutist Bill Douglass, who noted Garrett's emphasis on long, sustained tones. He recorded with Archie Shepp, and performed at San Francisco's Both/And club in a group with Andrew Hill, Sam Rivers, and Oliver Johnson, as well as Leon Thomas. He played concerts and recorded with Coltrane on the West Coast (1965). In Paris in 1971, he worked with Frank Wright and Jean-Luc Ponty, among others. In the late 1970s, he began an association with singer-multi-instrumentalist Zuzann Fasteau, whom he subsequently married. Working together as the Sea Ensemble, they toured widely, including the Democratic Republic of Congo, Senegal, Morocco, Yugoslavia, Haiti, and India.

DISC.: *We Move Together* (1974).—LP

Garrett, Kenny, jazz saxophonist and flutist; b. Detroit, Oct. 9, 1960. His father was an amateur tenor saxophonist. He intended to study film composing at Berklee but instead joined the big bands of Mercer Ellington and Thad Jones–Mel Lewis. After attending Rutgers Univ., he was a member of OTB, a band put together under the auspices of Blue Note Records. In the early 1980s, he played with Joanne Brackeen, Art Blakey, Woody Shaw, and Freddie Hubbard. In 1986 he began touring with Miles Davis, continuing until Davis's death in 1991. Other than performances with Sting in South Africa, he has since worked primarily as a leader. A stint in Indonesia (1996) inspired his composition "Delta-Bali Blues." He was voted Alto Saxist of the Year in *Down Beat*'s 1996 Readers Poll. In 1999 alone he played in several U.S. cities as well as Germany, Scotland, Tunisia, France, and Turkey. He played on soundtracks for *Love Jones* and *Great White Hype*, and acted and played in HBO's *Subway Stories*.

DISC.: *Introducing* (1984); *Garrett 5* (1988); *Prisoner of Love* (1989); *African Exchange Student* (1990); *Black Hope* (1992); *Triology* (1995); *Threshold* (1995); *Pursuance: The Music of John Coltrane* (1996) *Simply Said* (1999).—LP

Garrett, Lesley, English soprano; b. Thorne, Doncaster, April 10, 1955. She studied at the Royal Academy of Music in London and pursued postgraduate studies at the National Opera Studio. In 1979 she was co-winner of the Kathleen Ferrier Memorial Competition. After making her operatic debut with the English National Opera in London in 1980 as Alice in *Le comte Ory*, she sang Dorinda in Handel's *Orlando* that year at the Wexford Festival. In 1984 she made her first appearance at the Gyndebourne Festival as Damigella in *L'incoronazione de Poppea*. She returned to the English National Opera in 1984 as its principal soprano, winning praise for her appearances in such roles as Susanna in 1990, Zerlina in 1992, and Euridice in 1997. Her other roles of note included Despina, Adele, Oscar, Musetta, Janáček's Bystrouška, Weill's Jenny, and Tippett's Bella. As a guest artist, she appeared in Geneva, Florence, Moscow, St. Petersburg, and other European operatic centers. She also was engaged as a concert artist in her homeland and abroad.—NS/LK/DM

Garrido, Pablo, Chilean composer and ethnomusicologist; b. Valparaiso, March 26, 1905; d. Santiago, Sept. 14, 1982. He studied in Santiago, conducted concerts of Chilean music, and gave lectures. He publ. a valuable monograph, *Biografia de la Cueca Chilena* (Santiago, 1942). He composed an opera, *La sugestion* (Santiago, Oct. 18, 1961), a ballet, *El Guerrillero* (1963), *Rapsodia chilena* for Piano and Orch. (1938), Piano Concerto (1950), *Fantasia antillana* for Cello and Orch. (1950), *13 & 13* for String Quartet (1951), piano pieces, and songs based on Chilean folklore.—NS/LK/DM

Garrison, Jimmy (actually, **James Emory**), jazz bassist; father of **Matthew Justin Garrison;** b. Miami, Fla., March 3, 1934; d. N.Y., April 7, 1976. His family moved to Philadelphia when he was a child; there he studied clarinet. During his high school years, he switched to playing bass. He worked locally with Cal Massey, the Tommy Monroe Big Band (with John Coltrane as a guest in late 1956), and Coltrane and McCoy Tyner (1957). He moved to N.Y. (1958), where he played with Tony Scott, Curtis Fuller, Benny Golson, Lennie Tristano, Bill Evans (in the pianist's first trio after leaving Miles Davis, with Philly Joe Jones (1958), Kenny Dorham (1959–60), and Ornette Coleman (1961). He first played with Coltrane's group on the renowned Village Vanguard 1961 dates, sometimes as sole bassist, at other times with Reggie Workman. He was a mainstay of the Coltrane quartet from then on, with one interruption, until the saxophonist's death (1967). He formed trio with Hampton Hawes (1966), toured with Elvin Jones and Archie Shepp, and was active in teaching. He died of lung cancer in 1976. His widow and daughter are dancers; his son, Matthew Justin Garrison, is also a bassist.—LP

Garrison, Jon, American tenor; b. Higgensville, Mo., Dec. 11, 1944. He was educated at the Univ. of N.H. (B.A., 1966) and at N.Y.U. (M.A., 1968), and also pursued private vocal training with Arthur Hackett in Durham, N.H. (1965–66), and Raymond Buckingham (1969–75) and Bonnie Hamilton (1990–99) in N.Y. In 1974 he was engaged to sing a minor role at the Metropolitan Opera in N.Y., returning in 1975 to sing Rinuccio and in 1976 Tamino. In 1977 he appeared as Ferrando at the Santa Fe Opera, and in 1978 as Ramiro in *La Cenerentola* in Spoleto, Italy, and as Don Ottavio at the Metropolitan Opera. He made his debut as a soloist with the N.Y. Phil. under Kostelanetz's direction in 1979, and subsequently sang with the Cleveland Orch., the San Francisco Sym., the Boston Sym. Orch., the Philadelphia Orch., the Los Angeles Phil., the St. Louis Sym. Orch., and various other orchs. In 1982 he made his first appearance at the N.Y.C. Opera as Admete in *Alceste*, and subsequently sang there frequently until 1990. He appeared as Nadir at the Théâtre du Châtelet in Paris in 1983, and in 1984 as Des Grieux in Cincinnati. His recital debut followed in 1985 at Ore. State Univ. in Corvalis, the same year he sang Ferrando at the Metropolitan Opera, where he returned as Roméo in 1986. He portrayed Alfredo at the Washington (D.C.) Opera in 1988. In 1993 he was engaged as Lensky at the Pittsburgh Opera. After singing Desportes in *Die Soldaten* at the English National Opera in London in 1996, he appeared as Eisenstein at the Metropolitan Opera in 1998. He sang Pedro in MacMillan's *Inés de Castro* at the Scottish Opera in Glasgow in 1999.—NS/LK/DM

Garrison, Lucy McKim, American collector of slave songs; b. Philadelphia, Oct. 30, 1842; d. West Orange, N.J., May 11, 1877. During a visit to the S.C. Sea Islands in 1862, she collected the slave songs of the freedmen she met. With her husband, Wendell Phillips Garrison, and William Francis Allen and Charles Pickard Ware, she publ. the valuable book *Slave Songs of the United States* (1867).—NS/LK/DM

Garrison, Mabel, American soprano; b. Baltimore, April 24, 1886; d. N.Y., Aug. 20, 1963. She attended Western Md. Coll. and then pursued vocal training with Heinendahl and Minetti at the Peabody Cons. of Music in Baltimore (1909–11), and in N.Y. with Saenger (1912–14) and Witherspoon (1916). In 1908 she married the composer George Siemonn. On April 18, 1912, she made her operatic debut under her married name as Philine in *Mignon* with the Aborn Opera Co. in Boston. On Feb. 15, 1914, she first sang at the Metropolitan Opera in a concert; her stage debut there followed as a Flower Maiden in *Parsifal* on Nov. 26, 1914, with her formal debut coming the next day as Frasquita. She continued to sing at the Metropolitan Opera until her farewell as Lucia on Jan. 22, 1921. In 1921 she made guest appearances at the Berlin State Opera, the Vienna State Opera, and the Cologne Opera, and then launched a concert tour of the globe. After singing with the Chicago Opera (1925–26), she taught at Smith Coll. (1933–39). Among her finest roles were the Queen of the Night, Rosina, Gilda, Urbain, Martha, and the Queen of Shemakha. In her recitals, she often included songs by her husband, who frequently appeared as her accompanist.—NS/LK/DM

Garrison, Matt(hew Justin), jazz bassist; son of **Jimmy Garrison;** b. N.Y., June 2, 1970 After his father's death (1976), his mother Maya, a dancer, relocated to Rome, Italy, where he began to study piano and bass guitar. In 1988 he returned to the U.S. and lived and studied with his godfather, Jack DeJohnette, for two years; he also studied with Dave Holland. In 1989 he won the Louis Armstrong Award. He soon began gigging with Gary Burton, Bob Moses, Betty Carter, Mike Gibbs, and Lyle Mays. He has recorded and toured with many different modern bandleaders.—LP

Gary Lewis and The Playboys, 1960s era pop act (f. 1964). **MEMBERSHIP:** Gary Lewis, voc., drm. (b. N.Y., July 31, 1946); Alan Ramsey, gtr. (b. N.J., July 27, 1943); John West, gtr. (b. Unrichville, Ohio, July 31, 1939); David Walker, kybd. (b. Montgomery, Ala., May 12, 1943); David Costell, bs. (b. Pittsburgh, Pa., March 15, 1944).

Gary Lewis is the son of noted comedian and actor Jerry Lewis. Not knowing of his famous parentage, producer Snuff Garrett discovered his band at one of their regular gigs at Disneyland. Garrett and his cohort, musician Leon Russell, took the band under their wing and started producing them. The hits started coming immediately, fast and furious. Their debut single was a song with the sprightly beat and harmonies similar to the Beatles; "This Diamond Ring" topped the pop charts and went gold. It remains an evergreen on most oldies stations.

This began a phenomenal run for the band through the 1960s. The group had four more Top Ten hits in 1965, including "Count Me In" (#2), "Save Your Heart for Me" (#2 pop, #1 adult contemporary), "Everybody Loves a Clown" (#4), and "She's Just My Style" (#3). As a live attraction, they sold out houses around the world, and were especially popular in the Philippines,

where they sold out an 18,000-seat venue for 24 performances. They appeared on the *Ed Sullivan Show* five times between 1965 and 1967. In 1966, the group landed four more Top 20 hits: "Sure Gonna Miss Her" (#9), "Green Grass" (#8), "My Heart's Symphony" (#13), and "(You Don't Have To) Paint Me a Picture" (#15). Lewis was drafted, but put some material into the can before he went into the Army for two years. "Where Will the Words Come From" topped out at #21 and "Girls in Love" barely scratched the Top 40 at #39. A leftover from a 1965 session, "Sealed with a Kiss," rose to #19 in 1968.

By the time he got out of the service, pop music had passed him by. Although he had no more hits, his music remained in the pop culture consciousness. "My Heart's Symphony" and "Count Me In" made the U.K. Top Ten during the 1970s. "She's Just My Style" became the basis for an automobile advertisement late in the 1980s. In 1989, he played himself in the NBC movie *My Boyfriend's Back.* The group, although with new personnel save for Lewis, continues to do well on the oldies circuit.

DISC.: *This Diamond Ring* (1965); *A Session with Gary Lewis & The Playboys* (1965); *Everybody Loves a Clown* (1965); *She's Just My Style* (1966); *Playboys* (1967); *Listen* (1967); *(You Don't Have To) Paint Me a Picture* (1967); *New Directions* (1967); *Close Cover Before Playing* (1968); *Gary Lewis Now!* (1968); *Rhythm* (1969); *Rhythm of the Rain* (1969); *I'm on the Right Road Now* (1969); *Everybody Loves a Clown/She's Just My Style...* (1992); *Gary Lewis & The Playboys* (1992).—HB

Gary Puckett and The Union Gap, poprockers of the late 1960s. **MEMBERSHIP:** Gary Puckett, voc., gtr. (b. Hibbing, Minn., Oct. 17, 1942); Kerry Chater, bs.; Gary Withem, kybd.; Dwight Bement, sax.; Paul Wheatbread, drm.

Starting out in 1967 as a bar band, these young musicians took to wearing Civil War uniforms, a good match during their shows for the slightly overwrought, dramatic vocals of lead singer Gary Puckett. They started out as The Outcasts, but changed their name to The Union Gap, after a town in Wash. They were quickly signed by Columbia and by the end of 1967 they were on the charts with "Woman, Woman," which rose to #4 and went gold; the *Woman Woman* album hit #22. They followed this with "Young Girl," which stayed at #2 for three weeks, going gold, while the *Young Girl* album went gold and peaked at #21.

Puckett became the focal point of the group, which became more of a live band as the singles became increasingly orchestrated. By the time its third hit, "Lady Willpower," went gold and hit #2 in the summer of 1968, the group was known as Gary Puckett and The Union Gap. Three months later, "Over You" rose to #7 and went gold as well, their fourth gold single in a row. The *Incredible* album rose to #20. During 1968, they sold more records than any other recording act. By 1969, however, the group began to lose momentum. "Don't Give in to Him" peaked at #15. Their final hit, "This Girl Is a Woman Now," peaked at #9. By 1971, the group had disbanded. Chater continued writing, landing hits like "I Know a Heartache When I See One" with Jennifer Warnes. Puckett became a major player on the

1231

nostalgia circuit, touring with Flo and Eddie on the Happy Together Tour and opening for The Monkees reunion in the late 1980s. He continues to record, but strictly for fans.

DISC.: *Young Girl* (1968); *Incredible* (1968); *Woman, Woman* (1968); *The New Gary Puckett and The Union Gap Album* (1970); *The Gary Puckett Album* (1971); *Lady Willpower* (1972); *As It Stands* (1995); *Europa* (1998).—**HB**

Garzone, George, jazz saxophonist; b. Sept. 23, 1950, Cambridge, Mass. He received a bacherlor's degree from Berklee, where he met Joe Lovano, who became a close associate. Based in Boston for most of his life, he now spends about half his time in N.Y. He taught at Tufts Univ. (1985–87) and is now Associate Professor of Woodwinds at Berklee; he also teaches improvisation and jazz studies at the NEC. He is a co-founder of The Fringe, a cooperative pianoless trio that performs regularly in the Boston area and has toured Portugal. He has also toured with George Russell and worked with many other contemporary jazz players. During the 1990s, he has turned his attention to jazz theory, working on a system he calls the "Cross Intervallic Triadic Approach."

DISC.: *Return of the Neanderthal Man* (1989); *It's Time for the Fringe* (1992); *Four and Two's* (1996).—**LP**

Gascongne, Mathieu, French composer and priest who flourished in the early 16th century. He was a magister and priest in the Cambrai diocese (1518), and may also have been active at the French royal court. His extant works comprise eight masses, two Magnificats, 19 motets, and a number of chansons. Some of his sacred music appeared in anthologies publ. by Pierre Attaingnant (1534–35).—**LK/DM**

Gasdia, Cecilia, Italian soprano; b. Verona, Aug. 14, 1960. She studied in Verona. After winning the Maria Callas competition of the RAI in 1981, she made her operatic debut as Bellini's Giulietta in Florence. In 1982 she made her first appearance at Milan's La Scala as Anna Bolena, and also sang in Perugia and Naples. She made her debut at the Paris Opéra in 1983 as Anais in Rossini's *Moïse*. In 1985 she made her U.S. debut as Gilda in a concert performance of *Rigoletto* in Philadelphia. In 1986 she sang for the first time at the Chicago Lyric Opera and at the Metropolitan Opera in N.Y. During the 1991–92 season, she was engaged as Adina in Chicago, Nedda in Rome, and Elena in *La Donna del Lago* at La Scala. She portrayed Semiramide in Pesaro in 1994. In 1997 she sang Marguerite in Zürich. —**NS/LK/DM**

Gasparini, Francesco eminent Italian composer and pedagogue; b. Camaiore, near Lucca, March 5, 1668; d. Rome, March 22, 1727. He became a member of the Accademia Filarmonica in Bologna in 1685, then studied with Legrenzi in Venice in 1686. He subsequently went to Rome (1689), where he became a member of the Accademia di Santa Cecilia; he may have received further instruction from Corelli and Pasquini. In 1701 he became maestro di coro of the Ospedale della Pietà in

Venice. In 1713 Gasparini returned to Rome, where he became maestro di cappella of S. Lorenzo in Lucina in 1717. He was appointed to the same position at St. John Lateran in 1725, but ill health prevented him from assuming his duties. Gasparini distinguished himself as a composer of both secular and sacred music; he wrote about 50 operas in all. He was also an esteemed teacher, numbering Domenico Scarlatti, Quantz, and Benedetto Marcello among his students. He publ. the valuable treatise *L'armonico pratico al cimbalo* (Venice, 1708; many subsequent eds.; Eng. tr. by F. Stillings as *The Practical Harmonist at the Keyboard*, New Haven, 1963).

WORKS: DRAMATIC Opera (all 1st perf. in Venice unless otherwise given): *Il Roderico* (Rome, Jan. 25, 1694); *L'Ajace* (Rome, 1697); *Mirena e Floro* (Naples, 1699); *Tiberio Imperatore d'Oriente* (1702); *Gli imenei stabiliti dal caso* (Dec. 23, 1702); *Il più fedel fra I vassalli* (Feb. 3, 1703); *Il miglior d'ogni amore per il peggiore d'ogni odio* (Nov. 6, 1703); *La fede tradita e vendicata* (Jan. 5, 1704); *La maschera levata al vitio* (1704); *La Fredegonda* (Dec. 24, 1704); *Ambleto* (Carnival 1705); *Il principato custodito dalla frode* (Jan. 31, 1705); *Statira* (Feb. 2, 1705); *Antioco* (Oct. 30, 1705); *Flavio Anicio Olibrio* (Carnival 1707); *Anfitrione* (1707); *L'amor generoso* (1707); *Taican Rè della Cina* (1707); *Engelberta* (Carnival 1708); *Atenaide* (Vienna, Carnival 1709; Act 1 by A. S. Fiore, Act 2 by A. Caldara, and Act 3 by Gasparini); *Sesostri Rè d'Egitto* (Carnival 1709); *La ninfa Apollo* (Feb. 12, 1709); *Alciade, overo La violenza d'amore* (Bergamo, 1709; Act 1 by Gasparini, Act 2 by C. F. Pollarolo, and Act 3 by F. Ballarotti); *La principessa fedele* (1709); *Tamerlano* (1710); *L'amor tirannico* (1710); *Merope* (Dec. 26, 1711); *Costantino* (1711); *Amor vince l'odio, overo Timocrate* (Florence, Carnival 1715); *Il tartaro nella Cina* (Reggio Emilia, 1715); *Il comando non inteso ed ubbedito* (Florence, 1715); *Ciro* (Rome, Carnival 1716); *Teodosio ed Eudossa* (Braunschweig, Sept. 12, 1716; in collaboration with J. Fux and A. Caldara); *Il trace in catena* (Rome, Carnival 1716–17); *Intermezzi in derisione della setta maomettana* (Rome, Carnival 1717?); *Pirro* (Rome, Carnival 1717); *Il gran Cid* (Naples, Carnival 1717); *Democrito* (Turin, Carnival 1718); *Lucio Vero* (Rome, Carnival 1719); *Astianatte* (Rome, Carnival 1719); *L'oracolo del fato* (Vienna, 1719); *La pace fra Seleuco e Tolomeo* (Milan, Jan. 8, 1720); *Nino* (Reggio Emilia, 1720; Act 1 by G. M. Capelli, Act 2 by Gasparini, and Act 3 by A. M. Bononcini); *L'avaro* (Florence, 1720?); *Il Faramondo* (Rome, Dec. 26, 1720); *Dorinda* (Rome, Carnival 1723); *Gl'equivoci d'amore e d'innocenza* (1723); *Tigrane* (Rome, Jan. 12, 1724). **VOCAL: Oratorios:** *Santa Maria egittiaca, piacere, pentimento, e Lucifero* (n.d.); *Moisé liberato dal Nilo* (Vienna, 1703?); *L'Atalia* (n.d.); *La nascita di Cristo* (1724); *Le nozze di Tobia* (1724). **OTHER:** *Cantate da camera a voce sola*, op.1 (Rome, 1695); cantatas; arias; masses; motets.—**NS/LK/DM**

Gasparini, Quirino, Italian composer; b. Gandino, near Bergamo, 1721; d. Turin, Sept. 30, 1778. He studied with G. A. Fioroni in Milan, and later was a student of Martini. After pursuing his career in various Italian music centers, he was appointed maestro di cappella at Turin Cathedral in 1760. During Mozart's travels in Italy in 1771, he met Gasparini. Gasparini was held in high esteem by his contemporaries. He wrote the operas *Artaserse* (Milan, Dec. 26, 1756) and *Mitridate re di Ponto* (Turin, Jan. 31, 1767), the latter serving as inspiration for Mozart's opera. His motet *Adoramus te,*

K.327/Anh.A10 was attributed to Mozart until H. Spies established it as a work by Gasparini in 1922. His output included much sacred music and a number of instrumental pieces.—**LK/DM**

Gasparo da Salò (family name, **Bertolotti**),

Italian instrument maker; b. Polpenazzi (baptized in Salò, May 20), 1540; d. Brescia (buried), April 14, 1609. He went to Brescia in 1562, and settled there as a maker of viols, viole da gamba, and contrabass viols, which gained much celebrity; his violins were less valued. His pupils were his eldest son, Francesco, Giovanni Paolo Maggini, and Giacomo Lafranchini. Dragonetti's favorite double bass was an altered "viola contrabassa" of Gasparo's.

BIBL.: V. Rhò-Guerriero, *G. d.S.* (Rome, 1892); M. Butturini, *G. d.S.: Studio critico* (Salò, 1901); A. Mucchi, *G. d.S.* (Milan, 1940).—**NS/LK/DM**

Gassmann, Florian Leopold, important Bohe-

mian composer; b. Brux, May 3, 1729; d. Vienna, Jan. 20, 1774. He studied voice, violin, and harp with Johann Woborschil (Jan Voboril), the regens chori in Brux; his father opposed his interest in music, so he ran away from home, eventually making his way to Italy, where he may have studied with Padre Martini in Bologna. His first opera, *Merope*, was given in Venice in 1757. After serving Count Leonardo Veneri there, he was invited to Vienna to become ballet composer at the court in 1763. He soon established himself as an opera composer, gaining fame with his comic operas *L'amore artigiano* (Vienna, April 26, 1767) and *La Contessina* (Mahrisch-Neustadt, Sept. 3, 1770). In 1772 he was appointed court composer and also founded and served as 1st vice-president of the Tonkunstler-Sozietät, a benevolent society for musicians. In addition to his operas, he distinguished himself as an accomplished symphonist. He was highly esteemed by Mozart, Gerber, Burney, and Salieri, the last having been his student in Vienna. His 2 daughters, Maria Anna Fux (b. Vienna, 1771; d. there, Aug. 27, 1852) and (Maria) Therese Rosenbaum (b. Vienna, April 1, 1774; d. there, Sept. 8, 1837), were pupils of Salieri; both were active as singers.

WORKS: DRAMATIC Opera: *Merope* (Venice, Carnival 1757; only the overture and Act 1 extant); *Issipile* (Venice, Carnival 1758); *Gli Uccellatori*, dramma giocoso (Venice, Carnival 1759); *Filosofia ed amore*, dramma giocoso (Venice, Carnival 1760); *Catone in Utica* (Venice, 1761; only 1 aria extant); *Un Pazzo ne fa cento*, dramma giocoso (Venice, 1762); *L'Olimpiade* (Vienna, Oct. 18, 1764); *Il trionfo d'amore*, azione teatrale (Vienna, Jan. 25, 1765); *Achille in Sciro* (Venice, 1766); *Il Viaggiatore ridicolo*, dramma giocoso (Vienna, May 25, 1766); *L'amore artigiano*, dramma giocoso (Vienna, April 26, 1767); *Amore e Psiche* (Vienna, Oct. 5, 1767); *La notte critica*, dramma giocoso (Vienna, Jan. 5, 1768); *L'opera seria*, commedia per musica (Vienna, 1769); *Ezio* (Rome, Carnival 1770); *La Contessina*, drama giocoso (Mährisch-Neustadt, Sept. 3, 1770; ed. in Denkmäler der Tonkunst in Österreich, XLII-XLIV, Jg. XXI/1, 1914); *Il Filosofo inamorato*, dramma giocoso (Vienna, 1771); *Le Pescatrici*, dramma giocoso (Vienna, 1771); *Don Quischott von Mancia*, comedy (Vienna, 1771; Acts 1 and 2 by Paisiello, Act 3 by Gassmann); *I rovinati*, comedy (Vienna, June 23, 1772); *La casa di campagna*, dramma giocoso (Vienna, Feb. 23, 1773). **VOCAL: Sacred:** *La Betulia liberata*, oratorio (Vienna, March 29, 1772); masses; motets; offertories; graduals; hymns; etc. **Instrumental:** About 60 syms. (1 ed. by K. Geiringer, Vienna, 1933; 1 ed. by L. Somfai in Musica Rinata, XVIII, 1970); 27 opera overtures; Flute Concerto; 37 string quartets; 8 string quintets; 10 wind quintets; 37 wind trios; 7 string duos; etc.

BIBL.: F. Kosch, *F. L. G. als Kirchenkomponist* (diss., Univ. of Vienna, 1924); E. Leuchter, *Die Kammermusik F. L. G.s* (diss., Univ. of Vienna, 1926); E. Girach, *F. L. G.* (Reichenberg, 1930); G. Hill, *The Concert Symphonies of F. L. G. (1729–1774)* (diss., N.Y.U., 1975); idem, *A Thematic Catalog of the Instrumental Music of F. L. G.* (Hackensack, N.J., 1976).—**NS/LK/DM**

Gassner, Ferdinand Simon, Austrian violinist;

b. Vienna, Jan. 6, 1798; d. Karlsruhe, Feb. 25, 1851. From 1816, he was violinist at the National Theater in Mainz. In 1818 he became music director at Giessen Univ., which in 1819 made him Dr.Phil. and lecturer on music. In 1826 he joined the Court Orch. at Karlsruhe, where he became music director in 1830. He publ. the *Musikalischer Hausfreund* (Mainz, 1822–35) and ed. (1841–45) the *Zeitschrift für Deutschlands Musikvereine und Dilettanten.* He wrote *Partiturkenntniss, Ein Leitfaden zum Selbstunterricht* (1838; French ed., 1851, as *Traité de la partition*) and *Dirigent und Ripienist* (1846). He also contributed to the Supplement of Schilling's *Universallexikon der Tonkunst* (1842) and ed. an abridgment of the entire work (1849). He composed 2 operas, several ballets, 3 cantatas, songs, etc.—**NS/LK/DM**

Gast, Peter
See **Köselitz, Johann Heinrich**

Gastaldon, Stanislas, Italian composer; b. Turin,

April 7, 1861; d. Florence, March 7, 1939. At the age of 17 he began publishing nocturnes, *ballabili*, and other pieces for piano. He was music critic for the *Nuovo Giornale* in Florence. He wrote about 300 songs, some of which were popular (*La musica proibita, Ti vorrei rapire, Frate Anselmo, Donna Clara*). He was also fairly successful with his operas *Mala Pasqua* (Rome, 1890), *Il Pater* (Milan, 1894), *Stellina* (Florence, 1905), *Il sonetto di Dante* (Genoa, 1909), and *Il Reuccio di Caprilana* (Turin, 1913). He also wrote marches for military band, a piano fantasia, *La dansa delle scimmie*, etc.—**NS/LK/DM**

Gastinel, Léon-Gustave-Cyprien, French

composer; b. Villers, near Auxonne, Aug. 13, 1823; d. Fresnes-les-Rurgis, Oct. 20, 1906. He was a pupil of Halévy at the Paris Cons., taking 1st Grand Prix de Rome for his cantata *Vélasquez* in 1846. A successful composer of operas, he produced *Le Miroir* (1853), *L'Opéra aux fenêtres* (1857), *Titus et Bérénice* (1860), *Le Buisson vert* (1861), and *Le Barde* (Nice, 1896), and the ballet *Le Rêve* (Paris Opéra, 1890), and well as the stage works *La Kermesse, Eutatès, Ourania*, and *La Tulipe bleue.* Other works include 4 oratorios and 3 solemn masses, orch. compositions, chamber music, choruses, etc.

BIBL.: F. Boisson, *L. G.* (1893).—**NS/LK/DM**

Gastoldi, Giovanni Giacomo, eminent Italian

composer; b. Caravaggio, date unknown; d. c. 1622. He

was active mainly in Mantua. He was a sub-deacon (1572) and deacon (1573–74) at S. Barbara, later serving as maestro di contrappunto to the young priests (1579–87) and as maestro di cappella (1592–1608); then went to Milan. He contributed part of the score of *L'Idropica* for performance at the Mantuan court (June 2, 1608). He composed numerous sacred and secular vocal works, the finest being his ballettos, which include *Balletti* for 5 Voices, *con li suoi versi per cantare, sonare, & ballare; con una mascherata de cacciatori* for 6 Voices, *& un concerto de pastori* for 8 Voices (1591; ed. in Le Pupitre, X, Paris, 1968, and by H. Schmidt, N.Y., 1970) and *Balletti, con la intavolatura del liuto, per cantare, sonare, & ballare* for 3 Voices (1594).—**NS/LK/DM**

Gaston, E(verett) Thayer,

American music educator and music therapist; b. Woodward, Okla., July 4, 1901; d. Springfield, Mo., June 3, 1970. He took pre-med courses at Sterling (Kans.) Coll. (B.A., 1923), then studied music there (B.M., 1936) and at the Univ. of Kans. (M.A. in music education, 1938; Ph.D. in educational psychology, 1940). He was a prominent figure in the fields of music education and music therapy in the U.S.; was founder of the National Assn. for Music Therapy, serving as its president (1952–53). He prepared the *Gaston Test of Musicality* (1941; 4th ed., 1957) and ed. the textbook *Music in Therapy* (1968).

BIBL.: R. Johnson, *E. T. G.: Contributions to Music Therapy and Music Education* (diss., Univ. of Mich., 1973).—**NS/LK/DM**

Gastoué, Amédée (-Henri-Gustave- Noël),

French organist and music scholar; b. Paris, March 19, 1873; d. there, June 1, 1943. He studied piano and harmony with A. Deslandres (1890), harmony with Lavignac (1891), then organ with Guilmant and counterpoint and composition with Magnard. From 1896 to 1905 he was ed. of *Revue du Chant Grégorien*; in 1897 he began to contribute to the *Tribune de St.- Gervais*; became its ed. in 1904 and, in 1909, ed.-in-chief and director. He was prof. of Gregorian chant at the Schola Cantorum from its foundation (1896); also music critic of *La Semaine Littéraire* (from 1905). He was organist and maître de chapelle at St.-Jean-Baptiste-de-Belleville, Paris, where he also gave concerts; was a lecturer at the Catholic Univ. and the École des Hautes Études Sociales. In 1925 he became a member of the Académie des Beaux Arts.

WRITINGS: *Cours théorique et pratique de plain-chant romain grégorien* (1904); *Historie du chant liturgique à Paris* (vol. I: *Des Origines à la fin des temps carolingiens*, 1904; 2nd ed., 1917); *Les Origines du chant romain, l'antiphonaire grégorien* (1907); *Catalogue des manuscrits de musique byzantine de la Bibliothèque Nationale de Paris et des bibliothèques publiques de France* (1907); *Nouvelle méthode pratique de chant grégorien* (1908); *Traité d'harmonisation du chant grégorien* (1910); *L'Art grégorien* (1911; 3rd ed., 1920); *La Musique de l'eglise* (1911); *Variations sur la musique d'église* (1912); *Musique et liturgie:Le Graduel et l'Antiphonaire romain* (1913); *L'Orgue en France de l'antiquité au début de la période classique* (1921); *Les Primitifs de la musique française* (1922); *Le Cantique populaire en France: Ses sources, son histoire* (1924); *La Vie musicale de l'église* (1929); *La Liturgie et la musique* (1931); *Le Manuscrit de musique polyphonique du trésor d'Apt, XIVᵉ-XVᵉ siècles* (1936); *L'Église et la musique* (Paris, 1936).—**NS/LK/DM**

Gates, Bernard,

English bass; b. Westminster, c. 1685; d. North Aston, Oxfordshire, Nov. 15, 1773. He was one of the Children of the Chapel Royal. In 1708 he was appointed a Gentleman of the Chapel Royal. About 1727 he became Master of the Children, in 1731 lay vicar at Westminster Abbey, and in 1741 Master of the Choristers, positions he retained until 1757. Gates particularly distinguished himself in the music of Handel. —**LK/DM**

Gatti, Daniele,

Italian conductor; b. Milan, Nov. 6, 1961. He received training in conducting and composition at the Milan Cons. After making his debut as an opera conductor in Milan with *Giovanni d'Arco* in 1982, he appeared with opera houses and orchs. throughout Italy, including the orchs. of the RAI. In 1986 he became founder-conductor of the Stradivari Chamber Orch. He made his first appearance at Milan's La Scala in 1988 conducting Rossini's *L'Occasion fa il Ladro*. In 1991 he made his U.S. debut conducting *Madama Butterfly* in Chicago. In 1992 he became music director of the Orch. Sinfonica dell'Accademia Nazionale di Santa Cecilia in Rome, and also made his debut at the Royal Opera in London conducting *I Puritani*. During the 1993–94 season, he appeared as a guest conductor with the Chicago Sym. Orch., the Cincinnati Sym. Orch., the London Phil., the London Sym. Orch., the Philadelphia Orch., and the San Francisco Sym.; also toured Germany and South America with his Rome orch. In 1994 he was appointed principal guest conductor of the Royal Opera in London, and also made his debut as guest conductor with the Royal Phil. in the British capital. On Dec. 1, 1994, he made his first appearance at the Metropolitan Opera in N.Y. conducting *Madama Butterfly*. He made an auspicious U.S. debut with the N.Y. Phil. conducting Mahler's Sym. No. 6 (Feb. 22, 1996). In 1996 he became music director of the Royal Phil. in London.—**NS/LK/DM**

Gatti, Guido M(aggiorino),

eminent Italian writer on music, critic, and editor; b. Chieti, May 30, 1892; d. Grottaferrata, May 10, 1973. He took up violin training at 6 and piano studies at 12, and later studied engineering at the Univ. of Turin (1909–14). He was ed.-in-chief of *Riforma musicale* (1913–15; 1918). In 1920 he founded *Il pianoforte*, which was renamed the *Rassegna musicale* in 1928. He ed. it until it ceased publication in 1944, and then again from 1947 when it resumed publication in Rome. In 1962 it was renamed again as *Quaderni della Rassegna*. He also was director-general of the Teatro di Torino (1925–31), administrator of Lux films (1934–66), music critic of *Tempo* (1951–69), and ed. of *Studi musicali* (1972–73). In addition, he was ed. of several series, was music ed. of the *Dizionario Bompiani delle opere e dei personaggi* (1946–49) and the *Dizionario degli autori* (1956), and was a contributor of numerous articles to European and U.S. journals. Gatti was particularly influential in contemporary music circles.

WRITINGS: *I "Lieder" di Schumann* (Turin, 1914); *Figure di musicisti francesi* (Turin, 1915); *Giorgio Bizet* (Turin, 1915); *Musicisti moderni d'Italia e di fuori* (Bologna, 1920; 2nd ed., enl., 1925); *Débora e Jaèle di I. Pizzetti* (Milan, 1922); ed. with A. della Corte, *Dizionario di musica* (Turin, 1925; 6th ed., 1959); *Le barbier de Séville de Rossini* (Paris, 1925); *Ildebrando Pizzetti* (Turin, 1934;

2nd ed., 1955; Eng. tr., 1951); ed. with L. Dallapiccola, *F.B. Busoni: Scritti e pensieri sulla musica* (Florence, 1941; 2nd ed., rev., 1954); ed. with others, *L'opera di Gian Francesco Malipiero* (Treviso, 1952); *Cinquanta anni di opera a balletto in Italia* (Rome, 1954); with F. D'Amico, *Alfredo Casella* (Milan, 1958); *V. de Sabata* (Milan, 1958); ed. with A. Basso, *La musica: enciclopedia storica* (Turin, 1966) and *La musica: Dizionario* (Turin, 1968–71); ed. with B. Marziano, *Riccardo Gualino e la cultura torinese: Le manifestazioni del Teatro di Torino* (Turin, 1971).

BIBL.: C. Palandri, ed., *Gian Francesco Malipiero, il carteggio con G.M. G., 1914–1972* (Florence, 1997).—**NS/LK/DM**

Gatti, Luigi (Maria Baldassare),
Italian composer; b. Castro Lacizzi, June 11, 1740; d. Salzburg, March 1, 1817. He became vicemaestro of S. Barbara in Mantua in 1779, and also served as secondo maestro of the Teatro Scientifico in that city. In 1783 he was called to Salzburg as Kapellmeister to the court and cathedral, a position he retained until his death.

WORKS: DRAMATIC: O p e r a : *Alessandro nell'Indie* (Mantua, Jan. 24, 1768); *Nitteti* (Mantua, 1773); *Armida* (Mantua, Jan. 29, 1775); *Olimpiade* (Salzburg, Sept. 30, 1775); *Antigono* (Milan, Feb. 3, 1781); *Demofoonte* (Mantua, May 12, 1787). OTHER: Oratorios; masses; cantatas; instrumental music.

BIBL.: M. Gemacher, *L. G.: Seine Leben und seine Oratorien* (diss., Univ. of Vienna, 1959).—**LK/DM**

Gatti-Casazza, Giulio,
distinguished Italian operatic administrator; b. Udine, Feb. 3, 1868; d. Ferrara, Sept. 2, 1940. He was educated at the univs. of Ferrara and Bologna, and graduated from the Naval Engineering School at Genoa. He abandoned his career as engineer and became director of the opera in Ferrara in 1893. His ability attracted the attention of the Viscount di Modrone and A. Boito, who, in 1898, offered him the directorship of La Scala at Milan. During the 10 years of his administration, the institution came to occupy first place among the opera houses of Italy. From 1908 to 1935 he was general director of the Metropolitan Opera in N.Y., a tenure of notable distinction. During his administration, he engaged many celebrated musicians, produced over 175 works, including premieres by American as well as foreign composers, and expanded audiences through major tours and regular nationwide broadcasts. On April 3, 1910, Gatti-Casazza married **Frances Alda**. After their divorce in 1929, he married Rosina Galli, premiere danseuse and ballet mistress, in 1930. Gatti-Casazza's *Memories of the Opera* was posth. publ. in Eng. in 1941.—**NS/LK/DM**

Gatty, Nicholas Comyn,
English composer; b. Bradfield, Sept. 13, 1874; d. London, Nov. 10, 1946. He was educated at Downing Coll., Cambridge (B.A., 1896; Mus.B., 1898), then studied with Stanford at the Royal Coll. of Music. He was organist to the Duke of York's Royal Military School at Chelsea, and music critic of *Pall Mall Gazette* (1907–14). Gatty also acted as asst. conductor at Covent Garden.

WORKS: DRAMATIC O p e r a (all 1ˢᵗ perf. in London): *Greysteel* (1906); *Duke or Devil* (1909); *The Tempest* (April 17, 1920); *Prince Ferelon* (1921; received the Carnegie Award); *Macbeth*, 4-act opera (MS); *King Alfred and the Cakes*. OTHER:

Ode on Time for Soloists, Chorus, and Orch., after Milton; *3 Short Odes*; *Variations* for Orch. on *Old King Cole*; Piano Concerto; Piano Trio; String Quartet; waltzes for piano; songs.—**NS/LK/DM**

Gaubert, Philippe,
French conductor and composer; b. Cahors, July 3, 1879; d. Paris, July 8, 1941. He studied flute with Taffanel at the Paris Cons. and, in 1905, won the 2nd Prix de Rome. From 1919 to 1938 he was conductor of the Paris Cons. concerts, and from 1920 to 1941 also principal conductor at the Paris Opéra. He publ. a *Méthode complète de flûte* (8 parts, 1923).

WORKS: D R A M A T I C : O p e r a : *Sonia* (Nantes, 1913); *Naila* (Paris, April 7, 1927). O R C H . : *Rhapsodie sur des thèmes populaires* (1909); *Poème pastoral* (1911); *Le Cortège d'Amphitrite* (Paris, April 9, 1911); *Fresques*, symphonic suite (Paris, Nov. 12, 1923); *Les Chants de la mer*, 3 symphonic pictures (Paris, Oct. 12, 1929); Violin Concerto (Paris, Feb. 16, 1930); *Les Chants de la terre* (Paris, Dec. 20, 1931); *Poème romanesque* for Cello and Orch. (Paris, Jan. 30, 1932); *Inscriptions sur les portes de la ville*, 4 symphonic tableaux (Paris, Nov. 18, 1934); Sym. (Paris, Nov. 8, 1936); *Poème des champs et des villages* (Paris, Feb. 4, 1939). B a l l e t : *Philotis* (Paris, 1914). CHAMBER: *Médailles antiques* for Flute, Violin, and Piano; *Divertissement grec* for Flute and Harp; *Sur l'eau* for Flute and Piano; *Intermède champêtre* for Oboe and Piano; Violin Sonata. VOCAL: *Josiane*, oratorio (Paris, Dec. 17, 1921); songs. OTHER: Many transcriptions for flute.—**NS/LK/DM**

Gauk, Alexander,
Russian conductor, teacher, and composer; b. Odessa, Aug. 15, 1893; d. Moscow, March 30, 1963. He studied composition with Kalafati and Vitols, and conducting with N. Tcherepnin, at the Petrograd Cons. (graduated, 1917); then conducted at the State Opera and Ballet Theater there (1920–31). He was chief conductor of the Leningrad Phil. (1930–34), the U.S.S.R. State Sym. Orch. of Moscow (1936–41), and the All-Union Radio Sym. Orch. of Moscow (1953–63). He also taught conducting at the conservatories of Leningrad (1927–33), Tbilisi (1941–43), and Moscow (1939–63). His pupils included such distinguished conductors as Mravinsky, Melik-Pashayev, Simeonov, and Svetlanov. He championed the music of Russian composers; restored Rachmaninoff's 1st Sym. to the active Russian repertoire from orch. parts found in the archives of the Moscow Cons. He wrote a Sym., a Harp Concerto, a Piano Concerto, and songs.—**NS/LK/DM**

Gaul, Alfred (Robert),
English organist, teacher, and composer; b. Norwich, April 30, 1837; d. Birmingham, Sept. 13, 1913. He studied with Z. Buck in Norwich and completed his education at Cambridge (Mus.Bac., 1863). He then was active in various provincial English cities. He wrote an oratorio, *Hezekiah* (1861), several sacred cantatas, and many secular vocal works.—**NS/LK/DM**

Gaul, Harvey B(artlett),
American organist, conductor, music critic, and composer; b. N.Y., April 11, 1881; d. Pittsburgh, Dec. 1, 1945. He studied organ, harmony, and composition with George LeJeune in N.Y., then with Dudley Buck (1895). After further studies

with Alfred R. Gaul in Birmingham and Philip Ames in Durham (1906), he went to Paris to complete his training with Widor, Guilmant, and Decaux (organ) at the Cons. and with d'Indy (composition and orchestration) at the Schola Cantorum (1909–10). He was asst. organist at St. John's Chapel in N.Y. (1899–1901), and then organist and choirmaster at the Emmanuel Church in Cleveland (1901–09); also wrote music criticism for the *Cleveland News*. In 1910 he settled in Pittsburgh as organist of Calvary Church; served as music critic (1914–34) and arts ed. (1929–34) of the *Post-Gazette*; then conducted the Pittsburgh Civic String Orch. (1936–45) and the Savoyard Opera Co. (1939–45) and taught at the Univ. of Pittsburgh and the Carnegie Inst. of Technology. Gaul wrote more than 500 works, becoming best known for his church and organ music. He was also the author of a study of Stephen Foster, *The Minstrel of the Alleghenies* (Pittsburgh, 1952).—NS/LK/DM

Gaultier (Gautier, Gaulthier), Denis,

French lutenist and composer, cousin of **Ennemond Gaultier**; b. Marseilles?, 1603; d. Paris, late Jan. 1672. He spent most of his life in Paris as a lutenist. With his cousin, he was a leading composer of lute music and a major influence on the keyboard style of Froberger.

WORKS: *La Rhétorique des dieux* (Paris, c. 1652; ed. by A. Tessier in Publications de la Société Française de Musicologie, VI-VII, 1932); *Pièces de luth sur trois differens modes nouveaux* (Paris, c. 1670; reprint, 1978); *Livre de tablature des pièces de Mr. Gaultier Sr. de Neve et de Mr. Gaultier son cousin* (Paris, c. 1672; reprint, 1978).

BIBL.: E. Häffner, *Die Lautenstücke des D. G.* (Endingen, 1939); A. Souris and M. Rollin, eds., *OEuvres du vieux Gautier* (Paris, 1966).—NS/LK/DM

Gaultier (Gaulthier, Gautier), Ennemond,

French lutenist and composer, cousin of **Denis Gaultier**; b. Villette, Dauphoné, 1575; d. Neves, near Villette, Dec. 11, 1651. He was valet de chambre to Henri IV's queen (1600–31). Several of his lute works were publ. in collections of his day. See A. Souris and M. Rollin, eds., *OEuvres du vieux Gautier* (Paris, 1966).—NS/LK/DM

Gauthier, (Ida Joséphine Phoebe) Eva,

notable Canadian mezzo-soprano and teacher; b. Ottawa, Sept. 20, 1885; d. N.Y., Dec. 26, 1958. She began her training in Ottawa, where she had lessons in piano and harmony with J. Edgar Birch, and then in voice with Frank Buels. She gained experience as soloist at St. Patrick Church in Ottawa, and then made her professional debut at the Ottawa Basilica at the commemoration service for Queen Victoria in 1902. After pursuing her studies in Paris with Auguste-Jean Dubulle, and then with Jacques Bouhy, Emma Albani invited her to tour the British Isles with her in 1905. In 1906 she accompanied Albani on her farewell tour of Canada. In 1907 she was soloist in C. Harriss's *Coronation Mass for Edward VII* at the Queen's Hall in London. During this time, she also had vocal lessons with William Shakespeare in London. Following further studies with Giuseppe Oxilia in Milan (1907–08), she made her only stage appearance as Micaëla in Pavia in 1909. From 1910

to 1914 she toured extensively as a recitalist in Southeast Asia. After making her N.Y. recital debut in 1915, she appeared regularly there in imaginative programs, which included works by Stravinsky, Schoenberg, Ravel, Bartók, Hindemith, Kern, Berlin, and Gershwin, not to mention works by lesser-known composers of the past and even non-Occidental works. From 1936 she devoted herself principally to teaching.

BIBL.: N. Turbide, *Biographical Study of E. G. (1885–1958): First French-Canadian Singer of the Avant-garde* (diss., Univ. of Montreal, 1986).—NS/LK/DM

Gautier, (Jean-François-)Eugène,

French violinist, conductor, and composer; b. Vaugirard, near Paris, Feb. 27, 1822; d. Paris, April 1, 1878. He was a pupil of Habeneck (violin) and Halévy (composition) at the Paris Cons. In 1848 he became 2nd conductor at the Théâtre-Italien. In 1864 he became a prof. of harmony at the Cons. and, in 1872, a prof. of history. He composed 16 comic operas, an oratorio, *La Mort de Jesus*, a cantata, *Le 15 août*, an *Ave Maria*, etc.—NS/LK/DM

Gautier, Pierre,

French composer and opera director who was known as Pierre Gautier de Marseille; b. Provence, c. 1642; d. in a storm at sea off the coast of Sète, Dec. 1696. He learned to play the organ and harpsichord before going to Paris, where he studied with Chambonnières and was befriended by Hardelle. In 1670–71 he served as organist in La Ciotat. After returning to Paris, he moved in the circle of Lully. About 1681 he went to Marseilles, where he and his brother, the sculptor Jacques Gautier, explored the possibility of creating the first provincial opera company in France. In 1684 Lully granted Gautier a privilege to present operas in Marseilles and other locales in Provence. Gautier composed the opera *Le triomphe de la paix* for the inauguration of his opera company in Marseilles on Jan. 28, 1685. In 1687 his opera *Le jugement de soleil* was premiered there. When Gautier was imprisoned for the company's debts in 1688, his enterprise collapsed. Following a sojourn in Lyons, he returned to Marseilles in 1692 with the intention of building the city's first opera house. With Gautier as music director and his brother as director-in-chief, the new opera house opened in 1693 with a capacity of 1,000. The new enterprise flourished, and the company successfully mounted operas by Lully in Marseilles and on tour. After the company gave performances in Montpellier in Nov. 1696, Pierre and his brother met their tragic fate in a storm at sea on their return to Marseilles. Gautier's operas are not extant, but a number of his fine instrumental pieces have survived. A vol. of his "symphonies," actually 17 duos for Violin and Basso Continuo and 22 trios for 2 Violins and Basso Continuo, was publ. posthumously by Christophe Ballard in Paris in 1707.—LK/DM

Gautier de Coincy,

French trouvère; b. Coincy-l'Abbaye, 1177 or 1178; d. Soissons, Sept. 25, 1236. He entered the Benedictine monastery of St.-Médard in Soissons in 1193. He was made prior in Vic-sur-Aisne in 1214 and abbot in Soissons in 1233. His *Miracles de*

Mostre-Dame (1214–33) is an extensive verse narrative with songs. He also composed sacred chansons. He was an important contributor to the genre of sacred, Marian songs in vernacular settings.—**LK/DM**

Gavazzeni, Gianandrea, Italian conductor, writer on music, and composer; b. Bergamo, July 27, 1909; d. there, Feb. 5, 1996. He studied at the Accademia di Santa Cecilia in Rome (1921–25), and then took courses in piano with Renzo Lorenzoni and in composition with Ildebrando Pizzetti and Mario Pilati at the Milan Cons. (1925–31). While he devoted much time to musical journalism, he also pursued a conducting career from 1940. In 1948 he became a regular conductor at Milan's La Scala, where he served as artistic director from 1966 to 1968. He took La Scala companies on visits to the Edinburgh Festival (1957), to Moscow (1964), and to Montreal (1967). In 1957 he conducted *La Bohème* at the Lyric Opera of Chicago and in 1965 *Anna Bolena* at the Glyndebourne Festival. On Oct. 11, 1976, he made his Metropolitan Opera debut in N.Y. conducting *Il Trovatore*. He then pursued his career in Europe, where he was especially admired for his interpretations of the Italian operatic repertory. Among his numerous writings were *Donizetti* (Milan, 1937); *Musorgskij e la musica russa dell'800* (Florence, 1943); *Le feste musicali* (Milan, 1944); *Il suono è stanco* (Bergamo, 1950); *Quaderno del musicista* (Bergamo, 1952); *Musicisti d'Europa* (Milan, 1954); *La musica e il teatro* (Pisa, 1954); *La morte dell'opera* (Milan, 1954); *La casa di Arlecchino* (Milan, 1957); *Trent'anni di musica* (Milan, 1958); *Diario di Edimburgo e d'America* (Milan, 1960); *La campane di Bergamo* (Milan, 1963); *I nemici della musica* (Milan, 1965); *Carta da musica* (Milan, 1968); *Non eseguire Beethoven e altri scritti* (Milan, 1974). He composed the opera *Paolo e Virginia* (1932; Bergamo, 1935) and the ballet *Il furioso all'isola di S. Domingo* (1940).—**NS/LK/DM**

Gaveaux, Pierre, French singer and composer; b. Béziers, Oct. 9, 1760; d. Charenton, near Paris, Feb. 5, 1825. He was a choirboy at the Béziers Cathedral, where he later sang as a soloist. After composition lessons with Abbé Combés, the cathedral organist, he studied with Franz Beck. He settled in Paris, where he sang in opera from 1780. From 1793 he ran a music shop with his brother, and publ. his own works. In 1804 he became a singer at the imperial chapel, but was stricken with mental illness in 1812. In 1819 he entered an asylum. He composed more than 30 works for the stage, principally opéras-comiques. His most notable stage works were *Sophie et Moncars, ou L'intrigue portugaise* (Paris, Sept. 30, 1797) and *Léonore, ou L'amour conjugal* (Paris, Feb. 19, 1798). The latter was composed to a libretto by Bouilly, which was also set by Beethoven as *Fidelio*. Among Gaveaux's other works were Revolutionary pieces, overtures, and songs.—**NS/LK/DM**

Gaviniès, Pierre, noted French violinist and composer; b. Bordeaux, May 11, 1728; d. Paris, Sept. 8, 1800. He learned to play the violin as a child in the workshop of his father, a violin maker. In 1734, the family moved to Paris. Gaviniès made his first public appearance at a Concert Spirituel at the age of 13, and then reappeared at these concerts as a youth of 20. His success with the public was such that Viotti described him as "the French Tartini." From 1773 to 1777 he was director (with Gossec) of the Concert Spirituel. When the Paris Cons. was organized in 1795, he was appointed prof. of violin. His book of technical exercises, *Les 24 Matinées* (violin studies in all the 24 keys), demonstrates by its transcendental difficulty that Gaviniès must have been a virtuoso. He attracted numerous pupils, and is regarded as the founder of the French school of violin pedagogy. His compositions are of less importance; he wrote 3 sonatas for Violin accompanied by Cello (publ. posth.; the one in F minor is known as *Le Tombeau de Gaviniès*); his most celebrated piece is an air, *Romance de Gaviniès*, which has been publ. in numerous arrangements; he also wrote 6 sonatas for 2 Violins and 6 violin concertos, and a comic opera, *Le Prétendu* (Paris, Nov. 6, 1760).

BIBL.: C. Pipelet, *Éloge historique de P. G.* (Paris, 1802); L. de La Laurencie, *L'École française de violon de Lully à Viotti* (Paris, 1923).—**NS/LK/DM**

Gavoty, Bernard (Georges Marie), French writer on music and organist; b. Paris, April 2, 1908; d. there, Oct. 24, 1981. He studied philosophy and literature at the Sorbonne, and organ and composition at the Cons. in Paris. In 1942 he became organist at Saint-Louis des Invalides in Paris. Under the nom de plume Clarendon, he was music critic of the Paris newspaper *Le Figaro* from 1945 until his death. He publ. a series of lavishly illustrated monographs on contemporary celebrated musicians under the general title of *Les Grands Interprètes* (Geneva, 1953–55), and also made documentary films on famous musicians.

WRITINGS (all publ. in Paris unless otherwise given): *Louis Vierne: Vie et l'oeuvre* (1943); *Jehan Alain, musicien français (1911–1940)* (1945); *Les Français sont-ils musiciens?* (1948); *Souvenirs de Georges Enesco* (1955); with J.-Y. Daniel-Lesur, *Pour ou contre la musique moderne?* (1957); *La Musique adoucit les moeurs* (1959); with É. Vuillermoz; *Chopin amoureux* (1960); *Dix grands musiciens* (1963); *Vingt grand interprètes* (Lausanne, 1967); *L'Arme à gauche* (1971); *Parler, parler!* (1972); *Chopin* (1974); *Reynaldo Hahn: Le Musicien de la belle époque* (1976); *Alfred Cortot* (1977); *Anicroches* (1979); *Liszt: Le Virtuose, 1811–1848* (1980). —**NS/LK/DM**

Gavrilov, Andrei, outstanding Russian pianist; b. Moscow, Sept. 21, 1955. He studied piano with his mother, then entered the Central Music School in Moscow when he was 6 and studied with Tatiana Kestner; subsequently trained with Lev Naumov at the Moscow Cons. He won 1st prize at the Tchaikovsky Competition in Moscow in 1972, and thereafter pursued a distinguished career, making an impressive N.Y. recital debut in 1985. His superlative technique and interpretive insights are revealed in his remarkable performances of a comprehensive repertoire, ranging from the Baroque to the avant-garde.—**NS/LK/DM**

Gawrónski, Wojciech, Polish pianist, pedagogue, and composer; b. Seimony, near Vilnius, March 28, 1868; Kowanówko, near Posen, Aug. 5, 1910. He was a pupil at the Warsaw Music Inst. of Strobl (piano), Roguski (theory), and Noskowski (composition); he also studied privately with Minchejmer in Warsaw and Moszkowski in Berlin. He made successful concert tours in Poland and Russia, becoming particularly known for his performances of Chopin. After running his own music school in Orel (1895–1902), he taught in Warsaw and Łódź. He wrote three operas, *Samuel Zborowski*, *Marja*, and *Pojata*, as well as a Sym., 3 string quartets, piano pieces, and songs.—**NS/LK/DM**

Gay, John, English poet and dramatist, librettist of *The Beggar's Opera*; b. Barnstaple, Devon (baptized), Sept. 16, 1685; d. London, Dec. 4, 1732. *The Beggar's Opera* was premiered in London on Jan. 29, 1728, and was immensely popular for a century, chiefly because of its sharp satire and the English and Scots folk melodies it used. It has had a number of successful revivals. The government disliked it, and forbade the performance of its sequel, *Polly*, the score of which was printed in 1729. When *Polly* was finally performed in London on June 19, 1777, it was a fiasco, because the conditions satirized no longer prevailed.

BIBL.: C. Pearce, *Polly Peachum: The Story of "Polly" and "The Beggar's Opera"* (London, 1923); W. Schultz, *G.'s Beggar's Opera* (New Haven, Conn., 1923); O. Sherwin, *Mr. G.; Being a Picture of the Life and Times of the Author of The Beggar's Opera* (N.Y., 1929); C. Tolksdorf, *J. G.'s Beggar's Opera und Bert Brechts Dreigroschenoper* (Rheinberg, 1934).—**NS/LK/DM**

Gay, Maria (née **Pitchot**), Spanish contralto; b. Barcelona, June 13, 1879; d. N.Y., July 29, 1943. She studied sculpture and the violin; became a singer almost by chance, when Pugno, traveling in Spain, heard her sing and was impressed by the natural beauty of her voice. She sang in some of his concerts; also with Ysaÿe in Brussels; made her operatic debut there as Carmen (1902), a role that became her finest. She then studied in Paris with Ada Adiny, and when she returned to the operatic stage, made an international reputation. After tours in Europe, including appearances at London's Covent Garden (1906) and Milan's La Scala (1906–07), she made her American debut at the Metropolitan Opera in N.Y. as Carmen on Dec. 3, 1908, with Toscanini conducting. She sang with the Boston Opera Co. from 1910 to 1912 and with the Chicago Opera Co. from 1913 to 1927, when she retired from the stage. She and her husband, **Giovanni Zenatello**, whom she married in 1913, settled in N.Y. as teachers (1927).—**NS/LK/DM**

Gayarre, Julián (real name, **Gayarre Sebástian**), famous Spanish tenor; b. Valle de Roncal, Jan. 9, 1844; d. Madrid, Jan. 2, 1890. He received his training in Madrid and from Lamperti in Milan. In 1867 he made his operatic debut in Varese as Nemorino. After appearances in St. Petersburg (1873–75), he created the role of Enzo in *La Gioconda* at Milan's La Scala on April 8, 1876. Gayarre created a sensation at his debut at London's Covent Garden as Fernando in *La Favorite* on April 7, 1877, and was engaged to sing there until 1880, and again in 1886–87. On March 22, 1882, he created the title role in *Il Duca d'Alba* in Rome. In 1885 he

appeared at the Théâtre-Italien in Paris, returning there in 1886 to sing at the Opéra. During a performance of *Les Pêcheurs de perles* in Madrid on Dec. 8, 1889, he suffered a vocal breakdown which compelled him to abandon his career. Gayarre was one of the foremost lyrico-dramatic tenors of his time. His roles in Italian and French operas were outstanding.

BIBL.: F. Hernandel Girbal, *J. G.: El tenor de la voz de ángel* (Madrid, 1955).—**NS/LK/DM**

Gaye, Marvin (originally, **Gay, Marvin Jr.**), seminal soul singer and hitmaker of the 1960s–80s; b. Washington, D.C., April 2, 1939; d. Los Angeles, April 1, 1984. Raised in Washington, D.C., Marvin Gaye first sang solos with his father's church choir at the age of three. During high school, he studied piano while also learning to play drums. In the mid-1950s, he was a member of the local vocal group, The Rainbows, whose membership included Don Covay and Billy Stewart. Gaye made his first recordings in 1957 as a member of The Marquees, who were drafted to replace the original members of The Moonglows in 1958. Spotted performing with the group in 1961 by Berry Gordy Jr., Gaye was signed to the fledgling family of Motown labels. He initially served as a sessions drummer, later toured with The Miracles for six months, and co-wrote Martha and the Vandellas' "Dancing in the Streets" with William Stevenson.

Gaye started recording solo for the Tamla label in 1961, scoring his first near-smash rhythm-and-blues and moderate pop hit with "Stubborn Kind of Fellow," recorded with Martha and the Vandellas, in late 1962. A string of major hits in both the rhythm-and-blues and pop fields followed with "Hitch Hike" and "Pride and Joy" (which he co-wrote) and Holland-Dozier-Holland's "Can I Get a Witness." A more pop-oriented sound emerged in 1964 for the crossover hits "Try It Baby" (by Berry Gordy Jr.) and "You're a Wonderful One," the overlooked "Baby, Don't Do It," and the smash "How Sweet It Is to Be Loved by You," all written by Holland-Dozier-Holland.

Gaye began a series of recordings with Motown organization female singers in 1964 with Mary Wells. The duo produced the major two-sided hit "What's the Matter with You, Baby"/"Once Upon a Time." Gaye and Kim Weston had a minor hit in late 1964 with "What Good Am I without You" and a smash crossover hit in 1967 with "It Takes Two."

Established as a singles artist by 1965, Gaye continued his hit-making ways with "I'll Be Doggone" and "Ain't That Peculiar," both co-written by Smokey Robinson, and the definitive top-hit version of Barrett Strong and Norman Whitfield's "I Heard It Through the Grapevine," recorded a year earlier by Gladys Knight and the Pips. Subsequent crossover hits included "Too Busy Thinking About My Baby" and "That's the Way Love Is."

In 1967, Gaye began teaming with Tammi Terrell, recording three albums with her through 1969. Their smash rhythm-and-blues and pop hits of the period included four Nicholas Ashford/Valerie Simpson compositions, "Ain't No Mountain High Enough," "Your

Precious Love," "Ain't Nothing Like the Real Thing," and "You're All I Need to Get By," as well as "If I Could Build My World Around You." However, Gaye ceased touring after Terrell collapsed in his arms on stage in 1969. She died from a brain tumor on March 16, 1970, in Philadelphia.

After a protracted period of seclusion, Gaye re-emerged to demand more independence from the Motown organization. Eschewing the rigid singles format, he recorded and produced *What's Going On*, which featured sophisticated string and horn arrangements. The album, which revealed Gaye's growing social and spiritual concerns, was reluctantly released in mid-1971. With all songs either written or co-written by Gaye, the album ironically became one of Motown's best-selling albums, yielding top rhythm- and-blues and smash pop singles with "What's Going On," "Mercy, Mercy Me (the Ecology)," and "Inner City Blues (Make Me Wanna Holler)." Opening the door for other independent productions by Motown artists, most notably Stevie Wonder, *What's Going On* was the first "concept" album by a black artist and its success paved the way for other black artists to explore the form. Furthermore, in its poignant and passionate concern with urban decay, ecological crises, and spiritual impoverishment, the album helped expand soul music's boundaries into areas of social concern. He followed up the stunning success of *What's Going On* with the largely instrumental soundtrack to the movie *Trouble Man*, which yielded a smash crossover hit with the title song.

In 1973, Gaye co-wrote, co-produced, and recorded *Let's Get It On*. A dramatic contrast to his previous effort, the album shunned social commentary in favor of sensual, romantic material. The title song became a top rhythm-and-blues and pop hit, and the album also yielded the two-sided hit "Come Get to This"/"You Sure Love to Ball." Later that year, Gaye teamed with Diana Ross for an album and the hits "You're a Special Part of Me," "My Mistake (Was to Love You)" and "Don't Knock My Love."

In early 1974, Gaye returned to live performance at the Oakland (Calif.) Coliseum, which resulted in *Marvin Gaye Live!* Subsequent 1970s successes included the top R&B and major pop hit "I Want You" and the discofied "Got to Give It Up (Part I)," a top pop and R&B hit taken from his best-selling *Live at the London Palladium* album. During 1979, bankrupt and the subject of divorce proceedings, Marvin Gaye issued the embittered double-record set *Here, My Dear*, with royalties assigned to his ex-wife.

Gaye moved to Europe in 1980, eventually settling in Belgium. He negotiated his release from his Motown contract and signed with Columbia Records in 1982. His debut for the label, *Midnight Love*, was recorded in Belgium and became his best selling album, yielding a top R&B and smash pop hit with "Sexual Healing." He returned to the U.S. to tour in support of the album in 1983, but on April 1, 1984, while in the midst of recording material for a new album, he was shot to death by his father at his parents' home in L.A. The posthumous *Dream of a Lifetime* produced a rhythm-and-blues smash with "Sanctified Lady." Gaye was

inducted into the Rock and Roll Hall of Fame in 1987. In 1992, his daughter Nona launched her own recording career on Third Stone Records. Motown Records issued a tribute album to Gaye in 1995.

In a career that spanned the entire history of rhythm-and-blues, from 1950s doo-wop to 1980s soul, Gaye helped define the Motown sound and recorded some of the organization's most enduring hits of the 1960s and 1970s. Recording some of the label's most personal and engaging songs, Gaye made a graceful transition from early gospel-style recordings to a pop-oriented sound that emphasized his smooth, sensual tenor voice. The top sex symbol among black male singers throughout his career, he was one of soul music's most charismatic yet enigmatic figures and one of its most important stylists, influencing both black and white male vocalists.

Disc.: *Soulful Moods of M.G.* (1962); *That Stubborn Kinda Fellow* (1963); *Live on Stage* (1963); *When I'm Alone I Cry* (1964); *How Sweet It Is to Be Loved by You* (1965); *Hello Broadway* (1965); *A Tribute to the Great Nat King Cole* (1966); *Moods of M.G.* (1966); *In the Groove* (1968); *M.P.G.* (1969); *That's the Way Love Is* (1969); *What's Going On* (1971); *Trouble Man* (soundtrack; 1972); *Let's Get It On* (1973); *M.G. Live!* (1974); *I Want You* (1976); *Live at the London Palladium* (1977); *Here, My Dear* (1979); *Love Man* (1980); *In Our Lifetime: The Final Motown Sessions* (1981); *Midnight Love* (1982); *Dream of a Lifetime* (1985); *Romantically Yours* (1985); *The Last Concert Tour* (1991). **MARVIN GAYE AND MARY WELLS:** *Marvin and Mary Together* (1964). **MARVIN GAYE AND KIM WESTON:** *It Takes Two* (1966). **MARVIN GAYE AND TAMMI TERRELL:** *United* (1967); *You're All I Need to Get By* (1968); *Easy* (1969); *Greatest Hits* (1970). **MARVIN GAYE AND DIANA ROSS:** *Diana and Marvin* (1973).

Bibl.: David Ritz, *Divided Soul: The Life of M.G.* (N.Y., 1985); Sharon Davis, *I Heard It through the Grapevine: M.G., the Biography* (Edinburgh, 2000).—**BH**

Gayer (Ashkenasi), Catherine, American soprano; b. Los Angeles, Feb. 11, 1937. She studied at the Univ. of Calif. at Los Angeles and in Berlin. She made her operatic debut in Venice in the premiere of *Intolleranza* as the Companion on April 13, 1961; then joined the Deutsche Oper in West Berlin, and was made a Kammersängerin in 1970; also appeared at the East Berlin Komische Oper. She made guest appearances in Vienna, Salzburg, and Milan. She excelled in the modern operatic repertoire, but also was admired for her Queen of the Night, Constanze, Sophie, Gilda, Mélisande, and Zerbinetta.—**NS/LK/DM**

Gaztambide (y Garbayo), Joaquín (Romualdo), Spanish conductor and composer; b. Tudela, Navarre, Feb. 7, 1822; d. Madrid, March 18, 1870. He was a choirboy at Tudela Cathedral, where he began his musical training with Rubla. After studies in Pamplona with Guelbenzu, he completed his training at the Madrid Cons. with P. Albéniz (piano) and Carnicer (composition). He was active in Madrid as a theater manager and conductor. From 1862 he was director of the Madrid Cons. concert society, and in 1869–70 he toured South America with his own zarzuela company. He wrote over 40 zarzuelas, among the most notable being *Catalina* (Madrid, Oct. 23, 1854), *Los Magyares* (Madrid, April 12, 1857), *El juramento* (Madrid, Dec. 20, 1858), and *La conquista Madrid* (Madrid, Dec. 23, 1863).—NS/LK/DM

Gazzaniga, Giuseppe, Italian composer; b. Verona, Oct. 5, 1743; d. Crema, Feb. 1, 1818. He studied with Porpora, first in Venice and then at the Cons. di S. Onofrio a Capuana in Naples (1760–66); subsequently studied with Piccinni. He composed 47 operas, his *Don Giovanni Tenorio osia Il Convitato di pietra* (Venice, Feb. 5, 1787; ed. by S. Kunze, Kassel and Basel, 1974) anticipating Mozart's great masterpiece *Don Giovanni.* —NS/LK/DM

Gazzelloni, Severino, outstanding Italian flutist and teacher; b. Roccasecca, Frosinone, Jan. 5, 1919; d. Cassino, near Rome, Nov. 21, 1992. He studied with Giambattista Creati and at the Accademia di Santa Cecilia in Rome, graduating in 1942. In 1945 he made his formal debut in Rome, and then was 1st flutist in the RAI Orch. there for some 3 decades. He also pursued an international career as a soloist and recitalist of the first magnitude, excelling in an expansive repertoire ranging from the Baroque masters to the most demanding exponents of the contemporary avant-garde. Many composers wrote works especially for him. He taught at the Accademia di Santa Cecilia and at the Accademia Musicale Chigiana in Siena, as well as abroad.

BIBL.: G.-L. Petrucci and M. Benedetti, *S. G.: Il flauto del Novecento* (Naples, 1993).—NS/LK/DM

Gebauer, François René, French bassoonist, pedagogue, and composer, brother of **Michel Joseph Gebauer;** b. Versailles, March 15, 1773; d. Paris, July 28, 1845. He was a pupil of his brother and of Devienne. In 1788 he became a member of the band of the Swiss Guard in his native city. In 1790 he settled in Paris as a musician in the National Guard. After playing in theater orchs., he joined the orch. of the Opéra about 1799, remaining in it until 1826. He also played in the Imperial chapel orch. until 1830, and was a prof. at the Cons. (1795–1802; 1824–38). Gebauer composed 13 bassoon concertos and various chamber works, including solo bassoon pieces.—LK/DM

Gebauer, Michel Joseph, French oboist, bandmaster, and composer, brother of **François René Gebauer;** b. La Fere, Aisne, 1763; d. during Napoleon's retreat from Moscow, Dec. 1812. He became an oboist in the royal wind ensemble of the Swiss Guard in Versailles in 1777. In 1783 he joined the royal chapel there as a violist. In 1791 he went to Paris as a musician in the National Guard. He also was active as a theater musician and served as prof. of oboe at the Cons. (1795–1800). He then was director of music of the Consular (later Imperial) Guard, and also served as oboist in Napoleon's private chamber ensemble. Among his works were band pieces and chamber music. —LK/DM

Gebel, Georg, German composer; b. Brieg, Silesia, Oct. 25, 1709; d. Rudolstadt, Sept. 24, 1753. He studied

with his father. He was organist at St. Maria Magdalene in Breslau, and Kapellmeister to the Duke of Oels. In 1735 he joined Count Brühl's orch. at Dresden, where he met Hebenstreit, the inventor of the "Pantaleon," and learned to play that instrument. In 1747 he was appointed Kapellmeister to the Prince of Schwarzburg-Rudolstadt. He wrote a number of light operas (to German rather than Italian librettos, thus upholding the national tradition), and more than 100 syms., partitas, and concertos.—NS/LK/DM

Gebhard, Heinrich, German-American pianist, composer, and teacher; b. Sobernheim, July 25, 1878; d. North Arlington, N.J., May 5, 1963. As a boy of 8, he went with his parents to Boston, where he studied with Clayton Johns; after a concert debut in Boston (April 24, 1896), he went to Vienna to study with Leschetizky. He gave first American performances of works by d'Indy. His most notable interpretation was Loeffler's work for Piano and Orch., *A Pagan Poem,* which he played nearly 100 times with U.S. orchs.; also arranged the work for 2 pianos. His own works are in an impressionistic vein: *Fantasy* for Piano and Orch. (N.Y. Phil., Nov. 12, 1925, composer soloist); *Across the Hills,* symphonic poem (1940); *Divertimento* for Piano and Chamber Orch. (Boston, Dec. 20, 1927); String Quartet; *Waltz Suite* for 2 Pianos; *The Sun, Cloud and the Flower,* song cycle; and many piano pieces. His book *The Art of Pedaling* was publ. posth. with an introduction by Leonard Bernstein, who was one of his students (N.Y., 1963).—NS/LK/DM

Geck, Martin, German musicologist; b. Witten, March 19, 1936. He was educated at the Univ. of Kiel (Ph.D., 1962, with the diss. *Die Vokalmusik Dietrich Buxtehude und der frühe Pietismus;* publ. in Kassel, 1965). In 1976 he became a prof. at the Dortmund Padagogischen Hochschule. He was prof. of musicology at the Univ. of Dortmund from 1980.

WRITINGS: *Die Wiederentdeckung der Matthäuspassion im 19. Jahrhundert* (Regensburg, 1967); *Nicolaus Bruhns: Leben und Werk* (Cologne, 1968); *Die Bildnisse Richard Wagners* (Munich, 1970); *Deutsche Oratorien 1800 bis 1840: Verzeichnis der Quellen und Aufführungen* (Wilhelmshaven, 1971); *Musiktherapie als Problem der Gesellschaft* (Stuttgart, 1973; Swedish tr., Stockholm, 1977; Danish tr., Copenhagen, 1978); with J. Deathridge and E. Voss, *Wagner-Werk- Verzeichnis* (Mainz, 1986); with P. Schleuning, *"Geschrieben auf Bonaparte." Beethovens "Eroica": Revolution, Reaktion, Rezeption* (Reinbek bei Hamburg, 1989); *Johann Sebastian Bach* (Reinbek bei Hamburg, 1993); *Von Beethoven bis Mahler: Die Musik des deutsche Idealismus* (Stuttgart, 1993); with U. Tadday, *W. Feldmanns Versuch einer Geschichte des Dortmunder Conzerts aus dem Jahre 1830* (Hildesheim, 1994).—NS/LK/DM

Gédalge, André, eminent French pedagogue and composer; b. Paris, Dec. 27, 1856; d. Chessy, Feb. 5, 1926. He began to study music rather late in life, and entered the Paris Cons. at the age of 28. However, he made rapid progress, and obtained the 2nd Prix de Rome after a year of study (with Guiraud). He then elaborated a system of counterpoint, later publ. as *Traité de la fugue* (Paris, 1901; Eng. tr., 1964), which became a standard work. In 1905 he became a prof. of counterpoint and

fugue at the Paris Cons.; among his students were Ravel, Enesco, Koechlin, Roger-Ducasse, Milhaud, and Honegger. He also publ. *Les Gloires musicales du monde* (1898) and other pedagogic works. As a composer, he was less significant. Among his works are a pantomime, *Le Petit Savoyard* (Paris, 1891), an opera, *Pris au piège* (Paris, 1895), and 3 operas that were not performed: *Sita, La Farce du Cadi,* and *Hélène.* He also wrote 3 syms., several concertos, some chamber music, and songs.
—NS/LK/DM

Gedda (real name, **Ustinov**), **Nicolai (Harry Gustav),** noted Swedish tenor; b. Stockholm, July 11, 1925. Gedda was his mother's name, which he assumed in his professional life. His father was a Russian who went to Sweden after the Civil War. He studied at the opera school at the Stockholm Cons. On April 8, 1952, he made his operatic debut as Chapelou in *Le Postillon de Longjumeau* at the Royal Opera in Stockholm. In 1953 he made his debut at La Scala in Milan; in 1954 he sang Faust at the Paris Opéra and the Duke of Mantua at Covent Garden in London; in 1957 he sang Don José in *Carmen* at the Vienna State Opera. He made his U.S. debut as Faust with the Pittsburgh Opera on April 4, 1957; his Metropolitan Opera debut followed in N.Y. on Nov. 1, 1957, in that same role; he created the role of Anatol in Barber's *Vanessa* at the Metropolitan on Jan. 15, 1958. Because of his natural fluency in Russian and his acquired knowledge of German, French, Italian, and English, he was able to sing with total freedom the entire standard operatic repertoire. In 1980 and 1981 he made highly successful appearances in Russia, both in opera and on the concert stage. In 1986 he made his London recital debut. In 1991 he appeared as Christian II in a revival of Naumann's *Gustaf Wasa* in Stockholm. He sang in *Palestrina* at Covent Garden in 1997. His memoirs were publ. as *Gåvan är inte gratis* (Stockholm, 1978).
—NS/LK/DM

Gedda, Giulio Cesare, Italian conductor and composer; b. Turin, April 16, 1899; d. Callegno, near Turin, Sept. 7, 1970. He studied composition with Alfano in Turin. He played cello and organ, and began conducting in 1932. He wrote an opera, *L'amoroso fantasma* (Turin, 1933), 2 violin concertos (1930, 1954), a Viola Concerto (1940), a Cello Concerto, and Concerto for 4 Saxophones (1952). He ended his days in a mental institution.—NS/LK/DM

Gefors, Hans, Swedish composer; b. Stockholm, Dec. 8, 1952. He studied composition with Per-Gunnar Alldahl and Maurice Karkoff, with Ingvar Lidholm at the Stockholm Musikhögskolan (1972), and with Nrgård at the Århus Cons. He also wrote music criticism and worked as an ed. In 1988 he joined the faculty at the Univ. of Lund.

WORKS: DRAMATIC: O p e r a : *Poeten och glasmästaren,* chamber opera (1979; Århus, April 26, 1980); *Christina,* opera (1983–86; Stockholm, Oct. 18, 1986); *Der Park,* opera (1986–91); *Vargen kommer,* opera (1994–96). ORCH.: *Visviter* for String Orch. (1973); *Syndabocken,* theater music (1979); *Slits*

(1981; Hälsingborg, Feb. 18, 1982); *Twine* (1988; Nörrkoping, May 11, 1989); *Die Erscheinung im Park* (1990; Malmö, March 14, 1991); *Botho Strauss* (1991; Wiesbaden, April 25, 1992); Concerto for 5 Percussion and Sinfonietta (1993). CHAMBER: *Aprahishtita* for Cello, Piano, and Tape (1970–71); *Matutino* for Flute, Violin, Viola, Cello, and Piano (1973). VOCAL: *Reveille* for Voice and 5 Instruments (1974–75); *Orpheus singt,* cantata for Chorus and Orch. (1976–77; *Me morire en Paris* for Baritone and 4 Instruments (1979); Trio for Voice, Guitar, and Violin (1981); *Galjonsfiguren* for Soprano, Electric Guitar, and Tape (1983); *Lydias sånger* for Mezzo-soprano and Orch. (1996).
—NS/LK/DM

Gehlhaar, Rolf (Rainer), German-born American composer; b. Breslau, Dec. 30, 1943. He emigrated to the U.S. in 1953 and in 1958 became a naturalized American citizen. He took courses in philosophy, science, and music at Yale Univ. (B.A., 1965) and in music at the Univ. of Calif. at Berkeley (1965–67). From 1967 to 1970 he was the personal assistant to Stockhausen. In 1976 he settled in London. He founded the electronic music studio at Dartington Coll. in 1976, and that same year he served as director of the composition course in Darmstadt. In 1977 he was composer-in-residence at the New South Wales State Conservatorium of Music in Sydney. In 1978 he returned as director of the composition course in Darmstadt. He worked at IRCAM in Paris in 1979. In 1981 he worked there again and created the first composition utilizing digitally generated "3-dimensional" sounds, *Pas à pas...music for ears in motion.* In 1984 he commenced research on a computer-controlled interactive musical environment which resulted in his Sound=Space series. In 1995 he opened the Sound=Space Centre in London, the first permanent installation devoted to his creative workshops.

WORKS: CHAMBER: *Cello Solo* (1966); *Klavierstück 1–1* for Piano (1967); *Helix* for Quintet (1967); *Klavierstück 2–2* for 2 Pianos (1970); *Wege* for Amplified Piano and 2 Strings (1971); *Musi-Ken* for String Quartet (1972); *Spektra* for 4 Trumpets and 4 Trombones (1974); *Linear A* for Marimbaphone (1978); *Camera oscura* for Brass Quintet (1978); *Strangeness, Charm, and Colour* for Piano and 3 Brass (1978); *Fluid* for Clarinet, Violin, Cello, and Piano (1980); *Pixels* for 8 Instruments (1981); *Nairi* for Amplified Violin or Viola (1983); Suite for Piano (1990); *Grand Unified Theory of Everything (GUTE)* for Flute, Bass Clarinet, Alto Clarinet, and Piano (1992); *Angaghoutiun* for Piano Quartet (1994); *Amor* for Flute (1994); *Quantum Leap* for Piano (1994). M i x e d M e d i a : *Der, die oder das Klavier* for Piano and Film (1967); *Sound=Space,* interactive musical environment (1985); *Copernic Opera* for 15 Dancers in a Sound=Space (1986); *Eichung* for 3 Instruments in a Sound=Space (1986); *Sudden Adventures* for 2 Dancers in a Sound=Space (1988); *Head Pieces* for 2 Heads in a Sound=Space (1988). ELECTRONIC: *Beckenstück* for 6 Amplified Cymbals (1969); *Cybernet I* and *II,* interactive electronic environment (1971); *Solipse* for Cello and Tape Delay (1974); *5 Deutsche Tänze* for Tape (1975); *Rondell* for Trombone and Tape Delay (1975); *Polymorph* for Bass Clarinet or Clarinet and Tape Delay (1978); *Sub Rosa* for Tape (1980); *Pas à pas...music for ears in motion* for Live Electronics (1981); *Infra* for 10 Amplified Instruments (1985); *Origo* for 5 Amplified Instruments (1987); *Diagonal Flying* for Keyboards and Electronics (1989); *Strange Attractor* for Computer-controlled Piano (1991); *Chronik* for 2 Pianos, 2 Percussionists, and Electronics (1991); *Maree* for 6 Percussionists and Live Electronics (1991); *Cusps, Swallowtails, and Butterflies* for Tape, Amplified Cymbals, and

Live Electronics (1992). **ORCH.**: *Phase* for Orch. (1972); *Protoypen* for 4 Orch. Groups (1973); *Resonanzen* for 8 Orch. Groups (1976); *Lamina* for Trombone and Orch. (1977); *Tokamak* for Piano and Orch. (1982; rev. 1988). **VOCAL**: *Liebeslied* for Alto and Orch. (1974); *Isotrope* for Chorus (1977); *Particles* for Soprano, Chamber Orch., and Electronics (1977–78); *Worldline* for 4 Voices and Live Electronics (1980); *Das Mädchen aus der Ferne* for Soprano, Flute, and Piano (1983).—**NS/LK/DM**

Gehot, Jean or **Joseph,** Belgian violinist and composer; b. Brussels, April 8, 1756; d. in the U.S., c. 1820. He went to London after 1780, where he publ. *A Treatise on the Theory and Practice of Music* (1784), *The Art of Bowing the Violin* (1790), and *Complete Instructions for Every Musical Instrument* (1790). In 1792, he went to the U.S. and gave concerts in N.Y., presenting his *Overture in 12 movements, expressive of a voyage from England to America.* He then played violin at the City Concerts in Philadelphia, under the management of Reinagle and Capron. However, he failed to prosper in America. Most of his works were publ. in London, among them 17 string quartets, 12 string trios, and 24 "military pieces" for 2 Clarinets, 2 Horns, and Bassoon.—**NS/LK/DM**

Gehrkens, Karl (Wilson), American music educator; b. Kelleys Island, Ohio, April 19, 1882; d. Elk Rapids, Mich., Feb. 28, 1975. After graduation from Oberlin (Ohio) Coll. (B.A. 1905; M.A., 1912), he became a prof. of school music at the Oberlin Cons. of Music in 1907; retired in 1942. He was ed. of *School Music* from 1925 to 1934 and author or co-author of 9 books on music education. During his tenure as president of the Music Supervisors National Conference (1923), he coined the slogan "Music for every child, and every child for music."

BIBL.: F. Lendrim, *Music for Every Child: The Story of K.W. G.* (diss., Univ. of Mich., 1972).—**NS/LK/DM**

Geiringer, Karl (Johannes), eminent Austrian-American musicologist; b. Vienna, April 26, 1899; d. Santa Barbara, Calif., Jan. 10, 1989. He studied composition with Gál and Stohr, and musicology with Adler and Fischer in Vienna, and then continued his musicological studies with Sachs and Johannes Wolf in Berlin. He received his Ph.D. from the Univ. of Vienna with the diss. *Die Flankenwirbelinstrumente in der bildenden Kunst (1300–1550)* in 1923 (publ. in Tutzing, 1979). In 1930 he became librarian and museum curator of the Gesellschaft der Musikfreunde in Vienna. He left Austria in 1938 and went to London, where he worked for the BBC; also taught at the Royal Coll. of Music (1939–40). He then emigrated to the U.S., where he was a visiting prof. at Hamilton Coll., Clinton, N.Y. (1940–41). In 1941 he became a prof. at Boston Univ. and head of graduate studies in music, and in 1962 he was made a prof. at the Univ. of Calif., Santa Barbara; he retired in 1972. In 1955–56 he was president of the American Musicological Soc. In 1959 he was elected a Fellow of the American Academy of Arts and Sciences; also was an honorary member of the Österreichische Gesellschaft für Musikwissenschaft and of the American chapter of the Neue Bach-Gesellschaft; in addition, was a member of the

Joseph Haydn Inst. of Cologne. A music scholar and writer of great erudition, he contributed valuable publications on the Bach family, Haydn, and Brahms. He was general ed. of the Harbrace History of Musical Forms and of the Univ. of Calif., Santa Barbara, Series of Early Music.

WRITINGS: With H. Kraus, *Führer durch die Joseph Haydn Kollektion im Museum der Gesellschaft der Musikfreunde in Wien* (Vienna, 1930); *Joseph Haydn* (Potsdam, 1932); *Johannes Brahms: Leben und Schaffen eines deutschen Meisters* (Vienna, 1935; Eng. tr., 1936; rev. and enl. ed., 1981); *Musical Instruments: Their History in Western Culture from the Stone Age to the Present Day* (London, 1943; 3rd ed., rev. and enl., 1978, as *Instruments in the History of Western Music*); *Haydn: A Creative Life in Music* (N.Y., 1946; 3rd ed., 1983); *A Thematic Catalogue of Haydn's Settings of Folksongs from the British Isles* (Superior, Wisc., 1953); *The Bach Family: Seven Generations of Creative Genius* (N.Y., 1954); *Music of the Bach Family: An Anthology* (Cambridge, Mass., 1955); *Johann Sebastian Bach: The Culmination of an Era* (N.Y., 1966); *This I Remember* (Santa Barbara, Calif., 1993).

BIBL.: A. Silver, ed., *K. G.: A Checklist of His Publications in Musicology* (Santa Barbara, Calif., 1969); H.C. Robbins Landon and R. Chapman, *Studies in Eighteenth-Century Music: A Tribute to K. G. on His 70th Birthday* (N.Y. and London, 1970).—**NS/LK/DM**

Geiser, Walther, Swiss violist, conductor, pedagogue, and composer; b. Zofingen, May 16, 1897; d. Oberwil, near Basel, March 6, 1993. He was a student of Hirt (violin) and Suter (composition) at the Basel Cons. (1917–20), of Eldering (violin) in Cologne, and of Busoni (composition) at the Prussian Academy of Arts in Berlin (1921–23). From 1924 to 1963 he taught at the Basel Cons., and also was active as a violist and conductor, and was conductor of the Basel Bach Choir (1954–72). He generally followed a late Romantic path as a composer.

WORKS: 2 flute concertos (1921, 1963); Violin Concerto (1930); Horn Concerto (1934); *Konzertstück* for Organ and Chamber Orch. (1941); 4 orch. fantasies (1942, 1945, 1949, 1963); 2 syms. (1953, 1967); *Concerto da camera* for 2 Violins, Harpsichord, and String Orch. (1957); Piano Concerto (1959); chamber music; piano pieces; *Stabat Mater* for Baritone, Chorus, Orch., and Organ (1936); *Te Deum* for 4 Soloists, Chorus, Orch., and Organ (1960); choral music.—**NS/LK/DM**

Geisler, Paul, German conductor and composer; b. Stolp, Aug. 10, 1856; d. Posen, April 3, 1919. He was a pupil of his grandfather, who was a conductor at Marienburg, and also of Constantine Decker. As a conductor, Geisler was associated with the Leipzig musical theater (1881) and A. Neumann's traveling Wagner company (1882–83); for the following 2 years he was a conductor at Bremen. He lived in Leipzig and Berlin for most of his career before going to Posen, where he became director of the Cons. He wrote 7 operas, 2 cyclic cantatas, symphonic poems, incidental stage music, etc.—**NS/LK/DM**

Geissler, Fritz, German composer; b. Wurzen, near Leipzig, Sept. 16, 1921; d. Bad Saarow, Jan. 11, 1984. He studied at the Leipzig Hochschule für Musik, with Max

Dehnert and Wilhelm Weismann (1948–50), where he later taught (1962–70). He then joined the faculty of the Dresden Cons., where he was named a prof. in 1974. His music is dialectical and almost Hegelian in its syllogistic development and climactic synthesis. The ground themes are carefully adumbrated before their integration in a final catharsis, and formal dissonances are emancipated by a freely modified application of 12-tone writing.

WORKS: DRAMATIC: Opera: *Der Schatten*, fantastic opera (1975); *Die Stadtpfeifer* (1977); *Das Chagrinleder* (1978). **Ballet:** *Pigment* (1960); *Sommernachtstraum* (1965); *Der Doppelganger* (1969). Also *Der verrückte Jourdain*, a "Rossiniada" (1971). **ORCH.:** 2 chamber syms. (1954, 1970); *Italienische Lustspielouverture*, after Rossini (1958); *November 1918*, suite (1958); 9 syms.: No. 1 (1961), No. 2 (1963), No. 3 (1965–66), No. 4 for Strings (1968), No. 5 (1969), No. 6, *Sinfonia concertante*, for Wind Quintet and Strings (1971), No. 7 (1973), No. 8 for Soloists, Chorus, and Orch. (1974), and No. 9 (1978); *Sinfonietta giocosa* (1963); *The Adventures of the Good Soldier Schweik*, symphonic burlesque (1963); *Essay* (1969); *2 Symphonic Scenes* (1970); Piano Concerto (1970); *Beethoven-Variationen* (1971); Cello Concerto (1974); *Offenbach- Metamorphosen* (1977); Concerto for Flute, Strings, Harpsichord, and Percussion (1977); Concerto for Organ, Percussion, and Strings (1979). **CHAMBER:** String Quartet (1951); Suite for Wind Quintet (1957); Chamber Concerto for Harpsichord, Flute, and 10 Instruments (1967); *Ode to a Nightingale* for Nonet (1967–68); Viola Sonata (1969); Piano Trio (1970); piano pieces. **VOCAL:** *Gesang vom Menschen*, oratorio (1968); *Nachtelegien*, romance for High Voice and Instruments (1969); *Die Liebenden*, romance for Tenor and 2 Instrumental Groups (1969); *Schöpfer Mensch*, oratorio (1973); *Die Glocke von Buchenwald*, cantata (1974); *Die Flamme von Mansfeld*, oratorio (1978); choruses; songs.—**NS/LK/DM**

Geistinger, Marie (actually, **Maria Charlotte Cäcilia**), noted Austrian soprano; b. Graz, July 26, 1836; d. Klagenfurt, Sept. 30, 1903. She appeared on the stage while still a child. At 16, she sang the title role in *Die falsche Pepita* in Vienna. After singing in Berlin, Hamburg, Riga, and again in Berlin in juvenile comedy roles, she returned to Vienna in 1865 to sing the title role in Offenbach's *La Belle Helene* at the Theater an der Wien. During the following decade, she sang there regularly and acquired the status of queen of the Vienna musical theater. She became particularly well known for her roles in Offenbach's works, but also was acclaimed as Fantasca in Johann Strauss's *Indigo und die vierzig Rauber* in 1871. In 1874 she created the role of Rosalinde in Strauss's *Die Fledermaus*. In 1877 she was seen in dramatic roles at the Vienna Stadttheater. After appearances in Leipzig (1877–79), she returned to Vienna's Theater an der Wien. In 1881 she made her U.S. debut as Offenbach's Grande-Duchess in N.Y., subsequently starring in various productions there and in other cities. In 1884 she returned to Vienna and appeared at the Carltheater. She also had guest engagements in other Austrian and German music centers. In 1891, 1896, and 1899 she made return visits to the U.S. She retired from the stage in 1900.

BIBL.: E. Pirchan, *M. G.* (Vienna, 1947).—**NS/LK/DM**

Gelber, Bruno-Leonardo, esteemed Argentine pianist of Austrian and French-Italian descent; b. Buenos Aires, March 19, 1941. His parents were musicians and he took up the piano at a very early age; he was only 5 when he made his first public appearance, and at 6 became a pupil of Vincenzo Scaramuzza. When he was 7 he was stricken with poliomyelitis; while confined to his bed for a year, he continued to practice with his bed slid under the piano. At age 8, he made his formal recital debut; when he was 15 he attracted wide notice when he appeared as soloist in the Schumann Concerto under Lorin Maazel's direction in Buenos Aires. In 1960 he was awarded a French government grant and pursued his training in Paris with Marguerite Long. In 1961 he won 3rd prize in the Long-Thibaud competition. In subsequent years he toured all over the world, appearing as a soloist with the great orchs. and as a recitalist in the major music centers. He has won deserved accolades for his compelling performances of the Classical and Romantic repertory.—**NS/LK/DM**

Gelbrun, Artur, Polish-born Israeli composer and teacher; b. Warsaw, July 11, 1913; d. Tel Aviv, Dec. 24, 1985. He studied at the Warsaw Cons., then took courses with Molinari and Casella at the Accademia di Santa Cecilia in Rome; later studied composition with W. Burkhard and conducting with Scherchen in Zürich. He was an orch. and solo violinist in Warsaw, Lausanne, and Zürich (1936–47). In 1949 he emigrated to Israel and joined the staff of the Tel Aviv Academy of Music as prof. of conducting and composition.

WORKS: ORCH.: Suite (1947); *Prelude, Passacaglia and Fugue* (1954); *Variations* for Piano and Orch. (1955); *Prologue Symphonique* (1956); *5 Capriccios* (1957); 3 syms. (1957–58; 1961; *Jubilee*, 1973); Cello Concerto (1962); *Piccolo Divertimento* for Youth Orch. (1963; also perf. As a ballet); *4 Pieces* for Strings (1963); *Concerto-Fantasia* for Flute, Harp, and Strings (1963); Concertino for Chamber Orch. (1974); *Adagio* for Strings (1974); *Hommageà Rodin* (1979–81); Concerto for Oboe and Strings (1985; rev. and orchestrated by L. Biriotti, 1986). **Ballet:** *Hedva* (1951; concert premiere, Ein-Gev, May 27, 1951; stage premiere, St. Gallen, 1958); *Miadoux* (1966–67); *Prologue to the Decameron* (1968); *King Solomon and the Hoopoes* (1976). **CHAMBER:** String Trio (1945); String Quartet (1969); Wind Quintet (1971); Trio for Trumpet, Horn, and Trombone (1972); Piano Trio (1977); Septet for Harp, Flute, Clarinet, and String Quartet (1984); solo pieces; piano music. **VOCAL:** *Lieder der Mädchen* for Voice and Orch. (1945); *Song of the River* for Soprano and Orch. (1959); *Le Livre du Feu*, radiophonic oratorio (1964; Jerusalem, 1966); *Salmo e Alelujah* for Soprano and Orch. (1968); *Holocaust and Revival*, cantata for Narrator, Chorus, and Orch. (1977–78); songs.—**NS/LK/DM**

Geldof, Bob, songwriter, lead vocalist, and performing focal point for the Boomtown Rats; b. Dun Langhaire, Ireland, Oct. 5, 1954. Spearheading interest in young Irish rock and subsumed under the label *punk*, the Boomtown Rats won substantial success in Britain and Europe in the late 1970s, but they were virtually ignored in the United States. Bob Geldof later endeavored to raise money for African famine relief, first with the Band Aid single "Do They Know It's Christmas?" (purportedly the best- selling single ever in England), and later with the massive Live Aid concert staged in London and Philadelphia. Geldof's efforts reawakened the music scene to social concerns and served as an inspiration for other musical benefits such as Farm Aid. Bob Geldof launched a solo career in the late 1980s that fared little better than that of the Boomtown Rats.

Bob Geldof formed the Nightlife Thugs in 1975 after a stint as music reporter and editor with the *Georgia Straight* in Vancouver, British Columbia. The group soon evolved into the Boomtown Rats, with Geldof, Gerry Cott, Garry Roberts, Johnnie Fingers, Pete Briquette, and Simon Crowe. Establishing themselves in Ireland, the Boomtown Rats moved to London in 1976 and signed with Ensign Records. Conducting their first full-scale tour of England in 1977, the band recorded their debut album in Germany. "Looking After No. 1" became the first of a series of major British hits that included "She's So Modern" and "Rat Trap," from their second album, and the controversial "I Don't Like Mondays," their first and only (minor) American hit. With Geldof as songwriter and lead vocalist, the group garnered a reputation in Britain and Europe for their brash and cynical songs and arrogant stage presence. However, the group's albums after *A Tonic for the Troops* were less well received, and their American record company, Columbia, dropped the band in late 1985, leading to their dissolution in 1986.

After viewing a BBC television documentary on the famine in Ethiopia in 1984, Bob Geldof contacted Midge Ure of Ultravox and began booking an array of British rock stars to record a single to raise money to remedy the situation. Recruiting Sting, Boy George, Phil Collins, and members of U2, Ultravox, and Duran Duran, among others, the assemblage recorded "Do They Know It's Christmas?," written by Geldof and Ure, in November 1984. Released under the name Band Aid, the song became a major American hit and top British hit, selling more than seven million copies worldwide. The project inspired the adhoc group USA (United Support of Artists) for Africa in the United States, with superstars such as Bruce Springsteen, Bob Dylan, Paul Simon, Stevie Wonder, Michael Jackson, Prince, Lionel Richie, and Tina Turner recording the top hit "We Are the World," written by Jackson and Richie.

In 1985 Bob Geldof visited Africa and soon began organizing a huge simultaneous benefit concert linking London and Philadelphia. Staged on July 13, 1985, Live Aid was broadcast worldwide to an audience estimated to approach one billion viewers. Performers included Bob Dylan, Madonna, Crosby, Stills and Nash, Eric Clapton, Jimmy Page and Robert Plant, U2, The Who, Elvis Costello, and David Bowie. The concert ultimately raised more than $100 million for famine relief, a project overseen by Geldof for the next two years. He became an international celebrity, met with leaders of many nations, and was knighted by Queen Elizabeth II in 1986 and nominated for the Nobel Peace Prize in 1986 and 1987.

Never exploiting his fame for personal gain, Bob Geldof wrote his autobiography, *Is That All?*, published in 1986, and returned to music with his solo debut album, *Deep in the Heart of Nowhere*, and its minor American hit "This Is the World Calling." He recorded a follow-up album two years later and then lay low for a while, returning to tour America for the first time in 12 years in support of 1993's *The Happy Club*.

DISC.: BOB GELDOF: *Deep in the Heart of Nowhere* (1986); *The Happy Club* (1993). **THE BOOMTOWN RATS:** *The Boomtown Rats* (1977); *A Tonic for the Troops* (1979); *The Fine Art of Surfacing* (1979); *Mondo Bongo* (1981); *V Deep* (1982); *In the Long Grass* (1984); *Best (1977–1982)* (1987).—**BH**

Gelinek (also **Jelinek**), **Josef (Joseph),** Bohemian pianist, teacher, and composer; b. Seltsch, near Beroun, Dec. 3, 1758; d. Vienna, April 13, 1825. He studied philosophy at the Univ. of Prague, and also received training in organ and composition from Seger. After being ordained a priest in 1786, he settled in Vienna about 1789 and became a domestic chaplain, piano teacher, and tutor to the family of Count Philipp Kinsky. He later served as domestic chaplain to Prince Nikolaus II Esterházy. Following further training from Albrechtsberger, he was active as a pianist, teacher, and composer. He composed some 120 sets of keyboard variations, as well as fantasias and dances, some chamber music, and songs.—**NS/LK/DM**

Gellman, Steven (David), Canadian composer and teacher; b. Toronto, Sept. 16, 1947. He studied composition with Dolin at the Royal Cons. of Music of Toronto, then with Berio, Sessions, and Persichetti at the Juilliard School of Music in N.Y. (1965–68), with Milhaud at Aspen, Colo. (summers, 1965–66), and with Messiaen at the Paris Cons. (1974–76; premiers prix in analysis, 1975, and in composition, 1976). In 1976 he joined the faculty of the Univ. of Ottawa. He adopted an uncompromisingly modernistic idiom in most of his music, while safeguarding the formal design of Classical tradition.

WORKS: ORCH.: 2 piano concertos (1962, 1989); *Andante* for Strings (1963); *Mural* (1965); *Andante-Agitato* for Violin and Orch. (1966); *Movement* for Violin and Orch. (1967); *Symphony in 2 Movements* (Ottawa, July 15, 1971); *Odyssey* for Rock Group, Piano, and Orch. (Hamilton, Ontario, March 9, 1971); *Symphony II* (Toronto, Dec. 2, 1972); *Encore (Mythos I Revisited)* (1972); *Overture for Ottawa* (1972); *Chori* (1974; rev. 1976); *Animus-Anima* (Paris, April 28, 1976); *Awakening* (1982); *The Bride's Reception: A Symphonic Contemplation* (1981–83); *Universe Symphony* (1985; Toronto, Jan. 8, 1986); *Burnt Offerings* for Strings (1990); *Child-Play* for Chamber Orch. (1992). **CHAMBER:** *2 Movements* for String Quartet (1963); *Soliloquy* for Cello (1966; rev. 1982); *After Bethlehem* for String Quartet (1966); *Quartets: Poems of G.M. Hopkins* for Voice, Flute, Cello, and Harp (1966–67); *Mythos II* for Flute and String Quartet (1968); *Sonate pour sept* for Flute, Clarinet, Cello, Guitar, Piano, and 2 Percussionists (1975); *Wind Music* for 2 Trumpets, Horn, Trombone, and Bass Tuba (1978); *Dialogue I* for Horn (1978) and *II* for Flute and Piano (1979); *Transformation* for Flute and Piano (1980); *Trikáya* for Violin, Clarinet, Percussion, and Piano (1981); *Chiaroscuro* for Flute, Clarinet, Violin, Viola, Cello, Piano, and Percussion (1988); Concertino for Guitar and String Quartet (1988); *Musica Eterna* for String Quartet (1991). **P i a n o :** 2 sonatas (1964, 1973); *Fantasy* (1967); *Melodic Suite* (1971–72); *Veils* (1974); *Poème* (1977); *Waves and Ripples* (1979); *Fantasia on a Theme by Robert Schumann* (1983); *Keyboard Triptych* (Montreal, Oct. 19, 1986). **VOCAL:** *Love's Garden* for Soprano and Orch. (1988); *Canticles* for Chorus and Orch. (1989).—**NS/LK/DM**

Gelmetti, Gianluigi, Italian conductor; b. Rome, Sept. 11, 1945. He studied conducting at the Accademia di Santa Cecilia in Rome (diploma, 1965). His principal mentor was Ferrara (1962–67), but he also studied with Celibidache and in Vienna with Swarowsky. After serving as music director of the Orch. of the Pomeriggi Musicale in Milan (until 1980), he was chief conductor of the RAI Orch. in Rome (1980–84) and music director of the Rome Opera (1984–85). He was chief conductor of the Stuttgart Radio Sym. Orch. (from 1989) and music director of the Orchestre Philharmonique de Monte Carlo (1990–92).—**NS/LK/DM**

Geminiani, Francesco (Xaverio), eminent Italian violinist, composer, and music theorist; b. Lucca (baptized), Dec. 5, 1687; d. Dublin, Sept. 17, 1762. He studied with Carlo Ambrogio Lonati in Milan; then studied violin with Corelli and composition with A. Scarlatti in Rome. He was a violinist in the orch. of the Signoria theater in Lucca from 1707 to 1710; became concertmaster of the Naples Orch. in 1711. In 1714 he went to London, where he gained fame as a violin virtuoso, composer, and teacher. During the 1731–32 season, he presented a series of subscription concerts in London; in 1733–34 he maintained a concert room in Dublin, and also sold paintings; from 1737 to 1740 he was again in Dublin, giving concerts and teaching. He spent most of the succeeding years in England, but also made trips to the Continent. He returned to Ireland in 1759 as music master to Charles Coote (later the Earl of Bellamont) at Cootehill, County Cavan; that same year he went to Dublin, where he gave his last concert in 1760. Geminiani composed a number of fine sonatas and concertos in a distinctive and assured style. He also wrote the valuable treatise *The Art of Playing on the Violin* (1751), which effectively carried forward the Italian tradition of Corelli while setting the course for succeeding generations.

WRITINGS: *Rules for Playing in a True Taste...,* op.8 (London, 1748; with 4 tunes); *A Treatise of Good Taste in the Art of Musick* (London, 1749; facsimile ed. by R. Donnington, 1969; with 4 songs and 7 "Airs"); *The Art of Playing on the Violin,* op.9 (London, 1751; facsimile ed. by D. Boyden, London, 1952; with 12 works and 24 examples); *Guida armonica...,* op.10 (London, c. 1754); *The Art of Accompaniment...,* op.11 (2 parts, London, c. 1754); *A Supplement to the Guida Armonica* (London, c. 1754); *The Art of Playing the Guitar or Cittra...* (Edinburgh, 1760; with 11 sonatas). He also publ. a periodical, *The Harmonical Miscellany* (London, 1758; Part 1: 14 works "in the Tone Minor"; Part 2: 16 works "in the Tone Major").

WORKS: ORCH.: 6 Concerti grossi, op.2 (London, 1732; 2nd ed., rev., c. 1755; ed. by H. Moser, *Musik-Kränzlein,* Leipzig, n.d.); 6 Concerti grossi, op.3 (London, 1732; 2nd ed., rev., c. 1755; ed. by R. Hernried, London, 1935); 3 *Select Concertos* (London, 1734); 6 Concerti grossi, op.7 (London, 1746); *The Enchanted Forrest,* a piece in concerto grosso style (London, c. 1756); also arrangements of works by Corelli. **CHAMBER:** 12 *Sonate* for Violin, Violone, and Harpsichord, op.1 (London, 1716; rev. ed., 1739, as *Le prime sonate;* ed. by R. Finney, Northampton, Mass., 1935, and by W. Kolneder, Mainz, 1961); *XII Solos...compos'd by Sigr. Geminiani and Castrucci* for Flute, Violin, or Harpsichord (London, c. 1720; nos. 7 to 12 by Geminiani); 12 Sonate for Violin and Basso Continuo, op.4 (London, 1739); 6 *Sonates* for Cello and Basso Continuo, op.5 (Paris, 1746; also arranged for Violin and Basso Continuo as op.5, The Hague, 1746); *Six sonates transposées...avec des agréments* for Violin and Basso Continuo, op.6 (Paris, 1746); also arrangements of works by F. Mancini.

BIBL.: N. Careri, *F. G. (1687–1762)* (Oxford, 1993). —**NS/LK/DM**

Gencer, Leyla, Turkish soprano; b. Constantinople, Oct. 10, 1924. She studied at the Ankara Cons. with Elvira de Hidalgo; she also studied with Arangi-Lombardi in Istanbul. After making her operatic debut as Santuzza in Ankara in 1950, she completed her training in Italy with Apollo Granforte. In 1953 she sang in Naples, and then joined Milan's La Scala in 1956; she also appeared at the San Francisco Opera (1956–58). Her career was mainly concentrated in Europe, where she first sang at the Spoleto Festival (1959), the Salzburg Festival (1961), London's Covent Garden (1962), the Glyndebourne Festival (1962), and the Edinburgh Festival (1969). Among her admired roles were Donna Anna, Countess Almaviva, Anna Bolena, Norma, Elisabeth de Valois, and Maria Stuarda.—**NS/LK/DM**

Gendron, Maurice, French cellist, conductor, and pedagogue; b. Nice, Dec. 26, 1920; d. Grez-sur-Loing, Aug. 20, 1990. He studied cello with Stéphane Odero in Cannes, Jean Mangot at the Nice Cons. (premier prix, 1935), and Gérard Hekking at the Paris Cons. (premier prix, 1938); later he found mentors in conducting in Désormiere, Scherchen, and Mengelberg. In 1945 he acquired a following as a cello virtuoso when he appeared as soloist in Prokofiev's Cello Concerto in London; thereafter he played with major European orchs. He also was active as a conductor in France, and later was conductor with the Bournemouth Sinfonietta (1971–73). He served as a prof. at the Saarbrücken Hochschule für Musik (1953–70), and then at the Paris Cons. (1970–87).—**NS/LK/DM**

Genée, (Franz Friedrich) Richard, German conductor, composer, and librettist; b. Danzig, Feb. 7, 1823; d. Baden bei Wien, June 15, 1895. He received training from Stahlknecht in Berlin. In 1847 he began his career as a theater conductor in Danzig, and subsequently conducted in such cities as Mainz, Schwerin, and Amsterdam. In 1863 he became conductor at the Landestheater in Prague. He went to Vienna as conductor of the Theater an der Wien in 1868, where he displayed a gift for adapting foreign works for the Viennese stage. He also wrote librettos for Johann Strauss, Suppé, Millöcker, and other composers, often in collaboration with F. Zell. Although Genée composed numerous stage works, only his operettas *Der Seekadett* (Vienna, Oct. 24, 1876) and *Nanon, die Wirtin vom goldenen Lamm* (Vienna, March 10, 1877) had much success. After retiring from the Theater an der Wien in 1878, he continued to compose and write librettos for the rest of his life.

BIBL.: B. Hiltner-Hennenberg, *R. G.: Eine Bibliographie* (Frankfurt am Main, 1998).—**NS/LK/DM**

Generali (real name, Mercandetti), Pietro,

Italian composer; b. Masserano, Oct. 23, 1773; d. Novara, Nov. 3, 1832. He studied in Rome. He began to compose sacred music at an early age, but soon turned to opera. He traveled all over Italy as producer of his operas, and also went to Vienna and Barcelona. Returning to Italy, he became maestro di cappella at the Cathedral of Novara. He anticipated Rossini in the effective use of dynamics in the instrumental parts of his operas, and was generally praised for his technical knowledge. He wrote about 50 stage works, in both the serious and comic genres, but none survived in the repertoire after his death. The following were successful at their initial performances: *Pamela nubile* (Venice, April 12, 1804), *Le lagrime di una vedova* (Venice, Dec. 26, 1808), *Adelina* (Venice, Sept. 16, 1810), *L'Impostore* (Milan, May 21, 1815), *I Baccanali di Roma* (Venice, Jan. 14, 1816; his best work), *Il Servo padrone* (Parma, Aug. 12, 1818), and *Il divorzio persiano* (Trieste, Jan. 31, 1828).

BIBL.: Piccoli, *Elogio del maestro P. G.* (1833).—NS/LK/DM

Genesis, seminal British progressive-rock group of the late 1960s and 1970s. **MEMBERSHIP:** Peter Gabriel, lead voc. (b. London, England, Feb. 13, 1950); Tony Banks, kybd., voc. (b. East Heathly, Sussex, England, March 27, 1951); Steve Hackett, lead gtr., 12-string gtr. (b. London, England, Feb. 12, 1950); Mike Rutherford, bs., 12-string gtr., voc. (b. Guildford, England, Oct. 2, 1950); Anthony Phillips, gtr. (b. Putney, England, Dec. 1951); Chris Stewart, drm. Chris Stewart left almost immediately, to be replaced by John Silver in 1968, John Mayhew in 1969, and finally Phil Collins (b. London, England, Jan. 30, 1951) on drums and vocals in 1970; guitarist Steve Hackett replaced Anthony Phillips in the same year. Peter Gabriel left in June 1975; Hackett left in 1977.

Genesis favored a variety of keyboards and synthesizers in producing its sophisticated, richly textured music that set the style for other progressive- rock groups of the 1970s, such as Emerson, Lake and Palmer and Yes. Formed as a songwriters' collective, the group emphasized the songs rather than virtuoso musicianship. Building their reputation on the flamboyance and theatrics of lead vocalist Peter Gabriel, Genesis attempted to break through in America as a headline group rather than a supporting act in 1972. By 1975 the group had established itself with their early tour de force *The Lamb Lies Down on Broadway*, an elaborate album combining a story line with surreal lyrics; some critics hailed it as the definitive concept album. The band employed progressively more ambitious stage presentations for subsequent tours.

With Peter Gabriel's departure in 1975, Genesis began moving in a mainstream direction, with drummer Phil Collins taking over the lead vocal chores. Leaving behind their progressive pretensions with the 1977 departure of guitarist Steve Hackett, Genesis became an enormously popular touring and recording act in the 1980s, bolstered by the uncanny pop success of Phil Collins as a solo artist. Despite being criticized as boring, unimaginative, and repetitive, Genesis became one of the most popular and profitable rock groups in

the world, and Collins likewise achieved huge success as a singles artist. Meanwhile Gabriel has continued to produce provocative, personal music, achieving his greatest success with 1986's *So* and the hit song "Sledgehammer" and its innovative music video. Most recently he has become a champion of world music, founding the World Music Arts and Dance (WOMAD) festival.

Genesis was formed in January 1967 as a songwriters' collective by four students at England's Charterhouse School: Peter Gabriel, Tony Banks, Mike Rutherford, and Anthony Phillips. After sending a tape to producer-songwriter Jonathon King (1965's "Everyone's Gone to the Moon"), the group recorded their debut album, *In the Beginning* (rereleased as *From Genesis to Revelation*), for Mercury Records with King as producer. The group was released from its recording contract after a year and was joined by drummer John Mayhew in 1969. This lineup of Genesis recorded *Trespass* for the ABC subsidiary Impulse (released on Charisma in Great Britain). Phillips and Mayhew left the group in 1970, and Phil Collins was recruited to play drums and sing backup vocals. He had been a child actor, appearing as the Artful Dodger in the London production of *Oliver*, and had taken up drums at age 10. He had begun playing sessions at 14, and played with Flaming Youth in 1969. Several months later guitarist Steve Hackett joined Genesis.

For *Nursery Cryme*, on Charisma Records, Genesis featured extensive use of the mellotron (an early synthesizer). The album contained two Genesis favorites, "Musical Box" and "Return of the Giant Hogweed," and garnered rave reviews in Britain. The band then began experimenting with visuals and theatrics in performance that later became the group's early trademark. Peter Gabriel became the visual focus of Genesis, utilizing mime, costuming, and lengthy song introductions on stage. *Foxtrot* included Genesis favorites "Watcher of the Skies" and the 23-minute "Supper's Ready," which featured spectacular lighting and elaborate costuming by Gabriel in performance. In an effort to generate a following beyond its cult status in America, the group debuted in the United States as a headlining act in December 1972.

Genesis's first breakthrough into the American market came with 1973's *Selling England by the Pound*. Featuring songwriting developments on the themes of myth, legend, and fantasy, plus Banks's synthesizer work and several songs in odd time signatures, the album contained the group's first British hit, "I Know What I Like." With their reputation secure as a major British band by 1974, Genesis switched to Atlantic Records for the double-record concept album *The Lamb Lies Down on Broadway*. Written in its entirety by Peter Gabriel, the album traced the surreal contemporary adventures of its hero, Rael, in the harsh N.Y.C. environment. The subsequent British and American tours virtually duplicated the album in performance, with Gabriel portraying Rael through a series of odd costume changes.

In June 1975 Peter Gabriel, sensing a loss of creative momentum and weary from years of touring and recording, left Genesis. Inasmuch as Gabriel had been (incorrectly) assumed to be the band's musical leader and chief songwriter, critics began predicting its demise. Phil Collins took over on lead vocals for subsequent recordings. *A Trick of the Tail* proved surprisingly successful, as did *Wind and Wuthering*, which yielded their first (minor) American hit, "Your Own Special Way." In order to free Collins from his drumming duties, Genesis recruited former King Crimson and Yes drummer Bill Bruford for their 1976 tours. For their 1977 worldwide tour they used all new sound and lighting equipment, enlisting American drummer Chester Thompson. The 1976 and 1977 tours were documented on *Seconds Out*.

Phil Collins began working outside Genesis in 1976, recording six albums with the jazz fusion group Brand X through 1980. Former member Anthony Phillips launched a solo career in 1976, and in 1977 Steve Hackett dropped out of Genesis to pursue a solo career. He recorded six albums through 1983 and formed GTR with vocalist Max Bacon and former Asia and Yes guitarist Steve Howe in 1986.

Reduced to a trio after Hackett's departure, Genesis recorded the appropriately titled *And Then There Were Three*, with Rutherford playing all guitar and bass parts. Revealing a mainstream pop sound, the album yielded a major hit single with "Follow You, Follow Me." Genesis next recorded *Duke* and the best-selling *Abacab*, which produced major hits with "Misunderstanding" and "Abacab," respectively. Augmented by drummer Chester Thompson and new American guitarist Darryl Stuermer for tours, Genesis next released the double-record set *Three Sides Live*. All three members of the core band (Collins-Rutherford-Banks) have maintained their commitment to the group while pursuing various solo and other band projects from this period forward.

Phil Collins began recording as a solo artist in 1981, soon hitting with "I Missed Again" and "In the Air Tonight." He scored a near-smash in 1982–83 with a remake of the Supremes's "You Can't Hurry Love." His success seemed to bolster the career of Genesis, and 1983's *Genesis* yielded four hits, including the smash "That's All." Genesis toured in 1984, and thereafter Collins and Genesis alternated producing smash hits. Through 1986 Collins had three smash hits with "Easy Lover" (in duet with Philip Bailey), "Don't Lose My Number," and "Take Me Home," and top hits with "Against All Odds" (from the movie of the same name), "One More Night," "Sussudio," and "Separate Lives" (in duet with Marilyn Martin from the movie *White Nights*). Genesis scored five smash hits in 1986–87 with "Invisible Touch" (a top hit), "Throwing It All Away," "Land of Confusion," "Tonight, Tonight, Tonight," and "In Too Deep" from *Invisible Night*. Collins starred in the 1988 movie *Buster*, which yielded top hits for Collins with a remake of the Mindbenders' "Groovy Kind of Love" and "Two Hearts."

During the 1990s Genesis scored major hits with "No Son of Mine," "I Can't Dance," "Hold on My Heart," "Jesus Knows Me," and "Never a Time" from *We Can't Dance*. The American stadium tour in support of the album yielded the two-part live set *The Way We Walk* (the first volume, "The Shorts," celebrated their recent hits, while the second, "The Longs," featured re-cre-

ations of their more ambitious 1970s progressive tunes). Phil Collins recorded the socially conscious album *...But Seriously*, which yielded pop and easy-listening hits with the top "Another Day in Paradise," the smashes "I Wish It Would Rain Down," "Do You Remember?," and "Something Happened on the Way to Heaven," and the major "Hang in Long Enough." He scored a major hits in 1993–94 with "Both Sides of the Story" and "Everyday."

Peter Gabriel returned to recording with three solo albums—released in 1977, 1978, and 1980—all, oddly, with the same name, *Peter Gabriel*. Exploring electronic instrumentation and Third World music on these albums, Gabriel was at the forefront of rock's avant garde with his imaginative, complex arrangements and performance-artist persona in concert. He scored his first minor American hit in 1977 with "Solsbury Hill," and the third *Peter Gabriel* album included the moderate hit "Games without Frontiers," with backing vocals by Kate Bush, and "Biko," his tribute to South African activist Steve Biko, who died in prison in 1977.

In 1982 Peter Gabriel founded the World Music Arts and Dance organization in England, to promote contemporary non-Western music, or "world music." Over the years, the organization has presented more than 60 festivals in 12 countries, featuring acts from Jamaica, Africa, India, and Russia. That year the brooding, dense *Security* produced Gabriel's first major hit, "Shock the Monkey." He toured in 1983 and recorded five instrumental versions of previously released songs for the soundtrack to the movie *Birdy*. He finally made his commercial breakthrough in 1986 with the accessible *So* album, which yielded four hits: the top hit "Sledgehammer," the major hit "In Your Eyes," the near- smash hit "Big Time," and the minor hit "Don't Give Up," recorded with Kate Bush.

In 1986 Gabriel performed on the Amnesty International tour, and he later conducted his own international tour of arenas, introducing Senegal's most popular musician, Youssou N'Dour, to a new audience. He subsequently formed Real World Records for releases by Third World artists, and scored and recorded the music for the controversial 1989 Martin Scorsese movie *The Last Temptation of Christ* using musicians from Africa, India, Pakistan, and the Middle East. Gabriel managed moderate hits in 1992–93 with "Digging in the Dirt" and "Steam," and introduced his impressive CD-ROM *Peter Gabriel's Secret World* in late 1993.

In 1985 Mike Rutherford formed Mike and the Mechanics with vocalists Paul Young (b. Manchester, England, June 17, 1947) and Paul Carrack (b. Sheffield, England, April 22, 1951), keyboardist Adrian Lee (b. London, England, Sept. 9, 1947), and drummer Peter Van Hooke (b. London, England, June 4, 1950). Young had been lead vocalist with Sad Cafe, and Carrack had sung on Ace's smash 1975 hit "How Long" and Squeeze's moderate 1981 hit "Tempted." Mike and the Mechanics scored smash hits with "Silent Running (On Dangerous Ground)" and "All I Need Is a Miracle," and they toured the United States in 1986. They toured again in 1989, in support of *Living Years* and its top-hit title song.

DISC.: GENESIS: *In the Beginning* (1968; reissued as *From Genesis to Revelation*, 1974); *And Then There Was* (1987); *Trespass* (1970); *Nursery Cryme* (1971); *Foxtrot* (1972); *Best* (reissue of above two; 1976); *Nursery Cryme/Foxtrot* (1979); *Selling England by the Pound* (1973); *G. Live* (1974); *The Lamb Lies Down on Broadway* (1974); *A Trick of the Tail* (1976); *Wind and Wuthering* (1977); *Seconds Out* (1977); *...And Then There Were Three* (1978); *Duke* (1980); *Abacab* (1981); *Three Sides Live* (1982); *G.* (1983); *Invisible Touch* (1986); *We Can't Dance* (1991); *Live/The Way We Walk—Vol. One: The Shorts* (1992); *The Way We Walk—Vol. Two: The Longs* (1993). **THE LONDON SYMPHONY ORCH.:** *We Know What We Like: The Music of G.* (1987). **STEVE HACKETT:** *Voyage of the Acolyte* (1976); *Please Don't Touch* (1978); *Spectral Mornings* (1979); *Defector* (1980); *Cured* (1981); *Highly Strung* (1983); *Time Lapse* (1992); *Momentum* (1994); *Till We Have Faces* (1994); *Bay of Kings* (1994); *Blues with a Feeling* (1995). **GTR (WITH STEVE HACKETT):** *GTR* (1986). **BRAND X (WITH PHIL COLLINS):** *Unorthodox Behaviour* (1976); *Moroccan Roll* (1977); *Livestock* (1977); *Masques* (1978); *Product* (1979); *Do They Hurt?* (1980). **ANTHONY PHILLIPS:** *The Geese and the Ghost* (1977); *Wise After the Event* (1978); *Sides* (1980); *Private Parts and Pieces, Part III—Antiques* (1992); *1984* (1992); *Slow Dance* (1991); *Private Parts and Pieces, Vol. 8* (1993). **PETER GABRIEL:** *Peter Gabriel* (1977); *Peter Gabriel* (1978); *Peter Gabriel* (1980); *Peter Gabriel* (aka *Security*; 1982); *Plays Live* (1983); *Birdy* (soundtrack; 1985); *So* (1986); *Passion: Music for the Last Temptation of Christ* (soundtrack; 1989); *Shaking the Tree: 16 Golden Greats* (1990); *Revisited* (1992); *Us* (1992); *Secret World Live* (1994); *OVO: Millennium Show* (2000). **TONY BANKS:** *A Curious Feeling* (1979); *The Fugitive* (1983); *The Wicked Lady* (soundtrack; 1984); *Soundtracks* (1986); *Still* (1992). **PHIL COLLINS:** *Face Value* (1981); *Hello, I Must Be Going!* (1982); *No Jacket Required* (1985); *12"ers* (1988); *...But Seriously* (1989); *Serious Hits...Live!* (1990); *Both Sides* (1993). **MIKE RUTHERFORD:** *Smallcreep's Day* (1980); *Acting Very Strange* (1982). **MIKE AND THE MECHANICS:** *Mike + The Mechanics* (1985); *Living Years* (1988); *Word of Mouth* (1991); *Beggar on a Beach of Gold* (1995).

BIBL.: Armando Gallo, *G.: The Evolution of a Rock Band* (London, 1978); Steve Clarke, *G.: Turn It On Again* (London, 1984); Ray Coleman, *Phil Collins* (London, 1997); Spencer Bright, *Peter Gabriel: An Authorized Biography* (London, 1988). —BH

Gennrich, Friedrich, respected German musicologist; b. Colmar, March 27, 1883; d. Langen, Sept. 22, 1967. He studied Roman philology at the Univ. of Strasbourg, and took courses in musicology with F. Ludwig. In 1921 he went to Frankfurt am Main, where he taught musicology at the Univ. until 1964. He was a leading authority on music of the troubadours, trouvères, and Minnesinger.

WRITINGS: *Musikwissenschaft und romanische Philologie* (Halle, 1918); *Der musikalische Vortrag der altfranzösischen Chansons de geste* (Halle, 1923); *Die altfranzösiche Rotrouenge* (Halle, 1925); *Das Formproblem des Minnesangs* (Halle, 1931); *Grundriss einer Formenlehre des mittelalterlichen Liedes* (Halle, 1932); *Die Strassburger Schule für Musikwissenschaft* (Würzburg, 1940); *Abriss der frankonischen Mensuralnotation* (Nieder-Modau, 1946; 2nd ed., Darmstadt, 1956); *Abriss der Mensuralnotation des XIV. und der 1. Hälfte des XV. Jahrhunderts* (Nieder-Modau, 1948); *Melodien altdeutscher Lieder* (Darmstadt, 1954); *Franco von Köln,*

Ars Cantus Mensurabilis (Darmstadt, 1955); *Die Wimpfener Fragmente der Hessischen Landesbibliothek* (Darmstadt, 1958); *Der musikalische Nachlass der Troubadours* (Darmstadt, 1960). —NS/LK/DM

Gentele, Goeran, brilliant Swedish opera manager; b. Stockholm, Sept. 20, 1917; d. in an automobile accident near Olbia, Sardinia, July 18, 1972. He studied political science in Stockholm, and art at the Sorbonne in Paris. He was first engaged as an actor, then was stage director at the Royal Drama Theater (1941–52) and at the Royal Opera (1952–63) in Stockholm, where he was appointed director in 1963. In 1970 he was appointed general manager of the Metropolitan Opera in N.Y., effective June 1972. Great expectations for his innovative directorship in America were thwarted by his untimely death during a vacation in Italy. —NS/LK/DM

Genzmer, Harald, German composer and pedagogue; b. Blumenthal, Feb. 9, 1909. After piano and organ lessons in Marburg, he studied with Hindemith at the Berlin Hochschule für Musik. He taught at the Berlin Volksmusikschule (1938–45), and then was a prof. Of composition at the Freiburg im Breisgau Hochschule für Musik (1946–57) and the Munich Hochschule für Musik (1957–74). Hindemith proved a major influence on his music, which is especially notable for its display of skillful craftsmanship in a utilitarian manner.

WORKS: ORCH.: *Bremer Sinfonie* (1942); 3 numbered syms. (1957, 1958, 1986); 3 piano concertos (1948–74); Cello Concerto (1950); Flute Concerto (1954); Violin Concerto (1959); Concerto for Harp and Strings (1965); Viola Concerto (1967); 2 concertos for Trumpet and Strings (1968, 1985); Concerto for Cello and Winds (1969); *Sinfonia da camera* (1970); 2 organ concertos (1970, 1980); Concerto for Trumpet and Large Wind Orch. (1971–72); Chamber Concerto for Viola and Strings (1973); *Musik* (1977–78); *Sinfonia per Giovani* (1979); Concerto for 2 Clarinets and Strings (1983); *Lyrisches Konzert* for Cello and Orch. (1984); Concerto for 4 Horns and Orch. (1984); Concerto for Cello, Double Bass, and Strings (1985); *Cassation* for Strings (1987); Saxophone Concerto (1992). **Ballet:** *Kokua* (1951); *Der Zauberspiegel* (1965). **CHAMBER:** Trio for Violin, Cello, and Piano (1944); Trio for Flute, Viola, and Harp (1947); Quintet for Flute, Oboe, Clarinet, Horn, and Bassoon (1956–57); Sonata for Solo Violin (1957); Sonata for Cello and Harp (1963); Trio for Piano, Violin, and Cello (1964); Sextet for 2 Clarinets, 2 Horns, and 2 Bassoons (1966); Quartet for Violin, Viola, Cello, and Double Bass (1967); Quintet for 2 Trumpets, Horn, Trombone, and Tuba (1970); Sonata for Trumpet and Organ (1971); Trombone Sonata (1971); Trio for Flute, Horn or Cello, and Harpsichord or Piano (1973); Bassoon Sonata (1974); Sonata for Solo Flute (1975); Sonata for Trombone and Organ (1977); Sonata for Cello and Organ (1979); Sonata for 2 Flutes (1981); Vibraphone Sonata (1981); Sonata for Solo Cello (1982); *Mallet/Spiele* for Marimbaphone/Vibraphone (1966); Guitar Sonata (1986); *Konzert 1994* for Trumpet, Trombone, and Organ (1994); piano pieces; organ music. **VOCAL:** *Jiménez-Kantate* for Soprano, Chorus, and Orch. (1962); *Mistral- Kantate* for Soprano and Orch. (1969–70); *Deutsche Messe* for Chorus and Organ (1973); *Oswald von Wolkenstein,* cantata for Soprano, Baritone, Chorus, and Orch. (1975–76); *The Mystic Trumpeter,* cantata for Soprano or Tenor, Trumpet, and Strings (1978); *Geistliche Kantate* for

Soprano, Men's Chorus, Organ, and Percussion (1979); *Kantate 1981 nach engl. Barockgedichten* for Soprano, Chorus, and Orch. (1981).

BIBL.: M. Brück and R. Münster, *H. G.: Ausstellung zum 80. Geburtstag: Musiklesesaal, 8. September–17. November 1989* (Munich, 1989).—NS/LK/DM

Geoffrey, Jean-Nicolas, French organist and composer; b. place and date unknown; d. Perpignan, March 11, 1694. After holding various positions as an organist in Paris until 1690, he became organist at Perpignan Cathedral in 1692. His vast collection of harpsichord works reveals a composer of decided talent.—LK/DM

George, Earl, American composer, conductor, teacher, and music critic; b. Milwaukee, May 1, 1924. He studied composition with Hanson and Rogers and conducting with Paul White and Herman Genhart at the Eastman School of Music in Rochester, N.Y. (B.M., 1946; M.M., 1947; Ph.D., 1958). He also attended courses of Lopatnikoff and Martinů at the Berkshire Music Center in Tanglewood (summer, 1946), and continued his studies with the latter in N.Y. (1947). In 1947 he received the Gershwin Prize and in 1957 held a Guggenheim followship. From 1948 to 1956 he taught theory and composition at the Univ. of Minn., and in 1955–56 was a Fulbright lecturer at the Univ. of Oslo. He then was prof. of theory and composition at Syracuse Univ. (1959–88), where he was founder-conductor of the Univ. Singers (1963–69) and conductor of the Univ. Sym. Orch. (1971–80). He also was music critic of the Syracuse *Herald- Journal* from 1961. His works follow an astute median course of prudent American modernism.

WORKS: DRAMATIC: O p e r a : *Birthdays,* 2 operas individually titled *Pursuing Happiness* and *Another 4th of July* (Syracuse, April 23, 1976); *Genevieve* (Berea, Ohio, Feb. 10, 1984). **ORCH.:** *Passacaglia* (1944); *Adagietto* (1946); *Introduction and Allegro* (1946); Concerto for Strings (1948); *A Thanksgiving Overture* (1949); *A Currier and Ives Set* for Chamber Orch. (1953); Violin Concerto (1953); *Introduction, Variations, and Finale* (1957); *Some Night Music* for Strings (1957); Piano Concerto (1958); *Declamation* for Wind Ensemble (1965). **CHAMBER:** *Arioso* for Cello and Piano (1947); *3 Pieces* for Violin, Cello, and Piano (1949); String Quartet (1961); *Tuckets and Sennets* for Trumpet and Piano (1973); piano pieces, including a Sonata (1948). **VOCAL:** *Missa brevis* for Soloists, Chorus, and Orch. (1948); *Abraham Lincoln Walks at Midnight* for Soprano, Chorus, and Orch. (1949); *3 Poems of William Wordsworth* for Narrator, Chorus, and Piano (1960); *War Is Kind* for Men's Chorus, Trumpet, Percussion, and Piano (1966); *Voyages* for Soprano, Speaker, Chorus, and 5 Instrumentalists (1967); *Voices* for Soprano, Chorus, 2 Pianos, and Percussion (1974); *Hum-drum Heaven* for Soprano, Speaker, Chorus, and Piano (1978); choruses; song cycles.—NS/LK/DM

Georges, Alexandre, French organist and composer; b. Arras, Feb. 25, 1850; d. Paris, Jan. 18, 1938. He studied at the Niedermeyer School in Paris and later became a teacher of harmony there. He occupied various posts as organist in Paris churches, and was a successful organ teacher. As a composer, he was mainly interested in opera. The following were produced in Paris: *Le Printemps* (1888), *Poèmes d'amour* (1892), *Charlotte Corday* (March 6, 1901), *Miarka* (Nov. 7, 1905; his most successful work; revived and shortened, 1925), *Myrrha* (1909), and *Sangre y sol* (Nice, Feb. 23, 1912). He also wrote the oratorios *Notre Dame de Lourdes, Balthazar* and *Chemin de Croix*; the symphonic poems *Léila, La Naissance de Vénus* and *Le Paradis perdu*. He wrote some chamber music for unusual combinations: *À la Kasbah* for Flute and Clarinet, *Kosaks* for Violin and Clarinet, etc. He is best known, however, for his melodious *Chansons de Miarka* for Voice and Piano (also with Orch.) and his arrangement of *Chansons champenoises à la manière ancienne* by G. Dévignes.—NS/LK/DM

Georgescu, Dan Corneliu, Romanian composer; b. Craiova, Jan. 1, 1938. He studied at the Popular School for the Arts (1952–56) and with Ion Dumitrescu, Ciortea, Olah, and Mendelsohn at the Bucharest Cons. (1956–61). From 1962 to 1983 he was head of research at the Ethnography and Folklore Inst. of the Romanian Academy; then pursued research at the Inst. For the History of Art (from 1984). In 1987 he went to Berlin, and then was active in ethnomusicological pursuits at the Free Univ. from 1991. His output extends from traditional to electronic scores.

WORKS: ORCH.: *3 Pieces* (1959); *Motive maramureşene,* suite (1963); 4 pieces for Orch.: I, *Jocuri* (1963), II, *Dialogue rythmique* (1964), III, *Danses solennelles* (1965) and IV, *Collages* (1966); *Partita* (1966); *Alb-negru* (1967), *Zig-Zag* (1967), *Continuo* (1968) and *Rubato* (1969), a cycle of 4 pieces for various orch. groupings; 3 syms.: No. 1, *Armoniile simple* (1976), No. 2, *Orizontale* (1980), and No. 3, *Privirile culorilor* (1985). **B a l l e t :** *Model mioritic* (1973; Cluj, Oct. 1, 1975). **CHAMBER:** Piano Sonata (1958); Trio for Flute, Clarinet, and Bassoon (1959); *Chorals I, II and III* for Flute, Violin, Viola, Cello, and Piano (1970); 3 string quartets (1982; 1983–84; 1985); 2 *Contemplative Preludes* for Organ (1991). **VOCAL:** *Schite pentru o fresca,* cantata (1976). **ELECTRONIC:** *Crystal Silence* (1989). —NS/LK/DM

Georgescu, George, Romanian conductor; b. Sulina, Sept. 12, 1887; d. Bucharest, Sept. 1, 1964. After initial training in Bucharest, he went to Berlin and studied cello with H. Becker and conducting with Nikisch and Strauss. He began his conducting career in Berlin in 1918, and then returned to Bucharest as music director of the Phil. (1920–49) and the Opera (1922–26; 1932–34); from 1954 until his death he was music director of the George Enesco State Phil. He also made guest appearances throughout Europe.

BIBL.: T. Georgescu, *G. G.* (Bucharest, 1971).—NS/LK/DM

Georgiades, Thrasybulos, Greek musicologist; b. Athens, Jan. 4, 1907; d. Munich, March 15, 1977. He studied piano in Athens, then studied musicology with Rudolf von Ficker at the Univ. of Munich, where he received his Ph.D. in 1935 with the diss. *Englische Diskanttraktate aus der ersten Hälfte des 15. Jahrhunderts* (publ. in Würzburg, 1937); he also studied composition with Orff. In 1938 he became a prof. at the Athens Odeon, serving as its director from 1939 to 1941. He completed his Habilitation at the Univ. of Munich in 1947 with his *Bemerkungen zur antiken Quantitätsmetrik* (publ. in Hamburg, 1949, as *Der griechische Rhythmus. Musik, Reigen, Vers und Sprache*; 2nd ed., 1977; Eng. tr., N.Y., 1956). In 1948 he joined the faculty of the Univ. of Heidelberg; in 1956 he became a prof. at the Univ. of Munich, retiring in 1972. He contributed valuable papers to German music journals on ancient Greek, Byzantine, and medieval music. His other writings include *Volkslied als Bekenntnis* (Regensburg, 1947), *Musik und Sprache* (Berlin, 1954; Eng. tr., Cambridge, 1983), *Musik und Rhythmus bei den Griechen* (Hamburg, 1958), *Zum Ursprung der abendlandischen Musik* (Hamburg, 1958), *Musik und Schrift* (Munich, 1962), *Das musikalische Theater* (Munich, 1965), and *Schubert, Musik und Lyrik* (Göttingen, 1967).

BIBL.: D. Dorner, *Musik als Repräsentationsgeschehen: Ein musikphilosophischer Rekurs auf T. G.* (Frankfurt am Main, 1998). **—NS/LK/DM**

Georgiadis, Georges, Greek pianist and composer; b. Salonika, Sept. 8, 1912; d. Athens, May 8, 1986. He studied piano and composition at the Athens Cons. In 1943 he was appointed prof. of piano there. His music, cast in a traditional mold, was inspired chiefly by Greek folk resources. Among his compositions were a Concertino for Piano and Orch. (1959), *De la paix*, sym. (1960), 2 violin sonatas, songs, many piano pieces, and incidental music.**—NS/LK/DM**

Georgii, Walter, German pianist and pedagogue; b. Stuttgart, Nov. 23, 1887; d. Tübingen, Feb. 23, 1967. He studied piano in Stuttgart and theory in Leipzig, Berlin, and Halle. From 1914 to 1945 he taught piano in Cologne. He publ. *Weber als Klavierkomponist* (Leipzig, 1914), *Geschichte der Musik für Klavier zu 2 Hände* (Zürich, 1941; rev. ed., 1950), and *Klavierspielerbuchlein* (Zürich, 1953), as well as an anthology of piano music, *400 Jahre europaïscher Klavier Musik* (Cologne, 1950).**—NS/LK/DM**

Gerarde, Derick, Flemish composer who flourished from 1540 to 1580. He settled in England and was in the service of the Earl of Arundel in Nonesuch, Surrey. His distinguished output included some 90 motets, more than 120 secular vocal pieces, and about 45 instrumental works.**—LK/DM**

Gérardy, Jean, Belgian cellist; b. Spa, Dec. 6, 1877; d. there, July 4, 1929. At the age of 5 he began to study cello with R. Bellmann, and then was a pupil of Alfred Massau at the Liège Cons. from 1885 to 1889. In 1888 he played as a student in a trio with Ysaÿe and Paderewski, becoming a noted ensemble player. With Ysaÿe and Godowsky, he formed a trio and toured the U.S. in 1913–14. Gérardy's instrument was a Stradivari made in 1710.**—NS/LK/DM**

Gerber, Ernst Ludwig, celebrated German lexicographer; b. Sondershausen, Sept. 29, 1746; d. there, June 30, 1819. He studied organ and theory with his father, the organist and composer Heinrich Nikolaus Gerber. He then studied both law and music in Leipzig, becoming a skillful cellist and organist, in which latter capacity he became (1769) his father's assistant, and succeeded him in 1775. He visited Weimar, Kassel, Leipzig, and other cities, and gradually gathered together a large collection of musicians' portraits; to these he appended brief biographical notices, and finally conceived the plan of writing a biographical dictionary of musicians. Though his resources (in a small town without a public library, and having to rely in great measure on material sent him by his publisher, Breitkopf) were hardly adequate to the task he undertook, his *Historisch-biographisches Lexikon der Tonkünstler* (Leipzig, 2 vols., 1790–92; reprinted 1976) was so well received, and brought in such a mass of corrections and fresh material from all quarters, that he prepared a supplementary ed., *Neues historisch- biographisches Lexikon der Tonkünstler* (4 vols., 1812–14; reprinted 1966). Though the former was intended only as a supplement to Walther's dictionary, and both are, of course, out of date, they contain much material still of value, and have been extensively drawn upon by more recent writers. The Viennese Gesellschaft der Musikfreunde purchased his large library.**—NS/LK/DM**

Gerber, René, Swiss composer and teacher; b. Travers, June 29, 1908. He attended the Univ. of Zürich (1929) and studied with Andreae and Müller at the Zürich Cons. (1931–33) before completing his training in Paris (1934) with Dukas, Boulanger, Siohan, and Dupont. After serving as prof. of music at the Latin Coll. in Neuchâtel (1940–47), he was director of the Neuchâtel Cons. (1947–51). His works were marked by tonal and modal writing.

WORKS: DRAMATIC: Opera: *Roméo et Juliette* (1957–61); *Le Songe d'une nuit d'été* (1978–81). **ORCH.:** 2 concertos for Harp and Chamber Orch. (1931, 1969); Clarinet Concerto (1932); *Hommageà Ronsard* (1933); 2 piano concertos: No. 1 for Piano and Chamber Orch. (1933) and No. 2 for Piano and Orch. (1966–70); *Suite française I* (1933), *II* (1934), and *III* (1945) for Chamber Orch.; Concerto for Flute and Chamber Orch. (1934); Concerto for Bassoon and Chamber Orch. (1935–39); *Les Heures de France* (1937); Concerto for Trumpet and Chamber Orch. (1939); Violin Concerto (1941); *Trois Paysages de Breughel* (1942); *Le Terroir animé* (1944); *Trois Danses espagnoles* for Chamber Orch. (1944); 2 sinfoniettas for Strings (1949, 1968); *L'lmagier médiéval* (1952–74); *Lais Corinthiaca* (1957); *Suite brévinière* (1960); *Le Moulin de la Galette* (1970); Concerto for English Horn and Chamber Orch. (1976); *L'École de Fontainebleau* (1978–79); Concerto for Trumpet, Strings, and Percussion (1983); *The Old Farmer's Almanac* (1986). **CHAMBER:** Sonata for Solo Harp (1932); 4 string quartets (1933, 1934, 1941, 1947); Concertino for Winds, Piano, and Percussion (1935); *Ballet* for Flute and Piano (1943); Violin Sonata (1943); Trio for Violin, Cello, and Piano (1944); Flute Sonata (1945); Cello Sonata (1945); Trumpet Sonata (1948); Saxophone Sonata (1948); Suite for Flute, Oboe, and Piano (1948); Sonatine for Cor de chasse and Piano (1965); Trio for 2 Clarinets and Bassoon (1982; also for 3 Clarinets); *A Terpsychore* for Clarinet Ensemble (1993). **VOCAL:** *5 Impressions* for Voice, Wind Orch., 2 Harps, and Percussion (1942); *Le Tombeau de Botticelli* for Chorus and 11 Instruments (1967); *Trois Visions espagnoles* for Voice, 5 Winds,

Piano, and 2 Percussion (1973); *3 Poèmes de la Renaissance* for Contralto or Baritone, Violin, Cello, and Piano (1977); *3 Poèmes* for Soprano, Violin, Cello, and Piano (1988); other songs; noëls, etc.—**NS/LK/DM**

Gerber, Rudolf, learned German musicologist; b. Flehingen, Baden, April 15, 1899; d. Göttingen, May 6, 1957. He studied at the Univ. of Halle, and then at the Univ. of Leipzig (Ph.D., 1922, with the diss. *Die Arie in den Opern Johann Adolf Hasses*; publ. as *Der Operntypus Johann Adolf Hasses und seine textlichen Grundlagen*, Leipzig, 1925). In 1923 he became Abert's assistant at the Univ. of Berlin. He completed his Habilitation in 1928 at the Univ. of Giessen with his *Das Passionsrezitativ bei Heinrich Schütz und seine stilgeschichtlichen Grundlagen* (publ. in Gütersloh, 1929). In 1928 he joined its faculty, where he later was a prof. and head of its Music-Historical Inst. (1937–43). In 1943 he became a prof. at the Univ. of Göttingen. Among his other writings were *Johannes Brahms* (Potsdam, 1938), *Christoph Willibald Ritter von Gluck* (Potsdam, 1941; 2nd. ed., rev., 1950); and *Bachs Brandenburgische Konzerte* (Kassel, 1951). He also ed. works by Schütz, J.S. Bach, and Gluck.—**NS/LK/DM**

Gerbert, Martin, Freiherr von Hornau, eminent German music scholar; b. Hornau, near Horb am Neckar, Aug. 11, 1720; d. St.-Blasien, May 13, 1793. A student in the Benedictine monastery at St.-Blasien, he joined the order in 1737, became a priest in 1744, and then prof. of theology there. From 1759 to 1762 he made trips to Germany, France, and throughout Italy, collecting old MSS, particularly those on music history, of which he later made valuable use in his own works. He also visited Padre Martini in Bologna, corresponding with him from 1761 until Martini's death in 1784. In 1764 he was elected Prince-Abbot of the monastery at St.-Blasien. His writings on music are *De cantu et musica sacra* (2 vols., 1774; reprint, 1968), *Vetus liturgia alemannica* (2 vols., 1776; reprint, 1967), *Monumenta veteris liturgiae alemannicae* (2 vols., 1777–79), and *Scriptores ecclesiastici de musica sacra potissimum* (3 vols., 1784; reprint, 1905).

BIBL.: J. Bader, *Fürstabt M. G.* (Freiburg, 1875); A. Lamy, *M. G.* (Rheims, 1898); G. Pfeilschifter, *Die Korrespondenz des Fürstabtes M. G. von St. Blasien* (Vol. I, 1752–73; 1931); E. Hegar, *Die Anfänge der neueren Musikgeschichtsschreibung um 1770 bei G., Burney and Hawkins* (Strasbourg, 1932); G. Pfeilschifter, A. Allgeler, and W. Müller, eds., *Briefe und Akten des Fürstabts M. II. G. von St. Blasien, 1764–1793* (Karlsruhe, 1957).—**NS/LK/DM**

Gerelli, Ennio, Italian conductor and composer; b. Cremona, Feb. 12, 1907; d. there, Oct. 5, 1970. He studied at the Bologna Cons. He conducted ballet and opera in Italy, then was on the staff of La Scala in Milan (1935–40). In 1961 he founded the Camerata di Cremona. He also wrote some chamber music.—**NS/LK/DM**

Gergiev, Valery (Abissalovich), notable Russian conductor; b. Moscow, May 2, 1953. He received training in piano and conducting at the Ordzhoniskidze Coll. of Music, then pursued conducting studies with Ilya Musin at the Leningrad Cons. (graduated, 1977). In

1975 he won 1st prize in the All-Union Conductors' Competition in Moscow. In 1977 he captured 2nd prize in the Karajan competition in Berlin and was named asst. conductor at the Kirov Opera in Leningrad, where he made his debut conducting *War and Peace* in 1978; in 1979, was made permanent conductor there. He also served as chief conductor of the Armenian State Sym. Orch. in Yerevan (1981–85). In 1988 he was appointed artistic director and principal conductor of the Kirov Opera. From 1989 to 1992 he also was principal guest conductor of the Rotterdam Phil. He conducted the Kirov Opera on many tours abroad, including its first visit to the U.S. in 1992 when it appeared at the Metropolitan Opera in N.Y. On March 21, 1994, he made his Metropolitan Opera debut conducting *Otello*. In the autumn of 1994 he made a concert tour of the U.S. conducting the Kirov Orch. In 1995 he became music director of the Rotterdam Phil. In 1997 he became principal guest conductor of the Metropolitan Opera, where on Dec. 19 he conducted the first perf. of Buketoff's ed. of *Boris Godunov*. Gergiev's interpretative insights, backed by an assured conducting technique, make him one of the most admired conductors of his generation. While his idiomatic performances of the Russian repertoire are particularly compelling, he has demonstrated skills in a broad operatic and symphonic repertoire well beyond the Russian tradition. —**NS/LK/DM**

Gerhard, Roberto, eminent Catalonian-born English composer and teacher of Swiss-German and Alsatian descent; b. Valls, Sept. 25, 1896; d. Cambridge, Jan. 5, 1970. After training in piano with Granados (1915–16) and in composition with Pedrell (1916–20) in Barcelona, he pursued advanced studies in composition with Schoenberg in Vienna (1922–25) and Berlin (1925–28). Returning to Barcelona, he was made a prof. of music at the Ecola Normal de la Generalitat in 1931 and head of the music dept. of the Catalan Library in 1932, positions he held until the defeat of the Republic in the Spanish Civil War in 1939. He settled in Cambridge, where he held a research scholarship at King's Coll. In 1956 he taught at the Dartington Summer School of Music. In 1960 he was a visiting prof. of composition at the Univ. of Mich. in Ann Arbor. He taught at the Berkshire Music Center at Tanglewood in the summer of 1961. In 1960 he became a naturalized British subject. Gerhard was made a Commander of the Order of the British Empire in 1967 and was awarded an honorary doctor of music degree by the Univ. of Cambridge in 1968. In his early works, Gerhard followed traditional Spanish melodic and rhythmic patterns. The influence of Schoenberg is felt in his serial usage in the Wind Quintet (1928), but it was not until he settled in England that he began to reassess Schoenberg's 12-tone method with a detailed study of Hauer's and A. Hába's serial procedures. In 1952 he turned to the athematic procedures of Hába, which led to his composition of scores of great originality and merit. Among his finest works were the opera *The Duenna*, the ballet *Don Quixote*, and the 1st Sym.

WORKS: DRAMATIC: O p e r a : *The Duenna* (1945–47; BBC, 1947; rev. 1950; concert perf., Wiesbaden, June 27, 1951; stage perf., Madrid, Jan. 21, 1992; also *Interlude and Arias from*

1251

The Duenna for Mezzo-soprano and Orch., London, Sept. 18, 1961). **B a l l e t :** *Ariel* (1934; concert perf., Barcelona, May 18, 1936); *Soirées de Barcelone* (1936–38; unfinished; orch. suite, 1936–38; also for Piano, c. 1958; London, Jan. 12, 1985); *Don Quixote* (1940–41; 1947–49; London, Feb. 20, 1950; also *Dances from Don Quixote* for Piano, BBC, London, Nov. 26, 1947, and for Orch., 1958); *Alegrías* (1942; Birmingham, July 16, 1943; orch. suite, BBC, April 4, 1944); *Pandora* (1943–44; Cambridge, Jan. 26, 1944; orchestrated 1945; orch. suite, BBC, London, Feb. 1950). **ORCH.:** *Albada, Interludi i Danza* (1936; London, June 24, 1938); *Pedrelliana* (1941; final movement of subsequent work); 1 unnumbered sym.: *Homenage a Pedrell* (1941; BBC, London, 1954); 5 numbered syms.: No. 1 (1952–53; Baden-Baden, June 21, 1955), No. 2 (1957–59; London, Oct. 28, 1959; rev. 1967–68 as *Metamorphoses*), No. 3, *Collages* (1960; London, Feb. 8, 1961), No. 4, *New York* (N.Y., Dec. 14, 1967), and No. 5 (1969; unfinished); Violin Concerto (1942–43; rev. 1945, 1949; Florence, June 16, 1950); *Cadiz*, fantasia on a zarzuela by Chueca and Valverde (1943); *Gigantes y Cabezudos (Giants and Dwarfs)*, fantasia on a zarzuela by Fernández Caballero (c. 1943); *La Viejecita*, fantasia on a zarzuela by Fernandez Caballero (c. 1943); Concerto for Piano and Strings (1950); Concerto for Harpsichord, Strings, and Percussion (1955–56); *Lamparilla Overture*, after a zarzuela by Barbieri (1956); *Concerto for Orchestra* (Boston, April 25, 1965); *Epithalamion* (Valdagno, Sept. 17, 1966). **CHAMBER:** Piano Trio (1918); *2 Sardanas* for 11 Instruments (1928); Wind Quintet (1928); *Capriccio* for Flute (1949); 2 string quartets: No. 1 (1950–55; Dartington, Aug. 18, 1955) and No. 2 (1960–62); Cello Sonata (1956); Nonet for Wind Quintet, Trumpet, Trombone, Tuba, and Accordion (1956–57; BBC, London, Sept. 4, 1957); *Fantasia* for Guitar (1957); *Chaconne* for Violin (1959); *Concert for 8* for Flute, Clarinet, Mandolin, Guitar, Accordion, Percussion, Piano, and Double Bass (London, May 17, 1962); *Hymnody* for Flute, Oboe, Clarinet, Horn, Trumpet, Trombone, Tuba, 2 Percussion, and 2 Pianos (London, May 23, 1963); *Gemini* for Violin and Piano (1966); *Libra* for Flute, Clarinet, Guitar, Percussion, Piano, and Violin (1968); *Leo* for Flute, Clarinet, Horn, Trumpet, Trombone, 2 Percussion, Piano, Violin, and Cello (Hanover, N.H., Aug. 23, 1969). **P i a n o :** *Dos apunts* (2 sketches; 1921–22); *3 Impromptus* (1950). **VOCAL:** *L'Infantament Meravellos de Shahrazada*, song cycle for Soprano or Tenor and Piano (1917); *7 Haiku* for Soprano or Tenor, Flute, Oboe, Clarinet, Bassoon, and Piano (1922; rev. 1958); *14 Cançons Populars Catalanes* for Soprano or Tenor and Piano (1928; 6 orchestrated 1931; Vienna, June 16, 1932); *L'Alta Naixença del Rei en Jaume*, cantata for Soprano, Baritone, Chorus, and Orch. (1932; 1st complete perf., Barcelona, Nov. 17, 1984); *Cançons y Arietes* for Voice and Piano (1936); *Cancionero de Pedrell* for Soprano or Tenor and Piano (1941; also for Soprano or Tenor and 13 Instruments, 1941); *Por do Pasaré la Sierra* for Soprano or Tenor and Piano (1942); *7 Canciones de Vihuela* for High Voice and Piano (1942); *6 Tonadillas* for Soprano or Tenor and Piano (1942); *Sevillanas* for Soprano or Tenor and Piano (1943); *3 Toreras* for Medium Voice and Orch. (c. 1943; also for Voice and Piano); *Engheno Novo* for Voice and Orch. (c. 1943); *The Akond of Swat* for Mezzo-soprano or Baritone and 2 Percussion (1954; London, Feb. 7, 1956); *6 French Folksongs* for High Voice and Piano (1956); *Cantares* for Soprano or Tenor and Guitar (1956); *The Plague* for Speaker, Chorus, and Orch. (1963–64; London, April 1, 1964). **T a p e :** *Audiomobiles I-IV* (1958–59); *Lament for the Death of a Bullfighter* for Speaker and Tape (1959); 10 pieces (c. 1961); *Sculptures I-V* (1963). **OTHER:** Incidental music to plays, and film, radio, and television scores.

BIBL.: K. Potter, *The Life and Works of R. G.* (diss., Univ. of Birmingham, 1972); R. Paine, *Hispanic Traditions in Twentieth-Century Catalan Music with Particular Reference to G., Mompou, and Montsalvatge* (N.Y. and London, 1989); J. Homs, *R. G. i la seva obra* (Barcelona, 1991).—NS/LK/DM

Gerhardt, Elena, celebrated German-born English mezzo-soprano; b. Leipzig, Nov. 11, 1883; d. London, Jan. 11, 1961. She studied at the Leipzig Cons. (1899–1903) with Marie Hedmont. She made her public debut on her 20th birthday in a recital, accompanied by Nikisch; after appearing at the Leipzig Opera (1903–04), she toured Europe as a lieder artist with great success; made her English debut in London in 1906, and her American debut in N.Y., Jan. 9, 1912. In 1933 she settled in London, making appearances as a singer, and teaching. She compiled *My Favorite German Songs* (1915), ed. a selection of Hugo Wolf's songs (1932), and wrote an autobiography, *Recital* (London, 1953).—NS/LK/DM

Gericke, Wilhelm, noted Austrian conductor; b. Schwanberg, April 18, 1845; d. Vienna, Oct. 27, 1925. He studied with Dessoff at the Vienna Cons. (1862–65). After a number of engagements as guest conductor in provincial theaters, he became conductor of the municipal theater in Linz. In 1874 he joined the staff of the Vienna Court Opera as an asst. conductor. In 1880 he took charge of the Gesellschaft der Musikfreunde concerts, and also led the Singverein. From 1884 to 1889 he was conductor of the Boston Sym. Orch. Returning to Vienna, he once again served as conductor of the Gesellschaft der Musikfreunde concerts (1890–95). He was called again to America in 1898 to lead the Boston Sym. Orch., conducting its concerts until 1906; then returned to Vienna. Gericke did much to make it a fine ensemble, for he was a remarkably able conductor and a highly efficient drillmaster.—NS/LK/DM

Gerl, Franz Xaver, German bass and composer; b. Andorf, Nov. 30, 1764; d. Mannheim, March 9, 1827. He sang in the choir at Salzburg, and in 1789 became principal bass at the Theater auf der Wieden in Vienna, remaining on its roster until 1793. He created the role of Sarastro in Mozart's *Die Zauberflöte* in 1791; his wife, Barbara Reisinger (1770–1806), created the role of Papagena in that production. He composed several works for the stage, collaborating with Bendikt Schack. —NS/LK/DM

Gerlach, Theodor, German conductor and composer; b. Dresden, June 25, 1861; d. Kiel, Dec. 11, 1940. He studied with Wullner, then was a conductor in several provincial towns. He wrote an *Epic Symphony* (1891) and the opera *Matteo Falcone* (Hannover, 1898). Of particular interest were his experiments with "spoken opera," utilizing inflected speech, most notably in his *Liebeswogen* (Bremen, Nov. 7, 1903; rev. as *Das Seegespenst*, Altenburg, April 24, 1914). He also used the spoken word over an instrumental accompaniment in his *Gesprochene Lieder*.—NS/LK/DM

Gerle, Hans, German lutenist; b. Nuremberg, c. 1500; d. there, 1570. He was well known in his time, both as a performer on the lute and as a manufacturer of viols and lutes. His works in tablature are of considerable historic value: *Musica Teusch auf die Instrument der grossen unnd kleinen Geygen, auch Lautten* (Nuremberg, 1532; 2nd ed., 1537; 3rd ed., under the title *Musica und Tabulatur*, 1546), *Tabulatur auff die Laudten* (Nuremberg, 1533), and *Ein newes sehr künstlichs Lautenbuch* (Nuremberg, 1552; with pieces by Francesco da Milano, A. Rotta, Joan da Crema, Rosseto, and Gintzler). Reprints of his works have been ed. by W. Tappert in *Sang und Klang aus alter Zeit* (1906) and by H.D. Bruger in *Schule des Lautenspiels*, I/2, and *Alte Lautenkunst* I.—NS/LK/DM

Gerle, Robert, Hungarian-born American violinist, conductor, and teacher; b. Abbazia, Italy, April 1, 1924. He was educated at the Franz Liszt Academy of Music and the National Cons. in Budapest, receiving the Hubay Prize in 1942. He played in recital and with major orchs. in Europe, and eventually settled in the U.S., where he headed the string dept. of the Univ. of Okla. (1950–54). He then was on the staff of the Peabody Cons. of Music in Baltimore (1955–68), the Mannes Coll. of Music in N.Y. (1959–70), the Manhattan School of Music (1967–70), and Ohio State Univ. (1968–72). In 1972 he was named head of the Instrumental Program of the Univ. of Md., Baltimore County; was active as a conductor there and also continued his career as a violinist. He publ. *The Art of Practicing the Violin* (London, 1983) and *The Art of Bowing Practice: The Expressive Bow Technique* (London, 1991).—NS/LK/DM

German, Sir Edward (real name, **German Edward Jones**), admired English composer; b. Whitchurch, Salop, Feb. 17, 1862; d. London, Nov. 11, 1936. After studies with W.C. Hay in Shrewsbury (1880), he pursued his training at the Royal Academy of Music in London (1880–87) with Steggall (organ), Weist-Hill and Burnett (violin), Banister (theory), and Prout (composition and orchestration). He played violin in theater orchs., and soon began conducting them. From 1888 he was active with various London theaters, establishing his reputation as a composer with his incidental music. German scored his most notable stage success with the comic opera *Merrie England* (London, April 2, 1902). In 1928 he was knighted and in 1934 was awarded the Gold Medal of the Royal Phil. Soc. of London.

WORKS: DRAMATIC: Opera: *The Rival Poets* (1883–86); *The Emerald Isle* (London, April 27, 1901; completion of an unfinished work by Sullivan); *Merrie England* (London, April 2, 1902); *A Princess of Kensington* (London, Jan. 22, 1903); *Tom Jones* (1907; London, April 17, 1908); *Fallen Fairies* or *Moon Fairies* (London, Dec. 15, 1909). **Incidental Music:** *Richard III* (1889); *Henry VIII* (1892); *The Tempter* (1893); *Romeo and Juliet* (1895); *As You Like It* (1896); *Much Ado About Nothing* (1898); *Nell Gwyn* (1900); *The Conqueror* (1905). **ORCH.:** 2 syms. (1890; *Norwich*, 1893); *Marche Solonnelle* (1891); *Gypsy Suite* (1892); *The Leeds*, suite (1895); *English Fantasia: In Commemoration* (1897); *Hamlet*, symphonic poem (1897); *The Seasons*, suite (1899); *March Rhapsody* or *Rhapsody on March Themes* (1902); *Welsh Rhapsody* (1904); *The Irish Guards* for Military Band (1918); *Theme and 6 Diversions* (1919); *The Willow Song*, tone picture (1922); *Cloverely Suite* (1934). **OTHER:** Chamber music, many piano pieces, organ works, choral music, and songs.

BIBL.: W. Scott, *Sir E. G.: An Intimate Biography* (London, 1932); B. Rees, *A Musical Peacemaker: The Life and Works of Sir E. G.* (Bourne End, Buckinghamshire, 1987).—NS/LK/DM

Germani, Fernando, outstanding Italian organist and teacher; b. Rome, April 5, 1906; d. there, June 10, 1998. He was a student of Bajardi (piano), Dobici (theory), Respighi (composition), and Manari (organ) at the Accademia Nazionale di Santa Cecilia in Rome. He was only 15 when he became organist of the Augusteo Orch. in Rome, and he soon began to appear as a virtuoso. In 1927 he made his first tour of the U.S., and from 1936 to 1938 he taught at the Curtis Inst. of Music in Philadelphia. From 1932 to 1972 he taught at the Accademia Musicale Chigiana in Siena, and from 1935 to 1976 at the Rome Cons. In 1945 he played the entire Bach canon for organ, a feat he reprised several times in succeeding years. His subsequent tours took him all over the world. From 1948 to 1959 he held the position of 1st organist at St. Peter's Basilica in Rome. Germani was blessed with a brilliant technique, and his amazing memory allowed him to play the most difficult recitals without scores. While he was best known for his championship of the music of Bach, he also played works by Frescobaldi, Liszt, Franck, Reger, and other masters. He publ. an organ method (4 vols., 1942–52) and an ed. of Frescobaldi's organ and harpsichord music (3 vols., 1964). He also composed some organ music, including a *Toccata* (1937), which he featured at many of his recitals.

BIBL.: G. Wagner, *Anleitung zum Orgelspiel nach d. G.-Technik* (Heidelberg, 1976).—NS/LK/DM

Gernsheim, Friedrich, German pianist, conductor, and composer; b. Worms, July 17, 1839; d. Berlin, Sept. 11, 1916. He studied at the Leipzig Cons. with Moscheles (piano) and Hauptmann (theory), then was in Paris (1855–61). Returning to Germany, he became a prof. at the Cologne Cons. (1865–72). He then conducted choral concerts in Rotterdam (1872–80), subsequently teaching at the Stern Cons. in Berlin (1890–97). His works are marked by a Romantic flair, as an epigone of Schumann; he was also influenced by Brahms, who was his friend. He wrote 4 syms., overtures, a Piano Concerto, a Violin Concerto, 5 string quartets, 3 piano quartets, 2 piano trios, a String Quintet, 3 violin sonatas, 2 cello sonatas, choral works, songs, and piano pieces.

BIBL.: K. Holl, *F. G., Leben, Erscheinung und Werk* (Leipzig, 1928).—NS/LK/DM

Gero, Jhan (Jehan), Flemish composer who flourished in the 16th century. He was a fine madrigalist. He publ. 2 books of madrigals for 4 Voices (Venice, 1549), 2 books of madrigals for 3 Voices (Venice, 1553), and a book of madrigals for 2 Voices (Venice, 1541; modern ed. by S. Bernstein and J. Haar, N.Y., 1977). He also wrote motets. Gero was at one time confused with Johannes Gallus.—NS/LK/DM

Gérold, (Jean) Théodore, eminent Alsatian music scholar; b. Strasbourg, Oct. 26, 1866; d. Allenwiller, Feb. 15, 1956. He studied voice, violin, and theory at the

Strasbourg Cons., and musicology with Gustaf Jacobsthal and theology at the German Univ. of Strasbourg (Ph.D., 1910). In 1890 he went to Frankfurt am Main to study singing with Jules Stockhausen, and then took courses at the Paris Cons. He was a lecturer on music at the Univ. of Basel from 1914 to 1918. He returned to Strasbourg in 1919 to lecture on music at the new French Univ., from which in 1921 he received his doctorat *ès lettres*, and in 1931 his doctorat d'État. He retired from the Univ. in 1937, and occupied an ecclesiastical lecturing position in Allenwiller until his death.

WRITINGS: *Kleine Sänger-Fiebel: Sprachliche Übungen für Sänger* (Mainz, 1908; 2nd ed., 1911); *Das Liederbuch einer französischen Provinzdame um 1620* (Frankfurt am Main, 1912); *Chansons populaires des XVe et XVIe siècles avec leurs mélodies* (Strasbourg, 1913); *Clément Marot: Les Psaumes avec leurs mélodies* (Strasbourg, 1919); *La Musicologie médiévale* (Paris, 1921); *François Schubert* (Paris, 1923); *Jean Sébastien Bach* (Paris, 1925); *Les Pères de l'église et la musique* (Paris, 1931); *La Musique au moyen âge* (Paris, 1932); *Histoire de la musique des origines à la fin du XIVe siècle* (Paris, 1936); *Marie-Joseph Erb: Sa vie, son oeuvre* (Strasbourg and Paris, 1948).—NS/LK/DM

Gerschefski, Edwin,

American composer, pianist, and teacher; b. Meriden, Conn., June 10, 1909; d. Athens, Ga., Dec. 17, 1992. He studied piano with Bruce Simonds and composition at Yale Univ. (1926–31). Following further training in piano at the Matthay school in London (1931–33) and with Schnabel in Como (1935), he completed his studies in composition with Schillinger in N.Y. (1936–38). In 1940 he joined the faculty of Converse Coll. in Spartanburg, S.C., where he was dean of its music school (1945–59). He then was head of the music depts. at the univs. of N.Mex. (1959–60) and Ga. (1960–72), continuing on the faculty of the latter until 1976. In some of his works, he employed the Schillinger system of composition. He attracted particular notice for his settings of exact texts from newspapers, magazines, and business letters in several of his vocal scores.

WORKS: ORCH.: *Classic Symphony* (1931); Piano Concerto (1931); *Discharge in E* and *Streamline* for Band (1935); Violin Concerto (1951–52); *Toccata and Fugue* (1954); *Celebration* for Violin and Orch. (1964). **CHAMBER:** *Workout* for 2 Violins and 2 Violas (1933); Piano Quintet (1935); *8 Variations* for String Quartet (1937); Brass Septet (1938); *America*, variations for Winds (1962); *Rhapsody* for Violin, Cello, and Piano (1963); *The Alexander Suite* for 2 Cellos (1971); *Poem* for Cello and Piano (1973); various piano pieces, including 2 sonatas (1936, 1968). **VOCAL:** *Half Moon Mountain*, cantata for Baritone, Women's Chorus, and Orch., after a *Time* magazine article (1947–48; Spartanburg, S.C., April 30, 1948); *The Lord's Controversy with His People*, cantata for Soloist, Women's Chorus, and Small Orch. or Piano (1949); *Psalm C* for Soprano, Baritone, Chorus, Percussion, and Piano (1965); *Border Patrol* for Chorus and Piano, after a *Time* magazine article (1966); *Letter from BMI* for Chorus and Small Orch. (1981); songs. **OTHER:** Film music. —NS/LK/DM

Gershon, Russ (Ian),

jazz saxophonist, composer, and arranger; b. Aug. 11, 1959, Manhasset N.Y. He played violin, piano, and guitar as a child, then took up saxophone at age 17. He studied philosophy at Harvard Univ. while serving as jazz director and an on-air host at the school's radio station. After playing saxophone in several rock bands (1979–84), he attended Berklee (1984–85), studying with Bill Pierce, Ken Pullig, and Donald Brown, as well as privately with Bob Mover and Jerry Bergonzi. Inspired by Gil Evans, Sun Ra, and Charles Mingus, he began the Either/Orch. (1985) as an 11-person band; since 1990 it has comprised ten members. Drawing on his experiences in the rock world, he began leading the group on van tours of the U.S. (from 1988). He founded Accurate Records (1987), which has since released over 70 CDs by various artists. He taught jazz history at Harvard (1993–94) and has acted as artist-in-residence or visiting clinician at several educational institutions and festivals. He has done session work for rock and jazz groups, commercials, and film soundtracks.

DISC.: *Dial E* (1986); *Radium* (1987); *Half-Life of Desire* (1989); *Calculus of Pleasure* (1992); *Brunt* (1993).—LP

Gershwin, George (originally, Gershvin, Jacob),

vibrant American composer; brother of **Ira Gershwin**; b. N.Y., Sept. 26, 1898; d. Los Angeles, July 11, 1937. Gershwin forged a hybrid of Tin Pan Alley, theater music, jazz, and classical music in a remarkable, if abbreviated, career that found him writing successful popular songs, Broadway musicals, assorted serious compositions, and an opera, all of which have been embraced by performers ranging from symphony orchestras to jazz groups and nightclub singers. His music combined formal brilliance with rhythmic vitality and blues influences to create an original style distinctive in itself and broadly influential, making him the most significant American composer of the 20th century. His most notable accomplishments are found in different forms, including such song standards as "Swanee," "I Got Rhythm," and "The Man I Love," his revolutionary instrumental work *Rhapsody in Blue*, and his masterpiece, the opera *Porgy and Bess*.

Gershwin's parents, Morris and Rose Bruskin Gershvin (originally Gershovitz), were Russian immigrants. Gershwin gave little evidence of an interest in music until 1910, when the family acquired a piano, ostensibly for his older brother, Ira Gershwin, and he began to play it instead. By the age of 14, he was taking lessons from Charles Hambitzer, and he learned harmony and theory from Edward Kilenyi. (He continued to seek instruction throughout his career, notably working with Joseph Schillinger from 1932 to 1936.) Academic study, on the other hand, did not interest him; he dropped out of high school at 15 to take a job as a demonstration pianist with Jerome H. Remick, music publishers. Though he was writing music as early as 1913, his first song to be published was "When You Want 'Em You Can't Get 'Em (When You Got 'Em, You Don't Want 'Em)" (lyrics by Murray Roth) in March 1916. Three months later he placed his first song in a musical revue with the use of "Making of a Girl" (lyrics by Harold Atteridge) in *The Passing Show of 1916* (N.Y., June 22, 1916).

Gershwin left Remick in 1917 and was hired as rehearsal pianist for the revue *Miss 1917* (N.Y., Nov. 5, 1917). The cast also performed Sunday night concerts during the run, and at one of them, on Nov. 25, 1917,

Gershwin accompanied the show's star, Vivienne Segal, on two of his songs, "You-oo, Just You" and "There's More to the Kiss Than the X-X-X" (both lyrics by Irving Caesar). The performance brought him to the attention of music publishers T. B. Harms, where he was hired as a composer. This in turn led to a series of interpolations of Gershwin songs into revues and musicals. Among them was his first song with lyrics by his brother Ira, "The Real American Folk Song," sung in *Ladies First* (N.Y., Oct. 24, 1918). His first full score for a Broadway musical came in the spring of 1919 with *La, La, Lucille,* which had a modestly successful run of 104 performances.

Gershwin scored the first, and biggest, hit of his career with "Swanee" (lyrics by Caesar), which originally was used in *Demi- Tasse,* a revue that opened the Capitol movie theater in N.Y. on Oct. 24, 1919. It was then interpolated by Al Jolson into his touring musical *Sinbad* and recorded by him on Jan. 9, 1920. The result was a million- selling record, Jolson's most successful up to that point. The song also sold a million copies of sheet music. Gershwin's second show, the revue *Morris Gest's Midnight Whirl,* marked the beginning of his association with his most frequent lyricist of the next five years, B. G. De Sylva. The show, which also featured lyrics by John Henry Mears, ran 110 performances. Gershwin's lyricist for the first of the five successive editions of *George White's Scandals* that he scored was Arthur Jackson. The 1920 edition produced no hits but ran for 134 performances. Gershwin's next hit song, "Waiting for the Sun to Come Out," had lyrics by his brother writing under the pseudonym Arthur Francis. It was used in the musical *The Sweetheart Shop* (N.Y., Aug. 31, 1920) and recorded by Lambert Murphy, who had a hit with it in January 1921.

The team of Gershwin and De Sylva scored its first major hit with "Do It Again!," which was used in the play *The French Doll* (N.Y., Feb. 20, 1922) and recorded by Paul Whiteman and His Orch. for a best-seller in July 1922. That month, "Yankee Doodle Blues" (lyrics by Caesar and De Sylva) was used in the revue *Spice of 1922* (N.Y., July 6, 1922); a recording by Billy Murray and Ed Smalle became a hit in February 1923. With a run of only 88 performances, the 1922 edition of *George White's Scandals* was the least successful of those Gershwin scored, but it is memorable for featuring—at least on opening night—the short opera *Blue Monday* (libretto by De Sylva) and the song "(I'll Build a) Stairway to Paradise" (lyrics by De Sylva and "Arthur Francis"), which was recorded by Whiteman, whose orchestra played in the show, for a best-seller in January 1923.

Gershwin enjoyed success with his two shows of 1923, *The Rainbow,* which ran 113 performances in London, and his fourth *George White's Scandals,* which ran 168 performances, but no hit songs emerged from them. Also during the year, the Gershwin brothers wrote "The Sunshine Trail," a promotional song for a silent film of the same name, their first work for the screen.

Gershwin and De Sylva's early 1924 musical *Sweet Little Devil* was a modest success with a run of 120 performances and a hit in "Virginia (Don't Go Too Far),"

recorded by Carl Fenton and His Orch. Whiteman commissioned Gershwin to write a jazz-based instrumental work for his Feb. 12, 1924, performance at the Aeolian Hall in N.Y., "An Experiment in Modern Music." Gershwin responded with *Rhapsody in Blue,* on which he accompanied Whiteman's Palais Royale Orch. The piece became the most acclaimed of Gershwin's serious compositions, and generated a record hit as well, when the composer and the Whiteman Orch. cut a two-sided version of it on June 10.

Gershwin's score for the 1924 edition of *George White's Scandals* was his most successful, at a run of 192 performances, and his last. It featured "Somebody Loves Me" (lyrics by De Sylva and Ballard MacDonald), which became a best-selling record for Whiteman in December.

Gershwin had new shows on in London and N.Y. in the fall of 1924. *Primrose,* with a run of 255 performances in the West End, was a substantial hit, though its score was partially pieced together from earlier efforts. But *Lady, Be Good!,* featuring Fred and Adele Astaire, which ran 330 performances on Broadway, marked the full-fledged collaboration of the Gershwin brothers for the first time on such a successful venture. Whiteman had a hit with "Oh, Lady Be Good," and Cliff Edwards, who appeared in the show, had a hit with "Fascinating Rhythm," both in April 1925. That month, De Sylva and Ira Gershwin wrote lyrics for *Tell Me More,* which had a run of only 100 performances, though the British version, which opened in London on May 6, was much more successful. Thereafter, De Sylva teamed with Lew Brown and Ray Henderson, while the Gershwins became a permanent songwriting team.

Gershwin had four premieres in December 1925, three on successive days. The N.Y. Symphony Orch. performed his *Concerto in F* for piano at Carnegie Hall on Dec. 3. Twenty-five days later, the next Gershwin musical, *Tip- Toes,* opened for a run of 194 performances. Its hits included "Looking for a Boy" (for the Arden-Ohman Orch.; pianists Victor Arden and Phil Ohman appeared in the show), "That Certain Feeling" (for Whiteman), and "Sweet and Low-Down" (for Harry Archer and His Orch.). The next day, Whiteman performed *135th Street,* a revised version of *Blue Monday,* at Carnegie Hall. And the day after that saw the opening of the operetta *Song of the Flame,* on which Gershwin had collaborated with composer Herbert Stothart, with the lyrics written by Otto Harbach and Oscar Hammerstein II. The show ran 219 performances and generated hits in the title song (for Vincent Lopez and His Orch., among others) and "Cossack Love Song (Don't Forget Me)" (for the Ipana Troubadors).

The Gershwins' next show was nearly a year in coming, but *Oh, Kay!* was a substantial success, running 256 performances and producing five hit songs: "Someone to Watch over Me" (for Gertrude Lawrence, who starred in the show, with other popular recordings including a solo piano version by the composer); "Do-Do-Do" (for George Olsen and His Orch.); "Clap Yo' Hands" (for Roger Wolfe Kahn and His Orch.); "Maybe" (for Nat Shilkret and The Victor Orch.); and "Fidgety Feet" (for Fletcher Henderson and His Orch.).

Gershwin and Whiteman rerecorded *Rhapsody in Blue* on April 21, 1927, to take advantage of the higher-fidelity electronic recording process; the new version became a hit in September. The Gershwins's next musical, *Funny Face,* again starred the Astaires and was another success, with a run of 244 performances and three hit songs: "'S Wonderful" (for Frank Crumit), the title song (for the Arden-Ohman Orch.), and "My One and Only" (for Jane Green, though Fred Astaire, who sang it onstage, also had a popular recording).

Though Gershwin was the credited composer for the early 1928 Florenz Ziegfeld production of *Rosalie,* much of the score was made up of interpolations by Sigmund Romberg. The show was a smash, running 335 performances. No Gershwin hits emerged from it at first, though "How Long Has This Been Going On?" eventually became a standard and "The Man I Love," dropped during tryouts just as it had been for *Lady, Be Good!* three years earlier, finally became an independent hit in a recording by Marion Harris, among others, in March. The Gershwins' fall show, *Treasure Girl,* was a failure, which prevented "I've Got a Crush on You" from becoming a success at first.

Meanwhile, Gershwin continued to alternate his theater music with serious compositions, which also found a wide audience. In September and October 1928 he recorded his *Concerto in F* with the Whiteman Orch.; it became a popular recording in January 1929. His tone poem for Orch., *An American in Paris,* was premiered at Carnegie Hall in December 1928; on Feb. 4, 1929, Gershwin recorded the work with the Victor Symphony Orch., and it became a popular disc in June.

Show Girl, another Ziegfeld production, was more memorable for the relationship between its star, Ruby Keeler, and her husband, Al Jolson, than for its score. Jolson sometimes emerged from the audience to sing "Liza (All the Clouds'll Roll Away)" (lyrics also by Gus Kahn), and he made a hit recording of the song, but the show ran only 111 performances.

In 1930 the Gershwins revived their political satire, *Strike Up the Band,* which had closed out of town in 1927, and the revised show ran 191 performances on Broadway, with the title song becoming a hit for Red Nichols and His Five Pennies. *Girl Crazy* was a return to more lighthearted fare; it brought stardom to Ethel Merman and Ginger Rogers, ran 272 performances, and generated three hits: "Bidin' My Time" by The Foursome, who sang it onstage; plus "Embraceable You" and "I Got Rhythm," both of which earned their initial popularity in recordings by Red Nichols and His Orch. (the pit band for the show), while a fourth song from the show, "But Not for Me," would gain recognition later.

The Gershwins went to Calif. in November 1930 to write songs for a motion picture, *Delicious.* They returned to N.Y. in February 1931, and the film opened the following December. The near-title song "Delishious" was recorded by Nat Shilkret and the Victor Orch. that month and became a hit in January 1932. *Of Thee I Sing,* the Gershwins's second political satire, also opened in December 1931, and it became their most successful show ever, running 441 performances, though its highly integrated score resulted in there being only one outside

hit, the title song, which was recorded by Ben Selvin and His Orch. masquerading as The Knickerbockers.

Gershwin gave over much of 1932 to classical works, premiering the *Second Rhapsody* in January and the *Cuban Overture* in August. The Gershwins' *Pardon My English,* which opened in early 1933, was a failure, as was *Let 'Em Eat Cake,* a sequel to *Of Thee I Sing,* though "Mine" became a minor hit for Emil Coleman and His Orch. in November 1933. Gershwin undertook a North American concert tour in January and February 1934, during which he introduced *Variations on "I Got Rhythm,"* and he hosted a radio show, *Music by Gershwin,* in the spring and again in the fall. He then turned his full attention to *Porgy and Bess,* collaborating with Du Bose Heyward, author of the novel on which it was based, and with his brother.

Billed as a "folk opera," *Porgy and Bess* opened in a Broadway theater in 1935, and despite a score that contained such memorable songs as "Summertime" (lyrics by Heyward), "It Ain't Necessarily So" (lyrics by Ira Gershwin), and "I Loves You, Porgy" (lyrics by Ira Gershwin and Heyward), it was not financially successful and ran only 124 performances.

The Gershwins moved to L.A. in August 1936 to write songs for the movies. Their first effort was the Astaire-Rogers vehicle *Shall We Dance,* released in May 1937. Among the six songs featured were "Let's Call the Whole Thing Off" and "They Can't Take That Away from Me," both of which made the hit parade in recordings by Astaire. "They Can't Take That Away from Me" became Gershwin's only song to be nominated for an Academy Award.

The Gershwins had completed the songs for a second Astaire picture, *A Damsel in Distress,* and begun work on *The Goldwyn Follies* when George Gershwin was taken ill. He died of a brain tumor at the age of 38.

A Damsel in Distress was released in November 1937. It contained seven Gershwin songs, including "Nice Work If You Can Get It," which was recorded by Astaire and was in the hit parade for eight weeks. The score for *The Goldwyn Follies* was completed by Vernon Duke; when it was released in February 1938, four songs were credited to Gershwin, among them "Love Walked In," which topped the hit parade in May and June for Sammy Kaye and His Orch.

A Broadway revival of *Porgy and Bess* (N.Y., Jan. 22, 1942) was the most successful restaging in American musical theater history up to that time, with a run of 286 performances. This began the process by which the opera was recognized as Gershwin's greatest accomplishment. Swing bands revived Gershwin songs during the 1940s, including those of Harry James ("But Not for Me," 1942), Glenn Miller ("Rhapsody in Blue," 1943), and Tommy Dorsey ("Embraceable You," 1944). Dorsey also appeared in the second film version of *Girl Crazy* (1943), which starred Judy Garland and Mickey Rooney. *Rhapsody in Blue* (1945) was a Gershwin screen biography, notable for its music if not its historical accuracy.

Ira Gershwin and Kay Swift assembled unfinished and unused Gershwin music into songs for the film *The Shocking Miss Pilgrim,* released in January 1947. (Ira

Gershwin also contributed some unused music by his brother to the 1964 film *Kiss Me, Stupid*.) MGM used vintage Gershwin music as the basis for the musical *An American in Paris* (1951), and in addition to the success of the film—which won the Academy Award for Best Picture—the soundtrack album became a chart-topping hit.

The rise of popular singers in the wake of the demise of the big bands and the introduction of the long-playing record both enhanced Gershwin's song catalog, as performers frequently revived his work. For example, Ella Fitzgerald, in a precursor to her *Song Book* albums of the late 1950s and early 1960s, recorded *Ella Sings Gershwin* in September and October 1950, and Frank Sinatra included "A Foggy Day" from *A Damsel in Distress* and "They Can't Take That Away from Me" on his first Capitol Records album, *Songs for Young Lovers*, recorded in November 1953.

Meanwhile, individual Gershwin songs also earned hit revivals on the singles charts. "Love Walked In" reached the Top Ten in a version by The Hilltoppers in 1953, charting again in 1959 for The Flamingos and in 1960 for Dinah Washington. "I Got Rhythm" enjoyed a Top Ten revival in 1967 by The Happenings.

But it was *Porgy and Bess* that gained the most recognition after Gershwin's death. The show's second Broadway revival, opening March 10, 1953, was even more successful than the record-breaking first, running 305 performances. Columbia Records released the first attempt at a complete recording of the opera in 1955. Sam Cooke had a chart revival of "Summertime" in 1957, followed by charting versions in 1961 by The Marcels, 1962 by Rick Nelson, 1963 by the Chris Columbo Quintet, and, in 1966, a Top Ten version by Billy Stewart. The song was even given a bluesy reading by Janis Joplin on the chart-topping Big Brother and the Holding Company album *Cheap Thrills* in 1968.

Porgy and Bess was brought to the screen in 1959, at which time an avalanche of new recordings was released, including one by Ella Fitzgerald and Louis Armstrong and a Top 40 single of "I Loves You, Porgy" by Nina Simone. The first concert version of the complete opera was given at the Blossom Music Center in Cleveland by the Cleveland Orch. under the direction of Lorin Maazel on Aug. 16, 1975. The following spring, the Houston Grand Opera Company staged the work, and the production opened in N.Y. on Sept. 25, 1976. By the mid-1980s, *Porgy and Bess* was a part of the repertoire of several major opera companies.

On Broadway, two "new" Gershwin musicals have been created by wedding the scores from earlier shows (plus interpolations) to newly written librettos, resulting in long runs for *My One and Only* (based on *Funny Face*; 1983) and *Crazy for You* (based on *Girl Crazy*; 1992).

WORKS (only works for which Gershwin was a primary, credited composer are listed): **MUSICALS/REVUES** (dates refer to N.Y. openings unless otherwise noted): *La, La, Lucille* (May 26, 1919); *Morris Gest's Midnight Whirl* (Dec. 27, 1919); *George White's Scandals* (June 7, 1920); *George White's Scandals* (July 11, 1921); *George White's Scandals* (Aug. 28, 1922); *Our Nell* (Dec. 4, 1922); *The Rainbow* (London, April 3, 1923); *George White's Scandals* (June 18, 1923); *Sweet Little Devil* (Jan. 21, 1924);

George White's Scandals (June 30, 1924); *Primrose* (London, Sept. 11, 1924); *Lady, Be Good!* (Dec. 1, 1924); *Tell Me More* (April 13, 1925); *Tip-Toes* (Dec. 28, 1925); *Song of the Flame* (Dec. 30, 1925); *Oh, Kay!* (Nov. 8, 1926); *Funny Face* (Nov. 22, 1927); *Rosalie* (Jan. 10, 1928); *Treasure Girl* (Nov. 8, 1928); *Show Girl* (July 2, 1929); *Strike Up the Band* (Jan. 14, 1930); *Girl Crazy* (Oct. 14, 1930); *Of Thee I Sing* (Dec. 26, 1931); *Pardon My English* (Jan. 20, 1933); *Let 'Em Eat Cake* (Oct. 21, 1933); *My One and Only* (May 1, 1983); *Crazy for You* (Feb. 19, 1992). **OPERA:** *Porgy and Bess* (N.Y., Oct. 10, 1935). **INSTRUMENTAL:** *Blue Monday* (chamber opera performed as part of *George White's Scandals* [Aug. 28, 1922]; revised as *135th Street*, Carnegie Hall, Dec. 29, 1925, by Paul Whiteman and His Orch.); *Rhapsody in Blue* (for jazz band and orch.; Aeolian Hall, N.Y., Feb. 12, 1924, by Paul Whiteman and His Palais Royal Orch. with the composer at the piano); *Short Story* (for violin and piano; Feb. 8, 1925, the Univ. Club, N.Y., by Samuel Dushkin, violinist); *Concerto in F* (for piano and orch.; Dec. 3, 1925, Carnegie Hall, by the N.Y. Symphony Society with the composer at the piano, conducted by Walter Damrosch); *Preludes for Piano* (Dec. 4, 1926, Hotel Roosevelt, N.Y., by the composer); *An American in Paris* (tone poem for orch.; Dec. 13, 1928, Carnegie Hall, by the N.Y. Symphony Orch. conducted by Walter Damrosch); *Second Rhapsody* (for orch. with piano; Jan. 29, 1932, Symphony Hall, Boston, by the Boston Symphony Orch. with the composer at the piano, conducted by Serge Koussevitzky); *Cuban Overture* (for orch.; Aug. 16, 1932, Lewisohn Stadium, N.Y., by the N.Y. Philharmonic–Symphony Orch., conducted by Albert Coates); *Variations on "I Got Rhythm"* (Jan. 14, 1934, Symphony Hall, Boston, by the Reisman Symphonic Orch. with the composer at the piano, conducted by Charles Previn). **FILMS:** *Delicious* (1931); *Girl Crazy* (1932); *Shall We Dance* (1937); *A Damsel in Distress* (1937); *The Goldwyn Follies* (1938); *Girl Crazy* (1943); *Rhapsody in Blue* (1945); *The Shocking Miss Pilgrim* (1947); *An American in Paris* (1951); *Porgy and Bess* (1959); *Kiss Me, Stupid* (1964).

BIBL.: I. Goldberg, *G. G.: A Study in American Music* (N.Y., 1931, 2nd ed., rev., supplemented by E. Garson, 1958); M. Armitage, ed., *G. G.* (N.Y., 1938); D. Ewen, *A Journey to Greatness: The Life and Music of G. G.* (N.Y., 1956; 3rd ed., rev. as *G. G: His Journey to Greatness*, 1986); E. Jablonski and L. Stewart, *The G. Years* (Garden City, N.Y., 1958; 3rd ed., rev., 1996); M. Armitage, *G. G.: Man and Legend* (N.Y., 1958); R. Payne, *G.* (N.Y., 1960); R. Sirmay, ed., *The G. and Ira G. Song Book* (N.Y., 1960); E. Jablonski, *G. G.* (N.Y., 1962); R. Rushmore, *The Life of G. G.* (N.Y., 1966); R. Kimball and A. Simon, *The G.s* (N.Y., 1973); C. Schwartz, *G.: His Life and Music* (Indianapolis, 1973); Schwartz, *G. G.: A Selective Bibliography and Discography* (Detroit, 1974); A. Kendall, *G. G.: A Biography* (N.Y., 1987); E. Jablonski, *G: A Biography* (Garden City, N.Y., 1987); P. Kresh, *An American Rhapsody: The Story of G. G.* (N.Y., 1988); W. Rimler, *A G. Companion: A Critical Inventory & Discography, 1916–1984* (Ann Arbor, 1991); D. Rosenberg, *Fascinating Rhythm: The Collaboration of G. and Ira G.* (N.Y., 1991); J. Peyser, *The Memory of All That: The Life of G. G.* (N.Y., 1993); R. Greenberg, *G. G.* (London, 1998); G. Suriano, ed., *G. in His Time: A Biographical Scrapbook, 1919–1937* (N.Y., 1998).—**WR**

Gershwin, Ira (originally, Gershvin, Israel),

ingenious American lyricist; brother of **George Gershwin;** b. N.Y., Dec. 6, 1896; d. Beverly Hills, Aug. 17, 1983. Gershwin wrote lyrics primarily for the songs of his brother George Gershwin in a series of stage and movie musicals in the 1920s and 1930s. Witty and colloquial, Gershwin's lyrics ranked with those of Cole

Porter and Lorenz Hart as the most sophisticated of their time. With his brother, Gershwin wrote such hits as "I Got Rhythm," "They Can't Take That Away from Me," and "Love Walked In." Before and after his brother's death, Gershwin also collaborated with composers Vincent Youmans, Vernon Duke, Harry Warren, Harold Arlen, Kurt Weill, Aaron Copland, Jerome Kern, Arthur Schwartz, and Burton Lane on such songs as "Long Ago (And Far Away)" and "The Man That Got Away."

Gershwin's parents, Morris and Rose Burskin Gershvin (originally Gershovitz), were Russian immigrants. Gershwin attended the City Coll. of N.Y. from 1914 to 1916 and began contributing stories and light verse to periodicals. His first lyric to be heard onstage was "The Real American Folk Song (Is a Rag)" (music by George Gershwin), used in the Nora Bayes musical *Ladies First* (N.Y., Oct. 24, 1918). By the time of the Gershwins' next notable collaboration, George had achieved success with "Swanee," and Ira adopted the pseudonym Arthur Francis for his first song to be published, "Waiting for the Sun to Come Out," used in the musical *The Sweetheart Shop* (N.Y., Aug. 31, 1920). The song was recorded for a hit by Lambert Murphy in January 1921.

Still as Arthur Francis, Gershwin wrote lyrics to songs by Youmans and Paul Lannin for the musical *Two Little Girls in Blue*, which had a run of 135 performances, with "Oh Me! Oh My!" becoming a hit for Frank Crumit and the Paul Biese Trio in November 1921. By 1922, George Gershwin had begun writing songs for the annual revue *George White's Scandals*; in that year's edition, Ira Gershwin collaborated with B. G. De Sylva on the lyrics to "I'll Build a Stairway to Paradise," which became a best-selling instrumental record for Paul Whiteman and His Orch. in January 1923.

Gershwin abandoned his pseudonym in 1924 and he and his brother mounted their first successful Broadway show, *Lady, Be Good!* Featuring the dance team of Fred and Adele Astaire as well as Cliff Edwards, it ran 330 performances and generated two hits in the spring of 1925: "Fascinating Rhythm," recorded by Edwards, and "Oh, Lady Be Good," given its most successful recording as an instrumental by Whiteman, though Edwards had a popular vocal record. Also intended for the show was "The Man I Love," though it was cut and published independently. After being dropped from two other Gershwin shows, the song finally became a hit in March 1928 for Marion Harris (among others) and went on to become a standard.

The Gershwins were joined by De Sylva for the disappointing *Tell Me More*, which ran 100 performances; they bounced back with *Tip-Toes*, which ran 194 performances and contained three songs that became hits in the spring of 1926: "Looking for a Boy" by the Arden-Ohman Orch., "That Certain Feeling" by Whiteman, and "Sweet and Low-Down" by Harry Archer and His Orch., all recorded as instrumentals.

The run-up to the next Gershwin musical, *Oh, Kay!*, was dramatic for Ira: While it was being written, he came down with appendicitis, so Howard Dietz was brought in to write some lyrics; later, during rehearsals, on Sept. 14, 1926, he married Leonore Strunksy. (The

couple remained married until Gershwin's death. They had no children.) The show, which starred Gertrude Lawrence, was a hit, running 256 performances, and its score featured five songs that became hits in 1927: "Someone to Watch over Me" by Lawrence, among others; "Do, Do, Do" by George Olsen and His Orch.; "Clap Yo' Hands," an instrumental recording by Roger Wolfe Kahn and His Orch. and a vocal record by "Whispering" Jack Smith; "Maybe" by Nat Shilkret and the Victor Orch.; and "Fidgety Feet," an instrumental record by Fletcher Henderson and His Orch.

The Gershwins next attempted an antiwar political satire in *Strike Up the Band* (Long Branch, N.J., Aug. 29, 1927), which had a book by George S. Kaufman, but the show closed out of town. The more conventional *Funny Face*, featuring the Astaires, was a success, running 244 performances, with three songs emerging from it as hit records in 1928: "'S Wonderful" by Frank Crumit; the title song, by the Arden-Ohman Orch. (pianists Victor Arden and Phil Ohman appeared in the show); and "My One and Only" by Jane Green.

The Gershwins worked for impresario Florenz Ziegfeld on the extravaganza *Rosalie*, although Sigmund Romberg and P. G. Wodehouse had already written a score for the show. It ran 335 performances, its most memorable song being the Gershwins's "How Long Has This Been Going On?" Even more successful was the British musical *That's a Good Girl*, to which Gershwin and others contributed lyrics; it ran 363 performances. The Gershwins's own next musical, *Treasure Girl*, on the other hand, was a flop, now memorable only for introducing the standard "I've Got a Crush on You."

Show Girl, another Ziegfeld production, found the Gershwins collaborating with Gus Kahn, notably on "Liza (All the Clouds'll Roll Away)," given unscheduled performances by Al Jolson, whose wife, Ruby Keeler, was featured. The show ran 111 performances, and the song became a hit in a recording by Jolson in September 1929.

With a new book by Morrie Ryskind, *Strike Up the Band* finally reached Broadway at the start of 1930, where it became a hit, running 191 performances. The title song was a popular record for Red Nichols and His Five Pennies in February. Gershwin next contributed lyrics to the revue *The Garrick Gaieties* (N.Y., June 4, 1930), including "I Am Only Human After All" (music by Vernon Duke, lyrics also by E. Y. Harburg), which became a hit for the Colonial Club Orch. in July. The Gershwins returned to light musical comedy with *Girl Crazy*, which became the biggest success of the 1930–31 Broadway season, running 272 performances, establishing the careers of Ethel Merman and Ginger Rogers, and generating two immediate hits, "Embraceable You" and "I Got Rhythm," which made up the two sides of a popular record by Red Nichols in the fall of 1930. The score also featured "Bidin' My Time," which became a hit for The Foursome in November 1931, and "But Not for Me." Before the end of 1930, Gershwin had another hit as "Cheerful Little Earful" (music by Harry Warren, lyrics also by Billy Rose) was featured in the revue *Sweet and Low* (N.Y., Nov. 17, 1930) and given a popular recording by Tom Gerun and His Orch. in December.

By that time, Ira and George Gershwin had signed a contract with Fox Pictures and traveled to L.A. to write songs for their first film musical. *Delicious*, released at the end of 1931, featured four Gershwin songs, among them "Delishious," which became a hit for Nat Shilkret in January 1932. The Gershwins, however, had long since returned to N.Y. to concentrate on stage work. Their next effort was the ambitious satire on presidential politics, *Of Thee I Sing*, which ran 441 performances, produced a hit in the title song (recorded by Ben Selvin and His Orch. performing as The Knickerbockers), and became the first musical to win a Pulitzer Prize for Drama, the award shared by book writers Kaufman and Ryskind and lyricist Gershwin.

The Gershwins suffered two flops in 1933: *Pardon My English* and the sequel to *Of Thee I Sing, Let 'Em Eat Cake* (which nevertheless generated a hit in "Mine," recorded by Emil Coleman and His Orch. in November). They then separated temporarily, as George began work with DuBose Heyward on the opera *Porgy and Bess* and Ira collaborated with Harold Arlen and E. Y. Harburg on the revue *Life Begins at 8:40*. The revue was a hit, running 237 performances and featuring two hits: "You're a Builder-Upper," recorded by Leo Reisman and His Orch. with Arlen singing, and "Fun to Be Fooled" by Henry King and His Orch.

Gershwin re-joined his brother and Heyward and collaborated on lyrics to several of the songs in *Porgy and Bess*, including "I Got Plenty o' Nuthin'" and "I Loves You, Porgy," as well as writing all the lyrics to "It Ain't Necessarily So" and "There's a Boat Dat's Leavin' Soon for N.Y." Opening in a Broadway theater, *Porgy and Bess* ran a modestly successful 124 performances, though it gained in stature over time, eventually being recognized as one of George Gershwin's greatest achievements.

Gershwin and Duke wrote the songs for the *Ziegfeld Follies of 1936*. It ran 115 performances, its most memorable song being "I Can't Get Started." The Gershwins then signed to RKO, and on Aug. 10, 1936, they moved permanently to L.A. Their first effort was the Fred Astaire–Ginger Rogers film *Shall We Dance*, for which they wrote six songs, among them "Let's Call the Whole Thing Off," which reached the hit parade in May 1937, and "They Can't Take That Away from Me," which was in the hit parade in June, both in recordings by Astaire. "They Can't Take That Away from Me" earned an Academy Award nomination. The score also included "They All Laughed."

George Gershwin died of a brain tumor on July 11, 1937. Prior to his death, the brothers had completed the songs for their next film and begun work on another. *A Damsel in Distress*, also starring Astaire, contained seven songs, among them "Nice Work If You Can Get It," which was on the hit parade in November 1937, and "A Foggy Day." Ira teamed with Vernon Duke to complete the songs for *The Goldwyn Follies*. The final songs credited to the Gershwins included "Our Love Is Here to Stay" and "Love Walked In." The latter topped the hit parade in May 1938 for Sammy Kaye and His Orch., becoming one of the biggest hits of the year.

Gershwin's first major effort since the death of his brother came in 1941 with *Lady in the Dark*, on which he collaborated with Kurt Weill. A precursor to the more serious, integrated musicals that became common after *Oklahoma!* two years later, the show ran 467 performances and was memorable for star Gertrude Lawrence's performance of "The Saga of Jenny" and Danny Kaye's emergence as a star through his tongue-twisting rendition of the patter song "Tchaikowsky (And Other Russians)."

Porgy and Bess received its first Broadway revival on Jan. 22, 1942; the revival outdistanced the original production, running 286 performances. In August, Harry James and His Orch. had a hit recording of "But Not for Me." The following year the song was heard onscreen in the second film version of *Girl Crazy*, starring Judy Garland and Mickey Rooney. Also in 1943, Gershwin wrote the lyrics to music by Aaron Copland for the film *The North Star*.

The year 1944 began with a chart revival of "Embraceable You" by Tommy Dorsey and His Orch. with Jo Stafford and the Pied Pipers on vocals, a 1941 recording that had been reissued due to the musicians union recording ban. Gershwin collaborated with Jerome Kern on songs for the film *Cover Girl*, among them "Long Ago (And Far Away)," which became his single most successful song, attracting half-a-dozen chart recordings, the most popular of which was by Dick Haymes and Helen Forrest in April; the song was nominated for an Academy Award.

Gershwin had two projects with Kurt Weill in 1945. *The Firebrand of Florence*, a musical for which Gershwin also cowrote the libretto, was unsuccessful, and the team also wrote the songs for the 20th Century–Fox feature *Where Do We Go from Here? Park Avenue*, written with Arthur Schwartz, was another failure and marked Gershwin's last new Broadway musical. For the film *The Shocking Miss Pilgrim*, Gershwin and Kay Swift assembled some of George Gershwin's musical sketches into songs. Gershwin collaborated with Harry Warren on the last Fred Astaire Ginger Rogers film, *The Barkleys of Broadway*, in 1949.

An American in Paris, written by Alan Jay Lerner, directed by Vincente Minnelli, and starring Gene Kelly, brought the Gershwin brothers's music back into movie theaters in 1951 and, with the release of a soundtrack album, to the top of the charts at the start of 1952. For the film, Gershwin added new lyrics to such songs as "I Got Rhythm" and "'S Wonderful."

Revived on Broadway a second time, *Porgy and Bess* (N.Y., March 10, 1953) had its most successful run yet, continuing for 305 performances. In November 1953 The Hilltoppers took a revival of "Love Walked In" into the Top Ten. *Give a Girl a Break*, a new film musical on which Gershwin collaborated with Burton Lane, was released in December.

Gershwin retired at the end of 1954 after completing two films with Harold Arlen, both dramas with music: *A Star Is Born*, starring Judy Garland, who sang the Oscar-nominated "The Man That Got Away," and *The Country Girl*, starring Bing Crosby.

Porgy and Bess enjoyed another resurgence of interest in 1959 with the release of a film version of the opera along with several recordings, among them Nina Simone's Top 40 revival of "I Loves You, Porgy." Dinah Washington scored a Top 40 revival of "Love Walked In" in 1960. Ketty Lester had a chart revival of "But Not for Me" in 1962. In 1964, Gershwin contributed three new songs based on existing fragments of music by his brother for use in director Billy Wilder's satiric film *Kiss Me, Stupid,* starring Dean Martin. The Happenings revived "I Got Rhythm" for a Top Ten hit in 1967. In the 1980s and 1990s the Gershwins returned to Broadway with two new musicals, *My One and Only* and *Crazy for You,* that featured their songs. Gershwin's songs also enjoyed frequent concert and nightclub performances and recordings by a variety of singers, notably Michael Feinstein, who had served as Gershwin's secretary in his later years.

WORKS (only works for which Gershwin was a primary, credited lyricist are listed): **MUSICALS/REVUES** (all dates refer to N.Y. openings unless otherwise indicated): *Two Little Girls in Blue* (May 3, 1921); *Lady, Be Good!* (Dec. 1, 1924); *Tell Me More* (April 13, 1925); *Tip-Toes* (Dec. 28, 1925); *Oh, Kay!* (Nov. 8, 1926); *Funny Face* (Nov. 22, 1927); *Rosalie* (Jan. 10, 1928); *That's a Good Girl* (London, June 5, 1928); *Treasure Girl* (Nov. 8, 1928); *Show Girl* (July 2, 1929); *Strike Up the Band* (Jan. 14, 1930); *Girl Crazy* (Oct. 14, 1930); *Of Thee I Sing* (Dec. 26, 1931); *Pardon My English* (Jan. 20, 1933); *Let 'Em Eat Cake* (Oct. 21, 1933); *Life Begins at 8:40* (Aug. 27, 1934); *Porgy and Bess* (Oct. 10, 1935); *Ziegfeld Follies of 1936* (Jan. 30, 1936); *Lady in the Dark* (Jan. 23, 1941); *The Firebrand of Florence* (March 22, 1945); *Park Avenue* (Nov. 4, 1946); *My One and Only* (May 1, 1983); *Crazy for You* (Feb. 19, 1992). **FILMS:** *Delicious* (1931); *Girl Crazy* (1932); *Shall We Dance* (1937); *A Damsel in Distress* (1937); *The Goldwyn Follies* (1938); *Girl Crazy* (1943); *The North Star* (1943); *Cover Girl* (1944); *Where Do We Go from Here?* (1945); *The Shocking Miss Pilgrim* (1947); *The Barkleys of Broadway* (1949); *Give a Girl a Break* (1953); *A Star Is Born* (1954); *The Country Girl* (1954); *Porgy and Bess* (1959); *Kiss Me, Stupid* (1964).

WRITINGS: *Lyrics on Several Occasions* (N.Y., 1959); *The George and I. G. Song Book* (N.Y., 1960).

BIBL.: E. Jablonski and L. Stewart, *The G. Years* (Garden City, N.Y., 1958; 3rd ed., rev., 1976); R. Kimball and A. Simon, *The G.s* (N.Y., 1973); D. Rosenberg, *Fascinating Rhythm: The Collaboration of George and I. G.* (N.Y., 1991); R. Kimball, *The Complete Lyrics of I. G.* (N.Y., 1993); P. Furia, *I. G.: The Art of the Lyricist* (N.Y., 1996).—**WR**

Gerson-Kiwi, (Esther) Edith, German-born Israeli musicologist; b. Berlin, May 13, 1908; d. Jerusalem, July 15, 1992. She attended the Stern Cons. in Berlin (1918–25) and took a pianist's diploma at the Leipzig Hochschule für Musik (1930); she also studied harpsichord with Ramin in Leipzig and Landowska in Paris. She studied musicology with W. Gurlitt at the Univ. of Freiburg, Kroyer at the Univ. of Leipzig, and Besseler at the Univ. of Heidelberg (Ph.D., 1933, with the diss. *Studien zur Geschichte des Italienischen Liedmadrigals im 16. Jahrhundert*; publ. in Wurzburg, 1938). In 1935 she went to Palestine, where she was active in research and teaching; in 1969 she joined the faculty of the Univ. of Tel Aviv. She was a prolific and versatile writer; her subjects included Renaissance, Classical, Romantic, and contemporary music, and the ethnic music of the Middle East, on which she was an outstanding authority. Her books included *The Persian Doctrine of Dastgah Composition: A Phenomenological Study in the Musical Modes* (Tel Aviv, 1963), *The Legacy of Jewish Music through the Ages of Dispersion* (Jerusalem, 1963–64), and *Migrations and Mutations of the Music in East and West* (Tel Aviv, 1980).

BIBL.: S. Burstyn, ed., *Essays in Honor of E. G.-K.* (Tel Aviv, 1986).—**NS/LK/DM**

Gerstenberg, Walter, German musicologist; b. Hildesheim, Dec. 26, 1904; d. Tübingen, Oct. 26, 1988. He studied at the univs. of Berlin and Leipzig (Ph.D., 1929, with the diss. *Die Klavierkompositionen Domenico Scarlattis*; publ. in Regensburg, 1933; new ed., 1969), and then completed his Habilitation at the Univ. of Cologne in 1935 with his *Beiträge zur Problemgeschichte der evangelischen Kirchenmusik.* He taught at the univs. of Leipzig (1929–32) and Cologne (1932–38), and then was prof. of musicology at the univs. of Rostock (1941–48), Berlin (Free Univ., 1948–52), Tübingen (1952–58; 1959–70), and Heidelberg (1958). G. van Dadelsen and A. Holschneider ed. a Festschrift for his 60th birthday (Wolfenbüttel, 1964).

WRITINGS: *Die Zeitmasse und ihre Ordnungen in Bachs Musik* (Einbeck, 1951); *Zur Erkenntnis der Bachsen Musik* (Berlin, 1951); *Musikerhandschriften von Palestrina bis Beethoven* (Zürich, 1960); *Über Mozarts Klangwelt* (Tübingen, 1966).—**NS/LK/DM**

Gerster, Etelka, noted Hungarian soprano; b. Kaschau, June 25, 1855; d. Pontecchio, near Bologna, Aug. 20, 1920. She studied with Mathilde Marchesi in Vienna, then made her debut in Venice as Gilda in *Rigoletto,* Jan. 8, 1876. Her great success resulted in engagements in Berlin and Budapest in Italian opera under the direction of Carlo Gardini. She married Gardini on April 16, 1877. She then continued her successful career, making her London debut on June 23, 1877, as Amina in *La Sonnambula,* and her U.S. debut in the same role on Nov. 11, 1878, at the N.Y. Academy of Music. She returned to London for 2 more seasons (1878–80), then sang again in N.Y. from 1880 to 1883 and in 1887. After retiring, she taught singing in Berlin (1896–1917). She wrote the treatise *Stimmführer* (1906; 2nd ed., 1908).—**NS/LK/DM**

Gerster, Ottmar, German violinist, composer, and pedagogue; b. Braunfels, June 29, 1897; d. Leipzig, Aug. 31, 1969. He studied theory with Sekles at the Frankfurt am Main Cons. (1913–16), then violin with Adolf Rebner (1919–21). He played viola in string quartets (1923–27), and concurrently was concertmaster of the Frankfurt am Main Museumgesellschaft Orch. From 1927 to 1939 he taught violin and theory at the Folkwang-Schule in Essen; then was on the faculty of the Hochschule für Musik in Weimar (1947–52) and in Leipzig (1952–62). His music is marked by melodious polyphony in a neo-Classical vein; in his operas, he used folklike thematic material.

WORKS: DRAMATIC: Opera: *Madame Liselotte* (Essen, 1933); *Enoch Arden* (Düsseldorf, 1936); *Die Hexe von Passau*

(Düsseldorf, 1941); *Das Verzauberte Ich* (Wuppertal, 1949); *Der frohliche Sunder* (Weimar, 1963). **B a l l e t :** *Der ewige Kreis* (Duisburg, 1939). **O R C H.:** 3 syms.: *Kleine Sinfonie* (1931), *Thuringer Sinfonie* (1952) and *Leipziger Sinfonie* (1965); *Oberhessische Bauerntanze* (1937); Cello Concerto (1946); Piano Concerto (1956); Horn Concerto (1962). **C H A M B E R:** 2 string quartets (1923, 1954); String Trio (1957). **V O C A L:** *Ballade vom Manne Karl Marx (und der Veranderung der Welt)* for Baritone, Chorus, and Orch. (1961); many other choruses, some to words of political significance; songs.

> **BIBL.:** O. Goldhammer, *O. G.* (Berlin, 1953); R. Malth, *O. G.: Leben und Werk* (Leipzig, 1988).—**NS/LK/DM**

Gerstman, Blanche, South African pianist and composer of English descent; b. Cape Town, April 2, 1910; d. there, Aug. 11, 1973. She adopted the family name of her adoptive parents. She studied theory with Hely- Hutchinson and later with William Henry Bell at the South African Coll. of Music. She was subsequently active as a radio pianist; in 1950 she went to London, where she took additional courses at the Royal Coll. of Music with Howard Ferguson. Returning to South Africa in 1952, she taught at the Coll. of Music in Cape Town. She composed pleasurable piano pieces, singable choruses, and some playable chamber music. —**NS/LK/DM**

Gertler, André, Hungarian-born Belgian violinist and pedagogue; b. Budapest, July 26, 1907; d. Brussels, July 23, 1998. He was a student of Hubay (violin) and Kodály (composition) at the Budapest Academy of Music (graduated, 1925). He was only 13 when he began to make tours as a virtuoso. From 1925 to 1938 he appeared in recitals with his friend Bartók, whose music he championed. He was active in Belgium from 1928, and was 1st violinist in his own string quartet from 1931 to 1951. Gertler was a prof. at the Brussels Cons. (1940–54), the Cologne Hochschule für Musik (1954–59), and the Hannover Hochschule für Musik (1964–78). Although he was best known as an advocate of contemporary scores, he also played standard repertoire works and wrote cadenzas for Mozart's G major Violin Concerto, K.216, and Beethoven's Violin Concerto. —**NS/LK/DM**

Gervais, Charles-Hubert, French composer; b. Paris, Feb. 19, 1671; d. there, Jan. 15, 1744. He was in the service of the Duke of Chartres (later of Orléans) as his *ordinaire de la musique* by 1697. In 1700 he became his *maître de musique* and in 1712 his *intendant de la musique*. After his patron became Regent of France, he was made one of the four *sous-maîtres* of the Royal Chapel in 1723. He composed the operas *Méduse* (1697), *Penthée* (1705), and *Hypermnèstre* (Paris Opéra, Nov. 3, 1716), a ballet, *Les amours de Protée* (1720), 6 cantatas, 45 motets, and airs.—**LK/DM**

Gervaise, Claude, French composer who flourished in the 16th century. He was a violist and chamber musician to François I and Henri II. He composed many dances and chansons; 6 vols. of his *Danceries à 4 et 5 parties* were publ. by Attaignant from about 1545 to

1556, but only 3 vols. remain. A selection of his dances is included in Vol. 23 (Danceries) of *Les Maîtres Musiciens*, ed. by H. Expert (1908). Several chansons by Gervaise appear in 16th-century collections.—**NS/LK/DM**

Gerville-Réache, Jeanne, French contralto; b. Orthez, March 26, 1882; d. N.Y., Jan. 5, 1915. She was a student of Rosine Laborde and Pauline Viardot-García in Paris, where she made her operatic debut as Orféo at the Opéra-Comique in 1899. She continued to sing there until 1903, during which time she was chosen to create the role of Geneviève in *Pélleas et Mélisande* on April 30, 1902. In 1903–4 she appeared at Brussels's Théâtre Royal de la Monnaie, and then sang Orféo at London's Covent Garden in 1905. In 1907 she made her first appearance at the Manhattan Opera in N.Y. as Cieca, and sang there until 1910. She then appeared in Chicago, Boston, Philadelphia, and Montreal. Among her other roles were Dalila, Clytemnestra, and Hérodiade.—**NS/LK/DM**

Gesensway, Louis, Latvian-American violinist and composer; b. Dvinsk, Feb. 19, 1906; d. Philadelphia, March 11, 1976. The family moved to Canada when he was a child; he studied violin. In 1926 he joined the Philadelphia Orch., remaining with it until 1971. He was a prolific composer of some originality; he developed a system of "color harmony" by expanding and contracting the intervals of the diatonic scale into fractions, establishing a difference between enharmonically equal tones; such a scale in his projection contained 41 degrees.

> **WORKS: O R C H.:** Flute Concerto (Philadelphia, Nov. 1, 1946); *The 4 Squares of Philadelphia* for Narrator and Orch. (Philadelphia, Feb. 25, 1955); *Ode to Peace* (Philadelphia, April 15, 1960); *Commemoration Symphony* (1966–68; Philadelphia, Feb. 25, 1971); *A Pennsylvania Overture* (1972); Cello Concerto (1973). **C H A M B E R:** Concerto for 13 Brass Instruments (1942); Quartet for Clarinet and Strings (1950); Quartet for Oboe, Bassoon, Violin, and Viola (1951); Sonata for Solo Bassoon; Duo for Oboe and Guitar (1959); Duo for Viola and Bassoon (1960); Duo for Violin and Cello (1970).—**NS/LK/DM**

Gesius, Bartholomäus, German composer; b. Müncheberg, c. 1559; d. Frankfurt an der Oder, 1613. He was educated at the Univ. of Frankfurt an der Oder (1575–80). In 1582 he was in Müncheberg as Kantor. After living in Muskau and Wittenberg, he became Kantor at the Marienkirche in Frankfurt an der Oder in 1593. His *St. John Passion* (1588) is a significant work in the development of the Protestant Passion. Among his other works were another Passion, Latin pre-Reformation songs, Protestant hymns, occasional works, and music for school use.

> **BIBL.:** P. Blumenthal, *Der Kantor B. G. zu Frankfurt/Oder* (Frankfurt an der Oder, 1926).—**LK/DM**

Gesualdo, Carlo, Prince of Venosa and Count of Conza, Italian lutenist and composer; b. probably in Naples, c. 1560; d. there, Sept. 8, 1613. In 1590, his unfaithful wife and 1st cousin, Maria d'Avalos, and her lover were murdered at Gesualdo's orders. In 1594 he was at the court of the Estensi in Ferrara, where he married his 2nd wife, Leonora d'Este, the same year. Sometime after the death of the Duke of Ferrara, in 1597, Carlo returned to Naples, where he remained until death. Living in the epoch when the "new music" (the homophonic style) made its appearance, he was one of the most original musicians of the time. Like Rore, Banchieri, and Vincentino, he was a so-called chromaticist. His later madrigals reveal a distinctly individual style of expression and are characterized by strong contrasts, new (for their time) harmonic progressions, and a skillful use of dissonance; he was a master in producing tone color through the use of different voice registers and in expressing the poetic contents of his texts. He publ. 6 vols. of madrigals a 5 (1594–1611; modern ed. by F. Vatielli and A. Bizzelli, 1956–58). A complete edition of his works was ed. by W. Weisman and G. Watkins (10 vols., 1957–67).

BIBL.: F. Keiner, *Die Madrigale G. s von Venosa* (diss., Univ. of Leipzig, 1914); C. Gray and P. Heseltine, *C. G., Prince of Venosa, Musician and Murderer* (London, 1926); F. Vatielli, *Il Principe di Venosa e Leonora d'Este* (Milan, 1941); G. Watkins, *G., The Man and His Music* (London, 1973); A. Vaccaro, *C. G., principe di Venosa: L'uomo e i tempi* (Venosa, 1989; 2nd ed., rev. and aug., 1998).—**NS/LK/DM**

Geszty (real name, **Witkowsky**), **Sylvia,** Hungarian soprano; b. Budapest, Feb. 28, 1934. She studied at the Budapest Cons. In 1959 she made her operatic debut at the Hungarian State Opera in Budapest; was a member of the Berlin State Opera (1961–70), the Berlin Komische Oper (1963–70), the Hamburg State Opera (1966–72; 1973), and the Württemberg State Theater in Stuttgart (from 1970). She sang the Queen of the Night at London's Covent Garden in 1966, and repeated the role at the Salzburg Festival in 1967; at the Munich Opera Festival she also sang Zerbinetta, a favorite soubrette role, which she chose for her Glyndebourne Festival debut in 1971. She made her North American debut as Sophie in *Der Rosenkavalier* with the N.Y.C. Opera during its visit to Los Angeles on Nov. 19, 1973; she also appeared with the Berlin Städtische Oper, the Paris Opéra, La Scala in Milan, and the Teatro Colón in Buenos Aires, and in concerts and recitals.—**NS/LK/DM**

Getty, Gordon, American composer; b. Los Angeles, Dec. 20, 1933. He was the scion of the billionaire oil executive and art collector Jean Paul Getty. In 1945 he was taken to San Francisco, where he studied English literature at San Francisco State Coll. (graduated, 1956) and took courses at the San Francisco Cons. of Music. From his earliest attempts at composition, he proclaimed faith in the primacy of consonance and a revival of Romantic ideals. His preference lay with vocal music, and he possessed a natural gift for writing a fetching melodic line. For his songs and choruses, he selected the poems of Housman, Tennyson, Poe, and Dickinson. He also produced an opera, *Plump Jack*, based on the character of Shakespeare's Falstaff (excerpts only; San Francisco, March 13, 1985). The inevitable headline in one of several newspaper reviews was "Billionaire Has a Hit in Plump Jack!" Every critic's writing about Getty must deal with the inescapable suspicion that his music

is the accidental outgrowth of his material fortune, and must conquer conscious or subliminal prejudice in favor or disfavor of a work. Getty deserves full credit for braving this test courageously, ignoring bouquets and brickbats and persevering in writing his kind of music. Among his other works are the piano pieces *Homework Suite, 3 Diatonic Waltzes*, and *Tiefer und Tiefer* (all 1986), and a vocal work, *The White Election for Soprano and Piano*, to poems by Emily Dickinson (1986).—**NS/LK/DM**

Getz, Stan(ley), American jazz tenor saxophonist; b. Philadelphia, Feb. 2, 1927; d. Los Angeles, June 6, 1991. Getz was one of the major progenitors of the cool style of jazz in the 1950s; in the 1960s he helped to introduce Brazilian bossa nova on such popular albums as *Jazz Samba* and *Getz/Gilberto* and such tunes as "Desafinado" and "The Girl from Ipanema."

Getz's parents were Russian immigrants. His father, Alexander Getz, a tailor, had been named Gayetskis; his mother was the former Goldie Yampolsky. The family moved to the Bronx in N.Y. when he was young. He played several instruments as a child, starting on the string bass and then switching to bassoon before taking up the tenor saxophone. He was a member of the All-City Orch. while attending James Monroe H.S. At 15 he dropped out to join Dick Rogers's band, but he was forced to return to school until he was 16, when he left again to join Jack Teagarden. He played with Stan Kenton, 1944–45, and had brief stints with several other bands, including those of Jimmy Dorsey and Benny Goodman, first leading his own group in 1945 and first making his own records in 1946. On Nov. 7, 1946, he married singer Beverly Byrne, with whom he had two children. They divorced on Oct. 31, 1956.

Getz joined Woody Herman's Second Herd in September 1947 and achieved fame as a member of the "Four Brothers" saxophone section, named after the song of that title and also featuring Zoot Sims, Serge Chaloff, and Herbie Steward (replaced by Al Cohn). Getz's solo on the 1948 Herman recording of "Early Autumn" (music by Ralph Burns) added to his renown. In early 1949 he left Herman and again led his own small group. His career was bedeviled by drug addiction in the early 1950s, and he spent much of the late 1950s living in Europe. On Nov. 2, 1956, he married Monica Silfverskiold; they had two children and divorced on May 29, 1987.

Getz moved back to the U.S. in January 1961, to find the cool, restrained approach of his playing out of fashion in the face of the more aggressive work of John Coltrane and Ornette Coleman. He responded first with *Focus* (1962), on which he was accompanied by string arrangements written by Eddie Sauter, and then with *Jazz Samba*, recorded Feb. 13, 1962, on which he teamed with guitarist Charlie Byrd to play Brazilian tunes in the bossa nova style originated by Antonio Carlos Jobim. The LP was a remarkable commercial and critical success; it hit #1 in March 1963 and earned a Grammy nomination for Album of the Year, while the single "Desafinado" (music by Antonio Carlos Jobim) became a Top 40 hit and earned a Grammy nomination for Record of the Year, winning Getz his first Grammy for

Best Jazz Performance by a Soloist or Small Group, Instrumental.

Getz reached the pop charts with a series of albums, *Big Band Bossa Nova* in 1962, *Jazz Samba Encore!* in 1963, and *Reflections* in 1964, before exceeding the success of *Jazz Samba* with his duet album with João Gilberto, *Getz/Gilberto,* released in March 1964. Paced by a single release of "The Girl from Ipanema" (music by Antonio Carlos Jobim, Portuguese lyrics by Vinicuis De Moraes, English lyrics by Norman Gimbel) featuring Gilberto's wife, Astrud Gilberto, on vocals, that topped the easy-listening charts and hit the pop Top Ten, the LP went gold, winning two Grammys, for Album of the Year and Best Instrumental Jazz Performance by a Small Group or Soloist with Small Group. "The Girl from Ipanema" was named Record of the Year.

Getz's next album, *Getz Au Go Go,* a live album featuring Astrud Gilberto, made the charts in December 1964 and stayed there more than 10 months. His playing of the music of Eddie Sauter on the soundtrack of the film *Mickey One,* released in September 1965, earned him a Grammy nomination for Best Jazz Performance by a Large Group or Soloist with Large Group. His album *Sweet Rain* made the charts in September 1967 and earned a Grammy nomination for Best Instrumental Jazz Performance by a Small Group or Soloist with Small Group (7 or Fewer).

Getz again spent much of his time in Europe in the late 1960s and early 1970s. He commissioned Chick Corea to write for him and in 1972 recorded the resulting album, *Captain Marvel,* with a band including Corea. It was not released until 1975, when he signed a contract with Columbia Records, but it then made the charts. Getz earned two Grammy nominations in 1978, one for Best Jazz Instrumental Performance by a Soloist for *Stan Getz Gold* and another with Jimmy Rowles for Best Jazz Instrumental Performance by a Group for *The Peacocks.*

After performing more fusion-oriented music in the late 1970s and early 1980s, Getz returned to a more traditional approach. He became an artist in residence at Stanford Univ. in 1984. Suffering from liver cancer, he continued to record and perform. Getz earned two Grammy nominations in 1990, for Best Jazz Instrumental Performance by a Soloist for *Anniversary* and for Best Jazz Fusion Performance for *Apasionado,* winning his final Grammy for the track "I Remember You" from *Serenity* following his death at 64 in 1991.

DISC.: *Opus de Bop* (1945); *All Star Series* (1946); *Groovin' High* (1947); *In Retrospect* (1948); *Five Brothers* (1949); *Stan Getz and Tenor Sax Stars* (1949); *Stan Getz* (1949); *Stan Getz, Vol. 2* (1949); *The Brothers* (1949); *Long Island Sound* (1949); *Quartets* (1949); *Prezervation* (1949); *At Carnegie Hall* (1949); *The Sounds of Stan Getz* (1950); *Modern World* (1950); *Getz Age* (1950); *Roost Quartets* (1950); *Split Kick* (1950); *Chamber Music* (1951); *The Sound* (1951); *Jazz at Storyville* (1951); *Storyville, Vol. 1* (1951); *Storyville, Vol. 2* (1951); *Jazz at Storyville, Vol. 3* (1951); *Billie and Stan* (1952); *Moonlight in Vermont* (1952); *Live 1952, Vol. 1* (1952); *Plays* (1952); *Interpretatons by the Stan Getz Quintet* (1953); *More West Coast Jazz with Stan Getz* (1953); *The Melodic Stan Getz* (1953); *Interpretations* (1953); *Stan Getz Plays Blues* (1953); *Diz and Getz* (1953); *Stan Getz '57* (1953); *Stan Getz and the Cool Sounds* (1954); *Another Time, Another Place* (1954); *Eloquence* (1954); *Stan Getz at the Shrine* (1954); *At the Shrine Auditorium* (1954); *Hamp*

and Getz (1955); *Stan Getz Quintet* (1955); *West Coast Jazz* (1955); *Stan Getz in Stockholm* (1955); *For Musicians Only* (1956); *The Steamer* (1956); *The Soft Swing* (1957); *Award Winner: Stan Getz* (1957); *Stan Getz and J.J. Johnson at the Opera House* (1957); *Getz Meets Mulligan in Hi-Fi* (1957); *Stan Getz and the Oscar Peterson Trio* (1957); *Stan Getz with Cal Tjader* (1958); *Stan Meets Chet* (1958); *Jazz Giants '58* (1958); *Stockholm Sessions '58* (1958); *Imported from Europe* (1958); *Jazz Collector Edition* (1958); *Live in Europe* (1958); *Stan Getz at Large* (1960); *Cool Velvet* (1960); *Focus* (1961); *Stan Getz and Bob Brookmeyer* (1961): *Rhythms* (1961); *Jazz Samba* (1962); *Big Band Bossa Nova* (1962); *Jazz Samba Encore* (1963); *Getz/Gilberto* (1963); *Stan Getz with Guest Artist Laurindo Almeida* (1963); *Reflections* (1963); *Stan Getz and Bill Evans* (1964); *Getz Au Go Go Featuring Astrud Gilberto* (1964); *Getz/Gilberto #2* (1964); *Chick Corea/Bill Evans Sessions* (1964); *Mickey One* (soundtrack; 1965); *Look at Yesterday* (1965); *A Song After Sundown* (1966); *Stan Getz and Arthur Fiedler at Tanglewood* (1966); *Didn't We* (1966); *Quartet in Paris* (1966); *Voices* (1966); *Sweet Rain* (1967); *What the World Needs Now* (1967); *Marakesh Express* (1969); *Dynasty* (1971); *Communications '72* (1971); *Captain Marvel* (1972); *But Beautiful* (1974); *The Best of Two Worlds* (1975); *The Peacocks* (1975); *The Master* (1975); *Live at Montmartre* (1977); *Another World* (1977); *Children of the World* (1978); *Forest Eyes* (1979); *Stan Getz* (1979); *Live at Midem '80* (1980); *Autumn Leaves* (1980); *Stan Getz Live* (1980); *The Dolphin* (1981); *Spring Is Here* (1981); *Billy Highstreet Samba* (1981); *Pure Getz* (1982); *Blue Skies* (1982); *Live in Paris* (1982); *Poetry* (1983); *Line for Lyons* (1983); *The Stockholm Concert* (1983); *Voyage* (1986); *Serenity* (1987); *The Lyrical Stan Getz* (1988); *Just Friends* (1989); *Yours and Mine: Live at the Glasgow* (1989); *Soul Eyes* (1989); *Apasionado* (1989); *Live* (1990); *People Time* (1991).

BIBL.: A. Astrup, *The S. G. Discography* (Texarkana, Tex., 1978; 2nd ed., 1984); R. Palmer, *S. G.* (London, 1988); D. Maggin, *S. G.: A Life in Jazz* (N.Y., 1996); R. Kirkpatrick, *S. G.: An Appreciation of His Recorded Work* (Bath, 1992).—**WR**

Gevaert, François Auguste, eminent Belgian musicologist and composer; b. Huysse, near Audenarde, July 31, 1828; d. Brussels, Dec. 24, 1908. He was a pupil of De Somère (piano) and Mengal (composition) at the Ghent Cons. (1841–47), taking the Grand Prix de Rome for composition; from 1843 he was also organist at the Jesuit church. He lived in Paris (1849–50), and was commissioned to write an opera for the Théâtre-Lyrique. He then spent a year in Spain, his *Fantasía sobre motivos españoles* winning him the Order of Isabella la Católica. After visits to Italy and Germany, he returned to Ghent in 1852 and brought out 9 operas in quick succession. In 1857 his festival cantata *De nationale verjaerdag* won him the Order of Léopold. From 1867 to 1870 he was music director at the Paris Opéra, and from 1871 director of the Brussels Cons., succeeding Fétis. As conductor of the "Concerts du Conservatoire," he exerted a far-reaching influence through his historical concerts, producing works of all nations and periods. In 1873 he was elected a member of the Academy, succeeding Mercadante. In 1907 he was made a baron. In addition to his books, he ed. *Les Gloires de l'Italie* (a collection of vocal numbers from operas, oratorios, cantatas, etc., of the 17th and 18th centuries), *Recueil de chansons du XVᵉ siècle* (transcribed in modern notation), and *Vademecum de l'organiste* (classic transcriptions).

WORKS: 12 operas; 8 cantatas; a *Missa pro defunctis* and *Super flumina Babylonis* (both for Men's Chorus and Orch.);

overture, *Flandre au lion*; ballads (*Philipp van Artevelde*, etc.); songs (many in the collection *Nederlandsche Zangstukken*).

WRITINGS: *Leerboek van den Gregoriaenschen Zang* (1856); *Traité d'instrumentation* (1863; rev. and enl. as *Nouveau traité de l'instrumentation*, 1885; Ger. tr. By Riemann, 1887; Span. tr. by Neuparth, 1896; Russ. tr. by Rebikov, 1899); *Histoire et théorie de la musique de l'antiquité* (2 vols., 1875, 1881); *Les Origines du chant liturgique de l'église latine* (1890; Ger. tr. by Riemann); *Cours méthodique d'orchestration* (2 vols., 1890; complement of *Nouveau traité*); *La Melopée antique dans l'église latine* (1895); *Les Problèmes musicaux d'Aristote* (3 vols., 1899–1902); *Traité d'harmonie théorique et pratique* (2 vols., 1905, 1907).

BIBL.: F. Dufour, *Le Baron F.A. G.* (Brussels, 1909); E. Closson, *G.* (Brussels, 1928).—NS/LK/DM

Geyer, Stefi, Hungarian-born Swiss violinist and teacher; b. Budapest, Jan. 28, 1888; d. Zürich, Dec. 11, 1956. She studied with Hubay at the Royal Academy of Music in Budapest, and also toured in Europe and the U.S. at an early age. In 1919 she settled in Zürich and married **Walter Schulthess**. She taught at the Zürich Cons. (1923–53). She was an object of passion on the part of Bartók, who wrote a violin concerto for her (1907).—NS/LK/DM

Ghedini, Giorgio Federico, Italian composer and pedagogue; b. Cuneo, July 11, 1892; d. Nervi, March 25, 1965. He studied piano and organ with Evasio Lovazzano, cello with S. Grossi, and composition with G. Cravero at the Turin Cons., and then composition at the Liceo Musicale in Bologna with M.E. Bossi, graduating in 1911. He was prof. of harmony and composition at the conservatories in Turin (1918–37), Parma (1938–41), and Milan (from 1941), serving as director of the latter (1951–62). His works evolved from neo- Classicism to more advanced contemporary techniques.

WORKS: DRAMATIC: O p e r a : *Gringoire* (1915); *Maria d'Alessandria* (Bergamo, Sept. 9, 1937); *Re Hassan* (Venice, Jan. 26, 1939); *La pulce d'oro* (Genoa, Feb. 15, 1940); *Le Baccanti* (Milan, Feb. 21, 1948); *Billy Budd*, after Melville (Venice, Sept. 7, 1949); *Lord Inferno*, "harmonious comedy" for radio, after Beerbohm's *The Happy Hypocrite* (RAI, Oct. 22, 1952; rev. version as *L'Ipocrita felice*, Milan, March 10, 1956); *La Via della Croce* (Venice, April 9, 1961). B a l l e t : *Girotondo*, mime play for children (Venice, 1959). ORCH.: *Partita* (1926); *Concerto grosso* for Wind Quintet and Strings (1927); *Pezzo concertante* for 2 Violins, Viola obbligato, and Orch. (1931); *Marinaresca e baccanale* (1933; Rome, Feb. 2, 1936); *Sym.* (1938); *Architetture* (1940; Rome, Jan. 19, 1941); *Invenzioni* for Cello, Strings, Kettledrums, and Cymbals (1940); Piano Concerto (1946); *Musica Notturna* for Chamber Orch. (1947); Concerto for 2 Pianos and Chamber Orch. (1947; Milan, Jan. 24, 1948); *Il Belprato* for Violin and Strings (1947); *Canzoni* (1948); *L'Alderina* for Flute, Violin, and Orch. (1951); *L'Olmeneta* for 2 Cellos and Orch. (1951); *Musica da concerto* for Viola and Strings (1953); *Concentus Basiliensis* for Violin and Chamber Orch. (1954); *Vocalizzo da concerto* for Cello or Baritone and Orch. (1957); *Fantasie* for Piano and Strings (1958); *Sonata da concerto* for Flute, Strings, and Percussion (1958); *Divertimento* for Violin and Orch. (1960); *Studi per un affresco di battaglia* (1962); *Contrappunti* for Violin, Viola, Cello, and Strings (1962); *Musica concertante* for Cello and Strings (1962); *Appunti per un credo* for Chamber Orch. (1962); *Concert Overture* (1963). CHAMBER: Wind Quintet (1910); Piano Quartet (1917); Double Quartet for 5 Winds, 5 Strings, Harp,

and Piano (1921); Violin Sonata (1922); Cello Sonata (1924); 2 string quartets (1927, 1959); *Adagio e allegro da Concerto* for Flute, Clarinet, Horn, Viola, Cello, and Harp (1936); *Concertato* for Flute, Viola, and Harp (1942); *7 Ricercari* for Piano Trio (1943); *Canons* for Violin and Cello (1946); *Concentus* for String Quartet (1948); *Music* for Flute, Cello, and Piano (1963); piano pieces. VOCAL: *Le messa del Venerdi santo*, oratorio (1929; Perugia, Sept. 27, 1949); masses; cantatas; motets; choral pieces; songs.

BIBL.: N. Castiglioni, *G.F. G* (Milan, 1955).—NS/LK/DM

Gheluwe, Leon van, Belgian composer; b. Wanneghem-Lede, Sept. 15, 1837; d. Ghent, July 14, 1914. He studied in Ghent with Gevaert and others. He became a prof. at the Ghent Cons. (1869–71), and later was director of the École de Musique in Bruges (1871–1900). He wrote a Flemish opera, *Philippine van Vlaanderen* (Brussels, 1876), and a number of songs. —NS/LK/DM

Ghent, Emmanuel (Robert), Canadian-born American composer; b. Montreal, May 15, 1925. He studied medicine at McGill Univ. in Montreal (B.S., 1946; M.D., 1950), where he also received instruction in piano and bassoon. In 1951 he settled in the U.S. and completed his training in music with Shapey. In 1967 he held a Guggenheim fellowship. From 1969 he was active at the Bell Telephone Laboratories, where he prepared computer-generated works. His other works include mixed media scores and tape pieces. He also invented electronic devices capable of transmitting synchronization signals to musicians.—NS/LK/DM

Gheorghiu, Angela, admired Romanian soprano; b. Adjud, Sept. 7, 1965. She was a student of Mia Burbu at the George Enescu Lyceum in Bucharest, and then pursued training at the Bucharest Cons. (graduated, 1988). Following engagements in Romania, she made her first appearance at London's Covent Garden in 1992 as Zerlina. On Dec. 4, 1993, she made her Metropolitan Opera debut in N.Y. as Mimi. She returned to Covent Garden in 1994 as Violetta. In 1995 she was engaged as Gounod's Juliette at the Washington (D.C.) Opera and Verdi's Desdemona at the Salzburg Festival. In 1996 she returned to the Metropolitan Opera as Micaëla, and that same year married **Roberto Alagna**. She sang again at Covent Garden in 1997 as Adina. Her return to the Metropolitan Opera in 1998 to sing Juliette to Alagna's Roméo elicited critical accolades. They reprised those roles at the Lyric Opera in Chicago in 1999. Among her other esteemed roles are Liù, Nina in Massenet's *Chérubin*, Suzel in *L'Amico Fritz*, and Magda in *La Rondine*. —NS/LK/DM

Gheorghiu, Valentin, Romanian composer; b. Galați, March 21, 1928. He studied composition with Jora and Andricu at the Bucharest Cons., and then piano with Lazare Lévy and harmony at the Paris Cons. (1937–39). His works include 2 syms. (1949; 1953, rev. 1974), Piano Concerto (1959), *Imagini din copilarie*, suite for Orch. (1961), *Burlesca* for Piano and Orch. (1964), String Quartet (1946), Piano Sonata (1946), Cello Sonata (1950), Piano Trio (1950), and songs.—NS/LK/DM

Gherardello da Firenze, Italian composer; b. c. 1322; d. Florence, 1362 or 1363. He lived in Florence, where he became a clerk in 1343 and a priest in 1344 at the Cathedral. He later served as prior at S. Remigo. His extant works, 2 mass movements, ballate, madrigals, and the celebrated caccia *Tosto che l'alba del bel giorno appare,* have been ed. by N. Pirrotta in *The Music of Fourteenth-Century Italy,* Corpus Mensurabilis Musicae, VIII/1 (1964).—**LK/DM**

Gherardeschi, Filippo Maria, Italian composer; b. Pistola, 1738; d. Pisa, 1808. He was a student in Bologna of Padre Martini. He was made organist at Livorno Cathedral in 1761, and in 1763 he became maestro di cappella in Voltera. After serving as organist at Pisa Cathedral, he was maestro di cappella at Pistoia Cathedral and then at the Chiesa Conventuale dei Cavalieri di S. Stefano in Pisa from about 1766 until his death. From about 1768 until 1803 he also was director of music to the Grand Duke of Tuscany. He composed 7 operas, many works for the church, and chamber music. —**LK/DM**

Ghersem, Géry (de), Franco-Flemisch composer; b. Tournai, c. 1574; d. there, May 25, 1630. After serving as a choirboy at Tournai Cathedral, he went to Madrid and entered the Capilla Flamencia as a cantorcillo. In 1593 he was made cantor, and in 1598 asst. director. In 1604 he returned to Flanders and became director of the domestic chapel of the Archduke and chaplain of the oratory. His contemporaries held him in high esteem as a composer of sacred works and villancicos. A Mass for 7 Voices (Madrid, 1598) and the motet *Benedicam Dominum* for 8 Voices are extant.—**LK/DM**

Gheyn, Matthias van den, Flemish organist and composer; b. Tirlemont, Brabant, April 7, 1721; d. Louvain, June 22, 1785. From 1741, he was organist at St. Peter's, Louvain, and from 1745, town "carillonneur" he was celebrated in both capacities. He composed pieces for organ and for carillon.

WRITINGS: *Fondements de la basse continue* (lessons and sonatinas for organ and violin); *6 divertissements pour clavecin* (c. 1760).

BIBL.: S. van Elewyck, *M. v.d.G.* (Louvain, 1862). —**NS/LK/DM**

Ghezzo, Dinu, Romanian-born American composer, conductor, and teacher; b. Tuzla, July 2, 1941. He took courses in music education and conducting (diploma, 1964), and in composition (diploma, 1966), at the Bucharest Cons., and then completed his training at the Univ. of Calif. at Los Angeles (Ph.D. in composition, 1973). In 1978 he became a naturalized American citizen. From 1974 to 1976 he was an asst. prof. at Queens Coll. of the City Univ. of N.Y. He served as director of the New Repertory Ensemble of N.Y. from 1975 to 1988. In 1977 he became a prof. of music at N.Y.U. He also was composer-in- residence at the Univ. of Wisc. in Madison in 1995. His music is in a thoroughly contemporary style.

WORKS: ORCH.: *Thalla* for Piano and 17 Players (1974); Concertino for Clarinet and Symphonic Wind Ensemble (1975); *Celebrations* for Chamber Orch. and Tape (1980); *7 Short Pieces* for Chamber Orch. (1981); *Sketches* for Clarinet and Chamber Orch. (1981); *Echoes of Romania* for Strings (1990). **CHAMBER:** Clarinet Sonata (1967); String Quartet (1967); *Kanones II* for 6 Players (1978); *Aphorisms* for Clarinet and Piano (1981); Nonetto (1982); *Structures* for Cello and Piano (1982); *Sound Shapes I,* 5 studies for Wind Player (1984) and *II,* 5 pieces for Brass Player (1985); *From Here to...There* for 6 Players (1986); *Elegies* for Violin and Cello (1989). **MIXED MEDIA:** *Freedom* for Clarinet, Piano, Chamber Ensemble, and Tape (1990); *Ostrom I* for Quartet, Slides, and Tape (1990) and *II* for 6 to 18 Players (1990). **VOCAL:** *Letters to Walt Whitman* for Soprano, Clarinet, and Piano (1983); *2 Prayers* for Soprano and Tape (1988); *A Book of Songs* for Soprano, Chamber Group, and Tape (1989). —**NS/LK/DM**

Ghiaurov, Nicolai, outstanding Bulgarian bass; b. Lydjene, near Velingrad, Sept. 13, 1929. He was a student of Brambarov at the Sofia Cons., and then pursued his training at the Moscow Cons. (1950–55). After making his operatic debut as Don Basilio at the Moscow Opera Studio in 1955, he reprised that role for his Sofia debut in 1956. In 1957 he sang for the first time at the Paris Opéra, the Vienna State Opera, and at the Bolshoi Theater in Moscow, where he quickly established his reputation. In 1959 he made an impressive debut as Varlaam at Milan's La Scala, and in 1962 sang for the first time at London's Covent Garden as the Padre Guardino. In 1964 he made his first appearance at the Lyric Opera of Chicago as Gounod's Méphistophélès, which role he also chose for his Metropolitan Opera debut in N.Y. on Nov. 8, 1965. In subsequent years, he appeared with most of the principal opera houses of Europe and North America, as well as at many of the leading festivals. Ghiaurov's remarkable vocal and dramatic gifts placed him among the foremost bassos of his day. His other roles included Don Giovanni, Pimen, Ramfis, Boris Godunov, Philip II, Massenet's Don Quichotte, and Boito's Mefistofele. In 1981 he married **Mirella Freni.**—**NS/LK/DM**

Ghiglia, Oscar, Italian guitarist; b. Livorno, Aug. 13, 1938. He studied at the Accademia di Santa Cecilia in Rome (graduated, 1962), then took lessons with Segovia at the Accademia Musicale Chigiana in Siena. After winning a guitar competition in Paris in 1963, he received a scholarship to the Schola Cantorum, where he studied music history with Jacques Chailley (1963–64). He made his American and British debuts in 1966, and subsequently toured in America and in Europe.—**NS/LK/DM**

Ghis, Henri, French pianist and composer; b. Toulon, May 17, 1839; d. Paris, April 24, 1908. He studied at the Paris Cons. with Marmontel (piano), and received 1st prize in 1854. He also studied organ with Benoist, graduating in 1855. He became a fashionable piano teacher in Paris, numbering many aristocratic ladies (to whom he dedicated his pieces) among his pupils. He was also the first teacher of Ravel. He publ. salon music for piano: waltzes, mazurkas, polonaises, polkas, gavottes, caprices, etc., often with superinduced titles, as *Séduction, Menuet de la petite princesse, La Marquisette,* etc. However, he is mostly known for his popular arrangement of an early aria, which he publ. for piano as *Air Louis XIII* (1868); the actual melody was definitely not by Louis XIII, but in all probability an old French folk song.—**NS/LK/DM**

Ghiselin, Johannes, important Flemish composer who flourished in the late 15th and early 16th centuries. He also used the name Verbonnet as an alias. He was active at the court in Ferrara, and also a singer at S. Giovanni in Florence (1492–93); later was a singer to the King of France in Paris. He returned to Ferrara in 1503, but fled to the Netherlands after an outbreak of the plague in 1505. He was last reported in Bergen op Zoom in 1507. Petrucci publ. a vol. of Ghiselin's masses in 1503. His extant works include 9 masses, 13 motets, and secular vocal works. These compositions reveal him as a worthy contemporary of Josquin Desprez and Jacob Obrecht. A complete edition of his works was ed. by C. Gottwald in Corpus Mensurabilis Musicae, XXIII/1–4 (1961–68).

BIBL.: C. Gottwald, *J. G.—Johannes Verbonnet: Stilkritische Untersuchung zum Problem ihrer Identität* (Wiesbaden, 1962). —**NS/LK/DM**

Ghisi, Federico, Italian musicologist and composer; b. Shanghai, Feb. 25, 1901; d. Luzerna San Giovanni, July 18, 1975. His father was in the diplomatic corps in China. After the family settled in Italy in 1908, he studied harmony and counterpoint at the Milan Cons., and also piano privately with Faggioni; later he pursued training in chemistry at the Univ. of Pavia (graduated, 1923). While employed as a chemist, he took courses in composition with Ghedini at the Turin Cons. and in music history with Torrefranca at the Univ. of Florence (libera docenza, 1936). He then taught at the latter (1937–40), at the Università per Stranieri in Perugia (1945–74), and at the Univ. of Pisa (1963–70). Ghisi wrote many articles on Florence during the Renaissance era. Among his compositions were the operas *Il dono dei Re Magi* (1959) and *Il Vagabondo e la guardia* (1960), and the oratorio *L'ultima visione* (1967–72).

WRITINGS: *I canti carnascialeschi nelle fonti musicali del XV e XVI secolo* (Florence, 1937); *Le feste musicali della Firenze Medicea* (Florence, 1939); *Alle Fonti della Monodia:Nuovi brani della "Dafne" di J. Peri e "Il fuggilotio musicale" di G. Caccini* (Milan, 1940).—**NS/LK/DM**

Ghislanzoni, Antonio, Italian writer and dramatic poet; b. Barco, near Lecco, Nov. 25, 1824; d. Caprino-Bergamasco, July 16, 1893. He was intended for the church, but his fine baritone voice led him to adopt the career of a stage singer (Lodi, 1846), which he speedily abandoned, however, for literary work. He became the manager of *Italia Musicale,* and was for years the ed. of the Milan *Gazzetta Musicale,* to which he remained a faithful contributor until his death. He wrote over 80 opera librettos, that of *Aida* being the most famous. He publ. *Reminiscenze artistiche* (contains an episode entitled *La casa di Verdi a Sant' Agata*). —**NS/LK/DM**

Ghitalla, Armando, distinguished American trumpeter and teacher; b. Alfa, Ill., June 1, 1925. He studied at the Juilliard School of Music in N.Y. with William Vacchiano (1946–49). In 1949 he joined the Houston Sym. Orch., and in 1951 he was engaged by the Boston Sym. Orch., serving as its 1st trumpeter from 1965 to 1979. In 1979 he became prof. of trumpet at the Univ. of Mich. at Ann Arbor.—**NS/LK/DM**

Ghys, Joseph, Belgian violinist and composer; b. Ghent, 1801; d. St. Petersburg, Aug. 22, 1848. A pupil of Lafont at the Brussels Cons., he later taught in Amiens and Nantes, and, beginning in 1832, made concert tours in France, Belgium, Germany, Austria, and northern Europe. He wrote *Le Mouvement perpétuel* for Violin, with String Quartet, a Violin Concerto, and other music for the violin.—**NS/LK/DM**

Giacomelli, Geminiano, Italian composer; b. Piacenza, c. 1692; d. Loreto, Jan. 25, 1740. He studied with Capelli at Parma, and wrote his first opera, *Ipermestra,* in 1724. It was the first of 19 operas he wrote for Venice, Parma, Naples, and other Italian towns, the most popular being *Cesare in Egitto* (Milan, 1735). He was maestro di cappella at the court of Parma and the Chiesa della Steccata from 1719 to 1727, returning to both posts from 1732 to 1737. He was maestro di cappella for the church of S. Giovanni in Piacenza from 1727 to 1732, and also held a similar post at the Santa Casa in Loreto from 1738. His many church compositions include an oratorio, *La conversione di Santa Margherita,* and a setting of Psalm VIII for 2 Tenors and Bass.

BIBL.: C. Anguisola, *G. G. e Sebastiano Nasolini, musicisti piacentini* (Piacenza, 1935).—**NS/LK/DM**

Giacometti, Giovanni Battista, Italian instrumentalist whose fame gained him the name del Violino; b. Brescia, c. 1550; d. after 1603. He gained distinction as a lutenist, violist, and harpist in Rome. In 1586 he entered the service of the Gonzaga court in Mantua. Following sojourns to Florence (1589) and the Papal Chapel in Rome (1591), he was active at the Medici court in Florence. He excelled as a performer on the viola da gamba, harp, and violin.—**LK/DM**

Giacomini, Giuseppe, Italian tenor; b. Padua, Sept. 7, 1940. He received vocal instruction in Padua, Treviso, and Milan. In 1966 he made his operatic debut as Pinkerton in Vercelli, and then appeared frequently in Berlin and Vienna (from 1972), Hamburg (from 1973), Milan's La Scala (from 1974), and at the Paris Opéra (from 1975). In 1976 he made his U.S. operatic debut as Verdi's Alvaro in Cincinnati. He made his Metropolitan Opera debut in N.Y. in that same role on Nov. 27, 1976. In 1980 he portrayed Dick Johnson at his first appearance at London's Covent Garden. He was engaged as Radames in Chicago in 1988, and in 1993 he sang Otello in Monte Carlo. He portrayed Cavaradossi at the Bavarian State Opera in Munich in 1998.—**LK/DM**

Gialdini, Gialdino, Italian conductor and composer; b. Pescia, Nov. 10, 1843; d. there, March 6, 1919.

He was a pupil of T. Mabellini in Florence. His first opera, *Rosamunda* (prize opera in a competition instituted by the Pergola Theater, Florence), given in 1868, was unsuccessful. After producing 2 "opere buffe," *La Secchia rapita* (Florence, 1872) and *L'Idolo cinese* (1874), in collaboration with other musicians, he devoted himself to conducting. Later he again turned to dramatic composition, producing the operas *I due soci* (Bologna, Feb. 24, 1892), *La Pupilla* (Trieste, Oct. 23, 1896), and *La Bufera* (Pola, Nov. 26, 1910). He also publ. *Eco della Lombardia*, a collection of 50 folk songs.—**NS/LK/DM**

Gianneo, Luis, Argentine composer, conductor, and teacher; b. Buenos Aires, Jan. 9, 1897; d. there, Aug. 15, 1968. He studied harmony with Gaito and counterpoint and composition with Fornarini. From 1923 to 1943 he taught at the Inst. Musical in Tucumán, and then was a prof. of music at various schools in Buenos Aires. He was especially interested in the problems of musical education of the very young; in 1945 he organized and conducted the Orquesta Sinfónica Juvenil Argentina. From 1955 to 1960 he was director of the Buenos Aires Cons.

WORKS: B A L L E T : *Blanca nieves* (1939). O R C H . : *Turay-Turay*, symphonic poem (Buenos Aires, Sept. 21, 1929); 3 syms. (1938, 1945, 1963); *Obertura para una comedia infantil* (1939); Piano Concerto (1941); Sinfonietta (Buenos Aires, Sept. 20, 1943); Violin Concerto (Buenos Aires, April 13, 1944); *Variaciones sobre tema de tango* (1953). C H A M B E R : 4 string quartets (1936, 1944, 1952, 1958); 2 piano trios; String Trio; Violin Sonata; Cello Sonata; 3 piano sonatas (1917, 1943, 1957). V O C A L : *Cantica Dianae* for Chorus and Orch. (1949); *Angor Dei* for Soprano and Orch. (1962); *Poema de la Saeta* for Soprano and Orch. (1966); solo songs.—**NS/LK/DM**

Giannetti, Giovanni, Italian composer; b. Naples, March 25, 1869; d. Rio de Janeiro, Dec. 10, 1934. He studied in Naples, Trieste, and Vienna. In 1912–13 he was director of the Liceo Musicale, Siena, and in 1915 he was in Rome, where, from 1920, he was music director of the Teatro dei Piccoli, with which he toured Europe and South America.—**NS/LK/DM**

Giannettini, Antonio, Italian organist and composer; b. Fano, 1648; d. Munich, July 12, 1721. He went to Venice and sang bass in the choir of San Marco from 1674. He served as organist at SS. Giovanni e Paolo (1676–79), as well as at San Marco during periods between 1677 and 1686. In 1686 he became maestro di cappella at the Modena court. About 1702 he returned to Venice, and in 1707 he went back to Modena. He composed about 10 operas, of which *Medea in Atene* (Venice, 1675) became the best known. His other works included 9 oratorios, many cantatas, 12 motets, a Kyrie a 5, and Psalms a 4 with Instruments (Venice, 1717).

BIBL.: E. Luin, *A. G. e la musica a Modena alla fine del secolo 17* (Modena, 1931).—**NS/LK/DM**

Giannini, Dusolina, American soprano, daughter of **Ferruccio** and sister of **Vittorio Giannini;** b. Philadelphia, Dec. 19, 1900; d. Zürich, June 26, 1986. She received early musical training at home, then studied

voice with Sembrich in N.Y., where she made her concert debut on March 14, 1920. She made her operatic debut as Aida with the Hamburg Opera on Sept. 12, 1925, then sang in Berlin, Vienna, and London. She made her Metropolitan Opera debut in N.Y. as Aida on Feb. 12, 1936, and remained on its roster until 1941; she also appeared with other American opera houses. She sang again in Europe (1947–50), then taught voice. Giannini created the role of Hester in her brother's *The Scarlet Letter* (Hamburg, June 2, 1938).—**NS/LK/DM**

Giannini, Ferruccio, Italian-American tenor, father of **Dusolina** and **Vittorio Giannini;** b. Ponte d'Arnia, Nov. 15, 1868; d. Philadelphia, Sept. 17, 1948. He emigrated to the U.S. in 1885; studied with Eleodoro De Campi in Detroit. He made his debut in Boston in 1891, then toured the U.S. with the Mapleson Opera Co. (1892–94); made the first operatic recordings, which were issued by Emile Berliner in 1896. He later settled in Philadelphia, where he presented operas, concerts, and plays in his own theater.—**NS/LK/DM**

Giannini, Vittorio, American composer and teacher, son of **Ferruccio** and brother of **Dusolina Giannini;** b. Philadelphia, Oct. 19, 1903; d. N.Y., Nov. 28, 1966. Brought up in a musical family, he showed a precocious talent. He was sent to Italy at the age of 10, and studied at the Milan Cons. (1913–17). After returning to the U.S., he took private lessons with Martini and Trucco in N.Y.; in 1925 he entered the Juilliard graduate school, where he was a pupil of Rubin Goldmark in composition and Hans Letz in violin; in 1932 he won the American Prix de Rome; was in Rome for a period of 4 years. Upon his return to N.Y., he was appointed to the faculty of the Juilliard School of Music in 1939 as a teacher of composition and orchestration; in 1941 he also became an instructor in theory; furthermore, he was appointed prof. of composition at the Curtis Inst. of Music in Philadelphia in 1956. In 1965 became the first director of the N.C. School of the Arts in Winston-Salem. As a composer, Giannini was at his best in opera, writing music of fine emotional éclat, excelling in the art of bel canto and avoiding extreme modernistic usages; in his symphonic works, he also continued the rich Italian tradition; these qualities endeared him to opera singers, but at the same time left his music out of the mainstream of contemporary music making.

WORKS: DRAMATIC: O p e r a : *Lucedia* (Munich, Oct. 20, 1934); *Not all Prima Donnas are Ladies* (n.d.); *The Scarlet Letter* (1937; Hamburg, June 2, 1938); *Flora* (1937); *Beauty and the Beast* (CBS, Nov. 24, 1938; stage premiere, Hartford, Conn., Feb. 14, 1946); *Blennerhasset* (CBS, Nov. 22, 1939); *Casanova* (n.d.); *The Taming of the Shrew* (1952; concert premiere, Cincinnati, Jan. 31, 1953; television premiere, NBC, March 13, 1954); *Christus* (1956); *The Harvest* (Chicago, Nov. 25, 1961); *Rehearsal Call* (1961; N.Y., Feb. 15, 1962); *The Servant of 2 Masters* (1966; N.Y., March 9, 1967); *Edipus Rex* (unfinished). O R C H . : Concerto Grosso for Strings (1931); Suite (1931); Piano Concerto (1935); Sym., *In Memoriam Theodore Roosevelt* (1935; N.Y., Jan. 19, 1936, composer conducting); Sym., *I.B.M.* (1939); 5 numbered syms.: No. 1, *Sinfonia* (1950; Cincinnati, April 6, 1951), No. 2 (1955; St. Louis, April 16, 1956), No. 3 for Band (1958), No. 4 (N.Y., May 26, 1960), and No. 5 (1965); Organ Concerto (1937); *Prelude, Chorale,* and Fugue (1939); Violin Concerto (1944); Trumpet Concerto (1945); Frescobaldiana (1948); 3 divertimentos (1953, 1961, 1964); Prelude and Fugue for Strings (1955); Love's Labour Lost, suite for Chamber Orch. (1958); Psalm CXXX for Double Bass or Cello and Chamber Orch. (1963). **CHAMBER:** 2 violin sonatas (1926, 1945); String Quartet (1930); Piano Quintet (1931); Piano Trio (1931); Woodwind Quintet (1933); Sonata for Solo Violin (1945); piano pieces. **VOCAL:** Stabat mater for Chorus and Orch. (1920); Madrigal for 4 Solo Voices and String Quartet (1931); Primavera, cantata (1933); Requiem for Chorus and Orch. (1937); Lament for Adonis, cantata (1940); Canticle of Christmas for Baritone, Chorus, and Orch. (1951); Canticle of the Martyrs for Chorus and Orch. for the 500th anniversary of the Moravian Church (1956); The Medead for Soprano and Orch. (1960); Antigone for Soprano and Orch. (1962); numerous songs.

BIBL.: M. Mark, The Life and Works of V. G. (1903–1966) (diss., Catholic Univ. of America, 1970).—NS/LK/DM

Giardini, Felice de',

Italian violinist and composer; b. Turin, April 12, 1716; d. Moscow, June 8, 1796. He was a chorister at the Cathedral of Milan, and studied singing and harpsichord with Paladini and violin with Somis in Turin. As a young man he played in various theater orchs. in Rome and Naples, often improvising cadenzas at the end of operatic numbers. He acquired popularity in Italy and made a tour in Germany (1748), and then went to London (1750), where he made a series of successful appearances as a concert violinist. In 1752 he joined the Italian opera in London as concertmaster. He became its impresario in 1755, and was connected with the management, with interruptions, for some 40 years. He was concertmaster at the Pantheon Concerts (1774–80). From 1784 to 1789 he was in Italy. He then returned to London in 1790 and led 3 seasons of Italian opera. In 1796 he was engaged as a violinist in Russia and gave his initial concert in Moscow, on March 24, 1796, but soon became ill, and died shortly afterward. As a violinist, he was eclipsed in London by Salomon and Cramer, but he left his mark on musical society there. Among operas entirely by him were Rosmira (April 30, 1757), Siroe (Dec. 13, 1763), Enea e Lavinia (May 5, 1764) and Il Re pastore (March 7, 1765). He also wrote music for various pasticcios, several overtures, concertos, string quartets and violin sonatas.

BIBL.: S. McVeigh, The Violinist in London's Concert Life, 1750–1784; F. G. and His Contemporaries (diss., Oxford Univ., 1980).—NS/LK/DM

Giazotto, Remo,

Italian musicologist; b. Rome, Sept. 4, 1910. He studied piano and composition at the Milan Cons. (1931–33), his principal mentors being Torrefranca, Pizzetti, and Paribeni; he also took courses in literature and philosophy at the Univ. of Genoa. In 1932 he joined the staff of the Rivista Musicale Italiana, serving as its ed. (1945–49), and later as co-ed. of the Nuova Rivista Musicale Italiana (from 1967); he also was a prof. of music history at the Univ. of Florence (1957–69). The popular Adagio for Strings and Organ frequently attributed to Albinoni is almost totally the work of Giazotto.

WRITINGS: Il melodramma a Genova nel XVII e XVIII secolo (Genoa, 1942); Tomaso Albinoni, musico di violino, dilettante veneto (Milan, 1945); Busoni: La vita nell'opera (Milan, 1948); Poesia melodrammatica e pensiero critico nel Settecento (Milan, 1952); La musica a Genova nella vita pubblica e privata dal XIII al XVIII secolo (Genoa, 1952); La musica italiana a Londra negli anni di Purcell (Rome, 1955); Giovanni Battista Viotti (Milan, 1956); Musurgia nova (Milan, 1959); Vita di A. Stradella: Un "Orfeo assassinato" (2 vols., Milan, 1962); Vivaldi (Milan, 1965); Quattro secoli di storia dell'Accademia di Santa Cecilia (2 vols., Milan, 1970); Le due patri di Giulio Caccini, musico mediceo (1551–1618) (Florence, 1984); Puccini in Casa Puccini (Lucca, 1992).—NS/LK/DM

Gibb, Andy,

the Bee Gees' baby brother who followed them to the top of the charts (b. Manchester, England, March 5, 1958; d. Oxford, England, March 10, 1988). As notorious as a teen idol as he was a pop singer, Andy Gibb's short, tempestuous life earned him more ink in the tabloids than in Billboard. He was born into a musical family. His father, a big band leader and drummer, and his mother, a big band singer, kept the family moving around in search of gigs. They spent time in resorts such as Ibiza and the Isle of Man.

Shortly after Andy was born, the family moved to Australia. By the time he was four, his brothers were recording artists and performing on television. His brother Barry gave Andy his first guitar. By the time Andy was 13, he started performing. At 15, the family moved to the Isle of Man and Andy started playing out on a regular basis. A year later he was back in Australia, recording for the ATA label. His single "Words and Music" hit #5 on the Australian charts, and he started playing as an opening act for touring bands. His success in Australia came to the attention of his brother's manager, and soon the younger Gibb was signed to RSO Records along with his brothers. His debut, Flowing Rivers, spawned two gold, chart-topping hits, "I Just Want to Be Your Everything" and "(Love Is) Thicker Than Water." In addition to frequent radio play, he earned substantial coverage in the teen magazines owing to his good looks and youth (he was still shy of his 20th birthday). The album went platinum, topping out at #19.

After a club tour, Andy went into the studio and recorded Shadow Dancing. The title track spent seven weeks on the top of the charts, going platinum. This made Gibb the first solo artist to have his first three singles got to #1. "An Everlasting Love" went gold and rose to #5, while "(Our Love) Don't Throw it Away" hit #9 and also went gold.

Gibb married and had a daughter, but as his fame increased, family life seemed less appealing than jet-setting. He divorced his wife and took up with actress Victoria Principal, 14 years his senior. Hitting the road with his brothers on their Spirits Having Flown tour, he sang on their hits and did a spotlight on his own.

His third album, After Dark generated the #4 single "Desire," and the #12 "I Can't Help It." The album, however, only went gold, topping off at #21. Suddenly, as far as pop music was concerned, Andy was yesterday's news, to the point that, at 22, RSO released a greatest hits collection. Featuring a pair of previously unreleased duets with Olivia Newton John, "Time Is Time" (#11) and "Me (Without You)" (#40), the album sold disappointingly.

Gibb started exploring new frontiers. He took on the role of Frederic in the L.A. company of the revival of *The Pirates of Penzance*. This led to a co-hosting job on the syndicated music TV show *Solid Gold*. However, when his relationship with Principal faltered, he turned to cocaine and missed many tapings. He moved to N.Y., taking on the role of Joseph in the Broadway revival of *Joseph and the Amazing Technicolor Dreamcoat* in 1983. He was dismissed from this role for too many "sick days" as well. By 1985, his addiction caused him to seek help. Gibb checked into the Betty Ford Clinic. Cleaning up didn't improve his professional fortunes, however, and by 1987 he declared personal bankruptcy, claiming assets of $50,000 against debts of over a million.

Gibb continued playing and writing, however, and by late 1987 he had signed with Island records. He never got the chance to make that record, however. While writing in England, he came down with viral myocarditis (a viral infection causing the heart to swell) and died just five days after his 30th birthday.

DISC.: *Flowing Rivers* (1977); *Shadow Dancing* (1978); *After Dark* (1980).—**HB**

Gibbons, Christopher, English organist and composer, son of **Orlando Gibbons;** b. London (baptized), Aug. 22, 1615; d. there, Oct. 20, 1676. He was a pupil at the Chapel Royal. From 1638 to 1642 he was organist at Winchester Cathedral, and in 1660 he was appointed organist of the Chapel Royal, private organist to Charles II, and organist at Westminster Abbey. He received the degree of Mus.D. from Oxford in 1664, at the special request of the King. He wrote verse anthems, motets, and many string fantasies. He also collaborated with M. Locke in the music for Shirley's masque *Cupid and Death*. C. Rayner prepared the modern ed. *Christopher Gibbons: Keyboard Compositions*, in Corpus of Early Keyboard Music, XVIII (1967).

BIBL.: C. Rayner, *A Little-known 17th-century Composer, C. G.* (diss., Ind. Univ., 1963); J. Harley, *Orlando Gibbons and the Gibbons Family of Musicians* (Brookfield, Vt., 1999). —**NS/LK/DM**

Gibbons, Edward, English composer, brother of **Ellis** and **Orlando Gibbons;** b. Cambridge, 1568; d. probably in Exeter, c. 1650. He received a B.Mus. degree from both Oxford and Cambridge. After serving as a lay clerk at King's Coll., Cambridge, he became master of choristers in 1593, and kept the post until 1598. He then went to the Exeter Cathedral, where he served for many years, with the titles of "priest-vicar" and succentor, though he remained a layman. Little of his music is extant.

BIBL.: J. Harley, *Orlando Gibbons and the Gibbons Family of Musicians* (Brookfield, Vt., 1999).—**NS/LK/DM**

Gibbons, Ellis, English composer and organist, brother of **Edward** and **Orlando Gibbons;** b. Cambridge, 1573; d. May 1603. The only compositions of his which are known to exist are 2 madrigals included by Morley in his collection *The Triumphes of Oriana* (London, 1601): *Long live fair Oriana* and *Round about her charret.*

BIBL.: J. Harley, *Orlando Gibbons and the Gibbons Family of Musicians* (Brookfield, Vt., 1999).—**NS/LK/DM**

Gibbons, Orlando, celebrated English composer and organist, father of **Christopher** and brother of **Edward** and **Ellis Gibbons;** b. Oxford (baptized), Dec. 25, 1583; d. Canterbury, June 5, 1625. He was taken to Cambridge as a small child. In 1596 he became chorister at King's Coll. there, matriculating in 1598. He composed music for various occasions for King's Coll. (1602–03). In 1605 he was appointed organist of the Chapel Royal, retaining this position until his death. He received the degree of B.Mus. from Cambridge Univ. in 1606, and that of D.Mus. from Oxford in 1622. In 1619 he became chamber musician to the King and, in 1623, organist at Westminster Abbey. He conducted the music for the funeral of James I (1625), and died of apoplexy 2 months later. Gibbons's fame as a composer rests chiefly on his church music. He employed the novel technique of the "verse anthem" (a work for chorus and solo voices, the solo passages having independent instrumental accompaniment, for either organ or strings). Other works followed the traditional polyphonic style, of which he became a master. He was also one of the greatest English organists of the time. His madrigals and motets were ed. by E.H. Fellowes in The English Madrigal School, V (1921; 2nd ed., rev., 1964 by T. Dart), his services and anthems by P. Buck and others in Tudor Church Music, IV (1925), his keyboard music by G. Hendrie in Musica Britannica, XX (1962), and his verse anthems by D. Wulstan in Early English Church Music, III (1964).

WORKS: *Fantasies of 3 Parts...composed for viols* (1610); pieces for the virginal, in *Parthenia* (1611); *The First Set of Madrigals and Mottets of 5 Parts* (1612); 9 Fancies, appended to *20 konincklijke Fantasien op 3 Fiolen* by T. Lupo, Coperario, and W. Daman (Amsterdam, 1648).

BIBL.: E.H. Fellowes, *O. G., A Short Account of His Life and Work* (1925; 2nd ed., 1951, as *O. G. and His Family*); J. Harley, *O. G. and the Gibbons Family of Musicians* (Brookfield, Vt., 1999). —**NS/LK/DM**

Gibbs, Cecil Armstrong, English composer; b. Great Braddow, near Chelmsford, Aug. 10, 1889; d. Chelmsford, May 12, 1960. He studied at Trinity Coll., Cambridge (B.A., 1911; Mus.B., 1913), and also took courses in composition with Charles Wood and Vaughan Williams and in conducting with Boult at the Royal Coll. of Music in London, where he also taught (1921–39). In 1934 he received the Cobbett Gold Medal for his services to British chamber music. His style adhered to the Romantic school; he was best known for his songs, many to texts by Walter De la Mare.

WORKS: STAGE: *The Blue Peter*, comic opera (London, 1923); *The Sting of Love*, comic opera (1926); *When One Isn't There*, operetta (1927); *Twelfth Night*, opera (1946–47); *The Great Bell of Burley*, children's opera (1952); also incidental music. **ORCH.:** 3 syms.; Oboe Concerto; *Essex Suite* for String Quartet and Strings; *The Enchanted Wood*, dance phantasy for Piano and Strings (1919); *Fancy Dress*, dance suite (1935); *A Spring Garland*, suite for Strings (1937); Concertino for Piano and

Strings (1942); *Prelude, Andante, and Finale* for Strings (1946); *Dale and Fell*, suite for Strings (1954); *A Simple Concerto* for Piano and Strings (1955); *Threnody for Walter De la Mare* for String Quartet and Strings (1956); *A Simple Suite* for Strings (1957); *Shade and Shine*, suite for Strings (1958); *Suite* for Strings (1958–59); *Suite of Songs from the British Isles* (1959); *4 Orch. Dances* (1959). **CHAMBER:** 11 string quartets; 2 sonatas for Cello and Piano; *Country Magic*, piano trio (1922); *Lyric Sonata* for Violin and Piano (1928); Piano Trio (1940); Suite for Violin and Piano (1943); piano pieces. **C h o r a l :** *La Belle Dame sans merci* for Chorus and Orch. (1928); *The Birth of Christ* for Soloists, Chorus, and Orch. (1929); *The Highwayman* for Chorus and Orch. (1932); *The Ballad of Gil Morrice* for Chorus and Orch. (1934); *Deborah and Barak* for Soloists, Chorus, and Orch. (1936); *Odysseus* for Soloists, Chorus, and Orch. (1937–38); *The Passion According to St. Luke* for Chorus and Organ (1945); *Pastoral Suite* for Baritone, Chorus, and Orch. (1948–49); also anthems, motets, Psalms, part songs, carols, and about 150 songs.—NS/LK/DM

Gibbs, Georgia (originally, **Gibbons, Fredda**), white "cover girl" who topped the pop charts in the 1950s; b. Worcester, Mass., Aug. 17, 1920. Georgia Gibbs began recording in 1938, nearly 20 years before rock 'n' roll began to happen. Still, many rock historians point to her, and particularly her covers of LaVerne Baker's "Tweedle Dee" and Etta James's "The Wallflower," as emblematic of the white record business's exploitation of black artists.

Gibbs began singing with big bands in Boston as a teen, initially recording under her own name with Frankie Trumbaur and Artie Shaw. She worked as the "girl singer" on Jimmy Durante's Camel Caravan radio show. Announcer Garry Moore started introducing her as "her nibs, Miss Gibbs" a nickname that stuck through her career. In 1950, she had her first substantial solo hit with "If I Knew You Were Coming, I'd've Baked A Cake" (#5), landing nine more records in the Top 40 over the course of the next two years. This streak was capped off by the gold record "Kiss of Fire," a tango Gibbs took to the top of the charts for seven weeks. She started off 1953 with a #5 hit "Seven Lonely Days." Over the course of the next two years she charted half a dozen more hits produced by Hugo Peretti and Luigi Creatore, her A&R team at Mercury, capitalizing on her very mainstream, pop style, usually accompanied by big bands.

In 1955, Gibbs applied this approach on two current R&B hits that were beginning to show some action on the pop charts. First she covered Baker's "Tweedle Dee," taking it to #2, leaving Baker's version in the dust at #14. Two months later, she topped the charts with "Dance With Me Henry," a version of Etta James #1 R&B hit "The Wallflower" which in turn was a version of Hank Ballard's even raunchier 1954 #1 R&B hit "Work With Me Annie." Baker was so incensed at being undercut like this, she explored legal action and called her Congressman. He actually convened a federal hearing on the matter, but it resolved nothing.

Gibbs's career, however, stalled after that. "Sweet and Gentle," a version of a Cuban song and "I Want You to Be My Baby" rose to #12 and #14, respectively, both

in the summer of 1955. No subsequent songs broke the Top 20, though she did land four more in the Top 40 before dropping off the pop radar. After taking most of the 1960s off, Gibbs started performing occasionally during the 1970s and 1980s.

DISC.: *Ballin' the Jack* (1951); *Georgia Gibbs Sings Oldies* (1953); *The Man That Got Away* (1954); *Music and Memories* (1956); *Song Favorites* (1956); *Swingin' with Her Nibs* (1956); *Her Nibs* (1957); *Something's Gotta Give* (1964); *Like a Song* (1998); *Georgia Gibbs* (1998).—HB

Gibbs, Joseph, English organist and composer; b. Dec. 23, 1699; d. Ipswich, Dec. 12, 1788. He was organist at St. Nicholas's Church, Harwich, in Dedham, Essex, and finally at St. Mary Tower, Ipswich (from 1748). He publ. 8 violin sonatas (c. 1746) and 6 string quartets (c. 1777), and also wrote organ music.—LK/DM

Gibbs, Terry (originally, **Gubenko, Julius**), bebop-styled vibraphonist, percussionist, and leader; b. Brooklyn, N.Y., Oct. 13, 1924. He began by playing drums and timpani; won a Major Bowes radio amateur contest at age 12, and was a professional drummer before joining the army in World War II. Thereafter he played with Tommy Dorsey, Buddy Rich, Woody Herman, Benny Goodman, and Louie Bellson in the 1940s and 1950s, before starting his own group. He has usually led a small group but headed the big Dream Band (1959), which often had Mel Lewis on drums and was a forerunner of Lewis's big band with Thad Jones. During the 1960s–80s, he worked frequently with Steve Allen as a musical director. During the same period, he worked a lot in TV. For a number of years he featured female pianists such as Terry Pollard and Alice McLeod (Coltrane), most of whom doubled on vibes for duets with him. He has toured with Buddy DeFranco since the early 1980s. His son Gerry (Gerald Scott, b. N.Y., Jan. 15, 1964) is a drummer.

DISC.: *Good Vibes* (1951); *T. G.* (1953); *Swingin' with T. G.* (1956); *Mallets A-Plenty* (1956); *Vibrations* (1959); *Launching a New Sound in Music* (1959); *Dream Band, Vol. 1–3: Flying Home* (1959); *Steve Allen Presents* (1960); *Exciting T. G. Band* (1961); *Dream Band, Vol. 4–5: Big Cat* (1961); *Straight Ahead* (1962); *Explosion* (1962); *Jewish Melodies in Jazztime* (1963); *El Nutto* (1963); *Take It from Me* (1964); *Latino* (1964); *It's Time We Met* (1965); *Reza* (1966); *Bopstacle Course* (1974); *Smoke 'Em Up* (1978); *Live at the Lord* (1978); *Air Mail Special* (1981); *Chicago Fire* (1987); *Memories of You* (1991); *Kings of Swing* (1991).—LP/NS

Gibson, Debbie, the youngest artist to have written produced and performed a U.S. #1 single; b. Merrick, N.Y., Aug. 31, 1970. Deborah Gibson was a child prodigy, daughter of a TWA employee. Gibson more or less pressed her mother into service as a stage mother. Gibson started taking piano lessons from Billy Joel's old teacher Mortin Estrin when she was five years old, and wrote her first song at six. At this age, she started acting, initially in community theater. While still in grade school, she performed in the children's chorus at N.Y.'s renowned Metropolitan Opera, writing an opera of her own in fifth grade. Many commercials and industrial films also featured her voice.

At 12 years old, Gibson wrote "I Come from America," a song that won her $1000 in a songwriting contest and the interest of manager Doug Breitbart. Breitbart worked on developing Gibson's talents, setting her up with a home studio. By 16, Gibson was attending Calhoun H.S. by day, and playing out at clubs four nights a week. In her spare time, she wrote over 100 songs in her home studio. On the basis of these demos, Breitbart convinced Atlantic Records to sign her to a singles contract.

Her first single, 1986's "Only in My Dreams," a dance track that called to mind a more innocent Madonna, reached #4 on the charts and went gold. Following this auspicious debut, the even more dance oriented "Shake Your Love" also hit #4. The title track from her debut album, *Out of the Blue*, went to #3. The final single from the album, "Foolish Beat" became her first chart topper. Gibson was just a couple of months over 18, making her the youngest artist to have written, produced, and performed on a #1 single. After Gibson graduated with honors from Calhoun, the final single from the album, "Staying Together," stalled at #22. Nonetheless, the album hit #7 and went triple platinum.

Gibson became a teen phenomenon, her picture gracing the cover of magazines from *Teen Beat* to *Seventeen*. She was the girl next door who happened to have a mega-hit record, the suburban sweetheart. It was an image for which she was groomed: Her album cover featured her clutching a teddy bear. In anticipation of the release of her sophomore effort, *Electric Youth*, she became a commodity to the point that Revlon began marketing a perfume also called Electric Youth.

Electric Youth got off to a promising start. The first single, "Lost in Your Eyes" topped the charts for three weeks and went gold. The title track also went gold, but only reached #11. "No More Rhymes" faltered at #17, and the follow-up single didn't make it past #70. The album, however, spent five weeks at #1 and sold double platinum. Her third album, *Anything Is Possible*, didn't even make the Top 40, stalling at #41 while its lone hit, the title track, stalled at #26. Switching to EMI, her next album *Body, Mind Soul* did even worse.

Gibson turned back to theater, starring on Broadway in *Les Miserables* in 1992 and as Belle in the theatrical production of Disney's *Beauty and the Beast* in 1997–98. In 1995, she recorded an unlikely duet with the Circle Jerks on the Soft Boys song "I Wanna Destroy You." She also cut her own, self-released MOR album *Think With Your Heart*. She has since toured with other plays, as well as making a couple of movies. There are rumors that she might also star in her own sitcom.

DISC.: *Out of the Blue* (1987), *Electric Youth* (1989), *Anything Is Possible* (1990), *Body Mind Soul* (1993), *Think with Your Heart* (1995), *Deborah* (1997).—**HB**

Gibson, Sir Alexander (Drummond),

distinguished Scottish conductor; b. Motherwell, Feb. 11, 1926; d. London, Jan. 14, 1995. He studied piano at the Royal Scottish Academy of Music in Glasgow, and also was a student in music at the Univ. of Glasgow. He then held a piano scholarship at the Royal Coll. of Music in London, where he first studied conducting; he later received additional training in conducting from Markevitch at the Salzburg Mozarteum and from Kempen at the Accademia Musicale Chigiana in Siena. In 1951 he became a répétiteur and in 1952 a conductor at the Sadler's Wells Opera in London. After serving as assoc. conductor of the BBC Scottish Sym. Orch. in Glasgow (1952–54), he again conducted at the Sadler's Wells Opera (from 1954), where he later was music director (1957–59). In 1959 he made his first appearance at London's Covent Garden. From 1959 to 1984 he was principal conductor and artistic director of the Scottish National Orch. in Glasgow. In 1962 he founded Glasgow's Scottish Opera and was its artistic director until 1987. He also was principal guest conductor of the Houston Sym. Orch. (1981–83). In 1991 he became president of the Scottish Academy of Music and Drama in Glasgow. In 1967 he was made a Commander of the Order of the British Empire. He was knighted in 1977. Gibson was equally admired as an interpreter of the orch. and operatic repertoire.—**NS/LK/DM**

Giddings, Thaddeus P(hilander Woodbury),

American music educator; b. Anoka, Minn., Feb. 19, 1868; d. Clermont, Fla., March 4, 1954. He was educated at the Univ. of Minn. (1885–87) and at the Western Normal Music School in Lake Geneva, Wisc. (1890) and in Highland Park, Ill. (graduated, 1892). After serving as a supervisor of music in several Midwestern cities (from 1891), he held that position with the Minneapolis public schools (1910–42). He also taught public school music at the Univ. of Minn. (1915–28) and music education at the MacPhail Coll. of Music in Minneapolis (1923–42). With Joseph E. Maddy, he founded the National Music Camp in Interlochen, Mich., in 1928, remaining active with it until his death.

BIBL.: C. McDermid, *T.P. G.: A Biography* (diss., Univ. of Mich., 1967).—**LK/DM**

Gideon, Miriam,

American composer and teacher; b. Greeley, Colo., Oct. 23, 1906. She studied piano in N.Y. with Hans Barth and in Boston with Felix Fox, and pursued her education at Boston Univ. (B.A., 1926). Later she took courses in musicology at Columbia Univ. (M.A., 1946) and in composition at the Jewish Theological Seminary of America (D.S.M., 1970), and also studied with Saminsky and Sessions. She taught at Brooklyn Coll. (1944–54) and the City Coll. of the City Univ. of N.Y. (1947–55; 1971–76); she also was an assoc. prof. of music at the Jewish Theological Seminary (from 1955) and a teacher at the Manhattan School of Music (from 1967). In 1975 she was elected to the National Inst. of Arts and Letters. Her music was distinguished by its attractive modernism.

WORKS: DRAMATIC: Opera: *Fortunato* (1958). **ORCH.:** *Epigrams*, suite for Chamber Orch. (1941); *Lyric Piece* for Strings (1941; London, April 9, 1944); *Symphonia brevis (Two Movements for Orchestra)* (N.Y., May 16, 1953). **CHAMBER:** *Incantation on an Indian Theme* for Viola and Piano (1939); Flute Sonata (1943); String Quartet (1946); *Divertimento* for Woodwind Quartet (1948); *Fantasy on a Javanese Motive* for Cello and Piano (1948); Viola Sonata (1948); *Biblical Masks* for Violin and

Piano or Solo Organ (1960); Suite for Clarinet or Bassoon and Piano (1972); *Fantasy on Irish Folk Motives* for Oboe, Bassoon, Vibraphone, Glockenspiel, Tam-tam, and Viola (1975); Trio for Clarinet, Cello, and Piano (1978); *Eclogue* for Flute and Piano (1988); piano pieces, including a Sonata (1977). **VOCAL:** *Sonnets from Shakespeare* for High or Low Voice, Trumpet, and String Orch. or Quartet (1950; N.Y., April 1, 1951); *Songs of Youth and Madness* for High Voice and Orch. (N.Y., Dec. 5, 1977); choral pieces; many song cycles; solo songs.—**NS/LK/DM**

Giebel, Agnes, Dutch soprano of German descent; b. Heerlen, Aug. 10, 1921. She studied with Hilde Weselmann at the Folkwangschule in Essen. She began a career as a concert singer in 1947. She gained wide recognition for her radio broadcasts of the Bach cantatas over the RIAS in Berlin in 1950. At a later period, she promoted modern music; her performances of works by Schoenberg, Berg, Hindemith, and Henze were praised. She made several tours as a concert artist in the U.S. —**NS/LK/DM**

Gieburowski, Waclaw, eminent Polish musicologist; b. Bydgoszcz, Feb. 6, 1876; d. Warsaw, Sept. 17, 1943. He was a student of theology in Regensburg, where he also took courses in church music with Haberl. He then studied at the Univ. of Berlin with Wolf and Kretzschmar and at the Univ. of Breslau with Kinkeldey, where he took his Ph.D. with the diss. *Die Musica Magistri Szydlowitae, Ein polnischer Choraltraktat des 15. Jahrhunderts und seine Stellung in der Choraltheorie des Mittelalters* (1913; publ. Posen, 1915). He settled in Posen as choirmaster at the Cathedral in 1916; was a prof. of church music at the Univ. (1925–39). From 1928 to 1939 he publ. the valuable series Cantica Selecta Musices Sacrae in Polonia; restored to use many sacred works by Polish composers of the Renaissance; publ. several treatises on this subject; also composed several sacred choral works.—**NS/LK/DM**

Giegling, Franz, Swiss musicologist; b. Buchs, near Aarau, Feb. 27, 1921. He studied piano and theory at the Zürich Cons. with Cherbuliez. He received his Ph.D. from the Univ. of Zürich in 1947 with the valuable diss. *Giuseppe Torelli, Ein Beitrag zur Entwicklungsgeschichte des italienischen Konzerts* (publ. in Kassel, 1949). He was music critic of the *Neue Zürcher Zeitung* (1947–53), and subsequently worked for Radio Zürich and Radio Basel. Giegling was one of the eds. of the 6th edition of the Köchel catalogue of Mozart's works; he also contributed articles to *Die Musik in Geschichte und Gegenwart.*—**NS/LK/DM**

Gielen, Michael (Andreas), noted German conductor; b. Dresden, July 20, 1927. His father, Josef Gielen, was an opera director who settled in Buenos Aires in 1939; his uncle was **Eduard Steuermann.** Gielen studied piano and composition with Erwin Leuchter in Buenos Aires (1942–49). He was on the staff of the Teatro Colón there (1947–50), then continued his training with Polnauer in Vienna (1950–53). In 1951 he became a répétiteur at the Vienna State Opera, and later was its resident conductor (1954–60). He was principal conduc-

tor of the Royal Opera in Stockholm (1960–65), a regular conductor with the Cologne Radio Sym. Orch. (1965–69), and chief conductor of the Orchestre National de Belgique in Brussels (1968–73) and the Netherlands Opera in Amsterdam (1973–75). From 1977 to 1987 he was artistic director of the Frankfurt am Main Opera and chief conductor of its Museumgesellschaft concerts; also was chief guest conductor of the BBC Sym. Orch. in London (1979–82) and music director of the Cincinnati Sym. Orch. (1980–86). In 1986 he became chief conductor of the South-West Radio Sym. Orch. in Baden-Baden; he also was prof. of conducting at the Salzburg Mozarteum (from 1987). Gielen has acquired a fine reputation as an interpreter of contemporary music; he has also composed a number of works of his own, including a Violin Sonata (1946); a Trio for Clarinet, Viola, and Bassoon (1948); *Variations* for String Quartet (1949); *Music* for Baritone, Strings, Piano, Trombone, and Percussion (1954); *4 Songs of Stefan George* for Chorus and Instruments (1955); *Variations* for 40 Instruments (1959); *Pentaphonie* for Piano, 5 Soloists, and 5 Quintets (1960–63); String Quartet (1983); *Pflicht und Neigung* for 22 Players (1988); *Rückblick*, trio for 3 Cellos (1989); and *Weitblick*, sonata for Solo Cello (1991).

BIBL.: P. Giebig, ed., *M. G.: Dirigent, Komponist, Zeitgenosse* (Stuttgart, 1997).—**NS/LK/DM**

Gieseking, Walter (Wilhelm), celebrated German pianist; b. Lyons, Nov. 5, 1895; d. London, Oct. 26, 1956. He studied with Karl Leimer at the Hannover Cons., graduating in 1916. In 1912 he made his debut in Hannover, and from 1921 he made tours of Europe. In 1923 he made his British debut in London. He made his American debut at Aeolian Hall in N.Y. on Feb. 22, 1926, and after that appeared regularly in the U.S. and Europe with orchs. and in solo recitals. He became the center of a political controversy when he arrived in the U.S. in 1949 for a concert tour; he was accused of cultural collaboration with the Nazi regime, and public protests forced the cancellation of his scheduled performances at Carnegie Hall in N.Y. However, he was later cleared by an Allied court in Germany and was able to resume his career in America. He appeared again at a Carnegie Hall recital on April 22, 1953, and until his death continued to give numerous performances in both hemispheres. He was one of the most extraordinary pianists of his time. A superb musician capable of profound interpretations of both Classical and modern scores, his dual German-French background enabled him to project with the utmost authenticity the masterpieces of both cultures. He particularly excelled in the music of Mozart, Beethoven, Schubert, and Brahms; his playing of Debussy and Ravel was also remarkable; he was also an excellent performer of works by Prokofiev and other modernists. He composed some chamber music and made piano transcriptions of songs by Richard Strauss. His autobiography, *So Wurde ich Pianist*, was publ. posth. in Wiesbaden (1963).

BIBL.: B. Gavoty, *G.* (Geneva, 1955).—**NS/LK/DM**

Gifford, Helen (Margaret), Australian composer; b. Hawthorn, Victoria, Sept, 5, 1935. She studied with Roy Shepherd (piano) and Dorian Le Gallienne (harmony) at the Univ. of Melbourne Conservatorium of Music (Mus.Bac., 1958). From 1970 to 1982 she was active as a composer for the Melbourne Theatre Co. In 1974 was also composer-in-residence of the Australian Opera in Sydney.

WORKS: DRAMATIC: O p e r a : *Jo Being* (1974); *Regarding Faustus* (1983); *Iphigenia in Exile* (1985). **S t a g e :** Incidental music to plays. **ORCH.:** *Phantasma* for Strings (1963); *Chimaera* (1967); *Canzone: Hommage to Stravinsky* for Chamber Orch. (1968); *Imperium* (1969); *On Reflection* for 2 Violins and String Orch. (1972). **CHAMBER:** *Fantasy* for Flute and Piano (1958); Septet for Flute, Oboe, Bassoon, Harpsichord, Violin, Viola, and Cello (1962); *Skiagram* for Flute, Viola, and Vibraphone (1963); *Lyric* for Flute, Clarinet, and Cello (1964); String Quartet (1965); *Sonnet* for Flute, Guitar, and Harpsichord (1969); *Of Old Angkor* for Horn and Marimba (1970); *Company of Brass* for 9 Brass Instruments (1972); *Play* for 10 Instruments (1979); *Time and Time Again* for 6 Instruments (1981); *Going South* for 2 Trumpets, Horn, and 2 Trombones (1987); *A Plaint for Lost Worlds* for Piccolo, Clarinet, and Piano (1994). **P i a n o :** Sonata (1960); *Catalysis* (1964); *Cantillation* (1966); *The Spell* (1966); *Souvenence* (1973); *Toccato attacco* (1990). **VOCAL:** *The Wanderer* for Male Speaker and Ensemble (1962); *The Glass Castle* for Soprano and Women's Chorus (1968); *Bird Calls from an Old Land* for 5 Sopranos and Women's Chorus (1971); *Images for Christmas* for Speaker and Ensemble (1973); *Foretold at Delphi* for Soprano, Piccolo, Oboe, Arab Drum, and Pre- recorded Crumhorn (1978); *Music for the Adonia* for Soprano and 8 Instruments (1993); *Point of Ignition* for Voice and Orch. (1995).—**NS/LK/DM**

Gigault, Nicolas, French organist and composer; b. probably in Paris, c. 1627; d. there, Aug. 20, 1707. He acquired distinction as an organist at the Parisian churches of St. Honoré (1646–52), St. Nicolas-des-Champs (from 1652), St. Martin-des-Champs (from 1673), and Hôpital du Saint Esprit (from 1685). He publ. 2 vols. of music as *Livre de musique* (Paris, 1683, 1685; ed. by A. Guilmant and A. Pirro in Archives des maîtres de l'orgue, IV, Paris, 1902). The first vol. includes 20 noëls with variations, the earliest known works of their kind. The second vol., designated for the organ, includes 183 versets.—**LK/DM**

Gigli, Beniamino, celebrated Italian tenor; b. Recanati, March 20, 1890; d. Rome, Nov. 30, 1957. He was a chorister at Recanati Cathedral. He commenced serious vocal studies with Agnese Bonucci in Rome, and continued his training with Cotogni and Rosati as a scholarship student at the Liceo Musicale there. After winning 1st prize in the Parma competition in 1914, he made his operatic debut as Enzo in *La Gioconda* in Rovigo on Oct. 14, 1914; subsequently sang in various Italian theaters, including Milan's La Scala in 1918 as Boito's Faust, a role he repeated in his Metropolitan Opera debut in N.Y. on Nov. 16, 1920. He remained on the Metropolitan roster as one of its leading singers until 1932, then returned for the 1938–39 season. He made his Covent Garden debut in London as Andrea Chénier on May 27, 1930; sang there again in 1931, 1938, and 1946. He spent the years during World War II in Italy; then resumed his operatic appearances, making his farewell to the stage in 1953; however, he continued

to give concerts, making a final, impressive tour of the U.S. in 1955. Gigli's voice, with its great beauty and expressivity, made him one of the foremost tenors of his era; he was famous for such roles as the Duke of Mantua, Nemorino, Lionel, Des Grieux, Nadir, and Gounod's Faust, as well as for the leading roles in Puccini's operas. His memoirs were publ. in an Eng. tr. in London in 1957.

BIBL.: R. Rosner, *B. G.* (Vienna, 1929); D. Silvestrini, *B. G.* (Bologna, 1937); R. Gigli, *B. G. mio padre: A cura di Celso Minestroni* (Parma, 1986).—**NS/LK/DM**

Gigout, Eugène, esteemed French organist, pedagogue, and composer; b. Nancy, March 23, 1844; d. Paris, Dec. 9, 1925. He began his studies in the maîtrise of Nancy Cathedral. At age 11, he entered the École Niedermeyer in Paris and studied with Saint-Saëns and Loret. He then served on its faculty (1863–85; 1900–05); in 1885 he founded his own organ school. From 1911 he was a prof. of organ and improvisation at the Paris Cons. He also was active as a church organist in Paris and made successful tours of Europe as a recitalist. In 1895 he became a Chevalier of the Légion d'honneur. Gigout composed hundreds of organ pieces, both sacred and secular, as well as piano music, sacred organ pieces, and songs.

BIBL.: G. Fauré, *Hommage à E. G.* (Paris, 1923). —**NS/LK/DM**

Gilardi, Gilardo, Argentine composer; b. San Fernando, May 25, 1889; d. Buenos Aires, Jan. 16, 1963. He studied with Pablo Berutti, then devoted himself to teaching and composing. Two of his operas were produced at the Teatro Colón in Buenos Aires: *Ilse* (July 13, 1923) and *La leyenda de Urutau* (Oct. 25, 1934). He also wrote *Sinfonia ciclico* (1961), 3 piano trios, 2 string quartets, *Sonata Popular Argentina* for Violin and Piano (1939), and many dances and songs based on native melodies.—**NS/LK/DM**

Gilbert, Anthony (John), English composer and teacher; b. London, July 26, 1934. He studied composition with Milner, Goehr, and Seiber in London both privately and at Morley Coll. (1958–63). He studied conducting at Morley with Del Mar (1967–69) and received training in composition from Nono and Berio at the Dartington Summer School (1961, 1962) and from Schuller, Shifrin, Carter, and Sessions at the Berkshire Music Center in Tanglewood (summer, 1967). Gilbert studied piano with Denis Holloway at London's Trinity Coll. of Music before completing his training at the Univ. of Leeds (M.A., 1984; Mus.D., 1990). He taught at Goldsmiths' Coll., Univ. of London (1968–73). He served as composer-in-residence (1970–71) and visiting lecturer (1971–72) at the Univ. of Lancaster, and also taught at Morley Coll. (1971–74). In 1973 he joined the faculty of the Royal Northern Coll. of Music in Manchester. In 1978–79 he also was senior lecturer in composition at the New South Wales State Conservatorium of Music in Sydney, and in 1981 was composer-in-the-community of Bendigo, Australia. A modernist by nature, Gilbert nevertheless writes music in Classical forms and is not averse to representational music; on the purely structural side, he adopts various attenuated forms of serial music, and in thematic development uses disparate agglutinative blocks.

WORKS: DRAMATIC: O p e r a : *The Scene Machine* (1970; Kassel, April 1, 1971); *The Chakravaka-bird*, radio opera (1977; BBC, Jan. 1982). **ORCH.:** *Sinfonia* for Chamber Orch. (London, March 30, 1965); *Regions* for 2 Orchs. (1966); *Peal II* for Big Band (1968); Sym. (Cheltenham, July 12, 1973); *Ghost and Dream Dancing* (Birmingham, Sept. 19, 1974); *Crow-cry* for Chamber Orch. (1976; London, March 16, 1977); *Welkin* for Student Orch. (1976); *Towards Asavari* for Piano and Chamber Orch. (1978; Manchester, Jan. 26, 1979); *Koonapippi* for Youth Orch. (1981); *Little Fantasia on Gold- Digger Tunes* for Chamber Orch. (1981); *Dream Carousels* for Wind Band (1988; London, Feb. 26, 1989); *Tree of Singing Names* for Chamber Orch. (1989; rev. 1993); *Mozart Sampler with Ground* (1991); *Igorochki* for Concertini Recorders and Chamber Orch. (1992); *On Beholding a Rainbow*, violin concerto (1997). **CHAMBER:** *Brighton Piece* for Clarinet, Horn, Trumpet, Trombone, Cello, and 3 Percussion (1967); *9 or 10 Osannas* for Clarinet, Horn, Violin, Cello, and Piano (1967); *The Incredible Flute Music* for Flute and Piano (1968); *O'Grady Music* for Clarinet, Cello, and Toy Instruments (1971); *String Quartet with Piano Pieces* (1972); *Canticle I: Rock-song* for 2 Clarinets, Bass Clarinet, 2 Horns, 2 Trumpets, and Trombone (1973); *Vasanta with Dancing* for Flute Doubling Alto Flute, Oboe Doubling English Horn, Violin, Viola, Harp, Percussion, and Optional Dancer (1981); *Fanfarings 1 and 2* (1983), *3 and 4* (1986–87), *5* (1988), and *6* (1992) for Brass; *Quartet of Beasts* for Flute, Oboe, Bassoon, and Piano (1984); *6 of the Bestiary* for Saxophone Quartet (1985); *String Quartet II* (1987) and *III* (1987); *Ziggurat* for Bass Clarinet and Marimba (1994); *Farings* for Sopranino Recorder and Piano (1996); *Réflexions, Rose Nord* for Bass Clarinet and Vibraphone (1996); *Os* for Oboe and Vibraphone (1999). **P i a n o :** 2 sonatas (1962, 1966). **VOCAL:** *Love Poems* for Soprano, Clarinet, Cello, Accordion or Soprano, Bass Clarinet, and Chamber Organ (1970); *Inscapes* for Soprano, Speaker, and Small Ensemble (1975); *Chant of Cockeye Bob* for Children's Voices and Instruments (1981); *Beastly Jingles* for Soprano and Instrumental Ensemble (1984); *Certain Lights Reflecting* for Soprano and Orch. (Cheltenham, July 14, 1989); *Upstream River Rewa* for Narrator and Indo-European Ensemble (1991); *Vers de Lune* for Soprano and Small Ensemble (1999); also choruses, including *Handles to the Invisible* (1995).—**NS/LK/DM**

Gilbert, Henry F(ranklin Belknap),

remarkable American composer; b. Somerville, Mass., Sept. 26, 1868; d. Cambridge, Mass., May 19, 1928. He studied at the New England Cons. of Music in Boston and with E. Mollenhauer; from 1889 to 1892 he was a pupil of MacDowell (composition) in Boston. Rather than do routine music work to earn his livelihood (he had previously been a violinist in theaters, etc.), he took jobs of many descriptions, becoming, in turn, a real estate agent, a factory foreman, a collector of butterflies in Fla., etc., and composed when opportunity afforded. In 1893, at the Chicago World's Fair, he met a Russian prince who knew Rimsky-Korsakov and gave him many details of contemporary Russian composers whose work, as well as that of Bohemian and Scandinavian composers which was based on folk song, influenced Gilbert greatly in his later composition. In 1894 he made his first trip abroad and stayed in Paris, subsequently returning

to the U.S.; when he heard of the premiere of Charpentier's *Louise*, he became intensely interested in the work because of its popular character, and, in order to hear it, earned his passage to Paris, in 1901, by working on a cattle boat; the opera impressed him so much that he decided to devote his entire time thereafter to composition. In 1902 he became associated with Arthur Farwell, whose Wa-Wan Press publ. Gilbert's early compositions. From 1903 he employed Negro tunes and rhythms extensively in his works. The compositions of his mature period (from 1915) reveal an original style, not founded on any particular native American material but infused with elements from many sources, and are an attempt at "un-European" music, expressing the spirit of America and its national characteristics.

WORKS: DRAMATIC: O p e r a : *Uncle Remus* (c. 1906; unfinished); *Fantasy in Delft* (1915–20). **I n c i d e n t a l M u s i c :** *Cathleen ni Houlihan* (1903); *Pot of Broth* (1903); *Riders to the Sea* (1904; rev. 1913; symphonic prologue, Peterboro, N.H., Aug. 20, 1914); *The Twisting of the Rope* (1904); *The Redskin, or The Last of his Race* (1906; not extant). **ORCH.:** *2 Episodes* (c. 1895; Boston, Jan. 13, 1896); *Orlamonde*, symphonic poem (c. 1896; not extant); *Summer-day Fantasie* (c. 1899); *Gavotte* (n.d.); *Americanesque* (1902–08; Boston, May 24, 1911; retitled *Humoresque on Negro-Minstrel Tunes*); *Comedy Overture on Negro Themes* (1906; N.Y., Aug. 17, 1910); *3 American Dances* (c. 1906); *The Dance in Place Congo*, symphonic poem (c. 1908; rev. 1916; as a ballet, N.Y., March 23, 1918); *Strife* (1910–25); *6 Indian Sketches* (1911; rev. 1914; Boston, March 4, 1921); *Negro Rhapsody* (1912; Norfolk, Conn., June 5, 1913, composer conducting); *To Thee, America* for Chorus and Orch. (1914; Peterboro, N.H., Jan. 25, 1915); *The Island of the Fay*, symphonic poem (1923); *Dance for Jazz Band* (1924); *Symphonic Piece* (1925); *Nocturne* (1925–26; Philadelphia, March 16, 1928); Suite for Chamber Orch. (1926–27; Boston, April 28, 1928). **CHAMBER:** *Gavotte* for String Quartet; *Scherzino* for Piano Trio; *Quartette*; Waltz for String Quartet; *Tempo di rag* for Flute, Oboe, Cornet, Piano, 2 Violins, and Cello; String Quartet (1920); piano pieces. **VOCAL:** Many songs, including *Pirate Song*, after Stevenson, *Celtic Studies*, 4 songs after Irish poets, and *The Lament of Deirdre*. **OTHER:** *Pilgrim Tercentenary Pageant* for Band (1921; orch. suite, 1921; Boston, March 31, 1922).

BIBL.: K. Longyear, *H.F. G.: His Life and Works* (diss., Univ. of Rochester, 1968).—**NS/LK/DM**

Gilbert, Jean, (real name, Max Winterfeld)

German composer; b. Hamburg, Feb. 11, 1879; d. Buenos Aires, Dec. 20, 1942. He was trained in Kiel, Sondershausen, Weimar, and Berlin. In 1897 he began his career as a conductor at the Bremerhaven City Theater. Soon after, he went to Hamburg as conductor at the Carl-Schultze Theater. In 1900 he became conductor at the Centralhallen-Theater, where he brought out his first stage work, *Das Jungfernstift* or *Comtesse* (Feb. 8, 1901). After conducting in provincial music centers, he devoted himself to composing for the theater. He attained his first notable success with the musical comedy *Polnische Wirtschaft* (Cottbus, Dec. 26, 1909). Then followed an even greater success with *Die keusche Susanne* (Magdeburg, Feb. 26, 1910), which was subsequently performed throughout Germany, France, England, and Spain. In 1910 he went to Berlin, where he brought out *Autoliebchen* (March 16, 1912), *Puppchen* (Dec. 19, 1912),

Die Kino-Königen (March 8, 1913; rev. version of *Die elfte Muse*, Hamburg, Nov. 22, 1912), and *Die Tango-Prinzessin* (Oct. 4, 1913). He also had success with *Fräulein Tralala* (Königsberg, Nov. 15, 1913). During World War I, he continued to compose numerous stage works, including the Berlin favorites *Die Fräulein von Amt* (Sept. 2, 1915), *Blondinchen* (March 4, 1916), *Die Fahrt ins Glück* (Sept. 2, 1916), *Das Vagabundenmädel* (Dec. 2, 1916), and *Die Dose seiner Majestät* (Sept. 1, 1917). Also notable were *Arizonda* (Vienna, Feb. 1, 1916) and *Eheurlaub* (Breslau, Aug. 1, 1918). With the War over, Gilbert had a tremendous success with *Die Frau im Hermelin* (Berlin, Aug. 23, 1919) and *Katja, die Tänzerin* (Vienna, Jan. 5, 1922). Subsequent works included *Dorine und der Zufall* (Berlin, Sept. 15, 1922), *Die kleine Sünderin* (Berlin, Oct. 1, 1922), *Das Weib im Purpur* (Vienna, Dec. 21, 1923), *Geliebte seiner Hoheit* (Berlin, Sept. 24, 1924), *Uschi* (Hamburg, Jan. 24, 1925; later used in the pasticcio *Yvonne*, London, May 22, 1926), *Annemarie* (Berlin, July 2, 1915), and *Hotel Stadt Lemberg* (Hamburg, July 1, 1929). After the Nazis came to power in Germany in 1933, Gilbert lived in several European cities before emigrating to Buenos Aires in 1939. His son, Robert Gilbert (real name, David Robert Winterfeld; b. Berlin, Sept. 29, 1899; d. Minusio, March 20, 1978), was a librettist, lyricist, and composer. He collaborated with his father on several scores and also wrote many of his own. However, he became best known for his German-language adaptations of such American musicals as *Annie Get Your Gun* (1956), *My Fair Lady* (1961), *Hello, Dolly!* (1966), and *The Man of La Mancha* (1968).—NS/LK/DM

Gilbert, Kenneth, esteemed Canadian harpsichordist, organist, musicologist, and pedagogue; b. Montreal, Dec. 16, 1931. He received training in organ from Conrad Letendre in Montreal, where he also studied at the Cons. with Yvonne Hubert (piano) and Gabriel Cusson (harmony and counterpoint). After winning the Prix de Europe for organ in 1953, he pursued his training in Europe with Boulanger (composition), Litaize and Duruflé (organ), and Sylvia Spicket and Ruggero Gerlin (harpsichord) until 1955. From 1952 to 1967 he was organist and music director of Queen Mary Road United Church in Montreal. He devoted himself almost exclusively to harpsichord performances from 1965. After making his London recital debut in 1968, he pursued a global career. He also taught at the Montreal Cons. (1957–74), McGill Univ. (1964–72), and Laval Univ. (1969–76). In 1969–70 he was artist-in-residence at the Univ. of Ottawa. From 1971 to 1974 he was a guest prof. at the Royal Flemish Cons. of Music in Antwerp. He gave master classes in various European and American cities. In 1988 he became a teacher at the Salzburg Mozarteum. He also served as prof. of harpsichord at the Paris Cons. from 1988, the first Canadian to hold such a position there. Gilbert ed. the complete harpsichord works of François Couperin (4 vols., 1969–72), all 555 sonatas of Domenico Scarlatti (11 vols., 1971–84), and the complete harpsichord works of Rameau (1979). In 1986 he was made an Officer of the Order of Canada. He was elected to membership in the Royal Soc. of Canada in 1988.—NS/LK/DM

Gilbert, Pia, spirited German-born American composer and pedagogue; b. Kippenheim, June 1, 1921. She began her career as a dance accompanist in the N.Y. studios of Lotte Goslar, Doris Humphreys, and Martha Graham; then found her niche as a composer for dance and theater. She served in various capacities during her lengthy tenure as prof. in the dance dept. at the Univ. of Calif., Los Angeles (1947–85), including resident composer and music director of its dance company; in 1986 she joined the music faculty at the Juilliard School in N.Y. where she held the William Schuman Scholar's Chair in 2000. As a teacher, Gilbert is distinguished by her commitment to the musical literacy of dancers, as well as for her interdisciplinary approach. Her compositions, whether for dance, theater, or simply "music per se," are always subtly dramatic, and a certain sly humor invades several of her vocal works; *Vociano*, first performed by Jan DeGaetani at the 1978 Aspen (Colo.) Music Festival, is pleasing for its use of imaginary languages, and her later chamber opera, *Dialects* (1990–91; Bonn, May 21, 1991), is a modern-day recreation of the most playful of Futurist ideals. With A. Lockhart, she publ. *Music for the Modern Dance* (1961).

WORKS: DRAMATIC: Opera: *Dialects*, chamber opera (1990–91; Bonn, May 21, 1991). **Dance:** *In 2s It's Love* (1949); *Songs of Innocence and Experience* (1952); *Trio* for Piano, Dancer, and Lights (1956); *Valse* for Lotte Goslar (1959); *Bridge of the 7th Moon* (1960); *Freke-Phreec-Freake-Phreaque- Freak* (1969); *Irving, the Terrific* (1971); *Requiem for Jimmy Dean* (1972); *Legend* (1985). **Theater** (all 1st perf. by the Mark Taper Forum Theatre Group, Los Angeles): *The Deputy*, after R. Hochhuth (1966); *Murderous Angels*, after C.C. O'Brien (1970); *Tales from Hollywood*, after C. Hampton (1982). **ORCH.:** *Gestures* (1988). **CHAMBER:** *Transmutations* for Organ and Percussion (1975); *Spirals and Interpolations* for Small Ensemble (1976); *Interrupted Suite* for Clarinet and 3 Pianos (1978); *Tri, dispute, dialogue, diatribe* for Cello and Piano (1978); *Volatile* for Piano (1987). **VOCAL:** *Vociano* for Mezzo-soprano and Piano (1978); *Food* for Soprano, Baritone, Trumpet, Piano, and Snare Drum, to texts by John Cage (1981); *Bells* for Soprano and Piano (1983); *Das Lied der Gefallenen* for Voice and Piano, after L. Feuchtwanger (1984); *Quotations and Interludes* for Soprano, Clarinet, Violin, Piano, and Balloons (1990).—NS/LK/DM

Gilbert, Sir W(illiam) S(chwenck), English playwright and creator, with Sir Arthur (Seymour) Sullivan, of the famous series of comic operas; b. London, Nov. 18, 1836; d. Harrow Weald, Middlesex, May 29, 1911 (of cardiac arrest following a successful attempt to rescue a young woman swimmer from drowning). He was given an excellent education (at Boulogne and at King's Coll., London) by his father, who was a novelist. After a routine career as a clerk, Gilbert drifted into journalism, contributing drama criticism and humorous verse to London periodicals. His satirical wit was first revealed in a theater piece, *Dulcamara* (1866), in which he ridiculed grand opera. He met Sullivan in 1870, and together they initiated the productions of comic operas, which suited them so perfectly. Some plots borrow ludicrous situations from actual Italian and French operas; Gilbert's librettos, in rhymed verse, were nonetheless unmistakably English. This insularity of wit may explain the enormous popularity of the Gilbert & Sullivan operas in English-speaking countries, while they are practically unknown on the Continent. Despite the fact that the targets of Gilbert's ridicule were usually the upper classes of Great Britain, the operas were often performed at court. He was knighted in 1907. After 20 years of fruitful cooperation with Sullivan, a conflict developed, and the two severed their relationship for a time. A reconciliation was effected, but the subsequent productions fell short of their greatest successes. See the biography of Sullivan for complete details on the operas and a full bibliography.—NS/LK/DM

Gilberto, Astrud, Brazilian jazz-pop singer; wife of **João Gilberto;** b. Bahia, Brazil, March 30, 1940. Her husband João Gilberto was in the process of recording a bossa nova LP with himself on vocals and Stan Getz providing the main accompaniment. For one song, "The Girl from Ipanema," Astrud, who had had virtually no musical experience, was asked to sing some of the verses (she was a native of the Ipanema beach area). When the track was issued as a single, it was edited so that only Astrud's section was heard. "The Girl From Ipanema" was one of 1964's surprise smashes, reaching #5 on the American chart. Astrud's plaintive, even eerie vocal quality was riveting and widely imitated. Although there were no further U.S. hit singles, she became a cult figure in American jazz circles during the mid-1960s and rivaled her husband's status in their native country. In Britain, "The Girl From Ipanema" originally peaked at #29; it reentered the charts (#55, 1984) during a mini-boom in jazz, led by such acts as Sade, Everything But the Girl, and Working Week.

DISC.: *Boss of the Bossa Nova* (1963); *Warm World of A. G.* (1964); *Shadow of Your Smile* (1964); *Look to the Rainbow* (1965); *A Certain Smile, A Certain Sadness* (1966); *Beach Samba* (1967); *Deadly Affair* (soundtrack, 1967); *Windy* (1968); *I Haven't Got Anything Better to Do* (1969); *Gilberto with Stanley Turrentine* (1971); *A. G. Plus James Last* (1986).—**MM/LP**

Gilberto, João, Brazilian jazz-pop singer, guitarist, and composer, one of the leading figures in bossa nova; b. Juaseiro, Bahia, Brazil, June, 1931. His "Chega de Saudade" (1958) was one of the first bossa nova hits; by the early 1960s, he was considered a leading exponent of the bossa nova sound. This style, with its accompanying dance, sparked off a craze when introduced to U.S. audiences by Stan Getz and Charlie Byrd (1962). Getz teamed with Gilberto for *Getz/Gilberto* (1963); its standout track "The Girl From Ipanema" featured only his wife Astrud Gilberto's vocals when released in an edited version. João's material was largely composed by Antonio Carlos Jobim. After years off the concert stage, he began to perform at select festivals in the mid-1990s, including the N.Y. JVC Festival in 1998.

DISC.: *Brazil's Brilliant* (1960); *Gilberto and Jobim* (1960); *The Boss of the Bossa Nova* (1962); *Amoroso* (1977); *João Gilberto* (1988); *Live in Montreux* (1991); *João* (1992); *Farolito: Live in Mexico* (1999).—**MM/LP**

Gilboa, Jacob, Czech-born Israeli composer; b. Košice, May 2, 1920. He grew up in Vienna and went to Palestine in 1938. He studied composition with Tal in Jerusalem and Ben-Haim in Tel Aviv (1944–47), and then traveled to Germany and attended courses of new music with Stockhausen, Pousseur, Alois Kontarsky, and Caskel. His music represents a blend of oriental and Eastern Mediterranean idioms, basically lyrical, but technically ultramodern.

WORKS: CHAMBER: *7 Little Insects,* piano pieces for children (1955); Violin Sonata (1960); *Crystals* for Flute, Viola, Cello, Piano, and Percussion (1967); *Horizons in Violet and Blue,* ballet scene for 6 Players (1970); *Pastels* for 2 Prepared Pianos (1970); *3 Red Sea Impressions* for Violin, Piano, Harp, Electric Guitar, Organ, and Tape (1976); Cello Sonata (1981); String Quartet (1984); *Blossoms in the Desert* for Flute and Piano (1991). **VOCAL:** *Wild Flowers,* 4 lyrical pieces for Woman's Voice, Horn, Harp, and String Orch. (1957); *Passing Clouds* for Woman's Voice, Clarinet, Cello, and Piano (1958); *The 12 Jerusalem Chagall Windows* for Voices and Instruments (1966); *Thistles,* theater piece for Singing and Speaking Voices, Horn, Cello, Piano, and Percussion (1970); *From the Dead Sea Scrolls* for Chorus, Children's Chorus, 2 Organs, Tape, and Orch. (1971; Hamburg, Jan. 11, 1972); *14 Epigrams for Oscar Wilde* for Woman's Voice, Piano, and Tape (1973); *Bedu,* metamorphoses on a Bedouin call, for Man's Voice, Cello, Flute, and Piano (1975); *The Beth Alpha Mosaic* for Woman's Voice, Chamber Ensemble, and Tape (1975; Chicago, Jan. 24, 1976); *3 Vocalises for Peter Breughel* for Mezzo-soprano, Tape, and 13 Instruments (1979); *The Gray Colors of Käthe Kollwitz* for Woman's Voice, Synthesizer, Tape, and Chamber Ensemble (1990); *Lyric Triptych* for Alto, Girl's Chorus, Synthesizer, and Chamber Ensemble (1993). **ORCH.:** *Cedars* for Orch. (1971); *Gittit* for Chamber Orch. (1980); *7 Ornaments on a Theme of Ben-Haim* for Piano and Orch. (1981); *3 Lyric Pieces in the Mediterranean Style* for Chamber Orch. (1984). **OTHER:** *3 Strange Visions of Hieronymus Bosch* for Organ (1987).—**NS/LK/DM**

Gilchrist, William Wallace, American organist, conductor, teacher, and composer; b. Jersey City, N.J., Jan. 8, 1846; d. Easton, Pa., Dec. 20, 1916. He settled in Philadelphia and studied organ, singing, and composition with H. A. Clarke. He was active as an organist and choirmaster, and was founder-conductor of the Mendelssohn Glee Club (1874–1914) and conductor of the Philadelphia Sym. Soc. (1893–99). He also served as head of the vocal dept. at the Philadelphia Musical Academy (from 1882). In 1898 he was elected to the National Inst. Of Arts and Letters. He wrote 2 syms.: No. 1 (1891; Philadelphia, 1892) and No. 2 (unfinished; completed by W. Happich; Philadelphia, April 9, 1937), a symphonic poem, a piano quintet, oratorios, cantatas, and songs.

BIBL.: M. Schleifer, *W.W. G., 1846–1916: A Moving Force in the Musical Life of Philadelphia* (Metuchen, N.J., 1985).—**NS/LK/DM**

Gilels, Elizabeta, Russian violinist, sister of **Emil (Grigorievich) Gilels;** b. Odessa, Sept. 30, 1919. She studied with Stoliarsky at his school for gifted youths in Odessa and later graduated from the Moscow Cons., where she took lessons from A. Yampolsky. She received 3rd place in the Ysaÿe Competition (Brussels, 1937); taught at the Moscow Cons. (from 1967). She played duets with her husband, **Leonid Kogan;** their son, Pavel Kogan, was also a talented violinist.—**NS/LK/DM**

Gilels, Emil (Grigorievich), eminent Russian pianist, brother of **Elizabeta Gilels;** b. Odessa, Oct. 19, 1916; d. Moscow, Oct. 14, 1985. He entered the Odessa Cons. at the age of 5 to study with Yakov Tkatch, making his first public appearance at 9, followed by his formal debut at 13; after further studies with Bertha Ringbald at the Cons., he went to Moscow for advanced studies with Heinrich Neuhaus (1935–38). He won 1st prize at the Moscow Competition in 1933; after taking 2nd prize at the Vienna Competition in 1936, he won 1st prize at the Brussels Competition in 1938; that same year, he became a prof. at the Moscow Cons. Following World War II, he embarked upon an esteemed international career. He was the first Soviet musician to appear in the U.S. during the Cold War era, making his debut in Tchaikovsky's 1st Piano Concerto with Ormandy and the Philadelphia Orch. (Oct. 3, 1955). He subsequently made 13 tours of the U.S., the last in 1983. A member of the Communist party from 1942, he received various honors from the Soviet government. Gilels was one of the foremost pianists of his time. He was especially renowned for his performances of Beethoven, Schubert, Schumann, Chopin, Liszt, Tchaikovsky, and Brahms.

BIBL.: V. Delson, *E. G.* (Moscow, 1959); S. Hentova, *E. G.* (Moscow, 1967).—**NS/LK/DM**

Giles, Nathaniel, English organist and composer; b. Worcester, c. 1558; d. Windsor, Jan. 24, 1634. He studied at Oxford. He was organist at Worcester Cathedral from 1581 to 1585, when he became clerk, organist, and choirmaster at St. George's Chapel, Windsor; in 1597, became Gentleman and Master of the Children. He wrote 3 services for the church, many anthems, several motets, and 2 madrigals for 4 and 5 Voices. —**NS/LK/DM**

Gilibert, Charles, French baritone; b. Paris, Nov. 29, 1866; d. N.Y., Oct. 11, 1910. He studied at the Paris Cons. After making his operatic debut at the Paris Opéra-Comique in 1888, he sang in Brussels at the Théâtre Royal de la Monnaie (from 1889) and at London's Covent Garden (1894–1909). On Nov. 9, 1900, he made his debut with the Metropolitan Opera as Schaunard during the company's visit to Los Angeles. His formal debut with the company in N.Y. followed on Dec. 18, 1900, as the Duke of Verona, and he remained with the company until 1903. He then appeared at the Manhattan Opera House (1906–10). Among his other roles were Mozart's and Rossini's Bartolo, Masetto, Don Pasquale, and Monterone.—**NS/LK/DM**

Gille, Jacob Edvard, Swedish composer; b. Stockholm, Aug. 10, 1814; d. there, Nov. 8, 1880. He was a notary public, and learned to play the piano and organ. He served as choral master at the Catholic church in Stockholm, where he wrote 9 masses. As a composer he acquired a solid technique, his style of composition closely adhering to the German school. His works include 4 operas, 5 syms., 5 string quartets, 4 piano trios, 2 string trios, 3 piano sonatas, 3 organ sonatas, and many minor pieces.—**NS/LK/DM**

Gilles, Jean, French composer; b. Tarascon, near Avignon, Jan. 8, 1668; d. Toulouse, Feb. 5, 1705. He received music training in the choir school of the Cathedral of St. Sauveur at Aix-en-Provence, where he became 2nd instructor and organist in 1688. He later received an appointment as maître de musique at St. Étienne at Toulouse. His most famous work was *Messe des morts*, which contains an erudite fugue in its Requiem, attesting to Gilles's excellent technique. It became part of the regular services at funerals and was performed at services for Louis XV in 1774. He also wrote 32 choral motets and other sacred works.

BIBL.: M. Prada, *Un Maître de musique en Provence et en Languedoc: J. G., 1668–1705: L'Homme et l'oeuvre* (Beziers, 1986). —**NS/LK/DM**

Gillespie, Dizzy (actually, **John Birks**), bebop trumpeter, composer, leader, and singer, revered by musicians for his brilliance, personal warmth, sense of humor, and generosity in sharing his knowledge; b. Cheraw, S.C., Oct. 21, 1917; d. Englewood, N.J., Jan. 7, 1993. His father was a mason and weekend bandleader who played several instruments. To help out his family, Dizzy left school in the ninth grade to work. Two years later, he began to teach himself trombone and trumpet. He formed a trio (trumpet, piano, and drums) and was good enough to be accepted at the Laurinberg Inst. (N.C.); a full scholarship allowed him to concentrate on trumpet and piano. He left before his last year (1935) to rejoin his family in Philadelphia; he played there with Frankie Fairfax, earning his nickname at that time for his on- and offstage antics. He learned several Roy Eldridge solos from Charlie Shavers. He also became famous for his highly unorthodox bulging cheeks, resulting from a lack of training. (He was later diagnosed with a medical condition that prevented him from blowing in the recommended manner.) Moving to N.Y., he joined Teddy Hill's Band at the Savoy Ballroom (1937), replacing Eldridge, and made his first recordings (and first solo on "King Porter Stomp"); he toured Europe with Hill later that year. He joined Cab Calloway's big band (1939), where he was first exposed to Afro-Cuban music through bandmate Mario Bauza. It was the beginning of a lifelong association with Latin music. He met Charlie Parker in Kansas City (1940); shortly thereafter, Parker moved to N.Y. He, Dizzy, and others would go to Harlem clubs, especially Minton's, to jam and work on new ideas after Calloway's last set. In 1941 Calloway fired Dizzy for threatening him with a knife. He worked briefly with big bands led by Ella Fitzgerald, Claude Hopkins, Les Hite, Lucky Millinder, Charlie Barnet, Fletcher Henderson, and Benny Carter. He led a small band at the Downbeat Club in Philadelphia (1942) prior to joining Earl Hines for several months.

The 1940s saw Gillespie begin a lifelong pattern of switching between big bands and small groups. His big band work included stints with Duke Ellington (1943). Billy Eckstine (1944), and his own ensemble (1945–50). He co-led a small band at the Onyx Club, N.Y. with Oscar Pettiford, and had brief spells in other small bands, including John Kirby's Sextet. During this period he gained the reputation of being one of the leading and most articulate exponents of bebop. In 1945, Benny Goodman's group in Billy Rose's *7 Lively Arts* (a highbrow Broadway revue) was replaced by Tiny Grimes's group with Gillespie. Later that year, his group with Parker appeared at the Three Deuces, N.Y., and in Philadelphia. During the next few years his big band played in N.Y. and toured the eastern U.S. In 1947, Bauza introduced him to Cuban percussionist Chano Pozo, who joined the band; the group performed and recorded numbers such as "Tin Tin Deo" and "Manteca." Financial pressures forced Gillespie to temporarily give up the big band (1950), but he performed, recorded, and toured with big bands for the rest of his life. He resumed touring with a small group (with John Coltrane, 1950–51). He formed his own label, Dee Gee, in Detroit, one of the first to be owned by a jazz artist; but it went broke before he could recoup his investment. In 1953 someone accidentally fell on and bent his trumpet while it sat upright on a stand. After playing it he discovered he liked the sound and the fact that it was easier to hear oneself; he had trumpets built for him in that shape from then on.

In 1956 Gillespie became the first jazz musician appointed by the U.S. State Dept. to undertake a cultural mission. With the help of Quincy Jones, he formed a big band to tour the Middle East; a few months later he traveled on another sponsored tour to South America, cut short partly because of complaints about using taxpayer money to support a jazz band. His quintet performed a vast number of international engagements through the 1980s; he also toured with JATP. In 1963 he half-jokingly began a campaign to run as an independent candidate for president; he almost got on the ballot in Calif. and received many write-in votes despite his withdrawal beforehand. "Dizzy for President" campaign buttons were made up; proceeds from their sale eventually went to civil rights organizations. In 1971–72, he guested in an all-star touring line-up called the Giants of Jazz. His connection with the Latin world led to a number of visits to Cuba, despite the U.S. embargo; he became an important presence on the Cuban jazz scene, mentoring Paquito D'Rivera, Arturo Sandoval, and many others.

Gillespie appeared before four U. S. presidents at the White House, received numerous honors (including the Paul Robeson Award, 1972, and the National Medal of Art, 1989), and performed for governments throughout the world. In 1989–91, he toured with the so-called United Nations Band that crossed the U.S.; the tour introduced David Sanchez, and Danilo Perez to the wider public. Among his film appearances were *Jivin' in BebopM* (1946) and *Winter in Lisbon* (1990). He pursued his almost nonstop schedule as late as 1991, with concerts here and abroad, festival and TV appearances, and magazine interviews. After his death, the San Francisco Jazz Festival and his estate established the Dizzy Gillespie Jazz Education Fund. The singer Jeanie Bryson is his daughter.

DISC.: *Groovin' High* (1945); *Hot House* (1945); *Salt Peanuts* (1945); *Shaw Nuff* (1945); *One Bass Hit* (1946); *Live at the Spotlite* (1946); *Live at Carnegie Hall* (1947); *Bebop Enters Sweden* (1947); *At the Downbeat Club* (1947); *And His Big Band* (1948); *At Salle Pleyel* (1948); *School Days* (1951); *Champ* (1951); *In Paris* (1952);; *D. G./Stan Getz Sextet* (1953); *Concert in Paris* (1953); *And His Orch.* (1954); *Afro* (1954); *Tour de Force* (1955); *One Night in*

Washington (1955); World Statesman (1956); Dizzy in Greece (1956); Greatest Trumpet of Them All (1957); For Musicians Only (1957); And Stuff Smith (1957); At Newport (1957); Have Trumpet, Will Excite! (1959); Ebullient Mr. Gillespie (1959); Portrait of Duke Ellington (1960); Perceptions (1961); Gillespiana (1961); Electrifying Evening (1961); Carnegie Hall Concert (1961); An Electrifying Evening with the D. G. Quintet (1961); New Continent (1962); Dizzy on the French Riviera (1962); And the Double Six of Paris (1963); Something Old, Something New (1963); Cool World (1964); Reunion Big Band (1968); Big Four (1974); Trumpet Kings at Montreux '75 (1975); Big Seven (1975); Afro-Cuban Jazz Moods (1975); Gifted Ones (1977); Musician-Composer-Raconteur (1981); Meets Phil Woods (1986); Live at Royal Festival Hall (1989); Winter in Lisbon (soundtrack, 1990); Bebop and Beyond Plays (1991); To Diz with Love (1992); To Bird with Love: Live at the Blue Note (1992). C. PARKER: Bird & Diz (1950). C. PARKER, B. POWELL, C. MINGUS, M. ROACH: Greatest Jazz Concert Ever (1953). R. ELDRIDGE: Trumpet Battle (1954). S. ROLLINS: Duets (1957). C. COREA: Jazz for a Sunday Afternoon (1967). B. HACKETT, M. L. WILLIAMS: Giants (1974). M. ROACH: In Paris (1989).

BIBL.: Michael James, *D. G.* (London, 1959); Raymond Horricks, *D. G. and the Be-Bop Revolution* (Tunbridge Wells, U.K., 1984); Gene Lees, *Waiting for Dizzy* (Oxford,1987); Alyn Shipton, *Groovin' High: The Life of D. G.* (N.Y., 1999).—LP/JC

Gillis, Don, American composer; b. Cameron, Mo., June 17, 1912; d. Columbia, S.C., Jan. 10, 1978. He was educated at Tex. Christian Univ. (graduated, 1936) and at North Tex. State Univ. (M.M., 1943). In 1943 he joined NBC in Chicago, and then worked for the network in N.Y. (1944–54), mainly as a producer. In 1967–68 he was chairman of the music dept. at Southern Methodist Univ.; after serving as chairman of fine arts and director of media instruction at Dallas Baptist Coll. (1968–72), he was composer-in-residence and director of the inst. For media arts at the Univ. of S.C. (from 1973). His compositions, clothed in a conservative garb, were often enlivened by a whimsical bent.

WORKS: DRAMATIC: O p e r a : *The Park Avenue Kids* (Elkhart, Ind., May 12, 1957); *Pep Rally* (Interlochen, Mich., Aug. 15, 1957); *The Libretto* (1958; Norman, Okla., Dec. 1, 1961); *The Legend of Star Valley Junction* (1961–62; N.Y., Jan. 7, 1969); *The Gift of the Magi* (Forth Worth, Tex., Dec. 7, 1965); *World Premiere* (1966–67); *The Nazarene* (1967–68); *Behold the Man* (1973). **ORCH.:** *The Woolyworm* (1937); *Thoughts Provoked on Becoming a Prospective Papa,* suite (1937); 10 syms. (1939–67), including Sym. No. 5 1/2, the "Symphony for Fun" (1947); *The Panhandle,* suite (1937); *Intermission—10 Minutes* (1940); *Prairie Poem* (1943); *The Alamo* (1944); *A Short Overture to an Unwritten Opera* (1944); *To an Unknown Soldier* (1945); *Rhapsody for Harp and Orch.* (1946); *Tulsa: A Symphonic Portrait in Oil* (1950); *Dude Ranch,* suite (1967); 2 piano concertos; also band music. **CHAMBER:** 6 string quartets (1936–47); 3 suites for Woodwind Quintet (1938, 1939, 1939). **OTHER:** Vocal works; ballets; instrumental pieces.—NS/LK/DM

Gilly, Dinh, French baritone; b. Algiers, July 19, 1877; d. London, May 19, 1940. He studied at the Toulouse Cons. and with Cotogni in Rome. After completing his studies at the Paris Cons., he made his debut as the Priest in *Sigurd* at the Paris Opéra in 1899; continued to sing there until 1908. On Nov. 16, 1909, he made his debut with the Metropolitan Opera in N.Y. at the New Theatre as Albert in *Werther*; his formal debut at the Metropolitan Opera was as Alfio in *Cavalleria rusticana* on Nov. 24, 1909, and remained on its roster until 1914; he first appeared at London's Covent Garden as Amonasro in *Aida* on May 15, 1911; sang there until 1914 and again from 1919 to 1924. He also made appearances with the Beecham, Carl Rosa, and British National Opera companies. He made London his home and was active in later years as a teacher, numbering among his pupils John Brownlee.—**NS/LK/DM**

Gilman, Benjamin Ives, American psychologist and ethnomusicologist; b. N.Y., Feb. 19, 1852; d. Boston, March 18, 1933. He studied at Williams Coll. (A.B., 1872), Johns Hopkins Univ. (1881–82), the Univ. of Berlin (1882), and the Univ. of Paris (1886); also did graduate work in psychology at Harvard Univ. (1883–85). He lectured on the psychology of music at Princeton Univ., Columbia Univ., and at Harvard (1883); was asst. prof. of psychology at Clark Univ. (1892–93). He then became secretary of the Boston Museum of Fine Arts, where he remained until his retirement in 1925. In 1890 Mary Hemenway commissioned J. Walter Fewkes to record Zuni speech and song. Gilman was engaged to do the analysis, and he became the first ethnomusicologist to use the phonograph in analyzing ethnic music. In 1891 he and Fewkes worked together on Hopi transcriptions, for which Gilman invented a graphic notation. At the World's Columbian Exposition in Chicago in 1893, he recorded over 100 cylinders of music, including the earliest extant recordings of music from Java, Samoa, and Serbia. These cylinders were rediscovered in 1976 and provide evidence of change in this music during the 20th century. Gilman was internationally recognized in the field of ethnomusicological research; he also publ. studies on psychology, comparative musicology, museology, and art criticism. Among his important articles are "On Some Psychological Aspects of the Chinese Musical System," *Philosophical Review*, I (1892), and "Hopi Songs," *Journal of American Archaeology and Ethnology*, V (1908).—**NS/LK/DM**

Gilman, Lawrence, American music critic; b. Flushing, N.Y., July 5, 1878; d. Franconia, N.H., Sept. 8, 1939. He was self-taught in music. From 1901 to 1913 he was music critic of *Harper's Weekly*, from 1915 to 1923, music, dramatic, and literary critic of the *North American Review*, from 1921 to 1939, author of the program notes of the N.Y. Phil. and Philadelphia Orch. concerts, and from 1923 to 1939, music critic of the *N.Y. Herald Tribune*. He was a member of the National Inst. of Arts and Letters.

WRITINGS: *Phases of Modern Music* (1904); *Edward MacDowell* (1905; 2nd ed., rev. and enl., 1909, as *Edward MacDowell: A Study*); *The Music of To-Morrow* (1906); *Stories of Symphonic Music* (1907); *Aspects of Modern Opera* (1909); *Nature in Music* (1914); *A Christmas Meditation* (1916); *Music and the Cultivated Man* (1929); *Wagner's Operas* (1937); *Toscanini and Great Music* (1938).—**NS/LK/DM**

Gil-Marchex, Henri, French pianist; b. St. Georges d'Espérance (Isère), Dec. 16, 1894; d. Paris, Nov.

22, 1970. He studied at the Paris Cons., then with L. Capet and A. Cortot. He toured Europe, Russia, and Japan, and performed modern works at various festivals in Europe. From 1956 he was director of the Cons. at Poitiers.—**NS/LK/DM**

Gilmore, John (E.), avant-garde jazz saxophonist and percussionist; b. Summit, Miss., Sept. 28, 1931; d. Philadelphia, Pa., Aug. 20, 1995. He played tenor sax and clarinet in high school and then in an army band. After studying with Chicago guitarist George Eskridge, he spent one year with the Earl Hines band (1952). He began his association with Sun Ra in 1953, working almost exclusively with him until his death. Miles Davis hired him for a week in Philadelphia (1955), and considered adding him to his quintet before choosing John Coltrane instead. Gilmore and Coltrane became friends; Coltrane credited him with inspiring some of the ideas on "Chasin' the Trane," although this remark has been taken too literally. He toured with Art Blakey in 1964, including Europe, and made a U.S. tour with Freddie Hubbard. He played drums and percussion with Sun Ra.

DISC.: *Blowing in from Chicago* (1957); *Dizzy Reece/J. G.* (1970).—**LP**

Gilmore, Patrick S(arsfield), Irish-American bandmaster; b. Ballygar, County Galway, Dec. 25, 1829; d. St. Louis, Sept. 24, 1892. He went to Canada with an English band, but soon settled in Salem, Mass., where he conducted a military band. In 1859 in Boston he organized the famous Gilmore's Band. As bandmaster in the Federal army at New Orleans (1864), he gave a grand music festival with several combined bands, introducing the novel reinforcement of strong accents by cannon shots. He won wide renown through the *National Peace Jubilee* (1869) and the *World's Peace Jubilee* (1872), two monster music festivals held in Boston. In the former, he led an orch. of 1,000 and a chorus of 10,000, and in the latter an orch. of 2,000 and a chorus of 20,000. The orch. was reinforced by a powerful organ, cannon fired by electricity, anvils, and chimes of bells. After the 2nd jubilee, Gilmore went to N.Y., and, as a popular bandmaster, traveled throughout the U.S. and Canada, and also (1878) to Europe. He composed military music, dance music, and many arrangements for band. Some of his songs were popular. He claimed to be the composer of "When Johnny Comes Marching Home" (1863), a song that remained a favorite long after the Civil War. The song bears the name of Louis Lambert as composer; this may have been one of Gilmore's many aliases; at any rate, he introduced the song and started it on its way to popularity.

BIBL.: M. Darlington, *Irish Orpheus: The Life of P. G.* (Philadelphia, 1950).—**NS/LK/DM**

Gilse, Jan van, Dutch conductor and composer; b. Rotterdam, May 11, 1881; d. Oegstgeest, near Leiden, Sept. 8, 1944. He studied with Wüllner at the Cologne Cons. (1897–1902) and with Humperdinck in Berlin (1902–03). He was a conductor of the Bremen Opera (1905–08) and of the Dutch Opera at Amsterdam

(1908–09); was music director of the City of Utrecht (1917–22). He lived again in Berlin (1922–33), then was director of the Utrecht Cons. (1933–37). His music is heavily imbued with German Romanticism.

WORKS: DRAMATIC: Opera: *Frau Helga von Stavern* (1911); *Thijl* (1938–40; 1st complete perf., Amsterdam, Sept. 21, 1976; also a symphonic extract, *Funeral Music*, 1940). ORCH.: 5 syms.: No. 1 (1900–1901), No. 2 (1902–03), No. 3, *Erhebung* for Soprano and Orch. (1903; rev. 1928), No. 4 (1914), and No. 5 (1922–23; unfinished sketch only); Concert Overture (1900); *Variaties over een St. Nicolaasliedje* (Variations on a St. Nicholas Song; 1909; also for Piano); *3 Tanzkizzen* (Dance Sketches) for Piano and Small Orch. (1926); *Prologus brevis* (1928); *Kleine Vals* for Small Orch. (1936). CHAMBER: Nonet (1916); Trio for Flute, Violin, and Viola (1927). VOCAL: *Eine Lebensmesse*, oratorio (1904); 6 Songs for Soprano and Orch. (3 songs, 1915; 3 songs, 1923); *Der Kreis des Lebens*, oratorio (1928); other songs.—NS/LK/DM

Gilson, Paul, notable Belgian composer, pedagogue, and writer on music; b. Brussels, June 15, 1865; d. there, April 3, 1942. He studied with Auguste Cantillon (theory) and Charles Duyck (harmony) before pursuing his training at the Brussels Cons. (1887–89) with Gevaert (composition), where he won the Belgian Prix de Rome with his cantata *Sinai* (1889). His orch. work *La mer* (1892) placed him in the forefront of Belgian musical life. During the following decade, he composed his finest scores before concentrating on teaching and writing. He was prof. of harmony at the Brussels Cons. (1899–1909) and the Antwerp Cons. (1904–09), and then was inspector of music education in the Belgian schools (1909–30). He was music critic of *Le Soir* (1906–14), *Le Diapson* (1910–14), and of *Midi*. In 1925 a group of his students formed the Synthetistes to carry on his ideals, which led to the founding of the journal *Revue Musicale Belge*. Gilson's compositions reflect the considerable gifts of a traditionalist.

WRITINGS (all publ. in Brussels unless otherwise given): *Le tutti orchestral* (1913); *Traité d'harmonie* (1919); *Quintes, octaves, secondes et polytonie* (1921); *Manuel de musique militaire* (Antwerp, 1926); *Notes de musique et souvenirs* (1942).

WORKS: DRAMATIC: Opera: *Le démon* (1890; Mons, April 9, 1893); *Prinses Zonneschijn* (Antwerp, Oct. 10, 1903; as *La princesse Rayon de Soleil*, Brussels, Sept. 9, 1905); *Gens de mer* (Antwerp, Oct. 15, 1904; in French, Brussels, Dec. 16, 1929); *Rooversliefde* (Antwerp, Jan. 30, 1910). Ballet: *La captive* (1896–1900); *Les deux bossus* (1910–21). ORCH.: Concertino for Flute and Orch. (1882–1920); Suite (1885); *3 Pieces* (1885–92); *3 mélodies populaires flamandes* for Strings (1891–92); *Mélodies écossaises* for Strings (1891–92); Suites (1891–1941); *La mer* (Brussels, March 20, 1892); *Overture dramatique* (1900; Brussels, Jan. 13, 1901); 2 saxophone concertos (1902); *Thème et variations* or *Variations symphoniques* (1903; Brussels, Nov. 8, 1908); *Romance-fantaisie* for Violin and Orch. (1903); *Troisieme ouverture symphonique* (1903–04); *Concertstück* for Trumpet and Orch. (1905–06); *Andante et scherzo* for Cello and Orch. (1906); *Prélude symphonique: Le chant du coq* (1906); *Prélude pour le drame "Henry VIII" de Shakespeare* (1906–16; Brussels, May 26, 1918); *Symphonie inaugurale* (1909–10); *Suite à la manière ancienne* for Strings (1913–14); *Cavatina* (1921); *Epithalame* (1925); *Cinq paraphrases sur des chansons populaires flamanade* (1929); *Préludes hébraïques* (1934); *Caledonia* (1939); *Scherzando* for Piano and

Orch. (1941); numerous pieces for Wind or Brass Band. CHAMBER: 2 string quartets (1907; 1918–19); Trio for Oboe, Clarinet, and Bassoon (1934); suites; many piano pieces. VOCAL: Cantatas: *Au bois des elfes* (1887), *Sinai* (1889), *Et la lumière descend sur tous* (1896), *Hymne à l'art* (1897), *Ludus pro patria* (1905) and *La voix de la forêt* (1934). Oratorio: *Francesca da Rimini* (1892).

BIBL.: G. Brenta, *P. G.* (Brussels, 1965).—NS/LK/DM

Giltay, Berend, Dutch composer; b. Hilversum, June 15, 1910; d. Utrecht, March 21, 1975. He studied violin and viola with Dick Waleson and composition with Badings. He was a violinist with the Hilversum Radio Phil. and with various other Dutch orchs. From 1963 to 1966 he attended courses in electronic music at the Univ. of Utrecht and worked in Bilthoven at the Gaudeamus electronic studio.

WORKS ORCH.: Violin Concerto (1950); Concerto for Viola and Chamber Orch. (1955); Oboe Concerto (1956–57); *Sinfonia* (1956–57); Horn Concerto (c. 1958); *Concerto for Orchestra* (1960); *Kurucz Valtozatok Zenekarra*, variations (1966–67); Concerto for 2 Violins and Orch. (1966–67); *Gossauer Symphonie* (Utrecht, Oct. 3, 1972); *Kosmochromie I* for 4 Loudspeakers and Orch. (Utrecht, Feb. 22, 1974) and *II* for String Quartet, Chamber Orch., and Tape (1974). CHAMBER: *4 Miniatures* for Viola and Piano (1952); *Sonata a tre* for Oboe, Clarinet, and Bassoon (1953); Wind Quintet (1956); String Quintet (1957); 2 duos for 2 Violins (1962, 1966); *Divertimento* for 5 Flutes (1963); *Scherzo* for 2 Violins (1963); *6 studi concertante* for Viola (1963); *Elegy* for Alto Flute and 4 Flutes (1969); Trio for 2 Violins and Cello (1971). ELECTRONIC: *Phonolieten* for Tape (1965); *Polychromie I* for Tape (1966) and *II* for Piccolo, Flute and Alto Flute, 4 Flutes or other Instruments, and Tape (1972).—NS/LK/DM

Gimenez, Raul, Argentine tenor; b. Santa Fe, Sept. 14, 1950. He received training in Buenos Aires. Following his operatic debut there in 1980 at the Teatro Colón as Ernesto, he appeared in concert and opera in various South American music centers. In 1984 he made his European debut at the Wexford Festival as Filandro in Cimarosa's *La astuzie femminili*, and subsequently sang in Paris, Venice, Pesaro, Amsterdam, Rome, Aix-en-Provence, Zürich, and Geneva. He made his U.S. debut as Ernesto in Dallas in 1989, choosing that role for his first appearance at London's Covent Garden in 1990. He sang Rossini's Count Almaviva at his debut at the Vienna State Opera in 1990. In 1993 he sang for the first time at Milan's La Scala in *Tancredi*. In 1994 he portrayed Rossini's Don Ramiro in Dallas. Gimenez is highly regarded for his roles in Rossini operas, among them Almaviva, Argiro, Rodrigo, Count Alberto, Giocondo, and Florville.—NS/LK/DM

Giménez (Jiménez) (y Bellido), Jerónimo, Spanish conductor and composer; b. Seville, Oct. 10, 1854; d. Madrid, Feb. 19, 1923. He studied with Alard, Savard, and A. Thomas at the Paris Cons. He was conductor of the Sociedad de Conciertos in Madrid. He wrote over 100 zarzuelas.—NS/LK/DM

Gimpel, Bronislav, distinguished Austrian-born American violinist and teacher, brother of **Jakob**

Gimpel; b. Lemberg, Jan. 29, 1911; d. Los Angeles, May 1, 1979. He was a pupil of Pollack at the Vienna Cons. (1922–26) and of Flesch at the Berlin Hochschule für Musik (1928–29). In 1925 he appeared as soloist with the Vienna Sym. Orch. He was a laureate in the Wieniawski Competition in 1935. He was concertmaster of the Königsberg Radio Orch. (1929–31), the Göteborg Sym. Orch. (1931–37), and the Los Angeles Phil. (1937–42), and later was 1st violin in the American Artist Quartet; he also played in the New Friends of Music Piano Quartet and the Mannes Piano Trio (1950–56). Following tours of Europe as a soloist, where he also gave masterclasses in Karlsruhe (1959–61), he was 1st violin in the Warsaw Quintet (1962–67) and the New England Quartet (1967–73); he also was a prof. at the Univ. of Conn. (1967–73). Gimpel's remarkable technique made him a notable soloist, recitalist, and chamber music player.—NS/LK/DM

Gimpel, Jakob, esteemed Austrian-born American pianist and pedagogue, brother of **Bronislav Gimpel;** b. Lemberg, April 16, 1906; d. Los Angeles, March 12, 1989. He studied at the Lemberg Cons. before pursuing his training in Vienna with Steuermann (piano) and Berg (theory). After making his debut in Vienna in 1923, he gave concerts with extraordinary success in Germany until the advent of the Nazi regime forced him to go to Palestine. In 1938 he settled in the U.S. After World War II, he gave concerts on both sides of the Atlantic. He also devoted much time to teaching, and in 1971 he was made Distinguished Professor-in-Residence at Calif. State Univ. at Northridge. Gimpel was especially admired for his interpretations of the Romantic repertory. —NS/LK/DM

Ginastera, Alberto (Evaristo), greatly talented Argentine composer; b. Buenos Aires, April 11, 1916; d. Geneva, June 25, 1983. He was of Catalan-Italian descent. He took private lessons in music as a child; then entered the National Cons. of Music in Buenos Aires, where he studied composition with José Gil, Athos Palma, and José André; also took piano lessons with Argenziani. He began to compose in his early youth; in 1934 he won 1st prize of the musical society El Únisono for his *Piezas infantiles* for Piano. His next piece of importance was *Impresiones de la Puna* for Flute and String Quartet, in which he made use of native Argentine melodies and rhythms; he discarded it, however, as immature; he withdrew a number of his other works, some of them of certain value, for instance, his *Concierto argentino*, which he wrote in 1935, and *Sinfonia Porteña,* his 1st Sym. (which may be identical in its musical material with *Estancia*). Also withdrawn was his 2nd Sym., the *Sinfonía elegíaca,* written in 1944, even though it was successfully performed. In 1946–47 Ginastera traveled to the U.S. on a Guggenheim fellowship. Returning to Argentina, he served as director of the Cons. of the province of Buenos Aires in La Plata (1948–52; 1956–58); he then taught at the Argentine Catholic Univ. and also was a prof. at the Univ. of La Plata. In 1968 he left Argentina and lived mostly in Geneva. From his earliest steps in composition, Ginastera had an almost amorous attachment for the melodic and rhythmic

resources of Argentine folk music, and he evolved a fine harmonic and contrapuntal setting congenial with native patterns. His first significant work in the Argentine national idiom was *Panambí*, a ballet, composed in 1935 and performed at the Teatro Colón in Buenos Aires on July 12, 1940. There followed a group of *Danzas argentinas* for Piano, written in 1937; in 1938 he wrote 3 songs; the first one, *Canción al árbol del olvido,* is a fine evocation of youthful love; it became quite popular. In 1941 he was commissioned to write a ballet for the American Ballet Caravan, to be called *Estancia*; the music was inspired by the rustic scenes of the pampas; a suite from the score was performed at the Teatro Colón on May 12, 1943, and the complete work was brought out there on Aug. 19, 1952. A series of works inspired by native scenes and written for various instrumental combinations followed, all infused with Ginastera's poetic imagination and brought to realization with excellent technical skill. Soon, however, he began to search for new methods of musical expression, marked by modern and sometimes strikingly dissonant combinations of sound, fermented by asymmetrical rhythms. Of these works, one of the most remarkable is *Cantata para América Mágica*, scored for dramatic soprano and percussion instruments, to apocryphal pre-Columbian texts, freely arranged by Ginastera; it was first performed in Washington, D.C., on April 30, 1961, with excellent success. An entirely new development in Ginastera's evolution as composer came with his first opera, *Don Rodrigo* (1964), produced on July 24, 1964, at the Teatro Colón. In it he followed the general formula of Berg's *Wozzeck* in its use of classical instrumental forms, such as rondo, suite, scherzo, and canonic progressions; he also introduced *Sprechstimme*. In 1964 he wrote the *Cantata Bomarzo* on a commission from the Elizabeth Sprague Coolidge Foundation in Washington, D.C. He used the same libretto by Manuel Mujica Láinez in his opera *Bomarzo*, which created a sensation at its production in Washington, D. C., on May 19, 1967, by its unrestrained spectacle of sexual violence. It was announced for performance at the Teatro Colón on Aug. 9, 1967, but was canceled at the order of the Argentine government because of its alleged immoral nature. The score of *Bomarzo* reveals extraordinary innovations in serial techniques, with thematical employment not only of different chromatic sounds, but also of serial progressions of different intervals. His last opera, *Beatrix Cenci*, commissioned by the Opera Soc. of Washington, D.C., and produced there on Sept. 10, 1971, concluded his operatic trilogy. Among instrumental works of Ginastera's last period, the most remarkable was his 2nd Piano Concerto (1972), based on a tone-row derived from the famous dissonant opening of the finale of Beethoven's 9th Sym.; the 2nd movement of the concerto is written for the left hand alone. He was married to the pianist Mercedes de Toro in 1941. After their divorce in 1965, Ginastera married the Argentine cellist Aurora Natola, for whom he wrote the Cello Sonata, which she played in N.Y. on Dec. 13, 1979, and his 2nd Cello Concerto, which she performed in Buenos Aires on July 6, 1981.

WORKS: DRAMATIC: Opera: *Don Rodrigo* (1963–64; Buenos Aires, July 24, 1964); *Bomarzo* (1966–67; Washington, D.C., May 19, 1967); *Beatrix Cenci* (Washington, D.C., Sept. 10,

1971). **B a l l e t :** *Panambí* (1935; suite, Buenos Aires, Nov. 27, 1937; 1st complete perf., Buenos Aires, July 12, 1940); *Estancia* (1941; Buenos Aires, Aug. 19, 1952). **OTHER:** Film music. **ORCH.:** *Primer concierto argentino* (Montevideo, July 18, 1941; withdrawn); *Primera sinfonía (Porteña)* (1942; withdrawn); *Obertra pára el "Fausto" Criollo* (1943; Santiago, Chile, May 12, 1944); *Sinfonía elegíaca* (2nd Sym.; Buenos Aires, May 31, 1946; withdrawn); *Ollantay*, 3 symphonic movements after an Inca poem (1947; Buenos Aires, Oct. 29, 1949); *Variaciones concertantes* for Chamber Orch. (Buenos Aires, June 2, 1953); *Pampeana No. 3*, symphonic pastoral (Louisville, Ky., Oct. 20, 1954); Harp Concerto (1956; Philadelphia, Feb. 18, 1965); 2 piano concertos: No. 1 (Washington, D.C., April 22, 1961) and No. 2 (1972; Indianapolis, March 22, 1973); Violin Concerto (N.Y., Oct. 3, 1963); Concerto for Strings (1965; Caracas, May 14, 1966); *Estudios sinfónicos* (1967; Vancouver, March 31, 1968); 2 cello concertos: No. 1 (Hanover, N.H., July 7, 1968; rev. 1971–72 and 1977) and No. 2 (Buenos Aires, July 6, 1981); *Popul Vuh* (1975–83; unfinished; St. Louis, April 7, 1989); *Glosses sobre temes de Pau Casals* for String Orch. and String Quintet "in lontano" (San Juan, Puerto Rico, June 14, 1976; rev. for Full Orch. and 1st perf. in Washington, D.C., Jan. 24, 1978); *Iubilum* (1979–80; Buenos Aires, April 12, 1980). **CHAMBER:** *Impresiones de la Puna* for Flute and String Quartet (1942; withdrawn); *Dúo* for Flute and Oboe (1945); *Pampeana No. 1* for Violin and Piano (1947) and *No. 2* for Cello and Piano (1950); 4 string quartets: No. 1 (1948), No. 2 (1958), No. 3, with Soprano (1973), and No. 4, with Baritone, to the text of Beethoven's Heiligenstadt Testament (1974; unfinished); Piano Quintet (1963); *Puneña No. 2* for Cello (1976); Guitar Sonata (1976); Cello Sonata (N.Y., Dec. 13, 1979); *Fanfare* for 4 Trumpets in C (from *Iubilum*, 1980); *Serenade* for Cello, Flute, Oboe, Clarinet, Bassoon, Horn, Double Bass, Harp, and Percussion (1980). **KEYBOARD: P i a n o :** *Piezas infantiles* (1934); *Danzas argentinas* (1937); *3 piezas* (1940); *Malambo* (1940); *12 Preludios americanos* (1944); *Suite de Danzas criollas* (1946); *Rondó sobre temas infantiles argentinos* (1947); 3 sonatas (1952, 1981, 1982); *Pequeña danza* from *Estancia* (1955); *Toccata*, arranged from *Toccata per organo* by Domenico Zipoli (1972). **O r g a n :** *Toccata, Villancico y Fuga* (1947); *Variazioni e Toccata* (1980). **VOCAL:** 2 Canciones: No. 1, *Canción al árbol del ovido*, and No. 2, *Canción a la luna lunanca* (1938); *Cantos del Tucumán* for Voice, Flute, Violin, Harp, and 2 Indian Drums (1938); *Psalm 150* for Chorus, Boy's Chorus, and Orch. (1938; Buenos Aires, April 7, 1945); *5 Canciones populares argentinas* for Voice and Piano (1943); *Las horas de una estancia* for Voice and Piano (1943); *Hieremiae prophetae lamentatiónes* for Chorus (1946); *Cantata para América Mágica* for Dramatic Soprano and Percussion, to an apocryphal pre-Columbian text (1960; Washington, D.C., April 30, 1961); *Sinfonía Don Rodrigo* for Soprano and Orch. (Madrid, Oct. 31, 1964); *Cantata Bomarzo* for Speaker, Baritone, and Chamber Orch. (Washington, D.C., Nov. 1, 1964); *Milena*, cantata for Soprano and Orch., to texts from Kafka's letters (1971; Denver, April 16, 1973); *Serenata* for Cello, Baritone, and Chamber Ensemble, to texts of Pablo Neruda (1973; N.Y., Jan. 18, 1974); *Turbae ad Passionem Gregorianam* for Tenor, Baritone, Bass, Boy's Chorus, Mixed Chorus, and Orch. (1974; Philadelphia, March 20, 1975).

BIBL.: P. Suárez Urtubey, *A. G.* (Buenos Aires, 1967); *A. G.: A Catalogue of His Published Works* (London, 1976); F. Spangemacher, ed., *A. G.* (Bonn, 1984); G. Scarabino, *A. G.: Técnicas y estilo (1935–1950)* (Buenos Aires, 1996).—**NS/LK/DM**

Gingold, Josef, distinguished Russian-born American violinist and pedagogue; b. Brest-Litovsk, Oct. 28, 1909; d. Bloomington, Ind., Jan. 11, 1995. He went to the U.S. in 1920. He studied violin in N.Y. with Vladimir Graffman, and later in Brussels with Eugène Ysaÿe. He then served as 1st violinist in the NBC Sym. Orch. in N.Y. (1937–43); later was concertmaster of the Detroit Sym. Orch. (1943–46) and the Cleveland Orch. (1947–60). He taught at Case Western Reserve Univ. (1950–60) and was prof. of chamber music at the Meadowmount School of Music (1955–81). In 1960 he was appointed to the faculty of the Ind. Univ. School of Music in Bloomington; was made a distinguished prof. of music there in 1965. He also gave masterclasses at the Paris Cons. (1970–81), in Tokyo (1970), in Copenhagen (1979), and in Montreal (1980); held the Mischa Elman Chair at the Manhattan School of Music in N.Y. (1980–81). He was a guiding force in establishing the International Violin Competition of Indianapolis; was its first honorary chairman and president of the jury in 1982, positions he held again in 1986 and 1990. —**NS/LK/DM**

Ginguené, Pierre Louis, French historian of literature and writer on music; b. Rennes, April 25, 1748; d. Paris, Nov. 16, 1816. He studied at Rennes Coll., then went to Paris, where he was an original member of the Institut de France. He served in government posts, then wrote extensively on the history of French and Italian literature. He was an ardent advocate of Piccinni in the Gluck-Piccinni controversy; his attacks on Gluck are contained in his *Lettres et articles sur la musique, insérés dans les journaux sous le nom de Mélophile, pendant nos dernières querelles musicales, en 1780, 1781, 1782 et 1783* (Paris, 1783). He also wrote *Notice sur la vie et les ouvrages de Piccinni* (Paris, 1800), and contributed historical articles to the *Dictionnaire de musique* of the *Encyclopédie méthodique*.

BIBL.: D. Garat, *Notice sur la vie et les ouvrages de P.L. G.* (Paris, 1817).—**NS/LK/DM**

Ginsburg, Lev (Solomonovich), Russian cellist, music scholar, and pedagogue; b. Mogilev, Jan. 28, 1907; d. Moscow, Nov. 21, 1981. He studied cello, chamber music, and music history at the Moscow Cons. (graduated, 1931; kandidat degree, 1938, with the diss. *Luidzhi Bokkerini i evo rol' v razvitii violonchel'novo iskusstva* [Luigi Boccherini and his role in the development of the art of cello playing]; publ. in Moscow, 1938; Ph.D., 1947, with the diss. *Violonchel'noye iskusstvo ot evo istok ov do kontsa XVIII stoletiya* [The art of cello playing from its origin to the end of the XVIII century]). In 1936 he joined the faculty of the Moscow Cons., where he served as a prof. from 1950. He publ. the valuable *Istoriya violonchel'novo iskusstva* (History of the art of cello playing; vols. I and II, Moscow and Leningrad, 1950, 1957; vol. III, Moscow, 1965). His other works included monographs on Casals (Moscow, 1958; 2nd ed., enl., 1966), Ysaÿe (Moscow, 1959), Rostropovich (Moscow, 1963), and Tartini (Moscow, 1969), and collections of articles and essays.—**NS/LK/DM**

Giordani, Giuseppe, Italian composer, called **Giordanello;** b. Naples, Dec. 9, 1743; d. Fermo, Jan. 4,

1798. He studied with Fenaroli at the S. Loreto Cons. in Naples, where Cimarosa and Zingarelli were his fellow students. His 2nd opera, *Epponina*, was given in Florence in 1779. He continued to write operas for various Italian towns, but they were not outstanding, and few of the 30-odd he wrote have survived. He also wrote several oratorios and church music. From 1791 until his death he was maestro di cappella at the Fermo Cathedral. He is sometimes credited with *Il bacio* and other operas and works produced in London by Tommaso Giordani; Giuseppe was not related to Tommaso, and never left Italy. The famous song "Caro mio ben", popularized in London by Pacchierotti, was probably written by Giuseppe.—**NS/LK/DM**

Giordani, Tommaso, Italian composer; b. Naples, c. 1730; d. Dublin, Feb. 23 or 24, 1806. His family formed a strolling opera company, with the father as impresario and singer and the rest of the family, except Tommaso, as singers. Tommaso was probably a member of the orch. and the arranger of music. They left Naples about 1745 and moved northward, appearing in Italian towns, then in Graz (1748), Frankfurt am Main (1750), Amsterdam (1752), and Covent Garden, London (Dec. 17, 1753). They returned in 1756, at which time Tommaso first appeared as a composer, with his comic opera *La Comediante fatta cantatrice* (Covent Garden, Jan. 12, 1756). The Giordani company next went to Dublin, appearing there in 1764; Tommaso continued to be active both in Dublin and in London. He was conductor and composer at the King's Theatre, London, in 1769 and many following seasons, and in Dublin, where he lived after 1783. He was conductor and composer at the Smock Alley and Crow St. theaters, and also taught piano. In 1794 he was elected president of the Irish music fund. He played an important part in Irish music circles, and wrote altogether more than 50 English and Italian operas, including pasticcios and adaptations. The most notable were *L'Eroe cinese* (Dublin, 1766), *Il Padre e il figlio rivali* (London, 1770), *Artaserse* (London, 1772), *Il Re pastore* (London, 1778) and *Il bacio* (London, 1782). He also wrote several cantatas, including *Aci e Galatea* (London, 1777), an oratorio, *Isaac* (Dublin, 1767), songs for the original production of Sheridan's *The Critic* (Drury Lane, London, Oct. 29, 1779), many Italian and English songs that were long popular, concertos, string quartets, trios and many piano pieces.—**NS/LK/DM**

Giordano, Umberto, noted Italian composer; b. Foggia, Aug. 28, 1867; d. Milan, Nov. 12, 1948. He studied with Gaetano Briganti at Foggia and then with Paolo Serrao at the Naples Cons. (1881–90). His first composition performed in public was a symphonic poem, *Delizia* (1886); he then wrote some instrumental music. In 1888 he submitted a short opera, *Marina*, for the competition established by the publisher Sonzogno; Mascagni's *Cavalleria rusticana* received 1st prize, but *Marina* was cited for distinction. Giordano then wrote the opera *Mala vita*, which was performed in Rome, Feb. 21, 1892; it was only partly successful; it was then revised and presented under the title *Il voto in Milan* (Nov. 10, 1897). There followed the opera *Regina Diaz* (Rome, Feb. 21, 1894), which obtained a moderate

success. Then he set to work on a grand opera, *Andrea Chénier*; its premiere at La Scala in Milan (March 28, 1896) was a spectacular success and established Giordano as one of the best composers of Italian opera of the day. The dramatic subject gave Giordano a fine opportunity to display his theatrical talent, but the score also revealed his gift for lyric expression. Almost as successful was his next opera, *Fedora* (Teatro Lirico, Milan, Nov. 17, 1898), but it failed to hold a place in the world repertoire after the initial acclaim; there followed *Siberia* (La Scala, Dec. 19, 1903; rev. 1921; La Scala, Dec. 5, 1927). Two short operas, *Marcella* (Milan, Nov. 9, 1907) and *Mese Mariano* (Palermo, March 17, 1910), were hardly noticed and seemed to mark a decline in Giordano's dramatic gift; however, he recaptured public attention with *Madame Sans-Gêne*, produced at a gala premiere at the Metropolitan Opera in N.Y. on Jan. 25, 1915, conducted by Toscanini, with Geraldine Farrar singing the title role. With Franchetti, he wrote *Giove a Pompei* (Rome, July 5, 1921); he then produced *La cena delle beffe*, which was his last signal accomplishment; it was staged at La Scala, Dec. 20, 1924. He wrote one more opera, *Il Re* (La Scala, Jan. 10, 1929). During his lifetime, Giordano received many honors, and was elected a member of the Accademia Luigi Cherubini in Florence and of several other institutions. Although not measuring up to Puccini in musical qualities or to Mascagni in dramatic skill, Giordano was a distinguished figure in the Italian opera field for some four decades.

BIBL.: G. Paribeni, *Madame Sans-Gêne di U. G.* (Milan, 1923); D. Cellamare, *U. G.: La vita e le opere* (Milan, 1949); R. Giazotto, *U. G.* (Milan, 1949); G. Confalonieri, *U. G.* (Milan, 1958); D. Cellamare, *U. G.* (Rome, 1967); M. Morini, ed., *U. G.* (Milan, 1968).—**NS/LK/DM**

Giorgetti, Ferdinando, Italian composer and teacher; b. Florence, June 25, 1796; d. there, March 22, 1867. He was active as violinist before studying composition with Disma Mugolini. He later taught violin and viola, preparing a method for the latter (1856?). With Luigi Picchianti, he founded the first Italian music journal, *Rivista Musicale Fiorentina* (1840). He was an early champion of the Austro-German Classical style in Italy. His large output included works for the church and chamber music.—**LK/DM**

Giorni, Aurelio, Italian-American pianist, teacher, and composer; b. Perugia, Sept. 15, 1895; d. (suicide) Pittsfield, Mass., Sept. 23, 1938. He studied piano with Sgambati at the Accademia di Santa Cecilia in Rome (1909–11) and composition with Humperdinck in Berlin (1911–13). He emigrated to the U.S. in 1914 and was active mainly as a teacher; he was on the faculty at Smith Coll., the Philadelphia Cons. of Music, and the Hartford School of Music. He was also a fairly prolific composer; his Sym. in D minor was performed in N.Y. on April 25, 1937, but had such exceedingly bad reviews that he sank into a profound state of depression; several months later, he threw himself into the Housatonic River. Among his other works were *Orlando furioso*, symphonic poem (1926), Sinfonia concertante (1931), 3 trios, 2 string quartets, Cello Sonata, Violin Sonata, Piano Quartet, Piano Quintet, Flute Sonata, Clarinet

Sonata, 24 concert études for Piano, and songs.

BIBL.: E. Giorni Burns (his daughter), *The Broken Pedal* (Whittier, Calif., 1986).—NS/LK/DM

Giornovichi (real name, **Jarnowick**), **Giovanni Mane,** Italian violinist and composer; b. Raguso or Palermo, c. 1735; d. St. Petersburg, Nov. 23, 1804. He may have been a pupil of Antonio Lolli in Palermo. He gave successful concerts in Europe, and on the strength of his reputation, he was engaged as court musician to Catherine II (1783–86). He was in Russia again from 1789 to 1791, and then appeared in London (1791–96), Hamburg, and Berlin. He returned to Russia in 1803, and was a member of the Court Orch. in St. Petersburg until his death. In his old age he devoted himself to playing billiards for money. Among his works are 25 violin concertos (17 extant), 3 string quartets, and Fantasia e Rondo for Piano. He was probably the first to introduce the "romance" into the violin concerto as a slow movement, and he helped to set the rondo as the finale.—NS/LK/DM

Giorza, Paolo, Italian conductor and composer; b. Milan, Nov. 11, 1832; d. Seattle, May 5, 1914. After training with his father, he studied counterpoint with La Croix. He first became well known as a composer of light music, and then of ballet; later he was active as an opera conductor in North America. He wrote 2 operas, over 70 ballets, sacred music, marches, dances, and songs.—NS/LK/DM

Giovannelli, Ruggiero, Italian composer; b. Velletri, near Rome, c. 1560; d. Rome, Jan. 7, 1625. He settled in Rome and served as maestro di cappella of S. Luigi dei Francesi (1583–91), the Collegio Germanico (1591–94), and the Cappella Giulia of St. Peter's (1594–99). In 1595 he took holy order, and in 1599 he joined the Sistine Chapel as a singer, where he later held several positions, including that of maestro di cappella (1614–15) before retiring in 1624. Among his works were 2 vols. of motets (1593, 1604) and various other sacred compositions, and 6 vols. of madrigals (1585–1606).

BIBL.: A. Gabrieli, *R. G.: Musicista insigne* (Velletri, 1907); C. Winter, *R. G. (c. 1560–1625), Nachfolger Palestrinas zu St. Peter in Rom* (Munich, 1935).—NS/LK/DM

Giovanni da Cascia (Giovanni de Florentia), Italian composer who flourished in the 14th century. According to his younger contemporary Filippo Villani, in *Liber de civitatis Florentiae famosis civibus*, he was the initiator of the stylistic reform which spread from Florence shortly after 1300. He was organist and probably chorus master at S. Maria del Fiore at Florence. He lived at the court of Mastino II della Scala, Verona, c. 1329–51. His extant compositions include 16 madrigals and 3 cacce, MSS of which may be found in libraries at Florence and Paris and in the British Museum. For modern editions of his works, see N. Pirrotta, ed., *The Music of 14th Century Italy*, in Corpus Mensurabilis Musicae, VIII/1 (1954) and W. Marrocco, ed., *Italian Secular Music*, in Polyphonic Music of the Fourteenth Century, VI (1967).—NS/LK/DM

Gipps, Ruth (Dorothy Louisa), English conductor and composer; b. Bexhill-on-Sea, Sussex, Feb. 20, 1921; d. Eastbourne, East Sussex, Feb. 23, 1999. She studied oboe with Leon Goossens, piano with Kendall Taylor, and composition with Vaughan Williams at the Royal Coll. of Music in London (1937–42), and attended the Matthay Piano School (1942–43); obtained a B.Mus. in 1941 and a D.Mus. in 1948. She began her performing career as a pianist and oboist. After serving as director of the City of Birmingham Choir (1948–50), she was founder-conductor of the London Repertoire Orch. (1955–86). She also was founder-conductor of the London Chanticleer Orch. (from 1961), and music director of the Rondel Ensemble, a wind group. She taught at Trinity Coll., London (1959–66), the Royal Coll. of Music (1967–77), and Kingston Polytechnic (1977–79). In 1981 she was made a Member of the Order of the British Empire.

WORKS: ORCH.: Clarinet Concerto (1940); Oboe Concerto (1941; London, June 13, 1942); 5 syms.: No. 1 (1942; Birmingham, March 25, 1945), No. 2 (1945; Birmingham, Oct. 3, 1946), No. 3 (1965; London, March 19, 1966), No. 4 (1972; London, May 28, 1973) and No. 5 (1982; London, March 6, 1983); Violin Concerto (1943; London, Feb. 5, 1944); *Death on the Pale Horse* (Birmingham, Nov. 14, 1943); *Chanticleer*, overture (1944); *Song for Orchestra* (1948; Sutton Coldfield, Jan. 10, 1949); Piano Concerto (1948; Birmingham, March 21, 1949); *Cringlemire Garden* for Strings (Birmingham, Feb. 20, 1952); *Coronation Procession* (1953; Melbourne, Sept. 27, 1954); *The Rainbow*, pageant overture (1954; Birmingham, Oct. 6, 1964); Concerto for Violin, Viola, and Orch. (1957; London, Jan. 30, 1962); Horn Concerto (1968; London, Nov. 15, 1969); *Leviathan* for Double Bassoon and Chamber Orch. (1969; London, Feb. 13, 1971); *Ambarvalia* (1988); *Introduction and Carol: The Ox and the Ass* for Double Bass and Chamber Orch. (1988). **CHAMBER:** 2 oboe sonatas (1939, 1985); Trio for Oboe, Clarinet, and Piano (1940); *Sabrina*, string quartet (1940); Quintet for Oboe, Clarinet, Violin, Viola, and Cello (1941); *Brocade*, piano quartet (1941); *Rhapsody* for Clarinet and String Quartet (1942); Violin Sonata (1954); Clarinet Sonata (1955); String Quartet (1956); Horn Sonatina (1960); *Triton* for Horn and Piano (1970); Cello Sonata (1978); Wind Octet (1983); *The Riders of Rohan* for Tenor Trombone and Piano (1987). **OTHER:** Various vocal works.—NS/LK/DM

Giraldoni, Eugenio, notable Italian baritone, son of **Leone Giraldoni** and **Carolina Ferni-Geraldoni;** b. Marseilles, May 20, 1871; d. Helsinki, June 23, 1924. He received training from his mother. In 1891 he made his operatic debut as Escamillo in Barcelona, and then sang in various Italian music centers, including Milan's La Scala and Rome's Teatro Costanzi; at the latter he created the role of Scarpia on Jan. 14, 1900. On Nov. 28, 1904, he made his Metropolitan Opera debut in N.Y. as Barnaba, singing there for a season; he then pursued his career in Europe and South America. Among his other roles of distinction were Amonasro, Valentin, Boris Godunov, Rigoletto, and Gérard.—NS/LK/DM

Giraldoni, Leone, Italian baritone and pedagogue, father of **Eugenio Giraldoni;** b. Paris, 1824; d. Moscow, Oct. 1, 1897. He was a student of Ronzi in Florence. After making his operatic debut in Lodi in 1847, he sang in various Italian opera houses until his retirement in 1885. He then taught voice in his homeland, and later at the Moscow Cons. (from 1891). He created Verdi's Simone Boccanegra (Venice, March 12, 1857) and Renato (Rome, Feb. 17, 1859), and Donizetti's Duca d'Alba (Rome, March 22, 1882). His wife was **Carolina Ferni-Giraldoni.** He publ. *Guida teorico-practico ad uso dell'artista cantante* (Bologna, 1864). —NS/LK/DM

Girardi, Alexander, famous Austrian tenor and actor; b. Graz, Dec. 5, 1850; d. Vienna, April 20, 1918. He made his stage debut at the Kurtheater in Rohitsch-Sauerbrunn in 1869. After appearing in Krems, Karlsbad, Ischl, and Salzburg, he went to Vienna in 1870 and joined the Strampfertheater. In 1874 he became a member of the Theater an der Wien, acquiring renown in 1881 when he created the role of Marchese Sebastiani in Johann Strauss's *Der lustige Krieg.* In 1882 he had enormous success when he created the title role in Millöcker's *Der Bettelstudent.* After creating the role of Kálmán Zsupán in Strauss's *Der Zigeunerbaron* in 1885, he scored a resounding success in 1890 when he created the title role of Jonathan in Millöcker's *Der arme Jonathan.* Further acclaim came when he created the title role of Adam in Zeller's *Der Vogelhändler* in 1891. In 1894 he joined the Carltheater. In 1896 he became a member of the Deutsches Volkstheater, where he was active as an actor. From 1899 he was once more a favorite on the musical stages of Vienna. In 1902 he rejoined the Theater an der Wien, where he had triumphs creating the title roles in Eysler's *Bruder Straubinger* (1903) and *Pufferl* (1905). Returning to the Carltheater, his success continued as he created roles in Eysler's *Die Schützenliesel* (1905) and *Künstlerblut* (1906). In 1907 he went to Berlin as a member of the Thalia-Theater. In 1909 he returned to Vienna and joined the Raimundtheater. His last great success came at the Johann Strauss-Theater in 1912 when he created the role of Pali Rácz in Kálmán's *Der Zigeunerprimas.* Girardi continued to make appearances until the end of his life, being duly recognized as the foremost singer of the golden era of Vienna operetta. He is honored in Graz with a street named after him and in Vienna by the Girardigasse near the Theater an der Wien.

BIBL.: K. Nowak, *G.* (Berlin, 1908); A. Wutzky, *G.* (Vienna, 1943).—NS/LK/DM

Giraud, Fiorello, Italian tenor; b. Parma, Oct. 22, 1870; d. there, March 29, 1928. He was the son of the tenor Lodovico Giraud (1846–82). He studied with Babacini in Parma. He made his debut as Lohengrin in 1891 in Vercelli; then sang in Barcelona, Lisbon, and South America, and at La Scala in Milan. He created the role of Canio in Leoncavallo's *Pagliacci* (Milan, May 21, 1892). He was a fine interpreter of other verismo roles. —NS/LK/DM

Girdlestone, Cuthbert (Morton), English music scholar; b. Bovey-Tracey, Sept. 17, 1895; d. St. Cloud, France, Dec. 10, 1975. He was educated at the Sorbonne (licence ès lettres, 1915) and the Schola Cantorum in Paris, then entered Trinity Coll., Cambridge.

He became a lecturer at Cambridge in 1922, and from 1926 to 1960 was prof. of French at the Univ. of Durham, Newcastle division (later the Univ. of Newcastle upon Tyne). He publ. a valuable analysis of Mozart's piano concertos, *Mozart et ses concertos pour piano* (Paris, 1939; Eng. tr., 1948; 2nd ed., 1964), and the important monograph *Jean-Philippe Rameau: His Life and Work* (London, 1957; 2nd ed., rev., 1969). He further wrote *La Tragédie en musique (1673–1750) considérée comme genre littéraire* (Paris, 1972).

BIBL.: N. Suckling, ed., *Essays Presented to C.M. G.* (Newcastle upon Tyne, 1960).—NS/LK/DM

Giro, Manuel, Spanish composer; b. Lérida, Catalonia, Sept. 5, 1848; d. Barcelona, Dec. 20, 1916. He studied organ and composition at the cathedral school in Lérida and later in Barcelona and Paris. In 1884 he settled in Barcelona, where in 1885 he brought out his opera *Il rinegato Alonso García,* which proved a popular success. Another opera, *El sombrero de tres picos* (Madrid, 1893), was also well received. He further wrote ballets, choral music, chamber music, and piano pieces. —NS/LK/DM

Giroust, François, French composer; b. Paris, April 10, 1737; d. Versailles, April 28, 1799. He entered the Notre Dame choir school in Paris in 1745, where he studied with Louis Homet and Antoine Goulet. In 1756 he was ordained and was named maître de musique at Orléans Cathedral. Returning to Paris, he was maître de musique at the Saints-Innocents (1769–75). From 1775 he was sous-maître of the Royal Chapel, and from 1785 he also was surintendant de la musique de chambre. He was especially successful as a composer of grand motets. His other works included stage pieces, oratorios, masses, Masonic music, and patriotic pieces. —LK/DM

Gistelinck, Elias, Belgian composer; b. Beveren Leie, May 27, 1935. He received his training at the Brussels Cons. and the Paris Cons., then served as a producer for the Belgian Radio and Television (from 1961). He received the Italia Prize (1969) and a prize from the Fondation de France (1984).

WORKS: ORCH.: *Ad Maiorem Limburgiae Fodientium Gloriam* for Alto Saxophone, Bass Clarinet, and Strings (1970); *Drie Middelheimsculpturen* for Trumpet, Bass, Drums, Brass, and Winds (1972); *Weest gelukkig* for Tenor Saxophone, Trombone, Vibraphone, and Jazz Orch. (1974); *Muziek* for 3 Brass Groups and Percussion (1975); *Elegie voor Jan* (1976); *Drie bewigingen* for Jazz Quintet and Orch. (1985); Violin Concerto (1986); *Music for Halloween* (1988); Sinfonietta for Chamber Orch.(1988). **Ballet:** *Terpsychore en Euterpe* (1971); *De Bijen* (1972). **CHAMBER:** Trio for Oboe, Clarinet, and Bassoon (1962); Suite for Flute, Oboe, Clarinet, Horn, and Bassoon (1962); *5 Portraits* for Clarinet (1965); *Antieke alchemie* for String Quartet (1967); *Koan* for Clarinet Quartet (1971); *Cantus* for Oboe (1973); *Kleine treurmuziek voor "Che"* for Flute and Piano (1974); *Treurmuziek voor Ptak IV* for Violin, Cello, and Piano (1975); *So What, Brother* for Alto Saxophone (1981); *Lullaby for Nathaly* for Violin and Piano (1984); *Music for RGIP* for Violin and Piano (1987); *Memories of Childhood* for Trumpet and 4 Groups of Trumpets (1988); piano pieces. **OTHER:** Vocal works.—NS/LK/DM

Giteck, Janice, American composer and pianist; b. N.Y., June 27, 1946. She studied with Milhaud and Subotnick at Mills Coll. in Oakland, Calif. (B.A., 1968; M.A., 1969), and with Messiaen at the Paris Cons. (1969–70). She also studied electronic music with Lowell Cross and Anthony Gnazzo, Javanese gamelan with Daniel Schmidt, and West African drumming with Obo Addy. From 1979 she taught at the Cornish Inst. in Seattle. An interest in music therapy led her to psychology studies at Antioch Univ. in Seattle (M.A., 1986), and from 1986 to 1991 she worked as a music specialist at the Seattle Mental Health Inst. In 1999 she was one of four lead artists for ARTP (Artist's Regional Transit Project), a performance/media collective work sponsored by the Municipality of Metropolitan Seattle (Metro). Her early compositions, variously scored, reflect interest in the language and lore of American Indians; her best-known work is the ceremonial opera *A'agita* (orig. and sacrilegiously entitled *Wi'igita*), based on the legends and mythologies of the Pima and Papago, a native American tribe living in southwestern Ariz. and Mexico. She is currently composing a new piece on the theme of "love and rage" for ensembles in Portland, Syracuse, and Atlanta as part of the Reader's Digest/Meet the Composer Program.

WORKS: ORCH.: *Tree*, chamber sym. (1982); *Loo-wit* for Viola and Orch. (1983); *Hopi: Songs of the 4th World*, film score (1983); *Hearts and Hands*, film score (1987). CHAMBER: String Quartet No. 1 (1963); Quintet for Piano and Strings (1965); *Helixes* for Flute, Trombone, Violin, Cello, Guitar, Piano, and Percussion (1974); *Breathing Songs from a Turning Sky* for Flute, Clarinet, Bassoon, Cello, Piano, and Percussion (1979–80; rev. 1984); *Tapasya* for Viola and Percussion (1987). VOCAL: *How to Invoke a Garden/How to Invoke the Same Garden*, cantata for Soloists and 10 Instruments (1969); *Messalina*, mini-opera for Man's Voice, Cello, and Piano (1973); *Wi'igita*, later renamed *A'agita*, ceremonial opera for 3 Singing Actors, Dancing Actor, and 8 Instrumentalists/Actors (1976); *8 Sandbars on the Takano River* for 5 Women's Voices, Flute, Bassoon, and Guitar (1976); *Callin' Home Coyote*, burlesque for Tenor, Steel Drums, and String Bass (1977); *Far North Beast Ghosts the Clearing* for Chorus, after Swampy Creek Indians (1978); *Peter and the Wolves* for Trombonist/Actor and Prepared Tape (1978); *Pictures of the Floating World* for Chorus and 10 Instruments (1987). MIXED MEDIA: *Thunder, Like a White Bear Dancing*, ritual performance for Soprano, Flute, Piano, Hand Percussion, and Slide Projections, after the *Mide Picture Songs of the Ojibwa Indians* (1977). OTHER: *When the Crones Stop Counting* for 60 Flutes (1980).—NS/LK/DM

Giuffre, Jimmy (actually, **James Peter**), jazz wind player and composer, an effective and heartfelt improviser who has remained open to new trends and an original and gifted composer whose variety and depth is underestimated by most; b. Dallas, Tex., April 26, 1921. He studied at North Tex. State Teachers Coll. (bachelor's degree, 1942); played in a U.S. Army band; thereafter played in the bands of Boyd Raeburn, Jimmy Dorsey (1947), and Buddy Rich (1948). He wrote "Four Brothers" in 1947 for Woody Herman; the piece, which featured the four Lester Young–inspired saxophonists in the band, has sophisticated line writing within the tenor parts, with frequent crossings. (Ironically, he joined

Herman's band only in 1949). In the 1950s, he worked regularly at the Lighthouse in Hermosa Beach, Calif. His clarinet playing, which featured a soft style that emphasized the lower register, won him several polls in the late 1950s; as a result, he briefly gave up his other instruments (saxophone, flute). He formed a trio with guitarist Jim Hall and bassist Ralph Peña (1956), then Bob Brookmeyer and no bass. He became active as a teacher, serving on the faculty of the New School for Social Research, N.Y., Columbia Teachers Coll., and the School of Jazz in Lenox, Mass. (c. 1957–61); he also published a book on jazz phrasing.

Giuffre formed an innovative trio with Paul Bley (piano) and Steve Swallow (bass) that played venues in the U.S. and toured in Europe (1961–62). He then led a trio with Don Friedman and Barre Phillips (1964–65). In the 1970s, his trio with Kiyoshi Tokunaga (bass) and Randy Kaye (drums) drew on Middle Eastern, African, and Asian sounds and techniques; he was now playing bass clarinet, soprano, alto, and tenor saxophones, and flute and alto flute. He taught at New England Cons. (1978–92). By the early 1980s, he added bass flute to his repertoire and led a quartet with Peter Levin (keyboards; later Mark Rossi), Bob Nieske (bass), and Kaye. In 1989 his trio with Bley and Swallow reunited at Sweet Basil in Manhattan, producing a live recording. In the mid-1990s, he was forced to stop performing as a result of Parkinson's disease. For many years he has lived in Stockbridge, Mass.

Perhaps Giuffre's most famous piece is *The Train and the River*, a kind of folk-blues suite, performed by his trio in the 1957 TV special *The Sound of Jazz* and in the 1958 Newport Jazz Festival film *Jazz on a Summer's Day*. On "Tangents" (1954) he wrote out melodic bass and drum parts instead of having them "walk." His other compositions include "Pharoah" for brass (1956), "Hex" for jazz orch. (1960), "Mobiles" for clarinet and orch. (1961), "Orb," quintet for clarinet and strings (1969), other pieces for solo instrument and orch., and film scores.

DISC.: *Tenors West* (1955); *Tangents in Jazz* (1955); *J. G. Three* (1956); *The Giuffre Clarinet* (1956); *Music for Brass* (1957); *Western Suite* (1958); *Trav'lin' Light* (1958); *Four Brothers Sound* (1958); *Seven Pieces* (1959); *Lee Konitz Meets J. G.* (1959); *Easy Way* (1959); *Ad Lib* (1959); *Piece for Clarinet and String Orch.* (1960); *In Person* (1960); *Music for People, Birds, Butterflies and Mosquitoes* (1972); *Quiet Song* (1974); *River Chant* (1975); *Dragonfly* (1983); *Quasar* (1985); *Eiffel* (1987); *Liquid Dancers* (1989). P. BLEY AND S. SWALLOW: *Thesis* (1961); *Fusion* (1961); *Flight, Bremen 1961* (1961); *Emphasis, Stuttgart 1961* (1961); *Free Fall* (1962); *Diary of a Trio: Saturday* (1989); *Diary of a Trio: Sunday* (1989). S. ROGERS: *The Swinging Mr. Rogers* (1955).

WRITINGS: *Jazz Phrasing and Interpretation* (N.Y., 1969).—NS/MM/LP

Giuglini, Antonio, Italian tenor; b. Fano, 1827; d. Pesaro, Oct. 12, 1865. He studied with Cellini, making his debut in Fermo. He was highly successful in London when he sang at Her Majesty's Theatre in 1857; also sang at Drury Lane and the Lyceum there. In 1865 he was in St. Petersburg, where he displayed symptoms of mental aberrations. Upon his return to London, he was committed to an asylum; in the same year he was taken to Pesaro, where he died.—**NS/LK/DM**

Giuliani, Mauro (Giuseppe Sergio Pantaleo), famous Italian guitarist and composer; b. Bisceglie, near Bari, July 27, 1781; d. Naples, May 8, 1829. He was entirely self-taught, and at the age of 19 he undertook a highly successful tour in Europe. In 1806 he settled in Vienna, where he became associated with Hummel, Moscheles, and Diabelli; Beethoven became interested in him, and wrote some guitar music expressly for his performances. In 1823 he visited London, where he won extraordinary acclaim; a special publication, named after him *The Giulianiad* and devoted to reports about his activities, was initiated there, but only a few issues appeared. He publ. over 200 works for guitar. He also perfected a new guitar with a shorter fingerboard ("la ghitarra di terza").

BIBL.: T. Heck, *The Birth of the Classic Guitar and Its Cultivation in Vienna, Reflected in the Career and Compositions of M. G. (d. 1829)* (diss., Yale Univ., 1970); T. Heck, *M. G.: Virtuoso Guitarist and Composer* (Columbus, Ohio, 1995).—**NS/LK/DM**

Giulini, Carlo Maria, eminent Italian conductor; b. Barletta, May 9, 1914. He began to study the violin as a boy; at 16 he entered the Conservatorio di Musica di Santa Cecilia in Rome, where he studied violin and viola with Remy Principe, composition with Alessandro Bustini, and conducting with Bernardino Molinari; also received instruction in conducting from Casella at the Accademia Musicale Chigiana in Siena. He then joined the Augusteo Orch. in Rome in the viola section. He was drafted into the Italian army during World War II, but went into hiding as a convinced anti-Fascist; after the liberation of Rome by the Allied troops in 1944, he was engaged to conduct the Augusteo Orch. in a special concert celebrating the occasion. He then became asst. conductor of the RAI Orch. in Rome, and was made its chief conductor in 1946. In 1950 he helped to organize the RAI Orch. in Milan; in 1952 he conducted at Milan's La Scala as an assistant to Victor de Sabata; in 1954 he became principal conductor there; his performance of *La Traviata*, with Maria Callas in the title role, was particularly notable. In 1955 he conducted Verdi's *Falstaff* at the Edinburgh Festival, earning great praise. On Nov. 3, 1955, he was a guest conductor with the Chicago Sym. Orch. and later was its principal guest conductor (1969–72); during its European tour of 1971, he was joint conductor with Sir Georg Solti. From 1973 to 1976 he was principal conductor of the Vienna Sym. Orch., and in 1975 he took it on a world tour. On Oct. 24, 1975, he led it at a televised concert from the United Nations in N.Y. In 1978 he succeeded Zubin Mehta as music director of the Los Angeles Phil., and succeeded in maintaining it at a zenith of orchestral brilliance until 1984. His conducting style embodies the best traditions of the Italian school as exemplified by Toscanini, but is free from explosive displays of temper. He is above all a Romantic conductor who can identify his musical *Weltanschauung* with the musical essence of Mozart, Beethoven, Schubert, Schumann, Brahms, Bruckner, Verdi, and Mahler; he leads the classics with an almost abstract contemplation. In the music of the 20th century, he gives congenial interpretations of works by Debussy, Ravel, and Stravinsky; the expressionist school of composers lies outside of his deeply felt musicality, and he does not actively promote the experimental school of modern music. His behavior on the podium is free from self-assertive theatrics, and he treats the orch. as comrades-in-arms, associates in the cause of music, rather than subordinate performers of the task assigned to them. Yet his personal feeling for music is not disguised; often he closes his eyes in fervent self-absorption when conducting without score the great Classical and Romantic works.—**NS/LK/DM**

Giulini, Giorgio, Italian composer; b. Milan, 1716; d. there, 1780. He was the author of several instrumental works of considerable merit.—**NS/LK/DM**

Giuseppe, Enrico di
See **Di Giuseppe, Enrico**

Giustini, Lodovico, Italian organist and composer; b. Pistoia, Dec. 12, 1685; d. there, Feb. 7, 1743. He became organist of the Congregazione della Spirito Santo in 1725. He was the first to publ. sonatas for Cristofori's pianoforte (*12 Sonate da Cimbalo di piano e forte*, Florence, 1732).—**NS/LK/DM**

Gladys Knight and The Pips, one of the longest-lived family acts in rock music. **MEMBERSHIP:** Gladys Knight (b. Atlanta, Ga., May 28, 1944); Merald "Bubba" Knight (b. Atlanta, Ga., Sept. 4, 1942); William Guest (b. Atlanta, Ga., June 2, 1941); Edward Patten (b. Atlanta, Ga., Aug. 2, 1939).

Gladys Knight and the Pips have been together for more than 40 years, scoring smash R&B and major pop hits on six different labels. With the Pips functioning as an integral part of the group, Gladys Knight and the Pips featured the precise choreography of Cholly Atkins even before they (and he) joined the Motown organization. Despite the fact that Gladys Knight was favorably compared to Aretha Franklin, she and the Pips were treated as a second-line act at Motown, leading to their switch to Buddah Records in 1973. Developing a reputation as *the best* female-led soul group of the mid-1970s, Gladys Knight and the Pips became one of the few former Motown acts to retain (and even increase) their popularity and success after leaving the organization. Established as television and cabaret performers by 1974, Gladys Knight and the Pips recorded and toured the exclusive casino and supper-club circuit into the late 1980s, after which Knight performed and recorded solo.

Gladys Knight began singing with the gospel group the Morris Brown Choir in her native Atlanta, Ga., at age four, later touring with the group throughout the South. At age seven she won $2,000 on Ted Mack's *The Original Amateur Hour* television show, thereafter touring with Mack for a year. In 1952 Gladys joined several close relatives to sing informally at brother Merald's birthday party. Thus was born the first incarnation of the Pips, with Gladys, Brenda, and Merald "Bubba" Knight, and their cousins, Eleanor and William Guest.

The Pips began playing local engagements, then toured the nation with Jackie Wilson and Sam Cooke in 1957. Initial recordings for Brunswick proved unsuccessful. Eleanor and Brenda dropped out of the group in 1959, to be replaced by another cousin, Edward Patten, and Langston George. Finally, in 1961 the group scored their first hit (a top R&B and smash pop hit) with the Johnny Otis ballad "Every Beat of My Heart" on Vee Jay as the Pips and on Fury as Gladys Knight and the Pips. They hit with "Letter Full of Tears" on Fury in 1962, but the company soon went out of business. Gladys Knight returned to Atlanta for a year while the Pips did session work. Langston George left, and Knight rejoined the group in 1963, signing with Maxx Records, achieving a moderate pop and R&B hit with "Giving Up" in 1964.

The first signing to Motown's Soul label in 1965, Gladys Knight and the Pips languished with the company for several years before scoring a R&B smash and moderate pop hit in 1967 with "Everybody Needs Love." Later that year, under producer Norman Whitfield, the group had a top R&B and smash pop hit with "I Heard It through the Grapevine," only to see Marvin Gaye score an even bigger hit with the song a year later. Subsequent smash R&B and major pop hits on Soul include "The End of the Road," "The Nitty Gritty," "Friendship Train," and "You Need Love Like I Do (Don't You)." The group adopted a more mellow sound for later soul hits such as "If I Were Your Woman" (a pop near-smash), "I Don't Want to Do Wrong," "Make Me the Woman That You Go Home To," "Neither One of Us (Wants to Be the First to Say Goodbye)" (a pop smash), and Gladys's own "Daddy Could Swear, I Declare" through 1973.

Gladys Knight and the Pips' *Neither One of Us* album became a bestseller, but despite their consistent recording success and growing status as a live act, they felt they were not being treated as a front-line act by Motown, leading to their defection to Buddah Records in March 1973. Their debut Buddah album, *Imagination*, stayed on the album charts for more than a year and yielded three top R&B and smash pop hits with Tony Joe White's "Midnight Train to Georgia," Barry Goldberg and Gerry Goffin's "I've Got to Use My Imagination," and "Best Thing That Ever Happened to Me." The soundtrack to the movie *Claudine*, recorded under songwriter-producer Curtis Mayfield, included the pop and R&B smash "On and On." Subsequent major pop and smash R&B hits on Buddah included "I Feel a Song (In My Heart)," "The Way We Were"/"Try to Remember," and "Part Time Love." The R&B smashes "Love Finds Its Own Way," "Money," and "Baby Don't Change Your Mind" became only minor pop hits. With the group recording the soundtrack, Gladys Knight made her acting debut with then-husband Barry Hankerson in *Pipe Dreams* in 1976, but the project left the group in difficult financial straits for years.

In 1978 Gladys Knight signed with Columbia Records as a solo, whereas the Pips—"Bubba" Knight, William Guest, and Edward Patten—began recording for Casablanca Records. Allowed to work in clubs but prevented from recording together for more than two years by legal disputes, Gladys Knight and the Pips reunited for the Nicholas Ashford-Valerie Simpson-produced *About Love* and *Touch* albums for Columbia. They scored R&B smashes with "Landlord," "Save the Overtime (For Me)," and "You're Number One (In My Book)," but none of the songs was more than a minor pop hit. Gladys Knight joined Dionne Warwick, Elton John, and Stevie Wonder to record the top pop and R&B hit "That's What Friends Are For" in 1985, the year she starred with Flip Wilson in the short-lived CBS television situation comedy *Charlie and Company*. In 1986 she appeared in the HBO cable television special *Sisters in the Name of Love* with Dionne Warwick and Patti Labelle.

By 1987 Gladys Knight and the Pips had switched to MCA Records, where they managed R&B smashes with "Love Overboard" (a major pop hit) and "Lovin' on Next to Nothin'." In 1989 Gladys Knight began performing solo engagements, later recording *Good Woman* and *Just for You* for MCA. Gladys Knight and the Pips were inducted into the Rock and Roll Hall of Fame in 1996.

DISC.: *Everybody Needs Love* (1967); *Feelin' Bluesy* (1968); *Tastiest Hits* (1968); *Nitty Gritty* (1969); *If I Were Your Woman* (1971); *Standing Ovation* (1971); *Imagination* (1973); *Neither One of Us* (1973); *Help Me Make It Through the Night* (1973); *The Best of Gladys Knight & The Pips: The Columbia Years* (1974); *All the Great Hits* (1974); *I Feel a Song* (1974); *Claudine* (soundtrack; 1974); *The Best of Gladys Knight & The Pips* (1976); *Bless This House* (1976); *Still Together* (1977); *Memories* (1979); *About Love* (1980); *That Special Time of Year* (1980); *Touch* (1981); *Visions* (1983); *All Our Love* (1988); *Christmas Album* (1989); *Soul Survivors: The Best of Gladys Knight & The Pips, 1973–1983* (1990); *Greatest Hits* (1990); *Room in Your Heart* (1994); *The Best of Gladys Knight & The Pips: Anthology* (1995); *Blue Lights in the Basement* (1996); *The Lost Live Album* (1996); *The Ultimate Collection* (1997); *Live at the Roxy* (1998); *Essential Collection* (1999); *20th Century Masters: The Millennium Collection—The Best of Gladys Knight & The Pips* (2000); *Soul Grooves* (2000). **GLADYS KNIGHT:** *Good Woman* (1991); *Just for You* (1994).—**BH**

Glanert, Detlev, German composer; b. Hamburg, Sept. 6, 1960. He was 12 when he began to compose and receive lessons in trumpet and double bass. He pursued formal training in composition with Diether de la Motte (1981–82) and Gunther Friedrichs and Frank Michael Beyer (1982–84) in Hamburg, and with Hans Werner Henze in Cologne (1984–88).

WORKS: DRAMATIC: O p e r a : *Leviathan,* chamber opera (1985; Evian, May 13, 1986); *Leyla und Medjnun* (1987–88; Munich, May 28, 1988); *Der Spiegel des grossen Kaisers* (1989–93; Mannheim, 1995); *Josef Süss* (1998–99; Bremen, Oct. 13, 1999). **ORCH.:** 3 syms.: No. 1 (1985), No. 2, *Drei Gesänge aus Carmen von Wolf Wondratschek,* for Baritone and Orch. (1989–90), and No. 3 (1996); *Aufbruch* (1986); *Mitternachtstanz* for Timpani and Strings (1988; also for Solo Timpani, 1992); *Parergon* (1991); Piano Concerto (1993–94); *Musik* for Violin and Orch. (1995–96); *Katafalk* (1997). **CHAMBER:** *3 Pieces* for Viola and Piano (1981); Violin Sonata (1982); String Quartet (1984–86); Chamber Sym. for 9 Instruments (1985); *Norden* for Ensemble (1985); *4 Quartets* for 4 Double Basses (1986); *Serenade* for Cello and Piano (1986); *Yakub iki—Zeit des Wartens* for Violin, Cello, Piano, and

Clarinet (1989); *Mahler/Skizze* for 13 Instruments (1989); *Passa-caglia aus "Leyla und Medjnun"* for 13 Instruments (1990); *Mitternachtstanz* for Solo Timpani (1992; also for Timpani and String Orch., 1988); 2 chamber sonatas for 8 Instruments (*Vergessenes Bild*, 1994; *Gestalt*, 1995); *Chaconne*, octet (1996); Wind Quintet (1997). **P i a n o :** 4 *Fantasies* (1987–88). **VO-CAL:** 4 *Lieder nach Graffiti-Texten für Ensemble* for Soprano and 3 Instruments (1991); 3 *Sonette nach Gedichten von Wolf Wond-ratschek* for Baritone and Guitar (1992) *"Contemplated by a Portrait of a Divine,"* cantata for Soprano and 5 Instruments (1992); *Miserere* for Chorus (1995–96).—**LK/DM**

Glanville-Hicks, Peggy,

Australian-born American composer; b. Melbourne, Dec. 29, 1912; d. Sydney, June 25, 1990. She entered the Melbourne Cons. in 1927 as a composition student of Hart. In 1931 she went to London and studied with Benjamin (piano), Morris and Kitson (theory), Vaughan Williams (composition), Jacob (orchestration), and Lambert and Sargent (conducting); she then pursued further training with Boulanger in Paris and with Wellesz (musicology and advanced composition) in Vienna (1936–38). In 1938 she married **Stanley Bate,** but they divorced in 1948. In 1939 she went to the U.S. and in 1948 became a naturalized American citizen. From 1948 to 1958 she wrote music criticism for the *N.Y. Herald Tribune*, and also was active in contemporary music circles. In 1956 and 1958 she held Guggenheim fellowships. After living in Athens (1959–76), she returned to Australia. She utilized serial techniques in her music but not without explorations of early and non-Western modalities.

WORKS: DRAMATIC: O p e r a : *Caedmon* (1933); *The Transposed Heads* (1952–53; Louisville, April 3, 1954); *The Glit-tering Gate* (1957; N.Y., May 14, 1959); *Nausicaa* (1959–60; Athens, Aug. 19, 1961); *Carlos Among the Candles* (1962); *Sappho* (1963); *Beckett* (1989–90). **B a l l e t :** *Hylas and the Nymphs* (1935); *Postman's Knock* (1938); *Killer-of-Enemies* (1946); *The Masque of the Wild Man* (Spoleto, June 10, 1958); *Triad* (Spoleto, June 10, 1958); *Saul and the Witch of Endor* (CBS-TV, June 7, 1959; also for Orch. as *Drama*); *A Season in Hell* (1965; N.Y., Nov. 15, 1967); *Tragic Celebration: Jephthah's Daughter* (CBS-TV, Nov. 6, 1966). **ORCH.:** *Meditation* (1933); 2 sinfoniettas (1934, 1938); Piano Concerto (1936); Flute Concerto (1937); *Prelude and Scherzo* (1937); *Sinfonia da Pacifica* (1952–53; Melbourne, June 25, 1954); 3 *Gymnopédies* (1953); *Estruscan Concerto* for Piano and Chamber Orch. (1954; N.Y., Jan. 25, 1956); *Concerto Romantico* for Viola and Orch. (1956; N.Y., Feb. 19, 1957); *Tapestry* (1958). **CHAMBER:** String Quartet (1937); Sonatina for Alto Re-corder or Flute and Piano (1939); *Concerto da Camera* for Flute, Clarinet, Bassoon, and Piano (1946; Amsterdam, June 10, 1948); Sonata for Harp, Flute, and Horn (1950); Sonata for Solo Harp (1950–51); Sonata for Piano and Percussion (1951; N.Y., May 6, 1952); *Concertino Antico* for Harp and String Quartet (1955; Washington, D.C., Jan. 17, 1958); *Musica Antiqua* for 2 Flutes, Harp, Marimba, Timpani, and 2 Percussion (1957; Sydney, Jan. 21, 1982); *Prelude and Presto for Ancient American Instruments* (1957); *Girondelle for Giraffes* for 6 Instruments (1978). **VOCAL:** *Pastoral* for Women's Chorus and Clarinet or English Horn (1932–33); *Poem* for Chorus and Orch. (1933); *In Midwood Silence* for Soprano, Oboe, and String Quartet (1935); *Song in Summer* for Chorus and Orch. (1935); *Choral Suite* for Women's Chorus, Oboe, and Strings (1937); *Aria Concertante* for Tenor, Women's Chorus, Oboe, Piano, and Gong (1945); *Dance Cantata* for Tenor, Narrator, Speaking Chorus, and Orch. (1947); *Thomsoniana* for

Tenor or Soprano, Flute, Horn, Piano, and String Quartet (1949); *Letters from Morocco* for Tenor and Orch. (1952; N.Y., Feb. 22, 1953); songs. **OTHER:** Film scores.

BIBL.: D. Hayes, *P. G.-H.: A Bio-Bibliography* (Westport, Conn., 1990); W. Beckett, *P. G.-H.* (Pymble, Australia, 1992). —**NS/LK/DM**

Glareanus, Henricus or Heinrich Glarean (real name, Heinrich Loris; Latinized: Henricus Loritus),

Swiss music theorist; b. Mollis, Glarus canton, June 1488; d. Freiburg, March 28, 1563. He studied with Rubellus at Bern, and later with Cochläus at Cologne, where he was crowned poet laureate by Emperor Maximilian I in 1512, as the result of a poem he composed and sang to the Emperor. He first taught mathematics at Basel (1514). From 1517 to 1522 he was in Paris, where he taught philosophy. In 1522 he returned to Basel, where he stayed until 1529, and then he settled in Freiburg, where he was a prof. of poetry, then of theology. His first important work, *Isagoge in musicen*, publ. at Basel in 1516 (Eng. tr. in the *Journal of Music Theory*, III, 1959), dealt with solmization, intervals, modes, and tones. A still more important vol., the *Dodecachordon*, was publ. in 1547. In it, Glareanus advanced the theory that there are 12 church modes, corresponding to the ancient Greek modes, instead of the commonly accepted 8 modes. The 3rd part of the *Dodecachordon* contains many works by 15th- and 16th-century musicians. A copy of the *Dodecachordon*, with corrections in Glareanus's own handwriting, is in the Library of Congress, Washington, D.C. A German tr., with the musical examples in modern notation, was publ. by P. Bohn in vol. 16 of *Publikationen der Gesell-schaft für Musikforschung* (Leipzig, 1888) and an Eng. tr. and commentary by C. Miller was publ. in Musicologi-cal Studies and Documents, 6 (1965); facsimile ed. in *Monuments of Music and Music Literature in Facsimile*, 2/65 (N.Y., 1967). A complete index of Glareanus's works is contained in P. Lichtenthal's *Dizionario e bib-liografia della musica*, IV, pp. 274–76 (Milan, 1826). J. Wonegger publ. *Musicae epitome ex Glareani Dodekachordo* (1557; 2nd ed., 1559; in Ger. as *Uss Glareani Musik ein Usszug*, 1557).

BIBL.: O. Fritzsche, *Glarean, Sein Leben und seine Schriften* (Frauenfeld, 1890).—**NS/LK/DM**

Glasenapp, Carl Friedrich,

German music scholar; b. Riga, Oct. 3, 1847; d. there, April 14, 1915. He studied philology at Dorpat, and from 1875 was head-master at Riga. An ardent admirer of Wagner's art, he devoted his entire life to the study of the master's works, and was one of the principal contributors to the *Bayreuther Blätter* from their foundation. His great work is the monumental *Richard Wagners Leben und Wirken* (2 vols., Leipzig, 1876–77; 3rd ed., rev. and enl., as *Das Leben Richard Wagners*, 6 vols., Leipzig, 1894–1911; Eng. tr. by W. Ellis as *Life of Richard Wagner*, 6 vols., London, 1900–1908; Vols. I-III based on Glasenapp; reprinted N.Y., 1977, with new introduction by G. Buelow; 5th Ger. ed., rev., 1910–23). Though Glasenapp's work was considered the definitive biography in its time, its value is diminished by the fact that he publ. only materials approved by Wagner's family; as a result, it was super-seded by later biographies. His other works include *Wagner-Lexikon* with H. von Stein (1883), *Wagner-Encyklopädie* (2 vols., 1891), *Siegfried Wagner* (1906), and *Siegfried Wagner und seine Kunst* (1911), with sequels, *Schwarzschwanenreich* (1913) and *Sonnenflammen* (1919). He also ed. *Bayreuther Briefe, 1871–73* (1907) and *Familienbriefe an Richard Wagner, 1832–74* (1907).—NS/LK/DM

Gläser, Franz (Joseph), Bohemian composer and conductor; b Obergeorgenthal, April 19, 1798; d. Copenhagen, Aug. 29, 1861. He received training at the Prague Cons., then went to Vienna, where he was active as a composer of farces and pantomimes from 1817. In 1830 he went to Berlin, where he brought out his most successful opera, *Der Adlers Horst* (Dec. 29, 1832). In 1842 he settled in Copenhagen, and in 1845 he was named court conductor. His Danish operas, all premiered in Copenhagen, comprise *Bryllupet vet Comosøen* (The Wedding by Lake Como; Jan. 29, 1849), *Nokken* (The Water Sprites; Feb. 12, 1853), and *Den forgyldte svane* (The Golden Swan; March 17, 1854).

BIBL.: W. Neumann, *F. G.* (Leipzig, 1859); N. Pfeil, *F. G.* (Leipzig, 1870).—LK/DM

Glaser, Werner Wolf, German-born Swedish pianist, conductor, teacher, and composer; b. Cologne, April 14, 1910. He studied composition with Jarnach at the Cologne Hochschule für Musik, where he also received training in piano and conducting. He later studied composition with Hindemith at the Berlin Hochschule für Musik, art history at the Univ. of Bonn, and psychology at the Univ. of Berlin, receiving a Ph.D. After conducting the Chemnitz Opera orch. (1929–31) and serving as chorus master in Cologne (1931–33), he went to Copenhagen as a teacher at the Fredriksberg Cons. (1936–43). With I. Skovgaard, he founded the Lyngby School of Music in 1939. He settled in Sweden, becoming a naturalized citizen in 1951. He was conductor of the Södra Västmanland Orch. Soc. (1944–59) and was active as a music critic. With I. Andrén and G. Axén, he founded the Västerås School of Music in 1945, and was its director of studies from 1954 until his retirement in 1975. A man of wide interests, he studied modern art and literature, wrote poetry, and investigated the potentialities of music therapy. A prolific composer, he followed the neo-Classical line.

WORKS: DRAMATIC: O p e r a : *Kagekiyo,* chamber opera (1961); *Encounters,* chamber opera (Vasterås, Dec. 13, 1970); *A Naked King* (1971; Göteborg, April 6, 1973); *Cercatori,* chamber opera (1972); *The Boy and the Voice,* children's opera (1973); *Freedom Bells* (1980). **B a l l e t :** *Persefone* (1960); *Les Cinq Pas de l'homme* (1973). **ORCH.:** 13 syms. (1934; 1936; 1936; 1943; 1949; 1957; 1961; 1964; 1976; 1974–80; 1983; 1989; 1990); Flute Concerto (1934); Concertino for Alto Saxophone and Strings (1935); *Trilogia I* (1939) and *II* (1981); *3 Pieces* for Strings (1947); *Idyll, Elegy, and Fanfare* (1954); Concerto No. 2 (1957); *Music* for Strings (1957); *Concerto della Capella* for Winds, Percussion, and Piano (1960); *Le tre gradi* for Strings (1961); *Capriccio No. 3* for Piano and Orch. (1962); Concertino for Clarinet and Small Orch. (1962); Concerto for Violin, Winds, and Percussion (1962); Violin Concerto (1964); *4 Dance Scenes* (1964); *3 pezzi* for Oboe d'Amore and Chamber Orch. (1964);

Conflitti (1966); Oboe Concerto (1966); *Transformations* for Piano and Orch. (1966); *Modi gestus* for Strings (1966); *Syringa* for 3 Flutes and Strings (1966); Concerto for 20 Wind Instruments and Percussion (1966); *Paradosso* for 2 String Orchs. (1967); Concerto for Flute and Strings (1967); Horn Concerto (1969); *Arioso e Toccata No. 2* for Piano and Orch. (1969); *Canto* for Soprano Saxophone and Strings (1970); *3 Symphonic Dances* (1975); Cello Concerto (1976); *Adagio* for Strings (1977); *Divertimento No. 2* for Wind Quintet and Strings (1979) and *No. 3* (1983); Concerto for Soprano Saxophone and Strings (1980); Concerto for Tenor Saxophone and Strings (1981); *5 Serious Short Songs* for Strings (1984); *Concerto breve* for Violin, Strings, and Percussion (1986); *Nigeria* (1986); *5 Choreographic Scenes* for Chamber Orch. (1987); *Theme and Variations* (1987); Piano Concerto (1988); *Konzertstück* for Baritone Saxophone and Strings (1992); *Divertimento inverso* (1995). **CHAMBER:** 14 string quartets (1934; 1937; 1946; 1947; 1948; 1948; 1954; 1967; 1967; 1978; 1980; 1988; 1992–93; 1997); *Quartetto piccolo* for Strings (1938); Trio for 2 Violins and Cello (1947); Trio for Clarinet, Violin, and Cello (1948); Quartet for Saxophone, Violin, Viola, and Cello (1950); *Chamber Music* for Clarinet, Cello, and Piano (1952); Trio for Clarinet, Bassoon, and Piano (1953); Quartet for Flute, Clarinet, Cello, and Piano (1960); *Musica sacra* for Flute, Clarinet, Organ, and Strings (1960); *Intrada* for String Quartet (1964); Sonata for Solo Flute (1966); *Music* for Clarinet, Violin, and Double Bass (1967); 2 string trios (1969, 1975); 2 wind quintets (1970, 1970); Sonata for Solo Violin (1971); *Paysages sonores* for Piano Trio (1973); *Variations and Interlude* for 8 Cellos (1978); Trio for Flute, Oboe, and Cello (1978); Trio for Flute, Guitar, and Viola (1979); *3 Pieces* for 11 Saxophones (1982); 3 piano quintets (1984; 1991; 1993–94); Saxophone Quartet (1984); *Linda Quartet* for Baritone Saxophone and String Trio (1985); 2 trios for Flute, Cello, and Piano (1985, 1991); Oboe Sonata (1986); Baritone Saxophone Sonata (1986); *Trezze* for Oboe and String Quartet (1987); *Fantasia all antico* for Violin (1988); *Concerto da camera* for 6 Instruments (1990); Trio for Flute, Clarinet, and Cello (1992); Quartet for Oboe, Bassoon, Horn, and Piano (1993); Concerto for Saxophones and Piano (1996); Duo for Clarinet and Saxophone (1998); piano pieces; organ music. **VOCAL:** *Concerto lirico* for Soprano, Piano, Timpani, and Strings (1971); *Motetto dell'aqua* for Chorus, Flute, and Timpani (1998); cantatas; choruses; songs.—NS/LK/DM

Glass, Louis (Christian August), Danish composer; b. Copenhagen, March 23, 1864; d. there, Jan. 22, 1936. He was a pupil of his father, Christian Hendrik (1821–93), then at the Brussels Cons. of J. de Zarembski and J. Wieniawski (piano) and of J. Servais (cello). He appeared as both a pianist and a cellist.

WORKS: ORCH.: 6 syms.: No. 1 (1893), No. 2 (1898–99), No. 3, *Skavsymfoni* (Wood Sym.; 1901), No. 4 (1910–11), No. 5, *Sinfonia svastica* (1919), and No. 6, *Skoldungeaet* (Bird of the Scyldings; 1926); 2 overtures, *Der Volksfeind* and *Dänemark*; *Sommerliv,* suite; dance poem, *Artemis* (Copenhagen, Oct. 27, 1917); Oboe Concerto. **CHAMBER:** 4 string quartets; Piano Trio; 2 violin sonatas; numerous works for piano.—NS/LK/DM

Glass, Philip, outstanding American composer; b. Baltimore, Jan. 31, 1937. He began to play the violin when he was 6 and the flute at age 8. In his second year of high school, he sought admission to the Univ. of Chicago, was accepted, and studied mathematics and philosophy before graduating when he was 19. He also learned to play piano and studied the music of Ives and

Webern. He pursued training with Persichetti at the Juilliard School of Music in N.Y. (M.S., 1962), and also received instruction from Milhaud and Bergsma. In 1964 he was awarded a Fulbright scholarship and went to Paris to study with Nadia Boulanger. While there, he worked as a transcriber of the music of Ravi Shankar for a French filmmaker, which prompted him to pursue the study of Indian music. His research took him to North Africa, India, and the Himalayas, and upon his return to N.Y. he began to compose works with Eastern influences. His *Strung Out* for Amplified Violin (1968), an early example of minimalistic writing, was first heard at an all-Glass concert in N.Y. Although he would soon be regarded as a leading minimalist, Glass never claimed to have invented minimalism nor did he for long remain a rigorous adherent to its techniques. With the founding of the Philip Glass Ensemble in 1968, he soon acquired a devoted following via tours of the U.S. and overseas, as well as though many recordings. In some quarters, however, he was derided as a bane to music. There was no denying the widespread attention he received when his expansive opera *Einstein on the Beach*, a treatment of various aspects of the life of Albert Einstein, was first performed at the Avignon Festival on July 25, 1976, although it would be nearly a decade before the work received its full critical due. Glass secured his place among composers of dramatic scores with his successful opera *Satyagraha* (Sanskrit for "Truth Force"; Rotterdam, Sept. 5, 1980), which relates the early career of Mahatma Gandhi in South Africa. His opera *Akhnaten* (Stuttgart, March 24, 1984), whose protagonist is the monotheistic Pharoah Akhnaten, added further luster to his growing reputation. A commission from the Metropolitan Opera in N.Y. for the commemoration of the 500th anniversary of the discovery of America led to the composition of his opera *The Voyage*. This allegorical treatment of the compelling drive for exploration was premiered there on Oct. 12, 1992. While Glass continued to compose various dramatic scores, he also wrote much in other genres, including orch. pieces, chamber music, vocal works, and film scores. His *Low Symphony* (Munich, Aug. 30, 1992) and *Heroes Symphony* (1996) were notable for their effective utilization of music by David Bowie and Brian Eno. In 1998 the Philip Glass Ensemble celebrated its 30th anniversary.

WORKS: DRAMATIC: Opera: *Einstein on the Beach*, opera (Avignon, July 25, 1976); *A Madrigal Opera* (1979; Holland Festival, June 1980); *Satyagraha*, opera (Rotterdam, Sept. 5, 1980); *Akhnaten*, opera (1983; Stuttgart, March 24, 1984); *the CIVIL warS:A Tree is Best Measured When it is Down*, opera (Rome, March 1984); *The Juniper Tree*, opera (Cambridge, Mass., Dec. 11, 1985; in collaboration with Robert Moran); *The Making of the Representative for Planet 8*, opera, after Doris Lessing (1985–88; Houston, July 8, 1988); *The Fall of the House of Usher*, opera, after Poe (Cambridge, Mass., May 18, 1988); *1000 Airplanes on the Roof*, music theater piece (Vienna, July 5, 1988); *Hydrogen Jukebox*, music theater piece (concert perf., Philadelphia, April 29, 1990; stage perf., Charleston, S.C., May 26, 1990); *White Raven*, opera (1991; Lisbon, Spt. 26, 1998); *The Voyage*, opera (N.Y., Oct. 12, 1992); *Orphée*, opera (Cambridge, Mass., May 14, 1993); *La Belle et la bête*, opera (Gibellina, June 21, 1994); *Les Enfants terrible*, dance-opera (Zug, May 18, 1996); *The Marriages Between Zones Three, Four, and Five*, opera (Heidelberg,

May 10, 1997); *Monsters of Grace*, opera (1997; Los Angeles, April 15, 1998). Film Scores: *North Star* (1977); *Koyaanisqatsi* (1982); *Mishima* (1984); *Hamburger Hill* (1987); *Powaqqatsi* (1987); *The Thin Blue Line* (1988); *Mindwalk* (1990); *Candyman* (1992); *Compassion in Exile* (1992); *Anima Mundi* (1992); *A Brief History of Time* (1992); *Candyman II* (1995); *Jenipapo* (1995); *The Secret Agent* (1996); *Bent* (1997); *Kundun* (1997); *The Truman Show* (1998); *Dracula* (1998); *The Astronaut's Wife* (1998). Mixed Media: *The Photographer*, mixed media piece (1982). ORCH.: *Music in Similar Motion* (1969–81); *Company* for Strings (1983); *The Olympian: Lighting of the Torch and Closing* for the 23rd Olympiad (1984); *Phaedra* for Strings (1985; Dallas, Feb. 18, 1986); *In the Upper Room* for Chamber Orch. (1986); Violin Concerto (N.Y., April 5, 1987); *The Light* (Cleveland, Oct. 29, 1987); *The Canyon* (Rotterdam, Oct. 18, 1988); *Passages* for Chamber Orch. (1990); Concerto Grosso (Bonn, June 17, 1992); 4 syms.: No. 1, *Low Symphony*, after the music of David Bowie and Brian Eno (Munich, Aug. 30, 1992), No. 2 (N.Y., Oct. 15, 1994), No. 3 for Strings (1994; Künzelsau, Feb. 5, 1995), and No. 4, *Heroes Symphony*, after the music of David Bowie and Brian Eno (1996); *Echorus* for 2 Violins and Strings (1994–95); Concerto for Saxophone Quartet and Orch. (Stockholm, Sept. 1, 1995); *Music from The Secret Agent* for Chamber Orch. (1995); *Days and Nights in Rocinha* (1997; Vienna, Feb. 8, 1998). CHAMBER: *Head On* for Violin, Cello, and Piano (1967); *Piece in the Shape of a Square* for 2 Flutes (1967); *1+1* for Player and Amplified Table Top (1968); *Gradus* for Soprano Saxophone (1968); *Strung Out* for Amplified Violin (1968); *Another Look at Harmony—Part III* for Clarinet and Piano (1975); *Façades* for 2 Soprano Saxophones or 2 Flutes/Strings (1981); *Glassworks* for Chamber Ensemble (1981); 5 string quartets (n.d.; *Company*, 1983; *Mishima*, 1985; *Buczak*, 1989; 1991); *Prelude to Endgame* for Timpani and Double Bass (Cambridge, Mass., Dec. 12, 1984); *Arabesque in Memoriam* for Flute (1988); *France: From the Screens* for Violin (1991). KEYBOARD: Piano: *In Again Out Again* for 2 Pianos (1968); *2 Pages* (1968; also for Electric Keyboard); *Modern Love Waltz* (1978); *Mad Rush* (1979; also for Organ); *Opening* (1982); *Metamorphosis* (1988); *Wichita Vortex Sutra* (1988); *Now, So Long After That Time* (N.Y., June 13, 1994). Organ: *Music in Contrary Motion* (1969); *Dance No. 2* (1978) and *No. 4* (1979). VOCAL: *Hebeve Song* for Soprano, Clarinet, and Bassoon (1983); *3 Songs* for Chorus (1984); (6) *Songs from Liquid Days* for Voice and Instrument(s) (1986); *Itaipu* for Chorus and Orch. (Atlanta, Nov. 2, 1989); *Planctus* for Voice and Piano (1997).

BIBL.: W. Mertens, *American Minimal Music: La Monte Young, Terry Riley, Steve Reich, P. G.* (London, 1991); M. Altmann, *Sakrales Musiktheater im 20. Jahrhundert: Eine Studie zur Oper "Satyagraha" von P. G.* (Regensburg, 1993); R. Kostelanetz, ed., *Writings on G.: Essays, Interviews, Criticism* (Berkeley, 1997); J. Richardson, *Singing Archeology: P. G.'s Akhanaten* (Hanover, N.H., 1999).—NS/LK/DM

Glaz, Herta, Austrian-American contralto; b. Vienna, Sept. 16, 1908. She was trained in Vienna and made her operatic debut at the Breslau Opera in 1931, presaging a successful career, but in 1933 was forced to leave Germany. She toured Austria and Scandinavia as a concert singer; sang at the German Theater in Prague in 1935–36. In 1936 she took part in the American tour of the Salzburg Opera Guild, and subsequently sang at the Chicago Opera (1940–42). On Dec. 25, 1942, she made her debut with the Metropolitan Opera in N.Y. as

Amneris, remaining on its roster until 1956. She then taught voice at the Manhattan School of Music, retiring in 1977. Her husband was **Joseph Rosenstock.** —NS/LK/DM

Glazer, David, American clarinetist and teacher; b. Milwaukee, May 7, 1913. He studied at Milwaukee State Teachers Coll. (B.Ed., 1935) and the Berkshire Music Center in Tanglewood (summers, 1940–42). After teaching at the Longy School of Music in Cambridge, Mass. (1937–42), he played in the Cleveland Orch. (1946–51); then toured as a soloist with orchs. and as a chamber music artist; was active with the N.Y. Woodwind Quintet (1951–85). He also taught at the Mannes Coll. of Music, the N.Y. Coll. of Music, N.Y.U., and the State Univ. of N.Y. at Stony Brook.—NS/LK/DM

Glazunov, Alexander (Konstantinovich), eminent Russian composer and teacher; b. St. Petersburg, Aug. 10, 1865; d. Neuilly-sur-Seine, March 21, 1936. Of a well-to-do family (his father was a book publisher), he studied at a technical high school in St. Petersburg, and also took lessons in music with N. Elenkovsky. At 15, he was introduced to Rimsky-Korsakov, who gave him weekly lessons in harmony, counterpoint, and orchestration. He made rapid progress, and at the age of 16 completed his 1st Sym., which was conducted by Balakirev on March 29, 1882, in St. Petersburg. So mature was this score that Glazunov was hailed by Stasov, Cui, and others as a rightful heir to the masters of the Russian national school. The music publisher Belaiev arranged for publication of his works, and took him to Weimar, where he met Liszt. From that time Glazunov composed assiduously in all genres except opera. He was invited to conduct his syms. in Paris (1889) and London (1896–97). Returning to St. Petersburg, he conducted concerts of Russian music. In 1899 he was engaged as an instructor in composition and orchestration at the St. Petersburg Cons. He resigned temporarily during the revolutionary turmoil of 1905 in protest against the dismissal of Rimsky-Korsakov by the government authorities, but returned to the staff after full autonomy was granted to the Cons. by the administration. In 1905 Glazunov was elected director and retained this post until 1928, when he went to Paris. In 1929 he made several appearances as conductor in the U.S. He was the recipient of honorary degrees of Mus.D. from the univs. of Cambridge and Oxford (1907). Although he wrote no textbook on composition, his pedagogical methods left a lasting impression on Russian musicians through his many students who preserved his traditions. His music is often regarded as academic, yet there is a flow of rhapsodic eloquence that places Glazunov in the Romantic school. He was for a time greatly swayed by Wagnerian harmonies, but resisted this influence successfully; Lisztian characteristics are more pronounced in his works. Glazunov was one of the greatest masters of counterpoint among Russian composers, but he avoided extreme polyphonic complexity. The national spirit of his music is unmistakable; in many of his descriptive works, the programmatic design is explicitly

Russian. His most popular score is the ballet *Raymonda*. The major portion of his music was written before 1906, when he completed his 8th Sym.; after that he wrote mostly for special occasions. He also completed and orchestrated the overture to Borodin's *Prince Igor* from memory, having heard Borodin play it on the piano.

WORKS (all 1st perf. in St. Petersburg [Petrograd] unless otherwise given): **DRAMATIC: B a l l e t :** *Raymonda* (1896; Jan. 19, 1898); *The Ruses of Love* (1898; 1900); *The Seasons* (1899; Feb. 20, 1900). **OTHER:** *Introduction and Dance of Salome* for *Salome* by O. Wilde (1912); incidental music to *The King of the Jews* by K. Romanov (Jan. 9, 1914). **ORCH.:** 9 syms.: No. 1, in E major (1881; March 29, 1882; rev. 1885, 1929), No. 2, in F-sharp minor (1886; Paris, June 29, 1889), No. 3, in D major (Dec. 20, 1890), No. 4, in E-flat major (1893; Feb. 3, 1894), No. 5, in B-flat major (1895; London, Jan. 28, 1897), No. 6, in C minor (1896; Feb. 21, 1897), No. 7, in F major (1902; Jan. 3, 1903), No. 8, in E-flat major (Dec. 22, 1906), and No. 9, in D major (1910; completed by G. Yudin, 1948); *2 Overtures on Greek Themes* (1881, 1883); *2 Serenades* (1883, 1884); *Lyric Poem* (1884); *Stenka Razin,* symphonic poem (1885); *To the Memory of a Hero* (1885); *Characteristic Suite* (1885); *Idyll and Oriental Reverie* (1886); *The Forest,* symphonic poem (1887); *Mazurka* (1888); *Melody* and *Spanish Serenade* for Cello and Orch. (1888); *Slavonic Festival* (1888; from String Quartet No. 3); *Wedding March* (1889); *The Sea,* symphonic fantasy (1889); *Oriental Rhapsody* (1890); *The Kremlin,* musical picture (1891); *Spring,* musical picture (1891); *Chopiniana,* suite on themes by Chopin (1893); *Carnaval,* overture (1893); *2 Concert Waltzes* (1894); *2 Solemn Processionals* (1894, 1910); *Ballet Suite* (1894); *From Darkness to Light,* fantasy (1894); *Fantasy* (1895); *Suite* (1898) and *Characteristic Dance* (1900) from *Raymonda*; *Romantic Intermezzo* (1900); *Festival Overture* (1900); *Song of a Minstrel* for Cello and Orch. (1900; also for Cello, Piano, and Orch.); *March on a Russian Theme* (1901); *Ballade* (1902); *From the Middle Ages,* suite (1902; Jan. 3, 1903); *Ballet Scene* (1904); Violin Concerto (1904; March 4, 1905, L. Auer soloist); *Russian Fantasy* for Balalaika Orch. (March 11, 1906); *2 Preludes:* No. 1, In Memory of V. Stasov (1906) and No. 2, *In Memory of Rimsky-Korsakov* (1908); *The Song of Destiny,* overture (1908); *In Memory of N. Gogol* (1909); *Finnish Fantasy* (1909; March 27, 1910); *2 piano concertos* (1910; Nov. 11, 1917); *Finnish Sketches* (1912); *Karelian Legend,* musical picture (1914); *Paraphrase on National Anthems of the Allies* (1915); *Mazurka- Oberek* for Violin and Orch. (1917; orchestration by I. Yampolsky of work for Violin, Piano, and Orch.); *Variations* for Strings (1918); *Concerto- Ballata* for Cello and Orch. (1931; Paris, Oct. 14, 1933, Maurice Eisenberg soloist); Saxophone Concerto (1931; Nykoping, Nov. 25, 1934, Sigurd Rascher soloist); *Epic Poem* (1934). **CHAMBER:** 7 string quartets: No. 1, in D major (1882), No. 2, in F major (1884), No. 3, *Quatuor Slave,* in G major (1888), No. 4, in A minor (1894), No. 5, in D minor (1898), No. 6, in B- flat major (1921), and No. 7, in C major (1930); *5 Novelettes* for String Quartet (1886); *Elegy to the Memory of F. Liszt* for Cello and Piano (1886); *Reverie* for Horn and Piano (1890); Suite for String Quartet (1891); String Quintet (1895); *Meditation* for Violin and Piano (1891); *In modo religioso* for Brass Quartet (1892); *Elegy* for Viola and Piano (1893); *Mazurka-Oberek* for Violin and Piano (1917); *Elegy* for String Quartet (1928); Saxophone Quartet (1932). **P i a n o :** *Suite on the Theme "Sacha"* (1883); *Barcarolle and Novelette* (1889); *Prelude* and *2 Mazurkas* (1889); *Nocturne* (1889); *3 Études* (1890); *Little Waltz* (1892); *Grand Concert Waltz* (1893); *3 Miniatures* (1893); *Salon Waltz* (1893); *3 Pieces* (1894); *2 Impromptus* (1895); *Prelude and Fugue* (1899); *Theme and Variations* (1900); *2 sonatas* (both 1901); *4 Preludes and Fugues*

(1918–23); *Idylle* (1926); *Prelude and Fugue* (1926); *Suite* for 2 Pianos (1920). **VOCAL:** *Triumphal March* for Chorus and Orch. for the Chicago Columbian Exposition (1893); *Coronation Cantata* (1894); *Cantata in Memory of Pushkin's 100th Birthday* (1899); *Hymn to Pushkin* for Women's Chorus and Piano (1899); *Love* for Chorus (1907); *Prelude-Cantata for the 50th Anniversary of the St. Petersburg Cons.* (1912); 21 songs.

BIBL.: A. Ossovsky, *G.: His Life and Works* (St. Petersburg, 1907); V. Belaiev, *G.* (Vol. 1, Petrograd, 1922); V. Derzhanovsky, *A. G.* (Moscow, 1922); I. Glebov, *G.* (Leningrad, 1924); G. Fedorova, *G.* (Moscow, 1947; 2nd ed., 1961); H. Gunther, *A. G.* (Bonn, 1956); M. Ganina, *G.: Life and Works* (Leningrad, 1961); D. Gojowy, *A. G.: Sein Leben in Bildern und Dokumenten: Unter Ein beziehung des biographischen Fragments von G.s Schwiegersohn Herbert Günther* (Munich, 1986); D. Venturini, *A. G., 1865–1936: His Life and Works* (Delos, Ohio, 1992).—**NS/LK/DM**

Gleason, Frederick Grant, American organist, composer, and critic; b. Middletown, Conn., Dec. 17, 1848; d. Chicago, Dec. 6, 1903. He studied in Hartford with Dudley Buck, and later at the Leipzig Cons., in Berlin, and in London. Upon his return to the U.S., he was active as a church organist, teacher, and music critic. He wrote 2 operas, *Otho Visconti* (1877–90; Chicago, June 4, 1907) and *Montezuma*, as well as 4 cantatas, a symphonic poem, *Edris* (1896), a Piano Concerto, 3 piano trios, organ and piano pieces, songs, and 2 Episcopal church services.—**NS/LK/DM**

Gleason, Harold, American organist, musicologist, and teacher; b. Jefferson, Ohio, April 26, 1892; d. La Jolla, Calif., June 28, 1980. He studied music privately and took courses in civil engineering at the Calif. Inst. of Technology (1910–12), and then studied organ with Farnam in Boston (1917–18) and Bonnet in Paris (1922–23), and composition with Inch at the Eastman School of Music in Rochester, N.Y. After serving as a church organist in Calif. (1910–17), he was director of Boston's Music School Settlement (1917–18) and organist and choirmaster of N.Y.'s Fifth Ave. Presbyterian Church (1918–19). He then went to Rochester, N.Y., as George Eastman's personal organist and music director; he also was founder-director of the David Hochstein Memorial Music School (1919–29). From 1921 to 1953 he was head of the organ dept. at the Eastman School of Music, where he also was prof. of musicology (1932–50) and of music literature (1939–55), and director of graduate studies (1953–55). His wife was **Catharine Crozier**. He publ. *Method of Organ Playing* (1937; 7th ed., 1987), *Examples of Music before 1400* (1942; rev. ed., 1945), *Music Literature Outlines* (1949–55; rev. with W. Becker, 1979–81), and, with W. Marrocco, *Music in America* (1964).—**NS/LK/DM**

Glen, John, Scottish manufacturer of bagpipes and music researcher; b. Edinburgh, June 13, 1833; d. there, Nov. 29, 1904. His father, Thomas Glen (1804–73), the inventor of the "Serpentcleide," had established himself as a manufacturer of musical instruments, and the son succeeded to the business in 1866. He confined himself to the manufacture of bagpipes, of which he was soon recognized as the foremost manufacturer in Great Brit-

ain. He was equally noted for his research in Scottish music. He compiled *The Glen Collection of Scottish Dance Music, Strathspeys, Reels and Jigs...containing an Introduction on Scottish Dance Music* (2 vols., 1891, 1895) and *Early Scottish Melodies: including examples from MSS. and early printed works, along with a number of comparative tunes, notes on former annotators, English and other claims, and Biographical Notices, etc.* (1900).—**NS/LK/DM**

Glenn, Carroll, American violinist and teacher; b. Richmond, Va., Oct. 28, 1918; d. N.Y., April 25, 1983. She was only 4 years old when she began studies with her mother. After lessons with Felice de Horvath in Columbia, S.C., she entered the Juilliard School of Music in N.Y. at age 11 to study with Edouard Déthier, graduating when she was 15. In 1938 she won the Naumburg Award, which led to her N.Y. debut at Town Hall on Nov. 7 of that year. From 1941 she appeared as a soloist with many U.S. orchs. In 1943 she married **Eugene List**, with whom she frequently appeared in duo concerts. She also taught at the Eastman School of Music in Rochester, N.Y. (1964–75), the Manhattan School of Music (from 1975), and Queens Coll. of the City Univ. of N.Y. (from 1975). She actively sought rarely heard works for performance at her concerts.—**NS/LK/DM**

Glenn, (Evans) Tyree, jazz trombonist, vibraphonist, and singer; b. Corsicana, Tex., Nov. 23, 1912; d. Englewood, N.J., May 18, 1974. In his late teens he played with local Tex. bands, then with drummer Tommy Myles's band in Washington, D.C., and Va. (1934–36). He next worked in Charlie Echols's band in Los Angeles (1936), with Eddie Barefield on the West Coast, then Eddie Mallory's band (accompanying Ethel Waters); he remained with this band until 1939, with a break to recover from a band-coach crash. His next engagements were with the Benny Carter Big Band (1939), Cab Calloway (1939–46), and in Europe with the Don Redman Orch. He returned to N. Y. in 1947 and subbed for Lawrence Brown in Duke Ellington's band, shortly thereafter joining Ellington on a regular basis until 1951 (except for a period in 1950). After taking solo engagements in Scandinavia (1951), he returned to the U.S. (1952) and was active in studio, radio, and television work, occasionally undertaking acting roles. He led a quintet from 1955, usually featuring Harold Baker. He joined the Louis Armstrong All Stars (1965), remaining until Armstrong's illness (1968). He led a group at the Roundtable, N.Y. (1969), worked once more with Armstrong (1970–71), and deputized with Ellington (1971). He died of cancer.

DISC.: *At the Embers* (1957) *At the Roundtable* (1958); *Trombone Artistry* (1962).—**JC/LP**

Glennie, Evelyn (Elizabeth Ann), remarkable Scottish timpanist and percussionist; b. Aberdeen, July 19, 1965. Although she was born deaf, she nonetheless determined on a career in music; took up percussion training as a youth with Ron Forbes in Aberdeen, then studied at the Royal Academy of Music in London and with Keiko Abe in Japan. After playing in the National Youth Orch. of Scotland, she made her debut as a solo performer at London's Wigmore Hall in 1986. Her extraordinary talent brought her engagements with principal orchs. and festivals in Great Britain; subsequently toured extensively worldwide. In 1994 she appeared as soloist with Andrew Davis and the BBC Sym. Orch. at the traditional last night at the Proms in London, marking the close of its 100th anniversary season. She publ. the autobiography *Good Vibrations* (1990). In 1993 she was made a member of the Order of the British Empire. Glennie has done much to elevate the status of the timpanist and percussionist, and has also commissioned many new works.—**NS/LK/DM**

Glick, Srul Irving, Canadian composer, radio producer, conductor, and teacher; b. Toronto, Sept. 8, 1934. He studied composition with Weinzweig at the Univ. of Toronto (B.Mus., 1955; M.Mus., 1958), with Milhaud in Aspen, Colo. (summers, 1956–57), and with Louis Saguer and Max Deutsch in Paris (1959–60). From 1962 to 1986 he was a music producer for the CBC radio; he also taught theory and composition at the Royal Cons. of Music of Toronto (1963–69) and at York Univ. (1985–86). He served as conductor of the choir at the Beth Tikvah Synagogue in Toronto from 1969, and also led it on tours of Canada, Israel, and the U.S. After composing scores marked by a lyrical penchant with polytonal writing, he turned to a more contemporary idiom only to find his anchor later by combining classical and Jewish traditions of musical expression in a thoroughly personal idiom.

WORKS: ORCH.: *2 Essays* (1957); Sonata for Strings (1957); Sinfonietta (1958); *Sinfonia Concertante No. 1* for Strings (1961) and *No. 2; Lamentations,* for String Quartet and Orch. (1972); *Suite Hébraïque No. 1* (1961; also arranged for various forces); *Danse Concertante No. 1* for Small Orch. (1963); *Elegy* (1964); *Symphonic Dialogues* for Piano and Orch. (Toronto, Dec. 20, 1964); *Pan* (1966); 2 syms.: *No. 1* for Chamber Orch. (Toronto, April 24, 1966) and *No. 2* (1967; Toronto, Jan. 24, 1969); *Gathering In* for Strings (Montreal, March 26, 1970); *Psalm* (Hamilton, Oct. 17, 1971); *Symphonic Elegy, with Line Drawing and Funeral March* for Strings (Toronto, April 20, 1974); Violin Concerto, *Shir Hamaalot—Song of Ascension* (Victoria, British Columbia, Nov. 14, 1976); *Romance—Song of Joy* for Piano and Orch. (1978); Concerto for Viola and Strings (1981); *Lament and Cantorial Chant* for Viola and Strings (1985); *The Vision of Ezekiel,* fantasy for Violin and Orch. (1986); *Divertimento* for Strings (1987); *The Reawakening,* symphonic poem (1991). **Ballet:** *Heritage* (1967). **CHAMBER:** *Divertimento Sextet* for Flute, Clarinet, Bassoon, and String Trio (1958); Trio for Clarinet, Piano, and Cello (1958–59); *Petite Suite* for Flute (1960); String Trio (1963); *Danse Concertante No. 2* for Flute, Clarinet, Trumpet, Cello, and Piano (1964); Sonata for Jazz Quintet (1964); Sonatina for Jazz Sextet (1965); *Divertissement* for 7 Instruments and Conductor (1968); *Suite Hébraïque No. 2* for Clarinet, String Trio, and Piano (1969), *No. 3* for String Quartet (1975), *No. 4* for Alto Saxophone or Clarinet or Viola and Piano (1979), *No. 5* for Flute, Clarinet, Violin, and Cello (1980), and *No. 6* for Violin and Piano (1984); *Prayer and Dance* for Cello and Piano (1975); Flute Sonata (1983); *Devequt,* sonata (1982); String Quartet No. 1 (Toronto, June 25, 1984); *Dance Suite* for 2 Guitars (1986); *...from out of the depths; mourning music for the 6 million...* for String Quartet (1986); Oboe Sonata (1987); Trio for Flute, Viola, and Harp (1988); Cello Sonata (1989); Trio for Violin, Cello, and Piano (1990). **Piano:** *4 Preludes* (1958); *7 Preludes* (1959); *Ballade*

(1959); *Song and Caprice* (1960); *Nistar (Secret),* fantaisie elegiaque (1979). **VOCAL:** *Music for Passover* for Chorus and String Quartet or String Orch. (1963); *...i never saw another butterfly...* for Alto and Chamber Orch., after children's poems written in the Thereseinstadt concentration camp (1968); *Hashiriam asher L'Yisrael,* liturgical synagogal music for Chorus (1969–88; also for Chorus, Flute, Clarinet, and String Quartet); *Halleluyah* for Chorus (1970); *4 Songs* for Tenor and Orch. (1972); *Yiddish Suite No. 1* for Chorus and Cello or String Quartet (1979) and *No. 2, Time Cycle,* for Chorus, Flute, Clarinet, Harp, and String Quartet (1984); *I Breathe a New Song* for Cantor and Chorus (1981); *Northern Sketches* for Chorus, Piano, Violin, and Cello (1982); *The Hour Has Come,* sym. for Chorus and Orch. (1984; Toronto, Feb. 25, 1985); *Sing unto the Lord a New Song* for Chorus and Harp or Orch. (1986; Toronto, Jan. 25, 1987); *Canticle of Peace* for Chorus (1987); *If We Would But Listen,* cantata for Narrator, Tenor, Chorus, Flute, Clarinet, and String Quartet (1988); *Visions through Darkness: An Oratorio of Our Time* for Narrator, Mezzo-soprano, Tenor, Chorus, and Instruments (1988); *Songs of Creation* for Chorus, Brass Quintet, 4 Percussion, and Organ (1989); *The Flame Is Not Extinguished* for Tenor, Mezzo-soprano, Women's Chorus, and Piano (1990); many other sacred and secular vocal works.—**NS/LK/DM**

Glière, Reinhold (Moritsovich), eminent Russian composer and pedagogue; b. Kiev, Jan. 11, 1875; d. Moscow, June 23, 1956. Following training in Kiev (1891–94), he studied violin with Hrimaly at the Moscow Cons., where he also took courses with Arensky, Taneyev, and Ippolitov-Ivanov (1894–1900), graduating with a gold medal. He completed his studies in Berlin (1905–07). Returning to Russia, he became active as a teacher; was appointed prof. of composition at the Kiev Cons., and was its director from 1914 to 1920; then was appointed to the faculty of the Moscow Cons., a post he retained until 1941. He traveled extensively in European and Asiatic Russia, collecting folk melodies; he also conducted many concerts of his own works. He was a prolific composer, and was particularly distinguished in symphonic works, in which he revealed himself as a successor of the Russian national school. He never transgressed the natural borderline of traditional harmony, but he was able to achieve effective results. His most impressive work is his 3rd Sym., subtitled *Ilya Muromets,* an epic description of the exploits of a legendary Russian hero. In his numerous songs, Glière showed a fine lyrical talent. He wrote relatively few works of chamber music, most of them early in his career. In his opera *Shah-Senem,* he made use of native Caucasian songs. Glière was the teacher of 2 generations of Russian composers; among his students were Prokofiev and Miaskovsky. He received Stalin prizes for the String Quartet No. 4 (1948) and the ballet *The Bronze Knight* (1950).

WORKS: DRAMATIC: Opera: *Zemlya i nebo* (Earth and Sky; 1900); *Shah-Senem* (1923; Baku, 1926; rev. 1934); *Gyulsara,* music drama (1936; Moscow, 1937; in collaboration with Sadikov; rev. version as an opera, Tashkent, Dec. 25, 1949); *Leyli i Mejnun* (Tashkent, July 18, 1940); *Rashel,* after Maupassant's *Mademoiselle Fifi* (1942; Moscow, April 19, 1947). **Ballet:** *Khirzis* (Moscow, Nov. 30, 1912); *Ovechiy istochnik* (Sheep's Spring; 1922; rev. as *Komedianti* [The Comedians], 1930; Moscow, April 5, 1931); *Kleopatra* (1925; Moscow, Jan. 11, 1926); *Krasnïy mak* (The Red Poppy; 1926–27; Moscow, June 14, 1927;

rev. as *Krasniy tsvetok* [The Red Flower], 1949); *Medniy vsadnik* (The Bronze Horseman; 1948–49; Leningrad, March 14, 1949); *Taras Bulba* (1951–52); *Dog Kastilii* (1955). **OTHER:** Incidental music to plays. **ORCH.:** 3 syms.: No. 1 (1899–1900; Moscow, Jan. 3, 1903), No. 2 (1907–08; Berlin, Jan. 23, 1908, Koussevitzky conducting), and No. 3, *Ilya Muromets* (1909–11; Moscow, March 23, 1912); 3 symphonic poems: *The Sirens* (1908), *The Cossacks of Zaporozh* (1938), and *Zapovit* (1938); Concertos for Harp (Moscow, Nov. 23, 1938), Coloratura Soprano (Moscow, May 12, 1943), Cello (1946; Moscow, Feb. 18, 1947), Horn (1950; Moscow, Jan. 26, 1952), and Violin (1956; completed and orchestrated by Liatoshinsky); 7 overtures: *Holiday at Ferghana* (1940); *The Friendship of the Peoples* (1941); *Overture on Slav Themes* (1941); *For the Happiness of the Fatherland* (1942); *25 Years of the Red Army* (1943); *War Overture* (1943); *Victory* (1945). **Band:** *Fantasy for the Festival of the Comintern* (1924); *Red Army March* (1924); *Heroic March for the Buryiat-Mongolian A.S.S.R.* (1936); *Solemn Overture for the 20th Anniversary of the October Revolution* (1937). **CHAMBER:** 2 string sextets (1900, 1902); 4 string quartets (1900, 1905, 1928, 1948); String Octet (1900); *8 pieces* for Violin and Cello (1909); *12 pieces* for Cello and Piano (1910); *10 duos* for 2 Cellos (1911); numerous piano pieces. **VOCAL:** *Imitation of Ezekiel* for Narrator and Orch. (1919); *2 Poems* for Soprano and Orch. (1924); *A Toast* for Voice and Orch. (1939); numerous songs.

BIBL.: I. Boelza, *R.M. G.* (Moscow, 1955; 2nd ed., 1962); N. Petrova, *R.M. G.* (Leningrad, 1962).—NS/LK/DM

Glinka, Mikhail (Ivanovich), great Russian composer, often called "the father of Russian music" for his pioneering cultivation of Russian folk modalities; b. Novospasskoye, Smolensk district, June 1, 1804; d. Berlin, Feb. 15, 1857. A scion of a fairly rich family of landowners, he was educated at an exclusive school in St. Petersburg (1817–22). He also took private lessons in music; his piano teacher was a resident German musician, Carl Meyer; he also studied violin. When the pianist John Field was in St. Petersburg, Glinka had an opportunity to study with him, but he had only 3 lessons before Field departed. He began to compose even before acquiring adequate training in theory. As a boy, he traveled in the Caucasus, then stayed for a while at his father's estate. At 20 he entered the Ministry of Communications in St. Petersburg, and remained in government employ until 1828, at the same time constantly improving his general education by reading; he had friends among the best Russian writers of the time, including the poets Zhukovsky and Pushkin. He also took singing lessons with an Italian teacher, Belloli. In 1830 he went to Italy; he continued irregular studies in Milan (where he spent most of his Italian years), and also visited Rome, Naples, and Venice. He became enamored of Italian music, and his early vocal and instrumental compositions are thoroughly Italian in melodic and harmonic structure. In 1833 he visited Vienna, and then went to Berlin, where he took a course in counterpoint and general composition with Dehn; thus he was nearly 30 when he completed his theoretical education. In 1834 his father died, and Glinka went back to Russia to take care of the family affairs. In 1835 he was married; the marriage was unhappy, and he soon separated from his wife, finally divorcing her in 1846. The return to his native land led him to consider the composition of a truly national opera on a subject (suggested to him by Zhukovsky) depicting a historical episode in Russian history: the saving of the first czar of the Romanov dynasty by a simple peasant, Ivan Susanin. Glinka's opera was premiered in St. Petersburg on Dec. 9, 1836, under the title *A Life for the Czar*. The event was hailed by the literary and artistic circles of Russia as a milestone of Russian culture, and indeed the entire development of Russian national music received its decisive creative impulse from Glinka's patriotic opera. It remained in the repertoire of Russian theaters until the Revolution made it unacceptable, but it was revived, under the original title, *Ivan Susanin*, on Feb. 27, 1939, in Moscow, and thereafter was again accorded an honored place in the Russian repertory. Glinka's next opera, *Ruslan and Ludmila*, after Pushkin's fairy tale, was first performed in St. Petersburg on Dec. 9, 1842; this opera, too, became extremely popular in Russia. Glinka introduced into the score many elements of oriental music; one episode contains the earliest use of the whole-tone scale in an opera. Both operas retain the traditional Italian form, with arias, choruses, and orch. episodes clearly separated. In 1844 Glinka was in Paris, where he met Berlioz; he also traveled in Spain, where he collected folk songs; the fruits of his Spanish tour were 2 orch. works, *Jota Aragonesa* and *Night in Madrid*. On his way back to Russia, he stayed in Warsaw for 3 years. The remaining years of his life were spent in St. Petersburg, Paris, and Berlin. V. Shebalin et al. ed. his complete works (Moscow, 1955–69).

WORKS: DRAMATIC: Opera: *Rokeby*, opera (1824; sketches only); *Marina Rosheha*, opera (1834; sketches only); *Zhizn za tsarya* (A Life for the Czar), opera (1834–36; 1st perf. as *Ivan Susanin*, St. Petersburg, Dec. 9, 1836); *Ruslan i Lyudmila* (Ruslan and Ludmila), opera (1837–42; St. Petersburg, Dec. 9, 1842); *Dvumuzhnitsa* (The Bigamist), opera (1855; sketches only; not extant). **Stage:** *Moldavanka i tsïganka* (The Moldavian Girl and the Gypsy Girl), incidental music (1836); *Scene at the Monastery* (1837); *Knyaz Kholmsky* (Prince Kholmsky), incidental music (1840). **ORCH.:** 2 overtures (both c. 1822–26); *Andante Cantabile and Rondo* (c. 1823); Sym. (c. 1824; unfinished); *Symphony on 2 Russian Themes* (1834; unfinished; completed by V. Shebalin, 1938); *Valse-Fantaisie* (orig. for Piano, 1839; orchestrated 1845, not extant; reorchestrated 1856); *Capriccio brillante on the Jota Aragonesa* (1845; also known as *1st Spanish Overture*); *Kamarinskaya* (1848); *Recuerdos de Castila* (1848; expanded as *Souvenir d'une d'été à Madrid*, 1851; also known as *2nd Spanish Overture*); *Polonaise* (1855); *Concerto for Orchestra* (n.d.; unfinished). **CHAMBER:** Septet (c. 1823; unfinished); 2 string quartets (1824, unfinished; 1830); Viola Sonata (1825–28); *Divertimento brillante* on themes from Bellini's *La sonnambula* for Piano, 2 Violins, Viola, Cello, and Double Bass (1832); *Serenata* on themes from Donizetti's *Anna Bolena* for Piano, Harp, Bassoon, Horn, Viola, Cello, and Double Bass (1832); *Gran sestetto originale* for Piano and String Quintet (1832); *Trio pathétique* for Piano, Clarinet, and Bassoon (1832); more than 55 piano pieces. **VOCAL:** *Tarantella* for Reciter, Chorus, and Orch. (1841); choral pieces; numerous songs.

BIBL.: O. Fouque, *M.I. G. d'après ses mémoires et sa correspondance* (Paris, 1880); V. S.[asov], ed., *Zapiski M.I. G. i perepiska evo s rodnïmi i druzyami* (M. I. G.'s Memoirs and Correspondence with his Relations and Friends; St. Petersburg, 1887); N. Findeisen, *M.I. G.: Evo zhizn i tvorcheskaya deyatelnost (M.I. G.: His Life and Creative Activity)* (St. Petersburg, 1896); M. Calvocoressi, *G.: Biographie critique* (Paris, 1911); M. Montagu-Nathan, *G.* (London, 1916); B. Asafiev, *M.I. G.* (Moscow, 1947); T. Livanova, ed., *M.I. G.: Sbornik materialov i statyey* (M.I. G.: Collection of Material and Articles; Moscow, 1950); A. Ossovsky, ed., *M.I. G.: Issledovaniya i materialiï* (M.I. G.: Researches and Material; Leningrad and Moscow, 1950); E. Kann-Novikova, *M.I. G.: Novïye materialï i dokumenti* (M.I. G.: New Material and Documents; Moscow, 1950–55); A. Orlova and B. Asafiev, eds., *Letopis zhizni i tvorchestva G.* (Record of G.'s Life and Work; Moscow, 1952; Eng. tr., 1988); V. Kiselyou et al., eds., *Pamyati G. 1857–1957: Issledovaniya i materialï* (In Memory of G. 1857–1957: Research and Material; Moscow, 1958); D. Brown, *G.: A Biographical and Critical Study* (London, 1974). —NS/LK/DM

Gliński, Mateusz, Polish conductor, musicologist, and composer; b. Warsaw, April 6, 1892; d. Welland, Ontario, Jan. 3, 1976. He studied at the Warsaw Cons. with Barcewicz (violin) and Statkowski (composition), and then took courses in Leipzig with Reger (composition), Riemann and Schering (musicology), and Nikisch (conducting). He went to St. Petersburg in 1914, where he studied composition with Glazunov and Steinberg, and conducting with Nikolai Tcherepnin. In 1918 he went to Warsaw; from 1924 to 1939 was ed. of the periodical *Muzyka*. At the outbreak of World War II in 1939, he went to Rome, where he engaged in various activities as music critic and ed. In 1949 he established in Rome the Istituto Internazionale Federico Chopin. From 1959 to 1965 he taught at Assumption Univ. in Windsor, Ontario. In 1965 he established the Niagara Sym. Orch., which he conducted. His works include an opera, *Orlotko*, after Rostand's play *L'Aiglon* (1918–27), a symphonic poem, *Wagram* (1932), choral works, songs, and piano pieces. He publ. a monograph on *Scriabin* (Warsaw, 1933), *Chopin's Letters to Delfina Potocka* (Windsor, 1961), in which he subscribes to the generally refuted belief that these letters, which came to light in 1945, are indeed genuine, and *Chopin the Unknown* (Windsor, 1963).—NS/LK/DM

Globokar, Vinko, French composer, trombonist, conductor, and teacher; b. Anderny (of Slovenian descent), July 7, 1934. He studied at the Ljubljana Academy of Music (1949–54) and at the Paris Cons. (1955–59), where he received diplomas in trombone and chamber music. He pursued private instruction with René Leibowitz (composition and conducting, 1960–63), André Hodier (counterpoint), and Luciano Berio (composition, 1965). In 1965–66 he was active at the Center for Creative and Performing Arts at the State Univ. of N.Y. at Buffalo. From 1967 to 1976 he was a prof. at the Cologne Hochschule für Musik. He was head of vocal and instrumental research at IRCAM in Paris from 1973 to 1979. In 1983 he became a teacher and conductor in Florence, where he conducted programs of contemporary music with the Orch. Giovanile Italiana. A vol. of his writings was publ. as *Laboratorium: Texte zur Musik 1967–1997* (Saarbrücken, 1997). Globokar's mastery of improvisation as a trombonist has been reflected in his output as a composer. He has embraced a utilitarian view in which nothing is off limits in the compositional process or the means of expression.

WORKS: ORCH.: *Étude pour Folklora I* for 19 Instruments (1968) and *II* for Orch. (Frankfurt am Main, Aug. 26, 1968); *La ronde* for 4 Melody Instruments (1970); *La tromba e mobile* for Harmony Orch. (1970; Zagreb, May 17, 1979); *Ausstrahlungen* for 20 Players and Reed Soloist (Royan, April 8, 1971); *Das orchester* for Orch. (Bonn, Dec. 1, 1974); *Standpunke* for Orch. and Chorus (Donaueschingen, Oct. 22, 1977); *Der Käfig* for 36 Players and Improvising Soloist (Lugano, Feb. 7, 1980); *Miserere* for Orch., 5 Narrators, and Jazz Trio (WDR, Cologne, Nov. 27, 1982); *Hallo? Do you hear me?* for Orch., Chorus, Jazz Quintet, and Tape (1986; simultaneous radio broadcast, Helsinki, Stockholm, and Oslo, March 9, 1987); *L'Armonia drammatica* for Orch., Chorus, Vocal Soloists, and Tenor Saxophone (1987–90; Berlin, March 11, 1995); *Labour* for Orch. (1992; Cologne, Feb. 12, 1993); *Masse, Macht und Individuum* for Orch. and 4 Instrumental Soloists (Donaueschingen, Oct. 20, 1995); *Zlom* for 26 Players (1997; Saarbrücken, May 23, 1998). **CHAMBER:** *Fluide* for 9 Winds and 3 Percussion (1967); *Discours I* for Trombone and 4 Percussion (1967), *II* for 5 Trombones or Trombone and Tape (1967–68), *III* for 5 Oboes or Oboe and Tape (1969), *IV* for 3 Clarinets (1973–74), *V* for 4 Saxophones (1981), *VI* for String Quartet (1982), *VII* for Brass Quintet (1987; Florence, Nov. 14, 1988), *VIII* for Wind Quintet (1989–90; Metz, Nov. 18, 1990) and *IX* for 2 Pianos (Saarbrücken, May 21, 1993); *Correspondences* for 4 Players (1969); *Atemstudie* for Oboe (1972); *Notes* for Piano (1972); *Vendre le vent* for Piano, Percussion, and 9 Winds (1972); *Limites* for Violin or Viola (1973); *Res/as/ex/ins- pirer* for Wind Instrument (1973); *Voix instrumentalisée* for Bass Clarinet (1973); *Laboratorium* for 11 Players (1973–85); *Dedoublement* for Clarinet (1975); *Monolith* for Flute (1976); *Tribadabum extensif sur rythme fantôme* for 3 Percussionists (Romans, July 7, 1981); *Corporel* for Percussion (1984); *Par une forêt de symbôles* for 6 Players (Nice, Feb. 5, 1986); *Freu(n)de* for 6 Cellos (Graz, Oct. 22, 1987); *Dos a dos* for 2 Brass or 2 Wind Instruments (WDR, Cologne, Jan. 24, 1988); *Eisenberg* for 16 Players (Metz, Nov. 18, 1990); *Pendulum* for Cello (Oslo, Oct. 22, 1991); *Elégie balkanique* for Flute, Guitar, and Percussion (1992; Hamburg, Jan. 28, 1993); *Dialog über Wasser* for Acoustic Guitar and Electric Guitar (WDR, Cologne, March 26, 1994); *Dialog über Luft* for Accordion (Rumligen, Aug. 27, 1994); *Dialog über Erde* for Percussion (Barossa Festival, Australia, Oct. 2, 1994); *Skelet* for 4 Players (Flanders, Sept. 9, 1995); *Oblak semen* for Trombone (Nus, July 10, 1996); *Jururitu-baïoka* for Tuba and Piano (1996; Guebwiller, Sept. 1997); *Pensée écartelée* for Percussionist (Whitehaven, May 31, 1997). **ELECTRONIC:** *Drama* for Piano, Percussion, and Electronics (1971); *Koexistenz* for 2 Cellos and Electronics (1976); *Preoccupation* for Organ and Tape (Munich, May 16, 1980); *Réalités/Augenblicke* for 5 Voices, Tape, and Film (Montreuil, June 4, 1984); *Introspection d'un tubiste* for Tuba, Electronics, Tape, Lights, and Scenery (Avignon, July 25, 1983); *Kolo* for Chorus, Trombone, and Electronics (Cologne, Nov. 27, 1988); *Ombre* for Singing Percussionist, Tape, and Rhythm Machine (Tokyo, May 27, 1989); *Prestop I* for Clarinet and Electronics (Vittasaari, July 27, 1991) and *II* for Trombone and Electronics (Ljubljana, June 6, 1991); *Blinde Zeit* for 7 Players and Tape (1993; Brest, May 10, 1994); *Contrepoint barbare* for Violin, Cello, Accordion, and Tape (1996; Lyons, March 16, 1997). **MIXED MEDIA:** *Vorstellung* for Soloist and Film (1976); *Carrousel* for 4 Voices, 16 Instruments, and Actors (1976). **Vocal:** *Accord* for Soprano and 5 Soloists (1966); *Voie* for Chorus, Orch., and Reciter (1966; Zagreb, May 16, 1967); *Tramdeutung* for Chorus and 4 Instruments (1967; Rotterdam, Oct. 7, 1968); Concerto grosso for 5 Instrumental Soloists, 23 Players, Chorus, and Amateur Vocal Group (1969–75); *Airs de voyages vers* *l'intérieur* for 8 Voices, Trombone, and Clarinet (1972); *Toucher* for Reciting Percussionist (1973); *Un jour comme un autre* for Soprano and 5 Instruments (1975); *Jenseits der Sicherheit* for Voice (1981); *Sternbild der Grenze* for 18 Players, Baritone, Mezzo-soprano, and 5 Voices (Metz, Nov. 21, 1985); *Letters* for Soprano and 5 Instruments (London, June 29, 1994); *Second Thoughts* for 4 Women's Voices (Bremen, Sept. 15, 1995); *Réponse a "letters" après "second thoughts"* for Soprano, Flute, Accordion, and Percussion (Hannover, May 23, 1997).—**NS/LK/DM**

Glock, Sir William (Frederick), English music critic and broadcasting administrator; b. London, May 3, 1908. He was an organ scholar at Gonville and Caius Coll., Cambridge (1919–26), then took piano lessons with Artur Schnabel in Berlin (1930–33). He made some appearances as a concert pianist, but devoted most of his time and effort to criticism. In 1934 he joined the staff of the *Observer*; served as its chief music critic from 1939 to 1945. In 1949 he founded the magazine *The Score*, and ed. it until 1961. In 1948 he established the Summer School of Music at Bryanston, Dorset, which relocated to Dartington Hall, Devon, in 1953; he continued as its director until 1979. In 1959 he assumed the important post of controller of music of the BBC, retaining it until 1973. From 1976 to 1984 he was artistic director of the Bath Festival. He publ. *Notes in Advance: An Autobiography in Music* (Oxford, 1991). In 1964 he was made a Commander of the Order of the British Empire, and was knighted in 1970.—**NS/LK/DM**

Glodeanu, Liviu, Romanian composer; b. Dârja, Aug. 6, 1938; d. Bucharest, March 31, 1978. He studied at the Cluj Cons. and the Bucharest Cons., his principal teachers being Comes, Negrea, and Mendelsohn. In his music, he respected Romanian musical tradition while subtly employing modern means of expression.

WORKS: DRAMATIC: Opera: *Ulysse* (1967–72; Cluj, April 25, 1973); *Zamolxe* (1968–69; Cluj, April 25, 1973). **ORCH.:** Concerto for Strings and Percussion (1959); Piano Concerto (1960; Cluj, April 7, 1962); Symphonic Movement (1961); Flute Concerto (1962; Cluj, Jan. 6, 1965); Violin Concerto (1964–66; Cluj, Feb. 5, 1972); *Studii* (1967; Bucharest, Feb. 14, 1968); *Ricercare* (Cluj, April 15, 1971); Symphonies for Winds (1971; Bucharest, Feb. 18, 1972); *Pintea Viteazul* (Pintea the Brave), symphonic poem (1976; Cluj, April 1, 1978); Organ Concerto (Bucharest, April 20, 1978). **CHAMBER:** Clarinet Sonata (1959); 2 string quartets (1959, 1970); Violin Sonatina (1961–63); Inventions for Wind Quintet and Percussion (1963); *Mélopée* for Flute, Clarinet, Cello, and Tape (1971). **Piano:** 2 sonatas (1958, 1963). **VOCAL:** 4 cantatas (1958, 1959, 1960, 1961); *Ulysse* for Soprano or Tenor and Orch. (1967); *Un pămînt numit România,* oratorio for Baritone, Reciter, Chorus, and Orch. (Bucharest, May 21, 1977).—**NS/LK/DM**

Glorieux, François, Belgian pianist, composer, teacher, and conductor; b. Courtrai, Aug. 27, 1932. He studied at the Royal Cons. in Ghent (graduated, 1953), then toured as a pianist. He taught chamber music at the Royal Cons. in Ghent, and was head of the summer courses in piano at the Royal Cons. in Antwerp. He became especially successful in presenting entertaining improvisational recitals in 5 languages; also conducted

his own 25- member orch. from 1979. His compositions run the gamut from serious works to popular scores and arrangements, the last including pieces by Stan Kenton and Michael Jackson. He also prepared a new version of the Belgian national anthem (1981).

WORKS: ORCH.: *Manhattan* for Piano and Orch. (1973–74; Antwerp, March 28, 1974); *Walking on the Street* for Big Band (1975); *Contrasts* for Tenor Trombone and Orch. (1988). **Ballet:** *L'Énigme* (1964); *Ritus paganus* (1972); *The Dream* (1982). **ELECTRONIC:** *Hello Mister Joplin* for Synthesizers (1982). **VOCAL:** *Glorieux Hymn* for Organ or Synthesizer, Brass, Percussion, and Chorus ad libitum (1988). **OTHER:** *Rip van Winkel,* television musical (1969); *Evolution* for African Percussion Instruments, Piano, Electric Guitar, and Drums (1975); *Tribute to Stan Kenton* for Piano, Flute, Brass, Bass Guitar, and Percussion (1976); *Fanfare for Europe* for Brass and Percussion Ensemble (1977–78); *In memoriam Stan Kenton* for Piano, Flute, Brass, Bass Guitar, and Percussion (1979); *Tribute to Michael Jackson,* instrumental suite in 8 parts (1984–88); *The Legend of Bruce Lee* for Flute, Synthesizers, Brass, and Percussion (1986); *6 Pieces* for 8 Trumpets (1988); other chamber works; film scores.—**NS/LK/DM**

Glossop, Peter, English baritone; b. Sheffield, July 6, 1928. He was a student of Mosley, Rich, and Hislop. In 1952 he joined the chorus of the Sadler's Wells Opera in London, where he then was a principal member of the company (1953–62). In 1961 he won the Sofia Competition and made his debut at London's Covent Garden as Demetrius in *A Midsummer Night's Dream*, appearing there regularly until 1966. On Aug. 18, 1967, he made his Metropolitan Opera debut as Rigoletto during the company's visit to Newport, R.I. His formal debut at the Metropolitan Opera in N.Y. took place as Scarpia on June 5, 1971. He also sang with other opera houses in Europe and North America. Among his other roles were Nabucco, Iago, Simone Boccanegra, Falstaff, Wozzeck, and Billy Budd.—**NS/LK/DM**

Glover, Jane (Alison), English conductor and musicologist; b. Helmsley, Yorkshire, May 13, 1949. She was educated at St. Hugh's Coll., Oxford (B.A., M.A.; Ph.D., 1978, with a diss. on Cavalli). She was a junior research fellow (1973–75), lecturer in music (1976–84), and senior research fellow (1982–91) at St. Hugh's Coll., Oxford. In 1975 she made her professional conducting debut at the Wexford Festival with her own performing ed. of Cavalli's *Eritrea*. She was a lecturer in music at St. Anne's Coll. (1976–80) and at Pembroke Coll. (1979–84) at Oxford, and from 1979 she served on the music faculty at the Univ. of Oxford. From 1982 to 1985 she was music director of the Glyndebourne Touring Opera. In 1983 she became principal conductor of the London Choral Soc. from 1984 to 1991 she was artistic director of the London Mozart Players. In 1988 she made her first appearance at London's Covent Garden conducting *Die Entführung aus dem Serail,* and then at the English National Opera in London in 1989 with *Don Giovanni.* From 1989 to 1996 she was principal conductor of the Huddersfield Choral Soc. In 1995 she conducted Britten's *War Requiem* at the London Promenade Concerts.

She was engaged to conduct *Orfeo* at the English National Opera in 1997. As a guest conductor, she appeared with orchs. and opera companies around the world.—NS/LK/DM

Glover, John William, Irish composer; b. Dublin, June 19, 1815; d. there, Dec. 18, 1899. He studied in Dublin, and from 1848 taught vocal music at the Normal Training School of the Irish National Education Board and was also director of music in the Roman Catholic procathedral. He was noted for his promotion of choral music in Ireland. He ed. Moore's *Irish Melodies* (1859).

WORKS: DRAMATIC: O p e r a : *The Deserted Village,* after Goldsmith (London, 1880); 2 Italian operas to librettos by Metastasio. VOCAL: *St. Patrick at Tara,* cantata (1870); *Erin's Matin Song* (1873); *100 years ago,* ode to Thomas Moore (1879). OTHER: Concertos; piano pieces; songs; church music. —NS/LK/DM

Glover, Sarah Anna, English piano pedagogue; b. Norwich, Nov. 13, 1786; d. Malvern, Oct. 20, 1867. She was the originator of the tonic sol-fa system of notation, a method later modified and developed by John Curwen. She devised a pictorial chart called the "Norwich Sol-fa Ladder." She wrote *Scheme to Render Psalmody Congregational* (1835; 2nd ed., 1850), *Manual of the Norwich Sol-fa System* (1845), and *Manual containing a Development of the Tetrachordal System* (1850).—NS/LK/DM

Glover, William Howard, English conductor and composer; b. London, June 6, 1819; d. N.Y., Oct. 28, 1875. He played the violin in the Lyceum Theater orch. in London, and conducted opera in Manchester, Liverpool, and London. In 1868 he went to N.Y., where he was conductor at Niblo's Garden until his death.

WORKS: DRAMATIC: O p e r a : *Ruy Blas* (London, Oct. 21, 1861). O p e r e t t a : *Aminta* (London, Jan. 26, 1852); *Once Too Often* (London, Jan. 20, 1862); *Palomita, or The Veiled Songstress* (publ. in N.Y., 1875). OTHER: *Tam o' Shanter,* cantata (London, July 4, 1855, Berlioz conducting); overtures; piano music; songs.—NS/LK/DM

Gluck, Alma (née **Reba Fiersohn**), famous Romanian-born American soprano; b. Iaşi, May 11, 1884; d. N.Y., Oct. 27, 1938. She was taken to the U.S. as an infant and was educated in N.Y. In 1902 she married Bernard Gluck; although they were divorced in 1912, she used the name Alma Gluck throughout her professional career. After vocal training with Arturo Buzzi-Peccia in N.Y. (1906–9), she made her first appearance with the Metropolitan Opera as Massenet's Sophie during the company's visit to the New Theatre on Nov. 16, 1909. Her formal debut at the Metropolitan Opera took place as the Spirit in Gluck's *Orfeo ed Euridice* on Dec. 23, 1909. She remained on its roster until 1912, winning acclaim in such roles as Mimi, Nedda, and Gilda. After additional training with Sembrich in Berlin, she devoted herself to a distinguished concert career. During the 1913–15 and 1916–18 seasons, she was engaged to sing at the Sunday Concerts at the Metropolitan Opera. She became one of the leading recording artists of her day, excelling in both serious and popular

genres. She had a daughter with Bernard Gluck, (Abigail) Marcia Davenport, who became a noted novelist and writer on music. In 1914 she married **Efrem Zimbalist.** Their son, Efrem Zimbalist Jr., became a well-known actor. His daughter, Stefanie Zimbalist, also followed a thespian bent.—NS/LK/DM

Gluck, Christoph Willibald, Ritter von, renowned German composer; b. Erasbach, near Weidenwang, July 2, 1714; d. Vienna, Nov. 15, 1787. His father was a forester at Erasbach until his appointment as forester to Prince Lobkowitz of Eisenberg about 1729. Gluck received his elementary instruction in the village schools at Kamnitz and Albersdorf near Komotau, where he also was taught singing and instrumental playing. Some biographers refer to his study at the Jesuit college at Komotau, but there is no documentary evidence to support this contention. In 1732 he went to Prague to complete his education, but it is doubtful that he took any courses at the Univ. He earned his living by playing violin and cello at rural dances in the area; also sang at various churches. He met Bohuslav Čzernohorsky, and it is probable that Gluck learned the methods of church music from him. He went to Vienna in 1736, and was chamber musician to young Prince Lobkowitz, son of the patron of Gluck's father. In 1737 he was taken to Milan by Prince Melzi; this Italian sojourn was of the greatest importance to Gluck's musical development. There he became a student of G.B. Sammartini and acquired a solid technique of composition in the Italian style. After 4 years of study, he brought out his first opera, *Artaserse,* to the text of the celebrated Metastasio; it was premiered in Milan (Dec. 26, 1741) with such success that he was immediately commissioned to write more operas. There followed *Demetrio,* or *Cleonice* (Venice, May 2, 1742), *Demofoonte* (Milan, Jan. 6, 1743), *Il Tigrane* (Crema, Sept. 9, 1743), *La Sofonisba,* or *Siface* (Milan, Jan. 13, 1744), *Ipermestra* (Venice, Nov. 21, 1744), *Poro* (Turin, Dec. 26, 1744), and *Ippolito,* or *Fedra* (Milan, Jan. 31, 1745). He also contributed separate numbers to several other operas produced in Italy. In 1745 he received an invitation to go to London; on his way, he visited Paris and met Rameau. He was commissioned by the Italian Opera of London to write 2 operas for the Haymarket Theatre, as a competitive endeavor to Handel's enterprise. The first of these works was *La Caduta dei giganti,* a tribute to the Duke of Cumberland on the defeat of the Pretender; it was premiered on Jan. 28, 1746; the second was a pasticcio, *Artamene,* in which Gluck used material from his previous operas; it was premiered on March 15, 1746. Ten days later, he appeared with Handel at a public concert, despite the current report in London society that Handel had declared that Gluck knew no more counterpoint than his cook (it should be added that a professional musician, Gustavus Waltz, was Handel's cook and valet at the time). On April 23, 1746, Gluck gave a demonstration in London, playing on the "glass harmonica." He left London late in 1746 when he received an engagement as conductor with Pietro Mingotti's traveling Italian opera company. He conducted in Hamburg, Leipzig, and Dresden; on June 29, 1747, he produced a "serenata," *Le nozze d'Ercole e d'Ebe,* to celebrate a royal wedding; it was performed at the Saxon court, in Pillnitz. He then went to Vienna, where he staged his opera *Semiramide riconosciuta*, after Metastasio (May 14, 1748). He then traveled to Copenhagen, where he produced a festive opera, *La Contesa dei Numi* (March 9, 1749), on the occasion of the birth of Prince Christian; his next productions (all to Metastasio's texts) were *Ezio* (Prague, 1750), *Issipile* (Prague, 1752), *La clemenza di Tito* (Naples, Nov. 4, 1752), *Le Cinesi* (Vienna, Sept. 24, 1754), *La danza* (Vienna, May 5, 1755), *L'innocenza giustificata* (Vienna, Dec. 8, 1755), *Antigono* (Rome, Feb. 9, 1756), and *Il Re pastore* (Vienna, Dec. 8, 1756).

In 1750 Gluck married Marianna Pergin, daughter of a Viennese merchant, and for several years afterward conducted operatic performances in Vienna. As French influence increased there, he wrote several entertainments to French texts, containing spoken dialogue, in the style of opéra-comique; of these, the most successful were *Le Cadi dupé* (Dec. 1761) and *La Rencontre imprévue* (Jan. 7, 1764; perf. also under the title *Les Pèlerins de la Mecque*, his most popular production in this genre). His greatest work of the Vienna period was *Orfeo ed Euridice*, to a libretto by Calzabigi (in a version for castrato contralto; Oct. 5, 1762, with the part of Orfeo sung by Gaetano Guadagni). Gluck revised it for a Paris performance, produced in French on Aug. 2, 1774, with Orfeo sung by a tenor. There followed another masterpiece, *Alceste* (Vienna, Dec. 16, 1767), also to Calzabigi's text. In the preface to *Alceste*, Gluck formulated his aesthetic credo, which elevated the dramatic meaning of musical stage plays above a mere striving for vocal effects: "I sought to reduce music to its true function, that of seconding poetry in order to strengthen the emotional expression and the impact of the dramatic situations without interrupting the action and without weakening it by superfluous ornaments." Among other productions of the Viennese period were *Il trionfo di Clelia* (Vienna, May 14, 1763), *Il Parnaso confuso* (Schönbrunn Palace, Jan. 24, 1765), *Il Telemacco* (Vienna, Jan. 30, 1765), and *Paride ed Elena* (Vienna, Nov. 30, 1770).

The success of his French operas in Vienna led Gluck to the decision to try his fortunes in Paris, yielding to the persuasion of Francois du Roullet, an attaché at the French embassy in Vienna, who also supplied him with his first libretto for a serious French opera, an adaptation of Racine's *Iphigénie en Aulide* (Paris, April 19, 1774). He set out for Paris early in 1773, preceded by declarations in the Paris press by du Roullet and Gluck himself, explaining in detail his ideas of dramatic music. These statements set off an intellectual battle in the Paris press and among musicians in general between the adherents of traditional Italian opera and Gluck's novel French opera. It reached an unprecedented degree of acrimony when the Italian composer Nicola Piccinni was engaged by the French court to write operas to French texts, in open competition with Gluck; intrigues multiplied, even though Marie Antoinette never wavered in her admiration for Gluck, who taught her singing and harpsichord playing. However, Gluck and Piccinni themselves never participated in the bitter polemics unleashed by their literary and musical partisans. The sensational successes of the French version of Gluck's

Orfeo and of *Alceste* were followed by the production of *Armide* (Sept. 23, 1777), which aroused great admiration. Then followed his masterpiece, *Iphigénie en Tauride* (May 17, 1779), which established Gluck's superiority to Piccinni, who was commissioned to write an opera on the same subject but failed to complete it in time. Gluck's last opera, *Echo et Narcisse* (Sept. 24, 1779), did not measure up to the excellence of his previous operas. By that time, his health had failed; he had several attacks of apoplexy, which resulted in partial paralysis. In the autumn of 1779 he returned to Vienna, where he lived as an invalid. His last work was a *De profundis* for Chorus and Orch., written 5 years before his death.

Besides his operas, Gluck wrote several ballets, of which *Don Juan* (Vienna, Oct. 17, 1761) was the most successful; he also wrote a cycle of 7 songs to words by Klopstock, 7 trio sonatas, several overtures, etc. Wagner made a complete revision of the score of *Iphigénie en Aulide*; this arrangement was so extensively used that a Wagnerized version of Gluck's music became the chief text for performances during the 19th century. A complete ed. of Gluck's works was begun by the Barenreiter Verlag in 1951. A thematic catalogue was publ. by A. Wotquenne (Leipzig, 1904; Ger. tr. with suppl. by J. Liebeskind). See also C. Hopkinson, *A Bibliography of the Printed Works of C.W. von Gluck, 1714–1787* (2nd ed., N.Y., 1967).

BIBL.: F. Riedel, *Über die Musik des R.s C. v.G.* (Vienna, 1775); G. Leblond, *Mémoires pour servir à l'histoire de la révolution opérée dans la musique par M. le Chevalier G.* (Paris, 1781; Ger. tr., 1823; 2nd ed., 1837); J. Siegmeyer, *Über den R. G. und seine Werke* (Berlin, 1837); E. Miel, *Notice sur G.* (Paris, 1840); A. Schmid, *C.W. R. v.G.* (Leipzig, 1854); W. Neumann, *C.W. G.* (Kassel, 1855); J. Baudoin, *L'Alceste de G.* (Paris, 1861); A. Marx, *G. und die Oper* (Berlin, 1863); L. Nohl, *G. und Wagner* (Munich, 1870); G. Desnoiresterres, *G. et Piccinni* (Paris, 1875); E. Thoinan, *Notes bibliographiques sur la guerre musicale des G.istes et Piccinnistes* (Paris, 1878); H. Barbedette, *G.* (Paris, 1882); A. Reissmann, *C.W. v.G.* (Berlin, 1882); K. Bitter, *Die Reform der Oper durch G. und Wagner* (Braunschweig, 1884); H. Welti, *G.* (Leipzig, 1888); E. Newman, *G. and the Opera* (London, 1895); J. d'Udine, *G.* (Paris, 1906); J. Tiersot, *G.* (Paris, 1910); G. Scuderi, *C. G.: Orfeo* (Milan, 1924); R. Haas, *G. und Durazzo im Burgtheater* (Vienna, 1925); L. de la Laurencie, *G., Orphee: Etude et analyse musicale* (Paris, 1934); M. Cooper, *G.* (London, 1935); A. Einstein, *G.* (London, 1936); P. Landormy, *G.* (Paris, 1941); A. Della Corte, *G.* (Turin, 1942); W. Brandl, *C.W. R. v.G.* (Wiesbaden, 1948); A. Della Corte, *G. e i suoi tempi* (Florence, 1948); J.-G. Prod'homme, *G.* (Paris, 1948; rev. ed., 1985, by J. Faquet); R. Gerber, *C.W. R. v.G.* (Potsdam, 1950); R. Tenschert, *C.W. G.: Der grosse Reformator der Oper* (Freiburg, 1951); A. Abert, *C.W. G.* (Munich, 1959); P. Howard, *G. and the Birth of Modern Opera* (N.Y., 1964); W. Vetter, *C.W. G.* (Leipzig, 1964); P. Howard, *C.W. G.: A Guide to Research* (N.Y., 1987); N. de Palézieux, *C.W. G.: Mit Selbstzeugnissen und Bilddokumenten* (Reinbek, 1988); G. Croll and M. Woitas, eds., *Kongressbericht G. in Wien: Wien, 12.–16. November 1987* (Kassel, 1989); K. Hortschansky, ed., *C.W. G. und die Opernreform* (Darmstadt, 1989); B. Brown, *G. and the French Theatre in Vienna* (Oxford, 1991); P. Howard, *G.: An Eighteenth-Century Portrait in Letters and Documents* (Oxford, 1995); G. Tocchini, *I fratelli d'Orfeo: G. e il teatro musicale massonico tra Vienna e Parigi* (Florence, 1998).—NS/LK/DM

Glyn, Margaret H(enrietta), English musicologist; b. Ewell, Surrey, Feb. 28, 1865; d. there, June 3, 1946. She studied in London under C.J. Frost and Yorke Trotter, and became an authority on keyboard music of the Tudor period. She ed. organ and virginal music by Byrd, Orlando Gibbons, John Bull, and other composers, and publ. *The Rhythmic Conception of Music* (1907), *Analysis of the Evolution of Musical Form* (1909), *About Elizabethan Virginal Music and Its Composers* (1924; 2nd ed., 1934), and *Theory of Musical Evolution* (1924). She also composed a number of works for organ. —NS/LK/DM

Glynne, Howell, Welsh bass; b. Swansea, Jan. 24, 1906; d. in an automobile accident in Toronto, Nov. 24, 1969. He labored as a miner while pursuing vocal training with Davies and Warlich. He gained a place in the chorus of the Carl Rosa Opera Co., and in 1931 made his operatic debut with it as Sparafucile. He was a member of the Sadler's Wells Opera in London (1946–50; 1956–63); from 1947 he also appeared at London's Covent Garden, and was active as a concert artist. In 1964 he joined the faculty of the Univ. of Toronto. Among his best roles were Bartolo, Varlaam, and Baron Ochs.—NS/LK/DM

Gnattali, Radamés, Brazilian pianist, conductor, arranger, and composer; b. Pôrto Alegre, Jan. 27, 1906; d. Rio de Janeiro, Feb. 3, 1988. He was a pupil of Fontainha at the Pôrto Alegre Cons. After obtaining his degree from the Instituto de Belas-Artes in Pôrto Alegre (1924), he studied harmony with França at the Escola Nacional de Música in Rio de Janeiro. For some years he was director of the Rádio Nacional in Rio de Janeiro, and then was active as a performer, arranger, and composer. From 1967 to 1970 he worked for TV Globo in São Paulo as an arranger and conductor. In 1945 he was made a member of the Academia Brasiliera de Música. From his earliest years as a composer he wrote works in which jazz and indigenous rhythms and harmonies predominated.

Works: *Rapsódia Brasileira* for Orch. (1931); 4 piano concertos (1934, 1936, 1960, 1967); Cello Concerto (1941); 14 *Brasilianas* for Various Instruments or Orch. (1944 et seq.); 3 violin concertos (1947, 1962, 1969); *Variações* for Piano, Violin, and Orch. (1949); *Concêrto romântico* No. 1 (1949) and No. 2 (1964) for Piano and Orch.; 3 *Concêrtos cariocas* for Soloists and Orch. (1950–70); 3 *Sinfonias populares* (1955, 1962, 1969); Harp Concerto (1958); 2 string quartets; piano pieces, including 2 sonatas. —NS/LK/DM

Gnazzo, Anthony J(oseph), American composer; b. Plainville, Conn., April 21, 1936. He studied theory at the Hartt School of Music in Hartford, Conn. (B.A., 1957), mathematics at the Univ. of Hartford (B.A., 1963), and theory with Krenek, Berger, and Shapero at Brandeis Univ. (M.F.A., 1965; Ph.D., 1970). He was an instructor in electronic system design at the Univ. of Toronto (1965–66), and director of the tape-music center at Mills Coll. in Oakland, Calif. (1967–69); in 1974 he became an audio technician at the electronic music studio at Calif. State Univ. at Hayward. His compositions include text-sound pieces, electronic scores, environmental pieces, and kinetic sculpture.

Works: VOCAL: *Eden* for Narrator and 7 Instruments (1964); *Music for Large Vocal Groups* (1966; rev. 1969); *The Question,* oratorio for Chorus (1969); *Prime Source Nos. 1–23* (1971–79); *End Sheets* for Mixed Voices (1986); *A:10* for Mixed Voices (1991). **Piano:** *Music* for 2 Pianos and Electronic Sound (1964); *Music* for Piano and Instruments (1974); *Riding the Thorny Shrub of Hearing* for Piano (1992). **Tape:** *Stereo Radio I* and *II* (1970), *III* (1971), *IV* and *V* (1972); *Music for Cello and Tape I* (1971) and *II* (1974); *The Art of Canning Music* (1976); *Image/Delusion* (1980); *2-Pulse* (1983); *Museum Piece 1* (1990). **Mixed Media:** *Theater Piece I-XXVI* (1967–71); *10 Pieces for Pauline Oliveros* (1969); *Compound Skull Fracture* for Actor, Tape, and Slides (1975; in collaboration with J. Cuno); *Waiting for JB* (1980); *Lontano* for Narrator, Tape, and Slides (1982); *Visionary Romp* (1986); *Terra, Terra, Terra* (1991). **OTHER:** *Chamber Music* for 13 Instruments (1965); *Cross-cut for Paul Hertelendy* for 3 Electric Saws and String Orch. (1969); *Tighten Up* for 4 Rock Groups (1970); incidental music; dance scores; film and television music.—NS/LK/DM

Gnecchi, Vittorio, Italian composer; b. Milan, July 17, 1876; d. there, Feb. 1, 1954. He studied at the Milan Cons. His opera *Cassandra* was performed at Bologna on Dec. 5, 1905. Some years later, after the premiere of Strauss's *Elektra,* there was considerable discussion when Giovanni Tebaldini pointed out the identity of some 50 themes in the two works ("Telepatia Musicale," *Rivista Musicale Italiana,* XVII, 1909). Gnecchi also wrote the operas *Virtu d'amore* (1896) and *La rosiera,* after a comedy by Alfred de Musset (in Ger., Gera, Feb. 12, 1927; in It., Trieste, Jan. 24, 1931).—NS/LK/DM

Gnecco, Francesco, Italian composer; b. Genoa, c. 1769; d. Milan, 1810 or 1811. He was maestro di cappella at Savona Cathedral. He composed some 25 operas, of which *La prova d'un opera seria* (Milan, 1805) was particularly successful. His other works included sacred music and chamber pieces.—LK/DM

Gnessin, Mikhail (Fabianovich), Russian composer and pedagogue; b. Rostov-na-Donu, Feb. 2, 1882; d. Moscow, May 5, 1957. After lessons with O. Fritch in Rostov, he studied with Rimsky-Korsakov and Liadov at the St. Petersburg Cons. (1901–5; 1906–9). He later went to Moscow, where he was a prof. of composition at the Gnessin Academy (from 1923) and at the Cons. (from 1925); after serving as a prof. at the Leningrad Cons. (1935–44), he returned to Moscow and was head of the Gnessin State Inst. for Musical Education (1944–51). Most of his works composed after 1914 reflect his interest in Jewish themes. He publ. his reflections and reminiscences of Rimsky-Korsakov in Moscow in 1956.

Works: DRAMATIC: Opera: *Yunost Avraama* (Abraham's Youth) (1921–23). **ORCH.:** *Iz Shelli* (1908); *Mourning Dances from "Elegy to Adonais"* (1917); Symphonic Fantasy (1919); *The Jewish Orchestra at the Ball in Nothingtown* (1926). **CHAMBER:** *Requiem* for Piano Quintet (1914); *Variations on a Jewish Theme* for String Quartet (1917); *Songs of a Knight Errant* for String Quartet and Harp (1917); Violin Sonata (1928);

Adïgeya for Clarinet, Horn, and Piano Quartet (1933); *Elegia-pastoral* for Piano Trio (1940); Piano Trio (1943); Sonata-Fantasia for Piano Quartet (1945); *Theme with Variations* for Cello and Piano (1953); piano pieces. **VOCAL:** *Vrubel* for Voice and Orch. (1911); *The Conqueror Worm* for Voice and Orch. (1913); *1905–1917* for Chorus and Orch. (1926); choruses; about 50 songs; folk song arrangements. **OTHER:** incidental music; film scores.—**NS/LK/DM**

Gobbaerts, Jean-Louis, Belgian pianist and composer; b. Antwerp, Sept. 28, 1835; d. Saint-Gilles, near Brussels, May 5, 1886. He studied at the Brussels Cons. He wrote more than 1,000 light piano pieces, some quite popular, using the pseudonyms "Streabbog" (Gobbaerts reversed), "Ludovic," and "Lévi." His *Little Fairy Waltz* was a favorite of President Harry S. Truman. —**NS/LK/DM**

Gobbi, Tito, famous Italian baritone; b. Bassano del Grappa, near Venice, Oct. 24, 1913; d. Rome, March 5, 1984. He received vocal lessons from Barone Zanchetta in Bassano del Grappa before going to Rome to train with Giulio Crimi, then made his operatic debut as Count Rodolfo in *La Sonnambula* in Gubbio (1935). During the 1935–36 season, he was an understudy at Milan's La Scala, where he made a fleeting stage appearance as the Herald in Pizzetti's *Oreseolo* (1935). In 1936 he won 1st prize in the male vocal section of the Vienna International Competition; then went to Rome, where he sang Germont *père* at the Teatro Adriano (1937); that same year he made his first appearance at the Teatro Reale, in the role of Lelio in Wolf-Ferrari's *Le Donne curiose*; after singing secondary roles there (1937–39), he became a principal member of the company; appeared as Ford in *Falstaff* during its visit to Berlin in 1941. He also sang on the Italian radio and made guest appearances with other Italian opera houses; in Rieti in 1940 he first essayed the role of Scarpia, which was to become his most celebrated characterization. In 1942 he made his formal debut at La Scala as Belcore in *L'elisir d'amore*. In 1947 he appeared as Rigoletto in Stockholm, and in 1948 he sang in concerts in London and also made his U.S. debut as Figaro in *Il Barbiere di Siviglia* at the San Francisco Opera. In 1950 he made his Covent Garden debut in London as Renato in *Un ballo in maschera*. He made his first appearance at the Chicago Opera as Rossini's Figaro in 1954. On Jan. 13, 1956, he made his Metropolitan Opera debut in N.Y. as Scarpia. In subsequent years, his engagements took him to most of the principal music centers of the world. He was also active as an opera producer from 1965. In 1979 he bade farewell to the operatic stage. He was the brother-in-law of **Boris Christoff**. Gobbi was acclaimed as an actor as well as a singer; his mastery extended to some 100 roles. He publ. *Tito Gobbi: My Life* (1979) and *Tito Gobbi and His World of Italian Opera* (1984).—**NS/LK/DM**

Gockley, (Richard) David, American opera administrator; b. Philadelphia, July 13, 1943. He was educated at Brown Univ. (B.A., 1965), Columbia Univ. (M.B.A., 1970), and the New England Cons. of Music in Boston. Following engagements as an opera singer, he was on the staff of the Santa Fe Opera (1968–70) and of Lincoln Center for the Performing Arts in N.Y. (1970). In 1970 he joined the Houston Grand Opera as its business manager. After serving as its associate director in 1971–72, he was its general director from 1972. Under his guidance, it became one of America's finest opera companies. Gockley's tenure has been especially noteworthy for his championship of contemporary works, among them Adams's *Nixon in China* (1987) and Wallace's *Harvey Milk* (1995). He also promoted educational programs, introduced the use of surtitles, and inaugurated the touring Tex. Opera Theater.—**NS/LK/DM**

Godard, Benjamin (Louis Paul), French composer; b. Paris, Aug. 18, 1849; d. Cannes, Jan. 10, 1895. He took violin lessons with Richard Hammer and Vieuxtemps, and also was a composition student of Reber at the Paris Cons. (1863). He first gained wide notice as a composer with his sym. *Le Tasse* (1878), which won the Prix de la Ville de Paris. Although he continued to write major orch. works, he sought fame as a theater composer. However, his operas proved unsuccessful with only the *Berceuse* from *Jocelyn* (1888) remaining popular after his death. In 1887 he became prof. of the instrumental ensemble class at the Paris Cons. He was made a Chevalier of the Légion d'honneur in 1889.

WORKS: DRAMATIC: O p e r a : *Les Guelfes* (1880–82; Rouen, Jan. 17, 1902); *Pedro de Zalamea* (Antwerp, Jan. 31, 1884); *Jocelyn* (Brussels, Feb. 25, 1888); *Dante et Béatrice* (Paris, May 13, 1890); *La vivandiere* (unfinished; orchestration completed by P. Vidal; Paris, April 1, 1895). **ORCH.:** 2 piano concertos (1870, 1899); *Scènes poétiques* (1879); *Introduction and Allegro* for Piano and Orch. (1881); 2 violin concertos: No. 1, *Concerto romantique* (1887) and No. 2 (1892). **S y m s . :** *Le Tasse* for Soloists, Chorus, and Orch. (1878); No. 1 (n.d.); No. 2 (1880); *Symphonie gothique* (1883); *Symphonie orientale* (1884); *Symphonie descriptive* (n.d.); *Symphonie-ballet* (1882). **CHAMBER:** 5 violin sonatas (1865, 1875, 1878, 1881, n.d.); 2 piano trios (1880, 1884); 3 string quartets (1883, 1884, 1893); Cello Sonata (1887). **OTHER:** Numerous solo piano pieces and over 100 songs.

BIBL.: M. Clerjot, *B. G.* (Paris, 1902); M. Clavié, *B. G.* (Paris, 1906).—**NS/LK/DM**

Goddard, Arabella, French pianist of English descent; b. St.- Servan, St.-Malo, Jan. 12, 1836; d. Boulogne, April 6, 1922. She began study with Kalkbrenner in Paris at the age of 6, and made her first public appearance at the age of 14 in London at a Grand National Concert. After 3 years of study with the critic J.W. Davison (whom she married in 1859), she made tours of Europe. She later toured the U.S., Australia, and India (1872–76), retiring in 1882. She was particularly known for her performances of the late Beethoven sonatas at her recitals in London.—**NS/LK/DM**

Godefroid, (Dieudonné Joseph Guillaume) Félix, Belgian harpist and composer; b. Namur, July 24, 1818; d. Villers-sur-Mer, Calvados, July 12, 1897. He studied piano and solfège at his father's music school in Boulogne. After training in harp with Nadermann at the Paris Cons. (2nd prix, 1835), he completed his studies with Labarre and Parish-Alvars. He gained prominence as a harp virtuoso via tours of Germany, Spain, England, Holland, and other nations. He wrote much music for harp and a method, *Mes exercices*. He also composed an opera, *La harpe d'or* (Paris, 1858).—LK/DM

Godfrey, Dan(iel), English bandmaster, father of **Sir Dan(iel Eyers) Godfrey;** b. Westminster, Sept. 4, 1831; d. Beeston, Nottinghamshire, June 30, 1903. He was a pupil and Fellow of the Royal Academy of Music, in which he was later a prof. of military music. He was also bandmaster of the Grenadier Guards from 1856. He traveled with his band in the U.S. in 1872, retiring in 1896. He wrote popular waltzes (*Mabel, Guards, Hilda,* etc.), and made many arrangements for military band. —NS/LK/DM

Godfrey, Isidore, English conductor; b. London, Sept. 27, 1900; d. Sussex, Sept. 12, 1977. He was educated at the Guildhall School of Music in London. In 1925 he joined the D'Oyly Carte Opera Co. as a conductor, and from 1929 to 1968 served as its music director. In 1965 he was named an Officer of the Order of the British Empire.—NS/LK/DM

Godfrey, Sir Dan(iel Eyers), English conductor, son of **Dan(iel) Godfrey;** b. London, June 20, 1868; d. Bournemouth, July 20, 1939. He studied at the Royal Coll. of Music. He was conductor of the London Military Band (a civilian group actually) from 1889 to 1891. In 1893 he settled in Bournemouth as conductor of the Winter Gardens orch. He founded the Sym. Concerts there in 1894, and directed them until his retirement in 1934. He brought the concerts to a high level, and used all his efforts to promote the works of British composers. He was knighted in 1922 for his services to orch. music. He wrote his memoirs, *Memories and Music* (London, 1924).—NS/LK/DM

Godowsky, Leopold, famous Polish-born American pianist and pedagogue; b. Soshly, near Vilnius, Feb. 13, 1870; d. N.Y., Nov. 21, 1938. He played in public as a child in Russia. At the age of 14, he was sent to Berlin to study at the Hochschule für Musik, but after a few months there, proceeded to the U.S. He gave his first American concert in Boston on Dec. 7, 1884, and in 1885 he played engagements at the N.Y. Casino; in 1886, toured Canada with Ovide Musin. He then played in society salons in London and Paris, and became a protégé of Saint-Saëns. In 1890 he joined the faculty of the N.Y. Coll. of Music; in 1891 he became a naturalized American citizen. He taught at the Broad St. Cons. in Philadelphia (1894–95) and was head of the piano dept. of the Chicago Cons. (1895–1900). He then embarked on a European tour, giving a highly successful concert in Berlin (Dec. 6, 1900), where he remained as a teacher; from 1909 to 1914 he conducted a masterclass at the Vienna Academy of Music; made tours in the U.S. from 1912 to 1914, and settled permanently in the U.S. at the outbreak of World War I. After the war, he toured in Europe, South America, and Asia. In 1930 he suffered a stroke during a recording session. His subsequent career was greatly restricted. Godowsky was one of the outstanding masters of the piano; possessing a scientifically inclined mind, he developed a method of "weight and relaxation" applying it to his own playing, he became an outstanding technician of his instrument, extending the potentialities of piano technique to the utmost, with particular attention to the left hand. He wrote numerous piano compositions of transcendental difficulty, yet entirely pianistic in style; also arranged works by Weber, Brahms, and Johann Strauss. Particularly remarkable are his 53 studies on Chopin's études, combining Chopin's themes in ingenious counterpoint; among his original works, the most interesting are *Triakontameron* (30 pieces; 1920; no. 11 is the well-known *Alt Wien*) and *Java Suite* (12 pieces; 1924–25). He also wrote simple pedagogical pieces, e.g., a set of *46 Miniatures* for Piano, 4-hands, in which the pupil is given a part within the compass of 5 notes only (1918); ed. piano studies by Czerny, Heller, Köhler et al.; composed music for the left hand alone (*6 Waltz Poems, Prelude and Fugue,* etc.); and publ. an essay, "Piano Music for the Left Hand," *Musical Quarterly* (July 1935).

BIBL.: J. Nicholas, *G.—The Pianists' Pianist: A Biography of L. G.* (Hexham, 1989).—NS/LK/DM

Godron, Hugo, Dutch composer; b. Amsterdam, Nov. 22, 1900; d. Zoelmond, Dec. 6, 1971. He studied violin at the music school in Bussum, and composition with Sem Dresden in Amsterdam (1921–22). He taught composition and harmony at music schools in Bussum, Hilversum, and Utrecht; from 1939 to 1969 he was active as a sound engineer in Hilversum and Amsterdam. His music is generally joyful, almost playful, in character.

WORKS: ORCH.: Sinfonietta for Small Orch. (1932–33); *7 Miniatures* for Piano and Strings (1933); Piano Concerto (1938–39); *Sérénade occidentale* (1942–48); *Amabile Suite* for Clarinet, Piano, and Strings (1943); Concerto Grosso for Clarinet and Small Orch. (1944–45); *Concert Suite* for Piano and Strings (1945–47); *Miniatuur symphonie* (1949–50; orchestration of *Gardenia Suite* for Piano); 2 Polkas (1950–51; 1957–58); Suite for Harpsichord and Strings (1950); *Hommage à Chabrier* (1950–51); *Hommages classiques* for Flute, Piano, and Strings (1950); *Concerto for Orchestra* (1953–54); *Variations traditionnelles* for Small Orch. (1954); *Promenades*, suite (1954–55); *4 impresses* for Chamber Orch. (1956–57); *Aubade Gaudeamus*, suite for Piano, Strings, and Percussion (1966–68); *Hommage à Bizet* for Small Orch. (1971). **CHAMBER:** String Trio (1937); *Serenade* for Piano and Wind Quintet (1947); Sonatina for Flute, Violin, Viola, and Piano (1948); Piano Trio (1948); *Sonata facile* for Cello and Piano (1950); *Divertimento* for 2 Violins and Piano (1956); *Nouvelles* for Piano Trio (1963); *Quatuor bohémien* for Piano Quartet (1970); piano pieces. **OTHER:** *Assepoes* (radio fairy tale, Cinderella; 1946–47).—NS/LK/DM

Godwin, Joscelyn, English-born American musicologist, composer, and harpsichordist; b. Kelmscott, Jan. 16, 1945. He was educated at Christ Church Cathedral Choir School, Oxford (1952–58), Radley Coll. (1958–62), and Magdalene Coll., Cambridge (B.A., 1965; M.A., 1968). He became a Fellow of the Royal Coll. of Organists in 1965, and also studied at Cornell Univ. (Ph.D., 1969, with the diss. *The Music of Henry Cowell*).

He was an instructor in music at Cleveland State Univ. (1969–71), and then joined the faculty of Colgate Univ. (1982). He has lectured widely in the U.S. and the United Kingdom. In 1980 he became a naturalized American citizen. While his compositions are occasionally performed, and he himself performs frequently as a conductor and an instrumentalist (most recently the harpsichord), he is best known as the author, editor, and translator of numerous books and articles dealing with mysticism and ancient philosophies in relation to music.

WRITINGS: *Music, Mysticism and Magic: A Sourcebook* (London, 1986); *Harmonies of Heaven and Earth: The Spiritual Dimension of Music from Antiquity to the Avant-Garde* (London, 1987); *The Mystery of the Seven Vowels in Theory and Practice* (Grand Rapids, Mich., 1991); *Music and the Occult: French Musical Philosophies 1750–1950* (Rochester, N.Y., 1995); with M. Embach, *Johann Friedrich Von Dalberg (1760–1812): Schriftseller, Musiker, Domherr* (Mainz, 1998).—NS/LK/DM

Goeb, Roger (John),
American composer; b. Cherokee, Iowa, Oct. 9, 1914. He studied agriculture at the Univ. of Wisc., graduating in 1936, and in 1938 he went to Paris, where he took lessons with Boulanger at the École Normal de Musique. Returning to America in 1939, he was a pupil of Luening, pursued graduate work at N.Y.U., was a pupil of Elwell at the Cleveland Inst. of Music (M.Mus., 1942), and obtained his Ph.D. at the Univ. of Iowa (1945). He occupied teaching posts at the Univ. of Okla. (1942–44), Iowa State Univ. (1944–45), and the Juilliard School of Music (1947–50). He held 2 Guggenheim fellowships (1950, 1952); taught music at Stanford Univ. (1954–55); then was executive secretary of the American Composers' Alliance (1956–62). Personal misfortunes (both his wife and his son died of multiple sclerosis) caused him to interrupt his professional activities in 1964, but he resumed composition in 1979.

WORKS: ORCH.: 6 syms.: No. 1 (1941; withdrawn), No. 2 (1945), No. 3 (1950; N.Y., April 3, 1952, Stokowski conducting), No. 4 (1955; Pittsburgh, Feb. 24, 1956), No. 5 (1981) and No. 6 (1987); *Lyric Piece* for Trumpet and Orch. (1942); *Prairie Songs* for Small Orch. (1947); *Fantasy* for Oboe and Strings (1947); 4 Concertantes: No. 1 for Flute, Oboe, Clarinet, and Strings (1948), No. 2 for Bassoon or Cello and Strings (1950), No. 3 for Viola and Orch. (1951), and No. 4 for Clarinet, Timpani, 2 Percussion, Piano, and Strings (1951); *Romanza* for Strings (1948); 2 concertinos: No. 1 (1949) and No. 2 (Louisville, Nov. 28, 1956); *5 American Dances* (1952; 1–3 for Strings; 4 and 5 for Orch.); Violin Concerto (1953; N.Y., Feb. 1954); Piano Concerto (1954); 2 Sinfonias (1957, 1962); *Enconium* (1958); *Iowa Concerto* for Small Orch. (1959); *Divertissement* for Strings (1982); *Memorial* (1982); *Caprice* (1982); *Fantasia* (1983); *Essay* (1984); *Gambol* (1984). **CHAMBER:** 4 string quartets (1942, withdrawn; 1948; 1954; 1980); Sonata for Solo Viola (1942); Suite for Woodwind Trio (1946); Brass Septet (1949); Quintet for Trombone and String Quartet (1949); 4 wind quintets (1949, 1955, 1980, 1982); *2 Divertimenti* for Flute (1950); *3 Processionals* for Organ and Brass Quintet (1951); Piano Quintet (1955); Sonata for Solo Violin (1957); *Running Colors* for String Quartet (1961); Quartet for Oboe and String Trio (1964); Trio for Horn, Trumpet, and Trombone (1979); Quintet for Cello and String Quartet (1980); Octet for Clarinet, Bassoon, Horn, and Strings (1980); Flute Quartet (1983); *Black on White* for Clarinet and Strings (1985); *Nuances* for Clarinet and Viola (1986).—NS/LK/DM

Goebel, Reinhard,
esteemed German violinist; b. Siegen, Westphalia, July 31, 1952. He commenced violin lessons in his youth, receiving principal training in Cologne and Amsterdam from Maier, Gawriloff, and Leonhardt. In 1973 a passion for early music led him to organize the Musica Antiqua Köln, an ensemble dedicated to performing works on original instruments or modern replicas; after a major tour of Europe in 1978, the ensemble toured widely in North and South America, the Far East, and Australia, acquiring an international reputation through its exacting but spirited performances. Goebel plays a Jacobus Stainer violin built in 1665.—NS/LK/DM

Goedike, Alexander,
Russian pianist, pedagogue, and composer of German descent; b. Moscow, March 4, 1877; d. there, July 9, 1957. He studied with Safonov and G. Pabst (piano) and Arensky (composition) at the Moscow Cons. (graduated, 1898), where he was a prof. of piano from 1909.

WORKS: DRAMATIC: Opera: *Virineya* (1915); *At the Crossing* (1933); *Jacquerie* (1937); *Macbeth* (1944). **ORCH.:** Piano Concerto (1900); 3 syms. (1903, 1905, 1922); Organ Concerto (1929); Horn Concerto (1929); Trumpet Concerto (1930); Violin Concerto (1951). **CHAMBER:** Piano Quintet; 2 piano trios; String Quartet. **OTHER:** Pedagogic pieces for Piano.

BIBL.: V. Yakovlev, *A. G.* (Moscow, 1927); K. Adzhemov, *A. G.* (Moscow, 1960).—NS/LK/DM

Goehr, (Peter) Alexander,
prominent German-born English composer and teacher, son of **Walter Goehr;** b. Berlin, Aug. 10, 1932. He was a student of Richard Hall at the Royal Manchester Coll. of Music (1952–55), and then of Messiaen and Loriod in Paris (1955–56). After lecturing at Morley Coll. in London (1955–57), he was a music assistant at the BBC (1960–68). In 1968–69 he served as composer-in-residence at the New England Cons. of Music in Boston, and then was an assoc. prof. of music at Yale Univ. in 1969–70. From 1971 to 1976 he was the West Riding prof. of music at the Univ. of Leeds, and in 1975 he also was artistic director of the Leeds Festival. He subsequently was prof. of music at the Univ. of Cambridge from 1976 until his retirement in 1999. In 1980 he was a visiting prof. at the Beijing Cons. of Music. In 1989 he was made an honorary member of the American Academy and Inst. of Arts and Letters. He publ. *Finding the Key: Selecting Writings of Alexander Goehr* (London, 1998). Goehr's oeuvre has been notably influenced by Schoenberg, although he has succeeded in developing an individual mode of expression utilizing serial, tonal, and modal means.

WORKS: DRAMATIC: Ballet: *La Belle Dame Sans Merci* (1958). **Opera:** *Arden muss Sterben* or *Arden Must Die* (1966; Hamburg, March 5, 1967); *Behold the Sun* or *Die Wiedertäufer* (1981–84; Duisburg, April 19, 1985); *Arianna* (1994–95; London, Sept. 15, 1995). **Stage:** Music theater triptych consisting of *Naboth's Vineyard* (London, July 16, 1968), *Shadowplay* (London, July 8, 1970) and *Sonata about Jerusalem* (1970; Tel Aviv, Jan. 1971); *Kantan and Damask Drum* (Dortmund, Sept. 1999). **ORCH.:** *Fantasia* (1954; rev. 1959); *Hecuba's Lament* (1959–61; London, Aug. 24, 1961); Violin Concerto (1961–62; Cheltenham,

July 2, 1962); *Little Symphony* for Small Orch. (York, July 7, 1963); *Little Music* for Strings (Lucerne, Sept. 7, 1963); *Pastorals* (Donaueschingen, Oct. 1965); *3 Pieces from Arden Must Die* for Wind Band, Harp, and Percussion (1967; BBC Radio 3, Jan. 12, 1969); *Romanza* for Cello and Orch. (Brighton, April 28, 1968); *Konzertstück* for Piano and Small Orch. (Sydney, April 1969); Sym. in 1 Movement (1969; London, May 9, 1970; rev. 1981); Piano Concerto (Brighton, May 14, 1972); *Metamorphosis/Dance* (1973–74; London, Nov. 17, 1974); *Fugue on the Notes of the Fourth Psalm* for Strings (London, July 8, 1976); *Romanza on the Notes of the Fourth Psalm* for 2 Violins, 2 Violas Concertante, and Strings (1977; Edinburgh, Feb. 20, 1978); *Sinfonia* for Chamber Orch. (1979; London, Nov. 20, 1980); *Deux Etudes* (1980–81; Glasgow, Sept. 17, 1981); *Sym. with Chaconne* (1985–86; Manchester, Jan. 13, 1987); *Still Lands* for Small Orch. (1988–90; Peterborough, July 9, 1994); *Colossos or Panic: Symphonic Fragment after Goya* (1991–92; Boston, April 15, 1993); *Cambridge Hocket* for 4 Horns and Orch. (Cambridge, Nov. 6, 1993); *Schlussgesang* for Viola and Orch. (1996; Aldeburgh, June 21, 1997). **CHAMBER:** *Fantasias* for Clarinet and Piano (1954; London, Jan. 1956); 4 string quartets: No. 1 (1956–57; rev. version, London, June 15, 1988), No. 2 (Bristol, Oct. 26, 1967), No. 3 (1975–76; London, June 28, 1976) and No. 4, *In Memoriam John Ogdon* (Iowa City, Oct. 8, 1990); *Variations* for Flute and Piano (Hovingham, June 1959); Suite for Flute, Clarinet, Horn, Harp, Violin or Viola and Cello (Aldeburgh, June 29, 1961); Piano Trio (Bath, June 17, 1966); *Paraphrase on the Dramatic Madrigal Il Combattimento di Tancredi e Clorinda by Monteverdi* for Clarinet (Edinburgh, Aug. 27, 1969); *Concerto for Eleven* (1970; Brussels, Jan. 25, 1971); *Chaconne* for Winds (Leeds, Nov. 3, 1974); *Lyric Pieces* for Winds and Double Bass (London, Nov. 15, 1974); *Prelude and Fugue* for 3 Clarinets (Edinburgh, Sept. 1978); Cello Sonata (1984; BBC, 1986); *...a musical offering (J.S. B. 1985)...* for 14 Players (Edinburgh, Aug. 19, 1985); *Variations on Bach's Sarabande from the English Suite in E minor* for Winds and Timpani (1990; Huddersfield, Nov. 23, 1993); *Uninterrupted Movement* for Solo Cello, 4 Cellos, and Others (1995; Manchester, May 2, 1996); Quintet, *Five Objects Darkly*, for Bass Clarinet, Horn, Violin, Viola and Piano (1996; Los Angeles, Feb. 6, 1997); *En l'air, surterre* for Viola and Piano (1998); *Idées Fixes* for Chamber Ensemble (1998); Duos for 2 Violas, and Viola and Violin (1999). **P i a n o :** Sonata (1951–52); *Capriccio* (Cologne, April 1958); *3 Pieces* (1964; London, April 11, 1965); *Nonomiya* (Macclesfield, May 12, 1969); *...in real time* (1988–95). **VOCAL:** *The Deluge* cantata for Soprano, Contralto and Instrumental Ensemble (1957–58; London, Feb. 1959); *4 Songs from the Japanese* for Mezzo-soprano and Piano (1959; also for Mezzo-soprano and Orch., Cheltenham, July 1960); *Sutter's Gold*, cantata for Bass, Chorus, and Orch. (1959–60); 2 Choruses (London, Nov. 1962); *A Little Cantata of Proverbs* (1962); *In Theresienstadt* for Mezzo-soprano and Piano (1962–64; BBC Radio 3, March 27, 1992); *Virtutes* 9 songs and melodramas for Speaker, Chorus, and Instruments (Whitley, Surrey, May 29, 1963); *5 Poems and an Epigram of William Blake* for Chorus and Trumpet (London, July 14, 1964); *Warngedichte* for Mezzo-soprano and Piano (1966–67); *Psalm IV* for Soprano, Alto, Women's Chorus, Viola, and Organ (London, July 8, 1976); *Babylon the Great is Fallen* for Chorus and Orch. (London, Dec. 12, 1979); *Das Gesetz der Quadrille* for Mezzo-soprano or Baritone and Piano (Norwich, Oct. 18, 1979); *Behold the Sun* concert aria for High Soprano, Vibraphone Obbligato and Chamber Ensemble (1981; London, Feb. 9, 1982); *2 Imitations of Baudelaire* for Chorus (1985; 1st complete perf., London, June 29, 1987); *Eve Dreams in Paradise* for Mezzo-soprano, Tenor and Orch. (1987–88; Birmingham, March 14, 1989); *Carol for St. Steven* for

Chorus (Cambridge, Dec. 24, 1989); *Sing, Ariel* for Mezzo-soprano, 2 Sopranos and 5 Instruments (1989–90; Aldeburgh, June 23, 1990); *The Mouse Metamorphosed into a Maid* for Voice (1991; Columbia, S.C., April 12, 1992); *The Death of Moses* for Soprano, Contralto or Male Alto, Tenor, Baritone, Bass, Chorus, Children's Chorus or Semi-chorus of Sopranos and Altos and 13 Instrumentalists (1991–92; Seville, July 31, 1992); *I Said I Will Take Heed (Psalm 39),* Double Chorus and Wind Ensemble (1992–93; Amsterdam, May 14, 1993); *Lamento of Arianna* for Soprano and Ensemble, after Monteverdi (1994–95); *Cori di Pescatori*, 4 madrigals for 5 Men's Voices, after *Arianna* (1994–95); *Arianna Abbandonata* for Tenor and Guitar, after *Arianna* (1994–96); 3 Songs for Voice, Clarinet and Viola (London, July 14, 1996).

BIBL.: B. Northcott, ed., *The Music of A. G.: Interviews and Articles* (London, 1980).—**NS/LK/DM**

Goehr, Walter, German-born English conductor and composer, father of **(Peter) Alexander Goehr;** b. Berlin, May 28, 1903; d. Sheffield, Dec. 4, 1960. He studied theory with Schoenberg in Berlin, then was a conductor with the Berlin Radio (1925–31). In 1933 he went to England and was music director of the Columbia Graphophone Co. until 1939. From 1945 to 1948 he was conductor of the BBC Theatre Orch., and also conductor of the Morley Coll. concerts from 1943 until his death. He composed theater, radio, and film scores.—**NS/LK/DM**

Goepp, Philip H(enry), American organist, writer on music, teacher, and composer; b. N.Y., June 23, 1864; d. Philadelphia, Aug. 25, 1936. He studied in Germany (1872–77) and with J.K. Paine at Harvard Univ. (B.A., 1884). He then studied law at the Univ. of Pa. (graduated, 1888), and completed his musical training with David D. Wood. He was organist at Philadelphia's 1st Unitarian Church and a teacher of theory at Temple Univ.; he was also program annotator of the Philadelphia Orch. (1900–1921). He publ. *Annals of Music in Philadelphia* (1896) and *Symphonies and Their Meaning* (3 vols., 1898, 1902, 1913). Among his works were orch. music, chamber pieces, piano music, organ pieces, choral works, and songs.—**NS/LK/DM**

Goerne, Matthias, admired German baritone; b. Weimar, March 31, 1967. He sang in the children's choir of the Chemnitz Civic Opera before pursuing vocal studies with Hans Joachim Beyer in Leipzig (1985–91), Fischer-Dieskau in Berlin (1988–93), and Schwarzkopf in Zürich (1989–91). In 1987 he began his career as a soloist with orchs. and as a recitalist in Germany. Following an engagement as Lazarus in the *St. Matthew Passion* with the Leipzig Gewandhaus Orch. under Masur's direction in 1990, he appeared with many major orchs. In 1992 he made his operatic debut in the title role of Henze's *Der Prinz von Homburg* in Cologne. From 1993 to 1995 he sang at the Dresden State Opera. In 1994 he made his London recital debut at Wigmore Hall. He made his U.S. debut as a soloist as Christus in the *St. John Passion* with the Philadelphia Orch. under Rilling's direction in 1996, the same year he made his N.Y. recital debut at the Frick Collection. In 1997 he made his first appearance at the Salzburg Festival as Papageno. In 1998 he sang in recitals at the Edinburgh Festival and at N.Y.'s Alice Tully Hall, and on Dec. 14th of that year he made his Metropolitan Opera debut in N.Y. as Papageno. He sang *Die Winterreise* and *Schwanengesang* with Brendel as his accompanist at N.Y.'s Carnegie Hall in 1999, the same year he portrayed Wozzeck at the Zürich Opera. In addition to his esteemed interpretations of Schubert's lieder, Goerne has also won critical accolades for his Schumann, Wolf, and Mahler.—NS/LK/DM

Goethals, Lucien (Gustave Georges),

Belgian composer and teacher; b. Ghent, June 26, 1931. He studied with Rosseau at the Royal Cons. in Ghent (1947–56) and took courses at the Ghent Inst. for Psycho-Acoustics and Electronic Music at the Univ. of Ghent; he also worked in an electronic studio in Germany. In 1963 he organized the Belgian contemporary music group Spectra. From 1971 to 1991 he taught at the Ghent Cons. In 1981 he was awarded the Culture Prize of the City of Ghent. His compositions explore the problems of modernistic constructivism.

WORKS: DRAMATIC: Mixed Media: *Vensters*, audio-visual play for 2 Narrators, Cello, Piano, Percussion, Recorded Sounds, and Film Projections (Brussels, Sept. 16, 1967); *Hé*, audio-visual production for 10 Instruments, Tapes, and Film Projections (1971; in collaboration with H. Sabbe and K. Goeyvaerts). **ORCH.:** *5 Impromptus* for Chamber Orch. (1959); *Dialogos* for Strings, Wind Quintet, 2 String Quintets, Percussion, and Tape (1963); *Dialogos Suite* for Chamber Orch. (1963); *Sinfonia in Gris Mayor* for 2 Orchs., Percussion, and Tape (Brussels, June 14, 1966); *Enteuxis* for Strings, Oboe, and Flute (1968); *Concerto for Orchestra* (1972); *4 Pieces* (1976); Concerto for 2 Clarinets and Orch. (1980–83). **CHAMBER:** Violin Sonata (1959); *Rituele Suite* for Wind Quintet (1959); *Endomorfie I* for Violin, Piano and Tape (1964) and *II* for Flute, Oboe, Clarinet, Bassoon, 2 Trumpets, Trombone and Tuba (1964); *Cellotape* for Cello, Piano, Tape and Contact Microphone (1965); *Movimientos y acciones* for Flute, Clarinet, String Quartet, Chromatic Harp and Percussion (1965); *Mouvement* for String Quartet (1967); *Quebraduras* for Piano Quartet (1969); *Ensimismamientos* for Violin, Cello, Bassoon, Piano and Tape (1969); *Superposiciones* for Violin, Cello, Bassoon and Piano (1970); *Suma* for an undefined number of Instruments and Tape (1971); *3 paisajes sonores* for Flute, Oboe, Cello, Trombone, Double Bass and Harpsichord (1973); *Diferencias* for 10 Instruments (1974); *Musica con cantus firmus triste* for Flute, Violin, Viola and Cello (1978); *Rituel* for Cheng, Percussion and Tape (1979); Trio for Flute, Bass Clarinet and Piano (1980); *Beweging* for Clarinet Quartet (1981); *Duelos* for Xylorimba and Percussion (1984); piano pieces; organ music. **OTHER:** Vocal pieces; solo tape works.—NS/LK/DM

Goethe, Johann Wolfgang von, great German

man of letters; b. Frankfurt am Main, Aug. 28, 1749; d. Weimar, March 22, 1832. For his ideas on music, consult the complete critical ed. of his works by the Deutschen Akademie der Wissenschaften zu Berlin (1952 et seq.).

BIBL.: K. Mendelssohn-Bartholdy, *G. und Felix Mendelssohn-Bartholdy* (Leipzig, 1871; Eng. tr., 2nd ed., 1874); A. Julien, *G. et la musique: Ses jugements, son influence, les oeuvres qu'il a inspirées* (Paris, 1880); J. von Wasielewski, *G.'s Verhältnis zur Musik* (Leipzig, 1880); F. Hiller, *G.s musicalisches Leben* (Cologne, 1883); H. Blaze de Bury, *G. et Beethoven* (Paris, 1892); W. Nagel, *G. und Beethoven* (Langensalza, 1902); idem, *G. und Mozart* (Langensalza, 1904); J. Chantavoine, *G. musicien* (Paris, 1905); E. Segnitz, *G. und die Oper in Weimar* (Langensalza, 1908); W. Bode, *Die Tonkunst in G.s Leben* (2 vols., Berlin, 1912); R. Rolland, *G. et Beethoven* (Paris, 1930; Eng. tr., 1931); A. Della Corte, *La vita musicale di G.* (Turin, 1932); F. Küchler, *G.s Musikverständnis* (Leipzig, 1935); F. Sternfeld, *G. and Music* (N.Y., 1954); W. Gerstenberg, *G.s Dichtung und die Musik* (Leipzig, 1966); R. Spaethling, *Music and Mozart in the Life of G.* (Columbia, S.C., 1987).—NS/LK/DM

Goetschius, Percy, American music pedagogue;

b. Paterson, N.J., Aug. 30, 1853; d. Manchester, N.H., Oct. 29, 1943. He studied at the Stuttgart Cons., and taught various classes there. He then was on the faculty of Syracuse Univ. (1890–92) and at the New England Cons. of Music in Boston (1892–96). In 1905 he was appointed head of the dept. of music at the N.Y. Inst. of Musical Art, retiring in 1925.

WRITINGS: *The Material Used in Musical Composition* (Stuttgart, 1882; 14th ed., 1913); *The Theory and Practice of Tone-relations* (Boston, 1892; 17th ed., 1917); *Models of Principal Musical Forms* (Boston, 1895); *Syllabus of Music History* (1895); *The Homophonic Forms of Musical Composition* (N.Y., 1898; 10th ed., 1921); *Exercises in Melody Writing* (N.Y., 1900; 9th ed., 1923); *Applied Counterpoint* (N.Y., 1902); *Lessons in Music Form* (Boston, 1904); *Exercises in Elementary Counterpoint* (N.Y., 1910); with T. Tapper, *Essentials in Music History* (N.Y., 1914); *The Larger Forms of Musical Composition* (N.Y., 1915); *Masters of the Symphony* (Boston, 1929); *The Structure of Music* (Philadelphia, 1934). —NS/LK/DM

Goetz or Götz, Hermann (Gustav), admi-

rable German composer; b. Königsberg, Dec. 7, 1840; d. Hottingen, near Zürich, Dec. 3, 1876. He began composing as a youth, and at 17 commenced studies in piano and harmony with Louis Köhler. After training in mathematics and physics at the Univ. of Königsberg (1858–60), he pursued music studies with Bülow (piano and counterpoint), Stern (conducting and score reading), and H. Ulrich (composition) at the Stern Cons. in Berlin (1860–62), where he also studied organ. In 1862–63 he was director of the Berlin Meichsner Gesangverein. In 1863 he became organist and choirmaster at the Lutheran Church in Winterthur. He also was active as a pianist, conductor of oratorio and opera, and piano teacher. In 1870 he settled in Hottingen, although he continued to work as an organist in Winterthur until tuberculosis compelled him to give up his duties in 1872. He spent his last years composing, teaching, and writing music criticism. Goetz's most celebrated work was his comic opera *Der Widerspenstigen Zahmung*, after Shakespeare's *The Taming of the Shrew* (Mannheim, Oct. 11, 1874). It remains one of the finest scores in the genre of the 19th century. Among his orch works, his Sym. in F major and his 2nd Piano Concerto are commendable. His chamber music is also particularly noteworthy, especially his fine Piano Quartet and Piano Quintet, as are several of his choral pieces.

WORKS: DRAMATIC: *Die heilige drei Könige*, Neujahrspiel (1865; Winterthur, Jan. 6, 1866); *Der Widerspenstigen Zah-*

mung, comic opera, after Shakespeare (1868–72; Mannheim, Oct. 11, 1874); *Francesca von Rimini*, opera (1875–76; unfinished; completed by E. Frank; Mannheim, Sept. 30, 1877). ORCH.: 2 piano concertos: No. 1 (1861; Berlin, April 3, 1862) and No. 2 (Basel, Dec. 1, 1867); *Frühlings-Ouvertüre* (1864); 2 syms.: No. 1 in E minor (1866–67; Basel, March 3, 1867; score destroyed by the composer's widow) and No. 2 in F major (1873; Mannheim, Dec. 25, 1874; rev. 1875; Leipzig, Jan. 27, 1876); Violin Concerto (1868). CHAMBER: 2 fugues for String Quartet (1860–62); *Presto* for String Quartet (1860–62); *Ballade* for Piano, Violin and Cello (1861; unfinished); Piano Trio (1863); *3 leichte Stücke* for Violin and Piano (1863); String Quartet (1865); Piano Quartet (1867); Piano Quintet (1874). P i a n o : 2 sonatas for Piano, 4-Hands (c. 1857, 1865); *Alwinen-Polka* (c. 1860); *Fantasie* (1860); *Scherzo* (c. 1862); *Waldmärchen* (1863); *Lose Blätter* (1869); 2 sonatinas (1869); *Genrebilder* (1875–76). VOCAL: *Psalm 137* for Soprano, Chorus and Orch. (1864); *Schneewittchen* for Chorus and Orch. (1865; unfinished); *Es liegt so abendstill der See*, cantata for Tenor, Men's Chorus and Orch. (1865); *Nenie* for Chorus and Orch. (1874); choruses; songs.

BIBL.: E. Kreuzhage, *H. G.: Sein Leben und seine Werke* (Leipzig, 1916); G. Kruse, *H. G.* (Leipzig, 1920).—NS/LK/DM

Goetze, Walter W(ilhelm), German composer; b. Berlin, April 17, 1883; d. there, March 24, 1961. He was trained in Berlin. After working as a bassoonist and theater conductor, he had his first success as a theater composer with his *Parkettsitz Nr. 10* (Hamburg, Sept. 24, 1911). After bringing out such scores as *Zwischen zwölf und eins* (Leipzig, Feb. 9, 1913), *Der liebe Pepi* or *Der Bundesbruder* (Berlin, Dec. 23, 1914), and *Am Brunnen vor dem Tore* (Hannover, May 26, 1918), he had his finest success with *Ihre Hoheit die Tänzerin* (Stettin, May 8, 1919). Among the best of his subsequent works were *Adrienne* (Hamburg, April 24, 1926), *Henriette Sontag* (Altenberg, Jan. 20, 1929; rev. version as *Die göttliche Jette*, Berlin, Dec. 31, 1931), *Der goldene Pierrot* (Berlin, March 31, 1934), *Schach dem König!* (Berlin, May 16, 1935), and *Liebe im Dreiklang* (Heidelberg, Nov. 15, 1950; in collaboration with E. Malkowsky).—NS/LK/DM

Goeyvaerts, Karel (August), significant Belgian composer; b. Antwerp, June 8, 1923; d. there, Feb. 3, 1993. He studied at the Royal Flemish Cons. of Music in Antwerp (1943–47), with Milhaud and Messiaen at the Paris Cons. (1947–51), and at the summer courses in new music in Darmstadt (1951). In 1964 he joined the Inst. for Psycho-Acoustics and Electronic Music (IPEM) at the Univ. of Ghent. He worked as an ed. for electronic music at the Flemish Radio in Antwerp (1970–74) and for contemporary music at the Belgian Radio and TV in Brussels (1974–87). Goeyvaerts was one of the pioneers in Belgium of serialism, spatial music, and electronic techniques.

WORKS: ORCH.: 5 Pieces for Strings (1944); *Preludium, Fuga en Koraal* for Strings (1945); 2 violin concertos (1947, 1951); *Diafonie* (1957); *Jeux d'Été* for 3 Orchs. (1962); *De Passie* (1962); *Al naar gelang...* for 5 Orch. Groups and Tape ad libitum (1971); *...erst das Gesicht...dann die Hände...und zuletzt erst das Haar...* for Chamber Orch. (1975); *Litanie III* (1981). B a l l e t : *Cataclysme* (1963). CHAMBER: Trio for Violin, Clarinet and Cello (1946); 2 string quartets (1947, 1992); Violin Sonata (1948); *Tre Lieder per sonare a venti-sei* for Various Instrumental Combinations (1949);

Opus 2 for 13 Instruments (1951); *Opus 3 met gestreken en geslagen tonen* (with striking and rubbing sounds) for 9 Instruments (1952); *Pièce pour trois* for Flute, Violin and Piano (1960); *Parcours* for 2 to 6 Violins (1967); *Actief—Reactief* for 2 Oboes, 2 Trumpets and Piano (1968); Piano Quartet with Tape ad libitum (1971); *You'll Never Be Alone Any More* for Bass Clarinet and Tape (1974); *Voor tsjeng* for Cheng (Chinese Zither) (1974); *Ach Golgatha!* for Positive Organ, Harp and 3 Percussion (1975); *Pour que les fruits mûrissent cet été* for 14 Renaissance Instruments (1975); *Litanie II* for 3 Percussion (1980) and *V* for Harpsichord and Tape (1982); *After Shave* for Recorder, Violin, and Harpsichord (1982); *Instant OXO* for 3 Percussion (1982); *Zum Wassermann* for 14 Instruments (1985); *Avontuur* for Piano and 10 Winds (1985); *Aemstel- Kwartet* for Flute, Violin, Cello, and Harp (1985); *De zeven zegels* for String Quartet (1986); *De heilige stad* for 12 Instrumentalists (1986); *Veertien heilige kwinten met aureool* for Cheng (Chinese Zither) and Percussion (1986); *Ambachtelijk weefsel* for Shakuhachi and 2 Kōtōs (1989); *Chivas Regal* for Harpsichord and Percussion (1989); *Voor Harrie, Harry en René* for Flute, Bass Clarinet and Piano (1990); *...das Haar* for 10 Instruments (1990). P i a n o : *Nummer 1*, sonata for 2 Pianos (1951); *Stuk* for Piano and Tape (1964); *De schampere pianist* (1976); *Litanie I* (1979); *Pas à Pas* (1985). VOCAL: *Elegische Muziek* for Alto, Piano and Orch. (1950); *Improperia*, cantata for Alto, 2 Choruses, Flute, Oboe, Clarinet, Viola and Percussion (1959); *Goathemala* for Mezzo-soprano and Flute (1966); *Mass* in memory of Pope John XXIII, for Chorus, 2 Oboes, English Horn, 2 Bassoons, 2 Trumpets and 3 Trombones (1968); "...*Bélise dans un jardin*" for Chorus, Clarinet, Bass Clarinet, Bassoon, Violin, Viola and Cello (1971); *Het dagelijks leven van de Azteken* for Speaker and Percussion (1978); *Claus-ule* for Speaker and 8 Instruments (1979); *Litanie IV* for Soprano, Flute, Clarinet, Violin, Cello and Piano (1981); *De dunne bomen* for Soprano and Dance Group (1985); *Ode* for Counter-tenor, Baritone, Flute, and Bass Clarinet (1988); *...want de tijd is nabij* for Men's Chorus and String Orch. (1989); *Aquarius*, scenic cantata for 8 Sopranos, 16 Instrumentalists and 5 Dancers (1990; also for 8 Sopranos, 8 Baritones and Orch., 1991); choral pieces; songs. M i x e d M e d i a : *HE...!*, audiovisual manipulation for Pantomime, Projection, Tape, and 10 Instruments (1971; in collaboration with L. Goethals and H. Sabbe). OTHER: *Nummer 4 net dode tonen* for Tape (1952); *Nummer 5 met zuivere tonen* for Tape (1953); *Nummer 6* for 180 Sound Objects (1954); *Nummer 7 met convergerende en divergerende klankniveaus* for Electronics (1955); *Nachklänge aus dem Theater I/II* for Tape (1971); *Op acht paarden wedden* for Tape (1973); *Partiduur* for Tape (1974); *Honneurs funèbres a la tete musicale d'Orphée* for 6 Ondes Martenots (1976); *Muziek voor een koninklijk vuurwerk* for Tape (1976).—NS/LK/DM

Goffriller, Matteo, notable Italian instrument maker; b. Bressanone, c. 1659; d. Venice, Feb. 23, 1742. He settled in Venice in 1685, where he most likely learned his craft from Martin Kaiser whom he succeeded in the business in 1690. Goffriller was the first important master of instrument making in Venice. In addition to his superb cellos, he made remarkable violins and violas.—LK/DM

Gogorza, Emilio (Edoardo) de, American baritone and teacher; b. Brooklyn, May 29, 1874; d. N.Y., May 10, 1949. After singing as a boy soprano in England, he returned to the U.S. and studied with C. Moderati and E. Agramonte in N.Y. He made his debut in 1897 with Marcella Sembrich in a concert; sang throughout the country in concerts and with leading orchs. Beginning in 1925, he was an instructor of voice at the Curtis Inst. of Music in Philadelphia. He married **Emma Eames** in 1911.—**NS/LK/DM**

Go-Go's, The, the first all-woman band to make major inroads in rock, formed 1978. **MEMBERSHIP:** Belinda Carlisle, voc. (b. Los Angeles, Aug. 17, 1958); Jane Wiedlin, gtr., voc. (b. Oconomowoc, Wisc., May 20, 1958); Charlotte Caffey, lead gtr., kybd. (b. Los Angeles, Oct. 21, 1953); Gina Schock, drm. (b. Baltimore, Aug. 31); Kathy Valentine, bs. (b. Austin, Jan. 7).

Singer Belinda Carlisle, guitarist Jane Wiedlin, and lead guitarist Charlotte Caffey originally came together as The Misfits in the momentous days of late 1970s L.A. punk. At the time, Carlisle was known as Dottie Danger and Wiedlin as Jane Drano. Perhaps because the band's name already belonged to a group in N.Y. (featuring Glenn Danzig) or perhaps because as they played together more and more they sounded less and less punk, they changed their name to The Go-Go's. Part of that change had to do with adding drummer Gina Schock to the group. Unlike the rest of the band, she (and to an extent Caffey) had some previous playing experience, having toured the country with John Waters's starlet Edith Massey and her band Edie and the Eggs.

This Go-Go's lineup (with bassist Paula Olaverra) went to England. Two-tone ska stalwarts Madness took a shine to the band, and they opened for Madness all across England. They earned a following in England, to the extent that they recorded a single for Stiff Records called "We Got the Beat." The song became a minor hit as an import in the pop music underground. They parlayed that into gigs across the U.S. IRS Records signed them in 1981.

The group went into the studio with veteran producer Richard Gotterer, who had also produced Blondie's early albums (among others). The album, *Beauty and the Beat*, turned into one of the surprise hits of 1981, topping the charts for six weeks and selling double platinum. The initial single, "Our Lips Are Sealed," written by Wiedlin and Specials leader Terry Hall, rose to #20. The big hit was a recut version of "We Got the Beat" that spent three weeks at #2 and went gold. Far from their punk roots, the band sounded like a stripped-down version of a 1960s girl group; producer Gotterer had been around in those days, having also worked with Rick Derringer and the McCoys.

The Go-Go's followed this big hit up with *Vacation*. The title track went to #8, as did the album on its way to selling gold. It was not as strong an album, but clever marketing (especially through music videos) helped propel its sales.

The group took most of 1983 off while Caffey recovered from a broken wrist. Their 1984 release, *Talk Show*, sold poorly, reaching only #18. Still the record generated two more hits: "Head Over Heels" rose to #11 and "Turn to You" hit #32. Wiedlin left the band shortly after, kicking off her solo career by dueting with her longtime favorite band Sparks on the tune "Cool

Places" in 1983. The Go-Go's broke up officially in May of 1985, although they did have several reunions.

Wiedlin released an eponymous solo album that was widely ignored, though it had nice moments like the vaguely Celtic "My Traveling Heart." Her next album, *Fur*, did better and spawned the #9 hit "Rush Hour." Her 1990 project, *Tangled*, lived up to its name. It did include a collaboration with Cyndi Lauper, though even that was done "by mail." A couple of years later, she put together the band FroSTed, but that also went nowhere. She did, however, start acting. Wiedlin portrayed Joan of Arc in the film *Bill and Ted's Excellent Adventure* and supplied voices to the cartoons *Pinky and the Brain* and *King of the Hill* among others.

Valentine worked with several bands after The Go-Go's breakup, including one with Clem Burke from Blondie; a group called The World's Cutest Killers with Kelly Johnson of the hard rock band Girlschool; The Blue Bonnets, a more bluesy band; and a pop band called The Delphines. None did any major recording. Gina Schock's post Go-Go's band House of Schock put out an album in 1988 that didn't attract much attention. She also wrote for various television commercials and worked with Valentine in the Delphines.

Caffey formed The Graces with Meredith Brooks and Gia Ciambotti in 1987. The band released one album, *Perfect View*, that didn't do well. She collaborated with artists including former Bangle Susannah Hoffs, Courtney Love, and Jewel, all of them recording at least one of the songs. She also worked on all of Carlisle's solo albums in some way.

Carlisle had a great deal of post-Go-Go's success as a solo artist. She struck gold with her #13 album *Belinda*. Giving up all pretense of her punk past, this album cast Carlisle as an MOR vocalist, illustrated by the album's hit, the #3 "Mad About You." This direction became even more evident on her next album, the platinum *Heaven on Earth*. The track "Heaven Is a Place on Earth" topped the charts and the follow-up "I Get Weak" hit #2. "Circle in the Sand" went to #7. This should have solidified her stature in pop, but 1989's *Runaway Horses* didn't keep up the momentum, spawning the #11 single "Leave a Light On" and the #30 single "Summer Rain" on its way to reaching only #37 on the charts. It did sell gold, however. Her next two albums, *Live Your Life, Be Free* and *Real*, did not even make the charts.

In 1990, Wiedlin convinced the group to get back together temporarily to play some charity shows for her pet charity, PETA. They recorded a cover of "Cool Jerk" for their *Greatest Hits Record*. When Rhino put together the two CD compilation *Return to the Valley of the Go-Go's* in 1994, the group recorded three more songs. They enjoyed it so much, they started working together again and touring. In the year 2000 the band toured the county with two other 1980s bands, The B-52's and The Psychedelic Furs, and to record a new album.

DISC.: *Beauty & the Beat* (1981); *Vacation* (1982); *Talk Show* (1984); *Return to the Valley of the Go-Go's* (1994). **BELINDA CARLISLE:** *Belinda* (1986); *Heaven on Earth* (1988); *Runaway Horses* (1989); *Live Your Life Be Free* (1991); *Real* (1993); *A Woman and a Man* (1996). **JANE WIEDLIN:** *Jane Wiedlin* (1985); *Fur* (1988); *Tangled* (1990); *Cold* (with FroSTed; 1992). **HOUSE OF**

SCHOCK: *House of Schock* (1988). **THE GRACES:** *Perfect View* (1989).—HB

Goh, Taijiro, Japanese composer; b. Dairen, Manchuria, Feb. 15, 1907; d. Shizuoka, July 1, 1970. He studied in Tokyo. He organized the Soc. of Japanese Composers and created the Japan Women's Sym. Orch. (1963). His music follows the European academic type of harmonic and contrapuntal structure.

WORKS: DRAMATIC: O p e r a : *Madame Rosaria* (1943); *Tsubaki saku koro* (When Camellias Blossom; 1949; unfinished); *Tais* (1959; unfinished). B a l l e t : *Shimpi-shu* (Mysteries), ballet suite (1942); *Oni-Daiko* (Devil Drummers; 1956). C h o r e o g r a p h i c P l a y s : *Koku-sei-Ya* (1954); *Rashô-mon* (1954). ORCH.: 8 syms.: No. 1 (1925), No. 2 (1930), No. 3, *Kumo* (Clouds; 1938), No. 4 (1938), No. 5, *Nippon* (1939), No. 6, *Asia* (1939), No. 7, *Sokoku* (Motherland; 1942), and No. 8, *Chô jô Banri* (The Long Wall; 1945; only the 1st movement was completed); 3 violin concertos (1935, 1937, 1962); 2 piano concertos (1936, 1940); *Movement* for Cello, Temple Blocks, and Orch. (1937); *Theme and Variations* (1938); 2 overtures: *Otakebi* (War Cry; 1939) and *Over the Tan-Shan Southern Path* (1941); 3 symphonic marches: *Eiyû* (Hero; 1940), *Taiiku* (Gymnastics; 1940), and *Akeyuku Azia* (Asia Dawning; 1942); *Seija to Eiyu* (The Saint and the Hero), symphonic dance piece (1961). CHAMBER: *Theme and Variations* for String Trio (1933); 2 string quartets (1935, 1938); *Imayo* for Cello and Piano (1954). P i a n o : 5 sonatas (1915, 1919, 1920, 1927, 1927); *November in Manchuria*, rhapsody (1926); *Fantasy* (1927); *Variations* (1931); *8 Chinese Dances* (1941); *Katyusha*, choreographic poem (1954). VOCAL: *Nemuri no Serenade* (Serenade for Slumber) for Voice and Orch. (1944); *The Flow of the River Dalny* for Chorus and Orch. (1950); *Brasil*, symphonic poem for Narrator, Chorus, and Orch. (1967); other vocal works, including over 100 songs.—NS/LK/DM

Göhler, (Karl) Georg, German conductor and composer; b. Zwickau, June 29, 1874; d. Lübeck, March 4, 1954. He was a pupil of Vollhardt in Zwickau;,then studied at the Cons. and the Univ. of Leipzig (Ph.D., 1897, with a diss. on Cornelius Freundt). He then pursued a career as a conductor, becoming best known as a champion of Bruckner and Mahler. He wrote an opera, *Prinz Nachtwächter* (1922), several syms., Piano Concerto, Clarinet Concerto, 2 violin concertos, Cello Concerto, *Quartetto enimmatico* for Piano and Strings, String Trio, choral works, songs, and piano pieces.—NS/LK/DM

Goicoechea, Errasti Vicente, Spanish composer; b. Ibarra de Aramayona, Alava, April 5, 1854; d. Valladolid, April 9, 1916. He was a student of Felipe Forriti, and then entered the priesthood. In 1890 he became maestro de capilla at Valladolid Cathedral, where he was made canon in 1915. Goicoechea was a distinguished composer of church music.—LK/DM

Gold, Arthur, Canadian pianist; b. Toronto, Feb. 6, 1917; d. N.Y., Jan. 3, 1990. He studied with Josef and Rosina Lhevinne at the Juilliard School of Music in N.Y. Upon graduation, he formed a piano duo with Robert Fizdale with whom he gave numerous concerts in Europe and America, in programs of modern music, including works specially written for them by such celebrated composers as Barber, Milhaud, Poulenc, Auric, and Thomson. They also pioneered performances of works by Cage for prepared piano. With Fizdale, he publ. a successful book, *Misia* (N.Y., 1979), on the life of Maria Godebska, a literary and musical figure in Paris early in the century. Gold retired in 1982, and in a spirit of innocent but practical amusement he publ., with Fizdale, *The Gold and Fizdale Cookbook* (1983).—NS/LK/DM

Gold, Ernest (real name, **Ernest Goldner**), Austrian-born American composer and conductor; b. Vienna, July 13, 1921. He studied piano and violin at home, and later piano, conducting and composition at the Vienna Academy of Music (1937–38). He went to the U.S. in 1938 and became a naturalized American citizen in 1946. After harmony studies with Otto Cesana and conducting with Leon Barzin in N.Y., he moved to Hollywood, where he worked as an arranger and took lessons with Antheil (1946–48). Gold became particularly successful as a composer for films, winning an Academy Award for his score for *Exodus* (1960). He was music director of the Santa Barbara Sym. Orch. (1958–60) and founder-conductor of Los Angeles's Senior Citizens' Orch.

WORKS: ORCH.: 2 syms.: No. 1, *Pan American* (1941) and No. 2 (1947); Piano Concerto (1943); *Ballad* (1944); *Symphonic Preludes* (1944); *Allegorical Overture* (1947). F i l m : Many, including *The Defiant Ones* (1958), *On the Beach* (1959), *Exodus* (1960), *Inherit the Wind* (1960), *Judgment at Nuremberg* (1961), *It's a Mad, Mad, Mad, Mad World* (1963), *Ship of Fools* (1965), and *The Secret of Santa Vittoria* (1969). M u s i c T h e a t e r : *Too Warm for Furs* (1956); *I'm Solomon* (1968). B a n d : *Band in Hand* for Narrator and Band (1966); *Boston Pops March* (1966). OTHER: Chamber music; piano pieces; songs.—NS/LK/DM

Goldbeck, Robert, German-American pianist, teacher, and composer; b. Potsdam, April 19, 1839; d. St. Louis, May 16, 1908. He studied piano and harmony with his uncle, Louis Köhler, then continued his training with Henry Litolff in Braunschweig. After a period in Paris and London, he went to N.Y. (1857). In 1867 he went to Boston, where he helped Eben Tourjée organize the New England Cons. of Music. He subsequently went to Chicago and founded his own cons. (1868), and in 1873 he proceeded to St. Louis, where he became co-director of the Beethoven Cons., conductor of the Harmonic Soc., and later founder of the St. Louis Coll. of Music (1880). He lived in N.Y., Königsberg, London, St. Louis, and Chicago (from 1886), finally settling in St. Louis (1903). He wrote an opera, *Newport* (London, 1889), an operetta, *The Soldier's Return* (London, 1856), several *Morceaux symphoniques* for Piano and Orch., and various pedagogical pieces for piano. He publ. an *Encyclopedia of Music Education* (3 vols., 1903).—NS/LK/DM

Goldberg, Johann Gottlieb, German organist, harpsichordist, and composer; b. Danzig (baptized), March 14, 1727; d. Dresden, April 13, 1756. As a child, he was taken to Dresden by his patron, Count Hermann Karl von Keyserlingk. He is reported to have studied with Wilhelm Friedemann Bach, and later with J.S. Bach (1742–43), and in 1751 he became musician to Count Heinrich Bruhl, a post he held till his death. His name is immortalized through the set of 30 variations for keyboard by Bach, the so-called *Goldberg Variations*, which were believed to have been commissioned by Keyserlingk for Goldberg. Although this account is now doubted, it is known that Bach gave Goldberg a copy of the score. Goldberg's own compositions include 2 concertos, polonaises, a Sonata with Minuet and 12 variations for Harpsichord, 6 trios for Flute, Violin, and Bass, a Motet, and a Cantata.

BIBL.: E. Dadder, *J.G. G.:Leben und Werke* (Bonn, 1923).
—**NS/LK/DM**

Goldberg, Reiner, noted German tenor; b. Crostau, Oct. 17, 1939. He was a student of Arno Schellenberg at the Dresden Hochschule für Musik. In 1966 he began his career in Radebeul, and that same year made his Dresden debut as Luigi in *Il Tabarro*. In 1973 he became a member of the Dresden State Opera, and in 1977 of the (East) Berlin State Opera; he toured with both companies in Europe and abroad. In 1982 he made his debut at London's Covent Garden as Walther von Stolzing, in Paris as Midas in a concert perf. of *Die Liebe der Danae*, at the Salzburg Easter Festival as Erik, and at the Salzburg Summer Festival as Florestan. He also sang Parsifal on the soundtrack for the Syberberg film version of Wagner's opera. In 1983 he made his N.Y. debut as Guntram in a concert perf. of Strauss' opera. He sang for the first time at Milan's La Scala as Tannhäuser in 1984. In 1987 he first appeared at the Bayreuth Festival as Walther von Stolzing. He made his Metropolitan Opera debut in N.Y. on Jan. 27, 1992, as Florestan. As one of the leading Heldentenors of his day, Goldberg won considerable distinction for his portrayals of Siegmund, Tannhäuser, Siegfried, Erik, and Parsifal. His versatile repertoire also included Bacchus, Max, Hermann in *The Queen of Spades*, Faust, the Drum Major in *Wozzeck*, and Sergei in *Lady Macbeth of the District of Mtzensk*.—**NS/LK/DM**

Goldberg, Szymon, eminent Polish-born American violinist and conductor; b. Wocawek, June 1, 1909; d. Ôyama-machi, Japan, July 19, 1993. He played violin as a child in Warsaw. In 1917 he went to Berlin and took violin lessons with Carl Flesch. After a recital in Warsaw in 1921, he was engaged as concertmaster of the Dresden Phil. (1925–29). In 1929 he was appointed concertmaster of the Berlin Phil., but was forced to leave in 1934 despite Fürtwangler's vigorous attempts to safeguard the Jewish members of the orch.; he then toured Europe. He made his American debut in N.Y. in 1938. While on a tour of Asia, he was interned in Java by the Japanese from 1942 to 1945; eventually he went to the U.S. and became a naturalized American citizen in 1953. From 1951 to 1965 he taught at the Aspen Music School, being concurrently active as a conductor. In 1955 he founded the Netherlands Chamber Orch. in Amsterdam, which he led with notable distinction for 22 years; he also took

the ensemble on tours. From 1977 to 1979 he was conductor of the Manchester Camerata. He taught at Yale Univ. (1978–82), the Juilliard School in N.Y. (from 1978), the Curtis Inst. of Music in Philadelphia (from 1980), and the Manhattan School of Music in N.Y. (from 1981). From 1990 until his death he conducted the New Japan Phil. in Tokyo.

BIBL.: B. Gavoty, *S. G.* (Geneva, 1961).—**NS/LK/DM**

Goldberg, Theo, German-born Canadian composer and teacher; b. Chemnitz, Sept. 29, 1921. He received training in composition from Blacher at the Berlin Hochschule für Musik (1945–50). In 1954 he emigrated to Canada and in 1973 became a naturalized Canadian citizen. He taught school in Vancouver but pursued his education at Washington State Univ. in Pullman (M.A., 1969) and the Univ. of Toronto (D.Mus., 1972). From 1970 to 1987 he taught music education at the Univ. of British Columbia in Vancouver. In his output from 1975, he placed special emphasis on mixed media, tape, and computers.

WORKS: DRAMATIC: O p e r a : *Nacht mit Kleopatra*, opera-ballet (1950; Karlsruhe, Jan. 20, 1952); *Robinson und Freitag*, radio opera (1951); *Engel-Étude*, chamber opera (Berlin, Sept. 20, 1952); *Galatea Elettronica*, chamber opera (1969); *The Concrete Rose*, rock opera (1970); *Orphée aux enfers*, "opéra son et lumières" (1975); *Daedalus*, "opéra son et lumières" (1977). **ORCH.:** *Liebesliederwalzer Variations*, on a theme by Strauss (1952); Sinfonia Concertante for Flute, Clarinet, Trumpet, Violin, Cello and Orch. (1967); *Canadiana: Suite für Piano und Orchester nach Canadischen Volksweisen* (1971); *Songs of the Loon and the Raven* for Orch. and Tape (1975); *The Beaux' Stratagem* (1978); Flügelhorn Concerto, *Il Caro Sassone* (1981). **CHAMBER:** *Samogonski-Trio* for Baritone, Clarinet, Cello, and Piano (1951); Clarinet Quintet (1951); *3 Movements* for Bassoon and Buchla (1971); *Antithesis* for Saxophone and Tape (1974); *St. Francis' Sermon to the Birds* for Bassoon and Tape (1975). **OTHER:** *Orion*, sound images (1978); incidental music for stage, radio, and television; various multimedia pieces, among them *Variations of a Mandala* (1973), *The Magic Carpet* (1982), and *The Hoard of the Nibelungen, as performed by a company of Baenkelsaengers* (1988).—**NS/LK/DM**

Golde, Walter, American pianist, vocal teacher, and composer; b. Brooklyn, Jan. 4, 1887; d. Chapel Hill, N.C., Sept. 4, 1963. After piano training with Hugo Troetschel in Brooklyn, he studied at Dartmouth Coll., graduating in 1910. He then went to Vienna, where he took vocal lessons and studied counterpoint and composition with Robert Fuchs at the Cons. Returning to the U.S., he was accompanist to many famous musicians of the day. From 1944 to 1948 he headed the voice dept. of Columbia Univ., and in 1953 he was appointed director of the Inst. of Opera at the Univ. of N.C. He composed a number of attractive songs and piano pieces.
—**NS/LK/DM**

Goldenweiser, Alexander (Borisovich), Russian piano pedagogue and composer; b. Kishinev, March 10, 1875; d. Moscow, Nov. 26, 1961. He studied piano with Siloti and P. Pabst and composition with Arensky, Ippolitov-Ivanov, and Taneyev at the Moscow

Cons. In 1896 he made his debut as a pianist in Moscow. After teaching at the Moscow Phil. School (1904–6), he was a prof. at the Moscow Cons. from 1906 until his death; he also served as its rector (1922–24; 1939–42). Two generations of Russian pianists were his pupils, among them Kabalevsky and Berman. As a pedagogue, he continued the traditions of the Russian school of piano playing, seeking the inner meaning of the music while achieving technical brilliance. He was a frequent visitor at Tolstoy's house near Moscow, and wrote reminiscences of Tolstoy (Moscow, 1922). He publ. several essays on piano teaching, and also composed chamber music and piano pieces.—NS/LK/DM

Goldkette, Jean, French-born American pop-jazz bandleader, agent, and pianist; b. Valenciennes, France, March 18, 1899; d. Santa Barbara, Calif., March 24, 1962. After living in Greece and Russia, he and his family moved to the U.S. (1911). He began playing professionally in Chicago, then with Andrew Raymonds's band in Detroit (1921). He soon formed his own band; by the late 1920s his organization controlled over 20 bands, none of which involved him as performer. He is chiefly remembered as an employer of Bix Beiderbecke, Steve Brown, Jimmy and Tommy Dorsey, Ed Lang, Danny Polo, Joe Venuti, and others. He also appeared as piano soloist with the Detroit Sym. Orch. (1930). By the early 1930s had relinquished nominal interest in all his bands and activities on behalf of McKinney's Cotton Pickers; he worked as an agent for many years. While he reformed bands in the mid-1940s and 1950s, he was mainly active as a classical pianist. He moved to Santa Monica in 1961, and died a year later.—JC/LP

Goldman, Edwin Franko, eminent American bandmaster and composer, father of **Richard Franko Goldman;** b. Louisville, Jan. 1, 1878; d. N.Y., Feb. 21, 1956. He studied composition with Dvořák, and cornet with J. Levy and C. Sohst in N.Y. He became solo cornetist of the Metropolitan Opera orch. when he was 21, remaining there for 10 years. For the next 13 years, he taught cornet and trumpet. He formed his first band in 1911. In 1918 the Goldman Band outdoor concerts were inaugurated. His band was noted not only for its skill and musicianship but for its unusual repertoire, including modern works especially commissioned for the band. Goldman was a founder and first president of the American Bandmasters' Assn.; he received honorary D.Mus. degrees from Phillips Univ. and Boston Univ., and medals and other honors from governments and associations throughout the world. He wrote more than 100 brilliant marches, of which the best known is *On the Mall*; also other band music; solos for various wind instruments; studies and methods for cornet and other brass instruments; several songs. He was the author of *Foundation to Cornet or Trumpet Playing* (1914), *Band Betterment* (1934), and *The Goldman Band System* (1936).
—NS/LK/DM

Goldman, Richard Franko, distinguished American bandmaster, writer on music, teacher, and composer, son of **Edwin Franko Goldman;** b. N.Y., Dec.

7, 1910; d. Baltimore, Jan. 19, 1980. He graduated from Columbia Univ. in 1931, and later studied composition with Boulanger in Paris. He became an assistant of his father in conducting the Goldman Band in 1937. Upon his father's death in 1956, he succeeded him as conductor, and continued to conduct the band into the summer of 1979, when ill health forced him to retire and allow the band to dissolve. He taught at the Juilliard School of Music (1947–60), was a visiting prof. at Princeton Univ. (1952–56), and in 1968 he was appointed director of the Peabody Cons. of Music in Baltimore, serving as its president from 1969 to 1977. He was the N.Y. critic for the *Musical Quarterly* (1948–68) and ed. of the *Juilliard Review* (1953–58). He wrote many works for various ensembles: *A Sentimental Journey for Band* (1941), 3 duets for Clarinets (1944), Sonatina for 2 Clarinets (1945), Duo for Tubas (1948), Violin Sonata (1952), etc., as well as many arrangements for band. A progressive musician, Goldman experimented with modern techniques, and his music combined highly advanced harmony with simple procedures accessible to amateurs.

WRITINGS (all publ. in N.Y. unless otherwise given): *The Band's Music* (1938); *Landmarks of Early American Music, 1760–1800* (1943); *The Concert Band* (1946); *The Wind Band: Its Literature and Technique* (Boston, 1961); *Harmony in Western Music* (1965); D. Klotzman, ed., *Richard Franko Goldman: Selected Essays and Reviews, 1948–1968* (1980).—NS/LK/DM

Goldmann, Friedrich, German conductor, teacher, and composer; b. Siegmar-Schönau, April 27, 1941. After attending Stockhausen's seminar in Darmstadt (summer, 1959), he studied composition with Thilman at the Dresden Hochschule für Musik (1959–62), attended the masterclasses of Wagner-Régeny at the Akademie der Künste in East Berlin (1962–64), and took courses in musicology with Knepler and Meyer at Humboldt Univ. in East Berlin (1964–68). In 1973 he received the Hanns Eisler Prize, and later the German Democratic Republic's Arts Prize (1977) and the National Prize (1987). In 1978 he became a member of the Akademie der Künste in East Berlin, and in 1990 was made president of the German section of the ISCM. In 1988 he became conductor at the Berlin Hochschule der Künste, where he was prof. of composition and conducting from 1991.

WORKS: DRAMATIC: O p e r a : *R. Hot bzw. die Hitze* (1976). **ORCH.:** *Essay I–III* (1963–64; 1968; 1971); 4 syms. (1972–73; 1976; 1986; 1988–89); *Musik für Kammerorchester* (1973); Concerto for Trombone and 3 Instrumental Groups (1977); Violin Concerto (1977); Oboe Concerto (1978); Piano Concerto (1979); *Inclinatio temporum* (1981); *Exkursion: Musica per Orchestra con Henrico Sagittario* (1984); *SPANNUNGEN eingegrentz* (1988); *Klangszenen I* (1990) and *II* (1994). **CHAMBER:** Trio for Flute, Percussion, and Piano (1966–67); String Trio (1967); Sonata for Wind Quintet and Piano (1969–70); *So und So* for English Horn, Trombone, and Double Bass (1972); *Cellomusik* (1974); 2 string quartets (1975, 1997); *Zusammenstellung* for Wind Instruments (1976); Piano Trio (1978); *Für P.D.* for 15 Strings (1975); Oboe Sonata (1980); 2 ensemble concertos (1982, 1985); *Sonata a quattro* for 16 Players (1989); *zerbrechlich schwebend*, octet (1990); *Fast erstarrte Unruhe 1* for 6 Players (1991) and 2 for 9 Players (1992); Wind Quintet (1991); *Querstrebige Verbin-*

dungen for 13 Players (1992). **VOCAL:** *Odipus Tyrann: Kommentar* for Chorus and Orch. (1968–69); *Sing' Lessing* for Baritone, Flute, Oboe, Clarinet, Horn, Bassoon, and Piano (1978). **—NS/LK/DM**

Goldmark, Karl (actually, **Károly**), eminent Hungarian composer, uncle of **Rubin Goldmark**; b. Keszethely, May 18, 1830; d. Vienna, Jan. 2, 1915. He was born into a lower middle class Jewish family which numbered more than 20 children. After his family moved to Deutsch- Kreuz, he had a few violin lessons with a local chorister. His father then sent him to the Ödenburg music school in 1842, and subsequently to Vienna in 1844, where he had violin lessons with Jansa until 1845. After briefly attending the Vienna technical school, he continued his studies at the Vienna Cons. with J. Böhm (violin) and G. Preyer (harmony) until it was closed in the wake of the Revolutionary events of 1848. He was a violinist in the theater orch. in Öldenburg, and later in Ofen before returning to Vienna to play in the orchs. at the Josefsstädter and subsequently at the Carlstheater. During this time, he taught himself to play the piano and, during a sojourn in Budapest (1858–60), he studied composition on his own. From 1860 he made Vienna his home, where he established his reputation as a composer that year with his String Quartet. He also was active as a music critic, championing the cause of Wagner, and was active as conductor of the Eintracht Choral Soc. as well. On Dec. 26, 1865, the Vienna Phil. gave the first performance of his *Sakuntala Overture*, with notable success. His first opera, *Die Königen von Saba*, was premiered to great acclaim at the Vienna Court Opera on March 10, 1875. In his works for the stage, Goldmark was predominantly influenced by Wagner. In most of his other scores, he reveals the influence of Schumann, Mendelssohn, and Spohr. His career is recounted in his *Erinnerungen aus meinem Leben* (Vienna, 1922; 2nd ed., 1929; Eng. tr., 1927, as *Notes from the Life of a Viennese Composer*).

WORKS: DRAMATIC: Opera: *Die Königen von Saba* (Vienna, March 10, 1875); *Merlin* (Vienna, Nov. 19, 1886; rev. 1904); *Das Heimchen am Herd* (Vienna, March 21, 1896); *Die Kriegsgefangene* (Vienna, Jan. 17, 1899); *Götz von Berlichingen* (Budapest, Dec. 16, 1902; rev. 1903 and 1910); *Ein Wintermärchen* (Vienna, Jan. 2, 1908). **ORCH.:** 8 overtures: Overture (c. 1854), *Sakuntala* (Vienna, Dec. 26, 1865), *Penthesilea* (1879), *Im Frühling* (1888), *Der gefesselte Prometheus* (1889), *Sappho* (1893), *In Italien* (1904), and *Aus Jungendtagen* (1913); 2 syms. (1858–60; 1887); 2 scherzos (c. 1863, 1894); 2 symphonic poems: *Ländliche Hochzeit* (Vienna, March 5, 1876) and *Zrinyi* (1903; rev. 1907); Violin Concerto (1877; Nuremberg, Oct. 28, 1878). **CHAMBER:** 3 piano trios (n.d.; 1858–59; 1880); Piano Quartet (n.d.); 3 string quintets (n.d., 1862, 1879); String Quartet (1860); 2 suites for Violin and Piano (1869, 1893); Violin Sonata (1874); Cello Sonata (1892); *Ballade* for Violin and Piano (1913); *Romanze* for Violin and Piano (1913); Piano Quintet (publ. 1916); piano pieces. **VOCAL:** Choral works and songs.

BIBL.: O. Keller, *C. G.* (Leipzig, 1901); H. Schwarz, *Ignaz Brüll und sein Freundeskreis: Erinnerungen an Brüll, G. und Brahms* (Vienna, 1922); E. Kálmán, *K. G.* (Budapest, 1930); J. Klempá, *K. G.* (Budapest, 1930); L. Koch, *K. G.* (Budapest, 1930); M. Káldor and P. Várnai, *G. K. élete és müvészete* (Budapest, 1956). **—NS/LK/DM**

Goldmark, Rubin, American composer and teacher, nephew of **Karl (Károly) Goldmark;** b. N.Y., Aug. 15, 1872; d. there, March 6, 1936. He studied at the Vienna Cons. with A. Door (piano) and J.N. Fuchs (composition), and from 1891 to 1893 he was a student at the National Cons. in N.Y. with Joseffy (piano) and Dvořák (composition). He taught at the Colorado Springs Coll. Cons. (1895–1901). Returning to N.Y. in 1902, for the next 20 years he gave private lessons in piano and theory. In 1924 he was appointed head of the composition dept. of the Juilliard School in N.Y., and remained there until his death; among his pupils were Copland, Chasins, and Jacobi. He was active in promoting such musical clubs as The Bohemians (of N.Y.), of which he was a founder and president (1907–10), the Beethoven Assn., and the Soc. for the Publication of American Music. His Piano Quartet (1909; N.Y., Dec. 1, 1910) won the Paderewski Prize.

WORKS: ORCH: *Hiawatha*, overture (Boston, Jan. 13, 1900); *Samson*, tone poem (Boston, March 14, 1914); *A Negro Rhapsody* (N.Y., Jan. 18, 1923). **VOCAL:** *Requiem*, after Lincoln's Gettysburg Address (N.Y., Jan. 30, 1919); songs. **CHAMBER:** Piano Quartet (1909; N.Y., Dec. 13, 1910); Piano Trio; *The Call of the Plains* for Violin and Piano (1915); songs.

BIBL.: D. Tomatz, *R. G., Postromantic: Trial Balances in American Music* (diss., Catholic Univ. of America, 1966). **—NS/LK/DM**

Goldovsky, Boris, Russian-American pianist, conductor, opera producer, lecturer, and broadcaster, nephew of **Pierre Luboshutz;** b. Moscow, June 7, 1908. He studied piano with his uncle and took courses at the Moscow Cons. (1918–21). In 1921 he made his debut as a pianist with the Berlin Phil., and continued his studies with Schnabel and Kreutzer at the Berlin Academy of Music (1921–23). After attending Dohnányi's master class at the Budapest Academy of Music (graduated, 1930), he received training in conducting from Reiner at the Curtis Inst. of Music in Philadelphia (1932). He served as head of the opera depts. at the New England Cons. of Music in Boston (1942–64), the Berkshire Music Center at Tanglewood (1946–61), and the Curtis Inst. of Music (from 1977). In 1946 he founded the New England Opera Theater in Boston, which became the Goldovsky Opera Inst. in 1963; he also toured with his own opera company until 1984. He was a frequent commentator for the Metropolitan Opera radio broadcasts (from 1946) and also lectured extensively; he prepared Eng. trs. of various operas.

WRITINGS: *Accents on Opera* (1953); *Bringing Opera to Life* (1968); with A. Schoep, *Bringing Soprano Arias to Life* (1973); with T. Wolf, *Manual of Operatic Touring* (1975); with C. Cate, *My Road to Opera* (1979); *Good Afternoon, Ladies and Gentlemen!: Intermission Scripts from the Met Broadcasts* (1984); *Adult Mozart: A Personal Perspective* (4 vols., 1991–93).**—NS/LK/DM**

Goldsand, Robert, Austrian-American pianist and pedagogue; b. Vienna, March 17, 1911; d. Danbury, Conn., Sept. 16, 1991. He studied piano with Moriz Rosenthal and Emil von Sauer, and theory and composition with Camillo Horn and Joseph Marx in Vienna. After making his debut at age 10 in Vienna, he toured throughout Europe and Latin America; at 16, he made his U.S. debut in a recital at N.Y.'s Town Hall (March 21, 1927). In 1940 he settled in the U.S. and became a teacher at the Cincinnati Cons. while pursuing his concert career. From 1953 to 1990 he taught at the Manhattan School of Music in N.Y. He was best known for his judicious readings of the 19th-century repertory. —NS/LK/DM

Goldsbrough, Arnold (Wainwright), English organist, harpsichordist, and conductor; b. Gomersal, Oct. 26, 1892; d. Tenbury Wells, Dec. 14, 1964. After studies in Bradford, he took courses in double bass, conducting, and composition at the Royal Coll. of Music in London (1920–22). In 1923 he joined its faculty, and concurrently held various posts as an organist. In 1948 he founded his own orch. in London, with which he devoted himself to the performance of early music. In 1960 the orch. became the English Chamber Orch., which subsequently gained a distinguished reputation. —NS/LK/DM

Goldschmidt, Adalbert von, Austrian composer; b. Vienna, May 5, 1848; d. Hacking, near Vienna, Dec. 21, 1906. He studied at the Vienna Cons. From his earliest efforts in composition, he became an ardent follower of Wagner. At the age of 22, he wrote a cantata, *Die sieben Todsünden* (Berlin, 1875); this was followed by a music drama, *Helianthus* (Leipzig, 1884), for which he wrote both words and music. A dramatic trilogy, *Gaea* (1889–92), was his most ambitious work along Wagnerian lines. He also brought out a comic opera, *Die fromme Helene* (Hamburg, 1897), about 100 songs, and a number of piano pieces.

BIBL.: E. Friedegg, *Briefe an einen Komponisten: Musikalische Korrespondenz an A. v.G.* (Berlin, 1909).—NS/LK/DM

Goldschmidt, Berthold, German-born English composer and conductor; b. Hamburg, Jan. 18, 1903. He studied at the Univ. of Hamburg (1918–22) and took courses in composition (with Schreker) and in conducting at the Berlin State Academy of Music (1922–24). He participated as a répétiteur and celesta player in the premiere of Berg's opera *Wozzeck* in Berlin in 1925. After working as an asst. conductor at the Darmstadt Opera (1927–29), he was a conductor in Berlin with the Radio and the Städtische Oper (from 1931). With the Nazi takeover in 1933, he was dismissed. In 1935 he fled to England and in 1947 became a naturalized British subject. He made numerous appearances as a guest conductor in England. In 1959 he conducted the first complete British performance of Mahler's 3rd Sym. That same year he was consulted by Deryck Cooke on the latter's performing version of Mahler's 10th Sym. Goldschmidt conducted Cooke's first though incomplete reconstruction of the sym. in a London recording studio on Dec. 19, 1960. He conducted the first complete performance of the sym. at a London Promenade Concert on Aug. 13, 1964. Goldschmidt's inability to secure a performance of his opera *Beatrice Cenci* led him to cease composing in 1958. It was nearly 25 years before he broke his silence with his Clarinet Quartet of 1983. By the end of the 1980s he had been "discovered," and was composing again with renewed vigor. Several of his works were either lost during World War II (*Passacalia* for Orch. and *Requiem* for Chorus and Orch.) or were withdrawn by the composer (Sym. and Harp Concerto).

WORKS: DRAMATIC: O p e r a: *Der gewaltige Hahnrei* (1929–30; Mannheim, Feb. 14, 1932); *Beatrice Cenci* (1949; concert version, London, April 16, 1988; stage version, Magdeburg, Sept. 10, 1994). **B a l l e t:** *Chronica* for 2 Pianos (1938; orch. suite, 1958). **ORCH.:** Overture to Shakespeare's *Comedy of Errors* (1925); *Ciaccona Sinfonica* (1936); *Greek Suite* (1940–41); Sinfonietta (1945–46); Violin Concerto (1951–55; expansion of a Concertino, 1933); Cello Concerto (1952; expansion of a Concertino, 1933); Clarinet Concerto (1954); *Intrada* for Wind or Sym. Orch. (1985–86). **CHAMBER:** 4 string quartets (1926; 1936; 1988–89; 1992); Clarinet Quartet (1983); Piano Trio (1985); *Retrospective*, string trio (1991); *Fantasy* for Oboe, Cello, and Harp (1991); *Capriccio* for Violin (1992). **P i a n o:** 2 sonatas (1921, not extant; 1926); *Variations on a Palestine Shepherd's Song* (1934); *Scherzo* and *From the Ballet*, 2 pieces (1957–58). **VOCAL:** *Zwei Betrachtungen* for Chamber Chorus, Speaker, Piano, and Percussion (1931; renamed *Letzte Kapitel*, 1984); *Mediterranean Songs* for Voice and Orch. (1958); choruses; solo songs.

BIBL.: S. Hilger and W. Jacobs, eds., *B. G.* (Bonn, 1993). —NS/LK/DM

Goldschmidt, Harry, Swiss-born German musicologist; b. Basel, June 17, 1910; d. Dresden, Nov. 19, 1986. He was educated in Basel at the Cons. and the Univ. After working as a music critic in Basel (1933–49), he settled in East Berlin, where he received his Ph.D. in 1958 from the Humboldt Univ. In 1949–50 he was head of the music dept. of the East Berlin Radio, and then taught music history at the Hochschule für Musik (1950–55). From 1956 to 1965 he was director of the Central Inst. of Musicology. He publ. *Franz Schubert* (Berlin, 1954; 6th ed., 1976) and *Um die Sache der Musik:Vorträge und Aufsätze* (Leipzig, 1970; 2nd ed., aug., 1976). He also ed. *Beethoven-Studien* (Leipzig, I, 1974, II, 1977, and III, 1975), *Zu Beethoven:Aufsätze und Annotationen* (Berlin, 1979), and *Zu Beethoven, 2: Aufsätze und Dokumente* (Berlin, 1984).—NS/LK/DM

Goldschmidt, Otto (Moritz David), German pianist, conductor, and composer; b. Hamburg, Aug. 21, 1829; d. London, Feb. 24, 1907. He was at first a pupil of Jakob Schmitt and F.W. Grund in Hamburg, then of Mendelssohn, Bülow, Hauptmann, and Plaidy in Leipzig. In 1848 he played in London at a concert given by **Jenny Lind.** He accompanied her on her American tour (1851) and married her at Boston, Feb. 5, 1852. From 1852 to 1855 they lived in Dresden, and from 1858 until her death (1887), in London. He founded the Bach Choir in 1875, and conducted it until 1885. His works included an oratorio, *Ruth* (Hereford, 1867), a choral song, *Music*, for Soprano and Women's Chorus (Leeds, 1898), and piano music, including a Concerto, piano studies, 2 duets for 2 Pianos.—NS/LK/DM

Goldstein, Mikhail, Russian violinist, musicologist, teacher, and composer; b. Odessa, Nov. 8, 1917; d. Hamburg, Sept. 7, 1989. While still an infant, he took violin lessons with Stoliarsky in Odessa, where he made his debut at 5; at 13, he became a pupil of Yampolsky (violin) at the Moscow Cons., where he also studied with Miaskovsky (composition) and Saradzhev (conducting). After marrying a German woman, the Soviet authorities discriminated against him. In witty retaliation, he claimed to have found a sym. written in 1810 by one Ovsianiko-Kulikovsky. The sym. was hailed as a major find. When Goldstein admitted that it was actually a work of his own, he was denounced as an imposter attempting to appropriate a Russian treasure. With his career in eclipse, he went to East Berlin in 1967. After teaching violin in Jerusalem (1967–69), he became a prof. at the Hamburg Hochschule für Musik in 1969. He also was active as a concert artist. Goldstein pursued legitimate research in Russian and German musical biography of the 18th and 19th centuries.

WORKS: ORCH.: 4 syms. (1934, 1936, 1944, 1945); 2 violin concertos (1936, 1939); Piano Concerto (1940); *Niccòlo Paganini*, symphonic poem (1963); *Ukrainian Rhapsody* (1965); *Kinderszenen* (1966); *Hamburger Konzert* for Chamber Orch. (1975). **CHAMBER:** 3 string quartets (1932, 1940, 1975); Piano Trio (1933); 4 violin sonatas (1935, 1940, 1950, 1975); *Ukrainian Suite* for Violin and Piano (1952); Duo for Violin and Double Bass (1979); Quartet for 4 Violas (1982).—**NS/LK/DM**

Goléa, Antoine, Austrian-born French writer on music of Romanian descent; b. Vienna, Aug. 30, 1906; d. Paris, Oct. 12, 1980. He studied at the Bucharest Cons. (1920–28). After further training at the Sorbonne in Paris (1928–31), he settled in that city as a journalist. His wife was the soprano Colette Herzog (1923–86).

WRITINGS (all publ. in Paris unless otherwise given): *Pelléas et Mélisande, analyse poétique et musicale* (1952); *Esthétique de la musique contemporaine* (1954); *L'Avénement de la musique classique, de Bach à Mozart* (1955); *Recontres avec Pierre Boulez* (1958); *Georges Auric* (1958); *Recontres avec Olivier Messiaen* (1959); *La Musique dans la société européenne depuis le moyen âge jusqu'a nos jours* (1960); *L'Aventure de la musique au XXᵉ siècle* (1961); with A. Hodier and C. Samuel, *Panorma de l'art musical contemporaine* (1962); *Vingt ans de musique contemporaine* (1962); *J.-S. Bach* (1963); *Claude Debussy:L'homme et son oeuvre* (1965); *Richard Strauss* (1965); *Entretiens avec Wieland Wagner* (1967; German tr., 1968); *Histoire du ballet* (Lausanne, 1967); *Marcel Landowski: L'homme et son oeuvre* (1969); *Je suis un violoniste raté* (1973); *La Musique de la nuit des temps aux aurores nouvelles* (1977).—**NS/LK/DM**

Goleminov, Marin, Bulgarian composer and pedagogue; b. Kjustendil, Sept. 28, 1908. He studied at the Bulgarian State Academy of Music in Sofia (graduated, 1931), in Paris with d'Indy (composition) and Labé (conducting) at the Schola Cantorum, with Dukas (composition) at the École Normale de Musique, and aesthetics and music history at the Sorbonne (1931–34), and with J. Haas (composition) and H. Knappe and E. Erenberg (conducting) at the Munich Akademie der Tonkunst (1938–39). From 1943 he taught at the Bulgarian State Academy of Music, where he was a prof. of orchestration, composition, and conducting, and its rector. From 1965 to 1967 he was director of the National Opera. He received various honors from the Bulgarian government. In 1976 he was awarded the Gottfried von

Herder Prize of the Univ. of Vienna. In 1991 he became a member of the Bulgarian Academy of Sciences. He publ. books in Sofia on the sources of Bulgarian musical composition (1937), instrumentation (1947), orchestration (2 vols., 1953; 3rd ed., 1966), and on the creative process (1971). In his music, he utilized folk elements, particularly the asymmetrical rhythms of Bulgarian folk motifs, in a fairly modern but still quite accessible idiom.

WORKS: DRAMATIC: Opera: *Ivailo* (1958; Sofia, Feb. 13, 1959); *Zlatnata ptica* (The Golden Bird; Sofia, Dec. 20, 1961); *Zahari the Icon Painter* (1971; Sofia, Oct. 17, 1972); *Thracian Idols* (1981). **Ballet:** *Nestinarka* (1940; Sofia, Jan. 4, 1942); *The Daughter of Kaloyan* (Sofia, Dec. 23, 1973). **ORCH.:** *The Night*, symphonic poem (1932); *Prelude, Aria and Toccata* for Piano and Orch. (1947–53); 2 cello concertos (1949–50; 1992); *Poem* (1959); Concerto for String Quartet and String Orch. (1963; Moscow, Feb. 11, 1964); 4 syms.: No. 1, *Children's Symphony* (1963), No. 2 (1967; Sofia, March 6, 1968), No. 3, *Peace in the World* (1970; Sofia, April 21, 1971), and No. 4, *Shopophonia* (1978); Violin Concerto (1968); *Aquarelles* for Strings (1973); Piano Concerto (1975); *Diptyque* for Flute and Orch. (1982); Oboe Concerto (1983); *Concert* for Strings (1993). **CHAMBER:** 8 string quartets (1934; 1938; 1944; *Micro-quartet*, 1967; 1969; 1975; 1977; 1983); 2 wind quintets (1936, 1946); Trio for Oboe, Clarinet, and Bassoon (1964); Sonata for Solo Cello (1969); *Concert* for Brass Quintet (1978). **VOCAL:** *Father Paissy*, cantata (1966); *The Titan*, oratorio (Sofia, June 25, 1972); *Ballad of the April Insurrection* for Soloists, Chorus, and Orch. (1976); *Symphonic Impressions on the Picture of a Master* for Voice and Orch. (1982); Sym.-Cantata for Soloist, Chorus, and Orch. (1993); choruses; songs.

BIBL.: B. Arnaudova, *M. G.* (Sofia, 1968); S. Lazarov, *M. G.* (Sofia, 1971); R. Apostolova, *M. G.* (Sofia, 1988); L. Braschow-anowa and M. Miladinova, *M. G.: Biobibliografski ocherk* (Sofia, 1990).—**NS/LK/DM**

Golestan, Stan, Romanian-born French composer and music critic; b. Vaslui, June 7, 1875; d. Paris, April 21, 1956. He settled in Paris and studied composition and orchestration with d'Indy, Roussel, and Dukas at the Schola Cantorum (1895–1903). He then was a music critic for *Le Figaro*. In 1915 he won the Enesco Prize for composition.

WORKS: ORCH.: *La Dembovitza* (1902); *Lăutarul şi Cobzarul* (1902); Sym. (1910); *Rapsodie roumaine* (1912); *Rapsodie concertante* for Violin and Orch. (1920); *Concerto roumain* for Violin and Orch. (1933); *Concerto moldave* for Cello and Orch. (1936); Piano Concerto, *Sur les cîmes des Carpathiques* (1938). **CHAMBER:** Sonata for Piano and Violin (1906–08); 2 string quartets (1927, 1938); Sonatina for Flute and Piano (1932); *Ballade roumaine* for Harp (1932); *Arioso et Allegro de concert* for Viola and Piano (1933); *Eglogue* for Clarinet and Piano (1933); *Elégie et Danse rustique* for Oboe and Piano (1938). **Piano:** *Poèmes et paysages* (1922); *Thème, Variations et Danses* (1927). **VOCAL:** Songs.—**NS/LK/DM**

Golinelli, Stefano, Italian pianist, teacher, and composer; b. Bologna, Oct. 26, 1818; d. there, July 3, 1891. He studied piano and counterpoint in Bologna with Donelli, and also received instruction in composition from Vaccai. He pursued a highly successful career

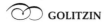

as a pianist via European tours. He also was a prof. of piano at the Liceo Musicale in Bologna (1840–70). Golinelli wrote over 200 works for piano, many quite effective.—LK/DM

Golitzin, Nikolai (Borisovich), Russian nobleman and patron of music, father of **Yuri (Nikolaievich) Golitzin;** b. St. Petersburg, Dec. 19, 1794; d. Tambov district, Nov. 3, 1866. He was a talented cello player, but his name is remembered mainly because of his connection with Beethoven, who dedicated the overture op.124 and the string quartets opp. 127, 130, and 132 to him. Golitzin was also responsible for the first performance of Beethoven's *Missa solemnis* (St. Petersburg Phil. Soc., April 7, 1824).—**NS/LK/DM**

Golitzin, Yuri (Nikolaievich), Russian conductor and composer, son of **Nikolai (Borisovich) Golitzin;** b. St. Petersburg, Dec. 11, 1823; d. there, Sept. 24, 1872. After training with Lomakin, he pursued his studies in Dresden and Leipzig. In 1842 he organized a serf choir; with it and his own orch., he made tours of Russia and Europe. Following a sojourn in England (1858–62), he resumed his career in Russia. He wrote 2 orch. fantasies, 2 masses, choral music, and piano pieces.—**LK/DM**

Göllerich, August, Austrian writer on music; b. Linz, July 2, 1859; d. there, March 16, 1923. He was a pupil of Liszt, and also studied composition with Bruckner. He acquired Ramann's music school in Nuremberg in 1890, and established branches in Erlangen, Fürth, and Ansbach. From 1896, he was conductor of the Musikverein and director of the Linz Cons. His wife, Gisela Pászthory-Voigt (also a pupil of Liszt), supervised the other schools. He publ. *A. Reissmann als Schriftsteller und Komponist* (1884), *Beethoven* (1904), and *Franz Liszt* (1908). His chief work, a biography of Bruckner (who himself selected Göllerich for this task), in 4 vols., was completed by Max Auer (1st vol., Regensburg, 1924; 2nd, 1928; remaining vols., 1932 and 1937).—**NS/LK/DM**

Gollmick, Adolf, German pianist, teacher, and composer, son of **Karl Gollmick;** b. Frankfurt am Main, Feb. 5, 1825; d. London, March 7, 1883. He studied with his father and other teachers in Frankfurt am Main, and in 1844 settled in London as a pianist and teacher. He composed 3 comic operas: *Dona Constanza, The Oracle,* and *Balthasar.* Other works include 2 "operatic cantatas": *The Blind Beggar's Daughter of Bethnal Green* and *The Heir of Lynne,* as well as several symphonic works, piano pieces, and songs.—**NS/LK/DM**

Gollmick, Karl, German writer on music and composer, father of **Adolf Gollmick;** b. Dessau, March 19, 1796; d. Frankfurt am Main, Oct. 3, 1866. He was of a musical family; his father, Friedrich Karl Gollmick (1774–1852), was an opera tenor. He studied theology in Strasbourg, and in 1817 he settled in Frankfurt am Main, where he taught French and served as chorus master.

He wrote mostly for piano; publ. potpourris, etc. His writings include *Kritische Terminologie für Musiker und Musikfreunde* (1833; 2nd ed., 1839), *Fétis als Mensch, Kritiker, Theoretiker und Komponist* (1852), and *Handlexikon der Tonkunst* (1858). He also wrote an autobiography (1866).—**NS/LK/DM**

Golovanov, Nikolai (Semyonovich), Russian conductor, composer, and pedagogue; b. Moscow, Jan. 21, 1891; d. there, Aug. 28, 1953. He studied choral conducting with Kastalsky at the Synodal School in Moscow, graduating in 1909, then entered the composition classes of Ippolitov-Ivanov and Vassilenko at the Moscow Cons. After graduation in 1914, he was engaged as asst. chorus master at the Bolshoi Theater in Moscow; was its chief conductor (1919–28; 1948–53). He was also chief conductor of the Moscow Phil. (1926–29), the U.S.S.R. All-Union Radio Sym. Orch. (1937–53), and the Stanislavsky Opera Theater (1938–53). He was awarded the Order of the Red Banner in 1935, and was 4 times recipient of the 1st Stalin Prize (1946, 1948, 1950, 1951). He wrote an opera, *Princess Yurata,* Sym., symphonic poem, *Salome,* after Oscar Wilde, numerous piano pieces, and songs. He was married to **Antonina Nezhdanova.**—**NS/LK/DM**

Golschmann, Vladimir, notable French-born American conductor of Russian descent; b. Paris, Dec. 16, 1893; d. N.Y., March 1, 1972. He studied violin and piano, and received training at the Paris Schola Cantorum in harmony, counterpoint, and composition. He played violin in orchs. in Paris, where he founded the Concerts Golschmann in 1919, at which he conducted many premieres of contemporary works; he also conducted opera and from 1920 was a conductor of ballet for Diaghilev. In 1923 he conducted in the U.S. for the first time with Les Ballets Suédois, and returned in 1924 as a guest conductor of the N.Y. Sym. Orch. A successful engagement as a guest conductor of the St. Louis Sym. Orch. in 1931 led to his appointment that year as its music director, a position he held with distinction for 27 years. In 1947 he became a naturalized American citizen. He later was music director of the Tulsa Phil. (1958–61) and the Denver Sym. Orch. (1964–70). Throughout his long career, he appeared as a guest conductor in North America and Europe. In addition to the 20th- century repertory, Golschmann's brilliance as an interpreter was at its best in the colorful works of the Romantic era.—**NS/LK/DM**

Golson, Benny, jazz saxophonist, composer, and arranger; b. Philadelphia, Jan. 26, 1929. He started on the piano; at 14, he picked up the tenor saxophone. In the mid-1940s he sat in on sessions on Philadelphia's Columbus Ave; here he jammed and gigged (from 1945) with John Coltrane, Jimmy Heath, Philly Joe Jones, Percy Heath, Red Garland, and Red Rodney. He played regularly with Ray Bryant and Gordon "Bass" Ashford in 1946. He attended and graduated from Howard Univ. (1950). He worked with Bullmoose Jackson (1951–53), Tadd Dameron (who influenced his composing), Lionel Hampton and Johnny Hodges (a 1954 tour that included

Coltrane), Earl Bostic, and Benny Goodman. In 1956 he joined the Dizzy Gillespie Big Band and toured South America. In 1957 he recorded his first album as a leader. After the Gillespie Orch. broke up (1958), he replaced Jackie McLean in Art Blakey's Jazz Messengers. He stayed with Blakey for about two years, serving as musical director and bringing in Lee Morgan, Jymie Merritt, and Bobby Timmons. This edition of the Messengers was regarded by many, including Blakey himself, to have been the best, producing the popular *Moanin'*, with four Golson compositions including "Blues March." (This piece was played at Blakey's memorial service in 1990.) Next he co-led the Jazztet with Art Farmer (1959–62), with whom he introduced the popular "Killer Joe." He, Max Roach, Kenny Burrell, Hank Jones, Dizzy Reece, and Joya Sherill opened in Manhattan in a play, *The Long Dream* (1960).

During the 1950s, Golson began to have his pieces recorded by other artists. In 1955 James Moody recorded "Blue Walk." Towards the end of the year, Miles Davis recorded "Stablemates" (Coltrane had brought it to the session). "Whisper Not" (words by Leonard Feather) was recorded by Ella Fitzgerald, Anita O'Day, and Mel Torme. In 1957 his "I Remember Clifford" was performed by the Gillespie Orch. at the Newport Jazz Festival and during a *Bandstand USA* broadcast from N.Y.'s Birdland; it was subsequently broadcast widely. From 1962 on Golson began devoting considerable time to arranging and composition. In 1965, after returning from Europe, he put away his saxophone and moved to Hollywood. Here he wrote scores and themes for David Janssen's feature film, *Where It's At*; television themes and scores for *M*A*S*H*, *Mission: Impossible*, *Room 222*, *The Partridge Family*, *Mannix*, *It Takes a Thief*, *Run for Your Life*, *Mod Squad*, *The Karen Valentine Show*, and various pilots; and music for the Academy Awards. He also scored specials for the BBC in London and feature films in Paris and Munich. He wrote music for innumerable American radio and television commercials, and did arrangements for Lou Rawls, Eartha Kitt, Connie Francis, Ella Fitzgerald, Eric Burdon, Nancy Wilson, Sammy Davis Jr., Diana Ross, "Mama" Cass Elliot, and Percy Faith.

In 1974, Golson resumed his playing career, freelancing extensively and recording with Curtis Fuller, Freddie Hubbard, Woody Shaw, and Pharaoh Sanders. In 1983 he reconstituted the Jazztet and appeared with it (as well as his own quartet) in festivals throughout the world. In 1987 the State Dept. sent him on a cultural tour of southeast Asia, after which Philip Morris International sent him on assignment to Thailand to write for the Bangkok Sym. Orch. Since 1989, he has lectured at William Paterson Coll. in Paterson, N.J., Stanford Univ., Rutgers Univ., and Berklee Coll. Since 1995 he has been musical director and member of the all-star saxophone repertory band, Roots, which toured extensively in Europe and has recorded four albums. Meanwhile, he has continued to write music, undertaking a number of ambitious projects, including a bass concerto (1993), premiered by Rufus Reid at Lincoln Center. He continues to do scoring, including the theme for *The Cosby Show*. In 1995, together with J. J. Johnson and Tommy Flanagan, he was given the Jazz Masters award by the National Endowment of the Arts.

DISC.: *N.Y. Scene* (1957); *Modern Touch* (1957); *Gone with Golson* (1959); *Gettin' with It* (1959); *Take a Number from 1 to 10* (1960); *Meet the Jazztet* (1960); *Turning Point* (1962); *Reunion* (1962); *Pop + Jazz = Swing* (one channel plays the standard, the other the original based on it; 1962); *Just Jazz* (1962); *Free* (1962); *Stockholm Sojourn* (1964); *Turn In, Turn On* (1967); *Killer Joe* (1977); *California Message* (1980); *One More Mem'ry* (1981); *Time Speaks* (1982); *This Is for You, John* (tribute to Coltrane, 1983); *Moment to Moment* (1983); *Live* (1991); *Up Jumped Benny* (1996); *Tenor Legacy* (with H. Ashby, J. Carter, B. Marsalis; 1997); *40 Years of B. G.* (with video concert and documentary; 1998).—**LP**

Goltermann, Georg (Eduard), German cellist, conductor, and composer; b. Hannover, Aug. 19, 1824; d. Frankfurt am Main, Dec. 29, 1898. He studied cello with A.C. Prell in Hannover; then studied cello with J. Menter and composition with I. Lachner in Munich. After touring as a cellist and serving briefly as a music director in Würzburg, he was asst. music director (1853–74) and music director (1874–98) of the Frankfurt am Main Stadttheater. He wrote a Sym., 3 overtures, 8 cello concertos, much piano music, and songs. —**NS/LK/DM**

Goltz, Christel, German soprano; b. Dortmund, July 8, 1912. She studied in Munich with Ornelli-Leeb. In 1935 she joined the chorus of the Fürth Opera, where she soon made her operatic debut as Agathe; from 1936 to 1950 she was a member of the Dresden State Opera; also sang with the Berlin State Opera and the Berlin City Opera. In 1951 she sang Salome at her debut at London's Covent Garden. From 1951 to 1970 she made many appearances with the Vienna State Opera; in 1952 she was named a Kammersängerin. On Dec. 15, 1954, she made her Metropolitan Opera debut in N.Y. as Salome, remaining on its roster for the season. She sang in many productions of modern operas.—**NS/LK/DM**

Golubev, Evgeny, Russian composer and pedagogue; b. Moscow, Feb. 16, 1910; d. there, Dec. 25, 1988. He studied composition with Miaskovsky at the Moscow Cons., graduating in 1936. He joined the faculty of his alma mater upon graduation and taught special courses in polyphonic composition. Several well-known Soviet composers were his students, among them Khrennikov, Eshpai, and Schnittke.

WORKS: BALLET: *Odysseus* (1965). **ORCH.:** 7 syms. (1933, 1937, 1942, 1947, 1960, 1966, 1972); 3 piano concertos (1944, 1948, 1956); Cello Concerto (1958); Viola Concerto (1962); Violin Concerto (1970). **CHAMBER:** 19 string quartets; 2 string quintets; 10 piano sonatas. **VOCAL:** 2 oratorios: *Return of the Sun* (1936) and *Heroes Are Immortal* (1946); many choruses. —**NS/LK/DM**

Golyscheff, Jefim, Russian composer and painter; b. Kherson, Sept. 20, 1897; d. Paris, Sept. 25, 1970. He studied violin in Odessa. In 1909, in the wake of anti-Jewish pogroms, he went to Berlin, where he studied chemistry as well as music theory; at the same time, he began to paint in the manner of Abstract Expressionism. He played a historic role in the development of the serial methods of composition; his String Trio, written about 1914 and publ. in 1925, contains passages described by him as "Zwölftondauer- Komplexen," in which 12 different tones are given 12 different durations in the main theme. As both a painter and a musician, he was close to the Dada circles in Berlin, and participated in futuristic experiments. On April 30, 1919, he presented at a Dada exhibition his *Anti-Symphonie*, subtitled *Musikalische Kreisguillotine*, with characteristic titles of its movements: 1, *Provocational Injections*; 2, *Chaotic Oral Cavity, or Submarine Aircraft*; and 3, *Clapping in Hyper F-sharp Major*. On May 24, 1919, he appeared at a Dada soirée with a piece entitled *Keuchmaneuver*. All this activity ceased with the advent of the Nazis in 1933. Golyscheff fled to Paris, but after the fall of France in 1940 he was interned by the Vichy authorities. His life was probably spared because of his expertise as a chemist; he was conscripted as a cement laborer. In 1956 he went to Brazil, where he devoted himself exclusively to painting. In 1966 he returned to Paris.—NS/LK/DM

Gombert, Nicolas, important Flemish composer; b. southern Flanders, possibly between Lille and St. Omer, c. 1495; d. c. 1560. He was one of the most eminent pupils of Josquin des Prez, on whose death he composed a funeral dirge. The details of his early life are obscure and uncertain. The physician Jerome Cardan reported that Gombert violated a boy and was sentenced to the galleys on the high seas. He is first positively accounted for in 1526, when his name appears on the list of singers at the court chapel of Charles V that was issued at Granada in that year; the restless Emperor traveled continually throughout his extensive domain—Spain, Germany, and the Netherlands—and his retinue was obliged to follow him in his round of his courts at Vienna, Madrid, and Brussels; Gombert probably was taken into the service of the Emperor on one of the latter's visits to Brussels. He is first mentioned as "maistre des enffans de la chapelle de nostre sr empereur" ("master of the boys of the royal chapel") in a court document dated Jan. 1, 1529; he remained in the Emperor's employ until 1538–40, during which time he took an active part in the various functions of the court, composing assiduously. After his retirement from his post in the royal chapel, he seems to have returned to his native Netherlands (Tournai), and there continued to compose until his death. He held a canonship at Notre Dame, Courtrai, from June 23, 1537, without having to take up residence there, and was also a canon at the Cathedral of Tournai from June 19, 1534. Despite his many trips abroad and the natural influence of the music of other countries, Gombert remained, stylistically, a Netherlander. The chief feature of his sacred works is his use of imitation, a principle which he developed to a high state of perfection. The parts are always in motion, and pauses appear infrequently; when they do occur, they are very short. In his handling of dissonance he may be regarded as a forerunner of Palestrina. His secular works, of which the earliest known printed examples (9 4-part chansons) are included in Attaignant's collection of 1529–49, are characterized by a refreshing simplicity and directness. Gombert's greatest contributions to the development of 16th-century music lay in his recognizing the peculiarities of Netherlandish polyphony and his developing and spreading it abroad. His extant works include 10 masses, over 160 motets, and 70 chansons, many of which appeared in contemporary (mostly Spanish) lute and guitar arrangements, a fact which shows the great vogue they had. Gombert's *Opera omnia*, ed. by J. Schmidt-Gorg, was publ. in Corpus Mensurabilis Musicae, VI/1–11 (1951–75).

BIBL.: H. Eppstein, *N. G. als Motettenkomponist* (Würzburg, 1935); J. Schmidt-Görg, *N. G., Kapellmeister Karls V: Leben und Werk* (Bonn, 1938).—NS/LK/DM

Gombosi, Otto (János), eminent Hungarian musicologist; b. Budapest, Oct. 23, 1902; d. Natick, Mass., Feb. 17, 1955. He studied piano with Kovács and composition with Weiner and Siklós at the Budapest Academy of Music, then musicology with Hornbostel, Sachs, and Wolf at the Univ. of Berlin (Ph.D., 1925, with the diss. *Jacob Obrecht: Eine stilkritische Studie*; publ. in Leipzig, 1925). From 1926 to 1928 he ed. the progressive Hungarian music periodical *Crescendo*. In 1939 he went to the U.S.; was a lecturer in music at the Univ. of Wash., Seattle (1940–46); then taught at Mich. State Univ. and the Univ. of Chicago (1949–51); from 1951 to 1955, was a prof. at Harvard Univ. He contributed numerous valuable papers to various periodicals, in Hungarian, German, Italian, and English; among his most important writings were *Bakfark Bálint élete és művei (Der Lautenist Valentine Bakfark)* (in Hungarian and German; Budapest, 1935) and *Tonarten und Stimmungen der antiken Musik* (Copenhagen, 1939).—NS/LK/DM

Gomes, (Antônio) Carlos, Brazilian composer; b. Campinas (of Portuguese parents), July 11, 1836; d. Belém, Sept. 16, 1896. He studied with his father, then at the Rio de Janeiro Cons., where he produced 2 operas, *A Noite do Castello* (Sept. 4, 1861) and *Joana de Flandres* (Sept. 15, 1863). The success of these works induced Emperor Don Pedro II to grant him a stipend for further study in Milan, where he soon made his mark with a humorous little piece entitled *Se sa minga* (a song from this work, "Del fucile ad ago," became popular), produced in 1867. After another piece in the same vein (*Nella Luna*, 1868), he made a more serious bid for fame with the opera *Il Guarany*, produced at La Scala on March 19, 1870, with brilliant success; this work, in which Amazon Indian themes are used, quickly went the round of Italy, and was given in London (Covent Garden) on July 13, 1872. Returning to Rio de Janeiro, Gomes brought out a very popular operetta, *Telegrapho elettrico*. His other operas are *Fosca* (La Scala, Milan, Feb. 16, 1873), *Salvator Rosa* (Genoa, March 21, 1874), *Maria Tudor* (La Scala, Milan, March 27, 1879), *Lo Schiavo* (Rio de Janeiro, Sept. 27, 1889), and *Condor* (La Scala, Milan, Feb. 21, 1891). He wrote the hymn *Il saluto del Brasile* for the centenary of American independence (Philadelphia, July 19, 1876), and the cantata *Colombo*, for the Columbus Festival (Oct. 12, 1892). In 1895 he was appointed director of the newly founded Belem Cons., but he died soon after arriving there. Besides his operas, he composed songs (3 books), choruses, and piano pieces.

BIBL.: S. Boccanera Júnior, *Um artista brasileiro: In memoriam* (Bahia, 1904); H.P. Vieira, *C. G.: Sua arte e sua obra* (São Paulo, 1934); I. Gomes Vaz de Carvalho, *A vida de C. G.* (Rio de Janeiro, 1935); It. tr., Milan, 1935); R. Seidl, *C. G., Brasileiro e patriota* (Rio de Janeiro, 1935); L.F. Vieira Souto, *A.C. G.* (Rio de Janeiro, 1936); J. Prito, *C. G.* (São Paulo, 1936); R. Almeida, *C. G.* (Rio de Janeiro, 1937); M. de Andrade, *C. G.* (Rio de Janeiro, 1939); P. Cerquera, *C. G.* (São Paulo, 1944); M. Góes, *C. G.: A força indômita* (Pará, Portugal, 1996).—**NS/LK/DM**

Gomes de Araújo, João, Brazilian composer; b. Pindamonhangaba, Aug. 5, 1846; d. São Paulo, Sept. 8, 1942. He studied at São Paulo and Milan. In 1905 he became a teacher at the São Paulo Cons., and remained there almost to the end of his long life. His works include 4 operas: *Edmea, Carminosa* (Milan, 1888), *Maria Petrowna* (1904; São Paulo, 1929), and *Helena* (São Paulo, 1910), as well as 6 syms., 6 masses, and vocal and instrumental works.—**NS/LK/DM**

Gomez, Eddie (Edgar), jazz-rock fusion bassist; b. Santurce, P.R., Oct. 4, 1944. After moving to N.Y., he took up the bass at age 12, and joined the Newport Jazz Festival Youth Band two years later (1959–61). After studies at N.Y.'s H.S. of Music and Art and the Juilliard School (1962–65), he played with Rufus Jones, Marian McPartland, Gary MacFarland, and Dixieland groups. He was associated with Paul Bley and Milford Graves in the early 1960s, and recorded for the ESP label with various groups. He is best known for his long tenure with Bill Evans (1966–79). He later brought his excellent technique to the electric bass, though he preferred playing amplified acoustic bass in fusion sessions. He co-founded the group Steps (later Steps Ahead, 1979–82). From 1988, he has led his own group, touring throughout the world, including a concert in Moscow in 1992. He has also continued to guest and do session work, and has appeared as a soloist with avant-garde classical ensembles, including the Kronos Quartet.

DISC.: *Down Stretch* (1976); *Gomez* (1984); *Discovery* (1985); *Trio* (1986); *Mezgo* (1986); *Street Smart* (1990); *Next Future* (1993). —**LP**

Gomez, Jill, British Guianan soprano; b. New Amsterdam, Sept. 21, 1942. She studied in London at the Royal Academy of Music and the Guildhall School of Music. After her operatic debut in a minor role in *Oberon* with the Cambridge Univ. Opera in 1967, she sang Adina with the Glyndebourne Touring Opera in 1968. In 1969 she made her first appearance at the Glyndebourne Festival as Mélisande. On Dec. 2, 1970, she created the role of Flora in Tippett's *The Knot Garden* at London's Covent Garden. She appeared as the Countess in Musgrave's *The Voice of Ariadne* with the English Opera Group in 1974. In 1977 she sang Tatiana at the Kent Opera. On March 25, 1979, she created the title role in the posthumous premiere of Prokofiev's *Maddalena* on the BBC. She appeared as the Governess in Britten's *The Turn of the Screw* at the English National Opera in London in 1984. She also sang opera in Glasgow, Cardiff, Zürich, Geneva, Frankfurt am Main, Lyons, and other cities. Among her other roles were Fiordiligi,

Donna Anna, Handel's Cleopatra, Berlioz's Teresa, Bizet's Leïla, and Britten's Helena. As a concert artist, she was engaged for many appearances in Europe and North America.—**NS/LK/DM**

Gomezanda, Antonio, Mexican pianist and composer; b. Lagos, Jalisco, Sept. 3, 1894; d. Mexico City, March 26, 1961. He studied composition in Berlin. Returning to Mexico, he taught piano at the National Cons. (1921–29) and at the Univ. of Mexico (1929–32). Among his works was an "Aztec ballet," *Xiuhtzitzquilo* (Berlin, Feb. 19, 1928).—**NS/LK/DM**

Gomez Martínez, Miguel Angel, Spanish conductor; b. Granada, Sept. 17, 1949. After piano studies with his mother, he enrolled at the Granada Cons. He also studied composition, piano, and violin at the Madrid Cons., and later attended the conducting classes of Boult and Leinsdorf at the Berkshire Music Center at Tanglewood; then studied with Markevitch in Madrid and Swarowsky in Vienna. He was music director of the St. Pölten Stadttheater (1971–72) and principal conductor of the Lucerne Stadttheater (1972–74). In 1973 he conducted at the Deutsche Opera in Berlin, and was subsequently its resident conductor (1974–77). In 1976 he was made resident conductor at the Vienna State Opera; also conducted in Berlin, Munich, Hamburg, London (at Covent Garden), Geneva, and Paris. In 1980 he made his U.S. debut, conducting at the Houston Grand Opera. From 1984 to 1987 he was principal conductor of the Orquestra Sinfónica de Radiotelevisión Española in Madrid. He was artistic director and chief conductor of the Teatro Lérico Nacional in Madrid from 1985 to 1991. In 1990 he became Generalmusikdirektor in Mannheim. He then served as chief conductor of the Finnish National Opera in Helsinki (1993–96), and of the Hamburg Sym. Orch. (1993–2000). —**NS/LK/DM**

Gomółka, Mikołaj, Polish composer; b. probably in Sandomierz, c. 1535; d. c. 1591. He was a chorister at the Polish court by 1545. After studies with Hans Klaus, he was a wind player at the court (1555–63). He then went to Sandomierz, where he was town councillor and head of the law court (1572–73). In 1578 he went to Kráków and was a musician in the service of various patrons. His major work was a collection of 150 melodies to words from the Psalms as tr. by the poet Jan Kochanowski and publ. as *Melodie na Psalterz polski* (Kraków, 1580; ed. in Wydawnictwo dawnej muzyke polskiej, XLVII-XLIX, 1963–66). His son, Michal Gomólka (b. Sandomierz, 1564; d. Jazlowiec, March 9, 1609), was also a musician.

BIBL.: J. Reiss, *Melodye psalmowe M. Gomołka* (Kráków, 1912); M. Perz, *M. G., monografia* (Kráków, 1969).—**NS/LK/DM**

Gondek, Juliana (Kathleen), American soprano; b. Pasadena, Calif., May 20, 1953. She was a student of Gwendolyn Koldofsky at the Univ. of Southern Calif. in Los Angeles (B.M., 1975; M.M., 1977), and pursued private vocal training with Kathleen Darragh in Los Angeles (1977–90) and with Marlena Malas in

N.Y. (1985–91). In 1980 she made her operatic debut as Ines in *Il Trovatore* with the San Diego Opera. She made her first appearance as a soloist with orch. when she sang with the Orchestre de la Suisse Romande in Geneva under Armin Jordan's direction in 1983. She won the gold medals at the Geneva (1983) and Francisco Viñas (Barcelona, 1984) competitions. In 1984 she made her first appearance at N.Y.'s Carnegie Recital Hall. From 1984 to 1991 she sang at the Newport (R.I.) Music Festival. In 1986 she was engaged as Mozart's Countess with the Netherlands Opera in Amsterdam. In 1987 she appeared as Alcina with the Opera Theatre of St. Louis, sang Bianca with the Greater Miami Opera, and was a soloist with the Indianapolis Sym. Orch. She sang with the San Francisco Sym. in 1988. On Sept. 25, 1990, she made her Metropolitan Opera debut in N.Y. as Marianne in *Der Rosenkavalier*, remaining on its roster until 1992. She portrayed Vitellia at the Edinburgh Festival and at Glasgow's Scottish Opera, and sang with the Toronto Sym. Orch. in 1991. In 1992 she was engaged as Elvira in *Don Giovanni* with the Seattle Opera, as Gismonda in *Ottone* at the Göttingen and Halle Handel festivals, and as soloist in Mahler's 4th Sym. with the N.Y. Phil under André Previn's direction. She returned to the Göttingen and Halle Handel festivals as Zenobia in *Radamisto* in 1993, and as Ginevra in *Ariodante* in 1995. After appearing as soloist in Gorecki's 3rd Sym. with the Minn. Orch. in Minneapolis under David Zinman's direction in 1993, she was engaged in 1994 to sing with the Freiburg Baroque Orch. and as Aspasia in *Mitridate, re di Ponto* at the Mostly Mozart Festival in N.Y. In 1997 she joined the artist faculty of the music dept. of the Univ. of Calif. at Los Angeles. In 1998 she sang Ginevra with the Dallas Opera, and in 1999 she was soloist in Britten's *Les Illuminations* with the Munich Chamber Orch. In 2000 she was engaged to sing Mozart's Countess at the Cologne Opera.—NS/LK/DM

Gönnenwein, Wolfgang,

German conductor, pedagogue, and operatic administrator; b. Schwäbisch-Hall, Jan. 29, 1933. He was educated at the Stuttgart Hochschule für Musik and at the univs. of Heidelberg and Tübingen. In 1959 he became conductor of the South German Madrigal Choir of Stuttgart, with which he toured Germany and Europe. In 1968 he was made prof. of choral conducting at the Stuttgart Hochschule für Musik, and in 1973 was named its director. He also was conductor of the Bach Choir of Cologne (1969–73) and later Intendant of the Württemberg State Theater in Stuttgart (1985–92).—NS/LK/DM

González-Avila, Jorge,

Mexican composer; b. Mérida, Yucatán, Dec. 10, 1925. He studied with Francisco Agea Hermosa (piano), R. Halffter (composition), Galindo (harmony), and Hernández Moncada (theory) at the National Cons. in Mexico City (1949–53), with Bal y Gay (1952), and with Chávez (1953). He then devoted himself mainly to teaching and composing. While his output included some orch., chamber, and vocal pieces, he concentrated his compositional skills on producing an extensive catalogue of solo piano music.—NS/LK/DM

Goodall, Sir Reginald,

notable English conductor; b. Lincoln, July 13, 1901; d. Barham, May 5, 1990. He studied piano, violin, and conducting at the Royal Coll. of Music in London, and later pursued his training in Munich and Vienna. In 1936 he made his debut conducting *Carmen* in London, and became a répétiteur at Covent Garden there. From 1936 to 1939 he was asst. conductor of the Royal Choral Soc. in London. His decision to join the British Union of Fascists just 5 days after Hitler invaded Poland in 1939 undoubtedly played a role in delaying his career opportunities. From 1944 to 1946 he was a conductor at the Sadler's Wells Opera in London, where he was chosen to conduct the premiere of Britten's *Peter Grimes* on June 7, 1945. From 1946 to 1961 he was on the conducting staff at Covent Garden, but then was relegated to the position of a répétiteur there from 1961 to 1971. Thereafter he again had the opportunity to conduct there. In 1968 he emerged as a major operatic conductor when he conducted a remarkable performance of *Die Meistersinger von Nürnberg* in English at the Sadler's Wells Opera. In 1973 he conducted an acclaimed traversal of the *Ring* cycle there in English. In subsequent years, he was ranked among the leading Wagnerian interpreters of the day. In 1975 he was made a Commander of the Order of the British Empire. He was knighted in 1985.

BIBL.: J. Lucas, *Reggie: The Life of R.G.* (London, 1993). —NS/LK/DM

Goode, Daniel (Seinfel),

American clarinetist, composer, teacher, and writer on music; b. N.Y., Jan. 24, 1936. After studies in philosophy at Oberlin Coll. in Ohio (B.A., 1957), he studied with Cowell and Luening at Columbia Univ. in N.Y. (M.A., 1962) and with Gaburo and Oliveros at the Univ. of Calif. at San Diego (1968–70). In 1983 he co-founded the DownTown Ensemble in N.Y.; also was a founding member of Gamelan Son of Lion. In 1971 he became an asst. prof. at Livingston Coll., Rutgers Univ.; in 1981, became a prof. at its Mason Gross School of the Arts. As a composer, Goode combines the techniques of process music with improvisation. His *Clarinet Songs* (1979–91), an evening-length suite comprised of 16 independent settings, explores non-traditional notations, circular breathing, and alternate, microtonal fingerings, all of which conspire to produce unusual, often striking timbres. A collection of his writings was publ. as *From Notebooks 1968-* (Lebanon, N.H., 1984).

WORKS: *Orbits* for 6 Moving Bodies and 2 Instrumentalists (1970); *Circular Thoughts* for Clarinet (1974); *Phrases of the Hermit Thrush* for Clarinet (1974; also for Clarinet and Orch., 1979); *The Thrush from Upper Dunakyn* for Bass Recorder (1974); *Cage's DREAM dreamed* for Piano (1977); *Stamping in the Dark* for an unspecified number of stamping individuals (1977); *Circular Thoughts* for Gamelan Ensemble (1978); *Clarinet Songs* for Clarinet (1979–91); *Eine Kleine Gamelan Music* for Gamelan Ensemble (1980); *40 Random Numbered Clangs* for Gamelan Ensemble (1980); *Wind Symphony* for Wind Band (1980); *Fiddle Studies* for Woodwind Quartet (1981); *Semaphores* for Gamelan Ensemble (1981); *Cape Breton Concerto* for 6 Traditional Fiddlers, Traditional (Cape Breton style) Piano, and Symphonic Band (1982); *The Red and White Cows* for unspecified instrumentation (1985; also for Violin, Viola, and Piano); *Shaking Music* for an unspecified number of moving instrumentalists (1986); *The Shouting Opera*, intermedia piece with slides, video, dance, music, computer speech, and audience participation (1986); *Diet Polka* for Accordion and Instruments obbligato (1987); *Tunnel- Funnel* for 15 Instruments (1988); *Flower Forms I, II, III* for Wind Ensemble (1988–90); *Clothesline* for Soprano and 8 Instruments (1992); *UFOs Made Me Do It* for Computer Voice (1992); *Nod Drama* for (unspecified) Mixed Ensemble (1993); *Pornography Made Me Do It again* for Computer Voices (1993); *Eight Thrushes, Accordion, and Bagpipe* for 10 Mixed Winds and Strings (1994).—NS/LK/DM

Goode, Richard (Stephen),

American pianist; b. N.Y., June 1, 1943. He was a pupil of Elvira Szigeti (1949–52) and Claude Frank (1952–54). He subsequently was an extension student at the Mannes Coll. of Music in N.Y. (1954–56), where he trained with Nadia Reisenberg (piano), Carl Schachter (theory), and Carl Bamberger (conducting). He studied with Serkin in Marlboro, Vt., and then privately (1960) and at the Curtis Inst. of Music in Philadelphia (1961–64), where he also studied with Horszowski. After attending the City Coll. of the City Univ. of N.Y. (1964–67), he completed his training at the Mannes Coll. of Music (1967–69; B.S., 1969). On Feb. 12, 1962, he made his formal debut in N.Y.; his European debut followed at the Festival of Two Worlds in Spoleto, Italy, in 1964. In 1967 he became a member of the Boston Sym. Chamber Players; from 1969 to 1979 he was a member of the Chamber Music Soc. of Lincoln Center in N.Y. His career as a solo artist was enhanced with his capture of the 1st prize at the Clara Haskil competition in 1973; in 1980 he was awarded the Avery Fisher Prize. He made various appearances as a soloist with orchs. and as a recitalist; also appeared with the Chamber Music Soc. of Lincoln Center again from 1983 to 1989. A non-specialist, he won praise as a virtuoso soloist, compelling recitalist, committed chamber music performer, and sensitive accompanist. His repertoire ranges from the standard literature to contemporary scores.—NS/LK/DM

Goodman (real name, Guttmann), Alfred,

German-American composer; b. Berlin, March 1, 1920; d. 1999. After training in Berlin, he went to England in 1939 and then to the U.S. in 1940, and subsequently served in the U.S. Army. Following studies with Cowell and Luening at Columbia Univ. (B.S., 1952; M.A., 1953), he returned to Germany in 1960 and was a composer and broadcaster with the Bavarian Radio in Munich; he later was its music adviser (1971–85). In 1973 he received his Ph.D. from the Free Univ. of Berlin, and then taught at the Munich Hochschule für Musik (from 1976). He publ. *Musik von A-Z* (Munich, 1971) and *Sachwörterbuch der Musik* (Munich, 1982).

WORKS: DRAMATIC: O p e r a : *The Audition* (1948–54; Athens, Ohio, July 27, 1954); *Der Läufer* (1969); *The Lady and the Maid* (1984). ORCH.: 2 syms. (1949, 1962); *Prelude '51* (1951); Sinfonietta (1952); *Uptown-Downtown* (1954); Clarinet Concerto (1959); *Mayfair Overture* (1961); *Capriccio Transatlantique* (1968); *Balkan Panorama* (1969); *A Yankee in Schwabing* (1969); *3 Essays* for Harpsichord and Strings (1972); *Pro Memoria* (1974). CHAMBER: 2 string quartets (1950, 1959); Trumpet Sonata (1950); Violin Sonata (1960); *Brass Quintet in 7 Rounds* (1963); *5 Sequences* for Woodwind Quartet (1969); *2 Soliloquies* for Double Bass (1976); *Across the Board* for Brass Ensemble

(1978); *Brassology for 11* (1984–85); *Direction L.A.* for 4 Trumpets and 4 Trombones (1985); piano pieces; organ music. VOCAL: Choral pieces; songs.—NS/LK/DM

Goodman, Benny (actually Benjamin David),

American bandleader and clarinetist; b. Chicago, May 30, 1909; d. N.Y., June 13, 1986. Goodman popularized swing music and was its most successful early practitioner. An accomplished clarinetist, Goodman dominated both his big band and smaller groups, combining a high level of jazz proficiency with enormous commercial appeal. Among the many major hits he scored in the 1930s and 1940s, the most popular were "And the Angels Sing," "Goodnight, My Love," "Goody Goody," and "Taking a Chance on Love."

Goodman was the ninth child of Russian immigrants David and Dora Rezinsky Goodman. His father was a tailor, and his early years were spent in extreme poverty. At the age of ten he began taking clarinet lessons at a synagogue, then joined the band at the settlement home Hull House and took lessons from Franz Schoepp. He first played professionally at the age of 12 and was soon performing in bands around Chicago, dropping out of high school at 14 to work full-time. In August 1925 he joined Ben Pollack's Orch., with which he stayed off and on for four years, making his first released recordings with the band in December 1926. His first recordings under his own name, "A Jazz Holiday" and "Wolverine Blues" (music and lyrics by Ferdinand "Jelly Roll" Morton, Benjamin F. Spikes, and John C. Spikes), were made in January 1928.

Goodman left Pollack in N.Y. in September 1929 and worked as a freelance musician during the early years of the Depression, doing recording sessions, many of them organized by Ben Selvin, as well as playing on the radio and in the pit orchs. of Broadway musicals. During this period he studied music theory with Joseph Schillinger. He also made occasional recordings under his own name and scored his first minor hit with "He's Not Worth Your Tears" in January 1931. In the fall of 1933 he began recording regularly for Columbia Records and scored hits in early 1934 with "Ain't Cha Glad?" (music by Fats Waller, lyrics by Andy Razaf), "Riffin' the Scotch" (music and lyrics by Johnny Mercer, Dick McDonough, Benny Goodman, and Buck Washington) with Billie Holiday on vocals, and "Ol' Pappy" (music by Jerry Livingston, lyrics by Marty Symes and Al J. Neiburg) with Mildred Bailey on vocals.

Goodman organized a permanent orchestra for a residence at Billy Rose's Music Hall in the spring of 1934. As he began the engagement on June 1, he was enjoying another hit with "I Ain't Lazy, I'm Just Dreamin'" (music and lyrics by Dave Franklin), and his recording of "Moon Glow" (music and lyrics by Will Hudson, Eddie DeLange, and Irving Mills) became a best-seller in July. Before the four-and-a-half month stand ended in October, he scored further hits with "Take My Word" and "Bugle Call Rag" (music and lyrics by Jack Pettis, Billy Meyers, and Elmer Schoebel).

In December 1934, Goodman's was one of three bands chosen to perform on the three-hour Saturday night radio program *Let's Dance*, broadcast over the

NBC network. The show lasted six months, and the exposure allowed him to achieve a series of hits that included "I'm a Hundred Percent for You" (music by Ben Oakland, lyrics by Mitchell Parish and Irving Mills) and "Blue Moon" (music by Richard Rodgers, lyrics by Lorenz Hart) in January 1935, "Music Hall Rag" in February, "Night Wind" (music by David A. Pollack, lyrics by Bob Rothberg) in March, and "I Was Lucky" (music by Jack Stern, lyrics by Jack Meskill) in April.

Goodman signed to RCA Victor Records and undertook a national tour in the summer of 1935. Initially problematic, it became a spectacular success starting on Aug. 21, 1935, opening night at the Palomar Ballroom near L.A., a date remembered as marking the birth of the Swing Era. In November he began a six- month residency at the Congress Hotel in Chicago, during which he enjoyed a series of Top Ten entries on the hit parade: "No Other One" (music and lyrics by Tot Seymour and Vee Lawnhurst) in November, "It's Been So Long" (music by Walter Donaldson, lyrics by Harold Adamson) in February 1936, and "Goody Goody" (music and lyrics by Johnny Mercer and Matty Malneck), which hit #1 in March.

Goodman again topped the hit parade with "The Glory of Love" (music and lyrics by Billy Hill) in July and with "These Foolish Things (Remind Me of You)" (music by Jack Strachey and Harry Link, lyrics by Erich Maschwitz writing under the pseudonym Holt Marvell) in August, and he reached the Top Ten with "You Can't Pull the Wool Over My Eyes" (music and lyrics by Milton Ager, Charles Newman, and Murray Mencher) in June, "You Turned the Tables on Me" (music by Louis Alter, lyrics by Sidney D. Mitchell) in October, and "Here's Love in Your Eyes" (music by Ralph Rainger, lyrics by Leo Robin) in November. The last title was performed in the motion picture, *The Big Broadcast of 1937*, released in October 1936, which marked the Goodman Orch.'s movie debut. The same month, the band began a residency at N.Y.'s Pennsylvania Hotel. Also in 1936, they launched a radio series, *The Camel Caravan*, which ran to the end of 1939.

In January 1937 trumpeter Harry James joined the Goodman Orch. He was featured on the band's next major hit, "Goodnight, My Love" (music by Harry Revel, lyrics by Mack Gordon), on which Ella Fitzgerald sang; the song topped the hit parade in February. Goodman's other hit parade entries for the year were "This Year's Kisses" (music and lyrics by Irving Berlin), which went to #1 in March, and "Afraid to Dream" (music by Harry Revel, lyrics by Mack Gordon) in September. During the year, the group made another film, *Hollywood Hotel*, released in December.

Goodman gave a historic jazz concert at Carnegie Hall on Jan. 16, 1938; its climax was a performance of "Sing, Sing, Sing" (music and lyrics by Louis Prima), and the studio recording of the song later was inducted into the Grammy Hall of Fame. Goodman made frequent appearances in the hit parade during the year, including: "Bob White" (music by Bernard Hanighen, lyrics by Johnny Mercer) and "You Took the Words Right Out of My Heart" (music by Ralph Rainger, lyrics by Leo Robin) in January; "It's Wonderful" (music by

Stuff Smith, lyrics by Mitchell Parish) in March; "Don't Be That Way" (music by Edgar Sampson) in April; "I Let a Song Go Out of My Heart" (music by Duke Ellington, lyrics by Henry Nemo, John Redmond, and Irving Mills), which hit #1 in July; "What Goes On Here in My Heart" (music by Ralph Rainger, lyrics by Leo Robin) in August; "I've Got a Date with a Dream" (music by Harry Revel, lyrics by Mack Gordon) in September; and "This Can't Be Love" (music by Richard Rodgers, lyrics by Lorenz Hart) and "What Have You Got That Gets Me" (music by Ralph Rainger, lyrics by Leo Robin) in December.

Goodman scored his biggest hit in more than two years in April 1939 with "And the Angels Sing," the music for which was written by his trumpeter, Ziggy Elman, who also contributed a memorable solo. Lyrics for the song, which went to #1 in May, were by Johnny Mercer. This recording also was inducted into the Grammy Hall of Fame. Goodman's only other hit parade entry for the year came in November with "I Didn't Know What Time It Was" (music by Richard Rodgers, lyrics by Lorenz Hart), one of the first records he released after returning to Columbia Records. The same month, he appeared with a sextet in the musical *Swingin' the Dream* (N.Y., Nov. 29, 1939), which had songs by James Van Heusen and Eddie DeLange; it ran 13 performances. From the score, he recorded "Darn That Dream," with a vocal by Mildred Bailey, and it topped the hit parade in March 1940. He was back in the hit parade in April with "How High the Moon" (music by Morgan Lewis, lyrics by Nancy Hamilton) and in May with "I Can't Love You Anymore" (music by Allie Wrubel, lyrics by Herb Magidson).

Goodman's orch. temporarily disbanded in July 1940 and he underwent an operation to correct a slipped disk. He reorganized his band in October. His next Top Ten hit came in April 1941 with his 1939 recording of "There'll Be Some Changes Made" (music by W. Benton Overstreet, lyrics by Billy Higgins); interest in the 1924 song had been sparked by its use in the film *Play Girl*, released in January 1941. Goodman returned to the radio during the year, broadcasting for Old Gold cigarettes. On March 21, 1942, he married Alice Hammond Duckworth, the sister of his musical advisor, John Hammond. They had two daughters.

Goodman returned to the Top Ten in April 1942 with "Somebody Else Is Taking My Place" (music and lyrics by Dick Howard, Russ Morgan, and Bob Ellsworth), which had a vocal by Peggy Lee, and with the instrumental "Jersey Bounce" (music by Bobby Plater, Tiny Bradshaw, and Edward Johnson). In May he appeared in the film *Syncopation*. Despite the onset of the musicians' union recording ban in August, he had stockpiled enough recordings that he was able to maintain a normal release schedule for nearly a year, and he scored Top Ten hits with "Take Me" (music by Rube Bloom, lyrics by Mack David) in August and "Idaho" (music and lyrics by Jesse Stone) in September, both with vocals by Dick Haymes, and with "Why Don't You Do Right" (music and lyrics by Joe McCoy) with vocals by Peggy Lee in January 1943, while "Taking a Chance on Love" (music by Vernon Duke, lyrics by John Latouche and

Ted Fetter) topped the charts in June 1943. He spent some of his time in Hollywood, appearing in the films *The Powers Girl* (January 1943), *Stage Door Canteen* (July 1943), and *The Gang's All Here* (December 1943).

Goodman again disbanded in March 1944 because of a dispute with his agent. In September he had a major role in the film *Sweet and Low-Down*. He appeared with a quintet in the Cole Porter revue *Seven Lively Arts* (N.Y., Dec. 7, 1944), which ran 182 performances. In April 1945 he had his first Top Ten album with *Hot Jazz*, which reissued some of his 1930s recordings for RCA Victor. He reorganized his big band and went back to recording for Columbia, scoring three Top Ten hits during 1945: "Gotta Be This or That" (music and lyrics by Sunny Skylar) in July; "It's Only a Paper Moon" (music by Harold Arlen, lyrics by E. Y. Harburg and Billy Rose) in September; and "I'm Gonna Love That Guy" (music and lyrics by Frances Ash) in October. In 1946 he reached the Top Ten of the singles charts with "Symphony" (music by Alex Alstone, English lyrics by Jack Lawrence) in January and "Blue Skies" (music and lyrics by Irving Berlin) in August, and his album *Benny Goodman Sextet Session* hit #1 in May.

During 1946 and into 1947, Goodman shared a radio show with musical comedian Victor Borge. He scored a Top Ten hit with "A Gal in Calico" (music by Arthur Schwartz, lyrics by Leo Robin) in January 1947. In October 1948 he appeared in the film *A Song Is Born*, and he scored his last Top Ten single with "On a Slow Boat to China" (music and lyrics by Frank Loesser) in December. With his band of 1948–49 he tried mixing bebop with his more familiar swing repertoire. In December 1949 he disbanded, thereafter assembling groups only for specific tours or recording sessions.

Discovering transcriptions of his January 1938 Carnegie Hall concert, Goodman released the album *Carnegie Hall Jazz Concert, Vols. 1 & 2* on Columbia in November 1950; it reached the Top Ten and stayed in the charts for a year, becoming the best-selling jazz album up to that time. Later, it was inducted into the Grammy Hall of Fame. Columbia followed it in the fall of 1952 with an album of air-checks, *Benny Goodman, 1937–1938, Jazz Concert No. 2*, which went to #1 in December.

Goodman rerecorded some of his better-known songs for the Capitol album *B.G. in Hi-Fi*, which hit the Top Ten in March 1955. He recorded the music for his film biography, *The Benny Goodman Story*, starring Steve Allen, and upon the film's release in February 1956 the soundtrack album hit the Top Ten. Increasingly, Goodman performed overseas, starting with a Far East tour in 1956–57, and in 1962 he undertook a tour of the U.S.S.R. that resulted in the chart LP *Benny Goodman in Moscow*. A studio reunion of the 1930s version of the Benny Goodman Quartet, featuring Gene Krupa, Teddy Wilson, and Lionel Hampton, resulted in the 1964 chart LP *Together Again!*

Goodman recorded less frequently in the last two decades of his life, but he returned to the charts in 1971 with *Benny Goodman Today*, a live album recorded in Stockholm. He continued to perform until his death from a heart attack in 1986 at the age of 77. After he died, his final album, *Let's Dance*, the soundtrack to a television special, earned a Grammy Award nomination for Best Jazz Instrumental Performance, Big Band.

WRITINGS: With Irving Kolodin, *The Kingdom of Swing* (N.Y., 1939); introduction by S. Baron, *B.: King of Swing: A Pictorial Biography Based on B. G.'s Personal Archives* (N.Y., 1979).

BIBL.: D. Connor and W. Hicks, *B. G. Off the Record: A Bio-Discography of B. G.* (Fairless Hills, Pa., 1958; rev. ed., *B. G. on the Record: A Bio-Discography of B. G.*, 1969; 2nd rev. ed. *The Record of a Legend: A Bio-Discography of B. G.*, 1984); S. Ayeroff, *B. G. for B-Flat Clarinet* (1980); Ayeroff, *B. G.* (1986); D. Connor, *B. G.: Listen to His Legacy* (Metuchen, N.J., 1988); B. Crowther, *B. G.* (London, 1988); J. Collier, *B. G. and the Swing Era* (N.Y., 1989); R. Firestone, *Swing, Swing, Swing: The Life & Times of B. G.* (N.Y., 1993); D. Connor, *B. G.: Wrappin' It Up* (Lanham, Md., 1996).—WR

Goodman, Roy, English conductor, violinist, and keyboard player; b. Guilford, Surrey, Jan. 26, 1951. After serving as a chorister at King's Coll., Cambridge (1959–64), he studied at the Royal Coll. of Music in London (1968–70) and the Berkshire Coll. of Education (1970–71). He then was director of music at the Univ. of Kent and of early music at the Royal Academy of Music in London, and then founded the Brandenburg Consort in 1975. From 1979 to 1986 he was co-director of the Parley of Instruments. He was principal conductor of the Hanover Band from 1986 to 1994, an orch. specializing in period instrument performances of scores from the Baroque and Classical eras. He also conducted operas from that period, especially those by Handel and Mozart. In 1988 he became music director of the European Union Baroque Orch. He also was music director of the Umeå Sym. Orch. in Sweden from 1996.—NS/LK/DM

Goodson, Katharine, English pianist; b. Watford, Hertfordshire, June 18, 1872; d. London, April 14, 1958. From 1886 to 1892 she was a pupil of O. Beringer at the Royal Academy of Music in London, and from 1892 to 1896 of Leschetizky in Vienna. She made her debut in London at a Saturday Popular Concert, Jan. 16, 1897, with signal success, then made tours of England, France, Austria, and Germany, which established her reputation. Her American debut, with the Boston Sym., took place on Jan. 18, 1907. She subsequently made many tours of the U.S., the Netherlands, Belgium, and Italy. In 1903 she married **Arthur Hinton.**—NS/LK/DM

Goo Goo Dolls, pop band, formed 1985. **MEMBERSHIP:** John Rzeznik, voc., gtr. (b. Buffalo, N.Y., Dec. 5, 1965); Robby Takac, bs., voc. (b. Buffalo, N.Y., Sept. 30, 1964); George Tutuska, drm.

They started playing together in high school in Buffalo with the even less likely name the Sex Maggots. They exchanged that unappealing name for their current sobriquet and started earning a reputation through the northeastern U.S. for bracing, loud shows and drunken reverie. This is not surprising because they idolized the punk band the Replacements. Their debut album had tunes like "Don't Beat My Ass (With A Baseball Bat)" and a song with a backwards masked message that asked "Hey mom, can I have another corn dog?" It also had covers of Cream and Blue Oyster Cult opuses and was alarmingly tuneful. After this self produced debut (picked up by Mercenary Records) the band signed with Metal Blade for *Jed*, a tighter album. *Hold Me Up* sharpened them even more, but the band still only had a cult following. For their 1993 album *Superstar Car Wash*, they worked with Replacements leader Paul Westerberg. Their song, "We Are the Normal" received some alternative play and raised the band's visibility a bit. However, it was 1995's *A Boy Named Goo* that proved to be their breakthrough, no small thanks to the #5 hit single "Name." The album went on to sell double platinum.

Just as the hit was breaking, Tutuska left the band. He was replaced by Mike Malinin (b. Washington, D.C., Oct. 10, 1967) for both the two-year tour that followed and the next recordings. These included tunes for soundtracks like *Ace Ventura: When Nature Calls*, *Batman and Robin*, and *City of Angels* which featured a tune Rzeznik wrote in a hotel room in one hour. That song, "Iris" inspired by a Calif. obituary listing, became the most- played cross-format song of all time, topping the pop charts; BMI awarded the song its "Most Played Song from a Film" award in 1998. It was also featured on the band's next album, *Dizzy Up the Girl*, which went triple platinum and topped out at #15, further helped by the #16 single "Black Balloon." Bouyed by its success, the Goo Goo Dolls spent most of 1999 touring in support of the album, and were a featured act in MTV's Millenium New Year's Eve program. Attesting to their mainstream acceptance, they appeared on TV's *Sesame Street* in early 2000 singing a new version of their hit "Slide," re-titled "Pride," along with a guitar-strumming Elmo.

DISC.: *First Release* (1987); *Goo Goo Dolls* (1987); *Jed* (1989); *Hold Me Up* (1990); *Superstar Car Wash* (1993); *A Boy Named Goo* (1995); *Dizzy Up the Girl* (1998).—HB

Goossens, prominent family of English musicians of Belgian descent:

(1) Eugène Goossens (I), conductor; b. Bruges, Feb. 25, 1845; d. Liverpool, Dec. 30, 1906. He studied violin at the Bruges Cons. and violin and composition at the Brussels Cons. In 1873 he went to London, where he appeared as an operetta conductor. He was 2nd conductor (1883–89) and principal conductor (1889–93) of the Carl Rosa Opera Co., then settled in Liverpool, where he was founder-conductor of the Goossens Male Voice Choir (from 1894).

(2) Eugène Goossens (II), violinist and conductor, son of the preceding; b. Bordeaux, Jan. 28, 1867; d. London, July 31, 1958. He studied in Bruges and at the Brussels Cons. (1883–86), and then went to England, where he worked as a violinist, répétiteur, and asst. conductor under his father with the Carl Rosa Opera Co. He also continued his studies at London's Royal Academy of Music (1891–92). After conducting various traveling opera companies, he served as principal conductor of the Carl Rosa Opera Co. (1899–1915), and later was a conductor with the British National Opera Co. He had the following 4 children, who became musicians.

(3) Sir (Aynsley) Eugene Goossens, distinguished conductor and composer; b. London, May 26, 1893; d. there, June 13, 1962. He first studied at the Bruges Cons. (1903–04), then at the Liverpool Coll. of Music. After winning a scholarship to the Royal Coll. of Music in London in 1907, he studied there with Rivarde (violin), Dykes (piano), and C. Wood and Stanford (composition). He was a violinist in the Queen's Hall Orch. (1912–15), then was asst. conductor to Beecham (1915–20). In 1921 he founded his own London orch., and he also conducted opera and ballet at Covent Garden (1921–23). After serving as music director of the Rochester (N.Y.) Phil. (1923–31), he greatly distinguished himself as music director of the Cincinnati Sym. Orch. from 1931 to 1947. He then was chief conductor of the Sydney (Australia) Sym. Orch. and director of the New South Wales Conservatorium (1947–56). In 1955 he was knighted. He was a discriminating interpreter of the late 19th and early 20th century repertoire of the Romantic and Impressionist schools. As a composer, he wrote in all genres; his style became a blend of impressionistic harmonies and neo-Classical polyphony; while retaining a clear tonal outline, he often resorted to expressive chromatic melos bordering on atonality. He publ. *Overture and Beginners: A Musical Autobiography* (London, 1951).

WORKS: DRAMATIC: *L'Ecole en Crinoline*, ballet (1921–22); *East of Suez*, incidental music to Maugham's play (London, Sept. 1922); *Judith*, opera after Arnold Benedict (1926–29; London, June 25, 1929, composer conducting); *Don Juan de Mañara*, opera after Arnold Benedict (1930–35; London, June 24, 1937, composer conducting). **ORCH.:** *Variations on a Chinese Theme* (1911); *Miniature Fantasy* for Strings (1911); *Perseus*, symphonic poem (1914); *Ossian*, symphonic prelude (1915); *2 Sketches* (1916; London, Jan. 3, 1917, composer conducting; also for String Quartet, London, March 10, 1916); *Kaleidoscope* (1917; 1920–26; suite, London, Aug. 15, 1933; also for Piano); *Tam O'Shanter: Scherzo* (1917–18; London, April 29, 1919, composer conducting); *4 Conceits* (Liverpool, Nov. 13, 1918, composer conducting; also for Piano, 1920); *Prelude to "Philip II"* (1918; London, Aug. 27, 1919, composer conducting); *The Hurdy- Gurdy Man* (1918–20); *Lyric Poem* for Violin and Orch. (1919; N.Y., Sept. 11, 1929; also for Violin and Piano, 1920); *The Eternal Rhythm* (London, Oct. 19, 1920, composer conducting); *Sinfonietta* (1922–23; London, Feb. 19, 1923, composer conducting); *Phantasy* for Strings (1923; Cincinnati, Feb. 6, 1942, composer conducting; also for String Sextet, Pittsfield, Mass., Sept. 29, 1923); Concertino for Double String Orch. (1926; rev. version, N.Y., Dec. 18, 1929; also for String Octet, London, Feb. 19, 1929); *Rhythmic Dance* (Rochester, N.Y., March 12, 1927, composer conducting); Oboe Concerto (London, Oct. 2, 1930); *Variations on "Cadet Roussel"* (1930; Bournemouth, Nov. 4, 1931; also for Voice and Piano, 1918); *3 Pictures* for Flute and Orch. (1935; Cincinnati, March 1936, composer conducting; also for Flute and Piano); *Intermezzo* from the opera *Don Juan de Mañara* (London, Oct. 12, 1936); *2 Nature Poems* (1937–38; Cincinnati, April 23, 1938, composer conducting); 2 syms.: No. 1 (Cincinnati, April 12, 1940, composer conducting) and No. 2 (BBC, London, Nov. 10, 1946); *Phantasy Concerto* for Piano and Orch. (1941–43; Cincinnati, Feb. 25, 1944, José Iturbi soloist, composer conducting); *Phantasy Concerto* for Violin and Orch. (1946–48; rev. 1958; London, Aug. 1959, composer conducting); *Divertisse-*

ment (1956–60; Sydney, June 22, 1963). C H A M B E R : *4 Sketches for Flute, Violin, and Piano or 2 Violins and Piano or Harp* (London, Nov. 1913); Suite for Flute, Violin, and Harp or 2 Violins and Harp or Piano (1914); *5 Impressions of a Holiday* for Flute or Violin, Cello, and Piano (1914; London, Feb. 1915); *Phantasy String Quartet* (London, June 28, 1915); String Quartet (London, Dec. 10, 1915); *2 Sketches* for String Quartet (London, March 10, 1916; also for String Orch., London, Jan. 3, 1917, composer conducting); *Rhapsody* for Cello and Piano (1916; London, Jan. 6, 1917); 2 violin sonatas: No. 1 (London, June 18, 1918) and No. 2 (1930; Bradford, Jan. 20, 1931); Piano Quintet (1919); *Lyric Poem* for Violin and Piano (1920; also for Violin and Orch., 1919; N.Y., Sept. 11, 1929); *Phantasy Sextet* for 3 Violins, Viola, and 2 Cellos (Pittsfield, Mass., Sept. 29, 1923; also for String Orch., Cincinnati, Feb. 6, 1942, composer conducting); Concertino for String Octet (1926; rev. version, London, Feb. 19, 1929); *3 Pictures* for Flute and Piano (1935; also for Flute and Orch., Cincinnati, March 1936, composer conducting). P i - a n o : Concert Study (1914); *Kaleidoscope*, suite (1917; also as a suite for Orch., London, Aug. 15, 1933); *Nature Poems* (1919); *4 Conceits* (1920; also for Orch., Liverpool, Nov. 13, 1918, composer conducting); *Hommage à Debussy* (1920); *2 Studies* (1923); *Capriccio* (1960). V O C A L : 2 Songs for Voice and Piano (1914); *Deux Proses Lyriques* for Voice and Piano (London, April 14, 1916); 4 Songs for Voice and Piano (1917); *Variations on "Cadet Roussel"* for Voice and Piano (1918); *Persian Idylls* for Voice and Piano (London, June 18, 1918); *2 Scotch Folk Songs* for Voice and Piano (1918); 3 Songs for Voice and Piano or String Quartet (1920–21); 4 Songs for Voice and Piano (1931); *Apocalypse*, oratorio (1951; Sydney, Nov. 22, 1954, composer conducting). O T H E R : *Fanfare for a Ceremony* for 4 Trumpets (London, Oct. 27, 1921); *Fanfare for Artists* for 4 Trumpets, 4 Trombones, Timpani, and Percussion (London, May 8, 1930).

(4) Marie (Henriette) Goossens, harpist; b. London, Aug. 11, 1894; d. Dorking, Surrey, Dec. 18, 1991. She studied at the Royal Coll. of Music in London. She made her debut in Liverpool in 1910, then was principal harpist at Covent Garden, the Diaghilev Ballet, the Queen's Hall Orch. (1920–30), the London Phil. (1932–39), the London Sym. Orch. (1940–59), and the London Mozart Players (from 1972). She was also prof. of harp at the Royal Coll. of Music (1954–67). In 1984 she was made an Officer of the Order of the British Empire. Her autobiography was publ. as *Life on a Harp String* (1987).

(5) Leon Goossens, eminent oboist; b. Liverpool, June 12, 1897; d. Tunbridge Wells, Feb. 13, 1988. He studied at the Royal Coll. of Music in London (1911–14). He played in the Queen's Hall Orch. (1914–24), and later in the orchs. of Covent Garden and the Royal Phil. Soc. He subsequently was principal oboe of the London Phil. (1932–39), and also prof. of oboe at the Royal Academy of Music (1924–35) and the Royal Coll. of Music (1924–39). In succeeding years, he appeared as a soloist with major orchs. and as a chamber music artist. In 1962 he suffered injuries to his lips and teeth as a result of an automobile accident, but after extensive therapy he was able to resume his virtuoso career. He commissioned works from several English composers, among them Elgar and Vaughan Williams. In 1950 he was made a Commander of the Order of the British Empire.

(6) Sidonie Goossens, harpist; b. Liscard, Cheshire, Oct. 19, 1899. She studied at the Royal Coll. of Music in London. She made her orch. debut in 1921, and later was principal harpist of the BBC Sym. Orch. in London (1930–80). She served as prof. of harp at the Guildhall School of Music there (from 1960). She was made a Member of the Order of the British Empire in 1974 and an Officer of the Order of the British Empire in 1981.

BIBL.: C. Rosen, *The G.* (London, 1993).—NS/LK/DM

Goovaerts, Alphonse (Jean Marie André),

Belgian musicologist; b. Antwerp, May 25, 1847; d. Brussels, Dec. 25, 1922. He was a member of a literary family, and as a youth he became greatly interested in Flemish literature and in church music. He arranged and publ. a collection of Flemish songs (1868–74); composed several pieces of church music, and performed them with a chorus he established in Antwerp; also made transcriptions for chorus of works by Palestrina and Flemish contrapuntists. He publ. several papers propounding a reform in church music, which aroused opposition from conservative circles (*La Musique de l'église*, 1876; in Flemish as *De kerkmuziek*). He also publ. a valuable book, *Histoire et bibliographie de la typographie musicale dans le Pays-Bas* (1880; awarded the gold medal of the Belgian Academy), a monograph on the Belgian music printer Pierre Phalèse, and other studies relating to Flemish music.—NS/LK/DM

Gorchakov (real name, Zweifel), Sergei,

Russian conductor, teacher, arranger, and composer; b. Moscow, Feb. 10, 1905; d. there, July 4, 1976. He studied conducting with Saradzhev at the Moscow Cons., graduating in 1929. From 1939 to 1952 he conducted the orch. of the All-Union Soviet Radio; from 1960 he taught orchestration at the Inst. of Military Band Conducting. He became particularly interested in the problem of orch. arrangements; in 1959 he submitted a diss. on specific problems of transcribing piano music for wind orchestra, for which he received the degree of candidate of arts and sciences. He also publ. a practical manual of orchestration for wind orch. (Moscow, 1962). He made numerous orch. arrangements of piano music; of these, particularly notable was his orchestration of Mussorgsky's *Pictures at an Exhibition.*—NS/LK/DM

Gorchakova, Galina,

compelling Russian soprano; b. Novokuznetsk, March 1, 1962. She was born into a musical family, her father being a baritone and her mother a soprano. She studied at the Novokuznetsk Academy of Music and Cons. From 1988 to 1990 she sang with the Sverdlovsk Opera. During this time, she also appeared as a guest artist throughout Russia. In 1990 she made her debut at the Kirov Opera in St. Petersburg as Yaroslavna in *Prince Igor*. She secured her position as one of the company's leading artists shortly thereafter with her stunning portrayal of Renata in *The Fiery Angel*. In 1991 she sang Renata again in a concert performance in London, and again in 1992 with the visiting Kirov Opera at the Metropolitan Opera in N.Y. In 1994 she made her San Francisco Opera debut as Prokofiev's Renata. On Jan. 4, 1995, she made her debut with the Metropolitan Opera as Cio-Cio-San. Later that year she sang in Rome, Los Angeles, Edinburgh, and

London, and appeared as Tosca at the Opéra de la Bastille in Paris. In 1996 she was engaged as Cio-Cio-San at Milan's La Scala and as Tosca at London's Covent Garden. In 1997 she appeared as Tchaikovsky's Tatiana at the Metropolitan Opera. In 1998 she sang Tosca at the Teatro Colón in Buenos Aires. She also pursued a highly successful career as a recitalist. In addition to her compelling interpretations of the Russian operatic repertoire, Gorchakova has won distinction in operas by Verdi and Puccini.—NS/LK/DM

Gorczycki, Grzegorz Gerwazy, important Polish composer; b. Bytom, Silesia, c. 1647; d. Kraków, April 30, 1734. He studied at the Univ. of Prague; was rector of the Congregatio Missionis in Chelmno (1674–76), and studied theology at the Univ. of Vienna (1689); he received a doctorate in philosophy from 1 of the 2 aforementioned Univs. He may have been in the service of King Jan III Sobieski (1674–96). He was chapel master at Wawel Cathedral in Kraków (1698–1734), where he caught a fatal cold while conducting at the coronation of August III and Maria Josepha (Jan. 17, 1734). He was a significant figure in Polish religious music. His works to Latin texts include motets, hymns, Psalms, and masses, some with instrumental accompaniment.—NS/LK/DM

Gordeli, Otar, Russian composer; b. Tiflis, Nov. 18, 1928. He studied composition with Andrei Balanchivadze; later took courses at the Moscow Cons., graduating in 1955. In 1959 he was appointed instructor at the Tbilisi Cons. In his music, he applied resources of native folk songs; his polyphonic structure was considerably advanced.

WORKS: Piano Concerto (1952); *The Seasons,* cantata for Narrator, Boy's Chorus, and Chamber Orch. (1955); Concertino for Flute and Orch. (1958); *Festive Overture* (1959); *Georgian Dance* for Orch. (1961); Sym. (1964); film music; jazz pieces.—NS/LK/DM

Gordigiani, Giovanni Battista, Italian singer, teacher, and composer, brother of **Luigi Gordigiani;** b. Modena, July 1795; d. Prague, March 2, 1871. He was trained at the Milan Cons. After appearing in opera in Florence (1817) and Pisa (1818), he pursued a career as a concert singer. In 1822 he settled in Prague, where he later became a voice teacher. Teresa Stolz was one of his pupils. Among his works were several operas, church music, and songs.—LK/DM

Gordigiani, Luigi, Italian composer, brother of **Giovanni Battista Gordigiani;** b. Florence, June 21, 1806; d. Modena, May 1, 1860. He is chiefly known for his more than 300 songs for voice and piano, canzonette and canti populari based on Italian folk tunes; Gordigiani wrote the words for many himself. He also publ. a collection of songs based on Tuscan folk poems. Other works include 10 operas, 3 cantatas, a ballet, and an oratorio.—NS/LK/DM

Gordon, Dexter (Keith), jazz saxophonist, whose powerful and charismatic approach made a strong impression on John Coltrane and many other musicians; b. Los Angeles, Feb. 27, 1923; d. Philadelphia, April 25, 1990. His father was a doctor whose patients included Duke Ellington and Lionel Hampton. He studied clarinet, and took up the alto saxophone at age 15; he then turned to the tenor saxophone, and soon began playing in a local band. He left school to work with Hampton (1940–43) and Louis Armstrong (1944); then moved to N.Y., where he played in Billy Eckstine's band (1944–46). He entered the army, where he assaulted an officer who insulted a photo of his wife; this led to a year in the stockade at Camp Polk, La., followed by a dishonorable discharge. Returning to Los Angeles, he appeared with Wardell Gray (1947–52), freelanced, and led various combos, covering jazz, rhythm and blues, rock and roll, and some uncategorizable styles. His sextet backed Helen Humes in 1950. The next decade saw his career disrupted by heroin use; he even had a role in a production of Jack Gelber's play about addiction, *The Connnection* (1960). In 1962 he moved to Copenhagen and continued his career in Europe. He returned to the U.S. to great acclaim (1976) and was elected a member of the Jazz Hall of Fame (1980). He received rave reviews and an Oscar nomination for his performance in Bertrand Tavernier's film *'Round Midnight* (1986), playing "Dale Turner," a Lester Young–like figure somewhat based on Bud Powell's life. He also had a small role in *Awakenings.*

DISC.: *Dexter Rides Again* (1945); *Long Tall Dexter* (1945); "The Duel" (with T. Edwards; 1947); "The Chase" (with Wardell Gray; 1947); *Quintet* (1947); *Hunt* (1947); *Daddy Plays the Horn* (1955); *Dexter Blows Hot and Cool* (1955); *Resurgence of D. G.* (1960); *Dexter Calling...* (1961); *Doin' Alright* (1961); *A Swingin' Affair* (1962); *Go!* (1962); *Our Man in Paris* (1963); *One Flight Up* (1964); *Gettin' Around* (1965); *The Panther!* (1970); *Jumpin' Blues* (1970); *At Montreux* (1970); *Blues á la Suisse* (1973); *Apartment* (1974); *Bouncin' with Dex* (1975); *More Than You Know* (1975); *Swiss Nights, Vol. 1, 2* (1975); *Homecoming* (1976); *Sophisticated Giant* (1977); *Manhattan Symphonie* (1978); *Nights at the Keystone, Vols. 1–3* (1978); *Gotham City* (1981); *'Round Midnight* (soundtrack, 1986); *Other Side of 'Round Midnight* (1986).

BIBL.: S. Britt, *Long Tall Dexter: A Critical Musical Biography of D. G.* (London). T. Sjøgren, *Long Tall Dexter: The Discography of D. G.* (Copenhagen, 1986).—NS/MM/LP

Gordon, Frank, jazz trumpeter and composer; b. Milwaukee, Wisc., Sept. 27, 1938. After graduating high school (1957) he went to N.Y. to study with Donald Byrd who, along with Cannonball Adderley, convinced him to go back to Milwaukee and enroll in the Univ. of Wisc. (1963). He moved to Chicago (1966) and studied at Roosevelt Univ., where he completed a bachelor's degree (1970); he subsequently earned a master's at Governors State Univ. in Park Forest, Ill. (1977). During these years in Chicago he joined the AACM and studied with Byrd, Bunky Green, Eddie Harris, and Muhal Richard Abrams (the last intermittently through 1985). He moved to N.Y. to join the Thad Jones/Mel Lewis Band (1976). He has recorded and/or toured in North America, Europe, Mexico, and Cuba with Harris, Abrams, Lena Horne, Illinois Jacquet, Charli Persip, Art Blakey, David Murray, Hank Mobley, Charlie Haden, Clifford Jordan, Quincy Jones, the Duke Ellington band,

Sam Rivers, and his own groups. He won four NEA grants to present concerts of his music; in November 1997 three of his compositions, commissioned by the AACM, were premiered by the S.E.M. String Ensemble in N.Y. He was a founding member of Ebony Brass. He has taught trumpet at Rutgers Univ. (from 1992) and the New School for Social Research. His clear and logical improvisation recalls Clifford Brown; his skilled composition for strings as well as jazz combos bears the influences of Wayne Shorter, Debussy, and Bartok. In 1999 he moved to Savannah, Ga. He appears in the films *Texas Tenor: The Illinois Jacquet Story*; *The Cotton Club*; *Thad Jones/Mel Lewis Live at the Domicile*; and *Lena Horne on Broadway*.

DISC.: *Clarion Echoes* (1985). M. Roach: *And the So What Brass Quintet*. Ebony Brass Quintet: *Brand New Bag*. E. Harris: *Excursions*. C. Persip: *Superband; Superband II*. T. Jones/M. Lewis Orch.: *It Only Happens Every Time; Live in Munich*.—**LP**

Gordon, Jacques, Russian-American violinist and teacher; b. Odessa, March 7, 1899; d. Hartford, Conn., Sept. 15, 1948. He made his debut in Odessa at age 7. After graduating from the Odessa Cons. (1913), he emigrated to the U.S., where he studied with Kneisel (violin) and Goetschius (theory) at N.Y.'s Inst. of Musical Art. He played in the Russian Sym. Orch. in N.Y. and then was concertmaster of the Chicago Sym. Orch. (1921–31); also played in the Berkshire String Quartet (1917–20). He founded the Gordon String Quartet (1930), and led it until 1947; also was conductor of the Hartford (Conn.) Sym. Orch. (1936–39). He taught at the American Cons. of Music in Chicago (from 1921) and at the Eastman School of Music in Rochester, N.Y. (from 1942).—**NS/LK/DM**

Gordon, James Carel Gerhard, flute maker; b. Cape Town, May 22, 1791; d. Lausanne, c. 1845. He was born of a Dutch captain and a Swiss mother. He joined the Swiss Guards of Charles X in Paris in 1814. He concurrently studied flute with Tulou, and worked on improvements of its mechanism more or less at the same time as Böhm, so that the priority of the invention became a matter of insoluble controversy. He escaped with his life during the attack on the Swiss Guards in the Revolution of 1830. He was pensioned and retired to Switzerland when his mind became deranged.

BIBL.: C. Welch, *History of the Boehm Flute* (London, 1896).
—**NS/LK/DM**

Gordon, Mack (originally, **Gittler, Morris**), Polish-born American lyricist; b. Warsaw, Poland, June 21, 1904; d. N.Y., March 1, 1959. Gordon was a prolific songwriter for the movies; he wrote songs used in at least 90 feature films, almost all of them released by the major Hollywood studios, between 1929 and 1956. Usually writing only the lyrics (though he also wrote music on occasion), he collaborated most often with composers Harry Revel, Harry Warren, James V. Monaco, and Josef Myrow. His slangy, conversational words to Revel's songs in the 1930s typified the upbeat philosophy Hollywood adopted to counter the Depression, but he hit his peak in his work with Warren in the early 1940s, defining the Swing Era with such novelty songs as "Chattanooga Choo Choo" and "I've Got a Gal in Kalamazoo," and such romantic ballads as "I Had the Craziest Dream" and "You'll Never Know" (which won him his sole Academy Award among nine nominations). His other biggest hits included "I Can't Begin to Tell You," "My Heart Tells Me," and "Good Night, My Love."

Gordon's family immigrated when he was a child and settled in N.Y. As a youth he sang in a minstrel show, then became an actor, comedian, and singer in vaudeville. In 1925 he and Anton F. Scibilia wrote lyrics to music by George David Weist for the shows *Flashes of the Gay White Way* and *World of Pleasure*. Weist had changed his name to Weiss by the time he and Gordon teamed up again for the revue *Padlocks of 1929*, but he was still credited as Weist for "White Way Blues," a song he cocomposed with Max Rich to Gordon's lyrics for the November 1929 film *The Song of Love*. Gordon and Rich wrote two other songs used in the movie; he and Rich had songs in two other films released before the end of the year. Also in 1929, Gordon met British composer Harry Revel (1905–58), who became his accompanist in vaudeville.

Gordon next wrote songs with composer Abner Silver for the June 1930 film *Swing High*. He had his first popular song with "Time on My Hands (You in My Arms)" (music by Vincent Youmans, lyrics also by Harold Adamson), which was used in the Florenz Ziegfeld-produced musical *Smiles* (N.Y., Nov. 18, 1930), then became a hit in equally successful recordings by the orchs. of Smith Ballew and Leo Reisman, albeit not until the fall of 1931.

Gordon and Revel commenced their eight-and-a-half-year songwriting partnership contributing songs to the musical *Meet My Sister* (N.Y., Dec. 30, 1930). They were then hired as the principal songwriters for what turned out to be the final edition of the *Ziegfeld Follies*, supervised by Ziegfeld himself; it ran 165 performances. Gordon and Revel's next few Broadway shows were failures, but they scored a hit together in December 1932 with the independently published "Underneath the Harlem Moon," the most popular recording of which was by Joe Rines and His Orch.

Gordon and Revel scored two more independent hits in June 1933, "An Orchid to You," recorded by Eddy Duchin and His Orch., and "It Was a Night in June," recorded by Anson Weeks and His Orch., after which they moved to Calif. to write for the movies. Their first assignment, for United Artists, was *Broadway Thru a Keyhole*, which opened in November. Then they signed to Paramount and wrote songs for *White Woman*, also released in November, and *Sitting Pretty*, released in December. The latter contained "Did You Ever See a Dream Walking?" (a best-seller for Eddy Duchin) and "Good Morning Glory" (a hit for Tom Coakley and His Palace Hotel Orch.).

Gordon and Revel were the primary songwriters for five movie musicals released by Paramount in 1934; four of them produced hit songs. *We're Not Dressing*, featuring Bing Crosby and Ethel Merman, opened in April and included five hits: "Good Night, Lovely Little

1325

Lady," "Love Thy Neighbor," "May I?" and "Once in a Blue Moon" for Crosby; and "She Reminds Me of You" for Eddy Duchin. *Shoot the Works*, released in July, featured "With My Eyes Wide Open I'm Dreaming," a hit for Leo Reisman. Crosby was also the star of the September release *She Loves Me Not*, and he recorded "Straight from the Shoulder" for a minor hit. *College Rhythm*, out in November, featured "Stay as Sweet as You Are," which became a best-seller for Jimmie Grier and His Orch. in December. Gordon and Revel also were loaned out to RKO to write songs for the Fred Astaire-Ginger Rogers film *The Gay Divorcee*, and upon its November release "Don't Let It Bother You" became a hit for Fats Waller.

Gordon and Revel had four Paramount film credits in 1935, although Revel wrote the music for only one of the songs for *Love in Bloom*, which opened in April; Gordon wrote both music and lyrics for the rest, including "Lookie, Lookie, Here Comes Cookie" and "My Heart Is an Open Book," which became hits for Glen Gray and the Casa Loma Orch. *Stolen Harmony*, also released in April, featured a minor hit for Guy Lombardo and His Royal Canadians, "Would There Be Love?" Ray Noble and His Orch. topped the hit parade in August with the title song from *Paris in the Spring*. The same month saw the release of *Two for Tonight*, starring Bing Crosby, who made hits out of "From the Top of Your Head to the Tip of Your Toes," "Without a Word of Warning," and "I Wish I Were Aladdin."

Gordon and Revel wrote songs for a final film at Paramount, *Collegiate*, released in January 1936 and containing the hits "I Feel Like a Feather in the Breeze," recorded by Jan Garber and His Orch., and "You Hit the Spot," recorded by Richard Himber and His Orch. They then signed a two-year contract with 20th Century–Fox at the unprecedented rate of $50,000 per film; their first assignment was to write for the studio's biggest star, Shirley Temple. *Poor Little Rich Girl*, released in June 1936, contained "When I'm with You," which topped the hit parade for Hal Kemp and His Orch. in August. That same month Gordon and Revel scored one of their few independent hits, when Kemp took "A Star Fell Out of Heaven" into the hit parade. The team's second Shirley Temple vehicle, *Stowaway*, released in December, gave them another hit with "Good Night, My Love," which went to #1 for Benny Goodman and His Orch. in February 1937.

Both *Poor Little Rich Girl* and *Stowaway* found Gordon writing for Alice Faye; he would write the bulk of her lyrics for the rest of her career. He and Revel were the principal songwriters for five Fox features released in 1937. Three contained hits. *Wake Up and Live* (in which Faye starred), released in April, contained two songs that went into the hit parade, "Never in a Million Years" for Bing Crosby and "There's a Lull in My Life" for Teddy Wilson and His Orch. with Billie Holiday on vocals. *You Can't Have Everything* (also starring Faye), released in August, contained "Afraid to Dream," which became a hit for Benny Goodman. And "Sweet Someone," a hit for Horace Heidt and His Orch., came from *Love and Hisses*, released in December.

Gordon and Revel earned screen credit as the primary songwriters for six films released in 1938, including *Love Finds Andy Hardy*, for which they were loaned to MGM. But their first hit came from an interpolation when "Sweet as a Song," one of the two songs they contributed to the February release *Sally, Irene and Mary* (starring Alice Faye) reached the hit parade for Horace Heidt. The other hits from their films of the year were "Where in the World" from *Josette*, recorded by Hal Kemp, "I've Got a Date with a Dream" from *My Lucky Star*, recorded by Benny Goodman, and the title song from *Thanks for Everything*, recorded by Artie Shaw and His Orch. On Jan. 14, 1939, following a first marriage that produced two children but ended in divorce, Gordon married movie actress Elizabeth Cooke. They too later divorced.

Gordon and Revel split up in 1939; their last song together, "I Never Knew Heaven Could Speak," from the May 1939 release *Rose of Washington Square*, starring Al Jolson and Alice Faye, was a hit for Bob Crosby and His Orch. Following the breakup, Gordon sometimes wrote his own music and also tried working with other partners. In December he and composer James Van Heusen had an independent hit with "Speaking of Heaven," recorded by Glenn Miller and His Orch. Another independent song, "In an Old Dutch Garden" (music by Will Grosz), recorded by Dick Jurgens and His Orch., was in the hit parade from February to April 1940. And "This Is the Beginning of the End," for which Gordon wrote music and lyrics, was featured in the April release *Johnny Apollo* and recorded by Tommy Dorsey and His Orch. with Frank Sinatra on vocals, though it did not become a hit song until later.

Gordon finally found a new partner in Harry Warren, who moved to 20th Century–Fox from Warner Bros. following his split with lyricist Al Dubin. Gordon and Warren's first film together, the Shirley Temple vehicle *Young People*, released in August 1940, was not a success, but *Down Argentine Way*, which opened in October, established the team, featuring "Down Argentina Way," a Top Ten hit for Bob Crosby and Gordon's first Oscar nominee, and "Two Dreams Met," a minor hit for Tommy Dorsey. It also marked the film debut of lively Brazilian performer Carmen Miranda and made a star out of Betty Grable, who had sung Gordon lyrics previously but who now began to alternate with Alice Faye as one of the lyricist's most frequent film singers.

Gordon and Warren wrote songs for four Fox features released in 1941, enjoying their greatest success with *Sun Valley Serenade*, released in September. The film, which featured Glenn Miller's orch., contained three hits, all recorded by Miller: the chart-topping, million-selling Academy Award nominee "Chattanooga Choo Choo"; "I Know Why (And So Do You)"; and "It Happened in Sun Valley." As a result, three of Gordon and Warren's films of 1942 also featured swing bands. *Orch. Wives*, released in September, reunited them with Miller, resulting in another million- selling #1 Oscar nominee, "I've Got a Gal in Kalamazoo," a Top Ten hit, "Serenade in Blue," and a third chart entry, "At Last." *Iceland*, released in October, featured Sammy Kaye and His Orch., who made a hit out of "There Will Never Be

Another You." And the November release *Springtime in the Rockies*, which starred Betty Grable and Carmen Miranda, gave a supporting role to Harry James and His Orch., as James made a #1, million-selling record out of "I Had the Craziest Dream."

"You'll Never Know" was a Gordon/Warren interpolation into the March 1943 Alice Faye vehicle *Hello, Frisco, Hello*. Dick Haymes had the most popular recording of the Academy Award-winning song, a million-seller that hit #1. *Sweet Rosie O'Grady*, a Betty Grable vehicle released in October 1943, had a full Gordon/Warren score, including "My Heart Tells Me," made into a chart-topping record by Glen Gray.

Warren left 20th Century–Fox at the end of 1943, and Gordon teamed with composer James V. Monaco for three films released in 1944, among them the Betty Grable vehicle *Pin Up Girl*, released in May, which contained "Once Too Often," a minor hit for Ella Fitzgerald, and *Sweet and Low-Down*, released in October, which contained "I'm Making Believe," a #1, million-selling hit for the Ink Spots and Ella Fitzgerald and Gordon's fifth Oscar nominee in as many years.

Songwriter and producer Billy Rose engineered a quick reunion of Warren and Gordon for *Billy Rose's Diamond Horseshoe*, starring Betty Grable and Dick Haymes, which was released in May 1945 and featured "I Wish I Knew" and "The More I See You," both of which became Top Ten hits for Haymes. With Monaco, Gordon's next film was *The Dolly Sisters*, again starring Betty Grable and released in November. From it, "I Can't Begin to Tell You" went to #1 and sold a million copies in a recording by Bing Crosby; it was nominated for a 1946 Academy Award.

Monaco died suddenly, but Gordon found his fourth and final major collaborator in Russian émigré Josef Myrow, with whom he wrote regularly for the last decade of his career. Their first film together was *Three Little Girls in Blue*, released in September 1946, which Gordon produced and which contained their first hit, "On the Boardwalk (In Atlantic City)," recorded by the Charioteers. Warren contributed the music for "This Is Always," made into a Top Ten hit by Harry James. The most memorable song from the film turned out to be a non-hit, "You Make Me Feel So Young," which later was interpolated into several other movies and was given its greatest exposure in a 1956 recording by Frank Sinatra. Gordon's biggest hit to emerge from a 1946 film, however, was "Mam'selle" (music by Edmund Goulding) from *The Razor's Edge*, which was given a million-selling, chart-topping treatment by Art Lund and also hit #1 for Sinatra.

Gordon and Myrow's second film was the Betty Grable vehicle *Mother Wore Tights*. Released in Aug. 1947, it featured "You Do," which had five Top Ten recordings, the most successful of which was by Dinah Shore, and was nominated for an Academy Award, as well as "Kokomo, Indiana," recorded by Vaughn Monroe for a Top Ten hit. Writing with Alfred Newman, Gordon earned another Oscar nomination for "Through a Long and Sleepless Night" from the July 1949 release *Come to the Stable* and got his ninth and final Oscar nod for "Wilhelmina" (music by Josef Myrow) from the

Betty Grable vehicle *Wabash Avenue*, released in April 1950. But his only chart record during this period was a revival of "With My Eyes Wide Open I'm Dreaming" by the Patti Page Quartet in January 1950, and 20th Century–Fox dropped him after 14 years. Gordon worked on a freelance basis thereafter.

Gordon was brought over to MGM by Harry Warren and the two wrote songs for the Judy Garland-Gene Kelly film *Summer Stock*, released in August 1950. Ray Anthony, a former member of Glenn Miller's orch., peaked in the Top Ten with his own orch.'s revival of "At Last" in April 1952. Don Cornell finally made a hit out of "This Is the Beginning of the End" in August.

I Love Melvin, a 1953 feature for which Gordon and Myrow wrote the songs, produced a Top Ten soundtrack album. Gordon's last film was *Bundle of Joy* starring Eddie Fisher and Debbie Reynolds and released in December 1956. He died at age 54 in 1959. After his death his most frequently revived songs were those he had written with Harry Warren: "At Last" was taken into the R&B Top Ten by Etta James in 1961; "Chattanooga Choo Choo" reached the Top 40 for Floyd Cramer in 1962 and Tuxedo Junction in 1978; and Chris Montez had Top 40 revivals of "The More I See You" and "There Will Never Be Another You" in 1966.

WORKS (only works for which Gordon was a primary, credited lyricist are listed): **MUSICALS/REVUES** (dates refer to N.Y. openings): *Flashes of the Gay White Way* (1925); *World of Pleasure* (1925); *Padlocks of 1929* (1929); *Ziegfeld Follies* (July 1, 1931); *Fast and Furious* (Sept. 15, 1931); *Marching By* (March 3, 1932); *Smiling Faces* (Aug. 30, 1932). **FILMS**: *The Song of Love* (1929); *Swing High* (1930); *Broadway Thru a Keyhole* (1933); *White Woman* (1933); *Sitting Pretty* (1933); *We're Not Dressing* (1934); *Shoot the Works* (1934); *The Old Fashioned Way* (1934); *The Gay Divorcee* (1934); *She Loves Me Not* (1934); *College Rhythm* (1934); *Love in Bloom* (1935); *Stolen Harmony* (1935); *Paris in the Spring* (1935); *Two for Tonight* (1935); *Collegiate* (1936); *Poor Little Rich Girl* (1936); *Stowaway* (1936); *Everybody Dance* (U.K., 1936); *Head over Heels* (U.K., 1936; U.S., 1937 as *Head over Heels in Love*); *Wake Up and Live* (1937); *This Is My Affair* (1937); *You Can't Have Everything* (1937); *Ali Baba Goes to Town* (1937); *Love and Hisses* (1937); *Rebecca of Sunnybrook Farm* (1938); *Josette* (1938); *Love Finds Andy Hardy* (1938); *My Lucky Star* (1938); *Hold That Co-ed* (1938); *Thanks for Everything* (1938); *Star Dust* (1940); *Young People* (1940); *Down Argentine Way* (1940); *That Night in Rio* (1941); *The Great American Broadcast* (1941); *Charlie Chan in Rio* (1941); *Sun Valley Serenade* (1941); *Week-End in Havana* (1941); *Song of the Islands* (1942); *Orchestra Wives* (1942); *Iceland* (1942); *Springtime in the Rockies* (1942); *Sweet Rosie O'Grady* (1943); *Pin Up Girl* (1944); *Sweet and Low-Down* (1944); *Irish Eyes Are Smiling* (1944); *Billy Rose's Diamond Horseshoe* (1945); *The Dolly Sisters* (1945); *Three Little Girls in Blue* (1946); *Mother Wore Tights* (1947); *When My Baby Smiles at Me* (1948); *Wabash Avenue* (1950); *Summer Stock* (1950); *I Love Melvin* (1953); *The Girl Next Door* (1953); *Bundle of Joy* (1956).—**WR**

Gordy, Berry Jr., founder and visionary behind Motown Records; b. Detroit, Nov. 28, 1929. Berry Gordy Jr., dropped out of high school to become a featherweight boxer. Upon his discharge from the Army in 1953, he set up a record store that soon went bankrupt. Subsequently working on a Ford Motor Company assembly line, Gordy began writing songs during the mid-1950s. His first song sale, to Decca, was "Reet Petite," Jackie Wilson's first, albeit minor, pop hit in 1957. Gordy's earliest major songwriting success came with "Lonely Teardrops," a top rhythm-and-blues and smash pop hit for Wilson in 1958. Gordy formed Jobete Music in 1958 and began producing records for Eddie Holland and Marv Johnson, who scored a smash R&B and pop hit with Gordy's "You Got What It Takes" in 1959.

Encouraged by songwriter friend William "Smokey" Robinson, Gordy borrowed money from his family to found Tammie Records, soon changed to Tamla Records. The label's first significant success occurred as distributor of Barrett Strong's "Money," on his sister's Anna label. Later in 1960, "Shop Around," cowritten by Gordy and Robinson, became Tamla's first smash hit for Robinson's Miracles, establishing the label as an important independent. Eddie Holland's brother Brian subsequently collaborated on early hits by the Marvelettes, as Robinson worked with Mary Wells for a series of hits in 1962 on the newly formed Motown label. Before year's end, the Contours hit with the raucous "Do You Love Me," written by Gordy, on yet another label, Gordy.

As the Motown family of labels developed local Detroit talent, Brian and Eddie Holland teamed with songwriter Lamont Dozier in 1963 to create a distinctive pop sound of widespread appeal. Initially working with the rough- sounding Martha and the Vandellas, Holland-Dozier-Holland (H-D-H) achieved massive songwriting and production success with the Supremes from 1964 to 1967. The team also wrote and produced major hits for Marvin Gaye and the Four Tops. In the meantime, Smokey Robinson was writing hits for Mary Wells, the Temptations, Marvin Gaye, and his own Miracles.

Recognized by 1964 as the largest independent record company through its success in the singles market, Motown diversified into an entertainment complex. The Jobete Music Company handled song publishing and copyrighting, while Hitsville, U.S.A. controlled the company's recording studios and International Talent Management trained artists in matters of deportment. Gordy's unprecedented concern with career management, coupled with the rigorous discipline imposed on artists, alienated some of his acts and led to the company's first defection in 1964 by Mary Wells. Nonetheless, Motown became respectable as acts originally aimed at teen audiences were groomed for the adult pop market. Thus, acts were introduced into the American supper club circuit and prime-time television while the company was establishing itself internationally.

During 1967, to create a higher degree of visibility for several of its singers, Motown renamed three of its acts: the Supremes became Diana Ross and the Supremes; the Miracles, Smokey Robinson and the Miracles; and Martha and the Vandellas, Martha Reeves and the Vandellas. Later Motown experimented with psychedelic soul for the Temptations under producer-songwriter Norman Whitfield. The team of Nicholas Ashford and Valerie Simpson also provided hits to Marvin Gaye and Tammi Terrell, and to Diana Ross's solo career.

Suffering the departure of the Holland-Dozier-Holland team in 1967, Gordy concentrated on the career of Diana Ross as a solo act beginning in 1970. Maintaining the company's success with the astounding popularity of the teen-oriented Jackson Five, Gordy moved the operation to Hollywood in 1971 and established Motown Industries, expanding his activities to a Broadway musical and films. Bolstered by the success of Marvin Gaye and Stevie Wonder as album- oriented singer-songwriters, Motown was nonetheless challenged in the pop and soul fields by Kenny Gamble and Leon Huff's Philadelphia International label by 1973, particularly by the O'Jays.

During the first half of the 1970s, Diana Ross was established as Motown's first all-around entertainer through her work in supper clubs and films, particularly with 1972's *Lady Sings the Blues*. Other films, including *Mahogany* and *The Wiz*, proved flops between 1975 and 1978. Moreover, Motown suffered a series of defections in the 1970s. Martha Reeves began recording solo for other labels in 1974 and the Four Tops switched to ABC/Dunhill. Gladys Knight and the Pips recorded for Buddah beginning in 1974 and, in 1975, the Jackson Five moved to Epic, as did Michael Jackson in 1978. The Miracles (without Smokey Robinson) switched to Columbia in 1977 and the Temptations went to Atlantic. Nonetheless, Motown maintained its position as an important independent label with the recordings of Diana Ross, Marvin Gaye, Stevie Wonder, the Commodores, and Rick James.

During the 1980s, Motown struggled to retain its prominence in popular music. Diana Ross moved to RCA in 1981 and Marvin Gaye signed with Columbia in 1982. The Temptations returned in 1980 and the Four Tops were back in the mid-1980s, later switching to Arista. The Gordy label introduced the popular DeBarge family in 1983. The company staged a successful 25th anniversary celebration in 1983, later broadcast on ABC-TV, and Motown Productions produced *Lonesome Dove*, one of the highest-rated mini-series of the decade, for CBS television in 1989. However, many former employees, including Eddie Holland and members of the Vandellas and Marvelettes, sued Motown, alleging failure to pay royalties.

Inducted into the Rock and Roll Hall of Fame in 1988, Gordy sold Motown Records to MCA and Boston Ventures in July for $61 million. Boston Ventures later bought out MCA's interest and sold Motown Records to the Dutch-based Polygram conglomerate for $325 million in August 1993. In late 1994, Warner Books published Gordy's self-serving biography *To Be Loved*.

BIBL.: David Morse, *Motown and the Arrival of Black Music* (N.Y., 1971); Peter Benjaminson, *The Story of Motown* (N.Y., 1979); Don Waller, *The Motown Story* (N.Y., 1985); Nelson George, *Where Did Our Love Go? The Rise and Fall of the Motown Sound* (N.Y., 1986); J. Randy Taraborrelli, *Motown: Hot Wax, City Cool and Solid Gold* (Garden City, N.Y., 1986); David Bianco, *Heat Wave: The Motown Fact Book* (Ann Arbor, Mich., 1988); Sharon Davis, *Motown: The History* (Enfield, Middlesex, 1988); Ben Fong-Torres, *The Motown Album: The Sound of Young America*

(N.Y., 1990); Raymona Gordy Singleton, *Berry, Me and Motown: The Untold Story* (Chicago, 1990); Berry Gordy, *To Be Loved: The Music, the Magic, the Memories of Motown: An Autobiography* (N.Y. 1994).—**BH**

Górecki, Henryk (Mikoaj), celebrated Polish composer; b. Czernica, Dec. 6, 1933. He received training at the Secondary Music School in Rybnik (1952–55), and then was a composition student of Szabelski at the State Higher School of Music in Katowice (1955–60). While a student there, he was honored with an all-Górecki concert on Feb. 27, 1958, which included premieres of five of his works. In 1960 his *Monologhi* for Soprano and 3 Instrumental Groups won first prize in the Polish Composers' Union competition. His *Scontri* for Orch. created a great stir at its premiere at the Warsaw Autumn Festival on Sept. 21, 1960. In 1961 he was active in Paris, where his 1st Sym. won first prize in the 2nd Youth Biennale. He also met Boulez there and Stockhausen in Cologne. Until 1963 Górecki followed a confirmed modernist course as a composer. With his *3 Pieces in Old Style* for String Orch. (Warsaw, April 30, 1964), he instituted a "white note" modal idiom, inspired by medieval Polish music, which was to become prominent in all of his later vocal scores. His *Do Matki* (Ad Matrem) for Soprano, Chorus, and Orch. (Warsaw, Sept. 24, 1972) consolidated this modal idiom for the ensuing decade; the work won 1st prize at the Rostrum of Composers in Paris in 1973. In 1973–74 Górecki was in Berlin under the auspices of the Deutscher Akademischer Austauschdienst. In the meantime, he joined the faculty of his alma mater in Katowice in 1965, where he was made a lecturer in 1968, assoc. prof. in 1972, and rector in 1975. In 1977 he was awarded the title of prof. by the Polish government. He composed what would later become his most famous score, the 3rd Sym., *Symphony of Lamentation Songs* for Soprano and Orch. (Royan, April 4, 1977). The three movements of the work (1, a Lamentation of the Holy Cross Monastery of the 15th century; 2, the prayer of 18-year-old Helena Wanda Blazusiakowna inscribed on her Gestapo cell wall in Zakopane during World War II; 3, a folk song of the Opole region) made a profound impression upon auditors in the waning years of an unlamented century marked by man's inhumanity to man. For Pope John Paul II's first visit as Pope to his Polish homeland in 1979, Górecki composed his *Beatus vir* for Baritone, Chorus, and Orch., which was premiered in the presence of the Pope in Kraków on June 9th of that year. Later that year, Górecki was compelled to resign his post as rector of the Katowice Cons. in the face of pressure from the Communist government. In the wake of the Communist regime's attempts to destroy the Solidarity movement, Górecki was moved to compose his *Miserere* for Chorus in 1981, a work finally premiered in Wocawek on Sept. 10, 1987. With the end of Communist rule in 1989, Górecki was free to pursue his career unfettered as one of Poland's foremost composers in a style notable both for its uniqueness and for its highly refined spirituality. In 1994 he received an honorary doctorate from the Univ. of Warsaw.

WORKS: **ORCH.:** *Pieśni o radości i rytmie* (Songs of Joy and Rhythm) for 2 Pianos and Chamber Orch. (1956; Katowice, Feb. 27, 1958; rev. 1959–60; London, July 8, 1990); 3 syms.: No. 1, *1959*, for Strings and Percussion (Warsaw, Sept. 14, 1959), No. 2, *Kopernikowska* (Copernican), for Soprano, Baritone, Chorus, and Orch. (1972; Warsaw, June 22, 1973), and No. 3, *Symfonia pieśni żałosnych* (Symphony of Lamentation Songs), for Soprano and Orch. (1976; Royan, April 4, 1977); *Scontri* (Collisions; Warsaw, Sept. 21, 1960); *Trzy utwory w dawnym stylu* (Three Pieces in Old Style) for Strings (1963; Warsaw, April 30, 1964); *Choros I* for Strings (Warsaw, Sept. 22, 1964); *Refren* (Refrain; Geneva, Oct. 27, 1965); *Muzyka staropolska* (Old Polish Music) for Brass and Strings (1967–69; Warsaw, Sept. 24, 1969); *Canticum graduum* (Düsseldorf, Dec. 11, 1969); *3 Dances* (Rybnik, Nov. 24, 1973); Concerto for Harpsichord and Strings (Katowice, March 2, 1980; also for Piano and Strings, Poznań, April 22, 1990); *Concerto-Cantata* for Flute and Orch. (1991–92; Amsterdam, Nov. 28, 1992). **CHAMBER:** *Variations* for Violin and Piano (1956; Katowice, Feb. 27, 1958); *Quartettino* for 2 Flutes, Oboe, and Violin (1956; Katowice, Feb. 27, 1958); *Sonatina in 1 Movement* for Violin and Piano (1956); Sonata for 2 Violins (1957; Katowice, Feb. 27, 1958); Concerto for 5 Instruments and String Quartet (1957; Katowice, Feb. 27, 1958); *3 Diagrams* for Flute (1959; Warsaw, Sept. 21, 1961); *Diagram IV* for Flute (1961); *Chorale in the Form of a Canon* for String Quartet (Warsaw, Feb. 7, 1961); *Genesis I: Elementi* for String Trio (Kraków, May 29, 1962) and *II: Canti strumentali* for 15 Players (Warsaw, Sept. 16, 1962); *Muzyczka I* for 2 Trumpets and Guitar (1967), *II* for 4 Trumpets, 4 Trombones, 2 Pianos, and Percussion (Warsaw, Sept. 23, 1967), *III* for Violas (Katowice, Oct. 20, 1967), and *IV* for Trombone, Clarinet, Cello, and Piano (Vienna, April 15, 1970); *3 Little Pieces* for Violin and Piano (1977; Katowice, Jan. 5, 1978); *Kołysanki I tańce* (Lullabies and Dances) for Violin and Piano (1982); *Recitativa i ariosa: "Lerchenmusik"* for Clarinet, Cello, and Piano (Lerchenborg, July 28, 1984; rev. version, Warsaw, Sept. 25, 1985; 2nd rev. version, Poznań, April 12, 1986); *Dla Ciebie, Anne-Lill* (For You, Anne-Lill) for Flute and Piano (1986; rev. version, Lerchenborg, Aug. 4, 1990); *Aria (scena operowa)* [Aria (operatic scene)] for Tuba, Piano, Tam-tam, and Bass Drum (Salzburg, May 28, 1987); 2 string quartets: No. 1, *Już się zmierzcha* (Already it is Dusk; 1988; Minneapolis, Jan. 21, 1989) and No. 2, *Quasi una fantasia* (1990–91; Cleveland, Oct. 27, 1991); *Małe Requiem dla pewnej Polki* (Little Requiem for a Polka) for Piano and 13 Instruments (Amsterdam, June 12, 1993); Piece for String Quartet (1993; N.Y., Jan. 20, 1994); *Valentine Piece* for Flute and Small Bell (N.Y., Feb. 14, 1996). **KEYBOARD: Piano:** *4 Preludes* (1955; Katowice, Jan. 30, 1970); *Toccata* for 2 Pianos (1955; Katowice, Feb. 27, 1958); Sonata (1956; rev. version, Lerchenborg, July 28, 1984; 2nd rev. version, 1990; Helsinki, March 17, 1991); *Z ptasiego gniazda* (From the Bird's Nest; 1956); *Kołysanka* (Lullaby; 1956–80); *Utwory różne* (Sundry Pieces; 1956–61; 1990); *5 Pieces* for 2 Pianos (1959); *Mazurkas* (1980); *Intermezzo* (Lerchenborg, Aug. 3, 1990). **Organ:** *Kantata* (1968; Kamień Pomorski, July 18, 1969). **VOCAL:** *3 Songs* for Medium Voice and Piano (1956); *2 Songs* for Medium Voice and Piano, after García Lorca (1956–80); *Epitafium* for Chorus and Instrumental Ensemble (Warsaw, Oct. 3, 1958); *Monologhi* for Soprano and 3 Instrumental Groups (1960; Berlin, April 26, 1968); *Genesis III*, monodrama for Soprano, Metal Percussion, and 6 Double Basses (1963); *Do Matki* (Ad Matrem) for Soprano, Chorus, and Orch. (1971; Warsaw, Sept. 24, 1972); *2 Sacred Songs* for Baritone and Orch. (1971; Poznań, April 6, 1976; also for Baritone and Piano); *Euntes ibant et flebant* (They Who Go Forth and Weep) for Chorus (1972–73; Wrocław, Aug. 31, 1975); *2 Little Songs* for Chorus of 4 Equal Voices (1972); *Amen* for Chorus (Poznań, April 5, 1975); *Beatus vir* for Baritone, Chorus, and Orch. (Kraków, June 9, 1979); *Szeroka woda* (Broad Waters) for Chorus (1979; Poznań, April 28, 1987); *Błogosławione pieśni malinowe* (Blessed Raspberry Songs) for Voice and Piano (1980); *Miserere* for Chorus (1981–87; Wocawek, Sept. 10, 1987); *Wieczór ciemny się uniża* (Dark Evening is Falling), 5 folk songs for Chorus (1981); *Wiso moja, Wiso szara* (My Vistula, Grey Vistula), folk song for Chorus (1981; Poznań, April 28, 1987); *O Domina Nostra: Medytacje o Jasnogórskiej Pani Naszej* (O Domina Nostra: Meditations on Our Lady of Jasna Góra) for Soprano and Organ (1982–85; Poznań, March 31, 1985; rev. version, London, July 7, 1990); Songs for Voice and Piano, after J. Słowacki (1983; Zakopane, Sept. 14, 1985); *Trzy kołysanki* (3 Lullabies) for Chorus (1984; rev. version, Lerchenborg, Aug. 2, 1991); *Ach, mój wianku lewandowy* (O, My Garland of Lavender), 7 folk songs for Chorus (1984); *Idzie chmura, pada deszcz* (Cloud Comes, Rain Falls), 5 folk songs for Chorus (1984); *Pieśni Maryjne* (Marian Songs) for Chorus (Warsaw, June 3, 1985); *Pod Twoją obronę* (Under Your Protection), Marian song for Chorus (1985); *Na Anioł Pański biją dzwony* (The Bells Ring Out for the Angelus Domini) for Chorus (1986); *Pieśni kościelne* (Church Songs) for Chorus (1986; Warsaw, April 1987); *Totus Tuus* for Chorus (Warsaw, July 19, 1987); *Przybądź Duchu Święty* (Come Holy Spirit) for Chorus (1988; Warsaw, Oct. 11, 1993); *Dobranoc* (Good Night) for Soprano, Alto Flute, 3 Tam-tams, and Piano (1988–90; London, May 6, 1990); *Trzy fragmenty do słów Stanisława Wyspiańskiego* (3 Fragments to Words by Stanisław Wyspiański) for Voice and Piano (Zakopane, Feb. 23, 1996). **BIBL.:** A. Thomas, *G.* (Oxford, 1997; Polish tr., Kraków, 1998).—NS/LK/DM

Gorin, Igor, Russian-born American baritone; b. Grodek, Ukraine, Oct. 26, 1908; d. Tucson, Ariz., March 24, 1982. His family moved to Vienna after the Russian Revolution, where he studied medicine and music. He entered the Cons., graduating in 1930, then made his professional operatic debut at the Volksoper the same year. In 1933 he went to the U.S., becoming a naturalized citizen in 1939. He launched a successful career as a radio singer, without forsaking his operatic ambitions. He made his debut at the Metropolitan Opera in N.Y. as Germont *père* in *La Traviata* (Feb. 10, 1964). In his last years he taught voice at the Univ. of Ariz. in Tucson. —NS/LK/DM

Gorini, Gino (actually, **Luigino,**) Italian pianist, teacher, and composer; b. Venice, June 22, 1914; d. there, Jan. 27, 1990. He studied with Tagliapietra (piano diploma, 1931) and Agostini (composition diploma, 1933) at the Venice Cons., and also had composition lessons with Malipiero. He was a prof. of piano at the Venice Cons. from 1940, and also made tours as a pianist in Italy and abroad. He publ. *La musica pianistica di G. Francesco Malipiero* (Florence, 1977).

WORKS: DRAMATIC: Film scores. **ORCH.:** *Maschere* for Small Orch. (1934); *Tre omaggi* (1934); Suite for Violin and Orch. (1934); *Due studi da concerto* for Piano and Orch. (1935); Flute Concerto (1935); Sym. (1936); *Introduzione e arioso* (1937); *Due Invenzioni* for Piano and Orch. (1937); Violin Concerto (1943); Piano Concerto (1948); *Serenata* for Strings, Harpsichord, and Percussion (1966); Concerto for Viola, Piano, and Orch. (1974). **CHAMBER:** *Contrasti* for 5 Instruments (1934); *Divertimento* for 8 Instruments (1935); Concertino for Chamber Group (1935); *Tempo di sonata* for Violin and Piano (1935); String Quartet (1937); Cello Sonata (1939); *Canto notturno* for Cello and Piano (1945); Piano Quintet (1948); Sonata for Solo Violin (1982). **Piano:** Sonata (1936); 10 *Preludi brevi* (1941); *Ricercare e Toccata* (1960).—NS/LK/DM

Goritz, Otto, German baritone; b. Berlin, June 8, 1873; d. Hamburg, April 11, 1929. He received his musical education from his mother, Olga Nielitz. He made his debut on Oct. 1, 1895, as Matteo (*Fra Diavolo*) at Neustrelitz, and his success led to an immediate engagement for 3 years. From 1898 to 1900 he was in Breslau, and from 1900 to 1903 in Hamburg. On Dec. 24, 1903, he made his American debut at the Metropolitan Opera in N.Y. as Klingsor in the first production of *Parsifal* outside Bayreuth; remained there until 1917. In 1924 he returned to Germany, where he sang in Berlin and Hamburg.—NS/LK/DM

Gorme, Eydie (originally, **Gormezano, Eydie**) and **Steve Lawrence** (originally, **Sidney Leibowitz**), one of the most durable and popular nightclub acts of the last half of the 20th century. Gorme, b. Bronx, N.Y., Aug. 16, 1931 was the daughter of Sephardic Jewish immigrants, a Sicilian tailor father and Turkish mother, and sang in the big bands of Tex Beneke and Tommy Tucker while attending N.Y.'s City Coll. and working as an interpreter at the U.N. She would also hang out at the Brill Building, singing on occasional demo sessions. In 1953, she auditioned for a job as a singer on Steve Allen's *Tonight Show*. While she had the voice and knew the repertoire, she was not the type they wanted. They were looking for a Marilyn Monroe, not a svelt Mediterranean. They hired her provisionally for two weeks; however, due to her success, she spent four years on the show. On the show, she was reunited with one of her Brill Building acquaintances, Steve Lawrence (b. Brooklyn, July 8, 1935). The son of a Brooklyn cantor, he started singing in the synagogue choir. As a boy tenor, Lawrence also did demo work at the Brill Building. At 16, he won an Arthur Godfrey television talent competition. By 1952, he was on the charts hitting #21 with a version of "Poinciana." His H.S. principal had to give him time off to make appearances; he was only 17 at the time. By 1953, he was singing on *The Tonight Show*.

Gorme and Lawrence worked together on *The Tonight Show* writing and singing. They also launched successful solo careers. In 1953, Lawrence followed up with "How Many Stars Have to Shine," taking it to #26. In 1954, Gorme recorded the Broadway tune "Fini" with the Neal Hefti Orch. and took it to #19. In 1956, she reached #39 with another Broadway tune, "Too Close for Comfort." Lawrence took an even-less-ethnic-than-Harry-Belafonte version of "The Banana Boat Song" to #18 during the winter of 1957. While working on *The Tonight Show*, Gorme and Lawrence started dating. The day after Gorme hit the Top 40 with "Love Me Forever," she and Lawrence were married, just before New Year's, 1958. Paul Newman and JoAnne Woodward, who were married on the same day in the same place, were witnesses. The song went to #24. The marriage lasted over 40 years.

In the spring of 1958, Lawrence recorded a lightweight remake of Buddy Knox's rockabilly tune "Party Doll." The Knox tune topped the charts; Lawrence's version only made #5. Around the same time, Gorme hit #11 with "You Need Hands." That summer, they hosted a summer replacement for *The Tonight Show*. Then Lawrence got drafted, serving as the official vocalist for the U.S. Army Band.

Through the early 1960s, while still in the Army, Lawrence had a series of MOR Top Ten hits with "Pretty Blue Eyes" (#9, 1960), "Footsteps" (#7, 1960) and "Portrait of My Love" (#9, 1961). Their album as a duo, *We Got Us*, won Best Performance by a Vocal Group (2 to 6) at the 3rd Annual Grammy Awards in 1960. After his Army service, Lawrence topped both the pop and adult contemporary charts in 1963 with "Go Away Little Girl," later a chart topper for Donny Osmond. Around the same time, Gorme was climbing the charts with her biggest hit, "Blame It on the Bossa Nova." These hits represented the pinnacles of their careers. By this time, they were working together as Steve and Eydie, becoming a highly successful nightclub act in places like Las Vegas. Eventually, they became one of the select acts to sign up with the Desert Inn to play that hotel exclusively in exchange for stock options in the hotel.

Although it didn't chart pop, Gorme won Best Vocal Performance, Female in 1966 at the 9th Annual Grammy Awards for the tune "If He Walked into My Life." Both appeared on Broadway, Lawrence earning a Tony nomination in the musical *What Makes Sammy Run* (1964–65) and the couple appearing in two years in the show *Golden Rainbow* (1968–70). Their 1975 television tribute to George Gershwin, *Our Love Is Here to Stay*, won two Emmy Awards. Their tribute to Irving Berlin three years later won seven. After over 40 years of performing together, they still sell out clubs nationwide. Gorme also continues to record solo, frequently in Spanish.

DISC.: Steve and Eydie: *S. & E. Sing the Golden Hits* (1960); *Two on the Aisle* (1963); *At the Movies* (1963); *That Holiday Feeling* (1964); *Together on Broadway* (1967); *Golden Rainbow* (soundtrack; 1968); *What It Was, Was Love* (soundtrack; 1969); *S. & E. & Friends Celebrate Gershwin* (1979); *We Got Us* (1984); *Alone Together* (1989). Steve Lawrence: *Here's S. L.* (1958); *Swing Softly with Me* (1959); *Portrait of My Love* (1961); *Winners!* (1963); *Academy Award Losers* (1964); *Everybody Knows* (1964); *S. L. Show* (1965); *What Makes Sammy Run?* (soundtrack; 1965); *Together on Broadway* (1967); *Golden Rainbow* (soundtrack; 1968); *Real True Lovin'* (1969); *Pretty Blue Eyes* (1985); *All About Love* (1987); *Come Waltz with Me* (1987); *People Will Say We're in Love* (1987); *S. L. Deluxe* (1987); *Swinging West* (1989); *About That Girl* (1991); *Songs Everybody Knows* (1991); *S. L. Sound* (1991). Eydie Gorme: *E. Swings the Blues* (1957); *Delight* (1957); *E. G. Vamps the Roaring 20's* (1958); *E. in Love* (1958); *Showstoppers* (1958); *Love Is a Season* (1958); *E. G. on Stage* (1959); *Come Sing with Me* (1961); *Blame It on the Bossa Nova* (1963); *Let the Good Times Roll* (1963); *Amor* (1964), *G. Country Style* (1964); *More Amor* (1965); *The Sound of Music* (1965); *Don't Go to Strangers* (1966); *Softly, As I Leave You* (1967); *Tonight I'll Say a Prayer* (1970); *Sings* (1987); *De Corazon a Corazon* (1988); *Canta en Espanol* (1989); *E. G. & Los Panchos* (1989); *Blanca Navidad* (1990); *Eso Es El Amor* (1992); *Muy Amigos T.H.* (1993); *Brillante* (1994); *24 Grandes Canciones* (1994); *Personalidad* (1996); *Corazon* (1998), *Eres Tu* (1999).—**HB**

Görner, Johann Gottlieb, German organist and composer, brother of **Johann Valentin Görner;** b. Penig, Saxony (baptized), April 16, 1697; d. Leipzig, Feb. 15, 1778. He settled in Leipzig and studied at the Thomasschule and the Univ. He was organist at the Univ. Church (from 1716), at St. Nicholas (from 1721), and at St. Thomas (from 1729). In 1723 Görner was also made music director of the Univ. Church, which appointment led to a dispute between Bach and the municipal authorities over musical responsibilities. All the same, relations between the two remained cordial. Görner retired from his duties in 1768. From 1723 to 1756 he also conducted the "second ordinary collegium musicum." He composed principally music for church use.—**LK/DM**

Görner, Johann Valentin, German composer, brother of **Johann Gottlieb Görner;** b. Penig, Saxony, Feb. 27, 1702; d. Hamburg, late July 1762. He was educated at the Univ. of Leipzig. After serving several German courts, he settled in Hamburg about 1729, and from 1756 was Cathedral music director. He composed *Sammlung neuer Oden und Lieder* (3 vols., 1742, 1744, 1752).—**LK/DM**

Gorodnitzki, Sascha, Russian-born American pianist and pedagogue; b. Kiev, May 24, 1904; d. N.Y., April 4, 1986. He was taken to the U.S. at an early age. After piano lessons with his mother, he studied with Edwin Hughes at N.Y.'s Inst. of Musical Art; he then was a pupil of J. Lhévinne (piano) and Goldmark (composition) at N.Y.'s Juilliard Graduate School (1926–32). In 1931 he made his formal debut as soloist with the N.Y. Phil., and then made tours throughout North America and Latin America. He also taught at the Juilliard Summer School from 1932, and then was a member of the piano faculty at the Juilliard School of Music from 1948 until his death. Among his outstanding students were Eugene Istomin and Garrick Ohlsson.—**NS/LK/DM**

Gorr, Rita (real name, **Marguerite Geirnaert**), noted Belgian mezzo-soprano; b. Zelzaete, Feb. 18, 1926. She was a student in Ghent of Poelfiet and in Brussels of Pacquot-d'Assy. After winning 1st prize in the Verviers Competition in 1946, she made her formal operatic debut as Fricka in Antwerp in 1949, and then sang in Strasbourg (1949–52). In 1952 she won 1st prize in the Lausanne Competition, which led to engagements at the Opéra-Comique and the Opéra in Paris that same year. In 1958 she appeared at the Bayreuth Festival for the first time. In 1959 she made her debut at London's Covent Garden as Amneris, where she sang regularly with notable success until 1971. In 1960 she sang at Milan's La Scala for the first time as Kundry. She made her Metropolitan Opera debut in N.Y. as Amneris on Oct. 17, 1962, and remained on its roster until 1967. Gorr was a remarkably versatile artist, excelling in the works of Wagner and Verdi as well as in the French repertory. Among her memorable roles were Fricka, Kundry, Ortrud, Azucena, Eboli, Amneris, Ulrica, Charlotte, Dalila, and Berlioz's Dido.—**NS/LK/DM**

Gosfield, Annie (actually, **Anne**), American composer, instrumentalist, improviser, and sampling specialist; b. Philadelphia, Sept. 11, 1960. She studied piano with Bernard Peiffer (1972–76) and Alexander Fiorillo (1976) and composition at North Tex. State Univ. (B.M., 1981) and at the Univ. of Southern Calif. (M.A., 1983). Gosfield is active in N.Y.'s downtown music scene, composing both acoustic and electronic music and frequently working with detuned, prepared, and electronically altered pianos. Her detuned sounds, microtonal scordatura, approximated micro-intervals, and almost-unisons combine to create chamber works of distinct (and quite evocative) harmonic richness. In some of her compositions, she recreates and incorporates the sounds of machines and mechanical instruments, while in still others she musically encapsulates idiosyncratic stories and experiences of her family through past generations. Her music has been widely performed, and she herself as appeared throughout the U.S. and Europe with her own ensemble in programs featuring her own works. She often collaborates with the guitarist Roger Kleier. Recent projects include a site-specific work performed at a factory in Nuremberg (EWA7, 1999), and an octet for strings and percussion inspired by industrial sounds (*Flying Sparks and Heavy Machinery*, 2000). She also presents composition workshops at conservatories and colleges across the U.S. and in Europe, most recently at the Calif. Inst. of the Arts (1999) and at Hartt Coll. in Hartford (2000). She has received grants and commissions from the NEA, the Rockefeller Foundation, Meet the Composer, the Siemens Corporation, the Jerome Foundation, The American Music Center, and NYFA, among others.

WORKS: *Nickolaievski Soldat* for Sampler, Electric Guitar, and Percussion (N.Y., Sept. 21, 1993); *Second Avenue Junkman* for Piano, Guitar, and Percussion (or Any Combination of Instruments) (N.Y., Sept. 21, 1993); *Sound of the Independent Speaker* for Sampler, Electric Guitar, and Percussion (N.Y., April 9, 1993); *Of Dice and Men* for Sampler, Electric Guitar, and Percussion (N.Y., Oct. 28, 1994); *Lost Night* for Trumpet, Trombone, Multiple Percussion, Sampling Keyboard, 2 Violins, Viola, Cello, and Contrabass (N.Y., Dec. 8, 1995); *The Manufacture of Tangled Ivory* for Percussion, Keyboards, Cello, Contrabass, and Electric Guitar (N.Y., May 1, 1995); *Across Town* for Sampler (Geneva, May 10, 1996); *Blue Serge* for Sampler (Lucerne, May 5, 1996); *Combustion Chamber* for Sampler, Electric Guitar, and Percussion (Ulm, Germany, May 20, 1996; in collaboration with R. Kleier); *Freud* for Sampler or Bowed Vibraphone and Electric Guitar (Kraków, Nov. 15, 1996; in collaboration with R. Kleier); *Geisten* for Sampler and Electric Guitar (Kraków, Nov. 15, 1996; in collaboration with R. Kleier); *In Rides the Dust* for Flute, Tenor Saxophone, Trumpet, Trombone, 2 Percussion, 2 Pianists (at 1 Piano), and Strings (Prague, Nov. 10, 1996; also for Flute, Tenor Saxophone, Trumpet, Trombone, Percussion, 2 Pianists (at 1 Piano), Electric Guitar, Cello, and Contrabass, N.Y., May 11, 1997); *Marble Hunt* for Sampler (Lucerne, May 5, 1996); *Bottom of the Barrelhouse* for Disklavier (N.Y., April 27, 1997); *Brooklyn, October 5, 1941* for Piano, Baseballs, and Catcher's Mitt (Dec. 13, 1997); *Cram Jin Quotient* for Electronically altered String Quartet (N.Y., Sept. 19, 1997); *Four Roses* for Sampler and Cello (N.Y., May 10, 1997); *Tone Bender* for 4 Pianists at 2 Prepared Pianos (N.Y., April 6, 1997); *Swell* for Piano, Guitar, Sampler, Violin, and Cello (or Any Combination of Instruments) (N.Y., May 2, 1997); *Tempi di Hangover* for Sampler (Venice, Nov. 11, 1997); *Bimini Place* for Piano and Electric Guitar (or Any Combination

of Instruments) (Alburquerque, May 2, 1998); *Bones* for Sampler, Electric Guitar, and Percussion (N.Y., Oct. 29, 1998; in collaboration with R. Kleier); *Brawl* for Saxophone Quartet (San Francisco, June 21, 1998); *Chivas* for Sampler and Electric Guitar (Albuquerque, May 2, 1998; in collaboration with R. Kleier); *Djerassi Suite* for Sampler and Electric Guitar (Albuquerque, May 2, 1998; in collaboration with R. Kleier); *Friday, Three A.M.* for Sampler (N.Y., Oct. 29, 1998); *EWA7* for Sampler, Electric Guitar, and 2 Percussion (Nuremberg, July 20, 1999); *It Almost Passed in a Dream* for Flute, Bass Marimba, Harmonic Canon, Adapted Guitar, and Cello (Harry Partch/Newband Instruments) (N.Y., Feb. 12, 1999); *Mentryville* for Prepared Piano (Valencia, Calif., March 21, 1999); *Shoot the Player Piano* for Video and Music (Minneapolis, Nov. 4, 1999); *Cranks and Cactus Needles* for Flute, Piano, Violin, and Cello (Luxembourg, Oct. 6, 2000); *Flying Sparks and Heavy Machinery* for String Quartet and Percussion Quartet (San Francisco, March 16, 2000); also various works for dance (1996–99).—**LK/DM**

Goss, Sir John, English organist and composer; b. Fareham, Hampshire, Dec. 27, 1800; d. London, May 10, 1880. A son of Joseph Goss, the Fareham organist, he became a child chorister of the Chapel Royal; then studied under Attwood. He was successively organist of Stockwell Chapel (1821), St. Luke's, Chelsea (1824), and St. Paul's Cathedral (1838–72). In 1856 he was appointed a composer to the Chapel Royal. He was knighted in 1872 and received the degree of Mus.Doc. from Cambridge Univ. in 1876. His music includes church services, anthems, chants, Psalms, etc.; some orch. pieces; songs and glees. He ed. a collection of hymns, *Parochial Psalmody* (1826–27), *Chants, Ancient and Modern* (1841), and, with W. Mercer, *Church Psalter and Hymnbook* (1855). He publ. *The Organist's Companion*, 4 vols. of voluntaries and interludes and *An Introduction to Harmony and Thorough-bass* (1833).—**NS/LK/DM**

Gossec, François-Joseph, significant South Netherlands composer; b. Vergnies, Jan. 17, 1734; d. Paris, Feb. 16, 1829. He showed musical inclinations at an early age; as a child, he studied at the collegiate church in Walcourt and sang in the chapel of St. Aldegonde in Maubeuge, and then joined the chapel of St. Pierre there, where he studied violin, harpsichord, harmony, and composition with Jean Vanderbelen. In 1742 he became a chorister at the Cathedral of Notre Dame in Antwerp; received some instruction with André-Joseph Blavier in violin and organ there. In 1751 he went to Paris, where he became a violinist and bass player in the private orch. of La Pouplinière. In addition to writing chamber music, he composed a number of syms. in the style of the Mannheim school. He wrote a fine *Missa pro defunctis*, which was given at the Jacobean monastery in the rue St. Jacques in 1760. After La Pouplinière's death in 1762, he became director of the private theater of Louis-Joseph de Bourbon, Prince of Condé, in Chantilly, where he remained until 1770. From about 1766 he also served as ordinaire de la musique to Louis-François de Bourbon, Prince of Conti. After several failures, he gained success as a composer for the theater with his opéra-comique *Les Pêcheurs* (Comédie-Italienne, Paris, April 23, 1766). Although he continued to compose for the theater until the turn of the century, only his ballets and incidental music won popular favor. In 1769 he organized the Concert des Amateurs, which he developed into one of the most distinguished ensembles of the day. He composed a number of syms. for its orch., and also introduced the music of other composers to Paris. He then was one of the directors of the Concert Spirituel (1773–77). Gossec was also active with the Paris Opéra, where he was maître de musique (1775–89) and sous-director (1780–89). From 1782 to 1784 he likewise was head of the Opéra. He served as director of the École Royale de Chant from 1784 to 1789. Gossec welcomed the French Revolution, and in 1789 was made co- director (with Sarette) of the Corps de Musique de la Garde Nationale. He composed many works to celebrate Revolutionary events, and in 1793 he brought out an arrangement of the Marseillaise for gargantuan chorus and orch. His devotion to the Revolution earned him the title of "Tyrtée [Tyrtaeus] de la Révolution." In 1795 he was made a member of the newly founded Académie des Beaux-Arts of the Institut de France. In 1804 he was one of the first individuals made a Chevalier of the Légion d'honneur by Napoleon. He was one of the inspectors and a prof. of composition at the Paris Cons. from its founding in 1795 until it was disbanded by Louis XVIII in 1816.

Gossec's historic role rests principally upon his creation of a French type of symphonic composition, in which he expanded the resources of instrumentation so as to provide for dynamic contrasts; he experimented with new sonorities in instrumental and choral writing; his string quartets attained a coherence of style and symmetry of form that laid the foundation of French chamber music. In his choral works, Gossec was a bold innovator, presaging in some respects the usages of Berlioz; his Te Deum (1790), written for a Revolutionary festival, is scored for 1,200 singers and 300 wind instruments; in his oratorio La Nativité (1774), he introduced an invisible chorus of angels placed behind the stage; in other works, he separated choral groups in order to produce special antiphonal effects.

WORKS: DRAMATIC (all 1st perf. in Paris unless otherwise given): *Le Périgourdin*, intermezzo (June 7, 1761); *Le Tonnelier*, opéra-comique (March 16, 1765); *Le Faux Lord*, opéra-comique (June 27, 1765); *Les Pêcheurs*, opéra-comique (April 23, 1766); *Toinon et Toinette*, opéra d'Hyl comique (June 20, 1767); *Le Double Déguisement*, opéra-comique (Sept. 28, 1767); *Les Agréments as et Sylvie*, pastorale (Dec. 10, 1768); *Sabinus*, tragédie lyrique (Versailles, Dec. 4, 1773); *Berthe*, opera (Brussels, Jan. 18, 1775; not extant); *Alexis et Daphné*, pastorale (Sept. 26, 1775); *Philémon et Baucis*, pastorale (Sept. 26, 1775); *Annette et Lubin*, ballet (1778); *La Fête de village*, intermezzo (May 26, 1778); *Mirza*, ballet (Nov. 18, 1779; rev. 1788); *La Fête de Mirza*, ballet-pantomime (Feb. 17, 1781); *Thesée*, tragédie lyrique (March 1, 1782); *Électre*, incidental music (1782); *Nitocris*, opera (1783); *Le Premier Navigateur, ou Le Pouvoir de l'amour*, ballet (July 26, 1785); *Athalie*, incidental music (Fontainebleau, Nov. 3?, 1785); *Rosine, ou L'Éposue abandonnée*, opera (July 14, 1786); *Le Pied de boeuf*, divertissement (June 17, 1787); *Les Sabots et le cerisier*, opera (1803). **ORCH.:** About 50 syms., other orch. pieces, and Revolutionary works for Wind Band. **CHAMBER:** 6 trio sonatas (c. 1753); 6 duos for Flutes or Violins (c. 1754); 6 duets for 2 Violins (1765); 6 trios for 2 Violins and Bass with Horns ad libitum (1766); 12 string quartets (2 books, 1769 and 1772). **VOCAL: Choral:** *Missa pro defunctis* (1760; publ. as *Messe des morts* in 1780); 2 oratorios: *La Nativité* (1774; ed. by D. Townsend, N.Y., 1966) and *L'Arche d'alliance* (1781; not extant); motets and other sacred works. **Revolutionary Works For Voices:** About 40 such pieces, including a *Te Deum* (1790); *Le Chant du 14 juillet* (1791); *Choeur à la liberté* (1792); *L'Offrande à la Liberté* (1792); *Hymne à la liberté* (1792); *Le Triomphe de la république, ou Le Camp de Grandpré* (1793); *Hymne à la liberté (Hymne à la nature)* (1793); *Hymne a l'humanite* (1795); *La Nouvelle au camp de l'assassinat...ou Le Cri de vengeance* (1799).

BIBL.: P. Hédouin, *G.: Sa vie et ses ouvrages* (Valenciennes, 1852); É. Gregoir, *Notice biographique sur F.-J. Gossé dit G., compositeur de musique* (Mons, 1878); F. Hellouin, *G. et la musique française à la fin du XVIIIᵉ siècle* (Paris, 1903); L. Dufrane, *G.: Sa vie, ses oeuvres* (Paris, 1927); F. Tonnard, *F.-J. G.: Musicien hennuyer de la Révolution française* (Brussels, 1938); B. Brook, *La Symphonie française* (Paris, 1962); R. Macdonald, *F.-J. G. and French Instrumental Music in the Second Half of the Eighteenth Century* (diss., Univ. of Mich., 1968); W. Thibaut, *F.-J. G., Chantre de la Révolution française* (Gilly, 1970); R. Mortier and H. Hasquin, eds., *Fêtes et musiques revolutionnaires: Grétry et G.* (Brussels, 1990).—NS/LK/DM

Gossett, Philip, esteemed American musicologist; b. N.Y., Sept. 27, 1941. He was educated at Amherst Coll. (B.A., 1963), Columbia Univ. (1961–62), and Princeton Univ. (M.F.A., 1965; Ph.D., 1970, with the diss. *The Operas of Rossini: Problems of Textual Criticism in Nineteenth-Century Opera*); held a Fulbright fellowship (1965–66) and a Guggenheim fellowship (1971–72). He joined the faculty at the Univ. of Chicago in 1968, where he was a prof. (from 1977) and chairman of the music dept. (1978–84). From 1995 to 1996 he was president of the American Musicological Soc. He ed. and tr. Rameau's *Traité de l'harmonie* as *Treatise on Harmony by Jean-Philippe Rameau* (N.Y., 1971); with C. Rosen, he ed. *Early Romantic Opera* (44 vols., N.Y., 1977–83); also ed. *Italian Opera 1810–1840* (58 vols., N.Y., 1984–); also served as general ed. of *The Works of Giuseppe Verdi*. He publ. *The Tragic Finale of Tancredi* (Pesaro, 1977), *Le Sinfonie di Rossini* (Pesaro, 1981), and *Anna Bolena and the Artistic Maturity of Gaetano Donizetti* (Oxford, 1985), for which he received the ASCAP-Deems Taylor Award in 1986.—NS/LK/DM

Gostuški, Dragutin, Serbian composer and musicologist; b. Belgrade, Jan. 3, 1923. He studied art history at the Univ. of Belgrade (Ph.D., 1965), and also took courses in composition and conducting at the Belgrade Academy of Music. He subsequently was active as a music critic. In 1952 he was engaged as a member of the staff of the Musicological Inst. of the Serbian Academy of Arts and Sciences; in 1974 he became its director. His works include a symphonic poem, *Belgrade* (Belgrade, June 11, 1951), *Concerto accelerato* for Violin and Orch. (Belgrade, Nov. 14, 1961), a fantastic ballet, *Remis* (1955; 1st stage perf., Zagreb, May 15, 1963), chamber music, piano pieces, and songs. —NS/LK/DM

Gotovac, Jakov, Croatian conductor and composer; b. Split, Oct. 11, 1895; d. Zagreb, Oct. 16, 1982. He studied law at the Univ. of Zagreb, and music with Antun Dobronić in Zagreb and with Joseph Marx in Vienna. In 1923 he was appointed conductor of the Croatian National Opera in Zagreb, retaining this post until 1958. He composed mostly for the theater; his instrumental music is imbued with the folkways of Croatia, enhancing the simple native materials by carefully proportioned modernistic mutations while preserving the impulsive asymmetrical patterns of the original songs.

WORKS: DRAMATIC: O p e r a : *Dubravka* (1928); *Morana* (Brno, Nov. 29, 1930); *Ero s onoga svijeta* (A Rogue from the World Beyond; Zagreb, Nov. 2, 1935; in Ger. as *Ero der Schelm*, Karlsruhe, April 3, 1938); *Kamenik* (The Quarry; Zagreb, Dec. 17, 1946); *Mila Gojsalica* (Zagreb, May 18, 1952); *Stanac* (Zagreb, Dec. 6, 1959); *Dalmaro* (Zagreb, Dec. 20, 1964); *Petar Svačiç*, opera-oratorio (1969). ORCH.: *Simfonijsko kolo* (Zagreb, Feb. 6, 1927); *Orači* (Ploughmen; 1937); *Pjesme i ples za Balkana* (Balkan Song and Dance) for Strings (1939); *Guslar* (Gusla Player; Zagreb, Oct. 7, 1940); *Bunjevacka igra* (1960); *Dalmatinsko pastirče* (Dalmatian Shepherd) for Recorders (1962). VOCAL: Choral pieces; songs.—NS/LK/DM

Gottlieb, Jack,

American composer and writer on music; b. New Rochelle, N.Y., Oct. 12, 1930. He studied composition with Robert Strassberg before pursuing training with Karol Rathaus at Queens Coll. in N.Y. (B.A., 1953), Aaron Copland and Boris Blacher at the Berkshire Music Center in Tanglewood (summers, 1954–55), Irving Fine at Brandeis Univ. (M.F.A., 1955), and Burrill Phillips and Robert Palmer at the Univ. of Ill. (D.M.A., 1964, with the diss. *The Music of Leonard Bernstein: A Study of Melodic Manipulations*). From 1958 to 1966 he was Bernstein's assistant at the N.Y. Phil. After serving as music director of Temple Israel in St. Louis (1970–73), he returned to N.Y. and was composer-in-residence at the School of Sacred Music at Hebrew Union Coll.-Jewish Inst. of Religion (1973–75). In 1977 he joined Amberson Enterprises, Inc., the company responsible for Bernstein's musical activities and archives. In 1979 he founded Theophilous Enterprises, Inc., for the publication of his own works. From 1991 to 1997 he was president of the American Soc. for Jewish Music. Gottlieb has written extensively on Bernstein's life and legacy, and ed. the rev. edition of the vol. *Leonard Bernstein's Young People's Concerts* (N.Y., 1992). He held a Yaddo residency (1960) and 9 MacDowell Colony residencies (1962–76). In 1975 he received an NEA award. In 1993 he was honored with the first Ahad Ha'am Award of the Center for Jewish Culture and Creativity of Philadelphia. Gottlieb's style of composition is distinctly American, generally conservative and tonal, but liberally laced with spiky rhythms and pungent dissonances.

WORKS: DRAMATIC: *Tea Party*, opera (1955; Athens, Ohio, Aug. 4, 1957); *Public Dance*, opera (1964; withdrawn); *The Song of Songs, Which is Solomon's*, operatorio (1968–76); *The Movie Opera* (1982; N.Y., Feb. 28, 1985; stage perf., N.Y., June 19, 1986; rev. 1994); *Death of a Ghost*, opera (N.Y., Dec. 13, 1988); *Bellwether*, musical (N.Y., April 7, 1989; withdrawn); *After the Flood*, musical fable (1990–91; rev. 1995); *Monkey Biz'niz*, musical diversion (1991–93; N.Y., Dec. 13, 1998). ORCH.: *Pieces of Seven* (Jacksonville, Fla., Oct. 23, 1962; withdrawn); *Articles of*

Faith (1965; Detroit, April 14, 1966). CHAMBER: Clarinet Quartet (1952; N.Y., May 29, 1953); *Pastorale and Dance* for Violin and Piano (1953; Waltham, Mass., May 17, 1954); String Quartet (1954; Waltham, Mass., April 25, 1955); *Twilight Crane* for Woodwind Quintet (1961; N.Y., March 24, 1962); *Fantasy on High Holy Day Themes* for Cello (Rye, N.Y., Sept. 30, 1998); *Sessionals* for Brass Quintet (Dobbs Ferry, N.Y., Oct. 10, 1998). KEYBOARD: P i a n o : Sonata (1960; N.Y., Feb. 9, 1963); *The Silent Flickers* for Piano, 4-Hands (1968; rev. 1996; also for Solo Piano, 1981). O r g a n : *Judge of the World* (Cincinnati, June 15, 1975); *The Voice of the Lord in the Storm* (1985). VOCAL: *Hoofprints*, 3 songs for Soprano and Piano (1954; rev. 1963; N.Y., March 8, 1964); *2 Blues* for Woman's Voice and Clarinet (1954; rev. 1963; N.Y., June 7, 1964); *Kids' Calls* for Chorus and Piano (1957; Urbana, Ill., Feb. 23, 1958); *In Memory of...*, cantata for Tenor, Chorus, and Organ (N.Y., March 18, 1960); *Songs of Loneliness* for Baritone and Piano (1962; Washington, D.C., March 7, 1964); *Love Songs for Sabbath*, Friday Evening Service for Cantor, Chorus, and Organ (N.Y., May 7, 1965); *Downtown Blues for Uptown Halls*, 3 songs for Woman's Voice, Clarinet, and Piano (1965; rev. 1977; N.Y., March 26, 1978); *Shout for Joy*, church or synagogue Psalms for Mostly Unison Chorus, Piano, 2 Flutes, and 3 Drums (1967; N.Y., Jan. 19, 1969); *New Year's Service for Young People* for Chorus and Organ (St. Louis, Oct. 1, 1970); *Verses from Psalm 118* for Chorus and Organ (St. Louis, June 6, 1973); *Sharing the Prophets*, musical happening for Soloists, Chorus, Piano, Double Bass, and Percussion (1975; N.Y., March 14, 1976); *Set Me as a Seal* for Chorus, Violin or Flute, and Piano (1976; rev. 1991); *4 Affirmations* for Alto or Baritone, Chorus, and Brass Sextet or Piano/Organ (N.Y., April 17, 1976; Nos. 1 and 3 withdrawn); *Psalmistry* for 4 or 2 Singers and 11 Players (1978–79; N.Y., Oct. 12, 1980); *Solitaire*, song cycle for Baritone and Piano (1988–91; N.Y., Feb. 25, 1992); *Scrapbook*, song cycle for Baritone and Piano (1988–91; N.Y., March 31, 1992); *Presidential Suite* for Chorus (1989; N.Y., Oct. 27, 1990); *The English Lesson* for Soprano, Mezzo-soprano or Alto, and Piano (1993); *yes is a pleasant country*, song cycle for High Voice and Piano, after e.e. cummings (N.Y., Nov. 22, 1998); *Grant us Peace*, anthem for Soloist, Chorus, and Organ or Piano (1999).
—NS/LK/DM

Gottlieb, (Maria) Anna,

Austrian singer and actress; b. Vienna, April 29, 1774; d. there, Feb. 4, 1856. She was reared in a theatrical family and made her first appearance in the theater as a child. At the age of 12, she created the role of Barbarina in Mozart's *Le nozze di Figaro* (Vienna, May 1, 1786). Mozart later chose her to create the role of Pamina in his *Die Zauberflöte* (Vienna, Sept. 30, 1791). She subsequently pursued a career mainly as a singer in Singspiels and musical parodies, and as an actress. She was a member of the Freihaustheater (1790–93) and of the Theater in der Leopoldstadt (1792–1809; 1813–28) in Vienna.—NS/LK/DM

Gottschalk, Louis Moreau,

celebrated American pianist and composer; b. New Orleans, May 8, 1829; d. Tijuca, near Rio de Janeiro, Dec. 18, 1869. His father, an English businessman, emigrated to New Orleans; his mother was of noble Creole descent, the granddaughter of a governor of a Haitian province. His talent for music was developed early; at the age of 4, he began studying violin with Félix Miolan, concertmaster of the opera orch., and piano with François Letellier, organist at the

St. Louis Cathedral; at the age of 7, he substituted for Letellier at the organ during High Mass, and the next year played violin at a benefit for Miolan. In 1841 he was sent to Paris, where he studied piano with Charles Hallé and Camille Stamaty and harmony with Pierre Maleden. He also later studied composition with Berlioz. On April 2, 1845, he gave a concert at the Salle Pleyel, which attracted the attention of Chopin. His piano compositions of the period, including *Bamboula*, *Le Bananier*, and *La Savane*, were influenced by Liszt and Chopin, but also inspired by childhood recollections of Creole and Negro dances and songs. In 1846–47 he appeared in a series of concerts with Berlioz at the Italian Opera, and in 1850 concertized throughout France and Switzerland, playing his own compositions. In 1851 he appeared in Madrid at the invitation of the Queen and was given the Order of Isabella; during his stay there, he developed the "monster concerts," for which he wrote a Sym. for 10 Pianos, *El Sitio de Zaragosa*, later transformed into *Bunker's Hill* by replacing the Spanish tunes with American ones.

Gottschalk returned to give a highly praised concert in N.Y. on Feb. 11, 1853, followed by many concerts throughout the U.S., Cuba, and Canada during the next 3 years. During the winter of 1855–56, he gave 80 concerts in N.Y. alone. His compositions from this period, including *La Scintilla*, *The Dying Poet*, and *The Last Hope*, written to display his talents, used many novel techniques of the "style pianola." After playing Henselt's Piano Concerto with the N.Y. Phil. on Jan. 10, 1857, he went to Cuba with the pubescent singer Adelina Patti. He then lived in the West Indies, writing works influenced by its indigenous music. In Havana, on Feb. 17, 1861, he introduced his most famous orch. work, *La Nuit des tropiques*. He also produced several grand "monster concerts" modeled after those of Jullien.

Though he was born in the antebellum South, Gottschalk's sympathies were with the North during the American Civil War; he had manumitted the slaves he inherited after his father's death in 1853. He resumed his U.S. concert career with a performance in N.Y. on Feb. 11, 1862, and from then until 1865 toured the North and the West with Max Strakosch, playing (by his estimation) over a thousand concerts. His notebooks from this era, posth. publ. as *Notes of a Pianist* (Philadelphia, 1881; reprint 1964), perceptively reveal life in Civil War America. After becoming involved in a scandal with a teenage girl in San Francisco, he was forced to flee to South America (Sept. 18, 1865); he appeared in concert throughout South America, and composed new works based on local melodies and rhythms. During a festival of his music in Rio de Janeiro on Nov. 25, 1869, he collapsed on stage after playing the appropriately titled *Morte!!*; he died within a month. His remains were exhumed and reburied with great ceremony in Brooklyn on Oct. 3, 1870.

Gottschalk was a prolific composer of bravura, pianistic works that enjoyed great popularity for some time even after his death; ultimately they slipped into the uniquitous centenary oblivion. As a pianist, he was one of the most adulated virtuosos of his era. His concerts, featuring his own compositions, emphasized his prodigious technique but were criticized by some as being superficial. A definitive catalog of his works is difficult to assemble, since many of the works referred to in his copious correspondence have not been found, there are revisions of one and the same work using different titles, and several works were publ. using the same opus number. Two catalogs of his music are R. Offergeld, *The Centennial Catalogue of the Published and Unpublished Compositions of Louis Moreau Gottschalk* (N.Y., 1970), and J. Doyle, *Louis Moreau Gottschalk 1829–1869: A Bibliographical Study and Catalog of Works* (Detroit, 1983). The latter is especially useful, since it lists each publ. work using the linguistic nominal variants. Gottschalk publ. some of his works using the pseudonyms Steven Octaves, Oscar Litti, A.B.C., and Paul Ernest. Among modern editions of his music, the most notable are *The Piano Works of Louis Moreau Gottschalk* (5 vols., N.Y., 1969), ed. by V. Lawrence and R. Jackson, and *The Little Book of Louis Moreau Gottschalk* (N.Y., 1976), ed. by R. Jackson and N. Ratliff.

WORKS: DRAMATIC: O p e r a : *Escenas campestres* (Havana, Feb. 17, 1860). ORCH.: *Grande Tarantelle* for Piano and Orch. (1858–64); 2 syms.: No. 1, *La Nuit des tropiques* (Havana, Feb. 17, 1860) and No. 2, *À Montevideo* (Montevideo, Nov. 1868); *Variations de concert sur l'hymne portugais du Roi D. Louis 1er* for Piano and Orch. (Rio de Janeiro, Oct. 31, 1869). OTHER: Chamber music, numerous solo piano pieces, and several vocal works.

BIBL.: H. Didimus, *Biography of L.M. G., the American Pianist and Composer* (Philadelphia, 1853); O. Hensel, *Life and Letters of L.M. G.* (Boston, 1870); L. Fors, *G.* (Havana, 1880); J. Cooke, *L.M. G.* (Philadelphia, 1928); F. Lange, *Vida y muerte de L.M. G. en Rio de Janeiro (1869)* (Mendoza, Argentina, 1951); V. Loggins, *Where the World Ends: The Life of L.M. G.* (Baton Rouge, 1958); J. Doyle, *The Piano Music of L.M. G. (1829–1869)* (diss., N.Y.U., 1960); J. Gray, *A Study and Edition of Recently Discovered Works of L.M. G.* (diss., Univ. of Rochester, 1971); W. Korf, *The Orchestral Music of L.M. G.* (diss., Univ. of Iowa, 1974); L. Rubin, *G. in Cuba* (diss., Columbia Univ., 1974); S. Starr, *Bamboula!: The Life and Times of L.M. G.* (Oxford, 1995).—NS/LK/DM

Gottwald, Clytus, German choral conductor, musicologist, and composer; b. Bad Salzbrunn, Silesia, Nov. 25, 1925. He received training in voice, choral conducting, and musicology at the Univ. of Tübingen, and also took courses in sociology, theology, and folklore. He completed his education at the Univ. of Frankfurt am Main (Ph.D., 1961, with the diss. *Johannes Ghiselen— Johannes Verbonnet: Stilkritische Untersuchung zum Problem ihrer Identität*; publ. in Wiesbaden, 1962). In 1960 he founded the Schola Cantorum Stuttgart, a polyphonic vocal ensemble he conducted in enterprising concerts until 1990. In addition to works of the 15th and 16th ceturies, he also conducted contemporary avant-garde scores. From 1969 to 1989 he was an ed. for new music for the South German Radio in Stuttgart. He contributed valuable articles to many journals and other publications on subjects ranging from early music to the avant-garde, from Josquin to John Cage. He ed. the complete works of Ghiselen in Corpus Mensurabilis Musicae, XXIII/1–4 (1961–68) and publ. *Codices musici* (series 1, *Die Handschriften der Württembergischen Landes-*

bibliothek Stuttgart, Wiesbaden, 1964; series 2, *Die Hand-schriften de ehemals Königlichen Hofbibliothek*, Wiesbaden, 1965), *Katalog der Musikalien in der Schermar-Bibliothek Ulm* (Wiesbaden, 1993), and *Manuscripta musica* (Wiesbaden, 1997). As a composer, he tended toward the experimental, producing a number of advanced vocal works.—**NS/LK/DM**

Goudimel, Claude, (also rendered as **Gaudimel, Gaudiomel, Godimel, Gondimel, Goudmel, Gudmel,** etc.), celebrated French composer and music theorist; b. Besançon, c. 1510; d. (killed in the St. Bartholomew massacre) Lyons, Aug. 27, 1572. In 1549 Goudimel studied at the Univ. of Paris. He publ. a book of chansons as a joint publisher with Du Chemin. He lived in Metz between 1557 and 1568, where he became a Huguenot. In 1568 he returned to Besancon, then lived in Lyons, where he perished. Most of his music was publ. by Du Chemin in Paris. Other contemporary publishers were Adrien Le Roy and Robert Ballard, who publ. his complete Huguenot psalter in 1564 under the title *Les CL Pseaumes de David, nouvellement mis en musique à quatre parties*; it was publ. in Geneva in 1565 as *Les Pseaumes mis en rime françoise par Clément Marot et Th. de Bèze, mis en musique à 4 parties*; it was reprinted in a facsimile ed. in Kassel, 1935. Goudimel also composed 5 masses, 1 publ. by Du Chemin (1554) and 4 by Le Roy and Ballard (1558), together with other sacred music. Two 4-part motets were included in T. Susato's *Ecclesiasticarum cantionum* (Antwerp, 1553–55). Publication of the Complete Works, under the direction of L. Dittmer and P. Pidoux (Inst. of Medieval Music), began in 1967 and concluded in 1983.

BIBL.: G. Becker, *Goudimel et son oeuvre* (1885); M. Brenet, *Claude Goudimel, Essai bio-bibliographique* (Besançon, 1898). —**NS/LK/DM**

Gould, Glenn (Herbert), remarkable and individualistic Canadian pianist; b. Toronto, Sept. 25, 1932; d. there, Oct. 4, 1982. His parents were musically gifted and fostered his precocious development, and he began to play piano, and even compose, in his childhood. At the age of 10, he entered the Royal Cons. of Music in Toronto, where he studied piano with Alberto Guerrero, organ with Frederick C. Silvester, and theory with Leo Smith, graduating in 1945 at the age of 13. He made his debut in Toronto on May 8, 1946. As he began practicing with total concentration on the mechanism of the keyboard, he developed mannerisms that were to become his artistic signature. He reduced the use of the pedal to a minimum in order to avoid harmonic "haze"; he cultivated "horizontality" in his piano posture, bringing his head down almost to the level of the keys. He regarded music as a linear art; this naturally led him to an intense examination of Baroque structures; Bach was the subject of his close study rather than Chopin; he also cultivated performances of Sweelinck, Gibbons, and other early keyboard masters. He played Mozart with emphasis on the early pianoforte techniques; he largely omitted the Romantic composers Chopin, Schumann, and Liszt from his repertoire, although he favored an early sonata by Richard Strauss. He found the late sonatas of Beethoven more congenial to his temperament, as well as the piano works of the modern Vienna school—Schoenberg, Berg, and Webern—perhaps because of their classical avoidance of purely decorative tonal formations. Actually, his selective but challenging repertoire ranged widely, from the 16th century to jazz. Following his U.S. debut in Washington, D.C., on Jan. 2, 1955, he evoked unequivocal praise at his concerts, but in 1964 he abruptly terminated his stage career and devoted himself exclusively to recording. This enabled him to perform unfettered by the presence of an audience and to select the best portions of the music he played in the studio, forming a mosaic unblemished by accidental mishaps. Certainly part of the interest he aroused with the public at large was due to mannerisms that marked his behavior on the stage. He used a 14-inch-high chair that placed his eyes almost at the level of the keyboard; he adopted informal dress; he had a rug put under the piano and a glass of distilled water within easy reach. He was in constant fear of bodily injury; he avoided shaking hands with the conductor after playing a concerto (he actually sued the Steinway piano company for a large sum of money when an enthusiastic representative shook his hand too vigorously). He also had an unshakable habit of singing along with his performance, even allowing his voice to be audible on his carefully wrought, lapidary recordings. Nonetheless, Gould acquired a devoted following, and a small coterie of friends, despite the fact that he was quite reclusive; he found release from his self-imposed isolation in editing a series of radio documentaries for the CBC, entitled "The Idea of North," three of which aired as "solitude tragedies." Symbolically, they were devoted to the natural isolation of the Canadian Arctic, the insular life of Newfoundland, and the religious hermetism of the Mennonite sect. Fittingly, upon his death in 1982, 7 days after a stroke from which he never recovered, it was learned that Gould had bequeathed his estate in equal portions to the A.S.P.C.A. (Assn. for the Prevention of Cruelty to Animals) and to the Salvation Army. In 1994 his life became the subject of a successful film, *Thirty-Two Short Films About Glenn Gould.* He was also made the invisible protagonist of Thomas Bernhart's immensely entertaining novel, *The Loser.* A selection of his writings is contained in T. Page, ed., *The Glenn Gould Reader* (N.Y., 1985). J. Roberts and G. Guertin ed. a selection of his letters (Oxford, 1992).

BIBL.: G. Paysant, *G. G.: Music and Mind* (Toronto, 1978; rev. ed., 1992); J. Cott, *Conversations with G. G.* (Boston, 1984); W. Matheis, *G. G.: Der Unheilige am Klavier* (Munich, 1987); O. Friedrich, *G. G.: A Life and Variations* (N.Y., 1989); A. Kazdin, *G. G. at Work: Creative Lying* (N.Y., 1989); J. Hagestedt, *Wie spielt G. G.?: Zu einer Theorie der Interpretation* (Munich, 1991); E. Angilette, *Philosopher at the Keyboard: G. G.* (Metuchen, N.J., 1992); M. Stegemann, *G. G.: Leben und Werk* (Munich, 1992); S. Hamel-Michaud, *G. G., mon bel et tendre amour* (Quebec, 1995); K. Bazzana, *G. G.: The Performer in the Work: A Study in Performance Practice* (Oxford, 1997); P. Ostwald, *G. G.: The Ecstasy and Tragedy of Genius* (N.Y., 1997).—**NS/LK/DM**

Gould, Morton, extraordinarily talented American composer and conductor; b. N.Y., Dec. 10, 1913. He composed his first work when he was only 6. At 8, he received a scholarship to the Inst. of Musical Art in N.Y. At 13, he also commenced piano lessons with Abby Whiteside, and later studied harmony and counterpoint with Vincent Jones. With the coming of the Great Depression, Gould was compelled to quit high school and earn his keep playing piano on the vaudeville circuit. He also played in movie theaters and toured in the Gould and Shefter piano duo. He worked as an arranger, composer, and conductor for WOR Radio (1934–42) and for CBS (1942–45) in N.Y. Gould secured his reputation as a composer with his *Spirituals* for orch., which he conducted in its premiere in N.Y. on Feb. 9, 1941. Several of his eminently accessible scores became notably popular via the radio, and many of his works were taken up by the leading American orchs. He toured widely as a guest conductor throughout North America and abroad, leading programs not only of his own works but also by other composers with aplomb. In 1986 he was elected a member of the American Academy and Inst. of Arts and Letters. From 1986 to 1994 he served as president of ASCAP. In 1994 he received a Kennedy Center Honor. He was awarded the Pulitzer Prize in Music in 1995 for his *String Music*. Gould's remarkable versatility as a composer was admirably revealed in various genres. While he was notably successful in producing works of broad appeal in a popular vein, he also wrote a number of scores in a more serious mode. He was especially masterful in creating works for the orch.

WORKS: DRAMATIC: Music Theater: *Billion Dollar Baby* (N.Y., Dec. 21, 1945); *Arms and the Girl* (N.Y., Feb. 2, 1950). **Ballet**: *Interplay* (N.Y., Oct. 17, 1945); *Fall River Legend* (N.Y., April 22, 1947; orch. suite, San Francisco, Jan. 6, 1949); *Fiesta* (Cannes, March 17, 1957); *Clarinade* (1964); *I'm Old Fashioned, Astaire Variations* (N.Y., June 16, 1983). **Film**: *Delightfully Dangerous* (1945); *Cinerama Holiday* (1955); *Windjammer* (1958). **Television:**: *World War I* (1964–65); *Holocaust* (1978; orch. suite, NBC-TV, April 1978; band suite, Tempe, Ariz., May 29, 1980, composer conducting); *Celebration '81* (1981). **ORCH.**: 3 *American Symphonettes* (1933, 1935, 1937); *Chorale and Fugue in Jazz* for 2 Pianos and Orch. (1934; N.Y., Jan. 2, 1936); Piano Concerto (1934; WOR Radio, N.Y., June 16, 1938); Violin Concerto (1938); *Foster Gallery* (1939; Pittsburgh, Jan. 12, 1940); *A Homespun Overture* (1939); *Latin-American Symphonette* (N.Y., Feb. 22, 1941); *Spirituals* (N.Y., Feb. 9, 1941); *Lincoln Legend* (N.Y., Nov. 1, 1942); *Cowboy Rhapsody* (1942); *American Salute* (1943); 6 syms.: No. 1 (Pittsburgh, March 5, 1943), No. 2, *On Marching Tunes* (N.Y., June 2, 1944), No. 3 (Dallas, Feb. 16, 1947, composer conducting; rev. version, N.Y., Oct. 28, 1948), No. 4, *West Point Symphony* for Band (West Point, N.Y., April 13, 1952, composer conducting), No. 5, *Symphony of Spirituals* (Detroit, April 1, 1976), and No. 6, *Centennial Symphony: Gala* for Band (Austin, Tex., April 9, 1983, composer conducting); Viola Concerto (1943); *Concerto for Orchestra* (Cleveland, Feb. 1, 1945); *Harvest* for Vibraphone, Harp, and Strings (St. Louis, Oct. 27, 1945); *Minstrel Show* (Indianapolis, Dec. 21, 1946); *Holiday Music* (1947); *Philharmonic Waltzes* (N.Y., Nov. 16, 1948); *Guajira* for Clarinet and Orch. (1949); *Serenade of Carols* (1949); *Big City Blues* (1950; also for Band); *Family Album*, suite (1951); *Tap Dance Concerto* (Rochester, N.Y., Nov. 16, 1952, composer conducting); *Inventions* for Piano Quartet and Orch. (N.Y., Oct. 19, 1953); *Dance Variations* for 2 Pianos and Orch. (N.Y., Oct. 24, 1953); *Showpiece* (Philadelphia, May 7, 1954); *Hoofer Suite* for Tap

Dancer and Orch. (1956); *Jekyll and Hyde Variations* (1956; N.Y., Feb. 2, 1957); *Cafe Rio* (1957); *Dialogues* for Piano and Strings (N.Y., Nov. 3, 1958); *Spirituals* for Harp and Strings (1961); *Calypso Souvenir* (1964); *Festive Music* (1964; Rock Island, Ill., Jan. 16, 1965, composer conducting); *Columbia: Broadsides* (Washington, D.C., July 14, 1967); *Venice* for Double Orch. and Brass Choirs (Seattle, May 2, 1967); *Vivaldi Gallery* for String Quartet and Divided Orch. (Seattle, March 25, 1968); *Soundings* (Atlanta, Sept. 18, 1969); *Concerto Grosso* (1969; N.Y., Dec. 4, 1988); *Troubadour Music* for 4 Guitars and Orch. (San Diego, March 1969); *Fire Music: Toccata* (1970); *Indian Attack* (1970); *Night Music* (1970); *Serenade* (1970); *American Ballads* (N.Y., April 24, 1976, composer conducting); *Chorales and Rags: Finale* (1977–82; N.Y., Nov. 13, 1988); *Cheers!*, celebration march (Boston, May 1, 1979; also for Band); *Burchfield Gallery* (Cleveland, April 9, 1981); *Celebration Strut* (NBC-TV, April 27, 1981); *Housewarming* (Baltimore, Sept. 16, 1982); *Apple Waltzes* (N.Y., Dec. 11, 1983, composer conducting); *Flourishes and Galop* (Louisville, Nov. 19, 1983); Flute Concerto (1983–84; Chicago, April 18, 1985); *Classical Variations on Colonial Themes* (1984–85; Pittsburgh, Sept. 11, 1986); *Flares and Declamations* (N.Y., Oct. 18, 1987); *Notes of a Remembrance* (1989; Washington, D.C., June 13, 1990); *Minute + Waltz Rag* (Baltimore, Oct. 25, 1990); *Diversions* for Tenor Saxophone and Orch. (N.Y., Nov. 28, 1990, composer conducting); *String Music* (Washington, D.C., March 10, 1994). **Band**: *Jericho Rhapsody* (1940); *Concertette* for Viola and Band (1943); *Fanfare for Freedom* (1943); *Ballad* (1946); *Big City Blues* (1950; also for Orch.); *Derivations* for Clarinet and Dance Band (1955; Washington, D.C., July 14, 1956; also for Clarinet and Piano); *Santa Fe Saga* (1956); *St. Lawrence Suite* (Massena, N.Y., Sept. 5, 1958, composer conducting); *Prisms* (Chicago, Dec. 17, 1962, composer conducting); *Formations* (1964); *Mini-Suite* (1968); *Cheers!*, celebration march (1979; also for Orch.). **CHAMBER**: Suite for Violin and Piano (1945); *Derivations* for Clarinet and Piano (1955; also for Clarinet and Dance Band); *Parade* for Percussion Trio (1956); *Benny's Gig*, 8 duos for Clarinet and Double Bass (1962); *Columbian Fanfares* for 3 Trumpets, 3 Trombones, and Tuba (1967); Tuba Suite for Tuba and 3 Horns (1967); Suite for Cello and Piano (1981; Miami, June 21, 1982); *Concerto Concertante* for Violin, Wind Quintet, and Piano (1981–82; Washington, D.C., Oct. 29, 1983); Duo for Flute and Clarinet (1982); *Cellos* for 8 Cellos or Multiples (Tempe, Ariz., June 9, 1984); *Recovery Music* for Clarinet (1984); *Festive Fanfare* for 2 Trumpets, 2 Trombones, Tuba, Timpani, and Percussion (1991); *Hail to a First Lady* for 2 Trumpets, 2 or 3 Trombones, Tuba, Timpani, and Percussion (1991). **Piano**: *Boogie Woogie Étude* (1943); *Dance Gallery* (1952); *Abby Variations* (1964); *At the Piano* (2 vols., 1964); *10 for Deborah* (1965); *Patterns* (1984; Madrid, May 14, 1985); *Pieces of China* (1985); *2 Pianos* for Piano Duet (1987); *Ghost Waltzes* (1991). **VOCAL**: *Of Time and the River* for Chorus (Princeton, N.J., Oct. 8, 1945); *Declaration* for 2 Narrators, Speaking Men's Chorus, and Orch. (1956; Washington, D.C., Jan. 20, 1957; orch. suite, Washington, D.C., Jan. 22, 1957); *Rhythm Gallery* for Narrator and Orch. (1959); *Come Up From the Valley, Children* for Voice and Piano (1964); *Salutations* for Narrator and Orch. (N.Y., April 27, 1966); *2 for Chorus* (1966); *Something to Do*, labor cantata for Soli, Narrator, Chorus, and Orch. (Washington, D.C., Sept. 4, 1976); *Quotations* for 2 Choruses and Wind Orch. (1983; N.Y., Jan. 28, 1984); *American Sing* for Soprano, Mezzo-soprano, Tenor, Bass, and Orch. (1984); *The Jogger and the Dinosaur* for Rapper and Orch. (Pittsburgh, April 4, 1993).

BIBL.: L. Evans, *M. G.: His Life and Music* (diss., Columbia Univ. Teachers Coll., 1978).—**NS/LK/DM**

Gould, Nathaniel Duren, American singing-school teacher and tune-book compiler; b. Bedford, Mass., Nov. 26, 1781; d. Boston, May 28, 1864. His father was the church builder Reuben Duren. After being adopted by a maternal uncle in 1792, he took the name Gould in 1806. He studied vocal music with Reuben Emerson. He organized his first singing school in Stoddard, N.H. (1798). He then formed the New Ipswich military band (1804), and was conductor of the Middlesex (Mass.) Musical Soc. (from 1805). From 1819 he lived mainly in Boston, where he was active as a teacher of vocal music and chirography. He publ. 8 anthologies for singing-school use, including *National Church Harmony* (1832; 4th ed., 1836). His study *Church Music in America* (Boston, 1853) remains a standard work in spite of its inaccuracies.

BIBL.: J. Ingalls, *N. D. G. 1781–1864* (thesis, Univ. of Lowell [Mass.], 1980).—NS/LK/DM

Goulet, Robert (originally, **Applebaum, Stanley**), American singer and actor; b. Lawrence, Mass., Nov. 26, 1933. Goulet's handsome appearance and resonant baritone typed him as a leading man of stage musicals after he made his Broadway debut in *Camelot*. Unfortunately, he entered his prime in the antiheroic, rock-dominated era of the 1960s, which meant that he was doomed to a career filled with successful appearances in swanky hotel/casinos and starring roles in road company revivals of Broadway shows from the 1940s and 1950s. Nevertheless, he charted 17 albums between 1962 and 1970, including the gold-selling *My Love Forgive Me*, also the title of his sole Top 40 hit.

Goulet's family moved to Edmonton, Alberta, Canada, when he was 14. He won a scholarship to the opera school of the Royal Cons. of Music in Toronto, and made his first professional appearance as a singer at 17 with the Summer Pops in Edmonton. He worked as a local disc jockey, appeared in Canadian productions of Broadway musicals, and had his own musical variety series, *Showtime*, on Canadian national television. He was cast as Lancelot in Alan Jay Lerner and Frederick Loewe's *Camelot* (N.Y., Dec. 3, 1960), a musical retelling of the King Arthur legend. The show ran 873 performances, and the cast album, featuring Goulet's singing of "If Ever I Would Leave You," topped the charts and went gold.

Goulet was signed by Columbia Records, which released his debut album, *Always You*, in early 1962; it stayed in the charts a year and a quarter. His second album, *Two of Us*, followed less than six months later and was in the charts more than a year. He also scored his first chart single, "What Kind of Fool Am I?" (music and lyrics by Leslie Bricusse and Anthony Newley) from the musical *Stop the World—I Want to Get Off*, in October. All this record activity won him the 1962 Grammy for Best New Artist. Also during the year, he voiced one of the characters in the animated film *Gay Purr-ee*.

Goulet's third album, *Sincerely Yours*, entered the charts at the start of 1963, reached the Top Ten, and remained on the charts nearly a year. Before 1962 was

over he had two more albums in the charts, *The Wonderful World of Love* and *Robert Goulet in Person*, the latter recorded live at the Chicago Opera House. Following his divorce from Louise Nicole, with whom he had had a daughter, he married musical comedy star Carol Lawrence, best known for her portrayal of Maria in *West Side Story*; they had two sons before divorcing.

Goulet starred in two comedy films in 1964, *Honeymoon Hotel* and *I'd Rather Be Rich*, but his movie career never took off, though he later starred in the 1970 film *Underground*, a World War II drama; had a cameo in Louis Malle's *Atlantic City* (1980); and played comic parts in *Scrooged* (1988) and *The Naked Gun 2: The Smell of Fear* (1991). It was his recording career that remained paramount in 1964, as he charted three more albums: *Manhattan Tower/The Man Who Loves Manhattan*, composed and conducted by Gordon Jenkins; *Without You*; and *My Love Forgive Me*. The last album, released in December, featured "My Love, Forgive Me (Amore, Scusami)" (music by Gino Mescoli, Italian lyrics by Vito Pallavicini, English lyrics by Sydney Lee), which was released as a single that peaked in the Top 40 in January 1965. The album hit the Top Ten and went gold.

Goulet was unable to repeat the success of *My Love Forgive Me*, though he charted another three albums in 1965: *Begin to Love*, *Summer Sounds* (its title song, with music and lyrics by Sid Tepper and Roy C. Bennett, a chart single), and *Robert Goulet on Broadway*. His albums continued to chart through 1970, though *I Remember You* (1966) was his last to reach the upper half of the charts.

From January to August 1966, Goulet starred in *Blue Light*, a dramatic television series about a spy during World War II. He returned to Broadway in John Kander and Fred Ebb's *The Happy Time* (N.Y., Jan. 19, 1968). It ran 286 performances, and he won the Tony Award for Actor in a Musical.

From the 1970s on, Goulet, living in Las Vegas and L.A., divided his time between appearances at hotel/casinos, guest-starring roles on television, and tours with national companies of Broadway musicals. In 1982 he married Vera Novak. In the early 1990s he toured in a production of *Camelot*, this time playing King Arthur. The revival returned him to Broadway in 1993.

DISC.: *Always You* (1961); *Two of Us* (1962); *Sincerely Yours...* (1963); *The Wonderful World of Love* (1963); *Robert Goulet in Person* (1963); *Manhattan Tower/The Man Who Loves Manhattan* (1964); *Without You* (1964); *My Love Forgive Me* (1964); *Begin to Love* (1965); *Summer Sounds* (1965); *Robert Goulet on Broadway* (1965); *Traveling On* (1966); *I Remember You* (1966); *Robert Goulet on Broadway, Vol. 2* (1967); *Woman, Woman* (1968); *Hollywood Mon Amour—Great Love Songs from the Movies* (1968); *Both Sides Now* (1969); *Souvenir D'Italie* (1969); *Greatest Hits* (1969); *I Wish You Love* (1970); *Close to You* (1992).—WR

Gounod, Charles (François), famous French composer; b. Paris, June 17, 1818; d. St. Cloud, Oct. 18, 1893. His father, Jean François Gounod, was a painter, winner of the 2nd Grand Prix de Rome, who died when Gounod was a small child. His mother, a most accomplished woman, supervised his literary, artistic, and musical education, and taught him piano. He completed his academic studies at the Lycée St. Louis; in 1836 he entered the Paris Cons., studying with Halévy, Le Sueur, and Paër. In 1837 he won the 2nd Prix de Rome with his cantata *Marie Stuart et Rizzio*; in 1839 he won the Grand Prix with his cantata *Fernand*. In Rome, he studied church music, particularly the works of Palestrina; composed a Mass for 3 Voices and Orch., which was performed at the church of San Luigi dei Francesi. In 1842, during a visit to Vienna, he conducted a Requiem of his own; upon his return to Paris, he became precentor and organist of the Missions Étrangères; studied theology for 2 years, but decided against taking Holy Orders; yet he was often referred to as l'Abbé Gounod; some religious choruses were publ. in 1846 as composed by Abbé Charles Gounod. Soon he tried his hand at stage music. On April 16, 1851, his first opera, *Sapho*, was produced at the Opéra, with only moderate success; he revised it much later, extending it to 4 acts from the original 3, and it was performed again on April 2, 1884; but it was unsuccessful. His second opera, *La Nonne sanglante*, in 5 acts, was staged at the Opéra on Oct. 18, 1854; there followed a comic opera, *Le Médecin malgré lui*, after Molière (Jan. 15, 1858), which also failed to realize his expectations. In the meantime, he was active in other musical ways in Paris; he conducted the choral society Orphéon (1852–60) and composed for it several choruses. Gounod's great success came with the production of *Faust*, after Goethe (Théâtre-Lyrique, March 19, 1859; perf. with additional recitatives and ballet at the Opéra, March 3, 1869); *Faust* remained Gounod's greatest masterpiece, and indeed the most successful French opera of the 19th century, triumphant all over the world without any sign of diminishing effect through a century of changes in musical tastes. However, it was widely criticized for the melodramatic treatment of Goethe's poem by the librettists, Barbier and Carré, and for the somewhat sentimental style of Gounod's music. The succeeding operas *Phiémon et Baucis* (Paris, Feb. 18, 1860), *La Colombe* (Baden-Baden, Aug. 3, 1860), *La Reine de Saba* (Paris, Feb. 29, 1862), and *Mireille* (Paris, March 19, 1864) were only partially successful, but with *Roméo et Juliette* (Paris, April 27, 1867), Gounod recaptured universal acclaim. In 1870, during the Franco-Prussian War, he went to London, where he organized Gounod's Choir, and presented concerts; when Paris fell, he wrote an elegiac cantata, *Gallia*, to words from the Lamentations of Jeremiah, which he conducted in London on May 1, 1871; it was later performed in Paris. He wrote some incidental music for productions in Paris: *Les Deux Reines*, to a drama by Legouvé (Nov. 27, 1872), and *Jeanne d'Arc*, to Barbier's poem (Nov. 8, 1873). In 1874, he returned to Paris; there he produced his operas *Cinq-Mars* (April 5, 1877), *Polyeucte* (Oct. 7, 1878), and *Le Tribut de Zamora* (April 1, 1881), without signal success. The last years of his life were devoted mainly to sacred works, of which the most important was *La Rédemption*, a trilogy, first performed at the Birmingham Festival in 1882; another sacred trilogy, *Mors et vita*, also written for the Birmingham Festival, followed in 1885. He continued to write religious works in close succession, including a *Te Deum* (1886), *La Communion des saints* (1889), *Messe dite le Clovis* (1890), *La Contemplation de Saint François au pied de la croix* (1890), and *Tantum ergo* (1892). A Requiem (1893) was left unfinished, and was arranged by Henri Büsser after Gounod's death. One of his most popular settings to religious words is *Ave Maria*, adapted to the 1st prelude of Bach's *Well-tempered Clavier*, but its original version was *Méditation sur le premier Prélude de Piano de J.S. Bach* for Violin and Piano (1853); the words were added later (1859). Other works are 2 syms. (1855), *Marche funèbre d'une marionnette* for Orch. (1873), *Petite symphonie* for Wind Instruments (1888), 3 string quartets, a number of piano pieces, and songs. Among his literary works were *Ascanio de Saint-Saëns* (1889), *Le Don Juan de Mozart* (1890; in Eng., 1895), and an autobiography, *Mémoires d'un artiste* (Paris, 1896; Eng. tr. by W. Hutchenson, N.Y., 1896).

BIBL.: M. de Bovet, *C. G.* (Paris, 1890; Eng. tr., London, 1891); L. Pagnerre, *C. G., Sa vie et ses oeuvres* (Paris, 1890); C. Saint-Saëns, *C. G. et le Don Juan de Mozart* (Paris, 1893); T. Dubois, *Notice sur C. G.* (Paris, 1894); P. Voss, *C. G.: Ein Lebensbild* (Leipzig, 1895); H. Tolhurst, *G.* (London, 1905); P. Hillemacher, *C. G.* (Paris, 1906); C. Bellaigue, *G.* (Paris, 1910); J.-G. Prod'homme and A. Dandelot, *G.: Sa vie et ses oeuvres* (2 vols., Paris, 1911); H. Soubiès and H. de Curzon, *Documents inedits sur le Faust de G.* (Paris, 1912); P. Landormy, *G.* (Paris, 1942); idem, *Faust de G.: Étude et analyse* (Paris, 1944); J. Harding, *G.* (London, 1973); M. Rustman, *Lyric Opera: A Study of the Contribution of C. G.* (diss., Univ. of Kans., 1986); S. Huebner, *The Operas of G.* (Oxford, 1990); M. Galland, ed., *C. G., Mireille: Dossier de presse parisienne (1864)* (Bietigheim, 1995).—NS/LK/DM

Gouvy, Louis Théodore, French composer; b. Goffontaine, near Saarbrucken, July 5, 1819; d. Leipzig, April 21, 1898. The son of French parents, he graduated from the college at Metz. He went to Paris to study law, but turned to music and presented a concert of his works in Paris in 1847. He also made frequent trips to Germany, where his music was received with great favor. He composed about 200 works, including an opera, *Der Cid* (1863), 7 syms. (1846–92), Wind Nonet, Wind Octet, Sextet for Flute and Strings, Piano Quintet, String Quintet, 5 string quartets, 5 piano trios, numerous piano pieces in an ingratiating salon manner, and songs.

BIBL.: O. Klauwell, *L.T. G., Sein Leben und seine Werke* (Berlin, 1902).—NS/LK/DM

Gow, Nathaniel, Scottish violinist, arranger, and music publisher, son of **Niel Gow**; b. Inver, near Dunkeld, May 28, 1763; d. Edinburgh, Jan. 19, 1831. He played the trumpet in Scottish bands, then changed to violin. In 1788 he opened a music shop in Edinburgh. He publ. numerous arrangements of Scottish tunes by his father and also his own arrangements of Scottish dances. He became a commercial music publisher in 1796, but was bankrupt by 1827. He also led a band for various aristocratic assemblies. Among his original pieces was an interesting instrumental composition, *Caller Herrin'*, based on a street vendor's cry.—NS/LK/DM

Gow, Niel, Scottish violinist and composer, father of **Nathaniel Gow;** b. Strathbrand, Perthshire, March 22,

1727; d. Inver, near Dunkeld, March 1, 1807. He played Scottish reels on the violin, and as a young man earned his living by performing at social gatherings in Edinburgh and London. He publ. a number of "Strathspey Reels" however, many of them were not original compositions but arrangements of old dance tunes. —NS/LK/DM

Graarud, Gunnar, Norwegian tenor; b. Holmestrand, near Christiania, June 1, 1886; d. Stuttgart, Dec. 6, 1960. He was a student in Berlin of Husler and Zawilowski. Following his operatic debut in Kaiserslautern in 1919, he sang at the Mannheim National Theater (1920–22), the Berlin Volksoper (1922–25), the Hamburg Opera (1926–28), the Bayreuth Festivals (from 1927), and the Vienna State Opera (1928–37). He also was a guest artist in London, Paris, Milan, and Salzburg. Among his best roles were Tristan, Siegmund, Parsifal, and Siegfried.—NS/LK/DM

Graben-Hoffmann, Gustav (Heinrich), (properly, **Gustav Heinrich Hoffmann,**) German composer; b. Bnin, near Posen, March 7, 1820; d. Potsdam, May 20, 1900. He studied with his father and with other teachers in Posen, then taught music in various localities in eastern Germany. In 1843 he settled in Berlin, and in 1850 he founded a Musikakademie für Damen. He then went to Leipzig, where he studied composition with Moritz Hauptmann. In 1869 he returned to Berlin, where he taught singing. He composed industriously; including a number of songs, which he was compelled to publ. at his own expense, despite economic hardships; of these, *500,000 Teufel* had a great vogue. He also publ. singing manuals: *Die Pflege der Singstimme* (1865), *Das Studium des Gesangs* (1872), and *Praktische Methode als Grundlage für den Kunstgesang* (1874).—NS/LK/DM

Grabner, Hermann, Austrian composer and music theorist; b. Graz, May 12, 1886; d. Bolzano, Italy, July 3, 1969. He took his degree in law at the Univ. of Graz. in 1909, then studied music with Reger and Sitt at the Leipzig Cons. He became a lecturer in theory at the Strasbourg Cons. in 1913. He served in the German army in World War I, and after the Armistice taught at the Mannheim Cons. From 1924 to 1938 he was prof. of composition at the Leipzig Cons. He then taught at the Hochschule für Musik (1938–45) and Cons. (1950–51) in Berlin. He wrote an opera, *Die Richterin* (Barmen, May 7, 1930), *Perkeo Suite* and *Burgmusik* for Wind Orch., Concerto for 3 Violins, organ pieces, songs, etc.

WRITINGS: *Die Funktionstheorie Hugo Riemanns und ihre Bedeutung für die praktische Analyse* (Munich, 1923); *Allgemeine Musiklehre* (Stuttgart, 1924; 5th ed., 1949); *Lehrbuch der musikalischen Analyse* (Leipzig, 1925); *Der lineare Satz; Ein Lehrbuch des Kontrapunktes* (Stuttgart, 1930; rev. ed., 1950); *Handbuch der Harmonielehre* (Berlin, 1944).—NS/LK/DM

Grabovsky, Leonid, Ukrainian composer; b. Kiev, Jan. 28, 1935. He studied at the Univ. of Kiev (1951–56) and took courses in composition with Revutsky and Liatoshinsky at the Kiev Cons. (1954–62;

diploma, 1962). After teaching at the latter (1961–63; 1966–68), he was active as a composer, editor, and translator. He was one of the earliest composers in the Soviet Union to espouse minimalism. His works also reveal Asian influences.

WORKS: DRAMATIC: O p e r a : *The Bear* (1963); *The Marriage Proposal* (1964). **ORCH.:** *Intermezzo* (1958); *Symphonic Frescoes on a Theme of Boris Prorokov* (1961); *Little Chamber Music No. 1* for 16 String Players (1966) and *No. 2* for Oboe, Harp, and 12 String Players (1971); *Homöomorphie IV* (1970); *Meditation and Pathetic Recitative* for Strings (1972); *On St. John's Eve*, symphonic legend (1976). **CHAMBER:** Sonata for Solo Violin (1959); Trio for Violin, Double Bass, and Piano (1964; rev. 1975); *Microstructures* for Oboe (1964; rev. 1975); *Constants* for Violin, 4 Pianos, and 6 Percussion Groups (1964); *Ornament* for Oboe, Harp or Guitar, and Viola (1969); *Concorsuono* for Horn (1977); *Concerto misterioso* for Flute, Clarinet, Bassoon, Antique Cymbals, Harpsichord, Harp, Violin, Viola, and Cello (1977). **P i a n o :** 4 2-part inventions (1962); *5 Character Studies* (1962); *Homöomorphie I-II* (1968) and *III* for 2 Pianos (1969); *Für Elise* (1988). **VOCAL:** *4 Ukrainian Songs* for Chorus and Orch. (1959); *Pastelle* for Mezzo-soprano, Violin, Viola, Cello, and Double Bass (1964; rev. 1975); *An Epitaph for Rainer Maria Rilke* for Soprano, Harp, Celesta, Guitar, and Bells (1965; rev. 1975); *La Mer* for Speaker, Chorus, Organ, and Orch. (1966–70); *Marginalia on Heisenbüttel* for Speaker, 2 Trumpets, Trombone, and Percussion (1967; rev. 1975); *Kogda* for Soprano, Violin, Clarinet, Piano, and Strings ad libitum (1987).—NS/LK/DM

Grace, Harvey, English organist and writer on music; b. Romsey, Jan. 25, 1874; d. Bromley, Kent, Feb. 15, 1944. He studied with M. Richardson at Southwark Cathedral, London, and was organist at various churches in London. From 1918 to his death, he was editor of the *Musical Times* and wrote editorials for it under the name "Feste" also ed. the *New Musical Educator* (London, 1934). He wrote organ music and prepared transcriptions for organ.

WRITINGS: *Music in Parish Churches* (London, 1917; 3rd ed., 1944); *French Organ Music, Past and Present* (N.Y., 1919); *The Complete Organist* (London, 1920; 4th ed., 1956); *The Organ Works of Bach* (London, 1922); *The Organ Works of Rheinberger* (London, 1925); *Ludwig van Beethoven* (London, 1927); *A Musician at Large* (collection of articles from the *Musical Times*; London, 1928); *A Handbook for Choralists* (London, 1928); with Sir W. Davies, *Music and Worship* (London, 1935; 2nd ed., 1948); *The Training and Conducting of Choral Societies* (London, 1938); *The Organ Works of Cesar Franck* (London, 1948).—NS/LK/DM

Gracis, Ettore, Italian conductor; b. La Spezia, Sept. 24, 1915; d. Treviso, April 12, 1992. He studied violin at the Parma Cons. and piano and composition at the Venice Cons., and also took courses in composition with Malipiero and Guarnieri at the Accademia Musicale Chigiana in Siena. He made his conducting debut in 1942; from that time, appeared with many opera houses of Italy. He also conducted sym. concerts. He was active in bringing out contemporary scores; conducted a number of works by Malipiero and other leading Italian composers.—NS/LK/DM

Grad, Gabriel, Lithuanian composer; b. Retovo, near Kovno, July 9, 1890; d. Tel Aviv, Dec. 9, 1950. He studied in Ekaterinoslav and in Berlin. He was founder-director of a Jewish music school in Kovno (1920–22). He went to Palestine in 1924, and then was founder-director of the Benhetov Cons. in Tel Aviv (from 1925). He wrote an opera, *Judith and Holofernes*, and about 250 other works, including chamber music, piano pieces, choruses, and songs, many of which were based on Jewish folk melodies.—**NS/LK/DM**

Grädener, Carl (Georg Peter), German cellist, conductor, teacher, and composer, father of **Hermann (Theodor Otto) Grädener;** b. Rostock, Jan. 14, 1812; d. Hamburg, June 10, 1883. He studied cello with Mattstedt in Altona, and then pursued training in law in Halle and Göttingen (1832–33). After serving as a cellist in Helsinki (1835–38), he was music director of the Univ. of Kiel (1838–48). He then went to Hamburg, where he was founder-director of a concert and vocal academy (1851–61). After serving as prof. of voice and composition at the Vienna Cons. (1862–65), he returned to Hamburg and taught at the Cons. until 1873. He publ. *Gesammelte Aufsätze* (Hamburg, 1872) and *System der Harmonielehre* (Hamburg, 1877). Among his compositions were the operas *König Harold* and *Der Mullerin Hochzeit*, 2 syms., the overture *Fiesco*, a Piano Concerto, a *Romance* for Violin and Orch., chamber music, and many piano pieces.—**NS/LK/DM**

Grädener, Hermann (Theodor Otto), German violinist, conductor, teacher, and composer, son of **Carl (Georg Peter) Grädener;** b. Kiel, May 8, 1844; d. Vienna, Sept. 18, 1929. He studied with his father, and then at the Vienna Cons. After serving as organist in Gumpendorf (1862–64), he was a violinist in the Vienna Court Orch. (from 1864). From 1877 to 1913 he taught theory at the Cons. of the Gesellschaft der Musikfreunde in Vienna, where he also was a prof. at the Univ. from 1882. He wrote the operas *Der Richter von Zalamea* and *Die heilige Zita*, 2 syms., a Piano Concerto, a Violin Concerto, a Cello Concerto, and various chamber pieces.—**NS/LK/DM**

Gradenwitz, Peter (Werner Emanuel), German-born Israeli musicologist and composer; b. Berlin, Jan. 24, 1910. He took courses in musicology, literature, and philosophy at the univs. of Berlin and Freiburg im Breisgau (1928–33). He also studied at the Berlin Hochschule für Musik and was a pupil in composition of Eisler and Rufer in Berlin, Weismann in Freiburg im Breisgau, and Milhaud in Paris (1934). Gradenwitz completed his training in musicology at the German Univ. in Prague (Ph.D., 1936, with the diss. *Johann Stamitz: Das Leben*; publ. in Brno, 1936; 2nd ed., greatly aug., as *Johann Stamitz: Leben, Umwelt, Werke*, 2 vols., Wilhelmshaven, 1984). In 1936 he settled in Palestine, and was active as a writer, lecturer, and concert organizer. He was founder, ed., and director of Israeli Music Publications, Ltd. (1949–82); also taught at the Univ. of Tel Aviv (1968–77). He lectured in Europe and the U.S. In 1980 he was made an honorary prof. at the Univ. of Freiburg im Breisgau, where he subsequently led annual seminars. He contributed numerous articles to various journals and other publications. Gradenwitz also composed, numbering among his works a Sym.; *Serenade* for Violin and Orch.; String Quartet; Trio for Flute, Viola, and Cello; *Palestinian* (later *Biblical*) *Landscapes* for Oboe and Piano; and songs.

WRITINGS: *Toldot hamusika* (Jerusalem, 1939; 8th ed., 1969); *The Music of Israel* (N.Y., 1949; 2nd ed., rev. and enl., 1996); *Olam hasimofonia* (Tel Aviv, 1945; 9th ed., 1974); *Olaf hapsantran* (Tel Aviv, 1952); *Die Musikgeschichte Israels* (Kassel, 1961); *Wege zur Musik der Gegenwart* (Stuttgart, 1963; 2nd ed., rev., 1974); *Wege zur Musik der Zeit* (Wilhelmshaven, 1974); *Musik zwischen Orient und Okzident: Eine Geschichte der Wechselbeziehungen* (Wilhelmshaven, 1977); *Das Heilige Land in Augenzeugenberichten* (Munich, 1984); *Leonard Bernstein: Eine Biographie* (Zürich, 1984; 2nd ed., 1990; Eng. tr., Oxford, 1986); *Kleine Kulturgeschichte der Klaviermusik* (Munich, 1986); *Literatur und Musik im Geselligen Kreis* (Stuttgart, 1991); *Arnold Schönberg und seine Meisterschüler: Berlin 1925–1933* (Vienna, 1998).—**NS/LK/DM**

Gradstein, Alfred, Polish composer; b. Czestochowa, Oct. 30, 1904; d. Warsaw, Sept. 9, 1954. He studied with Statkowski (composition) and Melcer (conducting) at the Warsaw Cons. (1922–25) and with Marx (composition) and Krauss (conducting) at the Vienna Academy of Music. From 1928 to 1947 he lived in Paris; then returned to Poland. He wrote a Piano Concerto (1932), chamber music, piano pieces, and many songs.—**NS/LK/DM**

Graener, Paul, significant German composer; b. Berlin, Jan. 11, 1872; d. Salzburg, Nov. 13, 1944. He studied composition with Albert Becker at the Veit Cons. in Berlin. He traveled in Germany as a theater conductor; in 1896 he went to London, where he taught at the Royal Academy of Music (1897–1902). He was then in Vienna as a teacher at the Neues Konservatorium; subsequently directed the Mozarteum in Salzburg (1910–13); after serving as prof. of composition at the Leipzig Cons. (1920–25), he was director of the Stern Cons. in Berlin (1930–33); thereafter he was vice-president of the Reichsmusikkamer (1933–41). His many songs reveal a penchant for folk-like melodies. His other works follow along traditional Romantic lines with some neo-Baroque aspects.

WORKS: DRAMATIC: Opera: *Don Juans letztes Abenteuer* (Leipzig, June 11, 1914); *Theophano* (Munich, June 5, 1918); *Schirin und Gertraude* (Dresden, April 28, 1920); *Hanneles Himmelfahrt* (Dresden, Feb. 17, 1927); *Friedemann Bach* (Schwerin, Nov. 13, 1931); *Der Prinz von Homburg* (Berlin, March 14, 1935); *Schwanhild* (Cologne, Jan. 4, 1941). **ORCH.:** Sym.; *Romantische Phantasie*; *Waldmusik*; *Gothische Suite*; Piano Concerto; Cello Concerto. **CHAMBER:** 6 string quartets; Piano Quintet; 3 violin sonatas.

BIBL.: G. Graener, *P. G.* (Leipzig, 1922); P. Grümmer, *Verzeichnis der Werke P. G.s* (Berlin, 1937).—**NS/LK/DM**

Graeser, Wolfgang, Swiss composer; b. Zürich, Sept. 7, 1906; d. (suicide) Nikolassee, June 13, 1928. He went to Berlin in 1921, where he studied violin with Karl Klingler and quickly acquired erudition in theory; he also made a serious study of various unrelated arts and sciences (mathematics, oriental languages, and painting). His signal achievement was an orchestration of Bach's *Kunst der Fuge* (Leipzig Thomaskirche, June 26, 1927). He publ. *Körpersinn* (Munich, 1927).

BIBL.: H. Zurlinden, *W. G.* (Munich, 1935).—**NS/LK/DM**

Graf, family of German musicians:

(1) Johann Graf, violinist and composer; b. Nuremberg (baptized), March 26, 1684; d. Rudolstadt, Feb. 2, 1750. He was a musician at the Deutschhauskirche in Nuremberg in his youth, and then studied violin and composition in Vienna. He served in the court bands in Mainz and Bamberg before being named Konzertmeister at the Schwarzburg-Rudolstadt court in 1722, where, from 1739, he was Kapellmeister. He wrote several violin sonatas and string quartets. He had 2 sons who were musicians.

(2) Christian Ernst Graf, violinist and composer; b. Rudolstadt, June 30, 1723; d. The Hague, July 17, 1804. He received training from his father, upon whose death he succeeded as Kapellmeister at the Schwarzburg-Rudolstadt court. In 1765 he was made Kapellmeister to Prince William of Orange at The Hague. Among his works were a Sym., a Violin Concerto, a Cello Concerto, chamber music, keyboard pieces, and songs.

(3) Friedrich Hartmann Graf, flutist and composer; b. Rudolstadt, Aug. 23, 1727; d. Augsburg, Aug. 19, 1795. He studied flute and composition with his father and timpani with Käsemann. After service as a military musician, he launched a career as a flutist in 1759. He was director of public concerts in Hamburg (1761–65), and then toured as a flute virtuoso. Following service at The Hague court (1769–72), he was made director of the Protestant Church and of St. Anna's Gymnasium in Augsburg in 1772. In 1783–84 he visited London, where he was co-director (with Wilhelm Cramer) of the Professional Concerts. In 1779 he was made a member of the Royal Swedish Academy of Music in Stockholm and in 1789 he was awarded an honorary doctorate in music by the Univ. of Oxford. He composed 2 syms., several flute concertos, 2 oratorios, 3 cantatas, and much chamber music.—**LK/DM**

Graf, Conrad, German-born Austrian piano maker; b. Riedlingen, Württemberg, Nov. 17, 1782; d. Vienna, March 18, 1851. He received training in cabinet making. In 1799 he settled in Vienna and later entered the employ of the piano maker Jakob Schelkle. In 1804 he married Schelkle's widow and opened his own piano workshop. In 1824 he was named Royal Court Piano and Keyboard Instrument Maker and in 1835 he won the gold medal at the first Vienna industrial products exhibition for his skill as a piano maker. His instruments were greatly admired by Beethoven, Chopin, Schumann, Liszt, and other musicians.

BIBL.: D. Wythe, *C. G. (1782–1851), Imperial Royal Court Fortepiano Maker in Vienna* (diss., N.Y.U., 1990).—**NS/LK/DM**

Graf, Hans, Austrian conductor; b. Linz, Feb. 15, 1949. He studied piano at the Bruckner Cons. in Linz (1957–59) and later took diplomas in piano and conducting at the Graz Hochschule für Musik (1971). He also

pursued training in conducting with Ferrara in Siena (1970, 1971) and Hilversum (1972), Celibidache in Bologna (1972), and Yansons in Weimar (1972) and Leningrad (1972–73). In 1975–76 he was music director of the Iraqi National Sym. Orch. in Baghdad. In 1979 he won 1st prize in the Karl Böhm conducting competition in Salzburg. He subsequently made appearances as a guest conductor with the Vienna Sym. Orch. (from 1980), the Vienna State Opera (from 1981), and at the Salzburg Festival (from 1983). From 1984 to 1994 he was music director of the Mozarteum Orch. and the Landestheater in Salzburg. In 1985 he made his first tour of the U.S. and Japan with the Mozarteum Orch. In 1987 he made his British debut as a guest conductor with the Royal Liverpool Phil. In 1995 he became principal conductor of the Calgary (Alberta) Phil. He concurrently served as music director of the Orchestre National Bordeaux Aquitaine from 1998. As a guest conductor, he has appeared with major orchs. in Europe, North America, and the Far East, and at various festivals. He has also conducted opera in Vienna, Berlin, Munich, Paris, and other major cities.—**NS/LK/DM**

Graf, Herbert, Austrian-born American opera producer and director, son of **Graf** b. Vienna, April 10, 1903; d. Geneva, April 5, 1973. He studied at the Univ. of Vienna with Adler; received his Ph.D. in 1925. He then was a producer at the opera houses in Münster, Breslau, Frankfurt am Main, and Basel. In 1934 he went to the U.S.; was associated with the Philadelphia Opera in 1934–35; in 1936 he was appointed producer of the Metropolitan Opera in N.Y.; in 1949 he also became head of the opera dept. at the Curtis Inst. of Music in Philadelphia. He later returned to Europe, where he was director of the Zürich Opera (1960–62) and the Grand Theatre in Geneva (1965–73). He publ. *The Opera and Its Future in America* (N.Y., 1941), *Opera for the People* (Minneapolis, 1951), and *Producing Opera for America* (Zürich, 1961).—**NS/LK/DM**

Graf, Max, Austrian music critic, teacher, and musicologist, father of **Herbert Graf**; b. Vienna, Oct. 1, 1873; d. there, June 24, 1958. He studied music history with Hanslick at the Univ. of Vienna (Ph.D., 1896, with the diss. *Die Musik der Frau in der Renaissancezeit*; publ. in Vienna, 1905), and also had lessons in theory with Bruckner. From 1900 to 1938 he wrote music criticism for the *Wiener Allgemeine Zeitung*; he lectured on musicology and aesthetics at the Cons. of the Gesellschaft der Musikfreunde (1902–09); then was on the staff of the Academy of Music (1909–38). In 1938, when Austria was incorporated into the Greater German Reich, he went to the U.S. He returned to Vienna in 1947. A brilliant writer in his homeland, he lapsed into speculative journalism in his books publ. in America, which are rendered worthless because of blatant inaccuracies.

WRITINGS: *Deutsche Musik im 19. Jahrhundert* (Berlin, 1898); *Wagner-Probleme und andere Studien* (Vienna, 1900); *Die innere Werkstatt des Musikers* (Stuttgart, 1910); *Richard Wagner im "Fliegenden Hollander"* (Vienna and Leipzig, 1911); *Vier Gespräche über deutsche Musik* (Regensburg, 1931); *Legend of a Musical City* (N.Y., 1945; 2nd ed., 1969); *Composer and Critic* (N.Y., 1946; 2nd ed., 1969); *Modern Music* (N.Y., 1946; 2nd ed.,

1969; Ger. ed., 1953, as *Geschichte und Geist der modernen Musik*); *From Beethoven to Shostakovich* (N.Y., 1947; 2nd ed., 1969); *Die Wiener Oper* (Vienna, 1955); *Jede Stunde war erfüllt: Ein Halbes Jahrhundert Musik und Theaterleben* (Vienna and Frankfurt am Main, 1957).—**NS/LK/DM**

Graf, Walter, Austrian ethnomusicologist; b. St. Pölten, June 20, 1903; d. Vienna, April 11, 1982. He studied musicology with Lach, Adler, and Wellesz, as well as anthropology, philosophy, psychology, and phonetics, at the Univ. of Vienna (Ph.D., 1932, with a diss. on German influences on Estonian folk song; Habilitation, 1952, with a study of the music of New Guinea; publ. in Vienna, 1950). He became lecturer (1958) and then asst. prof. (1962) at the Univ. of Vienna; from 1957 to 1963 he also was head of the Austrian Academy of Sciences recording archive, which he greatly expanded. In his articles, he continued Lach's anthropological concept of music; he also attempted to define the characteristics of sound that are important in the hearing and understanding of music. Among his writings are "Die ältesten deutschen Überlieferungen estnischer Volkslieder," *Musik des Ostens*, I (1962), *Die musikalische Klangforschung: Wege zur Erfassung der musikalischen Bedeutung der Klangfarbe* (Karlsruhe, 1969), and "Zur Rolle der Teiltonreihe in der Gestaltung klingend tradiertet Musik," *Festschrift Kurt Blaukopf* (Vienna, 1975).

BIBL.: E. Schenk, ed., *Musik als Gestalt und Erlebnis: Festschrift W. G. zum 65. Geburtstag* (Vienna, 1970).—**NS/LK/DM**

Graffigna, Achille, Italian composer; b. S. Martino dall' Argine, near Mantua, May 5, 1816; d. Padua, July 19, 1896. He studied with Alessandro Rolla in Milan. He wrote church music and theatrical cantatas, then devoted himself to opera. His *Ildegonda e Rizzardo* (La Scala, Milan, Nov. 3, 1841) was accepted with favor. In 1842 he went to Verona, where he produced *Eleonora di San Bonifacio* (March 11, 1843). There followed *Maria di Brabante* (Trieste, Oct. 16, 1852), *L'assedio di Malta* (Padua, July 30, 1853), *Gli Studenti* (Milan, Feb. 7, 1857), *Veronica Cibo* (Mantua, Feb. 13, 1858; rev. and produced at the Théâtre-Italien, Paris, March 22, 1865, as *La Duchessa di San Giuliano*), *Il Barbiere di Siviglia* (Padua, May 17, 1879; an homage to Rossini), *Il matrimonio segreto* (Florence, Sept. 8, 1883), and *La buona figliuola* (Milan, May 6, 1886).—**NS/LK/DM**

Graffman, Gary, eminent American pianist and music educator; b. N.Y., Oct. 14, 1928. He began playing the piano at a very early age and, when he was only 7, he was accepted as a student of Isabelle Vengerova at the Curtis Inst. of Music in Philadelphia (graduated, 1946). At 8, he appeared as soloist with Sevitzky and the Philadelphia Chamber String Sinfonietta. In 1946 he won the first regional Rachmaninoff Competition, which secured for him his first engagement with the Philadelphia Orch. under Ormandy's direction as soloist in Rachmaninoff's 2nd Piano Concerto on March 28, 1947. In 1947–48 he was a scholarship student at Columbia Univ. He made his Carnegie Hall recital debut in N.Y. on Dec. 27, 1948. After winning the Leventritt Award in 1949, he went to Europe on a Fulbright

scholarship in 1950. In 1951 he made his first tour of the U.S. Following additional studies with Horowitz in N.Y. and Serkin in Marlboro, Vt., he made his first tour of South America in 1955, followed by debut appearances in Europe in 1956, Asia and Australia in 1958, and South Africa in 1961. As a soloist, he was engaged by most of the leading orchs., and he also gave recitals in the principal music centers. His performances and recordings of concertos by Beethoven, Brahms, Chopin, Tchaikovsky, Rachmaninoff, and Prokofiev were particularly acclaimed by the public and critics alike. In 1979 his renowned career was tragically imperiled when he injured a finger of his right hand. In 1980 he joined the faculty of the Curtis Inst. of Music, where he was successively named artistic director in 1986, director in 1989, and president in 1995. He also pursued a successful career as a virtuoso in the left-hand piano repertoire, playing works by Strauss, Schmidt, Ravel, Korngold, Prokofiev, and Britten. On Feb. 4, 1993, he was soloist in the premiere of Rorem's 4th Piano Concerto for Left-Hand and Orch. with the Curtis Inst. of Music Sym. Orch. conducted by Previn. With Leon Fleischer, he gave the premiere of Bolcom's *Gaea* for Piano, 2 Left-Hands, and Orch. with Zinman and the Baltimore Sym. Orch. on April 13, 1996. Graffman is the author of the entertaining memoir *I Really Should Be Practicing* (Garden City, N.Y., 1981).—**NS/LK/DM**

Graham, Bill (originally, **Grajonca, Wolfgang**), rock music's most famous and influential concert producer from the mid-1960s through the 1980s; b. Berlin, Germany, Jan. 8, 1931; d. Oct. 25, 1991, near Vallejo, Calif. Bill Graham escaped the Nazi persecution of Jews as a child, fleeing first to France, then to the U.S. in 1941, where he was raised in the Bronx by a foster family. He formally changed his name to Bill Graham in 1949, when granted U.S. citizenship. He later served in the U.S. Army in the Korean War and graduated from N.Y.C. Coll. with a degree in business administration before moving to Calif. By 1960, he was an executive with the Allis-Chalmers farm equipment company in San Francisco.

In 1965, Bill Graham quit his position to take over management of the Mime Troupe, a radical street-theater improvisational group. On Nov. 6, 1965, Bill Graham staged a benefit concert for the Mime Troupe at San Francisco's Longshoreman's Hall with various Bay Area musicians. On Dec. 10, he promoted another benefit concert at the 1100-seat Fillmore Auditorium in one of San Francisco's black ghettos with the Jefferson Airplane, the Great Society (with Grace Slick), and the Warlocks (later the Grateful Dead). The financial and artistic success of the benefits, along with his subsequent production of the now-legendary Trips Festival at the Longshoreman's Hall in January 1966, encouraged Graham to regularly present rock shows at the Fillmore Auditorium. By year's end, he was also presenting concerts at the 5400-seat Winterland Arena and managing, if briefly, the Jefferson Airplane. The concerts became astoundingly successful and featured both little-known local talent and big-name outside acts.

Bill Graham presented his last show at the Fillmore Auditorium in July 1968. He opened Fillmore East in

N.Y. in March 1968 and assumed management of the Carousel Ballroom on San Francisco's Market Street in August. The old dance hall, which he renamed Fillmore West, had been run by the Jefferson Airplane and the Grateful Dead since early in the year. Over the next three years, Graham presented virtually every major rock act at the Fillmores, while giving little-known acts a chance to perform and booking a number of nonrock acts such as Miles Davis, Lenny Bruce, and the Staple Singers.

Graham's success with the Fillmores encouraged the establishment of similar venues across the country and marked the heyday of concert rock. He opened a talent booking agency in October 1968, and formed Fillmore and San Francisco Records in February 1969, recording Cold Blood and Elvin Bishop before dissolving the labels at the beginning of 1972. With the demise of the ballroom concert scene following the Woodstock Festival of August 1969, Graham announced his intention to close the Fillmores.

By July 1971, both Fillmore East and Fillmore West had been closed. Graham "retired" for a time, but was back in 1972, producing the Rolling Stones' tour. He booked acts into the Winterland Arena and produced the massive Watkins Glen Pop Festival in upstate N.Y. in 1973, the largest gathering of its kind. In 1974, he staged the Band's celebrated *Last Waltz* and produced George Harrison's tour, Bob Dylan's comeback tour, and the reunion of Crosby, Stills, Nash and Young. By 1978, the Winterland venue had also become obsolete, giving way to impersonal and lucrative festivals and stadium concerts. On New Year's Eve 1978, the New Riders of the Purple Sage, the Blues Brothers, and the Grateful Dead played the final performance at Winterland, a hall once castigated as overly large and acoustically unsound, but now sorely missed.

Bill Graham became the master of arena concert production, supervising the Rolling Stones' 1981 world tour and presenting the US Festival near San Bernardino in 1982. He reopened San Francisco's most successful nightclub, the Old Waldorf, as Wolfgang's in 1983. Withdrawing from the day-to-day operation of his organization, Graham appeared in small roles in the films *Apocalypse Now*, *The Cotton Club*, and *Gardens of Stone* during the 1980s. His organization financed outdoor amphitheaters in Sacramento (Cal Expo) and Palo Alto (Shoreline), which opened in 1983 and 1987, respectively. In 1985, he presided over the day-long Live Aid benefit in Philadelphia and later personally supervised the Amnesty International tours of 1986 and 1988. In 1987, Graham presented the first rock concert in Russia at Moscow's Izmajlovo Stadium with Santana, the Doobie Brothers, James Taylor, and Bonnie Raitt. Personal setbacks of the time included fires that destroyed his warehouse offices in 1985 and Wolfgang's in 1987.

In March 1988, the nightclub wing of the Bill Graham organization began presenting shows at the refurbished Fillmore Auditorium once again, but the hall was closed after October 1989's Loma Prieta earthquake. Graham presented three simultaneous benefit concerts for victims of the quake. He also made the final legal arrange-ments for and produced the Oliver Stone movie *The Doors* and performed the role of Lucky Luciano in the movie *Bugsym* starring Warren Beatty. In 1990, he helped produce the Gathering of the Tribes concert, which inspired 1991's Lollapalooza tour. However, on Oct. 25, 1991, Graham, companion Melissa Gold, and longtime pilot Steve Kahn were killed in a fiery helicopter crash near Vallejo, Calif.

In fitting tribute to the life and memory of Bill Graham, the Fillmore Auditorium reopened on April 27, 1994, after over $1 million in renovations. Mixing widely varying types of music, as Graham had in the early days of the Fillmore, the announced acts were American Music Club, Ry Cooder and David Lindley, and Smashing Pumpkins, with impromptu performances by Linda Perry and Joe Satriani. An effort to preserve Fillmore East failed in 1995.

Disc.: *Live at Bill Graham's Fillmore West* (1969); *Fillmore: The Last Days* (1972).

Writings: With Robert Greenfield, *Bill Graham Presents: My Life Inside Rock and Out* (N.Y., 1992).

Bibl.: John Glatt, *Rage and Roll: Bill Graham and the Selling of Rock* (Secaucus, N.J., 1993); Richard Kostelanetz, *Fillmore East: Memories of Rock Theater* (N.Y., 1995).—**BH**

Graham, Colin, English opera director and librettist; b. Hove, Sussex, Sept. 22, 1931. He attended the Royal Academy of Dramatic Art in London (1951–52). After working as a stage manager, he directed his first opera, Britten's *Noye's Fludde*, at the Aldeburgh Festival in 1958. In subsequent years, he worked closely with Britten, becoming an artistic director at the Aldeburgh Festival in 1968. He worked with the English Opera Group, serving as its director of productions from 1963 to 1975; from 1961 he was active at the Sadler's Wells (later English National) Opera in London, where he was director of productions from 1977 to 1982. He was also associated with London's Covent Garden (1961–73). In 1975 he created the English Music Theatre Co., with which he was active until 1978. In 1978 he was named director of production at the Opera Theatre of St. Louis, serving as its artistic director from 1985. Graham also pursued theological studies at the New Covenant School of Ministry in St. Louis, and was ordained in 1988. He staged the first British productions of *The Cunning Little Vixen* (1961), *From the House of the Dead* (1965), and *War and Peace* (1972). Among the 50 world premieres he directed were Britten's *Curlew River* (1964), *The Burning Fiery Furnace* (1966), *The Golden Vanity* (1967), *The Prodigal Son* (1968), *Owen Wingrave* (1972), and *Death in Venice* (1973), Bennett's *Mines of Sulphur* (1963) and *A Penny for a Song* (1967; librettist), Paulus's *The Postman Always Rings Twice* (1982; librettist), and Minoru Miki's *Joruri* (1985; librettist), and Susa's *The Dangerous Liaisons* (1994). Graham's early training in the dramatic arts, combined with his extraordinary command of every aspect of the music theater, have placed him among the leading masters of his craft.—**NS/LK/DM**

Graham, Susan, admired American mezzo-soprano; b. Roswell, N.Mex., July 23, 1960. She studied with Cynthia Hoffman at the Manhattan School of

Music in N.Y. (M.M., 1987). While still a student there, she attracted critical notice as Massenet's Chérubin, and then appeared with the operas in St. Louis and Seattle. During the 1989–90 season, she sang Annius in *La clemenza di Tito* at the Chicago Lyric Opera, Sonia in Argento's *The Aspern Papers* in Washington, D.C., Dorabella and Strauss's Composer in Santa Fe, and as soloist in *Das Knaben Wunderhorn* at N.Y.'s Carnegie Hall. In 1990–91 she appeared as Minerva in Monteverdi's *Il ritorno d'Ulisse in patria* at the San Francisco Opera and as Berlioz's Beatrice in Lyons. Her success in the Metropolitan Opera National Auditions led to her debut with the company in N.Y. during the 1991–92 season as the 2nd Lady in *Die Zauberflöte*, where she subsequently was engaged to sing Cherubino, Tebaldo in *Don Carlos*, Meg Page, Octavian, Ascanio, and Dorabella. From 1993 she sang at the Salzburg Festivals as well. During the 1993–94 season, she made her debut at London's Covent Garden as Chérubin. In 1995 she sang for the first time at Milan's La Scala as Berlioz's Marguerite and at the Vienna State Opera as Octavian, and on Sept. 15 of that year she created the title role in Goehr's *Arianna* at Covent Garden. She sang Beatrice in Santa Fe and Strauss's Composer at the Lyric Opera in Chicago in 1998. In 1999 she portrayed Ruggiero in *Alcina* in Paris. Her engagements as a concert artist have taken her to principal North American and European music centers, where she has appeared with many notable orchs.
—NS/LK/DM

Grahn, Ulf, Swedish composer; b. Solna, Jan. 17, 1942. He studied piano, violin, and composition with Hans Eklund at the Stockholm Citizen's School (1962–66), and then took various courses at the Stockholm Musikhögskolan (1966–70). In 1972 he and his wife, the pianist Barbro Dahlman, went to America, where he studied at the Catholic Univ. of America (M.M., 1973). With Dahlman, he founded the Contemporary Music Forum (1974), presenting programs of modern music by American and European composers. He served as its program director until 1984. After teaching at Northern Va. Community Coll. (1975–80), he joined the faculty of George Washington Univ. in Washington, D.C. (1983). He also served as artistic and managing director of the Lake Siljan Music Festival in Sweden (1988–89). In his music, Grahn maintains the golden mean of contemporary idioms, without doctrinaire deviations, scrupulously serving the tastes of the general audience.

WORKS: BALLET: *Lux* (1972; Stockholm, April 6, 1972). **ORCH.:** *Musica da camera* for Chamber Orch. (1964); *Fancy* (1965); *Lamento* for Strings (1967); 2 syms.: No. 1 (1967) and No. 2 (1983; Stockholm, June 20, 1984); *Hommage à Charles Ives* for Strings (1968; Trondheim, Feb. 13, 1969); Concerto for Double Bass and Chamber Orch. (1968; Santa Barbara, Calif., Feb. 7, 1973); *Joy* for Symphonic Band (1969; Stockholm, Feb. 2, 1970); *Ancient Music* for Piano and Chamber Orch. (1970; Copenhagen, March 20, 1972); *A Dream of a Lost Century* for Chamber Orch. (1971; Stockholm, June 1, 1972); *Concerto for Orchestra* (1973; Philadelphia, April 10, 1981); Concertino for Piano and Strings (1979); *Rondeau* for Chamber Orch. (1980); Guitar Concerto (Reston, Va., June 15, 1985); *As Time Passes By* (1993); *Pezzo* (1993); *A Tale* (1993). **CHAMBER:** Trio for Flute, Oboe, and Clarinet (1967); *This Reminds Me of...* for Flute, Clarinet, Horn, Trombone, and Percussion (1972; Washington, D.C., Dec. 15, 1975); *Soundscapes I* for Flute, Bass Clarinet, English Horn, and Percussion (Washington, D.C., Oct. 28, 1973), *II* for Instruments (1974), and *III* for Flute, Clarinet, Percussion, and Tape (1975); Chamber Concerto for Viola d'Amore and 10 Instruments (1975; Washington, D.C., Jan. 17, 1977); *Order-Fragments- Mirror* for Flute, Bass Clarinet, Percussion, and Piano (1975); Flute Sonata (1976); *Magnolias in Snow* for Flute and Piano (1976); String Quartet No. 2 (1979); *Floating Landscape* for 8 Flutes (1979); Piano Quartet (1980); *Summer Deviation* for Flute, Violin, Viola, Cello, and Piano (1981); *Images* for Bass Clarinet and Marimba (1981); *Eldorado* for Flute, Violin, Clarinet, Piano, and Baryton (1982); Violin Sonata (1983); *Nocturne* for Piano Trio and Tape (1987; Washington, D.C., March 7, 1988); *3 Dances with Interludes* for 6 Percussionists (1990); *Madrigal* for 4 Trombones (1991); *3 Water Colors* for Horn and Piano (1991); *Long shadows on the...* for Oboe and Guitar (1998). **P i a n o :** Sonata (1980). **VOCAL:** *Soundscapes IV* for Soprano, Flute, Bass Clarinet, Percussion, and Piano (1975); *Un Coup de dés* for Soprano and Chamber Ensemble (Washington, D.C., April 20, 1987).
—NS/LK/DM

Grainger, (George) Percy (Aldridge), celebrated Australian- born American pianist, composer, and folk song collector; b. Melbourne, July 8, 1882; d. White Plains, N.Y., Feb. 20, 1961. He studied with his mother and received piano lessons from Louis Pabst in Melbourne; he then was a pupil of Kwast (piano) and Knorr (composition) at the Hoch Cons. in Frankfurt am Main (1895–99); later he had additional piano lessons with Busoni in Berlin (1903). In 1901 he appeared as a pianist in London, and then played throughout Great Britain, Europe, Australia, New Zealand, and South Africa. In 1905 he joined the English Folk Song Soc. and became an ardent collector of folk songs. In 1914 he went to N.Y., where he made a sensational debut on Feb. 11, 1915. During service as an oboist in the U.S. Army Band (1917–19), he became a naturalized American citizen in 1918. He taught piano at the Chicago Musical Coll. during several summers between 1919 and 1928. In 1926 he toured Australia again. He married the Swedish poet and artist Ella Viola Ström in 1928 in a spectacular ceremony at the Hollywood Bowl, at which he conducted his *To a Nordic Princess*, written for his bride. In 1932–33 he was chairman of the music dept. at N.Y.U. In 1934–35 he again toured Australia, during which time he began organizing the Grainger Museum at the Univ. of Melbourne to house his MSS and personal effects and to serve as an ethnomusicological research center. He dedicated the museum in 1938. During World War II, he made numerous concert appearances for the Allied cause. After the War, he made his home in White Plains. Although Grainger was honored by election to the National Inst. of Arts and Letters in 1950, his last years were embittered by his belief that his work as a composer had been unjustly neglected. Always the eccentric, he directed that his skeleton be placed on display at the Grainger Museum, but his request was denied and he was buried in the ordinary manner. He prepared an autobiographical sketch as *The Aldridge-Grainger-Ström Saga* (1933), publ. the vol. *Music: A Commonsense View of All Types* (Sydney, 1934), and ed. 12 collections of music. Grainger's philosophy of life and art called for the widest communion of peoples. His profound study of folk music underlies the melodic and rhythmic structure of his own music. He made a determined effort to re-create in art music the free flow of instinctive songs of the people. He experimented with "gliding" intervals within the traditional scales and polyrhythmic combinations with independent strong beats in the component parts. In a modest way, he was a pioneer of electronic music. As early as 1937, he wrote a quartet for electronic instruments, notating the pitch by zigzags and curves. He introduced individual forms of notation and orch. scoring, rejecting the common Italian designations of tempi and dynamics in favor of colloquial English expressions.

WORKS: ORCH.: *English Dance* for Organ and Orch. (1899–1909; 1924–25); *Youthful Suite* (1899–1945); *Colonial Song* (1905–12; rev. c. 1928); *In a Nutshell*, suite (1905–16); *Mock Morris* for Strings (1910; also for Orch., 1914); *The Warriors* for 3 Pianos and Orch. (1912–16); *The Power of Rome and the Christian Heart* for Organ and Orch. (1918–43); *To a Nordic Princess* (1927–28); *Handel in the Strand* for Strings (1932); *Harvest Hymn* (1932); *The Immovable Do* (c. 1939). **Band::** *The Lads of Wamphray March* for Band (1906–07; rev. 1937–38); *Hill Song No. 2* for Band (1907; rev. 1911 and 1940–46); *Over the Hills and Far Away* for Piano and Band (1916–19); *Colonial Song* for Band (1918); *Marching Song of Democracy* for Band (1948). **CHAMBER:** *Walking Tune* for Wind Quartet (1900–1905); *Youthful Rapture* for Cello and Piano or Piano Trio, with 9 Instruments ad libitum (1901; 1929); *Hill Song No. 1* for 21 Instruments (1901–02; also for 22 or 23 Instruments, 1921; rev. 1923) and *No. 2* for 22 or 23 Wind Instruments and Cymbal (1907; rev. 1911 and 1940–46); *Free Music* for String Quartet (1907; also for Theremins, 1935–36); *Arrival Platform Humlet* for Viola (1908–12); *Mock Morris* for 3 Violins, Viola, and 2 Cellos (1910; also for Violin and Piano, 1910); *Handel in the Strand* for Piano Trio and Viola ad libitum (1911–12); *The Lonely Desert Man Sees the Tents of the Happy Tribes* for Various Instrumental Combinations (1911–14; 1949); *Colonial Song* for Piano Trio (1912); *Echo Song Trials* for Various Instrumental Combinations (1945); many keyboard pieces. **OTHER:** Choral works, pieces for Solo Voice and Piano or Other Instruments, and numerous folk song settings.

BIBL.: D. Parker, *P. A. G.: A Study* (N.Y., 1918); C. Scott, *P. G.: A Course in Contemporary Musical Biography* (N.Y., 1919); T. Slattery, *The Wind Music of P.A. G.* (diss., Univ. of Iowa, 1967); M. Tan, *The Free Music of P. G.* (diss., Juilliard School, 1971); T. Slattery, *P. G.: The Inveterate Innovator* (Evanston, Ill., 1974); T. Balough, *A Complete Catalogue of the Works of P. G.* (Nedlands, 1975); J. Bird, *P. G.: The Man and the Music* (London, 1976); L. Foreman, ed., *The P. G. Companion* (London, 1981); T. Balough, ed., *A Musical Genius from Australia: Selected Writings by and about P. G.* (Nedlands, 1982); D. Tall, ed., *P. G.: A Catalogue of the Music* (London, 1982); R. Simon, *P. G.: The Pictorial Biography* (N.Y., 1984); K. Dreyfus, ed., *The Farthest North of Human Kindness: Letters of P.G. 1901–14* (London, 1985); J. Blacking, *"A Commonsense View of All Music": Reflections on P. G.'s Contribution to Ethnomusicology and Music Education* (Cambridge, 1987); T. Lewis, *Source Guide to the Music of P. G.* (White Plains, N.Y., 1991); W. Mellers, *P. G.* (Oxford, 1992); M. Gillies, ed., *The All-Round Man: Selected Letters of P. G., 1914–1961* (Oxford, 1994).—**NS/LK/DM**

Gram, Hans, Danish-born American organist, writer on music, and composer; b. Copenhagen, May 20, 1754; d. Boston, April 28, 1804. He studied philosophy at the Univ. of Copenhagen, and also had some training in music. About 1785 he went to America, and settled in Boston, where he became organist of the Brattle St. Church. He contributed various musical pieces to the *Massachusetts Magazine*, including a curious composition entitled *The Death Song of an Indian Chief* for Voice, 2 Clarinets, 2 Horns, and Strings, which was publ. in the March 1791 issue; it was apparently the first orch. score publ. in the U.S. He also wrote *Sacred Lines for Thanksgiving Day* (1793) and some other vocal works for the same magazine. He was a co-ed. of *The Massachusetts Compiler* (Boston, 1795), a rather progressive collection on Psalmody, which also contained a music dictionary.—**NS/LK/DM**

Gram, Peder, Danish conductor and composer; b. Copenhagen, Nov. 25, 1881; d. there, Feb. 4, 1956. After graduation from the Univ. of Copenhagen, he studied theory at the Leipzig Cons. with Sitt and Krehl and conducting with Nikisch (1904–07). Returning to Copenhagen, he was chief conductor of the Danish Concert Soc. (1918–32) and head of the music dept. of the Danish Radio (1937–51). He publ. *Musikens formlaere i grundtraek* (1916), *Moderne musik* (1934), and *Analytisk harmonilaere* (1947), all in Copenhagen.

WORKS: ORCH.: *Romance* for Violin and Orch. (1909); *Symfonik fantasi* (1908); *Poème lyrique* (1911); 3 syms. (1913, 1925, 1954); Violin Concerto (1919); Overture (1921); *Festouverture* (1927); *Prolog til et drama af Shakespeare* (1928); *Intrada seria* (1946). **CHAMBER:** 3 string quartets (1907, 1928, 1941); Piano Trio (1914); Cello Sonata (1914); Oboe Sonatina (1935); Wind Quintet (1943); piano pieces. **VOCAL:** *Avalon* for Soprano and Orch. (1916); *Min ungdoms drm* for Tenor and Orch. (1921); songs.—**NS/LK/DM**

Gramatges, Harold, Cuban composer, pianist, and teacher; b. Santiago de Cuba, Sept. 26, 1918. He was a student of Ardévol and Roldan in Havana, and then of Copland (composition) and Koussevitzky (conducting) at the Berkshire Music Center in Tanglewood (summer, 1942). Returning to Havana, he was active in contemporary music circles. He also devoted time to teaching. After serving in the Cuban Embassy in Paris (1961–64), he returned to Havana and was director of the music dept. of the Casa de las Américas (1965–70). In 1970 he joined the music section of the Consejo Nacional de Cultura, and in 1976 the composition dept. of the music faculty of the Instituto Superior de Arte. His output represents an enlightened functionalist approach to composition in an effective modern style.

WORKS: DRAMATIC: *Icaro*, ballet (1943); *Mensaje al futuro*, ballet (1944); *Cantata a la paz*, theater piece (1987); incidental music. **ORCH.:** Sym. (1945); *Dos danzas cubanas* (1950); Sinfonietta (1955); *In memoriam (homenaje a Frank País)* (1961); *Para la dama duende* for Guitar and Orch. (1973). **CHAMBER:** Duo for Flute and Piano (1943); Trio for Clarinet, Cello, and Piano (1944); Concertino for Piano and Winds (1945); Quintet for Flute, Clarinet, Bassoon, Viola, and Double Bass (1950); Quintet for Flute, Oboe, Clarinet, Bassoon, and Trumpet (1957); *Movil II* for 7 Instruments (1970); *Diseños*, quintet for Winds and Percussion (1976); *Guirigay*, quintet (1985); piano pieces; guitar music. **VOCAL:** *La muerte del guerrillero* for Reciter and Orch. (1968–69); *Oda martiana* for Baritone and Orch. (1980); choral pieces; songs.—**NS/LK/DM**

Gramm (real name, **Grambasch**), **Donald (John),** American bass-baritone; b. Milwaukee, Feb. 26, 1927; d. N.Y., June 2, 1983. He studied piano and organ at the Wisc. Coll.-Cons. of Music (1935–44), and also studied voice with George Graham. He made his professional debut in Chicago at the age of 17 when he sang the role of Raimondo in *Lucia di Lammermoor*. He continued his vocal studies at the Chicago Musical Coll. and at the Music Academy of the West in Santa Barbara, where he was a student of Martial Singher. On Sept. 26, 1952, he made his debut at the N.Y.C. Opera as Colline in *La Bohème*, and continued to appear with the company for the rest of his life. On Jan. 10, 1964 he made his Metropolitan Opera debut in N.Y. as Truffaldino in *Ariadne auf Naxos*, and then sang major roles there until his death. He was extremely versatile in his roles; he sang Méphistophélès, Leporello, Mozart's Figaro, Falstaff in Verdi's opera, Baron Ochs, and Scarpia. He also distinguished himself as an interpreter of such difficult parts as Dr. Schön in Berg's *Lulu* and as Moses in Schoenberg's *Moses und Aron*.—NS/LK/DM

Grammann, Karl, German composer; b. Lübeck, June 3, 1844; d. Dresden, Jan. 30, 1897. He studied at the Leipzig Cons., and spent some years in Vienna, settling in Dresden in 1885. As a youth, he wrote 2 operas, *Die Schatzgräber* and *Die Eisjungfrau*, which were not produced. The following operas were staged with some success: *Melusine* (Wiesbaden, 1875), *Thusnelda und der Triumphzug des Germanicus* (Dresden, 1881), and *Das Andreasfest* (Dresden, 1882), and 2 short operas, *Ingrid* and *Das Irrlicht* (Dresden, 1894). His last opera, *Auf neutralem Boden*, was produced posth. (Hamburg, 1901). He further wrote several cantatas, syms., string quartets, violin sonatas, and other chamber music works.

BIBL.: F. Pfohl, *K. G. Ein Künstlerleben* (Berlin, 1910).—NS/LK/DM

Granados (y Campiña), Eduardo, Spanish conductor and composer, son of **Enrique Granados (y Campiña);** b. Barcelona, July 28, 1894; d. Madrid, Oct. 2, 1928. He studied in Barcelona with his father, then at the Madrid Cons. with Conrado del Campo. He taught at the Granados Academy in Barcelona, and was also active as a conductor, presenting many works by his father. He wrote several zarzuelas, of which the first, *Bufon y Hostelero*, was performed with some success in Barcelona (Dec. 7, 1917). His other stage works were *Los Fanfarrones*, comic opera, *La ciudad eterna*, mystery play, *Los Cigarrales*, operatic sketch, and musical comedies.—NS/LK/DM

Granados (y Campiña), Enrique, distinguished Spanish composer, pianist, and teacher, father of **Eduardo Granados (y Campiña);** b. Lérida, July 27, 1867; d. in the aftermath of the torpedoing of the S.S. *Sussex* by a German submarine in the English Channel, March 24, 1916. He went to Barcelona and studied piano with Francisco Jurnet at the Escolania de la Marcé and privately with Joan Baptista Pujol, and from 1883 took private composition lessons with Pedrell. In 1887 he went to Paris to pursue his training in piano with

Charles de Bériot. In 1889 he returned to Barcelona, and in 1890 made his recital debut there. He continued to make successful appearances as a pianist in subsequent years while pursuing his interest in composing. On Nov. 12, 1898, he scored a notable success as a composer with the premiere of his zarzuela *María del Carmen* in Madrid. In 1900 he organized the Sociedad de Conciertos Clasicos in Barcelona, and from 1901 taught there at his own Academia Granados. He secured his reputation as a composer with his imaginative and effective piano suite *Goyescas* (1911). He subsequently utilized music from the suite and from some of his vocal tonadillas to produce the opera *Goyescas*, which received its premiere at the Metropolitan Opera in N.Y. on Jan. 28, 1916, with the composer in attendance. It was on his voyage home that Granados perished. Although he was picked up by a lifeboat after the attack on the S.S. *Sussex*, he dove into the sea to save his drowning wife and both were lost. Granados' output reflected the influence of the Spanish and Romantic traditions, and the Castilian tonadilla. His finest scores are notable for their distinctive use of melody, rhythm, harmony, and color.

WORKS: DRAMATIC: *María del Carmen*, zarzuela (Madrid, Nov. 12, 1898); *Blancaflor* (Barcelona, Jan. 30, 1899); *Petrarca*, lyric drama (n.d.); *Picarol*, lyric drama (Barcelona, Feb. 23, 1901); *Follet*, lyric drama (Barcelona, April 4, 1903); *Gaziel*, lyric drama (Barcelona, Oct. 27, 1906); *Liliana*, lyric drama (Barcelona, July 9, 1911); *La cieguecita de Belén* or *El portalico de Belén* (1914); *Goyescas*, opera (1915; N.Y., Jan. 28, 1916); also *Miel de la Alcarria*, incidental music (n.d.) and *Ovillejos o La gallina ciega*, Sainte lírico (n.d.; unfinished). **ORCH.:** *Marcha de los vencidos* (Barcelona, Oct. 31, 1899); *Suite on Gallician Themes* (Barcelona, Oct. 31, 1899); *Dante*, or *La Divina Commedia* for Mezzo-soprano and Orch. (private perf., Barcelona, June 1908; rev. version, Barcelona, May 25, 1915); *Navidad* (1914; Madrid, May 31, 1916); undated scores: *Boires baixes: Suite árabe u oriental*; *Torrijos*. **CHAMBER:** Trio for Violin, Cello, and Piano (1894; Madrid, Feb. 15, 1895); Piano Quintet (Madrid, Feb. 15, 1895); Violin Sonata (c. 1910); *Serenade* for 2 Violins and Piano (Paris, April 4, 1914); *Madrigal* for Cello and Piano (Barcelona, May 2, 1915); undated scores: *Romanza* for Violin and Piano; Cello Sonata; 3 *Preludes* for Violin and Piano. **Piano:** *Danzas españolas* (1892–1900); *Goyescas*, 2 books (Book 1, Barcelona, March 11, 1911); numerous solo pieces. **VOCAL:** *Cant de les estrelles* for Chorus, Piano, and Organ (1910; Barcelona, March 11, 1911); *Elisenda* for Voice, Piano, Harp, String Quintet, Flute, Oboe, and Clarinet (1910; Barcelona, July 7, 1912); *L'Herba de amor* for Chorus and Organ (1914); songs.

BIBL.: G. Boladeres Ibern, *E. G.: Recuerdos de su vid y estudio critico de su obra por su antiguo discipulo* (Barcelona, 1921); H. Collet, *Albéniz et G.* (Paris, 1925; 2nd ed., 1948); J. Subirá, *E. G.: Su producción musical, su madrileñismo, su personalidad artística* (Madrid, 1926); A. Fernández-Cid, *G.* (Madrid, 1956); P. Vila San-Juan, *Papeles intimos de E. G.* (Barcelona, 1966); J. Riera, *E. G.: Estudio* (Lérida, 1967); A. Tarazona, *E. G.: El último romántico* (Madrid, 1975); A. Carreras i Granados, *G.* (Barcelona, 1988); M. Larrad, *The Goyescas of G.* (thesis, Univ. of Liverpool, 1988); C. Hess, *E. G.: A Bio-Bibliography* (N.Y., 1991); M. Larrad, *The Catalan Theater Works of E. G.* (diss., Univ. of Liverpool, 1991).—NS/LK/DM

Grancini, Michel'Angelo, Italian organist and composer; b. Milan, 1605; d. there, April 17, 1669. He spent his entire life in Milan. At age 17 he became organist at the Chiesa del Paradiso, and then served in that capacity at S. Sepolcro (1624–28) and at S. Ambrogio (from 1628). He also was organist (from 1630) and maestro di cappella (from 1650) at the Cathedral. Grancini composed a prolific body of sacred music, of which 19 vols. were publ. in Milan (1622–29). Some 200 works are in MSS at the Milan Cathedral.—NS/LK/DM

Grancino, family of Italian violin makers who were active in the 17th and early 18th centuries. **Andrea Grancino** established a workshop in Milan in 1646. His son, **Paolo Grancino,** worked in Milan between 1665 and 1692; he belonged to the Amati school, and several violins attributed to Amati are apparently his work. Paolo's son, **Giovanni Grancino,** began making violins in 1677; he is reputed to have been the best of the family. His sons, **Giovanni Battista Grancino** and **Francesco Grancino,** were active between 1715 and 1746. Their labels are marked Fratelli Grancini.—NS/LK/DM

Grandert, Johnny, Swedish composer; b. Stockholm, July 11, 1939. He studied under Lidholm at the Stockholm Musikhögskolan (1959–64), and also took music courses in Germany, Italy, and America but was mainly antodidact in music. He also was active as a painter. In 1972 he became principal and in 1986 director of music at the Norrtalje School of Music. The titles of his compositions betray a desire to puzzle and tantalize, but the music itself is not forbidding.

WORKS: DRAMATIC: O p e r a : *Gyllene jord* (1984). **ORCH.:** *The D. of B.* (1967); *Barypet,* concerto for Trumpet and Baritone Saxophone, with 16 Flutes, Percussion, and Strings (1968); *Skorogovorka* (Tongue Twister) for Wind Orch. and Percussion (1971); 7 syms.: No. 1 (1971), No. 2 (1973), No. 3, *Sinfonia Calamagrostis* (1972), No. 4 (1974; Stockholm, Nov. 29, 1975), No. 5 (1976; Swedish Radio, Feb. 22, 1977), No. 6 (1982; Helsinki, March 3, 1983), and No. 7 (1996); *Jerikos murar* for Flute, Slide Flute, 3 Bass Recorders, 3 Clarinets, 15 Trombones, Percussion, Organ, and Strings (1972); *Rodensiana* (1984); *Staccato* for Strings (1990). **CHAMBER:** *Chamber Music* for Chamber Ensemble (1961); 10 string quartets (1963–98); Nonet for Winds, Euphonium, and Cello (1964); *86 T* for Chamber Ensemble (1965); *10 an' 30* for Chamber Ensemble (1966); Octet for 3 Voices, Flute, Trombone, Viola, Double Bass, and Harp (1966); *Prego I* for Cello and Horn (1968); *Non omesso* for Chamber Ensemble (1969); *Non lo so* for Flute, Cello, and Piano (1970); *Pour Philippe,* wind quintet (1970); Quartet for Recorders (1972); Saxophone Quintet (1975); *Temptation,* essay for String Quartet (1979); *Midtwedt,* canon for 8 Violins (1986); *Isola Sale* for Chamber Ensemble (1989); Brass Quintet (1989); *Boureause* for Chamber Ensemble (1991); *Temper Tantrum* for Flute (1993–95). **VOCAL:** *Mirror 25* for Chorus and Orch. (1966); *Pour Pjotr* for Voice, Piano, Cello, Clarinet, and Percussion (1971). —NS/LK/DM

Grandi, Alessandro, significant Italian composer; b. c. 1577; d. Bergamo, 1630. He was maestro di cappella at the Accademia della Morte (1597–1604), the Accademia dello Spirito Santo (1610–15), and the cathedral in Ferrara (1615–17), then became a singer (1617) and 2nd maestro di cappella (1620) at S. Marco in Venice. He subsequently was maestro di cappella at S.

Maria Maggiore in Bergamo from 1627 until his death from the plague. His sacred music is of great importance; he excelled in the new concertato style. He also composed secular solo cantatas and arias, as well as concertato madrigals of great merit.

WORKS: VOCAL (all publ. in Venice unless otherwise noted): **S a c r e d :** *Il primo libro de* (21) *motetti* for 2 to 5 and 8 Voices, *con una messa* for 4 Voices and Basso Continuo (1610); *Il secondo libro de* (12) *motetti* for 2 to 4 Voices and Basso Continuo (1613; 2nd ed., aug., 1617); (16) *Motetti* for 5 Voices and Basso Continuo, *con le Letanie della beata vergine* (Ferrara, 1614; 3rd ed., aug., 1620, for 2 to 5 and 8 Voices and Basso Continuo [organ]); *Il terzo libro de* (26) *motetti* for 2 to 4 Voices, *con le Letanie della beata vergine* for 5 Voices and Basso Continuo (1614; not extant; 2nd ed., 1618); *Il quarto libro de* (17) *motetti* for 2 to 4 and 7 Voices and Basso Continuo (1616); *Celesti fiori...de suoi* (16) *concerti* for 2 to 4 Voices and Basso Continuo, *con alcune cantilene* (1619; 2nd ed., 1620, for 1 to 4 Voices); (18) *Motetti* for Voice and Basso Continuo (1621); (15) *Motetti* for 1 and 2 Voices and Basso Continuo, *con sinfonie* (1621); (14) *Motetti* for 1 and 2 Voices and Basso Continuo, *...libro II* (2nd ed., 1625); (19) *Motetti* for 1 and 2 Voices and Basso Continuo, *con sinfonie...libro III* (1629); *Salmi brevi* for 8 Voices and Basso Continuo (1629); *Messa, e salmi* for 3 Voices and Basso Continuo (1630); *Raccolta terza...de messa et salmi...* for 2 to 4 and 6 Voices ad libitum, Cornett, 4 Trombones, Violin, and Basso Continuo (1630); *Il sesto libro de* (19) *motetti* for 2 to 4 Voices and Basso Continuo (1630; 3rd ed., Antwerp, 1640, for 2 to 4 Voices and Basso Continuo); (2) *Messe* for 8 Voices and Basso Continuo (1637). **VOCAL: S e c u l a r :** (15) *Madrigali* for 2 to 4 Voices and Basso Continuo (1615); (42) *Cantade et arie* for Voice and Basso Continuo (2nd ed., 1620; not extant); (20) *Madrigali* for 2 to 4 Voices and Basso Continuo *...libro II* (1622); *Cantade et arie* for Voice and Basso Continuo *...libro III* (1626); *Arie, et cantade* for 2 and 3 Voices, 2 Violins, and Basso Continuo (1626; only 2nd-violin part extant); *Cantade et arie* for Voice and Basso Continuo *...libro IV* (1629; not extant).

BIBL.: M. Seelkopf, *Das geistliche Schaffen von A. G.* (diss., Julius-Maximilian Univ., Würzburg, 1973).—NS/LK/DM

Grandi, Margherita, (née **Margaret Garde**), Australian soprano; b. Hobart, Oct. 4, 1894; d. Milan, 1972. She studied at the Royal Coll. of Music in London, with Calvé in Paris, and with Russ in Milan. In 1919 she made her operatic debut under the stage name of Djema Vécla (an anagram of Calvé) at the Paris Opéra-Comique in *Werther.* In 1922 she created the title role in Massenet's *Amadis* in Monte Carlo. After marrying the scenic designer Giovanni Grandi, she sang under her married name. In 1932 she appeared as Aida at Milan's Teatro Carcano, and returned to that city to sing Elena in *Mefistofele* at La Scala in 1934. She sang at the Glyndebourne Festivals in 1939, 1947, and 1949. In 1946 she appeared at the Verona Arena. In 1947 she sang Tosca and Donna Anna at London's Cambridge Theatre. In 1949 she returned to London to create the role of Diana in Bliss's *The Olympians* at Covent Garden. She also made guest appearances in South America. In 1951 she retired from the operatic stage. Grandi's most acclaimed roles were Lady Macbeth and Tosca, which she projected in the grand manner.—NS/LK/DM

Grandjany, Marcel (Georges Lucien), distinguished French-born American harpist, pedagogue, and composer; b. Paris, Sept. 3, 1891; d. N.Y., Feb. 24, 1975. He was a student of Henriette Renié, taking the premier prix at the Paris Cons. in 1905. At age 17, he made his formal debut as soloist with the Lamoureux Orch. in Paris. In 1922 he made his first appearance in London and in 1924 made his debut in N.Y. From 1921 to 1935 he taught at the Fontainebleau Cons. In 1936 he settled in N.Y. and in 1945 became a naturalized American citizen. He taught at the Juilliard School of Music in N.Y. (1938–75), and also at the Montreal Cons. (1943–63). Among his works were a *Poème symphonique* for Harp, Horn, and Orch., other harp pieces, and songs. He publ. *First Grade Harp Pieces* (N.Y., 1964).—NS/LK/DM

Grandjean, Axel Karl William, Danish composer; b. Copenhagen, March 9, 1847; d. there, Feb. 11, 1932. He began his career as an opera singer, but gave up the stage for teaching and composition; also conducted several choral societies in Copenhagen. He wrote the operas *Colomba* (Copenhagen, Oct. 15, 1882), *Oluf* (Copenhagen, April 7, 1894), and others, as well as many choral works.—NS/LK/DM

Grandmaster Flash (originally, Saddler, Joseph), one of the creators and popularizers of hip hop culture who, with the Furious Five, established the basic tonal and political vocabulary of rap; b. Barbados, West Indies, Jan. 1, 1958.

Joseph Saddler, a.k.a. Grandmaster Flash, was probably the first renowned virtuoso of the turntables. His main innovation capitalized on the work of two other legendary Bronx deejays: D.J. Jones, noted for impeccable timing of his segues; and Kool Herc, known for his collection of obscure break beats. Even if Flash didn't invent the fast cut technique, keeping two copies of a record on the turntables and cutting back and forth between them to lengthen breaks and solos, he did master it.

Born in the West Indies, he came to the Bronx at a fairly early age. By his teens, he played records at parties, dances and impromptu gatherings—throw downs—in parks around the Bronx, often pirating the electricity from power cables until the police came to shut the party down. While studying electronics during the day, he continued deejaying by night, working local discos and working in his various techniques: quick cutting, scratching records, speed changes and back spinning.

Eventually Flash decided that this technique wouldn't stand on its own as entertainment, so he took another page from Kool Herc's book. He enlisted alliances with MC's, people who talked over the records, creating rhymes and exhorting people to dance. Early on he worked with Lovebug Starsky and Keith Wiggins. Wiggins, who became known as Cowboy, became the first member of Flash's crew, the Furious Five. Kurtis Blow joined for a while, but the crew solidified as Grandmaster Melle Mel (born Melvin Glover), his brother Nathaniel (a.k.a. Kid Creole), Rahiem (born Todd Williams) and Scorpio (born Eddie Morris, a.k.a. Mr. Ness). They started playing shows and even cut a couple of records for upstart labels that heard this

sound as a way to capitalize on the urban audience after the success of the Sugarhill Gang's "Rapper's Delight." The 12" "Super Rapping Theme" on Enjoy didn't sell well, nor did a couple the group cut for other companies under assumed names.

Joe Robinson, husband of Sylvia, who had a major hit with "Pillow Talk" on Robinson's Vibration Records, had released the Sugarhill Gang's record on his Sugarhill label. Robinson bought the Furious Five out of their Enjoy contract and put his wife (a quarter of a century veteran performer by that time) to work with them. "Freedom" (1980) went to #19 on the R&B charts. The group went on tour, previously unheard of for rappers. They followed this up in 1981 with "Birthday Party," a fun disc featuring the furious five playing kazoos. It went to #36 on the R&B chart.

The group put out a bunch of 12" singles during 1981: "Showdown" with the Sugarhill Gang and "It's Nasty," based on the Tom Tom Club's "Genius of Love" stood out in the hip-hop crowd. Flash finally went public with the turntables as a solo instrument that year with "The Adventures of Grandmaster Flash on The Wheels of Steel." Mixing bits and pieces of Chic's "Good Times" (the basis of the Sugarhill Gang's "Rapper's Delight"), Queen's "Another One Bites the Dust" and the section of Blondie's "Rapture" where Debbie Harry declaims "Flash is fast, Flash is cool," the record remains a tour de force of old school hip-hop. It only served as a set up to their next single, however. In 1982, they unleashed "The Message." Where rap had previously dealt mostly with MC concerns like partying, dancing and bragging, the message of "The Message" could make the blood run cold. A litany of social ills to which any of the members of the group and their Bronx peers could fall victim, it opened with the lines "Broken glass everywhere, people pissing on the street, they just don't care." The record went to #4 on the R&B charts.

During the recording of their next single, the anti-cocaine rap "White Lines," Flash had two major fallings out. He and Melle Mel had creative differences that led to two units called the Furious Five performing the next year. After the success of "The Message," Flash asked Joe Robinson to show him the money. When Robinson didn't, flash left Sugarhill. He signed to Elektra, but the luster and excitement weren't there, and younger rappers started to steal Flash's thunder. Add to that the coming of the sampler, a digital device that allowed digital devices to do simply what Flash had spent so many years perfecting, and Flash's descent began. He started to have drug problems. His first three records were lackluster affairs.

In 1987, Paul Simon convinced both Flash and the Five to reunite for a concert to raise funds for inner city health services. The concert went so well, the group went into the studio to record *On The Strength*, which included a version of Steppenwolf's "Magic Carpet Ride." In 1991, Flash appeared in the film *New Jack City*, and started his own production company Master Groove Records. Other artists started to pay homage to rap's early innovators. In 1992, Danish artist Nikolaj Steen recorded "The New Message" with Melle Mel and Scorpio. In 1995, Flash and Melle Mel guested on a cover of "White Lines." In 1994, they went out on tour with a bunch of other old school rappers, though without Cowboy, who died Sept. 8, 1989. Flash also did a show on N.Y. radio and even appeared in a fashion spread for designer Louis Vuitton. Late in the 1990s, he served as music director and deejay for HBO's *Chris Rock Show.*

DISC.: *The Message* (1982); *They Said It Couldn't Be Done* (1985); *The Source* (1986); *Da Bop Boom Bang* (1987); *On the Strength* (1988).—HB

Grandval, Marie Félicie Clémence de Reiset,

French composer; b. Saint-Rémy-des-Monts, Sarthe, Jan. 21, 1830; d. Paris, Jan. 15, 1907. She studied composition with Flotow and Saint-Saëns. Under various pen names, she wrote the operas *Le Sou de Lise* (Paris, 1859), *Les Fiancés de Rose* (Paris, May 1, 1863), *La Comtesse Eva* (Paris, Aug. 7, 1864), *La Pénitente* (Paris, May 13, 1868), *Piccolino* (Paris, Jan. 5, 1869), and *Mazeppa* (Bordeaux, 1892), as well as the oratorio *St. Agnès* (Paris, April 13, 1876), *La Forêt*, lyric poem for Soloists, Chorus, and Orch. (Paris, March 30, 1875), and songs. —NS/LK/DM

Granichstaedten, Bruno,

Austrian composer; b. Vienna, Sept. 1, 1879; d. N.Y., May 20, 1944. He began his career as a cabaret singer, and in 1908 turned to composing light opera. He produced 16 stage works before 1930, of which *Der Orlow* (Vienna, April 3, 1925) was the most successful. Other operettas are *Bub oder Mädel, Auf Befehl der Kaiserin, Evelyne, Walzerliebe*, etc. In 1938 he settled in the U.S.—NS/LK/DM

Grant, Amy,

contemporary Christian music superstar who rode the momentum to chart-topping pop (b. Augusta, Ga. Nov. 25, 1960). Born in Ga., Grant spent some of her childhood in Houston, Tex. before moving to Tenn. Her father practiced radiology in Nashville. While attending an exclusive private school for girls, she picked up the guitar and began attending services at a nondenominational church not far from Nashville's Music Row and the campus of Vanderbilt Univ. When she could not find any songs that appealed to her in her early teens, she began writing her own. She wrote and performed a Vespers service and the reaction was so positive she continued creating. This led to a job in a recording studio at 15, where she swept floors, bulk erased tapes, and cut demos. A producer working at the studio heard one of Grant's demos and played it over the phone to people at the Christian record company Word Records. Word was impressed and signed the teenaged girl.

Grant released her eponymous debut at the age of 18. Several more records followed, including two live recordings and Grant's records started to attract attention outside of Christian rock circles. One reason was Grant herself. A vivacious twenty-something who wore leopard print jackets, tight pants, and bare feet while performing on the Grammy Awards, she certainly was attractive enough for pop stardom. She had a voice that drew comparisons to Olivia Newton John and Karen Carpenter. Her music was powered by synthesizers and big drum sounds.

Her breakthrough in the Christian market came with the release of *Age to Age* in 1982. The album sold half a million right off the bat, making it the first Christian album to achieve platinum sales. It won Grant her first Grammy, for best female Gospel Performance, Contemporary. A single release, "Ageless Medley" won the Grammy for Best Gospel Performance, Female in 1983 (it would find its way onto her 1986 *Collection* album). She continued to sell well in the Christian market; her album *Straight Ahead* in 1985 hit #133. The track "Angels" won Grant yet another Best Gospel Performance Female Grammy. *Unguarded* also came out in 1985, and rose to #35. At the same time, Grant made her first foray onto the (secular) Top 40 pop charts with the #29 song "Find A Way." The album won yet another Best Gospel Performance Female, her fourth straight year of coming home with a Grammy.

By 1986, with a pop hit and several platinum albums behind her, Grant's shows had all the trappings of Big Rock: smoke, lights, and a massive sound system. It took semi trucks to move her show from venue to venue. She also had friends in high places, like Chicago frontman Peter Cetera. His single "Glory of Love" had just topped the charts. She had cut a song with him for his *Solitude/Solitaire* album. That became his next single, "The Next Time I Fall" which zoomed to the top of the charts. While it helped jumpstart her pop career, it landed her in hot water with her core fans in the Christian market, who accused her of selling out. It was something she would hear every time she made noise in the pop arena. In an attempt to reestablish her core audience, her 1988 album *Lead Me On* cut back on the pop trappings, leaning on acoustic guitar. A downright somber album, it nonetheless rose to #71 and won Grant her fifth Grammy, once again for Best Gospel Performance Female.

Although Grant had already topped the pop charts in tandem with Cetera, she really hadn't followed that up. In 1991, Grant made her major breakthrough to the pop market with *Hearts in Motion*. She cut a song "Baby Baby" in honor of her then-baby daughter, Millie. The tune reminded her of the fresh innocence of early Motown. Neither Word nor A&M heard the song, but she persevered and put it on the record. The tune topped both the pop and adult contemporary charts. She followed that up with "Every Heartbeat," which rose to #2. "That's What Love Is For" topped the adult contemporary charts and blasted to #7 on the pop charts. "Good for Me" reached #8. The final single from the album, "I Will Remember," made it to #20. The album hit #10, sold quintuple platinum, and spent well over a year on the charts.

Grant followed this with her second holiday album. *Home for Christmas* rose to #2, scored platinum, and remained a recurrent seller during the holiday season. She followed this with several projects, like *Music of the Spirit*, a semi-classical, multi-artist album of sacred music. Finally, she turned her attention back to mainstream pop with *House of Love* in 1994. While not nearly as successful as *Hearts in Motion*, it did generate the #18 single "Lucky One" and the #37 duet with Vince Gill, who she met at a concert the previous year, on the title track. The album hit #13 and went platinum. However, after the first leg of her concert tour supporting the album, Grant had to cancel the rest of her dates because of a torn retina.

This lent a note of irony to the title of her next album, 1997's *Behind the Eyes*. A more introspective, acoustic album, it was almost a more mature version of *Lead Me On*. Almost all of the songs were in the first person, and while the spirituality that infused all of her work bubbled through every song, none mentioned God. The album peaked during its first week of release at #8 and produced the hit "It Takes A Little Time." While Grant has taken the time to do charity work, including a two-hour concert to kick off the children's miracle network telethon in 1998, she spent the last years of the 1990s mostly dealing with her divorce from her husband of 16 years, Gary Chapman, host of the Nashville Network's *Country Music Today*. For the holiday season of 1999, she released another Christmas album, *A Christmas to Remember*.

DISC.: *Amy Grant* (1977); *My Father's Eyes* (1979); *Never Alone* (1980); *In Concert* (live; 1981); *Age to Age* (1982); *In Concert, Vol. 2* (live; 1982); *A Christmas Album* (1983); *Straight Ahead* (1984); *Unguarded* (1985); *Lead Me On* (1988); *Heart in Motion* (1991); *Home for Christmas* (1992); *Creation* (1993); *Gingham Dog & Calico Cat* (1993); *House of Love* (1994); *Behind the Eyes* (1997); *A Christmas to Remember* (1999).

BIBL.: Bob Italia, *Amy Grant: From Gospel to Pop* (Edina, 1992); Evan Keith, *Amy Grant* (N.Y., 1992); Bob Millard, *Amy Grant* (N.Y., 1986).—**HB**

Grant, Clifford (Scantlebury), Australian bass; b. Randwick, Sept. 11, 1930. He studied at the New South Wales State Conservatorium of Music in Sydney and with Otakar Kraus in London. In 1951 he made his operatic debut with the New South Wales Opera as Raimondo in *Lucia di Lammermoor*. After further appearances in Australia, he made his debut at the Sadler's Wells Opera in London in 1966 as Silva in *Ernani*, where he later sang Pogner, Sarastro, Hunding, the Commendatore, and Hagen. He also made his U.S. debut in 1966 at the San Francisco Opera as Lord Walton in *I Puritani*, and returned there to sing such roles as the King in *Aida*, Monterone, and Oroveso. He first sang at the Glyndebourne Festival as Nettuno in *Il Ritorno d'Ulisse* in 1972. His Covent Garden debut followed in London in 1974 as Mozart's Bartolo. On Nov. 19, 1976, he made his debut at the Metropolitan Opera in N.Y. as Phorcas in *Esclarmonde*. From 1976 to 1990 he pursued his operatic career in Australia. In 1993 he appeared as Alvise with England's Opera North.—**NS/LK/DM**

Grant, William Parks, American composer, educator, and music scholar; b. Cleveland, Jan. 4, 1910; d. Oxford, Miss., April 5, 1988. He was educated at Capital Univ. in Columbus, Ohio (B.M., 1932) and at Ohio State Univ. (M.A., 1933), and later completed his training with Howard Hanson and Harold Gleason at the Eastman School of Music in Rochester, N.Y. (Ph.D., 1948). He taught at the Northeast Jr. Coll. branch of La. State Univ. (1943–47), Temple Univ. (1947–53), and the Univ. of Miss. (1953–73). He publ. *Music for Elementary Teachers* (N.Y., 1951; rev. ed., 1960) and *Handbook of Musical Terms* (Metuchen, N.J., 1967). Grant served as music ed. of the critical edition of Mahler's 9th Sym., and also worked on the critical editions of Mahler's 2nd, 3rd, and 8th syms.

WORKS: DRAMATIC: Ballet: *The Dream of the Ballet-Master* (1934). **ORCH.:** 3 syms. (1930–38; 1941–43; 1953); *Masque of the Red Death* (1931–41); Horn Concerto (1940); Clarinet Concerto (1942–45); *Autumn Woodland Poem* for Strings (1945–46); Double Bass Concerto (1946); 3 suites for Strings (1946, 1952, 1959); *Rhythmic Overture* (1947); *Dramatic Overture* (1948); *Homage Ode* (1949); *Scherzo* for Flute and Orch. (1949); *A Mood Overture* (1950); 2 overtures (1955); *Character Sketches* (1963). **CHAMBER:** *Night Poems* for 2 Violins, Viola, and Cello (1940–42); *Poem* for Horn or Cello and Organ (1945); *Essay* for Horn or Cello and Organ (1948); 2 string quartets (1948–49; 1963); *Simplicity* for Violin and Piano (1949); *Laconic Suite* for 2 Trumpets, Horn, and Trombone (1949); *Prelude and Dance* for 3 Trumpets, 4 Horns, 3 Trombones, and Tuba (1951); *Soliloquy and Jubilation* for Flute, Oboe, Clarinet, Horn, and Bassoon (1952); *Instrumental Motet* for 2 Pardessus de Viole, Viola da Gamba, and Basse de Viole (1952); *Brevities* for 2 Trumpets, Horn, and Trombone (1952); Concert Duo for Tuba and Piano (1954); *Lento and Allegro* for 2 Trumpets, Horn, Trombone, and Tuba (1954–55); *Prelude and Canonic Piece* for Flute and Clarinet (1959); *Varied Obstinacy* for Alto or Tenor Saxophone and Tape (1971). **KEYBOARD: Piano:** 2 sonatas (1940, 1953). **Organ:** *Gothic Triptych* (1947). **VOCAL:** Choruses; songs. —**NS/LK/DM**

Grantham, Donald, American composer and teacher; b. Duncan, Okla., Nov. 9, 1947. He studied composition at the Univ. of Okla. (B.Mus., 1970) and then entered the Univ. of So. Calif. in Los Angeles in the composition classes of Robert Linn and Halsey Stevens (M.M. 1974; D.M.A., 1980). In the summers of 1973 and 1974 he studied with Boulanger at the American Cons. in Fontainebleau. After lecturing at the Univ. of Southern Calif. in Los Angeles (1974–75), he joined the faculty of the Univ. of Tex. at Austin in 1975, where he became a prof. in 1991. With K. Kennan, he was co-author of the 5th ed. of *The Technique of Orchestration* (Englewood Cliffs, N.J., 1997).

WORKS: DRAMATIC: Opera: *The Boor* (1989). **ORCH.:** *El album de los duendecitos* (1983); *Invocation and Dance* (1988); *To the Wind's 12 Quarters* (1993); *Fantasy on Mr. Hyde's Song* (1993); *Southern Harmony* (2000); *Exhilaration and Cry* (2000). **Wind Ensemble:** Concerto for Bass Trombone and Wind Ensemble (1979); *Bouncer* for Brass Quintet (1991); *Bum's Rush* (1994); *Fantasy Variations* (1995); *Fantasy on Mr. Hyde's Song* (1998); *J'ai ete au bal* (1999); *Kentucky Harmony* (2000). **CHAMBER:** Piano Trio (1971); Chamber Concerto for Harpsichord and String Quartet (1974); *4 caprichos de Francisco Goya* for Violin (1976); *Sonata in 1 Movement* for Bass Trombone and Piano (1979); *Duendecitos!* for Flute and Piano (1981); *Solitaire* for Flute (1995); Quintet, *Sacred Harp* (1998). **Piano:** *Fantasy Variations* for 2 Pianos (1996). **VOCAL:** *La noche en la isla* for Baritone and Chamber Orch. or Piano, after Pablo Neruda (1980); *To the King Celestial* for Soprano and Chamber Orch., after a 14th-century Eng. text (1981); *7 Choral Settings of Poems by Emily Dickinson* (1983); *4 Choral Settings of Poems by e.e. cummings* (1985); *A Collect for the Renewal of Life* for Chorus and Organ (1986); *3 Choral Settings of Poems by William Butler Yeats* (1986); *You Shall Go Out in Joy* for Chorus and Organ (1989);

Lascivious Love Songs for Mezzo-soprano and Woodwind Quintet for Piano (1990); *On This Day,* Christmas cantata for Soprano, Chorus, Children's Chorus, Percussion, and Harp (1993).—**NS/LK/DM**

Grappelli (Grappelly), Stephane, legendary, long-lived French jazz violinist and pianist, second only to Joe Venuti in importance in the history of jazz violin; b. Paris, Jan. 26, 1908; d. there, Nov. 30, 1997. Until the 1970s Grappelly was the preferred spelling. He began playing classical violin at 12, and piano in his early teens (he made several piano recordings in the 1930s). He turned to jazz violin in the late 1920s, working in cinemas and cafés, then with Grégor and His Grégoriens and Glickman's Orch. He soon led his own band and developed a musical partnership with Django Reinhardt, resulting in the formation of the enormously popular Quintet of the Hot Club of France (1934–39). He visited London with the QHCF (1938), then settled in Britain (1939) and worked with Arthur Young (1939–40) before becoming featured soloist with Barney Gilbraith at Lansdowne House (1940). After overcoming serious illness, he worked regularly at Hatchett's, London (1942) and toured variety halls with his Swingtette. He performed and recorded with Reinhardt again (1946–47), but thereafter they went their separate ways except for recording dates.

Grappelli became very active on the European touring circuit, with engagements in France (1947–48, included Bert Firman); London (Milroy Club, 1949); Rome (1951); and after recovery from an illness, Britain (1953). After another illness, he led at the Bagatelle Club, London (1954). He played further seasons in Rome, St. Tropez, Paris, and London (1955–58), before taking up a residency at Club St. Germain, Paris (1958). He made his U.S. debut at the 1969 Newport Jazz Festival. He was an active festival participant, and played the world's leading concert halls from the 1970s until his death. His extensive recording schedule consolidated his position as an international musical celebrity. He appeared regularly in concert with Yehudi Menuhin (from 1973), and (Nigel) Kennedy. He made his Carnegie Hall N.Y. debut (1974) and returned there for a special 80th-birthday concert.

DISC.: *Unique Piano Session* (1955); *Violins No End* (1957); *Improvisations* (1958); *Feeling + Finesse = Jazz* (1962); *Meets Barney Kessel* (1969); *Venupelli Blues* (with J. Venuti; 1969); *Paris Encounter* (with G. Burton; 1968); *Afternoon in Paris* (1971); *Jalousie: Music of the 30s* (with Y. Menuhin; 1972); *S. G./Bill Coleman* (1973); *Meets Earl Hines* (1974); *Steff and Slam* (with Slam Stewart; 1975); *Reunion, with George Shearing* (1976); *And Hank Jones* (1979); *And David Grisman* (1979); *Live at Tivoli Gardens, Copenhagen* (1979); *At the Winery* (1980); *Happy Reunion, with Martial Solal* (1980); *Live in San Francisco* (1982); *One on One, with McCoy Tyner* (1990); *Live* (1992); *So Easy to Remember* (1992); *And Michel Legrand* (1992); *85 & Still Swinging...* (1993); *It's Only a Paper Moon* (1994).

WRITINGS: *Mon Violon pour Tout Bagage* (autobiography).

BIBL.: M. Glaser, *S. G. Jazz Violin* (N.Y., 1981); R. Horricks, *S. G., or the Violin with Wings: A Profile* (N.Y., 1983); G. Smith, *S. G.: A Biography* (London, 1987).—**NS/JC-B**

Grasse, Edwin, American violinist and composer; b. N.Y., Aug. 13, 1884; d. there, April 8, 1954. Blind from infancy, he dictated his compositions to an accompanist. He studied violin with Hauser in N.Y., then went to Brussels for study with Thomson at the Cons., where he won 1st prize in 1900, and diplôme de capacité in 1901. He toured Europe and America. His works included *American Fantasie* for Violin and Orch., a Violin Sonata and other violin pieces, and organ pieces.—**NS/LK/DM**

Grassi, Eugène, French composer; b. Bangkok (of French parents), July 5, 1881; d. Paris, June 8, 1941. He went to France as a youth and studied with d'Indy; he revisited Siam from 1910 to 1913 to collect materials on indigenous music. His works reflect this study as well as, in harmonic idiom, the influence of Debussy. Among his compositions, all with oriental flavor, were *Le Réveil de Bouddha,* symphonic poem (Paris, Feb. 20, 1920), *Poème de l'univers* for Orch. (Paris, April 9, 1922), *Les Sanctuaires* (Paris, March 25, 1926), and songs in the impressionist manner.—**NS/LK/DM**

Grassini, Giuseppina (Maria Camilla), Italian contralto; b. Varese, April 8, 1773; d. Milan, Jan. 3, 1850. She studied in Varese with Domenico Zucchinetti and in Milan with Antonio Secchi. She made her operatic debut in Parma in 1789 in Guglielmi's *La Pastorella nobile.* Grassini sang at La Scala in Milan in 1790, and soon attained popularity on all the leading Italian stages. In 1800 she sang in Milan before Napoleon, and became his mistress; he took her with him to Paris, where she sang at national celebrations. She was in London from 1804 to 1806, then returned to Paris and sang at the French court. After Napoleon's abdication, she returned to Italy and sang from 1817 until 1823. She then taught voice in Milan, where her notable students included her nieces **Giudetta** and **Giulia Grisi,** as well as Pasta. She was noted for her beauty and her acting, as well as her voice.

BIBL.: A. Pougin, *Une Cantatrice "amie" de Napoleon: G. G.* (Paris, 1920); A. Gavoty, *La G.* (Paris, 1947).—**NS/LK/DM**

Grass Roots, The, one of the biggest American Top 40 bands of the late 1960s and early 1970s, formed 1964, in Los Angeles, Calif. **MEMBERSHIP:** Steve Barri (b. N.Y.C., Feb. 23, 1941); P.F. Sloan, voc. (b. Los Angeles, 1946); Rob Grill, voc., bs. (b. Los Angeles, Nov. 30, 1944); Warren Entner, gtr., voc. (b. Boston, July 7, 1944); Creed Bratton, gtr. (b. Sacramento, Calif., Feb. 8, 1943); Rick Coonce (real name, Erick Michael Coonce), drm. (b. Los Angeles, Aug 1, 1947).

The group was originally a vehicle for songwriters Steve Barri and P.F. Sloan, a West Coast–based writing team that specialized in pop songs. They had scored a huge hit with Barry McGuire's recording of their "Eve of Destruction" and were looking for a band to back their next creation, the song "Where Were You When I Needed You." They hired a local group called the Bedouins, renamed them the Grass Roots, and cut two songs, including the #28 "Where Were You When I Needed You." However, the band then disappeared, leaving the record company "rootless."

Meanwhile, a local L.A. band, the 13th Floor, was on the verge of signing with Dunhill. This band, including vocalists Rob Grill and Warren Entner, were offered the choice of starting cold or becoming the Grass Roots and picking up with a hit already under their belt. They opted for the latter, cutting a new version of an Italian hit. The song, "Live for Today" rose to #8 in the summer of 1967. The album of the same name only hit #75, setting the general tone for their history on LP. After trying to write their own material for 1967's *Feelings* album (with commercially disastrous results), the band recorded again with Barri, releasing "Midnight Confessions." Informed by an orchestrated Motown groove, it set the tone for the rest of the band's career. The record went to #5 and mined gold for the band. Even the album, *Golden Grass*, lived up to its name, going gold and hitting #25. "I'd Wait A Million Years" was another big hit in this mold, hitting #15 in 1969. After spending 1970 dealing with line-up changes, with Bratton leaving, replaced by Denny Provisor and Terry Furlong, the group came back strong in 1971 with a string of hits that included "Temptation Eyes" (#15, 1971), "Sooner Or Later" (#9, 1971) and "Two Divided By Love" (#16, 1971). This was the group's last great year of original hits, though they did hit the lower rungs of the Top 40 twice in 1972.

Grill continues to tour as the Grass Roots. Warren Entner went on to become a manager, representing some of the more lucrative hard rock bands including Ratt and Faith No More.

DISC.: *Where Were You When I Needed You?* (1966); *Let's Live for Today* (1967); *Feelings* (1968); *Lovin' Things* (1969); *Leavin' It All Behind* (1969); *Move Along* (1972); *A Lot of Mileage* (1973); *Grass Roots* (1975); *Powers of the Night* (1982); *Temptation Eyes* (1985).—HB

Grateful Dead, The, the ultimate head-trips band of the 1960s–mid- 1990s, spawners of the Deadhead movement, and one of the most successful live acts in the history of rock. **MEMBERSHIP:** Jerome "Jerry" Garcia, gtr., voc. (b. San Francisco, Calif., Aug. 1, 1942; d. Forest Knolls, Calif., Aug. 9, 1995); Bob Weir (Robert Hall), gtr., voc. (b. Atherton, Calif., Oct. 16, 1947); Ron "Pig Pen" McKernan, kybd. (b. San Bruno, Calif., Sept. 8, 1945; d. Corte Madera, Calif., March 8, 1973); Phil Lesh, bs. (b. Berkeley, Calif., March 15, 1940); Bill Kreutzmann, drm. (b. Palo Alto, Calif., May 7, 1946). The band's full-time lyricist beginning in 1969 was Robert Hunter (b. Arroyo Grande, Calif., June 23, 1941).

Other members included drummer Michael "Mickey" Hart (b. N.Y., Sept. 11, 1943); Tom Constanten, kybd. (b. Long Branch, N.J., March 19, 1944); Keith Godchaux, kybd. (b. Concord, Calif., July 19, 1948; d. Ross, Calif., July 23, 1980); Brent Mydland, kybd. (b. Munich, West Germany, Oct. 21, 1952; d. Lafayette, Calif., July 26, 1990); Vince Welnick, kybd. (b. Phoenix, Ariz., Feb. 21, 1951); and vocalist Donna Godchaux (b. Sheffield, Ala., Aug. 22, 1947).

Jerry Garcia grew up in San Francisco and Menlo Park, obtaining his first guitar, an electric guitar, at the age of 15. Dropping out of high school, he served a brief stint in the Army in 1959 before returning to the Palo Alto area and meeting Robert Hunter. He took up banjo in 1960 and formed a series of folk, jug-band, and bluegrass music groups with Hunter for local engagements beginning in early 1962. These included the Thunder Mountain Tub Thumpers, the Asphalt Jungle Boys (with John "Marmaduke" Dawson), and the Hart Valley Drifters (with David Nelson), which won an amateur bluegrass contest at the Monterey Folk Festival in 1963. The group subsequently became the Wildwood Boys and, by 1964, Garcia had formed Mother McCree's Uptown Jug Champions with harmonica player Ron "Pig Pen" McKernan and guitarists Bob Weir and Bob Matthews. By April 1965, Mother McCree's Uptown Jug Champions had gone electric and reemerged as the Warlocks, with Garcia, Weir, and McKernan. Adding drummer Bill Kreutzmann, the group replaced their first bassist with Phil Lesh, a classically trained trumpeter and composer of 12-tone and electronic music, in June.

Taking the name the Grateful Dead, the group played at Bill Graham's first rock event at the Fillmore Auditorium in November 1965 and, beginning in December, at author Ken Kesey's infamous "acid tests," chronicled in Tom Wolfe's *The Electric Kool-Aid Acid Test*. With financial benefactor and LSD manufacturer Augustus Stanley Owsley III acting as manager, the group performed at local venues such as the Fillmore Auditorium and the Avalon Ballroom, as well as for free in San Francisco's Golden Gate Park with the Jefferson Airplane and other area bands.

Moving into 710 Ashbury Street in the heart of the Haight-Ashbury district in June 1966, the Grateful Dead recorded a single for the local Scorpio label before briefly signing with MGM Records, which issued the live albums *Vintage Grateful Dead* and *Historic Dead* in the early 1970s. In January 1967, they appeared at the first "Human Be-In" in Golden Gate Park with the Jefferson Airplane and Quicksilver Messenger Service, soon signing with Warner Bros. Records.

Already a huge cult band, the Grateful Dead's debut album featured Pig Pen's gruff lead vocals on blues-based material such as "Good Morning, Little School Girl" and "Morning Dew," as well as group favorites such as "Beat It on Down the Line" and "New, New Minglewood Blues." Performing at the Monterey International Pop Festival in June 1967, the group added percussionist-drummer Mickey Hart in September, thus freeing Lesh from his strictly rhythmic function on bass. The Grateful Dead recorded their second album, *Anthem of the Sun*, over a six- month period, augmented by keyboardist Tom Constanten. By early 1968, Hart's father Lenny had become their manager.

The Grateful Dead added Robert Hunter as full-time nonperforming lyricist for 1969's *Aoxomoxoa*. It contained several band favorites such as "St. Stephen," "China Cat Sunflower," and "Mountains of the Moon," with lyrics by Hunter. The group performed at the Woodstock Music and Art Fair in August and the ill-fated Altamont Speedway affair in December. Also recorded that year was their first official live set, *Live Dead*, regarded as one of their better live recordings. It featured a 23-minute rendition of "Dark Star" and a rousing version of "Turn on Your Lovelight."

In 1970, the Grateful Dead dropped their blues- and improvisatory-based approach for a country-flavored, vocally rich, and much simplified sound that resulted in what many consider as the group's finest two albums, *Workingman's Dead* and *American Beauty*. Indeed, these two albums featured some of Robert Hunter's most striking efforts as a songwriter. Recorded with the assistance of old associates John Dawson and David Nelson, *Workingman's Dead* contained the group's first (albeit minor) hit, "Uncle John's Band," as well as "Easy Wind," "Casey Jones," "Cumberland Blues," and "New Speedway Boogie," their "official" statement about the December 1969 debacle at Altamont. *American Beauty*, recorded with the assistance of David Grisman and the New Riders of the Purple Sage, featured Garcia on pedal steel guitar. The album included a number of Grateful Dead classics such as Pig Pen's "Operator," Weir and Hunter's "Sugar Magnolia," Lesh and Hunter's "Box of Rain," and the Hunter-Garcia collaborations "Candyman," "Ripple," and "'Till the Morning Comes," as well as "Truckin'," the group's second minor hit and one of their major anthems. Their next Warner Bros. album, entitled simply *The Grateful Dead*, was a live set. It contained favorites such as "Bertha," "Wharf Rat," and "Playing in the Band," as well as Merle Haggard's "Mama Tried," John Phillips's "Me and My Uncle," and Chuck Berry's "Johnny B. Goode."

By 1970, the remarkably diffuse outside activities of the members of the Grateful Dead had started. While performing and recording with keyboardists Howard Wales and Merl Saunders, Jerry Garcia played sessions for Crosby, Stills, Nash and Young and the Jefferson Airplane. Garcia also played pedal steel guitar and banjo with Dave Torbert and former associates David Nelson and John "Marmaduke" Dawson in the countrified New Riders of the Purple Sage that spring. He remained with the New Riders into 1971, appearing on their debut Columbia album. The album included "I Don't Know You," "Whatcha Gonna Do," "Henry," "Dirty Business," and "All I Ever Wanted," all written by Dawson. The New Riders of the Purple Sage continued to record for Columbia with Garcia's replacement, Buddy Cage, through 1975. Their *Adventures of Panama Red* featured Peter Rowan's title song and "Lonesome L.A. Cowboy," and Robert Hunter's "Kick in the Head." The New Riders switched to MCA Records in 1975 and A&M Records in 1981. By 1983, Dawson was the only original member in the lineup, yet they continued to tour and record albums into the 1990s.

Mickey Hart quit the Grateful Dead for a solo career in February 1971. During the year, Pig Pen fell ill and seldom toured with the band. He was replaced by keyboardist-vocalist Keith Godchaux in October 1971. In 1972, Garcia and Weir each issued solo albums that served as effective companions to *Workingman's Dead* and *American Beauty*. Garcia played all instruments except drums on *Garcia*, which included "Sugaree" (a minor hit), "Deal," and "The Wheel," with songs credited to Garcia, Hunter, and drummer Bill Kreutzmann. Weir's *Ace*, essentially a Grateful Dead album, was recorded with Garcia, Lesh, Kreutzmann, Godchaux, and his vocalist wife Donna. It contained "Walk in the Sunshine" and "Mexicali Blues," written by Weir and

John Barlow, Weir's own "One More Saturday Night," and the classic Weir-Hunter collaboration, "Playing in the Band." Hart's 1972 *Rolling Thunder* was recorded with Garcia, Weir, Grace Slick, and Stephen Stills.

The Grateful Dead's two-month European tour of 1972, with Keith and Donna Godchaux (who had joined in March), yielded the multirecord set *Europe '72*. The album served as a live compendium of the songs of the Grateful Dead. In addition to featuring songs such as "China Cat Sunflower," "Sugar Magnolia," and "Truckin'," the album introduced "Jack Straw," "Tennessee Jed," "Ramble on Rose," and "Brown-Eyed Woman." The album proved a best-seller, remaining on the album charts for nearly six months. However, "Pig Pen" died of liver failure on March 8, 1973, at the age of 27.

In 1973, the Grateful Dead financed the establishment of their own independent record label, Grateful Dead Records. The label's first release, *Wake of the Flood*, contained more Hunter-Garcia songs such as "Row Jimmy," "Stella Blue," and "Mississippi Half- Step," as well as "Weather Report Suite," written, in part, with folk singer Eric Andersen. The following year, Round Records was founded for outside recordings by members of the group. By May, Round Records had issued Garcia's second solo album, with Peter Rowan's "Mississippi Moon" and Doctor John's "What Goes Around," and Robert Hunter's first, *Tales of the Great Rum Runners*, which included "It Must Have Been the Roses" and "Keys to the Rain."

During 1973 and 1974, the bluegrass aggregation Old and in the Way played around the San Francisco Bay Area. Comprising Jerry Garcia (banjo), Peter Rowan (guitar), David Grisman (mandolin), Vassar Clements (fiddle), and John Kahn (bass), the group recorded *Old and in the Way* for Round Records in October 1973. A modern bluegrass classic and one of Garcia's most successful endeavors, the album included Peter Rowan's "Land of the Navajo," "Midnight Moonlight," and "Panama Red." A second and third volume were issued in 1996 and 1997, respectively.

During 1974, the Grateful Dead utilized a massive $400,000 state-of-the-art sound system that emitted a loud, clear, and clean sound, rather than the usual distorted, bone-crushing noise normally associated with such a powerful system. That June, the group issued *Live from Mars Hotel*, which featured "U.S. Blues," "Unbroken Chain," "China Doll," and the Dead classic "Ship of Fools." Following a European tour, the Grateful Dead played five consecutive nights at San Francisco's Winterland in October before "retiring" from live performance for over a year. The shows later yielded the poorly mixed and poorly received *Steal Your Face* album. Filmed by seven camera crews, edited performances from this run were eventually released in film form in June 1977 as *The Grateful Dead Movie*.

In 1975, Round Records issued the Godchaux's *Keith and Donna*, *Seastones* (by Phil Lesh and composer-synthesizer wizard Ned Lagin), and Robert Hunter's *Tiger Rose*. Bob Weir assisted in the recording of the debut Round album by Kingfish, formed by Dave Torbert, a former member of the New Riders of the

Purple Sage. In 1976, Round issued *Diga* by The Diga Rhythm Band, featuring Mickey Hart and tabla player Zakir Hussain, and Garcia's third solo album *Reflections*, again essentially a Grateful Dead album, which featured Hunter's "It Must Have Been the Roses."

In June 1975, the Grateful Dead signed an agreement with United Artists for worldwide distribution of both Round and Grateful Dead Records. With the return of percussionist Mickey Hart, the Grateful Dead recorded *Blues for Allah*, a decidedly jazz-oriented venture that included the minor hit "The Music Never Stopped," by Weir and John Barlow, and the Hunter-Garcia-Kreutzmann collaboration "Franklin's Tower." In 1977, the Grateful Dead switched to Arista Records for a series of commercially oriented albums. For the first time, they used an outside producer, Keith Olsen of *Fleetwood Mac* fame, for *Terrapin Station*. Prominently featuring horns, strings, and vocal choruses, the album included "Estimated Prophet," "Samson and Delilah," and the extended cut "Terrapin."

Bob Weir's *Heaven Help the Fool*, produced by Olsen and recorded with guitarist Bobby Cochran and keyboardist Brent Mydland, was issued on Arista in early 1978, yielding the minor hit "Bombs Away." Soon thereafter, the Jerry Garcia Group's *Cats under the Stars* was released on Arista, again showcasing the lyrics of Robert Hunter. In September, the Grateful Dead spent $500,000 to ship 25 tons of equipment to Egypt so they could play at the foot of the Great Pyramids in a benefit performance for the Egyptian Dept. of Antiquities and the Faith and Hope Society, a charitable organization. Before year's end, the group's *Shakedown Street* was issued. Produced by Lowell George of Little Feat, the album evinced a sophisticated, almost discofied sound, as did *Go to Heaven*, produced by Gary Lyons. It included "Feel Like a Stranger" and "Althea," and yielded a minor hit with the Garcia-Hunter composition "Alabama Getaway."

In February 1979, Keith and Donna Godchaux left the Grateful Dead to pursue solo projects. Keith was replaced in April by keyboardist Brent Mydland, a former touring and recording partner of Bob Weir. Godchaux died on July 23, 1980, in Ross, Calif., of injuries suffered in a motorcycle accident two days prior.

Mickey Hart scored, in part, the music for the epic yet equivocal 1979 Vietnam War movie *Apocalypse Now*. Other recordings that were not used in the film (featuring exotic percussion instruments from Hart's extensive collection) surfaced in late 1980 as *The Rhythm Devils Play River Music*. Bobby and the Midnites, fronted by Bob Weir, debuted in June 1980 and signed with Arista Records. With guitarist Bobby Cochran, Dead keyboardist Brent Mydland, and jazz fusion drummer Billy Cobham, the group recorded two albums and toured through 1984. In 1981, the Grateful Dead issued two live sets, the acoustic *Reckoning* and the electric *Dead Set*, recorded in October 1980.

The Grateful Dead concentrated on live performing during the 1980s, as Jerry Garcia slipped into heroin addiction. By the mid-1980s, they had become one of the top-grossing touring rock acts and expanded their au-dience to a new, youthful generation of fans. During this time, Garcia recorded *Run for the Roses*, Weir recorded a second album with Bobby and the Midnites, and Hart recorded *Dafos* with percussionist Airto Moreira and vocalist Flora Purim. For a time, Robert Hunter performed in the Dinosaurs with Barry Melton, John Cipollina, Peter Albin, and Spencer Dryden, all veterans of psychedelic San Francisco bands. In July 1986, Jerry Garcia nearly died after collapsing in a diabetic coma. The Grateful Dead resumed touring in December, and Garcia and friends staged a three-week run at N.Y.'s Lunt-Fontaine Theater in October 1987 with "Garcia on Broadway."

The Grateful Dead emerged spectacularly in 1987. Their first studio album in seven years, *In the Dark*, was hailed as perhaps their best work since *Workingman's Dead* and *American Beauty*. It contained Weir's "Throwing Stones" and Mydland's "Tons of Steels," and yielded their first major hit with "Touch of Grey." The engaging MTV video of the song helped introduce them to a whole new generation of fans. They performed with Bob Dylan at six concerts in June, and recordings from the shows were issued in early 1989. Later that year, *Rolling Stone* magazine declared the Grateful Dead the single most successful touring band in rock history.

In 1984, the Grateful Dead set up the nonprofit philanthropic Rex Foundation to oversee contributions to environmental lobbies, social causes, and private ventures. By 1993, the organization had distributed over $4 million. The group's Sept. 24, 1988, concert at Madison Square Garden in N.Y. heralded their commitment to the issue of rain forest preservation, raising $500,000 for Cultural Survival, Greenpeace, and the Rainforest Action Network. In 1993, the Grateful Dead contributed about one-half of the cost of a liver transplant for legendary poster artist Stanley Mouse, who, with Alton Kelley, created the Grateful Dead skull-and-roses logo.

On July 26, 1990, keyboardist Brent Mydland was found dead of a drug overdose in his Lafayette, Calif., home. He was replaced temporarily by Bruce Hornsby and permanently by Vince Welnick of the Tubes in September 1990.

At the beginning of the 1990s, the Grateful Dead began releasing vintage live material on their own label, available only through mail-order. In 1991, they were honored with *Deadicated*, a benefit album of their songs by such artists as Los Lobos, Midnight Oil, Elvis Costello, Jane's Addiction, Dr. John, and Lyle Lovett. The Grateful Dead became the top concert attraction of 1991 and 1993. In 1992, The Grateful Dead had canceled an 18-date East Coast tour when Jerry Garcia was reported suffering from "exhaustion." He subsequently adopted a new vegetarian diet and initiated weight loss and exercise programs that improved his health significantly. In 1993, Grateful Dead Merchandising began issuing live material assembled by Grateful Dead archivist Dick Latvala as *Dick's Picks*. The Grateful Dead were inducted into the Rock and Roll Hall of Fame in 1994.

During the 1980s, Mickey Hart had immersed himself in the music of non- Western cultures and initiated a study of the myth and meaning of drumming. He presented and recorded the chants of Gyuto Tibetan Buddhist Monks, released in 1987, and produced albums by Babatunde Olatunji and Kitaro. In 1988, he released six discs of exotic music on Rykodisc as *The World*. The recordings included Sudanese folk music, traditional Jewish music, and the music of Egypt and India. Recognized as one of the world's leading ethnomusicologist by the late 1980s, Hart supervised the transfer of the entire catalog of Folkways Records to CD for the Smithsonian Inst. In the 1990s, his drum studies produced two books, *Drumming at the Edge of Magic*, a chronicle of his personal quest, and *Planet Drum*, a collection of world drum lore and legend. Each of the books had a companion CD, released on Rykodisc. Bob Weir also became an author in the 1990s, writing two children's books with his sister Wendy.

During the 1990s Jerry Garcia recorded *Blues from the Rainforest* with keyboardist Merl Saunders and accompanied David Grisman for "beat" wordsmith Ken Nordine's *Devout Catalyst*. He also performed and recorded with mandolinist Grisman and his own band, while continuing to perform with the Grateful Dead. He died unexpectedly on Aug. 9, 1995, in a Forest Knolls, Calif., treatment facility at the age of 53. After four agonizing months, the remaining members of the Grateful Dead officially disbanded the group.

During 1996, a number of Grateful Dead tribute albums were released, including *Fire on the Mountain* (by reggae artists such as the Wailing Soul, Toots Hibbert, and Steel Pulse), *Long Live the Dead* (by country artists Billy and Terry Smith), and jazz saxophonist David Murray's *Dark Star*. Before Garcia's death, Grateful Dead keyboard technician Bob Bralove had formed Second Sight with Vince Welnick, guitarist Henry Kaiser, and others, releasing an album on Shanachie Records. Also in 1995, Bob Weir had formed Ratdog with Welnick, harmonica player Matthew Kelly (from Kingfish), bassist Rob Wasserman, and drummer Jay Lane. Bill Kreutzmann moved to Kauai, where he formed the trio Backbone with guitarist-vocalist Rick Barnett and bassist Edd Cook. Mickey Hart became the first former member of the Grateful Dead to release an album of his own, *Mickey Hart's Mystery Box*, recorded with Weir, Bruce Hornsby, percussionists Airto Moreira and Zakir Hussain (among others), and the female vocal sextet the Mint Juleps, with lyrics by Robert Hunter.

Former members of the Grateful Dead launched the Furthur Festival in the summer of 1996, with Mickey Hart's Mystery Box and Bob Weir's Ratdog. By then Ratdog included Weir, Kelly, Wasserman, and Chuck Berry's longtime pianist Johnnie Johnson. That year, Vince Welnick formed the Missing Man Formation with guitarist Steve Kimock, bassist Bobby Vega, and former Tubes and Starship drummer Prairie Prince, releasing their debut album on Arista Records in 1998. The 1998 Furthur Festival tour featured the Other Ones, with Weir, Hart, Kimock, Phil Lesh, Bruce Hornsby, and saxophonist Dave Ellis, among others.

DISC.: *The Grateful Dead* (1967); *Anthem of the Sun* (1968); *Aoxomoxoa* (1969); *Live/Dead* (1969); *Workingman's Dead* (1970); *American Beauty* (1970); *Vintage Dead* (rec. 1966; rel. 1970); *Historic Dead* (rec. 1966; rel. 1971); *The Grateful Dead* (1971); *Europe '72* (1972); *Wake of the Flood* (1973); *History of the Grateful Dead—Bear's Choice* (rec. Feb. 1970; rel. 1973); *From the Mars Hotel* (1974); *Blues for Allah* (1975); *Steal Your Face* (rec. 1974; rel. 1976); *Terrapin Station* (1977); *Shakedown Street* (1978); *Go to Heaven* (1980); *Reckoning* (rec. 1980; rel. 1981); *Dead Set* (rec. 1980; rel. 1981); *Reckoning* (1986); *In the Dark* (1987); *Built to Last* (1989); *Without a Net* (rec. 1989, 1990; rel. 1990); *One from the Vault* (rec. 1975; rel. 1991); *Infrared Roses* (1991); *Two from the Vault* (rec. 1968; rel. 1992); *Dick's Picks Vol. 1* (rec. 1973; rel. 1993); *Dick's Picks Vol. 2* (rec. 1971; rel. 1994); *Dick's Picks Vol. 3* (rec. 1977; rel. 1995); *Hundred Year Hall* (rec. 1972; rel. 1995); *Dozin' at the Knick* (rec. 1990; rel. 1996); *Dick's Picks Vol. 4* (rec. 1970; rel. 1996); *Dick's Picks Vol. 5* (rec. 1979; rel. 1996); *Dick's Picks Vol. 6* (rec. 1983; rel. 1996); *Dick's Picks Vol. 7* (rec. 1974; rel. 1997); *Fallout from the Phil Zone* (1997); *Fillmore East* (rec. 1969; rel. 1997); *Fallout from the Phil Zone* (rec. 1969–95; rel. 1997); *Dick's Picks Vol. 8* (rec. 1970; rel. 1997); *Dick's Picks Vol. 9* (rec. 1990; rel. 1997); *Dick's Picks Vol. 10* (rec. 1977; rel. 1998). The Grateful Dead/John Oswald: *Grayfolded* (1995). **BOB DYLAN AND THE GRATEFUL DEAD:** *Dylan and the Dead* (rec. 1987; rel. 1988). **JERRY GARCIA AND HOWARD WALES:** *Hooteroll* (1971). **JERRY GARCIA:** *Garcia* (1972); *Compliments of Garcia* (1974); *Reflections* (1976); *Almost Acoustic* (1988); *Cats Under the Stars* (1978); *Run for the Roses* (1982). **JERRY GARCIA BAND:** *Jerry Garcia Band* (1991); *How Sweet It Is* (1997). **JERRY GARCIA AND MERL SAUNDERS:** *Live at the Keystone* (1973); *Live at the Keystone, Vol. 1* (1988); *Live at the Keystone, Vol. 2* (1988); *Keystone Encores, Vol. 1* (1988); *Keystone Encores, Vol. 2* (1988); *Blues from the Rainforest* (1991). **OLD AND IN THE WAY:** *Old and in the Way* (1974); *That High Lonesome Sound* (1996); *Breakdown* (1997). **JERRY GARCIA AND DAVID GRISMAN:** *Garcia/Grisman* (1991); *Not for Kids Only* (1993); *Shady Grove* (1996). **KEN NORDINE, JERRY GARCIA, AND DAVID GRISMAN:** *Devout Catalyst* (1992). **BOB WEIR:** *Ace* (1972); *Heaven Help the Fool* (1978). **BOBBY AND THE MIDNITES:** *Bobby and the Midnites* (1981); *Where the Beat Meets the Street* (1984). **MATTHEW KELLY:** *A Wing and a Prayer* (rec. 1973; rel. 1985). **KINGFISH:** *In Concert* (rec. 1976; rel. 1996); *Kingfish* (1976); *Live 'n' Kickin'* (1977); *Live at the Roxy* (1981); *Alive in '85* (1985); *A Wing and a Prayer* (1986); *A Night in New York* (rec. 1977; rel. 1997); *Relix's Best of Kingfish* (1997). **MICKEY HART:** *Rolling Thunder* (1972); *Diga* (with the Diga Rhythm Band; 1976); *Music to Be Born By* (1989); *At the Edge* (1990); *Planet Drum* (1991); *Mickey Hart's Mystery Box* (1996); *Supralingua* (1998). **THE RHYTHM DEVILS:** *Play River Music* (1980); *The Apocalypse Now Sessions* (1989). **MICKEY HART, AIRTO, AND FLORA PURIM:** *Dafos* (rec. 1982, 1983; rel. 1989). **MICKEY HART, HENRY WOLFF, AND NANCY HENNINGS:** *Yamantaka* (1983). **ROBERT HUNTER:** *Tales of the Great Rum Runners* (1974); *Tiger Rose* (1975); *Jack O' Roses* (1979); *Amagamalin Street* (1984); *Rock* (1984); *The Flight of the Marie Helena* (1985); *Liberty* (1987); *Promontory Rider* (1989); *A Box of Rain: Live* (1990); *Sentinel* (poetry; 1993). **KEITH AND DONNA GODCHAUX:** *Keith and Donna* (1975). **PHIL LESH AND NED LAGIN:** *Seastones* (1975). **SILVER (WITH BRENT MYDLAND):** *Silver* (1975). **SECOND SIGHT (WITH VINCE WELNICK AND BOB BRALOVE):** *Second Sight* (1996). **VINCE WELNICK AND THE MISSING MAN FORMATION:** *Vince Welnick and the Missing Man Formation* (1998). **BACKBONE (WITH BILL KREUTZMANN):** *Backbone* (1998).

WRITINGS: Mickey Hart, with Jay Stevens and Frederic Lieberman, *Drumming at the Edge of Magic: A Journey into the Spirit of Percussion* (San Francisco, 1990); Robert Hunter, *A Box of Rain* (N.Y., 1990); Mickey Hart, and Frederic Lieberman, with D. A. Sonneborn, *Planet Drum: A Celebration of Percussion and Rhythm* (N.Y., 1991); Bob and Wendy Weir, *Panther Dream* (N.Y., 1991); Jerry Garcia, *Paintings, Drawings and Sketches* (Berkeley, Calif., 1992); Bob and Wendy Weir, *Baru Bay, Australia* (N.Y., 1995).

BIBL.: Charles Reich and Jann Wenner, *Garcia: A Signpost to New Space* (San Francisco, 1972); Hank Harrison, *The Dead Book: A Social History of the G.D.* (N.Y., 1973); Hank Harrison, *The Dead* (Millbrae, Calif., 1980); Paul Grushkin, Cynthia Bassett, and Jonas Grushkin, *G.D.: The Official Book of the Dead Heads* (N.Y., 1983); Blair Jackson, *G.D.: The Music Never Stopped* (London, 1983); Jerilyn Lee Brandelius, *G.D. Family Album* (N.Y., 1989); Herb Greene, *Book of the Dead: Celebrating 25 Years with the G.D.* (N.Y., 1990); Hank Harrison, *The Dead: A Social History of the Haight-Ashbury Experience* (San Francisco, 1990); Jamie Jensen, *G.D.: Built to Last: Twenty-Five Years of the G.D.* (N.Y., 1990); William Ruhlmann, *The History of the G.D.* (N.Y., 1990); David Gans and Peter Simon, *Conversation with The Dead: The G.D. Interview Book* (Secaucus, N.J., 1991); Sandy Troy, *One More Saturday Night: Reflections with the G.D. Family and Dead Heads* (N.Y., 1991); Tom Constanten, *Between Rock and Hard Places: A Musical Autobiodyssey* (Eugene, Ore., 1992); Blair Jackson, *Goin' Down the Road: A G.D. Traveling Companion* (N.Y., 1992); David Shenk and Steve Silberman, *Skeleton Key: A Dictionary for Deadheads* (N.Y., 1994); Sandy Troy, *Captain Trips: A Biography of Jerry Garcia* (N.Y., 1994); David Gans and Peter Simon, *Playing in the Band: An Oral and Visual Portrait of the G.D.* (N.Y., 1985, 1996); Robert Greenfield, *Dark Star: An Oral Biography of Jerry Garcia* (N.Y., 1996); Rocky Scully with David Dalton, *Living with the Dead: Twenty Years on the Bus with Garcia and the G.D.* (Boston, 1996); David G. Dodd and Robert G. Weiner, *The G.D. and the Deadheads: An Annotated Bibliography* (Westport, Conn., 1997); Oliver Trager, *The American Book of the Dead: The Definitive Encyclopedia of the G.D.* (N.Y., 1997); Eric Wybenga, *Dead to the Core: An Almanac of the G.D.* (N.Y., 1997); Carol Brightman, *Sweet Chaos: The G.D.'s American Adventure* (N.Y., 1998).—**BH**

Grau, Maurice, Moravian-born American operatic impresario; b. Brünn, 1849; d. Paris, March 14, 1907. He was taken to N.Y. at 5. After studying at Columbia Univ. Law School, he turned to artist management and organized the American tours of many celebrated artists. He later became a partner in the successful theater management firm of Abbey, Schoeffel, and Grau. In 1890 they presented their own special season of Italian opera at the Metropolitan Opera in N.Y. with such stellar artists as Albani, Nordica, Patti, and Tamagno. In 1891 their firm secured the lease of the Metropolitan Opera. Upon Abbey's death in 1896, Grau took over the lease. After a hiatus (1897–98), Grau returned to run the Metropolitan Opera under the aegis of the Maurice Grau Opera Co. until 1903. His astute understanding of public taste led him to engage the most famous singers of the day. He showcased their talents in the French and Italian, and later Wagnerian, repertory with notable artistic and financial success. From 1897 to 1900 he also managed London's Covent Garden. In 1883 he married the opera singer Marie Durand.—**NS/LK/DM**

Graun, August Friedrich, German organist and composer, brother of **Carl Heinrich** and **Johann Gottlieb Graun;** b. Wahrenbrück, near Dresden, 1699; d. Merseburg, May 5, 1765. He was active as an organist and cantor at Merseburg, where he settled in 1729. Only one of his works is preserved, *Kyrie et Gloria* for 4 Voices with Instruments.—**NS/LK/DM**

Graun, Carl Heinrich, noted German composer, brother of **August Friedrich** and **Johann Gottlieb Graun;** b. Wahrenbrück, near Dresden, May 7, 1704; d. Berlin, Aug. 8, 1759. He studied voice with Grundig and Benisch, keyboard playing with Pezold, and composition with Johann Christoph Schmidt at the Dresden Kreuzschule (1713–21), and also sang in the chorus of the Dresden Court Opera. He became a tenor at the Braunschweig court in 1725. Graun was made Vice-Kapellmeister about 1727, and wrote several operas for the Court Theater. He then joined the court establishment of Crown Prince Ferdinand (later Frederick II the Great) in Ruppin in 1735, becoming his Kapellmeister in Rheinsberg in 1736. After Frederick became king, Graun went to Berlin as Royal Kapellmeister (1740); the new opera house was inaugurated with his opera *Cesare e Cleopatra* on Dec. 7, 1742; many others followed, several with librettos by the King. Graun enjoyed royal favor and public esteem throughout his career in Berlin, his only serious challenger being Hasse. His operas were firmly rooted in the Italian tradition; although not without merit, they vanished from the repertoire after he passed from the scene. His gifts were more strikingly revealed in his sacred music, particularly in his *Te Deum* (written to commemorate Frederick's victory at the battle of Prague in 1756) and his Passion oratorio, *Der Tod Jesu;* the latter, his finest and most famous work, was performed in Germany regularly until the end of the 19th century.

WORKS: DRAMATIC: Opera (all 1st perf. in Berlin unless otherwise given): *Sancio und Sinilde* (Braunschweig, Feb. 3, 1727); *Polydorus* (Braunschweig, 1726 or 1728); *Iphigenia in Aulis* (Braunschweig, 1731); *Scipio Africanus* (Wolfenbüttel, 1732); *Lo specchio della fedeltà* or *Timareta* (Braunschweig, June 13, 1733; music not extant); *Pharao Tubaetes* (Braunschweig, Feb. 1735); *Rodelinda, regina de' langobardi* (Potsdam, Dec. 13, 1741); *Venere e Cupido* (Potsdam, Jan. 6, 1742); *Cesare e Cleopatra* (Dec. 7, 1742); *Artaserse* (Dec. 2, 1743); *Catone in Utica* (Jan. 24, 1744); *La festa del Imeneo* (July 18, 1744); *Lucio Papirio* (Jan. 4, 1745); *Adriano in Siria* (Jan. 7, 1746); *Demofoonte, rè di Tracia* (Jan. 17, 1746; 3 arias by Frederick II); *Cajo Fabricio* (Dec. 2, 1746); *Le feste galanti* (April 6, 1747); *Il rè pastore* (Charlottenburg, Aug. 4, 1747; recitative, duet, and 2 choruses by Graun; remainder by Frederick II, C. Nichelmann, and J. Quantz); *L'Europa galante* (Schloss Monbijou, March 27, 1748); *Galatea ed Acide* (Potsdam, July 11, 1748; overture, 1 recitative, and 1 aria by Quantz; remainder by Frederick II); *Ifigenia in Aulide* (Dec. 13, 1748); *Angelica e Medoro* (March 27, 1749); *Coriolano* (Dec. 19, 1749); *Fetonte* (March 29, 1750); *Il Mitridate* (Dec. 18, 1750); *L'Armida* (March 27, 1751); *Britannico* (Dec. 17, 1751); *L'Orfeo* (March 27, 1752); *Il giudizio di Paride* (Charlottenburg, June 25, 1752); *Silla* (March 27, 1753; libretto by Frederick II); *Il trionfo della fedeltà* (Charlottenburg, Aug. 1753; major portion of the work by G. Benda and Hasse); *Semiramide* (March 27, 1754); *Montezuma* (Jan. 6, 1755; libretto by Frederick II); *Ezio* (April 1, 1755); *I fratelli nemici* (Jan. 9, 1756; libretto by Frederick II); *La Merope*

(March 27, 1756; libretto by Frederick II). VOCAL: S a - c r e d : *Cantata in obitum Friderici Guilielmi regis borussorum beati defuncti* (publ. in Berlin, 1741); *Der Tod Jesu* (Passion oratorio, Berlin, March 26, 1755; ed. by H. Serwer, Madison, Wisc., 1974); *Te Deum* (publ. in Leipzig, 1757); 4 masses; a number of settings of the Missa Brevis; 2 Magnificats; cantatas; motets; Psalms. He also composed much secular vocal music, including Italian and German cantatas, songs, arias, etc. OTHER: About 40 concertos, some 35 trio sonatas, keyboard music, etc.

BIBL.: C. Mennicke, *Hasse und die Brüder G. als Symphoniker* (Leipzig, 1906); M. Willer, *Die Konzertform der Brüder C. H. und Johann Gottlieb Graun* (Frankfurt am Main, 1995).—NS/LK/DM

Graun, Johann Gottlieb, distinguished German composer, brother of **August Friedrich** and **Carl Heinrich Graun**; b. Wahrenbrück, near Dresden, c. 1703; d. Berlin, Oct. 27, 1771. He began his musical studies while at the Dresden Kreuzschule; studied violin and composition with Pisendel in Dresden, then went to Prague, where he studied with Tartini. In 1726 he became Konzertmeister in Merseburg, where he numbered among his students Wilhelm Friedemann Bach. He was appointed Konzertmeister to Crown Prince Frederick (later Frederick II the Great) in Ruppin in 1732; continued in his service in Rheinsberg (1736–40), and then in Berlin in the newly founded Royal Opera under his brother Carl Heinrich, its Kapellmeister. He was a notable composer of instrumental music; he wrote about 95 sinfonias, 17 French overtures, 80 concertos (60 for violin), some 175 trio sonatas, and other chamber works.

BIBL.: C. Mennicke, *Hasse und die Brüder G. als Symphoniker* (Leipzig, 1906); M. Willer, *Die Konzertform der Brüder Carl Heinrich und J.C. G.* (Frankfurt am Main, 1995).—NS/LK/DM

Graunke, Kurt (Karl Wilhelm), German violinist, conductor, and composer; b. Stettin, Sept. 30, 1915. He studied violin with Gustav Havemann at the Berlin Hochschule für Musik, composition with Adolf Lessle and Hermann Grabner, violin with Hanns Weisse and Hans Dunschede, and conducting with Felix Husadel. During World War II, he studied in Vienna with Wolfgang Schneiderhan and played violin in the radio orch. In Munich in 1945 he founded his own orch., which he conducted for over 40 years and which made many recordings of scores for movies and television; it also gave several concerts each year, playing the world premieres of many works. His compositions are firmly rooted in Germanic modern Romanticism.

WORKS ORCH. (all 1st perf. in Munich): 8 syms.: No. 1 (May 14, 1969), No. 2 (Sept. 9, 1972), No. 3 for Strings (Nov. 7, 1975; also for Orch., May 12, 1976), No. 4 (Jan. 25, 1978), No. 5 (May 13, 1981), No. 6 (May 12, 1982), No. 7 (May 11, 1983), and No. 8 (Sept. 11, 1985); Violin Concerto (Sept. 17, 1959); *Air for Harp and Orch.*; 2 Symphonic Dances; *Novelette*; *Perpetuum mobile*; *Valse Anastasia*.—NS/LK/DM

Graupner, Catherine Comerford, English-born American actress and singer; b. c. 1769; d. Boston (buried), May 28, 1821. As the widow Mrs. Hillier, she appeared with a London theater group in Boston in 1794 at the Federal Street Theatre. In 1795 she was engaged at the Charleston, S.C., City Theatre. After her marriage to **Gottlieb Graupner** in 1796, she appeared regularly with him in Boston from 1797 until her death. She also was active as an actress and made appearances singing in oratorios. On Dec. 25, 1815, she sang in the first performance of the Handel and Haydn Soc.—LK/DM

Graupner, (Johann Christian) Gottlieb, German-born American oboist, music publisher, teacher, and composer; b. Verden, near Hannover, Oct. 6, 1767; d. Boston, April 16, 1836. He was the son of the oboist Johann Georg Graupner. He learned to play the oboe but also became proficient on many other instruments. After his honorable discharge as an oboist in a military regiment in Hannover (1788), he was active in London. He then emigrated to North America, where he was a member of the Charleston, S.C., City Theatre orch. by 1795. In 1796 he married **Catherine Comerford Graupner,** an actress and singer known as the widow Mrs. Hillier. They subsequently performed regularly together, settling in Boston in 1797. With Francis Mallet and Filippo Trajetta, he founded the American Conservatorio in 1801, which quickly turned to selling, hiring, and printing music. In 1802 Graupner became sole proprietor of the business, which developed into Boston's principal music publishing enterprise. He also was active as a theater musician and as a teacher. In 1808 he became a naturalized American citizen. In 1809 he helped to found the Philo-Harmonic Soc., which promoted the performance of the German orch. repertory until disbanding in 1824. In 1815 he was one of the founding members of the Handel and Haydn Soc. He publ. in Boston *Rudiments of the Art of Playing on the Piano Forte* (1806; 2nd ed., rev. and enl., 1819), *New Instructor for the Clarinet* (c. 1825), and *G. Graupner's Complete Preceptor for the German Flute* (1826). Among his extant compositions are *Governor Brooks' Grand March* for Flute and Piano (1820) and several songs.

BIBL.: K. Graupner Stone (his granddaughter), *History and Genealogy of the G. Family* (MS, 1906).—NS/LK/DM

Graupner, (Johann) Christoph, German composer; b. Kirchberg, Saxony, Jan. 13, 1683; d. Darmstadt, May 10, 1760. He studied music in Kirchberg with the cantor Michael Mylius and the organist Nikolaus Kuster, and later at the Thomasschule in Leipzig with Johann Kuhnau and Johann Schelle. He then went to Hamburg, where he became harpsichordist at the Oper-am-Gänsemarkt (1707–09) and also composed 5 operas. In 1709 he was called to Darmstadt as Vice-Kapellmeister to the Landgraf Ernst Ludwig; in 1712 he was appointed Kapellmeister, a post he held until his death. Graupner was a highly industrious composer, numbering 8 operas, some 1,400 church cantatas, 24 secular cantatas, about 100 syms., 50 concertos, 80 overtures, and many instrumental sonatas and keyboard works among his works. Several of his compositions were publ. during his lifetime, including *8 Partien auf das Clavier...erster Theil* (Darmstadt, 1718), the *Monatliche Clavier Früchte...meistenteils für Anfänger* (Darmstadt, 1722), and *Vier Partien auf das Clavier, unter* *der Benennung der Vier Jahreszeiten* (Darmstadt, 1733); he also brought out a *Neu vermehrtes Darmstädtisches Choralbuch* (Darmstadt, 1728). He was proficient as an engraver, and printed several keyboard pieces in his own workshop. His operas include *Dido, Königin von Carthago* (Hamburg, 1707), *Il fido amico, oder Der getreue Freund Hercules und Theseus* (Hamburg, 1708; not extant), *L'amore ammalato: Die Krankende Liebe, oder Antiochus und Stratonica* (Hamburg, 1708), *Bellerophon, oder Das in die preussisch Krone verwandelte Wagenstirn* (Hamburg, Nov. 28, 1708; not extant), *Der Fall des grossen Richters in Israel, Simson, oder Die abgekühlte Liebesrache der Deborah* (Hamburg, 1709; not extant), *Berenice und Lucilla, oder Das tugendhafte Lieben* (Darmstadt, March 4, 1710; not extant), *Telemach* (Darmstadt, Feb. 16, 1711; not extant), and *La costanza vince l'inganno* (Darmstadt, 1715). Denkmäler Deutscher Tonkunst, LI/LII (1926), contains 17 of his cantatas. An incomplete edition of his works was ed. by F. Noack (4 vols., Kassel, 1955–57).

BIBL.: F. Noack, *C. G.s Kirchenmusiken* (Leipzig, 1916); M. Witte, *Die Instrumentalkonzerte von C. G.* (diss., Univ. of Gottingen, 1963); C. Grosspietsch, *G.s Ouverturen und Tafelmusiken: Studien zur Darmstädter Hofmusik und thematischer Katalog* (N.Y., 1994).—NS/LK/DM

Graveure, Louis, (real name, Wilfred Douthitt),

English baritone; b. London, March 18, 1888; d. Los Angeles, April 27, 1965. He studied voice with Clara Novello-Davies. He sang in the operetta *The Lilac Domino* in N.Y. on Oct. 28, 1914. In 1915 he reappeared in N.Y. as Louis Graveure (after his mother's maiden name) and became a popular concert artist, singing all types of music. On Feb. 5, 1928, he gave a concert in N.Y. as a tenor; from 1931 to 1938 he was in Germany; from 1938 to 1940, in France; from 1940 to 1947, in England. In 1947 he returned to the U.S. and taught in various music schools.—NS/LK/DM

Gray, Alan,

English organist and composer; b. York, Dec. 23, 1855; d. Cambridge, Sept. 27, 1935. He took degrees in law and music from Trinity Coll., Cambridge (Mus.D., 1889). He was music director of Wellington Coll. (1883–92), conductor of the Cambridge Univ. Musical Soc. (1892–1912), and organist at Trinity Coll. (1892–1930). He wrote 5 cantatas, a *Coronation March*, chamber music, and many organ works. He was also an ed. for the Purcell Soc. Vaughan Williams was one of his students.—NS/LK/DM

Gray, Anne,

American writer on music of English descent; b. Vienna, Oct. 26, 1941. She was smuggled to London during World War II. In 1947 she was taken to N.Y. and in 1948 she became a naturalized American citizen. She studied music, speech, and drama at Hunter Coll. (B.A., 1963), English and education at San Diego State Univ. (M.A., 1968), and humanities at the Univ. of Calif. at San Diego (Ph.D., 1982). From 1968 to 1971 she was prof. of English at Mesa (Calif.) Coll. She wrote the useful and engaging tomes *The Popular Guide to Classical Music* (1994; 2nd ed., rev., 1996) and *The Popular Guide to Women in Classical Music* (2000).—NS/LK/DM

Gray, Cecil,

Scottish writer on music and composer; b. Edinburgh, May 19, 1895; d. Worthing, Sept. 9, 1951.

He studied at the Univ. of Edinburgh and with Bantock in Birmingham. He was co-ed. (with Philip Heseltine) of the periodical *The Sackbut* from 1920, as well as music critic for the *National* and *Athenaeum* (1925–30), the *Daily Telegraph* (1928–33), and the *Manchester Guardian* (1932). He composed the operas (to his own texts) *Deirdre, Temptation of St. Anthony*, and *The Trojan Women* and other works.

WRITINGS: *A Survey of Contemporary Music* (1924; 2nd ed., 1927); with P. Heseltine, *Carlo Gesualdo, Prince of Venosa; Musician and Murderer* (1926); *The History of Music* (1928); *Sibelius* (1931; 2nd ed., 1934); *Peter Warlock* (1934); *Sibelius: The Symphonies* (1935); *Predicaments, or Music and the Future* (1936); *The 48 Preludes and Fugues of Bach* (1938); *Contingencies and Other Essays* (1947); *Musical Chairs or Between Two Stools* (memoirs, 1948). —NS/LK/DM

Gray, Linda Esther,

Scottish soprano; b. Greenock, May 29, 1948. After training at the Royal Scottish Academy of Music in Glasgow, she went to London to pursue her studies at the Opera Centre and with Dame Eva Turner. During her student days, she made her first appearances in opera at the Sadler's Wells Theatre in London (1970). In 1972 she sang Mimi with the Glyndebourne Touring Opera Co., and then made her first appearance at the Glyndebourne Festival in 1973 as Mozart's 1st Lady. She then sang with the Scottish Opera in Glasgow. In 1978 she made her debut as Micaëla at the English National Opera in London, and in 1979 sang for the first time at the Welsh National Opera in Cardiff as Isolde. She made her debut at London's Covent Garden in 1980 as Gutrune, followed by her U.S. debut in Dallas in 1981 as Sieglinde. Although highly admired for her talent, she inextricably ceased singing in 1983. Among her other roles were Donna Elvira, Countess Almaviva, Leonore, Kundry, Aida, Tosca, and Ariadne.—NS/LK/DM

Gray, Wardell,

jazz saxophonist; b. Oklahoma City, Okla., Feb. 13, 1921; d. Las Vegas, May 25, 1955. After working in Detroit, he toured with The Earl Hines band (1943–45). He settled on the West Coast and had his first session as a leader (1946). He then performed with Benny Carter, Benny Goodman (1948), Count Basie (1948; again 1950–51), and Tadd Dameron (1947–51). But it was his remarkable recording sessions in 1946–50, especially those with Dexter Gordon, that made his reputation. His "Twisted" (1949) was set to lyrics by Annie Ross and became a hit in 1952. From 1951 until his death, he freelanced out of Los Angeles with various bands. He played with the same combination of lyricism, blues fervor, and facility as Lester Young (a major influence), but he also incorporated bop techniques, producing a unique and quite striking sound. His mysterious death appears to have resulted from a drug overdose in Los Angeles; his frightened companions drove to a desert area near Las Vegas and dropped his body there. He is the subject of a 1996 film by Abraham Ravett, *Forgotten Tenor*.

DISC.: "One for Prez" (1946); "Twisted" (1949); *W. G./Stan Hasselgard* (1947); *Way-Out Wardell* (1948); *Tenor Sax* (1949); *Central Ave.* (1949) *Easy Swing* (1949); *Chase and the Steeplechase*

(1952); *Live at the Haig* (1952); *W. G.'s Los Angeles Star* (1952); *Sextet* (1952); *Live in Hollywood* (1952).

WRITINGS: *Saxophone Solos,* transc. by Tom Washatka (1994).

BIBL.: D. Salemann, *W. G.: Solography, Discography, Band Routes, Engagements in Chronological Order* (Basel, 1986); C. Schlouch, *W. G.: A Discography.*—**LP**

Gray (Knoblaugh), Glen, pop-jazz saxophonist and leader; b. Roanoke, Ill., June 7, 1906; d. Plymouth, Mass., Aug. 23, 1963. He studied at Ill. Wesleyan Coll., but left and began playing local gigs. He played with a Detroit- based Jean Goldkette unit called the Orange Blossom Band. The band moved to take up a residency at the Casa Loma Hotel, Toronto. The band began to tour; while in N.Y. it was registered as The Casa Loma Orch. Inc. (1929). Gray was elected president of the company; he continued to play saxophone while Mel Jenssen fronted the band. Its underrated arrangements, especially those by Will Hudson, were highly regarded; they were recorded by Fletcher Henderson and others. From 1937 Gray fronted the band; he retired from touring (1950), but occasionally organized groups to re-record material associated with the band (from 1956). Alumni of his groups include Herb Ellis, Red Nichols, and Bobby Hackett. The original band appeared in the film *Girls Inc.* (1943).

DISC.: *Uncollected G. G. & The Casa Loma Band* (1939); *Hoagy Carmichael Songs* (1950).—**JC/LP**

Graziani, Bonifazio, Italian composer; b. probably in Marino, near Rome, 1604 or 1605; d. Rome, June 15, 1664. He served as maestro di cappella in Rome at the church of the Gesù and at the Seminario Romano from 1648. His output included 2 oratorios, *Adae* and *Fili prodigi,* and 25 vols. of polyphonic works, including masses, Psalms, and motets (Rome, 1650–78). His finest achievement was his motets for Solo Voice and Basso Continuo (6 vols., Rome, 1652–72).—**NS/LK/DM**

Graziani, Francesco, noted Italian baritone, brother of **Giuseppe** and **Lodovico Graziani**; b. Fermo, April 26, 1828; d. there, June 30, 1901. Following vocal training with Cellini, he made his operatic debut in *Gemma di vergy* in Ascoli Piceno in 1851. From 1853 to 1861 he sang at the Théâtre-Italien in Paris. On April 26, 1855, he made his first appearance at London's Covent Garden as Carlo in *Ernani.* He continued to sing there regularly during the next 25 years, making his farewell appearance in *La Traviata* on July 17, 1880. In 1854 he sang in the U.S. In 1861 he appeared for the first time in St. Petersburg, where he was chosen to create the role of Don Carlo in *La forza del destino* on Nov. 10, 1862. He continued to sing there until 1871. Graziani's roles in Verdi's operas were particularly remarkable, especially Rigoletto, Germont, Di Luna, Renato, and Amonasro. He also was a convincing exponent of roles in operas by Mozart, Rossini, and Donizetti.—**NS/LK/DM**

Graziani, Giuseppe, Italian bass, brother of **Francesco** and **Lodovico Graziani**; b. Fermo, Aug. 28, 1819; d. Porto S. Giorgio, March 6, 1905. After training in Naples with Mercadante, he devoted himself to a career as a concert artist.—**NS/LK/DM**

Graziani, Lodovico, Italian tenor, brother of **Francesco** and **Giuseppe Graziani**; b. Fermo, Nov. 14, 1820; d. there, May 15, 1885. He was a pupil of Cellini. In 1845 he made his operatic debut in Cambiaggio's *Don Procopio* in Bologna. In 1851 he sang at the Théâtre-Italien in Paris, and then in Venice, where he later created the role of Alfredo in *La Traviata* (March 6, 1853). He subsequently appeared at Milan's La Scala (1855, 1862) and in Vienna (1860). Among his other Verdi roles were Manrico, the Duke of Mantua, and Riccardo. —**NS/LK/DM**

Grazioli, Giovanni Battista (Ignazio), Italian organist and composer; b. Bogliaco, July 6, 1746; d. Venice, c. 1820. He was a pupil in Venice of Bertoni, where he later was 2nd organist (1782) and finally 1st organist (1785) at San Marco. He publ. 3 vols. of keyboard sonatas (Venice, Vols. 1 and 2, c. 1780; Vol. 3, c. 1785) and composed numerous sacred vocal works. —**LK/DM**

Greatorex, Thomas, English organist, conductor, teacher, and composer; b. North Wingfield, Derby, Oct. 5, 1758; d. Hampton, July 18, 1831. His father was the organist Anthony Greatorex (1730–1814). He was a pupil of Benjamin Cooke in London (1772). After serving in the household of the Earl of Sandwich (1774–76), he sang at the Concerts of Antient Music in London (from 1776) and was organist at Carlisle Cathedral (1781–84). Following studies with Santorelli in Italy (1786–88), he returned to London and became a highly popular singing teacher. From 1793 until his death he was conductor of the Concerts of Antient Music, and he also conducted festivals throughout England. In 1819 he became organist at Westminster Abbey. In 1822 he helped to organize the Royal Academy of Music in London, where he was a prof. of organ and piano. He publ. the collection *Parochial Psalmody* (1825), *A Selection of Tunes* (1829), *12 Glees* (1832), anthems, Psalms, and chants. His son, Henry Wellington Greatorex (b. Burton upon Trent, Dec. 24, 1813; d. Charleston, S.C., Sept. 10, 1858), was an organist and composer. He emigrated to the U.S. in 1836 and was a church organist in Hartford, Conn., N.Y., and Charleston. He publ. a *Collection of Sacred Music* (1851), which included hymn tunes by his grandfather and father, as well as 37 of his own. —**NS/LK/DM**

Greber, Jakob, German composer; b. place and date known; d. Mannheim (buried), July 5, 1731. He was trained in Italy and in 1703 went to London, where he brought out the first Italian opera, *Gli amori d'Ergasto* (April 9, 1705), for the opening of the New Queen's Theatre in the Haymarket. In 1707 he was appointed Kapellmeister to Duke Karl Philipp in Innsbruck, the governor of the Tirol. He continued in his patron's service when he became Elector Palatine in 1717, and was active in Neuburg, Heidelberg, and Mannheim. In addition to his works for the stage, Greber also composed solo cantatas.—**LK/DM**

Greco, Gaetano, Italian composer and pedagogue; b. Naples, c. 1657; d. there, c. 1728. He was a pupil of

Gennaro Ursino (composition) and Francesco Mirabella (violin). From 1695 to 1706, and again from 1710 to 1728, he taught at the Cons. dei Poveri de Gesu Cristo in Naples. He also served as maestro di cappella of the city of Naples from 1704 to 1720. Among Greco's notable students were Domenico Scarlatti, Porpora, Piccini, and Vinci. In his own compositions, Greco demonstrated a fine command of keyboard writing, producing admirable toccatas, fugues, and intavolature.—**LK/DM**

Greef, Arthur de, Belgian pianist and composer; b. Louvain, Oct. 10, 1862; d. Brussels, Aug. 29, 1940. He studied at the Brussels Cons. with L. Brassin (piano) and Gevaert (composition), then traveled as a pianist in Europe. In 1885 he became a prof. of piano at the Brussels Cons., retaining that post until 1930. His works include an opera in Flemish, *De Marketenster* (Louvain, 1879), Sym., Ballad for Strings, 2 piano concertos, 2 violin sonatas, *4 vieilles chansons flamandes* for Piano, a number of piano études, and songs.

BIBL.: B. Huys and E. Eikenes, *A. d.G.: En venn av Edvard Grieg* (Stavanger, 1994).—**NS/LK/DM**

Green, Al (originally, **Greene**), one of the premier soul singers of the first half of the 1970s; b. Forrest City, Ark., April 13, 1946. Al Green attained his R&B and pop successes on the basis of his affecting songwriting and high, sensual voice, and the production and arrangements of Memphis's Willie Mitchell. Pursuing a career as a preacher and gospel singer since the late 1970s, Green became one of gospel music's most popular artists in the 1980s and 1990s, and has occasionally returned to secular music.

Al Green began singing with the family gospel group The Greene Brothers when he was nine years old, remaining with them until he was 16. He toured with the group, making his first recordings with them for Fargo Records in 1960. His father was dismayed when he heard the young singer listening to Jackie Wilson's music, and he dismissed Al from the group. By now living in Grand Rapids, Mich., Al Green quickly formed his own pop group, The Creations, active from 1964 to 1967. Under the new name the Soul Mates, with Lee Virgins and brother Robert in 1967–1968, the group scored a smash R&B and moderate pop hit with "Back Up Train" on Hot Line Records.

Spotted by bandleader-producer Willie Mitchell in Midland, Tex., in 1969, Al Green signed with the Memphis-based Hi label. After several major R&B-only hits in 1970, he initiated a series of pop and R&B smashes with his own "Tired of Being Alone" in 1971. Writing his own material, either alone or in collaboration with Mitchell and Al Jackson (of Booker T. and the MGs), Green topped both the pop and R&B charts with "Let's Stay Together." *I'm Still in Love with You*, his most popular album, yielded two crossover smashes, "Look What You've Done to Me" and the title track. Subsequent crossover smashes through 1974 include "You Ought to Be with Me," "Call Me (Come Back Home)," "Here I Am (Come and Take Me)," "Livin' for You," "Sha-La-La (Make Me Happy)," and "L-O-V-E (Love)." R&B smashes continued through 1976 with "Let's Get

Married," "Oh Me, Oh My (Dreams in My Arms)," "Full of Fire," and "Keep Me Cryin'."

In 1974 Green was attacked by a former girlfriend, who poured hot grits on the star and then killed herself; this incident apparently inspired his conversion to Christianity. On Dec. 17, 1976, Green opened the Full Gospel Tabernacle, his own church in Memphis. However, he did not turn his back entirely on secular music; in 1977 he broke with Willie Mitchell, to produce his next recording, *The Belle Album*, which featured the hit "Belle." Two years later a second incident, a fall from stage that could have left him seriously injured, convinced Green that he must abandon his secular career. In the 1980s he recorded gospel albums and was eventually embraced by churchgoing record buyers, becoming one of gospel music's best-selling black male artists. Performing on the gospel circuit, Al Green returned to the pop charts in late 1988 with the near-smash hit "Put a Little Love in Your Heart," recorded with Annie Lennox of the Eurythmics. A 1992 secular album recorded in Memphis has yet to be released in the United States. In 1995 Al Green was inducted into the Rock and Roll Hall of Fame.

DISC.: AL GREENE: *Back Up Train* (1968). AL GREEN: *A. G.* (rec. 1967–68; rel. 1972); *Green Is Blues* (1969); *A. G. Gets Next to You* (1971); *Let's Stay Together* (1972); *I'm Still in Love with You* (1972); *Call Me* (1973); *Livin' for You* (1973); *Call Me/Livin' for You* (1986); *A. G. Explores Your Mind* (1974); *Greatest Hits, Vol. 1* (1975); *A. G. Is Love* (1975); *Full of Fire* (1976); *Have a Good Time* (1976); *Greatest Hits, Vol. 2* (1977); *The Belle Album* (1977); *Tired of Being Alone* (1977); *Can't Get Next to You* (1977); *Let's Stay Together* (1978); *Truth 'n' Time* (1978); *Tokyo Live* (1995); *Love Ritual* (rec. 1968–76; rel. 1978); *Your Heart's in Good Hands* (1995). GOSPEL ALBUMS: *The Lord Will Make a Way* (1980); *I'll Rise Again* (1983); *Precious Lord* (1985); *Trust in God* (1984); *He Is the Light* (1985); *Soul Survivor* (1987); *I Get Joy* (1989); *One in a Million* (1991); *Love Is Reality* (1992); *Gospel Soul* (1993); *Your Heart's in Good Hands* (1995).—**BH**

Green, Charlie (aka **Big Green; Long Boy**), jazz trombonist; b. Omaha, Nebr., c. 1900; d. N.Y., Feb. 1936. He worked with the Omaha Night Owls (c. 1920), then with Frank "Red" Perkins's band at various Omaha venues. After touring with carnival shows, he settled in N.Y. He worked with Fletcher Henderson (1924–27, occasionally thereafter). After a brief stint with June Clark's band at the Tango Gardens, he joined Fats Waller and James P. Johnson for the *Keep Shufflin'* revue (1928). He then recorded with Bessie Smith. In 1929 he played with Zutty Singleton (Lafayette Theatre) and Benny Carter. During the following year he worked occasionally with Elmer Snowden and Chick Webb. He played with Jimmie Noone at the Savoy, then briefly with McKinney's Cotton Pickers (1931); in 1932 he gigged with Sam Wooding and Don Redman. He worked regularly with Webb (1932–34) and again with Carter (1933). His last gigs were with Louis Metcalf's band and Kaiser Marshall's band (Ubangi Club). He froze to death on a Harlem doorstep when he was unable to get into his home and decided to spend the night outdoors. A rumor that he was still alive and living in Holland resulted from a confusion with American trombonist Jake Green, who had worked in Rotterdam during the 1930s.—JC/LP

Green, Elizabeth A(dine) H(erkimer),

American string and conducting pedagogue; b. Mobile, Ala., Aug. 21, 1906; d. Ann Arbor, Sept. 24, 1995. She began violin lessons at age 4 with her father, Albert Wingate Green, then studied at Wheaton (Ill.) Coll. (Mus.B., 1924; B.S., 1928). She had advanced training with Clarence Evans (viola) in Chicago and Jacques Gordon (violin) in Falls Village, Conn., and then pursued her education at Northwestern Univ. (M.Mus., 1939). She later received instruction in conducting from Malko in Chicago (1940–42), and completed violin studies with Galamian at the Meadowmount School in N.Y. (summers, 1948–53; 1955–56); still later she studied at Eastern Mich. Univ. (B.F.A., 1978). She taught at East H.S. in Waterloo, Iowa (1928–42), and also played in the Waterloo Sym. Orch. From 1942 to 1954 she taught in the Ann Arbor (Mich.) public schools, then at the Univ. of Mich., retiring in 1974. She became well-known as a teacher of string instruments and of conducting, and appeared as a conductor of various ensembles in the U.S. She publ. the widely consulted textbook *The Modern Conductor* (1961; 6th ed., 1997).

WRITINGS: *Orchestral Bowings and Routines* (1949; 2nd ed., 1957); *The Modern Conductor* (1961; 6th ed., 1997); *Teaching Stringed Instruments in Classes* (1966); with N. Malko, *The Conductor and His Score* (1975; 2nd ed., 1985, as *The Conductor's Score*); *The Dynamic Orchestra: Principles of Orchestral Performance for Instrumentalists, Conductors and Audiences* (1987); with others, *Miraculous Teacher: Ivan Galamian and the Meadowmount Experience* (1993).

BIBL.: D. Smith, *E.A.H. G.: A Biography* (diss., Univ. of Mich., 1986).—NS/LK/DM

Green, Grant, jazz guitarist, b. St. Louis, June 6,

1931; d. N.Y., Jan. 31, 1979. He began studying guitar while still in grade school; by 1944, he was gigging with local groups. He worked in both R&B and jazz groups through the 1950s, including recordings and performances with Jack McDuff. He was invited to N.Y. by Lou Donaldson in 1960 and recorded prolifically for Blue Note, both as a leader and sideman. For his first group of recordings he worked with Donaldson, Lee Morgan, Stanley Turrentine, Jimmy Forrest, Jack McDuff, and Larry Young. His later work moved from post-bop to a danceable style. His "street" funk cuts from this period have been widely sampled by recent rap and dance acts, evidence of his popularity amongst acid jazz audiences. His career was hampered from the late 1960s on due to drug addiction. His ex-daughter-in-law wrote a biography.

DISC.: *Sunday Mornin'* (1961); *Remembering* (1961); *Reaching Out* (1961); *Green Street* (1961); *Born to Be Blue* (1961); *Feelin' the Spirit* (1962); *Goin' West* (1962); *Oleo* (1962); *Am I Blue?* (1963); *Idle Moments* (with J. Henderson, B. Hutcherson, 1963); *Solid* (1964); *Street of Dreams* (1964); *Alive!* (1970); *Green Is Beautiful* (1970); *Live at the Lighthouse* (1972); *Main Attraction* (1976); *Easy* (1978). J. Forrest: *Black Forrest* (1959); *All the Gin Is Gone* (1959).

BIBL.: S. A. Green, *G. G.: Rediscovering the Forgotten Genius of Jazz Guitar* (San Francisco, 1999).—MM/LP

Green, John (Waldo), American pianist, conduc-

tor, arranger, and composer; b. N.Y., Oct. 10, 1908; d. Beverly Hills, May 15, 1989. He studied economics at Harvard Univ. (B.A., 1928), where he also received instruction in theory from W.R. Spalding; later studied piano with Hilsberg, orchestration with Deutsch, and conducting with Tours. Working as an arranger for Guy Lombardo, he produced his first hit song, *Coquette* (1928); while working as accompanist to Gertrude Lawrence, he wrote the popular *Body and Soul* (1930). He became an arranger for Paramount Pictures in Hollywood (1930); made recordings with his own dance band and performed on the radio. He settled in Hollywood as a member of the music staff of MGM Studios (1942), serving as head of its music dept. (1949–58). He prepared award-winning adaptations of the original scores for film versions of *Easter Parade* (1948), *An American in Paris* (1951), *West Side Story* (1961), and *Oliver!* (1968); he also wrote the score for the film *Raintree County* (1957). He was assoc. conductor of the Los Angeles Phil. (1959–61); also appeared as a guest conductor with several of the major U.S. orchs.—NS/LK/DM

Green, Ray (Burns), American composer; b. Cav-

endish, Mo., Sept. 13, 1909. He began piano study at 14, winning a composition scholarship to the San Francisco Cons., where he studied with Bloch (1927–33). After further studies with Elkus and Stricklen at the Univ. of Calif. at Berkeley (1933–35), he won a scholarship to Paris to study with Milhaud (composition) and Monteux (conducting). He returned to the U.S. (1937), where he was active with the WPA and served as director of the Federal Music Project of Northern Calif. (1939–41). He then was chief of music for the Veterans Administration in Washington, D.C. (1946–48), and subsequently executive director of the American Music Center in N.Y. (1948–61). He also founded his own music publishing company, American Music Editions (1951). His works are often modal in harmonic settings; rhythmic animation is much in evidence in his pieces based on American rural songs.

WORKS: DRAMATIC: Incidental music; dance scores. ORCH.: Piano Concertino (1937); *Prelude and Fugue* (1937); *Sunday Sing Symphony* for Flute, Clarinet, Bassoon, and Orch. (1939–40); *3 Short Symphonies* (1945–53; 1970; 1974); *3 Pieces for a Concert* for Chamber Orch. (1947); *Jig Theme and 3 Changes* for Piano and Strings (1948); Violin Concerto (1952); *Rhapsody* for Harp and Orch. (1953); band music. CHAMBER: Suite for Violin and Piano (1929); Suite for Viola and Piano (1930); *5 Epigrammic Portraits* for String Quartet (1933; rev. 1950–52); *5 Epigrammic Romances* for String Quartet (1933); String Quartet (1933); Wind Quintet (1933); *Holiday for 4* for Viola, Violin, Bassoon, and Piano (1936; rev. 1939); *Concertante* for Viola or Clarinet and Piano (1940; also for Viola and Orch., 1946); *Concert Set* for Trumpet, Piano, and Drums (1941). P i a n o : Sonata (1933); *12 Short Sonatas* (1948–62); other works. VO-CAL: Choral pieces.

BIBL.: S. Vise, *R. G.: His Life and Stylistic Elements of His Music from 1938–1962* (diss., Univ. of Mo., 1976).—NS/LK/DM

Greenawald, Sheri (Kay), American soprano; b. Iowa City, Nov. 12, 1947. She studied with Charles Matheson at the Univ. of Northern Iowa (B.A., 1968), with Maria DeVarady, Hans Heinz, and Daniel Ferro in N.Y., and with Audrey Langford in London. In 1974 she made her professional debut in Poulenc's *Les Mamelles de Tirésias* at N.Y.'s Manhattan Theater Club, and then sang with the San Francisco Opera, the Houston Grand Opera, the Santa Fe Opera, the Washington (D.C.) Opera et al. In 1980 she made her European debut as Mozart's Susanna with the Netherlands Opera. In 1991 she sang Pauline in the U.S. stage premiere of Prokofiev's *The Gambler* at the Lyric Opera in Chicago. After portraying Mélisande in Seattle in 1993, she appeared as the Marschallin at the Welsh National Opera in Cardiff in 1994. On Nov. 25, 1995, she made her Metropolitan Opera debut in N.Y. as Weill's Jenny. She sang in Susa's *Transformations* in St. Louis in 1997. She toured extensively as a concert artist. Among her many roles were Zerlina, Despina, Massenet's Sophie, Violetta, Mimi, and Britten's Ellen Orford. She also created roles in Pasatieri's *Signor Deluso* (1974) and *Washington Square* (1976), Floyd's *Bilby's Doll* (1976), and Bernstein's *A Quiet Place* (1983).—NS/LK/DM

Greenaway, Peter, Welsh film director, writer, painter, and librettist; b. Newport, April 5, 1942. He went to England and studied at the Walthamstow Coll. of Art. From 1965 to 1976 he worked as a film editor in the Central Office of Information. His first exhibition of paintings was mounted in 1964, and his first one-man show was held in Canterbury in 1989. As a film director and writer, he began producing short films in 1966 and feature-length films in 1978, all highly structured, visually complex, and elaborate; among the most well-known are *The Cook, The Thief, His Wife and Her Lover* (1990), *Prospero's Books* (1991), and *The Pillow Book* (1991). His book *The Falls* appeared in 1993. He collaborated with Louis Andriessen as librettist for the operas *Rosa* (Amsterdam, Nov. 2, 1994) and *Writing to Vemeer* (1997–99; Amsterdam, Dec. 1, 1999). Greenaway was made a Chevalier de l'Ordre des Arts et des Lettres of France in 1990.—NS/LK/DM

Greenberg, Noah, American conductor; b. N.Y., April 9, 1919; d. there, Jan. 9, 1966. He studied music privately, and then organized choruses in N.Y. In 1952 he founded the N.Y. Pro Musica Antiqua, an organization specializing in Renaissance and medieval music, performed in authentic styles and on copies of early instruments; he revived the medieval liturgical music dramas *The Play of Daniel* (1958) and *The Play of Herod* (1963); traveled with his ensemble in Europe in 1960 and 1963. It was primarily through the efforts of this group (later known as the N.Y. Pro Musica) that early music, in the U.S., became a viable idiom available to modern audiences. He held a Guggenheim fellowship in 1955 and Ford fellowships in 1960 and 1962.—NS/LK/DM

Green Day, the band that made 1990s punk pop formed in 1989. **MEMBERSHIP:** Billie Joe Armstrong, gtr., voc. (b. Rodeo, Calif., Feb. 17, 1972); Mike Dirnt (Michael Pritchard), bs. (b. Rodeo, Calif. May 4, 1972); Tre Cool (Frank Edwin Wright III), drm. (b. Germany, Dec. 9, 1972).

Armstrong and Dirnt had played together in a variety of garage bands since junior high. They formed a trio with drummer John Kiffmeyer called Sweet Children and signed a deal with Berkeley independent record company Lookout Records, releasing the *1000 Hours* EP. They changed their name to Green Day just before the record came out to avoid conflict with another local group recently signed to Warner Bros. They spent one day and laid down 10 songs for a full album, *39/Smooth* on Lookout. The album sold fairly well for a bunch of unknowns.

Kiffmeyer left the group to concentrate on college. A couple of years earlier, Armstrong played guitar and sang back-up on an album by a band called the Lookouts. He asked their drummer, Tre Cool, to fill in for Kiffmeyer, and he eventually replaced him, bringing the twisted tune "Dominated Love Song" to the band's second album, *Kerplunk*. That album sold even better than the first, moving 50,000 copies. Bigger record companies started to take notice, and finally Reprise bought them out of their Lookout contract and signed them.

Their major label debut, *Dookie,* sold 10 million copies, spending two weeks at #2. The band received four Grammy nominations. During summer 1994, they played both Lollapalooza and the Woodstock 25th Anniversary concert. The video for the song "Long View" became a staple at MTV, as did "Basket Case" and especially "When I Come Around." The latter two topped the Modern Rock charts. In the wake of the album's success, their early indie albums went gold. The group's follow-up album, *Insomniac* entered the charts at #2, selling two million copies. It didn't generate the same level of excitement at MTV or modern rock radio that *Dookie* did, and despite sales that would have blown most power punk pop bands away, the record company considered it a disappointment.

For *Nimrod,* the band expanded their horizons, adding violinist Petra Haden from the L.A. band That Dog, and horn players who had toured with No Doubt. Far more ambitious musically than anything they had previously recorded, the album went platinum and reached #10 on the charts. They played Woodstock '99 and announced plans for a Green Day movie, but nothing much has come of it as of this writing.

DISC.: *1000 Hours* (1990); *39/Smooth* (1991); *Kerplunk* (1992); *Dookie* (1994); *Insomniac* (1995); *Live* (1995); *Nimrod* (1997); *Foot in Mouth* (1998).—HB

Greene, (Harry) Plunket, Irish bass-baritone and teacher; b. Old Connaught House, County Wicklow, June 24, 1865; d. London, Aug. 19, 1936. He was a student of Hromada in Stuttgart, Vannuccini in Florence, and J.B. Welsh and A. Blume in London. On Jan. 21, 1888, he made his debut as a soloist in Handel's *Messiah* in Stepney. In 1890 he appeared at London's Covent Garden, but soon became a successful concert artist; from 1893 he appeared in recitals with Leonard Borwick, and that same year made his first tour of the

U.S. In 1899 he married Parry's daughter, Gwendolen. Greene devoted his later years to vocal pedagogy. He publ. the manual *Interpretation in Song* (London, 1912) and a book of reminiscences, *From the Blue Danube to Shannon* (London, 1934); also a biography of Stanford (London, 1935). He was a fine interpreter of Schumann and Brahms, and also sang in the premieres of works by Parry, Stanford, Elgar, and Vaughan Williams. —NS/LK/DM

Greene, Maurice, prominent English organist, teacher, and composer; b. London, Aug. 12, 1696; d. there, Dec. 1, 1755. He was a choirboy at St. Paul's Cathedral in London under Jeremiah Clarke and Charles King, and in 1710 he was articled to Richard Brind, the Cathedral organist. In 1714 he became organist at St. Dunstan-in-the-West, Fleet Street, and also at St. Andrew's Holborn, in 1718. In the latter year, he was appointed organist at St. Paul's Cathedral. In 1727 he was made organist and composer of the Chapel Royal. In 1730 he was awarded a doctorate in music from the Univ. of Cambridge, which also made him an honorary prof. of music. Greene became the Master of the King's Musick in 1735. As a teacher, he numbered William Boyce and John Stanley among his students. He was active in founding the Academy of Antient Music in 1710, and in 1731 he founded his own rival Apollo Soc. With Michael Festing et al., he founded the Soc. of Musicians, a charitable organization, in 1738. His valuable collection of English sacred music passed into the hands of Boyce, who made use of it in his *Cathedral Music.* Greene particularly distinguished himself as a composer of sacred music.

WORKS: *Florimel, or Love's Revenge,* dramatic pastorale (1734); *The Judgment of Hercules,* masque (1740; music not extant); *Phoebe,* pastoral opera (1747); 3 oratorios: *The Song of Deborah and Barak* (1732), *Jephtha* (1737), and *The Force of Truth* (1744; music not extant); about 100 anthems; services; canticles; *Ode for St. Cecilia's Day* (1730); 35 court odes; many cantatas; numerous songs; keyboard music.

BIBL.: E. Janifer, *The English Church Music of M. G. and His Contemporaries: A Study of Traditional and Contemporary Influences* (diss., Univ. of London, 1959); J. Moore, *The Church Music of M. G.* (diss., Univ. of Nottingham, 1961); H. Johnstone, *The Life and Works of M. G. (1696–1755)* (diss., Univ. of Oxford, 1967). —NS/LK/DM

Greenfield, Elizabeth Taylor, pioneering black American singer; b. Natchez, Miss., c. 1819; d. Philadelphia, March 31, 1876. She was born a slave but was freed in childhood and taken to Philadelphia, where she received her education thanks to the sponsorship of a Quaker widow. She taught herself to play the piano, guitar, and harp, and accompanied herself as a singer. After giving concerts in Buffalo and Rochester, N.Y. (1851), she appeared in England (1853). She then sang in Mich. (1855), Wisc. (1857), and Montreal (1863), and thereafter was active as a singer and teacher in Philadelphia.

BIBL.: A. LaBrew, *The Black Swan: E.T. G., Songstress* (Detroit, 1969). —LK/DM

Greenhouse, Bernard, esteemed American cellist and pedagogue; b. Newark, N.J., Jan. 3, 1916. He began his training with William Berce, and in 1933 he entered the Juilliard School of Music in N.Y. as a pupil of Salmond. After receiving a diploma from its graduate school in 1938, he pursued studies with Feuermann (1940–41), Alexanian (1944–46), and Casals (1946–47). He was 1st cellist in the CBS Sym. Orch. in N.Y. (1938–42), and also was a member of the Dorian String Quartet (1939–42). During his military service, he was solo cellist with the U.S. Navy Sym. Orch. and a member of the Navy String Quartet (1942–45). On Feb. 11, 1946, he made his recital debut at N.Y.'s Town Hall, where he gave annual recitals until 1957. He was a member of the Harpsichord Quartet (1947–51) and of the Bach Aria Group (1948–76), but it was as a founder-member of the Beaux Arts Trio (1955–87) that he won his greatest distinction. He taught at the Manhattan School of Music in N.Y. (1950–82), the Juilliard School of Music (1951–61), the Hartt School of Music in Hartford, Conn. (1956–65), the Ind. Univ. School of Music in Bloomington (summers, 1956–65), the State Univ. of N.Y. at Stony Brook (1960–85), the New England Cons. of Music in Boston (from 1986), and at Rutgers, the State Univ. of N.J. (from 1987). He also gave masterclasses around the globe. Greenhouse served as president of the Cello Soc. (1955–59; from 1987). In addition to the standard repertory, he performed much contemporary American music.

BIBL.: N. Delbanco, *The Beaux Arts Trio: A Portrait* (N.Y. and London, 1985). —NS/LK/DM

Greer, Sonny (William Alexander), jazz drummer who is famous for his long tenure with Duke Ellington; b. Long Branch, N.J., Dec. 13, 1902; d. N.Y., March 23, 1982. He played drums at high school, then worked with Wilbur Gardner, Mabel Ross, and in one of Harry Yerek's many orchs. While visiting Washington, D.C., he took a job playing at the Howard Theatre with the Marie Lucas Orch. He met Ellington in 1919, and did his first gig with him the following year. He would remain with the band until 1951. At that time he briefly joined Johnny Hodges's Small Band, then freelanced in N.Y., playing for various leaders, among them Louis Metcalf, Henry "Red" Allen (1952–53), Tyree Glenn (1959), Eddie Barefield, and J. C. Higginbotham. Other than a spell of inactivity because of a broken shoulder (1960), he continued to play throughout the 1960s. In 1967 he led a band at The Garden Café and took part in the filming of *The Night They Raided Minsky's.* He worked regularly with Brooks Kerr's trio during the 1970s.

Though some critics contend that Greer didn't "swing," Ellington's "Cottontail" shows that his style developed over the years and that he was especially effective on the ride cymbal. He was an innovator in the expansion of the drum kit; photographs from the early 1930s show him using orchestral chimes, timpani, temple blocks, and other additions to the set. —JC/LP

Grefinger, Wolfgang, important Austro-German composer; b. between 1470 and 1480; d. after 1515. He studied with Paul Hofhaimer. At the beginning of the 16th century he went to Vienna, where he attended the

Univ. (1509) and was ordained, serving as organist at St. Stephen's Cathedral. His historical significance rests upon his *Tenorlieder*, which are a vital link between the works of Erasmus Lapicida and Arnold von Bruck. He also composed sacred music, being especially admired for his 4-voice settings of hymns by Prudentius, *Cathemerinon: Hoc est Diurnarum rerum opus varium* (Vienna, 1515). He ed. the liturgical hymnbook *Psalterium pataviense antiphonis, responsoriis, hymnisque in notis musicalibus* (Vienna, 1512). His works were ed. by L. Nowak in *Das deutsche Gesellschaftslied in Österreich von 1480–1550* in Denkmäler der Tonkunst in Österreich, LXXII, Jg. XXXVII/2 (1930).—**NS/LK/DM**

Gregh, Louis French conductor, music publisher, and composer; b. Philippeville, Algeria, March 16, 1843; d. St. Mesme, Seine-et-Oise, Jan. 21, 1915. He settled in Paris, where he first found success as a composer of light theater scores with *Un lycée de jeunes filles* (Dec. 28, 1881). After bringing out the musical comedy *Le Présomptif in Brussels* (Dec. 12, 1883), he resumed composing for the Paris stage with *Grande vitesse, port dû* (Sept. 19, 1890), *Patatart, Patatart et cie* (Oct. 9, 1893), and *Le Capitaine Roland* (March 29, 1895). He also wrote ballets and incidental music to Beissier's play *Arlette* (1891). In later years, he was active with his own music publishing firm, which remained in the control of his family for three generations.—**NS/LK/DM**

Gregoir, Édouard (Georges Jacques), Belgian writer on music, pianist, and composer, brother of **Jacques (Mathieu Joseph) Gregoir;** b. Turnhout, Nov. 7, 1822; d. Wijneghem, near Antwerp, June 28, 1890. He was a piano student of Christian Rummel. After a brief career as a pianist, he settled in Antwerp in 1851 to pursue musical research. In addition to his many writings, he also contributed articles to various journals.

WORKS: 2 operas: *Willem Beukels* (Brussels, July 21, 1856) and *La belle bourbonnaise* (n.d.); incidental music; *Les croisades,* historical sym. (Antwerp, 1846); 2 overtures; *La vie,* oratorio (Antwerp, Feb. 6, 1848); *Le déluge,* symphonic oratorio (Antwerp, Jan. 31, 1849); part songs for Men's Voices; much keyboard music.

WRITINGS: *Essai historique sur la musique et les musiciens dans les Pays-Bas* (Brussels, 1861); *Galerie biographique des artistes-musiciens belges* (Brussels, 1862); *Biographie des artistes-musicales néeerlandais des XVIIIᵉ et XIXᵉ siècles* (Brussels, 1864); *Histoire de la facture et des facteurs d'orgues* (Antwerp, 1865); *Histoire de l'orgue* (Antwerp, 1865); *Schetsen van Nederlandsche toonkunstenaars* (Antwerp, c. 1865); *Notice historique sur les sociétés et écoles de musique d'Anvers* (Brussels, 1869); *Adriaan Willaert* (Brussels, 1869); *Recherches historiques concernant les journaux de musique depuis les temps les plus reculés jusqu'à nos jours* (Antwerp, 1872); *Documents historiques relatifs à l'art musical et aux artistes-musiciens* (Brussels, 1872–76); *Les artistes-musiciens belges au XIXᵉ siècle: Réponse à un critique de Paris* (Brussels, 1874); *Notice biographique sur F.J. Gossé dit Gossec* (Mons, 1878); *Les gloires de l'Opéra et la musiqueà Paris* (Brussels, 1878–81); *L'art musical en Belgique sous le règnes de Léopold I et Léopold II* (Brussels, 1879); *Grétry, célèbre compositeur belge* (Brussels, 1883); *Les tribulations d'un artiste-musicien à Paris en 1812: Pietro Belloni* (Brussels, 1884); *Les artistes-musiciens belges au XVIIIᵉ et au XIXᵉ siècle* (Brussels, 1885–90; suppl. 1887); *Souvenirs artistiques* (Brussels, 1888–89).—**NS/LK/DM**

Gregoir, Jacques (Mathieu Joseph), Belgian pianist and composer, brother of **Édouard (Georges Jacques) Gregoir;** b. Antwerp, Jan. 19, 1817; d. Brussels, Oct. 29, 1876. He studied with Henri Herz in Paris and with Rummel in Biebrich. He gave a number of successful piano recitals in Belgium, Germany, and Switzerland. He wrote salon pieces for piano and several practical methods of piano playing, and publ. duets for violin and piano in collaboration with Vieuxtemps. He also composed an opera, *Le Gondolier de Venise* (1848). —**NS/LK/DM**

Gregor, Bohumil, Czech conductor; b. Prague, July 14, 1926. He studied at the Prague Cons. with Alois Klima. After conducting at the 5th of May Theater in Prague (1947–49) and in Brno (1949–51), he served as music director in Ostrava (1958–62). From 1962 he was a regular guest conductor at the National Theater in Prague; he also appeared as a guest conductor throughout Europe; in 1969 he made his U.S. debut with the San Francisco Opera conducting *Jenůfa*. He was closely associated with the music of Janáček and other Czech composers.—**NS/LK/DM**

Gregor, Čestmír, Czech composer; b. Brno, May 14, 1926. He began his training with his father, Josef Gregor, who had been a student of Novák; later he studied with Kvapil (1950–54) and Kapr (1965–70) at the Janáček Academy of Music in Brno. From 1959 to 1972 he was director of music for the Czech Radio in Ostrava. In his works, he pursued an atonal style of composition.

WORKS: DRAMATIC: O p e r a : *Profesionální žena* (A Professional Woman; 1983). **B a l l e t :** *Závrat* (Vertigo; 1963; ballet version of the *Choreographic Symphony*); *Horko* (Heat; 1978). **ORCH.:** *Joyous Overture* (1951); *If All Girls of the World,* symphonic poem (1953); 3 syms. (*Country and People,* 1953; *Choreographic,* 1963; *Symphony of My City,* 1971; rev. 1973); *Once in Spring Evening,* suite for Chamber Orch. (1954); *No One is Alone,* piano concerto (1955); *May I Speak?,* overture (1956); *Tragic Suite* for Small Orch. (1957); *Concerto semplice* for Piano and Orch. (1958); Suite for Strings (1959); *Polyfonietta* (1961); *Daedalus's Children,* symphonic poem (1961); *If All Men of the World,* overture (1963); Violin Concerto (1965; rev. 1968); Cello Concerto, *Complimento à la musica di orgni giorno* (1974); Sinfonietta (1976); *Concerto da camera* for Clarinet and Strings (1977); *I've Joined the Army,* variations (1978); Piano Concerto (1979); *Symphonic Metamorphoses on a Blues Theme* (1986; rev. 1990). **CHAMBER:** Trio for Flute, Viola, and Bass Clarinet (1959); String Quartet (1965); *Amenities* for Violin and Piano (1987); 2 violin sonatas (1989); *Dolce Vita* for Violin and Piano (1990); 3 *Generations* for String Quartet (1991); *Auspicious Word,* bass clarinet sonata (1993). **P i a n o :** *Experiment* (1946); *Sonata brevis* (1946); *Ash Wednesday* (1962); 3 *Movements* (1966); *Sonata in 3 Tempi* (1966). **VOCAL:** 2 *Capricious Ballads* for Soprano and Piano (1975); *The Sea's Children,* choral cantata (1975). —**NS/LK/DM**

Gregor, Christian Friedrich, Silesian organist, music director, composer, and hymnologist; b. Dirsdorf, Silesia, Jan. 1, 1723; d. Zeist, the Netherlands, Nov. 6, 1801. Joining the Moravian Brethren in Herrnhut, Saxony, in 1742, he was ordained in 1756 and soon assumed leading positions in its management: was financial agent of Zinzendorf, member of the Unity Elders Conference (1764–1801), and bishop (1789–1801). He made numerous business trips to Germany, the Netherlands, England, Russia, and North America (Pa., 1770–72); while in Pa., he gave instruction in composition to Johann Friedrich Peter. During his stay at Herrnhut as organist, he compiled the first hymnal publ. by the Moravians (*Choral-Buch, enthaltend alle zu dem Gesangbuche der Evangelischen Brüder-Gemeinen vom Jahre 1778 gehörige Melodien*; Leipzig, 1784), and arranged the musical liturgies. He wrote 308 hymns (*Gesangbuch zum Gebrauch der evangelischen Brüder-Gemeinen*; Barby, 1778 et seq.), about 100 chorale tunes, and approximately 200 anthems and arias. The last are preserved in MS in the Moravian Church Archives at Bethlehem, Pa., and Winston-Salem, N.C. Several of his anthems were republ. frequently in 19th-century American tune books. —NS/LK/DM

Gregora, František, Bohemian double bass player, choral conductor, teacher, and composer; b. Netolice, Jan. 9, 1819; d. Písek, Jan. 27, 1887. He went to Vienna to study with Josef Dreschsler, and then entered the Cons. to study composition (with Gottfried Preyer) and double bass. From 1848 he pursued his career in Bohemia. He composed 17 double bass concertos and many other works for his instrument. Among his other works were much sacred music, part songs, and solo songs. He also publ. a valuable manual on harmony (Prague, 1876).—LK/DM

Gregory I, St., "the Great," Italian father of the church and Pope; b. Rome, c.540; d. there, March 12, 604. He became Pope in 590. According to a tradition dating back to about the 8th century, he was the principal figure in bringing about the codification of the plainsong or liturgical chant of the Roman Catholic Church, hence Gregorian chant. Gregory's actual role in the matter and the origin of Gregorian chant as it has come down to us remains a matter of much speculation among modern scholars.

BIBL.: G. Morin, *Les véritables origines du chant grégorien* (Maredsous, 1890; 2nd ed., 1904); A. Gastoué, *Les origines du chant romain* (Paris, 1907); A. Mocquereau, *Le nombre musical grégorien* (2 vols., Tournai, 1908, 1927; Eng. tr., 1932, 1951); P. Ferretti, *Estetica gregoriano* (2 vols.; Vol. I, Rome, 1834; Vol. II ed. by P. Ernetti, 1964); E. Jammers, *Der gregorianische Rhythmus* (Leipzig, 1937); W. Apel, *Gregorian Chant* (Bloomington, Ind., 1958); G. Murray, *Gregorian Chant According to the Manuscripts* (London, 1963); J. Rayburn, *Gregorian Chant: A History of the Controversy Concerning Its Rhythm* (N.Y., 1964); J. Deshusses, *Le sacramentaire grégorien* (Fribourg, 1971).—NS/LK/DM

Gregson, Edward, English composer, teacher, and conductor; b. Sunderland, July 23, 1945. He studied at the Royal Academy of Music in London (1963–67), where he was a student in composition of Alan Bush, and at the Univ. of London (B.Mus., 1977). He was a lecturer (1976–89), a reader (1989–93), and a prof. (1993–96) at Goldsmiths' Coll., Univ. of London. From 1989 to 1991 he was chairman of the Assn. of Professional Composers. In 1996 he became the principal of the Royal Northern Coll. of Music in Manchester, as well as an honorary prof. of music at the Univ. of Manchester. As a conductor, he has been particularly known for his advocacy of contemporary music. Gregson has won notable distinction as a composer of brass, wind band, and orch. scores.

WORKS: ORCH.: *Music for Chamber Orch.* (1968; BBC Radio 3, Nov. 4, 1977); Concerto for Horn and Brass Band (1971; also for Horn and Orch.); Concerto for Tuba and Brass Band (Manchester, April 24, 1976; also for Tuba and Orch., 1978; Edinburgh, June 11, 1983); *Flourish* (1978; rev. version, London, Nov. 14, 1986); *Metamorphoses* (London, June 1979); Trombone Concerto (London, July 25, 1979); Trumpet Concerto (London, April 20, 1983); *Greenwich Dances*, renamed *Contrasts* (London, May 7, 1983); *Celebration* (1991); *Blazon* (1992); Clarinet Concerto (Manchester, April 20, 1994); Concerto for Piano and Winds (1995). **B a n d :** *March Prelude* (1968); *Voices of Youth* (1968); *The Pacemakers* (1969); *Essay* (1970); *The Plantaganets* (1971); Concerto Grosso (1972); *Intrada* (1972); *Partita* (1972); *Prelude and Capriccio* (1972); *Fanfare* (1973); *Patterns* (1974); *A Swedish March* (1975); *Connotations* (1976); *Dances and Arias* (London, Oct. 7, 1984); *Occasion* (London, Oct. 4, 1986); *Of Men and Mountains* (Drachten, the Netherlands, Dec. 8, 1990) *Festivo* (Kortrikj, Belgium, July 14, 1985). **CHAMBER:** Oboe Sonata (1965); *Divertimento* for Trombone and Piano (1967); Brass Quintet (BBC Radio 3, Nov. 27, 1967); *Prelude and Capriccio* for Trumpet and Piano (1972); *Equale Dances* for Brass Quintet (Leeds, Dec. 1983); Sonata for 4 Trombones (1984; London, Jan. 8, 1985). **P i a n o :** *6 Little Pieces* (Amsterdam, Oct. 16, 1982; rev. 1993); Sonata (London, Feb. 18, 1983; rev. version, London, Nov. 21, 1986). **VOCAL:** *In the beginning,* cantata for Women's Voices and Piano (1966; rev. for Chorus and Piano, 1981; London, April 18, 1982); *Missa Brevis Pacem* for Baritone, Boy's Chorus, and Symphonic Wind Band (1987; Aldeburgh, April 9, 1988); *Make a Joyful Noise* for Chorus and Orch. (Croydon, Nov. 28, 1988); *A Welcome Ode* for Chorus and Optional Piano Duet/Percussion or Optional Organ/Percussion (Sunderland, Aug. 22, 1997). —NS/LK/DM

Greindl, Josef, German bass; b. Munich, Dec. 23, 1912; d. Vienna, April 16, 1993. He was a student in Munich of Paul Bender and Anna Bahr- Mildenburg. In 1936 he made his formal operatic debut as Hunding in Krefeld. After singing in Düsseldorf (1938–42), he was a member of the Berlin State Opera (from 1942); in 1949 he became a member of the Berlin Städtische (later Deutsche) Oper. In 1943 he made his first appearance at the Bayreuth Festival as Pogner, and returned to sing there regularly from 1951 to 1969. On Nov. 15, 1952, he made his Metropolitan Opera debut in N.Y. as Wagner's Heinrich, but remained on the roster for only a season. From 1956 to 1969 he sang at the Vienna State Opera. In 1963 he appeared at London's Covent Garden. In 1961 he was made a prof. at the Saarbrücken Hochschule für Musik, and in 1973 at the Vienna Hochschule für Musik. Greindl was equally convincing in dramatic and buffo roles. Among his other roles were Sarastro, Don Alfonso, Hans Sachs, and the Wanderer in *Siegfried.* —NS/LK/DM

Greiter, Matthaeus or **Matthias,** German poet and composer; b. Aichach, Bavaria, c. 1490; d. Strasbourg, Dec. 20, 1550. He was educated at the Univ. of Freiburg im Breisgau. After serving as a monk and cantor at the Strasbourg Minster, he converted to Protestantism in 1524 but remained at the Minster. He also taught music at the Gymnasium Argentinense. In 1546 he was charged with adultery, and was dismissed from his positions. In 1548 he resumed his position at the Gymnasium Argentinense. After reverting to Catholicism in 1549, he resumed his duties at the Minster in 1550 but died later that year of the plague. He wrote the texts and melodies of Psalm-Lieder for Lutheran services, and settings, for 4 voices, of German songs. He also wrote a tract, *Elementale musicum inventuti* (Strasbourg, 1544). A modern ed. of his works was publ. by H.-C. Müller, *Matthaeus Greiter: Sämtliche Weltliche Lieder*, in Das Chorwerk, LXXXVII (1962).—**NS/LK/DM**

Grell, (August) Eduard, German organist, conductor, and composer; b. Berlin, Nov. 6, 1800; d. Steglitz, near Berlin, Aug. 10, 1886. He studied with his father (piano and organ), J.C. Kaufmann (piano), G. Ritschl (voice and theory), and Zelter and Rungenhagen (composition), and later in Erfurt with M. Fischer (organ). In 1817 he became organist of Berlin's Nikolaikirche and a member of the Singakademie, where he later was asst. conductor (1832–53) and then conductor (1853–76). He also was organist at the Berlin Cathedral (1839–57). He composed 4 oratorios, a Te Deum, masses, cantatas, hymns, motets, etc. H. Bellermann ed. his essays as *Aufsätze und Gutachten* (Berlin, 1887).

BIBL.: H. Bellermann, *A. E. G.* (Berlin, 1899).—**NS/LK/DM**

Grenon, Nicolas, French composer; b. c. 1380; d. 1456. He became a clerk at Notre Dame Cathedral in 1399, and also was a canon at the Church of the Holy Sepulchre, where he later became a sub-deacon and then a deacon in 1401. From 1403 to 1408 he was master of the choirboys at Laon Cathedral, and in 1408–09 he was a singer and teacher at Cambrai Cathedral. He was in the service of John the Fearless, Duke of Burgundy, from 1412 to 1419. After a brief return to Cambrai Cathedral, he served as master of the choirboys at the Papal Chapel in Rome (1425–27) before settling in Cambrai. His extant works comprise a portion of a Gloria, 4 motets, and 5 chansons.—**LK/DM**

Grešák, Jozef, Slovak composer; b. Bardejov, Dec. 30, 1907; d. Piešťany, April 17, 1987. He studied piano and organ, but was mainly autodidact as a composer.

WORKS: DRAMATIC: *Prichod Slovákov* (The Arrival of the Slovaks), opera (1925); *Radúz and Mahuliena,* ballet (1954–55); *With Rosary,* opera (1970–73); *Zuzanka Hrašovie,* monodrama (1973; Bratislava, Jan. 15, 1975). **ORCH.:** Piano Concerto (1963); *Concertino-Pastorale* for Oboe, English Horn, Horn, and Orch. (1965); *Morceau I* for Violin and Orch. (1968); *Rotors II* (1969); *Concertant Symfonietta* (1975; Košice, May 5, 1976). **OTHER:** Chamber works; *The Emigrant Songs* for Soloists, Men's Chorus, and Orch. (1961) and other vocal pieces; piano music.—**NS/LK/DM**

Gresham-Lancaster, Scot, American composer, performer, and instrument designer; b. Redwood City,

Calif., April 19, 1954. He attended classes with Robert Sheff, Robert Ashley, and Terry Riley at Mills Coll. (1972–73) while still in high school, and then studied at Canada Coll. in Redwood City, Calif. (1973–74), Cabrillo Coll. in Aptos, Calif. (1974–75), San Francisco State Univ. (1975–76), and Va. Commonwealth Univ. (1976–77). In 1989 he became a lecturer at Calif. State Univ. at Hayward. He held composer residencies at Mills Coll. (1992) and at Amsterdam's Steim (1992, 1994, 1999), and also at the Djersassi Foundation in Calif. (1995). He has toured and recorded as a soloist and with the electroacoustic ensembles the Hub and Room, as well as with Alvin Curran, the Rova Sax Quartet, the Club Foot Orch., and the Dutch ambient group NYX. Gresham-Lancaster is a technical advisor to David Cope on the Plieades Project, an attempt to build and conduct research into SETI, using a 140-meter Galilaen feed radio telescope that would also serve as a large-scale musical instrument. Among his original instruments are a computer-controlled interactive filter bank (1984), "Uforce," a modified Nintendo game controller (1989), a digital elevation model control surface instrument (1989, with Bill Thibaut), Hub's 2nd generation computer network/music facilitating hardware (1990), an infrared remote control pulse accumulating device (1992), and a Tensegrity Harp (1994; after R. Buckminster Fuller).

WORKS: *Be Normal* for Instrumentalists, Tape, and Actors (1976); *Bozo's face makes a waltz* for Instrumentalists, Tape, and Actors (1976); *Styx* for Percussion Quartet and Electronics (1978); *Interlok* for 4 Guitarists and Electronics (1979; rev. 1982); *Allegory of the Beached Whale* for Bass Clarinet, Tenor Saxophone, and Electronics (1982); *Food Chain* for 4 Macintosh Computers and Sequencers (1985); *Whackers* for Computer and Selenoid-based Robot (1987); *McCall.DEM* for Computer, Electronics, and Digital Elevation Models (1989); *Human/Nature* for Piano (1990); *String Quartets in Baroque Forms* for String Quartet (1992); *A mighty wind blows through my soul* for String Orch. (1993); *VEX* for Computer Network, Electronics, and Disklavier (1994); *Whirlpool of Blood* for Voice, Long Tube, and Electronics (1994); *Machine* for String Orch. (1995); *Times Remembered* for 6 Computer-controlled CD Players and Digital Processors (1995); *5 Tones for Slonimsky* for Computer and Disklavier (1996); *The heart that wandered* for String Quartet (1996); *Giest Incidental Music* for String Quartet and Percussion (1998); *in the unlikely event of a water landing* for Cello Quartet and Neural Net Electronics (1999).—**LK/DM**

Gresnick, Antoine-Frédéric, Belgian composer; b. Liège (baptized), March 2, 1755; d. Paris, Oct. 16, 1799. After serving as a chorister at St. Lambert in Liège, he studied with Sala at S. Onofrio in Naples (1772–79). In 1786–87 he was in London, where his opera *Alceste* was first performed at the King's Theatre on Dec. 23, 1786. He was director of the Lyons theater orch. (1787–89) before settling in Paris in 1794, where he brought out 15 operas with varying success. He also wrote a Sinfonia (1771), a Harpsichord Concerto (1782), a Simphonie Concertante for Clarinet, Bassoon, and Orch. (c. 1797), and various vocal pieces.

BIBL.: P. Mercier, *A.-F. G., compositeur liégeois* (Louvain, 1977).—**NS/LK/DM**

Gretchaninoff, Alexander (Tikhonovich),

Russian-born American composer; b. Moscow, Oct. 25, 1864; d. N.Y., Jan. 3, 1956. He studied at the Moscow Cons. (1881–91) with Safonov (piano) and Arensky (composition), then studied composition at the St. Petersburg Cons. as a pupil of Rimsky-Korsakov (1891–1903). He was a prof. of composition at the Moscow Inst. from 1891 to 1922; then lived in Paris. He visited the U.S., where he appeared with considerable success as a guest conductor of his own works (1929–31); went to the U.S. again in 1939, settling in N.Y. He became a naturalized American citizen on July 25, 1946. He continued to compose until the end of his long life. A concert of his works was presented in his presence on the occasion of his 90th birthday at Town Hall in N.Y. (Oct. 25, 1954). Gretchaninoff's music is rooted in the Russian national tradition; influences of both Tchaikovsky and Rimsky-Korsakov are in evidence in his early works; toward 1910 he attempted to inject some impressionistic elements into his vocal compositions, but without signal success. His masterly sacred works are of historical importance, for he introduced a reform into Russian church singing by using nationally colored melodic patterns; in several of his masses, he employed instrumental accompaniment contrary to the prescriptions of the Russian Orthodox faith, a circumstance that precluded the use of these works in Russian churches. His *Missa oecumenica* represents a further expansion toward ecclesiastical universality; in this work, he makes use of elements pertaining to other religious music, including non-Christian. His instrumental works are competently written, but show less originality. His early *Lullaby* (1887) and the song *Over the Steppes* long retained their popularity, and were publ. in numerous arrangements. After the Revolution, Gretchaninov wrote a new Russian national anthem, *Hymn of Free Russia* (sung in N.Y. at a concert for the benefit of Siberian exiles, May 22, 1917), but it was never adopted by any political Russian faction. He publ. a book of reminiscences as *My Life* (Paris, in Russian, 1934; Eng. tr., 1951, with a complete catalogue of works as well as additions and an introduction by N. Slonimsky).

WORKS: DRAMATIC: O p e r a : *Dobrinya Nikititch* (Moscow, Oct. 27, 1903); *Sister Beatrice* (Moscow, Oct. 25, 1912; suppressed after 3 perfs. as being irreverent); *The Dream of a Little Christmas Tree*, children's opera (1911); *The Cat, the Fox, and the Rooster*, children's opera (1919); *The Castle Mouse*, children's opera (1921); *Marriage*, comic opera after Gogol (1945–46; Tanglewood, Aug. 1, 1948). **B a l l e t :** *Idylle forestière* (N.Y., 1925). **ORCH.:** Concert Overture in D minor (1892; St. Petersburg, March 1893); *Elegy in Memory of Tchaikovsky* (1893; St. Petersburg, Dec. 31, 1898, Rimsky-Korsakov conducting); 5 syms: No. 1 (1893; St. Petersburg, Jan. 26, 1895), No. 2 (1909; Moscow, March 14, 1909), No. 3 (1920–23; Kiev, May 29, 1924), No. 4 (1923–24; N.Y., April 9, 1942), and No. 5 (1936; Philadelphia, April 5, 1939); *Poème élégiaque* (Boston, March 29, 1946); *Festival Overture* (Indianapolis, Nov. 15, 1946); *Poème lyrique* (1948). **OTHER:** Incidental music for Ostrovsky's *Snegoruchka* (Moscow, Nov. 6, 1900); Tolstoy's *Tsar Feodor* (Moscow, Oct. 26, 1898) and *Death of Ivan the Terrible* (1899). **CHAMBER:** 4 string quartets; 2 trios; Violin Sonata; Cello Sonata; 2 clarinet sonatas; 2 *Miniatures* for Saxophone and Piano. **P i a n o :** 2 sonatas (n.d., 1944); *Petits tableaux musicaux* (1947); other works. **VOCAL:** *Liturgy of St. John Chrysostom* (Moscow, Oct. 19, 1898); *Laudate Deum* (Moscow, Nov. 24, 1915); *Liturgia domestica* (Moscow, March 30, 1918); *Missa oecumenica* for Soli, Chorus, and Orch. (Boston, Feb. 25, 1944); 84 choruses; 14 vocal quartets; 8 duets; 258 songs.—NS/LK/DM

Grétry, André-Ernest-Modeste,

greatly significant French composer of Walloon descent; b. Liège, Feb. 8, 1741; d. Montmorency, near Paris, Sept. 24, 1813. He was a choirboy and 2nd violinist at the collegiate church of St. Denis in Liège (1750–60), where his father served as violinist; he subsequently studied voice with Francois Leclerc, thoroughbass with H.F. Renkin, and composition with Henri Moreau. About 1754 an Italian opera company gave a season in Liège, and young Grétry thus received his first impulse toward dramatic music. His early works were instrumental; his first syms. were performed at the home of his patron, Canon Simon de Harlez; the latter helped him to obtain a scholarship to the Collège de Liège in Rome, where he studied harmony with G.B. Casali (1761–65). While in Rome, he composed mainly sacred music; however, he did write 2 intermezzos entitled *La Vendemmiatrice* for Carnival 1765. He was in Geneva in 1766 as a music teacher; there he met Voltaire, who advised him to go to Paris; before his departure, he produced the opéra-comique *Isabelle et Gertrude* (Dec. 1766), to a libretto by Favart, after Voltaire. He arrived in Paris in the autumn of 1767, where he sought the patronage of aristocrats and diplomats; the Swedish ambassador, the Count de Creutz, gave him the first encouragement by obtaining for him Marmontel's comedy *Le Huron*; it was performed with Grétry's music at the Comédie-Italienne (Aug. 20, 1768). From then on, he produced operas one after another, without interruption, even during the years of the French Revolution.

The merit of Grétry's operas lies in their melodies and dramatic expression. He was not deeply versed in the science of music; yet despite this lack of craftsmanship, he achieved fine effects of vocal and instrumental writing. His operas suffered temporary eclipse when Méhul and Cherubini entered the field, but public interest was revived by the magnificent tenor Elleviou in 1801. The changes in operatic music during the next 30 years caused the neglect of his works. Nevertheless, Gretry—the "Molière of music," as he was called—founded the school of French opéra-comique, of which Boieldieu, Auber, and Adam were worthy successors. He was greatly honored; he was elected a member of many artistic and learned institutions in France and abroad; the Prince-Bishop of Liège made him a privy councillor in 1784; a street in Paris was named for him in 1785; he was admitted to the Institut de France in 1795, as one of the first 3 chosen to represent the dept. of musical composition; he was also appointed inspector of the Paris Cons. in 1795, but resigned after just a few months. Napoleon made him a Chevalier of the Légion d'honneur in 1802, and granted him a pension of 4,000 francs in compensation for losses during the Revolution. His daughter, Lucille (real name, Angélique-Dorothée- Lucie; b. Paris, July 15, 1772; d.

there, Aug. 25, 1790), was a gifted musician; at the age of 13, with some assistance from her father, she composed an opera, *Le Mariage d'Antonio*, which was produced at the Opéra-Comique on July 29, 1786; her 2nd opera, *Toinette et Louis*, was produced on March 23, 1787. F.A. Gevaert, E. Fetis, A. Wotquenne, and others ed. a *Collection complète des oeuvres* (Leipzig, 1884–1936).

WORKS: DRAMATIC Opéras-comiques (all 1st perf. in Paris unless otherwise given): *Isabelle et Gertrude, ou Les Sylphes supposés* (Geneva, Dec. 1766); *Le Huron* (Aug. 20, 1768); *Lucile* (Jan. 5, 1769); *Le Tableau parlant* (Sept. 20, 1769); *Silvain* (Feb. 19, 1770); *Les Deux Avares* (Fontainebleau, Oct. 27, 1770); *L'Amitié à l'épreuve* (Fontainebleau, Nov. 13, 1770); *L'Ami de la maison* (Fontainebleau, Oct. 26, 1771); *Zémire et Azor* (Fontainebleau, Nov. 9, 1771); *Le Magnifique* (March 4, 1773); *La Rosière de Salency* (Fontainebleau, Oct. 23, 1773); *La Fausse Magie* (Feb. 1, 1775); *Matroco* (Nov. 3, 1777); *Le Jugement de Midas* (March 28, 1778); *Les Fausses Apparences, ou L'Amant jaloux* (Versailles, Nov. 20, 1778); *Les Événements imprévus* (Versailles, Nov. 11, 1779); *Aucassin et Nicolette, ou Les Moeurs du bon vieux temps* (Versailles, Dec. 30, 1779); *Théodore et Paulin* (Versailles, March 5, 1784); *Richard Coeur-de-lion* (Oct. 21, 1784); *Les Méprises par ressemblance* (Fontainebleau, Nov. 7, 1786); *Le Comte d'Albert* (Fontainebleau, Nov. 13, 1786); *Le Prisonnier anglais* (Dec. 26, 1787); *Le Rival confident* (June 26, 1788); *Raoul Barbe- bleue* (March 2, 1789); *Pierre le Grand* (Jan. 13, 1790); *Guillaume Tell* (April 9, 1791); *Cécile et Ermancé, ou Les Deux Couvents* (Jan. 16, 1792); *Basile, ou À trompeur, trompeur et demi* (Oct. 17, 1792); *Le Congrès des rois* (Feb. 26, 1794; in collaboration with others); *Joseph Barra* (June 5, 1794); *Callias, ou Nature et patrie* (Sept. 19, 1794); *Lisbeth* (Jan. 10, 1797); *Le Barbier du village, ou Le Revenant* (May 6, 1797); *Elisca, ou L'Amour maternel* (Jan. 1, 1799). Other: *La Vendemmiatrice*, 2 intermezzos (Rome, Carnival 1765); *Les Mariages samnites*, opéra (Jan. 1768?; rev. version, June 12, 1776); *Céphale et Procris, ou L'Amour conjugal*, opéra-ballet (Versailles, Dec. 30, 1773); *Amour pour amour*, 3 divertissements (Versailles, March 10, 1777); *Les Trois Âges de l'opéra*, prologue (April 27, 1778); *Andromaque*, opera (June 6, 1780); *Emilie, ou La Belle Esclave*, opéra-ballet (Feb. 22, 1781); *Colinette a la cour, ou La Double epreuve*, opéra (Jan. 1, 1782); *L'Embarras des richesses*, opera (Nov. 26, 1782); *Thalie au nouveau théâtre*, prologue (April 28, 1783); *La Caravane du Caire*, opéra-ballet (Fontainebleau, Oct. 30, 1783); *Panurge dans l'île des lanternes*, opera (Jan. 25, 1785); *Amphitryon*, opera (Versailles, March 15, 1786); *Aspasie*, opera (March 17, 1789); *Denys le tyran, maître d'école à Corinthe*, opera (Aug. 23, 1794); *La Fête de la raison*, later called *La Rosière républicaine, ou La Fête de la vertu*, opera (Sept. 2, 1794); *Anacréon chez Polycrate*, opera (Jan. 17, 1797); *Le Casque et les colombes*, opéra-ballet (Nov. 7, 1801); *Le Ménage*, later called *Delphis et Mopsa*, opera (Feb. 15, 1803). Several other stage works listed by Grétry were either never performed or were left unfinished.

WRITINGS: *Mémoires, ou Essais sur la musique* (Paris, 1789; 2nd ed., aug., 1797); *De la vérité, ce que nous fûmes, ce que nous, sommes, ce que nous devirons être* (Paris, 1801); *Reflexions d'un solitaire* (unfinished MS, 1801–13; ed. by L. Solvay and E. Closson, 4 vols., Brussels and Paris, 1919–22); *Méthode simple pour apprendre à préluder en peu de temps, avec toutes les ressources de l'harmonie* (Paris, 1903).

BIBL.: Comte de Livry, *Recueil de lettres écrites à G., ou à son sujet* (Paris, 1809); A.J. Grétry, *G. en famille ... précédées de son oraison funèbre par M. Bouilly* (Paris, 1814); F. Van Hulst, *G.* (Liège, 1842); L. de Saegher, *Notice biographique sur A. G.* (Brussels, 1869); E. Gregoir, *G.: Célèbre compositeur belge* (Brussels, 1883); J. Rongé and F. Delhasse, *G.* (Brussels, 1883); C. Gheude, *G.* (Liège, 1906); H. de Curzon, *G.* (Paris, 1907); E. Closson, *A.- M. G.* (Turnhout and Brussels, 1920); P. Long des Clavières, *La Jeunesse de G. et ses débuts à Paris* (Besançon, 1921); H. Wichmann, *G. und das musikalische Theater in Frankreich* (Halle, 1929); J. Bruyr, *G.* (Paris, 1931); J. Sauvenier, *A. G.* (Brussels, 1934); M. Degey, *A.-M. G.* (Brussels, 1939); S. Clercx, *G., 1741–1813* (Brussels, 1944); G. de Froidcourt, *G., Rouget de Lisle et la Marseillaise* (Liège, 1945); idem ed., *La Correspondance générale de G.* (Brussels, 1962); R. Jobe, *The Operas of A.- E.-M. G.* (diss., Univ. of Mich., 1965); D. Charlton, *G. and the Growth of Opéra Comique* (Cambridge, 1986); R. Mortier and H. Hasquin, eds., *Fêtes et musiques révolutionnaires: G. et Gossec* (Brussels, 1990); Y. Lenoir, ed., *A.-E.-M. G.: Lettres autographes conservées à la bibliothèque Royale Albert Ier* (Brussels, 1991); P. Vendrix, ed., *G. et l'Europe de l'opéra- comique* (Liège, 1992).—**NS/LK/DM**

Grevillius, Nils, Swedish conductor; b. Stockholm, March 7, 1893; d. Mariefred, Aug. 15, 1970. He was a violin student of Book at the Stockholm Cons. (1905–11), where he received 1st prize and the Prix Marteau, and later was a conducting student in Sondershausen and London. He began his career as concertmaster of the Royal Theater Orch. in Stockholm (1911–14). After serving as asst. conductor of the Stockholm Concert Soc. (1914–20), he conducted the Ballet Suédois in Paris (1922–23) and the Vienna Tonkünstlerverein (1923). Upon his return to Stockholm, he was conductor of the Royal Orch. (1924–53) and the Radio Orch. (1927–39), and also was court music director (1931–53).—**NS/LK/DM**

Grey, Madeleine, (real name, **Madeleine Nathalie Grumberg**), French mezzo-soprano; b. Villaines-la-Juhel, Mayenne, June 11, 1896; d. Paris, March 13, 1979. She was a student of Cortot (piano) and Hettich (voice) at the Paris Cons., and then devoted herself to a concert career. Fauré wrote his *Mirages* for her, and served as her accompanist at the cycle's premiere in Paris in 1919. Grey became particularly associated with the music of Ravel, who accompanied her in recordings of his *Chansons hébraïques* and *Chansons madécasses* in 1932. Canteloube dedicated his *Chants d'Auvergne* to her. Grey made many tours abroad, winning success in Italy, the U.S., and South America. She retired in 1952. While her command of diction and clarity of vocal timbre were especially suited to the French repertoire, she also championed works by Respighi, Malipiero, Villa Lobos, and other composers of her era.—**NS/LK/DM**

Grider, Rufus, American Moravian musician and historian; b. Bethlehem, Pa., 1817; d. date and place unknown (sometime after 1873 he wandered away from home and was never heard from again). Raised in the exceedingly rich musical culture of the American Moravians, Grider was a flutist in the Bethlehem orch. and a leading tenor; he was also a poet, artist, and antiquarian. His claim to remembrance stems from his unique and detailed portrayal of Moravian musical life in *Historical Notes on Music in Bethlehem, Pennyslvania, from 1741 to 1871* (Bethlehem, 1873).—**NS/LK/DM**

Griebling, Karen (Jean), American violist, violinist, conductor, teacher, and composer; b. Akron, Ohio, Dec. 31, 1957. She was trained at the Eastman School of Music in Rochester, N.Y. (B.M., 1980), the Univ. of Houston (M.M., 1982), and the Univ. of Tex. at Austin (D.M.A., 1986). She played in the Tex. Chamber Orch. (1980–81), the Houston Ballet Orch. (1980–82), the Corpus Christi Sym. Orch. (1985–86), and the Albany (N.Y.) Sym. Orch. (1986–87). In 1987 she joined the faculty of Hendrix Coll. in Conway, Ark., became a member of the Fort Smith Sym. Orch., and was made co-director of the Conway Civic Orch.; she also was a member of the Ark. String Quartet (from 1988). In 1990 she founded and became conductor of the Conway Chamber Orch.

WORKS: 6 string quartets (1970–92); Trio for 2 Violins and Viola (1973); Trio for Flute, Clarinet, and Bassoon (1976); 2 viola sonatas (1976, 1987); Oboe d'Amore Sonata (1980); *Johnny Appleseed*, ballet (1983); *Homage* for Winds (1983); Concerto Grosso (1985); *The House of Bernarda Alba*, opera (1986); *Gloria* for Chorus and Instrumental Ensemble (1988); *Sonata a Due* for Viola and Bass Trombone (1992); piano music; songs.
—NS/LK/DM

Grieg, Edvard (Hagerup), celebrated Norwegian composer; b. Bergen, June 15, 1843; d. there, Sept. 4, 1907. The original form of the name was Greig. His great-grandfather, Alexander Greig, of Scotland, emigrated to Norway about 1765, and changed his name to Grieg. Edvard Grieg received his first instruction in music from his mother, an amateur pianist. At the suggestion of the Norwegian violinist Ole Bull, young Grieg was sent to the Leipzig Cons. (1858), where he studied piano with Plaidy, Wenzel, and Moscheles, and theory with E.F. Richter, Robert Papperitz, Moritz Hauptmann, and Reinecke. He became immersed in the atmosphere of German Romanticism, with the esthetic legacy of Mendelssohn and Schumann; Grieg's early works are permeated with lyric moods related to these influences. In 1863 he went to Copenhagen, where he took a brief course of study with Niels Gade. In Copenhagen, he also met the young Norwegian composer Rikard Nordraak, with whom he organized the Euterpe Soc. for the promotion of national Scandinavian music, in opposition to the German influences dominating Scandinavian music. The premature death of Nordraak at the age of 23 (1866) left Grieg alone to carry on the project. After traveling in Italy, he returned to Norway, where he opened a Norwegian Academy of Music (1867), and gave concerts of Norwegian music; he was also engaged as conductor of the Harmonic Soc. in Christiania. In 1867 he married his cousin, the singer Nina Hagerup. At that time he had already composed his 2 violin sonatas and the first set of his *Lyric Pieces* for Piano, which used Norwegian motifs. On April 3, 1869, Grieg played the solo part in the world premiere of his Piano Concerto, which took place in Copenhagen. Thus, at the age of 25, he established himself as a major composer of his time. In 1874–75 he wrote incidental music to Ibsen's *Peer Gynt*; the 2 orch. suites arranged from this music became extremely popular. The Norwegian government granted him an annuity of 1,600 crowns, which enabled him to devote most of his time to composition. Performances of his works were given

in Germany with increasing frequency; soon his fame spread all over Europe. On May 3, 1888, he gave a concert of his works in London; he also prepared recitals of his songs with his wife. He revisited England frequently; received the honorary degree of Mus.Doc. from Cambridge (1894) and Oxford (1906). Other honors were membership in the Swedish Academy (1872), the French Academy (1890), etc. Despite his successes, Grieg was of a retiring disposition, and spent most of his later years in his house at Troldhaugen, near Bergen, avoiding visitors and shunning public acclaim. However, he continued to compose at a steady rate. His death, of heart disease, was mourned by all Norway; he was given a state funeral and his remains were cremated, at his own request, and sealed in the side of a cliff projecting over the fjord at Troldhaugen.

Grieg's importance as a composer lies in the strongly pronounced nationalism of his music; without resorting to literal quotation from Norwegian folk songs, he succeeded in re-creating their melodic and rhythmic flavor. In his harmony, he remained well within the bounds of tradition; the lyric expressiveness of his best works and the contagious rhythm of his dancelike pieces imparted a charm and individuality which contributed to the lasting success of his art. His unassuming personality made friends for him among his colleagues; he was admired by Brahms and Tchaikovsky. The combination of lyricism and nationalism in Grieg's music led some critics to describe him as "the Chopin of the North." He excelled in miniatures, in which the perfection of form and the clarity of the musical line are remarkable; the unifying purpose of Grieg's entire creative life is exemplified by his lyric pieces for piano. He composed 10 sets of these pieces in 34 years, between 1867 and 1901. His songs are distinguished by the same blend of Romantic and characteristically national inflections. In orch. composition, Grieg limited himself almost exclusively to symphonic suites, and arrangements of his piano pieces; in chamber music, his 3 violin sonatas, a Cello Sonata, and a String Quartet are examples of fine instrumental writing. F. Benestad was chairman of the Edvard Grieg Committee in Oslo from 1980, which oversaw the completion of Grieg's complete works in 20 vols. in 1995.

WORKS: DRAMATIC: Incidental music to Bjørnson's *Sigurd Jørsalfar* for Voice, Men's Chorus, and Orch., op.22 (Christiania, April 10, 1872), and to Ibsen's *Peer Gynt* for Solo Voices, Chorus, and Orch., op.23 (1874–75; Christiania, Feb. 24, 1876; rev. 1885 and 1891–92); *Szenen aus Olav Trygvason*, op.50 (1873; rev. and orchestrated 1889). **ORCH.:** Sym. in C minor (1864); *Im Herbst*, overture, op.11 (1866; rev. and orchestrated 1887; orig. for Piano, 4-Hands); *Trauermarsch zum Andenken an Richard Nordraak* for Military Band (1866; rev. 1878; orig. for Piano, 2-Hands); Piano Concerto in A minor, op.16 (1868; Copenhagen, April 3, 1869; rev. 1906–07); *Zwei nordische Weisen* for String Orch., op.63 (1869; orchestrated 1895; 1, *Im Volkston* [from the piano piece, op.17, no. 22]; 2, Kuhreigen [from the piano piece, op.17, no. 18]); *Drei Orchesterstücke aus Sigurd Jørsalfar*, op.56 (1872; rev. 1892); *Peer Gynt Suite* No. 1, op.46 (1874–75; rev. 1888); *Peer Gynt Suite* No. 2, op.55 (1874–75; rev. 1891 and 1892); *Zwei elegische Melodier* for String Orch., op.34 (1881; 1, *Herzwunden* [from the song, op.33, no. 3]; 2, *Letzter Frühling* [from the song, op.33, no. 2]); Piano Concerto in B minor (1882–83; unfinished); *Aus Holbergs Zeit*, suite for String Orch., op.40 (1884; orchestrated 1885; orig. for Piano, 2-Hands); *Altnorwegische Romanze mit Variationen*, op.51 (1891; orchestrated 1900; orig. for 2 Pianos); *Zwei Melodien* for String Orch., op.53 (1891; 1, *Norwegisch* [from the song, op.33, no. 12]; 2, *Erstes Begegnen* [from the song, op.21, no. 1]); *Lyrische Suite*, op.54 (1891; orchestrated 1904; based on the piano pieces, op.54, nos. 1, 2, 4, and 3); (4) *Symphonische Tänze*, op.64 (1896–97; also for Piano, 4-Hands); *Zwei lyrische Stücke* (1898; orig. for Piano, 2-Hands, op.68, nos. 4 and 5). **C H A M B E R :** String Quartet in D minor (1861; not extant); Violin Sonata No. 1, in F major, op.8 (1865); Violin Sonata No. 2, in G major, op.13 (1867); Intermezzo in A minor for Cello and Piano (1867); *Veed mandjaevningen* (Trial of Strength), march for Violin and Piano (1874; arranged from *Sigurd Jørsalfar*, op.22, no. 2); String Quartet in G minor, op.27 (1877–78); *Andante con moto* in C minor for Violin, Cello, and Piano (1878; 2nd movement from an unfinished piano trio); Cello Sonata in A minor, op.36 (1883); Violin Sonata No. 3, in C minor, op.45 (1886–87); String Quartet in F major (1891; unfinished). **P i a n o :** *Vier Stücke*, op.1 (1861); (6) *Poetiske tonebilder*, op.3 (1863); (4) *Humoresker*, op.6 (1865); Sonata in E major, op.7 (1865; rev. 1887); *Sørgemarsch over Rikard Nordraak* (Funeral March for Rikard Nordraak), in A minor (1866; also for Orch.); *Lyriske smaastykker* (Lyric Pieces), op.12 (1864–67); *Norske folkeviser og dandse*, op.17 (1869); *Folkelivsbilleder* (Pictures from Life in the Country), op.19 (1870–71); *Sex norske fjeldmelodier* (6 Norwegian Mountain Tunes, as arr. by Grieg; 1874–75; rev. 1886); *Ballade in Form von Variationen über eine norwegische Melodie* in G minor, op.24 (1875–76); *Fire albumblade*, op.28 (1864–78); *Improvisata over to norske folkeviser*, op.29 (1878); *Neue lyrische Stücke*, op.38 (1883); *Fra Holbergs tid* (From Holberg's Time), op.40 (1884; also for Orch.); *Klavierstücke nach eigenen Liedern*, op.41 (1884); *Lyrische Stücke*, op.43 (1886); *Norwegische Tänze*, op.35 (1887; arrangement of pieces for Piano, 4-Hands, op.35); *Walzer-Capricen* (1887; arrangement of pieces for Piano, 4-Hands, op.37); *Peer Gynt Suite* No. 1 (1888; arrangement of the orch. suite, op.46); *Lyrische Stücke*, op.47 (1885–88); *Altnorwegische Romanze mit Variationen*, op.51 (for two pianos, 1891) *Lyrische Stücke*, op.54 (1891; nos. 1 to 4 orchestrated as *Lyrische Suite*, 1904); *Gebet und Tempeltanz* (1893; arrangement from the Olav Trygvason scenes, op.50); *Peer Gynt Suite* No. 2 (1893; arrangement of the orch. suite, op.55); *Drei Orchesterstücke aus Sigurd Jørsalfar* (1893; arrangement of the orch. pieces, op.56); *Lyrische Stücke*, op.57 (1893); *Lyrische Stücke*, op.62 (1895); *Zwei nordische Weisen* (1896; arrangement of the orch. pieces, op.63); *Lyrische Stücke*, op.65 (1897); *Norske folkeviser*, op.66 (1897); *Drei Klavierstücke* (1891–98); *Lyrische Stücke*, op.68 (1898; nos. 4 and 5 also for Orch.); *Lyrische Stücke*, op.71 (1901); *Slåtter* (Norwegian Peasant Dances), op.72 (1902–03); *Stimmungen*, op.73 (1903–05). **P i a n o F o u r H a n d :** *Deux pièces symphoniques*, op.14 (1863–64); *I höst* (In Autumn), op.11 (1866; based on the song *Efteraarsstormen*, op.18, no. 4); *Sigurd Jørsalfar* (1874; 3 pieces from the incidental music, op.22); (4) *Norwegische Tänze*, op.35 (also for Piano, 2-Hands); (2) *Walzer-Capricen*, op.37 (1883; also for Piano, 2-Hands); *Peer Gynt Suite* No. 1 (1888; arrangement of the orch. suite, op.46); *Peer Gynt Suite* No. 2 (1893; arrangement of the orch. suite, op.55); *Drei Orchesterstücke aus Jørsalfar* (1893; arrangement of the orch. pieces, op.56); *Brudefølget dragger forbi* (The Bridal Procession Passes; 1893; arrangement of the piano piece, op.19, no. 2); *Zwei nordische Weisen* (1896; arrangement of the orch. pieces, op.63); (4) *Symphonische Tänze*, op.64 (1897; arrangement of the orch. pieces, op.64). **V O C A L : W i t h O r c h . :** Cantata for the unveiling of the Christie monument in Bergen, for Men's Voices and Military Band (1868); *Foran sydens kloster* (At a Southern Convent's Gate) for Soprano, Alto, Women's Voices, and Orch., op.20 (1871); *Bergliot*, melodrama for Declamation and Orch., op.42 (1871; orchestrated 1885); *Landkjending* (Land-sighting) for Baritone, Men's Chorus, Orch., and Organ ad libitum, op.31 (1872; rev. 1881); *Den bergtekne* (The Mountain Thrall) for Baritone, 2 Horns, and Strings, op.32 (1877–78); (6) Lieder for Voice and Orch. (1874–95). **C h o r a l** (all for Men's Voices unless otherwise given): *Børneskytten* (The Bear Hunt; 1867); *Aftenstemning* (Evening Mood; 1867); *Valgsang; Hvad siger de dog om dig* (Election Song: What Are They Saying about You; 1868); *Den norske sjømand* (The Norwegian Sailor; 1868–70); *Ved Welhavens baare* (At Welhaven's Bier; 1873); *Opsang til frihedsfolket i Norden* (Ballad of the Scandinavian Freedom Lovers; 1874); *Ved Halfdan Kjerulfs mindestotte* (At Halfdan Kjerulf's Monument), cantata for Tenor and Men's Voices (1874); *Album for mandssang*, arrangements of Norwegian folk songs, op.30 (1877–78); *Min dejligste tanke* (My Loveliest Thoughts; 1881); *Vort løsen* (Our Solution; 1881); *Sangerhilsen* (Salute in Song; 1883); *Holberg-kantate* for Baritone and Men's Voices (1884); *Flagvise* (Flag Song; 1893); *Vestanveir faedervise* (Wind from the West; 1896); *Kristianiensernes sangerhilsen* (Salute in Song from Kristiania) for Baritone and Chorus (1896); *Till Ole Bull: Hvor sodt at favnes* (To Ole Bull: How Sweet to Be Embraced; 1901); *Fire salmer* (4 Psalms) for Baritone and Mixed Voices, op.74 (1906); also a few unpubl. works. **S o n g s :** *Vier Lieder für Altstimme*, op.2 (1861); *Sex digte*, op.4 (1863–64); *Hjertets melodier* (The Heart's Melodies), op.5 (1863–64); *Romancer og ballader*, op.9 (1863–66); *Fire Romancer*, op.10 (1864); *Min lille fugl* (My Little Bird; 1865); *Romancer*, op.15 (1864–68); *Romancer og sange*, op.18 (1865–69); *Odalisken synger* (Song of the Odalisque; 1870); *Prinsessen* (The Princess; 1871); *Fire digte*, op.21 (1870–72); *Til Generalkonsul Tønsberg* (1873); *Sex digte*, op.25 (1876); *Fem digte*, op.26 (1876); *Tolv melodier*, op.33 (1873–80); *Romancer*, op.39 (1869–84); *Under juletraet* (Under the Christmas Tree; 1885); *Rejseminder: Fra fjeld og fjord* (Reminiscences: From Mountain and Fjord), op.44 (1886); *Sechs Lieder*, op.48 (1889); *Sechs Gedichte*, op.49 (1889); *Osterlied* (1889); *Norge*, op.58 (1893–94); *Elegiske digte*, op.59 (1893–94); *Digte*, op.60 (1893–94); *Sange*, op.61 (1894–95); *Haugtussa*, op.67 (1895); *Ave maria stella* (1899); *Fem digte*, op.69 (1900); *Fem digte*, op.70 (1900); *Efterladte sange*, I and II (1865–1905); also several unpubl. songs.

BIBL.: J. Foerster, *E.H. G.* (Prague, 1890); E. Closson, *E. G. et la musique scandinave* (Paris, 1892); D. Mason, *From G. to Brahms* (N.Y., 1902; 2nd ed., 1936); G. Schjelderup, *E. G. og hans vaerker* (Copenhagen, 1903); G. Capellen, *Die Freiheit oder Unfreiheit der Töne und Intervalle als Kriterium der Stimmführung nebst einem Anhang: G.-Analysen als Bestätigungsnachweis und Wegweiser der neuen Musiktheorie* (Leipzig, 1904; 2nd ed., 1917); H. Finck, *E. G.* (N.Y. and London, 1905; 2nd ed., rev. and aug., 1909, as *G. and His Music*); E. Lee, *E. G.* (London, 1908); G. Schjelderup and W. Niemann, *E. G.: Biographie und Würdigung seiner Werke* (Leipzig, 1908); E. Haraszti, *Das Nationalelement in G.s Musik* (Budapest, 1911); R. Stein, *G.: Eine Biographie* (Berlin, 1921); G. Hauch, ed., *Breve fra G.: Et udvalg* (Copenhagen, 1922); M. Beyer, ed., *Breve fra E. G. til Frants Beyer 1872–1907* (Christiania, 1923); P. de Stoecklin, *G.* (Paris, 1926); J. Röntgen, *G.* (The Hague, 1930); W. Bauer, *Die Harmonik in den Werken von E. G.* (diss., Univ. of Vienna, 1931); E. von Zschinsky-Troxler, ed., *E. G.: Briefe an die Verleger der Edition Peters 1866–1907* (Leipzig, 1932); Y. Rokseth, *G.* (Paris, 1933); D. Monrad Johansen, *E. G.* (Oslo, 1934; 3rd ed., 1956; Eng. tr., 1938); K. von Fischer, *G.s Harmonik und die nordländische Folklore* (Bern and Leipzig, 1938); K. Göllner, *Die Vokalmusik Norwegens als Grundlage des Schaffens*

E. G.s (diss., Univ. of Vienna, 1940); K. Fellerer, *E. G.* (Potsdam, 1942); A. Bakke, *E. G.* (Bern, 1943); *E. G. 1843–15. juni 1943: Til hundre- årsdagen for Hans Fødsel* (Bergen, 1943); F. Törnblom, *G.* (Stockholm, 1943); H. Ustvedt, *E. G.: Tondedikteren, nordmannen, demokraten* (Stockholm, 1943); L. Day, *G.* (N.Y., 1945); J. Grieg Cederblad, *E. G.* (Stockholm, 1946); A. Cherbuliez, *E. G.: Leben und Werk* (Zürich, 1947); G. Abraham, ed., *G.: A Symposium* (London, 1948); F. Bøe, *Trekk av E. G.s personlighet* (Oslo, 1949); J. Horton, *E. G.* (London, 1950); A. Vos, *Het leven van E. G. 1843–1907* (The Hague, 1951); D. Schjelderup-Ebbe, *A Study of G.'s Harmony: With Special Reference to His Contributions to Musical Impressionism* (Oslo, 1953); S. Jordan, *E. G.: En oversikt over hans liv og werker* (Bergen, 1954; suppl., 1959); H. Hurum, *I E. G.s verden* (Oslo, 1959); S. Torsteinson, *Troldhaugen: Nina og E. G.s hjem* (Oslo, 1959; 2nd ed., 1962); D. Schjelderup-Ebbe, *E. G. 1858–1867: With Special Reference to the Evolution of His Harmonic Style* (Oslo and London, 1964); B. Kortsen, *Four Unknown Cantatas by G.* (Bergen, 1972); J. Horton, *G.* (London, 1974); B. Schlotel, *G.* (London, 1986); C. Steel, *G.* (Kent, 1987); F. Benestad and D. Schjerlderup-Ebbe, *E. G.: Chamber Music: Nationalism-Universality-Individuality* (Oslo, 1993); E. Solås, *Ensom vandrer: Fantasier og refleksjoner i E. G.s landskap* (Oslo, 1993); B. Foster, *E. G.: The Choral Music* (Brookfield, Vt., 1999); H. Krellmann, *E. G.* (Reinbek, 1999).—NS/LK/DM

Grieg, Nina, (née **Hagerup**), Norwegian soprano; b. near Bergen, Nov. 24, 1845; d. Copenhagen, Dec. 9, 1935. Her father, Herman Hagerup, was a brother of Grieg's mother. Nina Hagerup studied singing with Helsted; she met **Edvard Grieg** in Copenhagen, and married him on June 11, 1867. Her interpretations of his songs elicited much praise from the critics.

BIBL.: I. Haavet, *N. G.: Kunstner og kunstnerhustru* (Oslo, 1998).—NS/LK/DM

Griend, Koos van de, Dutch pianist, conductor, music critic, and composer; b. Kampen, near Zwolle, Dec. 11, 1905; d. Amsterdam, Jan. 12, 1950. He studied in Amsterdam and in Berlin. Returning to Amsterdam in 1933, he developed energetic activities as a pianist, conductor, and music critic. He wrote 2 syms., a Cello Concerto, 3 string quartets, and a Quartet for 4 Horns.
—NS/LK/DM

Griepenkerl, Friedrich (Conrad), German pedagogue and writer on music; b. Peine, Dec. 10, 1782; d. Braunschweig, April 6, 1849. He was trained in philosophy in Göttingen, and also received lessons in piano, organ, and theory from Forkel. After teaching at the Fellenberg Inst. in Hofwyl (1808–16), he settled in Braunschweig and taught at the Catherine Academy (from 1816), the Carolinum (from 1821), and the Gymnasium (from 1828). He championed the cause of J. S. Bach.

WRITINGS (all publ. in Braunschweig): *Centifolien* (1820); *Lehrbuch der Ästhetik* (1826); *Lehrbuch der Logik* (1828; 2nd ed., 1831); *Briefe an einem jüngeren gelehrten Freund über Philosophie* (1832).—LK/DM

Griesbacher, Peter, German priest and composer; b. Egglham, March 25, 1864; d. Regensburg, Jan. 28, 1933. He studied theology, and was ordained a priest in 1886. From 1894 he was an instructor at the Franciscan church in Regensburg. He ed. various publications for Catholic church music, and also composed 40 masses, secular cantatas, and songs (about 250 opus numbers). He began as a composer in the strict style of contrapuntal writing, but his later works, in which he applied modern harmonies to Gregorian melodies, aroused considerable opposition. He publ. several manuals: *Lehrbuch des Kontrapunkts* (1910), *Kirchenmusikalische Stilistik und Formenlehre* (3 vols., 1912–13), and *Glockenmusik* (1926).

BIBL.: M. Tremmel, *P. G.* (Passau, 1935).—NS/LK/DM

Griffes, Charles Tomlinson, outstanding American composer; b. Elmira, N.Y., Sept. 17, 1884; d. N.Y., April 8, 1920. He began piano lessons at an early age with his sister; about 1899 he became a piano student of Mary Selena Broughton, an instructor at Elmira Coll. Thanks to Broughton's financial assistance, Griffes was able to go to Berlin in 1903 to pursue his training at the Stern Cons. with Ernst Jedliczka and Gottfried Galston (piano), Philippe Rufer and Humperdinck (composition), and Max Lowengard and Klatte (counterpoint). After private composition lessons with Humperdinck (1905–06), he again studied piano with Galston (1906–07). Upon his return to the U.S. in 1907, he was made director of music at the Hackley School in Tarrytown, N.Y. Until about 1911 Griffes' works followed along the path of German Romanticism. He then pursued his fascination with impressionism in a number of piano pieces and songs. His subsequent interest in the potentialities of the oriental scale resulted in such scores as his Japanese pantomime *Sho-jo* (1917) and the orch. version of his remarkable piano piece *The Pleasure-Dome of Kubla Khan* (1917). In his last works, such as his Piano Sonata (1917–18), he revealed a strong individual style tending toward extreme dissonance.

WORKS: DRAMATIC: *The Kairn of Koridwen*, dance drama (1916; N.Y., Feb. 10, 1917); *Sho-jo*, Japanese pantomime (Atlantic City, N.J., Aug. 5, 1917); *The White Peacock*, ballet (N.Y., June 22, 1919; arrangement of the piano piece, 1915); *Salut au monde*, festival drama (1919; N.Y., April 22, 1922). **ORCH.:** Overture (c. 1905); *Symphonische Phantasie* (1907); *The Pleasure-Dome of Kubla Khan* (1917; Boston, Nov. 28, 1919; arrangement of the piano piece, 1912); *Notturno für Orchester* (c. 1918; Philadelphia, Dec. 19, 1919); *Poem* for Flute and Orch. (1918; N.Y., Nov. 16, 1919); *Bacchanale* (Philadelphia, Dec. 19, 1919; arrangement of the *Scherzo* for Piano, 1913); *Clouds* (Philadelphia, Dec. 19, 1919; arrangement of the piano piece, 1916); *The White Peacock* (Philadelphia, Dec. 19, 1919; arrangement of the piano piece, 1915); *Nocturne* (1919; arrangement of the 2nd movement of the Piano Sonata, 1917–18). **CHAMBER:** Movement for String Quartet (1903); *3 Tone-Pictures: The Lake at Evening, The Vale of Dreams*, and *The Night Winds* for Woodwind and Harp (1915; also for Wind Quintet, String Quintet, and Piano, 1919; arrangements of the piano pieces, 1910–12); *Vivace (Allegro assai quasi presto)* for String Quartet (1917); *2 Sketches Based on Indian Themes: Lento e mesto* and *Allegro giocoso* for String Quartet (1918–19); *Allegro energico ma maestoso* for String Quartet (1919). **Piano:** *6 Variations* (1898); *Mazurka* (1898–1900); *4 Preludes* (1899–1900); 5 sonatas (c. 1904; c. 1910; c. 1911; c. 1912; 1917–18, N.Y., Feb. 26, 1918, 2nd movement orchestrated as *Nocturne*, 1919); *3 Tone-Pictures* (1910–12); (8) *Fantasy Pieces* (1912–15), including *Scherzo* (1913; orchestrated as *Bacchanale,* 1919); (4) *Roman Sketches: The White Peacock* (1915; orchestrated 1919), *Nightfall* (1916), *The Fountain of the Acqua Paola* (1916), and *Clouds* (1916; orchestrated 1919); *3 Preludes* (1919). **VOCAL:** (3) *Tone-Images* (1912–14); *2 Rondels* (c. 1914); *4 Impressions* (1914–16); *3 Poems* (1916); *5 Poems of Ancient China and Japan* (1916–17; N.Y., Nov. 1, 1917); *2 Poems* (1917–18); *3 Poems of Fiona MacLeod* (1918; N.Y., March 22, 1919; orchestrated 1918; Wilmington, Del., March 24, 1919).

BIBL.: J. Howard, *C.T. G.* (N.Y., 1923); E. Maisel, *C.T. G.: The Life of an American Composer* (N.Y., 1943); G. Conrey, *The Published Songs of C.T. G.: A Stylistic Examination* (diss., Chicago Musical Coll., 1955); D. Boda, *The Music of C. G.* (diss., Fla. State Univ., 1962); H. Pratt, *The Complete Piano Works of C.T. G.* (diss., Boston Univ., 1975); D. Anderson, *C.T. G.: An Annotated Bibliography-Discography* (Detroit, 1977); idem, *The Works of C.T. G.: A Descriptive Catalogue* (Ann Arbor, 1984); idem, *C.T. G.: A Life in Music* (Washington, D.C., 1993).—**NS/LK/DM**

Griffes, Elliot, American pianist, teacher, and composer; b. Boston, Jan. 28, 1893; d. Los Angeles, June 8, 1967. He studied at Ithaca Coll. (graduated, 1913), then with Horatio Parker at the Yale Univ. School of Music (1915–16), and with Chadwick, Stuart Mason, and Pattison at the New England Cons. of Music in Boston (1917–18); won a Juilliard scholarship (1922) and a Pulitzer scholarship (1931). He was active as a recitalist; also taught in various institutions, including Grinnell Coll. in Iowa (1920–22), the Brooklyn Settlement School (1923–24), the St. Louis School of Music (head of theory dept., 1935–36), and the Westchester Cons. in White Plains, N.Y. (director, 1942–43). He settled in Los Angeles as a composer of film scores. He wrote works in ingratiatingly Romantic colors.

WORKS: DRAMATIC: *The Blue Scarab,* operetta (1934); *Port of Pleasure,* opera (Los Angeles, June 29, 1963). **ORCH.:** *A Persian Fable* (1925); *Paul Bunyan, Colossus,* symphonic poem (1926–34); 2 syms.: No. 1 (1931) and No. 2, *Fantastic Pursuit,* for Strings (1941); *Yon Green Mountain,* suite (1943); *Montevallo,* concerto grosso for Organ, Piano, and Strings (1945). **CHAMBER:** 3 string quartets (1926, 1930, 1937); Violin Sonata (1931); *To the Sun,* symphonic fragment for Piano Trio (1940); Suite for Piano Trio (1941); *The Aztec Flute* for Flute and Piano Trio (1942); *The Fox and the Crow* for Chamber Ensemble (1950); piano pieces. **VOCAL:** Song cycles and solo songs.—**NS/LK/DM**

Griffiths, Paul, English music critic, writer on music, and librettist; b. Bridgend, Glamorgan, Wales, Nov. 24, 1947. He received his education at Lincoln Coll., Oxford. From 1971 he wrote music criticism for many publications. He was chief music critic of *The Times* of London from 1982 to 1992, and then of the *New Yorker* from 1992. He served as area ed. for 20th century music for the *New Grove Dictionary of Music and Musicians* (1980) and the *New Oxford Companion to Music* (1983). Among his books are *A Concise History of Avant-Garde Music* (1978; rev. ed., 1994, as *Modern Music: A Concise History*), *Modern Music: The Avant-Garde Since 1945* (1981; rev. ed., 1995, as *Modern Music and After*), *The Rake's Progress* (1982), *The String Quartet* (1983), *Bartók* (1984), *New Sounds, New Personalities: British Composers*

of the 1980s (1985), *An Encyclopedia of 20th Century Music* (1986), and *Stravinsky* (1992). He also wrote the librettos for Tan Dun's opera *Marco Polo* (1993–94) and Elliott Carter's opera *What Next?* (1999).—**NS/LK/DM**

Grignon, Juan Lamote de
See **Lamote de Grignon, Juan**

Grignon, Ricardo Lamote de
See **Lamote de Grignon y Ribas, Ricardo**

Grigny, Nicolas de, French organist and composer; b. Rheims (baptized), Sept. 8, 1672; d. there, Nov. 30, 1703. He was born into a musical family; his father and grandfather were organists in Rheims. After going to Paris, he served as organist at the abbey church of St. Denis (1693–95). He then returned to Rheims, where he became cathedral organist about 1697. He publ. *Premier livre d'orgue contenant une messe et les hymnes des principalles festes de l'année* (Paris, 1699; modern ed. by N. Dufourcq and N. Pierront, Paris, 1953).

BIBL.: W. Maul, *The Organ Works of N. d.G.* (diss., Univ. of Washington, 1965).—**NS/LK/DM**

Grigoriu, Theodor, Romanian composer; b. Galaţi, July 25, 1926. He studied violin with Enacovici at the Bucharest Cons. (1935–36), and, after private composition lessons with Jora (1949–54), he studied composition at the Moscow Cons. with Khatchaturian and Golubev (1954–55). In 1943 he won the George Enesco Prize for Composition, in 1975 the prize of the Romanian Academy, and in 1969, 1974, and 1985 prizes of the Romanian Composers's Union.

WORKS: DRAMATIC: Film scores. **ORCH.:** *Sinfonia cantabile* (1950; rev. 1966); *Dans tătar* (1953); *Theatrical Suite in the Classical Style* for Chamber Orch. (1956); *Symphonic Variations,* on a melody by Anton Pann (1955; Bucharest, Jan. 21, 1956); Concerto for Double Chamber Orch. and Solo Oboe (1957); *Hommage to Enesco* for 4 Groups of Violins (1960); *Melodic infinită* for Chamber String Orch. (1969); *Tristia* (1974); *Pastorale şi idile transilvane* (1984; 2nd version, 1986); Violin Concerto (1993; Indianapolis, May 1, 1994). **CHAMBER:** String Quartet (1943); Piano Trio (1943); *The River Arges Flows On,* suite for String Quartet (1953). **VOCAL:** 2 cantatas: *Cantata pentru 23 August* (1951) and *Oda orasului meu* (Ode to My City; 1963; rev. 1971); *Vis cosmic* (Cosmic Dream), symphonic poem for Vocalizing Tenor or Electronic Instrument and Orch. (1959; Bucharest, Oct. 28, 1965); *Elegie pontică* for Bass-Baritone, Women's Chorus, and Chamber Orch., after Ovid (Bucharest, June 24, 1969); *Vocalizele mării,* choral sym. (1984); songs.—**NS/LK/DM**

Grimaud, Hélène, French pianist; b. Aix-en-Provence, Nov. 7, 1964. She studied at the Aix-en-Provence Cons., with Pierre Barbizet at the Marseilles Cons., and with Jacques Rouvier at the Paris Cons. (1982–85; premier prix, 1985). Following her highly successful debut as a soloist with the Orchestre de Paris in 1988, she was engaged as a soloist with many of the world's foremost orchs., among them the Berlin Phil., the Gewandhaus Orch. of Leipzig, the London Sym.

Orch., the Israel Phil., the NHK Sym. Orch. of Tokyo, the Cleveland Orch., the Los Angeles Phil., the Philadelphia Orch., the San Francisco Sym., the Boston Sym. Orch., and the N.Y. Phil. As a recitalist, she has appeared throughout Europe and North America. In addition to her idiomatic interpretations of the French repertoire, Grimaud has won accolades for her performances of Beethoven, Schumann, Chopin, Liszt, Brahms, Strauss, and Rachmaninoff.—LK/DM

Grimes, Tiny (Lloyd), jazz guitarist and singer; b. Newport News, Va., July 7, 1916; d. N.Y., March 4, 1989. He started as a drummer, then worked as a pianist and dancer in Washington, D.C. (1935). He continued with this career until 1939 (with a residency at The Rhythm Club, N.Y., 1938); he then began playing guitar (originally a four-string tenor model). By the following year he was working professionally (on amplified guitar) with The Cats and a Fiddle, leaving in 1941. He went to Calif. and worked Art Tatum's trio until 1944, then led a trio at the Tondelayo Club, N.Y. He worked in Dizzy Gillespie's group, which replaced the Benny Goodman Quintet (1945) in Billy Rose's *7 Lively Arts* (a Broadway revue). His "Midnight Special" on Atlantic with Red Prysock was a R&B hit in 1948. He led The Rocking Highlanders (who wore kilts and tams) in N.Y. and Cleveland during the late 1940s; toured with his own group in the 1950s, then had residencies in Philadelphia. He led at the Village Gate, N.Y. (1962), Purple Manor (1963), and elsewhere. After an illness, he resumed playing at the Copra Lounge (1966). He toured France (1968, 1970) and worked with Earl Hines (1972). He led a group during the 1970s and starred at many jazz festivals. He was very active as a sideman throughout his career.

DISC.: *Blues Groove* (1958); *Callin' the Blues* (1958); *Big Time Guitar* (1962); *Profoundly Blue* (1973); *Some Groovy Fours* (with L. Glenn; 1974). Charlie Parker, "Romance without Finance," "Red Cross" (1944).—JC/LP

Grimm, Carl Hugo, American organist and composer; b. Zanesville, Ohio, Oct. 31, 1890; d. Cincinnati, Oct. 25, 1978. He studied music with his father, then held positions as organist in Cincinnati, where he also taught composition at the Cons. (1907–31).

WORKS: ORCH.: *Erotic Poem* (1927); *Thanatopsis* (1928); *Abraham Lincoln,* "character portrait" (1930); *Montana,* symphonic poem (Cincinnati, March 26, 1943); *An American Overture* (Cincinnati, Feb. 15, 1946); Trumpet Concerto (1948); Sym. (1950); *Pennsylvania Overture* (1954). **CHAMBER:** *Byzantine Suite* for 10 Instruments (1930); *Little Serenade* for Wind Quintet (1934); Cello Sonata (1945); many organ pieces; works for ensembles of multiple flutes. **VOCAL:** *Gothic Mass* (1970); many anthems; songs.—NS/LK/DM

Grimm, Friedrich Melchior, Baron von, German writer on music; b. Regensburg, Sept. 25, 1723; d. Gotha, Dec. 19, 1807. He went to Paris in 1750 and remained there until the Revolution, frequenting literary and musical circles and taking an active part in all controversies. His "Lettre sur Omphale" in the *Mercure de France* (1752) took the side of Italian opera in the

"guerre des bouffons," but some years later he upheld Gluck against the Italian faction supporting Piccinni. He ed. the *Correspondance littéraire, philosophique et critique,* which offers important data on French opera (16 vols., Paris, 1877–82). He befriended the Mozarts on their first visit to Paris (see the many references to him in E. Anderson, *Letters of Mozart and His Family,* London, 1938; 2nd ed., rev., 1966, by A. Hyatt King and M. Carolan; 3rd ed., rev., 1985). He also wrote a satire on J. Stamitz, *Le Petit Prophète de Boehmisch-Broda*; reproduced in Eng. in O. Strunk's *Source Readings in Music History* (N.Y., 1950).

BIBL.: Carlez, *G. et la musique de son temps* (1872); E. Scherer, *M. G.* (1887).—NS/LK/DM

Grimm, Heinrich, German composer; b. Holzminden, c. 1593; d. Braunschweig, July 10, 1637. He studied with Michael Praetorius, then studied theology at the Univ. of Helmstedt. In 1619 he became rector of the Magdeburg town school. In 1631, when the town was destroyed, he fled with his family to Braunschweig, where he became a cantor at the church of St. Catherine; subsequently was a cantor at St. Andreas's church (1632–37). He was an exponent of the concerted style, with thoroughbass, at that time still a novel technique in Germany. His extant works include masses, Psalms, Passions, motets, and several pedagogical works. He publ. *Unterricht, wie ein Knabe nach der alten Guidonischen Art zu solmisieren leicht angeführt werden kann* (Magdeburg, 1624) and *Instrumentum Instrumentorum, hoc est, Monochordum, vel potius Dodecachordum* (MS, 1629) and prepared a combined ed. of *Melopoeia seu melodiae condendae ratio* by Calvisius and *Pleiades Musicae* by Baryphonus (Magdeburg, 1630).

BIBL.: H. Lorenzen, *Der Cantor H. G. (1593–1637): Sein Leben und seine Werke mit Beitrag zur Musikgeschichte Magdeburgs und Braunschweigs* (diss., Univ. of Hamburg, 1940). —NS/LK/DM

Grimm, Julius Otto, German conductor and composer; Pernau, Latvia, March 6, 1827; d. Münster, Dec. 7, 1903. He studied philosophy at the Univ. of Dorpat and was a pupil of Moscheles and Hauptmann in Leipzig, where he was befriended by Brahms and Joachim. In 1860 he became conductor in Münster. He wrote a Sym. (1874), Suite for String Orch., song cycles, and piano pieces.

BIBL.: F. Ludwig, *J.O. G.* (Leipzig, 1925).—NS/LK/DM

Grimm, Karl, German cellist and composer; b. Hildburghausen, April 28, 1819; d. Freiburg, Jan. 9, 1888. He was for half a century 1st cellist at the Wiesbaden Opera. He composed many cello pieces, some of which attained considerable popularity.—NS/LK/DM

Grimm, (Karl Konstantin) Louis (Ludwig), German harpist and composer; b. Berlin, Feb. 17, 1820; d. there, May 23, 1882. He studied with Josef Hasselmans at the Stuttgart Cons. and Elias Parish Alvars in Leipzig. In 1844 he was made principal harpist of the royal chapel in Berlin, and in 1869 Königliche Concertmeister. He enjoyed a considerable reputation as a harp soloist. He also wrote various pieces for his instrument.—NS/LK/DM

Grisar, Albert, Belgian composer; b. Antwerp (of German-Belgian parents), Dec. 26, 1808; d. Asnières, near Paris, June 15, 1869. He studied for a short time (1830) with Reicha in Paris. Returning to Antwerp, he brought out his opera *Le Mariage impossible* (Brussels, March 4, 1833), and obtained a government subsidy for further study in Paris. On April 26, 1836, he produced *Sarah* at the Opéra-Comique; then *L'An mille* (June 23, 1837), *La Suisse à Trianon* (March 8, 1838), *Lady Melvil* (Nov. 15, 1838, with Flotow), *L'Eau merveilleuse* (Jan. 31, 1839, with Flotow), *Le Naufrage de la Méduse* (May 31, 1839, with Flotow and Pilati), *Les Travestissements* (Nov. 16, 1839), and *L'Opéra à la cour* (July 16, 1840, with Boieldieu Jr.). In 1840 he went to Naples for further serious study under Mercadante; returning to Paris in 1848, he brought out *Gilles ravisseur* (Feb. 21, 1848), *Les Porcherons* (Jan. 12, 1850), *Bonsoir, M. Pantalon* (Feb. 19, 1851), *Le Carillonneur de Bruges* (Feb. 20, 1852), *Les Amours du diable* (March 11, 1853), *Le Chien du jardinier* (Jan. 16, 1855), *Voyage autour de ma chambre* (Aug. 12, 1859), *Le Joaillier de St. James* (9 songs from *Lady Melvil*; Feb. 17, 1862), *La Chatte merveilleuse* (March 18, 1862), *Les Bégaiements d'amour* (Dec. 8, 1864), and *Les Douze Innocentes* (Oct. 19, 1865). He left, besides, 12 finished and unfinished operas; also dramatic scenes, over 50 romances, etc. His statue (by Brackeleer) was placed in the vestibule of the Antwerp Theater in 1870.

BIBL.: A. Pougin, *A. G.* (Paris, 1870).—NS/LK/DM

Grisart, Charles Jean Baptiste, French composer; b. Paris, Sept. 29, 1837; d. Compiègne, March 11, 1904. He is known for his light operas, the most popular of which were *La Quenouille de verre* (1873), *Les Trois Margots* (1877), *Le Pont d'Avignon* (1878), *Les Poupées de l'Infante* (1881), *Le Bossu* (1888), *Le Petit Bois* (1893), and *Voilà le roi!* (1894). He also wrote many piano pieces, masses, melodies, etc., and a quantity of transcriptions. —NS/LK/DM

Grisey, Gérard, French composer and teacher; b. Belfort, June 17, 1946; d. Paris, Nov. 11, 1998. He studied at the Trossingen Cons. (1963–65) and at the Paris Cons., where he was a student of Messiaen (1968–72). He also studied with Dutilleux at the École Normal de Musique in Paris (1968), and attended the summer courses at the Accademia Musicale Chigiana in Siena (1969) and of Ligeti, Stockhausen, and Xenakis in Darmstadt (1972). From 1972 to 1974 he held a scholarship at the Villa Medici in Rome, and then studied with Emile Leipp at the Univ. of Paris VI (1974–75). In 1980 he was active with IRCAM in Paris and was in Berlin on a Deutscher Akademischer Austauschdienst fellowship. From 1982 to 1986 he taught at the Univ. of Calif. at Berkeley, and in 1987 he joined the faculty of the Paris Cons. Grisey's music is obsessed with timbre as part of a "time-sound dynamic" found in the unique acoustic field in which his compositions reside. His use of instrumental color was metaphysical, intending to draw the listener's attention to one's own impressions of sounds, which Grisey described as being like a "cluster of forces that have their being in the realm of time," living like cells that come into being and then die.

WORKS: ORCH *Vagues, Chemins, le Souffle* for Clarinet and 2 Orchs. (1970–72); *D'eau et de pierre* for 2 Instrumental Groups (1972); *Dérives* for 2 Orch. Groups (1973–74; Paris, Oct. 31, 1974); *Les Espaces Acoustiques,* cycle of 6 pieces: *Prologue, Périodes, Partiels, Modulations, Transitoires,* and *Epilogue* (1974–85; *Modulations,* Paris, March 9, 1978; 1st complete perf., *Epilogue* excepted, Venice, Oct. 5, 1981; *Epilogue,* Venice, Sept. 28, 1985); *Le Temps et l'écume* for 4 Percussionists, 2 Synthesizers, and Chamber Orch. (1988–89; Radio France, Paris, Dec. 11, 1989). **CHAMBER:** *Echanges* for Prepared Piano and Double Bass (1968); *Charme* for Clarinet (1969); *Mégalithes* for Brass (1969); *Perichoresis* for 3 Chamber Groups (1969–70); *Périodes* for 7 Players (Rome, June 11, 1974); *Partiels* for Chamber Ensemble (1975; Paris, March 4, 1976); *Prologue* for Viola (1976; Paris, Jan. 16, 1978; also for Viola and Live Electronics, Darmstadt, Aug. 7, 1978); *Sortie vers la lumière du jour* for Electric Organ and 14 Players (Donaueschingen, Oct. 28, 1978); *Jour, contre-jour* for Electric Organ, 13 Players, and Tape (1978–79; Radio France, Paris, March 9, 1979); *Tempus ex machina* for 6 Percussionists (1979; Montreal, Nov. 13, 1980); *Solo pour deux* for Clarinet and Trombone (1981; Venice, Oct. 1, 1982); *Anubis-Nout* for Contrabass Clarinet (1983; Latina, June 16, 1984; also for Bass or Baritone Saxophone, Turin, May 22, 1990); *Talea* for Violin, Cello, Flute, Clarinet, and Piano (1986; Radio France, Paris, Jan. 13, 1987); *Accords perdue* for 2 Horns (1987; Abbazia di Fossanova, June 23, 1988); *Le Noir de l'Etoile* for 6 Percussionists and Tape (1989–90; Brussels, March 16, 1991); *Vortex Temporum I, II,* and *III* for Piano and 5 Instruments (1994–96; 1st complete perf., Witten, April 26, 1996); *Stèle* for 2 Percussionists (Radio France, Paris, Feb. 5, 1995). **VOCAL:** *Initiation* for Baritone, Trombone, and Double Bass (1970); *Les Chants de l'Amour* for Chorus and Synthesizer (1982–84; Paris, June 3, 1985); *L'Icône paradoxale* for 2 Women's Voices and Orch. (1993–94; Los Angeles, Jan. 18, 1996); *Quatre Chants pour franchir le Seuil* for Soprano and Chamber Orch. (1997–98; London, Feb. 3, 1999). **OTHER:** *Wolf Lieder: In der Frühe, Um Mitternacht, Das verlassene Mägdlein,* and *Nun wandre, Maria,* as orchestrated by Grisey for Mezzosoprano and Instrumental Ensemble (Radio France, Paris, Nov. 23, 1997).—LK/DM

Grishkat, Hans (Adolf Karl Willy), German conductor and pedagogue; b. Hamburg, Aug. 29, 1903; d. Stuttgart, Jan. 10, 1977. He studied at the Univ. of Tübingen and at the Hochschule für Musik in Stuttgart. In 1924 he organized the Reutlingen Chorale. In 1931 he formed the Swabian Chorale, and in 1936 the Grishkat Chorale in Stuttgart, gaining a fine reputation as a choral conductor in Germany. From 1945 to 1950 he led the Swabian Sym. Orch. in Reutlingen. In 1946 he was appointed instructor of choral conducting at the Hochschule für Musik in Stuttgart. From 1968 until his death he led the orch. conducting classes there.—NS/LK/DM

Grisi, Giuditta, Italian mezzo-soprano, sister of **Giulia Grisi;** b. Milan, July 28, 1805; d. Robecco d'Oglio, near Cremona, May 1, 1840. She studied at the Milan Cons., making her first appearance in Vienna in 1826. Afterward she sang with success in Italy and in Paris at the Théâtre-Italien under Rossini's management, retiring in 1838, after her marriage to Count Barni. Bellini wrote for her the part of Romeo in *I Capuleti ed i Montecchi* (Venice, March 11, 1830); her sister sang Juliet. —NS/LK/DM

Grisi, Giulia, celebrated Italian soprano, sister of **Giuditta Grisi;** b. Milan, July 28, 1811; d. Berlin, Nov. 29, 1869. She received training from her sister and from her aunt, Grassini. She also studied with Celli and Guglielmi, with Marliani in Milan, and with Giacomelli in Bologna. In 1828 she made her operatic debut as Emma in Rossini's *Zelmira* in Bologna. She soon won the admiration of Bellini, who wrote the role of Juliet for her in his *I Capuleti ed I Montecchi*, which role she created in Venice on March 11, 1830. In 1831 she made her debut at Milan's La Scala in Strepponi's *L'ullà di Bassor*, where she then created Adalgisa in Bellini's *Norma* (Dec. 26, 1831) and Adelia in Donizetti's *Ugo, conte di Parigi* (March 13, 1832). Dissatisfied with her La Scala contract and unable to break it legally, she fled to Paris. On Oct. 16, 1832, she made her debut there with phenomenal success at the Théâtre-Italien as Rossini's Semiramide. She sang there regularly from 1834 to 1846, creating Elvira in Bellini's *I Puritani* (Jan. 24, 1835), Elena in Donizetti's *Marin Faliero* (March 12, 1835), and Norina in the latter's *Don Pasquale* (Jan. 3, 1843). On April 18, 1834, she made her London debut as Rossini's Ninetta at the King's Theatre, and subsequently sang regularly in the British capital with remarkable success. On April 6, 1847, she appeared as Semiramide in the first production of the newly organized Royal Italian Opera at London's Covent Garden. She continued to sing there until her farewell appearance on July 24, 1861. In 1836 she married, but later separated from her husband. In 1839 she met the tenor Mario in London, with whom she became intimate. Although she was never divorced from her husband, she continued to live with Mario as his wife. They made a tour of the U.S. in 1854–55. Her outstanding vocal gifts were matched by her compelling dramatic talent. Her other famous roles included Alice in *Robert le diable*, Valentine, Anna Bolena, Lucrezia Borgia, and Leonora in *Il Trovatore*.

BIBL.: E. Forbes, *Mario and G.* (London, 1985). —NS/LK/DM

Grist, Reri, black American soprano; b. N.Y., Feb. 29, 1934. While still a child, she appeared as a dancer and singer in musicals. She was educated at N.Y.'s H.S. of Music and Art, and then at Queens Coll.; her voice teacher was Claire Gelda. In 1957 she sang Consuelo in the Broadway staging of *West Side Story*. In 1959 she made her operatic debut as Blöndchen at the Sante Fe Opera, and then sang with the N.Y.C. Opera. In 1960 she made her European debut in Cologne as the Queen of the Night, and then sang in Zürich as Zerbinetta. She appeared as Despina at the Glyndebourne Festival in 1962, the year she also made her debut at London's Covent Garden as the Queen of Shemakha. In 1965 she sang Blöndchen at the Salzburg Festival. On Feb. 25, 1966, she made her Metropolitan Opera debut in N.Y. as Rossini's Rosina, returning for the 1968–73 and 1977–78 seasons. Her operatic engagements also took her to many other music centers in North America and Europe. She also sang widely as a soloist with orchs. and as a recitalist. Among her other roles were Susanna, Adina, Norina, Gilda, Oscar, and Sophie.—NS/LK/DM

Griswold, Putnam, American bass-baritone; b. Minneapolis, Dec. 23, 1875; d. N.Y., Feb. 26, 1914. He went to London to study at the Royal Coll. of Music and with A. Randegger. After making his operatic debut at Covent Garden as Leonato in Stanford's *Much Ado About Nothing* (1901), he pursued his training in Paris with Bouhy, in Frankfurt am Main with Stockhausen, and in Berlin with Emerich. In 1904 he sang at the Berlin Royal Opera; after touring the U.S. with Savage's opera company as Gurnemanz in an English language production of *Parsifal* (1904–05), he returned to Berlin to sing with fine success at the Royal Opera (1906–11). On Nov. 23, 1911, he made his Metropolitan Opera debut in N.Y. as Hagen, and sang there until his death. He was highly admired as a Wagnerian, being notably successful as Wotan, King Marke, Pogner, and Daland. —NS/LK/DM

Grobe, Charles, German-American pianist, teacher, and composer; b. probably in Saxe-Weimar, c. 1817; d. Stroudsburg, Pa., Oct. 20, 1879. He emigrated to the U.S. about 1839. From 1840 to 1861 he was head of the music dept. at Wesleyan Female Coll. in Wilmington, Del. After running his own Musical and Educational Agency there (1862–70), he taught at Pennington (N.J.) Seminary and Female Collegiate Inst. (1870–74) and at Centenary Collegiate Inst. in Hackettstown, N.J. (1874–79). He publ. a *New Method for the Pianoforte* (1859) and *Concordia: A Collection of Vocal Music* (1861), both for female seminaries. He also contributed articles to many American music journals. Grobe was a prolific composer of piano music, producing a grand total of 1,998 opus numbers. He was particularly adept at creating "variations brillantes" on themes by the great German masters and on popular songs. Among his engaging titles were *Buds and Blossoms* (1851–67; 150 sets of variations) and *Beauties of Beethoven* (1857–60; 6 sets of variations). His *Music of the Union* (1861) was also a popular collection.

BIBL.: A. Kane Jr., *The Piano Music of C. G.* (thesis, Ohio Univ., 1973).—LK/DM

Grobe, Donald (Roth), American tenor; b. Ottawa, Ill., Dec. 16, 1929; d. Berlin, April 1, 1986. He attended the Mannes Coll. of Music in N.Y. and also received vocal coaching from Robert Long, Martial Singher, Robert Weede, and Marguerite von Winterfeldt. In 1952 he made his operatic debut as Borsa in *Rigoletto* in Chicago, and then sang in musicals, on television, and in concerts in N.Y. After singing opera in Krefeld/Mönchengladbach (1956–57) and Hannover (1957–60), he was a member of the Berlin Deutsche Oper, where he created the roles of Wilhelm in Henze's *Der Junge Lord* (1965) and Arundel in Fortner's *Elisabeth Tudor* (1972); in 1970, was made a Kammersänger. He also appeared at the Hamburg State Opera (1958–61; 1966–75) and the Bavarian State Opera in Munich (from 1967). On Nov. 22, 1968, he made his Metropolitan Opera debut in N.Y. as Froh in *Das Rheingold*. His other roles included Ferrando, Eisenstein, Hoffmann, Alwa in *Lulu*, and Flamand in *Capriccio*.—NS/LK/DM

Grob-Prandl, Gertrud, Austrian soprano; b. Vienna, Nov. 11, 1917; d. there, May 16, 1995. She was a student of Burian in Vienna. In 1938 she made her operatic debut as Santuzza at the Vienna Volksoper. After singing at the Zürich Opera (1946–47), she was a valued member of the Vienna State Opera (1947–64). She also appeared at London's Covent Garden (from 1951), in Milan, Berlin, and South America. She was known for her Wagnerian roles, most notably Ortrud, Brünnhilde, and Isolde.—NS/LK/DM

Grocheo, Johannes de, French music theorist who flourished in the 13th and early 14th centuries. He wrote the treatise *Ars musice* or *Theoria* (c. 1300), important as a source of information on secular music of the Middle Ages. It is printed in the original Latin with German tr. by J. Wolf in *Sammelbände der Internationalen Musik-Gesellschaft*, I (1899–1900); emendations were provided by H. Müller (op. cit., vol. IV).

BIBL.: E. Rohloff, *Studien zum Musiktraktat des J. d.G.* (Leipzig, 1930); E. Rohloff, *Die Quellenhandschriften zum Musiktraktat des J. d.G.* (Leipzig, 1972).—NS/LK/DM

Grofé, Ferde, (actually, **Ferdinand Rudolph von**), American composer, arranger, and pianist; b. N.Y., March 27, 1892; d. Santa Monica, Calif., April 3, 1972. He studied with Pietro Floridia. He was a violist in the Los Angeles Sym. Orch. (1909–19); he also played piano in film theaters, ragtime bands, and vaudeville. In 1917 he became an arranger and pianist for Paul Whiteman, for whom he prepared highly successful arrangements of *Avalon, Japanese Sandman,* and *Whispering*. His arrangement of Gershwin's *Rhapsody in Blue* for Whiteman in 1924 established Grofé's reputation. After his association with Whiteman ended in 1933, he conducted on the radio (1933–34) and taught at the Juilliard Graduate School in N.Y. (1939–42). In 1944 he won an Academy Award for his score for the film *Minstrel Man*. Of his many light orch. works, he remains best known for his *Grand Canyon Suite* (1931).

WORKS: ORCH.: *Mississippi: A Tone Journey* (1926); *Grand Canyon Suite* (Chicago, Nov. 22, 1931); *Tabloid Suite* (1933); *Killarney: An Irish Fantasy* (1934); *Hollywood Ballet* (1935); *Symphony in Steel* (1935; N.Y., Jan. 19, 1937); *Tin Pan Alley:The Melodic Decades* (1938); *Biography of an American* (1943); *Atlantic Crossing* (1950); *Lincoln's Gettysburg Address* (1954); *Hudson River Suite* (1956); *Niagara Falls Suite* (1960); *World's Fair Suite* (1963; N.Y., April 22, 1964); *Virginia City: Requiem for a Ghost Town* (Virginia City, Nev., Aug. 10, 1968); Piano Concerto (n.d.); pieces for Jazz Band and Brass Band. OTHER: Film scores, including *The King of Jazz* (1930), *Yankee Doodle Rhapsody* (1936), *Minstrel Man* (1944), and *Time out of Mind* (1946); piano pieces; songs; arrangements.—NS/LK/DM

Groh, Johann, German organist and composer; b. Dresden, c. 1575; d. probably in Weesenstein, Saxony, c. 1627. He was organist at the electoral school of St. Afra from 1604 to about 1621, and then was organist in the service of Rudolf von Bünau in Weesenstein. In addition to his vocal music, most of which was written for the church, he composed 36 intradas (Nuremberg, 1603) and 18 pavans and 12 galliards (Nuremberg, 1604; 2nd ed., 1612).—LK/DM

Grondahl, Launy, Danish conductor and composer; b. Ordrup, near Copenhagen, June 30, 1886; d.

Copenhagen, Jan. 21, 1960. He studied violin with Anton Bloch and Axel Gade, and theory with Ludolf Nielsen; later took music courses in Paris, Italy, Vienna, and elsewhere. Returning to Denmark, he became president of the Soc. of Young Musicians. From 1925 he conducted the Danish Radio Sym. Orch., serving as its chief conductor from 1931 to 1956. Among his compositions were a Violin Concerto (1917), Sym. (1919), Trombone Concerto (1924), Bassoon Concerto (1943), 2 string quartets, Violin Sonata, numerous piano pieces, and songs.—NS/LK/DM

Groot, Cor de, Dutch pianist, teacher, and composer; b. Amsterdam, July 7, 1914; d. there, May 26, 1993. He studied composition with Sem Dresden at the Amsterdam Cons. After winning the Vienna piano competition in 1936, he toured Europe and the U.S. He later was active as a piano teacher in The Hague and as a librarian and archivist in Hilversum.

WORKS: ORCH.: Piano Concerto (1931); *Concerto classico* for Piano and Orch. (1932); Concerto for 2 Pianos and Orch. (1939); Concerto for 2 Oboes and Orch. (1939); Piano Concertino (1939); Clarinet Concerto (1940); Flute Concerto (1940); Violin Concerto (1940); *Divertimento* (1949); *Wilhelmus ouverture* (1950); *Minuten Concerto* for Piano and Orch. (1950); *Ouverture energico* (1951); *Capriccio* for Piano and Orch. (1955); *Variations imaginaires* for Piano, Left-Hand and Orch. (1960–62); Concertino for Clarinet and Small Orch. (1971); *"Bis" (Evocation)* for Piano and Orch. (1972); *Les Chatons de Paris* for Accordion and Orch. (1978). CHAMBER: String Quartet (1947); *Serenade* for Oboe and Bassoon (1949); *Apparition* for Violin and Piano (1960); *2 Figures* for Oboe and Piano (1968); *Solitude* for Cello and Piano (1968); *Cloches dans le matin* for 1 or 2 Pianos (1972); *Invocation* for Cello and Piano (1974); *Satie-re* for 4 Pianos (1974); *Zit-liedjes en spring-dansjes* for Irish Harp (1982); *Music for the Party* for 2 Harps (1983).—NS/LK/DM

Grosheim, Georg Christoph, German writer on music and composer; b. Kassel, July 1, 1764; d. there, Nov. 18, 1841. He spent his entire life in Kassel. He was a pupil of Christian Kalkbrenner and Johannes Becker. He was a violist in the court orch. (1781–82) and ed. of the magazine on singing, *Euterpe* (1797–98). He wrote several books on music and an autobiography (Kassel, 1819). Grosheim composed 3 operas for Kassel: *Titania, oder Liebe durch Zauberei* (1792), *Das heilige Kleeblatt* (1793; Oct. 1794), and *Les Esclaves d'Alger* (Oct. 14, 1808; not extant).—NS/LK/DM

Grosjean, Ernest, French organist and composer, nephew of **Jean Romary Grosjean**; b. Vagney, Dec. 18, 1844; d. Versailles, Dec. 28, 1936. He studied in Paris with Boëly and Stamaty. He was organist at Verdun Cathedral from 1868 to 1916, then at St. Antoine, Versailles. From 1888 to 1914 was ed. of the *Journal des Organistes*. He wrote many works for organ and a *Théorie et pratique de l'accompagnement du plainchant*. —NS/LK/DM

Grosjean, Jean Romary, French organist and composer, uncle of **Ernest Grosjean;** b. Epinal, Jan. 12, 1815; d. St. Die, Feb. 13, 1888. He was organist at the St.

Dié Cathedral from 1839. He publ. a 2-vol. collection of organ works, *Album d'un organiste catholique*, which included some of his own compositions. He also ed. a complete collection of noëls and folk songs of Lorraine. —NS/LK/DM

Grossin, Estienne, French composer who flourished in the early 15th century. He entered the priesthood and served at the church of St. Merry and at Notre Dame Cathedral in Paris. His output included masses, motets, and chansons. See G. Reaney, *Early Fifteenth-century Music*, Corpus Mensurabilis Musicae, XI/3 (1966).—LK/DM

Grosskopf, Erhard, German composer; b. Berlin, March 17, 1934. He studied in Berlin with Pepping at the School for Church Music (1957–59) and with Blacher at the Hochschule für Musik (1959–64), and later worked at the Inst. for Electronic Music at the Univ. of Utrecht (1970–71). From 1968 he was active in avant-garde music circles in Berlin.

WORKS: *Sonata concertante No. 1* for Small Orch. (1966) and *No. 2* for Violin and Orch. (1967); *Konzertante Aspekte II* for Flute, Cello, Piano, and Orch. (1967); *Hörmusik* for Cello, 5 Orch. Groups, and Live Electronics (Berlin, Sept. 30, 1971); *Sun Music* for 3 Instrumental Groups (1972); *Quintett über den Herbstanfang* for Orch. (1982); String Quartet No. 1 (1983); Octet (1985); *Lichtknall: Eine apokalyptische Odyssee*, ballet (1987); *Lenzmusik I* for Violin, Clarinet, and Piano (1992); *Zeit der Windstille*, sym. (1993).—NS/LK/DM

Grossmann, Ferdinand, Austrian conductor, teacher, and composer; b. Tulln, July 4, 1887; d. Vienna, Dec. 5, 1970. He studied music in Linz, and later took a course in conducting with Weingartner in Vienna. In 1923 he founded a Volkskonservatorium in Vienna, and in 1946 he organized the Chamber Chorus of the Vienna Academy of Music, with which he toured in Europe and America. He composed a *German Mass* for Chorus (1952) and some chamber music.—NS/LK/DM

Grosz, Wilhelm, Austrian composer; b. Vienna, Aug. 11, 1894; d. N.Y., Dec. 10, 1939. He studied in Vienna with Richard Robert (piano), at the Cons. with Heuberger, Fuchs, and Schreker (theory and composition), and at the Univ. with Adler (musicology; Ph.D., 1920, with the diss. *Die Fugenarbeit in W.A. Mozarts Vokal- und Instrumentalwerken*). He was active mainly in Vienna, where he was conductor of the Kammerspiele in 1933–34. As a Jew, he sought refuge in London before emigrating to the U.S. in 1938.

WORKS: DRAMATIC: *Sganarell*, opera (Dessau, Nov. 21, 1925); *Der arme Reinhold*, dance fable (Berlin, Dec. 22, 1928); *Achtung, Aufnahme!*, musical comedy (Frankfurt am Main, March 23, 1930); incidental music for plays, films, and radio. ORCH.: 2 *Phantastische Stücke: Serenade* (1916) and *Tanz* (1917); *Overture to an Opera Buffa* (n.d.); *Symphonischer Tanz* for Piano and Orch. (1930); *Española*, jazz rhapsody (1937). CHAMBER: String Quartet (1915); *Jazzband* for Violin and Piano (1924); Violin Sonata (1925); piano pieces. VOCAL: Serious and light songs.—NS/LK/DM

Grout, Donald J(ay), eminent American musicologist; b. Rock Rapids, Iowa, Sept. 28, 1902; d. Ska-neateles, N.Y., March 9, 1987. He studied philosophy at Syracuse Univ. (A.B., 1923) and musicology at Harvard Univ. (A.M., 1932; Ph.D., 1939); he also received piano instruction in Boston, and took a course in French music in Strasbourg and in the history of opera in Vienna. After serving as a visiting lecturer at Mills Coll. in Oakland, Calif. (1935–36), he was on the faculties of Harvard Univ. (1936–42) and the Univ. of Tex. at Austin (1942–45); subsequently was a prof. of musicology at Cornell Univ. (1945–70). He held a Guggenheim Foundation grant in 1951. He served as president of the American Musicological Soc. (1952–54; 1960–62), and in 1966 became curator of the Accademia Monteverdiana in N.Y.

WRITINGS: *A Short History of Opera* (2 vols., N.Y., 1948; 3rd ed., 1988); *A History of Western Music* (N.Y., 1960; 4th ed., 1988); *Mozart in the History of Opera* (Washington, D.C., 1972); *Alessandro Scarlatti: An Introduction to His Operas* (Berkeley, 1979).

BIBL.: W. Austin, ed., *New Looks at Italian Opera: Essays in Honor of D.J. G.* (Ithaca, N.Y., 1968).—NS/LK/DM

Grove, Sir George, eminent English music and biblical scholar and lexicographer; b. Clapham, South London, Aug. 13, 1820; d. Sydenham, May 28, 1900. He graduated in 1839 from the Institution of Civil Engineers, and worked in various shops in Glasgow, and then in Jamaica and Bermuda. He returned to England in 1846, and became interested in music; without abandoning his engineering profession, he entered the Soc. of Arts, of which he was appointed secretary in 1850. In 1852 he became secretary of the Crystal Palace. He then was an ed., with William Smith, of the *Dictionary of the Bible*; traveled to Palestine in 1858 and 1861 in connection with his research; in 1865 he became director of the Palestine Exploration Fund. In the meantime, he accumulated a private music library; began writing analytical programs for Crystal Palace concerts; these analyses, contributed by Grove during the period 1856–96, established a new standard of excellence in musical exegesis. His enthusiasm for music led to many important associations; with Arthur Sullivan he went to Vienna in 1867 in search of unknown music by Schubert, and discovered the score of *Rosamunde*. In 1868 he became ed. of *Macmillan's Magazine*; remained on its staff for 15 years. He received many honors for his literary and musical achievements, among them the D.C.L., Univ. of Durham (1875), and LL.D., Univ. of Glasgow (1885). In 1883 he was knighted by Queen Victoria. When the Royal Coll. of Music was formed in London (1882), Grove was appointed director, and retained this post until 1894. He was the author of *Beethoven and His 9 Symphonies* (London, 1896; 3rd ed., 1898). His chief work, which gave him enduring fame, was the monumental *Dictionary of Music and Musicians*, which Macmillan began to publ. in 1879. It was first planned in 2 vols., but as the material grew, it was expanded to 4 vols., with an appendix, its publication being completed in 1889. Grove contributed voluminous articles on his favorite composers, Beethoven, Schubert, and Mendelssohn; he gathered a distinguished group of specialists to write the assorted entries. The 2nd edition was ed. by J. Fuller Maitland (5 vols., 1904–10), an American suppl. by W. Pratt and C. Boyd (1920; expanded, 1928), the 3rd

(1927–29) and 4th (1939–40) editions by H. Colles, and the 5th edition by E. Blom (1954). An entirely new 6th ed. was edited by S. Sadie as *The New Grove Dictionary of Music and Musicians* (20 vols., 1980). Sadie and J. Tyrrell edited an exhaustive revision with publication expected in 2000.

BIBL.: C. Graves, *The Life and Letters of Sir G. G.* (London, 1904); P. Young, *G. G., 1820–1900* (London, 1980).—**NS/LK/DM**

Grové, Stefans, South African composer and teacher; b. Bethlehem, Orange Free State, July 23, 1922. He studied with his mother and his uncle, David Roode, and learned to play the piano and organ. He continued his piano training in Cape Town at the South African Coll. of Music (diploma, 1948) and was a student in composition of W.H. Bell (1945–46). In 1953 he went to the U.S. on a Fulbright scholarship and pursued his studies at Harvard Univ., taking the M.A. in musicology and the M.Mus. under Piston in 1955; he also studied composition with Copland at the Berkshire Music Center in Tanglewood (summer, 1954). After teaching at Bard Coll. in Annandale-on-Hudson, N.Y. (1956–57), he was on the faculty of the Peabody Cons. of Music in Baltimore (1957–71). In 1972 he was a lecturer at the South African Coll. of Music, and then taught theory and composition at the Univ. of Pretoria from 1974. With the composition of his Violin Sonata on African motives (1984), he has pursued a style which is characterized by the incorporation of African elements in his music. These ethnic elements consist mainly of rhythmic and melodic procedures, resulting in complex rhythmic patterns with constant metric changes, as well as ostinato figures with constant changes.

WORKS: DRAMATIC: O p e r a : *Die bose Wind* (1983). **B a l l e t :** *Waratha* (1977); *Pinocchio* (1983). **ORCH.:** *Elegy* for Strings (1948); Overture (1953); Sinfonia concertante (1956); Violin Concerto (1959); Sym. (1962); *Partita* (1964); Concerto grosso for Violin, Cello, Piano, and Orch. (1974); *Maya*, concerto grosso for Violin, Piano, and Strings (1977); *Kettingrye* for Instrumentalists and Orch. (1978); *Vladimir's Round Table*, symphonic poem (1982); *Suite Concertato* for Harpsichord and Strings (1985); *Dance Rhapsody—An African City* (1985); *Concertato Overture on 2 Zulu Themes* (1988); *Overture Itubi*, festival dance for Youth Orch. (1992). **CHAMBER:** 2 string quartets (1946, 1955); String Trio (1948); Clarinet Sonata (1949); Trio for Violin, Cello, and Piano (1952); *Serenade* for Flute, Oboe, Viola, Bass Clarinet, and Harp (1952); Trio for Oboe, Clarinet, and Bassoon (1952); Cello Sonata (1953); Quintet for Harp and Strings (1954); *Divertimento* for Recorders (1955); Flute Sonata (1955); *Daarstelling* for Flute, Harpsichord, and Strings (1972); *Die nag van 3 April* for Flute and Harpsichord (1975); *Vir 'n winterdag* for Bassoon and Piano (1977); *Gesprek vir drie* for Oboe, Clarinet, and Percussion (1978); *Symphonia quattuor cordis* for Violin (1980); *Suite Juventuti* for Winds and Percussion (1982); *Jeu de Timbres* for Percussion (1983); Violin Sonata (1984); *Quintet—A City Serenade* for Flute or Alto Flute, Clarinet or Bass Clarinet, Viola, Cello, and Harp (1985); Trio for Violin, Horn, and Piano (1988); *Song of the African Spirits* for String Quartet (1993). **KEYBOARD: P i a n o :** *3 Inventions* (1951); *Stylistic Experiment*, 12 pieces (1971); *Tweespalt* for Piano, Left-hand (1975); *Songs and Dances from Africa*, 7 études (1988); *The Blus Dream Valley*, 4 fantasy pieces (1992). **O r g a n :** *Ritual* (1969); *Chorale Prelude on Psalm 42* (1974); *Rhapsodic Toccata* (1977);

Afrika Hymnus, concert fantasy (1991). **VOCAL:** *Cantata profana* for 2 Voices, Flute, Oboe, Harpsichord, and Cello (1959); Sym. for Chorus and Orch. (1975); *5 Ingrid Jonker Songs* for Soprano and Piano (1982); *Omnis Caterva Fidelium* for Children's Chorus and Piano (1985); *7 Songs on Bushman Poems* for Soprano, String Quartet, and Piano (1990); *Zulu Horizons* for Baritone and Orch. (1992).—**NS/LK/DM**

Groven, Eivind, Norwegian composer and musicologist; b. Lårdal, Telemark, Oct. 8, 1901; d. Oslo, Feb. 8, 1977. He studied at the Christiania Cons. (1923–25) and in Berlin. In 1931 he was appointed a consultant on folk music for Norwegian Radio, where he remained until 1946. In 1940 he received a state composer's pension. His many theoretical studies include *Naturskalaen* (The Natural Scale; Skein, 1927); *Temperering og renstemning* (Temperament and Non-tempered Tuning; Oslo, 1948; Eng. tr., 1970); *Eskimomelodier fra Alaska* (Eskimo Melodies from Alaska; Oslo, 1955). He collected about 1,800 Norwegian folk tunes, several of which he used as thematic foundation for his own compositions. In 1965 he patented an electronic organ, with special attachments for the production of non-tempered intervals.

WORKS: ORCH.: 5 symphonic poems: *Renaissance* (1935), *Historiske syner* (Historical Visions; 1936), *Fjelltonar* (Tunes from the Hills; 1938), *Skjebner* (The Fates; 1938), and *Bryllup i skogen* (Wedding in the Wood; 1939); 2 syms.: No. 1, *Innover viddene* (Toward the Mountains; 1937; rev. 1951) and No. 2, *Midnattstimen* (The Midnight Hour; 1946); *Hjalarljod*, overture (1950); Piano Concerto (1950); *Symfoniske slåtter* (Norwegian Folk Dances), 2 sets: No. 1 (1956) and No. 2, *Faldafeykir* (1967). **CHAMBER:** *Solstemning* (Sun Mood) for Flute or Flute and Piano (1946); *Balladetone* for 2 Hardanger Fiddles (1962); *Regnbogen* (The Rainbow) for 2 Hardanger Fiddles (1962). **VOCAL:** *Brudgommen* (The Bridegroom) for Soprano, 2 Altos, Tenor, Chorus, and Orch. (1928–31); *Naturens tempel* (The Temple of Nature) for Chorus and Orch. (1945); *Ivar Aasen*, suite for Soprano, Bass, Chorus, and Orch. (1946); *Soga om ein by* (The Story of a Town) for Soprano, Tenor, Bass, Chorus, and Orch. (1956); *Margjit Hjukse* for Chorus and Hardanger Fiddle (1963); *Draumkaede* for Soprano, Tenor, Baritone, Chorus, and Orch. (1965); *Ved foss og fjord* (By Falls and Fjord) for Men's Chorus and Orch. (1966); many songs.—**NS/LK/DM**

Groves, Sir Charles (Barnard), distinguished English conductor; b. London, March 10, 1915; d. there, June 20, 1992. He received training in piano and organ at the Royal Coll. of Music in London. In 1938 he joined the BBC as a chorus master, and then was assoc. conductor of the BBC Theatre Orch. (1942–44) and subsequently conductor of the BBC Northern Orch. in Manchester (1944–51). In 1951 he became conductor of the Bournemouth Municipal Orch.; after it was renamed the Bournemouth Sym. Orch. in 1954, he continued as its conductor until 1961. After serving as music director of the Welsh National Opera in Cardiff (1961–63), he was principal conductor of the Royal Liverpool Phil. from 1963 to 1977. He launched the career of several conductors through his sponsorship of the Liverpool International Conductors' Competition. In 1978–79 he was music director of the English National Opera in London, and later was principal conductor of the Guildford Phil. (from 1986). In 1958 he was made an Officer and in 1968 a Commander of the Order of the British Empire, and in 1973 he was knighted. Groves acquitted himself admirably as a conductor of the orch., operatic, and choral repertory.—NS/LK/DM

Grovlez, Gabriel (Marie), French conductor and composer; b. Lille, April 4, 1879; d. Paris, Oct. 20, 1944. He studied at the Paris Cons. with Descombes, Diémer, Fauré, Gédalge, and Lavignac, taking a premier prix in piano in 1899. He toured Europe as accompanist to Marteau. He concentrated his activities on Paris, where he was prof. of piano at the Schola Cantorum (1899–1909), and also choirmaster and conductor at the Opéra-Comique (1905–08). After serving as music director of the Théâtre des Arts (1911–13), he was director of the Opéra (1914–34); he also conducted opera abroad. In 1939 he became prof. of chamber music at the Cons. His works reflect the finest qualities of the Gallic tradition.

WORKS: DRAMATIC: O p e r a : *Coeur de rubis* (1906; Nice, 1922); *Le marquis do Carabas* (1926). B a l l e t : *La princesse au jardin* (1914; Paris, 1941); *Maïmouna* (1916; Paris, 1921); *Le vrai arbre de Robinson* (1921; N.Y., 1922). ORCH.: *Dans le jardin*, symphonic poem for Soprano, Women's Voices, and Orch. (1907); *La vengeance des fleurs*, symphonic poem (1910); *Madrigal lyrique* for Soprano and Orch. (1910); *Le reposoir des amants*, symphonic poem (1914); *Fantasia iberica* for Piano and Orch. (1941). OTHER: Piano pieces; many songs.—NS/LK/DM

Grozăvescu, Trajan, Romanian tenor; b. Lugoj, Nov. 21, 1895; d. (murdered) Vienna, Feb. 15, 1927. He studied in Bucharest and Cluj. After making his debut in Cluj as Pinkerton in 1920, he continued his vocal studies in Vienna with F. Steiner. He made appearances with the Vienna Volksoper, the Prague National Theater, and the Vienna State Opera. He was shot to death by his wife.

BIBL.: M. Demeter-Grozăvescu and I. Voledi, *T. G.* (Bucharest, 1965).—NS/LK/DM

Grua, Carlo (Alisio) Pietro, Italian composer, father of **Franz Paul (Francesco de Paula or Paolo) Grua;** b. probably in Milan, c. 1700; d. Mannheim (buried), April 11, 1773. He may have been the son of **Carlo Luigi Pietro Grua.** He was Kapellmeister at the court of the Elector Palatine in Mannheim (1734–73), where his operas *Meride* (Jan. 17, 1742) and *La clemenza di Tito* (Jan. 17, 1748) were first performed. He also wrote 5 oratorios and 2 Masses, but much of his output is not extant.—NS/LK/DM

Grua, Carlo Luigi Pietro, Italian composer; b. Florence, c. 1665; d. place and date unknown. He may have been the father of **Carlo (Alisio) Pietro Grua.** In 1691 he became an alto singer in the Hofkapelle of the Elector of Saxony in Dresden, where he served as vice-Kapellmeister in 1693–94, and where his opera *Camillo generoso* was premiered during Carnival 1693. In 1694 he was made vice-Kapellmeister of the Palatine court in Düsseldorf, where his opera *Telegono* was first performed during Carnival 1697. He retained his position until 1720, serving in Heidelberg after the Düsseldorf and Innsbruck musical establishments were com-

bined and moved there. He also composed 2 operas for Venice: *Il Pastor fido* (1721) and *Romol e Tazio* (1722). Among his other works were duets and sacred music.—NS/LK/DM

Grua, Franz Paul, (Francesco da Paula or **Paolo**), German composer of Italian descent, son of **Carlo (Alisio) Pietro Grua;** b. Mannheim (baptized), Feb. 1, 1753; d. Munich, July 5, 1833. He was a pupil of I. Fränzl (violin) and Holzbauer (composition) in Mannheim, where he became deputy violinist at the court of the elector Palatine in 1776. After further training with Padre Martini in Bologna (1777), he accompanied the Mannheim musical establishment in its relocation to Munich in 1778, where he was made vice-Kapellmeister in 1779 and Hofkapellmeister in 1784. He wrote the opera *Telemaco* (Munich, Carnival 1780) and much sacred music.—NS/LK/DM

Gruber, Franz Xaver, Austrian composer, great-great- grandfather of **H(einz) K(arl) Gruber;** b. Unterweizburg, near Hochburg, Nov. 25, 1787; d. Hallein, near Salzburg, June 7, 1863. He was born into an impoverished family but managed to study organ. In 1807 he became a teacher at the Nebenschule in Arnsdorf. He was also cantor and organist at St. Nicolas's in Oberndorf (1816–29). After teaching in Berndorf (1829–33), he served as regens chori in Hallein. While in Oberndorf, an asst. priest, Josef Mohr (1792–1848), brought him a Christmas poem to be set to music for Christmas Eve of 1818. Gruber's result was the celebrated Christmas carol *Stille Nacht, Heilige Nacht* (Silent Night, Holy Night), which was publ. in 1838.

BIBL.: K. Weinmann, *Stille nacht, Heilige Nacht* (Regensburg, 1918); J. Mühlmann, *F.X. G.* (Salzburg, 1966); A. Schmaus and L. Kriss-Rettenbeck, *Stille Nacht, Heilige Nacht* (Innsbruck, 1967).—NS/LK/DM

Gruber, H(einz) K(arl) "Nali," Austrian composer, conductor, chansonnier, and double bass player, great-great-grandson of **Franz Xaver Gruber;** b. Vienna, Jan. 3, 1943. After singing in the Vienna Boy's Choir (1953–57), he studied double bass with Planyavsky and Streicher, composition with Uhl and Ratz, and serial techniques with Jelinek at the Vienna Academy of Music (1957–63). In 1963–64 he attended a masterclass in composition there with Einem. He pursued his career in Vienna, where he joined the die reihe ensemble as a double bass player in 1961. From 1963 to 1969 he was principal double bass in the Niederösterreiches Tonkünstler Orch. In 1968 he co-founded with Schwertsik and Zykan the avant-garde group MOB art & tone ART, with which he was active until 1971. He played double bass in the Austrian Radio Sym. Orch. from 1969 to 1998. He then devoted much of his time to pursuing a career as a conductor and chansonnier. In 1979 he was awarded the music prize of the Austrian Ministry of Culture and Education. While Gruber's works are basically tonal in nature, he has developed an unbuttoned personal style in which serious and lighter elements are given free reign as the mood strikes him. His self-described "pandemonium" *Frankenstein!!* (1976–77) brought him international recognition. Among his later significant works were his 2 violin concertos (1977–78; 1988) and his Cello Concerto (1989).

WORKS: DRAMATIC: *Die Vertreibung aus dem Paradies*, melodrama (1966; ORF, Vienna, Feb. 11, 1969; rev. 1979); *Gomorra*, musical spectacle (1970–72; withdrawn; new version, 1984–91; Vienna, Jan. 18, 1993); *Reportage aus Gomorra* for 5 Singers and 8 Players (1975–76); *Frankenstein!!*, "pandemonium" for Baritone Channsonier and Orch. (1976–77; Liverpool, Nov. 25, 1978; also for Baritone Channsonier and 12 Instruments, Berlin, Sept. 30, 1979); *Bring me the head of Amadeus*, music for the television series *Not Mozart* (BBC2-TV, London, Nov. 17, 1991); *Gloria von Jaxtberg*, music theater (1992–93; Huddersfield, England, Nov. 11, 1994). **ORCH.:** *Concerto for Orchestra* (1960–64); *Manhattan Broadcasts* for Light Orch. (1962–64); *fürbass*, double bass concerto (1965); *Revue* for Chamber Orch. (1968); *Vergrösserung* (1970); *Arien* for Violin and Orch. (1974–75; withdrawn); 2 violin concertos: No. 1, *...aus Schatten duft gewebt* (1977–78; Berlin, Sept. 29, 1979; rev. 1992) and No. 2, *Nebelsteinmusik* (St. Florian, July 19, 1988); *Entmilitarisierte Zonen*, march paraphrases for Brass Band (Zagreb, May 17, 1979); *Charivari: An Austrian Journal* (1981; London, Aug. 23, 1983; rev. 1984); *Rough Music*, percussion concerto (1982–83; ORF, Vienna, Oct. 30, 1983); Concerto for Cello and Ensemble or Small Orch. (Tanglewood, Aug. 3, 1989); *Aerial*, trumpet concerto (1998–99; London, July 29, 1999). **CHAMBER:** Suite for 2 Pianos, Winds, and Percussion (1960); *Improvisationen* for Wind Quintet (1961); Concerto No. 1 for Flute, Vibraphone, Xylophone, and Percussion (1961) and No. 2 for Tenor Saxophone, Double Bass, and Percussion (1961); *4 Pieces* for Violin (1963; Vienna, May 20, 1966); *Gioco a Tre* for Violin, Cello, and Piano (1963); *2 Rhapsodies* for Cello and Piano (1964); *Spiel* for Wind Quintet (1967); *3 MOB Pieces* for 7 Interchangeable Instruments and Percussion (1968; rev. 1977; Graz, Oct. 14, 1979); *Bossa Nova* for Ensemble (1968); *Die wirkliche Wut über den verlorenen Groschen* for 5 Players (1972); *Festmusik* for Chamber Ensemble (1972); *Phantom-Bilder auf der Spur eines verdächtigten Themas* for 12 or 13 Players or Small Orch. (1977; London, March 7, 1979); *Anagramm* for 6 Cellos (ORF, Graz, Oct. 22, 1987). **Piano:** *Episoden* for 2 Pianos (1961); *Sechs Episoden aus einer unterbrochenen Chronik* (1967; Vienna, Feb. 20, 1968); *Luftschlösser* (Schloss Grafenegg, May 9, 1981). **VOCAL:** Mass for Chorus, 2 Trumpets, English Horn, Double Bass, and Percussion (1960); *Drei Lieder* for Baritone, Ensemble, and Tape (1961); *5 Kinderlieder* for Women's Chorus (1965; rev. 1980); *Zeitstimmung* for Baritone and Chamber Orch. (1995–96); other choruses and songs. **OTHER:** *Konjugationen* (for tape, 1963).—NS/LK/DM

Gruberová, Edita, Czech soprano; b. Bratislava, Dec. 23, 1946. She was a student in Prague of Maria Medvecká and in Vienna of Ruthilde Boesch. In 1968 she made her operatic debut as Rossini's Rosina at the Slovak National Theater in Bratislava. In 1970 she made her first appearance at the Vienna State Opera as the Queen of the Night, and subsequently sang there regularly. In 1973 she sang at the Glyndebourne Festival and in 1974 at the Salzburg Festival. On Jan. 5, 1977, she made her Metropolitan Opera debut in N.Y. as the Queen of the Night. She appeared as Giulietta in *I Capuleti e i Montecchi* at London's Covent Garden in 1984. After singing Lucia at Milan's La Scala in 1984, she reprised that role in Chicago in 1986 and in Barcelona in 1987. In 1989 she portrayed Violetta at the Metropolitan

Opera. She sang Donizetti's Elizabeth I in Vienna in 1990, and then appeared as Semiramide in Zürich in 1992. She returned to Vienna as Linda di Chamounix in 1997 and also sang Anna Bolena that year in Munich. She also toured widely as a concert singer. Among her other admired roles were Donna Anna, Gilda, and Ariadne.—NS/LK/DM

Gruenberg, Erich, Austrian-born English violinist; b. Vienna, Oct. 12, 1924. After studying in Vienna, he was awarded a scholarship to the Jerusalem Cons. in 1938; subsequently was engaged as concertmaster of the radio orch. there. In 1946 he went to London, and became a naturalized British subject in 1950. He served as concertmaster of the Boyd Neel Orch.; then of the Stockholm Phil. (1956–58), the London Sym. Orch. (1962–65), and the Royal Phil. (1972–76); also made appearances as a soloist and as a chamber music player. In 1994 he was made an Officer of the Order of the British Empire.—NS/LK/DM

Gruenberg, Louis, Russian-born American composer; b. near Brest Litovsk, Aug. 3, 1884; d. Los Angeles, June 9, 1964. He went with his family to the U.S. when he was 2. After piano lessons with Adele Margulies in N.Y., he went to Berlin in 1903 to study piano and composition with Busoni and Friedrich Koch. In 1912 he made his debut as a soloist with the Berlin Phil. under Busoni's direction, and then toured Europe and the U.S.; he also became an instructor at the Vienna Cons. that year. Upon winning the Flagler Prize in 1920 for his orch. piece *The Hill of Dreams*, he decided to settle in the U.S. and devote himself to composition. In 1923 he helped found the League of Composers and became a champion of contemporary music. The influence of jazz and spirituals resulted in one of his most successful scores, *The Daniel Jazz* for Tenor, Clarinet, Trumpet, and String Quartet (1924). In 1930 he was awarded the RCA Victor Prize for his 1st Sym. He then composed his most successful stage work, the opera *The Emperor Jones*, which was premiered at the Metropolitan Opera in N.Y. on Jan. 7, 1933. It received the David Bispham Medal. After serving as head of the composition dept. at the Chicago Musical Coll. (1933–36), Gruenberg settled in Calif. His film scores for *The Fight for Life* (1940), *So Ends our Night* (1941), and *Commandos Strike at Dawn* (1942) won him Academy Awards. He was elected a member of the National Inst. of Arts and Letters in 1947.

WORKS: DRAMATIC: *Signor Formica*, operetta (1910); *The Witch of Brocken*, operetta (1912); *Piccadillymädel*, operetta (1913); *The Bride of the Gods*, opera (1913); *Roly-boly Eyes*, musical (1919; in collaboration with E. Brown); *The Dumb Wife*, chamber opera (1923); *Hallo! Tommy!*, operetta (1920s); *Lady X*, operetta (c. 1927); *Jack and the Beanstalk*, opera (N.Y., Nov. 19, 1931); *The Emperor Jones*, opera (1931; N.Y., Jan. 7, 1933); *Helena's Husband*, opera (1936); *Green Mansions*, radio opera (CBS, Oct. 17, 1937); *Volpone*, opera (1945); *One Night of Cleopatra*, opera (n.d.); *The Miracle of Flanders*, musical legend (1954); *The Delicate King*, opera (1955); *Antony and Cleopatra*, opera (1955; rev. 1958 and 1961); ballets; pantomimes; incidental music; film scores: *The Fight for Life* (1940; orch. suite, 1954); *So Ends our Night* (1941); *Commandos Strike at Dawn* (1942); *An American Romance* (1944); *Counterattack* (1945); *Gangster* (1947); *Arch of Triumph* (1948);

Smart Women (1948); *All the King's Men* (1949); *Quicksand* (1950). **ORCH.**: 2 piano concertos (1915; 1938, rev. 1963); *The Hill of Dreams*, symphonic poem (1920; N.Y., Oct. 23, 1921); *The Enchanted Isle*, symphonic poem (c. 1920; rev. 1928; Worcester, Mass., Oct. 3, 1929); 6 syms.: No. 1 (1919; rev. 1928; Boston, Feb. 10, 1934), No. 2 (1941; rev. 1959 and 1963), No. 3 (1941–42; rev. 1964), No. 4 (1946; rev. 1964), and Nos. 5–6 (unfinished); *Vagabondia*, symphonic poem (1921–30; rev. 1957); *Jazz Suite* (1925; Cincinnati, March 22, 1929); *Moods* (c. 1929); *Prairie Song* (c. 1930; rev. 1954); *Serenade to a Beauteous Lady* (1934; Chicago, April 4, 1935); *Music to an Imaginary Legend* (1945); *Music to an Imaginary Ballet* (1945; rev. 1946); Violin Concerto (Philadelphia, Dec. 1, 1944); *Americana Suite* (1945; rev. 1964); *Dance Rhapsody* for Violin and Orch. (c. 1946); *Variations on a Pastoral Theme* (1947); *5 Country Sketches* (c. 1948); Cello Concerto (1949; rev. 1963); *Poem* for Viola and Orch. (c. 1951); *Harlem Rhapsody* (1953); Concerto for Strings and Piano (c. 1953; rev. 1955). **CHAMBER**: 3 violin sonatas (c. 1912, c. 1919, c. 1950); Suite for Violin and Piano (c. 1914); 2 string quartets (1914, 1937); 4 Bagatelles for Cello and Piano (1922); *4 Indiscretions* for String Quartet (c. 1924); *Poem* for Cello and Piano (c. 1925); *Jazzettes* for Violin and Piano (c. 1925); *4 Diversions* for String Quartet (c. 1930); 2 divertimentos: No. 1 for 2 Pianos and Percussion (c. 1930) and No. 2 for Violin, Horn, Cello, and Piano (1955); Piano Quintet (1937); *Poem* for Viola and Piano (c. 1951); Piano Trio (n.d.). **Piano**: *Jazzberries* (c. 1925); *Jazz Masks* (1929–31); *Jazz Epigrams* (1929); *3 Jazz Dances* (1931); etc. **VOCAL**: *The Daniel Jazz* for Tenor, Clarinet, Trumpet, and String Quartet (1924; N.Y., Feb. 22, 1925); *The Creation* for Baritone and 8 Instruments (1925; N.Y., Nov. 27, 1926); *An American Hymn* for Soloist, Men's Voices, and Orch. (1940s); *A Song of Faith*, oratorio for Speaker, Soloists, Chorus, Dancers, and Orch. (1952–62; Los Angeles, Nov. 1, 1981); solo songs; arrangements of spirituals.

BIBL.: R. Nisbett, *L.G.: His Life and Work* (diss., Ohio State Univ., 1979).—NS/LK/DM

Gruhn, (originally, Grunebaum,) Nora, English soprano of German descent; b. London, March 6, 1905. She studied at the Royal Coll. of Music in London and with Hermine Bosetti in Munich. She made her operatic debut in Kaiserslautern in 1928; sang with the Cologne Opera (1929–30); appeared at Covent Garden (1929–33; 1936–37) and Sadler's Wells (1946–48) in London. She sang the part of Gretel in an English production of Humperdinck's *Hansel und Gretel* reportedly more than 400 times.—NS/LK/DM

Grumiaux, Arthur, eminent Belgian violinist; b. Villers-Perwin, March 21, 1921; d. Brussels, Oct. 16, 1986. He studied violin and piano with Fernand Quinet at the Charleroi Cons. and violin with Alfred Dubois at the Royal Cons. in Brussels; also took private lessons in composition with Enesco in Paris. In 1940 he was awarded the Prix de Virtuosité from the Belgian government. In 1949 he was appointed prof. of violin at the Royal Cons. In 1973 he was knighted by King Baudouin for his services to music; he thus shared the title of baron with Paganini. His performances were characterized by a studied fidelity to the composer's intentions, assured technical command, and a discerning delineation of the inner structures of music.

BIBL.: L. and M. Winthrop, *A. G.: Gloire de l'école belge du violon* (Lausanne, 1996).—NS/LK/DM

Grümmer, Elisabeth, distinguished German soprano; b. Niederjeutz, near Diedenhofen, Alsace-Lorraine, March 31, 1911; d. Berlin, Nov. 6, 1986. She began her career as an actress; after being persuaded to study voice by Karajan, she had lessons with Schlender in Aachen. In 1940 she made her operatic debut in Aachen as the 1st Flowermaiden in *Parsifal*, and then sang her first major role there in 1941 as Octavian. After appearances in Duisburg (1942–44), she was a member of the Berlin Städtische Oper (from 1946). On June 29, 1951, she made her first appearance at London's Covent Garden as Eva in *Die Meistersinger von Nürnberg*. She then made debuts at the Vienna State Opera and the Salzburg Festival in 1953, at the Glyndebourne Festival in 1956, and at the Bayreuth Festival in 1957. On Feb. 17, 1967, she made her debut at the N.Y.C. Opera as the Marschallin, followed by her Metropolitan Opera debut in N.Y. as Elsa in *Lohengrin* on April 20, 1967. She then continued her career in Europe until retiring in 1972. In addition to opera, she toured extensively as a concert artist. From 1959 she was a prof. of voice at the (West) Berlin Hochschule für Musik. Grümmer's exquisite voice and admirable dramatic gifts made her an exemplary interpreter of the music of Mozart and Richard Strauss. Among her other outstanding roles were Pamina, Donna Anna, Ilia, and the Mozart and Strauss Countess.—NS/LK/DM

Grümmer, Paul, eminent German cellist, viola da gambist, and pedagogue; b. Gera, Feb. 26, 1879; d. Zug, Oct. 30, 1965. He studied with Klengel at the Leipzig Cons. and with Becker in Frankfurt am Main. He began his career as a cellist in 1898, appearing regularly in London from 1902. He became solo cellist of the Vienna Opera and Konzertverein (1905), and was a founding member of the Busch Quartet (1913); also toured with his own chamber orch. He taught at the Vienna Academy of Music (1907–13; 1940–46), the Cologne Hochschule für Musik (1926–33), and the Berlin Hochschule für Musik (1933–40). He publ. pedagogical works, including a *Viola da Gamba Schule* (Leipzig, 1928), and ed. Bach's unaccompanied cello suites (Vienna, 1944). His autobiography was publ. as *Begegnungen* (Munich, 1963).—NS/LK/DM

Grün, Jakob, Austrian violinist and teacher; b. Budapest, March 13, 1837; d. Baden, near Vienna, Oct. 1, 1916. He was a pupil of J. Böhm in Vienna and M. Hauptmann in Leipzig. In 1858 he became a member of the Weimar Court Orch. He went to Vienna in 1868, as concertmaster at the Court Opera (until 1897). From 1877 until his retirement in 1909 he was a prof. at the Vienna Cons.—NS/LK/DM

Grünbaum, (originally Müller,) Therese, famous Austrian soprano, daughter of **Wenzel Müller**; b. Vienna, Aug. 24, 1791; d. Berlin, Jan. 30, 1876. She studied with her father, and appeared on stage while still a child. In 1807 she went to Prague, and in 1816 she joined the Kärnthnertortheater in Vienna, remaining as a principal member there until 1826. While in Vienna, she gained fame for her Rossini roles; also created the role of Eglantine in Weber's *Euryanthe*. After appearances in Berlin (1828–30), she taught voice. She married the tenor Johann Christoff (b. Haslau, Oct. 28, 1785; d. Berlin, Oct. 10, 1870); a daughter, Caroline (b. Prague, March 18, 1814; d. Braunschweig, May 26, 1868), was also a soprano.—NS/LK/DM

Grund, Friedrich Wilhelm, German conductor and composer; b. Hamburg, Oct. 7, 1791; d. there, Nov. 24, 1874. He was brought up in a musical family, his father having been a theater conductor. He studied cello, but after a brief concert career devoted himself mainly to conducting. In 1819 he founded in Hamburg the Gesellschaft der Freunde des Religiösen Gesanges, which later became the Hamburg Singakademie. In 1828 he was engaged to lead the newly established Phil. Concerts, a post he held until 1862. In 1867 he organized (with Karl Grädener) the Hamburg Tonkünstlerverein. He wrote several operas, a cantata, *Die Auferstehung und Himmelfahrt Christi*, chamber music, and many piano pieces, which enjoyed considerable success and were praised by Schumann.—NS/LK/DM

Grundheber, Franz, German baritone; b. Trier, Sept. 27, 1937. He studied in Trier, Hamburg, at Ind. Univ., and at the Music Academy of the West in Santa Barbara. In 1966 he became a member of the Hamburg State Opera. In 1983 he sang Strauss's Mandryka at the Vienna State Opera, and in 1985 Strauss's Olivier at the Salzburg Festival. After appearing as Amonasro at the Savonlinna Festival in 1989, he sang Strauss's Barak at the Holland Festival in 1990. In 1992 he was engaged as Germont in Barcelona, and as Wozzeck in Paris and at London's Covent Garden. He also sang Wozzeck at the Lyric Opera in Chicago in 1994, and then appeared as Wagner's Dutchman at the Los Angeles Opera in 1995. In 1997 he returned to Covent Garden as Rigoletto, which role he sang at his Metropolitan Opera debut in N.Y. on March 8, 1999.—NS/LK/DM

Grunenwald, Jean-Jacques, distinguished French organist and composer; b. Cran-Gevrier, near Annecy (of Swiss parentage), Feb. 2, 1911; d. Paris, Dec. 19, 1982. He studied organ with Dupré at the Paris Cons., receiving 1st prize in 1935. He also studied composition with Henri Busser, obtaining another 1st prize in 1937. From 1936 to 1945 he was the assistant of Dupré at St.-Sulpice in Paris, and from 1955 to 1970 he was organist at St.-Pierre-de-Montrouge. He was a prof. at the Schola Cantorum in Paris from 1958 to 1961, and from 1961 to 1966 was on the faculty of the Geneva Cons. Through the years he played more than 1,500 concerts, presenting the complete organ works of Bach and César Franck. He also became famous for the excellence of his masterly improvisations, which rivaled those of his teacher Dupré. His compositions include *Fêtes de la lumière* for Orch. (1937), Piano Concerto (1940), *Concert d'été* for Piano and String Orch. (1944), lyric drama, *Sardanapale*, after Byron (1945–50), *Ouverture pour un Drame sacre* for Orch. (1954), *Cantate pour le Vendredi Saint* (1955), *Psalm 129 (De profundis)* for Chorus and Orch. (1959), *Fantaisie en dialogue* for Organ and Orch. (1964), Sonata for Organ (1964), and piano pieces.
—NS/LK/DM

Grüner-Hegge, Odd, Norwegian conductor and composer; b. Christiania, Sept. 23, 1899; d. there (Oslo), May 11, 1973. He studied piano and composition at the Christiania Cons. and conducting with Weingartner. In 1927 he began his conducting career; from 1931 he was a conductor with the Oslo Phil., subsequently serving as its chief conductor from 1945 to 1961; he then was manager of the Norwegian Opera in Oslo from 1961 to 1969. He also appeared as a guest conductor with many of the leading European orchs. Among his works were orch. scores, chamber music, and piano pieces.
—NS/LK/DM

Grünfeld, Alfred, Austrian pianist and composer, brother of **Heinrich Grünfeld**; b. Prague, July 4, 1852; d. Vienna, Jan. 4, 1924. He studied in Prague, and at Kullak's Academy in Berlin. He settled in Vienna in 1873, where he established himself as a pianist and teacher; also made tours in other European countries. He composed an operetta, *Der Lebemann* (Vienna, Jan. 16, 1903), and the comic opera *Die Schönen von Fogaras* (Dresden, 1907). He also made brilliant arrangements for piano of waltzes by Johann Strauss Jr., and also publ. piano studies and various other pieces.—NS/LK/DM

Grünfeld, Heinrich, Austrian cellist and teacher, brother of **Alfred Grünfeld**; b. Prague, April 21, 1855; d. Berlin, Aug. 26, 1931. He studied at the Prague Cons. He went to Berlin in 1876, and taught at Kullak's Academy; also played chamber music. He publ. a book of memoirs, *In Dur und Moll* (Berlin, 1924).—NS/LK/DM

Grusin, Dave, music business renaissance man: pianist, label head, and visionary; b. Littleton, Colo., June 26, 1934. While attending the Univ. of Colo., Dave Grusin got sucked into the jazz scene, working with jazz stalwarts like Terry Gibbs and Art Pepper. Yet he also had a pop side, and in 1959 he went to work as music director for MOR pop singer Andy Williams, a role he maintained through the mid-1960s, while continuing to play with Benny Goodman, Thad Jones, Milt Hinton, and Frank Foster. Later in the decade he expanded his horizons even more, taking on film scoring, including composing the incidental music between the Simon and Garfunkel songs of *The Graduate*. He also started to produce records for pop artists like Barbra Streisand and jazz players like Lee Ritenour. In 1976, Grusin founded GRP records with Larry Rosen. The company brought such noted artists as Diane Schuur and David Benoit to the public as well as furthering the careers of artists like Michael Brecker, Gary Burton, and Chick Corea. It was also the first record label to record all of its acts on digital equipment (rather than analog tape machines). Upon selling the company to MCA, Grusin and Rosen became pioneers in digital music on the World Wide Web, buying N2K, a multimedia company, and founding N2K Records and the Music Boulevard web site.

Through it all, Grusin continued to play and compose, working with the GRP All-Stars and creating scores for films ranging from *Tootsie* and *Havana* (for which he won an Oscar nomination) to *The Firm* and *The Fabulous Baker Boys*.

DISC.: *Subways Are for Sleeping* (1961); *Candy* (1961); *The Many Moods of Dave Grusin* (1962); *Kaleidoscope* (1964); *Discovered Again* (1977); *One of a Kind* (1977); *Mountain Dance* (1979); *A Flip of the Coin* (1980); *Dave Grusin and the GRP All-Stars/Live in Japan* (1980); *Out of the Shadows* (1982); *Night- Lines* (1983); *And the N.Y.-L.A. Dream Band* (1984); *Harlequin* (1985); *Cinemagic* (1987); *Zephyr* (1988); *Live in Japan* (1988); *Sticks and Stones* (1988); *The Fabulous Baker Boys* (1989); *Migration* (1989); *Bonfire of the Vanities* (1990); *The Gershwin Connection* (1991); *Homage to Duke* (1993); *The Orchestral Album* (1994); *Cure* (1995); *Two for the Road: The Music of Henry Mancini* (1996); *3 Days of the Condor* (1997); *Presents: West Side Story* (1997).—**HB**

Grützmacher, Friedrich (Wilhelm Ludwig),

renowned German cellist and pedagogue; b. Dessau, March 1, 1832; d. Dresden, Feb. 23, 1903. He began his musical training with his father, and then studied cello with Karl Drechsler and theory with Friedrich Schneider. When he was 16, he went to Leipzig, where his talent so impressed David that he secured for Grützmacher the position of 1st cellist in the Gewandhaus Orch. in 1849. He also taught at the Cons. from 1849. In 1860 he settled in Dresden as a member of the Hofkapelle, being named solo cellist in 1864. Among his students were Hugo Becker and Fitzenhagen. He composed concertos and other works for his instrument, as well as orch. pieces, chamber works, and songs. He also publ. *Hohe Schule des Violoncellspiels* (Leipzig, 1891). His brother, Leopold Grützmacher (b. Dessau, Sept. 4, 1835; d. Weimar, Feb. 26, 1900), was also a cellist. After studies with his brother and Drechsler, he played in the Gewandhaus Orch., the Schwerin Hofkapelle, the Prague Landestheater Orch., and the Meiningen ducal orch. In 1876 he became soloist and prof. at the Weimar Hofkapelle. He also was first cellist in the Bayreuth orch. He wrote 2 cellos concertos and salon pieces for cello. His son, Friedrich Grützmacher (b. Meiningen, July 20, 1866; d. Cologne, July 25, 1919), likewise was a cellist. He was a student of his father and of his uncle. In 1876 he made his debut in Weimar. After serving as 1st cellist in the Sondershausen Hofkapelle, he became soloist in the Budapest theater orch. He subsequently settled in Cologne in 1894 as soloist in the Gürzenich Orch. and Quartet, and as a prof. at the Cons. —**NS/LK/DM**

Gryce, Gigi (aka Quism, Basheer),

jazz saxophonist, arranger, and composer; b. Pensacola, Fla., Nov. 28, 1925; d. there, March 14, 1983. A great admirer of Tadd Dameron. He studied composition in Boston, gigging in local groups in Hartford and Boston from 1947. In 1952 he went to Paris, perhaps to study informally—he didn't do much jazz playing there. In 1953 he toured with Lionel Hampton's band and recorded with bandmate Clifford Brown. Later that year he and Brown worked in Atlantic City for Tadd Dameron, whom he greatly admired. He subsequently worked with Max Roach and Oscar Pettiford, then began leading his own bands. He co-led the Jazz Lab Quintet with Donald Byrd and did arrangements for Art Farmer (1950s). He was also a jazz music publisher. He recorded with Thelonious Monk (*Monk's Music* from 1957 as well as a quartet session under his own name),

Lee Morgan, and others before he quit performing in the early 1960s, possibly due to personal problems. During the 1970s, he changed his name simply to Quism. He became an elementary school teacher—so admired that the Bronx school where he taught is now named after him. Among his best-known pieces is "Nica's Tempo," now a standard; he also wrote "Stan's Blues" (formerly "Eleanor," after his first wife) and has also received credit for "Wildwood," both recorded by Stan Getz. His music was used by Fred Baker in his award-winning short *On the Sound* (1961) and in Baker's *Lenny Bruce without Tears* (1972).

DISC.: *Blue and Brown* (1953); *G. G. and His Big Band* (1953); *G. G. and His Orch.* (1953); *G. G.–Clifford Brown Sextet* (1953); *Bird Calls, Vol. 2* (1955); *Jordu* (1955); *Nica's Tempo* (1955); *Signals* (1955); *And the Jazz Lab Quintet* (1957); *At Newport* (1957); *Modern Jazz Perspective* (1957); *Quartet* (1958); *Jazz Lab* (1958); *Hap'nin's* (1960); *Jazz Lab Quintet* (1960); *Rat Race Blues* (1960); *Sayin' Somethin'!* (1960); *Reminiscin'* (1961).—**LP/MF**

Guadagni, Gaetano,

celebrated Italian castrato contralto, later soprano; b. Lodi or Vicenza, c. 1725; d. Padua, Nov. 1792. He was a contralto at the Basilica del Santo in Padua in 1746, and that same year he commenced his stage career at the Teatro San Moise in Venice. In 1748 he went to London and appeared at the Haymarket Theatre. Handel was so impressed with Guadagni's voice that he arranged contralto parts for him in *Messiah* and *Samson*, and also composed the role of Didimus in *Theodora* for him, which role Guadagni created at Covent Garden on March 16, 1750. Guadagni seems to have made his way to Lisbon in 1753 to study with Gioacchino "Gizziello" Conti. In 1754 he appeared at the Concert Spirituel in Paris, and also sang in Versailles. After another London sojourn in 1755, he sang throughout Europe. While in Vienna, he created the title role in Gluck's *Orfeo* on Oct. 5, 1762, and also sang in concerts. He then accompanied Gluck to Frankfurt am Main for the coronation of the emperor in 1764. After singing in Innsbruck (1765), Venice (1767–69), and once again at London's Haymarket Theatre (1770), he returned to his homeland. In 1772 he was granted the title of Cavaliere di San Marco in Venice. Following appearances in Munich in 1773 and 1775, he sang before Frederick the Great in Potsdam in 1776. In 1777 he settled in Padua, where he sang mainly at the Basilica del Santo. Guadagni was renowned for both his vocal and dramatic gifts. He composed several arias, including *Pensa a serbarmi, o cara* for Metastasio's *Ezio*. His sister, Maria Levinia Guadagni (b. Lodi, Nov. 21, 1735; d. Padua, c. 1790), was a singer and the wife of **Felice Alessandri**.—**NS/LK/DM**

Guadagnini,

family of famous Italian violin makers. **Lorenzo Guadagnini** (1689–1748) used the label "Laurentius Guadagnini, alumnus Antonius Stradivarius," and he may have studied with Stradivarius in Cremona shortly before the latter's death in 1737. Lorenzo's son, **Giovanni Battista Guadagnini** (b. Cremona, 1711; d. Turin, Sept. 18, 1786), received his training presumably from his father, and may have been with him at the shop of Stradivarius. He followed his father from Cremona to Piacenza (1740–49), worked in Milan

(1749–58), was in Parma (1759–71), and then settled in Turin. His violins are regarded as the finest of the Guadagninis. His 2 sons, **Giuseppe Guadagnini** (1736–1805) and **Gaetano Guadagnini** (1745–1831), continued the family tradition and manufactured some good instruments, but failed to approach the excellence of their father's creations. Violin-making remained the family's occupation through 4 more generations in Turin. The last representative, **Paolo Guadagnini**, perished in the torpedoing of an Italian ship, on Dec. 28, 1942.

BIBL.: E. Doring, *The G. Family of Violin Makers* (Chicago, 1949).—NS/LK/DM

Guadagno, Anton, Italian-born American conductor; b. Castellammare del Golfo, May 2, 1925. He studied at the Palermo Cons.; after obtaining degrees in conducting and composition at the Accademia di Santa Cecilia in Rome, he took 1st prize in conducting at the Salzburg Mozarteum; his principal conducting mentors were Ferrara, Molinari, C. Zecchi, and Karajan. Following engagements in Italy and South America, he emigrated to the U.S. and became a naturalized American citizen. In 1952 he made his U.S. debut conducting at a Carnegie Hall concert in N.Y. In 1958–59 he was an asst. conductor at the Metropolitan Opera in N.Y. From 1966 to 1972 he was music administrator of the Philadelphia Lyric Opera. In 1970 he made his London debut conducting *Andrea Chénier* at Drury Lane, and returned to London in 1971 to make his debut at Covent Garden conducting *Un ballo in maschera*. On Nov. 9, 1982, he made his formal debut at the Metropolitan Opera in N.Y. conducting the latter opera. He was artistic director of the Palm Beach (Fla.) Opera from 1984.—NS/LK/DM

Gualdo, John (Giovanni), Italian musician and wine merchant; b. place and date unknown; d. Philadelphia, Dec. 20, 1771. He arrived in Philadelphia from London in 1767 and opened a store. Among other things, he sold instruments and taught violin, flute, guitar, etc. He also arranged music and presented concerts, the first of which, given in Philadelphia on Nov. 16, 1769, was devoted largely to Gualdo's own compositions, and may well be regarded as the earliest "composer's concert" in America. He died insane. His *6 easy evening entertainments for 2 mandolins or 2 violins with a thorough bass for the harpsichord or violincello* are in MS in the Library of Congress, Washington, D.C. The printed op.2, *6 Sonates for 2 German flutes with a thorough bass* (his name appears as Giovanni Gualdo da Vandero), is in the British Museum.—NS/LK/DM

Guami, Francesco, distinguished Italian trombonist and composer, brother of **Gioseffo Guami;** b. Lucca, c. 1544; d. there, Jan. 30, 1602. He went to Munich about 1568 as a musician at the court chapel of Duke Albert V. About 1580 he is believed to have become Kapellmeister to Margrave Philipp II in Baden-Baden, although his name is not given in court records until 1587–88. He then returned to Italy, where he became maestro di cappella at San Marciliano in Venice about 1593. In 1596 he was made maestro di cappella at Udine Cathedral, but he seems not to have assumed his duties there. In 1598 he was appointed capo della musica of the Cappella Palatina in Lucca, and later was the first to serve there as maestro di cappella. He was highly esteemed as both an instrumentalist and as a composer of madrigals.

WORKS: VOCAL: S e c u l a r : *Il primo libro de' madrigali* for 4 and 5 Voices (Venice, 1588); *Il secondo libro de' madrigali* for 4, 5, and 6 Voices (Venice, 1593); *Il terzo libro de' madrigali* for 4 and 5 Voices (Venice, 1598). **S a c r e d :** *Laudate Dominum,* motet for 10 Voices (1585); Masses, all of which are lost. **OTHER:** *Ricercari a 2* (Venice, 1598).

BIBL.: P. Crabtree, *The Vocal Works of Gioseffo and F. G.* (diss., Univ. of Cincinnati, 1971).—NS/LK/DM

Guami, Gioseffo, renowned Italian organist and composer, brother of **Francesco Guami;** b. Lucca, c. 1540; d. there, 1611. He sang in the cappella grande at San Marco in Venice (1561–68), where he studied with Willaert and Annibale Padovano. He then went to Munich as 1st organist and capo delli concerti at the court chapel of Duke Albert V, where he was active until 1579; he also was in Italy with Lassus (1570–74). In 1579 he became organist at San Michele in Lucca. By 1585 he was maestro di cappella at the court of Prince Gian Andrea Doria in Genoa, but was once more in Lucca by 1587. After serving as 1st organist at San Marco in Venice (1588–91), he returned again to Lucca and was organist at the Cathedral from 1591 until his death. He was succeeded by his son Vincenzo. Guami was one of the most highly regarded musicians of his time. He was a master of the organ, but he also was praised as a string player and singer. He was a highly gifted composer, being especially esteemed for his motets.

WORKS: VOCAL: S a c r e d : *Sacrae cantiones* for 5 to 8 and 10 Voices (Venice, 1585); *Lamentationes Hieremiae prophetae* (Venice, 1588); *Sacrarum cantionum variis, et choris, et instrumentorum generibus concinendarum* (Milan, 1608); various other works, including the parody mass *In me transierunt* on a Lassus motet (1590). **S e c u l a r :** *Il primo libro di madrigali* for 5 Voices (Venice, 1565); *Il terzo libro de madrigali* for 5 Voices (Venice, 1584); *Il quarto libro de madrigali* for 5 and 6 Voices (Venice, 1591). **OTHER:** *Canzonetta francese a 4, 5, and 8* (Venice, 1601; may not be by Guami); also 2 fantasias a 4 (1588), a toccata for Organ (1593), and a number of canzonas.

BIBL.: A. Bonaccorsi, *Maestri di Lucca: I G. e altri musicisti* (Florence, 1967); P. Crabtree, *The Vocal Works of G. and Francesco G.* (diss., Univ. of Cincinnati, 1971).—NS/LK/DM

Guaraldi, Vince(nt Anthony), jazz pianist and composer; b. San Francisco, July 17, 1928; d. Menlo Park, Calif., Feb. 6, 1976. He played piano in high school and college in the San Francisco area. Around late 1949/early 1950, he began playing with Cal Tjader; he made his first recordings with Tjader in 1953. In 1955, he formed his own trio, which was popular among the San Francisco beatnik scene. During 1956, he toured with Woody Herman's Third Herd. He was a frequent contributor to West Coast sessions in the 1950s and 1960s, but became more identified with concept projects like the "Jazz Impressions." He is world famous for his themes for the *Peanuts* television specials during the

1960s, but these only hint at the hard swinging and attractive work he created. He last recorded in 1974, and two years later died of a heart attack while performing at a small club.

DISC.: *Modern Music from San Francisco* (1955); *Trio* (1956); *A Flower Is a Lovesome Thing* (1957); *Jazz Impressions of "Black Orpheus"* (1962); *Tour de Force* (1963); *V. G./Conte Candoli* (1963); *In Person* (1963); *Jazz Impressions of A Boy Named Charlie Brown* (1964); *Latin Side of V. G.* (1964); *Live at the El Matador* (1966).—**LP**

Guarducci, Tommaso, notable Italian castrato soprano; b. Montefiascone, c. 1720; d. after 1770. He was a pupil in Bologna of Bernacchi. From about 1745 he sang in many Italian music centers. In 1750 he became a prominent singer at the Spanish court; he also appeared at the Vienna court from 1752, while continuing his career in Italy. After singing at the King's Theatre in London (1766–68), he retired to his homeland in 1770.—**NS/LK/DM**

Guarino, Carmine, Italian composer; b. Rovigo, Oct. 1, 1893; d. Genoa, June 5, 1965. He studied violin and composition at the Naples Cons. His first opera, *Madama di Challant*, set in the tradition of Verdi, was premiered there on March 9, 1927, attracting favorable comments. He was also the composer of the first Italian radio opera, *Cuore di Wanda* (Radio Italiano, Dec. 20, 1931). Other works for the stage were an operetta, *Gaby* (San Remo, March 20, 1924); *Tabarano alla Corte di Nonesiste*, musical fable (1931); 2 operas: *Balilla* (Rome, March 7, 1935) and *Sogno di un mattino d'autunno* (Cluj, March 30, 1936); and a ballet, *El Samet, il silenzioso* (1958).—**NS/LK/DM**

Guarino, Piero, Italian pianist, conductor, pedagogue, and composer; b. Alexandria, Egypt, June 20, 1919; d. Rovereto, May 23, 1991. He studied piano and composition at the Athens Cons. (1936–39) before pursuing his training at the Accademia di Santa Cecilia in Rome; he completed advanced studies with Casella and Bonucci. From 1939 he was active as a pianist and conductor. After serving as director of the Alexandria Cons. (1950–60), he was director of the chamber orch. of the Accademia Musicale Napoletana (1962–73); he also taught at the Salzburg Mozarteum (1963–67) and the Perugia Cons. (1965–66). He then was director of the Sassari Cons. (1969–75) and the Parma Cons. (1975–89).

WORKS: DRAMATIC: O p e r a : *Vettura-letto* (chamber opera, 1969). **ORCH.:** Sym. for Strings (1946); Piano Concerto (1947); *Jeu parti* for Chamber Orch. (1966); *Omaggio a Clementi* for Student Orch. (1972). **CHAMBER:** *Gagliarda, Sarabanda e Giga* for Viola and Piano (1941); *Sonata da camera* for Cello and Piano (1943); *Introduzione, aria e finale* for Violin and Piano (1944); *12 Pezzi* for 10 Instruments (1945); Trio for Violin, Cello, and Piano (1945); *Divertimento su un Capriccio di Piatti* for 4 Cellos or 4 Groups of Cellos (1974); various piano pieces. **VOCAL:** *De Profundis* for 2 Women's Voices and String Orch. (1965); *Salve Regina* for Chorus (1977); *Schlaflied* for Women's Chorus (1978); *Quattro Haiku* for Soprano and Piano (1987).—**NS/LK/DM**

Guarneri, famous Italian family of violin makers. The Italian form of the name was **Guarnieri;** Guarneri was derived from the Latin spelling, **Guarnerius;** the labels invariably used the Latin form. **Andrea,** head of the family (b. Cremona, c. 1625; d. there, Dec. 7, 1698), was a pupil of Nicolo Amati; he lived in Amati's house from 1641 to 1646, and again from 1650 to 1654, when, with his wife, he moved to his own house in Cremona and began making his own violins, labeling them as "alumnus" of Amati and, after 1655, "ex alumnis," often with the additional words of "sub titolo Sanctae Theresiae." Andrea's son **Pietro Giovanni,** known as **Pietro da Mantova** (b. Cremona, Feb. 18, 1655; d. Mantua, March 26, 1720), worked in Cremona before settling in Mantua about 1638, where he also was active as a court musician; he also used the device "sub titolo Sanctae Theresiae." Another son of Andrea, **Giuseppe Giovanni Battista,** known as **Silius Andreae** (b. Cremona, Nov. 25, 1666; d. there, c. 1740), worked in his father's shop, which he eventually inherited in 1698; he made outstanding cellos as well as violins. Giuseppe's son **Pietro,** known as **Pietro da Venezia** (b. Cremona, April 14, 1695; d. Venice, April 7, 1762), left home about 1718 and settled in Venice, where he adopted some features of the Venetian masters Montagnana and Serafin. Another son of Giuseppe, **(Bartolomeo) Giuseppe Antonio,** known as **Giuseppe del Gesù,** from the initials IHS often appearing on his labels (b. Cremona, Aug. 21, 1698; d. there, Oct. 17, 1744), became the most celebrated member of the family; some of his instruments bear the label "Joseph Guarnerius Andreae Nepos Cremonae," which establishes his lineage as a grandson of Andrea. His violins are greatly prized, rivaling those of Stradivarius in the perfection of instrumental craftsmanship; he experimented with a variety of wood materials, and also made changes in the shapes of his instruments during different periods of his work. Such great virtuoso violinists as Paganini, Heifetz, Stern, Szeryng, and Grumiaux used his instruments.

BIBL.: G. de Piccolellis, *Liutai antichi e moderni, genealogia degli Amati et dei Guarnieri* (Florence, 1886); H. Petherick, *Joseph Guarnerius, His Work and His Master* (London, 1906); H. Wenstenberg, *Joseph Guarnerius del Gesù Abbildungen und Beschreibungen seiner Instrumente aus seinen drei Perioden* (Berlin, 1921); W. Hill, *Violin Makers of the G. Family, 1626–1762: Their Life and Work* (London, 1931).—**NS/LK/DM**

Guarnieri, Antonio, distinguished Italian conductor; b. Venice, Feb. 1, 1880; d. Milan, Nov. 25, 1952. He studied cello, piano, and composition in Venice. He began his career as a cellist in the Martucci Quartet. After making his conducting debut in Siena in 1904, he conducted in various Italian theaters. Following an engagement at the Vienna Court Opera (1912–13), he returned to Italy and founded the Società Sinfonica Italiana in Milan in 1915. In 1922 he made his first appearance at Milan's La Scala, where he subsequently was one of its principal conductors from 1929 until shortly before his death. Guarnieri was highly esteemed for his interpretations of the Italian operatic repertory.—**NS/LK/DM**

Guarnieri, (Mozart) Camargo, esteemed Brazilian composer, conductor, and teacher; b. Tietê, Feb. 1, 1907; d. São Paulo, Jan. 13, 1993. His father was an

Italian emigrant, his mother a Brazilian. After musical instruction from his parents, he went to São Paulo in 1922 and studied with Lamberto Baldi and Mário de Andrade; later he pursued his training with Koechlin (composition) and Rühlmann (conducting) in Paris (1938–39). Upon returning to São Paulo, he served as resident conductor of the Municipal Sym. Orch. and, from 1975, was conductor of the Univ.'s Sym. Orch.; he also was engaged in teaching. Between 1941 and 1981 he made a number of visits to the U.S., occasionally appearing as a conductor of his own works. His extensive catalogue of music, skillfully crafted in a tonal style, is basically reflective of Brazilian national elements.

WORKS: DRAMATIC: *Pedro Malazarte*, comic opera (1931); *O Homen Só*, opera (1960). **ORCH.:** *Suite Infantil* (1929); *Curuçá* (1930); 5 piano concertos (1931, 1946, 1964, 1968, 1970); 2 violin concertos (1940, 1953); *Encantamento* (1941); *Abertura Concertante* (1942); 7 syms. (1944, 1944, 1954, 1963, 1977, 1981, 1985); *Prólogo e Fuga* (1947); *Suite Brasiliana* (1950); *Chôro* for Violin and Orch. (1952), for Clarinet and Orch. (1956), for Piano and Orch. (1956), for Cello and Orch. (1961), for Flute and Orch. (1974), for Viola and Orch. (1975), and for Bassoon and Orch. (1990); *Variações sobre a Tema de Nordeste* for Piano and Orch. (1953); *Suite IV Centenário* (1954); *Suite Vila Rica* (1957); Piano Concertino (1961); *Seresta* for Piano and Chamber Orch. (1965); *Homenagem á Villa-Lobos* for Wind Orch. (1966); *Sequência: Coral e Ricercare* for Chamber Orch. (1966); *Abertura Festiva* (1971); *Saratí* for Piano and Orch. (1987); Sonatina for Violin and Chamber Orch. (1988). **CHAMBER:** 7 violin sonatas (1930, 1933, 1950, 1956, 1959, 1963, 1978); 3 string quartets (1932, 1944, 1962); 3 cello sonatas (1939, 1955, 1977); Viola Sonata (1950); Trio for Piano, Violin, and Cello (1989); numerous piano pieces. **VOCAL:** Cantatas; choral pieces; more than 300 songs.
—NS/LK/DM

Guarrera, Frank, American baritone; b. Philadelphia, Dec. 3, 1923. He studied voice with Richard Bonelli in Philadelphia. On Dec. 14, 1948, he made his Metropolitan Opera debut in N.Y. as Escamillo in *Carmen*, where he remained on its roster until 1976. He was invited by Toscanini to sing at La Scala in Milan; also made guest appearances in San Francisco, Chicago, Paris, and London. He was best known for his performances of Italian roles.**—NS/LK/DM**

Gubaidulina, Sofia (Asgatovna), remarkable Russian composer; b. Chistopol, Oct. 24, 1931. She received training in piano from Maria Piatnitskaya and in theory from Nazib Zhiganov at the Academy of Music (1946–49), and in piano from Leopold Lukomsky and Grigory Kogan, and in composition from Albert Leman at the Cons. (1949–54) in Kazan. She then studied composition with Nikolai Peiko and Vissarion Shebalin at the Moscow Cons. (1954–63), and later pursued research at the Moscow Electronic Music Studio (from 1968). In 1991 she settled in Germany. In 1999 she was awarded the Léonie Sonning Music Prize of Denmark. Gubaidulina's heritage—her grandfather was a mullah, her father was a Tatar, and her mother was of Russian, Polish, and Jewish descent—has played a significant role in her development as a composer. Claiming that "I am the place where East meets West,"

the spiritual quality of her works is reflected in the influence of the Muslim, Orthodox, Jewish, and Roman Catholic faiths. While she has pursued advanced compositional methods along avant-garde lines, she has done so in victorially divergent paths which have allowed her to retain a unique individuality.

WORKS: DRAMATIC: Opera-ballet-oratorio: *Oration for the Age of Aquarius* (1991). **Ballet:** *Volshebnaya svirel* (1960); *Flute of Tania* (1961); *Begushchaya po volnam* (1962). Film scores. **ORCH.:** 2 syms.: No. 1 (1958) and No. 2, *Stimmen...Verstummen* (Berlin, Sept. 4, 1986); Piano Concerto (1959); *Adagio and Fugue* for Violin and String Orch. (1960); *Intermezzo* for 8 Trumpets, 16 Harps, and Percussion (1961); *Triumph*, overture (1963); *Fairy Tale Poem* (1971); *Detto II* for Cello and Orch. (1972; Moscow, May 5, 1973); Concerto for Bassoon and Low Strings (1975; Moscow, May 6, 1976); Concerto for Orch. and Jazz Band (1976; Moscow, Jan. 16, 1978); *Te salutant* for Large Light Orch. (1978); *Introitus* for Piano and Chamber Orch. (Moscow, Feb. 22, 1978); *Offertorium* for Violin and Orch. (1980; Vienna, May 30, 1981; rev. version, Berlin, Sept. 24, 1982; final version, London, Nov. 2, 1986); *(Last) 7 Words* for Cello, Bayan, and Strings (Moscow, Oct. 20, 1982); *Antwort ohne Frage* for 3 Orchs. (1988); *Pro et Contra* (Louisville, Nov. 24, 1989); *Und: Das Feste ist in vollem Gange*, cello concerto (1993; La Palmas, Canary Islands, Jan. 31, 1994); *Zeitgestalten* (Birmingham, Nov. 29, 1994); *Music for Flute, Strings, and Percussion* (1994); Viola Concerto (1996; Chicago, April 17, 1997); *The Canticle of the Sun*, concerto for Cello, Chamber Chorus, and Percussion Orch. (1997; rev. 1998); *In the Shadow of the Tree* for Koto, Bass Koto, Zheng, and Orch. (1998; Tokyo, April 14, 1999); *Two Paths* for 2 Violas and Orch. (1998; N.Y., April 29, 1999). **CHAMBER:** *Variations* for String Quartet (1956); Piano Quintet (1957); *Allegro rustico* for Flute and Piano (1963); *5 Études* for Harp, Double Bass, and Percussion (1965); Percussion Sonata (1966); *Pantomime* for Double Bass and Piano (1966); *Concordanza* for 10 Instruments (Prague, May 23, 1971); 4 string quartets: No. 1 (1971; Cologne, March 24, 1979), No. 2 (Kuhmo, Finland, July 23, 1987), No. 3 (Edinburgh, Aug. 22, 1987), and No. 4 (1990); *Music for Harpsichord and Percussion* (Leningrad, April 5, 1972); *10 Preludes* for Cello (1974); *Quattro* for 2 Trumpets and 2 Trombones (1974); *Rumore e silenzio* for Percussion and Harpsichord or Celesta (1974); Double Bass Sonata (1975); *2 Ballads* for 2 Trumpets and Piano (1976); Trio for 3 Trumpets (1976); *Dots, Line, and Zigzag* for Bass Clarinet and Piano (1976); *On Tatar Folk Themes* for Domra and Piano (1977); Duo Sonata for 2 Bassoons (1977); *Misterioso* for 7 Percussion (1977); Quartet for 4 Flutes (1977); *Lamento* for Tuba and Piano (1977); *Muzika* for Harpsichord and Percussion (1977); *Song Without Words* for Trumpet and Piano (1977); *Detto I* for Organ and Percussion (1978); *Sounds of the Forest* for Flute and Piano (1978); Flute Sonatina (1978); *De Profundis* for Bayan (1978); *2 Pieces* for Horn and Piano (1979); *Jubilatio* for 4 Percussion (1979); *In croce* for Cello and Organ (1979); *Garten von Freuden und Traurigkeiten* for Flute, Harp, Viola, and Speaker ad libitum (1980); *Sonata: Rejoice!* for Violin and Cello (1981); *Descensio* for 9 Instruments (Paris, April 30, 1981); *Quasi Hoquetus* for Viola, Bassoon, and Piano (1984); Bayan Sonata (1985); *Silenzio*, 5 pieces for Accordion, Violin, and Cello (1991); *Der Seiltänzer*, violin sonata (Washington, D.C., Feb. 24, 1994); *In Erwartung* for Saxophone Quartet and 6 Percussionists (1994); *An Angel* for Alto and Double Bass (1994); *Quaternion* for 4 Cellos (1996). **KEYBOARD: Piano:** Sonatina (1952); *8 Preludes* (1955); *Chaconne* (1962); Sonata (1965); *Musical Toys*, 14 children's pieces

(1969); *Toccata-troncata* (1971); *Invention* (1974). **O r g a n** : *Light and Darkness* (1976). **VOCAL**: *Fazelija* for Soprano and Orch. (1956); *Night in Memphis* for Mezzo- soprano, Men's Chorus, and Orch. (1968; rev. 1988 and 1992); *Rubáiyát* for Baritone and Chamber Orch. (1969; Moscow, Dec. 24, 1976); *Stufen* for Speaking Chorus and Orch. (1972); *Laudatio Pacis* for Soprano, Alto, Tenor, Bass, Speaker, 2 Choruses, and Orch. (1975; in collaboration with M. Kopelent and P.-H. Dittrich); *Perception* for Soprano, Baritone, 2 Violins, 2 Violas, 3 Cellos, Double Bass, and Tape (1983; Lockenhaus, June 11, 1986); *Hommage à Marina Tsvetayeva* for Chorus (1984); *Hommage à T.S. Eliot* for Soprano and 8 Instruments (Cologne, March 25, 1987); *Witty Waltzing in the Style of Johann Strauss* for Soprano and 8 Instruments (Cologne, March 25, 1987); *Jauchzt vor Gott* for Chorus and Organ (1989); *Alleluia* for Boy Soprano, Chorus, and Orch. (1990); *Aus dem Stundenbuch* for Men's Chorus, Cello, and Orch. (1991); *Jetzt Immer Schnee* for Chamber Chorus and Chamber Ensemble (Amsterdam, June 12, 1993); *Galgenlieder a 3* for Mezzo-soprano, Double Bass, and Percussion (1995–96); *Galgenlieder a 5* for Mezzo-soprano, Flute, Percussion, Bayan, and Double Bass (1996); *Song Cycle* for Soprano and Double Bass (Huddersfield, Nov. 25, 1996); *St. John Passion* for Soloists, 2 Choruses, and Orch. (1999).—**NS/LK/DM**

Gubrud, Irene (Ann), American soprano; b. Canby, Minn., Jan. 4, 1947. She studied at St. Olaf Coll. in Northfield, Minn. (B.M., 1969), and with Marion Freschel at the Juilliard School of Music in N.Y. She won the Naumburg International Voice Competition (1980), and made her operatic debut as Mimi in St. Paul, Minn., in 1981; also toured widely as a recitalist. She was successful in a comprehensive repertoire, extending from early music to the avant-garde.—**NS/LK/DM**

Gudehus, Heinrich, distinguished German tenor; b. Altenhagen, near Celle, March 30, 1845; d. Dresden, Oct. 9, 1909. He was a student of Malvina Schnorr von Carolsfeld in Braunschweig and of Gustav Engel in Berlin. After making his operatic debut in Berlin as Nadori in *Jessonda* (Jan. 7, 1871), he sang in Lübeck, Freiburg, and Bremen. From 1880 to 1890 he was a principal member of the Dresden Court Opera. On July 28, 1882, he made his Bayreuth debut as Parsifal in its second staging, and returned there as Tristan in 1886 and as Walther von Stolzing in 1888. On June 4, 1884, he made his first appearance at London's Covent Garden in the latter role. He made his Metropolitan Opera debut in N.Y. on Nov. 28, 1890, as Tannhäuser, and remained on its roster for the season. After singing at the Berlin Royal Opera (1891–96), he settled in Dresden as a voice teacher. Among his other outstanding roles were Florestan, John of Leyden, Siegmund, Lohengrin, and Siegfried.—**NS/LK/DM**

Gudmundsen-Holmgreen, Pelle, noted Danish composer; b. Copenhagen, Nov. 21, 1932. He received training in violin. After private theory and composition lessons with Høffding (1951–53), he continued his training at the Royal Danish Cons. of Music in Copenhagen (1953–58), where he studied theory, composition, and music history with Høffding and Westergaard, and instrumentation with Holmboe. From 1967 to 1973 he taught composition at the Royal Cons. of

Music in Århus, and then devoted himself fully to composition. In 1973 he received the Carl Nielsen Prize. In 1980 he was awarded the Nordic Council Music Prize for his Sym. No. 3, *Antifoni*. After utilizing serial techniques, he developed an individual means of expression, a minimalist simplicity achieved through persistent repetition of notes and patterns.

WORKS: BALLET: *Den gamle mand* (1976); *Rituelle danse* (1976); *Flight* (1981). **ORCH.**: *Ouverture* for Strings (1955); *Lamento* for Chamber Orch. (1957); *Chronos* for Chamber Orch. (1962); 3 syms.: No. 1 (1962–65), No. 2, *På Rygmarven* (1966), and No. 3, *Antifoni* (1974–77); *Collegium Musicum Koncert* for Chamber Orch. (1964); *Mester Jakob/Frère Jacques* for Chamber Orch. (1964); *Repriser* for Chamber Orch. (1965); *5 Pieces* (1966); *Tricolore I* (1966), *II* (1966), *III* (1966), and *IV* (1969); *Segnali* for Wind Orch. (1966); *Rerepriser* for Chamber Orch. (1967); *Stykke for stykke* for Chamber Orch. (1968); *Kvartet for 18* for Wind Orch. (1968); *Spejl II* (1973); *Oktober* for Chamber Orch. (1977); *Mosaik* for Chamber Orch. (1979); *Triptykon*, percussion concerto (1985); *Naer og fjern* for Chamber Orch. (1987); *Concord* for Chamber Orch. (1988); Concerto Grosso for String Quartet and Orch. (1990); *Traffic* (1994). **CHAMBER:** *Variationer* for Cello (1954); Nonet for Woodwind Quintet, 2 Percussion, and Piano (1958); 8 string quartets: No. 1 (1959), No. 2, *Quartetto facile* (1959), No. 3, *5 små studier* (1959), No. 4 (1967), No. 5, *Step by Step* (1982), No. 6, *Parting* (1983), No. 7, *Parted* (1984), and No. 8, *Ground* (1986); *In Terra Pax* for Clarinet, 2 Percussion, and Piano (1961); *Kanon* for 9 Instruments (1967); *Plateaux pour deux* for Percussion and Cello (1970); *Terrasse* for Woodwind Quintet (1970); *Solo* for Electric Guitar (1971–72); *So Long* for Electric Guitar (1972); *Re-Cycling* for 7 Instruments (1975); *Kysset*, ritual dance for 5 Percussion and Electric Guitar (1976; also for 6 Percussion); *Passacaglia* for Clarinet, Piano, Percussion, Violin, and Cello (1977); Trio, *Møder og drømme* (1979); *Spejlstykker* for Clarinet, Cello, and Piano (1980); *reTurning* for Flute, Clarinet, Percussion, Harp, and Piano (1987); *Naer og fjern* for Wind Quintet, String Quartet, and Double Bass (1987). **KEYBOARD: P i a n o** : *Variations* (1959); *3 Epigrams* (1962); *Pictures at an Exhibition* (1968); *For Piano* (1992). **O r g a n** : *Mirror III* (1974). **VOCAL:** *Wandering* for Chorus (1956); *Je ne me tairai jamais. Jamais* for 12 Voices or Chorus, Narrator, and Chamber Ensemble (1966); *Statements* for Children's Chorus or Equal Voices (1969); *Examples* for Chorus (1970); *Yes-No* for Double Chorus (1973); *Light* for 5 Solo Voices or Chorus and Organ (1976); *Songs Without* for Mezzo-soprano or Contralto and Piano (1976); *Turn* for Soprano, Bass Flute, Guitar, and Harp (1993).—**NS/LK/DM**

Gueden, Hilde, noted Austrian soprano; b. Vienna, Sept. 15, 1917; d. Klosterneuburg, Sept. 17, 1988. She studied with Wetzelsberger at the Vienna Cons., then made her debut in operetta at the age of 16. She made her operatic debut as Cherubino in 1939 in Zürich, where she sang until 1941. After appearing in Munich (1941–42) and Rome (1942–46), she sang at the Salzburg Festival (1946); subsequently was a leading member of the Vienna State Opera until 1973. She first appeared at London's Covent Garden with the visiting Vienna State Opera in 1947; her Metropolitan Opera debut followed in N.Y. on Nov. 15, 1951, when she appeared as Gilda; she continued to sing there until 1960. In 1951 she was made an Austrian Kammersängerin. She maintained a wide-ranging repertoire, singing roles from Mozart to contemporary composers such as Britten and Blacher; she also was a fine operetta singer. She particularly excelled as Despina, Sophie, Zerbinetta, and Daphne. —**NS/LK/DM**

Guédron, Pierre, important French composer; b. Beauce province, Normandy, between 1570 and 1575; d. probably in Paris, 1619 or 1620. He was a chorister in the service of Cardinal de Guise, Louis II of Lorraine, by 1585. Following the cardinal's assassination in 1588, he entered the service of the royal chapel. He was given 1st place as maître des chanteurs de la chambre about 1590, then was made compositeur de la chambre du Roi (1601) and valet de chambre to the king and maître des enfants de la musique (1603). His son-in-law, Antoine Boësset, succeeded him in 1613 while he took up the post of intendant des musiques de la chambre du Roy et de la Reyne Mère (he is listed as surintendant in court records of 1617 and 1619). He was one of the most significant composers of airs de cour and ballets de cour of his era, some of which were included in a number of the ballets he wrote for the court.

WORKS: **BALLET** (all 1st perf. in Paris): *Ballet sur la naissance de Monseigneur le duc de Vendosme* (1602); *Ballet de la Reyne* (1609); *Ballet de Monseigneur le duc de Vendosme, ou Ballet d'Alcine* (1610); *Ballet du maître à danser* (c. 1612); *Ballet de Madame, soeur du Roy* (1613); *Ballet des Argonautes* (1614); *Ballet du triomphe de Minerve* (1615); *Ballet de Monsieur le Prince Condé* (1615); *Ballet du Roy, ou Ballet de la délivrance de Renaud* (1617); *Ballet des princes* (1618); *Ballet du Roy sur l'aventure de Tancrède en la forest enchantée* (1619). **VOCAL:** *Airs de cour* for 4 and 5 Voices (Paris, 1602; 1 part-book not extant); *Airs de cour* for 4 and 5 Voices (Paris, 1608); *Second livre d'airs de cour* for 4 and 5 Voices (Paris, 1613); *Troisième livre d'airs de cour* for 4 and 5 Voices (Paris, 1617); *Quatrième livre d'airs de cour* for 4 and 5 Voices (Paris, 1618; 1 part-book not extant); *Cinquième livre d'airs de cour* for 4 and 5 Voices (Paris, 1620; 4 part-books not extant). Airs were also arranged for voice and lute and were publ. in various contemporary anthologies; several were also arranged for instruments.

BIBL.: D. Royster, *P. G. and the Air de cour, 1600–1620* (diss., Yale Univ., 1972).—**NS/LK/DM**

Guelfi, Giangiacomo, Italian baritone; b. Rome, Dec. 21, 1924. He studied law in Florence and received vocal training from Ruffo. In 1950 he made his operatic debut as Rigoletto in Spoleto, and then sang at Milan's La Scala (from 1952); he also made appearances in Chicago (from 1954) and in London (from 1958). On Feb. 5, 1970, he made his Metropolitan Opera debut in N.Y. as Scarpia, remaining on its roster for only that season. In 1975 he sang Scarpia at London's Covent Garden.—**NS/LK/DM**

Guénin, Marie-Alexandre, French violinist, pedagogue, and composer; b. Maubeuge, Feb. 20, 1744; d. Étampes, Jan. 22, 1835. He began to study the violin at age 6, and about 1760 his father sent him to Paris to study with Capron and Gaviniès (violin) and Gossec (composition). He pursued his career in Paris, serving as first violinist in the orchs. Of the Opéra (1771–1801) and the Concert Spirituel (1771–83). In 1773 he made his debut as a soloist at the Concert Spirituel, and in 1777 he was made its asst. director. He also became music director to the Prince of Condé in 1777 and a violinist in the Musique du Chambre du Roy in 1778. In 1784 he joined the faculty of the École Royale de Chant et de Déclamation as a violin instructor. After it became the Cons. in 1795, he continued to teach there until 1802. About 1808 he went to Spain, where he was active in the service of Charles IV. After a sojourn in Marseilles, he was 2nd violin in the Musique du Roi (1814–16). He composed syms., trios, duos, sonatas, and other works which followed the models of Gossec and the Mannheim school.—**NS/LK/DM**

Guéranger, Dom Prosper Louis Pascal, French ecclesiastic scholar; b. Sable-sur-Sarthe, April 4, 1805; d. Solesmes, Jan. 30, 1875. As abbot of the Benedictine monastery at Solesmes, he carried out research and produced writings that gave the impetus to and laid the foundations for scholarly investigations leading to the restoration of Gregorian melodies. Dom Guéranger and the Benedictines of Solesmes played a role of prime importance in the accomplishment of this work. He wrote *Institutions liturgiques* (3 vols., 1840–53; 2nd ed., 4 vols., 1878–85), *L'Annee liturgique* (15 parts, 1840–1901; continued by Fromage), and *Ste. Cécile et la Société Romaine* (1873; 8th ed., 1898).

BIBL.: G. Guépin, *Prosper G.* (Le Mans, 1876); Chamard, *G. et l'abbé Bernier* (Angers, 1901); P. Delatte, *Dom G., abbé de Solesmes* (2 vols., Paris, 1909).—**NS/LK/DM**

Guerra-Peixe, César, Brazilian composer, violinist, and conductor; b. Petrópolis, March 18, 1914; d. Rio de Janeiro, Nov. 23, 1993. Following training in violin and theory locally (1925–30), he went to Rio de Janeiro and studied violin and theory (1932–37) and then composition with Newton Pádua at the Cons. Brasileiro (1934–43) and privately with Koellreuther (1944). He played violin in theater orchs. and in the National Sym. Orch. In 1946–47 he appeared as a conductor of his own works with the BBC in England. He taught composition privately, conducted many Brazilian orchs., and was director and music arranger for Tupi-TV in Rio de Janeiro. As a composer, he plunged headlong into the torrent of dodecaphony, but about 1949 he changed his orientation and reclaimed his Brazilian roots, nurtured by melorhythmic folksong resources.

WORKS: **ORCH.:** 2 syms.: No. 1 (1946) and No. 2, *Brasília*, for Narrator, Chorus, and Orch. (1960); *Instantâneos Sinfônicos 1 and 2* (1947); 2 divertimentos for Strings (1947); Suite for Strings (1949); *Abertura Solene* (1950); *Suite Sinfônica 1: Paulista* (1955) and *2: Pernambucana* (1955); *Ponteado* (1955); *Pequeño concerto* for Piano and Orch. (1956); *Museu de Inconfidência* (1972); Violin Concertino (1975); *Tribute to Portinari* (Rio de Janeiro, Oct. 15, 1993). **CHAMBER:** *Music* for Flute and Piano (1944); Nonet (1945); *Cuarto Mixto* for Flute, Clarinet, Violin, and Cello (1945); 2 string quartets (1947, 1958); 2 wind trios (1948, 1951); Violin Sonata (1950); Piano Trio (1960); Guitar Sonata (1969); *Dueto caracteristico* for Violin and Guitar (1970); Duo for Clarinet and Bassoon (1970); *Variações Opcionais* for Violin and Accordion (1977). **Piano:** *Música No. 1* (1945); 3 suites (1949, 1954, 1954); 2 sonatas (1950, 1967); 2 sonatinas (1950, 1969).—**NS/LK/DM**

Guerrero, Francisco, notable Spanish composer; b. Seville, Oct. 4?, 1528; d. there, Nov. 8, 1599. He studied with his brother, Pedro, and also taught himself to play the organ, cornet, harp, and vihuela. He was a contralto at Seville Cathedral (1542–46), during which time he studied with Morales (c. 1545). From 1546 to 1549 he was maestro de capilla at Jaén Cathedral. In 1549 he accepted a preband as a singer at Seville Cathedral. In 1551 and 1554 he was offered the post of maestro de capilla at Málaga Cathedral, but declined on both occasions; however, he accepted the post of associate to the maestro de capilla at Seville Cathedral in 1551. He was active in Yuste (1557 or 1558), Toledo (1561), Lisbon (1566), and Córdoba (1567) before touring Spain in the royal entourage in 1570–71. In 1574 he was made maestro de capilla at Seville Cathedral. In 1581–82 he was in Rome, and in 1588 in Venice. He then made a pilgrimage to the Holy Land (1588–89), which he recounted in his book *El viaje de Jerusalem que hizo Francisco Gerrero* (publ. posthumously, 1611). In 1589 he returned to Venice, and later that year he settled in Seville, where he died of the plague. Guerrero was greatly esteemed by his contemporaries. He was a significant composer of Spanish sacred music, being surpassed only by Victoria among the masters of his era. He composed 18 Masses and had some 150 other sacred works publ. in his lifetime. He also wrote numerous secular songs. Some of his secular works were included in anthologies. M. Querol Gavalda ed. his *Opera omnia* in Monumentos de la Música Española, XVI and XIX (1949–57; unfinished). L Merino ed. *The Masses of F. G.* (diss., Univ. of Calif., Los Angeles, 1972).

WORKS: VOCAL: *Sacrae cantiones, vulgo moteta nuncupata* for 4 and 5 Voices (Seville, 1555); *Psalmorum, liber primus: accedit Missa defunctorum* for 4 Voices (Rome, 1559; not extant); *Canticum beatae Mariae, quod Magnificat nuncupatur, per octomusicae modos variatum* for 4 and 5 Voices (Louvain, 1563); *Liber primus missarum* for 4 and 5 Voices (Paris, 1566); *Motetta* for 4 to 6 Voices (Venice, 1570); *Missarum liber secundus* for 4 to 6 Voices (Rome, 1582); *Liber vesperarum* for 4 to 6 and 8 Voices (Rome, 1584); *Passio D. N. Jesu Christi secundum Matthaeum et Joannem [more hispano]* for 5 Voices (Rome, 1585); (61) *Canciones y villanescas espirituales* for 3 to 5 Voices (Venice, 1589; with 18 contrafacta); *Motecta, liber secundus* for 4 to 6 and 8 Voices (Venice, 1589).

BIBL.: R. Mitjana y Gordon, *F. G. (1528–1599): Estudio crítico-biográfico* (Madrid, 1922).—NS/LK/DM

Guerrini, Guido, Italian composer and pedagogue; b. Faenza, Sept. 12, 1890; d. Rome, June 13, 1965. He studied with Torchi and Busoni at the Bologna Liceo Musicale. After teaching on its faculty (1920–24), he taught at the Parma Cons. (1925–28); he then was director of the Florence Cons. (1928–47), the Bologna Cons. (1947–49), and the Cons. di Santa Cecilia in Rome (1950–60). In addition to books on harmony and orchestration, he publ. *Ferrucio Busoni: La vita, la figura e l'opera* (Florence, 1941) and *Antonio Vivaldi: La vita e l'opera* (Florence, 1951). He was especially effective in composing orch., sacred, and chamber pieces.

WORKS: DRAMATIC: Opera: *Zalebi* (1915); *Nemici* (Bologna, Jan. 19, 1921); *La vigna* (1923–25; Rome, March 7, 1935); *L'arcangelo* (1930; Bologna, Nov. 26, 1949); *Enea* (Rome, Feb. 11, 1953). **ORCH.:** *Visioni dell'antico Egitto,* symphonic poem (1919); *L'ultimo viaggio d'Odisseo,* symphonic poem (1921); *Poemetto* for Cello and Orch. (1924); *Preludio a corale* for Organ and Orch. (1930); 3 Pieces for Piano, Percussion, and Strings (1931); *Danza degli spiriti* (1932); *7 Variations on a Sarabande by Corelli* for Piano and Strings (1940); *Canzone e ballo forlivese* for Chamber Orch. (1952); *7 Variations on an Allemande by John Bull* (1962–63). **CHAMBER:** 3 string quartets (1920, 1922, 1959); 2 piano trios (1920, 1926); Violin Sonata (1921); Piano Quintet (1927); String Quintet (1950); piano pieces. **VOCAL:** *Bacco ubbriaco* for Bass and Orch. (1938); *Il lamento di Job* for Bass, Piano, Tam-tam, and Strings (1938); *Missa pro defunctis* "alla memoria di G. Marconi" for Solo Voices, Chorus, and Orch. (1938–39); *La città beata, La città perduta* for Solo Voice or Voices, Chorus, and Orch. (1942); *Nativitas Cristi* for Solo Voices, Chorus, and Orch. (1952); *Vigiliae Sulamitis* for Mezzo-soprano and Orch. (1953); 4 Masses; many songs.

BIBL.: A. Damerini, *Profilo critico di G. G.: Biografia e bibliografia* (Milan, 1928); P. Fragapane, *G. G. e i suoi poemi sinfonici* (Florence, 1932); *Catalogo delle opere di G. G. al suo settantesimo anno di età e curriculum della sua vita e cura dell'interessato, come saluto e ricordo agli amici* (Rome, 1961). —NS/LK/DM

Guerrini, Paolo (Antigono), Italian music historian; b. Bagnolo Mella, Brescia, Nov. 18, 1880; d. Brescia, Nov. 19, 1960. He specialized in Italian sacred music. He ed. the periodical *Brixia Sacra* (1910–25), and in 1930 began publication of the historical studies *Memorie storiche della Diocesi di Brescia*; served further as archivist and librarian in Brescia. In 1936 he was appointed canon of the Brescia Cathedral. He revived and tr. into Italian the music books of Cardinal Katschthaler as *Storia della musica sacra* (Turin, 1910; 3rd ed., 1936). —NS/LK/DM

Guess Who, The, popular Canadian rock band that also gave rise to one-time member Randy Bachman's Bachman-Turner Overdrive. The Guess Who: **MEMBERSHIP:** Burton Cummings, lead voc., kybd., rhythm gtr. (b. Winnipeg, Manitoba, Canada, Dec. 31, 1947); Randy Bachman, lead gtr. (b. Winnipeg, Manitoba, Canada, Sept. 27, 1943); Jim Kale, bs. (b. Winnipeg, Manitoba, Canada, Aug. 11, 1943); Garry Peterson, drm. (b. Winnipeg, Manitoba, Canada, May 26, 1945). Many personnel changes beginning in 1970. Bachman-Turner Overdrive: **MEMBERSHIP:** Randy Bachman, voc., lead gtr; Tim Bachman, rhythm gtr. (b. Winnipeg, Manitoba, Canada); Robbie Bachman, drm. (b. Winnipeg, Manitoba, Canada, Feb. 18, 1953); C. F. Turner, bs., voc. (b. Winnipeg, Manitoba, Canada, Oct. 16, 1943). Tim Bachman left in 1973, to be replaced by Blair Thornton (b. Vancouver, British Columbia, Canada, July 23, 1950).

The Guess Who began their evolution in Winnipeg, Manitoba, Canada, in 1962, when Chad Allan (born Allan Kobel), Randy Bachman, Bob Ashley, Jim Kale, and Garry Peterson formed the Reflections. Changing their name to Chad Allan and the Expressions in 1964, they scored a top Canadian and major U.S. hit with "Shakin' All Over" in 1965. Burton Cummings joined the group in the summer of 1965 and Bob Ashley and Chad Allan dropped out of the group in 1966. Becoming the Guess Who, the group appeared on the Canadian television show *Where It's At* in 1967, recording over a dozen Canadian singles through 1968. They secured U.S. distribution of their recordings with RCA Records in 1969 and soon scored a smash hit with the Bachman-Cummings composition "These Eyes" from their debut RCA album. Their second RCA album, *Canned Wheat*, yielded the two-sided hit "Laughing"/"Undun" and the smash hit "No Time," another Bachman-Cummings collaboration.

The Guess Who became international stars with 1970's *American Woman* album and top two-sided single "American Woman"/"No Sugar Tonight." Randy Bachman left in July 1970, yet the Guess Who continued to score major hits through 1971 with "Hand Me Down World," "Share the Land," "Albert Flasher," and "Rain Dance." Experiencing a number of personnel changes, the Guess Who achieved two final hits in 1974 with "Clap for the Wolfman" (a smash) and "Dancin' Fool." The group disbanded in 1975.

Burton Cummings pursued a solo career in the late 1970s, managing a near- smash hit with "Stand Tall" in 1976. In 1979, Jim Kale reconstituted the Guess Who for a single album and subsequent touring. Burton Cummings and Randy Bachman toured as the Guess Who in 1987 and, by 1989, Garry Peterson had joined Kale's edition of the Guess Who.

After leaving the Guess Who, Randy Bachman formed Brave Belt with Chad Allan. After a sole album with Allan, Brave Belt regrouped with Bachman, his brothers Tim and Robbie, and C. Fred Turner. In 1972, the group became Bachman-Turner Overdrive, replacing Tim Bachman with Blair Thornton in 1973. Signed to Mercury Records, the group scored major hits with "Let It Ride" and "Takin' Care of Business" and a top hit with "You Ain't Seen Nothing Yet" in 1974. The hits continued in 1975 with "Roll on Down the Highway" and "Hey You." Randy Bachman departed in 1977 and the group continued to chart into 1979. Bachman formed Ironhorse, who achieved a modest hit with "Sweet Lui-Louise" in 1979. Randy and Tim Bachman regrouped with Fred Turner in 1984 for a sole album on *Compleat*.

DISC.: The Guess Who: *Sown and Grown in Canada* (1971); *The Guess Who Play the Guess Who* (1971); *Wheatfield Soul* (1969); *Canned Wheat Packed by the Guess Who* (1969); *American Woman* (1970); *Share the Land* (1970); *So Long, Bannatyne* (1971); *Rockin'* (1972); *Live at the Paramount* (1972) *Artificial Paradise* (1973); *Number 10* (1973); *Road Food* (1974); *Flavours* (1975); *Power in the Music* (1975); *The Way We Were* (1976); *Lacindy* (1994). **BURTON CUMMINGS:** *Burton Cummings* (1976); *My Own Way to Rock* (1977); *Dream of a Child* (1978). **RANDY BACHMAN:** *Axe* (1970); *Survivor* (1978). **BACHMAN-TURNER OVERDRIVE:** *Bachman-Turner Overdrive* (1973); *Bachman-Turner Overdrive II* (1973); *Not Fragile* (1974); *Four Wheel Drive* (1975); *Head On* (1975); *King Biscuit Flower Hour Concert* (1998).

BIBL.: Martin Melhuish, *Bachman-Turner Overdrive: Rock Is My Life, This Is My Song: The Authorized Biography* (Toronto, 1976).—**BH**

Guest, George (Hywel), esteemed Welsh organist, conductor, and teacher; b. Bangor, Feb. 9, 1924. He studied organ with Boyle in Chester and then was an

organ scholar under Orr at St. John's Coll., Cambridge (Mus.B., 1951). From 1951 to 1991 he was organist and choirmaster at St. John's Coll. He led the choir on various tours, and also appeared as an organ recitalist. He served as asst. lecturer (1953–56) and then as lecturer (1956–82) at the Univ. of Cambridge, and in 1960–61 he was a prof. at the Royal Academy of Music in London. From 1974 to 1991 he was organist at the Univ. of Cambridge. He served as president of the Royal Coll. of Organists (1978–80), the Cathedral Organists' Assn. (1980–82), and the Incorporated Assn. of Organists (1987–89). In 1987 he was made a Commander of the Order of the British Empire. His discriminating repertory as a choral conductor ranged from Palestrina to Britten. His years at Cambridge are highlighted in his book *A Guest at Cambridge* (Orleans, Mass., 1994). —**NS/LK/DM**

Guéymard, Louis, French tenor; b. Chapponay, Aug. 17, 1822; d. Paris, July 1880. Following his operatic debut in Lyons in 1845, he joined the Paris Opéra in 1848, where he was one of its principal singers until 1868 and where he created the roles of Jonas in *Le Prophéte* (1849), Arrigo in *Les Vêpres siciliennes* (1855), and Assad in *La Reine de Saba* (1862). He also sang at London's Covent Garden (1852) and in New Orleans (1873–74). His wife was the Belgian soprano Pauline Lauters- Guéymard (b. Brussels, Dec. 1, 1834; place and date of death unknown) who sang at the Paris Théâtre-Lyrique in 1854. She then was a member of the Paris Opéra (1857–76), where she created the roles of Balkis in *La Reine de Saba* (1862), Eboli in *Don Carlos* (1867), and Gertrude in Thomas's *Hamlet* (1868).—**NS/LK/DM**

Guézec, Jean-Pierre, French composer; b. Dijon, Aug. 29, 1934; d. Paris, March 9, 1971. He enrolled at the Paris Cons., where he attended classes of Messiaen, Milhaud, and Rivier. He received the premier prix in 1963. In 1969 he joined the faculty of the Paris Cons.

WORKS: Concerto for Violin and 14 Instruments (1960); *Concert en trois parties* for 11 Instruments (1961); *Suite pour Mondrian* for Orch. (1962); *Architectures colorées* for 15 Instruments (1964); *Ensemble multicolore 65* for 18 Instruments (1965); *Formes* for Orch. (1966); *Textures enchaînées* for 13 Wind Instruments (1967); *Assemblages* for 28 Instruments (1967); String Trio (1968); *Reliefs polychromés* for Chorus (1969); *Couleurs juxtaposées* for 2 Percussion Groups (1969); *Onze pour cinq* for Percussionists (1970).—**NS/LK/DM**

Guglielmi, Pietro Alessandro, noted Italian composer, father of **Pietro Carlo Guglielmi;** b. Massa di Carrara, Dec. 9, 1728; d. Rome, Nov. 18, 1804. He began his musical training with his father, Jacopo Guglielmi, then studied with Durante at the S. Maria di Loreto Cons. in Naples. His first opera, *Lo solachianello 'mbroglione*, was given in Naples in 1757. During the next decade, he wrote no fewer than 25 operas; these included such popular works as *Il ratto della sposa* (Venice, 1765) and *La Sposa fedele* (Venice, 1767), which, along with *L'impresa d'opera* (Venice, 1769), were performed throughout Europe with notable success. In 1767 he went to London, where he brought out several operas;

his wife, known as Maria Leli or Lelia Acchiapati (or Acchiappati), sang in his *Ezio* at the King's Theatre (Jan. 13, 1770). He returned to Italy in 1772, and continued to compose stage works with abandon; among the most popular were *La Villanella ingentilita* (Naples, Nov. 8, 1779), *La Quakera spiritosa* (1782), *Le vicende d'amore* (Rome, 1784), *La Virtuosa di Mergellina* (Naples, 1785), *La Pastorella nobile* (Naples, April 15, 1788), *La bella pescatrice* (Naples, Oct. 1789), and *La Serva innamorata* (Naples, 1790). His oratorios were also highly successful, and were often performed in stage versions; *La morte di Oloferne* (Rome, April 22, 1791) was a great favorite. In 1793 he was appointed maestro di cappella at S. Pietro in the Vatican; in 1797 he also assumed the post of maestro di cappella at S. Lorenzo Lucina. Guglielmi was one of the major Italian composers of his day. His productivity and facility were remarkable, making it possible for him to write for the stage or the church with equal aplomb.

WORKS: DRAMATIC:O p e r a / c o m i c (all 1st perf. in Naples unless otherwise given): *Lo solachianello 'mbroglione* (1757); *Il Filosofo burlato* (1758); *I capricci di una vedova* (1759); *La Moglie imperiosa* (1759); *I du soldati* (1760); *L'Ottavio* (1760); *Il finto cieco* (1761); *La Donna di tutti i caratteri* (1762); *La Francese brillante* (1763); *Li Rivali placati* (Venice, 1764); *Il ratto della sposa* (Venice, 1765); *La Sposa fedele* (Venice, 1767); *I Viaggiatori ridicoli tornati in Italia* (London, May 24, 1768); *L'impresa d'opera* (Venice, Carnival 1769); *Il Disertore* (London, May 19, 1770); *L'Amante che spende* (Venice, 1770); *Le pazzie di Orlando* (London, Feb. 23, 1771); *Il carnevale di Venezia, o sia La Virtuosa* (London, Jan. 14, 1772); *L'assemblea* (London, March 24, 1772); *Mirandolina* (Venice, Carnival 1773); *Il matrimonio in contrasto* (1776); *I fuoriusciti* (1777); *Il raggiratore di poca fortuna* (Aug. 1, 1779); *La Villanella ingentilita* (Nov. 8, 1779); *La Dama avventuriera* (1780); *La Serva padrona* (1780); *Le nozze in commedia* (Jan. 1781); *Mietitori* (Oct. 20, 1781); *La semplice ad arte* (May 12, 1782); *La Quakera spiritosa* (1783); *La Donna amante di tutti, e fedele a nessuno* (1783); *I finti amori* (1784); *La Virtuosa di Mergellina* (1785); *L'inganno amoroso* (June 12, 1786); *Le astuzie villane* (1786); *Lo scoprimento inaspettato* (Carnival 1787); *La Pastorella nobile* (April 15, 1788); *Gl'inganni delusi* (June 13, 1789); *La bella pescatrice* (Oct. 1789); *La Serva innamorata* (July 1790); *L'azzardo* (Oct. 9, 1790); *Le false apparenze* (1791); *La Sposa contrastata* (1791); *Il Poeta di campagna* (1792); *Amor tra le vendemmie* (1792); *La lanterna di Diogene* (Venice, 1793); *La Pupilla scaltra* (Venice, Jan. 8, 1795); *L'amore in villa* (Rome, 1797). **O p e r a / s e r i o u s :** *Tito Manlio* (Rome, Jan. 8, 1763); *L'Olimpiade* (Nov. 4, 1763); *Siroe re di Persia* (Florence, Sept. 5, 1764); *Farnace* (Rome, Feb. 4, 1765); *Tamerlano* (Venice, 1765); *Adriano in Siria* (Venice, Dec. 26, 1765); *Sesostri* (Venice, May 7, 1766); *Demofoonte* (Treviso, Oct. 8, 1766); *Antigono* (Milan, Jan. 1767); *Il Re pastore* (Venice, 1767); *Ifigenia in Aulide* (London, Jan. 16, 1768); *Alceste* (Milan, Dec. 26, 1768); *Ruggiero* (Venice, May 3, 1769); *Ezio* (London, Jan. 13, 1770); *Demetrio* (London, June 3, 1772); *Tamas Kouli-Kan nell'Indie* (Florence, Sept. 16, 1774); *Merope* (Turin, Carnival 1775); *Vologeso* (Milan, Dec. 26, 1775); *La Semiramide riconosciuta* (Aug. 12, 1776); *Artaserse* (Rome, Jan. 29, 1777); *Ricimero* (May 30, 1777); *Enea e Lavinia* (Nov. 4, 1785); *Laconte* (May 30, 1787); *Arsace* (Venice, Dec. 26, 1788); *Rinaldo* (Venice, Jan. 28, 1789); *Ademira* (May 30, 1789); *Alessandro nell'Indie* (Nov. 4, 1789); *Il trionfo di Camilla* (May 30, 1795); *La morte di Cleopatra* (June 22, 1796); *Ippolito* (Nov. 4, 1798); *Siface e Sofonisba* (May 30, 1802). **OTHER:** Many other stage works, as well as various other vocal works, including Masses, a Requiem, Credos, Offertories, Magnificats, and Misereres along with many instrumental sinfonias, 2 harpsichord concertos, 6 quartets for Harpsichord, 2 Violins, and Cello, 6 sonatas for Harpsichord or Piano, 5 piano sonatas, etc.

BIBL.: G. Bustico, *Pier A. G.: Appunti biografici* (Massa, 1898); idem, *Un musicista massese: Pier A. G.* (Barga, 1926).—NS/LK/DM

Guglielmi, Pietro Carlo, Italian composer, son of **Pietro Alessandro Guglielmi;** b. Rome or Naples, c. 1763; d. probably in Naples, Feb. 21, 1817. He studied voice, keyboard playing, and composition at the Cons. Santa Maria di Loreto in Naples. By 1794 he was in Madrid, where he brought out his first operas. In 1795 he returned to Italy and brought out operas for various cities. In 1809 he went to London as an opera composer. After returning to Naples in 1811, he served as maestro di cappella to the Archduchess Beatrice at Massa di Carrara from about 1813. He wrote over 40 dramatic scores, mainly comic operas, several of which were popular in their day. He also composed an oratorio, *La distruzione di Gerusalemme* (Naples, 1803).—NS/LK/DM

Guhr, Karl (Wilhelm Ferdinand), German conductor and composer; b. Militsch, Oct. 30, 1787; d. Frankfurt am Main, July 22, 1848. He studied in Breslau with Schnabel and Janitschek. From 1821 he was active as a conductor in Nuremberg, Wiesbaden, Kassel, and Frankfurt am Main, winning the admiration of Spontini, Wagner, Berlioz, and other contemporaries. He publ. the study *Über Paganinis Kunst die Violine zu spielen* (Mainz, 1831). Among his works were operas, a Sym., concertos, and chamber music.—LK/DM

Gui, Vittorio, eminent Italian conductor; b. Rome, Sept. 14, 1885; d. Florence, Oct. 16, 1975. He studied composition with Falchi at the Liceo Musicale di Santa Cecilia in Rome, and also attended the Univ. of Rome. On Dec. 7, 1907, he made his debut conducting *La Gioconda* at Rome's Teatro Adriano. After conducting in Naples, he appeared at Milan's La Scala (1923–25; 1932–34). In 1925 he was a founder and conductor of the Teatro di Torino. In 1928 he organized the Orch. Stabile in Florence, which served as the foundation of the famous Maggio Musicale Fiorentino, which he instituted in 1933; he also was a conductor at the Teatro Comunale there. In 1938–39 he conducted at London's Covent Garden, and returned there in 1952. He was chief conductor of the Glyndebourne Festivals from 1952 to 1960, and then was its artistic counsellor from 1960 to 1965. Gui continued to conduct in Italy until the close of his long life, making his final appearance only a few weeks before his death at the age of 90. He was one of the leading Italian conductors of his day, excelling not only in opera but also in symphonic music. He also composed the operas *David* (Rome, 1907) and *Fata Malerba* (Turin, May 15, 1927), the orch. works *Giulietta e Romeo* (1902), *Il tempo che fu* (1910), *Scherzo fantastico* (1913), *Fantasia bianca* (1919), and *Giornata di festa* (1921), chamber music, and songs. Gui publ. the study *Nerone di Arrigo Boito* (Milan, 1924) and a vol. of critical essays *Battute d'aspetto* (Florence, 1944).—NS/LK/DM

Guidetti, Giovanni Domenico, Italian ecclesiastic scholar; b. Bologna (baptized), Jan. 1, 1531; d. Rome, Nov. 30, 1592. After taking Holy Orders, he went to Rome, where he became Palestrina's pupil and in 1575 was appointed "cappellano" and chorister in the papal choir. From 1576 to 1581 he worked with Palestrina on a revised ed. of the Gradual and Antiphonary, but this work being forestalled by the publication of Leichtenstein's ed. (Venice, 1580), he obtained permission to publ. the services for everyday use: *Directorium chori ad usum sacro-sanctae basilicae Vaticanae* (Rome, 1582, and several reprints), *Cantus ecclesiaticus passionis Domini Nostri Jesu Christi* (Rome, 1586), and *Cantus ecclesiasticus officii majoris* (Rome, 1587; new ed., 1619). He also publ. *Praefationes in cantu firmo* (Rome, 1588). —NS/LK/DM

Guido d'Arezzo or **Guido Aretinus,** famous Italian music theorist; b. c.991; d. after 1033. He received his education at the Benedictine abbey at Pomposa, near Ferrara. He left the monastery in 1025, as a result of disagreements with his fellow monks, who were envious of his superiority in vocal teaching; he was then summoned by Bishop Theobald of Arezzo to the cathedral school there; it was because of this association that he became known as Guido d'Arezzo. In 1028 Pope John XIX called him to Rome to demonstrate his system of teaching. In his last years, he was a prior of the Camaldolite fraternity at Avellano. Guido's fame rests on his system of solmization, by which he established the nomenclature of the major hexachord Ut, Re, Mi, Fa, Sol, La, from syllables in the initial lines of the Hymn of St. John:

Ut queant laxis Resonare fibris

Mira gestorum Famuli tuorum,

Solve polluti Labii reatum,

Sancte Joannes.

No less epoch-making was Guido's introduction of the music staff of 4 lines, retaining the red *f*-line and the yellow *c*-line of his predecessors, and drawing between them a black *a*-line, above them a black *e*-line, and writing the plainsong notes (which he did not invent) in regular order on these lines and in the spaces:

Old yellow line e_____

New black line e_____

Old yellow line c_____

New black line a_____

Old red line f_____

He also added new lines above or below these, as occasion required; thus, Guido's system did away with all uncertainty of pitch. Another invention credited to Guido is the so-called Guidonian hand, relating the degrees of the overlapping hexachords to various places on the palm of the left hand, a device helpful in directing a chorus by indicating manually the corresponding positions of the notes. Opinions differ widely as to the attribution to Guido of all these innovations; some scholars maintain that he merely popularized the already- established ideas and that solmization, in particular, was introduced by a German abbot, Poncius Teutonicus, at the abbey of Saint-Maur des Fosses.

WRITINGS: *Aliae regulae* (foreword to an antiphoner; Pomposa, c. 1020–25); *Micrologus de disciplina artis musicae* (c. 1026; ed. by J. Smits van Waesberghe in Corpus Scriptorum de Musica, IV, 1955; Eng. tr. by W. Babb in C. Palisca, ed., *Hucbald, Guido, and John on Music: Three Medieval Treatises*, New Haven, 1979); *Regulae rhythmica* (c. 1025–27); *Epistola de ignoto cantu* (c. 1028–29; Eng. tr. in O. Strunk, *Source Readings in Music History*, N.Y., 1950; rev. ed., 1998, by L. Treitler).

BIBL.: L. Angeloni, *Sopra la vita, le opere ed il sapere di G. d'A.* (Paris, 1811); R. Kiesewetter, *G. von A.: Sein Leben und Wirken* (Leipzig, 1840); G. Ristori, *Biografia di G. Monaco d'A.* (Florence, 1867); M. Falchi, *Studi su G. Monaco di San Benedetto* (Florence, 1882); H. Wolking, *G.s Micrologus de disciplina artis musicae und seine Quellen* (Emsdetten, 1930); J. Smits van Waesberghe, *De musicopaedogogico et theoretico Guidone Aretino eiusque vita et moribus* (Florence, 1953); H. Oesch, *G. von A.* (Bern, 1954); C. Margueron, *Recherches sur Guittone d'A.* (Paris, 1966). —NS/LK/DM

Guignon, Jean-Pierre, (real name, **Giovanni Pietro Ghignone),** famous Italian-born French violinist and composer; b. Turin, Feb. 10, 1702; d. Versailles, Jan. 30, 1774. Following training from G.B. Somis in Turin, he went to Paris, where he made his debut at a Concert Spirituel in 1725. He subsequently appeared there regularly during the next 25 years. In 1730 he entered the service of the Prince of Carignan, and remained in his entourage until about 1750. In 1733 he was made ordinaire de la musique du roy, a position he retained until his retirement in 1762. In 1741 he became a naturalized French subject. In 1746 he was made teacher of the Dauphin, and shortly afterward persuaded the King to revive and bestow upon him the title of Roy et maître des ménétriers et joueurs d'instrumens tant hauts que bas et communauté des maîtres à dancer. As such, every professional musician in France was required to join a guild and pay a fee to Guignon as holder of the title. So much opposition resulted that his authority was curtailed in 1750, and in 1773 the position was abolished. Guignon greatly distinguished himself as a violinist. Among his compositions were 2 violin concertos, 6 sets of sonatas, and several duos. —NS/LK/DM

Guilfoyle, Ronan, Irish composer; b. Dublin, March 5, 1958. He began his studies in music in jazz, receiving training in bass and improvisation with Dave Holland in Banff, Canada. His performances as a jazz musician took him throughout Europe, Asia, and North America. He also taught improvisation for the International Council of UNESCO and was director of the jazz dept. of Newpark Music Centre in Dublin. In 1990 he began composing classical music, including scores often requiring performers to improvise.

WORKS: *Sequence of Events* for Bassoon, Trumpet, Trombone, Tenor Saxophone, and Drums (1990); Concerto for Jazz Guitar Trio and Orch. (1993; Dublin, Feb. 24, 1994); Violin Sonata (1994); *Concerto for Orchestra* (1995); *Devsirme* for Instrumental Ensemble or Jazz Quintet (1995); *Dice* for Soprano and Tenor Saxophones, Trombone, Bass Guitar, and Drums (1996); *A.K.A.* for Soprano Saxophone, Bass Guitar, and Drums (1996); *Obsessive* for Clarinet, Tenor Saxophone, Trombone, Bass Guitar, and Drums (1996); *T'Cha* for Soprano and Tenor Saxophones,

Trombone, Bass Guitar, and Drums (1996); *Transchumance* for Soprano and Tenor Saxophones, Trombone, Bass Guitar, and Drums (1996); *Music* for Clarinet and String Trio (1996); *Phantom City* for Soprano Saxophone, Accordion, Bass Guitar, and Drums (1997); *Toccata and Feud* for Piano (1998); *Music* for Soprano Saxophone and String Quartet (1998); *D/C* for Soprano Saxophone and English Horn.—**LK/DM**

Guillemain, Louis-Gabriel, French violinist and composer; b. Paris, Nov. 15, 1705; d. Chaville, near Paris, Oct. 1, 1770. He studied in Paris and then with G.B. Somis in Italy. By 1729 he was in Lyons, where he soon was made 1st violinist of the Dijon Academy of Music. Returning to Paris, he became a musicien ordinaire to Louis XV in 1737. He was notably successful at the court as both a violinist and composer. His ballet-pantomime *L'opérateur chinois* (Paris, Dec. 12, 1748) enjoyed extraordinary success. In later years, he was plagued by alcoholism and is believed to have taken his own life. He publ. 18 instrumental opus numbers (1734–62). His 12 trio syms., as well as several of his chamber sonatas, reveal a composer of discernable talent.

BIBL.: G. Castonguay, *The Orchestral Music of L.-G. G.* (diss., Clark Univ., Worcester, Mass., 1975).—**NS/LK/DM**

Guillou, Jean, prominent French organist, pianist, teacher, and composer; b. Angers, April 18, 1930. He began to study the piano at 5 and the organ at 10. When he was 12, he became organist at the church of St.-Serge in Angers. He then was a student at the Paris Cons. (1945–53) of Dupré, Duruflé, and Messiaen, where he took premiers prix in organ, harmony, counterpoint, and fugue. After serving as prof. of organ at the Istituto de Alta Cultura in Lisbon (1953–57), he went to Berlin to puruse his career. In 1963 he was named organist at St.-Eustache in Paris. He also pursued an international career as a recitalist, principally as an organist. In addition to teaching masterclasses in organ, he publ. a book on organ theory and design, *L'Orgue, Souvenir et Avenir* (Paris, 1978; 2nd ed., aug., 1989). Guillou's vast repertoire ranges from the Baroque to the contemporary periods. As a virtuoso organist, he has acquired a reputation for daring registration and rhythms, and for a mastery of improvisation.

WORKS: ORCH.: 5 organ concertos (1960, 1963, 1965, 1978, 1979); 2 piano concertos (1969, 1986); 3 syms.: No. 1 for Mezzo-soprano and Orch., *Judith-Symphonie* (1970), No. 2 for Strings (1974), and No. 3, *La Foule* (1977); *Concerto Heroïque* for Organ and Orch. (1985); Trombone Concerto (1990). **CHAMBER:** *Colloque* No. 1 for Flute, Oboe, Violin, and Piano (1956), No. 2 for Piano and Orch. (1964), No. 3 for Oboe, Harp, Celesta, Percussion, 4 Cellos, and 2 Double Basses (1964), No. 4 for Piano, Organ, and 2 Percussion (1966), and No. 5 for Piano and Organ (1969); Oboe Quartet (1971); Sonata for Trumpet and Organ (1972); Concerto for Violin and Organ (1982); *Fantaisie Concertante* for Cello and Organ (1991). **KEYBOARD: Piano:** 2 sonatas (1958, 1978). **Organ:** *Fantaisie* (1954); 18 Variations (1956); Sinfonietta (1958); *Toccata* (1963); *Symphonie Initiatique* for 2 Organs (1969); 7 *Sagas* (1970–83); *Scènes d'Enfants* (1974); *Jeux d'Orgue* (1978); *Sonate en Trio* (1984); *Hyperion* (1988); many transcriptions. **VOCAL:** *Andromede* for Soprano and Organ (1984); *Peace* for Chorus and Organ (1985); *Aube* for Chorus and Organ (1988).—**NS/LK/DM**

Guilmant, (Félix) Alexandre, eminent French organist and composer; b. Boulogne, March 12, 1837; d. Meudon, near Paris, March 29, 1911. He studied organ with his father, Jean-Baptiste Guilmant (1793–1890), and took harmony lessons with Gustave Carulli in Boulogne. In 1860 he took an advanced course in organ playing with Lemmens in Brussels. He then played organ in various churches in Paris, including St.-Sulpice (1862) and Notre Dame (1868); in 1871 he was appointed organist of Ste. Trinité, remaining at this post for 30 years. He was one of the founders of the Schola Cantorum (1894). In 1896 he was appointed prof. of organ at the Paris Cons.; also appeared as organ soloist with Paris orchs. And subsequently all over Europe and in the U.S. (1893–97). He was not only a virtuoso of the 1st rank, but a master in the art of improvisation. He formed a great school of students, among whom were René Vierné, Joseph Bonnet, Nadia Boulanger, Marcel Dupré, and the American organist William Carl. He was a prolific composer of works for organ, which include 8 sonatas, 2 syms. for Organ and Orch., 25 books of organ pieces, and 10 books of *L'Organiste liturgiste*; he also wrote Psalms, vespers, motets, etc. He ed. *Archives des maîtres de l'orgue* (10 vols., Paris, 1898–1914) and *École classique de l'orgue* (1898–1903).

BIBL.: *À la mémoire de A. G.* (by his friends of the Schola; Paris, 1911); F. Sabatier, *Pour une approche d'A. G.* (Paris, 1986). —**NS/LK/DM**

Guion, David (Wendell Fentress), American composer and teacher; b. Ballinger, Tex., Dec. 15, 1892; d. Dallas, Oct. 17, 1981. He studied piano with Godowsky in Vienna, but was autodidact in composition. He then held various teaching posts in Tex., and was active in collecting and arranging American folk songs. His best known work was his version of *Home on the Range* (1930). Among his other works were the African ballet suite, *Shingandi* (1929), several orch. suites, including *Texas* (1952), piano pieces, and songs. —**NS/LK/DM**

Guiraud, Ernest, French composer; b. New Orleans, June 23, 1837; d. Paris, May 6, 1892. He studied with his father, Jean Baptiste Guiraud, and produced his first opera, *Le Roi David*, in New Orleans at the age of 15. He then went to Paris, which was his home for the rest of his life. He studied at the Cons. with Marmontel (piano) and Halévy (composition), winning the Grand Prix de Rome in 1859 with his cantata *Bajazet et le joueur de flûte*. He stayed in Rome for 4 years, then returned to Paris, where his 1-act opera *Sylvie* was produced at the Opéra-Comique (May 11, 1864). He was appointed a prof. at the Cons. in 1876, numbering among his students Debussy, Gédalge, and Loeffler. He wrote the recitatives to Bizet's *Carmen* and completed the orchestration of Offenbach's *Les Contes d'Hoffmann*. His operas (all 1st perf. in Paris) include *En prison* (March 5, 1869), *Le Kobold* (July 2, 1870), *Madame Turlupin* (Nov. 23, 1872), *Piccolino* (April 11, 1876; his most popular stage work), *Galante aventure* (March 23, 1882), and *Fredegonde* (completed by Saint-Saëns; Dec. 18, 1895). He also wrote a ballet, *Gretna Green* (Paris, May 5, 1873), 2 suites for Orch. (c. 1871, 1886), and *Caprice* for Violin and Orch. (c. 1885). He publ. a treatise on instrumentation (Paris, 1892).—NS/LK/DM

Gulak-Artemovsky, Semyon Stepanovich, Russian baritone and composer; b. Gorodishche, Feb. 16, 1813; d. Moscow, April 17, 1873. He studied voice with Glinka in St. Petersburg. He sang at the Imperial Opera there (1842–64), then lived in Moscow. His opera *Zaporozhets za Dunayem* (A Cossack beyond the Danube) was produced in St. Petersburg on April 26, 1863, and subsequently acquired considerable popularity in Russia.

BIBL.: L. Kaufman, *S.S. G.-A.* (Kiev, 1962).—NS/LK/DM

Gulbranson, Ellen (née **Norgren**), Swedish soprano; b. Stockholm, March 4, 1863; d. Oslo, Jan. 2, 1947. She studied at the Stockholm Cons. and with M. and B. Marchesi in Paris. In 1886 she made her concert debut in Stockholm, and in 1889 her operatic debut at that city's Royal Opera as Amneris. She gained distinction as a Wagnerian, singing Brünnhilde at every Bayreuth Festival from 1896 to 1914; she also appeared as Kundry. She sang in Berlin from 1895 and in Vienna from 1896; in 1900 she appeared as Brünnhilde at London's Covent Garden, returning there in 1907–08. She also sang in other major music centers until her retirement in 1915.—NS/LK/DM

Gulda, Friedrich, remarkable Austrian pianist; b. Vienna, May 16, 1930; d. Weissenbach, Jan. 27, 2000. He began his training at the Grossmann Cons. After piano lessons with Felix Pazofsky (1938–42), he studied with Bruno Seidlhofer (piano) and Joseph Marx (composition) at the Vienna Academy of Music. At 14, he made his formal debut and at 16 won 1st prize at the Geneva Competition. Thereafter he pursued an outstanding international career. On Oct. 11, 1950, he made a brilliant U.S. debut at N.Y.'s Carnegie Hall. He was praised for his intellectual penetration of the music of Bach, Beethoven, and Mozart. He also became intensely fascinated by jazz, particularly in its improvisatory aspect, which he construed as corresponding to the freedom of melodic ornamentation in Baroque music. In 1956 he made an acclaimed appearance at N.Y.'s Birdland. He often included jazz numbers (with drums and slap bass) at the end of his recitals; he learned to play the saxophone, began to compose for jazz, and organized the Eurojazz Orch. As a further symptom of his estrangement from musical puritanism, he returned the 1970 Beethoven Bicentennial ring given to him by the Vienna Academy of Music in appreciation of his excellence in playing Beethoven's music, noting the failure of conservative classical music training. He composed and performed jazz pieces, among them *Music Nos. 1* and *2* for Piano and Big Band (1962, 1963), *Music* for 3 Jazz Soloists and Band (1962), Sym. in F for Jazz Band and Orch., *The Veiled Old Land* for Jazz Band (1964), *The Excursion* for Jazz Orch., celebrating the flight of the American spaceship Gemini 4 (1965), and Concertino for Players and Singers (1972). He made a bold arrange-

ment of Vienna waltzes in the manner of the blues, and also composed a jazz musical, *Drop-out oder Gustav der Letzte* (1970), freely after Shakespeare's *Measure for Measure*. He publ. a book of essays, *Worte zur Musik* (Munich, 1971).

BIBL.: E. Jantsch, *F. G.: Die Verantwortung des Interpreten* (Vienna, 1953); K. Geitel, *Fragen an F. G.* (Berlin, 1973). —NS/LK/DM

Guleghina, Maria, Russian soprano; b. Odessa, Aug. 9, 1959. She received vocal training at the Odessa Cons. In 1984 she won 1st prize in the All-Union Glinka Competition, and then sang at the Minsk Opera until 1990. She made her first appearance at Milan's La Scala as Amelia in 1986, and subsequently sang such roles there as Tosca, Lisa, and Elisabetta. In 1990 she sang Tosca at the Hamburg State Opera, which role she also portrayed at her Metropolitan Opera debut in N.Y. on March 30, 1991, and at the San Francisco Opera in 1992. In 1994 she sang Verdi's Elvira at the Barbican Hall in London, and in 1995 appeared as that composer's Odabella in Houston. In 1997 she was engaged as Tosca at the Metropolitan Opera and at London's Covent Garden. Following an appearance as Lady Macbeth at La Scala that year, she returned to the Metropolitan Opera as Lina in *Stiffelio* in 1998. In 1999 she sang Verdi's Lady Macbeth at the Opéra National de Paris. —NS/LK/DM

Gülke, Peter, German conductor and musicologist; b. Weimar, April 29, 1934. He was educated at the Franz Liszt Hochschule für Musik in Weimar, the Friedrich Schiller Univ. in Jena, and the Karl Marx Univ. in Leipzig (Ph.D., 1958, with the diss. *Liedprinzip und Polyphonie in der burgundischen Chanson des 15. Jahrhundert*), where he taught (1957–59). In 1959 he made his conducting debut in Rudolstadt, and then was music director of the theaters in Stendal (1964–65), Potsdam (1966–69), and Stralsund (1972–76). After conducting at the Dresden State Opera (1976–81), he was Generalmusikdirektor of the Mannheim National Theater (1981–83). In 1984 he became a lecturer in musicology at the Tech. Univ. in Berlin. He was Generalmusikdirektor in Wuppertal from 1986. In 1978 he brought out a performing edition of Schubert's Sym. in D major, D.936a, a work sometimes listed as that composer's Sym. No. 10. With D. Gülke, he ed. *Jean Jacques Rousseau: Ausgewählte Schriften zur Musik* (Leipzig, 1981). He also publ. *Brahms—Bruckner: Zwei Studien* (Kassel, 1989), *Franz Schubert und seine zeit* (Laaber, 1991), *Fluchtpunkt Musik: Reflexionen eines Dirigenten zwischen Ost und West* (Kassel and Stuttgart, 1994), *Im Zyklus eine Welt: Mozarts letzte Sinfonien* (Munich, 1997), and *"Triumph der neuen Tonkunst:" Mozarts späte Sinfonien und ihr Umfeld* (Kassel, 1998).—NS/LK/DM

Gulli, Franco, distinguished Italian violinist; b. Trieste, Sept. 1, 1926. He studied violin with his father, making his debut in 1933, then went to the Trieste Cons. He also studied in Siena and Paris, his teachers including Arrigo Serato and Joseph Szigeti. He married the pianist **Enrica Cavallo.** In 1947 they formed the noted

Gulli-Cavallo Duo, which made several successful tours. In 1968 he was soloist with the Dallas Sym. Orch.; subsequently played with several American orchs. In 1972 he was appointed prof. at the Ind. Univ. School of Music in Bloomington. An artist of integrity, Gulli secures fine performances of Classical and modern music faithful to the style of the period.—NS/LK/DM

Gumbert, Ferdinand, German composer; b. Berlin, April 22, 1818; d. there, April 6, 1896. After a short study of singing, he appeared at the Cologne Opera (1840–42). In 1842 he settled in Berlin as a voice teacher and also began to compose. His songs, written in a facile, eclectic style, enjoyed a considerable vogue. The song "An des Rheines grünen Ufern" was used as an insert in Lortzing's opera *Undine*. He produced several operettas in Berlin, including *Der kleine Ziegenhirt* (Jan. 21, 1854) and *Bis der Rechte kommt* (Nov. 20, 1856). He publ. *Musik, Gelesenes und Gesammeltes* (Berlin, 1860).

BIBL.: W. Neumann, *F. G.* (Kassel, 1856).—NS/LK/DM

Gumpelzhaimer, Adam, German composer, writer on music, and teacher; b. Trostberg, Upper Bavaria, 1559; d. Augsburg, Nov. 3, 1625. He studied music with Jodocus Entzenmüller at the Benedictine cloister of St. Ulrich and St. Afra in Augsburg, and was Kantor and Präzeptor of the school and church of St. Anna there from 1581. He was made a citizen of Augsburg in 1590. He publ. the treatise-textbook *Compendium musicae,* which went through 13 eds. It included compositions by Gumpelzhaimer as well as by other composers; the canons he wrote for it are particularly noteworthy. O. Mayr ed. *Adam Gumpelzhaimer: Ausgewählte Werke* in Denkmäler der Tonkunst in Bayern, XIX, Jg. X/2 (1909).

WORKS (all publ. in Augsburg): *Compendium musicae* (1591; 2nd ed., aug., 1595, as *Compendium musicae latino-germanicum;* 13th ed., 1681; facsimile, Ann Arbor, 1965); (27) *Neue teutsche geistliche Lieder...nach Art der welschen Villanellen* for 3 Voices (1591; 3rd ed., 1611, as *Lustgartlins teutsch und lateinischer geistlicher Lieder erster Theil);* (29) *Neue teutsche geistliche Lieder nach Art der welschen Canzonen* for 4 and 5 Voices (1594; 3rd ed., 1619, as *Wirtzgärtlins teutsch und lateinischer geistlicher Lieder, erster Theil);* *Contrapunctus* for 4 and 5 Voices (1595); (27) *Sacrorum concentuum...liber primus* for 8 Voices (1601); *Psalmus LI* for 8 Voices (1604); *Lustgärtlins* (28) *teutsch und lateinischer geistlicher Lieder ander Theil* for 3 Voices (1611); (25) *Sacrorum concentuum...cum duplici basso ad organorum usum...liber secundus* for 8 Voices (1614); *Zwai schöne Weihenacht Lieder* for 4 Voices (1618); *Wirtzgärtlins* (31) *teutsch und lateinischer geistlicher Lieder, ander Theil* for 4 and 5 Voices (1619); *Christliches Weihenacht Gesang* for 4 Voices (1620).

BIBL.: O. Mayr, *A. G.: Ein Beitrag zur Musikgeschichte der Stadt Augsburg im 16. und 17. Jahrhundert* (Augsburg, 1908). —NS/LK/DM

Gundry, Inglis, English composer; b. London, May 8, 1905; d. there, April 13, 2000. He studied law at Balliol Coll., Oxford (M.A, 1927) and at the Middle Temple (1927–29) before pursuing his musical training with Vaughan Williams, Gordon Jacob, and R.O. Morris at the Royal Coll. of Music in London (1935–38). In 1936 he won the Cobbett Prize. From 1946 he lectured on

music, and later was founder-music director of the Sacred Music Drama Soc. (1960–86). He publ. *Opera in a Nutshell* (1945), *The Nature of Opera as a Composite Art* (1947), and *Composers by the Grace of God: A Study of Music and Religion* (1989).

WORKS: OPERA: *Naaman: The Leprosy of War* (1936–37); *The Return of Odysseus* (1938); *The Partisans* (London, May 28, 1946); *Avon* (London, April 11, 1949); *The Tinners of Cornwall* (London, Sept. 30, 1953); *The Logan Rock* (Porthcurno, Aug. 15, 1956); *The Prince of Coxcombs* (London, Feb. 3, 1965); *The 3 Wise Men* (Kings Langley, Hertfordshire, Jan. 7, 1967); *The Prisoner Paul* (London, Oct. 16, 1970); *A Will of her Own* (1971–73; London, May 31, 1985); *The Rubicon* (1981–83); *Lindisfarne* (1984–86); *Claudia's Dream* (1986–89); *Galileo* (1992–93). **OTHER:** *Variations on an Indian Theme* for Orch. (1940); *5 Bells Suite* for Chorus and Orch. (1942); Harp Concerto; orch. suites; *Phantasy* for String Quartet; solo harp pieces, including a Solo Harp Concerto; *The Daytime of Christ,* oratorio; song cycles. —NS/LK/DM

Gungl, Joseph (József), famous Hungarian bandmaster and composer; b. Zsámbék, Dec. 1, 1810; d. Weimar, Jan. 31, 1889. He studied in Buda. He played the oboe in the band of an artillery regiment in the Austrian army, and later became its conductor. He wrote a number of marches and dances, which became extremely popular, and also traveled with his band all over Germany. In 1843 he established his own orch. in Berlin. He made an American tour in 1849, and then returned to Europe and lived mostly in Munich and Frankfurt am Main.—NS/LK/DM

Gunn, Glenn Dillard, American pianist, conductor, and music critic; b. Topeka, Kans., Oct. 2, 1874; d. Washington, D.C., Nov. 22, 1963. He studied at the Leipzig Cons. and in Chicago with Ziehn (theory). He taught at the Chicago Musical Coll. (1901–05). In 1915 he founded the American Sym. Orch., whose object was the performance of American works and the engagement of American soloists; in 1922 he founded the Glenn Dillard Gunn School of Music and Dramatic Art; in 1932 he became artistic director of the Chicago Cons. of Music. He was music critic for the *Chicago Tribune* (1910–15), the *Chicago Herald and Examiner* (1922–36), and the *Washington Times-Herald* (1940–54). He publ. *A Course of Lessons on the History and Aesthetics of Music* (Chicago, 1912) and *Music, Its History and Enjoyment* (N.Y., 1930).—NS/LK/DM

Gunn, John, Scottish cellist and writer on music; b. Edinburgh, c. 1765; d. there, c. 1824. In 1789 he went to London, where he taught cello and flute. He returned to Edinburgh in 1802.

WRITINGS: *40 Scotch Airs arranged as trios for flute, violin, and violoncello; The Art of Playing the German Flute on New Principles; The Theory and Practice of Fingering the Violoncello* (London, 1793); *An Essay, Theoretical and Practical, on the Application of Harmony, Thorough-Bass, and Modulation to the Violoncello* (Edinburgh, 1801); *An Historical Inquiry regarding the Performance on the Harp in the Highlands of Scotland from the earliest Times until it was discontinued about the year 1734* (Edinburgh, 1807).—NS/LK/DM

Gunsbourg, Raoul, Rumanian-French impresario; b. Bucharest, Dec. 25, 1859; d. Monte Carlo, May 31, 1955. After directing opera companies in Russia, he became the director of the Grand Theatre in Lille (1888–89), the Nice Opera (1889–91), and the Monte Carlo Opera (1893–1950), where he produced several of his own operas (he wrote the piano scores, and the orchestration was done by L. Jehin). Of these, *Le Vieil Aigle*, after Maxim Gorky's fable (Feb. 13, 1909), had a modicum of success.—NS/LK/DM

Guns N' Roses, perhaps the most controversial rock band since the Sex Pistols and certainly the most controversial to emerge in the late 1980s. **MEMBERSHIP:** Axl Rose (born William Bailey), lead voc. (b. Lafayette, Ind., Feb. 7, 1962); Slash (born Saul Hudson), lead gtr. (b. Stoke-on-Trent, Staffordshire, England, July 23, 1965); Izzy Stradlin (born Jeffrey Isbell), rhythm gtr. (b. Lafayette, Ind., April 8, 1962); Michael "Duff" McKagan, bs. (b. Seattle, Wash., Feb. 5, 1964); Steven Adler, drm. (b. Ohio, Jan. 22, 1965). Steven Adler left in 1990, to be replaced by Matt Sorum (b. Long Beach, Calif., Nov. 19, 1960); Dizzy (real name, Darren) Reed, kybd. (b. Hinsdale, Ill., June 18, 1963) also joined at this time. In November 1991 Izzy Stradlin left, to be replaced by Gilby Clarke (b. Cleveland, Ohio, Aug. 17, 1962).

Guns N' Roses produced angry, belligerent songs focused largely on the decadent side of life and its attendant rage, fear, and insecurity. Featuring the abrasive vocals of Axl Rose, rock's most notorious and volatile male performer of the 1990s, Guns N' Roses gained massive popularity with best-selling albums and insolent concert performances that sometimes led to riots. Along with Metallica, with whom they toured in 1992, Guns N' Roses challenged established heavy-metal bands such as Van Halen and reinvigorated the staid metal scene.

Axl Rose met guitarist Izzy Stradlin in 1984 in Los Angeles, where they formed a band variously known as Rose, Hollywood Rose, and LA Guns. In 1985 Guns N' Roses was formed by Rose and Stradlin; two members of Road Crew, Steven Adler and Slash; and Seattle-born Michael "Duff" McKagan. In 1986 Guns N' Roses recorded a four-song EP for the independent Uzi/Suicide label entitled *Live Like a Suicide*. Subsequently signed to Geffen Records, the group scored their first (top) hit with "Sweet Child o' Mine" in 1988, achieving their earliest notoriety as the opening act for Aerosmith's 1988 tour. Their debut album, *Appetite for Destruction*, stayed on the album charts for nearly three years and yielded the smash hits "Welcome to the Jungle" (used in the Clint Eastwood movie *Dead Pool*) and "Paradise City" and the minor hit "Nightrain." *G N'R Lies*, their next release, compiled the *Live Like a Suicide* EP and four songs recorded in 1988, producing the smash hit "Patience" while including "Used to Love Her" and the controversial "One in a Million."

Mired in personal and professional difficulties for a time (the band members were admitted alcohol and drug abusers), Guns N' Roses resumed recording in 1990, but Adler was dismissed, to be replaced by former Cult drummer Matt Sorum, and keyboardist Dizzy Reed was added. "You Could Be Mine," from the Arnold Schwarzenegger movie *Terminator 2*, became a major hit in 1991. In late 1991 Guns N' Roses issued the dark, sprawling albums *Use Your Illusion I* and *II* simultaneously. The ballads "Don't Cry" and "November Rain" and a remake of Paul McCartney's "Live and Let Die" became the hits from *Use Your Illusion I*, which contained "Don't Damn Me," the 10-minute "Coma," and the psychedelic "The Garden" (with Alice Cooper). *Use Your Illusion II* included the minor hit "Yesterdays," "Estranged," a version of Bob Dylan's "Knockin' on Heaven's Door" (used in the Tom Cruise movie *Days of Thunder*), and the antiwar "Civil War." In November 1991 Izzy Stradlin left Guns N' Roses and was replaced by Gilby Clarke of Kills for Thrills. In 1992 Guns N' Roses toured North America with the rival heavy-metal band Metallica.

In 1993 Guns N' Roses toured without their usual backing musicians, Izzy Stradlin returning for five overseas engagements in place of the injured Gilby Clarke. Their late 1993 album, *The Spaghetti Incident*, perhaps their finest work, contained covers of punk songs such as The New York Dolls' "Human Being," the Stooges' "Raw Power," Fear's "I Don't Care About You," and Johnny Thunders's "You Can't Put Your Arms Around a Memory," plus mass-murderer Charles Manson's "Look at Your Game, Girl" and the Skyliners' "Since I Don't Have You."

In 1992 Izzy Stradlin assembled his own band, The Ju Ju Hounds, with Georgia Satellites guitarist Rick Richards, recording an album for Geffen Records and touring in support of Keith Richards's X-Pensive Winos in early 1993. In 1994 Gilby Clarke recorded *Pawnshop Guitars* with Axl Rose, Slash, Duff McKagan, Matt Sorum, and others for Virgin Records. Slash later recorded and toured with Snakepit, which included Clarke, Sorum, Jellyfish vocalist Eric Dover, and Alice in Chains bassist Mike Inez.

DISC.: GUNS N' ROSES: *Appetite for Destruction* (1987); *G N' R Lies* (1988); *Use Your Illusion I* (1991); *Use Your Illusion II* (1991); *The Spaghetti Incident* (1993). **IZZY STRADLIN AND THE JU JU HOUNDS:** *Izzy Stradlin and the Ju Ju Hounds* (1992). **GILBY CLARKE:** *Pawnshop Guitars* (1994). **SLASH'S SNAKEPIT:** *It's Five O'Clock Somewhere* (1995).

BIBL.: Paul Elliot, *G. N' R.: The World's Most Outrageous Hard Rock Band* (London, 1990); Danny Sugerman, *Appetite for Destruction: The Days of G. N' R.* (N.Y., 1992).—BH

Günther, Mizzi, greatly talented Austrian soprano; b. Warnsdorf, Feb. 8, 1879; d. Vienna, March 18, 1961. After appearances in provincial theaters, she settled in Vienna and first gained attention as O Mimosa San in *Die Geisha* in 1901. Later that year she had her first starring role as Lotti in *Die drei Wünsche* at the Carltheater, then had her first great success as Lola Winter there in *Das süsse Mädel*. She joined the Theater an der Wien in 1905 singing Jessie in *Vergeltsgott*. On Dec. 30, 1905, she created the role of Hanna Glawari in Lehár's *Die lustige Witwe*, and thereafter was recognized as one of the leading operetta stars of her era. She went on to appear to great acclaim as Alice in *Die Dollarprinzessin* (1907) and as Lori in *Der Mann mit den drei Frauen*

(1908). In 1909 she became a member of the Johann Strauss-Theater, where she created the role of Mary Ann in Lehár's *Das Fürstenkind*. In 1911 she rejoined the Theater an der Wien and created the title role in Lehár's *Eva*. After again appearing at the Johann Strauss-Theater (from 1915), she once more sang at the Theater an der Wien (from 1919), where she created the role of Katja in *Katja, die Tänzerin* (1923). In subsequent years, she concentrated on character roles. She later appeared at the Raimundtheater and the Volksoper. As late as 1948 she was seen on the Vienna stage, marking some 50 years in the musical theater.—NS/LK/DM

Gunzenhauser, Stephen (Charles), American conductor; b. N.Y., April 8, 1942. He studied at the Oberlin (Ohio) Coll. Cons. of Music (B.Mus., 1963) and at the Salzburg Mozarteum (diploma, 1962); following further training at the New England Cons. of Music in Boston (M.Mus., 1965), he held 3 Fulbright grants and completed his education at the Cologne Hochschule für Musik (artist diploma, 1968). In 1967 he took 1st prize in the Santiago, Spain, conducting competition, and then was an asst. conductor to Markevitch and l'Orchestre National de l'Opéra de Monte Carlo (1968–69) and to Stokowski and the American Sym. Orch. in N.Y. (1969–70). He was music director of the Brooklyn Center Chamber Orch. (1970–72); then was artistic (1974–82) and administrative (1982–87) director of the Wilmington (Del.) Music School. In 1978 he became music director of the Del. Sym. Orch. in Wilmington; concurrently, was principal conductor (1978–81) and music director (from 1981) of the Lancaster (Pa.) Sym. Orch.—NS/LK/DM

Gura, Eugen, distinguished German bass-baritone, father of **Hermann Gura;** b. Pressern, near Saatz, Bohemia, Nov. 8, 1842; d. Aufkirchen, Bavaria, Aug. 26, 1906. He studied in Vienna and with Joseph Herger in Munich. In 1865 he made his operatic debut in Lortzing's *Der Waffenschmied* in Munich, where he sang until 1867. He then appeared in Breslau (1867–70) and Leipzig (1870–76). In 1876 he sang Donner and Gunther at the first Bayreuth Festival, and returned there regularly until 1892. In 1882 he sang the first British Hans Sachs and King Marke at London's Drury Lane. From 1882 to 1896 he sang at the Hamburg Opera. On Aug. 20, 1901, he made his farewell appearance in opera as Hans Sachs in Munich, the day before the official opening of the Prinzregententheater. Among his other notable roles were Wotan, Wolfram, Amfortas, Leporello, Iago, and Falstaff. He publ. *Erinnerungen aus meinem Leben* (Leipzig, 1905).—NS/LK/DM

Gura, Hermann, German baritone, son of **Eugen Gura;** b. Breslau, April 5, 1870; d. Bad Wiessee, Bavaria, Sept. 13, 1944. He studied with Hasselbeck and Zenger in Munich, making his debut as the Dutchman in Weimar in 1890; then sang throughout Europe (1890–96). He subsequently was a singer and producer at the Schwerin Hoftheater in Munich (1896–1908), then director of the Berlin Komische Opera (from 1911); also worked at London's Covent Garden as a producer in 1913. After producing opera in Helsinki from 1920 to 1927, he taught voice in Berlin.—NS/LK/DM

Guridi (Bidaola), Jésus, Spanish organist and composer; b. Vitoria, Alava province, Sept. 25, 1886; d. Madrid, April 7, 1961. He studied harmony with Valentín Arín, and then with José Sainz Besabé in Bilbao. He took courses in piano with Grovlez, organ with Decaux, composition with Sérieyx, and counterpoint and fugue with d'Indy at the Paris Schola Cantorum, and also studied organ and composition with Jongen in Liège; finally took a course in instrumentation with Neitzel in Cologne. He was an organist in Bilbao (1909–29) and also conducted the Bilbao Choral Soc. (1911–26). In 1939 he settled in Madrid, where he became prof. of organ at the Cons. in 1944. During his years in Bilbao, he promoted the cause of Basque folk music; publ. an album of 22 Basque songs. His zarzuelas make frequent use of Basque folk music; of these, *El caserío* (Madrid, 1926) attained enormous success in Spain. Other stage works include *Mirentxu*, idyll in 2 acts (Madrid, 1915), *Amaya*, lyric drama in 3 acts (Bilbao, 1920), and *La Meiga* (Madrid, 1928). He also wrote a symphonic poem, *Una aventura de Don Quijote* (1916), *Sinfonia pirenáica, Basque Sketches* for Chorus and Orch., an orch. suite, *10 Basque Melodies* (very popular in Spain), a number of a cappella choral works on Basque themes, 4 string quartets, pieces for piano, and songs.

BIBL.: J. de Arozamena, *J. G.* (Madrid, 1967).—NS/LK/DM

Gurlitt, Cornelius, German organist and composer; b. Altona, Feb. 10, 1820; d. there, June 17, 1901. He studied piano with Johann Peter Reinecke in Altona, and with Weyse in Copenhagen. In 1845 he made a journey through Europe, where he met Schumann, Lortzing, Franz, and other eminent composers. In 1864 he was appointed organist of the Altona Cathedral, retaining this post until 1898; also taught at the Hamburg Cons. (1879–87). He wrote an opera, *Die römische Mauer* (Altona, 1860); another opera, *Scheik Hassan*, was not performed. He also composed 3 violin sonatas, 3 cello sonatas, several cycles of songs, etc. He is chiefly remembered, however, for his numerous piano miniatures, in Schumann's style, a collection of which was publ. by W. Rehberg, under the title *Der neue Gurlitt* (2 vols., Mainz, 1931).—NS/LK/DM

Gurlitt, Manfred, German conductor, teacher, and composer, cousin of **Wilibald Gurlitt;** b. Berlin, Sept. 6, 1890; d. Tokyo, April 29, 1972. He was a student in Berlin of Mayer-Mahr and Breithaupt (piano), Kaun (theory and composition), and Humperdinck (composition). In 1911 he became an assistant at the Bayreuth Festivals, and also conducted opera in Essen and Augsburg. After serving as 1st conductor and opera director at the Bremen City Theater (1914–24), he returned to Berlin and was granted the title of Generalmusikdirektor, appeared as a guest conductor at the State Opera and on the radio, and taught at the Hochschule für Musik. After the Nazis proscribed his activities, he settled in Tokyo in 1939 as a conductor and teacher. He conducted his own opera company there from 1953.

WORKS: DRAMATIC: O p e r a : *Die Heilige* (Bremen, Jan. 27, 1920); *Wozzeck* (Bremen, April 22, 1926); *Soldaten* (Düsseldorf, Nov. 1930); *Nana* (Dortmund, 1933); *Nächtlicher Spuk*

(1937); *Warum?* (1940); *Nordische Ballade* (1944); *Wir schreiten aus* (1958). ORCH.: *Symphonische Musik* (1922); *Orchester-Gesänge* (1925); Chamber Concerto No. 1 for Piano and Chamber Orch. (1927) and No. 2 for Violin and Chamber Orch. (1929); Cello Concerto (1937); 2 syms.: No. 1, *Goya- Symphonie* (1938) and No. 2, *Shakespeare-Symphonie* for 5 Voices and Orch. (1954). VOCAL: *5 Gesänge* for Soprano and Chamber Orch. (1923); *Drei politische Reden aus der Französischen Revolution* for Baritone, Men's Chorus, and Orch. (1944); songs. OTHER: Chamber music and piano pieces.

BIBL.: H. Götz, *M. G.: Leben und Werk* (Frankfurt am Main, 1996).—NS/LK/DM

Gurlitt, Wilibald, eminent German musicologist and editor, cousin of **Manfred Gurlitt;** b. Dresden, March 1, 1889; d. Freiburg im Breisgau, Dec. 15, 1963. He studied musicology at the Univ. of Heidelberg with Philipp Wolfrum, and also with Riemann and Schering at the Univ. of Leipzig, where he received his Ph.D. in 1914 with the diss. *Michael Praetorius (Creuzbergensis): Sein Leben und seine Werke* (publ. in Leipzig, 1915). He subsequently was an assistant to Riemann. He served in World War I, and was taken prisoner in France. After the Armistice, he became a lecturer at the Univ. of Freiburg im Breisgau in 1919. He directed its dept. of musicology from 1920, and was made a full prof. in 1929, but was removed from his position by the Nazi regime in 1937. He resumed his professorship in 1945, retiring in 1958. Gurlitt's investigations of the organ music of Praetorius led him to construct (in collaboration with O. Walcker) a "Praetorius organ," which was to reproduce the tuning of the period. This gave impetus in Germany to performance of historic works on authentic or reconstructed instruments. Gurlitt's other interests included the problem of musical terminology, resulting in the publication of his *Handwörterbuch der musikalischen Terminologie*. In 1952 he revived the moribund *Archiv für Musikwissenschaft*. He edited the first 2 vols. of the 12th ed. of *Riemann's Musik-Lexikon* (Mainz, 1959 and 1961). He also publ. *Johann Sebastian Bach: Der Meister und sein Werk* (Berlin, 1936; 4th ed., 1959; Eng. tr., St. Louis, 1957). —NS/LK/DM

Gurney, Ivor (Bertie), English poet and composer; b. Gloucester, Aug. 28, 1890; d. Dartford, Kent, Dec. 26, 1937. He became a chorister at Gloucester Cathedral in 1900, where he studied with Brewer. After serving as asst. organist there (1906–11), he continued his studies as a scholarship student in composition with Stanford at the Royal Coll. of Music in London (1911–15). He then served in the British Army during World War I, and in 1917 was wounded and gassed at Passchendaele. Although he never recovered his mental and physical health, he resumed his studies at the Royal Coll. of Music in 1919 as a student of Vaughan Williams. In 1922 he was declared insane and spent the rest of his life in mental hospitals. Gurney was a gifted composer of songs, being principally influenced by Parry and German lieder. He set some of his own poems, as well as others, to music. In all, he publ. some 40 songs (4 vols., 1917–22). Among his other works were piano pieces and violin pieces.

BIBL.: C. Moore, *Maker and Lover of Beauty: I. G., Poet and Songwriter* (Rickmansworth, 1976); M. Hurd, *The Ordeal of I. G.* (Oxford, 1978); A. Boden, ed., *Stars in a Dark Night: The Letters of I. G. to the Chapman Family* (Gloucester, 1986); M. Pilkington, *G., Ireland, Quilter and Warlock* (London, 1989).—NS/LK/DM

Guschlbauer, Theodor, Austrian conductor; b. Vienna, April 14, 1939. He received training at the Vienna Academy of Music and in Salzburg. From 1961 to 1969 he was conductor of the Vienna Baroque Ensemble, and also chief conductor of the Salzburg Landestheater from 1966 to 1968. He was music director of the Lyons Opera from 1969 to 1975. From 1975 to 1983 he was Generalmusikdirektor in Linz, where he led both the Bruckner Orch. and the Landestheater. He was chief conductor of the Deutscher Oper am Rhein in Düsseldorf from 1983 to 1988, and also of the Strasbourg Phil. from 1983 to 1997. In 1997 he became chief conductor of the Rheinland-Pfalz State Phil. in Ludwigshafen. That same year, the French government honored him with the Légion d'honneur.—NS/LK/DM

Gusikoff, Michel, American violinist and composer, b. N.Y., May 15, 1893; d. there, July 10, 1978. He was the great-grandson of the Polish xylophonist and composer Michał Józef Guzikov (1806–1837). He studied violin with Mark Fonaroff and Kneisel, and composition with Goetschius. He was concertmaster of the St. Louis Sym. Orch., Russian Sym. Orch. in N.Y., N.Y. Sym. Orch., Philadelphia Orch., NBC Sym. Orch. in N.Y., Pittsburgh Sym. Orch., and Bell Telephone Hour Orch. Among his works were *American Concerto* or *Jazz Fantasy* for Violin and Orch. (1931), *Oh! Susanna* for String Quartet or String Orch. (1942), and violin pieces, including violin arrangements of Gershwin's songs. —NS/LK/DM

Gussakovsky, Apollon, Russian composer; b. Akhtyrka, 1841; d. St. Petersburg, March 9, 1875. He was educated as a chemist and served on the science faculty of the Univ. of St. Petersburg. He became acquainted with Balakirev as early as 1857, and became an associate of the nationalist school of Russian composers; both Balakirev and Mussorgsky thought highly of his talents. The majority of his works were written between 1857 and 1861; among these were *Allegro* for Orch., "Let There Be Light," the 1st movement of a projected sym. (St. Petersburg, Jan. 27, 1861), a String Quartet, "Foolish or Comical Scherzo," piano works, and songs. —NS/LK/DM

Gustafson, Nancy, American soprano; b. Evanston, Ill., June 27, 1956. She received vocal training in San Francisco. In 1983 she made her operatic debut as Woglinde at the San Francisco Opera, where she returned as Freia, Musetta, Antonia, and Elettra. She made her European operatic debut in Paris in 1985 as Rosalinde. Her first engagement with the Glyndebourne Opera was as Donna Elvira during the company's visit to Hong Kong in 1986. In 1988 she made her formal debut at the Glyndebourne Festival as Kát'a Kabanová, and also made her first appearance at London's Covent

Garden as Freia. She sang Violetta with the Scottish Opera in Glasgow and Marguerite at the Lyric Opera in Chicago in 1989. On March 28, 1990, she made her debut at the Metropolitan Opera in N.Y. as Musetta. That same year she also sang Freia in Munich, Eva at Milan's La Scala, and Amelia Boccanegra in Brussels. In 1993 she appeared at the London Promenade Concerts. After singing Floyd's Susannah in Houston in 1996, she returned to Covent Garden in 1997 as Eva. In 1998 she appeared as Mathilde in *Guillaume Tell* at the Vienna State Opera.—NS/LK/DM

Gutchë, Gene, (real name, **Romeo Maximilian Eugene Ludwig Gutsche**), German-born American composer; b. Berlin, July 3, 1907. He studied in Germany, Italy, and Switzerland; in 1925 he went to the U.S., where he later undertook additional academic work at the Univ. of Minn. with Donald Ferguson and at the Univ. of Iowa with Philip Greeley Clapp (Ph.D., 1953). He held 2 Guggenheim fellowships (1961, 1964). His music is marked by a fairly advanced idiom and a neo-Romantic treatment of programmatic subject matter. In some of his orch. works, he applies fractional tones by dividing the strings into 2 groups tuned at slightly differing pitches.

WORKS: ORCH.: 6 syms.: No. 1 (Minneapolis, April 11, 1950), No. 2 (1950–54), No. 3 (1952), No. 4 (1960; Albuquerque, March 8, 1962), No. 5 for Strings (Chautauqua, N.Y., July 29, 1962), and No. 6 (1968); *Rondo capriccioso* (1953; N.Y., Feb. 19, 1960); Piano Concerto (Minneapolis, June 19, 1956); Cello Concerto (1957); *Bongo Divertimento* for Solo Percussionist and Orch. (1962); *Timpani Concertante* (Oakland, Calif., Feb. 14, 1962); Violin Concerto (1962); *Genghis Khan*, symphonic poem (Minneapolis, Dec. 6, 1963); *Rites in Tenochtitlan* for Small Orch. (St. Paul, Jan. 26, 1965); *Gemini* (Minneapolis, July 26, 1966); *Classic Concerto* (St. Paul, Nov. 11, 1967); *Epimetheus USA* (Detroit, Nov. 13, 1969); *Icarus*, suite (1975); *Bi-Centurion* (1975; Rochester, N.Y., Jan. 8, 1976); *Perseus and Andromeda XX* (1976; Cincinnati, Feb. 25, 1977). **CHAMBER:** 4 string quartets; 3 piano sonatas. **VOCAL:** *Akhenaten* for Chorus and Orch. (St. Louis, Sept. 23, 1983); choruses.—NS/LK/DM

Gutheil-Schoder, Marie, prominent German mezzo-soprano; b. Weimar, Feb. 16, 1874; d. Bad Ilmenau, Oct. 4, 1935. She was largely self-taught, although she received some coaching from Richard Strauss in Weimar, where she made her operatic debut as the 1st Lady in *Die Zauberflöte* in 1891. After singing in Berlin and Leipzig, she was engaged by Mahler for the Vienna Court Opera (debut as Nedda, Feb. 16, 1900). In her early performances, she was criticized for her small voice; Mahler made note of her "disagreeable middle register," but he also declared that she was a musical genius; her strong dramatic characterizations made her a favorite there until 1926. She was successful as Carmen, Elektra, Eva, and the 3 principal soprano roles in *Les Contes d'Hoffmann*; her Mozart roles included Pamina, Elvira, Susanna, and Cherubino. Her only London appearance was at Covent Garden as Octavian in 1913; 3 years later she sang the role of the Composer, under Strauss's direction, in a Zürich production of the revised version of *Ariadne aux Naxos*. She was closely associated with the music of Schoenberg; she took part

in the premiere of his 2nd String Quartet (Vienna, Feb. 5, 1907), and later frequently performed in his *Pierrot Lunaire*; Schoenberg conceived the part of the Woman in his monodrama *Erwartung* as a "Gutheil part"; she appeared in its first performance (Prague, June 6, 1924). After her retirement, she was active as a teacher and producer in Vienna and Salzburg. She was successively married to the violinist and composer Gustav Gutheil and the Viennese photographer Franz Setzer. —NS/LK/DM

Guthrie, Woody (actually, **Woodrow Wilson**), American folk songwriter, singer, and guitarist; b. Okemah, Okla., July 14, 1912; d. N.Y., Oct. 3, 1967. As a folk- and country-based songwriter whose lyrical concerns embraced social issues, Guthrie was the primary influence on the generation of singer-songwriters who emerged in the early 1960s. His chief disciple was Bob Dylan but his songs and his approach were carried forward by numerous other performers, among them the Weavers, the Kingston Trio, Peter, Paul and Mary, the New Christy Minstrels, Joan Baez, and Bruce Springsteen. Guthrie's best-known songs include "This Land Is Your Land," "So Long, It's Been Good to Know Yuh," and "Oklahoma Hills."

Guthrie was the son of Charles Edward and Nora Belle Tanner Guthrie. In the year of his birth his father left his job as a court clerk to become a land speculator, initially with success. Both parents were musical, and Guthrie began singing and playing the harmonica at an early age. He enjoyed a comfortable childhood at first, but then his father went bankrupt and his mother, who suffered from the hereditary disease Huntington's chorea, had to be institutionalized. He was adopted by other families, later rejoining his father in Pampa, Tex., where he learned to play the guitar. By his late teens he was living on his own and traveling around the Southwest.

Guthrie married Mary Esta Jennings in Pampa on Oct. 8, 1933, and settled down, working as a sign painter; the couple had three children. But the disastrous economic conditions of the Depression and his own restlessness sent him back on the road by mid-decade. He settled in L.A. in 1937, launching the daily radio show *The Oklahoma and Woody Guthrie* on local station KFVD on July 19. Soon he was earning enough to send for his family. During the late 1930s he became increasingly involved with the union movement.

Guthrie had moved to N.Y. by 1940. In March he was interviewed for the Library of Congress, reminiscing about his childhood and singing songs. He appeared on several nationally broadcast radio shows and began writing a column, "Woody Sez," for the Communist publications *The Daily Worker* and *People's World*. (The columns were published in book form in 1975.) Contracted to RCA Victor, he recorded 11 of his songs for two three-disc 78-rpm albums, *Dust Bowl Ballads, Volume One* and *Volume Two*. These songs included "Talking Dust Bowl Blues," "Do Re Mi," the two-part "Tom Joad" (a musical retelling of John Steinbeck's novel *The Grapes of Wrath*), "Dusty Old Dust" (later retitled "So Long, It's Been Good to Know Yuh"), "I Ain't Got No Home in

This World Anymore," and "Vigilante Man." (Guthrie's compositions frequently feature original lyrics with melodies borrowed or adapted from previously existing songs.)

In May 1941, Guthrie was commissioned to write songs for a documentary film about the Bonneville and Grand Coulee Dams on the Columbia River and spent a month in Portland, Ore., where he composed such songs as "Roll On, Columbia" (later named the official folk song of the state of Wash.), "Grand Coulee Dam," and "Pastures of Plenty." The completed film, released in 1949, contained three of his songs.

Returning to N.Y. in June 1941, Guthrie joined the politically oriented group the Almanac Singers to record the album *The Soil and the Sea*. He toured the country with them in 1941, and in February 1942 he appeared on their final album, *Dear Mr. President*. He published his autobiography, *Bound for Glory*, in 1943, and then joined the merchant marines, serving through most of the rest of World War II. He appeared in the single performance of the Off- Broadway play *It's Up to You* (N.Y., March 31, 1945). "Oklahoma Hills," which he had written with his cousin, Jack Guthrie, became a #1 hit on what was then called the folk (later country) chart in July 1945 for Jack Guthrie and His Oklahomans.

Divorced from his first wife, Guthrie married dancer and dance instructor Marjorie Greenblatt Mazia on Nov. 13, 1945. They had four children, including Arlo Guthrie, who became a singer-songwriter and recorded many of his father's songs. In the late 1940s, Guthrie recorded extensively for the record labels run by Moses Asch, notably Folkways, committing to wax an extensive repertoire of original and traditional folk songs and children's music.

The Weavers, whose members included two former members of the Almanac Singers, scored a Top Ten hit with their recording of "So Long, It's Been Good to Know Yuh" in February 1951. Guthrie divorced his second wife and married Anneke Van Kirk in December 1953. They had one child and divorced in 1956. By then Guthrie was suffering from Huntington's chorea. He spent the last decade of his life hospitalized.

As the folk revival gathered steam in the late 1950s, Guthrie's songs began to be covered extensively by emerging performers. The Kingston Trio put "Hard, Ain't It Hard" on their gold-selling debut album *The Kingston Trio*, which topped the charts in November 1958; "Hard Travelin'" on their Top Ten *Make Way!* album, released in February 1961; "Pastures of Plenty" and "This Land Is Your Land" on their Top Ten *Goin' Places* album, released in June 1961; and "Reuben James" on their Top Ten *Close-Up* album, released in September 1961. That same month, the Limeliters released their Top Ten album *The Slightly Fabulous Limeliters*, which featured "Hard, Ain't It Hard" and "Hard Travelin'." Meanwhile, Hank Thompson revived "Oklahoma Hills" for a Top Ten country hit in May 1961.

Bob Dylan, who had befriended Guthrie upon his arrival in N.Y. in 1961, put his original tribute "Song to Woody" on his debut album, *Bob Dylan*, released in March 1962. In April the chart-topping, two-million-selling self-titled LP by Peter, Paul and Mary included

"This Train"; the trio also covered "This Land Is Your Land" on their Top Ten, gold- selling album *Moving*, released in January 1963. The previous month the song had reached the singles charts in renditions by the New Christy Minstrels and Ketty Lester. It also appeared on Trini Lopez's Top Ten, gold-selling album *Trini Lopez at PJ's*, released in July 1963. Meanwhile, Joan Baez covered "Pretty Boy Floyd" on her Top Ten, gold-selling *In Concert* LP, released in October 1962.

Guthrie's own recordings were reissued extensively during this period: Folkways released *Songs to Grow On, Volume 3*, and *Ballads of Sacco and Vanzetti* in 1961, *Woody Guthrie Sings Folk Songs* in 1962, and *Woody Guthrie Sings Folk Songs, Vol. 2*, and *Dust Bowl Ballads* in 1964, while Stinson Records, which had acquired part of the Asch catalog, released *Folk Songs by Woody Guthrie and Cisco Houston* and *More Songs by Woody Guthrie* in 1963. The major new release of the period was Elektra Records' three-LP box set collection *Woody Guthrie: Library of Congress Recordings*, issued in 1964 and a nominee for the year's Grammy Award for Best Folk Recording. In 1965, Macmillan published *Born to Win*, a collection of Guthrie's writings edited by Robert Shelton, the *New York Times* folk-music critic.

Guthrie died at 55 in 1967. Two memorial benefit concerts were held in the years immediately following his death, the first at Carnegie Hall on Jan. 20, 1968, featuring Bob Dylan, Pete Seeger, Arlo Guthrie, Judy Collins, and Richie Havens, and the second at the Hollywood Bowl on Sept. 12, 1970, featuring Seeger, Collins, Havens, Joan Baez, and Arlo Guthrie. Recordings of both shows were released in April 1972 under the title *A Tribute to Woody Guthrie, Part One* and *Part Two*, and charted briefly. In October 1976, *Bound for Glory*, a film based on Guthrie's autobiography, was released. His songs and life story were also brought to the stage in the Off-Broadway musical *Woody Guthrie* (N.Y., Nov. 26, 1979) and the regional theater revue *Woody Guthrie's American Song* (Haddam, Conn., July 31, 1991).

In 1988 the Smithsonian Institution financed its purchase of the Folkways catalog with the album *A Vision Shared—A Tribute to Woody Guthrie and Leadbelly*, in which Guthrie's songs were performed by John Mellencamp, Emmylou Harris, Bruce Springsteen (who had covered "This Land Is Your Land" on his chart-topping, multiplatinum album *Bruce Springsteen & The E-Street Band Live/1975–85* in 1986 and who titled his 1995 album *The Ghost of Tom Joad*), U2, Willie Nelson, Bob Dylan, and Pete Seeger.

In 1989, Guthrie's recording of "This Land Is Your Land" was inducted into the Grammy Hall of Fame. Guthrie's recordings were reissued by several labels in the 1980s and 1990s. In 2000, a traveling exhibit organized by the Smithsonian Institution toured the U.S. and included Guthrie's writings, songs, films, and recordings.

DISC.: All of the following were recorded during the 1930s and 1940s and recently reissued on CD. *Columbia River Collection* (1987); *Dust Bowl Ballads* (1988); *Library of Congress Recordings* (1988); *Struggle* (1990); *Long Ways to Travel: The Unreleased Folkways Masters* (1994); *Ballads of Sacco and Vanzetti* (1996); *This*

Land Is Your Land: The Asch Recordings, Vol. 1 (1997); Muleskinner Blues: The Asch Recordings, Vol. 2 (1997); Hard Travellin': The Asch Recordings, Vol. 3 (1999); Buffalo Skinners: The Asch Recordings, Vol. 4 (2000).

WRITINGS: On a Slow Train through California; Bound for Glory (N.Y., 1943); ed., American Folksong (N.Y., 1947); California to the N.Y. Island (1960); Hard-Hitting Songs for Hard-Hit People; W. G. Folk Songs (N.Y., 1963); R. Shelton, ed., Born to Win (N.Y., 1965); W. Sez (N.Y., 1975); Seeds of Man: An Experience Lived and Dreamed (N.Y., 1976).

BIBL.: R. Reuss, ed., A W. G. Bibliography, 1912–67 (N.Y., 1968); H. Yurchenco, A Mighty Hard Road: The Life of W. G. (N.Y., 1970); H. Wood, ed., A Tribute to W. G. (N.Y., 1972); H. Leventhal and M. Guthrie (his second wife), eds., The W. G. Songbook (N.Y., 1976); E. Robbin, W. G. and Me: An Intimate Reminiscence (Berkeley, Calif., 1979); J. Klein, W. G.: A Life (N.Y., 1980); D. Marsh and H. Leventhal, eds., Pastures of Plenty: A Self-Portrait (N.Y., 1990); J. Longhi, W., Cisco, & Me: Seamen Three in the Merchant Marine (Urbana, Ill., 1997).—**WR**

Gutiérrez, Gonzalo, Spanish organist and composer; b. c. 1540; d. Granada, 1605. He was appointed organist at the Cathedral of Granada in 1569, and held this post until his death.

BIBL.: J. Lopez Calo, La música en la catedral de Granada en el siglo XVI (Granada, 1963; vol. I, pp. 205–10; vol. II includes several of his works).—**NS/LK/DM**

Gutiérrez, Horacio, brilliant Cuban-born American pianist; b. Havana, Aug. 28, 1948. He studied in Havana, where he made his debut as soloist with the local orch. at age 11. In 1962 his family went to Los Angeles and in 1967 he became a naturalized American citizen. He completed his training at the Juilliard School of Music in N.Y. (1967–70). In 1970 he won 2nd prize at the Tchaikovsky Competition in Moscow, and then made successful debuts in N.Y. in 1972 and in London in 1974. In 1982 he was awarded the Avery Fisher Prize. He toured regularly throughout the world, appearing as a soloist with the foremost orchs., as a recitalist, and as a chamber music player.—**NS/LK/DM**

Gutiérrez Heras, Joaquín, Mexican composer; b. Tehuacán, Sept. 28, 1927. He attended classes in architecture at the National Univ. of Mexico and then studied composition with Blas Galindo and Rodolfo Halffter at the National Cons. of Mexico (1950–52). A scholarship from the French Inst. of Mexico enabled him to go to Paris, where he took courses in composition with Messiaen, Rivier, and Dandelot at the Paris Cons. (1952–53); on a Rockefeller Foundation scholarship, he studied composition with Bergsma and Persichetti at the Juilliard School of Music in N.Y. (1960–61). Upon his return to Mexico, he gave radio lectures and taught theory. As a composer, he professed a "voluntary lack of complexity."

WORKS: Divertimento for Piano and Orch. (1949); El deportista, satirical ballet (1957); Variations on a French Song for Piano or Harpsichord (1958–60); Chamber Cantata on Poems by Emilio Prados for Soprano, 2 Flutes, Harp, and 4 Strings (1961); Los Cazadores (The Hunters), symphonic scene (1962); Duo for Alto Flute and Cello (1964); Sonata simple for Flute and Piano (1965);

Trio for Oboe, Clarinet, and Bassoon (1965); 2 Pieces for 3 Brasses (1967); Night and Day Music for Wind Sym. Orch. (1973); De profundis for Chorus (1977); several scores for theater and film. —**NS/LK/DM**

Gutman, Natalia, Russian cellist; b. Moscow, June 14, 1942. At the age of 5, she became a pupil of Saposhnikov at the Gnessin Music School, later pursuing training with Rostropovich at the Moscow Cons. She made her first public appearance at the age of 9. After winning a medal at the Tchaikovsky Competition in Moscow in 1962, she took 1st prize in the German Radio Competition in Munich in 1967. She subsequently pursued a far-ranging career as a soloist with principal orchs. of Europe, North America, and Japan; also was active as a recitalist and chamber music player, frequently appearing in duo concerts with her husband **Oleg Kagan.** In addition to the standard cello repertory, Gutman acquired a fine reputation for her championship of contemporary music.—**NS/LK/DM**

Gutmann, Adolph, German pianist and composer; b. Heidelberg, Jan. 12, 1819; d. Spezia, Oct. 27, 1882. He lived mostly in Paris, where he studied with Chopin, and became a close friend of his. He publ. an album of Études caractéristiques which were quite popular in the 19th century, and much salon music for piano. He was also a successful performer whose virtuoso technique made him popular with audiences. —**NS/LK/DM**

Güttler, Ludwig, noted German trumpeter, conductor, and pedagogue; b. Sosa, June 13, 1943. He commenced music studies when he was 5, and began playing the trumpet at 14. After obtaining a degree in architecture, he studied trumpet with Armin Mennel at the Leipzig Hochschule für Musik (1961–65). From 1965 he was solo trumpeter of the Handel Festival Orch. in Halle, and later, of the Dresden Phil. (1969–81). In 1976 he founded the Leipziger Bach-Collegium, in 1978 the Blechbläserensemble Ludwig Güttler, and in 1985 the Virtuosi Saxoniae; made many tours with these groups, appearing as a trumpeter and conductor. In 1972 he joined the faculty of the Dresden Hochschule für Musik, taking charge of its master classes in wind instruments in 1982; also served as a guest teacher at the Weimar International Music Seminar (from 1977) and in Austria, Japan, and the U.S. Güttler discovered many scores for his instrument in various German archives, libraries, and castles, and made a special effort to bring them before the public. He won renown for his performances of Baroque and Classical works on period instruments. In 1978 he won the National Prize of the German Democratic Republic and in 1989 was awarded the Music Prize of the City of Frankfurt am Main. —**NS/LK/DM**

Guy, Barry (John), English double bass player and composer; b. London, April 22, 1947. He took up the double bass and played in a Dixieland jazz group before pursuing training in composition with Stanley Glasser at Goldsmiths' Coll. in London, where he completed his studies with Buxton Orr and Patric Standford at the Guildhall School of Music and Drama. In 1970 he founded the London Jazz Composers Orch. He also played double bass in several ensembles, ranging from early music groups to sym. orchs., and gave recitals. In 1991 he won the Royal Phil. Soc. of London award for chamber music and in 1994 he was co-winner of the Hilliard Ensemble composition prize. As a double bass player, his range extends from early music through jazz improvisation to the avant-garde. His compositions reflect similarly varied interests.

WORKS: DRAMATIC: *No Man's Land*, ballet after *Statements II* (1972–74; London, Nov. 13, 1974); *Eos*, ballet for Double Bass and Tape, after *Eos X* (1976–78; Bournemouth, Oct. 3, 1978); *Video Life*, dance piece for Double Bass and Tape (Rimini, Italy, Aug. 27, 1986); *Breaking the Surface*, film music (Channel 4 TV, June 18, 1986); *Kingdom*, ballet after *After the Rain* (1992; Geneva, Jan. 10, 1993). ORCH.: *Incontri* for Cello and Orch. (1970); *D* for Solo Amplified Strings (1972; London, Nov. 25, 1974); *Flagwalk* for Solo Strings (1974); *Anna* for Amplified Double Bass and Orch. (1974; London, Feb. 24, 1989); *Songs from Tomorrow* (Munich, Nov. 25, 1975); *Eos* for Double Bass and Orch. (Baden-Baden, Oct. 23, 1977; also as *Eos X* for Double Bass and Tape, 1976; London, June 20, 1977); *Statements II- Ex* for Amplified Double Bass and Orch. (Graz, Oct. 14, 1979; based on *Statements II* for Amplified Double Bass, 1972); *Voyages of the Moon* for Amplified Double Bass and Orch. (London, Nov. 8, 1983); *UM 1788* for 18 Solo Strings (Manchester, April 1, 1989); *After the Rain* for Strings (London, Feb. 23, 1992); *Concerto for Orchestra, Fallingwater* (London, Oct. 13, 1996). CHAMBER: *4 Miniatures* for Flute and Piano (1969); 3 string quartets, including No. 2 (1970) and No. 3 for Soprano and Amplified String Quartet, after Wilfred Owen (Southampton, Nov. 10, 1973); *Statements II* for Amplified Double Bass (1972; reworked as *Statements II-Ex* for Amplified Double Bass and Orch., Graz, Oct. 14, 1979); *Games (for all ages)* for Chamber Ensemble (Oxford, May 1973); *Play* for Chamber Ensemble (1976; Warsaw, Sept. 20, 1977); *Eos X* for Double Bass and Tape (1976; London, June 20, 1977; also as *Eos* for Double Bass and Orch., Baden-Baden, Oct. 23, 1977); *Details (From the Architecture of Antonio Gaudi)* for 2 Oboes, Bassoon, and Harpsichord (1977; Kingston Parish Church, Jan. 20, 1978); *Pfiff* for Cello, Percussion, and Piano (Graz, Oct. 15, 1979); *Bitz!* for Chamber Ensemble (1979; rev. 1981; London, May 7, 1984); *Circular* for 2 Oboes, 1 Oboist (London, Oct. 26, 1984); *Whistle and Flute* for Flute and Tape (1985; London, Jan. 6, 1986); *rondOH!* for Piano, Violin, and Double Bass (Canterbury, Oct. 10, 1985); *Look Up!* for 8 Cellos (1990; London, Jan. 16, 1991); *Bird Gong Game* for Improvising Soloist and Chamber Ensemble (Glasgow, March 20, 1992); *Mobile Herbarium* for Saxophone Quartet (Leicester, Nov. 19, 1992); *Celebration* for Violin (1994; London, Jan. 14, 1995); *Buzz* for Viol Consort (1994; London, March 7, 1995); *Redshift* for 2 Cellos (Manchester, April 30, 1998). VOCAL: *Hold Hands and Sing* for Chorus and Electronics (London, July 10, 1978); *Waiata* for Tenor and Medieval Instruments, 1 Player (London, Nov. 13, 1980; rev. for 2 Men's Voices Playing Various Renaissance Instruments, 1990); *The Road to Ruin* for 4 Voices and String Quartet, after Sassoon (Darmstadt, July 19, 1986); *Remembered Earth* for Tenor, Bass, Lute, Viola da Gamba, Synthesizer, and Tape (1992; also for Tenor, Bass, Soprano, Alto, Chorus, Baroque Violin, Double Bass, Oboe, and Harpsichord, 1999); *Up coup de dés* for 4 Men's Voices, after Mallarmé (1994).—LK/DM

Guy, Fred, jazz guitarist and banjoist, long associated with Duke Ellington; b. Burkesville, Ga., May 23, 1897; d. Chicago, Nov. 22, 1971. He was raised in N.Y.C. He first worked professionally playing the banjo with the Joseph C. Smith Orch. in the early 1920s, and then led his own band at The Oriental, N.Y. before joining Ellington on banjo (1925); he later switched to guitar (c. 1934). Guy credited guitarist Eddie Lang with encouraging him to take up the more modern instrument. Other than brief absences, he remained with Ellington until 1949. After that, he left full-time music and returned to his longtime home city of Chicago; he managed a local ballroom for over 20 years.—JC/LP

Guyonnet, Jacques, Swiss composer; b. Geneva, March 20, 1933. He studied at the Geneva Cons. (1950–58) and had courses in new music with Boulez at the summer sessions held in Darmstadt (1958–61). In 1959 he founded the Studio de Musique Contemporaine in Geneva; from 1976 to 1981 was president of the ISCM.

WORKS: DRAMATIC: *Entremonde*, ballet for Flute, Piano, 4 Percussionists, and Tape (1967); *Electric Sorcerers*, rock opera (1980–81). ORCH.: *Monades II* and *III* (1960, 1961); *En 3 éclats!* for Piano and Chamber Orch. (1964); *Stele in memoriam J.F. Kennedy* for Chamber Orch. and Tape (1964); *7 portes du temps* (1966–69); *A Single R* for Viola and Chamber Orch. (1971); *Die Wandlung* (1973); *Les Enfants du désert* for Strings (1974); *Zornagore* (1976); *Les profondeurs de la terre* (1977); *Ombre* (1979); *Les Dernières Demeures* (1979); *Harmonique- Souffle* for Chamber Orch. (1980). CHAMBER: *Monades I* for Chamber Ensemble (1958); *Polyphonie I* for Flute and Piano (1961) and *III* for Flute, Viola, and 2 Pianos (1964); *The Approach to the Hidden Man I* for Solo Cello and 6 Instruments (1966); *Let There Be Events!* for 17 Instrumental Soloists (1968–71); *Modèles I-II* for any number of Instrumental Soloists (1970); *Mémorial* for 4 Trumpets and 4 Trombones (1974); *Un soupir pour Aurore* for Cello and Piano (1990). PIANO: *Polyphonie II* for 2 Pianos (1959); *Chronicles* (1964–71). VOCAL: *The Approach to the Hidden Man II* for Mezzo-soprano, Chamber Orch., and Electronic Sound (1967); *Good Grief Jerry!* for Soprano and Chamber Orch. (1970–71); *Le Chant remémoré* for 4 Vocal Soloists and Orch. (1972). —NS/LK/DM

Guyot, Jean, South Netherlands composer, also known as **Jean de Châtelet** and **Johannes Castileti;** b. Châtelet, Hainaut, 1512; d. Liège, March 11, 1588. He was educated at the Univ. of Louvain (licencié-ès-arts, 1537). In 1546 he became chaplain and maître de chant at St. Paul's in Liège; about 1557 he became chaplain and maître de chant at St. Lambert Cathedral in Liège. After serving as Kapellmeister at the Imperial Court in Vienna (1563–64), he returned to St. Lambert Cathedral to take up his benefice but no longer served as maître de chant. Among his works are a Mass, 2 *Te Deums*, 20 motets, and 10 chansons.

BIBL.: C. Lyon, *J. G.* (Charleroi, 1876); B. Even, *J. G. de Châtelet et son oeuvre* (diss., Univ. of Liège, 1974).—NS/LK/DM

Guzikov, Michal Jozef, famous Polish xylophonist and composer; b. Szklow, Sept. 14, 1806; d. Aachen, Oct. 21, 1837. Of a Jewish musical family, he showed precocious talent, and with 4 relatives he traveled all over Europe. His virtuosity on the xylophone was extraordinary, and elicited praise from the public as well as from celebrated musicians, among them Mendelssohn. His programs consisted of arrangements of well-known works and also his own pieces. His most successful number was a transcription of Paganini's *La Campanella*.

BIBL.: M. Schlesinger, *Über G.* (Vienna, 1936). —NS/LK/DM

Gyrowetz, Adalbert (Mathias) (original name, **Vojtěch Matyáš Jirovec**), noted Bohemian composer and conductor; b. Budweis, Feb. 19, 1763; d. Vienna, March 19, 1850. He studied piano, violin, and composition with his father, a local choirmaster, and began to compose while a student at the Piarist Gymnasium in his native town; then studied philosophy and law in Prague. He subsequently became secretary to Count Franz von Funfkirchen, to whom he dedicated his first syms., a set of 6 in Haydnesque style (1783); was also a member of his private orch. In 1784 he went to Vienna, where he was befriended by Mozart; the latter arranged for one of his syms. to be performed in 1785. He then became secretary and music master to Prince Ruspoli, who took him to Italy. While in Rome (1786–87), he composed a set of 6 string quartets, the first of his works to be publ. After leaving Ruspoli's service, he studied with Sala in Naples. He made a brief visit to Paris in 1789, and then proceeded to London, where he met and befriended Haydn, who was also visiting the British capital. During his London sojourn, Gyrowetz was commissioned by the Pantheon to write an opera, *Semiramis*; however, before the work could be mounted, both the theater and his MS were destroyed by fire (1792). He returned to the Continent in 1793; in 1804 he became composer and conductor of the Vienna Hoftheater, where he produced such popular operas as *Agnes Sorel* (Dec. 4, 1806) and *Der Augenarzt* (Oct. 1,

1811). He also wrote *Il finto Stanislao* (Milan, July 5, 1818), to a libretto by Romani, which Verdi subsequently used for his *Un giorno di regno*. He likewise anticipated Wagner by writing the first opera on the subject of Hans Sachs's life in his *Hans Sachs im vorgerückten Alter* (Dresden, 1834). He retired from the Hoftheater in 1831, and his fame soon dissipated; he spent his last years in straitened circumstances and relative neglect, having outlived the great masters of the age. He composed a variety of stage works, including operas, Singspiels, and melodramas, as well as about 40 syms., 2 piano concertos (1796, 1800), and 3 concertantes (for Violin, Viola, and Cello, 1792; for 2 Violins and Viola, 1798; and for Flute, Oboe, Bassoon, Violin, and Cello, 1798). Among his sacred compositions are 11 masses, a Te Deum, a Tantum Ergo, and 2 vesper services. He also composed much chamber music, including about 45 string quartets (1788–1804) and some 46 piano trios (1790–1814). —NS/LK/DM

Gysi, Fritz, Swiss music critic and musicologist; b. Zofingen, Feb. 18, 1888; d. Zürich, March 5, 1967. He studied at the Basel Cons., and then took courses in musicology and art history at the univs. of Zürich, Berlin, and Bern (Ph.D., 1913, with the diss. *Die Entwicklung der kirchlichen Architektur in der deutschen Schweiz im 17. und 18. Jahrhundert*; publ. in Zürich, 1914); subsequently completed his Habilitation in music history at the Univ. of Zürich in 1921, where he was made a titular prof. in 1931. He was also a music critic for the *Basler Nachrichten* and the Basel *National-Zeitung* (from 1915) and the Zürich *Tagesanzeiger* (from 1928).

WRITINGS: *Mozart in seinen Briefen* (Zürich, 1919–21); *Max Bruch* (Zürich, 1922); *Claude Debussy* (Zürich, 1926); *Richard Wagner und die Schweiz* (Frauenfeld, 1929); *Richard Wagner und Zürich* (Zürich, 1933); *Richard Strauss* (Potsdam, 1934); *Hans Georg Nägeli* (Zürich, 1936).—NS/LK/DM

ISBN 0-02-865527-3